The Compact Oxford–Hachette French Dictionary

Lettres of Mme.

No peguin

may 17
8-10

The Compact Oxford–Hachette French Dictionary

Edited by

Marie-Hélène Corréard and Mary O'Neill

Oxford New York

OXFORD UNIVERSITY PRESS

Oxford University Press, Great Clarendon Street, Oxford OX2 6DP

Oxford New York
Athens Auckland Bangkok Bogota Bombay
Buenos Aires Calcutta Cape Town Dar es Salaam
Delhi Florence Hong Kong Istanbul Karachi
Kuala Lumpur Madras Madrid Melbourne
Mexico City Nairobi Paris Singapore
Taipei Tokyo Toronto Warsaw

and associated companies in
Berlin Ibadan

Oxford is a trade mark of Oxford University Press

First published 1995

British Library Cataloguing in Publication Data
Data available

Library of Congress Cataloging in Publication Data
Data available
ISBN 0-19-864535-X

20 19 18 17 16 15 14 13 12 11

Printed and bound in Great Britain by
Mackays of Chatham plc, Chatham, Kent

Contents

List of contributors	vi
Introduction	vii
The structure of French–English entries	viii
The structure of English–French entries	ix
Using this dictionary	x
Abbreviations and symbols	xiv
The pronunciation of French	xv
French–English dictionary	**1**
French correspondence	477
French advertisements	483
English–French dictionary	**485**
French Verbs	988
Numbers in French	1006
Index of lexical and grammar notes	1008

The Compact Oxford–Hachette French Dictionary

Chief Editor
Marie-Hélène Corréard

Associate Editor
Mary O'Neill

Editors
Jennifer Barnes
Marianne Chalmers
Gearóid Cronin
Laurence Delacroix
Françoise de Peretti
Frances Illingworth
Pascal Lecler
Martine Pierquin
Natalie Pomier
Susan Steinberg

Lexical usage notes and correspondence
Henri Béjoint
Richard Wakely

North American English
Kristin Clayton

Phonetics
Isabelle Vodoz

Data-capture
Alison Curr
Diane Diffley
Philip Gerrish
Patricia Moore

Administration
Isabelle Lemoine

Proofreading
Genevieve Hawkins
Gérard Kahn
Isabelle Lemoine

Design
Fran Holdsworth
Raynor Design
Jeffrey Tabberner

There are many people, not mentioned in the list of contributors, whose work is also represented in the present dictionary. We would like to thank the editorial team of the *Oxford–Hachette French Dictionary* on which the present publication is largely based and, in particular, Dr Valerie Grundy (Joint Chief Editor), for their contribution to the *Compact Oxford–Hachette French Dictionary*. We are also grateful to the numerous freelance translators and lexicographers who were involved in the parent project.

We are indebted to Sue Atkins who from the first has given us the benefit of her expertise in the field of lexicography and whose enthusiasm has been an inspiration.

Introduction

The *Compact Oxford–Hachette French Dictionary* represents a totally new concept in smaller format bilingual dictionaries. It is designed as a language aid for the English-speaking general dictionary user. It is innovative in that it makes use of the native speaker's knowledge of English, thus removing the need for phonetics or excessive grammatical information on the English–French side of the dictionary. Emphasis is placed on those areas of the foreign language where the user is likely to need most help, providing a level of essential detail which is often lacking in smaller dictionaries for reasons of space. Entries are clearly laid out, with numbered categories for different senses and parts of speech, as well as detailed treatment of important structures and usages.

A distinctive feature of the dictionary is the presentation of idiomatic phrases and English phrasal verbs which appear as independent categories within an entry to facilitate consultation. In addition to the generous coverage of proper nouns and abbreviations, users will find a unique feature in the form of helpful usage notes dealing with key topics such as age, clocktime, illnesses, forms of address etc, as well as detailed notes for important and often complex grammar words.

The French–English side is specially adapted for English speakers. The information concerning the scope of a translation is given in English where such information is deemed necessary. The reader will find a broad coverage of current French, including often difficult idiomatic usage, geared to the needs of a wide range of users, from students and adult learners of French to the enthusiastic tourist or business professional. The streamlined presentation of translations is designed to ensure that users are able to understand most of the language they are likely to encounter in a wide variety of contexts, both written and spoken.

As it is derived in the main from the larger *Oxford–Hachette French Dictionary*, the material in the English and French wordlists is up to date and authentic because it is corpus-based. A corpus is a database containing extracts from the text of books, newspapers, magazine articles etc, as well as transcripts of a variety of recordings of spoken language. In seconds, the corpus finds and displays all the contexts in which a particular word occurs. Displaying the word in context allows editors to focus on important uses and structures of the word and is an excellent indicator of frequency.

Designed with the specific requirements of the English-speaking user in mind, the *Compact Oxford–Hachette French Dictionary* is an efficient and unique linguistic resource for learners of French.

The structure of French–English entries

headword part of speech plus gender compounds in block at end of entry idioms in block at end of entry	**mur** /myʀ/ **I** *nm* wall; **rester** or **être entre quatre ~s** to be cooped up; **faire les pieds au ~** to do a handstand against the wall; to tie oneself up in knots. **II murs** *nm pl* (of business) premises; (of palace, embassy) confines; **être dans ses ~s** to own one's own house. ■ **~ portant** or **porteur** load-bearing wall; **~ du son** sound barrier; **~ de soutènement** retaining wall; **Mur des lamentations** Wailing Wall. IDIOMS **faire le ~** to go over the wall; **mettre qn au pied du ~** to call sb's bluff; **être au pied du ~** to be up against the wall.	IPA pronunciation swung dash as substitute for headword in examples
roman grammatical category number	**mûrir** /myʀiʀ/ [3] **I** *vtr* **1** to ripen [*fruit*]; **2** to mature [*person*]; to develop [*plan*]. **II** *vi* **1** [*fruit*] to ripen; **faire ~ des bananes** to ripen bananas; **2** [*person, talent*] to mature; [*plan, idea*] to evolve; [*passion*] to develop; **3** [*abscess*] to come to a head.	Arabic sense number example
field label	**musculation** /myskylasjɔ̃/ *nf* **(exercices de) ~** (gen) bodybuilding; (Med) exercises to strengthen the muscles; **salle de ~** weights room.	
	museau, *pl* **~x** /myzo/ *nm* **1** muzzle; snout; nose; **2**○ face.	register symbol ○ informal ◑ very informal ● vulgar or taboo
feminine form of headword	**mystérieux, -ieuse** /misteʀjø, øz/ *adj* mysterious.	
	mystifier /mistifje/ [2] *vtr* to hoodwink, to fool.	number of verb group, referring to the French verb tables at the end of the dictionary
level of language	**nounours**○ /nunuʀs/ *nm inv* (baby talk) teddy bear.	
	novateur, -trice /nɔvatœʀ, tʀis/ **I** *adj* innovative. **II** *nm,f* innovator, pioneer.	IPA pronunciation for feminine form
pejorative use	**paperasserie**○ /papʀasʀi/ *nf* (derogatory) paperwork.	
trademark symbol	**pédalo®** /pedalo/ *nm* pedalo (GB), pedal boat.	
	pochette-surprise, *pl* **pochettes-surprises** /pɔʃɛtsyʀpʀiz/ *nf*: *child's novelty consisting of several small surprise items in a cone.*	explanatory gloss where there is no direct translation equivalent
	poste² /pɔst/ *nf* post office; **envoyer par la ~** to send [sth] by post (GB), to mail (US). ■ **~ aérienne** airmail; **~ restante** poste restante (GB), general delivery (US).	North American translation
cross-reference	**priori** ▶ **a priori**.	
	QG /kyʒe/ *nm*: *abbr* ▶ **quartier**.	cross-reference

The structure of English–French entries

headword sense indicators	**patch I** *n* **1** (in clothes) pièce *f*; (on tyre, airbed) rustine® *f*; (on eye) bandeau *m*; **2** (of snow, ice) plaque *f*; (of damp, rust, sunlight) tache *f*; (of fog) nappe *f*; (of oil) flaque *f*; (of blue sky) coin *m*; **3** (area of ground) zone *f*; (for planting) carré *m*; a **~ of grass** un coin d'herbe; **4**○ (GB) (territory) territoire *m*; **5**○ (period) période *f*. **II** *vtr* rapiécer [*hole, trousers*]; réparer [*tyre*].	Arabic sense numbers translations
phrasal verb	■ **patch up**: ¶ **~ up [sth], ~ [sth] up** soigner [*person*]; rapiécer [*hole, trousers*]; réparer [*tyre*]; rafistoler○ [*marriage*]; ¶ **~ up [sth]** résoudre [*differences*].	phrasal verb pattern
roman grammatical category number typical subject collocates	**perform I** *vtr* **1** exécuter [*task*]; accomplir [*duties*]; procéder à [*operation*]; **2** jouer [*play*]; chanter [*song*]; exécuter [*dance, trick*]; **3** célébrer [*ceremony*]. **II** *vi* **1** [*actor, musician*] jouer; **2 to ~ well/badly** [*team*] bien/mal jouer; [*interviewee*] faire	part of speech typical object collocates swung dash as substitute for headword in examples
acronym	**PIN (number)** *n* (*abbr* = **personal identification number**) code *m* confidentiel (pour carte bancaire).	gender of translation
compounds in alphabetical order	**potato**: **~ chips** (US), **~ crisps** (GB), *n pl* chips *fpl*; **~ peeler** *n* éplucheurs-légumes *m inv*.	grammar information
abbreviation	**PR** *n* **1** (*abbr* = **public relations**) relations *fpl* publiques; **2** *abbr* ▶ **proportional representation**.	cross-reference to full form
idioms in block at end of entry	**pretty I** *adj* joli; **it was not a ~ sight** ce n'était pas beau à voir. **II**○ *adv* (very) vraiment; (fairly) assez; **~ good** pas mal du tout. IDIOMS **~ as a picture** ravissant; **to be sitting ~**○ avoir une bonne situation, se la couler douce○.	examples register symbol ○ informal ◑ very informal ● vulgar or taboo
North American usage	**privilege** *n* **1** (honour, advantage) privilège *m*; **tax ~s** avantages *mpl* fiscaux; **2** (prerogative) apanage *m*; **3 (US)** (in finance) option *f*.	
	profess *vtr* **1** (claim) prétendre (**to do** de faire; **that** que); **2** (declare openly) faire profession de	structures, complementation giving information on how to use the translation
field labels for specialist terms	**program I** *n* **1** (Comput) programme *m*; **to run**	
North American variant spelling	**programme** (GB), **program** (US) **I** *n* **1** (single broadcast) émission *f* (**about** sur); (schedule of	
feminine ending in translation	**promising** *adj* [*situation, result, future*] prometteur/-euse; [*artist, candidate*] qui promet;	
page number cross-reference to a lexical usage note	**psychotherapist** ▶ **1580** *n* psychothérapeute *mf*.	
	punt *n* **1** (boat) barque *f* (*à fond plat*); **2** (Irish pound) livre *f* irlandaise.	explanatory gloss
separate entry for complex compound	**purpose-built** *adj* (GB) [*premises, stadium*] construit spécialement; **a ~ apartment** ≈ un appartement indépendant.	

Using this dictionary

Task 1 You have to write to a hotel to book a room

Goal Translate: **I would like to book a double room**

1 Pick out the main words to be translated

like *book* *double room*

---

2 Look up *like* and choose the part of speech or grammatical category

like² *vtr*

like² *vtr* **1** aimer bien [*person*]: aimer (bien) [*artist, food, music, style*]; **to ~ A best** préférer A; **to be well ~d** être apprécié; **to want**

---

3 Study the different senses of *like* to find the one you want

2 (wish)

fasse attendre; **2 (wish)** vouloir, aimer; **I would ~ a ticket** je voudrais un billet; **I would** or **should ~ to do** je voudrais or j'aimerais faire; **would you ~ to come to dinner?** voudriez-vous venir dîner?; **we'd ~ her to**

---

4 Within this sense category, see if there are examples similar to what you want to translate

I would or **should ~ to do**

Note the translation

je voudrais or **j'aimerais faire**

fasse attendre; **2** (wish) vouloir, aimer; **I would ~ a ticket** je voudrais un billet; **I would** or **should ~ to do** je voudrais or j'aimerais faire; **would you ~ to come to dinner?** voudriez-vous venir dîner?; **we'd ~ her to**

---

5 Now look up *book* and choose the appropriate grammatical and sense categories. For the translation, look for the context (in square brackets) closest to your own

[*room*]

Note the translation

réserver

book I *n* **1** livre *m* (**about** sur; **of** de); **history ~** livre d'histoire; **to go by the ~** (figurative) suivre le règlement; **2** (exercise book) cahier *m*; **3** (of cheques, tickets, vouchers, stamps) carnet *m*; **~ of matches** pochette *f* d'allumettes.
II books *n pl* **1** (accounts) comptabilité *f*; **to keep the ~s** tenir les comptes; **2** (records of firm, business) registre *m*.
III *vtr* **1** réserver [*table*, **room**, *taxi, ticket*]; faire les réservations pour [*holiday*]; engager

III *vtr* **1 réserver** [*table, room, taxi, ticket*]; faire les réservations pour [*holiday*]; engager [*babysitter, entertainer*]; **to be fully ~ed** être complet/-ète; **2** (charge) [*policeman*] dresser un

---

6 Look up *double room* which you'll find listed in alphabetical order with other compounds of *double*

double: ~ room *n*

Note the translation

chambre *f* pour deux personnes

The *f* tells you that the French word *chambre* is feminine in gender

double: **~ room** *n* chambre *f* pour deux personnes; **~ saucepan** *n* (GB) ≈ bain-marie *m inv*; **~ spacing** *n* double interligne *m*.

double: **~ room** *n* **chambre *f* pour deux personnes**; **~ saucepan** *n* (GB) ≈ bain-marie *m inv*; **~ spacing** *n* double interligne *m*.

Result You can now write your sentence in French **je voudrais réserver une chambre pour deux personnes**

Task 2 On the telephone, you tell someone that you will contact him/her at a later date

Goal Translate:	**I'll call you back next Thursday**
1 *Call* and *back* work together in English, so look up *call* and scan the entry until you find the block with this type of verb **■ call back: ¶ ~ back 1** (on phone)	**■ call away: ~ [sb] away** appeler; **to be ~ed away** être obligé de s'absenter. **■ call back: ¶ ~ back 1** (on phone) rappeler; **2** (return) repasser; **¶ ~ [sb] back** rappeler [*person*]. **■ call for: ~ for [sth] 1** (shout) appeler à
2 Study the information to see what pattern your phrase matches **¶ ~ [sb] back** Note the translation **rappeler**	**■ call back: ¶ ~ back 1** (on phone) rappeler; **2** (return) repasser; **¶ ~ [sb] back** rappeler [*person*]. **■ call back: ¶ ~ back 1** (on phone) rappeler; **2** (return) repasser; **¶ ~ [sb] back rappeler** [*person*].
3 To find out how to form the future tense of *rappeler*, you must consult the French entry **rappeler**/ʀaple/**[19] I** *vtr* **~ qch . . .**	**rappeler** /ʀaple/ **[19] I** *vtr* **1 ~ qch à qn** to remind sb of sth; **rappelons-le** let's not forget; **2** to remind [sb] of; **vous me rappelez votre sœur** you remind me of your sister; **3** (on
4 The number 19 tells you where to find the model for conjugating *rappeler* in the French verb tables **je rappellerai**	**19 appeler** ll *before mute* e — j'appelle, -es, -e, -ent l — nous appelons, -ez
5 Consult the entry for *you*. You will see that there is a cross-reference to a boxed usage note Scan the note to find a model for your sentence *she knows you* = elle **vous** connaît = elle **te** connaît	**you** ◆ In English *you* is used to address every. . . **Remember that in French the object and indirect object pronouns are always placed before the verb:** *she knows **you*** = elle **vous** connaît = elle **te** connaît
6 Look up *Thursday*. You will see a cross-reference code number **▶584** Consult the usage note on **Dates, Days, and Months** and scan the typical examples of use to find a model for your phrase *last/next Monday* Note the translation lundi prochain	**thundery** *adj* orageux/-euse. **Thursday ▶584** *pr n* jeudi *m*. **thus** *adv* ainsi; **~ far** jusqu'à présent. *early on Monday* = lundi matin de bonne heure *late on Monday* = lundi soir tard *last/next Monday* = lundi dernier/prochain *the Monday before last* = l'autre lundi *last/next Monday* = lundi dernier/prochain
Result You can now translate your sentence into French.	**je te rappellerai jeudi prochain**

Task 3 You want to know what the weather forecast will be, so you consult a local newspaper under 'Météo'

Goal Work out what the following information means: **Temps plus frais avec éclaircies de courte durée**

1 Isolate the words which you need to translate

temps frais éclaircies durée

2 Look up *temps* and select the translation most appropriate to your context

1 weather

temps /tɑ̃/ *nm inv* **1** weather; **un beau ~** fine weather; **quel beau/sale ~!** what lovely/awful weather!; **le ~ est à la pluie** it looks like rain; **quel ~ fait-il?** what's the weather like?; **par tous les ~** in all weathers; **2** time;

Now look up *frais* and repeat step 2

1 cool; cold

frais, fraîche /fʀɛ, fʀɛʃ/ **I** *adj* **1** cool; cold; **'servir ~'** 'serve chilled'; **il fait ~ ce matin** it's cool this morning; (colder) it's chilly this morning; **2** [*news, snow*] fresh; [*paint*] wet; **de**

3 Look up *éclaircies*. You will find that nouns are generally given in the singular in the wordlist

éclaircie /eklɛʀsi/ *nf*

éclairagiste /eklɛʀaʒist/ *nm* (in theatre, films) electrician.
éclaircie /eklɛʀsi/ *nf* sunny spell.
éclaircir /eklɛʀsiʀ/ [3] **I** *vtr* **1** to lighten

Note the translation

sunny spell

éclaircie /eklɛʀsi/ *nf* sunny spell.

4 Look up *durée*. Scan the entry for potential translations. You notice that there is an example which resembles the phrase you have read

de courte ~

durée /dyʀe/ *nf* **1** (of reign, studies) length; (of contract) term; (of record, cassette) playing time; **pour** or **pendant (toute) la ~ de** for the duration of; **séjour d'une ~ de trois mois** three-month stay; **contrat à ~ déterminée** fixed-term contract; **de courte ~** [*peace*] short-lived; [*absence*] brief; [*loan*] short-term; **de longue ~** [*loan, contract*] long-term; [*absence*] long; **2 ~ (de vie)** life; **pile longue ~** long-life battery; **3** (Mus) (of note) value.

5 Study the context information in square brackets to see if there is anything to match yours

[*peace*] [*absence*] [*loan*]

fixed-term contract; **de courte ~** [*peace*] short-lived; **[*absence*]** brief; **[*loan*]** short-term; **de longue ~** [*loan, contract*] long-term; [*absence*]

There is no direct weather context but do any of the translations work for your phrase?

brief

short-lived; [*absence*] **brief**; [*loan*] short-term;

Result You now know what the weather will be like. **cooler weather with brief sunny spells**

Task 4 You are in a restaurant but you're not sure the menu caters for you

Goal Ask in French: **Do you have anything for vegetarians?**

1 If you need to know how to ask a question like this in French, look up *do*. Note that there is a cross-reference to a usage note on *do* and its grammatical uses

do I *v aux* ▶599|

do I *v aux* ▶599| **own up, did you or didn't you take my pen?** avoue, est-ce que c'est toi qui as pris mon stylo ou pas?; **didn't he look wonderful!** il était beau, hein?; **don't**

2 Scan the note. There is a heading which deals with questions. Study the information and examples—is there anything you can use as a model?

est-ce que + *subject* + *verb*
***do** you like Mozart?*
est-ce que tu aimes Mozart?

Remember that, as you will be using the formal 'vous' to translate 'you', you will need to adapt the model slightly

est-ce que vous avez . . .

Grammatical functions of *do*, auxiliary verb

In questions

In French there is no auxiliary verb in questions equivalent to ***do*** in English.

When the subject is a pronoun, use either of these structures: *verb* + *hyphen* + *subject* or, less formally, ***est-ce que*** + *subject* + *verb*:

***do** you like Mozart?* = aimes-tu Mozart?
= **est-ce que** tu aimes Mozart?

3 Now look up *anything*. Check the entry for the sense you need.

1 (in questions, conditional . . .)

anything *pron* **1** (in questions, conditional sentences) quelque chose; **if ~ happens to her** s'il lui arrive quoi que ce soit; **is there ~ to be done?** peut-on faire quelque chose?; **is there ~ in the rumour that...?** est-il vrai

Note the translation

quelque chose

anything *pron* **1** (in questions, conditional sentences) quelque chose; **if ~ happens to her** s'il lui arrive quoi que ce soit; **is there ~ to**

4 Look up *vegetarian*. In the entry, the noun and the adjective are merged but the information on the gender of the noun is given in brackets.

vegetarian *n, adj* végétarien/-ienne (*m/f*)

vegetarian *n, adj* végétarien/-ienne (*m/f*).
vegetarianism *n* végétarisme *m*.
vegetate *vi* végéter.
vegetation *n* végétation *f*.
vehemence *n* (of speech, action) véhémence *f*; (of feelings) intensité *f*.

Note the translation

vegetarian *n, adj* végétarien/-ienne (*m/f*).

Result You should now be able to ask your question.

est-ce que vous avez quelque chose pour les végétariens?

Abbreviations and symbols

abbr	abbreviation
adj	adjective
adv	adverb
Anat	anatomy
Aut	automobile
aux	auxiliary
Bot	botany
Comput	computing
conj	conjunction
Culin	culinary
dem pron	demonstrative pronoun
det	determiner
Econ	economy
excl	exclamation
f	feminine
Fr	French
GB	British English
gen	generally
indic	indicative
inv	invariable
m	masculine
Med	medicine
Mil	military
Mus	music
n	noun
nf	feminine noun
nm	masculine noun
nmf	masculine and feminine noun
nm,f	masculine and feminine noun
Naut	nautical
phr	phrase
pl	plural
Pol	politics
pp	past participle
pp adj	past participle adjective
pr n	proper noun
pref	prefix
prep	preposition
pres p adj	present participle adjective
pron	pronoun
qch	quelque chose (something)
qn	quelqu'un (somebody)
quantif	quantifier
rel pron	relative pronoun
sb	somebody
Sch	school
sg	singular
sth	something
subj	subjunctive
Tech	technology
Univ	university
US	American English
v	verb
v aux	auxiliary verb
vi	intransitive verb
v impers	impersonal verb
v refl	reflexive verb
vtr	transitive verb
Zool	zoology
†	dated
®	trademark
○	colloquial
◑	very colloquial
●	vulgar or taboo
~	swung dash used as a substitute for a headword
GB	British spelling only: US spelling varies
≈	indicates an approximate translation equivalent
▶	cross-reference

Note on proprietary status This dictionary includes some words which have, or are asserted to have, proprietary status as trademarks or otherwise. Their inclusion does not imply that they have acquired for legal purposes a non-proprietary or general significance, nor any other judgement concerning their legal status. In cases where the editorial staff have some evidence that a word has proprietary status this is indicated in the entry for that word by the symbol ®, but no judgement concerning the legal status of such words is made or implied thereby.

The pronunciation of French

Vowels

a	*as in* patte	/pat/		œ	*as in* leur	/lœʀ/
ɑ	pâte	/pɑt/		œ̃	brun	/bʀœ̃/
ɑ̃	clan	/klɑ̃/		ø	deux	/dø/
e	dé	/de/		u	fou	/fu/
ɛ	belle	/bɛl/		y	pur	/pyʀ/
ɛ̃	lin	/lɛ̃/				
ə	demain	/dəmɛ̃/				
i	gris	/gʀi/				
o	gros	/gʀo/				
ɔ	corps	/kɔʀ/				
ɔ̃	long	/lɔ̃/				

Semi-vowels

j	*as in* fille	/fij/
ɥ	huit	/ɥit/
w	oui	/wi/

Consonants

b	*as in* bal	/bal/	ŋ	*as in* dancing	/dɑ̃siŋ/
d	dent	/dɑ̃/	p	porte	/pɔʀt/
f	foire	/fwaʀ/	ʀ	rire	/ʀiʀ/
g	gomme	/gɔm/	s	sang	/sɑ̃/
k	clé	/kle/	ʃ	chien	/ʃjɛ̃/
l	lien	/ljɛ̃/	t	train	/tʀɛ̃/
m	mer	/mɛʀ/	v	voile	/vwal/
n	nage	/naʒ/	z	zèbre	/zɛbʀ/
ɲ	gnon	/ɲɔ̃/	ʒ	jeune	/ʒœn/

The symbols used in this dictionary for the pronunciation of French are those of the IPA (International Phonetic Alphabet). Certain differences in pronunciation are shown in the phonetic transcription, although many speakers do not observe them—e.g. the long 'a' /ɑ/ in *pâte* and the short 'a' /a/ in *patte*, or the difference between the nasal vowels 'un' /œ̃/ as in *brun* and 'in' /ɛ̃/ as in *brin*.

Transcription

Each entry is followed by its phonetic transcription between slashes, with a few exceptions.

Morphological variations

The phonetic transcription of the plural and feminine forms of certain nouns and adjectives does not repeat the root, but shows only the change in ending. Therefore, in certain cases, the presentation of the entry does not correspond to that of the phonetic transcription e.g. *électricien, -ienne* /elɛktʀisjɛ̃, ɛn/.

Phrases

Full phonetic transcription is given for adverbial or prepositional phrases which are shown in alphabetical order within the main headword e.g. *emblée, d'emblée* /dɑ̃ble/, *plain-pied, de plain-pied* /d(ə)plɛ̃pje/.

Consonants

Aspiration of 'h'

Where it is impossible to make a liaison this is indicated by /'/ immediately after the slash e.g. *haine* /'ɛn/.

Assimilation

A voiced consonant can become unvoiced when it is followed by an unvoiced consonant within a word e.g. *absorber* /apsɔʀbe/.

Vowels

Open 'e' and closed 'e'

A clear distinction is made at the end of a word between a closed 'e' and an open 'e' e.g. *pré* /pʀe/ and *près* /pʀɛ/, *complet* /kɔ̃plɛ/ and *combler* /kɔ̃ble/.

Within a word the following rules apply:

- 'e' is always open in a syllable followed by a syllable containing a mute 'e' e.g. *règle* /ʀɛgl/, *réglementaire* /ʀɛgləmɑ̃tɛʀ/
- in careful speech 'e' is pronounced as a closed 'e' when it is followed by a syllable containing a closed vowel (*y, i, e*) e.g. *pressé* /pʀese/
- 'e' is pronounced as an open 'e' when it is followed by a syllable containing an open vowel e.g. *pressant* /pʀɛsɑ̃/.

Mute 'e'

The pronunciation of mute 'e' varies considerably depending on the level of language used and on the region from which the speaker originates. As a general rule it is only pronounced at the end of a word in the South of France or in poetry and it is, therefore, not shown. In an isolated word the mute 'e' preceded by a single consonant is dropped e.g. *parfaitement* /paʀfɛtmɑ̃/, but *probablement* /pʀɔbabləmɑ̃/.

In many cases the pronunciation of the mute 'e' depends on the surrounding context. Thus one would say *une reconnaissance de dette* /ynʀəkɔnɛsɑ̃sdədɛt/, but, *ma reconnaissance est éternelle* /maʀkɔnɛsɑ̃sɛteteʀnɛl/. The mute 'e' is shown in brackets in order to account for this phenomenon.

Stress

There is no real stress as such in French. In normal unemphasized speech a slight stress falls on the final syllable of a word or group of words, providing that it does not contain a mute 'e'. This is not shown in the phonetic transcription of individual entries.

I.V.

French–English Dictionary

a, **A** /a, ɑ/ **I** *nm inv* (letter) a, A; **de A à Z** from A to Z; **démontrer qch à qn par A plus B** to demonstrate sth conclusively to sb.

II A *nf* (*abbr* = **autoroute**) motorway (GB), freeway (US).

à /a/ *prep*

■ **Note** You will find translations for expressions such as *machine à écrire*, *aller à la pêche*, *difficile à vivre etc* at the entries ***machine***, ***pêche***, ***difficile*** *etc*.
– For the uses of *à* with the verbs *aller*, *être*, *avoir*, *penser etc*, see the entries for these verbs.

1 to; **se rendre au travail** to go to work; **mener 3 ~ 2** to lead 3 (to) 2; **2** at; in; **~ la maison** at home; **~ Paris** in Paris; **au 74 de la rue Bossuet** at 74 rue Bossuet; **au printemps** in (the) spring; **~ midi** at midday; **~ quatre kilomètres d'ici** four kilometres[GB] from here; **~ 100 kilomètres-heure** at 100 kilometres[GB] per or an hour; **un timbre ~ trois francs** a three-franc stamp; **(de) huit ~ dix heures par jour** between eight and ten hours a day; **3** with; **le garçon aux cheveux bruns** the boy with dark hair; **4 il est ~ plaindre** he's to be pitied; **je suis ~ vous tout de suite** I'll be with you in a minute; **c'est ~ qui de jouer?** whose turn is it?; **5 ~ qui est cette montre?** whose is this watch?; **elle est ~ elle** it's hers; **6 ~ nous tous on devrait y arriver** between all of us we should be able to manage; **~ trois on est serrés** with three people it's a squash; **7 ~ ce qu'il paraît, ~ ce que l'on dit** apparently; **~ y bien réfléchir** when you really think about it; **8 ~ ta santé, ~ la tienne!** cheers!; **~ tes souhaits!** bless you!

abaisser /abese/ [1] **I** *vtr* **1** to reduce [*prices*] (**à** to; **de** by); to lower [*standards*] ; **2** to pull down [*lever*]; to lower [*safety curtain, window*].

II s'abaisser *v refl* (+ *v être*) **1** [*stage curtain*] to fall; **2 s'~ à faire** to stoop to doing.

abandon /abɑ̃dɔ̃/ *nm* **1** state of neglect; **être à l'~** [*house*] to be abandoned; [*garden*] to be neglected; **2** (of project, method) abandonment; (of right) relinquishment; **3** (from race, competition) withdrawal (**de** from); **vainqueur par ~** winner by default.

■ **~ du domicile conjugal** desertion of the marital home; **~ de poste** desertion (of one's post).

abandonner /abɑ̃dɔne/ [1] **I** *vtr* **1** (gen) to give up; (in school) to drop [*subject*]; **~ la partie** to throw in the towel; **2** (Sport) (from game, tournament) to withdraw; to retire; **3** to leave [*person, place*]; to abandon [*car, object*]; **4** to abandon [*child, animal*]; to desert [*home, wife, post, cause*]; **5** [*courage, chance*] to fail [*person*].

II *v refl* (+ *v être*) **s'~ au désespoir** to give in to despair.

abasourdir /abazuʀdiʀ/ [3] *vtr* to stun.

abat-jour /abaʒuʀ/ *nm inv* lampshade.

abats /aba/ *nm pl* offal; (of poultry) giblets.

abattement /abatmɑ̃/ *nm* **1** despondency; **2** reduction; **~ fiscal** tax allowance (GB) or deduction (US).

abattoir /abatwaʀ/ *nm* slaughterhouse.

abattre /abatʀ/ [61] **I** *vtr* **1** to shoot [sb] down [*person*]; to shoot [*animal*]; to slaughter [*cattle, sheep*]; **2** to pull down [*building*]; to knock down [*wall*]; to shoot down [*plane*]; [*person*] to fell [*tree*]; [*gale, storm*] to bring down [*tree, pylon*]; **3** to show [*card, hand*]; **~ ses cartes** to put one's cards on the table; **4** to demoralize; **5** to get through [*work*].

II s'abattre *v refl* (+ *v être*) **s'~ sur** [*storm*] to break over; [*rain*] to beat down on [*town, countryside*]; [*bird of prey*] to swoop down on.

abbaye /abei/ *nf* abbey.

abbé /abe/ *nm* **1** priest; **2** abbot.

abcès /apsɛ/ *nm inv* abscess; **crever** or **vider l'~** to resolve a crisis.

abdiquer /abdike/ [1] *vi* **1** [*sovereign*] to abdicate; **2** to surrender.

abdomen /abdɔmɛn/ *nm* abdomen, stomach.

abdominal, **~e**, *mpl* **-aux** /abdɔminal, o/ **I** *adj* abdominal.

II abdominaux *nm pl* **1** abdominal muscles; **2** (Sport) stomach exercises.

abeille /abɛj/ *nf* bee.

aberrant, **~e** /abɛʀɑ̃, ɑ̃t/ *adj* **1** absurd; **2** aberrant.

aberration /abɛʀasjɔ̃/ *nf* aberration.

abîme /abim/ *nm* **1** abyss; **2** (figurative) gulf.

abîmer /abime/ [1] **I** *vtr* to damage.

II s'abîmer *v refl* (+ *v être*) **1** [*object*] to get damaged; [*fruit*] to spoil; **2 s'~ la vue** to ruin one's eyesight.

abject, **~e** /abʒɛkt/ *adj* despicable, abject; **de façon ~e** despicably.

abjection /abʒɛksjɔ̃/ *nf* abjection.

ablation /ablasjɔ̃/ *nf* excision, removal.

abnégation /abnegasjɔ̃/ *nf* self-sacrifice.

aboiement /abwamɑ̃/ *nm* barking.

abois /abwa/ *nm pl* **aux ~** at bay; in desperate straits.

abolir /abɔliʀ/ [3] *vtr* to abolish.

abominable /abɔminabl/ *adj* abominable.

abondamment /abɔ̃damɑ̃/ *adv* [*drink*] a lot; [*illustrate*] amply; **rincer ~** rinse thoroughly.

abondance /abɔ̃dɑ̃s/ *nf* **1** (of information) wealth; (of resources) abundance; **2** affluence.

abondant, **~e** /abɔ̃dɑ̃, ɑ̃t/ *adj* [*food, harvest*] plentiful; [*source*] rich; [*illustrations*] numerous; [*hair*] thick; [*vegetation*] lush.

abonder /abɔ̃de/ [1] *vi* [*fruit, fish, game*] to be plentiful; [*examples*] to abound.
IDIOMS **~ dans le sens de qn** to agree wholeheartedly with sb.

abonné, **~e** /abɔne/ **I** *pp* ▶ **abonner**.
II *pp adj* **être ~** to subscribe (**à** to).
III *nm,f* **1** subscriber; **2** season ticket holder.

abonnement /abɔnmɑ̃/ *nm* **1** subscription; **2** (**carte d'**)**~** season ticket.

abonner /abɔne/ [1] **I** *vtr* **1 ~ qn à qch** (to magazine, TV channel) to take out a subscription to sth for sb; **2** (for theatre, concerts) to buy sb a season ticket for sth.
II s'abonner *v refl* (+ *v être*) **1** to subscribe (**à** to); **2** to buy a season ticket (**à** for).

abord /abɔʀ/ **I** *nm* **1** manner; **elle est d'un ~ difficile** she is rather unapproachable; **2 être d'un ~ aisé** [*subject, book*] to be accessible; **3 au premier ~** at first sight.
II d'abord *phr* first; **j'ai d'~ cru à une mauvaise plaisanterie** at first I thought it was a bad joke; **tout d'~** first of all.
III abords *nm pl* area around.

abordable /abɔʀdabl/ *adj* [*product, price*] affordable; [*text*] accessible.

abordage /abɔʀdaʒ/ *nm* (Naut) **1** collision; **2** (by pirates, enemy) boarding.

aborder /abɔʀde/ [1] **I** *vtr* **1** to tackle [*problem, subject*]; **2** to approach [*person, obstacle*]; **3** [*traveller, ship*] to reach [*place, shore*].
II *vi* [*traveller, ship*] to land.

aborigène /abɔʀiʒɛn/ **I** *adj* Aboriginal.
II *nmf* Aborigine.

aboutir /abutiʀ/[3] **I aboutir à** *v+prep* **1** [*street, stairs*] to lead to; [*person*] to end up in [*place*]; **2** to lead to [*agreement, result, breach*].
II *vi* [*negotiations, project*] to succeed; **ne pas ~** not to come off.

aboutissement /abutismɑ̃/ *nm* **1** culmination; **2** (successful) outcome.

aboyer /abwaje/ [23] *vi* [*dog*] to bark (**après** at); [*person*] to shout (**après** at).

abracadabrant, **~e** /abʀakadabʀɑ̃, ɑ̃t/ *adj* bizarre.

abrasif, **-ive** /abʀazif, iv/ *adj* abrasive.

abrégé /abʀeʒe/ *nm* **1** summary; **2** (book) concise guide.

abréger /abʀeʒe/ [15] *vtr* **1** to shorten [*word, expression*]; **2** to cut short [*visit, career*].

abreuver: **s'abreuver** /abʀøve/ [1] *v refl* (+ *v être*) [*animal*] to drink.

abreuvoir /abʀøvwaʀ/ *nm* **1** watering place; **2** drinking trough.

abréviation /abʀevjasjɔ̃/ *nf* abbreviation.

abri /abʀi/ *nm* **1** shelter; **2** shed; **3 personne n'est à l'~ d'un accident** accidents can happen to anybody.

abricot /abʀiko/ *nm* apricot.

abricotier /abʀikɔtje/ *nm* apricot tree.

abriter /abʀite/ [1] **I** *vtr* **1** [*building*] to shelter [*people, animals*]; **2** [*country, region*] to provide a habitat for [*animals, plant life*].
II s'abriter *v refl* (+ *v être*) to take shelter, to take cover.

abroger /abʀɔʒe/ [13] *vtr* to repeal.

abrupt, **~e** /abʀypt/ *adj* **1** [*hill, road*] steep; [*cliff*] sheer; **2** [*person, tone*] abrupt.

abruptement /abʀyptəmɑ̃/ *adv* **1** steeply; **2** suddenly; abruptly.

abruti, **~e** /abʀyti/ *nm,f* (offensive) moron○.

abrutir /abʀytiʀ/ [3] **I** *vtr* [*noise*] to deafen; [*heat*] to wear [sb] out; [*alcohol, medication, fatigue*] to have a numbing effect on; [*blow*] to stun.
II s'abrutir *v refl* (+ *v être*) **1** to become dull-witted; **2 s'~ de travail** to wear oneself out with work.

abrutissant, **~e** /abʀytisɑ̃, ɑ̃t/ *adj* [*music, noise*] deafening; [*heat*] exhausting; [*job*] mind-numbing.

absence /apsɑ̃s/ *nf* **1** absence; **briller par son ~** to be conspicuous by one's absence; **2** lack; **l'~ de pluie** the lack of rain.

absent, **~e** /apsɑ̃, ɑ̃t/ **I** *adj* **1 être ~** to be away; (for brief spell) to be out; **2** [*pupil, employee*] absent; **3** (missing) absent (**de** from); **4** absent-minded.
II *nm,f* absentee.

absenter: **s'absenter** /apsɑ̃te/ [1] *v refl* (+ *v être*) to go away; to go out.

absolu, **~e** /apsɔly/ **I** *adj* absolute; [*rule*] hard and fast.
II *nm* absolute.

absolument /apsɔlymɑ̃/ *adv* absolutely.

absolution /apsɔlysjɔ̃/ *nf* absolution (**de qch** for sth).

absolutisme /apsɔlytism/ *nm* absolutism.

absorbant, **~e** /apsɔʀbɑ̃, ɑ̃t/ *adj* **1** [*substance*] absorbent; **2** [*job, work*] absorbing.

absorber /apsɔʀbe/ [1] *vtr* **1** [*material, plant*] to absorb; **2** to take [*food, medicine*]; **3** to occupy [*mind*]; **4** [*company*] to take over; [*party, group*] to absorb.

absorption /apsɔʀpsjɔ̃/ *nf* **1** (of liquid, oxygen) absorption; **2** (of food, medicine) taking; **3** (of a business, company) takeover.

abstenir: **s'abstenir** /apstəniʀ/ [36] *v refl* (+ *v être*) **1** (from voting) to abstain; **2 s'~ de faire** to refrain from doing; **'pas sérieux s'~'** 'no time-wasters'.

abstention /apstɑ̃sjɔ̃/ *nf* abstention.

abstinence /apstinɑ̃s/ *nf* abstinence.

abstraction /apstʀaksjɔ̃/ *nf* abstraction; **faire ~ de** to set aside.

abstrait, **~e** /apstʀɛ, ɛt/ **I** *adj* abstract.
II *nm* (gen) abstract; (art) abstract art.

absurde /apsyʀd/ *adj, nm* absurd.

absurdité /apsyʀdite/ *nf* **1** absurdity; **2 dire des ~s** to talk nonsense.

abus /aby/ *nm inv* abuse; **il y a de l'~**○**!** that's a bit much○!

abuser /abyze/ [1] **I** *vtr* to fool; **se laisser ~** to be taken in.
II abuser de *v+prep* **1 ~ de l'alcool** to drink to excess; **~ des sucreries** to over-

indulge in sweet things; **2 ~ de** to exploit [*situation, credibility*]; **je ne voudrais pas ~ (de votre gentillesse)** I don't want to impose (on your kindness); **3 ~ de qn** to sexually abuse sb.
III *vi* to go too far.
IV **s'abuser** *v refl* (+ *v être*) **si je ne m'abuse** if I'm not mistaken.

abusif, -ive /abyzif, iv/ *adj* **1** excessive; **2** unfair; wrongful; **3** improper; **4** over-possessive.

acabit /akabi/ *nm* **de cet** or **du même ~** of that sort.

acacia /akasja/ *nm* **1** (European) **(faux) ~** locust tree, false acacia; **2** (tropical) acacia.

académicien, -ienne /akademisjɛ̃, ɛn/ *nm,f* **1** academician; **2** *member of the Académie française.*

académie /akademi/ *nf* (Sch) ≈ local education authority (GB), school district (US).

acajou /akaʒu/ *nm* mahogany.

acariâtre /akaʀjɑtʀ/ *adj* cantankerous.

accablant, ~e /akablɑ̃, ɑ̃t/ *adj* [*heat, silence*] oppressive; [*sadness*] overwhelming; [*evidence, testimony*] damning.

accabler /akable/ [1] *vtr* **1** [*bad news*] to devastate; **être accablé par** [*heat, grief*] to be overcome by; **2** [*testimony, inquiry, person*] to condemn.

accalmie /akalmi/ *nf* **1** lull; **2** slack period.

accaparant, ~e /akapaʀɑ̃, ɑ̃t/ *adj* very demanding.

accaparer /akapaʀe/ [1] *vtr* to corner [*market*]; to monopolize [*person, power*]; to preoccupy [*mind*].

accéder: **accéder à** /aksede/ [14] *v+prep* **1 ~ à** to reach [*place*]; **2 ~ à** to achieve [*fame, glory*]; to obtain [*job*]; to rise to [*high office*].

accélérateur /akseleʀatœʀ/ *nm* (Aut) accelerator.

accélération /akseleʀasjɔ̃/ *nf* acceleration.

accélérer /akseleʀe/ [14] **I** *vtr* to speed up [*rhythm, movement, process*]; **~ le pas** or **l'allure** to quicken one's step or pace.
II *vi* [*driver*] to accelerate.
III s'accélérer *v refl* (+ *v être*) [*movement*] to become faster; [*phenomenon*] to accelerate

accent /aksɑ̃/ *nm* **1** (of person, region) accent; **2** (on a letter) accent; **3** (on a syllable) **~ tonique** stress; **mettre l'~ sur qch** (figurative) to put the emphasis on sth; **4 ~ de sincérité** hint of sincerity.

accentuation /aksɑ̃tɥasjɔ̃/ *nf* (of crisis) escalation; (of inequality) heightening; (of problem) worsening; (of tendency) increase.

accentuer /aksɑ̃tɥe/ [1] **I** *vtr* **1** (gen) to emphasize, to accentuate; **2** to heighten [*tension*]; to increase [*tendency*]; **3** (in pronouncing) to stress.
II s'accentuer *v refl* (+ *v être*) to become more marked.

acceptable /aksɛptabl/ *adj* acceptable; passable; satisfactory.

acceptation /aksɛptasjɔ̃/ *nf* acceptance; **sous réserve d'~** subject to acceptance.

accepter /aksɛpte/ [1] *vtr* to accept [*invitation, person*]; to agree to [*condition, contract*].

accès /aksɛ/ *nm inv* **1** access; **d'un ~ facile/difficile** [*place*] easy/difficult to get to; **toutes les voies d'~ sont barrées** all approach roads are closed off; **'~ aux quais'** 'to the trains'; **'~ interdit'** 'no entry'; **l'~ à** access to [*profession, course*]; admission to [*club, school*]; **2 ~ de colère** fit of anger; **~ de fièvre** bout of fever; **par ~** by fits and starts.

accessible /aksesibl/ *adj* **1** [*place, book, information*] accessible; **2 ~ à** [*job*] open to; **3** [*price, fare*] affordable.

accession /aksesjɔ̃/ *nf* **~ à** accession to [*throne, power*]; attainment of [*independence*]; **~ à la propriété** home-buying.

accessoire /akseswaʀ/ **I** *adj* [*problem, detail*] incidental.
II *nm* **1** accessory; (for household appliance) attachment; **~s de toilette** toilet requisites; **2** (in the theatre) **~s** props.

accessoirement /akseswaʀmɑ̃/ *adv* **1** incidentally, as it happens; **2** if desired.

accident /aksidɑ̃/ *nm* **1** accident; **2** hitch; mishap; **~ de parcours**○ hitch; accident; **3 ~ de terrain** bit of uneven ground.
■ **~ corporel** accident involving injury; **~ domestique** accident in the home.

accidenté, ~e /aksidɑ̃te/ **I** *adj* **1** [*person*] injured; [*car*] involved in an accident; **2** [*road, ground*] uneven.
II *nm,f* accident victim.

accidentel, -elle /aksidɑ̃tɛl/ *adj* accidental.

accidentellement /aksidɑ̃tɛlmɑ̃/ *adv* **1** in an accident; **2** by accident, accidentally.

acclamation /aklamasjɔ̃/ *nf* cheering; **sous les ~s de** to the cheering of.

acclamer /aklame/ [1] *vtr* to cheer, to acclaim.

acclimater /aklimate/ [1] **I** *vtr* to acclimatize.
II s'acclimater *v refl* (+ *v être*) [*plant, animal*] to become acclimatized; [*person*] to adapt.

accointances /akwɛ̃tɑ̃s/ *nf pl* contacts.

accolade /akɔlad/ *nf* embrace.

accoler /akɔle/ [1] *vtr* **~ un bâtiment à** to build a building right next to.

accommodant, ~e /akɔmɔdɑ̃, ɑ̃t/ *adj* [*person*] accommodating.

accommoder /akɔmɔde/ [1] **I** *vtr* to prepare.
II *vi* [*eyes*] to focus.
III s'accommoder *v refl* (+ *v être*) **s'~ de qch** to make the best of sth; to put up with sth.

accompagnateur, -trice /akɔ̃paɲatœʀ, tʀis/ *nm,f* **1** (Mus) accompanist; **2** (with children) accompanying adult; (with tourists) courier.

accompagnement /akɔ̃paɲmɑ̃/ *nm* accompaniment; **~ musical** musical arrangement.

accompagner /akɔ̃paɲe/ [1] *vtr* **1** [*person*] to accompany, to go with, to come with; **2** to accompany [*phenomenon, event*]; **3** (Mus) to accompany (**à** on); **4** [*wine, vegetables*] to be served with.

accomplir /akɔ̃pliʀ/ [3] **I** *vtr* to accomplish

[*task*]; to fulfil[GB] [*obligation*]; to serve [*prison sentence*].

II **s'accomplir** *v refl* (+ *v être*) to be fulfilled.

accomplissement /akɔ̃plismɑ̃/ *nm* (of mission) accomplishment, fulfilment[GB]; (of ambition, aim) realization, achievement.

accord /akɔʀ/ *nm* **1** agreement; (tacit) understanding; **conclure un ~** to enter into an agreement; **d'~** all right, OK○; **je suis d'~** I agree (**avec** with); **se mettre** or **tomber d'~** to come to an agreement; **2** harmony; **3** (in grammar) **~ en genre/en nombre** gender/number agreement; **4** (Mus) chord.

accordéon /akɔʀdeɔ̃/ *nm* accordion; **plier qch en ~** to fold sth into pleats; **porte ~** folding door.

accordéoniste /akɔʀdeɔnist/ *nmf* accordion-player.

accorder /akɔʀde/ [1] **I** *vtr* **1 ~ qch à qn** to grant sb sth [*favour, loan, interview, permission, right*]; to give sb sth [*grant, reduction, chance*]; **2** to attach [*importance, value*] (**à** to); to pay [*attention*]; **3 il n'a pas entièrement tort, je te l'accorde** he's not entirely wrong, I'll give you that; **4** (Mus) to tune [*instrument*]; **5** to make [sth] agree [*word, adjective ending*].

II **s'accorder** *v refl* (+ *v être*) **1** to give oneself [*rest, time off*]; **2** to agree (**sur** about, on); **3** [*colours, clothes*] to go (together) well; **4** [*adjective, verb*] to agree (**avec** with).

accordeur /akɔʀdœʀ/ *nm* tuner.

accoster /akɔste/ [1] **I** *vtr* to accost [*person*].

II *vi* [*ship*] to dock.

accotement /akɔtmɑ̃/ *nm* verge; **~ non stabilisé** soft verge or shoulder.

accouchement /akuʃmɑ̃/ *nm* delivery; **~ par le siège** breech birth.

accoucher /akuʃe/ [1] *vi* to give birth.

accoucheur /akuʃœʀ/ *nm* **médecin ~** obstetrician.

accouder: **s'accouder** /akude/ [1] *v refl* (+ *v être*) to lean on one's elbows (**à, sur** on).

accoudoir /akudwaʀ/ *nm* arm-rest.

accouplement /akupləmɑ̃/ *nm* **1** mating; **2** (Tech) coupling.

accourir /akuʀiʀ/ [26] *vi* to run up.

accoutrement /akutʀəmɑ̃/ *nm* get-up○.

accoutrer /akutʀe/ [1] **I** *vtr* **~ qn de qch** to rig sb out in sth.

II **s'accoutrer** *v refl* (+ *v être*) to get oneself up (**de** in).

accoutumance /akutymɑ̃s/ *nf* (to a drug) addiction (**à** to).

accoutumé, **~e** /akutyme/ *adj* customary.

accoutumer /akutyme/ [1] **I** *vtr* to accustom (**à** to).

II **s'accoutumer** *v refl* (+ *v être*) to grow accustomed (**à** to).

accrédité, **~e** /akʀedite/ *adj* [*supplier, dealer*] authorized.

accréditer /akʀedite/ [1] *vtr* **1** to give credence to [*rumour*]; **2** to accredit [*ambassador*].

accro○ /akʀo/ *adj* hooked○ (**à** on).

accroc /akʀo/ *nm* **1** tear (**à** in); **2 se dérouler sans ~(s)** to take place without a hitch.

accrochage /akʀɔʃaʒ/ *nm* (between people) clash; (between vehicles) collision.

accrocher /akʀɔʃe/ [1] **I** *vtr* **1** to hang (**à** from); **2** to hook [sth] on (**à** to); **3** to catch [*stocking, sweater*] (**à** on); **4** to bump into [*vehicle*]; **5** to catch [*eye, attention*].

II **s'accrocher** *v refl* (+ *v être*) **1** (to ledge) to hang on; (to post) to cling (on) (**à** to); **2** [*person*] **s'~ à qn** to cling to sb; **3 l'hameçon s'est accroché à ma veste** the hook got caught in my jacket; **4**○ **s'~ pour faire** to try hard to do.

IDIOMS **avoir le cœur** or **l'estomac bien accroché** to have a strong stomach.

accroissement /akʀwasmɑ̃/ *nm* growth, increase (**de** in).

accroître /akʀwatʀ/ [72] *vtr*, **s'accroître** *v refl* (+ *v être*) to increase.

accroupir: **s'accroupir** /akʀupiʀ/ [3] *v refl* (+ *v être*) to squat (down); (hiding) to crouch (down).

accru, **~e** /akʀy/ *pp* ▶ **accroître**.

accueil /akœj/ *nm* **1** welcome, reception; **2** reception desk.

accueillant, **~e** /akœjɑ̃, ɑ̃t/ *adj* **1** hospitable, welcoming; **2** homely (GB), homey (US).

accueillir /akœjiʀ/ [27] *vtr* **1** to welcome; **2** to receive, to greet; **3** [*room, hotel*] to accommodate; **4** [*hospital, organization*] to cater for.

acculer /akyle/ [1] *vtr* **~ qn à la ruine/au désespoir** to drive sb to ruin/to despair.

accumulateur /akymylatœʀ/ *nm* storage battery.

accumulation /akymylasjɔ̃/ *nf* **1** accumulation; **une ~ de preuves** a mass of evidence; **2** storage.

accumuler /akymyle/ [1] **I** *vtr* **1** to store (up) [*things*]; to accumulate [*wealth, capital*]; to make a succession of [*mistakes*]; **2** to store (up) [*energy, heat*].

II **s'accumuler** *v refl* (+ *v être*) [*snow, rubbish*] to pile up; [*stocks, debts*] to accrue.

accusation /akyzasjɔ̃/ *nf* **1** accusation; (Law) charge; **2** prosecution.

accusé, **~e** /akyze/ **I** *pp* ▶ **accuser**.

II *pp adj* [*features*] strong; [*wrinkles*] deep; [*relief*] marked.

III *nm,f* defendant; **les ~s** the accused.

■ **~ de réception** acknowledgement (of receipt).

accuser /akyze/ [1] **I** *vtr* **1** to accuse [*person*]; to blame [*fate*]; [*evidence*] to point to [*person*]; [*judge*] to charge [*defendant*] (**de** with); **~ qn/qch de tous les maux** to put all the blame on sb/sth; **2** to show, to register [*fall, deficit*].

II **s'accuser** *v refl* (+ *v être*) **1** [*person*] to take the blame; **2** to become more marked.

IDIOMS **~ le coup** to be visibly shaken.

acerbe /asɛʀb/ *adj* acerbic.

acéré, **~e** /aseʀe/ *adj* sharp.

acétique /asetik/ *adj* acetic.

acharné, **~e** /aʃaʀne/ *adj* [*supporter*]

passionate; [*smoker*] incorrigible; [*work*] unremitting; [*struggle, discussion*] fierce.

acharnement /aʃaʀnəmɑ̃/ *nm* furious energy.

acharner: **s'acharner** /aʃaʀne/ [1] *v refl* (+ *v être*) **1** to persevere; **s'~ contre** to fight against [*project*]; **2 s'~ sur** [*person, animal*] to keep going at [*victim, prey*]; (figurative) to hound [*person*]; [*fate*] to dog [*person, project*].

achat /aʃa/ *nm* purchase.

acheminement /aʃ(ə)minmɑ̃/ *nm* transportation.

acheminer /aʃ(ə)mine/ [1] **I** *vtr* to transport.

II s'acheminer *v refl* (+ *v être*) **s'~ vers** to make one's way toward(s); to move toward(s).

acheter /aʃte/ [18] **I** *vtr* to buy; **~ qch à qn** to buy sth from sb; to buy sth for sb, to buy sb sth.

II s'acheter *v refl* (+ *v être*) **1 s'~ qch** to buy oneself sth; **2 cela s'achète où?** where can you get it?

acheteur, **-euse** /aʃtœʀ, øz/ *nm,f* buyer, purchaser.

achevé, **~e** /aʃve/ *adj* [*style, technique*] accomplished; [*model*] perfect.

achèvement /aʃɛvmɑ̃/ *nm* (gen) completion; (of discussions) conclusion.

achever /aʃve/ [16] **I** *vtr* **1** to finish [*work*]; to conclude [*discussions*]; to complete [*project, inquiry*]; to end [*life*]; **2** to destroy [*animal*]; to finish off [*person*]; **3**° [*scandal, bankruptcy*] to finish [sb] off.

II s'achever *v refl* (+ *v être*) to end.

acide /asid/ **I** *adj* acid, sharp.

II *nm* **1** acid; **2**° (drug) acid°.

acidité /asidite/ *nf* acidity, tartness, sharpness.

acidulé, **~e** /asidyle/ *adj* [*flavour*] slightly acid; [*perfume*] tangy.

acier /asje/ **I** *adj inv* steel(y).

II *nm* steel; **d'~** [*girder, column*] steel; [*nerves*] of steel; **avoir un moral d'~** to be made of stern stuff.

aciérie /asjeʀi/ *nf* steelworks.

acné /akne/ *nf* acne; **~ juvénile** teenage acne.

acolyte /akɔlit/ *nmf* henchman, acolyte.

acompte /akɔ̃t/ *nm* **1** down payment; deposit; **2** part payment.

à-côté, *pl* **~s** /akote/ *nm* **1** perk; **2** extra expense; **3** extra profit.

à-coup, *pl* **~s** /aku/ *nm* jolt; **par ~s** by fits and starts.

acoustique /akustik/ **I** *adj* acoustic.

II *nf* acoustics.

acquéreur /akeʀœʀ/ *nm* buyer, purchaser.

acquérir /akeʀiʀ/ [35] **I** *vtr* **1** to acquire; (by buying) to purchase; **2** to acquire [*reputation*]; **~ la certitude que** to become convinced that.

II s'acquérir *v refl* (+ *v être*) **s'~ facilement** to be easy to acquire.

acquiescer /akjese/ [12] *vi* to acquiesce; **~ d'un signe de tête** to nod in agreement.

acquis, **~e** /aki, iz/ **I** *pp* ▶ **acquérir**.

II *pp adj* **1** [*skills*] acquired; **2** [*principle, right*] accepted, established; **les avantages ~** the gains; **tenir qch pour ~** to take sth for granted.

III *nm inv* **1** acquired knowledge; **2 ~ sociaux** social benefits.

IDIOMS **bien mal ~ ne profite jamais** (Proverb) ill-gotten gains never prosper.

acquisition /akizisjɔ̃/ *nf* **1** purchase; **2** (for library) acquisition; **3** (of language, citizenship) acquisition.

acquit /aki/ *nm* receipt; **pour ~** received.

IDIOMS **par ~ de conscience** to put my/his etc mind at rest.

acquittement /akitmɑ̃/ *nm* (Law) acquittal.

acquitter /akite/ [1] **I** *vtr* (Law) to acquit.

II s'acquitter *v refl* (+ *v être*) **s'~ de son devoir** to do one's duty; **s'~ d'une dette** to pay off a debt; to repay a debt of gratitude.

acre /akʀ/ *nf* acre.

âcre /ɑkʀ/ *adj* [*taste*] sharp; [*smell*] acrid.

acrobate /akʀɔbat/ *nmf* acrobat.

acrobatie /akʀɔbasi/ *nf* acrobatics.

acte /akt/ *nm* **1** act; **~ manqué** Freudian slip; **être libre de ses ~s** to do as one wishes; **faire ~ de candidature** to put oneself forward as a candidate; **2** (Law) deed; **~ de naissance** birth certificate; **~ de vente** bill of sale; **3** (in play) act.

acteur, **-trice** /aktœʀ, tʀis/ *nm,f* **1** actor/actress; **2** protagonist.

actif, **-ive** /aktif, iv/ **I** *adj* (gen) active; [*market*] buoyant; **la vie active** working life.

II *nm* **l'~** the assets; **à mettre à l'~ de qn** a point in sb's favour[GB].

action /aksjɔ̃/ *nf* **1** action, act; **une bonne ~** a good deed; **2 l'~** action; **passer à l'~** to act; **en ~** in operation; **moyens d'~** courses of action; **3** effect; **l'~ de qn sur** sb's influence on; **4 ~ en justice** legal action; **5** (in finance) share.

actionnaire /aksjɔnɛʀ/ *nmf* shareholder.

actionner /aksjɔne/ [1] *vtr* to activate, to operate.

activement /aktivmɑ̃/ *adv* actively.

activer /aktive/ [1] **I** *vtr* **1** to speed up [*work*]; to stimulate [*digestion*]; **2** [*wind*] to stir up [*flames*]; **3** to stoke [*fire*].

II s'activer° *v refl* (+ *v être*) to hurry up.

activiste /aktivist/ *adj, nmf* activist.

activité /aktivite/ *nf* **1** activity; **~ professionnelle** occupation; **2 être en pleine ~** [*street*] to be bustling with activity; [*person*] to be very busy; **volcan en ~** active volcano.

actrice *nf* ▶ **acteur**.

actualiser /aktɥalize/ [1] *vtr* to update, to bring [sth] up to date.

actualité /aktɥalite/ **I** *nf* **1** current affairs; **l'~ culturelle** cultural events; **être à la une de l'~** to be in the headlines; **2** topicality; **d'~** topical; **toujours d'~** still relevant today.

II actualités *nf pl* **1** news; **2** newsreel.

actuel, **-elle** /aktɥɛl/ *adj* **1** present, current; **2** [*film, discussion*] topical.

actuellement /aktɥɛlmɑ̃/ *adv* **1** at the moment; **2** currently.

acuité /akɥite/ *nf* **1** acuity; **2** shrillness; **3** (of pain) intensity.

acupuncture /akypɔ̃ktyʀ/ *nf* acupuncture.

adage /adaʒ/ *nm* saying, adage.

adaptation /adaptasjɔ̃/ *nf* adaptation.

adapté, ~e /adapte/ *adj* **1** suitable; **~ à** [*solution*] suited to; **2** (for TV, stage) adapted (**à, pour** for; **de** from).

adapter /adapte/ [1] **I** *vtr* **1** to fit (**à** to); **2** to adapt [*equipment*]; **3** to adapt [*novel*].
II s'adapter *v refl* (+ *v être*) **1** [*tool, part*] to fit; **2** to adapt, to adjust (**à** to).

additif /aditif/ *nm* **1** additive; **2** rider (**à** to).

addition /adisjɔ̃/ *nf* **1** addition; **2** bill, check (US).

additionner /adisjɔne/ [1] *vtr* to add up.

adepte /adɛpt/ *nmf* **1** (of theory) supporter; (of person) disciple; **2** enthusiast.

adéquat, ~e /adekwa, at/ *adj* **1** appropriate, suitable; **2** adequate.

adhérence /adeʀɑ̃s/ *nf* (of tyre, sole) grip.

adhérent, ~e /adeʀɑ̃, ɑ̃t/ **I** *adj* [*substance*] which adheres (**à** to).
II *nm,f* (of club, organization) member.

adhérer: **adhérer à** /adeʀe/ [14] *v+prep* **1** [*glue*] to stick to; [*tyre*] to grip; **2** to join, to become a member of.

adhésif, -ive /adezif, iv/ *adj* adhesive.

adhésion /adezjɔ̃/ *nf* **1** membership; **2** support (**à** for).

adieu, *pl* **~x** /adjø/ *nm* goodbye, farewell.

adipeux, -euse /adipø, øz/ *adj* fatty.

adjacent, ~e /adʒasɑ̃, ɑ̃t/ *adj* adjacent.

adjectif /adʒɛktif/ *nm* adjective.

adjoindre /adʒwɛ̃dʀ/ [56] *vtr* to add; **~ une pièce au dossier** to add a document to the file.

adjoint, ~e /adʒwɛ̃, ɛ̃t/ *nm,f* assistant; deputy; **~ au maire** deputy mayor.

adjudant /adʒydɑ̃/ *nm* ≈ warrant officer.

adjuger /adʒyʒe/ [13] *vtr* to auction; **une fois, deux fois, adjugé!** going, going, gone!

adjurer /adʒyʀe/ [1] *vtr* to implore.

admettre /admɛtʀ/ [60] *vtr* **1** to accept, to admit [*fact*]; **2** to admit [*person, student*] (**dans** to); **être admis à un examen** to pass an exam; **3 ~ que** to suppose (that).

administrateur, -trice /administʀatœʀ, tʀis/ *nm,f* **1** administrator; **2** director; **3** trustee.
■ **~ de biens** property manager.

administratif, -ive /administʀatif, iv/ *adj* **1** [*staff, building*] administrative; **2** [*report*] official.

administration /administʀasjɔ̃/ *nf* **1** administration; **2** civil service; **~ judiciaire** receivership; **~ pénitentiaire** prison service; **3** management; **4** (of drugs, sacrament) administration, giving; (of proof) furnishing.

administré, ~e /administʀe/ *nm,f* constituent.

administrer /administʀe/ [1] *vtr* **1** to administer [*funds*]; to run [*company, country*]; **2** to administer, to give [*drug, sacrament*]; **~ une correction à qn** to give sb a hiding.

admirable /admiʀabl/ *adj* admirable.

admirateur, -trice /admiʀatœʀ, tʀis/ *nm,f* admirer.

admiratif, -ive /admiʀatif, iv/ *adj* admiring.

admiration /admiʀasjɔ̃/ *nf* admiration.

admirer /admiʀe/ [1] *vtr* to admire.

admis, ~e /admi, iz/ **I** *pp* ▶ **admettre**.
II *pp adj* [*practice*] accepted; [*candidate*] successful; **bien ~** widely accepted.

admissibilité /admisibilite/ *nf* (in exam) eligibility (*to take oral after written examination*).

admissible /admisibl/ *adj* **1** acceptable; **2** eligible.

admission /admisjɔ̃/ *nf* admission; **service des ~s** reception.

ADN /adeɛn/ *nm* (*abbr* = **acide désoxyribonucléique**) DNA.

adolescence /adɔlesɑ̃s/ *nf* adolescence.

adolescent, ~e /adɔlesɑ̃, ɑ̃t/ **I** *adj* adolescent, teenage.
II *nm,f* teenager, adolescent.

adonner: **s'adonner** /adɔne/ [1] *v refl* (+ *v être*) **s'~ à** to devote all one's time to; **il s'adonne à la boisson** he drinks too much.

adopter /adɔpte/ [1] *vtr* to adopt [*child, method*]; to pass [*law*].

adoptif, -ive /adɔptif, iv/ *adj* **1** [*child, country*] adopted; **2** [*parent*] adoptive.

adoption /adɔpsjɔ̃/ *nf* **1** adoption; **2** (of law) passing; **pays d'~** adopted country.

adorable /adɔʀabl/ *adj* adorable.

adoration /adɔʀasjɔ̃/ *nf* worship, adoration.

adorer /adɔʀe/ [1] *vtr* to adore, to worship.

adosser: **s'adosser** /adose/ [1] *v refl* (+ *v être*) **s'~ à/contre** to lean back on/against.

adoucir /adusiʀ/ [3] **I** *vtr* to soften [*skin, water*]; to moderate [*tone of voice*]; to soothe [*throat*]; to alleviate [*poverty*]; to ease [*suffering*]; to mitigate [*harshness*].
II s'adoucir *v refl* (+ *v être*) [*temperature*] to become milder; [*light*] to become softer; [*slope*] to become more gentle.

adoucissant, ~e /adusisɑ̃, ɑ̃t/ **I** *adj* [*lotion*] soothing.
II *nm* softener.

adoucisseur /adusisœʀ/ *nm* **~ d'eau** water softener.

adrénaline /adʀenalin/ *nf* adrenalin.

adresse /adʀɛs/ *nf* **1** address; **se tromper d'~** to get the wrong address; to pick the wrong person; **remarque lancée à l'~ de qn** remark directed at sb; **2** dexterity; **3** skill; **4** address, speech.

adresser /adʀese/ [1] **I** *vtr* **1** to direct [*criticism*] (**à** at); to make [*request, declaration, appeal*]; to deliver [*ultimatum*]; to present [*petition*]; to aim [*blow*]; **~ la parole à qn** to speak to sb; **2** to send [*letter*]; **3** to refer [sb] (**à** to).
II s'adresser *v refl* (+ *v être*) **1 s'~ à qn** to speak to sb; **2 s'~ à** to contact [*embassy*]; **s'~ au guichet 8** to go to window 8; **3 s'~ à**

[*measure*] to be aimed at; **4 s'~ à** to appeal to [*conscience*].

adroit, **~e** /adʀwa, at/ *adj* skilful[GB]; clever; **être ~ de ses mains** to be good with one's hands.

adroitement /adʀwatmɑ̃/ *adv* skilfully[GB].

aduler /adyle/ [1] *vtr* to worship, to adulate.

adulte /adylt/ *adj, nmf* adult.

adultère /adyltɛʀ/ **I** *adj* adulterous.
II *nm* adultery.

advenir /advəniʀ/ [36] *v impers* **1** to happen; **advienne que pourra** come what may; **2 ~ de** to become of.

adverbe /advɛʀb/ *nm* adverb.

adversaire /advɛʀsɛʀ/ *nmf* (gen) opponent; (Mil) adversary.

adverse /advɛʀs/ *adj* [*team*] opposing; **partie ~** opposite camp.

adversité /advɛʀsite/ *nf* adversity.

aérer /aeʀe/ [14] **I** *vtr* **1** to air; **2** to space out [*text*].
II s'aérer *v refl* (+ *v être*) to get some fresh air.

aérien, **-ienne** /aeʀjɛ̃, ɛn/ *adj* [*transport*] air; [*photography*] aerial; **métro ~** elevated section of the underground (GB), elevated railroad (US).

aéro-club, *pl* **~s** /aeʀoklœb/ *nm* flying club.

aérodrome /aeʀodʀom/ *nm* aerodrome (GB), (small) airfield.

aérodynamique /aeʀodinamik/ **I** *adj* aerodynamic.
II *nf* aerodynamics.

aérogare /aeʀogaʀ/ *nf* air terminal.

aéroglisseur /aeʀoglisœʀ/ *nm* hovercraft.

aéronautique /aeʀonotik/ *nf* aeronautics.

aérophagie /aeʀɔfaʒi/ *nf* aerophagia; **donner de l'~** to make the stomach bloated.

aéroport /aeʀɔpɔʀ/ *nm* airport.

aérosol /aeʀɔsɔl/ *nm* **1** aerosol; **2** spray.

aérospatiale /aeʀɔspasjal/ *nf* aerospace industry.

affable /afabl/ *adj* affable.

affabulation /afabylasjɔ̃/ *nf* fabrication.

affadir /afadiʀ/ [3] *vtr* to make [sth] tasteless.

affaiblir /afebliʀ/ [3] **I** *vtr* to weaken.
II s'affaiblir *v refl* (+ *v être*) to get weaker.

affaiblissement /afɛblismɑ̃/ *nm* **1** weakening; **2** weakened state.

affaire /afɛʀ/ **I** *nf* **1** affair; (political) crisis, affair; (moral) scandal; (legal) case; **2** affair; **j'ignore tout de cette ~** I don't know anything about the matter; **c'est une ~ d'argent** there's money involved; **et voilà toute l'~** and that's that; **c'est toute une ~, ce n'est pas une petite ~** it's quite a business; **c'est une autre ~** that's another matter; **3** (skill, trade) **il connaît bien son ~** he knows his job; **la mécanique, c'est leur ~** mechanics is their thing; **être à son ~** to be in one's element; **4** deal; **faire ~ avec** to do a deal with; **avoir ~ à** to be dealing with; **5** bargain; **j'ai fait une ~** I got a bargain; **la belle ~**○! big deal○!; **ça fera l'~** that'll do; **6** business, concern; **7** (question, problem) **une ~ délicate** a delicate matter; **c'est l'~ de quelques jours** it'll only take a few days; **l'~ se présente bien** things are looking good; **j'en fais mon ~** I'll deal with it; **on ne va pas en faire une ~ d'État**○! let's not make a big issue out of it!; **8** (difficulty) **être tiré d'~** to be out of danger; **se tirer d'~** to get out of trouble.
II affaires *nf pl* **1** business; **2** (personal) business affairs; **occupe-toi de tes ~s!** mind your own business!; **3** things, belongings.
■ **~s courantes** daily business; **~s publiques** public affairs.

affairement /afɛʀmɑ̃/ *nm* bustling activity.

affairer: **s'affairer** /afeʀe/ [1] *v refl* (+ *v être*) to bustle about (**à faire** doing).

affairiste /afeʀist/ *nmf* wheeler-dealer○.

affaisser: **s'affaisser** /afese/ [1] *v refl* (+ *v être*) **1** to subside; **2** [*shoulders, roof*] to sag; **3** to collapse; **4** [*head*] to droop.

affaler: **s'affaler** /afale/ [1] *v refl* (+ *v être*) **1** to collapse; **2**○ to fall.

affamé, **~e** /afame/ **I** *pp* ▸ **affamer**.
II *pp adj* **1** starving; **2 ~ de** hungry for.
IDIOMS **ventre ~ n'a pas d'oreilles** (Proverb) people don't listen when they're hungry.

affamer /afame/ [1] *vtr* to starve.

affectation /afɛktasjɔ̃/ *nf* **1** allocation (**à** to); **2** appointment (**à** to); posting (**à** to); **3** affectation.

affecter /afɛkte/ [1] *vtr* **1** to feign, to affect [*interest*]; to affect [*behaviour*]; to take on [*shape*]; **~ de faire/d'être** to pretend to do/to be; **~ de grands airs** to put on airs; **2** to allocate [*funds*] (**à** to); **3** to appoint (**à** to); to post (**à, en** to); **4** to affect [*country, market, person*].

affectif, **-ive** /afɛktif, iv/ *adj* **1** emotional; **2** affective.

affection /afɛksjɔ̃/ *nf* **1** affection; **prendre qn en ~, se prendre d'~ pour qn** to become fond of sb; **2** (Med) disease.

affectionner /afɛksjɔne/ [1] *vtr* to be fond of.

affectivité /afɛktivite/ *nf* feelings, affectivity.

affectueusement /afɛktɥøzmɑ̃/ *adv* affectionately, fondly.

affectueux, **-euse** /afɛktɥø, øz/ *adj* affectionate.

affermir /afɛʀmiʀ/ [3] **I** *vtr* **1** to strengthen [*authority, will*]; to consolidate [*power*]; to firm up [*muscles*]; **2** to sharpen up [*style*].
II s'affermir *v refl* (+ *v être*) **1** [*power*] to be consolidated; [*voice*] to become stronger; [*muscles*] to firm up; [*ground*] to become firmer; **2** [*style*] to become sharper.

affichage /afiʃaʒ/ *nm* **1** billsticking, billposting; **campagne d'~** poster campaign; **réveil à ~ numérique** digital alarm clock; **2** (Comput) display; **3** (of knowledge) display.
■ **~ à cristaux liquides** liquid crystal display, LCD.

affiche /afiʃ/ *nf* poster; (official) notice; **à l'~** [*film*] now showing; [*play*] on; **la pièce a tenu l'~ pendant deux ans** the play ran for two years; **quitter l'~** to come off.

■ **~ lumineuse** neon sign; **~ de théâtre** playbill.

affiché, ~e /afiʃe/ I *pp* ▶ **afficher**.
II *pp adj* **1** [*ad, picture*] (put) up; [*information*] posted (up); **2** [*result*] published; [*profits*] declared; **3** [*optimism, opinion*] declared; **4** (Comput) [*data*] displayed.

afficher /afiʃe/ [1] I *vtr* **1** to put up [*poster, notice*]; **2** to display [*prices, result*]; **~ complet** [*film, play*] to be sold out; [*hotel*] to be fully booked; [*car park*] to be full; **3** [*stock exchange, market*] to show [*rise*]; **4** to show [*film*]; to have [sth] on [*play*]; **5** to declare [*ambitions*]; to display [*scorn*]; to flaunt [*opinions, liaison*].
II **s'afficher** *v refl* (+ *v être*) **1** to flaunt oneself; **2** [*smile*] to appear (**sur** on).

affilée: **d'affilée** /dafile/ *phr* in a row, one after the other.

affiler /afile/ [1] *vtr* to sharpen.

affilier /afilje/ [2] I *vtr* to affiliate.
II **s'affilier** *v refl* (+ *v être*) to become affiliated.

affiner /afine/ [1] I *vtr* **1** to hone [*style*]; **2** to slim down [*waistline*].
II **s'affiner** *v refl* (+ *v être*) **1** [*judgment*] to become keener; [*style, taste*] to become (more) refined; **2** [*waistline*] to slim down.

affinité /afinite/ *nf* affinity.

affirmatif, -ive[1] /afiʀmatif, iv/ *adj* **1** affirmative; **faire un signe de tête ~** to nod agreement; **2** assertive.

affirmation /afiʀmasjɔ̃/ *nf* **1** assertion; **l'~ de soi** assertiveness; **2** (of feelings) affirmation.

affirmative[2] /afiʀmativ/ I *adj f* ▶ **affirmatif**.
II *nf* affirmative; **dans l'~** if the answer is yes.

affirmer /afiʀme/ [1] I *vtr* **1** to maintain; **~ faire** to claim to do; **pouvez-vous l'~?** can you be sure about it?; **2** to assert [*talent, authority*]; **3** to declare, to affirm [*will*].
II **s'affirmer** *v refl* (+ *v être*) [*tendency*] to become apparent; [*personality*] to assert itself.

affleurer /aflœʀe/ [1] *vi* [*reef*] to show on the surface; [*rock*] to come through the soil.

affliction /afliksjɔ̃/ *nf* affliction; **plonger qn dans l'~** to afflict sb deeply.

affligeant, ~e /afliʒɑ̃, ɑ̃t/ *adj* pathetic, depressing.

affliger /afliʒe/ [13] *vtr* **1** to afflict (**de** with); **2** to distress.

affluence /aflyɑ̃s/ *nf* crowd(s).

affluent /aflyɑ̃/ *nm* tributary.

affluer /aflye/ [1] *vi* [*people*] to flock (**à, vers** to); [*letters*] to pour in.

afflux /afly/ *nm inv* (of blood) rush; (of capital) influx.

affolant○, **~e** /afɔlɑ̃, ɑ̃t/ *adj* frightening.

affolement /afɔlmɑ̃/ *nm* panic.

affoler /afɔle/ [1] I *vtr* to throw [sb] into a panic.
II **s'affoler** *v refl* (+ *v être*) to panic; [*compass needle*] to spin.

affranchir /afʀɑ̃ʃiʀ/ [3] I *vtr* **1** to stamp [*letter*]; **2** to free [*slave, country*].
II **s'affranchir** *v refl* (+ *v être*) to free oneself (**de** from).

affranchissement /afʀɑ̃ʃismɑ̃/ *nm* **1** stamping; (cost) postage; **2** (of country) liberation; (of slaves) freeing.

affréter /afʀete/ [14] *vtr* to charter.

affreusement○ /afʀøzmɑ̃/ *adv* [*behave*] abominably; [*ugly, injured*] horribly.

affreux, -euse /afʀø, øz/ *adj* **1** hideous; **2** awful, dreadful.

affront /afʀɔ̃/ *nm* affront; **il m'a fait l'~ de refuser** he insulted me by refusing.

affrontement /afʀɔ̃tmɑ̃/ *nm* confrontation, clash.

affronter /afʀɔ̃te/ [1] *vtr* to face [*situation*]; to brave [*weather*].

affubler /afyble/ [1] *vtr* **~ qn de** to deck sb out in [*clothes*]; to saddle sb with [*nickname*].

affût /afy/ *nm* (in hunting) hide (GB), blind (US); **se tenir** or **être à l'~** to lie in wait; (figurative) to be on the lookout (**de** for).

affûter /afyte/ [1] *vtr* **1** to sharpen; **2** to grind.

afin /afɛ̃/ I **afin de** *phr* **~ de faire** in order to do.
II **afin que** *phr* so that.

AFNOR /afnɔʀ/ *nf* (*abbr* = **Association française de normalisation**) AFNOR (*French standards authority*).

AFP /aɛfpe/ *nf* (*abbr* = **Agence France-Presse**) AFP (*French news agency*).

africain, ~e /afʀikɛ̃, ɛn/ *adj* African.

Afrique /afʀik/ *pr nf* Africa.

agaçant, ~e /agasɑ̃, ɑ̃t/ *adj* annoying, irritating.

agacement /agasmɑ̃/ *nm* irritation.

agacer /agase/ [12] *vtr* to annoy, to irritate.

agate /agat/ *nf* **1** agate; **2** marble.

âge /ɑʒ/ *nm* **1** age; **faire son ~** to look one's age; **un homme d'un certain ~** a middle-aged man; **ne plus être en ~ de faire** to be too old to do; **2** old age; **avec l'~** as one gets older; **prendre de l'~** to grow old; **3** age, era.
■ **l'~ bête** or **ingrat** the awkward or difficult age; **l'~ mûr** maturity.

âgé, ~e /ɑʒe/ *adj* old.

agence /aʒɑ̃s/ *nf* **1** agency; **2** (of bank) branch.
■ **~ immobilière** estate agents (GB), real-estate agency (US); **~ de presse** news agency.

agencer /aʒɑ̃se/ [12] *vtr* **1** to lay out [*room*]; **2** to put together [*colours*].

agenda /aʒɛ̃da/ *nm* diary.

agenouiller: **s'agenouiller** /aʒnuje/ [1] *v refl* (+ *v être*) to kneel (down).

agent /aʒɑ̃/ *nm* **1** officer, official; **2** agent; **3** employee.
■ **~ artistique** theatrical agent; **~ de change** stockbroker; **~ de la circulation** traffic policeman; **~ commercial** sales representative; **~ de liaison** liaison officer; **~**

maritime shipping agent; **~ de police** policeman.

agglomération /aglɔmeʀasjɔ̃/ *nf* **1** town; (smaller) village; **l'~ lyonnaise** Lyons and its suburbs; **2** (Tech) agglomeration.

aggloméré /aglɔmeʀe/ *nm* chipboard.

agglutiner: **s'agglutiner** /aglytine/ [1] *v refl* (+ *v être*) [*onlookers*] to crowd together (**à** at); [*insects*] to cluster together.

aggravant, **~e** /agʀavɑ̃, ɑ̃t/ *adj* aggravating.

aggravation /agʀavasjɔ̃/ *nf* (of situation) worsening; (in debt) increase.

aggraver /agʀave/ [1] **I** *vtr* to aggravate, to make [sth] worse.

II s'aggraver *v refl* (+ *v être*) to get worse, to deteriorate.

agile /aʒil/ *adj* agile, nimble.

agilité /aʒilite/ *nf* agility.

agir /aʒiʀ/ [3] **I** *vi* **1** to act; **~ sous le coup de la colère** to act in anger; **2** to behave; **~ en lâche** to act like a coward; **3** [*medicine*] to take effect, to work; **~ sur le marché** to influence the market.

II s'agir de *v impers* (+ *v être*) **de quoi s'agit-il?** what is it about?; what's the matter?; **mais il ne s'agit pas de ça!** but that's not the point!; **il s'agit de ta santé!** it's your health that's at stake (here)!; **il s'agit de votre mari** it's about your husband; **s'agissant de** as regards; **il s'agit de faire vite** we must act quickly.

agissements /aʒismɑ̃/ *nm pl* activities, doings.

agitateur, **-trice** /aʒitatœʀ, tʀis/ *nm,f* agitator.

agitation /aʒitasjɔ̃/ *nf* **1** restlessness; **2** bustle (**de** in); activity; **3** unrest.

agité, **~e** /aʒite/ *adj* **1** [*sea*] rough; choppy; [*patient*] agitated; [*sleep*] troubled; [*period*] turbulent; [*night*] restless; **2** [*street*] bustling; [*life*] hectic.

agiter /aʒite/ [1] **I** *vtr* **1** to wave [*hand*]; to shake [*can*]; to shake up [*liquid*]; **2** to raise [*spectre*].

II s'agiter *v refl* (+ *v être*) **1** to fidget; (in bed) to toss and turn; **2** to sway (in the wind); **3** to bustle about; **4** to become restless.

agneau, *pl* **~x** /aɲo/ *nm* **1** lamb; **2** lambskin.

agnelle /aɲɛl/ *nf* ewe lamb.

agonie /agɔni/ *nf* death throes.

agoniser /agɔnize/ [1] *vi* to be dying.

agrafe /agʀaf/ *nf* **1** (for paper) staple; **2** (on waistband, bra) hook; **3** (Med) skin clip.

agrafer /agʀafe/ [1] *vtr* **1** to staple [sth] (together); **2** to fasten.

agrafeuse /agʀaføz/ *nf* stapler.

agraire /agʀɛʀ/ *adj* agrarian; **réforme ~** land reform.

agrandir /agʀɑ̃diʀ/ [3] **I** *vtr* **1** to enlarge [*town, photo*]; to extend [*house*]; to widen [*tunnel*]; **2** to expand [*organization*].

II s'agrandir *v refl* (+ *v être*) [*hole*] to get bigger; [*town, family, company*] to expand; [*eyes*] to widen.

agrandissement /agʀɑ̃dismɑ̃/ *nm* (of photo) enlargement.

agrandisseur /agʀɑ̃disœʀ/ *nm* enlarger.

agréable /agʀeabl/ *adj* nice, pleasant; **~ à l'œil** pleasing to the eye; **~ à vivre** [*person*] pleasant to be with.

agréer /agʀee/ [11] *vtr* **1** to agree to [*request*]; **veuillez ~ mes salutations distinguées** yours faithfully; yours sincerely; **2** to register [*taxi, doctor*]; to approve [*institution*]; **agent agréé** authorized dealer.

agrégation /agʀegasjɔ̃/ *nf* **1** *high-level competitive examination for recruitment of teachers*; **2** (of particles) aggregation.

agrégé, **~e** /agʀeʒe/ *nm,f*: *holder of the agrégation*.

agréger: **s'agréger** /agʀeʒe/ [15] *v refl* (+ *v être*) to aggregate.

agrément /agʀemɑ̃/ *nm* **1** charm; **plein d'~** very pleasant; full of charm; **sans ~** dull; unattractive; cheerless; **voyage d'~** pleasure trip; **2** (by official body) approval.

agrémenter /agʀemɑ̃te/ [1] *vtr* to liven up [*story*] (**de** with); to brighten up [*garden*] (**de** with).

agrès /agʀɛ/ *nm pl* (Sport) apparatus.

agresser /agʀese/ [1] *vtr* **1** to attack; **2** to mug; **3** to be aggressive with.

agresseur /agʀesœʀ/ *nm* **1** attacker; **2** (in war) aggressor.

agressif, **-ive** /agʀesif, iv/ *adj* **1** aggressive; **2** [*colour*] violent; [*sound*] ear-splitting; [*light, shampoo*] harsh; [*images*] disturbing.

agression /agʀesjɔ̃/ *nf* **1** attack; **2** mugging; **3** act of aggression.

agressivité /agʀesivite/ *nf* aggressiveness.

agricole /agʀikɔl/ *adj* **produit ~** farm produce; **coopérative ~** farming cooperative.

agriculteur, **-trice** /agʀikyltœʀ, tʀis/ *nm,f* farmer.

agriculture /agʀikyltyʀ/ *nf* farming.

agripper /agʀipe/ [1] **I** *vtr* to grab.

II s'agripper *v refl* (+ *v être*) to cling (**à** to).

agro-alimentaire, *pl* **~s** /agʀoalimɑ̃tɛʀ/ *adj* food-processing.

agronome /agʀɔnɔm/ *nmf* agronomist.

agronomie /agʀɔnɔmi/ *nf* agronomy.

agrume /agʀym/ *nm* citrus fruit.

aguerrir /ageʀiʀ/ [3] **I** *vtr* to harden [*person*].

II s'aguerrir *v refl* (+ *v être*) to become hardened.

aguets: **aux aguets** /ozagɛ/ *phr* **être aux ~** to be on one's guard.

aguicher /agiʃe/ [1] *vtr* **1** to lead [sb] on; **2** to attract [*customer*].

aguicheur, **-euse** /agiʃœʀ, øz/ *adj* alluring.

ah /ɑ/ *excl* oh!; **~ non alors!** certainly not!; **~, tu vois!** see!; **~ oui?**, **~ bon?** really?

ahuri, **~e** /ayʀi/ *adj* **1** dazed; **2** stunned, amazed.

ahurissant, **~e** /ayʀisɑ̃, ɑ̃t/ *adj* [*news, strength*] incredible; [*figure*] staggering.

aide[1] /ɛd/ **I** *nmf* assistant.

II **aide-** (*combining form*) **~-bibliothécaire** assistant librarian; **~-électricien** electrician's mate (GB) or helper (US); **~-soignant** nursing auxiliary (GB), nurse's aide (US).

aide² /ɛd/ *nf* **1** (from individual, group) help, assistance; (from state, government) assistance; **appeler à l'~** to call for help; **apporter son ~ à qn** to help sb: **2** (financial) aid; **~ au développement** foreign aid; **~ judiciaire** legal aid.

aider /ede/ [1] I *vtr* **1** to help (**à faire** to do); **se faire ~ par qn** to get help from sb; **2** to aid; to give aid to.
II **aider à** *v+prep* to help toward(s) [*understanding, funding*].
III **s'aider** *v refl* (+ *v être*) **1 s'~ de** to use [*dictionary, tool*]; **2** to help each other.

aïeul, **~e** /ajœl/ *nm,f* (literary) grandfather/grandmother.

aïeux /ajø/ *nm pl* (literary) ancestors.

aigle /ɛgl/ *nm, nf* eagle.

aiglefin /ɛgləfɛ̃/ *nm* haddock.

aigre /ɛgʀ/ *adj* **1** [*smell, taste*] sour; **2** [*tone, words*] sharp.

aigre-doux, **-douce**, *pl* **aigres-doux**, **aigres-douces** /ɛgʀədu, dus/ *adj* (Culin) [*fruit,taste*] bitter-sweet; [*sauce*] sweet and sour.

aigreur /ɛgʀœʀ/ *nf* **1** (of milk, fruit) sourness; (of wine) sharpness; **2** (Med) **~s d'estomac** heartburn; **3** (figurative) bitterness.

aigrir /egʀiʀ/ [3] *vtr* to embitter.

aigu, **-uë** /egy/ I *adj* **1** [*sound, voice, note*] high-pitched; **2** [*pain, symptom, problem*] acute; [*phase*] critical; **3** [*sense, perception*] keen.
II *nm* (Mus) (of stereo system) treble; (of voice) high notes .

aiguillage /egɥijaʒ/ *nm* (for trains) points (GB), switch (US); **une erreur d'~** a signalling[GB] error.

aiguille /egɥij/ *nf* **1** needle; **~ à coudre/à tricoter** sewing/knitting needle; **2** (of watch, chronometer) hand; (of gauge, speedometer) needle; (of weighing scales) pointer; **dans le sens/dans le sens inverse des ~s d'une montre** clockwise/anticlockwise.

aiguiller /egɥije/ [1] *vtr* **1** to direct [*person*]; to send [*mail*]; **2** (towards career) to guide [*person*]; **3** to steer [*conversation*].

aiguilleur /egɥijœʀ/ *nm* pointsman (GB), switchman (US).
■ **~ du ciel** air traffic controller.

aiguiser /egize/ [1] *vtr* **1** to sharpen [*knife*]; **2** to whet [*appetite*]; to arouse [*curiosity*].

ail, *pl* **~s** or **aulx** /aj, o/ *nm* garlic.

aile /ɛl/ *nf* (gen) wing; (of windmill) sail; (of car) wing (GB), fender (US); (of army) flank.
■ **~ delta** (of aircraft) delta wing; (Sport) hang-glider; **~ libre** (Sport) hang-glider.
IDIOMS **battre de l'~** to be in a bad way; **se sentir pousser des ~s** to feel exhilarated; **prendre un coup dans l'~** to suffer a setback; **voler de ses propres ~s** to stand on one's own two feet.

aileron /ɛlʀɔ̃/ *nm* (of bird) wing tip; (of shark) fin; (of plane) aileron; (of ship) fin.

ailier /elje/ *nm* (in football) winger; (in rugby) wing three-quarter.

ailleurs /ajœʀ/ I *adv* elsewhere; **nulle part ~** nowhere else.
II **d'ailleurs** *phr* besides, moreover.
III **par ailleurs** *phr* **ils se sont par ~ engagés à faire** they have also undertaken to do.
IDIOMS **être ~, avoir l'esprit ~** to be miles away.

ailloli = **aïoli**.

aimable /ɛmabl/ *adj* **1** [*person*] pleasant; **2** [*word*] kind; **3** [*remark*] polite.

aimant, **~e** /ɛmɑ̃, ɑ̃t/ I *adj* affectionate, loving.
II *nm* magnet.

aimer /eme/ [1] I *vtr* **1** to love [*person*]; **~ qn à la folie** to adore sb; **2** to like, to be fond of [*person, activity, thing*]; **~ faire** to like doing; **~ les voyages** to like travelling[GB]; **il aime autant le vin que la bière** he likes wine as much as he likes beer; **j'aime autant te dire que tu vas le regretter** I may as well tell you that you're going to regret it; **~ mieux** to prefer; **il n'a rien de cassé? j'aime mieux ça!** (in relief) nothing's broken? thank goodness!; **vous acceptez de me rembourser? j'aime mieux ça!** (threateningly) you agree to pay me back? that's more like it!
II **s'aimer** *v refl* (+ *v être*) **1** to love each other; **2** to like each other.

aine /ɛn/ *nf* groin.

aîné, **~e** /ene/ I *adj* elder; eldest.
II *nm,f* **1** elder son/daughter, elder child; **2** eldest son/daughter, eldest child; **3** elder or older brother/sister; **4** elder; oldest; **il est de vingt ans mon ~** he's twenty years older than me.

aînesse /enɛs/ *nf* **droit d'~** the law of primogeniture.

ainsi /ɛ̃si/ I *adv* **1** thus; **le mélange ~ obtenu** the mixture obtained in this way; **elle est ~** that's how or the way she is; **Charlotte, c'est ~ qu'on m'appelait** Charlotte, that's what they used to call me; **s'il en est ~** if that's how it is or the way it is; **le jury se compose ~** the panel is made up as follows; **~ soit-il** amen; **2** thus, so; **~, depuis 1989**... thus, since 1989...
II **ainsi que** *phr* **1** as well as; **2** as; **~ que nous en avions convenu** as we had agreed.

aïoli /ajɔli/ *nm*: *provençal garlic mayonnaise.*

air /ɛʀ/ *nm* **1** air; **le bon ~** clean air; **à l'~ libre** outside, outdoors; **concert en plein ~** open-air concert; **activités de plein ~** outdoor activities; **aller prendre l'~** to go out and get some fresh air; **on manque d'~ ici** it's stuffy in here; **regarder en l'~** to look up; **avoir le nez en l'~** to daydream; **être dans l'~** [*reform, idea*] to be in the air; **il y a un virus dans l'~** there's a virus going around; **en l'~** [*threat, words*] empty; [*plan, idea*] vague; **tout mettre en l'~**○ to make a dreadful mess; **de l'~**○! get lost○!; **2 il y a de l'~** (in room) there's a draught (GB) or draft (US); (outside) there's a breeze; **il n'y a pas d'~** there's no wind; **un courant d'~** a draught (GB) or draft (US); **3** manner; expression; **avoir un drôle d'~** to look odd; **avec un ~ résolu** in a resolute manner; **d'un ~ fâché** angrily; **il y a un ~ de famille entre vous deux** you two share a family likeness; **cela m'en a tout l'~** it seems or looks like it to me; **j'aurais l'~ de quoi?** I'd look a right idiot!; **il a l'~ de comprendre** he seems to understand; **cela a l'~ d'être une usine** it looks like a factory; **il a l'~ de vouloir faire beau** it looks as if it's going to be fine; **4** tune; **un ~ d'opéra** an aria.

IDIOMS **il ne manque pas d'~**○! he's got a nerve!; **brasser** or **remuer de l'~**○ to give the impression of being busy; **se donner des grands ~s** to put on airs; **j'ai besoin de changer d'~** I need a change of scene.

aire /ɛʀ/ *nf* **1** sphere, domain; **2** (surface) area; **3** eyrie.

■ **~ d'atterrissage** (for plane) landing strip; (for helicopter) landing pad; **~ de jeu** playground; **~ de loisirs** recreation area; **~ de services** motorway (GB) or freeway (US) service station; **~ de stationnement** parking area.

airelle /ɛʀɛl/ *nf* **1** bilberry; **2** cranberry.

aisance /ɛzɑ̃s/ *nf* **1** ease; **2** affluence, comfort.

aise /ɛz/ **I aises** *nf pl* **tenir à** or **aimer ses ~s** to like one's creature comforts; **il prenait ses ~s sur le canapé** he was stretched out on the sofa.

II à l'aise *phr* **être à l'~** or **à son ~** (physically) to be comfortable; (financially) to be comfortably off; (psychologically) to be at ease, to feel comfortable; **mettre qn mal à l'~** to make sb feel ill at ease; **à votre ~!** as you wish or like!

aisé, **~e** /eze/ *adj* **1** easy; **2** wealthy; **être ~** to be well-off.

aisément /ezemɑ̃/ *adv* easily.

aisselle /ɛsɛl/ *nf* armpit.

ajouré, **~e** /aʒuʀe/ *adj* **1** [*tablecloth*] openwork; [*edge, border*] hemstitched; **2** [*steeple, balcony*] with ornamental apertures.

ajournement /aʒuʀnəmɑ̃/ *nm* (of decision) postponement; (of trial) adjournment.

ajourner /aʒuʀne/ [1] *vtr* to postpone [*decision, plan*]; to adjourn [*debate, trial*].

ajout /aʒu/ *nm* addition.

ajouter /aʒute/ [1] **I** *vtr* to add (**à** to).

II ajouter à *v+prep* to add to [*confusion, disappointment*].

III s'ajouter *v refl* (+ *v être*) **s'~ à** to be added to.

ajuster /aʒyste/ [1] *vtr* **1** to adjust [*strap, price, timetable*]; to alter [*garment*] (**à** to); to calibrate [*weighing scales*]; **~ qch à** or **sur qch** to make sth fit sth; **corsage ajusté** close-fitting bodice; **2** to arrange [*hair*]; to straighten [*hat, tie*]; **3** to take aim at [*rabbit*]; **~ son tir** to adjust one's aim.

alaise = **alèse**.

alambic /alɑ̃bik/ *nm* still.

alangui, **~e** /alɑ̃gi/ *adj* **1** languid; **2** listless.

alarmant, **~e** /alaʀmɑ̃, ɑ̃t/ *adj* alarming.

alarme /alaʀm/ *nf* alarm; **sonner/donner l'~** to sound/to raise the alarm.

alarmer /alaʀme/ [1] **I** *vtr* to alarm.

II s'alarmer *v refl* (+ *v être*) to become alarmed (**de qch** about sth).

albâtre /albɑtʀ/ *nm* alabaster.

albatros /albatʀos/ *nm inv* albatross.

albinos /albinos/ *adj inv*, *nmf inv* albino.

album /albɔm/ *nm* **1** illustrated book; **~ de bandes dessinées** comic strip book; **2** album.

■ **~ à colorier** colouring[GB] book; **~ de famille** family album.

albumine /albymin/ *nf* albumin.

alchimie /alʃimi/ *nf* alchemy.

alcool /alkɔl/ *nm* **1** alcohol; **boire de l'~** to drink alcohol; **~ de poire** pear brandy; **sans ~** [*cocktail*] non-alcoholic; [*beer*] alcohol-free; **teneur en ~** alcohol content; **2** drink; **l'~ au volant** drink-driving; **3 un ~** a spirit; **il ne boit que des ~s forts** he only drinks spirits.

■ **~ à brûler** methylated spirits; **~ à 90°** = surgical spirit (GB), rubbing alcohol (US).

alcoolémie /alkɔlemi/ *nf* presence of alcohol in the blood.

alcoolique /alkɔlik/ *adj*, *nmf* alcoholic.

alcoolisé, **~e** /alkɔlize/ *adj* alcoholic; **une boisson non ~e** a non-alcoholic drink.

alcoolisme /alkɔlism/ *nm* alcoholism.

alcootest /alkɔtɛst/ *nm* **1** Breathalyzer®; **2** breath test.

alcôve /alkov/ *nf* alcove.

aléas /alea/ *nm pl* (gen) vagaries; (economic, financial) hazards.

aléatoire /aleatwaʀ/ *adj* **1** [*events, success*] unpredictable; [*profession*] insecure, risky; **2** [*number, access*] random.

alentour /alɑ̃tuʀ/ **I** *adv* **la ville et la région ~** the town and surrounding area.

II alentours *nm pl* surrounding area.

alerte /alɛʀt/ **I** *adj* [*person, mind*] alert; [*style, game*] lively.

II *nf* alert; **être en état d'~** to be in a state of alert; to be on the alert; **donner l'~** to raise the alarm; **~ générale** full alert.

■ **~ aérienne** air raid warning; **~ à la bombe** bomb scare.

alerter /alɛʀte/ [1] *vtr* to alert (**sur** to).

alèse /alɛz/ *nf* undersheet, mattress protector.

algèbre /alʒɛbʀ/ *nf* algebra.

Algérie /alʒeʀi/ *pr nf* Algeria.

algérien, **-ienne** /alʒeʀjɛ̃, ɛn/ *adj* Algerian.

algie /alʒi/ *nf* pain; **~ dentaire** toothache.

algue /alg/ *nf* **1** alga; **2** seaweed.

alias /aljas/ *adv* alias.

alibi /alibi/ *nm* **1** (Law) alibi; **2** excuse.

aliénation /aljenasjɔ̃/ *nf* alienation.

aliéné, **~e** /aljene/ *nm,f* insane person.

alignement /aliɲ(ə)mɑ̃/ *nm* **1** row, line; **2** alignment; **3 ~ de qch sur qch** [*currency,* *salaries, political party*] bringing into line of sth with sth.

aligner /aliɲe/ [1] I *vtr* **1** to line [sth] up; **2 ~ qch sur qch** to bring sth into line with sth; **3** to give a list of [*arguments, figures*]; **4** to line up [*players, team*].
II **s'aligner** *v refl* (+ *v être*) **1** [*houses, trees*] to be in a line; **2** [*people*] (gen) to line up; (soldiers) to fall into line; **3 s'~ sur** to align oneself with [*country, party, ideas*].

aliment /alimɑ̃/ *nm* (gen) food; (for farm animals) feed; (for plants) nutrient.

alimentaire /alimɑ̃tɛʀ/ *adj* [*needs, habits*] dietary; [*industry, shortage*] food; **produits** or **denrées ~s** foodstuffs; **régime ~** diet.

alimentation /alimɑ̃tasjɔ̃/ *nf* **1** diet; **2** feeding; **3** food; **magasin d'~** food shop, grocery store; **4** food industry; **5** supply, feeding (**de** of); **l'~ en eau** the water supply.

alimenter /alimɑ̃te/ [1] I *vtr* **1** to feed [*person, animal*]; **2** to feed, to supply [*engine, boiler*]; **~ une machine en papier** to feed paper into a machine; **3** to fuel [*conversation, hostility*].
II **s'alimenter** *v refl* (+ *v être*) **1** [*person*] to eat; [*animal*] to feed; **2** (with water, gas) **s'~ en** to be supplied with.

alinéa /alinea/ *nm* **1** indentation; **2** indented line; **3** paragraph.

aliter: **s'aliter** /alite/ [1] *v refl* (+ *v être*) to take to one's bed; **être alité** to be confined to bed.

allaitement /alɛtmɑ̃/ *nm* **1** breast-feeding; **2** suckling.

allaiter /alete/ [1] *vtr* **1** to breast-feed; **2** to suckle.

allant /alɑ̃/ *nm* drive, bounce; **être plein d'~** to have plenty of drive.

allécher /aleʃe/ [14] *vtr* to tempt (**avec** with).

allée /ale/ I *nf* **1** (in garden, wood) path; (leading to house) drive; (in town) avenue; **les ~s du pouvoir** the corridors of power; **2** aisle.
II **allées** *nf pl* **~s et venues** comings and goings.

allégation /alegasjɔ̃/ *nf* allegation.

allégé, **~e** /aleʒe/ I *pp* ▶ **alléger**.
II *pp adj* [*cheese, yoghurt, margarine*] low-fat; [*chocolate*] diet .

allégement /alɛʒmɑ̃/ *nm* **1** (in weight) lightening; **2** (of charges) reduction; (of restrictions, controls) relaxing; (of structures) simplification; **~ fiscal** tax relief.

alléger /aleʒe/ [15] I *vtr* **1** to lighten [*load, weight*]; **2** to reduce [*debt*] (**de** by); to cut [*taxes*]; to simplify [*mechanism*]; to relax [*control, restrictions*].
II **s'alléger** *v refl* (+ *v être*) **1** [*load*] to get lighter; **2** [*debt, taxation*] to be reduced; [*mechanism*] to be simplified; [*embargo*] to be relaxed.

allégorie /alegɔʀi/ *nf* allegory.

allègre /alɛgʀ/ *adj* [*style*] light; [*tone*] lighthearted; [*step, mood*] buoyant.

allégrement /alegʀəmɑ̃/ *adv* joyfully; (ironic) blithely.

allégresse /alegʀɛs/ *nf* joy.

allegro /alegʀo/ *adv* allegro.

alléguer /alege/ [14] *vtr* **1** to invoke; **2** to allege.

Allemagne /almaɲ/ *pr nf* Germany; **l'~ unie** unified Germany.

allemand, **~e** /almɑ̃, ɑ̃d/ I *adj* German.
II *nm* (language) German.

aller[1] /ale/ [9] I *v aux* **je vais apprendre l'italien** I'm going to learn Italian; **j'allais partir quand il est arrivé** I was about to leave when he arrived; **il va le regretter** he'll regret it; **il est allé voir l'exposition** he went to see the exhibition; **va leur parler** go and speak to them; **la situation va (en) se compliquant** the situation is getting more and more complicated.
II *vi* (+ *v être*) **1 comment vas-tu, comment ça va?** how are you?; **ça va (bien)** I'm fine; **~ beaucoup mieux** to be much better; **bois ça, ça ira mieux** drink this, you'll feel better; **les affaires vont bien** business is good; **ça va l'école?** how are things at school?; **qu'est-ce qui ne va pas?** what's the matter?; **ne pas ~ sans peine** or **mal** not to be easy; **ça devrait ~ de soi** it should be obvious; **ça va tout seul** it's as easy as pie; **ça va pas non**○, **ça va pas la tête?** are you mad (GB) or crazy○?; **2** to go; **où vas-tu?** where are you going?; **~ nager/au travail** to go swimming/to work; **~ chez le médecin** to go to the doctor's; **vas-y, demande-leur!** go on, ask them!; **allons-y!** let's go!; **allons!**, **allez!** come on!; **~ et venir** to pace up and down; to run in and out; **les nouvelles vont vite** news travels fast; **j'y vais** (answering phone, door) I'll get it; (when leaving)○ I'm off○; **la route va au village** the road leads to the village; **~ contre la loi** to break the law; to be against the law; **3 ça va**, **ça ira**○, **ça peut aller**○ that'll do; it'll do; **ça va comme ça** it's all right as it is; **ça ne va pas du tout** that's no good at all; **lundi ça (te) va?** would Monday suit you or be okay○?; **4 ~ à qn** to fit sb; **5 ~ à qn** to suit sb; **ta cravate ne va pas avec ta chemise** your tie doesn't go with your shirt; **6 ~ jusqu'à tuer** to go as far as to kill; **la voiture peut ~ jusqu'à 200 km/h** the car can do up to 200 kph; **~ jusqu'en 1914** to go up to 1914; **la période qui va de 1918 à 1939** the period between 1918 and 1939; **~ sur ses 17 ans** to be going on 17; **7 y ~ de sa petite larme** to shed a little tear.
III **s'en aller** *v refl* (+ *v être*) **1 s'en aller** to go, to leave, to be off; to go away; **2 la tache ne s'en va pas** the stain won't come out; **3** (formal) to pass away, to die.
IV *v impers* **1 il y va de ma réputation** my reputation is at stake; **2 il en va de même pour toi** that goes for you too; **3 40 divisé par 12, il y va 3 fois et il reste** 4 12 into 40 goes 3 times with 4 left over.

aller[2] /ale/ *nm* **1 j'ai pris le bus à l'~** I took the bus there; I took the bus here; **il n'arrête pas de faire des ~s et retours entre chez lui et son bureau** he keeps running to and fro from his house to the office; **2 ~ (simple)** single (ticket) (GB), one-way ticket (**pour** to); **(billet) ~ retour** return ticket, round trip (ticket) (US); **3** (Sport) **(match) ~** first leg.

allergie /alɛʀʒi/ *nf* (Med) allergy.

allergique /alɛʀʒik/ *adj* allergic (**à** to).

alliage /aljaʒ/ *nm* **1** alloy; **en ~** alloy; **2** (figurative) combination.

alliance /aljɑ̃s/ *nf* **1** wedding ring; **2** alliance.

allié, **~e** /alje/ I *pp* ▶ **allier**.
II *pp adj* allied; **le débarquement ~** the Allied landings.
III *nm,f* **1** ally; **les ~s** the Allies; **2** relative.

allier /alje/ [2] I *vtr* **1** to combine (**et**, **à** with); **2** (Tech) to alloy [*metals*] (**à**, **avec** with).
II **s'allier** *v refl* (+ *v être*) to form an alliance (**avec**, **à** with).

alligator /aligatɔʀ/ *nm* alligator.

allô /alo/ *excl* hello!, hallo!

allocation /al(l)ɔkasjɔ̃/ *nf* **1** allocation, granting; **2** benefit (GB), benefits (US).
■ **~ chômage** unemployment benefit (GB) or benefits (US); **~ logement** housing benefit or benefits (US); **~s familiales** family allowance.

allocution /al(l)ɔkysjɔ̃/ *nf* address; **une ~ télévisée** a televised address.

allongé, **~e** /alɔ̃ʒe/ *adj* **1** **être ~** [*person*] to be lying down; to be reclining; **2** elongated.

allonger /alɔ̃ʒe/ [13] I *vtr* **1** to lay [sb] down; **2** to lengthen [*dress, curtain*]; to extend [*list, holiday*]; **cette coiffure t'allonge le visage** that hairstyle makes your face look longer; **3** to stretch [sth] out [*arm*]; **4** to water [sth] down [*coffee, wine*].
II **s'allonger** *v refl* (+ *v être*) **1** to lie down; **2** to get longer.

allouer /alwe/ [1] *vtr* to allocate [*sum, allowance, budget*] (**à qn** to sb; **à qch** for sth); to grant [*loan*] (**à qn** to sb; **à qch** for sth); to allot [*time*] (**à qn** to sb; **à qch** for sth).

allumage /alymaʒ/ *nm* **1** (Aut) ignition; **2** (of lamp, heating) switching on.

allumé°, **~e** /alyme/ *adj* **1** mad°; **2** tipsy°.

allume-cigare(s) /alymsigaʀ/ *nm inv* cigar lighter.

allumer /alyme/ [1] I *vtr* **1** to light [*candle, gas*]; to light, to start [*fire*]; **2** to switch [sth] on, to turn [sth] on; **laisser ses phares allumés** to leave one's headlights on; **allume!** switch on or turn on the light!; **3** to stir [*imagination*]; to arouse [*desire*].
II **s'allumer** *v refl* (+ *v être*) **1** [*heating, radio, lighting*] to come on; **2** **son regard s'alluma** his face lit up.

allumette /alymɛt/ *nf* match, matchstick.

allumeur°, **-euse** /alymœʀ, øz/ *nm,f* tease.

allure /alyʀ/ *nf* **1** (of walker) pace; (of vehicle) speed; **ralentir son ~** to slow down; **à toute ~** at top speed; **à cette ~** at this rate; **2** (of animal) gait; **3** (of person) appearance; (of clothes) look; (of event) aspect; **4** style; **avoir de l'~** to have style.

allusif, **-ive** /alyzif, iv/ *adj* [*remark*] allusive; [*person*] indirect.

allusion /alyzjɔ̃/ *nf* allusion (**à** to); **faire ~ à** to allude to.

alluvial, **~e**, *mpl* **-iaux** /alyvjal, o/ *adj* alluvial.

alluvion /alyvjɔ̃/ *nf* alluvium; **des ~s** alluvia.

almanach /almana(k)/ *nm* almanac.

alors /alɔʀ/ I *adv* **1** then; **il avait ~ 18 ans** he was 18 at the time; **la mode d'~** the fashion in those days; **le premier ministre britannique d'~** the British Prime Minister at the time; **mes toiles/romans d'~** my paintings/novels of the time; **jusqu'~** until then; **2** then; **(mais) ~ cela change tout!** but that changes everything!; **et (puis) ~?** so what?; **3** so; **il y avait une grève des trains, ~ j'ai pris l'autobus** there was a train strike, so I took the bus; **4 ou ~** or else; **5**° so; **~ il me dit...** so he said to me...; **6 non mais ~!** honestly!; **ça ~!** good heavens!
II **alors que** *phr* **1** while; **2** when.
III **alors même que** *phr* even though.

alouette /alwɛt/ *nf* lark.

alourdir /aluʀdiʀ/ [3] I *vtr* **1** to weigh [sb] down [*person*]; to make [sth] tense [*atmosphere*]; **2** to increase [*tax, charges*].
II **s'alourdir** *v refl* (+ *v être*) [*eyelids*] to begin to droop; [*air*] to grow heavy.

alphabet /alfabɛ/ *nm* **1** alphabet; **2** ABC (book).

alphabétique /alfabetik/ *adj* alphabetical.

alphabétiser /alfabetize/ [1] *vtr* to teach [sb] to read and write; to promote literacy in.

alpin, **~e** /alpɛ̃, in/ *adj* alpine.

alpinisme /alpinism/ *nm* mountaineering.

alsacien, **-ienne** /alzasjɛ̃, ɛn/ I *adj* of Alsace.
II *nm* (language) Alsatian.

altération /alteʀasjɔ̃/ *nf* (of faculties) impairment (**de** of); (of foodstuff) spoiling (**de** of); (in environment) deterioration (**de** in); (of feeling) change (**de** in).

altérer /alteʀe/ [14] *vtr* **1** to affect [*taste, health*]; **2** to spoil [*foodstuff*]; to fade [*colour*]; **3** to distort [*text*]; to adulterate [*substance*].

alternance /altɛʀnɑ̃s/ *nf* **1** (gen) alternation; **en ~ avec** alternately with; **2** (in politics) **choisir l'~** to opt for a change in power.

alternateur /altɛʀnatœʀ/ *nm* alternator.

alternatif, **-ive**[1] /altɛʀnatif, iv/ *adj* (gen) alternate; [*current*] alternating.

alternative[2] /altɛʀnativ/ I *adj f* ▶ **alternatif**.
II *nf* alternative.

alternativement /altɛʀnativmɑ̃/ *adv* alternately, in turn.

alterner /altɛʀne/ [1] I *vtr* to alternate.
II *vi* **1** to alternate; **2 ~ avec qn pour faire** to take turns with sb (at) doing.

altesse /altɛs/ *nf* **1** (title) highness; **2** (person) prince/princess.

altier, **-ière** /altje, ɛʀ/ *adj* haughty.

altitude /altityd/ *nf* altitude; **prendre de l'~** to gain altitude; **en ~** high up (in the mountains).

alto /alto/ I *adj* alto.
II *nm* **1** (instrument) viola; **2** viola player (GB), violin (US); **3** (voice) alto.

altruiste /altʀɥist/ *adj* altruistic.

alu○ /aly/, **aluminium** /alyminjɔm/ *nm* aluminium (GB), aluminum (US).

alvéole /alveɔl/ *nf* **1** (in honeycomb) cell; **2** (in rock) cavity.

alvéolé, **~e** /alveɔle/ *adj* honeycombed.

amabilité /amabilite/ *nf* **1** kindness; **2** courtesy.

amadouer /amadwe/ [1] *vtr* to coax, to cajole.

amaigrir /amegʀiʀ/ [3] *vtr* to make [sb] thinner.

amaigrissant, **~e** /amegʀisɑ̃, ɑ̃t/ *adj* slimming.

amalgame /amalgam/ *nm* **1** (gen) mixture; (of ideas) hotchpotch (GB), hodgepodge (US); **2** (in dentistry, chemistry) amalgam.

amalgamer /amalgame/ [1] *vtr* **1** to lump together [*problems*]; to mix [*feelings, people*]; **2** to blend, to amalgamate [*ingredients*].

amande /amɑ̃d/ *nf* **1** almond; **2** kernel.

amandier /amɑ̃dje/ *nm* almond tree.

amant /amɑ̃/ *nm* lover.

amarre /amaʀ/ *nf* rope; **les ~s** moorings; **larguer les ~s** to cast off; to set off.

amarrer /amaʀe/ [1] *vtr* **1** to moor [*boat*]; **2** to tie (**à, sur** to).

amas /ama/ *nm inv* (of sand, objects) pile; (of scrap, ruins) heap.

amasser /amase/ [1] **I** *vtr* to amass, to accumulate [*fortune, books, papers*]; to acquire [*knowledge*]; to collect [*proof, evidence*].
II s'amasser *v refl* (+ *v être*) [*snow, objects*] to pile up; [*proof, evidence*] to build up.

amateur /amatœʀ/ **I** *adj inv* amateur; **radio ~** radio ham○.
II *nm* **1** (non-professional) amateur; **2** (of sport, photography) enthusiast; connoisseur; **3 il vend sa voiture, vous êtes ~?** he's selling his car, are you interested?

amazone /amazon/ *nf* horsewoman; **monter en ~** to ride sidesaddle.

Amazone /amazon/ **I** *nf* Amazon.
II *pr nm* **l'~** the Amazon (river).

ambassade /ɑ̃basad/ *nf* embassy.

ambassadeur /ɑ̃basadœʀ/ *nm* ambassador.

ambassadrice /ɑ̃basadʀis/ *nf* **1** ambassador; **2** ambassador's wife.

ambiance /ɑ̃bjɑ̃s/ *nf* atmosphere; **ça manque d'~ ici**○ it's not exactly lively here.

ambiant, **~e** /ɑ̃bjɑ̃, ɑ̃t/ *adj* **1** [*air*] surrounding; **à température ~e** at room temperature; **2** prevailing.

ambigu, **-uë** /ɑ̃bigy/ *adj* [*remark, situation*] ambiguous; [*character*] multifaceted; [*feeling, attitude*] ambivalent.

ambiguïté /ɑ̃bigɥite/ *nf* (of remark, situation) ambiguity; (of character) enigmatic nature; (of feelings) ambivalence.

ambitieux, **-ieuse** /ɑ̃bisjø, øz/ *adj* ambitious.

ambition /ɑ̃bisjɔ̃/ *nf* ambition; **avoir de l'~** to be ambitious.

ambitionner /ɑ̃bisjɔne/ [1] *vtr* to aspire to; **~ de faire** to aim to do.

ambivalent, **~e** /ɑ̃bivalɑ̃, ɑ̃t/ *adj* ambivalent.

ambre /ɑ̃bʀ/ *nm* **1 ~ (jaune)** amber; **2 ~ (gris)** ambergris.

ambré, **~e** /ɑ̃bʀe/ *adj* (in colour) amber.

ambulance /ɑ̃bylɑ̃s/ *nf* ambulance.

ambulancier, **-ière** /ɑ̃bylɑ̃sje, ɛʀ/ *nm,f* ambulance driver.

ambulant, **~e** /ɑ̃bylɑ̃, ɑ̃t/ *adj* [*artist*] itinerant; [*circus*] travelling[GB]; **vendeur ~** (in station) snack trolley man; **c'est un cadavre ~**○ he's/she's a walking skeleton○.

âme /ɑm/ *nf* soul; **Dieu ait son ~** God rest his/her soul; **socialiste dans l'~** a socialist to the core; **en mon ~ et conscience** in all honesty; **pas ~ qui vive** not a (single) soul; **errer comme une ~ en peine** to wander around like a lost soul; **~ sœur** soul mate.

amélioration /ameljɔʀasjɔ̃/ *nf* improvement (**de, dans** in).

améliorer /ameljɔʀe/ [1] *vtr*, **s'améliorer** *v refl* (+ *v être*) to improve.

amen /amɛn/ *nm inv* amen; **dire ~ à tout** to agree to everything.

aménagé, **~e** /amenaʒe/ **I** *pp* ▶ **aménager**.
II *pp adj* **1** converted; **2** equipped.

aménagement /amenaʒmɑ̃/ *nm* **1** (of region, town) development; **2** (of roads) construction; (of parks, green spaces) creation; **3** (of house, boat) fitting; **4** (of timetable) adjustment; **l'~ du temps de travail** flexible working hours.

aménager /amenaʒe/ [13] *vtr* **1** to convert; to do up [*house, attic*]; **2** to equip [*kitchen*]; to develop [*region*]; **3** to create [*parks, green spaces*]; to build [*road*]; to lay out [*garden*]; **4** to arrange [*timetable*]; to adjust [*regulations*].

amende /amɑ̃d/ *nf* fine.

amender /amɑ̃de/ [1] **I** *vtr* to amend [*law*].
II s'amender *v refl* (+ *v être*) to mend one's ways.

amener /amne/ [16] **I** *vtr* **1 ~ qn quelque part** to take sb somewhere; **2** (accompany) **~ qn (quelque part)** to bring sb (somewhere); **3** (controversial) **~ qch (à qn)** to bring (sb) sth; **4** to cause [*problems, illness*]; to bring [*rain, fame*]; **5** to bring up [*issue, subject*]; **~ qch sur le tapis**○ to bring sth up; **être bien amené** [*conclusion*] to be well-presented; **6 ~ qn à qch/faire** to lead sb to sth/to do.
II s'amener○ *v refl* (+ *v être*) **1** to come; **2** to turn up○ (**avec** with).

amenuiser: **s'amenuiser** /amənɥize/ [1] *v refl* (+ *v être*) [*supplies*] to dwindle; [*risk*] to lessen.

amer, **-ère** /amɛʀ/ *adj* bitter.

américain, **~e** /ameʀikɛ̃, ɛn/ **I** *adj* American; **à l'~e** (gen) in the American style; (Culin) à l'américaine.
II *nm* American English.

américaniser /ameʀikanize/ [1] **I** *vtr* to Americanize.
II s'américaniser *v refl* (+ *v être*) to become Americanized.

Amérique /ameʀik/ *pr nf* America.

amerrir /ameʀiʀ/ [3] *vi* [*hydroplane*] to land (on water); [*spacecraft*] to splash down.

amertume /amɛʀtym/ *nf* bitterness.

ameublement /amœbləmɑ̃/ *nm* **1** furniture; **2** furniture trade; **3** (of room, house) furnishing.

ameuter /amøte/ [1] *vtr* **1** [*person, noise*] to bring [sb] out; **2** to stir [sb] up.

ami, **~e** /ami/ **I** *adj* friendly.
II *nm,f* friend; **un ~ de longue date** a friend of long standing; **'un ~ qui vous veut du bien'** 'a well-wisher'; **en ~** as a friend; **un ~ des bêtes** an animal lover; ▶ **faux**[1].
IDIOMS **les bons comptes font les bons ~s** (Proverb) a debt paid is a friend kept; **c'est dans le malheur qu'on connaît ses ~s** (Proverb) a friend in need is a friend indeed.

amiable: **à l'amiable** /alamjabl/ *phr* [*separate*] on friendly terms; [*separation*] amicable; [*divorce*] by mutual consent; ▶ **constat**.

amiante /amjɑ̃t/ *nm* asbestos.

amical, **~e**[1], *pl* **-aux** /amikal, o/ *adj* friendly.

amicale[2] /amikal/ *nf* association.

amicalement /amikalmɑ̃/ *adv* **1** [*greet, receive*] warmly; [*compete*] in a friendly way; **2** (at end of letter) **(bien) ~** best wishes.

amidon /amidɔ̃/ *nm* starch.

amidonner /amidɔne/ [1] *vtr* to starch.

amincir /amɛ̃siʀ/ [3] *vtr* to make [sb] look slimmer.

amiral, *mpl* **-aux** /amiʀal, o/ *nm* admiral.

amitié /amitje/ **I** *nf* friendship; **par ~** out of friendship; **se lier d'~ avec qn** to strike up a friendship with sb.
II amitiés *nf pl* (at end of letter) kindest regards.

ammoniac /amɔnjak/ *nm* (gas) ammonia.

ammoniaque /amɔnjak/ *nf* ammonia.

amnésie /amnezi/ *nf* amnesia.

amnésique /amnezik/ **I** *adj* amnesic.
II *nmf* amnesiac.

amnistie /amnisti/ *nf* amnesty **(en faveur de** for); **loi d'~** amnesty law.

amnistier /amnistje/ [2] *vtr* to grant an amnesty to.

amoindrir /amwɛ̃dʀiʀ/ [3] *vtr* to reduce [*resistance*]; to weaken [*person*].

amonceler /amɔ̃sle/ [19] **I** *vtr* to pile up.
II s'amonceler *v refl* (+ *v être*) [*clouds, snow*] to build up; [*evidence, problems*] to pile up.

amoncellement /amɔ̃sɛlmɑ̃/ *nm* (of sand, earth) pile; (of wealth) mass.

amont /amɔ̃/ *nm* **1** (of river) upper reaches; **en ~** upstream **(de** from); **naviguer d'~ en aval** to sail downstream; **2** (in skiing) **ski ~** uphill ski .

amoral, **~e**, *mpl* **-aux** /amɔʀal, o/ *adj* amoral.

amorce /amɔʀs/ *nf* **1** (of discussion) initiation; **2** bait; **3** (of explosive) cap, primer; (of gun) cap.

amorcer /amɔʀse/ [12] *vtr* **1** to begin; **2** to prime.

amorphe /amɔʀf/ *adj* apathetic.

amortir /amɔʀtiʀ/ [3] *vtr* **1** to deaden [*noise*]; to absorb [*shock, impact*]; to break [*fall*]; **2** to pay off [*debt*]; **3 j'ai amorti mon ordinateur en quelques mois** my computer paid for itself in a few months.

amortissement /amɔʀtismɑ̃/ *nm* **1** (of noise) deadening; (of shock, impact) absorption; (of fall) cushioning; **2** (of debt) paying off; **3** (of equipment) depreciation.

amortisseur /amɔʀtisœʀ/ *nm* (Tech) shock absorber.

amour /amuʀ/ **I** *nm* love; **lettre d'~** love letter; **pour l'~ de l'art** for the sake of art; **c'était un ~ de jeunesse** it was a youthful romance; **faire l'~**○ **avec** to make love with.
II amours *nm pl* or *nf pl* **1** (Zool) mating; **2** love affairs; **les ~s de** the amorous adventures of; **à tes ~s!** (to somebody sneezing) bless you!
IDIOMS **vivre d'~ et d'eau fraîche** to live on love alone.

amouracher: **s'amouracher** /amuʀaʃe/ [1] *v refl* (+ *v être*) **s'~ de** to become infatuated with.

amourette /amuʀɛt/ *nf* passing infatuation.

amoureux, **-euse** /amuʀø, øz/ *adj* **1** in love **(de** with); **2 être ~ de peinture** to be a lover of painting.

amour-propre /amuʀpʀɔpʀ/ *nm* self-esteem; pride.

amovible /amɔvibl/ *adj* [*collar, cover*] detachable; [*shelf, partition*] removable.

ampère /ɑ̃pɛʀ/ *nm* amp, ampère.

amphi○ /ɑ̃fi/ *nm* (students' slang) lecture hall.

amphibie /ɑ̃fibi/ *adj* (Zool, Aut) amphibious.

amphithéâtre /ɑ̃fiteɑtʀ/ *nm* **1** (natural, ancient) amphitheatre[GB]; **2** (at university) lecture hall.

amphore /ɑ̃fɔʀ/ *nf* amphora.

ample /ɑ̃pl/ *adj* **1** [*coat, dress*] loose-fitting; [*skirt, sleeve*] full; [*gesture*] sweeping; **2** [*quantity*] ample; [*harvest*] abundant; [*details*] full.

amplement /ɑ̃pləmɑ̃/ *adv* fully; **c'est ~ suffisant** that's more than enough!

ampleur /ɑ̃plœʀ/ *nf* (of problem) size; (of project, subject, survey) scope; (of event, disaster, task) scale; (of damage, reaction) extent; **prendre de l'~** [*epidemic, rumour*] to spread.

ampli○ /ɑ̃pli/ *nm* amp○, amplifier.

amplificateur /ɑ̃plifikatœʀ/ *nm* amplifier.

amplifier /ɑ̃plifje/ [2] **I** *vtr* to amplify [*sound, current*]; to magnify [*rumour*].
II s'amplifier *v refl* (+ *v être*) [*sound*] to grow louder; [*trade*] to increase, grow; [*strike, rumour*] to intensify.

ampoule /ɑ̃pul/ *nf* **1 ~ (électrique)** (light) bulb; **~ de flash** flash bulb; **2** (Med) (drinkable) phial; (injectable) ampoule; **3** blister.

amputation /ɑ̃pytasjɔ̃/ *nf* **1** amputation; **2** drastic cut **(de** in).

amputer /ɑ̃pyte/ [1] *vtr* **1** (Med) to amputate [*limb*]; to perform an amputation on [*person*]; **2** to cut [sth] drastically [*budget*].

amulette /amylɛt/ *nf* amulet.

amusant, **~e** /amyzɑ̃, ɑ̃t/ *adj* **1** entertaining; **2** funny.

amuse-gueule /amyzgœl/ *nm inv* cocktail snack (GB), munchies (US).

amusement /amyzmɑ̃/ *nm* entertainment.

amuser /amyze/ [1] I *vtr* **1** to entertain; to amuse; **laisse-le, si ça l'amuse!** let him be, if that's what makes him happy!; **2** to distract.
II **s'amuser** *v refl* (+ *v être*) **1** to play; **pour s'~** for fun; **dépêche-toi, je n'ai pas le temps de m'~** (figurative) hurry up, I haven't got time to mess about°; **2 bien s'~** to have a good time.

amuseur, **-euse** /amyzœʀ, øz/ *nm,f* entertainer.

amygdale /amidal/ *nf* tonsil.

an /ɑ̃/ *nm* year; **en l'~ deux mille** in the year two thousand; **l'~ 55 avant J.-C./après J.-C.** 55 BC/AD; **avoir huit ~s** to be eight (years old); **les moins de dix-huit ~s** the under-eighteens.
IDIOMS **bon ~, mal ~** year in, year out.

anabolisant /anabolizɑ̃/ *nm* anabolic steroid.

anachronique /anakʀɔnik/ *adj* anachronistic.

anal, **~e**, *mpl* **-aux** /anal, o/ *adj* anal.

analogie /analɔʒi/ *nf* analogy.

analogue /analɔg/ *adj* similar (**à** to).

analphabète /analfabɛt/ *adj, nmf* illiterate.

analyse /analiz/ *nf* **1** analysis; **faire l'~ de qch** to analyse[GB] sth; **2** (Med) test; **~ de sang** blood test; **3** psychoanalysis.

analyser /analize/ [1] *vtr* **1** (gen) to analyse[GB]; **2** (Med) to test [*blood, urine*].

analyste /analist/ *nmf* analyst.

ananas /anana(s)/ *nm inv* pineapple.

anarchie /anaʀʃi/ *nf* anarchy.

anarchiste /anaʀʃist/ I *adj* anarchistic.
II *nmf* anarchist.

anatomie /anatɔmi/ *nf* anatomy.

ancêtre /ɑ̃sɛtʀ/ *nmf* **1** ancestor; **2**° old man/woman; **3** (figurative) ancestor; father.

anchois /ɑ̃ʃwa/ *nm inv* anchovy.

ancien, **-ienne**[1] /ɑ̃sjɛ̃, ɛn/ I *adj* **1** [*champion, president, capital*] former; **2** [*history, language*] ancient; **3** [*style, money, picture, book, building*] old; [*car*] vintage; [*piece of furniture*] antique; **4 c'est lui le plus ~** (in job, organization) he's been here longest.
II *nm* **1** (in tribe, congregation) elder; (in company) senior member; **les ~s** the older people; **2** old member; former student; **3 l'~** older property; (furniture) antiques.
■ **~ combattant** veteran; **l'Ancien Testament** the Old Testament.

ancienne[2]: **à l'ancienne** /alɑ̃sjɛn/ *phr* [*jam, piece of furniture*] traditional-style.

anciennement /ɑ̃sjɛnmɑ̃/ *adv* formerly.

ancienneté /ɑ̃sjɛnte/ *nf* **1** (of person) seniority; **trois ans d'~** three years' service; **2** (of tradition, relic) antiquity; (of building) age.

ancre /ɑ̃kʀ/ *nf* (Naut) anchor; **jeter/lever l'~** to cast/to weigh anchor.

ancrer /ɑ̃kʀe/ [1] I *vtr* **1** to anchor [*ship*]; **2** to fix [*idea*]; to establish [*custom*].
II **s'ancrer** *v refl* (+ *v être*) **1** to anchor; **2** [*idea*] to become fixed; [*custom*] to become established.

andouille /ɑ̃duj/ *nf* **1** (Culin) andouille; **2**° fool.

âne /ɑn/ *nm* **1** (Zool) donkey, ass; **2**° dimwit°; (Sch) dunce.
IDIOMS **faire l'~ pour avoir du son** to act dumb to find out more.

anéantir /aneɑ̃tiʀ/ [3] *vtr* **1** to ruin [*crops, harvest*]; to lay waste to [*town*]; to shatter [*hopes*]; **2** [*news*] to crush; [*strain*] to exhaust.

anéantissement /aneɑ̃tismɑ̃/ *nm* **1** (of town) destruction; (of crops, harvest) devastation; **2** (of hopes) shattering; (of a person) total collapse.

anecdote /anɛkdɔt/ *nf* anecdote; **pour l'~** as a matter of interest.

anémie /anemi/ *nf* **1** anaemia; **2** weakness.

anémique /anemik/ *adj* **1** anaemic; **2** weak.

anémone /anemɔn/ *nf* anemone.

ânerie /ɑnʀi/ *nf* **1** silly remark; **2** silly blunder.

ânesse /ɑnɛs/ *nf* she-ass, female donkey.

anesthésie /anɛstezi/ *nf* anaesthesia.

anesthésiste /anɛstezist/ *nmf* anaesthetist (GB), anesthesiologist (US).

aneth /anɛt/ *nm* dill.

ange /ɑ̃ʒ/ *nm* angel; **~ gardien** guardian angel.
IDIOMS **être aux ~s** to be in (one's) seventh heaven.

angélique[1] /ɑ̃ʒelik/ *adj* angelic.

angélique[2] /ɑ̃ʒelik/ *nf* angelica.

angelot /ɑ̃ʒlo/ *nm* cherub.

angine /ɑ̃ʒin/ *nf* throat infection; **~ de poitrine** angina pectoris.

anglais, **~e**[1] /ɑ̃glɛ, ɛz/ I *adj* English.
II *nm* (language) English.

Anglais, **~e** /ɑ̃glɛ, ɛz/ *nm,f* Englishman/Englishwoman.

anglaise[2] /ɑ̃glɛz/ I *adj f* ▸ **anglais** I.
II *nf* ringlet.

angle /ɑ̃gl/ *nm* **1** angle; **~ aigu/droit** acute/right angle; **2** corner.

Angleterre /ɑ̃glətɛʀ/ *pr nf* England.

angliciser /ɑ̃glisize/ [1] I *vtr* to anglicize.
II **s'angliciser** *v refl* (+ *v être*) to become anglicized.

anglo-américain, **~e**, *mpl* **~s** /ɑ̃glo amerikɛ̃, ɛn/ I *adj* **1** Anglo-American; **2** American English.
II *nm* American English.

anglo-normand, **~e**, *mpl* **~s** /ɑ̃glonɔʀmɑ̃, ɑ̃d/ *adj* Anglo-Norman.

Anglo-Normande /ɑ̃glonɔʀmɑ̃d/ *adj f* **les îles ~s** the Channel Islands.

anglophone /ɑ̃glɔfɔn/ I *adj* English-speaking.
II *nmf* English speaker; Anglophone.

anglo-saxon, **-onne**, *mpl* **~s** /ɑ̃glosaksɔ̃, ɔn/ *adj* Anglo-Saxon.

angoissant, **~e** /ɑ̃gwasɑ̃, ɑ̃t/ *adj* [*prospect*] alarming; [*film, silence*] frightening.

angoisse /ɑ̃gwas/ *nf* anxiety.

angoissé, **~e** /ɑ̃gwase/ *adj* [*voice, face, person*] anxious.

angoisser /ɑ̃gwase/ [1] **I** *vtr* to worry.
II° *vi* to be anxious, to be nervous.

anguille /ɑ̃gij/ *nf* eel.
IDIOMS **il y a ~ sous roche** there's something going on.

angulaire /ɑ̃gylɛʀ/ *adj* angular.

anguleux, -euse /ɑ̃gylø, øz/ *adj* [*features, face*] angular; [*elbow*] bony.

animal, ~e, *mpl* **-aux** /animal, o/ **I** *adj* animal.
II *nm* animal; **~ de compagnie** or **familier** pet; **~ domestique** domestic animal; **~ nuisible** pest.

animateur, -trice /animatœʀ, tʀis/ *nm,f* **1** (of group of holidaymakers, club) coordinator; (of study group, association) leader; (of project, festival) organizer; **2** presenter.

animation /animasjɔ̃/ *nf* **1** (of group, exhibition, festival) organization; (of sales) coordination; **2** life, liveliness; **mettre de l'~ dans une réception** to liven up a reception; **ville qui manque d'~** dull town; **3** (of street, market) hustle and bustle; (of people) excitement.

animé, ~e /anime/ *adj* **1** [*discussion, speaker, period*] lively; [*street*] bustling; **2 ~ de mauvaises intentions** spurred on by bad intentions.

animer /anime/ [1] **I** *vtr* **1** to lead [*discussion, group*]; to run [*course, show*]; to present [*programme*]; **2** to liven up [*town, story, meeting*].
II s'animer *v refl* (+ *v être*) **1** [*conversation*] to become lively; [*meeting*] to liven up; [*face*] to light up; [*speaker*] to become animated; **2** [*statue, object*] to come to life.

anis /ani/ *nm inv* **1** anise; **2** aniseed.

ankyloser: s'ankyloser /ɑ̃kiloze/ [1] *v refl* (+ *v être*) to get stiff.

annales /anal/ *nf pl* **1** annals; **ça restera dans les ~** that will go down in history; **2** (of exams) book of past papers.

anneau, *pl* **~x** /ano/ **I** *nm* ring.
II anneaux *nm pl* (Sport) rings; **aux ~x** on the rings.

année /ane/ *nf* year; **l'~ en cours** this year, the current year; **avec les ~s** over the years; **d'~ en ~** year by year; **d'une ~ à l'autre** from one year to the next; **ces dix dernières ~s** over the last ten years; **souhaiter la bonne ~ à qn** to wish sb a happy new year; **en début d'~** early in the year; **(dans) les ~s 80** (in) the eighties; **location à l'~** annual rent.
■ **~ bissextile** leap year; **~ civile** calendar year; **~ de référence** base year; **~ universitaire** academic year; **les Années folles** the Roaring Twenties.

année-lumière, *pl* **années-lumière** /anelymjɛʀ/ *nf* light-year.

annexe[1] /anɛks/ *adj* **1** [*room, building*] adjoining; **2** [*questions*] additional; [*file, document*] attached.

annexe[2] /anɛks/ *nf* **1** (building) annexe (GB), annex (US); **2** (document) appendix.

annexer /anɛkse/ [1] *vtr* to annex [*territory, country*].

annexion /anɛksjɔ̃/ *nf* annexation (**par** by).

anniversaire /aniversɛʀ/ **I** *adj* **date** or **jour ~ de** anniversary of.
II *nm* **1** birthday; **bon ~!** happy birthday!; **2** anniversary.

annonce /anɔ̃s/ *nf* **1** announcement; **à l'~ de leur départ** when their departure was announced; **2** advertisement, ad°; **une ~ publicitaire** an advert°; **petite ~** classified advertisement; **3** declaration; **faire une ~** (in bridge) to bid; **4** sign.

annoncer /anɔ̃se/ [12] **I** *vtr* **1** to announce; **elle nous a annoncé son départ** she informed us that she was leaving; **2** to forecast [*rain, event*]; **3** [*event, signal*] to herald.
II s'annoncer *v refl* (+ *v être*) **1** [*crisis, storm*] to be brewing; **2 la récolte 92 s'annonce excellente** the '92 harvest promises to be very good.

annonciateur, -trice /anɔ̃sjatœʀ, tʀis/ *adj* [*sign, signal*] warning.

Annonciation /anɔ̃sjasjɔ̃/ *nf* Annunciation.

annuaire /anɥɛʀ/ *nm* **1** directory; **2** yearbook.

annuel, -elle /anɥɛl/ *adj* (gen) annual, yearly; [*subscription*] annual, one-year; [*contract*] one-year.

annulaire /anylɛʀ/ *nm* ring finger.

annulation /anylasjɔ̃/ *nf* **1** (gen) (of measure) abolition; (of law, sanctions) repeal; **2** (Law) (of verdict) quashing; (of elections) cancellation[GB]; (of treaty) revocation; (of marriage) annulment.

annuler /anyle/ [1] **I** *vtr* **1** to cancel [*appointment, trip*]; to write off [*debt*]; to discount [*result of match*]; **2** (Law) to declare [sth] void [*elections*]; to quash [*verdict*].
II s'annuler *v refl* (+ *v être*) to cancel each other out.

anodin, ~e /anɔdɛ̃, in/ *adj* [*subject*] safe, neutral; [*question, joke*] innocent.

anomalie /anɔmali/ *nf* **1** anomaly; **2** abnormality; **3** fault.

ânon /anɔ̃/ *nm* **1** donkey foal; **2** little donkey.

anonymat /anɔnima/ *nm* **1** anonymity; **sortir de l'~** to reveal one's identity; to emerge from obscurity; **2** confidentiality.

anonyme /anɔnim/ *adj* anonymous.

anorexie /anɔʀɛksi/ *nf* anorexia.

anormal, ~e, *mpl* **-aux** /anɔʀmal, o/ *adj* abnormal.

ANPE /aɛnpeœ/ *nf* (*abbr* = **Agence nationale pour l'emploi**) *French national employment agency.*

anse /ɑ̃s/ *nf* (of cup, basket) handle.

antagoniste /ɑ̃tagɔnist/ *adj* [*groups*] opposing; [*interests*] conflicting.

antarctique /ɑ̃taʀktik/ *adj* Antarctic.

Antarctique /ɑ̃taʀktik/ *pr nm* **1** Antarctic; **océan ~** Antarctic Ocean; **2** Antarctica.

antécédent, ~e /ɑ̃tesedɑ̃, ɑ̃t/ **I** *adj* previous.
II *nm* **1** past history; **2** medical history; **3** (in grammar, mathematics) antecedent.

antenne /ɑ̃tɛn/ *nf* **1** (of radio, television) aerial; (of radar, satellite) antenna; **passer à l'~** [*programme, person*] to go on the air; **2** (of organization, service) branch; **~ régionale** regional branch; **3** (of insect, shrimp) antenna; **avoir des ~s** (figurative) to have a sixth sense.

antérieur, **~e** /ɑ̃teʀjœʀ/ *adj* **1** [*salary, situation, work*] previous; **2** [*limb, ligament*] anterior.

antérieurement /ɑ̃teʀjœʀmɑ̃/ *adv* previously; **~ à** prior to.

anthracite /ɑ̃tʀasit/ *adj inv* charcoal grey (GB), charcoal gray (US).

anthrax /ɑ̃tʀaks/ *nm inv* carbuncle.

anthropologie /ɑ̃tʀɔpɔlɔʒi/ *nf* anthropology.

anthropologiste /ɑ̃tʀɔpɔlɔʒist/, **anthropologue** /ɑ̃tʀɔpolɔg/ *nmf* anthropologist.

anthropophage /ɑ̃tʀɔpɔfaʒ/*nmf* cannibal.

antiaérien, **-ienne** /ɑ̃tiaeʀjɛ̃, ɛn/ *adj* antiaircraft.

antialcoolique /ɑ̃tialkɔlik/ *adj* anti-alcohol.

antiatomique /ɑ̃tiatɔmik/ *adj* (anti-)radiation; **abri ~** nuclear shelter.

antibiotique /ɑ̃tibjɔtik/ *adj, nm* antibiotic.

antibrouillard /ɑ̃tibʀujaʀ/ *adj inv* **phare ~** fog light.

antibruit /ɑ̃tibʀɥi/ *adj inv* soundproof.

antichambre /ɑ̃tiʃɑ̃bʀ/ *nf* anteroom.

antichar /ɑ̃tiʃaʀ/ *adj inv* antitank.

antichoc /ɑ̃tiʃɔk/ *adj inv* **1 casque ~** crash helmet; **2** [*watch*] shockproof.

anticipation /ɑ̃tisipasjɔ̃/ *nf* anticipation; **roman d'~** science fiction novel.

anticipé, **~e** /ɑ̃tisipe/ *adj* [*departure, election, liberation*] early.

anticiper /ɑ̃tisipe/ [1]
vtr to anticipate [*reaction, change, movement*].
II *vi* **1** to get ahead of oneself; **2** to think ahead.

anticonformiste /ɑ̃tikɔ̃fɔʀmist/ *adj, nmf* nonconformist.

anticonstitutionnel, **-elle** /ɑ̃tikɔ̃stitysjɔnɛl/ *adj* unconstitutional.

anticorps /ɑ̃tikɔʀ/ *nm inv* antibody.

anti-crevaison /ɑ̃tikʀəvɛzɔ̃/ *adj inv* **bombe ~** puncture sealant spray.

antidater /ɑ̃tidate/ [1] *vtr* to backdate.

antidérapant, **~e** /ɑ̃tideʀapɑ̃, ɑ̃t/ *adj* [*tyre*] nonskid; [*sole*] nonslip.

antidopage /ɑ̃tidɔpaʒ/ *adj* [*measure*] against doping; **contrôle ~** dope test.

antidote /ɑ̃tidɔt/ *nm* antidote (**contre** against; **à, de** for).

antigang /ɑ̃tigɑ̃g/ *adj inv* **brigade ~** crime squad.

antigel /ɑ̃tiʒɛl/ *adj inv, nm* antifreeze.

anti-inflammatoire, *pl* **~s** /ɑ̃tiɛ̃flamatwaʀ/ *adj, nm* anti-inflammatory.

antillais, **~e** /ɑ̃tijɛ, ɛz/ *adj* West Indian.

Antilles /ɑ̃tij/ *pr nf pl* **les ~** the West Indies; **les Petites/Grandes ~** the Lesser/Greater Antilles.

antilope /ɑ̃tilɔp/ *nf* antelope.

antimite /ɑ̃timit/ *adj, nm* moth-repellent.

antipathie /ɑ̃tipati/ *nf* antipathy (**pour** toward(s); **entre** between).

antipathique /ɑ̃tipatik/ *adj* unpleasant; **il m'est ~** I dislike him.

antipelliculaire /ɑ̃tipɛlikylɛʀ/ *adj* antidandruff.

antipode /ɑ̃tipɔd/ *nm* antipodes.

antipoison /ɑ̃tipwazɔ̃/ *adj inv* **centre ~** poisons unit.

antipollution /ɑ̃tipɔlysjɔ̃/ *adj inv* **la lutte ~** the fight against pollution.

antiquaire /ɑ̃tikɛʀ/ *nmf* antique dealer.

antique /ɑ̃tik/ *adj* ancient.

antiquité /ɑ̃tikite/ I *nf* antique; **un magasin d'~s** an antique shop.
II **antiquités** *nf pl* antiquities.

Antiquité /ɑ̃tikite/ *nf* antiquity; **dans l'~** in antiquity.

antireflet /ɑ̃tiʀəflɛ/ *adj inv* nonreflective; (in photography) antiglare.

antirides /ɑ̃tiʀid/ *adj inv* anti-wrinkle.

antirouille /ɑ̃tiʀuj/ *adj inv* **1** rust-proofing; **2** rust-removing.

antisémite /ɑ̃tisemit/ I *adj* anti-Semitic.
II *nmf* anti-Semite.

antitabac /ɑ̃titaba/ *adj inv* antismoking.

antiterroriste /ɑ̃titɛʀɔʀist/ *adj* **lutte ~** fight against terrorism.

antithèse /ɑ̃titɛz/ *nf* antithesis.

antituberculeux, **-euse** /ɑ̃titybɛʀkylø, øz/ *adj* **vaccin ~** tuberculosis vaccine.

antivenimeux, **-euse** /ɑ̃tivənimø, øz/ *adj* **produit ~** product for use against snake-bite.

antivol /ɑ̃tivɔl/ I *adj inv* **dispositif ~** anti-theft device.
II *nm* (of bicycle, motorbike) lock; (of car) anti-theft device.

anus /anys/ *nm inv* anus.

Anvers /ɑ̃vɛʀ/ *pr n* Antwerp.

anxiété /ɑ̃ksjete/ *nf* anxiety; **avec ~** anxiously.

anxieux, **-ieuse** /ɑ̃ksjø, øz/ *adj* [*person*] anxious; [*attitude*] concerned.

aorte /aɔʀt/ *nf* aorta.

août /u(t)/ *nm* August.

apaisant, **~e** /apɛzɑ̃, ɑ̃t/ *adj* **1** soothing; **2** calming; **3** conciliatory.

apaisement /apɛzmɑ̃/ *nm* **geste d'~** calming gesture.

apaiser /apeze/ [1] I *vtr* **1** to pacify, to appease; **2** to ease [*conflict*]; **3** to calm [*rage*].
II **s'apaiser** *v refl* (+ *v être*) **1** to die down; **2** to calm down.

apathie /apati/ *nf* **1** apathy; **2** stagnation.

apatride /apatʀid/ *adj* stateless.

APEC /apɛk/ *nf* (*abbr* = **Agence pour l'emploi des cadres**) *executive employment agency*.

apercevoir /apɛʀsəvwaʀ/ [5] I *vtr* **1** to make out; **2** to catch sight of.
II **s'apercevoir** *v refl* (+ *v être*) **1 s'~ que** to notice that, to realize that; **s'~ de** to notice

[*mistake*]; **2** to catch sight of each other; **3** to meet briefly.

aperçu /apɛʀsy/ *nm* **1** glimpse; **2** outline; **3** insight.

apéritif /apeʀitif/ *nm* drink.

apesanteur /apəzɑ̃tœʀ/ *nf* weightlessness.

à-peu-près /apøpʀɛ/ *nm inv* approximation.

aphone /afɔn/ *adj* voiceless; **être ~** to have lost one's voice.

aphte /aft/ *nm* mouth ulcer.

apiculteur, **-trice** /apikyltœʀ, tʀis/ *nm,f* beekeeper.

apiculture /apikyltyʀ/ *nf* beekeeping.

apitoiement /apitwamɑ̃/ *nm* pity (**sur** for).

apitoyer /apitwaje/ [23] **I** *vtr* to move [sb] to pity.
II s'apitoyer *v refl* (+ *v être*) **s'~ sur (le sort de) qn** to feel sorry for sb.

aplanir /aplaniʀ/ [3] *vtr* **1** to level; **2** to iron [sth] out.

aplati, **~e** /aplati/ *adj* **1** flattened; **2** [*nose*] flat.

aplatir /aplatiʀ/ [3] *vtr* **1** to flatten; **2** to smooth out [*cushion*]; to smooth down [*hair*]; **3** to press [*seams*].

aplomb /aplɔ̃/ **I** *nm* **1** confidence; **vous ne manquez pas d'~!** you've got a nerve!; **2** plumb, perpendicularity.
II d'aplomb *phr* **1 être d'~** to be straight, to be plumb vertical; **2**° **tu te sens d'~?** do you feel well?; **ça va te remettre d'~** it will put you back on your feet.

apnée /apne/ *nf* apn(o)ea; **plonger en ~** to dive without an aqualung.

apocalypse /apɔkalips/ *nf* apocalypse.

apocalyptique /apɔkaliptik/ *adj* apocalyptic.

apogée /apɔʒe/ *nm* **1** (of moon, satellite) apogee; **2** (of career, empire) peak.

apologie /apɔlɔʒi/ *nf* panegyric; apologia; **faire l'~ de** to justify; to praise.

apoplexie /apɔplɛksi/ *nf* apoplexy; **crise d'~** apoplectic fit.

a posteriori /apɔsteʀjɔʀi/ *phr* after the event.

apostolat /apɔstɔla/ *nm* **1** apostolate; **2** (figurative) apostolic mission.

apostrophe /apɔstʀɔf/ *nf* **1** apostrophe; **2** remark.

apostropher /apɔstʀɔfe/ [1] *vtr* to heckle.

apothéose /apɔteoz/ *nf* **1** (of show) high point; **2** (of career, work) culmination.

apothicaire† /apɔtikɛʀ/ *nm* apothecary‡; **comptes d'~** complicated calculations.

apôtre /apotʀ/ *nm* apostle.

apparaître /apaʀɛtʀ/ [73] **I** *vi* (+ *v être*) **1** [*person, problem*] to appear; [*sun, moon*] to come out; **2 laisser** or **faire ~** to show, to reveal; **3** to seem, to appear (to be).
II *v impers* **il apparaît que** it appears that.

apparat /apaʀa/ *nm* grandeur; **d'~** ceremonial.

appareil /apaʀɛj/ *nm* **1** device; **2** appliance; **3** telephone; **qui est à l'~?** who's calling please?; **4** aircraft, (aero)plane (GB), (air)plane (US); **5** system; **l'~ digestif** the digestive system; **6** apparatus; **l'~ du parti** the party apparatus.
■ **~ auditif** hearing aid; **~ (dentaire)** brace (GB), braces (US); **~ à sous** slot machine; **~ photographique** or **photo** camera.
IDIOMS **être dans son plus simple ~** to be in one's birthday suit.

appareillage /apaʀɛjaʒ/ *nm* **1** casting off; **2** equipment.

appareiller /apaʀeje/ [1] *vi* to cast off.

apparemment /apaʀamɑ̃/ *adv* **1** apparently; **2** seemingly.

apparence /apaʀɑ̃s/ *nf* appearance; **pour sauver les ~s** to keep up appearances.

apparent, **~e** /apaʀɑ̃, ɑ̃t/ *adj* **1** visible; **2** [*embarrassment*] apparent; **sans raison ~e** for no apparent reason; **3** seeming, apparent.

apparenté, **~e** /apaʀɑ̃te/ *adj* **1** [*person*] related (**à** to); **2** [*company*] allied.

apparenter: **s'apparenter** /apaʀɑ̃te/ [1] *v refl* (+ *v être*) **s'~ à** to resemble.

apparition /apaʀisjɔ̃/ *nf* **1** (of product, invention) appearance, advent; (of movement, problem) emergence; **2** apparition.

appartement /apaʀtəmɑ̃/ *nm* flat (GB), apartment; **~ témoin** show flat (GB) or apartment.

appartenance /apaʀtənɑ̃s/ *nf* affiliation (**à** to), membership (**à** of).

appartenir /apaʀtəniʀ/ [36] **I appartenir à** *v+prep* **1** to belong to; **2** to be a member of.
II *v impers* **il appartient à qn de faire** it is up to sb to do.

appât /apɑ/ *nm* **1** bait; **2** lure; **l'~ du gain** the lure of profit.

appâter /apɑte/ [1] *vtr* **1** to bait; **2** to lure.

appauvrir /apovʀiʀ/ [3] **I** *vtr* to impoverish.
II s'appauvrir *v refl* (+ *v être*) to become impoverished.

appauvrissement /apovʀismɑ̃/ *nm* impoverishment.

appeau, *pl* **~x** /apo/ *nm* decoy.

appel /apɛl/ *nm* **1** call; (urgent) appeal; **~ à** call for [*solidarity*]; appeal for [*calm*]; **~ au secours** call for help; cry for help; **lancer un ~ à** to call for; to appeal for; **faire ~ à** to appeal to [*person*]; to call [*fire brigade*]; to call in [*army*]; [*task*] to call for [*skills*]; **2** roll call; (Sch) registration; **3** (Mil) call up (GB), draft (US); **4** (Law) appeal; **faire ~** to appeal; **5** (Sport) take off.
■ **~ d'air** draught (GB), draft (US); **~ d'offres** invitation to tender; **~ de phares** flash of headlights (GB) or high beams (US).

appelé, **~e** /aple/ **I** *pp* ▶ **appeler**.
II *pp adj* **~ à qch/à faire** destined for sth/to do.
III *nm* (Mil) conscript, draftee (US).

appeler /aple/ [19] **I** *vtr* **1** to call; **il se fait ~ Robert** he likes to be called Robert; (as alias) he goes by the name of Robert; **~ (qn) à l'aide** to call (to sb) for help; **2** to phone (GB), to call; **3** to call [*doctor, taxi*]; to send for [*pupil*]; **~ qn sous les drapeaux** (Mil) to call sb up; **4 ~ qn à faire** to call on sb to do; **~ à la grève** to call for strike action; **~ qn à un poste** to appoint sb to a post; **5 mon travail m'appelle à beaucoup voyager** my work involves a lot of travel; **6** [*issue*] to call for [*attention*].

II **en appeler à** *v+prep* to appeal to.

III **s'appeler** *v refl* (+ *v être*) **comment t'appelles-tu?** what's your name?; **voilà ce qui s'appelle une belle voiture!** now, that's what you call a nice car!

IDIOMS **ça s'appelle 'reviens'**○! don't forget to give it back!; **~ les choses par leur nom**, **~ un chat un chat** to call a spade a spade.

appellation /apɛlɑsjɔ̃/ *nf* name, appellation.

appendice /apɛ̃dis/ *nm* (Anat) appendix.

appendicite /apɛ̃disit/ *nf* appendicitis.

appentis /apɑ̃ti/ *nm inv* lean-to.

appesantir: **s'appesantir** /apəzɑ̃tiʀ/ [3] *v refl* (+ *v être*) **s'~ sur** to dwell on.

appétissant, **~e** /apetisɑ̃, ɑ̃t/ *adj* appetizing.

appétit /apeti/ *nm* **1** appetite; **mettre qn en ~** to whet sb's appetite; **couper l'~ de qn** to take sb's appetite away; **2** appetite (**de** for), hunger (**de** for).

applaudir /aplodiʀ/ [3] I *vtr* to applaud.

II *vi* **1** to applaud, to clap; **~ à tout rompre** to bring the house down; **2** to approve; **~ des deux mains** to applaud or approve heartily.

applaudissement /aplodismɑ̃/ *nm* **1** applause; **2** acclaim.

applicable /aplikabl/ *adj* applicable (**à** to); **facilement ~** easy to implement.

applicateur /aplikatœʀ/ *nm* applicator.

application /aplikasjɔ̃/ *nf* **1** care; **il manque d'~** he doesn't apply himself; **2** implementation, enforcement; **mettre en ~** to apply [*theory*]; to implement [*law*]; **entrer en ~** to come into force; **3** (of device, program) **~s** applications; **4** (of ointment) application; **5** (Comput) application program.

applique /aplik/ *nf* wall light.

appliqué, **~e** /aplike/ *adj* **1** hardworking; **2** [*work*] careful; **3** [*science*] applied.

appliquer /aplike/ [1] I *vtr* **1** to apply [*ointment*] (**sur** to); to put [*stamp*] (**sur** on); **2** to implement [*policy*]; to apply [*law*]; **3** to apply [*technique, reasoning*] (**à** to).

II **s'appliquer** *v refl* (+ *v être*) **1** to take great care (**à faire** to do); **2 s'~ à qch/qn** [*law, remark*] to apply to sth/sb.

appoint /apwɛ̃/ *nm* **1** exact change; **faire l'~** to give the exact change; **2 d'~** [*role*] supporting; [*salary*] supplementary; [*heating*] additional.

appointements /apwɛ̃tmɑ̃/ *nm pl* salary.

apport /apɔʀ/ *nm* **1** provision; **2** contribution (**à** to); **~ de capitaux** capital contribution.

apporter /apɔʀte/ [1] *vtr* **1** to bring [*improvement, news*]; to bring in [*revenue*]; to bring about [*change*]; **~ qch à qn** to bring sb sth, to take sb sth; **2** to give [*support, explanation*] (**à** to); **~ son concours à qch** to help with sth.

apposer /apoze/ [1] *vtr* to affix (**sur** on).

apposition /apozisjɔ̃/ *nf* apposition.

appréciable /apʀesjabl/ *adj* **1** substantial; **2 c'est ~** it's nice.

appréciatif, **-ive** /apʀesjatif, iv/ *adj* **1** appreciative; **2** appraising.

appréciation /apʀesjasjɔ̃/ *nf* **1** (of quantity) estimate; **2** (financial) evaluation; **erreur d'~** misjudgment ; **3** (of quality) assessment; **être laissé à l'~ de qn** to be left to sb's discretion; **4** (of currency) appreciation.

apprécier /apʀesje/ [2] *vtr* **1** to appreciate [*art*]; to like [*person*]; **elle n'a pas apprécié** she wasn't exactly pleased; **2** (financially) to value; **3** to estimate [*distance*]; **4** to assess [*situation*].

appréhender /apʀeɑ̃de/ [1] *vtr* **1** to arrest; **2** to dread; **3** to comprehend, to understand.

appréhension /apʀeɑ̃sjɔ̃/ *nf* apprehension; **avec ~** apprehensively.

apprenant, **~e** /apʀənɑ̃, ɑ̃t/ *nm,f* learner.

apprendre /apʀɑ̃dʀ/ [52] *vtr* **1** to learn (**à faire** to do); **2** to learn [*truth*]; to hear (about) [*news*]; **3** to teach; **~ qch à qn** to teach sb sth; **4 ~ qch à qn** to tell sb sth.

apprenti, **~e** /apʀɑ̃ti/ *nm,f* **1** apprentice, trainee; **~ boulanger** baker's apprentice; **2** novice; **~ poète** novice poet.

IDIOMS **jouer les ~s sorciers** to open a Pandora's box.

apprentissage /apʀɑ̃tisaʒ/ *nm* **1** training, apprenticeship; **2** learning.

apprêté, **~e** /apʀete/ I *pp* ▶ **apprêter**.

II *pp adj* **1** affected; **2** [*hairstyle*] fussy.

apprêter /apʀɛte/ [1] I *vtr* to finish [*material*]; to size [*wall*]; to prime [*wood*].

II **s'apprêter** *v refl* (+ *v être*) **s'~ à faire** to get ready to do.

apprivoiser /apʀivwaze/ [1] *vtr* to tame.

approbateur, **-trice** /apʀɔbatœʀ, tʀis/ *adj* **sourire ~** smile of approval.

approbation /apʀɔbasjɔ̃/ *nf* approval.

approchant, **~e** /apʀɔʃɑ̃, ɑ̃t/ *adj* **quelque chose d'~** something similar.

approche /apʀɔʃ/ *nf* **1** approach (**de** of); **aux ~s de la ville** on the outskirts of town; **2** approach (**de** to); **d'~ difficile** [*book*] difficult to understand; [*person*] unapproachable.

approcher /apʀɔʃe/ [1] I *vtr* **1 ~ qch de la fenêtre** to move sth near to the window; **2** to go up to; to come up to; **3** to come into contact with, to rub shoulders with.

II **approcher de** *v+prep* to be (getting) close to.

III *vi* to approach.

IV **s'approcher** *v refl* (+ *v être*) **s'~ de** to go near; to come near.

approfondi, **~e** /apʀɔfɔ̃di/ I *pp* ▶ **approfondir**.

II *pp adj* detailed, in-depth.

approfondir /apʀɔfɔ̃diʀ/ [3] *vtr* **1** to go into [sth] in depth; **2 ~ ses connaissances en français** to improve one's knowledge of French; **3** to make [sth] deeper.

approfondissement /apʀɔfɔ̃dismɑ̃/ *nm* (in knowledge) improvement.

approprié, **~e** /apʀɔpʀije/ *adj* appropriate.

approprier: **s'approprier** /apʀɔpʀije/ [2] *v refl* (+ *v être*) **1** to take, to appropriate [*object, idea*]; **2** to seize [*power*].

approuver /apʀuve/ [1] *vtr* **1** to approve of; **je t'approuve d'avoir accepté** I think you were right to accept; **2** to approve [*budget*]; to pass [*bill*].

approvisionnement /apʀɔvizjɔnmɑ̃/ *nm* supply (**en** of).

approvisionner /apʀɔvizjɔne/ [1] **I** *vtr* **1** to supply (**en** with); **mal approvisionné** [*shop*] badly stocked; **2** to pay money into [*account*].
II s'approvisionner *v refl* (+ *v être*) **1 s'~ en** to get one's supplies of (**auprès de** from); **2** to stock up (**en** on, with).

approximatif, **-ive** /apʀɔksimatif, iv/ *adj* [*estimate, translation*] rough; **dans un anglais ~** in broken English.

approximation /apʀɔksimasjɔ̃/ *nf* **1** rough estimate; **2** approximation.

approximativement /apʀɔksimativmɑ̃/ *adv* approximately.

appui /apɥi/ *nm* **1** support; **à l'~ de** in support of [*theory*]; **prendre ~ sur** to lean on; **2 ~ (de fenêtre)** window sill.

appui-tête, *pl* **appuis-tête** /apɥitɛt/ *nm* headrest.

appuyé, **~e** /apɥije/ **I** *pp* ▶ **appuyer**.
II *pp adj* **1** [*look*] intent; **2** [*joke*] laboured[GB].

appuyer /apɥije/ [22] **I** *vtr* **1** to rest (**sur** on); to lean (**sur** on); **2** to press (**contre** against); **3** to support, to back up [*argument*] (**sur** with); to back, to support [*person*].
II *vi* **1 ~ sur** to press [*switch*]; to put one's foot on [*brake*]; **2 ~ sur** to stress, to emphasize [*word*].
III s'appuyer *v refl* (+ *v être*) **1** to lean (**sur** on; **contre** against); **2 s'~ sur** to rely on [*theory*]; to draw on [*report*]; [*study*] to be based on; **3**○ to get lumbered with○.

âpre /ɑpʀ/ *adj* **1** [*taste, cold*] bitter; **2** [*voice*] harsh; **3** [*struggle*] fierce; [*argument*] bitter.

âprement /ɑpʀəmɑ̃/ *adv* [*defend*] fiercely; [*argue*] bitterly.

après /apʀɛ/ **I** *adv* afterward(s), after; later; **peu/bien ~** shortly/long afterward(s); **je te le dirais ~** I'll tell you later; **une heure ~** one hour later; **peu ~ il y a un lac** a bit further on there's a lake; **et ~?** and then what?; so what○?
II *prep* after; **~ mon départ** after I leave; after I left; **~ coup** after the event, afterward(s); **j'irai ~ avoir fait la sieste** I'll go after I've had a nap; **il est toujours ~ son fils**○ he's always on at his son.
III d'après *phr* **1 d'~ moi** in my opinion; **d'~ lui/la météo** according to him/the weather forecast; **d'~ ce qu'elle a dit** from what she said; **d'~ ma montre** by my watch; **2** from; based on; **d'~ un dessin de Gauguin** from a drawing by Gauguin; **3 l'année d'~** the year after; **la fois/page d'~** the next time/page.
IV après que *phr* after; **~ qu'il a parlé** after he had spoken.
V après- (*combining form*) **l'~-guerre** the postwar years; **l'~-Thatcher** the post-Thatcher era.

après-demain /apʀɛdmɛ̃/ *adv* the day after tomorrow.

après-guerre, *pl* **~s** /apʀɛgɛʀ/ *nm* or *nf* postwar years.

après-midi /apʀɛmidi/ *nm inv* or *nf inv* afternoon.

après-rasage, *pl* **~s** /apʀɛʀazaʒ/ *adj inv*, *nm* after-shave.

après-ski /apʀɛski/ *nm inv* snowboot.

après-vente /apʀɛvɑ̃t/ *adj inv* after-sales.

âpreté /ɑpʀəte/ *nf* **1** (of struggle) fierceness; (of argument) bitterness; **2** (of fruit) bitterness.

a priori /apʀijɔʀi/ **I** *phr* a priori.
II *phr* **~, ça ne devrait pas poser de problèmes** on the face of it there shouldn't be any problems; **rejeter ~ une proposition** to reject a proposal out of hand.

à-propos /apʀɔpo/ *nm inv* **intervenir avec ~** to make an apposite remark; **agir avec ~** to do the right thing.

apte /apt/ *adj* **~ à qch/à faire** capable of sth/of doing; fit for sth/to do.

aptitude /aptityd/ *nf* aptitude (**à** for; **à faire** for doing); fitness (**à** for; **à faire** to do).

aquarelle /akwaʀɛl/ *nf* **1** watercolours[GB]; **l'~** watercolour[GB] painting; **2** watercolour[GB].

aquarelliste /akwaʀelist/ *nmf* watercolourist[GB].

aquarium /akwaʀjɔm/ *nm* aquarium, fish tank.

aquatique /akwatik/ *adj* **1** aquatic; **2 sport ~** water sport.

aqueduc /akdyk/ *nm* aqueduct.

aqueux, **~euse** /akø, øz/ *adj* aqueous.

aquilin /akilɛ̃/ *adj m* aquiline.

arabe /aʀab/ **I** *adj* **1** Arab; **2** Arabic.
II *nm* Arabic.

Arabe /aʀab/ *nmf* Arab.

arabesque /aʀabɛsk/ *nf* arabesque.

Arabie /aʀabi/ *pr nf* Arabia.
■ **~ Saoudite** Saudi Arabia.

arable /aʀabl/ *adj* arable.

arachide /aʀaʃid/ *nf* groundnut, peanut.

araignée /aʀeɲe/ *nf* spider.
■ **~ de mer** spider crab.
IDIOMS **avoir une ~ au plafond**○ to have a screw loose○.

aratoire /aʀatwaʀ/ *adj* ploughing (GB), plowing (US).

arbalète /aʀbalɛt/ *nf* crossbow.

arbitrage /aʀbitʀaʒ/ *nm* **1** refereeing, umpiring; **2** arbitration.

arbitraire /aʀbitʀɛʀ/ *adj* arbitrary.

arbitre /aʀbitʀ/ *nm* **1** referee, umpire; **2** arbitrator.

arbitrer /aʀbitʀe/ [1] **I** *vtr* **1** to referee, to umpire; **2** to arbitrate in.
II *vi* to arbitrate (**entre** between).

arborer /aʀbɔʀe/ [1] *vtr* **1** to wear [*smile*]; to

sport [*badge*]; **2** to parade [*opinion*]; **3** to bear [*banner*]; to fly [*flag*].

arborescent, **~e** /aʀbɔʀesɑ̃, ɑ̃t/ *adj* tree.

arboriculture /aʀbɔʀikyltyʀ/ *nf* arboriculture.

arbre /aʀbʀ/ *nm* **1** tree; **2** (Tech) shaft.
■ **~ généalogique** family tree; **~ de Noël** Christmas tree.

arbrisseau, *pl* **~x** /aʀbʀiso/ *nm* small tree.

arbuste /aʀbyst/ *nm* shrub.

arc /aʀk/ *nm* **1** (Sport) bow; **2** arc; **~ de cercle** arc of a circle; **3** arch.

arcade /aʀkad/ *nf* arcade; **~s** archways.
■ **~ sourcilière** arch of the eyebrow.

arcanes /aʀkan/ *nm pl* mysteries.

arc-bouter: **s'arc-bouter** /aʀkbute/ [1] *v refl* (+ *v être*) to brace oneself.

arceau, *pl* **~x** /aʀso/ *nm* **1** arch; **2** (in croquet) hoop; **3** (in car) roll bar.

arc-en-ciel, *pl* **arcs-en-ciel** /aʀkɑ̃sjɛl/ *nm* rainbow.

archaïque /aʀkaik/ *adj* archaic.

archaïsme /aʀkaism/ *nm* archaism.

archange /aʀkɑ̃ʒ/ *nm* archangel.

arche /aʀʃ/ *nf* arch; **~ de Noé** Noah's Ark.

archéologie /aʀkeɔlɔʒi/ *nf* archaeology.

archéologique /aʀkeɔlɔʒik/ *adj* archaeological.

archer /aʀʃe/ *nm* archer.

archet /aʀʃɛ/ *nm* (Mus) bow.

archétype /aʀketip/ *nm* archetype.

archevêché /aʀʃəveʃe/ *nm* **1** archdiocese; **2** archbishop's palace.

archevêque /aʀʃəvɛk/ *nm* archbishop.

archi○ /aʀʃi/ *pref* **~connu** really well-known; **~plein** chock-a-block○.

archipel /aʀʃipɛl/ *nm* archipelago.

architecte /aʀʃitɛkt/ *nmf* architect.

architecture /aʀʃitɛktyʀ/ *nf* **1** architecture; **2** structure.

archives /aʀʃiv/ *nf pl* archives, records.

arçon /aʀsɔ̃/ *nm* (in horse's saddle) tree; **cheval d'~s** pommel horse.

Arctique /aʀktik/ *pr nm*, *adj* Arctic.

ardemment /aʀdamɑ̃/ *adv* passionately.

ardent, **~e** /aʀdɑ̃, ɑ̃t/ *adj* **1** [*ember*] glowing; [*sun*] blazing; **2** [*faith*] burning; [*wish, patriot*] fervent; [*struggle*] fierce; [*speech*] impassioned; [*nature*] passionate.

ardeur /aʀdœʀ/ *nf* (of person) ardour[GB]; (of beliefs) fervour[GB]; (of beginner) enthusiasm.

ardoise /aʀdwaz/ I *adj inv* slate-grey (GB), slate-gray (US).
II *nf* **1** slate; **2**○ account.

ardu, **~e** /aʀdy/ *adj* **1** arduous; **2** taxing.

are /aʀ/ *nf* one hundred square metres[GB], are.

arène /aʀɛn/ *nf* **1** arena; **2** bullring; **3** **~s** amphitheatre[GB].

arête /aʀɛt/ *nf* **1** fishbone; **2** (of roof, mountain) ridge; (of prism) edge; (of nose) bridge.

argent /aʀʒɑ̃/ *nm* **1** money; **en avoir pour son ~** to get one's money's worth; **2** silver.
■ **~ liquide** cash; **~ de poche** pocket money.
IDIOMS **prendre pour ~ comptant** to take at face value.

argenté, **~e** /aʀʒɑ̃te/ *adj* **1** silver-plated; **2** (in colour) silvery.

argenterie /aʀʒɑ̃tʀi/ *nf* silverware, silver.

argentin, **~e** /aʀʒɑ̃tɛ̃, in/ *adj* Argentinian.

Argentine /aʀʒɑ̃tin/ *pr nf* Argentina.

argile /aʀʒil/ *nf* clay.

argot /aʀgo/ *nm* slang.

argotique /aʀgɔtik/ *adj* slang, slangy.

arguer /aʀge/ [1] I *vtr* **~ que** to claim that.
II **arguer de** *v+prep* to give [sth] as a reason (**pour faire** for doing).

argument /aʀgymɑ̃/ *nm* argument; **tirer ~ de qch** to use sth as an excuse.

argumentation /aʀgymɑ̃tasjɔ̃/ *nf* line of argument.

argumenter /aʀgymɑ̃te/ [1] *vi* to argue (**sur** about; **contre** against).

argus /aʀgys/ *nm inv*: *used car prices guide.*

aride /aʀid/ *adj* arid.

aridité /aʀidite/ *nf* aridity.

aristocrate /aʀistɔkʀat/ *nmf* aristocrat.

aristocratie /aʀistɔkʀasi/ *nf* aristocracy.

aristocratique /aʀistɔkʀatik/ *adj* aristocratic.

arithmétique /aʀitmetik/ I *adj* arithmetical.
II *nf* arithmetic.

armateur /aʀmatœʀ/ *nm* shipowner.

armature /aʀmatyʀ/ *nf* **1** (of tent) frame; **2** (in construction) framework.

arme /aʀm/ I *nf* **1** weapon; **charger une ~** to load a gun; **une ~ à double tranchant** a double-edged sword; **rendre les ~s** to surrender; **en ~s** armed; **passer qn par les ~s** to execute sb by firing squad; **à ~s égales** on equal terms; **faire ses premières ~s dans l'enseignement** to start out as a teacher; **2** branch of the armed services.
II **armes** *nf pl* coat of arms.
■ **~ blanche** *weapon with a blade*; **~ à feu** firearm.

armé, **~e**[1] /aʀme/ I *pp* ▶ **armer**.
II *pp adj* **1** armed (**de** with); **vol à main ~e** armed robbery; **2** equipped (**de** with; **contre** against); **bien ~ pour faire** well equipped to do.

armée[2] /aʀme/ *nf* army.
■ **~ de l'air** air force; **l'~ de réserve** the reserves; **l'~ de terre** the army.

armement /aʀməmɑ̃/ *nm* **1** (of country) armament; (of troop) arming; **2** arms, weapons; **3** (of rifle) cocking; (of camera) winding on; **4** (of ship) fitting out.

arménien, **-ienne** /aʀmenjɛ̃, ɛn/ *adj* Armenian.

armer /aʀme/ [1] I *vtr* **1** to arm (**de** with; **contre** against); **2** to reinforce [*concrete*] (**de** with); **3** to fit out [*ship*]; **4** to wind on [*camera*]; to cock [*rifle*].
II **s'armer** *v refl* (+ *v être*) to arm oneself.

armistice /aʀmistis/ *nm* armistice.

armoire /aʀmwaʀ/ *nf* **1** cupboard; **2** wardrobe.
■ **~ frigorifique** cold store; **~ à glace** wardrobe with a full length mirror; **c'est une ~ à glace**○ he/she is built like a tank○; **~ métallique** metal locker; **~ normande** large wardrobe (*in traditional Norman style*); **~ à pharmacie** medicine cabinet; **~ de toilette** bathroom cabinet.

armoiries /aʀmwaʀi/ *nf pl* arms.

armure /aʀmyʀ/ *nf* armour[GB].

armurerie /aʀmyʀʀi/ *nf* **1** gunsmith's; **2** gun room.

armurier /aʀmyʀje/ *nm* **1** gunsmith; **2** armourer[GB].

aromates /aʀɔmat/ *nm pl* herbs and spices.

aromatique /aʀɔmatik/ *adj* aromatic.

aromatiser /aʀɔmatize/ [1] *vtr* to flavour[GB].

arôme /aʀom/ *nm* **1** aroma; **2** flavouring[GB].

arpège /aʀpɛʒ/ *nm* arpeggio.

arpent /aʀpɑ̃/ *nm* **quelques ~s** a few acres.

arpenter /aʀpɑ̃te/ [1] *vtr* **1** to stride along; **2** to pace up and down; **3** to survey [*piece of land*].

arqué, ~e /aʀke/ *adj* [*brows*] arched; [*nose*] hooked; [*legs*] bandy.

arquebuse /aʀkəbyz/ *nf* arquebus.

arquer /aʀke/ [1] **I** *vtr* to bend [*bar*]; **~ le dos** to arch one's back.
II s'arquer *v refl* (+ *v être*) to become bowed.

arraché /aʀaʃe/ *nm* snatch; **obtenir à l'~** to snatch [*victory*]; **vol à l'~** bag snatching.

arrache-pied: **d'arrache-pied** /daʀaʃpje/ *phr* [*work*] flat out.

arracher /aʀaʃe/ [1] **I** *vtr* **1** to pull up or dig up [*weeds*]; to pull out [*tooth*]; to tear down [*poster*]; to rip out [*page*]; to tear off [*mask*]; to uproot [*tree*]; to blow off [*tiles*]; **2 ~ à qn** to snatch from sb [*bag, victory*]; to extract [sth] from sb [*promise*]; to get [sth] from sb [*smile*]; **3 ~ qn à** to uproot sb from [*home*]; to drag sb away from [*work*]; to rouse sb from [*thoughts*]; to rescue sb from [*poverty*].
II s'arracher *v refl* (+ *v être*) **1** to fight over; **2 s'~ à** to rouse oneself from [*thoughts*]; to tear oneself away from [*work*].
IDIOMS **c'est à s'~ les cheveux**○! it's enough to make you tear your hair out!; **~ les yeux à** or **de qn** to scratch sb's eyes out; **s'~ les yeux** to fight like cat and dog.

arracheur /aʀaʃœʀ/ *nm* **mentir comme un ~ de dents** to be a born liar.

arraisonner /aʀɛzɔne/ [1] *vtr* to board and inspect.

arrangeant, ~e /aʀɑ̃ʒɑ̃, ɑ̃t/ *adj* obliging.

arrangement /aʀɑ̃ʒmɑ̃/ *nm* arrangement.

arranger /aʀɑ̃ʒe/ [13] **I** *vtr* **1** to arrange, to organize; **2** to sort out; **pour ne rien ~, pour tout ~** to make matters worse; **3** to arrange [*flowers*]; **4** to tidy [*hair*]; to straighten [*skirt*]; **5** (Mus) to arrange; **6** to doctor [*facts*]; **7** to fix [*watch*]; **8** [*events*] to suit [*person*].
II s'arranger *v refl* (+ *v être*) **1** to get better, to improve; **2 s'~ avec qn** to arrange it with sb; **3** to manage; **4 on s'arrangera après** we'll sort it out later; **5**○ **elle ne sait pas s'~** she doesn't know how to make the most of herself.

arrangeur, -euse /aʀɑ̃ʒœʀ, øz/ *nm,f* (Mus) arranger.

arrestation /aʀɛstasjɔ̃/ *nf* arrest; **en état d'~** under arrest.

arrêt /aʀɛ/ *nm* **1** (gen) stopping; (of conflict) cessation; (of delivery) cancellation; (in production) halt; **2** stop; **sans ~** [*travel*] nonstop, without stopping; [*interrupt*] constantly; **à l'~** [*vehicle*] stationary; [*machine*] idle; [*electrical appliance*] off; **marquer un temps d'~** to pause; **être aux ~s** (Mil) to be under arrest; **3** stop; **un ~ de bus** a bus stop; **4** (Law) ruling.
■ **~ du cœur** heart failure; **~ sur image** freeze-frame, still; **~ de jeu** stoppage time; **jouer les ~s de jeu** to play injury time; **~ de mort** death sentence; **~ de travail** stoppage of work; sick leave; sick note.

arrêté, ~e /aʀete/ **I** *pp* ▶ **arrêter**.
II *pp adj* **1** [*matter*] settled; **2** [*ideas*] fixed.
III *nm* order, decree.

arrêter /aʀete/ [1] **I** *vtr* **1** to stop (**de faire** doing); **je n'arrête pas en ce moment!** I'm always on the go○ these days!; **être arrêté pour trois semaines** to be given a sick note for three weeks; **2** to switch off [*machine*]; to halt [*process*]; **3** to give up (**de faire** doing); **4** to arrest; **5** to decide on [*plan*].
II *vi* to stop; **arrête!** stop it!
III s'arrêter *v refl* (+ *v être*) **1** to stop; **2** to give up (**de faire** doing); **3** to end; **4 s'~ sur** to dwell on; **s'~ à** to focus on.

arrhes /aʀ/ *nf pl* deposit.

arrière /aʀjɛʀ/ **I** *adj inv* [*pocket*] back; [*door, wheel*] rear.
II *nm* **1** rear; **à l'~** (in car) in the back; (on plane, train, ship) at the rear; **en ~** backward(s); (position) behind; **pencher la tête en ~** to tilt one's head back; **remonter de deux ans en ~** to go back two years; **revenir en ~** [*person*] to turn back; (figurative) to take a backward step; (on tape) to rewind; **2** (Sport) fullback; **~ gauche** left back; **3** civilian zone; **4** civilian population.

arriéré, ~e /aʀjeʀe/ **I** *adj* **1** outdated; **2** backward; **3** behind the times; **4** retarded.
II *nm* arrears.

arrière-boutique, *pl* **~s** /aʀjɛʀbutik/ *nf* back of the shop.

arrière-cour, *pl* **~s** /aʀjɛʀkuʀ/ *nf* (enclosed) backyard.

arrière-garde, *pl* **~s** /aʀjɛʀgaʀd/ *nf* rearguard.

arrière-goût, *pl* **~s** /aʀjɛʀgu/ *nm* aftertaste.

arrière-grands-parents /aʀjɛʀgʀɑ̃paʀɑ̃/ *nm pl* great-grandparents.

arrière-pays /aʀjɛʀpei/ *nm inv* hinterland.

arrière-pensée, *pl* **~s** /aʀjɛʀpɑ̃se/ *nf* **1** ulterior motive; **2 sans ~** without reservation.

arrière-petits-enfants /aʀjɛʀpətizɑ̃fɑ̃/ *nm pl* great-grandchildren.

arrière-plan, *pl* **~s** /aʀjɛʀplɑ̃/ *nm* (of picture) background.

arrière-saison, *pl* **~s** /aʀjɛʀsɛzɔ̃/ *nf* late autumn (GB), late fall (US).

arrière-train, *pl* **~s** /aʀjɛʀtʀɛ̃/ *nm* hindquarters.

arrimage /aʀimaʒ/ *nm* (Naut) stowing.

arrimer /aʀime/ [1] *vtr* **1** to fasten; **2** (Naut) to stow.

arrivage /aʀivaʒ/ *nm* **1** delivery, consignment; **2** influx.

arrivant, **~e** /aʀivɑ̃, ɑ̃t/ *nm,f* **un nouvel ~** a newcomer.

arrivé, **~e**[1] /aʀive/ **I** *pp* ▶ **arriver**.
II *pp adj* **1 le premier ~** the first person to arrive; **2 être ~** to have made it (socially).

arrivée[2] /aʀive/ *nf* **1** arrival; **trains à l'~** arrivals; **2** (in race) finish; **3** (Tech) inlet.

arriver /aʀive/ [1] (+ *v être*) **I** *vi* **1** (gen) to arrive; (Sport) to finish; **~ à/de Paris** to arrive in/from Paris; **2** to come; **~ en courant** to come running up; **3 ~ à** to reach [*level, agreement*]; to find [*solution*]; to achieve [*goal*]; **~ (jusqu') à qn** to reach sb; **~ à son terme** to come to an end, to expire; **4 ~ à faire** to manage to do; **je n'y arrive pas** I can't do it; **je n'arrive à rien** I'm getting nowhere; **~ à ses fins** to achieve one's ends; **5 en ~ à** to come to; **j'en arrive à croire que...** I'm beginning to think that...; **6** to happen.
II *v impers* **qu'est-il arrivé?** what happened? (**à** to); **il m'arrive d'y aller, il arrive que j'y aille** I sometimes go there.

arrivisme /aʀivism/ *nm* ruthless ambition.

arriviste /aʀivist/ **I** *adj* ruthlessly ambitious.
II *nmf* upstart, arriviste (GB).

arrogance /aʀɔgɑ̃s/ *nf* arrogance.

arrogant, **~e** /aʀɔgɑ̃, ɑ̃t/ *adj* arrogant.

arroger: **s'arroger** /aʀɔʒe/ [13] *v refl* (+ *v être*) to appropriate [*title*]; to assume [*right, role*].

arrondi, **~e** /aʀɔ̃di/ **I** *adj* [*object*] rounded; [*face*] round.
II *nm* **1** (of face) roundness; (of shoulder) curve; **2** (of skirt) hemline.

arrondir /aʀɔ̃diʀ/[3] **I** *vtr* **1** to round off [*edge*]; **coiffure qui arrondit le visage** hairstyle that makes one's face look round; **2** to open wide [*eyes*]; **3** to round off [*figure*] (**à** to).
II s'arrondir *v refl* (+ *v être*) **1** [*object*] to become round(ed); [*eyes*] to widen; **2** [*face*] to fill out; **3** [*fortune*] to be growing.
IDIOMS **~ les angles** to smooth the rough edges.

arrondissement /aʀɔ̃dismɑ̃/ *nm* **1** arrondissement; **2** *administrative division in France*.

arrosage /aʀozaʒ/ *nm* **1** watering; **2**° drinks party.

arroser /aʀoze/ [1] **I** *vtr* **1** to water, to spray; **~ qch d'essence** to douse sth with petrol (GB) or gasoline (US); **on va se faire ~**°! we're going to get soaked!; **2** to baste [*meat*]; to sprinkle [*cake*] (**de** with); **3** to drink to; **4 repas arrosé au bourgogne** meal washed down with Burgundy.
II s'arroser° *v refl* (+ *v être*) **ça s'arrose** that calls for a drink.

arroseur /aʀozœʀ/ *nm* sprinkler.
IDIOMS **c'est l'~ arrosé** he's been hoisted by his own petard.

arrosoir /aʀozwaʀ/ *nm* watering can.

arsenal, *pl* **-aux** /aʀsənal, o/ *nm* **1** naval shipyard; **2** arsenal; **3**° gear; **tout un ~ de** a whole battery of.

arsenic /aʀsənik/ *nm* arsenic.

art /aʀ/ *nm* **1** art; **galerie d'~** art gallery; **2** art, skill; **avec ~** artistically; skilfully[GB]; **c'est tout un ~** it's an art in itself; **avoir l'~ de faire** to have a knack of doing.
■ **~ dramatique** drama; **~ lyrique** opera; **~ de vivre** art of living; **~s ménagers** home economics; **le Salon des Arts Ménagers** ≈ the Ideal Home Exhibition (GB), the Home Show (US); **~s plastiques** plastic arts.

artère /aʀtɛʀ/ *nf* **1** (Anat) artery; **2** arterial road; **3** main street.

artériel, **-ielle** /aʀteʀjɛl/ *adj* arterial.

arthrite /aʀtʀit/ *nf* arthritis.

arthrose /aʀtʀoz/ *nf* osteoarthritis.

artichaut /aʀtiʃo/ *nm* (globe) artichoke.
IDIOMS **avoir un cœur d'~** to be fickle (*in love*).

article /aʀtikl/ *nm* **1** (in paper, law) article; (in contract) clause; (in dictionary) entry; **2** (in grammar) article; **~ défini** definite article; **3** item; **~s de consommation courante** basic consumer goods; **faire l'~ à qn** to give sb the sales pitch.
IDIOMS **être à l'~ de la mort** to be at death's door.

articulaire /aʀtikylɛʀ/ *adj* articular.

articulation /aʀtikylasjɔ̃/ *nf* **1** (Anat) joint; **2** (of limbs) articulation; **3** (of lamp, sunshade) mobile joint; **4** (in phonetics) articulation; **5** (in sentence) link; **6** (of speech, essay) structure.

articuler /aʀtikyle/ [1] **I** *vtr* **1** to articulate; **articule!** speak clearly!; **2** to utter; **3** to connect [*component*] (**sur** to); **4** to structure [*ideas*].
II s'articuler *v refl* (+ *v être*) **s'~ autour de** to be based on, to hinge on.

artifice /aʀtifis/ *nm* **1** trick, ploy; **2** device; **les ~s du style** stylistic devices; **3** artifice; **sans ~** unpretentious.

artificiel, **-ielle** /aʀtifisjɛl/ *adj* **1** artificial; man-made; **2** [*pleasures*] superficial; [*gaiety*] forced.

artificiellement /aʀtifisjɛlmɑ̃/ *adv* artificially.

artificier /aʀtifisje/ *nm* **1** bomb disposal expert; **2** explosives manufacturer; **3** fireworks manufacturer.

artillerie /aʀtijʀi/ *nf* artillery; **~ navale** naval guns.

artilleur /aʀtijœʀ/ *nm* artilleryman, gunner.

artisan /aʀtizɑ̃/ *nm* **1** artisan, craftsman; **2** architect, author.

artisanal, **~e**, *mpl* **-aux** /aʀtizanal, o/ *adj* [*method*] traditional; **de fabrication ~e** hand-crafted; home-made.

artisanalement /aʀtizanalmɑ̃/ *adv* **fabriqué ~** hand-crafted; home-made.

artisanat /aʀtizana/ *nm* **1** craft industry, cottage industry; **2** artisans.
■ **~ d'art** arts and crafts.

artiste /aʀtist/ **I** *adj* **1** artistic; **2 il est un peu ~** he's a bit of a dreamer.
II *nmf* **1** artist; **~ peintre** painter; **2** (on stage) performer; (in music hall) artiste; **~ dramatique** actor; **~ lyrique** opera singer.

artistique /aʀtistik/ *adj* artistic.

as /ɑs/ *nm inv* **1** (Games) ace; **2** (in betting) **l'~** number one; **3**° ace°.
IDIOMS **être plein aux ~**° to be loaded°; **passer à l'~**° [*money*] to go down the drain; [*holidays*] to go by the board; **être fagoté comme l'~ de pique**° to look a mess.

AS /aɛs/ *nf*: *abbr* ▶ **association**.

ascendance /asɑ̃dɑ̃s/ *nf* descent, ancestry.

ascendant, ~e /asɑ̃dɑ̃, ɑ̃t/ **I** *adj* [*curve*] rising; [*movement*] upward; [*star*] ascending.
II *nm* **1** influence (**sur** over); **2** (Law) ascendant.

ascenseur /asɑ̃sœʀ/ *nm* lift (GB), elevator (US).
IDIOMS **renvoyer l'~** to return the favour[GB].

ascension /asɑ̃sjɔ̃/ *nf* **1** ascent; **faire l'~ de** to climb; **2** (figurative) rise.

Ascension /asɑ̃sjɔ̃/ *nf* Ascension.

ascensionnel, -elle /asɑ̃sjɔnɛl/ *adj* [*movement*] upward; [*speed*] climbing; **parachute ~** parascending.

ascète /asɛt/ *nmf* ascetic.

aseptique /asɛptik/ *adj* aseptic.

aseptisé, ~e /asɛptize/ *adj* [*art*] sanitized; [*world*] sterile; [*decor*] impersonal.

aseptiser /asɛptize/ [1] *vtr* to disinfect [*wound*]; to sterilize [*instrument*].

asexué, ~e /asɛksɥe/ *adj* asexual.

asiatique /azjatik/ *adj* Asian.

Asie /azi/ *pr nf* Asia; **~ Mineure** Asia Minor.

asile /azil/ *nm* **1** refuge; **chercher ~** to seek refuge; **2** (political) asylum; **3 ~ de vieillards** old people's home; **~ de nuit** night shelter.

asocial, ~e, *mpl* **-iaux** /asɔsjal, o/ **I** *adj* antisocial.
II *nm,f* social misfit.

aspect /aspɛ/ *nm* **1** side; **voir qch sous son ~ positif** to see the good side of sth; **2** aspect; **par bien des ~s** in many respects; **3** appearance.

asperge /aspɛʀʒ/ *nf* **1** asparagus; **2**° beanpole°, string bean (US).

asperger /aspɛʀʒe/ [13] *vtr* to spray; to splash.

aspérité /aspeʀite/ *nf* (in terrain) bump.

asphalte /asfalt/ *nm* asphalt.

asphyxie /asfiksi/ *nf* **1** asphyxiation; **2** paralysis.

asphyxier /asfiksje/ [2] **I** *vtr* **1** to asphyxiate [*person*]; **2** to paralyze [*network, company*].
II s'asphyxier *v refl* (+ *v être*) **1** to suffocate to death; **2** to gas oneself; **3** [*country*] to become paralyzed.

aspirant, ~e /aspiʀɑ̃, ɑ̃t/ **I** *adj* **ventilateur ~** extractor fan.
II *nm* (in army, air force) ≈ senior officer cadet; (in navy) ≈ midshipman cadet.

aspirateur /aspiʀatœʀ/ *nm* **1** vacuum cleaner, hoover® (GB); **2** (Med) aspirator.

aspiration /aspiʀasjɔ̃/ *nf* **1** aspiration (**à** for); **2** sucking up, drawing up; **3** inhalation; **4** (Med) vacuum extraction.

aspirer /aspiʀe/ [1] **I** *vtr* **1** to breathe in, to inhale ; **2** to suck [sth] up; **3 consonne aspirée** aspirated consonant.
II aspirer à *v+prep* **1** to yearn for; **2** to aspire to.

assagir: **s'assagir** /asaʒiʀ/ [3] *v refl* (+ *v être*) to quieten down (GB), to quiet down (US).

assaillant, ~e /asajɑ̃, ɑ̃t/ *nm,f* **1** attacker; **2** (Mil) **les ~s** the attacking forces.

assaillir /asajiʀ/ [28] *vtr* **1** to attack; **2** to plague; **~ qn de questions** to bombard sb with questions.

assainir /aseniʀ/ [3] *vtr* **1** to clean up; **2** to stabilize [*economy*]; to streamline [*company*].

assainissement /asenismɑ̃/ *nm* **1** cleaning up; **2** (of economy) stabilization; (of company) streamlining.

assaisonnement /asɛzɔnmɑ̃/ *nm* (Culin) seasoning; dressing.

assaisonner /asɛzɔne/ [1] *vtr* to season [*dish*]; to dress [*salad*].

assassin, ~e /asasɛ̃, in/ **I** *adj* **1** murderous; **2** [*campaign*] vicious.
II *nm* **1** murderer; **2** assassin.

assassinat /asasina/ *nm* **1** murder; **2** assassination.

assassiner /asasine/ [1] *vtr* **1** to murder; **2** to assassinate; **3**° to slate°.

assaut /aso/ *nm* attack, assault; **se lancer** or **monter à l'~ de** to launch an attack on; **prendre d'~** to storm; **les ~s du froid** the onslaught of cold weather.

assécher /aseʃe/ [14] *vtr* **1** to drain; **2** [*heat*] to dry up.

ASSEDIC /asedik/ *nf* (*abbr* = **Association pour l'emploi dans l'industrie et le commerce**) *organization managing unemployment contributions and payments.*

assemblage /asɑ̃blaʒ/ *nm* **1** (of motor) assembly (**de** of); **2** (of ideas) assemblage; (of objects) collection; (of colours) combination.

assemblée /asɑ̃ble/ *nf* **1** gathering; **2** meeting; **3** assembly.
■ **~ générale, AG** general meeting; **l'Assemblée nationale** the French National Assembly.

assembler /asɑ̃ble/ [1] **I** *vtr* to assemble, to put together.
II s'assembler *v refl* (+ *v être*) [*crowd*] to gather; [*ministers*] to assemble.
IDIOMS **qui se ressemble s'assemble** (Proverb) birds of a feather stick together.

asséner /asene/ [14] *vtr* **~ un coup à qn/qch** to deal sb/sth a blow; **réplique bien assénée** well-aimed retort.

assentiment /asɑ̃timɑ̃/ *nm* assent, consent.

asseoir /aswaʀ/ [41] **I** *vtr* **1** to sit [sb] down; (in

bed) to sit [sb] up; **faire ~ qn** to make sb sit down; (politely) to offer a seat to sb; **2** to seat, to bed [*foundations*]; **3** to establish [*reputation*]; **4** to base [*tax*] (**sur** on); **5°** to stagger, to astound.
II s'asseoir *v refl* (+ *v être*) to sit (down); (in bed) to sit up.

assermenté, **~e** /asɛʀmɑ̃te/ *adj* sworn, on oath.

assertion /asɛʀsjɔ̃/ *nf* assertion.

asservir /asɛʀviʀ/ [3] *vtr* **1** to enslave [*person*]; **2** to subjugate [*country*].

asservissement /asɛʀvismɑ̃/ *nm* **1** (of country, people) subjugation; **2** subjection; **maintenir un pays dans l'~** to keep a country enslaved; **3** subservience.

assesseur /asesœʀ/ *nm* magistrate's assistant.

assez /ase/ *adv* **1** enough; **~ fort** strong enough; **j'en aurai ~ de quatre** four will be quite enough (for me); **j'en ai ~** I've got enough; I'm fed up°; **2** quite; **~ souvent** quite often; **je suis ~ pressé** I'm in rather a hurry; **je suis ~ d'accord** I tend to agree.

assidu, **~e** /asidy/ *adj* **1** diligent; **2** [*care*] constant; **3** [*presence, visits*] regular; **4** devoted; **faire une cour ~e à qn** to court sb assiduously.

assiduité /asidɥite/ *nf* **1** diligence; **avec ~** [*work*] diligently; [*train*] assiduously; [*read*] regularly; **2** regular attendance; **3 ~s** assiduities.

assidûment /asidymɑ̃/ *adv* diligently; regularly; assiduously.

assiéger /asjeʒe/ [15] *vtr* to besiege.

assiette /asjɛt/ *nf* **1** (for food) plate; **2** (of horse rider) seat; **3 ~ (fiscale)** tax base; **4** (of vehicle) stability.
■ **~ anglaise** assorted cold meats; **~ en carton** paper plate; **~ creuse** soup plate; **~ à dessert** dessert plate; **~ plate** dinner plate; **~ à soupe** = **~ creuse**.
IDIOMS **ne pas être dans son ~** to be out of sorts.

assignation /asiɲasjɔ̃/ *nf* **1** allocation; **2** (Law) summons.

assigner /asiɲe/ [1] *vtr* **1** to assign [*task*]; to allocate [*funds*]; **2** to set [*date, objectif*]; **3** to ascribe [*value, role*] (**à** to); **4** (Law) **~ à comparaître** to summons; **~ qn à résidence** to put sb under house arrest.

assimilable /asimilabl/ *adj* **1** comparable (**à** to); **2** easily assimilated (**par** by).

assimilation /asimilasjɔ̃/ *nf* **1** comparison; **2** assimilation.

assimilé, **~e** /asimile/ *adj* similar.

assimiler /asimile/ [1] **I** *vtr* **1** to assimilate; **~ leur silence à un refus** to consider their silence tantamount to a refusal; **être assimilé cadre** to have executive status; **2 ~ qch/qn à** to liken sth/sb to.
II s'assimiler *v refl* (+ *v être*) **1 s'~ à** [*method*] to be comparable to; [*person*] to compare oneself to; **2** [*minority*] to become assimilated; [*substances*] to be assimilated.

assis, **~e** /asi, iz/ **I** *pp* ▶ **asseoir**.
II *pp adj* **1** seated; **être ~** to be sitting down; (in bed) to be sitting up; **reste ~** don't get up; (as reprimand) sit still; **on est mal ~ dans cette voiture** the seats in this car are uncomfortable; **2** [*reputation*] well-established; **3°** staggered.

assises /asiz/ *nf pl* **1** meeting; **2** (Law) assizes.

assistance /asistɑ̃s/ *nf* **1** assistance; aid; **~ judiciaire** legal aid; **porter** or **prêter ~ à qn** to assist sb; **2** audience; **3** attendance (**à** at).
■ **~ respiratoire** artificial respiration; **l'Assistance publique** ≈ welfare services.

assistant, **~e** /asistɑ̃, ɑ̃t/ *nm,f* assistant.
■ **~e maternelle** childminder (GB), babysitter (US); crèche worker; **~e sociale** social worker.

assisté, **~e** /asiste/ **I** *pp* ▶ **assister**.
II *pp adj* **1** assisted (**de** by); **2** receiving benefit (GB), on welfare (US); **3 ~ par ordinateur** computer-aided; **4 direction ~e** power steering.
III *nm,f*: *person receiving benefit* (GB) or *welfare* (US); **avoir une mentalité d'~** to think one can live on government handouts.

assister /asiste/ [1] **I** *vtr* to assist [*poor*]; to aid [*refugees, country*].
II assister à *v+prep* **1** to be at, to attend; **2** to witness.

associatif, **-ive** /asɔsjatif, iv/ *adj* **1** [*memory*] associative; **2 mouvement ~** associations; **vie associative** community life.

association /asɔsjasjɔ̃/ *nf* **1** association; **2** combination.
■ **~ sportive**, **AS** sports association.

associé, **~e** /asɔsje/ **I** *adj* [*member*] associate; [*companies*] associated.
II *nm,f* associate, partner.

associer /asɔsje/ [2] **I** *vtr* **1 ~ qn à** to include sb in [*success*]; to make sb a partner in [*business*]; to give sb a share of [*profits*]; **3 ~ qch à** to combine sth with; to associate sth with.
II s'associer *v refl* (+ *v être*) **1** to go into partnership, to link up (**à, avec** with); **s'~ pour faire** to join forces to do; **2 s'~ à** to join [*movement*]; to join in [*process, decision*]; to share in [*grief*]; **3** to combine.

assoiffé, **~e** /aswafe/ *adj* **1** thirsty; **2 ~ de** thirsting for.

assombrir /asɔ̃bʀiʀ/ [3] **I** *vtr* **1** to make [sth] dark, to darken; **2** to spoil, to cast a shadow over; **la tristesse assombrit son visage** his/her face clouded.
II s'assombrir *v refl* (+ *v être*) **1** [*sky*] to darken; **2** [*face*] to become gloomy.

assommer /asɔme/ [1] *vtr* **1** to knock [sb] senseless; **2°** to bore [sb] to tears°; **3° ~ qn** to get on sb's nerves; **4°** [*news*] to stagger; [*heat*] to overcome.

assorti, **~e** /asɔʀti/ *adj* **1** matching; **un couple bien ~** a well-matched couple; **2** assorted.

assortiment /asɔʀtimɑ̃/ *nm* **1** set; **2** assortment, selection; **3** (in shop) stock.

assortir /asɔʀtiʀ/ [3] **I** *vtr* **1** to match (**à** to;

avec with); **2 ~ qch de qch** to add sth to sth; **3** to stock [*shop*].
II **s'assortir** *v refl* (+ *v être*) **1 s'~ à** or **avec** to match; **2 s'~ de** to come with.
assoupir /asupiʀ/ [3] I *vtr* **1** to make [sb] drowsy; **2** to dull [*senses, passion*].
II **s'assoupir** *v refl* (+ *v être*) to doze off.
assouplir /asupliʀ/ [3] I *vtr* **1** to soften [*washing*]; **2** to make [sth] more supple [*body, leather*]; **2** to relax [*rule*]; to make [sth] less strict [*diet*].
II **s'assouplir** *v refl* (+ *v être*) **1** [*washing*] to get softer; **2** [*body, leather*] to become more supple; **3** [*person, rule*] to become more flexible.
assouplissant /asuplisɑ̃/ *nm* fabric softener.
assourdir /asuʀdiʀ/ [3] I *vtr* **1** to deafen; **2** to muffle.
II **s'assourdir** *v refl* (+ *v être*) to become muffled.
assourdissant, **~e** /asuʀdisɑ̃, ɑ̃t/ *adj* deafening.
assouvir /asuviʀ/ [3] *vtr* to satisfy [*hunger*]; to assuage [*anger*].
assouvissement /asuvismɑ̃/ *nm* **1** (of hunger) satisfying; (of anger) assuaging; **2** satisfaction.
assujetti, **~e** /asyʒeti/ *adj* **~ à** liable for [*tax*]; subject to [*rule*]; **être ~ à la sécurité sociale** to pay National Insurance contributions.
assujettir /asyʒetiʀ/ [3] I *vtr* **1** to subject (**à** to); **2** to subjugate, to subdue; **3** to secure.
II **s'assujettir** *v refl* (+ *v être*) [*person*] to submit (**à** to).
assujettissement /asyʒetismɑ̃/ *nm* **1** subjection; **2 ~ à l'impôt** liability to tax.
assumer /asyme/ [1] I *vtr* **1** to take [*responsibility*]; to hold [*post*]; to meet [*costs*]; **2** to come to terms with [*conditions, identity, past*]; to accept [*consequences*].
II **s'assumer** *v refl* (+ *v être*) **1** to take responsibility for oneself; **2** to come to terms with oneself.
assurable /asyʀabl/ *adj* insurable; **non ~** uninsurable.
assurance /asyʀɑ̃s/ *nf* **1** (self-)confidence, assurance; **avec ~** confidently; **2** assurance; **donner à qn l'~ que** to assure sb that; **3** insurance (policy); **4** insurance company; **5** insurance (premium); **6** insurance (sector); **7** benefit (GB), benefits (US).
■ **~ maladie** health insurance; sickness benefit (GB) or benefits (US); **~ mutuelle** mutual insurance company; **~s sociales** social insurance; **~ au tiers** third-party insurance; **~ tous risques** comprehensive insurance.
assurance-vie, *pl* **assurances-vie** /asyʀɑ̃svi/ *nf* life insurance.
assuré, **~e** /asyʀe/ I *pp* ▶ **assurer**.
II *pp adj* **1** sure, certain (**de faire** of doing); **75% des voix leur sont ~es** they are sure of 75% of the vote; **soyez ~ de ma reconnaissance** I am very grateful to you; **2** insured.
III *adj* **1** [*step, air*] confident; [*hand*] steady; **dit-il d'une voix ~e** he said confidently; **mal ~** [*step, voice*] faltering; [*gesture*] nervous; **2** certain, assured.
IV *nm,f* insured party.
■ **~ social** social insurance contributor.
assurément /asyʀemɑ̃/ *adv* **1** definitely; **2** most certainly.
assurer /asyʀe/ [1] I *vtr* **1 ~ à qn que** to assure sb that; **ce n'est pas drôle, je t'assure** believe me, it's no joke; **2 ~ qn de** to assure sb of [*support*]; **3** to insure [*property, goods*]; **4** to carry out [*maintenance*]; to provide [*service*]; **le service ne sera pas assuré demain** there will be no service tomorrow; **~ la liaison entre** to operate between; **~ la gestion de** to manage; **~ les fonctions de trésorier** to be treasurer; **5** to ensure [*victory*]; to secure [*right, post*] (**à qn** for sb); to assure [*position, future*]; to protect [*border*]; **~ un revenu à qn** to give sb an income; **~ ses vieux jours** to provide for one's old age; **6** to secure [*rope*]; to belay [*climber*]; **7** (Sport) **~ une balle** to play a safe ball.
II **s'assurer** *v refl* (+ *v être*) **1 s'~ de qch** to make sure of sth; **s'~ que** to make sure that; **2** to secure [*advantage, help*]; **s'~ les services de** to enlist the services of; **3** to take out insurance; **4** (figurative) **s'~ contre** to insure against [*eventuality, risk*].
assureur /asyʀœʀ/ *nm* **1** insurance agent; **2** insurance company.
astérisque /asteʀisk/ *nm* asterisk.
astéroïde /asteʀɔid/ *nm* asteroid.
asthmatique /asmatik/ *adj, nmf* asthmatic.
asthme /asm/ *nm* asthma.
asticot /astiko/ *nm* maggot.
asticoter○ /astikɔte/ [1] *vtr* to needle○.
astigmate /astigmat/ *adj* astigmatic.
astiquer /astike/ [1] *vtr* to polish.
astral, **~e**, *mpl* **-aux** /astʀal, o/ *adj* astral.
astre /astʀ/ *nm* star.
astreignant, **~e** /astʀɛɲɑ̃, ɑ̃t/ *adj* [*task*] demanding; [*discipline*] strict.
astreindre /astʀɛ̃dʀ/ [55] I *vtr* **~ qn à qch** [*person*] to force sth upon sb; [*rule*] to bind sb to sth; **~ qn à faire** to compel sb to do.
II **s'astreindre** *v refl* (+ *v être*) **s'~ à qch** to subject oneself to sth; **s'~ à faire** to force oneself to do.
astringent, **~e** /astʀɛ̃ʒɑ̃, ɑ̃t/ *adj* astringent.
astrologie /astʀɔlɔʒi/ *nf* astrology.
astrologue /astʀɔlɔg/ *nmf* astrologer.
astronautique /astʀɔnotik/ *nf* astronautics.
astronome /astʀɔnɔm/ *nmf* astronomer.
astronomie /astʀɔnɔmi/ *nf* astronomy.
astronomique /astʀɔnɔmik/ *adj* astronomical.
astuce /astys/ *nf* **1** cleverness; **2** shrewdness, astuteness; **3** trick; **4** pun; joke.
astucieux, **-ieuse** /astysjø, øz/ *adj* **1** clever; **2** shrewd, sharp.
asymétrie /asimetʀi/ *nf* asymmetry.
asymétrique /asimetʀik/ *adj* asymmetrical.

atelier /atəlje/ *nm* **1** (place) workshop; (artist's) studio; **2** working group; **3** (seminar) workshop.

atermoiement /atɛʀmwamɑ̃/ *nm* procrastination.

athée /ate/ **I** *adj* atheistic.
II *nmf* atheist.

athénien, -ienne /atenjɛ̃, ɛn/ *adj* Athenian.

athlète /atlɛt/ *nmf* athlete; **carrure d'~** athletic build.

athlétique /atletik/ *adj* athletic.

athlétisme /atletism/ *nm* athletics (GB), track and field events.

Atlantique /atlɑ̃tik/ *pr nm* **l'(océan) ~** the Atlantic (Ocean).

atlas /atlas/ *nm inv* atlas.

atmosphère /atmɔsfɛʀ/ *nf* atmosphere.

atmosphérique /atmɔsfeʀik/ *adj* atmospheric.

atoll /atɔl/ *nm* atoll.

atome /atom/ *nm* atom.
IDIOMS **avoir des ~s crochus avec qn**○ to get on well with sb.

atomique /atɔmik/ *adj* atomic.

atomiser /atɔmize/ [1] *vtr* **1** to annihilate [sth] with nuclear weapons; **2** to fragment [*sector, party*]; to annihilate [*competition*]; **3** (in physics) to atomize.

atomiseur /atɔmizœʀ/ *nm* spray, atomizer.

atomiste /atɔmist/ *nmf* nuclear scientist.

atone /atɔn/ *adj* **1** lifeless, apathetic; **2** [*syllable*] unstressed.

atours† /atuʀ/ *nm pl* finery.

atout /atu/ *nm* **1** trump (card); trumps; **c'est ~ cœur** hearts are trumps; **2** (figurative) asset; trump card; **mettre tous les ~s dans son jeu** to leave nothing to chance.

âtre /atʀ/ *nm* hearth.

atroce /atʀɔs/ *adj* atrocious, dreadful, terrible.

atrocité /atʀɔsite/ *nf* **1** atrocity; **2** monstrosity.

atrophier: **s'atrophier** /atʀɔfje/ [2] *v refl* (+ *v être*) to atrophy; **bras atrophié** wasted arm.

attabler: **s'attabler** /atable/ [1] *v refl* (+ *v être*) to sit down at (the) table.

attachant, ~e /ataʃɑ̃, ɑ̃t/ *adj* engaging.

attache /ataʃ/ *nf* **1** tie; string; rope; strap; **~s familiales** family ties; **2 avoir des ~s fines** to have delicate ankles and wrists.
■ **~ parisienne** paper fastener.

attaché, ~e /ataʃe/ *nm,f* attaché.
■ **~ d'administration** administrative assistant; **~ de presse** press attaché.

attachement /ataʃmɑ̃/ *nm* **1** (to person) attachment (**à** to); **2** (to principle, cause) commitment (**à** to).

attacher /ataʃe/ [1] **I** *vtr* **1** to tie [*person, hands, laces*] (**à** to); to tether [*horse, goat*]; to chain, to tie [*dog*] (**à** to); to lock [*bicycle*] (**à** to); to tie up [*person, parcel*]; **2** to fasten [*belt, garment*]; **3** to attach [*importance*] (**à** to); **4 les privilèges attachés à un poste** the privileges attached to a post.
II s'attacher *v refl* (+ *v être*) **1** to fasten, to do up; **2 s'~ à qn/qch** to become attached to sb/sth; **3 s'~ à faire** to set out to do.

attaquant, ~e /atakɑ̃, ɑ̃t/ *nm,f* (Mil, Sport) attacker; (in football) striker.

attaque /atak/ **I** *nf* **1** attack; (on bank) raid; **passer à l'~** to move into the attack; (figurative) to go on the attack; **~ à main armée** armed raid; **pas d'~s personnelles!** no personal comments!; **2** (Med) stroke; **~ cardiaque** heart attack.
II d'attaque○ *phr* on (GB) or in (US) form; **être d'~ pour faire** to feel up to doing.

attaquer /atake/ [1] **I** *vtr* **1** to attack; to raid [*bank*]; **2** (Law) to contest [*contract, will*]; **~ qn en justice** to bring a lawsuit against sb; **3** to make a start on [*work*]; to tackle [*problem*]; **4** (Mus) to strike up [*tune*]; to attack [*note*].
II *vi* **1** (in tennis, golf) to drive; [*runner*] to put on a spurt; **2** [*speaker*] to begin (brusquely).
III s'attaquer *v refl* (+ *v être*) **s'~ à** to attack [*person, policy*]; to tackle [*problem*].

attardé, ~e /ataʀde/ **I** *adj* **1** late; **2** old-fashioned; **3** retarded.
II *nm,f* mentally retarded person.

attarder: **s'attarder** /ataʀde/ [1] *v refl* (+ *v être*) **1** to stay until late; to linger; **2 s'~ sur** to dwell on [*point*].

atteindre /atɛ̃dʀ/ [55] **I** *vtr* **1** to reach [*place, age, level, target*]; to achieve [*aim*]; **2** [*projectile, marksman*] to hit [*target*]; **3** [*illness, misfortune*] to affect, to hit.
II atteindre à *v+prep* to reach [*perfection*]; to achieve [*success*].

atteint, ~e[1] /atɛ̃, ɛ̃t/ **I** *pp* ▶ **atteindre**.
II *pp adj* **1** affected (**de, par** by); **être ~ de** to be suffering from [*illness*]; **2** hit (**de, par** by).

atteinte[2] /atɛ̃t/ **I** *nf* **~ à** attack on; **porter ~ à** to undermine [*credibility, prestige*]; to damage [*reputation, honour*]; to endanger [*security*]; to infringe [*right*]; to threaten [*region*]; **~ à la vie privée** (Law) breach of privacy.
II hors d'atteinte *phr* **hors d'~** [*person*] beyond reach; [*target*] out of range; [*stay*] out of reach.

attelage /atlaʒ/ *nm* **1** (of horse) harness; (of oxen) yoke; (of wagon) coupling; (of trailer) towing attachment; (of rocket) docking or coupling device; **2** (animals) team; (of oxen) yoke; **3** horse-drawn carriage.

atteler /atle/ [19] **I** *vtr* to harness [*horse*]; to yoke [*oxen*]; to couple [*wagon*].
II s'atteler *v refl* (+ *v être*) **s'~ à une tâche** to get down to a job.

attelle /atɛl/ *nf* (Med) splint; **mettre des ~s à qn** to put splints on sb.

attenant, ~e /atnɑ̃, ɑ̃t/ *adj* adjacent.

attendre /atɑ̃dʀ/ [6] **I** *vtr* **1** to wait for [*person, event*]; **aller ~ qn à la gare** to (go and) meet sb at the station; **j'attends de voir pour le croire** I'll believe it when I see it; **se faire ~** to keep people waiting; **la réaction ne se fit pas ~** the reaction was instantaneous; **~ son jour** or **heure** to bide one's time; **il attend impatiemment leur départ** he can't wait for them to leave; **~ son tour** to wait one's turn;

en attendant mieux until something better turns up; **où étais-tu, on ne t'attendait plus!** where were you? we'd given up on you!; **2** to await, to be in store for [*person*]; **un délicieux repas m'attendait** a delicious meal awaited me; **3** to expect; **~ qch de qn/qch** to expect sth from sb/sth; **je les attends pour 5 heures** I'm expecting them at five; **elle attend un bébé** she's expecting a baby.

II *vi* to wait; (on phone) to hold; **faire ~ qn** to keep sb waiting; **sans plus ~** without further delay; **en attendant** in the meantime; all the same, nonetheless; **tu ne perds rien pour ~**○! I'll get you○, just you wait!

III s'attendre *v refl* (+ *v être*) **s'~ à qch** to expect sth; **s'~ à ce que qn fasse** to expect sb to do; **avec lui, il faut s'~ à tout** with him, anything can happen.

attendrir /atɑ̃dʀiʀ/ [3] **I** *vtr* **1** to touch, to move [*person*]; **se laisser ~** to soften; **sourire attendri** tender smile; **2** (Culin) to tenderize [*meat*].

II s'attendrir *v refl* (+ *v être*) to feel moved; **s'~ sur qn** to feel sorry for sb.

attendrissant, **~e** /atɑ̃dʀisɑ̃, ɑ̃t/ *adj* touching, moving; [*innocence*] endearing.

attendrissement /atɑ̃dʀismɑ̃/ *nm* **1** tenderness; **2** emotion.

attendu[1]: **attendu que** /atɑ̃dy/ *phr* **1** given or considering that; **2** (Law) whereas.

attendu[2], **~e** /atɑ̃dy/ *adj* **1** [*person, reaction, result*] expected; **2 le jour (tant) ~** the long-awaited day.

attentat /atɑ̃ta/ *nm* assassination attempt, attack; **~ à la bombe** bomb attack.

■ **~ à la pudeur** (Law) indecent assault.

attente /atɑ̃t/ *nf* **1** waiting; wait; **deux heures d'~** a two-hour wait; **mon ~ a été vaine** I waited in vain; **dans l'~ de vous lire** looking forward to hearing from you; **en ~** [*passenger*] waiting; [*file, application*] pending; [*call*] on hold; **2** expectation; **répondre à l'~ de qn** to come up to sb's expectations; **contre toute ~** against all expectations.

attenter /atɑ̃te/ [1] *v+prep* **~ à ses jours** to attempt suicide; **~ à la vie de qn** to make an attempt on sb's life.

attentif, **-ive** /atɑ̃tif, iv/ *adj* **1** attentive; **sous l'œil ~ de leur mère** under the watchful eye of their mother; **2** [*reading, work*] careful; [*examination*] close; [*care*] special.

attention /atɑ̃sjɔ̃/ **I** *nf* **1** attention; **faire ~ à qch** to mind [*cars, step*]; to watch out for [*black ice*]; to be careful of [*sun*]; to consider [*consequences*]; to take care of [*clothes, belongings*]; to watch [*diet, health*]; to pay attention to [*fashion, details*]; **faire ~ à qn** to pay attention to sb; to keep an eye on sb; to take notice of sb; **2** kind gesture; **être plein d'~s pour qn** to be very attentive to sb.

II *excl* **1** (cry) look out!, watch out!; (written) attention!; (in case of danger) warning!; (on road sign) caution!; **~ à la marche** mind the step; **2 ~, je ne veux pas dire**... don't get me wrong, I don't mean...

attentionné, **~e** /atɑ̃sjɔne/ *adj* attentive, considerate.

attentivement /atɑ̃tivmɑ̃/ *adv* **1** attentively; **2** carefully.

atténuantes /atenɥɑ̃t/ *adj f pl* **circonstances ~** (Law) mitigating circumstances.

atténuation /atenɥasjɔ̃/ *nf* (of pain, tension) alleviation, relief; (of nuisance) reduction; (of effect) mitigation; (of discipline) relaxation.

atténuer /atenɥe/ [1] **I** *vtr* to ease [*pain, distress*]; to lessen [*despair, impact*]; to smooth over [*differences*]; to weaken [*impression, effect*]; to soften [*blow*]; to reduce [*inequalities, seriousness*]; to relax [*severity*]; to dim [*light*]; to tone down [*colour*]; to make [sth] less strong [*smell, taste*]; to mitigate [*sentence*].

II s'atténuer *v refl* (+ *v être*) [*pain*] to ease; [*anger, grief, violence*] to subside; [*corruption, pessimism*] to lessen; [*tendency*] to become less pronounced; [*inequalities, gaps*] to be reduced; [*wrinkles, colour*] to fade; [*storm, noise*] to die down.

atterrant, **~e** /atɛʀɑ̃, ɑ̃t/ *adj* **1** appalling; **2** shattering.

atterré, **~e** /ateʀe/ *adj* **1** appalled; **2** shattered.

atterrer /ateʀe/ [1] *vtr* to leave [sb] aghast.

atterrir /ateʀiʀ/ [3] *vi* to land; **~ en catastrophe** to make a crash landing.

atterrissage /ateʀisaʒ/ *nm* landing; **~ sans visibilité** blind landing.

attestation /atɛstasjɔ̃/ *nf* **1** attestation; **2** certificate.

attester /atɛste/ [1] *vtr* **1** to vouch for; to testify to; **2** to prove, to attest to.

attifer○ /atife/ [1] *vtr* to rig [sb] out○.

attirail /atiʀaj/ *nm* gear, equipment.

attirance /atiʀɑ̃s/ *nf* attraction; **éprouver de l'~ pour** to be attracted to.

attirant, **~e** /atiʀɑ̃, ɑ̃t/ *adj* attractive.

attirer /atiʀe/ [1] **I** *vtr* **1** to attract [*person, capital*]; to draw, to attract [*crowd, attention*]; **~ qn dans un coin** to take sb into a corner; **~ qn dans un piège** to lure sb into a trap; **~ qn par des promesses** to entice sb with promises; **2** [*country, course, profession*] to appeal to; **3** to bring [*shame, criticism, anger*]; **~ des ennuis à qn** to cause sb problems.

II s'attirer *v refl* (+ *v être*) **s'~ le soutien de qn** to win sb's support; **s'~ la colère de qn** to incur sb's anger; **s'~ des ennuis** to get into trouble.

attiser /atize/ [1] *vtr* **1** to kindle [*feeling*]; to fuel [*discord*]; to stir up [*hatred*]; **2** to fan [*fire*].

attitré, **~e** /atitʀe/ *adj* **1** [*chauffeur*] official; **2** [*customer*] regular.

attitude /atityd/ *nf* **1** bearing; posture; **2** attitude.

attouchement /atuʃmɑ̃/ *nm* **1** molesting; **2** fondling; **3** (by healer) laying on of hands.

attractif, **-ive** /atʀaktif, iv/ *adj* attractive.

attraction /atʀaksjɔ̃/ *nf* attraction.

■ **~ terrestre** earth's gravity; **~ universelle** gravitation.

attrait /atʀɛ/ *nm* **1** appeal, attraction; lure; **avoir de l'~ pour qn** to appeal to sb; **2 l'~ de qn pour qch/qn** sb's liking for sth/sb.

attrape-nigaud, *pl* **~s** /atʀapnigo/ *nm* con°.

attraper /atʀape/ [1] *vtr* **1** to catch [*person, animal, ball, criminal*]; **se faire ~** to get caught; **attrapez-le!** stop him!; **2** to catch hold of [*rope, hand, leg*]; **3**° to catch [*cold, illness*]; to get [*sunstroke, headache*]; **4**° to tell [sb] off; **5**° to get [*fine, kick*].

attrayant, **~e** /atʀɛjɑ̃, ɑ̃t/ *adj* **1** attractive; **2** pleasant.

attribuable /atʀibɥabl/ *adj* attributable (**à** to).

attribuer /atʀibɥe/ [1] **I** *vtr* **1** to allocate [*seat, task*]; to grant [*right, custody*]; to award [*prize, grant*]; to lend [*importance*]; **~ qch à la fatigue** to put sth down to tiredness; **~ la responsabilité de qch à qn** to hold sb responsible for sth; **2 ~ qch à qn** to credit sb with sth [*quality*]; to attribute sth to sb [*work*].

II s'attribuer *v refl* (+ *v être*) **s'~ la meilleure part** to give oneself the largest share; **s'~ tout le mérite** to take all the credit.

attribut /atʀiby/ *nm* **1** (quality, symbol) attribute; **2** (in grammar) complement; **adjectif ~** predicative adjective; **nom ~** complement.

attribution /atʀibysjɔ̃/ **I** *nf* **1** allocation; **2** awarding.

II attributions *nf pl* (of individual) remit; (of court) competence.

attrister /atʀiste/ [1] *vtr* to sadden; **j'ai été attristé d'apprendre** I was sorry to hear.

attroupement /atʀupmɑ̃/ *nm* gathering; **causer un ~** to cause a crowd to gather.

attrouper: **s'attrouper** /atʀupe/ [1] *v refl* (+ *v être*) to gather.

au /o/ *prep* (= **à le**) ▶ **à**.

aubaine /obɛn/ *nf* **1** godsend; **2** bargain.

aube /ob/ *nf* **1** dawn; **2** (of priest) alb; (of choirboy) cassock.

aubépine /obepin/ *nf* hawthorn.

auberge /obɛʀʒ/ *nf* inn; **~ de jeunesse** youth hostel.

IDIOMS **tu n'es pas sorti de l'~**°**!** you're not out of the woods yet!

aubergine /obɛʀʒin/ *nf* aubergine, eggplant (US).

aubergiste /obɛʀʒist/ *nmf* innkeeper.

aucun, **~e** /okœ̃, yn/ **I** *adj* no, not any; **en ~e façon** in no way; **en ~ cas** under no circumstances.

II *pron* none; **je n'ai lu ~ de vos livres** I haven't read any of your books; **~ de ses arguments n'est convaincant** none of his arguments are convincing.

aucunement /okynmɑ̃/ *adv* in no way; **je ne suis ~ surpris** I'm not in the least surprised.

audace /odas/ *nf* **1** boldness; **2** daring; **3** audacity, nerve°; impudence; **il ne manque pas d'~** he's got a nerve°.

audacieux, **-ieuse** /odasjø, øz/ *adj* **1** bold; **2** audacious, daring.

au-dedans /odədɑ̃/ *adv* inside.

au-dehors /odəɔʀ/ *adv* **1** outside; **2** outwardly.

au-delà /od(ə)la/ **I** *nm* **l'~** the beyond, the hereafter.

II *adv* beyond; **je veux bien aller jusqu'à 1 000 francs mais pas ~** I'm quite prepared to go up to 1,000 francs but no more.

III au-delà de *phr* beyond; over.

au-dessous /odəsu/ **I** *adv* **1** below; **tu vois le dictionnaire, mon livre est ~** you see the dictionary, my book is underneath; **2** under; **les enfants de dix ans et ~** children of ten years and under.

II au-dessous de *phr* below; **~ du genou** below the knee; **être ~ de tout**° to be absolutely useless; to be despicable.

au-dessus /odəsy/ **I** *adv* above; **les enfants de 10 ans et ~** children of 10 and over; **la taille ~** the next size up.

II au-dessus de *phr* above; **~ de chez moi** in the apartment above mine; **deux étages ~ de chez moi** two floors up from me; **un pont ~ de la rivière** a bridge over or across the river; **se pencher ~ de la table** to lean across the table.

au-devant: **au-devant de** /odəvɑ̃də/ *phr* **aller ~ de qn** to go to meet sb; **aller ~ des désirs de qn** to anticipate sb's wishes; **aller ~ des ennuis** to let oneself in for trouble.

audible /odibl/ *adj* audible.

audience /odjɑ̃s/ *nf* **1** (Law) hearing; **lever l'~** to close the hearing; **salle d'~** courtroom; **2** (interview) audience; **3** (public) audience; **jouir d'une grande ~ auprès de** to be very popular with.

Audimat® /odimat/ *nm* audience ratings.

audiovisuel, **-elle** /odjɔvisɥel/ **I** *adj* **1** broadcasting; **2** audiovisual.

II *nm* **1** broadcasting; **2** audiovisual equipment; **3** audiovisual methods.

audit /odit/ *nm* audit.

auditeur, **-trice** /oditœʀ, tʀis/ *nm,f* listener.

auditif, **-ive** /oditif, iv/ *adj* [*nerve*] auditory; [*problems*] hearing; [*memory*] aural.

audition /odisjɔ̃/ *nf* **1** (sense) hearing; **2** audition; **3** (Law) hearing, examination.

auditionner /odisjɔne/ [1] *vtr, vi* to audition.

auditoire /oditwaʀ/ *nm* audience.

auge /oʒ/ *nf* **1** (for animal feed) trough; **2** mortar trough.

augmentation /ogmɑ̃tasjɔ̃/ *nf* increase; **une ~ (de salaire)** a pay rise (GB) or raise (US).

augmenter /ogmɑ̃te/ [1] **I** *vtr* to raise, to increase; to extend; **~ le loyer de qn** to put sb's rent up; **~ qn de 1 000 francs** to give sb a rise (GB) or raise (US) of 1,000 francs.

II *vi* to increase, to go up, to rise.

augure /ogyʀ/ *nm* **1** omen; **2** augury.

augurer /ogyʀe/ [1] *vtr* **que peut-on ~ de cette attitude?** what should we expect from this attitude?; **je n'augure rien de bon de cette rencontre** I can't see any good coming of this meeting.

auguste /ogyst/ *adj* august, noble.

aujourd'hui /oʒuʀdɥi/ *adv* **1** today; **~ en huit** a week (from) today; **2** today, nowadays; **la France d'~** present-day France.

aulne /on/ *nm* alder.

aumône /omon/ *nf* hand-out, alms; **faire l'~ à** to give alms to; **demander l'~** to ask for charity.

aumônerie /omonʀi/ *nf* chaplaincy.

aumônier /omonje/ *nm* chaplain.

aune /on/ *nm* = **aulne**.

auparavant /opaʀavɑ̃/ *adv* before; beforehand; previously; formerly.

auprès: **auprès de** /opʀɛdə/ *phr* **1** next to, beside; **il faut rester ~ de lui** you must stay with him; **il s'est rendu ~ de sa tante** he went to see his aunt; **2** compared with; **3 s'excuser ~ de qn** to apologize to sb; **renseigne-toi ~ de la mairie** ask for information at the town hall; **un sondage effectué ~ de 2 000 personnes** a poll carried out among 2,000 people; **représentant ~ de l'ONU** representative to the UN.

auquel ▶ **lequel**.

auréole /ɔʀeɔl/ *nf* **1** (stain) ring; **2** halo.

auréoler: **s'auréoler** /ɔʀeɔle/ [1] *v refl* (+ *v être*) **s'~ de** to take on an aura of; **auréolé de** basking in the glow of.

auriculaire /ɔʀikylɛʀ/ **I** *adj* auricular.

II *nm* little finger, pinkie.

aurifère /ɔʀifɛʀ/ *adj* **1** [*mineral*] auriferous; **2 valeurs ~s** gold stocks.

aurore /ɔʀɔʀ/ *nf* dawn; **se lever aux ~s** to get up with the lark; **~ boréale** Northern Lights, aurora borealis.

auscultation /ɔskyltasjɔ̃/ *nf* (Med) examination.

ausculter /ɔskylte/ [1] *vtr* (Med) to examine.

auspices /ospis/ *nm pl* auspices; **sous d'heureux ~** under favourable[GB] auspices.

aussi /osi/ **I** *adv* **1** too, as well, also; **il sera absent et moi ~** he'll be away and so will I; **2 ~ bien que** as well as; **~ âgé que** as old as; **c'est ~ bien** it's just as well; **3** so; **je ne savais pas qu'il était ~ vieux** I didn't know he was so old; **dans une ~ belle maison** in such a nice house.

II *conj* **1** so, consequently; **2**° **'on lui a volé son sac'—'quelle idée ~ de le laisser traîner!'** 'her bag was stolen'—'well, it was stupid to leave it lying about!'

aussitôt /osito/ **I** *adv* **1** immediately, straight away; **2 ~ arrivé** as soon as or the moment he arrived; **~ dit ~ fait** no sooner said than done.

II aussitôt que *phr* as soon as.

austère /ɔstɛʀ, ostɛʀ/ *adj* austere; stern; severe.

austérité /osteʀite/ *nf* austerity; severity.

austral, **~e**, *mpl* **~s** /ostʀal/ *adj* southern, south.

Australie /ostʀali/ *pr nf* Australia.

australien, **-ienne** /ostʀaljɛ̃, ɛn/ *adj* Australian.

autant /otɑ̃/ **I** *adv* **il n'a jamais ~ neigé** it has never snowed so much; **je t'aime toujours ~** I still love you as much; **essaie d'en faire ~** try and do the same; **triste ~ que désagréable** as sad as it is unpleasant; **je les hais tous ~ qu'ils sont** I hate every single one of them; **j'aime ~ partir tout de suite** I'd rather leave straight away; **~ dire que la réunion est annulée** in other words the meeting is cancelled[GB]; **~ parler à un mur** you might as well be talking to the wall; **~ que faire se peut** as much as possible, as far as possible; **~ que je sache** as far as I know; **~ que tu peux** as much as you can; as long as you can.

II autant de *quantif* **1 ~ de cadeaux** so many presents; **leurs promesses sont ~ de mensonges** their promises are just so many lies; **il y a ~ de femmes que d'hommes** there are as many women as (there are) men; **2 ~ de gentillesse** such kindness; **ce sera toujours ~ de fait** that'll be done at least; **je n'ai pas eu ~ de chance que lui** I haven't had as much luck as he has.

III d'autant *phr* **cela va permettre de réduire d'~ les coûts de production** this will allow an equivalent reduction in production costs; **d'~ plus!** all the more reason!; **d'~ mieux!** all the better!, even better!; **d'~ moins** even less, all the less; **d'~ que** all the more so as.

IV pour autant *phr* for all that; **sans pour ~ tout modifier** without necessarily changing everything; **pour ~ qu'ils se mettent d'accord** if they agree; **pour ~ que je sache** as far as I know.

autarcie /otaʀsi/ *nf* autarky; **vivre en ~** to be self-sufficient.

autel /otɛl/ *nm* altar; **mener** or **conduire à l'~** to give away.

auteur /otœʀ/ *nm* **1** author; **2** creator, originator; (of song) composer; (of crime) perpetrator; **film d'~** art film.

■ **~ dramatique** playwright.

auteur-compositeur, *pl* **auteurs-compositeurs** /otœʀkɔ̃pozitœʀ/ *nm* songwriter.

authenticité /otɑ̃tisite/ *nf* authenticity.

authentifier /otɑ̃tifje/ [2] *vtr* to authenticate.

authentique /otɑ̃tik/ *adj* [*story*] true; [*painting, document*] authentic, genuine; [*feeling*] genuine.

autiste /otist/ *nm,f* autistic person.

auto /auto/ **I** *adj inv* **assurance ~** car insurance (GB), automobile insurance (US).

II *nf* car, automobile (US).

■ **~ tamponneuse** bumper car, dodgem.

autobiographie /otobjogʀafi/ *nf* autobiography.

autobiographique /otobjogʀafik/ *adj* autobiographical.

autobus /otɔbys/ *nm inv* bus.

autocar /otɔkaʀ/ *nm* coach (GB), bus (US).

autochtone /otɔkton/ *adj, nmf* native.

autocollant, **~e** /otɔkɔlɑ̃, ɑ̃t/ **I** *adj* self-adhesive.

II *nm* sticker.

autocritique /otokʀitik/ *nf* self-criticism.

autocuiseur /otokɥizœʀ/ *nm* pressure cooker.

autodéfense /otodefɑ̃s/ *nf* **1** self-defence[GB]; **2** auto-immunity.

autodestruction /otodɛstʀyksjɔ̃/ *nf* self-destruction.

autodétruire: **s'autodétruire** /otodetʀɥiʀ/ [69] *v refl* (+ *v être*) [*person*] to destroy oneself; [*tape*] to self-destruct; [*missile*] to autodestruct.

autodidacte /otodidakt/ *nmf* self-educated person.

autodiscipline /otodisiplin/ *nf* self-discipline; **en ~** without supervision.

auto-école, *pl* **~s** /otoekɔl/ *nf* driving school.

autofinancement /otofinɑ̃smɑ̃/ *nm* self-financing.

autofocus /otofɔkys/ *nm inv* autofocus camera.

autogestion /otoʒɛstjɔ̃/ *nf* (of company) worker management, cooperative management; (of collectivity) collective management.

automate /otɔmat/ *nm* robot, automaton.

automatique /otɔmatik/ **I** *adj* **1** automatic; **2** inevitable.

II *nm* **1 l'~** STD, subscriber trunk dialling[GB]; **2** automatic (revolver); **3** automatic camera.

automatiquement /otɔmatikmɑ̃/ *adv* **1** automatically; **2**○ inevitably.

automatiser /otɔmatize/ [1] *vtr* to automate.

automatisme /otɔmatism/ *nm* automatism; automatic functioning; **acquérir des ~s** to acquire automatic reflexes.

automne /otɔn/ *nm* autumn (GB), fall (US).

automobile /otomɔbil/ **I** *adj* **1** [*industry, insurance*] car; **2** (Sport) [*racing*] motor; [*circuit*] motor racing.

II *nf* **1** (motor) car, automobile (US); **2** the motor (GB) or automobile (US) industry.

automobiliste /otomɔbilist/ *nmf* motorist.

autonome /otɔnɔm/ *adj* autonomous; independent; self-sufficient.

autonomie /otɔnɔmi/ *nf* **1** autonomy; **2** (of car, plane) range; **~ de vol** flight range.

autonomiste /otɔnɔmist/ *adj, nmf* separatist.

autoportrait /otopɔʀtʀɛ/ *nm* self-portrait.

autopsie /otɔpsi/ *nf* postmortem (examination), autopsy.

autoradio /otoʀadjo/ *nm* car radio.

autorisation /otɔʀizasjɔ̃/ *nf* **1** permission; authorization; **2** permit.

autorisé, **~e** /otɔʀize/ *adj* authorized; legal; accredited; permitted; **de source ~e** from official sources.

autoriser /otɔʀize/ [1] *vtr* **1** to allow, to authorize; **2 ~ qn à faire** to entitle sb to do; **rien ne vous autorise à agir ainsi** you have no right to behave like that; **3** to make [sth] possible.

autoritaire /otɔʀitɛʀ/ *adj, nmf* authoritarian.

autorité /otɔʀite/ *nf* **1** authority; **faire qch d'~** to do sth without consultation; **il n'a aucune ~ sur ses enfants** he has no control over his children; **faire ~** [*person*] to be an authority (**en, en matière de** on); [*work*] to be authoritative; **2** (person) authority, expert.

autoroute /otoʀut/ *nf* motorway (GB), freeway (US); **~ à péage** toll motorway.

autoroutier, **-ière** /otoʀutje, ɛʀ/ *adj* motorway (GB), freeway (US).

auto-stop /otostɔp/ *nm* hitchhiking; **faire de l'~** to hitchhike.

auto-stoppeur, **-euse**, *mpl* **~s** /otostɔpœʀ, øz/ *nm,f* hitchhiker.

autour /otuʀ/ **I** *adv* **un parterre de fleurs avec des pierres ~** a flowerbed with stones around it; **tout ~** all around.

II autour de *phr* **1** around, round (GB); **~ de la table** around the table; **2** around, about; **~ de 10 heures** around 10 o'clock; **3** about, on; **un débat ~ du thème du pouvoir** a debate on the theme of power.

autre /otʀ/ **I** *det* **1** other; **l'~ jour** the other day; **une ~ histoire** another story; **quelque chose/rien d'~** something/nothing else; **l'effet obtenu est tout ~** the effect produced is completely different; **2**○ **nous ~s/vous ~s** we/you; **nous ~s professeurs/Français** we teachers/French.

II *pron* **1 où sont les ~s?** where are the other ones?; where are the others?; **je t'ai pris pour un ~** I mistook you for someone else; **ils se respectent les uns les ~s** they respect each other; **chez lui c'est tout l'un ou tout l'~** with him it's all or nothing; **à d'~s**○**!** pull the other one (it's got bells on○)!; **2 prends-en un ~** have another one; **si je peux je t'en apporterai d'~s** if I can I'll bring you some more; **ils ont deux enfants et n'en veulent pas d'~s** they have two children and don't want any more.

III autre part *phr* somewhere else.

autrefois /otʀəfwa/ *adv* in the past; before, formerly; in the old days; **~ c'était possible** it used to be possible; **~, quand Paris s'appelait Lutèce** long ago, when Paris was called Lutetia; **les légendes d'~** old legends.

autrement /otʀəmɑ̃/ *adv* **1** differently, in a different way; **ça ne s'explique pas ~** there's no other explanation for it; **c'est comme ça, et pas ~** that's just the way it is; **on ne peut pas faire ~** there's no other way; **je n'ai pas pu faire ~ que de les inviter** I had no alternative but to invite them; **on ne peut y accéder ~ que par bateau** you can only get there by boat; **je ne l'ai jamais vue ~ qu'en jean** I've never seen her in anything but jeans; **~ dit** in other words; **2** otherwise; **3**○ **~ grave** (much) more serious; **~ aimable** (much) nicer; **il n'était pas ~ impressionné** he wasn't particularly impressed.

Autriche /otʀiʃ/ *pr nf* Austria.

autrichien, **-ienne** /otʀiʃjɛ̃, ɛn/ *adj* Austrian.

autruche /otʀyʃ/ *nf* ostrich.

IDIOMS **pratiquer la politique de l'~** to bury one's head in the sand.

autrui /otʀɥi/ *pron* others, other people.

auvent /ovɑ̃/ *nm* **1** canopy; **2** awning.

aux /o/ *prep* (= **à les**) ▶ **à**.

auxiliaire /oksiljɛʀ/ **I** *adj* **1** [*verb*] auxiliary; **2** [*equipment, service*] auxiliary; [*motor*] back-up; [*means*] additional; **3 maître ~** assistant teacher; **infirmier ~** nursing auxiliary (GB), nurse's aide (US).
II *nmf* assistant, helper.
III *nm* **1** aid; **2** auxiliary (verb).

auxquels, auxquelles ▶ **lequel**.

avachi, ~e /avaʃi/ *adj* [*suitcase, shoe*] which has lost its shape; [*chair*] shapeless.

avachir: s'avachir /avaʃiʀ/ [3] *v refl* (+ *v être*) [*chair*] to sag; [*person*] to let oneself go.

aval /aval/ *nm* **1** (of river) lower reaches; **en ~** downstream; **2** (in skiing) **ski ~** downhill ski; **3** approval.

avalanche /avalɑ̃ʃ/ *nf* avalanche.

avaler /avale/ [1] *vtr* **1** to swallow; **'ne pas ~'** (Med) 'not to be taken internally'; **j'ai avalé de travers** it went down the wrong way; **2** to inhale [*smoke, fumes*].

avance /avɑ̃s/ **I** *nf* **1** advance; **2** lead; **avoir/prendre de l'~ sur** to be/pull ahead of; **3 une ~ (sur salaire)** an advance (on one's salary).
II à l'avance *phr* in advance.
III d'avance *phr* in advance; **avoir cinq minutes d'~** to be five minutes early.
IV en avance *phr* **1** early; **être en ~** to be early; **2 être en ~ sur qn** to be ahead of sb; **3 il est en ~ pour son âge** he's advanced for his age.
V avances *nf pl* advances.

avancé, ~e[1] /avɑ̃se/ **I** *pp* ▶ **avancer**.
II *pp adj* [*ideas*] progressive; **la saison est bien ~e** it's late in the season; **je ne suis pas plus ~** I'm none the wiser; **te voilà bien ~!** that's done you a lot of good!

avancée[2] /avɑ̃se/ *nf* **1** (of roof, rock) overhang; **2** advance; **l'~ des connaissances en ce domaine** the advances made in this field of knowledge.

avancement /avɑ̃smɑ̃/ *nm* **1** promotion; **2** progress; **3 ~ de l'âge de la retraite** lowering of the retirement age.

avancer /avɑ̃se/ [12] **I** *vtr* **1** to move [sth] forward [*object*]; to push [sth] forward [*plate*]; **~ un siège à qn** to pull or draw up a seat for sb; **2** to bring forward [*trip, meeting*]; **3 ~ sa montre de cinq minutes** to put one's watch forward (by) five minutes; **4** to get ahead with [*work*]; **cela ne nous avance à rien** that doesn't get us anywhere; **5 ~ de l'argent à qn** [*bank*] to advance money to sb; **6** to put forward [*argument, theory*]; to propose [*figure*]; to make [*accusation*].
II *vi* **1** [*person, vehicle*] to move (forward); [*army*] to advance; **elle avança vers le guichet** she went up to the ticket office; **2** to make progress, to progress; **et votre projet? ça avance**○**?** and your project? how is it coming along?; **faire ~ la science** to further science; **3 ma montre avance de deux minutes** my watch is two minutes fast; **4** [*teeth, chin*] to stick out; [*peninsula, balcony*] to jut out.
III s'avancer *v refl* (+ *v être*) **1 s'~ vers qch** to move toward(s) sth; **s'~ vers qn** to go toward(s) sb; to come up to sb; **ne t'avance pas trop près du bord** don't go too near the edge; **2** to get ahead; **3** to jut out, to protrude; **4 je me suis un peu avancé en lui promettant le dossier pour demain** I shouldn't have committed myself by promising him/her I'd have the file ready for tomorrow.

avant[1] /avɑ̃/ **I** *adv* before; first; **bien ~** long before; **il l'a mentionné ~ dans l'introduction** he mentioned it earlier in the introduction; **je crois que la dame était ~** I think this lady was first.
II *prep* before; **~ mon retour** before I get back; before I got back; **~ le 1er juillet** before or by 1 July; **~ peu** shortly; **peu ~ 16 heures** a little before 4 pm; **~ tout, ~ toute chose** above all; first and foremost.
III d'avant *phr* **la séance d'~** the previous performance; **la fois d'~ nous nous étions déjà perdus** we got lost the last time as well.
IV avant de *phr* **~ de faire** before doing or one does.
V avant que *phr* before.
VI en avant *phr* forward(s); **en ~ toute!** full steam ahead!; **en ~ (la musique**○**)!** off we go!; **mettre en ~ le fait que** to point out the fact that; **se mettre en ~** to push oneself forward.
VII en avant de *phr* ahead of [*group*].

avant[2] /avɑ̃/ **I** *adj inv* [*wheel, seat, paw*] front.
II *nm* **1 l'~** the front; **aller de l'~** to forge ahead; **d'~ en arrière** backwards and forwards; **2** (Sport) forward.
III avant- (*combining form*) **l'~-1945/l'~-Thatcher** the pre-1945 period/the pre-Thatcher era.

avantage /avɑ̃taʒ/ *nm* **1** advantage; **tirer ~ de qch** to take advantage of sth; **paraître à son ~** to look one's best; **avoir ~ à faire** to be better off doing; **2** benefit; **~ fiscaux** tax benefits.

avantager /avɑ̃taʒe/ [13] *vtr* **1** [*person*] to favour[GB]; [*situation*] to be to the advantage of; **2** [*clothes, jewellery*] to show [sb/sth] off to advantage.

avantageusement /avɑ̃taʒøzmɑ̃/ *adv* favourably[GB]; **tirer ~ parti de qch** to use sth to one's advantage.

avantageux, -euse /avɑ̃taʒø, øz/ *adj* **1** [*conditions, offer*] favourable[GB], advantageous; [*rate, price*] attractive; [*product*] good value; **tirer un parti ~ de qch** to use sth to one's advantage; **2** [*description, outfit*] flattering; **3** [*air, tone*] conceited.

avant-bras /avɑ̃bʀa/ *nm inv* forearm.

avant-coureur, *pl* **~s** /avɑ̃kuʀœʀ/ *adj* **signes ~s** early warning signs.

avant-dernier, -ière, *pl* **~s** /avɑ̃dɛʀnje, ɛʀ/ **I** *adj* penultimate; **l'~ jour** the last day but one; **arriver ~** to come last but one.
II *nm,f* the last but one; **l'~ d'une famille de cinq enfants** the second youngest of five children.

avant-garde, *pl* **~s** /avɑ̃gaʀd/ *nf* **1** avant-garde; **2** vanguard; **à l'~** in the vanguard.

avant-goût, *pl* **~s** /avɑ̃gu/ *nm* foretaste.

avant-hier /avɑ̃tjɛʀ/ *adv* the day before yesterday.

avant-première, *pl* **~s** /avɑ̃pʀəmjɛʀ/ *nf* preview.

avant-propos /avɑ̃pʀɔpo/ *nm inv* foreword.

avant-scène, *pl* **~s** /avɑ̃sɛn/ *nf* **1** forestage; **2** (for spectators) box.

avant-veille, *pl* **~s** /avɑ̃vɛj/ *nf* two days before.

avare /avaʀ/ **I** *adj* mean, miserly; **~ de** sparing with; **il n'est pas ~ de compliments** he's generous with his compliments.
II *nmf* miser.

avarice /avaʀis/ *nf* meanness (GB), miserliness.

avarie /avaʀi/ *nf* damage.

avarier: **s'avarier** /avaʀje/ [2] *v refl* (+ *v être*) [*meat, fish*] to go rotten.

avatar /avataʀ/ *nm* **1** mishap; **2** change.

avec /avɛk/ **I**° *adv* **mon chapeau lui a plu, elle est partie ~** she liked my hat and went off with it.
II *prep* with; **viens ~ tes amis** bring your friends with you; **~ attention** carefully; **et ~ cela, que désirez-vous?** what else would you like?; **je fais tout son travail et ~ ça il n'est pas content!** I do all his work and he's still not happy!; **sa séparation d'~ sa femme** his separation from his wife.

avenant, **~e** /avnɑ̃, ɑ̃t/ **I** *adj* pleasant; **peu ~** rather unpleasant.
II à l'avenant *phr* in keeping.

avenir /avniʀ/ *nm* future; **dans un ~ proche** in the near future; **avoir de l'~** to have a future; **d'~** [*job*] with a future; [*technique, science*] of the future.

aventure /avɑ̃tyʀ/ *nf* **1** adventure; **partir à l'~** to set off in search of adventure; **2 il m'est arrivé une drôle d'~** something strange happened to me; **3** venture; **4** (love) affair.
IDIOMS **dire la bonne ~ à qn** to tell sb's fortune.

aventurer: **s'aventurer** /avɑ̃tyʀe/ [1] *v refl* (+ *v être*) to venture.

aventureux, **-euse** /avɑ̃tyʀø, øz/ *adj* adventurous.

aventurier, **-ière** /avɑ̃tyʀje, ɛʀ/ *nm,f* adventurer/adventuress.

avenu, **~e**[1] /avny/ *adj* **nul et non ~** null and void.

avenue[2] /avny/ *nf* avenue.

avéré, **~e** /aveʀe/ *adj* recognized, acknowledged; **il est ~ que** it is proven that.

avérer: **s'avérer** /aveʀe/ [14] *v refl* (+ *v être*) **s'~ utile** to prove useful; **il s'avère que** it turns out that.

averse /avɛʀs/ *nf* shower.

aversion /avɛʀsjɔ̃/ *nf* aversion; **avoir qn/qch en ~** to loathe sb/sth.

averti, **~e** /avɛʀti/ **I** *pp* ▶ **avertir**.
II *pp adj* **1** [*reader*] informed; **2** experienced.

avertir /avɛʀtiʀ/ [3] *vtr* **1** to inform; **2** to warn.

avertissement /avɛʀtismɑ̃/ *nm* **1** warning; **2** (Sport) caution; **3** (in book) foreword.

avertisseur /avɛʀtisœʀ/ *nm* **1** alarm; **2** (of car) horn.

aveu, *pl* **~x** /avø/ *nm* **1** confession; **2** admission.

aveuglant, **~e** /avœglɑ̃, ɑ̃t/ *adj* blinding.

aveugle /avœgl/ **I** *adj* **1** blind; **devenir ~** to go blind; **2** [*faith, love*] blind; [*violence, shooting*] indiscriminate.
II *nmf* blind person; **les ~s** the blind.

aveuglement /avœgləmɑ̃/ *nm* blindness.

aveuglément /avœglemɑ̃/ *adv* blindly.

aveugler /avœgle/ [1] *vtr* to blind.

aveuglette: **à l'aveuglette** /alavœglɛt/ *phr* **1** blindly; **avancer à l'~** to grope one's way along; **2** at random.

aviateur, **-trice** /avjatœʀ, tʀis/ *nm,f* airman/woman pilot.

aviation /avjasjɔ̃/ *nf* **1** aviation; **2** aircraft industry; **3** the air force.

aviatrice *nf* ▶ **aviateur**.

avide /avid/ *adj* **1** greedy; **2** [*reader*] avid; **~ de** avid for, eager for; **~ de sang** bloodthirsty.

avidité /avidite/ *nf* **1** greed; **2** eagerness.

avilir /aviliʀ/ [3] **I** *vtr* to demean.
II s'avilir *v refl* (+ *v être*) to demean oneself.

avilissant, **~e** /avilisɑ̃, ɑ̃t/ *adj* demeaning.

avilissement /avilismɑ̃/ *nm* degradation.

avion /avjɔ̃/ *nm* **1** (aero)plane (GB), airplane (US), aircraft; **aller à Rome en ~** to fly to Rome; **'par ~'** 'by air mail'; **2** flight; **ton ~ est à quelle heure?** what time is your flight?
■ **~ de chasse** fighter (plane); **~ à réaction** jet; **~ de tourisme** light passenger aircraft.

aviron /aviʀɔ̃/ *nm* **1** rowing; **faire de l'~** to row; **2** oar.

avis /avi/ *nm inv* **1** opinion; **je suis de ton ~** I agree with you; **de l'~ général** in most people's opinion; **changer d'~** to change one's mind; **2** advice; **sauf ~ contraire** unless otherwise informed; **3** (of jury, commission) recommendation; **4** notice; **~ à la population** public notice; public announcement; **lancer un ~ de recherche** to issue a description of a missing person/wanted person.
■ **~ au lecteur** foreword; **~ de passage** calling card (*left by postman etc*).
IDIOMS **deux ~ valent mieux qu'un** (Proverb) two heads are better than one.

avisé, **~e** /avize/ *adj* sensible; **être bien/mal ~** to be well-/ill-advised.

aviser /avize/ [1] **I** *vtr* to notify.
II *vi* to decide.
III s'aviser *v refl* (+ *v être*) **1 s'~ que** to realize that; **s'~ de** to notice; **2 ne t'avise pas de recommencer** don't dare do that again.

aviver /avive/ [1] **I** *vtr* **1** to intensify [*feeling*]; to increase [*interest*]; to stir up [*quarrel*]; to make [sth] more acute [*pain*]; **2** to liven up [*colour*]; **3** to kindle [*fire*].

II **s'aviver** *v refl* (+ *v être*) [*desire, anger*] to grow; [*pain, grief*] to become more acute.

avocat /avɔka/ *nm* **1** lawyer, solicitor (GB), attorney (at law) (US); **2** barrister (GB), (trial) lawyer (US); **~ de la défense** counsel for the defence, defense attorney (US); **~ de l'accusation** counsel for the prosecution; **3** (of idea) advocate; (of cause, person) champion; **se faire l'~ de qn/qch** to champion sb/sth; **4** avocado (pear).

avocate /avɔkat/ *nf* woman lawyer.

avoine /avwan/ *nf* oats.

avoir[1] /avwaʀ/ [8]

■ **Note** You will find translations for expressions such as *avoir raison, avoir beau, en avoir marre etc* at the entries ***raison, beau, marre*** etc.

I *v aux* to have; **j'ai perdu mon briquet** I've lost my lighter; **j'ai fini hier** I finished yesterday; **j'aurai fini demain** I'll have finished tomorrow; **il aurait aimé te parler** he would have liked to speak to you.

II *vtr* **1** to have (got) [*child, book, room, time*]; **j'ai mon stylo qui fuit** my pen is leaking; **elle avait les larmes aux yeux** there were tears in her eyes○; **2** to get [*object, job*]; to catch [*train, plane*]; (on the phone) **j'ai réussi à l'~** I managed to get through to him; **3** to wear, to have [sth] on; **4** to feel; **~ du chagrin** to feel sad; **qu'est-ce que tu as?** what's wrong or the matter with you?; **5 avoir faim/froid/20 ans** to be hungry/cold/20 years old; **6** to beat; to have○, to con○; **j'ai été eu** I've been had.

III **avoir à** *v+prep* to have to; **tu auras à rendre compte de tes actes** you'll have to account for your actions; **tu n'as pas à le critiquer** you shouldn't criticize him; **j'ai beaucoup à faire** I have or I've got a lot to do; **tu n'avais qu'à partir** you should have left; **tu n'as qu'à leur écrire** all you have to do is write to them.

IV **en avoir pour** *v+prep* **1 vous en avez pour combien de temps?** how long will it take you?; how long are you going to be?; **j'en ai pour cinq minutes** I'll be five minutes; **2 j'en ai eu pour 500 francs** it cost me 500 francs.

V **il y a** *v impers* **1** there is/there are; **il n'y a pas de raison de faire** there is no reason to do; **qu'est-ce qu'il y a?** what's wrong?; what's going on?; **il y a qu'elle m'énerve** she's getting on my nerves, that's what's wrong; **il y a à manger pour quatre** there's enough food for four; **il y en a toujours qui se plaignent** there's always someone who complains; **il n'y en a que pour leur chien** their dog comes first; **2 il y a longtemps** a long time ago; **il y a cinq ans que j'habite ici** I have been living here for five years; **il y a combien de temps qu'on ne s'est vus?** how long is it since we last met?; **3 combien y a-t-il jusqu'à la gare?** how far is it to the station?; **il y a au moins 15 kilomètres** it's at least 15 kilometres[GB] away.

avoir[2] /avwaʀ/ *nm* **1** credit; **2** credit note; **3** assets, holdings.

■ **~ fiscal** tax credit.

avoisinant, ~e /avwazinɑ̃, ɑ̃t/ *adj* neighbouring[GB].

avoisiner /avwazine/ [1] *vtr* **1** to be close to, to be about; **2** to be near.

avortement /avɔʀtəmɑ̃/ *nm* **1** (Med) abortion; **2** (of plan) collapse.

avorter /avɔʀte/ [1] *vi* **1** (Med) to have an abortion; **2** [*cow, ewe*] to abort, to miscarry; **2** [*plan*] to be aborted; [*uprising*] to fail.

avorton /avɔʀtɔ̃/ *nm* runt.

avouable /avwabl/ *adj* worthy; respectable.

avoué, ~e /avwe/ **I** *pp* ▶ **avouer**.

II *pp adj* [*enemy*] declared; [*intention*] avowed; [*terrorist*] self-confessed; **le mobile ~ du crime** the motive given for the crime.

III *nm* (Law) ≈ solicitor (GB), attorney(-at-law) (US).

avouer /avwe/ [1] **I** *vtr* to confess, to admit.

II *vi* to confess; to own up.

III **s'avouer** *v refl* (+ *v être*) **s'~ rassuré** to say one feels reassured; **s'~ coupable** to admit one's guilt; **s'~ vaincu** to admit defeat.

avril /avʀil/ *nm* April.

IDIOMS **en ~, ne te découvre pas d'un fil, en mai fais ce qu'il te plaît** (Proverb) ne'er cast a clout till May be out.

axe /aks/ *nm* **1** axis; **2** (Tech) axle; **3** major road; **4 dans l'~ du bâtiment** in a line with the building; **la cible est dans l'~ du viseur** the target is lined up in the sights.

axer /akse/ [1] *vtr* **1** to centre[GB] [*screw*]; to line up [*part*]; **2** to base, to centre[GB] (**sur** on); **~ ses recherches sur un thème** to focus one's research on a theme.

axiome /aksjom/ *nm* axiom.

ayant droit, *pl* **ayants droit** /ɛyɑ̃dʀwa/ *nm* **1** legal claimant, beneficiary; **2** assignee.

azalée /azale/ *nf* azalea.

azimut /azimyt/ *nm* **1** (in astronomy) azimuth; **2** (figurative) **défense tous ~s** total defence[GB]; **une offensive tous ~s** an all-out offensive; **arrestations tous ~s** extensive or wholesale arrests; **dans tous les ~s** everywhere, all over the place.

azimuté○**, ~e** /azimyte/ *adj* crazy○.

azote /azɔt/ *nm* nitrogen.

aztèque /astɛk/ *adj* Aztec.

azur /azyʀ/ *nm* azure.

azyme /azim/ *adj* unleavened.

Bb

b, **B** /be/ *nm inv* b, B; **le b a ba** the rudiments.
BA /bea/ *nf*: *abbr* ▶ **bon**.
baba /baba/ I○ *adj inv* **en être** or **rester** ~ to be flabbergasted○.
II *nm* ~ **(au rhum)** (rum) baba.
babillage /babijaʒ/ *nm* babbling.
babines /babin/ *nf pl* lips; **retrousser ses ~** [*dog*] to bare its teeth.
babiole /babjɔl/ *nf* **1** trinket; **2** trifle.
bâbord /babɔʀ/ *nm* port (side).
babouin /babwɛ̃/ *nm* baboon.
baby-foot /babifut/ *nm inv* table soccer.
bac /bak/ *nm* **1**○ *abbr* = **baccalauréat**; **2** ferry; **3** tub; **évier à deux ~s** double sink.
■ **~ à glace** ice tray; **~ à sable** sandpit (GB), sandbox (US).
baccalauréat /bakalɔʀea/ *nm* baccalaureate (*school-leaving certificate taken at 17–18*); **~ professionnel** vocational baccalaureate (*vocationally-oriented school-leaving certificate taken at 17–18*).
bâche /bɑʃ/ *nf* tarpaulin; **toile de ~** canvas sheet.
bachelier, **-ière** /baʃəlje, ɛʀ/ *nm,f*: *holder of the baccalaureate*.
bachotage○ /baʃɔtaʒ/ *nm* **faire du ~** to cram (for an exam).
bacille /basil/ *nm* bacillus.
bâcler /bakle/ [1] *vtr* to dash [sth] off [*piece of work*]; to rush through [*ceremony*]; **c'est du travail bâclé** it's a slapdash job.
bactérie /bakteʀi/ *nf* bacterium.
badaud, **~e** /bado, od/ *nm,f* **1** passerby; **2** onlooker.
badigeonner /badiʒɔne/ [1] *vtr* **1** to whitewash; **2** to paint; **3** to daub (**de** with); **4** (Culin) to brush (**de** with).
badin, **~e** /badɛ̃, in/ *adj* [*tone*] bantering; [*mood*] playful.
badiner /badine/ [1] *vi* to banter, to jest.
baffe○ /baf/ *nf* clout, slap.
baffle /bafl/ *nm* **1** speaker; **2** baffle.
bafouer /bafwe/ [1] *vtr* to scorn.
bafouiller /bafuje/ [1] *vtr*, *vi* [*person*] to mumble.
bagage /bagaʒ/ *nm* piece of luggage; **faire ses ~s** to pack.
IDIOMS **plier ~**○ to pack up and go; **partir avec armes et ~s** to up sticks and leave.
bagarre /bagaʀ/ *nf* fight, scuffle.
bagarrer○: **se bagarrer** /bagaʀe/ [1] *v refl* (+ *v être*) to fight.
bagarreur○, **-euse** /bagaʀœʀ, øz/ I *adj* aggressive.
II *nm,f* bruiser○, fighter.
bagatelle /bagatɛl/ *nf* **1** trifle, triviality; **2** trinket; **3 pour la ~ de** (ironic) for the trifling sum of.
bagnard /baɲaʀ/ *nm* convict.
bagne /baɲ/ *nm* penal colony.
bagnole○ /baɲɔl/ *nf* car.
bagou(t)○ /bagu/ *nm* **avoir du ~** to have the gift of the gab.
bague /bag/ *nf* **1** ring; **2** (around pipe) collar.
baguer /bage/ [1] *vtr* to ring [*bird, tree*].
baguette /bagɛt/ *nf* **1** baguette, French stick; **2** stick; **mener qn à la ~** to rule sb with a rod of iron; **3 ~ de chef d'orchestre** conductor's baton; **4** drumstick; **5** chopstick.
■ **~ magique** magic wand; **~ de sourcier** divining rod.
bahut /bay/ *nm* **1** sideboard; **2**○ (students' slang) school; **3**○ truck.
baie /bɛ/ *nf* **1** bay; **2** berry; **3 ~ (vitrée)** picture window.
baignade /bɛɲad/ *nf* swimming; **'~ interdite'** 'no swimming'.
baigner /beɲe/ [1] I *vtr* **1** to give [sb] a bath; **2** to bathe [*wound*].
II *vi* **~ dans l'huile** to be swimming in grease.
III **se baigner** *v refl* (+ *v être*) to go swimming.
IDIOMS **ça baigne**○ **(dans l'huile)** things are going fine.
baigneur, **-euse** /bɛɲœʀ, øz/ I *nm,f* swimmer.
II *nm* baby doll.
baignoire /bɛɲwaʀ/ *nf* **1** bathtub; **~ sabot** hip bath; **2** (in the theatre) ground-floor box.
bail, *pl* **baux** /baj, bo/ *nm* lease; **ça fait un ~**○ it's ages (**que** since).
bâillement /bajmɑ̃/ *nm* yawn.
bâiller /bɑje/ [1] *vi* **1** to yawn (**de** from, out of); **2** to gape (open).
bâillon /bɑjɔ̃/ *nm* gag.
bâillonner /bɑjɔne/ [1] *vtr* to gag.
bain /bɛ̃/ *nm* **1** bath; **2** swim; **3 grand/petit ~** deep/shallow pool.
■ **~ de bouche** mouthwash; **~ de foule** walkabout; **~ de jouvence** rejuvenating experience; **~ de soleil** (garment) suntop; **prendre un ~ de soleil** to sunbathe.
IDIOMS **se remettre dans le ~** to get back into the swing of things.
baïonnette /bajɔnɛt/ *nf* bayonet.
baiser /beze/ *nm* kiss; **bons ~s** love (and kisses).
baisse /bɛs/ *nf* **1** fall; **en ~** falling; **2** fading; **3** decline; **4** cut.
baisser /bese/ [1] I *vtr* **1** to lower [*blind*]; to wind [sth] down [*window*]; to pull down [*visor*]; to turn down [*collar*]; **~ les bras** (figurative) to give up; **~ le nez** (figurative) to hang one's head;

2 to turn down [*volume*]; to dim [*light*]; to cut [*prices*].
II *vi* to go down, to fall (**à** to; **de** by); [*light*] to fade; [*water*] to subside; [*sight*] to fail; [*hearing*] to deteriorate; **~ d'un ton**○ [*person*] to calm down.
III se baisser *v refl* (+ *v être*) **1** to bend down; **2** to duck; **3** to go down.

bajoue /baʒu/ *nf* cheek.

bal /bal/ *nm* **1** ball, dance; **2** dancehall.

balade /balad/ *nf* walk; ride.

balader○ /balade/ [1] **I** *vtr* **1** to take [sb] for a walk/drive; **2** to carry [sth] around.
II se balader *v refl* (+ *v être*) to go for a walk/ride/drive.
IDIOMS **envoyer qn ~**○ to send sb packing○.

baladeur /baladœʀ/ *nm* walkman®, personal stereo.

baladeuse /baladøz/ *nf* inspection lamp.

balafre /balafʀ/ *nf* **1** scar; **2** slash, gash.

balai /balɛ/ *nm* **1** broom; **passer le ~** to sweep the floor; **du ~**○! go away!; **2** (of windscreen wiper) blade.
■ **~ mécanique** carpet sweeper.

balai-brosse, *pl* **balais-brosses** /balɛbʀɔs/ *nm* stiff broom.

balaise○ = **balèze**.

balance /balɑ̃s/ *nf* **1** (weighing) scales; **faire pencher la ~** (figurative) to tip the scales; **2** balance.

Balance /balɑ̃s/ *pr nf* Libra.

balancelle /balɑ̃sɛl/ *nf* swing seat, garden hammock.

balancement /balɑ̃smɑ̃/ *nm* (of branches, body) swaying; (of arms, rope) swinging; (of head) lolling.

balancer /balɑ̃se/ [12] **I** *vtr* **1** to sway; **2** to swing; **3**○ to chuck○ (**sur** at); to chuck out○ [*old clothes, junk*]; **4**○ to bandy [sth] about [*figures*]; **5**○ to squeal on○.
II *vi* **1** to sway; **2** to hesitate.
III se balancer *v refl* (+ *v être*) **1** [*person*] to sway; [*boat*] to rock; **2**○ **je m'en balance** I couldn't care less.

balancier /balɑ̃sje/ *nm* **1** pendulum; **2** balancing pole.

balançoire /balɑ̃swaʀ/ *nf* **1** swing; **2** seesaw.

balayer /baleje/ [21] *vtr* **1** to sweep (up); **~ le sol** [*coat*] to brush the ground; **2** [*searchlight*] to sweep; [*machine-gun fire*] to rake; **3** to brush [sth] aside [*objections*]; **4** [*radar*] to scan.

balayette /balɛjɛt/ *nf* (short-handled) brush.

balayeur -euse /balɛjœʀ, øz/ *nm,f* roadsweeper.

balbutiement /balbysimɑ̃/ *nm* **les premiers ~s du cinéma** (figurative) the early days of the cinema.

balbutier /balbysje/ [2] *vtr*, *vi* to mumble.

balcon /balkɔ̃/ *nm* **1** balcony; **2** (in theatre, cinema) balcony, circle.

Bâle /bɑl/ *pr n* Basel.

Baléares /baleɑʀ/ *pr nf pl* **les (îles) ~** the Balearic Islands.

baleine /balɛn/ *nf* **1** whale; **2** whalebone; stay; rib.

balèze○ /balɛz/ *adj* **1** hefty○; **2** fantastic○.

balise /baliz/ *nf* **1** beacon; **2** signpost, waymark; **3** (Comput) tag.

baliser /balize/ [1] *vtr* **1** to mark [sth] out with beacons; **2** to signpost, to waymark.

balistique /balistik/ **I** *adj* ballistic.
II *nf* ballistics.

baliverne /balivɛʀn/ *nf* nonsense.

ballade /balad/ *nf* **1** ballad; **2** ballade.

balle /bal/ *nf* **1** ball; **renvoyer la ~ (à qn)** (figurative) to retort (to sb); **se renvoyer la ~** to keep up an animated discussion; to keep passing the buck; **2** (in ball games) shot; **faire des ~s** to knock the ball around; **~ de jeu** game point; **3** bullet; **4**○ franc.

ballerine /balʀin/ *nf* **1** ballerina; **2** ballet pump.

ballet /balɛ/ *nm* ballet; **~ aquatique** synchronized swimming.

ballon /balɔ̃/ *nm* **1** ball; **2** balloon; **3** wine glass; **4 ~ (alcootest)** Breathalyzer®.
■ **~ dirigeable** airship (GB), blimp (US); **~ d'eau chaude** hot water tank; **~ ovale** rugby; **~ d'oxygène** oxygen bottle; (figurative) life-saver; **~ rond** soccer; soccer ball.

ballonnement /balɔnmɑ̃/ *nm* bloating.

ballot○ /balo/ *nm* nerd○, fool.

ballottage /balɔtaʒ/ *nm*: *absence of an absolute majority in the first round of an election.*

ballotter /balɔte/ [1] *vtr* **1** [*sea*] to toss [sb/sth] around; [*movement*] to jolt; **2 être ballotté entre sa famille et son travail** to be torn between one's family and one's job.

ball-trap, *pl* **~s** /baltʀap/ *nm* clay pigeon shooting.

balluchon = **baluchon**.

balnéaire /balneɛʀ/ *adj* [*resort*] seaside.

balourdise /baluʀdiz/ *nf* clumsiness.

balsa /balza/ *nm* **1** balsa; **2** balsawood.

balsamine /balzamin/ *nf* balsam.

balte /balt/ *adj* Baltic; **les pays ~s** the Baltic States.

baluchon /balyʃɔ̃/ *nm* bundle.
IDIOMS **faire son ~** to pack one's bags (and leave).

balustrade /balystʀad/ *nf* **1** parapet; **2** railing; **3** balustrade.

bambin, **~e** /bɑ̃bɛ̃, in/ *nm,f* kid○, child.

bambou /bɑ̃bu/ *nm* **1** bamboo; **2 coup de ~**○ steep bill.

ban /bɑ̃/ **I** *nm* round of applause.
II bans *nm pl* banns.
IDIOMS **mettre qn au ~ de la société** to ostracize sb.

banal, **~e** /banal/ *adj* **1** commonplace, ordinary; **peu ~** unusual; **2** trivial, trite.

banalisation /banalizɑsjɔ̃/ *nf* **la ~ de l'informatique** the way in which computing has become a part of everyday life.

banaliser /banalize/ [1] *vtr* **1** to make [sth]

commonplace; **2 voiture banalisée** unmarked car.

banalité /banalite/ *nf* **1** ordinariness; **2** triteness; **3** trite remark.

banane /banan/ *nf* **1** banana; **2** quiff; **3** bumbag (GB), fanny pack (US).

bananier /bananje/ *nm* banana tree.

banc /bɑ̃/ *nm* **1** bench; **sur les ~s de l'école** at school; **2** (of fish) shoal.
■ **~ des accusés** dock; **au ~ des avocats** at the bar; **~ de brume** patch of mist; **~ d'église** pew; **~ d'essai** test bench; testing ground; **~ de sable** sandbank.

bancaire /bɑ̃kɛʀ/ *adj* **1** [*business*] banking; **2** [*card*] bank.

bancal, **~e** /bɑ̃kal/ *adj* **1** [*chair*] rickety; **2** [*solution*] unsatisfactory.

banco /bɑ̃ko/ *nm* (in cards) banco; **faire ~** to go banco.

bande /bɑ̃d/ *nf* **1** gang; **2** group; **~ de crétins!** you bunch of idiots!; **ils font ~ à part** they don't join in; **3** (of animals) pack; **4** (of material, paper) strip; band; **5** bandage; **6** broad stripe; (as edging) band; **7** (for recording) tape; (in cinematography) film.
■ **~ d'arrêt d'urgence**, **BAU** hard shoulder; **~ dessinée**, **BD**○ comic strip; comic book; **~ de fréquences** waveband; **~ originale** (of film) original soundtrack; **~ sonore** (of film) soundtrack.

bande-annonce, *pl* **bandes-annonces** /bɑ̃danɔ̃s/ *nf* trailer.

bandeau, *pl* **~x** /bɑ̃do/ *nm* **1** blindfold; **avoir un ~ sur les yeux** (figurative) to be blind; **2** eye patch; **3** headband.

bandelette /bɑ̃dlɛt/ *nf* **1** bandage; **2** (of silk, paper) small strip.

bander /bɑ̃de/ [1] *vtr* **1** to bandage; **2 ~ les yeux à qn** to blindfold sb.

banderole /bɑ̃dʀɔl/ *nf* banner.

bande-son, *pl* **bandes-son** /bɑ̃dsɔ̃/ *nm* soundtrack.

bandit /bɑ̃di/ *nm* **1** bandit; **~ de grand chemin** highwayman; **2** crook; **3** rascal.

banditisme /bɑ̃ditism/ *nm* **le ~** crime; **le grand/petit ~** organized/petty crime.

bandoulière /bɑ̃duljɛʀ/ *nf* shoulder strap.

banlieue /bɑ̃ljø/ *nf* **1** suburbs; **de ~** suburban; **2** suburb.

banlieusard, **~e** /bɑ̃ljøzaʀ, aʀd/ *nm,f* suburbanite.

banni, **~e** /bani/ *nm,f* exile.

bannière /banjɛʀ/ *nf* banner; **la ~ étoilée** the star-spangled banner.
IDIOMS **c'est la croix et la ~** it's hell (**pour faire** doing).

bannir /baniʀ/ [3] *vtr* **1** to banish (**de** from); **2** to ban.

banque /bɑ̃k/ *nf* **1** bank; **2** banking; **3** (in cards) bank; **tenir la ~** to be banker.
■ **~ d'affaires** merchant bank; **~ de données** data bank.

banqueroute /bɑ̃kʀut/ *nf* bankruptcy; **faire ~** to go bankrupt.

banquet /bɑ̃kɛ/ *nm* **1** banquet; **2** feast.

banquette /bɑ̃kɛt/ *nf* (in café) wall seat; (in car, train) seat.

banquier /bɑ̃kje/ *nm* banker.

banquise /bɑ̃kiz/ *nf* ice floe.

baptême /batɛm/ *nm* **1** baptism; christening; **2** (of ship) christening; (of church bell) blessing.
■ **~ de l'air** first flight; **~ du feu** baptism of fire.

baptiser /batize/ [1] *vtr* **1** to baptize, to christen; **2** to call, to name; to nickname; **3** to christen [*ship*]; to bless [*bell*].

baquet /bakɛ/ *nm* **1** tub; **2** bucket-seat.

bar /baʀ/ *nm* **1** bar; **2** sea bass.

baragouin○ /baʀagwɛ̃/ *nm* gibberish.

baragouiner○ /baʀagwine/ [1] *vtr* to gabble [*sentence*]; to speak [sth] badly [*language*].

baraka○ /baʀaka/ *nf* luck; **avoir la ~** to be lucky.

baraque /baʀak/ *nf* **1** shack; **2**○ pad○, house; dump○.

baraqué○, **~e** /baʀake/ *adj* hefty.

baraquement /baʀakmɑ̃/ *nm* **1** group of huts; **2** hut; **3** army camp.

baratin○ /baʀatɛ̃/ *nm* **1** sales pitch; **2** sweet-talk; **3** smooth talk○ (GB).

baratiner○ /baʀatine/ [1] **I** *vtr* **1** to give [sb] the spiel; **2** to chat [sb] up; **3** to try to persuade.
II *vi* to jabber (on).

barbant○, **~e** /baʀbɑ̃, ɑ̃t/ *adj* boring.

barbare /baʀbaʀ/ **I** *adj* **1** [*attitude*] barbaric; **2** [*horde*] barbarian.
II *nmf* barbarian.

barbe /baʀb/ **I** *nf* beard; **~ naissante** stubble; **c'est la ~**○**!** what a drag○!
II○ *excl* **la ~!** I've had enough!; **la ~ avec leurs consignes!** to hell with their orders○!
■ **~ à papa** candyfloss (GB), cotton candy (US).
IDIOMS **à la ~ de qn** under sb's nose.

barbelé /baʀbəle/ *nm* barbed wire (GB), barbwire (US).

barber○ /baʀbe/ [1] **I** *vtr* to bore [sb] stiff○.
II se barber *v refl* (+ *v être*) to be bored stiff○.

barbet /baʀbɛ/ *nm* water spaniel.

barbiche /baʀbiʃ/ *nf* **1** goatee (beard); **2** (on goat) (small) beard.

barbier /baʀbje/ *nm* barber.

barbiturique /baʀbityʀik/ *nm* barbiturate.

barboter /baʀbɔte/ [1] **I**○ *vtr* to filch○ (**à** from).
II *vi* to paddle.

barbouillage /baʀbujaʒ/ *nm* **1** daubing; **2** daub.

barbouiller /baʀbuje/ [1] **I** *vtr* **1** to smear (**de** with); **2** to daub (**de** with); **3 ~ des toiles** to do daubs, to dabble in painting; **~ du papier** to write drivel; **4 être** or **se sentir barbouillé** to feel queasy.
II se barbouiller *v refl* (+ *v être*) **se ~ le visage de qch** to get one's face all covered in sth.

barbu, **~e**[1] /baʀby/ *adj* bearded; **il est ~** he has a beard.

barbue[2] /baʀby/ *nf* brill.
barda° /baʀda/ *nm* baggage, gear°; (Mil) kit.
barde /baʀd/ *nf* thin slice of bacon, bard.
bardé, **~e** /baʀde/ *adj* covered (**de** in).
barder /baʀde/ [1] **I** *vtr* (Culin) to bard.
II° *v impers* **ça barde chez les voisins!** there's a row going on next door!
barème /baʀɛm/ *nm* scale; **~ de correction** marking scheme; **~ des prix** price list.
baril /baʀil/ *nm* barrel, cask; keg; drum.
barillet /baʀijɛ/ *nm* cylinder.
bariolé, **~e** /baʀjɔle/ *adj* **1** multicoloured[GB]; **2** gaudy; **3** motley.
barjaquer /baʀʒake/ [1] *vi* (Swiss Fr) to chatter.
baromètre /baʀɔmɛtʀ/ *nm* barometer.
baron /baʀɔ̃/ *nm* baron.
baronne /baʀɔn/ *nf* baroness.
baroque /baʀɔk/ *adj* **1** baroque; **2** bizarre.
baroudeur /baʀudœʀ/ *nm* **1** fighter, warrior; **2** adventurer.
barque /baʀk/ *nf* (small) boat.
IDIOMS **bien/mal mener sa ~** to manage things well/badly.
barquette /baʀkɛt/ *nf* punnet (GB), basket (US); tub; container.
barrage /baʀaʒ/ *nm* **1** dam; **2** roadblock; barricade; **faire ~ à** to block.
barre /baʀ/ *nf* **1** bar, rod; **2** (of chocolate) piece; **3** tiller, helm; **4** band, stripe; **5** stroke; **la ~ du t** the cross on the t; **6** (of goal) crossbar; (in high jump) bar; **7** (in ballet practice) barre; **8** (Law) bar; ≈ witness box (GB), witness stand (US); **9** mark; **franchir la ~ des 13%** to go over the 13% mark.
■ **~ fixe** horizontal bar; **~ oblique** slash.
IDIOMS **avoir un coup de ~**° to feel drained all of a sudden; **c'est le coup de ~ dans ce restaurant**° that restaurant is a rip-off°.
barreau, *pl* **~x** /baʀo/ *nm* **1** bar; **2** rung; **3** (Law) **le ~** the Bar.
barrer /baʀe/ [1] *vtr* **1** to block [*way*]; **'route barrée'** 'road closed'; **2** to cross out; **~ un chèque** to cross a cheque (GB) or check (US).
barrette /baʀɛt/ *nf* (hair) slide (GB), barrette (US).
barricade /baʀikad/ *nf* barricade.
barricader /baʀikade/ [1] *vtr* to barricade.
barrière /baʀjɛʀ/ *nf* **1** fence; **2** gate; **3** barrier.
barrique /baʀik/ *nf* barrel.
barrir /baʀiʀ/ [3] *vi* [*elephant*] to trumpet.
bar-tabac, *pl* **bars-tabac** /baʀtaba/ *nm* café (*selling stamps and cigarettes*).
bas, **basse**[1] /bɑ, bɑs/ **I** *adj* low; [*room*] low-ceilinged; [*land*] low-lying; **le ciel est ~** the sky is overcast; **à ~ prix** [*sell*] cheap; **un enfant en ~ âge** a very young child; **de ~ niveau** [*product*] low-grade; **être au plus ~** [*prices*] to have reached rock bottom.
II *adv* **1** low; **comment peut-on tomber si ~!** how can one sink so low!; **2 voir plus ~** see below; **3** quietly; **tout ~** [*speak*] in a whisper; [*sing*] softly; **4 être au plus ~** to be extremely weak; to be at one's lowest or at a very low ebb.
III *nm inv* **1** bottom; **le ~ du visage** the lower part of the face; **les pièces du ~** the downstairs rooms; **vers le ~** downward(s); **2** stocking.
IV en bas *phr* downstairs; down below; at the bottom.
■ **~ de gamme** *adj* low-quality; *nm* lower end of the market; **~ morceaux** (Culin) cheap cuts; **les ~ quartiers** the seedy districts (of a town); **basse saison** low season.
IDIOMS **avoir des hauts et des ~** to have one's ups and downs; **à ~ les tyrans!** down with tyranny!; **mettre qn plus ~ que terre** to tear sb to bits°.
basalte /bazalt/ *nm* basalt.
basané, **~e** /bazane/ *adj* **1** tanned; **2** swarthy.
bas-côté, *pl* **~s** /bɑkote/ *nm* **1** verge (GB), shoulder (US); **2** (side) aisle.
basculant, **~e** /baskylɑ̃, ɑ̃t/ *adj* **pont ~** bascule bridge; **camion à benne ~e** dump truck.
bascule /baskyl/ *nf* **1** rocker; **2** seesaw; **3** weighing machine.
basculer /baskyle/ [1] **I** *vtr* to transfer [*call*].
II *vi* **1** to topple over; **faire ~** to tip up [*skip*]; to tip out [*load*]; to knock [sb] off balance [*person*]; **2** (figurative) to change radically; **~ à droite** to swing over to the right.
base /bɑz/ *nf* **1** base (**de** of); **à ~ d'arsenic** arsenic-based; **le riz forme la ~ de leur alimentation** rice is their staple diet; **2** basis; **reposer sur des ~s solides** to rest on a firm foundation; **à la ~ de qch** at the root or heart of sth; **avoir des ~s en chimie** to have a basic grounding in chemistry; **salaire de ~** basic salary; **repartir sur de nouvelles ~s** to make a fresh start; **3** (in politics) **la ~** the rank and file.
■ **~ de données** database; **~ de lancement** launching site.
baser /bɑze/ [1] **I** *vtr* to base (**sur** on).
II se baser *v refl* (+ *v être*) **se ~ sur qch** to go by sth.
bas-fond, *pl* **~s** /bɑfɔ̃/ **I** *nm* **1** shallows; **2** dip.
II bas-fonds *nm pl* **1** dregs (of society); **2** seedy areas.
basilic /bazilik/ *nm* basil.
basilique /bazilik/ *nf* basilica.
basket /baskɛt/ *nm* **1** basketball; **2** trainer (GB), sneaker (US).
basketteur, **-euse** /baskɛtœʀ, øz/ *nm,f* basketball player.
basque /bask/ *adj*, *nm* Basque.
bas-relief, *pl* **~s** /bɑʀəljɛf/ *nm* bas-relief, low relief.
basse[2] /bɑs/ **I** *adj* ▶ **bas I**.
II *nf* (Mus) bass.
basse-cour, *pl* **basses-cours** /bɑskuʀ/ *nf* **1** poultry-yard; **2** poultry.
bassement /bɑsmɑ̃/ *adv* basely.
bassesse /bɑsɛs/ *nf* **1** baseness, lowness; **2** base or despicable act.

basset /basɛ/ *nm* basset (hound).

bassin /basɛ̃/ *nm* **1** pond; fountain; pool; **2** (in geography) basin; **3** pelvis; **4** bedpan.
■ **~ houiller** coal field.

bassine /basin/ *nf* bowl.

bassiste /basist/ *nmf* bass player.

bastide /bastid/ *nf* **1** (medieval) fortified town; **2** country house (*in Provence*).

bastonnade /bastɔnad/ *nf* beating.

bas-ventre, *pl* **~s** /bavɑ̃tʀ/ *nm* lower abdomen.

bataille /bataj/ **I** *nf* **1** battle; **2** fight; **3** ≈ beggar-my-neighbour[GB].
II en bataille *phr* [*hair*] dishevelled[GB]; [*eyebrows*] bushy.

batailleur, **-euse** /batajœʀ, øz/ **I** *adj* aggressive.
II *nm,f* fighter.

bataillon /batajɔ̃/ *nm* battalion; **Dupont?, inconnu au ~** (humorous) Dupont?, never heard of him.

bâtard, **~e** /bataʀ, aʀd/ **I** *adj* **1** [*dog*] mongrel; **2** [*work, style*] hybrid; [*status*] ill-defined; **3** (offensive) [*child*] bastard.
II *nm,f* **1** mongrel; **2** (offensive) bastard.

bateau, *pl* **~x** /bato/ **I** *adj inv* hackneyed.
II *nm* **1** boat, ship; **faire du ~** to go boating; to go sailing; **2 encolure ~** boat neck; **3** dropped kerb (GB) or curb (US).
■ **~ amiral** flagship; **~ de plaisance** pleasure boat; **~ pneumatique** rubber dinghy; **~ de sauvetage** lifeboat.

bateau-école, *pl* **bateaux-écoles** /batoekɔl/ *nm* training ship.

bateau-mouche, *pl* **bateaux-mouches** /batomuʃ/ *nm*: *large river boat for sightseeing*.

batelier, **-ière** /batəlje, ɛʀ/ *nm,f* boatman/boatwoman.

bâti, **~e** /bati/ **I** *pp* ▶ **bâtir**.
II *pp adj* **1** built; **terrain ~** developed site; **2 un homme bien ~** a well-built man.

batifoler /batifɔle/ [1] *vi* **1** to romp about; **2** to flirt.

bâtiment /batimɑ̃/ *nm* **1** building; **2** building trade; **3** ship.

bâtir /batiʀ/ [3] *vtr* **1** to build; **terrain à ~** building land; **2** to build [*fortune, reputation*] (**sur** on); **3** to tack [*hem*].

bâton /batɔ̃/ *nm* **1** stick; **2** vertical stroke; **3**○ ten thousand francs.
■ **~ de rouge (à lèvres)** lipstick; **~ de ski** ski stick.
IDIOMS **discuter à ~s rompus** to talk about this and that; **mettre des ~s dans les roues de qn** to put a spoke in sb's wheel.

bâtonnet /batɔnɛ/ *nm* stick.
■ **~ ouaté** cotton bud (GB), cotton swab (US); **~ de poisson** fish finger (GB), fish stick (US).

bâtonnier /batɔnje/ *nm* ≈ president of the Bar.

batracien /batʀasjɛ̃/ *nm* batrachian.

battage○ /bataʒ/ *nm* publicity, hype○; **faire du ~ autour de qch** to hype sth○.

battant, **~e** /batɑ̃, ɑ̃t/ **I** *adj* **~ neuf** brand new; **à deux heures ~es** on the stroke of two; **le cœur ~** with a beating heart.
II *nm,f* fighter.
III *nm* (of door) hinged section; **porte à deux ~s** double door.

batte /bat/ *nf* (Sport) bat (GB), paddle (US).

battement /batmɑ̃/ *nm* **1** beating; beat; fluttering; flutter; **2** break, gap; wait.

batterie /batʀi/ *nf* **1** percussion section; **2** drum kit; **3** battery.
■ **~ de cuisine** pots and pans.

batteur /batœʀ/ *nm* **1** percussionist; **2** drummer; **3** whisk.

battre /batʀ/ [61] **I** *vtr* **1** to beat [*opponent*]; to break [*record*]; **ne pas se tenir pour battu** not to admit defeat; **2** to beat [*person, animal, carpet*]; to thresh [*corn*]; **3** [*rain, sea*] to beat against; **4** to whisk [*eggs*]; to whip [*cream*]; **5** to shuffle [*cards*]; **7** (Mus) **~ la mesure** to beat time; **8** to scour [*countryside*].
II battre de *v+prep* **~ des ailes** to flap its wings; **~ des cils** to flutter one's eyelashes; **~ des mains** to clap (one's hands); **~ des paupières** to blink.
III *vi* **1** [*heart, pulse*] to beat; **2** [*door, shutter*] to bang.
IV se battre *v refl* (+ *v être*) to fight (**contre** against; **avec** with).
IDIOMS **~ en retraite devant qch** to retreat before sth; **~ son plein** to be in full swing.

battu, **~e**[1] /baty/ **I** *pp* ▶ **battre**.
II *pp adj* **1** [*child, wife*] battered; **2** tired.

battue[2] /baty/ *nf* (in hunting) beat.

BAU /beay/ *nf*: *abbr* ▶ **bande**.

baudet○ /bodɛ/ *nm* donkey, ass.

baudruche /bodʀyʃ/ *nf* balloon.

baume /bom/ *nm* balm, balsam.

baux /bo/ *nm pl* ▶ **bail**.

bavard, **~e** /bavaʀ, aʀd/ **I** *adj* **1** talkative; **2** indiscreet; **3** long-winded.
II *nm,f* **1** chatterbox; **2** blabbermouth○.

bavardage /bavaʀdaʒ/ *nm* **1** gossip; **2** idle chatter.

bavarder /bavaʀde/ [1] *vi* **1** to talk, to chatter; **2** to chat; **3** to gossip (**sur** about).

bave /bav/ *nf* dribble; spittle; slaver; slime.

baver /bave/ [1] *vi* **1** [*person*] to dribble; [*animal*] to slaver; **2** [*pen*] to leak; [*brush*] to drip; [*ink, paint*] to run.
IDIOMS **il leur en a fait ~**○ he gave them a hard time.

bavette /bavɛt/ *nf* **1** bib; **2** (Culin) flank; **3** mudflap.

baveux, **-euse** /bavø, øz/ *adj* [*omelette*] runny.

bavoir /bavwaʀ/ *nm* bib.

bavure /bavyʀ/ *nf* **1** smudge; **2** blunder.

bayer /baje/ [21] *vi* **~ aux corneilles** to gape.

bazar /bazaʀ/ *nm* **1** general store; **2**○ mess; **mettre le ~ dans** to mess up; **3**○ clutter; **4** bazaar.

bazarder○ /bazaʀde/ [1] *vi* **1** to throw out; **2** to sell off.

BCBG° /besebeʒe/ *adj* (*abbr* = **bon chic bon genre**) chic and conservative, Sloaney (GB).

BCG /beseʒe/ *nm* (*abbr* = **bacille bilié de Calmette et Guérin**) BCG.

bd *written abbr* = **boulevard 1**.

BD° /bede/ *nf*: *abbr* ▶ **bande**.

béant, **~e** /beɑ̃, ɑ̃t/ *adj* gaping.

béarnaise /beaʀnɛz/ *nf* Béarnaise sauce.

béat, **~e** /bea, at/ *adj* [*person*] blissfully happy; [*smile*] blissful, beatific; **~ d'admiration devant** wide-eyed with admiration at.

béatitude /beatityd/ *nf* beatitude.

beau (**bel** *before vowel or mute h*), **belle**[1], *mpl* **~x** /bo, bɛl/ **I** *adj* **1** beautiful; handsome; **avoir belle allure** [*person*] to cut a fine figure; [*car*] to be fine-looking; **se faire ~** to do oneself up; **peindre qch sous de belles couleurs** to make sth sound wonderful; **ce n'est pas (bien) ~ à voir**°! it's not a pretty sight!; **2** good; fine; nice; lovely; **un ~ geste** a noble gesture; **un bel avenir** a great future; **fais de ~x rêves!** sweet dreams!; **au ~ milieu de** right in the middle of; **c'est bien ~ tout ça, mais**° that's all well and good, but; **trop ~ pour être vrai** too good to be true; **3** [*sum*] tidy; [*salary*] very nice; **belle pagaille** absolute mess.

II *nm* **1 qu'est-ce que tu as fait de ~?** done anything interesting?; **2 le temps se met au ~** the weather is turning fine.

III avoir beau *phr* **j'ai ~ essayer, je n'y arrive pas** it's no good my trying, I can't do it.

IV bel et bien *phr* **1** well and truly; **2** definitely.

■ **~ fixe** fine weather; **~ parleur** smooth talker; **~x jours** fine weather; palmy days, good days; **belles années** happy years.

IDIOMS **faire le ~** [*dog*] to sit up and beg; **c'est du ~**°! (ironic) lovely!

beaucoup /boku/ **I** *adv* **1** a lot; much; **s'intéresser ~ à qch** to be very interested in sth; **c'est ~ dire** that's going a bit far; **c'est déjà ~ qu'elle soit venue** it's already quite something that she came; **~ moins de livres** far fewer books; **c'est ~ trop** it's far too much, it's much too much; **~ trop longtemps** far too long, much too long; **2 ~ de** a lot of, a great deal of; much, many; **il ne reste plus ~ de pain/de places** there isn't much bread left/aren't many seats left; **avec ~ de soin** very carefully; **3** many; **~ d'entre eux** many or a lot of them.

II de beaucoup *phr* by far.

III pour beaucoup *phr* **ta réussite est due pour ~ à** your success is largely due to; **être pour ~ dans** to have a lot to do with.

beau-fils, *pl* **beaux-fils** /bofis/ *nm* **1** son-in-law; **2** stepson.

beau-frère, *pl* **beaux-frères** /bofʀɛʀ/ *nm* brother-in-law.

beau-père, *pl* **beaux-pères** /bopɛʀ/ *nm* **1** father-in-law; **2** stepfather.

beauté /bote/ *nf* beauty; **de toute ~** exquisite; **se faire une ~** to do oneself up; **finir en ~** to end with a flourish.

beaux-arts /bozaʀ/ *nm pl* fine arts and architecture.

beaux-parents /bopaʀɑ̃/ *nm pl* parents-in-law.

bébé /bebe/ *nm* baby; **attendre un ~** to be expecting a baby.

bec /bɛk/ *nm* **1** beak; **donner des coups de ~** to peck (**dans** at); **il a toujours la cigarette au ~**° he's always got a cigarette stuck in his mouth; **2** (of jug) lip; (of teapot) spout; (of wind instrument) mouthpiece; **~ verseur** pourer (-spout).

IDIOMS **clouer le ~ à qn**° to shut sb up°; **se retrouver le ~ dans l'eau**° to be stuck, to be left high and dry; **tomber sur un ~**° to come across a snag.

bécane° /bekan/ *nf* bike, bicycle.

bécasse /bekas/ *nf* **1** woodcock; **2** featherbrain°.

bec-de-lièvre, *pl* **becs-de-lièvre** /bɛkdə ljɛvʀ/ *nm* harelip.

bêche /bɛʃ/ *nf* **1** spade; **2** garden fork.

bêcher /beʃe/ [1] *vtr* to dig (with a spade).

bêcheur°, **-euse** /bɛʃœʀ, øz/ *nm,f* stuck-up° person.

bedaine° /bədɛn/ *nf* paunch.

bée /be/ *adj f* **être bouche ~** to stand openmouthed or gaping.

beffroi /befʀwɑ/ *nm* belfry.

bégayer /begeje/ [21] *vtr*, *vi* to stammer.

bègue /bɛg/ *adj* **être ~** to stammer.

bégueule /begœl/ *adj* prudish.

béguin° /begɛ̃/ *nm* **avoir le ~ pour qn** to have a crush on sb.

beige /bɛʒ/ *adj*, *nm* beige.

beignet /bɛɲɛ/ *nm* **1** fritter; **2** doughnut, donut° (US).

bel *adj m* ▶ **beau I**, **IV**.

bêler /bɛle/ [1] *vi* to bleat.

belette /bəlɛt/ *nf* weasel.

belge /bɛlʒ/ *adj* Belgian.

Belgique /bɛlʒik/ *pr nf* Belgium.

bélier /belje/ *nm* **1** ram; **2** battering ram.

Bélier /belje/ *pr nm* Aries.

belle[2] /bɛl/ **I** *adj f* ▶ **beau I**.

II *nf* **1 ma ~** darling; **2** lady friend; **3** decider, deciding game.

III de plus belle *phr* with renewed vigour[GB]; **crier de plus ~** to shout louder than ever.

IV belles° *nf pl* stories.

■ **la Belle au Bois dormant** Sleeping Beauty.

IDIOMS **(se) faire la ~**° to do a bunk° (GB), to take a powder° (US); **en faire voir de ~s° à qn** to give sb a hard time.

belle-famille, *pl* **belles-familles** /bɛlfamij/ *nf* in-laws.

belle-fille, *pl* **belles-filles** /bɛlfij/ *nf* **1** daughter-in-law; **2** stepdaughter.

belle-mère, *pl* **belles-mères** /bɛlmɛʀ/ *nf* **1** mother-in-law; **2** stepmother.

belle-sœur, *pl* **belles-sœurs** /bɛlsœʀ/ *nf* sister-in-law.

belligérant /bɛliʒeʀɑ̃/ *nm* **1** belligerent, warring party; **2** combatant.

belliqueux, **-euse** /bɛlikø, øz/ *adj* aggressive.

belote /bəlɔt/ *nf* belote (*card game*).

bémol /bemɔl/ *nm* (Mus) flat; **mi ~** E flat.

bénédiction /benediksjɔ̃/ *nf* blessing.

bénéfice /benefis/ *nm* **1** profit; **2** benefit, beneficial effect; **3** advantage; **tirer ~ de qch** to gain advantage from sth.

bénéficiaire /benefisjɛʀ/ *nmf* beneficiary.

bénéficier: **bénéficier de** /benefisje/ [2] *v+prep* **~ de** to receive [*help*]; to enjoy [*immunity*]; to get [*special treatment*]; **faire ~ qn de qch** to give sb sth [*scholarship, good price*].

bénéfique /benefik/ *adj* beneficial.

benêt /bənɛ/ **I** *adj m* simple.

II *nm* half-wit.

bénévole /benevɔl/ **I** *adj* voluntary.

II *nmf* voluntary worker.

bénigne *adj f* ▸ **bénin**.

bénin, **-igne** /benɛ̃, iɲ/ *adj* [*illness, fault*] minor; [*tumour*] benign.

bénir /beniʀ/ [3] *vtr* to bless; **béni soit le ciel!** thank God!

bénit, **~e** /beni, it/ *adj* blessed; holy.

bénitier /benitje/ *nm* holy water font.

benjamin, **~e** /bɛ̃ʒamɛ̃, in/ *nm,f* youngest child.

benne /bɛn/ *nf* **1** skip (GB), dumpster® (US); **2** (colliery) wagon; **3** (cable) car.

béquille /bekij/ *nf* **1** crutch; **2** kickstand.

bercail○ /bɛʀkaj/ *nm* home.

berceau, *pl* **~x** /bɛʀso/ *nm* **1** cradle; **2** birthplace.

bercer /bɛʀse/ [12] **I** *vtr* to rock [*baby*].

II se bercer *v refl* (+ *v être*) **se ~ d'illusions** to delude oneself.

berceuse /bɛʀsøz/ *nf* **1** lullaby; **2** rocking chair.

béret /beʀɛ/ *nm* beret.

bergamote /bɛʀgamɔt/ *nf* bergamot; **thé à la ~** Earl Grey tea.

berge /bɛʀʒ/ *nf* (of river, canal) bank.

berger, **-ère** /bɛʀʒe, ɛʀ/ *nm,f* shepherd/shepherdess.

■ **~ allemand** Alsatian (GB), German shepherd; **~ des Pyrénées** Pyrenean mountain dog.

bergerie /bɛʀʒəʀi/ *nf* sheepfold.

berlue○ /bɛʀly/ *nf* **avoir la ~** to be seeing things.

bermuda /bɛʀmyda/ *nm* bermudas.

Bermudes /bɛʀmyd/ *pr nf pl* **les ~s** Bermuda.

berne /bɛʀn/ *nf* **en ~** at half-mast.

berner /bɛʀne/ [1] *vtr* to fool, to deceive.

besogne /bəzɔɲ/ *nf* job; **une basse ~** a menial chore.

besoin /bəzwɛ̃/ **I** *nm* need (**de** for; **de faire** to do); **répondre à un ~** to meet a need; **au ~** if need be; **avoir ~ de** to need; **j'ai bien ~ de ça**○! (ironic) that's all I need!; **est-il ~ de le dire?** need I remind you?; **pour les ~s de la cause** for the good of the cause; **être dans le ~** to be in need.

II besoins *nm pl* needs; **subvenir aux ~s de qn** to provide for sb; **~s en eau** water requirements.

IDIOMS **faire ses ~s**○ [*person*] to relieve oneself; [*animal*] to do its business.

bestial, **~e**, *mpl* **-iaux** /bɛstjal, o/ *adj* brutish, bestial.

bestialité /bɛstjalite/ *nf* brutishness.

bestiaux /bɛstjo/ *nm pl* **1** livestock; **2** cattle.

bestiole○ /bɛstjɔl/ *nf* **1** creepy-crawly○, bug; **2** animal.

bétail /betaj/ *nm* **1** livestock; **2** cattle.

bête /bɛt/ **I** *adj* stupid, silly; **ce n'est pas ~ ça!** that's not a bad idea!; **je suis restée toute ~** I was dumbfounded.

II *nf* creature; animal; **nos amis les ~s** our four-legged friends.

■ **~ à bon Dieu** ladybird (GB), ladybug (US); **~ curieuse** freak; **~ noire** bête noire (GB), pet hate.

IDIOMS **il est ~ comme ses pieds**○ he's as dumb as can be; **chercher la petite ~**○ to nitpick○; **reprendre du poil de la ~**○ to perk up; **travailler comme une ~**○ to work like crazy○.

bêtise /betiz/ *nf* **la ~** stupidity; **faire une ~** to do something stupid; **dire des ~s** to talk nonsense; **j'ai fait une ~ en acceptant** I was stupid to accept; **surtout pas de ~s!** be good now!; **se fâcher pour une ~** to get angry over nothing.

■ **~ de Cambrai** mint.

bêtisier /betizje/ *nm* collection of howlers○.

béton /betɔ̃/ *nm* concrete; **de** or **en ~** concrete; (figurative) watertight.

■ **~ armé** reinforced concrete.

bétonnière /betɔnjɛʀ/ *nf* concrete mixer.

betterave /bɛtʀav/ *nf* beet; **~ rouge** beetroot; **~ sucrière** sugar beet.

beugler /bøgle/ [1] *vi* **1** [*cow*] to moo; [*bull*] to bellow; **2**○ [*person*] to yell; [*loudspeaker*] to blare out.

beur○ /bœʀ/ *nmf* second-generation North African (*living in France*).

beurre /bœʀ/ *nm* butter; **~ doux** unsalted butter; **~ de saumon** salmon paste.

■ **~ blanc** *sauce made of butter, vinegar and shallots*; **~ d'escargot** garlic and parsley butter; **~ noir** black butter; **œil au ~ noir**○ black eye.

IDIOMS **faire son ~**○ to make a packet○; **compter pour du ~**○ to count for nothing; **vouloir le ~ et l'argent du ~**○ to want to have one's cake and eat it.

beurré○, **~e** /bœʀe/ *adj* drunk, plastered○.

beurrer /bœʀe/ [1] *vtr* to butter.

beurrier /bœʀje/ *nm* butter dish.

beuverie /bœvʀi/ *nf* drinking session.

bévue /bevy/ *nf* blunder.

biais /bjɛ/ **I** *nm inv* way; **par le ~ de qn** through sb; **par le ~ de qch** by means of sth.

II **de biais, en biais** *phr* **couper une étoffe en ~** to cut material on the cross; **jeter des regards en ~ à qn** to cast sidelong glances at sb.

bibelot /biblo/ *nm* ornament.

biberon /bibʀɔ̃/ *nm* (baby's) bottle (GB), (nursing) bottle (US).

bibine○ /bibin/ *nf* cheap wine, plonk○ (GB).

bible /bibl/ *nf* bible; **la Bible** the Bible.

bibliographie /biblijɔgʀafi/ *nf* bibliography.

bibliothécaire /biblijɔtekɛʀ/ *nmf* librarian.

bibliothèque /biblijɔtɛk/ *nf* **1** library; **2** bookcase.

biblique /biblik/ *adj* biblical.

bic® /bik/ *nm* biro®.

bicarbonate /bikaʀbɔnat/ *nm* bicarbonate.
■ **~ de soude** bicarbonate of soda.

bicentenaire /bisɑ̃tnɛʀ/ I *adj* two-hundred-year-old.
II *nm* bicentenary, bicentennial.

biceps /bisɛps/ *nm inv* biceps; **avoir des ~** to have muscular arms.

biche /biʃ/ *nf* doe; **ma ~**○ my pet (GB), honey (US).

bichonner○ /biʃɔne/ [1] *vtr* to pamper.

bicoque○ /bikɔk/ *nf* dump○, house.

bicyclette /bisiklɛt/ *nf* **1** bicycle; **2** cycling; **faire de la ~** to cycle.

bidasse○ /bidas/ *nm* soldier.

bidet /bidɛ/ *nm* **1** bidet; **2**○ nag, horse.

bidon /bidɔ̃/ I○ *adj inv* bogus; phoney○.
II *nm* **1** can; drum; flask; **2**○ stomach, paunch; **3**○ **c'est du ~** it is a load of hogwash○.

bidonville /bidɔ̃vil/ *nm* shanty town.

bidule○ /bidyl/ *nm* thingy○ (GB), thingamajig○.

bielle /bjɛl/ *nf* connecting rod.

bien /bjɛ̃/ I *adj inv* **1 être ~ dans un rôle** to be good in a part; **être ~ de sa personne** to be good-looking; **ce n'est pas ~ de mentir** it's not nice to lie; **ce serait ~** it would be nice; **ça fait ~ d'aller à l'opéra**○ it's the done thing to go to the opera; **les roses font ~** the roses look nice; **2** well; **ne pas se sentir ~** not to feel well; **t'es pas ~**○**!** you're out of your mind○!; **3 je suis ~ dans ces bottes** these boots are comfortable; **on est ~ au soleil!** isn't it nice in the sun!; **je me trouve ~ ici** I like it here; **4**○ **un quartier ~** a nice district; **des gens ~** respectable people; **un type ~** a gentleman.
II *adv* **1** well; [*function*] properly; [*interpret*] correctly; **~ joué!** well done!; **aller ~** [*person*] to be well; [*business*] to go well; **ça s'est ~ passé** it went well; **ni ~ ni mal** so-so; **il travaille ~** his work is good; **j'ai cru ~ faire** I thought I was doing the right thing; **c'est ~ fait pour elle!** it serves her right!; **tu ferais ~ d'y aller** it would be a good idea for you to go; **2** [*mix*] thoroughly; [*fill*] completely; [*listen*] carefully; **~ à droite** well over to the right; **3** [*presented*] well; [*furnished*] tastefully; [*live*] comfortably; **femme ~ faite** shapely woman; **aller ~ ensemble** to go well together; **aller ~ à qn** to suit sb; **~ prendre une remarque** to take a remark in good part; **4** [*nice, sad*] very; [*fear, enjoy*] very much; [*simple, true*] quite; **il y a ~ longtemps** a very long time ago; **merci ~** thank you very much; **c'est ~ dommage** it's a real pity; **~ rire** to have a good laugh; **c'est ~ compris?** is that clear?; **~ au contraire** on the contrary; **~ mieux** much or far better; **~ sûr** of course; **~ entendu** or **évidemment** naturally; **~ souvent** quite often; **5 je veux ~ t'aider** I don't mind helping you; **j'aimerais ~ essayer** I would love to try; **je le vois ~ habiter à Paris** I can just imagine him living in Paris; **6 il faut ~ que ça finisse** it has to come to an end; **il faudra ~ s'y habituer** we'll just have to get used to it; **7 ça montre ~ que** it just goes to show that; **je sais ~ que** I know that; **insiste ~** make sure you insist; **on verra ~** well, we'll see; **je t'avais ~ dit de ne pas le manger!** I told you not to eat it!; **il le fait ~ lui, pourquoi pas moi?** if he can do it, why can't I?; **tu peux très ~ le faire toi-même** you can easily do it yourself; **il se pourrait ~ qu'il pleuve** it might well rain; **que peut-il ~ faire à Paris?** what on earth can he be doing in Paris?; **8** definitely; **c'est ~ ce qu'il a dit** that's exactly what he said; **c'est ~ mardi aujourd'hui?** today is Tuesday, isn't it?; **tu as ~ pris les clés?** are you sure you've got the keys?; **c'est ~ de lui!** it's just like him!; **c'est ~ le moment!** (ironic) great timing!; **c'est ~ le moment de partir!** (ironic) what a time to leave!; **9** at least; **10 il y a ~ des années** a good many years ago; **~ des fois** often, many a time; **je te souhaite ~ du plaisir!** (ironic) I wish you joy of it!
III *nm* **1** good; **le ~ et le mal** good and evil; **ça fait du ~ aux enfants** it's good for the children; **vouloir le ~ de qn** to have sb's best interests at heart; **vouloir du ~ à qn** to wish sb well; **dire du ~/le plus grand ~ de qn** to speak well/very highly of sb; **parler en ~ de qn** to speak favourably[GB] of sb; **2** possession; **les ~s de ce monde** material possessions; **des ~s considérables** substantial assets.
IV *excl* **1 ~!** good!; **2 ~! ~!** all right! all right!
V **bien que** *phr* although.
■ **~s de consommation** consumer goods; **~s d'équipement ménager** household goods; **~s immobiliers** real estate; **~s mobiliers** personal property; **~s personnels** private property.

bien-être /bjɛ̃nɛtʀ/ *nm* **1** well-being; **2** welfare; **3** comforts.

bienfaisance /bjɛ̃fəzɑ̃s/ *nf* charity; **société de ~** charity.

bienfaisant, ~e /bjɛ̃fəzɑ̃, ɑ̃t/ *adj* beneficial, beneficent.

bienfait /bjɛ̃fɛ/ *nm* **1** kind deed; **~ du ciel** godsend; **2** beneficial effect.

bienfaiteur, -trice /bjɛ̃fɛtœʀ, tʀis/ *nm,f* benefactor/benefactress.

bien-fondé /bjɛ̃fɔ̃de/ *nm* (of idea) validity; (of claim) legitimacy.

bienheureux, **-euse** /bjɛ̃nøʀø, øz/ *nm,f* **les ~** the blessed.

bien-pensant, **~e**, *mpl* **~s** /bjɛ̃pɑ̃sɑ̃, ɑ̃t/ *adj* **1** right-thinking; **2** self-righteous.

bientôt /bjɛ̃to/ *adv* soon; **à ~** see you soon; **on est ~ arrivés?** are we nearly there?

bienveillance /bjɛ̃vɛjɑ̃s/ *nf* benevolence (**envers** to); **avec ~** benevolently.

bienveillant, **~e** /bjɛ̃vɛjɑ̃, ɑ̃t/ *adj* benevolent.

bienvenu, **~e**[1] /bjɛ̃vəny/ *adj* welcome.

bienvenue[2] /bjɛ̃vəny/ *nf* welcome (**à, dans** to).

bière /bjɛʀ/ *nf* **1** beer; **~ (à la) pression** draught (GB) or draft (US) beer; **2** coffin, casket (US). ■ **~ blonde** lager; **~ brune** ≈ stout; **~ rousse** brown ale.

bifteck /biftɛk/ *nm* steak.
IDIOMS **gagner son ~**○ to earn a living or crust (GB); **défendre son ~**○ to look out for number one○.

bifurcation /bifyʀkasjɔ̃/ *nf* (in road) fork.

bifurquer /bifyʀke/ [1] *vi* **1** [*road*] to fork; **2** [*driver*] to turn off; **3** (in career) to change tack.

bigame /bigam/ **I** *adj* bigamous.
II *nmf* bigamist.

bigarré, **~e** /bigaʀe/ *adj* **1** multicoloured[GB]; **2** [*crowd*] colourful[GB].

bigorneau, *pl* **~x** /bigɔʀno/ *nm* winkle.

bigot, **~e** /bigo, ɔt/ *nm,f* religious zealot.

bigoudi /bigudi/ *nm* roller, curler.

bijou, *pl* **~x** /biʒu/ *nm* **1** piece of jewellery (GB) or jewelry (US); **2** jewel; (figurative) gem.

bijouterie /biʒutʀi/ *nf* (shop) jeweller's (GB), jewelry store (US).

bijoutier, **-ière** /biʒutje, ɛʀ/ *nm,f* jeweller (GB), jeweler (US).

bilan /bilɑ̃/ *nm* **1** balance sheet; **déposer son ~** to file a petition in bankruptcy; **2** outcome; **3** (after disaster) toll; **4** assessment; **~ de santé** check-up; **5** report.

bilatéral, **~e**, *mpl* **-aux** /bilateʀal, o/ *adj* bilateral.

bilboquet /bilbɔkɛ/ *nm* cup-and-ball.

bile /bil/ *nf* bile.
IDIOMS **se faire de la ~**○ to worry (**pour** about).

bilingue /bilɛ̃g/ *adj* bilingual.

billard /bijaʀ/ *nm* **1** billiards; **2** billiard table. ■ **~ américain** pool; **~ anglais** snooker; **~ électrique** pinball machine.
IDIOMS **passer sur le ~**○ to have an operation.

bille /bij/ *nf* **1** (Games) marble; **2** (billiard) ball.

billet /bijɛ/ *nm* **1** (bank)note, bill (US); **2** ticket. ■ **~ doux** love letter.

billion /biljɔ̃/ *nm* billion (GB), trillion (US).

bimensuel /bimɑ̃sɥɛl/ *nm* fortnightly magazine (GB), semimonthly (US).

bimoteur /bimɔtœʀ/ *nm* twin-engined plane.

binaire /binɛʀ/ *adj* binary.

biner /bine/ [1] *vtr* to hoe.

biniou /binju/ *nm* Breton bagpipes.

binocles○ /binɔkl/ *nf pl* specs○, glasses.

binoculaire /binɔkylɛʀ/ *adj* binocular.

biochimie /bjoʃimi/ *nf* biochemistry.

biographie /bjɔgʀafi/ *nf* biography.

biologie /bjɔlɔʒi/ *nf* biology.

biophysique /bjofizik/ *nf* biophysics.

bip /bip/ *nm* beep; **~ sonore** tone.

bipartisme /bipaʀtism/ *nm* two-party system.

bipède /bipɛd/ *nm* biped.

biplace /biplas/ *adj, nm* two-seater.

biplan /biplɑ̃/ *nm* biplane.

bique○ /bik/ *nf* **1** nanny goat; **2 une vieille ~** an old bag○.

biréacteur /biʀeaktœʀ/ *nm* twin-engined jet.

bis[1] /bis/ *adv* bis.

bis[2], **~e**[1] /bi, biz/ *adj* greyish (GB) or grayish (US) brown.

bisaïeul, **~e** /bizajœl/ *nm,f* great-grandfather/-grandmother.

bisannuel, **-elle** /bizanɥɛl/ *adj* biennial.

biscornu, **~e** /biskɔʀny/ *adj* quirky.

biscotte /biskɔt/ *nf* continental toast.

biscuit /biskɥi/ *nm* biscuit (GB), cookie (US). ■ **~ à la cuillère** sponge finger (GB), ladyfinger (US); **~ salé** cracker; **~ de Savoie** sponge cake.

bise[2] /biz/ **I** *adj f* ▶ **bis**[2].
II *nf* **1**○ kiss; **faire la ~ à qn** to kiss sb on the cheeks; **2** North wind.

biseau, *pl* **~x** /bizo/ *nm* **1** bevel (edge); **tailler en ~** to bevel; **2** (tool) bevel.

bison /bizɔ̃/ *nm* **1** bison; **2** buffalo.

bisque /bisk/ *nf* (Culin) bisque.

bissectrice /bisɛktʀis/ *nf* bisector.

bissextile /bisɛkstil/ *adj* **année ~** leap year.

bistouri /bistuʀi/ *nm* (Med) bistoury.

bistro(t)○ /bistʀo/ *nm* bistro, café.

bit /bit/ *nm* bit.

BIT /beite/ *nm* (*abbr* = **Bureau international du travail**) ILO.

bitume /bitym/ *nm* **1** bitumen; **2** (on road) asphalt.

bivouac /bivwak/ *nm* bivouac.

bizarre /bizaʀ/ *adj* odd, strange.

bizarrement /bizaʀmɑ̃/ *adv* strangely.

blabla○ /blabla/ *nm inv* waffle○ (GB), hogwash○ (US).

blafard, **~e** /blafaʀ, aʀd/ *adj* pale.

blague○ /blag/ *nf* **1** joke; **~ à part** seriously; **2** fib○; **3** trick; **faire une ~ à qn** to play a trick on sb.

blaguer○ /blage/ [1] *vi* to joke; **il dit ça pour ~** he's kidding○.

blagueur○, **-euse** /blagœʀ, øz/ *nm,f* joker.

blaireau, *pl* **~x** /blɛʀo/ *nm* **1** badger; **2** shaving brush.

blâme /blɑm/ *nm* **1** criticism; **2** official warning.

blâmer /blɑme/ [1] *vtr* to criticize; to blame.

blanc, **blanche**[1] /blɑ̃, blɑ̃ʃ/ **I** *adj* [*person, dress, wall*] white; [*page*] blank; **~ cassé** off-white; **ne pas être ~** to have a less than spotless reputation.

II *nm* **1** white; **habillé/peint en ~** dressed in/painted white; **2** household linen; **3** white meat; **4** (egg) white; **5** white wine; **6** blank; (unintentional) gap; **laisser en ~** to leave [sth] blank; **j'ai eu un ~** my mind went blank; **7**○ correction fluid; **8** (Mil) **tirer à ~** to fire blanks.

III **blancs** *nm pl* (in chess, draughts) white.

Blanc, **Blanche** /blɑ̃, blɑ̃ʃ/ *nm,f* white man/woman.

blanc-bec, *pl* **blancs-becs** /blɑ̃bɛk/ *nm* greenhorn.

blanchâtre /blɑ̃ʃɑtʀ/ *adj* whitish.

blanche[2] /blɑ̃ʃ/ I *adj f* ▶ **blanc I**.

II *nf* (Mus) minim (GB), half note (US).

blanchir /blɑ̃ʃiʀ/ [3] I *vtr* **1** to whiten [*shoes*]; **~ (à la chaux)** to whitewash; **2** to blanch [*vegetables*]; **3** to clear [*name*]; **4** to launder [*money*].

II *vi* **1** to turn grey (GB) or gray (US); **2 faire ~** to blanch [*vegetables*].

III **se blanchir** *v refl* (+ *v être*) to clear oneself (**auprès de** in the eyes of).

blanchissage /blɑ̃ʃisaʒ/ *nm* **service de ~** laundry service.

blanchisserie /blɑ̃ʃisʀi/ *nf* laundry.

blanchisseur /blɑ̃ʃisœʀ/ *nm* **1** laundry worker; **2** (shop) laundry.

blanchisseuse /blɑ̃ʃisøz/ *nf* laundress.

blanquette /blɑ̃kɛt/ *nf* **~ de veau** blanquette of veal.

blasé, **~e** /blaze/ *adj* blasé.

blason /blazɔ̃/ *nm* coat of arms.

IDIOMS **redorer son ~** to restore one's reputation.

blasphème /blasfɛm/ *nm* blasphemy.

blasphémer /blasfeme/ [1] *vi* to blaspheme.

blatte /blat/ *nf* cockroach.

blé /ble/ *nm* wheat; **~ noir** buckwheat.

bled○ /blɛd/ *nm* village.

blême /blɛm/ *adj* pale.

blêmir /blemiʀ/ [3] *vi* to turn pale.

blessant, **~e** /blesɑ̃, ɑ̃t/ *adj* [*remark*] cutting.

blessé, **~e** /blese/ *nm,f* injured or wounded man/woman; casualty.

blesser /blese/ [1] I *vtr* **1** to hurt; **il a été blessé à la tête** he sustained head injuries; **2** to wound; **3** to hurt [*person, pride*]; **~ qn au vif** to cut sb to the quick.

II **se blesser** *v refl* (+ *v être*) to hurt oneself.

blessure /blesyʀ/ *nf* **1** injury; **2** wound.

blet, **blette**[1] /blɛ, blɛt/ *adj* overripe.

blette[2] /blɛt/ *nf* Swiss chard.

bleu, **~e** /blø/ I *adj* **1** blue; **2** [*steak*] very rare.

II *nm* **1** blue; **2** bruise; **se faire un ~** to bruise oneself; **3 ~ de travail** overalls; **4** blue cheese.

IDIOMS **avoir une peur ~e de qch** to be scared stiff○ of sth.

bleuâtre /bløɑtʀ/ *adj* bluish.

bleuet /bløɛ/ *nm* **1** (Bot) cornflower; **2** (Canadian Fr) blueberry.

bleuir /bløiʀ/ [3] *vtr, vi* to turn blue.

bleuté, **~e** /bløte/ *adj* bluish.

blindé, **~e** /blɛ̃de/ I *adj* armoured[GB].

II *nm* armoured[GB] vehicle.

blinder /blɛ̃de/ [1] *vtr* to put security fittings on [*door*]; to armour-plate[GB] [*car*].

blizzard /blizaʀ/ *nm* blizzard.

bloc /blɔk/ I *nm* **1** block (**de** of); **faire ~ avec/contre qn** to side with/unite against sb; **2** notepad; **~ de papier à lettres** writing pad.

II **à bloc** *phr* [*screw*] tightly; [*inflate*] fully.

III **en bloc** *phr* [*deny*] outright.

■ **~ opératoire** surgical unit.

blocage /blɔkaʒ/ *nm* blocking; **~ des salaires** wage freeze.

blockhaus /blɔkos/ *nm inv* blockhouse.

bloc-note, *pl* **blocs-notes** /blɔknɔt/ *nm* notepad.

blocus /blɔkys/ *nm inv* blockade.

blond, **~e** /blɔ̃, ɔ̃d/ I *adj* **1** blonde (GB), blond (US); **2** [*wheat*] golden; [*tobacco*] light; **bière ~e** lager.

II *nm,f* (female) blonde (GB), blond (US); (male) blond.

blondir /blɔ̃diʀ/ [3] *vi* [*person*] to go blonde (GB) or blond (US).

bloqué, **~e** /blɔke/ I *pp* ▶ **bloquer**.

II *pp adj* **1** blocked; **2** [*mechanism, door*] jammed; **elle/la voiture est ~e** she/the car is stuck; **il a le dos ~** his back has seized up; **3 être ~** [*activity, career*] to be at a standstill; [*situation*] to be deadlocked; **4 être ~** to have a (mental) block (**sur** about).

bloquer /blɔke/ [1] I *vtr* **1** to block [*road*]; (Mil) to blockade; **2** to lock [*steering wheel*]; to wedge [*door*]; (accidentally) to jam [*mechanism, door*]; **3** to stop [*vehicle, traveller*]; **4** to freeze [*account, prices*]; **5** to stop [*project*]; **6** to lump [sth] together [*days*].

II **se bloquer** *v refl* (+ *v être*) **1** [*brakes, door*] to jam; [*wheel, steering wheel*] to lock; **2** to retreat.

blottir: **se blottir** /blɔtiʀ/ [3] *v refl* (+ *v être*) **se ~ contre** to huddle up against; to snuggle up against.

blouse /bluz/ *nf* **1** overall; **2** coat; **~ blanche** white coat; **3** blouse.

blouson /bluzɔ̃/ *nm* **1** blouson; **~ d'aviateur** bomber jacket; **2 ~ noir** ≈ rocker.

blue-jean, *pl* **~s** /bludʒin/ *nm* jeans.

bluffer○ /blœfe/ [1] *vtr, vi* to bluff.

boa /bɔa/ *nm* boa.

bobard○ /bɔbaʀ/ *nm* fib○, tall story.

bobine /bɔbin/ *nf* (of film, cable) reel.

bobo○ /bobo/ *nm* (baby talk) **1** pain; **2** scratch.

bobsleigh /bɔbslɛg/ *nm* **1** bobsleigh, bobsled (US); **2** bobsleighing.

bocage /bɔkaʒ/ *nm* hedged farmland.

bocal, *pl* **-aux** /bɔkal, o/ *nm* jar; bowl.

bœuf /bœf, *pl* bø/ *nm* **1** bullock (GB), steer (US); **2** ox; **3** beef.

IDIOMS **faire un effet ~**○ to make a fantastic○ impression.

bohème /bɔɛm/ I *adj* bohemian.
II *nf* **la ~** bohemia; **vie de ~** bohemian lifestyle.

bohémien, **-ienne** /bɔemjɛ̃, ɛn/ *nm,f* **1** Romany; **2** tramp.

boire /bwaʀ/ [70] I *vtr* **1** to drink; **il m'a fait ~** he got me drunk; **2** [*plant*] to drink; [*paper*] to soak [sth] up.
II **se boire** *v refl* (+ *v être*) **ce vin se boit frais** this wine should be drunk chilled; **ce porto se boit bien** this port is very drinkable.
IDIOMS **~ comme un trou**○ to drink like a fish○; **il y a à ~ et à manger dans leur théorie** there's both good and bad in their theory.

bois /bwa/ I *nm inv* (gen) wood; **en ~** [*chair*] wooden; [*cheque*] dud○; **~ de charpente** timber; **~ mort** firewood.
II *nm pl* **1** antlers; **2** woodwind section.
IDIOMS **être de ~** to be insensitive; **il va voir de quel ~ je me chauffe**○ I'll show him.

boisé, **~e** /bwaze/ *adj* wooded.

boiserie /bwazʀi/ *nf* **~(s)** panelling[GB].

boisson /bwasɔ̃/ *nf* drink.

boîte /bwat/ *nf* **1** box; tin; **2** tin (GB), can; **petits pois en ~** canned peas; **3 ~ (de nuit)** nightclub; **4**○ firm; office.
■ **~ crânienne** cranium; **~ à gants** glove compartment; **~ à** or **aux lettres** post box (GB), mailbox (US); **~ à malice** bag of tricks; **~ à musique** musical box (GB), music box (US); **~ à ordures** rubbish bin (GB), garbage can (US); **~ à outils** toolbox; **~ postale, BP** PO Box; **~ de vitesses** gearbox.
IDIOMS **mettre qn en ~**○ to tease sb.

boiter /bwate/ [1] *vi* to limp.

boiteux, **-euse** /bwatø, øz/ I *adj* **1** lame; **2** [*chair*] wobbly; **3** [*argument, alliance*] shaky; [*verse*] lame.
II *nm,f* lame person.

boîtier /bwatje/ *nm* (gen) case; (for camera) body; (on telephone) casing.

boitiller /bwatije/ [1] *vi* to limp slightly.

bol /bɔl/ *nm* **1** bowl; **~ d'air** breath of fresh air; **2**○ luck; **coup de ~** stroke of luck.

bolide /bɔlid/ *nm* high-powered car; **comme un ~** at high speed.

bolognaise /bɔlɔɲɛz/ *adj inv* [*spaghetti*] Bolognese (GB), with meat sauce (US).

bombardement /bɔ̃baʀdəmɑ̃/ *nm* **1** (Mil) bombardment; **~ aérien** air raid; **2** bombing; shelling; **3** (with stones) pelting; (of questions) bombardment.

bombarder /bɔ̃baʀde/ [1] *vtr* **1** to bombard; **2** to bomb; to shell; **3 ~ qn de questions** to bombard sb with questions; **4**○ **~ qn à un poste** to catapult sb into a job.

bombardier /bɔ̃baʀdje/ *nm* **1** bomber; **2** bombardier.

bombe /bɔ̃b/ *nf* **1** bomb; **faire l'effet d'une ~** to come as a bombshell; **2 ~ (aérosol)** spray; **3** riding hat.
IDIOMS **partir à toute ~**○ to rush off; **arriver comme une ~** to come like a bolt out of the blue○.

bombé, **~e** /bɔ̃be/ *adj* **1** [*forehead*] domed; [*shape*] rounded; **2** [*road*] cambered.

bomber /bɔ̃be/ [1] I *vtr* **1 ~ le torse** to thrust out one's chest; (figurative) to swell with pride; **2**○ to spray-paint.
II *vi* **1** [*plank*] to bulge out; **2**○ to belt along○.

bon, **bonne**[1] /bɔ̃, bɔn/ I *adj* **1** good; **prends un ~ pull** take a warm jumper; **il a encore de bonnes jambes** he can still get around; **elle est (bien) bonne**○! that's a good one!; (indignantly) I like that!; **ça fait un ~ bout de chemin** it's quite a way; **voilà une bonne chose de faite!** that's that out of the way!; **nous sommes ~s derniers** we're well and truly last; **il n'est pas ~ à grand-chose** he's pretty useless; **il serait ~ qu'elle le sache** she ought to know; **à quoi ~?** what's the point?; **2** [*person, words*] kind; [*smile*] nice; **avoir ~ cœur** to be good-hearted; **3** [*time, answer*] right; **c'est ~, vous pouvez y aller** it's OK, you can go; **c'est tout juste ~ pour les chiens!** it's only fit for dogs!; **4** [*ticket*] valid; **tu es ~ pour la vaisselle, ce soir!** you're in line for the dishes tonight!; **5 bonne nuit/chance** good night/luck.
II *nm,f* **les ~s et les méchants** good people and bad people; (in films) the good guys and the bad guys○.
III *nm* **1 il y a du ~ dans cet article** there are some good things in this article; **2** coupon; voucher.
IV *excl* **1** good; **2** all right, OK; **3** (when intervening, interrupting) right, well.
V *adv* **ça sent ~!** that smells good!; **il fait ~** the weather's mild; **il fait ~ dans ta chambre** it's nice and warm in your room.
VI **pour de bon** *phr* **1** really; **tu dis ça pour de ~?** are you serious?; **2** for good.
■ **~ de commande** order form; **~ enfant** good-natured; **~ de garantie** guarantee slip; **~ marché** cheap; **~ mot** witticism; **~ à rien** good-for-nothing; **~ sens** common sense; **~ du Trésor** Treasury bond; **~ vivant** *adj* jovial; *nm* bon viveur; **bonne action** good deed; **bonne femme**○ (derogatory) woman, dame○ (US); wife, old lady○; **bonne pâte** good sort; **bonne sœur**○ nun; **bonnes œuvres** good works; **~s offices** good offices.

bonbon /bɔ̃bɔ̃/ *nm* sweet (GB), candy (US); **~ acidulé** acid drop (GB), sour ball (US).

bonbonne /bɔ̃bɔn/ *nf* **1** demijohn; (bigger) carboy; **2** (for gas) cylinder.

bonbonnière /bɔ̃bɔnjɛʀ/ *nf* sweet dish (GB), candy dish (US).

bond /bɔ̃/ *nm* **1** leap; **se lever d'un ~** to leap to one's feet; **2** (in time) jump; **faire un ~ en avant de 30 ans** to jump forward 30 years; **3** (in profits, exports) leap; (in prices) jump (**de** in); **la médecine a fait un ~ en avant avec cette découverte** this discovery was a medical breakthrough.
IDIOMS **saisir la balle au ~** to seize the opportunity; **faire faux ~ à qn** to let sb down.

bonde /bɔ̃d/ *nf* **1** (opening) (of swimming pool) outlet; (of pond) sluice; (of sink) plughole; (of barrel) bunghole; **2** (stopper) (in pool) outlet cover; (in pond) sluicegate; (in sink) plug; (in barrel) bung.

bondé, **~e** /bɔ̃de/ *adj* packed (**de** with).

bondir /bɔ̃diʀ/ [3] *vi* **1** to leap; **~ de joie** to jump for joy; **2 ~ sur qn/qch** to pounce on sb/sth; **3** [*animal*] to leap about; **4** to react furiously; **ça m'a fait ~** I was absolutely furious (about it).

bonheur /bɔnœʀ/ *nm* **1** happiness; **2** pleasure; **faire le ~ de qn** [*present*] to make sb happy; [*event, exhibition*] to delight sb; **3 avoir le ~ de faire** to have the pleasure of doing; **par ~** fortunately; **au petit ~ (la chance)** at random; **tu ne connais pas ton ~!** you don't realize how lucky you are!

IDIOMS **alors, tu as trouvé ton ~**○**?** did you find what you wanted?

bonhomme, *pl* **~s**, **bonshommes** /bɔnɔm, bɔ̃zɔm/ I *adj* good-natured.

II○ *nm* **1** fellow, chap○; **2** husband, old man○.

■ **~ de neige** snowman.

IDIOMS **aller** or **suivre son petit ~ de chemin** to go peacefully along.

boniments /bɔnimɑ̃/ *nm pl* stories; **raconter des ~ à qn** to give sb some story○ (**à propos de** about); to smooth-talk sb.

bonjour /bɔ̃ʒuʀ/ *nm, excl* hello; **bien le ~ à votre sœur** say hello to your sister for me.

IDIOMS **être simple comme ~**○ to be very easy.

bonne[2] /bɔn/ I *adj f* ▶ **bon I**.

II *nf* **1** maid, servant; **2 tu en as de ~s, toi!** you must be joking!

■ **~ d'enfants** nanny; **~ à tout faire** skivvy○ (GB), maid.

bonne-maman, *pl* **bonnes-mamans** /bɔn mamɑ̃/ *nf* grandma.

bonnement /bɔnmɑ̃/ *adv* **tout ~** (quite) simply.

bonnet /bɔnɛ/ *nm* **1** hat; (for baby) bonnet; **2** (on bra) cup.

■ **~ de bain** bathing cap; **~ de nuit** nightcap; (figurative) wet blanket○.

bonneterie /bɔnɛtʀi/ *nf* **1** hosiery; **2** hosiery shop.

bon-papa, *pl* **bons-papas** /bɔ̃papa/ *nm* granddad○, grandpapa○.

bonsaï /bɔ̃nzaj/ *nm* bonsai (tree).

bonshommes ▶ **bonhomme**.

bonsoir /bɔ̃swaʀ/ *nm, excl* good evening, good night.

bonté /bɔ̃te/ *nf* **1** kindness (**envers** toward(s)); **2** (of God) goodness.

bonus /bɔnys/ *nm inv* no-claims bonus.

bonze /bɔ̃z/ *nm* bonze.

boom /bum/ *nm* boom; **en plein ~** booming.

borborygme /bɔʀbɔʀigm/ *nm* rumbling, gurgling.

bord /bɔʀ/ *nm* **1** (of plate, bed) edge; (of road) side; (of river) bank; **au ~ de** on or at the edge of [*lake*]; on the brink of [*disaster*]; on the verge of [*bankruptcy*]; **le ~ de la mer** the seaside; **~ à ~** edge-to-edge; **2** (of cup) rim; (of hat) brim; **3 à ~** [*work*] on board; **par-dessus ~** overboard; **de ~** [*instruments, staff*] on board; **on fera**○ **avec les moyens du ~** we'll make do with what we've got; **4** (of ship, rig) side; **être du même ~** to be on the same side.

bordeaux /bɔʀdo/ I *adj inv* burgundy.

II *nm* Bordeaux; **~ rouge** claret.

border /bɔʀde/ [1] *vtr* **1** to line (**de** with); **2** [*plants*] to border [*lake*]; **3** [*path*] to run alongside [*house, land*]; **4** to tuck [sb] in; **5** to edge [*garment*] (**de** with).

bordereau, *pl* **~x** /bɔʀdəʀo/ *nm* form, slip; (from business, bank) note; (Comput) sheet.

bordure /bɔʀdyʀ/ I *nf* **1** (of sports ground, carpet) border; **2** (of road, platform) edge.

II **en bordure de** *phr* **1** next to [*park, canal, track*]; **2** on the edge of [*park*]; on the side of [*road*]; **3** just outside [*village*].

boréal, **~e**, *mpl* **-aux** /bɔʀeal, o/ *adj* boreal.

borgne /bɔʀɲ/ I *adj* **1** one-eyed; **2** [*hotel*] shady.

II *nmf* one-eyed man/woman.

borne /bɔʀn/ I *nf* **1 ~ (kilométrique)** kilometre[GB] marker; **2** boundary stone; **3** bollard (GB), post (US); **4**○ kilometre[GB]; **5** (for electricity) terminal.

II **bornes** *nf pl* **leur ambition est sans ~s** their ambition knows no bounds.

■ **~ d'incendie** fire hydrant; **~ téléphonique** emergency telephone; taxi stand telephone.

IDIOMS **dépasser les ~s** to go too far.

borné, **~e** /bɔʀne/ *adj* **1** narrow-minded; **2** [*existence*] narrow.

borner: **se borner** /bɔʀne/ [1] *v refl* (+ *v être*) **1 se ~ à faire** to content oneself with doing; **2 notre rôle se borne à analyser** our role is limited to analysing[GB].

bosquet /bɔskɛ/ *nm* grove.

bosse /bɔs/ *nf* **1** hump; **2** bump; **3** dent.

IDIOMS **avoir la ~ de**○ to have a flair for; **rouler sa ~** to knock about.

bosser○ /bɔse/ [1] *vi* to work.

bossu, **~e** /bɔsy/ *adj* hunchbacked.

bot /bo/ *adj m* **pied ~** club foot.

botanique /bɔtanik/ I *adj* botanical.

II *nf* botany.

botaniste /bɔtanist/ *nmf* botanist.

botte /bɔt/ *nf* **1** boot; **2** (of flowers) bunch; (of hay) bale.

■ **~s de caoutchouc** wellington boots; **~s de cheval** riding boots; **~s d'égoutier** waders.

botter /bɔte/ [1] *vtr* **1**○ **ça le botte!** he loves it, he really digs it○; **2** to kick.

bottillon /bɔtijɔ̃/ *nm* bootee.

bottin® /bɔtɛ̃/ *nm* telephone directory, phone book.

bottine /bɔtin/ *nf* ankle-boot.

bouc /buk/ *nm* **1** billy goat; **2** goatee.

■ **~ émissaire** scapegoat.

boucan○ /bukɑ̃/ *nm* din, racket○.

bouche /buʃ/ *nf* mouth; **il est arrivé la ~ en cœur** he came up smiling sweetly; **faire la fine ~ devant qch** to turn one's nose up at sth.
■ **~ d'aération** air vent; **~ d'égout** manhole; **~ d'incendie** fire hydrant; **~ de métro** tube (GB) or subway (US) entrance.

bouché, ~e[1] /buʃe/ **I** *pp* ▶ **boucher**[1].
II *pp adj* **1** oversubscribed; overcrowded; **2**○ dim○, stupid; **3 cidre ~** bottled cider.

bouche-à-bouche /buʃabuʃ/ *nm inv* mouth-to-mouth resuscitation.

bouche-à-oreille /buʃaɔʀɛj/ *nm inv* **le ~** word of mouth.

bouchée[2] /buʃe/ *nf* mouthful; **ne faire qu'une ~ d'un gâteau** to wolf a cake down; **pour une ~ de pain** for next to nothing; **mettre les ~s doubles** to double one's efforts.
■ **~ à la reine** vol-au-vent.

boucher[1] /buʃe/ [1] **I** *vtr* **1** to cork; **2** to block; to clog (up); **3** to fill [*crack*].
II se boucher *v refl* (+ *v être*) **1 se ~ le nez** to hold one's nose; **se ~ les oreilles** to put one's fingers in one's ears; **2** to get blocked; **3** [*ears*] to feel blocked.
IDIOMS **en ~ un coin à qn**○ to amaze sb.

boucher[2], **-ère** /buʃe, ɛʀ/ *nm,f* butcher.

boucherie /buʃʀi/ *nf* **1** butcher's shop; **2** butcher's trade; **3** slaughter.

bouchon /buʃɔ̃/ *nm* **1** cork, stopper; **2** (screw)-cap; **3** (of wax) plug; **4** traffic jam; **5** (in fishing) float.

boucle /bukl/ *nf* **1** buckle; **~ d'oreille** earring; **2** curl; **3** (of rope, in writing) loop.

bouclé, ~e /bukle/ *adj* curly.

boucler /bukle/ [1] **I** *vtr* **1** to fasten [*belt*]; **2**○ to lock [*door*]; **3**○ to cordon off [*district*]; to close [*border*]; **4**○ to complete [*investigation*]; **5**○ to lock [sb] up.
II *vi* [*hair*] to curl.
IDIOMS **la ~**○ to shut up; **~ la boucle** to come full circle.

bouclier /buklije/ *nm* shield.

Bouddha /buda/ *nm* Buddha.

bouddhisme /budism/ *nm* Buddhism.

bouder /bude/ [1] **I** *vtr* to stay away from [*show*]; to steer clear of [*goods*].
II *vi* to sulk.

boudeur, -euse /budœʀ, øz/ *adj* sulky.

boudin /budɛ̃/ *nm* (Culin) ≈ blood sausage; **~ blanc** ≈ white sausage.

boudiné, ~e /budine/ *adj* [*fingers, hand*] podgy.

boudiner /budine/ [1] *vtr* **être boudiné dans qch** to be squeezed into sth.

boudoir /budwaʀ/ *nm* **1** boudoir; **2** (Culin) boudoir biscuit.

boue /bu/ *nf* **1** (gen, figurative) mud; **2** silt.

bouée /bwe/ *nf* **1** rubber ring; **2** buoy.
■ **~ de sauvetage** or **de secours** lifebelt (GB), life preserver (US).

boueux, -euse /buø, øz/ *adj* muddy.

bouffant, ~e /bufɑ̃, ɑ̃t/ *adj* **1** baggy; **2** [*sleeves*] puffed; **3** [*hairstyle*] bouffant.

bouffe○ /buf/ *nf* **1** eating; **2** food, grub○; **3** meal.

bouffée /bufe/ *nf* **1** whiff; **2** (of tobacco, steam) puff; **une ~ d'air frais** a breath of fresh air; **~ d'orgueil** surge of pride.
■ **~ de chaleur** hot flush (GB), hot flash (US).

bouffer○ /bufe/ [1] **I** *vtr* **1** to eat; **2** to guzzle [*petrol*]; **3** to take up [*space*].
II *vi* to eat; (greedily) to stuff oneself○.
IDIOMS **se ~ le nez**○ to be at each other's throats.

bouffi, ~e /bufi/ *adj* puffy.

bouffon /bufɔ̃/ *nm* **1** clown, buffoon; **2** jester; **3** (in theatre) buffoon.

bougeoir /buʒwaʀ/ *nm* **1** candleholder; **2** candlestick.

bougeotte○ /buʒɔt/ *nf* **avoir la ~** to be restless.

bouger /buʒe/ [13] **I** *vtr* to move.
II *vi* **1** to move; **2**○ [*sector, company*] to be on the move; **3**○ **ville qui bouge** lively town; **4**○ to show signs of unrest.
III se bouger○ *v refl* (+ *v être*) **1** to get a move on○; **2** to put some effort in.

bougie /buʒi/ *nf* **1** candle; **2** (Tech) sparking plug (GB), spark plug.

bougon, -onne /bugɔ̃, ɔn/ *adj* grumpy.

bougonner /bugɔne/ [1] *vi* to grumble.

bougre○ /bugʀ/ *nm* **bon ~** good sort; **pauvre ~** poor devil.

bouillabaisse /bujabɛs/ *nf* bouillabaisse, fish soup.

bouillant, ~e /bujɑ̃, ɑ̃t/ *adj* boiling (hot).

bouille○ /buj/ *nf* face.

bouillie /buji/ *nf* **1** gruel; **en ~** mushy; **mettre en ~** to reduce [sth/sb] to a pulp; **2** baby cereal.

bouillir /bujiʀ/ [31] *vi* **1** to boil; **2** to be seething (**de** with).

bouilloire /bujwaʀ/ *nf* kettle.

bouillon /bujɔ̃/ *nm* **1** broth; **2** (Culin) stock; **3 bouillir à gros ~s** to boil fiercely.
■ **~ de culture** nutrient broth; (figurative) hotbed (**pour** of).

bouillonner /bujɔne/ [1] *vi* **1** to bubble; **2 ~ d'activité** to be bustling with activity.

bouillotte /bujɔt/ *nf* hot-water bottle.

boulanger, -ère /bulɑ̃ʒe, ɛʀ/ *nm,f* baker.

boulangerie /bulɑ̃ʒʀi/ *nf* bakery.

boule /bul/ *nf* **1** (in bowling) bowl; (in boules) boule; **2 mettre qch en ~** to roll sth up into a ball.
■ **~ de neige** snowball; **~ Quiès®** earplug.
IDIOMS **il a perdu la ~**○ he's gone mad; **mettre qn en ~**○ to make sb furious.

bouleau, *pl* **~x** /bulo/ *nm* birch.

boulet /bulɛ/ *nm* **1 ~ (de canon)** cannonball; **2** ball and chain; **3** (figurative) millstone.

boulette /bulɛt/ *nf* **1** (of bread, paper) pellet; **2 ~ de viande** meatball; **3**○ blunder.

boulevard /bulvaʀ/ *nm* **1** boulevard; **2 théâtre de ~** farce.

■ **~ périphérique** ring road (GB), beltway (US).

bouleversant, ~e /bulvɛʀsɑ̃, ɑ̃t/ *adj* deeply moving.

bouleversement /bulvɛʀsəmɑ̃/ *nm* upheaval.

bouleverser /bulvɛʀse/ [1] *vtr* **1** to move [sb] deeply; **2** [*experience*] to shatter; **3** to wreak havoc in [*place*]; to turn [sth] upside down [*house, files*]; **4** to disrupt [*schedule*]; **5** to change [*sth*] dramatically [*lifestyle, society*].

boulier /bulje/ *nm* abacus.

boulimie /bulimi/ *nf* bulimia.

boulon /bulɔ̃/ *nm* bolt.

boulot, -otte /bulo, ɔt/ **I** *adj* tubby.
II° *nm* **1** work; **2** job; **les petits ~s** casual jobs.

boulotter° /bulɔte/ [1] *vtr, vi* to eat.

boum[1] /bum/ *nm* **1** bang; **2**° **en plein ~** [*business*] booming; **faire un ~** [*birth rates*] to soar.

boum[2] /bum/ *nf* party.

bouquet /bukɛ/ *nm* **1 ~ (de fleurs)** bunch of flowers; bouquet; **2** (of firework display) final flourish; **c'est le ~**°! (figurative) that's the limit°!

bouquetin /buktɛ̃/ *nm* ibex.

bouquin° /bukɛ̃/ *nm* book.

bouquiner° /bukine/ [1] *vtr, vi* to read.

bouquiniste /bukinist/ *nmf* secondhand bookseller.

bourbier /buʀbje/ *nm* quagmire.

bourde /buʀd/ *nf* blunder.

bourdon /buʀdɔ̃/ *nm* **1** bumblebee; **2** tenor bell.

bourdonnement /buʀdɔnmɑ̃/ *nm* (of insect) buzzing; (of hive) humming; (of engine) hum; (of plane) drone.

bourdonner /buʀdɔne/ [1] *vi* to buzz; to hum; to drone.

bourg /buʀ/ *nm* market town.

bourgeois, ~e /buʀʒwa, az/ **I** *adj* bourgeois.
II *nm,f* **1** middle-class person; **2** (in Ancien Regime) bourgeois; **3** burgher.

bourgeoisie /buʀʒwazi/ *nf* **1** middle classes; **2** bourgeoisie.

bourgeon /buʀʒɔ̃/ *nm* bud; **en ~s** in bud.

bourgeonner /buʀʒɔne/ [1] *vi* to bud, to burgeon.

bourgogne /buʀgɔɲ/ *nm* (wine) Burgundy.

Bourgogne /buʀgɔɲ/ *pr nf* **la ~** Burgundy.

bourrade /buʀad/ *nf* **1** shove; **2** (sharp) nudge.

bourrage /buʀaʒ/ *nm* **~ de crâne** brainwashing.

bourrasque /buʀask/ *nf* (of wind) gust; (of snow) flurry.

bourratif, -ive /buʀatif, iv/ *adj* very filling, stodgy.

bourre° /buʀ/ *nf* **être à la ~** to be pushed for time.

bourreau, *pl* **~x** /buʀo/ *nm* executioner.

bourrelet /buʀlɛ/ *nm* **~ (de graisse)** roll of fat.

bourrer /buʀe/ [1] **I** *vtr* **1** to cram [sth] full; to fill [*pipe*]; **2**° **~ qn de** to stuff sb with [*food*]; to dose sb up with [*medicine*]; **3**° **~ qn de coups** to lay into sb°.
II *vi* to be filling.

bourricot /buʀiko/ *nm* donkey.

bourrique /buʀik/ *nf* **1** donkey; **2**° pig-headed person.

bourru, ~e /buʀy/ *adj* gruff.

bourse /buʀs/ *nf* **1** grant (GB), scholarship (US); **2** (on merit) scholarship; **3** purse; **pour les petites ~s** for limited budgets.

Bourse /buʀs/ *nf* **1** stock exchange; **2** shares.

boursier, -ière /buʀsje, ɛʀ/ **I** *adj* **semaine boursière** trading week; **le marché ~** share prices.
II *nm,f* **1** grant holder (GB), scholarship student (US); **2** (on merit) scholar (GB), scholarship student (US).

boursouflé, ~e /buʀsufle/ *adj* **1** blistered; **2** puffy; **3** [*body*] bloated.

boursoufler /buʀsufle/ [1] *vtr* **1** to cause [sth] to swell [*skin*]; **2** to blister [*paint*].

bousculade /buskylad/ *nf* **1** jostling; (accidental) crush; **2** rush.

bousculer /buskyle/ [1] **I** *vtr* **1** to push, to jostle [*person*]; to knock [sth] about [*chair*]; **2** to rush.
II se bousculer *v refl* (+ *v être*) to fall over each other (**pour faire** to do).

bouse /buz/ *nf* **une ~ (de vache)** a cowpat.

bousiller° /buzije/ [1] *vtr* **1** to botch [*work*]; **2** to wreck [*engine*]; to smash up [*car*]; to bust° [*mechanism*].

boussole /busɔl/ *nf* compass.

bout /bu/ *nm* **1** end; tip; (of shoe) toe; **au ~ du jardin** at the bottom of the garden; **aller jusqu'au ~** to go all the way; **aller (jusqu') au ~ de** to follow through [*idea, demand*]; **elle est à ~** she can't take any more; **je suis à ~ de forces** I can do no more; **ne me pousse pas à ~** don't push me; **être à ~ d'arguments** to have run out of arguments; **venir à ~ de** to overcome [*difficulty*]; to get through [*task, meal*]; **au ~ du compte** ultimately; **à ~ portant** at point-blank range; **2** (of bread, paper) piece; (of land) bit; **un petit ~ de femme**° a tiny woman.
■ **~ de chou**° sweet little thing°; **~ d'essai** screen test.
IDIOMS **tenir le bon ~**° to be on the right track; **ne pas être au ~ de ses peines** not to be out of the woods yet; **mettre les ~s**° to leave.

boutade /butad/ *nf* witticism.

bouteille /butɛj/ *nf* **1** (gen) bottle; (of gas) cylinder; **2 une bonne ~** a good bottle of wine.
IDIOMS **prendre de la ~**° to be getting on (a bit).

boutique /butik/ *nf* shop (GB), store (US).

boutoir /butwaʀ/ *nm* snout; **coup de ~** attack.

bouton /butɔ̃/ *nm* **1** button; **2** knob; button; **3** (Med) spot (GB), pimple (US); **4** (flower) bud.

■ **~ de fièvre** cold sore; **~ de manchette** cuff link; **~ de porte** doorknob.

bouton-d'or, *pl* **boutons-d'or** /butɔ̃dɔʀ/ *nm* buttercup.

boutonner /butɔne/ [1] *vtr*, **se boutonner** *v refl* (+ *v être*) to button up.

boutonneux, **-euse** /butɔnø, øz/ *adj* spotty (GB), pimply (US).

boutonnière /butɔnjɛʀ/ *nf* buttonhole.

bouture /butyʀ/ *nf* cutting; **faire des ~s** to take cuttings.

bouvreuil /buvʀœj/ *nm* bullfinch.

bovin, **~e** /bɔvɛ̃, in/ **I** *adj* bovine.
II *nm* bovine; **des ~s** cattle.

box, *pl* **boxes** /bɔks/ *nm* **1** lock-up garage; **2** (for horse) stall; **3** (in bar) alcove; (in dormitory) cubicle.
■ **~ des accusés** (Law) dock.

boxe /bɔks/ *nf* boxing; **~ française** savate.

boxer /bɔkse/ [1] *vi* (Sport) to box.

boxeur /bɔksœʀ/ *nm* (Sport) boxer.

boyau, *pl* **~x** /bwajo/ *nm* **1** gut; **2** catgut; **3** (for sausage) casing; **4** tubeless tyre (GB) or tire (US).

boycotter /bɔjkɔte/ [1] *vtr* to boycott.

bracelet /bʀaslɛ/ *nm* **1** bracelet; bangle; **2** wristband; **~ de montre** watchstrap.

bracelet-montre, *pl* **bracelets-montres** /bʀaslɛmɔ̃tʀ/ *nm* wristwatch.

braconner /bʀakɔne/ [1] *vi* to poach.

braconnier /bʀakɔnje/ *nm* poacher.

brader /bʀade/ [1] *vtr* **1** to sell cheaply; **2** to sell off.

braderie /bʀadʀi/ *nf* **1** street market; **2** discount store; **3** clearance sale.

braguette /bʀagɛt/ *nf* flies (GB), fly (US).

braille /bʀaj/ *nm* Braille.

brailler° /bʀaje/ [1] **I** *vtr* **1** to yell [*insults*]; **2** to bawl out [*song*].
II *vi* **1** to yell; **2** [*child, singer*] to bawl.

braire /bʀɛʀ/ [58] *vi* to bray.

braise /bʀɛz/ *nf* live embers.

bramer /bʀɑme/ [1] *vi* [*stag*] to bell.

brancard /bʀɑ̃kaʀ/ *nm* **1** stretcher; **2** (on cart) shaft.

brancardier /bʀɑ̃kaʀdje/ *nm* stretcher-bearer.

branche /bʀɑ̃ʃ/ *nf* **1** (of tree) branch; **2 céleri en ~s** sticks of celery; **3** field, sector; **4** (of family) branch; **5** (of candelabra) branch; (of spectacles) arm; (of star) point.

branché°, **~e** /bʀɑ̃ʃe/ *adj* trendy°.

branchement /bʀɑ̃ʃmɑ̃/ *nm* **1** (electrical) connection; **2** (for water) branch pipe; (for electricity) lead (GB), cable (US).

brancher /bʀɑ̃ʃe/ [1] **I** *vtr* **1** to plug [*sth*] in; **2** to connect (up) [*water, electricity*]; to connect [*house*]; **3**° **~ qn sur** to get sb onto [*topic*]; **4**° **je vais au cinéma, ça te branche?** I'm going to the cinema, are you interested?
II se brancher *v refl* (+ *v être*) **se ~ sur** to tune into.

branchie /bʀɑ̃ʃi/ *nf* (Zool) gill.

brandade /bʀɑ̃dad/ *nf* **~ (de morue)** brandade, dish of flaked salt cod.

brandir /bʀɑ̃diʀ/ [3] *vtr* to brandish.

branlant, **~e** /bʀɑ̃lɑ̃, ɑ̃t/ *adj* [*chair*] rickety; [*tooth*] loose; [*argument*] shaky.

branle /bʀɑ̃l/ *nm* **mettre qch en ~** to set [sth] in motion [*project, convoy*].

branler /bʀɑ̃le/ [1] *vi* [*wall*] to wobble; [*chair*] to be rickety; [*tooth*] to be loose.

braquage /bʀakaʒ/ *nm* **1**° robbery; **2** (Aut) (steering) lock.

braquer /bʀake/ [1] **I** *vtr* **1** to point [*gun, camera*] **(sur, vers** at); to turn or fix [*eyes*] **(sur, vers** on); **2 ~ à gauche/droite** to turn hard left/right; **3**° to point a gun at; **4**° to rob [*bank*]; **5**° **~ qn contre qch/qn** to turn sb against sth/sb; **ne le braque pas** don't get his back up.
II *vi* [*driver*] to turn the wheel full lock (GB) or all the way (US); **bien/mal ~** [*vehicle*] to turn well/badly.
III se braquer *v refl* (+ *v être*) to dig one's heels in.

braqueur° /bʀakœʀ/ *nm* robber.

bras /bʀa/ *nm inv* **1** arm; **au ~ de qn** on sb's arm; **~ dessus ~ dessous** arm in arm; **porter qch à bout de ~** (figurative) to keep sth afloat; **en ~ de chemise** in one's shirtsleeves; **2** manpower, labour[GB]; **3** (of river) branch; **~ de mer** sound; **4** (of armchair, record player) arm; (on stretcher) pole.
■ **~ droit** right hand man; **~ de fer** arm wrestling; (figurative) trial of strength.
IDIOMS **les ~ m'en tombent** I'm absolutely speechless; **avoir le ~ long** to have a lot of influence.

brasier /bʀazje/ *nm* inferno.

bras-le-corps: **à bras-le-corps** /abʀalkɔʀ/ *phr* [*lift*] bodily.

brassard /bʀasaʀ/ *nm* armband.

brasse /bʀas/ *nf* (Sport) breaststroke; **~ papillon** butterfly (stroke).

brassée /bʀase/ *nf* armful **(de** of).

brasser /bʀase/ [1] *vtr* **1** to toss around [*ideas*]; to shuffle around [*papers*]; to intermingle [*population*]; **il brasse des millions** he handles big money; **2** to brew [*beer*].
IDIOMS **~ de l'air**° to talk a lot of hot air°.

brasserie /bʀasʀi/ *nf* **1** brasserie; **2** brewery.

brassière /bʀasjɛʀ/ *nf* **1** baby's top; **2** crop top.

bravade /bʀavad/ *nf* bravado.

brave /bʀav/ *adj* **1** nice; **2** brave.

bravement /bʀavmɑ̃/ *adv* bravely; boldly.

braver /bʀave/ [1] *vtr* to defy [*person, order*]; to brave [*danger*].

bravo /bʀavo/ *excl* **1** bravo!; **2** well done!

bravoure /bʀavuʀ/ *nf* bravery.

break /bʀɛk/ *nm* estate car (GB), station wagon (US).

brebis /bʀəbi/ *nf inv* **1** ewe; **2 les ~** the flock, the faithful.

brèche /bʀɛʃ/ *nf* **1** hole, gap; **2** (Mil) breach.
IDIOMS **être sur la ~** to be on the go°.

bredouille /bRəduj/ *adj* empty-handed.

bredouiller /bRəduje/ [1] *vtr, vi* to mumble.

bref, brève[1] /bRɛf, bRɛv/ **I** *adj* brief; short.
II *adv* **(en) ~** in short.

breloque /bRəlɔk/ *nf* (on bracelet) charm.

Brésil /bRezil/ *pr nm* Brazil.

brésilien, -ienne /bReziljɛ̃, ɛn/ *adj* Brazilian.

Bretagne /bRətaɲ/ *pr nf* **la ~** Brittany.

bretelle /bRətɛl/ **I** *nf* **1** (gen) strap; **2** (for rifle) sling; **3** slip road (GB), ramp (US).
II bretelles *nf pl* braces.

breton, -onne /bRətɔ̃, ɔn/
I *adj* Breton.
II *nm* Breton.

breuvage /bRœvaʒ/ *nm* beverage.

brève[2] /bRɛv/ **I** *adj f* ▶ **bref I**.
II *nf* news flash.

brevet /bRəvɛ/ *nm* **1 ~ (d'invention)** patent; **2 ~ de secourisme** first aid certificate; **~ de pilote** pilot's licence[GB].

breveter /bRəvte/ [20] *vtr* **(faire) ~** to patent.

bréviaire /bRevjɛR/ *nm* breviary; (figurative) bible.

bribes /bRib/ *nf pl* bits; (of conversation) snatches; (of fortune) remnants.

bric: **de bric et de broc** /dəbRiked(ə)bRɔk/ *phr* [*furnished*] with bits and pieces.

bric-à-brac /bRikabRak/ *nm inv* bric-à-brac.

bricolage /bRikɔlaʒ/ *nm* DIY (GB), do-it-yourself.

bricole /bRikɔl/ *nf* **acheter une ~** to buy a little something; **des ~s** bits and pieces.

bricoler /bRikɔle/ [1] **I**° *vtr* **1** to tinker with; **2** to throw [*sth*] together.
II *vi* to do DIY (GB), to fix things (US).

bricoleur, -euse /bRikɔlœR, øz/ *nm,f* DIY enthusiast (GB), do-it-yourselfer.

bride /bRid/ *nf* **1** bridle; **2** (in sewing) button loop.
IDIOMS **partir à ~ abattue** to dash off; **avoir la ~ sur le cou** to have free rein.

bridé, ~e /bRide/ *adj* **yeux ~s** slanting eyes.

brider /bRide/ [1] *vtr* **1** to bridle [*horse*]; **2** to control [*person*]; to curb [*freedom*].

brièvement /bRijɛvmɑ̃/ *adv* briefly.

brièveté /bRijɛvte/ *nf* brevity.

brigade /bRigad/ *nf* **1** (Mil) brigade; **2** (in police) squad.

brigadier /bRigadje/ *nm* **1** (Mil) ≈ corporal; **2** fire chief.

brigand /bRigɑ̃/ *nm* brigand, bandit.

briguer /bRige/ [1] *vtr* to crave [*honour*]; to set one's sights on [*job*].

brillamment /bRijamɑ̃/ *adv* brilliantly.

brillant, ~e /bRijɑ̃, ɑ̃t/ **I** *adj* **1** bright; shiny; glistening; **2** brilliant.
II *nm* (cut) diamond, brilliant.

briller /bRije/ [1] *vi* **1** [*sun*] to shine; [*flame*] to burn brightly; [*gem*] to sparkle; [*tear*] to glisten; [*nose*] to be shiny; **2 ~ de** [*eyes*] to blaze with [*anger*]; to burn with [*fever*]; **3** [*person*] to shine; **elle brille par son esprit** she's extremely witty.

brimade /bRimad/ *nf* bullying.

brimer /bRime/ [1] *vtr* **1** to bully; **2 se sentir brimé** to feel picked on.

brin /bRɛ̃/ *nm* **1** (of parsley) sprig; (of straw) wisp; (of grass) blade; **2 un ~ de** a bit of; **faire un ~ de causette** to have a little chat.

brindille /bRɛ̃dij/ *nf* twig.

bringue° /bRɛ̃g/ *nf* **1** drinking party, booze-up° (GB); **2** rave-up°; **3** (girl) **(grande) ~** beanpole.

brinquebaler /bRɛ̃kbale/ [1] *vi* [*load*] to rattle about; [*vehicle*] to jolt along; [*person*] to be shaken.

brio /bRijo/ *nm* brilliance; (Mus) brio; **avec ~** brilliantly.

brioche /bRijɔʃ/ *nf* **1** brioche, (sweet) bun; **2**° paunch.

brique /bRik/ *nf* **1** brick; **2** (for milk etc) carton.

briquer /bRike/ [1] *vtr* **1** to polish [*sth*] up; **2** to scrub down [*boat*].

briquet /bRikɛ/ *nm* (cigarette) lighter.

brise /bRiz/ *nf* breeze; **bonne ~** fresh breeze.

brise-glace /bRizglas/ *nm inv* icebreaker.

brise-lames /bRizlam/ *nm inv* breakwater.

briser /bRize/ [1] **I** *vtr* **1** (gen) to break; to stop [*attempt*]; to break down [*resistance, taboo*]; to crush [*rebellion*]; **2** to shatter [*dream, image*]; to destroy [*country, career, person*]; **3** to shatter, to exhaust [*person*].
II se briser *v refl* (+ *v être*) **1** to break **(sur, contre** against); **2** [*dream*] to be shattered; **3** [*voice*] to break.

brisure /bRizyR/ *nf* **1** crack; **2** fragment.

britannique /bRitanik/ *adj* British.

Britannique /bRitanik/ *nmf* **un/une ~** a British man/woman; **les ~s** the British (people).

broc /bRo/ *nm* ewer.

brocante /bRɔkɑ̃t/ *nf* **1** bric-à-brac trade; **2** flea market.

brocanteur, -euse /bRɔkɑ̃tœR, øz/ *nm,f* bric-à-brac trader.

broche /bRɔʃ/ *nf* **1** brooch; **2** (for roasting) spit; **3** (in surgery) pin.

brocher /bRɔʃe/ [1] *vtr* to bind [sth] (with paper) [*book*]; **livre broché** paperback.

brochet /bRɔʃɛ/ *nm* (Zool) pike.

brochette /bRɔʃɛt/ *nf* **1** skewer; **2** kebab, brochette.

brochure /bRɔʃyR/ *nf* **1** booklet; **2** (travel) brochure.

brocoli /bRɔkɔli/ *nm* broccoli.

broder /bRɔde/ [1] *vtr, vi* to embroider.

broderie /bRɔdRi/ *nf* embroidery.

brodeuse /bRɔdøz/ *nf* embroiderer.

bromure /bRɔmyR/ *nm* bromide.

bronche /bRɔ̃ʃ/ *nf* **les ~s** the bronchial tubes.

broncher /bRɔ̃ʃe/ [1] *vi* **sans ~** without turning a hair.

bronchite /bRɔ̃ʃit/ *nf* bronchitis.

bronzage /bRɔ̃zaʒ/ *nm* (sun)tan.

bronze /bRɔ̃z/ *nm* bronze.

bronzer /bRɔ̃ze/ [1] **I** *vtr* to tan.

II *vi* to get a tan, to go brown.

brosse /bRɔs/ *nf* **1** brush; **donner un coup de ~ à qch** to give sth a brush; **avoir les cheveux (taillés) en ~** to have a crew cut; **2** (Belgian Fr) broom.

brosser /bRɔse/ [1] **I** *vtr* **1** to brush; to scrub; **2** to give a quick outline of.

II se brosser *v refl* (+ *v être*) to brush oneself down; **se ~ les dents** to brush one's teeth.

brouette /bRuɛt/ *nf* **1** wheelbarrow; **2** barrowful.

brouhaha /bRuaa/ *nm* hubbub.

brouillard /bRujaR/ *nm* fog; **être dans le ~**○ to be somewhat in the dark.

brouille /bRuj/ *nf* **1** quarrel; **2** rift.

brouiller /bRuje/ [1] **I** *vtr* **1** to make [sth] cloudy [*liquid*]; to blur [*text, vision*]; to cover (over) [*footprint*]; **~ les pistes** or **les cartes** to confuse or cloud the issue; **2** to jam [*signal*]; to interfere with [*reception*].

II se brouiller *v refl* (+ *v être*) **1** to fall out (**avec** with); **2** [*liquid*] to become cloudy; [*vision*] to become blurred; [*mind, memories*] to become confused; **avoir le teint brouillé** to look ill; **le temps se brouille** it's clouding over.

brouillon, -onne /bRujɔ̃, ɔn/ **I** *adj* **1** untidy; **2** disorganized; **3** muddled.

II *nm* **1** rough draft; **2 (papier) ~** rough paper.

broussaille /bRusaj/ *nf* **1** undergrowth; **2** scrub; **3** bushes.

broussailleux, -euse /bRusajø, øz/ *adj* **1** covered with bushes; **2** tousled.

brousse /bRus/ *nf* bush; **en pleine ~**○ in the sticks○.

brouter /bRute/ [1] *vtr* to nibble; to graze.

broutille /bRutij/ *nf* trifle; **ce n'est qu'une ~** it's nothing.

broyer /bRwaje/ [23] *vtr* **1** to grind [*wheat*]; **2** to crush.

IDIOMS **~ du noir** to brood.

bru /bRy/ *nf* daughter-in-law.

brugnon /bRyɲɔ̃/ *nm* nectarine.

bruine /bRɥin/ *nf* drizzle.

bruiner /bRɥine/ [1] *v impers* to drizzle.

bruire /bRɥiR/ [3] *vi* (literary) [*leaves*] to rustle; [*brook*] to babble; [*insect*] to hum.

bruissement /bRɥismɑ̃/ *nm* (literary) (of leaves) rustle; (of brook) babbling.

bruit /bRɥi/ *nm* **1** noise; **~ étouffé** thud; **un ~ de ferraille** a clang; **2** noise, din; **~ infernal** or **d'enfer** awful racket; **sans ~** silently; **3 le film a fait beaucoup de ~** the film attracted a lot of attention; **beaucoup de ~ pour rien** a lot of fuss about nothing; **4 ~ (de couloir)** rumour[GB].

bruitage /bRɥitaʒ/ *nm* sound effects.

brûlant, ~e /bRylɑ̃, ɑ̃t/ *adj* **1** [*tea*] boiling hot; [*sand, radiator*] burning hot; [*sun*] blazing; **2** [*person, forehead*] burning hot; **3** [*issue*] burning; **4** [*passion*] burning; [*eyes*] blazing.

brûlé, ~e /bRyle/ **I** *nm,f* **un grand ~** a third degree burns victim; **service des grands ~s** burns unit.

II *nm* **ça sent le ~** there's a smell of burning; (figurative) things are becoming unpleasant.

brûle-pourpoint: **à brûle-pourpoint** /abRylpuRpwɛ̃/ *phr* point-blank.

brûler /bRyle/ [1] **I** *vtr* **1** to burn [*papers*]; to set fire to [*house*]; **2** to burn [*fuel*]; to use [*electricity*]; **3** [*acid*] to burn; [*water*] to scald; **j'ai les yeux qui me brûlent** my eyes are stinging; **4**○ to ignore [*stop sign*]; **~ un feu (rouge)** to jump○ the lights.

II *vi* **1** [*wood*] to burn; [*forest, town*] to be on fire; **faire ~** to burn [*paper*]; **2 ~ (d'envie** or **d'impatience de faire)** to be longing to do.

III se brûler *v refl* (+ *v être*) to burn oneself.

brûlure /bRylyR/ *nf* **1** (Med) burn; **~s d'estomac** heartburn; **2** burn mark.

brume /bRym/ *nf* mist; fog; haze.

brumeux, -euse /bRymø, øz/ *adj* **1** hazy; misty; **2** [*idea*] hazy.

brun, ~e /bRœ̃, bRyn/ **I** *adj* brown, dark; dark-haired.

II *nm,f* dark-haired man/woman.

III *nm* brown; **~ clair/foncé** light/dark brown.

brunâtre /bRynɑtR/ *adj* brownish.

brunir /bRyniR/ [3] *vi* **1** [*skin*] to tan; **2** (Culin) to brown.

brushing /bRœʃiŋ/ *nm* blow-dry; **se faire faire un ~** to have a blow-dry.

brusque /bRysk/ *adj* **1** [*tone, person*] abrupt; **2** [*movement*] sudden; [*bend*] sharp.

brusquement /bRyskəmɑ̃/ *adv* **1** abruptly; **2** suddenly; sharply.

brusquer /bRyske/ [1] *vtr* **1** to be brusque with; **2** to rush.

brusquerie /bRyskəRi/ *nf* brusqueness.

brut, ~e[1] /bRyt/ *adj* **1** [*material*] raw; [*oil*] crude; [*stone*] rough; [*wool*] untreated; [*sugar*] unrefined; **2** [*cider, champagne*] dry; **3** [*salary, weight*] gross.

brutal, ~e *mpl* **-aux** /bRytal, o/ *adj* **1** [*blow*] violent; [*pain, death*] sudden; [*rise, fall*] dramatic; [*brake*] sharp; **2** [*tone*] brutal; [*gesture, temper*] violent; **3** stark.

brutalement /bRytalmɑ̃/ *adv* **1** [*repress*] brutally; [*close*] violently; **2** [*change*] dramatically; [*die, stop*] suddenly; [*brake*] sharply.

brutaliser /bRytalize/ [1] *vtr* to ill-treat.

brutalité /bRytalite/ *nf* **1** brutality; **2** suddenness.

brute[2] /bRyt/ **I** *adj f* ▶ **brut**.

II *nf* brute; **comme une ~** [*hit*] savagely.

Bruxelles /bRysɛl/ *pr n* Brussels.

bruyamment /bRɥijamɑ̃/ *adv* loudly; noisily.

bruyant, ~e /bRɥijɑ̃, ɑ̃t/ *adj* **1** noisy; loud; **2** resounding.

bruyère /bRyjɛR/ *nf* heather; briar; **terre de ~** heath.

bu, ~e /by/ *pp* ▶ **boire**.

buanderie /bɥɑ̃dRi/ *nf* laundry room.

buccal, ~e, *mpl* **-aux** /bykal, o/ *adj* oral.

bûche /byʃ/ *nf* **1** log (of wood); **2**○ tumble, fall; **3** (Culin) **~ de Noël** yule log.

bûcher[1]○ /byʃe/ [1] *vi* to slog away○.

bûcher[2] /byʃe/ *nm* **1 le ~** the stake; **2** (funeral) pyre.

bûcheron /byʃʀɔ̃/ *nm* lumberjack.

bûchette /byʃɛt/ *nf* **1** (for fire) stick; **2** counting rod.

bûcheur○, **-euse** /byʃœʀ, øz/ *adj* industrious.

bucolique /bykɔlik/ *adj* bucolic, pastoral.

budget /bydʒɛ/ *nm* budget; **le ~ de l'État** the Budget.

budgétaire /bydʒetɛʀ/ *adj* [*deficit*] budget; [*year*] financial (GB), fiscal (US).

buée /bɥe/ *nf* **1** condensation; **2** steam.

buffet /byfɛ/ *nm* **1** sideboard; **2** dresser; **3** (station) buffet; **4** (Culin) buffet.

buffle /byfl/ *nm* buffalo.

buis /bɥi/ *nm* **1** box tree; **2** boxwood.

buisson /bɥisɔ̃/ *nm* **1** bush; **2** shrub.

buissonnière /bɥisɔnjɛʀ/ *adj* **faire l'école ~** to play truant (GB), to play hooky○ (US).

bulbe /bylb/ *nm* (Bot) bulb.

bulgare /bylgaʀ/ *adj*, *nm* Bulgarian.

bulldozer /byldozœʀ/ *nm* bulldozer.

bulle /byl/ *nf* **1** bubble; **2** speech bubble.

bulletin /byltɛ̃/ *nm* **1** bulletin, report; **~ météorologique** weather forecast; **~ de santé** medical bulletin; **~ scolaire** or **de notes** school report (GB), report card (US); **2** certificate; **~ de naissance** birth certificate; **3** form; **~ de salaire** payslip; **~ de commande** order form; **~ de participation** entry form; **4** bulletin, official publication; **5** ballot or voting paper; **~ nul** spoiled ballot paper.

bulot /bylo/ *nm* whelk.

bureau, *pl* **~x** /byʀo/ *nm* **1** desk; **2** study; **3** office; **4** board.
■ **~ d'accueil** reception; **~ de change** bureau de change, foreign exchange office; **~ de poste** post office; **~ de tabac** tobacconist's; **~ de vote** polling station.

bureaucrate /byʀokʀat/ *nmf* bureaucrat.

bureaucratie /byʀokʀasi/ *nf* bureaucracy.

bureautique /byʀotik/ *nf* office automation.

burin /byʀɛ̃/ *nm* chisel.

buriné, **~e** /byʀine/ *adj* [*face*] craggy.

burlesque /byʀlɛsk/ **I** *adj* ludicrous; farcical.
II *nm* **le ~** the burlesque.

bus /bys/ *nm inv* bus.

buse /byz/ *nf* **1** buzzard; **2**○ clot○ (GB), clod○.

busqué, **~e** /byske/ *adj* [*nose*] hooked.

buste /byst/ *nm* **1** (in sculpture) bust; **2** (Anat) chest; **3** bust, breasts.

bustier /bystje/ *nm* **1** long-line bra; **2** bustier.

but /by(t)/ *nm* **1** goal; aim, purpose; **dans un ~ désintéressé** with no ulterior motive; **aller droit au ~** to go straight to the point; **2** (in football) goal; **3** (in archery) target.
IDIOMS **déclarer de ~ en blanc** to declare point-blank.

buté, **~e**[1] /byte/ *adj* stubborn, obstinate.

butée[2] /byte/ *nf* **1** (Tech) stop; **~ d'une porte** doorstop; **2** buttress.

buter /byte/ [1] **I** *vi* **~ contre qch** to trip over sth; to bump into sth; **~ sur** or **contre** to come up against [*obstacle*].
II se buter *v refl* (+ *v être*) to dig one's heels in.

butin /bytɛ̃/ *nm* **1** spoils; **2** (from robbery) haul; **3** (of research) fruits.

butiner /bytine/ [1] *vi* to gather pollen.

butte /byt/ *nf* mound.
IDIOMS **être en ~ à** to come up against [*difficulties*]; to be the butt of [*jokes*].

buvable /byvabl/ *adj* **1** to be taken orally; **2** drinkable.

buvard /byvaʀ/ *nm* **(papier) ~** blotting paper.

buvette /byvɛt/ *nf* refreshment area.

buveur, **-euse** /byvœʀ, øz/ *nm,f* drinker.

byzantin, **~e** /bizɑ̃tɛ̃, in/ *adj* Byzantine; **querelles ~es** hairsplitting quarrels.

BZH (*written abbr* = **Breizh**) Brittany.

c, **C** /se/ *nm inv* c, C; **c cédille** c cedilla.

c' ▶ **ce** II.

CA *written abbr* ▶ **chiffre**.

ça /sa/ *pron* **1** that; this; **c'est pour ~ qu'il est parti** that's why he left; **sans ~** otherwise; **tu te lèves toujours aussi tard que ~?** do you always get up this or that late?; **~, c'est bizarre** that's strange; **'tu la connais?'—'qui ~?'** 'do you know her?' —'who do you mean?'; **la rue a ~ de bien qu'elle est calme** one good thing about the street is that it's quiet; **2** it; that; **~ fait mal** it hurts; that hurts; **~ criait de tous les côtés** there was shouting everywhere; **voyager, ~ revient cher** travelling[GB] is expensive.
IDIOMS **~ alors!** well I never○!; **~, oui!** definitely!; **~, non!** no way!, absolutely not!; **elle est bête et méchante avec ~** she's stupid and what's more she's nasty; **et avec ~?** anything else?; **rien que ~!** (ironic) is that all!; **c'est ~!** that's right!; **~ va?** how are you?; how are things?; is that OK?; **~ y est, ~ recommence!** here we go again!; **~ y est, j'ai fini!** that's it, I've finished!

cabale /kabal/ *nf* **1** cabal; **2** (in religion) cabbala.

caban /kabɑ̃/ *nm* sailor's jacket.

cabane /kaban/ *nf* **1** hut; **2** shed; **3**○ prison.

cabanon /kabanɔ̃/ *nm* shed.

cabaret /kabaʀɛ/ *nm* cabaret.

cabas /kaba/ *nm* shopping bag.

cabillaud /kabijo/ *nm* cod.

cabine /kabin/ *nf* cabin; cab; booth; cubicle.
■ **~ d'essayage** fitting room; **~ de pilotage** cockpit; **~ téléphonique** phone box (GB), phone booth.

cabinet /kabinɛ/ **I** *nm* **1** (gen) office; (of doctor, dentist) surgery (GB), office (US); (of judge) chambers; **2** practice; **~ de médecins** medical practice; **ouvrir un ~** to set up in practice; **3** agency; **~ immobilier** estate agent's; **4** (Pol) cabinet; **~ ministériel** minister's personal staff; **5** (in museum) exhibition room.
II cabinets *nm pl* toilet.
■ **~ de toilette** bathroom.

cabinet-conseil, *pl* **cabinets-conseil** /kabinɛkɔ̃sɛj/ *nm* firm of consultants.

câble /kɑbl/ *nm* cable; rope; (of cable car) carrying cable.

câbler /kɑble/ [1] *vtr* **1** to install cable television in [*house, town*]; **2** to cable [*message*].

câblodistribution /kɑblodistʀibysjɔ̃/ *nf* cable television.

cabochard○, **~e** /kabɔʃaʀ, aʀd/ *adj* pigheaded○, stubborn.

caboche○ /kabɔʃ/ *nf* nut○, head.

cabosser /kabɔse/ [1] *vtr* to dent.

cabot○ /kabo/ *nm* dog, mutt○.

cabotin, ~e /kabɔtɛ̃, in/ *adj* **être ~** to like playing to the gallery.

cabrer /kabʀe/ [1] **I** *vtr* to make [sth] rear [*horse*].
II se cabrer *v refl* (+ *v être*) **1** [*horse*] to rear (**devant** at); **2** [*person*] to jib.

cabri /kabʀi/ *nm* (Zool) kid.

cabriole /kabʀijɔl/ *nf* (of clown, child, animal) caper; **~s** capering.

cabriolet /kabʀijɔlɛ/ *nm* **1** (Aut) convertible; **2** (carriage) cabriolet.

caca /kaka/ *nm* (baby talk) poo○ (GB), poop○ (US); **~ d'oie** (colour) greenish yellow.

cacahuète /kakawɛt/ *nf* peanut.

cacao /kakao/ *nm* cocoa.

cacatoès /kakatɔɛs/ *nm* cockatoo.

cachalot /kaʃalo/ *nm* sperm whale.

cache[1] /kaʃ/ *nm* **se servir d'un ~ pour apprendre une liste de vocabulaire** to cover up the answers while learning a list of vocabulary.

cache[2] /kaʃ/ *nf* hiding place; **~ d'armes** arms cache.

cache-cache /kaʃkaʃ/ *nm inv* hide and seek (GB), hide-and-go-seek (US).

cache-col /kaʃkɔl/ *nm inv* scarf.

cachemire /kaʃmiʀ/ *nm* cashmere; **motif ~** paisley pattern.

cache-nez /kaʃne/ *nm inv* scarf, muffler.

cache-pot /kaʃpo/ *nm inv* flowerpot holder, planter.

cacher /kaʃe/ [1] **I** *vtr* to hide; **~ son jeu** (figurative) to keep one's cards close to one's chest; **~ qch à qn** to conceal sth from sb; **pour ne rien vous ~** to be quite frank.
II se cacher *v refl* (+ *v être*) **1** to hide; (temporarily) [*person*] to go into hiding; **il ne s'en cache pas** he makes no secret of it; **2** [*sun, object*] to disappear.

cache-sexe /kaʃsɛks/ *nm inv* G-string.

cachet /kaʃɛ/ *nm* **1** tablet; **2** (for letter) stamp; seal; **~ de la poste** postmark; **3** style; cachet; **4** (of actor) fee.

cacheter /kaʃte/ [20] *vtr* to seal; **cacheté à la cire** sealed with wax.

cachette /kaʃɛt/ *nf* hiding place; **en ~** on the sly.

cachot /kaʃo/ *nm* **1** prison cell; **2** dungeon.

cachotterie /kaʃɔtʀi/ *nf* little secret; **faire des ~s à qn** to keep things from sb.

cachottier, -ière /kaʃɔtje, ɛʀ/ *adj* secretive.

cachou /kaʃu/ *nm* cachou.

cacophonie /kakɔfɔni/ *nf* cacophony.

cactus /kaktys/ *nm inv* cactus.

c-à-d (*written abbr* = **c'est-à-dire**) ie.

cadastral, **~e**, *mpl* **-aux** /kadastʀal, o/ *adj* cadastral; land.

cadastre /kadastʀ/ *nm* **1** land register; **2** land registry.

cadavre /kadavʀ/ *nm* **1** corpse, body; **2**○ dead bottle.

caddie /kadi/ *nm* **1** (Sport) caddie; **2** ®shopping trolley.

cadeau, *pl* **~x** /kado/ **I** *nm* present, gift; **faire un ~ à qn** to give sb a present; **il ne fait pas de ~x** (shopkeeper) he's not exactly cheap; (examiner, judge) he's very strict.
II **(-)cadeau** (*combining form*) gift; **papier(-)~** wrapping paper.
■ **~ empoisonné** poisoned chalice.

cadenas /kadna/ *nm* padlock.

cadence /kadɑ̃s/ *nf* **1** rhythm; **en ~** [*march*] in step; [*row*] rhythmically; **2** (of work) rate.

cadet, **-ette** /kadɛ, ɛt/ **I** *adj* **1** younger; **2** youngest.
II *nm,f* **1** younger son/daughter, younger child; **2** youngest child; **3** younger brother/sister; **4** junior, youngest; **5** (Sport) *athlete between the ages of 15 and 17.*
IDIOMS **c'est le ~ de mes soucis** it's the least of my worries.

cadran /kadʀɑ̃/ *nm* (of watch) face; (of meter) dial; **~ solaire** sundial.

cadre /kadʀ/ **I** *nm* **1** frame; **2** setting; surroundings; **3** **cela sort du ~ de mes fonctions** that's not part of my duties; **4** framework; **5** executive; **~ supérieur** senior executive; **les ~s moyens** middle management; **6** **faire partie des ~s** to be on the company's books; **7** (of bicycle) frame; **8** (on application form) space, box.
II **dans le cadre de** *phr* **1** on the occasion of; **2** (of negotiations) within the framework of; (of campaign, plan) as part of.

cadrer /kadʀe/ [1] **I** *vtr* to centre[GB] [*picture, scene*].
II *vi* to tally, to fit (**avec** with).

cadreur /kadʀœʀ/ *nm* (for a film) cameraman.

caduc, **caduque** /kadyk/ *adj* **1** obsolete; **2** (Law) null and void; **3** [*leaf*] deciduous.

cætera ▸ **et cætera**.

cafard /kafaʀ/ *nm* **1**○ depression; **avoir le ~** to be down in the dumps○; **un coup de ~** a fit of depression; **2** cockroach.

cafarder○ /kafaʀde/ [1] *vi* (schoolchildren's slang) to tell tales (GB), to tattle (US).

café /kafe/ *nm* **1** coffee; **~ vert** unroasted coffee; **~ en grains** coffee beans; **~ soluble** instant coffee; **2** café.
■ **~ crème** espresso with milk; **~ au lait** coffee with milk; **peau ~ au lait** coffee-coloured[GB] skin; **~ noir** black coffee.

caféine /kafein/ *nf* caffeine.

café-restaurant, *pl* **cafés-restaurants** /kafeʀɛstɔʀɑ̃/ *nm* café-restaurant.

cafétéria /kafeteʀja/ *nf* cafeteria.

cafetière /kaftjɛʀ/ *nf* **1** coffee pot; coffee maker; **2**○ head.

cafouillage○ /kafujaʒ/ *nm* bungling○.

cafouiller○ /kafuje/ [1] *vi* [*person*] to get flustered; [*machine*] to be on the blink○; [*organization*] to get in a muddle; **il a fait ~ nos projets** he messed up our plans.

cage /kaʒ/ *nf* **1** cage; **en ~** caged; **2**○ (Sport) goal.
■ **~ d'ascenseur** lift (GB) or elevator (US) shaft; **~ d'escalier** stairwell; **~ à lapins** rabbit hutch; **~ thoracique** rib cage.

cageot /kaʒo/ *nm* crate.

cagette /kaʒɛt/ *nf* tray.

cagibi /kaʒibi/ *nm* store cupboard.

cagnotte /kaɲɔt/ *nf* **1** kitty; **2** jackpot; **3** nest egg.

cagoule /kagul/ *nf* balaclava; hood.

cahier /kaje/ *nm* **1** notebook; (Sch) exercise book; **2** (in printing) section; **3** **~s** (in title of publication) journal, review; memoirs.
■ **~ de brouillon** rough book; **~ de textes** homework notebook.

cahin-caha○ /kaɛ̃kaa/ *adv* [*walk, advance*] with difficulty.

cahot /kao/ *nm* jolt; (figurative) **les ~s** the ups and downs.

cahotant, **~e** /kaɔtɑ̃, ɑ̃t/ *adj* [*road, career*] bumpy.

cahoter /kaɔte/ [1] *vi* [*vehicle*] to bounce along.

cahoteux, **~euse** /kaɔtø, -øz/ *adj* [*road*] rough, bumpy.

cahute /kayt/ *nf* hut, shack.

caïd /kaid/ *nm* **1** (in criminal underworld) boss; **jouer les ~s** to act tough; **2**○ (important person) big shot; star; (clever person) wizard.

caillasse /kajas/ *nf* stones.

caille /kaj/ *nf* (Zool) quail.

cailler /kaje/ [1] **I se cailler** *v refl* (+ *v être*) **1** [*milk*] to curdle; [*blood*] to congeal; **2**○ [*person*] to be freezing.
II○ *v impers* **ça caille** it's freezing.

caillot /kajo/ *nm* clot.

caillou, *pl* **~x** /kaju/ *nm* **1** pebble; **gros ~** stone; **2**○ nut○; **ne plus avoir un poil sur le ~** to be as bald as a coot○.

caillouteux, **-euse** /kajutø, øz/ *adj* stony.

caïman /kaimɑ̃/ *nm* cayman.

Caire /kɛʀ/ *pr n* **le ~** Cairo.

caisse /kɛs/ *nf* **1** crate; **2** (for plants) planter; **3** (of car) shell, body; **4**○ car; **vieille ~** old banger○; **5** (for money) till; cash register; cash box; **les ~s de l'État** the Treasury coffers; **voler la ~** to steal the takings; **6** cash desk; (in supermarket) checkout (counter); (in bank) cashier's desk; **7** fund.
■ **~ enregistreuse** cash register; **~ d'épargne** ≈ savings bank; **~ noire** slush fund; **~ à outils** toolbox.

caissette /kɛsɛt/ *nf* (gen) small box or case; (for fruit) crate.

caissier, **-ière** /kesje, ɛʀ/ *nm,f* cashier.

caisson /kɛsɔ̃/ *nm* **1** crate; **2** flotation tank; **~ de décompression** decompression chamber.

cajoler /kaʒɔle/ [1] *vtr* **1** to make a fuss of [*person*]; **2** to cuddle [*child*].

cajolerie /kaʒɔlʀi/ *nf* **1** cuddle;**2** compliment.

cajou /kaʒu/ *nm* **noix de ~** cashew nut.

cake /kɛk/ *nm* fruit cake.

cal /kal/ *nm* callus.

calamar /kalamaʀ/ *nm* squid.

calaminer: **se calaminer** /kalamine/ [1] *v refl* (+ *v être*) **être calaminé** to be coked up.

calamité /kalamite/ *nf* disaster, calamity.

calandre /kalɑ̃dʀ/ *nf* (Aut) (radiator) grille[GB].

calcaire /kalkɛʀ/ **I** *adj* [*water*] hard; [*soil*] chalky; [*rock*] limestone.
II *nm* **1** limestone; **2** fur (GB), sediment (US).

calciné, ~e /kalsine/ *adj* charred, scorched.

calciner /kalsine/ [1] *vtr* **1** to char; (in oven) to burn [sth] to a crisp; **2** (in chemistry) to calcine.

calcium /kalsjɔm/ *nm* calcium.

calcul /kalkyl/ *nm* **1** calculation; **faire le ~ de qch** to calculate sth; **'combien?'—'attends, il faut que je fasse le ~'** 'how much?'—'wait, I'll have to work it out'; **2** (subject) arithmetic; **~ mental** mental arithmetic; **3** calculation; **agir par ~** to act out of self-interest; **être un bon ~** to be a good move; **4** (Med) stone.

calculateur, -trice[1] /kalkylatœʀ, tʀis/ **I** *adj* calculating.
II *nm,f* calculating person.

calculatrice[2] /kalkylatʀis/ *nf* (pocket) calculator.

calculer /kalkyle/ [1] **I** *vtr* **1** to calculate, to work out; **2** to weigh up [*advantages, chances*]; to gauge [*results, efforts*]; **tout bien calculé** all things considered; **3 ~ son coup** to plan one's move.
II *vi* to calculate.

calculette /kalkylɛt/ *nf* pocket calculator.

cale /kal/ *nf* **1** wedge; (for wheel) chock; (for raising vehicle) block; **2** (Naut) (ship's) hold.

calé○**, ~e** /kale/ *adj* bright; **~ en qch** brilliant at sth.

calebasse /kalbas/ *nf* **1** (Bot) calabash, gourd; **2**○ nut○, head.

calèche /kalɛʃ/ *nf* barouche, calash.

caleçon /kalsɔ̃/ *nm* **1** boxer shorts; **~ long** long johns○; **2** (for woman) leggings.

calédonien, -ienne /kaledɔnjɛ̃, ɛn/ *adj* **1** New Caledonian; **2** Caledonian.

calembour /kalɑ̃buʀ/ *nm* pun, play on words.

calendes /kalɑ̃d/ *nf pl* calends; **renvoyer aux ~ grecques** to postpone indefinitely.

calendrier /kalɑ̃dʀije/ *nm* **1** calendar; **2** schedule; **3** dates.

cale-pied, *pl* **~s** /kalpje/ *nm* toe clip.

calepin /kalpɛ̃/ *nm* notebook.

caler /kale/ [1] **I** *vtr* **1** to wedge [*wheel*]; to steady [*piece of furniture*]; to support [*row of books*]; **bien calé dans mon fauteuil** ensconced in my armchair; **2**○ **ça cale l'estomac** it fills you up.
II *vi* **1** [*car*] to stall; **2** to give up; **~ sur un problème** to get stuck on a problem.
III se caler *v refl* (+ *v être*) to settle (**dans** in).

calfeutrer /kalføtʀe/ [1] **I** *vtr* to stop up [*crack*]; to draught proof [*door*].
II se calfeutrer *v refl* (+ *v être*) to shut oneself away.

calibre /kalibʀ/ *nm* **1** bore; calibre[GB]; diameter; **arme de gros ~** large-bore weapon; **2** (of eggs, fruit) size, grade; **3** gauge; **4** (of person) calibre[GB].

calibrer /kalibʀe/ [1] *vtr* **1** (Tech) to calibrate; **2** to grade, to size [*eggs, fruit*].

calice /kalis/ *nm* chalice.

calife /kalif/ *nm* caliph.

califourchon: **à califourchon** /akalifuʀʃɔ̃/ *phr* astride.

câlin, ~e /kɑlɛ̃, in/ **I** *adj* affectionate.
II *nm* cuddle.

câliner /kaline/ [1] *vtr* to cuddle.

calleux, -euse /kalø, øz/ *adj* calloused, rough-skinned.

callosité /kalozite/ *nf* callus.

calmant, ~e /kalmɑ̃, ɑ̃t/ **I** *adj* [*music, words*] soothing.
II *nm* sedative.

calmar /kalmaʀ/ *nm* squid.

calme /kalm/ **I** *adj* **1** [*sea, weather, situation*] calm; [*night*] still; [*place, life*] quiet; **2** [*person*] calm.
II *nm* **1** peace (and quiet); **2** calm; (of crowd) calmness; (of night) stillness; **lancer un appel au ~** to appeal for calm; **dans le ~** peacefully; **3** composure; **conserver son ~** to keep calm; **du ~!** calm down!; quiet!

calmement /kalməmɑ̃/ *adv* calmly.

calmer /kalme/ [1] **I** *vtr* **1** to calm down [*person*]; to calm [*stock market*]; to defuse [*situation*]; to tone down [*discussion*]; to subdue [*agitation, anger*]; to allay [*anxiety*]; **~ les esprits** to calm people down; **2** to ease [*pain*]; to dampen [*ardour*]; to take the edge off [*hunger*]; to quench [*thirst*].
II se calmer *v refl* (+ *v être*) **1** [*person, situation*] to calm down; [*agitation, storm*] to die down; [*debate*] to quieten (GB) or quiet (US) down; [*ardour, desire*] to cool; **les esprits se sont calmés** tempers have cooled; **2** [*pain*] to ease; [*noise*] to subside.

calomniateur, -trice /kalɔmnjatœʀ, tʀis/ *nm,f* slanderer.

calomnie /kalɔmni/ *nf* slander.

calomnier /kalɔmnje/ [2] *vtr* to slander.

calomnieux, -ieuse /kalɔmnjø, øz/ *adj* slanderous.

calorie /kalɔʀi/ *nf* calorie.

calorifère /kalɔʀifɛʀ/ *adj* heat-conveying.

calorique /kalɔʀik/ *adj* calorie; **ration/valeur ~** calorie intake/content.

calot /kalo/ *nm* (Mil) forage cap (GB), overseas cap (US).

calotte /kalɔt/ *nf* **1** skull cap; **2**○ slap; **3 ~ glaciaire** icecap.

calque /kalk/ *nm* **1** tracing; **2** tracing paper; **3** replica.

calquer /kalke/ [1] *vtr* **1** to copy [*behaviour*];

~ qch sur qch to model sth on sth; **2** to trace [*pattern, design*].

calumet /kalymɛ/ *nm* calumet; **~ de la paix** peace pipe.

calvados /kalvados/ *nm* calvados (*apple brandy distilled in Normandy*).

calvaire /kalvɛʀ/ *nm* **1** ordeal; **2** (monument) wayside cross; **3** Calvary.

calvinisme /kalvinism/ *nm* Calvinism.

calvitie /kalvisi/ *nf* baldness.

camaïeu /kamajø/ *nm* monochrome.

camarade /kamaʀad/ *nmf* **1** friend; **~ d'atelier** workmate; **2** comrade.

camaraderie /kamaʀadʀi/ *nf* comradeship, camaraderie.

Cambodge /kɑ̃bɔdʒ/ *pr nm* Cambodia.

cambouis /kɑ̃bwi/ *nm* dirty grease.

cambré, **~e** /kɑ̃bʀe/ *adj* [*back*] arched; [*foot, shoe*] with a high instep.

cambrer /kɑ̃bʀe/ [1] **I** *vtr* to curve, to arch.
II se cambrer *v refl* (+ *v être*) to arch one's back.

cambriolage /kɑ̃bʀijɔlaʒ/ *nm* burglary.

cambrioler /kɑ̃bʀijɔle/ [1] *vtr* to burgle (GB), to burglarize (US).

cambrioleur, **-euse** /kɑ̃bʀijɔlœʀ, øz/ *nm,f* burglar.

cambrousse○ /kɑ̃bʀus/ *nf* **la ~** the sticks○; **n'être jamais sorti de sa ~** to be a country bumpkin.

cambrure /kɑ̃bʀyʀ/ *nf* curve; (of foot) arch.
■ **~ des pieds** instep; **~ des reins** small of the back.

came /kam/ *nf* **1** (Tech) cam; **2**◑ drugs.

camé◑, **~e**[1] /kame/ *adj* **être ~** to be on drugs.

camée[2] /kame/ *nm* cameo.

caméléon /kameleɔ̃/ *nm* chameleon.

camelote○ /kamlɔt/ *nf* junk○.

camembert /kamɑ̃bɛʀ/ *nm* **1** (Culin) Camembert; **2**○ pie chart.

camer◑: **se camer** /kame/ [1] *v refl* (+ *v être*) to be on drugs.

caméra /kameʀa/ *nf* (cine-)camera (GB), movie camera (US).

Cameroun /kamʀun/ *pr nm* Cameroon.

caméscope® /kameskɔp/ *nm* camcorder.

camion /kamjɔ̃/ *nm* truck; **~ de déménagement** removal van.

camion-citerne, *pl* **camions-citernes** /kamjɔ̃sitɛʀn/ *nm* tanker.

camionnette /kamjɔnɛt/ *nf* van.

camionneur /kamjɔnœʀ/ *nm* truck driver.

camisole /kamizɔl/ *nf* camisole; **~ de force** straitjacket.

camomille /kamɔmij/ *nf* **1** camomile; **2** camomile tea.

camouflage /kamuflaʒ/ *nm* **1** (Mil) camouflage; **2** (figurative) concealing; disguising (**en** as).

camoufler /kamufle/ [1] *vtr* **1** (Mil) to camouflage; **2** to cover up [*crime, mistake, truth*]; to conceal [*intention, feelings*]; **3** to hide [*money*].

camp /kɑ̃/ *nm* **1** (gen) camp; **2** (Sport, Pol) side.
IDIOMS **ficher**○ or **foutre**◑ **le ~** to split○, to leave.

campagnard, **~e** /kɑ̃paɲaʀ, aʀd/ **I** *adj* country, rustic.
II *nm,f* country person.

campagne /kɑ̃paɲ/ *nf* **1** country; (open) countryside; **en rase ~** in the open countryside; **2** campaign; **faire ~** to campaign.

campanule /kɑ̃panyl/ *nf* campanula, bellflower.

campement /kɑ̃pmɑ̃/ *nm* camp, encampment.

camper /kɑ̃pe/ [1] **I** *vtr* to portray [*character*]; to depict [*landscape, scene*].
II *vi* to camp; **~ sur ses positions** (figurative) to stand firm.
III se camper *v refl* (+ *v être*) **se ~ devant qch/qn** to stand squarely in front of sth/sb; **bien campé sur ses jambes** standing firm.

campeur, **-euse** /kɑ̃pœʀ, øz/ *nm,f* camper.

camphre /kɑ̃fʀ/ *nm* camphor.

camping /kɑ̃piŋ/ *nm* **1** camping; **faire du ~ sauvage** to camp rough; **~ à la ferme** camping on a farm-based site; **2** campsite (GB), campground (US).

camping-car, *pl* **~s** /kɑ̃piŋkaʀ/ *nm* (controversial) camper.

camping-gaz® /kɑ̃piŋgaz/ *nm inv* camping stove.

campus /kɑ̃pys/ *nm inv* campus.

Canada /kanada/ *pr nm* Canada.

Canadair® /kanadɛʀ/ *nm* water bomber, air tanker.

canadien, **-ienne**[1] /kanadjɛ̃, ɛn/ *adj* Canadian.

canadienne[2] /kanadjɛn/ *nf* **1** sheepskin-lined jacket; **2** ridge tent.

canaille /kanɑj/ *nf* **1** villain; **2 la ~** the rabble.

canal, *pl* **-aux** /kanal, o/ *nm* **1** canal; **2** channel; **3** (Anat) duct.

canalisation /kanalizasjɔ̃/ *nf* **1** pipe; **2** mains.

canaliser /kanalize/ [1] *vtr* **1** to canalize [*river*]; **2** (figurative) to channel.

canapé /kanape/ *nm* **1** sofa; **~ convertible** sofa bed; **2** (Culin) canapé.

canaque /kanak/ *adj* Kanak.

canard /kanaʀ/ *nm* **1** duck; **~ laqué** Peking duck; **2**○ rag○, newspaper; **3** (Mus) wrong note; **4 mon ~**○ my darling.
IDIOMS **ça ne casse pas trois pattes à un ~**○ it's nothing to write home about.

canarder○ /kanaʀde/ [1] *vtr* to snipe at.

canari /kanaʀi/ *nm* **1** canary; **2 jaune ~** canary yellow.

cancan /kɑ̃kɑ̃/ *nm* **1**○ gossip; **2** (French) cancan.

cancaner○ /kɑ̃kane/ [1] *vi* to gossip.

cancanier, **-ière** /kɑ̃kanje, ɛʀ/ *adj* gossipy.

cancer /kɑ̃sɛʀ/ *nm* cancer.

Cancer /kɑ̃sɛʀ/ *pr nm* Cancer.

cancéreux, **-euse** /kɑ̃seʀø, øz/ *adj* [*cell*] cancerous; [*person*] with cancer.

cancérigène /kɑ̃seʀiʒɛn/ *adj* carcinogenic.
cancérologie /kɑ̃seʀɔlɔʒi/ *nf* cancer research; **service de ~** cancer ward.
cancérologue /kɑ̃seʀɔlɔg/ *nmf* cancer specialist.
cancre /kɑ̃kʀ/ *nm* dunce.
cancrelat /kɑ̃kʀəla/ *nm* cockroach.
candélabre /kɑ̃delabʀ/ *nm* candelabra (GB), candelabrum (US).
candeur /kɑ̃dœʀ/ *nf* ingenuousness.
candi /kɑ̃di/ *adj m* **fruit ~** candied fruit; **sucre ~** sugar candy.
candidat, ~e /kɑ̃dida, at/ *nm,f* **1** (Pol) candidate; **être ~ aux élections** to stand for election (GB), to run for office (US); **2** (for exam) candidate; **3** (for job etc) applicant (**à** for); **être ~ (à un poste)** to apply (for a post); **4** (Games) contestant (**à** in); **5** (aspirant) **pour la vaisselle, il n'y a pas beaucoup de ~s!** (humorous) when it comes to doing the dishes, there aren't many takers or volunteers.
candidature /kɑ̃didatyʀ/ *nf* **1** candidature, candidacy; **retirer sa ~** to stand down (GB), to drop out (US); **2** (for a post) application; **~ spontanée** unsolicited application; **faire acte de ~** to apply (**à** for).
candide /kɑ̃did/ *adj* ingenuous.
cane /kan/ *nf* (female) duck.
caneton /kantɔ̃/ *nm* duckling.
canette /kanɛt/ *nf* **1 ~ (de bière)** (small) bottle of beer; **2** can; **~ de bière** can of beer; **3** (of sewing machine) spool.
canevas /kanva/ *nm inv* **1** canvas; **2** tapestry work; **3** (figurative) framework.
caniche /kaniʃ/ *nm* poodle; **~ nain** toy poodle.
caniculaire /kanikylɛʀ/ *adj* scorching.
canicule /kanikyl/ *nf* **1** scorching heat; **2** heatwave.
canif /kanif/ *nm* penknife.
canin, ~e[1] /kanɛ̃, in/ *adj* canine; **exposition ~** dog show.
canine[2] /kanin/ *nf* canine (tooth).
caniveau, *pl* **~x** /kanivo/ *nm* gutter.
cannabis /kanabis/ *nm* cannabis.
canne /kan/ *nf* **1** (walking) stick; **2** (Bot) cane.
■ **~ à pêche** fishing rod; **~ à sucre** sugar cane.
canneberge /kanbɛʀʒ/ *nf* cranberry.
cannelé, ~e /kanle/ *adj* [*column, glass*] fluted.
cannelle /kanɛl/ *adj inv, nf* cinnamon.
cannelure /kanlyʀ/ *nf* (on column, pillar) flute; **~s** fluting.
cannette = **canette**.
cannibale /kanibal/ *adj, nmf* cannibal.
canoë /kanɔe/ *nm* **1** (Canadian) canoe; **2** canoeing.
canoë-kayak /kanɔekajak/ *nm* canoeing.
canon /kanɔ̃/ **I** *adj m inv* **droit ~** canon law.
II *nm* **1** (big) gun; cannon; **tirer un coup de ~** to fire a gun; **entendre des coups de ~** to hear cannon fire; **2** (of firearm) barrel; **fusil à ~ scié** sawn-off (GB) or sawed-off (US) shotgun; **3** (Mus) canon; **chanter en ~** to sing in a round; **4** (rule, principle) canon; **5** (in religion) canon; **6**° (verre) glass (of wine).
cañon /kanjɔ̃, kanjɔn/ *nm* canyon.
canonique /kanɔnik/ *adj* **droit ~** canon law; **d'âge ~** (humorous) of a venerable age.
canoniser /kanɔnize/ [1] *vtr* to canonize.
canonnade /kanɔnad/ *nf* cannonade.
canot /kano/ *nm* (small) boat, dinghy; **~ pneumatique** rubber or inflatable dinghy; **~ à rames** rowing boat; **~ de sauvetage** (on ship) lifeboat; (on plane) life raft.
canotage /kanɔtaʒ/ *nm* boating.
canotier /kanɔtje/ *nm* boater.
canson® /kɑ̃sɔ̃/ *nm* **(papier) ~** drawing paper.
cantaloup /kɑ̃talu/ *nm* cantaloupe melon.
cantate /kɑ̃tat/ *nf* cantata.
cantatrice /kɑ̃tatʀis/ *nf* (opera) singer.
cantine /kɑ̃tin/ *nf* **1** canteen (GB), cafeteria; **je ne mange jamais à la ~** (Sch) I never have school lunch; **2** tin trunk.
cantique /kɑ̃tik/ *nm* hymn, canticle.
canton /kɑ̃tɔ̃/ *nm* canton.
cantonais, ~e /kɑ̃tɔnɛ, ɛz/ *adj, nm* Cantonese.
cantonal, ~e[1], *mpl* **-aux** /kɑ̃tɔnal, o/ *adj* cantonal.
cantonale[2] /kɑ̃tɔnal/ *nf* **les ~s** cantonal elections.
cantonner /kɑ̃tɔne/ [1] **I** *vtr* **~ qn dans un lieu** to confine sb to a place; **~ qn dans le rôle de** to reduce sb to the role of.
II se cantonner *v refl* (+ *v être*) **se ~ dans un rôle** to restrict oneself to a role.
cantonnier /kɑ̃tɔnje/ *nm* road-mender.
cantonnière /kɑ̃tɔnjɛʀ/ *nf* pelmet.
canular /kanylaʀ/ *nm* hoax; **monter un ~ à qn** to hoax sb.
canule /kanyl/ *nf* cannula.
canyon = **cañon**.
caoutchouc /kautʃu/ *nm* **1** rubber; **2** rubber plant; **3** rubber band.
caoutchouteux, -euse /kautʃutø, øz/ *adj* rubbery.
cap /kap/ *nm* **1** (in geography) cape; **2** hurdle; **3** mark; **passer le ~ de la cinquantaine** to pass the fifty mark, to turn fifty; **4** course; **maintenir le ~** to hold one's course; **mettre le ~ sur** to head for.
Cap /kap/ *pr n* **le ~** Cape Town.
CAP /seape/ *nm*: *abbr* ▶ **certificat**.
capable /kapabl/ *adj* capable (**de faire** of doing); **il est ~ de tout pour garder sa place** he would do anything to keep his job; **ils sont bien ~s de nous mentir** I wouldn't put it past them to lie to us.
capacité /kapasite/ **I** *nf* **1** ability; **2** capacity.
II capacités *nfpl* (talent) abilities.
■ **~ en droit** *basic legal qualification*.
caparaçon /kapaʀasɔ̃/ *nm* caparison.

cape /kap/ *nf* cape; cloak; **film de ~ et d'épée** swashbuckler.
IDIOMS **rire sous ~** to laugh up one's sleeve.

capeline /kaplin/ *nf* wide-brimmed hat.

CAPES /kapɛs/ *nm* (*abbr* = **certificat d'aptitude professionnelle à l'enseignement secondaire**) *secondary school teaching qualification.*

capharnaüm /kafaʀnaɔm/ *nm* shambles○.

capillaire /kapilɛʀ/ **I** *adj* **1** capillary; **2 soins ~s** hair care.
II *nm* capillary.

capitaine /kapitɛn/ *nm* **1** (Mil) (in army, navy) ≈ captain; (in air force) ≈ flight lieutenant (GB), ≈ captain (US); **2** (Sport) captain.

capitainerie /kapitɛnʀi/ *nf* **1** port authority; **2** port authority buildings.

capital, **~e**[1], *mpl* **-aux** /kapital, o/ **I** *adj* **1** [*importance*] major; [*role, question*] key; **il est ~ de faire** it's essential to do; **2** [*letter*] capital; **3 peine ~e** capital punishment.
II *nm* **1** capital; **2 le ~ humain/industriel** human/industrial resources; **notre ~ santé** our health.
III capitaux *nm pl* capital, funds.

capitale[2] /kapital/ *nf* **1** capital (city); **2** capital (letter); **en ~s d'imprimerie** in block capitals.

capitaliser /kapitalize/ [1] *vtr* to capitalize.

capitalisme /kapitalism/ *nm* capitalism.

capitaliste /kapitalist/ *adj*, *nmf* capitalist.

capitonner /kapitɔne/ [1] *vtr* to pad.

capitulation /kapitylasjɔ̃/ *nf* capitulation (**devant** to).

capituler /kapityle/ [1] *vi* to capitulate (**devant** to).

caporal, *pl* **-aux** /kapɔʀal, o/ *nm* **1** (Mil) (in army) ≈ corporal; (in air force) ≈ corporal (GB), ≈ sergeant (US); **2** (tobacco) caporal.

caporal-chef, *pl* **caporaux-chefs** /kapɔʀalʃɛf, kapɔʀoʃɛf/ *nm* (in army) *rank between corporal and sergeant*; (in air force) *rank between corporal and sergeant* (GB) or *staff sergeant* (US).

capot /kapo/ **I** *adj inv* (Games) **être ~** not to win a trick.
II *nm* (Aut) bonnet (GB), hood (US).

capotage /kapɔtaʒ/ *nm* collapse.

capote /kapɔt/ *nf* **1** great-coat; **2** (of car, pram) hood (GB), top; **3**○ **~ (anglaise)** condom .

capoter /kapɔte/ [1] *vi* **1** to collapse; **2** [*car*] to overturn.

câpre /kɑpʀ/ *nf* caper.

caprice /kapʀis/ *nm* **1** (of person) whim; **céder aux ~s de qn** to indulge sb's whims; **c'est un ~ de la nature** (of plant, animal) it's a freak of nature; **2** tantrum; **faire un ~** to throw a tantrum.

capricieusement /kapʀisjøzmɑ̃/ *adv* capriciously; whimsically.

capricieux, -ieuse /kapʀisjø, øz/ *adj* [*person*] capricious; [*machine*] temperamental; [*weather*] changeable; [*destiny*] fickle.

capricorne /kapʀikɔʀn/ *nm* capricorn beetle.

Capricorne /kapʀikɔʀn/ *pr nm* Capricorn.

capsule /kapsyl/ *nf* **1** (of bottle) cap; top; **2** (Med) capsule; **3 ~ spatiale** space capsule; **4** (of firearm) cap.

capsuler /kapsyle/ [1] *vtr* to put a cap on [*bottle*]; **boisson capsulée** bottled drink.

capter /kapte/ [1] *vtr* **1** to get [*channel, programme*]; to pick up [*signal*]; **2** to catch [*attention*]; **3** to soak up [*light*]; **4** to collect [*water*].

captif, -ive /kaptif, iv/ *adj, nm,f* captive.

captivant, ~e /kaptivɑ̃, ɑ̃t/ *adj* enthralling; gripping; riveting; captivating.

captiver /kaptive/ [1] *vtr* [*beauty*] to captivate; [*music*] to enthrall; [*story, person*] to fascinate.

captivité /kaptivite/ *nf* captivity.

capture /kaptyʀ/ *nf* **1** capture; **2** catch; **une belle ~** a good catch.

capturer /kaptyʀe/ [1] *vtr* to capture.

capuche /kapyʃ/ *nf* hood; **à ~** with a hood.

capuchon /kapyʃɔ̃/ *nm* **1** (of garment) hood; **2** (of pen) cap.

capucin /kapysɛ̃/ *nm* Capuchin friar.

capucine /kapysin/ *nf* nasturtium.

caquet /kakɛ/ *nm* prattle; **rabattre le ~ à qn**○ to put sb in his/her place.

caqueter /kakte/ [20] *vi* [*hen*] to cackle; [*person*] to prattle.

car[1] /kaʀ/ *conj* because, for.

car[2] /kaʀ/ *nm* bus; **~ de police** police van; **~ (de ramassage) scolaire** school bus.

carabine /kaʀabin/ *nf* rifle.

carabiné○, **~e** /kaʀabine/ *adj* [*fever*] raging; [*headache*] ferocious; [*cold*] stinking○.

carabinier /kaʀabinje/ *nm* (in Italy) carabiniere.

Carabosse /kaʀabɔs/ *pr n* **la fée ~** the wicked fairy.

caracoler /kaʀakɔle/ [1] *vi* **1** to be well ahead; **2** [*horse*] to prance; [*rider*] to parade.

caractère /kaʀaktɛʀ/ *nm* **1** character; **~s d'imprimerie** block capitals; **en petits/gros ~s** in small/large print; **2** nature, temperament; **nous n'avons pas le même ~** we are different characters; **avoir mauvais ~** to be bad-tempered; **3** character; **il n'a aucun ~** he's got no backbone; **4** (of house, place) character; **5** characteristic; **6** nature; **à ~ commercial** of a commercial nature.
IDIOMS **avoir un ~ de chien** or **cochon**○, **avoir un sale ~** to have a vile temper; **avoir un ~ en or** to have a delightful nature.

caractériel, -ielle /kaʀakteʀjɛl/ *adj* [*problems*] emotional; [*person*] disturbed.

caractériser /kaʀakteʀize/ [1] **I** *vtr* to characterize.
II se caractériser *v refl* (+ *v être*) to be characterized (**par** by).

caractéristique /kaʀakteʀistik/ **I** *adj* characteristic.
II *nf* characteristics.

carafe /kaʀaf/ *nf* carafe; **vin en ~** wine by the carafe.

caraïbe /kaʀaib/ *adj* Caribbean.

Caraïbes /kaʀaib/ *pr nf pl* Caribbean (islands).
carambolage /kaʀɑ̃bɔlaʒ/ *nm* pile-up.
caramboler: **se caramboler** /kaʀɑ̃bɔle/ [1] *v refl* (+ *v être*) [*vehicles*] to collide.
caramel /kaʀamɛl/ *nm* **1** caramel; **2** toffee (GB), toffy (US); **~ mou** ≈ fudge.
carapace /kaʀapas/ *nf* shell, carapace.
carat /kaʀa/ *nm* carat; **or 18 ~s** 18-carat gold.
caravane /kaʀavan/ *nf* **1** caravan (GB), trailer (US); **2** (convoy) caravan.
caravaning /kaʀavaniŋ/ *nm* caravanning (GB), camping (*in a trailer*) (US).
caravelle /kaʀavɛl/ *nf* (boat) caravel.
carbonade /kaʀbɔnad/ *nf* carbonado.
carbone /kaʀbɔn/ *nm* **1** carbon; **2** carbon paper; **3** sheet of carbon paper.
carbonique /kaʀbɔnik/ *adj* carbonic; **neige ~** carbon dioxide snow, dry ice.
carbonisé, **~e** /kaʀbɔnize/ *adj* burned-out; charred; burned to a cinder.
carboniser /kaʀbɔnize/ [1] *vtr* **1** to carbonize; **2** to reduce [sth] to ashes; **3** to burn [sth] to a cinder.
carburant /kaʀbyʀɑ̃/ *nm* fuel.
carburateur /kaʀbyʀatœʀ/ *nm* carburettor (GB), carburetor (US).
carbure /kaʀbyʀ/ *nm* carbide.
carcan /kaʀkɑ̃/ *nm* **1** (device, punishment) iron collar; **2** **~ administratif** administrative constraints; **le ~ de la discipline** disciplinary rigidity.
carcasse /kaʀkas/ *nf* **1** carcass; **2**○ (of vehicle) shell; (of ship) skeleton.
carcéral, **~e**, *mpl* **-aux** /kaʀseʀal, o/ *adj* prison.
cardan /kaʀdɑ̃/ *nm* universal joint.
cardiaque /kaʀdjak/ *adj* **être ~** to have a heart condition; **crise ~** heart attack.
cardinal, **~e**, *mpl* **-aux** /kaʀdinal, o/ **I** *adj* cardinal.
II *nm* **1** cardinal; **2** cardinal number; **3** (Zool) cardinal (grosbeak), redbird (US).
cardiologie /kaʀdjɔlɔʒi/ *nf* cardiology; **service de ~** cardiology ward.
cardiologue /kaʀdjɔlɔg/ *nmf* cardiologist.
carême /kaʀɛm/ *nm* **le ~** Lent.
carence /kaʀɑ̃s/ *nf* **1** (Med) deficiency; **2** lack (**en** of); **3** **les ~s de la loi** the shortcomings of the law.
carène /kaʀɛn/ *nf* hull (*below the waterline*).
caressant, **~e** /kaʀɛsɑ̃, ɑ̃t/ *adj* **1** affectionate; **2** [*breeze*] soft.
caresse /kaʀɛs/ *nf* caress, stroke; **faire une ~** or **des ~s à** to stroke.
caresser /kaʀese/ [1] *vtr* **1** to stroke, to caress; **~ qn du regard** to look at sb lovingly; **2** to entertain [*hope, idea*]; to cherish [*dream*].
IDIOMS **~ qn dans le sens du poil** to stay on the right side of sb.
cargaison /kaʀgɛzɔ̃/ *nf* **1** cargo; **2**○ load.
cargo /kaʀgo/ *nm* (Naut) freighter, cargo ship; **~ mixte** passenger-cargo ship.

cari /kaʀi/ = **curry**.
caricatural, **~e**, *mpl* **-aux** /kaʀikatyʀal, o/ *adj* **1** grotesque; **2** caricatural.
caricature /kaʀikatyʀ/ *nf* caricature; **c'est une ~ de procès** (figurative) it's a mockery of a trial.
caricaturer /kaʀikatyʀe/ [1] *vtr* to caricature.
caricaturiste /kaʀikatyʀist/ *nmf* caricaturist, cartoonist.
carie /kaʀi/ *nf* **la ~ (dentaire)** (tooth) decay; **avoir une carie** to have a hole in one's tooth.
carié, **~e** /kaʀje/ *adj* decayed.
carier /kaʀje/ [2] **I** *vtr* to cause [sth] to decay [*tooth*].
II se carier *v refl* (+ *v être*) [*tooth*] to decay.
carillon /kaʀijɔ̃/ *nm* **1** (of church) (set of) bells; (tune) chimes; **2** (chiming) clock; (sound) chimes; **3** (door) chimes.
carillonner /kaʀijɔne/ [1] *vi* **1** [*bells*] to ring out, to peal out; **2** (at door) to ring (loudly).
caritatif, **-ive** /kaʀitatif, iv/ *adj* charitable; **une association caritative** a charity.
carlingue /kaʀlɛ̃g/ *nf* (of plane) cabin.
carmélite /kaʀmelit/ *nf* Carmelite nun.
carmin /kaʀmɛ̃/ *nm, adj inv* carmine.
carnage /kaʀnaʒ/ *nm* carnage, massacre; **ils ont fait un véritable ~** they massacred everyone.
carnassier, **-ière** /kaʀnasje, ɛʀ/ **I** *adj* carnivorous.
II *nm* carnivore.
carnaval, *pl* **~s** /kaʀnaval/ *nm* carnival; **jour du ~** carnival day.
carnavalesque /kaʀnavalɛsk/ *adj* grotesque.
carnet /kaʀnɛ/ *nm* **1** notebook; **2** (of tickets, vouchers, stamps) book.
■ **~ de chèques** chequebook (GB), checkbook (US); **~ de correspondance** (Sch) mark book; **~ de santé** health record.
carnivore /kaʀnivɔʀ/ **I** *adj* **1** [*animal*] carnivorous; **2** (of person) **être ~** to be a great meat-eater.
II *nm* carnivore.
carotide /kaʀɔtid/ *adj, nf* carotid.
carotte /kaʀɔt/ **I** *adj inv* carrot-coloured[GB], carroty.
II *nf* carrot.
IDIOMS **manier la ~ et le bâton** to use stick-and-carrot tactics.
carotter○ /kaʀɔte/ [1] *vtr* **~ qch à qn** to cheat sb out of sth.
caroube /kaʀub/ *nf* carob.
caroubier /kaʀubje/ *nm* carob tree.
carpe[1] /kaʀp/ *nm* carpus.
carpe[2] /kaʀp/ *nf* carp.
IDIOMS **il est resté muet comme une ~** he never said a word.
carpette /kaʀpɛt/ *nf* **1** rug; **2**○ doormat○.
carré, **~e** /kaʀe/ **I** *adj* **1** [*shape*] square; **il est ~ d'épaules** he has broad shoulders; **2** [*metre, root*] square.
II *nm* **1** square; **2** (of sky, ground) patch; (of chocolate) piece; **avoir une coupe au ~** to

have one's hair cut in a bob; **~ blanc** *'suitable for adults only' sign on French TV*; **3** (in mathematics) square; **4 ~ d'agneau** rack of lamb; **5** (in cards) **un ~ de dix** the four tens; **6** (Canadian Fr) (in a town) square.

carreau, *pl* **~x** /kaʀo/ *nm* **1** (floor) tile; (wall) tile; **2** window-pane; **faire les ~x** to clean the windows; **3** (on paper) square; (on fabric) check; **4** (in cards) diamonds; **avoir du ~** to be holding diamonds.
IDIOMS **rester sur le ~**° to be killed; to be left high and dry°; **se tenir à ~**° to watch one's step.

carrefour /kaʀfuʀ/ *nm* **1** junction; crossroads; **2** (figurative) crossroads.

carrelage /kaʀlaʒ/ *nm* **1** tiled floor; **2** tiles.

carreler /kaʀle/ [19] *vtr* to tile.

carrelet /kaʀlɛ/ *nm* plaice.

carreleur /kaʀlœʀ/ *nm* tiler.

carrément /kaʀemɑ̃/ *adv* **1 c'est ~ insultant** it's downright insulting; **la situation devient ~ inquiétante** quite frankly the situation is becoming worrying; **il vaut ~ mieux les jeter** it would be better just to throw them out; **2** completely; **dans un cas pareil, appelle ~ la police** in such a case, don't hesitate to call the police; **3** [*ask, say*] straight out; [*express*] clearly; **4 allez-y ~!** go straight ahead!

carrer: **se carrer** /kaʀe/ [1] *v refl* (+ *v être*) **se ~ dans un fauteuil** to ensconce oneself in an armchair.

carrière /kaʀjɛʀ/ *nf* **1** career; **faire ~ dans** to make a career in; **faire toute sa ~ dans qch** to spend one's whole career in sth; **2** quarry; **~ de sable** sandpit.

carriole /kaʀjɔl/ *nf* **1** cart; **2**° jalopy°, car.

carrosse /kaʀɔs/ *nm* (horse-drawn) coach.

carrosserie /kaʀɔsʀi/ *nf* **1** bodywork; **2** coachbuilding; **3** body repair work.

carrossier /kaʀɔsje/ *nm* coachbuilder.

carrure /kaʀyʀ/ *nf* **1** shoulders; **avoir une ~ imposante** to have broad shoulders; **2** calibre[GB].

cartable /kaʀtabl/ *nm* **1** schoolbag, satchel; **2** briefcase.

carte /kaʀt/ *nf* **1** card; **~ à jouer** playing card; **2** pass; **3** map; chart; **4 ~ génétique** genetic map; **5** menu; **manger à la ~** to order from the menu; **repas à la ~** à la carte meal.
■ **~ d'abonnement** season ticket; **~ d'adhérent** membership card; **~ bleue**® credit card; **~ grise** logbook; **~ d'identité** ID card; **~ de lecteur** library card; **~ orange**® season ticket (*in the Paris region*); **~ postale** postcard; **~ à puce** smart card; **~ de réduction** discount card; **~ de séjour** resident's permit; **~ vermeil**® senior citizen's railcard; **~ des vins** wine list; **~ de visite** visiting card; business card; **~ de vœux** greetings card.
IDIOMS **donner ~ blanche à qn** to give sb carte blanche or a free hand.

cartel /kaʀtɛl/ *nm* **1** cartel; **2** coalition.

carter /kaʀtɛʀ/ *nm* (of engine) crankcase; (of gearbox) casing.

cartilage /kaʀtilaʒ/ *nm* **1** (Anat, Zool) cartilage; **2** (Culin) gristle.

cartilagineux, **-euse** /kaʀtilaʒinø, øz/ *adj* **1** (Anat, Zool) cartilaginous; **2** (Culin) gristly.

cartomancie /kaʀtɔmɑ̃si/ *nf* fortune-telling.

cartomancien, **-ienne** /kaʀtɔmɑ̃sjɛ̃, ɛn/ *nm,f* fortune-teller.

carton /kaʀtɔ̃/ *nm* **1** cardboard; **en ~** [*folder*] cardboard; [*cups*] paper; **2** (cardboard) box; **3** card.
■ **~ à dessin** portfolio; **~ ondulé** corrugated cardboard.
IDIOMS **faire un ~**° to do great°.

cartonné, **~e** /kaʀtɔne/ *adj* **couverture ~e** (of book) hard cover.

cartonner° /kaʀtɔne/ [1] *vi* to score.

carton-pâte /kaʀtɔ̃pɑt/ *nm inv* pasteboard.

cartouche /kaʀtuʃ/ *nf* cartridge; (of gas) refill; **~ de cigarettes** carton of cigarettes.
IDIOMS **brûler ses dernières ~s** to play one's last card.

cartouchière /kaʀtuʃjɛʀ/ *nf* cartridge belt.

cas /kɑ/ **I** *nm inv* case; **auquel ~** in which case; **au ~ où il viendrait** in case he comes; **prends ta voiture, au ~ où** take your car, just in case; **en ~ de besoin** if necessary, if need be; **en ~ de décès** in the event of death; **si le ~ se présente** if the case arises; **le ~ échéant** if need be; **dans le ~ contraire, vous devrez...** should the opposite occur, you will have to...; **dans le meilleur/pire des ~** at best/worst; **c'est un ~ à envisager** it's a possibility we should bear in mind; **en aucun ~** under no circumstances, on no account; **c'est le ~ de le dire!** you can say that again!; **être dans le même ~ que qn** to be in the same position as sb; **n'aggrave pas ton ~** don't make things worse for yourself; **un ~ rare** a rare occurrence; **c'est un ~ de renvoi** it's grounds for dismissal.
II en tout cas, en tous les cas *phr* **1** in any case, at any rate; **2** at least.
■ **~ de conscience** moral dilemma; **~ limite** borderline case; **~ social** socially disadvantaged person.
IDIOMS **il a fait grand ~ de son avancement** he made a big thing of his promotion.

casanier, **-ière** /kazanje, ɛʀ/ *adj* [*person*] stay-at-home; [*existence*] unadventurous.

casaque /kazak/ *nf* (of jockey) jersey, silk.

cascade /kaskad/ *nf* **1** waterfall; **2** stunt; **3** series, spate.

cascadeur, **-euse** /kaskadœʀ, øz/ *nm,f* stuntman/stuntwoman.

case /kɑz/ *nf* **1** hut, cabin; **2** (in board games) square; **3** (on form) box.
■ **~ départ** (in board game) start; (figurative) square one; **retour à la ~ départ** back to square one.
IDIOMS **il lui manque une ~**° he's got a screw loose°.

caser° /kɑze/ [1] **I** *vtr* **1** to put, to stick°; **2** to marry off; **3** to put [sb] up; **4** to find a place or job for.

II se caser *v refl* (+ *v être*) to tie the knot○, to get married.

caserne /kazɛʀn/ *nf* barracks.
■ **~ de sapeurs-pompiers** fire station.

casher /kaʃɛʀ/ *adj inv* kosher.

casier /kɑzje/ *nm* **1** (in gym) locker; **~ (de rangement)** rack; **2** pigeonhole; **3** (in fishing) pot; **4 ~ judiciaire** police record.

casino /kazino/ *nm* casino.

casque /kask/ *nm* **1** helmet; crash helmet; safety helmet, hard hat; **2** (Mus) headphones; **3** hairdryer.

casqué, ~e /kaske/ *adj* helmeted.

casquer○ /kaske/ [1] *vi* **1** to foot the bill; **2** to take the rap○.

casquette /kaskɛt/ *nf* cap; **porter plusieurs ~s** (figurative) to wear several hats.

cassant, ~e /kasɑ̃, ɑ̃t/ *adj* **1** brittle; **2** curt, abrupt.

casse[1]○ /kɑs/ *nm* break-in, heist○ (US); **faire un ~** to break into a bank.

casse[2] /kɑs/ *nf* **1** breakage; **2** breaker's yard, scrap yard; **mettre à la ~** to scrap.

cassé, ~e /kase/ **I** *pp* ▶ **casser**.
II *pp adj* [*voice*] hoarse.

casse-cou /kasku/ *nmf inv* daredevil.

casse-croûte /kaskʀut/ *nm inv* snack.

casse-noisettes /kasnwazɛt/, **casse-noix** /kasnwa/ *nm inv* nutcrackers.

casse-pieds○ /kaspje/ *adj inv* **être ~** [*person*] to be a pain in the neck○; to be a bore; [*chore*] to be a drag○ or bore.

casser /kase/ [1] **I** *vtr* **1** to break [*object, bone*]; to crack [*nut*]; **~ les prix** to slash prices; **~ la figure**○ **à qn** to beat sb up○; **2**○ to demote [*soldier, employee*]; **3** to quash [*decision, ruling*].
II *vi* **1** to break; **2**○ [*couple*] to split up.
III se casser *v refl* (+ *v être*) **1** to break; **2 se ~ une** or **la jambe** to break one's leg; **se ~ la figure**○ [*pedestrian*] to fall over (GB) or down; [*venture*] to fail; [*people*] to have a scrap○; **il ne s'est pas cassé la tête**○ he didn't exactly strain himself; **se ~ la tête**○ **à faire** to go out of one's way to do; **3**○ to go away; **'bon, je me casse!'** 'right, I'm off○!'
IDIOMS **~ les pieds**○ **à qn** to annoy sb; **~ la croûte** to eat; **ça casse pas des briques**○ it's nothing to write home about○; **ça te prendra trois heures, à tout ~**○ it'll take you three hours at the very most.

casserole /kasʀɔl/ *nf* saucepan, pan.
IDIOMS **chanter comme une ~**○ to sing atrociously.

casse-tête /kastɛt/ *nm inv* **1** headache, problem; **2** puzzle.

cassette /kasɛt/ *nf* **1** tape, cassette; **2** casket.

casseur /kasœʀ/ *nm* **1** scrap dealer; **2** rioting demonstrator.

cassis /kasis/ *nm inv* **1** blackcurrant; **2** (in road) dip.

cassonade /kasɔnad/ *nf* soft brown sugar.

cassoulet /kasulɛ/ *nm*: *meat and (haricot) bean stew.*

cassure /kasyʀ/ *nf* **1** break; **2** split; **3** (in geology) fracture.

castagnettes /kastaɲɛt/ *nf pl* castanets.

caste /kast/ *nf* **1** caste; **2** (derogatory) (social) class.

castillan, ~e /kastijɑ̃, an/ *adj, nm* Castilian.

castor /kastɔʀ/ *nm* beaver.

castrer /kastʀe/ [1] *vtr* to castrate.

cataclysme /kataklism/ *nm* cataclysm.

catacombes /katakɔ̃b/ *nf pl* catacombs.

catadioptre /katadjɔptʀ/ *nm* reflector.

catalepsie /katalɛpsi/ *nf* catalepsy; **tomber en ~** to have a cataleptic fit.

catalogue /katalɔg/ *nm* catalogue[GB]; **acheter sur ~** to buy by mail order.

cataloguer /katalɔge/ [1] *vtr* **1** to catalogue[GB] [*objects*]; **2** to label [*people*].

catalyse /kataliz/ *nf* catalysis.

catalyser /katalize/ [1] *vtr* to catalyse[GB].

catamaran /katamaʀɑ̃/ *nm* catamaran.

cataplasme /kataplasm/ *nm* poultice.

catapulter /katapylte/ [1] *vtr* to catapult.

cataracte /kataʀakt/ *nf* cataract.

catastrophe /katastʀɔf/ *nf* disaster; **en ~** in a (mad) panic; **atterrissage en ~** crash landing.

catastropher /katastʀɔfe/ [1] *vtr* to devastate.

catastrophique /katastʀɔfik/ *adj* disastrous.

catch /katʃ/ *nm* wrestling.

catcheur, -euse /katʃœʀ, øz/ *nm,f* wrestler.

catéchisme /kateʃism/ *nm* catechism.

catégorie /kategɔʀi/ *nf* **1** category; **de première/deuxième ~** top-/low-grade; **2** (of staff) grade; **3** (in sociology) group; **4** (Sport) class.

catégorique /kategɔʀik/ *adj* **1** adamant; **2** categorical.

caténaire /katenɛʀ/ *adj, nf* catenary.

cathédrale /katedʀal/ *nf* cathedral.

cathode /katɔd/ *nf* cathode.

cathodique /katɔdik/ *adj* cathodic; **tube ~** cathode-ray tube.

catholicisme /katɔlisism/ *nm* (Roman) Catholicism.

catholique /katɔlik/ *adj, nmf* (Roman) Catholic; **ce n'est pas très ~**○ (humorous) it's a bit unorthodox; **ne pas avoir l'air très ~**○ to look a bit dubious.

cauchemar /koʃmaʀ/ *nm* nightmare; **faire un ~** to have a nightmare.

causant○**, ~e** /kozɑ̃, ɑ̃t/ *adj* talkative, chatty○.

cause /koz/ *nf* **1** cause; **il n'y a pas d'effet sans ~** there's no smoke without fire; **2** reason; **sans ~** groundless; **pour ~ de maladie** because of illness; **avoir pour ~ qch** to be caused by sth; **à ~ de** because of; **3** cause; **pour la ~ de la liberté** in the cause of freedom; **4** case; **être en ~** [*system, fact*] to be at issue; [*person*] to be involved; **être hors de ~** to be in the clear; **mettre en ~** to implicate; **mettre hors de ~** (gen) to clear; **remettre en ~** to call [sth] into question [*policy, right*]; to cast doubt on [*project, efficiency*]; to undermine [*efforts*]; **tout est remis en ~** everything has been thrown back into doubt; **remise en ~** (of system) reappraisal; **avoir gain de ~** to win one's case; **donner gain de ~ à** to decide in favour[GB] of.

IDIOMS **en toute connaissance de ~** in full knowledge of the facts.

causer /koze/ [1] **I** *vtr* **1** to cause; **~ des soucis** to give cause for concern; **2**○ to talk about; **~ travail** to talk shop.

II causer de *v+prep* to talk about.

III *vi* to talk **(avec qn** to sb; **à propos de** about); to chat.

causerie /kozʀi/ *nf* **1** talk; **2** chat.

causette○ /kozɛt/ *nf* chat; **faire la ~** to have a little chat.

causeur, -euse /kozœʀ, øz/ *nm,f* conversationalist.

caustique /kostik/ *adj* caustic.

cautériser /koteʀize/ [1] *vtr* to cauterize.

caution /kosjɔ̃/ *nf* **1** (when renting) deposit; (in finance) guarantee, security; (Law) bail; **2** support; **3 sujet à ~** open to doubt.

cautionner /kosjɔne/ [1] *vtr* **1** to give one's support to; **2** to stand surety for.

cavalcade /kavalkad/ *nf* **1** stampede, rush; **2** cavalcade.

cavale○ /kaval/ *nf* escape; **en ~** on the run.

cavaler○ /kavale/ [1] *vi* **1** to rush about; to run; **2** to be a womanizer.

cavalerie /kavalʀi/ *nf* cavalry.

cavaleur○**, -euse** /kavalœʀ, øz/ *adj* **être ~** to be a womanizer/man-chaser.

cavalier, -ière /kavalje, ɛʀ/ **I** *adj* **1** cavalier; **2 allée cavalière** bridle path.

II *nm,f* **1** (horse) rider; **être bon ~** to be a good rider; **2** (dancing) partner.

III *nm* **1** cavalryman; **2** (in chess) knight.

IDIOMS **faire ~ seul** to go it alone; (Sport) to be ahead.

cavalièrement /kavaljɛʀmɑ̃/ *adv* in a cavalier fashion.

cave /kav/ **I** *adj* (literary) [*eyes, cheeks*] hollow, sunken.

II *nf* cellar; **avoir une bonne ~** to have good wines.

caveau, *pl* **~x** /kavo/ *nm* vault.

caverne /kavɛʀn/ *nf* cavern.

caviar /kavjaʀ/ *nm* caviar.

cavité /kavite/ *nf* cavity; **~ buccale** oral cavity.

CB /sebe/ *nf* (*abbr* = **Citizens' Band) bande ~** CB.

CCP /sesepe/ *nm*: *abbr* ▶ **compte**.

CD /sede/ *nm* (*abbr* = **compact disc**) CD.

ce /sə/ **I (cet** /sɛt/ *before vowel or mute h*, **cette** /sɛt/, *pl* **ces** /se/) *adj* **1** this; that; **~ crayon(-ci)** this pencil; **~ livre(-là)** that book; **cette nuit** tonight; last night; **un de ces jours** one of these days; **2**○ **cet entretien, ça s'est bien passé?** how did the interview go?; **3 et pour ces dames?** what are the ladies having?; **4 il n'est pas de ces hommes qui disent** he's not the kind of man to say; **elle a eu cette chance que la corde a tenu** she was lucky in that the rope held; **5 cette arrogance!** what arrogance!; **j'ai un de ces rhumes!** I've got an awful cold!; **tu as de ces idées!** you've got some funny ideas!

II (c' /s/ *before e*) *pron* **qui est-~?** (person seen) who's that?; (on phone) who is it?; **~ faisant** in so doing; **c'est tout dire** that says it all; **fais ~ que tu veux** do what you like; **voilà ~ dont tu as besoin** that's what you need; **c'est ~ à quoi il a fait allusion** that's what he was alluding to; **il a fait faillite, ~ qui n'est pas surprenant** he's gone bankrupt, which is hardly surprising; **il tient à ~ que vous veniez** he's very keen that you should come; **~ que c'est grand!** it's so big!; **qu'est-~ que**○ **j'ai faim!** I'm starving!

CE /seə/ *nm*: *abbr* ▶ **cours**.

ceci /səsi/ *pron* this; **à ~ près** with one slight difference; **à ~ près que** except that; **cet hôtel a ~ de bien que**... one good thing about this hotel is that...

cécité /sesite/ *nf* blindness; **atteint de ~** blind.

céder /sede/ [14] **I** *vtr* **1** to give up [*seat, share*]; to yield [*right*] **(à** to); to make over [*property*] **(à** to); **~ le passage** to give way **(à** to); **~ la place** (figurative) to give way **(à** to); **2** to sell **(à qn** to sb).

II céder à *v+prep* to give in to, to yield to.

III *vi* **1** to give in; **2** [*beam*] to give way; [*handle*] to break off; [*door*] to yield.

cédille /sedij/ *nf* cedilla.

cèdre /sɛdʀ/ *nm* cedar.

CEE /seəə/ *nf*: *abbr* ▶ **communauté**.

ceindre /sɛ̃dʀ/ [55] (literary) **I** *vtr* **~ sa taille d'un ruban** to put or tie a ribbon around one's waist; **les reins ceints d'une serviette** with a towel round his/her waist.

II se ceindre *v refl* (+ *v être*) **se ~ la tête d'un bandeau** to put a headband on.

ceint, ~e /sɛ̃, sɛ̃t/ ▶ **ceindre**.

ceinture /sɛ̃tyʀ/ *nf* **1** belt; **2** waistband; **3** girdle; **4** waist; **avoir de l'eau jusqu'à la ~** to be waist-deep in water; **5** (Sport) waist hold; **~ noire** black belt; **6** ring.

■ **~ de sauvetage** lifebelt; **~ de sécurité** safety or seat belt.

IDIOMS **faire ~**○ to go without; **se serrer la ~** to tighten one's belt.

ceinturer /sɛ̃tyʀe/ [1] *vtr* **1** to encircle; **2** to collar○ [*thief*]; (Sport) to tackle.

ceinturon /sɛ̃tyʀɔ̃/ *nm* belt.

cela /səla/ *pron*

■ **Note** *Cela* and *ça* are equivalent in many cases. See the entry *ça* for more information.
– *Cela* is used in formal contexts and in the expressions shown below.

---

1 that; **quant à ~** as for that; **~ dit/fait** having said/done that; **2** it; that; **~ va sans dire** it or that goes without saying.

IDIOMS **voyez-vous ~!** did you ever hear of such a thing!

célébration /selebʀasjɔ̃/ *nf* celebration.

célèbre /selɛbʀ/ *adj* famous (**par** for); **tristement ~** notorious.

célébrer /selebʀe/ [14] *vtr* **1** to celebrate [*event, mass*]; to perform [*rite*]; **2** to praise [*person*]; to extol [*quality*].

célébrité /selebʀite/ *nf* **1** fame; **2** celebrity.

céleri /sɛlʀi/ *nm* **1** celery; **2** celeriac.

céleri-rave, *pl* **céleris-raves** /selʀiʀav/ *nm* celeriac.

célérité /seleʀite/ *nf* (formal) promptness; **avec ~** promptly.

céleste /selɛst/ *adj* celestial; heavenly; divine.

célibat /seliba/ *nm* **1** single status; **2** celibacy.

célibataire /selibatɛʀ/ **I** *adj* single.

II *nmf* bachelor; single woman; **mère ~** single mother.

celle ▶ **celui**.

celle-ci ▶ **celui-ci**.

celle-là ▶ **celui-là**.

celles-ci ▶ **celui-ci**.

celles-là ▶ **celui-là**.

cellier /selje/ *nm* cellar.

cellophane® /selɔfan/ *nf* cellophane®.

cellulaire /selylɛʀ/ *adj* cell; cellular.

cellule /selyl/ *nf* **1** cell; **2** unit; **~ familiale** family unit.

cellulite /selylit/ *nf* **1** cellulite; **2** cellulitis.

celluloïd® /selylɔid/ *nm* celluloid.

cellulose /selyloz/ *nf* cellulose.

celte /sɛlt/ *adj, nm* Celtic.

Celte /sɛlt/ *nmf* Celt.

celtique /sɛltik/ *adj, nm* Celtic.

celui /səlɥi/, **celle** /sɛl/, *mpl* **ceux** /sø/, *fpl* **celles** /sɛl/ *pron* the one; **le train du matin ou ~ de 17 heures?** the morning train or the 5 o'clock one?; **~ des deux qui finira le premier** the first one to finish; **ceux, celles** those; the ones; **ceux d'entre vous qui veulent partir** those of you who want to leave; **tous ceux qui sont absents** all those who are absent; **ceux qu'il a vendus** the ones he sold; **faire ~ qui n'entend pas** to pretend not to hear.

celui-ci /səlɥisi/, **celle-ci** /sɛlsi/, *mpl* **ceux-ci** /søsi/, *fpl* **celles-ci** /sɛlsi/ *pron* **1** this one; **ceux-ci, celles-ci** these; **2 je n'ai qu'une chose à dire et c'est celle-ci** I have only one thing to say and it's this; **3 elle essaya la fenêtre mais celle-ci était coincée** she tried the window but it was jammed; **il entra, suivi de son père et de son frère; ~ portait un paquet** he came in, followed by his father and his brother; the latter was carrying a parcel.

celui-là /səlɥila/, **celle-là** /sɛlla/, *mpl* **ceux-là** /søla/, *fpl* **celles-là** /sɛlla/ *pron* **1** that one; **ceux-là, celles-là** those (ones); **2 si je n'ai qu'un conseil à te donner, c'est ~** if I only have one piece of advice for you, it's this; **3** the former; **4 il fit une autre proposition, plus réaliste celle-là** he made another proposal, a more realistic one this time; **5**○ **il exagère, ~!** that guy's pushing it a bit○!; **~, alors!** (in admiration) what a man!; (in irritation) that man!; **regardez-moi ~: il n'est même pas rasé!** look at him! he hasn't even shaved!; **6**○ **elle est bien bonne, celle-là!** that's a good one!; **je ne m'attendais pas à celle-là** I didn't expect that!; **~ même** the very one.

cendre /sɑ̃dʀ/ *nf* ash; **cuites sous la ~** baked in the embers.

cendré, ~e /sɑ̃dʀe/ *adj* ash (grey (GB) or gray (US)); **blond ~** ash blond.

cendrier /sɑ̃dʀije/ *nm* ashtray.

Cendrillon /sɑ̃dʀijɔ̃/ *pr n* Cinderella.

Cène /sɛn/ *nf* **la ~** the Last Supper.

censé, ~e /sɑ̃se/ *adj* **être ~ faire** to be supposed to do.

censeur /sɑ̃sœʀ/ *nm* **1** censor; **2** critic; **3** (Sch) ≈ deputy head.

censure /sɑ̃syʀ/ *nf* **1** censorship; **2** board of censors; **3** censure.

censurer /sɑ̃syʀe/ [1] *vtr* **1** to censor; **2** to ban.

cent /sɑ̃/ **I** *adj* a hundred, one hundred.

II *nm* hundred; **un ~ d'œufs** a or one hundred eggs.

III pour cent *phr* per cent; **dix à vingt pour ~** between ten and twenty per cent.

IDIOMS **faire les ~ pas** to pace up and down; **être aux ~ coups**○ to be worried sick○; **attendre ~ sept ans**○ to wait for ages.

centaine /sɑ̃tɛn/ *nf* **1** hundred; **2** about a hundred; **3 dépasser la ~** to be over a hundred (years old).

centaure /sɑ̃tɔʀ/ *nm* centaur.

centenaire /sɑ̃tnɛʀ/ **I** *adj* hundred-year-old, centenarian.

II *nmf* **c'est une ~** she's a hundred years old.

III *nm* centenary, centennial.

centième /sɑ̃tjɛm/ *adj* hundredth.

centilitre /sɑ̃tilitʀ/ *nm* centilitre[GB].

centime /sɑ̃tim/ *nm* centime; **je n'ai pas un ~** I have no money.

centimètre /sɑ̃timɛtʀ/ *nm* **1** centimetre[GB]; **~ carré** square centimetre[GB]; **~ cube** cubic centimetre[GB]; **2 ne pas avancer d'un ~** not to move an inch; **3** tape measure.

central, ~e[1], *mpl* **-aux** /sɑ̃tʀal, o/ **I** *adj* **1** central; **court ~** (in tennis) centre[GB] court; **ordinateur ~** host computer; **2** main.

II *nm* **~ (téléphonique)** (telephone) exchange.

centrale[2] /sɑ̃tʀal/ *nf* **1** power station; **2** prison.

centralisateur, -trice /sɑ̃tʀalizatœʀ, tʀis/ *adj* centralizing.

centraliser /sɑ̃tʀalize/ [1] *vtr* to centralize.

centre /sɑ̃tʀ/ *nm* centre[GB]; **en plein ~** right in the centre[GB]; **il se prend pour le ~ du monde** he thinks the whole world revolves around him. ■ **~ d'accueil** reception centre[GB]; **~ commercial** shopping centre[GB]; **~ hospitalier** hospital complex; **~ sportif** sports centre[GB]; **~ universitaire** university.

centrer /sɑ̃tʀe/ [1] *vtr* to centre[GB]; **être centré sur qch** to be centred[GB] around sth.
centre-ville, *pl* **centres-villes** /sɑ̃tʀəvil/ *nm* town centre[GB], city centre[GB].
centrifuge /sɑ̃tʀifyʒ/ *adj* centrifugal.
centrifugeuse /sɑ̃tʀifyʒøz/ *nf* **1** juice extractor; **2** centrifuge.
centriste /sɑ̃tʀist/ *adj, nmf* centrist.
centuple /sɑ̃typl/ *nm* **dix mille est le ~ de cent** ten thousand is a hundred times one hundred; **au ~** a hundred times over.
centupler /sɑ̃typle/ [1] *vtr, vi* to increase a hundredfold.
cep /sɛp/ *nm* **~ (de vigne)** vine stock.
cèpe /sɛp/ *nm* cep.
cependant /səpɑ̃dɑ̃/ **I** *conj* yet, however.
II cependant que *phr* whereas, while.
céramique /seʀamik/ *nf* **1** ceramic; **2** ceramics.
cerbère /sɛʀbɛʀ/ *nm* minder; watchdog.
cerceau, *pl* **~x** /sɛʀso/ *nm* hoop; **pousser un ~** to bowl a hoop.
cercle /sɛʀkl/ *nm* **1** circle; **en ~** in a circle; **décrire des ~s** [*plane, bird*] to circle (overhead); **faire ~ autour de qn** to gather around sb; **le ~ de famille** the family circle; **2** circle, society; club; **3** hoop.
cercler /sɛʀkle/ [1] *vtr* to hoop [*barrel*]; **les noms cerclés en rouge** the names circled in red.
cercueil /sɛʀkœj/ *nm* coffin.
céréale /seʀeal/ *nf* cereal, grain.
cérébral, **~e**, *mpl* **-aux** /seʀebʀal, o/ **I** *adj* **1** cerebral; **2** intellectual.
II *nm,f* cerebral type.
cérémonial, *pl* **~s** /seʀemɔnjal/ *nm* ceremonial.
cérémonie /seʀemɔni/ **I** *nf* ceremony; **~ d'ouverture** opening ceremony; **tenue** or **habit de ~** ceremonial dress.
II cérémonies *nf pl* ceremony; **faire des ~s** to stand on ceremony; **sans ~s** [*dinner, invitation*] informal; [*receive*] informally.
cérémonieux, **-ieuse** /seʀemɔnjø, øz/ *adj* ceremonious; **d'un air ~** ceremoniously.
cerf /sɛʀ/ *nm* stag.
cerfeuil /sɛʀfœj/ *nm* chervil.
cerf-volant, *pl* **cerfs-volants** /sɛʀvɔlɑ̃/ *nm* **1** kite; **2** stag beetle.
cerise /s(ə)ʀiz/ **I** *adj inv* **(rouge) ~** cherry-red, cerise.
II *nf* cherry.
cerisier /s(ə)ʀizje/ *nm* **1** cherry (tree); **2** cherrywood.
cerne /sɛʀn/ *nm* ring.
cerné, **~e** /sɛʀne/ **I** *pp* ▶ **cerner**.
II *pp adj* **avoir les yeux ~s** to have rings under one's eyes.
cerneau, *pl* **~x** /sɛʀno/ *nm* **~ (de noix)** walnut half.
cerner /sɛʀne/ [1] *vtr* **1** to surround; **2** to define, to delimit [*issue, problem*]; to figure out [*person*]; to determine [*personality, needs*]; **3** to outline [*drawing*] (**de** with).
certain, **~e** /sɛʀtɛ̃, ɛn/ **I** *adj* **1 être ~ de** to be certain or sure of; **2** [*fact*] certain, sure; [*date, price, influence*] definite; [*rate*] fixed; **tenir pour ~** to be certain of; **c'est sûr et ~**○ it's definite; **un homme d'un âge ~** a man of advanced years.
II *det* **1 elle restera un ~ temps** she'll stay for some time or for a while; **un ~ nombre d'erreurs** a certain number of mistakes; **dans une ~e mesure** to a certain or to some extent; **d'une ~e manière** in a way; **2** (as intensifier) some; **il faut un ~ culot**○ **pour...** it takes some nerve○ to...; **il avait déjà un ~ âge** he was already getting on in years.
III certains, **certaines** *det pl* some; **à ~s moments** sometimes, at times.
IV certains, **certaines** *pron pl* some people; **~s d'entre eux** some of them.
certainement /sɛʀtɛnmɑ̃/ *adv* **1** most probably; **c'est ~ quelqu'un de très compétent** he/she must be a very competent person; **2** certainly; **mais ~!** certainly!, of course!
certes /sɛʀt/ *adv* admittedly; **ce ne sera ~ pas facile mais...** admittedly it won't be easy but...; **~ non!** certainly not!
certificat /sɛʀtifika/ *nm* **1** certificate; **2** testimonial.
■ **~ d'aptitude professionnelle, CAP** *vocational training qualification*; **~ de bonne vie et mœurs** ≈ character reference; **~ de décès** death certificate; **~ médical** medical certificate; **~ de naissance** birth certificate; **~ de résidence** proof of residence; **~ de scolarité** proof of attendance (*at school or university*); **~ de travail** *document from a previous employer giving dates and nature of employment*.
certifié, **~e** /sɛʀtifje/ *adj* **professeur ~** fully qualified teacher.
certifier /sɛʀtifje/ [2] *vtr* **1** to certify, to authenticate; **~ conforme** to authenticate; **copie certifiée conforme** certified copy; **2 elle m'a certifié que** she assured me that.
certitude /sɛʀtityd/ *nf* **1** certainty; **on sait avec ~ que** we know for certain that; **2** conviction; **avoir la ~ que/de faire** to be certain that/of doing.
cérumen /seʀymɛn/ *nm* earwax.
cerveau, *pl* **~x** /sɛʀvo/ *nm* **1** brain; **2** mind; **3** (person) brain○; **exode** or **fuite des ~x** brain drain; **la chasse aux ~x** talent hunting; **c'est un ~** he/she has an outstanding mind; **4** brains (**de** behind, of); nerve centre[GB].
IDIOMS **avoir le ~ fêlé**○ or **dérangé** to be cracked○ or deranged.
cervelas /sɛʀvəla/ *nm* saveloy.
cervelet /sɛʀvəlɛ/ *nm* cerebellum.
cervelle /sɛʀvɛl/ *nf* **1** brains; **~ de veau** (Culin) calf's brains; **2**○ **il n'a rien dans la ~** he's brainless; **~ d'oiseau** birdbrain○.
cervical, **~e**, *mpl* **-aux** /sɛʀvikal, o/ *adj* cervical.
ces ▶ **ce I**.

CES /seəɛs/ *nm* **1** *abbr* ▶ **collège**; **2** *abbr* ▶ **contrat**.

césar /sezaʀ/ *nm* **1** César (*film award*); **2 Jules César** Julius Caesar.

césarienne /sezaʀjɛn/ *nf* caesarian (section).

cessation /sesasjɔ̃/ *nf* suspension.

cesse /sɛs/ *nf* **sans ~** constantly; **un nombre sans ~ grandissant** an ever increasing number.

cesser /sese/ [1] I *vtr* to stop, to cease; to end; **~ toute activité** [*company*] to cease trading; **~ de faire** to stop doing; to give up doing.
II *vi* [*activity*] to cease; [*wind*] to drop; [*rain*] to stop; **faire ~** to put an end or a stop to, to end.

cessez-le-feu /seselfø/ *nm inv* ceasefire.

cession /sesjɔ̃/ *nf* transfer.

c'est-à-dire /setadiʀ/ *phr* **1** that is (to say); **2 ~ que** which means (that); **'le travail est trop dur'—'~?'** 'the work is too hard'—'what do you mean?'; **3 ~ que** well, actually; **'il ne se rend pas compte'—'~ qu'il est jeune'** 'he doesn't realize'—'well, you know, he's young'.

cet ▶ **ce** I.

CET /seəte/ *nm*: *abbr* ▶ **collège**.

cette ▶ **ce**.

ceux ▶ **celui**.

ceux-ci ▶ **celui-ci**.

ceux-là ▶ **celui-là**.

CFAO /seɛfao/ *nf* (*abbr* = **conception et fabrication assistées par ordinateur**) CADCAM.

chacal, *pl* **~s** /ʃakal/ *nm* jackal.

chacun, **~e** /ʃakœ̃, yn/ *pron* **1** each (one); **ils ont ~ sa** or **leur chambre** they each have their own room; **nous avons ~ pris notre veste** we all took our jackets; **2** everyone; **~ ses goûts** every man to his taste; **~ pour soi** every man for himself.

chagrin, **~e** /ʃagʀɛ̃, in/ I *adj* despondent.
II *nm* grief; **faire du ~ à qn** to cause sb grief; **avoir du ~** to be sad; **avoir un gros ~** to be very upset; **~ d'amour** unhappy love affair.

chagriner /ʃagʀine/ [1] *vtr* **1** to pain, to grieve; **2** to worry.

chahut /ʃay/ *nm* racket○; **faire du ~** [*party-goer*] to make a racket○; [*pupil*] to play up the teacher.

chahuter /ʃayte/ [1] I *vtr* to play up [*teacher*]; to heckle [*speaker*].
II *vi* to mess around.

chahuteur, **-euse** /ʃaytœʀ, øz/ *adj* disruptive.

chaîne /ʃɛn/ I *nf* **1** chain; **attacher qn avec des ~s** to chain sb up; **des catastrophes en ~** a series of disasters; **réaction en ~** chain reaction; **2** assembly line; **produire (qch) à la ~** to mass-produce (sth); **3** network; **~ de solidarité** support network; **4 ~ (de télévision)** (television) channel; **5 ~ hi-fi/stéréo** hi-fi/stereo system; **~ compacte** music centre[GB].
II **chaînes** *nf pl* snow chains.
■ **~ de fabrication** production line; **~ de montage** assembly line.

chaînette /ʃɛnɛt/ *nf* chain.

chaînon /ʃɛnɔ̃/ *nm* link; **~ manquant** missing link.

chair /ʃɛʀ/ I *adj inv* flesh-coloured[GB].
II *nf* flesh; meat; **bien en ~** plump; **~ à saucisses** sausage meat.
■ **~ de poule** gooseflesh, goose pimples; **donner la ~ de poule à qn** [*cold*] to give sb gooseflesh; [*fear*] to make sb's flesh creep.

chaire /ʃɛʀ/ *nf* **1** pulpit; **2** (at university) chair; **3** rostrum.

chaise /ʃɛz/ *nf* chair.
■ **~ haute** high-chair; **~ longue** deck-chair; **~ roulante** wheelchair.
IDIOMS **être assis entre deux ~s** to be in an awkward position.

châle /ʃɑl/ *nm* shawl.

chalet /ʃalɛ/ *nm* chalet.

chaleur /ʃalœʀ/ I *nf* **1** heat; warmth; **coup de ~** heat stroke; **on étouffe de ~, ici!** it's sweltering in here!; **~ animale** body heat; **2** (of person, welcome, colour) warmth; **3** (Zool) **(être) en ~** (to be) on heat.
II **chaleurs** *nf pl* **les grandes ~s** the hot season.

chaleureusement /ʃaløʀøzmɑ̃/ *adv* [*thank*] warmly.

chaleureux, **-euse** /ʃaløʀø, øz/ *adj* [*person, greeting*] warm; [*audience, applause*] enthusiastic.

challenge /ʃalɑ̃ʒ/ *nm*
(Sport) tournament; **2** trophy.

challenge(u)r /ʃalɑ̃ʒœʀ/ *nm* challenger.

chaloupe /ʃalup/ *nf* **1** rowing boat (GB), rowboat (US); **2** (motor) launch.

chalumeau, *pl* **~x** /ʃalymo/ *nm* blowtorch; welding torch.

chalut /ʃaly/ *nm* trawl; **pêcher (qch) au ~** to trawl (for sth).

chalutier /ʃalytje/ *nm* **1** trawler; **2** trawlerman.

chamailler○: **se chamailler** /ʃamaje/ [1] *v refl* (+ *v être*) to squabble.

chamailleur○, **-euse** /ʃamajœʀ, øz/ *adj* quarrelsome.

chamarré, **~e** /ʃamaʀe/ *adj* **1** richly ornamented; **2** brightly coloured[GB].

chambard○ /ʃɑ̃baʀ/ *nm* **1** din, racket○; **2** upheaval.

chambardement○ /ʃɑ̃baʀdəmɑ̃/ *nm* **1** shake-up○; **2** mess.

chambarder○ /ʃɑ̃baʀde/ [1] *vtr* to turn [sth] upside down [*house*].

chambouler○ /ʃɑ̃bule/ [1] *vtr* **1** to upset [*plans, routine*]; **2** to turn [sth] upside down [*house*]; to mess [sth] up [*papers*].

chambranle /ʃɑ̃bʀɑ̃l/ *nm* frame.

chambre /ʃɑ̃bʀ/ *nf* **1** bedroom; room; **~ pour une personne** single room; **~ pour deux personnes** double room; **~ à deux lits** twin room; **faire ~ à part** to sleep in separate rooms; **avez-vous une ~ de libre?** have you got any vacancies?; **2 musique de ~** chamber music; **3** (in parliament) house; **4** (in administration) chamber.
■ **~ à air** inner tube; **~ d'amis** guest

room; **~ de commerce** chamber of commerce; **~ à coucher** bedroom; bedroom suite; **~ d'hôte** ≈ room in a guest house; **'~s d'hôte'** 'bed and breakfast'; **~ noire** camera obscura; darkroom.

chambrée /ʃɑ̃bʀe/ *nf* (Mil) soldiers occupying barrack room.

chambrer /ʃɑ̃bʀe/ [1] *vtr* to bring [sth] to room temperature [*wine*].

chameau, *pl* **~x** /ʃamo/ *nm* **1** (Zool) camel; **2**○ nasty person.

chamelier /ʃaməlje/ *nm* camel driver.

chamelle /ʃamɛl/ *nf* she-camel.

chamois /ʃamwa/ *nm* (Zool) chamois.

champ /ʃɑ̃/ **I** *nm* field; (figurative) field, domain; **en pleins ~s** in open country; **le ~ est libre** the coast is clear; (figurative) the way is clear; **avoir le ~ libre** to have a free hand.

II à tout bout de champ○ *phr* all the time.

■ **~ de bataille** battlefield; **~ de courses** racetrack; **~ de foire** fairground.

champagne /ʃɑ̃paɲ/ *nm* champagne.

champagnisé /ʃɑ̃paɲize/ *nf* **vins ~s** sparkling wines.

champêtre /ʃɑ̃pɛtʀ/ *adj* [*scene*] rural; **bal ~** village dance; **déjeuner ~** country picnic.

champignon /ʃɑ̃piɲɔ̃/ *nm* **1** (Culin) mushroom; **~ vénéneux** toadstool; **aller aux ~s** to go mushroom picking; **2** (Bot, Med) fungus; **3**○ throttle, accelerator.

■ **~ atomique** mushroom cloud; **~ de Paris** button mushroom (GB), champignon (US).

champion, -ionne /ʃɑ̃pjɔ̃, ɔn/ *nm,f* champion; **le ~ en titre** the titleholder; **pays ~**○ **de la lutte contre la drogue** country which leads the field in the fight against drugs.

championnat /ʃɑ̃pjɔna/ *nm* championship.

chance /ʃɑ̃s/ *nf* **1** (good) luck; **pas de ~, tu as perdu!** hard luck, you've lost!; **coup de ~** stroke of luck; **avoir de la ~** to be lucky; **avoir la ~ de trouver une maison** to be lucky enough to find a house; **par ~** luckily, fortunately; **tenter** or **courir sa ~** to try one's luck; **2** chance (**de** of); **il y a de fortes ~s (pour) que** there's every chance that; **il a ses ~s** he stands a good chance; **mettre toutes les ~s de son côté** to take no chances; **'il va pleuvoir?'—'il y a des ~s'** 'is it going to rain?'—'probably'; **3** chance, opportunity; **la ~ de ma vie** the chance of a lifetime.

chancelant, ~e /ʃɑ̃slɑ̃, ɑ̃t/ *adj* **1** [*gait*] unsteady; [*object*] rickety, shaky; [*person*] staggering; **d'un pas ~** unsteadily; **2** [*courage, faith*] wavering; [*morale*] flagging; [*will*] faltering; [*empire*] tottering.

chanceler /ʃɑ̃sle/ [19] *vi* **1** [*person*] to stagger; [*object*] to wobble; **2** [*courage*] to waver; **3** [*empire*] to totter; [*health*] to be precarious.

chancelier /ʃɑ̃səlje/ *nm* **1** chancellor; **2** chancery.

chanceux, -euse /ʃɑ̃sø, øz/ *adj* lucky.

chancre /ʃɑ̃kʀ/ *nm* canker.

chandail /ʃɑ̃daj/ *nm* sweater, jumper (GB).

chandeleur /ʃɑ̃dlœʀ/ *nf* Candlemas.

chandelier /ʃɑ̃dəlje/ *nm* candlestick; candelabra[GB].

chandelle /ʃɑ̃dɛl/ *nf* **1** candle; **un dîner aux ~s** a candlelit dinner; **2** (Sport) shoulder stand.

IDIOMS **devoir une fière ~ à** to be hugely indebted to; **faire des économies de bouts de ~s** to make cheeseparing economies; **tenir la ~**○ to play gooseberry○.

change /ʃɑ̃ʒ/ *nm* **1** exchange rate; **2** (foreign) exchange; **perdre au ~** (figurative) to lose out.

changeant, ~e /ʃɑ̃ʒɑ̃, ɑ̃t/ *adj* changeable, fickle.

changement /ʃɑ̃ʒmɑ̃/ *nm* **1** change (**de** of); **2** change (**de** in); **~ en mieux/pire** change for the better/worse; **3** (of train, plane) change.

changer /ʃɑ̃ʒe/ [13] **I** *vtr* **1** to exchange [*object*] (**pour, contre** for); to change [*secretary, job*] (**pour, contre** for); **2** to change [*money*]; to cash [*traveller's cheque*]; **3** to change [*purchased item*] (**pour** for); **4 ~ qch de place** to move sth; **5** to change [*situation, appearance*]; **cette coiffure te change** you look different with your hair like that; **qu'est-ce que ça change?** what difference does it make?; **cela ne change rien au fait que** that doesn't alter the fact that; **on ne peut rien y ~** we can't do anything about it; **6 ~ qch/qn en** to turn sth/sb into; **7 cela nous change de la pluie** it makes a change from the rain; **pour ne pas ~** as usual; **8** to change [*baby*].

II changer de *v+prep* (gen) to change; **~ de train** to change trains; **~ d'avis** to change one's mind; **~ de domicile** to move house; **~ de trottoir** to cross over to the other side of the road; **nous avons changé de route au retour** we came back by a different route.

III *vi* to change; **~ en bien/mal** to change for the better/worse.

IV se changer *v refl* (+ *v être*) **1** to get changed, to change one's clothes; **2 se ~ en** to turn or change into.

chanoine /ʃanwan/ *nm* canon.

chanson /ʃɑ̃sɔ̃/ *nf* **1** song; **vedette de la ~** singing star; **2 c'est toujours la même ~**○ it's always the same old story; **je connais la ~**○ I've heard it all before; **3** (in literature) song, epic (poem).

chansonnette /ʃɑ̃sɔnɛt/ *nf* light-hearted song.

chansonnier, -ière /ʃɑ̃sɔnje, ɛʀ/ *nm,f* cabaret artist.

chant /ʃɑ̃/ *nm* **1** singing; **2** (of bird, whale) song; (of cock) crow(ing); (of cricket) chirp(ing); (of cicada) shrilling; **3** song; **4** ode; canto.

■ **~ du cygne** swansong; **~ grégorien** Gregorian chant; **~ de Noël** Christmas carol.

chantage /ʃɑ̃taʒ/ *nm* blackmail; **faire du ~ à qn** to blackmail sb.

chantant, ~e /ʃɑ̃tɑ̃, ɑ̃t/ *adj* [*voice, accent*] singsong.

chanter /ʃɑ̃te/ [1] **I** *vtr* **1** to sing; **2** to sing (of) [*exploit*]; **3**○ **qu'est-ce qu'il nous chante?** what's he talking about?

II chanter à○ *v+prep* **ça te chante d'y aller?** do you fancy○ going?

III *vi* **1** to sing; **~ juste/faux** to sing in tune/

out of tune; **2** [*bird*] to sing; [*cock*] to crow; [*cicada*] to shrill; **3 faire ~ qn** to blackmail sb.

chanteur, -euse /ʃɑ̃tœʀ, øz/ *nm,f* singer; (in band) vocalist.

chantier /ʃɑ̃tje/ *nm* **1** building site; **en ~** [*building*] under construction; **notre maison sera en ~ tout l'hiver** the work on our house will go on all winter; **mettre en ~** to undertake [*project*]; **2** builder's yard; **3**○ mess, shambles○.

chantonner /ʃɑ̃tɔne/ [1] *vtr, vi* to hum (to oneself).

chanvre /ʃɑ̃vʀ/ *nm* hemp.

chaos /kao/ *nm inv* chaos.

chaotique /kaɔtik/ *adj* chaotic.

chaparder○ /ʃapaʀde/ [1] *vtr* to pinch○ (**à qn** from sb).

chapeau, *pl* **~x** /ʃapo/ **I** *nm* **1** hat; **2** (of cake) top; (of lamp) shade.

II○ *excl* well done!

■ **~ haut de forme** top hat; **~ melon** bowler (hat) (GB), derby (hat) (US); **~ de roue** (Aut) hubcap; **démarrer sur les ~x de roues**○ [*car, driver*] to shoot off at top speed.

IDIOMS **tirer son ~ à** to take one's hat off to.

chapeauter○ /ʃapote/ [1] *vtr* [*person*] to head [*team*].

chapelet /ʃaplɛ/ *nm* **1** rosary; **2** (of onions, insults, islands) string; (of bombs) stick.

chapelle /ʃapɛl/ *nf* **1** chapel; **2** clique, coterie.

chapelure /ʃaplyʀ/ *nf* breadcrumbs.

chaperon /ʃapʀɔ̃/ *nm* **1** chaperon(e); **2 le Petit Chaperon rouge** Little Red Riding Hood.

chapiteau, *pl* **~x** /ʃapito/ *nm* **1** marquee (GB), tent; (of circus) big top; **2** (of pillar) capital.

chapitre /ʃapitʀ/ *nm* **1** (of book) chapter; **2** subject.

IDIOMS **avoir voix au ~** to have a say in the matter.

chaque /ʃak/ *det* each, every; **~ chose en son temps!** all in good time!

char /ʃaʀ/ *nm* **1** (Mil) tank; **2** chariot; **3** (in carnival) float.

■ **~ d'assaut** (Mil) tank; **~ à bœufs** oxcart; **~ à voile** (Sport) sand yacht; ice yacht.

charabia○ /ʃaʀabja/ *nm* gobbledygook○, double Dutch.

charade /ʃaʀad/ *nf* riddle.

charbon /ʃaʀbɔ̃/ *nm* coal; **~ de bois** charcoal.

IDIOMS **être sur des ~s ardents** to be like a cat on a hot tin roof.

charbonnier, -ière /ʃaʀbɔnje, ɛʀ/ *nm,f* coalman/coalwoman.

charcuter○ /ʃaʀkyte/ [1] *vtr* **se faire ~** [*patient*] to get hacked about.

charcuterie /ʃaʀkytʀi/ *nf* **1** cooked pork meats; **2** pork butcher's.

charcutier, -ière /ʃaʀkytje, ɛʀ/ *nm,f* pork butcher.

chardon /ʃaʀdɔ̃/ *nm* thistle.

charge /ʃaʀʒ/ **I** *nf* **1** burden, load; (of vehicle) load; (of ship) cargo, freight; **prendre qn en ~** [*taxi*] to take sb as a passenger; **prise en ~** (in taxi) minimum fare; **2 avoir la ~ de qn/qch** to be responsible for sb/sth; **avoir trois enfants à ~** to have three children to support; **prendre en ~** [*guardian*] to take charge of [*child*]; [*social security system*] to accept financial responsibility for [*sick person*]; to take care of [*fees, expenses*]; **se prendre en ~** to take care of oneself; **3 ~ de notaire** ≈ solicitor's office; **4** (legal) charge; evidence; **5** (Mil) charge; **6** (of explosives) charge.

II charges *nf pl* **1** expenses, costs; **2** (payable by tenant) service charges.

■ **~s locatives** service charges (*payable by a tenant*); **~s patronales** employer's social security contributions.

IDIOMS **revenir à la ~** to try again.

chargement /ʃaʀʒəmɑ̃/ *nm* **1** (goods) load; cargo; **2** (action) loading.

charger /ʃaʀʒe/ [13] **I** *vtr* **1** to load; **2** to charge [*battery*]; **3 ~ qn de faire** to give sb the responsibility of doing; **elle m'a chargé de vous transmettre ses amitiés** she asked me to give you her regards; **c'est lui qui est chargé de l'enquête** he is in charge of the investigation; **4** to bring evidence against [*accused*]; **5** [*police*] to charge at [*crowd*].

II se charger *v refl* (+ *v être*) **se ~ de** to take responsibility for; **je m'en charge** I'll see to it.

chargeur /ʃaʀʒœʀ/ *nm* **1** (Mil) magazine; **2** (of camera) cartridge; **3** (Comput) loader.

chariot /ʃaʀjo/ *nm* **1** trolley (GB), cart (US); **2** truck; **3** waggon[GB]; **4** (of typewriter) carriage.

charisme /kaʀism/ *nm* charisma.

charitable /ʃaʀitabl/ *adj* charitable; **tendre une main ~ à** to lend a helping hand to.

charité /ʃaʀite/ *nf* **1** charity; **faire la ~ à qn** to give sb charity; **2 par (pure) ~** out of the kindness of one's heart.

IDIOMS **~ bien ordonnée commence par soi-même** (Proverb) charity begins at home .

charlatan /ʃaʀlatɑ̃/ *nm* **1** quack○; **2** con man; **3** (politician) fraud.

charlot○ /ʃaʀlo/ *nm* clown; **arrête de faire le ~!** stop clowning!

charlotte /ʃaʀlɔt/ *nf* **1** (Culin) charlotte; **2** mobcap.

charmant, ~e /ʃaʀmɑ̃, ɑ̃t/ *adj* (gen, ironic) charming.

charme /ʃaʀm/ **I** *nm* **1** charm; **faire du ~ à qn** to make eyes at sb; **cela a le ~ de la nouveauté** it has (a certain) novelty value; **cela ne manque pas de ~** (lifestyle, novel) it's not without its charms; (proposition) it's not unattractive; **2** spell.

II charmes *nm pl* (euphemistic) physical attributes (euphemistic).

IDIOMS **se porter comme un ~** to be as fit as a fiddle.

charmer /ʃaʀme/ [1] *vtr* to charm.

charmeur, -euse /ʃaʀmœʀ, øz/ **I** *adj* winning, engaging.

II *nm,f* charmer; **~ de serpents** snake charmer.

charnel, **-elle** /ʃaʀnɛl/ *adj* [*pleasures, love*] carnal.

charnier /ʃaʀnje/ *nm* mass grave.

charnière /ʃaʀnjɛʀ/ *nf* **1** hinge; **2** (figurative) bridge (**entre** between); junction; **époque(-)~** transitional period; **rôle(-)~** pivotal role.

charnu, **~e** /ʃaʀny/ *adj* (gen) plump; [*lip*] fleshy, thick.

charogne /ʃaʀɔɲ/ *nf* rotting carcass; rotting corpse.

charpente /ʃaʀpɑ̃t/ *nf* (of roof) roof structure; (of building) framework; (of boat) structure; (of person) build.

charpentier /ʃaʀpɑ̃tje/ *nm* carpenter.

charpie /ʃaʀpi/ *nf* **réduire** or **mettre qch en ~** to tear sth to shreds.

charretier /ʃaʀtje/ *nm* carter.

IDIOMS **jurer comme un ~** to swear like a trooper.

charrette /ʃaʀɛt/ *nf* cart; **~ à bras** handcart, barrow.

charrier /ʃaʀje/ [2] **I** *vtr* **1** to carry, to haul; **2** [*river*] to carry [sth] along; **3**° to tease [sb] unmercifully.

II° *vi* to go too far; **faut pas ~!** that's a bit much! or a bit rich° (GB)!

charrue /ʃaʀy/ *nf* plough, plow (US).

IDIOMS **mettre la ~ avant les bœufs** to put the cart before the horse.

charte /ʃaʀt/ *nf* charter.

charter /ʃaʀtɛʀ/ *adj inv* [*plane, flight*] charter.

chasse /ʃas/ *nf* **1** hunting; shooting; **~ au trésor** treasure hunt; **la ~ est ouverte/fermée** it's the open/closed season; **2 ~ gardée** private hunting (ground); (figurative) preserve; **3 donner la ~ à**, **prendre en ~** to chase; **faire la ~ aux trafiquants** to hunt down traffickers.

■ **~ à courre** hunting; **~ d'eau** (toilet) flush; **tirer la ~** to pull the chain; **~ sous-marine** (Sport) harpoon fishing, harpooning.

IDIOMS **qui va à la ~ perd sa place** (Proverb) leave your place and you lose it.

chassé-croisé, *pl* **chassés-croisés** /ʃasekʀwaze/ *nm* continual coming and going (**entre** between).

chasse-neige /ʃasnɛʒ/ *nm inv* snowplough (GB), snowplow (US).

chasser /ʃase/ [1] **I** *vtr* **1** [*animal*] to hunt [*prey*]; **2** [*hunter*] to shoot (GB), to hunt; **3** [*person*] to chase away [*animal, intruder*]; [*rain*] to drive away [*tourists*]; to drive out [*enemy*]; to fire [*domestic servant*]; **4** to dispel [*smoke, doubt*].

II *vi* to go hunting; to go shooting (GB) or hunting (US).

chasseur, /ʃasœʀ/ *nm* **1** hunter **2** (Mil) fighter (aircraft); fighter pilot; **3** (in hotel) bellboy (GB), bellhop (US).

■ **~ alpin** *soldier trained for mountainous terrain*; **~ de têtes** head-hunter.

châssis /ʃɑsi/ *nm* **1** (of window) frame; **2** (Aut) chassis.

chaste /ʃast/ *adj* (gen) chaste; [*person*] celibate; [*ears*] innocent.

chasteté /ʃastəte/ *nf* chastity.

chat /ʃa/ *nm* **1** cat; tomcat; **2 jouer à ~** to play tag.

■ **~ de gouttière** ordinary cat; alley cat; **~ perché** off-ground tag.

IDIOMS **donner sa langue au ~** to give in; **il n'y a pas un ~** the place is deserted; **avoir un ~ dans la gorge** to have a frog in one's throat; **il ne faut pas réveiller le ~ qui dort** (Proverb) let sleeping dogs lie ; **s'entendre comme chien et ~** to fight like cat and dog.

châtaigne /ʃɑtɛɲ/ *nf* **1** (sweet) chestnut; **2**° clout°, punch.

châtaignier /ʃɑteɲe/ *nm* (sweet) chestnut tree.

châtain /ʃɑtɛ̃/ *adj m* [*hair*] brown.

château, *pl* **~x** /ʃato/ *nm* **1** castle; **2** palace; **3** mansion.

■ **~ de cartes** house of cards; **~ d'eau** water tower; **~ fort** fortified castle.

IDIOMS **mener la vie de ~** to live the life of Riley (GB), to live like a prince.

châtelain, **~e** /ʃɑtlɛ̃, ɛn/ *nm,f* **1** lord/lady of the manor; **2** owner of a manor.

châtier /ʃɑtje/ [2] *vtr* to punish [*offender, crime*].

IDIOMS **qui aime bien châtie bien** (Proverb) spare the rod and spoil the child.

chatière /ʃatjɛʀ/ *nf* catflap.

châtiment /ʃɑtimɑ̃/ *nm* punishment.

chaton /ʃatɔ̃/ *nm* **1** kitten; **2** catkin.

chatouille° /ʃatuj/ *nf* tickle; **faire des ~s à qn** to tickle sb.

chatouiller /ʃatuje/ [1] *vtr* **1** to tickle; **2** to titillate; **3**° to nettle.

IDIOMS **~ les côtes à qn** (euphemistic) to tan sb's hide.

chatouilleux, **-euse** /ʃatujø, øz/ *adj* **1** ticklish; **2** touchy.

chatoyer /ʃatwaje/ [23] *vi* to shimmer.

châtrer /ʃɑtʀe/ [1] *vtr* to castrate; to neuter [*cat*]; to geld [*horse*].

chatte /ʃat/ *nf* (female) cat.

chaud, **~e** /ʃo, ʃod/ **I** *adj* **1** hot; warm; **des vêtements ~s** warm clothing; **2** [*colour, voice, congratulations*] warm; [*supporter*] strong; **ils n'ont pas été très ~s pour faire** they were not very keen on doing; **3** [*region, period*] turbulent; [*discussion*] heated; **un des points ~s du globe** one of the flash points of the world; **4 quartier ~**° red light district.

II *adv* **il fait ~** it's warm; it's hot; **ça ne me fait ni ~ ni froid** it doesn't matter one way or the other to me.

III *nm* heat; **avoir ~** to be warm; to be hot; **nous avons eu ~** (figurative) we had a narrow escape; **se tenir ~** [*people, animals*] to keep warm.

IV à chaud *phr* **à ~** [*analyse*] on the spot; [*reaction*] immediate; **opérer à ~** to do an emergency operation.

■ **~ et froid** (Med) chill.

chaudement /ʃodmɑ̃/ *adv* (gen) warmly; [*recommend*] heartily.

chaudière /ʃodjɛʀ/ *nf* boiler.

chaudron /ʃodʀɔ̃/ *nm* cauldron.

chaudronnerie /ʃodʀɔnʀi/ *nf* **1** boilermaking; **2** boilerworks.

chaudronnier, -ière /ʃodʀɔnje, ɛʀ/ *nm,f* boilermaker.

chauffage /ʃofaʒ/ *nm* **1** heating; **mettre le ~** to turn the heating on; **2** heater.

chauffard○ /ʃofaʀ/ *nm* reckless driver, road hog○.

chauffe-eau /ʃofo/ *nm inv* water-heater; **~ électrique** immersion heater.

chauffer /ʃofe/ [1] **I** *vtr* **1** to heat [*house*]; to heat (up) [*object, meal*]; **~ du fer à blanc** to bring iron to a white heat; **2** [*sun*] to warm.
II *vi* **1** [*food*] to heat (up); [*engine*] to warm up; to overheat; [*oven, iron*] to heat up; **2** [*radiator*] to give out heat; **3**○ (figurative) **ça va ~!** there's going to be big trouble!
III se chauffer *v refl* (+ *v être*) **1 se ~ au soleil** to bask in the sun; **2 se ~ au charbon** to have coal-fired heating.

chaufferie /ʃofʀi/ *nf* **1** boiler room; **2** (in boat) stokehold.

chauffeur /ʃofœʀ/ *nm* **1** driver; **2** chauffeur.

chauffeuse /ʃoføz/ *nf* low armless easy chair.

chaume /ʃom/ *nm* **1** (in field) stubble; **2** thatch.

chaumière /ʃomjɛʀ/ *nf* **1** thatched cottage; **2** humble cottage; **faire jaser dans les ~s** (humorous) to cause tongues to wag.

chaussée /ʃose/ *nf* **1** roadway, highway; (in town) street; **2** (road) surface; **~ déformée** uneven road surface; **3** causeway.

chausse-pied, *pl* **~s** /ʃospje/ *nm* shoehorn.

chausser /ʃose/ [1] **I** *vtr* to put [sth] on [*shoes, spectacles*]; **chaussé de pantoufles** wearing slippers.
II *vi* **je chausse du 41** I take a (size) 41.
III se chausser *v refl* (+ *v être*) **1** to put (one's) shoes on; **2** to buy (one's) shoes.

chaussette /ʃosɛt/ *nf* sock; **en ~s** in one's socks or stockinged feet.
IDIOMS **laisser tomber qn comme une vieille ~**○ to cast sb off like an old rag.

chausson /ʃosɔ̃/ *nm* **1** slipper; **2** bootee; **3** ballet shoe.
■ **~ aux pommes** (Culin) apple turnover.

chaussure /ʃosyʀ/ *nf* shoe; **~ montante** ankle boot.
IDIOMS **trouver ~ à son pied** [*man, woman*] to find the right person.

chauve /ʃov/ *adj* bald.

chauve-souris, *pl* **chauves-souris** /ʃovsuʀi/ *nf* (Zool) bat.

chauvin, ~e /ʃovɛ̃, in/ **I** *adj* chauvinistic, jingoistic.
II *nm,f* chauvinist, jingoist.

chaux /ʃo/ *nf* lime; **blanchir à la ~** to whitewash.

chavirer /ʃaviʀe/ [1] **I** *vtr* to overwhelm.
II *vi* **1** [*boat*] to capsize; **2 faire ~ les cœurs** to be a heartbreaker; **3** [*objects*] to tip over.

chef /ʃɛf/ *nm* **1** leader; **2** superior, boss○; **3** head; (of sales department) manager; **architecte en ~** chief architect; **4 ~ cuisinier** or **de cuisine** chef; **5**○ ace; **se débrouiller comme un ~** to manage splendidly; **6 de mon/leur (propre) ~** on my/their own initiative; **7 au premier ~** primarily, first and foremost.
■ **~ d'accusation** (Law) count of indictment; **~ d'atelier** (shop) foreman; **~ d'équipe** foreman; (Sport) team captain; **~ d'État** head of state; **~ de famille** head of the family or household; **~ de gare** stationmaster; **~ de rayon** (in shop) department supervisor or manager; **~ de service** (gen) section or department head.

chef-d'œuvre, *pl* **chefs-d'œuvre** /ʃɛdœvʀ/ *nm* masterpiece.

chef-lieu, *pl* **chefs-lieux** /ʃɛfljø/ *nm* administrative centre.

chemin /ʃ(ə)mɛ̃/ *nm* **1** country road; lane; **~ (de terre)** dirt track; path; **2** way; **sur le ~ du retour** on the way back; **reprendre le ~ du bureau** to go back to work; **on a fait un bout de ~ ensemble** we walked along together for a while; **~ faisant, en ~** on or along the way; **cette femme fera du ~** that woman will go a long way; **l'idée fait son ~** the idea is gaining ground; **montrer le ~** to lead the way; **prendre le ~ de la faillite** to be heading for bankruptcy; **s'arrêter en ~** to stop off on the way; (figurative) to stop; **prendre le ~ des écoliers** to take the long way round (GB) or around (US).
■ **~ de fer** railway, railroad (US); rail; **~ de halage** towpath.

cheminée /ʃ(ə)mine/ *nf* **1** chimney; chimney stack; **2** fireplace; **3** mantelpiece; **4** (of ship) funnel.

cheminement /ʃ(ə)minmɑ̃/ *nm* **1** slow progression; **2 le ~ de sa pensée** his/her train of thought.

cheminer /ʃ(ə)mine/ [1] *vi* **1** to walk (along); **2** [*path*] **~ à travers** to wend its way through; **3** [*idea*] to progress, to develop.

cheminot /ʃ(ə)mino/ *nm* railway worker (GB), railroader (US).

chemise /ʃ(ə)miz/ *nf* **1** shirt; **2** vest (GB), undershirt (US); **3** folder.
■ **~ de nuit** nightgown; (for man) nightshirt.
IDIOMS **je m'en moque comme de ma première ~**○ I don't give two hoots○ (GB) or a hoot○ (US); **changer d'avis comme de ~**○ to change one's mind at the drop of a hat.

chemisier /ʃ(ə)mizje/ *nm* blouse.

chenal, *pl* **-aux** /ʃənal, o/ *nm* (of river, estuary) channel, fairway.

chenapan /ʃənapɑ̃/ *nm* (humorous) scallywag○, rascal.

chêne /ʃɛn/ *nm* **1** oak (tree); **2** oak; **table en ~** oak table.

chenet /ʃənɛ/ *nm* firedog, andiron.

chenil /ʃənil/ *nm* **1** (dog) kennel; **2** kennels.

chenille /ʃənij/ *nf* (Aut, Zool) caterpillar.

cheptel /ʃɛptɛl/ *nm* ~ **(vif)** livestock.

chèque /ʃɛk/ *nm* cheque (GB), check (US); **déposer un ~ à la banque** to pay in a cheque (GB) or check (US).
■ **~ bancaire** cheque (GB), check (US); **~ en blanc** blank cheque (GB) or check (US); **~ en bois**○ rubber cheque○ (GB) or check (US); **~ au porteur** bearer cheque (GB) or check (US); **~ postal** ≈ giro cheque (GB); **~ sans provision** bad cheque (GB) or check (US); **~ de voyage** traveller's cheque (GB) or check (US).

chéquier /ʃekje/ *nm* chequebook (GB), checkbook (US).

cher, chère[1] /ʃɛʀ/ **I** *adj* **1** dear (**à** to); beloved; **un être ~** a loved one; **selon une formule qui lui est chère** as his/her favourite[GB] saying goes; **2** (as term of address) dear; **~ monsieur** my dear sir; (in letter) **~s tous** dear all; **3** expensive; **pas ~** cheap.
II *nm,f* **mon ~/ma chère** my dear.
III *adv* **1** a lot (of money); **coûter plus/moins ~** to cost more/less; **acheter ~** to buy at a high price; **2** (figurative) [*pay, cost*] dearly.
IDIOMS **ne pas donner ~ de la peau de qn**○ not to rate sb's chances highly.

chercher /ʃɛʀʃe/ [1] **I** *vtr* **1** to look for [*person, object, excuse, trouble*]; to try to find [*answer, ideas*]; to try to remember [*name*]; **~ le sommeil** to try to get some sleep; **~ fortune** to seek one's fortune; **~ qn du regard** to look about for sb; **elle t'a giflé mais tu l'as bien cherché** she slapped you but you asked for it; **2 ~ à faire** to try to do; **3 aller ~ qn/qch** to go and get sb/sth; to pick sb/sth up; **4 où est-il allé ~ cela?** what made him think that?; **je me demande où il est allé ~ tous ces mensonges** I wonder how he thought up all these lies; **5 une maison dans ce quartier, ça va ~ dans les 800 000 francs** a house in this area must fetch (GB) or get (US) about 800,000 francs.
II se chercher *v refl* (+ *v être*) **1** to try to find oneself; **un écrivain qui se cherche** a writer who is feeling his way; **2 se ~ des excuses** to try to find excuses for oneself; **3**○ to be out to get each other○.

chercheur, -euse /ʃɛʀʃœʀ, øz/ *nm,f* researcher.
■ **~ d'or** gold-digger; **~ de trésor** treasure hunter.

chère[2] /ʃɛʀ/ **I** *adj f* ▶ **cher**.
II *nf* **faire bonne ~** to eat well.

chèrement /ʃɛʀmɑ̃/ *adv* **~ acquise** gained at great cost.

chéri, ~e /ʃeʀi/ **I** *pp* ▶ **chérir**.
II *pp adj* beloved; **l'enfant ~ de** the darling of.
III *nm,f* **1** darling; **2**○ boyfriend/girlfriend.

chérir /ʃeʀiʀ/ [3] *vtr* to cherish [*person*]; to hold [sth] dear [*idea*].

chérubin /ʃeʀybɛ̃/ *nm* **1** cherub; **2** (ironic) little angel.

chétif, -ive /ʃetif, iv/ *adj* [*child*] puny; [*plant*] scrawny.

cheval, *pl* **-aux** /ʃ(ə)val, o/ **I** *nm* **1** (Zool) horse; **à (dos de) ~** on horseback; **monter à ~** to ride a horse; **remède de ~** strong medicine; **fièvre de ~** raging fever; **miser sur le bon ~** to back the right horse; **2** (Sport) horse-riding; **3** horsemeat.
II à cheval sur *phr* **1** astride; **2** spanning; **3** in between; **4 être à ~ sur qch** to be a stickler for sth.
■ **~ à bascule** rocking horse; **~ de bataille** hobbyhorse; **~ de labour** carthorse (GB), drafthorse (US); **chevaux de bois** merry-go-round horses.
IDIOMS **monter sur ses grands chevaux** to get on one's high horse.

chevaleresque /ʃ(ə)valʀɛsk/ *adj* **1** [*literature*] courtly; **2** [*person*] chivalrous.

chevalerie /ʃ(ə)valʀi/ *nf* chivalry.

chevalet /ʃ(ə)valɛ/ *nm* **1** easel; **2** (on violin) bridge.

chevalier /ʃ(ə)valje/ *nm* knight; **~ servant** (humorous) devoted admirer.

chevalière /ʃ(ə)valjɛʀ/ *nf* signet ring.

cheval-vapeur, *pl* **chevaux-vapeur** /ʃ(ə)valvapœʀ, ʃ(ə)vovapœʀ/ *nm* horsepower.

chevauchée /ʃ(ə)voʃe/ *nf* ride.

chevaucher /ʃ(ə)voʃe/ [1] **I** *vtr* **1** to sit astride [*animal, chair*]; **2** to overlap.
II se chevaucher *v refl* (+ *v être*) to overlap.

chevelu, ~e /ʃəvly/ *adj* long-haired.

chevelure /ʃəvlyʀ/ *nf* hair; **une abondante ~** a mass of hair.

chevet /ʃəvɛ/ *nm* bedhead; **être au ~ de qn** to be at sb's bedside.

cheveu, *pl* **~x** /ʃəvø/ **I** *nm* hair; **être à un ~ de** to be within a hair's breadth of; **ne tenir qu'à un ~** to hang by a thread.
II cheveux *nm pl* hair.
IDIOMS **avoir un ~ sur la langue** to have a lisp; **venir comme un ~ sur la soupe** to come at an awkward moment; **se faire des ~x**○ **(blancs)** to worry oneself to death; **couper les ~x en quatre** to split hairs; **être tiré par les ~x** to be far-fetched.

cheville /ʃ(ə)vij/ *nf* **1** (Anat) ankle; **2** Rawlplug®; peg; dowel.
IDIOMS **il n'arrive pas à la ~ de Paul** he can't hold a candle to Paul; **être en ~ avec qn**○ to be in cahoots with sb○.

cheviller /ʃ(ə)vije/ [1] *vtr* to peg.
IDIOMS **avoir l'âme chevillée au corps** to have a tremendous hold on life.

chèvre[1] /ʃɛvʀ/ *nm* goat's cheese.

chèvre[2] /ʃɛvʀ/ *nf* (Zool) goat; nanny-goat.
IDIOMS **devenir ~**○ to go nuts●; **ménager la ~ et le chou** to sit on the fence.

chevreau, *pl* **~x** /ʃəvʀo/ *nm* **1** (Zool) kid; **2** (leather) kid.

chèvrefeuille /ʃɛvʀəfœj/ *nm* honeysuckle.

chevreuil /ʃəvʀœj/ *nm* **1** (Zool) roe (deer); (male) roebuck; **2** (Culin) venison.

chevron /ʃəvʀɔ̃/ *nm* **1** rafter; **2** herringbone pattern; (bigger) chevron design; **3** (Mil) chevron, stripe.

chevronné /ʃəvʀɔne/ *adj* [*person*] experienced, seasoned.

chevroter /ʃəvʀɔte/ [1] *vtr, vi* to quaver.

chevrotine /ʃəvʀɔtin/ *nf* buckshot.

chez /ʃe/ I *prep* **1 ~ qn** at sb's place; **rentre ~ toi** go home; **de ~ qn** [*telephone*] from sb's place; **fais comme ~ toi** make yourself at home; **2** (referring to shop, office) **aller ~ le boucher** to go to the butcher's; **ça ne vient pas de ~ nous** it doesn't come from our shop (GB) or store (US); **être convoqué ~ le patron** to be called in before the boss; **3** (referring to a region)**~ nous** where I come from; where I live; **un nom bien de ~ nous**○ (in France) a good old French name; **4** among; **~ l'animal** in animals; **5 ce que j'aime ~ elle, c'est son humour** what I like about her is her sense of humour[GB]; **c'est une obsession ~ elle!** it's an obsession with her!; **6** in; **~ Cocteau** in Cocteau.

II **chez-** (*combining form*) **son ~-soi** one's own home.

chic /ʃik/ I *adj* **1** smart (GB), chic; **2**○ chic, fashionable; **3**○ [*person*] nice.

II *nm* chic; **avoir le ~ pour faire** to have a knack for doing; **avec ~** with style.

chicane /ʃikan/ *nf* **1** chicane; (on road, ski slope) double bend; **en ~** on alternate sides; **2** bickering.

chicaner /ʃikane/ [1] *vi* to squabble.

chiche /ʃiʃ/ I *adj* **1** mean (GB), stingy; **2**○ **être ~ de faire** to be quite capable of doing.

II *excl* **'je vais le faire'—'~!'** 'I'll do it'—'I dare you!'

chichement /ʃiʃmɑ̃/ *adv* [*live*] frugally; [*give*] stingily; [*pay*] poorly.

chichi /ʃiʃi/ *nm* fuss; **ne fais pas de ~s pour moi!** don't go to any trouble!

chicorée /ʃikɔʀe/ *nf* **1** (plant) chicory; (salad vegetable) endive (GB), chicory (US); **2** (Culin) (powder) chicory; (drink) chicory coffee.

chien, chienne[1] /ʃjɛ̃, ʃjɛn/ I○ *adj* **ma chienne de vie** my awful life.

II *nm* **1** dog; **2** (of rifle) hammer.

III **de chien**○ *phr* [*job, weather*] rotten; **ça me fait un mal de ~** it hurts like hell○; **avoir un mal de ~ à faire** to have an awful time doing.

■ **~ d'aveugle** guide dog; **~ de berger** sheepdog; **~ de garde** guard dog; (figurative) watchdog; **~ de race** pedigree dog.

IDIOMS **être comme ~ et chat** to fight like cat and dog; **être couché en ~ de fusil** to be curled up; **avoir un air de ~ battu** to have a hangdog look; **ce n'est pas fait pour les ~s**○ it's there to be used.

chiendent /ʃjɛ̃dɑ̃/ *nm* couch grass; **brosse de ~** scrubbing brush.

chien-loup, *pl* **chiens-loups** /ʃjɛ̃lu/ *nm* Alsatian (GB), German shepherd.

chienne[2] /ʃjɛn/ I *adj f* ▶ **chien**.

II *nf* (animal) bitch.

chiffe /ʃif/ *nf* (figurative) **une vraie ~ molle** a real drip○.

chiffon /ʃifɔ̃/ *nm* **1** rag, (piece of) cloth; **parler ~s** to talk (about) clothes; **2** duster; **passer un coup de ~ sur qch** to give sth a quick dust.

chiffonner /ʃifɔne/ [1] I *vtr* **1** to crease, to crumple; **2**○ to bother [*person*].

II **se chiffonner** *v refl* (+ *v être*) to crease, to crumple.

chiffonnier, -ière /ʃifɔnje, ɛʀ/ I *nm,f* rag-and-bone man/woman.

II *nm* (piece of furniture) chiffonnier.

IDIOMS **se battre comme des ~s** to fight like cat and dog.

chiffre /ʃifʀ/ *nm* **1** figure; **2** (of safe) combination; **3** monogram.

■ **~ d'affaires, CA** turnover (GB), sales (US); **~ arabe** Arabic numeral; **~ romain** Roman numeral; **~ de vente** sales (figures).

chiffrer /ʃifʀe/ [1] I *vtr* **1** to put a figure on [*cost, loss*] (**à** at); to cost [*job*]; **~ à** to put the cost of [sth] at [*job*]; **2** to encode [*message*]; **3** to monogram.

II○ *vi* to add up; **ça chiffre vite** it soon adds up.

III **se chiffrer** *v refl* (+ *v être*) **se ~ à** to amount to, to come to.

chignon /ʃiɲɔ̃/ *nm* bun; chignon.

chimère /ʃimɛʀ/ *nf* **1** wild dream, pipe dream; **2** (in mythology) Chimaera.

chimérique /ʃimeʀik/ *adj* **1** [*plans, hopes*] wild; **2** [*animal*] fabulous.

chimie /ʃimi/ *nf* chemistry.

chimiothérapie /ʃimjoteʀapi/ *nf* chemotherapy.

chimique /ʃimik/ *adj* **1** chemical; [*fibre*] man-made; **2** [*food, taste*] synthetic.

chimiste /ʃimist/ *nmf* chemist; **ingénieur ~** chemical engineer.

chimpanzé /ʃɛ̃pɑ̃ze/ *nm* chimpanzee.

chiné, ~e /ʃine/ *adj* chiné.

chiner○ /ʃine/ [1] *vi* to bargain-hunt, to antique (US).

chinois, ~e /ʃinwa, az/ I *adj* **1** Chinese; **2**○ nitpicking○.

II *nm* Chinese.

IDIOMS **pour moi c'est du ~** it's double-Dutch (GB) or Greek to me.

chiot /ʃjo/ *nm* puppy, pup.

chiper○ /ʃipe/ [1] *vtr* to pinch○; **~ qch à qn** to pinch sth from sb.

chipie○ /ʃipi/ *nf* cow○.

chipoter○ /ʃipɔte/ [1] *vi* **1** to quibble (**sur** over); **2** to pick at one's food.

chips /ʃips/ *nf inv* crisp (GB), potato chip (US).

chique /ʃik/ *nf* plug or quid (GB) (of tobacco).

IDIOMS **couper la ~ à qn** to shut sb up○.

chiqué○ /ʃike/ *nm* **1 c'est du ~** it's a put-on or sham○; **2 faire du ~** to put on or give oneself airs.

chiquenaude /ʃiknod/ *nf* flick; **d'une ~** with a flick.

chiquer /ʃike/ [1] *vtr* **tabac à ~** chewing tobacco.

chiromancie /kiʀomɑ̃si/ *nf* palmistry.

chiropracteur /kiʀopʀaktœʀ/ *nm* chiropractor.

chirurgical, **~e**, *mpl* **-aux** /ʃiʀyʀʒikal, o/ *adj* surgical.

chirurgie /ʃiʀyʀʒi/ *nf* surgery.

chirurgien /ʃiʀyʀʒjɛ̃/ *nm* surgeon.

chirurgien-dentiste, *pl* **chirurgiens-dentistes** /ʃiʀyʀʒjɛ̃dɑ̃tist/ *nm* dental surgeon.

chlore /klɔʀ/ *nm* chlorine.

chlorhydrique /klɔʀidʀik/ *adj* hydrochloric.

chloroforme /klɔʀɔfɔʀm/ *nm* chloroform.

chlorophylle /klɔʀɔfil/ *nf* chlorophyll.

chlorure /klɔʀyʀ/ *nm* chloride.

choc /ʃɔk/ **I** *adj inv* **'prix ~!'** 'huge reductions'; **c'est l'argument ~!** there's no answer to that!

II *nm* **1** impact, shock; (between people) collision; (between cars) crash; (minor) bump; **sous le ~** under the impact; **2** (noise) crash, smash; thud; clang; chink; **3** (confrontation) (gen), (Mil) clash; (Sport) encounter; **unité de ~** (Mil) shock troops; **de ~** [*journalist, boss*] ace°; **4** (emotional, physical) shock; **être encore sous le ~** to be still in a state of shock.

chocolat /ʃɔkɔla/ *nm* chocolate; **~ noir** or **à croquer** plain (GB) or dark (US) chocolate; **~ en poudre** drinking chocolate.

chœur /kœʀ/ *nm* **1** choir; (in opera, play) chorus; (figurative) chorus (**de** of); **en ~** [*say*] in unison; [*laugh*] all together; **2** (in church) chancel, choir.

choir /ʃwaʀ/ [51] *vi* to fall; **laisser ~ qn** to drop sb.

choisir /ʃwaziʀ/ [3] *vtr* to choose (**entre** between); **c'est à toi de ~** it's up to you.

choix /ʃwa/ *nm inv* **1** choice; **arrêter son ~ sur** to settle or decide on; **un très grand ~ de...** a very wide choice or range or selection of...; **2 de ~** [*item*] choice; [*candidate*] first-rate; **les places de ~** the best seats; **un morceau de ~** (of meat) a prime cut; **de second ~** of inferior quality.

choléra /kɔleʀa/ *nm* cholera.

cholestérol /kɔlɛsteʀɔl/ *nm* cholesterol.

chômage /ʃomaʒ/ *nm* unemployment; **mettre qn au ~** to make sb redundant (GB), to lay sb off.

■ **~ partiel** short time (working); **~ technique** layoffs.

chômer /ʃome/ [1] *vi* **1** to be idle; **2** to be out of work.

chômeur, **-euse** /ʃomœʀ, øz/ *nm,f* unemployed person.

chope /ʃɔp/ *nf* beer mug, tankard.

choquer /ʃɔke/ [1] *vtr* **1** to shock [*person*]; to offend [*sight, sensibility*]; **le film risque de ~** the film might cause offence[GB]; **2** [*news*] to shake [*person*]; [*accident*] to shake [sb] (up).

choral, **~e**[1], *mpl* **~s** or **-aux** /kɔʀal, o/ *adj* choral.

chorale[2] /kɔʀal/ *nf* choir.

chorégraphe /kɔʀegʀaf/ *nmf* choreographer.

chorégraphie /kɔʀegʀafi/ *nf* choreography.

choriste /kɔʀist/ *nmf* chorister; member of the choir; member of the chorus.

chorus /kɔʀys/ *nm inv* chorus; **faire ~ avec qn** (figurative) to join in with sb.

chose /ʃoz/ **I**° *adj* **se sentir tout ~** to feel peculiar.

II *nf* **1** (object, abstract) thing; **de deux ~s l'une** it's got to be one thing or the other; **une ~ communément admise** a widely accepted fact; **2 en mettant les ~s au mieux/au pire** at best/at (the) worst; **mettre les ~s au point** to clear things up; **avant toute ~** before anything else; above all else; **3** matter; **la ~ en question** the matter in hand; **4**° **être un peu porté sur la ~** to like it°, to be keen on sex; **5**° **Chose m'a dit...** what's-his-name/what's-her-name told me...

chou, *pl* **~x** /ʃu/ *nm* **1** cabbage; **2** choux bun (GB), pastry shell (US); **3** dear, darling.

■ **~ de Bruxelles** Brussels sprout; **~ à la crème** cream puff; **~ rave** kohlrabi.

IDIOMS **bête comme ~** really easy; **faire ~ blanc**° to draw a blank; **faire ses ~x gras de qch**° to use sth to one's advantage; **aller planter ses ~x ailleurs** to go to pastures new; **rentrer dans le ~**° **de qn** to beat sb up; to give sb a piece of one's mind.

choucas /ʃuka/ *nm* jackdaw.

chouchou° /ʃuʃu/ *nm* **1** (teacher's) pet; (of adoring public) darling; **2** (for hair) scrunchie.

chouchouter° /ʃuʃute/ [1] *vtr* to pamper.

choucroute /ʃukʀut/ *nf* sauerkraut.

chouette /ʃwɛt/ **I**° *adj* great°, neat° (US); **être ~ avec qn** to be really nice to sb.

II *nf* **1** owl; **2 vieille ~** old harridan.

chou-fleur, *pl* **choux-fleurs** /ʃuflœʀ/ *nm* cauliflower.

choyer /ʃwaje/ [23] *vtr* to pamper.

chrétien, **-ienne** /kʀetjɛ̃, ɛn/ *adj, nm,f* Christian.

chrétienté /kʀetjɛ̃te/ *nf* **la ~** Christendom.

Christ /kʀist/ *pr n* **le ~** Christ.

christianisme /kʀistjanism/ *nm* Christianity.

chromatique /kʀɔmatik/ *adj* chromatic.

chrome /kʀom/ *nm* **1** chromium; **2** (of vehicle) **faire les ~s** to polish the chrome.

chromosome /kʀɔmozom/ *nm* chromosome.

chronique /kʀɔnik/ **I** *adj* chronic.

II *nf* (in newspaper) column, page; (on radio) programme[GB].

chronologie /kʀɔnɔlɔʒi/ *nf* chronology.

chronologique /kʀɔnɔlɔʒik/ *adj* chronological.

chronomètre /kʀɔnɔmɛtʀ/ *nm* stopwatch.

chronométrer /kʀɔnɔmetʀe/ [14] *vtr* to time.

chrysalide /kʀizalid/ *nf* chrysalis.

chrysanthème /kʀizɑ̃tɛm/ *nm* chrysanthemum.

chu ▸ **choir**.

chuchotement /ʃyʃɔtmɑ̃/ *nm* whisper.

chuchoter /ʃyʃɔte/ [1] *vtr, vi* to whisper.

chuintement /ʃɥɛ̃tmɑ̃/ *nm* (of steam) hiss; (of tyres) swish.
chuinter /ʃɥɛ̃te/ [1] *vi* [*steam*] to hiss gently; [*tyre*] to swish.
chut /ʃyt/ *excl* shh!, hush!
chute /ʃyt/ *nf* **1** (gen) fall; (of empire) collapse; (of hair) loss; (of pressure) drop (**de** in); **~ libre** free fall; **2** (of film) ending; (of story) punch line; **3** (of cloth, paper) offcut.
■ **~ d'eau** waterfall; **la ~ des reins** the small of the back.
chuter /ʃyte/ [1] *vi* to fall; to drop.
ci /si/ I *det* **cette page-~** this page; **ces jours-~** (past) these last few days; (future) in the next few days; (present) at the moment; **ces temps-~** lately; at the moment.
II *pron* this; **~ et ça** this and that.
ci-après /siapʀɛ/ *adv* (gen) below.
cible /sibl/ *nf* target.
cibler /sible/ [1] *vtr* to target.
ciboire /sibwaʀ/ *nm* ciborium.
ciboulette /sibulɛt/ *nf* (Bot) chive; (Culin) chives.
cicatrice /sikatʀis/ *nf* scar.
cicatriser /sikatʀize/ [1] *vtr*, **se cicatriser** *v refl* (+ *v être*) to heal.
ci-contre /sikɔ̃tʀ/ *adv* opposite.
ci-dessous /sidəsu/ *adv* below.
ci-dessus /sidəsy/ *adv* above.
ci-devant /sidəvɑ̃/ *adj inv* former.
cidre /sidʀ/ *nm* cider.
ciel /sjɛl/, *pl* (literary) **cieux** /sjø/, (*in art*) **ciels** *nm* **1** sky; **carte du ~** star chart; **les cieux étoilés** the starry skies; **à ~ ouvert** [*pool*] open-air; [*sewer*] open; **2 le ~, les cieux** heaven; **(juste) ~!** (good) heavens!; **c'est le ~ qui t'envoie** you're a godsend.
cierge /sjɛʀʒ/ *nm* (church) candle.
cieux ▶ **ciel** 1, 2.
cigale /sigal/ *nf* cicada.
cigare /sigaʀ/ *nm* cigar.
cigarette /sigaʀɛt/ *nf* cigarette; **~ sans filtre** cigarette without a filter.
ci-gît /siʒi/ *phr* here lies.
cigogne /sigɔɲ/ *nf* stork.
ci-inclus, ~e /siɛ̃kly, yz/ I *adj* enclosed.
II *adv* enclosed.
ci-joint, ~e /siʒwɛ̃, ɛ̃t/ I *adj* enclosed.
II *adv* enclosed.
cil /sil/ *nm* eyelash.
cime /sim/ *nf* (tree)top.
ciment /simɑ̃/ *nm* cement.
cimenter /simɑ̃te/ [1] *vtr* to cement; to concrete.
cimetière /simtjɛʀ/ *nm* cemetery, graveyard; churchyard.
cinéaste /sineast/ *nmf* film director.
ciné-club, *pl* **~s** /sineklœb/ *nm* film club.
cinéma /sinema/ *nm* **1 (salle de) ~** cinema (GB), movie theater (US); **2** cinema; film industry; **faire du ~** to be in films; **3**○ (figurative) **arrête ton ~** cut out the play-acting; stop making such a fuss○; **se faire tout un ~** to start imagining things.
■ **~ d'art et d'essai** cinema showing art films (GB), art house (US).
cinémathèque /sinematɛk/ *nf* film archive.
cinématographique /sinematɔgʀafik/ *adj* film (GB), movie (US).
cinéphile /sinefil/ *nmf* cinema enthusiast (GB) or buff○.
cinétique /sinetik/ *nf* kinetics.
cinglant, ~e /sɛ̃glɑ̃, ɑ̃t/ *adj* **1** [*wind*] biting; [*rain*] driving; **2** [*remark, irony*] scathing; [*defeat, failure*] crushing.
cinglé○**, ~e** /sɛ̃gle/ *adj* mad○, crazy○.
cingler /sɛ̃gle/ [1] I *vtr* **1** [*rain, wind*] to sting [*face*]; **2** (with whip) to lash.
II *vi* (Naut) **~ vers** to head for.
cinq /sɛ̃k/ *adj inv, pron, nm inv* five.
IDIOMS **en ~ sec**○ in a flash○.
cinquantaine /sɛ̃kɑ̃tɛn/ *nf* **1** about fifty; **2 avoir la ~** to be about fifty.
cinquante /sɛ̃kɑ̃t/ *adj inv, pron* fifty.
cinquantenaire /sɛ̃kɑ̃tnɛʀ/ *nm* fiftieth anniversary.
cinquantième /sɛ̃kɑ̃tjɛm/ *adj* fiftieth.
cinquième /sɛ̃kjɛm/ I *adj* fifth.
II *nf* **1** (Sch) *second year of secondary school, age 12–13*; **2** (Aut) fifth (gear).
cintre /sɛ̃tʀ/ *nm* **1** (clothes) hanger; **2** (in architecture) curve.
cintré, ~e /sɛ̃tʀe/ *adj* [*coat*] waisted; [*shirt*] tailored.
cirage /siʀaʒ/ *nm* (shoe) polish.
IDIOMS **être dans le ~**○ to be half-conscious.
circoncire /siʀkɔ̃siʀ/ [64] *vtr* to circumcise.
circoncision /siʀkɔ̃sizjɔ̃/ *nf* male circumcision.
circonférence /siʀkɔ̃feʀɑ̃s/ *nf* circumference.
circonflexe /siʀkɔ̃flɛks/ *adj* **accent ~** circumflex (accent).
circonscription /siʀkɔ̃skʀipsjɔ̃/ *nf* district.
■ **~ électorale** ≈ electoral constituency (GB) or district (US).
circonscrire /siʀkɔ̃skʀiʀ/ [67] *vtr* **1** to contain [*fire, epidemic*]; to limit [*subject, field*] (**à** to); **2** to define.
circonspection /siʀkɔ̃spɛksjɔ̃/ *nf* caution; **avec ~** cautiously.
circonstance /siʀkɔ̃stɑ̃s/ I *nf* **1** circumstance; **2** situation; **en toute ~** in any event; **en la ~** in this particular case; **pour la ~** for the occasion; **être à la hauteur des ~s** to be equal to the occasion.
II **de circonstance** *phr* [*poem*] for the occasion; **faire une tête de ~** to assume a suitable expression.
■ **~s atténuantes** (Law) extenuating or mitigating circumstances.
circuit /siʀkɥi/ *nm* **1** (Sport) circuit; **2** (in tourism) tour; **ne pas suivre les ~s touristiques** to go off the beaten track; **3** (figurative) **être mis hors ~** [*person*] to be put on the sidelines; **vivre en**

~ fermé to live in a closed world; **4** (Tech) circuit.

circulaire /siʀkylɛʀ/ *adj, nf* circular.

circulation /siʀkylasjɔ̃/ *nf* **1** traffic; **2** circulation; **la libre ~ des personnes** the free movement of people; **être en ~** [*banknotes, product*] to be in circulation; **disparaître de la ~** to go out of circulation; **3** (of air, gas, blood) circulation.

circulatoire /siʀkylatwaʀ/ *adj* [*problems*] circulatory.

circuler /siʀkyle/ [1] *vi* **1** [*train, bus*] to run; **2** [*person*] to get around; to move about; (by car) to travel; **3** [*rumour, information*] to circulate, to go around or about; **faire ~** to circulate; to spread [*rumour*]; **4** [*banknotes*] to circulate; **5** [*blood, air*] to circulate.

cire /siʀ/ *nf* wax.

ciré /siʀe/ *nm* oilskin.

cirer /siʀe/ [1] *vtr* to polish [*shoes, floor*].

cirque /siʀk/ *nm* **1** circus; **2**○ (figurative) racket○; **arrête ton ~!** stop your nonsense!; **c'est le ~ pour se garer à Oxford** it's a real performance parking in Oxford.

cirrhose /siʀoz/ *nf* cirrhosis.

cisaille /sizɑj/ *nf* pair of shears; **~s** shears.

ciseau, *pl* **~x** /sizo/ **I** *nm* **1** (Tech) chisel; **2** (Sport) scissors jump; **3** (Sport) scissors hold.
II ciseaux *nm pl* scissors; **tailler à grands coups de ~x** to cut boldly.

ciseler /sizle/ [17] *vtr* to chase [*metal*]; to chisel [*wood, stone*].

citadelle /sitadɛl/ *nf* citadel.

citadin, **~e** /sitadɛ̃, in/ **I** *adj* city.
II *nm,f* city-dweller.

citation /sitasjɔ̃/ *nf* (from author) quotation.

cité /site/ *nf* **1** (gen) city; town; **2** housing estate.
■ **~ universitaire** student halls of residence (GB), dormitories (US).

citer /site/ [1] *vtr* **1** to quote [*author, passage*]; **2** to name [*title, book*]; to cite [*person, example, fact*]; **3** (Law) to summon [*witness*]; **être cité en justice** to be issued with a summons.

citerne /sitɛʀn/ *nf* tank.

citoyen, **-enne** /sitwajɛ̃, ɛn/ *nm,f* citizen.

citrique /sitʀik/ *adj* citric.

citron /sitʀɔ̃/ **I** *adj inv* **(jaune) ~** lemon (yellow).
II *nm* **1** lemon; **2**○ head, nut○.
■ **~ givré** lemon sorbet (*served inside a lemon*); **~ vert** lime.

citronnade /sitʀɔnad/ *nf* lemon squash (GB), lemonade (US).

citronnelle /sitʀɔnɛl/ *nf* (Bot) citronella.

citronnier /sitʀɔnje/ *nm* lemon tree.

citrouille /sitʀuj/ *nf* **1** pumpkin; **2**○ head, nut○.

civet /sivɛ/ *nm* ≈ stew; **~ de lièvre** jugged hare.

civière /sivjɛʀ/ *nf* stretcher.

civil, **~e** /sivil/ **I** *adj* (gen) civilian; [*marriage*] civil; [*funeral*] non religious.
II *nm* civilian; **en ~** in civilian clothes; in plain clothes; **dans le ~** in civilian life.

civilisation /sivilizasjɔ̃/ *nf* civilization.

civiliser /sivilize/ [1] *vtr* to civilize.

civique /sivik/ *adj* civic; **avoir l'esprit ~** to have a sense of civic responsibility.

claie /klɛ/ *nf* **1** wicker rack; **2** fence, hurdle.

clair, **~e**[1] /klɛʀ/ **I** *adj* **1** [*colour*] light; [*complexion*] fair; **2** [*room*] bright, light; **3** [*weather, water*] clear; **4** [*text*] clear; **suis-je ~?** do I make myself clear?; **passer le plus ~ de son temps** to spend most of one's time (**à faire** doing).
II *adv* [*speak*] clearly; **il faisait ~** it was already light; **voir ~** to see well.
III *nm* **1** light; **en ~** (television channel) unscrambled; (Mil), (Comput) in clear; (starting sentence) to put it clearly; **mettre ses idées au ~** to get one's ideas straight; **tirer une affaire au ~** to get to the bottom of things; **2** light colours[GB].
■ **~ de lune** moonlight; **au ~ de lune** in the moonlight.
IDIOMS **c'est ~ comme de l'eau de roche** it's crystal clear.

claire[2] /klɛʀ/ *nf* oyster bed; **fine de ~** (Culin) claire oyster.

clairement /klɛʀmɑ̃/ *adv* clearly.

clairière /klɛʀjɛʀ/ *nf* clearing, glade.

clairon /klɛʀɔ̃/ *nm* **1** bugle; **2** bugler.

claironner /klɛʀɔne/ [1] *vtr* to shout [sth] from the rooftops.

clairsemé, **~e** /klɛʀsəme/ *adj* [*houses*] scattered; [*hair*] thin; [*population*] sparse.

clairvoyance /klɛʀvwajɑ̃s/ *nf* perceptiveness.

clairvoyant, **~e** /klɛʀvwajɑ̃, ɑ̃t/ *adj* perceptive.

clamer /klame/ [1] *vtr* to proclaim (**que** that).

clameur /klamœʀ/ *nf* roar.

clan /klɑ̃/ *nm* clan.

clandestin, **~e** /klɑ̃dɛstɛ̃, in/ *adj* [*organization, newspaper*] underground; [*immigration, employment*] illegal; **passager ~** stowaway.

clandestinité /klɑ̃dɛstinite/ *nf* **1** secret or clandestine nature; **dans la ~** [*live*] in hiding; [*operate*] in secret; **passer dans la ~** to go underground; **2 travailler dans la ~** to work illegally.

clap /klap/ *nm* clapperboard.

clapet /klapɛ/ *nm* **1** valve; **2**○ mouth, trap○.

clapier /klapje/ *nm* rabbit hutch.

clapoter /klapɔte/ [1] *vi* to lap.

clapotis /klapɔti/ *nm* lapping (**de** of).

claque[1] /klak/ *nm* **(chapeau) ~** opera hat.

claque[2] /klak/ *nf* **1** slap; **2**○ slap in the face; **3** (in theatre) claque.
IDIOMS **en avoir sa ~**○ to be fed up.

claqué○, **~e** /klake/ *adj* knackered◑ (GB), done in○.

claquement /klakmɑ̃/ *nm* (of door) bang; (of whip) crack; (of tongue) click; (of flag) flapping.

claquer /klake/ [1] **I** *vtr* **1** to slam [*door*]; **2**○ to exhaust [*person*]; **3**○ to blow○ [*money*].

II *vi* (gen) [*door*] to bang; (closing) to slam shut; [*flag*] to flap; **elle claque des dents** her teeth are chattering.

III **se claquer** *v refl* (+ *v être*) **1 se ~ un muscle** to pull or strain a muscle; **2**° to wear oneself out.

claquettes /klakɛt/ *nf pl* tap dancing; **faire des ~** to tap dance.

clarification /klaʀifikasjɔ̃/ *nf* clarification.

clarifier /klaʀifje/ [2] *vtr* to clarify.

clarinette /klaʀinɛt/ *nf* clarinet.

clarté /klaʀte/ *nf* **1** light; **2** (of water) clarity; (of complexion) fairness; **3** (of style) clarity.

classe /klas/ *nf* **1** (Sch) (group) class, form (GB); (level) year, form (GB), grade (US); **ses élèves n'auront pas ~** his/her class won't be having any lessons; **après la ~** after school; **2** (Sch) classroom; **3** (in society, transport) class; **les ~s sociales** social classes; **billet de seconde ~** second-class ticket; **4 avoir de la ~** to have class; **5** (Mil) **faire ses ~s** to do one's basic training.

■ **~ d'âge** age group; **~ de nature**, **~ verte** *educational schooltrip to the countryside*; **~s préparatoires (aux grandes écoles)** *preparatory classes for entrance to Grandes Écoles*.

classement /klasmɑ̃/ *nm* **1** classification; **2** filing; **faire du ~ dans ses papiers** to sort one's papers out; **3** grading; **~ trimestriel** (Sch) termly position (in class); **4** (Sport) ranking; **en tête du ~** in first place; **5** (of hotel, restaurant) rating; **6** (Law) **~ d'une affaire** closing of a case.

classer /klase/ [1] I *vtr* **1** to classify; **2** to file (away) [*documents*]; **3** (Law) to close [*case*]; **c'est une affaire classée** the matter is closed; **4** to list [*old building*]; **5** to class [*country, pupils*]; to rank [*song, player*]; **6**° to size [sb] up.

II **se classer** *v refl* (+ *v être*) to rank.

classeur /klasœʀ/ *nm* **1** ring binder; **2** file; **3** filing cabinet.

classicisme /klasisism/ *nm* **1** (in art) classicism; **2** (in clothes, tastes) traditionalism, conservatism.

classification /klasifikasjɔ̃/ *nf* classification.

classifier /klasifje/ [2] *vtr* to classify.

classique /klasik/ I *adj* **1** classical; **théâtre ~ français** French classical theatre; **faire des études ~s** (Sch) to do classics; **2** classic; [*method*] classic, standard; [*consequence*] usual; **de coupe ~** of classic cut; **c'est ~**°**!** it's typical!; **c'est le coup ~**°**!** it's the same old story!

II *nm* classic; **un ~ du genre** a classic of its kind.

claudiquer /klodike/ [1] *vi* to limp.

clause /kloz/ *nf* clause; **~ de conscience** conscience clause.

claustrophobe /klostʀɔfɔb/ *adj* claustrophobic.

claustrophobie /klostʀɔfɔbi/ *nf* claustrophobia.

clavecin /klavsɛ̃/ *nm* harpsichord.

clavicule /klavikyl/ *nf* collarbone.

clavier /klavje/ *nm* keyboard; **~ numérique** numeric keypad.

claviste /klavist/ *nmf* **1** typesetter; **2** keyboarder.

clé /kle/ I *nf* **1** (of lock, tin) key; **sous ~** under lock and key; **fermer à ~** to lock; **prix ~s en main** [*car*] on the road price (GB), sticker price (US); **2** (condition, solution) key (**de** to); **détenir la ~ du bonheur** to know the secret of true happiness; **3** spanner (GB), wrench; **4** (of flute) key; (of violin) peg; **~ de fa/de sol/d'ut** bass or F/treble or G/alto or C clef; **5** (Sport) armlock.

II **(-)clé** (*combining form*) **poste/mot(-)~** key post/word.

III **à la clé** *phr* at stake; **avec, à la ~, une récompense** with a reward thrown in.

■ **~ anglaise**, **~ à molette** adjustable spanner (GB) or wrench (US); **~ de voûte** keystone.

IDIOMS **prendre la ~ des champs** to escape.

clef = **clé**.

clémence /klemɑ̃s/ *nf* **1** leniency; **2** (of climate) mildness.

clément, **~e** /klemɑ̃, ɑ̃t/ *adj* **1** [*judge*] lenient; **2** [*temperature, winter*] mild.

clémentine /klemɑ̃tin/ *nf* clementine.

cleptomanie /klɛptɔmani/ *nf* kleptomania.

clerc /klɛʀ/ *nm* (Law) clerk.

clergé /klɛʀʒe/ *nm* clergy.

cliché /kliʃe/ *nm* **1** snapshot; **2** cliché.

client, **~e** /klijɑ̃, ɑ̃t/ *nm,f* (of shop) customer; (of solicitor) client; (of hotel) guest; (in taxi) fare.

IDIOMS **c'est à la tête du ~** it depends whether they like the look of you.

clientèle /klijɑ̃tɛl/ *nf* (of shop) customers; (of solicitor) clients; (of doctor) patients; **avoir une bonne ~** [*shop*] to have a lot of customers; **se faire une ~** to build up a clientele; **je vais lui retirer ma ~** I'll take my custom elsewhere.

cligner: **cligner de** /kliɲe/ [1] *v+prep* **~ des yeux** to blink; **~ de l'œil** to wink.

clignotant, **~e** /kliɲɔtɑ̃, ɑ̃t/ *nm* (Aut) indicator (GB), blinker (US).

clignoter /kliɲɔte/ [1] *vi* [*light*] to flash; to flash on and off; [*star*] to twinkle.

climat /klima/ *nm* climate.

climatique /klimatik/ *adj* climatic.

climatisation /klimatizasjɔ̃/ *nf* air-conditioning.

climatiser /klimatize/ [1] *vtr* to air-condition [*room*].

climatiseur /klimatizœʀ/ *nm* air-conditioner.

clin /klɛ̃/ *nm* **~ d'œil** wink; (figurative) allusion; **en un ~ d'œil** in a flash.

clinicien, **-ienne** /klinisjɛ̃, ɛn/ *nm,f* clinician.

clinique /klinik/ I *adj* clinical.

II *nf* private hospital; **~ vétérinaire** veterinary clinic.

clinquant, **~e** /klɛ̃kɑ̃, ɑ̃t/ *adj* [*jewellery, decor*] flashy°.

clip /klip/ *nm* **1** pop video; **2** clip brooch; **3** clip-on (earring).

clique /klik/ *nf* clique; **prendre ses ~s et ses claques** to pack up and go.

cliquer /klike/ [1] *vi* (Comput) to click (**sur** on).

cliqueter /klikte/ [20] *vi* [*keys*] to jingle; [*chain*] to rattle; [*machine*] to go clickety-clack; [*knitting needles*] to click.

clitoris /klitɔʀis/ *nm* clitoris.

clivage /klivaʒ/ *nm* divide; **~ d'opinion** division of opinion.

clochard, **~e** /klɔʃaʀ, aʀd/ *nm,f* tramp, down-and-out.

cloche /klɔʃ/ *nf* **1** bell; **2** (in horticulture) cloche; **3**○ clod○, idiot; **4** **~ à fromage** cover of cheese dish.
IDIOMS **entendre plusieurs sons de ~** to hear several versions; **sonner les ~s à qn** to bawl sb out○.

cloche-pied: **à cloche-pied** /aklɔʃpje/ *phr* **sauter à ~** to hop.

clocher[1]○ /klɔʃe/ [1] *vi* [*reasoning*] to be faulty; **il y a quelque chose qui cloche** there's something wrong.

clocher[2] /klɔʃe/ *nm* **1** steeple; church or bell tower; **2** (figurative) home town; **esprit de ~** parochial or small-town mentality; **querelle de ~** local quarrel.

clochette /klɔʃɛt/ *nf* **1** (little) bell; **2** (of flower) bell.

cloison /klwazɔ̃/ *nf* **1** partition; **2** screen; **~ extensible** folding room-divider; **~ étanche** watertight bulkhead; (figurative) watertight compartment.

cloisonner /klwazɔne/ [1] *vtr* **1** to partition [*room*]; to divide up [*space*]; **2** to divide up [*company, society*]; to compartmentalize [*administration*].

cloître /klwɑtʀ/ *nm* cloister.

cloîtrer /klwatʀe/ [1] **I** *vtr* **1** to shut [sb] away; **2** to cloister [*monk, nun*].
II se cloîtrer *v refl* (+ *v être*) to shut oneself away.

clone /klon/ *nm* clone.

clope○ /klɔp/ *nm* or *f* fag○ (GB), ciggy○, cigarette.

clopin-clopant○ /klɔpɛ̃klɔpɑ̃/ *phr* **aller ~** to hobble along.

clopinettes○ /klɔpinɛt/ *nf pl* **gagner des ~** to earn peanuts○.

cloporte /klɔpɔʀt/ *nm* woodlouse.

cloque /klɔk/ *nf* blister.

clore /klɔʀ/ [79] **I** *vtr* **1** to close [*debate*]; **2** to end, to conclude [*programme, conference*]; **3** to close [*eyes*]; **4** to conclude [*deal*].
II se clore *v refl* (+ *v être*) to end (**par** with).

clos, **~e** /klo, oz/ **I** *adj* [*system*] closed; [*area*] enclosed; **monde ~** self-contained world.
II *nm inv* fenced or enclosed field.

clôture /klotyʀ/ *nf* **1** fence; wire fence; wire-mesh fence; railings; **2** (of debate, session) close; (of subscription) closing; (of shop, office) closing; (of season) close; **discours de ~** closing speech.

clôturer /klotyʀe/ [1] *vtr* **1** to fence in [*land*]; **2** [*person*] to close [*debate, list, account*]; [*speech*] to end [*debate, festival*].

clou /klu/ **I** *nm* **1** nail; stud; **2** (of show) star attraction; (of evening) high point; **3** (Med) boil; **4**○ **mettre qch au ~** to pawn sth.
II clous *nm pl* **1** pedestrian crossing (GB), crosswalk (US); **2**○ **des ~s!** no way!
■ **~ de girofle** (Bot, Culin) clove.
IDIOMS **enfoncer le ~** to drive the point home.

clouer /klue/ [1] *vtr* to nail down [*lid*]; to nail together [*planks*]; **~ au sol** (figurative) to pin [sb] down; **être cloué au lit** to be confined to bed.

clown /klun/ *nm* clown; **faire le ~** to clown about.

club /klœb/ *nm* **1** club; **2** **~ de vacances** holiday camp.

cm (*written abbr* = **centimètre**) cm; **cm²** (square centimetre) cm²; **cm³** (cubic centimetre) (gen) cm³; (for engines) cc.

CM /seɛm/ *nm*: *abbr* ▸ **cours**.

CNRS /seɛnɛʀɛs/ *nm* (*abbr* = **Centre national de la recherche scientifique**) *national centre for scientific research.*

coaccusé, **~e** /koakyze/ *nm,f* codefendant.

coaguler /kɔagyle/ [1] *vi*, **se coaguler** *v refl* (+ *v être*) [*blood*] to coagulate.

coaliser: **se coaliser** /kɔalize/ [1] *v refl* (+ *v être*) (gen) to unite; (in politics) to form a coalition.

coalition /kɔalisjɔ̃/ *nf* coalition.

coasser /kɔase/ [1] *vi* to croak.

cobaye /kɔbaj/ *nm* guinea pig.

cobra /kɔbʀa/ *nm* cobra.

coca /kɔka/ *nm* or *f* coca extract.

cocagne /kɔkaɲ/ *nf* **mât de ~** ≈ greasy pole; **pays de ~** land of milk and honey.

cocaïne /kɔkain/ *nf* cocaine.

cocarde /kɔkaʀd/ *nf* **1** rosette; (on uniform) cockade; **2** (on side of plane) roundel; (on vehicle) official badge.

cocasse /kɔkas/ *adj* comical.

coccinelle /kɔksinɛl/ *nf* ladybird, ladybug (US).

coccyx /kɔksis/ *nm* coccyx.

coche /kɔʃ/ *nm* (stage)coach.
IDIOMS **manquer le ~** to miss the boat.

cocher[1] /kɔʃe/ [1] *vtr* to tick (GB), to check (US).

cocher[2] /kɔʃe/ *nm* coachman; cabman.

cochère /kɔʃɛʀ/ *adj f* **porte ~** carriage entrance.

cochon, **-onne** /kɔʃɔ̃, ɔn/ **I**○ *adj* **1** [*film, story*] dirty; [*person*] dirty-minded; **2** [*person*] messy, dirty.
II○ *nm,f* **1** pig○, slob○; **de ~** [*job*] botched; [*weather*] lousy○; **2** sex maniac.
III *nm* **1** (Zool) pig, hog; **2** (Culin) pork.
■ **~ d'Inde** Guinea pig; **~ de lait** suckling pig.

cochonnerie○ /kɔʃɔnʀi/ *nf* **1** junk○; **il ne mange que des ~s** he only eats junk food; **c'est de la ~ ce stylo** this pen is crap●; **2** mess; **faire des ~s** to make a mess; **3** **dire des ~s** to say smutty○ things.

cochonnet /kɔʃɔnɛ/ *nm* **1** (Zool) piglet; **2** (in bowls) jack.
cocker /kɔkɛʀ/ *nm* (cocker) spaniel.
cocktail /kɔktɛl/ *nm* **1** cocktail; **2** (figurative) mixture; **3** cocktail party.
coco /koko/ *nm* **1** coconut; **2**° darling, pet°.
cocon /kɔkɔ̃/ *nm* cocoon.
cocorico /kɔkɔʀiko/ *nm* (*also onomatopoeic*) cock-a-doodle-do.
cocotier /kɔkɔtje/ *nm* coconut palm.
cocotte /kɔkɔt/ *nf* **1**° (baby talk) hen; **2**° **ma ~** honey; **3** (Culin) casserole (GB), pot.
cocotte-minute®, *pl* **cocottes-minute** /kɔkɔtminyt/ *nf* pressure-cooker.
code /kɔd/ **I** *nm* **1** code; **2 se mettre en ~** to dip (GB) or dim (US) one's lights.
II codes *nm pl* (of vehicle) dipped (GB) or dimmed (US) (head)lights, low beam.
■ **~ confidentiel (d'identification)** personal identification number, PIN; **~ postal** post code (GB), zip code (US); **~ de la route** (Aut) highway code (GB), rules of the road (US); **passer son ~**° (Aut) to take the written part of a driving test.
coder /kɔde/ [1] *vtr* to code, to encode.
codétenu, **~e** /kodetny/ *nm,f* fellow prisoner.
codifier /kɔdifje/ [2] *vtr* to codify [*laws*]; to standardize [*language, custom*].
codirecteur, **-trice** /kodiʀɛktœʀ, tʀis/ *nm,f* joint manager; joint director.
coefficient /kɔefisjɑ̃/ *nm* **1** ratio; **2** margin; **3** (at school, university) *weighting factor in an exam*; **la chimie est au ~ 4** chemistry results are multiplied by 4; **4** (in arithmetic) coefficient; (in physics) coefficient; modulus.
coéquipier, **-ière** /koekipje, ɛʀ/ *nm,f* team mate.
cœur /kœʀ/ **I** *nm* **1** heart; **il a le ~ malade** he has a heart condition; **serrer qn sur** or **contre son ~** to hold sb close; **2** (Culin) heart; **3** figurative (of fruit, rock) core; (of problem, debate, region, building) heart; (of tree) heartwood; **au ~ de** (of region, town) in the middle of; (of building, problem, system) at the heart of; **au ~ de l'été** in the height of summer; **au ~ de l'hiver** in the dead of winter; **4** (person) **un ~ simple** a simple soul; **mon (petit) ~** sweetheart; **5** heart; **écouter son ~** to go with one's feelings; **aller droit au ~ de qn** to touch sb deeply; **avoir un coup de ~ pour qch** to fall in love with sth; **ça me fait mal au ~ de voir** it sickens me to see; **mon ~ se serre quand...** I feel a pang when...; **problème de ~** emotional problem; **6 parler à ~ ouvert** to speak openly; **7 avoir bon ~** to be kind-hearted; **ton bon ~ te perdra** you're too generous for your own good; **8** courage; **le ~ m'a manqué** my courage failed me; **redonner du ~ à qn** to give sb new heart; **9 je n'ai plus le ~ à rien** I don't feel like doing anything any more; **10** (Games) (card) heart; (suit) hearts.
II à cœur *phr* **avoir à ~ de faire** to be intent on doing; **prendre qch à ~** to take sth seriously.
III de bon cœur *phr* willingly; **il brossait le sol et y allait de bon ~** he was scrubbing the floor with a will; **rire de bon ~** to laugh heartily.
IV par cœur *phr* by heart; **connaître qn par ~** to know sb inside out.
IDIOMS **avoir mal au ~** to feel sick (GB) or nauseous (US); **avoir du ~ au ventre** to be brave; **être joli comme un ~** to be as pretty as a picture; **avoir le ~ sur la main** to be open-handed; **il ne le porte pas dans son ~** he's not his favourite[GB] person; **le ~ n'y est pas** my/your etc heart isn't in it; **si le ~ t'en dit** if you feel like it; **avoir qch sur le ~** to be resentful about sth.
coexister /koegziste/ [1] *vi* to coexist.
coffre /kɔfʀ/ *nm* **1** chest; **~ à jouets** toy box; **2** (for valuables) safe; (individual) safety deposit box; **la salle des ~s** the strongroom; **3** (of car) boot (GB), trunk (US).
IDIOMS **avoir du ~**° to have a powerful voice.
coffre-fort, *pl* **coffres-forts** /kɔfʀəfɔʀ/ *nm* safe.
coffret /kɔfʀɛ/ *nm* **1** casket; **~ à bijoux** jewellery (GB) or jewelry (US) box; **2** (of records, cassettes, books) boxed set.
cogiter /kɔʒite/ [1] *vi* (humorous) to cogitate, to think.
cognac /kɔɲak/ *nm* cognac.
cogner /kɔɲe/ [1] **I** *vtr* **1** to knock; **2**° to beat up.
II *vi* **1 ~ contre** [*shutter*] to bang against; [*branch*] to knock against; [*projectile*] to hit; **ma tête est allée ~ contre la vitre** my head hit the window; **~ à la porte** to bang on the door; **2**° [*boxer*] to hit out; **ça va ~** there's going to be a brawl; **3** [*heart, blood*] to pound.
III se cogner *v refl* (+ *v être*) to bump into something; **se ~ le genou contre** to bang one's knee against; **se ~ le pied contre une pierre** to stub one's toe on a stone.
cohabitation /koabitasjɔ̃/ *nf* **1** living with somebody; **2** *situation where the French President is in political opposition to the government.*
cohabiter /koabite/ [1] *vi* [*people*] to live together; [*things*] to coexist.
cohérence /kɔeʀɑ̃s/ *nf* **1** coherence; consistency; **2** (in physics) cohesion.
cohérent, **~e** /kɔeʀɑ̃, ɑ̃t/ *adj* coherent; consistent.
cohéritier, **-ière** /koeʀitje, ɛʀ/ *nm,f* joint heir.
cohésion /kɔezjɔ̃/ *nf* cohesion.
cohorte /koɔʀt/ *nf* **1**° crowd, group; **2** (in Roman legion) cohort.
cohue /kɔy/ *nf* crowd; **c'est la ~** it's a crush or scramble.
coi, **coite** /kwa, kwat/ *adj* **rester** or **se tenir ~** to remain quiet.
coiffant, **~e** /kwafɑ̃, ɑ̃t/ *adj* **gel ~** styling gel.
coiffe /kwaf/ *nf* (gen) headgear; (of nun) wimple.
coiffer /kwafe/ [1] **I** *vtr* **1 ~ qn** to do sb's

hair; to comb sb's hair; **se faire ~ par qn** to have one's hair done by sb; **elle est mal coiffée** her hair is untidy; **2 ~ qn d'un chapeau** to put a hat on sb; **coiffé d'une casquette** wearing a cap.

II se coiffer *v refl* (+ *v être*) **1** to do or comb one's hair; **2 se ~ de qch** to put sth on.

IDIOMS **~ qn au poteau**○ or **sur le fil**○ to beat sb by a whisker.

coiffeur, -euse[1] /kwafœʀ, øz/ *nm,f* hairdresser.

coiffeuse[2] /kwaføz/ *nf* dressing table.

coiffure /kwafyʀ/ *nf* **1** hairstyle; **2** hairdressing; **3** headgear.

coin /kwɛ̃/ **I** *nm* **1** corner; **à tous les ~s de rue** everywhere; **les ~s et les recoins** the nooks and crannies; **aux quatre ~s de la ville** all over the town; **aller au ~** (as punishment) to go and stand in the corner; **j'ai dû poser mon sac dans un ~** I must have put my bag down somewhere; **au ~ du feu** by the fire; **2** (of eye, mouth) corner; **un sourire en ~** a half-smile; **un regard en ~** a sidelong glance; **3** (of ground) plot; (of lawn) patch; **un ~ de paradis** an idyllic spot; **dans un ~ de ma mémoire** in my memory; **4** (in region) **un ~ de France** a part of France; **dans le ~** around here, in these parts; around there, in those parts; **le café du ~** the local café; **je ne suis pas du ~** I'm not from around here; **les gens du ~** the locals; **connaître les bons ~s pour manger** to know all the good places to eat; **5** (for photograph) corner; (for file) reinforcing corner; **6** (Tech) wedge.

II coin(-) *(combining form)* **~-repas/-salon** dining/living area.

coincé, ~e /kwɛ̃se/ **I** *pp* ▶ **coincer**.

II *pp adj* **1** stuck; trapped; **~ entre** [*house*] wedged between; **2**○ **j'ai le dos ~, je suis ~** my back has gone○; **3**○ (figurative) stuck○; **4**○ ill at ease; **5**○ uptight○.

coincer /kwɛ̃se/ [12] **I** *vtr* **1** to wedge [*object*]; to wedge [sth] open/shut [*door*]; [*snow*] to trap [*person*]; **2** to jam [*drawer, zip*]; **3** (in door) to catch [*finger*]; **4**○ to catch, to corner [*person*]; **se faire ~ par** to get caught or cornered by; **5**○ [*police*] to pick [sb] up○, to arrest; **6**○ to catch [sb] out [*person*].

II *vi* **1** [*zip, drawer*] to stick; **2**○ **ça coince** there's a problem.

III se coincer *v refl* (+ *v être*) **1** [*object*] to get stuck or jammed; **2 se ~ les doigts** to get one's fingers caught; **se ~ une vertèbre**○ to trap a nerve in one's back.

coïncidence /kɔɛ̃sidɑ̃s/ *nf* coincidence.

coïncider /kɔɛ̃side/ [1] *vi* (gen) to coincide; [*tastes*] to be similar.

coin-coin /kwɛ̃kwɛ̃/ *nm inv* quack.

coing /kwɛ̃/ *nm* quince.

coït /kɔit/ *nm* coitus; **~ interrompu** coitus interruptus.

coite ▶ **coi**.

coke[1] /kɔk/ *nm* (coal) coke.

coke[2]○ /kɔk/ *nf* (drug users' slang) (cocaine) coke○.

col /kɔl/ *nm* **1** collar; **2** (in mountains) pass; **3** (of bottle) neck; **4** (Anat) neck; **il s'est cassé le ~ du fémur** he broke his hip(bone).

■ **~ blanc** white-collar worker; **~ bleu** blue-collar worker.

cola /kɔla/ *nm* cola tree; **noix de ~** cola nut.

colchique /kɔlʃik/ *nm* autumn crocus.

coléoptère /kɔleɔptɛʀ/ *nm* beetle.

colère /kɔlɛʀ/ *nf* **1** anger, wrath; **être en ~** to be angry, to be mad○; **passer sa ~ sur qn** to take out or vent one's anger on sb; **sous le coup de la ~** in a fit of anger; **2** fit; tantrum; **faire** or **piquer**○ **une ~** to have a fit; to throw a tantrum.

coléreux, -euse /kɔleʀø, øz/ *adj* [*person*] quick-tempered.

colibri /kɔlibʀi/ *nm* hummingbird.

colifichet /kɔlifiʃɛ/ *nm* trinket; knick-knack.

colimaçon /kɔlimasɔ̃/ *nm* snail; **escalier en ~** spiral staircase.

colin /kɔlɛ̃/ *nm* (fish) hake; coley.

colin-maillard /kɔlɛ̃majaʀ/ *nm* **jouer à ~** to play blind man's buff.

colique /kɔlik/ *nf* **1** diarrhoea; **2** stomach pain; (in babies) colic.

colis /kɔli/ *nm* parcel.

■ **~ piégé** parcel bomb; **~ postal** parcel sent by mail.

colite /kɔlit/ *nf* colitis.

collaborateur, -trice /kɔlabɔʀatœʀ, tʀis/ *nm,f* **1** colleague; assistant; **2** employee; **3** (journalist) contributor; **4** (derogatory) collaborator.

collaboration /kɔlabɔʀasjɔ̃/ *nf* **1** (to newspaper) contribution; (work on project) collaboration; **2** (in Second World War) collaboration.

collaborer /kɔlabɔʀe/ [1] *vi* **1 ~ à** to contribute to [*newspaper*]; to collaborate on [*project*]; **2** (as working partner) to collaborate.

collage /kɔlaʒ/ *nm* **1** collage; (in photography) montage; **2 le ~ des affiches** putting up posters.

collant, ~e /kɔlɑ̃, ɑ̃t/ **I** *adj* **1** [*substance, object*] sticky; **2** [*dress*] skintight; **3**○ [*person*] clinging; [*salesman*] persistant.

II *nm* tights (GB), panty hose (US); **~ de danse** dance tights.

collatéral, ~e, *mpl* **-aux** /kɔlateʀal, o/ *adj* [*street, aisle*] side.

collation /kɔlasjɔ̃/ *nf* light meal.

colle /kɔl/ *nf* **1** glue; (wallpaper) paste; **2**○ poser○; **3**○ (Sch) (students' slang) detention; **4**○ **~ (orale)** (students' slang) oral test.

collecte /kɔlɛkt/ *nf* **1** collection; **faire une ~** to raise funds; **2** (prayer) collect.

collecter /kɔlɛkte/ [1] *vtr* to collect.

collectif, -ive /kɔlɛktif, iv/ **I** *adj* [*work*] collective; [*dismissals*] mass; [*heating*] shared; [*ticket*] group; **immeuble ~** block of flats (GB), apartment building (US).

II *nm* **1** collective; **2** action group.

collection /kɔlɛksjɔ̃/ *nf* **1** collection (**de** of); **~ de timbres** stamp collection; **faire ~ de qch** to collect sth; **2** (of books) (gen) series; (by same author) set; **3** (in fashion) collection.

collectionner /kɔlɛksjɔne/ [1] *vtr* **1** to collect; **2** (figurative) **~ les erreurs** to make one mistake after another.

collectionneur, **-euse** /kɔlɛksjɔnœʀ, øz/ *nm,f* collector.

collectivement /kɔlɛktivmɑ̃/ *adv* (gen) collectively; [*resign*] en masse, as a body.

collectivité /kɔlɛktivite/ *nf* **1** group; **~ professionnelle** professional body; **2** community.

■ **~ locale** local authority (GB), local government (US).

collège /kɔlɛʒ/ *nm* **1** secondary school (GB), junior high school (US) (*up to age 16*); **2** college; **~ électoral** (Pol) electoral college.

■ **~ d'enseignement secondaire**, **CES** secondary school (GB), junior high school (US) (*up to age 16*); **~ d'enseignement technique**, **CET** *technical secondary school in France* (*up to age 16*).

collégial, **~e**, *mpl* **-iaux** /kɔleʒjal, o/ *adj* [*church*] collegiate; [*system*] collegial.

collégien, **-ienne** /kɔleʒjɛ̃, ɛn/ *nm,f* schoolboy/schoolgirl.

IDIOMS **se faire avoir**○ **comme un ~** to be completely taken in.

collègue /kɔlɛg/ *nmf* colleague.

coller /kɔle/ [1] **I** *vtr* **1** to stick, to glue [*wood, paper*]; to paste up [*poster*]; to hang [*wallpaper*]; to stick [sth] on [*label*]; to stick down [*envelope*]; **2 ~ qch contre** or **à qch** to press sth against sth; **il la colla contre le parapet** he pushed her up against the parapet; **3**○ to stick○; **je leur ai collé la facture sous le nez** I stuck○ the bill (right) under their noses; **~ une amende/une gifle à qn** to fine/slap sb; **4**○ (in exam) **se faire ~** to fail; **5**○ to give [sb] detention [*pupil*].

II *vi* **1** to stick; **2**○ **~ à** to be consistent or fit with; **leurs témoignages ne collent pas** their evidence doesn't tally.

III se coller *v refl* (+ *v être*) **1 se ~ à** or **contre qn/qch** to press oneself against sb/sth; **2**○ **dès qu'il rentre, il se colle devant son ordinateur** as soon as he comes in he's glued○ to his computer.

collerette /kɔlʀɛt/ *nf* **1** ruff; **2** ruffle.

collet /kɔlɛ/ *nm* snare.

IDIOMS **être ~ monté** to be prim; **mettre la main au ~ de qn** to collar○ sb.

colleur, **-euse** /kɔlœʀ, øz/ *nm,f* **~ (d'affiches)** billposter, billsticker.

collier /kɔlje/ *nm* **1** necklace; **~ de perles** string of pearls; **~ de fleurs** garland of flowers; **2** (of animal) collar; **3** beard.

IDIOMS **donner un coup de ~** to get one's head down; to put one's back into it.

collimateur /kɔlimatœʀ/ *nm* **avoir qn dans le ~**○ to have it in for sb○.

colline /kɔlin/ *nf* hill.

collision /kɔlizjɔ̃/ *nf* **1** collision; **2** clash, conflict.

colloque /kɔl(l)ɔk/ *nm* conference, symposium (**sur** on).

collusion /kɔlyzjɔ̃/ *nf* collusion.

collyre /kɔliʀ/ *nm* eyedrops.

colmater /kɔlmate/ [1] *vtr* to plug, to seal off [*leak*]; to seal [*crack*].

colombage /kɔlɔ̃baʒ/ *nm* half-timbering; **ferme à ~s** half-timbered farmhouse.

colombe /kɔlɔ̃b/ *nf* **1** dove; **2 ma ~** my little love.

colombier /kɔlɔ̃bje/ *nm* dovecote.

colon /kɔlɔ̃/ *nm* **1** colonist; **2**○ (soldiers' slang) colonel.

côlon /kolɔ̃, kɔlɔ̃/ *nm* colon.

colonel /kɔlɔnɛl/ *nm* (Mil) (in army) ≈ colonel; (in air force) ≈ group captain (GB), ≈ colonel (US).

colonial, **~e**, *mpl* **-iaux** /kɔlɔnjal, o/ *adj, nm,f* colonial.

colonialisme /kɔlɔnjalism/ *nm* colonialism.

colonie /kɔlɔni/ *nf* (gen) colony; **~ (de vacances)** holiday camp (*for children*).

coloniser /kɔlɔnize/[1] *vtr* to colonize.

colonnade /kɔlɔnad/ *nf* colonnade.

colonne /kɔlɔn/ *nf* (gen) column; (of bed) (bed)-post; **~ d'air** air stream.

■ **~ vertébrale** (Anat) spinal column.

colorant, **~e** /kɔlɔʀɑ̃, ɑ̃t/ **I** *adj* colouring[GB].

II *nm* **1** colouring[GB] agent; **2** dye; **3** (in chemistry) stain; **4** (Culin) colouring[GB]; **5** hair colourant[GB].

coloration /kɔlɔʀasjɔ̃/ *nf* **1** colouring[GB]; dyeing; staining; tinting; **2** colour[GB]; **3** skin tone.

coloré, **~e** /kɔlɔʀe/ *adj* **1** (gen) coloured[GB]; [*face*] ruddy; florid; **2** [*life, crowd*] colourful[GB]; [*style*] lively.

colorer /kɔlɔʀe/ [1] **I** *vtr* to colour[GB]; to tint; to stain; to dye.

II se colorer *v refl* (+ *v être*) [*face*] to flush.

coloriage /kɔlɔʀjaʒ/ *nm* **1** colouring[GB]; **2** coloured[GB] picture; **3** picture for colouring[GB] in.

colorier /kɔlɔʀje/ [2] *vtr* to colour in (GB), to color (US).

coloris /kɔlɔʀi/ *nm inv* colour[GB]; shade.

colossal, **~e**, *mpl* **-aux** /kɔlɔsal, o/ *adj* colossal, huge.

colosse /kɔlɔs/ *nm* giant.

colporter /kɔlpɔʀte/ [1] *vtr* **1** to spread [*news*]; **2** to peddle [*goods*].

colporteur, **-euse** /kɔlpɔʀtœʀ, øz/ *nm,f* pedlar.

coltiner○ /kɔltine/ [1] **I** *vtr* to lug○ [*suitcase*].

II se coltiner *v refl* (+ *v être*) **1** to lug○ [*heavy object*]; **2** to get stuck with○ [*chore, person*].

col-vert, *pl* **cols-verts**, **colvert** /kɔlvɛʀ/ *nm* mallard (*inv*).

colza /kɔlza/ *nm* rape; **huile de ~** rapeseed oil.

coma /kɔma/ *nm* coma.

comateux, **-euse** /kɔmatø, øz/ *adj* comatose.

combat /kɔ̃ba/ *nm* **1** (Mil) fighting; **~s aériens** air battles; **mettre hors de ~** to disable; **2** (in politics) struggle; **livrer un ~** to campaign; **3** (Sport) bout; **(mettre) hors de ~** (to put) out of action.

■ **~ de coqs** cock fight; **~ singulier** single combat.

combatif, -ive /kɔ̃batif, iv/ *adj* **1** assertive; **2** aggressive.

combativité /kɔ̃bativite/ *nf* fighting spirit.

combattant, ~e /kɔ̃batɑ̃, ɑ̃t/ **I** *adj* **1 esprit ~** fighting spirit; **2** [*unit*] combat.
II *nm,f* combatant.

combattre /kɔ̃batʀ/ [61] *vtr, vi* to fight.

combien[1] /kɔ̃bjɛ̃/ **I** *adv* **1 ~ mesure le salon?** how big is the lounge?; **j'aimerais savoir ~ il a payé son costume** I'd like to know how much or what he paid for that suit; **~ êtes-vous/sont-ils?** how many of you/them are there?; **2** (to what extent) **je ne saurais te dire ~ il me manque** I can't tell you how much I miss him; **c'est cher mais ~ efficace!** it's expensive but so effective!
II combien de *det* **1** how many, how much; **c'est à ~ de kilomètres?** how far away is it?; **2 ~ de temps faut-il?** how long does it take?

combien[2] /kɔ̃bjɛ̃/ *nmf inv* **1 tu es le/la ~?** (in queue) how many people are before you?; **2 le ~ sommes-nous?** what's the date today?; **3** (for measurements) **tu chausses du ~?** what size shoes do you take?; **4 tu le vois tous les ~?** how often do you see him?

combinaison /kɔ̃binɛzɔ̃/ *nf* **1** combining; combination; **2** (of safe) combination; **3** (full-length) slip; **4** jumpsuit; **5** overalls (GB), coveralls (US).
■ **~ d'aviateur** flying suit; **~ de plongée** wetsuit.

combine○ /kɔ̃bin/ *nf* trick○; scheme; **marcher dans la ~** to be in on it○.

combiné /kɔ̃bine/ *nm* handset, receiver.

combiner /kɔ̃bine/ [1] **I** *vtr* **1** to combine; **2** to work out [*plan*].
II se combiner *v refl* (+ *v être*) **1** [*elements*] to combine; **2** [*colours*] to go together.

comble /kɔ̃bl/ **I** *adj* [*room*] packed.
II *nm* **1 le ~ de l'injustice/du mauvais goût** the height of injustice/of bad taste; **être au ~ de la joie** to be absolutely delighted; **pour ~ de malchance j'ai...** to crown it all, I...; **c'est un** or **le ~**○! that's the limit!; **2** roof space; **de fond en ~** from top to bottom; completely.
III combles *nm pl* attic.

combler /kɔ̃ble/ [1] *vtr* **1** to fill (in) [*ditch*]; **2** to fill in [*gaps*]; to make up [*deficit*]; **~ son retard** to make up (for) lost time; **3** to fulfil[GB] [*need, desire*]; **la vie m'a comblé** I've had a wonderful life; **~ qn** to fill sb with joy or delight; **c'est une femme comblée** she has everything she could possibly want or wish for.

combustible /kɔ̃bystibl/ **I** *adj* combustible.
II *nm* fuel; **~ nucléaire** nuclear fuel.

combustion /kɔ̃bystjɔ̃/ *nf* combustion.

comédie /kɔmedi/ *nf* **1** comedy; **2** play-acting; **jouer la ~** to put on an act; **3**○ scene; **faire une ~** to make a scene; **4**○ **quelle ~ pour avoir un visa!** what a palaver○ to get a visa!
■ **~ de boulevard** light comedy; **~ musicale** musical.

comédien, -ienne /kɔmedjɛ̃, ɛn/ **I** *adj* **il est (un peu) ~** (figurative) he puts it on; (hypocritical) he's a sham.
II *nm,f* actor/actress.

comestible /kɔmɛstibl/ **I** *adj* edible.
II comestibles *nm pl* food; **marchand de ~s** grocer.

comète /kɔmɛt/ *nf* comet.

comique /kɔmik/ **I** *adj* **1** [*character, style*] comic; **2** funny.
II *nmf* comic actor/actress; comedian.
III *nm* **1** clown; **2** comedy; **3 c'est d'un ~!** it's so funny!

comité /kɔmite/ *nm* **1** committee; **2** group; **un dîner en petit ~** an intimate little dinner.

commandant /kɔmɑ̃dɑ̃/ *nm* (in army) ≈ major; (in air force) ≈ squadron leader (GB), ≈ major (US).
■ **~ de bord** captain; **~ en second** (Mil) ≈ second-in-command.

commande /kɔmɑ̃d/ *nf* **1** order; **2** commission; **passer ~ de qch à qn** to commission sb to do sth; **3** (Tech) control; **levier de ~** control lever; **être aux** or **tenir les ~s** to be at the controls; (figurative) to be in control; **4** (on computer) command.

commandement /kɔmɑ̃dmɑ̃/ *nm* **1** (Mil) command; **2** (in religion) commandment.

commander /kɔmɑ̃de/ [1] **I** *vtr* **1** to order; **~ qch à qn** to order sth from sb; **2** to commission [*book, survey*]; **3** (in café) to order; **4** (Mil) to command, to be in command of [*army*]; **5 ~ qn** to order sb about; **6** to command; **les circonstances commandent la prudence** the circumstances call for caution; **7** [*machine*] to control [*mechanism*].
II commander à *v+prep* **1** to be in command of; **2** to order, to command.
III *vi* to give the orders, to be in charge.
IV se commander *v refl* (+ *v être*) **ça ne se commande pas** it's not something you can control.

commanditaire /kɔmɑ̃ditɛʀ/ *nmf* **1** sleeping partner (GB), silent partner (US); **2** backer, sponsor; **3 le ~ d'un assassinat** the person behind an assassination.

commanditer /kɔmɑ̃dite/ [1] *vtr* **1** to finance [*company*]; **2** to sponsor [*project*]; **3** to be behind [*crime*].

commando /kɔmɑ̃do/ *nm* commando.

comme /kɔm/ **I** *adv* how; **~ il a raison!** how right he is!
II *conj* **1** as; **ici ~ en Italie** here as in Italy; **il est paresseux, ~ sa sœur d'ailleurs** he's lazy, just like his sister; **fais ~ moi** do as I do; **~ toujours** as always; **jolie ~ tout** ever so pretty (GB), really pretty; **2** (in comparisons) **il est grand ~ sa sœur** he's as tall as his sister; **c'est tout ~**○ it comes to the same thing; **elle me traite ~ un enfant** she treats me like a child; **3** like; **un manteau ~ le tien** a coat like yours; **~ ça** like that; **puisque c'est ~ ça** if that's the way it is; **4** as if, as though; **~ pour faire** as if to do; **~ si je n'avais que ça à faire!** as if I had nothing better to do!; **il a fait ~ s'il ne me voyait pas** he pretended (that)

he hadn't seen me; **5**○ **elle a eu ~ un évanouissement** she sort of fainted; **6 avare ~ il est, il ne te donnera rien** he's so mean, he won't give you anything; **7** as; **travailler ~ jardinier** to work as a gardener; **8** as, since; **~ elle était seule** as or since she was alone; **9** as; **~ il traversait la rue** as he was crossing the road.

IDIOMS **~ quoi!** which just shows!; **~ ci ~ ça**○ so-so○.

commémoratif, -ive /kɔmemɔʀatif, iv/ *adj* [*plaque*] commemorative; [*ceremony*] memorial.

commémorer /kɔmemɔʀe/ [1] *vtr* to commemorate.

commencement /kɔmɑ̃smɑ̃/ *nm* beginning; **~s pénibles** difficult beginnings.

commencer /kɔmɑ̃se/ [12] **I** *vtr* **1** to start, to begin; **c'est lui qui a commencé!** (fight) he started it!; **tu commences bien l'année!** that's a good start to the year!; **2 ~ à** or **de faire** to start or begin to do; **ça commence à bien faire**○ or **à suffire!** it's getting to be a bit much!

II *vi* to start, to begin; **pour ~, c'est trop cher** for a start, it's too expensive; **vous êtes tous coupables à ~ par toi** you're all guilty starting with you.

III *v impers* **il commence à neiger** it's starting or beginning to snow.

comment /kɔmɑ̃/ *adv* **1** how; **~ faire?** how can it be done?; **~ allez-vous?** how are you?; **~ t'appelles-tu?** what's your name?; **~ se peut-il que...?** how can it be that...?; **~ ça se fait**○**?** how come○?; **2 ~? qu'est-ce que tu dis?** pardon? what did you say?; **~, peux-tu répéter?** sorry, could you say that again?; **Paul ~?** Paul who?; **3 ~ est leur maison/fils?** what's their house/son like?; **~ trouvez-vous ma robe?** what do you think of my dress?; **4 ~ cela?** what do you mean?; **~? tu voudrais des excuses?** what? you expect me to apologize?; **~ donc!** but of course!; **et ~ (donc)**○**!** and how○!; **'c'était bon?'—'et ~**○**!'** 'was it nice?'—'it certainly was!'

commentaire /kɔmmɑ̃tɛʀ/ *nm* **1** comment; **2** commentary.

commentateur, -trice /kɔmmɑ̃tatœʀ, tʀis/ *nm,f* commentator.

commenter /kɔmmɑ̃te/ [1] *vtr* **1** to comment on [*decision, event*]; **2** to give a commentary on [*film, visit*]; **3** to commentate on [*match*]; **4** to comment on [*text*].

commérage /kɔmeʀaʒ/ *nm* gossip.

commerçant, ~e /kɔmɛʀsɑ̃, ɑ̃t/ **I** *adj* [*street*] shopping; [*nation*] trading; **il n'est pas très ~** he's not interested in pleasing the customer.

II *nm,f* shopkeeper, storekeeper (US); retailer.

commerce /kɔmɛʀs/ *nm* **1** shop, store (US); **dans le ~** in the shops or stores (US); **2** business; **3** trade; **faire le ~ de** to trade in; **faire ~ de** to sell; **faire du ~** to be in business.

■ **~ de détail** retail trade; **~ extérieur** foreign trade; **~ de gros** wholesale trade.

commercial, ~e, *mpl* **-iaux** /kɔmɛʀsjal, o/ **I** *adj* **1** commercial; **carrière ~e** career in sales and marketing; **2** trade; **embargo ~** trade embargo.

II *nm,f* sales and marketing person.

commercialisation /kɔmɛʀsjalizasjɔ̃/ *nf* marketing.

commercialiser /kɔmɛʀsjalize/ [1] *vtr* to market.

commère /kɔmɛʀ/ *nf* gossip.

commettre /kɔmɛtʀ/ [60] *vtr* to make [*error*]; to commit [*crime*]; to carry out [*attack*].

commis /kɔmi/ *nm* **1** (in office) clerk; **2** shop assistant (GB), salesclerk (US); **~ voyageur** travelling[GB] salesman.

commisération /kɔmizeʀasjɔ̃/ *nf* commiseration.

commissaire /kɔmisɛʀ/ *nm* **1 ~ (de police)** ≈ police superintendent; **2** commissioner; **3** (of race, sports event) steward; (of exhibition) organizer.

commissaire-priseur, *pl* **commissaires-priseurs** /kɔmisɛʀpʀizœʀ/ *nm* auctioneer.

commissariat /kɔmisaʀja/ *nm* **~ (de police)** police station.

commission /kɔmisjɔ̃/ **I** *nf* **1** committee; **2** commission; **payé à la ~** paid on a commission basis; **3** errand; **4 faire la ~ à qn** to give sb the message.

II commissions○ *nf pl* shopping; **faire les ~s** to do one's or the shopping.

commissionnaire /kɔmisjɔnɛʀ/ *nm* **1** agent, broker; **2** (in bank) messenger.

commissure /kɔmisyʀ/ *nf* corner.

commode /kɔmɔd/ **I** *adj* **1** (gen) convenient; [*tool*] handy; **2** easy; **3 ne pas être (très) ~** to be strict; to be difficult (to deal with).

II *nf* chest of drawers.

commodément /kɔmɔdemɑ̃/ *adv* [*situated*] conveniently; [*get around*] easily.

commodité /kɔmɔdite/ *nf* convenience.

commotion /kɔmosjɔ̃/ *nf* **1** (Med) **~ (cérébrale)** concussion (*of the brain*); **2** (figurative) shock.

commuer /kɔmɥe/ [1] *vtr* to commute [*prison sentence*].

commun, ~e[1] /kɔmœ̃, yn/ **I** *adj* **1** common; [*policy, property*] joint; [*friend*] mutual; [*room, memories, experience*] shared; **d'un ~ accord** by mutual agreement; **pour le bien ~** for the common good; **après dix ans de vie ~e** after living together for ten years; **2** [*person, tastes*] common; [*face*] plain; **3 elle est d'une beauté peu ~e** she's uncommonly beautiful.

II *nm* ordinary; **le ~ des mortels** ordinary mortals; **hors du ~** exceptional.

III en commun *phr* [*work, write*] jointly, together; **avoir qch en ~** to have sth in common; **nous mettons tout en ~** we share everything.

communal, ~e, *mpl* **-aux** /kɔmynal, o/ *adj* [*budget, resources*] local council (GB), local government (US); [*building*] local council (GB), community (US); **chemin ~** ≈ public track; **terrain ~** common land.

communautaire /kɔmynotɛʀ/ *adj* **1** (referring

to the EC) [*budget, law*] Community; **2 la vie ~** life in a community.

communauté /kɔmynote/ *nf* **1** community; **2** commune; **vivre en ~** to live in a commune; **3** (Law) **~ (de biens)** joint ownership.
■ **Communauté économique européenne, CEE** European Economic Community, EEC.

commune² /kɔmyn/ **I** *nf* village; town.
II communes *nf pl* **la Chambre des ~s** the (House of) Commons.

communément /kɔmynemɑ̃/ *adv* generally, commonly.

communiant, ~e /kɔmynjɑ̃, ɑ̃t/ *nm,f* **(premier) ~** child taking his/her first communion.

communicatif, -ive /kɔmynikatif, iv/ *adj* **1** [*person*] talkative; **2** [*gaiety, enthusiasm*] infectious.

communication /kɔmynikasjɔ̃/ *nf* **1 ~ (téléphonique)** (telephone) call; **mettre qn en ~ avec qn** to put sb through to sb; **2** report; (at conference) paper; **faire une ~ sur** to give a paper on; **3 demander ~ d'un dossier à qn** to ask sb for a file; **4** (between people) communication, contact; **être en ~ avec qn** to be in touch or contact with sb; **5** (media) communications; **~ de masse** mass media; **6** (by phone, radio) **moyens/voies de ~** communications.

communier /kɔmynje/ [2] *vi* to receive Communion.

communion /kɔmynjɔ̃/ *nf* **1** Communion; **2** (figurative) communion.
■ **~ (privée)** first communion; **~ solennelle** *solemn declaration of faith made at the age of 11.*

communiqué /kɔmynike/ *nm* **1** communiqué, press release; **2** statement.

communiquer /kɔmynike/ [1] **I** *vtr* **1** to announce [*date, decision, result*]; to give [*address, details*]; **2** [*person*] to pass on [*document, disease*]; to convey [*idea, feeling*]; **3** (in physics) to transmit.
II *vi* **1** to communicate; **2** [*rooms*] to be adjoining.
III se communiquer *v refl* (+ *v être*) **1** [*people*] to pass on [sth] to each other; **2** [*fire, disease*] to spread (**à** to).

communisme /kɔmynism/ *nm* communism.

communiste /kɔmynist/ *adj, nmf* communist.

commutateur /kɔmytatœʀ/ *nm* switch.

commuter /kɔmyte/ [1] *vtr* to commute.

compact, ~e /kɔ̃pakt/ *adj* **1** [*fog, crowd*] dense; [*earth*] compact; **2** [*car*] compact; **3** [*opposition*] monolithic.

compagne /kɔ̃paɲ/ *nf* **1** (female) companion; **2** (female animal) mate.

compagnie /kɔ̃paɲi/ *nf* **1** company; **en ~ de** together with; **2 salut la ~!** hello everybody!; **3** (commercial) company; **4** theatre company.
■ **~ aérienne** airline.

compagnon /kɔ̃paɲɔ̃/ *nm* **1** companion; **2** partner; **3** mate; **4** journeyman; **5** (in freemasonry) fellow of the craft.
■ **~ d'armes** comrade-in-arms; **~ de route** fellow traveller^GB.

comparable /kɔ̃paʀabl/ *adj* comparable.

comparaison /kɔ̃paʀɛzɔ̃/ *nf* **1** comparison; **c'est sans ~ le plus confortable** it's far and away the most comfortable; **2** simile; **3 adjectif de ~** comparative adjective.

comparaître /kɔ̃paʀɛtʀ/ [73] *vi* (Law) to appear.

comparatif, -ive /kɔ̃paʀatif, iv/ *adj* comparative.

comparé, ~e /kɔ̃paʀe/ *adj* **1** [*literature, law*] comparative; **2 comparé à** compared to.

comparer /kɔ̃paʀe/ [1] **I** *vtr* to compare.
II se comparer *v refl* (+ *v être*) **1 se ~ à qn/qch** to compare oneself with sb/sth; **2** to be comparable; **ça ne se compare pas** there's no comparison.

comparse /kɔ̃paʀs/ *nmf* **1** (in theatre) extra; **rôle de ~** walk-on part; (derogatory) minor part; **2** sidekick○.

compartiment /kɔ̃paʀtimɑ̃/ *nm* compartment.

compartimenter /kɔ̃paʀtimɑ̃te/ [1] *vtr* **1 ~ un grenier** to divide up a loft with partitions; **tiroir compartimenté** drawer divided into compartments; **2** (figurative) to compartmentalize [*administration, science*].

comparution /kɔ̃paʀysjɔ̃/ *nf* (Law) appearance (**devant** before).

compas /kɔ̃pa/ *nm* compass.

compassion /kɔ̃pasjɔ̃/ *nf* compassion.

compatible /kɔ̃patibl/ *adj* compatible.

compatir /kɔ̃patiʀ/ [3] *vi* to sympathize.

compatissant, ~e /kɔ̃patisɑ̃, ɑ̃t/ *adj* compassionate.

compatriote /kɔ̃patʀiɔt/ *nmf* fellow-countryman/-countrywoman, compatriot.

compensation /kɔ̃pɑ̃sasjɔ̃/ *nf* compensation.

compensé, ~e /kɔ̃pɑ̃se/ *adj* **1 semelle ~e** wedge heel; **2** (Med) compensated.

compenser /kɔ̃pɑ̃se/ [1] **I** *vtr* to compensate for; to make up for; to offset.
II se compenser *v refl* (+ *v être*) **ses défauts et ses qualités se compensent** his/her good qualities make up for his/her faults.

compère /kɔ̃pɛʀ/ *nm* **1** partner; accomplice; **2** mate○ (GB), buddy○ (US); **3 joyeux ~** cheery fellow○.

compétence /kɔ̃petɑ̃s/ *nf* **1** ability; competence, skill; **2** (Law) competence; **relever de la ~ de qn** to fall within the competence of sb; **3** domain; **être** or **entrer dans les ~s de qn** to be in sb's domain.

compétent, ~e /kɔ̃petɑ̃, ɑ̃t/ *adj* **1** competent; **2** [*authority*] competent; [*department*] appropriate.

compétitif, -ive /kɔ̃petitif, iv/ *adj* competitive.

compétition /kɔ̃petisjɔ̃/ *nf* **1** competition; **en ~ pour** competing for; **2** competition; **faire de la ~** to compete; **sport de ~** competitive sport; **3 ~ (sportive)** sporting event.

compétitivité /kɔ̃petitivite/ *nf* competitiveness.

compiler /kɔ̃pile/ [1] *vtr* to compile.

complainte /kɔ̃plɛ̃t/ *nf* lament.

complaire: **se complaire** /kɔ̃plɛʀ/ [59] *v refl* (+ *v être*) **se ~ à faire** to take pleasure in doing; **se ~ dans le malheur** to wallow in misery.

complaisance /kɔ̃plɛzɑ̃s/ *nf* **1** kindness, readiness to oblige; **2** (derogatory) soft attitude (**à l'égard de** toward(s)); **décrire la situation sans ~** to give an objective assessment of the situation; **3** (derogatory) complacency, smugness.

complaisant, **~e** /kɔ̃plɛzɑ̃, ɑ̃t/ *adj* **1** obliging; **2** (derogatory) indulgent; **3** (derogatory) complacent, self-satisfied.

complément /kɔ̃plemɑ̃/ *nm* **1 ~ de salaire** extra payment; **2** (to funding, programme) supplement; **3 ~ de nom** possessive phrase; **~ d'objet direct/indirect** direct object/indirect.

complémentaire /kɔ̃plemɑ̃tɛʀ/ *adj* **1** [*training, information*] further; [*activity, amount*] supplementary; **2** complementary.

complet, **-ète** /kɔ̃plɛ, ɛt/ **I** *adj* **1** (gen) complete; [*failure*] total; [*inquiry, range*] full; [*survey*] comprehensive; **athlète ~** all-rounder; **2** [*train, hotel*] full; **le gouvernement au ~** the entire government; **être (réuni) au (grand) ~** to be all present.

II *nm* suit; **~ deux/trois pièces** two-/three-piece suit.

complètement /kɔ̃plɛtmɑ̃/ *adv* completely; [*read*] right through; **~ réveillé** fully awake; **je m'en moque ~** I couldn't care less.

compléter /kɔ̃plete/ [14] **I** *vtr* **1** to complete [*collection*]; to top up [*sum*]; to supplement [*knowledge*]; **pour ~ le tout** or **tableau**○ (ironic) to cap it all; **2** [*person*] to complement [*person*]; **3** to complete [*sentence*].

II se compléter *v refl* (+ *v être*) [*elements, people*] to complement each other.

complexe /kɔ̃plɛks/ **I** *adj* complex.

II *nm* **1** complex; **~ d'Œdipe** Oedipus complex; **il n'a pas de ~** he has no inhibitions; **2** complex; **un ~ sportif** a sports complex.

complexé○, **~e** /kɔ̃plekse/ *adj* **il est très ~** he has a lot of hang-ups○.

complexer /kɔ̃plekse/ [1] *vtr* to give [sb] a complex .

complexité /kɔ̃plɛksite/ *nf* complexity.

complication /kɔ̃plikasjɔ̃/ *nf* complication.

complice /kɔ̃plis/ **I** *adj* **1 être ~ de qch** to be a party to sth; **2** [*air*] of complicity.

II *nmf* **1** accomplice; **se faire le ~ de qch** to be a party to sth.

complicité /kɔ̃plisite/ *nf* **1** complicity; **2** bond.

compliment /kɔ̃plimɑ̃/ **I** *nm* compliment; **faire un ~ à qn** to compliment sb.

II compliments *nm pl* (gen) compliments; **(tous) mes ~s!** congratulations!; **mes ~s à votre mère** give my regards to your mother.

complimenter /kɔ̃plimɑ̃te/ [1] *vtr* to compliment.

compliqué, **~e** /kɔ̃plike/ *adj* **1** complicated; [*mind*] tortuous; **2** (Med) [*fracture*] compound.

compliquer /kɔ̃plike/ [1] **I** *vtr* to complicate.

II se compliquer *v refl* (+ *v être*) **1** to get or become more complicated; **2 se ~ la vie** or **l'existence** to make life difficult for oneself.

complot /kɔ̃plo/ *nm* plot.

comploter /kɔ̃plɔte/ [1] *vtr, vi* to plot.

comportement /kɔ̃pɔʀtəmɑ̃/ *nm* **1** (gen) behaviour[GB]; **2** (of sportsman, car) performance.

comporter /kɔ̃pɔʀte/ [1] **I** *vtr* **1** to include; **2** to comprise, to consist of; **3** to entail, to involve [*risk, disadvantage*].

II se comporter *v refl* (+ *v être*) **1** to behave, to act; **2** [*sportsman, car*] to perform.

composant /kɔ̃pozɑ̃/ *nm* **1** (Tech) component; **2** (in chemistry) constituent.

composante /kɔ̃pozɑ̃t/ *nf* **1** (gen) element; **2** component.

composé, **~e** /kɔ̃poze/ **I** *adj* **1** [*salad*] mixed; **2** [*manner*] affected.

II *nm* (in chemistry) compound.

composer /kɔ̃poze/ [1] **I** *vtr* **1** [*elements, people*] to make up; **composé de** made up of; **2** [*person*] to put [sth] together [*programme, menu*]; to select [*team*]; to make up [*bouquet*]; **3** [*artist*] to compose [*piece of music*]; to paint [*picture*]; **4** to dial [*number*]; **5** to typeset [*page*].

II se composer *v refl* (+ *v être*) **1 se ~ de** to be made up of ; **2** to assume [*attitude, expression*].

composite /kɔ̃pozit/ *adj* **1** heterogeneous; **2** (Tech) [*material*] composite.

compositeur, **-trice** /kɔ̃pozitœʀ, tʀis/ *nm,f* **1** (Mus) composer; **2** typesetter.

composition /kɔ̃pozisjɔ̃/ *nf* **1** (of government, delegation) make-up; (of team) line-up; (of product) ingredients; (of drug) composition; **2** (of government) formation; (of committee) setting up; (of team) selection; (of list, menu) drawing up; (of bouquet) making up; **de ma ~** of my invention; **3** (of piece of music, picture) composition (**de** by); (of letter) writing; **~ florale** flower arrangement; **4** (Sch) end-of-term test; **5** typesetting.

IDIOMS **être de bonne ~** to be good-natured.

compost /kɔ̃pɔst/ *nm* compost.

composter /kɔ̃pɔste/ [1] *vtr* to (date)stamp; to punch [*ticket*].

compote /kɔ̃pɔt/ *nf* (Culin) stewed fruit, compote; **mettre qn en ~** to beat sb black and blue.

compréhensible /kɔ̃pʀeɑ̃sibl/ *adj* **1** understandable; **2** comprehensible.

compréhensif, **-ive** /kɔ̃pʀeɑ̃sif, iv/ *adj* understanding.

compréhension /kɔ̃pʀeɑ̃sjɔ̃/ *nf* **1** understanding; **2** (of text, words) comprehension; (of language) understanding.

comprendre /kɔ̃pʀɑ̃dʀ/ [52] **I** *vtr* **1** to understand; **il ne comprend rien à rien** he hasn't got a clue; **c'est à n'y rien ~** it's completely baffling; **mal ~** to misunderstand; **être compris comme une menace** to be interpreted as a threat; **se faire ~** to make oneself understood; **je n'ai pas le temps, tu**

comprends you see, I haven't got time; **2** to consist of, to comprise; **3** to include.

II se comprendre *v refl* (+ *v être*) **1** [*people*] to understand each other or one another; **2 je me comprends** I know what I'm trying to say; **3** [*attitude*] to be understandable.

compresse /kɔ̃prɛs/ *nf* compress.

compresser /kɔ̃prese/ [1] *vtr* to compress.

compressible /kɔ̃presibl/ *adj* **1** [*gas*] compressible; **2** [*expenses, staff*] that can be cut back on.

compression /kɔ̃prɛsjɔ̃/ *nf* **1** (Tech) compression; **2** reduction; **3** cut.

comprimé /kɔ̃prime/ *nm* tablet.

comprimer /kɔ̃prime/ [1] *vtr* **1** to constrict; to squeeze [*tube*]; **2** (Med) to compress; **3** (Tech) **air comprimé** compressed air; **4** to cut [*expenditure*].

compris, ~e /kɔ̃pri, iz/ **I** *pp* ▶ **comprendre**.

II *pp adj* including; **service ~/non ~** service included/not included.

III tout compris *phr* in total, all in° (GB).

IV y compris *phr* including.

compromettant, ~e /kɔ̃prɔmetɑ̃, ɑ̃t/ *adj* compromising.

compromettre /kɔ̃prɔmɛtr/ [60] **I** *vtr* **1** to endanger, to jeopardize; **2** to compromise [*person*]; to damage [*reputation*].

II se compromettre *v refl* (+ *v être*) to compromise oneself.

compromis, ~e /kɔ̃prɔmi, iz/ **I** *adj* **1** [*career*] in jeopardy; **2** [*person*] compromised; [*reputation*] damaged.

II *nm* compromise (**entre** between).

comptabiliser /kɔ̃tabilize/ [1] *vtr* to count (the number of) [*mistakes, entries*].

comptabilité /kɔ̃tabilite/ *nf* **1** accountancy; **2** bookkeeping; **faire sa ~** to do one's accounts; **3** accounts department.

comptable /kɔ̃tabl/ **I** *adj* **1** [*year*] accounting; [*department*] accounts; **agent ~** accountant; **2** [*noun*] countable; **non ~** uncountable.

II *nmf* accountant; bookkeeper.

comptant /kɔ̃tɑ̃/ *adj inv, adv* cash.

compte /kɔ̃t/ **I** *nm* **1** count; **faire le ~ de qch** to work out [*expenditure*]; to count (up) [*people, objects*]; **le ~ est bon** that works out right; **comment fais-tu ton ~ pour faire...?** (figurative) how do you manage to do...?; **au bout du ~** in the end; **tout ~ fait** all things considered; **en fin de ~** at the end of the day; **2** (of money) amount; (of objects, people) number; **le ~ n'y est pas, il n'y a pas le ~** that's not the right amount; that's not the right number; **avoir son ~ d'heures de sommeil** to get the right amount of sleep; **il a son ~**° he's done for°; (drunk) he's had a drop too much; **nous avons eu notre ~ d'ennuis** (figurative) we've had more than our fair share of problems; **à ce ~-là** in that case; **3 prendre qch en ~, tenir ~ de qch** to take sth into account; **~ tenu de** considering; **4 être** or **travailler à son ~** to be self-employed; **pour le ~ de qn** on behalf of sb; **y trouver son ~** to get something out of it; **5** account; **faire ses ~s** to do one's accounts; **6** (in bank, with shop) account; **~ en banque** bank account; **mettre qch sur le ~ de qn** to charge sth to sb's account; (figurative) to put sth down to sb; **7 rendre ~ de qch à qn** to give an account of sth to sb; to account for sth to sb; **devoir rendre des ~s à qn** to be answerable to sb; **demander des ~s à qn** to ask for an explanation from sb; **8 se rendre ~ de** to realize; to notice; **9 dire qch sur le ~ de qn** to say sth about sb; **10** (Sport) (in boxing) count.

II à bon compte *phr* **s'en tirer à bon ~** to get off lightly.

■ **~ chèques** current account (GB), checking account (US); **~ chèque postal, CCP** post office account; **~ à rebours** countdown.

compte-gouttes /kɔ̃tgut/ *nm inv* dropper; **au ~** (figurative) sparingly.

compter /kɔ̃te/ [1] **I** *vtr* **1** to count; **on compte deux millions de chômeurs** there is a total of two million unemployed; **on ne compte plus ses victoires** he/she has had countless victories; **2 ~ une bouteille pour trois** to allow a bottle between three people; **je préfère ~ large** I prefer to be on the safe side; **3** (as fee, price) **~ qch à qn** to charge sb for sth; **4** to count, include; **tu m'as compté?** have you counted or included me?; **sans ~ les soucis** not to mention the worry; **5** to have; **notre club compte des gens célèbres** our club has some well-known people among its members; **6 ~ faire** to intend to do; **7 il comptait que je lui prête de l'argent** he expected me to lend him some money; **'je vais t'aider'—'j'y compte bien'** 'I'll help you'—'I should hope so too'; **8 il a toujours compté ses sous** he has always watched the pennies; **sans ~** [*give, spend*] freely; **ses jours sont ~s** his/her days are numbered.

II *vi* **1** to count; **~ sur ses doigts** to count on one's fingers; **2** to matter; **c'est l'intention qui compte** it's the thought that counts; **ça compte beaucoup pour moi** it means a lot to me; **4** to count; **ça ne compte pas, il a triché** it doesn't count, he cheated; **5 ~ au nombre de, ~ parmi** to be counted among; **6 ~ avec** to reckon with; to take [sb/sth] into account; **~ sans** not to take [sb/sth] into account; **7 ~ sur** to count on [*person, help*]; (for support) to rely on [*person, resource*]; (in anticipation) to reckon on [*sum, income*]; **ne compte pas sur moi** (responding to invitation) count me out.

III se compter *v refl* (+ *v être*) **leurs victoires se comptent par douzaines** they have had dozens of victories.

IV à compter de *phr* as from.

V sans compter que *phr* and what is more; especially as.

compte(-)rendu, *pl* **comptes(-)rendus** /kɔ̃trɑ̃dy/ *nm* (gen) report; (of book) review.

compteur /kɔ̃tœr/ *nm* meter; clock; **~ d'eau** water meter.

■ **~ kilométrique** ≈ milometer; **~ de vitesse** speedometer.

comptine /kɔ̃tin/ *nf* **1** counting rhyme; **2** nursery rhyme.

comptoir /kɔ̃twaʀ/ *nm* **1** (of café) bar; **2** (of shop) counter.

compulser /kɔ̃pylse/ [1] *vtr* to consult.

comte /kɔ̃t/ *nm* (title) count; earl.

comté /kɔ̃te/ *nm* **1** county; **2** earldom (*land*).

comtesse /kɔ̃tɛs/ *nf* countess.

con●, **conne** /kɔ̃, kɔn/ **I** *adj* **1** bloody◑ (GB) stupid; **2** dead○ easy.
II *nm,f* bloody◑ idiot (GB), stupid jerk○; **idée à la ~** lousy○ idea.

concasser /kɔ̃kase/ [1] *vtr* **1** (Culin, Tech) to crush; **2** (Mus) to mix.

concave /kɔ̃kav/ *adj* concave.

concéder /kɔ̃sede/ [14] *vtr* to concede.

concentration /kɔ̃sɑ̃tʀasjɔ̃/ *nf* concentration.
■ **~ urbaine** conurbation.

concentré, **~e** /kɔ̃sɑ̃tʀe/ **I** *pp* ▶ **concentrer**.
II *pp adj* **1 un air ~** a look of concentration; **2** concentrated; [*lait*] condensed.
III *nm* (Culin) **~ de tomate** tomato purée (GB) or paste (US).

concentrer /kɔ̃sɑ̃tʀe/ [1] **I** *vtr* to concentrate.
II se concentrer *v refl* (+ *v être*) to concentrate; [*attention*] to be concentrated (**sur** on).

concentrique /kɔ̃sɑ̃tʀik/ *adj* concentric.

concept /kɔ̃sɛpt/ *nm* concept.

conception /kɔ̃sɛpsjɔ̃/ *nf* **1** conception; **2** design; **3** idea; conception.

conceptualiser /kɔ̃sɛptɥalize/ [1] *vtr* to conceptualize.

concernant /kɔ̃sɛʀnɑ̃/ *prep* **1** concerning; **2** as regards, with regard to.

concerner /kɔ̃sɛʀne/ [1] *vtr* **1** to concern; **en ce qui me concerne** as far as I am concerned; **2** to affect.

concert /kɔ̃sɛʀ/ **I** *nm* **1** (Mus) concert; **2 ~ d'applaudissements** roar of applause.
II de concert *phr* **ils ont agi de ~** they worked together.

concertation /kɔ̃sɛʀtasjɔ̃/ *nf* **1** consultation; **2** cooperation.

concerté, **~e** /kɔ̃sɛʀte/ *adj* [*plan, action*] concerted.

concerter: **se concerter** /kɔ̃sɛʀte/ [1] *v refl* (+ *v être*) to consult each other.

concertiste /kɔ̃sɛʀtist/ *nmf* concert performer.

concerto /kɔ̃sɛʀto/ *nm* concerto.

concession /kɔ̃sesjɔ̃/ *nf* **1** concession; **film sans ~s** uncompromising film; **2** (awarding of right) concession (**de** of); **3** (right, contract) (of mine, site) concession; (of product) distributorship; (Aut) dealership.

concessionnaire /kɔ̃sesjɔnɛʀ/ *nmf* (commercial) agent; (Aut) dealer.

concevable /kɔ̃s(ə)vabl/ *adj* conceivable.

concevoir /kɔ̃s(ə)vwaʀ/ [5] **I** *vtr* **1** to design [*product, system*]; **2** to conceive [*child*]; **3** to understand [*attitude*]; **4** to see [*phenomenon, activity*] (**comme** as); **5** (formal) to conceive [*hatred*]; to have [*doubt*].
II se concevoir *v refl* (+ *v être*) **1** to be conceivable; **2** to be understandable.

concierge /kɔ̃sjɛʀʒ/ *nmf* caretaker (GB), superintendant (US).

concile /kɔ̃sil/ *nm* council.

conciliant, **~e** /kɔ̃siljɑ̃, ɑ̃t/ *adj* conciliatory.

conciliation /kɔ̃siljasjɔ̃/ *nf* conciliation; (of couple) reconciliation.

concilier /kɔ̃silje/ [2] **I** *vtr* to reconcile.
II se concilier *v refl* (+ *v être*) (formal) to win [*support*]; to win over [*person*].

concis, **~e** /kɔ̃si, iz/ *adj* concise.

concision /kɔ̃sizjɔ̃/ *nf* conciseness; **avec ~** concisely.

concitoyen, **-enne** /kɔ̃sitwajɛ̃, ɛn/ *nm,f* fellow-citizen.

conclave /kɔ̃klav/ *nm* conclave.

concluant, **~e** /kɔ̃klyɑ̃, ɑ̃t/ *adj* conclusive.

conclure /kɔ̃klyʀ/ [78] *vtr* **1** to conclude (**que** that); **2** to conclude [*deal, agreement*]; **'marché conclu!'** 'it's a deal!'; **3** [*person*] to conclude [*speech*] (**par** with); **4** [*concert*] to bring [sth] to a close.

conclusion /kɔ̃klyzjɔ̃/ **I** *nf* **1** conclusion; **~, il y a un problème**○ in other words, there's a problem; **tirer les ~s d'une expérience** to learn from an experience; **ne tire pas de ~s hâtives** don't jump to conclusions; **2** (of deal, treaty) conclusion; **3** (of speech, session) close; (of event) outcome.
II conclusions *nf pl* **1** (of analysis, autopsy) results; (of inquiry) findings; **2** (Law) (of expert) opinion; (of jury) verdict; (of plaintiff) pleadings, submissions.

concocter○ /kɔ̃kɔkte/ [1] *vtr* to concoct [*dish*]; to devise [*programme*].

concombre /kɔ̃kɔ̃bʀ/ *nm* cucumber.

concordance /kɔ̃kɔʀdɑ̃s/ *nf* concordance (**de** between); compatibility; **les ~s de vues entre eux** their like-minded attitudes.
■ **~ des temps** sequence of tenses.

concordant, **~e** /kɔ̃kɔʀdɑ̃, ɑ̃t/ *adj* [*facts*] corroborating; [*testimonies*] which are in agreement.

concorder /kɔ̃kɔʀde/ [1] *vi* [*results, evidence*] to tally; [*estimates*] to agree.

concourir /kɔ̃kuʀiʀ/ [26] **I** *vi* [*candidate*] to compete.
II concourir à *v+prep* **~ à qch/à faire** [*factors*] to combine to bring about sth/to do; [*people*] to work together toward(s) sth/to do; [*factor, person*] to help bring about sth/do.

concours /kɔ̃kuʀ/ *nm inv* **1** (gen) competition; (agricultural) show; **~ de beauté** beauty contest; **être hors ~** to be ineligible to compete; **2** competitive examination; **~ d'entrée** entrance examination; **3** help, assistance; support; cooperation.
■ **~ de circonstances** combination of circumstances; **~ hippique** (sport) show jumping; horse show.

concret, **-ète** /kɔ̃kʀɛ, ɛt/ *adj* **1** [*result*] concrete; [*presence*] tangible; **2** [*mind, person*] practical.

concrètement /kɔ̃kʀɛtmɑ̃/ *adv* **1** in concrete terms; **2** in practical terms.

concrétisation /kɔ̃kʀetizasjɔ̃/ *nf* (of alliance) concrete expression; (of hopes) fulfilment[GB]; (of ambition) achievement.

concrétiser /kɔ̃kʀetize/ [1] **I** *vtr* to make [sth] a reality [*plan, project*].
II se concrétiser *v refl* (+ *v être*) [*plan, dream*] to become a reality; [*offer*] to materialize.

concubin, ~e /kɔ̃kybɛ̃, in/ *nm,f* (Law) common law husband/wife.

concubinage /kɔ̃kybinaʒ/ *nm* cohabitation.

concupiscent, ~e /kɔ̃kypisɑ̃, ɑ̃t/ *adj* lecherous.

concurrence /kɔ̃kyʀɑ̃s/ *nf* competition; **faire (de la) ~ à qn** to compete with sb; **prix défiant toute ~** unbeatable price; **jusqu'à ~ de** up to a limit of.

concurrencer /kɔ̃kyʀɑ̃se/ [12] *vtr* to compete with.

concurrent, ~e /kɔ̃kyʀɑ̃, ɑ̃t/ **I** *adj* rival.
II *nm,f* (for a job) rival; (Sport) competitor; (in competitive examination) candidate.

concurrentiel, -ielle /kɔ̃kyʀɑ̃sjɛl/ *adj* competitive.

condamnable /kɔ̃danabl/ *adj* reprehensible.

condamnation /kɔ̃danasjɔ̃/ *nf* **1** (Law) conviction; sentence; **2** condemnation.

condamné, ~e /kɔ̃dane/ **I** *adj* **1** [*person*] terminally ill; **2** [*door*] sealed up.
II *nm,f* convicted prisoner; **~ à mort** condemned man/woman.

condamner /kɔ̃dane/ [1] *vtr* **1** (Law) to sentence; **~ qn à une amende** to fine sb; **~ qn à mort** to sentence sb to death; **~ qn pour vol** to convict sb of theft; **2** [*law*] to punish [*thieving, smuggling*]; **3** [*person, country*] to condemn [*act, decision*]; **4 il se voit condamné à un choix difficile** he's being forced to make a difficult choice; **~ qn à faire** to compel sb to do; **5** to seal up [*window*]; to shut up [*room*]; **6** (figurative) to spell death for [*society, industry*]; **7 les médecins l'ont condamné** the doctors have given up hope of saving him.

condensation /kɔ̃dɑ̃sasjɔ̃/ *nf* condensation.

condensé /kɔ̃dɑ̃se/ *nm* summary; digest.

condenser /kɔ̃dɑ̃se/ [1] *vtr*, **se condenser** *v refl* (+ *v être*) to condense.

condescendance /kɔ̃desɑ̃dɑ̃s/ *nf* condescension.

condescendant, ~e /kɔ̃desɑ̃dɑ̃, ɑ̃t/ *adj* condescending.

condiment /kɔ̃dimɑ̃/ *nm* (Culin) seasoning; condiment.

condisciple /kɔ̃disipl/ *nmf* fellow student.

condition /kɔ̃disjɔ̃/ **I** *nf* **1** condition; **à une ~** on one condition; **à ~ d'avoir le temps** provided (that) one has the time; **sous ~** [*freed*] conditionally; **sans ~(s)** [*acceptance*] unconditional; [*accept*] unconditionally; **imposer ses ~s** to impose one's own terms; **~ préalable** precondition; **2** (Law) (of contract, treaty) term; **3** condition; **être en mauvaise ~ (physique)** to be out of condition or unfit; **4** condition; **la ~ ouvrière** (the conditions of) working-class life; **5 ~ (sociale)** social status; **des personnes de toutes ~s** people from all walks of life.
II conditions *nf pl* **1** conditions; **dans ces ~s** in these conditions; in that case; **2** terms; **~s de financement** methods of financing.

conditionnel, -elle /kɔ̃disjɔnɛl/ **I** *adj* conditional.
II *nm* conditional.

conditionnement /kɔ̃disjɔnmɑ̃/ *nm* **1** (of person) conditioning; **2** packaging.

conditionner /kɔ̃disjɔne/ [1] *vtr* **1** to condition; **2** to package; **conditionné sous vide** vacuum-packed.

condoléances /kɔ̃dɔleɑ̃s/ *nf pl* condolences; **toutes mes ~** please accept my deepest sympathy.

condom /kɔ̃dɔm/ *nm* condom.

condor /kɔ̃dɔʀ/ *nm* condor.

conducteur, -trice /kɔ̃dyktœʀ, tʀis/ **I** *adj* **1** conductive; **2** [*principle*] guiding.
II *nm,f* **1** (of vehicle) driver; **2** (of machine) operator.
III *nm* conductor.

conductible /kɔ̃dyktibl/ *adj* conductive.

conduire /kɔ̃dɥiʀ/ [69] **I** *vtr* **1** to take [*person*]; (in car) to drive; **conduisez monsieur à sa chambre** show the gentleman to his room; **2** [*leader, guide, studies*] to lead (**à** to); **la route qui conduit à Oxford** the road that goes to Oxford; **~ qn au désespoir** to drive sb to despair; **3** to drive [*car, train*]; to ride [*motorbike*]; **4** to conduct [*research, negotiations*]; to pursue [*policy*]; to carry out [*project*]; to run [*business*]; **5** to carry [*water*]; to conduct [*electricity, heat*].
II se conduire *v refl* (+ *v être*) to behave.

conduit /kɔ̃dɥi/ *nm* **1** conduit; **2** (Anat) canal, duct.
■ **~ de fumée** flue; **~ de ventilation** ventilation shaft.

conduite /kɔ̃dɥit/ *nf* **1** behaviour[GB]; (of pupil) conduct; **2** (of inquiry) conducting; (of building works) supervision; (of company) management; (of nation) leadership; **3** (of vehicle) driving; (of motorbike) riding; **4** (Aut) **voiture avec ~ à gauche** left-hand drive car; **5** (exam) driving test; **6** pipe.

cône /kon/ *nm* cone.

confection /kɔ̃fɛksjɔ̃/ *nf* **1 la ~** the clothing industry; **2** making.

confectionner /kɔ̃fɛksjɔne/ [1] *vtr* (gen) to make; to prepare [*meal*].

confédération /kɔ̃fedeʀasjɔ̃/ *nf* confederation.
■ **la Confédération helvétique** Switzerland.

confédéré, ~e /kɔ̃fedeʀe/ *adj, nm* confederate.

conférence /kɔ̃feʀɑ̃s/ *nf* **1** lecture; **2** conference; **3** debate.
■ **~ de presse** press conference; **~ au sommet** summit meeting.

conférencier, **-ière** /kɔ̃feʀɑ̃sje, ɛʀ/ *nm,f* speaker; lecturer.

conférer /kɔ̃feʀe/ [14] *vtr* (gen) to give; to confer [*status, right*].

confesser /kɔ̃fese/ [1] **I** *vtr* **1** to confess [*sin*]; **2 ~ qn** to hear sb's confession.
II se confesser *v refl* (+ *v être*) **1** to go to confession; **se ~ à un prêtre** to make one's confession to a priest; **2 se ~ à un ami** to confide in a friend.

confesseur /kɔ̃fesœʀ/ *nm* confessor.

confession /kɔ̃fesjɔ̃/ *nf* **1** confession; **2** faith.
IDIOMS **on te donnerait le bon Dieu sans ~** you look as if butter wouldn't melt in your mouth.

confessionnal, *pl* **-aux** /kɔ̃fesjɔnal, o/ *nm* confessional.

confetti /kɔ̃feti/ *nm* confetti.

confiance /kɔ̃fjɑ̃s/ *nf* **1** trust; **en toute ~** with complete confidence; **de ~** [*person*] trustworthy; [*mission*] which requires (the utmost) trust; **avoir ~ en qn**, **faire ~ à qn** to trust sb; **mettre qn en ~** to win sb's trust; **2** (in ability) confidence; **faire ~ à** to have confidence in; **3** confidence; **~ en soi** (self-)confidence.

confiant, **~e** /kɔ̃fjɑ̃, ɑ̃t/ *adj* **1** confident; **2** (self-)confident; **3** trusting.

confidence /kɔ̃fidɑ̃s/ *nf* secret, confidence; **être dans la ~** to be in on the secret; **faire des ~s à qn sur qch** to confide in sb about sth.

confident, **~e** /kɔ̃fidɑ̃, ɑ̃t/ *nm,f* confidant/confidante.

confidentialité /kɔ̃fidɑ̃sjalite/ *nf* confidentiality.

confidentiel, **-ielle** /kɔ̃fidɑ̃sjɛl/ *adj* confidential.

confier /kɔ̃fje/ [2] **I** *vtr* **1 ~ qch à qn** to entrust sb with sth [*mission*]; to entrust sth to sb [*money, letters*]; **2 ~ qch à qn** to confide sth to sb [*intentions*]; **~ un secret à qn** to tell sb a secret.
II se confier *v refl* (+ *v être*) to confide (**à** in).

configuration /kɔ̃figyʀasjɔ̃/ *nf* **1** shape; **la ~ du terrain** the lie of the land; **la ~ des lieux** the layout of the premises; **2** configuration; **3** set-up.

confiné, **~e** /kɔ̃fine/ *adj* **1** [*atmosphere*] stuffy; [*air*] stale; **2** [*space*] confined, restricted.

confiner /kɔ̃fine/ [1] **I** *vtr* to confine.
II confiner à *v+prep* to border on.
III se confiner *v refl* (+ *v être*) **1** to shut oneself away or up; **2 se ~ dans un rôle** to restrict oneself to a role.

confins /kɔ̃fɛ̃/ *nm pl* boundaries; (of desert) edges.

confirmation /kɔ̃fiʀmasjɔ̃/ *nf* confirmation.

confirmer /kɔ̃fiʀme/ [1] **I** *vtr* to confirm [*order, fact*]; to uphold [*decision*]; to be evidence of [*attitude, quality*]; to affirm [*intention*].
II se confirmer *v refl* (+ *v être*) [*news*] to be confirmed; [*testimony*] to be corroborated.

confiscation /kɔ̃fiskasjɔ̃/ *nf* confiscation, seizure.

confiserie /kɔ̃fizʀi/ *nf* **1** confectioner's (shop); **2** confectionery.

confiseur, **-euse** /kɔ̃fizœʀ, øz/ *nm,f* confectioner.

confisquer /kɔ̃fiske/ [1] *vtr* to confiscate, to seize.

confit, **~e** /kɔ̃fi, it/ **I** *adj* (Culin) [*fruits*] crystallized; [*gherkin*] pickled.
II *nm* confit; **~ de canard** confit of duck.

confiture /kɔ̃fityʀ/ *nf* (Culin) jam, preserve; marmalade.
IDIOMS **donner de la ~ aux cochons** to cast pearls before swine.

conflictuel, **-elle** /kɔ̃fliktɥɛl/ *adj* [*subject*] controversial; [*tendency*] conflicting; [*relationship*] confrontational.

conflit /kɔ̃fli/ *nm* conflict.
■ **~ de générations** generation gap; **~ social** industrial strife; **~ du travail** industrial dispute.

confluence /kɔ̃flyɑ̃s/ *nf* confluence; (figurative) convergence.

confluent /kɔ̃flyɑ̃/ *nm* confluence.

confondre /kɔ̃fɔ̃dʀ/ [53] **I** *vtr* **1** to mix up, to confuse; **je l'ai confondu avec son cousin** I mistook him for his cousin; **tous secteurs confondus** all sectors taken together; **2** (literary) to merge; **3** (formal) to stagger; **leur ignorance me confondait** I found their ignorance staggering; **4** to expose [*traitor*].
II se confondre *v refl* (+ *v être*) **1** [*shapes, colours*] to merge; [*events, facts*] to become confused; **2** [*interests, hopes*] to coincide; **sa vie se confond avec son œuvre** his life and his work are one; **3** (formal) **se ~ en excuses** to apologize profusely.

conforme /kɔ̃fɔʀm/ *adj* **1 être ~ à** to be in keeping with [*law*]; to comply with [*regulations*]; **2 être ~ à l'original** to conform to the original.

conformément /kɔ̃fɔʀmemɑ̃/ *adv* **~ à** in accordance with.

conformer: **se conformer** /kɔ̃fɔʀme/ [1] *v refl* (+ *v être*) to conform to [*tradition*]; to comply with [*regulations*].

conformisme /kɔ̃fɔʀmism/ *nm* conformity.

conformité /kɔ̃fɔʀmite/ *nf* **1 ~ à la loi** compliance with the law; **en ~ avec** [*act*] in accordance with; **2** similarity; **vérifier la ~ de la traduction à l'original** to check that the translation is faithful to the original; **3** (of tastes, points of view) correspondence.

confort /kɔ̃fɔʀ/ *nm* comfort; **maison avec tout le ~** house with all mod cons○ (GB) or modern conveniences.

confortable /kɔ̃fɔʀtabl/ *adj* comfortable; **pas ~** uncomfortable.

confortablement /kɔ̃fɔʀtabləmɑ̃/ *adv* comfortably.

conforter /kɔ̃fɔʀte/ [1] *vtr* to consolidate [*position*]; to reinforce [*situation*].

confrère /kɔ̃fʀɛʀ/ *nm* (at work) colleague; (in association) fellow member.

confrérie /kɔ̃fʀeʀi/ *nf* brotherhood.

confrontation /kɔ̃fʀɔ̃tasjɔ̃/ *nf* **1** (of ideas, witnesses) confrontation; (of texts) comparison; **2** (between people) debate; clash.

confronter /kɔ̃fʀɔ̃te/ [1] *vtr* **1** to confront [*witnesses*]; **2** to compare [*texts*].

confus, ~e /kɔ̃fy, yz/ *adj* **1** confused; **2** [*feeling, fear*] vague; **3** sorry; embarrassed.

confusément /kɔ̃fyzemɑ̃/ *adv* [*explain*] confusedly; [*feel*] vaguely.

confusion /kɔ̃fyzjɔ̃/ *nf* **1** confusion; **2** embarrassment; **3** mix-up.

congé /kɔ̃ʒe/ *nm* **1** leave; **prendre quatre jours de ~** to take four days off; **être en ~ de maladie** to be on sick leave; **avoir ~ le lundi** to have Mondays off; **2** notice; **donner (son) ~ à qn** to give sb notice; **3 prendre ~ de qn** to take leave of sb.
■ **~s scolaires** school holidays (GB) or vacation (US).

congédier /kɔ̃ʒedje/ [2] *vtr* to dismiss.

congélateur /kɔ̃ʒelatœʀ/ *nm* freezer; (in refrigerator) freezer compartment.

congélation /kɔ̃ʒelasjɔ̃/ *nf* (gen) freezing; (of oil) congelation.

congeler /kɔ̃ʒle/ [17] **I** *vtr* to freeze; **produits congelés** frozen foods.
II se congeler *v refl* (+ *v être*) to freeze.

congénère /kɔ̃ʒenɛʀ/ *nmf* fellow creature.

congénital, ~e, *mpl* **-aux** /kɔ̃ʒenital, o/ *adj* congenital.

congère /kɔ̃ʒɛʀ/ *nf* snowdrift.

congestion /kɔ̃ʒɛstjɔ̃/ *nf* congestion.
■ **~ cérébrale** stroke; **~ pulmonaire** congestion of the lungs.

congestionner /kɔ̃ʒɛstjɔne/ [1] *vtr* **1 il est tout congestionné** he's all flushed; **2** to congest [*street*].

conglomérat /kɔ̃glɔmeʀa/ *nm* **1** conglomerate; **2** (figurative) conglomeration.

congolais, ~e /kɔ̃gɔlɛ, ɛz/ **I** *adj* Congolese.
II *nm* (Culin) (small) coconut cake.

congre /kɔ̃gʀ/ *nm* conger eel.

congrégation /kɔ̃gʀegasjɔ̃/ *nf* congregation; (humorous) assembly.

congrès /kɔ̃gʀɛ/ *nm* conference; **le Congrès** (US) Congress.

congressiste /kɔ̃gʀesist/ *nmf* (conference) delegate.

congruent, ~e /kɔ̃gʀyɑ̃, ɑ̃t/ *adj* [*idea, remark*] compatible (**à** with).

conifère /kɔnifɛʀ/ *nm* conifer.

conique /kɔnik/ *adj* cone-shaped.

conjecture /kɔ̃ʒɛktyʀ/ *nf* conjecture ; **vaines ~s** idle speculation.

conjecturer /kɔ̃ʒɛktyʀe/ [1] *vtr* (formal) to speculate (**que** that).

conjoint, ~e /kɔ̃ʒwɛ̃, ɛ̃t/ **I** *adj* [*action*] joint; [*questions*] linked.
II *nm,f* spouse; **les ~s** the husband and wife.

conjointement /kɔ̃ʒwɛ̃tmɑ̃/ *adv* **1** jointly; **2** at the same time.

conjonction /kɔ̃ʒɔ̃ksjɔ̃/ *nf* conjunction.

conjonctivite /kɔ̃ʒɔ̃ktivit/ *nf* conjunctivitis.

conjoncture /kɔ̃ʒɔ̃ktyʀ/ *nf* situation; circumstances.

conjoncturel, -elle /kɔ̃ʒɔ̃ktyʀɛl/ *adj* [*situation*] economic; **évolution conjoncturelle** current trends.

conjoncturiste /kɔ̃ʒɔ̃ktyʀist/ *nmf* economic forecaster.

conjugaison /kɔ̃ʒygɛzɔ̃/ *nf* **1** (of verb) conjugation; **2** (figurative) combination.

conjugal, ~e, *mpl* **-aux** /kɔ̃ʒygal, o/ *adj* [*love*] conjugal; [*life*] married.

conjugalement /kɔ̃ʒygalmɑ̃/ *adv* [*live*] as man and wife.

conjuguer /kɔ̃ʒyge/ [1] *vtr* **1** to conjugate [*verbe*]; **2** to combine [*efforts*].

conjuration /kɔ̃ʒyʀasjɔ̃/ *nf* **1** conspiracy; **2** (of evil spirits) conjuration.

conjuré, ~e /kɔ̃ʒyʀe/ *nm,f* conspirator.

conjurer /kɔ̃ʒyʀe/ [1] *vtr* **1** to avert [*crisis*]; to ward off [*danger*]; **2 je vous en conjure** I beg you.

connaissance /kɔnɛsɑ̃s/ *nf* **1** knowledge (**de** of); **mes ~s en grec** my knowledge of Greek; **à ma ~** to my knowledge; **prendre ~ d'un texte** to acquaint oneself with a text; **en ~ de cause** with full knowledge of the facts; **2** consciousness; **sans ~** unconscious; **3** acquaintance; **faire (plus ample) ~ avec qn** to get to know sb (better); **en pays de ~** among familiar faces; on familiar ground.

connaisseur, -euse /kɔnɛsœʀ, øz/ **I** *adj m* expert.
II *nm,f* connoisseur, expert.

connaître /kɔnɛtʀ/ [73] **I** *vtr* **1** to know; **il connaît l'informatique** he knows something about computers; **faire ~ à qn** to make [sth] known to sb [*decision*]; to introduce sb to [*music*]; **je l'ai connu en Chine** I met him in China; **tu connais la nouvelle?** have you heard the news?; **la mécanique, ça me connaît!** I know quite a bit about mechanics; **tu n'y connais rien** you don't know a thing about it; **2** to experience [*hunger, failure*]; to enjoy [*success*]; to have [*difficulties*]; **~ une situation difficile** to be in a difficult situation; **~ une forte croissance** to show a rapid growth.
II se connaître *v refl* (+ *v être*) **1** to know oneself; **quand il a bu, il ne se connaît plus** when he's drunk, he goes berserk; **2** to know each other; **ils se sont connus à Rome** they met in Rome; **3 s'y ~ en théâtre/en vin** to know all about theatre[GB]/wine.
IDIOMS **on connaît la chanson** or **musique!** we've heard it all before!; **~ qch comme sa poche** to know sth like the back of one's hand.

conne° ▸ **con** I, II.

connecter /kɔnɛkte/ [1] *vtr* to connect (**à** to).

connexion /kɔnɛksjɔ̃/ *nf* connection.

connivence /kɔnivɑ̃s/ *nf* connivance; **signe**

de ~ sign of complicity; **être** or **agir de ~ avec qn** to connive with sb.

connotation /kɔnɔtasjɔ̃/ *nf* connotation.

conque /kɔ̃k/ *nf* conch.

conquérant, **~e** /kɔ̃kerɑ̃, ɑ̃t/ **I** *adj* **1** conquering; **2** triumphant.
II *nm,f* conqueror.

conquérir /kɔ̃keriʀ/ [35] *vtr* to conquer [*nation*]; to capture [*market*]; to win [*friendship*]; to win over [*audience*].
IDIOMS **se croire en pays** or **terrain conquis** to lord it over everyone.

conquête /kɔ̃kɛt/ *nf* conquest.

conquis, **~e** /kɔ̃ki, iz/ ▶ **conquérir**.

consacré, **~e** /kɔ̃sakʀe/ *adj* **formule ~e** time-honoured[GB] expression; **artiste ~** recognized artist; **être ~ joueur de l'année** to be designated player of the year.

consacrer /kɔ̃sakʀe/ [1] **I** *vtr* **1** to devote (**à** to); **pouvez-vous me ~ un instant?** can you spare me a moment?; **2** to sanction; **3** to consecrate.
II se consacrer *v refl* (+ *v être*) **se ~ à** to devote oneself to.

consanguin, **~e** /kɔ̃sɑ̃gɛ̃, in/ *adj* [*marriage*] between blood relations.

consciemment /kɔ̃sjamɑ̃/ *adv* consciously.

conscience /kɔ̃sjɑ̃s/ *nf* **1** conscience; **avoir bonne/mauvaise ~** to have a clear/a guilty conscience; **j'ai la ~ tranquille** my conscience is clear; **2** awareness; **avoir ~ de** to be aware or conscious of; **prendre ~ de** to become aware of; **prise de ~** realization; **perdre ~** to lose consciousness.
■ **~ professionnelle** conscientiousness.

consciencieusement /kɔ̃sjɑ̃sjøzmɑ̃/ *adv* conscientiously.

consciencieux, **-ieuse** /kɔ̃sjɑ̃sjø, øz/ *adj* conscientious.

conscient, **~e** /kɔ̃sjɑ̃, ɑ̃t/ *adj* **1** aware; **2** conscious.

conscription /kɔ̃skʀipsjɔ̃/ *nf* conscription (GB), draft (US).

conscrit /kɔ̃skʀi/ *nm* conscript (GB), draftee (US).

consécration /kɔ̃sekʀasjɔ̃/ *nf* **1** (of author) recognition; **2** consecration.

consécutif, **-ive** /kɔ̃sekytif, iv/ *adj* consecutive; **~ à** resulting from; following.

consécutivement /kɔ̃sekytivmɑ̃/ *adv* consecutively.

conseil /kɔ̃sɛj/ *nm* **1** advice; **~ d'ami** piece of friendly advice; **quelques ~s de prudence** a few words of warning; **il est de bon ~** he always gives good advice; **~s d'entretien** cleaning or care instructions; **2** council; **3** consultant.
■ **~ d'administration** board of directors; **~ de classe** (Sch) staff meeting; **~ de discipline** disciplinary committee; **~ général** *council of a French department*; **~ de révision** medical board (*assessing fitness for military service*).

conseiller[1], **-ère** /kɔ̃seje, ɛʀ/ **I** *nm,f* **1** adviser[GB]; **2** counsellor[GB].
II *nm* councillor[GB].
■ **~ (principal) d'éducation** (Sch) chief supervisor; **~ d'État** member of the Council of State; **~ général** *councillor*[GB] *for a French department*; **~ municipal** town councillor[GB]; **~ d'orientation** careers adviser.

conseiller[2] /kɔ̃seje/ [1] *vtr* to recommend; to advise; **~ à qn de faire** to advise sb to do; **il est conseillé de faire** it is advisable to do.

consensuel, **-elle** /kɔ̃sɛ̃sɥɛl/ *adj* consensual, based on consensus.

consentant, **~e** /kɔ̃sɑ̃tɑ̃, ɑ̃t/ *adj* willing; (Law) consenting.

consentement /kɔ̃sɑ̃tmɑ̃/ *nm* consent (**à** to).

consentir /kɔ̃sɑ̃tiʀ/ [30] **I** *vtr* to grant; to allow; **~ un effort financier** to provide funding.
II consentir à *v+prep* **~ à qch/à faire** to agree to sth/to do.
IDIOMS **qui ne dit mot consent** (Proverb) silence means consent.

conséquence /kɔ̃sekɑ̃s/ *nf* consequence (**pour** for; **sur** to); **être lourd de ~s** to have serious consequences; **sans ~(s)** of no consequence; **ne pas tirer à ~** to be of no consequence; **avoir pour ~ le chômage** to result in unemployment; **en ~ (de quoi)** as a result (of which); **agir en ~** to act accordingly; **avoir des qualifications et un salaire en ~** to have qualifications and a corresponding salary.

conséquent, **~e** /kɔ̃sekɑ̃, ɑ̃t/ **I** *adj* **1** substantial; **2** consistent.
II par conséquent *phr* therefore, as a result.

conservateur, **-trice** /kɔ̃sɛʀvatœʀ, tʀis/ **I** *adj* **1** conservative; **2 produit ~** preservative.
II *nm,f* **1** conservative; **2** (museum) curator; **3** librarian.

conservation /kɔ̃sɛʀvasjɔ̃/ *nf* conservation; preservation; **lait longue ~** long-life milk (GB).

conservatisme /kɔ̃sɛʀvatism/ *nm* conservatism.

conservatoire /kɔ̃sɛʀvatwaʀ/ *nm* academy; **~ de musique** conservatoire.

conserve /kɔ̃sɛʀv/ **I** *nf* **1 la ~, les ~s** canned food; **boîte de ~** can; **2** preserve.
II de conserve *phr* [*act*] in concert; [*sail*] in convoy.

conserver /kɔ̃sɛʀve/ [1] *vtr* **1** to keep; to retain; **~ l'anonymat** to remain anonymous; **2** (Culin) to preserve; (in vinegar) to pickle; **3** [*activity*] to keep [sb] young; **homme bien conservé** well-preserved man.

conserverie /kɔ̃sɛʀvəʀi/ *nf* **1** cannery, canning plant; **2** canning industry.

considérable /kɔ̃sideʀabl/ *adj* considerable, significant; **l'enjeu est ~** the stakes are high.

considérablement /kɔ̃sideʀabləmɑ̃/ *adv* considerably, significantly.

considération /kɔ̃sideʀasjɔ̃/ *nf* **1** consideration; **prendre qch en ~** to consider sth, to take sth into account; **en ~ de** in view of; **sans ~ de** irrespective of; **2** consideration, factor; **~s commerciales** commercial considerations; **3** respect, esteem.

considérer /kɔ̃sideʀe/ [14] **I** *vtr* **1** to consider,

to take into account; **à tout bien ~** all things considered; **2** to consider, to regard; **~ qn/qch comme (étant)** to consider sb/sth to be, to regard sb/sth as being; **3 être bien considéré** to be highly regarded.
II se considérer *v refl* (+ *v être*) **se ~ (comme) 1** to consider oneself (to be); **2** to regard one another as being.

consigne /kɔ̃siɲ/ *nf* **1** orders, instructions; **passer la ~ à qn** to pass the word on to sb; **'~s à suivre en cas d'incendie'** 'fire regulations'; **2** left luggage office (GB), baggage checkroom (US); **3** (on bottle) deposit.
■ **~ automatique** left luggage lockers (GB), baggage lockers (US).

consigné, **~e** /kɔ̃siɲe/ *adj* [*bottle*] returnable.

consigner /kɔ̃siɲe/ [1] *vtr* **1** to record, to write down; **2** to confine [*soldier*] (**dans**, **à** to); to give [sb] detention [*pupil*]; **3** to charge a deposit on [*bottle*].

consistance /kɔ̃sistɑ̃s/ *nf* **1** consistency; **avoir de la/manquer de ~** to be quite thick/to be too runny; **prendre ~** to thicken; **2** substance, weight; **sans ~** [*person*] spineless; [*rumour*] groundless.

consistant, **~e** /kɔ̃sistɑ̃, ɑ̃t/ *adj* [*meal, investment*] substantial; [*dish*] nourishing; [*argument*] solid.

consister /kɔ̃siste/ [1] *vi* **1 ~ en** or **dans** to consist in; **~ à faire** to consist in doing; **en quoi consiste mon erreur?** where have I gone wrong?; **2 ~ en** to consist of, to be made up of; **en quoi consiste cette aide?** what form does this aid take?

consolant, **~e** /kɔ̃sɔlɑ̃, ɑ̃t/ *adj* comforting.

consolation /kɔ̃sɔlasjɔ̃/ *nf* consolation.

console /kɔ̃sɔl/ *nf* console.

consoler /kɔ̃sɔle/ [1] **I** *vtr* to console; **si ça peut te ~** if it is any comfort to you.
II se consoler *v refl* (+ *v être*) to find consolation; **se ~ de** to get over.

consolidation /kɔ̃sɔlidasjɔ̃/ *nf* consolidation, strengthening.

consolider /kɔ̃sɔlide/ [1] **I** *vtr* to consolidate, to strengthen.
II se consolider *v refl* (+ *v être*) **1** to grow stronger, to be consolidated, to be strengthened; **2** to consolidate.

consommables /kɔ̃sɔmabl/ *nm pl* consumables.

consommateur, **-trice** /kɔ̃sɔmatœʀ, tʀis/ *nm,f* **1** consumer; **2** (in bar) customer.

consommation /kɔ̃sɔmasjɔ̃/ *nf* **1** consumption; **faire une grande ~ de** to use a lot of; **la trop forte ~ de graisses** excessive intake of fats; **de ~** [*goods, society*] consumer; **2** drink; **3** consummation.

consommé, **~e** /kɔ̃sɔme/ **I** *adj* [*skill*] consummate.
II *nm* consommé.

consommer /kɔ̃sɔme/ [1] *vtr* **1** to consume; to use; **2** to eat [*food*]; to drink [*tea, wine*]; to take [*drugs*]; **3** (formal) to consummate [*marriage*]; **une rupture consommée** a complete break.

consonance /kɔ̃sɔnɑ̃s/ *nf* consonance; **mot aux ~s étrangères** foreign-sounding word.

consonne /kɔ̃sɔn/ *nf* consonant.

conspirateur, **-trice** /kɔ̃spiʀatœʀ, tʀis/ **I** *adj* conspiratorial.
II *nm,f* conspirator.

conspiration /kɔ̃spiʀasjɔ̃/ *nf* conspiracy.

conspirer /kɔ̃spiʀe/ [1] **I** *vi* to conspire, to plot (**contre** against).
II conspirer à *v+prep* to conspire to bring about; **~ à faire** to conspire to do.

conspuer /kɔ̃spɥe/ [1] *vtr* to boo.

constamment /kɔ̃stamɑ̃/ *adv* constantly.

constance /kɔ̃stɑ̃s/ *nf* **1** consistency; constancy; **2** steadfastness.

constant, **~e**[1] /kɔ̃stɑ̃, ɑ̃t/ *adj* **1** constant; consistent; **2** continuous; continual.

constante[2] /kɔ̃stɑ̃t/ *nf* constant.

constat /kɔ̃sta/ *nm* (Law) certified or official report.
■ **~ (à l')amiable** *accident report drawn up by the parties involved*; **~ d'huissier** bailiff's report.

constatation /kɔ̃statasjɔ̃/ *nf* **1** observation; **2** (of inquiry) **~s** findings.

constater /kɔ̃state/ [1] *vtr* **1** to notice, to note; **~ (par) soi-même** to see for oneself; **2** to ascertain, to establish; **3** to record.

constellation /kɔ̃stɛlasjɔ̃/ *nf* **1** constellation; **2** cluster.

constellé, **~e** /kɔ̃stɛlle/ *adj* **~ de** spangled with; riddled with; spotted with.

consternant, **~e** /kɔ̃stɛʀnɑ̃, ɑ̃t/ *adj* **1** distressing; **2** appalling.

consternation /kɔ̃stɛʀnasjɔ̃/ *nf* consternation, dismay.

consterner /kɔ̃stɛʀne/ [1] *vtr* to fill [sb] with consternation, to dismay.

constipé, **~e** /kɔ̃stipe/ *adj* **1** constipated; **2**° **avoir l'air ~** to look uptight.

constiper /kɔ̃stipe/ [1] *vtr* to make [sb] constipated.

constituant, **~e** /kɔ̃stitɥɑ̃, ɑ̃t/ **I** *adj* constituent.
II *nm* constituent.

constitué, **~e** /kɔ̃stitɥe/ *adj* **1 personne bien/mal ~e** person of sound/unsound constitution; **2** constituted.

constituer /kɔ̃stitɥe/ [1] **I** *vtr* **1** to be, to constitute [*crime, reason*]; **2** to form, to set up [*team, commission*]; **3** to make up [*whole*]; **4** (Law) to settle (**à, pour** on); **~ qn héritier** to appoint sb as heir.
II se constituer *v refl* (+ *v être*) **1** to build up [*network, reserve*]; to get oneself [*alibi*]; **2 se ~ en** to form [*party, company*]; **3 se ~ prisonnier** to give oneself up.

constitution /kɔ̃stitysjɔ̃/ *nf* **1** (of company) setting up; (of capital) accumulation; (of application) preparing; **~ de stocks** stockpiling; **2** constitution.

constitutionnel, **-elle** /kɔ̃stitysjɔnɛl/ *adj* constitutional.

constructeur, **-trice** /kɔ̃stʀyktœʀ, tʀis/ *nm,f* **1** (car) manufacturer; **2** builder.

constructible /kɔ̃stʀyktibl/ *adj* [*land*] building.

constructif, **-ive** /kɔ̃stʀyktif, iv/ *adj* constructive.

construction /kɔ̃stʀyksjɔ̃/ *nf* **1** construction; building; **matériaux de ~** building materials; **en (cours de) ~** under construction; **de ~ japonaise** Japanese built; **2 la ~** the construction industry; **~ navale** shipbuilding.

construire /kɔ̃stʀɥiʀ/ [69] **I** *vtr* to build; to construct; **se faire ~ une villa** to have a villa built.

II se construire *v refl* (+ *v être*) **1 ça s'est beaucoup construit par ici** there's been a lot of building here; **2 se ~ avec le subjonctif** to take the subjunctive.

consul /kɔ̃syl/ *nm* consul.

consulaire /kɔ̃sylɛʀ/ *adj* consular.

consulat /kɔ̃syla/ *nm* consulate.

consultant, **~e** /kɔ̃syltɑ̃, ɑ̃t/ *nm,f* consultant.

consultatif, **-ive** /kɔ̃syltatif, iv/ *adj* consultative.

consultation /kɔ̃syltasjɔ̃/ *nf* **1** consultation; **après ~ des experts** after consulting the experts; **~ électorale** election; **2** surgery hours (GB), office hours (US); **aller à la ~** to go to the doctor's; **~ des nourrissons** baby clinic.

consulter /kɔ̃sylte/ [1] **I** *vtr* to consult; **~ le peuple** to hold a general election.

II *vi* [*doctor*] to see patients.

III se consulter *v refl* (+ *v être*) to consult together; **se ~ du regard** to exchange glances.

consumer /kɔ̃syme/ [1] **I** *vtr* **1** [*fire*] to consume; **2** (literary) **la maladie qui la consume** the illness which is eating away at her.

II se consumer *v refl* (+ *v être*) **1** to burn; **2** literary to waste away; **se ~ en vains efforts** to weary oneself in vain efforts.

contact /kɔ̃takt/ *nm* **1** contact; **prendre ~ avec** to make contact with; **garder le ~** to keep in touch; **entrer en ~ avec** to get in touch with; **elle est devenue plus sociable à ton ~** she's become more sociable through spending time with you; **2 mettre/couper le ~** to switch on/switch off the ignition.

contacter /kɔ̃takte/ [1] *vtr* to contact, to get in touch with.

contagieux, **-ieuse** /kɔ̃taʒjø, øz/ *adj* **1** contagious; **2** [*laughter*] infectious.

contagion /kɔ̃taʒjɔ̃/ *nf* **1** contagion; **2** (of laughter) infectiousness; **craindre la ~ de certaines idées** to fear that certain ideas might catch on.

contamination /kɔ̃taminasjɔ̃/ *nf* contamination.

contaminer /kɔ̃tamine/ [1] *vtr* to contaminate; to infect.

conte /kɔ̃t/ *nm* tale, story; **~ de fées** fairy tale.

contemplatif, **-ive** /kɔ̃tɑ̃platif, iv/ *adj* contemplative.

contemplation /kɔ̃tɑ̃plasjɔ̃/ *nf* contemplation.

contempler /kɔ̃tɑ̃ple/ [1] *vtr* to survey; to contemplate; to look at.

contemporain, **~e** /kɔ̃tɑ̃pɔʀɛ̃, ɛn/ *adj, nm,f* contemporary.

contenance /kɔ̃t(ə)nɑ̃s/ *nf* **1** (of container) capacity; **2** bearing, attitude; **essayer de se donner une ~** to try to appear composed; **perdre ~** to lose one's composure; **faire bonne ~** to put on a brave face.

contenant /kɔ̃t(ə)nɑ̃/ *nm* container.

conteneur /kɔ̃t(ə)nœʀ/ *nm* container.

contenir /kɔ̃t(ə)niʀ/ [36] **I** *vtr* **1** to contain [*substance, error*]; **2** [*container*] to hold [*litres*]; [*hall*] to accommodate [*spectators*]; **3** to contain [*crowd, anger*].

II se contenir *v refl* (+ *v être*) to contain oneself.

content, **~e** /kɔ̃tɑ̃, ɑ̃t/ **I** *adj* happy, pleased, glad; **~ de soi** pleased with oneself; **non ~ de ne rien faire, il...** not content with doing nothing, he...

II *nm* **avoir son ~ de** to have had one's fill of.

contentement /kɔ̃tɑ̃tmɑ̃/ *nm* contentment, satisfaction.

contenter /kɔ̃tɑ̃te/ [1] **I** *vtr* to satisfy [*customer, curiosity*]; **facile à ~** easy to please.

II se contenter *v refl* (+ *v être*) **se ~ de qch/de faire** to content oneself with sth/with doing.

contentieux, **-ieuse** /kɔ̃tɑ̃sjø, øz/ **I** *adj* contentious.

II *nm* **1** bone of contention; **2** legal department; **3** litigation.

contenu, **~e** /kɔ̃t(ə)ny/ **I** *pp* ▶ **contenir**.

II *pp adj* restrained; suppressed.

III *nm* contents; content.

conter /kɔ̃te/ [1] *vtr* (literary) to tell, to recount.

contestable /kɔ̃tɛstabl/ *adj* questionable.

contestataire /kɔ̃tɛstatɛʀ/ **I** *adj* antiestablishment, anti-authority.

II *nmf* protester.

contestation /kɔ̃tɛstasjɔ̃/ *nf* **1** protest (**de** against); **2** challenging; **être sujet à ~**, **prêter à ~** to be questionable; **sans ~ possible** beyond dispute; **2 la ~** dissent; **3** dispute.

conteste: **sans conteste** /sɑ̃kɔ̃tɛst/ *phr* unquestionably.

contesté, **~e** /kɔ̃tɛste/ *adj* controversial.

contester /kɔ̃tɛste/ [1] **I** *vtr* to question; to contest; to dispute; to challenge.

II *vi* **1** to raise objections; **2** to protest.

conteur, **-euse** /kɔ̃tœʀ, øz/ *nm,f* storyteller.

contexte /kɔ̃tɛkst/ *nm* context.

contigu, **-uë** /kɔ̃tigy/ *adj* [*rooms*] adjoining.

contiguïté /kɔ̃tigɥite/ *nf* contiguity.

continence /kɔ̃tinɑ̃s/ *nf* (formal) continence.

continent, **~e** /kɔ̃tinɑ̃, ɑ̃t/ **I** *adj* continent.

II *nm* **1** continent; **2** mainland.

continental, **~e**, *mpl* **-aux** /kɔ̃tinɑ̃tal, o/ *adj* **1** continental; **2** mainland.

contingence /kɔ̃tɛ̃ʒɑ̃s/ *nf* **1** contingency; **2 les ~s** contingencies.

contingent, **~e** /kɔ̃tɛ̃ʒɑ̃, ɑ̃t/ I *adj* contingent.
II *nm* **1** contingent; (Mil) conscripts, draft (US); **2** quota; **3** (Law), (figurative) share.

contingenter /kɔ̃tɛ̃ʒɑ̃te/ [1] *vtr* to fix a quota for [*imports*].

continu, **~e** /kɔ̃tiny/ *adj* continuous; **de façon ~e** continuously.

continuation /kɔ̃tinɥasjɔ̃/ *nf* continuation; **bonne ~!** all the best!

continuel, **-elle** /kɔ̃tinɥɛl/ *adj* continual.

continuellement /kɔ̃tinɥɛlmɑ̃/ *adv* continually.

continuer /kɔ̃tinɥe/ [1] I *vtr* to continue.
II *vi* to continue, to go on; **~ à** or **de faire** to continue doing.

continuité /kɔ̃tinɥite/ *nf* continuity.

continûment /kɔ̃tinymɑ̃/ *adv* continuously.

contondant, **~e** /kɔ̃tɔ̃dɑ̃, ɑ̃t/ *adj* blunt.

contorsion /kɔ̃tɔʀsjɔ̃/ *nf* contortion.

contorsionner: **se contorsionner** /kɔ̃tɔʀsjɔne/ [1] *v refl* (+ *v être*) to tie oneself in knots.

contorsionniste /kɔ̃tɔʀsjɔnist/ *nmf* contortionist.

contour /kɔ̃tuʀ/ *nm* **1** outline, contour; **2 ~s** (of road, river) twists and turns.

contourner /kɔ̃tuʀne/ [1] *vtr* to go round; to by-pass [*town*]; to get round [*problem*].

contraceptif, **-ive** /kɔ̃tʀasɛptif, iv/ I *adj* contraceptive.
II *nm* contraceptive.

contraception /kɔ̃tʀasɛpsjɔ̃/ *nf* contraception.

contracter /kɔ̃tʀakte/ [1] I *vtr* **1** to tense [*muscle*]; to tighten [*throat*]; **2** to incur [*debt*]; to take out [*loan*]; to enter into [*agreement*]; **3** to contract [*disease*].
II **se contracter** *v refl* (+ *v être*) [*muscle, substance, word*] to contract; [*face, person*] to tense up; [*throat*] to tighten.

contraction /kɔ̃tʀaksjɔ̃/ *nf* **1** tenseness; **2** contraction.

contractuel, **-elle** /kɔ̃tʀaktɥɛl/ I *adj* contractual; **personnel ~** contract staff.
II *nm,f* **1** contract employee; **2** traffic warden (GB), meter reader (US).

contradiction /kɔ̃tʀadiksjɔ̃/ *nf* contradiction; **être en ~ avec** to contradict.

contradictoire /kɔ̃tʀadiktwaʀ/ *adj* contradictory; **~ à** in contradiction to.

contraignant, **~e** /kɔ̃tʀɛɲɑ̃, ɑ̃t/ *adj* restrictive.

contraindre /kɔ̃tʀɛ̃dʀ/ [54] I *vtr* **1 ~ qn à faire** to force or compel sb to do; **2** to restrain, to curb.
II **se contraindre** *v refl* (+ *v être*) **se ~ à** to force oneself to.

contraint, **~e**[1] /kɔ̃tʀɛ̃, ɛ̃t/ *adj* **1 ~ et forcé** (Law) under duress; **2** strained, forced.

contrainte[2] /kɔ̃tʀɛ̃t/ *nf* **1** pressure; coercion; **sous la ~** under duress; **2** constraint; **3 sans ~** without restraint, freely.

contraire /kɔ̃tʀɛʀ/ I *adj* **1** opposite; contrary; [*interests*] conflicting; **être ~ aux usages** to be contrary to custom; **dans le cas ~** (should it be) otherwise; **2** adverse.
II *nm* **le ~** the opposite, the contrary (**de** of); **ne dites pas le ~** don't deny it; **au ~!** on the contrary!; **au ~ de tes amis** unlike your friends.

contrairement /kɔ̃tʀɛʀmɑ̃/ *adv* **~ à ce qu'on pourrait penser/à une opinion ré pandue** contrary to what one might think/to popular belief; **~ à qn/à la France** unlike sb/France.

contrariant, **~e** /kɔ̃tʀaʀjɑ̃, ɑ̃t/ *adj* **1** [*person*] contrary; **2** [*event*] annoying.

contrarier /kɔ̃tʀaʀje/ [2] *vtr* **1** to upset; **2** to annoy; **3** to frustrate, to thwart.

contrariété /kɔ̃tʀaʀjete/ *nf* vexation.

contraste /kɔ̃tʀast/ *nm* contrast; **faire ~ avec** to contrast with.

contrasté, **~e** /kɔ̃tʀaste/ *adj* **1** contrasting; **2** [*photo*] with good contrast; **3** [*results*] uneven; [*week, year*] of sharp contrasts.

contraster /kɔ̃tʀaste/ [1] I *vtr* to contrast [*colours*]; to give contrast to [*photo*].
II *vi* to contrast (**avec** with).

contrat /kɔ̃tʀa/ *nm* contract; (figurative) agreement, arrangement.
■ **~ emploi solidarité**, **CES** part time low-paid work for the long-term unemployed.

contravention /kɔ̃tʀavɑ̃sjɔ̃/ *nf* **1** parking ticket; speeding ticket; fine; **2** minor offence[GB]; **être en ~ (à la loi)** to be in breach of the law.

contre[1] /kɔ̃tʀ/ I *prep* **1** against; **22% ~ 18% hier** 22% as against 18% yesterday; **10 voix ~ 8** 10 votes to 8; **allongés l'un ~ l'autre** lying side by side; **2** versus; **3** (in exchange) for; **échange-la ~ une bleue** exchange it for a blue one.
II **par contre** *phr* on the other hand.

contre[2] /kɔ̃tʀ/ I *nm* **1 le pour et le ~** the pros and cons; **2** (Sport) counter-attack; **faire un ~** to counter-attack.
II *pref* counter; **~ attaque/espionnage** counter-attack/intelligence; **~-allée** service road; **~-courant** counter-current; **à ~-courant** against the current; against the tide; **~-expertise** second opinion; **~-indication** contraindication; **~-indiqué** (Med) contraindicated; (gen) inadvisable; **~-interrogatoire** cross examination; **~-jour** backlighting; **à ~-jour** against the light; **~-pied** opposite; **prendre le ~-pied de ce que dit qn** to say the opposite of what sb says; **~-valeur** exchange value.

contrebalancer /kɔ̃tʀəbalɑ̃se/ [12] *vtr* **1** to counterbalance; **2** to offset.

contrebande /kɔ̃tʀəbɑ̃d/ *nf* **1** smuggling; **faire de la ~** to be involved in smuggling; **2** smuggled goods, contraband.

contrebandier, **-ière** /kɔ̃tʀəbɑ̃dje, ɛʀ/ *nm,f* smuggler.

contrebas: **en contrebas** /ɑ̃kɔ̃tʀəba/ *phr* (down) below; **en ~ de** below.

contrebasse /kɔ̃tʀəbas/ *nf* **1** double bass; **2** double bass player.

contrecarrer /kɔ̃tʀəkaʀe/ [1] *vtr* **1** to thwart, to foil; **2** to counteract.

contrecœur: **à contrecœur** /kɔ̃tʀəkœʀ/ *phr* reluctantly.

contrecoup /kɔ̃tʀəku/ *nm* effects; after-effects; **par ~** as a result.

contredanse○ /kɔ̃tʀədɑ̃s/ *nf* parking ticket.

contredire /kɔ̃tʀədiʀ/ [65] **I** *vtr* to contradict.
II se contredire *v refl* (+ *v être*) **1** to contradict oneself; **2** to contradict each other.

contrée /kɔ̃tʀe/ *nf* **1** (literary) land, clime; **2** region.

contrefaçon /kɔ̃tʀəfasɔ̃/ *nf* **1** forging, counterfeiting; forgery, counterfeit; **2** pirating; pirated copy.

contrefaire /kɔ̃tʀəfɛʀ/ [10] *vtr* **1** to forge, to counterfeit; **2** (literary) to imitate; **3** to disguise.

contrefort /kɔ̃tʀəfɔʀ/ *nm* **1** foothills; **2** buttress; **3** (of shoe) back.

contremaître, **-esse** /kɔ̃tʀəmɛtʀ, kɔ̃tʀəmɛtʀɛs/ *nm,f* foreman/forewoman.

contrepartie /kɔ̃tʀəpaʀti/ *nf* **1** equivalent (**en** in); **2** compensation; **en ~** in compensation (**de** for); in return (**de** for); **c'est la ~ de la liberté** it is the price you have to pay for freedom; **mais la ~ est que le salaire est élevé** but this is offset by the high salary.

contreplaqué /kɔ̃tʀəplake/ *nm* plywood.

contrepoids /kɔ̃tʀəpwa/ *nm* counterweight, counterbalance.

contrepoison /kɔ̃tʀəpwazɔ̃/ *nm* antidote.

contrer /kɔ̃tʀe/ [1] *vtr* to counter; to block.

contresens /kɔ̃tʀəsɑ̃s/ *nm* **1** misinterpretation; **2** mistranslation; **3 à ~** in the opposite direction; the wrong way; against the grain.

contretemps /kɔ̃tʀətɑ̃/ *nm inv* **1** setback, contretemps; **2 à ~** (Mus) on the off-beat; out of time; (figurative) at the wrong moment.

contrevenant, **~e** /kɔ̃tʀəvənɑ̃, ɑ̃t/ *nm,f* offender.

contrevenir: **contrevenir à** /kɔ̃tʀəvəniʀ/ [36] *v+prep* to contravene.

contribuable /kɔ̃tʀibɥabl/ *nmf* taxpayer.

contribuer: **contribuer à** /kɔ̃tʀibɥe/ [1] *v+prep* to contribute to; to pay one's share of; **cela y a beaucoup contribué** it was a major factor.

contribution /kɔ̃tʀibysjɔ̃/ *nf* **1** contribution (**aux frais** toward(s) the costs; **à une entreprise** to an undertaking); **mettre qn à ~** to call upon sb's services; **2 ~s** taxes; tax office.

contrit, **~e** /kɔ̃tʀi, it/ *adj* contrite, apologetic.

contrition /kɔ̃tʀisjɔ̃/ *nf* (literary) contrition.

contrôle /kɔ̃tʀol/ *nm* **1** control (**de** of; **sur** over); **prendre/perdre le ~** to take/lose control; **2** check; **~ de police** police check; **~ des billets** ticket inspection; **3** (Sch) test; **~ de géographie** geography test; **4** check-up; **5** monitoring; **sous ~ médical** under medical supervision.
■ **~ continu (des connaissances)** continuous assessment; **~ fiscal** tax investigation; **~ de soi** self-control; **~ technique (des véhicules)** MOT (test).

contrôler /kɔ̃tʀole/ [1] **I** *vtr* **1** to control; **2** to monitor; **3** to check; to inspect; to test; to verify; **~ que** to make sure that.
II se contrôler *v refl* (+ *v être*) to control oneself.

contrôleur, **-euse** /kɔ̃tʀolœʀ, øz/ *nm,f* inspector; **~ aérien** air-traffic controller.

contrordre /kɔ̃tʀɔʀdʀ/ *nm* **1 ordres et ~s** conflicting orders; **sauf ~** unless I/you etc hear to the contrary; **2** counter command.

controverse /kɔ̃tʀɔvɛʀs/ *nf* controversy (**sur** about).

controversé, **~e** /kɔ̃tʀɔvɛʀse/ *adj* controversial.

contumace /kɔ̃tymas/ *nf* **condamner qn par ~** to sentence sb in absentia.

contusion /kɔ̃tyzjɔ̃/ *nf* bruise.

contusionner /kɔ̃tyzjɔne/ [1] *vtr* to bruise.

convaincant, **~e** /kɔ̃vɛ̃kɑ̃, ɑ̃t/ *adj* **1** convincing; **2** persuasive.

convaincre /kɔ̃vɛ̃kʀ/ [57] **I** *vtr* **1** to convince (**de** of; **que** that); to persuade (**de faire** to do); **2 ~ qn de fraude** to prove sb guilty of fraud.
II se convaincre *v refl* (+ *v être*) to convince oneself (**de** of).

convaincu, **~e** /kɔ̃vɛ̃ky/ **I** *pp* ▶ **convaincre**.
II *pp adj* **1** convinced; **d'un ton ~** with conviction; **2** [*supporter*] staunch.

convalescence /kɔ̃valesɑ̃s/ *nf* convalescence; **être en ~** to be convalescing.

convalescent, **~e** /kɔ̃valesɑ̃, ɑ̃t/ *adj, nm,f* convalescent.

convecteur /kɔ̃vɛktœʀ/ *nm* convector heater.

convenable /kɔ̃vnabl/ *adj* **1** suitable; **2** reasonable; **tout juste ~** barely acceptable; **3** decent; proper; respectable.

convenablement /kɔ̃vnabləmɑ̃/ *adv* properly; reasonably well; decently.

convenance /kɔ̃vnɑ̃s/ *nf* **1 pour ~ personnelle** for personal reasons; **à votre ~** at your convenience; **2 ~s** (social) conventions.

convenir /kɔ̃vniʀ/ [36] **I** *vtr* **1** to admit (**que** that); **2** to agree (**que** that).
II convenir à *v+prep* to suit; to be suitable for; **c'est tout à fait ce qui me convient** it's exactly what I need.
III convenir de *v+prep* **1** to admit, to acknowledge; **2** to agree on; **~ de faire** to agree to do.
IV *v impers* **1 il convient de faire/que vous fassiez** one/you should do or ought to do; **2** (formal) **il est convenu que** it is agreed that; **ce qu'il est convenu d'appeler le réalisme** what is commonly called realism; **comme convenu** as agreed.

convention /kɔ̃vɑ̃sjɔ̃/ *nf* **1** agreement; **2** convention; **de ~** conventional.

conventionné, **~e** /kɔ̃vɑ̃sjɔne/ *adj* [*doctor, costs*] national health service; [*clinic*] registered; **médecin non ~** private doctor.

conventionnel, **-elle** /kɔ̃vɑ̃sjɔnɛl/ *adj* **1** conventional; **2** contractual.

convenu, **~e** /kɔ̃v(ə)ny/ I *pp* ▶ **convenir**.
II *pp adj* **1** [*date, terms*] agreed; **2** [*phrase*] conventional; [*smile*] polite.

convergence /kɔ̃vɛʀʒɑ̃s/ *nf* convergence.

convergent, **~e** /kɔ̃vɛʀʒɑ̃, ɑ̃t/ *adj* convergent.

converger /kɔ̃vɛʀʒe/ [13] *vi* to converge (**vers** on); **tous les regards convergèrent sur elle** all eyes turned toward(s) her.

conversation /kɔ̃vɛʀsasjɔ̃/ *nf* conversation; **avoir de la ~** to be a good conversationalist; **anglais de ~** conversational English; **dans la ~ courante** in everyday speech.

converser /kɔ̃vɛʀse/ [1] *vi* to converse (**avec** with).

conversion /kɔ̃vɛʀsjɔ̃/ *nf* **1** conversion (**à** to; **en** into); **2** (in skiing) kick-turn.

converti, **~e** /kɔ̃vɛʀti/ I *pp* ▶ **convertir**.
II *nm,f* convert.

convertible /kɔ̃vɛʀtibl/ *adj* **1** convertible (**en** into, to); **2 canapé ~** sofa-bed.

convertir /kɔ̃vɛʀtiʀ/ [3] I *vtr* to convert (**à** to; **en** into, to).
II **se convertir** *v refl* (+ *v être*) to convert, to become a convert (**à** to).

convertisseur /kɔ̃vɛʀtisœʀ/ *nm* converter.

convexe /kɔ̃vɛks/ *adj* convex.

conviction /kɔ̃viksjɔ̃/ *nf* conviction; **avoir la ~ que** to be convinced that.

convier /kɔ̃vje/ [2] *vtr* to invite [*person*] (**à** to; **à faire** to do).

convive /kɔ̃viv/ *nmf* guest.

convivial, **~e**, *mpl* **-iaux** /kɔ̃vivjal, o/ *adj* **1** convivial; **2** user-friendly.

convivialité /kɔ̃vivjalite/ *nf* **1** friendliness; conviviality; **2** user-friendliness.

convocation /kɔ̃vɔkasjɔ̃/ *nf* **1** (of meeting) convening; (of person) summoning; (for interview) invitation; (Mil) calling up; **2** notice to attend; (Law) summons; (Mil) call-up papers; **~ aux examens** notification of examination timetables.

convoi /kɔ̃vwa/ *nm* **1** convoy; **'~ exceptionnel'** (Aut) 'wide or dangerous load'; **2** train.

convoiter /kɔ̃vwate/ [1] *vtr* to covet.

convoitise /kɔ̃vwatiz/ *nf* **la ~** covetousness; **~ de** lust for; **regarder qch avec ~** to look longingly at sth.

convoquer /kɔ̃vɔke/ [1] *vtr* to call, to convene [*meeting*]; to send for [*pupil*]; to summon [*witness*]; to call up [*soldier*]; **être convoqué à un examen** to be asked to attend an exam.

convoyer /kɔ̃vwaje/ [23] *vtr* to escort.

convoyeur, **-euse** /kɔ̃vwajœʀ/ I *nm,f* **1** prison escort; **2** courier; **~ de fonds** security guard.
II *nm* **1** conveyor; **2 navire ~** escort ship.

convulser /kɔ̃vylse/ [1] *vtr* (formal) to contort [*face*]; to grip [*stomach*].

convulsif, **-ive** /kɔ̃vylsif, iv/ *adj* **1** convulsive; **2** [*laughter*] nervous.

convulsion /kɔ̃vylsjɔ̃/ *nf* convulsion.

convulsionner /kɔ̃vylsjɔne/ [1] *vtr* to convulse.

coopérant /kɔɔpeʀɑ̃/ *nm* cultural/technical/medical aide.

coopérateur, **-trice** /kɔɔpeʀatœʀ, tʀis/ *nm,f* **1** collaborator; **2** member of a cooperative.

coopératif, **-ive** /kɔɔpeʀatif, iv/ I *adj* cooperative.
II **coopérative** *nf* cooperative.

coopération /kɔɔpeʀasjɔ̃/ *nf* **1** cooperation; **2** cultural/technical aid.

coopérer /kɔɔpeʀe/ [14] *vi* to cooperate (**à** on, in).

coopter /kɔɔpte/ [1] *vtr* to co-opt.

coordinateur, **-trice** /kɔɔʀdinatœʀ, tʀis/ I *adj* coordinating.
II *nm,f* coordinator.

coordination /kɔɔʀdinasjɔ̃/ *nf* **1** coordination; **2** joint committee.

coordonné, **~e** /kɔɔʀdɔne/ I *pp* ▶ **coordonner**.
II *pp adj* coordinated; coordinating.
III **coordonnés** *nm pl* (in fashion) coordinates.

coordonnées /kɔɔʀdɔne/ *nf pl* **1** (on graph, map) coordinates; **2** information (**de** about); **3** address and telephone number.

coordonner /kɔɔʀdɔne/ [1] *vtr* to coordinate.

copain, **copine** /kɔpɛ̃, in/ I *adj* pally○ (GB), chummy○.
II *nm,f* **1** friend; **2** boyfriend/girlfriend.

copeau, *pl* **~x** /kɔpo/ *nm* shaving.

Copenhague /kɔpɛnag/ *pr n* Copenhagen.

copie /kɔpi/ *nf* **1** copying; copy; **2** (Sch) paper.

copier /kɔpje/ [2] *vtr* **1** to copy; **2** (Sch) **~ sur qn** to copy or crib from sb.

copieur, **-ieuse** /kɔpjœʀ, øz/ I *nm,f* (Sch) cheat.
II *nm* photocopier.

copieusement /kɔpjøzmɑ̃/ *adv* heartily; lavishly; copiously; **un repas ~ arrosé** a meal with lots to drink.

copieux, **-ieuse** /kɔpjø, øz/ *adj* [*meal*] hearty; [*portion*] generous; [*notes*] copious.

copilote /kopilɔt/ *nmf* co-pilot; co-driver.

copinage○ /kɔpinaʒ/ *nm* cronyism.

copine ▶ **copain**.

coprésidence /kopʀezidɑ̃s/ *nf* joint presidency; joint chairmanship.

coprésident, **~e** /kopʀezidɑ̃, ɑ̃t/ *nm,f* joint president; co-chair.

coproduction /kopʀɔdyksjɔ̃/ *nf* co-production.

copropriétaire /kopʀɔpʀijetɛʀ/ *nmf* **1** owner (*of an apartment in a jointly-owned building*); **2** joint owner, co-owner.

copropriété /kopʀɔpʀijete/ *nf* joint ownership; co-ownership; **immeuble en ~** block of individually owned apartments.

copuler /kɔpyle/ [1] *vi* to copulate (**avec** with).

coq /kɔk/ *nm* cockerel, rooster; cock; **au chant du ~** at cockcrow; **le ~ du village** the local Casanova.
■ **~ de bruyère** grouse.
IDIOMS **être comme un ~ en pâte** to be in

clover; **sauter du ~ à l'âne** to hop from one subject to another.

coque /kɔk/ *nf* **1** (of boat) hull; (of hydroplane) fuselage; (of car) body; **2** cockle; **3** (of nut) shell.

coquelicot /kɔkliko/ *nm* poppy.

coqueluche /kɔklyʃ/ *nf* **1** whooping-cough; **2**° idol.

coquet, **-ette** /kɔkɛ, ɛt/ *adj* **1** **être ~** to be particular about one's appearance; **2** pretty; **3**° [*sum*] tidy°.

coquetier /kɔktje/ *nm* eggcup.

coquettement /kɔkɛtmɑ̃/ *adv* coquettishly; stylishly; prettily.

coquetterie /kɔkɛtʀi/ *nf* **1** interest in one's appearance; vanity; **par ~** out of vanity; **2** coquetry; **~s** coquettish ways.

coquillage /kɔkijaʒ/ *nm* **1** shellfish; **2** shell.

coquille /kɔkij/ *nf* **1** shell; **2** scallop-shaped dish; **~ de saumon** scalloped salmon (GB), salmon served in a shell; **3** misprint; **4** (Med) spinal jacket.
■ **~ de beurre** butter curl; **~ Saint-Jacques** scallop; scallop shell.

coquillette /kɔkijɛt/ *nf* small macaroni.

coquin, **~e** /kɔkɛ̃, in/ **I** *adj* **1** mischievous; **2** naughty, saucy.
II *nm,f* rascal.

cor /kɔʀ/ *nm* **1** (Mus) horn; **~ d'harmonie** French horn; **2** (Med) corn.
IDIOMS **réclamer** or **demander qch à ~ et à cri** to clamour[GB] for sth.

corail, *pl* **-aux** /kɔʀaj, o/ *adj inv*, *nm* coral.

Coran /kɔʀɑ̃/ *pr nm* **le ~** the Koran.

corbeau, *pl* **~x** /kɔʀbo/ *nm* **1** crow; **grand ~** raven; **noir ~** raven black; **2**° writer of a poison-pen letter.

corbeille /kɔʀbɛj/ *nf* **1** basket; **~ à papier** wastepaper basket; **2** dress circle.

corbillard /kɔʀbijaʀ/ *nm* hearse.

cordage /kɔʀdaʒ/ *nm* **1** rope; **~s** rigging; **2** (of racket) stringing.

corde /kɔʀd/ *nf* **1** rope; **à semelles de ~** rope-soled; **2** skipping rope; **3** (of bow, racket, instrument) string.
■ **~ à linge** clothes line; **~ lisse** climbing rope; **~ à nœuds** knotted (climbing) rope; **~ raide** tightrope; **~ de rappel** abseiling rope; **~s vocales** vocal chords.
IDIOMS **mériter la ~** to deserve to be hanged; **pleuvoir** or **tomber des ~s** to be raining cats and dogs°; **tirer sur la ~** to push one's luck; **ce n'est pas dans mes ~s**° it's not my line; **faire jouer la ~ sensible** to tug at the heartstrings; **prendre un virage à la ~** to hug a bend; **usé jusqu'à la ~** threadbare.

cordée /kɔʀde/ *nf* roped party (of climbers).

cordelière /kɔʀdəljɛʀ/ *nf* cord.

cordial, **~e**, *mpl* **-iaux** /kɔʀdjal, o/ *adj* cordial; warm-hearted; warm.

cordialement /kɔʀdjalmɑ̃/ *adv* warmly; **détester qn ~** to dislike sb heartily; **~ (vôtre** or **à vous)** yours sincerely.

cordialité /kɔʀdjalite/ *nf* warmth; friendliness.

cordillère /kɔʀdijɛʀ/ *nf* cordillera; **la Cordillère des Andes** the Andes Cordillera.

cordon /kɔʀdɔ̃/ *nm* **1** cord; string; lace; **2** flex (GB), cord (US); **3** cordon; **4** row; **5** ribbon.
■ **~ ombilical** umbilical cord.

cordonnerie /kɔʀdɔnʀi/ *nf* **1** shoemaking; **2** shoe repairing; **3** cobbler's.

cordonnier /kɔʀdɔnje/ *nm* cobbler.

Corée /kɔʀe/ *pr nf* Korea.

coréen, **-éenne** /kɔʀeɛ̃, ɛn/ **I** *adj* Korean.
II *nm* Korean.

Corfou /kɔʀfu/ *pr n* Corfu.

coriace /kɔʀjas/ *adj* tough.

coriandre /kɔʀjɑ̃dʀ/ *nf* coriander.

Corinthe /kɔʀɛ̃t/ *pr n* Corinth; **raisins de ~** currants.

cormoran /kɔʀmɔʀɑ̃/ *nm* cormorant.

corne /kɔʀn/ *nf* **1** horn; antler; **à ~s** horned; **donner un coup de ~ à qn** to butt sb; **blesser d'un coup de ~** to gore; **2** (Mus) horn; **3** **faire une ~** to turn down the corner (of a page); **4**° **avoir de la ~ aux pieds** to have calluses on one's feet.
■ **~ d'abondance** horn of plenty, cornucopia; **~ de brume** foghorn; **~ à chaussures** shoehorn.

cornée /kɔʀne/ *nf* cornea.

corneille /kɔʀnɛj/ *nf* crow.

cornemuse /kɔʀnəmyz/ *nf* bagpipes.

corner /kɔʀne/ [1] **I** *vtr* to turn down the corner of [*page*]; **page cornée** dog-eared page.
II *vi* to hoot (GB), to honk.

cornet /kɔʀnɛ/ *nm* **1** (paper) cone; **2** (ice-cream) cone, cornet (GB); **3** **~ à la crème** cream horn.
■ **~ à dés** dice cup; **~ à pistons** cornet.

cornette /kɔʀnɛt/ *nf* cornet, wimple.

corniche /kɔʀniʃ/ *nf* **1** cornice; **2** moulding (GB), molding (US); **3** ledge (of rock); **4** cliff road.

cornichon /kɔʀniʃɔ̃/ *nm* **1** gherkin; **2**° nitwit°.

Cornouailles /kɔʀnuɑj/ *pr nf* Cornwall.

cornu, **~e** /kɔʀny/ **I** *adj* horned.
II **cornue** *nf* (for distilling) retort.

corollaire /kɔʀɔlɛʀ/ *nm* corollary.

corolle /kɔʀɔl/ *nf* **1** corolla; **2** **en ~** [*skirt*] flared.

coron /kɔʀɔ̃/ *nm* miners' terraced houses.

coronaire /kɔʀɔnɛʀ/ *adj* coronary.

corporatif, **-ive** /kɔʀpɔʀatif, iv/ *adj* corporate.

corporation /kɔʀpɔʀasjɔ̃/ *nf* corporation.

corporel, **-elle** /kɔʀpɔʀɛl/ *adj* [*needs*] bodily; [*punishment*] corporal.

corps /kɔʀ/ *nm inv* body; **(combat) ~ à ~** hand-to-hand combat; **se donner ~ et âme à** to give oneself body and soul to; **faire ~ avec** [*person*] to stand solidly behind; [*building*] to be joined to; **prendre ~** to take shape.
■ **~ du délit** corpus delicti; **~ enseignant** teaching profession; **~ et biens** (to sink) with all hands; **~ expéditionnaire** expeditionary force; **~ gras** fatty substance;

~ médical medical profession; **~ simple** element.
IDIOMS **tenir au ~** to be nourishing.

corpulence /kɔrpylɑ̃s/ *nf* stoutness, corpulence; **de forte ~** of stout build.

corpulent, **~e** /kɔrpylɑ̃, ɑ̃t/ *adj* stout, corpulent.

corpuscule /kɔrpyskyl/ *nm* corpuscle.

correct, **~e** /kɔrɛkt/ *adj* **1** [*calculation*] correct; [*copy*] accurate; **2** [*outfit*] proper; [*conduct*] correct; **3**○ [*result, wine*] reasonable, decent; **4** [*person*] polite; fair, correct.

correctement /kɔrɛktəmɑ̃/ *adv* **1** correctly; **2** properly; **3** decently; reasonably well.

correcteur, **-trice** /kɔrɛktœr, tris/ **I** *adj* corrective.
II *nm,f* **1** examiner (GB), grader (US); **2** proofreader.
■ **~ automatique d'orthographe** automatic spell checker.

correction /kɔrɛksjɔ̃/ *nf* **1** correcting; proofreading; marking (GB), grading (US); **2** correction; **3** thrashing; **4** correctness; good manners; **manquer de ~** to have no manners.

correctionnel, **-elle**[1] /kɔrɛksjɔnɛl/ *adj* **peine correctionnelle** penalty (imposed by court); **tribunal ~** magistrate's court.

correctionnelle[2] /kɔrɛksjɔnɛl/ *nf* magistrate's court.

corrélation /kɔrelasjɔ̃/ *nf* correlation (**entre** between); **être en (étroite) ~ avec qn** to be (closely) related or connected to sth.

correspondance /kɔrɛspɔ̃dɑ̃s/ *nf* **1** letters; mail; correspondence (**entre** between); **faire sa ~** to write some letters; **vendu par ~** available by mail order; **faire des études par ~** to do a correspondence course; **2** correspondence (**entre** between); **3** connection; **trains/vols en ~** connecting trains/flights.

correspondant, **~e** /kɔrɛspɔ̃dɑ̃, ɑ̃t/ **I** *adj* corresponding.
II *nm,f* correspondent; (Sch) pen pal.

correspondre /kɔrɛspɔ̃dr/ [6] **I correspondre à** *v+prep* to correspond to; to match; to suit [*tastes*]; **ça ne correspond pas du tout à la réalité** it bears no relation to reality.
II *vi* to correspond (**avec** with), to write (**avec** to).
III se correspondre *v refl* (+ *v être*) to correspond.

corrida /kɔrida/ *nf* **1** bullfight; **2**○ (real) performance.

corridor /kɔridɔr/ *nm* corridor.

corrigé /kɔriʒe/ *nm* (Sch) correct version.

corriger /kɔriʒe/ [13] **I** *vtr* **1** to correct; to proofread [*manuscript*]; to mark (GB), to grade (US) [*exam papers*]; to redress [*situation*]; to improve [*manners*]; **2** to adjust [*position*]; to modify [*theory*]; **~ le tir** (Mil) to alter one's aim; (figurative) to adjust one's tactics; **3** to give [sb] a hiding○; to spank [*child*].
II se corriger *v refl* (+ *v être*) **1** to correct oneself; **2** to mend one's ways; **se ~ d'un défaut** to cure oneself of a fault.

corroborer /kɔrɔbɔre/ [1] *vtr* to corroborate.

corroder /kɔrɔde/ [1] *vtr* to corrode.

corrompre /kɔrɔ̃pr/ [53] *vtr* **1** to bribe; **2** to corrupt.

corrompu, **~e** /kɔrɔ̃py/ **I** *pp* ▶ **corrompre**.
II *pp adj* corrupt.

corrosif, **-ive** /kɔrozif, iv/ *adj* **1** [*substance*] corrosive; **2** [*humour*] caustic.

corrosion /kɔrozjɔ̃/ *nf* corrosion.

corrupteur, **-trice** /kɔryptœr, tris/ **I** *adj* corrupting.
II *nm,f* **1** person who offers a bribe; **2** corrupter.

corruption /kɔrypsjɔ̃/ *nf* **1** corruption; **2** bribery.

corsage /kɔrsaʒ/ *nm* **1** blouse; **2** bodice.

corsaire /kɔrsɛr/ *nm* **1** corsair; **2** pedal pushers.

corse /kɔrs/ *adj*, *nm* Corsican.

Corse /kɔrs/ *pr nf* Corsica.

corsé, **~e** /kɔrse/ *adj* [*coffee*] strong; [*wine*] full-bodied; [*sauce, story*] spicy; [*problem*] tough; [*bill*] steep.

corser /kɔrse/ [1] **I** *vtr* **1** to make [sth] more difficult [*exercise*]; **pour ~ l'affaire** (just) to complicate matters; **2** to make [sth] spicier [*sauce*].
II se corser *v refl* (+ *v être*) to get more complicated.

corset /kɔrsɛ/ *nm* corset.

corso /kɔrso/ *nm* **~ fleuri** procession of floral floats.

cortège /kɔrtɛʒ/ *nm* **1** procession; **2** (literary) **~ de** stream of [*memories*]; spate of [*troubles*].

corvée /kɔrve/ *nf* chore; (Mil) fatigue (duty); **être de ~ pour faire** to have been roped into doing.

cosaque /kɔzak/ *nm* Cossack.

cosinus /kɔsinys/ *nm inv* cosine.

cosmétique /kɔsmetik/ *adj*, *nm* cosmetic.

cosmique /kɔsmik/ *adj* cosmic.

cosmonaute /kɔsmɔnot/ *nmf* cosmonaut.

cosmopolite /kɔsmɔpɔlit/ *adj* cosmopolitan.

cosse /kɔs/ *nf* (of pea) pod; (of grain) husk.

cossu, **~e** /kɔsy/ *adj* [*person*] well-to-do; [*interior*] plush; [*house*] smart.

costaud○ /kɔsto/ **I** *adj* strong, sturdy; hefty○.
II *nm* sturdily built man.

costume /kɔstym/ *nm* **1** suit; **2** costume; **répétition en ~** dress rehearsal.
■ **~ de bain**† swimming costume.

costumer: **se costumer** /kɔstyme/ [1] *v refl* (+ *v être*) **se ~ en** to dress up as; **soirée costumée** fancy-dress party.

costumier, **-ière** /kɔstymje, ɛr/ *nm,f* wardrobe master/mistress; costumier.

cotation /kɔtasjɔ̃/ *nf* quotation.

cote /kɔt/ *nf* **1** (of stocks, commodities) quotation; (stock exchange) list; **2** (of stamp) quoted value; **3** (at races) odds; **4** (of person, film) rating; **avoir**

la ~° **auprès de** to be popular with; to be well thought of by; **5** (on plan) dimension; **6** (on map) spot height.
■ **~ d'alerte** flood level; (figurative) danger level; **~ d'amour** or **de popularité** popularity rating.

côte /kot/ **I** *nf* **1** coast; **2** hill; **dans une ~** on a hill; **3** rib; **4** chop; **~ de bœuf** rib roast.
II côte à côte *phr* side by side.
■ **Côte d'Azur** French riviera.
IDIOMS **se tenir les ~s** to split one's sides with laughter.

coté, **~e** /kɔte/ **I** *pp* ▶ **coter**.
II *pp adj* **être (très) ~** to be (very) well thought of.

côté /kote/ **I** *nm* **1** side; **du ~ droit/gauche** on the righthand/lefthand side; **prendre** or **voir les choses du bon ~** to look on the bright side of things; **chambre ~ rue** room overlooking the street; **avoir ses bons ~s** to have one's good points; **par certains ~s** in some respects; **~ santé** healthwise; **de mon ~, je pense que**... for my part, I think that...; **d'un ~...d'un autre ~**... on the one hand...on the other hand...; **2** way, direction; **viens de ce ~** come this way; **de tous ~s** [*come*] from all directions; [*run, ask*] all over the place; **du ~ de Nice** [*live, happen*] near Nice; **aller du ~ de Dijon** to head for Dijon.
II à côté *phr* **1** nearby; **les gens d'à ~** the people next door; **à ~ de** next to; **la ballon est passé à ~ (du but)** the ball went wide (of the goal); **répondre à ~** (by mistake) to miss the point; (on purpose) to sidestep the question; **2** by comparison; **à ~ du film** compared to the film; **3** on the side; **elle est étudiante et travaille à ~** she's a student and works on the side.
III de côté *phr* **1** sideways; **2** aside; **mettre qch de ~** to put sth aside [*money, object*].
IV aux côtés de *phr* **aux ~s de qn** [*to be*] at sb's side; [*to work*] alongside sb.

coteau, *pl* **~x** /kɔto/ *nm* **1** hillside; **2** hill; **3** (sloping) vineyard.

Côte-d'Ivoire /kotdivwaʀ/ *pr nf* Ivory Coast.

côtelé, **~e** /kotle/ *adj* **velours ~** corduroy, cord.

côtelette /kotlɛt/ *nf* (Culin) chop.

coter /kɔte/ [1] *vtr* **1** to quote, to list [*shares*]; to price [*car*]; **2** to rate [*film*]; to mark [*homework*].

coterie /kɔtʀi/ *nf* circle, clique.

côtier, **-ière** /kotje, ɛʀ/ *adj* [*town, navigation*] coastal; [*fishing*] inshore.

cotisation /kɔtizasjɔ̃/ *nf* **1** contribution; **2** subscription.

cotiser /kɔtize/ [1] **I** *vi* **1** to pay one's contributions; **2** to pay one's subscription (**à** to).
II se cotiser *v refl* (+ *v être*) to club together (GB), to go in together.

coton /kɔtɔ̃/ *nm* **1** cotton; **2** thread; **3** cotton wool (GB), cotton (US).
■ **~ hydrophile** cotton wool (GB), absorbent cotton (US).
IDIOMS **filer un mauvais ~** to be in a bad way; **élever un enfant dans du ~** to give a child a very sheltered upbringing; **j'ai les jambes en ~** (after shock) my legs have turned to jelly; (after illness) I am a bit wobbly on my legs.

cotonnade /kɔtɔnad/ *nf* cotton fabric.

cotonneux, **-euse** /kɔtɔnø, øz/ *adj* [*fog*] like cotton-wool; [*cloud*] fleecy.

cotonnier, **-ière** /kɔtɔnje, ɛʀ/ **I** *adj* cotton.
II *nm* cotton plant.

côtoyer /kotwaje/ [23] **I** *vtr* to walk alongside [*river*]; to move in [*milieu*]; to mix with [*people*]; to be in close contact with [*death, danger*].
II se côtoyer *v refl* (+ *v être*) [*people*] to mix.

cotte /kɔt/ *nf* overalls.
■ **~ de mailles** coat of mail.

cou /ku/ *nm* neck; **avoir des ennuis** or **problèmes jusqu'au ~** to be up to one's neck in problems; **être endetté jusqu'au ~** to be up to one's eyes in debt.

couchage /kuʃaʒ/ *nm* **1** sleeping arrangements; **2** bedding; **un studio avec ~ pour six** a studio that sleeps six.

couchant /kuʃɑ̃/ **I** *adj* **soleil ~** setting sun; **au soleil ~** at sunset.
II *nm* **1** sunset; **2** (literary) west.

couche /kuʃ/ *nf* **1** layer; (of paint) coat; **2** class, sector; **les ~s laborieuses** the working classes; **3** nappy (GB), diaper (US); **4 ~s** childbirth.

couché, **~e** /kuʃe/ **I** *pp* ▶ **coucher**.
II *pp adj* [*grass*] flattened; [*writing*] sloping.

couche-culotte, *pl* **couches-culottes** /kuʃkylɔt/ *nf* disposable nappy (GB) or diaper (US).

coucher /kuʃe/ [1] **I** *nm* bedtime; **à l'heure du ~** at bedtime.
II *vtr* **1** to put [sb] to bed; to lay out [*wounded person*]; **2** to lay [sth] on its side; to lay [sth] down; **3** to flatten [*grass*].
III *vi* to sleep; **~ sous les ponts** to sleep rough (GB) or outdoors; **ça m'a fait ~ tard** it meant I went to bed late.
IV se coucher *v refl* (+ *v être*) **1** to lie (down); **2** to go to bed; **3** [*stem*] to bend; [*boat*] to list; **se ~ sur** [*cyclist*] to lean forward over [*handlebars*]; **4** [*sun*] to set.
■ **~ de soleil** sunset; **au ~ du soleil** at sunset.

couchette /kuʃɛt/ *nf* couchette, berth.

couci-couça° /kusikusa/ *adv* so-so°.

coucou /kuku/ **I** *nm* **1** cuckoo; **2** cowslip; **3**° (old) crate°, plane; **4** cuckoo clock.
II° *excl* **1** cooee!; **2** peekaboo!

coude /kud/ *nm* **1** elbow; **2** (in river, pipe) bend.
■ **le ~ à ~** solidarity; **travailler ~ à ~** to work shoulder to shoulder.
IDIOMS **se serrer** or **se tenir les ~s** to stick together; **lever le ~**° to drink a bit.

coudé, **~e** /kude/ **I** *pp* ▶ **couder**.
II *adj* bent at an angle.
III coudée *nf* **avoir les** or **ses ~es franches** to have elbow room.

cou-de-pied, *pl* **cous-de-pied** /kudpje/ *nm* instep.

couder /kude/ [1] *vtr* to bend.

coudre /kudʀ/ [76] *vtr* to sew; to sew [sth] on; to stitch [sth] on; to stitch (up).
IDIOMS **leur histoire est cousue de fil blanc** you can see right through their story.

couenne /kwan/ *nf* (bacon) rind.

couette /kwɛt/ *nf* **1** duvet, **2 ~s** bunches (GB), pigtails.

couffin /kufɛ̃/ *nm* Moses basket (GB), bassinet (US).

couiner /kwine/ [1] *vi* to squeak, to squeal.

coulant, **~e** /kulɑ̃, ɑ̃t/ *adj* [*cheese*] runny; [*person*] easy-going; [*style*] flowing.

coulée /kule/ *nf* (of lava) flow; (of paint) drip; **~e de boue** mudslide.

couler /kule/ [1] **I** *vtr* **1** to cast [*metal, statue*]; to pour [*concrete*]; **2** to sink [*ship*]; **3**° to put [sth] out of business; to bring [sb] down.
II *vi* **1** [*blood*] to flow; [*paint, cheese*] to run; **faire ~ qch** to run [*water, bath*]; **2** [*tap, pen*] to leak; [*nose*] to run; **3** [*boat*] to sink; [*company*] to go under.
III se couler *v refl* (+ *v être*) **se ~ dans/entre** to slip into/between.

couleur /kulœʀ/ *nf* **1** colour[GB]; **de quelle ~ est le mur?** what colour[GB] is the wall?; **de ~** [*person*] coloured[GB]; **sans ~** colourless[GB]; **plein de ~** colourful[GB]; **tu as pris des ~s!** you've got some colour[GB] in your cheeks!; **2** paint; **3 les ~s** (washing) coloureds[GB]; (flag) the colours[GB]; **4** (in cards) suit; **jouer dans la ~** to follow suit; **5** light; **sous des ~s trompeuses** in a false light; **sous ~ de faire** while pretending to do.
■ **~ locale** local colour[GB].
IDIOMS **ne pas voir la ~ de qch**° never to get a sniff of sth°; **il m'en a fait voir de toutes les ~s**° he put me through the mill.

couleuvre /kulœvʀ/ *nf* grass snake.
IDIOMS **avaler des ~s**° to believe anything one is told.

coulissant, **~e** /kulisɑ̃, ɑ̃t/ *adj* sliding.

coulisse /kulis/ *nf* **1 les ~s**, **la ~** the wings; **en ~** backstage; (figurative) behind the scenes; **2** runner; **porte à ~** sliding door; **3** (in sewing) casing.

coulisser /kulise/ [1] *vi* to slide.

couloir /kulwaʀ/ *nm* **1** corridor (GB), hallway; passage; **bruits de ~s** rumours[GB]; **2** lane; **~ (de circulation** or **réservé)** bus (and taxi) lane; **~ aérien** air (traffic) lane.

coup /ku/ *nm* **1** knock; blow; **~ à la porte** knock at the door; **~ de marteau** hammer blow; **à ~s de bâton** with a stick; **donner un ~ de qch à qn** to hit sb with sth; **donner un ~ de poing/pied/couteau à qn** to punch/kick/stab sb; **en avoir pris un ~**° to have taken (quite) a punishing; **porter un ~ (sévère) à** (figurative) to deal [sb/sth] a (severe) blow; **sa fierté en a pris un ~** it was a blow to his/her pride; **ça m'a donné un (sacré) ~**° it gave me an awful shock; **sous le ~ de la colère** in (a fit of) anger; **être sous le ~ d'une forte émotion** to be in a highly emotional state; **2** (noise) knock; bang; thump, thud; **au douzième ~ de minuit** on the last stroke of midnight; **sur le ~ de dix heures**° around ten; **~ de sifflet** whistle blast; **3 un (petit) ~ de brosse/chiffon** a (quick) brush/wipe; **un ~ de peinture** a lick of paint; **4** (in tennis, golf, cricket) stroke; shot; (in chess) move; (with dice) throw; (in boxing) punch; **tous les ~s sont permis** no holds barred; **~ défendu** foul; **5 ~ de feu/fusil** (gun)shot/(rifle) shot; **tuer qn d'un ~ de fusil** to shoot sb dead; **6**° job°, racket°; trick°; **monter un ~** to plan a job°; **il a raté son ~**° he blew it°; **réussir son ~** to pull it off; **être dans le ~** to be in on it; to be up to date; **qui a fait le ~?** who did it?; **ce n'est pas la première fois qu'il me fait le ~** it's not the first time he's done that to me; **7** time; **du premier ~** first time; **à chaque ~**, **à tous les ~s** every time; **ce ~-ci** this time; **du ~**° as a result; **après ~** afterward(s); **~ sur ~** in succession; **tout d'un ~**, **tout à ~** suddenly, all of a sudden; **d'un ~**, **d'un seul ~** just like that; **en un seul ~** in one go°; **sur le ~** at the time; instantly, on the spot; **pleurer un bon ~** to have a good cry; **boire à petits ~s** to sip; **8 à ~s de subventions** by means of subsidies; **9**° drink.
■ **~ bas** blow or punch below the belt; **~s et blessures** assault and battery; **~ dur** blow; **~ franc** free kick; **~ monté** put-up job.
IDIOMS **tenir le ~** [*shoes*] to last out; [*repair*] to hold; [*person*] to hold on; **en mettre un ~**° to give it all one's got°; **être aux cent ~s**° to be worried sick°, to be in a state°; **faire les quatre cents ~s**° to be a real tearaway; **attraper le ~ pour faire**° to get the knack of doing.

coupable /kupabl/ **I** *adj* guilty (**de qch** of sth; **d'avoir fait** of doing); [*negligence*] culpable; [*indifference*] shameful.
II *nmf* culprit.

coupant, **~e** /kupɑ̃, ɑ̃t/ *adj* sharp.

coup-de-poing, *pl* **coups-de-poing** /kudpwɛ̃/ *nm* **~ américain** knuckle-duster (GB), brass knuckles (US).

coupe /kup/ *nf* **1** cutting; cutting out; cut; **2** haircut; **faire une ~ à qn** to give sb a haircut; **3** (Sport) cup; **la ~ du Monde** the World Cup; **4** (fruit) bowl; (champagne) glass; **5** section; **~ transversale** cross section.
■ **~ en brosse** crew cut; **~ claire** drastic cut-back.
IDIOMS **la ~ est pleine** enough is enough; **être sous la ~ de qn** to be under sb's control.

coupe-circuit /kupsiʀkɥi/ *nm inv* fuse.

coupe-faim /kupfɛ̃/ *nm inv* appetite suppressant.

coupe-feu /kupfø/ *nm inv* firebreak.

coupe-gorge /kupgɔʀʒ/ *nm inv* rough place; rough area.

coupe-papier /kuppapje/ *nm inv* paper knife.

couper /kupe/ [1] **I** *vtr* **1** to cut; to cut down; to chop; to cut out; to cut off; **se faire ~ les cheveux** to have one's hair cut; **~ qch en**

tranches to slice sth; **~ la journée** to break up the day; **2** [*road*] to cut across; [*line*] to intersect with; **~ la route à qn** to cut in on sb; **3** to cut off [*road, supplies*]; to spoil [*appetite*]; to take the edge off [*hunger*]; to turn off [*water*]; **~ le contact** to switch off the ignition; **~ la fièvre à qn** to bring sb's temperature down; **~ le souffle à qn** to take sb's breath away; **~ la parole à qn** to interrupt sb; **4 ~ qn de qn/qch** to cut sb off from sb/sth; **5** to dilute [*wine*]; **6** (in tennis) to slice [*ball*]; (in cards) to cut [*pack*]; to trump [*card*].

II *vi* **attention ça coupe!** be careful, it's sharp; **~ à travers champs** to cut across country.

III se couper *v refl* (+ *v être*) **1** to cut oneself; **2** to give oneself away.

IDIOMS **c'est ton tour de faire à manger, tu n'y couperas pas** it's your turn to cook, you won't get out of it; **j'en mettrais ma main à ~** or **au feu** I'd stake my life on it.

couperet /kupʀɛ/ *nm* cleaver; (of guillotine) blade; **la nouvelle est tombée comme un ~** the news came as a bolt from the blue.

couperose /kupʀoz/ *nf* broken veins.

coupe-vent /kupvɑ̃/ *nm inv* **1** windcheater (GB), windbreaker (US); **2** windbreak.

couple /kupl/ *nm* **1** couple; pair; **2** relationship.

couplet /kuplɛ/ *nm* **1** verse; **2** couplet.

coupole /kupɔl/ *nf* cupola, dome.

coupon /kupɔ̃/ *nm* **1** remnant; **2** ticket voucher; **3** multiuse ticket (*in travel pass*); **4** coupon.

coupure /kupyʀ/ *nf* **1** cut; **~ d'électricité** or **de courant** power cut; **2** break; **3** gap (**entre** between); **4** (bank)note (GB), bill (US).

■ **~ de journal** or **de presse** (newspaper) cutting or clipping.

cour /kuʀ/ *nf* **1** courtyard; (school) playground; (farm) yard; **2** (of sovereign) court; (of celebrity) entourage; **3** courtship; **faire la ~ à** to court; **4** (Law) court.

■ **~ d'arrivée** arrivals area; **~ de départ** departures area; **~ intérieure** inner courtyard; **~ martiale** court-martial; **~ de récréation** playground.

courage /kuʀaʒ/ *nm* **1** courage, bravery; **avoir du ~** to be brave or courageous; **2** energy; **je n'ai même pas le ~ de me doucher** I don't even have the energy to have a shower; **bon ~!** good luck!; **perdre ~** to lose heart; **reprendre ~** to take fresh heart; **je n'ai pas eu le ~ de dire non** I didn't have the heart to say no.

courageusement /kuʀaʒøzmɑ̃/ *adv* **1** courageously, bravely; **2** with a will.

courageux, -euse /kuʀaʒø, øz/ *adj* courageous, brave; **je ne me sens pas très ~ aujourd'hui** I haven't got much energy today.

couramment /kuʀamɑ̃/ *adv* **1** fluently; **2** [*used*] widely; **cela se fait ~** it's very common; **ça se dit ~** it's a common expression.

courant[1] /kuʀɑ̃/ *prep* **~ janvier** some time in January.

courant[2], **~e** /kuʀɑ̃, ɑ̃t/ **I** *adj* **1** [*word, practice, mistake*] common; **2** [*language*] everyday; [*procedure*] usual, ordinary; [*size*] standard; **3** [*month, price*] current; **le 15 du mois ~** the 15th of this month.

II *nm* **1** current; **il n'y a plus de ~** the power has gone off; **2** trend; **un ~ politique** a political trend; **3** movement; **les ~s de population** population movements; **4 dans le ~ de** in the course of.

III au courant *phr* **être au ~ de** to know about [*news*]; to be up to date on [*technique*]; **mettre qn au ~** to put sb in the picture; to bring sb up to date; **tenir qn au ~** to keep sb posted.

■ **~ d'air** draught (GB), draft (US).

courbature /kuʀbatyʀ/ *nf* ache; **avoir des ~s** to be stiff.

courbaturé, ~e /kuʀbatyʀe/ *pp adj* stiff; aching.

courbe /kuʀb/ **I** *adj* curved.

II *nf* **1** curve; **2** bend.

■ **~ de niveau** contour line; **~ de température** temperature chart.

courber /kuʀbe/ [1] **I** *vtr* to bend; **~ le dos** (figurative) to bow down.

II *vi* **~ sous le poids** to be bowed down under the weight.

courbette /kuʀbɛt/ *nf* (low) bow; **faire des ~s** (figurative) to bow and scrape.

courbure /kuʀbyʀ/ *nf* curve.

coureur, -euse /kuʀœʀ, øz/ *nm,f* runner; **~ automobile** racing driver; **~ cycliste** racing cyclist; **~ de jupons** philanderer.

courge /kuʀʒ/ *nf* gourd; (vegetable) marrow.

courgette /kuʀʒɛt/ *nf* courgette (GB), zucchini (US).

courir /kuʀiʀ/ [26] **I** *vtr* **1** to compete in [*trials*]; **2 ~ le monde** to roam the world; **j'ai couru tout Paris pour trouver ton cadeau** I searched the whole of Paris for your present; **3 ~ les cocktails** to do the round of the cocktail parties; **~ les boutiques** to go round the shops (GB) or stores (US); **4 ~ un (grand) danger** to be in (great) danger; **~ un (gros) risque** to run a (big) risk; **faire ~ un risque à qn** to put sb at risk; **5**○ **~ les filles** to chase after girls.

II *vi* **1** to run; to race; **~ après qn/qch** to run after sb/sth; to chase after sb/sth; **les voleurs courent toujours** the thieves are still at large; **~ à la catastrophe** to be heading for disaster; **2** [*rumour*] to go around; **faire ~ un bruit** to spread a rumour[GB].

IDIOMS **tu peux toujours ~**○! you can go whistle for it○!; **laisser ~**○ to let things ride.

couronne /kuʀɔn/ *nf* **1** crown; **2 ~ de fleurs** garland; wreath; **~ de lauriers** laurel wreath; **3** ring-shaped loaf; **4** (in Paris) **la petite/grande ~** *the inner/outer suburbs.*

couronnement /kuʀɔnmɑ̃/ *nm* coronation; **c'est le ~ de leur carrière** it's their crowning achievement.

couronner /kuʀɔne/ [1] *vtr* to crown; **et pour ~ le tout** and to crown it all.

courre /kuʀ/ *vtr* **chasse à ~** hunting.

courrier /kuRje/ *nm* **1** mail, post (GB); **faire son ~** to write some letters; **par retour du ~** by return (of post) (GB), by return mail; **2 ~ des lecteurs** letters to the editor; **~ du cœur** problem page; **~ électronique** electronic mail.

courroie /kuRwɑ/ *nf* **1** strap; **2** (on machine) belt.

cours /kuR/ *nm inv* **1** lesson, class; **avoir ~** to have a class; **faire ~** to teach; **2** course book, textbook; **3** school; **~ de théâtre** drama school; **4** price; exchange rate; **avoir ~** to be legal tender; (figurative) [*theory, pratice*] to be current; **5** (of river) course; **6** (of tale, events) course; (of ideas) flow; **les choses suivent leur ~** things are taking their course; **la vie reprend son ~** life returns to normal; **donner libre ~ à** to give free rein to [*imagination*]; to give vent to [*anger*]; **au** or **dans le ~ de** in the course of, during; **en ~** [*month, week*] current; [*process, project*] under way; [*work, negotiations*] in progress; **en ~ de journée** in the course of the day; **en ~ de route** along the way.

■ **~ d'eau** watercourse; **~ élémentaire première année**, **CE1** *second year of primary school, age 7–8*; **~ moyen première année**, **CM1** *fourth year of primary school, age 9–10*; **~ particulier(s)** private tuition (GB), private tutoring (US); **~ préparatoire**, **CP** *first year of primary school, age 6–7*.

course /kuRs/ *nf* **1** running; run; racing; race; **faire la ~ avec qn** to race sb; **la ~ aux voix** the race for votes; **c'est la course tous les matins pour me préparer** I'm always in a rush in the morning to get ready; **2** (in taxi) journey; **c'est 50 francs la ~** the fare is 50 francs; **3** errand; **~s** shopping; **faire une ~** to run an errand; **faire les ~s** to do the shopping; **4** (of star, planet) path; (of clouds) passage; (of rocket, projectile) flight path.

■ **~ de haies** (in athletics) hurdles; (for horses) steeplechase; **~ d'obstacles** obstacle race; (figurative) obstacle course; **~ de taureaux** bullfight; bull run; **~ de vitesse** (in athletics) sprint; (on motorbikes) speedway race.

IDIOMS **ne plus être dans la ~** to be out of touch; **être à bout de ~** to be worn out.

coursier, **-ière** /kuRsje, ɛR/ *nm,f* messenger.

court, **~e** /kuR, kuRt/ **I** *adj* **1** short; **de ~e durée** short-lived; short-term; **avoir le souffle ~** to get out of breath easily; **prendre au plus ~** to take the shortest route; **2** [*defeat, victory, majority*] narrow.

II *adv* **couper qch ~** to cut sth short; **couper ~ à qch** to put paid to sth; **s'arrêter ~** to stop short.

III *nm* **~ de tennis** tennis court.

■ **~ métrage** short (film); **~e échelle**: **faire la ~e échelle à qn** to give sb a leg up°.

IDIOMS **être à ~ de** to be short of [*money*]; **prendre qn de ~** to catch sb on the hop° (GB) or unprepared.

court-circuit, *pl* **~s** /kuRsiRkɥi/ *nm* short-circuit.

courtier, **-ière** /kuRtje, ɛR/ *nm,f* broker.

courtisan /kuRtizɑ̃/ *nm* courtier.

courtisane /kuRtizan/ *nf* courtesan.

courtiser /kuRtize/ [1] *vtr* to woo.

courtois, **~e** /kuRtwa, az/ *adj* courteous; courtly.

courtoisie /kuRtwazi/ *nf* courtesy.

couru, **~e** /kuRy/ **I** *pp* ▶ **courir**.

II *pp adj* **1** [*place*] popular; **2 vingt partants, tous ~s** twenty starters, all ran.

IDIOMS **c'est ~ d'avance**° it's a foregone conclusion.

cousin, **~e** /kuzɛ̃, in/ *nm,f* cousin; **~ germain** first cousin.

coussin /kusɛ̃/ *nm* cushion.

cousu, **~e** /kuzy/ ▶ **coudre**.

coût /ku/ *nm* cost; **~ de la vie** cost of living.

coûtant /kutɑ̃/ *adj* **prix ~** cost price.

couteau, *pl* **~x** /kuto/ *nm* **1** knife; **donner un coup de ~ à qn** to stab sb; **~ à cran d'arrêt** flick knife (GB), switchblade (US); **2** razor shell (GB) or clam (US); **3** knife edge.

IDIOMS **être à ~x tirés avec qn** to be at daggers drawn with sb; **avoir le ~ sous la gorge** to have a pistol to one's head.

coûter /kute/ [1] **I** *vtr* to cost; **~ la vie à qn** to cost sb his/her life.

II *vi* to cost; **~ cher** to be expensive; **~ cher à qn** to cost sb a lot; (figurative) to cost sb dearly; **ça m'a coûté de m'excuser** it was hard for me to apologize.

III *v impers* **il t'en coûtera d'avoir fait cela** you will pay for doing this; **coûte que coûte, quoi qu'il en coûte** at all costs.

IDIOMS **il n'y a que le premier pas qui coûte** the first step is the hardest; **~ les yeux de la tête** to cost an arm and a leg°.

coûteux, **-euse** /kutø, øz/ *adj* costly.

coutume /kutym/ *nf* custom; **avoir ~ de faire** to be in the habit of doing; **comme de ~** as usual.

IDIOMS **une fois n'est pas ~** it does no harm just this once.

coutumier, **-ière** /kutymje, ɛR/ *adj* customary.

couture /kutyR/ **I** *adj inv* designer.

II *nf* **1** sewing; dressmaking; **faire de la ~** to sew; **2** seam.

IDIOMS **sous toutes les ~s** from every angle; **battre qn à plates ~s** to beat sb hollow.

couturier /kutyRje/ *nm* dress designer; **grand ~** couturier.

couturière /kutyRjɛR/ *nf* dressmaker.

couvée /kuve/ *nf* brood; clutch.

couvent /kuvɑ̃/ *nm* convent.

couver /kuve/ [1] **I** *vtr* **1** to sit on [*eggs*]; **la poule couve** the hen is brooding; **2** to overprotect; **~ qn/qch du regard** to look fondly at sb/sth; to gaze longingly at sb/sth; **3** to be coming down with [*illness*].

II *vi* [*rebellion*] to brew; [*fire, anger*] to smoulder (GB), to smolder (US).

couvercle /kuvɛRkl/ *nm* **1** lid; **2** screwtop.

couvert, **~e** /kuvɛʀ, ɛʀt/ **I** *pp* ▶ **couvrir**.
II *pp adj* **1** covered (**de** in, with); **être ~ de diplômes** to have a lot of qualifications; **2** [*pool*] indoor; [*market, passage*] covered; **3** [*sky*] overcast.
III *nm* **1** place setting; **mettre le ~** to lay the table; **un ~ en argent** a silver knife, fork and spoon; **2** cover charge.
IV à couvert *phr* under cover; **se mettre à ~** to take cover.
V sous le couvert de *phr* under the pretence[GB] of; **sous ~ de la plaisanterie** under the guise of a joke.

couverture /kuvɛʀtyʀ/ *nf* **1** blanket; rug (GB), lap robe (US); **2** (of book) cover; **3** (in press) coverage; **4** roofing, roof; **5** (of risk) cover.
IDIOMS **tirer la ~ à soi** to turn a situation to one's own advantage.

couveuse /kuvøz/ *nf* incubator.

couvre-feu, *pl* **~x** /kuvʀəfø/ *nm* curfew.

couvre-lit, *pl* **~s** /kuvʀəli/ *nm* bedspread.

couvreur /kuvʀœʀ/ *nm* roofer.

couvrir /kuvʀiʀ/ [32] **I** *vtr* **1** to cover [*furniture, wall, fire, card*]; to roof [*house*]; **~ qn de qch** (with blows, jewels, compliments) to shower sb with sth; **2** [*sound*] to drown out; **3** [*transmitter, inspector*] to cover [*region*]; **4** to wrap [sb] up; to cover [sb] up; **5** to cover up for [*mistake, person*]; **6** (with gun) to cover [*soldier*]; **7** to cover [*distance*]; **8** [*book, journalist*] to cover [*story, event*]; **9** [*sum*] to cover [*expenses*]; **~ les besoins de qn** to meet sb's needs; **~ une enchère** to make a higher bid.
II se couvrir *v refl* (+ *v être*) **1** to wrap up; to put on a hat; **2** [*sky*] to become overcast; **3 se ~ de** to become covered with; **4** (against accusations) to cover oneself; (against blows) to protect oneself.

CP /sepe/ *nm*: *abbr* ▶ **cours**.

CPAO /sepeao/ *nf*: (*abbr* = **conception de programmes assistée par ordinateur**) computer-aided software engineering, CASE.

crabe /kʀab/ *nm* crab; **marcher en ~** to sidle along.

crachat /kʀaʃa/ *nm* spit.

cracher /kʀaʃe/ [1] **I** *vtr* **1** to spit out; **c'est le portrait de sa mère tout craché**○ she's the spitting image of her mother; **2** to belch (out) [*flames, smoke*].
II *vi* **1** to spit; **je ne cracherais pas dessus**○ I wouldn't turn up my nose at it; **2** [*tap, pen*] to splutter; [*radio*] to crackle.

cracheur /kʀaʃœʀ/ *nm* **~ de feu** fire-eater.

crachin /kʀaʃɛ̃/ *nm* drizzle.

crachoir /kʀaʃwaʀ/ *nm* **1** spittoon; **2 tenir le ~ à qn**○ to talk on and on at sb.

craie /kʀɛ/ *nf* chalk.

craindre /kʀɛ̃dʀ/ [54] *vtr* **1** to fear, to be afraid of; **je crains que non** I'm afraid not; **2** to be sensitive to [*cold*]; [*plant*] to dislike [*sun*].

crainte /kʀɛ̃t/ *nf* fear; **par ~ de qch/de faire** for fear of sth/of doing; **avoir des ~s au sujet de qn** to be worried about sb; **n'ayez ~, soyez sans ~** have no fear.

craintif, **-ive** /kʀɛ̃tif, iv/ *adj* timorous, timid.

cramoisi, **~e** /kʀamwazi/ *adj* crimson (**de** with).

crampe /kʀɑ̃p/ *nf* cramp; **~s d'estomac** stomach cramps.

crampon /kʀɑ̃pɔ̃/ *nm* crampon; **chaussures à ~s** (for football) boots with studs (GB) or cleats (US); (for running) spiked shoes.

cramponner: **se cramponner** /kʀɑ̃pɔne/ [1] *v refl* (+ *v être*) to hold on tightly; **se ~ à** to cling to.

cran /kʀɑ̃/ **I** *nm* **1** notch; (in belt) hole; **monter d'un ~** to move up a notch; **2** nick; **3**○ **avoir du ~** to have guts○; **4** (in hair) wave.
II à cran *phr* **être à ~, avoir les nerfs à ~** to be on edge.
■ **~ d'arrêt** flick knife (GB), switchblade (US); **~ de sûreté** safety catch.

crâne /kʀɑn/ *nm* **1** skull; **2**○ head; **ne rien avoir dans le ~** to have no brains; **avoir le ~ dur** to be thick(-skulled)○; **bourrer le ~ à qn**○ to brainwash sb.

crâner○ /kʀɑne/ [1] *vi* to show off.

crânien, **-ienne** /kʀɑnjɛ̃, ɛn/ *adj* cranial; **boîte crânienne** cranium.

crapaud /kʀapo/ *nm* **1** toad; **2** (in diamond) flaw.

crapule /kʀapyl/ *nf* crook.

crapuleux, **-euse** /kʀapylø, øz/ *adj* villainous.

craqueler: **se craqueler** /kʀakle/ [19] *v refl* (+ *v être*) to crack.

craquement /kʀakmɑ̃/ *nm* **1** creaking sound, creak; **2** cracking sound, crack.

craquer /kʀake/ [1] **I** *vtr* **1** to split [*trousers*]; **2** to strike [*match*].
II *vi* **1** [*seam*] to split; [*branch*] to crack; [*bag*] to burst; **2** [*floor*] to creak; [*snow*] to crunch; **3**○ [*firm*] to collapse; [*person*] to crack up○.

crasse /kʀas/ *nf* **1** grime, filth; **2**○ dirty or mean trick.

crasseux, **-euse** /kʀasø, øz/ *adj* filthy, grimy.

cratère /kʀatɛʀ/ *nm* crater.

cravache /kʀavaʃ/ *nf* whip; **donner un coup de ~ à** to whip.

cravate /kʀavat/ *nf* tie.

crawl /kʀol/ *nm* crawl; **nager le ~** to do or swim the crawl.

crayon /kʀɛjɔ̃/ *nm* pencil; **~ à bille** ballpoint pen; **~ noir** lead pencil; **~ optique** light pen.

crayonner /kʀɛjɔne/ [1] *vtr* **1** to make a pencil sketch of; **2** to scribble down.

créance /kʀeɑ̃s/ *nf* **1** debt (*owed by a debtor*); **2** letter of credit; **3** credence; **perdre ~ auprès de qn** to lose credibility with sb.

créancier, **-ière** /kʀeɑ̃sje, ɛʀ/ *nm,f* creditor.

créateur, **-trice** /kʀeatœʀ, tʀis/ *nm,f* creator; designer.

créatif, **-ive** /kʀeatif, iv/ *adj* creative.

création /kʀeasjɔ̃/ *nf* **1** creation; **la ~ d'emplois** job creation; **la ~ d'une entreprise** the setting up of a company; **la ~ d'un nouveau**

produit the development of a new product; **tous les livres de la ~** all the books in the world; **2** (work of art, garment) creation; (play) first production; (commercial) new product.

créativité /kʀeativite/ *nf* creativity.

créature /kʀeatyʀ/ *nf* creature.

crécelle /kʀesɛl/ *nf* rattle; **voix de ~** shrill voice.

crèche /kʀɛʃ/ *nf* **1** crèche (GB), day-nursery; **2** (at Christmas) crib (GB), crèche (US).

crédibilité /kʀedibilite/ *nf* credibility (**auprès de** with).

crédible /kʀedibl/ *adj* credible.

crédit /kʀedi/ *nm* **1** funds; **les ~s de la recherche** research funding or budget; **2** credit; **accorder un ~** to grant credit terms or facilities; **faire ~ à qn** to give sb credit; **votre ~ est de 1 500 francs** you are 1,500 francs in credit; **porter une somme au ~ d'un compte** to credit sb's account with a sum of money; **mettre** or **porter qch au ~ de qn** (figurative) to give sb credit for sth.

créditer /kʀedite/ [1] *vtr* to credit (**de** with).

créditeur, **-trice** /kʀeditœʀ, tʀis/ **I** *adj* **être ~** to be in credit.

II *nm,f* customer in credit.

credo /kʀedo/ *nm* creed.

crédule /kʀedyl/ *adj* gullible, credulous.

crédulité /kʀedylite/ *nf* gullibility, credulity.

créer /kʀee/ [11] **I** *vtr* **1** (gen) to create; to develop [*new product*]; to set up [*company*]; **2** (in theatre) to create [*role*]; to put on [sth] (for the first time) [*play*].

II se créer *v refl* (+ *v être*) **se ~ des problèmes** to bring trouble on oneself; **se ~ une clientèle** [*doctor, notary*] to build up a practice.

crémaillère /kʀemajɛʀ/ *nf* trammel, chimney hook.

IDIOMS **pendre la ~** to have a house-warming (party).

crémation /kʀemasjɔ̃/ *nf* cremation.

crématoire /kʀematwaʀ/ *nm* crematorium; **four ~** crematorium furnace.

crème[1] /kʀɛm/ *adj inv* cream.

crème[2] /kʀɛm/ *nf* **1** cream; **2** cream dessert; **3**○ **la ~ des linguistes** the very best linguists.

■ **~ anglaise** ≈ custard; **~ Chantilly** whipped cream; **~ glacée** dairy ice cream; **~ de marrons** chestnut purée; **~ renversée** caramel custard.

crémerie /kʀɛmʀi/ *nf* cheese shop (GB) or store (US).

crémeux, **-euse** /kʀemø, øz/ *adj* creamy.

crémier, **-ière** /kʀemje, ɛʀ/ *nm,f* cheese seller.

créneau, *pl* **~x** /kʀeno/ *nm* **1** parallel parking; **2** gap; **tu as un ~ demain?** do you have any free time tomorrow?; **3** (in fortifications) **les ~x** crenellations.

■ **~ horaire** time slot.

créole /kʀeɔl/ **I** *adj* creole.

II *nm* Creole.

crêpe[1] /kʀɛp/ *nm* **1** crepe; **2** black veil.

crêpe[2] /kʀɛp/ *nf* pancake, crêpe; **s'aplatir comme une ~**○ to grovel.

crêper /kʀepe/ [1] *vtr* to backcomb (GB), to tease [*hair*].

IDIOMS **se ~ le chignon**○ to scratch each other's eyes out.

crépi /kʀepi/ *nm* rendering.

crépir /kʀepiʀ/ [3] *vtr* to render; **mur crépi** rendered wall.

crépitement /kʀepitmɑ̃/ *nm* crackling, crackle; sizzling.

crépiter /kʀepite/ [1] *vi* [*fire*] to crackle; [*oil*] to sizzle; [*rain*] to patter.

crépon /kʀepɔ̃/ *nm* crepe paper.

crépu, **~e** /kʀepy/ *adj* frizzy.

crépuscule /kʀepyskyl/ *nm* twilight, dusk.

crescendo /kʀeʃɛndo/ **I** *adv* **aller ~** [*noise*] to intensify.

II *nm* crescendo.

cresson /kʀesɔ̃, kʀəsɔ̃/ *nm* watercress.

crête /kʀɛt/ *nf* **1** (of cock) comb; (of bird) crest; **2** (of mountain, wave) crest; (of roof) ridge.

crétin, **~e** /kʀetɛ̃, in/ *nm,f* moron○.

creuser /kʀøze/ [1] **I** *vtr* **1** to dig a hole in [*ground*]; to hollow out [*trunk, fruit*]; to drill a hole in [*tooth*]; to dig into [*rock*]; **2** to dig [*hole, canal, grave*]; to sink [*well*]; to plough (GB), to plow (US) [*furrow*]; **3** [*wrinkles*] to furrow [*face*]; **elle avait le visage creusé par la faim** her face was gaunt with hunger; **~ les reins** to arch one's back; **4** to deepen, to increase [*deficit, inequalities*]; **~ l'écart entre** to widen the gap between; **5** to go into [sth] in depth [*question, subject*].

II se creuser *v refl* (+ *v être*) [*cheeks*] to become hollow; [*wrinkles*] to deepen; [*gap*] to widen.

IDIOMS **ça creuse**○ it really gives you an appetite; **se ~ (la tête** or **la cervelle)**○ to rack one's brains.

creuset /kʀøzɛ/ *nm* **1** crucible; **2** (figurative) melting pot.

creux, **-euse** /kʀø, øz/ **I** *adj* **1** [*trunk, tooth, sound, cheeks*] hollow; [*stomach, speech*] empty; [*analysis*] shallow; **un plat ~** a shallow dish; **assiette creuse** soup dish; **2** [*day, period*] slack, off-peak.

II *adv* **sonner ~** to make a hollow sound.

III *nm* **1** hollow; **le ~ des reins** the small of the back; **le ~ de l'aisselle** the armpit; **au ~ de l'estomac** in the pit of the stomach; **le ~ de la vague** the trough of the wave; **être au ~ de la vague** (figurative) to be at rock bottom; **2**○ **avoir un petit ~** to feel peckish○ (GB), to have the munchies○.

crevaison /kʀəvɛzɔ̃/ *nf* puncture.

crevasse /kʀəvas/ *nf* **1** crevasse; **2** crack, fissure; **3** chapped skin.

crevasser /kʀəvase/ [1] *vtr* to cause [sth] to crack [*ground, wall*]; to chap [*skin*].

crève-cœur /kʀɛvkœʀ/ *nm inv* heartbreak.

crever /kʀəve/ [16] **I** *vtr* **1** to puncture, to burst; **~ les yeux de qn** to blind sb; to poke

sb's eyes out; **ça crève les yeux** it's blindingly obvious; **ça crève le cœur** it's heartbreaking; **2**° **~ un cheval** to ride a horse into the ground.
II *vi* **1** to burst; to burst open; **2** to die; **~ de faim/froid** to be starving/freezing; **3 ~ d'envie** to be eaten up or consumed with envy; **~ d'orgueil** to be terribly full of oneself.
III **se crever** *v refl* (+ *v être*) **se ~ un tympan** to burst an eardrum; **il s'est crevé un œil** he put his eye out.
IDIOMS **marche ou crève** sink or swim.

crevette /kʀəvɛt/ *nf* **~ grise** shrimp; **~ rose** prawn.

cri /kʀi/ *nm* **1** cry; shout; scream; **un ~ de détresse** a cry for help; **un ~ aigu** a shriek; **à grands ~s** loudly; **pousser les hauts ~s** to protest loudly; **2** (of bird) call.

criant, **~e** /kʀijɑ̃, ɑ̃t/ *adj* **1** clear, striking; **2** blatant, glaring.

criard, **~e** /kʀiaʀ, aʀd/ *adj* [*voice*] shrill; [*colour*] garish.

crible /kʀibl/ *nm* (for minerals) screen; (for sand) riddle; **passer au ~** (figurative) to sift through.

cribler /kʀible/ [1] *vtr* **1 ~ qn/qch de balles** to riddle sb/sth with bullets; **~ qn de flèches/coups** to rain arrows/blows on sb; **2 ~ qn de reproches** to heap reproaches on sb; **3** to screen [*minerals*].

cric /kʀik/ *nm* (for car) jack.

cricket /kʀikɛ(t)/ *nm* cricket.

criée /kʀije/ *nf* **(vente à la) ~** auction.

crier /kʀije/ [2] **I** *vtr* **1** to shout (**à qn** to sb); **2** to proclaim; to protest [*innocence*].
II **crier à** *v+prep* **on a crié au génie quand il a proposé sa théorie** he was proclaimed a genius when he put forward his theory; **on a crié au scandale quand**... there was an outcry when...
III *vi* **1** to shout; to cry; to scream; **~ de joie** to shout for joy; **2** [*animal*] to give a cry; [*monkey*] to chatter; [*gull*] to cry; [*pig*] to squeal.
IDIOMS **~ comme un damné** to squeal like a stuck pig.

crieur, **-ieuse** /kʀijœʀ, øz/ *nm,f* **~ de journaux** news vendor.

crime /kʀim/ *nm* **1** crime; **~ d'État** crime against the State; **2** murder; **~ crapuleux** murder for money.

criminalité /kʀiminalite/ *nf* crime; **~ informatique** computer crime.

criminel, **-elle** /kʀiminɛl/ **I** *adj* criminal.
II *nm,f* **1** criminal; **2** murderer.

crin /kʀɛ̃/ *nm* horsehair; **à tout ~** (figurative) dyed-in-the-wool.

crinière /kʀinjɛʀ/ *nf* mane.

crique /kʀik/ *nf* cove.

criquet /kʀikɛ/ *nm* locust.

crise /kʀiz/ *nf* **1** crisis; **~ d'adolescence** adolescent crisis; **~ agricole** crisis in the agricultural industry; **en (pleine) ~** in (the middle of a) crisis; **la ~** the economic crisis, the slump; **2** shortage; **~ de l'emploi** job shortage; **3** (Med) attack; **~ d'appendicite** appendicitis; **~ de rhumatisme** bout of rheumatism; **~ de toux** coughing fit; **4** fit; **~ de colère** fit of rage; **~ de larmes** crying fit; **faire une ~** to have a tantrum; to have a fit°.
■ **~ cardiaque** heart attack; **~ de foie** indigestion; **~ de nerfs** hysterics.

crisper /kʀispe/ [1] **I** *vtr* **l'angoisse crispait son visage** his/her face was tense with worry.
II **se crisper** *v refl* (+ *v être*) [*hands*] to clench; [*face, person*] to tense (up); [*smile*] to freeze.

crisser /kʀise/ [1] *vi* [*shoes, chalk*] to squeak; [*snow*] to crunch; [*tyres, brakes*] to screech; [*pen*] to scratch.

cristal, *pl* **-aux** /kʀistal, o/ *nm* **1** crystal; **2** piece of crystalware.
■ **cristaux (de soude)** washing soda.

cristallin, **~e** /kʀistalɛ̃, in/ **I** *adj* **1** crystalline; **2** crystal clear.
II *nm* (of eye) (crystalline) lens.

cristalliser /kʀistalize/ [1] *vtr, vi, v refl* (+ *v être*) to crystallize.

critère /kʀitɛʀ/ *nm* **1** criterion; **~s de gestion/de confort** standards of management/comfort; **le prix n'est pas un ~ de qualité** price is no indication of quality; **le ~ déterminant** the crucial factor; **2** specification; **remplir les ~s d'âge et de diplôme** to meet the requirements as far as age and qualifications are concerned.

critérium /kʀiteʀjɔm/ *nm* (Sport) heat; (in cycling) rally.

critiquable /kʀitikabl/ *adj* questionable.

critique[1] /kʀitik/ **I** *adj* critical (**à l'égard de, envers** of).
II *nmf* critic.

critique[2] /kʀitik/ *nf* **1** criticism; **accabler qn de ~s** to heap criticism on sb; **faire une ~ à qn** to criticize sb; **la ~ est aisée** it's easy to criticize; **2** review; **faire la ~ d'un film** to review a film; **3 la ~ littéraire** literary criticism.

critiquer /kʀitike/ [1] *vtr* **1** to criticize; **2** to make a critical study of [*work*].

croasser /kʀɔase/ [1] *vi* to caw.

croc /kʀo/ *nm* fang.

croche /kʀɔʃ/ *nf* quaver (GB), eighth note (US); **double ~** semiquaver (GB), sixteenth note (US); **triple ~** demisemiquaver (GB), thirty-second note (US).

croche-pied°, *pl* **~s** /kʀɔʃpje/ *nm* **faire un ~ à qn** to trip sb up.

crochet /kʀɔʃɛ/ *nm* **1** hook; **2** picklock; **3** crochet hook; **faire du ~** to crochet; **4 mettre entre ~s** to put [sth] in square brackets; **5 faire un ~** to make a detour (**par** via); **6** (in boxing) hook; **7 un (radio) ~** a talent contest; **8** fang.
IDIOMS **vivre aux ~s° de qn** to sponge off sb°.

crocheter /kʀɔʃte/ [18] *vtr* **1** to crochet; **2** to pick [*lock*].

crochu, **~e** /kʀɔʃy/ *adj* [*nose*] hooked; [*hands*] clawed.

crocodile /kʀɔkɔdil/ *nm* crocodile.

croire /kʀwaʀ/ [71] **I** *vtr* **1** to believe; **faire ~ à qn** to make sb believe; **2** to think; **j'ai cru mourir** I thought I was dying; **je crois savoir que** I happen to know that; **il faut ~ qu'il avait vraiment besoin de repos** it would seem that he really needed a rest; **il est malin, faut pas**° **~!** he's clever, believe me!; **je ne suis pas celui que vous croyez** I'm not what you think I am; **tu ne crois pas si bien dire** you don't know how right you are; **on croirait de la soie** it looks like silk; **3 si l'on en croit l'auteur, à en ~ l'auteur** if we are to believe the author; **crois-en mon expérience** take my word for it.

II croire à *v+prep* **~ à** to believe [*story*]; to believe in [*ghosts*]; **~ à la médecine** to have faith in doctors.

III croire en *v+prep* **~ en** to believe in [*god*].

IV se croire *v refl* (+ *v être*) **il se croit beau** he thinks he's handsome; **tu te crois où?** where do you think you are?

croisade /kʀwazad/ *nf* crusade.

croisé, **~e**[1] /kʀwaze/ **I** *pp* ▶ **croiser**.

II *pp adj* **1** [*legs*] crossed; [*arms*] folded; **2** crossbred; **3** [*agreements*] reciprocal.

III *nm* **1** crusader; **2** twill.

croisée[2] /kʀwaze/ *nf* **1** junction (**de** of); **à la ~ des chemins** at the crossroads; **2** window.

croisement /kʀwazmɑ̃/ *nm* **1** crossroads; crossing, junction; **2** (of threads, straps) crossing; **3** crossbreeding; hybrid, cross(breed).

croiser /kʀwaze/ [1] **I** *vtr* **1** to cross; **~ les bras** to fold one's arms; **2 ~ qn/qch** to pass sb/sth (coming the other way); **3** to meet; **mon regard croisa le sien** our eyes met; **4** to cross (-breed).

II se croiser *v refl* (+ *v être*) [*cars*] to pass each other; [*letters*] to cross in the post (GB) or mail (US); [*roads*] to intersect; [*lines*] to cross.

croisière /kʀwazjɛʀ/ *nf* cruise; **régime de ~** cruising speed.

croisillon /kʀwazijɔ̃/ *nm* crosspiece; **~s** lattice work.

croissance /kʀwasɑ̃s/ *nf* growth; **en pleine ~** [*child*] growing; [*sector*] fast-growing.

croissant, **~e** /kʀwasɑ̃, ɑ̃t/ *nm* **1** croissant; **2** crescent; **~ de lune** crescent moon.

croître /kʀwatʀ/ [72] *vi* **1** to grow; **faire ~** to grow; **2** [*noise*] to get or grow louder; [*day*] to get longer; **aller croissant** to be increasing.

croix /kʀwa/ *nf* cross; **bras en ~** arms out on either side of the body.

IDIOMS **ton argent, tu peux faire une ~ dessus**° you can kiss your money goodbye; **faire une ~ sur son passé** to leave the past behind; **un jour à marquer d'une ~** a red-letter day, a day to remember.

croquant, **~e** /kʀɔkɑ̃, ɑ̃t/ *adj* crunchy.

croque-madame /kʀɔkmadam/ *nm inv*: *toasted ham and cheese sandwich topped with a fried egg*.

croque-monsieur /kʀɔkməsjø/ *nm inv*: *toasted ham and cheese sandwich*.

croque-mort°, *pl* **~s** /kʀɔkmɔʀ/ *nm* undertaker.

croquer /kʀɔke/ [1] **I** *vtr* **1** to crunch; **2**° to squander; **3** to sketch; **belle à ~** as pretty as a picture.

II *vi* **1** to be crunchy; **2 ~ dans une pomme** to bite into an apple.

croquet /kʀɔkɛ/ *nm* **1** croquet; **2** *small crunchy almond biscuit*.

croquette /kʀɔkɛt/ *nf* croquette.

croquis /kʀɔki/ *nm* sketch; **faire un ~ de la situation** to give an outline of the situation.

cross(-country) /kʀɔs(kuntʀi)/ *nm inv* **1** cross country race; **2** motocross event.

crosse /kʀɔs/ *nf* **1** (of rifle) butt; **2** (of cane) crook; **3** (Sport) stick.

crotte /kʀɔt/ *nf* dropping; **c'est de la ~ de chien** it's dog mess.

▪ **~ en chocolat** (Culin) chocolate drop.

crottin /kʀɔtɛ̃/ *nm* **1** dung; **2** (*small round*) goat's cheese.

crouler /kʀule/ [1] *vi* **1** to collapse; to crumble; **2 ~ sous** to be weighed down by [*parcels, debts, work*]; **~ sous les applaudissements** to resound with applause; **~ sous le poids de** [*table*] to groan under the weight of [*books*].

croupe /kʀup/ *nf* (of horse) croup; **monter en ~** to ride pillion.

croupi, **~e** /kʀupi/ *adj* stagnant.

croupier /kʀupje/ *nm* croupier.

croupion /kʀupjɔ̃/ *nm* **1** (of bird) rump; **2** (Culin) parson's nose.

croupir /kʀupiʀ/ [3] *vi* **1** [*water*] to stagnate; **2 ~ en prison** to rot in jail; **~ dans l'ignorance** to wallow in ignorance.

croustillant, **~e** /kʀustijɑ̃, ɑ̃t/ *adj* **1** crispy; crunchy; **2** [*story, details*] spicy.

croustiller /kʀustije/ [1] *vi* [*bread*] to be crusty; [*chocolate*] to be crunchy.

croûte /kʀut/ *nf* **1** (of bread) crust; (of cheese) rind; **une ~ de pain** a crust; **casser la ~**° to have a bite to eat; **2** (Culin) **pâté en ~** pâté en croute or in pastry; **3** (Med) scab; **4**° daub, bad painting.

croûton /kʀutɔ̃/ *nm* **1** crust; **2** (Culin) crouton.

croyance /kʀwajɑ̃s/ *nf* belief.

croyant, **~e** /kʀwajɑ̃, ɑ̃t/ *adj* **être ~** to be a believer.

CRS /seeʀɛs/ (*abbr* = **compagnie républicaine de sécurité**) *nm* **un ~** *a member of the French riot police*; **compagnie de ~** ≈ riot squad.

cru, **~e**[1] /kʀy/ **I** *adj* **1** raw; uncooked; [*milk*] unpasteurized; **se faire manger** or **dévorer tout ~**° to be eaten alive°; **2** [*light, colour*] harsh; **3** [*language*] crude.

II *nm* vineyard; vintage; vintage year; **du meilleur ~** [*collection*] vintage; **du ~** [*wine, author*] local.

cruauté /kʀyote/ *nf* **1** cruelty (**envers** to); **2** act of cruelty.

cruche /kʀyʃ/ *nf* **1** jug (GB), pitcher (US); jugful (GB), pitcherful (US); **2**° dope°.

crucial, **~e**, *mpl* **-iaux** /kʀysjal, o/ *adj* crucial.

crucifier /kʀysifje/ [2] *vtr* to crucify.

crucifix /kʀysifi/ *nm* crucifix.

crucifixion /kʀysifiksjɔ̃/ *nf* crucifixion.

cruciverbiste /kʀysivɛʀbist/ *nmf* crossword fan.

crudité /kʀydite/ *nf* **1** **~s** raw vegetables, crudités; **2** (of colour) garishness; (of light) harshness; **3** (of language) crudeness.

crue[2] /kʀy/ **I** *adj f* ▶ **cru I**.
II *nf* rise in water level; flood; **en ~** in spate.

cruel, **-elle** /kʀyɛl/ *adj* cruel (**envers, avec** to).

cruellement /kʀyɛlmɑ̃/ *adv* **1** cruelly; **2** **manquer ~ de qch** to be desperately short of sth; **3** terribly; **la pénurie de carburant se fait ~ sentir** the fuel shortage is being sorely felt; **être ~ ramené à la réalité** to be brought back to earth painfully.

crûment /kʀymɑ̃/ *adv* **1** bluntly; **2** crudely.

crustacé /kʀystase/ *nm* shellfish.

crypte /kʀipt(ə)/ *nf* crypt.

crypté, **~e** /kʀipte/ *adj* coded; encrypted; [*broadcast*] scrambled.

cube /kyb/ **I** *adj* cubic.
II *nm* **1** cube; **2** building block.

cubique /kybik/ *adj* **1** [*root*] cubic; **2** **de forme ~** cube-shaped.

cucul○ /kyky/ *adj* corny○; silly; twee (GB), cutsey (US).

cueillette /kœjɛt/ *nf* **1** (of fruits, flowers) picking; **2** crop.

cueillir /kœjiʀ/ [27] *vtr* **1** to pick [*fruit, flowers*]; **2** to gather [*information*]; **3**○ to pick up○, to arrest [*criminal*]; to pick up○ [*friend*].

cuiller, **cuillère** /kɥijɛʀ/ *nf* spoon; spoonful; **~ à café** teaspoon; coffee spoon.
IDIOMS **il n'y va pas avec le dos de la ~**○ he doesn't do things by halves; **en deux coups de ~ à pot** in two shakes of a lamb's tail○.

cuillerée /kɥij(ə)ʀe/ *nf* spoonful.

cuir /kɥiʀ/ *nm* **1** leather; **2** rawhide; hide.
■ **~ chevelu** scalp.

cuirasse /kɥiʀas/ *nf* **1** breast-plate; **2** armour[GB] plating.

cuirassé /kɥiʀase/ *nm* battleship.

cuirassier /kɥiʀasje/ *nm* cuirassier; **le premier ~** the first armoured[GB] division.

cuire /kɥiʀ/ [69] **I** *vtr* **1** to cook; to bake; to roast; **~ à la vapeur** to steam; **~ à l'étuvée** to braise; **à ~** [*apple*] cooking; **2** to fire [*porcelain*].
II *vi* **1** [*food*] to cook; to be cooking; **laissez ~ à petit feu** allow to simmer gently; **2**○ **on cuit sur la plage** it's baking (hot) on the beach; **3** [*graze*] to sting; **ça me cuit** it stings.

cuisant, **~e** /kɥizɑ̃, ɑ̃t/ *adj* **1** [*defeat, regret*] bitter; [*remark*] stinging; **2** [*pain*] burning; [*cold*] biting.

cuisine /kɥizin/ *nf* **1** kitchen; **2** galley; **3** kitchen furniture; **4** cooking; **faire la ~** to do the cooking; **5**○ intrigues.

cuisiner /kɥizine/ [1] *vtr, vi* to cook.

cuisinier, **-ière**[1] /kɥizinje, ɛʀ/ *nm,f* cook; chef.

cuisinière[2] /kɥizinjɛʀ/ *nf* cooker.

cuissarde /kɥisaʀd/ *nf* wader; thighboot.

cuisse /kɥis/ *nf* **1** thigh; **2** (Culin) (of chicken) thigh; (of venison) haunch; **des ~s de grenouille** frogs' legs.

cuisseau, *pl* **~x** /kɥiso/ *nm* **~ de veau** haunch of veal.

cuisson /kɥisɔ̃/ *nf* **1** cooking; baking; roasting; **2** (of pottery) firing.

cuissot /kɥiso/ *nm* (of venison) haunch.

cuistot○ /kɥisto/ *nm* cook.

cuit, **~e**[1] /kɥi, kɥit/ *pp* ▶ **cuire**.
IDIOMS **c'est ~**○ we've had it○; **c'est du tout ~**○ it's a piece of cake○; it's in the bag○; **ce n'est pas du tout ~**○ it's not all cut and dried; **elle attend que ça (lui) tombe tout ~**○ she expects things to fall straight into her lap.

cuite[2] /kɥit/ *nf* **tenir/prendre une ~** to be/to get plastered○.

cuivre /kɥivʀ/ **I** *nm* **1** **~ (rouge)** copper; **2** **~ (jaune)** brass.
II **cuivres** *nm pl* **1** copperware; **2** brass; **3** (Mus) **les ~s** the brass.

cul /ky/ *nm* **1**◑ bottom, arse● (GB), ass◑ (US); **2** (of bottle) bottom; **~ sec**○! bottoms up○!

culasse /kylas/ *nf* **1** cylinder head; **2** breech-block.

culbute /kylbyt/ *nf* somersault; **faire une ~ dans l'escalier** to tumble down the stairs.

culbuter /kylbyte/ [1] **I** *vtr* to knock [sb/sth] over.
II *vi* [*person*] to take a tumble; [*vehicle*] to overturn.

cul-de-jatte, *pl* **culs-de-jatte** /kydʒat/ *nmf* person who has had both legs amputated.

cul-de-sac, *pl* **culs-de-sac** /kydsak/ *nm* **1** cul-de-sac; **2** dead end.

culinaire /kylinɛʀ/ *adj* culinary; **préparation ~** dish.

culminant, **~e** /kylminɑ̃, ɑ̃t/ *adj* **point ~** (of mountain) highest point or peak; (of career) peak; (of crisis) height; (of holiday, evening) high point.

culminer /kylmine/ [1] *vi* **1** **~ au-dessus de qch** to tower above sth; **2** [*inflation, unemployment*] to reach its peak.

culot○ /kylo/ *nm* cheek○; **y aller au ~** to bluff.

culotte /kylɔt/ *nf* **1** pants (GB), panties (US); **2** **en ~(s) courte(s)** in short trousers (GB) or pants (US).

culotté○, **~e** /kylɔte/ *adj* cheeky.

culpabiliser /kylpabilize/ [1] **I** *vtr* to make [sb] feel guilty.
II *vi* to feel guilty.

culpabilité /kylpabilite/ *nf* guilt.

culte /kylt/ *nm* **1** cult; **~ du soleil** sun worship; **2** religion.

cultivateur, **-trice** /kyltivatœʀ, tʀis/ *nm,f* farmer.

cultiver /kyltive/ [1] **I** *vtr* to grow; to cultivate.

II se cultiver *v refl* (+ *v être*) to improve one's mind.

culture /kyltyʀ/ **I** *nf* **1** cultivation; **la ~ du blé** wheat growing; **2** crop; **~ d'hiver** winter crop; **3** (in biology) culture; **~ in vitro** in vitro culture; **4** (of society) culture; **~ de masse** mass culture; **5** knowledge; **~ classique** classical education; **6** arts; **subventionner la ~** to subsidize the arts.
II cultures *nf pl* cultivated land.
■ **~ physique** physical exercise.

culturel, -elle /kyltyʀɛl/ *adj* cultural.

culturisme /kyltyʀism/ *nm* body-building.

cumin /kymɛ̃/ *nm* cumin; **pain au ~** bread with cumin seeds.

cumul /kymyl/ *nm* **1 ~ d'avantages** accumulation of advantages; **~ de fonctions** holding of several posts concurrently; **2** (Law) **~ des peines** ≈ sentences to be served consecutively.

cumuler /kymyle/ [1] *vtr* **1** to hold [sth] concurrently [*offices*]; to draw [sth] concurrently [*salaries*]; **2** to accumulate [*handicaps, degrees*]; **3** to combine [*results*]; to add up [*amounts*].

cumulus /kymylys/ *nm inv* cumulus.

cupide /kypid/ *adj* grasping.

cupidité /kypidite/ *nf* avarice, greed, cupidity.

cure /kyʀ/ *nf* **faire une ~** to go for a course of treatment in a spa.
■ **~ d'amaigrissement** slimming course (GB), reducing treatment (US); **~ de désintoxication** detoxification; **~ de sommeil** sleep therapy.

curé /kyʀe/ *nm* (parish) priest.

cure-dents /kyʀdɑ̃/ *nm inv* toothpick.

curée /kyʀe/ *nf* **1** portion of quarry (*fed to hounds*); **2** (figurative) scramble for the spoils.

curer /kyʀe/ [1] **I** *vtr* to clean out [*pipe, pond*].
II se curer *v refl* (+ *v être*) **se ~ les ongles** to clean one's nails; **se ~ les dents** to pick one's teeth.

curetage /kyʀtaʒ/ *nm* (Med) D and C, dilation and curettage.

curieusement /kyʀjøzmɑ̃/ *adv* **1** oddly, strangely; **2** oddly enough.

curieux, -ieuse /kyʀjø, øz/ **I** *adj* **1** inquisitive, curious; **2** strange; **3 esprit ~** person with an enquiring mind; **être ~ d'apprendre** to be keen to learn.
II *nm,f* onlooker.

curiosité /kyʀjozite/ *nf* **1** curiosity; **2** curiosity, curio.

curiste /kyʀist/ *nmf* person having hydrotherapy.

curriculum vitae /kyʀikylɔmvite/ *nm inv* curriculum vitae, résumé (US).

curry /kyʀi/ *nm* **1** curry powder; **2** curry; **~ d'agneau** lamb curry.

curseur /kyʀsœʀ/ *nm* cursor.

cursus /kyʀsys/ *nm inv* course

cutané, ~e /kytane/ *adj* [*irritation*] skin.

cutter /kytœʀ/ *nm* Stanley knife®.

cuve /kyv/ *nf* **1** vat; tank; **2** (for photos) developing tank.

cuvée /kyve/ *nf* vatful; **la ~ 1959** the 1959 vintage; **~ du patron** house wine.

cuver○ /kyve/ [1] *vtr* **~ son vin** to sleep it off○.

cuvette /kyvɛt/ *nf* **1** bowl; **~ des wc** lavatory bowl or pan; **2** (in land) basin.

CV /seve/ *nm* **1** (*abbr* = **curriculum vitae**) CV (GB), résumé (US); **2** (*written abbr* = **cheval-vapeur**) HP.

cyclable /siklabl/ *adj* **piste ~** cycle track.

cycle /sikl/ *nm* **1** cycle; **~ infernal** vicious cycle; **2** series; **3** (Sch) **premier ~** *first two years of a university degree course leading to a diploma*; **deuxième ~** *final two years of a university degree course*; **troisième ~** postgraduate (GB) or graduate (US) studies; **4** (bi)cycle.

cyclique /siklik/ *adj* cyclic.

cyclisme /siklism/ *nm* cycling; cycle racing.

cycliste /siklist/ **I** *adj* [*club*] cycling; [*race*] cycle; **coureur ~** racing cyclist.
II *nmf* cyclist; **short de ~** cycling shorts.

cyclomoteur /siklomɔtœʀ/ *nm* moped.

cyclone /siklon/ *nm* **1** cyclone; **2** (in weather) depression; **arriver comme un ~** (figurative) to sweep in like a whirlwind.

cyclotourisme /sikloturism/ *nm* cycle touring.

cygne /siɲ/ *nm* swan; **~ mâle** cob; **~ femelle** pen; **jeune ~** cygnet.

cylindre /silɛ̃dʀ/ *nm* **1** cylinder; **2** roller.

cylindrée /silɛ̃dʀe/ *nf* capacity, size; **~ de 1200 cm³** 1200 cc engine.

cylindrique /silɛ̃dʀik/ *adj* cylindrical.

cymbale /sɛ̃bal/ *nm* cymbal; **coup de ~s** clash of cymbals.

cynique /sinik/ **I** *adj* cynical.
II *nmf* cynic.

cynisme /sinism/ *nm* cynicism.

cyprès /sipʀɛ/ *nm* cypress.

cystite /sistit/ *nf* cystitis; **avoir une ~** to have cystitis.

Dd

d, **D** /de/ *nm inv* d, D.

d' ▶ **de**.

DAB /deabe/ *nm*: (*abbr* = **distributeur automatique de billets**) automatic teller machine, ATM.

dactylo /daktilo/ *nmf* (*abbr* = **dactylographe**) typist.

dactylographie /daktilɔgʀafi/ *nf* typing.

dactylographier /daktilɔgʀafje/ [2] *vtr* to type (out).

dada○ /dada/ *nm* **1** horsie○; **2** hobby; **3** hobby-horse.

dadais○ /dadɛ/ *nm inv* clumsy youth.

daigner /deɲe/ [1] *vtr* to deign (**faire** to do).

daim /dɛ̃/ *nm* **1** (fallow) deer; **2** venison; **3** buckskin; **4** suede.

dallage /dalaʒ/ *nm* paving.

dalle /dal/ *nf* **1** slab; **2** flagstone; **3** concrete foundation slab.

IDIOMS **avoir la ~**○ to be ravenous; **que ~**◑ nothing at all, zilch○.

daller /dale/ [1] *vtr* to pave.

dalmatien /dalmasjɛ̃/ *nm* (dog) Dalmatian.

daltonien, **-ienne** /daltɔnjɛ̃, ɛn/ *adj* colour[GB]-blind.

daltonisme /daltɔnism/ *nm* colour[GB]-blindness.

dam /dɑ(m)/ *nm* **au grand ~ de** to the great displeasure of.

dame /dam/ **I** *nf* **1** lady; **~ de compagnie** live-in companion; **2** (in cards, chess) queen; (in draughts) King.

II dames *nf pl* draughts (GB), checkers (US).

damier /damje/ *nm* draughtboard (GB), checkerboard (US).

damnation /danasjɔ̃/ *nf* damnation.

damner /dɑne/ [1] **I** *vtr* to damn; **faire ~**○ **qn** to drive sb mad○.

II se damner *v refl* (+ *v être*) to damn oneself; **se ~ pour qn/qch**○ to sell one's soul for sb/sth.

dancing /dɑ̃siŋ/ *nm* dance hall.

dandiner: **se dandiner** /dɑ̃dine/ [1] *v refl* (+ *v être*) [*duck*] to waddle; **se ~ d'un pied sur l'autre** to shift from one foot to the other.

Danemark /danmaʀk/ *pr nm* Denmark.

danger /dɑ̃ʒe/ *nm* danger; **courir un (grand) ~** to be in (great) danger.

■ **~ public** danger to the public; (figurative) menace.

dangereux, **-euse** /dɑ̃ʒʀø, øz/ *adj* dangerous.

danois, **~e** /danwa, az/ **I** *adj* Danish.

II *nm* **1** Danish; **2** Great Dane.

dans /dɑ̃/ *prep* **1** in; **être ~ la cuisine** to be in the kitchen; **être ~ les affaires** to be in business; **être ~ un avion/bateau** to be on a plane/boat; **2** into; **entrer ~ une pièce** to go into a room; **monter ~ un avion** to get on a plane; **3 boire ~ un verre** to drink out of a glass; **prendre qch ~ un placard** to take sth out of a cupboard; **4 ~ deux heures** in two hours; **fait ~ les deux heures** done within two hours; **~ huit jours** in a week's time; **je t'appellerai ~ la journée** I'll phone you during the day; **5 ~ les 30 francs/50 ans** about 30 francs/50 years old.

danse /dɑ̃s/ *nf* **1** dance; **2** dancing; **faire de la ~** to take dancing classes.

■ **~ classique** classical ballet.

danser /dɑ̃se/ [1] *vtr*, *vi* to dance.

IDIOMS **ne pas savoir sur quel pied ~** not to know what to do.

danseur, **-euse** /dɑ̃sœʀ, øz/ *nm,f* dancer; **~ étoile** principal dancer; **en danseuse** (Sport) standing on the pedals.

DAO /deao/ *nm*: (*abbr* = **dessin assisté par ordinateur**) computer-aided design, CAD.

dard /daʀ/ *nm* **1** (Zool) sting; **2** spear.

dare-dare○ /daʀdaʀ/ *adv* double quick.

darne /daʀn/ *nf* (fish) steak.

dartre /daʀtʀ/ *nf* scurf patch.

datation /datasjɔ̃/ *nf* **1** dating; **2** date.

date /dat/ *nf* **1** date; **~ limite** deadline; **~ limite de vente** sell-by date; **2** time; **un ami de longue ~** a longstanding friend; **le dernier scandale en ~** the latest scandal.

dater /date/ [1] **I** *vtr* to date; **à ~ du 31 juillet** as from 31 July.

II *vi* **1 ~ de** to date from; **2** to be dated.

dation /dasjɔ̃/ *nf* payment in kind.

datte /dat/ *nf* (Bot, Culin) date.

dattier /datje/ *nm* date palm.

daube /dob/ *nf* casserole; **bœuf en ~** beef casserole.

dauphin /dofɛ̃/ *nm* **1** dolphin; **2** heir apparent; **3** dauphin.

dauphinois, **~e** /dofinwa, az/ *adj* from the Dauphiné region.

daurade /dɔʀad/ *nf* (sea) bream.

davantage /davɑ̃taʒ/ *adv* **1** more; **2** longer; **rester ~** to stay longer.

DCA /desea/ *nf* (*abbr* = **défense contre les aéronefs**) anti-aircraft defence[GB].

de (**d'** *before vowel or mute h*) /də, d/

■ **Note** You will find translations for expressions such as *d'abord*, *de travers*, *pomme de terre*, *chemin de fer* etc at the entries ***abord***, ***travers***, ***pomme*** and ***chemin*** etc.

I *prep* **1** from; **venir ~ Paris** to come from Paris; **il est ~ père italien** his father is Italian; **du matin au soir** from morning till night; **2** by; **un poème ~ Victor Hugo** a poem by Victor Hugo; **avoir un enfant ~ qn** to have a child by sb; **3** of; **les**

chapeaux ~ Paul Paul's hats; **la porte ~ la chambre** the bedroom door; **le 20 du mois** the 20th of the month; **deux heures d'attente** a two-hour wait; **c'est bien ~ lui** it's just like him; **4 trois personnes ~ tuées** three people killed; **deux heures ~ libres** two hours free; **5** than; **plus/moins ~ 10** more/less than 10; **6** in; **d'un ton monocorde** in a monotone; **d'un goût douteux** in dubious taste; **7** with; **pousser qch du pied** to push sth aside with one's foot; **8 travailler ~ nuit** to work at night; **ne rien faire ~ la journée** to do nothing all day; **9 être content ~ faire** to be happy to do; **~ la voir ainsi me peinait** seeing her like that upset me.

II *det* **de, de l', de la, du** some; any; **voulez-vous ~ la bière?** would you like some beer?; **je n'ai pas d'argent** I haven't got any money; **voulez-vous du riz ou des pâtes?** would you like rice or pasta?

dé /de/ *nm* **1** dice; **les ~s sont jetés** the die is cast; **2 ~ (à coudre)** thimble.

déambulateur /deɑ̃bylatœʀ/ *nm* zimmer® (frame) (GB), walker (US).

déambuler /deɑ̃byle/ [1] *vi* to wander (about).

débâcle /debɑkl/ *nf* **1** (Mil) rout; **2** (figurative) collapse.

déballer /debale/ [1] *vtr* **1** to unpack; **2** to display.

débandade /debɑ̃dad/ *nf* **1** stampede; **2** disarray.

débarbouiller /debaʀbuje/ [1] **I** *vtr* to wash.

II **se débarbouiller** *v refl* (+ *v être*) to wash one's face.

débarcadère /debaʀkadɛʀ/ *nm* landing stage, jetty.

débardeur /debaʀdœʀ/ *nm* tank top.

débarquement /debaʀkəmɑ̃/ *nm* **1** (of goods) unloading; **2** (of passengers) disembarkation; **3** (Mil) landing.

débarquer /debaʀke/ [1] **I** *vtr* to unload [*goods*].

II *vi* **1** to disembark; **2** (Mil) to land; **3**° to turn up° (**chez qn** at sb's place); **4**° **il débarque toujours** he never has a clue° (what's going on).

débarras /debaʀa/ *nm inv* **1** junk room; **2 bon ~**°! good riddance!

débarrasser /debaʀase/ [1] **I** *vtr* **1** to clear (out); **2 ~ [qn] de** to free [sb] from [*complex*]; **~ qn (de son manteau)** to take sb's coat.

II **se débarrasser** *v refl* (+ *v être*) **se ~ de** to get rid of; to dispose of.

IDIOMS **~ le plancher**° to clear off°.

débat /deba/ *nm* debate.

débattre /debatʀ/ [61] **I** *vtr* to negotiate; **prix à ~** price negotiable.

II **débattre de** or **sur** *v+prep* **1** to discuss; **2** to debate.

III **se débattre** *v refl* (+ *v être*) to struggle.

débauche /deboʃ/ *nf* **1** debauchery; **2** profusion.

débauché, ~e /deboʃe/ **I** *pp* ▶ **débaucher**.

II *nm,f* debauchee.

débaucher /deboʃe/ [1] *vtr* **1** to corrupt; **2** to lay [sb] off; **3**° to tempt [sb] away.

débile /debil/ **I**° *adj* daft°.

II *nmf* **~ mental** (Med) retarded person.

débilité /debilite/ *nf* **1** (Med) debility; **2**° (of film, remark) stupidity.

■ **~ mentale** mental retardation.

débiner° /debine/ [1] **I** *vtr* to badmouth°.

II **se débiner** *v refl* (+ *v être*) to clear off°; to make oneself scarce°.

débit /debi/ *nm* **1** debit; **la somme est inscrite au ~** the sum has been debited; **2** (when speaking) delivery; **3** (of river) rate of flow; **4** (of liquid) flow; (of gas) output.

■ **~ de boissons** bar.

débiter /debite/ [1] *vtr* **1** to debit; **2** to reel [sth] off; **~ des bêtises** to talk a lot of nonsense; **3** to cut [sth] up.

débiteur, -trice /debitœʀ, tʀis/ **I** *adj* **compte ~** debit account; **pays ~** debtor nation.

II *nm,f* debtor.

déblaiement /deblɛmɑ̃/ *nm* clearing.

déblayage /deblɛjaʒ/ *nm* **1** clearing; **2** sorting out.

déblayer /debleje/ [21] *vtr* **1** to clear away [*earth, snow*]; **2** to clear [*place*].

débloquer /deblɔke/ [1] **I** *vtr* **1** to unlock [*steering wheel*]; to unjam [*mechanism*]; **2** to unfreeze [*wages, prices*]; to end the deadlock in [*situation*]; **3** to make [sth] available [*credit, subsidies*]; to create [*post*]; **4** to clear [*street*].

II° *vi* to be off one's rocker°.

déboires /debwaʀ/ *nm pl* **1** disappointments; **2** trials, difficulties; **3** setbacks.

déboiser /debwaze/ [1] *vtr* to deforest.

déboîter /debwate/ [1] **I** *vtr* **1** (Med) to dislocate; **2** to disconnect [*tubes*].

II *vi* [*car*] to pull out.

III **se déboîter** *v refl* (+ *v être*) **se ~ le genou** to dislocate one's knee.

débonnaire /debɔnɛʀ/ *adj* **1** good-humoured[GB]; **2** kindly.

débordant, ~e /debɔʀdɑ̃, ɑ̃t/ *adj* **1** [*imagination*] overactive; **2 ~ de** brimming with [*energy*]; bursting with [*health*].

débordé, ~e /debɔʀde/ **I** *pp* ▶ **déborder**.

II *pp adj* **1** overwhelmed; **2** overloaded.

débordement /debɔʀdəmɑ̃/ *nm* (of protest) flood; (of enthusiasm) excess.

déborder /debɔʀde/ [1] **I** *vtr* **1** [*problem, feeling*] to go beyond; **2 se laisser ~** to let oneself be overwhelmed; **3** (Mil, Sport) to outflank.

II **déborder de** *v+prep* to be brimming over with; to be bursting with.

III *vi* **1** [*river*] to overflow; **2** [*liquid*] to overflow; to boil over; **la coupe déborde** it's the last straw; **3** to jut out; **4** (in colouring book) to go over the lines.

débouché /debuʃe/ *nm* **1** market (**pour** for); **~s à l'exportation** export outlets; **2** job opportunity; **3 avoir un ~ sur la mer** to have access to the sea.

déboucher /debuʃe/ [1] **I** *vtr* **1** to unblock; **2** to open; to uncork.

II *vi* **1** to appear (suddenly); **2 ~ sur** [*street*] to open onto; [*studies, talks*] to lead to.
III **se déboucher** *v refl* (+ *v être*) **1** to come unblocked; **2** [*ears*] to pop; **3 se ~ les oreilles/le nez** to unblock one's ears/nose.

déboucheur /debuʃœʀ/ *nm* drain clearing product.

débouler /debule/ [1] **I** *vtr* to charge down.
II *vi* **1** to tumble down; **2**○ to turn up.

déboulonner /debulɔne/ [1] *vtr* to unbolt.

débourser /debuʀse/ [1] *vtr* to pay out.

déboussoler○ /debusɔle/ [1] *vtr* to throw○, to confuse.

debout /dəbu/ **I** *adj inv, adv* **1** standing; [*object*] upright; **rester ~** to stand; **se mettre ~** to stand up; **je ne tiens plus ~** I'm falling asleep on my feet; **2 ton histoire tient ~**○ your story seems likely; **3 tu es déjà ~!** you're already up!; **rester ~** to stay up.
II *excl* get up!

déboutonner /debutɔne/ [1] **I** *vtr* to unbutton.
II **se déboutonner** *v refl* (+ *v être*) to come undone.

débraillé, ~e /debʀaje/ *adj* [*person*] dishevelled[GB]; [*clothes, style*] sloppy.

débrancher /debʀɑ̃ʃe/ [1] *vtr* to unplug [*appliance*]; to disconnect [*alarm system*]; to pull out [*plug*].

débrayage /debʀɛjaʒ/ *nm* (Aut) declutching.

débrayer /debʀeje/ [21] *vi* **1** (Aut) to declutch; **2** to stop work.

débridé, ~e /debʀide/ *adj* unbridled.

débris /debʀi/ *nm inv* **1** fragment; **des ~ de verre** broken glass; **2** piece of wreckage; **3** rubbish (GB), garbage (US).

débrouillard, ~e /debʀujaʀ, aʀd/ *adj* resourceful.

débrouiller /debʀuje/ [1] **I** *vtr* **1** to disentangle [*threads*]; **2** to solve [*riddle*].
II **se débrouiller** *v refl* (+ *v être*) **1** to manage; **se ~ avec qn** to sort it out with sb; **2** to get by; **il se débrouille bien en espagnol** he speaks good Spanish.

débusquer /debyske/ [1] *vtr* to flush [sb/sth] out.

début /deby/ **I** *nm* beginning; start.
II **débuts** *nm pl* **1** debut; **à mes ~s** when I started out; **2** early stages.

débutant, ~e /debytɑ̃, ɑ̃t/ **I** *adj* [*driver, skier*] novice; [*engineer*] recently qualified; **pour adultes ~s** for adult beginners.
II *nm,f* beginner.

débuter /debyte/ [1] *vi* **1** [*day, novel*] to begin, to start; [*person*] to start off; **2** to start out (**comme** as); **3** [*performer*] to make one's debut.

deçà /dəsa/ **I** *adv* **~, delà** here and there.
II **en deçà** *phr* **1** on this side; **2** below.

décacheter /dekaʃte/ [20] *vtr* to unseal.

décade /dekad/ *nf* **1** 10-day period; **2** (controversial) decade.

décadence /dekadɑ̃s/ *nf* **1** decadence; **2** decline.

décadent, ~e /dekadɑ̃, ɑ̃t/ *adj* **1** decadent; **2** in decline.

décaféiné, ~e /dekafeine/ *adj* decaffeinated.

décalage /dekalaʒ/ *nm* **1** gap; **2** discrepancy; **3** interval, time-lag; **4** shift.
■ **~ horaire** time difference.

décalcifier: **se décalcifier** /dekalsifje/ [1] *v refl* (+ *v être*) to be decalcified.

décalcomanie /dekalkɔmani/ *nf* transfer (GB), decal (US).

décaler /dekale/ [1] **I** *vtr* **1** to bring forward [*date, departure time*]; **2** to put (GB) or move (US) back [*date, departure time*]; **3** to move [sth] forward [*object*]; **4** to move [sth] back [*object*].
II **se décaler** *v refl* (+ *v être*) **se ~ sur la droite** to move or shift to the right.

décalquer /dekalke/ [1] *vtr* **1** to trace (**sur** from); **2** to transfer (**sur** onto).

décamper○ /dekɑ̃pe/ [1] *vi* to run off, to clear off○.

décanter /dekɑ̃te/ [1] **I** *vtr* to allow [sth] to settle [*liquid*]; to clarify [*waste water*].
II **se décanter** *v refl* (+ *v être*) **1** [*liquid*] to settle; **2** [*situation, ideas*] to become clearer.

décapant, ~e /dekapɑ̃, ɑ̃t/ *adj* **1** scouring; **2**○ [*humour*] abrasive, caustic.

décaper /dekape/ [1] *vtr* **1** to clean; **2** to strip [*furniture*]; **~ avec un abrasif** to scour; **3**○ [*alcohol, soap*] to be harsh.

décapitation /dekapitasjɔ̃/ *nf* decapitation; beheading.

décapiter /dekapite/ [1] *vtr* to behead; to decapitate.

décapotable /dekapɔtabl/ *adj* **une (voiture) ~** a convertible.

décapsuler /dekapsyle/ [1] *vtr* to take the top off.

décapsuleur /dekapsylœʀ/ *nm* bottle-opener.

décarcasser○: **se décarcasser** /dekaʀkase/ [1] *v refl* (+ *v être*) to put oneself to a lot of trouble.

décathlon /dekatlɔ̃/ *nm* decathlon.

décatir: **se décatir** /dekatiʀ/ [3] *v refl* (+ *v être*) to become decrepit.

décéder /desede/ [14] *vi* (+ *v être*) to die.

déceler /desle/ [17] *vtr* **1** to detect; **2** to reveal [*anomaly, feeling*]; **3** to indicate [*presence*].

décélération /deseleʀasjɔ̃/ *nf* deceleration.

décembre /desɑ̃bʀ/ *nm* December.

décemment /desamɑ̃/ *adv* decently.

décence /desɑ̃s/ *nf* decency.

décennal, ~e, *mpl* **-aux** /desenal, o/ *adj* ten-year.

décennie /deseni/ *nf* decade.

décent, ~e /desɑ̃, ɑ̃t/ *adj* **1** decent; **2** proper; **3** reasonable.

décentraliser /desɑ̃tʀalize/ [1] *vtr* to decentralize.

décentrer /desɑ̃tʀe/ [1] *vtr* to move away from the centre[GB].

déception /desɛpsjɔ̃/ *nf* disappointment.

décerner /desɛʀne/ [1] *vtr* to award.

décès /desɛ/ *nm inv* death.

décevant, **~e** /desəvɑ̃, ɑ̃t/ *adj* disappointing.

décevoir /desəvwaʀ/ [5] *vtr* **1** to disappoint; **2** to fail to fulfil[GB] [*hope*].

déchaîné, **~e** /deʃene/ I *pp* ▶ **déchaîner**.
II *pp adj* [*public opinion*] stirred up; **~ contre** furious with.

déchaîner /deʃene/ [1] I *vtr* to rouse [*feelings*]; to excite [*people*].
II **se déchaîner** *v refl* (+ *v être*) **1** [*sea, wind*] to rage; [*feelings*] to burst out; **2** [*crowd*] to go wild.

déchanter /deʃɑ̃te/ [1] *vi* to become disenchanted; **elle a dû ~** she was brought down to earth.

décharge /deʃaʀʒ/ *nf* **1** (of firearm) discharge; **2** **~ municipale** (municipal) dump; **3** **~ électrique** electric shock; **4** (Law) acquittal.

décharger /deʃaʀʒe/ [13] I *vtr* **1** to unload [*vessel, goods, passengers*]; **2** to unload [*firearm*]; **3** to fire [*gun*]; **4** **~ qn de** to relieve sb of [*task, obligation*]; **5** to discharge [*appliance, battery*]; **6** to unburden [*conscience*].
II **se décharger** *v refl* (+ *v être*) **1** **se ~ de qch** to off-load sth (**sur qn** onto sb); **2** [*battery*] to run down.

décharné, **~e** /deʃaʀne/ *adj* [*body*] emaciated; [*finger*] bony.

déchausser /deʃose/ [1] I *vtr* **~ qn** to take sb's shoes off.
II **se déchausser** *v refl* (+ *v être*) **1** to take off one's shoes; **2** to work loose due to receding gums.

dèche○ /dɛʃ/ *nf* **être dans la ~** to be broke○.

déchéance /deʃeɑ̃s/ *nf* **1** decline; **2** degeneration.

déchet /deʃɛ/ I *nm* **1** scrap; **2** waste; **3** wreck.
II **déchets** *nm pl* waste material, waste.

déchiffrer /deʃifʀe/ [1] *vtr* **1** to decipher; **2** (Mus) to sight-read.

déchiqueté, **~e** /deʃikte/ I *pp* ▶ **déchiqueter**.
II *pp adj* jagged, ragged.

déchiqueter /deʃikte/ [20] *vtr* **1** to tear [sth] to shreds; **2** [*machine, animal*] to tear to pieces; **3** to blow [sb] to pieces.

déchirant, **~e** /deʃiʀɑ̃, ɑ̃t/ *adj* **1** heart-rending; **2** agonizing.

déchirement /deʃiʀmɑ̃/ *nm* **1** heartbreak; **2** rift (**entre** between).

déchirer /deʃiʀe/ [1] I *vtr* **1** to tear up [*paper, material*]; **2** to tear [*garment*]; **3** to split [*group, country*]; **déchiré entre X et Y** torn between X and Y; **4** to torment.
II **se déchirer** *v refl* (+ *v être*) **1** to tear; **2** **se ~ un muscle** to tear a muscle; **3** to tear each other apart.

déchirure /deʃiʀyʀ/ *nf* (gen), (Med) tear.

déchoir /deʃwaʀ/ [51] I *vtr* (Law) to strip [sb] of.
II *vi* to demean oneself.

déchu, **~e** /deʃy/ I *pp* ▶ **déchoir**.
II *pp adj* [*monarch*] deposed; [*angel*] fallen.

décibel /desibɛl/ *nm* decibel.

décidé, **~e** /deside/ I *pp* ▶ **décider**.
II *pp adj* determined; resolute.

décidément /desidemɑ̃/ *adv* really.

décider /deside/ [1] I *vtr* **1** to decide; **c'est décidé** it's settled; **2** to persuade (**à faire** to do).
II **décider de** *v+prep* to decide on [*date, place*]; to fix [*price*].
III **se décider** *v refl* (+ *v être*) **1** to make up one's mind; **être décidé à faire** to be determined to do; **2** **se ~ pour** to decide on.

décimal, **~e**[1], *mpl* **-aux** /desimal, o/ *adj* decimal.

décimale[2] /desimal/ *nf* decimal.

décimer /desime/ [1] *vtr* to decimate.

décisif, **-ive** /desizif, iv/ *adj* **1** decisive; **2** conclusive.

décision /desizjɔ̃/ *nf* **1** decision; **2** decisiveness.

décisionnel, **-elle** /desizjɔnɛl/ *adj* **pouvoir ~** power to make decisions.

déclamer /deklame/ [1] *vtr* to declaim.

déclaration /deklaʀasjɔ̃/ *nf* **1** statement; declaration; **faire sa ~ à qn** to declare one's love to sb; **2** notification; **3** (Law) statement; **~ de vol/perte** report of theft/loss.
■ **~ d'impôts** (income-)tax return.

déclaré, **~e** /deklaʀe/ *adj* [*enemy*] avowed; [*hatred*] professed.

déclarer /deklaʀe/ [1] I *vtr* **1** to declare [*independence, intentions*]; **il a été déclaré coupable** he was found guilty; **2** to declare [*goods, revenue*]; to report [*theft*]; to register [*birth, death*]; **non déclaré** undeclared; illegal.
II **se déclarer** *v refl* (+ *v être*) **1** [*fire, epidemic*] to break out; [*fever*] to start; **2** **se ~ pour/contre** to come out for/against; **3** to declare one's love (**à qn** to sb).

déclasser /deklase/ [1] *vtr* **1** to downgrade; **2** to jumble [sth] up.

déclenchement /deklɑ̃ʃmɑ̃/ *nm* (of mechanism) release; (of illness) onset; (of reaction) start; (of conflict, strike) outbreak.

déclencher /deklɑ̃ʃe/ [1] I *vtr* **1** to spark (off) [*protest*]; to prompt [*decision*]; to cause [*reaction, explosion*]; to start [*avalanche*]; **2** to launch [*offensive*]; to begin [*hostilities*]; to start [*strike, debate*]; **3** to set off [*mechanism*].
II **se déclencher** *v refl* (+ *v être*) **1** to go off; to be activated; **2** [*war*] to break out; [*crisis, offensive*] to begin.

déclic /deklik/ *nm* **1** trigger; **2** (of camera) click.

déclin /deklɛ̃/ *nm* decline.

déclinaison /deklinɛzɔ̃/ *nf* declension.

décliner /dekline/ [1] I *vtr* **1** to decline; to turn [sth] down; **~ toute responsabilité** to disclaim all responsibility; **2** **~ son identité** to give one's name; **3** to decline.
II *vi* [*light, talent*] to fade; [*health*] to deteriorate; [*enthusiasm*] to wane; [*sun*] to go down.
III **se décliner** *v refl* (+ *v être*) to decline.

déclivité /deklivite/ *nf* gradient.

décocher /dekɔʃe/ [1] *vtr* to shoot [*arrow*].

décoction /dekɔksjɔ̃/ *nf* brew, decoction.

décoder /dekɔde/ [1] *vtr* to decode.
décodeur /dekɔdœʀ/ *nm* decoder.
décoiffer /dekwafe/ [1] *vtr* **~ qn** to ruffle sb's hair; **elle est toute décoiffée** her hair is in a mess.
décoincer /dekwɛ̃se/ [12] *vtr* to unjam [*mechanism, door*]; to free [*key*]; to get [sth] back to normal [*neck, back*].
décolérer /dekɔleʀe/ [14] *vi* **ne pas ~** to stay angry.
décollage /dekɔlaʒ/ *nm* **1** take-off; **2** peeling off.
décoller /dekɔle/ [1] **I** *vtr* to peel off [*sticker*].
II *vi* [*plane*] to take off.
III se décoller *v refl* (+ *v être*) to come off.
décolleté, ~e /dekɔlte/ **I** *adj* low-cut.
II *nm* low neckline.
décolleuse /dekɔløz/ *nf* steam stripper.
décolonisation /dekɔlɔnizasjɔ̃/ *nf* decolonization.
décolorant, ~e /dekɔlɔʀɑ̃, ɑ̃t/ *adj* bleaching.
décoloration /dekɔlɔʀasjɔ̃/ *nf* **1** discoloration; **2** fading.
décolorer /dekɔlɔʀe/ [1] *vtr* **1** to bleach; **2** to cause to fade.
décombres /dekɔ̃bʀ/ *nm pl* rubble.
décommander /dekɔmɑ̃de/ [1] **I** *vtr* to call [sth] off.
II se décommander *v refl* (+ *v être*) to cry off (GB), to beg off.
décomposer /dekɔ̃poze/ [1] **I** *vtr* **1** to break down [*argument, water*]; to disperse [*light*]; **2** to distort [*features*].
II se décomposer *v refl* (+ *v être*) **1** to decompose; **2** to fall apart.
décomposition /dekɔ̃pozisjɔ̃/ *nf* **1** decomposition; **2** disintegration.
décompte /dekɔ̃t/ *nm* **1** discount; **2** count; **faire le ~ de** to count [sth] up [*votes, points*]; **3** (itemized) statement.
décompter /dekɔ̃te/ [1] *vtr* **1** to deduct (**de** from); **2** to count [*votes, points*].
déconcentrer /dekɔ̃sɑ̃tʀe/ [1] *vtr* to distract.
déconcerter /dekɔ̃sɛʀte/ [1] *vtr* to disconcert.
déconfit, ~e /dekɔ̃fi, it/ *adj* crestfallen.
déconfiture /dekɔ̃fityʀ/ *nf* (of person) failure; (of party, team) defeat.
décongeler /dekɔ̃ʒle/ [17] *vtr, vi* to defrost.
déconnecter /dekɔnɛkte/ [1] *vtr* **1** to disconnect [*appliance*]; **2** to dissociate (**de** from).
déconner◑ /dekɔne/ [1] *vi* **1** to kid around○; to talk crap◑ **sans ~!** no kidding○!; **faut pas ~!** come off it○!; **2** to mess around○; to piss around◑ (GB); **3** to play up○, to act up○.
déconseiller /dekɔ̃seje/ [1] *vtr* to advise against.
déconsidérer /dekɔ̃sideʀe/ [14] *vtr* to discredit.
décontenancer /dekɔ̃tnɑ̃se/ [12] *vtr* to disconcert.
décontracté, ~e /dekɔ̃tʀakte/ **I** *pp* ▶ **décontracter**.
II *pp adj* **1** relaxed; **2** casual; **3** laid-back○.
décontracter /dekɔ̃tʀakte/ [1] *vtr*, **se décontracter** *v refl* (+ *v être*) to relax.
décontraction /dekɔ̃tʀaksjɔ̃/ *nf* **1** relaxation; **2** ease; **3** casual attitude.
déconvenue /dekɔ̃vəny/ *nf* disappointment.
décor /dekɔʀ/ *nm* **1** decor; **2** setting; **j'ai besoin de changer de ~** I need a change of scene; **aller dans le ~**○ to drive off the road; **3** set; **film tourné en ~ naturel** film shot on location.
décorateur, -trice /dekɔʀatœʀ, tʀis/ *nm,f* **1** interior decorator; **2** window dresser; **3** set designer.
décoratif, -ive /dekɔʀatif, iv/ *adj* **1** ornamental; **2** decorative.
décoration /dekɔʀasjɔ̃/ *nf* **1** decorating; **2** (gen), (Mil) decoration; **3** interior design; **4** set design.
décorer /dekɔʀe/ [1] *vtr* (gen), (Mil) to decorate.
décortiquer /dekɔʀtike/ [1] *vtr* to shell [*nut*]; to peel [*prawn*].
découcher /dekuʃe/ [1] *vi* to spend the night away from home.
découdre /dekudʀ/ [76] **I** *vtr* to undo, to unpick (GB) [*hem, seam*].
II *vi* **en ~** to have a fight (**avec** with).
découler /dekule/ [1] *vi* **1** to follow (**de** from); **2** to result (**de** from).
découpage /dekupaʒ/ *nm* **1** cut-out; **2** (for filming) shooting script.
■ **~ électoral** division into constituencies (GB), districting (US).
découper /dekupe/ [1] *vtr* to cut up [*tart*]; to carve [*roast*]; to divide up [*land, territory*]; to cut out [*article, photo*].
découragement /dekuʀaʒmɑ̃/ *nm* discouragement, despondency.
décourager /dekuʀaʒe/ [13] *vtr* **1** to dishearten; **2** to discourage (**de faire** from doing); **3** to deter.
décousu, ~e /dekuzy/ **I** *pp* ▶ **découdre**.
II *pp adj* [*garment, hem*] which has come undone.
III *adj* [*story*] rambling; [*conversation*] casual.
découvert, ~e[1] /dekuvɛʀ, ɛʀt/ **I** *pp* ▶ **découvrir**.
II *pp adj* **1** bare; **avoir la tête ~e** to be bareheaded; **2** [*truck*] open; [*car*] open-topped.
III *nm* overdraft; **être à ~** to be overdrawn.
découverte[2] /dekuvɛʀt/ *nf* discovery; **partir à la ~ de qch** to set off to explore sth.
découvrir /dekuvʀiʀ/ [32] **I** *vtr* **1** to discover; **faire ~ qch à qn** to introduce sb to sth; **2** to expose [*plot*]; **3** to show [*arm, back*]; **4** to leave [sth] exposed [*border, chess piece*].
II se découvrir *v refl* (+ *v être*) **1** to remove one's hat; **2 elle s'est découvert un talent** she found she had a talent; **3** to kick off one's bedclothes.
décrasser /dekʀase/ [1] *vtr* to get [sb/sth] clean.
décrépit, ~e /dekʀepi, it/ *adj* [*person*] decrepit; [*building*] dilapidated; [*wall*] crumbling.

décrépitude /dekʀepityd/ *nf* decrepitude.

décret /dekʀɛ/ *nm* decree.

décréter /dekʀete/ [14] *vtr* **1** to order; **2** to decree (**que** that); **3** to declare (**que** that).

décrier /dekʀije/ [2] *vtr* to disparage.

décrire /dekʀiʀ/ [67] *vtr* **1** to describe; **2** to follow.

décrocher /dekʀɔʃe/ [1] **I** *vtr* **1** to take down [*picture*]; **2** to uncouple [*wagon*]; **3** **~ son téléphone** to pick up the receiver; to take the phone off the hook; **4**° to get [*contract, diploma*].
II *vi* to give up.
IDIOMS **~ le gros lot** to hit the jackpot.

décroître /dekʀwatʀ/ [72] *vi* [*level*] to fall; [*moon*] to wane; [*day*] to get shorter; [*light, noise*] to fade; [*inflation*] to go down; [*influence*] to decline.

décrypter /dekʀipte/ [1] *vtr* **1** to decipher [*signs*]; **2** to interpret [*statement*].

déçu, **~e** /desy/ *pp* ▶ **décevoir**.

déculpabiliser /dekylpabilize/ [1] *vtr* to free of guilt.

décupler /dekyple/ [1] *vtr*, *vi* to increase tenfold.

dédaigner /dedeɲe/ [1] *vtr* to despise.

dédaigneux, **-euse** /dedɛɲø, øz/ *adj* disdainful, scornful.

dédain /dedɛ̃/ *nm* contempt, disdain.

dédale /dedal/ *nm* **1** (of buildings) maze; **2** (of laws, formalities) labyrinth.

dedans /dədɑ̃/ **I** *adv* inside.
II en dedans *phr* inside.

dédicace /dedikas/ *nf* **1** dedication (**à qn** to sb); **2** inscription.

dédicacer /dedikase/ [12] *vtr* **1** to dedicate [*book*] (**à** to); **2** to sign [*book, photo*].

dédier /dedje/ [2] *vtr* **1** to dedicate [*novel*] (**à** to); **2** to devote [*life*] (**à** to).

dédire: **se dédire** /dediʀ/ [65] *v refl* (+ *v être*) to back out.

dédommagement /dedɔmaʒmɑ̃/ *nm* compensation.

dédommager /dedɔmaʒe/ [13] *vtr* **1** to compensate; **être dédommagé de** to get compensation for; **2** **~ qn de qch** to make it up to sb for sth.

dédouaner /dedwane/ [1] *vtr* to clear through customs.

dédoubler /deduble/ [1] **I** *vtr* **1** to split [sth] in two [*group*]; **2** to separate [sth] into strands [*cable*].
II se dédoubler *v refl* (+ *v être*) [*nail*] to split; [*image*] to split in two; [*cable*] to come apart.

déductible /dedyktibl/ *adj* deductible; **~ des impôts** tax-deductible.

déduction /dedyksjɔ̃/ *nf* deduction.

déduire /dedɥiʀ/ [69] **I** *vtr* **1** to deduce; **2** to infer; **3** to deduct.
II se déduire *v refl* (+ *v être*) **1** to be inferred; **2** to be deduced; **3** to be deducted.

déesse /deɛs/ *nf* goddess.

défaillance /defajɑ̃s/ *nf* failure; **~ cardiaque** heart failure.

défaillant, **~e** /defajɑ̃, ɑ̃t/ *adj* **1** [*motor, system*] faulty; **2** [*service, organization*] inefficient; **3** [*health, memory*] failing; [*person*] fainting.

défaillir /defajiʀ/ [28] *vi* **1** to faint; **se sentir ~** to feel faint; **~ de bonheur** to be overwhelmed with joy; **2** [*health, memory*] to fail; **soutenir qn sans ~** to show unflinching support for sb.

défaire /defɛʀ/ [10] **I** *vtr* to undo; to untie; **le lit n'était pas défait** the bed hadn't been slept in.
II se défaire *v refl* (+ *v être*) **1** to come undone; **2** [*alliance, friendship*] to break up; **3** **se ~ de** to get rid of; to part with; to rid oneself of; **4** [*face*] to fall; **avoir la mine défaite** to look haggard.

défaite /defɛt/ *nf* defeat.

défaut /defo/ **I** *nm* **1** fault, failing; **se mettre en ~** to put oneself in the wrong; **prendre qn en ~** to catch sb out; **2** defect; flaw; **présenter des ~s** to be faulty; **~ de fabrication** manufacturing fault; **~ de prononciation** speech impediment; **3** shortage; **faire ~** [*money, resources*] to be lacking; **le courage leur a fait ~** their courage failed them; **4** (Law) **par ~** in absentia.
II à défaut de *phr* **à ~ de (quoi)** failing (which); **à ~ de mieux** for want of anything better; **à ~ de pouvoir acheter, elle loue** since she can't buy, she has to rent.

défaveur /defavœʀ/ *nf* **il s'est trompé de 30 francs en ma ~** he overcharged me 30 francs; **mon âge a joué en ma ~** my age went against me.

défavorable /defavɔʀabl/ *adj* [*situation*] unfavourable[GB] (**à** to); [*person*] opposed (**à** to).

défavorisé, **~e** /defavɔʀize/ *adj* **1** underprivileged; **2** disadvantaged.

défection /defɛksjɔ̃/ *nf* **1** defection; **2** non-appearance; **3** (of friends) desertion.

défectueux, **-euse** /defɛktɥø, øz/ *adj* [*material*] faulty, defective; [*reasoning*] flawed.

défendre /defɑ̃dʀ/ [6] **I** *vtr* **1** **~ à qn de faire** to forbid sb to do; **2** to defend [*person, country, interests*]; **3** to fight for [*right*]; to stand up for [*friend, principle*]; **~ une cause** to champion a cause; **4** (Law, Sport) to defend.
II se défendre *v refl* (+ *v être*) **1** to defend oneself; to stand up for oneself; **2** to be tenable; **3** to protect oneself; **4**° to get by; **se ~ en français** to be quite good at French; **5** **se ~ d'être vexé** to deny being offended; **on ne peut se ~ de penser que...** one can't help thinking that...

défense /defɑ̃s/ *nf* **1** **'~ de fumer'** 'no smoking'; **~ d'en parler devant lui** don't mention it in front of him; **2** (Med, Mil, Sport) defence[GB]; **assurer la ~ du pays** to defend the country; **3** protection; **sans ~** helpless; unprotected; **la ~ de l'environnement** the protection of the environment; **la ~ de la langue française** the preservation of the French language; **prendre la ~ de** to stand up for; **4** (Zool) tusk.

défenseur /defɑ̃sœʀ/ *nm* defender.

défensive /defɑ̃siv/ *nf* **sur la ~** on the defensive.

déférence /defeʀɑ̃s/ *nf* deference; **marques de ~** marks of respect.

déferlement /defɛʀləmɑ̃/ *nm* (of praise, images) flood; (of passion) surge; (of words) torrent.

déferler /defɛʀle/ [1] *vi* **1** [*wave*] to break (**sur** on); **2** [*violence*] to erupt; **3 ~ sur** [*people*] to pour into [*country, town*].

défi /defi/ *nm* **1** challenge; **mettre qn au ~ de faire** to challenge sb to do; **2** act of defiance; **air de ~** defiant look.

défiance /defjɑ̃s/ *nf* distrust, mistrust.

déficience /defisjɑ̃s/ *nf* deficiency; **~ cardiaque** heart failure.

déficient, **~e** /defisjɑ̃, ɑ̃t/ *adj* **1** (Med) deficient; **2** [*system, inspection*] inadequate.

déficit /defisit/ *nm* **1** deficit; **2** (Med) deficiency.

déficitaire /defisitɛʀ/ *adj* showing a deficit; showing a loss; showing a shortfall.

défier /defje/ [2] *vtr* **1** to challenge [*rival*]; **~ qn du regard** to stare defiantly at sb; **2** to defy [*danger, death*]; **prix défiant toute concurrence** unbeatable price.

défigurer /defigyʀe/ [1] *vtr* to disfigure.

défilé /defile/ *nm* **1** parade; **2** (protest) march; **3** (of visitors, candidates) stream; **4** gorge.
■ **~ aérien** flypast (GB), flyover (US); **~ militaire** march-past; **~ de mode** fashion show.

défiler /defile/ [1] **I** *vi* **1** to parade; [*protesters*] to march; **2** [*people*] to come and go; **3** [*images, landscape*] to unfold; **~ rapidement** to flash past; **4** (Comput) to scroll.
II se défiler○ *v refl* (+ *v être*) to wriggle out of it.

définir /definiʀ/ [3] *vtr* to define.

définitif, **-ive** /definitif, iv/ **I** *adj* [*accounts, report*] final; [*edition*] definitive; [*refusal*] flat; **rien de ~** nothing definite.
II en définitive *phr* at the end of the day.

définition /definisjɔ̃/ *nf* **1** (gen) definition; **2** (in crossword) clue.

définitivement /definitivmɑ̃/ *adv* for good.

déflagration /deflagʀasjɔ̃/ *nf* detonation.

défoncer /defɔ̃se/ [12] *vtr* to break down [*door*]; to smash in [*back of a car*]; **les camions ont défoncé la route** the lorries have ruined the road surface.

déformation /defɔʀmasjɔ̃/ *nf* **1** distortion; **2** deformity; **3 c'est de la ~ professionnelle** it's a habit that comes from the job.

déformé, **~e** /defɔʀme/ *adj* [*face, image, truth*] distorted; [*object, mind*] warped; [*body, limb*] misshapen; [*garment*] shapeless; **chaussée ~e** uneven (road) surface.

déformer /defɔʀme/ [1] **I** *vtr* **1** to bend [sth] (out of shape); **2** to distort [*image, features*]; **3** to distort [*facts*]; **on a déformé mes propos** my words have been twisted.
II se déformer *v refl* (+ *v être*) to lose its shape.

défoulement /defulmɑ̃/ *nm* letting off steam.

défouler /defule/ [1] **I** *vtr* **ça me défoule** it helps me (to) unwind.
II se défouler *v refl* (+ *v être*) **1** to let off steam; **2 se ~ sur qn** to take it out on sb; **3** to let one's hair down○.

défraîchi, **~e** /defʀeʃi/ *adj* [*garment, curtain*] worn; [*material, beauty*] faded.

défrayer /defʀeje/ [21] *vtr* **1 ~ la chronique** to be the talk of the town; **2 ~ qn** to pay sb's expenses.

défricher /defʀiʃe/ [1] *vtr* to clear, to reclaim.

défroisser /defʀwase/ [1] *vtr* to smooth out [*dress, paper*].

défunt, **~e** /defœ̃, œ̃t/ **I** *adj* **1** former; **2** late.
II *nm,f* **le ~** the deceased.

dégagé, **~e** /degaʒe/ *adj* **1** [*road, sky*] clear; [*forehead*] bare; **2** [*look*] casual.

dégagement /degaʒmɑ̃/ *nm* **1** clearing; **2** (in football) clearance.

dégager /degaʒe/ [13] **I** *vtr* **1** to free; **~ qn d'une responsabilité** to relieve sb of a responsibility; **~ la balle** to clear the ball; **~ des crédits** to make funds available; **2** to unblock [*nose, sinus*]; **2** to clear [*office, way*]; **'dégagez, s'il vous plaît'** 'move along please'; **dégage**○! get lost○!; **3** to find [*idea, sense*]; **~ les grands axes d'une politique** to highlight the main points of a policy; **4** to emit [*odour, gas*]; **~ de la chaleur** to give off heat.
II se dégager *v refl* (+ *v être*) **1** to free oneself/itself; **2** [*weather, sky*] to clear; **3 se ~ de** to come out of; **4** to become clear.

dégaine○ /degɛn/ *nf* odd appearance.

dégainer /degene/ [1] *vtr* to draw [*gun*].

dégarnir /degaʀniʀ/ [3] **I** *vtr* to empty [*shelf, fridge*].
II se dégarnir *v refl* (+ *v être*) **1** to be going bald; **2** [*street, hall*] to empty.

dégât /degɑ/ *nm* damage.

dégel /deʒɛl/ *nm* thaw.

dégeler /deʒle/ [17] **I** *vtr* **1** to improve [*relations*]; **~ l'atmosphère** to break the ice; **2** to unfreeze [*credit*].
II *vi* to thaw (out).
III se dégeler *v refl* (+ *v être*) **1** [*relations, situation*] to thaw; **2** [*audience*] to warm up.

dégénérer /deʒeneʀe/ [14] *vi* **1** [*incident*] to get out of hand; **~ en** to degenerate into; **2** [*plant, species*] to degenerate.

dégénérescence /deʒeneʀesɑ̃s/ *nf* degeneration.

dégingandé, **~e** /deʒɛ̃gɑ̃de/ *adj* lanky.

dégivrage /deʒivʀaʒ/ *nm* **1** (of windscreen) de-icing; **2** (of fridge) defrosting.

dégivrer /deʒivʀe/ [1] *vtr* **1** to de-ice [*windscreen*]; **2** to defrost [*fridge*].

déglingué○, **~e** /deglɛ̃ge/ *adj* dilapidated.

déglutir /deglytiʀ/ [3] *vtr, vi* to swallow.

dégonfler /degɔ̃fle/ [1] **I** *vtr* to deflate [*tyre*].
II *vi* [*swelling, bump*] to go down.

III se dégonfler *v refl* (+ *v être*) **1** [*rubber ring*] to deflate; [*tyre, balloon*] to go down; **2**○ to chicken out○, to lose one's nerve.

dégot(t)er○ /degɔte/ [1] *vtr* to find.

dégouliner /deguline/ [1] *vi* **1** to trickle; **2** to drip (**de** with).

dégoupiller /degupije/ [1] *vtr* **~ une grenade** to pull the pin out of a grenade.

dégourdi, ~e /deguʀdi/ *adj* smart.

dégourdir /deguʀdiʀ/ [3] **I** *vtr* **1** to loosen up [*limbs, person*]; **2 ~ des enfants** to bring children out of themselves.

II se dégourdir *v refl* (+ *v être*) **se ~ les jambes** to stretch one's legs.

dégoût /degu/ *nm* disgust.

dégoûtant, ~e /degutɑ̃, ɑ̃t/ *adj* **1** filthy; **2**○ disgusting; revolting.

dégoûté, ~e /degute/ *adj* disgusted; **ne pas être ~** to have a strong stomach; **faire le ~** to turn one's nose up.

dégoûter /degute/ [1] *vtr* **1** to disgust; **2** to make [sb] feel sick; **3 ~ qn de qch/de faire** to put sb off sth/off doing.

dégradant, ~e /degʀadɑ̃, ɑ̃t/ *adj* degrading.

dégradation /degʀadasjɔ̃/ *nf* **1** damage; **2** deterioration.

dégradé, ~e /degʀade/ **I** *adj* **tons ~s** shaded tones; **coupe ~e** layered cut.

II *nm* (in colours) gradation.

dégrader /degʀade/ [1] **I** *vtr* **1** to damage; **2** (Mil) to cashier [*officer*]; **3** to degrade [*person*].

II se dégrader *v refl* (+ *v être*) to deteriorate.

dégrafer /degʀafe/ [1] **I** *vtr* to undo.

II se dégrafer *v refl* (+ *v être*) to come undone.

dégraisser /degʀese/ [1] *vtr* **1** to trim the fat off; **2**○ to streamline [*workforce*]; **3** to dry-clean.

degré /dəgʀe/ *nm* **1** degree; **par ~s** gradually; **à un moindre ~** to a lesser extent; **jusqu'à un certain ~** up to a point; **susceptible au plus haut ~** extremely touchy; **brûlures du premier ~** first-degree burns; **équation du premier ~** first-degree equation; **~ de parenté** degree of kinship; **2** step; **enseignement du second ~** secondary education; **c'est à prendre au deuxième ~** it is not to be taken literally; **les ~s de l'échelle sociale** the rungs of the social ladder; **3 ce vin fait 12°** this wine contains 12% alcohol.

■ **~ Celsius** degree Celsius; **~ Fahrenheit** degree Fahrenheit.

dégressif, -ive /degʀesif, iv/ *adj* [*tax*] graduated; **tarifs ~s** tapering charges.

dégriffé, ~e /degʀife/ *adj* **robe/veste ~e** marked-down designer dress/jacket.

dégringolade○ /degʀɛ̃gɔlad/ *nf* **1** fall; **2** (in prices) collapse.

dégringoler○ /degʀɛ̃gɔle/ [1] **I** *vtr* to race down [*stairs, hill*].

II *vi* **1** [*person*] to take a tumble; [*books*] to tumble down; **2** to drop sharply.

dégriser /degʀize/ [1] *vtr* **1** to sober [sb] up; **2** to bring [sb] to his/her senses.

dégrossi, ~e /degʀosi/ *adj* **mal ~** [*person*] coarse.

dégrossir /degʀosiʀ/ [3] *vtr* to break the back of [*task*].

déguerpir /degɛʀpiʀ/ [3] *vi* to leave; **faire ~ qn** to drive sb off.

déguisé, ~e /degize/ *adj* **1** in fancy dress; in disguise; **2** [*party*] fancy-dress; **3** [*attempt*] concealed; [*compliment*] disguised; **une façon ~e de faire** a roundabout way of doing.

déguisement /degizmɑ̃/ *nm* **1** costume; **2** disguise.

déguiser /degize/ [1] **I** *vtr* **1** to dress [sb] up (**en** as); **2** to disguise.

II se déguiser *v refl* (+ *v être*) **1** to dress up; **2** to disguise oneself.

dégustation /degystasjɔ̃/ *nf* tasting.

déguster /degyste/ [1] *vtr* to savour[GB] [*drink, victory*]; to enjoy [*performance*].

déhanchement /deɑ̃ʃmɑ̃/ *nm* **1** swaying hips; **2** lopsidedness.

déhancher: se déhancher /deɑ̃ʃe/ [1] *v refl* (+ *v être*) to wiggle one's hips.

dehors /dəɔʀ/ **I** *adv* outside; **mettre qn ~** to throw sb out; to fire sb; to expel sb.

II *excl* get out!

III en dehors de *phr* **1** outside; **2** apart from.

déjà /deʒa/ *adv* **1** already; **2** before, already; **je te l'ai ~ dit** I've told you before; **3**○ **c'est ~ un joli salaire!** that's a pretty good salary!; **il s'est excusé, c'est ~ quelque chose** at least he apologized, that's something; **elle est ~ assez riche (comme ça)!** she's rich enough as it is; **c'est combien, ~?** how much was it again?

déjeuner¹ /deʒœne/ [1] *vi* to have lunch.

déjeuner² /deʒœne/ *nm* lunch.

déjouer /deʒwe/ [1] *vtr* to frustrate [*precaution, manoeuvre*]; to foil [*plan, conspiracy*], to evade [*surveillance, inspection*].

delà /dəla/ *adv* **deçà** or **de-ci, ~** here and there.

délabré, ~e /delabʀe/ *adj* [*house, equipment*] dilapidated; [*health*] damaged.

délabrement /delabʀəmɑ̃/ *nm* **1** dilapidation; **2 le ~ de ta santé/de l'économie** the poor state of your health/the economy.

délabrer /delabʀe/ [1] **I** *vtr* to ruin [*house, equipment*].

II se délabrer *v refl* (+ *v être*) [*house*] to become run-down; [*business, country*] to go to rack and ruin; [*health*] to deteriorate.

délacer /delase/ [12] *vtr* to undo; to unlace.

délai /delɛ/ *nm* **1 dans un ~ de 24 heures** within 24 hours; **respecter un ~** to meet a deadline; **dans les meilleurs ~s** as soon as possible; **sans ~** immediately, without delay; **2** extension; **demander un ~** to ask for extra time.

■ **~ de livraison** delivery or lead time.

délaisser /delese/ [1] *vtr* **1** to abandon [*activity*]; **2** to neglect [*friends*].

délassement /delɑsmɑ̃/ *nm* relaxation; **mon ~ préféré** my favourite[GB] way of relaxing.

délasser /delɑse/ [1] *vtr, v refl* (+ *v être*) to relax; **ça délasse** it's relaxing.

délateur, -trice /delatœʀ, tʀis/ *nm,f* informer.

délation /delɑsjɔ̃/ *nf* informing.

délavé, ~e /delave/ *adj* **1** [*colour, sky*] washed-out; [*jeans, poster*] faded; **2** waterlogged.

délayer /deleje/ [21] *vtr* to thin [*paint*]; to mix [*flour*].

délectation /delɛktasjɔ̃/ *nf* delight.

délecter: **se délecter** /delɛkte/ [1] *v refl* (+ *v être*) **se ~ à faire/en faisant** to delight in doing; **se ~ à l'avance de qch/de faire** to be thoroughly looking forward to sth/to doing.

délégation /delegasjɔ̃/ *nf* delegation.

délégué, ~e /delege/ *nm,f* delegate.
■ **~ syndical** union representative.

déléguer /delege/ [14] *vtr* **1** to appoint [sb] as a delegate; **2** to delegate [*responsibility, power*].

délestage /delɛstaʒ/ *nm* **1** unloading of the ballast; **2** diversion (*to relieve a road of heavy traffic*).

délester /delɛste/ [1] *vtr* **1** to get rid of the ballast from; **2** to divert traffic away from.

délibération /delibeʀasjɔ̃/ *nf* deliberation; **mettre qch en ~** to debate sth.

délibéré, ~e /delibeʀe/ **I** *adj* [*act, violation*] deliberate; [*choice, policy*] conscious; **de propos ~** deliberately, on purpose.
II *nm* (Law) deliberation.

délibérément /delibeʀemɑ̃/ *adv* [*wound, provoke*] deliberately; [*accept, choose*] consciously.

délibérer /delibeʀe/ [14] **I délibérer de** or **sur** *v+prep* to discuss.
II *vi* to be in session.

délicat, ~e /delika, at/ *adj* **1** [*dish*] subtle; [*person*] refined; **manières ~es** refinement; **2** tactful; **3** thoughtful; **des procédés peu ~s** unscrupulous means; **4** [*balance, task*] delicate; [*business, file, moment*] sensitive; [*mission, tactic*] tricky; **5** [*skin*] delicate.

délicatement /delikatmɑ̃/ *adv* **1** delicately; **2** tactfully.

délicatesse /delikatɛs/ *nf* **1** delicacy; **la ~ de ses traits** his/her fine features; **un style sans ~** a coarse style; **2** sensitivity; **3** delicacy, trickiness.

délice /delis/ *nm* delight.

délicieusement /delisjøzmɑ̃/ *adv* **1** deliciously; **2** delightfully.

délicieux, -ieuse /delisjø, øz/ *adj* **1** delicious; **2** [*feeling, music*] delightful; [*joy*] exquisite.

délictueux, -euse /deliktɥø, øz/ *adj* criminal.

délié, ~e /delje/ **I** *adj* **1** [*waist*] slender; **2** [*movement*] loose; **3** [*mind*] nimble.
II *nm* upstroke.
IDIOMS **avoir la langue ~e** to have the gift of the gab○.

délier /delje/ [2] *vtr* to untie; **~ qn de** to release sb from [*promise*].
IDIOMS **~ la langue à qn** to loosen sb's tongue.

délimiter /delimite/ [1] *vtr* **1** to mark the boundary of; **2** to form the boundary of; **3** to define [*role, border*]; to define the scope of [*subject, issue*].

délinquance /delɛ̃kɑ̃s/ *nf* crime; **la ~ juvénile** juvenile delinquency.

délinquant, ~e /delɛ̃kɑ̃, ɑ̃t/ **I** *adj* delinquent.
II *nm,f* offender.

déliquescence /delikesɑ̃s/ *nf* decline.

déliquescent, ~e /delikesɑ̃, ɑ̃t/ *adj* declining.

délirant, ~e /deliʀɑ̃, ɑ̃t/ *adj* **1** [*welcome*] ecstatic; **2**○ [*scenario*] crazy○.

délire /deliʀ/ *nm* **1** (Med) delirium; **2**○ madness; **3** frenzy; **salle en ~** ecstatic audience.

délirer /deliʀe/ [1] *vi* **1** (Med) to be delirious; **2**○ to be mad.

délit /deli/ *nm* offence[GB].

délivrance /delivʀɑ̃s/ *nf* **1** (of captive) release; (of country) deliverance; **2** relief; **3** (of passport) issue; (of degree) award.

délivrer /delivʀe/ [1] *vtr* **1** to free, to liberate; **~ qn de** to relieve sb of; **2** to issue [*passport*].

déloger /delɔʒe/ [13] *vtr* **1** to evict [*tenant*]; **2** to flush out [*rebels, game*]; **3** to remove [*dust*].

déloyal, ~e, *mpl* **-aux** /delwajal, o/ *adj* [*person*] disloyal (**envers** to); [*competition*] unfair; [*method*] underhand.

delphinarium /dɛlfinaʀjɔm/ *nm* dolphinarium.

deltaplane /dɛltaplan/ *nm* **1** hang-glider; **2** hang-gliding.

déluge /delyʒ/ *nm* downpour; **~ de** flood of [*tears, complaints*]; **le Déluge** the Flood.
IDIOMS **ça remonte au ~** it goes back to the year dot or one; **après moi le ~** I don't care what happens after I'm gone.

déluré, ~e /delyʀe/ *adj* **1** smart, resourceful; **2** forward.

démagogie /demagɔʒi/ *nf* demagoguery, demagogy; **faire de la ~** to try to gain popularity.

démagogique /demagɔʒik/ *adj* demagogic.

démagogue /demagɔg/ *nmf* demagogue.

demain /dəmɛ̃/ *adv* tomorrow; **à ~!** see you tomorrow; **l'Europe de ~** the Europe of the future.
IDIOMS **~ il fera jour** tomorrow is another day; **ce n'est pas ~ la veille!** that's not going to happen in a hurry!

démancher: **se démancher** /demɑ̃ʃe/ [1] *v refl* (+ *v être*) [*tool*] to come off its handle.

demande /dəmɑ̃d/ *nf* **1** request, application, claim (**de** for); **gratuit sur (simple) ~** free on request; **~ de dommages et intérêts** claim for damages; **~ de divorce** petition for divorce; **faire une ~ de mutation** to apply for a transfer; **2** (in economics) demand; **3** application form.
■ **~ d'emploi** job application; **'~s d'emploi'** 'situations wanted'; **~ en mariage** marriage proposal.

demandé, **~e** /dəmɑ̃de/ *adj* **très ~** [*destination*] very popular; [*product*] in great demand.

demander /dəmɑ̃de/ [1] **I** *vtr* **1** to ask for [*advice, money, help*]; to apply for [*nationality*]; to claim [*damages*]; **~ le divorce** to sue for divorce; **~ en mariage** to propose to; **on demande un plombier** plumber wanted; **fais ce qu'on te demande!** do as you're told!; **il n'en demandait pas tant** he didn't expect all that; **je ne demande pas mieux** there's nothing I would like better; **2 ~ qch à qn** to ask sb sth; **il m'a demandé de tes nouvelles** he asked after you; **je ne t'ai rien demandé○!** I wasn't talking to you!; **3** to send for [*priest*]; to dial [*number*]; **le patron vous demande** the boss wants to see you; (on phone) the boss wants to speak to you; **4** to call for [*reforms, sentence*]; to require [*effort, qualification*]; to need [*attention*]; **~ à être revu** [*text*] to need revision.
II se demander *v refl* (+ *v être*) to wonder

demandeur[1], **-euse** /dəmɑ̃dœʀ, øz/ **I** *adj* **le pays est très ~ de matières premières** raw materials are very much in demand in the country.
II *nm,f* applicant.
■ **~ d'asile** asylum-seeker; **~ d'emploi** job-seeker.

demandeur[2], **-eresse** /dəmɑ̃dœʀ, d(ə)ʀɛs/ *nm,f* (Law) plaintiff.

démangeaison /demɑ̃ʒɛzɔ̃/ *nf* itch.

démanger /demɑ̃ʒe/ [13] *vtr* **ça me démange** it itches, it's itching; **l'envie de le gifler me démangeait** I was itching to slap him; **la main me démange○** I feel like hitting somebody.

démantèlement /demɑ̃tɛlmɑ̃/ *nm* dismantling (**de** of).

démanteler /demɑ̃tle/ [17] *vtr* to dismantle; to break up.

démantibuler○ /demɑ̃tibyle/ [1] *vtr* to bust○, to break up.

démaquillage /demakijaʒ/ *nm* make-up removal.

démaquillant, **~e** /demakijɑ̃, ɑ̃t/ **I** *adj* [*milk*] cleansing.
II *nm* make-up remover.

démaquiller: **se démaquiller** /demakije/ [1] *v refl* (+ *v être*) to remove one's make-up.

démarcation /demaʀkasjɔ̃/ *nf* demarcation.

démarchage /demaʀʃaʒ/ *nm* door-to-door selling; **~ électoral** canvassing; **~ téléphonique** cold calling.

démarche /demaʀʃ/ *nf* **1** walk; **2** step; **faire une ~ auprès de qn** to approach sb; **faire des ~s pour obtenir qch** to take steps to obtain sth; **3** reasoning; **~ de la pensée** thought process.

démarcher /demaʀʃe/ [1] *vtr* **1** to sell door-to-door; **2** to canvass.

démarcheur, **-euse** /demaʀʃœʀ, øz/ *nm,f* (door-to-door) salesman.

démarquer /demaʀke/ [1] **I** *vtr* **1** to mark down [*goods*]; **2** (Sport) to free [sb] from a marker.
II se démarquer *v refl* (+ *v être*) **1 se ~ de** to distance oneself from; **2** (Sport) to get free of one's marker.

démarrage /demaʀaʒ/ *nm* **1** starting up; **2** spurt.
■ **~ en côte** hill start.

démarrer /demaʀe/ [1] **I** *vtr* to start (up).
II *vi* **1** [*vehicle*] to pull away; [*engine*] to start; [*driver*] to drive off; [*business*] to start up; [*campaign*] to get under way; [*person*] to start off; **2** (Sport) to put on a spurt.

démarreur /demaʀœʀ/ *nm* (in car) starter.

démasquer /demaske/ [1] **I** *vtr* to unmask [*person*]; to uncover [*plot*].
II se démasquer *v refl* (+ *v être*) to remove one's mask; (figurative) to drop one's mask.

démêlé /demele/ *nm* wrangle; **avoir des ~s avec la justice** to get into trouble with the law.

démêler /demele/ [1] *vtr* **1** to disentangle; to untangle; **2** to sort out [*situation*].

démêloir /demelwaʀ/ *nm* wide-toothed comb.

démembrement /demɑ̃bʀəmɑ̃/ *nm* **1** break-up, dismemberment; **2** (of estate) division.

démembrer /demɑ̃bʀe/ [1] *vtr* to divide up, to dismember.

déménagement /demenaʒmɑ̃/ *nm* **1** moving house; move; **2** removal; **entreprise de ~s** removals firm (GB), moving company (US).

déménager /demenaʒe/ [13] **I** *vtr* **1** to move [*furniture*]; to relocate [*offices*]; **2** to clear [*room*].
II *vi* **1** to move (house); **2○** to push off○; **3○** to be off one's rocker○.

déménageur /demenaʒœʀ/ *nm* **1** removal (GB) or moving (US) man; **2** furniture remover (GB) or mover (US).

démence /demɑ̃s/ *nf* **1** insanity; **2** dementia.

démener: **se démener** /dem(ə)ne/ [16] *v refl* (+ *v être*) **1** to thrash about; **2** to put oneself out, to exert oneself.

dément, **~e** /demɑ̃, ɑ̃t/ *adj* **1** insane, mad; **2○** terrific○.

démenti /demɑ̃ti/ *nm* denial.

démentiel, **-ielle** /demɑ̃sjɛl/ *adj* insane.

démentir /demɑ̃tiʀ/ [30] *vtr* **1** to deny; **2** [*person*] to refute [*statement*]; [*fact*] to give the lie to [*statement*]; to contradict [*forecast*]; to belie [*appearance*].

démerder◑: **se démerder** /demɛʀde/ [1] *v refl* (+ *v être*) to manage (**pour faire** to do); **se ~ avec ses problèmes** to sort out one's own problems.

démériter /demeʀite/ [1] *vi* to prove oneself unworthy.

démesure /deməzyʀ/ *nf* **1** (of ambition) excesses; **2** excessive size.

démesuré, **~e** /deməzyʀe/ *adj* excessive, immoderate.

démesurément /deməzyʀemɑ̃/ *adv* excessively, inordinately.

démettre /demɛtʀ/ [60] **I** *vtr* **1** to dislocate [*joint*]; **2** to dismiss [*employee*].
II se démettre *v refl* (+ *v être*) **1 se ~**

l'épaule to dislocate one's shoulder; **2** to resign.

demeurant: **au demeurant** /odəmœʀɑ̃/ *phr* as it happens, for all that.

demeure /dəmœʀ/ **I** *nf* **1** residence; **2 mettre qn en ~ de faire** to require sb to do; (Law) to give sb formal notice to do.
II à demeure *phr* permanently; [*installations*] permanent.
IDIOMS **il n'y a pas péril en la ~** there's no rush.

demeuré, **~e** /dəmœʀe/ **I** *adj* retarded.
II *nm,f* simpleton.

demeurer /dəmœʀe/ [1] **I** *vi* **1** (+ *v avoir*) to reside, to live; **2** (+ *v être*) to remain.
II *v impers* **il n'en demeure pas moins que** nonetheless, the fact remains that.

demi, **~e**[1] /d(ə)mi/ **I et demi**, **et demie** *phr* and a half; **trois et ~** three and a half; **il est trois heures et ~e** it's half past three.
II *nm,f* half.
III *nm* **1** glass of beer; **2** (Sport) **~ de mêlée/d'ouverture** scrum/stand-off half.
IV à demi *phr* half; **à ~ éveillé** half awake; **à ~ satisfait** not entirely satisfied.
V demi- (*combining form*) **1** half; **une ~-pomme** half an apple; **2** partial; **une ~-victoire** a partial victory.

demi-cercle, *pl* **~s** /d(ə)misɛʀkl/ *nm* semicircle; **en ~** [*stand*] in a semicircle; [*object*] semicircular.

demi-douzaine, *pl* **~s** /d(ə)miduzɛn/ *nf* **une ~ (de)** half a dozen.

demie[2] /d(ə)mi/ **I** *adj* ▶ **demi I**.
II *nf* (in telling time) **il est déjà la ~** it's already half past.

demi-écrémé, **~e**, *mpl* **~s** /d(ə)miekʀeme/ *adj* semi-skimmed.

demi-finale, *pl* **~s** /d(ə)mifinal/ *nf* semifinal.

demi-frère, *pl* **~s** /d(ə)mifʀɛʀ/ *nm* half-brother.

demi-heure, *pl* **~s** /d(ə)mijœʀ/ *nf* half an hour.

demi-journée, *pl* **~s** /d(ə)miʒuʀne/ *nf* half a day.

démilitariser /demilitaʀize/ [1] *vtr* to demilitarize.

demi-litre, *pl* **~s** /d(ə)militʀ/ *nm* half a litre[GB].

demi-mal /d(ə)mimal/ *nm* **il n'y a que ~** it's not as bad as all that.

demi-mesure, *pl* **~s** /d(ə)mim(ə)zyʀ/ *nf* half-measure.

demi-mot: **à demi-mot** /ad(ə)mimo/ *phr* **j'ai compris à ~** I didn't need to have it spelt out.

déminer /demine/ [1] *vtr* to clear [sth] of mines.

demi-pension /d(ə)mipɑ̃sjɔ̃/ *nf* half board.

demi-pensionnaire, *pl* **~s** /d(ə)mipɑ̃sjɔnɛʀ/ *nmf* (Sch) pupil who has school lunches.

démis, **~e** /demi, iz/ **I** *pp* ▶ **démettre**.
II *pp adj* dislocated.

demi-saison, *pl* **~s** /d(ə)misɛzɔ̃/ *nf* **manteau de ~** lightweight coat.

demi-sel /d(ə)misɛl/ *adj* [*butter*] slightly salted.

demi-sœur, *pl* **~s** /d(ə)misœʀ/ *nf* half-sister.

démission /demisjɔ̃/ *nf* **1** resignation (**de** from); **2** (figurative) failure to take responsibility.

démissionnaire /demisjɔnɛʀ/ *adj* resigning.

démissionner /demisjɔne/ [1] *vi* **1** to resign (**de** from); **2** to abdicate one's responsibilities.

demi-tarif, *pl* **~s** /d(ə)mitaʀif/ **I** *adj* half-price.
II *adv* half-price.
III *nm* half-price ticket; **voyager à ~** to travel half-fare.

demi-tour, *pl* **~s** /d(ə)mituʀ/ *nm* half-turn; **faire ~** to turn back.

démobiliser /demɔbilize/ [1] *vtr* **1** to demobilize; **2** to demotivate.

démocrate /demɔkʀat/ **I** *adj* democratic.
II *nmf* democrat.

démocratie /demɔkʀasi/ *nf* democracy.

démocratique /demɔkʀatik/ *adj* democratic.

démocratiser /demɔkʀatize/ [1] **I** *vtr* to democratize.
II se démocratiser *v refl* (+ *v être*) **1** to become more democratic; **2** to become more accessible.

démodé, **~e** /demɔde/ *adj* old-fashioned.

démoder: **se démoder** /demɔde/ [1] *v refl* (+ *v être*) to go out of fashion.

démographie /demɔgʀafi/ *nf* demography.

démographique /demɔgʀafik/ *adj* demographic.

demoiselle /d(ə)mwazɛl/ *nf* **1** young lady; **2** single woman.
■ **~ de compagnie** female companion; **~ d'honneur** bridesmaid.

démolir /demɔliʀ/ [3] *vtr* **1** to demolish; to wreck; to destroy; **2**○ to tear to pieces; to beat up○; to exhaust.

démolisseur, **-euse** /demɔlisœʀ, øz/ *nm,f* **1** demolition worker; **2** demolition contractor (GB), wrecker (US).

démolition /demɔlisjɔ̃/ *nf* demolition.

démon /demɔ̃/ *nm* demon, devil; **avoir le ~ du jeu** to have a passion for gambling.
■ **~ de midi** ≈ middle-age lust.

démoniaque /demɔnjak/ *adj* demonic.

démonstrateur, **-trice** /demɔ̃stʀatœʀ, tʀis/ *nm,f* (for products) demonstrator.

démonstratif, **-ive** /demɔ̃stʀatif, iv/ *adj* demonstrative.

démonstration /demɔ̃stʀasjɔ̃/ *nf* **1** display; **~ de courage** display of courage; **~s d'amitié** a show of friendship; **2** demonstration; **faire la ~ d'un appareil** to demonstrate an appliance; **3** (of theory) demonstration, proof.

démontable /demɔ̃tabl/ *adj* [*furniture*] that can be taken apart.

démonté, **~e** /demɔ̃te/ *adj* [*sea*] stormy.

démonte-pneu, *pl* **~s** /demɔ̃t(ə)pnø/ *nm* tyre-lever (GB), tire iron (US).

démonter /demɔ̃te/ [1] **I** *vtr* **1** to dismantle, to take [sth] to pieces [*machine*]; to remove [*wheel*]; to take off [*door*]; **2**° to fluster; **ne pas se laisser ~** to remain unruffled.

II se démonter *v refl* (+ *v être*) **1** [*furniture*] to come apart; **2**° [*person*] to become flustered.

démontrer /demɔ̃tʀe/ [1] *vtr* to demonstrate, to prove; **~ qch par a plus b** to prove sth conclusively.

démoralisant, **~e** /demɔʀalizɑ̃, ɑ̃t/ *adj* demoralizing.

démoraliser /demɔʀalize/ [1] **I** *vtr* to demoralize.

II se démoraliser *v refl* (+ *v être*) to get demoralized.

démordre: **démordre de** /demɔʀdʀ/ [6] *v+prep* **il n'en démord pas** he sticks by it, he's sticking to it.

démouler /demule/ [1] *vtr* to turn [sth] out of the tin (GB) or pan (US) [*cake*]; to remove [sth] from the mould (GB) or mold (US) [*statue*].

démultiplier /demyltiplije/ [2] *vtr* **1** to reduce [*speed*]; **2** to increase [*powers, capacity*].

démuni, **~e** /demyni/ *adj* **1** destitute; penniless; **~ de** devoid of, without [*talent*]; **2** out of stock.

démunir /demyniʀ/ [3] **I** *vtr* to divest (**de** of).

II se démunir *v refl* (+ *v être*) **se ~ de qch** to leave oneself without sth; **je ne veux pas me ~** I don't want to leave myself short.

démystifier /demistifje/ [2] *vtr* **1 ~ qn** to dispel sb's illusions; **2** to demystify.

démythifier /demitifje/ [2] *vtr* to demythologize.

dénaturé, **~e** /denatyʀe/ *adj* **1** [*alcohol*] denatured; **2** [*tastes*] warped; [*parents*] unnatural.

dénaturer /denatyʀe/ [1] *vtr* **1** to denature; **2** to distort [*facts*]; **3** to spoil [*taste, sauce*].

dénégation /denegasjɔ̃/ *nf* denial.

dénicher /deniʃe/ [1] *vtr* **1**° to dig out° [*object*]; to track down [*person*]; to find [*right address*]; **2** to flush out [*thief, animal*]; **3** to take [sth] from the nest.

dénier /denje/ [2] *vtr* to deny.

deniers /dənje/ *nm pl* money; **~s publics** or **de l'État** public funds.

dénigrement /denigʀəmɑ̃/ *nm* denigration.

dénigrer /denigʀe/ [1] *vtr* to denigrate.

dénivellation /denivɛlasjɔ̃/ *nf* **1** difference in level; **2** gradient.

dénombrable /denɔ̃bʀabl/ *adj* countable; **non ~** uncountable.

dénombrement /denɔ̃bʀəmɑ̃/ *nm* count.

dénombrer /denɔ̃bʀe/ [1] *vtr* to count.

dénominateur /denɔminatœʀ/ *nm* denominator.

dénomination /denɔminasjɔ̃/ *nf* name, designation.

dénommer /denɔme/ [1] *vtr* to name.

dénoncer /denɔ̃se/ [12] **I** *vtr* to denounce.

II se dénoncer *v refl* (+ *v être*) to give oneself up.

dénonciation /denɔ̃sjasjɔ̃/ *nf* denunciation.

dénoter /denɔte/ [1] *vtr* denote.

dénouement /denumɑ̃/ *nm* **1** denouement; **2** outcome.

dénouer /denwe/ [1] **I** *vtr* **1** to undo [*knot*]; **2** to unravel [*intrigue*]; to resolve [*crisis*].

II se dénouer *v refl* (+ *v être*) **1** [*laces*] to come undone; **2** [*crisis*] to resolve itself.

dénoyauter /denwajote/ [1] *vtr* to stone (GB), to pit (US).

dénoyauteuse /denwajotøz/ *nf* fruit-stoner (GB), fruit-pitter (US).

denrée /dɑ̃ʀe/ *nf* **1** foodstuff; **~ de base** staple; **2** commodity.

dense /dɑ̃s/ *adj* dense; concentrated; heavy.

densité /dɑ̃site/ *nf* **1** density; **à forte ~** [*area*] densely populated; **2** denseness.

dent /dɑ̃/ *nf* **1** tooth; **à pleines** or **belles ~s** with relish; **rire de toutes ses ~s** to laugh heartily; **ne rien avoir à se mettre sous la ~** to have nothing to eat; **2** (of comb) tooth; (of fork) prong; (of stamp) serration; **en ~s de scie** [*blade*] serrated; [*results*] which go up and down; **3** crag.

■ **~ de lait** milk tooth; **~ de sagesse** wisdom tooth.

IDIOMS **avoir une ~ contre qn** to bear sb a grudge; **avoir les ~s longues** to be ambitious.

dentaire /dɑ̃tɛʀ/ *adj* dental; **faire ~**° or **des études ~s** to study to be a dentist.

denté, **~e** /dɑ̃te/ *adj* **1** toothed; **2** dentate.

dentelé, **~e** /dɑ̃t(ə)le/ *adj* [*coast*] indented; [*crest*] jagged; [*stamp*] perforated; [*leaf*] dentate.

dentelle /dɑ̃tɛl/ *nf* lace.

IDIOMS **il ne fait pas dans la ~** he's not one to bother with niceties.

dentellière /dɑ̃təljɛʀ/ *nf* lacemaker.

dentelure /dɑ̃tlyʀ/ *nf* (of stamp) perforation; (of crest) jagged outline; (of leaf) serration.

dentier /dɑ̃tje/ *nm* dentures.

dentifrice /dɑ̃tifʀis/ *nm* toothpaste.

dentiste /dɑ̃tist/ *nmf* dentist.

dentition /dɑ̃tisjɔ̃/ *nf* dentition.

dénuder /denyde/ [1] **I** *vtr* to strip.

II se dénuder *v refl* (+ *v être*) **1** to strip (off); **2** to become bare.

dénué, **~e** /denɥe/ *adj* **~ de** lacking in; **~ de sens** senseless; **~ de fondement** groundless.

dénuement /denymɑ̃/ *nm* **1** destitution; **2** bareness.

déodorant, **~e** /deodɔʀɑ̃, ɑ̃t/ **I** *adj* deodorant.

II *nm* deodorant.

déontologie /deɔ̃tɔlɔʒi/ *nf* (professional) ethics.

déontologique /deɔ̃tɔlɔʒik/ *adj* [*code*] of ethics.

dépannage /depanaʒ/ *nm* repair.

dépanner /depane/ [1] *vtr* **1** to fix [*car, machine*]; to fix the car of [*driver*]; **2** to tow away; **3**° to help [sb] out.

dépanneur, **-euse**[1] /depanœʀ, øz/ *nm,f* engineer.

dépanneuse[2] /depanøz/ *nf* breakdown truck (GB), tow truck (US).

dépareillé, **~e** /depaʀeje/ *adj* **1** odd; **articles ~s** oddments; **2** incomplete.

déparer /depaʀe/ [1] *vtr* to spoil, to mar.

départ /depaʀ/ *nm* **1** departure; **~ des grandes lignes** (platforms for) main line departures; **téléphone avant ton ~** phone before you leave; **vols quotidiens au ~ de Nice** daily flights from Nice; **être sur le ~** to be about to leave; **il n'y a qu'un ~ du courrier par jour** the post (GB) or mail (US) only goes once a day; **2** resignation; **le ~ en retraite** retirement; **3** (Sport) start; **donner le (signal du) ~ aux coureurs** to start the race; **prendre un nouveau ~** (figurative) to make a fresh start; **4** start; **au ~** at first; at the outset; **de ~** initial; [*language*] source; [*salary*] starting.

départager /depaʀtaʒe/ [13] *vtr* to decide between [*competitors*].

département /depaʀtəmɑ̃/ *nm* department.

départemental, **~e**, *mpl* **-aux** /depaʀtəmɑ̃tal, o/ *adj* [*election*] local, regional; [*road*] secondary.

départir: **se départir** /depaʀtiʀ/ [30] *v refl* (+ *v être*) **se ~ de** to lose [*calm, smile*]; to swerve from [*opinion*]; to abandon [*reserve*]; to break [*silence*].

dépassé, **~e** /depɑse/ *adj* **1** outdated, outmoded; **2**○ overwhelmed.

dépassement /depɑsmɑ̃/ *nm* **1** overtaking (GB), passing (US); **2** exceeding; excess.

dépasser /depɑse/ [1] **I** *vtr* **1** to overtake (GB), to pass (US) [*car, pedestrian*]; to go past [*place*]; to spread beyond [*borders*]; **2** to exceed [*figure, dose, limit, expectations*]; **elle le dépasse de cinq centimètres** she's five centimetres[GB] taller than him; **~ qch en hauteur** to be taller than sth; **il a dépassé la cinquantaine** he's over or past fifty; **~ la mesure** or **les bornes** or **les limites** to go too far; **3** to be ahead of, to outstrip [*rival*]; **~ qn en bêtise** to surpass sb in stupidity; **ça me dépasse!** it's beyond me!
II *vi* to jut or stick out; [*underskirt*] to show.

dépatouiller○: **se dépatouiller** /depatuje/ [1] *v refl* (+ *v être*) to get by; **se ~ de** to pull oneself out of [*situation*].

dépaysement /depeizmɑ̃/ *nm* **1** change of scenery; **2** disorientation.

dépayser /depeize/ [1] *vtr* **1** to provide [sb] with a pleasant change of scenery; **2** to disorient.

dépecer /dep(ə)se/ [16] *vtr* to tear apart, to cut up.

dépêche /depɛʃ/ *nf* dispatch.

dépêcher /depeʃe/ [16] **I** *vtr* to dispatch (**à** to).
II se dépêcher *v refl* (+ *v être*) to hurry up.

dépeigné, **~e** /depeɲe/ *adj* dishevelled[GB].

dépeindre /depɛ̃dʀ/ [55] *vtr* to depict (**comme** as).

dépénaliser /depenalize/ [1] *vtr* to decriminalize.

dépendance /depɑ̃dɑ̃s/ *nf* **1** dependence, dependency; **maintenir qn dans la ~** to keep sb dependent; **2** outbuilding; **3** dependency, dependent territory.

dépendant, **~e** /depɑ̃dɑ̃, ɑ̃t/ *adj* dependent (**de** on); **~s l'un de l'autre** interdependent; **une personne âgée ~e** an elderly dependant.

dépendre /depɑ̃dʀ/ [6] **I** *vtr* to take down [*painting*].
II dépendre de *v+prep* **1** to depend on; **2** to be dependent on; **3** [*organization*] to come under the control of; [*employee*] to be responsible to; **4** [*environment*] to be the responsibility of; **5** [*territory*] to be a dependency of; **6** [*building, land*] to belong to.

dépens /depɑ̃/ *nm pl* **1 aux ~ de** at the expense of; **2 vivre aux ~ des autres** to live off other people.

dépense /depɑ̃s/ *nf* **1** spending, expenditure; **regarder à la ~** to watch one's spending; **~s publiques** public expenditure; **2** expense; **réduire ses ~s** to cut down on expenses; **3** outlay; **une ~ de 300 francs** an outlay of 300 francs; **4** consumption; **~ d'énergie physique** expenditure of physical energy.

dépenser /depɑ̃se/ [1] **I** *vtr* to spend [*money, time*]; to use up [*energy, fuel*].
II se dépenser *v refl* (+ *v être*) **1** to get (enough) exercise; **2 se ~ pour faire** to put a lot of energy into doing.

dépensier, **-ière** /depɑ̃sje, ɛʀ/ *adj* extravagant.

déperdition /depɛʀdisjɔ̃/ *nf* loss; **~ de chaleur** heat loss.

dépérir /depeʀiʀ/ [3] *vi* [*person*] to waste away; [*plant*] to wilt; [*economy*] to be on the decline.

dépérissement /depeʀismɑ̃/ *nm* deterioration; wilting; decline.

dépersonnaliser /depɛʀsɔnalize/ [1] *vtr* to depersonalize.

dépêtrer: **se dépêtrer** /depetʀe/ [1] *v refl* (+ *v être*) **se ~ de** to extricate oneself from.

dépeuplement /depœpləmɑ̃/ *nm* depopulation.

dépeupler /depœple/ [1] *vtr* to depopulate [*region*]; to empty [*streets*]; to reduce the wildlife in [*forest, river*].

déphasé, **~e** /defɑze/ *adj* **1**○ out of step; **2** out of phase.

dépilation /depilasjɔ̃/ *nf* hair removal, depilation.

dépilatoire /depilatwaʀ/ *adj* depilatory, hair-removing.

dépistable /depistabl/ *adj* detectable.

dépistage /depistaʒ/ *nm* screening (**de** for); **test de ~ du sida** Aids test; **~ précoce** early detection.

dépister /depiste/ [1] *vtr* **1** to track down [*criminal, game*]; **2** to detect [*illness*].

dépit /depi/ **I** *nm* pique; **par ~** out of pique.
II en dépit de *phr* in spite of; **en ~ du bon sens** in a very illogical way.

dépité, **~e** /depite/ *adj* piqued (**de** at).

déplacé, **~e** /deplase/ *adj* inappropriate; **c'est ~** it's out of place; it's uncalled for.

déplacement /deplasmɑ̃/ *nm* **1** trip; **ça vaut le ~!** it's worth the trip!; **frais de ~** travelling[GB] expenses; **2** moving; shifting; transfer (**vers** to); **3** displacement.
■ **~ de vertèbre** slipped disc.

déplacer /deplase/ [12] **I** *vtr* to move [*object, person*]; to displace [*population*]; to shift [*attention*]; to change [*issue*]; to shift the emphasis of [*discussion*].
II se déplacer *v refl* (+ *v être*) **1** to move; **se ~ une vertèbre** to slip a disc; **2** to get about; to travel; **se ~ avec difficulté** to have difficulty getting about; **3** [*doctor*] to go out on call.

déplaire /deplɛʀ/ [59] **I** *vi* **1 le spectacle a déplu** the show was not well received; **2 elle déplaît** she is not liked.
II déplaire à *v+prep* **cela m'a déplu** I didn't like it; **la situation n'est pas pour me ~** the situation quite suits me.
III *v impers* **il me déplairait de vous voir partir** (formal) I should be sorry to see you go; **ne vous en déplaise** (ironic) whether you like it or not.

déplaisant, ~e /deplɛzɑ̃, ɑ̃t/ *adj* unpleasant, disagreeable.

déplâtrer /deplɑtʀe/ [1] *vtr* to remove the cast from [*limb*].

dépliant /deplijɑ̃/ *nm* **1** leaflet; **2** fold-out page.

déplier /deplije/ [2] *vtr* to unfold [*newspaper*]; to open out [*map*].

déploiement /deplwamɑ̃/ *nm* **1** display; array; **2** deployment.

déplorable /deplɔʀabl/ *adj* **1** regrettable; **2** appalling, deplorable.

déplorer /deplɔʀe/ [1] *vtr* to deplore.

déployer /deplwaje/ [23] **I** *vtr* **1** to display [*talent, wealth*]; to expend [*energy*]; **2** to deploy [*troops*]; **3** to spread [*wings*]; to unfurl [*sail*].
II se déployer *v refl* (+ *v être*) [*police*] to fan out.

déplumer: **se déplumer** /deplyme/ [1] *v refl* (+ *v être*) [*bird*] to lose its feathers.

dépoli, ~e /depɔli/ *adj* **verre ~** frosted glass.

dépolitiser /depɔlitize/ [1] *vtr* to depoliticize.

dépolluer /depɔlɥe/ [1] *vtr* to rid [sth] of pollution, to clean up.

dépollution /depɔlysjɔ̃/ *nf* cleanup.

dépopulation /depɔpylasjɔ̃/ *nf* depopulation.

déportation /depɔʀtasjɔ̃/ *nf* **1** internment in a concentration camp; **2** deportation, transportation.

déporté, ~e /depɔʀte/ *nm,f* **1** prisoner interned in a concentration camp; **2** transported convict.

déporter /depɔʀte/ [1] **I** *vtr* **1** to send [sb] to a concentration camp; **2** to deport; **3** to make [sth] swerve [*vehicle*].
II se déporter *v refl* (+ *v être*) to swerve.

déposant, ~e /depozɑ̃, ɑ̃t/ *nm,f* **1** depositor; **2** (Law) deponent.

déposer /depoze/ [1] **I** *vtr* **1** to dump [*rubbish*]; to lay [*wreath*]; to drop off, to leave [*parcel, passenger*]; to deposit [*money*]; **~ les armes** to lay down one's arms; **2** to register [*trademark*]; to submit [*file, offer*]; to lodge [*complaint*]; **~ son bilan** to file a bankruptcy petition; **3** [*river*] to deposit [*alluvium*]; **4** to depose [*sovereign*].
II *vi* **1** (Law) to make a statement, to testify; **2** [*wine*] to leave a sediment.
III se déposer *v refl* (+ *v être*) [*dust*] to settle; [*deposit*] to collect.

dépositaire /depozitɛʀ/ *nmf* **1** agent; **~ agréé** authorized dealer; **2** trustee; **3** (of secret) guardian.
■ **~ de journaux** newsagent (GB), newsdealer (US).

déposition /depozisjɔ̃/ *nf* (Law) statement; deposition; evidence.

déposséder /depɔsede/ [14] *vtr* to dispossess.

dépossession /depɔsɛsjɔ̃/ *nf* dispossession.

dépôt /depo/ *nm* **1** warehouse; depot; **2** outlet; **l'épicerie fait ~ de pain** the grocer's sells bread; **3** (of trademark) registration; (of bill) introduction; **4 date limite de ~ des déclarations d'impôt** deadline for income tax returns; **5** deposit; **6** police cells.
■ **~ de bilan** voluntary liquidation; **~ de munitions** munitions store; **~ d'ordures** (rubbish) tip or dump (GB), garbage dump (US).

dépotoir /depɔtwaʀ/ *nm* **1** dump; **2**° shambles°.

dépôt-vente, *pl* **dépôts-ventes** /depovɑ̃t/ *nm* secondhand shop (GB) or store (*where goods are sold on commission*).

dépouille /depuj/ *nf* **1** skin, hide; **2** body; **~ mortelle** mortal remains; **3 ~s** spoils.

dépouillé, ~e /depuje/ *adj* **1** [*style*] spare; **2** [*tree*] bare.

dépouillement /depujmɑ̃/ *nm* **1** (of votes) counting, count; (of mail) going through; **2** asceticism; **3** (of style) sobriety.

dépouiller /depuje/ [1] **I** *vtr* **1** to skin [*animal*]; **2** to lay [sth] bare [*region*]; **3** to rob; **~ qn de ses biens** to strip sb of his/her possessions; **4** to count [*votes*]; to go through [*mail*].
II se dépouiller *v refl* (+ *v être*) **1 se ~ de** to shed [*clothes*]; to divest oneself of [*possessions*]; (figurative) to cast off [*arrogance*]; **2** [*tree*] to shed its leaves; [*style*] to become spare.

dépourvu, ~e /depuʀvy/ **I** *adj* **~ de** devoid of [*interest, charm*]; without [*heating*].
II *nm* **prendre qn au ~** to take sb by surprise.

dépoussiérer /depusjeʀe/ [14] *vtr* to dust; (figrative) to revamp.

dépravation /depʀavasjɔ̃/ *nf* depravity.

dépraver /depʀave/ [1] *vtr* to deprave.

dépréciation /depʀesjasjɔ̃/ *nf* depreciation.

déprécier /depʀesje/ [2] *vtr* **1** to depreciate; **2** to disparage, to depreciate.

déprédations /depʀedasjɔ̃/ *nf pl* damage; **commettre des ~s** to cause damage.

dépressif, -ive /depʀesif, iv/ *adj, nm,f* depressive.

dépression /depʀesjɔ̃/ *nf* depression; **~ nerveuse** nervous breakdown.

dépressurisation /depʀesyʀizasjɔ̃/ *nf* **1** depressurization; **2** loss of pressure.

déprimant, ~e /depʀimɑ̃, ɑ̃t/ *adj* depressing.

déprime° /depʀim/ *nf* depression; **faire de la ~** to get depressed.

déprimer /depʀime/ [1] **I** *vtr* to depress.
II° *vi* to be depressed.

déprogrammer /depʀɔgʀame/ [1] *vtr* to cancel.

depuis /dəpɥi/ **I** *adv* since; **~ je n'ai plus de nouvelles** since then I haven't had any news.
II *prep* **1** since; **elle fait de la danse ~ l'âge de 6 ans** she has been dancing since she was 6 years old; **~ quand vis-tu là-bas?** how long have you been living there?; **~ le début jusqu'à la fin** from start to finish; **2** for; **~ dix ans** for ten years; **il pleut ~ trois jours** it's been raining for three days; **~ quand?** how long?; **~ longtemps** for a long time; **je le savais ~ longtemps** I had known for a long time; **~ peu** recently; **~ toujours** always; **3** from; **~ ma fenêtre** from my window **~ le premier jusqu'au dernier** from first to last.
III depuis que *phr* since, ever since; **il pleut ~ que nous sommes arrivés** it's been raining ever since we arrived.

députation /depytasjɔ̃/ *nf* deputation.

député /depyte/ *nm* **1** (in politics) deputy; (in GB) member of Parliament; **2** representative, delegate.

député-maire, *pl* **députés-maires** /depytemɛʀ/ *nm* deputy and mayor.

députer /depyte/ [1] *vtr* to send as a representative; **~ qn pour faire** to delegate sb to do.

déracinement /deʀasinmɑ̃/ *nm* **1** uprooting; **2** rootlessness.

déraciner /deʀasine/ [1] *vtr* **1** to uproot; **2** to eradicate [*prejudice*].

déraillement /deʀɑjmɑ̃/ *nm* derailment.

dérailler /deʀɑje/ [1] *vi* **1** to be derailed; **faire ~ un train** to derail a train; **2**° to lose one's marbles°; to talk through one's hat°.

dérailleur /deʀɑjœʀ/ *nm* derailleur.

déraisonnable /deʀɛzɔnabl/ *adj* unreasonable.

déraisonner /deʀɛzɔne/ [1] *vi* to talk nonsense.

dérangé, ~e /deʀɑ̃ʒe/ *adj* **1** upset; **2**° deranged.

dérangeant, ~e /deʀɑ̃ʒɑ̃, ɑ̃t/ *adj* disturbing.

dérangement /deʀɑ̃ʒmɑ̃/ *nm* **1** trouble, inconvenience; **2 ~ intestinal** stomach upset; **3 être en ~** [*lift, phone*] to be out of order.

déranger /deʀɑ̃ʒe/ [13] **I** *vtr* to disturb [*person*]; to upset [*routine, plans*]; to affect [*mind*]; **excusez-moi de vous ~** (I'm) sorry to bother you; **est-ce que la fumée vous dérange?** do you mind if I smoke?; **et alors, ça te dérange que je sorte?** so, what's it to you if I go out?
II se déranger *v refl* (+ *v être*) **1** to go out, to come out; **je me suis dérangé pour rien, c'était fermé** I wasted my time going there, it was shut; **2** to get up; to move; **3** to put oneself out.

dérapage /deʀapaʒ/ *nm* **1** skid; **2** blunder; **3** loss of control.

déraper /deʀape/ [1] *vi* **1** [*prices, discussion*] to get out of control; **2** [*knife*] to slip; **3** to skid; **4** [*skier*] to sideslip.

dératisation /deʀatizasjɔ̃/ *nf* pest control (*for rats*).

derechef /dəʀəʃɛf/ *adv* (formal) once again.

déréglé, ~e /deʀegle/ *adj* [*mind*] unbalanced; [*life*] irregular; [*mechanism*] out, disturbed; **avoir le sommeil ~** to have a disrupted sleep pattern.

dérèglement /deʀɛgləmɑ̃/ *nm* **1** (in machine) fault; **2** disorder.

déréglementer /deʀegləmɑ̃te/ [1] *vtr* to deregulate.

dérégler /deʀegle/ [14] *vtr* to affect [*weather, organ*]; to upset [*process, mechanism*]; **~ la radio** to lose the station on the radio; **~ la télévision** to lose the channel on the TV; **~ le réveil** to set the alarm clock wrong.

dérider /deʀide/ [1] **I** *vtr* to cheer [sb] up.
II se dérider *v refl* (+ *v être*) to start smiling.

dérision /deʀizjɔ̃/ *nf* scorn, derision; **tourner qn/qch en ~** to ridicule sb/sth.

dérisoire /deʀizwaʀ/ *adj* pathetic; trivial, derisory.

dérivatif, -ive /deʀivatif, iv/ **I** *adj* derivative.
II *nm* **1** diversion (**à** from); **2** (Med) derivative.

dérivation /deʀivasjɔ̃/ *nf* diversion (GB), detour.

dérive /deʀiv/ *nf* drift; **à la ~** adrift.

dérivé, ~e /deʀive/ *nm* by-product; **~s du pétrole** petroleum by-products.

dériver /deʀive/ [1] **I dériver de** *v+prep* **1** to stem from; **2** to be derived from.
II *vi* to drift.

dériveur /deʀivœʀ/ *nm* **1** (sailing) dinghy; **2** (in fishing) drifter.

dermatologie /dɛʀmatɔlɔʒi/ *nf* dermatology.

derme /dɛʀm/ *nm* dermis.

dernier, -ière[1] /dɛʀnje, ɛʀ/ **I** *adj* **1** last; [*floor, shelf*] top; **je les veux jeudi ~ délai** I want them by Thursday at the latest; **2** latest; **les dernières nouvelles** the latest news; **ces ~ temps** recently; **3 c'est de la dernière impolitesse** it's the height of rudeness; **du ~ ridicule** utterly ridiculous; **c'était la dernière chose à faire** it was the worst possible thing to do; **le ~ choix** the poorest quality.
II *nmf* last; **arriver le ~** to arrive last; **c'est le ~ qui me reste** it's my last one; **c'est bien le ~ de mes soucis** that is the least of my worries; **être le ~ de la classe** to be bottom of the class; **le petit ~** the youngest child; **ce ~** the latter; **dans ce ~ cas** in the latter case; **le ~ des imbéciles sait cela** any fool knows that; **le ~ des ~s** the lowest of the low.
III en dernier *phr* last; **j'irai chez eux en ~** I'll go to them last.
■ **~ cri** latest fashion; **dernière demeure**

final resting place; **dernières volontés** last requests.

dernière[2] /dɛʀnjɛʀ/ *nf* **1 la ~** the latest; **2** last performance.

dernièrement /dɛʀnjɛʀmɑ̃/ *adv* recently, lately.

dernier-né, **dernière-née**, *mpl* **derniers-nés** /dɛʀnjene, dɛʀnjɛʀne/ *nm,f* **1** youngest (child); **2** latest model.

dérobade /deʀɔbad/ *nf* evasion.

dérobé, **~e** /deʀɔbe/ I *adj* [*door, stairs*] concealed.

II **à la dérobée** *phr* furtively.

dérober /deʀɔbe/ [1] I *vtr* (literary) **1** to steal; **2** to hide.

II **se dérober** *v refl* (+ *v être*) **1** to be evasive; **2** to shirk responsibility; **3 se ~ à** to shirk [*duty*]; to evade [*question*]; **4** [*ground, knees*] to give way.

dérogation /deʀɔgasjɔ̃/ *nf* **1** (special) dispensation; **2** infringement (**à** of).

déroger: **déroger à** /deʀɔʒe/ [13] *v+prep* to infringe [*law, right*]; to depart from [*principles, policy*]; to ignore [*obligation*]; to break with [*tradition*].

dérouiller○ /deʀuje/ [1] *vi* to get a beating.

déroulement /deʀulmɑ̃/ *nm* **1 le ~ des événements** the sequence of events; **veiller au bon ~ de** to make sure [sth] goes smoothly; **~ de carrière** career development; **le ~ de l'intrigue** the unfolding of the plot; **2** uncoiling, unwinding.

dérouler /deʀule/ [1] I *vtr* to unroll [*carpet*]; to uncoil [*rope*]; to unwind [*wire, film*].

II **se dérouler** *v refl* (+ *v être*) **1** to take place; **2** [*negotiations*] to proceed, to go; [*events, story*] to unfold.

déroutant, **~e** /deʀutɑ̃, ɑ̃t/ *adj* puzzling.

déroute /deʀut/ *nf* crushing defeat, rout; **mettre en ~** to rout, to defeat; **en ~** in disarray.

dérouter /deʀute/ [1] *vtr* **1** to puzzle; **2** to divert.

derrière[1] /dɛʀjɛʀ/ I *prep* behind; **~ les apparences** beneath the surface; **il faut toujours être ~ lui** or **~ son dos** you have to keep after him.

II *adv* behind; (of room) at the back; (in car) in the back.

derrière[2] /dɛʀjɛʀ/ *nm* **1** (of house, object) back; **de ~** [*bedroom, door*] back; **2**○ behind○, backside○.

des /de/ I *det* ▶ **un** I.

II *det* ▶ **de** (*note*).

dès /dɛ/ I *prep* from; **~ (l'âge de) huit ans** from the age of eight; **~ maintenant** straight away; **~ le départ** (right) from the start; **je vous téléphone ~ mon arrivée** I'll phone you as soon as I arrive; **~ Versailles il y a des embouteillages** there are traffic jams from Versailles onwards; **vous serez pris en charge ~ l'aéroport** you'll be taken care of as soon as you get to the airport.

II **dès que** *phr* as soon as.

III **dès lors** *phr* **1** from then on, from that time on, henceforth; **2** therefore, consequently.

IV **dès lors que** *phr* **1** once, from the moment that; **2** since.

désabusé, **~e** /dezabyze/ *adj* disillusioned; cynical.

désaccord /dezakɔʀ/ *nm* disagreement; **être en ~** to disagree (**avec** with; **sur** over).

désaccordé, **~e** /dezakɔʀde/ *adj* (Mus) out-of-tune.

désaffecté, **~e** /dezafɛkte/ *adj* disused.

désaffection /dezafɛksjɔ̃/ *nf* disaffection (**pour** with).

désagréable /dezagʀeabl/ *adj* unpleasant, disagreeable.

désagréablement /dezagʀeabləmɑ̃/ *adv* unpleasantly.

désagrégation /dezagʀegasjɔ̃/ *nf* disintegration, break-up, collapse.

désagréger: **se désagréger** /dezagʀeʒe/ [15] *v refl* (+ *v être*) to disintegrate, to collapse, to break up.

désagrément /dezagʀemɑ̃/ *nm* inconvenience.

désaltérant, **~e** /dezalteʀɑ̃, ɑ̃t/ *adj* thirst-quenching.

désaltérer /dezalteʀe/ [14] I *vtr* **~ qn** to quench sb's thirst.

II **se désaltérer** *v refl* (+ *v être*) to quench one's thirst.

désamorcer /dezamɔʀse/ [12] *vtr* to defuse [*explosive, crisis*]; to drain [*pump*].

désappointer /dezapwɛ̃te/ [1] *vtr* to disappoint.

désapprobateur, **-trice** /dezapʀɔbatœʀ, tʀis/ *adj* disapproving; **d'un air ~** disapprovingly.

désapprobation /dezapʀɔbasjɔ̃/ *nf* disapproval.

désapprouver /dezapʀuve/ [1] *vtr* to disapprove of.

désarçonner /dezaʀsɔne/ [1] *vtr* **1** to throw [*rider*]; **2** to take [sb] aback.

désargenté○, **~e** /dezaʀʒɑ̃te/ *adj* hard up○, penniless.

désarmant, **~e** /dezaʀmɑ̃, ɑ̃t/ *adj* disarming.

désarmé, **~e** /dezaʀme/ I *pp* ▶ **désarmer**.

II *pp adj* **1** [*soldier, country*] disarmed; **2** [*ship*] laid up.

désarmement /dezaʀməmɑ̃/ *nm* **1** disarmament; **2** (of ship) laying up.

désarmer /dezaʀme/ [1] I *vtr* **1** to disarm; **2** to lay up [*ship*].

II *vi* **1** to disarm; **2** [*person*] to give up the fight; [*anger*] to abate.

désarroi /dezaʀwa/ *nm* distress; confusion; **au grand ~ de** much to the distress of; **jeter qn dans le ~** to throw sb into confusion.

désarticulé, **~e** /dezaʀtikyle/ *adj* [*chair*] wrecked; [*puppet*] with broken joints.

désastre /dezastʀ/ *nm* disaster.

désastreux, **-euse** /dezastʀø, øz/ *adj* disastrous.

désavantage /dezavɑ̃taʒ/ *nm* **1** disadvantage;

se montrer à son ~ to show oneself in an unfavourable[GB] light; **2** drawback, disadvantage.

désavantager /dezavɑ̃taʒe/ [13] *vtr* to put [sb/sth] at a disadvantage, to disadvantage.

désavantageux, -euse /dezavɑ̃taʒø, øz/ *adj* unfavourable[GB], disadvantageous.

désaveu /dezavø/ *nm* **1** denial; **2** rejection.

désavouer /dezavwe/ [1] *vtr* **1** to deny; **2** to disown.

désaxé, ~e /dezakse/ I *pp* ▶ **désaxer**.
II *pp adj* deranged.
III *nm,f* deranged person.

désaxer /dezakse/ [1] *vtr* **1** to put [sth] out of true [*wheel*]; **2** to unbalance [*person*].

desceller /desele/ [1] I *vtr* to work [sth] free.
II **se desceller** *v refl* (+ *v être*) to work loose.

descendance /desɑ̃dɑ̃s/ *nf* **1** descendants; **2†** descent.

descendant, ~e /desɑ̃dɑ̃, ɑ̃t/ I *adj* [*curve*] downward; [*scale*] falling.
II *nm,f* descendant (**de** of).

descendre /desɑ̃dʀ/ [6] I *vtr* (+ *v avoir*) **1** to take [sb/sth] down (**à** to), to bring [sb/sth] down (**de** from); **2** to lower [*shelf, blind*]; to wind [sth] down [*window*]; **3** to go down, to come down; **~ la rivière en pagayant/à la nage** to paddle/to swim down the river; **4**° to bump off° [*person*]; to shoot down [*plane*]; **5**° to down [*bottle*].
II *vi* (+ *v être*) **1** to go down (**à** to), to come down (**de** from); [*night*] to fall; **tu es descendu à pied?** did you walk down?; **la route descend en pente douce/raide** the road slopes down gently/drops steeply; **2 ~ de** to step off [*step*]; to climb down from [*wall, tree*]; to get off [*train, bike, horse*]; to get out of [*car*]; **~ à la prochaine gare** to get off at the next station; **3** [*temperature, prices*] to drop, to go down; [*tide*] to go out; **4 ~ dans le Midi** to go down to the South (of France); **5 ~ dans un hôtel** to stay at a hotel; **6 ~ de** to be descended from.

descente /desɑ̃t/ *nf* **1** descent; **la ~ a pris une heure** it took an hour to come down; **faire la ~ d'une rivière en péniche** to go down a river in a barge; **2 à ma ~ du train** when I got off the train; **accueillir qn à sa ~ d'avion** to meet sb off the plane; **3 ~ de police** police raid; **la police a fait une ~ dans l'immeuble** the police raided the building; **4** (in skiing) downhill (event).
■ **~ de lit** (bedside) rug; **~ d'organe** prolapse.

descriptif, -ive /deskʀiptif, iv/ *adj* descriptive.

description /deskʀipsjɔ̃/ *nf* description; **faire une ~ de qch** to give a description of sth, to describe sth.

déségrégation /desegʀegasjɔ̃/ *nf* desegregation.

désembuer /dezɑ̃bye/ [1] *vtr* to demist (GB), to defog (US).

désemparé, ~e /dezɑ̃paʀe/ I *pp* ▶ **désemparer**.
II *pp adj* **1** distraught, at a loss; **2** [*plane, ship*] in distress.

désemparer /dezɑ̃paʀe/ [1] I *vtr* to throw [sb] into confusion.
II *vi* **sans ~** without let-up.

désemplir /dezɑ̃pliʀ/ [3] *vi* **ne pas ~** to be always full.

désenchanté, ~e /dezɑ̃ʃɑ̃te/ *adj* disillusioned, disenchanted (**de** with).

désenchantement /dezɑ̃ʃɑ̃tmɑ̃/ *nm* disillusionment, disenchantment.

désenclaver /dezɑ̃klave/ [1] *vtr* to open up [*region*].

désendettement /dezɑ̃dɛtmɑ̃/ *nm* **1** reduction of the debt; **2** rescuing from debt.

désenfler /dezɑ̃fle/ [1] *vi* to become less swollen, to go down.

désengager: **se désengager** /dezɑ̃gaʒe/ [13] *v refl* (+ *v être*) to withdraw (**de** from).

désensibiliser /desɑ̃sibilize/ [1] *vtr* to desensitize.

déséquilibre /dezekilibʀ/ *nm* **1** unsteadiness; **en ~** [*table*] unstable; [*person*] off balance; **2** imbalance; **3** derangement.

déséquilibré, ~e /dezekilibʀe/ I *pp* ▶ **déséquilibrer**.
II *pp adj* (Med) unbalanced.
III *nm,f* lunatic.

déséquilibrer /dezekilibʀe/ [1] *vtr* **1** to make [sb] lose their balance; to make [sth] unstable; **2** to destabilize [*country*]; **3** (Med) to unbalance [*person*].

désert, ~e /dezɛʀ, ɛʀt/ I *adj* **1** uninhabited; **île ~e** desert island; **2** deserted.
II *nm* desert.

déserter /dezɛʀte/ [1] *vtr, vi* to desert.

déserteur /dezɛʀtœʀ/ *nm* deserter.

désertion /dezɛʀsjɔ̃/ *nf* **1** desertion; **2** defection.

désertique /dezɛʀtik/ *adj* **1** [*climate, region*] desert; **2** barren.

désespérant, ~e /dezɛspeʀɑ̃, ɑ̃t/ *adj* [*person, situation*] hopeless; [*news*] heart-breaking; **d'une lenteur ~e** appallingly slow.

désespéré, ~e /dezɛspeʀe/ I *pp* ▶ **désespérer**.
II *pp adj* [*person*] in despair; [*situation*] hopeless; [*attempt*] desperate; **cri ~** cry of despair.
III *nm,f* desperate person.

désespérément /dezɛspeʀemɑ̃/ *adv* despairingly; desperately; hopelessly.

désespérer /dezɛspeʀe/ [14] I *vtr* to drive [sb] to despair; **il ne désespère pas qu'elle revienne un jour** he has not given up hope that she will come back one day.
II **désespérer de** *v+prep* **~ de qn** to despair of sb; **il ne désespère pas de le sauver** he hasn't given up hope of saving him.
III *vi* to despair, to lose hope; **c'est à ~** it's hopeless.
IV **se désespérer** *v refl* (+ *v être*) to despair.

désespoir /dezespwaʀ/ *nm* despair; **mettre** or

réduire qn au ~ to drive sb to despair; **en ~ de cause** in desperation.

déshabillé /dezabije/ *nm* negligee.

déshabiller /dezabije/ [1] I *vtr* to undress.
II **se déshabiller** *v refl* (+ *v être*) **1** to undress; **2** to take one's coat off.

déshabituer /dezabitɥe/ [1] *vtr* **~ qn du tabac** to get sb out of the habit of smoking.

désherbant /dezɛʀbɑ̃/ *nm* weedkiller.

désherber /dezɛʀbe/ [1] *vtr* to weed.

déshérité /dezeʀite/ I *pp* ▶ **déshériter**.
II *pp adj* underprivileged; disadvantaged; deprived.
III *nm,f* **les ~s** the underprivileged.

déshériter /dezeʀite/ [1] *vtr* to disinherit.

déshonneur /dezɔnœʀ/ *nm* disgrace.

déshonorant, **~e** /dezɔnɔʀɑ̃, ɑ̃t/ *adj* dishonourable[GB], degrading.

déshonorer /dezɔnɔʀe/ [1] I *vtr* to bring disgrace on [*family*]; to bring [sth] into disrepute [*profession*].
II **se déshonorer** *v refl* (+ *v être*) to disgrace oneself.

déshumaniser /dezymanize/ [1] *vtr* to dehumanize.

déshydratation /dezidʀatasjɔ̃/ *nf* **1** dehydration; **2** drying.

déshydrater /dezidʀate/ [1] *vtr* to dehydrate.

desiderata /dezideʀata/ *nm pl* wishes.

désignation /deziɲasjɔ̃/ *nf* designation.

désigner /deziɲe/ [1] *vtr* **1** [*word*] to designate; [*triangle, colour*] to represent; **2** to point out; **3** to choose, to designate (**comme**, **en qualité de** as); **être tout désigné pour** to be just right for.

désillusionner /dezil(l)yzjɔne/ [1] *vtr* to disillusion.

désinence /dezinɑ̃s/ *nf* ending.

désinfectant, **~e** /dezɛ̃fɛktɑ̃, ɑ̃t/ I *adj* disinfecting.
II *nm* disinfectant.

désinfecter /dezɛ̃fɛkte/ [1] *vtr* to disinfect.

désintégration /dezɛ̃tegʀasjɔ̃/ *nf* disintegration; (of rock) crumbling.

désintégrer: **se désintégrer** /dezɛ̃tegʀe/ [14] *v refl* (+ *v être*) to disintegrate.

désintéressé, **~e** /dezɛ̃teʀese/ I *pp* ▶ **désintéresser**.
II *pp adj* [*person, act*] selfless, unselfish; [*advice*] disinterested.

désintéressement /dezɛ̃teʀɛsmɑ̃/ *nm* disinterestedness.

désintéresser: **se désintéresser** /dezɛ̃teʀese/ [1] *v refl* (+ *v être*) **se ~ de** to lose interest in.

désintérêt /dezɛ̃teʀɛ/ *nm* lack of interest (**pour** in).

désintoxication /dezɛ̃tɔksikasjɔ̃/ *nf* detoxification.

désintoxiquer /dezɛ̃tɔksike/ [1] *vtr* to detoxify; **se faire ~** to undergo detoxification.

désinvolte /dezɛ̃vɔlt/ *adj* casual, offhand.

désinvolture /dezɛ̃vɔltyʀ/ *nf* casual manner; **avec ~** casually.

désir /deziʀ/ *nm* wish, desire; **vos ~s sont des ordres** your wish is my command; **prendre ses ~s pour des réalités** to delude oneself.

désirable /deziʀabl/ *adj* desirable.

désirer /deziʀe/ [1] *vtr* to want; **s'il le désire** if he wants; **effets non désirés** unwanted effects; **que désirez-vous?** what would you like? **laisser à ~** to leave something to be desired.

désireux, **-euse** /deziʀø, øz/ *adj* anxious (**de faire** to do).

désistement /dezistəmɑ̃/ *nm* withdrawal.

désister: **se désister** /deziste/ [1] *v refl* (+ *v être*) to stand down (GB), to withdraw.

désobéir /dezɔbeiʀ/ [3] *v+prep* to be disobedient; **~ à qn** to disobey sb.

désobéissance /dezɔbeisɑ̃s/ *nf* disobedience.

désobéissant, **~e** /dezɔbeisɑ̃, ɑ̃t/ *adj* disobedient.

désobligeant, **~e** /dezɔbliʒɑ̃, ɑ̃t/ *adj* discourteous.

désobliger /dezɔbliʒe/ [13] *vtr* to offend.

désodorisant, **~e** /dezɔdɔʀizɑ̃, ɑ̃t/ I *adj* deodorant.
II *nm* deodorant.

désodoriser /dezɔdɔʀize/ [1] *vtr* to freshen.

désœuvré, **~e** /dezœvʀe/ *adj* at a loose end° (GB), at loose ends° (US).

désœuvrement /dezœvʀəmɑ̃/ *nm* lack of anything to do; **par ~** for lack of anything better to do.

désolation /dezɔlasjɔ̃/ *nf* **1** grief; **2** desolation.

désolé, **~e** /dezɔle/ I *pp* ▶ **désoler**.
II *pp adj* **1** sorry; **j'en suis ~** I'm sorry about that; **2** desolate.

désoler /dezɔle/ [1] I *vtr* **1** to upset, to distress; **2** to depress; **tu me désoles!** I despair of you!
II **se désoler** *v refl* (+ *v être*) to be upset (**de qch** about).

désopilant, **~e** /dezɔpilɑ̃, ɑ̃t/ *adj* hilarious.

désordonné, **~e** /dezɔʀdɔne/ *adj* [*person*] untidy; [*thinking*] muddled; [*meeting*] disorderly; [*movements*] uncoordinated; [*behaviour, existence*] wild.

désordre /dezɔʀdʀ/ I° *adj inv* **faire ~** to look untidy or messy; **être très ~** to be very untidy.
II *nm* **1** untidiness; mess; **pièce en ~** untidy room; **quel ~!** what a mess!; **il a tout mis en ~** he made such a mess; **2** chaos; **en ~** in chaos; **semer le ~** to cause chaos; **3 dans le ~** in any order; **gagner dans le ~** (at races) to win with a combination forecast; **4** disorder; **~s sociaux** social disorder; **~s mentaux** mental disorders.

désorganisé, **~e** /dezɔʀganize/ *adj* disorganized.

désorienter /dezɔʀjɑ̃te/ [1] *vtr* **1** to disorientate[GB]; **2** to confuse, to bewilder.

désormais /dezɔʀmɛ/ *adv* **1** from now on; **2** from then on.

désosser /dezɔse/ [1] *vtr* (Culin) to bone.

despote /dɛspɔt/ *nm* despot.

despotique /dɛspɔtik/ *adj* despotic.

desquelles ▶ **lequel**.

desquels ▶ **lequel**.

dessaisir /desɛziʀ/ [3] **I** *vtr* **1 ~ qn de** to relieve sb of [*responsibility*]; **~ un juge d'un dossier** to take a judge off a case; **2 ~ qn de** to divest sb of [*property*].
II se dessaisir *v refl* (+ *v être*) **se ~ de** to relinquish.

dessaler /desale/ [1] *vtr* **1** to desalinate; **2** (Culin) to desalt.

dessécher /deseʃe/ [14] **I** *vtr* **1** to dry [sth] out; **arbre desséché** withered tree; **2** to harden [*person, heart*].
II se dessécher *v refl* (+ *v être*) [*hair, lips*] to become dry; [*vegetation*] to wither; [*ground*] to dry out.

dessein /desɛ̃/ *nm* design; intention; **à ~** deliberately; **dans le ~ de faire** with a view to doing.

desseller /desele/ [1] *vtr* to unsaddle.

desserrer /deseʀe/ [1] **I** *vtr* **1** to loosen [*belt, screw*]; to release [*brake*]; to undo [*knot*]; **2** to relax [*grip, credit*].
II se desserrer *v refl* (+ *v être*) [*screw*] to work loose; [*knot*] to come undone.
IDIOMS **il n'a pas desserré les dents** he never once opened his mouth.

dessert /desɛʀ/ *nm* dessert.

desserte /desɛʀt/ *nf* **1** (transport) service; **la ~ d'une ville par les transports en commun** public transport services to and from a city; **la ~ aérienne des Antilles** flights to and from the Antilles; **2** sideboard.

desservir /desɛʀviʀ/ [30] *vtr* **1** [*train*] to serve [*town*]; **2** to lead to [*room, floor*]; **3** to serve; **l'hôpital dessert la moitié du pays** the hospital serves half of the country.

dessin /desɛ̃/ *nm* **1** drawing; **~ industriel** technical drawing; **tu veux que je te fasse un ~○?** do I have to spell it out for you?; **2** design; **3** pattern; **4** outline.
■ **~ animé** cartoon.

dessinateur, **-trice** /desinatœʀ, tʀis/ *nm,f* **1** draughtsman (GB), draftsman (US); **2** designer.
■ **~ de bande dessinée** (strip) cartoonist; **~ humoristique** cartoonist.

dessiner /desine/ [1] **I** *vtr* **1** to draw; **2** to design [*material, decor*]; to draw up [*plans*].
II *vi* to draw.
III se dessiner *v refl* (+ *v être*) **1** [*future, possibility*] to take shape; **2 se ~ à l'horizon** to appear on the horizon; **il se dessinait nettement dans la lumière** he was clearly outlined in the light.

dessoûler /desule/ [1] *vtr* to sober up.

dessous[1] /dəsu/ **I** *adv* underneath.
II en dessous *phr* **1** underneath; **il habite juste en ~** he lives on the floor below; **2 agir en ~** to act in an underhand way; **3 la taille en ~** the next size down.
III en dessous de *phr* below; **les enfants en ~ de 13 ans** children under 13.

dessous[2] /dəsu/ **I** *nm inv* (of plate, tongue) underside; (of arm) inside (part); **le ~ du pied** the sole of the foot; **l'étagère de** or **du ~** the shelf below; the bottom shelf; **les voisins du ~** the people who live on the floor below.
II *nm pl* **1** underwear; **2** inside story.

dessous-de-plat /d(ə)sudpla/ *nm inv* **1** table mat; **2** plate stand; **3** trivet.

dessous-de-table /d(ə)sudtabl/ *nm inv* backhanders○ (GB), bribes.

dessous-de-verre /d(ə)sudvɛʀ/ *nm inv* coaster.

dessus[1] /dəsy/ *adv* on top; **un gâteau avec du chocolat ~** a cake with chocolate on top; **le prix est marqué ~** the price is on it; **passe ~** go over it; **compte ~** count on it; **'ton rapport est fini?'—'non, je travaille** or **suis ~'** 'is your report finished?'—'no, I'm working on it'.

dessus[2] /dəsy/ *nm inv* (of shoe) upper; (of table, head) top; (of hand) back; **les voisins du ~** the people who live on the floor above; **le drap de ~** the top sheet.
IDIOMS **reprendre le ~** to regain the upper hand; (after illness) to get back on one's feet.

dessus-de-lit /d(ə)sydli/ *nm inv* bedspread.

déstabiliser /destabilize/ [1] *vtr* to unsettle [*person*]; to destabilize [*country*].

destin /dɛstɛ̃/ *nm* **1** fate; **2** destiny.

destinataire /dɛstinatɛʀ/ *nmf* **1** addressee; **2** beneficiary; **3** payee.

destination /dɛstinasjɔ̃/ **I** *nf* **1** destination; **2** purpose.
II à destination de *phr* [*plane, train*] bound for.

destinée /dɛstine/ *nf* destiny.

destiner /dɛstine/ [1] **I** *vtr* **1 ~ qch à qn** to design sth for sb; **être destiné à faire** to be designed or intended to do; to be destined to do; **2 l'argent destiné à mes enfants** the money intended for my children; **la lettre ne leur était pas destinée** the letter wasn't (meant) for them.
II se destiner *v refl* (+ *v être*) **elle se destine à une carrière de juriste** she's decided on a legal career.

destituer /dɛstitɥe/ [1] *vtr* to discharge [*officer*]; to depose [*monarch*].

destitution /dɛstitysjɔ̃/ *nf* (of officer) discharge; (of politician) deposition.

destructeur, **-trice** /dɛstʀyktœʀ, tʀis/ *adj* destructive.

destruction /dɛstʀyksjɔ̃/ *nf* destruction.

désuet, **-ète** /dezɥɛ, ɛt/ *adj* [*decor, charm*] old-world, quaint; [*manner, style*] old-fashioned; [*word*] obsolete.

désunion /dezynjɔ̃/ *nf* **1** division; **2** discord.

désunir /dezyniʀ/ [3] *vtr* to divide, to break up.

détachable /detaʃabl/ *adj* detachable.

détachant /detaʃɑ̃/ *nm* stain remover.

détaché, **~e** /detaʃe/ **I** *pp* ▶ **détacher**.

II *pp adj* **1** detached, unconcerned; **2** [*teacher, diplomat*] on secondment (GB), transferred.

détachement /detaʃmɑ̃/ *nm* **1** detachment (**de** from); **2** (Mil) detachment; **3** secondment.

détacher /detaʃe/ [1] **I** *vtr* **1** to untie [sb/sth] (**de** from); **2** to unfasten; to undo; to untie; **3** to tear off [*coupon*]; to take down [*poster*]; **4** **~ qn de** to turn or drive sb away from [*person, family*]; **5** **~ les yeux** or **le regard de qch** to take one's eyes off sth; **6** to second (GB), to transfer; **7** to articulate [*word, syllable*]; to detach [*note*]; **8** to remove the stain(s) from.

II se détacher *v refl* (+ *v être*) **1** [*prisoner, animal*] to break loose; [*boat*] to come untied; **2** to come undone; **3** [*coupon, page*] to come out; [*wallpaper, poster*] to come away, to peel; **4** to grow away from [*person*]; **5** [*pattern, title*] to stand out; **6** **se ~ de** to detach oneself from; to pull away from.

détail /detaj/ *nm* **1** detail; **2** breakdown; **~ des dépenses** breakdown of expenses; **analyse de ~** detailed analysis; **un point de ~** a minor detail; **3** retail; **acheter (qch) au ~** to buy (sth) retail.

détailler /detaje/ [1] *vtr* **1** to detail; to itemize; **2** to scrutinize.

détaler° /detale/ [1] *vi* **1** [*rabbit*] to bolt; **2**° to decamp, to leave.

détartrage /detaʀtʀaʒ/ *nm* **1** (of kettle) descaling; **2** (of teeth) scaling.

détartrer /detaʀtʀe/ [1] *vtr* **1** to descale [*kettle*]; **2** to scale [*teeth*].

détaxe /detaks/ *nf* **1** tax removal; **2** tax refund; **3** export rebate.

détecter /detɛkte/ [1] *vtr* to detect.

détection /detɛksjɔ̃/ *nf* detection.

détective /detɛktiv/ *nm* detective.

déteindre /detɛ̃dʀ/ [55] *vi* **1** [*garment, material*] to fade; **2** [*colour, garment*] to run; **3** (figurative) to rub off (**sur** on).

détendre /detɑ̃dʀ/ [6] **I** *vtr* **1** to release [*spring*]; **2** to slacken [*rope, spring*]; **3** to relax [*muscle*]; to calm [*atmosphere, mind*]; **4** to entertain [*audience*].

II *vi* **1** to be relaxing; **2** to be entertaining.

III se détendre *v refl* (+ *v être*) **1** [*rope, spring*] to slacken; **2** [*person, muscle*] to relax.

détendu, **~e** /detɑ̃dy/ **I** *pp* ▸ **détendre**.

II *pp adj* **1** relaxed; **2** slack.

détenir /det(ə)niʀ/ [36] *vtr* **1** to keep [*objects*]; to hold [*power, capital, record*]; to possess [*arms*]; to have [*secret, evidence*]; **2** to detain [*suspect*].

détente /detɑ̃t/ *nf* **1** relaxation; **2** détente; **3** (on gun) trigger.

IDIOMS **être lent** or **dur à la ~**° to be slow on the uptake.

détention /detɑ̃sjɔ̃/ *nf* **1** (of passport, drugs, record) holding; (of arms, secret) possession; **2** detention; **~ préventive** or **provisoire** custody.

détenu, **~e** /detəny/ *nm,f* prisoner.

détergent, **~e** /detɛʀʒɑ̃, ɑ̃t/ **I** *adj* detergent; **produit ~** detergent.

II *nm* detergent.

détérioration /deteʀjɔʀasjɔ̃/ *nf* **1** damage (**de** to); **2** wear and tear; **3** deterioration (**de** in).

détériorer /deteʀjɔʀe/ [1] **I** *vtr* to damage.

II se détériorer *v refl* (+ *v être*) [*economy, situation, weather*] to deteriorate; [*foodstuff*] to go bad.

déterminant, **~e** /detɛʀminɑ̃, ɑ̃t/ *adj* [*role, factor*] decisive.

détermination /detɛʀminasjɔ̃/ *nf* determination.

déterminé, **~e** /detɛʀmine/ **I** *pp* ▸ **déterminer**.

II *pp adj* **1** [*person*] determined; **2** [*duration, objective*] given.

déterminer /detɛʀmine/ [1] *vtr* **1** to determine [*reason, responsibility*]; **2** to work out [*policy, terms*]; **il est mort dans des circonstances mal déterminées** the circumstances in which he died are not yet clear; **3** to determine [*attitude, decision*]; **4** **~ qn à faire** to make sb decide to do.

déterrer /deteʀe/ [1] *vtr* to dig [sb/sth] up.

détestable /detɛstabl/ *adj* [*style, weather*] appalling; [*habits*] revolting; [*person*] hateful.

détester /detɛste/ [1] *vtr* **1** to detest, to loathe [*person*]; **2** to hate; **ne pas ~ faire** not to be averse to doing.

détonateur /detɔnatœʀ/ *nm* **1** detonator; **2** (figurative) catalyst.

détonation /detɔnasjɔ̃/ *nf* detonation.

détonner /detɔne/ [1] *vi* to be out of place.

détordre /detɔʀdʀ/ [6] *vtr* to straighten [*iron bar*]; to unwind [*cable*].

détour /detuʀ/ *nm* **1** detour; **ça vaut le ~** it's worth the trip; **2** roundabout means; **3** circumlocution; **il me l'a dit sans ~s** he told me straight; **4** (in road, river) bend; **au ~ de la conversation** in the course of the conversation.

détourné, **~e** /detuʀne/ **I** *pp* ▸ **détourner**.

II *pp adj* [*reference*] oblique; [*means*] indirect.

détournement /detuʀnəmɑ̃/ *nm* **1** misappropriation; **2** hijacking; **3** (of traffic, river) diversion.

■ **~ de mineur** (Law) corruption of a minor.

détourner /detuʀne/ [1] **I** *vtr* **1** to divert [*attention*]; **~ de** to distract [sb] from [*goal*]; **2** **~ les yeux** or **le regard** or **la tête** to look away; **3** to divert [*traffic, river, flight*]; **~ la conversation** to change the subject; **4** to hijack [*plane, ship*]; to misappropriate [*funds*].

II se détourner *v refl* (+ *v être*) **1** **se ~ de** to turn away from [*friend, religion*]; **2** to look away.

détraqué°, **~e** /detʀake/ *nm,f* deranged person.

détraquer /detʀake/ [1] **I** *vtr* **1** to bust° [sth]; to make [sth] go wrong; **2**° [*medicine*] to upset [*stomach*]; to damage [*health*].

II se détraquer *v refl* (+ *v être*) [*mechanism*] to break down; [*timepiece*] to go wrong; [*weather*] to break.

détremper /detʀɑ̃pe/ [1] *vtr* to saturate [*ground*]; to soak [*garment*].

détresse /detʀɛs/ *nf* distress.

détriment: **au détriment de** /odetʀimɑ̃də/ *phr* to the detriment of.

détritus /detʀity(s)/ *nm pl* refuse, rubbish (GB), garbage (US).

détroit /detʀwɑ/ *nm* straits; **le ~ de Gibraltar** the Straits of Gibraltar.

détromper /detʀɔ̃pe/ [1] **I** *vtr* to set [sb] straight.

II se détromper *v refl* (+ *v être*) **détrompez-vous!** don't you believe it!

détrôner /detʀone/ [1] *vtr* to dethrone.

détruire /detʀɥiʀ/ [69] *vtr* to destroy.

dette /dɛt/ *nf* debt; **~ publique/extérieure** national/foreign debt; **~ de jeu** gambling debt; **avoir une ~ envers qn** to be indebted to sb.

DEUG /dœg/ *nm* (*abbr* = **diplôme d'études universitaires générales**) *university diploma taken after two years' study*.

deuil /dœj/ *nm* **1** bereavement; **2** mourning, grief; **jour de ~ national** day of national mourning; **3** mourning (clothes).

IDIOMS **faire son ~ de qch**° to kiss sth goodbye°.

deux /dø/ **I** *adj inv* **1** two; **~ fois** twice; **des ~ côtés de la rue** on either side or both sides of the street; **tous les ~ jours** every other day; **à nous ~** I'm all yours; (to enemy) it's just you and me now; **2** a few, a couple of; **l'arrêt de bus est à ~ pas** the bus stop is a stone's throw away; **3** second; **le deux mai** the second of May (GB), May second (US).

II *pron* **elles sont venues toutes les ~** they both came.

III *nm inv* two.

IDIOMS **faire ~ poids, ~ mesures** to have double standards; **un tiens vaut mieux que ~ tu l'auras** (Proverb) a bird in the hand is worth two in the bush; **en ~ temps, trois mouvements** very quickly; **en moins de ~**° very quickly; **lui et moi, ça fait ~** we're two different people; **je n'ai fait ni une ni ~** I didn't have a second's hesitation.

deuxième /døzjɛm/ **I** *adj* second; **dans un ~ temps nous étudierons**... subsequently, we will study...; **c'est à prendre au ~ degré** it is not to be taken literally.

II *nmf* second.

■ **~ classe** second class, standard class (GB); (Mil) private.

deuxièmement /døzjɛmmɑ̃/ *adv* secondly.

deux-points /døpwɛ̃/ *nm inv* colon.

deux-roues /døʀu/ *nm inv* two-wheeled vehicle.

dévaler /devale/ [1] *vtr* to hurtle down; to tear down.

dévaliser /devalize/ [1] *vtr* **1** to rob [*person, bank, safe*]; **2** to clean out° [*shop, larder*].

dévalorisation /devalɔʀizasjɔ̃/ *nf* (of currency) depreciation.

dévaloriser /devalɔʀize/ [1] **I** *vtr* **1** to depreciate; **2** to belittle.

II se dévaloriser *v refl* (+ *v être*) **1** to lose value; to lose prestige; **2** to put oneself down.

dévaluation /devalɥasjɔ̃/ *nf* devaluation.

dévaluer /devalɥe/ [1] *vtr* to devalue.

devancer /dəvɑ̃se/ [12] *vtr* **1** to be ahead of, to outstrip [*competitor*]; **2 les pompiers ont devancé la police sur les lieux de l'accident** the fire brigade got to the scene of the accident ahead of the police; **3** to anticipate [*demand, desire*]; to forestall [*attack, criticisms*]; **4 ~ l'appel** to enlist for military service before call-up.

devant[1] /dəvɑ̃/ **I** *prep* **1** in front of; **il l'a dit ~ moi** he said it in front of me; **tous les hommes sont égaux ~ la loi** all men are equal in the eyes of the law; **fuir ~ le danger** to run away from danger; **hésiter ~ le danger** to hesitate in the face of danger; **le bus est passé ~ moi sans s'arrêter** the bus went straight past me without stopping; **2** outside; **il attendait ~ la porte** he was waiting outside the door; he was waiting by the door; **3** ahead of; **la voiture ~ nous** the car ahead or in front of us; **laisser passer quelqu'un ~ (soi)** to let somebody go first; **avoir du temps ~ soi** to have plenty of time; **avoir toute la vie ~ soi** to have one's whole life ahead of one.

II *adv* **1 'où est la poste?'—'tu es juste ~'** 'where's the post office?'—'you're right in front of it'; **2 pars ~, je te rejoins** go ahead, I'll catch up with you; **3** (of hall, theatre) at the front; (in car) in the front.

devant[2] /dəvɑ̃/ *nm* front; **de ~** [*teeth, room*] front.

IDIOMS **prendre les ~s** to take the initiative.

devanture /dəvɑ̃tyʀ/ *nf* **1** (shop)front; **2** shop or store (US) window; **en ~** on display, in the window.

dévastation /devastasjɔ̃/ *nf* devastation, havoc.

dévaster /devaste/ [1] *vtr* **1** [*army*] to lay waste to; [*storm, fire*] to destroy; **2** [*burglar*] to wreck.

développement /devlɔpmɑ̃/ *nm* **1** development; **pays en voie de ~** developing nation or country; **2** (in photography) developing.

développer /devlɔpe/ [1] **I** *vtr* to develop.

II se développer *v refl* (+ *v être*) [*body, ability*] to develop; [*plant, company, town*] to grow; [*practice, habit*] to become widespread.

devenir[1] /dəvniʀ/ [36] *vi* (+ *v être*) to become; **qu'est-ce que je vais ~?** what is to become of me?; **et Paul, qu'est-ce qu'il devient?** and what is Paul up to these days?

devenir[2] /dəvniʀ/ *nm* future.

dévergonder: **se dévergonder** /devɛʀgɔ̃de/ [1] *v refl* (+ *v être*) to be going to the bad.

déverser /devɛʀse/ [1] **I** *vtr* to pour [*liquid*] **(dans** in); to drop [*bombs*] **(sur** on); to dump [*refuse, sand*] **(sur** on); to discharge [*effluent*] **(dans** into); to disgorge [*crowd*] **(dans** onto); **~ du pétrole** to dump oil; to spill oil.

II se déverser *v refl* (+ *v être*) [*river*] to flow **(dans** into); [*sewer, crowd*] to pour **(dans** into).

dévêtir /devɛtiʀ/ [33] **I** *vtr* to undress.

II se dévêtir *v refl* (+ *v être*) to get undressed.

déviation /devjasjɔ̃/ *nf* **1** diversion (GB), detour (US); **2** departure, deviation (**par rapport à** from); **3** (of compass) deviation; **4** (of light) deflection.

dévider /devide/ [1] *vtr* **1** to unwind [*thread, cable*]; **2** to pour out [*story, memories*].

dévier /devje/ [2] **I** *vtr* to deflect [*ball, trajectory*]; to divert [*traffic*].
II *vi* **1** [*bullet, ball*] to deflect; [*vehicle*] to veer off course; **2** **~ de** to deviate from [*plan*]; **3** [*tool*] to slip; **4** [*conversation*] to drift.

devin /dəvɛ̃/ *nm* soothsayer, seer; **je ne suis pas ~!** I'm not psychic○!

deviner /dəvine/ [1] *vtr* **1** to guess [*secret*]; to foresee, to tell [*future*]; **2** to sense [*danger*]; **3** to make out, to discern.

devinette /dəvinɛt/ *nf* riddle.

devis /d(ə)vi/ *nm inv* estimate, quote.

dévisager /devizaʒe/ [13] *vtr* to stare at.

devise /dəviz/ *nf* **1** currency; **2** (foreign) currency; **3** motto.

deviser /dəvize/ [1] *vi* to converse.

dévisser /devise/ [1] *vtr* to unscrew.

dévitaliser /devitalize/ [1] *vtr* to do root canal work on.

dévoiler /devwale/ [1] *vtr* **1** to unveil; **2** to reveal; to uncover.

devoir[1] /dəvwaʀ/ [44] **I** *v aux* **1** to have to; **je dois aller au travail** I've got to or I must go to work; **il a dû accepter** he had to accept; **il aurait dû partir** he should have left; **dois-je prendre un parapluie?** do I need to or should I take an umbrella?; **dussé-je en mourir** (literary) even if I die for it; **2 il a dû accepter** he must have accepted; **elle doit avoir 13 ans** she must be about 13 years old; **il devait le savoir** he must have known; **3 cela devait arriver** it was bound or it had to happen; **un incident qui devait avoir de graves conséquences** an incident which was to have serious consequences; **ils doivent arriver vers 10 heures** they're due to arrive around 10 o'clock.
II *vtr* to owe; **il me doit des excuses** he owes me an apology; **je te dois d'avoir gagné** it's thanks to you that I won.
III se devoir *v refl* (+ *v être*) **1 je me dois de le faire** it's my duty to do it; **2 les époux se doivent fidélité** spouses owe it to each other to be faithful; **3 un homme de son rang se doit d'avoir un chauffeur** a man of his standing has to have a chauffeur.
IV comme il se doit *phr* **1 agir comme il se doit** to behave in the correct way; **2 comme il se doit, elle est en retard!** as you might expect, she's late!

devoir[2] /dəvwaʀ/ *nm* **1** duty; **se faire un ~ de faire** to make it one's duty to do; **il est de mon ~ de** it's my duty to; **2** test; homework; **faire ses ~s** to do one's homework.

dévolu, ~e /devɔly/ *nm* **jeter son ~ sur** to set one's heart on [sth]; to set one's cap at [sb].

dévorant, ~e /devɔʀɑ̃, ɑ̃t/ *adj* [*hunger*] voracious; [*flames, passion*] all-consuming.

dévorer /devɔʀe/ [1] *vtr* **1** to devour [*food, book*]; **~ qn de baisers** to smother sb with kisses; **2** [*obsession*] to consume.

dévot, ~e /devo, ɔt/ **I** *adj* devout.
II *nm,f* sanctimonious person.

dévotion /devosjɔ̃/ *nf* **1** devoutness; **2** (religious) devotion (**à** to); **2** passion (**pour** for).

dévoué, ~e /devwe/ *adj* devoted (**à** to).

dévouement /devumɑ̃/ *nm* devotion.

dévouer: **se dévouer** /devwe/ [1] *v refl* (+ *v être*) **1** to devote or dedicate oneself; **2** to put oneself out.

dévoyer /devwaje/ [23] **I** *vtr* to deprave [sb], to lead [sb] astray.
II se dévoyer *v refl* (+ *v être*) to go astray.

dextérité /dɛksteʀite/ *nf* dexterity, skill.

diabète /djabɛt/ *nm* diabetes.

diabétique /djabetik/ *adj, nmf* diabetic.

diable /djɑbl/ **I** *nm* **1** devil; **avoir un mal du ~** or **de tous les ~s à faire** to have a devil or a hell○ of a job doing; **en ~** diabolically; fiendishly; **un (petit) ~** a little devil; **2** two-wheeled trolley (GB), hand truck (US).
II *excl* gosh! (GB), my God!; **pourquoi/comment ~** why/how on earth.
IDIOMS **habiter au ~** or **à tous les ~s** to live miles from anywhere; **que le ~ t'emporte!** to hell with you!; **ce n'est pas le ~!** it's not that difficult!; **ce serait tenter le ~** that would be asking for it; **avoir le ~ au corps** to be like someone possessed; **tirer le ~ par la queue** to live from hand to mouth.

diablement /djɑbləmɑ̃/ *adv* terrifically, fiendishly.

diabolique /djabɔlik/ *adj* **1** diabolic; [*system, invention*] fiendish; **2** [*person*] demonic; [*scheme, smile*] devilish; **3** [*precision, skill*] uncanny.

diaboliquement /djabɔlikmɑ̃/ *adv* fiendishly, diabolically.

diabolo /djabɔlo/ *nm* **1** (Games) diabolo; **2 ~ menthe** mint cordial and lemonade (GB) or soda (US).

diadème /djadɛm/ *nm* **1** tiara; **2** diadem.

diagnostic /djagnɔstik/ *nm* (gen, Med) diagnosis.

diagnostique /djagnɔstik/ *adj* diagnostic.

diagnostiquer /djagnɔstike/ [1] *vtr* to diagnose.

diagonal, ~e[1], *mpl* **-aux** /djagɔnal, o/ *adj* diagonal.

diagonale[2] /djagɔnal/ *nf* diagonal; **lire qch en ~** to skim through sth.

diagramme /djagʀam/ *nm* graph.

dialecte /djalɛkt/ *nm* dialect.

dialogue /djalɔg/ *nm* dialogue[GB].

dialoguer /djalɔge/ [1] *vi* to have talks.

dialoguiste /djalɔgist/ *nmf* screenwriter, dialogist.

dialyse /djaliz/ *nf* dialysis.

diamant /djamɑ̃/ *nm* diamond; **~ de vitrier** glazier's diamond.

diamantaire /djamɑ̃tɛʀ/ *nm* **1** diamond cutter; **2** diamond merchant.

diamétralement /djametʀalmɑ̃/ *adv* diametrically.

diamètre /djamɛtʀ/ *nm* diameter.

diapason /djapazɔ̃/ *nm* **1** (note) diapason; **2** tuning fork.
IDIOMS **se mettre au ~** to fall in step; **être au ~** to be in tune.

diaphane /djafan/ *adj* (literary) diaphanous.

diaphragme /djafʀagm/ *nm* diaphragm.

diapo○ /djapo/ *nf* slide.

diaporama /djapoʀama/ *nm* slide show.

diapositive /djapozitiv/ *nf* slide, transparency.

diarrhée /djaʀe/ *nf* diarrhoea.

diatribe /djatʀib/ *nf* diatribe.

dichotomie /dikɔtɔmi/ *nf* dichotomy.

dico○ /diko/ *nm* dictionary.

dictateur /diktatœʀ/ *nm* dictator.

dictature /diktatyʀ/ *nf* dictatorship.

dictée /dikte/ *nf* dictation.

dicter /dikte/ [1] *vtr* **1** to dictate (**à qn** to sb); **2** to motivate.

diction /diksjɔ̃/ *nf* (gen) diction; (in cinema, theatre) elocution.

dictionnaire /diksjɔnɛʀ/ *nm* dictionary; **~ analogique** ≈ thesaurus.

dicton /diktɔ̃/ *nm* saying.

didacticiel /didaktisjɛl/ *nm* educational software program.

didactique /didaktik/ *adj* **1** [*work, tone*] didactic; **2** [*term, language*] technical, specialist.

dièse /djɛz/ *adj, nm* sharp; **do ~** C sharp.

diesel /djezɛl/ *nm* diesel.

diète /djɛt/ *nf* **1** (Med) light diet; **2** (political assembly) diet.

diététicien, **-ienne** /djetetisjɛ̃, ɛn/ *nm,f* dietitian.

diététique /djetetik/ **I** *adj* dietary.
II *nf* dietetics; **magasin de ~** health food shop (GB) or store (US).

dieu, *pl* **~x** /djø/ *nm* **1** god; **2 sur le terrain c'est un ~** he's brilliant on the sports field.
IDIOMS **être beau comme un ~** to look like a Greek god; **nager comme un ~** to be a superb swimmer; **être dans le secret des ~x** to be privy to the secrets of those on high.

Dieu /djø/ *nm* God; **~ soit loué** or **béni!** thanks be to God!; **c'est pas ~ possible**○**!** good God, it's not possible!
IDIOMS **se prendre pour ~ le père** to think one is God Almighty; **chaque jour que ~ fait** day in, day out; **il vaut mieux s'adresser à ~ qu'à ses saints** (Proverb) always go straight to the top; **c'est la maison du bon ~ ici!** it's open house here!

diffamation /difamasjɔ̃/ *nf* slander; (Law) libel.

diffamatoire /difamatwaʀ/ *adj* (gen) slanderous, defamatory; (Law) libellous[GB]; **écrit ~** libel.

diffamer /difame/ [1] *vtr* (gen) to slander, to defame; (Law) to libel.

différé, **~e** /difeʀe/ **I** *pp* ▸ **différer**.
II *pp adj* **1** postponed; **2** [*payment*] deferred; **3** [*programme*] pre-recorded.
III *nm* recording; **match en ~** recording of the match.

différemment /difeʀamɑ̃/ *adv* differently.

différence /difeʀɑ̃s/ *nf* difference; **à une ~ près** with one difference; **à la ~ de** unlike; **à la ~ que, à cette ~ que** with the difference that; **le droit à la ~** the right to be different.

différenciation /difeʀɑ̃sjasjɔ̃/ *nf* differentiation.

différencier /difeʀɑ̃sje/ [2] **I** *vtr* **1** to differentiate; **rien ne les différencie** there's no way of telling them apart; **2** to make [sb/sth] different.
II se différencier *v refl* (+ *v être*) **1** [*person, organization*] to differentiate oneself (**de** from); **2** to differ (**de** from); **3** to become different (**de** from).

différend /difeʀɑ̃/ *nm* disagreement.

différent, **~e** /difeʀɑ̃, ɑ̃t/ *adj* **1** different (**de** from); **2** different, various; **pour ~es raisons** for various reasons.

différentiel, **-ielle** /difeʀɑ̃sjɛl/ *adj* differential.

différer /difeʀe/ [14] **I** *vtr* to postpone [*departure, meeting*]; to defer [*payment*].
II *vi* to differ.

difficile /difisil/ *adj* **1** (gen) difficult; [*victory*] hard-won; **le plus ~ reste à faire** the worst is yet to come; **2** [*person, personality*] difficult; **être ~ à vivre** to be difficult to live with; **3** fussy (**sur** about); **tu le trouves beau? tu n'es pas ~!** do you think he's good-looking? you're easy to please!

difficilement /difisilmɑ̃/ *adv* with difficulty; **~ supportable** hard to bear.

difficulté /difikylte/ *nf* **1** difficulty (**à faire** in doing); **2** difficulty; **avoir des ~s scolaires** to have problems at school.

difforme /difɔʀm/ *adj* [*body, limb*] deformed; [*object, building*] strangely shaped; [*tree*] twisted.

difformité /difɔʀmite/ *nf* deformity.

diffus, **~e** /dify, yz/ *adj* [*light, heat*] diffuse; [*feeling*] vague.

diffuser /difyze/ [1] *vtr* **1** to broadcast; **2** to spread; **~ le signalement de qn** to send out a description of sb; **3** to distribute [*article, book*]; **4** to diffuse [*light, heat*].

diffusion /difyzjɔ̃/ *nf* **1** broadcasting; **la ~ du film** the showing of the film; **2** dissemination, diffusion; **3** (commercial) distribution; **4** (of newspaper) circulation; **à large ~** with a wide circulation.

digérer /diʒeʀe/ [14] *vtr* **1** to digest; **bien/mal ~** to have good/bad digestion; **2**○ to swallow [*insult*]; to stomach [*defeat*].

digeste /diʒɛst/ *adj* easily digestible.

digestif, **-ive** /diʒɛstif, iv/ **I** *adj* digestive.
II *nm* liqueur (*taken after dinner*); brandy.

digestion /diʒɛstjɔ̃/ *nf* digestion.

digicode® /diʒikɔd/ *nm* digital (access) lock.

digital, **~e**, *mpl* **-aux** /diʒital, o/ *adj* digital.

digne /diɲ/ *adj* **1** dignified; **2** worthy; **~ de confiance** or **de foi** trustworthy; **~ de ce nom** worthy of the name.

dignement /diɲmɑ̃/ *adv* **1** with dignity; **2** fittingly.

dignitaire /diɲitɛʀ/ *nm* dignitary.

dignité /diɲite/ *nf* **1** dignity; **avoir sa ~** to have one's pride; **2** (title) dignity.

digression /digʀesjɔ̃/ *nf* digression.

digue /dig/ *nf* **1** sea wall; **2** dyke (GB), dike (US); **3** harbour[GB] wall.

dilapider /dilapide/ [1] *vtr* to squander.

dilatation /dilatasjɔ̃/ *nf* **1** (of gas) expansion; **2** (Med) dilation.

dilater /dilate/ [1] *vtr* **1** to dilate [*pupil, cervix*]; to distend [*stomach*]; **2** to expand [*gas*].

dilemme /dilɛm/ *nm* dilemma.

dilettante /dilɛtɑ̃t/ *nmf* (gen) amateur, dilettante; **écrire des romans en ~** to be an amateur novelist.

diligence /diliʒɑ̃s/ *nf* **1** stagecoach; **2** haste.

diligent, ~e /diliʒɑ̃, ɑ̃t/ *adj* diligent.

diluant /dilɥɑ̃/ *nm* thinner.

diluer /dilɥe/ [1] *vtr* **1** to dilute; **2** to thin [sth] down.

diluvien, -ienne /dilyvjɛ̃, ɛn/ *adj* **pluies diluviennes** torrential rain.

dimanche /dimɑ̃ʃ/ *nm* Sunday; **peintre du ~** weekend painter.

IDIOMS **ce n'est pas tous les jours ~** not every day is a holiday.

dimension /dimɑ̃sjɔ̃/ *nf* **1** dimension; **film en trois ~s** 3-D film; **2** size; **3** dimension, aspect; **4** (of problem, situation) dimensions.

diminuer /diminɥe/ [1] **I** *vtr* **1** to reduce [*quantity, duration, costs, risks*]; to lower [*rate, salary*]; **2** to dampen [*enthusiasm, courage*]; **3** to belittle [*person, achievement*]; **4** to weaken [*person*]; to sap [*strength*].

II *vi* **1** [*cost, unemployment*] to come or go down; [*buying power*] to be reduced; [*salary*] to fall; [*gap*] to close; [*growth, deficit, difference*] to decrease; [*production, sales, demand*] to fall off; [*candle, bottle*] to go down; **les jours diminuent** the days are getting shorter; **2** [*activity, interest, violence*] to fall off; [*pressure, tension*] to decrease; [*noise, flames, rumours, rage*] to die down; [*strength*] to diminish; [*courage*] to fail; [*ardour*] to cool; [*temperature*] to go down.

diminutif, -ive /diminytif, iv/ **I** *adj* diminutive.

II *nm* **1** diminutive; **2** pet name.

diminution /diminysjɔ̃/ *nf* (gen) decrease (**de** in); (controlled) reduction (**de** in); (in production, trade) fall-off (**de** in).

dinde /dɛ̃d/ *nf* **1** turkey/turkey hen; **2** (Culin) turkey.

dindon /dɛ̃dɔ̃/ *nm* turkey (cock).

IDIOMS **être le ~ de la farce** to be fooled or duped.

dindonneau, *pl* **~x** /dɛ̃dɔno/ *nm* turkey; **un rôti de ~** turkey roast.

dîner[1] /dine/ [1] *vi* to have dinner.

IDIOMS **qui dort dîne** (Proverb) when you're asleep you don't feel hungry.

dîner[2] /dine/ *nm* dinner.

dînette /dinɛt/ *nf* doll's tea set; **jouer à la ~** to play at tea parties.

dingo○ /dɛ̃go/ *adj inv* crazy○.

dingue○ /dɛ̃g/ **I** *adj* **1** [*person*] crazy○; **être ~ de qch** to be crazy○ about sth; **2** [*noise, success*] wild; [*price, speed*] ridiculous.

II *nmf* **1** nutcase○; **2 un ~ de musique** a music freak○.

dinosaure /dinozɔʀ/ *nm* dinosaur.

diocèse /djɔsɛz/ *nm* diocese.

dioxyde /dijɔksid/ *nm* dioxide; **~ de carbone** carbon dioxide.

diphtérie /difteʀi/ *nf* diphtheria.

diphtongue /diftɔ̃g/ *nf* diphthong.

diplomate /diplɔmat/ **I** *adj* diplomatic.

II *nmf* diplomat.

diplomatie /diplɔmasi/ *nf* diplomacy.

diplomatique /diplɔmatik/ *adj* diplomatic.

diplôme /diplom/ *nm* **1** certificate, diploma; **il n'a aucun ~** he hasn't got any qualifications; **2** (at university) degree; diploma; **3** (in army, police) staff exam.

diplômé, ~e /diplome/ **I** *adj* **une infirmière ~e** a qualified nurse.

II *nm,f* graduate.

dire[1] /diʀ/ [65] **I** *vtr* **1** to say [*words, prayer*]; to read [*lesson*]; to tell [*story, joke*]; **~ qch entre ses dents** to mutter sth; **j'ai mon mot à ~ là-dessus** I've got something to say about that; **2** to tell; **c'est ce qu'on m'a dit** so I've been told; **faire ~ à qn que** to let sb know that...; **je me suis laissé ~ que...** I heard that...; **tenez-vous le pour dit!** I don't want to have to tell you again!; **c'est moi qui vous le dis**○ I'm telling you; **c'est pas pour ~, mais..**○ I don't want to make a big deal of it, but○...; **à qui le dites-vous**○**!** don't I know it!; **je ne vous le fais pas ~**○**!** you don't need to tell me!; **ne pas se le faire ~ deux fois**○ not to need to be told twice; **dis donc, où tu te crois**○**?** hey! where do you think you are?; **3** to say (**que** that); **on dit que...** it is said that...; **si l'on peut ~** if one might say so; **on peut ~ qu'elle a du toupet celle-là!** she's really got a nerve○!; **autant ~ que** you might as well say that; **si j'ose ~** if I may say so; **ce n'est pas à moi de le ~** it's not for me to say; **c'est (tout) ~!** need I say more?; **cela dit** having said that; **tu peux le ~**○**!** you can say that again○!; **à vrai ~** actually; **entre nous soit dit** between you and me; **soit dit en passant** incidentally; **c'est ~ si j'ai raison** it just goes to show I'm right; **c'est beaucoup ~** that's going a bit far; **c'est peu ~** that's an understatement; **c'est vite dit** that's easy for you to say; **ce n'est pas dit** I'm not that sure; **voilà qui est bien dit!** well said!; **comment ~?** how shall I put it?; **pour ainsi ~** so to speak; **autrement dit** in other words; **comme dirait l'autre**○ as they say; **il n'y a pas à ~, elle est belle**○ you have to admit, she's beautiful; **4** [*law*] to state (**que** that); [*measuring device*] to show (**que** that); **vouloir ~** to mean; **quelque chose me dit que** something tells me that; **5 ~ à qn de faire** to tell sb to do; **6** to think;

que diriez-vous d'une promenade? how about a walk?; **on dirait un fou** you'd think he was mad; **on dirait de l'estragon** it looks like tarragon; it tastes like tarragon; **ça ne me dit rien de faire** I don't feel like doing; **notre nouveau jardinier ne me dit rien (qui vaille)** I don't think much of our new gardener.

II **se dire** *v refl* (+ *v être*) **1** to tell oneself (**que** that); **il faut (bien) se ~ que**... one must realize that...; **2** to exchange [*insults, compliments*]; **se ~ adieu** to say goodbye to each other; **3** to claim to be; **4 ça ne se dit pas** you can't say that.

III **se dire** *v impers* **il ne s'est rien dit d'intéressant à la réunion** nothing of interest was said during the meeting.

dire[2] /diʀ/ I *nm* **au ~ de** according to.

II **dires** *nm pl* statements; **selon les ~s de** according to.

direct /diʀɛkt/ I *adj* **1** [*contact, descendent, tax*] direct; [*superior*] immediate; **2** [*route, access*] direct; **train ~** through train; **ce train est ~ pour Lille** this train is nonstop to Lille; **3** direct, frank.

II *nm* **1** live broadcasting; **en ~ de** live from; **2** jab; **~ du gauche** left jab; **3** express (train).

directement /diʀɛktəmɑ̃/ *adv* **1** [*travel, go*] straight; **2** [*concern, affect*] directly; **3** directly.

directeur, -trice[1] /diʀɛktœʀ, tʀis/ I *adj* **principe ~** guiding principle; **idée directrice d'un ouvrage** central theme of a book.

II *nm,f* **1** headmaster/headmistress (GB), principal (US); (of private school) principal; **2** (of hotel, cinema) manager/manageress; **3** director; head (**de** of).

■ **~ de banque** bank manager; **~ général** managing director (GB), chief executive officer (US); **~ de journal** newspaper editor; **~ de prison** prison governor (GB), warden (US); **~ sportif** (team) manager; **~ d'usine** plant manager.

direction /diʀɛksjɔ̃/ *nf* **1** direction; **il a pris la ~ du nord** he headed north; **en ~ de** toward(s); **indiquer la ~ à qn** to tell sb the way; **prenez la ~ Nation** take the train going to 'Nation'; **2** (gen) management; supervision; (of newspaper) editorship; (of movement) leadership; **orchestre sous la ~ de** orchestra conducted by; **3** management; **la ~ et les ouvriers** management and workers; **4** manager's office; head office; **5** (Aut) steering.

directionnel, -elle /diʀɛksjɔnɛl/ *adj* directional.

directive /diʀɛktiv/ *nf* directive.

directorial, ~e, *mpl* **-iaux** /diʀɛktɔʀjal, o/ *adj* managerial.

directrice[2] /diʀɛktʀis/ ▶ **directeur**.

dirigeable /diʀiʒabl/ *adj, nm* dirigible.

dirigeant, ~e /diʀiʒɑ̃, ɑ̃t/ I *adj* [*class*] ruling; [*role*] leading.

II *nm* leader.

diriger /diʀiʒe/ [13] I *vtr* **1** to be in charge of [*people*]; to run [*service, newspaper, party*]; to manage [*company, theatre*]; to lead [*discussion, investigation*]; to direct [*operation*]; to supervise [*research*]; **2** to steer; to pilot; **il vous dirigera dans la ville** he'll guide you around the town; **3** to turn [*light, jet*] (**sur** on); to point [*gun, telescope*] (**sur** at); to direct [*criticism*] (**contre** against); **4** to dispatch [*goods*]; to direct [*convoy*]; **5** (Mus) to conduct; **6** to direct [*actors*]; to manage [*theatre company*].

II **se diriger** *v refl* (+ *v être*) **se ~ vers** to make for; **se ~ droit sur** to head or make straight for; **avoir du mal à se ~ dans le noir** to have difficulty finding one's way in the dark.

discale /diskal/ *adj f* **hernie ~** slipped disc.

discernement /disɛʀnəmɑ̃/ *nm* judgment.

discerner /disɛʀne/ [1] *vtr* **1** to detect [*sign, smell, expression*]; to make out [*shape, noise*]; **2** to make out [*motives, intentions*]; **~ le vrai du faux** to discriminate between truth and untruth.

disciple /disipl/ *nmf* **1** follower; **2** disciple.

disciplinaire /disiplinɛʀ/ *adj* disciplinary.

discipline /disiplin/ *nf* **1** discipline; **2** discipline, specialism; **3** (Sch) subject; **4** sport.

discipliner /disipline/ [1] *vtr* **1** to discipline; **2** to control [*troops*]; to discipline [*thoughts, feelings*]; **3** to keep [sth] under control [*hair*].

disco /disko/ I *adj inv* disco; **soirée ~** disco night.

II *nm* disco music.

discontinu, ~e /diskɔ̃tiny/ *adj* [*movement*] intermittent; [*line*] broken.

discordance /diskɔʀdɑ̃s/ *nf* **1** (of opinions) conflict; **2** (of colours) clash; **3** (of sounds) dissonance.

discordant, ~e /diskɔʀdɑ̃, ɑ̃t/ *adj* **1** [*sound, instrument*] discordant; [*voice*] strident; **2** [*colours*] clashing; **3** [*personalities, opinions*] conflicting.

discorde /diskɔʀd/ *nf* discord, dissension.

discothèque /diskɔtɛk/ *nf* **1** music library; **2** record collection; **3** discotheque.

discours /diskuʀ/ *nm inv* **1** speech (**sur** on); **2** talk; **assez de ~, des actes!** let's have less talk and more action!; **3** views; (political) position; **il tient toujours le même ~** his views haven't changed; **4** (in linguistics) speech; discourse.

discrédit /diskʀedi/ *nm* disrepute; **jeter le ~ sur** to discredit.

discréditer /diskʀedite/ [1] I *vtr* to discredit.

II **se discréditer** *v refl* (+ *v être*) to discredit oneself.

discret, -ète /diskʀɛ, ɛt/ *adj* **1** [*person*] unassuming; [*garment, colour*] sober; [*hint, charm*] subtle; [*lighting*] subdued; [*smile, surveillance, perfume*] discreet; [*place*] quiet; **2** discreet (**sur** about); **3** not inquisitive.

discrètement /diskʀɛtmɑ̃/ *adv* **1** discreetly; **2** soberly; **3** quietly.

discrétion /diskʀesjɔ̃/ I *nf* discretion; **dans la plus grande ~** in the greatest secrecy.

II **à discrétion** *phr* unlimited; **il y avait à boire et à manger à ~** you could drink and eat as much as you like.

III à la discrétion de *phr* at the discretion of.

discrimination /diskʀiminasjɔ̃/ *nf* discrimination.

discriminatoire /diskʀiminatwaʀ/ *adj* discriminatory (**à l'encontre de** against).

disculper /diskylpe/ [1] **I** *vtr* to exculpate.
II se disculper *v refl* (+ *v être*) to vindicate oneself (**auprès de qn** in the eyes of).

discussion /diskysjɔ̃/ *nf* **1** discussion (**sur** about); **le texte est en ~** the text is under discussion; **relancer la ~** to revive the debate; **2** argument.

discutable /diskytabl/ *adj* questionable; debatable.

discuté, ~e /diskyte/ **I** *pp* ▶ **discuter.**
II *pp adj* controversial.

discuter /diskyte/ [1] **I** *vtr* **1** to discuss, to debate; **2** to question.
II discuter de *v+prep* to discuss.
III *vi* **1** to talk (**avec qn** to sb); **2** to argue; **il a dit trois heures et il n'y a pas à ~** he said three o'clock and that's all there is to it.
IV se discuter *v refl* (+ *v être*) **ça se discute, ça peut se ~** that's debatable.

diseur, -euse /dizœʀ, øz/ *nm,f* **~ de bonne aventure** fortune-teller.

disgrâce /disgʀɑs/ *nf* disgrace.

disgracieux, -ieuse /disgʀasjø, øz/ *adj* ugly; unsightly.

disjoncter /disʒɔ̃kte/ [1] *vi* **ça a disjoncté** the trip switch has gone.

dislocation /dislɔkasjɔ̃/ *nf* **1** dismemberment; breaking up; **2 ~ (articulaire)** dislocation (of a joint).

disloquer /dislɔke/ [1] *vtr* **1** to dismember [*empire, state*]; **2** to dislocate [*shoulder, arm*]; **3** to break up [*furniture*].

disparaître /dispaʀɛtʀ/ [73] *vi* **1** to disappear; to vanish; **disparaissez!** out of my sight!; **des centaines de personnes disparaissent chaque année** hundreds of people go missing every year; **2** [*pain, smell*] to go; [*stain*] to come out; [*difficulty*] to disappear; [*fever*] to subside; **faire ~** to get rid of [*pain, dandruff*]; to remove [*stain*]; to make [sth] extinct [*species*]; **3** (euphemistic) to die; to die out; to become extinct; **voir ~** to witness the end of [*civilisation, culture*].

disparate /dispaʀat/ *adj* ill-assorted; mixed.

disparité /dispaʀite/ *nf* disparity (**de** in); difference (**entre** between).

disparition /dispaʀisjɔ̃/ *nf* **1** disappearance; (of species) extinction; **en voie de ~** dying; **une espèce en voie de ~** an endangered species; **2** (euphemistic) death.

disparu, ~e /dispaʀy/ **I** *pp* ▶ **disparaître.**
II *pp adj* **1** missing; **porté ~** (Mil) missing in action; **2** [*civilisation, traditions*] lost; [*species*] extinct; **3** (euphemistic) dead.
III *nm,f* **1** missing person; **neuf morts, un ~** nine dead, one missing; **2** (euphemistic) **les ~s** the dead.

dispense /dispɑ̃s/ *nf* **1** exemption (**de** from); **2** certificate of exemption.

dispenser /dispɑ̃se/ [1] **I** *vtr* **1** to give [*lessons, advice*]; to hand out [*gifts*] (**à** to); to bestow [*honours*] (**à** on); **2 ~ qn de (faire) qch** to exempt sb from (doing) sth; to excuse sb from (doing) sth; **se faire ~ d'un cours** to be excused from a lesson; **je vous dispense de (tout) commentaire** I don't need any comment from you.
II se dispenser *v refl* (+ *v être*) **se ~ de (faire) qch** to spare oneself (the trouble of doing) sth.

disperser /dispɛʀse/ [1] **I** *vtr* to scatter [*objects, family*]; to disperse [*crowd, smoke*]; to break up [*gathering, collection*]; **~ ses efforts** to spread oneself too thin.
II se disperser *v refl* (+ *v être*) to disperse; to scatter; to break up.

disponibilité /dispɔnibilite/ **I** *nf* availability.
II disponibilités *nf pl* available funds.

disponible /dispɔnibl/ *adj* available (**auprès de** from).

dispos, ~e /dispo, oz/ *adj* **frais et ~** fresh as a daisy.

disposé, ~e /dispoze/ **I** *pp* ▶ **disposer.**
II *pp adj* **1** arranged; laid out; **2 ~ à faire** willing to do; **3 être bien ~** to be in a good mood; **être bien ~ l'égard de** or **envers qn** to be well-disposed toward(s) sb.

disposer /dispoze/ [1] **I** *vtr* **1** to arrange [*objects*]; to position [*people*]; **2 ~ de** to have; **les machines dont nous disposons** the machines we have at our disposal.
II se disposer *v refl* (+ *v être*) **1 se ~ à faire** to be about to do; **2 se ~ en cercle autour de qn** to form a circle around sb.

dispositif /dispozitif/ *nm* **1** device; system; **2** operation; **~ policier/financier** police/financial operation.

disposition /dispozisjɔ̃/ **I** *nf* **1** arrangement; layout; position; **2** disposal; **c'est à ta ~** it's at your disposal; **se tenir à la ~ de qn** to be at sb's disposal; **à la ~ du public** for public use; **3** measure, step.
II dispositions *nf pl* aptitude.

disproportionné, ~e /dispʀɔpɔʀsjɔne/ *adj* [*effort, demand*] disproportionate; [*head*] out of proportion with one's body.

dispute /dispyt/ *nf* argument (**sur** about).

disputé, ~e /dispyte/ *adj* **1** keenly contested; **2** controversial.

disputer /dispyte/ [1] **I** *vtr* **1** to compete in [*competition*]; to compete for [*cup*]; to play [*match*]; to run [*race*]; to take part in [*fight*]; **2**° to tell [sb] off; **se faire ~** to get told off.
II se disputer *v refl* (+ *v être*) **1** to argue (**sur** about; **pour** over); **nous nous sommes disputés** we had an argument; **2** to fight over [*inheritance, bone*]; to contest [*seat*]; **3** [*tournament*] to take place.

disquaire /diskɛʀ/ *nmf* record dealer.

disqualifier /diskalifje/ [2] **I** *vtr* to disqualify; **se faire ~ (par)** to be disqualified (by); **se**

faire ~ d'office to put oneself out of the running.

II se disqualifier *v refl* (+ *v être*) to discredit oneself (**en faisant** by doing).

disque /disk/ *nm* **1** record; **passer un ~** to play a record; **2** disc; disk; **3** (Sport) discus.

■ **~ dur** hard disk; **~ numérique** digital disk; **~ souple** flexi-disc; floppy disk; **~ de stationnement** parking disc.

disquette /diskɛt/ *nf* diskette, floppy disk.

dissection /disɛksjɔ̃/ *nf* dissection.

disséminer /disemine/ [1] **I** *vtr* to spread [*germs, ideas*]; to disperse [*pollen*].

II se disséminer *v refl* (+ *v être*) [*people*] to scatter; [*germs, ideas*] to spread.

dissension /disɑ̃sjɔ̃/ *nf* **1** dissension; **2** disagreement (**au sein de** within).

disséquer /diseke/ [14] *vtr* to dissect.

dissertation /disɛʀtasjɔ̃/ *nf* essay.

dissidence /disidɑ̃s/ *nf* **1** dissent; dissidence; rebellion; **2 la ~** the dissidents.

dissident, ~e /disidɑ̃, ɑ̃t/ **I** *adj* dissident.

II *nm,f* **1** dissident; **2** dissenter.

dissimulateur, -trice /disimylatœʀ, tʀis/ *adj* secretive.

dissimulation /disimylasjɔ̃/ *nf* concealment.

dissimulé, ~e /disimyle/ **I** *pp* ▶ **dissimuler**.

II *pp adj* concealed; **mal ~** ill-concealed; **fierté non ~e** undisguised pride.

dissimuler /disimyle/ [1] *vtr* to conceal (**qch à qn** sth from sb); **ne pas ~** not to try to conceal.

dissipation /disipasjɔ̃/ *nf* **1** (of misunderstanding) clearing up; **2** (of fog, clouds) clearing; **3** (of attention) wandering; **4** restlessness.

dissipé, ~e /disipe/ *adj* [*pupil*] badly-behaved; [*life*] dissipated.

dissiper /disipe/ [1] **I** *vtr* **1** to dispel [*doubt*]; to clear up [*misunderstanding*]; to disperse [*smoke*]; **2** to distract [*person*].

II se dissiper *v refl* (+ *v être*) **1** [*threat*] to recede; [*doubt*] to vanish; [*misunderstanding*] to be cleared up; [*mist*] to clear; **2** to behave badly.

dissocier /disɔsje/ [2] *vtr* to separate (**de** from).

dissolu, ~e /disɔly/ *adj* [*life*] dissolute; [*morals*] loose.

dissolution /disɔlysjɔ̃/ *nf* dissolution.

dissolvant, ~e /disɔlvɑ̃, ɑ̃t/ **I** *adj* solvent; **produit ~** solvent.

II *nm* **1** nail varnish; solvent; **2** solvent.

dissonance /disɔnɑ̃s/ *nf* dissonance.

dissonant, ~e /disɔnɑ̃, ɑ̃t/ *adj* [*voice*] dissonant; [*colours*] clashing.

dissoudre /disudʀ/ [75] **I** *vtr* **1** to dissolve [*assembly*]; to disband [*movement*]; **2** to dissolve [*substance*].

II se dissoudre *v refl* (+ *v être*) **1** [*organization*] to disband; **2** [*substance*] to dissolve.

dissuader /disɥade/ [1] *vtr* **1** to dissuade (**de faire** from doing); to put [sb] off (**de faire** doing); **2** to deter; **~ l'ennemi** to deter the enemy.

dissuasif, -ive /disɥazif, iv/ *adj* **1** dissuasive; deterrent; **2** prohibitive.

dissuasion /disɥazjɔ̃/ *nf* (Mil) deterrence.

dissymétrie /disimetʀi/ *nf* asymmetry.

distance /distɑ̃s/ *nf* **1** distance; **Paris est à quelle ~ de Londres?** how far is Paris from London?; **j'ai couru sur une ~ de deux kilomètres** I ran for two kilometres[GB]; **à une ~ de 10 kilomètres** 10 kilometres[GB] away; **être à faible ~ de** not to be far (away) from; **prendre ses ~s avec** to distance oneself from; **tenir** or **garder ses ~s** to stand aloof; **tenir la ~** [*runner*] to stay the course; **à ~** from a distance; **commande à ~** remote control; **2** gap; **à une semaine de ~** one week apart.

distancer /distɑ̃se/ [12] *vtr* to outdistance; to outrun; **se faire** or **se laisser ~** to get left behind.

distant, ~e /distɑ̃, ɑ̃t/ *adj* **1** [*place, noise*] distant; **un village ~ de trois kilomètres** a village three kilometres[GB] away; **~s de trois kilomètres** three kilometres[GB] apart; **2** [*person*] distant; [*attitude*] reserved; [*relations*] cool; **3 à une époque ~e de la nôtre** in the distant past.

distiller /distile/ [1] *vtr* to distil[GB].

distillerie /distilʀi/ *nf* **1** distillery; **2** distilling.

distinct, ~e /distɛ̃, ɛ̃kt/ *adj* **1** distinct (**de** from); **2** [*sound*] distinct; [*voice*] clear; **de façon ~e** clearly; **3** [*firm*] separate.

distinctif, -ive /distɛ̃ktif, iv/ *adj* [*mark*] distinguishing; [*feature*] distinctive.

distinction /distɛ̃ksjɔ̃/ *nf* **1** distinction; **établir une ~ entre** to draw a distinction between; **sans ~** without discrimination; indiscriminately; **2** honour[GB]; **~ honorifique** award; **3** distinction, refinement.

distingué, ~e /distɛ̃ge/ *adj* distinguished.

distinguer /distɛ̃ge/ [1] **I** *vtr* **1** to distinguish between; **~ A de B** to distinguish A from B; **il est difficile de les ~** it's difficult to tell them apart; **2** to distinguish, to make out; **3** to discern; **4** to set [sb] apart; to make [sth] different (**de** from); **aucune caractéristique physique ne les distingue** physically, they have no distinguishing features; **5** to single out [sb] for an honour[GB].

II *vi* **~ entre A et B** to distinguish between A and B.

III se distinguer *v refl* (+ *v être*) **1 se ~ de** to differ from; to set oneself apart from; **2** to distinguish oneself; **3** to be distinguishable; **4** to draw attention to oneself; **il vaut mieux éviter de se ~** it's best not to be conspicuous.

distorsion /distɔʀsjɔ̃/ *nf* distortion.

distraction /distʀaksjɔ̃/ *nf* **1** leisure, entertainment; **les ~s sont rares ici** there's not much to do around here; **2** recreation; **3** absent-mindedness; **mes professeurs me reprochent ma ~** my teachers tell me off for not paying attention.

distraire /distʀɛʀ/ [58] **I** *vtr* **1** to amuse; to entertain; **2 ~ qn de qch** to take sb's mind off sth; **3** to distract (**de** from; **par** by).

II se distraire *v refl* (+ *v être*) **1** to amuse

oneself; to enjoy oneself; **que fais-tu pour te ~?** what do you do for entertainment?; **2 j'ai besoin de me ~** I need to take my mind off things.

distrait, **~e** /distʀɛ, ɛt/ *adj* [*person*] absent-minded; inattentive; [*air*] distracted; [*look*] vague; **regarder qn d'un œil ~** to look vaguely at sb.

distraitement /distʀɛtmɑ̃/ *adv* absent-mindedly; **regarder ~ qch** to look vaguely at sth; **écouter ~** to listen with half an ear.

distrayant, **~e** /distʀɛjɑ̃, ɑ̃t/ *adj* entertaining.

distribuer /distʀibɥe/ [1] *vtr* **1** to distribute (**à** to); to allocate (**à** to); **~ les cartes** to deal; **~ le courrier** to deliver the mail; **~ les récompenses** to give out the awards; **2** to supply [*water, heat*].

distributeur, **-trice** /distʀibytœʀ, tʀis/ **I** *adj* distributing.

II *nm,f* distributor; **~ exclusif** sole distributor.

III *nm* **1** dispenser; vending machine; **~ de tickets** ticket machine; **~ de billets (de banque)** cash dispenser; **~ de boissons** drinks vending machine; **2** retailing group.

distribution /distʀibysjɔ̃/ *nf* **1** retailing; **2** (in commerce) distribution; **3** (of water, electricity) supply; **4** distribution, handing out; allocation; **5** distribution, layout; **6** (of actors) casting; cast.

diurétique /djyʀetik/ *adj*, *nm* diuretic.

divaguer /divage/ [1] *vi* **1** to rave; **la fièvre le fait ~** he's delirious; **2** to ramble; to talk nonsense; **3** to stray.

divan /divɑ̃/ *nm* divan; couch.

divergence /divɛʀʒɑ̃s/ *nf* divergence; difference.

divergent, **~e** /divɛʀʒɑ̃, ɑ̃t/ *adj* divergent.

diverger /divɛʀʒe/ [13] *vi* to diverge (**de** from); to differ (**de** from).

divers, **~e** /divɛʀ, ɛʀs/ *adj* **1** various; **à ~es reprises** on various occasions; **les gens les plus ~** all sorts of people; **2** miscellaneous.

diversifier /divɛʀsifje/ [2] *vtr* to widen the range of; to diversify.

diversion /divɛʀsjɔ̃/ *nf* **1** (Mil) diversion; **une manœuvre de ~** a diversionary move; **2** (literary) diversion, distraction.

diversité /divɛʀsite/ *nf* diversity; variety.

divertir /divɛʀtiʀ/ [3] **I** *vtr* to entertain; to amuse.

II *vi* (literary) to entertain.

III se divertir *v refl* (+ *v être*) to amuse oneself; **pour se ~** for fun; to take one's mind off things.

divertissant, **~e** /divɛʀtisɑ̃, ɑ̃t/ *adj* amusing; entertaining; enjoyable.

divertissement /divɛʀtismɑ̃/ *nm* entertainment; recreation.

dividende /dividɑ̃d/ *nm* dividend.

divin, **~e** /divɛ̃, in/ *adj* divine; **le ~ Enfant** the Holy Child.

diviniser /divinize/ [1] *vtr* to deify.

divinité /divinite/ *nf* deity; divinity.

diviser /divize/ [1] **I** *vtr* to divide; **~ pour régner** divide and rule.

II se diviser *v refl* (+ *v être*) **1** to become divided (**sur** over); **2** to be divided; **3** to be divisible; **4** to divide; to fork.

divisible /divizibl/ *adj* divisible.

division /divizjɔ̃/ *nf* division.

divorce /divɔʀs/ *nm* divorce (**d'avec** from); **prononcer le ~ entre deux époux** to grant a divorce to a couple; **gagner le ~** to win a divorce suit.

divorcé, **~e** /divɔʀse/ *nm,f* divorcee.

divorcer /divɔʀse/ [12] *vi* to get divorced; **elle veut ~** she wants a divorce.

divulguer /divylge/ [1] *vtr* to disclose.

dix /dis, *but before consonant* di, *before vowel* diz/ *adj inv*, *pron* ten.

IDIOMS **ne rien savoir faire de ses ~ doigts** to be useless; **un de perdu, ~ de retrouvés** (Proverb) there's plenty more fish in the sea.

dix-huit /dizɥit/ *adj inv*, *pron* eighteen.

dix-huitième /dizɥitjɛm/ *adj* eighteenth.

dixième /dizjɛm/ **I** *adj* tenth.

II *nf* (Sch) *second year of primary school, age 7–8.*

dix-neuf /diznœf/ *adj inv*, *pron* nineteen.

dix-neuvième /diznœvjɛm/ *adj* nineteenth.

dix-sept /dis(s)ɛt/ *adj inv*, *pron* seventeen.

dix-septième /dis(s)ɛtjɛm/ *adj* seventeenth.

dizaine /dizɛn/ *nf* **1** ten; **2** about ten; **ça a duré une bonne ~ d'années** it went on for over ten years; **des ~s de personnes** dozens of people.

do /do/ *nm inv* (Mus) (note) C; (in sol-fa) doh.

docile /dɔsil/ *adj* [*animal, person*] docile; [*hair*] manageable.

docilement /dɔsilmɑ̃/ *adv* obediently; meekly.

dock /dɔk/ *nm* **1** dock; **2** warehouse.

docteur /dɔktœʀ/ *nm* doctor; **jouer au ~** to play doctors and nurses; **~ en droit** Doctor of Law.

doctorat /dɔktɔʀa/ *nm* PhD, doctorate (**ès, en** in).

doctrinaire /dɔktʀinɛʀ/ *adj* [*attitude*] doctrinaire; [*tone*] sententious.

doctrinal, **~e**, *mpl* **-aux** /dɔktʀinal, o/ *adj* doctrinal; ideological.

doctrine /dɔktʀin/ *nf* doctrine.

document /dɔkymɑ̃/ *nm* **1** document (**sur** on); **~ sonore** audio material; **avec ~s à l'appui** with documentary evidence; **2** document, paper.

documentaire /dɔkymɑ̃tɛʀ/ **I** *adj* documentary; **centre ~** information centre[GB]; **à titre ~** for your information.

II *nm* documentary (**sur** on, about).

documentaliste /dɔkymɑ̃talist/ *nmf* information officer; (school) librarian.

documentation /dɔkymɑ̃tasjɔ̃/ *nf* **1** material (**sur** on); **2** research; **3** brochures; **4 centre de ~** resource centre[GB].

documenter /dɔkymɑ̃te/ [1] **I** *vtr* to provide [sb] with information.

II **se documenter** *v refl* (+ *v être*) **se ~ sur qch** to research sth.

dodeliner /dɔdline/ [1] *vi* **il dodelinait de la tête** his head was nodding.

dodo /dodo/ *nm* (baby talk) **faire ~** to sleep.

dodu, **-e** /dɔdy/ *adj* plump.

dogmatique /dɔgmatik/ *adj* dogmatic.

dogme /dɔgm/ *nm* dogma.

dogue /dɔg/ *nm* mastiff.

doigt /dwa/ *nm* finger; **petit ~** little finger (GB), pinkie; **bout des ~s** fingertips; **du bout des ~s** (figurative) reluctantly; **connaître une ville sur le bout des ~s** to know a city like the back of one's hand; **montrer du ~** to point at; (figurative) to point the finger at; **mettre le ~ sur qch** to put one's finger on sth.

■ **~ de pied** toe.

IDIOMS **se brûler les ~s** to get one's fingers burned; **être à deux ~s de** to be a whisker away from; **filer entre les ~s** [*money, thief*] to slip through one's fingers; [*time*] to slip away from sb; **mon petit ~ me dit que** a little bird tells me that; **se faire taper sur les ~s** to get one's knuckles rapped; **lever le ~** to put one's hand up.

doigté /dwate/ *nm* **1** tact; **avoir du ~** to be tactful; **2** (of pianist) fingering.

dollar /dɔlaʀ/ *nm* dollar.

domaine /dɔmɛn/ *nm* **1** estate; **2** field, domain; **3** territory.

dôme /dom/ *nm* dome.

domestique /dɔmɛstik/ I *adj* **1** [*staff, animal*] domestic; **les travaux ~s** housework; **2** [*market*] domestic, home.

II *nmf* servant.

domestiquer /dɔmɛstike/ [1] *vtr* **1** to domesticate [*animal*]; **2** to harness [*electricity*].

domicile /dɔmisil/ I *nm* place of residence; (of company) registered address; **dernier ~ connu** last known address.

II **à domicile** *phr* **travail à ~** working at or from home; **donner des soins à ~** to give home care; **'livraisons à ~'** 'home deliveries'.

domicilié, **~e** /dɔmisilje/ *adj* **1 être ~ à Arras** to live in Arras; **2 j'habite à Paris, mais je suis ~e à Rennes** I live in Paris, but my official address is in Rennes.

dominance /dɔminɑ̃s/ *nf* dominance.

dominant, **~e** /dɔminɑ̃, ɑ̃t/ *adj* **1** [*colour, gene*] dominant; [*wind, tendency*] prevailing; [*feature, idea*] main; **2** [*class*] ruling

dominateur, **-trice** /dɔminatœʀ, tʀis/ *adj* [*person*] domineering; [*attitude*] overbearing.

domination /dɔminasjɔ̃/ *nf* domination; **être sous la ~ de** to be dominated by.

dominer /dɔmine/ [1] I *vtr* **1** to dominate; to tower above; **de là, on domine toute la vallée** from there you get a view of the whole valley; **il est tellement grand qu'il domine tout le monde** he's so tall that he towers over everyone; **2** to dominate [*match, market, sector*]; to overshadow [*opponent*]; **3** [*theme*] to dominate; **4** to master [*subject*]; to overcome [*fear*]; to control [*anger*]; **~ la situation** to be in control of the situation.

II *vi* **1** to rule, to hold sway; **2** to be in the lead; **3** [*impression*] to prevail; [*taste*] to stand out.

III **se dominer** *v refl* (+ *v être*) to control oneself.

dominical, **~e**, *mpl* **-aux** /dɔminikal, o/ *adj* [*walk, mass*] Sunday.

domino /dɔmino/ *nm* domino.

dommage /dɔmaʒ/ *nm* **1 c'est (vraiment) ~** it's a (great) shame or pity; **2** damage; **3** (Law) tort.

■ **~s corporels** personal injury; **~s et intérêts** damages.

dommages-intérêts /dɔmaʒɛ̃teʀɛ/ *nm pl* damages.

dompter /dɔ̃te/ [1] *vtr* to tame [*wild animal*]; to bring [sb] to heel [*unruly person*]; to subdue [*insurgents*]; to overcome [*passion*].

dompteur, **-euse** /dɔ̃tœʀ, øz/ *nm,f* tamer.

DOM-TOM /dɔmtɔm/ *nm pl* (*abbr* = **départements et territoires d'outre-mer**) *French overseas departments and territories.*

don /dɔ̃/ *nm* **1** donation; **faire ~ de** to give (**à** to); **~ de soi** self-sacrifice; **2** gift (**de qch** for sth); **avoir le ~ de faire** to have a talent for doing.

■ **~ du sang** blood donation.

donation /dɔnasjɔ̃/ *nf* **1** donation; **2** (Law) gift.

donc /dɔ̃k/ *conj* so, therefore; **j'étais ~ en train de lire, lorsque...** so I was reading, when...; **je disais ~ que...** as I was saying...; **tais-toi ~!** be quiet, will you?; **entrez ~!** do come in!; **mais où est-il ~ passé?** where on earth has he gone?

donjon /dɔ̃ʒɔ̃/ *nm* keep, donjon.

don Juan, *pl* **dons Juans** /dɔ̃ʒɥɑ̃/ *nm* **un ~** a Casanova.

Don Juan /dɔ̃ʒɥɑ̃/ *pr n* **1** Don Juan; **2** (Mus) Don Giovanni.

donne /dɔn/ *nf* (in cards) deal; **mauvaise** or **fausse ~** misdeal.

donné, **~e**[1] /dɔne/ I *pp* ▶ **donner**.

II *pp adj* **1 il n'est pas ~ à tout le monde de faire** not everyone can do; **2** given; **à un moment ~** at one point; all of a sudden; **3** cheap.

III **étant donné (que)** *phr* given (that).

donnée[2] /dɔne/ *nf* **1** fact, element; **2** data.

donner /dɔne/ [1] I *vtr* **1** to give [*present, headache, advice, answer, permission*] (**à** to); to deal [*cards*] (**à** to); to give [*party, dinner*] (**pour** for); to give [*lesson, talk*] (**à, devant** to); **~ pour les œuvres** to give to charity; **~ l'heure à qn** to tell sb the time; **je lui donne 40 ans** I'd say he/she was 40; **~ faim à qn** to make sb feel hungry; **elle donne sa fille à garder à mes parents** she has my parents look after her daughter; **j'ai donné ma voiture à réparer** I've taken my car in to be repaired; **les sondages le donnent en tête** the polls put him in the lead; **2** to show [*film*]; to put on [*play*]; to give [*performance*]; **3** to produce, to yield [*fruit,* *juice*]; to produce [*results*]; **leur intervention n'a rien donné** their intervention didn't have any effect; **4** to show [*signs*] (**de** of; **à** to); **5**° to inform on [*accomplice*] (**à** to).

II *vi* **1 le poirier va bien ~ cette année** the pear tree will yield a good crop this year; **2** [*radio*] to be playing; **3 ne plus savoir où ~ de la tête** (figurative) not to know which way to turn; **4 ~ sur** [*room, window*] to overlook; [*door*] to give onto; **~ au nord** to face or look north; **la cuisine donne dans le salon** the kitchen leads into the living-room; **5 ~ dans** to tend toward(s); **6 ~ de soi-même** or **de sa personne** to give of oneself.

III **se donner** *v refl* (+ *v être*) **1 se ~ à** to devote oneself to; **2 se ~ le temps de faire** to give oneself time to do; **se ~ les moyens de faire** to find the means to do; **3 se ~ pour but de faire** to make it one's aim to do; **4 se ~ de grands airs** to put on airs; **5 se ~ des coups** to exchange blows; **se ~ le mot** to pass the word on.

IDIOMS **donnant donnant: je garde ton chat à Noël, tu gardes le mien à Pâques** fair's fair: I keep your cat at Christmas, you keep mine at Easter; **avec lui, c'est donnant donnant** he never does anything for nothing.

donneur, **-euse** /dɔnœʀ, øz/ *nm,f* **1** (Med) donor; **2** (Games) dealer; **3 les ~s de bons conseils** people who like to give advice.

don Quichotte /dɔ̃kiʃɔt/ *pr n* Don Quixote.

dont /dɔ̃/ *rel pron* **1** whose, of which; **la jeune fille ~ on nous disait qu'elle avait 20 ans** the girl who they said was 20; **Sylvaine est quelqu'un ~ on se souvient** Sylvaine is somebody (that) you remember; **l'époque ~ je vous parle** the time I'm talking about; **la maladie ~ il souffre** the illness which he's suffering from, the illness that he has; **des renseignements ~ nous ne sommes pas certains** information which we are not sure about; **la façon ~ il a été traité** the way he has been treated; **2 il y a eu plusieurs victimes ~ mon père** there were several victims, one of whom was my father; **des boîtes ~ la plupart sont vides** boxes, most of which are empty.

dopage /dɔpaʒ/ *nm* **1** (of horses) doping; **2** illegal drug-taking.

doper /dɔpe/ [1] *vtr* to dope.

dorade /dɔʀad/ *nf* (sea) bream.

doré, **~e** /dɔʀe/ I *pp* ▶ **dorer**.

II *pp adj* **1** [*paint, paper*] gold; [*frame*] gilt; [*dome*] gilded; [*hair*] golden; [*skin*] tanned; [*bread, chicken*] golden brown; **~ à l'or fin** gilded; **2** [*exile*] luxurious; **jeunesse ~e** gilded youth.

III *nm* gilt.

dorénavant /dɔʀenavɑ̃/ *adv* from now on; henceforth.

dorer /dɔʀe/ [1] I *vtr* **1** to gild; **2** (Culin) to glaze; **3** [*sun*] to turn [sth] to gold.

II *vi* (Culin) to brown.

III **se dorer** *v refl* (+ *v être*) **se ~ au soleil** to sunbathe.

dorloter /dɔʀlɔte/ [1] *vtr* to mollycoddle; to pamper.

dormeur, **-euse** /dɔʀmœʀ, øz/ I *nm,f* sleeper; **c'est un gros ~** he sleeps a lot.

II *nm* **1** edible crab; **2** nurse shark.

dormir /dɔʀmiʀ/ [30] *vi* **1** to sleep; **~ d'un sommeil léger** to be in a light sleep; **~ debout** (figurative) to be dead on one's feet; **ça m'empêche de ~** it keeps me awake; **il n'en dort plus** he's losing sleep over it; **les manuscrits dormaient dans un tiroir** the manuscripts were gathering dust in a drawer; **2** [*money*] to lie idle.

IDIOMS **ne ~ que d'un œil** to sleep with one eye open; **~ sur ses deux oreilles**, **~ tranquille** to rest easy; **~ comme un loir** to sleep like a log; **~ à poings fermés** to be fast asleep.

dorsal, *mpl* **-aux** /dɔʀsal, o/ *adj* [*pain*] back; [*fin*] dorsal.

dortoir /dɔʀtwaʀ/ I *nm* dormitory.

II **(-)dortoir** (*combining form*) **ville-~** dormitory town.

dorure /dɔʀyʀ/ *nf* gilt.

doryphore /dɔʀifɔʀ/ *nm* Colorado beetle.

dos /do/ *nm inv* **1** back; **avoir le ~ rond** or **voûté** to stoop; **mal de ~** backache; **voir qn de ~** to see sb from behind; **robe décolletée dans le ~** dress with a low back; **dans** or **derrière le ~ de qn** when sb's back is turned; **ils sont arrivés, sac au ~** they arrived, with their rucksacks on their backs; **il n'a rien sur le ~**° he's wearing hardly anything; **tourner le ~ à** to have one's back to; to turn one's back to; (figurative) to turn one's back on; **2** (of book) spine; (of blade) blunt edge.

IDIOMS **courber le ~** to bow and scrape; **mettre qch sur le ~ de**° to blame sth on; **il a bon ~ le réveil**°! it's easy to blame it on the alarm-clock!

dosage /dozaʒ/ *nm* **1** amount; measurement; **2** mix; mixing; **3** proportions.

dos-d'âne /dodɑn/ *nm inv* hump; **pont en ~** humpback bridge.

dose /doz/ *nf* **1** dose; **forcer la ~**° to go a bit far°; **2** measure.

doser /doze/ [1] *vtr* **1** to measure; **2** to use [sth] in a controlled way.

dossard /dosaʀ/ *nm* number (*worn by an athlete*).

dossier /dosje/ *nm* **1** file, dossier; **~ médical** medical records; **~ d'inscription** (Sch) registration form; **sélection sur ~** selection by written application; **2** (Law) file; case; **3 le ~ brûlant de la pollution** the controversial problem of pollution; **4** file, folder; **5** (of chair) back.

dot /dɔt/ *nf* dowry.

dotation /dɔtasjɔ̃/ *nf* allocation; endowment.

doté, **~e** /dɔte/ I *pp* ▶ **doter**.

II *pp adj* **richement ~** [*foundation*] richly endowed; [*daughter*] with a large dowry.

doter /dɔte/ [1] I *vtr* **1 ~ qn de qch** to alloc-

ate sth to sb; **2 ~ qn/qch de** to equip sb/sth with; **3 ~ qn/qch de** to endow sb/sth with.
II se doter *v refl* (+ *v être*) **se ~ de** to acquire [*income*]; to create, set up [*service*].

douane /dwan/ *nf* **1** customs; **2** (on goods) duty.

douanier, -ière /dwanje, ɛʀ/ **I** *adj* customs.
II *nm* customs officer.

double /dubl/ **I** *adj* double; **à ~ effet** dual or double action; **l'avantage est ~** the advantage is twofold; **valise à ~ fond** suitcase with a false bottom; **~ nationalité** dual nationality; **avoir le don de ~ vue** to have second sight; **en ~ exemplaire** in duplicate.
II *adv* double.
III *nm* **1** double; **leur piscine fait le ~ de la nôtre** their swimming-pool is twice as big as ours; **2** copy; **un ~ des clés** a spare set of keys; **3** (in tennis) doubles; **faire un ~** to play a doubles match.

doublé, ~e /duble/ **I** *pp* ▶ **doubler**.
II *pp adj* **1** [*coat*] lined (**de** with); **2** [*film*] dubbed; **3 un imbécile ~ d'un lâche** a coward as well as a fool.

doublement /dubləmɑ̃/ *adv* in two ways; **il est ~ coupable** he's doubly guilty.

doubler /duble/ [1] **I** *vtr* **1** to double; **2** to line (**de** with); **3** to dub [*film*]; to stand in for [*actor*]; **4** to overtake (GB), to pass (US); **'défense de ~'** 'no overtaking' (GB), 'no passing' (US).
II *vi* to double; **~ de valeur** to double in value.
III se doubler *v refl* (+ *v être*) **se ~ de qch** to be coupled with sth.

doublure /dublyʀ/ *nf* **1** lining; **2** (for actor) double.

douce ▶ **doux**.

douceâtre /dusɑtʀ/ *adj* sickly sweet.

doucement /dusmɑ̃/ *adv* **1** gently; **holà! ~ avec le vin!** hey! go easy on the wine!; **2** quietly; **3** slowly.

doucereux, -euse /dusʀø, øz/ *adj* [*manner, person*] smooth; [*words*] sugary; [*smile*] unctuous.

douceur /dusœʀ/ **I** *nf* **1** softness; mildness; mellowness; smoothness; gentleness; **~ de vivre** relaxed rhythm of life; **employer la ~ avec** to use the gentle approach with; **avec ~** gently; **2** sweet (GB), candy (US).
II en douceur *phr* **1** smoothly; **atterrissage en ~** smooth landing; **2 shampooing qui lave en ~** mild shampoo.

douche /duʃ/ *nf* shower; **~ froide** cold shower; letdown○.

doucher /duʃe/ [1] **I** *vtr* **1** to give [sb] a shower; **2**○ to dampen [*enthusiasm*]; to cool off [*person*].
II se doucher *v refl* (+ *v être*) to take a shower.

doué, ~e /dwe/ *adj* **1** gifted, talented (**en** in, at); **être ~ pour** to have a gift for; **être ~ pour les chiffres** to have a good head for figures; **2 ~ de** endowed with, gifted with.

douille /duj/ *nf* **1** cartridge (case); **2** (light) socket.

douillet, -ette /dujɛ, ɛt/ *adj* **1** oversensitive to pain; **2** cosy (GB), cozy (US).

douleur /dulœʀ/ *nf* **1** pain; **médicament contre la ~** painkiller; **2** grief; **accablé de ~** grief-stricken.

douloureuse[1] /duluʀøz/ **I** *adj f* ▶ **douloureux**.
II○ *nf* bill.

douloureusement /duluʀøzmɑ̃/ *adv* **1** grievously; terribly; **2** painfully.

douloureux, -euse[2] /duluʀø, øz/ *adj* **1** painful; **2** [*event*] distressing; [*question*] painful; [*expression*] sorrowful.

doute /dut/ **I** *nm* doubt; **laisser qn dans le ~** to leave sb in a state of uncertainty; **mettre qch en ~** to call sth into question; **dans le ~, j'ai préféré ne rien dire** not being sure I didn't say anything; **j'ai des ~s!** I have my doubts!; **un ~ subsiste** there is still some doubt; **il fait peu de ~ que** there's little doubt that; **nul ~ que** there's no doubt that.
II sans doute *phr* probably; **sans aucun ~** without any doubt.

douter /dute/ [1] **I** *vtr* **1 ~ que** to doubt that or whether **2 ~ de qch** to have doubts about sth; **je n'ai jamais douté de toi** I never doubted you; **elle l'affirme mais j'en doute** she says it's true but I have my doubts; **elle ne doute de rien**○**!** (ironic) she's so sure of herself!
II *vi* to doubt.
III se douter *v refl* (+ *v être*) **se ~ de** to suspect; **je m'en doutais!** I thought so!; **je m'en doute, je m'en serais douté!** (ironic) obviously!; **je me doute (bien) qu'il devait être furieux** I can (well) imagine that he was furious; **nous étions loin de nous ~ que** we didn't have the least idea that.

douteux, -euse /dutø, øz/ *adj* **1** uncertain; **il est ~ qu'il ait pu s'échapper** it is unlikely that he was able to escape; **2** ambiguous; **3** dubious; **4** [*deal, character*] shady.

douve /duv/ *nf* moat.

Douvres /duvʀ/ *pr n* Dover.

doux, douce /du, dus/ *adj* [*light, voice, substance*] soft; [*wine, cider*] sweet; [*cheese, tobacco, shampoo, weather, punishment*] mild; [*person, face, slope*] gentle.
IDIOMS **filer ~**○ to keep a low profile; **se la couler douce**○ to take it easy; **en douce**○ on the sly.

douzaine /duzɛn/ *nf* **1** dozen; **à la ~** by the dozen; **2** about twelve, a dozen or so; **il y en a à la ~** there are dozens of them.

douze /duz/ *adj inv, pron* twelve.

douzième /duzjɛm/ *adj* twelfth.

doyen, -enne /dwajɛ̃, ɛn/ *nm,f* **1 ~ (d'âge)** oldest person; **2** the (most) senior member; **3** dean.

draconien, -ienne /dʀakɔnjɛ̃, ɛn/ *adj* draconian; very strict.

dragée /dʀaʒe/ *nf* **1** sugared almond; **2** sugar-coated pill.

dragon /dʀagɔ̃/ *nm* **1** dragon; **2** (Mil) dragoon.

draguer /dʀage/ [1] *vtr* **1**○ to come on to○; **2** to dredge, to drag [*river, canal*]; **3** (Mil) to sweep [*mines*].

dragueur○, **-euse** /dʀagœʀ, øz/ *nm,f* **c'est un drôle de ~**○ he's a terrible flirt.
■ **~ de mines** (Mil) minesweeper.

drain /dʀɛ̃/ *nm* drain.

drainage /dʀɛnaʒ/ *nm* **1** drainage; **2** (Med) draining (off).

drainer /dʀɛne/ [1] *vtr* **1** to drain; **2** (figurative) to siphon off [*capital*] (**vers** to); to attract [*audience*] (**vers** to).

dramatique /dʀamatik/ **I** *adj* **1** tragic; **ce n'est pas ~ si tu ne viens pas** it's not the end of the world if you don't come; **2** dramatic; **art ~** drama; **auteur ~** playwright.
II *nf* play, drama.

dramatiser /dʀamatize/ [1] *vtr* to dramatize.

dramaturge /dʀamatyʀʒ/ *nmf* playwright.

drame /dʀam/ *nm* **1** tragedy; **tourner au ~** to take a tragic turn; **tu ne vas pas en faire un ~!** don't make a scene about it!; **2** drama; play; **~ lyrique** opera.

drap /dʀa/ *nm* **1** sheet; **2** woollen[GB] cloth.
■ **~ de plage** beach towel.
IDIOMS **se mettre dans de beaux ~s** to land oneself in a fine mess.

drapeau, *pl* **~x** /dʀapo/ *nm* flag; **être sous les ~x** to be doing military service; **être appelé sous les ~x** to be called up; **~ tricolore** tricolour[GB].

drap-housse, *pl* **draps-housses** /dʀaus/ *nm* fitted sheet.

dressage /dʀɛsaʒ/ *nm* **1** training; (of horse) breaking in; **2** dressage.

dresser /dʀese/ [1] **I** *vtr* **1** to train [*animal*]; to break in [*horse*]; to teach [sb] how to behave [*person*]; **2** to put up [*tent, scaffolding, statue*]; **3** to raise [*head*]; to prick up [*ears*]; **4** to lay out [*buffet*]; **5** to draw up [*list*]; **~ un procès-verbal à qn** to give sb a ticket; **6 ~ qn contre** to set sb against.
II se dresser *v refl* (+ *v être*) **1** to stand up; **se ~ sur la pointe des pieds** to stand on tiptoe; **2 se ~ contre** to rebel against; **3** [*statue, obstacle*] to stand; to tower up.

dresseur, **-euse** /dʀɛsœʀ, øz/ *nm,f* trainer.

dribbler /dʀible/ [1] *vi* to dribble.

drogue /dʀɔg/ *nf* drug; **la ~** drugs; **c'est devenu une ~** it has become an addiction.

drogué, **~e** /dʀɔge/ *nm,f* drug-addict.

droguer /dʀɔge/ [1] **I** *vtr* **1** [*doctor*] to dope; to dish out○ drugs to; **2** to dope [*animal, sportsman*]; to drug [*victim*]; to doctor [*drink*].
II se droguer *v refl* (+ *v être*) **1** to dope oneself (**à, de** with); **2** to take drugs; **se ~ à l'héroïne** to be on heroin.

droguerie /dʀɔgʀi/ *nf* hardware shop (GB) or store (US).

droguiste /dʀɔgist/ *nmf* owner of a hardware shop (GB) or store (US).

droit, **~e**[1] /dʀwa, at/ **I** *adj* **1** [*line, road, nose*] straight; [*writing*] upright; **se tenir ~** to stand up straight; to sit up straight; **s'écarter du ~ chemin** to stray from the straight and narrow; **2** right; **du côté ~** on the right-hand side; **3** [*person*] straight(forward), upright; **4** [*skirt*] straight; [*jacket*] single-breasted; **5** [*angle, prism*] right.
II *adv* straight; **continuez tout ~** carry straight on; **aller ~ à la catastrophe** to be heading straight for disaster; **marcher** or **filer**○ **~** to toe the line; **venir tout ~ de** [*quote*] to come straight out of.
III *nm* **1** right; **de quel ~ est-ce que tu me juges?** what gives you the right to judge me?; **être dans son (bon) ~** to be within one's rights; **de (plein) ~** by right(s); **cela leur revient de ~** it's theirs by right; **avoir ~ à** to be entitled to; **il a eu ~ à une amende** (ironic) he got a fine; **avoir le ~ de faire** to be allowed to do; to have the right to do; **avoir le ~ de vie ou de mort sur qn** to have (the) power of life and death over sb; **il s'imagine qu'il a tous les ~s** he thinks he can do whatever he likes; **être en ~ de** to be entitled to; **2 le ~** law; **faire son ~** to study law; **3** fee; **4** (in boxing) right; **direct du ~** straight right.
■ **~ d'antenne** broadcasting right; **(prisonnier de) ~ commun** nonpolitical prisoner; **~ d'entrée** entrance fee; **~ de passage** right of way (GB), easement (US); **~ de regard sur** a say in; **~s d'auteur** royalties; **~s de douane** customs duties; **les ~s de l'homme** human rights; **~s de succession** inheritance tax.
IDIOMS **se tenir ~ comme un i** or **un piquet** to hold oneself very erect.

droite[2] /dʀwat/ *nf* **1** right; **la porte de ~** the door on the right; **tourner à ~** to turn right; **à ta ~** on your right; **demander à ~ et à gauche** to ask everywhere; to ask everybody; **2 voter à ~** to vote for the right; **de ~** right-wing; **3** straight line.

droitier, **-ière** /dʀwatje, ɛʀ/ *nm,f* right-hander.

droiture /dʀwatyʀ/ *nf* honesty, uprightness.

drôle /dʀol/ *adj* **1** funny, odd; **c'est un ~ de type** he's an odd guy; **se sentir (tout) ~** to feel a bit funny○; **faire (tout) ~ à qn** to give sb a funny feeling; **faire une ~ de tête** to make a bit of a face; **2** funny, amusing; **vous êtes ~, vous!** (ironic) don't make me laugh!; **3**○ **un ~ de courage** a lot of courage.
IDIOMS **j'en ai entendu de ~s** I heard some funny things; **en faire voir de ~s à qn** to lead sb a merry dance.

drôlement /dʀolmɑ̃/ *adv* **1**○ really; **2** oddly.

dromadaire /dʀɔmadɛʀ/ *nm* dromedary.

dru, **~e** /dʀy/ **I** *adj* **1** [*hair*] thick; **2** [*shower*] heavy.
II *adv* **1** [*grow*] thickly; **2 la pluie tombait ~** it was raining heavily.

druide /dʀɥid/ *nm* druid.

DST /deɛste/ *nf* (*abbr* = **Direction de la surveillance du territoire**) French counter-intelligence agency.

du /dy/ *det* ▶ **de**.

dû, **due**, *mpl* **dus** /dy/ **I** *pp* ▶ **devoir**[1].

II *pp adj* **1** owed, owing, due (**à** to); **en bonne et due forme** in due form; **2** **~ à** due to.
III *nm* **réclamer son ~** to claim one's due; **payer son ~** to pay one's dues.
IDIOMS **chose promise chose due** a promise is a promise.

dualité /dɥalite/ *nf* duality.

dubitatif, -ive /dybitatif, iv/ *adj* sceptical (GB), skeptical (US).

duc /dyk/ *nm* duke.

duché /dyʃe/ *nm* **1** dukedom; **2** duchy.

duchesse /dyʃɛs/ *nf* duchess.

duel /dɥɛl/*nm* duel (**à** with); (figurative) battle.

dune /dyn/ *nf* dune.

duo /dyo, dɥo/ *nm* **1** duet; **en ~** as a duo; **2** double act (GB), duo (US); **3**° pair.

dupe /dyp/ I *adj* **être ~** to be taken in or fooled (**de** by).
II *nf* dupe; **un marché de ~s** a fool's bargain.

duper /dype/ [1] *vtr* to fool; **facile à ~** gullible.

duplex /dyplɛks/ *nm inv* maisonette (GB), duplex apartment (US).

duplicata /dyplikata/ *nm inv* duplicate.

duplicité /dyplisite/ *nf* duplicity; **avec ~** duplicitously.

duquel ▸ **lequel**.

dur, ~e /dyʀ/ I *adj* **1** [*ground, toothbrush, bread*] hard; [*meat*] tough; [*brush, cardboard*] stiff; [*plastic*] rigid; **2** [*zip, handle, pedal*] stiff; [*steering*] heavy; **3** **elle est ~e à la tâche** she's a hard worker; **4** [*sound, tone, light, colour*] harsh; **5** [*face, expression*] severe; **6** [*parents, boss*] hard; harsh; [*policy*] hardline; **la droite/gauche ~e** the hard Right/Left; **7** [*living conditions*] harsh; [*credit terms*] tough; **8** [*job*] hard; tough; [*climate, necessity*] harsh; [*competition, sport*] hard, tough; **le plus ~ est passé** the hardest part is over; **9** [*exam*] hard, difficult; **10** [*water*] hard.
II *nm,f* **1** tough nut°; **jouer les ~s** to act tough; **2** hardliner.
III *adv* [*work, hit*] hard.
IV *nm* **construction en ~** permanent structure.
V **à la dure** *phr* **élevé à la ~e** brought up the hard way.
IDIOMS **~ d'oreille**° hard of hearing; **avoir la tête ~e** to be stubborn; to be dense; **avoir la vie ~e** [*habit*] to die hard; **mener la vie ~e à qn** to give sb a hard time; **en faire voir de ~es à qn** to give sb a hard time.

durable /dyʀabl/ *adj* [*impression*] lasting; [*interest*] enduring; [*situation*] long-standing; [*material*] durable.

durant /dyʀɑ̃/ *prep* **1** for; **des heures ~** for hours and hours; **deux jours ~** for two whole days; **2** during.

durcir /dyʀsiʀ/ [3] I *vtr* **1** to harden [*ground, features, position*]; **2** to step up [*strike action*]; **~ sa politique en matière de** to take a harder line on.
II *vi* [*clay, artery*] to harden; [*cement, glue*] to set; [*bread*] to go hard.
III **se durcir** *v refl* (+ *v être*) **1** [*clay, arteries, face*] to harden; **2** [*tone*] to become harsher; [*conflict*] to intensify.

durée /dyʀe/ *nf* **1** (of reign, studies) length; (of contract) term; (of record, cassette) playing time; **pour** or **pendant (toute) la ~ de** for the duration of; **séjour d'une ~ de trois mois** three-month stay; **contrat à ~ déterminée** fixed-term contract; **de courte ~** [*peace*] short-lived; [*absence*] brief; [*loan*] short-term; **de longue ~** [*loan, contract*] long-term; [*absence*] long; **2** **~ (de vie)** life; **pile longue ~** long-life battery; **3** (Mus) (of note) value.

durement /dyʀmɑ̃/ *adv* **1** badly; **2** harshly; **3** [*look*] severely; **4** [*hit*] hard.

durer /dyʀe/ [1] *vi* **1** to last; **pourvu que ça dure** long may it last; **2** to go on; **ça ne peut plus ~** it can't go on any longer; **faire ~** to prolong [*meeting*]; **faire ~ le plaisir** (ironic) to prolong the agony; **3** [*conference, festival*] to run (**de** from; **à** to).

dureté /dyʀte/ *nf* **1** (of material, face) hardness; (of meat) toughness; (of brush) stiffness; **2** (of expression, tone, climate) harshness; (of look) severity; **avec ~** [*look*] severely; [*punish*] harshly; **3** (of task) difficulty.

durillon /dyʀijɔ̃/ *nm* callus.

durite /dyʀit/ *nf* radiator hose.

DUT /deyte/ *nm* (*abbr* = **diplôme universitaire de technologie**) *two-year diploma from a university institute of technology*.

duvet /dyvɛ/ *nm* **1** (of bird) down; **2** sleeping bag.

duveteux, -euse /dyvtø, øz/ *adj* downy (GB), fuzzy.

dynamique /dinamik/ I *adj* dynamic, lively.
II *nf* **1** dynamics; **2** process.

dynamiser /dinamize/ [1] *vtr* **1** to make [sb/sth] more dynamic; **2** to revitalize.

dynamisme /dinamism/ *nm* dynamism; **être plein de ~** to be very dynamic.

dynamite /dinamit/ *nf* dynamite.

dynastie /dinasti/ *nf* dynasty.

dysenterie /disɑ̃tʀi/ *nf* dysentery.

dysfonctionnement /disfɔ̃ksjɔnmɑ̃/ *nm* **1** (Med) dysfunction; **2** malfunctioning.

dyslexie /dislɛksi/ *nf* dyslexia.

Ee

e, **E** /ə/ *nm inv* e, E; **e dans l'o** a and o joined together.

eau, *pl* **~x** /o/ **I** *nf* **1** water; **l'~ de source** spring water; **2** water; **l'~ de la rivière** the water in the river; **prendre l'~** [*shoe*] to let in water; **être à l'~** [*boat*] to be launched; (figurative) [*project, plan*] to have gone down the drain; **être en ~** (figurative) to be dripping with sweat; **mettre à l'~** to launch [*ship*]; **se jeter à l'~** to throw oneself into the water; (figurative) to take the plunge; **tomber à l'~** to fall into the water; (figurative) to fall through; **nettoyer le sol à grande ~** to sluice the floor down; **3** rain; **4** water; **émeraude de la plus belle ~** emerald of the finest quality.

II eaux *nf pl* **1** water; waters; **~x troubles** muddy waters; (figurative) troubled waters; **2** (Med) waters.

■ **~ bénite** holy water; **~ de chaux** limewater; **~ douce** fresh water; **~ de Javel** ≈ (chloride) bleach; **~ lourde** heavy water; **~ de mer** seawater; **~ oxygénée** hydrogen peroxide; **~ plate** plain water; still mineral water; **~ de rose** rose water; **à l'~ de rose** [*novel, film*] sentimental; **~ de vaisselle** dishwater; **~ vive** white water; **~x et forêts** forestry commission; **~x usées** waste water.

IDIOMS **mettre l'~ à la bouche de qn** to make sb's mouth water; **c'est l'~ et le feu** they are like chalk and cheese; **être de la même ~** to be of the same ilk; **ou dans ces ~x-là**○ or thereabouts; **vivre d'amour et d'~ fraîche** to live on love alone.

EAU *written abbr* ▶ **Émirats**.

eau-de-vie, *pl* **eaux-de-vie** /odvi/ *nf* brandy, eau de vie; **à l'~** in brandy.

eau-forte, *pl* **eaux-fortes** /ofɔrt/ *nf* etching.

ébahir /ebaiʀ/ [3] **I** *vtr* to dumbfound.

II s'ébahir *v refl* (+ *v être*) to be dumbfounded (**de, devant** by).

ébattre: **s'ébattre** /ebatʀ/ [61] *v refl* (+ *v être*) to frolic (about); to frisk about; to splash about.

ébauche /eboʃ/ *nf* **1** (for sculpture) rough shape; (for picture) preliminary sketch; (of novel, reform) preliminary draft; **2** (of sculpture) rough-hewing; (of picture) sketching out; (of novel, reform) drafting; **être encore à l'état d'~** to be still at an early stage; **3 l'~ d'un sourire** a hint of a smile; **l'~ d'un geste** an arrested gesture.

ébaucher /eboʃe/ [1] **I** *vtr* to sketch out [*picture, solution*]; to draft [*novel, plan*]; to rough-hew [*statue*]; to begin [*conversation*].

II s'ébaucher *v refl* (+ *v être*) [*solution, novel*] to begin to take shape; [*friendship*] to begin to develop; [*talks*] to start; [*image*] to begin to form.

ébène /ebɛn/ *nf* ebony.

ébéniste /ebenist/ *nmf* cabinetmaker.

éberluer /ebɛʀlɥe/ [1] *vtr* to dumbfound.

éblouir /ebluiʀ/ [3] *vtr* to dazzle.

éblouissant, **~e** /ebluisɑ̃, ɑ̃t/ *adj* dazzling.

éblouissement /ebluismɑ̃/ *nm* **1** dazzle; **2** (figurative) dazzling experience; **3** dizzy spell.

éborgner /ebɔʀɲe/ [1] *vtr* **~ qn** to blind sb in one eye; (humorous) to poke sb's eye out.

éboueur /ebuœʀ/ *nm* dustman (GB), garbageman (US).

ébouillanter /ebujɑ̃te/ [1] *vtr* **1** to scald; **2** to blanch [*vegetables*].

éboulement /ebulmɑ̃/ *nm* (of wall, cliff) collapse; **~ (de rochers)** rockfall; **~ (de terrain)** mudslide.

éboulis /ebuli/ *nm inv* mass of fallen rocks; heap of fallen earth.

ébouriffer /ebuʀife/ [1] *vtr* to tousle; to ruffle.

ébranler /ebʀɑ̃le/ [1] **I** *vtr* **1** to rattle [*windowpane*]; to shake [*house*]; to weaken [*building*]; **2** to shake [*person, country, confidence*]; to undermine [*health*].

II s'ébranler *v refl* (+ *v être*) [*train*] to move off.

ébrécher /ebʀeʃe/ [14] *vtr* to chip [*cup*]; to make a nick in [*blade*]; to damage [*saw*].

ébriété /ebʀijete/ *nf* intoxication.

ébrouer: **s'ébrouer** /ebʀue/ [1] *v refl* (+ *v être*) **1** [*horse*] to snort; **2** [*person, dog*] to shake oneself/itself; [*bird*] to flap its wings.

ébruiter /ebʀɥite/ [1] **I** *vtr* to divulge.

II s'ébruiter *v refl* (+ *v être*) [*news*] to get out.

ébullition /ebylisjɔ̃/ *nf* (Culin) boiling; **porter à ~** to bring to the (GB) or a (US) boil.

IDIOMS **être en ~** [*crowd*] to be in a fever of excitement; [*country, brain*] to be in a ferment.

écaille /ekaj/ *nf* **1** (on fish, reptile) scale; (on oyster) shell; **2** tortoiseshell; **lunettes en ~** horn-rimmed glasses; **3** flake; **4** (of bud, onion) scale.

écailler[1] /ekaje/ [1] **I** *vtr* **1** (Culin) to scale [*fish*]; to open [*oyster*]; **2 ~ qch** to chip [sth] off.

II s'écailler *v refl* (+ *v être*) to flake away.

écailler[2], **-ère** /ekaje, ɛʀ/ *nm,f* oyster seller.

écarlate /ekaʀlat/ *adj* scarlet.

écarquiller /ekaʀkije/ [1] *vtr* **~ les yeux** to open one's eyes wide.

écart /ekaʀ/ **I** *nm* **1** (between objects) distance, gap; (between dates) interval; (between ideas) gap; (between versions) difference; **2** difference; **~ des salaires** pay differential; **3 faire un ~** [*horse*] to shy; [*car*] to swerve; [*person*] to leap aside; **4** lapse; **il fait des ~s de régime** he doesn't stick to his diet; **~s de langage** bad language; **5** (in cards) discard.

II à l'écart *phr* **être à l'~** to be isolated; **se tenir à l'~** to stand apart; (aloofly) to keep oneself to oneself; not to join in; **mettre qn à**

l'~ to push sb aside; (as censure) to ostracize sb; **entraîner qn à l'~** to take sb aside.
III à l'écart de *phr* away from; **tenir qn à l'~ de** to keep sb away from [*place*]; to keep sb out of [*activity, talks*].

écarté, ~e /ekaʀte/ **I** *pp* ▶ **écarter**.
II *pp adj* **1** [*fingers*] spread; [*arms*] wide apart; [*knees, legs*] apart; [*eyes*] widely set; [*teeth*] widely spaced; **2** [*place*] isolated.

écarteler /ekaʀtəle/ [17] *vtr* (kill) to quarter [sb].

écartement /ekaʀtəmɑ̃/ *nm* distance, space.

écarter /ekaʀte/ [1] **I** *vtr* **1** to move [sth] further apart [*objects*]; to open [*curtains*]; to spread [*fingers, legs*]; to part [*lips, leaves*]; **2** to move [sth] aside [*chair*]; to remove [*obstacle*]; to push [sb] aside; to move [sb] on; **3 ~ qn de son devoir** to distract sb from his duty; **4** to dispel [*suspicion*]; to eliminate [*risk*]; to eliminate, to push [sb] aside [*rival*]; **5** to reject [*idea, application*]; to rule out [*possibility*].
II s'écarter *v refl* (+ *v être*) **1** [*crowd, clouds*] to part; [*shutters*] to open; **2** to move away; **3 s'~ de** to move away from [*direction, standard*]; to stray from [*path, subject*].

ecchymose /ekimoz/ *nf* bruise.

ecclésiastique /eklezjastik/ **I** *adj* ecclesiastical; **ordres ~s** holy orders.
II *nm* cleric.

écervelé, ~e /esɛʀvəle/ *nm,f* featherbrain.

échafaud /eʃafo/ *nm* **1** scaffold; **2** guillotine.

échafaudage /eʃafodaʒ/ *nm* **1** scaffolding; **2** stack.

échafauder /eʃafode/ [1] *vtr* **1** to put [sth] together [*plan*]; to develop [*theory*]; to build up [*fortune*]; **2** to stack [sth] up.

échalas /eʃala/ *nm inv* **1** cane, stake; **2**° beanpole°.

échalote /eʃalɔt/ *nf* shallot.

échancré, ~e /eʃɑ̃kʀe/ *adj* **1** [*dress*] low-cut; [*briefs*] high-cut; **trop ~** [*sleeve*] cut too wide; **2** [*blouse*] open-necked; **3** [*coast*] indented; [*leaf*] jagged.

échange /eʃɑ̃ʒ/ **I** *nm* **1** exchange; **elles ont fait l'~ de leurs manteaux** they've swapped coats; **2** trade; **~s commerciaux** trade; **3** (cultural, linguistic) exchange; **4** (Sport) rally; **5** (in chess) exchange.
II en échange *phr* in exchange, in return.
III en échange de *phr* in exchange for, in return for.
■ **~ de bons procédés** quid pro quo; **~ standard** replacement by a reconditioned part.

échanger /eʃɑ̃ʒe/ [13] *vtr* **1** to exchange; **~ des insultes** to trade insults; **'ni repris ni échangés'** 'no exchanges or returns'; **2** (Sport) **~ des balles** to rally.

échangeur /eʃɑ̃ʒœʀ/ *nm* interchange (GB), grade separation (US).

échantillon /eʃɑ̃tijɔ̃/ *nm* sample.

échappatoire /eʃapatwaʀ/ *nf* way out.

échappement /eʃapmɑ̃/ *nm* (Aut) (**tuyau d'**)~ exhaust (pipe); (expulsion) release.

échapper /eʃape/ [1] **I échapper à** *v+prep* **1** to get away from; (cleverly) to elude; **2** to escape [*death, failure*]; (to manage) to avoid [*accident, punishment*]; **3** to escape from [*social background*]; to shake off [*anxiety*]; **je sens qu'il m'échappe** [*partner*] I feel he is drifting away from me; [*child*] I feel he's growing away from me; **4 ~ à qn** or **des mains de qn** to slip out of sb's hands; **5 un soupir m'a échappé** I let out a sigh; **6** to escape; **le titre m'échappe** the title escapes me; **cela m'échappe** it's beyond me; **7** to defy [*logic*]; **~ à la règle** to be an exception to the rule.
II s'échapper *v refl* (+ *v être*) **1** to run away; to fly away; to escape; to get away; **2** [*gas, smoke*] to escape; [*water*] to leak; **3** to get away; **s'~ pour quelques jours** to get away for a few days; **4 laisser s'~** to shed [*tears*]; to let out [*sigh, words*].
IDIOMS **l'~ belle** to have a narrow escape.

écharde /eʃaʀd/ *nf* splinter.

écharpe /eʃaʀp/ *nf* **1** scarf; **2** sash; **3** (Med) sling.

écharper /eʃaʀpe/ [1] *vtr* **~ qn/qch** to tear sb/sth to pieces.

échasse /eʃɑs/ *nf* stilt.

échassier /eʃasje/ *nm* wading bird.

échauder /eʃode/ [1] *vtr* **1** to put [sb] off; **2** to scald.
IDIOMS **chat échaudé craint l'eau froide** (Proverb) once bitten, twice shy.

échauffement /eʃofmɑ̃/ *nm* (Sport) warm-up.

échauffer /eʃofe/ [1] *vtr* **1** (Sport) to warm up; **2** to stir [*imagination*]; to stir up [*person, debate*]; **3** to start [sth] fermenting.
IDIOMS **~ les oreilles de qn** to vex sb.

échéance /eʃeɑ̃s/ *nf* **1** (of debt) due date; (of share, policy) maturity date; (of loan) redemption date; **arriver à ~** [*payment*] to fall due; [*investment, policy*] to mature; **2** expiry date; **3 à longue/brève ~** [*forecast*] long-/short-term; [*strengthen, change*] in the long/short term; **4** payment; repayment; **5** date; deadline.

échéancier /eʃeɑ̃sje/ *nm* **1** schedule of due dates; **2** schedule of repayments.

échéant: **le cas échéant** /ləkazeʃeɑ̃/ *phr* if need be, should the case arise.

échec /eʃɛk/ **I** *nm* **1** failure; setback; **faire ~ à qn** to thwart sb; **2** defeat; (Mil) reverse; **3 faire ~ au roi** to check the king; **~ et mat** checkmate.
II échecs *nm pl* **les ~s** chess; chess set; chessmen.

échelle /eʃɛl/ *nf* **1** ladder; **~ coulissante** extending ladder (GB), extension ladder (US); **faire la courte ~ à qn** to give sb a leg up; **2** (of map, model) scale; **3** scale; **à l'~ humaine** on a human scale; **4** (figurative) (social) scale, ladder; (professional) hierarchy, ladder; **~ des salaires** pay scale; **5** (Mus) scale; **6**° (in stocking) ladder.

échelon /eʃlɔ̃/ *nm* **1** rung; **2** grade; **sauter les ~s** to get accelerated promotion; **3** level.

échelonner /eʃlɔne/ [1] **I** *vtr* **1** to space [sth] out [*objects*]; **2** to spread [*payments, work*]; to stagger [*holidays*]; **3** to grade [*exercises*]; to build up [*arguments*].

II **s'échelonner** *v refl* (+ *v être*) **1** to be positioned at intervals; **2** [*payments, work*] to be spread (**sur** over); [*holidays, departures*] to be staggered (**sur** over).

écheveau, *pl* **~x** /eʃvo/ *nm* **1** hank, skein; **2** (figurative) tangle.

échevelé, **~e** /eʃəvle/ *adj* **1** tousled; **2** [*rhythm*] frenzied; [*romanticism*] unbridled.

échine /eʃin/ *nf* **1** (Anat) spine; **2** (Culin) ≈ spare rib.

IDIOMS **courber l'~ devant** to submit to; **avoir l'~ souple** to be a toady.

échiquier /eʃikje/ *nm* **1** chessboard; **2** chequered (GB) or checkered (US) pattern.

Échiquier /eʃikje/ *pr nm* **l'~** the Exchequer, the Treasury.

écho /eko/ *nm* **1** echo; **faire ~ à qch**, **se faire l'~ de qch** to echo sth; **2** response; **nous n'avons eu aucun ~ des pourparlers** we have heard nothing about the talks.

échographie /ekogʀafi/ *nf* (Med) scan; **passer une ~** to have a scan.

échoir /eʃwaʀ/ [51] I *vi* (+ *v être*) [*rent*] to fall due; [*draft*] to be payable.

II **échoir à** *v+prep* **~ à qn** to fall to sb's share.

échoppe /eʃɔp/ *nf* stall.

échouer /eʃwe/ [1] I *vtr* to beach [*boat*].

II **échouer à** *v+prep* to fail [*exam, test*].

III *vi* **1** [*person, attempt*] to fail; **~ face à un adversaire** to lose to an opponent; **faire ~** to cause [sth] to fail [*talks, plan*]; **2** to end up (**dans** in); **3** to run aground.

IV **s'échouer** *v refl* (+ *v être*) [*boat*] to run aground; [*whale*] to be beached.

échu, **~e** /eʃy/ I *pp* ▶ **échoir**.

II *adj* expired; **payer à terme ~** to pay in arrears.

éclabousser /eklabuse/ [1] *vtr* **1** to splash; to spatter; **2 il a été éclaboussé par ces rumeurs** the rumours[GB] have damaged his reputation.

éclair /eklɛʀ/ I *adj inv* **rencontre ~** brief meeting; **visite ~** flying visit; **attaque ~** lightning strike; **guerre ~** blitzkrieg; **repas ~** quick meal.

II *nm* **1** flash of lightning; **passer comme un ~** to flash past; **2** (of explosion, diamonds) flash; (of eyes) glint; **3** (of lucidity, triumph) moment; **il a eu un ~ de génie** he had a brainwave (GB) or brainstorm (US); **4** (Culin) éclair.

éclairage /eklɛʀaʒ/ *nm* lighting; light; **~ au gaz** gaslight; **sous cet ~** (figurative) in that light.

éclairagiste /eklɛʀaʒist/ *nm* (in theatre, films) electrician.

éclaircie /eklɛʀsi/ *nf* sunny spell.

éclaircir /eklɛʀsiʀ/ [3] I *vtr* **1** to lighten [*colour*]; to lighten the colour[GB] of [*paint, hair*]; to improve [*complexion*]; **2** to shed light on [sth].

II **s'éclaircir** *v refl* (+ *v être*) **1** [*weather*] to clear; **l'horizon s'éclaircit** (figurative) the outlook is getting brighter; **2** [*colour*] to fade; [*complexion*] to improve; [*hair*] to get lighter; **3** [*situation, mystery*] to become clearer; **4** [*crowd, forest*] to thin out; **5 s'~ les cheveux** to lighten one's hair; **s'~ la voix** or **la gorge** to clear one's throat.

éclaircissant /eklɛʀsisɑ̃/ *adj m* **produit ~** hair lightener.

éclaircissement /eklɛʀsismɑ̃/ *nm* **1** explanation; **2** clarification.

éclairé, **~e** /ekleʀe/ *adj* [*person, advice*] enlightened; [*art lover*] well-informed.

éclairer /ekleʀe/ [1] I *vtr* **1** to light [*street, room*]; [*sun*] to light up [*place, object*]; [*accessory*] to set off [*garment*]; **2** to give [sb] some light; to light the way for [sb]; **3** [*remark*] to throw light on [*text, situation*]; **4** to enlighten [sb].

II *vi* to give light.

III **s'éclairer** *v refl* (+ *v être*) **1** [*screen, face*] to light up; **2 s'~ à l'électricité** to have electric lighting; **3** [*situation*] to become clearer; [*matter*] to be cleared up.

éclaireur, **-euse** /eklɛʀœʀ, øz/ *nm,f* **1** scout (GB), Boy Scout (US); **2** guide (GB), Girl Guide (US); **3** (Mil) scout.

éclat /ekla/ *nm* **1** splinter; **un ~ d'obus** a piece of shrapnel; **voler en ~s** to shatter; **2** (of light, star) brightness; (of lighthouse, spotlight) glare; (of snow, diamond) sparkle; **3** (of colour, material) brilliance; (of flower) brightness; (of hair, plumage) shine, sheen; (of metal) lustre[GB]; (of complexion) radiance; (on shoe, table) shine; **4** (of face, smile) radiance; (of eyes) sparkle; **sans ~** [*eyes*] dull; [*beauty*] lifeless; **5** splendour[GB]; **avec ~** [*announce*] dramatically; [*celebrate*] with great pomp; **manquer d'~** [*ceremony, speech*] to lack sparkle; **6** scene; **faire un ~** to make a scene.

■ **~ de colère** fit of anger; **~ de rire** roar of laughter; **des ~s de voix** raised voices.

IDIOMS **rire aux ~s** to roar with laughter.

éclatant, **~e** /eklatɑ̃, ɑ̃t/ *adj* **1** [*light*] dazzling; [*sun*] blazing; **2** [*colour, plumage*] bright; **dents d'une blancheur ~e** sparkling white teeth; **3** [*beauty, smile*] radiant; [*victory, success*] brilliant; **4** [*proof, display*] striking; **5** [*laughter, voice*] ringing.

éclaté, **~e** /eklate/ *adj* (gen) fragmented; [*family*] divided.

éclatement /eklatmɑ̃/ *nm* **1** (of pipe) bursting; **2** (of spleen, liver) rupture; **2** (of grenade) explosion; (of tyre) blow-out; **3** break-up.

éclater /eklate/ [1] *vi* **1** [*tyre, bubble*] to burst; [*shell, firework*] to explode; [*bottle*] to shatter; **faire ~** to burst [*bubble, balloon*]; to detonate [*bomb, grenade*]; to let off [*firework*]; **2** [*pipe, boil*] to burst; **3** [*laughter, firing*] to break out; [*shot*] to ring out; **4** [*scandal, news*] to break; [*truth*] to come out; **5** [*war*] to break out; [*storm*] to break; [*crisis*] to erupt; **6** [*anger*] to erupt; **laisser ~ sa joie** to be wild with joy; **7** [*coalition*] to break up (**en** into); [*party*] to split;

8 to lose one's temper; **~ de rire** to burst out laughing.

éclectique /eklɛktik/ *adj* eclectic.

éclipse /eklips/ *nf* eclipse.

éclipser /eklipse/ [1] **I** *vtr* **1** to eclipse; **2** to obscure; **3** to outshine.

II s'éclipser○ *v refl* (+ *v être*) to slip away.

éclopé, ~e /eklɔpe/ *adj* injured, lame.

éclore /eklɔʀ/ [79] *vi* **1** [*chick, egg*] to hatch; [*flower*] to bloom; **faire ~ un œuf** to incubate an egg; **2** [*idea*] to dawn; [*talent*] to bloom.

écluse /eklyz/ *nf* lock.

écœurant, ~e /ekœʀɑ̃, ɑ̃t/ *adj* **1** [*food, smell*] sickly; [*dish*] over-rich; **2** nauseating; **3** (humorous) sickening; **tu es vraiment ~** you make me sick.

écœurement /ekœʀmɑ̃/ *nm* nausea; **jusqu'à l'~** ad nauseam.

écœurer /ekœʀe/ [1] *vtr* **1** to make [sb] feel sick; **2** (figurative) to sicken.

école /ekɔl/ *nf* **1** school; **être à l'~** to be at (GB) or in (US) school; **la grande/petite ~** primary/nursery school; **2** education system; **3** (**grande**) **~** *higher education institution with competitive entrance examination*; **une ~ de commerce** a business school; **4** training (**de** in); **être à bonne ~** to be in good hands; **5** (in art) school; **faire ~** to gain a following.

■ **~ élémentaire** primary school; **~ hôtelière** hotel management school; **~ d'infirmières** nursing college; **~ libre** independent education; independent school; **~ maternelle** nursery school; **~ militaire** military academy; **~ normale** primary teacher training college; **~ primaire** primary school; **~ publique** state school (GB), public school (US); state education (GB), public education (US); **École nationale d'administration, ENA** *Grande École for top civil servants*; **École normale supérieure, ENS** *Grande École from which the educational élite is recruited*.

écolier, -ière /ekɔlje, ɛʀ/ *nm,f* schoolchild, schoolboy/schoolgirl.

écologie /ekɔlɔʒi/ *nf* ecology.

écologique /ekɔlɔʒik/ *adj* **1** [*balance, catastrophe*] ecological; [*speech*] on the environment; **2** [*impact, interest*] environmental; **3** [*product*] environment-friendly.

écologiste /ekɔlɔʒist/ **I** *adj* **1** [*candidate*] Green; **2** [*measure*] ecological.

II *nmf* **1** environmentalist; **2** Green (candidate); **3** ecologist.

écomusée /ekomyze/ *nm* ≈ open air museum.

éconduire /ekɔ̃dɥiʀ/ [69] *vtr* to turn [sb] away.

économat /ekɔnɔma/ *nm* **1** bursar's office; **2** (function) office of bursar.

économe /ekɔnɔm/ **I** *adj* economical; **~ de son temps** sparing with one's time.

II *nm* (Culin) potato peeler.

économie /ekɔnɔmi/ **I** *nf* **1** (of country) economy; **2** economics; **3** saving; **faire l'~ de** to save the cost of [*trip, meal*]; **4** economy, thrift; **par ~** to save money; **5** economy, succinctness; **s'exprimer avec une grande ~ de paroles** to express oneself succinctly.

II économies *nf pl* savings; **faire des ~s** to save up; to save money.

■ **~ d'entreprise** managerial economics; **~ de marché** free market (economy).

IDIOMS **il n'y a pas de petites ~s** every little helps.

économique /ekɔnɔmik/ *adj* **1** [*policy, crisis*] economic; **2** economical.

économiser /ekɔnɔmize/ [1] *vtr* **1** to save (up) [*money*]; **~ ses forces** to pace oneself; **2** to save [*petrol, water, energy*]; **3** to economize.

économiste /ekɔnɔmist/ *nmf* economist.

écoper /ekɔpe/ [1] **I** *vtr* to bail out.

II écoper○ **de** *v+prep* to get [*fine, punishment*].

III○ *vi* to take the rap○.

écorce /ekɔʀs/ *nf* (of tree) bark; (of fruit) peel; (of chestnut) skin.

■ **~ terrestre** earth's crust.

écorché, ~e /ekɔʀʃe/ **I** *adj* **~** (**vif**) hypersensitive.

II *nm* **1** (Anat) écorché; **2** cutaway (diagram).

écorcher /ekɔʀʃe/ [1] *vtr* **1** to skin; to flay; **2** to graze [*face, leg*]; **3** to mispronounce [*word*]; to murder [*song, language*].

écorchure /ekɔʀʃyʀ/ *nf* graze.

écossais, ~e /ekɔsɛ, ɛz/ **I** *adj* [*character, landscape*] Scottish; [*whisky*] Scotch; [*language*] Scots; [*skirt*] tartan.

II *nm* **1** Scots; **2** (Scottish) Gaelic; **3** tartan (cloth).

Écossais, ~e /ekɔsɛ, ɛz/ *nm,f* Scotsman/Scotswoman, Scot.

Écosse /ekɔs/ *pr nf* Scotland.

écosser /ekɔse/ [1] *vtr* to shell.

écoulement /ekulmɑ̃/ *nm* **1** (of water, traffic) flow; (of time) passing; **2** (Med) discharge; **~ de sang** bleeding; **3** (of banknotes, drugs) circulation.

écouler /ekule/ [1] **I** *vtr* **1** to sell [*product, stock*]; **les stocks sont écoulés** stocks are exhausted; **2** to pass [*banknote, drugs*]; to fence [*stolen goods*].

II s'écouler *v refl* (+ *v être*) **1** [*time, life*] to pass; **la semaine écoulée** the past week; **2** [*river*] to flow; **3** [*oil, water*] to escape; **4** [*water*] to drain away; **5** [*product*] to move.

écourter /ekuʀte/ [1] *vtr* to cut short [*stay*]; to shorten [*speech*].

écoute /ekut/ *nf* **1 l'~ de** listening to [*poem, cassette, person*]; **être à l'~ de** to be listening to [*programme*]; to be (always) ready to listen to [*problems*]; **2** audience; **un taux d'~ de 15%** audience ratings of 15%; **heure de grande ~** peak listening time; peak viewing time; **3** (Tech) **un appareil d'~** a listening device; **un centre d'~(s)** monitoring centre[GB]; **je suis sur ~(s)** my phone is being tapped.

écouter /ekute/ [1] **I** *vtr* **1** to listen to [sb/sth]; **~ qn chanter/parler** to listen to sb singing/talking; **écoute, ne sois pas ridicule!** come on, don't be ridiculous!; **~ aux portes** to eavesdrop; **2** to listen to [*explanation, witness, advice*]; **3 ~ son cœur** to follow one's own inclination.

II **s'écouter** *v refl* (+ *v être*) **1 s'~ parler** to like the sound of one's own voice; **2** to cosset oneself; **3 si je m'écoutais** if it was up to me.

écouteur /ekutœʀ/ *nm* **1** (on phone) earpiece; **2** earphones; **3** headphones.

écoutille /ekutij/ *nf* (Naut) hatch.

écrabouiller○ /ekʀabuje/ [1] *vtr* **1** to squash; to flatten; **2** to crush○.

écran /ekʀɑ̃/ *nm* **1** screen; **porter une œuvre à l'~** to adapt a work for the cinema; **crever l'~** to have a great screen presence; **2** cinema (GB), movie theater (US); **3** screen; (on machine) display; **une vedette du petit ~** a TV star; **4** screen; **crème ~ total** sun block; **5** screen; (nuclear) shielding.

■ **~ antibruit** soundproofing; **~ de cheminée** firescreen; **~ de contrôle** monitor; **~ de fumée** screen of smoke; (figurative) smokescreen; **~ solaire** sunscreen.

écrasant, **~e** /ekʀazɑ̃, ɑ̃t/ *adj* **1** [*weight*] enormous; **2** [*heat*] sweltering; [*defeat, debt*] crushing; [*victory*] resounding; [*responsibility*] heavy.

écraser /ekʀaze/ [1] **I** *vtr* **1** to crush [*finger, person*]; to squash [*insect*]; [*driver*] to run over [*person, animal*]; **se faire ~** to get run over; **il écraserait tout le monde pour réussir** he would walk over anyone to succeed; **2** to squash [*box, fruit*]; to flatten [*vegetation*]; **3** (Culin) to mash [*fruit, vegetables*]; **4** to squash; **~ sa cigarette** to stub out one's cigarette; **~ une larme** to wipe away a tear; **5** to press [*nose, face*] (**contre** against); **6** to crush [*rebellion*]; to thrash○ [*opponent*]; **7** to outshine [sb]; **8** to put [sb] down; **9** [*grief, pain*] to overwhelm; [*fatigue, heat*] to overcome.

II **s'écraser** *v refl* (+ *v être*) **1** [*car, train*] to crash; [*driver, motorcyclist*] to have a crash; [*insect*] to splatter (**contre** on); **s'~ (au sol)** [*plane*] to crash (to the ground); **2**○ to shut up○; **3**○ to keep one's head down.

écrémer /ekʀeme/ [14] *vtr* to skim; **du lait écrémé** skimmed milk.

écrevisse /ekʀəvis/ *nf* crayfish (GB), crawfish (US).

écrier: **s'écrier** /ekʀije/ [2] *v refl* (+ *v être*) to exclaim; **s'~ que** to cry that.

écrin /ekʀɛ̃/ *nm* (for jewellery) case.

écrire /ekʀiʀ/ [67] **I** *vtr* **1** to write; **2** to spell.

II *vi* to write; **essaie de mieux ~** try to improve your writing.

III **s'écrire** *v refl* (+ *v être*) **1** to be written; **2** to be spelled.

écrit, **~e** /ekʀi, it/ **I** *adj* written; **c'était ~** it was bound to happen.

II *nm* **1** work, piece of writing; **2** document; **par ~** in writing; **3** written examination; written work.

IDIOMS **les paroles s'envolent, les ~s restent** never put anything in writing; (as security) get it in writing.

écriteau, *pl* **~x** /ekʀito/ *nm* sign.

écritoire /ekʀitwaʀ/ *nf* writing case.

écriture /ekʀityʀ/ **I** *nf* **1** handwriting; **2** (in printing) hand; **3** (text) writing; **4** script; **~ phonétique** phonetic script; **5** (activity) writing; **6** style.

II **écritures** *nf pl* accounts; **tenir les ~s** to do the books.

Écriture /ekʀityʀ/ *nf* **les (saintes) ~s** the Scriptures; **l'~ sainte** Holy Writ.

écrivain /ekʀivɛ̃/ *nm* writer; **~ public** letter-writer.

écrou /ekʀu/ *nm* (Tech) nut.

écrouer /ekʀue/ [1] *vtr* (Law) to commit [sb] to prison.

écroulé, **~e** /ekʀule/ *adj* **1** overwhelmed; **~**○ **de rire** doubled up with laughter; **2** [*building, bridge*] in a state of collapse.

écrouler: **s'écrouler** /ekʀule/ [1] *v refl* (+ *v être*) [*wall, person, regime*] to collapse; [*hope*] to fade; [*dream, illusion*] to crumble.

écru, **~e** /ekʀy/ *adj* **1** [*canvas*] unbleached; [*wool*] undyed; [*silk*] raw; **2** ecru.

ECU /eky/ *nm*: (*abbr* = **European currency unit**) ECU.

écu /eky/ *nm* **1** (in EU) ecu; **2** ≈ crown; **3** shield; **4** escutcheon.

écueil /ekœj/ *nm* **1** reef; **2** (figurative) pitfall.

écuelle /ekɥɛl/ *nf* **1** bowl; **2** bowlful.

éculé, **~e** /ekyle/ *adj* hackneyed.

écume /ekym/ *nf* **1** (on water) foam; (on stock, jam) scum; (on beer, soapy water) froth; (on metal) dross; **2** (at mouth) foam, froth.

écumer /ekyme/ [1] **I** *vtr* **1** to skim; **2** to scour.

II *vi* **1** [*sea*] to foam; [*wine*] to froth; **2** to foam; **~ de rage** to be foaming with rage.

écumoire /ekymwaʀ/ *nf* skimming ladle, skimmer.

écureuil /ekyʀœj/ *nm* squirrel.

écurie /ekyʀi/ *nf* **1** stable; **2** (Sport) stable; **3** (figurative) pigsty.

écusson /ekysɔ̃/ *nm* **1** (Mil) flash (GB); **2** (of school) crest, badge; (of club, movement) badge; (of car) insignia; **3** (in heraldry) coat of arms.

écuyer, **-ère** /ekɥije, ɛʀ/ **I** *nm,f* **1** horseman/horsewoman; **2** riding instructor; **3** bareback rider.

II *nm* **1** squire; **2** equerry.

eczéma /egzema/ *nm* eczema; **~ du nourrisson** infantile eczema.

éden /edɛn/ *nm* paradise.

Éden /edɛn/ *pr nm* Eden; **le jardin d'~** the Garden of Eden.

édenté, **~e** /edɑ̃te/ *adj* **1** toothless; **2** gap-toothed; **3** [*comb*] broken.

EDF /œdeɛf/ *nf* (*abbr* = **Électricité de France**) *French electricity board.*

édicter /edikte/ [1] *vtr* to enact [*law*]; to lay down [*rule*].

édifice /edifis/ *nm* **1** building; **2** structure.

édifier /edifje/ [2] *vtr* **1** to build [sth]; **2** to build [*empire*]; to create [*work*]; **3** to edify; **4** to enlighten.

Édimbourg /edɛ̃buʀ/ *pr n* Edinburgh.

édit /edi/ *nm* edict.

éditer /edite/ [1] *vtr* **1** to publish [*book, author*]; to release [*record*]; **2** to edit; **3** (Comput) to edit.

éditeur, **-trice** /editœʀ, tʀis/ **I** *nm,f* editor.
II *nm* **1** publisher; **2** (Comput) editor.

édition /edisjɔ̃/ **I** *nf* **1** (of book) publication; (of record) release; **2** (book, print) edition; (record) release; **3** publishing; **société d'~** publishing firm; **4** editing; **5** edition; **~ du soir** evening edition.
II éditions *nf pl* **les ~s de la Roulotte** la Roulotte (Publishing Compan).

éditorial, **~e**, *mpl* **-iaux** /editɔʀjal, o/ **I** *adj* [*policy, service*] editorial.
II *nm* editorial, leader.

édredon /edʀədɔ̃/ *nm* eiderdown.

éducateur, **-trice** /edykatœʀ, tʀis/ **I** *adj* educational.
II *nm,f* youth worker.

éducatif, **-ive** /edykatif, iv/ *adj* educational.

éducation /edykasjɔ̃/ *nf* **1** education; **~ permanente/sexuelle** continuing/sex education; **2** education; **faire l'~ de qn** to educate sb; **3** training; **4** manners.
■ **Éducation nationale**, **EN** Ministry of Education; (system) state education.

édulcorant /edylkɔʀɑ̃/ *nm* sweetener.

édulcorer /edylkɔʀe/ [1] *vtr* **1** to sweeten; **2** to tone down [*letter, remark*].

éduquer /edyke/ [1] *vtr* to educate [*person*]; to train [*dog*].

effaçable /efasabl/ *adj* [*cassette*] erasable; [*stain*] removable.

effacé, **~e** /efase/ *adj* retiring.

effacement /efasmɑ̃/ *nm* **1** deletion; **2** (of cassette) erasure; **3** self-effacement.

effacer /efase/ [12] **I** *vtr* **1** to rub out; to remove; to delete; to erase; **2** to wipe [*tape*]; to clear [*screen, file*]; to clean [*blackboard*]; **3** [*sun*] to fade [*colour*]; [*rain*] to erase [*tracks*]; [*snow*] to cover (up) [*tracks*]; [*cream*] to remove [*wrinkles*]; **4** to blot out [*memory, image*]; to remove [*differences*]; **on efface tout et on recommence** let's start afresh; **5** to write off [*debt, losses*].
II s'effacer *v refl* (+ *v être*) **1 ça s'efface** you can rub it out; **2** [*inscription, drawing*] to fade; **3** [*memory*] to fade; [*impression*] to wear off; [*fear*] to disappear; **4** to step aside; **5** to stay in the background; **s'~ devant un rival** to give way to a rival.

effaceur /efasœʀ/ *nm* **~ (d'encre)** correction pen.

effarant, **~e** /efaʀɑ̃, ɑ̃t/ *adj* astounding.

effarer /efaʀe/ [1] *vtr* to alarm; **effaré de/par** alarmed at/by.

effaroucher /efaʀuʃe/ [1] *vtr* **1** to frighten [sb/sth] away; **2** to alarm.

effectif, **-ive** /efɛktif, iv/ **I** *adj* real; **devenir ~** [*measure*] to come into effect.
II *nm* (of school) number of pupils; (of university) number of students; (of company) workforce; (of army) strength.

effectivement /efɛktivmɑ̃/ *adv* **1** indeed; **2** actually, really.

effectuer /efɛktɥe/ [1] *vtr* to do [*work, repairs*]; to make [*payment, change, choice, trip*]; to carry out [*transaction*]; to conduct [*survey*]; to serve [*sentence*].

efféminé, **~e** /efemine/ *adj* effeminate.

effervescence /efɛʀvesɑ̃s/ *nf* **1** effervescence; **2** turmoil.

effervescent, **~e** /efɛʀvesɑ̃, ɑ̃t/ *adj* **1** effervescent; **2** (figurative) [*crowd*] seething; [*personality*] effervescent.

effet /efɛ/ **I** *nm* **1** effect; **n'avoir aucun ~** [*criticism, suggestion*] to have no effect; [*medicine*] not to work; **prendre ~** [*measure, law*] to take effect; **sous l'~ de l'alcool** under the influence of alcohol; **2** impression; **être du plus mauvais ~** to be in the worst possible taste; **faire un drôle d'~** [*alcohol, experience*] to make one feel strange; **un ~ de surprise** an element of surprise; **3** effect; **couper tous ses ~s à qn** to steal sb's thunder; **4 à cet ~** for that purpose; **5 l'~ Doppler** the Doppler effect.
II en effet *phr* indeed; **'tu n'étais pas chez toi hier soir?'—'en ~'** 'you weren't home yesterday evening?'—'no, I wasn't'.
III effets *nm pl* things, clothes.
■ **~ de serre** greenhouse effect; **~s secondaires** (Med) side effects.

efficace /efikas/ *adj* [*action, method, remedy*] effective; [*person, device*] efficient.

efficacement /efikasmɑ̃/ *adv* efficiently; effectively.

efficacité /efikasite/ *nf* (of action, remedy) effectiveness; (of person, device) efficiency.

effigie /efiʒi/ *nf* **1** effigy; **à l'~ de** [*medal, stamp*] with the head of; **2** logo.

effilé, **~e** /efile/ *adj* **1** [*almonds*] flaked; **2** [*figure*] slender.

effiler /efile/ [1] **I** *vtr* **1** to sharpen; **2** to string [*green beans*].
II s'effiler *v refl* (+ *v être*) to fray.

effilocher /efilɔʃe/ [1] **I** *vtr* to shred.
II s'effilocher *v refl* (+ *v être*) **1** [*material*] to fray; **2** [*trust, love*] to dwindle (away).

efflanqué, **~e** /eflɑ̃ke/ *adj* emaciated.

effleurer /eflœʀe/ [1] *vtr* to touch lightly, to brush (against); to graze; **l'idée ne m'a même pas effleuré** the idea didn't even cross my mind.

effluent /eflyɑ̃/ *nm* effluent; **~s radioactifs** radioactive discharge.

effluve /eflyv/ *nm* **1** unpleasant smell; **2** fragrance.

effondrement /efɔ̃dʀəmɑ̃/ *nm* **1** collapse; **2** subsidence.

effondrer: **s'effondrer** /efɔ̃dʀe/ [1] *v refl* (+ *v être*) **1** [*roof, person, regime*] to collapse; [*dream*] to crumble; [*hopes*] to fall; [*popularity*] to fall drastically; **2** to collapse; **être effondré par la nouvelle** to be distraught at the news.

efforcer: **s'efforcer** /efɔʀse/ [12] *v refl* (+ *v être*) to try hard (**de faire** to do).

effort /efɔʀ/ *nm* **1** effort; **fais un petit ~ d'imagination!** use a bit of imagination!; **avec mon dos, je ne peux pas faire d'~** with this back of mine, I can't do anything strenuous; **allons, encore un petit ~!** come on, one more try!; come on, you're almost there!; **2** (in physics) stress; strain.

effraction /efʀaksjɔ̃/ *nf* (Law) breaking and entering.

effrayant, **~e** /efʀɛjɑ̃, ɑ̃t/ *adj* **1** [*sight, ugliness*] frightening; [*thinness, paleness*] dreadful; **2**° [*heat, price*] terrible.

effrayer /efʀeje/ [21] *vtr* **1** to frighten; to alarm; **2** [*difficulty, price*] to put [sb] off.

effréné, **~e** /efʀene/ *adj* [*rhythm, competition*] frenzied; [*ambition*] wild.

effriter /efʀite/ [1] **I** *vtr* to crumble; to break up.

II s'effriter *v refl* (+ *v être*) **1** to crumble (away); **2** [*majority, support*] to crumble; [*popularity*] to dwindle (away); [*currency*] to fall.

effroi /efʀwɑ/ *nm* dread, terror.

effronté, **~e** /efʀɔ̃te/ *adj* [*child, remark, look*] cheeky; [*adult*] shameless; cheeky.

effronterie /efʀɔ̃tʀi/ *nf* cheek, effrontery.

effroyable /efʀwɑjabl/ *adj* dreadful.

effroyablement /efʀwɑjabləmɑ̃/ *adv* **1** horribly; **2**° terribly.

effusion /efyzjɔ̃/ *nf* effusion; **avec ~** effusively.

■ **~ de sang** bloodshed.

égal, **~e**, *mpl* **-aux** /egal, o/ **I** *adj* **1** equal (**à** to); **à travail ~, salaire ~** equal work for equal pay; **à prix ~, je préfère celui-là** if the price is the same, I'd rather have that one; **~ à lui-même, il...** true to form, he...; **2** [*ground*] level; [*light*] even; [*colour*] uniform; [*weather*] settled; [*pulse, breathing*] steady; **d'un pas ~** at an even pace; **3 ça m'est ~** I don't mind either way; (dismissively) I don't care.

II *nm,f* equal; **traiter d'~ à ~ avec qn** to deal with sb as an equal; **à l'~ de son prédécesseur** just like his predecessor.

IDIOMS **rester ~ à soi-même** to be one's usual self; **combattre à armes ~es** to be on an equal footing.

également /egalmɑ̃/ *adv* **1** also, too; **2** equally.

égaler /egale/ [1] *vtr* **1** to equal [*record*]; to be as good as [*person*]; to be as high as [*price*]; **2 leur intelligence égale leur charme** they're as clever as they're charming; **3 trois plus trois égalent six** three plus three equals six or is six.

égalisation /egalizasjɔ̃/ *nf* **1** levelling[GB] out; **2** (Sport) **le penalty a permis l'~** the penalty evened (GB) or tied (US) the score.

égaliser /egalize/ [1] **I** *vtr* **1** to level [*ground*]; to level out [*prices, income*]; **2** to make [sth] the same size [*planks*].

II *vi* (Sport) to equalize (GB), to tie (US).

égaliseur /egalizœʀ/ *nm* **~ graphique** graphic equalizer.

égalitaire /egalitɛʀ/ *adj, nmf* egalitarian.

égalité /egalite/ *nf* **1** equality; **2** (Sport) **être à ~** to be level (GB), to be tied (US); **~!** deuce!; **3** (in mathematics) equality.

égard /egaʀ/ **I** *nm* **1** consideration; **sans ~ pour** without regard for; **2 à l'~ de qn** toward(s) sb; **à l'~ de qch** regarding sth; **à cet ~** in this respect.

II égards *nm pl* **avec des ~s** with respect; **être plein d'~s envers qn** to be attentive to sb's every need.

égaré, **~e** /egaʀe/ *adj* **1** stray; **2** [*look*] wild, distracted.

égarement /egaʀmɑ̃/ *nm* **1** distraction, madness; **2** confusion; **3** erratic behaviour[GB].

égarer /egaʀe/ [1] **I** *vtr* **1** to lead [sb] astray; **la colère vous égare** you're letting your anger get the better of you; **2** to mislay.

II s'égarer *v refl* (+ *v être*) **1** to get lost; **2** (figurative) [*mind*] to wander; [*person*] to ramble.

égayer /egeje/ [21] *vtr* to enliven [*conversation*]; to lighten [*style*]; to brighten [*day, life*]; to cheer [sb] up; to brighten [sth] up.

égérie /eʒeʀi/ *nf* muse.

égide /eʒid/ *nf* aegis; **sous l'~ de** under the aegis of.

églantier /eglɑ̃tje/ *nm* wild rose, dog-rose.

églantine /eglɑ̃tin/ *nf* wild rose, dog-rose.

églefin /egləfɛ̃/ *nm* haddock.

église /egliz/ *nf* church; **aller à l'~** to go to church.

Église /egliz/ *nf* Church; **homme d'~** cleric.

ego /ego/ *nm inv* ego.

égocentrique /egosɑ̃tʀik/ *adj, nmf* egocentric.

égoïsme /egɔism/ *nm* selfishness.

égoïste /egɔist/ *adj* selfish.

égorger /egɔʀʒe/ [13] *vtr* **~ qn** to cut sb's throat.

égosiller: **s'égosiller** /egozije/ [1] *v refl* (+ *v être*) **1** to shout oneself hoarse; **2** to sing at the top of one's voice; **3** to yell.

égout /egu/ *nm* sewer.

égoutter /egute/ [1] **I** *vtr* to drain [*dishes, vegetables*].

II *vi* [*dishes, rice*] to drain; [*washing*] to drip.

III s'égoutter *v refl* (+ *v être*) [*dishes, rice, vegetables*] to drain; [*washing*] to drip dry.

égouttoir /egutwaʀ/ *nm* draining rack (GB), (dish) drainer (US).

égratigner /egʀatiɲe/ [1] **I** *vtr* **1** to scratch, to graze; **2** to hurt, offend.

II s'égratigner *v refl* (+ *v être*) to scratch oneself; to graze oneself.

égratignure /egʀatiɲyʀ/ *nf* **1** scratch; graze; **2** (on car, table) scratch.

Égypte /eʒipt/ *pr nf* Egypt.

égyptien, **-ienne** /eʒipsjɛ̃, ɛn/ **I** *adj* Egyptian.

II *nm* Egyptian.

éhonté, **~e** /eɔ̃te/ *adj* [*liar, lie*] brazen; [*demand*] shameless.

Éire /ɛʀ/ *pr n* Éire, Republic of Ireland.

éjaculer /eʒakyle/ [1] *vi* to ejaculate.

éjectable /eʒɛktabl/ *adj* **siège ~** ejector seat (GB), ejection seat (US).

éjecter /eʒɛkte/ [1] *vtr* **1** (in accident) to throw [sb/sth] out; **2**○ to chuck○ [sb] out; **3** (Tech) to eject.

élaboration /elabɔʀasjɔ̃/ *nf* (of plan, strategy) development; (of solution) working out; (of document) drafting; (of newspaper) putting together.

élaboré, **~e** /elabɔʀe/ *adj* [*cuisine, treatment*] sophisticated.

élaborer /elabɔʀe/ [1] *vtr* to work [sth] out; to draw [sth] up; to put [sth] together.

élaguer /elage/ [1] *vtr* to prune.

élan /elɑ̃/ *nm* **1** (Sport) run up; **saut sans ~** standing jump; **2** momentum; **continuer sur son ~** to continue at the same pace; **3** impetus; **4** enthusiasm; **~ patriotique** patriotic fervour[GB]; **5** impulse; **~ de tendresse** surge of tenderness; **6** (Zool) elk.

élancé, **~e** /elɑ̃se/ *adj* slender.

élancement /elɑ̃smɑ̃/ *nm* throbbing pain.

élancer: **s'élancer** /elɑ̃se/ [12] *v refl* (+ *v être*) **1** to dash forward; **2** [*person, car*] to shoot off○; **3 s'~ vers le ciel** [*tree, spire*] to soar up toward(s) the sky.

élargi, **~e** /elaʀʒi/ *adj* [*format*] enlarged; [*government*] expanded.

élargir /elaʀʒiʀ/ [3] **I** *vtr* **1** to widen [*road*]; to let out [*garment*]; **2** to stretch [*shoes, sweater*]; **3** to extend [*contacts, audience, law*]; to broaden [*knowledge, activities, debate*]; to increase [*majority, electorate*]; to expand [*sector*].

II s'élargir *v refl* (+ *v être*) [*group, family*] to expand; [*margin, gap*] to increase; [*debate, road*] to widen; [*person*] to fill out; [*hips*] to become broader; [*garment*] to stretch.

élastique /elastik/ **I** *adj* **1** [*waistband*] elasticated (GB), elasticized (US); **2** [*gas, fibre*] elastic; **3** [*rule, timetable*] flexible; [*budget*] elastic.

II *nm* **1** rubber band; **2** (in haberdashery) elastic; **3** (Sport) bungee cord; **4** French skipping.

IDIOMS **les lâcher avec un ~**○ to be tight-fisted.

élastomère /elastɔmɛʀ/ *nm* elastomer.

électeur, **-trice** /elɛktœʀ, tʀis/ *nm,f* voter.

élection /elɛksjɔ̃/ *nf* **1** election; **~ partielle** by-election (GB), off-year election (US); **2** choice; **mon pays d'~** my chosen country.

électoral, **~e**, *mpl* **-aux** /elɛktɔʀal, o/ *adj* [*programme, reform, promise*] electoral; [*poster, period*] election; [*victory, campaign*] election, electoral.

électorat /elɛktɔʀa/ *nm* electorate, voters.

électricien, **-ienne** /elɛktʀisjɛ̃, ɛn/ *nm,f* electrician.

électricité /elɛktʀisite/ *nf* electricity.

électrifier /elɛktʀifje/ [2] *vtr* to bring electricity to [*village*]; to electrify [*railtracks*].

électrique /elɛktʀik/ *adj* **1** [*installation, appliance*] electrical; **réseau ~** electricity network; **2** (figurative) [*atmosphere*] electric.

électrisant, **~e** /elɛktʀizɑ̃, ɑ̃t/ *adj* electrifying.

électriser /elɛktʀize/ [1] *vtr* **1** to charge [sth] with electricity; **2** to electrify.

électro(-) /elɛktʀo/ *pref* electro; **~cardiogramme** electrocardiogram.

électrochoc /elɛktʀoʃɔk/ *nm* **~s** electroshock therapy, EST.

électrocuter /elɛktʀɔkyte/ [1] **I** *vtr* to electrocute.

II s'électrocuter *v refl* (+ *v être*) to be electrocuted.

électrode /elɛktʀɔd/ *nf* electrode.

électrogène /elɛktʀɔʒɛn/ *adj* **groupe ~** (electricity) generator.

électrolyse /elɛktʀɔliz/ *nf* electrolysis.

électroménager /elɛktʀomenaʒe/ **I** *adj m* **appareil ~** electrical domestic or household appliance.

II *nm* **1** electrical domestic or household appliances; **2** electrical goods industry.

électron /elɛktʀɔ̃/ *nm* electron.

électronicien, **-ienne** /elɛktʀɔnisjɛ̃, ɛn/ *nm,f* electronics engineer.

électronique /elɛktʀɔnik/ **I** *adj* **1** [*circuit*] electronic; **2** [*microscope*] electron.

II *nf* electronics.

électrophone /elɛktʀɔfɔn/ *nm* record player.

élégamment /elegamɑ̃/ *adv* [*dress*] elegantly; [*behave*] courteously.

élégance /elegɑ̃s/ *nf* elegance; **avec ~** [*dress*] elegantly; [*lose*] gracefully; [*behave*] honourably[GB]; [*resolve problem*] neatly.

élégant, **~e** /elegɑ̃, ɑ̃t/ **I** *adj* elegant; **ce n'est pas très ~ de ta part** it's not very decent of you.

II *nm,f* dandy/elegant lady.

élément /elemɑ̃/ **I** *nm* **1** (in structure, ensemble) element; (in device) component; (in mixture) ingredient; **~ moteur** driving force; **2** factor, element; **l'~-clé de** the key element in; **3** (of furniture) unit; **4** fact; **disposer de tous les ~s** to have all the facts; **5 bon ~** good pupil; good player; **~s rebelles** rebel elements; **6** (chemical) element.

II éléments *nm pl* **1 (premiers) ~s** basics; **2** elements.

élémentaire /elemɑ̃tɛʀ/ *adj* **1** [*principle*] basic; **2** elementary.

éléphant /elefɑ̃/ *nm* elephant.

éléphante /elefɑ̃t/ *nf* (cow) elephant.

éléphanteau, *pl* **~x** /elefɑ̃to/ *nm* (elephant) calf.

éléphantesque /elefɑ̃tɛsk/ *adj* elephantine, enormous.

élevage /elvaʒ/ *nm* **1** livestock farming; **~ de moutons** sheep farming; **faire de l'~ de porcs** to breed pigs; **d'~** [*oysters*] farmed; [*pheasant*] captive-bred; **2** farm; **un ~ de visons** a mink farm; **3** stock (**de** of).

élévateur /elevatœʀ/ *nm* elevator.

élévation /elevasjɔ̃/ *nf* **1** rise (**de** in); **2** (to rank) elevation; **3** (in architecture) elevation; **4 ~ de terrain** rise in the ground.

élève /elɛv/ *nmf* (gen) student; (Sch) pupil; **~ officier** trainee officer.

élevé, **~e** /elve/ *adj* **1** [*level, price, rank*] high;

2 [*plateau*] high; **3** [*sentiment*] fine; [*principles*] high; [*ideal*] lofty; [*language*] elevated.

élever /elve/ [16] I *vtr* **1** to put up, to erect; **2** to raise [*temperature, level*]; **~ la voix** or **le ton** to raise one's voice; **~ le débat** to raise the level of the debate; **3** to lift, to raise [*load*]; **4 la poésie élève l'âme** poetry is elevating; **5** to raise [*objection*]; to voice [*doubts*]; **6** to bring [sb] up; **c'est mal élevé** it's bad manners (**de faire** to do); **7** to rear [*cattle*]; to keep [*bees, fowl*].
II **s'élever** *v refl* (+ *v être*) **1** [*temperature, rate*] to rise; **2 s'~ à** [*profits, expenses*] to come to; [*turnover, death toll*] to stand at; **3** to rise; **s'~ dans les airs** or **le ciel** [*smoke*] to rise up into the air; [*bird*] to soar into the air; **4** to be heard; **5 s'~ contre qch** to protest against sth; **6** [*statue*] to stand; **s'~ au-dessus de qch** to rise above sth.

éleveur, -euse /elvœʀ, øz/ *nm,f* breeder.

elfe /ɛlf/ *nm* elf.

élider /elide/ [1] *vtr*, **s'élider** *v refl* (+ *v être*) to elide.

éligible /eliʒibl/ *adj* eligible for office.

élimé /elime/ I *pp* ▶ **élimer**.
II *pp adj* **vêtement élimé** threadbare garment.

élimer /elime/ [1] I *vtr* to wear [sth] thin.
II **s'élimer** *v refl* (+ *v être*) to wear thin.

éliminatoire /eliminatwaʀ/ *adj* [*question, match*] qualifying; [*mark*] eliminatory.

éliminer /elimine/ [1] *vtr* to eliminate [*candidate, toxins*]; to rule out [*possibility*].

élire /eliʀ/ [66] *vtr* to elect **se faire ~** to be elected; **~ domicile** to take up residence.

élision /elizjɔ̃/ *nf* elision.

élite /elit/ *nf* **l'~** the elite; **d'~** [*troops*] elite, crack; [*athlete, student*] high-flying.

élitisme /elitism/ *nm* elitism.

élixir /eliksiʀ/ *nm* elixir.

elle /ɛl/ *pron f* she; it; **~s** they; **~, ~ ne dit rien** she never says a word; **je les vois plus souvent qu'~** I see them more often than she does; I see them more often than (I see) her; **à cause d'~** because of her; **le bol bleu est à ~** the blue bowl is hers.

elle-même, *pl* **elles-mêmes** /ɛlmɛm/ *pron* herself; itself; **elles-mêmes** themselves; **'Madame Dubois?'—'~'** 'Mrs Dubois?'—'speaking'.

elles *pron* ▶ **elle**.

ellipse /elips/ *nf* **1** ellipsis; **2** (in mathematics) ellipse.

elliptique /eliptik/ *adj* **1** elliptical; **2** elliptic.

élocution /elɔkysjɔ̃/ *nf* diction; **défaut d'~** speech impediment.

éloge /elɔʒ/ *nm* **1** praise; **faire l'~ de** to sing the praises of; **être tout à l'~ de qn** to do sb great credit; **2** eulogy; **~ funèbre** funeral oration.

élogieux, -ieuse /elɔʒjø, øz/ *adj* full of praise; laudatory.

éloigné, ~e /elwaɲe/ *adj* **1** distant; **~ de tout** remote; **deux usines ~es de cinq kilomètres** two factories five kilometres[GB] apart; **2** [*memories*] distant; [*event*] remote; **~ dans le temps** distant (in time); **dans un passé peu ~** not (so) long ago; **3** [*cousin*] distant; **4 leurs opinions sont ~es** their points of view are poles apart; **très ~ de la réalité** far removed from reality.

éloignement /elwaɲmɑ̃/ *nm* **1** distance; **2** remoteness; **avec l'~, l'événement prend tout son sens** in retrospect, the full significance of the event becomes apparent.

éloigner /elwaɲe/ [1] I *vtr* **1** to move [sb/sth] away (**de** from); **2 ils font tout pour l'~ de moi** they are doing everything to drive us apart; **~ une menace** to remove a threat.
II **s'éloigner** *v refl* (+ *v être*) **1** to move away; **ne t'éloigne pas trop** don't go too far away; **2 s'~ de** to move away from [*party line*]; to stray from [*subject*].

élongation /elɔ̃gasjɔ̃/ *nf* (Med) pulled muscle; (treatment) traction.

éloquence /elɔkɑ̃s/ *nf* eloquence.

éloquent, ~e /elɔkɑ̃, ɑ̃t/ *adj* eloquent; **le score est ~** the score speaks for itself.

élu, ~e /ely/ *nm,f* **1** elected representative; **2** beloved; **3** (in religion) **les ~s** the elect.

élucider /elyside/ [1] *vtr* to solve [*crime, problem*]; to clarify [*circumstances*].

élucubrations /elykybʀasjɔ̃/ *nf pl* rantings.

éluder /elyde/ [1] *vtr* to evade.

Élysée /elize/ *pr nm* **1 (palais de l')~** Élysée Palace (*the official residence of the French President*); **2** Elysium.

émacier: **s'émacier** /emasje/ [2] *v refl* (+ *v être*) to become emaciated.

émail, *pl* **-aux** /emaj, o/ *nm* enamel.

émaillé, ~e /emaje/ *adj* [*utensil*] enamel; [*metal*] enamelled.

émailler /emaje/ [1] *vtr* **1** to enamel; **2 discours émaillé d'allusions** speech sprinkled with allusions.

émanation /emanasjɔ̃/ *nf* emanation; **~s de gaz** gas fumes.

émancipation /emɑ̃sipasjɔ̃/ *nf* emancipation.

émanciper /emɑ̃sipe/ [1] I *vtr* to emancipate [*people*]; to liberate [*country*].
II **s'émanciper** *v refl* (+ *v être*) to become emancipated; **femme émancipée** liberated woman.

émaner /emane/ [1] I *vi* **~ de** to emanate from; to come from.
II *v impers* **il émane d'elle un charme fou** she exudes charm.

émasculer /emaskyle/ [1] *vtr* to emasculate.

émaux ▶ **émail**.

emballage /ɑ̃balaʒ/ *nm* packaging; wrapping; packing.
■ **~ sous vide** vacuum packing.

emballer /ɑ̃bale/ [1] I *vtr* **1** to pack, to wrap; **2**° **être emballé par** to be taken with.
II **s'emballer** *v refl* (+ *v être*) **1** [*horse*] to bolt; **2**° to get carried away; **3** to get all worked up°; **4**° [*engine*] to race; **5** [*prices, inflation*] to shoot up; [*currency*] to shoot up in value.

embarcadère /ɑ̃baʀkadɛʀ/ *nm* pier; wharf.

embarcation /ɑ̃baʀkasjɔ̃/ *nf* boat.

embardée /ɑ̃baʀde/ *nf* (of car) swerve; (of boat) yaw.

embargo /ɑ̃baʀgo/ *nm* embargo.

embarquement /ɑ̃baʀkəmɑ̃/ *nm* boarding; **port d'~** port of embarkation.

embarquer /ɑ̃baʀke/ [1] **I** *vtr* **1** to load [*goods*]; to take [sb] on board; **2**○ to take [*object*]; [*police*] to pick up [*criminal*]; **3**○ **~ qn dans un projet** to get sb involved in a project.
II *vi* **1** to board; **2** to sail (**pour** for).
III s'embarquer *v refl* (+ *v être*) **1** to board; **2**○ **s'~ dans** to launch into [*explanation*].

embarras /ɑ̃baʀa/ *nm inv* **1** embarrassment; **2 ~ d'argent** or **financiers** financial difficulties; **3** awkward position; difficult situation; **4 je conçois votre ~** I understand your dilemma; **n'avoir que l'~ du choix** to have too much to choose from.

embarrassant, **~e** /ɑ̃baʀasɑ̃, ɑ̃t/ *adj* **1** awkward; embarrassing; **2** cumbersome.

embarrassé, **~e** /ɑ̃baʀase/ **I** *pp* ▶ **embarrasser**.
II *pp adj* **1** embarrassed; **être bien ~ pour répondre** to be at a loss for an answer; **2** [*room*] cluttered; **~ d'une grosse valise** weighed down with a large suitcase; **3** (Med) [*stomach*] upset.

embarrasser /ɑ̃baʀase/ [1] **I** *vtr* **1** to embarrass; **2** to clutter [sth] (up); **cette armoire m'embarrasse plutôt qu'autre chose** this wardrobe is more of a nuisance than anything else.
II s'embarrasser *v refl* (+ *v être*) **s'~ de** to burden oneself with [*baggage, person*]; to worry about [*details*].

embauche /ɑ̃boʃ/ *nf* appointment (GB) (**de** of), hiring (US) (**de** of); **salaire d'~** starting salary.

embaucher /ɑ̃boʃe/ [1] *vtr* **1** to take on (GB), to hire; **2**○ to recruit.

embaumer /ɑ̃bome/ [1] **I** *vtr* **1** [*smell*] to fill [*place*]; [*place*] to smell of [*wax*]; **2** to embalm.
II *vi* to be fragrant; **ça embaume!** what a pleasant smell!

embaumeur, **-euse** /ɑ̃bomœʀ, øz/ *nm,f* embalmer.

embellir /ɑ̃beliʀ/ [3] **I** *vtr* **1** to improve [sth]; to make [sb] more attractive; **2** to embellish [*story, truth*].
II *vi* to become more attractive.

embellissement /ɑ̃belismɑ̃/ *nm* **1** (of house) improving; **travaux d'~** improvements; **2** (of facts) embellishment.

emberlificoté○, **~e** /ɑ̃bɛʀlifikɔte/ *adj* [*text*] muddled; [*situation*] confused.

emberlificoter○ /ɑ̃bɛʀlifikɔte/ [1] **I** *vtr* **1** to entangle; **2** to take [sb] in○.
II s'emberlificoter *v refl* (+ *v être*) to get entangled; to get tangled up (**dans** in).

embêtant, **~e** /ɑ̃betɑ̃, ɑ̃t/ *adj* **1** annoying; **c'est ~ ça!** that's a real nuisance!; **2** annoying, irritating; **3** boring.

embêtement /ɑ̃betmɑ̃/ *nm* problem.

embêter /ɑ̃bete/ [1] **I** *vtr* **1** to bother; **2** to pester; to annoy; **3** to bore.
II s'embêter *v refl* (+ *v être*) **1** to be bored; **un hôtel quatre étoiles! tu ne t'embêtes pas**○**!** a four-star hotel! you're doing all right for yourself!; **2 s'~ à faire** to go to all the bother of doing.

emblée: **d'emblée** /dɑ̃ble/ *phr* **1** straightaway; **2** at first sight.

emblématique /ɑ̃blematik/ *adj* emblematic; symbolic.

emblème /ɑ̃blɛm/ *nm* emblem.

embobiner /ɑ̃bɔbine/ [1] *vtr* **1**○ to hoodwink; **2** (in sewing) to wind.

emboîter /ɑ̃bwate/ [1] **I** *vtr* to fit [sth] together; **~ qch dans** to fit sth into.
II s'emboîter *v refl* (+ *v être*) [*part*] to fit (**dans** into); [*parts*] to fit together.
IDIOMS **~ le pas à qn** to fall in behind sb.

embolie /ɑ̃bɔli/ *nf* embolism.

embonpoint /ɑ̃bɔ̃pwɛ̃/ *nm* stoutness; **avoir de l'~** to be stout.

embouché, **~e** /ɑ̃buʃe/ *adj* **mal ~** coarse; in a foul mood.

embouchure /ɑ̃buʃyʀ/ *nf* (of river) mouth; (of instrument) mouthpiece; (of pipe) opening.

embourber: **s'embourber** /ɑ̃buʀbe/ [1] *v refl* (+ *v être*) **1** to get stuck in the mud; **2** to get bogged down.

embourgeoiser: **s'embourgeoiser** /ɑ̃buʀʒwaze/ [1] *v refl* (+ *v être*) [*person*] to become middle-class; [*area*] to become gentrified.

embout /ɑ̃bu/ *nm* (of cigar, cane) tip; (of hosepipe) nozzle; (of pipe) mouthpiece.

embouteillage /ɑ̃butɛjaʒ/ *nm* **1** traffic jam; **2** tailback.

emboutir /ɑ̃butiʀ/ [3] *vtr* **1** to stamp, to press [*part, metal*]; **2**○ to crash into [*vehicle*].

embranchement /ɑ̃bʀɑ̃ʃmɑ̃/ *nm* **1** junction; **2** side road; **3** (on railways) branch line; **3** (Bot, Zool) branch.

embrancher /ɑ̃bʀɑ̃ʃe/ [1] **I** *vtr* to link [sth] up (**à, sur** with).
II s'embrancher *v refl* (+ *v être*) [*road, diversion*] to link up (**sur** with).

embrasé, **~e** /ɑ̃bʀaze/ *adj* **1** burning; **2** glowing.

embraser /ɑ̃bʀaze/ [1] **I** *vtr* **1** to set [sth] ablaze; **2** to set [sth] alight [*country*].
II s'embraser *v refl* (+ *v être*) **1** to catch fire; **2** to erupt into violence; **3** [*sky*] to be set ablaze; **4** to burn with desire.

embrasser /ɑ̃bʀase/ [1] **I** *vtr* **1** to kiss; **je t'embrasse** lots of love; **2** to embrace; to hug; **3** to take up [*career, cause*]; **4** to cover [*subject, period*].
II s'embrasser *v refl* (+ *v être*) **1** to kiss (each other); **2** to embrace; to hug.
IDIOMS **~ qn comme du bon pain** to hug sb warmly.

embrasure /ɑ̃bʀazyʀ/ *nf* **~ de fenêtre** window; **~ de porte** doorway.

embrayage /ɑ̃bʀɛjaʒ/ *nm* **1** clutch; **2** (Tech)

engaging; (in car) letting out the clutch; **3** clutch pedal.

embrayer /ɑ̃bʀeje/ [21] *vi* [*driver*] to engage the clutch; (Tech) to engage.

embrigader /ɑ̃bʀigade/ [1] *vtr* **1** to recruit; **2** (Mil) to brigade.

embrocher /ɑ̃bʀɔʃe/ [1] *vtr* (Culin) to put [sth] on a spit; to skewer.

embrouiller /ɑ̃bʀuje/ [1] **I** *vtr* **1** to tangle [*wires*]; **2** to confuse [*matter, person*].
II s'embrouiller *v refl* (+ *v être*) **1** to become tangled; **2** [*ideas, person*] to become confused; **s'~ dans** to get tangled up in [*explanations*].

embroussaillé, **~e** /ɑ̃bʀusaje/ *adj* [*path*] overgrown; [*hair*] bushy.

embrumé, **~e** /ɑ̃bʀyme/ *adj* **1** misty; **2** [*mind*] befuddled; [*look*] glazed.

embruns /ɑ̃bʀœ̃/ *nm pl* spray.

embryon /ɑ̃bʀijɔ̃/ *nm* embryo.

embûche /ɑ̃byʃ/ *nf* **1** trap; **dresser des ~s** to set traps; **2** hazard; pitfall; **semé d'~s** hazardous; (figurative) fraught with pitfalls.

embuer /ɑ̃bɥe/ [1] **I** *vtr* to mist up, to fog up.
II s'embuer *v refl* (+ *v être*) [*window*] to mist up, to fog up; [*eyes*] to mist over.

embuscade /ɑ̃byskad/ *nf* ambush.

éméché○, **~e** /emeʃe/ *adj* tipsy.

émeraude[1] /emʀod/ *adj inv, nm* emerald green.

émeraude[2] /emʀod/ *nf* emerald.

émergence /emɛʀʒɑ̃s/ *nf* emergence.

émerger /emɛʀʒe/ [13] *vi* **1** to emerge; **2**○ to surface.

émeri /emʀi/ *nm* emery.

émérite /emeʀit/ *adj* **1** outstanding; **2 professeur ~** emeritus professor.

émerveillement /emɛʀvɛjmɑ̃/ *nm* wonder; **il fait l'~ de ses professeurs** his teachers are greatly impressed by him.

émerveiller /emɛʀveje/ [1] **I** *vtr* **~ qn** to fill sb with wonder.
II s'émerveiller *v refl* (+ *v être*) **s'~ de** or **devant qch** to marvel at sth.

émetteur, **-trice** /emetœʀ, tʀis/ **I** *adj* **1** [*station*] broadcasting; **2** [*bank*] issuing.
II *nm* **1** transmitter; **2** (of loan, card) issuer; **3** (in linguistics) sender.

émettre /emɛtʀ/ [60] *vtr* **1** to express [*opinion, wish*]; to put forward [*hypothesis*]; **2** to utter [*cry*]; to produce [*sound, heat*]; **3** to issue [*document, currency*]; **4** to float [*loan*]; **5** to broadcast [*programme*]; **6** [*boat*] to send out [*signal*]; **7** to emit [*radiation*].

émeu /emø/ *nm* (Zool) emu.

émeute /emøt/ *nf* riot.

émietter /emjete/ [1] **I** *vtr* **1** to crumble [sth]; **2** to split [sth] up [*estate, fortune*].
II s'émietter *v refl* (+ *v être*) to crumble.

émigrant, **~e** /emigʀɑ̃, ɑ̃t/ *nm,f* emigrant.

émigration /emigʀasjɔ̃/ *nf* emigration.

émigré, **~e** /emigʀe/ *nm,f* emigrant; émigré.

émigrer /emigʀe/ [1] *vi* **1** to emigrate; **travailleur émigré** emigrant worker; **2** [*bird*] to migrate.

émincer /emɛ̃se/ [12] *vtr* to slice [sth] thinly.

éminence /eminɑ̃s/ *nf* **1** hillock; **2** (Anat) protuberance.

Éminence /eminɑ̃s/ *nf* Eminence.
■ **~ grise** éminence grise, grey (GB) or gray (US) eminence.

éminent, **~e** /eminɑ̃, ɑ̃t/ *adj* distinguished, eminent.

émirat /emiʀa/ *nm* emirate.

Émirats /emiʀa/ *pr nm pl* **~ arabes unis, EAU** United Arab Emirates.

émis, **~e** /emi, iz/ *pp* ▸ **émettre**.

émissaire /emisɛʀ/ *nm* emissary.

émission /emisjɔ̃/ *nf* **1** programme[GB]; **2** (of document, currency) issue; **3** (of waves, signals) emission.

emmagasiner /ɑ̃magazine/ [1] *vtr* **1** to store; **2** to stockpile [*goods*]; to store [*energy*]; to store up [*knowledge*].

emmanchure /ɑ̃mɑ̃ʃyʀ/ *nf* armhole.

emmêler /ɑ̃mɛle/ [1] **I** *vtr* **1** to tangle; **2** to confuse [*matter*].
II s'emmêler *v refl* (+ *v être*) to get tangled up; **s'~ les pieds dans** to get one's feet caught in.

emménagement /ɑ̃menaʒmɑ̃/ *nm* moving in.

emménager /ɑ̃menaʒe/ [13] *vi* to move in; **~ dans** to move into.

emmener /ɑ̃mne/ [16] *vtr* **1** to take (**à, jusqu'à** to); **veux-tu que je t'emmène en voiture?** do you want a lift (GB) or a ride (US)?; **2**○ (controversial) to take [*umbrella, book*]; **3** to take [sb] away; **4** to lead [*team, troop*].

emmerder◑ /ɑ̃mɛʀde/ [1] **I** *vtr* to annoy, to hassle○; **~ le monde** to be a pain○ (in the arse● (GB) or ass◑ (US)); **je les emmerde** to hell○ with them.
II s'emmerder *v refl* (+ *v être*) **1** to be bored stiff○; **2 s'~ à faire** to go to the trouble or bother of doing; **t'emmerdes pas avec ça!** don't bother with that!; **tu t'emmerdes pas!** you're doing all right for yourself!; (as reprimand) you've got a nerve or a bloody cheek○! (GB).

emmitoufler /ɑ̃mitufle/ [1] **I** *vtr* to wrap [sb/sth] up warmly.
II s'emmitoufler *v refl* (+ *v être*) to wrap (oneself) up warmly.

emmurer /ɑ̃myʀe/ [1] *vtr* to wall [sb/sth] in.

émoi /emwa/ *nm* agitation, turmoil.

émonder /emɔ̃de/ [1] *vtr* to prune.

émotif, **-ive** /emɔtif, iv/ *adj* emotional.

émotion /emosjɔ̃/ *nf* emotion; **donner des ~s à qn**○ to give sb a fright.

émotivité /emɔtivite/ *nf* **enfant d'une grande ~** highly emotional child.

émousser /emuse/ [1] **I** *vtr* **1** to blunt; **2** to dull [*curiosity, sensitivity*].
II s'émousser *v refl* (+ *v être*) **1** to become blunt; **2** [*curiosity*] to become dulled.

émoustiller /emustije/ [1] *vtr* **1** to exhilarate; **2** to titillate.

émouvant, **~e** /emuvɑ̃, ɑ̃t/ *adj* moving.

émouvoir /emuvwaʀ/ [43] **I** *vtr* to move; to touch; **se laisser ~ par les larmes de qn** to be swayed by sb's tears; **~ l'opinion** to cause a stir.
II s'émouvoir *v refl* (+ *v être*) **1** to be touched or moved; **2 s'~ de** to become concerned about; to be bothered by; **il n'y a pas de quoi s'~** there's nothing to get excited about.

empailler /ɑ̃pɑje/ [1] *vtr* **1** to seat [sth] (with straw); **2** to stuff.

empailleur, **-euse** /ɑ̃pɑjœʀ, øz/ *nm* **1** taxidermist; **2** chair seater.

empaler /ɑ̃pale/ [1] **I** *vtr* to impale.
II s'empaler *v refl* (+ *v être*) to become impaled.

empaqueter /ɑ̃pakte/ [20] *vtr* to package; to wrap [sth] up.

emparer: **s'emparer** /ɑ̃paʀe/ [1] *v refl* (+ *v être*) **1 s'~ de** to take over [*town, record*]; to seize [*power, person*]; to gain possession of [*ball*]; to get hold of [*rumour, microphone*]; **2 s'~ de** [*stupor, feeling*] to take hold of [sb/sth].

empâter: **s'empâter** /ɑ̃pɑte/ [1] *v refl* (+ *v être*) to become puffy; to put on weight; to thicken out.

empêchement /ɑ̃pɛʃmɑ̃/ *nm* **1** unforeseen difficulty; **j'ai un ~** something's cropped up; **2** (Law) impediment.

empêcher /ɑ̃peʃe/ [1] **I** *vtr* to prevent, to stop; **~ qn de faire** to prevent or stop sb (from) doing.
II s'empêcher *v refl* (+ *v être*) **je n'ai pas pu m'~ de rire** I couldn't help laughing.
III *v impers* **(il) n'empêche** all the same; **il n'empêche que** the fact remains that.

empêcheur, **-euse** /ɑ̃pɛʃœʀ, øz/ *nm,f* **~ de tourner en rond** spoilsport.

empereur /ɑ̃pʀœʀ/ *nm* emperor.

empesé, **~e** /ɑ̃pəze/ *adj* [*collar*] starched; [*person, manner*] starchy.

empester /ɑ̃pɛste/ [16] **I** *vtr* to stink [sth] out (GB), to stink up (US).
II *vi* to stink.

empêtrer: **s'empêtrer** /ɑ̃petʀe/ [1] *v refl* (+ *v être*) **s'~ dans** to get entangled in [*briars*]; to get tangled up in [*lies*]; to get mixed up in [*business*].

emphase /ɑ̃fɑz/ *nf* **1** grandiloquence; **2** emphasis.

emphatique /ɑ̃fatik/ *adj* **1** grandiloquent; **2** emphatic.

empiècement /ɑ̃pjɛsmɑ̃/ *nm* (of garment) yoke.

empiéter /ɑ̃pjete/ [14] *vi* to encroach (**sur** upon).

empiffrer○: **s'empiffrer** /ɑ̃pifʀe/ [1] *v refl* (+ *v être*) to stuff oneself.

empiler /ɑ̃pile/ [1] **I** *vtr* to pile [sth] (up).
II s'empiler *v refl* (+ *v être*) to pile up; **s'~ dans** to pile into.

empire /ɑ̃piʀ/ *nm* **1** empire; **2** (commercial) empire.

Empire /ɑ̃piʀ/ *nm* **l'~** the Empire.
■ **l'~ du Milieu** the Middle Kingdom; **l'~ d'Orient** the Byzantine Empire; **l'~ (romain) d'Occident** the Western (Roman) Empire.

empirer /ɑ̃piʀe/ [1] *vi* to get worse.

empirique /ɑ̃piʀik/ *adj* empirical.

emplacement /ɑ̃plasmɑ̃/ *nm* **1** site; **2** parking space.

emplâtre /ɑ̃plɑtʀ/ *nm* (Med) medicated plaster.

emplette /ɑ̃plɛt/ *nf* purchase.

emplir /ɑ̃pliʀ/ [3] *vtr*, **s'emplir** *v refl* (+ *être*) to fill (**de** with).

emploi /ɑ̃plwɑ/ *nm* **1** job; **2** employment; **3** use; **l'~ d'armes** the use of weapons; **téléviseur couleur à vendre, cause double ~** colour[GB] TV for sale, surplus to requirements; **4** usage.
■ **~ du temps** timetable.
IDIOMS **avoir la tête de l'~** to look the part.

employé, **~e** /ɑ̃plwaje/ *nm,f* employee.
■ **~ de banque** bank clerk; **~ de bureau** office clerk; **~ municipal** local authority employee.

employer /ɑ̃plwaje/ [23] **I** *vtr* to employ [*person*]; to use [*word, product*].
II s'employer *v refl* (+ *v être*) **1** to be used; **2 s'~ à faire** to apply oneself to doing.

employeur, **-euse** /ɑ̃plwajœʀ, øz/ *nm,f* employer.

empocher /ɑ̃pɔʃe/ [1] *vtr* to pocket.

empoigner /ɑ̃pwaɲe/ [1] *vtr* to grab (hold of).

empoisonnant○, **~e** /ɑ̃pwazɔnɑ̃, ɑ̃t/ *adj* annoying; irritating.

empoisonné, **~e** /ɑ̃pwazɔne/ **I** *pp* ▶ **empoisonner**.
II *pp adj* [*foodstuff*] poisoned; [*atmosphere, relations*] sour; [*quarrel*] venomous.

empoisonnement /ɑ̃pwazɔnmɑ̃/ *nm* **1** poisoning; **2**○ trouble.

empoisonner /ɑ̃pwazɔne/ [1] **I** *vtr* to poison; **~ la vie de qn** to make sb's life a misery.
II s'empoisonner *v refl* (+ *v être*) to poison oneself; **il s'est empoisonné avec une huître pas fraîche** he got food poisoning from eating a bad oyster; **s'~ la vie** ○ to make one's life a misery.

empoisonneur, **-euse** /ɑ̃pwazɔnœʀ, øz/ *nm,f* **1** poisoner; **2**○ nuisance.

emporté, **~e** /ɑ̃pɔʀte/ *adj* **être ~**, **avoir un caractère ~** to be quick-tempered.

emportement /ɑ̃pɔʀtəmɑ̃/ *nm* fit of anger; **avec ~** angrily.

emporte-pièce /ɑ̃pɔʀtəpjɛs/ *nm inv* **1** (Tech) punch; **découper qch à l'~** to punch sth; **jugement à l'~** rash judgment; **2** pastry cutter.

emporter /ɑ̃pɔʀte/ [1] **I** *vtr* **1** to take [*object*]; **pizzas à ~** takeaway pizzas (GB), pizzas to go (US); **2** [*ambulance*] to take [sb] away; [*boat, plane*] to carry [sb] away; **3** [*wind, river*] to sweep [sb/sth] away; [*shell, bullet*] to take [sth] off [*ear, leg*]; **4 une leucémie l'a emporté** he died of leukaemia; **5** to take [*position*]; **6 l'~**

to win; to prevail; **l'~ sur qn** to beat sb; **l'~ sur qch** to overcome sth.
II **s'emporter** *v refl* (+ *v être*) to lose one's temper.

empoté○, **~e** /ɑ̃pɔte/ *adj* clumsy, awkward.

empourprer: **s'empourprer** /ɑ̃puʀpʀe/ [1] *v refl* (+ *v être*) [*sky*] to turn crimson; [*face*] to flush.

empreindre /ɑ̃pʀɛ̃dʀ/ [55] **I** *vtr* **1** to imprint; **2** to imbue.
II **s'empreindre** *v refl* (+ *v être*) to become marked (**de** with), to become imbued (**de** with).

empreinte /ɑ̃pʀɛ̃t/ *nf* **1** footprint; track; **2** stamp, mark.
■ **~s digitales** fingerprints; **~s génétiques** genetic fingerprints.

empressé, **~e** /ɑ̃pʀese/ *adj* **1** [*care, help*] prompt; **2** [*admirer*] attentive.

empressement /ɑ̃pʀɛsmɑ̃/ *nm* **1** eagerness; **avec ~** eagerly; **2** attentiveness.

empresser: **s'empresser** /ɑ̃pʀese/ [1] *v refl* (+ *v être*) **s'~ de faire** to hasten to do; **s'~ autour** or **auprès de qn** to fuss over sb.

emprise /ɑ̃pʀiz/ *nf* hold, influence.

emprisonnement /ɑ̃pʀizɔnmɑ̃/ *nm* imprisonment; **peine d'~** prison sentence.

emprisonner /ɑ̃pʀizɔne/ [1] *vtr* **1** to imprison (**à, dans** in); **2** to keep [sb] prisoner.

emprunt /ɑ̃pʀœ̃/ *nm* **1** loan; **faire un ~** to take out a loan; **~ public** public sector loan; **2** borrowing; **d'~** [*car, name*] borrowed; **3** loan; **un ~ fait à un musée** a loan from a museum; **4** (of idea, word) borrowing.

emprunté, **~e** /ɑ̃pʀœ̃te/ *adj* awkward.

emprunter /ɑ̃pʀœ̃te/ [1] *vtr* **1** to borrow; **2** to imitate [*voice*]; **3** to take [*road*].

empuantir /ɑ̃pyɑ̃tiʀ/ [3] *vtr* to stink out (GB), to stink up (US).

ému, **~e** /emy/ **I** *pp* ▶ **émouvoir**.
II *pp adj* moved (**par** by); touched (**par** by); nervous; **trop ~ pour parler** too overcome to speak.
III *adj* [*words, look*] full of emotion; [*memory*] fond.

émulation /emylasjɔ̃/ *nf* competitiveness.

émule /emyl/ *nmf* imitator; **être l'~ de qn** to model oneself on sb; **il a fait de nombreux ~s** many people modelled themselves on him.

émulsifiant /emylsifjɑ̃/ *nm* emulsifier.

émulsion /emylsjɔ̃/ *nf* emulsion.

en /ɑ̃/ **I** *prep* **1** in; into; to; **vivre ~ ville** to live in town; **aller ~ Allemagne** to go to Germany; **monter ~ voiture** to get into a car; **~ hiver/1991** in winter/1991; **~ semaine** during the week; **voyager ~ train** to travel by train; **2 il est toujours ~ manteau** he always wears a coat; **~ bras de chemise** in shirt sleeves; **3** as; **je vous parle ~ ami** I'm speaking (to you) as a friend; **agir ~ traître** to act like a traitor; **4** into; **traduire ~ anglais** to translate into English; **5 c'est ~ or** it's (made of) gold; **le même ~ bleu/plus grand** the same in blue/only bigger; **être bon ~ histoire** to be good at history; **~ hauteur, le mur fait trois mètres** the wall is three metres[GB] high; **6** (used with gerund) **je l'ai croisé ~ sortant** I met him as I was leaving; **prends un café ~ attendant** have a cup of coffee while you're waiting; **~ arrivant chez moi, je leur ai téléphoné** when I got back home, I telephoned them; **l'enfant se réveilla ~ hurlant** the child woke up screaming; **ouvrez cette caisse ~ soulevant le couvercle** open this box by lifting the lid; **elle a fait une erreur ~ acceptant ce poste** she made a mistake in accepting the job; **tu aurais moins chaud ~ enlevant ta veste** you'd be cooler if you took your jacket off.
II *pron* **1** (indicating means) **il sortit son épée et l'~ transperça** he took out his sword and ran him/her through; **2** (indicating cause) **ça l'a tellement bouleversé qu'il ~ est tombé malade** it distressed him so much that he fell ill (GB) or became sick (US); **3** (representing person) **ils aiment leurs enfants et ils ~ sont aimés** they love their children and they are loved by them; **4** (representing thing) **'veux-tu du vin?'—'oui, j'~ veux'** 'would you like some wine?'—'yes, I'd like some'; **il n'~ reste pas beaucoup** there isn't much (of it) left; there aren't many left; **je m'~ souviens** I remember (it); **j'~ suis fier** I'm proud of it; **5** (representing place) **il entra dans le café comme j'~ sortais** he entered the café as I was coming out; **6**○ **tu ~ as un beau chapeau!** what a nice hat you've got!; **on s'~ souviendra de ce dimanche!** we won't forget this Sunday in a hurry!

ENA /ena/ *nf*: *abbr* ▶ **école**.

énarque /enaʀk/ *nmf* graduate of the ENA.

encadré /ɑ̃kadʀe/ *nm* (in newspaper) box; **~ publicitaire** display ad.

encadrement /ɑ̃kadʀəmɑ̃/ *nm* **1** supervision; **2** supervisory staff; managerial staff; (Mil) officers; **3** (of picture) frame.

encadrer /ɑ̃kadʀe/ [1] *vtr* **1** to supervise [*staff*]; to train [*soldier*]; **2** to flank [*person*]; to frame [*face, window*]; **~ de rouge** to outline [sth] in red; **3** to frame [*picture*].

encaissé, **~e** /ɑ̃kese/ *adj* [*valley, river*] steep-sided.

encaisser /ɑ̃kese/ [1] *vtr* **1** to cash [*cheque, sum of money*]; **2**○ to take [*blow, defeat*]; **je ne peux pas ~ ton frère** I can't stand your brother.
IDIOMS **~ le coup**○ to take it all in one's stride.

encart /ɑ̃kaʀ/ *nm* insert; **~ publicitaire** promotional insert.

en-cas /ɑ̃ka/ *nm inv* snack.

encastrer /ɑ̃kastʀe/ [1] **I** *vtr* to build in [*oven, refrigerator*]; to fit [*sink, hotplate*]; **baignoire encastrée (dans le sol)** sunken bath; **route encastrée dans la montagne** road set into the mountain.
II **s'encastrer** *v refl* (+ *v être*) to fit (**dans** into).

encaustique /ɑ̃kɔstik/ *nf* wax polish; **passer à l'~** to wax.

enceinte /ɑ̃sɛ̃t/ **I** *adj f* [*woman*] pregnant.
II *nf* **1 (mur d')~** surrounding wall; **2** (of

prison, palace) compound; (of courthouse, church) interior; **dans l'~ même de l'aéroport** within the airport compound.

encens /ɑ̃sɑ̃/ *nm inv* incense.

encenser /ɑ̃sɑ̃se/ [1] *vtr* **1** to cense; **2** (figurative) to sing the praises of [*person*]; to acclaim [*work of art*].

encercler /ɑ̃sɛʀkle/ [1] *vtr* **1** to surround, to encircle; **2** (with pen) to circle.

enchaînement /ɑ̃ʃɛnmɑ̃/ *nm* **1** (of events) chain; **2** sequence; **3** (in music, sport) transition; **4** routine.

enchaîner /ɑ̃ʃɛne/ [1] **I** *vtr* to chain up [*person, animal*]; **~ à** to chain to.

II *vi* to go on; **~ avec une nouvelle chanson** to move on to a new song.

III s'enchaîner *v refl* (+ *v être*) [*shots, sequences in film*] to follow on.

enchantement /ɑ̃ʃɑ̃tmɑ̃/ *nm* **1** delight; **2** enchantment, spell; **comme par ~** as if by magic.

enchanter /ɑ̃ʃɑ̃te/ [1] *vtr* **1** to delight; **ça ne m'enchante guère** it doesn't exactly thrill me; **enchanté (de faire votre connaissance)!** how do you do!; **2 forêt enchantée** enchanted forest.

enchanteur, -eresse /ɑ̃ʃɑ̃tœʀ, tʀɛs/ **I** *adj* enchanting.

II *nm,f* enchanter/enchantress.

enchère /ɑ̃ʃɛʀ/ **I** *nf* bid; **faire une ~** to bid, to make a bid.

II enchères *nf pl* **vente aux ~s** auction.

enchevêtrement /ɑ̃ʃ(ə)vɛtʀəmɑ̃/ *nm* (of threads, branches) tangle; (of colours, streets) labyrinth; (of ideas) muddle.

enchevêtrer /ɑ̃ʃ(ə)vetʀe/ [1] **I** *vtr* **1** to tangle [sth] up [*threads*]; **2 être enchevêtré** [*sentence, plot*] to be muddled; [*problem, case*] to be complicated.

II s'enchevêtrer *v refl* (+ *v être*) **1** [*branches, threads*] to get tangled; **2** [*phrases, ideas*] to become muddled; **3** [*person*] **s'~ dans** to get tangled up in.

enclave /ɑ̃klav/ *nf* enclave.

enclencher /ɑ̃klɑ̃ʃe/ [1] **I** *vtr* **1** (figurative) to set [sth] in motion [*process*]; **2** to set [*timer*]; to engage [*mechanism*].

II s'enclencher *v refl* (+ *v être*) **1** [*process, cycle*] to get under way; **2** [*mechanism*] to engage.

enclin, ~e /ɑ̃klɛ̃, in/ *adj* inclined (**à** to; **à faire** to do).

enclos /ɑ̃klo/ *nm inv* (gen) enclosure; (for animals) pen.

enclume /ɑ̃klym/ *nf* (Tech, Anat) anvil.

encoche /ɑ̃kɔʃ/ *nf* notch.

encoignure /ɑ̃kwaɲyʀ/ *nf* corner.

encolure /ɑ̃kɔlyʀ/ *nf* **1** (of garment) neckline; **2** collar size; **3** (of animal) neck.

encombrant, ~e /ɑ̃kɔ̃bʀɑ̃, ɑ̃t/ *adj* **1** [*piece of furniture*] bulky; [*parcel, suitcase*] cumbersome; **2** [*person, matter*] troublesome.

encombre: **sans encombre** /sɑ̃zɑ̃kɔ̃bʀ/ *phr* without a hitch.

encombré, ~e /ɑ̃kɔ̃bʀe/ *adj* [*road, sky*] congested (**de** with); [*room*] cluttered.

encombrement /ɑ̃kɔ̃bʀəmɑ̃/ *nm* **1** traffic congestion; **2** (of switchboard, airwaves) jamming; **3** (of room) cluttering; **4** (of courts) congestion; **5** (of piece of furniture) bulk.

encombrer /ɑ̃kɔ̃bʀe/ [1] **I** *vtr* **1** [*object, people*] to clutter up [*room*]; **2** [*object, person*] to obstruct [*road, path*]; **3** to jam [*switchboard, frequency*]; to clutter up [*mind*].

II s'encombrer *v refl* (+ *v être*) **s'~ de** to burden oneself with; **s'~ l'esprit** to clutter up one's mind (**de** with).

encontre: **à l'encontre de** /alɑ̃kɔ̃tʀədə/ *phr* **1** contrary to; **2** counter to; **3** against; **4** toward(s).

encorder: **s'encorder** /ɑ̃kɔʀde/ [1] *v refl* (+ *v être*) to rope up.

encore /ɑ̃kɔʀ/ **I** *adv* **1** still; **il était ~ étudiant quand il s'est marié** he was still a student when he got married; **il n'est ~ que midi** it's only midday; **tu en es ~ là?** haven't you got (GB) or gotten (US) beyond that by now?; **hier ~ elle allait bien** only yesterday she was fine; **qu'il soit impoli passe ~, mais**... the fact that he's rude is one thing, but...; **2 pas ~** not yet; **il n'est pas ~ rentré** he hasn't come home yet; he still hasn't come home; **cela ne s'est ~ jamais vu** it has never been seen before; **3** again; **les prix ont ~ augmenté** prices have gone up again; **~ toi!** you again!; **~!** encore!, more!; **~ une fois** once more, once again; **qu'est-ce que j'ai ~ fait?** what have I done now?; **4** more; **j'en veux ~** I want some more; **mange ~ un peu** have some more to eat; **c'est ~ mieux** it's even better; **5 ~ un gâteau?** another cake?; **pendant ~ trois jours** for another three days; **qu'est-ce qu'il te faut ~?** what more do you need?; **et puis quoi ~○!** what next○!; **6 ~ faut-il qu'elle accepte** but she still has to accept; **si ~ il était généreux!** if he were at least generous!; **7** only, just; **il y a ~ trois mois** only or just three months ago.

II et encore *phr* if that; **c'est tout au plus mangeable, et ~!** it's only just edible, if that!

III encore que *phr* even though.

encourageant, ~e /ɑ̃kuʀaʒɑ̃, ɑ̃t/ *adj* encouraging.

encouragement /ɑ̃kuʀaʒmɑ̃/ *nm* encouragement.

encourager /ɑ̃kuʀaʒe/ [13] *vtr* **1** to encourage (**à faire** to do); **2** to cheer [sb] on.

encourir /ɑ̃kuʀiʀ/ [26] *vtr* to incur.

encrasser /ɑ̃kʀase/ [1] *vtr* **1** to clog [sth] (up) [*filter, engine, artery*]; to make [sth] sooty [*chimney*]; **2** to dirty; (Aut) to foul up [*spark plugs*].

encre /ɑ̃kʀ/ *nf* ink; **~ d'imprimerie** printer's ink.

■ **~ de Chine** Indian (GB) or India (US) ink; **~ sympathique** invisible ink.

IDIOMS **cela a fait couler beaucoup d'~** a lot of ink has been spilled over this; **se faire un sang d'~** to be worried sick.

encrier /ɑ̃kʀije/ *nm* inkwell; ink pot.

encyclopédie /ɑ̃siklɔpedi/ *nf* encyclopedia.

endémique /ɑ̃demik/ *adj* endemic.

endetté, **~e** /ɑ̃dete/ *adj* in debt.

endettement /ɑ̃dɛtmɑ̃/ *nm* debt; **~ public/extérieur** national/foreign debt.

endetter /ɑ̃dete/ [1] **I** *vtr* to put [sb] into debt. **II s'endetter** *v refl* (+ *v être*) to get into debt (**auprès de** with).

endiablé, **~e** /ɑ̃djɑble/ *adj* **1** [*rhythm*] furious; **2** [*child*] boisterous.

endiguer /ɑ̃dige/ [1] *vtr* to confine [*river*]; to contain [*demonstrators, group*]; to curb [*speculation, dissatisfaction*].

endimanché, **~e** /ɑ̃dimɑ̃ʃe/ *adj* in one's Sunday best.

endive /ɑ̃div/ *nf* chicory (GB), endive (US); **deux ~s** two heads of chicory.

endoctriner /ɑ̃dɔktʀine/ [1] *vtr* to indoctrinate.

endolori, **~e** /ɑ̃dɔlɔʀi/ *adj* aching.

endolorir /ɑ̃dɔlɔʀiʀ/ [3] *vtr* to make [sb/sth] ache.

endommager /ɑ̃dɔmaʒe/ [13] *vtr* to damage.

endormi, **~e** /ɑ̃dɔʀmi/ *adj* **1** [*person, animal*] sleeping, asleep; **2** (figurative) [*village, mind, pupil*] sleepy.

endormir /ɑ̃dɔʀmiʀ/ [30] **I** *vtr* **1** [*person*] to send [sb] to sleep [*child*]; [*person, substance*] to put [sb] to sleep [*patient*]; **2** (from boredom) [*person, lecture*] to send [sb] to sleep [*person*] (**avec** with); **3** to dupe [*person, opinion, enemy*] (**avec** with); **4** to lessen [*vigilance*]; to allay [*suspicion*]; to numb [*faculties*]. **II s'endormir** *v refl* (+ *v être*) **1** to fall asleep; **2** to get to sleep; **3** (figurative) to sit back.

endossable /ɑ̃dosabl/ *adj* [*cheque*] endorsable; **non ~** non-endorsable.

endosser /ɑ̃dose/ [1] *vtr* **1** to put on [*jacket*]; **2** to take on [*role, responsibility*]; to shoulder [*consequences*]; **3** to endorse [*cheque*].

endroit /ɑ̃dʀwɑ/ **I** *nm* **1** place; **par ~s** in places; **à quel ~?** where?; **2** (of fabric, pullover) right side; **à l'~** (of object) the right way up; (of garment) the right way round (GB) or around (US). **II à l'endroit de** *phr* toward(s).

enduire /ɑ̃dɥiʀ/ [69] **I** *vtr* to coat (**de** with). **II s'enduire** *v refl* (+ *v être*) **s'~ de** to put [sth] on.

enduit /ɑ̃dɥi/ *nm* **1** coating; **2** filler.

endurance /ɑ̃dyʀɑ̃s/ *nf* **1** (of person) stamina; **~ à** resistance to; **2** (of vehicle, engine, machine) endurance.

endurant, **~e** /ɑ̃dyʀɑ̃, ɑ̃t/ *adj* [*person, athlete*] tough; [*engine, vehicle*] hard-wearing.

endurcir /ɑ̃dyʀsiʀ/ [3] **I** *vtr* **1** [*sport, hard work*] to strengthen [*body, character*]; **~ qn contre** to build up sb's resistance to; **2** [*ordeal*] to harden [*person*]. **II s'endurcir** *v refl* (+ *v être*) **1** to become stronger; **2** to become hardened; **s'~ contre** to become inured to.

endurer /ɑ̃dyʀe/ [1] *vtr* **1** to endure; **faire ~ qch à qn** to put sb through sth; **2** to put up with.

énergétique /enɛʀʒetik/ *adj* **1** [*needs, resources*] energy; **2** [*food*] high-calorie.

énergie /enɛʀʒi/ *nf* **1** energy; **faire des économies d'~** to save energy; **2** energy; **avec l'~ du désespoir** driven on by despair; **avec ~** [*work*] energetically; [*protest*] strongly.

énergique /enɛʀʒik/ *adj* **1** [*person, gesture*] energetic; [*handshake*] vigorous; [*face, expression*] resolute; **2** [*policy, action*] tough; [*objection, protest*] strong; [*refusal*] firm; [*intervention*] forceful.

énergumène /enɛʀgymɛn/ *nmf* oddball.

énervé, **~e** /enɛʀve/ *adj* **1** irritated; **2** nervous; [*child*] overexcited.

énervement /enɛʀvəmɑ̃/ *nm* **1** irritation; **dans un moment d'~** in a moment of exasperation; **2** agitation; **elle pleura d'~** she was so on edge that she cried.

énerver /enɛʀve/ [1] **I** *vtr* **1** to put [sb] on edge; **2 ~ qn** to get on sb's nerves, to irritate sb. **II s'énerver** *v refl* (+ *v être*) to get worked up (**pour** over).

enfance /ɑ̃fɑ̃s/ *nf* childhood; **la petite ~** early childhood.
IDIOMS **c'est l'~ de l'art** it's child's play.

enfant /ɑ̃fɑ̃/ *nmf* child; infant; **c'est une ~ terrible** she's an unruly child; **être ~ unique** to be an only child; **un ~ du peuple** a child of the people.
■ **~ de chœur** altar boy; **ce n'est pas un ~ de chœur** (figurative) he's no angel.

enfanter /ɑ̃fɑ̃te/ [1] *vtr* to give birth to.

enfantillage /ɑ̃fɑ̃tijaʒ/ *nm* childishness.

enfantin, **~e** /ɑ̃fɑ̃tɛ̃, in/ *adj* **1** simple, easy; **2** [*class*] infant (GB), for young children; **mode ~e** children's fashion; **3** childish, childlike.

enfer /ɑ̃fɛʀ/ *nm* **1** Hell; **2** (figurative) hell (**de** of); **aller/conduire à un train d'~**○ to go/drive hell for leather○; **voiture/soirée d'~**○ hell of a○ car/party.

enfermer /ɑ̃fɛʀme/ [1] **I** *vtr* **1** to shut [sth] in [*animal*]; to lock [sth] up [*money, jewellery*]; to lock [sb] up, to put [sb] away○ [*criminal, insane person*]; **elle est bonne à ~**○ she's stark raving mad○; **2 ~ qn dans un rôle** to confine sb to a role; **~ qn dans une situation** to trap sb in a situation. **II s'enfermer** *v refl* (+ *v être*) **1** (gen) to lock oneself in; (accidentally) to get locked in; (in order to be alone) to shut oneself away; **ne reste pas enfermé toute la journée!** don't stay cooped up indoors all day!; **2 s'~ dans** to retreat into; **s'~ dans le mutisme** to remain obstinately silent; **s'~ dans ses préjugés** to be stubbornly prejudiced.

enferrer: **s'enferrer** /ɑ̃fere/ [1] *v refl* (+ *v être*) (figurative) to tie oneself up in knots; **s'~ dans des mensonges** to get tangled up in lies.

enfiévré, **~e** /ɑ̃fjevʀe/ *adj* [*imagination*] fevered; [*atmosphere*] feverish.

enfilade /ɑ̃filad/ *nf* (of traps) succession; (of houses, tables) row.

enfiler /ɑ̃file/ [1] **I** *vtr* **1** to slip on; **2** to thread [*piece of thread, needle*].
II s'enfiler *v refl* (+ *v être*) **1**○ to guzzle down; (figurative) to devour; **2**○ to get landed○ with [*chore*]; **3 s'~ dans** [*corridor, street*] to take.

enfin /ɑ̃fɛ̃/ *adv* finally; lastly; **~ et surtout** last but not least; **~ seuls!** alone at last!; **~, puisque tu y tiens** oh well, as you insist; **mais ~, cessez de vous disputer!** for heaven's sake, stop arguing!; **il pleut tous les jours, ~ presque** it rains every day, well almost; **(mais) ~, que signifie toute cette histoire?** what on earth does it all mean?

enflammé, **~e** /ɑ̃flame/ *adj* **1** burning; **2** [*person, declaration*] passionate; [*speech*] impassioned, fiery; **3** (Med) [*throat, wound*] inflamed; **4** [*cheeks, face*] burning (**de** with); [*sky*] ablaze, blazing.

enflammer /ɑ̃flame/ [1] **I** *vtr* **1** to set fire to [*object, material*]; **2** to inflame [*public opinion, mind*]; to fire [*imagination*]; to fuel [*anger*].
II s'enflammer *v refl* (+ *v être*) **1** [*house, paper*] to go up in flames; [*petrol, wood*] to catch fire; **2** [*eyes*] to blaze; [*imagination*] to be fired (**de** with; **à la vue de** by); [*country, people*] to explode; **s'~ pour qn** to become passionate about sb; **s'~ pour qch** to get carried away by sth.

enfler /ɑ̃fle/ [1] **I** *vtr* **1** (figurative) to exaggerate [*story, event*]; **2** (literary) to swell.
II *vi* **1** [*part of body*] to swell (up); [*river, sea*] to swell; **2** [*rumour, anger*] to spread.
III s'enfler *v refl* (+ *v être*) [*anger*] to mount; [*voice*] to rise; [*rumour*] to grow.

enflure /ɑ̃flyʀ/ *nf* (Med) swelling.

enfoncer /ɑ̃fɔ̃se/ [12] **I** *vtr* **1** to push in [*cork, stake*]; **~ ses mains dans ses poches** to dig one's hands into one's pockets; **~ son doigt** to stick one's finger (**dans** into); **~ un clou dans qch** to knock a nail into sth; **2** to break down [*door*]; to break through [*enemy lines*]; **~ des portes ouvertes** to state the obvious; **3** to smash in [*side of car*]; **4 ne m'enfonce pas davantage** don't rub it in.
II s'enfoncer *v refl* (+ *v être*) **1 s'~ dans la neige/le sable** to sink in the snow/the sand; **il s'enfonça dans son fauteuil** he sank back into his armchair; **s'~ dans l'erreur** to make error after error; **s'~ dans l'eau** to sink; **les piquets s'enfoncent facilement** the posts go in easily; **s'~ une épine dans le doigt** to get a thorn in one's finger; **s'~ dans la forêt** to go into the forest; **2**○ to make things worse for oneself.

enfouir /ɑ̃fwiʀ/ [3] **I** *vtr* **1** to bury; **2 ~ son visage dans les coussins** to bury one's face in the cushions; **~ qch dans un sac** to shove sth into a bag.
II s'enfouir *v refl* (+ *v être*) **s'~ sous les couvertures** to burrow under the blankets.

enfourcher /ɑ̃fuʀʃe/ [1] *vtr* to mount [*horse*]; to get on [*motorbike*].

enfourner /ɑ̃fuʀne/ [1] *vtr* **1** to put [sth] in the oven; **2**○ to stuff down.

enfreindre /ɑ̃fʀɛ̃dʀ/ [55] *vtr* to infringe, to break.

enfuir: **s'enfuir** /ɑ̃fɥiʀ/ [9] *v refl* (+ *v être*) **1** (gen) to run away (**de** from); [*bird*] to fly away; to escape (**de** from); **2** [*time*] to fly.

enfumer /ɑ̃fyme/ [1] *vtr* to fill [sth] with smoke; **tu nous enfumes avec tes cigares!** you're smoking us out with your cigars!

engagé, **~e** /ɑ̃gaʒe/ *nm,f* enlisted man/woman.

engageant, **~e** /ɑ̃gaʒɑ̃, ɑ̃t/ *adj* [*person, manner*] welcoming; [*dish, place*] inviting.

engagement /ɑ̃gaʒmɑ̃/ *nm* **1** commitment; **prendre l'~ de faire** to undertake to do; **2** involvement; **3** (Mil) enlistment.

engager /ɑ̃gaʒe/ [13] **I** *vtr* **1** to hire [*staff*]; to enlist [*soldier*]; to engage [*artist*]; **2** to begin [*process, reform policy*]; **nous avons engagé la conversation** we struck up a conversation; **~ le combat** to go into combat; **~ une action judiciaire** to take legal action; **3** to commit [*person*]; **cela ne t'engage à rien** this doesn't commit you to anything; **4** to stake [*reputation, honour*]; **~ sa parole** to give one's word; **5 ~ qch dans** to put sth in; **6** to lay out [*capital*]; **~ des dépenses** to undertake expenditure; **7 ~ qn à faire** to urge sb to do; **8** (Sport) **~ qn dans une compétition** to enter sb for a competition; **9** to pawn [*valuable object*].
II s'engager *v refl* (+ *v être*) **1** to promise (**à faire** to do); **s'~ vis-à-vis de qn** to take on a commitment to sb; **2 s'~ dans un projet** to embark on a project; **s'~ dans la bataille** to go into action; **3** to get involved; **4 s'~ sur une route** to go into a road; **5** [*lawsuit, process, negotiations*] to begin; **6 s'~ dans l'armée/la police** to join the army/the police; **s'~ dans une compétition** to enter a competition.

engelure /ɑ̃ʒlyʀ/ *nf* chilblain.

engendrer /ɑ̃ʒɑ̃dʀe/ [1] *vtr* **1** to engender; **2** [*woman*] to give birth to; [*man*] to father.

engin /ɑ̃ʒɛ̃/ *nm* **1** device; **qu'est-ce que c'est que cet ~○?** what's that contraption?; **2** vehicle; **3** piece of equipment.

englober /ɑ̃glɔbe/ [1] *vtr* to include.

engloutir /ɑ̃glutiʀ/ [3] *vtr* **1** [*sea, storm, fog*] to engulf, to swallow up; **2**○ to gulp [sth] down; **3** [*person*] to squander [*money*]; [*project*] to swallow up [*money*].

engoncé, **~e** /ɑ̃gɔ̃se/ *adj* **il était ~ dans une veste trop étroite** he was squeezed into a tight jacket.

engorger /ɑ̃gɔʀʒe/ [13] *vtr* **1** to block (up) [*pipes, drains*]; **2** to clog up [*roads*]; **3** (Med) to congest [*organ*].

engouement /ɑ̃gumɑ̃/ *nm* (for thing, activity) passion; (for person) infatuation; **l'~ du public pour** the general craze for.

engouer: **s'engouer** /ɑ̃gwe/ [1] *v refl* (+ *v être*) **s'~ de** to develop a passion for [*artist, painting*].

engouffrer /ɑ̃gufʀe/ [1] **I**° *vtr* to gobble up [*sandwich*].
II s'engouffrer *v refl* (+ *v être*) (into a room) to rush; (into a taxi, an underground station) to dive (**dans** into).

engourdir /ɑ̃guʀdiʀ/ [3] **I** *vtr* **1** to make [sb/sth] numb; **2** to make [sb/sth] drowsy.
II s'engourdir *v refl* (+ *v être*) [*limb*] to go numb; [*mind*] to grow dull.

engourdissement /ɑ̃guʀdismɑ̃/ *nm* **1** (physical) numbness; (mental) drowsiness; **2** (of body) numbing; (of mind) dulling.

engrais /ɑ̃gʀɛ/ *nm inv* manure; fertilizer.

engraisser /ɑ̃gʀese/ [1] **I** *vtr* **1** to fatten [*cattle*]; **2** to fertilize [*soil*]; **3**° to make [sb] rich.
II *vi* to get fat.
III s'engraisser° *v refl* (+ *v être*) **s'~ (sur le dos de qn)** to grow fat° (off sb's back).

engranger /ɑ̃gʀɑ̃ʒe/ [13] *vtr* to gather in [*harvest*]; (figurative) to store [*data*].

engrenage /ɑ̃gʀənaʒ/ *nm* **1** gears; **2** (figurative) (of violence) spiral.

engueuler° /ɑ̃gœle/ [1] **I** *vtr* to tell [sb] off [*child*]; to give [sb] an earful° [*adult*].
II s'engueuler *v refl* (+ *v être*) to have a row (**avec qn** with sb).

enhardir: **s'enhardir** /ɑ̃aʀdiʀ/ [3] *v refl* (+ *v être*) to become bolder.

énième /ɛnjɛm/ *adj* umpteenth.

énigmatique /enigmatik/ *adj* enigmatic.

énigme /enigm/ *nf* **1** enigma, mystery; **découvrir le mot de l'~** to discover the answer to the mystery; **2** riddle; **parler par ~s** to speak in riddles.

enivrant, **~e** /ɑ̃nivʀɑ̃, ɑ̃t/ *adj* intoxicating.

enivrer /ɑ̃nivʀe/ [1] **I** *vtr* **1** to make [sb] drunk; **2 ~ qn** [*success*] to go to sb's head.
II s'enivrer *v refl* (+ *v être*) to get drunk.

enjambée /ɑ̃ʒɑ̃be/ *nf* stride; **avancer/s'éloigner à grandes ~s** to stride forward.

enjamber /ɑ̃ʒɑ̃be/ [1] *vtr* [*person*] to step over [*obstacle*].

enjeu, *pl* **~x** /ɑ̃ʒø/ *nm* (Games) stake; **analyser l'~ des élections** to analyse[GB] what is at stake in the elections; **un ~ économique** an economic issue.

enjoindre /ɑ̃ʒwɛ̃dʀ/ [56] *vtr* **~ à qn de faire** to enjoin sb to do.

enjôler /ɑ̃ʒole/ [1] *vtr* to beguile; **se laisser ~ par** to be taken in or beguiled.

enjôleur, **-euse** /ɑ̃ʒolœʀ, øz/ *adj* bewitching.

enjoliver /ɑ̃ʒɔlive/ [1] *vtr* to embellish.

enjoliveur /ɑ̃ʒɔlivœʀ/ *nm* hubcap.

enjoué, **~e** /ɑ̃ʒwe/ *adj* [*character*] cheerful; [*tone*] light-hearted.

enlacer /ɑ̃lase/ [12] **I** *vtr* to embrace; [*snake*] to wrap itself around [*prey*].
II s'enlacer *v refl* (+ *v être*) [*people*] to embrace; [*body*] to intertwine.

enlaidir /ɑ̃lediʀ/ [3] *vtr* to spoil [*landscape*]; to make [sb] look ugly [*person*].

enlevé, **~e** /ɑ̃lve/ *adj* [*rhythm, piece of music*] lively.

enlèvement /ɑ̃lɛvmɑ̃/ *nm* kidnapping[GB], abduction.

enlever /ɑ̃lve/ [16] **I** *vtr* **1** to take [sth] away, to remove [*piece of furniture, book*]; to take [sth] down [*curtains, pictures*]; to take [sth] off [*garment*]; to move, to remove [*vehicle*]; **2** to remove [*stain, paint*]; **3** to take [sb/sth] away [*people, object*]; **~ à qn l'envie de partir** to put sb off going; **cela n'enlève rien à l'estime que j'ai pour elle** it doesn't make me think any the less of her; **4** to kidnap; [*lover*] to carry [sb] off ; **5** to carry [sth] off [*trophy, prize*]; to capture [*market*].
II s'enlever *v refl* (+ *v être*) **1** [*varnish, wallpaper*] to come off; [*stain*] to come out; **2** [*part, section*] to be detachable; **3**° **enlève-toi de là** get off°.

enlisement /ɑ̃lizmɑ̃/ *nm* sinking; (figurative) (in negotiations) stalemate.

enliser /ɑ̃lize/ [1] **I** *vtr* to get [sth] stuck (**dans** in).
II s'enliser *v refl* (+ *v être*) **1** [*boat, vehicle*] to get stuck (**dans** in); **2** (figurative) [*inquiry, negotiations*] to drag on; **être enlisé dans** to be embroiled in [*conflict, difficulties*].

enluminure /ɑ̃lyminyʀ/ *nf* illumination.

enneigé, **~e** /ɑ̃neʒe/ *adj* [*summit*] snowy; [*road*] covered in snow.

enneigement /ɑ̃nɛʒmɑ̃/ *nm* **bulletin d'~** snow report.

ennemi, **~e** /ɛnmi/ **I** *adj* **1** (Mil) enemy; **2** (gen) hostile.
II *nm,f* enemy; **se faire des ~s** to make enemies.
III *nm* (Mil) enemy; **passer à l'~** to go over to the enemy.

ennui /ɑ̃nɥi/ *nm* **1** boredom; **tromper l'~** to escape from boredom; **c'est à mourir d'~** it's enough to bore you stiff or to death; **quel ~!** what a bore!; **2** problem; **avoir des ~s** to have problems; **j'ai des ~s avec la police** I'm in trouble with the police; **créer des ~s à qn** to make trouble for sb; **s'attirer des ~s** to run into trouble.

ennuyé, **~e** /ɑ̃nɥije/ *adj* **1** bored; **2** embarrassed; **j'étais très ~ de laisser les enfants seuls** I felt awful about leaving the children on their own; **3 j'aurais été très ~ si je n'avais pas eu la clé** I would have been in real trouble if I hadn't had the key.

ennuyer /ɑ̃nɥije/ [22] **I** *vtr* **1** to bore; **2** to bother; **si ça ne vous ennuie pas trop** if you don't mind; **3** to annoy; **4** to hassle°.
II s'ennuyer *v refl* (+ *v être*) **1** to be bored; **2** to get bored; **3 s'~ de** to miss [*friend, parents*].

ennuyeux, **-euse** /ɑ̃nɥijø, øz/ *adj* **1** boring; **2** tedious; **3** annoying.
IDIOMS **être ~ comme la pluie** to be as dull as ditchwater.

énoncé /enɔ̃se/ *nm* **1** (of exam subject) wording (**de** of); **l'~ d'une théorie** the exposition of a theory; **2** (of fact) statement (**de** of); **3** (Law) **à**

l'~ du verdict when the verdict was pronounced.

énoncer /enɔ̃se/ [12] *vtr* to pronounce [*verdict*]; to set out, to state [*facts, principles*]; to expound [*theory*].

enorgueillir: **s'enorgueillir** /ɑ̃nɔʀgœjiʀ/ [3] *v refl* (+ *v être*) to pride oneself (**de** on).

énorme /enɔʀm/ *adj* **1** [*object, person*] huge, enormous; [*expense*] huge, vast; **2** [*success, effort*] tremendous; [*mistake*] terrible; [*lie*] outrageous; [*laugh*] hearty.

énormément /enɔʀmemɑ̃/ *adv* tremendously, immensely.

énormité /enɔʀmite/ *nf* **1** (of figure, size) hugeness; (of mistake, lie) enormity; **2** outrageous remark.

enquérir: **s'enquérir** /ɑ̃keʀiʀ/ [35] *v refl* (+ *v être*) **s'~ de** to enquire about sth.

enquête /ɑ̃kɛt/ *nf* **1** (Law) inquiry, investigation (**sur** into); (into a death) inquest (**sur** into); **~ de police** police investigation; **~ judiciaire** judicial inquiry; **2** (by journalist) investigation (**sur** into); **3** (by sociologist) survey (**sur** about).

enquêter /ɑ̃kete/ [1] *vi* [*policeman*] to carry out an investigation, to investigate; [*expert, commission*] to hold an inquiry.

enquêteur, **-trice** /ɑ̃ketœʀ, tʀis/ *nm,f* **1** investigating officer; **2** pollster; **3** interviewer.

enquiquinant°, **~e** /ɑ̃kikinɑ̃, ɑ̃t/ *adj* **1** annoying; **elle est ~e, celle-là!** she's a real pain°!; **2** boring.

enquiquiner° /ɑ̃kikine/ [1] **I** *vtr* **1 ~ qn** to get on sb's nerves; **2** to pester sb.

II s'enquiquiner *v refl* (+ *v être*) **s'~ à faire** to go to the trouble of doing.

enraciner: **s'enraciner** /ɑ̃ʀasine/ [1] *v refl* (+ *v être*) **1** to take root; **2** (figurative) [*person*] to put down roots; [*custom, idea*] to take root.

enragé, **~e** /ɑ̃ʀaʒe/ *adj* **1** fanatical; **2** enraged; **3** (Med) rabid.

IDIOMS **manger de la vache ~e**° to go through hard times.

enrager /ɑ̃ʀaʒe/ [13] *vi* to be furious; **faire ~ qn** to tease sb.

enrayer /ɑ̃ʀeje/ [21] **I** *vtr* **1** to check [*epidemic, development*]; to curb [*inflation, unemployment*]; to stop [sth] escalating [*crisis, violence*]; **2** to jam; **~ le mécanisme** to jam the mechanism; (figurative) to put a spanner (GB) or wrench (US) in the works.

II s'enrayer *v refl* (+ *v être*) to get jammed.

enregistrement /ɑ̃ʀəʒistʀəmɑ̃/ *nm* **1** (of music, video) recording; **2** (of data) recording; (of order) taking down; **3** (Law) registration; **4** (of baggage) check-in.

enregistrer /ɑ̃ʀəʒistʀe/ [1] *vtr* **1** to record [*cassette, album*]; **2** to note [*progress, failure*]; to record [*rise, drop*]; **3** to make a record of [*expenses*]; to take [*order*]; to record [*data*]; to set [*record*]; **4** to register [*birth, claim*]; **5** to check in [*baggage*]; **6 c'est enregistré, j'enregistre**° I've made a mental note of it.

enrhumer: **s'enrhumer** /ɑ̃ʀyme/ [1] *v refl* (+ *v être*) to catch a cold.

enrichir /ɑ̃ʀiʃiʀ/ [3] **I** *vtr* **1** to make [sb] rich [*person*]; to bring wealth to [*country*]; **2** to enrich, to enhance [*collection, book*] (**de** with); **3** (Tech) to enrich.

II s'enrichir *v refl* (+ *v être*) **1** [*person*] to become or grow rich; **2** to be enriched (**de** with).

enrichissant, **~e** /ɑ̃ʀiʃisɑ̃, ɑ̃t/ *adj* [*experience*] rewarding; [*relationship*] fulfilling.

enrober /ɑ̃ʀɔbe/ [1] *vtr* **1** to coat (**de** with); **2** (figurative) to wrap up [*news*] (**de** in).

enrôlement /ɑ̃ʀolmɑ̃/ *nm* (in the army) enlistment (**dans** in); (in political party) enrolment[GB] (**dans** in); **~ forcé** impressment.

enrôler /ɑ̃ʀole/ [1] **I** *vtr* (gen) to recruit; (Mil) to enlist, to recruit.

II s'enrôler *v refl* (+ *v être*) to enrol[GB], to enlist.

enrouer: **s'enrouer** /ɑ̃ʀwe/ [1] *v refl* (+ *v être*) [*voice*] to go hoarse; [*person*] to make oneself hoarse; **d'une voix ~e** hoarsely.

enrouler /ɑ̃ʀule/ [1] **I** *vtr* **1** to wind; **2** to wrap.

II s'enrouler *v refl* (+ *v être*) **1** [*thread, tape*] to wind; **2** [*person, animal*] to curl up.

enrubanner /ɑ̃ʀybane/ [1] *vtr* to decorate [sth] with ribbon.

ENS /œɛnɛs/ *nf*: *abbr* ▶ **école**.

ensabler: **s'ensabler** /ɑ̃sɑble/ [1] *v refl* (+ *v être*) **1** [*vehicle*] to get stuck in the sand; [*boat*] to get stranded (*on a sandbank*); **2** [*canal, harbour*] to silt up.

ensanglanter /ɑ̃sɑ̃glɑ̃te/ [1] *vtr* **1** to cover [sth] with blood; **2** to bring bloodshed to [*country*].

enseignant, **~e** /ɑ̃seɲɑ̃, ɑ̃t/ **I** *adj* **corps ~** teaching profession; **syndicat ~** teachers' trade union.

II *nm,f* (Sch) teacher; (at university) lecturer.

enseigne /ɑ̃sɛɲ/ *nf* **1** (shop) sign; **~ lumineuse** neon sign; **2** (Mil, Naut) ensign.

IDIOMS **nous sommes logés à la même ~** we are in the same boat.

enseignement /ɑ̃sɛɲmɑ̃/ *nm* **1** education; **l'~ supérieur** higher education; **2** teaching; **méthodes d'~** teaching methods; **3** lesson; **~s d'un échec** lessons learnt from failure.

■ **~ par correspondance** or **à distance** distance learning; **~ général** mainstream education; **~ professionnel** vocational training; **~ religieux** religious instruction.

enseigner /ɑ̃seɲe/ [1] *vtr* to teach; **~ qch à qn** to teach sth to sb, to teach sb sth.

ensemble /ɑ̃sɑ̃bl/ **I** *adv* **1** together; **ils iraient bien ~ ces deux-là**°! they'd make a fine pair, those two°!; **2** at the same time.

II *nm* **1** group; **un ~ de personnes** a group of people; **une vue d'~** an overall view; **plan d'~ d'une ville** general plan of a town; **dans l'~** by and large; **dans l'~ de** throughout; **dans son** or **leur ~** as a whole; **2** set; **3** unity, cohesion; **former un bel ~** to form a harmonious whole; **4** (of gestures) coordination; (of sounds) unison; **un mouvement d'~** a coordinated movement; **5** (in mathematics) set; **théorie des ~s** set theory; **6** (Mus) ensemble; **7** (of offices) complex; **~ hôtelier** hotel complex; **~ industriel** industrial estate (GB) or park (US); **8** (set of clothes) outfit; suit.

ensevelir /ɑ̃səvəliʀ/ [3] *vtr* to bury.

ensoleillé, **~e** /ɑ̃sɔleje/ *adj* sunny.

ensoleillement /ɑ̃sɔlɛjmɑ̃/ *nm* **l'~ moyen de la région est de 2 000 heures par an** on average the region gets 2,000 hours of sunshine a year.

ensommeillé, **~e** /ɑ̃sɔmeje/ *adj* [*person, voice*] sleepy, drowsy.

ensorcelé, **~e** /ɑ̃sɔʀsəle/ *adj* [*house, forest*] enchanted.

ensorceler /ɑ̃sɔʀsəle/ [19] *vtr* **1** to cast or to put a spell on; **2** to bewitch, to enchant.

ensorceleur, **-euse** /ɑ̃sɔʀsəlœʀ, øz/ **I** *adj* **1** bewitching; **2** magic.
II *nm,f* charmer.

ensuite /ɑ̃sɥit/ *adv* **1 très bien, mais ~?** fine, but then what?; **il ne me l'a dit qu'~** he only told me later or subsequently; **2** secondly.

ensuivre: **s'ensuivre** /ɑ̃sɥivʀ/ [19] *v refl* (+ *v être*) to follow, to ensue.

entacher /ɑ̃taʃe/ [1] *vtr* to mar [*relations*].

entaille /ɑ̃taj/ *nf* **1** cut; (deeper) gash; **2** (on an object) gash; notch.

entailler /ɑ̃taje/ [1] **I** *vtr* to cut into; (deeply) to make a gash in.
II s'entailler *v refl* (+ *v être*) **s'~ le doigt** to cut one's finger, to gash one's finger.

entame /ɑ̃tam/ *nf* **1** (Culin) first slice; **2** (in cards) lead.

entamer /ɑ̃tame/ [1] *vtr* **1** to start [*day, activity*]; to initiate [*procedure*]; to open [*meeting, negotiations*]; **2** to undermine [*credibility, morale*]; to shake [*resolve, determination*]; **3** to eat into [*savings*]; **4** to cut into [*loaf, roast*]; to open [*bottle, jar*]; to start eating [*desert*]; **5** to cut into [*skin, wood*]; **6** to eat into [*metal*].

entartrer /ɑ̃taʀtʀe/ [1] **I** *vtr* to fur up (GB), to scale up.
II s'entartrer *v refl* (+ *v être*) to scale; [*teeth*] to be covered in tartar.

entasser /ɑ̃tase/ [1] **I** *vtr* **1** to pile [*books, clothes*]; **2** to hoard [*money, old things*]; **3** to pack, to cram [*people, objects*] (**dans** into).
II s'entasser *v refl* (+ *v être*) [*objects*] to pile up; [*people*] to squeeze (**dans** into; **sur** onto).

entendement /ɑ̃tɑ̃dmɑ̃/ *nm* understanding; **cela dépasse l'~** it's beyond belief.

entendre /ɑ̃tɑ̃dʀ/ [6] **I** *vtr* **1** to hear [*noise, word*]; **faire ~ un cri** to give a cry; **je n'en ai jamais entendu parler** I've never heard of it; **je ne veux plus en ~ parler** I don't want to hear another word about it; **vous entendrez parler de moi!** (threateningly) you haven't heard the last of it!; **on n'entend plus parler de lui** his name is not mentioned any more; **2** [*judge, police*] to hear [*witness*]; **à t'~, tout va bien** according to you, everything is fine; **elle ne veut rien ~** she won't listen; **3** to understand; **il agit comme il l'entend** he does as he likes; **elle a laissé ~ que** she intimated that; **ils ne l'entendent pas de la sorte** or **de cette oreille** they don't see it that way; **4** to mean; **qu'entends-tu par là?** what do you mean by that?; **5 ~ faire** to intend doing; **j'entends qu'on fasse ce que je dis** I expect people to do what I say.
II s'entendre *v refl* (+ *v être*) **1** to get on or along; **2** to agree (**sur** on); **on leur dit la vérité ou pas? il faudrait s'~** shall we tell them the truth or not? let's get it straight; **3** [*noise*] to be heard; **4** to hear oneself; [*two or more people*] to hear each other; **5 phrase qui peut s'~ de plusieurs façons** sentence which can be taken in several different ways; **6 s'y ~ en meubles anciens** to know about antiques.

entendu, **~e** /ɑ̃tɑ̃dy/ **I** *pp* ▶ **entendre**.
II *pp adj* **1 c'est une affaire ~e** it's settled; **'tu viens demain?'—'~!'** 'will you come tomorrow?'—'OK°!'; **2 d'un air ~** with a knowing look.
III bien entendu *phr* of course.

entente /ɑ̃tɑ̃t/ *nf* **1** harmony; **vivre en bonne ~ avec qn** to be on good terms with sb; **2** understanding; **3** arrangement; **~ commerciale** trade arrangement.

entériner /ɑ̃teʀine/ [1] *vtr* **1** to ratify; **2** to confirm.

enterré, **~e** /ɑ̃teʀe/ *adj* buried; **mort et ~** dead and buried; **~ (depuis longtemps)** (figurative) long-forgotten.

enterrement /ɑ̃tɛʀmɑ̃/ *nm* **1** burial; **2** funeral; **faire une tête d'~°** to look gloomy.

enterrer /ɑ̃teʀe/ [1] **I** *vtr* to bury.
II s'enterrer° *v refl* (+ *v être*) to go and hole up°.
IDIOMS **~ sa vie de garçon** to have a stag party.

entêtant, **~e** /ɑ̃tetɑ̃, ɑ̃t/ *adj* [*aroma*] heady; [*music*] insistent.

en-tête, *pl* **~s** /ɑ̃tɛt/ *nm* heading.

entêtement /ɑ̃tɛtmɑ̃/ *nm* stubbornness, obstinacy.

entêter: **s'entêter** /ɑ̃tete/ [1] *v refl* (+ *v être*) **1** to be stubborn; **2** to persist.

enthousiasme /ɑ̃tuzjasm/ *nm* enthusiasm.

enthousiasmer /ɑ̃tuzjasme/ [1] **I** *vtr* to fill [sb] with enthusiasm.
II s'enthousiasmer *v refl* (+ *v être*) to get enthusiastic (**pour** about).

enthousiaste /ɑ̃tuzjast/ *adj* enthusiastic.

enticher: **s'enticher** /ɑ̃tiʃe/ [1] *v refl* (+ *v être*) **s'~ de** to become infatuated with [*person*].

entier, **-ière** /ɑ̃tje, ɛʀ/ **I** *adj* **1** whole; **manger un pain ~** to eat a whole or an entire loaf; **(pendant) des heures entières** for hours on end; **lait ~** full-fat milk; **2** [*success, satisfaction*] complete; **avoir l'entière responsabilité de qch** to have full responsibility for sth; **3** [*object, reputation*] intact; **le mystère reste ~** the mystery remains unsolved; **4 être tout ~ à son travail** to be completely absorbed in one's work; **avoir un caractère ~** to be thoroughgoing.

II *nm* (in mathematics) integer.

entièrement /ɑ̃tjɛʀmɑ̃/ *adv* entirely, completely; **~ équipé** fully equipped.

entonner /ɑ̃tɔne/ [1] *vtr* to start singing [*song*]; to launch into [*subject*].

entonnoir /ɑ̃tɔnwaʀ/ *nm* **1** funnel; **2** crater.

entorse /ɑ̃tɔʀs/ *nf* **1** (Med) sprain; **se faire une ~ à la cheville** to sprain one's ankle; **2** (figurative) infringement (**à** of); **faire une ~ au règlement** to bend the rules.

entortiller /ɑ̃tɔʀtije/ [1] I *vtr* **1** to wind (**autour de qch** round[GB] sth); **2** to tangle up.
II **s'entortiller** *v refl* (+ *v être*) [*thread, wool*] to get entangled (**dans** in).

entourage /ɑ̃tuʀaʒ/ *nm* **1** family circle; **2** circle (of friends); **on dit dans son ~ que** people close to him/her say that.

entouré, **~e** /ɑ̃tuʀe/ I *pp* ▶ **entourer**.
II *adj* **1** [*person*] popular; **2 nos patients sont très ~s** our patients are well looked after.

entourer /ɑ̃tuʀe/ [1] I *vtr* **1** [*buildings, fence, people*] to surround; **entouré de** [*place*] surrounded by or with; **2 ~ qch de qch** to put sth around sth; **~ qch de mystère** to shroud sth in mystery; **3** to rally round (GB) or around (US) [*sick person*].
II **s'entourer** *v refl* (+ *v être*) **1 s'~ d'objets** to surround oneself with things; **s'~ de précautions** to take every possible precaution; **2 s'~ d'un châle** to wrap oneself (up) in a shawl.

entournure /ɑ̃tuʀnyʀ/ *nf* **être gêné aux ~s** (figurative) to be in an awkward position; (financially) to feel the pinch○.

entracte /ɑ̃tʀakt/ *nm* intermission.

entraider: **s'entraider** /ɑ̃tʀede/ [1] *v refl* (+ *v être*) to help each other or one another.

entrailles /ɑ̃tʀɑj/ *nf pl* (of animal) innards, entrails.

entrain /ɑ̃tʀɛ̃/ *nm* **1** (of person) spirit, go○ (GB); **retrouver son ~** to cheer up; **2** (of party, discussion) liveliness; **être plein d'~** to be very lively; **sans ~** half-hearted.

entraînant, **~e** /ɑ̃tʀɛnɑ̃, ɑ̃t/ *adj* lively.

entraînement /ɑ̃tʀɛnmɑ̃/ *nm* **1** training, coaching; **terrain/jours d'~** training ground/days; **2** practice[GB]; **avoir de l'~** to be highly trained; **l'~ à la lecture** reading practice[GB]; **3** training session.

entraîner /ɑ̃tʀene/ [1] I *vtr* **1** to lead to; **une panne a entraîné l'arrêt de la production** a breakdown brought production to a standstill; **2** [*river, current*] to carry [sth/sb] away [*boat, swimmer*]; **il a entraîné qn/qch dans sa chute** he dragged sb/sth down with him; **3** to take [*person*]; **~ qn sur la piste de danse** to take sb onto the dance floor; **~ qn à faire** [*person*] to make sb do; [*circumstances*] to lead sb to do; **4** (figurative) to carry [sb] away [*person, group*]; **5** to train, to coach [*athlete, team*] (**à** for); to train [*horse, soldier*] (**à** for); **un joueur bien entraîné** a well-trained player; **6** [*engine, piston etc*] to drive [*machine, wheel, turbine*].
II **s'entraîner** *v refl* (+ *v être*) **1** [*player, soldiers*] to train (**à** for); **2** to prepare oneself (**à qch** for sth).

entraîneur /ɑ̃tʀɛnœʀ/ *nm* (of player, athlete) coach.

entrave /ɑ̃tʀav/ I *nf* hindrance (**à** to); (on freedom) restriction (**à** of); **s'exprimer sans ~** to speak freely.
II **entraves** *nf pl* (on animal) hobble; (on convict) shackles.

entraver /ɑ̃tʀave/ [1] *vtr* **1** to hinder, to impede; **~ la carrière de qn** to hinder sb in his/her career; **2** to hobble [*animal*]; to shackle [*convict*].

entre /ɑ̃tʀ/ *prep*

■ **Note** You will find translations for expressions such as *entre parenthèses, lire entre les lignes etc* at the entries ***parenthèse, lire[1]*** *etc.*

1 between; **~ midi et deux** at lunchtime; **'doux ou très épicé?'—'~ les deux'** 'mild or very spicy?'—'in between'; **~ son travail et l'informatique, il n'a pas le temps de sortir** what with work and his computer he doesn't have time to go out; **2** among; **organiser une soirée ~ amis** to organize a party among friends; **chacune d'~ elles** each of them; **~ hommes** as one man to another; **~ nous** between you and me, between ourselves; **nous sommes ~ nous** there's just the two of us; we're among friends; **les enfants sont souvent cruels ~ eux** children are often cruel to each other.

entrebâillement /ɑ̃tʀəbɑjmɑ̃/ *nm* (of door, shutter, window) gap (**de** in).

entrebâiller /ɑ̃tʀəbɑje/ [1] *vtr* to half-open [*door, curtains*].

entrechoquer /ɑ̃tʀəʃɔke/ [1] I *vtr* to clatter [*saucepans*]; to clink [*glasses*]; to knock [sth] together [*pebbles, spoons*].
II **s'entrechoquer** *v refl* (+ *v être*) **1** [*glasses*] to clink; **2** [*ideas, interests*] to clash.

entrecôte /ɑ̃tʀəkot/ *nf* **1** entrecôte (steak); **2** rib steak.

entrecouper /ɑ̃tʀəkupe/ [1] I *vtr* to punctuate (**de** by).
II **s'entrecouper** *v refl* (+ *v être*) [*lines, roads*] to intersect.

entrecroiser /ɑ̃tʀəkʀwaze/ [1] *vtr* to intertwine.

entrée /ɑ̃tʀe/ *nf* **1** entrance (**de** to); **se retrouver à l'~ du bureau** to meet outside the office; **2** (on motorway) (entry) slip road (GB), on-ramp (US); **3** (in house) (gen) hall; (in hotel, public place) lobby; (door, gateway) entry; **4 l'~ dans la récession** the beginning of the recession; **d'~ (de jeu)** from the very start; **d'~ de jeu, il m'a proposé un marché** he offered me a deal straight off or right off; **5 l'~ d'un pays dans une organisation** the entry of a country into an organization; **'~ libre'** 'admission free'; **'~ interdite'** 'no entry'; **6** ticket; **deux ~s gratuites** two free tickets; **7** (of person) entrance; **réussir son ~** [*actor*] to enter on cue; **faire son ~ dans le monde** to enter society; **8** (Culin) starter; **9** (in bookkeeping) **~s** receipts.

■ **~ des artistes** stage door; **~ en matière** introduction.

entrefaites: **sur ces entrefaites** /syʀsezɑ̃tʀəfɛt/ *phr* at that moment, just then.

entrefilet /ɑ̃tʀəfilɛ/ *nm* brief article.

entrejambes /ɑ̃tʀəʒɑ̃b/ *nm inv* crotch.

entrelacer /ɑ̃tʀəlase/ [12] *vtr*, **s'entrelacer** *v refl* (+ *v être*) to intertwine, to interlace.

entremêler /ɑ̃tʀəmele/ [1] I *vtr* to mix [*objects*]; to interweave [*threads*].

II **s'entremêler** *v refl* (+ *v être*) (gen) to be mixed; [*hair, branches*] to get tangled.

entremets /ɑ̃tʀəmɛ/ *nm* dessert.

entremetteur, **-euse** /ɑ̃tʀəmɛtœʀ, øz/ *nm,f* **1** matchmaker; **2** go-between.

entremise /ɑ̃tʀəmiz/ *nf* intervention; **il l'a su par mon ~** he heard of it through me.

entreposer /ɑ̃tʀəpoze/ [1] *vtr* to store.

entrepôt /ɑ̃tʀəpo/ *nm* **1** warehouse; **2** stockroom.

entreprenant, **~e** /ɑ̃tʀəpʀənɑ̃, ɑ̃t/ *adj* (gen) enterprising; **être ~** (man) to be forward with the ladies.

entreprendre /ɑ̃tʀəpʀɑ̃dʀ/ [52] *vtr* **1** to start, to undertake [*research, repairs*]; **~ de faire** to set about doing; to undertake to do; **2 ~ qn sur un sujet** to engage sb in conversation about sth.

entrepreneur, **-euse** /ɑ̃tʀəpʀənœʀ, øz/ *nm,f* **1** builder; **2** contractor; **~ de pompes funèbres** undertaker, mortician (US); **3** owner-manager (*of a small firm*).

entreprise /ɑ̃tʀəpʀiz/ *nf* **1** firm, business; **petites et moyennes ~s** small and medium businesses; **~ de pompes funèbres** undertaker's (GB), funeral home (US); **2** business, industry; **la libre ~** free enterprise; **3** undertaking, enterprise; venture.

entrer /ɑ̃tʀe/ [1] I *vtr* (+ *v avoir*) **1** to bring [sth] in; to take [sth] in; **~ qch en fraude dans un pays** to smuggle sth into a country; **2** (in computing) to enter.

II *vi* (+ *v être*) **1** (gen) to get in, to enter; (viewed from outside) to go in; (viewed from within) to come in; **entrez!** come in!; **fais-la ~** show her in; **'défense d'~'** (on door) 'no entry'; (on gate, fence) 'no trespassing'; **je ne fais qu'~ et sortir** I can only stay a minute; **2** to fit; **la clé n'entre pas dans la serrure** the key doesn't fit in the lock; **je n'arrive pas à faire ~ la pièce dans la fente** I can't get the coin into the slot; **3 ~ dans** to enter [*period, debate*]; to join [*opposition, company, army, party*]; **~ à** to enter [*school, charts*]; to get into [*university*]; **~ en** to enter into [*discussions, negotiations*]; **~ dans la vie de qn** to come into sb's life; **il m'a fait ~ au ministère** he got me into the ministry; **je ne sais pas comment cette idée lui est entrée dans la tête** I don't know how he/she got that idea into his/her head; **~ dans la légende** [*person*] to become a legend; [*fact*] to become legendary; **cela n'entre pas dans mes attributions** it's not part of my duties; **~ en fusion** to begin to melt; **~ dans une colère noire** to fly into a blind rage.

entresol /ɑ̃tʀəsɔl/ *nm* mezzanine; **à l'~** on the mezzanine.

entre-temps /ɑ̃tʀətɑ̃/ *adv* meanwhile, in the meantime.

entretenir /ɑ̃tʀətniʀ/ [36] I *vtr* **1** to look after [*garment, carpet, house*]; to maintain [*road, building*]; **~ sa forme** to keep in shape; **2** to support [*family*]; to keep [*mistress*]; **3** to keep [sth] going [*conversation, fire*]; to keep [sth] alive [*friendship*]; **~ des liens étroits avec** to have close ties with; **4 ~ qn de qch** to speak to sb about sth.

II **s'entretenir** *v refl* (+ *v être*) **1 s'~ de qch** to discuss sth; **2 s'~ facilement** [*house, fabric*] to be easy to look after.

entretien /ɑ̃tʀətjɛ̃/ *nm* **1** (of house, garden) upkeep; (of car, road, building) maintenance; (of garment, plant, skin) care; **2** cleaning; **3** (gen) discussion; (for a job) interview; (in newspaper) interview; (in politics) talks.

entrevoir /ɑ̃tʀəvwaʀ/ [46] *vtr* **1** to catch a glimpse of; (indistinctly) to make out; **2** to glimpse [*truth, solution*]; **3** to foresee [*difficulty, improvement*]; **laisser ~ qch** [*result, sign*] to point to sth.

entrevue /ɑ̃tʀəvy/ *nf* (gen) meeting; (political) talks.

entrouvert, **~e** /ɑ̃tʀuvɛʀ, ɛʀt/ *adj* [*door*] ajar, half open; [*lips*] parted.

entrouvrir /ɑ̃tʀuvʀiʀ/ [32] I *vtr* to open [sth] a little.

II **s'entrouvrir** *v refl* (+ *v être*) (gen) [*door, country*] to half-open; [*lips*] to part.

énumération /enymeʀasjɔ̃/ *nf* **1** listing; **2** catalogue[GB].

énumérer /enymeʀe/ [14] *vtr* to enumerate, to list.

envahir /ɑ̃vaiʀ/ [3] *vtr* [*troops, crowd*] to invade; [*animal, plant*] to overrun; [*goods*] to flood [*market*].

envahisseur /ɑ̃vaisœʀ/ *nm* invader.

enveloppe /ɑ̃vlɔp/ *nf* **1** (for letter) envelope; **sous ~** in an envelope; **2** (for parcel) wrapping; (of grains) husk; (of peas, beans) pod.

■ **~ budgétaire** budget; **~ matelassée** padded envelope.

enveloppé, **~e** /ɑ̃vlɔpe/ *adj* [*person*] plump.

envelopper /ɑ̃vlɔpe/ [1] I *vtr* **1** [*person*] to wrap [sb/sth] (up); [*sheet*] to cover; **2** [*fog, silence, night*] to envelop; [*mist*] to veil; [*mystery, secrecy*] to surround.

II **s'envelopper** *v refl* (+ *v être*) to wrap oneself (up).

envenimer /ɑ̃vnime/ [1] I *vtr* to inflame [*debate*]; to aggravate [*situation*].

II **s'envenimer** *v refl* (+ *v être*) [*dispute*] to worsen; [*situation*] to turn ugly.

envergure /ɑ̃vɛʀgyʀ/ *nf* **1** (of plane) wingspan; **2** (figurative) (of person) stature; (of project, enterprise) scale; **un projet d'~** a substantial project; **d'~ internationale** [*organization*] of international scope; **sans ~** [*project*] limited; [*person*] of no account.

envers[1] /ɑ̃vɛʀ/ *prep* toward(s), to.

IDIOMS **~ et contre tous/tout** in spite of everyone/everything.

envers[2] /ɑ̃vɛʀ/ **I** *nm inv* (of sheet of paper) back; (of piece of cloth) wrong side; (of garment) inside; (of coin) reverse; **l'~ du décor** (figurative) the other side (of the picture).

II à l'envers *phr* **1** the wrong way; **2** upside down; **3** inside out; **4** back to front; **5** the wrong way round (GB) or around (US); **mettre ses chaussures à l'~** to put one's shoes on the wrong feet; **6 passer un film à l'~** to run a film backward(s).

enviable /ɑ̃vjabl/ *adj* enviable.

envie /ɑ̃vi/ *nf* **1** (gen) urge (**de faire** to do); (for food) craving (**de** for); **~ folle** insane urge; **ce n'est pas l'~ qui me manque** don't think I haven't thought of it!; **avoir ~ de qch** to feel like sth; **avoir ~ de dormir** to want to go to bed; **mourir d'~ de faire** to be dying○ to do; **donner (l')~ à qn de faire** to make sb want to do; **2** envy; **il te fait ~ ce jouet?** would you like that toy?; **3** birthmark.

IDIOMS **avoir une ~ pressante** to need to go to the toilet.

envier /ɑ̃vje/ [2] *vtr* to envy; **j'envie ta façon de voir** I envy you your outlook.

envieux, **-ieuse** /ɑ̃vjø, øz/ **I** *adj* envious.

II *nm,f* envious person; **faire des ~** to make people jealous.

environ /ɑ̃viʀɔ̃/ *adv* about; **tous les deux ans ~** about every two years.

environnant, **~e** /ɑ̃viʀɔnɑ̃, ɑ̃t/ *adj* surrounding.

environnement /ɑ̃viʀɔnmɑ̃/ *nm* environment.

environner /ɑ̃viʀɔne/ [1] *vtr* to surround.

environs /ɑ̃viʀɔ̃/ *nm pl* **être des ~** to be from the area; **aux ~ de** (place) in the vicinity of; (time, moment) around; (amount) in the region of.

envisager /ɑ̃vizaʒe/ [13] *vtr* **1** to plan (**de faire** to do); **2** to envisage [*hypothesis, situation*]; to foresee [*problem, possibility*]; **~ l'avenir avec sérénité** to view the future with confidence; **~ le pire** to imagine the worst; **3** to consider.

envoi /ɑ̃vwa/ *nm* **1 tous les ~s de colis sont suspendus** parcel post is suspended; **faire un ~ de** to send [*flowers, books*]; **2 demander l'~ (immédiat) de troupes** to ask for troops to be dispatched (immediately); **3 l'~ de la fusée** the rocket launch; **donner le coup d'~ de** to kick off [*match, campaign*]; to open [*festival*].

■ **~ en nombre** bulk dispatch (GB) or mailing (US); **~ recommandé** registered post (GB) or mail (US); **~ contre remboursement** cash on delivery.

envol /ɑ̃vɔl/ *nm* (of bird, imagination) flight; (of plane) takeoff.

envolée /ɑ̃vɔle/ *nf* **1** flight of fancy; **2** (in prices) surge (**de** in); (of political party) rise.

envoler: **s'envoler** /ɑ̃vɔle/ [1] *v refl* (+ *v être*) **1** [*bird*] to fly off (**pour** to); [*plane, passenger*] to take off (**pour** for); [*paper, hat*] to be blown away; **2** [*prices*] to soar; **3** to vanish; **mon portefeuille ne s'est tout de même pas envolé**○ my wallet didn't just disappear; **4**○ to do a runner○, to escape.

envoûtement /ɑ̃vutmɑ̃/ *nm* **1** bewitchment; **2** spell.

envoûter /ɑ̃vute/ [1] *vtr* to bewitch; **~ son auditoire** to hold the audience spellbound.

envoyé, **~e** /ɑ̃vwaje/ **I** *adj* **ça c'est (bien) ~**○! well said!

II *nm,f* envoy; **~ spécial** special correspondent.

envoyer /ɑ̃vwaje/ [24] **I** *vtr* **1** to send (**à** to); **~ des signaux de fumée** to send smoke signals; **~ qn étudier à Genève** to send sb off to study in Geneva; **2** to throw [*pebble*]; to fire [*missile*] (**sur** at); **~ qch dans l'œil de qn** to hit sb in the eye with sth; **~ le ballon dans les buts** to put the ball in the net; **3 ~ un coup de pied à qn** to kick sb.

II s'envoyer *v refl* (+ *v être*) **1** to exchange; **s'~ des baisers** to blow each other kisses; **2**○ to guzzle [*drink*]; to wolf down [*meal*].

IDIOMS **~ qn promener**○ to send sb packing○; **tout ~ promener**○ to drop the lot○; **il ne me l'a pas envoyé dire**○ and he told me in no uncertain terms.

enzyme /ɑ̃zim/ *nm* or *f* enzyme.

éolienne /eɔljɛn/ *nf* (aeolian) windmill.

épais, **épaisse** /epɛ, ɛs/ **I** *adj* **1** (gen) thick; **il n'est pas bien ~ ce petit**○**!** he's a skinny little fellow!; **2** [*mind, intelligence*] dull; **3** [*night, silence*] deep.

II *adv* a lot, much.

épaisseur /epɛsœʀ/ *nf* **1** thickness; **couper qch dans (le sens de) l'~** to cut sth sideways; **dans l'~ de la nuit** (figurative) in the depths of night; **2** layer.

épaissir /epesiʀ/ [3] **I** *vtr* **1** to thicken; **2** to thicken [*waist*]; **3** to deepen [*mystery*].

II *vi* **1** [*sauce*] to thicken; [*jelly*] to set; **faire ~** cook until the mixture thickens; **2** to put on weight.

III s'épaissir *v refl* (+ *v être*) [*sauce, waist, mist*] to thicken; [*mystery*] to deepen.

épancher: **s'épancher** /epɑ̃ʃe/ [1] *v refl* (+ *v être*) to open one's heart (**auprès de** to).

épanoui, **~e** /epanwi/ *adj* [*flower*] in full bloom; [*smile, face*] beaming; [*person, personality*] well-adjusted; [*figure*] ample.

épanouir /epanwiʀ/ [3] **I** *vtr* **1** [*sun*] to open (out) [*flower*]; [*joy*] to light up [*face*]; **2** (figurative) to make [sb/sth] blossom.

II s'épanouir *v refl* (+ *v être*) [*flower*] to bloom; [*face*] to light up; [*person*] to blossom; **permettre aux gens de s'~** to enable people to fulfil[GB] their potential.

épanouissement /epanwismɑ̃/ *nm* **1** (of flower) blooming; **2** (of person) (gen) development; (of talent) flowering; **favoriser/empêcher l'~ de qn/qch** to foster/to hamper the development of sb/sth.

épargne /epaʀɲ/ *nf* savings; **un compte (d') ~** a savings account.

épargner /epaʀɲe/ [1] **I** *vtr* **1** to save [*money*]; **2** to spare [*place, person, institution*]; **3 ~ qch à qn** to spare sb sth.
II *vi* to save.
III s'épargner *v refl* (+ *v être*) to save oneself [*wait, effort*].

éparpiller /epaʀpije/ [1] **I** *vtr* to scatter; (figurative) to dissipate [*strength, talents*].
II s'éparpiller *v refl* (+ *v être*) [*crowd, ashes*] to scatter.

épars, ~e /epaʀ, aʀs/ *adj* scattered.

épatant○**, ~e** /epatɑ̃, ɑ̃t/ *adj* marvellous[GB].

épate○ /epat/ *nf* **faire de l'~** to show off.

épaté, ~e /epate/ *adj* **1 nez ~** pug nose, flat nose; **2**○ amazed (**de** by).

épater○ /epate/ [1] *vtr* **1** to impress; **ça t'épate, hein?** surprised, aren't you?; **2** to amaze.

épaule /epol/ *nf* shoulder; **rentrer la tête dans les ~s** to hunch one's shoulders.
IDIOMS **changer son fusil d'~** to change one's tactics; **avoir la tête sur les ~s** to have one's head screwed on○.

épauler /epole/ [1] **I** *vtr* **1** to help; **je ne suis pas épaulé** I don't get any support; **2** to take aim with [*rifle*].
II *vi* to take aim.

épaulette /epolɛt/ *nf* **1** shoulder-pad; **2** (shoulder-)strap; **3** (Mil) epaulette.

épave /epav/ *nf* **1** wreck; **2** (car) (gen) wreck; (after accident) write-off○; **3** (person) wreck.

épée /epe/ *nf* sword; **c'est un coup d'~ dans l'eau** (figurative) it was a complete waste of effort.

épeler /eple/ [19] *vtr* to spell [*word*].

éperdu, ~e /epɛʀdy/ *adj* [*need, desire*] overwhelming; [*scream*] frantic; [*glance*] desperate; [*flight*] headlong; [*love, recognition*] boundless.

éperdument /epɛʀdymɑ̃/ *adv* [*scream*] frantically; [*in love*] madly; **je me moque ~ de ce qu'il pense** I couldn't care less about what he thinks.

éperon /epʀɔ̃/ *nm* spur; **donner des ~s** to spur on a horse.

épervier /epɛʀvje/ *nm* (Zool) sparrowhawk.

éphèbe /efɛb/ *nm* **1** (humorous) Adonis; **2** ephebe.

éphémère /efemɛʀ/ *adj* [*happiness*] fleeting; [*success, product, insect*] short-lived.

épi /epi/ *nm* **1** (of corn) ear; (of flower) spike; **~ de maïs** corn cob; **2** (unmanageable) tuft of hair (GB), cow-lick (US).

épice /epis/ *nf* spice.

épicé, ~e /epise/ *adj* **1** (gen) spicy; (with pepper, chili) hot; **2** [*story*] spicy.

épicentre /episɑ̃tʀ/ *nm* epicentre[GB].

épicer /epise/ [12] *vtr* to spice; (figurative) to add spice to.

épicerie /episʀi/ *nf* **1** grocer's (shop) (GB), grocery (store) (US); **~ fine** delicatessen; **2** grocery trade; **3** groceries.

épicier, -ière /episje, ɛʀ/ *nm,f* grocer.

épidémie /epidemi/ *nf* (Med), (figurative) epidemic.

épiderme /epidɛʀm/ *nm* skin.

épidermique /epidɛʀmik/ *adj* skin; [*sensitivity*] extreme; **réaction ~** gut reaction.

épier /epje/ [2] *vtr* **1** to spy on [*person, behaviour*]; **il épie tous mes faits et gestes** he watches my every move; **2** to be on the lookout for.

épilation /epilasjɔ̃/ *nf* removal of unwanted hair.

épilepsie /epilɛpsi/ *nf* epilepsy; **crise d'~** epileptic fit.

épiler /epile/ [1] *vtr* to remove unwanted hair from; to wax [*leg*]; to pluck [*eyebrows*].

épilogue /epilɔg/ *nm* epilogue[GB]; (figurative) outcome.

épiloguer /epilɔge/ [1] *vi* to go on and on (**sur** about).

épinard /epinaʀ/ *nm* spinach.
IDIOMS **ça met du beurre dans les ~s**○ it brings in a nice bit of extra money.

épine /epin/ *nf* thorn; **~ dorsale** spine.
IDIOMS **ôter à qn une ~ du pied** to take a weight off sb's shoulders.

épineux, -euse /epinø, øz/ *adj* [*stem*] prickly; [*problem, situation*] tricky; [*question*] vexed; [*character*] prickly.

épingle /epɛ̃gl/ *nf* pin; **~ de** or **à nourrice, ~ de sûreté** safety pin.
IDIOMS **monter qch en ~** to blow sth up out of proportion; **être tiré à quatre ~s**○ to be immaculately dressed; **tirer son ~ du jeu** to get out while the going is good.

épingler /epɛ̃gle/ [1] *vtr* **1** to pin; **2**○ to collar○; **se faire ~** to be collared○.

épinière /epinjɛʀ/ *adj f* **moelle ~** spinal cord.

épique /epik/ *adj* epic; **c'était ~**○ (humorous) it was quite something○.

épisode /epizɔd/ *nm* episode; **roman à ~s** serialized novel.

épisodique /epizɔdik/ *adj* sporadic.

épitaphe /epitaf/ *nf* epitaph; **en ~** as an epitaph.

épithète /epitɛt/ *nf* attributive adjective.

éploré, ~e /eplɔʀe/ *adj* **1** grief-stricken; **2** tearful.

éplucher /eplyʃe/ [1] *vtr* to peel [*fruit, vegetable*]; (figurative) to go through [sth] with a fine-tooth comb [*article, accounts*].

épluchure /eplyʃyʀ/ *nf* **~ de pomme** piece of apple peel; **~s** peelings.

éponge /epɔ̃ʒ/ *nf* **1** sponge; **donner un coup d'~ à qch** to sponge sth (down); **2** terry-towelling[GB].
IDIOMS **passer l'~** to forget the past; **passer l'~ sur qch** to forget all about sth.

éponger /epɔ̃ʒe/ [13] *vtr* to mop up [*liquid*]; to mop [*sweat, forehead, surface*]; to absorb [*deficit*]; to pay off [*debts*].

épopée /epɔpe/ *nf* **1** epic; **2** saga.

époque /epɔk/ *nf* **1** time; **à l'~ où** at the time when; **vivre avec son ~** to move with the times; **quelle ~!** what's the world coming to!; **à mon ~** in my day; **2** (historical) era; **3 en**

costume **d'~** in period costume; **des meubles d'~** antique furniture.

époumoner○: **s'époumoner** /epumɔne/ [1] *v refl* (+ *v être*) to shout oneself hoarse.

épouse /epuz/ *nf* wife, spouse.

épouser /epuze/ [1] *vtr* **1** to marry [*person*]; **2** to adopt [*cause, idea*].

épousseter /epuste/ [20] *vtr* to dust.

époustoufler○ /epustufle/ [1] *vtr* to amaze; **époustouflé de** flabbergasted at.

épouvantable /epuvɑ̃tabl/ *adj* **1** (gen) dreadful; **2** appalling.

épouvantail /epuvɑ̃taj/ *nm* **1** scarecrow; **2**○ (ugly person) fright; **3** spectre[GB].

épouvante /epuvɑ̃t/ *nf* **1** terror; **2** horror.

épouvanter /epuvɑ̃te/ [1] *vtr* **1** to terrify; **2** to horrify.

époux /epu/ **I** *nm inv* husband.
II *nm pl* **les ~** the (married) couple; **les jeunes ~** the newly weds.

éprendre: **s'éprendre** /epʀɑ̃dʀ/ [52] *v refl* (+ *v être*) **s'~ de qn** to become enamoured of sb.

épreuve /epʀœv/ *nf* **1** ordeal; **2** test; **mettre à rude ~** to put [sb] to a severe test [*person*]; to be very hard on [*car, shoes*]; to tax [*patience, nerves*]; to put a strain on [*friendship, relationship*]; **à toute ~** unfailing; **l'~ du feu** ordeal by fire; **à l'~ du feu/des balles** fire-/bullet-proof; **3** (part of an) examination; **~ écrite/orale** written/oral examination; **4** (Sport) **~ d'athlétisme** athletics event; **5** (photograph, print) proof.

épris, **~e** /epʀi, iz/ *adj* in love (**de** with); **être ~ de voyages** to have a great love of travelling[GB].

éprouvant, **~e** /epʀuvɑ̃, ɑ̃t/ *adj* gruelling[GB]; trying.

éprouver /epʀuve/ [1] *vtr* **1** to feel [*regret, love*]; to have [*sensation, doubt, difficulty*]; **~ de la jalousie** to be jealous; **2** to test; **une technique éprouvée** a tried and tested technique; **3** [*death, event*] to distress [*person*]; [*storm, crisis*] to hit [*region*].

éprouvette /epʀuvɛt/ *nf* **1** test tube; **2** sample.

EPS /œpeɛs/ *nf* (*abbr* = **éducation physique et sportive**) PE.

épuisé, **~e** /epɥize/ **I** *pp* ▶ **épuiser**.
II *pp adj* **1** exhausted, worn out; **2** [*publication, livre*] out of print; [*item*] out of stock; **notre stock est ~** we're sold out.

épuisement /epɥizmɑ̃/ *nm* **1** exhaustion; **2 jusqu'à ~ des stocks** while stocks last.

épuiser /epɥize/ [1] **I** *vtr* **1** to exhaust, to wear [sb] out; **2** to exhaust [*subject, mine*]; **3** to impoverish [*soil*].
II s'épuiser *v refl* (+ *v être*) **1** to exhaust oneself; **2** [*stocks, provisions*] to be running out.

épuisette /epɥizɛt/ *nf* **1** landing net; **2** shrimp net.

épuration /epyʀasjɔ̃/ *nf* **1** (of gas, liquid) purification; (of oil) refining; (of sewage) treatment; **2** purge.

épurer /epyʀe/ [1] *vtr* **1** to purify [*water, gas*]; **2** to purge [*party*]; **3** to expurgate [*text*].

équateur /ekwatœʀ/ *nm* equator.

équation /ekwasjɔ̃/ *nf* equation.

équerre /ekɛʀ/ *nf* **1** set square; **2** flat T-bracket; **3** flat angle bracket; **en** or **d'~** at right angles.

équestre /ekɛstʀ/ *adj* equestrian; **centre ~** riding school.

équilibre /ekilibʀ/ *nm* **1** balance; **garder l'~** to keep one's balance; **être en ~ sur** [*object*] to be balanced on; [*person*] to balance on; **l'~ des forces** the balance of power; **2** equilibrium; **manquer d'~** to be unstable; **retrouver son ~** to get back to normal.

équilibrer /ekilibʀe/ [1] *vtr* to balance; **un enfant équilibré** a well-balanced child.

équilibriste /ekilibʀist/ *nmf* acrobat.

équinoxe /ekinɔks/ *nm* equinox.

équipage /ekipaʒ/ *nm* **1** crew; **2** horse and carriage.

équipe /ekip/ *nf* team; shift; crew; **travailler en ~** to work as a team; **~ de secours** rescue team; **~ de tournage** film crew; **l'~ de nuit** the night shift.

équipé, **~e**[1] /ekipe/ **I** *pp* ▶ **équiper**.
II *pp adj* **bien/mal ~** well-/ill-equipped; **cuisine ~e** fitted kitchen.

équipée[2] /ekipe/ *nf* escapade; **une folle ~** a wild escapade.

équipement /ekipmɑ̃/ *nm* **1** equipment; kit; **2 ~s** facilities.

équiper /ekipe/ [1] **I** *vtr* to equip [*hospital, vehicle*] (**de** with); to provide [*town*] (**de** with); to fit out [*person*] (**de** with).
II s'équiper *v refl* (+ *v être*) to equip oneself.

équipier, **-ière** /ekipje, ɛʀ/ *nm,f* **1** team member; **2** crew member.

équitable /ekitabl/ *adj* [*person*] fair-minded; [*decision*] fair.

équitation /ekitasjɔ̃/ *nf* (horse-)riding.

équité /ekite/ *nf* equity; **en toute ~** in all fairness.

équivalence /ekivalɑ̃s/ *nf* **1** equivalence; **2 titre admis en ~** recognized qualification.

équivalent, **~e** /ekivalɑ̃, ɑ̃t/ *adj* **1** equivalent; **2** identical.

équivaloir /ekivalwaʀ/ [45] **I équivaloir à** *v+prep* to be equivalent to [*quantity*]; to amount to [*effect*].
II s'équivaloir○ *v refl* (+ *v être*) **les deux solutions s'équivalent** there isn't much to choose between the two solutions.

équivoque /ekivɔk/ **I** *adj* **1** ambiguous; **2** [*reputation*] dubious; [*behaviour*] questionable.
II *nf* ambiguity; **sans ~** [*reply*] unequivocal; [*condemn*] unequivocally.

érable /eʀabl/ *nm* **1** maple (tree); **2** maple (wood); **sirop d'~** maple syrup.

érafler /eʀafle/ [1] **I** *vtr* to scratch.
II s'érafler *v refl* (+ *v être*) to scratch oneself.

érailler /eʀɑje/ [1] **s'érailler** *v refl* (+ *v être*) to become hoarse.

ère /ɛʀ/ *nf* **1** era; **en l'an 10 de notre ~** in the year 10 AD; **2** age; **à l'~ atomique** in the nuclear age.

érection /eʀɛksjɔ̃/ *nf* erection.

éreinter○ /eʀɛ̃te/ [1] **I** *vtr* to exhaust.
II s'éreinter *v refl* (+ *v être*) to wear oneself out.

ergot /ɛʀgo/ *nm* **1** (of cock) spur; (of dog) dew-claw; **2** ergot.

ergoter /ɛʀgɔte/ [1] *vi* to split hairs (**sur, à propos de** over).

ériger /eʀiʒe/ [13] **I** *vtr* to erect [*statue, building*].
II s'ériger *v refl* (+ *v être*) **s'~ en** to set oneself up as.

ermite /ɛʀmit/ *nm* **1** hermit; **2** recluse; **vivre en ~** to live the life of a recluse.

éroder /eʀɔde/ [1] *vtr* to erode; to undermine [*argument*].

érosion /eʀozjɔ̃/ *nf* erosion.

érotique /eʀɔtik/ *adj* erotic.

érotisme /eʀɔtism/ *nm* eroticism.

errance /ɛʀɑ̃s/ *nf* restless wandering.

errant, **~e** /ɛʀɑ̃, ɑ̃t/ *adj* **1** wandering; **2** rootless; **chien ~** stray dog.

errer /ɛʀe/ [1] *vi* [*person, gaze*] to wander; [*animal*] to roam.

erreur /ɛʀœʀ/ *nf* **1** mistake; **~ de jugement** error of judgment; **~ de traduction** mistranslation; **induire qn en ~** to mislead sb; **sauf ~ de ma part** if I'm not mistaken; **il n'y a pas d'~ possible** there's no mistake; **2** (Law) error.

erroné, **~e** /ɛʀɔne/ *adj* incorrect, erroneous.

ersatz /ɛʀzats/ *nm* ersatz; **~ de café** ersatz coffee.

érudit, **~e** /eʀydi, it/ *nm,f* scholar, erudite person.

érudition /eʀydisjɔ̃/ *nf* erudition, scholarship; **avec ~** eruditely.

éruption /eʀypsjɔ̃/ *nf* eruption; **entrer en ~** to erupt.

ès /ɛs/ *prep* **licence ~ lettres** ≈ arts degree, B.A. (degree).

escabeau, *pl* **~x** /ɛskabo/ *nm* **1** stepladder; **2** kitchen steps.

escadrille /ɛskadʀij/ *nf* squadron.

escadron /ɛskadʀɔ̃/ *nm* (Mil) company; **~ de la mort** death squad.

escalade /ɛskalad/ *nf* **1** (Sport) climbing; ascent; **2** escalation.

escalader /ɛskalade/ [1] *vtr* to scale [*wall*]; to climb [*mountain*].

escale /ɛskal/ *nf* **1** stopover; **~ technique** (for plane) refuelling[GB] stop; (for ship) overhaul; **2** (for ship) port of call; (for plane) stopover.

escalier /ɛskalje/ *nm* **1** staircase; **2** stairs.
■ **~ mécanique** or **roulant** escalator; **~ de service** backstairs.

escalope /ɛskalɔp/ *nf* escalope; **~ de dinde** turkey escalope.

escamotable /ɛskamɔtabl/ *adj* [*landing gear*] retractable; [*ladder*] foldaway.

escamoter /ɛskamɔte/ [1] *vtr* **1** [*magician*] to make [sth] disappear; **2 ~ un lit** to fold a bed away; **3** to evade [*issue*].

escapade /ɛskapad/ *nf* escapade; **faire une ~** to run away.

escargot /ɛskaʀgo/ *nm* snail; **avancer comme un ~** to go at a snail's pace; **~ de mer** winkle, periwinkle.

escarmouche /ɛskaʀmuʃ/ *nf* skirmish.

escarpé, **~e** /ɛskaʀpe/ *adj* **1** steep; **2** craggy.

escarpement /ɛskaʀpəmɑ̃/ *nm* **1** steep slope; **2** steepness.

escarpin /ɛskaʀpɛ̃/ *nm* court shoe (GB), pump (US).

escarre /ɛskaʀ/ *nf* bedsore.

escient /ɛsjɑ̃/ *nm* **à bon ~** wittingly; **à mauvais ~** ill-advisedly.

esclaffer: **s'esclaffer** /ɛsklafe/ [1] *v refl* (+ *v être*) to guffaw.

esclandre /ɛsklɑ̃dʀ/ *nm* scene.

esclavage /ɛsklavaʒ/ *nm* **1** slavery; **2** (figurative) tyranny.

esclavagisme /ɛsklavaʒism/ *nm* slavery.

esclave /ɛsklav/ *nmf* slave.

escompte /ɛskɔ̃t/ *nm* discount; **~ de 3%** 3% discount.

escompter /ɛskɔ̃te/ [1] *vtr* to anticipate; **~ faire** to count on doing, to hope to do.

escorte /ɛskɔʀt/ *nf* **1** escort; **2** (figurative) accompaniment.

escorter /ɛskɔʀte/ [1] *vtr* to escort.

escrime /ɛskʀim/ *nf* fencing.

escrimer○: **s'escrimer** /ɛskʀime/ [1] *v refl* (+ *v être*) **s'~ à faire** to knock○ oneself out trying to do.

escrimeur, **-euse** /ɛskʀimœʀ, øz/ *nm,f* fencer.

escroc /ɛskʀo/ *nm* swindler, crook.

escroquer /ɛskʀɔke/ [1] *vtr* to swindle; **~ qch à qn** to swindle sb out of sth.

escroquerie /ɛskʀɔkʀi/ *nf* **1** fraud, swindling; **tentative d'~** attempted fraud; **c'est de l'~!** it's daylight robbery; **2** swindle.

ésotérique /ezɔteʀik/ *adj* esoteric; **cercle ~** closed circle.

espace /ɛspas/ *nm* **1** space; **2 ~ de loisirs** leisure complex; **3** gap; **4 en l'~ de** in the space of; **l'~ d'un instant** for a moment.
■ **~ publicitaire** advertising space; **~ vert** open space; **~ vital** living space.

espacer /ɛspase/ [12] **I** *vtr* to space [sth] out.
II s'espacer *v refl* (+ *v être*) to become less frequent.

espadon /ɛspadɔ̃/ *nm* swordfish.

espadrille /ɛspadʀij/ *nf* espadrille.

Espagne /ɛspaɲ/ *pr nf* Spain.
IDIOMS **bâtir des châteaux en ~** to build castles in the air.

espagnol, **~e** /ɛspaɲɔl/ **I** *adj* Spanish.
II *nm* **l'~** Spanish.

espalier /ɛspalje/ *nm* **1** espalier; **2** fruit-wall.

espèce /ɛspɛs/ **I** *nf* **1** species; **l'~ humaine** mankind; **2** kind; **de la pire ~** of the worst kind.

II **espèces** *nfpl* **en ~s** in cash.

espérance /ɛsperɑ̃s/ *nf* hope; **~ de vie** life expectancy.

espérer /ɛspeʀe/ [14] I *vtr* **1 ~ qch** to hope for sth; **2** to expect; **je n'en espérais pas tant** it's more than I expected; **je ne t'espérais plus** I had given up on you.
II *vi* to hope; **on peut toujours ~!** you can always hope!

espiègle /ɛspjɛgl/ *adj* mischievous; **d'un air ~** mischievously.

espion, -ionne /ɛspjɔ̃, ɔn/ *nm,f* spy.

espionnage /ɛspjɔnaʒ/ *nm* espionage, spying; **film/roman d'~** spy film/story.

espionner /ɛspjɔne/ [1] *vtr* to spy on; **~ pour le compte de qn** to spy for sb.

esplanade /ɛsplanad/ *nf* esplanade.

espoir /ɛspwaʀ/ *nm* hope; **rendre ~** to rekindle hope; **reprendre ~** to feel hopeful again; **dans l'~ de te lire bientôt** hoping to hear from you soon; **avec ~** hopefully.

esprit /ɛspʀi/ *nm* **1** mind; **avoir l'~ mal placé** to have a dirty mind°; **avoir l'~ d'aventure** to be adventurous; **avoir un ~ de synthèse** to be good at synthesizing information; **avoir l'~ de contradiction** to be contrary; **dans mon ~ c'était facile** the way I saw it, it was easy; **cela ne t'est jamais venu à l'~?** didn't it ever occur to you?; **avoir l'~ ailleurs** to be miles away; **conforme à l'~ de l'entreprise** in accordance with the company ethic; **les choses de l'~** spiritual matters; **2** wit; **avoir de l'~** to be witty; **faire de l'~** to try to be witty; **~ d'à-propos** ready wit; **3 dans un ~ de vengeance** in a spirit of revenge; **ils ont l'~ de famille** they're a very close family; **4 l'un des plus grands ~s de son temps** one of the greatest minds of his/her time; **calmer les ~s** to calm people down; **les ~s sont échauffés** feelings are running high; **5** spirit; **croire aux ~s** to believe in ghosts.
■ **~ de corps** solidarity; **~ d'équipe** team spirit.
IDIOMS **perdre ses ~s** to faint; **les grands ~s se rencontrent** great minds think alike.

esquimau, -aude, *mpl* **~x** /ɛskimo, od/ I *adj* Eskimo; **chien ~** husky.
II *nm* **1** Eskimo; **2** ®chocolate-covered ice lolly (GB), ice-cream bar (US).

esquinter° /ɛskɛ̃te/ [1] *vtr* **1** to damage; **2** (in fight) to hurt [*person*].

esquisse /ɛskis/ *nf* **1** sketch; **2** outline.

esquisser /ɛskise/ [1] I *vtr* to sketch [*portrait*]; to outline [*programme*].
II **s'esquisser** *v refl* (+ *v être*) [*solution*] to emerge.

esquiver /ɛskive/ [1] I *vtr* to dodge, duck [*blow*]; to sidestep [*issue*].
II **s'esquiver** *v refl* (+ *v être*) **1** to slip away; **2** to shy away.

essai /esɛ/ I *nm* **1** trial; **être à l'~** to undergo trials; **~ sur route** road test; **2** test; **faire des ~s** to do tests; **3** try; **un coup d'~** a try; **faire un ~** to have a try; **prendre qn à l'~** to give sb a try-out; **4** essay (**sur** on); **5** (in rugby) try.
II **essais** *nm pl* (Sport) qualifying round.

essaim /esɛ̃/ *nm* swarm.

essayage /esɛjaʒ/ *nm* fitting; **cabine d'~** fitting room.

essayer /eseje/ [21] I *vtr* **1** to try; **~ sa force** to test one's strength; **2** to test [*weapon, plane, product*]; to run trials on [*car, machine*]; **3** to try on [*clothes, shoes*]; to try [*size, colour*]; to try out [*car*].
II *vi* to try; **~ à la poste** to try the post office; **j'essaierai que tout se passe bien** I'll try to make sure everything goes all right.
III **s'essayer** *v refl* (+ *v être*) **s'~ à** to have a go at, to try one's hand at.

essence /esɑ̃s/ *nf* **1** petrol (GB), gasoline (US); **2** essential oil; **3** tree species.
■ **~ à briquet** lighter fuel (GB), lighter fluid (US); **~ ordinaire** ≈ 2-star petrol (GB), regular gasoline (US); **~ sans plomb** unleaded (petrol) (GB), unleaded gasoline (US); **~ super** ≈ 4-star petrol (GB), premium gasoline (US).

essentiel, -ielle /esɑ̃sjɛl/ I *adj* essential; **rôle ~** key role.
II *nm* **c'est l'~** that's the main thing; **aller à l'~** to get to the heart of the matter; **l'~ des voix** the bulk of the vote; **pour l'~** mainly; **en voyage je n'emporte que l'~** when I travel I only take the bare minimum.

essentiellement /esɑ̃sjɛlmɑ̃/ *adv* **1** mainly; **2** essentially.

essieu, *pl* **~x** /esjø/ *nm* axle.

essor /esɔʀ/ *nm* (of technology, area) development; (of fashion, sport) increasing popularity; **être en plein ~** to be booming.

essorage /esɔʀaʒ/ *nm* **1** wringing; **2** spin-drying.

essorer /esɔʀe/ [1] *vtr* **1** to wring; **2** to spin-dry [*washing*]; to spin [*lettuce*].

essoreuse /esɔʀøz/ *nf* spin-drier (GB), spin-dryer; **~ à salade** salad spinner.

essoufflement /esufləmɑ̃/ *nm* breathlessness; (figurative) loss of impetus.

essouffler /esufle/ [1] I *vtr* to leave [sb] breathless; **être essoufflé** to be out of breath.
II **s'essouffler** *v refl* (+ *v être*) **1** to get breathless; **2** to run out of steam.

essuie-glace, *pl* **~s** /esɥiglas/ *nm* windscreen wiper (GB), windshield wiper (US).

essuie-mains /esɥimɛ̃/ *nm inv* hand towel.

essuie-tout /esɥitu/ *nm inv* kitchen paper.

essuyer /esɥije/ [22] I *vtr* **1** to dry [*glass, hands*]; to wipe [*table*]; **~ la vaisselle** to dry up; **~ ses larmes** to wipe away one's tears; **2** to run into [*storm*]; to suffer [*defeat, losses, insults*]; to meet with [*failure, refusal*].
II **s'essuyer** *v refl* (+ *v être*) to dry oneself, to towel off (US); **s'~ les mains** to dry one's hands.

est /ɛst/ I *adj inv* east; eastern.
II *nm* **1** east; **un vent d'~** an easterly wind; **l'~ du Japon** eastern Japan; **2 l'Est** the East; **de l'Est** eastern.

estafette /ɛstafɛt/ *nf* **1** ®van; **2** (Mil) dispatch rider.

estampe /ɛstɑ̃p/ *nf* **1** engraving; **2** print.

esthète /ɛstɛt/ *nmf* aesthete.

esthéticienne /ɛstetisjɛn/ *nf* beautician.

esthétique /ɛstetik/ **I** *adj* [*quality, sense*] aesthetic; [*monument, decor*] aesthetically pleasing; [*pose, gesture*] graceful.
II *nf* aesthetics; **~ industrielle** industrial design.

estimation /ɛstimasjɔ̃/ *nf* estimate; valuation; assessment.

estime /ɛstim/ *nf* respect.

estimer /ɛstime/ [1] *vtr* **1** to feel; **~ nécessaire de faire** to consider it necessary to do; **2** to think highly of [*friend, artist*]; **3** to value [*painting*]; to assess [*damage*]; **~ qn à sa juste valeur** to recognize sb's real worth; **une vitesse estimée à 150 km/h** an estimated speed of 150 kph; **4** to reckon.

estival, **~e**, *mpl* **-aux** /ɛstival, o/ *adj* **1** summer; **2** summery.

estivant, **~e** /ɛstivɑ̃, ɑ̃t/ *nm,f* summer visitor.

estomac /ɛstɔma/ *nm* stomach; **avoir l'~ bien accroché** to have a strong stomach; **leur refus m'est resté sur l'~**○ their refusal left a nasty taste in my mouth.
IDIOMS **avoir l'~ dans les talons**○ to be famished.

estomaquer○ /ɛstɔmake/ [1] *vtr* to flabbergast.

estomper /ɛstɔ̃pe/ [1] **I** *vtr* to blur [*shape*]; to gloss over [*details*].
II s'estomper *v refl* (+ *v être*) [*landscape*] to become blurred; [*hatred, memories*] to fade.

estrade /ɛstʀad/ *nf* platform.

estragon /ɛstʀagɔ̃/ *nm* tarragon.

estropié, **~e** /ɛstʀɔpje/ *nm,f* cripple.

estropier /ɛstʀɔpje/ [2] **I** *vtr* **1** to maim; **2** (figurative) to make a hash of [*song, poem*].
II s'estropier *v refl* (+ *v être*) to maim oneself.

estuaire /ɛstɥɛʀ/ *nm* estuary.

esturgeon /ɛstyʀʒɔ̃/ *nm* sturgeon.

et /e/ *conj* and; **~ voilà qu'il sort un couteau de sa poche!** and next thing he whips a knife out of his pocket!; **~ moi de répondre**... so I replied...; **~ si on allait au cinéma?** how about going to the cinema?; **~ alors?**, **~ après?** so what?

étable /etabl/ *nf* cowshed.

établi, **~e** /etabli/ **I** *pp* ▶ **établir**.
II *pp adj* **1** [*reputation, use*] established; **2** [*power, regime*] ruling; [*order*] established.
III *nm* workbench.

établir /etabliʀ/ [3] **I** *vtr* **1** to set up [*home*]; **2** to establish [*rule, link, reputation, identity, innocence, fact*]; to introduce [*tax, discipline*]; to set up [*government*]; to set [*record, standard*]; **3** to draw up [*list, plan, budget, file*]; to make out [*cheque, bill*]; to prepare [*quote*]; to make [*diagnostic*]; to draw [*parallel*].
II s'établir *v refl* (+ *v être*) **1** [*person*] to settle (**à, en** in); **s'~ à son compte** to set up one's own business; **2** [*links*] to develop.

établissement /etablismɑ̃/ *nm* **1** organization; **~ bancaire** banking institution; **2** (of relations, regime) establishment; (of tax, sanctions) introduction; **3** premises.
■ **~ scolaire** school; **~ spécialisé** institution.

étage /etaʒ/ *nm* **1** floor; **le premier ~** the first floor (GB), the second floor (US); **le dernier ~** the top floor; **à l'~** upstairs; **2** (of tower) level; (of aquaduct, cake) tier.

étager /etaʒe/ [13] **I** *vtr* to plant [sth] in tiers [*flowers*]; to stagger [*increases*].
II s'étager *v refl* (+ *v être*) [*gardens*] to rise in terraces.

étagère /etaʒɛʀ/ *nf* shelf.

étain /etɛ̃/ *nm* **1** tin; **2** pewter; **3** piece of pewter ware.

étal /etal/ *nm* **1** (market) stall; **2** butcher's block.

étalage /etalaʒ/ *nm* **1** window display; **2** display; **faire ~ de ses connaissances** to flaunt one's knowledge.

étalagiste /etalaʒist/ *nmf* window dresser.

étalement /etalmɑ̃/ *nm* (of holidays) staggering; (of payments) spreading.

étaler /etale/ [1] **I** *vtr* **1** to spread out [*sheet*]; to spread [*rug*]; to roll [sth] out [*pastry*]; **2** to scatter; **3** to spread [*butter, glue*]; to apply [*paint, ointment*]; **4** to spread [*work, payments*]; to stagger [*departures, holidays*]; **5** to flaunt [*wealth, knowledge*]; to display [*merchandise*]; **~ au grand jour** to bring [sth] out into the open.
II s'étaler *v refl* (+ *v être*) **1** [*butter, paint*] to spread; **2** [*person*] to sprawl, to spread out; **3**○ to go sprawling○; **s'~ de tout son long** to fall flat on one's face; **s'~** or **se faire ~ à un examen** to fail an exam.

étalon /etalɔ̃/ *nm* **1** stallion; **2** standard; **~ monétaire** monetary standard.

étalon-or /etalɔ̃ɔʀ/ *nm inv* gold standard.

étamine /etamin/ *nf* stamen.

étanche /etɑ̃ʃ/ *adj* **1 ~ (à l'eau)** waterproof; watertight; **~ (à l'air)** airtight; **2** (figurative) impenetrable.

étanchéité /etɑ̃ʃeite/ *nf* **~ (à l'eau)** waterproofness; watertightness; **~ (à l'air)** airtightness.

étancher /etɑ̃ʃe/ [1] *vtr* to quench [*thirst*].

étang /etɑ̃/ *nm* pond.

étant /etɑ̃/ ▶ **donné** III.

étape /etap/ *nf* **1** stop; **2** (in journey) stage; (in race) leg; **3** (figurative) stage, step; **brûler les ~s** to go too far too fast.

état /eta/ **I** *nm* **1** condition; **mettre qn hors d'~ de nuire** to put sb out of harm's way; **leur ~ de santé est excellent** their (state of) health is excellent; **l'~ des routes** road conditions; the state of the roads; **en mauvais ~** in poor condition; **maintenir qch en ~ de marche** to keep sth in working order; **hors d'~ de marche** [*car*] off the road, not running; [*machine*] out of order; **j'ai laissé les choses en l'~** I left everything as it was; **à**

l'~ brut in its raw state; **2** state; **être dans un drôle**○ **d'~** to be in a hell of a state○; **ne pas être dans son ~ normal** not to be oneself; **être dans un ~ second** to be in a trance; **ce n'est encore qu'à l'~ de projet** it's still only at the planning stage; **à l'~ pur** in its pure state; **3** statement.

II faire ~ de *phr* **1** to cite [*document, law*]; **2** to mention [*conversation*]; **3** to state [*benefits*]; to air [*ideas*]; **4** to make a point of mentioning [*success, courage*].

■ **~ d'alerte** state of alert; **en ~ d'alerte** on the alert; **~ d'âme** qualm; feeling; **~ de choc** state of shock; **~ civil** registry office (GB); civil status; **~ d'esprit** state or frame of mind; **~ de fait** fact; **~ des lieux** inventory and statement of state of repair; **~s de service** service record.

IDIOMS **être/se mettre dans tous ses ~s**○ to be in/to get into a state○.

État /eta/ *nm* **1** state, State; **2** state, government.

étatique /etatik/ *adj* [*financing, management*] state (GB), public (US); [*control*] state.

état-major, *pl* **états-majors** /etamaʒɔʀ/ *nm* **1** (Mil) staff; **2** headquarters.

États-Unis /etazyni/ *pr nm pl* **~ (d'Amérique)** United States (of America).

étau, *pl* **~x** /eto/ *nm* vice (GB), vise (US); (figurative) stranglehold **(autour de** on); **l'~ se resserre** the net is tightening.

étayer /eteje/ [21] *vtr* **1** to prop up; **2** (figurative) to support [*theory*].

été /ete/ *nm* summer; **~ comme hiver** all year round.

éteindre /etɛ̃dʀ/ [55] **I** *vtr* **1** to put out [*fire, cigarette*]; to blow out [*candle*]; **2** to switch off, to turn off [*light, TV, oven*]; to turn off [*gas*]; **3** to subdue [*desire, passion*].

II s'éteindre *v refl* (+ *v être*) **1** [*cigarette, fire, light*] to go out; [*radio*] to go off; **2** (euphemistic) to pass away or on; **3** [*desire, passion*] to fade; [*anger*] to subside.

éteint, **~e** /etɛ̃, ɛ̃t/ **I** *pp* ▶ **éteindre**.

II *pp adj* **1** [*gaze*] dull; **2** [*volcano*] extinct; [*star*] extinct, dead.

étendard /etɑ̃daʀ/ *nm* standard, flag.

étendre /etɑ̃dʀ/ [6] **I** *vtr* **1** to stretch [*arms, legs*]; **2** to spread (out) [*tarpaulin, cloth*]; **~ le linge** to hang out the washing; **3 se faire ~**○ **à un examen** to flunk○ an exam; **4** to spread [*paint*]; **5** to extend [*power, embargo*].

II s'étendre *v refl* (+ *v être*) **1** [*land, forest*] to stretch (**sur** over); **2** [*strike, epidemic*] to spread (**à** to); [*town*] to expand, to grow; **3** [*law, measure*] **s'~ à** to apply to; **4** [*period, work*] to stretch (**sur** over), to last; **5** to lie down; **6 s'~ sur** to dwell on.

étendu, **~e**[1] /etɑ̃dy/ **I** *pp* ▶ **étendre**.

II *pp adj* [*city*] sprawling; [*region, plain*] vast; [*vocabulary, knowledge, damage*] extensive.

étendue[2] /etɑ̃dy/ *nf* **1** expanse; **2** size; **3** scale, extent; range.

éternel, **-elle** /etɛʀnɛl/ *adj* endless; eternal.

éternellement /etɛʀnɛlmɑ̃/ *adv* **1** forever; **2** permanently; **3** perpetually, continually; **4** eternally.

éterniser: **s'éterniser** /etɛʀnize/ [1] *v refl* (+ *v être*) [*meeting, conversation*] to drag on; [*visitor*] to stay for ages○.

éternité /etɛʀnite/ *nf* eternity.

éternuer /etɛʀnɥe/ [1] *vi* to sneeze.

éther /etɛʀ/ *nm* ether.

éthéré, **~e** /eteʀe/ *adj* ethereal.

éthique /etik/ **I** *adj* ethical.

II *nf* **1** ethics; **2** code of ethics.

ethnie /ɛtni/ *nf* ethnic group.

ethnique /ɛtnik/ *adj* ethnic.

ethnologie /ɛtnɔlɔʒi/ *nf* ethnology.

éthylique /etilik/ *adj*, *nmf* [*poisoning*] alcoholic.

étincelant, **~e** /etɛ̃slɑ̃, ɑ̃t/ *adj* [*sun*] blazing; [*star*] twinkling; [*gemstone, glass*] sparkling; [*feathers, colour*] brilliant; **~ de propreté** sparkling clean.

étinceler /etɛ̃sle/ [19] *vi* to twinkle; to sparkle.

étincelle /etɛ̃sɛl/ *nf* spark; **jeter des ~s** to glitter; **ça va faire des ~s**○ that will make sparks fly; **faire des ~s** to do brilliantly.

étioler: **s'étioler** /etjɔle/ [1] *v refl* (+ *v être*) to wilt.

étiqueter /etikte/ [20] *vtr* to label.

étiquette /etikɛt/ *nf* **1** label; **2** tag; **porter une ~** to be labelled[GB]; **candidat sans ~** independent candidate; **3** etiquette.

étirer /etiʀe/ [1] **I** *vtr* to stretch; **~ les jambes** to stretch one's legs out.

II s'étirer *v refl* (+ *v être*) **1** [*person*] to stretch; **2** [*procession, road*] to stretch out.

étoffe /etɔf/ *nf* **1** fabric; **2** (figurative) substance; **avoir l'~ d'un grand homme** to have the makings of a great man.

étoffer /etɔfe/ [1] **I** *vtr* to expand.

II s'étoffer *v refl* (+ *v être*) to put on weight.

étoile /etwal/ *nf* star.

■ **l'~ du berger** the evening star; **~ filante** shooting star; **~ de mer** starfish; **~ polaire** Pole Star.

IDIOMS **coucher** or **dormir à la belle ~** to sleep out in the open.

étoilé, **~e** /etwale/ *adj* **1** starry; **2** [*glass, windscreen*] crazed.

étole /etɔl/ *nf* stole.

étonnamment /etɔnamɑ̃/ *adv* surprisingly.

étonnant, **~e** /etɔnɑ̃, ɑ̃t/ *adj* **1** surprising; **pas ~ qu'il soit malade**○ no wonder he's ill; **2** amazing.

étonnement /etɔnmɑ̃/ *nm* surprise; **à mon grand ~** to my amazement.

étonner /etɔne/ [1] **I** *vtr* to surprise.

II s'étonner *v refl* (+ *v être*) to be surprised.

étouffant, **~e** /etufɑ̃, ɑ̃t/ *adj* **1** stifling; **2** oppressive.

étouffé, **~e**[1] /etufe/ *adj* **1** [*sound, voice*] muffled; **2** [*sob*] choked; [*laughter*] suppressed; [*sigh*] discreet.

étouffée[2] /etufe/ *nf* **à l'~** braised; **cuire à l'~** to braise.

étouffement /etufmɑ̃/ *nm* asphyxiation.

étouffer /etufe/ [1] I *vtr* **1** to stifle [*creativity*]; to suppress [*protest*]; **2** to hush up [*scandal*]; **3** to suffocate [*person*]; to choke [*plant*]; **la générosité ne les étouffe pas** generosity is not their middle name; **4** to smother [*fire*]; **5** to stifle [*yawn*]; to hold back [*sigh*]; **6** to deaden [*noise*].
II *vi* to feel stifled; **on étouffe ici**○! it's stifling in here!; **mourir étouffé** to die of suffocation.
III **s'étouffer** *v refl* (+ *v être*) to choke.

étourderie /eturdəri/ *nf* absent-mindedness; **une faute d'~** a careless mistake.

étourdi, **~e** /eturdi/ I *adj* **1** absent-minded; **2** unthinking.
II *nm,f* scatterbrain.

étourdir /eturdir/ [3] I *vtr* **1** to stun, to daze; **2 ~ qn** [*noise*] to make sb's head spin.
II **s'étourdir** *v refl* (+ *v être*) **s'~ de paroles** to become intoxicated with words.

étourdissant, **~e** /eturdisɑ̃, ɑ̃t/ *adj* [*noise*] deafening; [*speed*] dizzying.

étourdissement /eturdismɑ̃/ *nm* **avoir un ~** to feel dizzy.

étourneau, *pl* **~x** /eturno/ *nm* **1** starling; **2**○ scatterbrain○.

étrange /etrɑ̃ʒ/ I *adj* strange; **chose ~ elle n'a pas répondu** strangely enough she didn't answer.
II *nm* **1** strangeness; **2 l'~** the bizarre.

étrangement /etrɑ̃ʒmɑ̃/ *adv* **1** curiously; **vous me rappelez ~ un ami** it's strange but you remind me of a friend; **2** surprisingly.

étranger, **-ère** /etrɑ̃ʒe, ɛr/ I *adj* **1** foreign; **2 ~ à** [*person*] not involved in [*case*]; outside [*group*]; [*fact*] with no bearing on [*problem*]; **se sentir ~** to feel like an outsider; **3** unfamiliar (**à** to).
II *nm,f* **1** foreigner; **2** outsider; **3** stranger.
III *nm* **à l'~** abroad.

étrangeté /etrɑ̃ʒte/ *nf* strangeness.

étranglé, **~e** /etrɑ̃gle/ *adj* **1** [*voice*] choked; [*sound*] muffled; **2** [*street*] narrow.

étranglement /etrɑ̃gləmɑ̃/ *nm* **1** strangulation; **2** (of road, valley) narrow section.

étrangler /etrɑ̃gle/ [1] I *vtr* **1** to strangle; **2** to choke.
II **s'étrangler** *v refl* (+ *v être*) **1** to strangle oneself; **2** to choke.

étrangleur, **-euse** /etrɑ̃glœr, øz/ *nm,f* strangler.

être[1] /ɛtr/ [7] *vi* (+ *v avoir*)

■ **Note** You will find translations for fixed phrases using *être* such as *être en train de, être sur le point de, quoi qu'il en soit, étant donné* etc at the entries ***train***, ***point***, ***quoi***, ***donné*** etc.

1 to be; **nous sommes pauvres** we are poor; **l'eau est froide** the water is cold; **j'étais chez moi** I was at home; **elle sera à Nice** she'll be in Nice; **quand je serai riche** when I'm rich; **2** (as auxiliary verb) **elles sont tombées** they have fallen; they fell; **elle s'était vengée** she took her revenge; she had taken her revenge; **votre voiture est réparée** your car has been repaired; **3** (to go) **je n'ai jamais été en Chine** I've never been to China; **j'ai été manger au restaurant** I went to eat in the restaurant; **4** (with *ce*) **est-ce leur voiture?** is it their car?; **c'est grave?** is it serious?; **qui est-ce?** who is he/she?; who is that?; who is it?; **est-ce que tu parles russe?** do you speak Russian?; **qu'est-ce que c'est?** what is it?; **ce sont mes enfants** these are my children; they are my children; **c'est cela** that's right; **sortir par ce temps, c'est de la folie** going out in this weather is sheer madness; **c'est à désespérer** it's hopeless; **c'est à Pierre/lui de choisir** it's Pierre's/his turn to choose; it's up to Pierre/to him to choose; **ne serait-ce qu'en faisant** if only by doing; **5** (with *il*) **il est facile de critiquer** it is easy to criticize; **il n'est pas jusqu'à l'Antarctique qui ne soit pollué** even the Antarctic is polluted; **il n'en est rien** this isn't at all the case; **6** (with *en*) **où en étais-je?** where was I?; **je ne sais plus où j'en suis** I'm lost; **'où en es-tu de tes recherches?'—'j'en suis à mi-chemin/au début'** 'how far have you got in your research?'—'I'm halfway through/at the beginning'; **j'en suis à me demander si**... I'm beginning to wonder whether...; **j'en étais à ne pouvoir distinguer le vrai du faux** I got to the point where I couldn't distinguish between truth and falsehood; **~ en uniforme** to be wearing a uniform; **7** (with *y*) **j'y suis** I'm with you, I get it○; **je n'y suis pas** I don't get it; **nous partons, vous y êtes?** we're leaving, do you understand?; we're leaving, are you ready?; **tu n'y es pas, c'est plus compliqué que ça** you don't realize, it's a lot more complicated than that; **8** (with *à* and *de*) **ce livre est à moi/à mon frère** this book is mine/my brother's; **à qui est ce chien?** who does this dog belong to?, whose dog is this?; **je suis à vous tout de suite** I'll be with you right away; **je suis à vous** I'm all yours; **~ à ce qu'on fait** to have one's mind on what one is doing; **elle est d'un ridicule!** she's so ridiculous!; **le plus simple serait de tout recommencer** the simplest thing to do would be to start all over again.

être[2] /ɛtr/ *nm* **1 ~ humain** human being; **les ~s animés et inanimés** animate and inanimate things; **un ~ sans défense** a defenceless[GB] creature; **2** person; **un ~ cher** or **aimé** a loved one; **un ~ sensible** a sensitive soul; **3 de tout son ~** with one's whole being; **blessé au plus profond de son ~** hurt to the core.

étreindre /etrɛ̃dr/ [55] I *vtr* to embrace, to hug [*friend*]; to clasp [*opponent*].
II **s'étreindre** *v refl* (+ *v être*) to embrace (each other).

étreinte /etrɛ̃t/ *nf* embrace; grip; **l'ennemi resserrait son ~** (figurative) the army was tightening its grip.

étrenner /etrene/ [1] *vtr* to use [sth] for the first time.

étrennes /etrɛn/ *nf pl* **1** gift; **2** money.

étrier /etrije/ *nm* stirrup.

IDIOMS **mettre à qn le pied à l'~** (figurative) to get sb started.

étriper○ /etʀipe/ [1] **I** *vtr* (figurative) **~ qn** to skin sb alive.

II s'étriper *v refl* (+ *v être*) to murder each other.

étriqué, **~e** /etʀike/ *adj* [*jacket*] skimpy; [*life*] restricted.

étroit, **~e** /etʀwa, at/ **I** *adj* **1** narrow; **avoir l'esprit ~** to be narrow-minded; **2** [*links*] close; **en ~e collaboration** closely.

II à l'étroit *phr* **nous sommes un peu à l'~** we're a bit cramped; **je me sens un peu à l'~ dans cette jupe** this skirt feels a bit too tight.

étroitement /etʀwatmɑ̃/ *adv* closely.

étroitesse /etʀwatɛs/ *nf* narrowness; **~ d'esprit** narrow-mindedness.

étude /etyd/ **I** *nf* **1** study; **~ réalisée par** study carried out by; **2** survey; **3 (mise à l')~** consideration; **à l'~** under consideration; **4** (of lawyer) office; **5** (Sch) study room (GB), study hall (US); **6** study period.

II études *nf pl* studies; **faire des ~s** to be a student; **je n'ai pas fait d'~s (supérieures)** I didn't go to university or college.

■ **~ de marché** market research.

étudiant, **~e** /etydjɑ̃, ɑ̃t/ *nm,f* student; **~ en droit** law student.

étudier /etydje/ [2] **I** *vtr* to study [*drawing, map, language, phenomenon*]; to examine [*file, situation*]; to learn [*lesson*]; to design [*new engine*].

II *vi* **1** to be a student; **2** to be studying.

étui /etɥi/ *nm* case; **~ à revolver** holster.

étuve /etyv/ *nf* **1** steam room; **le grenier est une ~** (figurative) the attic is like an oven; **2** incubator.

étymologie /etimɔlɔʒi/ *nf* etymology.

étymologique /etimɔlɔʒik/ *adj* etymological.

eucalyptus /økaliptys/ *nm inv* eucalyptus.

eucharistie /økaʀisti/ *nf* **1** Eucharist; **2** Sacrament.

eunuque /ønyk/ *nm* eunuch.

euphémisme /øfemism/ *nm* euphemism; **par ~** euphemistically.

euphorie /øfɔʀi/ *nf* euphoria.

euphorique /øfɔʀik/ *adj* **1** euphoric; **2** [*market*] bullish.

euphorisant, **~e** /øfɔʀizɑ̃, ɑ̃t/ **I** *adj* stimulating; uplifting; euphoriant.

II *nm* (Med) stimulant.

eurasien, **-ienne** /øʀazjɛ̃, ɛn/ *adj* Eurasian.

eurochèque /øʀoʃɛk/ *nm* Eurocheque.

euromarché /øʀomaʀʃe/ *nm* Euromarket.

Europe /øʀɔp/ *pr nf* Europe; **l'~ communautaire** the European community.

européen, **-éenne** /øʀɔpeɛ̃, ɛn/ *adj* European.

Eurotunnel /øʀotynɛl/ *nm* Eurotunnel.

Eurovision /øʀovizjɔ̃/ *nf* Eurovision; **en ~** through Eurovision.

euthanasie /øtanazi/ *nf* euthanasia.

eux /ø/ *pron* **1** they; **~ seuls ont le droit de parler** they alone have the right to speak; **je sais que ce n'est pas ~ qui ont fait ça** I know they weren't the ones who did it; **2** them; **les inviter, ~, quelle idée!** invite THEM, what an idea!; **à cause d'~** because of them; **ce sont des amis à ~** they're friends of theirs; **c'est à ~** it's theirs.

eux-mêmes /ømɛm/ *pron* themselves; **les experts ~ reconnaissent que...** even the experts admit that...

évacuation /evakɥasjɔ̃/ *nf* **1** evacuation; **2** discharge; **il y a un problème d'~ de l'eau** the water doesn't drain away.

évacuer /evakɥe/ [1] *vtr* **1** to evacuate; **2** to drain off [*waste water*]; **3** (figurative) to shrug off [*problem*].

évader: **s'évader** /evade/ [1] *v refl* (+ *v être*) **1** to escape; **faire ~ qn** to help sb to escape; **2** (figurative) to get away (**de** from).

évaluation /evalɥasjɔ̃/ *nf* **1** (of collection, house) valuation; **faire l'~ de** to value; **2** (of costs, damages) assessment; estimate, appraisal (US); **3** (of staff) appraisal.

évaluer /evalɥe/ [1] *vtr* **1** to estimate [*size, length*]; to assess [*risks, damages, costs*]; **2** to value [*inheritance*]; **3** to assess [*employee, student*].

Évangile /evɑ̃ʒil/ *nm* Gospel; **ce n'est pas parole d'~** it's not gospel (truth).

évanouir: **s'évanouir** /evanwiʀ/ [3] *v refl* (+ *v être*) **1** to faint; **évanoui** unconscious; **2** [*feeling*] to fade.

évanouissement /evanwismɑ̃/ *nm* **1** blackout, fainting fit; **2** fading.

évaporation /evapɔʀasjɔ̃/ *nf* evaporation.

évaporé, **~e** /evapɔʀe/ **I** *adj* giddy, birdbrained○.

II *nm,f* birdbrain○.

évaporer: **s'évaporer** /evapɔʀe/ [1] *v refl* (+ *v être*) **1** to evaporate; **2**○ to vanish.

évaser /evaze/ [1] **I** *vtr* to flare.

II s'évaser *v refl* (+ *v être*) [*duct*] to open out; [*skirt*] to be flared.

évasif, **-ive** /evazif, iv/ *adj* evasive; **d'un air ~** evasively.

évasion /evazjɔ̃/ *nf* escape; **~ des capitaux** flight of capital.

Ève /ɛv/ *pr nf* Eve; **en tenue d'~** in her birthday suit.

IDIOMS **elle ne le connaît ni d'~ ni d'Adam** she doesn't know him from Adam.

évêché /eveʃe/ *nm* **1** diocese; **2** bishop's palace.

éveil /evɛj/ *nm* awakening; **donner l'~** to arouse suspicions.

éveiller /eveje/ [1] **I** *vtr* **1** to arouse [*curiosity, suspicions*]; to stimulate [*intelligence*]; to awaken [*conscience*]; **sans ~ l'attention** without attracting attention; **un enfant éveillé** a bright child; **2** to wake (up) [*sleeper*]; **être éveillé** to be awake.

II s'éveiller *v refl* (+ *v être*) **1** to wake up, to awake; **2** [*imagination*] to start to develop.

événement /evenmɑ̃/ *nm* event.

éventail /evɑ̃taj/ *nm* **1** fan; **2** range.

éventaire /evɑ̃tɛʀ/ *nm* stall.

éventer: **s'éventer** /evɑ̃te/ [1] *v refl* (+ *v être*) **1** to fan oneself; **2** [*perfume, coffee*] to go off; [*wine*] to pass its best; [*beer, lemonade*] to go flat.

éventrer /evɑ̃tʀe/ [1] *vtr* **1** [*person*] to disembowel; [*bull*] to gore; **2** to rip open; to burst open.

éventualité /evɑ̃tɥalite/ *nf* **1** eventuality; **2** possibility; **dans l'~ de** in the event of.

éventuel, -elle /evɑ̃tɥɛl/ *adj* possible.

éventuellement /evɑ̃tɥɛlmɑ̃/ *adv* **1** possibly; **2** if necessary.

évêque /evɛk/ *nm* bishop (**de** of).

évertuer: **s'évertuer** /evɛʀtɥe/ [1] *v refl* (+ *v être*) to try one's best (**à faire** to do), to strive (**à faire** to do).

éviction /eviksjɔ̃/ *nf* **1** ousting (**de** from); **2** (Law) eviction.

évidemment /evidamɑ̃/ *adv* of course.

évidence /evidɑ̃s/ **I** *nf* **1** obviousness; **2** obvious fact; **se rendre à l'~** to face the facts; **de toute ~, à l'~** obviously.
II en évidence *phr* **laisser qch en ~** to leave sth in an obvious place; **mettre en ~** to highlight [*feature*].

évident, ~e /evidɑ̃, ɑ̃t/ *adj* obvious; **ce n'est pas ~**○ not necessarily; it's not so easy.

évider /evide/ [1] *vtr* to hollow out; to scoop out.

évier /evje/ *nm* sink.

évincer /evɛ̃se/ [12] *vtr* to oust [*rival*].

éviter /evite/ [1] *vtr* **1** to avoid [*obstacle, pedestrian*]; **~ de faire** to avoid doing; **~ qch à qn** to save sb sth; **~ à qn de faire** to save sb (from) doing; **2** to dodge [*bullet, blow*].

évocateur, -trice /evɔkatœʀ, tʀis/ *adj* **1** evocative; **2** significant.

évocation /evɔkasjɔ̃/ *nf* **1** evocation; reminiscence; **2** mention (**de** of).

évolué, ~e /evɔlɥe/ *adj* **1**○ **il n'est pas très ~!** he's not very bright!; **2** civilized; **3** evolved.

évoluer /evɔlɥe/ [1] *vi* **1** to evolve, to change; **2** to develop; **faire ~ la situation** to bring about some change in the situation; **3** to glide.

évolutif, -ive /evɔlytif, iv/ *adj* progressive.

évolution /evɔlysjɔ̃/ *nf* **1** evolution; **2** development; **3** progress (**de** of); **4** progression; **5** change; **être en pleine ~** to be undergoing rapid change.

évoquer /evɔke/ [1] *vtr* **1** to recall; **2** to mention, to bring up; **3** to bring back [*memory*]; to conjure up [*image*]; to be reminiscent of [*childhood*]; **4** to evoke.

ex /ɛks/ **I**○ *nmf inv* ex.
II *nm* **1** (*written abbr* = **exemple**) eg; **2** (*written abbr* = **exemplaire**) copy; **25 ~** 25 copies.

ex- /ɛks/ *pref* **~actrice/champion** former actress/champion.

exacerber /ɛgzasɛʀbe/ [1] *vtr* to exacerbate.

exact, ~e /ɛgza(kt), akt/ *adj* **1** correct; **2** accurate; **3** exact; **4** punctual.

exactement /ɛgzaktəmɑ̃/ *adv* exactly.

exaction /ɛgzaksjɔ̃/ **I** *nf* exaction.
II exactions *nf pl* barbaric acts, acts of violence; atrocities.

exactitude /ɛgzaktityd/ *nf* **1** correctness; **2** accuracy; **3** exactness; **4** punctuality.

ex æquo /ɛgzeko/ **I** *adj inv* equally placed.
II *adv* **ils sont premiers/deuxièmes ~** they've tied for first/second place.

exagéré, ~e /ɛgzaʒeʀe/ *adj* **1** exaggerated; **2** excessive; **d'une sensibilité ~e** oversensitive.

exagérément /ɛgzaʒeʀemɑ̃/ *adv* excessively.

exagérer /ɛgzaʒeʀe/ [14] **I** *vtr* to exaggerate.
II *vi* to go too far.

exaltant, ~e /ɛgzaltɑ̃, ɑ̃t/ *adj* thrilling; inspiring.

exaltation /ɛgzaltasjɔ̃/ *nf* **1** elation; **parler avec ~** to speak elatedly; **2** stimulation; **3** glorification.

exalté, ~e /ɛgzalte/ **I** *pp* ▸ **exalter**.
II *pp adj* impassioned.
III *nm,f* fanatic.

exalter /ɛgzalte/ [1] **I** *vtr* **1** to glorify; **2** to heighten; **3** to elate, to thrill.
II s'exalter *v refl* (+ *v être*) to enthuse.

examen /ɛgzamɛ̃/ *nm* **1** (Sch, Univ) examination, exam○; **passer un ~** to take or to sit (for) (GB) an exam○; **réussir à un ~** to pass an exam○; **~ de rattrapage** retake, resit (GB); **2** (Med) examination; **3** examination; consideration; review; **à l'~** on examination; **être en cours d'~** to be under review; to be under consideration; **4** inspection; **mettre qn en ~** (Law) to investigate sb.
■ **~ blanc** mock (exam○); **~ de conscience** self-examination.

examinateur, -trice /ɛgzaminatœʀ, tʀis/ *nm,f* examiner.

examiner /ɛgzamine/ [1] *vtr* **1** to examine; to review; **~ qch de près** to have a close look at sth; **~ qn de la tête aux pieds** to look sb up and down; **2** (Med) to examine [*patient, wound*].

exaspération /ɛgzaspeʀasjɔ̃/ *nf* **1** exasperation; **2** intensification.

exaspérer /ɛgzaspeʀe/ [14] *vtr* **1** to exasperate, to infuriate; **2** to exacerbate.

exaucer /ɛgzose/ [12] *vtr* to grant.

excavatrice /ɛkskavatʀis/ *nf* excavator.

excédent /ɛksedɑ̃/ *nm* surplus (**sur** over); **~ de bagages** excess baggage.

excédentaire /ɛksedɑ̃tɛʀ/ *adj* surplus.

excéder /ɛksede/ [14] *vtr* **1** to exceed (**de** by); **2** to infuriate.

excellence /ɛksɛlɑ̃s/ *nf* excellence.

Excellence /ɛksɛlɑ̃s/ *nf* **Son ~, l'ambassadeur de France** His/Her Excellency, the French Ambassador.

excellent, ~e /ɛksɛlɑ̃, ɑ̃t/ *adj* excellent.

exceller /ɛksele/ [1] *vi* to excel (**dans** in; **à faire** in doing).

excentré, ~e /ɛksɑ̃tʀe/ *adj* **1** [*area*] outlying; **2 être ~** [*axis*] to be off-centre[GB].

excentricité /ɛksɑ̃tʀisite/ *nf* eccentricity.

excentrique /ɛksɑ̃tʀik/ I *adj* **1** eccentric; **2** [*area*] outlying.
II *nmf* eccentric.

excepté, **~e** /ɛksɛpte/ I *pp* ▶ **excepter**.
II *prep* except; **il l'a dit à tout le monde ~ à moi** he told everybody except me.
III **excepté que** *phr* except that.

excepter /ɛksɛpte/ [1] *vtr* **si l'on excepte** except for, apart from.

exception /ɛksɛpsjɔ̃/ *nf* exception; **faire ~** to be an exception; **à l'~ de**, **~ faite de** except for, with the exception of; **sauf ~** with the occasional exception; **d'~** [*person*] exceptional; [*law, tribunal*] emergency.

exceptionnel, **-elle** /ɛksɛpsjɔnɛl/ *adj* **1** [*leave*] exceptional; [*permission*] special; [*price*] bargain; [*meeting*] extraordinary; **2** [*circumstances, person*] exceptional.

exceptionnellement /ɛksɛpsjɔnɛlmɑ̃/ *adv* exceptionally.

excès /ɛksɛ/ *nm inv* excess; **commettre des ~** to go too far; **faire des ~ de boisson** to drink excessively; **des ~ de langage** bad language; **tomber dans l'~ inverse** to go to the opposite extreme; **~ de confiance/zèle** overconfidence/overzealousness.
■ **~ de vitesse** speeding; **faire un ~ de vitesse** to break the speed limit.

excessif, **-ive** /ɛksesif, iv/ *adj* **1** excessive; **être d'un optimisme ~** to be overoptimistic; **2** extreme; **il est ~** he is a man of extremes.

excessivement /ɛksesivmɑ̃/ *adv* excessively.

excision /ɛksizjɔ̃/ *nf* **1** excision; **2** female circumcision.

excitant, **~e** /ɛksitɑ̃, ɑ̃t/ I *adj* **1** [*substance*] stimulating; **2** exciting; thrilling.
II *nm* stimulant; **prendre des ~s** to take stimulants.

excitation /ɛksitasjɔ̃/ *nf* **1** excitement; **2** arousal; **3** stimulation.

excité, **~e** /ɛksite/ I *adj* **1** [*crowd*] frenzied, in a frenzy; [*atmosphere*] frenzied; **2** [*person*] thrilled, excited; **3** (sexually) aroused; (from alcohol) elated.
II *nm,f* **1** rowdy; **2** fanatic; **3** neurotic.
IDIOMS **être ~ comme une puce**○ to be like a cat on a hot tin roof.

exciter /ɛksite/ [1] I *vtr* **1** to arouse, to stir up [*anger*]; to kindle [*desire*]; **2** to thrill; **3** to arouse; **4** to tease [*animal*]; to get [sb] excited [*child*]; [*coffee*] to get [sb] hyped up [*person*]; **5** to stimulate [*palate*]; to excite [*nerve*].
II **s'exciter** *v refl* (+ *v être*) to get excited; **s'~ à propos de qn/qch** to rave about○ sb/sth.

exclamatif, **-ive** /ɛksklamatif, iv/ *adj* exclamatory.

exclamation /ɛksklamasjɔ̃/ *nf* cry, exclamation.

exclamer: **s'exclamer** /ɛksklame/ [1] *v refl* (+ *v être*) to exclaim.

exclu, **~e** /ɛkskly/ I *pp* ▶ **exclure**.
II *pp adj* excluded (**de** from); **c'est exclu!** it's out of the question!; **se sentir ~** to feel left out.

exclure /ɛksklyʀ/ [78] *vtr* **1** to exclude [*person*]; to rule out [*possibility*]; **2** to expel [*member, student*]; to oust [*leader, boss*].

exclusif, **-ive** /ɛksklyzif, iv/ *adj* exclusive; **concessionaire ~** sole agent.

exclusion /ɛksklyzjɔ̃/ I *nf* **1** exclusion; **2** expulsion; **3** suspension.
II **à l'exclusion de** *phr* with the exception of.

exclusivité /ɛksklyzivite/ *nf* exclusive rights; **en ~** [*publish*] exclusively; [*product*] exclusive.

excommunier /ɛkskɔmynje/ [2] *vtr* to excommunicate.

excrément /ɛkskʀemɑ̃/ *nm* excrement.

excrétion /ɛkskʀesjɔ̃/ *nf* excretion.

excroissance /ɛkskʀwasɑ̃s/ *nf* **1** (Med) growth, excrescence; **2** (in botany) outgrowth.

excursion /ɛkskyʀsjɔ̃/ *nf* excursion, trip.

excuse /ɛkskyz/ *nf* **1** excuse (**à qch** for sth); **2** apology; **mille ~s** I'm terribly sorry.

excuser /ɛkskyze/ [1] I *vtr* to forgive; to pardon; to excuse; **excusez-moi** I'm sorry; **vous êtes tout excusé** it's quite all right; **rien n'excuse la cruauté** there is no excuse for cruelty.
II **s'excuser** *v refl* (+ *v être*) to apologize.

exécrable /ɛgzekʀabl/ *adj* loathsome; dreadful; detestable.

exécrer /ɛgzekʀe/ [14] *vtr* to loathe.

exécutant, **~e** /ɛgzekytɑ̃, ɑ̃t/ *nm,f* **1** (Mus) performer; **2 il dit n'avoir été qu'un ~** he claims he was only obeying orders.

exécuter /ɛgzekyte/ [1] I *vtr* **1** to carry out [*task, mission*]; to do [*exercise*]; **2** to carry out [*orders, threat*]; to fulfil[GB] [*promise, contract*]; to enforce [*law, ruling*]; to implement [*treaty*]; **3** to execute [*prisoner*]; to kill [*victim*]; **4** (Mus) to perform.
II **s'exécuter** *v refl* (+ *v être*) to comply.

exécutif, **-ive** /ɛgzekytif, ive/ I *adj* executive.
II *nm* executive.

exécution /ɛgzekysjɔ̃/ *nf* **1** execution, carrying out; enforcement; fulfilment[GB]; **mettre à ~** to carry out [*threat*]; to implement [*programme*]; **travaux en cours d'~** work in progress; **veiller à la bonne ~ d'une tâche** to see that a job is done well; **d'~ facile** [*movement*] easy to do; [*piece of music*] easy to play; **2** execution; **~ capitale** capital punishment.

exemplaire /ɛgzɑ̃plɛʀ/ I *adj* **1** exemplary; **élève ~** model pupil; **2** (Law) [*punishment*] exemplary.
II *nm* **1** copy; print; **~ gratuit** complimentary copy; **2** specimen.

exemple /ɛgzɑ̃pl/ I *nm* **1** example; **sans ~** unprecedented; **être l'~ de la gentillesse** to be a model of kindness; **donner qn en ~** to hold sb up as an example; **2** warning (**pour** to).
II **par exemple** *phr* for example; **ça par ~!** how amazing!; well, honestly!

exempt, **~e** /ɛgzɑ̃, ɑ̃t/ *adj* exempt; **~ d'impôt** tax-free.

exempter /ɛgzɑ̃te/ [1] *vtr* **1** to exempt; **2** to preserve (**de** from).

exemption /ɛgzɑ̃psjɔ̃/ *nf* exemption.

exercer /ɛgzɛʀse/ [12] **I** *vtr* **1** to exercise [*right*]; to exert [*authority*]; to have [*effect*]; **2** to exercise [*profession*]; to practise[GB] [*art, medicine*]; **3** to train [*mind*]; to exercise [*body*].
II s'exercer *v refl* (+ *v être*) **1** [*athlete*] to train; [*musician*] to practise[GB]; **s'~ au calme** to make an effort to stay calm; **2** [*influence, force*] to be exerted.

exercice /ɛgzɛʀsis/ *nm* exercise; **faire un ~** to do an exercise; **faire de l'~** to get some exercise; **dans l'~ de ses fonctions** in the course of one's duty; while at work; **être en ~** [*civil servant*] to be in office; [*doctor*] to be in practice; **en ~** [*minister, president*] incumbent; **entrer en ~** to take up one's duties; **être à l'~** (Mil) to be at drill.

exergue /ɛgzɛʀg/ *nm* **1** epigraph; **2** inscription.

exhaler /ɛgzale/ [1] **I** *vtr* to exhale.
II s'exhaler *v refl* (+ *v être*) [*perfume*] to waft (**de** from).

exhaustif, **-ive** /ɛgzostif, iv/ *adj* exhaustive.

exhiber /ɛgzibe/ [1] **I** *vtr* to flaunt [*wealth*]; to show [*animal*]; to expose [*body*].
II s'exhiber *v refl* (+ *v être*) **1** to expose oneself; **2** to flaunt oneself.

exhibition /ɛgzibisjɔ̃/ *nf* **1** (of animals) show; exhibition; **2** (Sport) demonstration, display; **3** (of wealth) parade; (of emotion) display.

exhibitionnisme /ɛgzibisjɔnism/ *nm* exhibitionism.

exhibitionniste /ɛgzibisjɔnist/ *adj, nmf* exhibitionist.

exhortation /ɛgzɔʀtasjɔ̃/ *nf* exhortation; **~ au calme** call for calm.

exhorter /ɛgzɔʀte/ [1] *vtr* to motivate; **~ qn à faire** to urge or exhort sb to do.

exhumer /ɛgzyme/ [1] *vtr* **1** to exhume; **2** to excavate.

exigeant, **~e** /ɛgziʒɑ̃, ɑ̃t/ *adj* demanding.

exigence /ɛgziʒɑ̃s/ *nf* demand (**de qch** for sth).

exiger /ɛgziʒe/ [13] *vtr* **1** to demand [*answer, reforms*]; **2** to require; **comme l'exige la loi** as required by law; **'expérience exigée'** 'experience required'.

exigu, **-uë** /ɛgzigy/ *adj* [*room*] cramped; [*entrance*] narrow; [*space*] confined.

exiguïté /ɛgzigɥite/ *nf* smallness.

exil /ɛgzil/ *nm* exile; **en ~** in exile.

exilé, **~e** /ɛgzile/ *nm,f* exile.

exiler /ɛgzile/ [1] **I** *vtr* to exile.
II s'exiler *v refl* (+ *v être*) to go into exile.

existence /ɛgzistɑ̃s/ *nf* **1** existence; **2**° life.

existentialisme /ɛgzistɑ̃sjalism/ *nm* existentialism.

exister /ɛgziste/ [1] *vi* to exist; **ce risque existe** this is a very real risk; **si le paradis existe** if there is such a place as heaven; **la maison existe encore** the house is still standing.

exode /ɛgzɔd/ *nm* exodus; **~ rural** rural depopulation.

exonération /ɛgzɔneʀasjɔ̃/ *nf* exemption (**de** from).

exonérer /ɛgzɔneʀe/ [14] *vtr* to exempt (**de** from).

exorbitant, **~e** /ɛgzɔʀbitɑ̃, ɑ̃t/ *adj* [*price*] exorbitant; [*demands*] outrageous; [*power*] inordinate.

exorbité, **~e** /ɛgzɔʀbite/ *adj* bulging.

exorciser /ɛgzɔʀsize/ [1] *vtr* to exorcize.

exotique /ɛgzɔtik/ *adj* exotic.

exotisme /ɛgzɔtism/ *nm* exoticism.

expansif, **-ive** /ɛkspɑ̃sif, iv/ *adj* communicative, outgoing.

expansion /ɛkspɑ̃sjɔ̃/ *nf* **1** growth; **en (pleine) ~** (rapidly) growing; (rapidly) increasing; **2** expansion.

expatriation /ɛkspatʀijasjɔ̃/ *nf* expatriation.

expatrié, **~e** /ɛkspatʀije/ *adj, nm,f* expatriate.

expatrier /ɛkspatʀije/ [2] **I** *vtr* to deport.
II s'expatrier *v refl* (+ *v être*) to emigrate (**en, à** to).

expectative /ɛkspɛktativ/ *nf* **rester dans l'~** to wait and see.

expédient /ɛkspedjɑ̃/ *nm* expedient; **user d'~s** to resort to expedients; **vivre d'~s** to live by one's wits.

expédier /ɛkspedje/ [2] *vtr* **1** to send; to post (GB), to mail (US); to dispatch; **~ qch à qn** to send sb sth; **~ par avion** to send [sth] by air mail; **2** to get rid of [*person*]; to polish off [*work, meal*]; **~ un procès en une heure** to get a trial over within one hour.

expéditeur, **-trice** /ɛkspeditœʀ, tʀis/ **I** *adj* [*office*] forwarding.
II *nm,f* sender; **retour à l'~** return to sender.

expéditif, **-ive** /ɛkspeditif, iv/ *adj* [*person*] brisk; [*method*] cursory; **un jugement ~** a hasty verdict; **une justice expéditive** summary justice.

expédition /ɛkspedisjɔ̃/ *nf* expedition; **~ punitive** punitive strike.

expérience /ɛkspeʀjɑ̃s/ *nf* **1** experience; **avoir de l'~** to be experienced; **j'en ai fait l'~ à mes dépens** I learned that lesson at my own expense; **2** experiment; **faire une ~** to carry out an experiment.

expérimental, **~e**, *mpl* **-aux** /ɛkspeʀimɑ̃tal, o/ *adj* experimental.

expérimentation /ɛkspeʀimɑ̃tasjɔ̃/ *nf* experimentation.

expérimenté, **~e** /ɛkspeʀimɑ̃te/ *adj* experienced.

expérimenter /ɛkspeʀimɑ̃te/ [1] *vtr* to test; to try out.

expert /ɛkspɛʀ/ *nm* **1** expert (**en** on); **l'avis d'un ~** expert advice; **2** adjuster.

expert-comptable, *pl* **experts-comptables** /ɛkspɛʀkɔ̃tabl/ *nm* ≈ chartered accountant (GB), certified public accountant (US).

expertise /ɛkspɛʀtiz/ *nf* **1** valuation (GB),

appraisal (US); assessment; **rapport d'~** expert's report; **2** expertise.

expertiser /ɛkspɛʀtize/ [1] *vtr* **1** to value (GB), to appraise (US) [*jewellery*]; to assess [*damages*]; **2** to authenticate [*painting*].

expier /ɛkspje/ [2] *vtr* to atone for, to expiate (**par** with).

expiration /ɛkspiʀasjɔ̃/ *nf* **1** exhalation; **2** expiry (GB), expiration (US).

expirer /ɛkspiʀe/ [1] **I** *vtr* to exhale.
II *vi* **1** [*contract*] to expire; **2** to breathe out.

explicatif, -ive /ɛksplikatif, iv/ *adj* explanatory.

explication /ɛksplikasjɔ̃/ *nf* explanation; **nous avons eu une bonne ~** we've talked things through.
■ **~ de texte** textual analysis.

explicite /ɛksplisit/ *adj* [*text, film*] explicit; [*answer*] definite.

expliciter /ɛksplisite/ [1] *vtr* to clarify, to explain.

expliquer /ɛksplike/ [1] **I** *vtr* **1** to explain; **2** (Sch) to analyse[GB] [*text*].
II s'expliquer *v refl* (+ *v être*) **s'~ qch** to understand sth; **tout finira par s'~** everything will become clear; **je m'explique** let me explain.

exploit /ɛksplwa/ *nm* exploit, feat.

exploitant, ~e /ɛksplwatɑ̃, ɑ̃t/ *nm,f* **~ agricole** farmer.

exploitation /ɛksplwatasjɔ̃/ *nf* **1** exploitation; **2 ~ agricole** farm; **~ commerciale** business concern; **3** (of land, forest) exploitation; (of airline, shipping line) operation.

exploiter /ɛksplwate/ [1] *vtr* **1** to exploit [*person*]; **~ une situation** to capitalize on a situation; **2** to work [*mine*]; to mine [*coal, iron*]; to exploit [*forest*]; to run [*firm*]; to operate [*network, airline*]; to use [*patent*]; **3** to make the most of [*gift, knowledge*].

explorateur, -trice /ɛksplɔʀatœʀ, tʀis/ *nm,f* explorer.

exploration /ɛksplɔʀasjɔ̃/ *nf* exploration.

explorer /ɛksplɔʀe/ [1] *vtr* to explore.

exploser /ɛksploze/ [1] *vi* to explode; to blow up; **faire ~** to blow up; to explode; to cause [sth] to blow up; **faire ~**○ **qn** to make sb blow up○.

explosif, -ive /ɛksplozif, iv/ **I** *adj* explosive.
II *nm* explosive; **un attentat à l'~** bomb attack.

explosion /ɛksplozjɔ̃/ *nf* **1** explosion; **2** outburst; **3** (in market) boom.

export /ɛkspɔʀ/ *nm* export.

exportateur, -trice /ɛkspɔʀtatœʀ, tʀis/ **I** *adj* [*country*] exporting; [*market, company*] export.
II *nm,f* exporter.

exportation /ɛkspɔʀtasjɔ̃/ *nf* export; **faire l'~ de qch** to export sth.

exporter /ɛkspɔʀte/ [1] *vtr* to export.

exposé, ~e /ɛkspoze/ **I** *pp* ▶ **exposer**.
II *pp adj* **1** exposed; **côte ~e au vent** coast exposed to the wind; **maison ~e au sud** south-facing house; **2** on show; on display.
III *nm* **1 ~ de** account of; **faire un** or **l'~ des faits** to give a statement of the facts; **2** (Sch) talk; **faire un ~** to give a talk.

exposer /ɛkspoze/ [1] **I** *vtr* **1** to exhibit [*art*]; to display, to put [sth] on display [*goods*]; **2** to state [*facts*]; to outline [*idea, plan*]; to list [*complaints*]; to explain [*situation*]; to expound [*argument*]; **3** to risk [*life, reputation*]; **4** to expose [*skin, body*] (**à** to); **ne reste pas exposé au soleil** stay out of the sun.
II s'exposer *v refl* (+ *v être*) **1** to put oneself at risk; **s'~ à** to lay oneself open to [*criticsm*]; **2 s'~ au soleil** to go out in the sun.

exposition /ɛkspozisjɔ̃/ *nf* **1** (of art) exhibition; (of animals, plants) show; (for trade) fair; **~ universelle** world fair; **2** (in shop) display; **3** (of situation, facts) exposition; **4** (of house) aspect; **5** (to light, radiation) exposure.

exprès[1] /ɛkspʀɛ/ *adv* **1** deliberately, on purpose; **'la porte se referme toute seule'—'c'est fait ~'** 'the door shuts itself'—'that's what it's meant to do!'; **comme par un fait ~** as ill-luck would have it; **2** specially.

exprès[2], **-esse** /ɛkspʀɛs/ **I** *adj* express.
II exprès *adj inv* **envoyer qch en** or **par ~** to send sth special delivery or express.

express /ɛkspʀɛs/ **I** *adj inv* express; [*lunch*] quick.
II *nm inv* **1** express (train); **2** espresso.

expressément /ɛkspʀesemɑ̃/ *adv* expressly.

expressif, -ive /ɛkspʀesif, iv/ *adj* expressive.

expression /ɛkspʀesjɔ̃/ *nf* expression; **avec ~** [*recite, sing*] with feeling; **réduire qch à sa plus simple ~** (figurative) to reduce sth to a minimum.
■ **~ corporelle** self-expression through movement.

expressionnisme /ɛkspʀesjɔnism/ *nm* expressionism.

expressivité /ɛkspʀesivite/ *nf* expressiveness.

exprimer /ɛkspʀime/ [1] **I** *vtr* **1** to express; **2** to squeeze [*liquid*].
II s'exprimer *v refl* (+ *v être*) **1** to express oneself; **si j'ose m'~ ainsi** if I may put it that way; **2** to be expressed.

exproprier /ɛkspʀɔpʀije/ [2] *vtr* **~ qn** to put a compulsory purchase order on sb's property.

expulser /ɛkspylse/ [1] *vtr* **1** to evict; **2** to deport; **3** to expel; **4** (Sport) to send [sb] off.

expulsion /ɛkspylsjɔ̃/ *nf* **1** eviction; **2** deportation; **3** expulsion.

expurger /ɛkspyʀʒe/ [13] *vtr* to purge.

exquis, ~e /ɛkski, iz/ *adj* exquisite; delightful.

exsangue /ɛgzɑ̃g/ *adj* bloodless.

exsuder /ɛksyde/ [1] **I** *vtr* to exude.
II *vi* to ooze (**de** from).

extase /ɛkstaz/ *nf* ecstasy; **être en ~ devant** to be in ecstasy or raptures over.

extasier: s'extasier /ɛkstazje/ [2] *v refl* (+ *v être*) to go into ecstasy or raptures.

extatique /ɛkstatik/ *adj* ecstatic.

extensible /ɛkstɑ̃sibl/ *adj* **1** extensible; **2** extendable.

extensif, -ive /ɛkstɑ̃sif, iv/ *adj* **1** extensive; **2** extended.

extension /ɛkstɑ̃sjɔ̃/ *nf* extension; **faire des mouvements d'~ et de flexion** to stretch and bend; **prendre de l'~** [*industry*] to expand; [*strike*] to spread, to extend.

exténuer /ɛkstenɥe/ [1] **I** *vtr* to exhaust.
II s'exténuer *v refl* (+ *v être*) to wear oneself out (**à faire** doing).

extérieur, ~e /ɛksteʀjœʀ/ **I** *adj* **1** outside; **question ~e au sujet** irrelevant point; **2** outer; **3** foreign; **4** outward.
II *nm* **1** outside; **à l'~** outside, outdoors; **d'~** outdoor; **2** exterior, appearance; **3 en ~** [*filmed*] on location.

extérieurement /ɛksteʀjœʀmɑ̃/ *adv* **1** on the outside; **2** outwardly.

extérioriser /ɛksteʀjɔʀize/ [1] *vtr* to show [*feelings*].

extermination /ɛkstɛʀminasjɔ̃/ *nf* extermination.

exterminer /ɛkstɛʀmine/ [1] *vtr* to exterminate; to wipe out.

externat /ɛkstɛʀna/ *nm* **1** (Sch) day school; **2** (Med) **faire son ~** to be a nonresident student doctor (in a hospital) (GB), to be an extern (US).

externe /ɛkstɛʀn/ **I** *adj* external; outside; exterior.
II *nmf* **1** (Sch) day pupil; **2** (Med) non-residential medical student (GB), extern (US).

extincteur /ɛkstɛ̃ktœʀ/ *nm* fire extinguisher.

extinction /ɛkstɛ̃ksjɔ̃/ *nf* **1** (Med) **avoir une ~ de voix** to have lost one's voice; **2** extinction; **espèce en voie d'~** endangered species; **3 après l'~ de l'incendie** after the fire was put out; **après l'~ des feux** after lights out.

extirper /ɛkstiʀpe/ [1] *vtr* **1** to eradicate; **2**° to drag [*person*] (**de** out of, from).

extorquer /ɛkstɔʀke/ [1] *vtr* to extort (**à qn** from sb).

extorsion /ɛkstɔʀsjɔ̃/ *nf* extortion; **~ de fonds** extortion (of money).

extra /ɛkstʀa/ **I** *adj inv* **1**° great°; **2** [*product*] of superior quality; **huile d'olive ~ vierge** extra virgin olive oil.
II *nm inv* **1** extra; **se payer un petit ~** to have a little treat; **2 faire des ~** to do a few extra jobs; **3** extra worker.

extraction /ɛkstʀaksjɔ̃/ *nf* **1** (of oil, gas) extraction; (of coal, diamonds) mining; (of marble, slate) quarrying; **2** (of bullet, tooth) extraction.

extrader /ɛkstʀade/ [1] *vtr* to extradite.

extradition /ɛkstʀadisjɔ̃/ *nf* extradition.

extraire /ɛkstʀɛʀ/ [58] *vtr* **1** to extract [*mineral*]; to mine [*gold, coal*]; to quarry [*slate, marble*]; **2** to extract; to pull out; to remove.

extrait /ɛkstʀɛ/ *nm* **1** (from book, film) extract, excerpt; (from speech) extract; **2** essence, extract; **~ de viande/de légumes** meat/vegetable extract.
■ **~ (d'acte) de naissance** birth certificate; **~ de casier judiciaire (de qn)** copy of (sb's) criminal record; **~ de compte** abstract of accounts.

extralucide /ɛkstʀalysid/ *adj* clairvoyant.

extraordinaire /ɛkstʀaɔʀdinɛʀ/ *adj* **1** extraordinary, amazing, remarkable; **et si par ~...** and if by some extraordinary twist of fate...; **c'est quand même ~!** it's incredible!; **2** [*expenses, measures*] extraordinary.

extrapoler /ɛkstʀapɔle/ [1] *vtr, vi* to extrapolate.

extrascolaire /ɛkstʀaskɔlɛʀ/ *adj* extracurricular.

extraterrestre /ɛkstʀatɛʀɛstʀ/ *nmf* extraterrestrial, alien.

extravagance /ɛkstʀavagɑ̃s/ *nf* **1** eccentricity; **2** extravagance; **faire des ~s** to do extravagant things.

extravagant, ~e /ɛkstʀavagɑ̃, ɑ̃t/ *adj* **1** eccentric; **2** extravagant; **3** exorbitant.

extraverti, ~e /ɛkstʀavɛʀti/ *adj, nm,f* extrovert.

extrême /ɛkstʀɛm/ **I** *adj* **1** furthest; **dans l'~ nord/sud du pays** in the extreme North/South of the country; **2** extreme; **3** drastic.
II *nm* extreme; **c'est pousser la logique à l'~** that's taking logic to extremes; **courageux à l'~** extremely brave; **à l'~ inverse** at the other extreme.

extrêmement /ɛkstʀɛmmɑ̃/ *adv* extremely.

Extrême-Orient /ɛkstʀɛmɔʀjɑ̃/ *pr nm* **l'~** the Far East.

extrémiste /ɛkstʀemist/ *adj, nmf* extremist.

extrémité /ɛkstʀemite/ *nf* **1** end; (of finger) tip; (of mast) top; (of town, field) edge; **aux deux ~s** at both ends; **2 (en) être à la dernière ~** to be close to death; **3** extreme.

exubérance /egzybeʀɑ̃s/ *nf* exuberance.

exubérant, ~e /egzybeʀɑ̃, ɑ̃t/ *adj* exuberant.

exulter /egzylte/ [1] *vi* to be exultant, to exult.

exutoire /egzytwaʀ/ *nm* outlet; **servir d'~ à** to be an outlet for.

f, **F** /ɛf/ *nm inv* **1** f, F; **2 F3** 2-bedroom flat (GB) or apartment; **3** (*written abbr* = **franc**) **50 F** 50 F.

fa /fa/ *nm inv* (Mus) (note) F; (in sol-fa) fa.

fable /fɑbl/ *nf* **1** tale; **2** fable; **3** tall story.

fabricant /fabʀikɑ̃/ *nm* manufacturer.

fabrication /fabʀikasjɔ̃/ *nf* making; manufacture; **~ en série** mass production.
■ **~ assistée par ordinateur**, **FAO** computer-aided manufacturing, CAM.

fabrique /fabʀik/ *nf* factory.

fabriquer /fabʀike/ [1] *vtr* **1** to make; to manufacture; **fabriqué en série** mass-produced; **2** to forge [*papers*]; to invent [*alibi*]; **qu'est-ce que tu fabriques**○**?** what are you up to?

fabuler /fabyle/ [1] *vi* **1** to make things up; **2** to confabulate.

fabuleux, **-euse** /fabylø, øz/ *adj* [*beauty, wealth*] fabulous; [*sum*] fantastic; [*creature*] mythical.

fac○ /fak/ *nf* **1** faculty; **2** university.

façade /fasad/ *nf* **1** (of building) front; **~ nord** north side; **2** façade.

face /fas/ **I** *nf* **1** face; **2** side; **le côté ~ d'une pièce** the heads side of a coin; **la ~ cachée de la politique** the underside of politics; **3 faire ~** to face up to things; **se faire ~** to face each other; to be opposite one another; to confront each other; **faire ~ à** to face [*place*]; (figurative) to face [*adversary, challenge*]; to cope with [*spending*]; to meet [*demand*]; to measure up to [*competition*].
II de face *phr* [*photo*] fullface; [*lighting*] frontal; **aborder un problème de ~** to tackle a problem head-on.
III en face *phr* **il habite en ~** he lives opposite; **voir les choses en ~** to see things as they are; **je leur ai dit la vérité en ~** I told them the truth straight out; **l'équipe d'en ~** the opposing team.
IV en face de *phr* **1 en ~ de l'église** opposite the church (GB), across from the church; **2 en ~ de difficultés imprévues** faced with unexpected difficulties; **3** compared with.
V face à *phr* **1 mon lit est ~ à la fenêtre** my bed faces the window; **2 ~ à cette situation** in view of this situation.
IDIOMS **se voiler la ~** not to face facts.

face-à-face /fasafas/ *nm inv* **1** one-to-one debate (GB), one-on-one debate (US); **2** encounter.

facétie /fasesi/ *nf* **1** facetious remark; **2** practical joke.

facétieux, **-ieuse** /fasesjø, øz/ *adj* mischievous.

facette /fasɛt/ *nf* facet; **à plusieurs ~s** multifaceted.

fâché, **~e** /fɑʃe/ **I** *pp* ▶ **fâcher**.
II *pp adj* angry; **être ~ avec qn** to have fallen out with sb.

fâcher: **se fâcher** /fɑʃe/ [1] *v refl* (+ *v être*) **1** to get angry (**contre** with); **2** to fall out (**avec** with).
IDIOMS **se ~ tout rouge**○ to be hopping mad○.

fâcheux, **-euse** /fɑʃø, øz/ *adj* [*influence*] detrimental; [*delay, move*] unfortunate; [*effect*] unpleasing; [*news, event*] distressing.

facial, **~e**, *mpl* **-iaux** /fasjal, o/ *adj* facial.

faciès /fasjɛs/ *nm inv* **1** facies; **2** face.

facile /fasil/ **I** *adj* **1** easy; **avoir la larme ~** to be quick to cry; **2** easy-going.
II○ *adv* easily; **il a soixante ans ~** he's easily sixty.

facilement /fasilmɑ̃/ *adv* **1** easily; **elle rit ~** she's quick to laugh; **2**○ **j'ai mis ~ deux heures pour venir** it took me a good two hours to get here.

facilité /fasilite/ **I** *nf* **1** (of work) easiness; (of use, maintenance) ease; **2** fluency.
II facilités *nf pl* **1 donner toutes ~s pour faire** to afford every opportunity to do; **2 ~s (de paiement)** easy terms.

faciliter /fasilite/ [1] *vtr* to make [sth] easier (**à** for).

façon /fasɔ̃/ **I** *nf* **1** way; **de toute ~, de toutes les ~s** anyway; **en aucune ~** in no way; **de ~ à faire** in order to do; in such a way as to do; **de ~ (à ce) qu'elle fasse** so (that) she does; **elle nous a joué un tour à sa ~** she played a trick of her own on us; **je vais leur dire ma ~ de penser** I'll tell them exactly what I think; **~ de parler** so to speak; **2 un peigne ~ ivoire** an imitation ivory comb; **doublure ~ soie** silk-look lining; **3 on m'a donné le tissu et j'ai payé la ~** the cloth was a present and I paid for the making-up.
II façons *nf pl* **en voilà des ~s!** what a way to behave!; **sans ~s** [*meal*] informal; [*person*] unpretentious; **non merci, sans ~s** no thank you, really.

façonner /fasɔne/ [1] *vtr* **1** to manufacture; to make; **2** to hew [*wood*]; to fashion [*clay*]; to sleek [*leather*]; **3** to shape, to mould (GB), to mold (US).

fac-similé, *pl* **~s** /faksimile/ *nm* facsimile.

facteur, **-trice** /faktœʀ, tʀis/ **I** *nm,f* postman/postwoman.
II *nm* factor; **le ~ chance** the element of chance; **mettre en ~s** to factorize.

factice /faktis/ *adj* [*smile*] forced; [*jewellery*] imitation; [*flower, beauty*] artificial.

factieux, **-ieuse** /faksjø, øz/ *nm,f* dissident.

faction /faksjɔ̃/ *nf* **1** faction; **2** (Mil) guard duty.

factrice ▶ **facteur** I.

factuel, **-elle** /faktɥɛl/ *adj* factual.

facture /faktyʀ/ *nf* **1** bill; invoice; **2** craftsmanship; technique.

facturer /faktyʀe/ [1] *vtr* **1** to invoice [*goods*]; **2** to charge for [*transport*].

facultatif, -ive /fakyltatif, iv/ *adj* optional.

faculté /fakylte/ *nf* **1** (mental) faculty; ability; **2** option; **3** (at university) faculty; **4** (Law) right.

fadaises /fadɛz/ *nf pl* twaddle○, silly chatter.

fade /fad/ *adj* [*person, book*] dull; [*food, taste*] tasteless; [*colour*] drab.

fadeur /fadœʀ/ *nf* (of taste) blandness; (of style) dreariness.

fagot /fago/ *nm* bundle of firewood.

fagoter○: **se fagoter** /fagɔte/ [1] *v refl* (+ *v être*) to do oneself up○; **mal fagoté** badly dressed.

faible /fɛbl/ **I** *adj* **1** (gen) weak; [*sight*] poor; [*constitution*] frail; **être ~ avec qn** to be too soft on sb; **2** [*proportion, increase*] small; [*income, speed*] low; [*means, impact*] limited; [*chance*] slim; **de ~ profondeur** shallow; **3** [*noise, glow*] faint; [*lighting*] dim; [*wind, rain*] light; **4** [*result*] poor; [*argument*] feeble; **5** [*pupil, class*] slow; **~ d'esprit** feeble-minded; **6 le mot est ~!** that's putting it mildly!

II *nmf* weak-willed person.

III *nm* weakness; **avoir un ~ pour qn** to have a soft spot for sb.

faiblement /fɛbləmɑ̃/ *adv* weakly; [*influence, increase*] slightly; [*lit*] dimly.

faiblesse /fɛblɛs/ *nf* **1** weakness; (of invalid) frailty; **avoir une ~** to feel faint; **sans ~** [*repress*] ruthlessly; **2** inadequacy; **3** (of voice) faintness; (of lighting) dimness.

faiblir /fɛbliʀ/ [3] *vi* **1** [*person, pulse*] to get weaker; [*sight, memory*] to be failing; **2** [*person, currency*] to weaken; **3** [*athlete*] to flag; [*plot, game*] to decline; [*interest*] to wane; [*hope*] to fade; [*return, rate*] to dwindle; [*speed*] to slacken; **4** [*storm*] to abate; [*noise*] to grow faint; [*lighting*] to grow dim.

faïence /fajɑ̃s/ *nf* **1** earthenware; **2** piece of earthenware.

IDIOMS **se regarder en chiens de ~** to look daggers at each other.

faille /fɑj/ *nf* **1** (in geology) fault; **2** flaw; **sans ~** unfailing; **3** rift.

faillir /fajiʀ/ [28] *vi* **1 elle a failli le gifler** she almost or (very) nearly slapped him; **2 sans ~** unfailingly; **~ à ses engagements** to fail in one's commitments.

faillite /fajit/ *nf* **1** bankruptcy; **2** failure.

faim /fɛ̃/ *nf* hunger (**de** for); **avoir ~** to be hungry; **mourir de ~** to die of starvation; (figurative) to be starving; **je suis resté sur ma ~** I was disappointed.

fainéant, ~e /feneɑ̃, ɑ̃t/ *adj* lazy.

fainéantise /feneɑ̃tiz/ *nf* laziness.

faire /fɛʀ/ [10]

■ **Note** You will find translations for expressions such as *faire la cuisine*, *faire jour*, *faire peur*, *faire semblant* etc, at the entries ***cuisine***, ***jour***, ***peur***, ***semblant*** etc.

I *vtr* **1** to make; **~ son lit/une faute** to make one's bed/a mistake; **il fera un bon médecin** he'll make a good doctor; **l'armée en a fait un homme** the army made a man of him; **~ des jaloux** to make people jealous; **deux et deux font quatre** two and two is four; **2** to do; **~ de la recherche/une licence** to do research/a degree; **j'ai à ~** I have things to do; **que fait-il?** what does he do?; what is he doing?; **qu'as-tu fait du billet?** what have you done with the ticket?; **que veux-tu que j'y fasse?** what do you want me to do about it?; **~ médecine/du violon** to do or study medicine/to study or play the violin; **~ une école de commerce** to go to business school; **~ un numéro de téléphone/une lettre** to dial a number/to write a letter; **~ du tennis/de la couture** to play tennis/to sew; **~ un poulet** to do or cook a chicken; **~ qch à 30 francs** to sell sth for 30 francs; **3** to do [*distance, journey*]; to go round [*shops*]; to do○ [*region, museums*]; **j'ai fait tous les tiroirs mais je ne l'ai pas trouvé** I went through all the drawers but I couldn't find it; **4**○ to have [*diabetes, complex*]; **5 ~ le malade/l'ignorant** to pretend to be ill/not to know; **6 leur départ ne m'a rien fait** their departure didn't affect me at all; **ça y fait**○ it has an effect; **pour ce que ça fait**○**!** for all the good it does!; **7** to say; **'bien sûr,' fit-elle** 'of course,' she said; **le canard fait 'coin-coin'** ducks go 'quack'; **8 ça m'a fait rire** it made me laugh; **~ manger un bébé** to feed a baby; **fais voir** show me; **fais-leur prendre un rendez-vous** get them to make an appointment; **~ traverser la rue à un vieillard** to help an old man across the road; **9 ~ réparer sa voiture** to have or get one's car repaired; **il a fait construire une maison** he had a house built; **10 je n'en ai rien à ~**○ I couldn't care less; **ça ne fait rien!** it doesn't matter!; **qu'est-ce que ça peut bien te ~**○**?** what is it to you?; **il sait y ~** he's got the knack; **il ne fait que pleuvoir** it never stops raining; **je ne fais qu'obéir aux ordres** I'm only obeying orders.

II *vi* **1** to do, to act; **fais comme tu veux** do as you like; **fais comme chez toi** make yourself at home; **2** to look; **~ jeune** to look young; **3 ça fait 15 ans que j'habite ici** I've been living here for 15 years; **ça fait 2 mètres de long** it's 2 metres[GB] long; **ça fait cher** it is expensive; **4** to go (to the toilet); **tu as fait?** have you been?; **5**○ **~ avec** to make do with; to put up with.

III se faire *v refl* (+ *v être*) **1 se ~ un café** to make oneself a coffee; **se ~ comprendre** to make oneself understood; **2** to get, to become; **il se fait tard** it's getting late; **3 s'en ~** to worry; **il ne s'en fait pas!** he's not the sort of person to worry about things!; (as criticism) he's got a nerve!; **4 se ~ à** to get used to; **je ne m'y fais pas** I can't get used to it; **5 ça se fait encore ici** it's still done here; **ça ne se fait pas** it's not the done thing; **6** [*colour, style*] to be in (fashion); **7 c'est ce qui se fait de mieux** it's the best there is; **le pont se fera bien un jour** the bridge will be built one day; **8 comment se fait-il que...?** how is it that...?, how come...?

faire-part /fɛʀpaʀ/ *nm inv* announcement.

faire-valoir /fɛʀvalwaʀ/ *nm inv* **être le ~ de** [*actor*] to be a foil for.

faisable /fəzabl/ *adj* **c'est ~** it can be done.

faisan /fəzɑ̃/ *nm* (cock) pheasant.

faisane /fəzan/ *nf* **(poule) ~** hen pheasant.

faisceau, *pl* **~x** /fɛso/ *nm* **1** beam; **~ lumineux** beam of light; **2** bundle.

fait, **~e** /fɛ, fɛt/ **I** *pp* ▶ **faire**.
II *pp adj* **1** done; **bien ~** well done; **c'en est ~ de** that's the end of; **c'est bien ~ (pour toi)**○! it serves you right!; **2 ~ de** or **en** made (up) of; **idée toute ~e** ready-made idea; **elle est bien ~e** she's got a great figure; **la vie est mal ~e** life is unfair; **3 ~ pour qch/pour faire** meant for sth/to do; **4** [*programme, device*] designed; **bien ~** well-designed; **5**○ done for; **6 un fromage bien ~** a ripe cheese.
III *nm* **1** fact; **le ~ est là** or **les ~s sont là, il t'a trompé** the fact (of the matter) is that he cheated you; **les ~s et gestes de qn** sb's movements; **2 de ce ~** because of this or that; **du ~ de qch** due to sth; **être le ~ de qn** to be due to sb; **3** event; **le film part de ~s réels** the film is based on real-life events; **4** point; **aller droit au ~** to go straight to the point.
IV au fait /ofɛt/ *phr* by the way.
V de fait *phr* **1** [*situation*] de facto; **2** [*exist, result in*] effectively; **3** indeed.
VI en fait *phr* in fact, actually.
VII en fait de *phr* as regards.
■ **~ d'actualité** news item; **~ divers** (short) news item; **~ de société** fact of life.
IDIOMS **être au ~ de** to be informed about; **mettre qn au ~** to inform sb; **être sûr de son ~** to be sure of one's facts; **prendre qn sur le ~** to catch sb in the act.

faîte /fɛt/ *nm* **1** (of mountain) summit; (of house) rooftop; (of tree) top; **2** ridgepole; **3** (of fame) pinnacle.

falaise /falɛz/ *nf* cliff.

fallacieux, **-ieuse** /falasjø, øz/ *adj* [*argument*] fallacious; [*pretext*] false.

falloir /falwaʀ/ [50] **I** *v impers* **1 il faut qch/qn** we need sth/sb **(pour faire** to do); **ce qu'il faut** what is needed; **il va ~ deux jours/du courage** it will take two days/courage; **il me faut (absolument) ce livre!** I've got to have that book!; **2 'tu vas payer?'—'il faut bien!'** 'are you going to pay?'—'I have to!'; **il ne faut pas la déranger** she mustn't be disturbed; **faudrait pas me prendre pour un imbécile**○! do you think I'm a fool?; **fallait le dire plus tôt**○! why didn't you say so before?; **il fallait le faire** it had to be done; **faut le faire**○! (admiring) it takes a bit of doing!; (critical) would you believe it?; **il ne fallait pas!** (receiving gift) you shouldn't have!; **comme il faut** [*behave*] properly.
II s'en falloir *v refl* (+ *v être*) **peu s'en faut** very nearly; **il s'en faut de beaucoup** very far from it; **elle a perdu, mais il s'en est fallu de peu** she lost, but only just.
IDIOMS **il faut ce qu'il faut!** there's no point in skimping!; **en moins de temps qu'il ne faut pour le dire** before you could say Jack Robinson.

falsification /falsifikasjɔ̃/ *nf* **1** falsification; **2** forging.

falsifier /falsifje/ [2] *vtr* **1** to falsify, to tamper with [*document*]; to distort, to falsify [*facts*]; **2** to forge.

famé, **~e** /fame/ *adj* **un quartier mal ~** a disreputable or seedy area.

famélique /famelik/ *adj* emaciated, scrawny.

fameux, **-euse** /famø, øz/ *adj* **1** much talked-about; **2** famous; **3** excellent.

familial, **~e**, *mpl* **-iaux** /familjal, o/ *adj* **1** [*meal, life, firm*] family; **la cellule ~e** the family unit; **2 voiture ~e** estate car (GB), station wagon (US).

familiariser /familjaʀize/ [1] **I** *vtr* to familiarize.
II se familiariser *v refl* (+ *v être*) to familiarize oneself **(avec** with).

familiarité /familjaʀite/ *nf* familiarity.

familier, **-ière** /familje, ɛʀ/ **I** *adj* **1** [*face, landscape*] familiar; **2** [*word*] informal, colloquial; **3** [*attitude*] informal; [*person, gesture*] familiar; **4 animal ~** pet.
II *nm* **1** close friend; **2** regular.

familièrement /familjɛʀmɑ̃/ *adv* **1** commonly; **2** informally; **3** with undue familiarity.

famille /famij/ *nf* **1** family; **air de ~** family resemblance; **c'est de ~** it runs in the family; **2** body; **une ~ politique** a political persuasion; **3** (Zool) family.

famine /famin/ *nf* famine; **salaire de ~** starvation wages.

fana○ /fana/ *nmf* fanatic; **un ~ de cinéma** a film buff.

fanatique /fanatik/ **I** *adj* [*believer*] fanatical; [*admiration, love*] ardent.
II *nmf* **1** fanatic; **2**○ enthusiast, freak○.

fanatisme /fanatism/ *nm* fanaticism.

faner /fane/ [1] **I** *vtr* **1** to wither [*plant*]; **2** to fade [*colour*]; **3** to toss [*grass*].
II *vi* **1** to wither; **2** to make hay.
III se faner *v refl* (+ *v être*) **1** [*plant*] to wither, to wilt; **2** [*beauty, colour*] to fade.

fanfare /fɑ̃faʀ/ *nf* brass band; **annoncer qch en ~** to trumpet sth; **réveiller qn en ~** to wake sb up with a great commotion.

fanfaron, **-onne** /fɑ̃faʀɔ̃, ɔn/ *nm,f* boaster, swaggerer; **faire le ~** to boast.

fantaisie /fɑ̃tɛzi/ *nf* **1** imaginativeness; **être plein de ~** to be full of marvellous[GB] ideas; **manquer de ~** [*person*] to be staid; [*life*] to be dull; **2** whim, fancy; **vivre selon sa ~** to do as one pleases; **3 s'offrir une petite ~** to spoil oneself; **un bijou ~** a piece of costume jewellery (GB) or jewelry (US).

fantaisiste /fɑ̃tɛzist/ *adj* **1** [*person, timetable*] unreliable; [*figures*] doubtful; **2** [*idea*] far-fetched; [*procedure*] odd.

fantasmatique /fɑ̃tasmatik/ *adj* fantastical.

fantasme /fɑ̃tasm/ *nm* fantasy.

fantasque /fɑ̃task/ *adj* [*character*] unpredictable; [*tale*] fanciful.

fantassin /fɑ̃tasɛ̃/ *nm* infantryman, footsoldier.

fantastique /fɑ̃tastik/ **I** *adj* fantastic; **le cinéma ~** fantasy films.
II *nm* **le ~** fantasy.

fantoche /fɑ̃tɔʃ/ *adj* puppet.

fantôme /fɑ̃tom/ **I** *nm* ghost.
II (-)fantôme (*combining form*) [*train, city*] ghost; **cabinet-~** shadow cabinet (GB); **image(-)~** (on screen) ghost; **société(-)~** (Law) dummy company.

FAO /ɛfao/ *nf* **1** (*abbr* = **Food and Agriculture Organization**) FAO; **2** (Comput) (*abbr* = **fabrication assistée par ordinateur**) CAM.

faon /fɑ̃/ *nm* (Zool) fawn.

farandole /faʀɑ̃dɔl/ *nf* **1** farandole; **2** ≈ conga.

farce /faʀs/ *nf* **1** practical joke; **magasin de ~s et attrapes** joke shop (GB), novelty store (US); **2** joke; **3** (in theatre) farce; **4** stuffing, forcemeat.

farceur, **-euse** /faʀsœʀ, øz/ *nm,f* practical joker.

farcir /faʀsiʀ/ [3] **I** *vtr* **1** (Culin) to stuff (**de** with); **2**° to cram (**de** with).
II se farcir° *v refl* (+ *v être*) **1** to get stuck with°; **2** to put up with; **3** to polish off°.

fard /faʀ/ *nm* make-up; **sans ~** [*beauty*] natural; [*truth*] simple.
■ **~ à joues** blusher; **~ à paupières** eye-shadow.
IDIOMS **piquer un ~**° to go as red as a beetroot (GB), to turn as red as a beet (US).

fardeau, *pl* **~x** /faʀdo/ *nm* burden.

farder /faʀde/ [1] **I** *vtr* to disguise [*truth*].
II se farder *v refl* (+ *v être*) [*actor*] to make up; [*woman*] to use make-up.

farfelu°, **~e** /faʀfəly/ *adj* [*scheme, idea*] hare-brained°; [*story*] far-fetched; [*person*] scatter-brained°; [*show*] bizarre.

farine /faʀin/ *nf* **1** flour; **2** baby cereal.
■ **~ d'avoine** oatmeal; **~ de poisson** fish meal.
IDIOMS **se faire rouler dans la ~**° to be had°.

farineux, **-euse** /faʀinø, øz/ *adj* [*food*] starchy; [*potato*] floury; [*fruit*] mealy.

farouche /faʀuʃ/ *adj* **1** [*child, animal*] timid, shy; [*adult*] unsociable; **2** [*look, appearance, warrior*] fierce; **3** [*enemy, hatred*] bitter; [*adversary, determination*] fierce; [*supporter*] staunch; [*ambition*] driving; [*will*] iron; **4** [*landscape*] wild.

farouchement /faʀuʃmɑ̃/ *adv* [*opposed, independent*] fiercely; [*refuse*] doggedly.

fascicule /fasikyl/ *nm* **1** booklet; **2** fascicule.

fascinant, **~e** /fasinɑ̃, ɑ̃t/ *adj* [*person, film*] fascinating; [*charm, music*] spellbinding; [*beauty*] bewitching.

fascination /fasinasjɔ̃/ *nf* fascination.

fasciner /fasine/ [1] *vtr* [*speaker, music*] to hold [sb] spellbound; [*sea, person*] to fascinate; [*look, show*] to mesmerize.

fascisme /faʃism/ *nm* fascism.

faste /fast/ **I** *adj* auspicious.
II *nm* splendour[GB], pomp; **avec ~** with pomp.

fastidieux, **-ieuse** /fastidjø, øz/ *adj* tedious, tiresome.

fastueux, **-euse** /fastɥø, øz/ *adj* sumptuous.

fatal, **~e** /fatal/ *adj* **1** inevitable; **2** fatal, disastrous; **3** [*moment, day*] fateful.

fatalement /fatalmɑ̃/ *adv* inevitably.

fatalisme /fatalism/ *nm* fatalism.

fataliste /fatalist/ **I** *adj* fatalistic.
II *nmf* fatalist.

fatalité /fatalite/ *nf* **1 la ~** fate; **2** mischance; **3** inevitability.

fatidique /fatidik/ *adj* fateful.

fatigant, **~e** /fatigɑ̃, ɑ̃t/ *adj* **1** [*sport, journey*] tiring; [*climate*] wearing; **2** [*work*] arduous; **3** [*person, lecture*] tiresome; [*film, conversation*] tedious.

fatigue /fatig/ *nf* **1** tiredness; **être mort de ~, tomber de ~** to be dead tired; **2** (Med) fatigue; **~ visuelle** eyestrain.

fatigué, **~e** /fatige/ **I** *pp* ▶ **fatiguer**.
II *pp adj* **1** [*voice*] strained; [*eyes, smile*] weary; **2** [*garment*] worn.

fatiguer /fatige/ [1] **I** *vtr* **1** to make [sb/sth] tired; to strain [*eyes*]; to weaken [*heart*]; to tire [*horse*]; **2** to tire [sb] out; **3** to wear [sb] out; **4** to wear out [*engine*].
II *vi* **1**° to get tired; **2** [*engine, car*] to be labouring[GB].
III se fatiguer *v refl* (+ *v être*) **1** to get tired; **2** to tire oneself out; **3 se ~ les yeux** to strain one's eyes; **4 se ~ à faire** to bother doing.

fatras /fatʀa/ *nm inv* jumble.

faubourg /fobuʀ/ *nm* **1** working class area (*on the outskirts*); **2** *part of a town outside its walls or former walls*.

fauché°, **~e** /foʃe/ *adj* broke°, penniless.

faucher /foʃe/ [1] *vtr* **1** to mow, to cut; to scythe; **2** [*car, bullet*] to mow [sb] down; **3**° to pinch° (GB), to steal.

faucheuse /foʃøz/ *nf* mowing machine.

faucille /fosij/ *nf* sickle.

faucon /fokɔ̃/ *nm* falcon, hawk (US).

faudra /fodʀa/ ▶ **falloir**.

faufiler /fofile/ [1] **I** *vtr* to baste.
II se faufiler *v refl* (+ *v être*) **1 se ~ à l'extérieur** to slip out; **se ~ à travers** to thread one's way through; **2 se ~ dans** [*mistakes*] to creep into [*text*]; **3** [*route*] to snake in and out (**entre** between).

faune¹ /fon/ *nm* faun.

faune² /fon/ *nf* **1** wildlife, fauna; **la ~ marine** marine life; **2** (derogatory) set, crowd.

faussaire /fosɛʀ/ *nmf* forger.

fausse ▶ **faux**¹ I.

faussement /fosmɑ̃/ *adv* **1** falsely, wrongfully; **2** deceptively.

fausser /fose/ [1] *vtr* to distort [*result, mechanism*]; to warp [*mind*]; to damage [*lock*]; to bend [*key, axle*]; to buckle [*blade*].
IDIOMS **~ compagnie à qn** to give sb the slip.

faut /fo/ ▶ **falloir**.

faute /fot/ *nf* **1** mistake, error; **il a fait un (parcours) sans ~** he's never put a foot wrong; **2** (gen) misdemeanour[GB]; (Law) civil wrong; **être en ~** to be at fault; **prendre qn en ~** to catch sb out; **3** fault; **~ professionnelle** professional misconduct; **~ de service** act of negligence; **c'est (de) ma ~** it's my fault; **par la ~ de qn** because of sb; **rejeter la ~ sur qn** to lay the blame on sb; **4 ~ de temps** through lack of time; **~ de preuves** for lack of evidence; **~ de mieux** for want of anything better; **~ de quoi** otherwise, failing which; **sans ~** without fail; **5** (Sport) foul; (in tennis) fault.

fauteuil /fotœj/ *nm* **1** chair, armchair; **2** (in theatre) seat; **3 ~ de député** seat in parliament.

fauteur /fotœʀ/ *nm* **~ de troubles** troublemaker; **~ de guerre** warmonger.

fautif, -ive /fotif, iv/ **I** *adj* **1** at fault; **2** [*memory*] faulty; [*reference*] inaccurate.
II *nm,f* culprit.

fauve /fov/ **I** *adj* tawny.
II *nm* **1** wild animal; **2** big cat; **3** (colour) fawn.

fauvette /fovɛt/ *nf* warbler.

faux[1], fausse /fo, fos/ **I** *adj* **1** [*result, number, idea*] wrong; [*impression*] false; **2** [*beard, tooth, eyelashes*] false; **3** [*wood, marble, diamonds*] imitation; fake; [*door, drawer*] false; **4** forged; **5** [*freedom, need*] false; [*policeman, bishop*] bogus; [*candour, humility*] feigned; **c'est un ~ problème** it's not really a problem at all; **6** [*hope*] false; [*fear*] groundless; **7** [*pretext, promise, accusation*] false; **8** deceitful.
II *adv* [*play, sing*] out of tune; **sonner ~** to have a hollow ring.
III à faux *phr* **porter à ~** [*beam*] to be off balance.
IV *nm inv* **1 le ~** falsehood; **2** fake; forgery.
■ **fausse couche** (Med) miscarriage; **fausse facture** bogus invoice; **fausse fenêtre** blind window; **fausse joie** ill-founded joy; **faire une fausse joie à qn** to raise sb's hopes in vain; **fausse note** jarring note; **fausse piste** wrong track; **~ ami** *foreign word which looks deceptively like a word in one's own language*; **~ frais** extras, incidental expenses; **~ jeton**○ two-faced person; **~ pas** slip; mistake; faux pas; **~ pli** crease; **~ témoignage** perjury.

faux[2] /fo/ *nf inv* scythe.

faux-filet, *pl* **~s** /fofilɛ/ *nm* sirloin.

faux-fuyant, *pl* **~s** /fofɥijɑ̃/ *nm* **chercher un ~** to try to evade the issue.

faux-monnayeur, *pl* **~s** /fomɔnɛjœʀ/ *nm* forger, counterfeiter.

faux-semblant, *pl* **~s** /fosɑ̃blɑ̃/ *nm* **les ~s** pretence[GB].

faveur /favœʀ/ **I** *nf* favour[GB]; **régime** or **traitement de ~** preferential treatment; **le jugement a été rendu en sa ~** the court decided in his/her favour[GB]; **des mesures en ~ des handicapés** measures to help the disabled; **intervenir en ~ de qn** to intervene on sb's behalf.
II à la faveur de *phr* thanks to; **à la ~ de la nuit** under cover of darkness.

favorable /favɔʀabl/ *adj* favourable[GB]; **être ~ à qch** to be in favour[GB] of sth.

favorablement /favɔʀabləmɑ̃/ *adv* favourably[GB].

favori, -ite /favɔʀi, it/ **I** *adj, nm,f* favourite[GB].
II favoris *nm pl* sideburns.

favoriser /favɔʀize/ [1] *vtr* **1** to favour[GB]; **les milieux favorisés** the privileged classes; **2** to encourage, to promote.

favorite ▶ **favori** I.

favoritisme /favɔʀitism/ *nm* favouritism[GB].

fax /faks/ *nm inv* **1** fax; **2** fax machine.

fayot[1]○ /fajo/ *nm* bean.

fayot[2]○, **-otte** /fajo, ɔt/ *nm,f* creep○, crawler○.

FB (*written abbr* = **franc belge**) BFr.

fébrile /febʀil/ *adj* **1** [*emotion, gesture*] feverish; [*person*] nervous; **2** (Med) feverish.

fébrilité /febʀilite/ *nf* **1** agitation; **avec ~** agitatedly; **2** nervousness.

fécal, ~e, *mpl* **-aux** /fekal, o/ *adj* faecal.

fécond, ~e /fekɔ̃, ɔ̃d/ *adj* **1** fertile; **2** fruitful; **année ~e en incidents** eventful year.

fécondation /fekɔ̃dasjɔ̃/ *nf* (of female) impregnation; (of plant) pollination; (of egg, ovum) fertilization.

féconder /fekɔ̃de/ [1] *vtr* to impregnate [*female*]; to inseminate [*animal*]; to pollinate [*plant*]; to fertilize [*egg, ovum*].

fécondité /fekɔ̃dite/ *nf* **1** fertility; **2** (of author) productivity.

fécule /fekyl/ *nf* starch.

féculent /fekylɑ̃/ *nm* starch; starchy food.

fédéral, ~e, *mpl* **-aux** /federal, o/ *adj* federal.

fédération /fedeʀasjɔ̃/ *nf* federation.

fée /fe/ *nf* fairy; **~ du logis** perfect housewife.
IDIOMS **avoir des doigts de ~** to have nimble fingers.

féerique /fe(e)ʀik/ *adj* [*beauty*] enchanting; [*landscape, moment*] enchanted.

feindre /fɛ̃dʀ/ [55] *vtr* to feign; **~ de faire/d'être** to pretend to do/to be.

feint, ~e[1] /fɛ̃, ɛ̃t/ *adj* [*emotion*] feigned; [*smile*] false; **non ~** genuine.

feinte[2] /fɛ̃t/ *nf* **1** feint; **faire une ~** (in football, rugby) to dummy (GB), to fake (US); **2**○ trick, ruse; **faire une ~ à qn** to trick or con○ sb.

feinter /fɛ̃te/ [1] *vi* (in fencing) to make a feint; (in boxing) to feint; (in football, rugby) to dummy (GB), to fake (US).

fêlé○, **~e** /fɛle/ *adj* cracked○.

fêler /fɛle/ [1] *vtr*, **se fêler** *v refl* (+ *v être*) to crack.

félicitations /felisitasjɔ̃/ *nf pl* congratulations; **être reçu avec les ~ du jury** to pass with distinction.

féliciter /felisite/ [1] **I** *vtr* to congratulate.
II se féliciter *v refl* (+ *v être*) **se ~ de qch** to be very pleased about sth.

félin, **~e** /felɛ̃, in/ **I** *adj* **1** feline; **exposition ~e** cat show; **2** [*grace*] feline; [*eyes*] catlike.
II *nm* feline; **les ~s** felines, the cat family.

fêlure /fɛlyʀ/ *nf* crack.

femelle /fəmɛl/ **I** *adj* **1** female; **éléphant ~** cow elephant; **moineau ~** hen sparrow; **cygne ~** pen; **2** [*socket*] female.
II *nf* female; (in pair) mate.

féminin, **~e** /feminɛ̃, in/ **I** *adj* [*sex, occupation*] female; [*magazine, lingerie, record*] women's; [*team, club*] ladies'; [*appearance*] feminine.
II *nm* feminine; **au ~** in the feminine.

féminiser /feminize/ [1] **I** *vtr* to open [sth] up to women [*profession*].
II se féminiser *v refl* (+ *v être*) [*profession*] to become more open to women; to become predominantly female.

féministe /feminist/ *adj, nmf* feminist.

féminité /feminite/ *nf* femininity.

femme /fam/ *nf* **1** woman; **2** wife.
■ **~ de chambre** chambermaid; **~ au foyer** housewife; **~ d'intérieur** homemaker; **~ de lettres** woman of letters; ▶ **bon, jeune**.
IDIOMS **souvent ~ varie** (Proverb) woman is fickle.

fémur /femyʀ/ *nm* thighbone; **se casser le col du ~** to break one's hip.

fenaison /fənɛzɔ̃/ *nf* **1** haymaking time; **2** haymaking.

fendiller /fɑ̃dije/ [1]**I** *vtr* to chap [*lips*]; to craze [*earth*]; to crack [*wood*].
II se fendiller *v refl* (+ *v être*) [*lips*] to chap; [*earth*] to craze over; [*wood*] to crack.

fendre /fɑ̃dʀ/ [6] **I** *vtr* **1** to chop [*wood*]; to slit [*material*]; **2** to crack [*wall, stone*]; to split [*lip*]; to split [sth] open [*skull*]; **3 ~ le cœur à qn** to break sb's heart; **4 ~ l'air** to slice through the air; **~ la foule** to push one's way through the crowd.
II se fendre *v refl* (+ *v être*) **1** to crack; **2** [*heart*] to break; **3**○ to cough up○ [*money*]; **tu ne t'es pas fendu!** that didn't break the bank!
IDIOMS **se ~ la pêche**○ to split one's sides○; **avoir la bouche fendue jusqu'aux oreilles** to be grinning from ear to ear.

fenêtre /fənɛtʀ/ *nf* window.
■ **~ à battants** casement window; **~ à guillotine** sash window.
IDIOMS **jeter l'argent par les ~s** to throw money away.

fenouil /fənuj/ *nm* fennel.

fente /fɑ̃t/ *nf* **1** slit; (for coin, card) slot; (of jacket) vent; **2** crack; (in wood) split; (in rock) crevice.

féodal, **~e**, *mpl* **-aux** /feɔdal, o/ *adj* feudal.

fer /fɛʀ/ *nm* **1** iron; **2 de ~** [*discipline, fist, will*] iron; **3** (on shoe) steel tip; **4** branding iron; **5 croiser le ~ avec** to cross swords with.
■ **~ à cheval** horseshoe; **~ forgé** wrought iron; **~ à repasser (à vapeur)** (steam) iron.
IDIOMS **croire dur comme ~** to believe wholeheartedly; **il faut battre le ~ tant qu'il est chaud** (Proverb) strike while the iron is hot; **tomber les quatre ~s en l'air** to fall flat on one's back.

fer-blanc, *pl* **fers-blancs** /fɛʀblɑ̃/ *nm* tinplate.

férié, **~e** /feʀje/ *adj* **jour ~** public holiday (GB), holiday (US).

ferme[1] /fɛʀm/ **I** *adj* **1** [*ground, flesh*] firm; **2** [*step, voice*] firm; [*gesture, style*] confident; **3** [*market, order, price*] firm; **4** (Law) **peine de prison ~** custodial sentence.
II *adv* [*argue, campaign*] vigorously; [*believe*] firmly; **tenir ~** to stand one's ground.
IDIOMS **attendre de pied ~** to be ready and waiting.

ferme[2] /fɛʀm/ *nf* farm, farmhouse.

fermement /fɛʀməmɑ̃/ *adv* firmly.

ferment /fɛʀmɑ̃/ *nm* ferment.

fermentation /fɛʀmɑ̃tasjɔ̃/ *nf* **1** fermentation; **2** (political, racial) ferment.

fermenter /fɛʀmɑ̃te/ [1] *vi* **1** [*beer, yeast*] to ferment; **2** (figurative) to be in ferment.

fermer /fɛʀme/ [1] **I** *vtr* **1** to close, to shut [*door, book, eyes*]; to clench [*fist*]; to draw [*curtain*]; to turn off [*tap, gas, radio*]; to switch off [*electricity*]; to do up [*jacket*]; **~ à clé** to lock (up); **2** to close; (definitively) to close [sth] down.
II *vi* to close (down).
III se fermer *v refl* (+ *v être*) **1** [*door*] to shut; [*flower*] to close up; [*coat, bracelet*] to fasten; **2** [*person*] to clam up; [*face*] to harden.
IDIOMS **~ les yeux sur** to turn a blind eye to.

fermeté /fɛʀməte/ *nf* firmness.

fermeture /fɛʀmətyʀ/ *nf* **1** (of business) closing; (definitive) closure, closing down; (of account) closing; **2** (on handbag) clasp; (on garment) fastening.
■ **~ éclair®**, **~ à glissière** zip (GB), zipper (US).

fermier, **-ière** /fɛʀmje, ɛʀ/ **I** *adj* free-range.
II *nm,f* farmer.

fermoir /fɛʀmwaʀ/ *nm* (on necklace, bag) clasp.

féroce /feʀɔs/ *adj* **1** [*animal*] ferocious; [*repression*] savage; [*person*] fierce; **2** [*battle*] fierce; **3** [*appetite*] voracious; [*desire*] violent.

férocité /feʀɔsite/ *nf* **1** (of animal) ferociousness; **2** (of remark) savagery; **3** (of person, look) fierceness.

ferraille /feʀɑj/ *nf* **1** scrap metal; **2** scrapheap; **3**○ small change.

ferrailleur /feʀɑjœʀ/ *nm* scrap (metal) dealer.

ferrer /feʀe/ [1] *vtr* **1** to shoe [*horse*]; **2** to hook [*fish*].

ferreux, **-euse** /feʀø, øz/ *adj* [*metal*] ferrous.

ferronnerie /feʀɔnʀi/ *nf* **1** ironworks; **2** wrought iron work; **3** iron work.

ferronnier /feʀɔnje/ *nm* **1** iron craftsman; **2** iron work merchant.

ferroviaire /feʀɔvjɛʀ/ *adj* [*transport, collision, traffic*] rail; [*station, tunnel, company*] railway (GB), railroad (US).

fertile /fɛʀtil/ *adj* **1** [*ground*] fertile; **2** [*imagination*] fertile; [*year*] productive.

fertilité /fɛʀtilite/ *nf* fertility.

fervent, ~e /fɛʀvɑ̃, ɑ̃t/ *adj* [*believer*] fervent; [*admirer*] ardent.

ferveur /fɛʀvœʀ/ *nf* (of prayer) fervour[GB]; (of love) ardour[GB].

fesse /fɛs/ *nf* buttock.
IDIOMS **avoir chaud aux ~s**○ to have a narrow escape○; **coûter la peau des ~s**○ to cost an arm and a leg○.

fessée /fese/ *nf* smack on the bottom, spanking.

festin /fɛstɛ̃/ *nm* feast.

festival /fɛstival/ *nm* festival; **pièce hors ~** play on the fringe.

festivités /fɛstivite/ *nf pl* festivities.

festoyer /fɛstwaje/ [23] *vi* to feast.

fête /fɛt/ *nf* **1** public holiday (GB), holiday (US); **2** (saint's) name-day; **ça va être ma ~**○! I'm going to cop it○!; **3** festival; **4** (day of) celebration; **5** party; **faire la ~** to live it up○; **être à la ~** to have a field day; **6** fête, fair, celebrations.
■ **~ foraine** funfair; **~ des Mères** Mothers' Day; **~ des Pères** Fathers' Day; **~ du travail** May Day, Labour Day (GB).
IDIOMS **faire sa ~ à qn**○ to give sb a working over○.

fêter /fete/ [1] *vtr* to celebrate [*event*]; to fete [*champion*].

fétiche /fetiʃ/ I *adj* lucky; **jour/chiffre ~** lucky day/number.
II *nm* **1** mascot; **2** fetish.

fétide /fetid/ *adj* **1** [*smell*] foul; [*place*] foul-smelling; **2** [*person*] repulsive.

feu¹, ~e /fø/ *adj* late; **~ la reine, la ~e reine** the late queen.

feu², *pl* ~x /fø/ *nm* **1** fire; ▶ **huile**; **2** light; **sous le ~ des projecteurs** under the glare of the spotlights; (figurative) in the spotlight; **3** (on vehicle) light; **4** traffic light; **~ orange** amber (GB) or yellow (US) light; **j'ai le ~ vert de mon patron** my boss has given me the go-ahead; **5** (on cooker) ring (GB), burner (US); **faire cuire à petit ~** cook over a gentle heat; **6 avez-vous du ~?** have you got a light?; **7 elle avait les joues en ~** her cheeks were burning or on fire; **8** passion; **avoir un tempérament de ~** to have a fiery temperament; **dans le ~ de la discussion** in the heat of the discussion; **9 ~!** fire!; **faire ~** to fire (**sur** at); **coup de ~** shot; **10** (Mil) action; **aller au ~** to go into action.
■ **~ d'artifice** fireworks display; firework; **~ de cheminée** chimney fire; open fire; **~ follet** will-o'-the-wisp; **~ de joie** bonfire; **~ de paille** flash in the pan; **~ de signalisation**, **~ tricolore** traffic light; **~x de croisement** dipped (GB) or dimmed (US) headlights; **~x de détresse** warning lights; **~x de route** headlights.
IDIOMS **il n'y a pas le ~**○! there's no rush!; **ne pas faire long ~**○ not to last long; **il n'y a vu que du ~**○ he fell for it; **mourir à petit ~** to die a slow death; **avoir le ~ aux fesses**○ to be in a rush.

feuillage /fœjaʒ/ *nm* **1** foliage, leaves; **2** leafage.

feuille /fœj/ *nf* **1** (Bot) leaf; **2** (of paper, metal) sheet; **~ d'aluminium** aluminium (GB) or aluminum (US) foil.
■ **~ de chou**○ rag○, newspaper; **avoir les oreilles en ~ de chou** to have cauliflower ears; **~ d'impôts** tax return; **~ de maladie** *a form for reclaiming medical expenses from the social security office*; **~ de paie** payslip (GB), pay stub (US).

feuillet /fœjɛ/ *nm* **1** (in book) leaf; **2** page.

feuilleté, ~e /fœjte/ I *adj* **pâte ~e** puff pastry.
II *nm* savoury[GB] pasty (*made with puff pastry*).

feuilleter /fœjte/ [20] *vtr* to leaf through [sth].

feuilleton /fœjtɔ̃/ *nm* serial; soap (opera).

feutre /føtʀ/ *nm* **1** felt; **2** felt hat; **3** felt-tip (pen).

feutré, ~e /føtʀe/ *adj* [*atmosphere*] hushed; [*sound*] muffled.

fève /fɛv/ *nf* **1** broad bean; **2** lucky charm (*hidden in Twelfth Night cake*).

février /fevʀije/ *nm* February.

fiable /fjabl/ *adj* reliable.

fiançailles /fjɑ̃saj/ *nf pl* engagement.

fiancé, ~e /fjɑ̃se/ *nm,f* fiancé/fiancée.

fiancer: se fiancer /fjɑ̃se/ [12] *v refl* (+ *v être*) to get engaged (**à, avec** to).

fibre /fibʀ/ *nf* **1** fibre[GB]; **2 avoir la ~ maternelle** to have a strong maternal streak.

ficeler /fisle/ [19] *vtr* to tie up [*parcel*]; **bien ficelé** [*novel*] well structured.

ficelle /fisɛl/ *nf* **1** string; **2** trick; **la ~ est un peu grosse** it's a bit obvious; **3** thin baguette.
IDIOMS **tirer sur la ~** to push one's luck.

fiche¹○ /fiʃ/ *vtr*, **se fiche** *v refl* (+ *v être*) ▶ **ficher I 3, 4, 5; II 2, 3, 4**.

fiche² /fiʃ/ *nf* **1** index card; slip; **~ médicale** medical card; **2** form; **~ d'inscription** enrolment[GB] form; **3** plug; **prise à trois ~s** three-pin plug; **4** (Comput) plug.
■ **~ d'état civil** *record of personal details for administrative purposes*; **~ de paie** payslip (GB), pay stub (US).

ficher /fiʃe/ [1] I *vtr* **1** to put [sth] on a file; to open a file on [sb]; **être fiché (par la police)** to be on police files; **2** to drive [*stake, nail*] (**dans** into); **3**○ to do; **qu'est-ce que tu fiches?** what the heck○ are you doing?; **n'en avoir rien à ~** not to give a damn○; **4**○ **~ un coup à qn** to wallop sb; (figurative) to be a real blow to sb; **~ la paix à qn** to leave sb alone; **5**○ **~ qch quelque part** to chuck○ sth somewhere; **où est-ce qu'il a bien pu ~ mon journal?** where the hell○ has he put my newspaper?; **~ qn dehors** or **à la porte** to kick sb out○.
II **se ficher** *v refl* (+ *v être*) **1** [*arrow, knife*] to stick (**dans** in); **2**○ **se ~ en colère** to fly off the handle○; **se ~ dedans** to screw up○; **3**○ **se ~ de qn** to make fun of sb; **se ~ du monde** to have a hell of a nerve○; **4**○ **se ~ de ce que qn fait** not to give a damn○ (about) what sb does.

fichier /fiʃje/ *nm* file; (in library) index.

fichu○ /fiʃy/ **I** *pp* ▶ **ficher** I 3, 4, 5, II 2, 3, 4.
II *adj* **1** [*weather, job*] rotten○; [*rain*] dreadful; [*car, TV*] damned○; **avoir un ~ caractère** to have a nasty temper; **2** [*person, car*] done for○; **s'il pleut c'est ~** if it rains that's the end of that; **3 être bien ~** to be well designed; [*book*] to be well laid out; **je suis mal ~** I feel lousy○; **4 être ~ de faire** to be quite capable of doing.

fictif, -ive /fiktif, iv/ *adj* [*character*] imaginary; [*identity*] false.

fiction /fiksjɔ̃/ *nf* **1** fiction; **2** (on TV) drama.

fidèle /fidɛl/ **I** *adj* **1** [*person, dog*] faithful (**à** to); **être ~ au poste** to be always there; **2** loyal (**à** to); **3** true (**à** to); **4** [*translation, account*] faithful (**à** to).
II *nmf* **1** loyal supporter; **2** faithful friend; **3 les ~s** the faithful.

fidèlement /fidɛlmɑ̃/ *adv* **1** faithfully; **2** loyally.

fidélité /fidelite/ *nf* **1** fidelity (**à** to); **2** loyalty (**à** to); **3** (of translation) accuracy.

fief /fjɛf/ *nm* **1** fief; **2** (figurative) territory; (of party) stronghold.

fier[1], **fière** /fjɛʀ/ *adj* proud; **avoir fière allure** to cut a fine figure.

fier[2]: **se fier** /fje/ [2] *v refl* (+ *v être*) **1 se ~ à** to trust [*person, promise*]; **2 se ~ à** to rely on [*person, memory, instrument*]; to trust to [*chance*].

fierté /fjɛʀte/ *nf* pride; **tirer ~ de qch** to take pride in sth.

fièvre /fjɛvʀ/ *nf* **1** (high) temperature; **avoir de la ~** to have a (high) temperature; **2** frenzy; **3** fervour[GB]; **~ électorale** election fever.
■ **~ de cheval**○ raging fever.

fiévreux, -euse /fjevʀø, øz/ *adj* **1** feverish; **2** frantic.

figer /fiʒe/ [13] **I** *vtr* to congeal [*grease*]; to thicken [*sauce*]; to clot [*blood*].
II se figer *v refl* (+ *v être*) **1** [*smile, person*] to freeze (**de** with); **2** [*grease, sauce*] to congeal; [*blood*] to clot; (figurative) to freeze.

fignoler /fiɲɔle/ [1] **I** *vtr* **1** to put the finishing touches to; **2** to take great pains over.
II *vi* to fiddle about.

figue /fig/ *nf* fig; **~ de Barbarie** prickly pear.

figuier /figje/ *nm* fig tree.

figurant, ~e /figyʀɑ̃, ɑ̃t/ *nm,f* (in films) extra; (in theatre) bit player.

figuratif, -ive /figyʀatif, iv/ *adj* figurative, representational.

figuration /figyʀasjɔ̃/ *nf* **faire de la ~** (in films) to be an extra; (figurative) to have a token role.

figure /figyʀ/ *nf* **1** face; **elle a changé de ~** her face fell; **2 faire ~ d'amateur** to look like an amateur; **reprendre ~ humaine** to look half-human again; **3** (in history, politics) figure; **4** (in drawing) figure.
IDIOMS **prendre ~** to take shape; **faire bonne ~** to keep an air of composure; to make the right impression; to do well.

figurer /figyʀe/ [1] **I** *vtr* to represent.
II *vi* [*name, object*] to appear (**dans** in).
III se figurer *v refl* (+ *v être*) to imagine; **j'avais compris, figurez-vous!** I'd gathered that!

figurine /figyʀin/ *nf* figurine.

fil /fil/ **I** *nm* **1** thread; ▶ **coudre**; **2** yarn; **3** string; **~ de pêche** (fishing) line; **~ de fer** wire; **4** wire; (on microphone, appliance) flex (GB), cord (US); (on phone) lead; **coup de ~**○ (phone) call; **au bout du ~**○ on the phone; **5** thread; **perdre le ~ des événements** to lose track of events; **6** (of web) thread; **7** (of razor) edge.
II au fil de *phr* **au ~ des ans** over the years; **au ~ de la conversation** in the course of the conversation; **aller au ~ de l'eau** to go with the flow.
■ **~ conducteur** (of electricity, heat) conductor; (of novel) thread; (of inquiry) lead; **~ directeur** guiding principle; **~ de terre** earth wire (GB), ground wire (US).
IDIOMS **ne tenir qu'à un ~** to hang by a thread.

filament /filamɑ̃/ *nm* filament.

filature /filatyʀ/ *nf* **1** textile mill; **2** spinning; **3 prendre qn en ~** to tail sb○.

file /fil/ *nf* **1 ~ (d'attente)** queue (GB), line (US); **2** line; **~ indienne** single file; **à la ~** in a row; **3** lane; **se garer en double ~** to double-park.

filer /file/ [1] **I** *vtr* **1** to spin [*wool, cotton*]; **2** to spin [*web, cocoon*]; **3** to get a run in [*tights*]; **4** to tail○ [sb]; **~ le train à qn**○ to be on sb's tail○; **5**○ to give [sth] (**à** to).
II○ *vi* **1** to go off, to leave; **2** to rush; **3** [*time*] to fly by; [*prisoner*] to get away; **~ entre les mains** to slip through one's fingers.
IDIOMS **~ comme le vent** or **une flèche** to go like the wind.

filet /filɛ/ *nm* **1** net; **~ à provisions** string bag; **coup de ~** (police) raid; **2** fillet; **3** (of water) trickle; (of smoke) wisp; **~ de citron** dash of lemon juice.

filial, ~e[1], *mpl* **-iaux** /filjal, o/ *adj* filial.

filiale[2] /filjal/ *nf* subsidiary; **~ commune** joint subsidiary.

filiation /filjasjɔ̃/ *nf* filiation.

filière /filjɛʀ/ *nf* **1** (Sch) course of study; **2** (Econ) field; **3 suivre la ~ habituelle** to climb up the usual career ladder; **4** official channels; **5 ~ (clandestine) de la drogue** drugs ring.

filiforme /filifɔʀm/ *adj* spindly; threadlike.

filigrane /filigʀan/ *nm* **1 être en ~ dans** to be implicit in; **2** filigree.

filin /filɛ̃/ *nm* rope.

fille /fij/ *nf* **1** daughter; **2** girl; **~ mère** unmarried mother.

fillette /fijɛt/ *nf* **1** little girl; **2**○ half bottle.

filleul /fijœl/ *nm* godson, godchild.

filleule /fijœl/ *nf* goddaughter, godchild.

film /film/ *nm* **1** film, movie (US); **~ muet** silent film; **2** course, sequence; **3** (thin) film.
■ **~ d'animation** cartoon; **~ policier** detective film.

filmer /filme/ [1] *vtr* to film.

filon /filɔ̃/ *nm* vein, seam; **exploiter un ~** to mine a seam.

fils /fis/ *nm inv* son; **Dupont ~** Dupont Junior.

filtre /filtʀ/ *nm* filter; **cigarette avec/sans ~** filter-tip/untipped cigarette.

filtrer /filtʀe/ [1] **I** *vtr* **1** to filter; **2** to screen [*visitors, calls*].
II *vi* **1** [*information*] to leak out; [*idea*] to filter through; **2** [*liquid*] to filter through.

fin[1], **fine** /fɛ̃, fin/ **I** *adj* **1** [*rain, sand, brush*] fine; [*slice, layer*] thin; **2** [*beans*] quality; **3** [*ankle, waist*] slender; [*features*] fine; [*wine*] fine; [*dish*] delicate; **4** [*person*] perceptive; [*mind*] shrewd; [*taste, humour*] subtle; **vraiment c'est ~!** that's really clever!; **jouer au plus ~ avec qn** to try to outsmart sb; **avoir l'air ~**○ to look a fool; **5 avoir l'ouïe ~e** to have a keen sense of hearing; **6 au ~ fond de** in the remotest part of [*country*]; **le ~ mot de l'histoire** the truth of the matter.
II *adv* **1 être ~ prêt** to be all set; **2** [*write, grind*] finely; [*slice*] thinly.
III *nm* **le ~ du ~** the ultimate (**de** in).
■ **~ renard** sly customer○; **~e mouche** = **~ renard**; **~es herbes** mixed herbs.

fin[2] /fɛ̃/ *nf* **1** end, ending; **à la ~ des années 70** in the late '70s; **c'est la ~ de tout** it's the last straw; **tu vas te taire à la ~**○**!** for God's sake, be quiet!; **chômeur en ~ de droits** unemployed person no longer entitled to benefit; **2** end, death; **3** end, aim, purpose; **à toutes ~s utiles** for whatever purpose it may serve.
■ **~ de série** oddment.

final, **~e**[1], *mpl* **-aux** /final, o/ *adj* final.

finale[2] /final/ *nf* (Sport) final.

finalement /finalmɑ̃/ *adv* **1** in the end, finally; **2** in fact, actually.

finance /finɑ̃s/ **I** *nf* **1 la ~** finance; **2** financiers.
II finances *nf pl* **les ~s** finances; **moyennant ~s** for a consideration.

financement /finɑ̃smɑ̃/ *nm* financing.

financer /finɑ̃se/ [12] *vtr* to finance.

financier, **-ière** /finɑ̃sje, ɛʀ/ **I** *adj* financial.
II *nm* **1** financier; **2** small cake.

finement /finmɑ̃/ *adv* **1** finely; **2** cleverly.

finesse /finɛs/ *nf* **1** (of thread, writing) fineness; (of layer, paper) thinness; (of blade) keenness; **2** (dish, piece of jewellery) delicacy; (of face) fineness; (of waist) slenderness; **3** (of remark, person) perceptiveness; (of actor, acting) sensitivity; **4** (of senses) keenness, sharpness; **5 les ~s d'une langue** the subtleties of a language.

fini, **~e** /fini/ **I** *pp* ▶ **finir**.
II *pp adj* **1 être ~** to be over, to be finished; **~ de rire, il faut travailler maintenant!** the party's over, it's time to get down to work!; **2 produits ~s** finished products.
III *nm* finish.

finir /finiʀ/ [3] **I** *vtr* **1** to finish (off), to complete [*work*]; to end [*day, speech*]; **2** to use up [*supplies*]; to finish [*dessert, main course*].
II *vi* **1** to finish, to end; [*contract, lease*] to run out, to expire; **le film finit bien** the film has a happy ending; **ça va mal ~!** it'll end in tears!; **il finira mal ce garçon** that boy will come to a bad end; **2 ~ par faire** to end up doing; **ils finiront bien par céder** they're bound to give in in the end; **3 en ~ avec qch/qn** to have done with sth/sb; **finissons-en!** let's get it over with!; ▶ **queue**.

finition /finisjɔ̃/ *nf* **1** finishing; **travaux de ~** finishing; **2** finish.

finlandais, **~e** /fɛ̃lɑ̃dɛ, ɛz/ *adj* Finnish.

Finlandais, **~e** /fɛ̃lɑ̃dɛ, ɛz/ *nm,f* Finn.

Finlande /fɛ̃lɑ̃d/ *pr nf* Finland.

finnois, **~e** /finwa, az/ **I** *adj* Finnish.
II *nm* (language) Finnish.

fiole /fjɔl/ *nf* phial.

fioriture /fjɔʀityʀ/ *nf* embellishment.

fioul /fjul/ *nm* fuel oil; **~ domestique** heating oil.

firme /fiʀm/ *nf* firm.

fisc /fisk/ *nm* tax office.

fiscal, **~e**, *mpl* **-aux** /fiskal, o/ *adj* fiscal, tax.

fiscalité /fiskalite/ *nf* **1** taxation; **2** tax system.

fission /fisjɔ̃/ *nf* fission.

fissure /fisyʀ/ *nf* **1** crack; **2** (Anat) fissure; **3** (figurative) rift, division.

fissurer /fisyʀe/ [1] *vtr* to crack, to fissure.

fiston○ /fistɔ̃/ *nm* sonny○, son.

fixation /fiksasjɔ̃/ *nf* **1** fixing; fastening; **2** (of date, price, rate) setting; **3** (on ski) binding; **4** fixation.

fixe /fiks/ *adj* **1** fixed; **2** permanent.

fixé, **~e** /fikse/ **I** *pp* ▶ **fixer**.
II *pp adj* **1 tu es ~ maintenant!** you've got the picture now○!; **2 nous ne sommes pas encore très ~s** we haven't really decided yet.

fixement /fiksəmɑ̃/ *adv* fixedly.

fixer /fikse/ [1] **I** *vtr* **1** to fix (**à** to); **2** to set [*date, price, terms*]; **~ son choix sur** to decide on; **3** to fix [*colour, emulsion*]; to establish [*boundaries*]; **4** to focus [*attention*]; to stare at [*person, object*].
II se fixer *v refl* (+ *v être*) **1** [*part*] to be attached (**à** to); **2** to set oneself [*goal, limit*]; **3** [*person, population*] to settle.

flacon /flakɔ̃/ *nm* **1** (small) bottle; **2** decanter; **3** (in laboratory) flask.

flagada○ /flagada/ *adj inv* weary.

flagellation /flaʒɛlasjɔ̃/ *nf* (gen) flogging; (as religious punishment) flagellation.

flageller /flaʒɛle/ [1] *vtr* to flog; (as religious punishment) to flagellate.

flageoler /flaʒɔle/ [1] *vi* **avoir les jambes qui flageolent** to feel wobbly.

flageolet /flaʒɔlɛ/ *nm* flageolet.

flagrant, **~e** /flagʀɑ̃, ɑ̃t/ *adj* [*difference*] obvious; [*injustice*] flagrant; [*lie*] blatant; **en ~ délit** in flagrante delicto; **prendre qn en ~ délit** to catch sb red-handed.

flair /flɛʀ/ *nm* **1** sense of smell, nose; **2** intuition.

flairer /flɛʀe/ [1] *vtr* **1** to sniff [*object*]; **le chien a flairé une piste** the dog has picked up a scent; **2** [*animal*] to scent; [*person*] to smell; **3** to sense [*danger*].

flamand, **~e** /flamɑ̃, ɑ̃d/ **I** *adj* Flemish.

II *nm* Flemish.

flamant /flamɑ̃/ *nm* flamingo.

flambant /flɑ̃bɑ̃/ *adv* **~ neuf** brand new.

flambeau, *pl* **~x** /flɑ̃bo/ *nm* torch.

flambée /flɑ̃be/ *nf* **1** fire; **faire une ~** to light a fire; **2** (of violence, hatred) flare-up; (of prices) explosion (**de** in).

flamber /flɑ̃be/ [1] **I** *vtr* to singe [*chicken*]; to flambé [*omelette, pancake*] (**à** in).

II *vi* to burn.

flamboyant, **~e** /flɑ̃bwajɑ̃, ɑ̃t/ *adj* **1** [*fire, light*] blazing; [*colour*] flaming; **2 gothique ~** Flamboyant Gothic.

flamme /flɑm/ *nf* **1** flame; **en ~s** on fire; **2** (literary) love, passion.

IDIOMS **descendre en ~s** to shoot down; **être tout feu tout ~** to be wildly enthusiastic.

flan /flɑ̃/ *nm* (Culin) **1** ≈custard; **2** custard tart (GB) or flan (US).

IDIOMS **en rester comme deux ronds de ~**○ to be dumbfounded.

flanc /flɑ̃/ *nm* **1** (of person) side; (of animal) flank, side; **être sur le ~**○ to be exhausted; **2** (of mountain, ship) side.

flancher○ /flɑ̃ʃe/ [1] *vi* **1** to lose one's nerve; **2** to crack up; **3** [*heart, engine*] to give out; [*memory*] to let [sb] down.

flanelle /flanɛl/ *nf* flannel; **~ de coton** flannelette.

flâner /flɑne/ [1] *vi* **1** to stroll; **2** to dawdle; to loaf○ around.

flâneur, **-euse** /flɑnœʀ, øz/ *nm,f* stroller.

flanquer /flɑ̃ke/ [1] **I** *vtr* **1** to flank (**de** by); **il est toujours flanqué de son adjoint** his assistant never leaves his side; **2**○ to give [*blow, fine*]; **~ qch par terre** to throw sth to the ground; to drop sth; to knock sth to the ground; **~ la frousse**○ **à qn** to give sb a fright; **~ qn dehors** (from a job) to fire sb; (from a place) to chuck○ sb out.

II se flanquer○ *v refl* (+ *v être*) **se ~ dans** to run into; **se ~ par terre** to fall flat on one's face.

flapi○, **~e** /flapi/ *adj* worn out.

flaque /flak/ *nf* **1 ~ (d'eau)** puddle; **2 ~ d'huile** pool of oil.

flash, *pl* **~es** /flaʃ/ *nm* **1** flash; **2 ~ (d'information)** news headlines; **~ publicitaire** advert (GB), commercial (US).

flasque[1] /flask/ *adj* [*skin, flesh*] flabby.

flasque[2] /flask/ *nf* flask.

flatter /flate/ [1] **I** *vtr* **1** to flatter; **2 leur visite a flatté tout le village** the whole village felt honoured[GB] by their visit; **3** to pat [*animal*].

II se flatter *v refl* (+ *v être*) to pride oneself (**de** on).

flatterie /flatʀi/ *nf* flattery; **de basses ~s** toadying.

flatteur, **-euse** /flatœʀ, øz/ **I** *adj* **1** [*portrait*] flattering; **2** [*person, remarks*] sycophantic.

II *nm,f* sycophant.

flatulence /flatylɑ̃s/ *nf* wind, flatulence.

fléau, *pl* **~x** /fleo/ *nm* **1** scourge; **2** (figurative) curse, plague; **3** (person) pest.

flèche /flɛʃ/ *nf* **1** arrow; **partir en ~** to shoot off; **monter en ~** [*prices*] to soar; **2** barbed remark; **3** spire.

flécher /fleʃe/ [14] *vtr* to signpost.

fléchette /fleʃɛt/ *nf* **1** dart; **2** (game) darts.

fléchir /fleʃiʀ/ [3] **I** *vtr* **1** to bend; **2** to sway; to weaken.

II *vi* **1** [*knees*] to bend; [*legs*] to give way; **2** [*attention, concentration*] to flag; [*courage*] to waver; [*will, resistance*] to weaken; [*production, demand*] to fall off.

flegmatique /flɛgmatik/ *adj* phlegmatic.

flegme /flɛgm/ *nm* phlegm, composure.

flemmard○, **~e** /flemaʀ, aʀd/ **I** *adj* bone idle.

II *nm,f* lazybones○, lazy devil○.

flemme○ /flɛm/ *nf* laziness; **j'ai la ~ d'y aller** I'm too lazy to go there.

flétan /fletɑ̃/ *nm* halibut.

flétrir /fletʀiʀ/ [3] **I** *vtr* to blacken [*name, reputation*].

II se flétrir *v refl* (+ *v être*) [*plant*] to wither; [*flower, beauty*] to fade; [*fruit*] to shrivel.

fleur /flœʀ/ *nf* **1** flower; **être en ~s** [*garden*] to be full of flowers; [*plant, shrub*] to be in bloom or flowering; [*tree, lilac*] to be in blossom; **à ~s** flowery; **2 à ~ d'eau** [*rock*] just above the water.

■ **~ des champs** wild flower; **~ de lys** fleur-de-lis, heraldic lily.

IDIOMS **être ~ bleue** to be starry-eyed or romantic; **avoir une sensibilité à ~ de peau** to be hypersensitive; **avoir les nerfs à ~ de peau** to be a bundle of nerves; **faire une ~ à qn**○ to do sb a favour[GB].

fleuret /flœʀɛ/ *nm* (sword) foil.

fleurette /flœʀɛt/ *nf* (Culin) **crème ~** whipping cream.

IDIOMS **conter ~† à qn** to woo† sb.

fleuri, **~e** /flœʀi/ **I** *pp* ▶ **fleurir**.

II *pp adj* **1** [*garden*] full of flowers; [*tree*] in blossom; in bloom; **2** [*table*] decorated with flowers; **3** [*wallpaper*] flowery.

fleurir /flœʀiʀ/ [3] **I** *vtr* to decorate [sth] with flowers [*house, table*].

II *vi* **1** [*rose bush*] to flower; [*cherry tree*] to blossom; **2** [*new buildings*] to spring up; [*posters*] to appear; **3** to thrive, to flourish.

fleuriste /flœʀist/ *nmf* **1** florist; **2** flower shop, florist's.

fleuron /flœʀɔ̃/ *nm* jewel (in the crown).

fleuve /flœv/ **I** *nm* river.

II (-)fleuve (*combining form*) interminable.

flexible /flɛksibl/ *adj* **1** [*blade, tube*] flexible; [*body*] supple; **2** [*person, timetable*] flexible; **3** [*person*] malleable.

flexion /flɛksjɔ̃/ *nf* (of object) bending; (of arm, leg) flexing.

flibustier /flibystje/ *nm* **1** (pirate) freebooter; **2** swindler.

flic° /flik/ *nm* cop°, policeman.

flipper[1] /flipœʀ/ *nm* (Games) **1** pinball machine; **2** (device in machine) flipper; **3** (game) pinball.

flipper[2]° /flipe/ [1] *vi* **1** to freak out°; **2** to be depressed.

flirter /flœʀte/ [1] *vi* to flirt.

flocon /flɔkɔ̃/ *nm* (of snow) flake; (of dust) speck; (of wool) bit; **~s d'avoine** oat flakes (GB), oatmeal (US); **~s de pomme de terre** instant mashed potato mix.

flop° /flɔp/ *nm* flop.

flopée° /flɔpe/ *nf* **(toute) une ~ de gamins** masses of kids.

floraison /flɔʀɛzɔ̃/ *nf* flowering.

floral, **~e**, *mpl* **-aux** /flɔʀal, o/ *adj* floral.

flore /flɔʀ/ *nf* flora.

florilège /flɔʀilɛʒ/ *nm* anthology.

florin /flɔʀɛ̃/ *nm* (unit of Dutch currency) guilder.

florissant, **~e** /flɔʀisɑ̃, ɑ̃t/ *adj* **1** [*activity*] thriving; [*theatre*] fashionable; **2** [*complexion*] ruddy.

flot /flo/ **I** *nm* **1** (of letters, refugees) flood; (of questions, visitors) stream; (of criticism) torrent; **2** (literary) tide; **les ~s** (literary) the billows (literary).
II à flot *phr* **couler à ~(s)** to flow.

flottant, **~e** /flɔtɑ̃, ɑ̃t/ *adj* [*wood, line*] floating; [*clothes, hair*] flowing.

flotte /flɔt/ *nf* **1** fleet; **2**° rain; **3**° water.

flottement /flɔtmɑ̃/ *nm* **1** wavering; **2** (of currency) floating.

flotter /flɔte/ [1] **I** *vi* **1** to float; **~ à la dérive** to drift; **2** [*mist*] to drift; [*flag*] to fly; **~ au vent** to flutter in the wind, to stream in the wind; **elle flotte dans ses vêtements** her clothes are hanging off her; **3** [*currency*] to float.
II° *v impers* to rain.

flotteur /flɔtœʀ/ *nm* **1** (on fishing line, net, hydroplane) float; **2** (of toilet) ballcock.

flou, **~e** /flu/ **I** *adj* **1** [*outline*] blurred; **2** (figurative) vague, hazy.
II *nm* **1** (of photograph, shape, outline) fuzziness; **2** (figurative) vagueness.
■ **~ artistique** soft focus; (figurative) artistry.

fluctuant, **~e** /flyktɥɑ̃, ɑ̃t/ *adj* [*prices, opinions*] fluctuating; [*person*] fickle.

fluet, **-ette** /flyɛ, ɛt/ *adj* [*body, person*] slight; [*arm*] frail; [*voice*] thin, reedy.

fluide /flɥid/ **I** *adj* **1** [*oil, paint*] fluid; **2** [*style*] fluent; [*traffic*] moving freely.
II *nm* **1** (in physics) fluid; **2** (of clairvoyant) (psychic) powers.

fluidité /flɥidite/ *nf* **1** (in physics) fluidity; **2** (of style, diction) fluency.

fluo° /flyo/ *adj inv* fluorescent.

fluor /flyɔʀ/ *nm* fluorine; **dentifrice au ~** fluoride toothpaste.

fluorescent, **~e** /flyɔʀɛsɑ̃, ɑ̃t/ *adj* fluorescent.

flûte /flyt/ **I** *nf* **1** (Mus) flute; **petite ~** piccolo; **2** (champagne) flute; **3** French stick.
II° *excl* damn°!, darn it°!
■ **~ à bec** recorder; **~ de Pan** panpipes; **~ traversière** (transverse) flute.

flûtiste /flytist/ *nmf* flautist, flutist (US).

fluvial, **~e**, *mpl* **-iaux** /flyvjal, o/ *adj* fluvial, river.

flux /fly/ *nm inv* **1** flow; **2** (in physics) flux; **3** (Econ) flow; **4** flood tide; **le ~ et le reflux** flood tide and ebb tide; (figurative) the ebb and flow; **5** influx.

FMI /ɛfɛmi/ *nm*: *abbr* ▸ **fonds**.

foc /fɔk/ *nm* jib.

focal, **~e**, *mpl* **-aux** /fɔkal, o/ *adj* focal.

focaliser /fɔkalize/ [1] *vtr* to focus [*rays*]; to focalize [*electron beam*].

fœtus /fetys/ *nm inv* foetus.

fofolle ▸ **foufou**.

foi /fwa/ *nf* **1** faith; **avoir la ~** to be a believer; **2 ma ~ oui** well yes; **en toute bonne ~ je crois que** in all sincerity, I believe that; **je crois qu'il est de bonne ~** I think he is genuine; **il est de mauvaise ~** he doesn't mean a word of it; **3 sur la ~ de témoins** on the evidence of witnesses; **qui fait** or **faisant ~** [*text, signature*] authentic; **sous la ~ du serment** under oath.
IDIOMS **sans ~ ni loi** fearing neither God nor man.

foie /fwa/ *nm* liver; **crise de ~** indigestion; **~ gras** foie gras.

foin /fwɛ̃/ *nm* hay; **tas de ~** haystack; **la saison des ~s** the haymaking season.

foire /fwaʀ/ *nf* **1** fair; **~ du livre** book fair; **2** fun fair; **3**° bedlam; **faire la ~**° to live it up°; ▸ **larron**.

fois /fwa/ **I** *nf inv* **1** (with numerals) **une ~** once; **deux ~** twice; **trois ~** three times; **quatre ~ trois font douze** four times three is twelve; **l'autre ~** last time; **tant de ~** so many times; **une (bonne) ~ pour toutes** once and for all; **une ~ sur deux** half the time; **une ~ sur trois** every third time; **deux ~ sur cinq** two times out of five; **pour une ~** for once; **une ~ encore** once more; **toutes les ~ que** every time (that); **deux ~ plus petit** half as big; **c'est dix ~ trop lourd!** it's far too heavy!; **régler en trois ~** to pay in three instalments[GB]; **2** (with ordinals) time; **pour la énième ~** for the hundredth time; **la première ~ que je vous ai parlé** when I first talked to you.
II à la fois *phr* **deux à la ~** two at a time; **porter trois valises à la ~** to carry three suitcases at the same time; **elle est à la ~ intelligente et travailleuse** she's both clever and hardworking.
III des fois° *phr* sometimes; **tu n'as pas vu mon chien, des ~?** you wouldn't have seen my dog, by any chance?
IV des fois que° *phr* in case.
IDIOMS **il était une ~** once upon a time there was.

foisonner /fwazɔne/ [1] *vi* **1** to abound; **2 ~ de** or **en** to have an abundance of.

fol ▸ **fou** I.

folâtrer /fɔlɑtʀe/ [1] *vi* [*person*] to romp about; [*animal*] to frisk.

folichon°, **-onne** /fɔliʃɔ̃, ɔn/ *adj* **ne pas être ~** to be far from brilliant.

folie /fɔli/ *nf* **1** madness; **aimer qn/qch à la ~** to be mad (GB) or crazy about sb/sth; **2** act of folly; **elle a fait une ~ en acceptant** she was mad to accept; **3** extravagance.
■ **~ douce** sheer madness; **~ des grandeurs** delusions of grandeur.

folk /fɔlk/ *nm* folk music.

folklo° /fɔlklo/ *adj* eccentric, crazy°; **ça va être ~!** it'll be some laugh°!

folklore /fɔlklɔʀ/ *nm* **1** folklore; **2**° razzmatazz°.

folklorique /fɔlklɔʀik/ *adj* **1** [*music*] folk; [*costume*] traditional; **2**° eccentric.

folle ▶ **fou** I, II.

follement /fɔlmɑ̃/ *adv* **s'amuser ~** to have a terrific time; **un spectacle ~ drôle** a terribly funny show.

follet /fɔlɛ/ *adj m* **feu ~** will-o'-the-wisp.

fomenter /fɔmɑ̃te/ [1] *vtr* to instigate.

foncé, **~e** /fɔ̃se/ **I** *pp* ▶ **foncer**.
II *pp adj* [*colour*] dark; [*pink, mauve*] deep.

foncer /fɔ̃se/ [12] **I** *vtr* **1** to make [sth] darker or deeper [*colour*]; **2** to line.
II *vi* **1**° [*person, vehicle*] to tear along°; **fonce!** get a move on°!; **2**° **~ vers/dans** to rush toward(s)/into; **~ sur qch/vers la sortie** to make a dash for sth/for the exit; **~ sur qn** to charge at sb; **~ tête baissée dans la bagarre** to rush headlong into the fray; **~ à New York** to dash over to New York; **il n'est pas du genre à ~** he's not the type to rush into things; **fonce!** go for it°!; **3** [*colour*] (gen) to darken; [*pink, mauve*] to deepen; [*fabric*] to go darker.

fonceur°, **-euse** /fɔ̃sœʀ, øz/ *nm,f* go-getter°.

foncier, **-ière** /fɔ̃sje, ɛʀ/ *adj* [*income*] from land; **impôt ~** property tax.

foncièrement /fɔ̃sjɛʀmɑ̃/ *adv* fundamentally.

fonction /fɔ̃ksjɔ̃/ *nf* **1** (in administration, company) post; duties; **dans l'exercice de leurs ~s** while carrying out their duties; **occuper la ~ de** to hold the position of; **quitter ses ~s** to leave one's job; **voiture de ~** company car; **occuper d'importantes ~s** to hold important office; **2 en ~ de** according to; **3** function; **avoir pour ~ de faire** to be designed to do; **faire ~ de** to serve as; **4** (in chemistry) function; **~ acide** acid function; **5** profession; **~ enseignante** teaching profession; **6** (Tech) (on machine) function; **7** (in grammar) function.
■ **~ publique** civil service.

fonctionnaire /fɔ̃ksjɔnɛʀ/ *nmf* civil servant; (higher ranking) government official.

fonctionnel, **-elle** /fɔ̃ksjɔnɛl/ *adj* functional.

fonctionnement /fɔ̃ksjɔnmɑ̃/ *nm* **1** (of institution) functioning; **2** (of machinery) working; **mauvais ~** malfunction; **en ~** in service; **en état de ~** in working order.

fonctionner /fɔ̃ksjɔne/ [1] *vi* to work; **~ à l'essence** to run on petrol (GB) or gas (US).

fond /fɔ̃/ **I** *nm* **1** (of vessel, lake, valley) bottom; (of cupboard, wardrobe) back; **vider les ~s de bouteilles** to empty out all the old bottles; **~ de la mer** seabed; **~ de l'océan** ocean floor; **toucher le ~** (in water) to touch the bottom; (figurative) to hit rock bottom; **2** (of shop, yard) back; (of corridor, room) far end; **la chambre du ~** the back bedroom; **au ~ des bois** deep in the woods; **de ~ en comble** from top to bottom; **3 les problèmes de ~** the basic problems; **un débat de ~** an in-depth debate; **au ~** or **dans le ~, le problème est simple** basically, the problem is simple; **dans le ~, tu as raison** you're right, really; **4** (of text) content; **5 regarder qn au ~ des yeux** (lovingly) to look deep into sb's eyes; (suspiciously) to give sb a searching look; **elle a un bon ~** she's very good at heart; **il a un mauvais ~** he's got a nasty streak; **6** background; **7 un ~ de porto** a drop of port; **8 il y a 20 mètres de ~** the water is 20 metres[GB] deep; **9** (Sport) **épreuve de ~** long-distance event.
II à fond *phr* **1 connaître son domaine à ~** to be an expert in one's field; **être à ~ pour**° to support wholeheartedly; **respirer à ~** to breathe deeply; **mettre la radio à ~** to turn the radio right up; **2**° **rouler à ~** to drive at top speed.
■ **~ d'artichaut** artichoke bottom; **~ de teint** foundation (GB), make-up base (US).

fondamental, **~e**, *mpl* **-aux** /fɔ̃damɑ̃tal, o/ *adj* **1** basic, fundamental; **2** essential.

fondamentalement /fɔ̃damɑ̃talmɑ̃/ *adv* **1** fundamentally; **2** radically.

fondant, **~e** /fɔ̃dɑ̃, ɑ̃t/ *adj* **1** [*ice*] melting; **2** [*pear*] which melts in the mouth.

fondateur, **-trice** /fɔ̃datœʀ, tʀis/ *nm,f* founder; **groupe ~** founding group.

fondation /fɔ̃dasjɔ̃/ **I** *nf* foundation.
II fondations *nf pl* foundations; **creuser les ~s de** to lay the foundations of.

fondé, **~e** /fɔ̃de/ **I** *pp* ▶ **fonder**.
II *pp adj* justifiable, well-founded, legitimate; **vos reproches ne sont pas ~s** your criticisms are unfounded; **non ~, mal ~** [*accusation*] groundless.
■ **~ de pouvoir** (of company) authorized representative; (of bank) senior banking executive.

fondement /fɔ̃dmɑ̃/ *nm* foundation; **être sans** or **dénué de ~** to be unfounded.

fonder /fɔ̃de/ [1] **I** *vtr* **1** to found; **2** to base; **~ ses espoirs sur** to place one's hopes in.
II se fonder *v refl* (+ *v être*) **se ~ sur** [*theory, method*] to be based on; [*person*] to go on.

fonderie /fɔ̃dʀi/ *nf* **1** foundry; **2** casting.

fondre /fɔ̃dʀ/ [6] **I** *vtr* **1** to melt down [*metal*], to smelt [*mineral*]; **2** to cast [*statue*].
II *vi* **1** [*snow, butter*] to melt; **2** [*sugar*] to dissolve; **3** [*savings*] to melt away; **4** (from illness) [*person*] to waste away; **5** (emotionally) to soften; **~ en larmes** to dissolve into tears.
III se fondre *v refl* (+ *v être*) **se ~ dans** [*person, figure*] to blend in with.

fonds /fɔ̃/ I *nm inv* **1** (in gallery, museum) collection; **2** fund.
II *nm pl* funds; **rentrer dans ses ~** to recover outlay.
■ **~ de commerce** business; **Fonds monétaire international, FMI** International Monetary Fund, IMF.

fondu, ~e[1] /fɔ̃dy/ I *pp* ▶ **fondre**.
II *pp adj* [*butter*] melted; [*metal*] molten; [*sugar*] dissolved.

fondue[2] /fɔ̃dy/ *nf* (Culin) fondue; **~ au fromage** or **savoyarde** cheese fondue; **~ bourguignonne** fondue bourguignonne (*meat dipped in hot oil*).

fontaine /fɔ̃tɛn/ *nf* **1** fountain; **2** drinking fountain; **3** spring.

fonte /fɔ̃t/ *nf* **1** cast iron; **2** melting down, smelting; **3** thawing; **~ des neiges** thaw.

fonts /fɔ̃/ *nm pl* **~ baptismaux** font.

foot○ /fut/ *nm* = **football**.

football /futbol/ *nm* football (GB), soccer.
■ **~ américain** american football (GB), football (US).

footballeur, -euse /futbolœʀ, øz/ *nm,f* football (GB) or soccer player.

footing /futiŋ/ *nm* jogging; **faire un ~** to go for a jog.

forage /fɔʀaʒ/ *nm* drilling.

forain, -aine /fɔʀɛ̃, ɛn/ I *adj* fairground.
II *nm* stallkeeper; **les ~s** fairground people.

forçat /fɔʀsa/ *nm* **1** convict; **2** galley slave.

force /fɔʀs/ I *nf* **1** strength; **~s** strength; **avoir de la ~** to be strong; **reprendre des ~s** to regain one's strength; **c'est au-dessus de mes ~s** it's too much for me; **de toutes ses ~s** with all one's might; **c'est ce qui fait leur ~** that's where their strength lies; **ils sont de ~ égale aux échecs** they are evenly matched at chess; **2** force; **de ~** by force; **faire manger de ~** to force to eat; **entrer de ~ dans un lieu** to force one's way into a place; **3 ~ de vente** sales force; **~s** (Mil) forces; **d'importantes ~s de police** large numbers of police.
II **à force**○ *phr* **à ~, elle l'a cassé** she ended up breaking it.
III **à force de** *phr* **réussir à ~ de travail** to succeed by dint of hard work; **il est aphone à ~ de crier** he's been shouting so much (that) he's lost his voice.
■ **~ de dissuasion** (Mil) deterrent force; **~ de frappe** nuclear weapons; **~ de la nature** (real) Goliath; **~s de l'ordre** forces of law and order.

forcé, ~e /fɔʀse/ I *pp* ▶ **forcer**.
II *pp adj* **1** (gen) forced; [*consequence*] inevitable; **2** [*gaiety, comparison*] forced; **3**○ **c'est ~!** there's no way around it○!; **c'est ~ qu'il/elle fasse** he's/she's bound to do.

forcément /fɔʀsemɑ̃/ *adv* inevitably; **pas ~** not necessarily; **'j'ai faim'—'~, tu n'as pas déjeuné!'** 'I'm hungry'—'well, it's hardly surprising, you had no lunch!'

forcené, ~e /fɔʀsəne/ I *adj* [*rhythm*] furious; [*activity*] frenzied.
II *nm,f* **1** maniac; **2** crazed gunman.

forcer /fɔʀse/ [12] I *vtr* **1** to force; **~ qn à qch** to force sb into sth; **2 ~ la porte de qn** to force one's way into sb's house; **3** to break through [*fence, enclosure*]; **~ le passage/l'entrée** to force one's way through/in.
II **forcer sur** *v+prep* to overdo [*wine, salt, colour*].
III *vi* **1** to overdo it; **2 serrez sans ~** do not tighten too much; **ne force pas!** don't force it!
IV **se forcer** *v refl* (+ *v être*) to force oneself; **il se force pour manger** it's a real effort for him to eat.
IDIOMS **~ la main à qn** to force sb's hand.

forer /fɔʀe/ [1] *vtr* to drill; **~ un puits** to sink a well.

forestier, -ière /fɔʀɛstje, ɛʀ/ *adj* **1** [*area*] forested; **chemin ~** forest path; **exploitation forestière** (place) forestry plantation; **2** (Culin) with mushrooms.

foret /fɔʀɛ/ *nm* drill.

forêt /fɔʀɛ/ *nf* forest; **~ tropicale** rain forest.
IDIOMS **c'est l'arbre qui cache la ~** you can't see the wood for the trees.

forfait /fɔʀfɛ/ *nm* **1** fixed rate; **~ hebdomadaire** weekly rate; **un ~ de 15 francs** a fixed price of 15 francs; **2** package; **~ avion-auto** fly-drive package; **3** pass; **~ skieur** ski pass; **4** (of player) withdrawal; **déclarer ~** to give up; (Sport) to withdraw.

forfaitaire /fɔʀfɛtɛʀ/ *adj* **prix ~** contract or all-inclusive price; **tarif ~** flat fare or fee; **somme ~** lump sum; **indemnité ~** basic allowance.

forge /fɔʀʒ/ *nf* **1** forge; **2** ironworks.

forgé, ~e /fɔʀʒe/ I *pp* ▶ **forger**.
II *pp adj* [*object, metal*] wrought.

forger /fɔʀʒe/ [13] *vtr* **1** to forge; **2** to form [*character*].

forgeron /fɔʀʒəʀɔ̃/ *nm* blacksmith.
IDIOMS **c'est en forgeant qu'on devient ~** (Proverb) practice makes perfect.

formaliser: **se formaliser** /fɔʀmalize/ [1] *v refl* (+ *v être*) to take offence[GB] (**de** to).

formalisme /fɔʀmalism/ *nm* **1** (derogatory) formality; **2** (in art, philosophy) formalism.

formalité /fɔʀmalite/ *nf* formality; **les ~s à accomplir pour obtenir un visa** the necessary procedure to obtain a visa; **par pure ~** as a matter of form.

format /fɔʀma/ *nm* format, size; **de grand/très grand ~** large/extra large.

formateur, -trice /fɔʀmatœʀ, tʀis/ *adj* formative.

formation /fɔʀmasjɔ̃/ *nf* **1** education; training; **avoir une ~ littéraire** to have an arts background; **en ~** undergoing training; **2** training course; **3** (of government, team) forming; **4** group.
■ **~ continue, ~ permanente** adult continuing education; **~ professionnelle** professional training; **~ sur le tas** on-the-job training.

forme /fɔʀm/ I *nf* **1** shape; form; **sous ~ de** in the form of; **sans ~** shapeless; **2** (of government, contract) form; (of payment) method; **3** form; **pour la ~** as a matter of form; **4** (in grammar) form; **5** form; **en ~** on form; **en pleine ~** in great shape.
II **formes** *nf pl* **1** (of person) figure; **2** (of object, building) lines; **3 faire qch dans les ~s** to do sth in the correct manner; **y mettre les ~s** to be tactful.

formé, **~e** /fɔʀme/ I *pp* ▶ **former**.
II *pp adj* **1** made up; formed; **2** educated; trained; **3** [*writing, sentence*] formed.

formel, **-elle** /fɔʀmɛl/ *adj* **1** [*refusal, denial, person*] categorical; [*promise*] definite; [*order*] strict; **être ~ sur qch** [*person*] to be definite about sth; [*law*] to be clear on sth; **2 c'est purement ~** it's just a formality.

formellement /fɔʀmɛlmɑ̃/ *adv* **1** [*deny*] categorically; [*prohibit, forbid*] strictly; **2** officially; **~ identifié** clearly identified.

former /fɔʀme/ [1] I *vtr* **1** to form [*circle, rectangle*]; **2** to form, to constitute; **formez des groupes de cinq** get into groups of five; **3** to train [*staff*]; to educate [*person, tastes*]; to develop [*intelligence*]; **4** to form [*abscess, film*].
II **se former** *v refl* (+ *v être*) **1** to form; **2** to be formed; **3** to train, to be trained (**à** in); **4** [*character, style*] to develop; [*person*] to educate oneself; **5** [*idea*] to form.

formidable /fɔʀmidabl/ *adj* **1** [*force*] tremendous; [*explosion*] enormous; **2**○ [*party, book*] great○; [*person*] marvellous[GB]; **3**○ incredible.

formol /fɔʀmɔl/ *nm* formalin.

formulaire /fɔʀmylɛʀ/ *nm* form.

formulation /fɔʀmylasjɔ̃/ *nf* **1** formulation; **2** wording.

formule /fɔʀmyl/ *nf* **1** expression; **~ toute faite** set phrase; **2** (in travel, tourism) option; **~ à 75F** (in restaurant) set menu at 75F; **3** method; **4** concept; **5** (in science) formula; **6** (of car) **~ un** Formula One; **7** (of programme, magazine) format.
■ **~ magique** magic words; (figurative) magic formula.

formuler /fɔʀmyle/ [1] *vtr* (gen) to express; to put [sth] into words [*idea*].

fort, **~e** /fɔʀ, fɔʀt/ I *adj* **1** strong; **armée ~e de 10 000 hommes** 10,000-strong army; **~ d'un chiffre d'affaires en hausse** boasting an increased turnover; **s'attaquer à plus ~ que soi** to take on someone bigger than oneself; **2** [*noise*] loud; [*light*] bright; [*heat, activity*] intense; [*cramp*] bad; [*temperature, fever, rate*] high; [*fear, anger*] deep; [*blow, jolt*] hard; [*rain*] heavy; [*spice*] hot; [*slope*] steep; [*amount, majority*] large; [*lack, shortage*] great; [*drop, increase*] sharp; [*difference*] big; **~e émigration** high level of emigration; **3** (at school subject) good (**en, à** at; **pour faire** at doing); **4** [*person*] stout; [*hips*] broad; [*bust*] large; [*thighs*] big; **5**○ **c'est un peu ~!** that's a bit much○!
II *adv* **1** extremely, very; **2** [*doubt*] very much; **avoir ~ à faire**○ to have a lot to do; **3** [*knock, hit, rub*] hard; [*squeeze*] tight; [*breathe*] deeply; [*speak*] loudly; [*feel*] strongly; **y aller un peu ~**○ to go a bit too far; **4** well; **il ne va pas très ~** he's not very well.
III *nm* **1** fort; **2** strong person.
IV **au plus fort de** *phr* **au plus ~ de l'été** at the height of summer.
■ **~ en thème**○ (Sch) swot○ (GB), grind○ (US); **~e tête** rebel.
IDIOMS **c'est plus ~ que moi/qu'elle** I/she just can't help it.

fortement /fɔʀtəmɑ̃/ *adv* [*encourage, criticize*] strongly; [*rise, increase*] sharply; [*centralized, industrialized*] highly; [*shaken*] deeply; [*damaged*] badly; [*displease, dislike*] greatly; [*armed*] heavily; **il est ~ question de démolir l'usine** demolition of the factory is being seriously considered.

forteresse /fɔʀtəʀɛs/ *nf* stronghold.

fortifiant /fɔʀtifjɑ̃/ *nm* (Med) tonic.

fortification /fɔʀtifikasjɔ̃/ *nf* fortification.

fortifier /fɔʀtifje/ [2] *vtr* **1** to strengthen [*nails, hair*]; **2** [*meal*] to fortify; [*holiday, vitamins*] to do [sb] good; **3** to reinforce [*construction*].

fortuit, **~e** /fɔʀtɥi, it/ *adj* [*meeting*] accidental; [*incident, discovery*] fortuitous.

fortune /fɔʀtyn/ *nf* **1** fortune; **faire ~** to make a fortune; **2 de ~** makeshift.
IDIOMS **faire contre mauvaise ~ bon cœur** to put on a brave face.

fortuné, **~e** /fɔʀtyne/ *adj* wealthy.

fosse /fos/ *nf* **1** pit; **2** grave; **3** sandpit.
■ **~ commune** communal grave; **~ septique** septic tank.

fossé /fose/ *nm* **1** (gen) ditch; (of castle) moat; **2** (figurative) gap; rift.

fossette /fɔsɛt/ *nf* dimple.

fossile /fɔsil/ *adj, nm* fossil.

fossiliser /fɔsilize/ [1] *vtr*, **se fossiliser** *v refl* (+ *v être*) to fossilize.

fossoyeur /fɔswajœʀ/ *nm* gravedigger; (figurative) destroyer (**de** of).

fou (**fol** *before vowel or mute h*), **folle** /fu, fɔl/ I *adj* **1** mad; **devenir ~** to go mad; **un tueur ~** a crazed killer; **2** [*person, idea*] mad (GB), crazy; [*look*] wild; [*party, story*] crazy; **réaliser ses rêves les plus ~s** to see one's wildest dreams come true; **être ~ furieux**○ to be raving mad; **être ~ à lier**○ to be stark raving mad○; **entre eux c'est l'amour ~** they're madly in love; **~ de qn** crazy about sb; **3** mad, huge; **un monde ~** a huge crowd; **à une vitesse folle** at a crazy speed; **avoir un mal ~ à faire** to find it incredibly difficult to do; **c'est ~ ce que le temps passe vite!** it's amazing how time flies!; **4** [*vehicle, horse*] runaway; [*curl, lock of hair*] stray; [*rush, flight*] headlong; **avoir le ~ rire** to have a fit of the giggles.
II *nm,f* madman/madwoman; **envoyer qn chez les ~s**○ to send sb to the nuthouse○; **courir comme un ~** to run like mad; **c'est un ~ d'art contemporain** he's mad about contemporary art; **quelle bande de ~s!** what a bunch of lunatics!

III *nm* **1** fool, court jester; **2** (in chess) bishop.
IDIOMS **faire les ~s**° to fool about; **plus on est de ~s plus on rit**° the more the merrier.

foudre /fudʀ/ *nf* lightning; **coup de ~** love at first sight; **avoir le coup de ~ pour** to be really taken with.

foudroyant, ~e /fudʀwajɑ̃, ɑ̃t/ *adj* [*attack, progress*] lightning, sudden; [*success*] meteoric; [*look*] furious; [*death*] sudden.

foudroyer /fudʀwaje/ [23] *vtr* **1** to strike [*tree*]; **mort foudroyé** struck dead by lightning; **~ qn du regard** to look daggers at sb°; **2** [*bad news*] to devastate.

fouet /fwɛ/ *nm* **1** whip; **dix coups de ~** ten lashes of the whip; **le grand air m'a donné un coup de ~** the fresh air invigorated me; **se heurter de plein ~** to collide head-on; **2** (Culin) whisk; **~ mécanique** hand whisk.

fouetter /fwɛte/ [1] *vtr* **1** to whip, to flog [*person*]; to whip [*animal*]; **2 la pluie leur fouettait le visage** the rain lashed their faces; **3** (Culin) to whisk (GB), to beat (US).
IDIOMS **il n'y a pas de quoi ~ un chat**° it's no big deal°; **avoir d'autres chats à ~**° to have other fish to fry.

foufou°, **fofolle** /fufu, fɔfɔl/ *adj* scatter-brained.

fougère /fuʒɛʀ/ *nf* **1** fern; **2** bracken.

fougue /fug/ *nf* enthusiasm.

fougueux, -euse /fugø, øz/ *adj* spirited, enthusiastic.

fouille /fuj/ *nf* **1** (of place, person, baggage) search; **2** excavation.

fouillé, ~e /fuje/ **I** *pp* ▶ **fouiller**.
II *pp adj* [*study, portrait, piece of work*] detailed; [*style*] elaborate.

fouiller /fuje/ [1] **I** *vtr* **1** to search; to frisk; **2** to dig [*site*].
II *vi* **~ dans** (gen) to rummage through; to search [*memory*]; to delve into [*past*].

fouillis /fuji/ *nm inv* mess; jumble.

fouine /fwin/ *nf* **1** (Zool) stone marten; **2** snooper.

fouiner /fwine/ [1] *vi* **1** to forage about; **2 ~ dans** to rummage through [*objects, papers*]; to poke one's nose into [*life, past*].

fouineur, -euse /fwinœʀ, øz/ *adj* inquisitive.

foulard /fulaʀ/ *nm* scarf, headscarf.

foule /ful/ *nf* **1** crowd; mob; **il y avait ~ à la réunion** there were masses of people at the meeting; **attirer les ~s** to be a crowd-puller; **venir en ~ à** to flock to; **2** mass.

foulée /fule/ *nf* (of horse, athlete) stride; **courir dans la ~ de qn** (Sport) to tail sb; **dans la ~ de leurs prédécesseurs** (figurative) in the wake of their predecessors; **dans la ~ il a...** while he was at it, he...

fouler /fule/ [1] **I** *vtr* to tread [*grapes*].
II se fouler *v refl* (+ *v être*) **1** (Med) **se ~ le poignet** to sprain one's wrist; **2**° to strain oneself; **tu ne t'es pas foulé** you didn't kill yourself°.

foulure /fulyʀ/ *nf* sprain; **une ~ du poignet** a sprained wrist.

four /fuʀ/ *nm* **1** oven; **cuire au ~** to roast, to bake; **2** furnace; kiln.
■ **~ à chaleur tournante** fan(-assisted) oven; **~ crématoire** crematory (furnace); **~ à micro-ondes** microwave oven.
IDIOMS **il fait noir comme dans un ~** it's pitch dark in here.

fourbi° /fuʀbi/ *nm* **1** gear°; **2** shambles°.

fourbu, ~e /fuʀby/ *adj* exhausted.

fourche /fuʀʃ/ *nf* fork; **faire une ~** to fork.

fourcher /fuʀʃe/ [1] *vi* **ma langue a fourché** it was a slip of the tongue.

fourchette /fuʀʃɛt/ *nf* **1** fork; **2** (of prices, temperature) range; (of income) bracket; **~ horaire** period.
IDIOMS **avoir un bon coup de ~**° to have a hearty appetite.

fourchu, ~e /fuʀʃy/ *adj* [*branch*] forked; **cheveux ~s** split ends.

fourgon /fuʀgɔ̃/ *nm* **1** van; **2** (of train) goods wagon (GB), freight car (US).
■ **~ à bestiaux** cattle truck; **~ cellulaire** police van (GB), patrol wagon (US).

fourgonnette /fuʀgɔnɛt/ *nf* (small) van.

fourmi /fuʀmi/ *nf* (Zool) ant; **travail de ~** laborious task.
IDIOMS **avoir des ~s dans les jambes** to have pins and needles in one's legs.

fourmilier /fuʀmilje/ *nm* anteater.

fourmilière /fuʀmiljɛʀ/ *nf* **1** ant hill; **2** hive of activity.

fourmillement /fuʀmijmɑ̃/ *nm* **1 un ~ de gens** a mass of people; **2** tingling sensation.

fourmiller /fuʀmije/ [1] **I fourmiller de** *v+prep* to be chock-full of [*mistakes*]; to be swarming with [*visitors*]; to be teeming with [*animals*].
II *vi* to abound (**dans** in).

fournaise /fuʀnɛz/ *nf* blaze; **la ville est une ~ en été** the town is baking hot in summer.

fourneau, *pl* **~x** /fuʀno/ *nm* **1** (Tech) furnace; **2** stove.

fournée /fuʀne/ *nf* batch.

fourni, ~e /fuʀni/ **I** *pp* ▶ **fournir**.
II *pp adj* [*beard*] bushy; [*hair*] thick; [*grass*] lush; [*timetable*] busy.

fournir /fuʀniʀ/ [3] **I** *vtr* to supply [*document, equipment*]; to provide [*energy*]; to contribute [*effort*]; to produce [*proof*]; **~ qn en** to supply sb with [*goods*].
II se fournir *v refl* (+ *v être*) **se ~ chez** or **auprès de** to get [sth] from.

fournisseur, -euse /fuʀnisœʀ, øz/ **I** *adj* **pays ~** exporting country.
II *nm* supplier; **premier ~ de** largest supplier of; **~ de drogue** drug dealer.

fourniture /fuʀnityʀ/ *nf* **1** supply, provision (**de** of); **2 ~s** equipment; **~s scolaires/de bureau** school/office stationery; **~s de laboratoire** laboratory equipment.

fourrage /fuʀaʒ/ *nm* forage; **~ sec** fodder; **~ ensilé** silage.

fourré, ~e /fuʀe/ **I** *pp* ▶ **fourrer**.
II *pp adj* **1** (Culin) filled (**à** with); **2** fur-lined;

lined (**de, en** with); **3**° **toujours ~ au café** always hanging about at the café; **où étais-tu ~?** where have you been hiding?
III *nm* thicket.

fourrer /fuʀe/ [1] **I** *vtr* **1**° to stick°; **~ qch dans la tête de qn** to put sth into sb's head; **2** (Culin) to fill (**avec, de** with); **3** to line [*garment*] (**avec, de** with).
II se fourrer° *v refl* (+ *v être*) **1 se ~ dans un coin** to get into a corner; **aller se ~ dans** [*object*] to get stuck in; **2 se ~ une idée dans la tête** to get an idea into one's head.

fourre-tout /fuʀtu/ *adj inv* **sac ~** holdall (GB), carryall (US).

fourrière /fuʀjɛʀ/ *nf* pound; **mettre une voiture à la ~** to impound a car.

fourrure /fuʀyʀ/ *nf* fur, coat; **~ polaire** fleece.

foutre◑ /futʀ/ [6] **I** *vtr* **1 qu'est-ce que ça peut leur ~?** what the hell° has it got to do with them?; **n'en avoir rien à ~** not to give a damn°; **2 ~ qch quelque part** to stick° sth somewhere.
II se foutre *v refl* (+ *v être*) **1 il ne s'est pas foutu de toi!** he's been very generous!; **se ~ du monde** to have a bloody (GB) or hell of a◑ (US) nerve; **2** not to give a damn° (**de** about).
IDIOMS **~ le camp** to bugger off° (GB), to split° (US).

foutu◑, **~e** /futy/ **I** *pp* ▶ **foutre**.
II *pp adj* **1** (*before n*) bloody awful◑ (GB), damned (US); **2 être ~** [*person, garment*] to have had it°; [*machine*] to be knackered◑ (GB), to be shot° (US); **3 être mal ~** to be unattractive; to feel lousy°; **4 être ~ de faire** to be totally capable of doing.

fox-terrier, *pl* **~s** /fɔkstɛʀje/ *nm* fox terrier.

foyer /fwaje/ *nm* **1** home; **fonder un ~** to get married; **2** household; **3** hostel (**de, pour** for); **4** club; **5** hearth; **6** (of resistance) pocket; (of intrigue) hotbed; **un ~ d'incendie** a fire; **7** (of rebellion) seat; (of epidemic) source; **8** (in optics) focus; **lunettes à double ~** bifocals.

fracas /fʀaka/ *nm inv* (of falling object) crash; (of waves) roar; (of town, battle) din.

fracassant, **~e** /fʀakasɑ̃, ɑ̃t/ *adj* [*noise*] deafening; [*news*] sensational; [*success*] stunning.

fracasser /fʀakase/ [1] **I** *vtr* to smash [*shop window, skull*].
II se fracasser *v refl* (+ *v être*) to crash (**contre, sur** against).

fraction /fʀaksjɔ̃/ *nf* **1** (in mathematics) fraction; **2** (of sum of money) part; (of company) section; (of electorate) proportion; **en une ~ de seconde** in a split second.

fractionner /fʀaksjɔne/ [1] *vtr* to divide up [*work, group*]; to split [*party*]; to stagger [*deliveries*]; to spread [*payments*].

fracture /fʀaktyʀ/ *nf* fracture; **~ du poignet** fractured wrist.

fracturer /fʀaktyʀe/ [1] **I** *vtr* **1** to fracture [*bone*]; **2** to break down [*door*]; to break [*window*]; to force [*safe*].
II se fracturer *v refl* (+ *v être*) **se ~ la cheville** to break one's ankle.

fragile /fʀaʒil/ *adj* **1** fragile; **2** [*person*] frail; [*eye*] sensitive; [*heart*] weak.

fragiliser /fʀaʒilize/ [1] *vtr* to weaken.

fragilité /fʀaʒilite/ *nf* **1** fragility; **2** (Med) (of person) frailty.

fragment /fʀagmɑ̃/ *nm* **1** (of cup, bone) fragment; **2** (of book, novel) passage.

fragmentaire /fʀagmɑ̃tɛʀ/ *adj* [*knowledge*] patchy; [*view*] incomplete.

fragmentation /fʀagmɑ̃tasjɔ̃/ *nf* **1** (figurative) division; splitting up; **2** (of rock) fragmentation.

fragmenter /fʀagmɑ̃te/ [1] *vtr* to break up [*substance*]; to divide up [*work*].

fraîche ▶ **frais** I, V.

fraîchement /fʀɛʃmɑ̃/ *adv* **1** freshly, newly; **2** coldly; **elle a été ~ accueillie** she was given a cool reception.

fraîcheur /fʀɛʃœʀ/ *nf* **1** coolness; coldness; **la ~ du soir** the cold evening air; **2** freshness.

frais, **fraîche** /fʀɛ, fʀɛʃ/ **I** *adj* **1** cool; cold; **'servir ~'** 'serve chilled'; **il fait ~ ce matin** it's cool this morning; (colder) it's chilly this morning; **2** [*news, snow*] fresh; [*paint*] wet; **de fraîche date** recent; **3** [*complexion, face*] fresh; **4** [*troops, horses*] fresh; **de l'argent ~** more money.
II *adv* **il fait ~** it's cool.
III *nm* **prendre le ~** to get some fresh air; **mettre au ~** to put in a cool place; to put to cool.
IV *nm pl* **1** expenses; **aux ~ de l'entreprise** paid for by the company; **faire des ~** to spend a lot of money; **rentrer dans ses ~** to cover one's expenses; **faire les ~ de qch** to bear the brunt of sth; **2** fees; **3** (in bookkeeping) costs.
V à la fraîche *phr* in the cool of the morning; in the cool of the evening.
■ **~ d'annulation** cancellation fees; **~ de déplacement** (of employee) travel expenses; (for repairman) call-out charge; **~ d'expédition** (for parcel) postage and packing; (for goods) freight; **~ d'inscription** (gen) registration fees; (for school) school fees (GB), tuition fees (US); (at university) tuition fees, academic fees (GB); **~ de port** postage.
IDIOMS **être ~ comme une rose** to be as fresh as a daisy.

fraise /fʀɛz/ *nf* **1** strawberry; **~ des bois** wild strawberry; **2** (tool, instrument) reamer; milling-cutter; (of dentist) drill.
IDIOMS **ramener sa ~**° to stick one's nose in°.

fraiseur, **-euse** /fʀɛzœʀ, øz/ *nm,f* (worker) cutter.

fraisier /fʀɛzje/ *nm* **1** strawberry plant; **2** strawberry gateau.

framboise /fʀɑ̃bwaz/ *nf* **1** raspberry; **2** raspberry liqueur.

framboisier /fʀɑ̃bwazje/ *nm* raspberry cane; raspberry bush.

franc[1], **franche** /fʀɑ̃, fʀɑ̃ʃ/ **I** *adj* **1** [*person*] frank, straight; [*reply*] straight; [*laughter, expression*] open, honest; **jouer ~ jeu** to play fair; **2** duty-free; **~ de port** postage paid.

II *adv* **parler ~** to be perfectly frank.
III *nm* (unit of currency) franc; **~ lourd** new franc.

franc², franque /fʀɑ̃, fʀɑ̃k/ *adj* Frankish.

Franc, Franque /fʀɑ̃, fʀɑ̃k/ *nm,f* (in history) Frank.

français, ~e /fʀɑ̃sɛ, ɛz/ **I** *adj* French; **à la ~e** French-style.
II *nm* French.

Français, ~e /fʀɑ̃sɛ, ɛz/ *nm,f* Frenchman/ Frenchwoman.

France /fʀɑ̃s/ *pr nf* France.

franche ▸ franc¹ I.

franchement /fʀɑ̃ʃmɑ̃/ *adv* **1** frankly, candidly; **je lui ai demandé ~** I asked him straight out; **2** [*lean*] firmly; [*enter*] boldly; **3** really; **il m'a franchement agacé** he really annoyed me; **4** (in exasperation) **~!** really!, honestly!

franchir /fʀɑ̃ʃiʀ/ [3] *vtr* to cross [*line*]; to get over [*fence*]; to cover [*distance*].

franchise /fʀɑ̃ʃiz/ *nf* **1** frankness, sincerity; **2** exemption; **3** (in insurance) excess (GB), deductible (US); **4** (granted to commercial distributor) franchise. ■ **~ de bagages** baggage allowance; **~ postale** (on envelope) 'postage paid'.

franc-jeu /fʀɑ̃ʒø/ *nm* fair play.

franc-maçon, -onne, *pl* **francs-maçons, franc-maçonnes** /fʀɑ̃masɔ̃, ɔn/ **I** *adj* Masonic.
II *nm,f* Freemason.

franc-maçonnerie, *pl* **~s** /fʀɑ̃masɔnʀi/ *nf* **la ~** Freemasonry.

franco /fʀɑ̃ko/ *adv* **1 ~ de port** postage paid, carriage paid; **2**○ **y aller ~** to go right ahead; (when explaining) to go straight to the point.

francophone /fʀɑ̃kɔfɔn/ **I** *adj* French-speaking; **littérature ~** literature in the French language.
II *nmf* French speaker.

franc-parler /fʀɑ̃paʀle/ *nm* **avoir son ~** to speak one's mind.

franc-tireur, *pl* **francs-tireurs** /fʀɑ̃tiʀœʀ/ *nm* sniper.

frange /fʀɑ̃ʒ/ *nf* **1** (on rug, curtain, garment) fringe; **2** (hair) fringe (GB), bangs (US).

frangin○ /fʀɑ̃ʒɛ̃/ *nm* brother.

frangine○ /fʀɑ̃ʒin/ *nf* sister.

franglais /fʀɑ̃glɛ/ *nm* Franglais.

franque ▸ franc².

franquette○: **à la bonne franquette** /alabɔnfʀɑ̃kɛt/ *phr* **recevoir qn à la bonne ~** to have sb over for an informal meal.

frappé, ~e /fʀape/ **I** *pp* **▸ frapper**.
II *pp adj* [*champagne*] chilled; [*cocktail*] frappé; [*coffee*] iced.

frapper /fʀape/ [1] **I** *vtr* **1** (gen) to hit, to strike; **~ le sol du pied** to stamp one's foot; **~ à coups de pied** to kick; **~ à coups de poing** to punch; **~ un grand coup** (gen) to hit hard; (on door) to knock; **2** to strike [*coin*]; **3** [*unemployment, epidemic*] to hit [*region, population*]; **les taxes qui frappent les produits français** duties imposed on French goods; **4** to strike; **j'ai été frappé de voir que...** I was amazed to see that...
II *vi* **1** to hit, to strike; **~ dans ses mains** to clap one's hands; **2** to knock (**à** on, at); **on a frappé** there was a knock at the door; **3** to strike; **les gangsters ont encore frappé**○ the gangsters have struck again.

frasque /fʀask/ *nf* escapade; **faire des ~s** to get up to mischief.

fraternel, -elle /fʀatɛʀnɛl/ *adj* fraternal, brotherly.

fraterniser /fʀatɛʀnize/ [1] *vi* to fraternize (**avec** with).

fraternité /fʀatɛʀnite/ *nf* fraternity, brotherhood.

fraude /fʀod/ *nf* **1** (Law) fraud; **~ fiscale** tax fraud; **~ électorale** vote or election rigging; **entrer** or **passer en ~** [*person*] to enter illegally; **2** (in school) cheating.

frauder /fʀode/ [1] *vi* (on public transport) to travel without a ticket; (in cinema) to slip in without paying.

fraudeur, -euse /fʀodœʀ, øz/ *nm,f* **1** swindler; **2** tax evader; **3** (in exam) cheat.

frauduleux, -euse /fʀodylø, øz/ *adj* fraudulent.

frayer /fʀɛje/ [21] **I** *vtr* **~ un passage à qn à travers la foule** to clear a path for sb through the crowd; **~ le chemin** or **la voie à qch** (figurative) to pave the way for sth.
II **se frayer** *v refl* (+ *v être*) **se ~ un chemin dans** or **à travers** to make one's way through.

frayeur /fʀɛjœʀ/ *nf* **1** fear; **2** fright.

fredonner /fʀədɔne/ [1] *vtr* to hum.

freezer /fʀizœʀ/ *nm* icebox.

frégate /fʀegat/ *nf* **1** (Naut) frigate; **2** (Zool) frigate bird.

frein /fʀɛ̃/ *nm* brake; **donner un coup de ~** to slam on the brakes; **mettre un ~ à** to curb.
IDIOMS **ronger son ~** to champ at the bit.

freiner /fʀɛne/ [1] **I** *vtr* **1** to slow down [*vehicle, parachute*]; **2** to impede [*person, advance, enemy*]; **3** to curb [*inflation, consumption*].
II *vi* **1** to brake; **~ à bloc** or **à fond** to slam on the brakes; **2** (in skiing, iceskating) to slow down.

frelaté, ~e /fʀəlate/ *adj* [*alcohol*] adulterated; [*taste*] unnatural.

frêle /fʀɛl/ *adj* frail.

frelon /fʀəlɔ̃/ *nm* hornet.

frémir /fʀemiʀ/ [3] *vi* **1** [*leaf*] to quiver; [*water*] to ripple; **2** (with emotion) [*lip*] to tremble; [*person*] to quiver (**de** with); to shudder (**de** with); **3** (Culin) to start to come to the boil.

frémissement /fʀemismɑ̃/ *nm* **1** quiver, tremor; **2** (with emotion) (of lip, hand) trembling; (of person, hand) quiver, shudder.

frêne /fʀɛn/ *nm* ash (tree).

frénésie /fʀenezi/ *nf* frenzy; **avec ~** [*struggle*] frantically; [*applaud*] wildly.

frénétique /fʀenetik/ *adj* [*struggle, activity*] frenzied; [*player*] frenetic.

frénétiquement /fʀenetikmɑ̃/ *adv* frantically, frenziedly, wildly.

fréquemment /fʀekamɑ̃/ *adv* frequently.

fréquence /fʀekɑ̃s/ *nf* frequency.

fréquent, **~e** /fʀekɑ̃, ɑ̃t/ *adj* **1** frequent; **2** common.

fréquentable /fʀekɑ̃tabl/ *adj* respectable.

fréquentation /fʀekɑ̃tasjɔ̃/ *nf* **1** company; **c'est une mauvaise ~ pour toi** that's not the sort of person you should associate with; **2 ~ des théâtres** theatregoing[GB].

fréquenté, **~e** /fʀekɑ̃te/ **I** *pp* ▶ **fréquenter**.
II *pp adj* popular, busy; **lieu bien ~** place that attracts the right sort of people.

fréquenter /fʀekɑ̃te/ [1] **I** *vtr* **1** to associate with [*person*]; to move in [*milieu*]; **2** to attend [*school, classes*]; to visit [*museum*]; to go to [*restaurant*]; to frequent [*clubs*].
II se fréquenter *v refl* (+ *v être*) [*friends*] to see one another.

frère /fʀɛʀ/ *nm* brother.

fresque /fʀɛsk/ *nf* **1** fresco; **2** panorama.

fret /fʀɛt/ *nm* freight.

frétillement /fʀetijmɑ̃/ *nm* wriggling, wagging.

frétiller /fʀetije/ [1] *vi* [*fish*] to wriggle; **~ de la queue** [*dog*] to wag its tail.

fretin /fʀətɛ̃/ *nm* **(menu) ~** small fry.

friable /fʀijabl/ *adj* [*rock, biscuit*] crumbly.

friand, **~e** /fʀijɑ̃, ɑ̃d/ **I** *adj* **être ~ de qch** to be very fond of sth.
II *nm* (Culin) puff; **~ au fromage** cheese puff.

friandise /fʀijɑ̃diz/ *nf* **1** delicacy; **2** sweet (GB), candy (US).

fric○ /fʀik/ *nm* dough○, money; **être bourré de ~** to be loaded○.

friche /fʀiʃ/ *nf* waste land; **en ~** [*piece of land*] uncultivated, waste.

friction /fʀiksjɔ̃/ *nf* **1** (Med) rub; **2** friction.

frictionner /fʀiksjɔne/ [1] **I** *vtr* to give [sb] a rub [*person*]; to rub [*head, feet*].
II se frictionner *v refl* (+ *v être*) to rub oneself down.

frigidaire® /fʀiʒidɛʀ/ *nm* refrigerator.

frigide /fʀiʒid/ *adj* frigid.

frigo○ /fʀigo/ *nm* fridge○.

frigorifier /fʀigɔʀifje/ [2] *vtr* to freeze.

frigorifique /fʀigɔʀifik/ *adj* refrigerated.

frileux, **-euse** /fʀilø, øz/ *adj* **1** sensitive to the cold; **2** [*attitude, policy*] cautious.

frime○ /fʀim/ *nf* **1 pour la ~** for show; **2 c'est de la ~** it's all an act.

frimousse○ /fʀimus/ *nf* little face.

fringale○ /fʀɛ̃gal/ *nf* **j'ai la ~** I'm absolutely starving○.

fringuer○: **se fringuer** /fʀɛ̃ge/ [1] *v refl* (+ *v être*) to dress.

friper /fʀipe/ [1] *vtr*, **se friper** *v refl* (+ *v être*) to crease, to crumple.

fripouille○ /fʀipuj/ *nf* **1** crook○; **2 (petite) ~!** (little) monkey!

frire /fʀiʀ/ [64] *vtr, vi* to fry.

frisé, **~e**[1] /fʀize/ **I** *pp* ▶ **friser**.
II *pp adj* [*hair*] curly; [*person*] curly-haired.

frisée[2] /fʀize/ *nf* curly endive.

friser /fʀize/ [1] **I** *vtr* **1** to curl [*hair, moustache*]; **se faire ~** to have one's hair curled; **2** to border on; **cela frise les 10%** it's approaching 10%.
II *vi* to curl; [*person*] to have curly hair.

frisquet○, **-ette** /fʀiskɛ, ɛt/ *adj* chilly.

frisson /fʀisɔ̃/ *nm* **1** shiver, shudder; **j'ai des ~s** I keep shivering; **grand ~** great thrill; **2** (of leaves) rustling; (of water) rippling.

frissonner /fʀisɔne/ [1] *vi* **1** (with cold) to shiver; (with fear) to shudder; (with pleasure) to tremble; **2** (literary) [*leaves*] to tremble; **3** [*water, milk*] to simmer.

frite /fʀit/ *nf* (Culin) chip (GB), French fry (US).

friteuse /fʀitøz/ *nf* chip pan (GB), deep fat fryer (US).

friture /fʀityʀ/ *nf* **1** (Culin) frying (**à** in); **2** (for frying) fat; oil; **3** fried food; **4** (fish) **petite ~** ≈ whitebait; **5** (on radio) crackling.

frivole /fʀivɔl/ *adj* frivolous.

frivolité /fʀivɔlite/ *nf* **1** frivolousness; **2** trivial matter.

froid, **~e** /fʀwa, fʀwad/ **I** *adj* **1** (in temperature) cold; **2** [*person*] cold; [*manner*] cool; **être ~ avec qn** to be cool toward(s) sb.
II *adv* **il fait ~** it's cold.
III *nm* **1** cold; **coup de ~** chill; **prendre ~** to catch a cold; **2** coldness; **ils sont en ~ avec moi** relations between them and me are strained; **jeter un ~** to cast a chill (**dans, sur** over).
IV à froid *phr* **démarrage à ~** cold start.
IDIOMS **il fait un ~ de canard**○ it is bitterly cold; **donner ~ dans le dos** to send a shiver down the spine; **ne pas avoir ~ aux yeux** to be fearless.

froidement /fʀwadmɑ̃/ *adv* **1** coolly; **abattre ~** to shoot down in cold blood [*person*]; **2 regarder les choses ~** to look at things with a cool head.

froideur /fʀwadœʀ/ *nf* (gen) coldness; (of reception) coolness.

froisser /fʀwase/ [1] **I** *vtr* **1** to crease [*fabric*]; to crumple [*paper*]; **2** to offend, to hurt [*person*]; **3** (Med) to strain.
II se froisser *v refl* (+ *v être*) **1** to crease; **2** to be hurt (**de** by); **3** (Med) to strain.

frôler /fʀole/ [1] **I** *vtr* **1** [*person*] to brush (against); **2** [*bullet, stone, car*] to miss narrowly; to brush against [*object, wall*]; **il a frôlé la mort** he came close to dying.
II se frôler *v refl* (+ *v être*) [*people*] to brush against each other.

fromage /fʀɔmaʒ/ *nm* cheese; **~ blanc** or **frais** fromage frais; **~ maigre** low-fat cheese; **~ à tartiner** cheese spread; **~ de tête** brawn (GB), head cheese (US).

fromager /fʀɔmaʒe/ *nm* **1** cheesemaker; **2** cheese seller.

fromagerie /fʀɔmaʒʀi/ *nf* cheese shop; **(rayon) ~** cheese counter.

froment /fʀɔmɑ̃/ *nm* wheat; **farine de ~** wheat flour.

fronce /fʀɔ̃s/ *nf* gather; **jupe à ~s** gathered skirt.

froncement /fʀɔ̃smɑ̃/ *nm* **avoir un léger ~ de sourcils** to frown slightly.

froncer /fʀɔ̃se/ [12] *vtr* **1** to gather [*pleats*]; **2 ~ les sourcils** to frown.

fronde /fʀɔ̃d/ *nf* **1** (weapon) sling; **2** (toy) catapult (GB), slingshot (US); **3** revolt.

frondeur, **-euse** /fʀɔ̃dœʀ, øz/ *adj* rebellious; anti-authoritarian.

front /fʀɔ̃/ **I** *nm* **1** forehead; **2** (Mil) front; **3** façade.
II de front *phr* **ils marchaient à quatre de ~** they were walking four abreast; **mener plusieurs tâches de ~** to have several jobs on the go.
IDIOMS **avoir le ~ de faire** to have the face or effrontery to do.

frontal, **~e**, *mpl* **-aux** /fʀɔ̃tal, o/ *adj* [*attack*] frontal; [*collision*] head-on.

frontalier, **-ière** /fʀɔ̃talje, ɛʀ/ *adj* border; **travailleur ~** person who works across the border.

frontière /fʀɔ̃tjɛʀ/ *nf* **1** frontier, border; **~ naturelle** natural boundary; **hors de nos ~s** abroad; **2 ~s entre les disciplines** boundaries between disciplines.

fronton /fʀɔ̃tɔ̃/ *nm* pediment.

frottement /fʀɔtmɑ̃/ *nm* **1** rubbing; **2** (in physics, mechanics) friction.

frotter /fʀɔte/ [1] **I** *vtr* **1** to rub; **2** to scrub; to polish [*silver*].
II *vi* to rub (**sur** on; **contre** on, against).
III se frotter *v refl* (+ *v être*) **1 se ~ les yeux** to rub one's eyes; **2** to scrub oneself; **3 se ~ à** to take on [*person*].
IDIOMS **qui s'y frotte s'y pique** if you go looking for trouble, you'll find it.

frottis /fʀɔti/ *nm inv* (Med) smear.

frousse○ /fʀus/ *nf* fright; **avoir la ~** to be scared (**de** of).

fructifier /fʀyktifje/ [2] *vi* [*capital*] to yield a profit; [*business*] to flourish.

fructueux, **-euse** /fʀyktɥø, øz/ *adj* **1** [*relationship, meeting*] fruitful; [*attempt, career*] successful; [*work*] productive; **2** (financially) profitable.

frugal, **~e**, *mpl* **-aux** /fʀygal, o/ *adj* [*person, meal*] frugal.

fruit /fʀɥi/ *nm* fruit; **voulez-vous un ~?** would you like some fruit?
■ **~ confit** candied or glacé fruit; **~ de la passion** passion fruit; **~ sec** dried fruit; **~s de mer** seafood.

fruité, **~e** /fʀɥite/ *adj* [*alcohol, aroma*] fruity.

fruste /fʀyst/ *adj* unsophisticated.

frustrant, **~e** /fʀystʀɑ̃, ɑ̃t/ *adj* frustrating.

frustré, **~e** /fʀystʀe/ **I** *adj* frustrated.
II *nm,f* malcontent.

frustrer /fʀystʀe/ [1] *vtr* **1 ~ qn** to thwart sb; **2 ~ qn de qch** to deprive sb of sth; to cheat sb (out) of sth; **3** to defraud [*creditors*]; **4** (in psychoanalysis) to frustrate.

fuel /fjul/ *nm* = **fioul**.

fugace /fygas/ *adj* fleeting; [*symptom*] elusive.

fugitif, **-ive** /fyʒitif, iv/ **I** *adj* **1** [*prisoner*] escaped; **2** fleeting, elusive.
II *nm,f* fugitive.

fugue /fyg/ *nf* **1 faire une ~** to run away; **2** (Mus) fugue.

fugueur, **-euse** /fygœʀ, øz/ *nm,f* runaway (child).

fuir /fɥiʀ/ [29] **I** *vtr* **1** to flee [*country, oppression*]; to flee from [*battle*]; **2** to avoid [*discussion, person*]; to steer clear of [*problem, crowd*]; to stay out of [*sun*].
II *vi* **1** [*person*] to flee; [*animal*] to run away; **~ à toutes jambes** to run for it; **faire ~** to scare [sb] off [*person*]; **2** [*tap, gas, pen*] to leak; **3 ~ devant ses responsabilités** not to face up to one's responsibilities.

fuite /fɥit/ *nf* **1** (gen) flight; (of prisoner) escape; **prendre la ~** to flee; to escape; **~ de capitaux** outflow of capital; **2** (of information) leak; **3** (of liquid, gas) leak.

fulgurant, **~e** /fylgyʀɑ̃, ɑ̃t/ *adj* [*attack*] lightning; [*progression*] dazzling; [*imagination*] brilliant; **ses progrès ont été ~s** he/she has made terrific progress.

fulminer /fylmine/ [1] *vi* to fulminate.

fumant, **~e** /fymɑ̃, ɑ̃t/ *adj* **1** smoking, steaming; **2**○ terrific○; **faire un coup ~** to pull off a real coup (**à qn** on sb).

fumé, **~e**[1] /fyme/ **I** *pp* ▶ **fumer**.
II *pp adj* **1** (Culin) smoked; **2** [*lenses*] tinted; [*glass*] smoked.

fume-cigarette /fymsigaʀɛt/ *nm inv* cigarette holder.

fumée[2] /fyme/ *nf* **1** smoke; **~s** (from factory) fumes; **partir en ~** (figurative) to go up in smoke; **2** steam.
IDIOMS **il n'y a pas de ~ sans feu** (Proverb) there's no smoke without fire.

fumer /fyme/ [1] **I** *vtr* **1** to smoke; **2** (Culin) to smoke.
II *vi* **1** [*person, chimney*] to smoke; **2** [*soup*] to steam; [*acid*] to give off fumes.
IDIOMS **~ comme un pompier** or **sapeur** to smoke like a chimney.

fumet /fymɛ/ *nm* (Culin) (of meat) aroma; (of wine) bouquet; (of sauce) fumet.

fumeur, **-euse**[1] /fymœʀ, øz/ *nm,f* smoker; **zone non ~s** non-smoking area.

fumeux, **-euse**[2] /fymø, øz/ *adj* [*theory, ideas*] woolly (GB), wooly (US).

fumier /fymje/ *nm* manure; **tas de ~** dunghill.

fumigène /fymiʒɛn/ *adj* **grenade ~** smoke grenade.

fumiste○ /fymist/ *nm,f* **1** shirker; **2** phoney○.

fumoir /fymwaʀ/ *nm* smoking-room.

funambule /fynɑ̃byl/ *nmf* tightrope walker; **un numéro de ~(s)** a tightrope act.

funèbre /fynɛbʀ/ *adj* **1 cérémonie/service ~** funeral ceremony/service; **2** gloomy.

funérailles /fyneʀɑj/ *nf pl* funeral.

funéraire /fyneʀɛʀ/ *adj* [*ceremony*] funeral; [*monument*] funerary.

funeste /fynɛst/ *adj* [*error*] fatal; [*decision, day*] fateful; [*consequence*] dire.

funiculaire /fynikylɛʀ/ *nm* funicular.

fur: **au fur et à mesure** /ofyʀeaməzyʀ/ *phr* as one goes along; **la championne joue de mieux en mieux au ~ et à mesure des rencontres** the champion is playing better and better with each match; **le chemin se rétrécissait au ~ et à mesure qu'on avançait** the path grew progressively narrower as we went along.

furet /fyʀɛ/ *nm* ferret.

fureter /fyʀte/ [18] *vi* to rummage, to ferret around (**dans** in).

fureur /fyʀœʀ/ *nf* **1** rage, fury; **2** frenzy; **avec ~** frenziedly; **~ de vivre** lust for life; **ce sport fait ~ en ce moment** that sport is all the rage at the moment.

furibond, **~e** /fyʀibɔ̃, ɔ̃d/ *adj* furious.

furie /fyʀi/ *nf* rage, fury.

furieusement /fyʀjøzmɑ̃/ *adv* **1** furiously, violently; **2**° **j'ai ~ envie de dormir** I'm dying to go to sleep.

furieux, **-ieuse** /fyʀjø, øz/ *adj* **1** furious, angry; **être ~ contre qn** to be furious with sb; **2**° [*desire*] terrible; **3** [*battle*] intense; [*storm, torrent*] raging.

furoncle /fyʀɔ̃kl/ *nm* boil.

furtif, **-ive** /fyʀtif, iv/ *adj* **1** furtive; **marcher d'un pas ~** to creep along; **2** fleeting.

fusain /fyzɛ̃/ *nm* **1** spindle tree; **2** charcoal; **3** charcoal crayon; **4** charcoal drawing.

fuseau, *pl* **~x** /fyzo/ *nm* **1** spindle; **en ~** tapering; **2** lace bobbin; **3 ~(x) (de ski)** ski pants; **4 ~ horaire** time zone.

fusée /fyze/ *nf* **1** rocket; **2** (Aut) stub axle.
IDIOMS **partir comme une ~** to set off like a rocket.

fuselage /fyzlaʒ/ *nm* fuselage.

fuselé, **~e** /fyzle/ *adj* tapering, spindle-shaped.

fuser /fyze/ [1] *vi* to ring out; **les rires fusaient** laughter came from all sides.

fusible /fyzibl/ *nm* fuse.

fusil /fyzi/ *nm* **1** gun, shotgun; (Mil) rifle; **2** sharpening steel; **3** gas igniter.

fusilier /fyzi(l)je/ *nm* rifleman, fusilier; **~ marin** marine.

fusillade /fyzijad/ *nf* **1** gunfire; **2** shoot-out.

fusiller /fyzije/ [1] *vtr* **1** to shoot; **2**° to wreck.
IDIOMS **~ qn du regard** to look daggers at sb.

fusil-mitrailleur, *pl* **fusils-mitrailleurs** /fyzimitʀajœʀ/ *nm* light machine gun.

fusion /fyzjɔ̃/ *nf* **1** (of metal, ice) melting; **roche en ~** molten rock; **2** (in biology, physics) fusion; **3** (of companies, parties, professions) merger; (of systems, cultures) fusion (**entre** of); (of peoples) mixing (**entre** of).

fusionner /fyzjɔne/ [1] *vtr, vi* to merge.

fût /fy/ *nm* **1** cask, barrel; **2** drum.

futaie /fytɛ/ *nf* forest of tall trees.

futé, **~e** /fyte/ **I** *adj* [*person, animal*] wily, crafty; [*smile, reply*] crafty; **ce n'est pas très ~** that isn't or wasn't very clever.
II *nm,f* **(petit) ~** cunning little devil.

futile /fytil/ *adj* [*reasons*] trivial; [*person, remark*] superficial.

futilité /fytilite/ **I** *nf* superficiality.
II futilités *nf pl* **1** banalities; **2** trifles; trifling activities; **3** trivial details.

futur, **~e** /fytyʀ/ **I** *adj* future; **les ~es mères** expectant mothers; **mon ~ mari** my husband-to-be.
II *nm* future.

futuriste /fytyʀist/ *adj* **1** futuristic; **2** (in art) futurist.

fuyant, **~e** /fɥijɑ̃, ɑ̃t/ *adj* **1** [*look*] shifty; **2** [*horizon*] receding.

fuyard, **~e** /fɥijaʀ, aʀd/ *nm,f* **1** runaway; **2** deserter.

Gg

g, G /ʒe/ *nm inv* **1** g, G; **2** (*written abbr* = **gramme**) **250 g** 250 g.

gabardine /gabaʀdin/ *nf* gabardine.

gabarit /gabaʀi/ *nm* **1** (of vehicle) size; **2**○ (of person) calibre[GB]; (physical) build; **3** (Tech) template; (device) gauge[GB].

gâcher /gɑʃe/ [1] *vtr* **1** to waste [*food, talent*]; throw away [*life*]; **2** to spoil [*party*].

gâchette /gɑʃɛt/ *nf* **1** (of gun) tumbler; **2** (controversial) trigger; **avoir la ~ facile** to be trigger-happy; **3** (on lock) tumbler.

gâchis /gɑʃi/ *nm inv* **1** waste; **2** mess.

gadget /gadʒɛt/ *nm* gadget.

gadin○ /gadɛ̃/ *nm* **ramasser un ~** to fall flat on one's face.

gadoue○ /gadu/ *nf* mud.

gaélique /gaelik/ *adj, nm* Gaelic.

gaffe○ /gaf/ *nf* blunder; clanger○ (GB), blooper○ (US); **faire ~** to watch out.

gaffeur○, **-euse** /gafœʀ, øz/ *nm,f* blunderer.

gag /gag/ *nm* **1** (in film, show) gag; **2** joke.

gaga○ /gaga/ *adj inv* **1** gaga○; **2** daft○ (GB), silly.

gage /gaʒ/ **I** *nm* **1** security; **laisser sa montre en ~** to leave one's watch as security; **mettre qch en ~** to pawn sth; **être le ~ de qch** to be a guarantee of sth; **2** (Games) forfeit; **3** pledge.
II gages† *nm pl* wages; **tueur à ~s** hired killer.

gager /gaʒe/ [13] *vtr* (formal) to wager, to bet.

gageure /gaʒyʀ/ *nf* challenge.

gagnant, ~e /gaɲɑ̃, ɑ̃t/ **I** *adj* [*number, team*] winning; **jouer** or **partir ~** to be on to a winner.
II *nm,f* winner; winning horse; winning ticket.

gagne-pain /gaɲpɛ̃/ *nm inv* livelihood.

gagne-petit /gaɲpəti/ *nmf inv* low-wage earner.

gagner /gaɲe/ [1] **I** *vtr* **1** to win; **~ d'une longueur** to win by a length; **pour lui, rien n'est encore gagné** (figurative) he's not there yet, he's still got a long way to go; **c'est gagné!** we've done it!; **à tous les coups on gagne!** every one a winner!; **2** to earn; **il gagne bien sa vie** he makes a good living; **c'est toujours ça de gagné!** well, that's something anyway!; **3** to gain [*reputation, advantage, time*]; **~ de la vitesse** to gather speed; **4** to save [*time*]; **~ de la place en faisant** to make more room by doing; **5** to win [sb] over (**à** to); **6** to reach, to get to [*place*]; **7** [*blaze, disease, unrest*] to spread to [*place*]; **8** [*fear, discouragement*] to overcome; **9** to beat [sb] (**à** at); **~ qn de vitesse** to outstrip sb.
II *vi* **1** to win; **2 le film gagne à être vu en version originale** the film is best seen in the original version; **3** to gain (**en** in); **4 y ~** to come off better; **y ~ en** to gain in [*comfort*]; **5** [*sea*] to encroach (**sur** on).

gagneur, -euse /gaɲœʀ, øz/ *nm,f* winner.

gai, ~e /gɛ/ *adj* **1** [*person, humour*] happy; [*smile, expression*] cheerful; [*conversation, work*] light-hearted; **2** (ironic) **c'est ~** great!; **3** merry, tipsy.

gaiement /gɛmɑ̃/ *adv* **1** cheerfully, merrily; gaily; **2** (ironic) happily; **allons-y ~** let's get on with it.

gaieté /gete/ *nf* gaiety, cheerfulness.

gain /gɛ̃/ *nm* **1** earnings; **mes ~s au jeu** my gambling gains; **2** (on stock exchange) gain; **3** saving; **c'est un ~ de temps considérable** it saves a considerable amount of time.

gaine /gɛn/ *nf* **1** (for dagger) sheath; **2** girdle; **3** (Tech) sheathing; casing; **4** (Bot) sheath.

gainer /gene/ [1] *vtr* **1** [*dress*] to sheathe [*body*]; **2** (Tech) to sheathe.

gala /gala/ *nm* gala; **tenue de ~** evening dress.

galant, ~e /galɑ̃, ɑ̃t/ *adj* **1** gallant, gentlemanly; **2** [*rendezvous*] romantic; **en ~e compagnie** in the company of a gentleman.

galaxie /galaksi/ *nf* galaxy.

galbe /galb/ *nm* curve.

galbé, ~e /galbe/ *adj* [*column*] with entasis; [*table leg*] curved.

gale /gal/ *nf* **1** scabies; **2** (on dog, cat) mange; (on sheep) scab; **3** (Bot) scab.
IDIOMS **il est mauvais** or **méchant comme la ~**○ he's a nasty piece of work○.

galère /galɛʀ/ *nf* **1** galley; **2**○ hell○.
IDIOMS **être dans la même ~** to be in the same boat.

galérer○ /galeʀe/ [14] *vi* **1** to have a hard time; **2** to slave away.

galerie /galʀi/ *nf* **1** gallery; **2** tunnel.
■ **~ marchande** shopping arcade; **~ de toit** roof rack; **Galerie des Glaces** hall of mirrors.
IDIOMS **amuser la ~**○ to play to the gallery; **pour épater la ~**○ (in order) to impress the crowd.

galet /galɛ/ *nm* **1** pebble; **2** (Tech) roller.

galette /galɛt/ *nf* **1** round flat biscuit, cookie (US); **2** pancake.
■ **~ des Rois** Twelfth Night cake (*containing bean or lucky charm*).

galeux, -euse /galø, øz/ *adj* [*person*] with scabies; [*dog*] mangy; [*sheep*] scabby; [*tree*] covered with scab.

Galles /gal/ *pr nf pl* **le pays de ~** Wales.

gallois, ~e /galwɑ, ɑz/ **I** *adj* Welsh.
II *nm* (language) Welsh.

Gallois, ~e /galwɑ, ɑz/ *nm,f* Welshman/Welshwoman; **les ~** the Welsh.

gallon /galɔ̃/ *nm* gallon.

galoche /galɔʃ/ *nf* clog; **menton en ~** protruding chin.

galon /galɔ̃/ *nm* **1** (for trimming) braid; **2** (Mil) stripe; **prendre du ~** to be promoted.

galonné, **~e** /galɔne/ *adj* **1** trimmed with braid; **2** (Mil) [*soldier*] of officer class; [*sleeve*] displaying the insignia of rank.

galop /galo/ *nm* **1** gallop; **petit ~** canter; **grand ~** full gallop; **au ~!** gallop!; (figurative) hurry up!; **s'enfuir au (triple) ~**○ to run off double-quick; **2** (Mus) galop.

IDIOMS **chassez le naturel il revient au ~** (Proverb) what's bred in the bone will come out in the flesh.

galoper /galɔpe/ [1] *vi* **1** to gallop; **ne laisse pas ~ ton imagination** don't let your imagination run away with you; **2**○ [*child*] to charge (around).

galopin /galɔpɛ̃/ *nm* (little) rascal.

gamba /gɑ̃ba, *pl* as/ *nf* large (Mediterranean) prawn.

gambader /gɑ̃bade/ [1] *vi* to gambol.

gamelle /gamɛl/ *nf* (of soldier) dixie (GB), mess kit; (of camper) billycan (GB), tin dish; (of worker) lunchbox; (for pet) dish.

IDIOMS **prendre une ~**○ to fall flat on one's face○; (figurative) to come a cropper.

gamin, **~e** /gamɛ̃, in/ **I** *adj* [*air, look*] youthful; [*attitude*] childish.

II *nm,f* kid○; **~ des rues** street urchin.

gamme /gam/ *nf* **1** (Mus) scale; **2** range; **produit (de) bas de ~** low quality product; cheap product; **viser le haut de ~** to aim at the top end of the market.

gammée /game/ *adj f* **croix ~** swastika.

ganglion /gɑ̃glijɔ̃/ *nm* ganglion; **avoir des ~s**○ to have swollen glands.

gangrène /gɑ̃gʀɛn/ *nf* **1** (Med) gangrene; **2** (figurative) canker.

gangrener /gɑ̃gʀəne/ [16] **I** *vtr* to corrupt [*country, society*].

II se gangrener *v refl* (+ *v être*) **1** (Med) to become gangrenous; **2** (figurative) to become corrupt.

gangster /gɑ̃gstɛʀ/ *nm* **1** gangster; **2** swindler.

gant /gɑ̃/ *nm* glove.

■ **~ de boxe** boxing glove; **~ de crin** massage glove; **~ de ménage** rubber glove; **~ de toilette** ≈ (face) flannel (GB), wash cloth (US).

IDIOMS **son tailleur lui va comme un ~** her suit fits her like a glove; **mettre** or **prendre des ~s avec qn** to handle sb with kid gloves; **jeter/relever le ~** to throw down/to take up the gauntlet; ▶ **velours**.

ganté, **~e** /gɑ̃te/ *adj* [*hand*] gloved; [*person*] wearing gloves.

garage /gaʀaʒ/ *nm* **1** garage; **2** garage, filling station.

■ **~ à vélos** bicycle shed; bicycle storage area.

garagiste /gaʀaʒist/ *nmf* **1** garage owner; **2** car mechanic.

garant, **~e** /gaʀɑ̃, ɑ̃t/ **I** *adj* **être** or **se porter ~ de qch/qn** to vouch for sth/sb.

II *nm,f* guarantor.

III *nm* guarantee.

garanti, **~e**[1] /gaʀɑ̃ti/ **I** *pp* ▶ **garantir**.

II *adj* **1** with a guarantee; **être ~ de six mois** to have a six-month guarantee; **2** guaranteed.

garantie[2] /gaʀɑ̃ti/ *nf* **1** guarantee, warranty; **2** (in finance) security; guarantee; **en ~** as security; **3** (in insurance) cover; **montant des ~s** sum insured; **4** guarantee (**de** of); **5** (Law) guarantee.

garantir /gaʀɑ̃tiʀ/ [3] *vtr* **1** to guarantee; **~ qch à qn** to guarantee sb sth; **2** to safeguard [*right, security*]; **3** to guarantee [*loan, investment, product*].

garçon /gaʀsɔ̃/ *nm* **1** boy; **2** young man; **un brave** or **gentil ~** a nice chap (GB) or guy (US); **être beau** or **joli ~** to be good-looking; **3** bachelor; **4 ~ (de café)** waiter.

■ **~ d'ascenseur** lift (GB) or elevator (US) attendant; **~ d'écurie** stableboy; **~ d'honneur** best man; **~ manqué** tomboy.

garçonne /gaʀsɔn/ *nf* **être coiffée à la ~** to have an urchin (hair)cut.

garçonnet /gaʀsɔnɛ/ *nm* little boy; **taille/rayon ~** boys' size/department.

garçonnière /gaʀsɔnjɛʀ/ *nf* bachelor flat (GB) or apartment.

garde[1] /gaʀd/ *nm* **1** guard; **2** (for invalid, patient) carer; (in prison) warder.

■ **~ champêtre** ≈ local policeman (*appointed by the municipality*); **~ du corps** bodyguard; **~ forestier** forest warden; **Garde des Sceaux** French Minister of Justice.

garde[2] /gaʀd/ *nf* **1** nurse; **2** guard; **la vieille ~** the old guard; **3** guard; **monter la ~** to mount guard; **monter la ~ auprès de qn** to keep watch over sb; to stand guard over sb; **être sous la ~ de qn** to be guarded by sb; to be looked after by sb; **être de ~** [*doctor*] to be on call; [*soldier*] to be on guard duty; **4** guard, on-guard position; **en ~!** on guard!; **mettre qn en ~** to warn sb; **prendre ~** to watch out (**à** for); to be careful; **sans y prendre ~** inadvertently; **5** hilt; **6 (page de) ~** endpaper.

■ **~ à vue** (Law) ≈ police custody; **placer qn en ~ à vue** to hold sb for questioning.

garde-à-vous /gaʀdavu/ *nm inv* **se mettre au ~** to stand to attention.

garde-barrière, *pl* **~s** /gaʀdbaʀjɛʀ/ *nmf* level-crossing keeper (GB), gateman (*at grade crossing*) (US).

garde-chasse, *pl* **~s** /gaʀdəʃas/ *nm* game warden; gamekeeper.

garde-côte, *pl* **~s** /gaʀdəkot/ *nm* coastguard ship.

garde-fou, *pl* **~s** /gaʀdəfu/ *nm* **1** parapet; **2** safeguard.

garde-frontière, *pl* **gardes-frontières** /gaʀdfʀɔ̃tjɛʀ/ *nm* border guard.

garde-malade, *pl* **gardes-malades** /gaʀdmalad/ *nmf* home nurse.

garde-manger /gaʀdmɑ̃ʒe/ *nm inv* meat safe.

garde-meubles /gaʀdəmœbl/ *nm inv* furniture storage warehouse.

garder /gaʀde/ [1] **I** *vtr* **1** to keep [*money, object*]; to keep on [*hat, sweater*]; to keep on [*employee*]; **2** [*soldier*] to guard; [*person*] to look after.
II se garder *v refl* (+ *v être*) **1 se ~ de faire** to be careful not to do; **2** [*foodstuff*] to keep.

garderie /gaʀdəʀi/ *nf* **1** day nursery; **2** after-school child-minding facility.

garde-robe, *pl* **~s** /gaʀdəʀɔb/ *nf* wardrobe.

gardien, -ienne[1] /gaʀdjɛ̃, ɛn/ *nm,f* **1** (in premises) security guard; (in apartment block) caretaker (GB), janitor (US); (in park) keeper; (in prison) warder; (in museum, car park) attendant; **2** (Sport) keeper.
■ **~ de but** goalkeeper; **~ de nuit** night watchman; **~ de la paix** police officer.

gardiennage /gaʀdjɛnaʒ/ *nm* (of premises) security; (of apartment block) caretaking.

gardienne[2] /gaʀdjɛn/ *nf* **1** ▸ **gardien**; **2** caretaker; **3 ~ (d'enfant)** childminder (GB), daycare lady (US).

gardon /gaʀdɔ̃/ *nm* roach.
IDIOMS **être frais comme un ~** to be as fresh as a daisy.

gare /gaʀ/ **I** *nf* (railway) station.
II *excl* **~ (à toi)!** (warning) watch out!; (threat) careful!, watch it○!
■ **~ de marchandises** goods station (GB), freight station (US); **~ maritime** harbour[GB] station; **~ routière** coach station (GB), bus station (US).
IDIOMS **sans crier ~** without any warning.

garenne /gaʀɛn/ *nf* (rabbit) warren.

garer /gaʀe/ [1] **I** *vtr* to park.
II se garer *v refl* (+ *v être*) **1** to park; **2** [*vehicle*] to pull over.

gargariser: **se gargariser** /gaʀgaʀize/ [1] *v refl* (+ *v être*) **1** to gargle; **2**○ **se ~ de** to revel in.

gargarisme /gaʀgaʀism/ *nm* **1** gargling; **2** mouthwash.

gargouille /gaʀguj/ *nf* **1** gargoyle; **2** waterspout.

gargouiller /gaʀguje/ [1] *vi* [*water, fountain*] to gurgle; [*stomach*] to rumble.

garnement /gaʀnəmɑ̃/ *nm* tearaway (GB), brat○.

garni, ~e /gaʀni/ **I** *pp* ▸ **garnir**.
II *adj* **bien ~** [*wallet*] full; [*fridge*] well-stocked; [*buffet*] copious; **une assiette bien ~e** a plateful.

garnir /gaʀniʀ/ [3] *vtr* **1** [*books, objects*] to fill [*room*]; [*person*] to stock [*shelves, freezer*]; **2** to stuff [*cushion*]; **3** (Culin) to decorate [*table, cake*]; to garnish [*meat, fish*].

garnison /gaʀnizɔ̃/ *nf* garrison.

garniture /gaʀnityʀ/ *nf* **1** (Culin) side dish; (for dessert) decoration; (for meat, fish) garnish; **2** (on hat, garment) trimming.
■ **~ de cheminée** mantelpiece ornaments.

garrigue /gaʀig/ *nf* garrigue, scrubland (*in southern France*).

garrot /gaʀo/ *nm* **1** (Med) tourniquet; **2** (Zool) withers; **le cheval mesure 1,50 m au ~** ≈ the horse is 15 hands; **3** (Tech) (of rope) tightening peg; **4** garrotte.

gars○ /ga/ *nm inv* **1** lad (GB), boy; **2** chap○ (GB), guy○ (US).

Gascogne /gaskɔɲ/ *pr nf* **la ~** Gascony; **le golfe de ~** the Bay of Biscay.

gascon, -onne /gaskɔ̃, ɔn/ *adj* Gascon.

Gascon, -onne /gaskɔ̃, ɔn/ *nm,f* Gascon.
IDIOMS **faire une offre de ~** to raise false hopes.

gas-oil /gazwal/ *nm* diesel (oil) (GB), fuel oil (US).

gaspillage /gaspijaʒ/ *nm* **1** wasting; **quel ~!** what a waste!; **2** squandering.

gaspiller /gaspije/ [1] *vtr* **1** to waste [*time, food*]; **2** to squander [*resources, talent*].

gastronome /gastʀɔnɔm/ *nmf* gourmet, gastronome.

gastronomie /gastʀɔnɔmi/ *nf* gastronomy.

gâteau, *pl* **~x** /gɑto/ *nm* cake; gâteau.
■ **~ apéritif** cocktail biscuit; **~ de cire** honeycomb; **~ de riz** ≈ rice pudding; **~ sec** biscuit (GB), cookie (US); **~ de semoule** semolina pudding.
IDIOMS **c'est du ~**○**!** it's a piece of cake○!; **c'est pas du ~**○**!** it's no picnic!

gâter /gɑte/ [1] **I** *vtr* to spoil [*person, landscape, pleasure*]; to ruin [*teeth*].
II se gâter *v refl* (+ *v être*) **1** to go bad; to rot; **2** to take a turn for the worse.

gâteux, -euse /gɑtø, øz/ **I** *adj* **1** senile; **2 il est ~ avec sa fille**○ he's dotty about his daughter○.
II *nm,f* senile person.

gauche[1] /goʃ/ *adj* **1** left; **2** [*person, manner*] awkward; [*style*] clumsy.
IDIOMS **se lever du pied ~**○ to get out of bed on the wrong side (GB), to get up on the wrong side of the bed (US).

gauche[2] /goʃ/ *nf* **1** left; **à ~** [*drive*] on the left; [*go, look*] to the left; [*turn*] left; **de ~** [*page*] left-hand; **2** Left; **de ~** [*government, idea*] left-wing.
IDIOMS **passer l'arme à ~**○ to kick the bucket○; **jusqu'à la ~**○ completely, thoroughly; **mettre de l'argent à ~**○ to put money aside.

gaucher, -ère /goʃe, ɛʀ/ *adj* left-handed.

gauchiste /goʃist/ *adj, nmf* leftist.

gaufre /gofʀ/ *nf* **1** waffle; **2** honeycomb.

gaufrette /gofʀɛt/ *nf* wafer.

gaufrier /gofʀije/ *nm* waffle iron.

Gaule /gol/ *pr nf* Gaul.

gaulois, ~e /golwa, az/ **I** *adj* Gallic.
II *nm* Gaulish.

Gaulois, ~e /golwa, az/ *nm,f* Gaul.

gaver /gave/ [1] **I** *vtr* **1** to force-feed [*geese*]; **2** to stuff [sb] with food.
II se gaver *v refl* (+ *v être*) **1** to stuff oneself; **2 se ~ de** to devour [*novels*].

gay /gɛ/ *adj inv, nm* gay, homosexual.

gaz /gaz/ I *nm inv* gas; **se chauffer au ~** to have gas heating.
II *nm pl* **1** (Aut) air-fuel mixture; **rouler à pleins ~**○ to go at full throttle; **2** (Med) wind.
■ **~ carbonique** carbon dioxide; **~ d'échappement** exhaust fumes; **~ de ville** mains gas.
IDIOMS **il y a de l'eau dans le ~**○ there's trouble brewing.

gaze /gɑz/ *nf* gauze.

gazéifier /gazeifje/ [2] *vtr* **1** to carbonate [*drink*]; **2** to gasify.

gazelle /gazɛl/ *nf* gazelle.

gazer /gaze/ [1] I *vtr* to gas.
II○ *vi* **ça gaze?** how're things○?; **ça gaze** things are fine.

gazette /gazɛt/ *nf* **1** newspaper; **2 la ~ du quartier** the local gossip.

gazeux, -euse /gazø, øz/ *adj* **1** [*drink*] fizzy; **2** gaseous.

gazinière /gazinjɛʀ/ *nf* gas cooker (GB), gas stove.

gazoduc /gazɔdyk/ *nm* gas pipeline.

gazole /gazɔl/ *nm* diesel (oil) (GB), fuel oil (US).

gazon /gazɔ̃/ *nm* **1** grass, turf; **2** lawn.

gazouiller /gazuje/ [1] *vi* to twitter; to babble.

GDF /ʒedeɛf/ (*abbr* = **Gaz de France**) *French gas board.*

geai /ʒɛ/ *nm* jay.

géant, ~e /ʒeɑ̃, ɑ̃t/ I *adj* **1** huge, enormous; **2** (Bot, Zool) giant.
II *nm,f* giant/giantess.

geignard, ~e /ʒɛɲaʀ, aʀd/ *adj* [*person*] moaning; [*child*] whining.

geindre /ʒɛ̃dʀ/ [55] *vi* **1** (in pain) to moan, to groan; to whimper; (complainingly) to whine; **2** [*violin*] to wail; [*chair*] to creak.

gel /ʒɛl/ *nm* **1** frost; **résistant au ~** frost-resistant; **2 ~ des prix/salaires** price/wage freeze; **3 après le ~ du projet** after the project had been put on ice; **4** gel.

gélatine /ʒelatin/ *nf* gelatine (GB), gelatin (US)

gelé, ~e[1] /ʒəle/ I *pp* ▶ **geler**.
II *adj* **1** [*water, ground*] frozen; [*toe*] frost-bitten; **j'ai les oreilles ~es** my ears are frozen; **2** [*prices, negotiations*] frozen.

gelée[2] /ʒəle/ *nf* **1** (from fruit) jelly; (from meat, fish) gelatinous stock; **œuf en ~** egg in aspic; **2** gel; **3** frost.
■ **~ blanche** hoarfrost; **~ royale** royal jelly.

geler /ʒəle/ [17] I *vtr* **1** to freeze; to nip [*plant*]; **2** to freeze [*salaries*]; to suspend [*plan, production*].
II *vi* [*water, ground, finger, foot*] to freeze; [*plant*] to be frosted.
III **se geler**○ *v refl* (+ *v être*) to be freezing.
IV *v impers* **il gèle** it's freezing.

gélule /ʒelyl/ *nf* capsule.

Gémeaux /ʒemo/ *pr nm pl* Gemini.

gémir /ʒemiʀ/ [3] *vi* **1** [*person*] to moan; to whimper; **2** [*floorboards, chair*] to creak.

gémissement /ʒemismɑ̃/ *nm* **1** moan; **2** (of floorboards) creak.

gemme /ʒɛm/ *nf* **1** gem, gemstone; **2** resin.

gênant, ~e /ʒɛnɑ̃, ɑ̃t/ *adj* **1** [*box, piece of furniture*] cumbersome; [*problem, noise*] annoying; [*odour*] unpleasant; **2** embarrassing.

gencive /ʒɑ̃siv/ *nf* gum.

gendarme /ʒɑ̃daʀm/ *nm* **1** (Mil) gendarme, French policeman; **la peur du ~** the fear of authority; **2 quel ~!** what a bossy person!; **3** dried sausage.
■ **~ couché** road hump.

gendarmerie /ʒɑ̃daʀm(ə)ʀi/ *nf* **1** ≈ police station; **2** ≈ police quarters; **3 ~ (nationale)** gendarmerie.

gendre /ʒɑ̃dʀ/ *nm* son-in-law.

gène /ʒɛn/ *nm* gene.

gêne /ʒɛn/ *nf* **1** embarrassment; **2** discomfort; **3** inconvenience; **4** poverty.

gêné, ~e /ʒɛne/ I *pp* ▶ **gêner**.
II *adj* **1** embarrassed; **2** short of money.

généalogie /ʒenealɔʒi/ *nf* genealogy.

généalogique /ʒenealɔʒik/ *adj* genealogical; **arbre ~** family tree.

gêner /ʒɛne/ [1] I *vtr* **1** to disturb; to bother; **2** [*smoke, noise*] to bother; **3** to embarrass; **4** [*car*] to block [*traffic*]; [*belt*] to restrict [*breathing*]; **5** [*person*] to get in the way of [*discussion, progress*]; **6** [*pebble, belt*] to hurt.
II **se gêner** *v refl* (+ *v être*) **1** to get in each other's way; **2 pourquoi se ~?** why hesitate?; **je vais me ~**○ see if I don't; **ne vous gênez pas pour moi** don't mind me.

général, ~e[1], *mpl* **-aux** /ʒeneʀal, o/ I *adj* **1** general; **de l'avis ~** in most people's opinion; **dans l'intérêt ~** in the public interest; **2 en ~, de façon ~e** generally, in general; **en règle ~e** as a rule.
II *nm* general.

générale[2] /ʒeneʀal/ *nf* **1** dress rehearsal; **2** general's wife.

généralisation /ʒeneʀalizasjɔ̃/ *nf* **1** (of policy) general implementation; (of language) general use; **2** generalization; **3** (of illness, strike) spread.

généralisé, ~e /ʒeneʀalize/ *adj* [*conflict, pessimism*] widespread; [*process*] general; [*cancer*] generalized.

généraliser /ʒeneʀalize/ [1] I *vtr* to bring [sth] into general use.
II *vi* to generalize.
III **se généraliser** *v refl* (+ *v être*) [*technique*] to become standard; [*tax*] to become widely applicable; [*strike, illness*] to spread.

généraliste /ʒeneʀalist/ *adj* [*journal, engineer*] non-specialized; [*conception*] broad; **(médecin) ~** GP, general practitioner.

généralité /ʒeneʀalite/ *nf* generality.

génération /ʒeneʀasjɔ̃/ *nf* generation.

générer /ʒeneʀe/ [14] *vtr* to generate.

généreusement /ʒeneʀøzmɑ̃/ *adv* generously; liberally.

généreux, -euse /ʒeneʀø, øz/ *adj* **1** [*person,*

nature] generous; [*idea, gesture*] noble; **2** [*portion*] generous; **poitrine généreuse** large bust.

générique /ʒeneʀik/ **I** *adj* generic.
II *nm* credits; **le ~ de début/fin** opening/closing credits.

générosité /ʒeneʀɔzite/ *nf* **1** generosity; **2** generosity of spirit.

genèse /ʒənɛz/ *nf* **1** (of plan) genesis; (of state) birth; **2 la Genèse** Genesis.

genêt /ʒənɛ/ *nm* (Bot) broom.

génétique /ʒenetik/ **I** *adj* genetic.
II *nf* genetics.

Genève /ʒənɛv/ *pr n* Geneva.

génial, **~e**, *mpl* **-iaux** /ʒenjal, o/ *adj* **1** brilliant; **2**° great°.

génie /ʒeni/ *nm* **1** genius; **idée de ~** brainwave; **2** spirit; genie; **3** engineering; **~ civil** civil engineering; civil engineers.

genièvre /ʒənjɛvʀ/ *nm* **1** juniper; **2** juniper berry; **3** Dutch gin.

génisse /ʒenis/ *nf* heifer.

génital, **~e**, *mpl* **-aux** /ʒenital, o/ *adj* genital.

génocide /ʒenɔsid/ *nm* genocide.

genou, *pl* **~x** /ʒ(ə)nu/ **I** *nm* knee; **sur les ~x de qn** on sb's lap.
II à genoux *phr* **se mettre à ~x** to kneel down; to go down on one's knees; **être à ~x devant qn** (figurative) to worship sb.
IDIOMS **faire du ~ à qn**° to play footsie° with sb; **être sur les ~x**° to be on one's last legs; **mettre qn sur les ~x**° to wear sb out.

genouillère /ʒənujɛʀ/ *nf* (Sport) knee pad; (Med) knee support; (for animal) knee boot.

genre /ʒɑ̃ʀ/ *nm* **1** sort, kind, type; **tu vois le ~!** you know the type!; **un peu dans le ~ de ta robe** a bit like your dress; **2 pour se donner un ~** (in order) to make oneself look different; **3** (in grammar) gender; **4** genre; **5** (Bot, Zool) genus.
■ **le ~ humain** mankind.

gens /ʒɑ̃/ *nm pl* **1** people; **les ~ sans histoires** ordinary people; **2** servants; retinue.
■ **~ d'église** clergymen; **~ de lettres** writers; **~ de maison** servants; **~ du monde** polite society; **~ de théâtre** actors; **~ du voyage** travelling[GB] people.

gentiane /ʒɑ̃sjan/ *nf* **1** gentian; **2** gentian liqueur.

gentil, **-ille** /ʒɑ̃ti, ij/ *adj* **1** kind, nice; **sois ~, réponds au téléphone** do me a favour[GB], answer the phone; **2** good; **sois ~** be a good boy; **3 c'est bien ~ tout ça, mais**... that's all very well, but...

gentille ▸ **gentil**.

gentillesse /ʒɑ̃tijɛs/ *nf* **1** kindness; **2** (ironic) **échanger des ~s** to exchange insults; **dire des ~s sur** to say unpleasant things about.

gentiment /ʒɑ̃timɑ̃/ *adv* **1** kindly; **2** quietly.

géographie /ʒeɔgʀafi/ *nf* geography.

geôlier, **-ière** /ʒolje, ɛʀ/ *nm,f* jailer.

géologie /ʒeɔlɔʒi/ *nf* geology.

géomètre /ʒeɔmɛtʀ/ *nmf* land surveyor.

géométrie /ʒeɔmetʀi/ *nf* geometry; **à ~ variable** [*doctrine*] flexible.

géométrique /ʒeɔmetʀik/ *adj* [*form*] geometric; [*demonstration*] geometrical.

Géorgie /ʒeɔʀʒi/ *pr nf* **1** (in US) Georgia; **2** (in Europe) Georgia.
■ **~ du Sud** South Georgia.

géorgien, **-ienne** /ʒeɔʀʒjɛ̃, ɛn/ **I** *adj* Georgian.
II *nm* (language) Georgian.

gérance /ʒeʀɑ̃s/ *nf* management; **mettre en ~** to appoint a manager for [*shop, company*]; to appoint a managing agent for [*property*]

géranium /ʒeʀanjɔm/ *nm* geranium.

gérant, **~e** /ʒeʀɑ̃, ɑ̃t/ *nm,f* manager; (of property) (managing) agent.

gerbe /ʒɛʀb/ *nf* **1** bouquet; wreath; **2** (of water) spray; **3** (of wheat) sheaf.

gercer /ʒɛʀse/ [12] **I** *vtr* to chap [*skin, lips*].
II *vi* to become chapped.

gerçure /ʒɛʀsyʀ/ *nf* (in skin, lips) crack.

gérer /ʒeʀe/ [14] *vtr* **1** to manage [*production, time, database*]; to run [*business, country*]; **2** to handle [*situation, information*].

gériatrie /ʒeʀjatʀi/ *nf* **1** geriatrics; **2** geriatric ward.

germain, **~e** /ʒɛʀmɛ̃, ɛn/ *adj* **1** (**cousin**) **~** first cousin; **2** Germanic.

germanique /ʒɛʀmanik/ *adj, nm* Germanic.

germaniste /ʒɛʀmanist/ *nmf* Germanist.

germanophone /ʒɛʀmanɔfɔn/ **I** *adj* German-speaking.
II *nmf* German speaker.

germe /ʒɛʀm/ *nm* (of embryo, seed) germ; (of egg) germinal disc; (of potato) sprout; **~s de soja** bean sprouts.

germer /ʒɛʀme/ [1] *vi* **1** [*wheat*] to germinate; **2** [*idea, suspicion*] to form.

gérondif /ʒeʀɔ̃dif/ *nm* gerund, gerundive.

gésier /ʒezje/ *nm* gizzard.

gésir /ʒeziʀ/ [37] *vi* (formal) **elle gisait sur son lit** she was lying on her bed; **ci-gît Luc Pichon** here lies Luc Pichon.

geste /ʒɛst/ *nm* **1** movement; gesture; **joindre le ~ à la parole** to suit the action to the word; **2** gesture, act; **un ~ symbolique** a token gesture.

gesticuler /ʒɛstikyle/ [1] *vtr* **1** to gesticulate; **2** to fidget.

gestion /ʒɛstjɔ̃/ *nf* **1** management; **2** (of situation, information) handling; **3** (classroom) management.
■ **~ administrative** administration; **~ des stocks** stock (GB) or inventory (US) control.

gestionnaire /ʒɛstjɔnɛʀ/ *nmf* administrator.
■ **~ de fichiers** file-management system.

gestuel, **-elle**¹ /ʒɛstɥɛl/ *adj* gestural; **peinture gestuelle** action painting.

gestuelle² /ʒɛstɥɛl/ *nf* body language.

geyser /ʒezɛʀ/ *nm* geyser.

ghetto /geto/ *nm* ghetto.

gibbon /ʒibɔ̃/ *nm* gibbon.

gibecière /ʒibsjɛʀ/ *nf* gamebag.

gibier /ʒibje/ *nm* game; **gros ~** big game; (figurative) big time criminals; **être un ~ facile pour les escrocs** to be easy prey for conmen.

giboulée /ʒibule/ *nf* shower; **les ~s de mars** ≈ April showers (GB).

giclée /ʒikle/ *nf* spurt; squirt.

gicler /ʒikle/ [1] *vi* [*blood, water*] to spurt; [*juice*] to squirt.

gifle /ʒifl/ *nf* slap in the face.

gifler /ʒifle/ [1] *vtr* **1** to slap across the face; **2** [*rain, wind*] to lash.

gigantesque /ʒigɑ̃tɛsk/ *adj* huge, gigantic.

gigogne /ʒigɔɲ/ *adj* **lit ~** hideaway bed; **tables ~s** nest of tables.

gigot /ʒigo/ *nm* leg of lamb; **~ de mouton** leg of mutton.

gigoter /ʒigɔte/ [1] *vi* **1** to wriggle; **2** to fidget.

gilet /ʒilɛ/ *nm* **1** cardigan; **2** waistcoat (GB), vest (US).
■ **~ pare-balles** bulletproof vest; **~ de sauvetage** lifejacket.

gin /dʒin/ *nm* gin; **~ tonic** gin and tonic.

gingembre /ʒɛ̃ʒɑ̃bʀ/ *nm* ginger.

girafe /ʒiʀaf/ *nf* (Zool) giraffe.

giratoire /ʒiʀatwaʀ/ *adj* gyratory.
■ **sens ~** roundabout (GB), traffic circle (US).

girofle /ʒiʀɔfl/ *nm* clove; **un clou de ~** a clove.

giroflée /ʒiʀɔfle/ *nf* wallflower.

girolle /ʒiʀɔl/ *nf* chanterelle.

girouette /ʒiʀwɛt/ *nf* windvane.

gisement /ʒizmɑ̃/ *nm* (of oil, minerals) deposit.

gît ▸ **gésir**.

gitan, **~e** /ʒitɑ̃, an/ *nm,f* Gypsy[GB].

gîte /ʒit/ *nm* **1** shelter; **2** (Culin) **~ (à la noix)** ≈ top rump; **3** (of hare) form.
■ **~ rural** self-catering cottage.

givrant /ʒivʀɑ̃/ *adj m* **brouillard ~** freezing fog.

givre /ʒivʀ/ *nm* (on ground, plant) frost; (on windscreen, propeller) ice.

givré, **~e** /ʒivʀe/ *adj* **1** [*window*] frosty; [*tree*] frost-covered; [*snow*] frozen; **2**° crazy; **3** (Culin) [*glass*] frosted.

givrer /ʒivʀe/ [1] *vi*, **se givrer** *v refl* (+ *v être*) to frost over.

glaçage /glasaʒ/ *nm* (Culin) (on meat) glazing; (on dessert) icing; glazing.

glace /glas/ *nf* **1** ice; **de ~** [*reception*] frosty; [*face*] stony; **2** ice cream; **3** mirror; **4** sheet of glass; (of shop window) glass; (of car) window.
IDIOMS **rester de ~** to remain unmoved.

glacé, **~e** /glase/ *adj* **1** [*rain, water*] ice-cold; [*hands*] frozen; [*person*] freezing; **thé ~** iced tea; **2** [*cake*] iced; **3** [*atmosphere*] frosty, icy; [*smile*] chilly; **4** [*paper*] glossy.

glacer /glase/ [12] **I** *vtr* **1** to freeze [*body*]; to chill [sb] to the bone; **2** to intimidate; **~ qn d'effroi**, **~ le sang de qn** to make sb's blood run cold.
II se glacer *v refl* (+ *v être*) [*expression*] to freeze.

glaciaire /glasjɛʀ/ *adj* glacial; **calotte ~** icecap.

glacial, **~e**, *mpl* **~s** or **-iaux** /glasjal, o/ *adj* **1** icy; **2** [*person, reception*] frosty; [*silence*] stony; [*look*] icy.

glacier /glasje/ *nm* **1** glacier; **2** ice-cream maker; **3** ice-cream parlour[GB].

glacière /glasjɛʀ/ *nf* coolbox (GB), cooler, ice chest (US).

glaçon /glasɔ̃/ *nm* **1** ice cube; **2** (in river) block of ice; (on branch) icicle.

glaïeul /glajœl/ *nm* gladiolus.

glaire /glɛʀ/ *nf* **1** mucus; **2** albumen.

glaise /glɛz/ *nf* clay.

glaive /glɛv/ *nm* double-edged sword.

gland /glɑ̃/ *nm* **1** acorn; **2** (Anat) glans; **3** tassel.

glande /glɑ̃d/ *nf* (Anat) gland.

glapir /glapiʀ/ [3] *vi* **1** [*pup*] to yap; [*fox*] to bark; **2** [*person*] to shriek.

glas /glɑ/ *nm inv* toll, knell; **sonner le ~** (figurative) to sound the death knell.

glauque /glok/ *adj* [*waters, light*] murky; [*street*] squalid.

glissade /glisad/ *nf* slide; skid.

glissant, **~e** /glisɑ̃, ɑ̃t/ *adj* slippery.

glissement /glismɑ̃/ *nm* **1** sliding; **2** (in sense) shift; (among voters) swing (**à** to); (in prices) fall.

glisser /glise/ [1] **I** *vtr* **1** to slip (**dans** into); **2** to slip in [*remark, criticism*]; **~ qch à l'oreille de qn** to whisper sth in sb's ear.
II *vi* **1** to be slippery; **2** to slip; **3** to slide; to glide; **4 ~ sur** to have no effect on; to skate over.
III se glisser *v refl* (+ *v être*) **1** to slip (**dans** into); to sneak (**dans** into); **2** to creep into.

glissière /glisjɛʀ/ *nf* slide; **~ (de sécurité)** crash barrier; **fermeture à ~** zip (GB), zipper (US).

global, **~e**, *mpl* **-aux** /glɔbal, o/ *adj* [*sum, number of people*] total; [*result, cost*] overall; [*agreement, vision, solution*] global; [*study*] comprehensive.

globalement /glɔbalmɑ̃/ *adv* on the whole.

globe /glɔb/ *nm* **1 ~ (terrestre)** earth, globe; **parcourir le ~** to globe-trot; **2** round glass lampshade; glass case; **3** (in architecture) dome.
■ **~ oculaire** eyeball.

globule /glɔbyl/ *nm* globule, corpuscle; blood cell.
■ **~ blanc** white cell; **~ polaire** polar body; **~ rouge** red cell.

gloire /glwaʀ/ *nf* **1** glory, fame; **2** credit; **faire qch pour la ~** to do sth (just) for the sake of it; **3** glory, praise; **4 tirer ~ de** to pride oneself on; **5** celebrity; star.

glorieux, **-ieuse** /glɔʀjø, øz/ *adj* glorious.

glorifier /glɔʀifje/ [2] **I** *vtr* to glorify.
II se glorifier *v refl* (+ *v être*) to glory; to boast.

glose /gloz/ *nf* gloss; note.

glossaire /glɔsɛʀ/ *nm* glossary.

glotte /glɔt/ *nf* glottis.

gloussement /glusmɑ̃/ *nm* (of hen) clucking; (of person) chuckle.

glousser /gluse/ [1] *vi* [*hen*] to cluck; [*person*] to chuckle.

glouton, -onne /glutɔ̃, ɔn/ *adj* [*person*] gluttonous; [*appetite*] voracious.

gloutonnerie /glutɔnʀi/ *nf* gluttony.

glu /gly/ *nf* **1** bird lime; **2** glue.

gluant, ~e /glyɑ̃, ɑ̃t/ *adj* **1** sticky; **2** slimy.

glucide /glysid/ *nm* carbohydrate.

glycémie /glisemi/ *nf* **taux de ~** blood sugar level.

glycérine /gliseʀin/ *nf* glycerin.

glycine /glisin/ *nf* wisteria.

gnome /gnom/ *nm* gnome.

gnon○ /ɲɔ̃/ *nm* dent; bruise; **prendre un ~** to get hit.

gnostique /gnɔstik/ *adj, nmf* gnostic.

go: tout de go /go/ *phr* [*say*] straight out.

goal○ /gol/ *nm* goalkeeper, goalie○.

gobelet /gɔblɛ/ *nm* cup; tumbler; beaker; **~ en carton** paper cup.

gober /gɔbe/ [1] *vtr* **1** to suck [*egg*]; to swallow [sth] whole; **2**○ to fall for○ [*story*].

godasse○ /gɔdas/ *nf* shoe.

godet /gɔdɛ/ *nm* **1** goblet; **2** pot; **3** (for dice) shaker.

goéland /gɔelɑ̃/ *nm* gull.

goémon /gɔemɔ̃/ *nm* **1** wrack; **2** seaweed fertilizer.

gogo○**: à gogo** /gogo/ *phr* galore; **vin à ~** wine galore.

goguenard, ~e /gɔgnaʀ, aʀd/ *adj* quietly ironic.

goguette○**: en goguette** /ɑ̃gɔgɛt/ *phr* **partir en ~** to go on a spree.

goinfre○ /gwɛ̃fʀ/ *nmf* greedy pig○.

goinfrer○**: se goinfrer** /gwɛ̃fʀe/ [1] *v refl* (+ *v être*) to stuff oneself○.

goître /gwatʀ/ *nm* goitre[GB].

golden /gɔldɛn/ *nf inv* Golden Delicious (apple).

golf /gɔlf/ *nm* **1** golf; **2** golf course.

golfe /gɔlf/ *nm* gulf; bay.

gommage /gɔmaʒ/ *nm* **1** erasing; **2** gumming; **3** scrub; **~ du visage** facial scrub.

gomme /gɔm/ **I** *nf* **1** eraser, rubber (GB); **2** gum; **3** (Med) gumma.

II à la gomme○ *phr* [*idea*] pathetic, useless; [*machine*] useless; [*plan*] hopeless.

IDIOMS **mettre (toute) la ~**○ to step on it○; to give it full throttle○; to turn it up full blast.

gommer /gɔme/ [1] *vtr* **1** to rub [sth] out; **2** to smooth out [*wrinkle*]; to erase [*past, boundaries*]; to iron out [*difference*]; **3** to gum; **papier gommé** gummed paper.

gond /gɔ̃/ *nm* hinge; **sortir de ses ~s** to come off its hinges; to fly off the handle○.

gondole /gɔ̃dɔl/ *nf* **1** gondola; **2** sales shelf, gondola.

gondoler: se gondoler /gɔ̃dɔle/ [1] *v refl* (+ *v être*) [*paper*] to crinkle; [*wood*] to warp.

gondolier /gɔ̃dɔlje/ *nm* gondolier.

gonflable /gɔ̃flabl/ *adj* inflatable.

gonflé, ~e /gɔ̃fle/ **I** *pp* ▶ **gonfler**.

II *adj* **1** [*tyre, balloon*] inflated; [*cheeks*] puffed out; **2** swollen; bloated; puffy; **muscles ~s** bulging muscles; **yeux ~s de sommeil** eyes heavy with sleep; **éponge ~e d'eau** sponge saturated with water; **3**○ **être ~** to have guts○; (critical) to have a nerve○.

gonfler /gɔ̃fle/ [1] **I** *vtr* **1** to blow up; to inflate [*balloon, tyre*]; to fill [*lungs, sail*]; to puff out [*cheeks*]; **être gonflé à bloc** to be fully inflated; to be raring○ to go; **2** to flex [*muscle*]; to make [sth] bulge [*pocket, bag*]; to saturate [*sponge*]; to make [sth] swollen [*river*]; to swell [*bud*]; **la limonade gonfle l'estomac** lemonade makes you feel bloated; **3 il est gonflé d'orgueil** he's full of his own importance; **4** to increase [*profits*]; to push up [*prices*]; to inflate [*statistics*]; to exaggerate [*importance*].

II *vi* **1** (gen) to swell (up); (Culin) to rise; **2** [*sum, numbers*] to increase.

gonflette○ /gɔ̃flɛt/ *nf* (derogatory) **faire de la ~** to pump iron○, to go body-building.

gonfleur /gɔ̃flœʀ/ *nm* (air) pump.

gong /gɔ̃g/ *nm* **1** gong; **2** (in boxing) bell.

goret /gɔʀɛ/ *nm* **1** piglet; **2**○ (child) little pig○.

gorge /gɔʀʒ/ *nf* **1** throat; **avoir mal à la ~** to have a sore throat; **je suis pris à la ~, je n'ai plus un sou** I'm in a fix○, I haven't got a penny; **tenir qn à la ~** to have sb by the throat; (figurative) to have a stranglehold over sb; **avoir la ~ serrée** or **nouée** to have a lump in one's throat; to have one's heart in one's mouth; **à ~ déployée, à pleine ~** [*sing*] at the top of one's voice; [*laugh*] uproariously; **ta remarque m'est restée en travers de la ~** I found your comment hard to swallow or very hard to take; **2** bosom, breast; **3** gorge.

IDIOMS **faire des ~s chaudes de qn/qch** to laugh sb/sth to scorn.

gorgé, ~e[1] /gɔʀʒe/ *adj* **~ de nourriture** glutted with food; **~ d'eau** [*land*] waterlogged; [*sponge*] saturated with water; **fruit ~ de soleil** fruit bursting with sunshine.

gorgée[2] /gɔʀʒe/ *nf* sip; gulp.

gorille /gɔʀij/ *nm* **1** gorilla; **2**○ bodyguard.

gosier /gozje/ *nm* throat, gullet.

gosse○ /gɔs/ *nmf* **1** kid○; **sale ~** brat○; **2 il est beau ~** he's a good-looking fellow.

gothique /gɔtik/ *adj, nm* Gothic.

gouache /gwaʃ/ *nf* **1** gouache, poster paint; **2** gouache (painting).

gouaille /gwɑj/ *nf* cheek, cheekiness.

goudron /gudʀɔ̃/ *nm* tar.

goudronner /gudʀɔne/ [1] *vtr* to tarmac.

gouffre /gufʀ/ *nm* **1** chasm, abyss; **le ~ de Padirac** the caves of Padirac; **2 le pays est au bord du ~** the country is on the brink of the abyss.

goujat /guʒa/ *nm* boor; **en ~, comme un ~** boorishly.

goujon /guʒɔ̃/ *nm* (Zool) gudgeon; **taquiner le ~**○ to do the odd bit of fishing.

goulet /gulɛ/ *nm* **1** narrows; **2** gully.

■ ~ **d'étranglement** bottleneck.

goulot /gulo/ *nm* (of bottle) neck; **boire au ~** to drink from the bottle.

goulu, ~e /guly/ *adj* greedy.

goupiller○: **se goupiller** /gupije/ [1] *v refl* (+ *v être*) **ça s'est mal goupillé** it turned out badly.

goupillon /gupijɔ̃/ *nm* **1** bottle brush; **2** holy water sprinkler.

gourd, ~e[1] /guʀ, guʀd/ *adj* numb.

gourde[2] /guʀd/ **I**○ *adj* dumb○, gormless○ (GB).
II *nf* **1** flask; gourd; **2**○ dope○.

gourdin /guʀdɛ̃/ *nm* bludgeon, cudgel.

gourmand, ~e /guʀmɑ̃, ɑ̃d/ *adj* **1** fond of good food; (critical) greedy; **il est ~ (de sucreries)** he has a sweet tooth; **2** grasping.

gourmandise /guʀmɑ̃diz/ **I** *nf* weakness for sweet things; weakness for good food; greed.
II gourmandises *nf pl* sweets (GB), candies (US).

gourmet /guʀmɛ/ *nm* gourmet.

gourmette /guʀmɛt/ *nf* chain bracelet.

gourou /guʀu/ *nm* guru.

gousse /gus/ *nf* pod; **~ d'ail** clove of garlic.

gousset /gusɛ/ *nm* **1** (pocket) fob; **2** (gen, Tech) gusset.

goût /gu/ *nm* **1** taste; palate; **2** taste; **avoir un ~ sucré** to taste sweet; **donner du ~ à qch** to give sth flavour[GB]; **3** taste; **de bon ~** in good taste; **s'habiller sans ~** to have no dress sense; **avoir le mauvais ~ de faire** to be tactless enough to do; **4** liking; **ne pas être du ~ de tout le monde** not to be to everyone's liking; not to be everyone's cup of tea; **elle reprend ~ à la vie** she's starting to enjoy life again; **être au ~ du jour** to be trendy; **faire qch par ~** to do sth for pleasure; **5** taste; **mes ~s artistiques** my taste in art; **chacun ses ~s** each to his own.
IDIOMS **tous les ~s sont dans la nature** (Proverb) it takes all sorts to make a world.

goûter[1] /gute/ [1] **I** *vtr* **1** to taste, to try; **2** to enjoy [*peace, solitude*].
II goûter à *v+prep* **1** to try [*food, drink*]; **2** to have a taste of [*freedom, power*]; **~ aux joies de qch** to sample the joys of sth.

goûter[2] /gute/ *nm* **1** snack; **2** children's party.

goutte /gut/ **I** *nf* **1** drop (**de** of); **~ de pluie** raindrop; **~ à ~** drop by drop; **à grosses ~s** [*rain*] heavily; [*perspire*] profusely; **2** (Med) gout.
II gouttes *nf pl* (Med) drops.
IDIOMS **se ressembler comme deux ~s d'eau** to be as alike as two peas in a pod; **avoir la ~ au nez** to have a runny nose.

goutte-à-goutte /gutagut/ *nm inv* (Med) drip.

gouttelette /gutlɛt/ *nf* droplet.

goutter /gute/ [1] *vi* to drip (**de** from).

gouttière /gutjɛʀ/ *nf* gutter; drainpipe.

gouvernail /guvɛʀnaj/ *nm* **1** rudder; **2** helm; **tenir le ~** to be at the helm.

gouvernant, ~e[1] /guvɛʀnɑ̃, ɑ̃t/ **I** *adj* [*class, party*] ruling.
II gouvernants *nm pl* **les ~s** the government.

gouvernante[2] /guvɛʀnɑ̃t/ *nf* **1** governess; **2** housekeeper.

gouverne /guvɛʀn/ *nf* **pour votre ~** for your information.

gouvernement /guvɛʀnəmɑ̃/ *nm* government.

gouvernemental, ~e, *mpl* **-aux** /guvɛʀnəmɑ̃tal, o/ *adj* government; governmental.

gouverner /guvɛʀne/ [1] *vtr* **1** to govern, to rule; **2** [*money*] to rule; **3** to steer [*ship*].

gouverneur /guvɛʀnœʀ/ *nm* governor.

goyave /gɔjav/ *nf* guava.

grabataire /gʀabatɛʀ/ *adj* bedridden.

grabuge○ /gʀabyʒ/ *nm* **il va y avoir du ~** there's going to be trouble.

grâce /gʀɑs/ **I** *nf* **1** (of person, gesture) grace; (of landscape) charm; (of style) elegance; **2 de bonne ~** with (a) good grace; **3** favour[GB]; **faire à qn la ~ d'accepter** to do sb the honour[GB] of accepting; **donner le coup de ~ à qn** to deal sb the death blow; **4** mercy; (Law) (free) pardon; **~ présidentielle** presidential pardon; **je vous fais ~ des détails** I'll spare you the details; **5** (divine) grace; **~ à Dieu!** thank God!
II grâce à *phr* thanks to.

Grâce /gʀɑs/ *nf* Grace; **votre ~** your Grace.

gracier /gʀasje/ [2] *vtr* to pardon, to reprieve.

gracieusement /gʀasjøzmɑ̃/ *adv* **1** free of charge; **2** gracefully.

gracieux, -ieuse /gʀasjø, øz/ *adj* **1** graceful; **2** gracious.

gracile /gʀasil/ *adj* slender.

grade /gʀad/ *nm* rank; **monter en ~** to be promoted; **en prendre pour son ~**○ to be hauled over the coals.

gradé, ~e /gʀade/ *nm,f* noncommissioned officer.

gradin /gʀadɛ̃/ *nm* (in hall) tier; (in arena) terrace; **les ~s** the terraces (GB), the bleachers (US).

gradué, ~e /gʀadɥe/ *adj* **règle ~e** ruler; **verre ~** measuring cup.

graduel, -elle /gʀadɥɛl/ *adj* gradual.

graduer /gʀadɥe/ [1] *vtr* **1** to increase [*difficulty*]; to grade (GB), to graduate (US) [*exercises*]; **2** to graduate [*instrument*].

graffiti /gʀafiti/ *nm pl* graffiti.

grain /gʀɛ̃/ *nm* **1** grain; **nourri au ~** corn-fed (GB) or grain-fed; **2** (of cereal, salt, sand) grain; **~ de poivre** peppercorn; **~ de café** coffee bean; **~ de moutarde** mustard seed; **~ de cassis** blackcurrant; **~ de raisin** grape; **3** speck; **4 un ~ de folie** a touch of madness; **5 le ~** the grain; **à gros ~** coarse grained; **6** heavy shower.
■ **~ de beauté** beauty spot, mole.
IDIOMS **avoir un ~**○ to be loony○; **mettre son ~ de sel**○ to put one's oar in○.

graine /gʀɛn/ *nf* seed; birdseed; **monter en ~** [*vegetable*] to run to seed; [*child*] to shoot up;

ton fils, c'est de la mauvaise ~ your son is a bad lot○.
IDIOMS **prends-en de la ~**○ let that be an example to you.

graisse /gʀɛs/ *nf* **1** (gen) fat; (of seal, whale) blubber; **2** (Tech) grease.

graisser /gʀɛse/ [1] *vtr* to grease [*pan*]; to lubricate [*mechanism*]; **~ la patte à qn**○ to grease sb's palm.

graisseux, **-euse** /gʀɛsø, øz/ *adj* (gen) greasy; (Med) fatty.

grammaire /gʀamɛʀ/ *nf* grammar.

grammatical, **~e**, *mpl* **-aux** /gʀamatikal, o/ *adj* grammatical.

gramme /gʀam/ *nm* gram; **il n'a pas un ~ de bon sens** he hasn't an ounce of common sense.

grand, **~e** /gʀɑ̃, gʀɑ̃d/ **I** *adj* **1** [*person, tree, tower*] tall; [*arm, stride, journey*] long; [*margin, angle*] wide; [*place, object, fire*] big; **plus ~ que nature** larger than life; **2** [*crowd, family, fortune*] large, big; **pas ~ monde** not many people; **il fait ~ jour** it's broad daylight; **laver à ~e eau** to wash [sth] in plenty of running water; to wash [sth] down; **3** [*dreamer, collector, friend*] great; [*cheat, gambler*] big; [*drinker, smoker*] heavy; **c'est un ~ timide** he's very shy; **4** [*discovery, news, expedition*] great; [*date*] important; [*role*] major; [*problem, decision*] big; **5** main; **les ~es lignes d'une politique** the broad lines of a policy; **6** [*company, brand*] leading; **les ~es industries** the big industries; **7** [*painter, wine*] great; [*heart, spirit*] noble; **8** [*brother, sister*] elder; [*pupil*] senior (GB), older; **les ~es classes** the senior forms (GB), the upper classes (US); **assez ~ pour faire** old enough to do; **9** [*height, length, value, distance*] great; [*size, quantity*] large; [*speed*] high; [*kilometre, hour*] good; **10** [*kindness, friendship, danger, interest*] great; [*noise*] loud; [*cold*] severe; [*heat*] intense; [*wind*] strong, high; [*storm*] big, violent; **à ma ~e surprise** much to my surprise; **ça te ferait le plus ~ bien** it would do you a world of good; **à ~s cris** loudly; ▶**remède**; **11** [*family, name*] great; **la ~e bourgeoisie** the upper middle class; **12** [*reception, plan*] grand; **13** [*word*] big; [*phrase*] high-sounding; **faire de ~s gestes** to wave one's arms about; **et voilà, tout de suite les ~s mots** there you go, straight off the deep end.
II *nm,f* big boy/girl; (Sch) senior (GB) or older pupil.
III *adv* wide; **ouvrir tout ~ les bras** to throw one's arms open; **ouvrir ~ ses oreilles** to prick up one's ears; **voir ~** to think big.
IV *nm* **les ~s de ce monde** the great and the good; the world's leaders.
V en grand *phr* [*open*] wide; **faire les choses en ~** to do things on the grand scale.
■ **~ banditisme** organized crime; **~ bassin** main pool; **le ~ capital** big money; **~ couturier** couturier; **~ duc** eagle owl; **~ écart** (Sport) splits; **le ~ écran** the big screen; **~ ensemble** high-density housing complex; **le ~ large** the high seas; **~ magasin** department store; **~ mât** mainmast; **le ~ monde** high society; **le Grand Nord** the Far North; **Grand Pardon** Day of Atonement; **~ prêtre** high priest; **~ prix** grand prix; **le ~ public** the general public; **produit ~ public** consumer product; **la ~e banlieue** the outer suburbs; **la ~e cuisine** haute cuisine; **~e distribution** volume retailing; **la Grande Guerre** the First World War; **la ~e muraille de Chine** the Great Wall of China; **~e personne** grown-up, adult; **~e puissance** superpower; **~e roue** big wheel (GB), Ferris wheel (US); **~e surface** supermarket; **~es eaux** fountains; **dès qu'on la gronde, ce sont les ~es eaux** the minute you tell her off, she turns on the waterworks; **~es lignes** main train routes; **~es marées** spring tides; **~es ondes** long wave; **les ~s blessés** the seriously injured; **~s espaces** open spaces; **~s fauves** big cats; **Grands Lacs** Great Lakes; **~s singes** great apes.

grand-angle, *pl* **grands-angles** /gʀɑ̃tɑ̃gl, gʀɑ̃zɑ̃gl/ *adj* wide-angle.

grand-chose /gʀɑ̃ʃoz/ *pron* **pas ~** not much, not a lot; **ça ne sert pas à ~** it's not much use; **il n'y a plus ~ à faire** there isn't much left to do.

grand-duché, *pl* **grands-duchés** /gʀɑ̃dyʃe/ *nm* grand duchy.

Grande-Bretagne /gʀɑ̃dbʀətaɲ/ *pr nf* Great Britain.

grandement /gʀɑ̃dmɑ̃/ *adv* greatly; a great deal; extremely.

grandeur /gʀɑ̃dœʀ/ *nf* **1** size; **~ nature** [*reproduction*] full-scale; [*portrait*] life-size; **2** scale; **3** greatness; **par ~ d'âme** out of generosity of spirit.

grandiloquent, **~e** /gʀɑ̃dilɔkɑ̃, ɑ̃t/ *adj* pompous, grandiloquent.

grandiose /gʀɑ̃djoz/ *adj* [*site, building, decor*] grandiose; [*success, party*] spectacular; [*gesture, character*] grand.

grandir /gʀɑ̃diʀ/ [3] **I** *vtr* **1** to magnify; **2** to make [sb] look taller; **3** to exaggerate; **4 sortir grandi d'une épreuve** to come out of an ordeal with increased stature.
II *vi* **1** to grow; to grow up; **2** [*company*] to expand; [*crowd, anxiety*] to grow; [*noise*] to become louder and louder.
III se grandir *v refl* (+ *v être*) to make oneself (look) taller.

grand-mère, *pl* **grands-mères** /gʀɑ̃mɛʀ/ *nf* grandmother.

grand-oncle, *pl* **grands-oncles** /gʀɑ̃tɔ̃kl, gʀɑ̃zɔ̃kl/ *nm* great-uncle.

grand-père, *pl* **grands-pères** /gʀɑ̃pɛʀ/ *nm* grandfather.

grands-parents /gʀɑ̃paʀɑ̃/ *nm pl* grandparents.

grand-tante, *pl* **grand(s)-tantes** /gʀɑ̃tɑ̃t/ *nf* great-aunt.

grange /gʀɑ̃ʒ/ *nf* barn.

granit(e) /gʀanit/ *nm* granite; **dalle de ~** granite slab.

granité, **~e** /gʀanite/ *adj* [*surface, leather, paper*] grained.

granulé /gʀanyle/ *nm* granule.

granuleux, **-euse** /gʀanylø, øz/ *adj* **1** [*rock*] granular; **2** [*paper*] grained; [*skin*] grainy.

graphie /gʀafi/ *nf* **1** written form; **2** spelling.

graphique /gʀafik/ **I** *adj* **1** [*work*] graphic; **2** [*screen*] graphic; [*software*] graphics.
II *nm* graph; **~ à bandes** or **en colonnes** bar chart or graph.

graphisme /gʀafism/ *nm* **1** style of drawing; **2** handwriting; **3** graphic design.

graphite /gʀafit/ *nm* graphite.

graphologie /gʀafɔlɔʒi/ *nf* graphology.

grappe /gʀap/ *nf* (of fruit) bunch; (of flowers) cluster.

grappiller /gʀapije/ [1] *vtr* to pick up [*fruit*]; to glean [*information*].

grappin /gʀapɛ̃/ *nm* grappling irons.
IDIOMS **mettre le ~ sur qn**○ to get sb in one's clutches.

gras, **grasse** /gʀɑ, gʀɑs/ **I** *adj* **1** [*substance*] fatty; [*fish*] oily; [*cheese*] full fat; [*paper, hair*] greasy; **2** coarse, vulgar; **3** (in printing) bold; **4** loose, phlegmy.
II *adv* **cuisiner ~** to use a lot of fat in cooking; **manger ~** to eat fatty foods.
III *nm* **1** (from meat) fat; **2** grease; **3** (of arm, calf) **le ~** the fleshy part (**de** of).

grassement /gʀɑsmɑ̃/ *adv* [*pay*] handsomely; [*mark*] generously; [*feed*] lavishly.

gratifiant, **~e** /gʀatifjɑ̃, ɑ̃t/ *adj* gratifying; **travail ~** rewarding job.

gratifier /gʀatifje/ [2] *vtr* **1 ~ qn de qch** to give sb sth; **2** to gratify.

gratin /gʀatɛ̃/ *nm* **1** gratin (*breadcrumbs and cheese*); **2**○ **le ~** the upper crust○.

gratiné, **~e** /gʀatine/ *adj* **1** (Culin) au gratin; **2**○ [*person, style*] weird; [*problem*] mind-bending○.

gratiner /gʀatine/ [1] *vtr* **(faire) ~ un plat** to brown a dish.

gratis /gʀatis/ **I** *adj inv* free.
II *adv* free (GB), for free.

gratitude /gʀatityd/ *nf* gratitude; **avoir de la ~ pour qn** to be grateful to sb.

gratte-ciel /gʀatsjɛl/ *nm inv* skyscraper.

gratter /gʀate/ [1] **I** *vtr* **1** to scratch; to scrape (off); **2** to make [sb] itch; **ça me gratte partout** I'm itching all over.
II *vi* **~ à la porte** to scratch at the door.
III se gratter *v refl* (+ *v être*) to scratch; **se ~ la tête** to scratch one's head.

grattoir /gʀatwaʀ/ *nm* **1** (tool) scraper; **2** (on matchbox) striking strip.

gratuit, **~e** /gʀatɥi, it/ *adj* **1** [*place, service*] free; **2** [*violence, comment*] gratuitous; [*accusation*] spurious; [*exercise*] pointless; **3** [*compliment*] disinterested.

gratuité /gʀatɥite/ *nf* **1 la ~ de l'enseignement** free education; **2** unwarranted or gratuitous nature.

gratuitement /gʀatɥitmɑ̃/ *adv* **1** free (GB), for free (US); **2** [*work, repair*] for nothing; **3** gratuitously.

gravats /gʀava/ *nm pl* rubble.

grave /gʀav/ **I** *adj* **1** [*problem, injury*] serious; **2** [*expression*] grave, solemn; **3** [*voice*] deep; [*note*] low; [*sound*] low-pitched.
II graves *nm pl* **les ~s** the bass.

graveleux, **-euse** /gʀavlø, øz/ *adj* smutty; indecent.

gravement /gʀavmɑ̃/ *adv* **1** gravely, solemnly; **2** seriously.

graver /gʀave/ [1] *vtr* to engrave.

graveur, **-euse** /gʀavœʀ, øz/ *nm,f* engraver.

gravier /gʀavje/ *nm* **du ~** gravel.

gravillon /gʀavijɔ̃/ *nm* grit; **un ~** a bit of grit.

gravir /gʀaviʀ/ [3] *vtr* to climb up.

gravitation /gʀavitasjɔ̃/ *nf* gravitation; **~ universelle** Newton's law of gravitation.

gravité /gʀavite/ *nf* **1** seriousness; **2** solemnity; **3** (in physics) gravity.

graviter /gʀavite/ [1] *vi* to orbit.

gravure /gʀavyʀ/ *nf* **1 la ~** engraving; **2** engraving; **3** print, reproduction.

gré /gʀe/ *nm* **1 contre le ~ de qn** against sb's will; **de plein ~** willingly; **de ~ ou de force** one way or another; **2** (formal) **savoir ~ à qn de qch** to be grateful to sb for sth; **3 j'ai flâné au ~ de mon humeur** I strolled where the mood took me.

grec, **grecque**[1] /gʀɛk/ **I** *adj* **1** [*island, art*] Greek; **2** [*profile*] Grecian.
II *nm* Greek; **le ~ ancien/moderne** Ancient/Modern Greek.

Grec, **Grecque** /gʀɛk/ *nm,f* Greek.

Grèce /gʀɛs/ *pr nf* Greece; **~ antique** Ancient Greece.

grecque[2] /gʀɛk/ **I** *adj f* ▶ **grec**.
II *nf* **1** Greek key; **2** (Culin) **à la ~** à la grecque.

greffe /gʀɛf/ *nf* **1** (of organ) transplant; (of skin) graft; **2** (in agriculture) grafting; graft.

greffer /gʀefe/ [1] **I** *vtr* **1** to transplant [*organ*]; to graft [*tissue*]; **2** to graft [*tree*].
II se greffer *v refl* (+ *v être*) **se ~ sur qch** [*problem, event*] to come along on top of sth.

greffier, **-ière** /gʀefje, ɛʀ/ *nm,f* clerk of the court (GB), court clerk (US).

grégaire /gʀegɛʀ/ *adj* gregarious; **instinct ~** herd instinct.

grêle /gʀɛl/ **I** *adj* **1** skinny; spindly; **2** [*voice*] reedy; [*sound*] thin.
II *nf* **1** hail; **2 recevoir une ~ de coups** to be showered with blows.

grêlé, **~e** /gʀɛle/ *adj* pockmarked.

grêler /gʀɛle/ [1] *v impers* to hail; **il grêle** it's hailing.

grêlon /gʀɛlɔ̃/ *nm* hailstone.

grelot /gʀəlo/ *nm* small bell.

grelotter /gʀəlɔte/ [1] *vi* to shiver.

grenade /gʀənad/ *nf* **1** grenade; **2** pomegranate.

Grenade /gʀənad/ **I** *pr n* Granada.

II *pr nf* **la ~** Grenada.

grenadier /gʀənadje/ *nm* **1** grenadier; **2** pomegranate tree.

grenadine /gʀənadin/ *nf* **(sirop de) ~** grenadine.

grenaille /gʀənaj/ *nf* **1** steel filings; **2** lead shot.

grenat /gʀəna/ *adj inv* dark red.

grenier /gʀənje/ *nm* attic, loft; **~ à grain** granary.

grenouille /gʀənuj/ *nf* frog; **cuisses de ~** frogs' legs.

grès /gʀɛ/ *nm inv* **1** sandstone; **2** (piece of) stoneware.

grésiller /gʀezije/ [1] *vi* **1** [*radio*] to crackle; **2** [*butter, oil*] to sizzle.

grève /gʀɛv/ *nf* **1** strike; **mouvement de ~** industrial action; **2** shore.

■ **~ de la faim** hunger strike; **~ sur le tas** sit-down strike; **~ tournante** staggered strike; **~ du zèle** work-to-rule.

grever /gʀəve/ [16] *vtr* to be a burden on [*country*]; to put a strain on [*budget*].

gréviste /gʀevist/ *nmf* striker.

gribouiller○ /gʀibuje/ [1] I *vtr* to scribble.

II *vi* to doodle.

grief /gʀijɛf/ *nm* grievance; **je ne t'en fais pas ~** I don't hold it against you.

grièvement /gʀijɛvmɑ̃/ *adv* [*injured*] seriously; [*burned*] badly; [*affected*] severely.

griffe /gʀif/ *nf* **1** claw; **toutes ~s dehors** ready to pounce; **tomber entre les ~s de qn** to fall into sb's clutches; **2** (on garment) label; **3** signature stamp; **4** (in jewellery) claw.

griffer /gʀife/ [1] I *vtr* to scratch; **~ qn au visage** to scratch sb on the face.

II **se griffer** *v refl* (+ *v être*) to scratch oneself.

griffonner /gʀifɔne/ [1] *vtr* **1** to scrawl; **2** to sketch.

griffure /gʀifyʀ/ *nf* scratch.

grignoter /gʀiɲɔte/ [1] I *vtr* **1** to nibble; **2** to encroach on [*territory*]; to conquer [*corner of market*]; **3** to fritter away [*inheritance*].

II *vi* **1** [*rodent*] to gnaw; **2** [*person*] to nibble.

gri-gri, *pl* **gris-gris** /gʀigʀi/ *nm* lucky charm, talisman.

gril /gʀil/ *nm* **1** grill (GB), broiler (US); **2** grill pan (GB), broiler (US).

grillade /gʀijad/ *nf* **manger des ~s** to eat grilled meat.

grillage /gʀijaʒ/ *nm* wire netting; chicken wire; wire mesh.

grillagé, **~e** /gʀijaʒe/ *adj* [*enclosure*] fenced with wire; [*door*] covered with wire mesh.

grille /gʀij/ *nf* **1** railings; (iron) gate; (of sink, sewer) drain; (of air vent) grille; (in oven, fridge) shelf; (in fireplace, stove) grate; **2** (in crossword) grid; **3** (on TV, radio) programme[GB]; **4** (for assessing results) model; **5** (in administration) scale.

grillé, **~e** /gʀije/ I *pp* ▶ **griller**.

II *pp adj* **1** [*meat*] grilled; [*bread*] toasted; [*almonds*] roasted; **2** crispy, well-browned; **3**○ burned out; **l'ampoule est ~e** the bulb has blown; **4**○ [*spy*] exposed.

grille-pain /gʀijpɛ̃/ *nm inv* toaster.

griller /gʀije/ [1] I *vtr* **1** to grill [*meat*]; to toast [*bread*]; to roast [*almonds*]; **2** to burn out [*appliance*]; to blow [*bulb*]; **3**○ to jump○ [*light*]; to ignore [*give way sign*]; **4**○ to give the game away about [sb]; **5**○ **~ un adversaire** to manage to get ahead of one's opponent.

II *vi* **1** to grill; **faire ~** to grill; to toast; to roast; **2** [*bulb*] to blow.

grillon /gʀijɔ̃/ *nm* cricket.

grimace /gʀimas/ *nf* **1** grimace; funny face; **2** grotesque.

grimacer /gʀimase/ [12] *vi* to grimace.

grimer /gʀime/ [1] I *vtr* to make [sb] up.

II **se grimer** *v refl* (+ *v être*) to make oneself up.

grimpant, **~e** /gʀɛ̃pɑ̃, ɑ̃t/ *adj* [*plant*] climbing.

grimper /gʀɛ̃pe/ [1] I *vtr* to climb [*stairs*].

II *vi* **1** **~ aux arbres** to climb (up) trees; **grimpe sur mon dos** get on my back; **2**○ [*road*] to be steep; **3**○ [*temperature, prices*] to climb.

grimpeur, **-euse** /gʀɛ̃pœʀ, øz/ *nm,f* rock climber.

grinçant, **~e** /gʀɛ̃sɑ̃, ɑ̃t/ *adj* **1** [*lock*] creaking; [*music*] grating; **2** [*tone*] scathing; [*joke*] caustic; [*laugh*] nasty.

grincement /gʀɛ̃smɑ̃/ *nm* **1** (of door) creaking; (of chalk) squeaking; (of violin) screeching; **2** creak; squeak; screech.

grincer /gʀɛ̃se/ [12] *vi* [*door*] to creak; [*violin*] to screech; [*chalk*] to squeak; **~ des dents** to grind one's teeth; (figurative) to gnash one's teeth.

grincheux, **-euse** /gʀɛ̃ʃø, øz/ *adj* grumpy (GB), grouchy○.

gringalet /gʀɛ̃galɛ/ *nm* runt.

griotte /gʀijɔt/ *nf* morello cherry.

grippe /gʀip/ *nf* flu; **~ intestinale** gastric flu (GB), intestinal flu (US).

IDIOMS **prendre qn/qch en ~**○ to take a sudden dislike to sb/sth.

grippé, **~e** /gʀipe/ *adj* **être ~** to have flu (GB), to have the flu.

gris, **~e** /gʀi, iz/ I *adj* **1** grey (GB), gray (US); **2** dreary; dull; **3** tipsy.

II *nm inv* grey (GB), gray (US).

IDIOMS **faire ~e mine** to be none too pleased.

grisaille /gʀizaj/ *nf* **1** dullness; **2** (of weather) greyness (GB), grayness (US).

grisant, **~e** /gʀizɑ̃, ɑ̃t/ *adj* **1** [*speed, pleasure*] exhilarating; [*success, danger*] intoxicating; **2** [*perfume*] heady.

grisâtre /gʀizɑtʀ/ *adj* [*colour, sky*] greyish (GB), grayish (US); [*morning*] dull.

griser /gʀize/ [1] I *vtr* **1** [*speed*] to exhilarate; [*success*] to intoxicate; **se laisser ~ par le pouvoir** to let power go to one's head; **2** [*perfume*] to intoxicate.

II **se griser** *v refl* (+ *v être*) **se ~ de** to get drunk on.

grisou /gʀizu/ *nm* firedamp; **coup de ~** firedamp explosion.

grive /gʀiv/ *nf* thrush.

grivois, ~e /gʀivwa, az/ *adj* bawdy; coarse.

grivoiserie /gʀivwazʀi/ *nf* **1** suggestiveness; **2** suggestive remark.

grizzli, grizzly /gʀizli/ *nm* grizzly bear.

grognement /gʀɔɲəmɑ̃/ *nm* grunt; growl.

grogner /gʀɔɲe/ [1] *vi* **1** to groan; (figurative) to grumble; **2** [*pig*] to grunt; [*dog*] to growl.

grognon /gʀɔɲɔ̃, ɔn/ *adj* grumpy (GB), grouchy○.

groin /gʀwɛ̃/ *nm* snout.

grommeler /gʀɔmle/ [19] *vi* **1** to grumble (**contre** about); **2** [*boar*] to snort.

grondement /gʀɔ̃dmɑ̃/ *nm* (of avalanche) rumble; (of torrent, machine) roar; (of crowd) angry murmur.

gronder /gʀɔ̃de/ [1] **I** *vtr* to tell [sb] off.
II *vi* **1** [*thunder*] to rumble; [*machine, wind*] to roar; **2** [*rebellion*] to be brewing.

groom /gʀum/ *nm* bellboy (GB), bellhop (US).

gros, grosse /gʀo, gʀos/ **I** *adj* **1** big, large; **2** thick; **3** fat; **4** [*customer, market*] big; [*damage*] considerable; **5** [*problem, mistake*] serious, big; [*disappointment, flaw*] big, major; **6** big; [*cold*] bad; [*sobs*] loud; [*voice, sigh*] deep; [*rain, snowfall*] heavy; [*drinker, smoker*] heavy.
II *adv* **1** [*write*] big; **2** [*bet, lose*] a lot of money; (figurative) a lot.
III *nm inv* **1 le ~ de** the majority of [*spectators, passengers*]; the bulk of [*work*]; most of [*winter, deficit*]; **2** wholesale trade; **3 la pêche au ~** game fishing.
IV en ~ *phr* **1** roughly; **en ~ je suis d'accord avec toi** basically, I agree with you; **2** wholesale; **3** in big letters.
■ **~ bétail** large livestock; **~ bonnet**○ big shot○; **~ lot** first prize; **gagner** or **décrocher le ~ lot** to hit the jackpot; **~ mot** swearword; **~ œuvre** shell (of a building); **~ plan** close-up; **~ sel** cooking salt; **~ titre** headline; **grosse caisse** bass drum; **grosse légume**○ = **~ bonnet**; **grosse tête**○ brain○.
IDIOMS **en avoir ~ sur le cœur** or **la patate**○ to be very upset; **c'est un peu ~ comme histoire!** that's a bit of a tall story!

groseille /gʀozɛj/ *nf* redcurrant; **~ à maquereau** gooseberry.

groseillier /gʀozeje/ *nm* redcurrant bush; **~ à maquereau** gooseberry bush.

grosse ▶ **gros**.

grossesse /gʀosɛs/ *nf* pregnancy; **robe de ~** maternity dress.
■ **~ nerveuse** phantom pregnancy (GB), false pregnancy.

grosseur /gʀosœʀ/ *nf* **1** size; **2** (of thread) thickness; **3** (Med) lump.

grossier, -ière /gʀosje, ɛʀ/ *adj* **1** [*person, gesture*] rude; [*language*] bad; **2** [*laugh, features*] coarse; **3** [*imitation*] crude; [*material*] coarse; **4** [*cleaning*] cursory; [*sketch, idea*] rough; [*work*] crude; **5** [*ignorance*] crass; [*error*] glaring.

grossièrement /gʀosjɛʀmɑ̃/ *adv* **1** [*calculate*] roughly; **2** [*built*] crudely; **3** [*speak*] rudely; **4 se tromper ~** to be utterly mistaken.

grossièreté /gʀosjɛʀte/ *nf* **1** rudeness; **2** dirty word; **3** coarseness.

grossir /gʀosiʀ/ [3] **I** *vtr* **1** to enlarge [*image*]; **2** to increase [*numbers*]; to boost [*profits*]; **3** to exaggerate [*incident*]; **4** to make [sb] look fat; **5** to swell [*river*].
II *vi* **1** to put on weight; **2** (gen) to grow; [*river*] to swell; **3** [*storm*] to get worse; [*rumour*] to grow.

grossissant, ~e /gʀosisɑ̃, ɑ̃t/ *adj* **1** magnifying; **2** [*tide*] swelling.

grossiste /gʀosist/ *nmf* wholesaler.

grosso modo /gʀosomodo/ *adv* roughly.

grotesque /gʀɔtɛsk/ **I** *adj* ridiculous.
II *nm* **1 être d'un ~ absolu** to be utterly ridiculous; **2 le ~** the grotesque.

grotte /gʀɔt/ *nf* **1** cave; **2** grotto.

grouiller /gʀuje/ [1] **I** *vi* to swarm about; to mill about; **~ d'asticots** to be crawling with maggots.
II se grouiller○ *v refl* (+ *v être*) to get a move on○.

groupe /gʀup/ *nm* **1** group (**de** of); **par ~s de deux** in pairs, in twos; **2** (of objects) group; cluster; **3** (Econ) group; **~ financier** financial group.
■ **~ d'autodéfense** vigilante group; **~ électrogène** (electricity) generator; **~ de presse** newspaper group; **~ sanguin** blood group; **~ scolaire** school; **~ des Sept, G7** Group of Seven, G7 countries; **~ de travail** working party.

groupement /gʀupmɑ̃/ *nm* **1** association, group; **2** grouping.

grouper /gʀupe/ [1] **I** *vtr* to put together [*bills, cheques*].
II se grouper *v refl* (+ *v être*) **1** to gather; **se ~ par trois** to form groups of three; **2** to form a group; **restez groupés** keep together.

groupuscule /gʀupyskyl/ *nm* (very) small group.

gruau, *pl* **~x** /gʀyo/ *nm* **1** gruel; **2** fine wheat flour.

grue /gʀy/ *nf* **1** (Tech) crane; **2** (Zool) crane.
IDIOMS **faire le pied de ~**○ to hang around.

grumeau, *pl* **~x** /gʀymo/ *nm* lump; **faire des ~x** [*sauce*] to go lumpy.

gruyère /gʀyjɛʀ/ *nm* Gruyère, Swiss cheese.

Guadeloupe /gwadlup/ *pr nf* **la ~** Guadeloupe.

gué /ge/ *nm* ford; **passer un ruisseau à ~** to ford a stream.

guenille /gənij/ *nf* rag; **en ~s** in rags.

guenon /gənɔ̃/ *nf* female monkey.

guépard /gepaʀ/ *nm* cheetah.

guêpe /gɛp/ *nf* wasp.
IDIOMS **pas folle la ~**○! I'm/she's etc not just a pretty face○!

guêpier /gepje/ *nm* **1** wasps' nest; **2** tight corner; **dans quel ~ es-tu allé te fourrer**○**?** what kind of mess have you got (GB) or gotten (US) yourself into?

guêpière /gepjɛʀ/ *nf* basque, bodyshaper with suspenders (GB) or garters (US).

guère /gɛʀ/ *adv* hardly; **il n'avait ~ le choix** he didn't really have a choice.

guéridon /geʀidɔ̃/ *nm* pedestal table.

guérilla /geʀija/ *nf* guerilla warfare.

guérir /geʀiʀ/ [3] **I** *vtr* **1** to cure [*person, disease*]; to heal [*wound*]; **2 ~ qn de** to cure sb of [*habit*].

II *vi* to recover; to heal; to get better.

III se guérir *v refl* (+ *v être*) **se ~ de** to overcome [*shyness*].

guérison /geʀizɔ̃/ *nf* (of sick person) recovery; (of wound) healing.

guérisseur, -euse /geʀisœʀ, øz/ *nm,f* healer.

guérite /geʀit/ *nf* **1** sentry box; **2** (for toll road) booth.

guerre /gɛʀ/ *nf* war; warfare; **les pays en ~** the warring nations; **elle lui fait la ~ pour qu'il range sa chambre** she's fighting a running battle with him to try and get him to tidy his room.

■ **~ chimique** chemical war; chemical warfare; **~ éclair** blitzkrieg, lightning war; **~ mondiale** world war; **Première/Deuxième Guerre mondiale** World War I/II; **~ nucléaire** nuclear war; nuclear warfare; **~ de 14** 1914–18 war; **~ de Sécession** American Civil War; **~ de tranchée** trench warfare; **~ d'usure** war of attrition.

IDIOMS **à la ~ comme à la ~** in time of hardship you have to make the best of things; **c'est de bonne ~** it's only fair; **être sur le pied de ~** to be on a war footing; **de ~ lasse, elle renonça** realizing that she was fighting a losing battle, she gave up.

guerrier, -ière /geʀje, ɛʀ/ **I** *adj* warlike; **exploits ~s** war deeds.

II *nm,f* warrior.

guet /gɛ/ *nm* **1** lookout; **faire le ~** to be on the lookout; **2** (Mil) watch.

guet-apens, *pl* **guets-apens** /gɛtapɑ̃/ *nm* ambush; (figurative) trap.

guêtre /gɛtʀ/ *nf* **1** (Sport) leggings; **2** gaiter.

guetter /gete/ [1] *vtr* **1** to watch [*prey, criminal, reaction*]; to watch out for [*sign*]; to look out for [*postman*]; **2** to threaten; **la folie le guette** he is on the brink of madness.

gueule /gœl/ *nf* **1**● face; **il a la ~ de l'emploi** he really looks the part; **2**● mouth; **(ferme) ta ~!** shut your face○ (GB) or mouth○!; **3**● look; **le gâteau a une drôle de ~** the cake looks weird; **4** (of animal) mouth; **5** (of tunnel, cannon) mouth.

■ **~ de bois**○ hangover.

IDIOMS **faire la ~**● to be sulking.

gueuler● /gœle/ [1] **I** *vtr* to yell; to bawl out.

II *vi* to yell, to bawl; to kick up a real fuss; **~ après qn** to have a go at sb○; **~ contre qch** to moan about sth.

gui /gi/ *nm* mistletoe.

guichet /giʃɛ/ *nm* **1** window; (in bank) counter; (in museum, station) ticket office; (in theatre, cinema) box office; **la pièce se jouera à ~s fermés** the play is sold out; **2** (in door, wall) grille.

■ **~ automatique** automatic teller machine.

guichetier, -ière /giʃtje, ɛʀ/ *nm,f* ticket clerk.

guide /gid/ *nm* guide.

guide-interprète, *pl* **guides-interprètes** /gidɛ̃tɛʀpʀɛt, gidzɛ̃tɛʀpʀɛt/ *nmf* tour guide and interpreter.

guider /gide/ [1] **I** *vtr* **1** to show [sb] the way; **~ jusque** to take [sb] to; **2** [*star, sign*] to guide; [*scent, tracks*] to lead; **3** to guide [*plane, missile*]; **4** to guide [*student*].

II se guider *v refl* (+ *v être*) **se ~ sur qch** to set one's course by sth.

guidon /gidɔ̃/ *nm* handlebars.

guigne○ /giɲ/ *nf* bad luck; **avoir la ~** to be dogged by bad luck.

guignol /giɲɔl/ *nm* **1** puppet show, ≈ Punch and Judy show; **c'est du ~** it's farcical; **2** (derogatory) clown; **faire le ~** to clown around.

guillemets /gijmɛ/ *nm pl* inverted commas (GB), quotation marks.

guillotine /gijɔtin/ *nf* guillotine.

guillotiner /gijɔtine/ [1] *vtr* to guillotine.

guimauve /gimov/ *nf* **1** (Bot) (marsh) mallow; **2** (confectionery) marshmallow.

guimbarde /gɛ̃baʀd/ *nf* **1**○ old banger (GB) or crate○; **2** Jew's harp.

guindé, ~e /gɛ̃de/ *adj* formal.

guinée /gine/ *nf* guinea.

guingois: **de guingois** /degɛ̃gwa/ *phr* **être de ~** to be lopsided.

guirlande /giʀlɑ̃d/ *nf* garland; tinsel; paper chain.

■ **~ électrique** set or string of fairy lights.

guise /giz/ *nf* **1 'à votre ~'** 'just as you like or please'; **2 en ~ de** by way of.

guitare /gitaʀ/ *nf* guitar.

guitariste /gitaʀist/ *nmf* guitarist.

gustatif, -ive /gystatif, iv/ *adj* [*organ*] taste.

guttural, ~e, *mpl* **-aux** /gytyʀal, o/ *adj* guttural.

Guyana /gɥijana/ *pr nf* Guyana; **République de ~** Republic of Guyana.

Guyane /gɥijan/ *pr nf* **~ (française)** (French) Guyana; **~ hollandaise** Dutch Guiana.

gym○ /ʒim/ *nf* physical education; (Sport) gymnastics.

gymnase /ʒimnɑz/ *nm* gymnasium.

gymnaste /ʒimnast/ *nmf* gymnast.

gymnastique /ʒimnastik/ *nf* **1** gymnastics; **2** exercises; **~ de l'esprit** mental exercise.

■ **~ aquatique** aquagym; **~ corrective** ≈ physiotherapy exercises.

gynécologie /ʒinekɔlɔʒi/ *nf* gynaecology.

gynécologue /ʒinekɔlɔg/ *nmf* gynaecologist.

gyrophare /ʒiʀɔfaʀ/ *nm* flashing light, emergency rotating light.

gyroscope /ʒiʀɔskɔp/ *nm* gyroscope.

h, **H** /aʃ/ *nm inv* **1** h, H; **2** (*written abbr* = **heure**) **9 h 10** 9.10.

ha /ˈa/ (*written abbr* = **hectare**) ha.

habile /abil/ *adj* clever, skilful[GB].

habilement /abilmɑ̃/ *adv* cleverly, skilfully[GB].

habileté /abilte/ *nf* skill; skilfulness[GB].

habiliter /abilite/ [1] *vtr* to authorize (**à faire** to do).

habillé, **~e** /abije/ *adj* [*dress*] smart; [*dinner*] formal.

habillement /abijmɑ̃/ *nm* clothing.

habiller /abije/ [1] **I** *vtr* **1** to dress (**de** in); to dress [sb] up (**en** as); **2** to clothe; to provide [sb] with clothing; **3** to make [sb's] clothes; **4** [*clothes*] to suit [*person*]; **un rien l'habille** she looks good in anything.
II s'habiller *v refl* (+ *v être*) **1** to get dressed; to dress up; **s'~ en pirate** to dress up as a pirate; **s'~ long/court** to wear long/short clothes; **2 s'~ chez** to get one's clothes from.

habit /abi/ *nm* **1 ~s** clothes; **2** tails, morning coat; morning dress; **3** outfit, costume; **4** (of monk, nun) habit.
■ **~ de cheval** riding clothes; **~ ecclésiastique** clerical dress; **~ de lumière** matador's costume; **~s du dimanche** Sunday best.

habitable /abitabl/ *adj* **1** habitable; **2 surface ~** living space.

habitacle /abitakl/ *nm* **1** (of plane) cockpit; (of rocket) cabin; **2** binnacle.

habitant, **~e** /abitɑ̃, ɑ̃t/ *nm,f* inhabitant; resident; **loger chez l'~** to stay as a paying guest.

habitat /abita/ *nm* **1** (Bot, Zool) habitat; **2** settlement; **3** housing.

habitation /abitasjɔ̃/ *nf* **1** house, dwelling; **2** home; **3** living; **immeuble d'~** block of flats (GB), apartment building (US).
■ **~ à loyer modéré, HLM** ≈ council flat (GB), low-rent apartment (US); ≈ block of council flats (GB), low-rent apartment building (US).

habité, **~e** /abite/ *adj* **1** inhabited; **2** [*rocket*] manned.

habiter /abite/ [1] **I** *vtr* **1** to live in [*house, country*]; **2** (formal) [*feeling*] to dwell in.
II *vi* **~ à** or **en** to live in [*paris, suburbs*].

habitude /abityd/ **I** *nf* **1** habit; **par ~** out of habit; **ce n'est pas dans mes ~s d'être en retard** it's not like me to be late; **ils ont l'~ de se coucher tôt** they usually go to bed early; **avoir ses (petites) ~s** to have got (GB) or gotten (US) into a routine; to have one's own way of doing things; **comme à leur ~** as they usually do; **avoir l'~ de** to be used to; **2** custom.
II d'habitude *phr* usually.

habitué, **~e** /abitɥe/ *nm,f* regular.

habituel, **-elle** /abitɥɛl/ *adj* usual.

habituellement /abitɥɛlmɑ̃/ *adv* usually, generally.

habituer /abitɥe/ [1] **I** *vtr* **1** to get [sb/sth] used (**à** to; **à faire** to doing); **2** to teach (**à faire** to do).
II s'habituer *v refl* (+ *v être*) to get used or accustomed (**à** to).

hâbleur, **-euse** /ˈɑblœʀ, øz/ *adj* boastful.

hache /ˈaʃ/ *nf* axe (GB), ax (US).
IDIOMS **enterrer la ~ de guerre** to bury the hatchet; **déterrer la ~ de guerre** to go on the warpath.

haché, **~e** /ˈaʃe/ *adj* **1** [*meat*] minced; **2** [*speech*] disjointed.

hache-légumes /ˈaʃlegym/ *nm inv* vegetable chopper.

hacher /ˈaʃe/ [1] *vtr* to mince [*meat*]; to chop [*onion*].

hachette /ˈaʃɛt/ *nf* hatchet.

hache-viande /ˈaʃvjɑ̃d/ *nm inv* mincer.

hachis /ˈaʃi/ *nm inv* mince; **~ de persil** chopped parsley.
■ **~ Parmentier** ≈ shepherd's pie.

hachisch /ˈaʃiʃ/ *nm* hashish.

hachoir /ˈaʃwaʀ/ *nm* **1** mincer; **2** (food) chopper.

hachurer /ˈaʃyʀe/ [1] *vtr* to hatch.

haddock /ˈadɔk/ *nm* smoked haddock.

hagard, **~e** /ˈagaʀ, aʀd/ *adj* [*person*] dazed; [*eyes*] wild.

haie /ˈɛ/ *nf* **1** hedge; **2** (Sport) hurdle; fence; **course de ~s** hurdle race; steeple chase; **3** line, row; **faire une ~ d'honneur** to form a guard of honour[GB].

haillon /ˈɑjɔ̃/ *nm* rag; **en ~s** in rags.

haine /ˈɛn/ *nf* hatred; **s'attirer la ~ de qn** to earn sb's hatred; **par ~ de qch** out of hatred for sth.

haineux, **-euse** /ˈɛnø, øz/ *adj* full of hatred.

haïr /ˈaiʀ/ [25] *vtr* to hate.

haïssable /ˈaisabl/ *adj* detestable, hateful.

halage /ˈalaʒ/ *nm* towing; **chemin de ~** towpath.

hâle /ˈɑl/ *nm* (sun)tan.

hâlé, **~e** /ˈɑle/ *adj* tanned.

haleine /alɛn/ *nf* **1** breath; **2** breathing; **hors d'~** out of breath; **à perdre ~** until one is out of breath; **un travail de longue ~** a long-drawn-out job.

haler /ˈale/ [1] *vtr* to tow [*boat*]; to haul in [*chain*].

haletant, **~e** /ˈaltɑ̃, ɑ̃t/ *adj* [*person*] panting; [*voice*] breathless.

haleter /ˈalte/ [18] *vi* **1** to gasp for breath; to pant; **2** [*machine*] to puff; [*chest*] to heave.

hall /ˈol/ *nm* entrance hall (GB), lobby (US); **~ (de gare)** concourse.

halle /ˈal/ *nf* covered market.

hallucinant°, **~e** /alysinɑ̃, ɑ̃t/ *adj* astounding.

hallucination /alysinasjɔ̃/ *nf* hallucination; **avoir des ~s** to hallucinate; (figurative) to be seeing things.

halluciné°, **~e** /alysine/ *nm,f* crank.

hallucinogène /alysinɔʒɛn/ *adj* hallucinogenic.

halo /ˈalo/ *nm* halo; **entouré d'un ~ de mystère** shrouded in mystery.

halogène /alɔʒɛn/ *adj* halogen.

halte /ˈalt/ **I** *nf* **1** stop; **faire une ~** to stop somewhere; **2** stopping place.

II *excl* stop!; (Mil) halt!

halte-garderie, *pl* **haltes-garderies** /ˈaltəgaʀdəʀi/ *nf* ≈ playgroup.

haltère /altɛʀ/ *nm* dumbbell; barbell; **faire des ~s** to do weightlifting.

haltérophilie /alteʀɔfili/ *nf* weightlifting.

hamac /ˈamak/ *nm* hammock.

hameau, *pl* **~x** /ˈamo/ *nm* hamlet.

hameçon /amsɔ̃/ *nm* hook; **mordre à l'~** to take the bait.

hampe /ˈɑ̃p/ *nf* **1** (for flag) pole; (of weapon) shaft; **2** (Culin) flank.

hanche /ˈɑ̃ʃ/ *nf* (of person) hip; (of horse) haunch.

handicap /ˈɑ̃dikap/ *nm* handicap.

handicapé, **~e** /ˈɑ̃dikape/ **I** *adj* **1** disabled, handicapped; **2 être ~** to be at a disadvantage.

II *nm,f* disabled person.

handicaper /ˈɑ̃dikape/ [1] *vtr* to handicap.

handisport /ɑ̃dispɔʀ/ *adj* wheelchair.

hangar /ˈɑ̃gaʀ/ *nm* shed; warehouse; hangar.

hanneton /ˈantɔ̃/ *nm* cockchafer (GB), June bug (US).

hanter /ˈɑ̃te/ [1] *vtr* to haunt.

hantise /ˈɑ̃tiz/ *nf* dread.

happer /ˈape/ [1] *vtr* to catch [*insect*]; **happé par** [*arm*] caught up in [*machine*]; [*person*] hit by [*train*]; (figurative) swallowed up by [*crowd*].

haranguer /ˈaʀɑ̃ge/ [1] *vtr* to harangue.

haras /ˈaʀa/ *nm inv* stud farm.

harasser /ˈaʀase/ [1] *vtr* to exhaust.

harcèlement /ˈaʀsɛlmɑ̃/ *nm* harassment.

harceler /ˈaʀsəle/ [17] *vtr* **1** to pester (**de** with); **2** to harass.

hardes /ˈaʀd/ *nf pl* (literary) rags.

hardi, **~e** /ˈaʀdi/ *adj* bold, daring.

hardiesse /ˈaʀdjɛs/ *nf* boldness, daring.

hareng /ˈaʀɑ̃/ *nm* herring; **~ saur** smoked herring.

hargne /ˈaʀɲ/ *nf* aggression; **avec ~** aggressively.

hargneux, **-euse** /ˈaʀɲø, øz/ *adj* aggressive.

haricot /ˈaʀiko/ *nm* (Bot) bean; **~ blanc** haricot bean; **~ vert** French bean.

IDIOMS **c'est la fin des ~s**° we've had it°.

harmonica /aʀmɔnika/ *nm* mouth organ, harmonica.

harmonie /aʀmɔni/ *nf* **1** harmony; **2** brass band.

harmonieux, **-ieuse** /aʀmɔnjø, øz/ *adj* harmonious; [*movements*] graceful; [*couple*] well-suited.

harmoniser /aʀmɔnize/ [1] **I** *vtr* **1** to coordinate [*colours*]; **2** to harmonize; to make [sth] consistent; to bring into line (**avec** with); **3** (Mus) to harmonize.

II s'harmoniser *v refl* (+ *v être*) **bien s'~** [*colours*] to go together well.

harnachement /ˈaʀnaʃmɑ̃/ *nm* **1** harness; harnessing; **2**° get-up°.

harnacher /ˈaʀnaʃe/ [1] *vtr* **1** to harness [*horse*]; **2**° to rig out° [*person*].

harnais /ˈaʀnɛ/ *nm inv* harness.

harpe /ˈaʀp/ *nf* harp.

harpie /ˈaʀpi/ *nf* harpy.

harpon /ˈaʀpɔ̃/ *nm* harpoon.

harponner /ˈaʀpɔne/ [1] *vtr* **1** to harpoon [*whale*]; **2**° to waylay [*passerby*]; to nab° [*thief*].

hasard /ˈazaʀ/ *nm* chance; **par ~** by chance; **par un malencontreux ~** by an unfortunate accident; **par un curieux ~** by a curious coincidence; **par un heureux ~** by a stroke of luck; **ce n'est pas un ~ si...** it's no accident that...; **le ~ a voulu que...** as luck would have it,...; **au ~** [*choose*] at random; [*walk*] aimlessly; [*answer*] off the top of one's head; **au ~ de mes promenades** on my walks; **comme par ~, il a oublié son argent** (ironic) surprise, surprise, he's forgotten his money; **à tout ~** just in case, on the off chance; **les ~s de la vie** the fortunes of life.

IDIOMS **le ~ fait bien les choses** fate is a great provider.

hasarder /ˈazaʀde/ [1] **I** *vtr* **1** to venture [*advice*]; **2** (literary) to risk [*life*].

II se hasarder *v refl* (+ *v être*) to venture (**à faire** to do).

hasardeux, **-euse** /ˈazaʀdø, øz/ *adj* **1** risky; **2** hazardous.

hâte /ˈɑt/ *nf* **1** haste; **en toute ~** in great haste; **à la ~** hastily; **2 j'ai ~ de partir/qu'elle parte** I can't wait to leave/for her to leave.

hâter /ˈɑte/ [1] **I** *vtr* to hasten; **~ le pas** to quicken one's step.

II se hâter *v refl* (+ *v être*) to hurry, to rush.

hâtif, **-ive** /ˈɑtif, iv/ *adj* **1** [*judgment*] hasty, hurried; **2** [*plant*] early.

hâtivement /ˈɑtivmɑ̃/ *adv* hurriedly, hastily.

hausse /ˈos/ *nf* increase (**de** in), rise (**de** in); **être en ~** [*prices, temperature*] to be rising; [*goods*] to be going up in price; **en ~ de 10%** up 10%.

haussement /ˈosmɑ̃/ *nm* **~ d'épaules** shrug.

hausser /ˈose/ [1] **I** *vtr* to raise; **~ les épaules** to shrug one's shoulders.

II se hausser *v refl* (+ *v être*) **se ~ au**

niveau de to rise up to the level of; **se ~ sur la pointe des pieds** to stand on tiptoe.

haut, **~e**[1] /'o, 'ot/ I *adj* **1** high; tall; **la partie ~e d'un mur** the top part of a wall; **l'étagère la plus ~e** the top shelf; **à ~e voix** [*speak*] loudly; [*read*] aloud, out loud; **à ~ risque** very risky; **au plus ~ point** immensely; **2** [*rank, society, quality*] high; [*person, post*] high-ranking; [*responsibility*] big; **bénéficier de ~es protections** to have friends in high places; **~e surveillance** close supervision; **3** (in geography) upper; **la ~e Égypte** Upper Egypt; **4 de la plus ~e antiquité** from earliest antiquity; **le ~ Moyen Âge** the early Middle Ages.

II *adv* **1** high; **un personnage ~ placé** a high-ranking person; **plus ~ sur la page** higher up on the page; **'voir plus ~'** see above; **de ~** from above; **2** (in time) far back; **3** loud(ly); **dire qch tout ~** to say sth aloud or out loud; **n'avoir jamais un mot plus ~ que l'autre** never to raise one's voice.

III *nm* **1** top; **le ~ du corps** the top half of the body; **l'étagère du ~** the top shelf; **les pièces du ~** the upstairs rooms; **parler du ~ d'un balcon** to speak from a balcony; **2 faire 50 mètres de ~** to be 50 metres[GB] high.

IV **en haut** *phr* upstairs; on an upper floor; **en ~ de** at the top of.

■ **~ en couleur** [*character*] colourful[GB]; **~ fait** heroic deed; **~ fonctionnaire** senior civil servant; **~ lieu de** centre[GB] of or for; **en ~ lieu** in high places; **~e mer** open sea; **~es eaux** high water; **~es sphères** high social circles; **~es terres** highlands; **~s fourneaux** blast furnace.

IDIOMS **marcher la tête ~e** to walk with one's head held high; **voir les choses de ~** to have a detached view of things; **tomber de ~** to be dumbfounded; **regarder qn de ~ en bas** to look sb up and down; **avoir** or **connaître des ~s et des bas** to have one's ups and downs; **~ les mains!** hands up!; **gagner ~ la main** to win hands down; **prendre qch de ~** to react indignantly.

hautain, **~e** /'otɛ̃, ɛn/ *adj* haughty.

hautbois /'obwa/ *nm inv* **1** oboe; **2** oboist.

haut-de-forme, *pl* **hauts-de-formes** /'odfɔʀm/ *nm* top hat.

haute[2] /'ot/ I *adj f* ▶ **haut I**.

II○ *nf* **les gens de la ~** the upper crust.

haute(-)fidélité, *pl* **hautes(-)fidélités** /'otfidelite/ *nf* hi-fi, high fidelity.

hautement /'otmɑ̃/ *adv* highly.

hauteur /'otœʀ/ I *nf* **1** height; **prendre de la ~** [*plane*] to climb; **dans le sens de la ~** upright; **à ~ d'homme** at head height; **à ~ des yeux** at eye level; **2** hill; **gagner les ~s** to reach high ground; **3** haughtiness; **4** (of voice) pitch.

II **à la hauteur de** *phr* **1 arriver à la ~ de** to come up to; to draw level with; **raccourcir une jupe à la ~ des genoux** to shorten a dress to the knee; **2** (figurative) **être à la ~** to measure up; **être à la ~ de sa tâche** to be equal to one's job; **être à la ~ du talent de qn** to do justice to sb's talent.

IDIOMS **tomber de toute sa ~** to fall headlong; **se dresser de toute sa ~** to draw oneself up to one's full height.

haut-fond, *pl* **hauts-fonds** /'ofɔ̃/ *nm* shallows.

haut(-)fourneau, *pl* **hauts(-)fourneaux** /'ofuʀno/ *nm* blast furnace.

haut-le-cœur /'olkœʀ/ *nm inv* retching, heaving; **avoir un ~** to retch.

haut-le-corps /'olkɔʀ/ *nm inv* start, jump.

haut-parleur, *pl* **~s** /'opaʀlœʀ/ *nm* loudspeaker.

hauturier, **-ière** /'otyʀje, ɛʀ/ *adj* [*fishing*] deep-sea.

havane /'avan/ I *adj inv* tobacco-brown.

II *nm* **1** Havana tobacco; **2** Havana cigar.

hâve /'ɑv/ *adj* (formal) haggard, gaunt.

havre /'ɑvʀ/ *nm* haven.

havresac /'avʀəsak/ *nm* haversack.

Haye /'ɛ/ *pr n* **la ~** the Hague.

hebdomadaire /ɛbdɔmadɛʀ/ *adj, nm* weekly.

hébergement /ebɛʀʒəmɑ̃/ *nm* **1** accommodation; **2** housing.

héberger /ebɛʀʒe/ [13] *vtr* to put [sb] up; to accommodate; to take [sb] in; to provide shelter for.

hébété, **~e** /ebete/ *adj* [*look*] stupid; **~ par** stupefied by [*alcohol, work*]; **~ de douleur** numb with grief.

hébraïque /ebʀaik/ *adj* Hebrew.

hébreu, *pl* **~x** /ebʀø/ I *adj m* Hebrew.

II *nm* Hebrew.

IDIOMS **pour moi, c'est de l'~** it's all Greek to me.

HEC /aʃəse/ *nf* (*abbr* = **Hautes études commerciales**) *major business school*.

hécatombe /ekatɔ̃b/ *nf* massacre, slaughter.

hectare /ɛktaʀ/ *nm* hectare.

hecto /ɛkto/ I *nm* (*abbr* = **hectogramme**) hectogram.

II **hecto(-)** (*combining form*) hecto.

hédoniste /edɔnist/ *adj* hedonistic.

hégémonie /eʒemɔni/ *nf* hegemony.

hein○ /'ɛ̃/ *excl* what○?, sorry?

hélas /'elas/ *excl* alas; **~ non!** unfortunately not!

héler /'ele/ [14] *vtr* to hail.

hélice /elis/ *nf* **1** (screw) propeller; **2** helix.

hélicoptère /elikɔptɛʀ/ *nm* helicopter.

héliporté, **~e** /elipɔʀte/ *adj* helicopter-borne.

hélitreuiller /elitʀœje/ [1] *vtr* to winch [sb] to safety (*by helicopter*).

hellène /ellɛn/ *adj* Hellenic.

helvétique /ɛlvetik/ *adj* Helvetic, Swiss; **la Confédération ~** Switzerland.

hématologie /ematɔlɔʒi/ *nf* haematology.

hématome /ematom/ *nm* **1** bruise; **2** haematoma.

hémicycle /emisikl/ *nm* semicircular auditorium.

hémisphère /emisfɛʀ/ *nm* hemisphere.

hémistiche /emistiʃ/ *nm* hemistich; **coupe à l'~** caesura.

hémoglobine /emɔglɔbin/ *nf* haemoglobin.

hémophile /emɔfil/ I *adj* haemophilic.
II *nmf* haemophiliac.

hémorragie /emɔʀaʒi/ *nf* **1** haemorrhage, bleeding; **2** (of capital) outflow.

hémorroïdes /emɔʀɔid/ *nf pl* piles, haemorrhoids.

henné /'ene/ *nm* henna.

hennir /'eniʀ/ [3] *vi* to neigh, to whinny.

hennissement /'enismɑ̃/ *nm* neigh, whinny.

hépatique /epatik/ I *adj* hepatic.
II *nmf* person with a liver complaint.

hépatite /epatit/ *nf* hepatitis.

héraldique /eʀaldik/ I *adj* heraldic.
II *nf* heraldry.

héraut /'eʀo/ *nm* herald.

herbacé, **~e** /ɛʀbase/ *adj* herbaceous.

herbage /ɛʀbaʒ/ *nm* pasture.

herbe /ɛʀb/ I *nf* **l'~** grass; **une ~** (Culin) a herb; **mauvaise ~** weed.
II **en herbe** *phr* **1** [*wheat*] in the blade; **2** [*musician*] budding.
■ **~s folles** wild grass.
IDIOMS **couper l'~ sous le pied de qn** to pull the rug from under sb's feet.

herbeux, **-euse** /ɛʀbø, øz/ *adj* grassy.

herbicide /ɛʀbisid/ I *adj* herbicidal.
II *nm* weed killer.

herbier /ɛʀbje/ *nm* herbarium.

herbivore /ɛʀbivɔʀ/ I *adj* herbivorous.
II *nm* herbivore.

herboriser /ɛʀbɔʀize/ [1] *vi* to collect plants, to botanize.

herboriste /ɛʀbɔʀist/ *nmf* herbalist.

herboristerie /ɛʀbɔʀistɔʀi/ *nf* **1** herb trade; **2** herbalist's shop (GB) or store (US).

hère /'ɛʀ/ *nm* (literary) **un pauvre ~** a poor wretch.

héréditaire /eʀeditɛʀ/ *adj* hereditary; (figurative) [*enemy*] traditional.

hérédité /eʀedite/ *nf* **1** heredity; **2** (of title) hereditary nature.

hérésie /eʀezi/ *nf* **1** heresy; **2** (humorous) sacrilege.

hérétique /eʀetik/ I *adj* heretical.
II *nmf* heretic.

hérissé, **~e** /'eʀise/ *adj* [*hair*] bristling, standing up on end; **~ de** spiked with [*nails*]; **question ~e de difficultés** question fraught with difficulties.

hérisser /'eʀise/ [1] I *vtr* **1** [*bird*] to ruffle (up) [*feathers*]; **2 ~ qch de** to spike sth with; **3**° **ça me hérisse** it makes my hackles rise.
II **se hérisser** *v refl* (+ *v être*) **1** [*hair*] to stand on end; **2**° [*person*] to bristle.

hérisson /'eʀisɔ̃/ *nm* hedgehog.

héritage /eʀitaʒ/ *nm* **1** inheritance; **faire un ~** to come into an inheritance; **une tante à ~** a wealthy aunt; **laisser qch en ~** to bequeath sth (**à** to); **recevoir qch en ~** to inherit sth; **2** heritage.

hériter /eʀite/ [1] I *vtr* to inherit.
II **hériter de** *v+prep* to inherit.
III *vi* to inherit; to come into an inheritance; **~ de qn** to receive an inheritance from sb.

héritier, **-ière** /eʀitje, ɛʀ/ *nm,f* heir/heiress (**de** to).

hermétique /ɛʀmetik/ *adj* **1** hermetic; airtight; watertight; **2** [*milieu*] impenetrable; [*poetry, author*] abstruse; [*face*] inscrutable.

hermétiquement /ɛʀmetikmɑ̃/ *adv* [*sealed*] hermetically.

hermétisme /ɛʀmetism/ *nm* **1** abstruseness; **2** hermeticism.

hermine /ɛʀmin/ *nf* **1** stoat; **2** ermine.

hernie /'ɛʀni/ *nf* **1** hernia; **2** (in tyre) bulge.

héroï-comique, *pl* **~s** /eʀɔikɔmik/ *adj* mock-heroic.

héroïne /eʀɔin/ *nf* **1** heroine; **2** heroin.

héroïque /eʀɔik/ *adj* [*person, act*] heroic; [*poem*] epic.

héroïsme /eʀɔism/ *nm* heroism.

héron /'eʀɔ̃/ *nm* heron.

héros /'eʀo/ *nm inv* hero; **mourir en ~** to die a hero's death.

herse /'ɛʀs/ *nf* **1** harrow; **2** portcullis.

hertzien, **-ienne** /ɛʀtzjɛ̃, ɛn/ *adj* [*wave*] Hertzian; [*station*] radio-relay.

hésitant, **~e** /ezitɑ̃, ɑ̃t/ *adj* **1** hesitant; **2** [*start*] shaky.

hésitation /ezitasjɔ̃/ *nf* **1** indecision, hesitancy; **il a eu une seconde d'~** he hesitated for a second; **2** hesitation.

hésiter /ezite/ [1] *vi* to hesitate (**sur** over; **devant** before); **elle hésite encore** she's still undecided; **il n'y a pas à ~** it's got to be done; **j'hésite sur la décision à prendre** I'm not sure which decision to take; **j'hésite entre plusieurs possibilités** I can't decide between several possibilities; **~ à faire** to be hesitant or reluctant to do.

hétéroclite /eteʀɔklit/ *adj* [*population, work*] heterogeneous; [*objects*] miscellaneous.

hétérogène /eteʀɔʒɛn/ *adj* mixed, heterogeneous.

hétérosexuel, **-elle** /eteʀɔsɛksɥɛl/ *adj, nm,f* heterosexual.

hêtre /'ɛtʀ/ *nm* **1** beech (tree); **2** beechwood.

heure /œʀ/ *nf* **1** hour; **24 ~s sur 24** 24 hours a day; **dans l'~ qui a suivi** within the hour; **d'~ en ~** [*increase*] by the hour; **toutes les deux ~s** every two hours; **à trois ~s d'avion de Paris** three hours away from Paris by plane; **à trois ~s de marche de Paris** a three-hour walk from Paris; **faire du 60 à l'~**° to do 60 km per hour; **payé à l'~** paid by the hour; **200 francs de l'~** 200 francs an hour; **une petite ~** an hour at the most; **une bonne ~** a good hour; **2** time; **quelle ~ est-il?** what time is it?; **il est 10 ~s** it's 10 (o'clock); **il est 10 ~s 20** it's 20 past 10; **il est 10 ~s moins 20** it's 20 to 10; **mettre sa montre à l'~** to set one's watch; **l'~ tourne**

time is passing; **l'~ d'arrivée** the arrival time; **~s d'ouverture** opening times; **être à l'~** to be on time; **'sandwiches à toute ~'** 'sandwiches available at any time'; **à une ~ avancée (de la nuit)** late at night; **de bonne ~** early; **il doit être loin à l'~ qu'il est** he must be a long way off by now; **c'est son ~** it's his/her usual time; **il ne viendra pas à l'~ qu'il est** he won't come this late; **à l'~ où je te parle** while I'm speaking to you; **de la première ~** from the very beginning; **à la première ~** at first light; **de dernière ~** last-minute; **ta dernière ~ est arrivée** your time has come; **à l'~ actuelle, pour l'~** at the present time; **l'~ du déjeuner** lunchtime; **aux ~s des repas** at mealtimes; **l'~ est grave** the situation is serious; **il est peintre à ses ~s** he paints in his spare time; **à la bonne ~!** well done!; **3** era, age; **vivre à l'~ des satellites** to live in the satellite era.

■ **~ d'affluence** peak hour; **~ d'été** summer time (GB), daylight saving(s) time; **~ H** (Mil), (figurative) zero hour; **~ d'hiver** winter time (GB), standard time; **~ de pointe** rush hour; **~s supplémentaires** overtime.

heureusement /œʀøzmɑ̃/ *adv* **1** fortunately; **2** (formal) [*concluded*] successfully; [*expressed*] nicely.

heureux, **-euse** /œʀø, øz/ *adj* **1** happy; **~ en ménage** happily married; **très ~ de faire votre connaissance** (very) pleased to meet you; **2** [*ending*] happy; [*proportions*] pleasing; [*choice*] fortunate; [*surprise*] pleasant; **3** [*winner*] lucky; **'il a réussi!'—'encore ~!'** 'he succeeded!'—'just as well!'

IDIOMS **être ~ comme un roi** or **un pape** to be as happy as a lark; **attendre un ~ événement** to be expecting a baby.

heurt /'œʀ/ *nm* **1** collision; **2** (figurative) (between people) clash; **sans ~s** [*do*] smoothly; [*relationship*] smooth.

heurté, **~e** /'œʀte/ *adj* [*style, rhythm*] jerky; [*colours*] clashing.

heurter /'œʀte/ [1] **I** *vtr* **1** [*object*] to hit; [*person*] to collide with, to bump into; **2** (figurative) to offend [*person, morality*]; to go against [*convention*]; to hurt [*feelings*].

II *vi* **~ contre** to strike.

III se heurter *v refl* (+ *v être*) to collide; (figurative) to clash; **se ~ à** to bump into [*table*]; to come up against [*refusal, problem*].

heurtoir /'œʀtwaʀ/ *nm* (door) knocker.

hévéa /evea/ *nm* rubber tree.

hexagonal, **~e**, *mpl* **-aux** /ɛgzagɔnal, o/ *adj* **1** hexagonal; **2**○ [*policy*] inward-looking.

hexagone /ɛgzagon/ *nm* **1** hexagon; **2**○ **l'Hexagone** France.

hiatus /'jatys/ *nm inv* **1** hiatus; **2** (figurative) break; discrepancy.

hiberner /ibɛʀne/ [1] *vi* to hibernate.

hibou, *pl* **~x** /'ibu/ *nm* owl.

hic○ /'ik/ *nm* snag; **voilà le ~** there's the snag.

hideur /'idœʀ/ *nf* hideousness.

hideux, **-euse** /'idø, øz/ *adj* hideous.

hier /jɛʀ/ *adv* yesterday; **ça ne date pas d'~** it's nothing new.

hiérarchie /'jeʀaʀʃi/ *nf* hierarchy.

hiérarchique /'jeʀaʀʃik/ *adj* hierarchical; **mon supérieur ~** my immediate superior; **par la voie ~** through the correct channels.

hiérarchiser /'jeʀaʀʃize/ [1] *vtr* to organize [sth] into a hierarchy [*structure*]; to prioritize [*tasks*]; **~ les salaires** to establish a wages hierarchy.

hiératique /jeʀatik/ *adj* hieratic.

hiéroglyphe /'jeʀɔglif/ *nm* hieroglyph; **les ~s** hieroglyphics.

hi-fi /'ifi/ *adj inv*, *nf inv* hi-fi.

hilarant, **~e** /ilaʀɑ̃, ɑ̃t/ *adj* hilarious; **gaz ~** laughing gas.

hilare /ilaʀ/ *adj* **être ~** to be laughing; **un visage ~** a merry face.

hilarité /ilaʀite/ *nf* mirth, hilarity.

hindou, **~e** /ɛ̃du/ *adj*, *nm,f* Hindu.

hindouisme /ɛ̃duism/ *nm* Hinduism.

hippique /ipik/ *adj* equestrian; **concours ~** showjumping event (GB), horse show; **club ~** riding school.

hippocampe /ipɔkɑ̃p/ *nm* sea horse, hippocampus.

hippodrome /ipɔdʀom/ *nm* racecourse (GB), racetrack (US).

hippopotame /ipɔpɔtam/ *nm* hippopotamus.

hirondelle /iʀɔ̃dɛl/ *nf* swallow.

hirsute /'iʀsyt/ *adj* dishevelled[GB], unkempt.

hispanique /ispanik/ *adj*, *nmf* Hispanic.

hisse /'is/ *excl* **oh ~!** heave-ho!

hisser /'ise/ [1] **I** *vtr* to hoist [*flag*].

II se hisser *v refl* (+ *v être*) to heave oneself up.

histoire /istwaʀ/ *nf* **1** history; **entrer dans l'~** to go down in history; **l'~ jugera** posterity will be the judge; **2** story; **tout ça, c'est des ~s**○! that's all fiction!; **une ~ à dormir debout** a tall story; **raconter des ~s** to tell fibs; **c'est une ~ de fous** it's absolutely crazy!; **3** matter, business; **~ d'amour** love affair; **~ de famille** family matter; **c'est sûrement une ~ d'argent** there must be money involved; **il m'est arrivé une drôle d'~** a funny thing happened to me; **4** fuss; trouble; **en voilà des ~s!** what a fuss!; **elle fait toujours des ~s** she's always making a fuss; **ça va faire des ~s** it will cause trouble; **je ne veux pas d'~s avec le propriétaire** I don't want any trouble with the landlord; **c'est une femme à ~s** she's a troublemaker; **une vie sans ~s** an uneventful life; **ça a été toute une ~ pour faire** it was a terrible job doing; **au travail, et pas d'~s**○! get on with it, no messing about○!; **5**○ **~ de rire** or **s'amuser** just for fun.

historien, **-ienne** /istɔʀjɛ̃, ɛn/ *nm,f* historian.

historique /istɔʀik/ **I** *adj* **1** historical; **2** historic; **3 passé ~** past historic.

II *nm* **faire l'~ du cinéma** to trace the history of the cinema.

hit-parade, *pl* **~s** /'itpaʀad/ *nm* charts.

hiver /ivɛʀ/ *nm* winter; **été comme ~** in summer and winter alike.

hivernage /ivɛʀnaʒ/ *nm* wintering.

hivernal, **~e**, *mpl* **-aux** /ivɛʀnal, o/ *adj* **1** winter; **2** wintry.

HLM /aʃɛlɛm/ *nm* or *f*: *abbr* ▶ **habitation**.

hochement /'ɔʃmɑ̃/ *nm* **~ de tête** nod; shake of the head.

hocher /'ɔʃe/ [1] *vtr* **~ la tête** to nod; to shake one's head.

hochet /'ɔʃɛ/ *nm* rattle.

hockey /'ɔkɛ/ *nm* hockey.

holà /'ɔla/ *excl* hey (there)!
IDIOMS **mettre le ~ à qch** to put an end or a stop to sth.

hold-up, *pl* **~** or **~s** /'ɔldœp/ *nm* hold-up.

hollandais, **~e** /'ɔlɑ̃dɛ, ɛz/ **I** *adj* Dutch.
II *nm* Dutch.

Hollandais, **~e** /'ɔlɑ̃ dɛ, ɛz/ *nm,f* Dutchman/ Dutchwoman; **les ~** the Dutch.

Hollande /'ɔlɑ̃d/ *pr nf* Holland.

holocauste /ɔlɔkost/ *nm* **1** holocaust; **2** (figurative) (total) sacrifice.

homard /'ɔmaʀ/ *nm* lobster.

homélie /ɔmeli/ *nf* homily.

homéopathie /ɔmeɔpati/ *nf* homeopathy.

homéopathique /ɔmeɔpatik/ *adj* homeopathic; **à doses ~s** (figurative) in small doses.

homérique /ɔmeʀik/ *adj* Homeric.

homicide /ɔmisid/ **I** *adj* homicidal.
II *nm* homicide; (Law) manslaughter; (premeditated) murder.

hommage /ɔmaʒ/ *nm* homage, tribute; **rendre ~ à** to pay tribute to; **présenter ses ~s** to pay one's respects.

hommasse /ɔmas/ *adj* mannish.

homme /ɔm/ *nm* man; **l'~** man; mankind; **un ~ à la mer!** man overboard!; **comme un seul ~** as one; **l'~ du jour** the man of the moment; **leur ~ de confiance** their right-hand man; **il n'est pas ~ à se venger** he's not the type to want revenge.
■ **~ d'affaires** businessman; **~ des cavernes** caveman; **~ d'équipage** crewman; **~ d'esprit** wit; **~ d'État** statesman; **~ à femmes** womanizer; **~ au foyer** house-husband; **~ de main** hired hand; **~ du monde** man-about-town, socialite; **~ de paille** front, straw man (US); **~ de peine** labourer[GB]; **~ de terrain** man with practical experience; **~ à tout faire** handyman; **~ de troupe** private; **~s en blanc** surgeons.
IDIOMS **un ~ averti en vaut deux** (Proverb) forewarned is forearmed.

homme-grenouille, *pl* **hommes-grenouilles** /ɔmgʀənuj/ *nm* frogman.

homogène /ɔmɔʒɛn/ *adj* homogeneous.

homogénéiser /ɔmɔʒeneize/ [1] *vtr* to homogenize.

homogénéité /ɔmɔʒeneite/ *nf* homogeneity.

homologue /ɔmɔlɔg/ **I** *adj* homologous.
II *nmf* counterpart, opposite number.

homologuer /ɔmɔlɔge/ [1] *vtr* **1** to approve [*product*]; **2** (Sport) to recognize officially [*record*].

homonyme /ɔmɔnim/ *nm* **1** homonym; **2** namesake.

homosexualité /omɔsɛksɥalite/ *nf* homosexuality.

homosexuel, **~elle** /omɔsɛksɥɛl/ *adj*, *nm,f* homosexual.

honnête /ɔnɛt/ *adj* **1** honest; **2** [*person*] decent; [*life*] respectable; [*intention*] honourable[GB]; **3** fair, reasonable.

honnêtement /ɔnɛtmɑ̃/ *adv* **1** [*say, manage*] honestly; [*reply*] frankly; [*behave*] properly, honourably[GB]; [*judge*] fairly; [*admit*] freely; **2** fairly, reasonably; **s'acquitter ~ d'une tâche** to do a decent job; **travail ~ payé** reasonably well-paid job.

honnêteté /ɔnɛtte/ *nf* honesty; **avec ~** honestly.

honneur /ɔnœʀ/ *nm* **1** honour[GB]; **à qui ai-je l'~?** (formal) to whom do I have the honour[GB] of speaking?; **à toi l'~!** you do the honours[GB]!; **j'ai l'~ de vous informer que** I beg to inform you that; **j'ai l'~ de solliciter** I would respectfully request; **d'~** [*stairs*] main; **2** credit; **c'est tout à leur ~** it's all credit to them; **3 mettre qn à l'~** to honour[GB] sb; **être à l'** or **en ~** to be in favour[GB]; **faire** or **rendre ~ à qn** to honour[GB] sb; **faire ~ à un repas** to do justice to a meal; **faire les ~s de la maison à qn** to show sb around the house; **avoir les ~s de la presse** to be mentioned in the press; **en quel ~**○**?** (ironic) any particular reason why?
IDIOMS **en tout bien tout ~** with no hidden motive.

honnir /'ɔniʀ/ [3] *vtr* (literary) to execrate.
IDIOMS **honni soit qui mal y pense** evil unto him who evil thinks.

honorabilité /ɔnɔʀabilite/ *nf* integrity.

honorable /ɔnɔʀabl/ *adj* **1** honourable[GB]; **2** [*score*] creditable; [*salary*] decent.

honorablement /ɔnɔʀabləmɑ̃/ *adv* **1** honourably[GB]; **~ connu** highly respected; **2** decently.

honoraire /ɔnɔʀɛʀ/ **I** *adj* [*member*] honorary.
II honoraires *nm pl* fee, fees.

honorer /ɔnɔʀe/ [1] *vtr* **1** to honour[GB] [*god, person, memory*]; **~ qn de sa confiance** to honour[GB] sb with one's trust; **2** to honour[GB] [*promise, debt*]; **3** to be a credit to [*country, profession*].

honorifique /ɔnɔʀifik/ *adj* honorary.

honoris causa /ɔnɔʀiskoza/ *phr* honorary.

honte /'ɔ̃t/ *nf* **1** shame; **avoir ~ de** to be ashamed of; **faire ~ à qn** to make sb ashamed; **sans ~** (formal) shamelessly; **sans fausse ~** quite openly; **2** disgrace; **faire la ~ de** to be a disgrace to; **quelle ~!** what a disgrace!

honteusement /'ɔ̃tøzmɑ̃/ *adv* **1** shamefully; **2** shamelessly.

honteux, **-euse** /'ɔ̃tø, øz/ *adj* **1** disgraceful; **2** ashamed (**de** of).

hôpital, *pl* **-aux** /ɔpital, o/ *nm* hospital.
■ **~ de jour** outpatient clinic.

IDIOMS **c'est l'~ qui se moque de la charité** it's the pot calling the kettle black.

hoquet /'ɔkɛ/ *nm* hiccup; **avoir le ~** to have hiccups.

hoqueter /'ɔkte/ [20] *vi* [*person*] to hiccup; [*engine*] to sputter.

horaire /ɔʀɛʀ/ I *adj* per hour, hourly; **tranche** or **plage ~** time-slot.
II *nm* timetable, schedule; **les ~s libres** or **à la carte** flexitime.

horde /'ɔʀd/ *nf* horde.

horizon /ɔʀizɔ̃/ *nm* horizon; **à l'~** on the horizon; **changer d'~** to have a change of scene.

horizontal, ~e[1], *mpl* **-aux** /ɔʀizɔ̃tal, o/ *adj* horizontal.

horizontale[2] /ɔʀizɔ̃tal/ *nf* horizontal; **à l'~** in a horizontal position.

horloge /ɔʀlɔʒ/ *nf* clock.

horloger, -ère /ɔʀlɔʒe, ɛʀ/ *nm,f* watchmaker.

horlogerie /ɔʀlɔʒʀi/ *nf* **1** watchmaking; **2** watchmaker's (shop).

hormis /'ɔʀmi/ *prep* (formal) save, except (for).

hormone /ɔʀmɔn/ *nf* hormone; **~ de croissance** growth hormone.

horodateur /ɔʀɔdatœʀ/ *nm* parking ticket machine.

horoscope /ɔʀɔskɔp/ *nm* horoscope.

horreur /ɔʀœʀ/ *nf* **1** horror; **être saisi d'~** to be horror-struck; **quelle ~!** how horrible!; **2 dire des ~s de** or **sur qn** to say awful things about sb; **3** loathing; **avoir ~ de qn/de faire** to loathe sb/doing; **le poisson cru me fait ~** I loathe raw fish.

horrible /ɔʀibl/ *adj* **1** horrible; **2** revolting; **3** hideous.

horriblement /ɔʀibləmɑ̃/ *adv* [*damaged*] horribly; [*cold*] terribly.

horrifier /ɔʀifje/ [2] *vtr* to horrify.

horripiler /ɔʀipile/ [1] *vtr* to exasperate, to drive [sb] up the wall○.

hors /'ɔʀ/

■ **Note** When *hors* and *hors de* are followed by a noun without the article, refer to the noun entry. Thus *hors service* and *hors d'usage* are at the entries *service* and *usage*.

I *prep* (literary) apart from, save.
II **hors de** *phr* out of, outside; **~ d'ici!** get out of here!
■ **~ tout** overall; **longueur ~ tout** overall length.
IDIOMS **être ~ de soi** to be beside oneself; **cela m'a mis ~ de moi** it infuriated me.

hors-bord /'ɔʀbɔʀ/ I *adj* [*motor*] outboard.
II *nm inv* powerboat, speedboat; **faire du ~** to go speedboating.

hors-d'œuvre /'ɔʀdœvʀ/ *nm inv* starter, hors d'oeuvre.

hors-jeu /'ɔʀʒø/ *nm inv* **(pour) ~** for offside.

hors-la-loi /'ɔʀlalwa/ *nm inv* outlaw.

hors-piste /'ɔʀpist/ *nm inv* off-piste skiing.

hors-texte /'ɔʀtɛkst/ *nm inv* (in book) plate.

hortensia /ɔʀtɑ̃sja/ *nm* hydrangea.

horticulteur, -trice /ɔʀtikyltœʀ, tʀis/ *nm,f* horticulturist.

hospice /ɔspis/ *nm* home; **~ de vieillards** old people's home.

hospitalier, -ière /ɔspitalje, ɛʀ/ *adj* **1** hospital; **centre ~** hospital; **2** hospitable.

hospitalisation /ɔspitalizasjɔ̃/ *nf* hospitalization; **~ à domicile** home (medical) care.

hospitaliser /ɔspitalize/ [1] *vtr* to hospitalize.

hospitalité /ɔspitalite/ *nf* hospitality; **demander l'~** to ask for shelter.

hospitalo-universitaire, *pl* **~s** /ɔspitaloynivɛʀsitɛʀ/ *adj* **centre ~** teaching hospital.

hostellerie /ɔstɛlʀi/ *nf* (country) inn.

hostie /ɔsti/ *nf* Host.

hostile /ɔstil/ *adj* hostile (**à** to).

hostilité /ɔstilite/ *nf* hostility; **les ~s** (Mil) hostilities.

hôte /ot/ I *nm* **1** host; **2** occupant.
II *nmf* guest.

hôtel /otɛl/ *nm* hotel.
■ **~ particulier** town house; **~ de passe** hotel used by prostitutes; **~ des ventes** saleroom; **~ de ville** ≈ town hall.

hôtelier, -ière /otəlje, ɛʀ/ I *adj* [*industry*] hotel; [*school*] hotel management.
II *nm,f* hotelier.

hôtellerie /otɛlʀi/ *nf* **1** hotel business; **2** (country) inn.

hôtesse /otɛs/ *nf* (at home, at exhibition) hostess; (in company) receptionist; (in train, boat) stewardess.
■ **~ d'accueil** receptionist; **~ de l'air** air hostess.

hotte /'ɔt/ *nf* **1** basket; **2** hood.
■ **~ aspirante** extractor hood (GB), ventilator (US); **la ~ du Père Noël** Santa Claus's sack.

houblon /'ublɔ̃/ *nm* hop, hops.

houe /'u/ *nf* hoe.

houille /'uj/ *nf* coal.
■ **~ blanche** hydroelectric power.

houiller, -ère[1] /'uje, ɛʀ/ *adj* [*industry*] coal; [*area*] coalmining.

houillère[2] /'ujɛʀ/ *nf* **1** coalmine; **2** colliery.

houle /'ul/ *nf* swell.

houlette /'ulɛt/ *nf* (of shepherd) crook; **sous la ~ de** (figurative) under the leadership of.

houleux, -euse /'ulø, øz/ *adj* **1** [*sea*] rough; **2** [*meeting*] stormy.

houppe /'up/ *nf* **1** (of hair) tuft; (of threads) tassel; **2** powder puff.

houppelande /'uplɑ̃d/ *nf* greatcoat.

houppette /'upɛt/ *nf* powder puff.

hourra /'uʀa/ *nm* cheer; **pousser des ~s** to cheer.

houspiller /'uspije/ [1] *vtr* to scold; **se faire ~** to be scolded.

housse /'us/ *nf* cover, slipcover; dustcover; garment bag.

houx /'u/ *nm inv* holly.

HT (*written abbr* = **hors taxes**) exclusive of tax.

hublot /'yblo/ *nm* (in plane) window; (in boat) porthole.

huche /'yʃ/ *nf* **1** chest; **2 ~ à pain** bread bin.

huées /'ɥe/ *nf pl* booing; **partir sous les ~** to be booed off.

huer /'ɥe/ [1] *vtr* to boo.

huile /ɥil/ *nf* **1** oil; **2** oil painting; **3**° big shot°, bigwig°.
■ **~ de coude** (humorous) elbow grease; **~ solaire** suntan oil.
IDIOMS **tout/ça baigne dans l'~**° everything/it is going smoothly; **jeter** or **verser de l'~ sur le feu** to add fuel to the fire.

huiler /ɥile/ [1] *vtr* to oil.

huileux, -euse /ɥilø, øz/ *adj* oily.

huis /'ɥi/ *nm inv* **à ~ clos** (Law) in camera; (figurative) behind closed doors.

huissier /ɥisje/ *nm* **1 ~ (de justice)** bailiff; **2** porter; usher.

huit /'ɥit, but before consonant 'ɥi/ **I** *adj inv* eight; **~ jours** a week; eight days; **mardi en ~** a week on Tuesday; **donner ses ~ jours à qn** to give sb a week's notice.
II *pron* eight.
III *nm inv* **1** eight; **2** a figure of eight.

huitaine /'ɥitɛn/ *nf* **1** about a week; **sous ~** within a week; **2** about eight.

huitième /'ɥitjɛm/ **I** *adj* eighth.
II *nf* (Sch) *fourth year of primary school, age 9–10.*

huître /ɥitʀ/ *nf* oyster.

hululer /'ylyle/ [1] *vi* to hoot.

humain, ~e /ymɛ̃, ɛn/ **I** *adj* **1** human; **pertes ~es** loss of life; **2** [*regime*] humane; [*person*] human, understanding.
II *nm* human (being).
IDIOMS **l'erreur est ~e** to err is human.

humainement /ymɛnmɑ̃/ *adv* **1** humanly; **2** humanely.

humaniser /ymanize/ [1] **I** *vtr* to humanize.
II s'humaniser *v refl* (+ *v être*) to become more human.

humaniste /ymanist/ *adj, nmf* humanist.

humanitaire /ymanitɛʀ/ *adj* humanitarian.

humanité /ymanite/ *nf* humanity; **avec ~** humanely.

humble /œ̃bl/ **I** *adj* humble.
II humbles *nm pl* **les ~s** the common people.

humblement /œ̃bləmɑ̃/ *adv* humbly.

humecter /ymɛkte/ [1] *vtr* to moisten, to dampen.

humer /'yme/ [1] *vtr* to sniff; to smell.

humérus /ymeʀys/ *nm inv* humerus.

humeur /ymœʀ/ *nf* **1** mood; **être de bonne/mauvaise ~** to be in a good/bad mood; **être/ne pas être d'~ à faire** to be in the mood/in no mood to do; **2** temper; **être d'~ égale** to be even-tempered; **être d'~ inégale** to be moody; **3** bad temper; **geste d'~** bad-tempered gesture; **avec ~** bad-temperedly.

humide /ymid/ *adj* **1** damp; **2** [*climate*] humid; [*season*] rainy; **il fait froid et ~** it's cold and damp; **il fait une chaleur ~** it's muggy.

humidificateur /ymidifikatœʀ/ *nm* humidifier.

humidifier /ymidifje/ [2] *vtr* to humidify.

humidité /ymidite/ *nf* **1** dampness, damp; **2** humidity.

humiliant, ~e /ymiljɑ̃, ɑ̃t/ *adj* humiliating.

humiliation /ymiljasjɔ̃/ *nf* humiliation.

humilier /ymilje/ [2] *vtr* to humiliate.

humilité /ymilite/ *nf* **1** humility; **2** (of task) humble nature.

humoriste /ymɔʀist/ *nmf* **1** humorist; **2** joker.

humoristique /ymɔʀistik/ *adj* humorous; **dessin ~** cartoon.

humour /ymuʀ/ *nm* humour[GB]; **avoir de l'~** to have a sense of humour[GB]; **il n'a pas su apprécier l'~ de la situation** he couldn't see the funny side of it; **faire de l'~** to make jokes.

huppé, ~e /'ype/ *adj* **1**° [*person*] upper-crust; **2** [*bird*] crested.

hurlement /'yʀləmɑ̃/ *nm* (of animal) howl, howling; (of person) yell, howl; (of siren) wail, wailing; **pousser un ~ de douleur** to howl with pain.

hurler /'yʀle/ [1] **I** *vtr* **1** to yell; **2** [*radio*] to blare out.
II *vi* **1** to yell; (with pain, anger) to howl; **2** [*siren*] to wail; [*wind*] to roar; [*radio*] to blare.
IDIOMS **~ avec les loups** to follow the crowd; **~ à la mort** to bay at the moon.

hurluberlu, ~e /yʀlybɛʀly/ *nm,f* oddball°.

hussarde /'ysaʀd/ *nf* **à la ~** roughly.

hutte /'yt/ *nf* hut.

hybride /ibʀid/ *adj, nm* hybrid.

hybrider /ibʀide/ [1] *vtr* to cross, to hybridize.

hydratant, ~e /idʀatɑ̃, ɑ̃t/ *adj* moisturizing.

hydratation /idʀatasjɔ̃/ *nf* **1** hydration; **2** moisturizing.

hydrate /idʀat/ *nm* hydrate; **~ de carbone** carbohydrate.

hydrater /idʀate/ [1] **I** *vtr* **1** to hydrate; **2** to moisturize [*skin*].
II s'hydrater *v refl* (+ *v être*) **bien s'~** to take plenty of fluids.

hydraulique /idʀolik/ **I** *adj* hydraulic.
II *nf* hydraulics.

hydravion /idʀavjɔ̃/ *nm* seaplane, hydroplane.

hydro /idʀo/ *pref* hydro; **~électrique** hydroelectric.

hydrocarbure /idʀokaʀbyʀ/ *nm* hydrocarbon.

hydrocution /idʀɔkysjɔ̃/ *nf* immersion hypothermia.

hydrofuge /idʀɔfyʒ/ *adj* water-repellent.

hydrogène /idʀɔʒɛn/ *nm* hydrogen.
■ **~ lourd** deuterium.

hydroglisseur /idʀɔglisœʀ/ *nm* hydroplane.

hydromel /idʀɔmɛl/ *nm* mead.

hydrophile /idʀɔfil/ *adj* absorbent.

hydroptère /idʀɔptɛʀ/ *nm* hydrofoil.

hydroxyde /idʀɔksid/ *nm* hydroxide.

hyène /ˈjɛn/ *nf* hyena.

hygiaphone® /iʒjafɔn/ *nm* grill (*perforated communication panel*).

hygiène /iʒjɛn/ *nf* hygiene; **bonne ~ alimentaire** healthy diet.
■ **~ corporelle** personal hygiene; **~ mentale** mental health.

hygiénique /iʒjenik/ *adj* **1** hygienic; **2** [*lifestyle*] healthy; **promenade ~** constitutional.

hymen /imɛn/ *nm* **1** hymen; **2** (literary) nuptial bond.

hymne /imn/ *nm* hymn; **~ national** national anthem.

hyperactif, **-ive** /ipɛʀaktif, iv/ *adj* hyperactive.

hyperbole /ipɛʀbɔl/ *nf* **1** hyperbola; **2** hyperbole.

hyperclassique /ipɛʀklasik/ *adj* [*situation, reaction*] absolutely classic; **roman** or **film ~** great classic.

hyperdoué, **~e** /ipɛʀdwe/ *adj* exceptionally gifted.

hypermarché /ipɛʀmaʀʃe/ *nm* hypermarket (GB), large supermarket.

hypermétrope /ipɛʀmetʀɔp/ *adj* longsighted.

hypernerveux, **-euse** /ipɛʀnɛʀvø, øz/ *adj* highly strung.

hypersensible /ipɛʀsɑ̃sibl/ *adj* hypersensitive.

hypertendu, **~e** /ipɛʀtɑ̃dy/ *adj* **1**° extremely tense; **2** (Med) suffering from high blood pressure.

hypertension /ipɛʀtɑ̃sjɔ̃/ *nf* **~ (artérielle)** high blood pressure.

hypertrophie /ipɛʀtʀɔfi/ *nf* **1** (Med) enlargement; **2** (of town) overdevelopment.

hypertrophier: **s'hypertrophier** /ipɛʀtʀɔfje/ [2] *v refl* (+ *v être*) **1** (Med) to hypertrophy; **2** [*town*] to become overdeveloped.

hypnose /ipnoz/ *nf* hypnosis.

hypnotique /ipnɔtik/ *adj*, *nm* hypnotic.

hypnotiser /ipnɔtize/ [1] **I** *vtr* to hypnotize; (figurative) to mesmerize.
II s'hypnotiser *v refl* (+ *v être*) **s'~ sur** to become obsessed by [*detail, problem*].

hypnotiseur, **-euse** /ipnɔtizœʀ, øz/ *nm,f* hypnotist.

hypocondriaque /ipɔkɔ̃dʀijak/ *adj*, *nmf* hypochondriac.

hypocrisie /ipɔkʀizi/ *nf* hypocrisy.

hypocrite /ipɔkʀit/ **I** *adj* hypocritical.
II *nmf* hypocrite.

hypodermique /ipɔdɛʀmik/ *adj* hypodermic.

hypophyse /ipɔfiz/ *nf* pituitary gland.

hypotension /ipɔtɑ̃sjɔ̃/ *nf* **~ (artérielle)** low blood pressure.

hypoténuse /ipɔtenyz/ *nf* hypotenuse.

hypothécaire /ipɔtekɛʀ/ *adj* mortgage.

hypothèque /ipɔtɛk/ *nf* mortgage; **prendre une ~ sur l'avenir** (figurative) to mortgage one's future.

hypothéquer /ipɔteke/ [14] *vtr* to mortgage; (figurative) to endanger.

hypothèse /ipɔtɛz/ *nf* hypothesis; **se refuser à la moindre ~** to refuse to speculate.

hypothétique /ipɔtetik/ *adj* hypothetical.

hystérie /isteʀi/ *nf* hysteria; **~ collective** mass hysteria.

hystérique /isteʀik/ *adj* hysterical.

Ii

i, **I** /i/ *nm inv* i, I.
IDIOMS **mettre les points sur les i** to make things crystal clear.

ibérique /ibeʀik/ *adj* Iberian.

iceberg /ajsbɛʀg, isbɛʀg/ *nm* iceberg.

ici /isi/ *adv* **1** here; **c'est ~ que**... this is where...; **par ~** this way; around here; **les gens d'~** the locals; **je vois ça d'~!** I can just picture it!; **vous êtes ~ chez vous!** make yourself at home!; **2 jusqu'~** until now; until then; **d'~ peu** shortly; **d'~ demain** by tomorrow; **d'~ deux jours** two days from now; **d'~ là** by then; **il l'aime bien, mais d'~ à ce qu'il l'épouse**... he likes her, but as for marrying her...

ici-bas /isibɑ/ *adv* here below.

icône /ikon/ *nf* icon.

iconographie /ikɔnɔgʀafi/ *nf* **1** iconography; **2** illustrations.

id. *written abbr* = **idem**.

idéal, **~e**, *mpl* **-aux** /ideal, o/ **I** *adj* ideal.
II *nm* ideal; **dans l'~** ideally.

idéaliser /idealize/ [1] *vtr* to idealize.

idéalisme /idealism/ *nm* idealism.

idée /ide/ *nf* **1** idea; **avoir de l'~** to be inventive; **avoir une ~ derrière la tête** to have something in mind; **2** idea; thought; **j'ai ma petite ~ sur le sujet** I have my own theory about that; **se faire des ~s** to imagine things; **avoir les ~s larges** to be broad-minded; **changer d'~** to change one's mind; **avoir de la suite dans les ~s** to be single-minded; not to be easily deterred; **3** idea; **as-tu une ~ du temps qu'il faut pour y aller?** do you have any idea how long it takes to get there?; **4 avoir dans l'~ que** to have an idea that; **avoir dans l'~ de faire** to plan to do; **ça ne leur viendrait jamais à l'~** it would never occur to them; **tu ne m'ôteras pas de l'~ que**... I still think that...
■ **~ fixe** idée fixe, obsession; **~ force** key idea; **~ de génie** brainwave○; **~ noire** dark thought; **~ reçue** received idea.

idem /idɛm/ *adv* ditto.

identification /idɑ̃tifikasjɔ̃/ *nf* identification.

identifier /idɑ̃tifje/ [2] **I** *vtr* to identify.
II s'identifier *v refl* (+ *v être*) **1** to become identified (**à** with); **2** to identify (**à** with).

identique /idɑ̃tik/ *adj* **1** identical (**à** to); **2** unchanged.

identité /idɑ̃tite/ *nf* **1** identity; **2** similarity; **~ de vues** similar views.

idéologie /ideɔlɔʒi/ *nf* ideology.

idiomatique /idjɔmatik/ *adj* idiomatic.

idiome /idjom/ *nm* idiom.

idiot, **~e** /idjo, ɔt/ **I** *adj* stupid.
II *nm* idiot; **faire l'~** to behave like an idiot; (as deception) to act dumb.

idiotie /idjɔsi/ *nf* **1** stupid thing; **2** rubbish (GB), garbage (US); **3** stupidity.

idiotisme /idjɔtism/ *nm* idiom.

idolâtrer /idɔlɑtʀe/ [1] *vtr* to idolize.

idole /idɔl/ *nf* idol.

idylle /idil/ *nf* **1** love affair; **2** (in literature) idyll.

idyllique /idilik/ *adj* idyllic.

if /if/ *nm* **1** yew (tree); **2** yew (wood).

ignare /iɲaʀ/ *adj* ignorant.

ignifuge /iɲifyʒ/ *adj* fireproofing.

ignifuger /iɲifyʒe/ [13] *vtr* to fireproof.

ignoble /iɲɔbl/ *adj* **1** [*person, conduct*] vile; **2** [*place*] squalid; [*food*] revolting.

ignominie /iɲɔmini/ *nf* **1** ignominy; **2** dreadful thing.

ignorance /iɲɔʀɑ̃s/ *nf* ignorance.

ignorant, **~e** /iɲɔʀɑ̃, ɑ̃t/ *adj* ignorant.

ignoré, **~e** /iɲɔʀe/ *adj* unknown (**de** to); ignored (**de** by).

ignorer /iɲɔʀe/ [1] **I** *vtr* **1 j'ignore comment/si** I don't know how/whether; **~ tout de qch** to know nothing of or about sth; **~ l'existence de** to be unaware of the existence of; **il ignorait la peur** he didn't know what fear was; **2** to ignore [*person*].
II s'ignorer *v refl* (+ *v être*) **c'est un poète qui s'ignore** he is a poet without knowing it.

iguane /igwan/ *nm* iguana.

il /il/ **I** *pron m* he; it; **~s** they; **Pierre a-t-~ téléphoné?** has Pierre phoned?; **~ a été réparé** it has been repaired.
II *pron* it; **~ pleut** it's raining; **~ m'arrive de faire** I sometimes do.

île /il/ *nf* island.
■ **l'~ de Beauté** Corsica; **~ flottante** (Culin) floating island.

illégal, **~e**, *mpl* **-aux** /ilegal, o/ *adj* illegal.

illégalité /ilegalite/ *nf* **1** illegality; **2** breach of the law.

illégitime /ileʒitim/ *adj* [*child*] illegitimate.

illettré, **~e** /iletʀe/ *adj, nm,f* illiterate.

illettrisme /iletʀism/ *nm* illiteracy.

illicite /ilisit/ *adj* illicit; unlawful.

illico○ /iliko/ *adv* straightaway; **~ presto** pronto○.

illimité, **~e** /ilimite/ *adj* unlimited.

illisible /ilizibl/ *adj* **1** illegible; **2** [*book*] unreadable.

illogique /ilɔʒik/ *adj* illogical.

illumination /ilyminasjɔ̃/ **I** *nf* **1** floodlighting; **2** flash of inspiration.
II illuminations *nf pl* (in town) illuminations; (on tree) lights.

illuminé, **~e** /ilymine/ **I** *adj* **1** [*monument*] floodlit; **2** [*face*] radiant.
II *nm,f* **1** visionary; **2** crank.

illuminer /ilymine/ [1] **I** *vtr* **1** to illuminate; to floodlight; **2** [*smile*] to light up [*face*]; [*faith, passion*] to illuminate [*life*].
II s'illuminer *v refl* (+ *v être*) to light up.

illusion /ilyzjɔ̃/ *nf* illusion; **se faire des ~s** to delude oneself; **il ne fait pas ~** he doesn't fool anyone.

illusionner: **s'illusionner** /ilyzjɔne/ [1] *v refl* (+ *v être*) to delude oneself.

illusionniste /ilyzjɔnist/ *nmf* conjurer, illusionist.

illusoire /ilyzwaʀ/ *adj* illusory.

illustrateur, **-trice** /ilystʀatœʀ, tʀis/ *nm,f* illustrator.

illustration /ilystʀasjɔ̃/ *nf* illustration.

illustre /ilystʀ/ *adj* illustrious; **un ~ inconnu** a perfect nobody.

illustrer /ilystʀe/ [1] **I** *vtr* to illustrate.
II s'illustrer *v refl* (+ *v être*) to distinguish oneself.

îlot /ilo/ *nm* **1** islet; **2 ~s de végétation** isolated patches of vegetation.

ils ▶ **il**.

image /imaʒ/ *nf* **1** picture; **2** (on film) frame; **3** reflection, image; **4** picture (**de** of); **à l'~ de ses prédécesseurs**... just like his/her predecessors...; **5** image; **les ~s d'un poème** the imagery of a poem.
■ **~ d'Épinal** *simplistic print of traditional French life*; (figurative) clichéd image; **~ de marque** brand image; corporate image; (public) image.

imagé, **~e** /imaʒe/ *adj* [*style*] colourful[GB].

imagerie /imaʒʀi/ *nf* **1** imagery; **2** print trade; **3** imaging.

imaginable /imaʒinabl/ *adj* conceivable, imaginable.

imaginaire /imaʒinɛʀ/ *adj* imaginary.

imaginatif, **-ive** /imaʒinatif, iv/ *adj* imaginative.

imagination /imaʒinasjɔ̃/ *nf* imagination; **des chiffres qui dépassent** or **défient l'~** mind-boggling° figures.

imaginer /imaʒine/ [1] **I** *vtr* **1** to imagine, to picture; **2** to suppose; **3** to devise, to think up; **que vas-tu ~?** how can you think such a thing?
II s'imaginer *v refl* (+ *v être*) **1** to imagine, to picture; **2 s'~ à 60 ans** to picture oneself at 60; **3** to think (**que** that).

imbattable /ɛ̃batabl/ *adj* unbeatable.

imbécile /ɛ̃besil/ **I** *adj* idiotic.
II *nmf* fool; **faire l'~** to play the fool.

imbécillité /ɛ̃besilite/ *nf* stupidity.

imberbe /ɛ̃bɛʀb/ *adj* beardless.

imbiber /ɛ̃bibe/ [1] **I** *vtr* to soak.
II s'imbiber *v refl* (+ *v être*) **s'~ de** to become soaked with.

imbriquer: **s'imbriquer** /ɛ̃bʀike/ [1] *v refl* (+ *v être*) **1** [*slates*] to overlap; **2** [*chapters*] to be interwoven; [*issues*] to be interlinked; [*parts*] to interlock.

imbu, **~e** /ɛ̃by/ *adj* full (**de** of); **~ de sa personne** full of oneself.

imbuvable /ɛ̃byvabl/ *adj* **1** undrinkable; **2**° unbearable.

imitateur, **-trice** /imitatœʀ, tʀis/ *nm,f* **1** impressionist; **2** (of painting) imitator.

imitation /imitasjɔ̃/ *nf* imitation; (of person) impression; **numéro d'~** impressions; **sac ~ crocodile** imitation crocodile handbag.

imiter /imite/ [1] *vtr* **1** to imitate; to forge [*signature*]; **2** to do an impression of [sb]; **3 il part, je vais l'~** he's leaving and I'm going to do the same.

immaculé, **~e** /imakyle/ *adj* immaculate.

immangeable /ɛ̃mɑ̃ʒabl/ *adj* inedible.

immanquablement /ɛ̃mɑ̃kabləmɑ̃/ *adv* inevitably.

immatériel, **-ielle** /imateʀjɛl/ *adj* **1** immaterial; **2** (Law) intangible.

immatriculation /imatʀikylasjɔ̃/ *nf* registration; **numéro d'~** registration (GB) or license (US) number.

immatriculer /imatʀikyle/ [1] *vtr* to register; to register (GB) or license (US) [*car*].

immédiat, **~e** /imedja, at/ **I** *adj* immediate.
II *nm* **l'~** the present; **dans l'~** for the time being.

immédiatement /imedjatmɑ̃/ *adv* immediately.

immense /imɑ̃s/ *adj* (gen) huge; [*pain, regret*] immense; [*joy, courage*] great.

immensité /imɑ̃site/ *nf* (of place) immensity; (of knowledge) breadth.

immergé, **~e** /imɛʀʒe/ *adj* [*body, object*] submerged; [*reefs*] sunken.

immerger /imɛʀʒe/ [13] *vtr* to immerse [*object*]; to bury [sth] at sea.

immersion /imɛʀsjɔ̃/ *nf* **1** (of body, object) immersion; (of corpse) burial at sea; **2** flooding; **3** (Sch) immersion.

immettable° /ɛ̃metabl/ *adj* unwearable.

immeuble /imœbl/ *nm* **1** building; **2** (Law) real asset.

immigrant, **~e** /imigʀɑ̃, ɑ̃t/ *adj, nm,f* immigrant.

immigration /imigʀasjɔ̃/ *nf* immigration.

immigré, **~e** /imigʀe/ *adj, nm,f* immigrant.

immigrer /imigʀe/ [1] *vi* to immigrate.

imminent, **~e** /iminɑ̃, ɑ̃t/ *adj* imminent.

immiscer: **s'immiscer** /imise/ [12] *v refl* (+ *v être*) to interfere (**dans** in).

immobile /imɔbil/ *adj* (gen) motionless; [*vehicle*] stationary; [*stare*] fixed.

immobilier /imɔbilje/ *nm* **l'~** property (GB), real estate (US).

immobiliser /imɔbilize/ [1] **I** *vtr* **1** to bring [sth] to a standstill [*vehicle*]; to stop [*machine, horse*]; **2** to immobilize [*person, limb*]; **3** to tie up [*capital*].
II s'immobiliser *v refl* (+ *v être*) to come to a halt; (deliberately) to stop.

immobilisme /imɔbilism/ *nm* opposition to change.

immobilité /imɔbilite/ *nf* **1** immobility; **2** stillness.

immodéré, **~e** /imɔdeʀe/ *adj* **1** excessive; **2** immoderate.

immoler /imɔle/ [1] *vtr* to sacrifice (**à** to).

immonde /imɔ̃d/ *adj* **1** filthy; **2** revolting.

immondices /imɔ̃dis/ *nf pl* refuse (GB), trash (US).

immoral, **~e**, *mpl* **-aux** /imɔʀal, o/ *adj* immoral.

immortaliser /imɔʀtalize/ [1] *vtr* to immortalize.

immortalité /imɔʀtalite/ *nf* immortality.

immortel, **-elle** /imɔʀtɛl/ *adj* immortal.

immotivé, **~e** /imɔtive/ *adj* [*anger, act*] unmotivated; [*fear*] groundless.

immuable /imɥabl/ *adj* **1** immutable; **2** unchanging; **3** perpetual.

immuniser /imynize/ [1] *vtr* **1** to immunize; **2** (figurative) **~ qn contre** to make sb immune to.

immunitaire /imynitɛʀ/ *adj* (Med) immune.

immunité /imynite/ *nf* immunity.

impact /ɛ̃pakt/ *nm* impact; mark.

impair, **~e** /ɛ̃pɛʀ/ **I** *adj* [*number*] odd; [*day, year*] odd-numbered.
II *nm* indiscretion, faux pas.

imparable /ɛ̃paʀabl/ *adj* **1** unstoppable; **2** unanswerable; **3** irrefutable.

impardonnable /ɛ̃paʀdɔnabl/ *adj* unforgivable.

imparfait, **~e** /ɛ̃paʀfɛ, ɛt/ **I** *adj* imperfect.
II *nm* **l'~** the imperfect (tense).

impartial, **~e**, *mpl* **-iaux** /ɛ̃paʀsjal, o/ *adj* impartial.

impartir /ɛ̃paʀtiʀ/ [3] *vtr* to give; **dans les temps impartis** within the given time.

impasse /ɛ̃pas/ *nf* **1** dead end, cul-de-sac (GB); **2** deadlock.

impassible /ɛ̃pasibl/ *adj* impassive.

impatience /ɛ̃pasjɑ̃s/ *nf* impatience; **brûler d'~ de faire** to be dying to do.

impatient, **~e** /ɛ̃pasjɑ̃, ɑ̃t/ *adj* impatient.

impatienter /ɛ̃pasjɑ̃te/ [1] **I** *vtr* to irritate.
II s'impatienter *v refl* (+ *v être*) to get impatient.

impayable○ /ɛ̃pɛjabl/ *adj* **elle est ~** she's priceless.

impayé, **~e** /ɛ̃pɛje/ *adj* unpaid.

impeccable /ɛ̃pɛkabl/ *adj* perfect; impeccable; spotless.

impeccablement /ɛ̃pɛkabləmɑ̃/ *adv* impeccably.

impénétrable /ɛ̃penetʀabl/ *adj* **1** impenetrable; **2** inscrutable.

impénitent, **~e** /ɛ̃penitɑ̃, ɑ̃t/ *adj* [*drinker*] inveterate; [*bachelor*] confirmed.

impensable /ɛ̃pɑ̃sabl/ *adj* unthinkable, unimaginable.

imper○ /ɛ̃pɛʀ/ *nm* raincoat, mac○ (GB).

impératif, **-ive** /ɛ̃peʀatif, iv/ **I** *adj* imperative.
II *nm* **1** (of situation) imperative; (for quality) necessity (**de** for); (of timetable) constraint; **2** (in grammar) imperative.

impératrice /ɛ̃peʀatʀis/ *nf* empress.

imperceptible /ɛ̃pɛʀsɛptibl/ *adj* imperceptible.

imperfection /ɛ̃pɛʀfɛksjɔ̃/ *nf* **1** imperfection; **2** flaw.

impérial, **~e**[1], *mpl* **-iaux** /ɛ̃peʀjal, o/ *adj* imperial.

impériale[2] /ɛ̃peʀjal/ *nf* **autobus à ~** double-decker bus.

impérialisme /ɛ̃peʀjalism/ *nm* imperialism.

impérieux, **-ieuse** /ɛ̃peʀjø, øz/ *adj* **1** imperious; **2** pressing.

impérissable /ɛ̃peʀisabl/ *adj* imperishable.

imperméabiliser /ɛ̃pɛʀmeabilize/ [1] *vtr* to waterproof.

imperméabilité /ɛ̃pɛʀmeabilite/ *nf* **1** waterproofness; **2** impermeability.

imperméable /ɛ̃pɛʀmeabl/ **I** *adj* **1** [*material*] waterproof; [*ground*] impermeable; **2** impervious.
II *nm* raincoat.

impersonnel, **-elle** /ɛ̃pɛʀsɔnɛl/ *adj* impersonal.

impertinence /ɛ̃pɛʀtinɑ̃s/ *nf* **1** impertinence; **2** impertinent remark.

impertinent, **~e** /ɛ̃pɛʀtinɑ̃, ɑ̃t/ *adj* impertinent.

imperturbable /ɛ̃pɛʀtyʀbabl/ *adj* imperturbable, unruffled.

imperturbablement /ɛ̃pɛʀtyʀbabləmɑ̃/ *adv* [*continue, listen*] unperturbed.

impétueusement /ɛ̃petɥøzmɑ̃/ *adv* impetuously.

impétueux, **-euse** /ɛ̃petɥø, øz/ *adj* (gen) impetuous; [*torrent*] raging.

impie /ɛ̃pi/ *adj* impious.

impitoyable /ɛ̃pitwajabl/ *adj* merciless, pitiless; relentless; ruthless.

impitoyablement /ɛ̃pitwajabləmɑ̃/ *adv* mercilessly.

implacable /ɛ̃plakabl/ *adj* implacable; tough; harsh.

implacablement /ɛ̃plakabləmɑ̃/ *adv* relentlessly; ruthlessly.

implantation /ɛ̃plɑ̃tasjɔ̃/ *nf* establishment; setting up; installation; settlement; implantation.

implanté, **~e** /ɛ̃plɑ̃te/ *adj* **1** [*factory, party*] established; [*population*] settled; **2** [*roots*] established; **dents mal ~es** crooked teeth.

implanter /ɛ̃plɑ̃te/ [1] **I** *vtr* **1** to establish [*factory*]; to build [*supermarket*]; to open [*agency*]; to introduce [*product, fashion*]; to instil[GB] [*ideas*]; **2** (Med) to implant.
II s'implanter *v refl* (+ *v être*) [*company, product*] to establish itself; [*factory*] to be built; [*person*] to settle; [*party, doctrine*] to gain a following.

implication /ɛ̃plikasjɔ̃/ *nf* **1** involvement; **2** implication (**sur** for); **3** commitment.

implicite /ɛ̃plisit/ *adj* implicit.

impliquer /ɛ̃plike/ [1] *vtr* **1** to implicate (**dans** in); **2** to involve [*staff*] (**dans** in); **3** to involve (**de faire** doing); **4** to mean.

implorer /ɛ̃plɔʀe/ [1] *vtr* **1** to beseech, to implore; **2** to beg for.

imploser /ɛ̃ploze/ [1] *vi* to implode.

impoli, **~e** /ɛ̃pɔli/ *adj* rude, impolite.

impolitesse /ɛ̃pɔlitɛs/ *nf* rudeness, impoliteness; **avec ~** rudely.

impondérable /ɛ̃pɔ̃deʀabl/ *adj*, *nm* imponderable.

impopulaire /ɛ̃pɔpylɛʀ/ *adj* unpopular.

importance /ɛ̃pɔʀtɑ̃s/ *nf* **1** importance; **sans ~** unimportant; **quelle ~?** what does it matter?; **2** size; (of damage) extent; **prendre de l'~** to increase in size; **d'une certaine ~** sizeable; **3 prendre de l'~** [*person*] to become more important.

important, **~e** /ɛ̃pɔʀtɑ̃, ɑ̃t/ **I** *adj* **1** important; **2** significant; considerable; sizeable; large; [*delay*] lengthy; **3 prendre un air ~** to adopt a self-important manner.
II *nm,f* **faire l'~**, **jouer les ~s** to act important°.

importateur, **-trice** /ɛ̃pɔʀtatœʀ, tʀis/ **I** *adj* importing.
II *nm,f* importer.

importation /ɛ̃pɔʀtasjɔ̃/ *nf* **1** importation; **2** import.

importer /ɛ̃pɔʀte/ [1] **I** *vtr* (gen) to import; to introduce [*species*].
II *v impers* **peu importe** or **qu'importe que...** it doesn't matter or what does it matter if...; **'lequel?'—'n'importe'** 'which one?'—'it doesn't matter'; **n'importe quel enfant** any child; **n'importe qui** anybody, anyone; **n'importe lequel** any; **n'importe où** anywhere; **n'importe quand** anytime; **prends n'importe quoi** take anything; **elle dit n'importe quoi** she talks nonsense; **c'est fait n'importe comment** it's done any old how°.

importun, **~e** /ɛ̃pɔʀtœ̃, yn/ **I** *adj* **1** troublesome; tiresome; **visiteur ~** unwelcome visitor; **2** [*visit*] ill-timed; [*remark*] ill-chosen; [*question*] awkward.
II *nm,f* unwelcome visitor; tiresome individual.

importuner /ɛ̃pɔʀtyne/ [1] *vtr* **1** to bother (**de** with); **2** to disturb.

imposable /ɛ̃pozabl/ *adj* [*person*] liable to tax; [*income*] taxable.

imposant, **~e** /ɛ̃pozɑ̃, ɑ̃t/ *adj* imposing; impressive.

imposé, **~e** /ɛ̃poze/ *adj* **1** fixed; **2** set.

imposer /ɛ̃poze/ [1] **I** *vtr* **1** [*person*] to impose [*sanctions, deadline*]; to lay down [*rule*]; **elle nous a imposé le silence** she made us be quiet; **2** to impose [*idea, opinion*]; to set [*fashion*]; **3** to command [*respect, admiration*]; **4** to tax.
II en imposer *v+prep* **elle en impose par son calme** her calm is impressive; **elle en impose à ses élèves** she inspires respect in her pupils.
III s'imposer *v refl* (+ *v être*) **1** [*choice, solution*] to be obvious; [*caution, change*] to be called for; **une visite au Louvre s'impose** a visit to the Louvre is a must; **2** to impose [sth] on oneself; **s'~ de travailler le soir** to make it a rule to work in the evening; **3** to impose (**à qn** on sb); **4 s'~ comme leader** to establish oneself as the leader; **s'~ dans un domaine** to make a name for oneself in a field; **s'~ sur un marché** to establish itself in a market; **5** [*person*] to make one's presence felt; [*will*] to impose itself.

imposition /ɛ̃pozisjɔ̃/ *nf* taxation.

impossibilité /ɛ̃pɔsibilite/ *nf* impossibility; **être dans l'~ de faire** to be unable to do; **mettre qn dans l'~ de faire** to make it impossible for sb to do.

impossible /ɛ̃pɔsibl/ **I** *adj* impossible.
II *nm* **l'~** the impossible; **faire** or **tenter l'~** to do everything one can.
IDIOMS **~ n'est pas français** there's no such word as 'can't'.

imposteur /ɛ̃pɔstœʀ/ *nm* impostor.

imposture /ɛ̃pɔstyʀ/ *nf* **1** deception; **2** fraud.

impôt /ɛ̃po/ *nm* tax; **après ~** after tax.
■ **~ foncier** property tax; **~ sur le revenu** income tax; **~s locaux** local taxes.

impotent, **~e** /ɛ̃pɔtɑ̃, ɑ̃t/ **I** *adj* infirm.
II *nm,f* person with impaired mobility.

impraticable /ɛ̃pʀatikabl/ *adj* **1** impassable; **2** unworkable.

imprécis, **~e** /ɛ̃pʀesi, iz/ *adj* [*outline, memory*] vague; [*concept*] hazy; [*aim*] inaccurate; [*results*] imprecise; [*person*] vague.

imprécision /ɛ̃pʀesizjɔ̃/ *nf* imprecision; vagueness; inaccuracy.

imprégner /ɛ̃pʀeɲe/ [14] **I** *vtr* to impregnate [*material, wood*] (**de** with).
II s'imprégner *v refl* (+ *v être*) **s'~ de** to become soaked with [*water*]; to immerse oneself in [*language*].

imprenable /ɛ̃pʀənabl/ *adj* **avec vue ~** with unobstructed view guaranteed.

imprésario /ɛ̃pʀesaʀjo/ *nm* agent, impresario.

impression /ɛ̃pʀesjɔ̃/ *nf* **1** impression; **faire bonne ~** to make a good impression; **j'ai l'~ d'être surveillé** I feel I am being watched; **2** printing; **faute d'~** misprint; **3** pattern; **4** (of film) exposure.

impressionnable /ɛ̃pʀesjɔnabl/ *adj* **1** sensitive; **2** impressionable.

impressionnant, **~e** /ɛ̃pʀesjɔnɑ̃, ɑ̃t/ *adj* **1** impressive; **2** disturbing.

impressionner /ɛ̃pʀesjɔne/ [1] *vtr* **1** to impress; **ne te laisse pas ~ par les examinateurs** don't be overawed by the examiners; **2** [*image*] to disturb; **3** to act on [*retina, film*].

impressionnisme /ɛ̃pʀesjɔnism/ *nm* Impressionism.

imprévisible /ɛ̃pʀevizibl/ *adj* unpredictable.

imprévu, **~e** /ɛ̃pʀevy/ **I** *adj* **1** unforeseen; **2** unexpected.
II *nm* **1** hitch; **2 l'~** the unexpected; **plein d'~** [*person, film*] quirky; [*trip*] with a few

surprises; **un métier plein d'~** a job which is never dull; **3** unforeseen expense.

imprimante /ɛ̃pʀimɑ̃t/ *nf* printer.

imprimé, **~e** /ɛ̃pʀime/ **I** *pp* ▶ **imprimer**.
II *pp adj* printed (**de** with).
III *nm* **1** form; **2** printed matter; **3** print; **un ~ à fleurs** a floral print.

imprimer /ɛ̃pʀime/ [1] *vtr* **1** to print [*text*]; **2** to put [*stamp, seal*] (**sur** on); **3** to leave an imprint of [sth] (**dans, sur** in); **4** [*time, age*] to etch [*wrinkles*].

imprimerie /ɛ̃pʀimʀi/ *nf* **1** printing; **atelier d'~** printing shop; **2** printing works; **3** printers, print workers.

imprimeur /ɛ̃pʀimœʀ/ *nm* printer.

improbable /ɛ̃pʀɔbabl/ *adj* unlikely, improbable.

improductif, **-ive** /ɛ̃pʀɔdyktif, iv/ *adj* unproductive; **capitaux ~s** idle capital.

impromptu, **~e** /ɛ̃pʀɔ̃pty/ **I** *adj* impromptu.
II *adv* impromptu.
III *nm* impromptu.

impropre /ɛ̃pʀɔpʀ/ *adj* [*term, usage*] incorrect; **~ à** unfit for [*human consumption*].

improprement /ɛ̃pʀɔpʀəmɑ̃/ *adv* incorrectly.

improvisation /ɛ̃pʀɔvizasjɔ̃/ *nf* improvisation.

improvisé, **~e** /ɛ̃pʀɔvize/ *adj* [*speech*] improvised; [*meal*] impromptu; [*means*] makeshift; [*solution*] ad hoc; [*cook*] stand-in.

improviser /ɛ̃pʀɔvize/ [1] **I** *vtr* to improvise [*meal, speech*]; to concoct [*excuse, alibi*]; **~ un hôpital** to set up a makeshift hospital.
II *vi* to improvise.
III s'improviser *v refl* (+ *v être*) **1 s'~ cuisinier** to act as a cook; **2 un camp pour réfugiés ne s'improvise pas** you can't create a refugee camp just like that.

improviste: **à l'improviste** /alɛ̃pʀɔvist/ *phr* unexpectedly.

imprudemment /ɛ̃pʀydamɑ̃/ *adv* [*speak*] carelessly; [*act*] unwisely.

imprudence /ɛ̃pʀydɑ̃s/ *nf* **1** carelessness; **2 commettre une ~** to do something foolish.

imprudent, **~e** /ɛ̃pʀydɑ̃, ɑ̃t/ *adj* [*person, words*] careless; [*action*] rash.

impudence /ɛ̃pydɑ̃s/ *nf* **1** impudence; **2** impudent behaviour[GB].

impudent, **~e** /ɛ̃pydɑ̃, ɑ̃t/ *adj* impudent.

impudeur /ɛ̃pydœʀ/ *nf* immodesty; shamelessness.

impudique /ɛ̃pydik/ *adj* obscene; indecent; shameless.

impuissance /ɛ̃pɥisɑ̃s/ *nf* **1** impotence; **~ à faire** inability to do; **2** (Med) impotence.

impuissant, **~e** /ɛ̃pɥisɑ̃, ɑ̃t/ *adj* **1** powerless, helpless; **2** (Med) impotent.

impulsif, **-ive** /ɛ̃pylsif, iv/ *adj* impulsive.

impulsion /ɛ̃pylsjɔ̃/ *nf* **1** (gen) impulse; (Tech) pulse; **2** (figurative) impetus.

impunément /ɛ̃pynemɑ̃/ *adv* with impunity.

impuni, **~e** /ɛ̃pyni/ *adj* unpunished.

impunité /ɛ̃pynite/ *nf* impunity.

impur, **~e** /ɛ̃pyʀ/ *adj* **1** [*thoughts*] impure; **2** [*air*] dirty; [*blood*] tainted; **3** [*ore*] impure; **4** unclean.

impureté /ɛ̃pyʀte/ *nf* impurity.

imputable /ɛ̃pytabl/ *adj* attributable (**à** to).

imputer /ɛ̃pyte/ [1] *vtr* to attribute (**à** to), to impute (**to** à).

inabordable /inabɔʀdabl/ *adj* **1** [*coast*] inaccessible; [*person*] unapproachable; **2** [*prices*] prohibitive.

inacceptable /inaksɛptabl/ *adj* unacceptable.

inaccessible /inaksesibl/ *adj* **1** inaccessible; **2** [*person*] unapproachable.

inaccoutumé /inakutyme/ *adj* unusual.

inachevé, **~e** /inaʃve/ *adj* unfinished.

inactif, **-ive** /inaktif, iv/ *adj* idle; [*person*] inactive; [*population*] non-working.

inactivité /inaktivite/ *nf* inactivity.

inadaptation /inadaptasjɔ̃/ *nf* **1** inappropriateness; **2** maladjustment.

inadapté, **~e** /inadapte/ *adj* **1** [*child*] maladjusted; **2** [*method, means*] inappropriate; [*tool*] unsuitable; [*system, law*] ill-adapted; **3** [*person*] ill-equipped (**à** for).

inadéquat, **~e** /inadekwa, at/ *adj* inadequate; unsuitable.

inadmissible /inadmisibl/ *adj* **1** intolerable; **2** unacceptable.

inadvertance: **par inadvertance** /paʀ inadvɛʀtɑ̃s/ *phr* inadvertently.

inaltérable /inalteʀabl/ *adj* **1** [*substance*] unalterable, non-corroding; [*colour*] fade-resistant; **2** [*character*] constant; [*principle*] immutable; [*hope*] steadfast; [*humour*] unfailing.

inaltéré, **~e** /inalteʀe/ *adj* [*substance*] unaltered; [*sky, air*] pure.

inamovible /inamɔvibl/ *adj* [*official*] irremovable.

inanimé, **~e** /inanime/ *adj* [*matter*] inanimate; [*person*] unconscious; lifeless.

inanition /inanisjɔ̃/ *nf* starvation.

inaperçu, **~e** /inapɛʀsy/ *adj* **passer ~** to go unnoticed.

inappréciable /inapʀesjabl/ *adj* **1** [*support*] invaluable; [*advantage*] inestimable; **2** imperceptible.

inapte /inapt/ *adj* unfit; **~ (au service)** unfit (for military service).

inaptitude /inaptityd/ *nf* unfitness (**à qch** for sth; **à faire** for doing).

inarticulé, **~e** /inaʀtikyle/ *adj* inarticulate.

inassouvi, **~e** /inasuvi/ *adj* [*appetite*] insatiable; [*thirst*] unquenchable; [*person, desire*] unsatisfied.

inattaquable /inatakabl/ *adj* **1** (Mil) unassailable; **2** irreproachable; **3** irrefutable; **4** rustproof [*metal*].

inattendu, **~e** /inatɑ̃dy/ *adj* unexpected.

inattentif, **-ive** /inatɑ̃tif, iv/ *adj* **1** inattentive; distracted; **2** heedless.

inattention /inatɑ̃sjɔ̃/ *nf* inattention; **moment d'~** lapse of concentration; **faute d'~** careless mistake.

inaudible /inodibl/ *adj* inaudible.

inaugural, **~e**, *mpl* **-aux** /inogyRal, o/ *adj* **1** [*ceremony*] inauguration; [*speech*] inaugural; **2** [*flight, voyage*] maiden.

inauguration /inogyRasjɔ̃/ *nf* (of statue) unveiling; (of building) inauguration; (of exhibition) opening; (of policy) launching.

inaugurer /inogyRe/ [1] *vtr* **1** to unveil [*statue, plaque*]; to open [*motorway, school*]; **2** to open [*conference*]; to inaugurate [*series of articles*]; **3** to mark the start of [*period*]; **4**○ to christen○ [*car*].

inavouable /inavwabl/ *adj* shameful.

inavoué, **~e** /inavwe/ *adj* [*crime, vice*] unconfessed; [*reason, aim*] undisclosed; [*fear*] hidden; [*love*] undeclared.

incalculable /ɛ̃kalkylabl/ *adj* **1** innumerable; **2** incalculable.

incandescent, **~e** /ɛ̃kɑ̃dɛsɑ̃, ɑ̃t/ *adj* incandescent; white-hot; glowing.

incapable /ɛ̃kapabl/ *adj* **1** **~ de faire** incapable of doing; unable to do; **2** incompetent.

incapacité /ɛ̃kapasite/ *nf* **1** inability; **être dans l'~ de faire** to be unable to do; **2** incompetence; **3** disability; **4** (Law) incapacity.

incarcération /ɛ̃kaRseRasjɔ̃/ *nf* imprisonment.

incarcérer /ɛ̃kaRseRe/ [14] *vtr* to imprison, to jail.

incarnation /ɛ̃kaRnasjɔ̃/ *nf* incarnation.

incarné, **~e** /ɛ̃kaRne/ *adj* **1** incarnate; **c'est la bêtise ~e** he/she is stupidity itself; **2** [*nail*] ingrowing.

incarner /ɛ̃kaRne/ [1] **I** *vtr* **1** to embody; **2** to play, to portray.
II s'incarner *v refl* (+ *v être*) to become incarnate.

incartade /ɛ̃kaRtad/ *nf* misdemeanour[GB].

incassable /ɛ̃kasabl/ *adj* unbreakable.

incendiaire /ɛ̃sɑ̃djɛR/ **I** *adj* **1** [*bomb*] incendiary; **2** [*statement*] inflammatory.
II *nmf* arsonist.

incendie /ɛ̃sɑ̃di/ *nm* fire; **~ criminel** arson.

incendier /ɛ̃sɑ̃dje/ [2] *vtr* **1** to burn (down), to torch; **2**○ to haul [sb] over the coals.

incertain, **~e** /ɛ̃sɛRtɛ̃, ɛn/ *adj* **1** [*date, origin*] uncertain; [*effect*] unknown; [*outlines*] blurred; [*colour*] indeterminate; [*smile, feeling*] vague; **2** [*result, profit*] uncertain; [*weather*] unsettled; **3** [*person*] uncertain; [*step, voice*] hesitant.

incertitude /ɛ̃sɛRtityd/ *nf* uncertainty; **vivre dans l'~ du lendemain** to live from day to day.

incessamment /ɛ̃sesamɑ̃/ *adv* very shortly.

incessant, **~e** /ɛ̃sɛsɑ̃, ɑ̃t/ *adj* [*noise, rain*] incessant; [*activity*] unceasing; [*criticism*] unremitting.

inceste /ɛ̃sɛst/ *nm* incest.

incestueux, **-euse** /ɛ̃sɛstɥø, øz/ *adj* incestuous.

inchangé, **~e** /ɛ̃ʃɑ̃ʒe/ *adj* unchanged.

incidemment /ɛ̃sidamɑ̃/ *adv* **1** in passing; **2** by chance.

incidence /ɛ̃sidɑ̃s/ *nf* **1** impact; **2** incidence.

incident, **~e** /ɛ̃sidɑ̃, ɑ̃t/ *nm* **1** incident; **en cas d'~** if anything should happen; **2 ~ (de parcours)** hitch; **~ technique** technical hitch; **l'~ est clos** the matter is closed.

incinérateur /ɛ̃sineRatœR/ *nm* **1** incinerator; **2** crematorium (GB), crematory (US).

incinération /ɛ̃sineRasjɔ̃/ *nf* **1** incineration; **2** cremation.

incinérer /ɛ̃sineRe/ [14] *vtr* **1** to burn; to incinerate; **2** to cremate.

incise /ɛ̃siz/ *nf* **1** (Mus) phrase; **2** parenthetical clause.

inciser /ɛ̃size/ [1] *vtr* to make an incision in [*skin*].

incisif, **-ive**[1] /ɛ̃sizif, iv/ *adj* [*criticism*] incisive; [*portrait*] telling; [*look*] piercing.

incision /ɛ̃sizjɔ̃/ *nf* incision.

incisive[2] /ɛ̃siziv/ **I** *adj f* ▶ **incisif**.
II *nf* incisor.

incitation /ɛ̃sitasjɔ̃/ *nf* **1** incentive; **2** (Law) incitement.

inciter /ɛ̃site/ [1] *vtr* [*person, situation*] to encourage; [*event, decision*] to prompt; **~ qn à la prudence** to make sb cautious; **~ à la haine raciale** to stir up racial hatred.

inclinable /ɛ̃klinabl/ *adj* adjustable.

inclinaison /ɛ̃klinɛzɔ̃/ *nf* (of hill) incline; (of wall, seat) angle; (of roof) slope; (of boat) list.

inclination /ɛ̃klinasjɔ̃/ *nf* **1** inclination; **2** nod; bow.

incliné, **~e** /ɛ̃kline/ *adj* **1** [*ground*] sloping; [*roof*] steep; **2** [*wall*] leaning.

incliner /ɛ̃kline/ [1] **I** *vtr* to tilt [*sunshade*]; to tip up [*bottle*]; **~ le buste** to lean forward.
II s'incliner *v refl* (+ *v être*) **1** to lean forward; (politely) to bow; **2 s'~ devant qch** to bow to sth, to accept sth; **3** to give in○ (**devant** to); **4 s'~ devant le courage de qn** to admire sb's courage.

inclure /ɛ̃klyR/ [78] *vtr* **1** to include; **2** to enclose.

inclus, **~e** /ɛ̃kly, yz/ **I** *pp* ▶ **inclure**.
II *pp adj* **1 20 personnes, enfants ~** 20 people, including children; **jusqu'à jeudi ~** up to and including Thursday (GB), through Thursday (US); **2** enclosed.

inclusion /ɛ̃klyzjɔ̃/ *nf* inclusion.

incohérence /ɛ̃kɔeRɑ̃s/ *nf* **1** incoherence; **2** discrepancy.

incohérent, **~e** /ɛ̃kɔeRɑ̃, ɑ̃t/ *adj* [*talk, behaviour*] incoherent; [*attitude*] illogical.

incollable /ɛ̃kɔlabl/ *adj* **1**○ impossible to catch out; **2 riz ~** easy-cook rice.

incolore /ɛ̃kɔlɔR/ *adj* colourless[GB]; [*glass*] clear.

incomber /ɛ̃kɔ̃be/ [1] **I incomber à** *v+prep* [*task*] to fall to; [*responsibility*] to lie with.
II *v impers* **il incombe à qn de faire** it is incumbent upon sb to do.

incommode /ɛ̃kɔmɔd/ *adj* **1** inconvenient; awkward; **2** uncomfortable.

incommodé, **~e** /ɛ̃kɔmɔde/ **I** *pp* ▶ **incommoder**.
II *pp adj* unwell, indisposed.

incommoder /ɛ̃kɔmɔde/ [1] *vtr* to bother.

incomparable /ɛ̃kɔ̃paʀabl/ *adj* incomparable.

incompatible /ɛ̃kɔ̃patibl/ *adj* incompatible.

incompétence /ɛ̃kɔ̃petɑ̃s/ *nf* (gen) incompetence; (Law) incompetency.

incompétent, **~e** /ɛ̃kɔ̃petɑ̃, ɑ̃t/ *adj* incompetent.

incomplet, **-ète** /ɛ̃kɔ̃plɛ, ɛt/ *adj* incomplete.

incompréhensible /ɛ̃kɔ̃pʀeɑ̃sibl/ *adj* incomprehensible.

incompréhension /ɛ̃kɔ̃pʀeɑ̃sjɔ̃/ *nf* **1** incomprehension; **2** lack of understanding.

incompressible /ɛ̃kɔ̃pʀɛsibl/ *adj* **1** incompressible; **2** [*costs*] fixed; **3** (Law) **peine ~** sentence without possibility of remittance.

incompris, **~e** /ɛ̃kɔ̃pʀi, iz/ **I** *adj* **un artiste ~** an artist whose work is not understood.

II *nm,f* misunderstood person.

inconcevable /ɛ̃kɔ̃svabl/ *adj* inconceivable.

inconditionnel, **-elle** /ɛ̃kɔ̃disjɔnɛl/ **I** *adj* unconditional.

II *nm,f* devoted admirer; fan; **les ~s de la mode** dedicated followers of fashion.

inconduite /ɛ̃kɔ̃dɥit/ *nf* (gen) misbehaviour[GB]; (Law) misconduct.

inconfortable /ɛ̃kɔ̃fɔʀtabl/ *adj* **1** uncomfortable; **2** awkward.

incongru, **~e** /ɛ̃kɔ̃gʀy/ *adj* [*behaviour*] unseemly; [*remark*] incongruous.

incongruité /ɛ̃kɔ̃gʀɥite/ *nf* **1** incongruity; **2** faux-pas; incongruous remark.

inconnu, **~e** /ɛ̃kɔny/ **I** *adj* unknown (**de** to); [*territories*] unexplored.

II *nm,f* **1** unknown (person); **2** stranger.

III *nm* **l'~** the unknown.

inconsciemment /ɛ̃kɔ̃sjamɑ̃/ *adv* **1** subconsciously; **2** unintentionally, unconsciously.

inconscience /ɛ̃kɔ̃sjɑ̃s/ *nf* **1** recklessness; **2** (Med) unconsciousness.

inconscient, **~e** /ɛ̃kɔ̃sjɑ̃, ɑ̃t/ **I** *adj* **1** unthinking; foolhardy; **être ~ de** to be unaware of; **2** (Med) unconscious; **3** [*act, gesture*] unconscious, automatic.

II *nm,f* **c'est un ~** he's irresponsible.

III *nm* **l'~** the unconscious.

inconséquence /ɛ̃kɔ̃sekɑ̃s/ *nf* (of reasoning) inconsistency; (of behaviour) fecklessness.

inconséquent, **~e** /ɛ̃kɔ̃sekɑ̃, ɑ̃t/ *adj* [*person, behaviour*] inconsistent.

inconsidéré, **~e** /ɛ̃kɔ̃sideʀe/ *adj* **1** [*remark, act*] ill-considered; [*loan*] ill-advised; **2** [*consumption*] excessive.

inconsistance /ɛ̃kɔ̃sistɑ̃s/ *nf* lack of substance; lack of character.

inconsistant, **~e** /ɛ̃kɔ̃sistɑ̃, ɑ̃t/ *adj* [*argument, plot*] flimsy; [*programme*] lacking in substance; [*person*] characterless.

inconsolable /ɛ̃kɔ̃sɔlabl/ *adj* inconsolable.

inconstant, **~e** /ɛ̃kɔ̃stɑ̃, ɑ̃t/ *adj* fickle.

incontestable /ɛ̃kɔ̃tɛstabl/ *adj* unquestionable, indisputable.

incontesté, **~e** /ɛ̃kɔ̃tɛste/ *adj* [*victory*] undisputed; [*fact*] uncontested.

incontinence /ɛ̃kɔ̃tinɑ̃s/ *nf* incontinence.

incontinent, **~e** /ɛ̃kɔ̃tinɑ̃, ɑ̃t/ *adj* incontinent.

incontournable /ɛ̃kɔ̃tuʀnabl/ *adj* [*issue*] that must be addressed; [*facts*] that cannot be ignored.

incontrôlable /ɛ̃kɔ̃tʀolabl/ *adj* **1** unverifiable; **2** uncontrollable.

inconvenance /ɛ̃kɔ̃vnɑ̃s/ *nf* impropriety.

inconvenant, **~e** /ɛ̃kɔ̃vnɑ̃, ɑ̃t/ *adj* unsuitable; improper, unseemly.

inconvénient /ɛ̃kɔ̃venjɑ̃/ *nm* drawback, disadvantage; **si vous n'y voyez pas d'~** if you have no objection.

incorporer /ɛ̃kɔʀpɔʀe/ [1] *vtr* **1** (Culin) to blend; **2** to incorporate [*chapter*]; **3** (Mil) to enlist (GB), to induct (US).

incorrect, **~e** /ɛ̃kɔʀɛkt/ *adj* **1** [*term, interpretation, argument*] incorrect; [*adjustment*] faulty; [*forecast*] inaccurate; **2** [*behaviour*] improper; [*term*] unsuitable; [*person*] impolite; **3** unfair.

incorrection /ɛ̃kɔʀɛksjɔ̃/ *nf* **1** (of style, language) incorrectness; (of behaviour) impropriety; **2** inaccuracy.

incorrigible /ɛ̃kɔʀiʒibl/ *adj* incorrigible.

incorruptible /ɛ̃kɔʀyptibl/ *adj* incorruptible.

incrédule /ɛ̃kʀedyl/ *adj* **1** incredulous; **2** (in religion) unbelieving.

incrédulité /ɛ̃kʀedylite/ *nf* incredulity.

increvable /ɛ̃kʀəvabl/ *adj* **1°** [*person*] tireless; **2** puncture-proof.

incriminer /ɛ̃kʀimine/ [1] *vtr* [*person*] to accuse; [*evidence*] to incriminate; **l'article incriminé** the offending article.

incroyable /ɛ̃kʀwajabl/ *adj* incredible, unbelievable; **~ mais vrai** strange but true.

incrustation /ɛ̃kʀystasjɔ̃/ *nf* **1** inlaying; **2** inlay; **3** encrustation.

incruster /ɛ̃kʀyste/ [1] **I** *vtr* **1** to inlay; **2 robe incrustée de diamants** dress encrusted with diamonds.

II s'incruster *v refl* (+ *v être*) [*pebble, shell*] to become embedded.

incubation /ɛ̃kybasjɔ̃/ *nf* incubation.

incuber /ɛ̃kybe/ [1] *vtr* to incubate, to hatch.

inculpation /ɛ̃kylpasjɔ̃/ *nf* (Law) charge.

inculpé, **~e** /ɛ̃kylpe/ *nm,f* ≈ accused; **les ~s** the accused.

inculper /ɛ̃kylpe/ [1] *vtr* (Law) to charge.

inculquer /ɛ̃kylke/ [1] *vtr* to inculcate (**à** in), to instil[GB] (**à** in).

inculte /ɛ̃kylt/ *adj* uncultivated.

incurable /ɛ̃kyʀabl/ *adj*, *nmf* incurable.

incursion /ɛ̃kyʀsjɔ̃/ *nf* incursion, foray.

incurver /ɛ̃kyʀve/ [1] *vtr*, **s'incurver** *v refl* (+ *v être*) to curve, to bend.

Inde /ɛ̃d/ *pr nf* India.

indécence /ɛ̃desɑ̃s/ *nf* (gen) indecency; (of remark) impropriety; **ce luxe, quelle ~!** such luxury is quite obscene.

indécent, **~e** /ɛ̃desɑ̃, ɑ̃t/ *adj* indecent; [*luxury*] obscene; **avoir une chance ~e** to be disgustingly lucky.

indéchiffrable /ɛ̃deʃifʀabl/ *adj* **1** indecipherable; **2** [*mystery*] incomprehensible.

indécis, ~e /ɛ̃desi, iz/ **I** *adj* **1 il est encore ~** he hasn't decided yet; **2** indecisive; **3** [*results*] uncertain.
II *nm,f* **1** indecisive person; **2** (in opinion poll) 'don't know'; (in election) floating voter.

indécision /ɛ̃desizjɔ̃/ *nf* **1** indecision, uncertainty; **2** indecisiveness.

indécrottable° /ɛ̃dekʀɔtabl/ *adj* hopeless°.

indéfendable /ɛ̃defɑ̃dabl/ *adj* indefensible.

indéfini, ~e /ɛ̃defini/ *adj* **1** [*number*] indeterminate; **2** [*sadness*] undefined; [*unease*] vague; [*duration*] indeterminate, indefinite; **3** (in grammar) indefinite.

indéfiniment /ɛ̃definimɑ̃/ *adv* indefinitely.

indéfinissable /ɛ̃definisabl/ *adj* undefinable.

indélébile /ɛ̃delebil/ *adj* indelible.

indélicat, ~e /ɛ̃delika, at/ *adj* **1** tactless; **2** dishonest.

indélicatesse /ɛ̃delikatɛs/ *nf* **1** indelicacy, tactlessness; **2** dishonesty; **3** act of dishonesty.

indemne /ɛ̃dɛmn/ *adj* unscathed, unharmed.

indemnisation /ɛ̃dɛmnizasjɔ̃/ *nf* **1** indemnification; **2** indemnity, compensation.

indemniser /ɛ̃dɛmnize/ [1] *vtr* to indemnify; **se faire ~** to receive compensation.

indemnité /ɛ̃dɛmnite/ *nf* **1** (Law) indemnity, compensation; **2** allowance.
■ **~ de chômage** unemployment benefit; **~ journalière** sick pay; **~ de licenciement** severance pay; **~ de logement** housing allowance.

indéniable /ɛ̃denjabl/ *adj* undeniable, unquestionable.

indentation /ɛ̃dɑ̃tasjɔ̃/ *nf* indentation.

indépendamment /ɛ̃depɑ̃damɑ̃/ **I** *adv* independently.
II indépendamment de *phr* **1** regardless of; **2** in addition to.

indépendance /ɛ̃depɑ̃dɑ̃s/ *nf* independence.

indépendant, ~e /ɛ̃depɑ̃dɑ̃, ɑ̃t/ **I** *adj* **1** independent; **2** [*room*] separate; **maison ~e** detached house.
II *nm,f* **1** freelance, self-employed person; **2** independent (candidate).

indépendantiste /ɛ̃depɑ̃dɑ̃tist/ **I** *adj* [*organization*] (pro-)independence.
II *nmf* **1** freedom fighter; **2** member of an independence movement.

indescriptible /ɛ̃dɛskʀiptibl/ *adj* indescribable.

indésirable /ɛ̃deziʀabl/ *adj* [*person*] undesirable; **effets ~s** (Med) adverse reactions.

indestructible /ɛ̃dɛstʀyktibl/ *adj* indestructible.

indéterminé, ~e /ɛ̃detɛʀmine/ *adj* [*form, quantity*] indeterminate; [*reason, number*] unspecified; **l'origine de l'incendie reste ~e** the cause of the fire has not yet been identified.

index /ɛ̃dɛks/ *nm inv* **1** index; **mettre qch/qn à l'~** to blacklist sth/sb; **2** forefinger; **3** (Tech) pointer.

indexation /ɛ̃dɛksasjɔ̃/ *nf* **1** indexation, index-linking; **2** (of documents) indexing.

indexer /ɛ̃dɛkse/ [1] *vtr* **1** to index-link; **~ qch sur qch** to index sth to sth; **2** to index.

indicateur, -trice /ɛ̃dikatœʀ, tʀis/ **I** *adj* **panneau** or **poteau ~** signpost.
II *nm* **1** informer; **2** indicator; **~ de tendance** market indicator; **3** (street) directory; **4** timetable; **5** gauge, indicator.

indicatif, -ive /ɛ̃dikatif, iv/ **I** *adj* indicative.
II *nm* **1** (in grammar) indicative; **2 ~ (téléphonique)** dialling[GB] code; **~ de département** area code; **3** theme tune.

indication /ɛ̃dikasjɔ̃/ *nf* **1** indication; **il n'y a pas d'~ d'origine** the place of origin is not indicated; **2** information; **sauf ~ contraire** unless otherwise indicated; **3** (for use) instruction; **4** indication, clue.

indice /ɛ̃dis/ *nm* **1** sign, indication; **2** (in inquiry) clue; **3** (Econ) index; **4 l'~ d'écoute** audience ratings.

indicible /ɛ̃disibl/ *adj* inexpressible.

indien, -ienne /ɛ̃djɛ̃, ɛn/ *adj* **1** Indian; **2** (North American) Indian.

indifféremment /ɛ̃difeʀamɑ̃/ *adv* **1** equally; **2 servir ~ de salon ou de bureau** to be used either as a living room or a study.

indifférence /ɛ̃difeʀɑ̃s/ *nf* indifference.

indifférent, ~e /ɛ̃difeʀɑ̃, ɑ̃t/ *adj* **1** indifferent; **laisser qn ~** to leave sb cold; **2** irrelevant.

indifférer /ɛ̃difeʀe/ [14] *vtr* to leave [sb] indifferent.

indigène /ɛ̃diʒɛn/ **I** *adj* **1** [*fauna, flora*] indigenous; **2** [*population, custom*] local; native.
II *nmf* local; native.

indigeste /ɛ̃diʒɛst/ *adj* indigestible.

indigestion /ɛ̃diʒɛstjɔ̃/ *nf* **1** indigestion; **avoir une ~** to have (an attack of) indigestion; **2 avoir une ~ de qch** to be fed up° with sth.

indignation /ɛ̃diɲasjɔ̃/ *nf* indignation (**devant** at).

indigne /ɛ̃diɲ/ *adj* **1** [*conduct*] disgraceful; [*mother, son*] bad; **2 ~ de qn** unworthy of sb; **~ de faire** not fit to do.

indigné, ~e /ɛ̃diɲe/ *adj* indignant (**de** at).

indigner /ɛ̃diɲe/ [1] **I** *vtr* to make [sb] indignant, to outrage [sb].
II s'indigner *v refl* (+ *v être*) to be indignant (**de** about).

indigo /ɛ̃digo/ *adj inv, nm* indigo.

indiqué, ~e /ɛ̃dike/ **I** *pp* ▶ **indiquer**.
II *pp adj* **1** [*treatment*] recommended; **le moyen tout ~ d'échouer** the sure way to fail; **2 à l'heure ~e** at the specified time; **le village est très mal indiqué** the village is very badly signposted.

indiquer /ɛ̃dike/ [1] *vtr* **1** [*person*] to point out, to point to; [*signpost*] to show the way to; **pouvez-vous m'~ la banque la plus proche?** can you tell me where the nearest bank is?; **2** to indicate (**que** that); **3 je peux t'~ un bon médecin** I can give you the name of a good doctor; **4** to give; **l'heure indi-**

quée sur le programme est fausse the time given on the programme[GB] is wrong; **on m'a indiqué la marche à suivre** I've been told the procedure; **5** [*meter, signpost, map*] to show; **le restaurant n'est pas indiqué** there are no signs to the restaurant.

indirect, **~e** /ɛ̃diʀɛkt/ *adj* indirect.

indiscipliné, **~e** /ɛ̃disipline/ *adj* undisciplined, unruly.

indiscret, **-ète** /ɛ̃diskʀɛ, ɛt/ *adj* **1** [*question*] indiscreet; [*person*] inquisitive; **à l'abri des regards ~s** away from prying eyes; **2** indiscreet; **il est ~** he can't keep a secret.

indiscrétion /ɛ̃diskʀesjɔ̃/ *nf* **1** inquisitiveness; **sans ~, combien gagnez-vous?** if you don't mind my asking, how much do you earn?; **2** lack of discretion; **être d'une grande ~** to be very indiscreet; **3** indiscreet remark.

indiscutable /ɛ̃diskytabl/ *adj* indisputable, unquestionable.

indiscutablement /ɛ̃diskytabləmɑ̃/ *adv* unquestionably.

indispensable /ɛ̃dispɑ̃sabl/ **I** *adj* essential; **être ~ à qn** to be indispensable to sb.

II *nm* **l'~** essentials; **n'emporte que l'~** only take the essentials with you.

indisposé, **~e** /ɛ̃dispoze/ *adj* unwell, indisposed.

indisposer /ɛ̃dispoze/ [1] *vtr* **1** to annoy; **2** to upset [sb], to make [sb] feel ill.

indisposition /ɛ̃dispozisjɔ̃/ *nf* indisposition.

indissociable /ɛ̃disɔsjabl/ *adj* inseparable (**de** from).

indissoluble /ɛ̃disɔlybl/ *adj* indissoluble.

indistinct, **~e** /ɛ̃distɛ̃, ɛ̃kt/ *adj* indistinct.

individu /ɛ̃dividy/ *nm* **1** individual; **2** human being, person; **3 un sinistre ~** a sinister individual or character; **un ~ armé** an armed man; **4** (in scientific study) subject.

individualisé, **~e** /ɛ̃dividɥalize/ *adj* [*training*] tailored to individual needs, individualized (US); [*salary*] negotiated on an individual basis.

individualiser /ɛ̃dividɥalize/ [1] **I** *vtr* **1** to tailor [sth] to individual needs; **2** to individualize.

II s'individualiser *v refl* (+ *v être*) to become more individual.

individualiste /ɛ̃dividɥalist/ *adj* individualistic.

individuel, **-elle** /ɛ̃dividɥɛl/ *adj* (gen) individual; [*responsibility*] personal; [*car, property*] private; [*room*] single; **maison individuelle** (detached) house.

individuellement /ɛ̃dividɥɛlmɑ̃/ *adv* individually.

indivisible /ɛ̃divizibl/ *adj* indivisible.

indochinois, **~e** /ɛ̃dɔʃinwa, az/ *adj* Indochinese.

indo-européen, **-éenne**, *mpl* **~s** /ɛ̃do øʀɔpeɛ̃, ɛn/ *adj* Indo-European.

indolence /ɛ̃dɔlɑ̃s/ *nf* laziness, indolence.

indolent, **~e** /ɛ̃dɔlɑ̃, ɑ̃t/ *adj* lazy, indolent.

indolore /ɛ̃dɔlɔʀ/ *adj* painless.

indomptable /ɛ̃dɔ̃tabl/ *adj* indomitable; uncontrollable; untamable.

indompté, **~e** /ɛ̃dɔ̃te/ *adj* unsubdued, untamed.

indonésien, **-ienne** /ɛ̃dɔnezjɛ̃, ɛn/ **I** *adj* Indonesian.

II *nm* Indonesian.

indu, **~e** /ɛ̃dy/ *adj* **1** [*hour*] ungodly°, unearthly; [*remark, reaction*] inappropriate, unseemly; **2** [*profit*] unwarranted, unjustified.

indubitable /ɛ̃dybitabl/ *adj* indubitable; **il est ~ que** there is no doubt that.

induction /ɛ̃dyksjɔ̃/ *nf* induction.

induire /ɛ̃dɥiʀ/ [69] *vtr* **1** [*event, measures*] to lead to, to bring about; **2** to infer, to conclude (**de** from); **3** to induce (**à faire** to do); **~ qn en erreur** to mislead sb; **4** to induce [*current*].

indulgence /ɛ̃dylʒɑ̃s/ *nf* **1** (of parent, audience) indulgence; **2** (of jury) leniency.

indulgent, **~e** /ɛ̃dylʒɑ̃, ɑ̃t/ *adj* **1** [*parent, audience*] indulgent; **2** [*jury*] lenient.

industrialiser /ɛ̃dystʀijalize/ [1] **I** *vtr* to industrialize.

II s'industrialiser *v refl* (+ *v être*) to become industrialized.

industrie /ɛ̃dystʀi/ *nf* **1** industry; **l'~ hôtelière** the hotel trade; **2** industrial concern.

industriel, **-ielle** /ɛ̃dystʀijɛl/ **I** *adj* industrial; **pain ~** factory-baked bread.

II *nm,f* industrialist, manufacturer.

industriellement /ɛ̃dystʀijɛlmɑ̃/ *adv* industrially.

inébranlable /inebʀɑ̃labl/ *adj* **1** unshakeable, unwavering; **2** immovable.

inédit, **~e** /inedi, it/ *adj* [*book*] (previously) unpublished; [*situation*] (totally) new.

ineffable /inefabl/ *adj* ineffable, unutterable.

inefficace /inefikas/ *adj* **1** ineffective; **2** inefficient.

inefficacité /inefikasite/ *nf* **1** ineffectiveness, inefficacy; **2** inefficiency.

inégal, **~e**, *mpl* **-aux** /inegal, o/ *adj* unequal; uneven; irregular; [*mood*] changeable, erratic; **avec un bonheur ~** with mixed success.

inégalable /inegalabl/ *adj* incomparable, matchless.

inégalé, **~e** /inegale/ *adj* unequalled[GB], unrivalled[GB].

inégalement /inegalmɑ̃/ *adv* **1** unequally; **2** unevenly.

inégalité /inegalite/ *nf* **1** disparity (**de** in); **2** inequality; **3** (of mood) changeability; (of surface) unevenness.

inéluctable /inelyktabl/ *adj, nm* inevitable, ineluctable.

inénarrable /inenaʀabl/ *adj* hilarious.

inenvisageable /inɑ̃vizaʒabl/ *adj* inconceivable.

inepte /inɛpt/ *adj* [*person*] inept; [*judgment*] inane; [*remark*] idiotic.

ineptie /inɛpsi/ *nf* **1** inanity; **2** idiotic remark; **3** (action) stupid thing.

inépuisable /inepɥizabl/ *adj* inexhaustible.

inerte /inɛʀt/ *adj* **1** inert; **2** apathetic.

inertie /inɛʀsi/ *nf* **1** inertia; **2** apathy, inertia.

inespéré, **~e** /inɛspeʀe/ *adj* [*victory*] unhoped for; **c'est une occasion ~e de faire** this is a heaven-sent opportunity to do.

inestimable /inɛstimabl/ *adj* [*fortune, value*] inestimable; [*damage*] incalculable; [*painting*] priceless; [*help*] invaluable.

inévitable /inevitabl/ *adj* inevitable; unavoidable.

inexact, **~e** /inegza, akt/ *adj* inaccurate.

inexactitude /inegzaktityd/ *nf* **1** inaccuracy; **2** unpunctuality.

inexcusable /inɛkskyzabl/ *adj* inexcusable.

inexistant, **~e** /inegzistɑ̃, ɑ̃t/ *adj* [*means, help*] nonexistent.

inexorable /inɛgzɔʀabl/ *adj* inexorable.

inexpérience /inɛkspeʀjɑ̃s/ *nf* inexperience.

inexpérimenté, **~e** /inɛkspeʀimɑ̃te/ *adj* inexperienced.

inexplicable /inɛksplikabl/ *adj* inexplicable.

inexploitable /inɛksplwatabl/ *adj* [*mine*] unworkable; [*information*] unusable.

inexploité, **~e** /inɛksplwate/ *adj* unexploited; untapped.

inexpressif, **-ive** /inɛkspʀesif, iv/ *adj* inexpressive.

inexprimable /inɛkspʀimabl/ *adj* inexpressible.

in extremis /inɛkstʀemis/ *phr* at the last minute.

inextricable /inɛkstʀikabl/ *adj* inextricable.

infaillible /ɛ̃fajibl/ *adj* infallible.

infaisable /ɛ̃fəzabl/ *adj* unfeasible, impossible.

infamant, **~e** /ɛ̃famɑ̃, ɑ̃t/ *adj* **1** [*remark*] defamatory; **2** [*act*] infamous.

infâme /ɛ̃fɑm/ *adj* **1** [*food, smell*] revolting; **2** [*person*] despicable; [*treachery*] base; [*crime*] odious.

infamie /ɛ̃fami/ *nf* **1** infamy; **2** infamous act; **3** slanderous remark.

infanterie /ɛ̃fɑ̃tʀi/ *nf* infantry.

infantile /ɛ̃fɑ̃til/ *adj* **1** [*illness*] childhood; [*mortality*] infant; [*psychology*] child; **2** [*person, behaviour*] infantile, childish.

infarctus /ɛ̃faʀktys/ *nm inv* heart attack.

infatigable /ɛ̃fatigabl/ *adj* [*person, spirit*] tireless.

infatué, **~e** /ɛ̃fatɥe/ *adj* **être ~ de sa personne** or **soi-même** to be full of oneself.

infect, **~e** /ɛ̃fɛkt/ *adj* foul; revolting.

infecter /ɛ̃fɛkte/ [1] **I** *vtr* **1** (Med) to infect; **2** (figurative) to poison.

II s'infecter *v refl* (+ *v être*) to become infected, to go septic.

infectieux, **-ieuse** /ɛ̃fɛksjø, øz/ *adj* infectious.

infection /ɛ̃fɛksjɔ̃/ *nf* **1** (Med) infection; **2** (figurative) **c'est une ~!** it stinks to high heaven°!

inférieur, **~e** /ɛ̃feʀjœʀ/ **I** *adj* **1** lower; [*size*] smaller; [*length*] shorter; **~ à la moyenne** below average; **être en nombre ~** to be fewer in number; **2** inferior; **3** (in mathematics) **si a est ~ à b** if a is less than b.

II *nm,f* inferior.

infériorité /ɛ̃feʀjɔʀite/ *nf* inferiority.

infernal, **~e**, *mpl* **-aux** /ɛ̃fɛʀnal, o/ *adj* **1** [*noise, heat*] infernal; **cycle ~** unstoppable chain of events; **2** [*situation*] diabolical; **ce gosse est ~°** that child is a monster.

infertile /ɛ̃fɛʀtil/ *adj* barren, infertile.

infester /ɛ̃fɛste/ [1] *vtr* to infest, to overrun; **infesté d'orties** overrun with nettles; **infesté de puces** flea-ridden.

infidèle /ɛ̃fidɛl/ **I** *adj* **1** [*husband*] unfaithful; [*friend*] disloyal; **2** [*translation*] inaccurate.

II *nmf* infidel.

infidélité /ɛ̃fidelite/ *nf* **1** infidelity; **faire des ~s à** to be unfaithful to; **2** disloyalty; **3** inaccuracy.

infiltration /ɛ̃filtʀasjɔ̃/ *nf* **1 ~s d'eau** water seepage; **il y a des ~s dans le mur** water is seeping into the wall; **2** (of spies) infiltration; **3** (Med) injection.

infiltrer /ɛ̃filtʀe/ [1] **I** *vtr* to infiltrate [*organization*].

II s'infiltrer *v refl* (+ *v être*) **1** [*liquid*] to seep (**dans** into); [*light, cold*] to filter in; **le doute s'infiltra dans mon esprit** I began to have doubts; **2** [*person*] **s'~ dans** to infiltrate [*group, place*].

infime /ɛ̃fim/ *adj* tiny, minute.

infini, **~e** /ɛ̃fini/ **I** *adj* infinite; **avec d'~es précautions** with infinite care.

II *nm* **l'~** infinity.

infinité /ɛ̃finite/ *nf* **l'~** infinity; **une ~ de** an endless number of.

infinitésimal, **~e**, *mpl* **-aux** /ɛ̃finitezimal, o/ *adj* infinitesimal.

infinitif, **-ive** /ɛ̃finitif, iv/ *nm* infinitive; **à l'~** in the infinitive.

infirme /ɛ̃fiʀm/ **I** *adj* (gen) disabled; (because of age) infirm.

II *nmf* disabled person; **les ~s** the disabled.

infirmer /ɛ̃fiʀme/ [1] *vtr* (gen, Law) to invalidate.

infirmerie /ɛ̃fiʀməʀi/ *nf* (gen) infirmary; sick room; sick bay.

infirmier /ɛ̃fiʀmje/ *nm* male nurse.

infirmière /ɛ̃fiʀmjɛʀ/ *nf* nurse.

infirmité /ɛ̃fiʀmite/ *nf* (gen) disability; (through old age) infirmity.

inflammable /ɛ̃flamabl/ *adj* flammable.

inflammation /ɛ̃flamasjɔ̃/ *nf* (Med) inflammation.

inflammatoire /ɛ̃flamatwaʀ/ *adj* (Med) inflammatory.

inflation /ɛ̃flasjɔ̃/ *nf* inflation.

inflationniste /ɛ̃flasjɔnist/ *adj* inflationary.

infléchir /ɛ̃fleʃiʀ/ [3] *vtr*, **s'infléchir** *v refl* (+ *v être*) to soften; to deflect.

inflexible /ɛ̃flɛksibl/ *adj* inflexible.

inflexion /ɛ̃flɛksjɔ̃/ *nf* **1** change; **2** slight drop.

infliger /ɛ̃fliʒe/ [13] *vtr* **1** to inflict [*defeat*]; **2** to impose [*fine*].

influençable /ɛ̃flyɑ̃sabl/ *adj* impressionable.

influence /ɛ̃flyɑ̃s/ *nf* influence; **avoir une ~ néfaste** [*factor*] to have a detrimental effect.
influencer /ɛ̃flyɑ̃se/ [12] *vtr* to influence [*person*]; to affect [*situation*].
influent, **~e** /ɛ̃flyɑ̃, ɑ̃t/ *adj* influential.
influer: **influer sur** /ɛ̃flye/ [1] *v+prep* to have an influence on.
influx /ɛ̃fly/ *nm inv* **~ nerveux** nerve impulse.
informateur, **-trice** /ɛ̃fɔʀmatœʀ, tʀis/ *nm,f* **1** (gen) informant; **2** (police) informer.
informaticien, **-ienne** /ɛ̃fɔʀmatisjɛ̃, ɛn/ *nm,f* computer scientist.
information /ɛ̃fɔʀmasjɔ̃/ *nf* **1** information; **une ~** a piece of information; **2** (in newspaper, on television) **une ~** a piece of news, a news item; **écouter les ~s** to listen to the news; **l'~** reporting; **contrôler l'~** to control the media; **3** (in computer science) data, information.
informatique /ɛ̃fɔʀmatik/ **I** *adj* [*system, equipment*] computer.
II *nf* computer science, computing.
informatiser /ɛ̃fɔʀmatize/ [1] *vtr* to computerize.
informe /ɛ̃fɔʀm/ *adj* shapeless.
informer /ɛ̃fɔʀme/ [1] **I** *vtr* to inform; **de source bien informée** from a reliable source.
II s'informer *v refl* (+ *v être*) **1** to keep oneself informed; **2 s'~ de qch** to enquire about sth; **3 s'~ sur qn** to make enquiries about sb.
infortune /ɛ̃fɔʀtyn/ *nf* misfortune; **compagnon d'~** companion in adversity.
infortuné, **~e** /ɛ̃fɔʀtyne/ *adj* ill-fated.
infra /ɛ̃fʀa/ *adv* below; **voir ~** see below.
infraction /ɛ̃fʀaksjɔ̃/ *nf* offence[GB]; **être en ~** to be in breach of the law.
infranchissable /ɛ̃fʀɑ̃ʃisabl/ *adj* [*obstacle*] insurmountable; [*border*] impassable.
infrarouge /ɛ̃fʀaʀuʒ/ *adj, nm* infrared; **missile guidé par ~** heat-seeking missile.
infrastructure /ɛ̃fʀastʀyktyʀ/ *nf* **1** facilities; **~ hôtelière** hotel facilities; **2** (Econ) infrastructure.
infructueux, **-euse** /ɛ̃fʀyktɥø, øz/ *adj* fruitless.
infuser /ɛ̃fyze/ [1] *vi* [*tea*] to brew, to infuse; [*herbal tea*] to infuse.
infusion /ɛ̃fyzjɔ̃/ *nf* **1** herbal tea; **2** infusion.
ingénier: **s'ingénier** /ɛ̃ʒenje/ [2] *v refl* (+ *v être*) to do one's utmost (**à faire** to do).
ingénierie /ɛ̃ʒeniʀi/ *nf* engineering.
ingénieur /ɛ̃ʒenjœʀ/ *nm* engineer.
ingénieux, **-ieuse** /ɛ̃ʒenjø, øz/ *adj* ingenious.
ingéniosité /ɛ̃ʒenjozite/ *nf* ingenuity.
ingénu, **~e** /ɛ̃ʒeny/ *adj* ingenuous.
ingénuité /ɛ̃ʒenɥite/ *nf* ingenuousness; **en toute ~** in all innocence.
ingérence /ɛ̃ʒeʀɑ̃s/ *nf* interference (**dans** in).
ingérer /ɛ̃ʒeʀe/ [14] **I** *vtr* to ingest.
II s'ingérer *v refl* (+ *v être*) to interfere (**dans** in).
ingestion /ɛ̃ʒɛstjɔ̃/ *nf* ingestion.
ingrat, **~e** /ɛ̃gʀa, at/ *adj* **1** ungrateful; **2** [*book*] tedious and unrewarding; [*face, landscape*] unattractive; **3** [*task, role*] thankless; [*land, soil*] unproductive.
ingratitude /ɛ̃gʀatityd/ *nf* ingratitude (**envers** to).
ingrédient /ɛ̃gʀedjɑ̃/ *nm* ingredient.
ingurgiter /ɛ̃gyʀʒite/ [1] *vtr* to gulp down [*food*].
inhabitable /inabitabl/ *adj* uninhabitable.
inhabité, **~e** /inabite/ *adj* uninhabited.
inhabituel, **-elle** /inabitɥɛl/ *adj* unusual (**de la part de** for).
inhalateur /inalatœʀ/ *nm* inhaler.
inhalation /inalasjɔ̃/ *nf* inhalation.
inhaler /inale/ [1] *vtr* to inhale.
inhérent, **~e** /ineʀɑ̃, ɑ̃t/ *adj* inherent (**à** in).
inhiber /inibe/ [1] *vtr* to inhibit.
inhibition /inibisjɔ̃/ *nf* inhibition.
inhospitalier, **-ière** /inɔspitalje, ɛʀ/ *adj* inhospitable.
inhumain, **~e** /inymɛ̃, ɛn/ *adj* inhuman.
inhumation /inymasjɔ̃/ *nf* **1** burial; **2** funeral.
inhumer /inyme/ [1] *vtr* to bury.
inimaginable /inimaʒinabl/ *adj* **1** unimaginable; **2** unthinkable.
inimitable /inimitabl/ *adj* inimitable.
ininflammable /inɛ̃flamabl/ *adj* nonflammable.
inintelligible /inɛ̃teliʒibl/ *adj* unintelligible.
inintéressant, **~e** /inɛ̃teʀesɑ̃, ɑ̃t/ *adj* uninteresting.
ininterrompu, **~e** /inɛ̃tɛʀɔ̃py/ *adj* **1** [*process*] uninterrupted; [*drop*] continuous; [*traffic*] endless; **2** [*procession*] unbroken.
iniquité /inikite/ *nf* iniquity.
initial, **~e**[1], *mpl* **-iaux** /inisjal, o/ *adj* initial.
initiale[2] /inisjal/ *nf* initial.
initiateur, **-trice** /inisjatœʀ, tʀis/ *nm,f* **1** originator; instigator; **2** instructor.
initiation /inisjasjɔ̃/ *nf* **1** introduction (**à** to); **2** initiation.
initiative /inisjativ/ *nf* initiative; **avoir l'esprit d'~** to have initiative.
initié, **~e** /inisje/ *nm,f* **1** initiate; **2** insider trader.
initier /inisje/ [2] **I** *vtr* **1** to introduce (**à** to); **2** to initiate (**à** into); **3** to initiate [*project*].
II s'initier *v refl* (+ *v être*) **s'~ à qch** to learn sth.
injecter /ɛ̃ʒɛkte/ [2] *vtr* to inject; **yeux injectés de sang** bloodshot eyes.
injection /ɛ̃ʒɛksjɔ̃/ *nf* injection; **en ~(s)** by injection.
injonction /ɛ̃ʒɔ̃ksjɔ̃/ *nf* injunction, command.
injure /ɛ̃ʒyʀ/ *nf* insult, abuse; **faire ~ à qn** to insult sb.
injurier /ɛ̃ʒyʀje/ [1] *vtr* to insult, to swear at.
injurieux, **-ieuse** /ɛ̃ʒyʀjø, øz/ *adj* [*remark*] abusive; [*attitude*] insulting.
injuste /ɛ̃ʒyst/ *adj* unfair (**envers** to).

injustement /ɛ̃ʒystəmɑ̃/ *adv* unjustly; unfairly.

injustice /ɛ̃ʒystis/ *nf* injustice; (of person) unfairness; **une ~** an injustice; **réparer une ~** to right a wrong.

injustifiable /ɛ̃ʒystifjabl/ *adj* unjustifiable.

inlassable /ɛ̃lasabl/ *adj* [*person*] tireless; [*curiosity*] insatiable; [*efforts*] unremitting.

inné, **~e** /inne/ *adj* innate.

innocemment /inɔsamɑ̃/ *adv* innocently.

innocence /inɔsɑ̃s/ *nf* innocence.

innocent, **~e** /inɔsɑ̃, ɑ̃t/ *adj* innocent.

innocenter /inɔsɑ̃te/ [1] *vtr* to prove [sb] innocent.

innocuité /inɔkɥite/ *nf* harmlessness; **en toute ~** without any risks.

innombrable /innɔ̃bʀabl/ *adj* **1** countless; **2** [*crowd*] vast.

innommable /innɔmabl/ *adj* unspeakable; foul.

innovateur, **-trice** /inɔvatœʀ, tʀis/ *nm,f* innovator.

innover /inɔve/ [1] *vi* to innovate (**en matière de** in).

inoculer /inɔkyle/ [1] *vtr* to inoculate.

inodore /inɔdɔʀ/ *adj* [*substance*] odourless[GB].

inoffensif, **-ive** /inɔfɑ̃sif, iv/ *adj* harmless.

inondation /inɔ̃dasjɔ̃/ *nf* **1** flood; **2** flooding.

inonder /inɔ̃de/ [1] *vtr* to flood.

inopérant, **~e** /inɔpeʀɑ̃, ɑ̃t/ *adj* ineffective.

inopiné, **~e** /inɔpine/ *adj* unexpected.

inopportun, **~e** /inɔpɔʀtœ̃, yn/ *adj* **1** inappropriate; **2** ill-timed.

inoubliable /inublijabl/ *adj* unforgettable.

inouï, **~e** /inwi/ *adj* [*event*] unprecedented; [*success, violence*] incredible; **c'est ~** that's unheard of.

inox /inɔks/ *nm inv* stainless steel.

inoxydable /inɔksidabl/ *adj* [*metal*] non-oxidizing; **acier ~** stainless steel.

inqualifiable /ɛ̃kalifjabl/ *adj* unspeakable.

inquiet, **-iète** /ɛ̃kjɛ, ɛt/ *adj* **1** anxious; **2** worried.

inquiétant, **~e** /ɛ̃kjetɑ̃, ɑ̃t/ *adj* **1** worrying; **2** frightening.

inquiéter /ɛ̃kjete/ [14] **I** *vtr* **1** to worry; **2 les douaniers ne l'ont pas inquiété** the customs officers didn't bother him; **il a pu quitter le pays sans être inquiété** he was able to leave the country without any trouble.

II s'inquiéter *v refl* (+ *v être*) **1** to worry, to get worried; **2 s'~ de qch** to enquire about sth.

inquiétude /ɛ̃kjetyd/ *nf* **1** anxiety, concern; **être un sujet d'~** to give cause for concern; **2** worry; **il n'y a pas d'~ à avoir** there's nothing to worry about.

inquisiteur, **-trice** /ɛ̃kizitœʀ, tʀis/ **I** *adj* inquisitive.

II *nm,f* inquisitor.

inquisition /ɛ̃kizisjɔ̃/ *nf* inquisition.

insaisissable /ɛ̃sezisabl/ *adj* [*person, character*] elusive; [*nuance*] imperceptible.

insalubre /ɛ̃salybʀ/ *adj* insanitary.

insanité /ɛ̃sanite/ *nf* **1** rubbish; **c'est une ~** it's rubbish; **2** insanity.

insatiable /ɛ̃sasjabl/ *adj* insatiable.

insatisfaction /ɛ̃satisfaksjɔ̃/ *nf* dissatisfaction (**quant à** with).

insatisfait, **~e** /ɛ̃satisfɛ, ɛt/ **I** *adj* [*person*] dissatisfied (**de** with); [*desire*] unsatisfied.

II *nm,f* **c'est un ~** he's never satisfied.

inscription /ɛ̃skʀipsjɔ̃/ *nf* **1** (in school) enrolment[GB]; (at university) registration; **2 l'~ au club coûte 200 francs** the membership fee for the club costs 200 francs; **~ électorale** registration as a voter; **3** inscription; **~s racistes** racist graffiti.

inscrire /ɛ̃skʀiʀ/ [67] **I** *vtr* **1** to enrol[GB] [*pupil*]; to register [*student*]; **~ qn sur une liste** to enter sb's name on a list; **2** to write down [*name, date*].

II s'inscrire *v refl* (+ *v être*) **1** to enrol[GB]; to register; **s'~ au chômage** to register as unemployed; **s'~ à un parti** to join a party; **2 s'~ dans le cadre de** to be in line with; **s'~ dans une stratégie** to be part of a strategy; **3 s'~ en faux contre qch** to dispute the validity of sth.

inscrit, **~e** /ɛ̃skʀi, it/ **I** *pp* ▶ **inscrire**.

II *nm,f* registered student; registered voter.

insecte /ɛ̃sɛkt/ *nm* insect.

insecticide /ɛ̃sɛktisid/ *nm* insecticide.

insécurité /ɛ̃sekyʀite/ *nf* insecurity.

insémination /ɛ̃seminasjɔ̃/ *nf* insemination; **~ artificielle** artificial insemination.

inséminer /ɛ̃semine/ [1] *vtr* to inseminate.

insensé, **~e** /ɛ̃sɑ̃se/ *adj* **1** insane; **2**○ [*crowd, traffic jam*] phenomenal.

insensibiliser /ɛ̃sɑ̃sibilize/ [1] *vtr* (Med) to anaesthetize.

insensibilité /ɛ̃sɑ̃sibilite/ *nf* insensitivity.

insensible /ɛ̃sɑ̃sibl/ *adj* **1** impervious (**à** to); **2** insensitive.

insensiblement /ɛ̃sɑ̃sibləmɑ̃/ *adv* imperceptibly.

inséparable /ɛ̃sepaʀabl/ *adj* inseparable.

insérer /ɛ̃seʀe/ [14] **I** *vtr* to insert (**dans** in).

II s'insérer *v refl* (+ *v être*) (gen) to be inserted; **cette mesure s'insère dans un contexte de rigueur** this measure is to be seen in the context of austerity.

insertion /ɛ̃sɛʀsjɔ̃/ *nf* **1** insertion; **2** integration.

insidieux, **-ieuse** /ɛ̃sidjø, øz/ *adj* insidious.

insigne /ɛ̃siɲ/ **I** *adj* [*honour, favour, privilege*] great.

II *nm* badge.

insignifiant, **~e** /ɛ̃siɲifjɑ̃, ɑ̃t/ *adj* insignificant.

insinuation /ɛ̃sinɥasjɔ̃/ *nf* insinuation.

insinuer /ɛ̃sinɥe/ [1] **I** *vtr* to insinuate (**que** that).

II s'insinuer *v refl* (+ *v être*) **s'~ dans**

[*person*] to worm one's way into; [*liquid*] to seep into; **le doute s'insinuait dans leur esprit** doubt crept into their minds.

insipide /ɛ̃sipid/ *adj* insipid.

insistance /ɛ̃sistɑ̃s/ *nf* insistence; **avec ~** insistently.

insistant, **~e** /ɛ̃sistɑ̃, ɑ̃t/ *adj* insistent.

insister /ɛ̃siste/ [1] *vi* **1** to insist; **j'ai dû ~ pour qu'il vienne** I had to press him to come; **'ça ne répond pas'—'insiste'** 'there's no reply!'—'keep on trying'; **2 ~ sur** to stress, to lay stress on [*danger, need*]; to put the emphasis on [*presentation, spelling*]; **3 ~ sur** to pay particular attention to [*defect, stain*].

insolation /ɛ̃sɔlasjɔ̃/ *nf* sunstroke.

insolence /ɛ̃sɔlɑ̃s/ *nf* **1** insolence; **2** insolent remark.

insolent, **~e** /ɛ̃sɔlɑ̃, ɑ̃t/ *adj* **1** [*child, tone*] insolent; **2** [*rival, winner*] arrogant; **3** [*joy*] unashamed; [*luxury*] ostentatious.

insolite /ɛ̃sɔlit/ *adj*, *nm* unusual; **goût de l'~** taste for the unusual.

insoluble /ɛ̃sɔlybl/ *adj* insoluble.

insolvabilité /ɛ̃sɔlvabilite/ *nf* insolvency.

insolvable /ɛ̃sɔlvabl/ *adj* insolvent.

insomniaque /ɛ̃sɔmnjak/ *adj*, *nmf* insomniac.

insomnie /ɛ̃sɔmni/ *nf* insomnia.

insondable /ɛ̃sɔ̃dabl/ *adj* [*mystery*] unfathomable.

insonorisation /ɛ̃sɔnɔʀizasjɔ̃/ *nf* soundproofing.

insonoriser /ɛ̃sɔnɔʀize/ [1] *vtr* to soundproof.

insouciance /ɛ̃susjɑ̃s/ *nf* carefreeness; **vivre dans l'~** to lead a carefree life.

insouciant, **~e** /ɛ̃susjɑ̃, ɑ̃t/ *adj* carefree.

insoumis, **~e** /ɛ̃sumi, iz/ *adj* [*people*] unsubdued; **soldat ~** draft dodger.

insoumission /ɛ̃sumisjɔ̃/ *nf* **1** insubordination; **2** (Mil) avoidance of the draft.

insoupçonné, **~e** /ɛ̃supsɔne/ *adj* unsuspected.

insoutenable /ɛ̃sutnabl/ *adj* **1** [*pain*] unbearable; **2** [*pace*] impossible; **3** [*opinion*] untenable.

inspecter /ɛ̃spɛkte/ [1] *vtr* to inspect.

inspecteur, **-trice** /ɛ̃spɛktœʀ, tʀis/ *nm,f* inspector.

■ **~ de police** ≈ detective constable (GB); **~ du travail** health and safety inspector.

inspection /ɛ̃spɛksjɔ̃/ *nf* **1** inspection; **2** inspectorate.

inspiration /ɛ̃spiʀasjɔ̃/ *nf* inspiration; brainwave○.

inspirer /ɛ̃spiʀe/ [1] **I** *vtr* **1** to inspire [*person*]; **être bien/mal inspiré de faire** to be well-/ill-advised to do; **un roman inspiré des vieux contes populaires** a novel based on old folk tales; **2** to appeal to; **ça ne m'inspire pas** that doesn't appeal to me; **3 ~ la méfiance/le dégoût à qn** to inspire distrust/disgust in sb; **il ne m'inspire pas confiance** I don't have much confidence in him.

II *vi* to breathe in, to inhale.

III s'inspirer *v refl* (+ *v être*) **1 s'~ de** to draw one's inspiration from; **2 s'~ de qn** to follow sb's example.

instabilité /ɛ̃stabilite/ *nf* (gen) instability; (of weather) changeability.

instable /ɛ̃stabl/ *adj* (gen) unstable; [*weather*] unsettled.

installateur, **-trice** /ɛ̃stalatœʀ, tʀis/ *nm,f* fitter.

installation /ɛ̃stalasjɔ̃/ **I** *nf* **1** installation, putting in; **~ électrique** electric wiring; **2** system; **~ électrique** wiring; **3** move; **depuis mon ~ à Paris** since I moved to Paris; **4 notre ~ est temporaire** we're not permanently settled.

II installations *nf pl* facilities.

■ **~s militaires** military installations.

installé, **~e** /ɛ̃stale/ **I** *pp* ▶ **installer**.

II *pp adj* [*person*] living (**à** in); [*organization, company*] based (**à** in); **être bien ~ dans un fauteuil** to be ensconced or comfortably installed in an armchair; **ils sont bien ~s dans leur nouvelle maison** they're very snug in their new home; **c'est un homme ~** (figurative) he's very nicely set up.

installer /ɛ̃stale/ [1] **I** *vtr* **1** to install, to put in [*central heating, sink*]; to put up [*shelves*]; to connect [*gas*]; to set up [*factory*]; **2** to put [*guest*] (**dans** in); **~ qn dans un fauteuil** to sit sb in an armchair; **il a été installé dans ses fonctions** he took up his duties; **~ qn à un poste** to appoint sb to a post.

II s'installer *v refl* (+ *v être*) **1** [*recession*] to set in; [*illness*] to take hold; **le doute commence à s'~ dans leur esprit** they're beginning to have doubts; **2 s'~ à son compte** to set up one's own business; **des usines étrangères vont s'~ dans la région** foreign companies are going to open factories in the area; **3** to settle; **partir s'~ à l'étranger** to go and live abroad; **je viendrai te voir quand tu seras installé** I'll come and see you when you're settled in; **s'~ dans un fauteuil** to settle into an armchair; **s'~ au soleil** to sit in the sun; **s'~ pour travailler/à son bureau** to settle down to work/at one's desk; **installe-toi, j'arrive!** make yourself at home, I'm coming!

instamment /ɛ̃stamɑ̃/ *adv* insistently.

instance /ɛ̃stɑ̃s/ *nf* **1** authority; **les ~s d'un parti politique** the leaders of a political party; **2 en ~ de départ** on the point of departure; **être en ~ de divorce** to be engaged in divorce proceedings.

instant, **~e** /ɛ̃stɑ̃, ɑ̃t/ *nm* moment, instant; **à tout** or **chaque ~** all the time; **ne pas perdre un ~** not to waste any time; **par ~s** at times; **pour l'~** for the moment; **il devrait arriver d'un ~ à l'autre** he should arrive any minute now; **à l'~ même où** just when.

instantané, **~e** /ɛ̃stɑ̃tane/ **I** *adj* instantaneous; [*drink, soup*] instant.

II *nm* snapshot.

instar: **à l'instar de** /alɛ̃staʀdə/ *phr* following the example of.

instaurer /ɛ̃stoʀe/ [1] *vtr* to establish [*regime, dialogue*]; to impose [*curfew*].

instigateur, -trice /ɛ̃stigatœʀ, tʀis/ *nm,f* **1** instigator; **2** originator.

instigation /ɛ̃stigasjɔ̃/ *nf* **à l'~ de qn** at sb's instigation.

instiller /ɛ̃stile/ [1] *vtr* to instil[GB] (**à, dans** into).

instinct /ɛ̃stɛ̃/ *nm* instinct; **d'~** instinctively.

instinctif, -ive /ɛ̃stɛ̃ktif, iv/ *adj* instinctive.

instituer /ɛ̃stitɥe/ [1] *vtr* to institute.

institut /ɛ̃stity/ *nm* **1** institute; **2 ~ de beauté** beauty salon or parlour[GB].
■ **Institut universitaire de formation des maîtres, IUFM** *primary teacher training college*; **Institut universitaire de technologie, IUT** university institute of technology.

instituteur, -trice /ɛ̃stitytœʀ, tʀis/ *nm,f* (primary school) teacher.

institution /ɛ̃stitysjɔ̃/ *nf* **1** institution; **2** private school.

institutionnel, -elle /ɛ̃stitysjɔnɛl/ *adj* institutional.

institutrice ▶ **instituteur**.

instructeur /ɛ̃stʀyktœʀ/ *nm* (gen, Mil) instructor.

instructif, -ive /ɛ̃stʀyktif, iv/ *adj* (gen) instructive; [*book*] informative; [*experience*] enlightening.

instruction /ɛ̃stʀyksjɔ̃/ **I** *nf* **1** (gen) education; (Mil) training; **manquer d'~** to be uneducated; **2** (Law) *preparation of a case for eventual judgment.*
II instructions *nf pl* instructions.
■ **~ civique** civics; **~ religieuse** religious instruction.

instruire /ɛ̃stʀɥiʀ/ [69] **I** *vtr* **1** to teach [*child*]; to train [*soldiers*]; **~ qn de qch** to inform sb of sth; **2** (Law) **~ une affaire** to prepare a case for judgment.
II s'instruire *v refl* (+ *v être*) to learn.

instruit, ~e /ɛ̃stʀɥi, it/ **I** *pp* ▶ **instruire**.
II *pp adj* [*person*] educated.

instrument /ɛ̃stʀymɑ̃/ *nm* (gen, Mus) instrument; **être l'~ de qn** to be sb's tool; **être l'~ de la vengeance de qn** to be the instrument of sb's revenge.
■ **~s de bord** controls.

instrumentation /ɛ̃stʀymɑ̃tasjɔ̃/ *nf* instrumentation.

insu: **à l'insu de** /alɛ̃sydə/ *phr* **à l'~ de qn** without sb knowing.

insubordination /ɛ̃sybɔʀdinasjɔ̃/ *nf* insubordination.

insubordonné, ~e /ɛ̃sybɔʀdɔne/ *adj* (gen) rebellious; (Mil) insubordinate.

insuffisamment /ɛ̃syfizamɑ̃/ *adv* **1** insufficiently; **2** inadequately.

insuffisance /ɛ̃syfizɑ̃s/ *nf* **1** insufficiency, shortage; **2** poor standard; **l'~ de la production** the shortfall in production; **3** (Med) insufficiency.

insuffisant, ~e /ɛ̃syfizɑ̃, ɑ̃t/ *adj* **1** insufficient; **2** inadequate.

insuffler /ɛ̃syfle/ [1] *vtr* to instil[GB] (**à** into); **~ la vie à qn** to breathe life into sb.

insulaire /ɛ̃sylɛʀ/ *adj* [*population*] island; [*mentality*] insular.

insultant, ~e /ɛ̃syltɑ̃, ɑ̃t/ *adj* insulting (**pour** to).

insulte /ɛ̃sylt/ *nf* insult; **faire à qn l'~ de refuser** to insult sb by refusing.

insulter /ɛ̃sylte/ [1] *vtr* to insult; to shout abuse at; [*attitude*] to be an insult to.

insupportable /ɛ̃sypɔʀtabl/ *adj* unbearable.

insurgé, ~e /ɛ̃syʀʒe/ *nm,f* insurgent, rebel.

insurger: **s'insurger** /ɛ̃syʀʒe/ [13] *v refl* (+ *v être*) **1** to rise up (**contre** against); **2** to protest.

insurmontable /ɛ̃syʀmɔ̃tabl/ *adj* insurmountable.

insurrection /ɛ̃syʀɛksjɔ̃/ *nf* insurrection, uprising.

intact, ~e /ɛ̃takt/ *adj* intact.

intangible /ɛ̃tɑ̃ʒibl/ *adj* [*laws*] inviolable.

intarissable /ɛ̃taʀisabl/ *adj* [*imagination*] inexhaustible; [*gossip*] endless; [*source*] never-ending.

intégral, ~e, *mpl* **-aux** /ɛ̃tegʀal, o/ *adj* **1** [*payment*] full, in full; **2** [*tan*] all-over; **3** [*text*] unabridged; **version ~e** uncut version.

intégralement /ɛ̃tegʀalmɑ̃/ *adv* [*pay*] in full; [*refuse*] completely.

intégralité /ɛ̃tegʀalite/ *nf* **l'~ de leur salaire** their entire salary.

intégrante /ɛ̃tegʀɑ̃t/ *adj f* **faire partie ~ de qch** to be an integral part of sth.

intégration /ɛ̃tegʀasjɔ̃/ *nf* integration (**à, dans** into).

intègre /ɛ̃tɛgʀ/ *adj* [*person, character, life*] honest.

intégrer /ɛ̃tegʀe/ [14] **I** *vtr* **1** to insert (**à, dans** into); **2** to integrate [*population*]; **3**° **il vient d'~ Harvard** he has just got into Harvard; **4** [*solution, budget*] to include.
II s'intégrer *v refl* (+ *v être*) **1** [*population*] to integrate; **2** [*building*] to fit in (**à, dans** with).

intégrisme /ɛ̃tegʀism/ *nm* fundamentalism.

intégrité /ɛ̃tegʀite/ *nf* integrity.

intellect /ɛ̃telɛkt/ *nm* intellect.

intellectuel, -elle /ɛ̃telɛktɥɛl/ **I** *adj* [*work*] intellectual; [*effort*] mental.
II *nm,f* intellectual.

intelligence /ɛ̃teliʒɑ̃s/ *nf* **1** intelligence; **2 agir d'~ avec qn** to act in agreement with sb; **faire des signes d'~ à qn** to make signs of complicity to sb.

intelligent, ~e /ɛ̃teliʒɑ̃, ɑ̃t/ *adj* intelligent; clever.

intelligible /ɛ̃teliʒibl/ *adj* intelligible (**à** to); **parler à haute et ~ voix** to speak loudly and clearly.

intempéries /ɛ̃tɑ̃peʀi/ *nf pl* bad weather.

intempestif, -ive /ɛ̃tɑ̃pɛstif, iv/ *adj* untimely; [*curiosity, zeal*] misplaced.

intemporel, -elle /ɛ̃tɑ̃pɔʀɛl/ *adj* timeless.

intenable /ɛ̃t(ə)nabl/ *adj* **1** [*situation*] unbearable; **2** [*child*] difficult.

intendance /ɛ̃tɑ̃dɑ̃s/ *nf* (Sch) administration; **l'~ ne suit pas** the backup is not forthcoming.

intendant, ~e /ɛ̃tɑ̃dɑ̃, ɑ̃t/ **I** *nm,f* (Sch) bursar.
II *nm* (Mil) quartermaster; paymaster.

intense /ɛ̃tɑ̃s/ *adj* (gen) intense; [*red, green*] vivid; [*traffic*] heavy.

intensif, -ive /ɛ̃tɑ̃sif, iv/ *adj* intensive.

intensifier /ɛ̃tɑ̃sifje/ [2] *vtr*, **s'intensifier** *v refl* (+ *v être*) to intensify.

intensité /ɛ̃tɑ̃site/ *nf* intensity.

intenter /ɛ̃tɑ̃te/ [1] *vtr* **~ un procès à qn** to sue sb.

intention /ɛ̃tɑ̃sjɔ̃/ *nf* intention; **c'est l'~ qui compte** it's the thought that counts; **à l'~ de qn** [*remark*] aimed at sb; [*party*] in sb's honour[GB].

intentionné, ~e /ɛ̃tɑ̃sjɔne/ *adj* **bien/mal ~** well-/ill-intentioned.

intentionnel, -elle /ɛ̃tɑ̃sjɔnɛl/ *adj* intentional.

interaction /ɛ̃tɛʀaksjɔ̃/ *nf* interaction.

interallié, ~e /ɛ̃tɛʀalje/ *adj* (Mil) joint allied.

intercalaire /ɛ̃tɛʀkalɛʀ/ **I** *adj* **feuille** or **feuillet ~** insert.
II *nm* divider.

intercaler /ɛ̃tɛʀkale/ [1] **I** *vtr* to insert (**dans** into).
II s'intercaler *v refl* (+ *v être*) [*appointment*] to fit; [*example, page*] to be inserted.

intercéder /ɛ̃tɛʀsede/ [14] *vi* to intercede (**en faveur de qn** on sb's behalf).

intercepter /ɛ̃tɛʀsɛpte/ [1] *vtr* to intercept.

interchangeable /ɛ̃tɛʀʃɑ̃ʒabl/ *adj* interchangeable.

interclasse /ɛ̃tɛʀklas/ *nm* break (between classes).

interdiction /ɛ̃tɛʀdiksjɔ̃/ *nf* **1** banning; **'~ de dépasser'** 'no overtaking' (GB), 'no passing' (US); **'~ de stationner'** 'no parking'; **2** ban; **lever une ~** to lift a ban.
■ **~ de séjour** prohibition on residence.

interdire /ɛ̃tɛʀdiʀ/ [65] *vtr* to ban; **interdit d'antenne** banned from broadcasting; **~ à qn de faire, ~ que qn fasse** to forbid sb to do.

interdisciplinaire /ɛ̃tɛʀdisiplinɛʀ/ *adj* (Sch) cross-curricular; (at university level) interdisciplinary.

interdit, ~e /ɛ̃tɛʀdi, it/ **I** *pp* ▶ **interdire**.
II *pp adj* prohibited, forbidden; **entrée ~e** no entry or admittance; **film ~ aux moins de 13 ans** film unsuitable for children under 13; **être ~ de séjour** (Law) to be subject to a prohibition on residence; (figurative) to be banned.
III *adj* dumbfounded.
IV *nm* proscription; taboo.

intéressant, ~e /ɛ̃teʀɛsɑ̃, ɑ̃t/ **I** *adj* **1** interesting; **2** [*prices, conditions*] attractive; **il est plus ~ de payer au comptant qu'à crédit** it's better to pay in cash rather than by credit.
II *nm,f* **faire l'~** or **son ~** to show off.

intéressé, ~e /ɛ̃teʀese/ **I** *pp* ▶ **intéresser**.
II *pp adj* **1** interested (**par** in); **se dire ~ par qch** to express an interest in sth; **2** attentive; **3 les parties ~es** those concerned; **les personnes ~es aux bénéfices** people with a share in the profits; **4** [*person*] self-interested; [*action*] motivated by self-interest; **il est ~** he acts out of self-interest; **ses conseils étaient ~s** he/she had a selfish motive for giving that advice.
III *nm,f* person concerned; **le principal ~** the person most directly concerned.

intéresser /ɛ̃teʀese/ [1] **I** *vtr* **1** to interest; **ça ne m'intéresse pas** I'm not interested; **2** [*problem, decision*] to concern; **3 ~ les salariés aux bénéfices** to offer a profit-sharing scheme to employees.
II s'intéresser *v refl* (+ *v être*) **s'~ à** (gen) to be interested in; to take an interest in.

intérêt /ɛ̃teʀɛ/ *nm* **1** interest (**pour** in); **porter un grand ~ à qch** to take a great interest in sth; **recherche digne d'~** worthwhile research; **l'~ supérieur de la nation** the higher good of the country; **elle a tout ~ à partir** it is in her best interest to leave; **je ne vois pas l'~ de cette réforme** I can't see the point of this reform; **par ~** [*act*] out of self-interest; [*marry*] for money; **2** (financial) interest; **prêt sans ~s** interest-free loan; **des ~s dans le sucre** interests in sugar.

interférence /ɛ̃tɛʀfeʀɑ̃s/ *nf* interference.

interférer /ɛ̃tɛʀfeʀe/ [14] *vi* to interfere (**avec** with).

intérieur, ~e /ɛ̃teʀjœʀ/ **I** *adj* **1** [*wall, temperature*] internal, interior; [*courtyard*] inner; [*sea*] inland; [*pocket*] inside; [*border*] internal; **le côté ~** the inside; **2** domestic; **sur le plan ~** on the domestic front; **3** [*regulations*] internal.
II *nm* (of box, newspaper, cupboard) inside; (of car, house, country) interior; **à l'~** inside; indoors; **à l'~ des terres** inland; **d'~** [*game, plant*] indoor; **être fier de son ~** to be proud of one's home.

intérim /ɛ̃teʀim/ *nm* **1** interim (period); **président par ~** acting president; **assurer l'~ de** to stand in for; **2** temporary work; **société** or **agence d'~** temporary employment agency; **travailler en ~** to temp○.

intérimaire /ɛ̃teʀimɛʀ/ *adj* [*committee*] interim; [*minister*] acting, interim; [*job, staff*] temporary.

intérioriser /ɛ̃teʀjɔʀize/ [1] *vtr* to internalize.

interjection /ɛ̃tɛʀʒɛksjɔ̃/ *nf* interjection.

interligne /ɛ̃tɛʀliɲ/ *nm* line space.

interlocuteur, -trice /ɛ̃tɛʀlɔkytœʀ, tʀis/ *nm,f* **1 mon ~** the person I am talking to; **2** (in negotiations) representative; **3 Louis est notre seul ~** Louis is our only contact.

interloquer /ɛ̃tɛʀlɔke/ [1] *vtr* to take [sb] aback.

interlude /ɛ̃tɛʀlyd/ *nm* interlude.

intermède /ɛ̃tɛʀmɛd/ *nm* interlude.

intermédiaire /ɛ̃tɛʀmedjɛʀ/ **I** *adj* [*rate, stage*] intermediate; **avez-vous la taille ~?** do you have a size in between?
II *nmf* (in negotiations) go-between; (in industry) middleman.
III *phr* **par l'~ de** through.

interminable /ɛ̃tɛʀminabl/ *adj* **1** interminable, never-ending; **2** endless.

intermittence /ɛ̃tɛʀmitɑ̃s/ *nf* **1 par ~** [*rain*] on and off; [*work*] intermittently; **2** (Med) remission.

intermittent, ~e /ɛ̃tɛʀmitɑ̃, ɑ̃t/ *adj* [*rain, fever*] intermittent; [*noise, efforts*] sporadic.

internat /ɛ̃tɛʀna/ *nm* **1** boarding school; **2** period as houseman (GB), internship (US).

international, ~e, *mpl* **-aux** /ɛ̃tɛʀnasjɔnal, o/ *adj* international.

interne /ɛ̃tɛʀn/ **I** *adj* (gen) internal; [*training*] in-house; [*ear*] inner; **à usage ~** for internal use.

II *nmf* **1** (Sch) boarder; **je suis ~** I'm a boarder; **2 ~ (en médecine)** houseman (GB), intern (US).

internement /ɛ̃tɛʀnəmɑ̃/ *nm* **1** (Pol) internment; **2** (Med) committal (to a psychiatric institution).

interner /ɛ̃tɛʀne/ [1] *vtr* to intern [*political prisoner*]; to commit [*mental patient*]; **il est bon à ~** (humorous) he ought to be locked up.

interpellation /ɛ̃tɛʀpelasjɔ̃/ *nf* **procéder à des ~s** to take people in for questioning.

interpeller /ɛ̃tɛʀpəle/ [1] *vtr* **1** to call out to; to shout at; **2** to question; (in police station) to take [sb] in for questioning.

interphone® /ɛ̃tɛʀfɔn/ *nm* **1** intercom; **2** entry phone.

interposer: s'interposer /ɛ̃tɛʀpoze/ [1] *v refl* (+ *v être*) to intervene; **par personne interposée** through an intermediary.

interprétariat /ɛ̃tɛʀpʀetaʀja/ *nm* interpreting; **école d'~** interpreting school.

interprétation /ɛ̃tɛʀpʀetasjɔ̃/ *nf* **1** (gen, Mus) interpretation (**de** of); **2** (profession) interpreting.

interprète /ɛ̃tɛʀpʀɛt/ *nmf* **1** interpreter; **2** performer; **les ~s d'une pièce** the cast of a play; **3** spokesperson; **se faire l'~ de qn** to act as sb's spokesperson.

interpréter /ɛ̃tɛʀpʀete/ [14] *vtr* **1** to play [*role, sonata*]; to sing [*song*]; **2** to interpret; **mal ~ qch** to misinterpret sth.

interrogateur, -trice /ɛ̃tɛʀɔgatœʀ, tʀis/ *adj* enquiring; **d'un air ~** enquiringly.

interrogatif, -ive /ɛ̃tɛʀɔgatif, iv/ *adj* interrogative.

interrogation /ɛ̃tɛʀɔgasjɔ̃/ *nf* **1** (of witness) questioning (**sur** about); **2** (in grammar) question; **3** (Sch) test; **~ orale** oral test; **4** (in computing) query.

interrogatoire /ɛ̃tɛʀɔgatwaʀ/ *nm* (gen) interrogation; (by police) questioning.

interroger /ɛ̃tɛʀɔʒe/ [13] **I** *vtr* **1** (gen) to question (**sur** about); to ask; [*police*] to question, to interrogate [*suspect*]; [*journalist*] to put questions to (**sur** on); (figurative) to search [*memory*]; to examine [*conscience*]; **être interrogé comme témoin** (Law) to be called as a witness; **2** to query [*computer*]; **~ son répondeur** to check one's calls; **3** (Sch) to test (**sur** on).

II s'interroger *v refl* (+ *v être*) **s'~ sur** to wonder about.

interrompre /ɛ̃teʀɔ̃pʀ/ [53] **I** *vtr* **1** to interrupt [*programme, meal, conversation*]; to break off [*dialogue*]; to disrupt [*traffic*]; [*person*] to cease [*activity*]; **~ son repas pour faire** to stop eating to do; **ne m'interrompts pas tout le temps!** stop interrupting all the time!; **2** to put an end to [*career, holiday*]; to stop [*treatment*]; to terminate [*pregnancy*].

II s'interrompre *v refl* (+ *v être*) **1** [*person, conversation*] to break off; **2** [*rain*] to stop.

interrupteur /ɛ̃teʀyptœʀ/ *nm* switch.

interruption /ɛ̃teʀypsjɔ̃/ *nf* **1** break (**de** in); **sans ~** continuously; **2** ending (**de** of); **l'~ du dialogue entre** the breaking off of the dialogue[GB] between.

intersection /ɛ̃tɛʀsɛksjɔ̃/ *nf* intersection.

interstice /ɛ̃tɛʀstis/ *nm* (in floor) crack; (in shutters, blinds) chink.

intertitre /ɛ̃teʀtitʀ/ *nm* (in film) insert title.

intervalle /ɛ̃tɛʀval/ *nm* **1** space; **à ~s réguliers** at regular intervals; **2** interval; **dans l'~** meanwhile, in the meantime.

intervenir /ɛ̃tɛʀvəniʀ/ [36] *vi* **1** [*changes*] to take place; [*agreement*] to be reached; **2** [*speaker*] to speak (**dans** in); **3** (in emergency) [*police*] to intervene; **le chirurgien a décidé d'~** the surgeon decided to operate; **4 ~ auprès de qn pour qn** to intercede with sb on sb's behalf.

intervention /ɛ̃tɛʀvɑ̃sjɔ̃/ *nf* **1** intervention; **~ de l'armée** military intervention; **2** speech; lecture; **3 ~ (chirurgicale)** operation.

intervertir /ɛ̃tɛʀvɛʀtiʀ/ [3] *vtr* to invert [*objects, words*].

intestin /ɛ̃tɛstɛ̃/ *nm* bowel, intestine.

intestinal, ~e, *mpl* **-aux** /ɛ̃tɛstinal, o/ *adj* intestinal.

intime /ɛ̃tim/ **I** *adj* **1** [*life, diary*] private; [*friend, relationship*] intimate; [*hygiene*] personal; **avoir des relations ~s avec qn** to be on intimate terms with sb; **2** [*gathering*] intimate; [*conversation*] private; [*dinner, wedding*] quiet; **3** [*room*] cosy (GB), cozy (US); **4** [*knowledge*] intimate; **j'ai la conviction ~ que...** I firmly believe that...

II *nmf* close friend.

intimement /ɛ̃timmɑ̃/ *adv* intimately; **je suis ~ convaincu que...** I'm absolutely convinced that...

intimer /ɛ̃time/ [1] *vtr* **~ à qn l'ordre de faire** to order sb to do.

intimidation /ɛ̃timidasjɔ̃/ *nf* intimidation; **d'~** [*measures, remarks*] intimidatory.

intimider /ɛ̃timide/ [1] *vtr* to intimidate; **se laisser ~ par** to be intimidated by.

intimité /ɛ̃timite/ *nf* **1** intimacy; **2** privacy; **dans la plus stricte ~** in the strictest privacy; **dans l'~ il est beaucoup plus chaleureux** in private he is much warmer; **3** private life; **4** (of house, setting) cosiness.

intitulé /ɛ̃tityle/ *nm* title, heading.

intituler /ɛ̃tityle/ [1] **I** *vtr* to call.

II s'intituler *v refl* (+ *v être*) to be called, to be entitled.

intolérable /ɛ̃tɔleʀabl/ *adj* intolerable; deeply shocking.

intolérance /ɛ̃tɔleʀɑ̃s/ *nf* intolerance; (Med) allergy (**à** to).

intolérant, **~e** /ɛ̃tɔleʀɑ̃, ɑ̃t/ *adj* intolerant.

intonation /ɛ̃tɔnasjɔ̃/ *nf* intonation.

intouchable /ɛ̃tuʃabl/ *adj*, *nmf* untouchable.

intoxication /ɛ̃tɔksikasjɔ̃/ *nf* **1** (Med) poisoning; **2** (figurative) disinformation.

intoxiquer /ɛ̃tɔksike/ [1] **I** *vtr* to poison; (figurative) to brainwash.
II s'intoxiquer *v refl* (+ *v être*) to poison oneself.

intraduisible /ɛ̃tʀadɥizibl/ *adj* **1** untranslatable; **2** inexpressible.

intraitable /ɛ̃tʀɛtabl/ *adj* inflexible; **je serai ~ là-dessus** I will not budge on this.

intransigeance /ɛ̃tʀɑ̃ziʒɑ̃s/ *nf* intransigence.

intransigeant, **~e** /ɛ̃tʀɑ̃ziʒɑ̃, ɑ̃t/ *adj* [*attitude*] uncompromising; [*person*] intransigent; [*supporter*] staunch.

intraveineuse /ɛ̃tʀavenøz/ *nf* intravenous injection.

intrépide /ɛ̃tʀepid/ *adj* intrepid, bold.

intrépidité /ɛ̃tʀepidite/ *nf* boldness, intrepidity; **avec ~** boldly.

intrigant, **~e** /ɛ̃tʀigɑ̃, ɑ̃t/ *nm,f* schemer.

intrigue /ɛ̃tʀig/ *nf* **1** intrigue; **2** plot; **une ~ policière** a detective story.

intriguer /ɛ̃tʀige/ [1] *vtr* to intrigue; **elle m'intrigue** I find her intriguing.

intrinsèque /ɛ̃tʀɛ̃sɛk/ *adj* intrinsic.

introduction /ɛ̃tʀɔdyksjɔ̃/ *nf* **1** (gen) introduction (**à**, **de** to); **2** (of key, probe) insertion.

introduire /ɛ̃tʀɔdɥiʀ/ [69] **I** *vtr* **1** to insert [*object*] (**dans** into); **2** to usher [sb] in [*visitor*]; (surreptitiously) to smuggle (**dans** into); **3** to introduce [*person*] (**auprès de** to); **4** to introduce [*product, idea*] (**dans** into).
II s'introduire *v refl* (+ *v être*) **s'~ dans** to get into; **s'~ dans une maison par effraction** to break into a house.

introduit, **~e** /ɛ̃tʀɔdɥi, it/ *pp* ▸ **introduire**.

introspection /ɛ̃tʀɔspɛksjɔ̃/ *nf* introspection.

introverti, **~e** /ɛ̃tʀɔvɛʀti/ *nm,f* introvert.

intrus, **~e** /ɛ̃tʀy, yz/ *nm,f* intruder.

intrusion /ɛ̃tʀyzjɔ̃/ *nf* **1** (gen) intrusion (**dans** into); **2** interference (**dans** in).

intuitif, **~ive** /ɛ̃tɥitif, iv/ *adj* intuitive.

intuition /ɛ̃tɥisjɔ̃/ *nf* intuition; **avoir l'~ de** to have an intuition about.

inusable /inyzabl/ *adj* hardwearing.

inusité, **~e** /inyzite/ *adj* uncommon, not in common use.

inutile /inytil/ *adj* useless; pointless; needless; **(il est) ~ de faire** there's no point in doing; **~ de dire que** needless to say; **~ de me demander si** it's no use asking me whether; **sans risques ~s** without unnecessary risks.

inutilement /inytilmɑ̃/ *adv* unnecessarily; needlessly; in vain.

inutilisable /inytilizabl/ *adj* unusable.

inutilité /inytilite/ *nf* (of expense, action) pointlessness.

invalide /ɛ̃valid/ **I** *adj* disabled.
II *nmf* disabled person; **~ de guerre** registered disabled ex-serviceman.

invalider /ɛ̃valide/ [1] *vtr* to invalidate.

invalidité /ɛ̃validite/ *nf* (Med) disability; (Law) invalidity.

invariable /ɛ̃vaʀjabl/ *adj* invariable.

invasion /ɛ̃vazjɔ̃/ *nf* (Mil), (figurative) invasion.

invective /ɛ̃vɛktiv/ *nf* abuse; **se répandre en ~s** to pour out abuse.

invendu, **~e** /ɛ̃vɑ̃dy/ *adj* unsold.

inventaire /ɛ̃vɑ̃tɛʀ/ *nm* **1** stocktaking (GB), inventory (US); **2** stocklist (GB), inventory (US); **3** (of wardrobe, suitcase) list of contents; (of collection) inventory.

inventer /ɛ̃vɑ̃te/ [1] **I** *vtr* to invent; to devise; **histoire inventée** made-up story; **je n'invente rien** I'm not making it up.
II s'inventer *v refl* (+ *v être*) **ça ne s'invente pas** that has to be true.
IDIOMS **il n'a pas inventé la poudre**○ he is not very bright.

inventeur, **-trice** /ɛ̃vɑ̃tœʀ, tʀis/ *nm,f* inventor.

inventif, **-ive** /ɛ̃vɑ̃tif, iv/ *adj* **1** inventive; **2** resourceful.

invention /ɛ̃vɑ̃sjɔ̃/ *nf* **1** invention; **2** fabrication; **c'est de l'~ pure** it's a complete fabrication.

inventorier /ɛ̃vɑ̃tɔʀje/ [2] *vtr* to make out a stocklist (GB) or an inventory (US) of [*goods*]; to draw up an inventory of [*belongings, valuables*].

inverse /ɛ̃vɛʀs/ **I** *adj* (gen) [*direction, effect*] opposite; **dans l'ordre ~** (referring to list) in reverse order.
II *nm* (gen) **l'~** the opposite; **à l'~** conversely; **à l'~ de ce qu'il croyait** contrary to what he thought.

inversement /ɛ̃vɛʀsəmɑ̃/ *adv* (gen) conversely.

inverser /ɛ̃vɛʀse/ [1] *vtr* **1** to invert [*position, words*]; to reverse [*tendency, roles, order*]; **image inversée** mirror image; **2** to reverse [*electric current*].

inversion /ɛ̃vɛʀsjɔ̃/ *nf* inversion; reversal.

invertébré, **~e** /ɛ̃vɛʀtebʀe/ *adj* invertebrate.

invertir /ɛ̃vɛʀtiʀ/ [3] *vtr* to reverse; to switch [sth] round [*words*].

investigateur, **-trice** /ɛ̃vɛstigatœʀ, tʀis/ *nm,f* investigator.

investigation /ɛ̃vɛstigasjɔ̃/ *nf* investigation; **d'~** investigative.

investir /ɛ̃vɛstiʀ/ [3] **I** *vtr* **1** to invest [*capital*]; **2** to invest [*person, ambassador*] (**de** with); **3** [*police*] to go into; [*tourists, demonstrators*] to take over; **4** [*army*] to besiege.
II s'investir *v refl* (+ *v être*) **s'~ dans** to put a lot of oneself into; to invest emotionally in.

investissement /ɛ̃vɛstismɑ̃/ *nm* (gen) investment; (Mil) investing.

investisseur /ɛ̃vɛstisœʀ/ *nm* investor.

investiture /ɛ̃vɛstityʀ/ *nf* investiture.

invétéré, **~e** /ɛ̃veteʀe/ *adj* [*drinker, thief*] inveterate; [*liar*] compulsive; [*hatred*] deep-rooted.

invincible /ɛ̃vɛ̃sibl/ *adj* [*people*] invincible; [*argument*] irrefutable.

inviolable /ɛ̃vjɔlabl/ *adj* (gen) inviolable; [*door, safe*] impregnable.

invisible /ɛ̃vizibl/ *adj* **1** invisible; **la route était ~ depuis la maison** the road could not be seen from the house; **2** [*danger*] unseen.

invitation /ɛ̃vitasjɔ̃/ *nf* invitation (**à** to).

invité, **~e** /ɛ̃vite/ *nm,f* guest; **~ de marque** distinguished guest.

inviter /ɛ̃vite/ [1] *vtr* to invite (**à** to); **~ qn à s'asseoir** to invite or ask sb to sit down; **ceci invite à penser que**... this suggests that...

invivable /ɛ̃vivabl/ *adj* unbearable.

invocation /ɛ̃vɔkasjɔ̃/ *nf* invocation.

involontaire /ɛ̃vɔlɔ̃tɛʀ/ *adj* [*reaction*] involuntary; [*mistake*] unintentional; [*witness*] unwitting.

invoquer /ɛ̃vɔke/ [1] *vtr* to invoke.

invraisemblable /ɛ̃vʀɛsɑ̃blabl/ *adj* **1** [*story*] unlikely; [*explanation*] implausible; **2**° fantastic, incredible.

invraisemblance /ɛ̃vʀɛsɑ̃blɑ̃s/ *nf* **1** unlikelihood; **2** improbability.

invulnérable /ɛ̃vylneʀabl/ *adj* invulnerable.

iode /jɔd/ *nm* iodine.

irascible /iʀasibl/ *adj* [*person*] quick-tempered.

iris /iʀis/ *nm inv* **1** (flower) iris; **2** (of eye) iris; **3** (of camera) iris diaphragm.

irisé, **~e** /iʀize/ *adj* [*stone, glass, plumage*] iridescent.

irlandais, **~e** /iʀlɑ̃dɛ, ɛz/ **I** *adj* Irish.
II *nm* Irish.

Irlandais, **~e** /iʀlɑ̃dɛ, ɛz/ *nm,f* Irishman/ Irishwoman.

Irlande /iʀlɑ̃d/ *pr nf* Ireland; **la République d'~** the Republic of Ireland; **l'~ du Nord** Northern Ireland.

ironie /iʀɔni/ *nf* irony; **l'~ du sort** the irony of fate; **faire de l'~** to be ironic.

ironique /iʀɔnik/ *adj* ironic.

irradier /iʀadje/ [2] **I** *vtr* to irradiate; **déchets irradiés** radioactive waste.
II *vi* to radiate (**dans** through).

irrattrapable /iʀatʀapabl/ *adj* irretrievable.

irréalisable /iʀealizabl/ *adj* [*dream*] impossible; [*plan*] unworkable.

irrécupérable /iʀekypeʀabl/ *adj* **1** irrecoverable; **2** damaged beyond repair; **3** [*delinquent*] beyond help.

irréductible /iʀedyktibl/ **I** *adj* [*will*] implacable.
II *nmf* diehard.

irréel, **-elle** /iʀeɛl/ *adj* unreal.

irréfléchi, **~e** /iʀefleʃi/ *adj* [*action, remark*] ill-considered.

irréfutable /iʀefytabl/ *adj* irrefutable.

irrégularité /iʀegylaʀite/ *nf* irregularity; **les ~s du sol** the uneven ground.

irrégulier, **-ière** /iʀegylje, ɛʀ/ *adj* **1** [*shape, pulse*] irregular; [*writing, results, ground*] uneven; **2** [*procedure, transaction*] irregular; **immigré en situation irrégulière** illegal immigrant; **3** [*athlete, pupil*] whose performance is uneven.

irrémédiable /iʀ(ʀ)emedjabl/ *adj* [*loss, mistake*] irreparable.

irremplaçable /iʀɑ̃plasabl/ *adj* irreplaceable.

irréparable /iʀepaʀabl/ **I** *adj* [*car*] beyond repair; [*damage, crime*] irreparable.
II *nm* **commettre l'~** to go beyond the point of no return.

irrépressible /iʀepʀesibl/ *adj* (gen) irrepressible; [*tears*] uncontrollable.

irréprochable /iʀepʀɔʃabl/ *adj* [*life, employee*] irreproachable, beyond reproach; [*work*] perfect; [*taste, manners*] impeccable.

irrésistible /iʀezistibl/ *adj* irresistible; [*person, joke*] hilarious.

irrésolu, **~e** /iʀʀezɔly/ *adj* **1** [*person*] indecisive; **2** unsolved.

irrespirable /iʀɛspiʀabl/ *adj* [*air*] unbreathable; [*atmosphere*] stifling.

irresponsable /iʀɛspɔ̃sabl/ *adj* irresponsible.

irrévérencieux, **-ieuse** /iʀʀeveʀɑ̃sjø, øz/ *adj* irreverent.

irréversible /iʀevɛʀsibl/ *adj* irreversible; non-reversible.

irrévocable /iʀevɔkabl/ *adj* irrevocable.

irrigation /iʀigasjɔ̃/ *nf* **1** (of land) irrigation; **2** (Med) supply of blood (**de** to).

irriguer /iʀige/ [1] *vtr* to irrigate.

irritable /iʀitabl/ *adj* irritable.

irritation /iʀitasjɔ̃/ *nf* (gen, Med) irritation.

irriter /iʀite/ [1] **I** *vtr* **1** to irritate, to annoy; **2** (Med) to irritate.
II s'irriter *v refl* (+ *v être*) **1** to get annoyed (**de** about, over), to get angry (**de** about, over); **2** (Med) to become irritated, to become inflamed.

irruption /iʀypsjɔ̃/ *nf* **faire ~ dans** to burst into [*room*].

islam /islam/ *nm* **l'~** Islam.

islamique /islamik/ *adj* Islamic.

isolation /izɔlasjɔ̃/ *nf* insulation; **~ acoustique** soundproofing.

isolement /izɔlmɑ̃/ *nm* **1** (of village, region) remoteness; (of house) isolated location; **2** (of patient, country, politician) isolation; (of prisoner) solitary confinement.

isoler /izɔle/ [1] **I** *vtr* **1** to isolate [*sick person, dissident*]; to put [sb] in solitary confinement [*prisoner*]; **2** to isolate [*gene, substance*]; **3** to soundproof; to insulate; **4** to insulate [*wire*].
II s'isoler *v refl* (+ *v être*) to isolate oneself; **s'~ dans un coin pour lire une lettre** to withdraw into a corner to read a letter.

isoloir /izɔlwaʀ/ *nm* voting or polling (GB) booth.

issu, **~e**[1] /isy/ *adj* **1 être ~ de** to come from; **2 être ~ de** to result from.

issue[2] /isy/ *nf* **1** exit; **'sans ~'** 'no exit'; **2** solution (**à** to); **situation sans ~** situation with no solution; **3** outcome; **à l'~ de** at the end

of; **à l'~ de trois jours de pourparlers** at the close of three days of talks.
■ **~ de secours** emergency exit.

isthme /ism/ *nm* isthmus.

Italie /itali/ *pr nf* Italy.

italien, -ienne /italjɛ̃, ɛn/ **I** *adj* Italian. **II** *nm* Italian.

italique /italik/ *nm* italics (*pl*); **mettre qch en ~(s)** to put sth in italics.

itinéraire /itinerer/ *nm* **1** (gen) route; (detailed) itinerary; **2** (figurative) career.
■ **~ bis** alternative route; **~ de délestage** relief route.

itinérant, ~e /itinerɑ̃, ɑ̃t/ *adj* [*exhibition*] touring; [*life, staff*] peripatetic; [*circus*] travelling[GB].

IUFM /iyɛfɛm/ *nm*: *abbr* ▶ **institut**.

IUT /iyte/ *nm*: *abbr* ▶ **institut**.

ivoire /ivwaʀ/ *adj inv, nm* ivory.

ivre /ivʀ/ *adj* **1** intoxicated, drunk; **2 ~ de bonheur** drunk with happiness; **~ de rage** wild with rage.

ivresse /ivʀɛs/ *nf* **1** intoxication; **2** exhilaration.
■ **~ des profondeurs** decompression sickness.

ivrogne /ivʀɔɲ/ *nmf* drunkard.

Jj

j, J /ʒi/ *nm inv* j, J; **le jour J** D-day; **jour J moins dix** ten days to D-day.

j' ▶ **je**.

jabot /ʒabo/ *nm* **1** (of bird) crop; **2** (of shirt) jabot.

jacasser /ʒakase/ [1] *vi* to chatter.

jachère /ʒaʃɛʀ/ *nf* **(terre en) ~** fallow land.

jacinthe /ʒasɛ̃t/ *nf* hyacinth; **~ des bois** bluebell.

jackpot /(d)ʒakpɔt/ *nm* **1** jackpot; **2** slot machine.

jacquet /ʒakɛ/ *nm* backgammon.

jacter○ /ʒakte/ [1] *vi* to jaw○, to talk.

jade /ʒad/ *nm* **1** jade; **2** piece of jade.

jadis /ʒadis/ *adv* formerly, in the past; **les mœurs de ~** the customs of long ago.

jaguar /ʒagwaʀ/ *nm* jaguar.

jaillir /ʒajiʀ/ [3] *vi* [*liquid*] to gush out; [*tears*] to flow; [*flame*] to shoot up; [*laughter*] to burst out; [*idea, truth*] to emerge.

jais /ʒɛ/ *nm inv* **1** jet; **2 (noir) de ~** jet-black.

jalon /ʒalɔ̃/ *nm* **1** marker; **2** (figurative) **poser les ~s de** to prepare the ground for; **~ important** milestone.

jalonner /ʒalɔne/ [1] *vtr* **1** [*trees*] to line [*road*]; [*incidents*] to punctuate [*career*]; **2** to mark out [*road*].

jalousement /ʒaluzmɑ̃/ *adv* jealously; enviously.

jalouser /ʒaluze/ [1] *vtr* to be jealous of.

jalousie /ʒaluzi/ *nf* **1** jealousy; **2** slatted blind.

jaloux, -ouse /ʒalu, uz/ **I** *adj* jealous **(de** of); **avec un soin ~** with meticulous care.
II *nm,f* jealous man/woman; **faire des ~** to make people jealous.

jamais /ʒamɛ/ *adv* **1** never; **~ plus!** never again!; **rien n'est ~ certain** nothing is ever certain; **sait-on ~?** you never know; **~ de la vie!** never!; **c'est le moment ou ~** it's now or never; **2** ever; **plus belle que ~** prettier than ever; **si ~** if; **3 à ~, à tout ~** forever; **4 ne... ~ que** only; **il ne fait ~ que son devoir** he is only doing his duty.

jambe /ʒɑ̃b/ *nf* leg; **avoir de bonnes ~s** to have strong legs; **avoir des ~s de 20 ans** to have the legs of a 20-year-old; **aller** or **courir à toutes ~s** to run as fast as one's legs can carry one; **j'ai les ~s comme du coton**○ I feel weak at the knees; **traîner la ~**○ to trudge along.
IDIOMS **cela me fait une belle ~**○ a fat lot of good○ that does me; **il ne tient plus sur ses ~s** he can hardly stand up; **prendre ses ~s à son cou** to take to one's heels; **avoir qn dans les ~s** to have sb under one's feet; **tenir la ~ à qn** to keep talking to sb; **par-dessus** or **par-dessous la ~** in a slipshod manner.

jambon /ʒɑ̃bɔ̃/ *nm* ham.
■ **~ blanc** or **de Paris** cooked ham; **~ de pays** cured ham.

jambonneau, *pl* **~x** /ʒɑ̃bɔno/ *nm* knuckle of ham.

jante /ʒɑ̃t/ *nf* **1** rim; **2** wheel.

janvier /ʒɑ̃vje/ *nm* January.

Japon /ʒapɔ̃/ *pr nm* Japan.

japonais, ~e /ʒapɔnɛ, ɛz/ **I** *adj* Japanese.
II *nm* Japanese.

jappement /ʒapmɑ̃/ *nm* yapping.

japper /ʒape/ [1] *vi* to yap.

jaquette /ʒakɛt/ *nf* **1** morning coat; **2** dust jacket; **3** (on tooth) crown.

jardin /ʒaʀdɛ̃/ *nm* garden (GB), yard (US); **faire son ~** to work in one's garden (GB) or in the yard (US); **chaise de ~** garden chair (GB), patio chair (US).
■ **~ d'acclimatation** = **~ zoologique**; **~ d'agrément** ornamental or pleasure garden; **~ d'enfants** kindergarten; **~ potager** vegetable garden; **~ public** park; **~ zoologique** zoo.

jardinage /ʒaʀdinaʒ/ *nm* gardening.

jardiner /ʒaʀdine/ [1] *vi* to do some gardening; **il aime ~** he enjoys gardening.

jardinier, -ière[1] /ʒaʀdinje, ɛʀ/ **I** *adj* garden.
II *nm,f* gardener; **~ paysagiste** landscape gardener.

jardinière[2] /ʒaʀdinjɛʀ/ *nf* **1** jardinière; **2 ~ d'enfants** kindergarten teacher.

jargon /ʒaʀgɔ̃/ *nm* **1** jargon; **~ administratif** officialese; **2** gibberish.

jarre /ʒaʀ/ *nf* (earthenware) jar.

jarret /ʒaʀɛ/ *nm* **1** (of human) ham, hollow of the knee; **2** (of animal) hock; **3** (Culin) **~ de veau** knuckle of veal.

jarretelle /ʒaʀtɛl/ *nf* suspender (GB), garter (US).

jars /ʒaʀ/ *nm inv* gander.

jaser /ʒaze/ [1] *vi* to gossip **(sur** about); **ça fait ~** it sets people talking.

jasmin /ʒasmɛ̃/ *nm* jasmine.

jaspe /ʒasp/ *nm* jasper.

jatte /ʒat/ *nf* bowl, basin.

jauge /ʒoʒ/ *nf* gauge; **~ d'huile** dipstick.

jauger /ʒoʒe/ [13] *vtr* **1** to get the measure of [*candidate*]; **2** to measure [*capacity*]; to measure the capacity of [*tank*].

jaunâtre /ʒonɑtʀ/ *adj* yellowish.

jaune /ʒon/ **I** *adj* yellow; **~ orange** orangy[GB] yellow; **~ d'or** golden yellow; **~ paille** straw-coloured[GB]; **~ poussin** bright yellow; **teint ~** sallow complexion.
II *nm* **1** yellow; **2 ~ (d'œuf)** (egg) yolk; **3** blackleg (GB), scab.
IDIOMS **rire ~**○ to give a forced laugh.

Jaune /ʒon/ *nmf* (offensive) East Asian.

jaunir /ʒoniʀ/ [3] I *vtr* to turn [sth] yellow, to make [sth] go yellow; **jauni par la nicotine** nicotine-stained.
II *vi* to go yellow.

jaunisse /ʒonis/ *nf* jaundice; **il va en faire une ~**○! that'll put his nose out of joint!

java /ʒava/ *nf* **1** popular dance; **2**○ rave-up○; **faire la ~** to rave it up○.

javanais, ~e /ʒavanɛ, ɛz/ I *adj* Javanese.
II *nm* Javanese.

Javel /ʒavɛl/ *nf* **(eau de) ~** ≈ bleach.

javelliser /ʒavelize/ [1] *vtr* to chlorinate.

javelot /ʒavlo/ *nm* javelin.

J-C (*written abbr* = **Jésus-Christ**) **avant ~** BC; **après ~** AD.

je (**j'** *before vowel or mute h*) /ʒ(ə)/ *pron* I.

jean /dʒin/ *nm* **1** (pair of) jeans; **2** denim.

jeannette /ʒanɛt/ *nf* **1** sleeve board; **2** ≈ Brownie.

je-ne-sais-quoi /ʒənsɛkwa/ *nm inv* **avoir un ~** to have a certain something.

jérémiades /ʒeʀemjad/ *nf pl* moaning.

jerrican /ʒeʀikan/ *nm* jerrycan.

jersey /ʒɛʀzɛ/ *nm* **1** jersey; **2** stocking stitch.

jésuite /ʒezɥit/ *adj, nm* Jesuit.

Jésus /ʒezy/ *pr n* Jesus; **le petit ~** baby Jesus.

jet[1] /ʒɛ/ *nm* **1** throwing; throw; **à un ~ de pierre** a stone's throw away (**de** from); **2** jet; spurt; burst; **passer au ~** to hose down; **premier ~** (figurative) first sketch; **d'un seul ~** [*write*] in one go.
■ **~ d'eau** fountain; hosepipe.

jet[2] /dʒɛt/ *nm* jet (plane).

jetable /ʒətabl/ *adj* disposable.

jetée /ʒəte/ *nf* pier; jetty.

jeter /ʒəte/ [20] I *vtr* **1** to throw; to hurl; to throw away or out; **~ qch à qn** to throw sth to sb [*ball*]; to throw sth at sb [*stone*]; **~ qn dehors/par la fenêtre** to throw sb out/out of the window; **~ quelques idées sur le papier** (figurative) to jot down a few ideas; **bon à ~** fit for the bin (GB) or the garbage (US); **2** to give [*cry, light*]; to cast [*glance, shadow*]; **~ un vif éclat** to shine brightly; **3** to lay [*foundations*]; **4** to create [*confusion*]; to cause [*consternation*]; to sow [*terror*]; **~ l'émoi dans la ville** to throw the town into turmoil.
II **se jeter** *v refl* (+ *v être*) **1 se ~ du haut d'un pont** to throw oneself off a bridge; **se ~ sur** to fall upon [*opponent*]; to pounce on [*prey, newspaper*]; **se ~ au cou de qn** to fling oneself around sb's neck; **se ~ à l'eau** to jump into the water; (figurative) to take the plunge; **(aller) se ~ contre un arbre** to crash into a tree; **se ~ tête baissée dans qch** to rush headlong into sth; **2** [*river*] to flow (**dans** into).

jeton /ʒ(ə)tɔ̃/ *nm* (for machine) token; (in board games) counter; (at casino) chip.

jeu, *pl* **~x** /ʒø/ *nm* **1 le ~** play; **un ~** a game; **faire un ~** to play a game; **par ~** for fun; **entrer en ~** to come into the picture; **se prendre** or **se piquer au ~** to get hooked; **se prendre à son propre ~** to be caught at one's own game; **mettre en ~** to bring [sth] into play; to stake; **hors ~** offside; **ils ont beau ~ de me critiquer** it's easy for them to criticize me; **2 le ~** gambling; **ton avenir est en ~** your future is at stake; **3** (in cards) hand; **avoir du ~** to have a good hand; **cacher bien son ~** (figurative) to keep it quiet; **4** (of cards) deck; **~ d'échecs** chess set; **5** (of actor) acting; (of musician) playing; (of sportsman) game; **6** (of keys, spanners) set; **7** (Tech) play; **il y a du** or **trop de ~** there's too much play.
■ **~ d'argent** game played for money; **~ de construction** construction set; **~ de hasard** game of chance; **~ de massacre** ≈ coconut shy (GB); **~ de mots** pun; **~ de l'oie** ≈ snakes and ladders (GB); **~ de société** board game; party game; **~ télévisé** (TV) game show; **~x Olympiques**, **JO** Olympic Games.
IDIOMS **jouer le ~** to play the game; **jouer le grand ~** to pull out all the stops○; **c'est pas de** or **du ~**○! that's not fair!; **faire le ~ de qn** to play into sb's hands.

jeu-concours, *pl* **jeux-concours** /ʒøkɔ̃kuʀ/ *nm* competition.

jeudi /ʒødi/ *nm* Thursday.
■ **~ de l'Ascension** Ascension day; **~ saint** Maundy Thursday.
IDIOMS **ça aura lieu la semaine des quatre ~s**○! it won't happen, not in a month of Sundays!

jeun: **à jeun** /aʒœ̃/ *phr* **1** on an empty stomach; **soyez à ~** don't eat or drink anything; **2**○ sober.

jeune /ʒœn/ I *adj* **1** (gen) young; [*industry*] new; [*face, hairstyle*] youthful; **elle n'est plus très ~** she's not so young any more; **nos ~s années** our youth; **le ~ âge** youth; **le ~ marié** the groom; **la ~ mariée** the bride; **2** younger; **mon ~ frère** my younger brother.
II *nmf* young person; **un ~** a young man; **les ~s** young people.
III *adv* **s'habiller ~** to wear young styles; **faire ~** to look young.
■ **~ femme** young woman; **~ fille** girl; **~ homme** young man; **~ loup** up-and-coming executive; **~ premier** romantic lead.

jeûne /ʒøn/ *nm* **1** fasting; fast; **2** period of fasting.

jeûner /ʒøne/ [1] *vi* to fast.

jeunesse /ʒœnɛs/ *nf* **1** youth; **une seconde ~** a new lease of life; **une erreur de ~** a youthful indiscretion; **il n'est plus de la première ~** (humorous) he's no longer in the first flush of youth; **2** young people; **la ~ étudiante** students.
IDIOMS **il faut que ~ se passe** youth will have its course; **les voyages forment la ~** travel broadens the mind.

jf *written abbr* = **jeune femme** or **fille**; ▶**jeune**.

jh *written abbr* = **jeune homme**; ▶**jeune**.

joaillerie /ʒɔajʀi/ *nf* **1** jeweller's shop (GB), jewelry store (US); **2** jewellery (GB), jewelry (US).

joaillier, -ière /ʒɔalje, ɛʀ/ *nm,f* jeweller (GB), jeweler (US).

Joconde /ʒɔkɔ̃d/ *pr n* **la ~** the Mona Lisa.

joggeur, -euse /dʒɔgœʀ, øz/ *nm,f* jogger.

joie /ʒwa/ *nf* joy; **au comble de la ~** overjoyed; **faire la ~ de qn** to make sb happy; **se faire une ~ de faire** to look forward to doing; to be delighted to do.
IDIOMS **s'en donner à cœur ~** to enjoy oneself to the full; (figurative) to have a field day.

joignable /ʒwaɲabl/ *adj* **il n'est pas ~ en ce moment** he's not available at the moment.

joindre /ʒwɛ̃dʀ/ [56] **I** *vtr* **1** to get hold of, to reach [*person*]; **2** to enclose [*cheque*] (**à** with); to attach [*card*] (**à** to); **~ sa voix à** to add one's voice to; **3** to link [*points, places*]; to put [sth] together [*planks, feet*]; **~ l'intelligence à la simplicité** to be intelligent without being pretentious.
II se joindre *v refl* (+ *v être*) **1 se ~ à** to join [*person, group*]; to join in [*conversation*]; to mix with [*feeling*]; **2** [*lips*] to meet; [*hands*] to join.
IDIOMS **~ les deux bouts**○ to make ends meet.

joint /ʒwɛ̃/ *nm* (in wood) joint; (of tap) washer; (on pipes) seal.

jointure /ʒwɛ̃tyʀ/ *nf* joint.

joli, ~e /ʒɔli/ **I** *adj* (gen) nice; [*face*] pretty; [*sum*] tidy; [*situation*] good; **faire ~** to look nice; **c'est ~ de dire du mal de ses parents** (ironic) that's a fine thing, saying nasty things about one's parents.
II *nm* **c'est du ~!** (ironic) very nice!
■ **~ cœur** smooth talker; **faire le ~ cœur** to play Romeo.
IDIOMS **être ~ à croquer** or **comme un cœur** to be as pretty as a picture.

joliment /ʒɔlimɑ̃/ *adv* **1** prettily, nicely; **2**○ [*happy, well*] really; [*handle*] nicely; **il s'est fait ~ recevoir** (ironic) he got a fine reception.

jonc /ʒɔ̃/ *nm* rush.

joncher /ʒɔ̃ʃe/ [1] *vtr* [*papers, leaves*] to be strewn over [*ground*].

jonction /ʒɔ̃ksjɔ̃/ *nf* **1** junction; **2** link-up; **point de ~** meeting point.

jongler /ʒɔ̃gle/ [1] *vi* to juggle.

jongleur, -euse /ʒɔ̃glœʀ, øz/ *nm,f* juggler.

jonque /ʒɔ̃k/ *nf* junk.

jonquille /ʒɔ̃kij/ *nf* daffodil.

jouable /ʒwabl/ *adj* **1** feasible; **le coup est** or **c'est ~** it's feasible; **le pari est ~** the gamble might pay off; **2** [*piece of music*] playable; **une pièce qui n'est pas ~** a play that's impossible to stage.

joue /ʒu/ *nf* **1** cheek; **2** (Mil) **en ~!** aim!; **mettre qn en ~** to take aim at sb.

jouer /ʒwe/ [1] **I** *vtr* **1** [*children, musician*] to play; **2** to back [*horse*]; to stake [*money*]; to risk [*reputation, life*]; **c'est joué d'avance** it's a foregone conclusion; **tout n'est pas encore joué** the game isn't over yet; **~ le tout pour le tout** to go for broke○; **3 qu'est-ce qu'on joue au théâtre/cinéma?** what's on at the theatre/cinema?; **4 ~ les imbéciles** to play dumb; **~ la surprise** to pretend to be surprised.
II jouer à *v+prep* **~ à** to play [*tennis, game*]; to play with [*doll*]; **à quoi jouez-vous?** what are you playing?; (figurative) what are you playing at?; **~ à qui perd gagne** to play 'loser takes all'; **~ à la marchande** to play shops.
III jouer de *v+prep* **1** to play [*instrument*]; **2** to use [*influence*].
IV *vi* **1** to play (**avec** with); **arrête de ~ avec ta bague!** stop fiddling with your ring!; **à toi de ~!** your turn!; (figurative) the ball's in your court!; **bien joué!** well played!; (figurative) well done!; **2** to gamble; **~ avec** to gamble with [*life, health*]; **~ aux courses** to bet on the horses; **~ sur** to bank on [*credulity*]; **3** to act; **il joue bien** he's a good actor; **4** [*argument, clause*] to apply; [*age, qualification*] to matter; **~ en faveur de qn** to work in sb's favour[GB]; **faire ~ ses relations** to make use of one's connections.
V se jouer *v refl* (+ *v être*) **1** [*future, peace*] to be at stake; [*drama*] to be played out; **2 se ~ de** to make light of [*problem*]; to make light work of [*obstacle*].

jouet /ʒwɛ/ *nm* **1** toy; **2** plaything; **être le ~ des vagues** to be at the mercy of the waves.

joueur, -euse /ʒwœʀ, øz/ **I** *adj* **1** playful; **2 être ~/joueuse** to be a gambling man/woman.
II *nm,f* **1** player; **une joueuse de tennis** a woman tennis player; **être beau/mauvais ~** to be a good/bad loser; **2** gambler.

joufflu, ~e /ʒufly/ *adj* [*person*] chubby-cheeked; [*face*] chubby.

joug /ʒu/ *nm* yoke.

jouir: **jouir de** /ʒwiʀ/ [3] *v+prep* to enjoy; to enjoy the use of [*property*]; [*place*] to have [*view, climate*]; **~ de toutes ses facultés** to have the use of all one's faculties.

jouissance /ʒwisɑ̃s/ *nf* **1** (Law) use; **2** pleasure.

joujou, *pl* **~x** /ʒuʒu/ *nm* (baby talk) toy; **faire ~** to play (**avec** with).

jour /ʒuʀ/ *nm* **1** day; **quel ~ sommes-nous?** what day is it today?; **un ~ ou l'autre** some day; **~ pour ~** to the day; **de ~ en ~** from day to day; **à ce ~** to date; **à ~** up to date; **mettre à ~** to bring up to date [*work*]; to revise [*edition*]; **mise à ~** updating (**de** of); **de nos ~s** nowadays; **d'un ~ à l'autre** [*expected*] any day now; [*change*] from one day to the next; **du ~ au lendemain** overnight; **mode du ~** latest fashion; **d'un ~** [*fashion*] passing; [*queen*] for a day; **vivre au ~ le ~** to live one day at a time; **le ~ se lève** it's getting light; **au lever du ~** at daybreak; **le petit ~** the early morning; **se lever avec le ~** to get up at the crack of dawn; **de ~** [*work*] days; [*travel*] in the daytime; **2** daylight; light; **il fait ~** it's daylight; **en plein ~** in broad daylight; **se faire ~** [*truth*] to come to light; **mettre au ~** to unearth [*remains*]; to bring [sth] to light [*truth*]; **éclairer qch d'un ~ nouveau** to shed new light on sth; **je t'ai vu sous ton vrai ~** I saw you in your true

colours[GB]; **3** (figurative) **donner le ~ à qn** to bring sb into the world; **voir le ~** [*person*] to come into the world; [*work of art*] to see the light of day; **mes ~s sont comptés** my days are numbered; **des ~s difficiles** hard times; **les beaux ~s reviennent** spring will soon be here; **4** (in wall) gap; **~s** openwork (embroidery).
■ **~ de l'An** New Year's Day; **~ férié** bank holiday (GB), legal holiday (US); **~ de fermeture** closing day; **~ ouvrable** working day.
IDIOMS **être dans un bon ~** to be in a good mood.

journal, *pl* **-aux** /ʒuʀnal, o/ *nm* **1** newspaper; **2** magazine; **3** news (bulletin); **4** journal.
■ **~ de bord** logbook; **~ intime** diary; **Journal officiel** *government publication listing new acts, laws etc.*

journalier, **-ière** /ʒuʀnalje, ɛʀ/ *adj* daily.

journalisme /ʒuʀnalism/ *nm* journalism.

journaliste /ʒuʀnalist/ *nmf* journalist.

journalistique /ʒuʀnalistik/ *adj* journalistic; **style ~** journalese.

journée /ʒuʀne/ *nf* day; **~ de repos** day off; **dans la ~** during the day; **la ~ d'hier/de mardi** yesterday/Tuesday; **faire des ~s de huit heures** to work an eight-hour day; **être payé à la ~** to be paid by the day.

journellement /ʒuʀnɛlmɑ̃/ *adv* **1** daily; **2** all the time.

joute /ʒut/ *nf* **1** (figurative) jousting, battle; **~ oratoire** or **verbale** sparring match; **2** joust.

jouter /ʒute/ [1] *vi* to joust (**contre** against, with).

jouvence /ʒuvɑ̃s/ *nf* **fontaine de ~** Fountain of Youth.

jouxter /ʒukste/ [1] *vtr* to adjoin.

jovial, **~e**, *mpl* **~s** or **-iaux** /ʒɔvjal, o/ *adj* jovial.

jovialité /ʒɔvjalite/ *nf* joviality.

joyau, *pl* **~x** /ʒwajo/ *nm* jewel, gem.

joyeusement /ʒwajøzmɑ̃/ *adv* merrily, cheerfully.

joyeux, **-euse** /ʒwajø, øz/ *adj* merry, cheerful, joyful.

jubilation /ʒybilasjɔ̃/ *nf* joy, jubilation.

jubilé /ʒybile/ *nm* jubilee.

jubiler /ʒybile/ [1] *vi* to be jubilant.

jucher /ʒyʃe/ [1] *vtr*, **se jucher** *v refl* (+ *v être*) to perch (**sur** on).

judaïsme /ʒydaism/ *nm* Judaism.

judas /ʒyda/ *nm inv* peephole.

Judée /ʒyde/ *pr nf* Judaea; **arbre de ~** Judas tree.

judiciaire /ʒydisjɛʀ/ *adj* judicial.

judicieux, **-ieuse** /ʒydisjø, øz/ *adj* judicious, sensible.

judo /ʒydo/ *nm* judo.

judoka /ʒydoka/ *nmf* judoka.

juge /ʒyʒ/ *nm* judge; **être à la fois ~ et partie** to be judge and jury; **tu es seul ~** only you can tell.
■ **~ d'instruction** examining magistrate; **~ de touche** linesman.

jugé: **au jugé** /oʒyʒe/ *phr* [*value*] by guesswork; [*shoot*] blind; **avancer au ~** to follow one's nose.

jugement /ʒyʒmɑ̃/ *nm* judgment; **n'avoir aucun ~** to lack judgment; **passer en ~** [*case*] to come to court.

jugeote○ /ʒyʒɔt/ *nf* common sense.

juger /ʒyʒe/ [13] **I** *vtr* **1** to judge [*person, competition*]; **mal ~ qn** to misjudge sb; **2** to consider; **~ qn intelligent** to consider sb intelligent; **~ utile de faire** to consider it useful to do; **3** (Law) to try [*case, accused*]; to judge [*case*]; **le tribunal jugera** the court will decide.
II juger de *v+prep* **1** to assess; **j'en jugerai par moi-même** I'll judge for myself; **pour autant qu'on puisse en ~** as far as one can judge; **à en ~ par** judging by; **2 jugez de ma colère** imagine my anger.

juguler /ʒygyle/ [1] *vtr* to stamp out [*epidemic, uprising*]; to curb [*inflation*].

juif, **juive** /ʒɥif, ʒɥiv/ **I** *adj* Jewish.
II *nm,f* Jew.

juillet /ʒɥijɛ/ *nm* July; **le 14 ~** Bastille Day.

juin /ʒɥɛ̃/ *nm* June.

juive ▶ **juif**.

jumeau, **-elle**[1], *mpl* **~x** /ʒymo, ɛl/ *adj, nm,f* twin.

jumelage /ʒymlaʒ/ *nm* twinning.

jumelé, **~e** /ʒymle/ *adj* twin; double.

jumeler /ʒymle/ [19] *vtr* to twin.

jumelle[2] /ʒymɛl/ *nf*, **jumelles** *nf pl* binoculars; **à la ~** through binoculars.
■ **~s de théâtre** opera glasses.

jument /ʒymɑ̃/ *nf* mare.

jumping /dʒœmpiŋ/ *nm* showjumping.

jungle /ʒœ̃gl/ *nf* jungle.

junte /ʒœ̃t/ *nf* junta.

jupe /ʒyp/ *nf* skirt.
IDIOMS **il est toujours dans les ~s de sa mère** he's tied to his mother's apron strings.

jupe-culotte, *pl* **jupes-culottes** /ʒypkylɔt/ *nf* culottes.

jupon /ʒypɔ̃/ *nm* petticoat.
IDIOMS **courir le ~** to womanize.

juré, **~e** /ʒyʀe/ **I** *pp* ▶ **jurer**.
II *pp adj* **1** on oath; sworn-in; **2** [*enemy*] sworn.
III *nm* juror; **les ~s** the members of the jury.

jurer /ʒyʀe/ [1] **I** *vtr* to swear (**de faire** to do); **on leur a fait ~ le secret** they were sworn to secrecy; **jure-le moi!** swear!; **je te jure que ça fait mal** I can tell you it hurts; **~ de tuer qn** to vow to kill sb; **ah mais je te jure**○**!** honestly○!
II jurer de *v+prep* to swear to; **j'en jurerais** I would swear to it.
III *vi* **1** to swear (**après, contre** at); **2** [*colours*] to clash; **3 ne ~ que par** to swear by.
IV se jurer *v refl* (+ *v être*) **1** to swear [sth] to one another; **2** to vow (**de faire** to do).

IDIOMS **il ne faut ~ de rien** (Proverb) never say never.

juridiction /ʒyʀidiksjɔ̃/ *nf* **1** jurisdiction; **2** courts.

juridique /ʒyʀidik/ *adj* legal; **vide ~** gap in the law.

jurisprudence /ʒyʀispʀydɑ̃s/ *nf* case law.

juriste /ʒyʀist/ *nmf* **1** jurist; **2** lawyer.

juron /ʒyʀɔ̃/ *nm* swearword; **dire des ~s** to swear.

jury /ʒyʀi/ *nm* **1** jury; **président du ~** foreman of the jury; **2** panel of judges; **3** board of examiners.

jus /ʒy/ *nm inv* **1** juice; **2** (from meat) juices; gravy; **3**° **un ~** a coffee; **4**° juice°, electricity; **prendre le ~** to get a shock.

jusque (**jusqu'** *before vowel*) /ʒysk/ **I** *prep* **1** **aller jusqu'à Paris** to go as far as Paris; to go all the way to Paris; **courir jusqu'au bout du jardin** to run right down to the bottom of the garden (GB) or the end of the yard (US); **suivre qn ~ dans sa chambre** to follow sb right into his/her room; **la nouvelle est arrivée jusqu'à nous** the news has reached us; **descendre jusqu'à 100 mètres de profondeur** to go down to a depth of 100 metres[GB]; **jusqu'où comptez-vous aller?** how far do you intend to go?; **2** **jusqu'à**, **jusqu'en** until, till; **jusqu'à présent** or **maintenant**, **jusqu'ici** (up) until now; **jusqu'à quand?** until when?, how long?; **3** **monter jusqu'à 20°** to go up to 20°; **4** to the point of; **pousser la cruauté jusqu'au sadisme** to carry cruelty to the point of sadism; **aller jusqu'à faire** to go so far as to do; **5** even; **des détritus ~ sous la table** rubbish everywhere, even under the table; **ils sont venus, jusqu'au dernier** every last one of them came.

II jusqu'à ce que *phr* until.

jusque-là /ʒyskəla/ *adv* **1** until then, up to then; **2** up to here; up to there.

IDIOMS **en avoir ~ de qch/qn**° to have had it up to here with sth/sb°; **s'en mettre ~**° to stuff one's face°.

juste /ʒyst/ **I** *adj* **1** [*person*] just, fair; **2** [*cause*] just; [*anger*] righteous; [*claim*] legitimate; [*word, answer*] right, correct; **3** [*balance, watch*] accurate; **~ milieu** happy medium; **à ~ raison** or **titre** with good reason; **dire des choses ~s** to make some valid points; **apprécier qn à sa ~ valeur** to get a fair picture of sb; **4** (Mus) [*piano, voice*] in tune; [*note*] true; **5** **c'est un peu ~** (in width, time) it's a bit tight; (in quantity) it's barely enough.

II *adv* **1** [*sing*] in tune; [*ring*] true; [*guess*] right; **elle a vu ~** she was right; **viser ~** to aim straight; (figurative) to hit the nail on the head; **2** just; **~ à temps** just in time; **3** (**tout**) **~** only just; **j'arrive ~** I've only just arrived; **c'est tout ~ s'il sait lire** he can hardly read.

III au juste *phr* exactly.

IV *nm* righteous man; **les ~s** the righteous.

justement /ʒystəmɑ̃/ *adv* **1** precisely; **2** just; **3** correctly; **4** justifiably.

justesse /ʒystɛs/ **I** *nf* **1** correctness; **avec ~** correctly; **2** accuracy; **avec ~** accurately.

II de justesse *phr* [*succeed*] only just; **il en a réchappé de ~** he had a narrow escape.

justice /ʒystis/ *nf* **1** justice; **rendre la ~** to dispense justice; **il faut leur rendre** or **faire cette ~ qu'ils sont...** one has to acknowledge that they are...; **en toute ~** in all fairness; **ce n'est que ~** it is only fair; **se faire ~** to take the law into one's own hands; to take one's own life; **2** **la ~** the law; the legal system; the courts; **être livré à la ~** to be handed over to the law; **aller en ~** to go to court; **action en ~** legal action.

justicier, **-ière** /ʒystisje, ɛʀ/ *nm,f* righter of wrongs.

justificatif, **-ive** /ʒystifikatif, iv/ **I** *adj* [*document*] supporting; **pièce justificative** documentary evidence.

II *nm* documentary evidence; **~ de domicile** proof of domicile; **~ de frais** receipt.

justification /ʒystifikasjɔ̃/ *nf* **1** justification; **2** explanation; documentary evidence.

justifier /ʒystifje/ [2] **I** *vtr* to justify [*method, absence*]; to vindicate [*guilty party*]; to explain [*ignorance*]; **les faits ont justifié nos craintes** events proved our fears to have been justified; **tu essaies toujours de la ~** you are always making excuses for her.

II justifier de *v+prep* to give proof of [*residence, identity*].

III se justifier *v refl* (+ *v être*) **1** to make excuses; (in court) to clear oneself; **2** [*decision*] to be justified (by).

jute /ʒyt/ *nm* jute; (**toile de**) **~** hessian.

juteux, **-euse** /ʒytø, øz/ *adj* **1** [*fruit*] juicy; **2**° profitable, juicy°.

juvénile /ʒyvenil/ *adj* [*smile*] youthful; [*delinquence*] juvenile.

juxtaposer /ʒykstapoze/ [1] *vtr* to juxtapose.

juxtaposition /ʒykstapozisjɔ̃/ *nf* juxtaposition.

k, K /ka/ *nm inv* k, K.

kaki /kaki/ **I** *adj inv* khaki.
II *nm* **1** persimmon; **2** khaki.

kaléidoscope /kaleidɔskɔp/ *nm* kaleidoscope.

kangourou /kɑ̃guʀu/ **I** *adj inv* **poche ~** front pocket; **slip ~** pouch-front briefs.
II *nm* **1** kangaroo; **2** ®baby carrier.

karaté /kaʀate/ *nm* karate.

kart /kaʀt/ *nm* go-kart.

karting /kaʀtiŋ/ *nm* go-karting; **faire du ~** to go karting.

kasher /kaʃɛʀ/ *adj inv* kosher.

kayak /kajak/ *nm* kayak; **faire du ~** to go canoeing.

képi /kepi/ *nm* kepi.

kermesse /kɛʀmɛs/ *nf* fete.

kF *written abbr* = **kilofranc**.

kibboutz, *pl* **-tzim** /kibuts, kibutsim/ *nm* kibbutz.

kick /kik/ *nm* kick-start.

kidnapper /kidnape/ [1] *vtr* to kidnap; **se faire ~** to be kidnapped.

kidnappeur, -euse /kidnapœʀ, øz/ *nm,f* kidnapper.

kif-kif○ /kifkif/ *adj inv* **c'est ~ (bourricot)** it's all the same.

kilo[1] /kilo/ *pref* kilo.

kilo[2] /kilo/ *nm* (*abbr* = **kilogramme**) kilo; **prendre des ~s** to put on weight.

kilofranc /kilɔfʀɑ̃/ *nm* 1,000 French francs.

kilogramme /kilɔgʀam/ *nm* kilogram.

kilométrage /kilɔmetʀaʒ/ *nm* ≈ mileage.

kilomètre /kilɔmɛtʀ/ *nm* kilometre[GB].

kilomètre-heure *pl* **kilomètres-heure** /kilɔmɛtʀœʀ/ *nm* kilometre[GB] per hour.

kilométrique /kilɔmetʀik/ *adj* [*distance*] in kilometres[GB]; [*price*] per kilometre[GB].

kilo-octet /kilɔɔktɛ/ *nm* kilobyte.

kilotonne /kilɔtɔn/ *nf* kiloton.

kilowattheure /kilɔwatœʀ/ *nm* kilowatt-hour.

kimono /kimɔno/ *nm* **1** kimono; **2** ≈ judo suit.

kinésithérapeute /kineziteʀapøt/ *nmf* physiotherapist (GB), physical therapist (US).

kinésithérapie /kineziteʀapi/ *nf* physiotherapy (GB), physical therapy (US).

kiosque /kjɔsk/ *nm* kiosk.
■ **~ à musique** bandstand.

kiwi /kiwi/ *nm* kiwi.

klaxon® /klaksɔn/ *nm* (car) horn.

klaxonner /klaksɔne/ [1] *vi* to sound one's horn (GB), to honk the horn.

kleptomane /klɛptɔman/ *adj, nmf* kleptomaniac.

knock-out /nɔkaut/ **I** *adj inv* knocked out.
II *nm* knockout.

Ko (*written abbr* = **kilo-octet**) KB.

KO /kao/ **I** *adj inv* (*abbr* = **knocked out**) **1** KO'd○; **mettre qn ~** to KO○ sb; **2**○ exhausted.
II *nm* (*abbr* = **knockout**) KO○.

koala /kɔala/ *nm* koala (bear).

krach /kʀak/ *nm* (on stock exchange) crash.

kraft /kʀaft/ *nm* **(papier) ~** brown paper.

K-way® /kawe/ *nm* windcheater (GB), windbreaker (US).

kyrielle /kiʀjɛl/ *nf* **une ~ de** a string of.

kyste /kist/ *nm* cyst.

l, **L** /ɛl/ *nm inv* **1** (letter) l, L; **2** (*written abbr* = **litre**) **20 l** 20 l.

l' ▶ **le**.

la¹ *det, pron* ▶ **le**.

la² /la/ *nm* (Mus) (note) A; (in sol-fa) lah; **donner le ~** to give an A; (figurative) to set the tone.

là /la/ *adv* **1** there; here; **viens ~** come here; **~ où je travaille** where I work; **j'habite par ~** I live over there; **pas par ici, par ~** not this way, that way; **de ~ au village** from there to the village; **rester ~ à ne rien faire** to hang around doing nothing; **2** then; **d'ici ~** between now and then; by then; **et ~, le téléphone a sonné** and then the phone rang; **en ce temps-~** in those days; **ce jour-~** that day; **3 s'il en est (arrivé) ~, c'est que**... if he's got to that point, it's because...; **nous n'en sommes pas encore ~** we haven't got that far yet; we haven't reached that point yet; **alors ~ tu exagères!** now you're going too far!; **~, c'est fini, ne pleure plus** there now, it's over, don't cry; **~ c'est différent** that's a different matter; **que vas-tu chercher ~?** what are you thinking of?; **il a fallu en passer par ~** there was no alternative; **qu'entendez-vous par ~?** what do you mean by that?; **si tu vas par ~** if you are saying that; **de ~** hence; from that.

là-bas /laba/ *adv* over there.

labo○ /labo/ *nm* lab○.

laborantin, **~e** /labɔʀɑ̃tɛ̃, in/ *nm,f* laboratory assistant.

laboratoire /labɔʀatwaʀ/ *nm* laboratory.
■ **~ d'analyses médicales** medical laboratory; **~ de langues** language laboratory; **~ orbital** skylab; **~ pharmaceutique** pharmaceutical company.

laborieux, **-ieuse** /labɔʀjø, øz/ *adj* **1** [*work, process*] arduous; [*style*] laboured^GB; [*victory*] hard-won; **2 les classes laborieuses** the working classes.

labour /labuʀ/ *nm* ploughing (GB), plowing (US); **cheval de ~** plough (GB) or plow (US) horse.

labourer /labuʀe/ [1] *vtr* to plough (GB), to plow (US).

labyrinthe /labiʀɛ̃t/ *nm* **1** maze; **2** labyrinth; **3** (figurative) labyrinth, maze.

lac /lak/ *nm* **1** lake; **2** reservoir.

lacer /lase/ [12] *vtr* to lace up [*shoes, corset*].

lacérer /laseʀe/ [14] *vtr* to lacerate [*skin, flesh*]; to slash [*garment, poster*].

lacet /lasɛ/ *nm* **1** lace; **chaussures à ~s** lace-up shoes; **nouer ses ~s** to do up one's laces; **2** (in road) hairpin bend; **une route en ~s** a twisting road.

lâche /lɑʃ/ **I** *adj* **1** [*person, crime*] cowardly; **2** [*belt*] loose; **3** [*regulation*] lax.
II *nmf* coward.

lâchement /lɑʃmɑ̃/ *adv* **ils se sont ~ enfuis** they fled like cowards.

lâcher¹ /lɑʃe/ [1] **I** *vtr* **1** to drop [*object*]; to let go of [*rope, branch*]; **lâche-moi** let go of me; (figurative)○ give me a break○; **~ prise** to lose one's grip; **2** to utter [*word*]; to reveal [*information*]; to let out [*scream*]; **3** to let [sb/sth] go [*person, animal*]; **il ne m'a pas lâché une seconde** he didn't leave me to myself for a second; **4** to drop [*friend, associate, activity*]; **la peur ne la lâche plus depuis** she's been living in constant terror ever since; **5** (Sport) to break away from [*rival competitor*].
II *vi* [*rope*] to give way; [*brakes*] to fail; **ses nerfs ont lâché** he/she went to pieces.

lâcher² /lɑʃe/ *nm* (of balloons, birds) release.

lâcheté /lɑʃte/ *nf* **1** cowardice; **par ~** out of cowardice; **2** cowardly act.

laconique /lakɔnik/ *adj* [*style*] laconic; [*reply*] terse.

lacrymal, **~e**, *mpl* **-aux** /lakʀimal, o/ *adj* lachrymal.

lacrymogène /lakʀimɔʒɛn/ *adj* [*grenade, bomb*] teargas; **gaz ~** teargas.

lacté, **~e** /lakte/ *adj* **1** [*product*] milk; **2** [*liquid*] milky; **la voie ~e** the Milky Way.

lacune /lakyn/ *nf* (in manuscript) lacuna; (in knowledge, law) gap.

lacustre /lakystʀ/ *adj* **cité ~** lake dwelling.

là-dedans /lad(ə)dɑ̃/ *adv* in here; in there; **il y a tout un symbolisme ~** there's a lot of symbolism in it; **et moi ~ qu'est-ce que je fais○?** and where do I come in?

là-dessous /lad(ə)su/ *adv* under here; under there; **il y a qch de louche ~**○ there's something fishy○ about all this.

là-dessus /lad(ə)sy/ *adv* **1** (on a surface) on here; on there; **2 qu'as-tu à dire ~?** what have you got to say about it?; **3 ~ il a raccroché** with that he hung up; **nous nous sommes quittés ~** we parted at that point.

ladite ▶ **ledit**.

lagon /lagɔ̃/ *nm* lagoon.

lagune /lagyn/ *nf* lagoon.

là-haut /lao/ *adv* **1** up here; up there; **tout ~** (all the) way up there; **2** upstairs; **3** in heaven.

laïc /laik/ *nm* layman.

laïcité /laisite/ *nf* secularism; secularity.

laid, **~e** /lɛ, lɛd/ *adj* **1** ugly; **2** disgusting.

laideur /lɛdœʀ/ *nf* ugliness.

lainage /lɛnaʒ/ *nm* **1** woollen^GB material; **2** woollen^GB garment.

laine /lɛn/ *nf* wool; **de** or **en ~** woollen^GB, wool.
■ **~ peignée** worsted; **~ à repriser** darning wool; **~ de verre** glass wool; **~ vierge** new wool (GB), virgin wool.

laineux, -euse /lɛnø, øz/ *adj* woolly.

laïque /laik/ **I** *adj* [*school*] nondenominational (GB), public (US); [*state, mind*] secular.
II *nmf* layman/laywoman; **les ~s** lay people.

laisse /lɛs/ *nf* (for dog) lead (GB), leash (US).

laissé-pour-compte, **laissée-pour-compte**, *mpl* **laissés-pour-compte** /lesepuʀkɔ̃t/ *nm,f* **les laissés-pour-compte** (gen) the forgotten people; **les laissés-pour-compte de la révolution technologique** the casualties of the technological revolution.

laisser /lese/ [1] **I** *vtr* **1** to leave; **~ la liberté à qn** to let sb go free; **~ la vie à qn** to spare sb's life; **je te laisse** I must go; **~ le choix à qn** to give sb the choice; **laisse ce jouet à ton frère** let your brother have the toy; **tu y laisseras ta santé** you'll ruin your health; **laisse-le, ça lui passera** ignore him, he'll get over it; **cela me laisse sceptique** I'm sceptical (GB) or skeptical (US); **2** (literary) **cela ne laisse pas d'étonner** it is a continual source of amazement.
II *v aux* **~ qn/qch faire** to let sb/sth do; **laisse-moi faire** let me do it; leave it to me; **ils s'entretuent et on laisse faire** they're killing each other and we just sit back and do nothing; **laisse faire!** so what!
III se laisser *v refl* (+ *v être*) **se ~ bercer par les vagues** to be lulled by the waves; **il se laisse insulter** he puts up with insults; **elle n'est pas du genre à se ~ faire** she won't be pushed around; **c'est parce que tu te laisses faire** it's because you're too soft; **il ne veut pas se ~ faire** he won't let you touch him; **se ~ aller** to let oneself go.

laisser-aller /leseale/ *nm inv* **1** scruffiness; **2** sloppiness.

laissez-passer /lesepase/ *nm inv* pass.

lait /lɛ/ *nm* milk; **~ démaquillant** cleansing milk.
■ **~ de chaux** whitewash; **~ concentré non sucré** evaporated milk; **~ concentré sucré** sweetened condensed milk; **~ demi-écrémé** low-fat milk; **~ écrémé** skimmed milk (GB), skim or nonfat milk (US); **~ maternel** breastmilk; **~ de poule** eggnog.
IDIOMS **si on lui pressait le nez il en sortirait du ~**○ he's/she's still wet behind the ears.

laitage /lɛtaʒ/ *nm* dairy product.

laitance /lɛtɑ̃s/ *nf* (Culin, Zool) soft roe.

laiterie /lɛtʀi/ *nf* **1** dairy; **2** dairy industry.

laiteux, -euse /lɛtø, øz/ *adj* [*liquid, white*] milky; [*complexion*] creamy.

laitier, -ière /lɛtje, ɛʀ/ **I** *adj* [*industry, product*] dairy; [*production, cow*] milk.
II *nm,f* milkman/milkwoman.

laiton /lɛtɔ̃/ *nm* brass.

laitue /lɛty/ *nf* lettuce.

laïus○ /lajys/ *nm inv* speech.

lama /lama/ *nm* **1** (animal) llama; **2** (religious leader) lama.

lambda /lɑ̃bda/ **I**○ *adj inv* [*person, reader*] average.
II *nm inv* lambda.

lambeau, *pl* **~x** /lɑ̃bo/ *nm* **1** (of cloth) rag; (of paper, hide) strip; (of flesh) bit; **mettre qch en ~x** to tear sth to pieces; **2** (figurative) (of fortune, inheritance) remnants; **fortune qui part en ~x** fortune which is being frittered away.

lambris /lɑ̃bʀi/ *nm inv* panelling[GB]; marble walls; (on ceiling) mouldings (GB), moldings (US).

lambrisser /lɑ̃bʀise/ [1] *vtr* to panel; **pièce lambrissée** panelled[GB] room.

lame /lam/ *nf* **1** (of knife, saw, screwdriver) blade; **2** knife; **3** sword; **une fine ~** an expert swordsman; **4** (of metal, wood) strip; (on blind) slat; **5** (wave) breaker.
■ **~ de fond** ground swell; (figurative) upheaval; **~ de rasoir** razor blade.

lamé /lame/ *nm* lamé; **en ~** lamé.

lamelle /lamɛl/ *nf* **1** (of wood, metal) small strip; **2** (Culin) (of cheese, truffle) sliver; **découper en fines ~s** to slice thinly; **3** (Bot) (of mushroom) gill.

lamentable /lamɑ̃tabl/ *adj* [*programme, match, result*] pathetic, awful.

lamentablement /lamɑ̃tabləmɑ̃/ *adv* [*fail*] miserably; [*cry*] piteously.

lamentation /lamɑ̃tasjɔ̃/ *nf* wailing.

lamenter: **se lamenter** /lamɑ̃te/ [1] *v refl* (+ *v être*) to moan; **se ~ sur son propre sort** to feel sorry for oneself.

laminer /lamine/ [1] *vtr* to roll.

lampadaire /lɑ̃padɛʀ/ *nm* **1** standard (GB) or floor (US) lamp; **2** streetlight.

lampe /lɑ̃p/ *nf* **1** lamp, light; **2** (light) bulb.
■ **~ à bronzer** sun lamp; **~ de chevet** bedside light; **~ électrique** torch (GB), flashlight (US); **~ à pétrole** paraffin (GB) or kerosene (US) lamp; **~ de poche** pocket torch (GB), flashlight (US); **~ témoin** indicator light; **~ tempête** hurricane lamp.

lampée○ /lɑ̃pe/ *nf* gulp.

lampion /lɑ̃pjɔ̃/ *nm* paper lantern.

lance /lɑ̃s/ *nf* (gen) spear; (in jousting) lance.
■ **~ d'arrosage** garden hose nozzle; **~ d'incendie** fire hose nozzle.

lancée /lɑ̃se/ *nf* **sur ma ~** while I was at it; **continuer sur sa ~** (gen) to continue to forge ahead; (when making speech) to continue in the same vein.

lance-flammes /lɑ̃sflam/ *nm inv* flamethrower.

lancement /lɑ̃smɑ̃/ *nm* **1** (of ship, company, offensive) launching; (of programme, process) setting up; **2** (of product, book, film) launch; (of loan) floating; (of actor, writer) promotion; **3** (of missile, satellite) launching; launch.

lance-pierres /lɑ̃spjɛʀ/ *nm inv* catapult.
IDIOMS **payer qn avec un ~**○ to pay sb peanuts○.

lancer[1] /lɑ̃se/ [12] **I** *vtr* **1** to throw [*ball, pebble, javelin*]; **~ le poids** to put the shot; **2** to launch [*rocket, ship*]; to fire [*arrow*]; to drop [*bomb*]; to launch [*offensive, singer*]; to start up [*engine*]; to take [sth] to full speed [*vehicle*]; **3** to throw out [*smoke, flames*]; to give [*look, scream*]; to put about [*rumour*]; to issue [*ultimatum*]; to send out [*invitation*]; **4** to hurl [*insult*]; to make [*accusation*]; to crack [*joke*]; **lança-t-il** he said.

II○ *vi* to throb; **mon doigt me lance** my finger is throbbing.

III se lancer *v refl* (+ *v être*) **1 se ~ dans des dépenses** to get involved in expense; **se ~ dans les affaires** to go into business; **2 se ~ dans le vide** to jump; **3** to throw [sth] to each other [*ball*]; to throw [sth] at each other [*stone*]; to exchange [*insults*].

lancer² /lɑ̃se/ *nm* **1** (Sport) **~ du disque** discus event; **~ du poids** shot put (event); **troisième ~** third throw; **2 le ~, la pêche au ~** rod and reel fishing.

lance-roquettes /lɑ̃sʀɔkɛt/ *nm inv* rocket launcher.

lancinant, ~e /lɑ̃sinɑ̃, ɑ̃t/ *adj* [*pain*] shooting; [*music, rhythm*] insistent.

landau /lɑ̃do/ *nm* pram (GB), baby carriage (US).

lande /lɑ̃d/ *nf* moor.

langage /lɑ̃gaʒ/ *nm* language.

■ **~ administratif** official jargon; **~ journalistique** journalese; **~ des sourds-muets** sign language.

lange /lɑ̃ʒ/ *nm* **1** swaddling clothes; **2** nappy (GB), diaper (US).

langer /lɑ̃ʒe/ [13] *vtr* **1** to wrap [sb] in swaddling clothes [*baby*]; **2** to put a nappy (GB) or diaper (US) on [*baby*].

langoureux, -euse /lɑ̃guʀø, øz/ *adj* languorous.

langouste /lɑ̃gust/ *nf* spiny lobster.

langoustine /lɑ̃gustin/ *nf* langoustine.

langue /lɑ̃g/ *nf* **1** (Anat) tongue; **tirer la ~** to stick out one's tongue; (for doctor) to put out one's tongue; (figurative) to be dying of thirst; to struggle financially; **2** language; speech; **3 les ~s vont aller bon train** people will talk; **mauvaise ~** malicious gossip; **4 ~ de terre** spit of land.

■ **~ de bois** political cant; **~ maternelle** mother tongue; **~ verte** slang.

IDIOMS **avoir la ~ bien pendue**○ to be very talkative; **avoir qch sur le bout de la ~** to have sth on the tip of one's tongue.

languette /lɑ̃gɛt/ *nf* (on shoe) tongue; (on satchel, bag) strap; (of bread, ham) long narrow strip; **découpez en ~s** cut in strips.

langueur /lɑ̃gœʀ/ *nf* languor; **des yeux pleins de ~** languid eyes.

languir /lɑ̃giʀ/ [3] **I** *vi* **1** [*conversation*] to languish; [*economy*] to be sluggish; **2 je languis de vous revoir** I'm longing to see you; **faire ~ qn** to keep sb in suspense.

II se languir *v refl* (+ *v être*) to pine (**de qn** for sb).

languissant, ~e /lɑ̃gisɑ̃, ɑ̃t/ *adj* [*person*] listless; [*conversation*] desultory.

lanière /lanjɛʀ/ *nf* (gen) strap; (of whip) lash; **découper en ~s** to cut up into strips.

lanterne /lɑ̃tɛʀn/ *nf* **1** lantern; **2** (Aut) sidelight (GB), parking light (US).

IDIOMS **être la ~ rouge** to bring up the rear; **éclairer la ~ de qn** to enlighten sb.

laper /lape/ [1] *vtr* to lap (up) [*soup, milk*].

lapider /lapide/ [1] *vtr* **1** to stone [sb] to death [*person*]; **2** to throw stones at [*person*].

lapin /lapɛ̃/ *nm* **1** (animal, meat) rabbit; **~ de garenne** wild rabbit; **coup du ~** rabbit punch; (in accident) whiplash injury; **cage** or **cabane à ~s** rabbit hutch; (figurative)○ tower block; **2** rabbit(skin).

IDIOMS **poser un ~ à qn**○ to stand sb up; **se faire tirer comme des ~s**○ to be picked off like flies; **c'est un chaud ~**○ he's a randy devil.

lapine /lapin/ *nf* doe rabbit.

laps /laps/ *nm inv* **~ de temps** period of time.

lapsus /lapsys/ *nm inv* slip; **~ révélateur** Freudian slip.

laquais /lakɛ/ *nm inv* lackey.

laque /lak/ *nf* **1** hairspray; **2** lacquer; gloss paint (GB), enamel (US).

laqué, ~e /lake/ *adj* **1** [*paint*] gloss; **2** (Culin) **canard ~** Peking duck.

laquelle /lakɛl/ ▶ **lequel**.

laquer /lake/ [1] **I** *vtr* to lacquer; to paint [sth] in gloss (GB) or enamel (US).

II se laquer *v refl* (+ *v être*) **se ~ les cheveux** to put hairspray on one's hair.

larbin○ /laʀbɛ̃/ *nm* (derogatory) servant.

lard /laʀ/ *nm* ≈ fat streaky bacon.

IDIOMS **je ne sais pas si c'est du ~ ou du cochon**○ I don't know what to think.

larder /laʀde/ [1] *vtr* (Culin) to lard; **~ qn de coups de couteau** (figurative) to stab sb repeatedly.

lardon /laʀdɔ̃/ *nm* (Culin) bacon cube.

large /laʀʒ/ **I** *adj* **1** [*shoulders, hips*] broad; [*avenue, river, bed*] wide; [*coat*] loose-fitting; [*trousers*] loose; [*skirt, cloak*] full; [*jumper*] big; [*gesture, movement*] sweeping; [*smile*] broad; [*curve*] long; **~ de trois mètres** three metres[GB] wide; **2** [*advance, profit*] substantial; [*choice, public*] wide; [*coalition*] broad; [*extract, majority*] large; **au sens ~** in a broad sense; **3** [*person*] generous; **4** [*life*] comfortable; **5 avoir les idées ~s, être ~ d'esprit** to be broad-minded.

II *adv* **1** [*plan*] on a generous scale; [*calculate, measure*] on the generous side; **2 s'habiller ~** to wear loose-fitting clothes.

III *nm* **1 faire quatre mètres de ~** to be four metres[GB] wide; **2** open sea; **au ~** offshore; **prendre le ~** to sail; (figurative)○ to make oneself scarce○.

IDIOMS **ne pas en mener ~**○ to be worried stiff○.

largement /laʀʒəmɑ̃/ *adv* **1** widely; **se prononcer ~ en faveur de qch** to come out largely in favour[GB] of sth; **2** largely, to a large extent; **être ~ responsable de qch** to be largely responsible for sth; **3 arriver ~ en tête** to be a clear winner; **~ en dessous de la limite** well under the limit; **il dépasse ~ les autres** he's much taller than the others; **4 tu**

as ~ le temps you've got plenty of time; **c'est ~ suffisant** that's more than enough; **5** easily; **une chaîne en or vaudrait ~ le double** a gold chain would easily be worth twice as much; **6** [*contribute, compensate*] generously.

largesse /larʒɛs/ *nf* generous gift; **répandre ses ~s** to give lavishly.

largeur /larʒœr/ *nf* **1** width, breadth; (in geometry) breadth; **être déchiré sur toute la ~** to be torn right across; **dans le sens de la ~** widthwise; **2 ~ d'esprit** or **de vues** broadmindedness.

largo /largo/ *adj, adv* largo.

largué°, **~e** /large/ *adj* **1** lost, out of one's depth; **2** out of touch.

larguer /large/ [1] *vtr* **1** (Mil) to drop [*bomb, missile*]; to drop [*parachutist*]; to release [*satellite, space shuttle*]; **2** to unfurl [*sail*]; **~ les amarres** to cast off; (figurative) to set off; **3**° to give up [*studies, apartment*]; to chuck° [*boyfriend, girlfriend*].

larme /larm/ *nf* **1** tear; **elle a ri aux ~s** she laughed till she cried; **pleurer à chaudes ~s** to cry as though one's heart would break; **avoir la ~ à l'œil** to be a bit weepy; **2**° drop.

larmoyant, **~e** /larmwajɑ̃, ɑ̃t/ *adj* **1** [*eyes*] full of tears; **2** [*voice*] whining; [*speech*] maudlin.

larmoyer /larmwaje/ [23] *vi* **1** [*eyes*] to water; **2** [*person*] to whine.

larron /larɔ̃/ *nm* **1** (humorous) scoundrel; **2** thief.
IDIOMS **s'entendre comme ~s en foire** to be as thick as thieves; **l'occasion fait le ~** (Proverb) opportunity makes the thief.

larvaire /larvɛr/ *adj* (figurative) embryonic.

larve /larv/ *nf* **1** (Zool) larva; **2** (person) wimp°; worm.

laryngé, **~e** /larɛ̃ʒe/ *adj* laryngeal.

laryngite /larɛ̃ʒit/ *nf* laryngitis.

larynx /larɛ̃ks/ *nm inv* larynx.

las, **lasse** /lɑ, lɑs/ *adj* weary.

lasagnes /lazaɲ/ *nf pl* lasagna.

lascar° /laskar/ *nm* fellow; (of child) devil, rascal.

lascif, **-ive** /lasif, iv/ *adj* (literary) [*person, look*] lascivious; [*temperament*] lustful.

laser /lazɛr/ *nm* laser.

lassant, **~e** /lasɑ̃, ɑ̃t/ *adj* **1** [*speech*] tedious; [*reproaches*] tiresome; **2** tiring.

lasser /lɑse/ [1] **I** *vtr* **1** to bore [*person, audience*]; **2** to weary [*person, audience*].
II se lasser *v refl* (+ *v être*) [*person*] to grow tired; **sans se ~** without tiring; patiently.

lassitude /lasityd/ *nf* weariness; **avec ~** wearily.

lasso /laso/ *nm* lasso; **prendre au ~** to lasso.

latence /latɑ̃s/ *nf* latency.

latent, **~e** /latɑ̃, ɑ̃t/ *adj* [*danger, illness*] latent; [*anxiety, jealousy*] underlying.

latéral, **~e**, *mpl* **-aux** /lateral, o/ *adj* [*door, exit*] side; [*tunnel, aisle*] lateral.

latéralement /lateralmɑ̃/ *adv* [*arrive*] from the side; [*place*] sideways.

latin, **~e** /latɛ̃, in/ **I** *adj* **1** [*writers, texts*] Latin; **2** [*temperament*] Latin; [*culture*] Mediterranean; **3 langues ~es** Romance languages.
II *nm* Latin.
IDIOMS **c'est à y perdre son ~** one can't make head or tail of it.

Latin, **~e** /latɛ̃, in/ *nm,f* Latin; **les ~s** the Latin people.

latino-américain, **~e**, *mpl* **~s** /latinoamerikɛ̃, ɛn/ *adj* Latin-American.

latitude /latityd/ *nf* latitude.
IDIOMS **avoir toute ~ de faire** to be entirely free to do.

latte /lat/ *nf* **1** lath; (of floor) board; **2** (of bed base) slat.

laudatif, **-ive** /lodatif, iv/ *adj* laudatory.

lauréat, **~e** /lɔrea, at/ *nm,f* **1** (of competition) winner; **2** (in exam) successful candidate.

laurier /lɔrje/ **I** *nm* **1** (Bot) laurel; **~ commun** bay (tree); **2** (Culin) **feuille de ~** bay leaf.
II lauriers *nm pl* laurels; **s'endormir sur ses ~s** to rest on one's laurels.

laurier-rose, *pl* **lauriers-roses** /lɔrjeroz/ *nm* oleander.

lavable /lavabl/ *adj* washable; **~ en machine** machine washable.

lavabo /lavabo/ *nm* washbasin, washbowl.

lavage /lavaʒ/ *nm* **1** washing; cleaning; **2** (washing machine cycle) wash.
■ **~ de cerveau** brainwashing; **faire un ~ d'estomac à qn** to pump sb's stomach (out).

lavande /lavɑ̃d/ *adj inv, nf* lavender.

lavandière /lavɑ̃djɛr/ *nf* washerwoman.

lave /lav/ *nf* lava; **coulée de ~** lava flow.

lave-glace, *pl* **~s** /lavglas/ *nm* windscreen (GB) or windshield (US) washer.

lave-linge /lavlɛ̃ʒ/ *nm inv* washing machine.

lavement /lavmɑ̃/ *nm* (Med) enema.

laver /lave/ [1] **I** *vtr* **1** to wash [*clothes, child, car*]; **~ son linge** to do one's washing; **~ la vaisselle** to do the dishes; **~ qch à grande eau** to wash sth down; **~ qch à la brosse** to scrub sth; **2** to clean [*wound*]; **3** to clear; **~ qn d'une accusation** to clear sb of an accusation; **4** (literary) to wash away [*sins*].
II se laver *v refl* (+ *v être*) **1** to wash; **se ~ les mains** to wash one's hands; **se ~ les dents** to brush one's teeth; **2** to be washable; **3 se ~ d'un affront** to take revenge for an insult.
IDIOMS **je m'en lave les mains** I'm washing my hands of it.

laverie /lavri/ *nf* **~ (automatique)** launderette, laundromat® (US).

lavette /lavɛt/ *nf* **1** dishcloth; **2**° (derogatory) wimp°.

laveur, **-euse** /lavœr, øz/ *nm,f* cleaner.

lave-vaisselle /lavvɛsɛl/ *nm inv* dishwasher.

lavis /lavi/ *nm inv* **1** (technique) wash; **2** wash drawing.

lavoir /lavwaʀ/ *nm* wash house.

laxatif, -ive /laksatif, iv/ **I** *adj* laxative.
II *nm* laxative.

laxisme /laksism/ *nm* laxity.

laxiste /laksist/ *adj* lax.

layette /lɛjɛt/ *nf* baby clothes, layette.

le, la[1] (**l'** *before vowel or mute h*), *pl* **les** /lə, la, l, lɛ/ **I** *det* **1** the; **la table de la cuisine** the kitchen table; **les Dupont** the Duponts; **2 ~ sel de mer** sea salt; **elle aime les chevaux** she likes horses; **arriver sur** or **vers les 11 heures** to arrive about 11 o'clock; **dans les 20 francs** about 20 francs; ; **3 elle s'est cogné ~ bras** she banged her arm; **la jupe/fille de ma sœur** my sister's skirt/daughter; **4** a, an; **50 francs ~ kilo** 50 francs a kilo; **5 l'imbécile!** the fool!; (**oh**) **la jolie robe!** what a pretty dress!
II *pron* him; her; it; them; **je ne les comprends pas** I don't understand them.
III *pron neutre* **je ~ savais** I knew; I knew it; **je ~ croyais aussi, mais**... I thought so too, but...; **je te l'avais bien dit** I told you; **espérons-~!** let's hope so!

lé /le/ *nm* **1** (of cloth, wallpaper) width; **2** (of skirt) panel.

LEA /ɛləa/ *nf pl* (*abbr* = **langues étrangères appliquées**) *university language course with emphasis on business and management.*

leadership /lidœʀʃip/ *nm* **1** leading role; **2** supremacy.

lèche-bottes○ /lɛʃbɔt/ **I** *nmf inv* crawler○ (GB), bootlicker○.
II *nm* crawling○ (GB), bootlicking○; **faire du ~** to be a crawler (GB) or bootlicker○.

lécher /leʃe/ [1] **I** *vtr* **1** to lick [*spoon, plate*]; **2** [*flames*] to lick; [*sea*] to lap against; **3**○ to polish [*piece of work*].
II se lécher *v refl* (+ *v être*) **se ~ les doigts** to lick one's fingers.

lèche-vitrines /lɛʃvitʀin/ *nm inv* window-shopping.

leçon /ləsɔ̃/ *nf* **1** lesson; **~ particulière** private lesson; **2** lesson; **elle m'a fait la ~** she lectured me; **je n'ai de ~s à recevoir de personne** nobody is going to tell me what to do; **la ~ de la fable** the moral of the story.

lecteur, -trice /lɛktœʀ, tʀis/ **I** *nm,f* **1** (gen) reader; **2** teaching assistant.
II *nm* **1** (in computing) reader; **~ optique** optical scanner or reader; **~ de disquettes** disk drive; **2** player; **~ de cassettes** cassette player; **~ laser** CD player.

lecture /lɛktyʀ/ *nf* **1** (of book, newspaper) reading; **faire la ~ à qn** to read to sb; **2** reading, interpretation; **3** reading material; **tu as pris de la ~?** have you brought something to read?; **4** (of music, X-ray, disk) reading; **5** (of parliamentary bill) reading; **6** (of cassette, CD) play; playing.

ledit, ladite, *pl* **lesdits, lesdites** /lədi, ladit, ledi, ledit/ *adj* the aforementioned.

légal, ~e, *mpl* **-aux** /legal, o/ *adj* legal; lawful.

légalement /legalmɑ̃/ *adv* **1** legally; **2** lawfully.

légaliser /legalize/ [1] *vtr* **1** to legalize; **2** to authenticate.

légalité /legalite/ *nf* **1** legality; **2** lawfulness.

légataire /legatɛʀ/ *nmf* legatee; **~ universel** sole legatee.

légendaire /leʒɑ̃dɛʀ/ *adj* legendary.

légende /leʒɑ̃d/ *nf* **1** legend; **entrer dans la ~** to become legendary; **2** (accompanying picture) caption; (on map) key; **3** tall story.

léger, -ère /leʒe, ɛʀ/ **I** *adj* **1** light; **se sentir plus ~** (figurative) to have a great weight off one's mind; **2** (Culin) [*meal, cooking*] light; **3** [*person, movement*] nimble; [*step*] light; **4** [*laugh*] gentle; [*blow, knock*] soft; [*error, delay*] slight; [*fear*] mild; [*taste, smell, hope*] faint; [*wind, rain, mist*] light; [*layer, cloud*] thin; [*injury*] minor; **5** [*coffee, tea, drink*] weak; [*perfume, wine*] light; [*tobacco*] mild (GB), light (US); **6** [*action*] ill-considered; [*remark*] thoughtless, careless; [*argument, proof*] weak, flimsy; **7**○ **c'est un peu ~** it's a bit skimpy; **8** [*woman*] loose; [*way of life*] loose, lax; [*husband, mood*] fickle; **9** (Mil) [*weapon, division*] light.
II *adv* [*travel*] light; **cuisiner/manger ~** to cook/to eat light meals.
III à la légère *phr* (gen) without thinking; [*accuse*] rashly; **prendre qch à la légère** not to take sth seriously.

légèrement /leʒɛʀmɑ̃/ *adv* **1** [*move, push*] gently; [*perfume*] lightly, slightly; [*tremble, injured, tinged*] slightly; **être habillé ~** to be dressed for warm weather; **2** (Culin) [*eat*] lightly; **3** [*walk, run*] lightly, nimbly; **4** [*act, speak*] without thinking.

légèreté /leʒɛʀte/ *nf* **1** lightness; **2** (of person, movements) lightness, nimbleness; (of gait, style) lightness; **3** thoughtlessness; casualness; **4** (of character) fickleness; **la ~ de ses mœurs** his/her loose morals.

légion /leʒjɔ̃/ *nf* **1** (Mil) legion; **2** army; **ils sont ~** they are legion.
■ **la Légion** (**étrangère**) the Foreign Legion.

légionnaire /leʒjɔnɛʀ/ **I** *nmf* member of the Legion of Honour[GB].
II *nm* (Roman) legionary; (in Foreign Legion) legionnaire.

législatif, -ive /leʒislatif, iv/ *adj* legislative; **élections législatives** ≈ general election.

législation /leʒislasjɔ̃/ *nf* legislation; **~ du travail** labour[GB] law.

législature /leʒislatyʀ/ *nf* **1** term of office; **2** legislature.

légiste /leʒist/ *nm* jurist.

légitime /leʒitim/ *adj* **1** [*child, right*] legitimate; [*union, heir*] lawful; **2** [*grievance, action*] legitimate; [*anger*] justifiable; **3** [*salary*] fair; [*reward*] just.
■ **~ défense** self-defence[GB].

légitimité /leʒitimite/ *nf* **1** legitimacy; **2** (of an act) lawfulness.

legs /lɛg/ *nm inv* **1** (Law, gen) legacy; (of personal belongings) bequest; (to museum, foundation) bequest; **2** (figurative) legacy.

léguer /lege/ [14] *vtr* **1** (in one's will) to leave sth; **2** to hand down [*traditions*]; to pass on [*flaw, defect, quality*].

légume /legym/ *nm* vegetable; **~s secs** pulses.

légumineuse /legyminøz/ *nf* leguminous plant.

leitmotiv /lajtmɔtiv/ *nm* leitmotiv.

lendemain /lɑ̃dəmɛ̃/ **I** *nm* **1 le ~, la journée du ~** the following day; **dès le ~** the (very) next day; **le ~ de l'accident** the day after the accident; **du jour au ~** overnight; **2 au ~ de** (in the period) after; **au ~ de la guerre** just after the war; **3 le ~** tomorrow, the future; **sans ~** [*happiness, success*] short-lived.

II lendemains *nm pl* **1** outcome; consequences; **2** future; **des ~s difficiles** difficult days ahead.

lénifiant, ~e /lenifjɑ̃, ɑ̃t/ *adj* [*medicine, remark*] soothing.

lent, ~e[1] /lɑ̃, ɑ̃t/ *adj* slow; [*film, vehicle*] slow-moving; [*poison*] slow-acting; **avoir l'esprit ~** to be slow-witted.

lente[2] /lɑ̃t/ *nf* (Zool) nit.

lentement /lɑ̃t(ə)mɑ̃/ *adv* slowly; **qui va ~ va sûrement** (Proverb) slowly but surely.

lenteur /lɑ̃tœʀ/ *nf* slowness; **avec ~** slowly.

lentille /lɑ̃tij/ *nf* **1** (Bot, Culin) lentil; **2** lens; **~s de contact** contact lenses.

léopard /leɔpaʀ/ *nm* **1** leopard; **2** leopardskin.

lèpre /lɛpʀ/ *nf* leprosy.

lépreux, -euse /lepʀø, øz/ *nm,f* leper.

lequel /ləkɛl/, **laquelle** /lakɛl/, **lesquels** *mpl*, **lesquelles** *fpl* /lekɛl/, (with *à*) **auquel**, **auxquels** *mpl*, **auxquelles** *fpl* /okɛl/, (with *de*) **duquel** /dykɛl/, **desquels** *mpl*, **desquelles** *fpl* /dekɛl/ **I lequel, laquelle, lesquels, lesquelles** *adj* who; which; **il m'a présenté son cousin, ~ cousin vit en Grèce** he introduced me to his cousin, who lives in Greece; **auquel cas** in which case.

II *rel pron* who; which; **les gens contre lesquels ils luttaient** the people (who) they were fighting against; **la table sur laquelle tu as posé la tasse** the table (which) you put the cup on.

III *pron* which; **lesquels sont les plus compétents?** which are the most competent?; **'j'ai vu un film de Chaplin hier'—'~?'** 'I saw a Charlie Chaplin film yesterday'—'which one?'

les ▶ **le**.

lesbienne /lɛsbjɛn/ *nf* lesbian.

lesdites ▶ **ledit**.

lesdits ▶ **ledit**.

lèse-majesté /lɛzmaʒɛste/ *nf inv* lese-majesty.

léser /leze/ [14] *vtr* to wrong [*person*]; to prejudice [*interests*].

lésiner /lezine/ [1] *vi* **ne pas ~ sur** to be liberal with [*ingredients, money, compliments*]; **ne pas ~ sur la dépense** to spare no expense.

lésion /lezjɔ̃/ *nf* (Med) lesion; **~ pulmonaire** pulmonary lesion.

lesquels, lesquelles ▶ **lequel**.

lessivable /lesivabl/ *adj* washable.

lessive /lesiv/ *nf* **1** washing powder; washing liquid; **2** washing.

lessiver /lesive/ [1] *vtr* **1** to wash; **2**○ **être lessivé** (humorous) to be washed out○.

lest /lɛst/ *nm* **1** ballast; **jeter** or **lâcher du ~** to jettison ballast; **lâcher du ~** (figurative) to make concessions; **2** (on fishing net) weight.

leste /lɛste/ *adj* **1** [*person, animal*] agile, nimble; **2** [*joke, remark*] risqué.

lester /lɛste/ [1] *vtr* **1** to ballast; **2**○ to stuff sth.

létal, ~e, *mpl* **-aux** /letal, o/ *adj* lethal; **dose ~e** lethal dose.

léthargie /letaʀʒi/ *nf* lethargy.

léthargique /letaʀʒik/ *adj* **1** [*person*] lethargic; [*industry, economy*] sluggish; **2** (Med) lethargic.

Lettonie /lɛtɔni/ *pr nf* Latvia.

lettre /lɛtʀ/ **I** *nf* **1** (of alphabet) letter; **~ minuscule** small letter; **~ majuscule** or **capitale** capital letter; **~ d'imprimerie** block letter; **en toutes ~s** in full; **c'est écrit en toutes ~s dans le rapport** it's down in black and white in the report; **les Romains furent des urbanistes avant la ~** the Romans were city planners before the concept was invented; **2** letter; **~ de réclamation** letter of complaint; **~ de rupture** letter ending a relationship; **une petite ~** a note; **3** letter; **à la ~, au pied de la ~** [*apply, follow*] to the letter; **il prend tout ce qu'on lui dit à la ~** he takes everything you say literally.

II lettres *nf pl* **1** (university subject) French; (more general) arts (GB), humanities (US); **étudiant en ~s** student reading French (GB), student majoring in French (US); arts (GB) or humanities (US) student; **2** letters; **femme de ~s** woman of letters; **les gens de ~s** writers; **avoir des ~s** to be well read.

▣ **~ ouverte** open letter; **~ recommandée** registered letter; **~s classiques** French and Latin; **~s modernes** French language and literature.

IDIOMS **passer comme une ~ à la poste**○ [*reform*] to go through smoothly; [*excuse*] to be accepted without any questions.

lettré, ~e /letʀe/ **I** *adj* [*person*] well-read; [*milieu*] literary.

II *nm,f* man/woman of letters.

leu: **à la queue leu leu** /alakøløløl/ *phr* in single file.

leucémie /løsemi/ *nf* leukaemia.

leucocyte /løkɔsit/ *nm* leucocyte (GB), leukocyte (US).

leur, (*pl* **leurs**) /lœʀ/ **I** *pron* them; **il ~ a expliqué le fonctionnement de l'appareil** he told them how the machine worked; **il ~ a fallu faire** they had to do.

II *det* their; **un de ~s amis** a friend of theirs; **pendant ~ absence** while they were away.

III le leur, la leur, les leurs *pron* theirs; **c'est le ~** it's theirs; **il est des ~s** he's one of them; **ils m'ont demandé d'être des ~s**

they asked me to come along; **ils vivent loin des ~s** they live far away from their families.

leurre /lœʀ/ *nm* **1** illusion; **2** (in fishing, hunting) lure; **3** (Mil) decoy.

leurrer /lœʀe/ [1] I *vtr* to delude; **se laisser ~** to let oneself be taken in.
II **se leurrer** *v refl* (+ *v être*) to delude oneself (**de** with; **au sujet de** about).

levain /ləvɛ̃/ *nm* (fermenting agent) starter; (for bread) leaven (GB), sourdough (US).

levant /ləvɑ̃/ I *adj m* **soleil ~** rising sun; **au soleil ~** at sunrise.
II *nm* east; **au ~** in the east; **du ~ au couchant** from east to west.

levé, **~e**[1] /ləve/ I *pp* ▶ **lever**[1].
II *pp adj* **1 voter à main ~e** to vote by a show of hands; **2** up; **elle est toujours la première ~e** she's always the first up.

levée[2] /ləve/ *nf* **1** (of embargo, sentence, martial law) lifting; (of siege) raising; (of measures) suspension; (of diplomatic immunity) removal; (of secrecy, anonymity, taboo) ending; (of session) close; **2** (of mail) collection; **3** (embankment) levee.
■ **~ de boucliers** outcry.

lève-glace, *pl* **~s** /lɛvglas/ *nm* **~ électrique** (option) electric windows; (mechanism) electric window mechanism.

lever[1] /ləve/ [16] I *vtr* **1** to raise; **~ la main** or **le doigt** (for permission to speak) to put up one's hand; **~ la main sur qn** to raise a hand to sb; **~ les bras au ciel** to throw up one's hands; **lève les pieds quand tu marches!** don't drag your feet!; **~ les yeux** or **la tête** to look up; **2** to lift [*object*]; to raise [*barrier*]; **~ son verre** to raise one's glass; **~ le rideau** to raise the curtain; **3** (out of bed) to get [sb] up [*child, sick person*]; **4** to lift [*embargo, restriction*]; to raise [*siege*]; to dispel [*doubt*]; to end [*taboo, secret*]; to remove [*obstacle*]; to close [*session*]; **5** to raise [*funds*]; to levy [*tax*]; **6** to flush out [*game, partridges*]; **~ un lièvre** to start a hare.
II *vi* **1** (Culin) [*dough*] to rise; **2** [*seedlings, corn*] to come up.
III **se lever** *v refl* (+ *v être*) **1** to get up; **il faut se ~ de bonne heure**○ **pour comprendre ce qu'il dit** (figurative) you need to be pretty○ clever to understand what he says; **2** to stand up; **se ~ de table** to leave the table; **'accusé, levez-vous!'** 'the accused will stand'; **3** [*person, people*] to rise up; **4** [*sun*] to rise; **le jour se lève** it's getting light; **5** [*wind*] to rise; [*breeze*] to get up; **6** [*fog, mist*] to clear; [*weather*] to clear up.

lever[2] /ləve/ *nm* **1 être là au ~ des enfants** to be there when the children get up; **2 au ~ du jour** at daybreak; **au ~ du soleil** at sunrise.

lève-tard /lɛvtaʀ/ *nmf inv* late riser.

lève-tôt /lɛvto/ *nmf inv* early riser, early bird○.

levier /ləvje/ *nm* lever; **soulever qch avec un ~** to lever sth up.
■ **~ de changement de vitesse** (Aut) gear lever (GB), gear stick (US); **~ de commande** control stick; **~ de frein à main** (Aut) hand brake.

lévitation /levitasjɔ̃/ *nf* levitation.

levraut /ləvʀo/ *nm* leveret.

lèvre /lɛvʀ/ *nf* **1** lip; **avoir le sourire aux ~s** to be smiling; **être sur toutes les ~s** to be on everyone's lips; **du bout des ~s** [*eat*] half-heartedly; [*reply*] grudgingly; **2** (of vulva) labium; **3** (of wound, crater) lip, edge.
IDIOMS **être suspendu aux ~s de qn** to hang on sb's every word.

lévrier /levʀije/ *nm* greyhound; **~ afghan** Afghan hound.

levure /ləvyʀ/ *nf* yeast; **~ chimique** baking powder.

lexical, **~e**, *mpl* **-aux** /lɛksikal, o/ *adj* lexical.

lexique /lɛksik/ *nm* **1** glossary; (bilingual) vocabulary (book); **2** lexicon, lexis.

lézard /lezaʀ/ *nm* **1** lizard; **2** lizard(skin).

lézarde /lezaʀd/ *nf* crack.

lézarder /lezaʀde/ [1] I *vtr* to crack.
II○ *vi* **~ au soleil** to bask in the sun.
III **se lézarder** *v refl* (+ *v être*) to crack.

liaison /ljɛzɔ̃/ *nf* **1** link; **la ~ Calais–Douvres** the Calais–Dover line or route; **2 ~ radio** radio contact; **~ satellite** satellite link; **3 assurer la ~ entre différents services** to liaise between different services; **travailler en ~ avec** to work in collaboration with; **4** (between ideas) connection; **5** (love) affair; **6** (between words) liaison.

liane /ljan/ *nf* creeper, liana.

liant, **~e** /ljɑ̃, ɑ̃t/ *adj* sociable.

liasse /ljas/ *nf* (of banknotes) wad; (of letters, papers, documents) bundle.

Liban /libɑ̃/ *pr nm* Lebanon.

libellé /libɛlle/ *nm* wording.

libeller /libɛlle/ [1] *vtr* **1** to draw up [*contract, legal document*]; **2** (formal) to word [*letter, article, request*]; **3** to make out [*cheque, money order*].

libellule /libɛllyl/ *nf* dragonfly.

libéral, **~e**, *mpl* **-aux** /libeʀal, o/ *adj* **1** liberal; **2** (in politics) Liberal; **3** free-market.

libéralisation /libeʀalizasjɔ̃/ *nf* (gen) liberalization; **~ des mœurs** relaxation of moral standards.

libéraliser /libeʀalize/ [1] I *vtr* to liberalize.
II **se libéraliser** *v refl* (+ *v être*) [*country, attitudes*] to become more liberal.

libéralisme /libeʀalism/ *nm* liberalism.

libérateur, **-trice** /libeʀatœʀ, tʀis/ I *adj* liberating.
II *nm,f* liberator.

libération /libeʀasjɔ̃/ *nf* **1** (of prisoner, hostage) release; **2** (of country, population) liberation; **3** liberation; **~ des femmes** women's liberation; **4** relief; **5** (of prices) deregulation; (of trade) freeing; **6** (of energy) release.

Libération /libeʀasjɔ̃/ *nf* (of 1944) **la ~** the Liberation.

libéré, **~e** /libeʀe/ I *pp* ▶ **libérer**.
II *pp adj* **1** [*man, woman*] liberated; **2** [*country,*

area, town] free; **3** [*post, premises*] vacant; **4** [*person, company*] free (**de** from).

libérer /libeʀe/ [14] **I** *vtr* **1** to liberate [*country, town*]; to free [*companion, hostage*]; **2** to release [*prisoner, hostage*]; to free [*slave, animal*]; **3** to allow [sb] to go [*employee, pupil*]; **4** to liberate [*person, imagination*]; (of post, duties) to relieve [*minister, employee*]; **~ qn de l'emprise de qn** to get sb away from sb's influence; **5** to release [*emotion*]; to give free rein to [*imagination*]; **6** to relieve [*mind, person*]; **~ sa conscience** to unburden oneself; **7** to vacate [*apartment, office*]; **~ le passage** to clear the way; **~ la chambre avant midi** (in hotel) to check out before noon; **8** to free [*arm, hand*]; to release [*spring, catch*]; **9** to liberalize [*economy, trade*]; to deregulate [*prices*]; **~ les loyers** to lift rent controls; **10** to release [*gas, energy*].

II se libérer *v refl* (+ *v être*) **1** to free oneself/ itself; **se ~ d'une dette** to pay a debt; **2 j'essaierai de me ~ mercredi** I'll try and be free on Wednesday.

libertaire /libɛʀtɛʀ/ *adj, nmf* libertarian.

liberté /libɛʀte/ *nf* **1** (gen) freedom; **Statue de la ~** Statue of Liberty; **élever des animaux en ~** to raise animals in a natural habitat; **espèce vivant en ~** species in the wild; **être en ~** to be free; **l'assassin est toujours en ~** the killer is still at large; **prendre la ~ de faire** to take the liberty of doing; **prendre des ~s avec qn** to take liberties with sb; **~ de pensée** freedom of thought; **2** (Law) **mettre qn en ~ conditionnelle** to release sb on parole; **mise en ~ provisoire** provisional release; **mise en ~ surveillée** release on probation.

libertin, **~e** /libɛʀtɛ̃, in/ *adj, nm,f* libertine.

libidineux, **-euse** /libidinø, øz/ *adj* libidinous, lustful.

libido /libido/ *nf* libido.

libraire /libʀɛʀ/ *nmf* bookseller.

librairie /libʀɛʀi/ *nf* **1** bookshop (GB), bookstore; **2** bookselling business.

librairie-papeterie, *pl* **librairies-papeteries** /libʀɛʀipapɛtʀi/ *nf* stationer's and bookshop (GB) or bookstore.

libre /libʀ/ *adj* **1** [*person, country*] free; **~ à elle de partir** it's up to her whether she goes or not; **être ~ de ses actes** to do as one wishes; **2** [*person*] free and easy; [*manner*] free; [*opinion*] candid; [*morality*] easygoing; **3** [*hand, thumb*] free; [*road, way*] clear; **4** [*person, room*] available; [*seat*] free; '**~ de suite**' 'available immediately'; **5** [*WC*] vacant; **la ligne n'est pas ~** (on telephone) the number is engaged (GB) or busy (US).

■ **~ arbitre** free will; **~ entreprise** free enterprise.

IDIOMS **être ~ comme l'air** to be as free as a bird.

libre-échange /libʀeʃɑ̃ʒ/ *nm* free trade.

librement /libʀəmɑ̃/ *adv* freely; **parlez-moi ~** you can speak freely.

libre-service, *pl* **libres-services** /libʀə sɛʀvis/ **I** *adj inv* self-service.

II *nm* **1 le ~** self-service; **2** self-service shop (GB) or store (US); self-service restaurant.

■ **~ bancaire** automatic teller.

lice /lis/ *nf* lists; **être en ~** to have entered the lists.

licence /lisɑ̃s/ *nf* **1** (bachelor's) degree; **~ en droit** law degree; **préparer une ~ d'anglais** to do a degree in English; **2** (Law) licence[GB]; **produit sous ~** licensed product; **3** (Sport) **avoir sa ~ de tennis** to be a member of the national tennis federation.

licencié, **~e** /lisɑ̃sje/ **I** *pp* ▶ **licencier**.

II *pp adj* [*student*] graduate.

III *nm,f* **1** graduate (GB), college graduate (US); **2** (Sport) member (*of a sports federation*); **3 ~ (économique)** redundant employee (GB), laid-off worker.

licenciement /lisɑ̃simɑ̃/ *nm* dismissal; **~ (économique)** redundancy (GB), lay-off; **~ collectif** mass redundancy; **~ sec** compulsory redundancy (*without compensation*).

licencier /lisɑ̃sje/ [2] *vtr* **1** to make [sb] redundant (GB), to lay [sb] off; **2** to dismiss (GB), to let [sb] go.

licencieux, **-ieuse** /lisɑ̃sjø, øz/ *adj* licentious.

lichen /likɛn/ *nm* lichen.

licite /lisit/ *adj* lawful.

licorne /likɔʀn/ *nf* unicorn.

lie /li/ *nf* **1** dregs, lees; **2** (figurative) dregs.

lie-de-vin /lidvɛ̃/ *adj inv* wine, wine-coloured[GB].

liège /ljɛʒ/ *nm* cork; **bouchon en ~** cork.

liégeois, **~e** /ljeʒwa, az/ *adj* of Liège; **café/ chocolat ~** *iced coffee/chocolate topped with whipped cream.*

lien /ljɛ̃/ *nm* **1** strap; string; (figurative) bond; **2** connection, link; **3** (gen) link, tie; (emotional) tie, bond; **~s économiques** economic links; **~s de parenté** family ties; **être uni par les ~s du mariage** to be joined or united in marriage.

lier /lje/ [1] **I** *vtr* **1** to tie [sb/sth] up; **il avait les mains liées** his hands were tied; **2** to bind; **ils sont très liés** they are very close; **3** to link [*ideas, events*]; **tous ces problèmes sont liés** these problems are all linked; **4 ~ amitié avec qn** to strike up a friendship with sb; **5** (Mus) to slur [*notes*].

II se lier *v refl* (+ *v être*) [*people*] to make friends.

lierre /ljɛʀ/ *nm* ivy.

liesse /ljɛs/ *nf* jubilation; **en ~** jubilant.

lieu /ljø/ **I** *nm* **1** (*pl* **~s**) **~ (noir)** coley, black pollock; **2** (*pl* **~x**) place; **sur le ~ de travail** in the workplace; **~ de passage** thoroughfare; **en tous ~x** everywhere; **en ~ et place de qn** [*sign, act*] on behalf of sb; **en premier ~** in the first place; **en dernier ~** lastly; **avoir ~** to take place; **tenir ~ de** to serve as [*bedroom, study*]; **il y a ~ de s'inquiéter** there is cause for anxiety; **s'il y a ~** if necessary; **cela n'a pas ~ d'être** it shouldn't be so; **donner ~ à** to cause [*scandal*].

II au lieu de *phr* instead of.

III lieux *nm pl* **1** parts; **repérer les ~x** to

have a scout around; **sur les ~x** [*be present*] at the scene; [*arrive*] on the scene; **2** premises; **visiter les ~x** to visit the premises.

■ **~ commun** platitude; **~ public** public place.

lieue /ljø/ *nf* league; **~ marine** league.

IDIOMS **j'étais à cent** or **mille ~s d'imaginer** I never for a moment imagined.

lieutenant /ljøtnɑ̃/ *nm* **1** (Mil) (in army) ≈ lieutenant (GB), ≈ first lieutenant (US); (in air force) ≈ flying officer (GB), ≈ first lieutenant (US); **2** (on boat) first officer.

lieutenant-colonel, *pl* **lieutenants-colonels** /ljøtnɑ̃kɔlɔnɛl/ *nm* (in army) ≈ lieutenant-colonel; (in air force) ≈ wing commander (GB), ≈ lieutenant colonel (US).

lièvre /ljɛvʀ/ *nm* **1** (Zool) hare; **2** (Sport) pacemaker.

IDIOMS **courir plusieurs ~s à la fois** to try to do too many things at once.

lifting /liftiŋ/ *nm* face-lift.

ligament /ligamɑ̃/ *nm* ligament.

ligaturer /ligatyʀe/ [1] *vtr* (Med) to tie.

ligne /liɲ/ *nf* **1** line; **~ blanche** (Aut) white line; **~ de départ/d'arrivée** (Sport) starting/finishing line; **lire les ~s de la main de qn** to read sb's palm; **~ droite** straight line; (driving) straight piece of road; **la dernière ~ droite avant l'arrivée** the home straight; **2** (in writing) line; **je vous écris ces quelques ~s pour vous dire**... this is just a quick note to tell you...; **à la ~!** new paragraph!; **3** (in public transport) service; route; (of train, underground) line; **~ de chemin de fer** railway line; **~s intérieures** domestic flights; **4** cable; **~ aérienne** overhead cable; **5** (telephone) line; **obtenir la ~** to get through; **6** figure; **garder la ~** to stay slim; **retrouver la ~** to get back one's figure; **7** (of body) contours; (of face) shape; (of hills) outline; **la ~ aérodynamique d'une voiture** the aerodynamic lines of a car; **8** (of clothes, furniture, style) look; **9** line; **une ~ de produits de beauté** a line of beauty products; **10** outline; **raconter un événement dans ses grandes ~s** to give an outline of events; **11** (of political party) line; **12** fishing line; **pêche à la ~** angling; **13** line; row; **les ~s ennemies** (Mil) the enemy lines; **14** (in computing) **en ~** on line; **15** (of ancestry) line.

■ **~ de but** (Sport) goal line; **~ de conduite** line of conduct; **se donner comme ~ de conduite de faire** to make it a rule to do; **~ de démarcation** (Mil) demarcation line; **~ de mire** line of sight; **~ de tir** line of fire; **~ de visée** = **~ de mire**.

IDIOMS **être en première ~** (gen), (Mil) to be in the front line; (figurative) to be in the firing line; **entrer en ~ de compte** to be taken into account.

lignée /liɲe/ *nf* **1** descendants; lineage; **de haute ~** of noble descent; **2** tradition.

lignite /liɲit/ *nm* brown coal, lignite.

ligoter /ligɔte/ [1] *vtr* to truss [sb] up [*person*]; **~ qn à qch** to tie sb to sth.

ligue /lig/ *nf* league.

liguer /lige/ [1] **I** *vtr* **~ des gens/nations contre** to unite people/countries against.

II se liguer *v refl* (+ *v être*) [*people*] to join forces.

lilas /lila/ *adj inv*, *nm* lilac.

lilliputien, **-ienne** /lilipysjɛ̃, ɛn/ *adj*, *nm,f* Lilliputian.

limace /limas/ *nf* (Zool) slug.

limaille /limaj/ *nf* filings.

limande /limɑ̃d/ *nf* dab; **filet de ~** fillet of dab.

limande-sole, *pl* **limandes-soles** /limɑ̃d sɔl/ *nf* lemon sole.

lime /lim/ *nf* **1** (Tech) file; **~ à ongles** nail file; **2** (Bot) lime; **3** (Zool) lima.

limer /lime/ [1] **I** *vtr* **1** to file [*nail, metal*]; to file down [*key, rough edge*]; **2** to file through [*bars of cage*].

II se limer *v refl* (+ *v être*) **se ~ les ongles** to file one's nails.

limier /limje/ *nm* **1** bloodhound; **2**○ sleuth.

limitatif, **-ive** /limitatif, iv/ *adj* limiting, restrictive.

limitation /limitasjɔ̃/ *nf* (of power, liberty) limitation, restriction; (of prices, interest rates) control; **~ de vitesse** (Aut) speed limit.

limite /limit/ [1] **I** *nf* **1** border; **2** (of estate, piece of land) boundary; (of sea, forest, village) edge; **3** limit; **connaître ses ~s** to know one's (own) limitations; **tout de même, il y a des ~s**○! there are limits, you know!; **vraiment, il dépasse les ~s!** he's really going too far!; **à la ~, je préférerais qu'il refuse** I'd almost prefer it if he refused; **4 à la ~ de** on the verge of; **activités à la ~ de la légalité** activities bordering on the illegal; **5 dans une certaine ~** up to a point, to a certain extent; **dans la ~ de, dans les ~s de** within the limits of; **dans la ~ du possible** as far as possible.

II (-)limite (*combining form*) **âge(-)~** maximum age; **date(-)~** deadline; **date(-)~ de vente** sell-by date; **vitesse(-)~** maximum speed.

■ **~ d'âge** age limit.

limité, **~e** /limite/ **I** *pp* ▶ **limiter**.

II *pp adj* [*conversation, resources, interest, choice*] limited.

limiter /limite/ [1] **I** *vtr* to limit, to restrict [*power, duration, number*]; **cela limite nos possibilités** that rather limits our scope; **~ les dégâts** to minimize the damage.

II se limiter *v refl* (+ *v être*) **1 se ~ à deux verres de bière par jour** to limit oneself to two glasses of beer a day; **je me limiterai à quelques observations** I'll confine myself to a few observations; **2 se ~ à** to be limited to; **la vie ne se limite pas au travail** there's more to life than work.

limitrophe /limitʀɔf/ *adj* [*country, region*] adjacent; [*city*] border.

limoger /limɔʒe/ [13] *vtr* to dismiss [*high official*].

limon /limɔ̃/ *nm* **1** silt; **2** (on horse-drawn carriage) shaft.

limonade /limɔnad/ *nf* lemonade (GB), lemon soda (US).

limousine /limuzin/ *nf* (Aut) limousine.

limpide /lɛ̃pid/ *adj* **1** clear, limpid; **2** (figurative) [*explanation, style*] clear, lucid.

limpidité /lɛ̃pidite/ *nf* **1** clarity; **2** (figurative) clarity, lucidity.

lin /lɛ̃/ *nm* **1** flax; **2** linen.

linceul /lɛ̃sœl/ *nm* shroud.

linéaire /lineɛʀ/ *adj* linear.

linge /lɛ̃ʒ/ *nm* **1** linen; **~ sale** dirty linen; **~ de couleur** coloureds[GB]; **2** washing; **corde** or **fil à ~** clothes line; **3 ~ (de corps)** underwear; **4** cloth.
■ **~ de maison** household linen; **~ de toilette** bathroom linen.
IDIOMS **être blanc comme un ~** to be as white as a sheet.

lingerie /lɛ̃ʒʀi/ *nf* **1** linen room; **2 ~ (féminine)** lingerie; **~ fine** fine lingerie.

lingot /lɛ̃go/ *nm* ingot; **~ de métal** metal ingot; **~ d'or** gold ingot (*weighing 1 kg*).

linguiste /lɛ̃gɥist/ *nmf* linguist.

linguistique /lɛ̃gɥistik/ **I** *adj* linguistic.
II *nf* linguistics.

linteau, *pl* **~x** /lɛ̃to/ *nm* lintel.

lion /ljɔ̃/ *nm* lion; **la part du ~** the lion's share; **~ de mer** sealion.
IDIOMS **se battre** or **se défendre comme un ~** to fight like a tiger; **avoir mangé du ~**○ to be full of beans○ (GB), to be full of pep○ (US).

Lion /ljɔ̃/ *pr nm* Leo.

lionceau, *pl* **~x** /ljɔ̃so/ *nm* lion cub.

lionne /ljɔn/ *nf* lioness.

lipide /lipid/ *nm* lipid.

liquéfier /likefje/ [2] *vtr*, **se liquéfier** *v refl* (+ *v être*) to liquefy.

liqueur /likœʀ/ *nf* liqueur.

liquidation /likidasjɔ̃/ *nf* **1** (Law) (of company, property) liquidation; (of debts, accounts) settlement; **2** clearance; **~ totale (du stock)** total clearance.

liquide /likid/ **I** *adj* **1** liquid; **miel ~** clear honey; **2 argent ~** cash.
II *nm* **1** liquid; **2** cash.
■ **~ correcteur** correction fluid, white-out (fluid) (US); **~ de frein** brake fluid.

liquider /likide/ [1] *vtr* **1** to settle [*accounts*]; to liquidate [*company, business*]; **2** to clear [*goods, stock*]; **3**○ to settle [*problems, quarrels*]; **4**○ to liquidate○ [*enemy, witness*]; **5**○ to demolish [*meal*]; to empty [*glass*]; to clear [*plate*].

liquidité /likidite/ *nf* **1** liquidity; **2 des ~s** liquid assets.

lire[1] /liʀ/ [66] *vtr* to read; **~ entre les lignes** to read between the lines; **un auteur qui est très lu** a popular author; **~ qch en diagonale** to skim through sth; **~ sur les lèvres de qn** to lip-read what sb is saying; **~ dans les pensées de qn** to read sb's mind.

lire[2] /liʀ/ *nf* lira.

lis /lis/ *nm inv* lily.

liseré /lizʀe/ *nm*, **lisééré** /lizeʀe/ *nm* (on dress) edging; piping.

liseron /lizʀɔ̃/ *nm* bindweed, convolvulus.

liseuse /lizøz/ *nf* **1** bed jacket; **2** small reading lamp.

lisible /lizibl/ *adj* **1** [*writing, manuscript*] legible; **2** [*author, novel*] readable.

lisière /lizjɛʀ/ *nf* **1** (of wood, field) edge; (of village) outskirts; **2** (on piece of fabric) selvage.

lisse /lis/ *adj* [*skin, surface, hair*] smooth; [*tyre*] worn.

lisser /lise/ [1] *vtr* to smooth [*hair, garment*]; to stroke [*beard*]; **l'oiseau lisse ses plumes** the bird is preening its feathers or itself.

liste /list/ *nf* (gen) list; (at election) list (of candidates) (GB), ticket (US).
■ **~ d'attente** waiting list; **~ électorale** electoral roll; **~ de mariage** wedding list.
IDIOMS **être sur ~ rouge** to be ex-directory (GB), to have an unlisted number (US).

lit /li/ *nm* **1** bed; **~ à une place** or **d'une personne** single bed; **~ à deux places** or **de deux personnes** double bed; **aller** or **se mettre au ~** to go to bed; **tirer qn du ~** to drag sb out of bed; **au ~!** bedtime!; **~ métallique** iron bedstead; **le ~ était tout défait** the bedclothes were rumpled; **le ~ n'était pas défait** the bed had not been slept in; **un hôtel de 300 ~s** a 300-bed hotel; **2** (Law) marriage; **3** (Culin) bed; **4** (of river) bed; **la rivière est sortie de son ~** the river has overflowed its banks.
■ **~ de camp** camp bed (GB), cot (US); **~ pliant** folding bed; **~ en portefeuille** apple-pie bed; **~s superposés** bunk bed.
IDIOMS **comme on fait son ~ on se couche** (Proverb) as you make your bed so you must lie in it.

litanie /litani/ *nf* litany.

literie /litʀi/ *nf* bedding.

lithographie /litɔgʀafi/ *nf* **1** lithography; **2** lithograph.

litière /litjɛʀ/ *nf* **1** (for cattle) litter; (for horses) bedding; (for cats) cat litter; **2** (mode of transport) litter.

litige /litiʒ/ *nm* dispute; **statuer sur un ~** to give a ruling on a case; **point de ~** bone of contention; point at issue; **les parties en ~** the litigants.

litigieux, **-ieuse** /litiʒjø, øz/ *adj* [*case, point, argument*] contentious.

litote /litɔt/ *nf* (humorous) understatement; (in rhetoric) litotes.

litre /litʀ/ *nm* **1** (measure) litre[GB]; **2** (bottle) litre[GB] bottle.

littéraire /liteʀɛʀ/ **I** *adj* [*work, criticism*] literary; **études ~s** arts studies.
II *nm,f* **1** literary person; **2** arts or liberal arts (US) student.

littéral, **~e**, *mpl* **-aux** /liteʀal, o/ *adj* literal.

littéralement /liteʀalmɑ̃/ *adv* [*mean, translate*] literally; [*quote*] verbatim.

littérature /liteʀatyʀ/ *nf* literature.

littoral, **~e**, *mpl* **-aux** /litɔʀal/ **I** *adj* [*navigation, waters, town*] coastal.

II *nm* coast.

liturgie /lityʀʒi/ *nf* liturgy.

livide /livid/ *adj* [*person, face*] deathly pale; (literary) [*dawn, complexion, light*] livid.

livraison /livʀɛzɔ̃/ *nf* **1** (of goods) delivery; **'~s à domicile'** 'we deliver'; **'Livraisons'** 'deliveries only'; **il est venu prendre ~ de la commande** he came to pick up the order; **2** (goods delivered) delivery.

livre[1] /livʀ/ *nm* book; **c'est mon ~ de chevet** it's my bedside reading; (figurative) it's my bible; **l'industrie du ~** the book trade.

■ **~ blanc** blue book; **~ de bord** logbook; **~ de cuisine** cookery book; **~ d'or** visitors' book; **~ de poche**® paperback; **~ scolaire** schoolbook.

livre[2] /livʀ/ *nf* **1** pound; **~ sterling** pound sterling; **~ irlandaise** Irish pound, punt; **2** (unit of weight) half a kilo; (in UK) pound.

livrée /livʀe/ *nf* livery.

livrer /livʀe/ [1] **I** *vtr* **1** [*shopkeeper, retailer*] to deliver [*goods*]; **~ qn** to deliver sb's order; **2** to hand [sb] over [*criminal*]; to betray [*accomplice, secret*]; to pass [sth] on [*document*]; **3 être livré à soi-même** to be left to one's own devices; **4 il nous livre un peu de lui-même** he reveals something of himself.

II se livrer *v refl* (+ *v être*) **1 se ~ à un trafic de drogue** to engage in drug trafficking; **2 se ~ à** [*criminal*] to give oneself up to; **3 se ~ à un ami** to confide in a friend.

IDIOMS **~ bataille (à qn)** to fight (sb).

livret /livʀɛ/ *nm* **1** booklet; **2** libretto.

■ **~ de caisse d'épargne** ≈ savings book (GB), bankbook (*for a savings account*) (US); **~ de famille** family record book (*of births, marriages and deaths*); **~ scolaire** school report book.

livreur, **-euse** /livʀœʀ, øz/ *nm,f* delivery man/ woman.

lobe /lɔb/ *nm* lobe; **~ de l'oreille** ear lobe.

lobotomie /lɔbɔtɔmi/ *nf* lobotomy.

local, **~e**, *pl* **-aux** /lɔkal, o/ **I** *adj* [*newspaper, industry, authorities*] local; [*pain, showers*] localized; **22 heures heure ~e** 22.00 local time.

II *nm* **1** place; **les scouts ont besoin d'un ~** the scouts need a place to meet; **2 ~ commercial** commercial premises; **locaux habitables** residential units; **dans les locaux du lycée** on school premises; **les locaux du journal** the newspaper offices.

localement /lɔkalmɑ̃/ *adv* on a local level; **appliquer la crème ~** apply the cream locally.

localiser /lɔkalize/ [1] *vtr* **1** to locate [*person, noise*]; **2** to confine, to localize [*fire*].

localité /lɔkalite/ *nf* locality.

locataire /lɔkatɛʀ/ *nmf* tenant; **être ~** to be renting.

location /lɔkasjɔ̃/ *nf* **1** (by owner) renting out; (by tenant) renting; **agence de ~** rental agency; **mettre en ~** to rent out, to let (GB); **2** rented accommodation; **3** rent; **4** (of equipment) hire; **~ de voitures** car hire, car rental; **contrat de ~** rental agreement; **~ de vidéos** video rental; **5** (of theatre seats) reservation, booking (GB); **~ des places à partir du 3 juin** tickets will be available from 3 June.

location-vente, *pl* **locations-ventes** /lɔkasjɔ̃vɑ̃t/ *nf* 100% mortgage scheme.

locomotion /lɔkɔmɔsjɔ̃/ *nf* locomotion.

locomotive /lɔkɔmɔtiv/ *nf* **1** engine, locomotive; **~ à vapeur** steam engine; **2** (figurative) driving force; powerhouse.

locuteur, **-trice** /lɔkytœʀ, tʀis/ *nm,f* speaker.

locution /lɔkysjɔ̃/ *nf* phrase; idiom.

logarithme /lɔgaʀitm/ *nm* logarithm, log.

loge /lɔʒ/ *nf* **1** (caretaker's dwelling) lodge; **2** (of actor) dressing room; (in theatre) box; **3** (in freemasonry) Lodge; **4** loggia.

IDIOMS **être aux premières ~s**○ to be in an ideal position.

logé, **~e** /lɔʒe/ **I** *pp* ▶ **loger**.

II *pp adj* housed; **être ~, nourri, blanchi** to have bed, board and one's laundry done.

logement /lɔʒmɑ̃/ *nm* **1** accommodation; **~ individuel** flat (GB), apartment (US); house; **2** housing; **la crise du ~** the housing crisis.

■ **~ social** local authority housing (GB), public housing (US).

loger /lɔʒe/ [13] **I** *vtr* **1** to house [*student, refugee*]; **2** to put [sb] up [*friend*]; to provide accommodation for [*refugees, trainees*]; **3** [*hotel*] to have accommodation for; **4** to put; **je n'ai pas pu ~ tous mes meubles dans le salon** I couldn't fit all my furniture in the living room; **5 ~ une balle dans la tête de qn** to shoot sb in the head.

II *vi* **1** to live; **2** to stay; **~ à l'hôtel** to stay at a hotel.

III se loger *v refl* (+ *v être*) **1 avec cette somme, je dois me nourrir et me ~** with that I have to pay for food and accommodation; **2 se ~ dans qch** to get stuck in sth; [*dust*] to collect in sth; **la balle est venue se ~ dans le genou** the bullet lodged in his/her knee; **se ~ une balle dans la tête** to shoot oneself in the head.

logeur, **-euse** /lɔʒœʀ, øz/ *nm,f* lodger.

loggia /lɔdʒja/ *nf* loggia.

logiciel, **-ielle** /lɔʒisjɛl/ *nm* **1** software; **~ de base** system(s) software; **2** program.

logique /lɔʒik/ **I** *adj* **1** logical; **il n'est pas ~ avec lui-même** he is not consistent; **2**○ reasonable; **ce serait ~ qu'ils soient en colère** one could understand why they would be angry.

II *nf* logic; **manquer de ~** to be illogical; **défier toute ~** to defy all logic; **c'est dans la ~ des choses** it's in the nature of things; **en toute ~** logically.

logiquement /lɔʒikmɑ̃/ *adv* logically.

logis /lɔʒi/ *nm inv* (literary) home, dwelling.

logistique /lɔʒistik/ *nf* logistics.

logo /lɔgo/ *nm* logo.

loi /lwa/ *nf* **1** law; **voter une ~** to pass a law; **2 la ~** the law; **enfreindre la ~** to break the law; **d'après la ~ française** under French law; **tomber sous le coup de la ~** to be or constitute an offence[GB]; **faire la ~** (figurative) to lay down the law; **3** rule; law; **la ~ du milieu** the law of the underworld; **~ du silence** code of silence; conspiracy of silence; **c'est la ~ des séries** things always happen in a row.

■ **~ d'amnistie** *act granting amnesty to some offenders*; **~ communautaire** community law; **~ divine** divine law; **~ de la jungle** law of the jungle.

loin /lwɛ̃/ **I** *adv* **1** a long way, far (away); **c'est ~** it's a long way; **c'est trop ~** it's too far; **il habite plus ~** he lives further or farther away; **du plus ~ qu'il m'aperçut** as soon as he saw me; **voir plus ~** (in text) see below; **plus ~ dans le roman** at a later point in the novel; **2** (in time) **tout cela est bien ~** that was all a long time ago; **aussi ~ que je me souvienne** as far back as I can remember; **l'été n'est plus très ~ maintenant** summer isn't far off now; **le temps n'est pas si ~ où**... it's not so long since...; **3** (figurative) **de là à dire qu'il est incompétent, il n'y a pas ~** that comes close to saying he's incompetent; **tu sembles si ~** you seem so distant; you seem miles away; **il n'est pas bête, ~ s'en faut!** he's not stupid, far from it!; **ça va beaucoup plus ~** it goes much further; **votre fille est brillante, elle ira ~** your daughter is brilliant, she'll go far.

II loin de *phr* **1** (in space) far from; **est-ce encore ~ d'ici?** is it much further or farther from here?; **2** (in time) far from; **il n'est pas ~ de 11 heures** it's not far off 11 o'clock; **cela ne fait pas ~ de quatre ans que je suis ici** I've been here for almost four years now; **3** (figurative) far from, a long way from; **je me sens ~ de tout cela** I feel detached from all that; **~ de moi cette idée!** nothing could be further from my mind!; **avec l'imprimante, il faut compter pas ~ de 10000 francs** if you include the printer, you're talking about 10,000 francs or thereabouts.

III de loin *phr* from a distance; **je ne vois pas très bien de ~** I can't see very well at a distance; **c'est de ~ ton meilleur roman** it's by far your best novel.

IV au loin *phr* **(tout) au ~** (far away) in the distance.

V de loin en loin *phr* **1 on pouvait voir des maisons de ~ en ~** you could see houses scattered here and there; **les arbres étaient plantés de ~ en ~** the trees were planted at wide intervals; **2** every now and then.

IDIOMS **~ des yeux, ~ du cœur** (Proverb) out of sight, out of mind.

lointain, **~e** /lwɛ̃tɛ̃, ɛn/ **I** *adj* **1** [*country, past*] distant; **2** [*link, connection*] remote; [*cause*] indirect; **3** [*person, manner*] distant.

II *nm* background; **dans le ~** [*see, hear*] in the distance.

loir /lwaʀ/ *nm* (edible) dormouse.

loisir /lwaziʀ/ *nm* **1** spare time; **(tout) à ~** at (great) leisure; **2 avoir tout ~ de faire** to have plenty of time to do; **3** leisure activity.

lombaire /lɔ̃bɛʀ/ *nf* lumbar vertebra.

londonien, **-ienne** /lɔ̃dɔnjɛ̃, ɛn/ *adj* of London.

Londres /lɔ̃dʀ/ *pr n* London.

long, **longue** /lɔ̃, lɔ̃g/ **I** *adj* **1** long; **plus/trop ~ de deux mètres** two metres[GB] longer/too long; **au ~ cours** [*voyage, navigation*] ocean; [*captain*] fully-licensed; **2** [*moment, life, journey, film, silence*] long; [*friendship*] long-standing; **être ~ (à faire)** [*person*] to be slow (to do); **je ne serai pas ~** I won't be long; I will be brief; **être en longue maladie** to be on extended sick leave; **il guérira, mais ce sera ~** he will get better, but it's going to take a long time; **être ~ à la détente**○ to be slow on the uptake○; **pendant de longues heures** for hours; **3** [*vowel*] long.

II *adv* **1 en dire ~/trop ~/plus ~** to say a lot/too much/more (**sur qch/qn** about sth/sb); **je pourrais t'en dire ~ sur lui** I could tell you a thing or two about him; **2 s'habiller ~** to wear longer skirts.

III *nm* **1 un câble de six mètres de ~** a cable six metres[GB] long, a six-metre[GB] long cable; **en ~** [*cut, split*] lengthwise; **en ~ et en large** [*tell*] in great detail; **marcher de ~ en large** to pace up and down; **en ~, en large et en travers**○ [*tell*] at great length; **le ~ du mur** along the wall; up or down the wall; **tomber de tout son ~** to fall flat (on one's face).

IV à la longue *phr* in the end, eventually.

■ **~ métrage** feature-length film.

long-courrier, *pl* **~s** /lɔ̃kuʀje/ *nm* **1** ocean-going ship; **2** long-haul aircraft.

longe /lɔ̃ʒ/ *nf* (for horse) tether; rein.

longer /lɔ̃ʒe/ [13] *vtr* **1** [*person, train*] to go along [*forest, coast*]; to follow [*river*]; [*boat*] to sail along [*coast*]; **2** [*garden, road*] to run alongside [*lake, field*].

longévité /lɔ̃ʒevite/ *nf* longevity.

longiligne /lɔ̃ʒiliɲ/ *adj* lanky, rangy.

longitude /lɔ̃ʒityd/ *nf* longitude.

longitudinal, **~e**, *mpl* **-aux** /lɔ̃ʒitydinal, o/ *adj* longitudinal, lengthwise.

longtemps /lɔ̃tɑ̃/ *adv* [*wait, sleep*] (for) a long time; **il t'a fallu ~?** did it take you long?; **il n'en a plus pour ~** (ill person) he won't last much longer; **~ avant/après** long before/after; **je peux le garder plus ~?** can I keep it a bit longer?; **il n'y a pas ~ qu'il travaille ici** he hasn't worked or been working here long; **ça fait ~ que tu attends?** have you been waiting long?; **il y a** or **ça fait ~ qu'il n'a pas téléphoné** he hasn't phoned for ages○; **il est mort depuis ~** he died a long time ago; **il n'y a pas si ~ c'était encore possible** it was still possible until quite recently.

longue ▸ **long** I, IV.

longuement /lɔ̃gmɑ̃/ *adv* [*hesitate, talk*] for a long time; [*explain, interview*] at length; **j'y ai ~ réfléchi** I've given it a lot of thought.

longueur /lɔ̃gœʀ/ **I** *nf* **1** length; **la maison est tout en ~** the house is long and narrow; **2** (in race) length; **avoir une ~ d'avance sur qn** (Sport) to be one length ahead of sb; (figurative) to be ahead of sb; **3** (Sport) (in swimming) length; **faire des ~s** to do lengths; **le saut en ~** the long or broad (US) jump; **4** length; **traîner en ~** [*film, book*] to go on forever.

II longueurs *nf pl* (in film, book, speech) overlong passages.

III à longueur de *phr* **à ~ de journée** all day long; **à ~ d'année** all year round; **à ~ de temps** all the time; **à ~ d'émissions** programme[GB] after programme[GB].

■ **~ d'onde** wavelength.

longue-vue, *pl* **longues-vues** /lɔ̃gvy/ *nf* telescope.

looping /lupiŋ/ *nm* loop; **faire un ~** to loop the loop.

lopin /lɔpɛ̃/ *nm* **~ (de terre)** patch of land, plot (of land).

loquace /lɔkas/ *adj* talkative, loquacious.

loque /lɔk/ **I** *nf* (person) **~ (humaine)** (human) wreck.

II loques *nf pl* rags; **tomber en ~s** to fall to pieces.

loquet /lɔkɛ/ *nm* latch.

lorgner○ /lɔʀɲe/ [1] *vtr* to give [sb] the eye○ [*person*]; to cast longing glances at [*jewel, cake*]; to have one's eye on [*inheritance, job*].

lorgnette /lɔʀɲɛt/ *nf* **1** opera-glasses; **2** spyglass.

lorgnon /lɔʀɲɔ̃/ *nm* **1** lorgnette; **2** pince-nez.

lorrain, **~e** /lɔʀɛ̃, ɛn/ **I** *adj* of Lorraine.

II *nm* Lorraine dialect.

lors: **lors de** /lɔʀ/ *phr* **1** during; **2** at the time of.

lorsque (**lorsqu'** *before vowel or mute h*) /lɔʀsk(ə)/ *conj* when.

losange /lɔzɑ̃ʒ/ *nm* rhomb, lozenge; **en ~** diamond-shaped.

lot /lo/ *nm* **1** (of inheritance, misfortune) share; (of land) plot; **2** (in lottery) prize; **gagner le gros ~** to hit the jackpot; **3** (of objects for sale) (gen) batch; (at auction) lot; **4** (of person) **être au-dessus du ~** to be above the average; **5** (in computing) batch; **6** fate, lot.

loterie /lɔtʀi/ *nf* raffle; (in fair) tombola (GB), raffle (US); (large scale) lottery; **cet examen est une vraie ~** this exam is a real game of chance.

loti, **~e** /lɔti/ *adj* **bien/mal ~** well/badly off; **mieux/plus mal ~** best/worst off.

lotion /losjɔ̃/ *nf* lotion; **~ après rasage** aftershave (lotion).

lotissement /lɔtismɑ̃/ *nm* housing estate (GB), subdivision (US).

loto /lɔto/ *nm* lotto; **le ~ national** national lottery.

lotte /lɔt/ *nf* monkfish, angler fish; (freshwater) burbot.

lotus /lɔtys/ *nm inv* lotus.

louable /luabl/ *adj* [*intention, effort*] commendable, praiseworthy.

louage /luaʒ/ *nm* **voiture de ~** rented car (GB), rental car (US).

louange /luɑ̃ʒ/ *nf* praise; **chanter les ~s de qn/de qch** to sing sb's/sth's praises.

louche /luʃ/ **I** *adj* [*person, past, affair*] shady; [*place*] seedy.

II *nf* ladle; ladleful.

loucher /luʃe/ [1] **I** *vi* to have a squint.

II loucher sur○ *v+prep* **~ sur les filles/gâteaux** to eye the girls/cakes.

louer /lue/ [1] *vtr* **1** [*owner, landlord*] to let (GB), to rent out [*house*]; to hire out [*premises*]; to rent out [*equipment, film*]; **'à ~'** 'for rent', 'to let' (GB); **2** [*tenant, hirer*] to rent [*house*]; to hire [*room*]; to rent [*equipment, film*]; **3** to hire [*staff*]; **~ les services de qn** to hire the services of sb; **4** to praise; **Dieu soit loué** thank God.

loufoque○ /lufɔk/ *adj* crazy○.

louis /lwi/ *nm inv* (coin) louis; **~ d'or** (gold) louis.

loukoum /lukum/ *nm* Turkish delight.

loup /lu/ *nm* **1** wolf; **le grand méchant ~** the big bad wolf; **à pas de ~** stealthily; **crier au ~** to cry wolf; **2 ~ (de mer)** (sea) bass; **3** domino, mask.

■ **(vieux) ~ de mer** old salt, old tar.

IDIOMS **avoir une faim de ~** to be ravenous; **être connu comme le ~ blanc** to be known to everybody; **hurler avec les ~s** to follow the herd or crowd; **se jeter dans la gueule du ~** to stick one's head in the lion's mouth; **elle a vu le ~** (humorous) she's lost her virginity; **les ~s ne se mangent pas entre eux** (Proverb) (there is) honour[GB] among thieves; **quand on parle du ~ (on en voit la queue)** (Proverb) speak of the devil; **l'homme est un ~ pour l'homme** (Proverb) dog eat dog.

loupe /lup/ *nf* magnifying glass; **examiner qch à la ~** to look at sth through a magnifying glass; (figurative) to put sth under the microscope.

louper○ /lupe/ [1] **I** *vtr* **1** to miss [*train, opportunity, visitor*]; **la prochaine fois, ils ne te louperont pas** next time they'll get you; **il n'en loupe pas une** he's always opening his big mouth; **2** to flunk○ [*exam*]; to screw up○ [*sauce, piece of work*].

II *vi* **j'avais dit que ça se casserait, ça n'a pas loupé** I said it would break, and sure enough it did; **tu vas tout faire ~** you'll mess everything up.

loup-garou, *pl* **loups-garous** /lugaʀu/ *nm* werewolf.

lourd, **~e**[1] /luʀ, luʀd/ **I** *adj* **1** [*person, object, metal*] heavy; **2** [*stomach, head, steps*] heavy; [*gesture*] clumsy; **il a les yeux ~s de sommeil** his eyes are heavy with sleep; **3** [*meal, food*] heavy; [*wine*] heady; **~ à digérer** heavy on the stomach; **4** [*hair*] thick; **5** [*equipment, weapons*] heavy; **6** [*fine, taxation*] heavy; **7** [*defeat, responsibility*] heavy; [*mistake*] serious; **8** [*administration, structure*] unwieldy; [*staff numbers*] large; **9** [*person, animal*] ungainly; [*body, object, architecture*] heavy; [*building*] cumbersome, ponderous; **10** [*person*] oafish; [*voice*] thick; [*joke*] flat; [*style*] clumsy; **11** [*atmosphere, silence*] heavy; [*heat*] sultry;

12 être ~ de dangers to be fraught with danger; **être ~ de menaces** to be charged with menace.

II *adv* **1 peser ~** to weigh heavy; **peser/ne pas peser ~** (figurative) to carry a lot of/not to carry very much weight; **2** (of weather) **il fait ~** it's close; **3**° **pas ~** not a lot, not much; **dix personnes, ça ne fait pas ~** ten people, that's not a lot.

IDIOMS **avoir le cœur ~** to have a heavy heart; **avoir la main ~e** to be heavy-handed; **avoir la main ~e avec le sel/le parfum** to overdo the salt/the perfume.

lourdaud, **~e** /luʀdo, od/ *adj* [*person*] oafish; [*mind*] dull; [*speech*] clumsy.

lourde[2] /luʀd/ *adj f* ▶ **lourd** I.

lourdement /luʀdəmɑ̃/ *adv* **1** heavily; **se tromper ~** to be gravely mistaken; **2 marcher ~** to walk clumsily; **insister ~ sur** to keep going on about.

lourdeur /luʀdœʀ/ *nf* **1** (of organization) complexity; **2** heaviness; **avoir des ~s d'estomac** to feel bloated; **3** (of style) clumsiness; (in a text) clumsy expression; **4** (of prison sentence) heaviness; **5** weight; **6** (of person) oafishness; (of joke) poorness; (of architecture) ungainliness; **7** (of weather) closeness; (of atmosphere) heaviness.

loutre /lutʀ/ *nf* **1** otter; **2** otterskin.

louve /luv/ *nf* she-wolf.

louveteau, *pl* **~x** /luvto/ *nm* (Zool) wolf cub.

louvoyer /luvwaje/ [23] *vi* **1** [*ship*] to beat to windward, to tack; **2** (figurative) to manoeuvre (GB), to maneuver (US); (in argument) to beat around the bush.

lover: **se lover** /lɔve/ [1] *v refl* (+ *v être*) [*snake*] to coil itself up; [*person*] to curl up.

loyal, **~e**, *mpl* **-aux** /lwajal, o/ *adj* **1** [*friend*] true; [*servant*] loyal, faithful; **2** [*procedure, conduct*] honest; [*competition, game*] fair.

loyalement /lwajalmɑ̃/ *adv* faithfully, fairly, honestly.

loyaliste /lwajalist/ *adj, nmf* loyalist.

loyauté /lwajote/ *nf* **1** loyalty; **2** honesty.

loyer /lwaje/ *nm* rent; **~ de 3 000 francs** rent of 3,000 francs.

lubie /lybi/ *nf* whim; **avoir des ~s** to have whims.

lubrifiant, **~e** /lybʀifjɑ̃, ɑ̃t/ *nm* lubricant.

lubrifier /lybʀifje/ [2] *vtr* to lubricate.

lubrique /lybʀik/ *adj* [*person*] lecherous; [*look, dance*] lewd.

lucarne /lykaʀn/ *nf* (small) window; (in roof) skylight.

lucide /lysid/ *adj* [*person, policy*] clear-sighted; (Med) lucid; [*analysis*] lucid.

lucidité /lysidite/ *nf* **1** lucidity; **moments de ~** lucid moments; **2** (of person) clear-headedness; (of mind) clarity; **juger en toute ~** to judge without any illusions.

luciole /lysjɔl/ *nf* firefly.

lucratif, **-ive** /lykʀatif, iv/ *adj* lucrative.

ludique /lydik/ *adj* [*activity*] play.

ludothèque /lydɔtɛk/ *nf* toy library.

luette /lyɛt/ *nf* uvula.

lueur /lɥœʀ/ *nf* **1** (faint) light; **les ~s de la ville** the city lights; **pas la moindre ~ d'espoir** not the faintest glimmer of hope; **à la ~ d'une bougie** by candlelight; **à la ~ des événements d'hier** in the light of yesterday's events; **2** glow; **les dernières ~s du soleil couchant** the dying glow of the sunset; **3** gleam, flash.

luge /lyʒ/ *nf* **1** toboggan (GB), sled (US); **2** (sport) luge.

lugubre /lygybʀ/ *adj* [*landscape, thought*] gloomy; [*sound, singing*] mournful.

lui /lɥi/ *pron* **I** *pron m* **1** he; **elle lit, ~ regarde la télévision** she's reading, he's watching TV; **~ seul a le droit de parler** he alone has the right to talk; **~ c'est ~ et moi c'est moi**° he and I are different; **2** him; **à cause de ~** because of him; **je les vois plus souvent que ~** I see them more often than he does; I see them more often than I see him; **ce sont des amis à ~** they're friends of his; **il n'a pas encore de voiture à ~** he doesn't have his own car yet; **c'est à ~** it's his, it belongs to him; it's his turn; **c'est à ~ de choisir** it's up to him to choose.

II *pron mf* it; **le parti lance un appel, apportez-~ votre soutien** the party is launching an appeal—give it your support; **l'Espagne a signé, le Portugal, ~, n'a pas encore donné son accord** Spain has signed while Portugal hasn't yet agreed.

III *pron f* her; **je ~ ai annoncé la nouvelle** I told her the news.

lui-même /lɥimɛm/ *pron* **1** (referring to person) himself; **'M. Greiner?'—'~'** (on phone) 'Mr Greiner?'—'speaking'; **2** (referring to object, idea, concept) itself.

luire /lɥiʀ/ [69] *vi* [*sun, polished surface*] to shine; [*embers*] to glow; **~ de sueur** to glisten with sweat; **leur regard luisait de colère** their eyes blazed with anger.

luisant, **~e** /lɥizɑ̃, ɑ̃t/ *adj* [*polished surface*] shining; [*wet surface*] glistening; [*eyes*] gleaming.

lumbago /lœ̃bago/ *nm* back pain.

lumière /lymjɛʀ/ **I** *nf* **1** light; **~ naturelle/électrique** natural/electric light; **la ~ du soleil** sunlight; **la ~ du jour** daylight; **il y a une ~ très particulière dans cette région** there's a very special quality to the light in this region; **les ~ de la ville** the city lights; **à la ~ d'une chandelle** by candlelight; **2** (figurative) light; **à la ~ des récents événements** in the light of recent events; **faire (toute) la ~ sur une affaire** to bring the truth about a matter to light; **3** (person) **ce n'est pas une ~** he'll never set the world on fire.

II lumières *nf pl* **1** (of vehicle) lights; **2**° **j'ai besoin de vos ~s** I need to pick your brains; **aider qn de ses ~s** to give sb the benefit of one's wisdom.

Lumières /lymjɛʀ/ *nf pl* **le siècle des ~** the Age of Enlightenment.

luminaire /lyminɛʀ/ *nm* light (fitting).

lumineux, **-euse** /lyminø, øz/ *adj* **1** luminous; **panneau ~** electronic display (board); **enseigne lumineuse** neon sign; **rayon/point ~** ray/spot of light; **2 idée lumineuse** brilliant idea, brainwave○; **3** [*complexion, smile, gaze*] radiant.

luminosité /lyminozite/ *nf* brightness, luminosity.

lump /lœ̃mp/ *nm* lumpfish; **œufs de ~** lumpfish roe.

lunaire /lynɛʀ/ *adj* lunar.

lunatique /lynatik/ *nmf* moody person.

lunch /lœ̃ʃ/ *nm* buffet (lunch); buffet (supper).

lundi /lœ̃di/ *nm* Monday; **le ~ noir** Black Monday.

lune /lyn/ *nf* moon; **pleine ~** full moon; **nuit sans ~** moonless night.
■ **~ de miel** honeymoon; **~ rousse** ≈ April moon.
IDIOMS **être dans la ~**○ to have one's head in the clouds; **avoir l'air de tomber de la ~** to look blank; **demander la ~**○ to cry for the moon; **promettre la ~**○ to promise the earth or the moon; **décrocher la ~** to do the impossible.

luné○, **~e** /lyne/ *adj* **bien ~** cheerful; **mal ~** grumpy.

lunette /lynɛt/ **I** *nf* lavatory seat.
II lunettes *nf pl* **1** glasses; **2** (protective) goggles; **~s de natation** swimming goggles.
■ **~ arrière** (Aut) rear window; **~s noires** dark glasses; **~s de soleil** sunglasses.

lunule /lynyl/ *nf* (on nail) half-moon.

lurette○ /lyʀɛt/ *nf* **il y a belle ~ qu'elle a tout dépensé** she spent it all ages○ ago.

luron /lyʀɔ̃/ *nm* fellow; **gai** or **joyeux** or **sacré ~** jolly fellow.

lustre /lystʀ/ **I** *nm* **1** (gen) (decorative) ceiling light; (made of glass) chandelier; **2** sheen; **3** (of place, institution) prestigious image; **donner un nouveau ~ à** to give fresh appeal to.
II lustres○ *nm pl* **depuis des ~s** for a long time, for ages○.

lustré, **~e** /lystʀe/ *adj* **1** glossy; (through wear) shiny; **2** [*fabric*] glazed.

lustrer /lystʀe/ [1] *vtr* to polish [*shoes, mirror*]; to make [sth] shine [*hair*].

luth /lyt/ *nm* **1** (Mus) lute; **2** (Zool) leatherback.

lutin /lytɛ̃/ *nm* **1** goblin; **2** (child) imp; **petit ~** little imp.

lutte /lyt/ *nf* **1** conflict; struggle; **~ d'influence** power struggle; **livrer à une ~ sans merci à qn** to engage in a ruthless battle against sb; **2** fight; struggle; **la ~ contre le cancer** the fight against cancer; **3** (Sport) wrestling.
■ **~ armée** armed conflict; **~ de classes** class war; **~ d'intérêts** clash of interests.

lutter /lyte/ [1] *vi* **1** [*people, country*] to struggle; **~ contre qn** to fight against sb; **2** [*person, group*] to fight; **~ contre** to fight [*crime, pollution, unemployment*]; to fight against [*violence*]; to contend with [*noise, bad weather*]; **aider le malade à ~ contre la maladie** to help the sick person fight back; **Louis luttait contre le sommeil** Louis was struggling to stay awake.

lutteur, **-euse** /lytœʀ, øz/ *nm,f* **1** (gen) fighter; **2** (Sport) wrestler.

luxation /lyksasjɔ̃/ *nf* (Med) dislocation.

luxe /lyks/ *nm* luxury; **s'offrir le ~ de faire** to afford the luxury of doing; (figurative) to give oneself the satisfaction of doing; **il peut se payer ce ~** he can afford it; **je l'ai nettoyé et ce n'était pas du ~**○ I gave it a much needed clean; **avoir des goûts de ~** to have expensive tastes.

Luxembourg /lyksɑ̃buʀ/ *pr nm* Luxembourg.

luxembourgeois, **~e** /lyksɑ̃buʀʒwa, az/ **I** *adj* of Luxembourg.
II *nm*: *German dialect spoken in Luxembourg.*

Luxembourgeois, **~e** /lyksɑ̃buʀʒwa, az/ *nm,f* **1** native of Luxembourg; **2** inhabitant of Luxembourg.

luxer /lykse/ [1] **I** *vtr* to dislocate.
II se luxer *v refl* (+ *v être*) **se ~ l'épaule** to dislocate one's shoulder.

luxueux, **-euse** /lyksɥø, øz/ *adj* [*apartment*] luxurious; [*magazine*] glossy.

luxure /lyksyʀ/ *nf* lust.

luxuriant, **~e** /lyksyʀjɑ̃, ɑ̃t/ *adj* luxuriant.

luzerne /lyzɛʀn/ *nf* alfalfa, lucerne (GB).

lycée /lise/ *nm* secondary school (*school preparing students aged 15–18 for the baccalaureate*).

lycéen, **-éenne** /liseɛ̃, ɛn/ *nm,f* secondary school student.

lymphatique /lɛ̃fatik/ *adj* **1** lethargic; **2** (Anat) lymphatic.

lymphe /lɛ̃f/ *nf* lymph.

lyncher /lɛ̃ʃe/ [1] *vtr* to lynch.

lynx /lɛ̃ks/ *nm inv* lynx.
IDIOMS **avoir un œil** or **des yeux de ~** to have very keen eyesight.

lyonnais, **~e**[1] /ljɔnɛ, ɛz/ *adj* of Lyons.

lyonnaise[2] /ljɔnɛz/ *nf* **1** (Culin) **à la ~** à la lyonnaise; **2** *regional game of boules.*

lyophiliser /ljɔfilize/ [1] *vtr* to freeze-dry.

lyre /liʀ/ *nf* lyre.

lyrique /liʀik/ *adj* **1** (Mus) [*song, composer*] operatic; [*singer, season*] opera; **opéra ~** lyric opera; **2** [*poetry, poet*] lyric; [*content, tone*] lyrical.

lyrisme /liʀism/ *nm* lyricism; **avec ~** lyrically.

lys /lis/ *nm inv* lily.

Mm

m, M /ɛm/ *nm inv* **1** m, M; **2** (*written abbr* = **mètre**) **30 m** 30 m.
m' ▶ **me**.
M. (*written abbr* = **Monsieur**) Mr; **~ Bon** Mr Bon.
ma ▶ **mon**.
MA /ɛma/ *nmf* (*abbr* = **maître auxiliaire**) *secondary teacher without tenure*.
macabre /makabʀ/ *adj* macabre.
macadam /makadam/ *nm* tarmac®.
macaque /makak/ *nm* **1** macaque; **2**○ ugly man.
macaron /makaʀɔ̃/ *nm* **1** macaroon; **2** lapel badge; sticker.
macédoine /masedwan/ *nf* mixed diced vegetables.
macérer /maseʀe/ [14] *vi* [*plant, fruit, vegetable*] to soak, to steep; [*meat*] to marinate; [*gherkin*] to pickle; **faire ~** to steep, to soak.
mâche /mɑʃ/ *nf* corn salad, lamb's lettuce.
mâcher /mɑʃe/ [1] *vtr* to chew.
IDIOMS **~ la besogne** or **le travail à qn** to break the back of the work for sb; **il ne mâche pas ses mots** he doesn't mince his words.
machette /maʃɛt/ *nf* machete.
machiavélique /makjavelik/ *adj* Machiavellian.
machin○ /maʃɛ̃/ *nm* **1** thing, thingummy○, whatsit○; **qu'est-ce que c'est que ce ~-là?** what on earth's that?; **2** old fogey.
Machin○, **~e** /maʃɛ̃, in/ *nm,f* what's-his-name○/what's-her-name○.
machinal, **~e**, *mpl* **-aux** /maʃinal, o/ *adj* [*gesture, reaction*] mechanical; **jeter un coup d'œil ~** to glance absent-mindedly.
machinalement /maʃinalmɑ̃/ *adv* mechanically, without thinking.
machination /maʃinasjɔ̃/ *nf* plot.
machine /maʃin/ *nf* **1** machine; **taper à la ~** to type; **coudre à la ~** to machine-sew; **faire deux ~s**○ **(de linge)** to do two loads of washing; **2** (Naut) engine; **faire ~ arrière** to go astern; (figurative) to back-pedal.
■ **~ à calculer** calculating machine; **~ à coudre** sewing machine; **~ à écrire** typewriter; **~ à laver** washing machine; **~ à laver la vaisselle** dishwasher; **~ à sous** slot machine, one-armed bandit; **~ à vapeur** steam engine.
machine-outil, *pl* **machines-outils** /maʃinuti/ *nf* machine tool.
machinerie /maʃinʀi/ *nf* **1** machinery; **2** machine room; (Naut) engine room.
machiniste /maʃinist/ *nmf* **1** stagehand; scene shifter; **2** driver.
machisme /ma(t)ʃism/ *nm* male chauvinism.
machiste /ma(t)ʃist/ *adj, nm* male chauvinist.
mâchoire /mɑʃwaʀ/ *nf* jaw.
IDIOMS **bâiller/rire à s'en décrocher la ~** to yawn/to laugh one's head off.
mâchonner /mɑʃɔne/ [1] *vtr* to chew.
mâchouiller○ /mɑʃuje/ [1] *vtr* to chew (on).
maçon /masɔ̃/ *nm* bricklayer; builder; mason.
maçonnerie /masɔnʀi/ *nf* building; bricklaying; masonry-work.
maçonnique /masɔnik/ *adj* masonic.
maculer /makyle/ [1] *vtr* to smudge (**de** with); **~ qch de sang/boue** to spatter sth with blood/mud.
madame, *pl* **mesdames** /madam, medam/ *nf* **1** (addressing a woman whose name you do not know) **Madame** (in letter) Dear Madam; **bonsoir ~** good evening!; **occupez-vous de ~** (in shop) could you attend to this lady, please?; **mesdames et messieurs bonsoir** good evening ladies and gentlemen; **2** (addressing a woman whose name you know, for example Bon) Mrs, Ms; **bonjour, ~** good morning, Mrs Bon; **Chère Madame** (in letter) Dear Mrs Bon or Ms Bon; **3** (polite form of address) **oui, Madame** yes, madam.
Madeleine /madlɛn/ *pr n* Madeleine.
IDIOMS **pleurer comme une ~** to cry one's eyes out.
mademoiselle, *pl* **mesdemoiselles** /madmwazɛl, medmwazɛl/ *nf* **1** (addressing a woman whose name you do not know) **Mademoiselle** (in letter) Dear Madam; **bonjour, ~** good morning; **occupez-vous de ~** (in shop) could you attend to this lady, please?; **mesdames, mesdemoiselles, messieurs** ladies and gentlemen; **2** (addressing a woman whose name you know, for example Bon) Miss, Ms; **bonjour, ~** good morning, Miss Bon; **Chère Mademoiselle** (in letter) Dear Miss Bon or Ms Bon; ; **3** (polite form of address) **oui, Mademoiselle** yes, madam.
madère /madɛʀ/ *nm* madeira.
madone /madɔn/ *nf* madonna.
madras /madʀas/ *nm inv* madras cotton.
madrier /madʀije/ *nm* beam.
maestria /maɛstʀija/ *nf* brilliance, panache.
maf(f)ia /mafja/ *nf* mafia; **la Mafia** the Mafia.
maf(f)ieux, **-ieuse** /mafjø, øz/ *adj* mafia.
maf(f)ioso, *pl* **-iosi** /mafjozo, zi/ *nm* mafioso.
magasin /magazɛ̃/ *nm* **1** shop, store; **grand ~** department store; **faire les ~s** to go shopping; **2** warehouse; **avoir en ~** to have in stock.
magasinier, **-ière** /magazinje, ɛʀ/ *nm,f* **1** stock controller; **2** warehouse keeper.
magazine /magazin/ *nm* magazine.
mage /maʒ/ *nm* magus; **les rois ~s** the (Three) Wise Men.

maghrébin, **~e** /magʀebɛ̃, in/ *adj* North African, Maghrebi.

magicien, **-ienne** /maʒisjɛ̃, ɛn/ *nm,f* **1** magician/enchantress; **2** conjuror; **3** (figurative) wizard.

magie /maʒi/ *nf* **1** magic; **2** conjuring.

magique /maʒik/ *adj* **1** magic; **formule ~** magic words; **2** (figurative) magical.

magistère /maʒistɛʀ/ *nm*: *high-level University degree.*

magistral, **~e**, *mpl* **-aux** /maʒistʀal, o/ *adj* **1** brilliant; **réussir un coup ~** to bring off a masterstroke; **2** magisterial; **3** (humorous) [*telling off*] tremendous.

magistrat /maʒistʀa/ *nm* magistrate.

magistrature /maʒistʀatyʀ/ *nf* **1** magistracy; **2** public office.

magma /magma/ *nm* **1** magma; **2** (figurative) jumble.

magnanime /maɲanim/ *adj* magnanimous.

magnat /maɲa/ *nm* magnate, tycoon.

magnésie /maɲezi/ *nf* magnesia.

magnétique /maɲetik/ *adj* magnetic.

magnétiser /maɲetize/ [1] *vtr* to magnetize; (figurative) to hypnotize.

magnétiseur, **-euse** /maɲetizœʀ, øz/ *nm,f* healer.

magnétisme /maɲetism/ *nm* magnetism.

magnéto○ /maɲeto/ *nm*: *abbr* = **magnétophone**.

magnétophone /maɲetɔfɔn/ *nm* tape recorder.

magnétoscope /maɲetɔskɔp/ *nm* video recorder, VCR.

magnificence /maɲifisɑ̃s/ *nf* magnificence.

magnifier /maɲifje/ [1] *vtr* **1** to idealize; **2** to glorify.

magnifique /maɲifik/ *adj* magnificent; gorgeous.

magnitude /maɲityd/ *nf* (of earthquake) strength.

magnolia /maɲɔlja/ *nm* magnolia (tree).

magot○ /mago/ *nm* pile○ (of money).

magouille○ /maguj/ *nf* **1** wangling○, fiddling○; **2** trick; **~s politiques** political skulduggery; **~s électorales** election rigging.

magouiller○ /maguje/ [1] *vi* to wangle○, to fiddle○.

magouilleur, **-euse** /magujœʀ, øz/ *nm,f* fiddler○, cheat.

magret /magʀɛ/ *nm* **~ de canard** duck breast.

Mahomet /maɔme/ *pr n* Mohammed.

mai /mɛ/ *nm* May; **le premier ~** May Day.

maigre /mɛgʀ/ **I** *adj* **1** [*person*] thin; **2** [*meat*] lean; [*cheese*] low-fat; **3** [*day*] without meat; **faire** or **manger ~** to abstain from meat; **4** [*talents, savings*] meagre[GB]; [*applause*] scant; **5** [*lawn, hair*] sparse; **un ~ filet d'eau** a trickle of water.

II *nmf* thin man/woman; **c'est une fausse ~** she looks thinner than she is.

IDIOMS **~ comme un clou**○ or **un coucou**○ as thin as a rake.

maigrement /mɛgʀəmɑ̃/ *adv* [*paid*] poorly.

maigreur /mɛgʀœʀ/ *nf* **1** thinness; **d'une grande ~** very thin; **2** meagreness[GB].

maigrichon, **-onne** /mɛgʀiʃɔ̃, ɔn/ *adj* skinny, scrawny.

maigrir /mɛgʀiʀ/ [3] *vi* to lose weight; **pour ~** [*pill*] slimming (GB), reducing (US).

mail /maj/ *nm* **1** mall; **2** pall-mall.

mailing /mɛliŋ/ *nm* (controversial) **1** direct mail advertising; **2** mail shot; **3** mailing pack.

maille /maj/ *nf* **1** stitch; **une ~ qui file** (in tights) a ladder; **2** mesh; **passer à travers les ~s** to slip through the net; **3** (in fence) link.

IDIOMS **avoir ~ à partir avec qn** to have a brush with sb.

maillet /majɛ/ *nm* mallet.

maillon /majɔ̃/ *nm* link; **~ de la chaîne** a link in the chain.

maillot /majo/ *nm* **1 ~ (de corps)** vest (GB), undershirt (US); **2** (of footballer) shirt; (of cyclist) jersey; **3** swimsuit.

■ **~ de bain** swimsuit; **le ~ jaune** the leader in the Tour de France.

main /mɛ̃/ *nf* **1** hand; **se donner** or **se tenir la ~** to hold hands; **saluer qn de la ~** to wave at sb; **la ~ dans la ~** hand in hand; **haut les ~s!** hands up!; **demander la ~ de qn** to ask for sb's hand in marriage; **avoir qch bien en ~(s)** to hold sth firmly; (figurative) to have sth well in hand; **si tu lèves la ~ sur elle** if you lay a finger on her; **à la ~** [*sew*] by hand; [*adjust*] manually; **fait ~** handmade; **vol à ~ armée** armed robbery; **donner un coup de ~ à qn** to give sb a hand; **2 une ~ secourable** a helping hand; **une ~ criminelle** someone with criminal intentions; **3 avoir qch sous la ~** to have sth to hand; **cela m'est tombé sous la ~** I just happened to come across it; **mettre la ~ sur qch** to get one's hands on sth; **je n'arrive pas à mettre la ~ dessus** I can't lay my hands on it; **je l'ai eu entre les ~s mais** I did have it but; **être entre les ~s de qn** [*power*] to be in sb's hands; **prendre en ~s** to take [sth/sb] in hand; **à ne pas mettre entre toutes les ~s** [*book*] not for general reading; **tomber entre les ~s de qn** to fall into sb's hands; **les ~s vides** empty-handed; **je le lui ai remis en ~s propres** I gave it to him/her in person; **de la ~ à la ~** [*sell*] privately; [*be paid*] cash (in hand); **4 écrit de la ~ du président** written by the president himself; **de ma plus belle ~** in my best handwriting; **5 avoir le coup de ~** to have the knack; **se faire la ~** to practise[GB]; **6** (in cards) hand; deal; **7 à ~ droite/gauche** on the right/left.

■ **~ courante** handrail.

IDIOMS **j'en mettrais ma ~ au feu** or **à couper** I'd swear to it; **d'une ~ de fer** with an iron rod; **il n'y est pas allé de ~ morte**○! he didn't pull his punches!; **avoir la ~ leste** to be always ready with a slap; **laisser les ~s libres à qn** to give sb a free hand or rein; **faire ~ basse sur** to help oneself to [*goods*]; to take over [*market, country*]; **en venir aux ~s** to come to blows; **avoir la ~ heureuse** to be lucky; **mettre la dernière ~ à** to put the finishing touches to.

mainate /mɛnat/ *nm* mynah bird.

main-d'œuvre, *pl* **mains-d'œuvre** /mɛ̃dœvʀ/ *nf* labour[GB].

main-forte /mɛ̃fɔʀt/ *nf inv* **prêter ~ à qn** to come to sb's aid.

mainmise /mɛ̃miz/ *nf* seizure.

maint, **~e** /mɛ̃, mɛ̃t/ *det* many, many a; **à ~es reprises** many times.

maintenance /mɛ̃tnɑ̃s/ *nf* maintenance.

maintenant /mɛ̃t(ə)nɑ̃/ *adv* now; **commence dès ~** start straightaway; **~ les choses se font différemment** nowadays people do things differently.

maintenir /mɛ̃t(ə)niʀ/ [36] **I** *vtr* **1** to keep; to maintain; to keep up; **~ les prix** to keep prices stable; **~ qch debout** to keep sth upright; **2** to support [*wall, ankle*]; **3** to stand by [*decision*]; **~ que** to maintain that; **~ sa candidature** [*job candidate*] to go through with one's application; [*politician*] not to withdraw one's candidacy.

II se maintenir *v refl* (+ *v être*) [*trend*] to persist; [*price, situation*] to remain stable; [*weather*] to remain fair; [*political system*] to remain in force; [*currency*] to hold steady; [*person*] to remain in good health.

maintien /mɛ̃tjɛ̃/ *nm* **1** maintaining; **notre but c'est le ~ des prix** our aim is to keep prices stable; **assurer le ~ de l'ordre** to maintain order; **2** support; **3** deportment.

maire /mɛʀ/ *nm* mayor.

■ **~ adjoint** deputy mayor.

mairie /mɛʀi/ *nf* **1** town council (GB) or hall (US); **être élu à la ~ de** to be elected mayor of; **2** town hall.

mais /mɛ/ *conj* but; **incroyable ~ vrai** strange but true; **~ ne t'inquiète donc pas!** don't you worry about it!; **il est bête, ~ bête**○! he's so incredibly stupid!; **~ où est-il passé?** where on earth○ has he got to?; **~ vas-tu te taire!** can't you just shut up○?; **~, vous pleurez!** good heavens, you're crying!; **~ j'y pense** now that I come to think of it.

maïs /mais/ *nm inv* **1** maize (GB), corn (US); **2** sweetcorn; **épi de ~** corn on the cob.

maison /mɛzɔ̃/ **I** *adj inv* [*product*] home-made.

II *nf* **1** house; **2** home; **3** family, household; **faire la jeune fille de la ~** (humorous) to do the honours[GB]; **gens de ~** domestic staff; **c'est une ~ de fous!** it's a madhouse!; **4 ~ d'Orange** House of Orange; **5** firm; **avoir 15 ans de ~** to have been with the firm for 15 years; **'la ~ ne fait pas crédit'** 'no credit given'.

■ **~ d'arrêt** prison; **~ bourgeoise** *imposing town house*; **~ de campagne** house in the country; **~ close** brothel; **~ de correction** institution for young offenders; **~ de la culture** ≈ community arts centre[GB]; **~ des jeunes et de la culture, MJC** ≈ youth club; **~ de jeu** gaming house; **~ de maître** manor; **~ mère** headquarters; main branch; **~ normande** half-timbered house; **~ de passe** brothel; **~ de poupée** doll's (GB) or doll (US) house; **~ de retraite** old people's or retirement home; **~ de santé** nursing home; **la Maison Blanche** the White House.

IDIOMS **c'est gros comme une ~**○ it sticks out a mile; **avoir un pied dans la ~** to have a foot in the door; **c'est la ~ du bon Dieu** it's open house.

maisonnée /mɛzɔne/ *nf* household; family.

maître, **-esse**[1] /mɛtʀ, ɛs/ **I** *adj* **1 être ~ de soi** to have self-control; **être ~ chez soi** to be master in one's own house; **être ~ de son véhicule** to be in control of one's vehicle; **se rendre ~ d'une ville** to take over a city; **2** main; key; major.

II *nm,f* **1** teacher; **2** (of house) master/mistress; **3** (of animal) owner; **un chien et son ~** a dog and its master.

III *nm* **1** ruler; **être (le) seul ~ à bord** to be in sole command; **être le ~ du pays** to rule the country; **être son propre ~** to be one's own master/mistress; **régner en ~ absolu** to reign supreme (**sur** over); **2** master; **le ~ du suspense** the master of suspense; **être passé ~ dans l'art de qch/de faire** to be a past master of sth/at doing; **en ~** masterfully; **coup de ~** masterstroke; **3** Maître (*form of address given to members of the legal profession*).

■ **~ d'armes** (Sport) fencing instructor; **~ d'hôtel** maître d'hôtel (GB), maître d' (US); **~ d'œuvre** project manager; **~ à penser** mentor; **maîtresse femme** strong-minded woman.

IDIOMS **trouver son ~** to meet one's match.

maître-assistant, **~e**, *mpl* **maîtres-assistants** /mɛtʀasistɑ̃, ɑ̃t/ *nm,f* ≈ senior lecturer (GB), senior instructor (US).

maître-chanteur, *pl* **maîtres-chanteurs** /mɛtʀəʃɑ̃tœʀ/ *nm* blackmailer.

maître-nageur, *pl* **maîtres-nageurs** /mɛtʀənaʒœʀ/ *nm* **1** swimming instructor; **2** pool attendant.

■ **~ sauveteur** lifeguard.

maîtresse[2] /mɛtʀɛs/ **I** *adj f* ▶ **maître I**.

II *nf* **1** ▶ **maître II**; **2** mistress.

maîtrise /mɛtʀiz/ *nf* **1** mastery; **avec ~** masterfully; **2** perfect command (**de** of); **3 ~ (de soi)** self-control; **4** master's degree.

maîtriser /mɛtʀize/ [1] **I** *vtr* **1** to control [*feelings*]; to bring [sth] under control [*fire*]; to overcome [*opponent*]; to get on top of [*problem*]; **2** to master [*language*].

II se maîtriser *v refl* (+ *v être*) to have self-control.

maïzena® /maizena/ *nf* cornflour.

majesté /maʒɛste/ *nf* majesty; **Sa Majesté** His/Her Majesty.

majestueux, **-euse** /maʒɛstɥø, øz/ *adj* majestic; stately.

majeur, **~e** /maʒœʀ/ **I** *adj* **1 être ~** to be over 18 or of age; **2** main, major; **en ~e partie** for the most part; **3** (Mus) major.

II *nm* middle finger.

major /maʒɔʀ/ *nm* **1 sortir ~ de sa promotion** to come first in one's year; **2** (Mil) *French rank above that of warrant officer* (GB) or *chief warrant officer* (US); (Mil, Naut) *French rank above that of fleet chief petty officer* (GB) or *chief warrant officer* (US).

majoration /maʒɔʀasjɔ̃/ *nf* increase.

majordome /maʒɔʀdɔm/ *nm* butler.

majorer /maʒɔʀe/ [1] *vtr* to increase.

majoritaire /maʒɔʀitɛʀ/ *adj* majority.

majoritairement /maʒɔʀitɛʀmɑ̃/ *adv* **1** by a majority (vote); **2 province ~ catholique** predominantly Catholic province.

majorité /maʒɔʀite/ *nf* **1** majority; **avoir la ~** to have a majority; **ils sont en ~** they are in the majority; **ce sont, en ~, des enfants** they are, for the most part, children; **2 la ~** the government, the party in power.

majuscule /maʒyskyl/ I *adj* capital.

II *nf* capital (letter).

mal, *mpl* **maux** /mal, mo/ I *adj inv* **1** wrong; **qu'a-t-elle fait de ~?** what has she done wrong?; **2** bad; **ce ne serait pas ~ de déménager** it wouldn't be a bad idea to move out; **3**○ **il n'est pas mal** [*film*] it's not bad; [*man*] he's not bad(-looking).

II *nm* **1** trouble, difficulty; **avoir du ~ à faire** to find it difficult to do; **se donner du ~** to take trouble; **ne te donne pas ce ~!** don't bother!; **donne-toi un peu de ~!** make some effort!; **2** pain; **faire ~** to hurt, to be painful; **se faire ~** to hurt oneself; **j'ai ~** it hurts; **avoir ~ partout** to ache all over; **elle avait très ~** she was in pain; **avoir ~ à la tête** to have a headache; **avoir ~ à la gorge** to have a sore throat; **j'ai ~ au genou** my knee hurts; **j'ai ~ au cœur** I feel sick (GB) or nauseous; **3** illness, disease; **4 être en ~ de** to be short of [*inspiration*]; to be lacking in [*affection*]; **5** harm; **faire du ~ à** to harm, to hurt; **il n'y a pas de ~** there's no harm done; **une douche ne te ferait pas de ~** (humorous) a shower wouldn't do you any harm; **6 le ~** evil; **qu'elle parte, est-ce vraiment un ~?** is it really a bad thing that she is leaving?; **penser à ~** to have evil intentions; **sans penser à ~** without meaning any harm; **dire du ~ de qn/qch** to speak ill of sb/sth.

III *adv* **1** badly; not properly; **elle travaille ~** her work isn't good; **~ faire** to do wrong; **tu t'y prends ~** you're going about it the wrong way; **je t'entends ~** I can't hear you very well; **~ entretenu** neglected; **2** with difficulty; **on voit ~ comment** it's difficult to see how; **3** [*diagnosed, addressed*] wrongly; **j'avais ~ compris** I had misunderstood; **~ informé** ill-informed; **4 se trouver ~** to faint; **être ~ (assis** or **couché** or **installé)** not to be comfortable; **être au plus ~** to be critically ill.

IV **pas mal** *phr* **1** [*travel, read*] quite a lot; **2 tu ne ferais pas ~ d'y aller** you would be well-advised to go; **3 il ne s'en est pas ~ tiré** (in exam) he coped quite well; (in dangerous situation) he got off lightly.

■ **~ de l'air** airsickness; **~ des grands ensembles** *social problems attendant on high-density housing*; **~ de mer** seasickness; **~ du pays** homesickness; **~ du siècle** world-weariness; **~ des transports** travel sickness.

IDIOMS **entre** or **de deux maux il faut choisir le moindre** (Proverb) it's a matter of choosing the lesser of two evils.

malade /malad/ I *adj* [*person*] ill, sick; [*animal*] sick; [*organ, plant*] diseased; **tomber ~** to fall ill or sick, to get sick (US); **être ~ en voiture/en avion** to get carsick/airsick; **j'en suis ~**○ (figurative) it makes me sick; **~ d'inquiétude** worried sick.

II *nmf* **1** sick man/woman; **2** patient.

■ **~ imaginaire** hypochondriac; **~ mental** mentally ill person.

IDIOMS **être ~ comme un chien**○ to be as sick as a dog.

maladie /maladi/ *nf* **1** illness, disease; **il va en faire une ~**○ (figurative) he'll have a fit○; **2**○ mania; **avoir la ~ du rangement** to have a mania for tidiness.

■ **~ professionnelle** occupational disease; **~ sexuellement transmissible**, **MST** sexually transmitted disease, STD; **~ du sommeil** sleeping sickness.

maladif, **-ive** /maladif, iv/ *adj* [*child*] sickly; [*jealousy*] pathological.

maladresse /maladʀɛs/ *nf* **1** clumsiness, awkwardness; **2** tactlessness; **3** blunder.

maladroit, **~e** /maladʀwa, wat/ I *adj* **1** clumsy; **2** tactless.

II *nm,f* **1** clumsy person; **2** tactless person.

maladroitement /maladʀwatmɑ̃/ *adv* **1** clumsily, awkwardly; **2** tactlessly; ineptly.

mal-aimé, **~e**, *mpl* **~s** /malɛme/ *adj* **être ~** to be starved of affection.

malaise /malɛz/ *nm* **1** dizzy turn; **avoir un ~** to feel faint; **2** (figurative) uneasiness; unrest (**chez** among).

■ **~ cardiaque** mild heart attack.

malaisé, **~e** /malɛze/ *adj* difficult (**à faire, de faire** to do).

malaxer /malakse/ [1] *vtr* **1** to cream [*butter*]; to knead [*dough*]; **2** to mix [*cement*].

malchance /malʃɑ̃s/ *nf* bad luck, misfortune; **par ~** as ill luck would have it.

malchanceux, **-euse** /malʃɑ̃sø, øz/ *adj* unlucky.

maldonne /maldɔn/ *nf* misdeal; (figurative) misunderstanding.

mâle /mɑl/ I *adj* **1** male; [*elephant*] bull; [*antelope, rabbit*] buck; [*sparrow*] cock; **cygne ~** cob; **canard ~** drake; **2** manly.

II *nm* **1** male; **2** (humorous) he-man○.

malédiction /malediksjɔ̃/ *nf* curse.

maléfice /malefis/ *nm* evil spell.

maléfique /malefik/ *adj* evil.

malencontreusement /malɑ̃kɔ̃tʀøzmɑ̃/ *adv* inopportunely; inappropriately; unfortunately.

malencontreux, **-euse** /malɑ̃kɔ̃tʀø, øz/ *adj* unfortunate.

malentendant, **~e** /malɑ̃tɑ̃dɑ̃, ɑ̃t/ *nm,f* **les ~s** the hearing-impaired.

malentendu /malɑ̃tɑ̃dy/ *nm* misunderstanding.

malfaçon /malfasɔ̃/ *nf* defect (*caused by bad workmanship*).

malfaisant, **~e** /malfəzɑ̃, ɑ̃t/ *adj* [*person*] evil; [*influence*] harmful.

malfaiteur /malfɛtœʀ/ *nm* criminal.

malformation /malfɔʀmasjɔ̃/ *nf* malformation (**de** of).

malgache /malgaʃ/ *adj, nm* Malagasy.

malgré /malgʀe/ *prep* in spite of, despite; **~ cela**, **~ tout** nevertheless; **~ moi** against my wishes; reluctantly.

malhabile /malabil/ *adj* clumsy.

malheur /malœʀ/ *nm* **1 le ~** misfortune, adversity; **avoir sa part de ~** to have one's share of misfortune; **faire le ~ de qn** to bring sb nothing but unhappiness; **2** misfortune; accident; **un grand ~** a tragedy; **un ~ est si vite arrivé!** accidents can so easily happen!; **raconter ses ~s à qn** to tell sb one's troubles; **le grand ~!** (ironic) so what!; **3** misfortune; **ceux qui ont le ~ de faire** those who are unfortunate enough to do; **j'ai eu le ~ de le leur dire** I made the mistake of telling them; **par ~**, **le ~ a voulu que** as bad luck would have it; **si par ~ la guerre éclatait** if, God forbid, war should break out; **porter ~** to be bad luck; **le ~, c'est que...** the trouble is,...
IDIOMS **faire un ~**○ to be a sensation; to go wild; **un ~ n'arrive jamais seul** (Proverb) it never rains but it pours; **à quelque chose ~ est bon** (Proverb) every cloud has a silver lining.

malheureusement /maløʀøzmɑ̃/ *adv* unfortunately.

malheureux, **-euse** /maløʀø, øz/ **I** *adj* **1** [*person, life*] unhappy, miserable; [*victim, choice, word*] unfortunate; [*candidate*] unlucky; **si c'est pas ~**○ **de voir**... isn't it awful to see...; **c'est ~ que** it's a pity or shame that; **2**○ [*sum*] paltry, pathetic.
II *nm,f* **1** poor wretch; **le ~!** poor man!; **ne fais pas cela, malheureuse!** don't do that, for heaven's sake!; **2** poor person; **les ~** the poor.
IDIOMS **être ~ comme les pierres** to be as miserable as sin.

malhonnête /malɔnɛt/ *adj* dishonest.

malhonnêteté /malɔnɛtte/ *nf* dishonesty.

malice /malis/ *nf* **1** mischief; **avec ~** mischievously; **2**† malice; **être sans ~** to be harmless.

malicieux, **-ieuse** /malisjø, øz/ *adj* mischievous.

malin, **maligne** /malɛ̃, maliɲ/ **I** *adj* **1** clever; **j'ai eu l'air ~!** (ironic) I looked like a total fool!; **2**○ **ce n'est pas bien ~** it's not exactly difficult; **3** malicious; **prendre un ~ plaisir à faire** to take malicious pleasure in doing; **4** (Med) malignant.
II *nm,f* **c'est un ~** he's a crafty one.
IDIOMS **à ~, ~ et demi** (Proverb) there's always someone who will outwit you.

malingre /malɛ̃gʀ/ *adj* [*person, tree*] sickly; [*body*] puny.

malintentionné, **~e** /malɛ̃tɑ̃sjɔne/ *adj* malicious.

malle /mal/ *nf* **1** trunk; **2** (of car) **~ (arrière)** boot (GB), trunk (US).

malléabilité /maleabilite/ *nf* malleability.

mallette /malɛt/ *nf* briefcase.

malmener /malməne/ [16] *vtr* **1** to manhandle; **2** to give [sb] a rough ride.

malnutrition /malnytʀisjɔ̃/ *nf* malnutrition.

malodorant, **~e** /malɔdɔʀɑ̃, ɑ̃t/ *adj* foul-smelling.

malotru, **~e** /malɔtʀy/ *nm,f* boor.

Malouines /malwin/ *pr nf pl* **les (îles) ~** the Falklands.

malpoli, **~e** /malpɔli/ *adj* rude.

malpropre /malpʀɔpʀ/ *nmf* **se faire renvoyer comme un ~** to be chucked out○.

malsain, **~e** /malsɛ̃, ɛn/ *adj* unhealthy.

maltraiter /maltʀɛte/ [1] *vtr* to mistreat [*person*]; to misuse [*language*].

malus /malys/ *nm inv* loaded premium.

malveillance /malvɛjɑ̃s/ *nf* **1** malice; **2** (Law) malicious intent.

malveillant, **~e** /malvɛjɑ̃, ɑ̃t/ *adj* malicious.

malvenu, **~e** /malvəny/ *adj* out of place.

malversation /malvɛʀsasjɔ̃/ *nf* **1** malpractice; **2** embezzlement.

maman /mɑmɑ̃/ *nf* mum○ (GB), mom○ (US), mummy○ (GB), mommy○ (US), mother.

mamelle /mamɛl/ *nf* udder; teat.

mamelon /mamlɔ̃/ *nm* **1** nipple; **2** hillock.

mamie○ /mami/ *nf* granny○, grandma○.

mammaire /mamɛʀ/ *adj* mammary.

mammifère /mamifɛʀ/ *nm* mammal.

mammouth /mamut/ *nm* mammoth.

mam'selle○, **mam'zelle**○ /mamzɛl/ *nf* miss.

mamy = **mamie**.

manager[1] /manaʒœʀ/ = **manageur**.

manager[2] /manaʒe/ [13] *vtr* to manage.

manageur /manaʒœʀ/ *nm* manager.

manche[1] /mɑ̃ʃ/ *nm* **1** (of tool) handle; (of violin) neck; **2**○ clumsy idiot.
■ **~ à balai** broomhandle; broomstick; joystick.

manche[2] /mɑ̃ʃ/ *nf* **1** sleeve; **sans ~s** sleeveless; **2** (Sport) round; (in cards) hand; (in bridge) game; (in tennis) set.
IDIOMS **avoir qn dans la ~** to have sb in one's pocket; **se faire tirer par la ~** to need coaxing; **c'est une autre paire de ~s**○ it's a different ball game○.

Manche /mɑ̃ʃ/ *pr nf* **la ~** the (English) Channel; **le tunnel sous la ~** the Channel tunnel.

manchette /mɑ̃ʃɛt/ *nf* **1** (double) cuff; **2** oversleeve; **3** headline.

manchon /mɑ̃ʃɔ̃/ *nm* muff.

manchot, **-otte** /mɑ̃ʃo, ɔt/ **I** *adj* one-armed; one-handed; **il est ~** he's only got one arm; **ne**

pas être ~○ to be pretty good with one's hands○.
II *nm* penguin.
mandarin /mɑ̃daʀɛ̃/ *nm* **1** mandarin; **2** Mandarin (Chinese).
mandarine /mɑ̃daʀin/ *nf* mandarin orange.
mandat /mɑ̃da/ *nm* **1 ~ (postal)** money order; **2** term of office; **exercer son ~** to be in office; **3** mandate; **donner ~ à qn de faire** to authorize sb to do.
■ **~ d'amener** summons; **~ d'arrêt** (arrest) warrant; **~ d'expulsion** expulsion order; eviction order; **~ de perquisition** search warrant.
mandataire /mɑ̃datɛʀ/ *nmf* **1** representative, agent; **2** proxy.
mandat-carte, *pl* **mandats-cartes** /mɑ̃dakaʀt/ *nm* postal order.
mandater /mɑ̃date/ [1] *vtr* to appoint [sb] as one's representative; to give a mandate to.
mandat-lettre, *pl* **mandats-lettres** /mɑ̃dalEtʀ/ *nm* postal order.
mandibule /mɑ̃dibyl/ *nf* mandible.
mandoline /mɑ̃dɔlin/ *nf* mandolin.
mandrin /mɑ̃dʀɛ̃/ *nm* (of drill) chuck.
manège /manɛʒ/ *nm* **1** merry-go-round; **2** riding school; **~ (couvert)** indoor school or arena; **3** (little) trick, (little) game; **j'ai bien observé ton ~** I know what you are up to.
mânes /mɑn/ *nm pl* manes.
manette /manɛt/ *nf* **1** lever; joystick; **2** (figurative) **~s** controls.
mangeable /mɑ̃ʒabl/ *adj* edible.
mangeoire /mɑ̃ʒwaʀ/ *nf* manger; trough; feeding tray.
manger[1] /mɑ̃ʒe/ [13] **I** *vtr* **1** to eat; **il n'y a rien à ~ dans la maison** there's no food in the house; **2** to use up [*savings*]; to go through [*inheritance*]; to take up [*time*]; **3** [*rust, acid*] to eat away; **mangé aux mites** moth-eaten; **se faire ~ par les moustiques** to be eaten alive by mosquitoes; **4 ~ ses mots** to mumble.
II *vi* to eat; **~ au restaurant** to eat out; **~ à sa faim** to eat one's fill; **donner à ~ à qn** to feed sb; to give [sb] something to eat; **faire à ~** to cook; **inviter qn à ~** to invite sb for a meal; to invite sb out for a meal; **~ chinois** to have a Chinese meal; **on mange mal ici** the food is not good here.
III se manger *v refl* (+ *v être*) **ça se mange?** can you eat it?; **le gaspacho se mange froid** gazpacho is served cold.
IDIOMS **~ la consigne** or **commission** to forget one's orders.
manger[2] /mɑ̃ʒe/ *nm* food; **apporter son ~** to bring one's own food.
mangeur, **-euse** /mɑ̃ʒœʀ, øz/ *nm,f* **bon/gros ~** good/big eater.
■ **mangeuse d'hommes** man-eater.
mangouste /mɑ̃gust/ *nf* **1** mongoose; **2** mangosteen.
mangue /mɑ̃g/ *nf* mango.
maniabilité /manjabilite/ *nf* manoeuvrability (GB), maneuverability (US).
maniable /manjabl/ *adj* [*object, car*] easy to handle; [*book*] manageable in size.
maniaque /manjak/ **I** *adj* particular, fussy.
II *nmf* **1** fusspot (GB), fussbudget (US); **2** fanatic; **c'est un ~ de l'ordre** he's obsessive about tidiness; **3** maniac; **4** (Med) manic.
■ **~ sexuel** sex maniac.
maniaquerie /manjakʀi/ *nf* fussiness.
manie /mani/ *nf* **1** habit (**de faire** of doing); **avoir la ~ de tout garder** to be a compulsive hoarder; **c'est une vraie ~** it's an absolute obsession; **2** quirk, idiosyncrasy; **3** (Med) mania.
maniement /manimɑ̃/ *nm* handling; (of machine) operation; (of language) command; **d'un ~ aisé** [*tool*] to be easy to handle.
■ **~ d'armes** arms drill.
manier /manje/ [2] **I** *vtr* to handle; **bien ~ le pinceau** (figurative) to be a good painter.
II se manier *v refl* (+ *v être*) **se ~ aisément** [*tool*] to be easy to handle; [*car*] to handle well.
IDIOMS **~ la fourchette avec entrain**○ (humorous) to have a hearty appetite; **il sait ~ la brosse à reluire**○ he's good at buttering people up○.
manière /manjɛʀ/ *nf* **1** way; **d'une ~ ou d'une autre** in one way or another; **d'une certaine ~** in a way; **leur ~ de vivre/penser** their way of life/thinking; **de toutes les ~s possibles** in every possible way; **de telle ~ que** in such a way that; **de ~ à faire** so as to do; **de ~ à ce que** so that; **à ma ~** my (own) way; **de quelle ~ peut-on résoudre le problème?** how can one solve the problem?; **de toute ~, de toutes ~s** anyway, in any case; **la ~ forte** strong-arm tactics, force; **utiliser la ~ douce** to use kid gloves; **2** style; **à la ~ de qn/qch** in the style of sb/sth; **3** manners; **il n'a pas de ~s** he has no manners; **faire des ~s** to stand on ceremony.
maniéré, **~e** /manjeʀe/ *adj* affected.
manifestant , **~e** /manifɛstɑ̃, ɑ̃t/ *nm,f* demonstrator.
manifestation /manifɛstasjɔ̃/ *nf* **1** demonstration (**contre** against; **pour** for); **2** event; **~s sportives** sporting events; **3** (of phenomenon) appearance; **4** (of solidarity, feeling) expression, manifestation.
■ **~ silencieuse** vigil; **~ de soutien** rally (**en faveur de** for).
manifeste /manifɛst/ **I** *adj* obvious, manifest.
II *nm* manifesto.
manifester /manifɛste/ [1] **I** *vtr* to show, to demonstrate [*courage*]; to express [*desire, fears*]; **~ sa présence** to make one's presence known.
II *vi* to demonstrate (**contre** against; **en faveur de** for); **appeler à ~ le 5 juin** to call a demonstration for 5 June.
III se manifester *v refl* (+ *v être*) **1** [*symptom*] to manifest itself; [*phenomenon*] to appear; [*illness, worry*] to show itself; **2** [*witness*] to come forward; [*person*] to appear; to get in touch.
manigance /manigɑ̃s/ *nf* little scheme.

manigancer /manigɑ̃se/ [12] *vtr* **~ quelque chose** to be up to something; **~ un mauvais coup** to hatch up a scheme.

manipulateur, **-trice** /manipylatœʀ, tʀis/ *nm,f* **1** technician; **2** manipulator.

manipulation /manipylasjɔ̃/ *nf* **1** (of object) handling; **2** manipulation; **~s électorales** electoral rigging; **3** (Sch) experiment.

manipuler /manipyle/ [1] *vtr* **1** to handle [*object*]; to use [*words*]; **2** to massage [*figures*]; to manipulate [*person*].

manitou /manitu/ *nm* **1**○ **grand ~** big noise○; **2** manitou.

manivelle /manivɛl/ *nf* handle.
IDIOMS **donner le premier tour de ~** to start filming.

manne /man/ *nf* godsend; **~ céleste** manna from Heaven.

mannequin /mankɛ̃/ *nm* **1** (fashion) model; **2** dummy.

manœuvre[1] /manœvʀ/ *nm* unskilled worker.

manœuvre[2] /manœvʀ/ *nf* manoeuvre (GB), maneuver (US); **faire la ~** [*locomotive*] to shunt; **champ de ~** military training area; **fausse ~** mistake.

manœuvrer /manœvʀe/ [1] **I** *vtr* **1** to manoeuvre (GB), to maneuver (US) [*vehicle*]; **2** to operate [*machine*]; **3** to manipulate [*person*].
II *vi* to manoeuvre (GB), to maneuver (US).

manoir /manwaʀ/ *nm* manor (house).

manomètre /manɔmɛtʀ/ *nm* pressure gauge, manometer.

manquant, **~e** /mɑ̃kɑ̃, ɑ̃t/ *adj* missing.

manque /mɑ̃k/ **I** *nm* **1 ~ de** lack of; shortage of; **~ de chance, il est tombé malade** just his luck, he fell ill; **2** gap; **en ~ d'affection** in need of affection; **être en (état de) ~** [*drug addict*] to be suffering from withdrawal symptoms.
II à la manque○ *phr* **une idée à la ~** a useless idea.

manqué, **~e** /mɑ̃ke/ **I** *pp* ▸ **manquer**.
II *pp adj* [*attempt*] failed; [*opportunity*] missed; **c'est un poète ~** he should have been a poet.

manquement /mɑ̃kmɑ̃/ *nm* **~ à la discipline** breach of discipline; **~ à une promesse** failure to keep a promise.

manquer /mɑ̃ke/ [1] **I** *vtr* **1** to miss; **un film à ne pas ~** a film not to be missed; **tu l'as manquée de cinq minutes** you missed her/it by five minutes; **2** to make a mess of [*photo, solo*]; to fail [*exam*]; **~ son coup**○ to fail; **3**○ **la prochaine fois je ne le manquerai pas** next time I won't let him get away with it.
II manquer à *v+prep* **1 ~ à qn** to be missed by sb; **la Bretagne/ma tante me manque** I miss Brittany/my aunt; **2 ~ à sa parole** to break one's word.
III manquer de *v+prep* **1** to lack; **on ne manque de rien** we don't want for anything; **elle ne manque pas de charme** she's not without charm; **il ne manque pas de culot**○**!** he's got a nerve!; **on manque d'air ici** it's stuffy in here; **2 je ne manquerai pas de vous le faire savoir** I'll be sure to let you know; **'remercie-le de ma part'—'je n'y manquerai pas'** 'thank him for me'—'I won't forget'; **et évidemment, ça n'a pas manqué**○**!** and sure enough that's what happened!; **3 il a manqué (de) casser un carreau** he almost broke a windowpane.
IV *vi* **1 les vivres vinrent à ~** supplies ran out; **le courage leur manqua** their courage failed them; **les mots me manquent pour exprimer ma joie** I can't find the words to express my joy; **ce n'est pas l'envie qui m'en manque** it's not that I don't want to; **2** [*person*] to be absent; to be missing.
V *v impers* **il lui manque un doigt** he's got a finger missing; **il nous manque deux joueurs pour former une équipe** we're two players short of a team; **ça manque d'animation ici!** it's not very lively here!; **il ne manquerait plus que ça**○**!** that would be the last straw!
VI se manquer *v refl* (+ *v être*) **1** to bungle one's suicide attempt; **2** to miss each other.

mansarde /mɑ̃saʀd/ *nf* attic room.

mansardé, **~e** /mɑ̃saʀde/ *adj* [*room*] attic.

mante /mɑ̃t/ *nf* **~ religieuse** praying mantis; (figurative) man-eater.

manteau, *pl* **~x** /mɑ̃to/ *nm* coat.
■ **~ de cheminée** mantelpiece.
IDIOMS **sous le ~** illicitly.

mantille /mɑ̃tij/ *nf* mantilla.

manucure /manykyʀ/ **I** *nmf* manicurist.
II *nf* manicure.

manuel, **-elle** /manɥɛl/ **I** *adj* manual.
II *nm* manual; (Sch) textbook.
■ **~ de conversation** phrase book; **~ d'utilisation** instruction manual.

manuellement /manɥɛlmɑ̃/ *adv* manually.

manufacture /manyfaktyʀ/ *nf* **1** factory; **2** manufacture.

manufacturer /manyfaktyʀe/ [1] *vtr* to manufacture.

manu militari /manymilitaʀi/ *adv* forcibly.

manuscrit, **~e** /manyskʀi, it/ **I** *adj* handwritten.
II *nm* manuscript.

manutention /manytɑ̃sjɔ̃/ *nf* handling.

manutentionnaire /manytɑ̃sjɔnɛʀ/ *nm* warehouseman.

mappemonde /mapmɔ̃d/ *nf* **1** map of the world (in two hemispheres); **2** globe.

maquereau, *pl* **~x** /makʀo/ *nm* mackerel.

maquette /makɛt/ *nf* scale model.

maquillage /makijaʒ/ *nm* **1** making-up; **2** make-up.
■ **~ de théâtre** greasepaint.

maquiller /makije/ [1] **I** *vtr* **1** to make [sb] up; **2** to doctor [*truth*]; **~ un crime en accident** to disguise a crime as an accident.
II se maquiller *v refl* (+ *v être*) **1** to put make-up on; **2** to wear make-up.

maquilleur, **-euse** /makijœʀ, øz/ *nm,f* make-up artist.

maquis /maki/ *nm inv* maquis; **prendre le ~** to go underground.

maquisard, **~e** /makizaʀ, aʀd/ *nm,f* member of the Resistance.

marabout /maʀabu/ *nm* **1** marabou; **2** marabout.

maraîcher, **-ère** /maʀɛʃe, ɛʀ/ **I** *adj* **produits ~s** market garden produce (GB), truck (US).
II *nm,f* market gardener (GB), truck farmer (US).

marais /maʀɛ/ *nm inv* marsh; swamp.
■ **~ salant** saltern.

marasme /maʀasm/ *nm* stagnation; **être dans le ~** to be in the doldrums.

marathon /maʀatɔ̃/ *nm* marathon.

marathonien, **-ienne** /maʀatɔnjɛ̃, ɛn/ *nm,f* marathon runner.

marâtre /maʀɑtʀ/ *nf* cruel mother.

marauder /maʀode/ [1] *vi* **1** to pilfer; **2** [*taxi*] to cruise for fares; [*person*] to prowl around.

maraudeur, **-euse** /maʀodœʀ, øz/ *nm,f* petty thief.

marbre /maʀbʀ/ *nm* **1** marble; **2** marble top; **3** marble statue.
IDIOMS **rester de ~** to remain stony-faced; **la nouvelle les laissa de ~** they were completely unmoved by the news.

marbrer /maʀbʀe/ [1] *vtr* **1** to marble; **2 peau marbrée** mottled skin.

marbrier, **-ière**[1] /maʀbʀije, ɛʀ/ *nm* marble mason.

marbrière[2] /maʀbʀijɛʀ/ *nf* marble quarry.

marbrure /maʀbʀyʀ/ *nf* **1** marbling; **2** mottling.

marc /maʀ/ *nm* marc.
■ **~ de café** coffee grounds.

marcassin /maʀkasɛ̃/ *nm* young wild boar.

marchand, **~e** /maʀʃɑ̃, ɑ̃d/ **I** *adj* [*quality*] marketable; [*sector*] trade; [*value*] market.
II *nm,f* shopkeeper; stallholder; **~ d'armes/de bestiaux** arms/cattle dealer; **~ de charbon/vins** coal/wine merchant.
■ **~ ambulant** hawker; **~ de couleurs** ironmonger (GB), hardware merchant; **~ de glaces** ice cream vendor; **~ en gros** wholesaler; **~ de journaux** newsagent; newsvendor; **~ des quatre saisons** costermonger (GB), fruit and vegetable merchant; **~ de sable** sandman; **~ de tableaux** art dealer; **~ de tapis** carpet salesman.

marchandage /maʀʃɑ̃daʒ/ *nm* haggling; **faire du ~** to haggle.

marchander /maʀʃɑ̃de/ [1] *vtr* **1** to haggle over; **2** (figurative) **~ sa peine** not to put oneself out; **il n'a pas marchandé ses éloges** he was not sparing in his praise.

marchandise /maʀʃɑ̃diz/ *nf* goods, merchandise; **tromper** or **voler qn sur la ~** to swindle sb.

marche /maʀʃ/ *nf* **1** walking; walk; pace, step; **faire de la ~** to go walking; **à 10 minutes de ~** 10 minutes' walk away; **2** march; **fermer la ~** to bring up the rear; **ouvrir la ~** to be at the head of the march; **3** (of vehicle) progress; (of events) course; (of time, progress) march; **bus en ~** moving bus; **dans le sens contraire de la ~** facing backward(s); **4** (of mechanism) operation; (of organization) running; **en état de ~** in working order; **mettre en ~** to start (up) [*engine, machine*]; to switch on [*TV*]; **se mettre en ~** to start up; **5** step; **les ~s** the stairs.
■ **~ arrière** reverse; **faire ~ arrière** to reverse; (figurative) to backpedal; **~ avant** forward; **~ à suivre** procedure.
IDIOMS **prendre le train en ~** to join halfway through; to climb onto the bandwagon.

marché /maʀʃe/ *nm* **1** market; **~ aux fleurs** flower market; **faire son ~** to do one's shopping at the market; **2** deal; **conclure un ~ avec qn** to strike a deal with sb; **~ conclu!** it's a deal!; **bon/meilleur ~** cheap/cheaper; **par-dessus le ~**° to top it all.
■ **~ de l'emploi** job market; **~ extérieur** foreign market; **~ intérieur** domestic market; internal market; **~ libre** free market; **~ noir** black market; **~ aux puces** flea market; **~ du travail** labour[GB] market; **Marché commun** Common Market.
IDIOMS **faire bon ~ de qch** to set little value on sth.

marchepied /maʀʃəpje/ *nm* **1** step; **2** steps.

marcher /maʀʃe/ [1] *vi* **1** to walk; [*demonstrators*] to march; **2** to tread (**dans** in; **sur** on); **se laisser ~ sur les pieds** (figurative) to let oneself be walked over; **3** [*mechanism, system*] to work; **ma radio marche mal** my radio doesn't work properly; **faire ~ qch** to get sth to work; **~ au gaz** to run on gas; **les bus ne marchent pas le dimanche** the buses don't run on Sundays; **4**° **~ (bien)/~ mal** [*work, relationship*] to go well/not to go well; [*film, student*] to do well/not to do well; [*actor*] to go down well/not to go down well; **comment marchent les affaires?** how is business?; **5**° **je marche** I'll go for it; **c'est trop risqué, je ne marche pas** it's too risky, count me out; **ça marche!** it's a deal!; **6**° to fall for it; **7 faire ~ qn** to pull sb's leg; **elle fait ~ sa mère comme elle veut** she's got her mother wrapped round her little finger; **faire ~ son monde**° to be good at giving orders.
IDIOMS **il ne marche pas, il court**°**!** he's as gullible as they come; **~ sur la tête de qn**° to walk all over sb.

marcheur, **-euse** /maʀʃœʀ, øz/ *nm,f* walker.

mardi /maʀdi/ *nm* Tuesday; **~ gras** Shrove Tuesday.

mare /maʀ/ *nf* **1** pond; **~ aux canards** duck pond; **2 ~ de** pool of [*blood, mud*].

marécage /maʀekaʒ/ *nm* **1** marsh, swamp; **2** (figurative) quagmire.

marécageux, **-euse** /maʀekaʒø, øz/ *adj* **1** [*ground*] marshy, swampy; [*plant*] marsh; **2** (figurative) [*ground, situation*] sticky°.

maréchal, *pl* **-aux** /maʀeʃal, o/ *nm* ≈ field marshal (GB), general of the army (US).
■ **~ de France** marshal of France.

maréchal-ferrant, *pl* **maréchaux-ferrants** /maʀeʃalfɛʀɑ̃, maʀeʃofɛʀɑ̃/ *nm* farrier.

maréchaussée /maʀeʃose/ *nf* mounted police.

marée /maʀe/ *nf* **1** tide; **la ~ monte/**

descend the tide is coming in/is going out; **à ~ haute/basse** at high/low tide; **la ~ montante/descendante** the rising/ebbing tide; **2** fresh fish.

■ **~ noire** oil slick.

IDIOMS **contre vents et ~s** come hell or high water; against all odds.

marelle /marɛl/ *nf* hopscotch.

marémoteur, **-trice** /maremɔtœr, tris/ *adj* tidal; **usine marémotrice** tidal power station.

marennes /maren/ *nf inv* Marennes oyster.

mareyeur, **-euse** /marɛjœr, øz/ *nm,f* fish wholesaler.

margarine /margarin/ *nf* margarine.

marge /marʒ/ **I** *nf* **1** margin; **2** leeway; **on a 10 minutes de ~** we've got 10 minutes to spare; **3** scope; **tu devrais me laisser plus de ~ de décision** you should allow me more scope for making decisions; **4** profit margin; mark-up.

II en marge de *phr* **vivre en ~ de la société** to live on the fringes of society; **vivre en ~ de la loi** to live outside the law; **se sentir en ~** to feel like an outsider.

■ **~ bénéficiaire** profit margin; **~ d'erreur** margin of error; **~ de manœuvre** room for manoeuvre (GB) or maneuver (US); **~ de sécurité** safety margin.

marginal, **~e**, *mpl* **-aux** /marʒinal, o/ **I** *adj* **1** marginal; **2** [*artist*] fringe; **3** on the margins of society.

II *nm,f* dropout; **les marginaux** the fringe elements of society.

marginaliser /marʒinalize/ [1] *vtr* to marginalize.

marginalité /marʒinalite/ *nf* **la ~** the fringes of society.

marguerite /margərit/ *nf* daisy.

IDIOMS **effeuiller la ~** to play he/she loves me, he/she loves me not.

mari /mari/ *nm* husband.

mariage /marjaʒ/ *nm* **1** marriage; **né d'un premier ~** from a previous marriage; **~ de raison** marriage of convenience; **faire un ~ d'amour** to marry for love; **faire un riche ~** to marry into money; **2** wedding; **3** (figurative) (of colours) marriage; (of companies) merger; (of parties) alliance; (of techniques) fusion.

■ **~ blanc** marriage in name only; **~ civil** civil wedding; **~ religieux** church wedding.

IDIOMS **c'est le ~ de la carpe et du lapin**○ it's a mismatch.

Marianne /marjan/ *pr n* Marianne (*female figure personifying the French Republic*).

marié, **~e** /marje/ **I** *pp* ▶ **marier**.

II *pp adj* married.

III *nm,f* **le (jeune) ~** the (bride)groom; **la (jeune) ~e** the bride; **les (jeunes) ~s** the newlyweds.

marier /marje/ [2] **I** *vtr* to marry (**à, avec** to).

II se marier *v refl* (+ *v être*) **1** to get married (**avec qn** to sb); **2** [*colours*] to blend.

marijuana /marirwana/ *nf* marijuana.

marin, **~e**[1] /marɛ̃, in/ **I** *adj* **1** [*life*] marine; [*salt*] sea; [*drilling*] offshore; [*boat*] seaworthy; **2 pull ~** seaman's jersey; **costume ~** sailor suit.

II *nm* sailor.

■ **~ d'eau douce** fair-weather sailor; **~ pêcheur** fisherman.

IDIOMS **avoir le pied ~** to be a good sailor, not to get seasick.

marine[2] /marin/ **I** *adj inv* navy (blue).

II *nm* marine.

marine[3] /marin/ *nf* **1** navy; **de ~** [*instrument*] nautical; **2** seascape.

mariner /marine/ [1] *vtr, vi* to marinate.

marinier /marinje/ *nm* bargeman.

marinière /marinjɛr/ *nf* smock.

marionnette /marjɔnɛt/ *nf* **1** puppet; **2 ~s** puppet show.

■ **~ à fils** marionette; **~ à gaine** glove puppet.

marionnettiste /marjɔnetist/ *nmf* puppeteer.

maritalement /maritalmɑ̃/ *adv* [*live*] as man and wife.

maritime /maritim/ *adj* [*climate, commerce*] maritime; [*area*] coastal; [*company*] shipping.

marivaudage /marivodaʒ/ *nm* gallant sophisticated banter.

marjolaine /marʒɔlɛn/ *nf* marjoram.

marmelade /marməlad/ *nf* stewed fruit; **en ~** cooked to a mush.

marmite /marmit/ *nf* **1** (cooking-)pot; **2** potful.

IDIOMS **faire bouillir la ~**○ to bring home the bacon.

marmiton /marmitɔ̃/ *nm* chef's assistant.

marmonner /marmɔne/ [1] *vtr* to mumble, to mutter.

marmot○ /marmo/ *nm* kid○, brat○.

marmotte /marmɔt/ *nf* **1** marmot; **2** (figurative) sleepyhead○.

IDIOMS **dormir comme une ~** to sleep like a log.

maroquinerie /marɔkinri/ *nf* **1** leather shop; **2** leather industry; leather trade; **(articles de) ~** leather goods.

maroquinier /marɔkinje/ *nm* trader in fine leather goodss.

marotte /marɔt/ *nf* **1** pet subject, hobby horse; pet or favourite[GB] hobby; **2** puppet.

marquant, **~e** /markɑ̃, ɑ̃t/ *adj* [*fact*] memorable; [*memory*] lasting; [*personality*] outstanding.

marque /mark/ *nf* **1** brand, make; **de ~ japonaise** Japanese; **de ~** [*product*] branded; [*guest*] distinguished; [*person*] eminent; **2** mark; sign; **~ de doigts** fingermarks; **~s d'usure** signs of wear; **on voit encore les ~s (de coups)** you can still see the bruises; **~ de pas** footprint; **~ du pluriel** plural marker; **laisser sa ~** to make one's mark; **3** (Sport) score; **à vos ~s, prêts, partez!** on your marks, get set, go!.

■ **~ déposée** registered trademark; **~ de fabricant** or **fabrication** manufacturer's brand name; **~ de fabrique** trademark; **~ d'infamie** stigma.

marqué, **~e** /maʀke/ I *pp* ▶ **marquer**.
II *pp adj* **1 il a le corps ~ de traces de coups** he's bruised all over; **elle est restée ~e par la guerre** the war left its mark on her; **une époque ~e par les conflits sociaux** a period marked by social unrest; **visage ~** worn face; **2** [*difference*] marked.

marquer /maʀke/ [1] I *vtr* **1** to mark [*goods*]; to brand [*cattle*]; to mark out [*site*]; **2** to mark, to signal [*beginning, end*]; **3** to mark [*body, object*]; **4** (figurative) [*event, work*] to leave its mark on [*person*]; **c'est quelqu'un qui m'a beaucoup marqué** he/she was a strong influence on me; **5** to write [sth] down [*information*]; to mark [*price*]; **marquez cela sur mon compte** put it on my account; **qu'est-ce qu'il y a de marqué?** what does it say?; **6** to show; **~ la mesure** (Mus) to beat time; **il faut ~ le coup** let's celebrate; **7 ~ un temps (d'arrêt)** to pause; **~ un silence** to fall silent; **8** (Sport) to score [*goal*]; to mark [*opponent*].
II *vi* **1** to leave a mark (**sur** on); **2** (Sport) to score.

marqueterie /maʀkɛtʀi/ *nf* **1** marquetry; **2** inlay.

marqueur /maʀkœʀ/ *nm* marker pen.

marquis, **~e**[1] /maʀki, iz/ *nm,f* marquis/marchioness.

marquise[2] /maʀkiz/ *nf* glass canopy (GB), marquee (US).

marraine /maʀɛn/ *nf* **1** godmother; **2** sponsor.
■ **~ de guerre** *soldier's wartime female penfriend*.

marrant○, **~e** /maʀɑ̃, ɑ̃t/ *adj* funny; **ce n'est pas ~** it's not much fun; it's a real pain○.

marre○ /maʀ/ *adv* **en avoir ~** to be fed up○ (**de** with).

marrer○: **se marrer** /maʀe/ [1] *v refl* (+ *v être*) **1** to have a great time; **2** to have a good laugh.

marron, **-onne** /maʀɔ̃, ɔn/ I *adj* crooked.
II *adj* brown; **~ clair/foncé** light/dark brown.
III *nm* **1** chestnut; **~ (d'Inde)** horse chestnut; **2** brown.
■ **~ glacé** marron glacé; **~s chauds** roast chestnuts.

marronnier /maʀɔnje/ *nm* chestnut (tree).

mars /maʀs/ *nm inv* March.
IDIOMS **arriver comme ~ en carême** to come as sure as night follows day.

marseillais, **~e** /maʀsɛjɛ, ɛz/ *adj* of Marseilles; **une histoire ~e** ≈ a tall story.

Marseillaise /maʀsɛjɛz/ *nf* Marseillaise (*French national anthem*).

marsouin /maʀswɛ̃/ *nm* porpoise.

marteau, *pl* **~x** /maʀto/ *nm* hammer; (of judge) gavel; (on door) knocker.

martel† /maʀtɛl/ *nm* **se mettre ~ en tête** to get worried.

marteler /maʀtəle/ [17] *vtr* **1** to hammer, to pound; **2** to rap out [*words*].

martial, **~e**, *mpl* **-iaux** /maʀsjal, o/ *adj* [*art, law*] martial; [*music, step*] military.

martinet /maʀtinɛ/ *nm* **1** (Zool) swift; **2** whip.

martingale /maʀtɛ̃gal/ *nf* **1** (on jacket) half belt; **2** (for horse) martingale.

martin-pêcheur, *pl* **martins-pêcheurs** /maʀtɛ̃pɛʃœʀ/ *nm* kingfisher.

martre /maʀtʀ/ *nf* **1** marten; **2** sable.

martyr, **~e**[1] /maʀtiʀ/ I *adj* martyred; **enfant ~** battered child.
II *nm,f* martyr (**d'une cause** to a cause).

martyre[2] /maʀtiʀ/ *nm* **1** martyrdom; **2** agony; **souffrir le ~** to suffer agony.

martyriser /maʀtiʀize/ [1] *vtr* **1** to torment [*victim, animal*]; to batter [*child*]; **2** to martyr.

marxisme /maʀksism/ *nm* Marxism.

mas /mɑ/ *nm inv* farmhouse (*in Provence*).

mascarade /maskaʀad/ *nf* **1** farce; **~ de justice** travesty of justice; **2** masked ball, masquerade.

mascotte /maskɔt/ *nf* mascot.

masculin, **~e** /maskylɛ̃, in/ I *adj* [*population, sex, part*] male; [*sport*] man's; [*magazine, team*] men's; [*face, noun*] masculine.
II *nm* masculine.

masochisme /mazɔʃism/ *nm* masochism.

masochiste /mazɔʃist/ I *adj* masochistic.
II *nmf* masochist.

masque /mask/ *nm* **1** mask; **2** face-pack; **3** expression; **prendre un ~ tragique** to put on a tragic expression.
■ **~ à gaz** gas mask; **~ de plongée** diving mask; **~ de soudeur** face shield.
IDIOMS **jeter le ~** to show one's true colours[GB].

masqué, **~e** /maske/ I *pp* ▶ **masquer**.
II *pp adj* **1** [*bandit*] masked; **2** (figurative) concealed.

masquer /maske/ [1] I *vtr* **1** to conceal [*defect*]; to hide [*landscape*]; to mask [*problem, smell*]; **2** to block [*opening, light*].
II **se masquer** *v refl* (+ *v être*) to hide [sth] from oneself [*truth*].

massacrante /masakʀɑ̃t/ *adj f* **être d'humeur ~** to be in a foul mood.

massacre /masakʀ/ *nm* **1** massacre, slaughter; **2**○ (figurative) massacre; **3**○ botch(-up).
IDIOMS **faire un ~**○ [*actor*] to be a roaring○ success; [*gambler*] to make a killing.

massacrer /masakʀe/ [1] I *vtr* **1** to massacre, to slaughter; **2**○ (figurative) to slaughter○ [*opponent*]; to massacre [*piece of music*]; to botch [*job*]; to criticize, to savage (GB), to trash US [*play, actor*].
II **se massacrer** *v refl* (+ *v être*) to slaughter one another.

massage /masaʒ/ *nm* massage; **faire un ~ à qn** to give sb a massage.

masse /mas/ *nf* **1** mass; **~ rocheuse** rocky mass; **une ~ humaine** a mass of humanity; **2 une ~ de** a lot of; **des ~s de**○ masses of; **départs en ~** mass exodus; **3 la ~, les ~s** the masses; **culture de ~** mass culture; **4** sledgehammer.
■ **~ d'armes** mace; **~ monétaire** money supply; **~ salariale** (total) wage bill.
IDIOMS **(se laisser) tomber comme une ~**

to collapse; **dormir comme une ~** to sleep like a log○.

massepain /maspɛ̃/ *nm* marzipan cake.

masser /mase/ [1] **I** *vtr* **1** to assemble, to mass; **2** to massage.

II se masser *v refl* (+ *v être*) **1** to mass; **2 se ~ les jambes** to massage one's legs.

masseur, -euse /masœʀ, øz/ *nm,f* masseur/ masseuse.

massicot /masiko/ *nm* (for paper) guillotine.

massif, -ive /masif, iv/ **I** *adj* **1** [*features*] heavy; [*person*] heavily built; [*silhouette*] massive; **2** [*dose, crowd*] massive; [*redundancies*] mass; **3** [*gold, oak*] solid.

II *nm* **1** massif; **2** (of flowers) clump; **3** (flower) bed.

massivement /masivmɑ̃/ *adv* [*demonstrate*] in great numbers; [*inject*] in massive doses; [*absorb*] in large quantities; [*approve*] overwhelmingly.

mass media /masmedja/ *nm pl* mass media.

massue /masy/ *nf* (gen, Sport) club, bludgeon.

mastic /mastik/ **I** *adj inv* putty-coloured[GB].

II *nm* (for windows) putty; (for holes) filler; (for trees) grafting wax.

mastiquer /mastike/ [1] *vtr* **1** to chew; **2** to putty [*window*]; to fill in [*crack*].

mastoc○ /mastɔk/ *adj inv* huge.

mastodonte /mastɔdɔ̃t/ *nm* **1** mastodon; **2** (figurative) (person) colossus, hulk○; (animal) monster; (object) huge thing.

masturber /mastyʀbe/ [1] *vtr*, **se masturber** *v refl* (+ *v être*) to masturbate.

m'as-tu-vu○ /matyvy/ *nmf inv* show-off.

masure /mazyʀ/ *nf* hovel.

mat, ~e /mat/ **I** *adj* **1** [*paint*] matt (GB), matte (US); **2** [*complexion*] olive; **3** [*sound*] dull.

II *nm* **(échec et) ~!** checkmate!

mât /mɑ/ *nm* **1** mast; **2** pole; climbing pole; **~ de drapeau** flagpole.

■ **~ de cocagne** greasy pole.

matador /matadɔʀ/ *nm* matador.

matamore /matamɔʀ/ *nm* braggart; **faire le ~** to swagger.

match /matʃ/ *nm* (in team sports) match (GB), game (US); (in boxing, wrestling, tennis) match; **~ nul** draw (GB), tie (US); **faire ~ nul** to draw (GB), to tie (US).

■ **~ de classement** league match.

matelas /matla/ *nm inv* mattress; **~ pneumatique** air bed.

matelassé, ~e /matlase/ **I** *pp* ▶ **matelasser**.

II *pp adj* [*material*] quilted; [*door*] padded.

matelasser /matlase/ [1] *vtr* to pad [*door*]; to quilt [*jacket*].

matelot /matlo/ *nm* **1** sailor; **2** ≈ ordinary seaman (GB), ≈ seaman apprentice (US).

matelote /matlɔt/ *nf* **1** fish stew; **2** hornpipe.

mater /mate/ [1] *vtr* to put down [*uprising*]; to bring [sb/sth] into line [*rebels*]; to take [sb/sth] in hand [*child, horse*].

matérialisation /materjalizasjɔ̃/ *nf* **1** (of plan, hopes) realization; **2** (of roads) marking.

matérialiser /materjalize/ [1] **I** *vtr* **1** to realize [*dream*]; to fulfil[GB] [*hope*]; to make [sth] happen [*plan*]; **2** to mark; **'chaussée non matérialisée sur 3 km'** 'no road markings for 3 km'.

II se matérialiser *v refl* (+ *v être*) to materialize.

matérialisme /materjalism/ *nm* materialism.

matérialiste /materjalist/ **I** *adj* materialistic.

II *nmf* materialist.

matériau, *pl* **~x** /materjo/ *nm* material; **~x de construction** building materials.

matériel, -ielle /materjɛl/ **I** *adj* [*cause, conditions*] material; [*means*] practical; [*obstacle*] tangible; **sur le plan ~** in practical terms.

II *nm* **1** equipment; **~ agricole** farm machinery; **2** material.

■ **~ informatique** hardware.

matériellement /materjɛlmɑ̃/ *adv* **1 c'est ~ possible** it can be done; **c'est impossible ~** it's a physical impossibility; **2** financially.

maternel, -elle[1] /matɛʀnɛl/ *adj* **1** [*instinct*] maternal; [*love*] motherly; **2 conseils ~s** mother's advice; **3** [*line, aunt*] maternal; **du côté ~** on the mother's side.

maternelle[2] /matɛʀnɛl/ *nf* nursery school.

maternellement /matɛʀnɛlmɑ̃/ *adv* in a motherly way.

materner /matɛʀne/ [1] *vtr* **1** to mother; **2** to mollycoddle.

maternité /matɛʀnite/ *nf* **1** motherhood; **2** pregnancy; **de ~** [*leave*] maternity; **3** maternity hospital.

mathématicien, -ienne /matematisjɛ̃, ɛn/ *nm,f* mathematician.

mathématique /matematik/ *adj* **1** mathematical; **2** (figurative) **c'est ~** it follows; it's dead certain.

mathématiquement /matematikmɑ̃/ *adv* **1** mathematically; **2** logically.

mathématiques /matematik/ *nf pl* mathematics.

matheux○**, -euse** /matø, øz/ *nm,f* mathematician.

maths○ /mat/ *nf pl* maths○ (GB), math○ (US).

matière /matjɛʀ/ *nf* **1** material; **fournir la ~ d'un roman** to provide the material for a novel; **2** matter; **en ~ d'emploi** as far as employment is concerned; **~ à réflexion** food for thought; **3** (Sch) subject.

■ **~s fécales** faeces; **~s grasses** fat; **~ grise** grey (GB) or gray (US) matter; **~ plastique** plastic; **~ première** raw material.

Matignon /matiɲɔ̃/ *pr n*: *offices of the French Prime Minister*.

matin /matɛ̃/ *nm* morning; **travailler le ~** to work in the morning; **5 heures du ~** 5 (o'clock) in the morning; **de bon ~** early in the morning.

IDIOMS **être du ~** to be a morning person; **un de ces quatre ~s**○ one of these days.

matinal, ~e, *mpl* **-aux** /matinal, o/ *adj*

[*walk*] morning; [*hour*] early; **être ~** to be an early riser, to be up early.

mâtiné, **~e** /mɑtine/ *adj* **un anglais ~ de français** a mixture of English and French.

matinée /matine/ *nf* **1** morning; **2** matinée.
IDIOMS **faire la grasse ~** to have a lie-in (GB), to sleep in.

matines /matin/ *nf pl* matins.

matou /matu/ *nm* tomcat.

matraquage /matʀakaʒ/ *nm* **1** bludgeoning; **2** (figurative) **~ publicitaire** hype○.

matraque /matʀak/ *nf* club; truncheon (GB), billy (US); cosh (GB), blackjack (US); **c'est le coup de ~**○ (figurative) it costs a fortune.

matraquer /matʀake/ [1] *vtr* **1** to club; to cosh (GB), to blackjack (US); **2** [*media*] to bombard [*public*] (**de** with); **3**○ to rip [sb] off○.

matriarcal, **~e**, *mpl* **-aux** /matʀijaʀkal, o/ *adj* matriarchal.

matrice /matʀis/ *nf* **1** matrix; **2** die.

matricule /matʀikyl/ *nm* reference number; (Mil) service number.

matrimonial, **~e**, *mpl*, **-iaux** /matʀimɔnjal, o/ *adj* marriage, matrimonial.

matrone /matʀɔn/ *nf* matronly woman.

maturation /matyʀasjɔ̃/ *nf* ripening; maturing.

maturité /matyʀite/ *nf* maturity; **manquer de ~** to be immature.

maudire /modiʀ/ [80] *vtr* to curse.

maudit, **~e** /modi, it/ I *pp* ▶ **maudire**.
II *adj* **1**○ blasted○; **2** cursed (**de** by); **~s soient-ils** a curse on them.
III *nm,f* damned soul; **les ~s** the damned.

Maure /mɔʀ/ *nmf* Moor.

Mauresque /mɔʀɛsk/ *nf* Moorish woman.

mausolée /mozɔle/ *nm* mausoleum.

maussade /mosad/ *adj* [*mood*] sullen; [*weather*] dull; [*landscape*] bleak.

mauvais, **~e** /mɔvɛ, ɛz/ I *adj* **1** bad, poor; [*lawyer, doctor*] incompetent; [*wage*] low; **avoir une ~e opinion de qn** to have a poor opinion of sb; **du ~ tabac/alcool** cheap tobacco/alcohol; **2** [*address*] wrong; **3** [*day, moment*] bad; [*method*] wrong; **il ne serait pas ~ de faire** it wouldn't be a bad idea to do; **4** bad; [*surprise*] nasty; [*taste, smell*] unpleasant, nasty; **par ~ temps** in bad weather; **ça a ~ goût** it tastes horrible; **5** [*cold, wound*] nasty; [*sea*] rough; **6** [*person, smile*] nasty; [*intentions, thoughts*] evil; [*instinct*] base; **préparer un ~ coup** to be up to mischief.
II *adv* **sentir ~** to smell; **sentir très ~** to stink; **il fait ~** the weather is bad.
III *nm* **il n'y a pas que du ~ dans le projet** the project isn't all bad.
■ **~ esprit** scoffing person; scoffing attitude; **faire du ~ esprit** to scoff; **~ garçon** tough guy; **~ plaisant** person with a warped sense of humour[GB]; **~ traitements** ill-treatment; **faire subir des ~ traitements à qn** to ill-treat sb; **~e herbe** weed; **~es rencontres** bad company.

IDIOMS **la trouver** or **l'avoir ~e**○ to be furious.

mauve[1] /mov/ *adj, nm* mauve.

mauve[2] /mov/ *nf* mallow.

mauviette /movjɛt/ *nf* wimp○.

maux ▶ **mal**.

maxi- /maksi/ *pref* **~-jupe** maxi-skirt; **~-bouteille** one-and-a-half litre[GB] bottle.

maxillaire /maksilɛʀ/ I *adj* maxillary.
II *nm* jawbone.

maxima ▶ **maximum**.

maximal, **~e**, *mpl* **-aux** /maksimal, o/ *adj* maximum.

maximaliser /maksimalize/ [1] *vtr* to maximize.

maximaliste /maksimalist/ *adj* uncompromising; hard-line.

maxime /maksim/ *nf* maxim.

maximiser /maksimize/ [1] *vtr* to maximize.

maximum, *pl* **~s** or **maxima** /maksimɔm, maksima/ I *adj* maximum.
II *nm* **1** maximum; **un prêt jusqu'à un ~ de...** a loan for a maximum amount of...; **10 francs au grand ~** 10 francs at the very most; **au ~** [*work*] to the maximum; [*reduce*] as much as possible; **obtenir le ~ d'avantages** to get as many advantages as possible; **faire le ~** to do one's utmost; **2** (Law) maximum sentence.

mayonnaise /majɔnɛz/ *nf* mayonnaise.

mazagran /mazagʀɑ̃/ *nm*: *thick china goblet for coffee.*

mazout /mazut/ *nm* (fuel) oil; **chauffage au ~** oil-fired heating.

me (**m'** *before vowel or mute h*) /m(ə)/ *pron* **1** me; **tu ne m'as pas fait mal** you didn't hurt me; **2** myself; **je ~ lave (les mains)** I wash (my hands); **je m'en veux** I'm angry with myself.

Me *written abbr* = **maître** III 3.

méandre /meɑ̃dʀ/ *nm* **1** meander; **2** (figurative) **~s** twists and turns; **les ~s de l'administration** the maze of officialdom.

mec○ /mɛk/ *nm* guy○; **mon ~** my man○.

mécanicien, **-ienne** /mekanisjɛ̃, ɛn/ I *adj* mechanical.
II *nm,f* mechanic.
III *nm* (of train) engine driver (GB), (locomotive) engineer (US); (of plane) flight engineer; (of boat) engineer.

mécanique /mekanik/ I *adj* mechanical; [*toy*] clockwork; [*razor*] hand; **industrie ~** engineering industry.
II *nf* **1** mechanics; **un génie de la ~** a mechanical genius; **une merveille de ~** a marvel of engineering; **2**○ machine.

mécaniquement /mekanikmɑ̃/ *adv* mechanically; **fabriqué ~** machine-made.

mécaniser /mekanize/ [1] *vtr*, **se mécaniser** *v refl* (+ *v être*) to mechanize.

mécanisme /mekanism/ *nm* mechanism.

mécano○ /mekano/ *nm* mechanic.

mécanographe /mekanɔgʀaf/ *nmf* punch-card operator.

mécénat /mesena/ *nm* patronage.

mécène /mesɛn/ *nm* patron of the arts.

méchamment /meʃamɑ̃/ *adv* **1** spitefully, maliciously; viciously; **traiter qn ~** to treat sb badly; **2**° [*damage*] badly; [*good*] terribly.

méchanceté /meʃɑ̃ste/ *nf* **1** nastiness; **par pure ~** out of pure spite; **sans ~** without malice; **2** maliciousness, viciousness; **3** malicious act; malicious remark.

méchant, **~e** /meʃɑ̃, ɑ̃t/ **I** *adj* **1** [*person*] nasty, malicious; [*animal*] vicious; [*flu, business*] nasty, bad; **ce n'est pas une ~e femme** she's not such a bad woman; **2**° fantastic°, terrific°.

II *nm,f* **1** villain, baddie°; **2** naughty boy/girl.

mèche /mɛʃ/ *nf* **1** (of hair) lock; ; **2** (in hair) streak; **3** (of candle) wick; **4** (Med) packing; **5** (of explosive) fuse; **6** (drill) bit.

IDIOMS **être de ~ avec qn**° to be in cahoots° with sb; **vendre la ~** to let the cat out of the bag.

méchoui /meʃwi/ *nm* North African style barbecue; spit-roast lamb.

méconnaissable /mekɔnɛsabl/ *adj* unrecognizable.

méconnaître /mekɔnɛtʀ/ [73] *vtr* to misread [*situation*]; to be mistaken about [*cause, intention*].

méconnu, **~e** /mekɔny/ *adj* [*artist, work*] neglected; [*talent*] undervalued; [*value*] unrecognized.

mécontent, **~e** /mekɔ̃tɑ̃, ɑ̃t/ *adj* [*customer, employer*] dissatisfied; [*voter*] discontented; **pas ~** rather pleased.

mécontentement /mekɔ̃tɑ̃tmɑ̃/ *nm* **1** dissatisfaction; **2** discontent; **3** annoyance; **4** displeasure.

Mecque /mɛk/ *pr n* **la ~** Mecca.

médaille /medaj/ *nf* **1** medal; **~ d'or** gold medal; **2** coin; **3** medallion.

médaillon /medajɔ̃/ *nm* **1** locket; **2** (in art, architecture) medallion.

médecin /mɛdsɛ̃/ *nm* doctor; **~ traitant** general practitioner, GP (GB).

■ **~ de garde** duty doctor, doctor on duty; **~ légiste** forensic surgeon.

médecine /mɛdsin/ *nf* medicine.

■ **~ scolaire** ≈ school health service; **~ du travail** ≈ occupational medicine; **~s douces** or **parallèles** alternative medicine.

média /medja/ **I** *nm* medium.

II médias *nm pl* **les ~s** the media.

médian, **~e** /medjɑ̃, an/ *adj* median.

médiateur, **-trice** /medjatœʀ, tʀis/ *nm,f* **1** mediator; **2** ombudsman.

médiathèque /medjatɛk/ *nf* multimedia library.

médiation /medjasjɔ̃/ *nf* mediation; **tenter une ~** to make an attempt at mediation.

médiatique /medjatik/ *adj* [*exploitation*] by the media; [*success*] media; **geste ~** publicity stunt.

médiatiser /medjatize/ [1] *vtr* to give [sth] publicity in the media.

médiatrice /medjatʀis/ *nf* ▶ **médiateur**.

médical, **~e**, *mpl* **-aux** /medikal, o/ *adj* medical.

médicament /medikamɑ̃/ *nm* medicine, drug.

médication /medikasjɔ̃/ *nf* medication.

médicinal, **~e**, *mpl* **-aux** /medisinal, o/ *adj* medicinal.

médico-légal, **~e**, *mpl* **-aux** /medikolegal, o/ *adj* forensic; **certificat ~** autopsy report; **institut ~** forensic science laboratory.

médiéval, **~e**, *mpl* **-aux** /medjeval, o/ *adj* medieval.

médiocre /medjɔkʀ/ *adj* mediocre; [*actor*] mediocre, second-rate; [*pupil, intelligence*] below-average; [*soil, light, return, food*] poor; [*interest, success, ambition, attraction*] limited; [*life*] humdrum; [*income*] meagre[GB].

médiocrement /medjɔkʀəmɑ̃/ *adv* rather badly.

médiocrité /medjɔkʀite/ *nf* **1** mediocrity; **la ~ de ces élèves** the mediocre standard of these pupils; **2** meagreness[GB].

médire /mediʀ/ [65] *v+prep* **~ de** to speak ill of.

médisance /medizɑ̃s/ *nf* malicious gossip.

médisant, **~e** /medizɑ̃, ɑ̃t/ *adj* malicious.

méditation /meditasjɔ̃/ *nf* meditation.

méditer /medite/ [1] **I** *vtr* **1** to contemplate (**de faire** doing); **2** to mull over; **longuement médité** [*plan*] carefully considered.

II *vi* to meditate; **~ sur** to meditate on [*existence*]; to ponder on or over [*problem*].

Méditerranée /mediteʀane/ *pr nf* **la (mer) ~** the Mediterranean (Sea).

médium /medjɔm/ *nm* **1** medium; **2** (Mus) middle register.

méduse /medyz/ *nf* jellyfish.

méduser /medyze/ [1] *vtr* to dumbfound.

meeting /mitiŋ/ *nm* meeting; **~ aérien** air show.

méfait /mefɛ/ **I** *nm* misdemeanour[GB]; crime.

II méfaits *nm pl* (of alcohol, tobacco) detrimental effect.

méfiance /mefjɑ̃s/ *nf* mistrust, suspicion; **éveiller la ~ de qn** to arouse sb's suspicions; **~ de qn envers qn/qch** sb's wariness of sb/sth.

méfiant, **~e** /mefjɑ̃, ɑ̃t/ *adj* suspicious; **elle est d'un naturel** or **caractère ~** she's always very wary.

méfier: **se méfier** /mefje/ [2] *v refl* (+ *v être*) **1 se ~ de qn/qch** not to trust sb/sth; **sans se ~** quite trustingly; **2 se ~ de qch** to be wary of sth; **méfie-toi!** be careful!; watch it!.

méga /mega/ *pref* mega; **~hertz** megahertz; **~watt** megawatt.

mégalomane /megalɔman/ *adj, nmf* megalomaniac.

mégaphone /megafɔn/ *nm* **1** loudhailer; **2** megaphone.

mégarde: **par mégarde** /paʀmegaʀd/ *phr* inadvertently.

mégère /meʒɛʀ/ *nf* shrew.

mégot /mego/ *nm* **1** cigarette butt or end; **2** (cigar) stub.

meilleur, ~e[1] /mɛjœʀ/ **I** *adj* **1** better (**que** than); **2** best; **le ~ des deux** the better of the two; **au ~ prix** [*buy*] at the lowest price; [*sell*] at the highest price.
II *nm,f* **le ~, la ~e** the best one.
III *adv* better; **il fait ~ qu'hier** the weather is better than it was yesterday.
IV *nm* **le ~** the best bit; **donner le ~ de soi-même** to give of one's best; **pour le ~ et pour le pire** for better or for worse.

meilleure[2] /mɛjœʀ/ *nf* **ça c'est la ~!** that's the best one yet!; **j'en passe et des ~s!** that's the least of it, I could go on!

mélancolie /melɑ̃kɔli/ *nf* (gen) melancholy; (Med) melancholia.

mélancolique /melɑ̃kɔlik/ *adj* (gen) melancholy; (Med) melancholic.

mélange /melɑ̃ʒ/ *nm* (of teas, tobaccos) blend; (of products, ideas) combination; (of colours, feelings) mixture; **c'est un ~ (coton et synthétique)** it's a mix (of cotton and synthetic fibres[GB]); **bonheur sans ~** unadulterated happiness.

mélanger /melɑ̃ʒe/ [13] **I** *vtr* **1** to blend [*teas, oils, tobaccos*]; to mix [*colours, shades*]; **2** to put together [*styles, people, objects*]; **3** to mix up; **~ les cartes** to shuffle (the cards); **mais non! tu mélanges tout!** no! you're getting it all mixed up.
II se mélanger *v refl* (+ *v être*) **1** [*teas, oils, tobaccos*] to blend; [*colours, shades*] to mix, to blend together; **2** [*memories, ideas*] to get muddled.

mélangeur /melɑ̃ʒœʀ/ *nm* mixer; **robinet ~** mixer tap (GB), mixer faucet (US).

mélanome /melanom/ *nm* melanoma.

mélasse /melas/ *nf* black treacle (GB), molasses.

mêlée /mele/ *nf* **1** mêlée; **~ générale** free-for-all; **2** (Sport) scrum; **3** (figurative) fray.

mêler /mele/ [1] **I** *vtr* **1** to mix [*products, colours*]; to blend [*ingredients, cultures*]; to combine [*influences*]; **2 être mêlé à un scandale** to be involved in a scandal.
II se mêler *v refl* (+ *v être*) **1** [*cultures, religions*] to mix; [*smells, voices*] to mingle; **2 se ~ à** to mingle with [*crowd*]; to mix with [*people*]; to join in [*conversation*]; **3 se ~ de** to meddle in; **mêle-toi de tes affaires**○ mind your own business; **de quoi je me mêle**○! what's it got to do with you?

méli-mélo, *pl* **mélis-mélos** /melimelo/ *nm* jumble, mess.

mélo○ /melo/ *adj* slushy○, schmaltzy○; **feuilleton ~** soap (opera).

mélodie /melɔdi/ *nf* **1** melody, tune; **2** melodiousness.

mélodieux, -ieuse /melɔdjø, øz/ *adj* melodious.

mélodique /melɔdik/ *adj* melodic.

mélodrame /melɔdʀam/ *nm* melodrama.

mélomane /melɔman/ *nmf* music lover.

melon /məlɔ̃/ *nm* **1** melon; **2** bowler (hat) (GB), derby (hat) (US).

membrane /mɑ̃bʀan/ *nf* **1** (Anat) membrane; **2** (in loudspeaker) diaphragm.

membre /mɑ̃bʀ/ *nm* **1** member; **les pays ~s** the member countries; **2** limb; **~ postérieur** hind limb.

même /mɛm/ **I** *adj* **1** same; **la ~ robe qu'hier** the same dress as yesterday; **2 c'est l'intelligence ~** he's/she's intelligence itself; **3 le jour ~ où** the very same day that; **c'est cela ~** that's it exactly.
II *adv* **1** even; **je ne m'en souviens ~ plus** I can't even remember now; **2** very; **c'est ici ~ que je l'ai rencontré** I met him at this very place.
III de même *phr* **agir** or **faire de ~** to do the same; **cette remarque ne s'adresse pas qu'à lui, il en est** or **va de ~ pour** the same is true of.
IV de même que *phr* **le prix du café, de ~ que celui du tabac, a augmenté de 10%** the price of coffee, as well as that of tobacco, has risen by 10%.
V même si *phr* even if.
VI *pron* **le ~, la ~, les ~s** the same; **ce sac est le ~ que celui de Pierre** this bag is the same as Pierre's.

mémé○ /meme/ *nf* **1** gran○, granny○; **2** old granny○.

mémento /memɛ̃to/ *nm* guide.

mémère○ /memɛʀ/ *nf* **1** old granny○; **2** granny○.

mémo○ /memo/ *nm* note.

mémoire[1] /memwaʀ/ **I** *nm* **1** memo; **2** dissertation.
II mémoires *nm pl* memoirs.

mémoire[2] /memwaʀ/ *nf* **1** memory; **si j'ai bonne ~** if I remember rightly; **ne pas avoir de ~** to have a bad memory; **des faits qui sont dans toutes les ~s** facts that everyone remembers; **de ~ d'homme** in living memory; **en ~ de** to the memory of, in memory of; **d'illustre ~** [*character, event*] illustrious; **pour ~** for the record; for reference; **2** (Comput) memory; storage; **mettre des données en ~** to input data.
■ **~ de maîtrise** dissertation (*which constitutes part of the French master's degree*); **~ morte** read-only memory, ROM; **~ vive** random access memory, RAM.

mémorable /memɔʀabl/ *adj* memorable.

mémorial, ~e, *mpl* **-iaux** /memɔʀjal, o/ *nm* memorial.

mémoriser /memɔʀize/ [1] *vtr* to memorize.

menaçant, ~e /mənasɑ̃, ɑ̃t/ *adj* menacing; **dire des paroles ~es** to make threats.

menace /mənas/ *nf* threat; **~s en l'air** idle threats; **sous la ~** under duress; **sous la ~ d'une arme** at gunpoint.

menacer /mənase/ [12] *vtr* **1** to threaten [*person*]; **2** to pose a threat to; **être menacé** [*stability, economy*] to be in jeopardy; [*life*] to be in danger; [*calm*] to be threatened; [*career*] to be on the line; [*population*] to be at risk.

ménage /menaʒ/ *nm* **1** household; **rien ne va plus dans leur ~** their relationship doesn't work any more; **se mettre en ~ avec qn** to set up home with sb; **scènes de ~** domestic rows; **monter son ~** to buy the household goods; **2** housework; **faire le ~** to do the cleaning; **faire des ~s** to do domestic cleaning work.
IDIOMS **faire bon ~** to be compatible.

ménagement /menaʒmɑ̃/ *nm* **avec ~s** gently; **sans ~s** [*say*] bluntly; [*push*] roughly, unceremoniously.

ménager[1] /menaʒe/ [13] **I** *vtr* **1** to handle [sb] carefully; to deal carefully with [sb]; to be gentle with [sb]; to be careful with [sth]; **~ la susceptibilité de qn** to humour[GB] sb; **~ sa santé** to look after one's health; **2** to be careful with [*clothes, savings*]; **il ne ménage pas ses efforts** or **sa peine** he spares no effort; **3 ~ un passage** to make an opening; **4** to organize [*meeting*].
II se ménager *v refl* (+ *v être*) to take it easy.

ménager[2], **-ère**[1] /menaʒe, ɛʀ/ *adj* [*jobs*] domestic; [*equipment*] household; **appareils ~s** domestic appliances; **travaux ~s** housework.

ménagère[2] /menaʒɛʀ/ *nf* **1** housewife; **2** canteen of cutlery.

ménagerie /menaʒʀi/ *nf* menagerie.

mendiant, **~e** /mɑ̃djɑ̃, ɑ̃t/ *nm,f* beggar.

mendicité /mɑ̃disite/ *nf* begging.

mendier /mɑ̃dje/ [2] **I** *vtr* to beg for; **~ qch auprès de qn** to beg sb for sth.
II *vi* to beg.

mener /məne/ [16] **I** *vtr* **1 ~ qn quelque part** to take sb somewhere; to drive sb somewhere; **2** to lead [*people, country*]; to run [*company*]; **il ne se laisse pas ~ par sa grande sœur** he won't be bossed about° by his sister; **se laisser ~ par son seul intérêt** to be motivated by pure self-interest; **3** (Sport) to lead; **4 ~ au village** [*road*] to go or lead to the village; **5 ~ à** to lead to; **cela mène à tout** it leads to all kinds of things; **cette histoire peut te ~ loin** it could be a very nasty business; **~ à bien** to complete [sth] successfully; to bring [sth] to a successful conclusion; to handle [sth] successfully; **6** to carry out [*study, reform*]; to pursue [*policy*]; to run [*campaign*]; **~ une enquête** to hold an investigation; to head an investigation; **~ sa vie comme on l'entend** to live as one pleases; **~ une grève de la faim** to be on hunger strike.
II *vi* (Sport) to be in the lead.
IDIOMS **~ la danse** or **le jeu** to call the tune; **~ la grande vie** to live it up.

ménestrel /menɛstʀɛl/ *nm* minstrel.

meneur, **-euse** /mənœʀ, øz/ *nm,f* leader; **qualités de ~** leadership qualities.

menhir /meniʀ/ *nm* menhir.

méninge /menɛ̃ʒ/ **I** *nf* (Anat) meninx.
II méninges° *nf pl* brains°; **se creuser les ~s** to rack one's brains.

méningite /menɛ̃ʒit/ *nf* meningitis.

ménisque /menisk/ *nm* meniscus.

ménopause /menɔpoz/ *nf* menopause.

menotte /mənɔt/ **I** *nf* tiny hand.
II menottes *nf pl* handcuffs; **passer les ~s à qn** to handcuff sb.

mensonge /mɑ̃sɔ̃ʒ/ *nm* **1** lie; **2 le ~** lying.

mensonger, **-ère** /mɑ̃sɔ̃ʒe, ɛʀ/ *adj* [*accusations*] false; [*advertising*] misleading; [*campaign*] dishonest.

mensualisé, **~e** /mɑ̃sɥalize/ *adj* [*salary, employee*] paid monthly.

mensualité /mɑ̃sɥalite/ *nf* monthly instalment[GB].

mensuel, **-elle** /mɑ̃sɥɛl/ **I** *adj* monthly.
II *nm* monthly magazine.

mensuellement /mɑ̃sɥɛlmɑ̃/ *adv* once a month, monthly.

mensurations /mɑ̃syʀasjɔ̃/ *nf pl* measurements.

mental, **~e**, *mpl* **-aux** /mɑ̃tal, o/ *adj* mental; **handicapé ~** mentally handicapped person.

mentalité /mɑ̃talite/ *nf* mentality; **belle ~!** the mentality of some people!

menteur, **-euse** /mɑ̃tœʀ, øz/ **I** *adj* [*person*] untruthful; [*statement*] full of lies.
II *nm,f* liar.

menthe /mɑ̃t/ *nf* **1** mint; **~ poivrée** peppermint; **~ verte** spearmint; **2** mint tea; **3 ~ (à l'eau)** mint cordial.

menthol /mɛ̃tɔl/ *nm* menthol.

mentholé, **~e** /mɛ̃tɔle/ *adj* mentholated; [*sweet, cigarette*] menthol.

mention /mɑ̃sjɔ̃/ *nf* **1** mention; **faire ~ de qch** to mention sth; **2** (Sch) **~ passable** *pass with 50 to 60%*; **~ assez bien** *pass with 60 to 70%*; **~ bien** *pass with 70 to 80%*; **~ très bien** *pass with 80% upwards*; **3** note; **rayer la ~ inutile** or **les ~s inutiles** delete as appropriate.

mentionner /mɑ̃sjɔne/ [1] *vtr* to mention; **ci-dessus mentionné** mentioned above.

mentir /mɑ̃tiʀ/ [30] **I** *vi* **1** to lie, to tell lies; **2** [*figures*] to be misleading.
II se mentir *v refl* (+ *v être*) **1** to fool oneself; **2** to lie to one another.

menton /mɑ̃tɔ̃/ *nm* chin.

menu, **~e** /məny/ **I** *adj* **1** [*person*] slight; [*foot, piece*] tiny; [*writing*] small; **2** [*jobs*] small; [*worries, expenses*] minor; [*details*] minute; **~ fretin** small fry.
II *adv* [*write*] small; [*chop*] finely.
III *nm* menu; **~ gastronomique/touristique** gourmet/middle-price menu.
IV par le menu *phr* in (great) detail.

menuet /mənɥɛ/ *nm* minuet.

menuiserie /mənɥizʀi/ *nf* woodwork; **un atelier de ~** a joiner's workshop.

menuisier /mənɥizje/ *nm* joiner (GB), finish carpenter.

méprendre: **se méprendre** /mepʀɑ̃dʀ/ [52] *v refl* (+ *v être*) to be mistaken; **elles se ressemblent tellement, c'est à s'y ~** they're so much alike, it's hard to tell them apart.

mépris /mepʀi/ *nm inv* contempt; **au ~ de la loi** regardless of the law.

méprisable /meprizabl/ *adj* contemptible; despicable.

méprisant, ~e /meprizɑ̃, ɑ̃t/ *adj* [*gesture*] contemptuous; [*person*] disdainful.

méprise /mepriz/ *nf* mistake.

mépriser /meprize/ [1] *vtr* to despise [*person, wealth*]; to scorn [*danger, offer*].

mer /mɛr/ *nf* **1** sea; **une ~ d'huile** a glassy sea; **en pleine ~** out at sea; **prendre la ~** to go to sea; **la ~ monte** the tide is coming in; **2** seaside.
IDIOMS **ce n'est pas la ~ à boire** it's not all that difficult.

mercantile /mɛrkɑ̃til/ *adj* mercenary.

mercenaire /mɛrsənɛr/ *adj, nmf* mercenary.

mercerie /mɛrsəri/ *nf* haberdasher's shop (GB), notions store (US).

merci[1] /mɛrsi/ *nm, excl* thank you.

merci[2] /mɛrsi/ *nf* mercy; **on est toujours à la ~ d'un accident** there's always the risk of an accident.

mercredi /mɛrkrədi/ *nm* Wednesday.

mercure /mɛrkyr/ *nm* mercury.

mercurochrome®/mɛrkyrokrom/*nm*Mercurochrome®, antiseptic.

merde● /mɛrd/ *nf, excl* shit◐.

mère /mɛr/ **I** *nf* **1** mother; **2**○ **la ~ Michel** old mother Michel; **3 ~ supérieure** Mother Superior.
II (-)mère (*combining form*) **cellule/maison ~** parent cell/company.
■ **~ célibataire** single mother; **~ de famille** mother; housewife; **~ porteuse** surrogate mother; **~ poule** mother hen.

merguez /mɛrgɛz/ *nf inv* spicy sausage.

méridien /meridjɛ̃/ *nm* meridian.

méridional, ~e, *mpl* **-aux** /meridjɔnal, o/ **I** *adj* southern.
II *nm,f* Southerner.

meringue /mərɛ̃g/ *nf* meringue.

merisier /mərizje/ *nm* **1** wild cherry tree; **2** cherry wood.

mérite /merit/ *nm* **1** merit; **2** credit; **au ~** according to merit; **avoir du ~ à faire** to deserve credit for doing; **vanter les ~s de** to sing the praises of.

mériter /merite/ [1] **I** *vtr* to deserve; **~ réflexion** to be worth considering.
II se mériter *v refl* (+ *v être*) **c'est quelque chose qui se mérite** it's something that has to be earned.

méritoire /meritwar/ *adj* praiseworthy, commendable.

merlan /mɛrlɑ̃/ *nm* whiting.

merle /mɛrl/ *nm* blackbird.

mérou /meru/ *nm* grouper.

mérovingien, -ienne /merovɛ̃ʒjɛ̃, ɛn/ *adj* Merovingian.

merveille /mɛrvɛj/ **I** *nf* marvel, wonder; **faire ~** or **des ~s** to work wonders.
II à merveille *phr* wonderfully; **se porter à ~** to be in excellent health.

merveilleux, -euse /mɛrvɛjø, øz/ **I** *adj* marvellous[GB], wonderful.
II *nm* **le ~** the fabulous.

mes ▶ mon.

mésange /mezɑ̃ʒ/ *nf* tit; **~ charbonnière** great tit.

mésaventure /mezavɑ̃tyr/ *nf* misadventure; **connaître une ~** to have an unfortunate experience.

mesdames ▶ madame.

mesdemoiselles ▶ mademoiselle.

mésentente /mezɑ̃tɑ̃t/ *nf* dissension; disagreement.

mesquin, ~e /mɛskɛ̃, in/ *adj* **1** petty-minded; petty; **2** [*person*] mean (GB), cheap○ (US).

mesquinerie /mɛskinri/ *nf* **1** meanness; **2** stinginess; **3** mean trick; **4** mean remark.

message /mesaʒ/ *nm* message; **~ publicitaire** commercial.

messager, -ère /mesaʒe, ɛr/ *nm,f* **1** messenger; **2** envoy.

messagerie /mesaʒri/ *nf* **1** freight forwarding; **2 ~ vocale** voice messaging.

messe /mɛs/ *nf* mass; **~s basses**○ whispering.

messie /mesi/ *nm* messiah.

messieurs ▶ monsieur.

mesure /məzyr/ *nf* **1** measure; **prendre des ~s** to take measures; to take steps; **par ~ de sécurité** as a safety precaution; **2** measurement; **c'est du sur ~** it's made to measure; **tu as un emploi sur ~** the job is tailor-made for you; **c'est une adversaire à ta ~** she is a match for you; **pour faire bonne ~** for good measure; **3 unité de ~** unit of measurement; **instrument de ~** measuring device; **deux ~s de lait pour une ~ d'eau** two parts milk to one of water; **4** moderation; **parler avec ~** to weigh one's words; **dépasser la ~** to go too far; **5** (Mus) bar; **c'est une ~ à trois temps** it's in three time; **battre la ~** to beat time; **6 être en ~ de rembourser** to be in a position to reimburse; **dans la ~ du possible** as far as possible; **dans une certaine ~** to some extent; **dans la ~ où** insofar as.

mesurer /məzyre/ [1] **I** *vtr* **1** to measure; **~ le tour de cou de qn** to take sb's neck measurement; **2** to measure [*productivity, gap*]; to assess [*difficulties, risks, effects*]; to consider [*consequences*]; **~ sa force contre qn** to pit one's strength against sb; **~ ses paroles** to weigh one's words; **3 le temps nous est mesuré** our time is limited; **ne pas ~ ses efforts** to try one's utmost.
II *vi* **~ 20 mètres carrés** to be 20 metres[GB] square; **elle mesure 1,60 m** she's 1.60 m tall.
III se mesurer *v refl* (+ *v être*) **1 se ~ en mètres** to be measured in metres[GB]; **2 se ~ à** or **avec qn** to pit one's strength against sb.

métairie /metɛri/ *nf* tenanted farm.

métal, *pl* **-aux** /metal, o/ *nm* metal; **pièce de** or **en ~** metal coin; **~ jaune** gold.

métallique /metalik/ *adj* **1** metal; **c'est ~**

it's made of metal; **2** metallic; **le bruit ~ des clés** the clink of keys.

métallisé /metalize/ *adj* [*green, blue*] metallic.

métallurgie /metalyRʒi/ *nf* **1** metalworking industry; **2** metallurgy.

métallurgiste /metalyRʒist/ *nm* **1** metalworker; **2** metallurgist.

métamorphose /metamɔRfoz/ *nf* metamorphosis.

métamorphoser /metamɔRfoze/ [1] **I** *vtr* to transform [sb/sth] completely.

II se métamorphoser *v refl* (+ *v être*) **se ~ en** to metamorphose into.

métaphore /metafɔR/ *nf* metaphor.

métaphysique /metafizik/ *nf* metaphysics.

métastase /metastɑz/ *nf* metastasis.

métayer, -ère /meteje, ɛR/ *nm,f* tenant farmer (GB), sharecropper (US).

météo /meteo/ *nf* weather forecast; **~ marine** shipping forecast.

météore /meteɔR/ *nm* meteor.

météorite /meteɔRit/ *nm* or *nf* meteorite.

météorologie /meteɔRɔlɔʒi/ *nf* meteorology; **la ~ nationale** the Meteorological Office (GB), the Weather Service (US).

météorologique /meteɔRɔlɔʒik/ *adj* meteorological; **conditions ~s** weather conditions.

méthane /metan/ *nm* methane.

méthode /metɔd/ *nf* **1** method; **procéder avec ~** to proceed methodically; **2** (of music) method; (for languages) course book (GB), textbook (US); **3** way; **j'ai ma ~ pour le convaincre** I've got a way of convincing him; **~ miracle** magic formula.

méthodique /metɔdik/ *adj* methodical.

méthodisme /metɔdism/ *nm* Methodism.

méticuleux, -euse /metikylø, øz/ *adj* meticulous; painstaking.

méticulosité /metikylozite/ *nf* meticulousness.

métier /metje/ *nm* **1** job; profession; trade; craft; **faire son ~ de mère** to do one's job as a mother; **avoir 20 ans de ~** to have 20 years' experience; **c'est le ~ qui rentre!** you learn by your mistakes!; **2 ~ à tisser** weaving loom.

métis, -isse /metis/ *nm,f* person of mixed race.

métissage /metisaʒ/ *nm* (of people) miscegenation; (of plants, animals) crossing; **~ culturel** cultural cross-fertilization.

métrage /metRaʒ/ *nm* **1** (of material) length; **2 long ~** feature(-length) film.

mètre /mɛtR/ *nm* **1** metre[GB]; **le 60 ~s** the 60 metres[GB]; **piquer un cent ~s**° to break into a run; **2** rule (GB), yardstick (US); **~ ruban** or **de couturière** tape measure.

métrique /metRik/ *adj* metric.

métro /metRo/ *nm* underground (GB), subway (US).

IDIOMS **~, boulot, dodo**° the daily grind.

métronome /metRɔnɔm/ *nm* metronome.

métropole /metRɔpɔl/ *nf* **1** metropolis; **2** major city; **3** Metropolitan France.

métropolitain, ~e /metRɔpɔlitɛ̃, ɛn/ *adj* **1** [*network*] underground (GB), subway (US); **2** [*culture, investor*] from Metropolitan France.

mets /mɛ/ *nm inv* dish, delicacy.

metteur /mɛtœR/ *nm* **~ en scène** director; **~ en pages** make-up man.

mettre /mɛtR/ [60] **I** *vtr* **1** to put; **je mets les enfants à la crèche** I send the children to a creche; **mets ton écharpe** put your scarf on; **~ le linge à sécher** to put the washing out to dry; to put in [*heating, shower*]; to put up [*curtains, shelves*]; **faire ~ le téléphone** to have a telephone put in; **2** to wear; **3 ~ qn en colère** to make sb angry; **tu me mets hors de moi** you infuriate me; **4 ~ la radio** to put the radio on; **mets moins fort!** turn it down!; **~ le réveil** to set the alarm; **5** to put up [*sign*]; **qu'est-ce que je dois ~?** what shall I put?; **je t'ai mis un mot** I've left you a note; **~ en musique** to set to music; **~ en anglais** to put into English; **6 y ~ du sien** to put oneself into it; **combien pouvez-vous ~?** how much can you afford?; how much can you put in?; **elle a mis une heure** it took her an hour (**pour faire** to do); **~ un temps fou**° to take ages°; **7** (Sch) **je vous ai mis trois sur vingt** I've given you three out of twenty; **8**° **mettons dix dollars** let's say ten dollars; **mettons qu'il vienne, qu'est-ce que vous ferez?** supposing he comes, what will you do?

II *vi* **~ bas** [*animal*] to give birth; to calve; to lamb; to foal.

III se mettre *v refl* (+ *v être*) **1 se ~ devant la fenêtre** to stand in front of the window; **se ~ au lit** to go to bed; **se ~ debout** to stand up; **ne plus savoir où se ~** not to know where to put oneself; **où est-ce que ça se met?** where does this go?; **2** to spill [sth] on oneself; **3 je ne sais pas quoi me ~** I don't know what to put on; **4 se ~ à l'anglais** to take up English; **il va se ~ à pleuvoir** it's going to start raining; **5 se ~ en tort** to put oneself in the wrong; **je préfère me ~ bien avec lui** I prefer to get on the right side of him; **se ~ à l'aise** to make oneself comfortable.

meuble /mœbl/ **I** *adj* [*soil*] loose.

II *nm* **un ~** a piece of furniture; **des ~s** furniture; **~ hi-fi** hi-fi unit.

IDIOMS **sauver les ~s** to salvage something.

meublé /mœble/ *nm* furnished flat (GB) or apartment.

meubler /mœble/ [1] *vtr* to furnish (**de, avec** with); **la plante meuble bien la pièce** the plant makes the room look more cosy (GB) or cozy (US).

meugler /møgle/ [1] *vi* to moo.

meule /møl/ *nf* **1** millstone; **2** grindstone; **3 ~ de foin** haystack; **~ de paille** rick of straw.

meunier, -ière[1] /mønje, ɛR/ *nm,f* miller.

meunière[2] /mønjɛR/ *nf* **1** miller's wife; **2** (Culin) **sole ~** sole meunière.

meurtre /mœRtR/ *nm* murder.

meurtrier, -ière /mœRtRije, ɛR/ **I** *adj* [*fighting, repression*] bloody; [*explosion, accident*] fatal;

[*epidemic*] deadly; [*arm*] lethal; [*road*] very dangerous.
II *nm,f* murderer.

meurtrir /mœʀtʀiʀ/ [3] *vtr* **1** to hurt; **2** to bruise; **3** to wound [*self-esteem*].

meurtrissure /mœʀtʀisyʀ/ *nf* bruise.

meute /møt/ *nf* pack of hounds; **la ~ des journalistes** the pack of journalists.

mexicain, ~e /mɛksikɛ̃, ɛn/ *adj* Mexican.

Mexico /mɛksiko/ *pr n* Mexico City.

Mexique /mɛksik/ *pr nm* Mexico.

mezzanine /medzanin/ *nf* mezzanine.

MF /ɛmɛf/ *nf* (*abbr* = **modulation de fréquence**) frequency modulation, FM.

mi /mi/ *nm inv* (Mus) (note) E; (in sol-fa) mi, me.

mi- /mi/ *pref* **à la ~-mai/saison** in mid-May/-season; **à ~-parcours** in the middle; **~-chinois, ~-français** half Chinese, half French.

miam-miam° /mjammjam/ *excl* yum-yum°!, yummy°!

miauler /mjole/ [1] *vi* to miaow (GB), to meow.

mi-bas /mibɑ/ *nm inv* knee sock, long sock.

mica /mika/ *nm* mica.

mi-carême /mikaʀɛm/ *nf*: *Thursday of the third week in Lent.*

miche /miʃ/ *nf* round loaf.

mi-chemin: **à mi-chemin** /amiʃmɛ̃/ *phr* halfway; (figurative) halfway through.

micmac° /mikmak/ *nm* **1** shady° goings-on; **2** mess°.

micro¹ /mikʀo/ *pref* **~analyse** microanalysis; **~biologie** microbiology.

micro² /mikʀo/ *nm* microphone, mike°; **~ caché** bug.

microbe /mikʀɔb/ *nm* **1** germ, microbe; **2**° squirt°.

microclimat /mikʀoklima/ *nm* microclimate.

microcosme /mikʀɔkɔsm/ *nm* microcosm.

micro-cravate, *pl* **micros-cravates** /mikʀo kʀavat/ *nm* lapel-microphone.

microfilm /mikʀɔfilm/ *nm* microfilm.

micro-ondes /mikʀoɔ̃d/ *nm inv* microwave°.

micro-organisme, *pl* **~s** /mikʀoɔʀganism/ *nm* microorganism.

microphone /mikʀɔfɔn/ *nm* microphone.

microscope /mikʀɔskɔp/ *nm* microscope.

microscopique /mikʀɔskɔpik/ *adj* microscopic; (figurative) tiny.

microsillon /mikʀɔsijɔ̃/ *nm* **(disque) ~** microgroove record.

midi /midi/ *nm* **1** twelve o'clock, midday, noon; **je fais mes courses entre ~ et deux**° I go shopping in my lunch hour; **2** lunchtime; **3 le Midi** the South of France.

midinette /midinɛt/ *nf* feather-brained young girl, bimbo°.

mie /mi/ *nf* bread without the crusts; **de la ~ (de pain)** fresh breadcrumbs.

miel /mjɛl/ *nm* honey.
IDIOMS **être tout sucre tout ~** to be as nice as pie°.

mielleux, -euse /mjɛlø, øz/ *adj* [*tone*] unctuous, honeyed; [*person*] fawning.

mien, mienne /mjɛ̃, mjɛn/ I *det* **ces idées, je les ai faites miennes** I adopted these ideas.
II **le mien, la mienne, les miens, les miennes** *pron* mine.

miette /mjɛt/ *nf* crumb; **réduire en ~s** to smash [sth] to bits [*vase*]; to shatter [*happiness, hopes*]; **elle n'en perd pas une ~**° she's taking it all in.

mieux /mjø/ I *adj inv* better; **le ~, la ~, les ~** the best; the nicest; the most attractive; **le ~ des deux** the better one; **ce qu'il y a de ~** the best.
II *adv* **1** better; **je ne peux pas te dire ~** that's all I can tell you; **qui dit ~?** any other offers?; any advance on that bid?; **de ~ en ~** better and better; **tu n'as pas d'argent? de ~ en ~** you've no money now? that's absolutely great°!; **on la critiquait à qui ~ ~** each person criticized her more harshly than the last; **2 le ~, la ~, les ~** the best; (of two) the better; **cela s'est passé le ~ du monde** it all went fine.
III *nm inv* **le ~ est de refuser** the best thing is to refuse; **il y a un/du ~** there is an/some improvement; **je ne demande pas ~ que de rester ici** I'm perfectly happy staying here; **fais pour le ~, fais au ~** do whatever is best; **tout va pour le ~** everything's fine; **cela prendra trois semaines, au ~** it'll take at least three weeks; **elle est au ~ avec sa voisine** she is on very good terms with her neighbour[GB].

mièvre /mjɛvʀ/ *adj* [*person*] vapid; [*smile*] sickly; [*novel*] soppy.

mièvrerie /mjɛvʀəʀi/ *nf* (of person, smile) vapidity; (of novel) soppiness.

mi-figue /mifig/ *adj inv* **~ mi-raisin** [*smile*] half-hearted; [*compliment*] ambiguous; [*remark*] half-humourous[GB].

mignon, -onne /miɲɔ̃, ɔn/ *adj* **1** cute; **2** sweet, kind.

migraine /migʀɛn/ *nf* splitting headache; migraine.

migrateur, -trice /migʀatœʀ, tʀis/ *adj* migratory.

migration /migʀasjɔ̃/ *nf* migration.

migratoire /migʀatwaʀ/ *adj* migratory.

migrer /migʀe/ [1] *vi* to migrate.

mijaurée /miʒoʀe/ *nf* **ne fais pas ta ~** don't put on such airs.

mijoter /miʒɔte/ [1] I *vtr* **1** (Culin) to prepare [*dish*]; **2**° to cook up [*revenge*].
II *vi* (Culin) to simmer.
IDIOMS **laisser qn ~ dans son jus**° to let sb stew in his/her own juice.

mil /mil/ *adj inv* = **mille** I.

milice /milis/ *nf* militia; **~ de quartier** local vigilante group.

milieu, *pl* **~x** /miljø/ I *nm* **1** middle; **au beau** or **en plein ~** right in the middle; **2** middle; **au ~ de la nuit** in the middle of or halfway through the night; **3** middle ground; **c'est vrai**

ou faux, il n'y a pas de ~ it's either right or wrong, there's no in-between; **4** environment; **en ~ rural** in the country; **5** background, milieu; **le ~ de l'édition** the world of publishing; **le ~** the underworld.
II **au milieu de** *phr* **1** among; **être au ~ de ses amis** to be with one's friends; **2** surrounded by; **au ~ du désastre** in the midst of disaster.

militaire /militɛʀ/ I *adj* [*hospital, authorities, attitude*] military; [*doctor*] army.
II *nm* serviceman; **un ~ de carrière** a career soldier.

militant, ~e /militɑ̃, ɑ̃t/ I *adj* militant.
II *nm,f* (of organization) active member, activist; (for cause) campaigner.

militantisme /militɑ̃tism/ *nm* political activism.

militarisation /militaʀizasjɔ̃/ *nf* militarization.

militariste /militaʀist/ *adj* militaristic.

militer /milite/ [1] *vi* **1** to campaign (**pour** for); **2** to be a political activist.

mille /mil/ I *adj inv* a thousand, one thousand; **deux/trois ~** two/three thousand.
II *nm inv* **1** a thousand, one thousand; **2** bull's eye; **taper dans le ~** to hit the bull's-eye; (figurative) to hit the nail on the head.
III *nm* **1 ~ (marin** or **nautique)** (nautical) mile; **2** (air) mile.
IV **pour mille** *phr* per thousand.
IDIOMS **je ne gagne pas des ~ et des cents** I don't earn very much; **je vous le donne en ~** you'll never guess (in a million years).

millefeuille /milfœj/ *nm* millefeuille (*a pastry filled with custard and cream*).

millénaire /milenɛʀ/ I *adj* **1 un arbre ~** a one thousand year old tree; **2** [*tradition*] age-old.
II *nm* **1 pendant des ~s** for thousands of years; **2** millennium, millenary.

mille-pattes /milpat/ *nm inv* centipede, millipede.

millésime /milezim/ *nm* vintage, year.

millet /mijɛ/ *nm* millet; **~ des oiseaux** birdseed, millet.

milli /mili/ *pref* milli; **~litre** millilitre[GB]; **~mètre** millimetre[GB].

milliard /miljaʀ/ *nm* billion.

milliardaire /miljaʀdɛʀ/ *nmf* multimillionaire, billionaire.

millième /miljɛm/ *adj* thousandth.

millier /milje/ *nm* **1** thousand; **2 un ~** about a thousand.

million /miljɔ̃/ *nm* million; **être riche à ~s** to be worth millions.

millionième /miljɔnjɛm/ *adj* millionth.

millionnaire /miljɔnɛʀ/ I *adj* **être ~** [*firm, company*] to be worth millions; [*person*] to be a millionaire.
II *nmf* millionaire; **un ~ en dollars** a dollar millionaire.

mime /mim/ *nm* mime.

mimer /mime/ [1] *vtr* **1** to mime; **2** to mimic.

mimétisme /mimetism/ *nm* **1** (Zool) mimicry; **2 par ~** through unconscious imitation.

mimique /mimik/ *nf* funny face.

mimosa /mimoza/ *nm* mimosa.

minable○ /minabl/ I *adj* **1** [*salary, person*] pathetic; **2** [*place, clothes*] crummy○; [*existence*] miserable.
II *nmf* **1** pathetic○ character; **2** loser○.

minaret /minaʀɛ/ *nm* minaret.

minauder /minode/ [1] *vi* **1** to mince about; **2** to simper.

mince /mɛ̃s/ I *adj* **1** [*person, leg*] slim, slender; [*neck, arm*] slender; [*face, nose*] thin; [*slice, blade*] thin; [*volume*] slim; **2** [*consolation*] small; [*chance*] slim; **ce n'est pas une ~ affaire** that's no small task; that's no trivial matter.
II○ *excl* **~ (alors)!** (surprised) wow○!; (disappointed) damn○!

minceur /mɛ̃sœʀ/ *nf* (of person, legs) slimness, slenderness; (of neck, arms) slenderness; (of face, nose) thinness; (of slice, blade) thinness.

mincir /mɛ̃siʀ/ [3] *vi* to lose weight.

mine /min/ I *nf* **1** expression; **faire triste ~** to have a gloomy expression; **faire ~ d'accepter** to pretend to accept; **elle nous a dit, ~ de rien, que**○ she told us, casually, that; **il est doué, ~ de rien**○ it may not be obvious, but he's very clever; **2 avoir mauvaise ~** to look a bit off-colour[GB]; **avoir bonne ~** [*person*] to look well; **j'aurais bonne ~!** I would look really stupid!; **3** lead; **crayon à ~ dure/grasse** hard/soft pencil; **4** mine; **~ d'or** gold mine; **5** (Mil) mine.
II **mines** *nf pl* **faire des ~s** to simper.
IDIOMS **ne pas payer de ~**○ not to look anything special○.

miner /mine/ [1] *vtr* **1** to sap [*morale, energy*]; to undermine [*health*]; **2** (Mil) to mine.

minerai /minʀɛ/ *nm* ore; **~ de fer** iron ore.

minéral, ~e, *mpl* **-aux** /mineʀal, o/ I *adj* [*water*] mineral; [*chemistry*] inorganic.
II *nm* mineral.

minéralogique /mineʀalɔʒik/ *adj* **plaque ~** number plate (GB), license plate (US).

minerve /minɛʀv/ *nf* (Med) surgical collar (GB), neck brace (US).

minet /minɛ/ *nm* **1** pussycat; **2**○ pretty boy○.

minette /minɛt/ *nf* **1** pussycat; **2**○ cool chick○.

mineur, ~e /minœʀ/ I *adj* **1** (Law) under 18; **2** [*detail*] minor; **3** (Mus) **en ré ~** in D minor.
II *nm,f* (Law) person under 18.
III *nm* miner; **~ de fond** pit worker.

mini- /mini/ *pref* mini; **~-révolution** mini-revolution.

miniature /minjatyʀ/ *adj, nf* miniature.

minier, -ière /minje, ɛʀ/ *adj* mining.

mini-golf, *pl* **~s** /minigɔlf/ *nm* mini-golf.

mini-jupe, *pl* **~s** /miniʒyp/ *nf* mini-skirt.

minimal, ~e, *mpl* **-aux** /minimal, o/ *adj* minimal, minimum.

minime /minim/ I *adj* [*damages, difference*] negligible; [*chance*] slim.
II *nmf* (Sport) junior (*7 to 13 years old*).

minimiser /minimize/ [1] *vtr* to minimize, to play down.

minimum, *pl* **~s** or **minima** /minimɔm, minima/ I *adj* minimum.
II *nm* **1** minimum; **en faire un ~** to do as little as possible; **un ~ de bon sens** a certain amount of common sense; **il faut au ~ deux heures pour faire le trajet** the journey takes at least two hours; **2** (Law) minimum sentence.
■ **~ vital** subsistence level.

minipilule /minipilyl/ *nf* low-dose combined pill.

ministère /ministɛʀ/ *nm* **1** ministry; (in UK, US) department; **2** (Law) **le ~ public** the public prosecutor's office; **3** (religious) ministry.

ministériel, -ielle /ministeʀjɛl/ *adj* ministerial, cabinet.

ministre /ministʀ/ *nm* **1** minister; (in UK) Secretary of State; (in US) Secretary; **2** (of religion) minister.

Minitel® /minitɛl/ *nm* Minitel (*terminal linking phone users to a database*).

minivague /minivag/ *nf* soft perm.

minois /minwɑ/ *nm inv* fresh young face; **joli petit ~** pretty little face.

minoritaire /minɔʀitɛʀ/ *adj* minority.

minorité /minɔʀite/ *nf* **1** minority; **être mis en ~** to be defeated; **2** (age) minority; **~ pénale** (Law) ≈ legal infancy.

minoterie /minɔtʀi/ *nf* **1** flour mill; **2** flour-milling (industry).

minou /minu/ *nm* pussycat.

minuit /minɥi/ *nm* midnight.

minuscule /minyskyl/ I *adj* [*person, thing*] tiny; [*quantity*] tiny, minute.
II *nf* small letter; (in printing) lower-case letter.

minutage /minytaʒ/ *nm* (precise) timing.

minute /minyt/ *nf* minute; **il peut arriver d'une ~ à l'autre** he may arrive any minute now; **la ~ de vérité** the moment of truth.

minuter /minyte/ [1] *vtr* **1** to time; **2** to work out the timing of; **l'opération doit être minutée à la seconde** the operation requires split-second timing.

minuterie /minytʀi/ *nf* **1** time-switch; **2** automatic lighting.

minuteur /minytœʀ/ *nm* timer.

minutie /minysi/ *nf* meticulousness; **travail d'une grande ~** meticulous work.

minutieux, -ieuse /minysjø, øz/ *adj* meticulous; [*description*] detailed.

mioche° /mjɔʃ/ *nmf* kid°; **sale ~** horrible brat°.

mirabelle /miʀabɛl/ *nf* **1** mirabelle (*small yellow plum*); **2** plum brandy.

miracle /miʀɑkl/ I *adj inv* **un médicament ~** a wonder drug; **une méthode ~** a magic formula.
II *nm* **1** miracle; **faire un ~** to work a miracle; (figurative) to work miracles; **tenir du ~** to be a miracle; **comme par ~** as if by magic; **2** miracle play.

miraculeux, -euse /miʀakylø, øz/ *adj* miraculous; [*cure*] miracle; [*product, remedy*] which works wonders.

mirador /miʀadɔʀ/ *nm* watchtower.

mirage /miʀaʒ/ *nm* mirage.

mi-raisin /miʀɛzɛ̃/ *adj inv* ▶ **mi-figue**.

miraud°, ~e /miʀo, od/ *adj* shortsighted.

mirifique /miʀifik/ *adj* (ironic) fabulous°.

mirobolant°, ~e /miʀɔbɔlɑ̃, ɑ̃t/ *adj* fabulous°.

miroir /miʀwaʀ/ *nm* mirror; **~ aux alouettes** lure.

miroitement /miʀwatmɑ̃/ *nm* (of glass) sparkling; (of water) shimmering.

miroiter /miʀwate/ [1] *vi* **faire ~ qch à qn** to hold out the prospect of sth to sb.

mis, ~e[1] /mi, miz/ I *pp* ▶ **mettre**.
II *pp adj* **être bien ~** to be well-dressed.

misanthrope /mizɑ̃tʀɔp/ I *adj* misanthropic.
II *nmf* misanthropist, misanthrope.

mise[2] /miz/ *nf* **une ~ de cinq francs** a five-franc bet.
■ **~ de fonds** investment; **~ en plis** set.
IDIOMS **être de ~** [*conduct*] to be proper.

miser /mize/ [1] I *vtr* to bet (**sur** on).
II *vi* **1 ~ sur le 2** (in casino) to place a bet on the 2; **2 ~ sur sa chance** to count on one's luck; **~ sur qn** to place all one's hopes in sb.

misérable /mizeʀabl/ I *adj* **1** [*person*] destitute, poor; [*life, country*] poor, wretched; **2** [*salary*] meagre[GB].
II *nmf* **1** pauper; **2** scoundrel.

misère /mizɛʀ/ *nf* **1** destitution; **réduire qn à la ~** to reduce sb to poverty; **2** misery, wretchedness; **3** trouble, woe; **on a tous nos petites ~s** we all have our troubles; **4 être payé une ~** to be paid a pittance.

miséreux, -euse /mizeʀø, øz/ *nm,f* destitute person; **les ~** the destitute.

miséricorde /mizeʀikɔʀd/ *nf, excl* mercy.

misogyne /mizɔʒin/ I *adj* misogynous.
II *nmf* misogynist.

misogynie /mizɔʒini/ *nf* misogyny.

missel /misɛl/ *nm* missal.

missile /misil/ *nm* missile.

mission /misjɔ̃/ *nf* mission.

missionnaire /misjɔnɛʀ/ *adj, nmf* missionary.

missive /misiv/ *nf* missive.

mistral /mistʀal/ *nm* mistral.

mitaine /mitɛn/ *nf* fingerless mitt.

mite /mit/ *nf* (clothes) moth.

mi-temps[1] /mitɑ̃/ *nm inv* part-time job; **2 elle travaille à ~** she works part-time.

mi-temps[2] /mitɑ̃/ *nf inv* (Sport) half-time; **en deuxième ~** in the second half.

miteux, -euse /mitø, øz/ *adj* [*place*] seedy; [*clothes*] shabby.

mitigé, ~e /mitiʒe/ *adj* [*reception*] lukewarm; [*success*] qualified.

mitonner /mitɔne/ [1] *vtr* to cook [sth] lovingly.

mitoyen, **-enne** /mitwajɛ̃, ɛn/ *adj* [*hedge*] dividing; **mur ~** party wall.

mitraille /mitʀaj/ *nf* **1** hail of bullets; **2**○ small change.

mitrailler /mitʀaje/ [1] *vtr* **1** to machine-gun; **2 ~ qn de questions** to fire questions at sb; **3**○ to take photo after photo of [sb/sth].

mitraillette /mitʀajɛt/ *nf* submachine gun.

mitrailleuse /mitʀajøz/ *nf* machine gun.

mixage /miksaʒ/ *nm* sound mixing.

mixer[1] /mikse/ [1] *vtr* to mix.

mixer[2] /miksɛʀ/ = **mixeur**.

mixeur /miksœʀ/ *nm* **1** mixer; **2** blender.

mixité /miksite/ *nf* (gen) mixing of sexes; (Sch) coeducation.

mixte /mikst/ *adj* **1** [*school*] coeducational; [*class*] mixed; **2** [*couple, marriage*] mixed; [*economy*] mixed; [*commission*] joint; **société ~** joint venture.

mixture /mikstyʀ/ *nf* **1** concoction; **2** (in pharmacy) mixture; **3** mishmash○.

MJC /ɛmʒise/ *nf* (*abbr* = **maison des jeunes et de la culture**) ≈ youth club.

MLF /ɛmɛlɛf/ *nm* (*abbr* = **mouvement de libération des femmes**) ≈ Women's Lib.

Mlle (*written abbr* = **Mademoiselle**) Ms, Miss.

Mlles (*written abbr* = **Mesdemoiselles**) Misses.

mm (*written abbr* = **millimètre**) mm.

MM. (*written abbr* = **Messieurs**) Messrs.

Mme (*written abbr* = **Madame**) Ms, Mrs.

Mmes (*written abbr* = **Mesdames**) Ms, Mrs.

mnémotechnique /mnemɔtɛknik/ *adj* mnemonic.

Mo (*written abbr* = **mégaoctet**) Mb, MB.

mob○ /mɔb/ *nf* moped.

mobile /mɔbil/ **I** *adj* (gen) mobile; [*leaf*] loose; [*feast*] movable.

II *nm* **1** motive; **2** mobile.

mobilier, **-ière** /mɔbilje, ɛʀ/ **I** *adj* **biens ~s** movable property; **valeurs mobilières** securities.

II *nm* furniture; **~ de bureau** office furniture.

mobilisateur, **-trice** /mɔbilizatœʀ, tʀis/ *adj* rousing; stimulating.

mobilisation /mɔbilizasjɔ̃/ *nf* mobilization; **~ générale** mobilization; all-out effort.

mobiliser /mɔbilize/ [1] **I** *vtr* to mobilize [*soldier*]; to call up [*civilian*].

II se mobiliser *v refl* (+ *v être*) to rally, to mobilize.

mobilité /mɔbilite/ *nf* mobility.

mobylette® /mɔbilɛt/ *nf* moped.

mocassin /mɔkasɛ̃/ *nm* moccasin, loafer.

moche○ /mɔʃ/ *adj* **1** [*person*] ugly; [*garment*] ghastly; [*colour*] awful; **2** [*incident*] dreadful; **3** [*act*] nasty.

IDIOMS **~ comme un pou** as ugly as sin.

modalité /mɔdalite/ **I** *nf* modality.

II modalités *nf pl* terms; practical details; **~s d'inscription** (Sch) enrolment[GB] procedure.

mode[1] /mɔd/ *nm* **1** way, mode; **~ de paiement** method of payment; **2** (in grammar) mood.

■ **~ dialogué** (Comput) conversational mode; **~ d'emploi** instructions for use.

mode[2] /mɔd/ *nf* **1** fashion; **lancer une ~** to start a trend; **une ~ passagère** a fad; **à la ~** [*garment, club*] fashionable; [*singer*] popular; **2** fashion industry.

modèle /mɔdɛl/ **I** *adj* (gen) model; [*conduct*] perfect, exemplary.

II *nm* **1** (gen) model; **prendre ~ sur qn** to do as sb does/did; **~ à suivre** somebody to look up to; **2** model; **grand/petit ~** large-/small-size; **le ~ au-dessus** the next size up; **3** (of garment) model; **essaie ce ~** try this style; **4 ~ de signature** specimen signature; **5** (for artist) model; **6** pattern; **~ déposé** registered pattern.

■ **~ réduit** scale model; **~ réduit d'avion** model plane.

modeler /mɔdle/ [17] *vtr* to model [*clay*]; to mould (GB) or mold (US) [*character*].

modélisme /mɔdelism/ *nm* modelling, model-making.

modération /mɔdeʀasjɔ̃/ *nf* **1** moderation; **2** (in price, tax) reduction; **3** (of sentence, law) mitigation.

modéré, **~e** /mɔdeʀe/ *adj* [*party, speed, words*] moderate; [*price*] reasonable; [*temperament*] even; [*enthusiasm*] mild.

modérément /mɔdeʀemɑ̃/ *adv* **1** relatively; **2** slightly.

modérer /mɔdeʀe/ [14] **I** *vtr* to curb [*expenses, feelings*]; to moderate [*language*]; to reduce [*speed*].

II se modérer *v refl* (+ *v être*) to exercise self-restraint.

moderne /mɔdɛʀn/ *adj* modern.

modernisation /mɔdɛʀnizasjɔ̃/ *nf* modernization.

moderniser /mɔdɛʀnize/ [1] *vtr* to modernize; to update.

modernité /mɔdɛʀnite/ *nf* modernity.

modeste /mɔdɛst/ *adj* [*sum, apartment, person*] modest; [*cost*] moderate; [*background*] humble.

modestie /mɔdɛsti/ *nf* modesty.

modicité /mɔdisite/ *nf* lowness; **la ~ des prix** the low prices.

modification /mɔdifikasjɔ̃/ *nf* modification.

modifier /mɔdifje/ [2] *vtr* (gen) to change; to alter [*engine*]; to amend [*bill*].

modique /mɔdik/ *adj* [*sum, resources*] modest.

modiste /mɔdist/ *nf* milliner.

modulation /mɔdylasjɔ̃/ *nf* modulation.

■ **~ de fréquence**, **MF** frequency modulation, FM.

module /mɔdyl/ *nm* **1** (gen, Sch) module; **2** (kitchen) unit.

moduler /mɔdyle/ [1] *vtr* **1** to modulate; **2** to adjust [*price*]; to adapt [*policy*].

moelle /mwal/ *nf* marrow; **~ osseuse** bone marrow.
■ **~ épinière** spinal cord.

moelleux, -euse /mwalø, øz/ *adj* **1** [*carpet*] thick; [*bed*] soft; [*nest*] cosy (GB), cozy (US); **2** [*wine*] mellow.

mœurs /mœʀ(s)/ *nf pl* (gen) customs; (of social group) lifestyle; **entrer dans les ~** to become part of everyday life; **l'évolution des ~** the change in attitudes; **les ~ des renards** the habits of foxes; **des ~ relâchées** or **dissolues** loose morals; **la police des ~**, **les Mœurs**○ the vice squad; **une affaire de ~** a sex case.
IDIOMS **autres temps, autres ~** other days, other ways.

mohair /mɔɛʀ/ *nm* mohair; **de** or **en ~** mohair.

moi[1] /mwa/ *pron* **1** I, me; **c'est ~** it's me; **2** me; **pour ~ il est fou** personally, I think he's mad; **des amis à ~** friends of mine; **c'est à ~** it's mine; it's my turn.

moi[2] /mwa/ *nm* **le ~** the self; **le vrai ~**○ the real me.

moignon /mwaɲɔ̃/ *nm* stump.

moi-même /mwamɛm/ *pron* myself.

moindre /mwɛ̃dʀ/ *adj* **1** lesser; **considérer qch comme un ~ mal** to consider sth as the lesser of two evils; **à ~ prix** more cheaply; **2 le ~** the least; **c'est la ~ des choses** it's the least I/you etc could do; **je n'en ai pas la ~ idée** I haven't got the slightest idea.

moine /mwan/ *nm* monk.
IDIOMS **l'habit ne fait pas le ~** (Proverb) you can't judge a book by its cover.

moineau, *pl* **~x** /mwano/ *nm* sparrow.

moins[1] /mwɛ̃/ **I** *prep* **1** minus; **2 il est huit heures ~ dix** it's ten (minutes) to eight; **il était ~ une**○ it was a close shave○.
II *adv* (comparative) less; (superlative) **le ~** the least; **~ bien payé** less well-paid; **le ~ difficile** the less difficult; the least difficult; **de ~ en ~** less and less; **~ je sors, ~ j'ai envie de sortir** the less I go out, the less I feel like going out; **il n'en est pas ~ vrai que** it's nonetheless true that; **il ressemble à son frère en ~ gros** he looks like his brother, only thinner; **~ longtemps** not so long; **à tout le ~, pour le ~** to say the least; **j'ai un an de ~ que lui** I'm a year younger than he is; **il y avait deux fourchettes en ~ dans la boîte** there were two forks missing from the box.
III moins de *quantif* **~ de livres** fewer books; **~ de sucre** less sugar; **il est ~ de 3 heures** it's not quite 3 o'clock; **les ~ de 20 ans** people under 20.
IV à moins de *phr* unless.
V à moins que *phr* unless.
VI au moins *phr* at least.
VII du moins *phr* at least.

moins[2] /mwɛ̃/ *nm inv* minus.
■ **~ que rien** good-for-nothing, nobody.

moiré, ~e /mwaʀe/ *adj* [*material*] moiré; [*silk, paper*] watered.

mois /mwa/ *nm inv* **1** month; **au ~ de juin** in June; **2** monthly salary.

moisi /mwazi/ *nm* mould (GB), mold (US).

moisir /mwaziʀ/ [3] *vi* [*foodstuff*] to go mouldy (GB) or moldy (US); [*object, plant*] to become mildewed; **on va pas ~ ici**○**!** we're not going to hang around here all day!

moisissure /mwazisyʀ/ *nf* **1** mould (GB), mold (US); **2** mildew.

moisson /mwasɔ̃/ *nf* **1** harvest; **2** (of prizes, medals) haul.

moissonner /mwasɔne/ [1] *vtr* to harvest.

moissonneuse /mwasɔnøz/ *nf* reaper.

moissonneuse-batteuse, *pl* **moissonneuses-batteuses** /mwasɔnøzbatøz/ *nf* combine harvester.

moite /mwat/ *adj* [*heat*] muggy; [*walls*] damp; [*skin*] sweaty.

moiteur /mwatœʀ/ *nf* (of air) mugginess; (of skin) sweatiness.

moitié /mwatje/ *nf* half; **à ~ vide** half empty; **dormir à ~**○ to be half asleep.

moitié-moitié /mwatjemwatje/ *adv* half-and-half.

moka /mɔka/ *nm* **1** mocha; **2** mocha cake.

molaire /mɔlɛʀ/ *nf* molar.

molécule /mɔlekyl/ *nf* molecule.

moleskine /mɔlɛskin/ *nf* **1** imitation leather, Leatherette®; **2** moleskin.

molester /mɔlɛste/ [1] *vtr* to manhandle [sb], to rough [sb] up○.

molette /mɔlɛt/ *nf* (of spanner) adjusting knob.

mollasson○**, -onne** /mɔlasɔ̃, ɔn/ *adj* sluggish.

molle ▶ **mou** I.

mollement /mɔlmɑ̃/ *adv* **1** idly; **2** [*work*] without much enthusiasm; [*protest, support*] half-heartedly; [*answer*] rather unconvincingly.

mollesse /mɔlɛs/ *nf* **1** softness; **2** (of flesh) flabbiness; **3** (of person) listlessness; **4** (of person, reply) lack of conviction; (of opposition) weakness.

mollet /mɔlɛ/ **I** *adj m* **œuf ~** soft-boiled egg.
II *nm* (Anat) calf; **des ~s de coq** legs like sticks.

molleton /mɔltɔ̃/ *nm* **1** flannel; flannelette; **2** (table) felt; **3** (ironing board) cover.

molletonner /mɔltɔne/ [1] *vtr* to line with fleece.

mollir /mɔliʀ/ [3] *vi* **1** [*courage*] to fail; [*enthusiasm*] to cool; [*resistance*] to grow weaker; [*person*] to soften; **2** [*knees*] to give way; [*arm*] to go weak.

mollusque /mɔlysk/ *nm* mollusc (GB), mollusk (US).

molosse /mɔlɔs/ *nm* huge dog.

môme○ /mom/ *nmf* kid○; brat○.

moment /mɔmɑ̃/ *nm* **1** moment; **le ~ venu** when the time comes/came; **il devrait arriver d'un ~ à l'autre** he should arrive any minute now; **à un ~ donné** at some point; at a given moment; **à ce ~-là** at that time; just then; in that case; **au ~ où** at the time (when); **au ~ où il quittait son domicile** as he was leaving his home; **jusqu'au ~ où** until; **du ~ que** as long as, provided; **ce n'est pas le ~** now is not the time; **il arrive toujours au bon** or **mauvais ~!** he certainly picks his moment to call!; **2** moment; **un ~!** just a moment!; **3 ça va prendre un ~** it will take a while; **au bout d'un ~** after a while; **savoir profiter du ~ présent** to live every moment to the full; **par ~s** at times; **les ~s forts du film** the film's highlights; **dans ses meilleurs ~s, il fait penser à Orson Welles** at his best, he reminds one of Orson Welles; **à mes ~s perdus** in my spare time.

momentané, **~e** /mɔmɑ̃tane/ *adj* momentary.

momentanément /mɔmɑ̃tanemɑ̃/ *adv* for a moment, momentarily.

momie /mɔmi/ *nf* mummy.

momifier /mɔmifje/ [2] *vtr*, **se momifier** *v refl* (+ *v être*) to mummify.

mon, **ma**, *pl* **mes** /mɔ̃, ma, mɛ/ *det* my; **j'ai ~ idée** I have my own ideas about that; **à ~ arrivée** when I arrive; when I arrived.

monacal, **~e**, *mpl* **-aux** /mɔnakal, o/ *adj* monastic.

monarchie /mɔnaʀʃi/ *nf* monarchy.

monarchiste /mɔnaʀʃist/ *adj*, *nmf* monarchist.

monarque /mɔnaʀk/ *nm* monarch.

monastère /mɔnastɛʀ/ *nm* monastery.

monceau, *pl* **~x** /mɔ̃so/ *nm* (of rubbish, rubble) pile.

mondain, **~e** /mɔ̃dɛ̃, ɛn/ **I** *adj* [*life, ball*] society; [*conversation*] polite.
II *nm,f* socialite.

mondanités /mɔ̃danite/ *nf pl* **1** society events; **2 se faire des ~** to stand on ceremony.

monde /mɔ̃d/ *nm* **1** world; **pas le moins du ~** not in the least; **se porter le mieux du ~** to be absolutely fine; **aller** or **voyager de par le ~** to travel the world; **c'est le bout du ~!**, **c'est au bout du ~!** it's in the back of beyond!; **ce n'est pas le bout du ~!** it's not such a big deal!; **à la face du ~** for all the world to see; **en ce bas ~** here below; **elle n'est plus de ce ~** she's no longer with us; **la perfection n'est pas de ce ~** there is no such thing as perfection; **je n'étais pas encore au ~** I wasn't yet born; **2** world; **le ~ médical** the medical world; **le ~ animal** the animal kingdom; **un ~ nous sépare** we are worlds apart; **3** people; **il n'y a pas grand ~** there aren't many people; **tout le ~** everybody; **tout mon petit ~** my family and friends; **4** society; **le beau** or **grand ~** high society.
IDIOMS **se faire un ~ de qch** to get all worked up about sth; **depuis que le ~ est ~** since the beginning of time; **c'est le ~ à l'envers!** whatever next!; **c'est un ~**° ! that's a bit much!

mondial, **~e**, *mpl* **-iaux** /mɔ̃djal, o/ *adj* [*record, congress, economy*] world; [*problem, success*] worldwide; **seconde guerre ~e** Second World War.

mondialement /mɔ̃djalmɑ̃/ *adv* **être ~ connu** to be known all over the world.

mondialisation /mɔ̃djalizasjɔ̃/ *nf* globalization; **la ~ d'un conflit** the worldwide spread of a conflict.

mondovision /mɔ̃dɔvizjɔ̃/ *nf* satellite broadcasting.

monème /mɔnɛm/ *nm* moneme.

monétaire /mɔnetɛʀ/ *adj* [*system, stability*] monetary; [*market*] money.

monétariste /mɔnetaʀist/ *adj*, *nmf* monetarist.

monétique /mɔnetik/ *nf* electronic banking.

mongol, **~e** /mɔ̃gɔl/ **I** *adj* Mongolian.
II *nm* Mongolian.

Mongolie /mɔ̃gɔli/ *pr nf* Mongolia.

mongolien, **-ienne** /mɔ̃gɔljɛ̃, ɛn/ (controversial) **I** *adj* **être ~** to have Down's syndrome.
II *nm,f* Down's syndrome child.

moniteur, **-trice** /mɔnitœʀ, tʀis/ **I** *nm,f* **1** (Aut, Sport) instructor; **2** (in holiday camp) group leader (GB), counselor (US).
II *nm* **1** (TV) monitor; **2** (Comput) monitor system.
■ **~ cardiaque** heart monitor.

monnaie /mɔnɛ/ *nf* **1** currency; **fausse ~** forged or counterfeit currency; **2** change; **faire de la ~** to get some change; **3** coin; **battre ~** to mint or strike coins; **4 l'hôtel de la Monnaie**, **la Monnaie** the Mint; **5** (Econ) money.
■ **~ d'échange** trading currency; bargaining chip; **~ de papier** paper money.
IDIOMS **rendre à qn la ~ de sa pièce** to pay sb back in his/her own coin; **c'est ~ courante** it's commonplace.

monnayable /mɔnɛjabl/ *adj* **1** [*banknote*] convertible; **2** [*talent*] marketable.

monnayer /mɔnɛje/ [21] *vtr* **1** to convert [sth] into cash; **2** to capitalize on [*talent, experience*]; **~ qch contre qch** to exchange sth for sth.

mono[1] /mono/ *pref* mono; **~chrome** monochrome; **~lingue** monolingual; **~syllabe** monosyllable.

mono[2] /mono/ *nf* (in hi-fi) mono; **en ~** in mono.

monocle /mɔnɔkl/ *nm* monocle.

monocoque /mɔnɔkɔk/ *adj* [*boat*] monohull; [*car*] monocoque.

monocorde /mɔnɔkɔʀd/ *adj* [*voice, speech*] monotonous; [*instrument*] single-string; **sur un** or **d'un ton ~** in a monotone.

monocylindrique /monosilɛ̃dʀik/ *adj* single-cylinder.

monogame /mɔnɔgam/ **I** *adj* monogamous.
II *nmf* monogamist.

monogamie /mɔnɔgami/ *nf* monogamy.

monoï /mɔnɔj/ *nm inv* coconut oil (*used in cosmetics*).

monologue /mɔnɔlɔg/ *nm* monologue[GB]; **le ~ d'Hamlet** Hamlet's soliloquy.
■ **~ intérieur** stream of consciousness.

mononucléose /mɔnonykleoz/ *nf* mononucleosis; **~ infectieuse** glandular fever.

monoparental, **~e**, *mpl* **-aux** /mɔnopaʀɑ̃tal, o/ *adj* **famille ~e** single-parent family.

monoplace[1] /mɔnɔplas/ *nm* single-seater (aircraft).

monoplace[2] /mɔnɔplas/ *nf* one-seater (car).

monopole /mɔnɔpɔl/ *nm* monopoly.

monopoliser /mɔnɔpɔlize/ [1] *vtr* to monopolize.

monoski /mɔnɔski/ *nm* **1** monoski; **2** monoskiing.

monothéiste /mɔnɔteist/ **I** *adj* monotheistic.
II *nmf* monotheist.

monotone /mɔnɔtɔn/ *adj* monotonous.

monotonie /mɔnɔtɔni/ *nf* monotony.

monoxyde /mɔnɔksid/ *nm* monoxide.

Monseigneur, *pl* **Messeigneurs** /mɔ̃sɛɲœʀ, mesɛɲœʀ/ *nm* **1** Your Highness; Your Eminence; **2 ~ le duc de Parme** His Grace, the duke of Parma.

monsieur, *pl* **messieurs** /məsjø, mesjø/ *nm* **1 Monsieur** Dear Sir; **bonjour, ~** good morning; **2 bonjour, ~** good morning, Mr X; **cher Monsieur** Dear Mr X; **3** man; **le simple/double messieurs** the men's singles/doubles; **c'était un (grand) ~!** he was a (true) gentleman!; **4 'Monsieur a sonné?'** 'you rang sir?'; **tu comprends, Monsieur a ses habitudes!** His Lordship is rather set in his ways you see!
■ **~ Tout le Monde** the man in the street.

monstre /mɔ̃stʀ/ **I**° *adj* [*task, success, publicity*] huge; [*nerve*] colossal.
II *nm* **1** monster; **un ~ d'orgueil** a monstrously arrogant person; **2** freak (of nature).
■ **~ marin** sea monster; **~ sacré** superstar.

monstrueusement /mɔ̃stʀyøzmɑ̃/ *adv* horrendously.

monstrueux, **-euse** /mɔ̃stʀyø, øz/ *adj* **1** [*crime, cruelty*] monstrous; **2** hideous; **d'une laideur monstrueuse** hideously ugly; **3** [*error*] colossal.

monstruosité /mɔ̃stʀyozite/ *nf* **1** (of conduct) monstrousness; **2** atrocity; **3** monstrosity; **dire des ~s** to say preposterous things; **4** deformity.

mont /mɔ̃/ *nm* mountain.
■ **le ~ Blanc** Mont Blanc; **~ de Vénus** (Anat) mons veneris.

montage /mɔ̃taʒ/ *nm* **1** set-up; **2** (of machine) assembly; (of tent) putting up; **chaîne de ~** assembly line; **3** (of film) editing; **salle de ~** cutting room; **4** (of gem) setting.
■ **~ photo** photomontage; **~ sonore** sound montage.

montagnard, **~e** /mɔ̃taɲaʀ, aʀd/ **I** *adj* [*people, plant*] mountain; [*custom*] highland; **la vie ~e** life in the mountains.
II *nm,f* mountain dweller.

montagne /mɔ̃taɲ/ *nf* **1** mountain; **pays de ~s** mountainous country; **2 la ~** the mountains; **de ~** [*road, animal*] mountain; **il neige en haute ~** it's snowing on the upper slopes; **3** mountain (**de** of).
■ **les ~s Rocheuses** the Rocky Mountains; **~s russes** big dipper, roller coaster.
IDIOMS **se faire une ~ de qch** to get really worked up about sth; **c'est la ~ qui accouche d'une souris** a great deal of effort leading to nothing much.

montagneux, **-euse** /mɔ̃taɲø, øz/ *adj* mountainous.

montant, **~e** /mɔ̃tɑ̃, ɑ̃t/ **I** *adj* **1** [*cabin, group*] going up; **2** [*path, road*] uphill; [*curve*] rising; **3** [*neck*] high; [*socks*] long; **chaussures ~es** ankle boots.
II *nm* **1** sum; **le ~ des pertes** the total losses; **d'un** or **pour un ~ de** [*deficit, savings*] amounting to; [*cheque*] to the amount of; [*goods*] for a total of; **2** (of door, window) upright, jamb; transom; (of scaffolding) pole; (of ladder) upright; **~ de lit** bedpost.

mont-de-piété, *pl* **monts-de-piété** /mɔ̃d pjete/ *nm* pawnshop, pawnbroker's.

monte-charge /mɔ̃tʃaʀʒ/ *nm inv* goods lift (GB) or elevator (US).

montée /mɔ̃te/ *nf* **1** (up slope, stairs) climb; (of mountain) ascent; **2** (of plane) climb, ascent; **3** rising; rise; **la ~ des eaux** the rise in the water level; **une brusque ~ d'adrénaline** a rush of adrenaline; **la ~ de lait se produit deux jours après la naissance** the milk comes in two days after the birth; **4** (in prices, value) rise; (in danger, risk) increase; **5** hill; **une légère ~** a slight slope.

monter /mɔ̃te/ [1] **I** *vtr* (+ *v avoir*) **1** to take [sb/sth] up (**à** to); to take [sb/sth] upstairs; to bring [sb/sth] up (**de** from); to bring [sb/sth] upstairs; **2** to put [sth] up (**sur** on); to raise [*shelf*]; **3** to get [sth] up; **impossible de ~ le piano par l'escalier** it's impossible to get the piano up the stairs; **4** to go up [sth]; to come up [sth]; **~ la colline à bicyclette** to cycle up the hill; **5** to turn up [*volume, gas*]; **6 ~ les blancs en neige** beat or whisk the egg whites until stiff; **7 ~ qn contre qn** to turn or set sb against sb; **8** to ride [*horse*]; **9** to mount, to cover [*mare, cow*]; **10** to assemble [*appliance, unit*]; to put up [*tent, scaffolding*]; to set [*gem*]; **~ un film** to edit a film; **11** to hatch [*plot*]; to mount [*attack*]; to set up [*company*]; to stage [*play*]; **monté de toutes pièces** [*story*] fabricated from beginning to end; **12 ~ son ménage** to set up home.
II *vi* (+ *v être*) **1** to go up (**à** to); to go upstairs; to come up (**à** to); to come upstairs; [*plane*] to climb; [*bird*] to fly up; [*sun, mist*] to rise; **tu es monté à pied?** did you walk up?; did you come up on foot?; **il est monté au col en voiture** he drove up to the pass; **~ sur** to get onto [*footpath*]; to climb onto [*stool*]; **~ à l'échelle** to climb (up) the ladder; **faites-les ~** send them up; **2 ~ dans une voiture/dans un train** to get in a car/on a train; **~ à bord** to get on board; **~ sur** to get on [*bike, horse*]; **3** [*road*] to go uphill, to climb; [*ground*] to rise; **~ jusqu'à** [*path, wall*] to go up to; **~ en lacets** to wind its way up; **4** [*garment, snow*] to come up (**jusqu'à** to); ; **5** [*temperature, price*] to rise, to go up (**à** to; **de** by); [*tide*] to come in; [*melody*] to rise; **ça va faire ~ le dollar** it'll push the dollar up; **6 ~ à** or **sur Paris** to go

up to Paris; **7 ~ (à cheval)** to ride; **~ à bicyclette** to ride a bicycle; **8** (Mil) **~ à l'assaut** or **l'attaque** to mount an attack (**de** on); **9** (Games) to play a higher card; **10** [*employee*] to rise, to move up; [*artist*] to rise; **11** [*anger, emotion*] to mount; [*sobs*] to rise; [*tears*] to well up; **le ton monta** the conversation became noisier; the discussion became heated; **12 ~ à la gorge de qn** to rise (up) in sb's throat; **~ à la tête de qn** to go to sb's head; **13** (Aut, Tech) **~ à 250 km/h** to go up to 250 kph.

III se monter *v refl* (+ *v être*) **se ~ à** [*bill*] to amount to.

IDIOMS **se ~ la tête**○ to get worked up○.

monteur, **-euse** /mɔ̃tœʀ, øz/ *nm,f* **1** fitter; **2** (in film-making) editor; **3** paste-up artist.

montgolfière /mɔ̃gɔlfjɛʀ/ *nf* **1** hot-air balloon; **2** (hot-air) ballooning.

monticule /mɔ̃tikyl/ *nm* **1** hillock; **2** mound (**de** of).

montrable /mɔ̃tʀabl/ *adj* [*person*] presentable; [*images*] suitable for viewing.

montre /mɔ̃tʀ/ *nf* watch; **trois heures ~ en main** three hours exactly.

Montréal /mɔ̃ʀeal/ *pr n* Montreal.

montrer /mɔ̃tʀe/ [1] **I** *vtr* **1** to show; **~ qch à qn** to show sb sth; **2** to show [*feelings, knowledge*]; to reveal [*intentions*]; **3** [*person*] to point out [*track, place, object*]; [*sign*] to point to [*direction*]; [*survey, table*] to show [*trend, results*]; **~ qn du doigt** to point at sb; to point the finger at sb.

II se montrer *v refl* (+ *v être*) **1** to show oneself to be; to prove (to be); **il faut se ~ optimiste** we must try to be optimistic; **2** [*person*] to show oneself; [*sun*] to come out; **elle n'osait pas se ~ avec lui** she didn't dare be seen with him.

IDIOMS **~ le poing à qn** to shake one's fist at sb; **~ les dents** to bare one's teeth; **~ le bout de son** or **du nez** to show one's face; to peep through.

montreur, **-euse** /mɔ̃tʀœʀ, øz/ *nm,f* **~ de marionnettes** puppeteer; **~ d'ours** bear tamer.

monture /mɔ̃tyʀ/ *nf* **1** (for rider) mount; **2** (of glasses) frames; (of ring) setting.

monument /mɔnymɑ̃/ *nm* **1** monument; **2** (historic) building; **visiter les ~s de Paris** to see the sights of Paris; **3 être un ~ de bêtise** to be monumentally stupid; **un des ~s de la littérature européenne** a masterpiece of European literature.

■ **~ historique** ancient monument; **~ aux morts** war memorial.

monumental, **~e**, *mpl* **-aux** /mɔnymɑ̃tal, o/ *adj* monumental.

moquer: **se moquer** /mɔke/ [1] *v refl* (+ *v être*) **1** to make fun (**de** of); **2 se ~ de** not to care about; **je me moque qu'ils viennent ou pas** I don't care whether they come or not; **3 se ~ du monde** to take people for fools.

moquerie /mɔkʀi/ *nf* **1** mocking remark; **2** mockery.

moquette /mɔkɛt/ *nf* fitted carpet (GB), wall-to-wall carpet.

moqueur, **-euse** /mɔkœʀ, øz/ *adj* mocking.

moral, **~e**[1], *mpl* **-aux** /mɔʀal, o/ **I** *adj* **1** moral; **n'avoir aucun sens ~** to have no sense of right and wrong; **2** [*torture*] mental; [*courage, support*] moral; **force ~e** moral fibre[GB]; **3** [*work, person*] moral; [*conduct*] ethical.

II *nm* **1** morale; **avoir bon ~**, **avoir le ~** to be in good spirits; **avoir le ~ à zéro**○ to feel very down; **remonter le ~ de qn** to raise sb's spirits; **saper le ~ de qn** to undermine sb's morale; **2** mind; **au ~ comme au physique** mentally and physically.

morale[2] /mɔʀal/ *nf* **1** morality; **contraire à la ~** immoral; **leur ~** their moral code; **2** moral; **faire la ~ à qn** to give sb a lecture; **3 la ~** moral philosophy, ethics.

moralement /mɔʀalmɑ̃/ *adv* **1** morally, ethically; **2** psychologically.

moralisateur, **-trice** /mɔʀalizatœʀ, tʀis/ *adj* moralizing, moralistic.

moralisation /mɔʀalizasjɔ̃/ *nf* (of masses) moral improvement; (of regime, press) cleaning up.

moraliser /mɔʀalize/ [1] *vtr* to clean up; to reform.

moraliste /mɔʀalist/ *nmf* **1** moralist; **2** moralizer; **3** moral philosopher.

moralité /mɔʀalite/ *nf* **1** morals, moral standards; **2** (of action) morality; **3** moral; **~, ne faites confiance à personne** the moral is, don't trust anybody.

morbide /mɔʀbid/ *adj* morbid.

morceau, *pl* **~x** /mɔʀso/ *nm* **1** piece, bit; **~ de sucre** sugar lump; **coupez la viande en ~x** cut the meat into cubes; **manger un ~**○ to have a snack; **2** (of meat) cut; **bas ~** cheap cut; **3** (Mus) piece; **~ de piano** piano piece; **4** (from book) extract; **5**○ **le chapitre 8 est un gros ~**○ chapter 8 is quite substantial.

IDIOMS **recoller les ~x** to patch things up.

morceler /mɔʀsəle/ [19] *vtr* to divide [sth] up; to split [sth] up].

mordant, **~e** /mɔʀdɑ̃, ɑ̃t/ **I** *adj* **1** caustic, scathing; **2** [*cold*] biting.

II *nm* **1** sarcasm; **avec ~** sarcastically; **2**○ (of person, team) zip○.

mordiller /mɔʀdije/ [1] *vtr* to nibble at; to chew.

mordoré, **~e** /mɔʀdɔʀe/ *adj* golden brown.

mordre /mɔʀdʀ/ [6] **I** *vtr* **1** to bite; **2** [*file*] to bite; [*acid, rust*] to eat into.

II mordre à *v+prep* **~ à l'appât** or **l'hameçon** to take the bait.

III *vi* **1 ~ dans une pomme** to bite into an apple; **2 ~ sur** to go over [*white line*]; to encroach on [*territory*]; **3**○ to fall for it○.

IV se mordre *v refl* (+ *v être*) **se ~ la langue** to bite one's tongue.

IDIOMS **je m'en suis mordu les doigts** I could have kicked myself.

mordu, **~e** /mɔʀdy/ **I**○ *adj* **1 être ~ de qch** to be mad○ about sth; **2** smitten.

II° *nm,f* fan; **les ~s du ski** skiing fans.

morfondre: **se morfondre** /mɔʀfɔ̃dʀ/ [6] *v refl* (+ *v être*) **1 se ~ à attendre** or **en attendant** to wait dejectedly; **2** to pine.

morgue /mɔʀg/ *nf* **1** morgue; (hospital) mortuary; **2** arrogance.

moribond, **~e** /mɔʀibɔ̃, ɔ̃d/ **I** *adj* [*person*] dying; [*civilization*] moribund.
II *nm,f* dying man/woman.

morille /mɔʀij/ *nf* morel (mushroom).

mormon, **~e** /mɔʀmɔ̃, ɔn/ *adj, nm,f* Mormon.

morne /mɔʀn/ *adj* **1** [*person, attitude, silence*] gloomy; [*face*] glum; [*look*] doleful; **2** [*landscape, life*] dreary; [*weather*] dismal.

morose /mɔʀoz/ *adj* morose; gloomy.

morosité /mɔʀozite/ *nf* gloom.

morphème /mɔʀfɛm/ *nm* morpheme.

morphine /mɔʀfin/ *nf* morphine.

morphologie /mɔʀfɔlɔʒi/ *nf* morphology.

mors /mɔʀ/ *nm inv* bit; **prendre le ~ aux dents** to take the bit between its/one's teeth.

morse /mɔʀs/ *nm* **1** walrus; **2 (code) ~** Morse code.

morsure /mɔʀsyʀ/ *nf* **1** bite; **~ de chien** dogbite; **2 la ~ du froid** the biting cold.

mort[1] /mɔʀ/ *nf* death; **mourir de sa belle ~** to die peacefully in old age; **il n'y a pas eu ~ d'homme** there were no fatalities; **être à deux doigts de la ~** to be at death's door; **trouver la ~** (literary) to die; **mettre qn à ~** to put sb to death; **mise à ~** (of condemned) killing; (of bull) dispatch; **à ~** [*fight*] to the death; [*war*] ruthless; [*brake, squeeze*] like mad°; [*beat*] to death; [*wounded*] fatally.
■ **~ cérébrale** brain death; **~ subite** sudden death; **~ subite du nourrisson** cot death (GB), crib death (US).
IDIOMS **la ~ dans l'âme** with a heavy heart.

mort[2], **~e** /mɔʀ, mɔʀt/ **I** *pp* ▶ **mourir**.
II *pp adj* **1** dead; **2 je suis ~ de froid** I'm freezing to death; **je suis ~**° I'm dead tired; **mes orteils sont comme ~s** my toes have gone numb; **3** [*district*] dead; [*season*] slack; **eaux ~es** stagnant water; **4** [*civilization*] dead; [*city*] lost.
III *nm,f* dead person, dead man/woman; **les ~s** the dead.
IV *nm* **1** fatality; **il y a eu 12 ~s** there were 12 dead; **2** body; **faire le ~** to play dead; to lie low.
IDIOMS **ne pas y aller de main ~e**° not to pull any punches.

mortalité /mɔʀtalite/ *nf* mortality.

mort-aux-rats /mɔʀɔʀa/ *nf inv* rat poison.

mortel, **-elle** /mɔʀtɛl/ **I** *adj* **1** [*blow, illness*] fatal; [*poison, gas*] lethal; [*venom*] deadly; **2** [*cold, silence*] deathly; [*anguish*] mortal; **3** [*enemy*] mortal; **4** [*person, meeting*] deadly boring; **5** [*being*] mortal.
II *nm,f* mortal.

mortellement /mɔʀtɛlmɑ̃/ *adv* **1** [*injured*] fatally; **2** [*boring*] deadly.

morte-saison, *pl* **mortes-saisons** /mɔʀt(ə)sɛzɔ̃/ *nf* off season.

mortier /mɔʀtje/ *nm* mortar.

mortifier /mɔʀtifje/ [2] *vtr* to mortify.

mort-né, **~e**, *mpl* **~s** /mɔʀne/ *adj* **1** stillborn; **2** [*plan*] abortive.

mortuaire /mɔʀtɥɛʀ/ *adj* **cérémonie ~** funeral ceremony; **veillée ~** wake.

morue /mɔʀy/ *nf* cod.

morve /mɔʀv/ *nf* nasal mucus.

morveux, **-euse** /mɔʀvø, øz/ *adj* snotty-nosed°; **se sentir ~** to feel embarrassed.

mosaïque /mɔzaik/ *nf* mosaic.

Moscou /mɔsku/ *pr n* Moscow.

moscovite /mɔskɔvit/ *adj* of Moscow.

Moscovite /mɔskɔvit/ *nmf* Muscovite.

mosquée /mɔske/ *nf* mosque.

mot /mo/ *nm* **1** word; **faire du ~ à ~** to translate word for word; **à ~s couverts** in veiled terms; **au bas ~** at least; **pour eux, l'amitié n'est pas un vain ~** they take friendship seriously; **il est bête et le ~ est faible!** he's stupid and that's putting it mildly!; **2** word; **dire un ~ à qn**, **toucher un ~ à qn**° to have a word with sb; **il ne dit jamais un ~ plus haut que l'autre** he never raises his voice; **avoir son ~ à dire** to be entitled to one's say; **avoir toujours le ~ pour rire** to be a born joker; **3** note; **je t'ai laissé un ~** I left you a note.
■ **~ d'esprit** witticism; **~ de la fin** closing words; **avoir le ~ de la fin** to have the last word; **~ d'ordre** watchword; **~ d'ordre de grève** strike call; **~ de passe** password; **~s croisés** crossword; **~s doux** sweet nothings.
IDIOMS **avoir des ~s avec qn** to have words with sb; **ne pas avoir peur des ~s** to call a spade a spade; **manger ses ~s** to mumble; **se donner** or **passer le ~** to pass the word around.

motard, **~e** /mɔtaʀ, aʀd/ **I**° *nm,f* motorcyclist, biker°.
II *nm* police motorcyclist.

mot-clé, *pl* **mots-clés** /mokle/ *nm* key word.

moteur, **-trice**[1] /mɔtœʀ, tʀis/ **I** *adj* **1** [*force, principle*] driving; **la voiture a quatre roues motrices** the car has four-wheel drive; **2** (Med) **troubles ~s** motor problems.
II *nm* **1** motor; **2** engine; **3 être le ~ de qch** to be the driving force behind sth.

motif /mɔtif/ *nm* **1** grounds; **il y a des ~s d'espérer** there are grounds for hope; **2** reason; **3** motive; **4** pattern; **à ~ floral** with a floral pattern; **5** (in music, novel) motif.

motion /mɔsjɔ̃/ *nf* motion; **~ de censure** motion of censure.

motivant, **~e** /mɔtivɑ̃, ɑ̃t/ *adj* [*salary*] attractive; [*work*] rewarding.

motivation /mɔtivasjɔ̃/ *nf* **1** motivation; **2** motive; **~s profondes** deeper motives.

motivé, **~e** /mɔtive/ *adj* **1** motivated; **il est peu ~** he lacks motivation; **2** [*complaint*] justifiable.

motiver /mɔtive/ [1] *vtr* **1** to motivate; **2** to lead to [*decision, action*]; **motivé par** caused by.

moto /moto/ *nf* **1** (motor)bike; **à ~** by motorbike; **2** motorcycling.
motocross /motokRɔs/ *nm inv* motocross, scramble (GB).
motoculture /motokyltyR/ *nf* rotary cultivation.
motocycle /motosikl/ *nm* motorcycle.
motocyclette /motosiklɛt/ *nf* motorcycle.
motocyclisme /motosiklism/ *nm* motorcycle racing.
motocycliste /motosiklist/ I *adj* [*rally*] motorcycle.
II *nmf* motorcyclist.
motoneige /motonɛʒ/ *nf* snowmobile.
motoriser /mɔtɔRize/ [1] *vtr* to motorize; **être motorisé**○ to have transport (GB) or transportation (US).
motrice[2] /mɔtRis/ I *adj f* ▶ **moteur I**.
II *nf* (of train) engine.
motte /mɔt/ *nf* **~ (de terre)** clod (of earth); **~ de gazon** sod, piece of turf; **~ (de beurre)** slab of butter; **acheter du beurre en ~** to buy butter by weight.
mou (**mol** *before vowel or mute h*), **molle** /mu, mɔl/ I *adj* **1** [*substance, cushion*] soft; [*material*] limp; [*blow*] dull; **2** [*features*] weak; [*stomach*] flabby; **3** [*person*] listless; [*growth*] sluggish; **4** [*parent*] soft; **5** [*speech, resistance*] feeble, weak.
II *nm* **1** wimp○; **2** (in butchery) lights (GB), lungs (US); **3 donner du ~** to let (the rope) out a bit; **laisser/donner du ~ à qn**○ to let sb have/to give sb a bit of leeway.
mouchard, **~e** /muʃaR, aRd/ I○ *nm,f* **1** grass○ (GB), informer; **2** sneak○.
II *nm* **1** tachograph; **2** spyhole.
moucharder○ /muʃaRde/ [1] *vtr* **1 ~ qn** to inform on sb; to squeal○ on sb; **2** (GB) to sneak○.
mouche /muʃ/ *nf* **1** fly; **2** patch, beauty spot; **3** bull's eye; **faire ~** to hit the bull's eye; (figurative) to be right on target; **4** (Sport) (on foil) button.
■ **~ à miel** bee; **~ verte** greenbottle; **~ du vinaigre** fruit fly.
IDIOMS **on entendrait une ~ voler** you could hear a pin drop; **quelle ~ les a piqués**○**?** what's got (GB) or gotten (US) into them?; **prendre la ~** to fly off the handle.
moucher /muʃe/ [1] I *vtr* **~ qn** to blow sb's nose; (figurative)○ to put sb in their place.
II **se moucher** *v refl* (+ *v être*) to blow one's nose.
IDIOMS **il ne se mouche pas du pied** or **du coude**○ he's full of airs and graces.
moucheron /muʃRɔ̃/ *nm* midge.
moucheté, **~e** /muʃte/ *adj* **1** [*material*] flecked; [*plumage, fish*] speckled; [*coat*] spotted; [*horse*] dappled; **2** (Sport) [*foil*] buttoned.
mouchoir /muʃwaR/ *nm* handkerchief; tissue (GB).
moudre /mudR/ [77] *vtr* to grind.
moue /mu/ *nf* pout; **faire la ~** to pout; (doubtfully) to pull a face.
mouette /mwɛt/ *nf* (sea) gull.
mouf(f)ette /mufɛt/ *nf* skunk.
moufle /mufl/ *nf* mitten.
mouiller /muje/ [1] I *vtr* **1** to wet; to get [sth] wet; **2** to drop [*anchor*]; to lay [*mine*].
II *vi* to anchor, to drop anchor.
III **se mouiller** *v refl* (+ *v être*) **1** to get wet; **2**○ to stick one's neck out○.
moulage /mulaʒ/ *nm* **1** casting; **faire un ~ de qch** to take a cast of sth; **2** (of grain) milling.
moulant, **~e** /mulɑ̃, ɑ̃t/ *adj* skin-tight, tight-fitting.
moule[1] /mul/ *nm* **1** mould (GB), mold (US); **2** tin, pan (US); (for jellies) mould (GB), mold (US); **~ à gaufre** waffle iron.
moule[2] /mul/ *nf* mussel.
mouler /mule/ [1] *vtr* **1** to mould (GB), to mold (US) [*substance*]; to cast [*bronze*]; to mint [*medal*]; **2** to take a cast of; **3** [*garment*] to hug.
moulin /mulɛ̃/ *nm* mill.
■ **~ à paroles**○ chatterbox; **~ à vent** windmill.
IDIOMS **apporter de l'eau au ~ de qn** to fuel sb's arguments; **on ne peut être à la fois au four et au ~** one can't be in two places at once; **on y entre comme dans un ~**○ one can just slip in; **se battre contre des ~s à vent** to tilt at windmills.
mouliner /muline/ [1] *vtr* to grind, to mill [*pepper, coffee*].
moulinet /mulinɛ/ *nm* **1** (in fishing) reel; **2 faire des ~s avec les bras** to wave one's arms about.
moulinette® /mulinɛt/ *nf* (small) vegetable mill.
moulu, **~e** /muly/ I *pp* ▶ **moudre**.
II *pp adj* [*coffee, pepper*] ground.
III○ *adj* **~ (de fatigue)** worn out; **~ (de coups)** beaten black and blue.
moulure /mulyR/ *nf* moulding (GB), molding (US).
moumoute○ /mumut/ *nf* **1** toupee; **2** sheepskin jacket.
mourant, **~e** /muRɑ̃, ɑ̃t/ *adj* [*person, animal*] dying; [*company*] moribund; [*light*] fading; [*voice*] faint.
mourir /muRiR/ [34] I *vi* (+ *v être*) **1** to die; **~ de froid** to die of exposure; to die of cold; **je meurs de soif/de froid** I'm dying of thirst/freezing to death; **c'était à ~ (de rire)**! it was hilarious!; **~ debout** to be active to the end; **2** (literary) [*light, day*] to fade away; [*flames*] to die down; [*sound, conversation*] to die away.
II **se mourir** *v refl* (+ *v être*) (literary) [*person, civilization*] to be dying; [*flames*] to die down.
IDIOMS **partir c'est ~ un peu** to say goodbye is to die a little; **je ne veux pas ~ idiot**○ I want to know; **tu n'en mourras pas**○! it won't kill you!
mouroir /muRwaR/ *nm* (derogatory) old people's home, twilight home.
mouron /muRɔ̃/ *nm* pimpernel.
mousquetaire /muskətɛR/ *nm* musketeer.
mousqueton /muskətɔ̃/ *nm* **1** snap clasp; **2** (in climbing) carabiner.
moussant, **~e** /musɑ̃, ɑ̃t/ *adj* [*gel*] foaming.
mousse[1] /mus/ *nm* ship's apprentice.

mousse² /mus/ *nf* **1** moss; **2** foam; (from soap) lather; (on milk, coffee) froth; (on beer) head; **3** **~ au chocolat** chocolate mousse; **4** foam rubber; **bas en ~** stretch stockings.

■ **~ carbonique** (fire) foam; **~ à raser** shaving foam.

IDIOMS **pierre qui roule n'amasse pas ~** (Proverb) a rolling stone gathers no moss.

mousseline /muslin/ *nf* **1** muslin; **2** chiffon.

mousser /muse/ [1] *vi* [*beer*] to foam; [*detergent, soap*] to lather.

IDIOMS **se faire ~**○ to sing one's own praises.

mousseux, **-euse** /musø, øz/ *adj* **1** [*wine*] sparkling; [*beer*] fizzy; **2** [*lace*] frothy.

mousson /musɔ̃/ *nf* monsoon.

moustache /mustaʃ/ **I** *nf* moustache (GB), mustache (US).

II moustaches *nf pl* (Zool) whiskers.

moustachu, **~e** /mustaʃy/ *adj* [*person*] with a moustache (GB) or mustache (US).

moustiquaire /mustikɛʀ/ *nf* mosquito net.

moustique /mustik/ *nm* mosquito.

moût /mu/ *nm* (from grape, potato) must; (from hops, barley) wort.

moutarde /mutaʀd/ *adj inv*, *nf* mustard.

IDIOMS **la ~ me monte au nez**○! I'm beginning to see red!

mouton /mutɔ̃/ **I** *nm* **1** sheep; **2** mutton; **3** sheepskin; **4** (derogatory) sheep; **ce sont des ~s de Panurge** they follow one another like sheep.

II moutons *nm pl* **1** small fleecy clouds; **2** whitecaps; **3** fluff.

■ **~ à cinq pattes** rare bird.

IDIOMS **il frise comme un ~** his hair goes all frizzy; **revenons à nos ~s**○ let's get back to the point.

mouture /mutyʀ/ *nf* **1** (of coffee) grind; **2 première/nouvelle ~** first/new version.

mouvance /muvɑ̃s/ *nf* sphere of influence.

mouvant, **~e** /muvɑ̃, ɑ̃t/ *adj* **1** [*ground*] unstable; **2** [*group*] shifting; **reflets ~s** shimmering reflections; **3** [*situation, opinion*] changing.

mouvement /muvmɑ̃/ *nm* **1** movement; **faire un ~** to move; **tu es libre de tes ~s** you can come and go as you please; **2** movement; **~ perpétuel** perpetual motion; **le ~ de personnel dans une entreprise** staff changes in a company; **accélérer le ~** to speed up; **3** bustle; **suivre le ~** (figurative) to follow the crowd; **4** impulse, reaction; **un ~ de colère** a surge of anger; **5 le ~ étudiant** the student protest movement; **~ de grève** strike, industrial action; **6 le ~ des idées** the evolution of ideas; **être dans le ~** to move with the times; **un milieu en ~** a changing environment; **7** (Econ) **le ~ du marché** market fluctuations; **~ de hausse** upward trend; **8** (of symphony, poem) movement; **9** (of timepiece) movement; **~ d'horlogerie** clockwork mechanism.

mouvementé, **~e** /muvmɑ̃te/ *adj* **1** [*life, week, trip*] eventful, hectic; [*meeting*] lively; **2** [*terrain*] rough.

mouvoir /muvwaʀ/ [43] (formal) **I** *vtr* **1** [*person*] to move; [*energy, mechanism*] to drive; **2** [*feeling, desire*] to drive.

II se mouvoir *v refl* (+ *v être*) to move.

moyen, **-enne¹** /mwajɛ̃, ɛn/ **I** *adj* **1** [*height, size*] medium; [*town*] medium-sized; [*price*] moderate; **2** [*student, result*] average; **3** [*income*] middle; [*level*] intermediate; **4** average; **le Français ~** the average Frenchman; **5** average, mean.

II *nm* **1** means, way; **tous les ~s sont bons** any means will do; **employer les grands ~s** to resort to drastic measures; **2** (of expression, production) means; (of investigation, payment) method; **3** way; **(il n'y a) pas ~ de lui faire comprendre qu'il a tort** it's impossible to make him realize he's wrong.

III au moyen de *phr* by means of.

IV par le moyen de *phr* by means of, through.

V moyens *nm pl* **1** means; **faute de ~s** through lack of money; **je n'ai pas les ~s de faire** I can't afford to do; **avoir de petits ~s** not to be very well off; **2** resources; **donner à qn les ~s de faire** to give sb the means to do; **se débrouiller par ses propres ~s** to manage on one's own; **3** ability; **perdre ses ~s** to go to pieces.

■ **~ de locomotion** or **transport** means of transport (GB) or transportation (US); **Moyen Âge** Middle Ages.

moyenâgeux, **-euse** /mwajɛnɑʒø, øz/ *adj* **1** medieval; **2** antiquated.

moyen-courrier, *pl* **~s** /mwajɛ̃kuʀje/ *nm* medium-haul airliner.

moyennant /mwajenɑ̃/ *prep* **~ finances** for a fee; **~ quoi** in view of which; in return for which.

moyenne² /mwajɛn/ **I** *adj f* ▶ **moyen**.

II *nf* **1** average; **2** half marks (GB), 50%; **j'ai eu tout juste la ~** I barely passed; **3** average; **la ~ d'âge** the average age; **en ~** on average; **4** (Aut) average speed.

moyennement /mwajɛnmɑ̃/ *adv* [*intelligent, wealthy*] moderately; [*understand*] moderately well; [*like*] to a certain extent.

Moyen-Orient /mwajɛnɔʀjɑ̃/ *pr nm* Middle East.

moyeu, *pl* **~x** /mwajø/ *nm* hub.

MST /ɛmɛste/ *nf*: *abbr* ▶ **maladie**.

mû ▶ **mouvoir**.

mucoviscidose /mykovisidoz/ *nf* cystic fibrosis.

mucus /mykys/ *nm inv* mucus.

mue¹ ▶ **mouvoir**.

mue² /my/ *nf* **1** (of insect) metamorphosis; (of reptile) sloughing of the skin; (of bird, mammal) moulting (GB), molting (US); (of stag) casting; **2** (of snake, insect) slough, sloughed skin; **3** breaking (GB) or changing (US) of voice; **4** (literary) transformation.

muer /mɥe/ [1] **I** *vtr* (literary) to transform.

II *vi* **1** [*insect*] to metamorphose; [*snake*] to slough its skin; [*bird, mammal*] to moult (GB), to molt (US); **2 sa voix mue, il mue** his voice is breaking (GB) or changing (US).

III se muer *v refl* (+ *v être*) **1** to be transformed; **2** to transform oneself.

muet, -ette /mɥɛ, ɛt/ **I** *adj* **1** dumb; speechless; **2** [*witness, reproach*] silent; **3** [*vowel, consonant*] mute, silent; **4** [*film*] silent; [*role*] nonspeaking.

II *nm,f* mute.

mufle /myfl/ **I** *adj* boorish, loutish.

II *nm* **1** (Zool)muffle; muzzle; **2** boor, lout.

muflerie /myflǝʀi/ *nf* boorishness.

mugir /myʒiʀ/ [3] *vi* **1** to low; to bellow; **2** [*wind*] to howl; [*siren*] to wail; [*torrent*] to roar.

muguet /mygɛ/ *nm* lily of the valley.

mulâtre /mylɑtʀ/ *adj, nm* mulatto.

mulâtresse /mylɑtʀɛs/ *nf* mulatto.

mule /myl/ *nf* **1** female mule; **2** (slipper) mule.

mulet /mylɛ/ *nm* **1** (male) mule; **2** grey mullet (GB), mullet (US).

muletier, -ière /myltje, ɛʀ/ **I** *adj* **sentier** or **chemin ~** mule track.

II *nm* muleteer, mule skinner○ (US).

mulot /mylo/ *nm* fieldmouse.

multi /mylti/ *pref* multi; **~colore** multicoloured[GB]; **~media** multimedia.

multifonction /myltifɔ̃ksjɔ̃/ *adj inv* (gen) multipurpose; (Comput) multifunction.

multiforme /myltifɔʀm/ *adj* [*aspect*] multiform; [*life, danger*] many-sided.

multipare /myltipaʀ/ *adj* multiparous.

multipartite /myltipaʀtit/ *adj* **1** [*treaty*] multipartite; **2** [*elections*] multi-party.

multiple /myltipl/ **I** *adj* **1** [*reasons, occasions*] numerous, many; [*births*] multiple; **après de ~s spéculations** after much speculation; **à choix ~** multiple-choice; **2** [*causes, facets*] many, various; **3** (in science) multiple.

II *nm* multiple.

multipliable /myltiplijabl/ *adj* multiplicable.

multiplicateur, -trice /myltiplikatœʀ, tʀis/ *adj* multiplying.

multiplication /myltiplikasjɔ̃/ *nf* **1 ~ de** increase in the number of; **2** (in mathematics, science) multiplication.

multiplicité /myltiplisite/ *nf* multiplicity.

multiplier /myltiplije/ [2] **I** *vtr* **1** to multiply (**par** by); **2** to increase [*risks, fortune*]; to increase the number of [*trains, accidents*].

II se multiplier *v refl* (+ *v être*) **1** [*branches, villas*] to grow in number; [*incidents, arrests*] to be on the increase; [*difficulties*] to increase; [*rows*] to become more frequent; **2** [*animals, germs*] to multiply.

multipropriété /myltipʀɔpʀijete/ *nf* time-sharing.

multirisque /myltiʀisk/ *adj* **assurance ~** comprehensive insurance.

multisalle /myltisal/ *adj inv* **cinéma ~** cinema complex (GB), multiplex (US).

multitude /myltityd/ *nf* **1 une ~ de** a mass of [*tourists, objects*]; a lot of [*reasons, ideas*]; **2** multitude, throng.

municipal, ~e, *mpl* **-aux** /mynisipal, o/ *adj* [*council*] local, town; [*council*] city; [*park, pool*] municipal; **arrêté ~** bylaw.

municipales /mynisipal/ *nf pl* local elections.

municipalité /mynisipalite/ *nf* **1** municipality; **2** town council; city council.

munir /myniʀ/ [3] **I** *vtr* **1** to provide (**de** with); **2 ~ un bâtiment d'un escalier de secours** to put a fire escape on a building; **muni de** fitted with.

II se munir *v refl* (+ *v être*) **se ~ de** to bring; to take.

munitions /mynisjɔ̃/ *nf pl* ammunition, munitions.

muqueuse /mykøz/ *nf* mucous membrane.

mur /myʀ/ **I** *nm* wall; **rester** or **être entre quatre ~s** to be cooped up; **faire les pieds au ~** to do a handstand against the wall; to tie oneself up in knots.

II murs *nm pl* (of business) premises; (of palace, embassy) confines; **être dans ses ~s** to own one's own house.

■ **~ portant** or **porteur** load-bearing wall; **~ du son** sound barrier; **~ de soutènement** retaining wall; **Mur des lamentations** Wailing Wall.

IDIOMS **faire le ~** to go over the wall; **mettre qn au pied du ~** to call sb's bluff; **être au pied du ~** to be up against the wall.

mûr, ~e[1] /myʀ/ *adj* **1** ripe; **2** mature; **l'âge ~** middle age; **après ~e réflexion** after careful consideration; **3** ready; **il est ~ pour des aveux** he's ready to confess; **4** [*situation*] at a decisive stage; **5 être ~** [*abscess*] to have come to a head.

IDIOMS **en voir des vertes et des pas ~es**○ to go through a lot; **en dire des vertes et des pas ~es**○ to tell some dirty jokes; to say a lot of nasty things.

muraille /myʀɑj/ *nf* great wall.

mural, ~e, *mpl* **-aux** /myʀal, o/ *adj* [*covering, map*] wall; [*plant*] climbing; **peinture ~e** mural.

mûre[2] /myʀ/ **I** *adj f* ▶ **mûr**.

II *nf* blackberry.

mûrement /myʀmɑ̃/ *adv* **~ réfléchi** carefully thought through.

murène /myʀɛn/ *nf* moray eel.

murer /myʀe/ [1] **I** *vtr* to build a wall around [sth]; to brick [sth] up; to block [sth] off; to wall [sb] up.

II se murer *v refl* (+ *v être*) **se ~ chez soi** to shut oneself away.

muret /myʀɛ/ *nm*, **murette** /myʀɛt/ *nf* low wall.

mûrier /myʀje/ *nm* mulberry tree.

mûrir /myʀiʀ/ [3] **I** *vtr* **1** to ripen [*fruit*]; **2** to mature [*person*]; to develop [*plan*].

II *vi* **1** [*fruit*] to ripen; **faire ~ des bananes** to ripen bananas; **2** [*person, talent*] to mature; [*plan, idea*] to evolve; [*passion*] to develop; **3** [*abscess*] to come to a head.

murmure /myʀmyʀ/ *nm* **1** murmur; **2 ~s**

mutterings; **3** (of wind) whisper; (of spring) murmur, babbling; **4** rumour[GB].

murmurer /myʀmyʀe/ [1] **I** *vtr* **1** to murmur; **2** to say; **on murmure qu'il est riche** he is rumoured[GB] to be rich.
II *vi* **1** [*person*] to murmur; [*wind*] to whisper; [*spring, stream*] to babble; **2** to mutter; **obéir sans ~** to obey without a murmur; **3** to spread rumours[GB].

musaraigne /myzaʀɛɲ/ *nf* (Zool) shrew.

musarder /myzaʀde/ [1] *vi* to wander around.

musc /mysk/ *nm* musk.

muscade /myskad/ *nf* nutmeg; **noix de ~** nutmeg.

muscle /myskl/ *nm* muscle.

musclé, **~e** /myskle/ *adj* **1** muscular; **2** [*style*] sinewy; [*music, speech*] powerful; [*reaction*] strong; [*intervention, match*] tough; **3** (Econ) competitive.

muscler /myskle/ [1] **I** *vtr* **1 ~ les bras** to develop the arm muscles; **2** to strengthen.
II se muscler *v refl* (+ *v être*) to develop one's muscles.

musculaire /myskylɛʀ/ *adj* [*tissue*] muscle; [*weakness*] muscular.

musculation /myskylasjɔ̃/ *nf* **(exercices de) ~** (gen) bodybuilding; (Med) exercises to strengthen the muscles; **salle de ~** weights room.

musculature /myskylatyʀ/ *nf* musculature.

muse /myz/ *nf* **1** Muse; **les neuf ~s** the Muses; **2** (figurative) muse.

museau, *pl* **~x** /myzo/ *nm* **1** muzzle; snout; nose; **2**○ face.

musée /myze/ *nm* museum; art gallery (GB), art museum (US); **~ de cire** waxworks, wax museum; **une ville ~** a city of great historical and artistic importance.

museler /myzəle/ [19] *vtr* to muzzle.

muselière /myzəljɛʀ/ *nf* muzzle.

musette[1] /myzɛt/ *nm* **1** accordion music; **2** dance (*where accordion music is played*).

musette[2] /myzɛt/ *nf* **1** haversack; **2** lunchbag; **3** (Zool) common shrew.

muséum /myzeɔm/ *nm* **~ (d'histoire naturelle)** natural history museum.

musical, **~e**, *mpl* **-aux** /myzikal, o/ *adj* [*event*] musical; [*critic*] music; [*choice*] of music.

music-hall, *pl* **~s** *nm* /mysikol/ music hall; **spectacle de ~** variety show.

musicien, **-ienne** /myzisjɛ̃, ɛn/ **I** *adj* musical.
II *nm,f* musician.

musique /myzik/ *nf* **1** music; **travailler en ~** to work with music in the background; **mettre en ~** to set [sth] to music; **faire de la ~** to play an instrument; **2 une ~ triste** a sad piece of music; **une ~ de film** a film score.
IDIOMS **connaître la ~**○ to know the score○; **je ne peux pas aller plus vite que la ~**○ I can't go any faster than I'm already going; **être réglé comme du papier à ~**○ [*person*] to be as regular as clockwork; [*conference, project*] to go very smoothly.

musqué, **~e** /myske/ *adj* **1** musky; **2** (Zool) **bœuf ~** musk ox; **rat ~** muskrat.

musulman, **~e** /myzylmɑ̃, an/ *adj, nm,f* Muslim.

mutant, **~e** /mytɑ̃, ɑ̃t/ *adj, nm,f* mutant.

mutation /mytasjɔ̃/ *nf* **1** transfer; **2** transformation; **en pleine ~** undergoing radical transformation; **3** mutation.

muter /myte/ [1] **I** *vtr* to transfer [*official*] (**à** to).
II *vi* to mutate.

mutilation /mytilasjɔ̃/ *nf* mutilation.

mutilé, **~e** /mytile/ *nm,f* disabled person; **~ de guerre** disabled war veteran.

mutiler /mytile/ [1] **I** *vtr* to mutilate.
II se mutiler *v refl* (+ *v être*) to inflict an injury on oneself.

mutin, **~e** /mytɛ̃, in/ **I** *adj* mischievous.
II *nm* mutineer; rioter.

mutiner: **se mutiner** /mytine/ [1] *v refl* (+ *v être*) to mutiny; to riot.

mutinerie /mytinʀi/ *nf* mutiny; riot.

mutisme /mytism/ *nm* silence.

mutuel, **-elle**[1] /mytɥɛl/ *adj* mutual.

mutuelle[2] /mytɥɛl/ *nf* mutual insurance company.

mutuellement /mytɥɛlmɑ̃/ *adv* mutually; **s'aider ~** to help each other.

myocarde /mjɔkaʀd/ *nm* myocardium.

myope /mjɔp/ *adj* short-sighted.
IDIOMS **~ comme une taupe**○ as blind as a bat.

myopie /mjɔpi/ *nf* short-sightedness.

myosotis /mjɔzɔtis/ *nm inv* forget-me-not.

myriade /miʀjad/ *nf* myriad.

myrrhe /miʀ/ *nf* myrrh.

myrte /miʀt/ *nm* myrtle.

myrtille /miʀtij/ *nf* bilberry, blueberry.

mystère /mistɛʀ/ *nm* **1** mystery; **auteur ~** mysterious author; **2** secrecy; **il n'est un ~ pour personne que** it's an open secret that; **3** (in religion) mystery; **4** rite.

mystérieux, **-ieuse** /misteʀjø, øz/ *adj* mysterious.

mysticisme /mistisism/ *nm* mysticism.

mystification /mistifikasjɔ̃/ *nf* **1** hoax; **2** myth.

mystifier /mistifje/ [2] *vtr* to hoodwink, to fool.

mystique /mistik/ **I** *adj* mystical.
II *nmf* mystic.
III *nf* **1** mysticism; **2** mystique; **3** blind belief.

mythe /mit/ *nm* myth.

mythique /mitik/ *adj* mythical.

mythologie /mitɔlɔʒi/ *nf* mythology.

mythologique /mitɔlɔʒik/ *adj* mythological.

mythomane /mitɔman/ *adj, nmf* mythomaniac.

mythomanie /mitɔmani/ *nf* mythomania.

Nn

n, **N** /ɛn/ **I** *nm inv* **1** n, N; **2 n°** (*written abbr* = **numéro**) no.
II N *nf* (*abbr* = **nationale**) **sur la N7** on the N7.

n' ▶ **ne**.

nabab /nabab/ *nm* **1** (wealthy man) mogul; **2** (in India) nabob.

nabot, **~e** /nabo, ɔt/ *nm,f* (offensive) dwarf.

nacelle /nasɛl/ *nf* **1** (of hot-air balloon) gondola; **2** carrycot (GB), carrier (US); **3** (of worker) cradle.

nacre /nakʀ/ *nf* mother-of-pearl.

nacré, **~e** /nakʀe/ *adj* pearly.

nage /naʒ/ *nf* **1** swimming; **200 mètres quatre ~s** 200 metres[GB] medley; **traverser à la ~** to swim across; **2 être en ~** to be in a sweat.
■ **~ sur le dos** backstroke; **~ indienne** sidestroke; **~ libre** freestyle.

nageoire /naʒwaʀ/ *nf* **1** (of fish) fin; **2** (of seal) flipper.

nager /naʒe/ [13] **I** *vtr* to swim; **~ le crawl** to do the crawl.
II *vi* **1** to swim; **2** (figurative) **~ dans le bonheur** to bask in contentment; **~ dans l'opulence** to live a life of luxury; **elle nage dans sa robe** her dress is far too big for her; **3**○ to be absolutely lost; **je nage en Latin** Latin is beyond me.
IDIOMS **~ entre deux eaux** to run with the hare and hunt with the hounds.

nageur, **-euse** /naʒœʀ, øz/ *nm,f* swimmer.

naguère /nagɛʀ/ *adv* **1** quite recently; **2** formerly.

naïf, **naïve** /naif, iv/ **I** *adj* naïve.
II *nm,f* innocent, gullible fool.

nain, **~e** /nɛ̃, nɛn/ **I** *adj* [*tree*] dwarf; [*dog*] miniature.
II *nm,f* dwarf.

naissance /nɛsɑ̃s/ *nf* **1** (gen) birth; (of rumour) start; **de ~** [*Italian, French*] by birth; [*deaf*] from birth; **donner ~ à** to give birth to [*child*]; to give rise to [*rumour*]; **à la ~** at birth; **à ma ~** when I was born; **2 à la ~ du cou** at the base of the neck.

naissant, **~e** /nɛsɑ̃, ɑ̃t/ *adj* new.

naître /nɛtʀ/ [74] *vi* (+ *v être*) **1** to be born; **elle est née le 5 juin** she was born on 5 June; **le bébé doit ~ à la fin du mois** the baby is due at the end of the month; **les bébés qui viennent de ~** newborn babies; **l'enfant à ~** the unborn baby or child; **je l'ai vu ~** (figurative) I have known him since he was born; **2** (figurative) [*movement, idea*] to be born; [*company*] to come into existence; [*love, friendship*] to spring up; [*day*] to break; [*suspicion*] to arise; **~ de** to arise out of; **faire ~** to give rise to [*hope*]; to arouse [*suspicion*]; **voir ~** to see the birth of [*newspaper, the cinema, century*].

naïve ▶ **naïf**.

naïvement /naivmɑ̃/ *adv* naively.

naïveté /naivte/ *nf* naivety.

naja /naʒa/ *nm* cobra.

nanisme /nanism/ *nm* dwarfism.

nanti, **~e** /nɑ̃ti/ **I** *adj* well-off.
II nantis *nm pl* **les ~s** the well-off.

naphtaline /naftalin/ *nf* mothballs; **boule de ~** mothball.

napoléonien, **-ienne** /napɔleɔnjɛ̃, ɛn/ *adj* Napoleonic.

napolitain, **~e** /napɔlitɛ̃, ɛn/ **I** *adj* Neapolitan.
II *nm* the Neapolitan dialect.

nappe /nap/ *nf* **1** tablecloth; **2** (of oil, gas) layer; (of water, fire) sheet; (of fog) blanket; **~ de mazout** oil slick.

napper /nape/ [1] *vtr* (Culin) to coat; to glaze.

napperon /napʀɔ̃/ *nm* mat.

narcisse /naʀsis/ *nm* (flower) narcissus.

narcissisme /naʀsisism/ *nm* narcissism.

narco(-) /naʀko/ *pref* drug; **~-dollars/-trafiquant** drug money/trafficker.

narcotique /naʀkɔtik/ *adj, nm* narcotic.

narguer /naʀge/ [1] *vtr* to taunt [*person*]; to flout [*authority*].

narguilé /naʀgile/ *nm* hookah.

narine /naʀin/ *nf* nostril.

narquois, **~e** /naʀkwa, az/ *adj* mocking.

narrateur, **-trice** /naʀatœʀ, tʀis/ *nm,f* narrator.

narratif, **-ive** /naʀatif, iv/ *adj* narrative.

narration /naʀasjɔ̃/ *nf* narration; **interrompre sa ~** to break off one's account.

narrer /naʀe/ [1] *vtr* (literary) to relate.

nasal, **~e**, *mpl* **-aux** /nazal, o/ *adj* [*sound, blockage*] nasal; **hémorragie ~e** heavy nosebleed.

naseau, *pl* **~x** /nazo/ *nm* nostril.

nasillard, **~e** /nazijaʀ, aʀd/ *adj* [*voice*] nasal; [*instrument*] tinny.

nasillement /nazijmɑ̃/ *nm* **1** (of person) nasal twang; **2** (of radio) tinny sound; **3** (of duck) quack.

nasiller /nazije/ [1] *vi* **1** to speak with a nasal voice; **2** [*duck*] to quack.

nasse /nas/ *nf* **1** keepnet; **2** (figurative) net.

natal, **~e**, *mpl* **~s** /natal/ *adj* native.

nataliste /natalist/ *adj* [*policy*] pro-birth.

natalité /natalite/ *nf* (**taux de**) **~** birthrate.

natation /natasjɔ̃/ *nf* swimming; **faire de la ~** to go swimming.

natif, **-ive** /natif, iv/ *adj* **~ de** native of.

nation /nasjɔ̃/ *nf* nation.
■ **les Nations unies** the United Nations.

national, **~e**[1], *mpl* **-aux** /nasjɔnal, o/ **I** *adj* national.
II *nm* national.

nationale[2] /nasjɔnal/ *nf* trunk road (GB), ≈ A road (GB), highway (US).

nationaliser /nasjɔnalize/ [1] *vtr* to nationalize.

nationalisme /nasjɔnalism/ *nm* nationalism.

nationalité /nasjɔnalite/ *nf* nationality.

nativité /nativite/ *nf* **1** nativity; **2** Nativity scene.

natte /nat/ *nf* **1** plait, braid (US); **2** mat; **3** plaited loaf.

naturalisation /natyʀalizasjɔ̃/ *nf* naturalization.

naturalisé, **~e** /natyʀalize/ *adj* naturalized; **Grec ~** naturalized Greek.

naturaliser /natyʀalize/ [1] *vtr* to naturalize [*foreigner, species*]; to assimilate [*word, custom*]; **elle est naturalisée française** she's acquired French nationality.

naturalisme /natyʀalism/ *nm* naturalism.

nature /natyʀ/ **I** *adj inv* **1** [*yoghurt*] plain; [*tea*] black; **2**○ [*person*] natural.
II *nf* **1** (gen) nature; **contre ~** against nature; **protection de la ~** protection of the environment; **en pleine ~** in the heart of the countryside; **lâcher qn dans la ~** to leave sb in the middle of nowhere; (figurative) to let sb loose; **2 de ~ à faire** likely to do; **des offres de toute ~** offers of all kinds; **3 peindre d'après ~** to paint from life; **plus vrai que ~** more real than life; **4 en ~** [*pay*] in kind; **avantages en ~** fringe benefits.
■ **~ humaine** human nature; **~ morte** still life; ▶ **petit**.
IDIOMS **partir** or **disparaître dans la ~**○ to vanish into thin air.

naturel, **-elle** /natyʀɛl/ **I** *adj* natural.
II *nm* **1** nature, disposition; **être d'un ~ craintif** to be timid by nature; **2 il manque de ~** he's not very natural; **avec le plus grand ~** in the most natural way; **3 au ~** [*rice*] plain; [*tuna*] in brine.

naturellement /natyʀɛlmɑ̃/ *adv* naturally.

naturisme /natyʀism/ *nm* naturism (GB), nudism.

naturiste /natyʀist/ *nmf* naturist (GB), nudist.

naufrage /nofʀaʒ/ *nm* (Naut) shipwreck, sinking; **faire ~** [*ship*] to be wrecked; [*sailor*] to be shipwrecked; [*company*] to collapse.

naufragé, **~e** /nofʀaʒe/ **I** *adj* shipwrecked; **retrouver le navire ~** to find the wreck of the ship.
II *nm,f* survivor (of a shipwreck); castaway.

nauséabond, **~e** /nozeabɔ̃, ɔ̃d/ *adj* sickening, nauseating.

nausée /noze/ *nf* nausea; **avoir la ~** to feel sick (GB) or nauseous.

nautique /notik/ *adj* [*science*] nautical; [*sports*] water.

nautisme /notism/ *nm* water sports.

naval, **~e**, *mpl* **~s** /naval/ *adj* **1** [*industry*] shipbuilding; **2** (Mil) naval.

navet /navɛ/ *nm* **1** turnip; **2** rubbishy film (GB), turkey○ (US).

navette /navɛt/ *nf* **1** shuttle; shuttle service; **faire la ~** (gen) to travel back and forth; (to work) to commute; **2** (in weaving) shuttle.
■ **~ spatiale** space shuttle.

navigabilité /navigabilite/ *nf* **1** (of river) navigability; **2** (of boat) seaworthiness; (of plane) airworthiness.

navigable /navigabl/ *adj* navigable.

navigant, **~e** /navigɑ̃, ɑ̃t/ *adj* **personnel ~** (on plane) flying personnel; (Naut) seagoing personnel; **mécanicien ~** flight engineer.

navigateur, **-trice** /navigatœʀ, tʀis/ *nm,f* **1** navigator; **2** sailor.
■ **~ solitaire** solo yachtsman.

navigation /navigasjɔ̃/ *nf* **1** navigation; **2** (Comput) browsing.
■ **~ de plaisance** boating; yachting.

naviguer /navige/ [1] *vi* **1** [*ship, sailor*] to sail; [*pilot, plane*] to fly; **en état de ~** [*ship*] seaworthy; **2** to navigate; **3** (Comput) to browse.

navire /naviʀ/ **I** *nm* ship.
II navire- (*combining form*) **~-école/-usine** training/factory ship; **~s-citernes** tankers.
■ **~ amiral** flagship; **~ de commerce** merchant ship; **~ de guerre** warship.

navrant, **~e** /navʀɑ̃, ɑ̃t/ *adj* **1** depressing; **2** distressing.

navré, **~e** /navʀe/ *adj* **je suis vraiment ~** I am terribly sorry; **avoir l'air ~** to look sad or upset; **d'un ton ~** sadly; apologetically.

navrer /navʀe/ [1] *vtr* (literary) to upset.

nazi, **~e** /nazi/ *adj, nm,f* Nazi.

nazisme /nazism/ *nm* Nazism.

ne /nə/ (**n'** *before vowel or mute h*) *adv*

■ **Note** In cases where *ne* is used with *pas, jamais, guère, rien, plus, aucun, personne* etc, one should consult the corresponding entry.
– *ne + verb + que* is treated in the entry below.

je n'ai que 100 francs I've only got 100 francs; **tu n'avais qu'à le dire!** you only had to say so!; **elle ne fait que (de) se plaindre** she does nothing but complain; **il n'y a que lui pour être aussi désagréable** only he can be so unpleasant; **tu n'es qu'un raté** you're nothing but a loser○; **je n'ai que faire de tes conseils** you can keep your advice.

né, **~e** /ne/ **I** *pp* ▶ **naître**.
II *pp adj* **bien ~** highborn; **Madame Masson ~e Roux** Mrs Masson née Roux.
III (-)né (*combining form*) **musicien(-)/écrivain(-)~** born musician/writer.

néanmoins /neɑ̃mwɛ̃/ *adv* nevertheless.

néant /neɑ̃/ *nm* **1 le ~** nothingness; **le ~ de ma vie** the emptiness of my life; **réduire à ~** to destroy [*argument, hopes*]; **2 'revenus: ~'** 'income: nil'.

nébuleuse[1] /nebyløz/ *nf* (in astronomy) nebula.

nébuleux, **-euse**[2] /nebylø, øz/ *adj* **1** [*sky*] cloudy; **2** [*idea*] nebulous.

nécessaire /nesesɛʀ/ **I** *adj* necessary (**à** for); **croire ~ de faire** to believe it necessary to do;

plus qu'il n'est ~ more than is necessary; **il est ~ que tu y ailles** you have to go, it is necessary for you to go; **les voix ~s pour renverser le gouvernement** the votes needed in order to overthrow the government.

II *nm* **1 faire le ~** to do what is necessary; **as-tu fait le ~ pour les billets?** did you see about the tickets?; **2** essentials; **le strict ~** the bare essentials.

■ **~ de couture** sewing kit; **~ à ongles** manicure set; **~ de toilette** toiletries.

nécessairement /nesesɛʀmɑ̃/ *adv* necessarily; **'y aura-t-il des licenciements?'—'pas ~/oui, ~'** 'will there be redundancies?'—'not necessarily/yes, it is unavoidable'; **passe-t-on ~ par Oslo?** do you have to go via Oslo?

nécessité /nesesite/ *nf* **1** necessity; **le téléphone est devenu une ~** the telephone has become a necessity; **~ urgente** urgent need; **~ de qch/de faire/d'être** need for sth/to do/to be; **~ pour qn de qch/de faire** sb's need for sth/to do; **de première ~** vital; **par ~** out of necessity; **sans ~** unnecessarily; **être dans la ~ de faire** to have no choice but to do; **2** need; **être dans la ~** to be in need.

IDIOMS **~ fait loi** (Proverb) necessity knows no law.

nécessiter /nesesite/ [1] *vtr* to require; **la situation nécessite qu'elle intervienne** the situation calls for her intervention.

nécessiteux, **-euse** /nesesitø, øz/ I *adj* needy.

II *nm,f* needy person; **les ~** the needy.

nécrologie /nekʀɔlɔʒi/ *nf* **1** deaths column; **2** obituary.

nécrologique /nekʀɔlɔʒik/ *adj* obituary.

nectar /nɛktaʀ/ *nm* nectar.

néerlandais, **~e** /neɛʀlɑ̃dɛ, ɛz/ I *adj* Dutch.

II *nm* Dutch.

Néerlandais, **~e** /neɛʀlɑ̃dɛ, ɛz/ *nm,f* Dutchman/Dutchwoman; **les ~** the Dutch.

nef /nɛf/ *nf* nave; **~ latérale** side aisle.

néfaste /nefast/ *adj* harmful (**à** to).

négatif, **-ive**[1] /negatif, iv/ I *adj* negative.

II *nm* negative.

négation /negasjɔ̃/ *nf* **1** negation; **2** (in grammar) negative.

négative[2] /negativ/ I *adj f* ▶ **négatif** I.

II *nf* **répondre par la ~** to reply in the negative; **dans la ~, nous aviserons** if not, we will think again.

négativement /negativmɑ̃/ *adv* negatively.

négligé, **~e** /negliʒe/ I *adj* [*person, appearance*] sloppy; [*hair*] unkempt; [*house*] neglected; [*work*] careless; [*injury*] untreated.

II *nm* negligée.

négligeable /negliʒabl/ *adj* [*amount*] negligible; [*person*] insignificant; **non ~** [*sum*] considerable; [*detail*] significant.

négligemment /negliʒamɑ̃/ *adv* **1** nonchalantly; **2** carelessly.

négligence /negliʒɑ̃s/ *nf* **1** negligence; **2** oversight.

négligent, **~e** /negliʒɑ̃, ɑ̃t/ *adj* [*employee*] negligent, careless; [*glance*] casual.

négliger /negliʒe/ [13] I *vtr* (gen) to neglect; to leave untreated [*cold*]; to ignore [*rule*]; **ne rien ~ pour réussir** to try everything possible to succeed; **une offre qui n'est pas à ~** an offer which is worth considering; **~ de faire** to fail to do.

II **se négliger** *v refl* (+ *v être*) **1** not to take care over one's appearance; **2** not to look after oneself.

négoce /negɔs/ *nm* trade; **faire du ~ avec** to trade with.

négociable /negɔsjabl/ *adj* negotiable.

négociant, **~e** /negɔsjɑ̃, ɑ̃t/ *nm,f* merchant; wholesaler.

négociateur, **-trice** /negɔsjatœʀ, tʀis/ *nm,f* negotiator.

négociation /negɔsjasjɔ̃/ *nf* negotiation; **la table de ~** the negotiating table.

négocier /negɔsje/ [2] *vtr, vi* to negotiate.

nègre /nɛgʀ/ I *adj* [*art*] African.

II *nm* **1** (offensive) Negro; **2** ghostwriter.

négresse /negʀɛs/ *nf* (offensive) Negress.

négroïde /negʀɔid/ *adj* Negroid.

neige /nɛʒ/ *nf* snow; **~ fondue** slush; sleet; **aller à la ~** to go skiing; **blancs battus en ~** stiffly beaten eggwhites.

IDIOMS **être blanc comme ~** to be completely innocent; **fondre comme ~ au soleil** to melt away.

neiger /neʒe/ [13] *v impers* to snow; **il neige** it's snowing.

neigeux, **-euse** /nɛʒø, øz/ *adj* [*peak*] snow-covered; [*weather*] snowy.

nénuphar /nenyfaʀ/ *nm* waterlily.

néo /neo/ *pref* neo.

néologisme /neɔlɔʒism/ *nm* neologism.

néon /neɔ̃/ *nm* **1** neon; **2** neon light.

néophyte /neɔfit/ *nmf* neophyte.

néo-zélandais, **~e** /neozelɑ̃dɛ, ɛz/ *adj* New Zealand.

Néo-Zélandais, **~e** /neozelɑ̃dɛ, ɛz/ *nm,f* New Zealander.

népalais, **~e** /nepalɛ, ɛz/ I *adj* Nepali.

II *nm* Nepali.

néphrétique /nefʀetik/ *adj* nephritic; **coliques ~s** renal colic.

népotisme /nepɔtism/ *nm* nepotism.

nerf /nɛʀ/ **1** nerve; **être malade des ~s** to suffer from nerves; **2** spirit, go°; **redonner du ~ à qn** to put new heart into sb; **allez, du ~°!** come on, buck up°!

■ **~ de bœuf** pizzle.

IDIOMS **jouer avec les ~s de qn** to be deliberately annoying; **ses ~s ont lâché** he/she went to pieces; **avoir les ~s à fleur de peau** to have frayed nerves; **avoir les ~s en pelote°** or **en boule°** or **à vif** to be really wound up; **être sur les ~s, avoir ses ~s°** to be on edge; **taper°** or **porter sur les ~s de qn** to get on sb's nerves; **être à bout de ~s** to be at the end of one's tether or rope (US); **passer ses ~s sur° qn/qch** to take it out on sb/sth; **l'argent est le ~ de la guerre** money is the sinews of war.

nerveusement /nɛʀvøzmɑ̃/ *adv* **1** [*wait*] nervously; **2 être épuisé ~** to be suffering from nervous exhaustion.

nerveux, **-euse** /nɛʀvø, øz/ **I** *adj* **1** [*person*] tense; **2** [*hand*] sinewy; **3** [*engine*] responsive; [*horse, style*] vigorous; **4** (Anat) [*cell*] nerve; [*system*] nervous.
II *nm,f* nervous person.

nervosité /nɛʀvozite/ *nf* **1** nervousness; **2** excitability; **3** (of engine) responsiveness.

nervure /nɛʀvyʀ/ *nf* **1** (of leaf) nervure; **2** (of vault) rib.

n'est-ce pas /nɛspa/ *adv* **c'est joli, ~?** it's pretty, isn't it?; **tu es d'accord, ~?** you agree, don't you?; **~ qu'il est gentil?** isn't he nice?

net, **nette** /nɛt/ **I** *adj* **1** [*price, weight*] net; **2** [*change, increase*] marked; [*drop*] sharp; [*tendency*] distinct; **3** [*victory, memory*] clear; [*situation*] clear-cut; [*handwriting*] neat; [*break*] clean; **en avoir le cœur ~** to be clear in one's mind about it; **4** [*house, garment, hands*] clean; (figurative) [*conscience*] clear; **faire place nette** to clear everything away; **personne pas nette** (figurative) unsavoury[GB] person.
II *adv* [*stop*] dead; [*kill*] outright; [*refuse*] flatly; [*say*] straight out; **la corde a cassé ~** the rope snapped.

nettement /nɛtmɑ̃/ *adv* **1** [*increase, deteriorate*] markedly; [*dominate*] clearly; [*prefer*] definitely; **2** [*see, say*] clearly; [*refuse*] flatly; [*remember*] distinctly.

netteté /nɛtte/ *nf* **1** (of image, features) sharpness; (of result, statement) definite nature; **2** (of place) cleanness; (of work) neatness.

nettoyage /netwajaʒ/ *nm* **1** cleanup; **~ de printemps** spring-cleaning; **2** cleaning; (of skin) cleansing; **~ à sec** dry-cleaning; **3 opération de ~**○ (by army, police) mopping-up operation.
IDIOMS **faire le ~ par le vide**○ to have a good clearout○.

nettoyant /nɛtwajɑ̃/ *nm* cleaning agent.

nettoyer /netwaje/ [23] *vtr* **1** (gen) to clean; to clean up [*garden*]; to clean out [*river*]; to clean off [*stain*]; **faire ~ qch à sec** to have sth dry-cleaned; **2** (figurative) [*police*] to clean up [*town*]; [*burglar*] to clean out○ [*apartment*].

neuf[1] /nœf/ *adj inv, pron, nm inv* nine.

neuf[2], **neuve** /nœf, nœv/ **I** *adj* new; **tout ~** brand new; **'état ~'** 'as new'.
II *nm inv* new; **habillé de ~** dressed in new clothes; **refaire qch à ~** to redo sth completely; **faire du ~ avec du vieux** to revamp things.
IDIOMS **faire peau neuve** to undergo a transformation.

neurasthénie /nøʀasteni/ *nf* depression.

neurasthénique /nøʀastenik/ *adj, nmf* depressive.

neuro /nøʀo/ *pref* neuro.

neurovégétatif, **-ive** /nøʀoveʒetatif, iv/ *adj* [*trouble*] vegetative; **système ~** autonomic nervous system.

neutraliser /nøtʀalize/ [1] *vtr* to neutralize.

neutralité /nøtʀalite/ *nf* neutrality.

neutre /nøtʀ/ *adj* (gen) neutral; [*pronoun, insect*] neuter.

neutron /nøtʀɔ̃/ *nm* neutron.

neuvième /nœvjɛm/ **I** *adj* ninth.
II *nf* (Sch) *third year of primary school, age 8–9.*

neveu, *pl* **~x** /n(ə)vø/ *nm* nephew.

névralgie /nevʀalʒi/ *nf* neuralgia.

névralgique /nevʀalʒik/ *adj* **1** (Med) neuralgic; **2** (figurative) **point ~** key point.

névrose /nevʀoz/ *nf* neurosis.

névrosé, **~e** /nevʀoze/ *adj, nm,f* neurotic.

New York /njujɔʀk/ *pr n* **1** New York City; **2 l'État de ~** New York (State).

new yorkais, **~e**, *mpl* **~**, *fpl* **~es** /njujɔʀ kɛ, ɛz/ *adj* of New York.

New Yorkais, **~e**, *mpl* **~**, *fpl* **~es** /njujɔʀ kɛ, ɛz/ *nm,f* New Yorker.

nez /ne/ *nm* nose; **~ en trompette** turned-up nose; **ça sent le parfum à plein ~**○ there's a strong smell of perfume; **je n'ai pas mis le ~ dehors**○ I didn't set foot outside; **mettre le ~ à la fenêtre**○ to show one's face at the window; **lever le ~** to look up; **tu as le ~ dessus**○ it's staring you in the face; **avoir du ~**, **avoir le ~ fin** (figurative) to be shrewd; **rire au ~ de qn** to laugh in sb's face.
IDIOMS **mener qn par le bout du ~**○ to have sb under one's thumb; **avoir qn dans le ~**○ to have it in for sb; **avoir un coup** or **verre dans le ~**○ to have had one too many○; **au ~ (et à la barbe) de qn** right under sb's nose; **filer** or **passer sous le ~ de qn** to slip through sb's fingers; **se casser le ~**○ to fail, to come a cropper○.

NF /ɛnɛf/ *adj, nf* (*abbr* = **norme française**) French manufacturing standard; **label ~** *label showing a product has been manufactured to standard.*

ni /ni/ *conj* nor, or; **elle ne veut ~ ne peut changer** she doesn't want to change, nor can she; **elle ne veut pas le voir ~ lui parler** she doesn't wish to see him or talk to him; **~...~** neither...nor; **~ l'un ~ l'autre** neither of them; **il ne m'a dit ~ oui ~ non** he didn't say yes or no; **~ plus ~ moins** no more and no less.
IDIOMS **~ vu ~ connu**○ on the sly○; **c'est ~ fait ~ à faire**○ it's a botched○ job; **il n'a fait ~ une ~ deux**○ he didn't have a second's hesitation.

niais, **~e** /njɛ, njɛz/ *adj* stupid.

niaiserie /njɛzʀi/ *nf* **1** stupidity; **2** stupid or inane remark; **débiter des ~s** to talk rubbish or twaddle○.

nicaraguayen, **-enne** /nikaʀagwajɛ̃, ɛn/ *adj* Nicaraguan.

niche /niʃ/ *nf* **1** kennel, doghouse (US); **2** recess; (for statue) niche; **3**○ trick.

nichée /niʃe/ *nf* (of birds, children) brood; (of mice) litter.

nicher /niʃe/ [1] **I** *vi* **1** [*bird*] to nest; **2**○ [*person*] to live.
II se nicher *v refl* (+ *v être*) **1** [*bird*] to nest; **2** [*person, cottage*] to nestle.

nickel /nikɛl/ I° *adj* spotless.
II *nm* nickel.

nicotine /nikɔtin/ *nf* nicotine.

nid /ni/ *nm* nest.
■ **~ d'aigle** eyrie; **~ d'ange** snuggle suit; **~ d'hirondelle** bird's nest; **~ à poussière** dust trap; **~ de résistance** pocket of resistance.

nid-d'abeilles, *pl* **nids-d'abeilles** /nida bɛj/ *nm* honeycomb weave.

nid-de-poule, *pl* **nids-de-poule** /nidpul/ *nm* pothole.

nidification /nidifikasjɔ̃/ *nf* nesting.

nièce /njɛs/ *nf* niece.

nième /ɛnjɛm/ = **énième**.

nier /nje/ [2] *vtr* to deny [*fact, existence*]; to repudiate [*debt*].

nigaud, **~e** /nigo, od/ I *adj* silly.
II *nm,f* (silly) twit° (GB), goof° (US).

nigérian, **~e** /niʒerjɑ̃, an/ *adj* Nigerian.

nigérien, **-ienne** /niʒerjɛ̃, ɛn/ *adj* of Niger.

nihiliste /niilist/ *adj, nmf* nihilist.

nimbe /nɛ̃b/ *nm* nimbus, halo.

nimber /nɛ̃be/ [1] *vtr* [*sun*] to halo (**de** with); [*mist*] to swathe.

nipper°: **se nipper** /nipe/ [1] *v refl* (+ *v être*) to get rigged out° in one's Sunday best.

nippes° /nip/ *nf pl* rags°, old clothes.

nippon, **-onne** /nipɔ̃, ɔn/ *adj* Japanese.

nitouche° /nituʃ/ *nf* **sainte ~** goody-goody°.

niveau, *pl* **~x** /nivo/ *nm* **1** level; **~ d'huile** oil level; **au ~ du sol** at ground level; **être de ~** to be level; **arrivé au ~ du bus, il**... when he drew level with the bus he...; **bâtiment sur deux ~x** two-storey (GB) or two-story (US) building; **2** (figurative) (gen) level; (of knowledge, education) standard; **'~ bac + 3'** baccalaureate or equivalent plus 3 years' higher education; **à ~** up to the required standard; **de haut ~** [*athlete*] top; [*candidate*] high-calibre[GB]; **au plus haut ~** [*discussion, intervention*] top-level; **au ~ des investissements** (controversial) as regards investment.
■ **~ de langue** register; **~ social** social status; **~ sonore** sound level; **~ de vie** standard of living.

niveler /nivle/ [19] *vtr* **1** to level [*ground*]; to flatten [*bump*]; **2** to bring [sth] to the same level [*income, salaries*]; **~ par le bas/haut** to level down/up.

nivellement /nivɛlmɑ̃/ *nm* **1** (of ground) levelling[GB]; **2** (economic) standardization; (social) levelling[GB]-out.

nobiliaire /nɔbiljɛr/ *adj* nobiliary.

noble /nɔbl/ I *adj* (gen) noble; [*family*] aristocratic; [*person*] of noble birth.
II *nmf* nobleman/noblewoman; **les ~s** the nobility .

noblement /nɔbləmɑ̃/ *adv* **1** nobly; **2** handsomely.

noblesse /nɔblɛs/ *nf* nobility; **la petite ~** the gentry.

noce /nɔs/ *nf* **1**° party; **faire la ~**° (figurative) to live it up°, to party°; **aujourd'hui je n'étais pas à la ~** (figurative) today was no picnic; **2** wedding party; **3 ~s** wedding; **en premières ~s, il a épousé**... his first wife was...

noceur°, **-euse** /nɔsœr, øz/ *nm,f* party animal°.

nocif, **-ive** /nɔsif, iv/ *adj* noxious, harmful.

noctambule /nɔktɑ̃byl/ I *adj* [*walker*] late-night.
II *nmf* night owl.

nocturne¹ /nɔktyrn/ I *adj* [*attack*] night; [*animal*] nocturnal; **la vie ~** nightlife.
II *nm* **1** nocturnal bird; **2** (Mus) nocturne.

nocturne² /nɔktyrn/ *nf* **1** (in sport) evening fixture; **2** (of shop) late-night opening.

noël /nɔɛl/ *nm* **1** Christmas carol; **2** Christmas present.

Noël /nɔɛl/ *nm* Christmas; **'Joyeux ~'** 'Merry Christmas'; **de ~** [*tree, gift*] Christmas.

nœud /nø/ *nm* **1** (gen) knot; **faire un ~ de cravate** to tie a tie; **2** (of matter) crux; (of play) core.
■ **~ coulant** slipknot; **~ papillon** bow tie; **~ de vipères** nest of vipers.

noir, **~e**¹ /nwar/ I *adj* **1** (gen) black; [*eyes*] dark; [*person, race*] black; **être ~ de crasse** to be black with grime; **être ~ de coups** to be black and blue; **être ~ de monde** to be swarming with people; **2** [*street, alleyway*] dark; **il fait ~** it's dark; **3** [*year*] bad, bleak; [*poverty*] dire; [*idea*] gloomy, dark; **4** [*look*] black; [*plot, design*] evil, dark; **entrer** or **se mettre dans une colère ~e** to fly into a towering rage.
II *nm* **1** (colour) black; **2 avoir du ~ sur le visage** to have a black mark on one's face; **3** darkness; **4 au ~** [*sell*] on the black market; **travailler au ~** to work without declaring one's earnings; to moonlight°; **5**° **un (petit) ~** an espresso.
IDIOMS **voir tout en ~** to look on the black side (of things).

Noir, **~e** /nwar/ *nm,f* black man/woman.

noirâtre /nwarɑtr/ *adj* blackish.

noiraud, **~e** /nwaro, od/ *adj* swarthy.

noirceur /nwarsœr/ *nf* (gen) blackness; (of hair, night, eyes) darkness.

noircir /nwarsir/ [3] I *vtr* **1** [*coal*] to make [sth] dirty; [*smoke*] to blacken; [*ink*] to stain [sth] black; **2** (figurative) **~ du papier** to scribble away; **~ la situation** to paint a black picture of the situation; **~ qn** to blacken sb's name.
II *vi* [*banana*] to go black; [*wall*] to get dirty; [*metal*] to tarnish; [*person*] to get brown.
III **se noircir** *v refl* (+ *v être*) [*sky*] to darken; [*weather*] to become threatening; **se ~ le visage** to blacken one's face.

noire² /nwar/ I *adj f* ▶ **noir** I.
II *nf* (Mus) crotchet (GB), quarter note (US).

noise /nwaz/ *nf* **chercher ~** or **des ~s à qn** to pick a quarrel with sb.

noisetier /nwaztje/ *nm* hazel (tree).

noisette /nwazɛt/ I *adj inv* hazel.

II *nf* **1** hazelnut; **2 ~ de beurre** small knob of butter.

noix /nwa/ *nf inv* **1** walnut (GB), English walnut (US); **à la ~**○ [*story, artist*] crummy○; **2 ~ de beurre** knob of butter.

■ **~ de cajou** cashew nut; **~ de coco** coconut; **~ (de) muscade** nutmeg.

nom /nɔ̃/ **I** *nm* **1** name; **petit ~** first name; **~ et prénom** full name; **connu sous le ~ de** known as; **donner un ~ à** to name; **sans ~** unspeakable; **George Sand, de son vrai ~ Aurore Dupin** George Sand, whose real name was Aurore Dupin; **parler en son propre ~** to speak for oneself; **2** noun.

II au nom de *phr* **1** in the name of; **2** on behalf of.

■ **~ de baptême** Christian name; **~ d'emprunt** pseudonym; **~ de famille** surname; **~ de jeune fille** maiden name.

IDIOMS **traiter qn de tous les ~s (d'oiseaux)**○ to call sb all the names under the sun; **appeler les choses par leur ~** to call a spade a spade.

nomade /nɔmad/ **I** *adj* nomadic.

II *nmf* nomad; **vie de ~** nomadic existence.

nombre /nɔ̃bʀ/ *nm* number; **un ~ à deux chiffres** a two-digit number; **un certain ~ de** some; **être en ~ inférieur/supérieur** [*players*] to be fewer/greater in number; [*group*] to be smaller/bigger; **dans le ~**○ **il y aura bien quelqu'un qui me prêtera de l'argent** surely one of them will lend me some money; **ils étaient au ~ de 30** there were 30 of them; **écrasé sous le ~** (of people) overcome by sheer weight of numbers; (of letters) overwhelmed by the sheer volume; **sans ~** [*enemies*] countless; [*problems*] endless; **bon ~ de** a good many; **~ de fois** many times.

nombreux, **-euse** /nɔ̃bʀø, øz/ *adj* [*population, collection*] large; [*people, objects*] numerous, many; **ils étaient peu ~** there weren't many of them; **ils ont répondu ~ à l'appel** a great many people responded to the appeal; **ils arrivent toujours plus ~** they are arriving in ever greater numbers; **les touristes deviennent trop ~** the number of tourists is becoming excessive.

nombril /nɔ̃bʀil/ *nm* navel; **elle se prend pour le ~ du monde**○ she thinks she's God's gift to mankind.

nombrilisme○ /nɔ̃bʀilism/ *nm* navel-gazing○.

nombriliste○ /nɔ̃bʀilist/ *adj* [*person*] egocentric; [*policy*] inward-looking.

nomenclature /nɔmɑ̃klatyʀ/ *nf* nomenclature; (in dictionary) word list.

nominal, **~e**, *mpl* **-aux** /nɔminal, o/ *adj* (gen) nominal; [*list*] of names.

nominatif, **-ive** /nɔminatif, iv/ **I** *adj* [*list*] of names; [*invitation*] personal; [*share, security*] registered.

II *nm* nominative.

nomination /nɔminasjɔ̃/ *nf* **1** appointment; **~ aux affaires étrangères** appointment to the Foreign Affairs Office; **2** letter of appointment; **3** (controversial) nomination.

nommément /nɔmemɑ̃/ *adv* specifically, by name.

nommer /nɔme/ [1] **I** *vtr* **1** to appoint; **être nommé à Paris** to be posted to Paris; **2** to name [*person*]; to call [*thing*]; **le nommé Durand** the man named Durand; **pour ne ~ personne** to name or mention no names.

II se nommer *v refl* (+ *v être*) **1** to be called; **2** to give one's name.

non /nɔ̃/ **I** *adv* **1** no; **'tu y vas?'—'~'** 'are you going?'—'no, I'm not'; **répondez par oui ou par ~** answer yes or no; **ah, ça ~!** definitely not!; **'il était content?'—'que ~**○**!'** 'was he pleased?'—'not at all!'; **faire ~ de la tête** to shake one's head; **2 je pense que ~** I don't think so; **je te dis que ~** no, I tell you; **il paraît que ~** apparently not; **cela marche? elle affirme que ~** does it work? she claims it doesn't; **tu trouves ça drôle? moi ~** do you think that's funny? I don't; **~ sans raison** not without reason; **~ moins difficile** just as difficult; **qu'il soit d'accord ou ~** whether he agrees or not; **tu viens, oui ou ~?** are you coming or not?; **c'est difficile, ~?** it's difficult, isn't it?; **sois un peu plus poli, ~ mais**○**!** be a bit more polite, for heaven's sake!; **3** non; **~ alcoolisé** nonalcoholic; **~ négligeable** considerable; **objet ~ identifié** unidentified object.

II *nm inv* **1** no; **2** 'no' vote.

III non plus *phr* **je ne suis pas d'accord ~ plus** I don't agree either; **il n'a pas aimé le film, moi ~ plus** he didn't like the film and neither did I.

IV non(-) (/nɔn/ *before vowel or mute h*) (*combining form*) **~-agression** nonaggression; **~-fumeur** nonsmoker; **~-syndiqué** non union member.

nonagénaire /nɔnaʒenɛʀ/ **I** *adj* **être ~** to be in one's nineties.

II *nmf* ninety-year old.

non-aligné, **~e**, *mpl* **~s** /nɔnaliɲe/ *nm,f* nonaligned country.

nonante /nɔnɑ̃t/ *adj inv, pron* ninety.

non-assistance /nɔnasistɑ̃s/ *nf* **~ à personne en danger** failure to render assistance.

nonchalance /nɔ̃ʃalɑ̃s/ *nf* nonchalance; **avec ~** nonchalantly.

nonchalant, **~e** /nɔ̃ʃalɑ̃, ɑ̃t/ *adj* nonchalant; (child) apathetic.

non-figuratif, **-ive**, *mpl* **~s** /nɔ̃figyʀatif, iv/ *nm,f* abstract artist.

non-lieu, *pl* **~x** /nɔ̃ljø/ *nm* (Law) dismissal (of a charge); **il y a eu ~** the judge dismissed the case.

nonpareilles /nɔ̃paʀɛj/ *nf pl* (Culin) hundreds and thousands.

non-recevoir /nɔ̃ʀəsəvwaʀ/ *nm* **fin de ~** flat refusal.

non-reconduction, *pl* **~s** /nɔ̃ʀəkɔ̃dyksjɔ̃/ *nf* (of contract) nonrenewal; (of person) failure to reappoint.

non-respect /nɔ̃ʀɛspɛ/ *nm* **~ de** failure to comply with [*clause*]; failure to respect [*person*].

non-sens /nɔ̃sɑ̃s/ *nm inv* **1** nonsense; **2** (in translation) meaningless phrase.

non-voyant, **~e**, *mpl* **~s** /nɔ̃vwajɑ̃, ɑ̃t/ *nm,f* visually handicapped person.

nord /nɔʀ/ **I** *adj inv* north; northern.
II *nm* **1** north; **un vent de ~** a northerly wind; **le vent du ~** the north wind; **le ~ de l'Europe** northern Europe; **2 le Nord** the North; **la Corée du Nord** North Korea.
IDIOMS **il ne perd pas le ~**○! he' s got his head screwed on○!

nord-africain, **~e**, *mpl* **~s** /nɔʀafʀikɛ̃, ɛn/ *adj* North African.

nord-américain, **~e**, *mpl* **~s** /nɔʀameʀikɛ̃, ɛn/ *adj* North American.

nord-est /nɔʀ(d)ɛst/ **I** *adj inv* northeast; northeastern.
II *nm* northeast; **vent de ~** northeasterly wind.

nordique /nɔʀdik/ *adj* Nordic.

nord-ouest /nɔʀ(d)wɛst/ **I** *adj inv* northwest; northwestern.
II *nm* northwest; **vent de ~** northwesterly wind.

Nord-Sud /nɔʀsyd/ *adj inv* [*dialogue, relations, conflicts*] North-South.

normal, **~e**[1], *mpl* **-aux** /nɔʀmal, o/ *adj* normal; **ne pas être dans son état ~** not to be oneself; **il est ~ que** it is natural that; **il n'est pas ~ que** it is not right that.

normale[2] /nɔʀmal/ *nf* **1** average; **2** norm; **retour à la ~** return to normal.

normalement /nɔʀmalmɑ̃/ *adv* normally.

normalien, **-ienne** /nɔʀmaljɛ̃, ɛn/ *nm,f* student at an École normale supérieure.

normalisation /nɔʀmalizasjɔ̃/ *nf* **1** normalization; **2** standardization.

normaliser /nɔʀmalize/ [1] *vtr* **1** to normalize [*relations*]; **2** to standardize [*sizes*].

normalité /nɔʀmalite/ *nf* normality.

normand, **~e** /nɔʀmɑ̃, ɑ̃d/ **I** *adj* [*conquest*] Norman; [*coast*] Normandy; [*team*] from Normandy.
II *nm* Norman (French).

Normand, **~e** /nɔʀmɑ̃, ɑ̃d/ *nm,f* Norman.
IDIOMS **une réponse de ~** a noncommittal reply.

norme /nɔʀm/ *nf* (gen) norm; (Tech) standard.

Norvège /nɔʀvɛʒ/ *pr nf* Norway.

norvégien, **-ienne** /nɔʀveʒjɛ̃, ɛn/ **I** *adj* Norwegian.
II *nm* Norwegian.

nos ▶ **notre**.

nostalgie /nɔstalʒi/ *nf* nostalgia (**de** for).

nostalgique /nɔstalʒik/ *adj* nostalgic (**de** for).

notabilité /nɔtabilite/ *nf* notability.

notable /nɔtabl/ **I** *adj* [*fact*] notable; [*progress*] significant.
II *nm* notable.

notablement /nɔtabləmɑ̃/ *adv* significantly.

notaire /nɔtɛʀ/ *nm* notary public.

notamment /nɔtamɑ̃/ *adv* **1** notably; **2** in particular.

notation /nɔtasjɔ̃/ *nf* **1** notation; **2** (of pupil) marking (GB), grading (US); (of employee, staff) grading.

note /nɔt/ *nf* **1** bill (GB), check (US); **faire la ~ de qn** to write out sb's bill (GB) or check (US); **2** (Mus) note; (figurative) note, touch; **une ~ triste** a sad note; **forcer la ~** to overdo it; **3** mark (GB), grade (US); **~ éliminatoire** fail mark (GB) or grade (US); **c'est une bonne ~ pour lui** (figurative) that's a point in his favour[GB]; **4** (written) note; **prendre qch en ~** to make a note of sth; **prendre (bonne) ~ de qch** (figurative) to take (due) note of sth.
■ **~ de frais** expense account; **~ d'honoraires** bill; **~ de service** memorandum, memo○.

noter /nɔte/ [1] *vtr* **1** to write down [*idea, address*]; **c'est (bien) noté?** have you got that?; **2** to notice [*change*]; **ceci est à ~** this should be noted; **notez (bien) que je n'ai rien à lui reprocher** mind you I haven't got anything particular against him; **il faut quand même ~** it has to be said; **3** to mark (GB), to grade (US) [*exercise*]; to give a mark (GB) or grade (US) to [*pupil*]; to grade [*employee*].

notice /nɔtis/ *nf* **1** note; **2** instructions.

notification /nɔtifikasjɔ̃/ *nf* (gen) notification; (Law) notice.

notifier /nɔtifje/ [2] *vtr* **~ qch à qn** (gen) to notify sb of sth; (Law) to give sb notice of sth.

notion /nɔsjɔ̃/ *nf* **1** notion; **perdre la ~ de** to lose all sense of; **2 ~s** basic knowledge.

notoire /nɔtwaʀ/ *adj* [*fact, position*] well-known; [*swindler, stupidity*] notorious.

notoirement /nɔtwaʀmɑ̃/ *adv* **1** manifestly; **2** notoriously.

notoriété /nɔtɔʀjete/ *nf* **1** fame; (of product) reputation; **il est de ~ (publique) que** it's common knowledge that; **2** (person) celebrity.

notre, *pl* **nos** /nɔtʀ, no/ *det* our; **à nos âges** at our age; **c'était ~ avis à tous** we all felt the same; **nos enfants à nous**○ our children.

nôtre /notʀ/ **I** *det* **nous avons fait ~s ces idées** we've adopted these ideas; **cette terre est ~** this land is our land.
II le nôtre, la nôtre, les nôtres *pron* ours; **soyez des ~s!** won't you join us?; **les ~s** our own people; (team, group) our side.

nouer /nwe/ [1] **I** *vtr* **1** (gen) to tie; to knot [*tie*]; to tie up [*parcel*]; **~ ses bras autour du cou de qn** to put one's arms around sb's neck; **avoir la gorge nouée** to have a lump in one's throat; **2** to establish [*relations*]; to engage in [*dialogue*].
II se nouer *v refl* (+ *v être*) **1** [*plot*] to take shape; **2** [*diplomatic relations*] to be established; [*dialogue, friendship*] to begin.

noueux, **-euse** /nuø, øz/ *adj* gnarled.

nougat /nuga/ *nm* nougat.

nouille /nuj/ *nf* **1 ~s** noodles, pasta; **2**○ noodle○, idiot.

nounou○ /nunu/ *nf* nanny (GB), nurse.

nounours○ /nunuʀs/ *nm inv* (baby talk) teddy bear.

nourri, ~e /nuʀi/ *adj* [*gunfire*] heavy; [*applause*] sustained.

nourrice /nuʀis/ *nf* **1** childminder (GB), babysitter (US); **2** wet nurse.

nourrir /nuʀiʀ/ [3] **I** *vtr* **1** to feed [*person, animal*]; to nourish [*skin, leather*]; **bien nourri** well-fed; **mal nourri** undernourished; **~ au sein/au biberon** to breast-/to bottle-feed; **mon travail ne me nourrit pas** I don't make enough to live on; **2** (figurative) to harbour[GB] [*hopes*]; to feed [*fire*]; to fuel [*passion, discussion*].
II se nourrir *v refl* (+ *v être*) [*animal*] to feed (**de** on); [*person*] to eat; **se ~ de** to live on [*vegetables*]; to feed on [*illusions*].

nourrissant, ~e /nuʀisɑ̃, ɑ̃t/ *adj* nourishing.

nourrisson /nuʀisɔ̃/ *nm* infant.

nourriture /nuʀityʀ/ *nf* **1** food; **2** diet.

nous /nu/ *pron* **1** (subject) we; (object) us; **~ le savons** we know; **donne-~ l'adresse** give us the address; **entre ~, il n'est pas très intelligent** between ourselves or you and me, he isn't very intelligent; **une maison à ~** a house of our own; **la voiture est à ~** the car is ours; **pensons à ~** let's think of ourselves; **2** (with reflexive verb) **~ ~ soignons** we look after ourselves; **~ ~ aimons** we love each other; **~ ~ levons tôt** we get up early.

nous-même, *pl* **nous-mêmes** /numɛm/ *pron* ourselves.

nouveau (**nouvel** *before vowel or mute h*), **nouvelle**[1], *mpl* **~x** /nuvo, nuvɛl/ **I** *adj* (gen) new; [*attempt, attack*] fresh; **tout ~** brand-new; **se faire faire un ~ costume** to have a new suit made; to have another suit made; **procéder à de nouvelles arrestations** to make further arrests; **une nouvelle fois** once again; **les ~x élus** the newly-elected members; **les ~x mariés** the newlyweds; **la nouvelle venue** the newcomer; **c'est une façon très nouvelle d'aborder le problème** it's a very novel approach to the problem.
II *nm,f* (in school) new boy/girl; (in company) new employee; (in army) new recruit.
III *nm* **1 téléphone-moi s'il y a du ~** give me a call if there is anything new to report; **j'ai du ~ pour toi** I've got some news for you; **2 il nous faut du ~** we want something new.
IV à nouveau, de nouveau *phr* (once) again.
IDIOMS **tout ~ tout beau** the novelty will soon wear off.

nouveau-né, ~e, *mpl* **~s** /nuvone/ **I** *adj* newborn.
II *nm,f* newborn baby.

nouveauté /nuvote/ *nf* **1** novelty; **ce n'est pas une ~!** that's nothing new!; **2** (gen) new thing; (book) new publication; (record) new release; (car, machine) new model.

nouvel ▶ **nouveau** I.

nouvelle[2] /nuvɛl/ **I** *adj f* ▶ **nouveau** I.
II *nf* **1** ▶ **nouveau II**; **2** news; **une ~** a piece of news; **tu connais la ~?** have you heard the news?; **première ~**○! that's news to me!; **recevoir des ~s de qn** (to hear from sb; (through somebody else) to hear news of sb; **il m'a demandé de tes ~s** he asked after you; **je viens aux ~s**○ I've come to see what's happening; **aux dernières ~s**○**, il se porte bien** the last I heard he was doing fine; **il aura de mes ~s**○! he'll be hearing from me!; **goûte ce petit vin, tu m'en diras des ~s**○ have a taste of this wine, it's really good!; **3** short story.

nouvellement /nuvɛlmɑ̃/ *adv* [*published*] recently; [*built*] newly.

novateur, -trice /nɔvatœʀ, tʀis/ **I** *adj* innovative.
II *nm,f* innovator, pioneer.

novembre /nɔvɑ̃bʀ/ *nm* November.

novice /nɔvis/ **I** *adj* inexperienced, green.
II *nmf* novice.

noyade /nwajad/ *nf* drowning; **il y a eu 20 ~s** there were 20 people drowned.

noyau, *pl* **~x** /nwajo/ *nm* **1** stone (GB), pit (US); **2** small group; **~x d'agitateurs** small groups of agitators; **~x de résistance** pockets of resistance; **3** nucleus.

noyauter /nwajote/ [1] *vtr* to infiltrate.

noyé, ~e /nwaje/ **I**○ *adj* **je suis ~** I can't cope.
II *nm,f* drowned person.

noyer[1] /nwaje/ [23] **I** *vtr* (gen) to drown; to flood [*village, engine*]; **~ qn sous un flot de paroles** to talk sb's head off.
II se noyer *v refl* (+ *v être*) to drown; (suicide) to drown oneself; **mourir noyé** to die by drowning; **se ~ dans des détails** to get bogged down in details.
IDIOMS **se ~ dans un verre d'eau** to make a mountain out of a molehill.

noyer[2] /nwaje/ *nm* **1** walnut (tree); **2** (wood) walnut.

nu, ~e /ny/ **I** *adj* [*person*] naked; [*wall, tree, coastline*] bare; [*truth*] plain; **tête ~e** bareheaded; **pieds ~s** barefoot; **torse ~** stripped to the waist.
II *nm* (in art) nude.
III à nu *phr* **être à ~** to be exposed; **mettre à ~** to strip [*electric wire*]; to expose [*person, vice*]; **mettre son cœur à ~** to open one's heart.

nuage /nyaʒ/ *nm* cloud; **sans ~s** [*sky*] cloudless; [*happiness*] unclouded; **~ de lait** dash of milk.
IDIOMS **être dans les ~s**○ to have one's head in the clouds; **descendre de son ~** to come back to earth.

nuageux, -euse /nyaʒø, øz/ *adj* [*sky*] cloudy; **masse nuageuse** cloudmass.

nuance /nyɑ̃s/ *nf* **1** (of colour) shade; **2** (of meaning) nuance; **sans ~** [*commentary*] clearcut; [*personality*] straightforward; (derogatory) unsubtle; **3** (difference) slight or subtle difference; **à cette ~ près que** with the small reservation that; **4** (Mus) nuance.

nuancer /nyɑ̃se/ [12] *vtr* **1** to qualify [*opinion*]; to modify [*view of situation*]; **peu nuancé** unsubtle; **2** to moderate [*remarks, statements*].

nucléaire /nykleɛʀ/ **I** *adj* nuclear.

II *nm* **le ~** nuclear energy; nuclear technology.

nudité /nydite/ *nf* **1** nakedness, nudity; **2** (of place, wall) bareness.

nuée /nye/ *nf* **1** (of insects) swarm; (of people) horde; **2** (in meteorology) dense cloud..

nues /ny/ *nf pl* **tomber des ~**○ to be flabbergasted○; **porter qn aux ~** to praise sb to the skies.

nuire /nɥiʀ/ [69] **I nuire à** *v+prep* to harm [*person*]; to be harmful to [*health, interests, reputation*]; to damage [*crops*]; to take away from [*pleasure, quality*].

II se nuire *v refl* (+ *v être*) **1** to do each other a lot of harm; **2** to do oneself a lot of harm.

IDIOMS **trop parler nuit** you should know when to keep your mouth shut.

nuisance /nɥizɑ̃s/ *nf* nuisance.

nuisible /nɥizibl/ *adj* [*substance, waste*] dangerous; [*influence*] harmful; **insecte ~** (insect) pest; **~ à** detrimental to.

nuit /nɥi/ *nf* night; **cette ~** last night; tonight; **une ~ d'hôtel** a night in a hotel; **voyager de ~** to travel by night; **avant la ~** before dark; **à la ~ tombante**, **à la tombée de la ~** at nightfall; **il fait ~** it's dark; **il faisait ~ noire**, **il faisait une ~ d'encre** it was pitch dark; **ça se perd dans la ~ des temps** it is lost in the mists of time.

■ **~ blanche** sleepless night; **~ bleue** *night of terrorist bomb attacks*.

IDIOMS **c'est le jour et la ~** they're as different as chalk and cheese; **attends demain pour donner ta réponse: la ~ porte conseil** wait till tomorrow to give your answer: sleep on it first.

nul, **nulle** /nyl/ **I** *adj* **1**○ [*person*] hopeless; [*piece of work*] worthless; [*film*] trashy○; **2** (Law) [*contract*] void; [*will*] invalid; [*elections*] null and void; [*vote*] spoiled; **3** (Sport) **match ~** tie, draw (GB); nil-all draw; **4** [*difference*] nil.

II *adj* **~ homme/pays** no man/country; **~ autre que vous** no-one else but you; **sans ~ doute** without any doubt.

III○ *nm,f* idiot○; **c'est un ~** he's a dead loss○.

IV *pron* no-one; **~ n'ignore que** everyone knows that.

V nulle part *phr* nowhere.

nullement /nylmɑ̃/ *adv* not at all.

nullité /nylite/ *nf* **1** (Law) nullity; **frapper de ~** to render void; **2** (of argument) invalidity; (of book, film)○ worthlessness; **3**○ (person) idiot○.

numéraire /nymeʀɛʀ/ *nm* cash.

numéral, **~e**, *mpl* **-aux** /nymeʀal, o/ **I** *adj* numeral.

II *nm* numeral.

numérique /nymeʀik/ *adj* (gen) numerical; [*display*] digital; **clavier ~** keypad.

numériquement /nymeʀikmɑ̃/ *adv* numerically.

numéro /nymeʀo/ *nm* **1** number; **~ de téléphone** telephone number; **2** (magazine) issue; **suite au prochain ~** to be continued; **3** (in show) act; (song) number; **4**○ (person) **quel ~!** what a character!

■ **~ d'abonné** customer's number; **~ d'appel** telephone number; **~ d'appel gratuit** freefone number (GB), toll-free number (US); **~ vert** = **~ d'appel gratuit**.

IDIOMS **tirer le bon/mauvais ~** to be lucky/unlucky.

numérotation /nymeʀɔtasjɔ̃/ *nf* numbering; **~ téléphonique** telephone numbering system; **~ abrégée** abbreviated dialling[GB].

numéroter /nymeʀɔte/ [1] *vtr* to number; **compte numéroté** numbered account.

numismatique /nymismatik/ **I** *adj* numismatic.

II *nf* numismatics.

nu-pied, *pl* **~s** /nypje/ *nm* sandal.

nuptial, **~e**, *mpl* **-iaux** /nypsjal, o/ *adj* [*mass*] nuptial; [*room*] bridal; **cérémonie ~e** wedding.

nuque /nyk/ *nf* nape (of the neck).

nurse /nœʀs/ *nf* nanny (GB), nurse.

nu-tête /nytɛt/ *adv* bareheaded.

nutritif, **-ive** /nytʀitif, iv/ *adj* [*meal*] nutritious; [*skin cream*] nourishing; [*value*] nutritive.

nutrition /nytʀisjɔ̃/ *nf* nutrition.

nymphe /nɛ̃f/ *nf* nymph.

nymphomane /nɛ̃fɔman/ *adj, nf* nymphomaniac.

Oo

o, O /o/ *nm inv* o, O.

oasis /ɔazis/ *nf inv* oasis.

obédience /ɔbedjɑ̃s/ *nf* persuasion; **elle est d'~ marxiste** she is a Marxist.

obéir /ɔbeiʀ/ [3] *v+prep* **1** to obey; **~ à** to obey [*order, rules*]; to follow [*standards, feelings*]; **~ à qn** to obey sb; **2** [*brakes, vehicle*] to respond.
IDIOMS **~ à qn au doigt et à l'œil** to obey sb slavishly.

obéissance /ɔbeisɑ̃s/ *nf* obedience; **~ passive** blind obedience.

obéissant, ~e /ɔbeisɑ̃, ɑ̃t/ *adj* obedient.

obélisque /ɔbelisk/ *nm* obelisk.

obèse /ɔbɛz/ *adj* obese.

objecter /ɔbʒɛkte/ [1] *vtr* to object.

objecteur /ɔbʒɛktœʀ/ *nm* objector; **~ de conscience** conscientious objector.

objectif, -ive /ɔbʒɛktif, iv/ **I** *adj* objective.
II *nm* **1** objective; **se donner qch pour ~** to set oneself sth as an objective; **2** lens; **3** target.

objection /ɔbʒɛksjɔ̃/ *nf* objection.

objectivement /ɔbʒɛktivmɑ̃/ *adv* **1** objectively; **2** clearly.

objectivité /ɔbʒɛktivite/ *nf* objectivity.

objet /ɔbʒɛ/ **I** *nm* **1** object; **~ fragile** fragile item; **~s personnels** personal possessions; **2** (of debate, research) subject; (of hatred, desire) object; (of disagreement) source; **faire l'~ de** to be the subject of [*inquiry, research*]; to be subjected to [*ridicule, surveillance*]; to be the object of [*desire, hatred, struggle*]; **3** purpose, object; **la linguistique a pour ~** the purpose of linguistics is; **'~: réponse à votre lettre du...'** 're: your letter of...'; **être sans ~** [*fears*] to be groundless; **4** (Law) **~ d'un litige** matter at issue; **~ d'un procès** subject of an action.
II -objet (*combining form*) as an object; **femme-~** woman as an object.
■ **~s trouvés** lost property; **aller aux ~s trouvés** to go to lost property (GB) or to lost and found (US); **~ volant non identifié, ovni** unidentified flying object, UFO.

obligation /ɔbligasjɔ̃/ *nf* **1** obligation, responsibility; duty; **ce n'est pas une ~ de les inviter** you don't have to invite them; **2** necessity; **se voir** or **trouver dans l'~ de faire** to be forced to do; **3** (Econ) bond; **4** (Law) obligation.
■ **~s militaires, OM** military service.

obligatoire /ɔbligatwaʀ/ *adj* **1** compulsory; **2**○ inevitable.

obligatoirement /ɔbligatwaʀmɑ̃/ *adv* inevitably, necessarily.

obligeamment /ɔbliʒamɑ̃/ *adv* obligingly, very kindly.

obligeance /ɔbliʒɑ̃s/ *nf* **avoir l'~ de** to be kind enough to.

obliger /ɔbliʒe/ [13] **I** *vtr* **1 ~ qn à** [*person, police, event*] to force sb to; [*authorities, rules*] to make it compulsory for sb to; [*duty, caution*] to compel sb to; **je suis obligé de partir** I have to go; **je suis bien obligé de vous croire** I have no choice but to believe you; **2** (Law) [*lease, contract*] to bind [sb] legally; **3 ~ qn** to oblige sb.
II s'obliger *v refl* (+ *v être*) **s'~ à faire** to force oneself to do.

oblique /ɔblik/ *adj* slanting; sidelong; oblique.

obliquer /ɔblike/ [1] *vi* **~ vers la droite/gauche** to bear right/left.

oblitération /ɔbliteʀasjɔ̃/ *nf* (of stamp) cancelling[GB]; **(cachet d')~** postmark.

oblong, -ongue /ɔblɔ̃, ɔ̃g/ *adj* oblong.

obnubiler /ɔbnybile/ [1] *vtr* to obsess.

obole /ɔbɔl/ *nf* small donation.

obscène /ɔpsɛn/ *adj* obscene.

obscur, ~e /ɔpskyʀ/ *adj* **1** dark; **2** obscure; **3** lowly; **4** vague.

obscurcir /ɔpskyʀsiʀ/ [3] **I** *vtr* **1** to make [sth] dark [*place*]; **2** to blur [*situation*]; to obscure [*view*].
II s'obscurcir *v refl* (+ *v être*) **1** [*sky, place*] to darken; **2** [*gaze*] to become sombre[GB]; [*situation*] to become confused.

obscurément /ɔpskyʀemɑ̃/ *adv* **1** [*feel*] vaguely; **2** [*live*] in obscurity.

obscurité /ɔpskyʀite/ *nf* **1** darkness; **2** vagueness.

obsédant, ~e /ɔpsedɑ̃, ɑ̃t/ *adj* [*memory, dream, music*] haunting; [*rhythm*] insistent; [*problem*] nagging.

obsédé, ~e /ɔpsede/ *nm,f* **~ (sexuel)** sex maniac; **un ~ du ski** a ski freak○.

obséder /ɔpsede/ [14] *vtr* [*memory, dream*] to haunt; [*idea, problem*] to obsess.

obsèques /ɔpsɛk/ *nf pl* funeral.

obséquieux, -ieuse /ɔpsekjø, øz/ *adj* obsequious.

observateur, -trice /ɔpsɛʀvatœʀ, tʀis/ **I** *adj* observant.
II *nm,f* observer.

observation /ɔpsɛʀvasjɔ̃/ *nf* **1** observation; **mission d'~** observer mission; **2** observation, remark; comment; **3** reproach.

observatoire /ɔpsɛʀvatwaʀ/ *nm* **1** observatory; **2** look-out post.

observer /ɔpsɛʀve/ [1] **I** *vtr* **1** to watch, to observe; **2** to notice, to observe [*phenomenon, reaction*]; **faire ~ qch à qn** to point sth out to sb; **3** to observe [*rules, usage, treaty*]; to keep to [*diet*]; to maintain [*strategy, policy, strike*]; **~ le silence** to keep or remain quiet; **4** to watch [*words, manners*].

II **s'observer** *v refl* (+ *v être*) **1** to watch each other; **2** to keep a check on oneself.

obsession /ɔpsɛsjɔ̃/ *nf* obsession.

obsessionnel, -elle /ɔpsɛsjɔnɛl/ *adj* obsessional.

obsolète /ɔpsɔlɛt/ *adj* obsolete.

obstacle /ɔpstakl/ *nm* **1** obstacle; **faire ~ aux négociations** to obstruct the negotiations; **2** (in horseriding) fence.

obstétricien, -ienne /ɔpstetʀisjɛ̃, ɛn/ *nm,f* obstetrician.

obstétrique /ɔpstetʀik/ *nf* obstetrics.

obstination /ɔpstinasjɔ̃/ *nf* obstinacy; **avec ~** stubbornly.

obstiné, ~e /ɔpstine/ I *pp* ▶ **obstiner**.
II *pp adj* **1** stubborn; **2** dogged.

obstinément /ɔpstinemɑ̃/ *adv* obstinately.

obstiner: **s'obstiner** /ɔpstine/ [1] *v refl* (+ *v être*) to persist; **s'~ à ne pas faire** to refuse obstinately to do.

obstruction /ɔpstʀyksjɔ̃/ *nf* obstruction, blockage.

obstruer /ɔpstʀye/ [1] **I** *vtr* to obstruct, to block.
II **s'obstruer** *v refl* (+ *v être*) to get or become blocked.

obtempérer /ɔptɑ̃peʀe/ [14] *v+prep* to comply (**à** with).

obtenir /ɔptəniʀ/ [36] *vtr* to get, to obtain; to secure [*silence*].

obtention /ɔptɑ̃sjɔ̃/ *nf* getting, obtaining.

obturation /ɔptyʀasjɔ̃/ *nf* **1** blocking (up); **2 vitesse d'~** shutter speed.

obturer /ɔptyʀe/ [1] *vtr* to block up.

obtus, ~e /ɔpty, yz/ *adj* obtuse.

obus /oby/ *nm inv* shell; **un éclat d'~** a piece of shrapnel.

occasion /ɔkazjɔ̃/ *nf* **1** occasion; **à l'~** some time; **à l'~ de** on the occasion of; **à** or **en plusieurs ~s** on several occasions; **les grandes ~s** special occasions; **2** opportunity, chance; **être l'~ de qch** to give rise to sth; **j'ai encore raté une bonne ~ de me taire** I should have kept my mouth shut; **3** second-hand buy; **4** bargain.

occasionnel, -elle /ɔkazjɔnɛl/ *adj* occasional.

occasionner /ɔkazjɔne/ [1] *vtr* to cause.

occident /ɔksidɑ̃/ *nm* **1** west; **2 l'Occident** the West.

occidental, ~e, *mpl* **-aux** /ɔksidɑ̃tal, o/ *adj* western.

Occidental, ~e, *mpl* **-aux** /ɔksidɑ̃tal, o/ *nm,f* Westerner.

occitan, ~e /ɔksitɑ̃, an/ **I** *adj* of the langue d'oc.
II *nm* langue d'oc.

occlusion /ɔklyzjɔ̃/ *nf* (Med) occlusion; **~ intestinale** obstruction of the bowels.

occulte /ɔkylt/ *adj* **1** occult; **2** secret.

occulter /ɔkylte/ [1] *vtr* **1** to eclipse; **2** to obscure [*issue*]; to conceal [*truth*].

occupant, ~e /ɔkypɑ̃, ɑ̃t/ **I** *adj* [*forces*] occupying.
II *nm,f* (of house) occupier; (of house, vehicle) occupant.

occupation /ɔkypasjɔ̃/ *nf* **1** (pastime) occupation; **2** occupation, job; **3** occupancy; **4** (of country, factory) occupation.

occupé, ~e /ɔkype/ I *pp* ▶ **occuper**.
II *pp adj* **1** [*person, life*] busy; **2** [*seat*] taken; [*phone*] engaged (GB), busy; [*toilet*] engaged; **3** (Mil) [*country*] occupied.

occuper /ɔkype/ [1] **I** *vtr* **1** to live in, to occupy [*flat, house*]; to be in [*shower, cell*]; to sit in, to occupy [*seat*]; **2** to take up, to occupy [*space*]; to take up, to fill [*time*]; **le sport occupe une grande place dans ma vie** sport plays a large part in my life; **3** to occupy [*person, mind*]; **ça m'occupe!** it keeps me busy!; **le sujet qui nous occupe** the matter which we are dealing with; **4** to have [*employment*]; to hold [*job, office*]; **5** [*strikers, army*] to occupy [*place*]; **~ les locaux** to stage a sit-in.
II **s'occuper** *v refl* (+ *v être*) **1** to keep oneself busy or occupied; **trouver à s'~** to find sth to do; **2 s'~ de** to see to, to take care of [*dinner, tickets*]; **3 s'~ de** to be dealing with [*file, matter*]; **4 s'~ de** to take care of [*child, animal, plant*]; to attend to [*customer*]; **5 s'~ de** to be in charge of [*finance, library*]; to work with [*children*]; **6 s'~ des affaires des autres**○ to poke one's nose into other people's business○; **occupe-toi de tes affaires**○ or **de ce qui te regarde**○**!** mind your own business○!; **ne t'occupe pas de ça!, t'occupe**○**!** keep your nose out○! (GB), keep your butt out○! (US).

occurrence /ɔkyʀɑ̃s/ *nf* **1** case, instance; **en l'~** in this case; **2** occurrence.

océan /ɔseɑ̃/ *nm* ocean.

océanique /ɔseanik/ *adj* oceanic.

ocre /ɔkʀ/ *adj inv, nm* ochre[GB].

octave /ɔktav/ *nf* octave.

octobre /ɔktɔbʀ/ *nm* October.

octogénaire /ɔktɔʒenɛʀ/ **I** *adj* **être ~** to be in one's eighties.
II *nmf* octogenarian.

octroyer /ɔktʀwaje/ [23] *vtr* **~ à qn** to grant sb [*pardon, favour*]; to award sb [*grant*]; to allocate sb sth [*budget*].

oculaire /ɔkylɛʀ/ *adj* **troubles ~s** eye trouble; **témoin ~** eyewitness.

oculiste /ɔkylist/ *nmf* oculist, ophthalmologist.

ode /ɔd/ *nf* ode.

odeur /ɔdœʀ/ *nf* smell; **avoir une mauvaise ~** to smell.

odieux, -ieuse /ɔdjø, øz/ *adj* **1** horrible; **2** obnoxious (**avec qn** to sb).

odorant, ~e /ɔdɔʀɑ̃, ɑ̃t/ *adj* which has a smell.

odorat /ɔdɔʀa/ *nm* sense of smell; **l'organe de l'~** the olfactory organ.

œdème /edɛm/ *nm* (Med) oedema.

œdipe /edip/ *nm* Oedipus complex.

œil, *pl* **yeux** /œj, jø/ *nm* eye; **ouvrir l'~** to keep one's eyes open; **fermer les yeux sur qch** to turn a blind eye to sth; **les yeux fermés**

with one's eyes closed; **acheter qch les yeux fermés** to buy sth with complete confidence; **il faut l'avoir à l'~** you have to keep an eye on him/her; **avoir l'~ à tout** to be vigilant; **jeter un ~ à** or **sur qch** to have a quick look at sth; **aux yeux de tous** openly; **être agréable à l'~** to be nice to look at; **jeter un coup d'~ à qch** to glance at sth; **cela vaut le coup d'~** it's worth seeing; **avoir le coup d'~** to have a good eye; **regarder qch d'un ~ neuf** to see sth in a new light; **voir qch d'un mauvais ~** to take a dim view of sth; **à mes yeux** in my opinion.

■ **~ poché**○ black eye; **~ de verre** glass eye.

IDIOMS **mon ~**○**!** my eye○, my foot○; **à l'~**○ for nothing, for free○; **faire les gros yeux à qn** to glare at sb; **dévorer qch/qn des yeux** to gaze longingly at sth/sb; **faire les yeux doux à qn** to make eyes at sb; **tourner de l'~**○ to faint; **cela me sort par les yeux**○ I've had it up to here○; **avoir bon pied bon ~** to be as fit as a fiddle; **sauter aux yeux** to be obvious.

œil-de-bœuf, *pl* **œils-de-bœuf** /œjdəbœf/ *nm* (window) bull's-eye.

œillade /œjad/ *nf* **1** wink; **2** glance.

œillère /œjɛʀ/ *nf* blinker; **avoir des ~s** (figurative) to have a blinkered attitude.

œillet /œjɛ/ *nm* **1** carnation; **2** (in shoe, tarpaulin) eyelet; (in belt, bracelet) hole; (made of metal) grommet.

œsophage /ezɔfaʒ/ *nm* oesophagus.

œuf /œf, *pl* ø/ *nm* egg; **~s de cabillaud** cod's roe.

■ **~ à la coque** boiled egg; **~ dur** hard-boiled egg; **~ mollet** soft-boiled egg; **~ sur le plat** fried egg; **~s brouillés** scrambled eggs; **~s à la neige** floating islands.

œuvre /œvʀ/ *nf* **1** (artistic, literary) work; **~s complètes** complete works; **2 être à l'~** to be at work; **se mettre à l'~** to get down to work; **voir qn à l'~** to see sb in action; **mettre en ~** to implement [*programme, reform*]; to display [*ingenuity*]; **tout mettre en ~ pour faire** to make every effort to do.

■ **~ d'art** work of art; **~ de bienfaisance** or **de charité** charity.

IDIOMS **être à pied d'~** to be ready to get down to work.

off○ /ɔf/ *adj inv* **1** off-screen; **voix ~** voice-over; **2** alternative.

offense /ɔfɑ̃s/ *nf* insult; **faire ~ à qn** to offend sb.

offenser /ɔfɑ̃se/ [1] **I** *vtr* to offend.

II s'offenser *v refl* (+ *v être*) to take offence[GB] (**de** at).

offensif, -ive[1] /ɔfɑ̃sif, iv/ *adj* (Mil) offensive.

offensive[2] /ɔfɑ̃siv/ *nf* (Mil), (figurative) offensive.

office /ɔfis/ **I** *nm* **1 remplir son ~** [*object*] to fulfil[GB] its purpose; **faire ~ de table** to serve as a table; **2 ~ religieux** service; **3** butlery.

II d'office *phr* **d'~** without consultation; **nos propositions ont été rejetées d'~** our proposals were dismissed out of hand; **commis d'~** [*lawyer*] appointed by the court.

■ **~ du tourisme** tourist information office.

officialiser /ɔfisjalize/ [1] *vtr* to make [sth] official.

officiel, -ielle /ɔfisjɛl/ **I** *adj* official; **être en visite officielle** to be on a state visit.

II *nm* official.

officier[1] /ɔfisje/ [2] *vi* to officiate.

officier[2] /ɔfisje/ *nm* officer.

officieux, -ieuse /ɔfisjø, øz/ *adj* unofficial; **à titre ~** unofficially.

offrande /ɔfʀɑ̃d/ *nf* offering; **en ~** as an offering.

offrant /ɔfʀɑ̃/ *nm* **vendre qch au plus ~** to sell sth to the highest bidder.

offre /ɔfʀ/ *nf* **1** offer; **répondre à une ~ d'emploi** to reply to a job advertisement; **'locations: ~s'** 'accommodation to let' (GB), 'rentals' (US); **2** (Econ) supply.

■ **~ d'achat** bid; **~ publique d'achat, OPA** takeover bid.

offrir /ɔfʀiʀ/ [4] **I** *vtr* **1 ~ qch à qn** to give sth to sb; **2** to buy (**à qn** for sb); **3** to offer [*role, credit*]; **4** to offer, to give [*choice*]; to offer [*resignation*]; to present [*problems*].

II s'offrir *v refl* (+ *v être*) **1 s'~** to buy oneself [*hat, flowers*]; **ils ne peuvent pas s'~ le théâtre** they can't afford to go to the theatre[GB]; **je me suis offert le restaurant** I treated myself to a meal out; **s'~ un jour de vacances** to give oneself a day off; **2** [*solution*] to present itself; **s'~ en spectacle** to make an exhibition of oneself.

offusquer /ɔfyske/ [1] **I** *vtr* to offend.

II s'offusquer *v refl* (+ *v être*) to be offended (**de** by); to take offence[GB] (**de** at).

ogive /ɔʒiv/ *nf* rib.

ogre /ɔgʀ/ *nm* ogre; **manger comme un ~** to eat like a horse.

oie /wa/ *nf* goose; **~ blanche** naïve young girl.

oignon /ɔɲɔ̃/ *nm* **1** onion; **2** (of flower) bulb.

IDIOMS **occupe-toi de tes ~s**○ mind your own business○.

oiseau, *pl* **~x** /wazo/ *nm* bird; **un (drôle d')~** an oddball○.

IDIOMS **trouver l'~ rare**○ to find the one person in a million; **petit à petit l'~ fait son nid** (Proverb) with time and effort you achieve your goals.

oiseux, -euse /wazø, øz/ *adj* [*words*] idle; [*argument*] pointless.

oisif, -ive /wazif, iv/ **I** *adj* idle; **vie oisive** life of idleness.

II *nm,f* idler; **les ~s** the idle rich.

oisillon /wazijɔ̃/ *nm* fledgling.

oisiveté /wazivte/ *nf* idleness.

IDIOMS **l'~ est (la) mère de tous les vices** (Proverb) the devil makes work for idle hands (to do).

olé○: **olé olé** /ɔleɔle/ *phr* [*joke*] naughty; [*person*] racy○.

olfactif, -ive /ɔlfaktif, iv/ *adj* olfactory.

oligo-élément, *pl* **~s** /ɔligoelemɑ̃/ *nm* trace element.

olive /ɔliv/ *nf* olive.

olivier /ɔlivje/ *nm* **1** olive tree; **2** olive wood.

olympique /ɔlɛ̃pik/ *adj* Olympic.

ombrager /ɔ̃bʀaʒe/ [13] *vtr* [*leaves*] to shade; **route ombragée** shady road.

ombrageux, **-euse** /ɔ̃bʀaʒø, øz/ *adj* tetchy.

ombre /ɔ̃bʀ/ *nf* **1** shade; **tu leur fais de l'~** you're (standing) in their light; (figurative) you're putting them in the shade; **rester dans l'~ de qn** to be in sb's shadow; **2** shadow; **n'être plus que l'~ de soi-même** to be a shadow of one's former self; **3** darkness; **4 laisser certains détails dans l'~** to be deliberately vague about certain details; **rester dans l'~** to stay behind the scenes; **5** hint; **une ~ de tristesse passa dans son regard** a look of sadness crossed his/her face; **sans l'~ d'une preuve** without the slightest shred of evidence.

■ **~ chinoise** shadow puppet; **~ à paupières** eye shadow.

IDIOMS **jeter une ~ au tableau** to spoil the picture.

ombrelle /ɔ̃bʀɛl/ *nf* parasol, sunshade.

omelette /ɔmlɛt/ *nf* omelette.

omettre /ɔmɛtʀ/ [60] *vtr* to leave out, to omit; **~ de faire** to fail or omit to do.

omission /ɔmisjɔ̃/ *nf* omission; **mentir par ~** to lie by omission.

omnibus /ɔmnibys/ *nm inv* slow or local train.

omnipotent, **~e** /ɔmnipɔtɑ̃, ɑ̃t/ *adj* omnipotent, all-powerful.

omniprésent, **~e** /ɔmnipʀezɑ̃, ɑ̃t/ *adj* omnipresent.

omniscient, **~e** /ɔmnisjɑ̃, ɑ̃t/ *adj* omniscient.

omnisports /ɔmnispɔʀ/ *adj inv* **salle ~** sports hall; **club ~** (multi-)sports club.

omnivore /ɔmnivɔʀ/ **I** *adj* omnivorous.

II *nmf* omnivore.

omoplate /ɔmɔplat/ *nf* shoulder blade.

OMS /oɛmɛs/ *nf* (*abbr* = **Organisation mondiale de la santé**) WHO.

on /ɔ̃/ *pron* **1 ~ a refait la route** the road was resurfaced; **~ a prétendu que** it was claimed that; **il pleut des cordes, comme ~ dit** it's raining cats and dogs, as they say; **2** we; **mon copain et moi, ~ va en Afrique** my boyfriend and I are going to Africa; **qu'est-ce qu'~ mange ce soir?** what's for dinner tonight?; **3** you; **alors, ~ se promène?** so you're taking a stroll then?; **4 ~ fait ce qu'~ peut!** one does what one can!; **toi, ~ ne t'a rien demandé** nobody asked you for your opinion; **5** they; **~ ne m'a pas demandé mon avis** they didn't ask me for my opinion; **6 ~ t'appelle** someone's calling you; **7 ~ ne peut pas vivre avec 2 000 francs par mois** you can't live on 2,000 francs a month.

once /ɔ̃s/ *nf* ounce; **sans une ~ de méchanceté** without an ounce of malice.

oncle /ɔ̃kl/ *nm* uncle; **~ d'Amérique** (figurative) rich uncle.

onctueux, **-euse** /ɔ̃ktɥø, øz/ *adj* **1** smooth, creamy; **2** unctuous.

onctuosité /ɔ̃ktɥozite/ *nf* smoothness.

onde /ɔ̃d/ *nf* wave; **grandes ~s** long wave; **sur les ~s** on the air.

ondée /ɔ̃de/ *nf* shower.

on-dit /ɔ̃di/ *nm inv* **les ~** hearsay.

ondulé, **~e** /ɔ̃dyle/ *adj* [*hair, shape*] wavy; [*cardboard*] corrugated.

onduler /ɔ̃dyle/ [1] *vi* [*hair*] to fall in waves; [*body*] to sway.

onéreux, **-euse** /ɔneʀø, øz/ *adj* [*expense*] onerous, heavy; [*purchase*] expensive.

ongle /ɔ̃gl/ *nm* nail; **se faire les ~s** to do one's nails.

IDIOMS **jusqu'au bout des ~s** through and through.

onglet /ɔ̃glɛ/ *nm* **1** tab; **avec ~s** with thumb-index; **2** (Culin) *prime cut of beef.*

onguent /ɔ̃gɑ̃/ *nm* ointment, salve.

onirique /ɔniʀik/ *adj* [*scene, atmosphere*] dream-like; [*symbol*] dream.

onomatopée /ɔnɔmatɔpe/ *nf* onomatopoeia.

ONU /ɔny, oɛny/ *nf* (*abbr* = **Organisation des Nations unies**) UN, UNO.

onyx /ɔniks/ *nm inv* onyx.

onze /ɔ̃z/ *adj inv, pron* eleven.

onzième /ɔ̃zjɛm/ **I** *adj* eleventh.

II *nf* (Sch) *first year of primary school, age 6–7.*

OPA /opea/ *nf* (*abbr* = **offre publique d'achat**) takeover bid.

opacité /ɔpasite/ *nf* **1** opacity; **2** (figurative) impenetrability.

opaque /ɔpak/ *adj* **1** opaque; **2** (figurative) [*text*] opaque; [*night*] dark; [*wood, fog*] impenetrable.

OPEP /ɔpɛp/ *nf* (*abbr* = **Organisation des pays producteurs de pétrole**) OPEC.

opéra /ɔpeʀa/ *nm* **1** opera; **2** opera house.

opérateur, **-trice** /ɔpeʀatœʀ, tʀis/ *nm,f* operator; **~ de saisie** keyboarder.

opération /ɔpeʀasjɔ̃/ *nf* **1 ~ (chirurgicale)** operation, surgery; **2** calculation; **faire des ~s** (Sch) to do sums; **3** (Tech) operation; **4** process; **5** transaction.

opérationnel, **-elle** /ɔpeʀasjɔnɛl/ *adj* operational.

opératoire /ɔpeʀatwaʀ/ *adj* **1** [*technique*] surgical; [*risk*] in operating; **les suites ~s** the after-effects of surgery; **2** operative.

opérer /ɔpeʀe/ [14] **I** *vtr* **1** to operate on [*patient, organ*]; **~ qn de l'appendicite** to remove sb's appendix; **se faire ~** to have an operation, to have surgery; **2** to make [*choice, distinction*]; **3** to bring about [*change*].

II *vi* **1** to operate; **il faut ~** an operation is necessary; **2** [*cure, charm*] to work (**sur** on); **3** to proceed; **leur façon d'~** the way they go about things; **4** [*thief*] to operate.

III s'opérer *v refl* (+ *v être*) to take place.

opérette /ɔpeʀɛt/ *nf* operetta, light opera.

ophtalmologiste /ɔftalmɔlɔʒist/ *nmf* ophthalmologist.

opiner /ɔpine/ [1] *vi* **~ du bonnet** or **de la tête** to nod in agreement.

opiniâtre /ɔpinjɑtʀ/ *adj* [*resistance*] dogged; [*work*] relentless; [*person*] tenacious.

opinion /ɔpinjɔ̃/ *nf* **1** opinion; **il se moque de l'~ des autres** he doesn't care what other people think; **mon ~ est faite** my mind is made up; **2 l'~ (publique)** public opinion.

opium /ɔpjɔm/ *nm* opium.

opportun, **~e** /ɔpɔʀtœ̃, yn/ *adj* opportune, appropriate.

opportunisme /ɔpɔʀtynism/ *nm* opportunism.

opportuniste /ɔpɔʀtynist/ **I** *adj* opportunistic.
II *nmf* opportunist.

opportunité /ɔpɔʀtynite/ *nf* **1** appropriateness; **2** opportunity.

opposant, **~e** /ɔpozɑ̃, ɑ̃t/ *nm,f* opponent.

opposé, **~e** /ɔpoze/ **I** *adj* **1** [*direction*] opposite; **2** [*opinion*] opposite; [*parties, forces, sides*] opposing; [*interests, aims*] conflicting; **3** opposed (**à** to).
II à l'opposé *phr* **1 à l'~ de mes frères** in contrast to my brothers; **2 il est parti exactement à l'~** he went off in exactly the opposite direction.

opposer /ɔpoze/ [1] **I** *vtr* **1** to put up [*resistance, argument*]; **~ un refus à qn** to refuse sb; **2 ~ à** to match or pit [sb] against [*person, team*]; **3** [*dispute, problem*] to divide [*people*]; **4** to compare (**à** to, with).
II s'opposer *v refl* (+ *v être*) **1 s'~ à qch** to be opposed to sth; **2 s'~ à** to stand in the way of [*progress, change*]; **3** to contrast (**with** à); **4** [*ideas, opinions*] to conflict; [*people*] to disagree; [*supporters*] to be divided; **5** [*teams, opponents*] to confront each other.

opposition /ɔpozisjɔ̃/ *nf* **1** opposition; **par ~ à** in contrast with or to; **2** (Law) objection; **faire ~ à un chèque** to stop a cheque (GB) or check (US).

oppresser /ɔpʀese/ [1] *vtr* to oppress; **se sentir oppressé** to feel breathless.

oppresseur /ɔpʀesœʀ/ *nm* oppressor.

oppression /ɔpʀesjɔ̃/ *nf* oppression.

opprimer /ɔpʀime/ [1] *vtr* **1** to oppress [*people*]; **2** to stifle [*conscience*].

opter /ɔpte/ [1] *vi* to opt (**pour** for).

opticien, **-ienne** /ɔptisjɛ̃, ɛn/ *nm,f* optician.

optimal, **~e**, *mpl* **-aux** /ɔptimal, o/ *adj* optimum.

optimisme /ɔptimism/ *nm* optimism.

optimiste /ɔptimist/ **I** *adj* optimistic (**sur** about).
II *nmf* optimist.

option /ɔpsjɔ̃/ *nf* option; **en ~** optional.

optionnel, **-elle** /ɔpsjɔnɛl/ *adj* optional.

optique /ɔptik/ **I** *adj* **1** (Anat) optic; **2** (Tech) optical.
II *nf* **1** optics; **2** perspective; **3** optical components.

opulence /ɔpylɑ̃s/ *nf* opulence.

opulent, **~e** /ɔpylɑ̃, ɑ̃t/ *adj* **1** wealthy; affluent; **2** ample.

or[1] /ɔʀ/ *conj* and yet; **~, ce jour-là, il était sorti sans son parapluie** now, on that particular day, he went out without his umbrella.

or[2] /ɔʀ/ **I** *adj inv* [*colour, paint*] gold; [*hair*] golden.
II *nm* **1** gold; **en ~** gold; [*husband*] marvellous[GB]; [*opportunity*] golden; **2** gilding.

oracle /ɔʀakl/ *nm* oracle.

orage /ɔʀaʒ/ *nm* storm.

orageux, **-euse** /ɔʀaʒø, øz/ *adj* **1** stormy; thundery; **2** [*discussion*] stormy.

oraison /ɔʀɛzɔ̃/ *nf* prayer; **~ funèbre** funeral oration.

oral, **~e**, *mpl* **-aux** /ɔʀal, o/ **I** *adj* **1** oral; **2** (Med) **par voie ~e** orally.
II *nm* (Sch) oral (examination).

orange[1] /ɔʀɑ̃ʒ/ *adj inv* orange; [*light*] amber (GB), yellow (US).

orange[2] /ɔʀɑ̃ʒ/ *nf* orange.

oranger /ɔʀɑ̃ʒe/ *nm* orange tree; **fleur d'~** orange blossom.

orangeraie /ɔʀɑ̃ʒʀɛ/ *nf* orange grove.

orangerie /ɔʀɑ̃ʒʀi/ *nf* orangery.

orang-outan, *pl* **orangs-outans** /ɔʀɑ̃utɑ̃/ *nm* orang-utang (GB), orangutan (US).

orateur, **-trice** /ɔʀatœʀ, tʀis/ *nm,f* **1** speaker; **2** orator.

orbite /ɔʀbit/ *nf* **1** orbit; **mettre sur ~** to put [sth] into orbit; **2** eye-socket.

orchestral, **~e**, *mpl* **-aux** /ɔʀkɛstʀal, o/ *adj* orchestral.

orchestration /ɔʀkɛstʀasjɔ̃/ *nf* orchestration.

orchestre /ɔʀkɛstʀ/ *nm* **1** orchestra; **2** band; **3** orchestra pit; **4** orchestra stalls (GB), orchestra (US).

orchidée /ɔʀkide/ *nf* orchid.

ordinaire /ɔʀdinɛʀ/ **I** *adj* **1** ordinary; [*quality*] standard; [*reader, tourist*] average; [*crockery*] everyday; **journée peu ~** unusual day; **2** [*existence*] humdrum; **très ~** [*meal, wine*] very average; [*person*] very ordinary.
II *nm* **sortir de l'~** to be out of the ordinary.
III à l'ordinaire, **d'ordinaire** *phr* usually.

ordinateur /ɔʀdinatœʀ/ *nm* computer; **~ central** mainframe; **conception assistée par ~** computer-aided design.

ordination /ɔʀdinasjɔ̃/ *nf* ordination.

ordonnance /ɔʀdɔnɑ̃s/ *nf* prescription.

ordonner /ɔʀdɔne/ [1] *vtr* **1** to order; **2** to put [sth] in order; **3** to ordain; **il a été ordonné prêtre** he has been ordained.

ordre /ɔʀdʀ/ *nm* **1** order; **je n'ai d'~ à recevoir de personne** I don't take orders from anybody; **j'ai des ~s** I'm acting under orders; **à vos ~s!** (Mil) yes, sir!; **jusqu'à nouvel ~** until further notice; **2** order; **par ~ alphabétique** in alphabetical order; **3** tidiness, orderliness; **être en ~** [*house*] to be tidy; [*accounts*] to be in order; **mettre de l'~ dans ses idées** to get one's ideas straight; **4** order; **rappeler qn à l'~** to reprimand sb; **tout est rentré dans l'~** everything is back to normal; **rétablir l'~ (public)** to restore law and order;

5 nature; **c'est dans l'~ des choses** it's in the nature of things; **de l'~ de 30%** in the order of 30% (GB), on the order of 30% (US); **de premier ~** first-rate; **c'est du même ~** it's the same kind of thing; **6** (in religion) order; **entrer dans les ~s** to take (holy) orders; **7 libellez le chèque à l'~ de X** make the cheque (GB) or check (US) payable to X.

■ **~ du jour** agenda; **être à l'~ du jour** to be on the agenda; (figurative) to be talked about.

ordure /ɔʀdyʀ/ **I** *nf* filth.

II ordures *nf pl* **1** refuse (GB), garbage (US); **2** filth.

ordurier, -ière /ɔʀdyʀje, ɛʀ/ *adj* filthy.

orée /ɔʀe/ *nf* **1** edge; **2** (figurative) start.

oreille /ɔʀɛj/*nf* **1** ear; **dresser l'~** to prick up one's ears; **c'est arrivé à leurs ~s** they got to hear of it; **n'écouter que d'une ~** to half-listen; **ouvre-bien les ~s!** listen carefully; **arrête de crier, tu me casses les ~s**○ stop yelling, you're bursting my eardrums; **2** hearing; **avoir l'~ fine** to have keen hearing; **3 à l'abri des ~s indiscrètes** where no-one can hear.

IDIOMS **tirer les ~s à qn** to tell sb off; **se faire tirer l'~ pour faire** to drag one's feet about doing; **rougir jusqu'aux ~s** to blush to the roots of one's hair.

oreiller /ɔʀɛje/ *nm* pillow.

oreillons /ɔʀɛjɔ̃/ *nm pl* mumps.

ores: **d'ores et déjà** /dɔʀzedeʒa/ *phr* already.

orfèvre /ɔʀfɛvʀ/ *nmf* goldsmith; **être ~ en la matière** to be an expert in the field.

orfèvrerie /ɔʀfɛvʀəʀi/ *nf* **1** goldsmith's art; **2** goldsmith's and silversmith's.

organe /ɔʀgan/ *nm* **1** (Anat) organ; **2 ~ de presse** press organ.

organigramme /ɔʀganigʀam/ *nm* organization chart.

organique /ɔʀganik/ *adj* organic.

organisateur, -trice /ɔʀganizatœʀ, tʀis/ *nm,f* organizer.

organisation /ɔʀganizasjɔ̃/ *nf* organization.

organiser /ɔʀganize/ [1] **I** *vtr* to organize.

II s'organiser *v refl* (+ *v être*) **1** [*opposition*] to get organized; **2** to organize oneself; **3** [*fight, help*] to be organized; **4 s'~ autour de** [*plot*] to be built round .

organisme /ɔʀganism/ *nm* **1** body; **2** organism; **3** organization, body.

orgasme /ɔʀgasm/ *nm* orgasm.

orge /ɔʀʒ/ *nf* barley.

orgelet /ɔʀʒəlɛ/ *nm* stye.

orgie /ɔʀʒi/ *nf* orgy.

orgue /ɔʀg/ *nm* organ; **tenir l'~** to be at the organ.

orgueil /ɔʀgœj/ *nm* pride; **être l'~ de qn** to be sb's pride and joy.

orgueilleux, -euse /ɔʀgœjø, øz/ *adj* overproud.

orient /ɔʀjɑ̃/ *nm* **1** east; **2 l'Orient** the East.

oriental, ~e, *mpl* **-aux** /ɔʀjɑ̃tal, o/ *adj* eastern; oriental.

Oriental, ~e, *mpl* **-aux** /ɔʀjɑ̃tal, o/ *nm,f* Asian; **les Orientaux** Asians.

orientation /ɔʀjɑ̃tasjɔ̃/ *nf* **1** (of house) aspect; (of aerial) angle; (of projector) direction; **2** (of inquiry, research, policy) direction; **3** (Sch) **changer d'~** to change courses.

orienter /ɔʀjɑ̃te/ [1] **I** *vtr* **1** to adjust [*aerial, lamp*]; **2 ~ la conversation sur** to bring the conversation around to; **3** to direct [*person*]; **~ qn vers un spécialiste** to send sb to a specialist; **4** (Sch) to give career advice.

II s'orienter *v refl* (+ *v être*) **1** to get or find one's bearings; **2 s'~ vers** [*person*] to turn toward(s); **s'~ vers les carrières scientifiques** to go in for a career in science.

orifice /ɔʀifis/ *nm* **1** orifice; **2** (of pipe) mouth; (of tube) neck.

originaire /ɔʀiʒinɛʀ/ *adj* **1** [*plant, animal*] native; **famille ~ d'Asie** Asian family; **2** [*state*] original; [*deformity*] inherent.

original, ~e, *mpl* **-aux** /ɔʀiʒinal, o/ **I** *adj* **1** original; **2** eccentric.

II *nm* original.

originalité /ɔʀiʒinalite/ *nf* **1** originality; **sans ~** unoriginal; **2** eccentricity.

origine /ɔʀiʒin/ *nf* origin; **être d'~ modeste** to come from a modest background; **dès l'~** right from the start; **à l'~** originally; **d'~** original.

originel, -elle /ɔʀiʒinɛl/ *adj* original.

oripeaux /ɔʀipo/ *nm pl* faded finery.

orme /ɔʀm/ *nm* **1** elm (tree); **2** elm (wood).

ormeau, *pl* **~x** /ɔʀmo/ *nm* **1** young elm tree; **2** abalone.

ornement /ɔʀnəmɑ̃/ *nm* **1** ornament; **2** decorative detail.

ornemental, ~e, *mpl* **-aux** /ɔʀnəmɑ̃tal, o/ *adj* ornamental.

orner /ɔʀne/ [1] *vtr* to decorate [*house*]; to trim [*hat*].

ornière /ɔʀnjɛʀ/ *nf* rut; **sortir de l'~** to get out of a tricky○ situation.

ornithologie /ɔʀnitɔlɔʒi/ *nf* ornithology.

ornithorynque /ɔʀnitɔʀɛ̃k/ *nm* (duck-billed) platypus, duckbill (US).

orphelin, ~e /ɔʀfəlɛ̃, in/ *nm,f* orphan.

IDIOMS **défendre la veuve et l'~** to defend the weak.

orphelinat /ɔʀfəlina/ *nm* orphanage.

orque /ɔʀk/ *nm* or *f* killer whale.

orteil /ɔʀtɛj/ *nm* toe; **gros ~** big toe.

orthodoxe /ɔʀtɔdɔks/ **I** *adj* **1** orthodox; **2** Orthodox.

II *nmf* Orthodox.

orthographe /ɔʀtɔgʀaf/ *nf* spelling.

orthographier /ɔʀtɔgʀafje/ [2] *vtr* to spell; **mal orthographié** misspelled.

orthopédie /ɔʀtɔpedi/ *nf* orthopedics.

orthophoniste /ɔʀtɔfɔnist/ *nmf* speech therapist.

ortie /ɔʀti/ *nf* (stinging) nettle; **se piquer aux ~s** to get stung in the nettles.

os /ɔs, *pl* o/ *nm inv* bone; **en chair et en ~** in the flesh.
IDIOMS **il y a un ~**○ there's a hitch; **jusqu'à l'~**○ completely; **tomber sur un ~**○ to come across a snag; **être trempé jusqu'aux ~**○ to be soaked to the skin○.

oscillation /ɔsilasjɔ̃/ *nf* **1** oscillation; **2** swinging; rocking; **3** fluctuation.

osciller /ɔsile/ [1] *vi* **1** [*pendulum*] to swing; [*boat*] to rock; [*head*] to roll from side to side; **2** [*currency*] to fluctuate; **3** to vacillate.

osé, ~e /oze/ *adj* **1** risqué; **2** [*behaviour*] daring; [*words*] outspoken.

oseille /ozɛj/ *nf* **1** sorrel; **2**○ dough○, money.

oser /oze/ [1] *vtr* to dare; **si j'ose dire** if I may say so.

osier /ozje/ *nm* **1** osier; **2** osier, wicker.

osmose /ɔsmoz/ *nf* osmosis.

ossature /ɔsatyʀ/ *nf* skeleton; **~ du visage** bone structure.

osselet /ɔslɛ/ *nm* **1** small bone; **2 les ~s** jacks.

ossements /ɔsmɑ̃/ *nm pl* remains.

osseux, -euse /ɔsø, øz/ *adj* **1** bony; **2** [*disease*] bone.

ostensible /ɔstɑ̃sibl/ *adj* obvious.

ostentatoire /ɔstɑ̃tatwaʀ/ *adj* ostentatious.

ostéopathe /ɔsteɔpat/ *nmf* osteopath.

ostracisme /ɔstʀasism/ *nm* ostracism; **être frappé d'~** to be ostracized.

ostréiculture /ɔstʀeikyltyʀ/ *nf* oyster farming.

otage /ɔtaʒ/ *nm* hostage; **être pris en ~** to be taken hostage.

OTAN /ɔtɑ̃/ *nf* (*abbr* = **Organisation du traité de l'Atlantique Nord**) NATO.

otarie /ɔtaʀi/ *nf* eared seal, otary.

ôter /ote/ [1] **I** *vtr* **1** to take off [*clothes, glasses*]; to remove [*bones, stain*]; **2 ~ qch à qn** to take sth away from sb; **on ne m'ôtera pas de l'idée que...** I'm still convinced that...; **3 4 ôté de 9, il reste 5** 9 minus or take away 4 leaves 5.
II s'ôter *v refl* (+ *v être*) **1 s'~ qch de l'esprit** or **la tête** to get sth out of one's mind or head; **2 ôte-toi de là!** move!

otite /ɔtit/ *nf* inflammation of the ear; **avoir une ~** to have earache.

oto-rhino-laryngologiste, *pl* **~s** /otoʀinolaʀɛ̃gɔlɔʒist/ *nmf* ENT specialist.

ou /u/ *conj* or; **~ (bien)... ~ (bien)...** either... or...

où /u/ **I** *adv* where; **~ es-tu?** where are you?; **je l'ai perdu je ne sais ~** I've lost it somewhere or other; **par ~ êtes-vous passés pour venir?** which way did you come?; **~ en êtes-vous?** where have you got to?; **tu vois ~ je veux en venir?** you see what I am getting at?; **~ allons-nous?** what are things coming to!
II *rel pron* **1** where; **le quartier ~ nous habitons** the area we live in; **trouver un endroit ~ dormir** to find a place or somewhere to sleep; **d'~ s'élevait de la fumée** out of which smoke was rising; **~ qu'ils aillent** wherever they go; **2 la misère ~ elle se trouvait** the poverty in which she was living; **au train** or **à l'allure ~ vont les choses** (at) the rate things are going; **le travail s'est accumulé, d'~ ce retard** there is a backlog of work, hence the delay; **3** when; **il fut un temps ~** there was a time when; **le matin ~ je l'ai rencontré** the morning I met him; **juste au moment ~ j'allais partir** at the very moment I was about to leave.

ouailles /waj/ *nf pl* flock; **une de mes ~** one of my flock.

ouate /wat/ *nf* **1** cotton wool (GB), cotton (US); **2** wadding.

oubli /ubli/ *nm* **1 l'~ de qch** forgetting sth; (of duty) neglect of sth; **2** omission; **3** oblivion; **tomber dans l'~** to be completely forgotten, to sink into oblivion.

oublier /ublije/ [2] **I** *vtr* **1** to forget [*name, date, fact*]; to forget about [*worries, incident*]; **j'ai oublié mes clés chez elle** I've left my keys at her house; **se faire ~** to keep a low profile, to lie low○; **2** to leave out, to forget [*person, detail*]; **3** to forget, to neglect [*duty, friend*].
II s'oublier *v refl* (+ *v être*) **1** to be forgotten; **2** to leave oneself out.

oubliettes /ublijɛt/ *nf pl* oubliette.
IDIOMS **mettre** or **jeter qch aux ~** to consign sth to oblivion.

ouest /wɛst/ **I** *adj inv* west; western.
II *nm* **1** west; **2 l'Ouest** the West; **de l'Ouest** western.

ouf /uf/ **I** *nm* **faire ~** to breathe a sigh of relief.
II *excl* phew!

oui /wi/ **I** *adv* yes; **alors c'est ~?** so the answer is yes?; **acceptera-t-il ~ ou non de me rencontrer?** will he agree to meet me or not?; **découvrir si ~ ou non** to discover whether or not; **dire ~ à qch** to welcome sth; to agree to sth; **faire ~ de la tête** to nod; **lui, prudent? un lâche, ~!** him, cautious? a coward, more like○!; **c'est bientôt fini, ~?** are you going to stop that or not?; **je crois que ~** I think so.
II *nm inv* **1** yes; **2** 'yes' vote; **le ~ l'a emporté** the ayes have it.
IDIOMS **pour un ~ (ou) pour un non** [*get angry*] for the slightest thing; [*change one's mind*] at the drop of a hat.

ouï-dire /widiʀ/ *nm inv* hearsay; **par ~** by hearsay.

ouïe /wi/ *nf* **1** hearing; **être tout ~** to be all ears; **2** (of fish) gill.

ouïr† /wiʀ/ [38] *vtr* **j'ai ouï dire que** word has reached me that.

ouistiti /wistiti/ *nm* **1** marmoset; **2**○ **un (drôle de) ~** a funny character.

ouragan /uʀagɑ̃/ *nm* hurricane.

ourler /uʀle/ [1] *vtr* to hem.

ourlet /uʀlɛ/ *nm* hem; **faire un ~ à** to put a hem on.

ours /uʀs/ *nm inv* **1** bear; **2 il est un peu ~** he's a bit surly.
■ **~ blanc** polar bear; **~ en peluche** teddy bear; **~ polaire** = **~ blanc**.

IDIOMS **vendre la peau de l'~ avant de l'avoir tué** (Proverb) to count one's chickens before they're hatched.

ourse /uʀs/ *nf* she-bear.

oursin /uʀsɛ̃/ *nm* (sea) urchin.

ourson /uʀsɔ̃/ *nm* bear cub.

outil /uti/ *nm* tool; **~ de travail** work tool.

outrage /utʀaʒ/ *nm* insult; **faire ~ à** to be an insult to.

■ **~ à agent** *verbal assault of a policeman*; **~ à magistrat** contempt of court.

outrager /utʀaʒe/ [13] *vtr* to offend.

outrance /utʀɑ̃s/ *nf* excess; **manger à ~** to eat excessively.

outrancier, -ière /utʀɑ̃sje, ɛʀ/ *adj* extreme.

outre[1] /utʀ/ I *prep* in addition to.

II *adv* **passer ~** to pay no heed.

III **outre mesure** *phr* unduly.

IV **en outre** *phr* in addition.

outre[2] /utʀ/ *nf* goatskin; **être plein comme une ~**○ to be full to bursting.

outre-Atlantique /utʀatlɑ̃tik/ *adv* across the Atlantic; **d'~** American.

outre-Manche /utʀəmɑ̃ʃ/ *adv* across the Channel; **d'~** British.

outremer /utʀəmɛʀ/ *adj inv, nm* ultramarine.

outre-mer /utʀəmɛʀ/ *adv* overseas.

outrepasser /utʀəpase/ [1] *vtr* to exceed [*rights*]; to overstep [*limits, orders*].

outrer /utʀe/ [1] *vtr* **1** to outrage; **être outré** to be outraged; **2** to exaggerate.

ouvert, ~e /uvɛʀ, ɛʀt/ I *pp* ▶ **ouvrir**.

II *pp adj* **1** open; **grand ~** wide open; **(la) bouche ~e** with one's mouth open; open-mouthed; **être ~ aux idées nouvelles** to be open to new ideas; **2** [*light, gas*] on; [*tap*] running; **3 ~ à** [*centre, service*] open to; **4** [*series, question*] open-ended.

ouvertement /uvɛʀtəmɑ̃/ *adv* openly; blatantly.

ouverture /uvɛʀtyʀ/ *nf* **1** opening; **heures d'~** opening hours; **à l'~** at opening time; **2** openness; **~ d'esprit** open-mindedness; **~ à l'Ouest** opening-up to the West; **3** (Mus) overture.

ouvrable /uvʀabl/ *adj* [*day*] working; [*hours*] business.

ouvrage /uvʀaʒ/ *nm* **1** work; **se mettre à l'~** to get down to work; **2** book, work; **3** piece of work; **~ de broderie** piece of embroidery.

IDIOMS **mettre** or **avoir du cœur à l'~** to work with a will.

ouvre-boîtes /uvʀəbwat/ *nm inv* tin-opener (GB), can-opener.

ouvre-bouteilles /uvʀəbutɛj/ *nm inv* bottle-opener.

ouvreur, -euse /uvʀœʀ, øz/ *nm,f* usher/usherette.

ouvrier, -ière /uvʀije, ɛʀ/ I *adj* of the workers; **classe ouvrière** working class.

II *nm,f* worker; workman.

ouvrir /uvʀiʀ/ [32] I *vtr* to open; to draw back [*bolt*]; to undo [*collar, shirt, zip*]; to intitiate [*dialogue, lesson*]; to turn on [*radio, heating*]; to open up [*possibilities, market*]; to cut open [*cheek*]; **ne pas ~ la bouche** not to say a word; **~ ses oreilles** to keep one's ears open; **~ les bras à qn** to welcome sb with open arms; **~ l'esprit à qn** to open sb's mind.

II *vi* **1** to open the door; **ouvre-moi!** let me in!; **se faire ~** to be let in; **2** to open; **3** to be opened.

III **s'ouvrir** *v refl* (+ *v être*) [*door, window, parachute*] to open; [*shirt, dress*] to come undone; [*dialogue, process*] to be initiated; [*country, economy, institution*] to open up; [*person*] to open up [*passage*]; [*ground, scar*] to open up; [*person*] to cut open [*head, foot*]; **s'~ les veines** to slash one's wrists; **s'~ à qn** to open one's heart to sb.

ovaire /ɔvɛʀ/ *nm* ovary.

ovale /ɔval/ *adj, nm* oval.

ovation /ɔvasjɔ̃/ *nf* **1** ovation; **il a fini son discours sous les ~s de la foule** he finished his speech to wild applause from the crowd; **2** accolade.

ovni /ɔvni/ *nm* (*abbr* = **objet volant non identifié**) unidentified flying object, UFO.

ovulation /ɔvylasjɔ̃/ *nf* ovulation.

ovule /ɔvyl/ *nm* **1** (Anat) ovum; **2** (Bot) ovule; **3** (Med) pessary.

oxydable /ɔksidabl/ *adj* liable to rust.

oxydation /ɔksidasjɔ̃/ *nf* oxidation.

oxyde /ɔksid/ *nm* oxide; **~ de carbone** carbon monoxide.

oxyder /ɔkside/ [1] *vtr*, **s'oxyder** *v refl* (+ *v être*) to oxidize.

oxygène /ɔksiʒɛn/ *nm* **1** oxygen; **à ~** [*mask, tent*] oxygen; **2** air.

oxygéné, ~e /ɔksiʒene/ I *pp* ▶ **oxygéner**.

II *pp adj* **eau ~e** hydrogen peroxide.

oxygéner /ɔksiʒene/ [14] I *vtr* to oxygenate.

II **s'oxygéner** *v refl* (+ *v être*) [*person*] to get some fresh air.

ozone /ozɔn/ *nf* ozone; **la couche d'~** the ozone layer.

p, P /pe/ *nm inv* p, P.
pacha /paʃa/ *nm* pasha; **mener une vie de ~**° to live the life of Riley.
pacificateur, -trice /pasifikatœʀ, tʀis/ **I** *adj* [*action*] placatory; [*role*] peacemaking.
II *nm,f* peacemaker.
pacifier /pasifje/ [1] *vtr* to establish peace in.
pacifique /pasifik/ **I** *adj* peaceful.
II *nmf* peace-loving person.
Pacifique /pasifik/ *pr nm* **l'océan ~, le ~** the Pacific (Ocean).
pacifiste /pasifist/ *adj, nmf* pacifist.
pacotille /pakɔtij/ *nf* **de la ~** cheap rubbish, junk°; **héroïsme de ~** bogus heroism.
pacte /pakt/ *nm* pact.
pactole /paktɔl/ *nm* gold mine; **ramasser le ~**° to make a fortune.
pagaie /pagɛ/ *nf* (Naut) paddle.
pagaille° /pagaj/ **I** *nf* mess; **semer la ~** [*strike*] to cause chaos.
II en pagaille *phr* **1** in a mess; **2 pêcher du poisson en ~** to catch loads° of fish.
page[1] /paʒ/ *nm* page (boy).
page[2] /paʒ/ *nf* **1** page; **en première ~** on the front page; **tourner la ~** to turn over a new leaf; **2** chapter; **une ~ sombre de leur existence** a dark chapter in their lives.
■ **~ de publicité** commercial break.
IDIOMS **être à la ~** to be up to date.
pagination /paʒinasjɔ̃/ *nf* **1** pagination; **2** paging.
paginer /paʒine/ [1] *vtr* to paginate.
pagne /paɲ/ *nm* **1** loincloth; **2** grass skirt.
pagode /pagɔd/ *nf* pagoda.
paie /pɛ/ *nf* pay; **bulletin** or **fiche** or **feuille de ~** payslip.
IDIOMS **ça fait une ~ que je ne l'ai pas vu**° it's ages° since I've seen him.
paiement /pɛmɑ̃/ *nm* payment.
païen, -ïenne /pajɛ̃, ɛn/ *adj, nm,f* pagan.
paillard, ~e /pajaʀ, aʀd/ *adj* bawdy.
paillasse /pajas/ *nf* **1** straw mattress; **2** lab bench; **3** draining board.
paillasson /pajasɔ̃/ *nm* doormat.
paille /paj/ **I** *adj inv* **jaune ~** straw yellow.
II *nf* straw; **~ de riz** rice straw; **~ de fer** steel wool.
IDIOMS **être sur la ~**° to be penniless; **tirer à la courte ~** to draw lots.
pailleté, ~e /pajte/ *adj* **1** sequined, spangled (US); **2** [*material*] glittery.
paillette /pajɛt/ *nf* **1** sequin, spangle (US); **robe à ~s** sequined or spangled (US) dress; **2** glitter; **3** (of rock) splinter; **4 savon en ~s** soap flakes; **5** straw.
pain /pɛ̃/ *nm* **1** bread; **des miettes de ~** breadcrumbs; **2** loaf; **un petit ~** a (bread) roll; **3** (Culin) **~ de légumes/viande** vegetable/meat loaf; **4** (of soap, wax) bar.
■ **~ blanc** white bread; **manger son ~ blanc (le premier)** to have it easy at the start; **~ de campagne** farmhouse bread; farmhouse loaf; **~ complet** wholemeal bread; wholemeal loaf; **~ d'épices** gingerbread; **~ grillé** toast; **une tranche de ~ grillé** a piece of toast; **~ au lait** milk roll; **~ de mie** sandwich loaf; **~ de seigle** rye bread; rye loaf; **~ de son** bran loaf.
IDIOMS **se vendre comme des petits ~s** to sell like hot cakes; **ça ne mange pas de ~**° it doesn't cost anything; **je ne mange pas de ce ~-là**° I won't have anything to do with it.
pair, ~e[1] /pɛʀ/ **I** *adj* [*number*] even.
II *nm* **1** peer; **c'est une cuisinière hors ~** she's an excellent cook; **2 aller** or **marcher de ~ avec qch** to go hand in hand with sth.
III au pair *phr* **travailler au ~** to work as an au pair.
paire[2] /pɛʀ/ *nf* pair; **donner une ~ de gifles à qn** to box sb's ears.
IDIOMS **les deux font la ~!** they're two of a kind!
paisible /pɛzibl/ *adj* [*life, district*] peaceful, quiet; [*person, water*] calm; [*sleep*] peaceful.
paisiblement /pɛzibləmɑ̃/ *adv* peacefully, peaceably.
paître /pɛtʀ/ [74] *vi* to graze.
IDIOMS **envoyer ~ qn**° to send sb packing°.
paix /pɛ/ *nf inv* peace; **être en ~ avec soi-même** to be at peace with oneself; **avoir la ~** to get some peace; **laisser qn en ~** to leave sb alone; **la ~**°**!** be quiet!
palabre /palabʀ/ *nm* or *f* endless discussion.
palabrer /palabʀe/ [1] *vi* to discuss endlessly.
palace /palas/ *nm* luxury hotel.
palais /palɛ/ *nm inv* **1** palate; **2** palace; **3** (Law) **~ (de justice)** law courts .
■ **~ des sports** sports centre[GB].
palatal, ~e, *mpl* **-aux** /palatal, o/ *adj* palatal.
pale /pal/ *nf* (of propeller, oar) blade.
pâle /pɑl/ *adj* pale; **vert ~** pale green.
IDIOMS **être ~ comme un linge** to be as white as a sheet; **faire ~ figure à côté de** to pale into insignificance beside.
palefrenier, -ière /palfʀənje, ɛʀ/ *nm,f* groom.
paléontologie /paleɔ̃tɔlɔʒi/ *nf* paleontology.
palet /palɛ/ *nm* **1** (in ice hockey) puck; **2** quoit.
palette /palɛt/ *nf* **1** palette; **2** range; **une ~ d'activités** a range of activities; **3** (of pork, mutton) ≈ shoulder.
pâleur /pɑlœʀ/ *nf* **1** paleness; **2** pallor.
pâlichon°**, -onne** /pɑliʃɔ̃, ɔn/ *adj* [*person*] peaky° (GB), peaked (US).

palier /palje/ *nm* **1** landing; **mon voisin de ~** my neighbour[GB] on the same floor; **2** level; plateau; **3** (Sport) **~ (de décompression)** (decompression) stage; **avancer par ~s** to proceed by stages.

palière /paljɛʀ/ *adj f* **porte ~** entry door.

pâlir /pɑliʀ/ [3] *vi* **1** to fade; **2** to grow or turn pale; **faire ~ qn d'envie** to make sb green with envy.

palissade /palisad/ *nf* fence.

palliatif, -ive /paljatif, iv/ **I** *adj* palliative.
II *nm* palliative.

pallier /palje/ [2] *vtr* to compensate for.

palmarès /palmaʀɛs/ *nm inv* **1** honours[GB] list; list of (award) winners; **2** record of achievements; **3** hit parade; **4** bestsellers list.

palme /palm/ *nf* **1** palm leaf; **2** palm (tree); **3** (for diver) flipper; **4** (Mil) ≈ bar; **5** prize; **remporter la ~** to take the prize.

palmé, ~e /palme/ *adj* **1** [*feet*] webbed; **2** [*leaf*] palmate.

palmeraie /palməʀɛ/ *nf* palm grove.

palmier /palmje/ *nm* **1** palm (tree); **2** large pastry biscuit.

palombe /palɔ̃b/ *nf* wood pigeon.

pâlot○**, -otte** /pɑlo, ɔt/ *adj* peaky○ (GB), peaked (US).

palourde /paluʀd/ *nf* clam.

palper /palpe/ [1] *vtr* **1** (Med) to palpate; **2** to feel.

palpitant, ~e /palpitɑ̃, ɑ̃t/ *adj* **1** thrilling; **2** [*heart*] fluttering; [*body*] twitching; **3** panting.

palpitation /palpitasjɔ̃/ *nf* **1** (Med) palpitation; **2** twitching.

palpiter /palpite/ [1] *vi* **1** [*heart*] to beat; to flutter; [*body*] to twitch; [*vein*] to pulse; **2** (literary) [*person, water*] to quiver; [*light, flame*] to flicker.

paludisme /palydism/ *nm* malaria.

pâmer†**: se pâmer** /pɑme/ [1] *v refl* (+ *v être*) **se ~ (d'admiration) devant qch** to swoon over sth.

pamphlet /pɑ̃flɛ/ *nm* satirical tract.

pamphlétaire /pɑ̃fletɛʀ/ *nmf* pamphleteer.

pamplemousse /pɑ̃pləmus/ *nm* grapefruit.

pan /pɑ̃/ **I** *nm* **1** (of cliff, house) section; (of life) part; (of darkness) patch; **~ de vitre** glass panel; **2** (of tower) side; **~s d'un manteau** coat-tails.
II *excl* (*also onomatopoeic*) (from shot) bang!; (from fist) thump!; (from spanking) whack!

pan- /pɑ̃, pan/ *pref* Pan; **~-russe** Pan-Russian; **~-européen** Pan-European.

panacée /panase/ *nf* panacea.

panache /panaʃ/ *nm* **1** panache; **2** plume.

panaché, ~e /panaʃe/ **I** *adj* [*bouquet, salad*] mixed; [*tulip, ivy*] variegated.
II *nm* shandy (GB), shandygaff (US).

panacher /panaʃe/ [1] *vtr* to mix [*colours, flowers, styles*].

panaris /panaʀi/ *nm inv* whitlow.

pancarte /pɑ̃kaʀt/ *nf* **1** notice (GB), sign (US); **2** placard (GB), sign (US).

pancréas /pɑ̃kʀeas/ *nm inv* pancreas.

panda /pɑ̃da/ *nm* panda.

panégyrique /paneʒiʀik/ *nm* panegyric.

paner /pane/ [1] *vtr* to coat with breadcrumbs.

panier /panje/ *nm* **1** basket; **2** (in dishwasher) rack; **3** (Sport) basket; **marquer un ~** to score a basket.
■ **~ à linge** linen basket; **~ à salade** salad shaker; Black Maria (GB), paddy wagon (US).
IDIOMS **être un ~ percé**○ to spend money like water; **ils sont tous à mettre dans le même ~**○ they are all about the same; **mettre tous ses œufs dans le même ~**○ to put all one's eggs in one basket; **le haut** or **dessus du ~**○ the pick of the bunch; **mettre** or **jeter au ~** to throw [sth] out; to get rid of [sth].

panique /panik/ *nf* panic; **mouvement de ~** panic; **semer** or **jeter la ~** to spread panic; **être pris de ~** to panic.

paniquer○ /panike/ [1] **I** *vtr* to throw [sb] into a panic.
II *vi* to panic.

panne /pan/ *nf* (of vehicle, machine) breakdown; (of engine) failure; **~ de courant** power failure; **tomber en ~ sèche** or **d'essence** to run out of petrol (GB) or gas (US); **être en ~ de**○ to be out of [*coffee, washing powder*]; to have run out of [*ideas*].

panneau, *pl* **~x** /pano/ *nm* **1** sign; board; **2** notice board; **3** panel.
■ **~ indicateur** signpost; **~ publicitaire** hoarding (GB), billboard; **~ de signalisation routière** road sign; **~ solaire** solar panel.
IDIOMS **tomber** or **donner dans le ~**○ to fall for it○.

panoplie /panɔpli/ *nf* **1** outfit; **2** display of weapons; **3** (of objects) array; (of measures, means) range.

panorama /panɔʀama/ *nm* **1** panorama; **2** (of art, culture) survey.

panoramique /panɔʀamik/ *adj* **1** [*view, visit*] panoramic; **2** [*windscreen*] wrap-around; **3** [*screen*] wide.

panse /pɑ̃s/ *nf* **1** (of cow) paunch; **2**○ belly○; **3** (of jug) belly.

pansement /pɑ̃smɑ̃/ *nm* dressing; **~ (adhésif)** plaster (GB), Band-Aid®.

panser /pɑ̃se/ [1] *vtr* **1** to dress [*wound*]; to put a dressing on [*arm, leg*]; **2** [*time*] to heal [*hurt pride*].

pantalon /pɑ̃talɔ̃/ *nm* trousers (GB), pants (US); **~ de pyjama** pyjama (GB) or pajama (US) bottoms.

pantelant, ~e /pɑ̃tlɑ̃, ɑ̃t/ *adj* [*person*] panting; [*flesh*] quivering.

panthère /pɑ̃tɛʀ/ *nf* **1** panther; **2** panther skin.

pantin /pɑ̃tɛ̃/ *nm* puppet.

pantois, ~e /pɑ̃twa, az/ *adj* flabbergasted.

pantomime /pɑ̃tɔmim/ *nf* **1** mime; **2** mime show.

pantoufle /pɑ̃tufl/ *nf* slipper.

panure /panyʀ/ *nf* breadcrumbs.

paon /pɑ̃/ *nm* peacock; **faire le ~** to strut around like a peacock.

paonne /pan/ *nf* peahen.

papa /papa/ *nm* dad○, daddy○, father; **fils** or **fille à ~** spoiled little rich kid○.

pape /pap/ *nm* **1** pope; **2** (figurative) high priest.
IDIOMS **être sérieux comme un ~** to be solemn-faced.

paperasse○ /papʀas/ *nf* **1** bumph○ (GB), documents; **2** paperwork.

paperasserie○ /papʀasʀi/ *nf* (derogatory) paperwork.

papeterie /papɛtʀi/ *nf* **1** stationer's (shop), stationery shop (GB) or store (US); **2** stationery; **3** papermaking industry; **4** paper mill.

papetier, -ière /paptje, ɛʀ/ **I** *adj* papermaking.
II *nm,f* **1** papermaker; **2** stationer.

papi○ /papi/ *nm* granddad○, grandpa○.

papier /papje/ *nm* **1** paper; **2** paper; **~s (d'identité)** (identity) papers or documents; **3**○ (newspaper) article, piece○.
■ **~ absorbant** kitchen towel, paper towel (US); **~ alu**○, **~ (d')aluminium** (aluminium (GB) or aluminum (US)) foil, kitchen foil; **~ brouillon** rough paper (GB), scrap paper; **~ cadeau** gift wrap; **~ à cigarettes** cigarette paper; **fin comme du ~ à cigarettes** wafer-thin; **~ d'emballage** wrapping paper; **~ hygiénique** toilet paper or tissue; **~ journal** newsprint; **~ à lettres** writing paper; **~ peint** wallpaper; **~ de verre** sandpaper, glasspaper; **~s gras** litter.
IDIOMS **être dans les petits ~s de qn**○ to be in sb's good books; ▶ **musique**.

papier-calque, *pl* **papiers-calque** /papjekalk/ *nm* tracing paper.

papillon /papijɔ̃/ *nm* **1** butterfly; **~ de nuit** moth; **2**○ parking ticket; **3 (brasse) ~** butterfly (stroke); **4** (Tech) wing nut.

papillonner /papijɔne/ [1] *vi* **1** to flit about; **2** to flirt incessantly.

papillote /papijɔt/ *nf* **1** (Culin) foil parcel; (on cutlet) frill; **2** (for hair) curlpaper; **3** chocolate sweet (GB), chocolate candy (US).

papilloter /papijɔte/ [1] *vi* **1** [*light*] to flicker; **2** [*person*] to blink.

papoter○ /papɔte/ [1] *vi* to chatter.

paprika /papʀika/ *nm* paprika.

papy = **papi**.

Pâque /pɑk/ *nf* **la ~ juive** Passover.

paquebot /pakbo/ *nm* liner .

pâquerette /pɑkʀɛt/ *nf* daisy.
IDIOMS **être au ras des ~s**○ to be very basic.

Pâques /pɑk/ *nm, nf pl* Easter.

paquet /pakɛ/ *nm* **1** (of sugar, washing powder) packet (GB), package (US); (of cigarettes, coffee) packet (GB), pack (US); **2** parcel; **3** (of clothes) bundle; (of letters) packet; **4**○ masses; **5**○ packet○ (GB), bundle○ (US).
■ **~ de muscles**○ muscleman; **~ de nerfs**○ bundle of nerves○.
IDIOMS **mettre le ~**○ to pull out all the stops.

par /paʀ/ **I** *prep* **1 il a pris ~ les champs** he cut across the fields; **elle est arrivée ~ la droite** she came from the right; **le peintre a terminé** or **fini ~ la cuisine** the painter did the kitchen last; **2 ~ le passé** in the past; **~ une belle journée d'été** on a beautiful summer's day; **ils sortent même ~ moins 40°** they go outdoors even when it's minus 40°; **3** per; **~ jour/an** a day/year; **~ personne** per person; **4** by; **être pris ~ son travail** to be taken up with one's work; **régler** or **payer ~ carte de crédit** to pay by credit card; **deux ~ deux** [*work*] in twos; [*walk*] two by two; **5** in; **~ étapes** in stages; **~ endroits** in places; **6 l'accident est arrivé ~ sa faute** it was his/her fault that the accident happened; **~ jalousie** out of jealousy; **7** through; **tu peux me faire passer le livre ~ ta sœur** you can get the book to me via your sister; **entre ~ le garage** come in through the garage.
II de par *phr* (formal) **1** throughout, all over; **voyager de ~ le monde** to travel all over the world; **2 de ~ leurs origines** by virtue of their origins.

parabole /paʀabɔl/ *nf* **1** parable; **2** parabola.

parachever /paʀaʃve/ [16] *vtr* **1** to complete; **2** to put the finishing touches to.

parachute /paʀaʃyt/ *nm* **1** parachute; **2** parachuting.

parachuter /paʀaʃyte/ [1] *vtr* **1** to parachute; **2**○ **je n'ai pas envie d'être parachuté en Normandie** I don't want to be shunted off○ to Normandy.

parachutisme /paʀaʃytism/ *nm* parachuting.

parachutiste /paʀaʃytist/ **I** *adj* [*troops, regiment*] parachute.
II *nmf* **1** parachutist; **2** paratrooper.

parade /paʀad/ *nf* **1** (Mil) parade; **2** (in fencing) parry; **3 un enthousiasme de ~** a show of enthusiasm; **faire ~ de** to flaunt; **4** (by animal) display.

parader /paʀade/ [1] *vi* to strut about.

paradis /paʀadi/ *nm inv* **1** heaven; **2** paradise.
■ **~ fiscal** tax haven; **~ terrestre** Garden of Eden.
IDIOMS **tu ne l'emporteras pas au ~**○ you'll live to regret it.

paradisiaque /paʀadizjak/ *adj* heavenly.

paradoxal, ~e, *mpl* **-aux** /paʀadɔksal, o/ *adj* paradoxical.

paradoxe /paʀadɔks/ *nm* paradox.

paraffine /paʀafin/ *nf* **1** paraffin (GB), kerosene (US); **2** paraffin wax.

parages /paʀaʒ/ *nm pl* neighbourhood[GB]; **elle est dans les ~** she is around somewhere.

paragraphe /paʀagʀaf/ *nm* **1** paragraph; **2** section mark.

paraître /paʀɛtʀ/ [73] **I** *vi* **1** to come out, to be published; **'à ~'** 'forthcoming titles'; **2** to appear, to seem, to look; **3** [*person, sun*] to appear; [*scar*] to show; **elle ne laisse rien ~ de ses sentiments** she doesn't let her feelings show at all; **4** to appear; **~ en public** to

appear in public; **~ à son avantage** to look one's best.
II *v impers* **il paraît qu'il a menti** apparently he lied; **oui, il paraît** so I hear; **à ce qu'il paraît** apparently.

parallèle[1] /paʀalɛl/ I *adj* **1** parallel (**à** to); **2** [*market, police*] unofficial; [*medicine*] alternative; [*universe*] parallel.
II *nm* **1** parallel; **mettre deux événements en ~** to draw a parallel between two events; **2** (in geography) parallel.

parallèle[2] /paʀalɛl/ *nf* parallel line.

parallèlement /paʀalɛlmɑ̃/ *adv* **1 ~ à** parallel to; **2** at the same time.

parallélisme /paʀalelism/ *nm* **1** parallelism; **2** (Aut) (wheel) alignment.

paralyser /paʀalize/ [1] *vtr* **1** (Med) to paralyse[GB]; **2** to paralyse[GB] [sth]; to bring [sth] to a halt.

paralysie /paʀalizi/ *nf* paralysis; **être frappé de ~** to be paralysed[GB].

paralytique /paʀalitik/ *adj*, *nmf* paralytic.

paramédical, **~e**, *mpl* **-aux** /paʀamedikal, o/ *adj* paramedical.

paramètre /paʀamɛtʀ/ *nm* parameter.

paranoïaque /paʀanɔjak/ *adj*, *nmf* paranoiac.

paranormal, **~e**, *mpl* **-aux** /paʀanɔʀmal, o/ *adj* paranormal.

parapente /paʀapɑ̃t/ *nm* **1** paraglider; **2** paragliding.

paraphe /paʀaf/ *nm* **1** initials; **2** (of pen) flourish; **3** signature.

parapher /paʀafe/ [1] *vtr* **1** to initial; **2** to put a flourish to; **3** to sign.

paraphrase /paʀafʀɑz/ *nf* paraphrase.

paraplégique /paʀapleʒik/ *adj*, *nmf* paraplegic.

parapluie /paʀaplɥi/ *nm* umbrella.

parascolaire /paʀaskɔlɛʀ/ *adj* extracurricular.

parasitaire /paʀazitɛʀ/ *adj* parasitic(al).

parasite /paʀazit/ I *adj* [*organism*] parasitic(al); [*idea*] intrusive.
II *nm* **1** parasite; **2** (on TV, radio) **~s** interference.

parasiter /paʀazite/ [1] *vtr* **1** to live as a parasite on [*plant, animal*]; **2** to cause interference on [*radio, TV*].

parasol /paʀasɔl/ *nm* beach umbrella; sun umbrella.

paratonnerre /paʀatɔnɛʀ/ *nm* lightning rod.

paravent /paʀavɑ̃/ *nm* screen.

parc /paʀk/ *nm* **1** park; **2** playpen; **3** (for animals) pen; **4** (of facilities) (total) number; (of capital goods) stock; **~ automobile** fleet of cars; (nationwide) number of cars (on the road); **~ immobilier** housing stock.
■ **~ d'attractions** amusement or theme park; **~ de loisirs** theme park; **~ national** national park ; **~ naturel** nature park.

parce: **parce que** /paʀs(ə)k(ə)/ *phr* because; **c'est bien ~ que c'est toi!** only because it's you!

parcelle /paʀsɛl/ *nf* **1** plot (of land); **2 une ~ de bonheur** a bit of happiness.

parchemin /paʀʃəmɛ̃/ *nm* parchment.

parcheminé, **~e** /paʀʃəmine/ *adj* **1** [*paper*] with a parchment finish; **2** [*skin*] papery; [*face, hand*] shrivelled[GB].

par-ci /paʀsi/ *adv* **~ par-là** here and there.

parcimonie /paʀsimɔni/ *nf* parsimony.

parcimonieux, **-ieuse** /paʀsimɔnjø, øz/ *adj* sparing; stingy.

parcmètre /paʀkmɛtʀ/ *nm* parking meter.

parcourir /paʀkuʀiʀ/ [26] *vtr* **1** to travel all over [*country*]; **~ la ville** to go all over town; **2** to cover [*distance*]; **le chemin de fer parcourt toute la région** the railway runs right across the region; **3** to glance through [*letter*]; to scan [*horizon*].

parcours /paʀkuʀ/ *nm inv* **1** (of bus, traveller) route; (of river) course; **~ balisé** or **fléché** waymarked trail; **2** (Sport) course; **~ de golf** round of golf; **3** career; **son ~** (of artist) the development of his/her art; **incident de ~** hitch.

par-delà /paʀdəla/ *prep* (literary) beyond.

par-derrière /paʀdɛʀjɛʀ/ *adv* **1 passer ~** to go round (GB) or to the back; **ils m'ont attaqué ~** they attacked me from behind; **2 critiquer qn ~** to criticize sb behind his/her back.

par-dessous /paʀdəsu/ *prep, adv* underneath.

pardessus /paʀdəsy/ *nm inv* overcoat.

par-dessus /paʀdəsy/ I *adv* **1 pose ton sac dans un coin et mets ton manteau ~** put your bag in a corner and put your coat on top of it; **2 le mur n'est pas haut, passe ~** the wall isn't high, climb over it.
II *prep* **1 saute ~ le ruisseau** jump over the stream; **2 ce que j'aime ~ tout** what I like best of all.

par-devant /paʀdəvɑ̃/ *adv* **1 passer ~** to come round by the front; **2 il te fait des sourires ~ mais dit du mal de toi dans ton dos** he's all smiles to your face but says nasty things about you behind your back.

pardon /paʀdɔ̃/ *nm* **1** forgiveness; pardon; **je te demande ~** I'm sorry; **2 ~!** sorry!; **~? qu'est-ce que tu as dit?** sorry, what did you say?; **~ madame/monsieur, je cherche**... excuse me please, I'm looking for...

pardonner /paʀdɔne/ [1] I *vtr* to forgive [*mistake, lapse*]; **pardonnez-moi, mais**... excuse me, but...
II *vi* **ne pas ~** [*illness, error*] to be fatal.
IDIOMS **faute avouée est à moitié pardonnée** (Proverb) a fault confessed is half redressed.

pare-balles /paʀbal/ *adj inv* bulletproof.

pare-brise /paʀbʀiz/ *nm inv* windscreen (GB), windshield (US).

pare-chocs /paʀʃɔk/ *nm inv* bumper.

pareil, **-eille** /paʀɛj/ I *adj* **1** similar; **les deux chapeaux sont presque ~s** the two hats are almost identical; **c'est toujours ~ avec toi** it's always the same with you; **à nul autre ~** without equal; **2** such; **je n'ai jamais dit une**

chose pareille I never said any such thing; **je n'ai jamais rien vu de ~** I've never seen anything like it.

II *nm,f* equal; **un homme sans ~** a man without equal; **d'un dynamisme sans ~** incredibly dynamic; **pour moi c'est du ~ au même**○ it makes no difference to me.

III○ *adv* **1 faire ~** to do the same; **2**○ (Canadian Fr) **je l'ai fait ~** I did it all the same.

pareillement /paʀɛjmɑ̃/ *adv* **1** (in) the same way; **2** too; **vous le pensez et moi ~** you think so and so do I.

parent, **~e** /paʀɑ̃, ɑ̃t/ I *adj* [*languages*] similar (**de** to); **~ avec** [*person*] related to.

II *nm,f* **1** relative, relation; **2** (Zool) parent.

III *nm* **1** parent; **mes ~s** my parents; **2 ~s** forebears.

■ **~ pauvre** poor relation.

parental, **~e**, *mpl* **-aux** /paʀɑ̃tal, o/ *adj* parental.

parenté /paʀɑ̃te/ *nf* **1** (between people) blood relationship; **2** (between projects, stories) connection; **3** relations.

parenthèse /paʀɑ̃tɛz/ *nf* **1** bracket; **ouvrir une ~** (figurative) to digress; **(soit dit) par ~** or **entre ~s** incidentally; **2** interlude.

parer /paʀe/ [1] I *vtr* **1** to ward off; **2** to protect (**contre** against); **3** to adorn; **4 ~ qn/qch de qch** to attribute sth to sb/sth.

II **parer à** *v+prep* **~ à toute éventualité** to be prepared for all contingencies; **~ au plus pressé** to deal with the most urgent matters first.

III **se parer** *v refl* (+ *v être*) **1** to take precautions (**contre** against); **2** to adorn oneself (**de** with); **3 se ~ de** to be bedecked with.

paresse /paʀɛs/ *nf* laziness.

paresser /paʀɛse/ [1] *vi* to laze; to laze around.

paresseux, **-euse** /paʀɛsø, øz/ I *adj* lazy.

II *nm,f* lazy person.

III *nm* (Zool) sloth.

parfaire /paʀfɛʀ/ [10] *vtr* to complete [*education, works*]; to perfect [*technique*].

parfait, **~e** /paʀfɛ, ɛt/ I *adj* **1** perfect; **2** [*likeness*] exact; [*discretion*] absolute; **3** [*tourist*] archetypal; [*example*] classic.

II *nm* (in grammar) perfect.

parfaitement /paʀfɛtmɑ̃/ *adv* [*happy, capable*] perfectly; [*know*] perfectly well; [*tolerate, accept*] fully.

parfois /paʀfwa/ *adv* sometimes.

parfum /paʀfœ̃/ *nm* **1** perfume; **2** (of flower, fruit) scent; (of bath salts) fragrance; (of wine) bouquet; (of coffee) aroma; **3** flavour[GB]; **4 un ~ de scandale** a whiff of scandal.

IDIOMS **mettre qn au ~**○ to put sb in the picture.

parfumé, **~e** /paʀfyme/ I *pp* ▶ **parfumer**.

II *pp adj* **1** [*flower*] sweet-scented; [*tea*] flavoured[GB]; [*fruit, air*] fragrant; **2** [*handkerchief*] scent; **3 glace ~e au café** coffee-flavoured[GB] ice cream.

parfumer /paʀfyme/ [1] I *vtr* **1 les fleurs parfument la pièce** the room is fragrant with flowers; **2** to put scent on [*handkerchief*]; to put scent in [*bath*]; **3** to flavour[GB].

II **se parfumer** *v refl* (+ *v être*) **1** to wear perfume; **2** to put perfume on.

parfumerie /paʀfymʀi/ *nf* perfumery.

pari /paʀi/ *nm* **1** bet; **2** betting; **3** gamble.

parier /paʀje/ [2] *vtr* to bet; **~ qch avec qn** to bet sb sth; **~ sur** to bet on, to back; **il y a fort** or **gros à ~ que** it's a safe bet that; **je l'aurais parié!** I knew it!

parieur, **-ieuse** /paʀjœʀ, øz/ *nm,f* **1** better (GB), bettor (US); **2** gambler.

Paris /paʀi/ *pr n* Paris.

parisien, **-ienne** /paʀizjɛ̃, ɛn/ *adj* Parisian, Paris.

paritaire /paʀitɛʀ/ *adj* joint.

parité /paʀite/ *nf* parity; **à ~** at parity.

parjure /paʀʒyʀ/ I *nmf* perjurer.

II *nm* perjury.

parking /paʀkiŋ/ *nm* car park (GB), parking lot (US).

par-là /paʀla/ *adv* **par-ci ~** here and there.

parlant, **~e** /paʀlɑ̃, ɑ̃t/ *adj* **1** [*gesture*] eloquent; [*comparison*] vivid; [*evidence, result, figure*] which speaks for itself; **2 le cinéma ~** the talkies○; **un film ~** a talking picture; **horloge ~e** speaking clock.

Parlement /paʀləmɑ̃/ *nm* Parliament.

parlementaire /paʀləmɑ̃tɛʀ/ I *adj* parliamentary.

II *nmf* **1** Member of Parliament; **2** negotiator.

parlementer /paʀləmɑ̃te/ [1] *vi* to negotiate.

parler[1] /paʀle/ [1] I *vtr* **1** to speak; **~ (l')italien** to speak Italian; **2 ~ affaires/politique** to talk (about) business/politics.

II **parler à** *v+prep* **~ à qn** to talk or speak to sb; **moi qui vous parle, je n'aurais jamais cru ça**○! I'm telling you, I'd never have believed it!

III **parler de** *v+prep* **1 ~ de qch/qn** to talk about sth/sb (**à qn, avec qn** to sb); to mention sth/sb; **~ de tout et de rien, ~ de choses et d'autres** to talk about this and that; **les journaux en ont parlé** it was in the papers; **faire ~ de soi** to get oneself talked about; to make the news; **on en parle** there's talk of it; **qui parle de vous expulser?** who said anything about throwing you out?; **ta promesse, parlons-en!** some promise!; **n'en parlons plus!** let's drop it; that's the end of it; **il va ~ de toi à son chef** he'll put in a word for you with his boss; **on m'a beaucoup parlé de vous** I've heard a lot about you; **je ne veux pas qu'on m'en parle** I don't want to hear about it; **2 ~ de** [*book, film*] to be about.

IV *vi* **1** to talk, to speak; **~ vite/en russe** to speak or talk fast/in Russian; **parle plus fort** speak up, speak louder; **2** to speak; **économiquement parlant** economically speaking; **~ en connaissance de cause** to know what one is talking about; **une prime? tu parles**○! a bonus? you must be joking○!; **tu parles si je viens**○! you bet I'm coming○!; **3** to talk; **~ pour ne rien dire** to talk for the sake of talking; **il s'écoute ~** he loves the sound of his own voice; **parlons peu mais parlons bien** let's get down to business.

V se parler *v refl* (+ *v être*) **1** to talk or speak (to each other); **2** to be on speaking terms; **3** to be spoken.

IDIOMS **trouver à qui ~** to meet one's match.

parler² /paʀle/ *nm* **1** way of talking; **2** dialect.

parloir /paʀlwaʀ/ *nm* (in school, hospital) visitors' room; (in prison) visiting room; (in convent) parlour[GB].

parme /paʀm/ *adj inv, nm* mauve.

Parmentier /paʀmɑ̃tje/ *pr n* **hachis ~** cottage pie, shepherd's pie.

parmi /paʀmi/ *prep* **1** among, amongst; **2 demain il sera ~ nous** he'll be with us tomorrow; **3 choisir ~ huit destinations** to choose from eight destinations.

parodie /paʀɔdi/ *nf* **1** parody; **2** mockery; **une ~ de procès** a travesty of justice.

parodier /paʀɔdje/ [2] *vtr* to parody.

paroi /paʀwa/ *nf* **1** (of tunnel) side; (of cave) wall; (of tube, pipe) inner surface; **2** (of house) wall; **3 ~ rocheuse** rock face; **la ~ nord** the north face; **4** (Anat) wall; **~ utérine** uterine wall.

paroisse /paʀwas/ *nf* parish.

paroissial, ~e, *mpl* **-iaux** /paʀwasjal, o/ *adj* parish.

paroissien, -ienne /paʀwasjɛ̃, ɛn/ *nm,f* parishioner.

parole /paʀɔl/ *nf* **1** speech; **avoir la ~ facile** to have the gift of the gab○; **2 avoir droit à la ~** to have the right to speak; **laisser la ~ à qn** to let sb speak; **temps de ~** speaking time; **3** word; **~s en l'air** empty words; **une ~ blessante** a hurtful remark; **sur ces bonnes ~s, je m'en vais** on that (philosophical) note, I'm off; **4** word; **donner sa ~** to give one's word; **tenir ~** to keep one's word; **~ d'honneur!** cross my heart!, I promise!; **ma ~!** (upon) my word!; **5** words; **c'est ~ d'évangile** it's gospel truth; **~s** words, lyrics; **film sans ~s** silent film.

parolier, -ière /paʀɔlje, ɛʀ/ *nm,f* **1** lyric writer; **2** librettist.

paroxysme /paʀɔksism/ *nm* (of pleasure) paroxysm; (of battle) climax; (of ridiculousness) height.

parquer /paʀke/ [1] *vtr* **1** to pen [*cattle*]; **2** to coop up [*people*]; **3** to park [*car*].

parquet /paʀkɛ/ *nm* **1** parquet (floor); **2** (Law) **le ~** ≈ the prosecution.

parrain /paʀɛ̃/ *nm* **1** godfather; **2** (of candidate) sponsor; (of organization) patron.

parrainage /paʀɛnaʒ/ *nm* (of candidate, project) sponsorship; (of organization) patronage.

parrainer /paʀene/ [1] *vtr* **1** to be patron of [*organization*]; **2** to sponsor [*programme, race*].

parricide /paʀisid/ *nm* parricide.

parsemer /paʀsəme/ [16] *vtr* **parsemez-la de persil haché** sprinkle some chopped parsley over it; **une pelouse parsemée de fleurs** a lawn dotted with flowers.

part /paʀ/ **I** *nf* **1** (of cake) slice; (of meat, rice) helping; (of market, legacy) share; **vouloir une ~ du gâteau** to want a slice or share of the cake; **avoir sa ~ de misères** to have one's (fair) share of misfortunes; **2** proportion; **une grande ~ de** a high proportion or large part of; **une ~ de chance** an element of chance; **pour une bonne** or **grande ~** to a large or great extent; **à ~ entière** [*member*] full; [*science*] in its own right; **3** share; **faire sa ~ de travail** to do one's share of the work; **prendre ~ à** to take part in; **il m'a fait ~ de ses projets** he told me about his plans; **faire ~ d'une naissance** to announce a birth; **4 de toute(s) ~(s)** from all sides; **de ~ et d'autre** on both sides, on either side; **de ~ en ~** [*pierce*] right or straight through; **5 pour ma/notre ~** for my/our part; **d'une ~..., d'autre ~...** on (the) one hand... on the other hand; **prendre qch en bonne/mauvaise ~** to take sth in good part/take sth badly.

II à part *phr* **1** [*file*] separately; **mettre qch à ~** to put sth to one side; **prendre qn à ~** to take sb aside or to one side; **2 une salle à ~** a separate room; **blague à ~** joking aside; **3 être un peu à ~** [*person*] to be out of the ordinary; **un cas à ~** a special case; **4** apart from; **à ~ ça, quoi de neuf○?** apart from that, what's new?

III de la part de *phr* **1 de la ~ de** [*write, act*] on behalf of; **2 de la ~ de qn** from sb; **donne-leur le bonjour de ma ~** say hello to them for me; **sans engagement de votre ~** with no obligation on your part; **de leur ~, rien ne m'étonne** nothing they do surprises me.

IDIOMS **faire la ~ des choses** to put things in perspective.

partage /paʀtaʒ/ *nm* **1** dividing, sharing; **recevoir qch en ~** to be left sth (in a will); **2** distribution; **3** sharing (**de** with), division (**de** with); **régner/gouverner sans ~** to reign/to govern absolutely; **une victoire sans ~** a total victory; **4** division (**en** into), partition (**en** into).

■ **~ de poste** job sharing

partagé, ~e /paʀtaʒe/ **I** *pp* ▶ **partager.**

II *pp adj* **1** [*opinion, unions*] divided (**sur** on); **2** [*reactions, feelings*] mixed; **3 être ~** to be torn (**entre** between); **4** [*grief*] shared; **les torts sont ~s** they are both to blame; **5** [*affection*] mutual; **amour ~** requited love.

partager /paʀtaʒe/ [13] **I** *vtr* **1** to share [*toys, food*]; **2** to divide [*country, room*]; **3** to divide [sth] (up), to split [*inheritance, estate, work*]; **4** to share; **ils partagent le même goût de l'aventure** they share a love of adventure; **faire ~ qch à qn** to let sb share in sth; **il sait nous faire ~ ses émotions** he knows how to get his feelings across; **5** [*issue*] to divide, to split [*public opinion*].

II se partager *v refl* (+ *v être*) **1** to share [*money, work, responsibility*]; **2** to be divided (**en** into), to be split (**en** into); **3** [*costs, responsibility*] to be shared; [*cake*] to be cut (up) (**en** into).

partance /paʀtɑ̃s/ *nf* **en ~** about to take off;

about to sail; about to leave; **être en ~ pour** or **vers** to be bound for.

partant°, **~e** /paʀtɑ̃, ɑ̃t/ *adj* **être ~** to be game° (**pour faire** to do).

partenaire /paʀtənɛʀ/ I *nmf* partner; **qui était le ~ d'Arletty?** who played opposite Arletty?

II *nm* partner; **nos ~s de l'UE** our partners in the EU.

partenariat /paʀtənaʀja/ *nm* partnership.

parterre /paʀtɛʀ/ *nm* **1** (in garden) bed; **2** stalls (GB), orchestra (US); **3 un ~ de journalistes** a panel of journalists.

parti, **~e**[1] /paʀti/ I° *adj* **être ~** to be tight°.

II *nm* **1** group; party; **les ~s de l'opposition** the opposition parties; **2** option; **prendre ~** to commit oneself; **prendre ~ contre qn** to side against sb; **prendre le ~ de qn** to side with sb; **prendre le ~ de qch** to opt for sth; **3**† **bon ~** suitable match.

■ **~ pris** bias; **~ pris de réalisme** bias toward(s) realism.

IDIOMS **prendre son ~ de qch** to come to terms with sth; **tirer ~ de** to take advantage of [sth]; to turn [sth] to good account.

partial, **~e**, *mpl* **-iaux** /paʀsjal, o/ *adj* biased[GB].

partialité /paʀsjalite/ *nf* bias.

participant, **~e** /paʀtisipɑ̃, ɑ̃t/ *nm,f* participant (**à** in).

participation /paʀtisipasjɔ̃/ *nf* **1** participation (**à** in); involvement (**à** in); **2** contribution; **~ aux frais** (financial) contribution.

■ **~ aux bénéfices** profit-sharing.

participe /paʀtisip/ *nm* participle; **~ passé** past participle.

participer: **participer à** /paʀtisipe/ [1] *v+prep* **1 ~ à** to participate in, to take part in; to be involved in; **~ à la joie de qn** to share sb's joy; **2 ~ à** to contribute to; **~ aux bénéfices** to share in the profits.

particularité /paʀtikylaʀite/ *nf* **1** special feature; **2** (of disease, situation) particular nature; (of custom) uniqueness.

particule /paʀtikyl/ *nf* particle; **nom à ~** aristocratic name.

particulier, **-ière** /paʀtikylje, ɛʀ/ I *adj* **1** particular; **il a ceci de ~ qu'il aime son indépendance** the thing is with him that he likes his independence; **2** [*rights, privileges, role*] special; [*example, objective*] specific; **3** [*car, secretary*] private; **4** [*case, situation*] unusual; [*talent, effort*] special; [*habits*] odd; [*accent, style*] distinctive, unusual; **c'est quelqu'un de très ~** he's/she's somebody out of the ordinary; he's/she's weird.

II **en particulier** *phr* **1** in private; **2** individually; **3** in particular, particularly.

III *nm* (**simple**) **~** private individual; **vendre de ~ à ~** to sell privately.

particulièrement /paʀtikyljɛʀmɑ̃/ *adv* **1** particularly, exceptionally; **2** particularly, in particular.

partie[2] /paʀti/ I *adj f* ▶ **parti** I.

II *nf* **1** part; (of amount, salary) proportion, part; **la majeure ~ des gens** most people; **en ~** partly, in part; **en grande ~** to a large or great extent; **faire ~ des premiers** to be among the first; **cela fait ~ de leurs avantages** that's one of their advantages; **faire ~ intégrante de qch** to be an integral part of sth; **il a plu une ~ de la journée** it rained for part of the day; **2** line (of work); **il est de la ~** it's in his line (of work); **3** game; **une ~ de tennis** a game of tennis; **faire une ~** to have a game; **gagner la ~** to win the game; to win the day; **je fête mes trente ans, j'espère que tu seras de la ~** I'm having a thirtieth birthday party, I hope you can come; **ce n'est que ~ remise** maybe next time; **4** (in contract, negotiations) party; **les ~s en présence** the parties involved; **être ~ prenante dans** to be actively involved in; **5** (Mus) part.

■ **~ de chasse** hunting party; **~ civile** plaintiff; **~ de pêche** fishing trip; **~ de plaisir** fun.

IDIOMS **avoir affaire à forte ~** to have a tough opponent; **prendre qn à ~** to take sb to task.

partiel, **-ielle** /paʀsjɛl/ *adj* [*payment*] part; [*destruction, agreement*] partial; **des solutions partielles** incomplete solutions.

partiellement /paʀsjɛlmɑ̃/ *adv* partly, partially.

partir /paʀtiʀ/ [30] I *vi* (+ *v être*) **1** to leave, to go; **~ à pied** to leave on foot; **j'espère que je ne vous fais pas ~?** I hope I'm not driving you away?; **~ en courant** to run off; **~ sans laisser d'adresse** to disappear without trace; **2** to go; **~ loin/à Paris** to go far away/to Paris; **~ en week-end** to go away for the weekend; **~ à la pêche** to go fishing; **elle est partie se reposer** she's gone for a rest; **~ en tournée** to set off on tour (GB) or on a tour; **~ en retraite** to retire; **3** [*person, vehicle, train*] to leave; [*plane*] to take off; [*motor*] to start; **je pars** I'm off, I'm leaving; **les coureurs sont partis** the runners are off; **à vos marques, prêts, partez!** on your marks, get set, go!; **4** [*bullet, arrow*] to be fired; [*cork*] to shoot out; [*capsule*] to shoot off; [*retort*] to slip out; **le coup de feu est parti** the gun went off; **il était tellement énervé que la gifle est partie toute seule** he was so angry that he slapped him/her before he could stop himself; **5** [*path, road*] to start; **~ favori** to start favourite[GB]; **~ battu d'avance** to be doomed from the start; **~ de rien** to start from nothing; **c'est parti!** go!; **et voilà, c'est parti, il pleut°!** here we go, it's raining!; **être bien parti** to have got (GB) or gotten (US) off to a good start; **être bien parti pour gagner** to seem all set to win; **c'est mal parti°** things don't look too good, it doesn't look too promising; **il a l'air parti pour réussir°** he seems to be heading for success; **6 ~ de** to start from [*idea*]; **~ du principe que** to work on the assumption that; **~ d'une bonne intention** to be well-meant; **7** [*stain*] to come out; [*smell*] to go; [*enamel, button*] to come off; **8** [*parcel, application*] to be sent (off); **9 quand il est parti on ne l'arrête plus°** once he starts or gets going there's no stopping him; **~ dans des explications** to launch into explanations.

II à partir de *phr* from; **à ~ de 16 heures/de 2 000 francs** from 4 o'clock onwards/2,000 francs; **à ~ du moment où** as soon as; as long as; **les enfants ne sont admis qu'à ~ de huit ans** children under eight are not admitted; **fabriqué à ~ d'un alliage** made from an alloy; **faire une étude à ~ de statistiques** to base a study on statistics.

partisan, **~e** /partizɑ̃, an/ **I** *adj* **1** partisan; **2 ~ de qch/de faire** in favour[GB] of sth/of doing; **être ~ du moindre effort**○ to be lazy; to go for the easy option.

II *nm,f* (gen) supporter, partisan; (Mil) partisan.

partitif, **-ive** /partitif, iv/ *adj* partitive.

partition /partisjɔ̃/ *nf* (Mus) score.

partout /partu/ *adv* **1** everywhere; **avoir mal ~** to be sore all over; **un peu ~ dans le monde** more or less all over the world; **~ où je vais** wherever I go; **2 il est le premier ~** he's the best at everything; **3** (Sport) **trois (points** or **buts) ~** three all.

IDIOMS **fourrer son nez ~**○ to stick one's nose into everything○.

parure /paryr/ *nf* **1** finery; **2** set of jewels; **3** set; **~ de table** set of table linen.

parution /parysjɔ̃/ *nf* publication (**de** of).

parvenir: **parvenir à** /parvənir/ [36] *v+prep* (+ *v être*) **1 ~ à** to reach [*place, stage, person*]; **faire ~ qch à qn** to send sth to sb; to get sth to sb; **2 ~ à** to reach [*agreement, solution*]; to achieve [*balance, objective*]; **3 ~ à faire** to manage to do.

parvenu, **~e** /parvəny/ *nm,f* upstart.

parvis /parvi/ *nm inv* (of church) square.

pas[1] /pa/ *adv* **1 je ne prends ~ de sucre** I don't take sugar; **ils n'ont ~ le téléphone** they haven't got a phone; **il n'y a ~ de café dans le placard** there isn't any coffee in the cupboard; **ce n'est ~ une raison pour crier comme ça!** that's no reason to shout like that!; **je ne pense ~** I don't think so; **elle a aimé le film, mais lui ~** she liked the film but he didn't; **2** (in expressions, exclamations) **~ du tout** not at all; **~ le moins du monde** not in the least; **~ vraiment** not really; **~ tant que ça, ~ plus que ça** not all that much; **~ d'histoires!** I don't want any arguments or fuss!; **~ de chance!** hard luck!; **~ possible!** I can't believe it!; **~ vrai**○**?** isn't that so?

pas[2] /pa/ *nm inv* **1** step; **l'hiver arrive à grands ~** winter is fast approaching; **marcher à ~ de loup** to move stealthily; **marcher à ~ feutrés** to walk softly; **faire ses premiers ~** to take one's first steps; **faire le premier ~** to make the first move; **suivre qn ~ à ~** to follow sb everywhere; **de là à dire qu'il s'en fiche**○**, il n'y a qu'un ~** there's only a fine line between that and saying he doesn't care; **j'habite à deux ~ (d'ici)** I live very near here; **2** pace; **marcher d'un bon ~** to walk at a brisk pace; **ralentir le ~** to slow down; **marcher au ~** to march; (on horseback) to walk; **'roulez au ~'** 'dead slow' (GB), '(very) slow' (US); **mettre qn au ~** to bring sb to heel; **partir au ~ de course** to rush off; **j'y vais de ce ~** I'm on my way now; **3** footstep; **4** footprint; **revenir sur ses ~** to retrace one's steps; **marcher sur les ~ de qn** to follow in sb's footsteps; **5** step; **apprendre les ~ du tango** to learn how to tango.

IDIOMS **se tirer d'un mauvais ~** to get out of a tight corner; **faire** or **sauter le ~** to take the plunge; **prendre le ~ sur qch/qn** to overtake sth/sb.

pascal, **~e**, *mpl* **~s** or **-aux** /paskal, o/ **I** *adj* [*weekend*] Easter; [*candle, lamb*] paschal.

II *nm* pascal.

passable /pasabl/ *adj* **1** [*film, party*] fairly good; [*production, results*] reasonable; **2** (Sch) (in assessment) fair.

passablement /pasabləmɑ̃/ *adv* [*drunk, annoyed*] rather; [*drink, worry*] quite a lot.

passage /pasaʒ/ *nm* **1** traffic; **interdire le ~ des camions dans la ville** to ban trucks from (driving through) the town; **une rue où il y a beaucoup de ~** a street where there's a lot of traffic; **2** stay; **ton ~ dans la ville a été bref** your stay in the town was brief; **après un bref ~ dans la fonction publique** after a short spell in the civil service; **3 attendre le ~ du boulanger** to wait for the baker's van to come; **je peux te prendre au ~** I can pick you up on the way; **des hôtes de ~** short-stay guests; **se servir au ~** to help oneself; (figurative) to take a cut (of the profits); to pocket some of the profits; **4 '~ interdit, voie privée'** 'no entry, private road'; **pour empêcher le ~ de l'air** in order to prevent draughts (GB) or drafts (US); **pour céder le ~ à l'ambulance** in order to let the ambulance go past; **5 leur troisième ~ à l'Olympia** the third time they've played the Olympia; **chaque ~ de votre chanson à la radio** every time your song is played on the radio; **6** (of person) way; (of avalanche, lava) path; **barrer le ~ à qn** to bar sb's way; **prévoir le ~ de câbles** to plan the route of cables; **7** transition (from sth) to sth; **~ à la phase suivante** progression to the next phase; **8** alley; passageway; **9** (in novel, symphony) passage; (in film) sequence.

■ **~ à l'acte** acting out; **~ à niveau** level crossing (GB), grade crossing (US); **~ pour piétons** pedestrian crossing; **~ à tabac** beating; **~ à vide** bad patch; unproductive period.

passager, **-ère** /pasaʒe, ɛr/ **I** *adj* [*situation, crisis*] temporary; [*feeling*] passing; [*shower*] brief; [*unease*] slight, short-lived; [*affair*] fleeting.

II *nm,f* passenger; **~ clandestin** stowaway.

passant, **~e** /pasɑ̃, ɑ̃t/ **I** *adj* [*street*] busy.

II *nm,f* passer-by.

III *nm* (on belt, watchstrap) loop.

passe[1]○ /pɑs/ *nm* **1** master key; **2** pass.

passe[2] /pɑs/ *nf* **1** (Sport) pass; **2** (of conjurer, bullfighter) pass; **3 être dans une ~ difficile** to be going through a difficult patch; **être en ~ de faire** to be (well) on the way to doing.

passé, ~e /pɑse/ I *pp* ▶ **passer**.
II *pp adj* **1** [*years, experiences*] past; **~ de mode** dated; **il était cinq heures ~es** it was past five o'clock; **2 l'année passée** last year; **3** [*colour, material*] faded.
III *nm* **1** past; **dans** or **par le ~** in the past; **2** past (tense).
IV *prep* after; **~ 8 heures il s'endort dans son fauteuil** come eight o'clock he goes to sleep in his armchair.
■ **~ antérieur** past anterior; **~ composé** present perfect; **~ simple** past historic.

passe-droit, *pl* **~s** /pasdʀwɑ/ *nm* preferential treatment.

passe-montagne, *pl* **~s** /pasmɔ̃taɲ/ *nm* balaclava.

passe-partout /paspaʀtu/ I *adj inv* [*expression*] catch-all; [*garment*] for all occasions.
II *nm inv* **1** master key; **2** two-man saw; **3** mount.

passe-passe /paspas/ *nm inv* **tour de ~** conjuring trick; (figurative) sleight of hand.

passe-plat, *pl* **~s** /paspla/ *nm* serving hatch.

passeport /paspɔʀ/ *nm* passport.

passer /pɑse/ [1] I *vtr* **1** to cross [*river, border*]; to go through [*door, customs*]; to get over [*hedge, obstacle*]; **il m'a fait ~ la frontière** he got me across the border; **2 ~ qch à la douane** to get sth through customs; **3** to go past, to pass; **quand vous aurez passé le feu, tournez à droite** turn right after the lights; **le malade ne passera pas la nuit** the patient won't last the night; **4 ~ le doigt sur la table** to run one's finger over the table-top; **~ la tête à la fenêtre** to stick one's head out of the window; **elle m' a passé le bras autour des épaules** she put her arm around my shoulders; **5** to pass [*object*] (**à** to); to pass [sth] on [*instructions, disease*] (**à** to); **~ sa colère sur ses collègues** to take one's anger out on one's colleagues; **6** to lend; to give; **7 tu peux me ~ Chris?** can you put Chris on?; **je vous le passe** I'm putting you through; **8** to take, to sit [*examination*]; to have [*interview*]; **faire ~ un test à qn** to give sb a test; **9** to spend [*time*] (**à faire** doing); **dépêche-toi, on ne va pas y ~ la nuit**○! hurry up, or we'll be here all night!; **10 elle leur passe tout** she lets them get away with murder; **passez-moi l'expression** if you'll pardon the expression; **11** to skip [*page, paragraph*]; **je vous passe les détails** I'll spare you the details; **j'en passe et des meilleures**○ and so on and so forth, I could go on; **12 ~ l'aspirateur** to vacuum; **13** to filter [*coffee*]; to strain [*fruit juice, sauce*]; to purée [*vegetables*]; **14** to slip [sth] on [*garment, ring*]; to slip into [*dress*]; **15** to play [*record, cassette*]; to show [*film, slides*]; to place [*ad*] (**dans** in); **16** to sign [*contract*]; to enter into [*agreement*]; to place [*order*]; to pass [*law, decree*]; **17** (Aut) **~ la troisième/la marche arrière** to go into third gear/into reverse; **18** (Games) **~ son tour** to pass.
II *vi* (+ *v être*) **1** to go past or by, to pass; **~ sur un pont** to go over a bridge; **l'autobus vient juste de ~** the bus has just gone; **le facteur n'est pas encore passé** the postman hasn't come yet; **~ à côté de** [*person*] to pass; [*road*] to run alongside; **nous sommes passés près de chez toi** we were near your house; **~ à pied/à bicyclette** to walk/cycle past; **2 je ne fais que ~** I've just popped in (GB) or dropped by for a minute; **il est passé déposer un dossier** he came by to drop off a file; **~ dans la matinée** [*plumber*] to come by in the morning; **passe nous voir** come and see us; **~ prendre qn/qch** to pick sb/sth up; **3** to go; **passons au salon** let's go into the lounge; **les contrebandiers sont passés en Espagne** the smugglers have crossed into Spain; **4** to get through; **tu ne passeras pas, c'est trop étroit** you'll never get through, it's too narrow; **il est passé au rouge** he went through the red lights; **il m'a fait signe de ~** he waved me on; **vas-y, ça passe!** go on, there's plenty of room!; **~ par-dessus bord** to fall overboard; **il est passé par la fenêtre** he fell out of the window; he got in through the window; **5 ~ par** to go through; **nous sommes passés par Édimbourg** we went via Edinburgh; **~ par l'opératrice** to go through the operator; **je ne sais jamais ce qui te passe par la tête** I never know what's going on in your head; **des reptiles à l'homme, en passant par le singe** from reptiles to man, including apes; **6**○ **il accuse le patron, ses collègues, bref, tout le monde y passe** he's accusing the boss, his colleagues — basically, everyone in sight; **que ça te plaise ou non, il va falloir y ~** whether you like it or not, there's no alternative; **on ne peut pas faire autrement que d'en ~ par là** there is no other way around it; **je sais, j'en suis déjà passé par là** I know all about that, I've been there○; **7 ~ sur** to pass over [*question, mistake*]; **je préfère ~ sur ce point** I'd rather not dwell on that point; **~ à côté d'une question** to miss the point; **laisser ~ qch** to overlook sth; **laisser ~ une occasion** to miss an opportunity; **8 notons en passant que** we should note in passing that; **soit dit en ~** incidentally; **9** [*comments, speech*] to go down well; [*law, measure, candidate*] to get through; [*attitude, doctrine*] to be accepted; **je ne me sens pas bien, ce doit être le concombre qui passe mal** I don't feel well, it must be the cucumber; **que je sois critiqué, passe encore, mais calomnié, non!** criticism is one thing, but I draw the line at slander; **~ au premier tour** to be elected in the first round; **~ dans la classe supérieure** to move up to the next year; **(ça) passe pour cette fois**○ I'll let it go this time; **10 ~ à l'ennemi** to go over to the enemy; **~ sous contrôle de l'ONU** to be taken over by the UN; **~ de main en main** to be passed around; **~ constamment d'un sujet à l'autre** to flit from one subject to another; **~ à un taux supérieur** to go up to a higher rate; **11 ~ pour un imbécile** to look a fool; **~ pour un génie** to pass as a genius; **~ pour de l'intelligence** to pass for intelligence; **il passe pour l'inventeur de l'ordinateur** he's supposed to have invented computers; **se faire ~ pour malade** to pretend to be ill; **il se fait ~ pour mon frère** he passes himself off as my

brother; **12** [*pain, crisis*] to pass; **quand l'orage sera** or **aura passé** when the storm is over; **ça passera** [*bad mood*] it'll pass; [*hurt*] you'll get over it; **la première réaction passée** once we/they calmed down; **~ de mode** to go out of fashion; **cette mode est vite passée** that fashion was short-lived; **faire ~ à qn l'envie de faire** to cure sb of the desire to do; **ce médicament fait ~ les maux d'estomac** this medicine relieves stomach ache; **cette mauvaise habitude te passera** it's a bad habit you'll grow out of; **13** [*performer, group*] (on stage) to be appearing; (on TV, radio) to be on; [*show, film*] to be on; [*music*] to be playing; **14 ~ avant/après** to come before/after; **la santé passe avant tout** health comes first; **il fait ~ sa famille avant ses amis** he puts his family before his friends; **15**° **où étais-tu (encore) passé?** where (on earth) did you get to?; **où est passé mon livre?** where has my book got to?; **16** [*time*] to pass, to go by; **je ne vois pas le temps ~** I don't know where the time goes; **17** to turn to; **passons aux choses sérieuses** let's turn to serious matters; **~ à l'étape suivante** to move on to the next stage; **nous allons ~ au vote** let's vote now; **~ à l'offensive** to take the offensive; **18 ~ de père en fils** to be handed down from father to son; **l'expression est passée dans la langue** the expression has become part of the language; **ça finira par ~ dans les mœurs** it'll eventually become common practice; **19** to be promoted to; **elle est passée maître dans l'art de mentir** she's an accomplished liar; **20** [*money, amount*] to go on or into; [*product, material*] to go into; **toutes mes économies y sont passées** all my savings went into it; **21**° **y ~** to die; **22** [*colour, material*] to fade; **~ au soleil** to fade in the sun; **23** [*coffee*] to filter; **24 ~ en marche arrière** to go into reverse; **la troisième passe mal** third gear is a bit stiff; **~ de seconde en troisième** to go from second into third; **25** (in bridge, poker) to pass.

III se passer *v refl* (+ *v être*) **1** to happen; **tout se passe comme si le franc avait été dévalué** it's as if the franc had been devalued; **2** to take place; **la scène se passe au Vietnam** the scene is set in Vietnam; **3** [*examination, negotiations*] to go; **tout s'est passé très vite** it all happened very fast; **ça va mal se ~ pour toi** you're going to be in trouble; **ça ne se passera pas comme ça!** I won't leave it at that!; **4** [*period*] to go by, to pass; **deux ans se sont passés depuis** that was two years ago; **nos soirées se passaient à regarder la télévision** we spent the evenings watching television; **5 se ~ de** to do without [*object, activity, person*]; to go without [*meal, sleep*]; **se ~ de commentaires** to speak for itself; **6 se ~ la langue sur les lèvres** to run one's tongue over one's lips; **se ~ la main sur le front** to put a hand to one's forehead; **7 ils se sont passé des documents** they exchanged some documents.

IDIOMS **qu'est-ce qu'elle nous a passé**°! she really went for us°!

passereau, *pl* **~x** /pasʀo/ *nm* passerine.

passerelle /pasʀɛl/ *nf* **1** footbridge; **2** link (**entre** between); **3** (to boat) gangway; (to plane) steps.

passe-temps /pastɑ̃/ *nm inv* pastime, hobby.

passeur, **-euse** /pasœʀ, øz/ *nm,f* **1** ferryman/ferrywoman; **2** smuggler; (for drugs) courier, mule°; **3** (Sport) passer.

passible /pasibl/ *adj* (Law) **~ de** [*crime*] punishable by; [*person*] liable to.

passif, **-ive** /pasif, iv/ **I** *adj* passive.

II *nm* **1** passive (voice); **2** debit; **mettre qch au ~ de qn** to count sth amongst sb's failures.

passion /pasjɔ̃/ *nf* passion; **avec ~** passionately; **sans ~** dispassionately; without enthusiasm.

Passion /pasjɔ̃/ *nf* Passion.

passionnant, **~e** /pasjɔnɑ̃, ɑ̃t/ *adj* exciting, fascinating, riveting.

passionné, **~e** /pasjɔne/ **I** *adj* [*love*] passionate; [*debate, argument*] impassioned; **être ~ de** or **pour qch** to have a passion for sth.

II *nm,f* enthusiast.

passionnel, **-elle** /pasjɔnɛl/ *adj* [*debate*] passionate; [*crime*] of passion.

passionnément /pasjɔnemɑ̃/ *adv* passionately.

passionner /pasjɔne/ [1] **I** *vtr* **1** to fascinate; **la botanique le passionne** he has a passion for botany; **2** to inflame [*debate*].

II se passionner *v refl* (+ *v être*) to have a passion (**pour** for).

passivité /pasivite/ *nf* passivity.

passoire /paswaʀ/ *nf* **1** colander; **2** strainer.

pastel /pastɛl/ **I** *adj inv* [*shade*] pastel; **bleu ~** pastel blue.

II *nm* pastel.

pastèque /pastɛk/ *nf* watermelon.

pasteur /pastœʀ/ *nm* **1** minister, pastor; **2** priest; **3** shepherd.

pasteuriser /pastœʀize/ [1] *vtr* to pasteurize.

pastiche /pastiʃ/ *nm* pastiche.

pastille /pastij/ *nf* **1** pastille, lozenge; **~ contre la toux** cough drop; **2 ~ de chocolat** chocolate drop; **~ de menthe** peppermint; **3** spot; **4** (of cloth, rubber) patch; (of plastic) disc.

pastoral, **~e**[1], *mpl* **-aux** /pastɔʀal, o/ *adj* pastoral.

pastorale[2] /pastɔʀal/ *nf* (Mus) pastoral.

patate /patat/ *nf* **1**° spud°; **~ douce** sweet potato; **2**° blockhead°, idiot.

IDIOMS **ça m'est resté sur la ~**° it left me feeling bitter.

patati° /patati/ *excl* **~, patata** and so on and so forth.

pataud, **~e** /pato, od/ *adj* clumsy.

pataugeoire /patoʒwaʀ/ *nf* paddling pool (GB), baby pool (US).

patauger /patoʒe/ [13] *vi* **1** to splash about; to paddle; **2** to flounder.

pâte /pɑt/ **I** *nf* **1** pastry; dough; batter; **2** paste.

II pâtes *nf pl* **~s (alimentaires)** pasta.

■ **~ d'amandes** marzipan; **~ à beignets** batter; **~s de fruit(s)** fruit jellies; **~ à**

modeler modelling[GB] clay, Plasticine®; **~ à tartiner** spread.
IDIOMS **mettre la main à la ~** to pitch in.
pâté /pɑte/ *nm* **1** pâté; **~ de campagne** farmhouse pâté (GB), coarse pâté; **2** pie; **~ en croûte** ≈ pie; **3 ~ de maisons** block (of houses); **4** (ink)blot; **5** sandcastle.
pâtée /pɑte/ *nf* dog food; cat food; swill.
patelin○ /patlɛ̃/ *nm* small village.
patente /patɑ̃t/ *nf*: *licence*[GB] *to exercise a trade or profession.*
patenté, **~e** /patɑ̃te/ *adj* licensed, authorized.
patère /patɛʀ/ *nf* peg, hook.
paternel, **-elle** /patɛʀnɛl/ *adj* **1** paternal; **mon oncle ~** my paternal uncle; **2** fatherly.
paternité /patɛʀnite/ *nf* **1** fatherhood; (Law) paternity; **2** authorship.
pâteux, **-euse** /pɑtø, øz/ *adj* **1** [*substance*] doughy; [*gruel*] mushy; **2** [*voice*] thick; **j'ai la bouche pâteuse** my mouth feels all furry.
pathétique /patetik/ *adj* moving.
pathologie /patɔlɔʒi/ *nf* pathology.
pathologique /patɔlɔʒik/ *adj* pathological.
patibulaire /patibylɛʀ/ *adj* sinister-looking.
patiemment /pasjamɑ̃/ *adv* patiently.
patience /pasjɑ̃s/ *nf* **1** patience; **2** (Games) patience (GB), solitaire (US).
IDIOMS **prendre son mal en ~** to resign oneself to one's fate.
patient, **~e** /pasjɑ̃, ɑ̃t/ *adj, nm,f* patient.
patienter /pasjɑ̃te/ [1] *vi* to wait; **faire ~ qn** to make sb wait.
patin /patɛ̃/ *nm* **1** skate; **2** (Tech) (on piece of furniture) furniture glide; (on helicopter) skid; (on sledge) runner.
■ **~ à glace** ice skate; ice-skating; **~ de frein** (Aut) brake block; **~ à roulettes** roller skate; roller-skating.
patinage /patinaʒ/ *nm* skating.
patine /patin/ *nf* patina; finish, sheen.
patiner /patine/ [1] **I** *vtr* to apply a finish to.
II *vi* **1** to skate; **2** (Aut) [*wheel*] to spin; [*clutch*] to slip; **faire ~ l'embrayage** to slip the clutch.
III se patiner *v refl* (+ *v être*) to acquire a patina.
patineur, **-euse** /patinœʀ, øz/ *nm,f* skater.
patinoire /patinwaʀ/ *nf* ice rink.
pâtir /pɑtiʀ/ [3] *vi* **~ de** to suffer as a result of.
pâtisserie /pɑtisʀi/ *nf* **1** cake shop, pâtisserie; **2** pastry, cake.
pâtissier, **-ière** /pɑtisje, ɛʀ/ *nm,f* confectioner, pastry cook.
patois /patwa/ *nm inv* patois, dialect.
patraque○ /patʀak/ *adj* **être ~** to be under the weather○.
patriarcal, **~e**, *mpl* **-aux** /patʀijaʀkal, o/ *adj* patriarchal.
patriarche /patʀijaʀʃ/ *nm* patriarch.
patrie /patʀi/ *nf* homeland, country.
patrimoine /patʀimwan/ *nm* **1** (of person, family) patrimony; (of firm) capital; **~ immobilier** property holdings; **2** heritage.
■ **~ génétique** gene pool.
patriote /patʀijɔt/ **I** *adj* patriotic.
II *nmf* patriot; **en ~** patriotically.
patriotique /patʀijɔtik/ *adj* patriotic.
patriotisme /patʀijɔtism/ *nm* patriotism.
patron, **-onne** /patʀɔ̃, ɔn/ **I** *nm,f* boss○.
II *nm* **1** (sewing) pattern; **2** large; **grand ~** extra-large.
■ **~ d'industrie** captain of industry; **~ de pêche** skipper, master.
patronage /patʀɔnaʒ/ *nm* **1** patronage; **2**† ≈ youth club.
patronal, **~e**, *mpl* **-aux** /patʀɔnal, o/ *adj* [*organization*] employers'; [*contributions*] employer.
patronat /patʀɔna/ *nm* employers.
patronne ▸ **patron I**.
patronyme /patʀɔnim/ *nm* patronymic.
patrouille /patʀuj/ *nf* patrol.
patrouiller /patʀuje/ [1] *vi* to be on patrol.
patte /pat/ *nf* **1** leg; paw; foot; **~ de devant** foreleg; **~ de derrière** hind leg; **donner la ~** to give its paw; **retomber sur ses ~s** to fall on its feet; **2**○ leg, foot; **tu es toujours dans mes ~s** you are always getting under my feet; **marcher à quatre ~s** to walk on all fours; to crawl; **traîner la ~** to limp; **en avoir plein les ~s** to be dead on one's feet○; **3**○ hand; **on reconnaît ta ~** one can recognize your hand; **bas les ~s**○**!** keep your hands to yourself!; hands off○!; **4** tab; (on shelving unit) lug; (on garment) flap; (on collar) tab; (on shoe) tongue; **5** sideburn.
■ **~s d'éléphant** flares; **~ folle**○ gammy leg (GB), game leg (US); **~s de mouche** spidery scrawl.
IDIOMS **faire ~ de velours** to draw in its claws; to switch on the charm; **montrer ~ blanche** to prove one is acceptable; **avoir un fil à la ~** to be tied down; **se tirer dans les ~s** to pull dirty tricks on each other.
patte-d'oie, *pl* **pattes-d'oie** /patdwɑ/ *nf* **1** crow's-foot; **2** junction.
pâturage /pɑtyʀaʒ/ *nm* **1** pasture; **2** (Law) pasturage.
pâture /pɑtyʀ/ *nf* **1** feed; **être jeté en ~** (figurative) to be thrown to the lions or wolves; **2** pasture.
paume /pom/ *nf* palm (of the hand).
paumé○, **~e** /pome/ **I** *adj* **1** [*person*] mixed up (GB), out of it○ (US); **2** [*place*] godforsaken, jerkwater (US).
II *nm,f* misfit.
paumer○ /pome/ [1] **I** *vtr, vi* to lose.
II se paumer *v refl* (+ *v être*) to get lost.
paupière /popjɛʀ/ *nf* eyelid.
paupiette /popjɛt/ *nf* **~ de veau** stuffed escalope of veal.
pause /poz/ *nf* **1** break; **faire une ~** to take a break; **2** (in process) pause; **3** (Mus) rest.
pauvre /povʀ/ **I** *adj* **1** poor; **2** sparse; **minerai ~ en métal** ore with a low metal content; **3** [*smile*] weak; **un ~ type**○ a poor chap○ (GB) or guy○; a dead loss○; **~ de moi!** poor me!

II° *nmf* **le/la ~!** poor man/woman!; poor thing!
III *nm* **un ~** a poor man; **~ d'esprit** half-wit.

pauvrement /povʀəmɑ̃/ *adv* poorly.

pauvreté /povʀəte/ *nf* **1** poverty; **2** shabbiness; **3** (debate) poor quality; (of argument) thinness; **~ de moyens** lack of means.

pavaner: **se pavaner** /pavane/ [1] *v refl* (+ *v être*) to strut (about).

pavé /pave/ *nm* cobblestone; **se retrouver sur le ~** to find oneself out on the street.
IDIOMS **lancer un ~ dans la mare** to set the cat among the pigeons; **sous les ~s, la plage** beneath the harsh reality lies a brighter tomorrow; **tenir le haut du ~** to head the field.

paver /pave/ [1] *vtr* to lay [sth] with cobblestones.

pavillon /pavijɔ̃/ *nm* **1** (detached) house; **2** (for exhibition) pavilion; (of hospital) wing;**3** (of ear) auricle; **4** (of loudspeaker) horn; **5** (Naut) flag.

pavoiser /pavwaze/ [1] **I** *vtr* to decorate [sth] with flags.
II° *vi* to crow.

pavot /pavo/ *nm* poppy.

payant, **~e** /pɛjɑ̃, ɑ̃t/ *adj* **1** [*person*] paying; **2** [*show*] not free; **chaîne ~e** subscription channel; **3**° lucrative, profitable.

paye /pɛj/ = **paie**.

payement /pɛjmɑ̃/ = **paiement**.

payer /peje/ [21] **I** *vtr* **1** to pay for [*ticket, purchase, service*]; to pay [*bill, debt, tax, interest, salary, supplier, employee*]; **il est payé pour le savoir!** he knows that to his cost!; **~ qch à qn**° to buy sb sth; **je te paie le restaurant** I'll treat you to a meal; **2** to pay for [*mistake, carelessness*]; **~ pour les autres** to take the rap°.
II *vi* **1** [*efforts, sacrifice*] to pay off; [*profession, activity*] to pay; **2**° to be funny.
III se payer *v refl* (+ *v être*) **1** [*service, goods*] to have to be paid for; **2**° to treat oneself to [*holiday, meal*]; to get [*cold, bad mark*]; to get landed with [*job*]; **se ~ une cuite** to get plastered°; **se ~ un arbre** to crash into a tree.
IDIOMS **se ~ du bon temps**° to have a good time; **se ~ la tête**° **de qn** to take the mickey° out of sb (GB), to razz° sb (US).

payeur, **-euse** /pɛjœʀ, øz/ **I** *adj* **organisme ~** paying authority.
II *nm* **mauvais ~** bad debtor.

pays /pei/ *nm* **1** country; **2 la Bourgogne est le ~ du bon vin** Burgundy is the home of good wine; **gens/produit du ~** local people/product.
IDIOMS **voir du ~** to do some travelling[GB].

paysage /peizaʒ/ *nm* landscape, scenery.

paysager, **-ère** /peizaʒe, ɛʀ/ *adj* **1** environmental; **2** [*garden*] landscaped; **3** [*office*] open-plan.

paysagiste /peizaʒist/ *nmf* **(jardinier) ~** landscape gardener.

paysan, **-anne** /peizɑ̃, an/ **I** *adj* [*life*] rural; [*ways*] peasant; [*soup, bread*] country.
II *nm,f* **1** ≈ small farmer; **2** (derogatory) peasant.

Pays-Bas /peibɑ/ *pr nm pl* **les ~** The Netherlands.

PC /pese/ *nm* **1** (Pol) (*abbr* = **parti communiste**) CP, Communist Party; **2** (Comput) (*abbr* = **personal computer**) PC; **3** (*abbr* = **poste de commandement**) (of police force) division; (Mil) CP.

PCV /peseve/ *nm* (*abbr* = **paiement contre vérification**) reverse charge call (GB), collect call (US).

PDG /pedeʒe/ *nm* (*abbr* = **président-directeur général**) chairman and managing director (GB), chief executive officer, CEO.

péage /peaʒ/ *nm* **1** toll; **2** tollbooth.

peau, *pl* **~x** /po/ *nf* **1** skin; **n'avoir que la ~ sur les os** to be all skin and bone; **changer de ~** to turn over a new leaf; **2** leather; **gants de ~** leather gloves; **3** peel; **4**° life; **risquer sa ~** to risk one's life; **faire la ~ à qn** to kill sb; **tenir à sa ~** to value one's life; **vouloir la ~ de qn** to want sb dead; ▶ **vieux**.
IDIOMS **je n'aimerais pas être dans sa ~** I wouldn't like to be in his/her shoes; **être bien dans sa ~**° to feel good about oneself; **avoir qn dans la ~**° to be crazy about sb; **prendre une/deux balles dans la ~**° to be shot once/twice; **rétrécir comme une ~ de chagrin** to shrink away to nothing.

peaufiner /pofine/ [1] *vtr* to put the finishing touches to [*work, text*].

peccadille /pekadij/ *nf* peccadillo.

pêche /pɛʃ/ *nf* **1** peach; **2** fishing; **~ en mer** sea fishing; **aller à la ~** to go fishing; **la ~ a été bonne?** did you catch anything?; **3**° clout°; **4**° **avoir la ~** to be feeling great.
■ **~ à la ligne** angling.

péché /peʃe/ *nm* sin; **ce serait un ~ de rater ça**° it would be a crime to miss that; **le chocolat, c'est mon ~ mignon** I've got a weakness for chocolate.

pécher /peʃe/ [14] *vi* to sin; **~ par ignorance** to err through ignorance; **~ par excès de confiance** to be overconfident; **le roman pèche sur un point** the novel has one shortcoming.

pêcher[1] /pɛʃe/ [1] **I** *vtr* **1** to go fishing for; **2** to catch; **3**° to get; **où est il allé ~ cette idée?** where did he get that idea from?
II *vi* to fish; **~ à la mouche** to fly-fish; **~ à la ligne** to angle.

pêcher[2] /pɛʃe/ *nm* peach tree.

pécheresse /peʃʀɛs/ *nf* sinner.

pécheur /peʃœʀ/ *nm* sinner.

pêcheur /pɛʃœʀ/ *nm* fisherman.
■ **~ de baleines** whaler; **~ de perles** pearl diver.

pectoral, *pl* **-aux** /pɛktɔʀal, o/ *nm* pectoral muscle.

pécule /pekyl/ *nm* savings, nest egg°.

pécuniaire /pekynjɛʀ/ *adj* financial.

pédagogie /pedagɔʒi/ *nf* **1** education, pedagogy; **2** teaching skills; **3** teaching method.

pédagogique /pedagɔʒik/ *adj* [*activity*] educational; [*system*] education; [*material, method*] teaching; **formation ~** teacher training.

pédagogue /pedagɔg/ *nmf* **1** teacher; **2** educationalist.

pédale /pedal/ *nf* (of bicycle, piano) pedal; (of sewing machine) treadle.

IDIOMS **perdre les ~s**○ to lose one's grip.

pédaler /pedale/ [1] *vi* to pedal.

pédalier /pedalje/ *nm* (of bicycle) chain transmission; (of piano) pedals.

pédalo® /pedalo/ *nm* pedalo (GB), pedal boat.

pédant, ~e /pedɑ̃, ɑ̃t/ **I** *adj* pedantic.

II *nm,f* pedant.

pédantisme /pedɑ̃tism/ *nm* pedantry.

pédérastie /pedeʀasti/ *nf* **1** pederasty; **2** homosexuality.

pédestre /pedɛstʀ/ *adj* **randonnée ~** ramble.

pédiatre /pedjatʀ/ *nmf* paediatrician.

pédiatrie /pedjatʀi/ *nf* paediatrics.

pédicure /pedikyʀ/ *nmf* chiropodist (GB), podiatrist (US).

pedigree /pedigʀe/ *nm* pedigree.

peeling /piliŋ/ *nm* exfoliation.

pègre /pɛgʀ/ *nf* underworld.

peigne /pɛɲ/ *nm* comb.

peigner /peɲe/ [1] **I** *vtr* to comb [*hair, wool*].

II se peigner *v refl* (+ *v être*) to comb one's hair.

peignoir /pɛɲwaʀ/ *nm* dressing gown (GB), robe (US); **~ de bain** bathrobe.

peinard○, **~e** /penaʀ, aʀd/ *adj* [*job*] cushy○; [*place*] snug.

peindre /pɛ̃dʀ/ [55] **I** *vtr* **1** to paint; **2** to depict.

II *vi* to paint.

III se peindre *v refl* (+ *v être*) **se ~ sur** [*embarrassment, joy*] to be written on.

peine /pɛn/ **I** *nf* **1** sorrow, grief; **avoir de la ~** to feel sad or upset; **faire de la ~ à qn** [*person*] to hurt sb; [*event, remark*] to upset sb; **2** effort, trouble; **c'est ~ perdue** it's a waste of effort; **se donner de la ~ pour faire** to go to a lot of trouble to do; **il n'est pas au bout de ses ~s** his troubles are far from over; he's still got a long way to go; **ce n'est pas la ~ de crier** there's no need to shout; **ce n'est pas la ~ d'aller voir ce film** that film's not worth seeing; **pour ta ~** for your trouble; **3** difficulty; **sans ~** easily; **avec ~** with difficulty; **avoir de la ~ à faire** to have difficulty (in) doing, to find it hard to do; **4** (Law) penalty, sentence; **~ de prison** prison sentence; **'défense de fumer sous ~ d'amende'** 'no smoking, offenders will be fined'.

II à peine *phr* hardly, barely; **il était à ~ arrivé qu'il pensait déjà à repartir** no sooner had he arrived than he was thinking of leaving again.

■ **~ capitale** capital punishment; **~ de cœur** heartache; **~ de mort** death penalty.

peiner /pene/ [1] **I** *vtr* to sadden, to upset; **être peiné** to be sad, to be upset.

II *vi* [*person*] to struggle; [*machine, car*] to labour[GB].

peintre /pɛ̃tʀ/ *nm* painter.

peinture /pɛ̃tyʀ/ *nf* **1** paint; **'~ fraîche'** 'wet paint'; **2** paintwork; **3** painting; **~ au pistolet** spray painting; **je ne peux pas le voir en ~**○ I can't stand the sight of him; **4** portrayal.

■ **~ murale** mural.

peinturlurer /pɛ̃tyʀlyʀe/ [1] *vtr* to daub.

péjoratif, -ive /peʒɔʀatif, iv/ *adj* pejorative, derogatory.

Pékin /pekɛ̃/ *pr n* Beijing, Peking.

pékinois, ~e /pekinwɑ, az/ **I** *adj* of Beijing, Pekinese.

II *nm* **1** (language) Pekinese; **2** (Zool) Pekinese.

pelage /pəlaʒ/ *nm* coat, fur.

pêle-mêle /pɛlmɛl/ *adv* higgledy-piggledy.

peler /pəle/ [17] **I** *vtr* to peel.

II *vi* **1** [*skin, nose*] to peel; **2**○ **~ (de froid)** to freeze.

pèlerin /pɛlʀɛ̃/ *nm* pilgrim.

pèlerinage /pɛlʀinaʒ/ *nm* pilgrimage.

pèlerine /pɛlʀin/ *nf* cape.

pélican /pelikɑ̃/ *nm* pelican.

pelle /pɛl/ *nf* shovel; spade; **à la ~**○ by the dozen.

■ **~ à tarte** pie server.

pelleteuse /pɛltøz/ *nf* mechanical digger.

pellicule /pelikyl/ **I** *nf* film; **~ couleur** colour[GB] film.

II pellicules *nf pl* dandruff.

pelote /p(ə)lɔt/ *nf* **1** (of wool) ball; **2** (Sport) **~ basque** pelota.

peloton /p(ə)lɔtɔ̃/ *nm* **1** platoon; **~ d'exécution** firing squad; **2** (in cycling) pack; **dans le ~ de tête** in the leading pack; among the leaders.

pelotonner: **se pelotonner** /p(ə)lɔtɔne/ [1] *v refl* (+ *v être*) **1** to snuggle up; **2** to huddle up.

pelouse /p(ə)luz/ *nf* lawn; **'~ interdite'** 'keep off the grass'.

peluche /p(ə)lyʃ/ *nf* **1** plush; **jouet en ~** cuddly toy (GB), stuffed animal (US); **2** fluff.

pelure /p(ə)lyʀ/ *nf* (of vegetable, fruit) peel; (of onion) skin.

pelvis /pɛlvis/ *nm inv* pelvis.

pénal, ~e, *mpl* **-aux** /penal, o/ *adj* criminal.

pénalisation /penalizasjɔ̃/ *nf* **1** (Sport) penalty; **2 ~ (fiscale)** taxation.

pénaliser /penalize/ [1] *vtr* to penalize.

pénalité /penalite/ *nf* penalty.

penaud, ~e /pəno, od/ *adj* sheepish.

penchant /pɑ̃ʃɑ̃/ *nm* **1** fondness; **2** weakness; **3** tendency.

penché, ~e /pɑ̃ʃe/ **I** *pp* ▶ **pencher**.

II *pp adj* [*tree, tower*] leaning; [*writing*] slanting.

pencher /pɑ̃ʃe/ [1] **I** *vtr* to tilt; to tip [sth] up; **~ la tête en avant** to bend one's head forward(s).

II *vi* **1** [*tower, tree, wall*] to lean; [*boat*] to list; [*picture*] to slant, to tilt; **2 ~ pour** to incline toward(s) [*opinion, theory*]; to be in favour[GB] of [*solution*].

III **se pencher** *v refl* (+ *v être*) **1** to lean; **'défense de se ~ au-dehors'** 'do not lean out of (GB) or out (US) the window'; **2** to bend down; **3 se ~ sur** to look into [*problem, past*].

pendable /pɑ̃dabl/ *adj* **jouer un tour ~ à qn** to play a rotten trick on sb.

pendaison /pɑ̃dɛzɔ̃/ *nf* hanging.

pendant[1] /pɑ̃dɑ̃/ I *prep* for; **je t'ai attendu ~ des heures** I waited for you for hours; **~ les trois premières années** for the first three years; **~ combien de temps avez-vous vécu à Versailles?** how long did you live in Versailles?; **il a été malade ~ tout le trajet** he was sick throughout the journey; **~ ce temps(-là)** meanwhile.

II **pendant que** *phr* while; **~ que tu y es** while you're at it.

pendant[2] /pɑ̃dɑ̃/ *nm* **~ (d'oreille)** drop earring.

pendentif /pɑ̃dɑ̃tif/ *nm* pendant.

penderie /pɑ̃dʀi/ *nf* **1** wardrobe; **2** walk-in cupboard (GB) or closet.

pendre /pɑ̃dʀ/ [6] I *vtr* **1** to hang [*person*]; **2** to hang [*picture, curtains*]; to hang up [*clothes, key*].

II *vi* **1** [*object, clothes*] to hang (**à** from); [*arms, legs*] to dangle; **2** [*strips, lock of hair*] to hang down; [*cheek, breasts*] to sag.

III **se pendre** *v refl* (+ *v être*) **1** to hang oneself; **2 se ~ à** to hang from [*branch*]; **se ~ au cou de qn** to throw one's arms around sb's neck.

IDIOMS **ça te pend au nez**○ you've got it coming to you.

pendu, **~e** /pɑ̃dy/ I *pp* ▶ **pendre**.

II *pp adj* **1** [*person*] hanged; **2** [*object*] hung (**à** on), hanging (**à** from); **être ~ aux lèvres de qn** to hang on sb's every word; **être toujours ~ au téléphone** to spend all one's time on the telephone.

III *nm,f* hanged man/woman.

IV *nm* **jouer au ~** to play hangman.

pendule[1] /pɑ̃dyl/ *nm* pendulum.

pendule[2] /pɑ̃dyl/ *nf* clock.

IDIOMS **remettre les ~s à l'heure** to set the record straight.

pénétration /penetʀasjɔ̃/ *nf* **1** penetration; **2** seepage.

pénétré, **~e** /penetʀe/ I *pp* ▶ **pénétrer**.

II *pp adj* earnest, intense; **être ~ de** to be imbued with [*feeling*]; **être ~ de son importance** to be full of one's own importance.

pénétrer /penetʀe/ [14] I *vtr* **1** [*rain*] to soak or seep into [*ground*]; [*sun*] to penetrate [*foliage*]; **le froid m'a pénétré jusqu'aux os** the cold went right through me; **2** to fathom [*secret, thoughts*]; **3** to penetrate; **4** [*idea, fashion*] to reach [*group*].

II *vi* **~ dans** or **à l'intérieur de** to enter, to get into; to penetrate; **faire ~ la pommade en massant doucement** rub the ointment into your skin.

III **se pénétrer** *v refl* (+ *v être*) **se ~ d'une idée** to get an idea firmly rooted in one's mind.

pénible /penibl/ *adj* [*effort, impression*] painful; [*work*] hard; [*journey*] difficult; [*person*] tiresome.

péniblement /peniblәmɑ̃/ *adv* [*walk*] with difficulty; [*reach*] barely.

péniche /peniʃ/ *nf* barge.

pénicilline /penisilin/ *nf* penicillin.

péninsule /penɛ̃syl/ *nf* peninsula.

pénis /penis/ *nm inv* penis.

pénitence /penitɑ̃s/ *nf* **1** penance; **2** punishment.

pénitencier /penitɑ̃sje/ *nm* prison, penitentiary (US).

pénitent, **~e** /penitɑ̃, ɑ̃t/ *adj, nm,f* penitent.

pénitentiaire /penitɑ̃sjɛʀ/ *adj* [*institution*] penal; [*regime*] prison.

pénombre /penɔ̃bʀ/ *nf* half-light.

pense-bête, *pl* **pense-bêtes** /pɑ̃sbɛt/ *nm* reminder.

pensée /pɑ̃se/ *nf* **1** thought; **être perdu dans ses ~s** to be lost in thought; **2** mind; **en ~, par la ~** in one's mind; **nous serons avec vous par la ~** we'll be with you in spirit; **3** thinking; **~ claire** clear thinking; **4** (Bot) pansy.

penser /pɑ̃se/ [1] I *vtr* **1** to think (**de** of, about); **~ du bien de qn** to think well of sb; **je n'en pense rien** I have no opinion about it; **qu'est-ce que tu penserais d'un week-end en Normandie?** what would you say to a weekend in Normandy?; **2** to think; **c'est bien ce que je pensais!** I thought as much!; **je (le) pense, je pense que oui** I think so; **tu penses vraiment ce que tu dis?** do you really mean what you're saying?; **tout laisse** or **porte à ~ que** there's every indication that; **vous pensez si j'étais content!** you can imagine how pleased I was!; **'il s'est excusé?'—'penses-tu!'** 'did he apologize?'—'you must be joking!'; **3 ça me fait ~ qu'il faut que je leur écrive** that reminds me that I must write to them; **4 ~ faire** to be thinking of doing, to intend to do; **5** to think [sth] up [*plan, device*]; **c'est bien pensé!** it's well thought out!

II **penser à** *v+prep* **1** to think of, to think about; **il suffisait d'y ~** it just required some thinking; **ne pensez plus à rien** empty your mind; **sans ~ à mal** without meaning any harm; **tu n'y penses pas!** you can't be serious!; **n'y pensons plus!** let's forget about it!; **2** to remember; **mais j'y pense, c'est ton anniversaire aujourd'hui!** now I come to think of it, it's your birthday today!; **il me fait ~ à mon père** he reminds me of my father; **3 ~ à faire** to be thinking of doing.

III *vi* to think; **façon de ~** way of thinking; **je lui ai dit ma façon de ~!** I gave him/her a piece of my mind!; **~ tout haut** to think out loud.

penseur /pɑ̃sœʀ/ *nm* thinker.

pensif, **-ive** /pɑ̃sif, iv/ *adj* pensive, thoughtful.

pension /pɑ̃sjɔ̃/ *nf* **1** pension; **2** boarding house; **prendre qn en ~** to take sb as a lodger; **3** boarding school.

■ **~ alimentaire** alimony; **~ complète** full board; **~ de famille** family hotel.

pensionnaire /pɑ̃sjɔnɛʀ/ *nmf* **1** (in hotel) resident; **2** (in prison) inmate; **3** (Sch) boarder.

pensionnat /pɑ̃sjɔna/ *nm* boarding school.

pentagone /pɛ̃tagɔn/ *nm* pentagon.

pente /pɑ̃t/ *nf* slope; **toit en ~** sloping roof.
IDIOMS **être sur la mauvaise ~, être sur une ~ savonneuse** [*person*] to be on the slippery slope (GB), to be going astray; [*company, economy*] to be going downhill; **remonter la ~** to get back on one's feet.

Pentecôte /pɑ̃tkot/ *nf* Pentecost; **à la ~** at Whitsun.

pénultième /penyltjɛm/ *nf* penultimate (syllable).

pénurie /penyʀi/ *nf* shortage.

pépé° /pepe/ *nm* **1** grandpa°; **2** old man.

pépère° /pepɛʀ/ *adj* [*life, job*] cushy°; [*place*] nice.

pépier /pepje/ [2] *vi* to chirp.

pépin /pepɛ̃/ *nm* **1** pip; **sans ~s** seedless; **2**° slight problem; **3**° brolly° (GB), umbrella.

pépinière /pepinjɛʀ/ *nf* **1** nursery; **2** (figurative) breeding-ground.

pépiniériste /pepinjeʀist/ *nmf* nurseryman/nurserywoman.

pépite /pepit/ *nf* nugget.

perçant, ~e /pɛʀsɑ̃, ɑ̃t/ *adj* **1** [*cry, voice*] shrill; [*gaze*] piercing; **2** [*vision*] sharp.

percée /pɛʀse/ *nf* **1** opening; **2** breakthrough.

percement /pɛʀsəmɑ̃/ *nm* (of tunnel) boring; (of road) cutting; building.

perce-neige /pɛʀsənɛʒ/ *nm inv* or *nf inv* snowdrop.

perce-oreille, *pl* **~s** /pɛʀsɔʀɛj/ *nm* earwig.

percepteur /pɛʀsɛptœʀ/ *nm* tax inspector.

perceptible /pɛʀsɛptibl/ *adj* **1** [*sound*] perceptible; **2** [*tax*] payable.

perception /pɛʀsɛpsjɔ̃/ *nf* **1** tax office; **2** perception.

percer /pɛʀse/ [12] **I** *vtr* **1** to pierce [*body, surface*]; to burst [*abscess, eardrum*]; **2 ~ un trou dans** to make a hole in; **3** to make [*window, door*]; to bore, to build [*tunnel*]; to build [*road*]; **4** to pierce [*silence, air*]; to break through [*clouds*]; **5** to penetrate [*secret*]; to uncover [*plot*]; **~ qn à jour** to see through sb; **6 ~ ses dents** to be teething; **~ une dent** to cut a tooth.
II *vi* **1** [*sun*] to break through; [*plant*] to come up; [*tooth*] to come through; **2** (Mil, Sport) to break through; **3** [*actor, writer*] to become known.

perceuse /pɛʀsøz/ *nf* drill.

percevoir /pɛʀsəvwaʀ/ [5] *vtr* **1** to collect [*tax*]; to receive [*pension, rent*]; **2** to perceive [*smell, change*]; to feel [*vibration*]; **être perçu comme** to be seen as.

perche /pɛʀʃ/ *nf* **1** (gen) pole; (of ski tow) T-bar; **saut à la ~** pole-vaulting; (for microphone) boom; **2**° **(grande) ~** beanpole°; **3** (Zool) perch.
IDIOMS **tendre la ~ à qn** to throw sb a line.

percher /pɛʀʃe/ [1] **I** *vtr* **~ qch sur une étagère** to stick sth up on a shelf.
II *vi* to perch; to roost
III se percher *v refl* (+ *v être*) **1** to perch; **2 voix haut perchée** high-pitched voice.

perchiste /pɛʀʃist/ *nmf* **1** pole-vaulter; **2** boom operator; **3** ski-lift attendant.

perchoir /pɛʀʃwaʀ/ *nm* **1** perch; **2**° (Pol) Speaker's Chair.

percolateur /pɛʀkɔlatœʀ/ *nm* (espresso) coffee machine.

percussionniste /pɛʀkysjɔnist/ *nmf* percussionist.

percussions /pɛʀkysjɔ̃/ *nf pl* **les ~** percussion instruments; percussion section; drums.

percutant, ~e /pɛʀkytɑ̃, ɑ̃t/ *adj* **1** [*criticism*] hard-hitting; [*person*] forceful; [*slogan*] punchy°; **2** [*sound*] percussive.

percuter /pɛʀkyte/ [1] **I** *vtr* [*car, driver*] to hit.
II *vi* **~ contre** [*vehicle*] to crash into; [*shell*] to explode against.
III se percuter *v refl* (+ *v être*) [*vehicles*] to collide.

perdant, ~e /pɛʀdɑ̃, ɑ̃t/ **I** *adj* losing; **être ~** to have lost out.
II *nm,f* loser.

perdition /pɛʀdisjɔ̃/ *nf* **1 lieu de ~** den of iniquity; **2 en ~** [*country, company*] in trouble; [*ship*] in distress.

perdre /pɛʀdʀ/ [6] **I** *vtr* **1** to lose; **~ de vue** to lose sight of; **leurs actions ont perdu 9%** their shares have dropped 9%; **sans ~ le sourire, elle a continué** still smiling, she went on; **2** to shed [*leaves, flowers*]; **3** to miss [*chance*]; **tu n'as rien perdu (en ne venant pas)** you didn't miss anything (by not coming); **4** to waste [*day, years*]; **perdre son temps** to waste one's time; **5 je perds mes chaussures** my shoes are too big; **je perds mon pantalon** my trousers are falling down; **6** to bring [sb] down; **cet homme te perdra** that man will be your undoing.
II *vi* to lose; **j'y perds** I lose out.
III se perdre *v refl* (+ *v être*) **1** to get lost; **se ~ dans ses pensées** to be lost in thought; **2** [*tradition*] to die out.
IDIOMS **~ la raison** or **l'esprit** to go out of one's mind.

perdreau, *pl* **~x** /pɛʀdʀo/ *nm* (young) partridge.

perdrix /pɛʀdʀi/ *nf inv* partridge.

perdu, ~e /pɛʀdy/ **I** *pp* ▶ **perdre**.
II *pp adj* **1** lost; **chien ~** stray dog; **balle ~e** stray bullet; **c'est ~ d'avance** it's hopeless; **2** [*day, opportunity*] wasted; **c'est du temps ~** it's a waste of time; **à tes moments ~s** in your spare time; **3** [*harvest*] ruined; **il est ~** there's no hope for him; **4** [*person*] lost.
III *adj* remote, isolated; **vivre dans un coin ~** to live in a godforsaken spot.
IDIOMS **se lancer à corps ~ dans** to throw oneself headlong into; **ce n'est pas ~ pour tout le monde** somebody will do all right out of it; **crier/courir comme un ~** to shout/to run like a madman.

père /pɛʀ/ *nm* father; **Dupont ~** Dupont senior; **le ~**° **Dupont** old° Dupont.
■ **le ~ Noël** Santa Claus.

pérégrinations /peʀegʀinasjɔ̃/ *nf pl* travels, peregrinations.

péremption /peʀɑ̃psjɔ̃/ *nf* **date de ~** use-by date.

péréquation /peʀekwasjɔ̃/ *nf* adjustment.

perfection /pɛʀfɛksjɔ̃/ *nf* perfection; **à la ~** to perfection.

perfectionné, **~e** /pɛʀfɛksjɔne/ *adj* advanced.

perfectionnement /pɛʀfɛksjɔnmɑ̃/ *nm* improvement.

perfectionner /pɛʀfɛksjɔne/ [1] **I** *vtr* to perfect [*technique*]; to refine [*art*].
II se perfectionner *v refl* (+ *v être*) to improve.

perfectionniste /pɛʀfɛksjɔnist/ *adj, nmf* perfectionist.

perfide /pɛʀfid/ *adj* perfidious, treacherous.

perfidie /pɛʀfidi/ *nf* perfidy, treachery.

perforation /pɛʀfɔʀasjɔ̃/ *nf* perforation.

perforer /pɛʀfɔʀe/ [1] *vtr* **1** to pierce; to perforate; **2** to punch; **carte perforée** punch card.

performance /pɛʀfɔʀmɑ̃s/ *nf* **1** result, performance; **2** achievement.

performant, **~e** /pɛʀfɔʀmɑ̃, ɑ̃t/ *adj* [*car, equipment*] high-performance; [*person, techniques*] efficient; [*company*] competitive.

perfusion /pɛʀfyzjɔ̃/ *nm* (Med) drip (GB), IV (US).

péricliter /peʀiklite/ [1] *vi* to be going downhill.

péridurale /peʀidyʀal/ *nf* epidural.

péril /peʀil/ *nm* (literary) peril, danger; **à ses risques et ~s** at his/her own risk; **il n'y a pas ~ en la demeure** what's the hurry?

périlleux, **-euse** /peʀijø, øz/ *adj* perilous, dangerous.

périmé, **~e** /peʀime/ *adj* **1** out-of-date; **son passeport est ~** his/her passport has expired; **ce yaourt est ~** this yoghurt has passed its use-by date; **2** [*idea, custom, institution*] outdated.

périmètre /peʀimɛtʀ/ *nm* **1** perimeter; **2** area.

périnatal, **~e**, *mpl* **~s** /peʀinatal/ *adj* perinatal.

périnée /peʀine/ *nm* perineum.

période /peʀjɔd/ *nf* period; era; **en ~ de crise** at times of crisis.

périodique /peʀjɔdik/ **I** *adj* **1** [*fever*] recurring; **2 serviette ~** sanitary towel (GB), sanitary napkin (US).
II *nm* periodical.

péripétie /peʀipesi/ *nf* **1** incident; **2** event; **3** adventure; **4 les ~s d'une intrigue** the twists and turns of a plot.

périphérie /peʀifeʀi/ *nf* periphery.

périphérique /peʀifeʀik/ **I** *adj* (gen) peripheral; [*area*] outlying; **radio ~** *broadcasting station situated outside the territory to which it transmits.*
II *nm* ring road (GB), beltway (US).

périphrase /peʀifʀɑz/ *nf* circumlocution.

périple /peʀipl/ *nm* journey; voyage.

périr /peʀiʀ/ [3] *vi* to die, to perish.

périscope /peʀiskɔp/ *nm* periscope.

périssable /peʀisabl/ *adj* **1** perishable; **2** ephemeral.

Péritel® /peʀitɛl/ *nf* **prise ~** scart socket; scart plug.

perle /pɛʀl/ *nf* **1** pearl; **~ de culture** cultured pearl; **~ fine** real pearl; **2** (figurative) gem; **~ rare** real treasure; **3**° howler°.

perler /pɛʀle/ [1] *vi* [*drop, tear*] to appear.

permanence /pɛʀmanɑ̃s/ **I** *nf* **1** permanence; **2** persistence; **3 ~ téléphonique** manned line; **assurer** or **tenir une ~** to be on duty; to hold a surgery (GB), to have office hours (US); **4** permanently manned office; **5** (Sch) (private) study room (GB), study hall (US).
II en permanence *phr* **1** permanently; **2** constantly.

permanent, **~e**[1] /pɛʀmanɑ̃, ɑ̃t/ **I** *adj* **1** [*staff, exhibition*] permanent; [*committee*] standing; **2** [*tension, danger*] constant; [*show*] continuous; [*disability*] permanent.
II *nm,f* **1** permanent employee; **2** permanent member.

permanente[2] /pɛʀmanɑ̃t/ *nf* perm.

perméable /pɛʀmeabl/ *adj* permeable.

permettre /pɛʀmɛtʀ/ [60] **I** *vtr* **1 ~ à qn de faire** to allow sb to do; **(vous) permettez! j'étais là avant!** excuse me! I was here first!; **il est menteur comme c'est pas permis**° he's an incredible liar; **2 ~ à qn de faire** to allow or enable sb to do; **si le temps le permet** weather permitting; **si mon emploi du temps (me) le permet** if my schedule allows or permits; **leurs moyens ne le leur permettent pas** they can't afford it; **autant qu'il est permis d'en juger** as far as one can tell.
II se permettre *v refl* (+ *v être*) **1 je peux me ~ ce genre de plaisanterie avec lui** I can get away with telling him that kind of joke; **puis-je me ~ une remarque?** might I say something?; **se ~ de faire** to take the liberty of doing; **2 je ne peux pas me ~ d'acheter une nouvelle voiture** I can't afford to buy a new car.

permis, **~e** /pɛʀmi, iz/ **I** *pp* ▶ **permettre**.
II *pp adj* permitted.
III *nm inv* permit, licence[GB].
■ **~ de chasse** hunting permit; **~ de conduire** driver's licence[GB]; driving test; **~ de séjour** residence permit; **~ de travail** work permit.

permissif, **-ive** /pɛʀmisif, iv/ *adj* permissive.

permission /pɛʀmisjɔ̃/ *nf* **1** permission; **la ~ de minuit** permission to stay out late; **2** (Mil) leave; **partir en ~** to go on leave.

permutation /pɛʀmytasjɔ̃/ *nf* (Mil) exchange of posts.

permuter /pɛʀmyte/ [1] *vtr* to switch [sth] around [*letters, labels*].

pernicieux, **-ieuse** /pɛʀnisjø, øz/ *adj* pernicious.

pérorer /peʀɔʀe/ [1] *vi* to hold forth.

Pérou /peʀu/ *pr nm* Peru.
IDIOMS **ce n'est pas le ~** it's not a fortune.

perpendiculaire /pɛʀpɑ̃dikylɛʀ/ *adj, nf* perpendicular (**à** to).

perpétrer /pɛʀpetʀe/ [14] *vtr* to perpetrate.

perpétuel, -elle /pɛʀpetɥɛl/ *adj* **1** perpetual; **2** [*post, secretary*] permanent; **réclusion perpétuelle** life imprisonment.

perpétuer /pɛʀpetɥe/ [1] *vtr* to perpetuate.

perpétuité /pɛʀpetɥite/ *nf* perpetuity; **à ~** (Law) [*imprisonment*] life; [*burial plot*] in perpetuity.

perplexe /pɛʀplɛks/ *adj* perplexed, baffled.

perplexité /pɛʀplɛksite/ *nf* perplexity, confusion.

perquisition /pɛʀkizisjɔ̃/ *nf* search.

perquisitionner /pɛʀkizisjɔne/ [1] *vtr* to search [*house*].

perron /peʀɔ̃/ *nm* flight of steps.

perroquet /peʀɔkɛ/ *nm* parrot.

perruche /peʀyʃ/ *nf* budgerigar (GB), budgie° (GB), parakeet (US).

perruque /peʀyk/ *nf* wig.

persan, ~e /pɛʀsɑ̃, an/ *adj* Persian.

perse /pɛʀs/ *adj* Persian.

persécuter /pɛʀsekyte/ [1] *vtr* to persecute.

persécution /pɛʀsekysjɔ̃/ *nf* persecution.

persévérance /pɛʀseveʀɑ̃s/ *nf* perseverance.

persévérer /pɛʀseveʀe/ [14] *vi* **1** to persevere; **2** to persist.

persienne /pɛʀsjɛn/ *nf* (louvred[GB]) shutter.

persiflage /pɛʀsiflaʒ/ *nm* mockery, persiflage.

persil /pɛʀsi(l)/ *nm* parsley.

persillade /pɛʀsijad/ *nf* chopped parsley and garlic.

persique /pɛʀsik/ *adj* Persian; **le golfe Persique** the Persian Gulf.

persistance /pɛʀsistɑ̃s/ *nf* persistence; **avec ~** persistently.

persistant, ~e /pɛʀsistɑ̃, ɑ̃t/ *adj* [*heat, problem*] continuing; [*smell, snow*] lingering; [*cough, symptom*] persistent; **arbre à feuilles ~es** evergreen.

persister /pɛʀsiste/ [1] *vi* [*symptom, pain*] to persist; [*inflation*] to continue; [*doubt*] to remain; **je persiste à croire que** I still think that.

personnage /pɛʀsɔnaʒ/ *nm* **1** character; **se composer un ~** to adopt a persona; **2** figure; **un ~ haut placé** a high-placed person.

personnaliser /pɛʀsɔnalize/ [1] *vtr* to add a personal touch to.

personnalité /pɛʀsɔnalite/ *nf* **1** personality; **2** important person.

personne[1] /pɛʀsɔn/ *pron* anyone, anybody; **je n'ai parlé à ~** I didn't talk to anyone; **~ n'est parfait** nobody's perfect.

personne[2] /pɛʀsɔn/ *nf* person; **dix ~s** ten people; **les ~s âgées** the elderly; **une ~ de confiance** someone trustworthy; **bien fait de sa ~** good-looking; **le respect de la ~ (humaine)** respect for the individual; **il s'en occupe en ~** he's dealing with it personally; **c'est la cupidité en ~** he/she is greed personified.
■ **~ à charge** dependant; **~ civile** or **morale** artificial person, legal entity.

personnel, -elle /pɛʀsɔnɛl/ **I** *adj* **1** [*friend, effects*] personal; [*papers*] private; **adresse personnelle** home or private address; **2** individual; **3** selfish; **4** [*pronoun*] personal.
II *nm* staff; workforce; employees, personnel.

personnellement /pɛʀsɔnɛlmɑ̃/ *adv* personally.

personnifier /pɛʀsɔnifje/ [2] *vtr* to personify.

perspective /pɛʀspɛktiv/ *nf* **1** (in art) perspective; **2** view; **3** perspective, angle; **4** prospect.

perspicace /pɛʀspikas/ *adj* perceptive, perspicacious.

perspicacité /pɛʀspikasite/ *nf* insight, perspicacity.

persuader /pɛʀsɥade/ [1] *vtr* to persuade; **j'en suis persuadé** I'm convinced of it.

persuasif, -ive /pɛʀsɥazif, iv/ *adj* persuasive.

perte /pɛʀt/ *nf* **1** loss; **être en ~ de vitesse** to be losing speed; to be slowing down; **à ~ de vue** as far as the eye can see; **2** waste; **3** ruin; **courir** or **aller à sa ~** to be heading for a fall; **vouloir la ~ de qn** to try to bring about sb's downfall.
■ **~ sèche** dead loss.

pertinemment /pɛʀtinamɑ̃/ *adv* **1** perfectly well; **2** pertinently.

pertinence /pɛʀtinɑ̃s/ *nf* pertinence; **avec ~** pertinently.

pertinent, ~e /pɛʀtinɑ̃, ɑ̃t/ *adj* pertinent.

perturbant, ~e /pɛʀtyʀbɑ̃, ɑ̃t/ *adj* disturbing.

perturbateur, -trice /pɛʀtyʀbatœʀ, tʀis/ *adj* disruptive.

perturbation /pɛʀtyʀbasjɔ̃/ *nf* **1** disruption; **2** disturbance; **3** upheaval.

perturber /pɛʀtyʀbe/ [1] *vtr* to disrupt [*traffic, market, meeting*]; to interfere with [*development*]; to disturb [*sleep*].

pervenche /pɛʀvɑ̃ʃ/ *nf* **1** periwinkle; **2**° (female) traffic warden (GB), meter maid° (US).

pervers, ~e /pɛʀvɛʀ, ɛʀs/ **I** *adj* **1** wicked; **2** perverted; **3** [*effect*] pernicious.
II *nm,f* pervert.

perversion /pɛʀvɛʀsjɔ̃/ *nf* perversion.

perversité /pɛʀvɛʀsite/ *nf* perversity.

pervertir /pɛʀvɛʀtiʀ/ [3] *vtr* to corrupt.

pesamment /pəzamɑ̃/ *adv* [*fall*] heavily; [*walk*] with a heavy step.

pesant, ~e /pəzɑ̃, ɑ̃t/ *adj* **1** heavy; **2** cumbersome; **3** [*atmosphere, silence*] oppressive.
IDIOMS **valoir son ~ d'or** to be worth its weight in gold.

pesanteur /pəzɑ̃tœʀ/ *nf* **1** (of style) heaviness; (of mind) dullness; (of bureaucracy) inertia; **2** gravity.

pèse-personne, *pl* **~s** /pɛzpɛʀsɔn/ *nm* bathroom scales.

peser /pəze/ [16] I *vtr* **1** to weigh; **2** to weigh up; **~ le pour et le contre** to weigh up the pros and cons; **~ ses mots** to choose one's words carefully; **tout bien pesé** all things considered.
II *vi* **1** to weigh; **je pèse 70 kg** I weigh 70 kg; **~ lourd** to weigh a lot; **2** to carry weight; **~ dans/sur une décision** to have a decisive influence in/on a decision; **3 ~ sur** [*suspicion, risks*] to hang over [*person, project*]; **4** [*tax, debts*] to weigh [sb/sth] down [*person, country*]; **5** [*person, decision*] to influence (greatly) [*policy, situation*].

pessimisme /pesimism/ *nm* pessimism.

pessimiste /pesimist/ I *adj* pessimistic.
II *nmf* pessimist.

peste /pɛst/ *nf* **1** plague; **2**° pest°.
IDIOMS **je me méfie de lui comme de la ~**° I don't trust him an inch.

pester /pɛste/ [1] *vi* **~ contre qn/qch** to curse sb/sth.

pesticide /pɛstisid/ I *adj* pesticidal.
II *nm* pesticide.

pestilentiel, -ielle /pɛstilɑ̃sjɛl/ *adj* pestilential.

pet° /pɛ/ *nm* fart°.

pétale /petal/ *nm* petal.

pétanque /petɑ̃k/ *nf* petanque (*game of bowls played in France*).

pétarader /petaʀade/ [1] *vi* to backfire, to sputter.

pétard /petaʀ/ *nm* banger (GB), firecracker (US); **un ~ mouillé** (figurative) a damp squib; **être en ~**° to be hopping mad° (GB), to be real mad° (US).

péter /pete/ [14] I° *vtr* to bust° [*machine*]; to snap [*thread*].
II *vi* **1**° to fart°; **2**° [*balloon, pipe, seam*] to burst; [*explosive*] to go off; [*situation*] to blow up; [*machine*] to bust°; [*thread*] to snap.
IDIOMS **~ le feu**° to be full of beans°.

pétillant, ~e /petijɑ̃, ɑ̃t/ *adj* sparkling.

pétiller /petije/ [1] *vi* [*drink*] to fizz; [*firewood*] to crackle; [*eyes*] to sparkle.

petit, ~e /p(ə)ti, it/ I *adj* **1** small, little; short; **une toute ~e pièce** a tiny room; **se faire tout ~** (figurative) to try to make oneself inconspicuous; **2** [*walk, distance*] short; **par ~es étapes** in easy stages; **3** young, little; **le ~ nouveau** the new boy; **c'est notre ~ dernier** he's our youngest; **4** [*eater*] light; [*wage*] low; [*cry, worry*] little; [*hope*] slight; [*detail, defect*] minor; [*job*] modest; [*civil servant*] low-ranking; **5** (figurative) little; **de bons ~s plats** tasty dishes; **envoie-moi un ~ mot** drop me a line; **une ~e trentaine de personnes** under thirty people.
II *adv* **tailler ~** to be small-fitting; **~ à ~** little by little.
■ **~ ami** boyfriend; **~ bois** kindling; **~ coin**° (euphemistic) loo° (GB), bathroom (US); **~ déjeuner** breakfast; **~ noir**° coffee; **~ nom**° first name; **~ pois** (garden) pea, petit pois; **~ pot** jar of baby food; **~ rat (de l'Opéra)** *pupil at Paris Opéra's ballet school*; **~ salé** streaky salted pork; **~e amie** girlfriend; **~e annonce** classified advertisement; **~e nature** weakling; **~e reine** cycling; **~e souris** tooth fairy; **~e voiture** toy car; **~s chevaux** ≈ ludo.

petit-cousin, petite-cousine, *mpl* **petits-cousins** /p(ə)tikuzɛ̃n, p(ə)titkuzin/ *nm,f* second cousin.

petite-fille, *pl* **petites-filles** /p(ə)titfij/ *nf* granddaughter.

petitesse /p(ə)titɛs/ *nf* **1** pettiness; **2** small size.

petit-fils, *pl* **petits-fils** /p(ə)tifis/ *nm* grandson.

pétition /petisjɔ̃/ *nf* petition.

petit-lait /p(ə)tilɛ/ *nm* whey.
IDIOMS **ça se boit comme du ~**°! it slips down nicely!

petits-enfants /p(ə)tizɑ̃fɑ̃/ *nm pl* grandchildren.

petit-suisse, *pl* **petits-suisses** /p(ə)tisɥis/ *nm* individual fromage frais.

pétri, ~e /petʀi/ *adj* **~ de** steeped in [*ignorance*]; puffed up with [*pride*]; full of [*contradictions*].

pétrifier /petʀifje/ [2] *vtr* **1** to petrify; **2** (figurative) to transfix.

pétrin /petʀɛ̃/ *nm* dough trough.
IDIOMS **être dans le ~** to be in a fix°.

pétrir /petʀiʀ/ [3] *vtr* **1** to knead [*dough*]; **2** to mould (GB), mold (US) [*personality*].

pétrole /petʀɔl/ *nm* oil, petroleum; **~ brut** crude oil.

pétrolier /petʀɔlje/ I *adj* oil.
II *nm* oil tanker.

pétulance /petylɑ̃s/ *nf* exuberance.

pétulant, ~e /petylɑ̃, ɑ̃t/ *adj* exuberant.

peu /pø/

■ **Note** See the entries *avant, depuis, d'ici* and *sous* for the use of *peu* with these words.

I *adv* **1** not much; **il parle ~** he doesn't talk much; **elle gagne assez ~** she doesn't earn very much; **elle gagne très ~** she earns very little; **deux semaines c'est trop ~** two weeks isn't long enough; **si ~ que ce soit** however little; **très ~ pour moi**°! thanks, but no thanks!; **2** not very; **~ soigneux** not very tidy; **assez ~ connu** little-known; **elle n'est pas ~ fière** she's more than a little proud.
II *pron* few, not many; **~ leur font confiance** few or not many people trust them.
III **de peu** *phr* only just.
IV **peu de** *quantif* **~ de mots** few words; **~ de temps** little time; **c'est ~ de chose** it's not much.
V *nm* **le ~ de** the little [*trust, freedom*]; the few [*books, friends*]; the lack of [*interest, enthusiasm*].
VI **un peu** *phr* **1** a little, a bit; **reste encore un ~** stay a little longer; **mange un ~ plus** eat a bit more; **parle un ~ plus fort** speak a little louder; **un ~ plus/moins de** a few more/slightly fewer [*books*]; a little more/slightly

less [*time*]; **un ~ beaucoup** more than a bit; **2** just; **répète un ~ pour voir**○! you just try saying that again!; **'tu le ferais toi?'—'un ~ (que je le ferais)**○**!'** 'would you do it?'—'I sure would○!'; **pour un ~ ils se seraient battus** they very nearly had a fight.
VII peu à peu *phr* gradually, little by little.
VIII pour peu que *phr* if; **pour ~ qu'il ait bu, il va nous raconter sa vie** if he's had anything at all to drink, he'll tell us his life story.
peuplade /pœplad/ *nf* small tribe.
peuple /pœpl/ *nm* people.
peupler /pœple/ [1] **I** *vtr* **1** to populate [*country*]; to stock [*forest, pond*]; **2** [*animals, plants*] to colonize [*region, island*]; [*spectators, students*] to fill [*hall, street*].
II se peupler *v refl* (+ *v être*) [*town, region*] to fill up (**de** with).
peuplier /pøplije/ *nm* poplar.
peur /pœʀ/ *nf* fear; fright, scare; **être mort** or **vert**○ **de ~** to be scared to death; **une ~ panique s'empara de lui** he was panic-stricken; **avoir ~** to be afraid; **j'en ai bien ~** I'm afraid so; **il n'a ~ de rien** he's not afraid of anything, he's fearless; **faire ~ à qn** to frighten sb; **maigre à faire ~** terribly thin.
peureux, -euse /pœʀø, øz/ *adj* fearful.
peut-être /pøtɛtʀ/ *adv* perhaps, maybe.
phalange /falɑ̃ʒ/ *nf* phalanx.
phallique /falik/ *adj* phallic.
phallocrate /falɔkʀat/ *nm* male chauvinist, phallocrat.
phallus /falys/ *nm inv* phallus.
pharaon /faʀaɔ̃/ *nm* pharaoh.
phare /faʀ/ *nm* **1** headlight; **2** lighthouse.
pharmaceutique /faʀmasøtik/ *adj* pharmaceutical.
pharmacie /faʀmasi/ *nf* **1** chemist's (shop) (GB), drugstore (US), pharmacy; **2** medicine cabinet; **3** (science) pharmacy.
pharmacien, -ienne /faʀmasjɛ̃, ɛn/ *nm,f* (dispensing) chemist (GB), pharmacist.
pharynx /faʀɛ̃ks/ *nm inv* pharynx.
phase /fɑz/ *nf* **1** stage; **2** phase.
phénoménal, ~e, *mpl* **-aux** /fenɔmenal, o/ *adj* phenomenal.
phénomène /fenɔmɛn/ *nm* **1** phenomenon; **des ~s de racisme** manifestations of racism; **2**○ **c'est un ~** he/she's quite a character; **3** (in circus) freak.
philanthropie /filɑ̃tʀɔpi/ *nf* philanthropy.
philatéliste /filatelist/ *nmf* stamp collector, philatelist.
philo○ /filo/ *nf* (students' slang) philosophy.
philosophe /filɔzɔf/ **I** *adj* philosophical.
II *nmf* philosopher.
philosophie /filɔzɔfi/ *nf* philosophy; **avec ~** philosophically.
philosophique /filɔzɔfik/ *adj* philosophical.
phobie /fɔbi/ *nf* phobia (**de** about).
phonétique /fɔnetik/ **I** *adj* phonetic.
II *nf* phonetics.
phonographe /fɔnɔgʀaf/ *nm* gramophone (GB), phonograph (US).
phoque /fɔk/ *nm* **1** seal; **2** sealskin.
IDIOMS **souffler comme un ~**○ to puff and pant.
phosphate /fɔsfat/ *nm* phosphate.
phosphore /fɔsfɔʀ/ *nm* phosphorus.
phosphorescent, ~e /fɔsfɔʀesɑ̃, ɑ̃t/ *adj* phosphorescent.
photo /fɔto/ *nf* **1** photography; **2** photo, photograph, picture.
■ **~ d'identité** passport photo
photocomposition /fɔtokɔ̃pozisjɔ̃/ *nf* filmsetting (GB), photocomposition (US).
photocopie /fɔtokɔpi/ *nf* photocopy.
photocopier /fɔtokɔpje/ [2] *vtr* to photocopy.
photocopieuse /fɔtokɔpjøz/ *nf* photocopier.
photogénique /fɔtoʒenik/ *adj* photogenic.
photographe /fɔtogʀaf/ *nmf* **1** photographer; **2 aller chez le ~** to go to the camera shop (GB) or store (US).
photographie /fɔtogʀafi/ *nf* **1** photography; **2** photograph, picture.
photographier /fɔtogʀafje/ [2] *vtr* to photograph, to take a photo of.
photographique /fɔtogʀafik/ *adj* photographic.
photomaton® /fɔtomatɔ̃/ *nm* photo booth.
photosensible /fɔtosɑ̃sibl/ *adj* photosensitive.
photosynthèse /fɔtosɛ̃tɛz/ *nf* photosynthesis.
phrase /fʀɑz/ *nf* **1** sentence; **2** phrase; **avoir une ~ malheureuse** to say the wrong thing; **faire de grandes ~s** to use flowery language; **~ toute faite** stock phrase; **3** (Mus) phrase.
phréatique /fʀeatik/ *adj* **nappe ~** ground water.
physicien, -ienne /fizisjɛ̃, ɛn/ *nm,f* physicist.
physiologie /fizjɔlɔʒi/ *nf* physiology.
physiologique /fizjɔlɔʒik/ *adj* physiological.
physionomie /fizjɔnɔmi/ *nf* **1** face; **2** (figurative) (of country) face; (of area) appearance, look.
physionomiste /fizjɔnɔmist/ *nmf* **c'est un bon ~** he has a good memory for faces.
physiothérapie /fizjɔteʀapi/ *nf* physiotherapy (GB), physical therapy (US).
physique[1] /fizik/ **I** *adj* physical.
II *nm* **1** physical appearance; **2** physique; **avoir un ~ séduisant** to look attractive; **au ~** physically.
IDIOMS **avoir le ~ de l'emploi** to look the part.
physique[2] /fizik/ *nf* physics.
physiquement /fizikmɑ̃/ *adv* physically.
phytothérapie /fitoteʀapi/ *nf* herbal medicine.
piaffer /pjafe/ [1] *vi* **1** [*horse*] to paw the ground; **2** [*person*] to be impatient (**de faire** to do); **~ d'impatience** to be champing at the bit.
piailler /pjɑje/ [1] *vi* **1** [*bird*] to chirp; **2**○ [*person*] to squeal.

pianiste /pjanist/ *nmf* **1** pianist; **2** piano player.

piano /pjano/ **I** *nm* piano; **jouer qch au ~** to play sth on the piano.
II *adv* **1** (Mus) piano; **2**○ gently; **vas-y ~** take it easy.
■ **~ à queue** grand piano.

pianoter /pjanɔte/ [1] *vi* **1** to tinkle on the piano; **2 ~ sur une table** to drum one's fingers on a table.

pic /pik/ **I** *nm* **1** peak; **2** pick; **3** woodpecker.
II à pic *phr* [*cliff*] sheer; [*ravine*] very steep.
IDIOMS **tomber à ~** to come just at the right time

pichenette /piʃnɛt/ *nf* flick.

pichet /piʃɛ/ *nm* jug (GB), pitcher.

picorer /pikɔʀe/ [1] *vi* [*bird*] to peck about; [*person*] to nibble.

picotement /pikɔtmɑ̃/ *nm* tingling; tickling; smarting.

picoter /pikɔte/ [1] **I** *vtr* to sting, to make [sth] sting [*eyes, nose*]; to tickle [*throat*]; to sting [*skin, limb*].
II *vi* [*throat*] to tickle; [*eyes*] to sting.

pie /pi/ **I** *adj inv* [*cow*] black and white; **~ noir** [*horse*] piebald.
II *nf* **1** magpie; **2**○ chatterbox○.

pièce /pjɛs/ **I** *nf* **1** room; **maison de quatre ~s** four-room(ed) house; **2** coin; **~ de monnaie** coin; **3** play; **~ de théâtre** play; **4** bit, piece; **en ~s** in bits; **mettre en ~s** to pull [sth/sb] to pieces; **5** part; **~ de rechange** spare part; **6** patch; **7** document; **juger (avec) ~s à l'appui** to judge on the basis of supporting documents; **juger sur ~s** to judge on the actual evidence; **c'est inventé de toutes ~s** (figurative) it's a complete fabrication; **8** (gen) piece, item; (in chess set, puzzle) piece; **~ de collection** collector's item; **travailler à la ~** to do piecework; **on n'est pas aux ~s**○ we're not in a sweat-shop.
II -pièces (*combining form*) **1 un trois-~s cuisine** a three-roomed apartment with kitchen; **2 un (maillot) deux-~s** a two-piece swimsuit.
■ **~ à conviction** exhibit; **~ d'eau** ornamental lake; ornamental pond; **~ détachée** spare part; **en ~s détachées** in kit form; dismantled; **~ d'identité** identity papers; **~ maîtresse** showpiece; key element; **~ montée** layer cake.

pied /pje/ *nm* **1** foot; **être ~s nus** to be barefoot(ed); **sauter à ~s joints** to jump with one's feet together; (figurative) to jump in with both feet; **coup de ~** kick; **à ~** on foot; **promenade à ~** walk; **taper du ~** to stamp one's foot; to tap one's foot; **mettre ~ à terre** to dismount; **de la tête aux ~s** from head to foot; **portrait en ~** full-length portrait; **avoir un ~**○ **dans l'édition** to have a foothold in publishing; **avoir conscience de là où on met les ~s**○ to be aware of what one is letting oneself in for; **sur un ~ d'égalité** on an equal footing; **2** (of hill, stairs) foot, bottom; (of glass) stem; (of lamp) base; (of camera) stand; **3** (of celery, lettuce) head; **~ de vigne** vine; **4** (measurement) foot.
■ **~ à coulisse** calliper rule.
IDIOMS **être sur ~** [*person*] to be up and about; [*business*] to be up and running; **mettre sur ~** to set up; **j'ai ~** I can touch the bottom; **perdre ~** to go out of one's depth; to lose ground; **être à ~ d'œuvre** to be ready to get down to work; **elle joue au tennis comme un ~**○ she's hopeless at tennis; **faire un ~ de nez à qn** to thumb one's nose at sb; **faire un ~ de nez aux conventions** to cock a snook at conventions; **faire du ~ à qn** to play footsy with sb○; **faire des ~s et des mains**○ **pour obtenir** to work really hard at getting; **ça lui fera les ~s**○ that will teach him a lesson; **c'est le ~**○ that's terrific○; **mettre à ~** to suspend; **lever le ~**○ to slow down.

pied-à-terre /pjetatɛʀ/ *nm inv* pied-à-terre.

pied-bot, *pl* **pieds-bots** /pjebo/ *nm* club-footed person.

pied-de-biche, *pl* **pieds-de-biche** /pjed biʃ/ *nm* crowbar.

pied-de-poule, *pl* **pieds-de-poule** /pjed pul/ *adj inv* houndstooth.

piédestal, *pl* **-aux** /pjedɛstal, o/ *nm* pedestal.

pied-noir○, *pl* **pieds-noirs** /pjenwaʀ/ *nmf* (*French colonial born in Algeria*).

piège /pjɛʒ/ *nm* **1** trap; **tendre un ~ à qn** to set a trap for sb; **il s'est laissé prendre au ~** he walked into the trap; **2** pitfall.

piéger /pjeʒe/ [15] *vtr* **1** to trap [*animal, criminal*]; **2** to trick, to trap [*person*]; **3** to booby-trap [*letter, parcel, car*].

pierre /pjɛʀ/ *nf* stone; rock; **poser la première ~** to lay the foundation stone.
IDIOMS **jeter la ~ à qn** to accuse sb; **faire d'une ~ deux coups** to kill two birds with one stone.

piété /pjete/ *nf* piety; **de ~** devotional.

piétiner /pjetine/ [1] **I** *vtr* **1** to trample [sth] underfoot; **2** to trample on.
II *vi* **1 ~ d'impatience/de rage** to hop up and down with impatience/with fury; **2** to shuffle along; to trudge along; **3** to make no headway.

piéton, -onne /pjetɔ̃, ɔn/ **I** *adj* pedestrianized.
II *nm,f* pedestrian; **passage pour ~s** pedestrian crossing.

piétonnier, -ière /pjetɔnje, ɛʀ/ *adj* pedestrianized.

piètre /pjɛtʀ/ *adj* [*actor, writer*] very mediocre; [*health, results*] very poor; **c'est une ~ consolation** that's small comfort; **avoir ~ allure** to cut a sorry figure.

pieu, *pl* **~x**[1] /pjø/ *nm* stake.

pieusement /pjøzmɑ̃/ *adv* **1** piously; **2** devotedly; **3** religiously.

pieuvre /pjœvʀ/ *nf* octopus.

pieux[2], **pieuse** /pjø, øz/ **I** *adj* **1** pious, religious; **avoir une pensée pieuse pour qn** to remember sb in one's prayers; **2** [*affection, silence*] reverent.
II *nm pl* ▶ **pieu**.

■ ~ **mensonge** white lie.

pif° /pif/ *nm* **1** nose, conk° (GB), schnozzle° (US); **2** intuition; **j'ai eu du ~** I had a hunch°; **au ~** [*measure*] roughly; [*find*] by chance; [*decide*] just like that.

pige /piʒ/ *nf* **travailler à la ~, faire des ~s** to do freelance work.

pigeon /piʒɔ̃/ *nm* **1** pigeon; **2**° sucker°.
■ ~ **ramier** wood pigeon, ring dove; ~ **vole** Simon says; ~ **voyageur** carrier pigeon.

piger° /piʒe/ [13] *vtr* to understand.

pigment /pigmɑ̃/ *nm* pigment.

pignon /piɲɔ̃/ *nm* **1** gable; **2** gearwheel; **3** pine kernel.
IDIOMS **avoir ~ sur rue** to be well-established.

pilaf /pilaf/ *nm* pilau; **riz ~** pilau rice.

pile[1]° /pil/ *adv* **1 s'arrêter ~** to stop dead; **2** exactly; **à 10 heures et demie ~** at ten-thirty sharp or on the dot°; **être ~ à l'heure** to be right on time; **tu tombes ~** you're just the person I wanted to see.

pile[2] /pil/ *nf* **1** pile; stack; **2 ~ (électrique)** battery; **à ~s** battery-operated; **3** pier; **4** (of coin) **le côté ~** the reverse side; **jouer à ~ ou face** to play heads or tails; **ils ont décidé à ~ ou face** they tossed for it.
■ ~ **bouton** button battery; ~ **solaire** solar cell.

piler /pile/ [1] **I** *vtr* to grind [*nuts*]; to crush [*garlic, glass*].
II° *vi* [*car*] to pull up short; [*driver*] to slam on the brakes.

pileux, -euse /pilø, øz/ *adj* **système ~** hair.

pilier /pilje/ *nm* **1** pillar; **2** (figurative) mainstay; **3** (in rugby) prop forward.

pillage /pijaʒ/ *nm* **1** pillage, plundering; looting; **2** pillaging.

pillard, ~e /pijaʀ, aʀd/ **I** *adj* pillaging, plundering; thieving.
II *nm,f* looter; pillager.

piller /pije/ [1] *vtr* to pillage [*town*]; to loot [*shop*]; to ransack [*house*]; to raid [*fridge*]; to plunder [*temple*].

pilon /pilɔ̃/ *nm* **1** pestle; **2** (of poultry) drumstick.

pilonner /pilɔne/ [1] *vtr* **1** (Mil) to bombard; **2**° to give [sb] a pounding° [*opponent*].

pilori /pilɔʀi/ *nm* stocks; **mettre qn au ~** (figurative) to pillory sb.

pilotage /pilɔtaʒ/ *nm* piloting.

pilote /pilɔt/ **I** *nm* pilot.
II (-)pilote (*combining form*) **projet(-)~** pilot project; **hôpital(-)~** experimental hospital.
■ ~ **automobile** racing driver; ~ **d'essai** test pilot.

piloter /pilɔte/ [1] *vtr* to pilot [*plane, ship*]; to drive [*car*].

pilotis /pilɔti/ *nm inv* stilts.

pilule /pilyl/ *nf* pill.
IDIOMS **avaler la ~**° to grin and bear it; **faire passer la ~**° to sweeten the pill; **se dorer la ~**° to sunbathe.

pimbêche /pɛ̃bɛʃ/ *nf* stuck-up madam°.

piment /pimɑ̃/ *nm* **1** capsicum; **2** hot pepper; **3** spice.
■ ~ **rouge** hot red pepper, chilli; ~ **vert** green chilli pepper.

pimenter /pimɑ̃te/ [1] *vtr* **1** to put chillies[GB] in; **2** to give a bit of spice to.

pimpant, ~e /pɛ̃pɑ̃, ɑ̃t/ *adj* spruce, smart.

pin /pɛ̃/ *nm* pine (tree); **pomme de ~** pine cone.

pinailler° /pinɑje/ [1] *vi* to split hairs, to quibble (**sur** about).

pince /pɛ̃s/ *nf* **1** (pair of) pliers; (pair of) tongs; **2** dart; **faire des ~s à la taille** to put darts in at the waist; **un pantalon à ~s** pleat front trousers (GB) or pants (US); **3** (of crab) pincer, claw; **4** crowbar.
■ ~ **à cheveux** hair grip; ~ **coupante** wire cutters; ~ **à dessin** bulldog clip; ~ **à épiler** tweezers; ~ **à linge** clothes peg; ~ **à sucre** sugar tongs; ~ **à vélo** bicycle clip.

pincé, ~e[1] /pɛ̃se/ *adj* **1** [*smile*] tight-lipped; **prendre un air ~** to become stiff or starchy; **2** [*lips*] thin; [*nostrils*] pinched.

pinceau, *pl* **~x** /pɛ̃so/ *nm* (paint) brush.

pincée[2] /pɛ̃se/ **I** *adj f* ▶ **pincé**.
II *nf* (of pepper, salt) pinch.

pincement /pɛ̃smɑ̃/ *nm* **1** pinch; **avoir un ~ de cœur** to feel a twinge of sadness; **2** (of string) plucking.

pince-nez /pɛ̃sne/ *nm inv* pince-nez.

pincer /pɛ̃se/ [12] **I** *vtr* **1** [*person*] to pinch; [*crab*] to nip; **2**° to nab°, to catch [*thief*]; **3 ~ les lèvres** to purse one's lips; **4** to pluck [*string*]; **5** [*wind, cold*] to sting [*face*].
II° *vi* **ça pince dur** it's bitterly cold.
III se pincer *v refl* (+ *v être*) to pinch oneself; **se ~ le nez** to hold one's nose; **elle s'est pincée en refermant le tiroir** she caught her fingers closing the drawer.
IDIOMS **en ~**° **pour qn** to be stuck° on sb, to be in love with sb.

pince-sans-rire /pɛ̃ssɑ̃ʀiʀ/ *nmf inv* **c'est un ~** he has a deadpan sense of humour[GB].

pincettes /pɛ̃sɛt/ *nf pl* tweezers; **il n'est pas à prendre avec des ~s**° he's like a bear with a sore head.

pinède /pinɛd/ *nf* pine forest.

pingouin /pɛ̃gwɛ̃/ *nm* **1** auk; **2** penguin.

ping-pong®, *pl* **~s** /piŋpɔ̃ŋ/ *nm* table tennis, ping-pong®.

pingre /pɛ̃gʀ/ **I** *adj* stingy, niggardly.
II *nmf* skinflint.

pin-pon /pɛ̃pɔ̃/ *nm* (*also onomatopoeic*) *sound of a two-tone siren*.

pin's /pins/ *nm inv* lapel badge.

pinson /pɛ̃sɔ̃/ *nm* chaffinch.
IDIOMS **être gai comme un ~** to be as happy as a lark.

pintade /pɛ̃tad/ *nf* guinea fowl.

pinte /pɛ̃t/ *nf* **1** pint (GB) (= 0,57 litre); **2** ≈ quart (US) (= 0,94 litre); **3** pot, tankard.

pinter○: **se pinter** /pɛ̃te/ [1] *v refl* (+ *v être*) to get plastered○ or drunk.

pin-up○ /pinœp/ *nf inv* glamour[GB] girl, sexy girl.

pioche /pjɔʃ/ *nf* **1** mattock; pickaxe (GB), pickax (US); **2** (Games) stock.

piocher /pjɔʃe/ [1] *vtr* **1** to dig [sth] over [*soil*]; **2**○ to swot up on○ (GB), to work on [*subject*]; to cram for○ [*exam*]; **3** (Games) to take [sth] from the stock [*card, domino*].

piolet /pjɔlɛ/ *nm* ice axe (GB), ice pick (US).

pion, pionne /pjɔ̃, pjɔn/ **I**○ *nm,f* (Sch) *student paid to supervise pupils.*
II *nm* **1** (in games) (gen) counter; (in chess) pawn; (in draughts) draught (GB), checker (US); **2** (figurative) pawn.

pionnier, -ière /pjɔnje, ɛʀ/ *adj, nm,f* pioneer.

pipe /pip/ *nf* pipe; **fumer la ~** to smoke a pipe.
IDIOMS **casser sa ~**○ to kick the bucket○; **se fendre la ~**○ to laugh one's head off○.

pipeau, *pl* **~x** /pipo/ *nm* (reed-)pipe.
IDIOMS **c'est du ~**○ it's no great shakes○; **c'est pas du ~**○ it's for real○.

pipelette○ /piplɛt/ *nf* gossip(monger).

piper /pipe/ [1] *vtr* **1**○ **ne pas ~ (mot)** not to say a word (**de** about); **2** (Games) to load [*dice*]; to mark [*cards*].

pipi○ /pipi/ *nm* wee○ (GB), pee○; wee-wee○.
IDIOMS **c'est du ~ de chat** (drink) it's gnat's piss○; (show, book) it's as dull as dishwater.

piquant, ~e /pikɑ̃, ɑ̃t/ **I** *adj* **1** [*stem, thistle*] prickly; [*needle, nail*] sharp; [*beard*] bristly; **2** [*mustard, sauce*] hot; [*wine, cheese*] sharp; **3** [*adventure*] spicy, piquant.
II *nm* **1** (of stem, thistle) prickle; (of hedgehog, cactus) spine; (of barbed wire) spike, barb; **2** (of story) spiciness; (of situation) piquancy.

pique[1] /pik/ *nm* (Games) spades.

pique[2] /pik/ *nf* **1** cutting remark; **2** pike; (of picador) lance.

piqué, ~e /pike/ *pp adj* **1** [*wood*] worm-eaten; [*linen, mirror, fruit*] spotted; [*paper, book*] foxed; **2**○ [*person*] dotty○, eccentric.

pique-assiette○ /pikasjɛt/ *nmf inv* sponger○, freeloader○.

pique-nique, *pl* **~s** /piknik/ *nm* picnic.

piquer /pike/ [1] **I** *vtr* **1** [*wasp, jellyfish, nettle, smoke*] to sting; [*mosquito, flea, spider, snake*] to bite; [*thistle, rosebush*] to prick; **2**○ to give [sb] an injection; **faire ~ un animal** to have an animal put down; **3** [*mildew, rust*] to spot [*linen, mirror*]; to fox [*paper, book*]; **4 ses yeux la piquaient** her eyes were stinging; **ça me pique partout** I'm itchy all over; **5**○ to pinch○ (GB), to steal [*book, idea*]; to pinch○ (GB), to borrow [*pencil, pullover*]; **6** to catch; **ils se sont fait ~ à tricher pendant l'examen** they got caught cheating during the exam; **7 cette remarque m'a piquée** this remark wounded me; **~ qn au vif** to cut sb to the quick; **8** to arouse [*curiosity, interest*]; **9**○ **~ un fou rire** to have a fit of the giggles; **~ une crise de nerfs** to throw a fit○; **~ un cent mètres** to break into a run; **10 ~ une tête (dans l'eau)** to dive (into the water).
II *vi* **1** [*beard*] to be bristly; [*garment, wool*] to be scratchy; [*throat, eyes*] to sting; **2** [*bird*] to swoop down; [*plane*] to dive; **~ du nez** to nod off, to doze off; [*plane*] to go into a nosedive; **3**○ **arrête de ~ dans le plat** stop picking (things out of the dish); **4**○ **le taureau piqua droit sur nous** the bull came straight for us.
III se piquer *v refl* (+ *v être*) **1** to prick oneself; **se ~ aux orties** to get stung by nettles; **2** to inject oneself; **3 se ~ d'être philosophe** to like to pretend one is a philosopher; **se ~ de pouvoir réussir seul** to claim that one can manage on one's own.
IDIOMS **quelle mouche t'a piqué**○**?** what's eating○ you?; **son article n'était pas piqué des hannetons**○ his/her article didn't pull any punches.

piquet /pikɛ/ *nm* **1** stake; **2** peg; **3** (in skiing) gate pole; **4** (of sunshade) pole; **5** picket; **~ de grève** (strike) picket, picket line.
IDIOMS **rester planté comme un ~**○ to stand like a dummy.

piquette○ /pikɛt/ *nf* plonk○ (GB), cheap wine.

piqûre /pikyʀ/ *nf* **1** injection, shot; **faire une ~ à qn** to give sb an injection; **2** (of thorn, pin) prick; (of nettle, bee) sting; (of mosquito) bite; **3** stitch; stitching .
■ **~ de rappel** (Med) booster (injection).

pirate /piʀat/ *nm* pirate.
■ **~ de l'air** hijacker, skyjacker; **~ informatique** computer hacker.

pirater /piʀate/ [1] *vtr* to pirate.

piraterie /piʀatʀi/ *nf* piracy.
■ **~ aérienne** hijacking, skyjacking; **~ informatique** computer hacking.

pire /piʀ/ **I** *adj* **1** worse (**que** than); **2** worst; **les ~s mensonges** the most wicked lies; **le ~ des imbéciles** the biggest fool.
II *nm* **le ~** the worst; **au ~** at the very worst.

pirogue /piʀɔg/ *nf* dugout canoe, pirogue.

pirouette /piʀwɛt/ *nf* pirouette; **s'en tirer par une ~** to dodge the question skilfully.

pis /pi/ **I** *adj inv* worse.
II *adv* worse; **tant ~** too bad.
III *nm inv* (of cow) udder.

pis-aller /pizale/ *nm inv* stopgap; makeshift solution.

piscine /pisin/ *nf* swimming pool; **~ couverte** indoor swimming pool.

pisse◑ /pis/ *nf* piss◑.

pissenlit /pisɑ̃li/ *nm* dandelion.
IDIOMS **manger les ~s par la racine**◑ to be pushing up the daisies○.

pisser◑ /pise/ [1] **I** *vtr* **~ le sang** [*person, nose, injury*] to pour with blood.
II *vi* to pee○, to piss◑.
IDIOMS **il pleut comme vache qui pisse** it's pissing down◑; **ne plus se sentir ~** to be full of oneself; **ça lui a pris comme une envie de ~** he/she had a sudden urge to do it; **laisse ~!** forget it!

pissotière○ /pisɔtjɛʀ/ *nf* street urinal, pissoir (US).

pistache /pistaʃ/ *nf* pistachio.

piste /pist/ *nf* **1** trail; **être sur une fausse ~** to be on the wrong track; **2** (in police investigation) lead; **3** (in stadium) track; (in horseracing) racecourse (GB), racetrack (US); (in motor racing) racetrack; (in iceskating) rink; (in circus) ring; (in skiing) slope; (in cross-country skiing) trail; **~ de danse** dance floor; **entrer en ~** (at circus) to come into the ring; (figurative) to enter the fray; **en ~!** (figurative) get cracking○!; **être en ~** (figurative) to be in the running; **4** track, path; (in desert) trail; **5** (in airport) runway; **6** (on record, cassette) track.
■ **~ cyclable** cycle lane; cycle path.

pistil /pistil/ *nm* pistil.

pistolet /pistɔlɛ/ *nm* **1** pistol, gun; **~ d'alarme** alarm gun; **tirer au ~** to fire a pistol; **2** (Tech) gun; **~ à peinture** spray gun.

piston /pistɔ̃/ *nm* **1** (Tech) piston; **moteur à ~s** piston engine; **2**○ contacts; **avoir du ~** to have connections or contacts in the right places.

pistonner○ /pistɔne/ [1] *vtr* to pull strings for [*candidate*].

piteux, -euse /pitø, øz/ *adj* **1** [*results*] poor, pitiful; **2** [*air*] crestfallen.

pitié /pitje/ *nf* pity, mercy; **avoir ~ de qn** to feel sorry for sb; **prendre qn en ~** to take pity on sb; **il fait ~ (à voir)** he's a pitiful sight; **par ~, tais-toi!** for pity's sake, be quiet!

piton /pitɔ̃/ *nm* **1** hook; **2** (in climbing) piton; **3** (of mountain) peak.

pitoyable /pitwajabl/ *adv* **1** pitiful; **2** pathetic.

pitre /pitʀ/ *nm* clown, buffoon.

pitrerie /pitʀəʀi/ *nf* clowning.

pittoresque /pitɔʀɛsk/ *adj* picturesque; colourful[GB].

pivert /pivɛʀ/ *nm* green woodpecker.

pivoine /pivwan/ *nf* peony.
IDIOMS **être rouge comme une ~** to be as red as a beetroot (GB) or a beet (US).

pivot /pivo/ *nm* **1** (Tech) pivot; **2** (of economy, strategy, group) linchpin; (of plot) kingpin; **3** (Sport) (player) pivot, post; **4** (of tooth) post and core.

pivoter /pivɔte/ [1] *vi* [*person, animal*] to pivot, to turn; [*wall, panel*] to pivot; [*door, table*] to revolve; [*armchair, chair*] to swivel.

PJ /peʒi/ *nf* **1** (*abbr* = **police judiciaire**) *detective division of the French police force*; **2** (*abbr* = **pièce(s) jointe(s)**) enc.

PL (*written abbr* = **poids lourd**) HGV (GB), heavy truck (US).

placard /plakaʀ/ *nm* **1** cupboard; **mettre au ~** to put [sth] on ice [*plan*]; to shunt [sb] aside [*person*]; **2** poster, bill; (in newspaper) **~ publicitaire** display advertisement.

place /plas/ *nf* **1** room, space; **2** (in theatre, cinema, bus) seat; **remettre qch à sa ~** to put sth back in its place; **il reste une ~ en première** there's one seat left in first class; **payer sa ~** (in cinema, theatre) to pay for one's ticket; (on train) to pay one's fare; **prenez ~** take your seats; **sur ~** to/on the scene; **3** (in ranking, hierarchy) place; **obtenir la deuxième ~** to take second place; **il est dans les premières ~s** he's up toward(s) the top; **la ~ d'un mot dans une phrase** the position of a word in a sentence; **il faut savoir rester à sa ~** you must know your place; **remettre qn à sa ~** to put sb in his/her place; **tenir une grande ~ dans la vie de qn** to play a large part in sb's life; **4 à la ~ de** instead of, in place of; **(si j'étais) à ta ~** if I were in your position; **je ne peux pas le faire à ta ~!** I can't do it for you!; **5 en ~** [*system, structures*] in place; [*troops*] in position; [*leader, party, regime*] ruling; **ne plus tenir en ~** to be restless or fidgety; **mettre en ~** to put [sth] in place [*programme*]; to put [sth] in position [*team*]; to establish, to set up [*network, institution*]; **6** (in town) square; **la ~ du village** the village square; **la ~ du marché** the marketplace; **7** (Econ) market; **~ financière** financial market; **8** job; **perdre sa ~** to lose one's job; **il y a des ~s à prendre** there are good job opportunities; **9 être dans la ~** to be on the inside; **avoir un pied dans la ~** to have a foot in the door.

placebo /plasebo/ *nm* placebo; **l'effet ~** the placebo effect.

placement /plasmɑ̃/ *nm* **1** investment; **2 assurer le ~ des diplômés** to ensure that graduates find employment; **3** (of child) fostering.

placenta /plasɛ̃ta/ *nm* placenta.

placer /plase/ [12] **I** *vtr* **1** to put, to place [*object*]; to seat [*person*]; **~ un service sous la responsabilité de qn** to make sb responsible for a department; **~ qn/être placé devant un choix difficile** to present sb/to be faced with a difficult choice; **~ sa confiance en qn** to put one's trust in sb; **~ ses espoirs en qn** to pin one's hopes on sb; **mal placé** [*pride*] misplaced; **2** to place, to find a job for [*person*]; **3** to invest [*money*]; **4** to slip in [*remark, anecdote*]; **je n'arrive pas à en ~ une**○ **avec elle!** I can't get a word in edgeways (GB) or edgewise (US) with her!; **5** to place [sb] in care [*child*].
II se placer *v refl* (+ *v être*) **1 se ~ près de** to sit next to; **2 il s'est placé dans les premiers** (in class) he got one of the top places; **avoir des amis haut placés** to have friends in high places.

placide /plasid/ *adj* placid, calm.

placidité /plasidite/ *nf* placidity, calmness.

plafond /plafɔ̃/ *nm* **1** ceiling; (of tent, vehicle, tunnel) roof; **2** ceiling, limit; **crever le ~** to go through the ceiling.

plafonner /plafɔne/ [1] *vtr* to put a ceiling on [*prices, salaries, production*].

plafonnier /plafɔnje/ *nm* (gen) flush-fitting ceiling light; (in car) interior light.

plage /plaʒ/ *nf* **1** beach; **2** range; **~ de prix** price range.
■ **~ arrière** rear window shelf; **~ horaire** time slot.

plagiaire /plaʒjɛʀ/ *nmf* plagiarist.

plagiat /plaʒja/ *nm* plagiarism.

plagier /plaʒje/ [2] *vtr* to plagiarize.

plaid /plɛd/ *nm* tartan rug (GB), plaid blanket (US).

plaider /plede/ [1] **I** *vtr* to plead [*case*].
II *vi* **1** to plead; **2 ~ en faveur de qn** [*circumstances, qualities*] to speak in favour[GB] of sb.

plaideur, -euse /plɛdœʀ, øz/ *nm,f* litigant.

plaidoirie /plɛdwaʀi/ *nf* plea.

plaidoyer /plɛdwaje/ *nm* **1** speech for the defence[GB]; **2** plea.

plaie /plɛ/ *nf* **1** wound; sore; cut; **2**○ **cet enfant, quelle ~**○**!** that child is such a pain○!
IDIOMS **mettre le doigt sur la ~** to put one's finger on the problem.

plaignant, ~e /plɛɲɑ̃, ɑ̃t/ *nm,f* plaintiff, complainant.

plaindre /plɛ̃dʀ/ [54] **I** *vtr* to pity, to feel sorry for [*person, animal*].
II se plaindre *v refl* (+ *v être*) **1** to complain; **2** [*injured person*] to moan.

plaine /plɛn/ *nf* plain.

plain-pied: **de plain-pied** /dəplɛ̃pje/ *phr* **une maison de ~** a single-storey (GB) or single-story (US) house.

plainte /plɛ̃t/ *nf* **1** (gen, Law) complaint; **déposer une ~ contre qn** to lodge a complaint against sb; **2** moan, groan.

plaintif, -ive /plɛ̃tif, iv/ *adj* plaintive.

plaire /plɛʀ/ [59] **I plaire à** *v+prep* **1 elle plaît aux hommes** men find her attractive; **elle m'a plu tout de suite** I liked her straight away; **il a tout pour ~** he is attractive in every way; **2 mon nouveau travail me plaît** I like my new job; **c'est un modèle qui plaît beaucoup** it's a very popular model.
II se plaire *v refl* (+ *v être*) **1** [*people, couple*] to like each other; **2 ils se plaisent ici** they like it here; **3 il se plaît à dire qu'il est issu du peuple** he likes to say that he's a son of the people.
III *v impers* **s'il te plaît, s'il vous plaît** please.

plaisance /plɛzɑ̃s/ *nf* **la navigation de ~** boating; **bateau de ~** pleasure boat.

plaisant, ~e /plɛzɑ̃, ɑ̃t/ *adj* **1** pleasant; **2** amusing, funny.

plaisanter /plɛzɑ̃te/ [1] *vi* to joke (**sur, de** about).

plaisanterie /plɛzɑ̃tʀi/ *nf* joke; **la ~ a assez duré!** this has gone on long enough!

plaisantin /plɛzɑ̃tɛ̃/ *nm* **1** practical joker; **petit ~!** wise guy○!; **2** skiver○.

plaisir /plɛziʀ/ *nm* pleasure; **prendre un malin ~ à faire** to take a wicked delight in doing; **j'ai appris avec ~ que** I was delighted to hear that; **à ~** [*lie, exaggerate, worry*] for the sake of it; **faire ~ à qn** to please sb; **faites-moi le ~ de vous taire!** would you please shut up○!; **faire durer le ~** to make the pleasure last; (ironic) to prolong the agony.

plan, ~e /plɑ̃, plan/ *nm* **1** (of town, underground) map; (in building) plan, map; **2** plan; **tirer des ~s** to draw up plans; **3** (of machine) blueprint; **4** (of essay, book) outline, framework; **5** (in cinematography) shot; **premier ~** foreground; **second ~** middle-distance; **6** level; **au premier ~ de l'actualité** at the forefront of the news; **de second ~** second-rate; **sur le ~ politique** from a political point of view; **7** plan, programme[GB]; **c'est (pas) le bon ~**○ it's (not) a good idea.
■ **~ d'eau** artificial lake; **~ d'épargne** savings plan.
IDIOMS **laisser qn en ~**○ to leave sb in the lurch, to leave sb high and dry; **laisser qch en ~**○ to leave sth unfinished; **il a tout laissé en ~** he dropped everything.

planche /plɑ̃ʃ/ *nf* **1** (gen) plank; (for kneading dough, washing) board; **faire la ~** to float on one's back; **2** plate.
■ **~ à roulettes** (Sport) skateboard; **~ de salut** lifeline; **~ à voile** windsurfing board.
IDIOMS **monter sur les ~s** to go on the stage, to tread the boards; **avoir du pain sur la ~**○ to have one's work cut out.

plancher[1]○ /plɑ̃ʃe/ [1] *vi* (students' slang) to work (**sur** on).

plancher[2] /plɑ̃ʃe/ *nm* **1** floor; **2** (Econ) floor, minimum; **atteindre un ~** [*prices, share values*] to bottom out.
■ **le ~ des vaches**○ land, terra firma.

plancton /plɑ̃ktɔ̃/ *nm* plankton.

planer /plane/ [1] *vi* **1** [*plane, bird*] to glide; [*bird of prey*] to hover; **2 laisser ~ le doute** to allow uncertainty to persist; **3**○ [*dreamer*] to have one's head in the clouds.

planète /planɛt/ *nf* planet.

planeur /planœʀ/ *nm* **1** glider; **2** gliding.

planification /planifikasjɔ̃/ *nf* planning.

planifier /planifje/ [2] *vtr* to plan.

planning○ /planiŋ/ *nm* (controversial) schedule.
■ **~ familial** family planning service.

planque○ /plɑ̃k/ *nf* **1** (for person) hideout; **2** (for object) hidey-hole○ (GB), stash○ (US).

planqué○ /plɑ̃ke/ *nm* (soldiers' slang) skiver.

planquer○ /plɑ̃ke/ [1] **I** *vtr* to hide [*person*]; to hide [sth] away [*object*].
II se planquer *v refl* (+ *v être*) **1** to hide; to go into hiding; **2** to skive.

plant /plɑ̃/ *nm* young plant.

plantaire /plɑ̃tɛʀ/ *adj* (Anat) plantar.

plantation /plɑ̃tasjɔ̃/ *nf* **1** plantation; **2** (of flowers) bed; (of vegetables) patch.

plante /plɑ̃t/ *nf* **1** plant; **~ verte** houseplant; **~ grasse** succulent; **soigner par les ~s** to use herbal medicine; **2 ~ (des pieds)** sole (of the foot).

planter /plɑ̃te/ [1] **I** *vtr* **1** to plant [*flowers, shrub, vegetables, garden*]; **2** to drive in [*stake*]; to knock in [*nail*]; **~ un couteau dans** to stick a knife into; **3** to pitch [*tent*]; **~ le décor** to set the scene; **4 ~ (là)** to drop [*tool*]; to abandon [*car*].
II se planter *v refl* (+ *v être*) **1**○ **aller se ~ devant qch** to go and stand in front of sth; **2**○ to crash; **se ~ en vélo** to have a bicycle accident; **3**○ to get it wrong; **il s'est planté en histoire** he made a mess of the history exam.

plantureux, -euse /plɑ̃tyʀø, øz/ *adj* [*dinner*] lavish; [*bosom*] ample; [*woman*] buxom.

plaque /plak/ *nf* (of ice, dampness) patch; (on skin) blotch; (of glass, metal) plate; (of marble, chocolate) slab; (on door of surgery, solicitor's office) brass plate; (of policeman) badge.
■ **~ d'égout** manhole cover; **~ d'immatriculation** or **minéralogique** number plate (GB), license plate (US).
IDIOMS **être à côté de la ~**○ to be completely mistaken.

plaqué, **~e** /plake/ *adj* **~ or** gold-plated; **~ acajou** with a mahogany veneer.

plaquer /plake/ [1] **I** *vtr* **1 ~ qn contre qch** to pin sb against sth; **2**○ to leave [*job, spouse, partner*]; **tout ~** to chuck it all in○ (GB), to chuck everything○ (US); **3** (in rugby) to tackle; **4** (Mus) to strike [*agreement*].
II se plaquer *v refl* (+ *v être*) **se ~ contre un mur** to flatten oneself against a wall.

plaquette /plakɛt/ *nf* **1** (of butter) packet; **2** (of pills) ≈ blister strip.
■ **~ de frein** brake shoe.

plastic /plastik/ *nm* plastic explosive; **attentat au ~** bomb attack.

plastifier /plastifje/ [2] *vtr* to coat [sth] with plastic.

plastique[1] /plastik/ *nm* plastic; **c'est du ~** it's plastic.

plastique[2] /plastik/ *nf* (of object, statue) formal beauty; (of person) physique.

plastiquer /plastike/ [1] *vtr* to carry out a bomb attack on.

plastron /plastʀɔ̃/ *nm* **1** shirt front; **2** (of fencer) plastron.

plat, **~e** /pla, plat/ **I** *adj* **1** flat; **2** [*boat*] flat-bottomed; [*watch, lighter*] slimline; [*hair*] limp; **3** [*style, description*] lifeless; **faire de ~es excuses à qn** to apologize abjectly to sb.
II *nm* **1** dish; **2** course.
III à plat *phr* **1 poser qch à ~** to lay sth down flat; **à ~ ventre** flat on one's stomach; **tomber à ~** [*joke*] to fall flat; **2** [*tyre*] flat; [*battery*] flat (GB), dead; **3**○ **être à ~** [*person*] to be run down.
■ **~ du jour** today's special; **~ de résistance** main course.
IDIOMS **mettre les pieds dans le ~**○ to put one's foot in it; **faire tout un ~ de qch**○ to make a big deal about sth.

platane /platan/ *nm* plane tree.

plateau, *pl* **~x** /plato/ *nm* **1** tray (**de** of); **2 ~ de tournage** film set; **3** (in geography) plateau; **4** (of weighing scales) pan.

plate-bande, *pl* **plates-bandes** /platbɑ̃d/ *nf* border, flower bed.

plate-forme, *pl* **plates-formes** /platfɔʀm/ *nf* platform; **~ pétrolière** oil rig.

platement /platmɑ̃/ *adv* **s'excuser ~** to apologize abjectly.

platine[1] /platin/ *adj inv*, *nm* platinum.

platine[2] /platin/ *nf* (record player) turntable.

platitude /platityd/ *nf* **1** (of remark, text) banality; **2** platitude.

platonique /platɔnik/ *adj* platonic.

plâtre /plɑtʀ/ *nm* **1** plaster; **2** (Med) plaster cast.
IDIOMS **battre qn comme ~**○ to beat the living daylights out of sb○; **essuyer les ~s** to put up with the initial problems.

plâtrer /plɑtʀe/ [1] *vtr* **1** to plaster [*wall*]; **2** (Med) **~ le bras de qn** to put sb's arm in plaster or in a cast.

plausible /plozibl/ *adj* plausible.

playback /plɛbak/ *nm inv* miming, lip syncing; **chanter en ~** to lip-sync (a song).

plébiscite /plebisit/ *nm* plebiscite.

plein, **~e** /plɛ̃, plɛn/ **I** *adj* **1** full; **2 un ~ panier** a basketful (**de** of); **prendre à ~es mains** to pick up a handful of [*earth, sand, coins*]; **3** [*brick, wall, partition*] solid; [*cheeks, face*] plump; [*shape*] rounded; **4** [*power, agreement, effect*] full; [*success, satisfaction, confidence*] complete; **5** [*day, month*] whole, full; [*moon*] full; **6 en ~e poitrine/réunion/forêt** (right) in the middle of the chest/meeting/forest; **en ~ jour** in broad daylight; **en ~ été** at the height of summer; **7** (Zool) **~e** [*female animal*] pregnant; [*cow*] in calf; **8**○ sloshed○, drunk; **9 veste ~e peau** jacket made out of full skins.
II *adv* **1 avoir des billes ~ les poches** to have one's pockets full of marbles; **il a des idées ~ la tête** he's full of ideas; **2 être orienté ~ sud** to face due south.
III *nm* **faire le ~ de** to fill up with [*water, petrol*]; **le ~ s'il vous plaît** fill it up please.
IV plein de○ *quantif* **~ de** lots of, loads○ of [*things, friends*].
V à plein *phr* fully.
VI tout plein○ *phr* really; **mignon tout ~** really sweet.
IDIOMS **en avoir ~ les jambes**○ to be worn out; **en avoir ~ le dos**○ to be fed up.

plein-air /plɛnɛʀ/ *nm inv* (Sch) (outdoor) games.

plein-temps, *pl* **pleins-temps** /plɛ̃tɑ̃/ *nm* full-time job.

plénitude /plenityd/ *nf* **un sentiment de ~** a blissful feeling.

pléonasme /pleɔnasm/ *nm* pleonasm.

pléthorique /pletɔʀik/ *adj* excessive; **aux effectifs ~s** [*company*] overstaffed.

pleurer /plœʀe/ [1] **I** *vtr* to mourn [*friend*]; to lament [*absence*].
II *vi* **1** to cry, to weep; **c'est une histoire bête à ~** this story is too stupid for words; **2** [*eyes*] to water; **3 ~ sur qch/qn** to shed tears over sth/sb; **arrête de ~ sur ton sort!** stop feeling sorry for yourself!; **4**○ [*person*] to whine.
IDIOMS **elle n'a plus que ses yeux pour ~** all she can do is cry or weep.

pleureur /plœʀœʀ/ *adj m* **saule ~** weeping willow.

pleurnicher○ /plœʀniʃe/ [1] *vi* to snivel.

pleurs /plœʀ/ *nm pl* tears; **en ~** in tears; **il y aura des ~ et des grincements de dents** there will be wailing and gnashing of teeth.

pleuvoir /pløvwaʀ/ [39] **I** *v impers* to rain; **il pleut** it's raining; **il pleut à torrents** it's pouring with rain; **il pleut des cordes**○ it's coming down in buckets.

II *vi* [*blows, bombs*] to rain down; [*questions, criticisms*] to come thick and fast.

pli /pli/ *nm* **1** (in cloth, curtain, sheet of paper) fold; (in trousers) crease; (in skirt) pleat; **2** (of stomach, double chin) fold; **3** (Games) trick; **faire un ~** to take a trick; **4** letter; **sous ~ cacheté** in a sealed envelope.
IDIOMS **ça ne fait pas un ~**○ there's no doubt about it; **c'est un ~ à prendre** it's something you've got to get used to; **il a pris un mauvais ~** he's got into a bad habit.

plier /plije/ [2] **I** *vtr* **1** to fold [*paper, garment, umbrella*]; to fold up [*tent, chair*]; **2** to bend [*stem, arm*]; **3** to submit (**à** to).
II *vi* **1** [*tree, branch, joint*] to bend; [*plank, floor*] to sag; **2** to give in.
III se plier *v refl* (+ *v être*) **1** to fold; **2 se ~ à** to submit to.
IDIOMS **être plié (en deux**○ or **quatre**○) to be doubled up with laughter.

plinthe /plɛ̃t/ *nf* skirting board (GB), baseboard (US).

plisser /plise/ [1] **I** *vtr* **1** to pleat [*cloth*]; **2** to crease [*garment*]; **3 ~ le front** to knit one's brows; **~ les yeux** to screw up one's eyes.
II *vi* [*stocking*] to wrinkle; [*skirt, jacket*] to be creased or puckered.
III se plisser *v refl* (+ *v être*) **1** [*garment, cloth*] to crease or get creased; **2** [*nose*] to wrinkle.

pliure /plijyʀ/ *nf* fold; **la ~ du genou** the back of the knee.

plomb /plɔ̃/ *nm* **1** lead; **sans ~** [*petrol*] unleaded; **soleil de ~** burning sun; **ciel de ~** leaden sky; **2** (in hunting) **un ~** a lead pellet; **du ~** lead shot; **3** fuse; **faire sauter les ~s** to blow the fuses.
IDIOMS **avoir du ~ dans l'aile**○ to be in a bad way○; **cela va leur mettre du ~ dans la cervelle**○ that will knock some sense into them.

plombage /plɔ̃baʒ/ *nm* (in dentistry) filling.

plomber /plɔ̃be/ [1] *vtr* **1** to fill [*tooth*]; **2** to seal.

plombier /plɔ̃bje/ *nm* plumber.

plonge○ /plɔ̃ʒ/ *nf* washing up, dishwashing (US).

plongée /plɔ̃ʒe/ *nf* **1** (skin) diving; **2** scuba diving; **3** snorkelling[GB]; **~ sous-marine** deep-sea diving; **faire de la ~** to go diving; **3** (in cinematography) high-angle shot.

plongeoir /plɔ̃ʒwaʀ/ *nm* **1** diving-board; **2** springboard.

plongeon /plɔ̃ʒɔ̃/ *nm* **1** dive; **2** fall.

plonger /plɔ̃ʒe/ [13] **I** *vtr* to plunge.
II *vi* **1** to dive; **2** [*bird*] to swoop down; **3** [*business, trade*] to flounder.
III se plonger *v refl* (+ *v être*) **1** to plunge; **2** to bury oneself (**dans** in); **être plongé dans ses pensées** to be deep in thought.

plongeur, -euse /plɔ̃ʒœʀ, øz/ *nm,f* **1** diver; **2** dishwasher.

plot /plo/ *nm* **1** (electrical) contact; **2** (of wood) block.

ployer /plwaje/ [23] **I** *vtr* to bend [*knee, branch*]; to bow [*head*].
II *vi* [*branch, person*] to bend; **~ sous un fardeau** to be weighed down by a burden.

pluie /plɥi/ *nf* **1** rain; **sous une ~ battante** in driving rain; **2** (of missiles, insults) hail; (of sparks, compliments) shower.
■ **~s acides** acid rain.
IDIOMS **il n'est pas né de la dernière ~**○ he wasn't born yesterday○; **parler de la ~ et du beau temps** to make small talk; **faire la ~ et le beau temps** to call the shots○; **après la ~ le beau temps** (Proverb) every cloud has a silver lining (Proverb).

plume /plym/ *nf* **1** (Zool) feather; **2** (pen) nib; **écrire au fil de la ~** to write as the thoughts come into one's head; **vivre de sa ~** to earn a living by one's pen.
IDIOMS **elle y a laissé des ~s**○ she did not come off unscathed; **voler dans les ~s de qn**○ to fly at sb.

plumeau, *pl* **~x** /plymo/ *nm* **1** feather duster; **2** tuft.

plumer /plyme/ [1] *vtr* **1** to pluck [*bird*]; **2**○ **se faire ~** to be ripped off○ or fleeced○.

plumier /plymje/ *nm* pencil box.

plupart: **la plupart** /laplypaʀ/ *nf inv* **la ~ des gens/oiseaux** most people/birds; **la ~ du temps** most of the time, mostly.

pluridisciplinaire /plyʀidisiplinɛʀ/ *adj* multidisciplinary.

pluriel, -elle /plyʀjɛl/ **I** *adj* plural.
II *nm* plural.

plus[1] /ply, plys, plyz/ **I** *prep* plus.
II *adv* **1** (comparative) more; (superlative) **le ~** the most; **il travaille ~ (que moi)** he works more (than I do); **~ j'y pense, moins je comprends** the more I think about it, the less I understand; **~ ça va** as time goes on; **qui ~ est** furthermore, what's more; **de ~ en ~** more and more; **~ petit** smaller; **le ~ petit** the smallest; **le ~ vite** the fastest; **trois heures ~ tôt/tard** three hours earlier/later; **deux fois ~ cher** twice as expensive; **il est on ne peut ~ désagréable** he's as unpleasant as can be; **il est ~ ou moins artiste** he's an artist of sorts; **il a été ~ ou moins poli** he wasn't particularly polite; **un livre des ~ intéressants** a most interesting book; **2** (in negative constructions) **elle ne fume ~** she doesn't smoke any more; **il n'y a ~ d'œufs** there are no more eggs; **il n'y a ~ aucun problème** there's no longer any problem; **~ jamais ça!** never again!; **~ que trois jours avant Noël!** only three days left or to go until Christmas!
III plus de *quantif* **deux fois ~ de livres que** twice as many books as; **deux fois ~ de vin** twice as much wine; **il a gagné le ~ d'argent** he won the most money; **les gens de ~ de 60 ans** people over 60; **il était déjà bien ~ de onze heures** it was already well past eleven o'clock.
IV au plus *phr* at the most; **tout au ~** at the very most.
V de plus *phr* **1** furthermore, moreover,

what's more; **2 donnez-moi deux pommes de ~** give me two more apples; **une fois de ~** once more, once again.

VI en plus *phr* **en ~ (de cela)** on top of that; **les taxes en ~** plus tax, tax not included.

■ **Note** *A note on pronunciation*:
– *plus/le plus* used in comparison (meaning more/the most) is pronounced [ply] before a consonant and [plyz] before a vowel. It is pronounced [plys] when at the end of a clause. In the *plus de* and *plus que* structures both [ply] and [plys] are generally used.
– *plus* used in *ne plus* (meaning no longer/not any more) is always pronounced [ply] except before a vowel, in which case it is pronounced [plyz]: *il n'habite plus ici* [plyzisi].

plus² /plys/ *nm inv* **1 le signe ~** the plus sign; **2**° plus°.

plusieurs /plyzjœʀ/ **I** *adj* several; **une ou ~ personnes** one or more people.
II *pron* **~ ont déjà signé** several people have already signed.

plus-value, *pl* **~s** /plyvaly/ *nf* **1** (of property) increase in value; (sales profit) capital gain; **2** surcharge; **3** (Econ) surplus value.
■ **~ financière** capital gain.

plutôt /plyto/ *adv* **1** rather; **pourquoi lui ~ qu'un autre?** why him rather than anybody else?; **passe ~ le matin** call round (GB) or come by (US) in the morning preferably; **2** instead; **~ mourir (que d'accepter)!** I'd rather or sooner die (than accept)!; **demande ~ à Corinne** ask Corinne instead; **j'ai ~ tendance à ne pas m'en faire** I'm more the kind not to worry; **3** rather; **dis ~ que tu n'as pas envie de le faire** why don't you just say that you don't want to do it?; **4** rather; **la nouvelle a été ~ bien/mal accueillie** the news went down rather well/badly.

pluvieux, -ieuse /plyvjø, øz/ *adj* wet, rainy.

PME /peɛmə/ *nf pl* (*abbr* = **petites et moyennes entreprises**) small and medium enterprises, SMEs.

PMI /peɛmi/ *nf pl* (*abbr* = **petites et moyennes industries**) small and medium-sized industries.

PMU /peɛmy/ *nm* (*abbr* = **Pari mutuel urbain**) *French state-controlled betting system*; **un ~** a betting office.

PNB /peɛnbe/ *nm* (*abbr* = **produit national brut**) gross national product, GNP.

pneu /pnø/ *nm* tyre (GB), tire (US).

pneumatique /pnømatik/ *adj* **1** (Tech) pneumatic; **2** (gen) inflatable.

pneumonie /pnømɔni/ *nf* pneumonia.

poche¹ /pɔʃ/ *nm* **(livre de) ~** paperback.

poche² /pɔʃ/ *nf* **1** (in garment, bag) pocket; **en ~** in one's pocket; **il est revenu le contrat en ~** (figurative) he came back with the contract in the bag°; **son diplôme en ~, il est parti aux États-Unis** armed with his diploma, he set off for the States; **il avait 1 000 francs en ~** he had 1,000 francs on him; **avoir de l'argent plein les ~s**° to be loaded°; **s'en mettre plein** or **se remplir les ~s**° to line one's pockets; **faire les ~s de qn** to pick sb's pocket; **2 ~ de gaz/d'air** gas/air pocket; **3 avoir des ~s sous les yeux** to have bags under one's eyes; **4** (Zool) (of kangaroo) pouch.
■ **~ revolver** hip pocket.
IDIOMS **mettre qn dans sa ~**° to get sb on one's side; **c'est dans la ~**° it's in the bag°; **en être de sa ~**° to be out of pocket; **ne pas avoir les yeux dans sa ~**° not to miss a thing°; **connaître un endroit comme sa ~**° to know a place like the back of one's hand.

pocher /pɔʃe/ [1] **I** *vtr* **1** (Culin) to poach; **2 ~ un œil à qn** to give sb a black eye.
II *vi* [*garment*] to seat at the back; to go baggy at the knees.

pochette /pɔʃɛt/ *nf* **1** (for pencils) case; (for credit cards etc) wallet; (for make-up, glasses) pouch; (for document) folder; (for record) sleeve; **2** (of matches) book; **3** clutch bag.

pochette-surprise, *pl* **pochettes-surprises** /pɔʃɛtsyʀpʀiz/ *nf*: *child's novelty consisting of several small surprise items in a cone.*

pochoir /pɔʃwaʀ/ *nm* stencil; **exécuté au ~** stencilled[GB].

podium /pɔdjɔm/ *nm* **1** (gen) podium; **2** catwalk (GB), runway (US).

poêle¹ /pwal/ *nm* **1** stove; **2** (on coffin) pall.

poêle² /pwal/ *nf* frying pan; **œuf à la ~** fried egg.

poème /pɔɛm/ *nm* poem; **c'est tout un ~**° it's quite something.

poésie /pɔezi/ *nf* **1** poetry; **2** poem; **3** poetic quality **(de** of).

poète /pɔɛt/ *nm* **1** poet; **2** dreamer.

poétique /pɔetik/ *adj* poetic.

poids /pwɑ/ *nm inv* **1** weight; **peser son ~** to be very heavy; **argument de ~** weighty argument; **adversaire de ~** opponent to be reckoned with; **2** burden; **être un ~ pour qn** to be a burden on sb; **avoir un ~ sur la conscience** to have a guilty conscience; **3** influence; **4 des ~ en laiton** brass weights; **5** (in athletics) shot; **lancer le ~** to put the shot.
■ **~ et haltères** weightlifting; **~ léger** lightweight; **~ lourd** (Sport) heavyweight; heavy truck; **~ mort** dead weight.
IDIOMS **avoir** or **faire deux ~ deux mesures** to have double standards.

poignant, ~e /pwaɲɑ̃, ɑ̃t/ *adj* **1** poignant; **2** heart-rending, harrowing.

poignard /pwaɲaʀ/ *nm* dagger; **coup de ~** stab.

poignarder /pwaɲaʀde/ [1] *vtr* **1** to stab, to knife; **2** to stab [sb] to death.

poigne /pwaɲ/ *nf* **avoir de la ~** to have a strong grip; **homme à ~** strong man.

poignée /pwaɲe/ *nf* **1** handful; **2** (of door, drawer, bag) handle; (of sword) hilt.
■ **~ de main** handshake; **échanger une ~ de main** to shake hands.

poignet /pwaɲɛ/ *nm* **1** wrist; **à la force du ~** [*succeed*] by sheer hard work; **2** (of shirt) cuff.

poil /pwal/ *nm* **1** (on body, animal) hair; **à ~○** stark naked; **perdre ses ~s** to moult (GB) or molt (US); **caresser dans le sens du ~** to stroke [sth] the way the fur lies; to butter [sb] up○; **de tout ~○** of all kinds; **ça marche au ~○** it works like a dream; **2○** (of irony) touch; (of commonsense) shred; **un ~ trop petit** a shade too small; **à un ~ près** by a whisker; **3** (of carpet) pile; (of cloth) nap; (of brush) bristle.
■ **~ à gratter** itching powder.
IDIOMS **être de bon/mauvais ~○** to be in a good/bad mood; **hérisser le ~○ de qn** to put sb's back up○; **avoir un ~ dans la main○** to be bone idle.

poilu, ~e /pwaly/ **I** *adj* hairy.
II○ *nm*: *French soldier in World War I.*

poinçon /pwɛ̃sɔ̃/ *nm* **1** (tool) punch; **2** (on gold) die, stamp; hallmark.

poinçonner /pwɛ̃sɔne/ [1] *vtr* **1** to punch, to clip; **2** to hallmark.

poinçonneuse /pwɛ̃sɔnøz/ *nf* **1** ticket-punch; **2** punching machine.

poindre /pwɛ̃dʀ/ [56] *vi* [*day*] to break; [*sun, plant*] to peep through.

poing /pwɛ̃/ *nm* fist; **coup de ~** punch; **montrer le ~** to shake one's fist; **être pieds et ~s liés** (figurative) to have one's hands tied.
IDIOMS **dormir à ~s fermés** to sleep like a log.

point /pwɛ̃/ **I** *nm* **1** point; **un ~ de rencontre** a meeting point; **~ de vente** (sales) outlet; **2** (at sea) position; **faire le ~** to take bearings; (analyse) to take stock of the situation; **3 être sur le ~ de faire** to be just about to do, to be on the point of doing; **j'en suis toujours au même ~** I'm still exactly where I was; **au ~ où j'en suis, ça n'a pas d'importance!** I'm past caring!; **4 il m'agace au plus haut ~** he annoys me intensely; **je ne le pensais pas bête à ce ~** I didn't think he was that stupid; **si tu savais à quel ~ il m'agace!** if you only knew how much he annoys me!; **à tel ~ que** to such an extent that; **douloureux au ~ que** so painful that; **5** (on agenda) item, point; **un ~ de détail** a minor point; **en tout ~, en tous ~s** in every respect or way; **6** dot; **un ~ de colle** a spot of glue; **un ~ de rouille** a speck of rust; **~ d'intersection** point of intersection; **7** (Games, Sport) point; **compter les ~s** to keep (the) score; **8** (Sch) mark (GB), point (US); **être un bon ~ pour** to be a plus point for; **être un mauvais ~ pour qn/qch** to be a black mark against sb/sth; **9** full stop (GB), period (US); **mettre un ~ final à qch** (figurative) to put a stop or an end to sth; **tu vas te coucher un ~ c'est tout○!** you're going to bed and that's final!; **10** (Med) pain; **avoir un ~ à la poitrine** to have a pain in the chest; **11** (in sewing, knitting) stitch; **faire un ~ à qch** to put a few stitches in sth.
II à point *phr* **1 à ~ nommé** just at the right moment; **2** (Culin) **(cuit) à ~** [*meat*] medium rare.
III au point *phr* **être au ~** [*system, machine*] to be well designed; [*show, programme*] to be well put together; **mettre au ~** to perfect [*system, method*]; to develop [*vaccine, machine*]; **faire la mise au ~** (in photography) to focus; **faire une mise au ~** (figurative) to set the record straight.
■ **~ chaud** trouble or hot spot; **~ de côté** (pain) stitch; **~ de départ** starting point; **nous revoilà à notre ~ de départ** (figurative) we're back to square one; **~ d'eau** water tap (GB) or faucet (US); **~ d'exclamation** exclamation mark; **~ faible** weak point; **~ fort** strong point; **~ d'interrogation** question mark; **~ du jour** daybreak; **~ de mire** (Mil) target; (figurative) focal point; **~ mort** neutral; **être au ~ mort** (in car) to be in neutral; [*business, trade*] to be at a standstill; [*negotiations*] to be in a state of deadlock; **~ noir** (Med) blackhead; (of situation) problem; **~ de repère** landmark; point of reference; **~ de suture** (Med) stitch; **~ de vue** point of view; viewpoint; **du ~ de vue du sens** as far as meaning is concerned; **~s de suspension** suspension points.
IDIOMS **être mal en ~** to be in a bad way.

pointage /pwɛ̃taʒ/ *nm* **1** (gen) checking; (on list) ticking off (GB), checking off (US); **le ~ des voix** the tally of the votes; **2** (of employee) clocking in; **une feuille de ~** a time sheet.

pointe /pwɛ̃t/ **I** *nf* **1** (of knife) point; (of shoe) toe; (of hair) end; (of railing) spike; (of spear) tip, point; **en ~** pointed; **tailler un buisson en ~** to shape a shrub into a point; **2 de ~** [*technology*] advanced, state-of-the-art; [*sector, industry*] high-tech; [*company*] leading; **à la ~ du progrès** state-of-the-art; **3** high; **une vitesse de ~ de 200 km/h** a maximum or top speed of 200 kph; **heure de ~** rush hour; **aux heures de ~** at peak time; **4** (of garlic) touch; (of accent, irony) hint; **5** blocked shoe; **6 lancer des ~s à qn** to direct cutting remarks at sb.
II pointes *nf pl* **faire des ~s** to dance on points.
■ **~ du pied** tiptoe; **aborder une question sur la ~ des pieds** to broach a matter carefully.

pointer /pwɛ̃te/ [1] **I** *vtr* **1** to tick off (GB), to check off (US) [*names, figures*]; to check [*list*]; to time [*athlete*]; **2** to point [*weapon*]; **~ le doigt vers** to point at; **~ son museau** [*animal*] to peep out; **~ son nez○** to show one's face.
II *vi* **1** [*employee*] to clock in; **~ à l'agence pour l'emploi** to sign on at the unemployment office; **2** [*spire*] to rise up; **3** [*sun, plant*] to come up; [*day, dawn*] to break.
III se pointer○ *v refl* (+ *v être*) [*person*] to turn up (**à** at).

pointillé, ~e /pwɛ̃tije/ **I** *adj* dotted (**de** with).
II *nm* dotted line.

pointilleux, -euse /pwɛ̃tijø, øz/ *adj* [*person*] fussy (**sur** about), pernickety.

pointu, ~e /pwɛ̃ty/ *adj* **1** (gen) pointed; [*scissors*] with a sharp point; **2** [*check*] close, thorough; **3** [*question, approach*] precise.

pointure /pwɛ̃tyʀ/ *nf* (of glove, shoe) size.

point-virgule, *pl* **points-virgules** /pwɛ̃viʀgyl/ *nm* semicolon.

poire /pwaʀ/ *nf* **1** pear; **en forme de ~** pear-shaped; **2**○ mug○ (GB), sucker○.
IDIOMS **couper la ~ en deux** to split the difference; **garder une ~ pour la soif** to save something for a rainy day.

poireau, *pl* **~x** /pwaʀo/ *nm* leek.

poireauter○ /pwaʀote/ [1] *vi* to hang about○.

poirier /pwaʀje/ *nm* **1** pear (tree); **2 faire le ~** to do a headstand.

pois /pwa/ *nm inv* **1** (Bot, Culin) pea; **petit ~** (garden) pea; **2** dot; **à ~** polka dot, spotted.
■ **~ cassé** split pea; **~ chiche** chickpea; **~ de senteur** sweet pea.

poison /pwazɔ̃/ *nm* **1** poison; **2**○ **quel ~ cet enfant!** that child is a pest!

poisse○ /pwas/ *nf* **1** rotten luck○; **2** drag○.

poisseux, -euse /pwasø, øz/ *adj* [*hands, table*] sticky; [*atmosphere*] muggy; [*restaurant*] greasy.

poisson /pwasɔ̃/ *nm* fish; **les ~s d'eau douce/de mer** freshwater/saltwater fish.
■ **~ d'argent** silverfish; **~ d'avril** April fool's joke; **~ rouge** goldfish.
IDIOMS **être comme un ~ dans l'eau** to be in one's element.

poissonnerie /pwasɔnʀi/ *nf* fishmonger's (shop) (GB), fish shop (US).

poissonnier, -ière /pwasɔnje, ɛʀ/ *nm,f* fishmonger (GB), fish vendor (US).

Poissons /pwasɔ̃/ *pr nm pl* Pisces.

poitrail /pwatʀaj/ *nm* breast.

poitrine /pwatʀin/ *nf* **1** chest; **tour de ~** chest size; **2** breasts; **tour de ~** bust size.
■ **~ fumée/salée** ≈ smoked/unsmoked streaky bacon.

poivre /pwavʀ/ *nm* pepper; **~ en grains** whole peppercorns.

poivré, ~e /pwavʀe/ *adj* [*sauce*] peppery; [*joke*] racy.

poivrer /pwavʀe/ [1] *vtr* to add pepper to [*sauce*].

poivrier /pwavʀije/ *nm* **1** pepper-pot (GB), pepper shaker (US); **2** (Bot) pepper tree.

poivron /pwavʀɔ̃/ *nm* sweet pepper, capsicum.

poivrot○, **~e** /pwavʀo, ɔt/ *nm,f* drunk, drunkard.

poker /pɔkɛʀ/ *nm* poker; **coup de ~** gamble.

polaire /pɔlɛʀ/ *adj* [*region, wildlife*] polar; [*landscape, cold*] arctic.

polar○ /pɔlaʀ/ *nm* detective novel.

polariser /pɔlaʀize/ [1] *vtr*, **se polariser** *v refl* (+ *v être*) **1** to polarize; **2** to focus.

pôle /pol/ *nm* **1** pole; **2** centre[GB].

polémique /pɔlemik/ **I** *adj* [*book, statement*] polemical.
II *nf* debate; **de violentes ~s** fierce debate.

poli, ~e /pɔli/ **I** *pp* ▶ **polir**.
II *pp adj* [*metal, style*] polished.
III *adj* polite (**avec qn** to sb).
IV *nm* shine; **donner du ~ à qch** to polish sth up.

police /pɔlis/ *nf* **1** police; police force; **2** security service; **3 faire la ~** to keep order; **4** (in insurance) policy.
■ **~ judiciaire, PJ** *detective division of the French police force*; **~ des mœurs** or **mondaine** vice squad; **~ secours** ≈ emergency services.

policier, -ière /pɔlisje, ɛʀ/ **I** *adj* (gen) police; [*novel*] detective.
II *nm* policeman; **femme ~** policewoman.

poliment /pɔlimɑ̃/ *adv* politely.

poliomyélite /pɔljomjelit/ *nf* poliomyelitis.

polir /pɔliʀ/ [3] *vtr* to polish [*stone, metal*]; to polish (up) [*style*].

polisson, -onne /pɔlisɔ̃, ɔn/ **I** *adj* **1** naughty; **2** saucy.
II *nm,f* naughty child.

politesse /pɔlitɛs/ *nf* politeness; **tu pourrais avoir la ~ de t'excuser** you might have the decency to apologize; **rendre la ~ à qn** to return the compliment; **se faire des ~s** to exchange pleasantries.
IDIOMS **brûler** or **griller la ~ à qn** to push in ahead of sb.

politicien, -ienne /pɔlitisjɛ̃, ɛn/ **I** *adj* (purely) political.
II *nm,f* politician.

politique[1] /pɔlitik/ *adj* (gen) political; [*behaviour, act*] calculating.

politique[2] /pɔlitik/ *nf* **1** politics; **faire de la ~** [*militant*] to be involved in politics; **2** policy; **notre ~ des prix** our pricing policy.
IDIOMS **pratiquer la ~ de l'autruche** to stick one's head in the sand; **pratiquer la ~ du pire** to envisage the worst-case scenario.

politiser /pɔlitize/ [1] *vtr* to politicize.

pollen /pɔl(l)ɛn/ *nm* pollen.

polluer /pɔl(l)ɥe/ [1] *vtr* to pollute.

pollution /pɔl(l)ysjɔ̃/ *nf* pollution.

polo /pɔlo/ *nm* **1** polo shirt; **2** (Sport) polo.

polochon○ /pɔlɔʃɔ̃/ *nm* bolster; **bataille (à coups) de ~s** pillow fight.

poltron, -onne /pɔltʀɔ̃, ɔn/ *nm,f* coward.

polycopier /pɔlikɔpje/ [2] *vtr* to duplicate.

polygame /pɔligam/ *adj* polygamous.

polyglotte /pɔliglɔt/ *adj, nmf* polyglot.

polytechnicien, -ienne /pɔlitɛknisjɛ̃, ɛn/ *nm,f*: *graduate of the École Polytechnique*.

Polytechnique /pɔlitɛknik/ *nf*: *Grande École of Science and Technology*.

polyvalence /pɔlivalɑ̃s/ *nf* **1** versatility; **2** (of employee) flexibility.

pommade /pɔmad/ *nf* (Med) ointment.
IDIOMS **passer de la ~**○ **à qn** to butter sb up○.

pomme /pɔm/ *nf* **1** apple; **2** (of watering can) rose; (of shower) shower-head; (of walking stick) pommel, knob; **3**○ mug○ (GB), sucker○; **ça va encore être pour ma ~** I'm in for it again○.
■ **~ d'Adam** Adam's apple; **~ d'api** ≈ small apple; **~ de pin** pine cone; **~ de terre** potato; **~s frites** chips (GB), (French) fries.

IDIOMS **tomber dans les ~s**○ to faint, to pass out○.

pommeau, *pl* **~x** /pɔmo/ *nm* knob; pommel.

pommette /pɔmɛt/ *nf* cheekbone.

pommier /pɔmje/ *nm* **1** apple tree; **2** apple, apple-wood.

pompe /pɔ̃p/ *nf* **1** pump; **2**◑ shoe; **3** pomp; **4**○ (Sport) press-up (GB), push-up.
■ **~ à essence** petrol pump (GB), gas pump (US); **~ à incendie** fire engine; **~s funèbres** undertaker's (GB), funeral director's.
IDIOMS **avoir un coup de ~**○ to be knackered◑ (GB) or pooped○.

pomper /pɔ̃pe/ [1] *vtr* **1** to pump [*liquid, air*]; **2**○ (students' slang) to copy (**sur** from).
IDIOMS **~ l'air**○ **à qn** to get on sb's nerves.

pompette○ /pɔ̃pɛt/ *adj* tipsy○, drunk.

pompeux, **-euse** /pɔ̃pø, øz/ *adj* pompous.

pompier, **-ière** /pɔ̃pje, ɛʀ/ **I** *adj* pompous.
II *nm* fireman, firefighter; **appeler les ~s** to call the fire brigade (GB) or department (US).

pompiste /pɔ̃pist/ *nmf* petrol (GB) or gas (US) pump attendant.

pompon /pɔ̃pɔ̃/ *nm* (on hat) pompom, bobble; (on slipper) pompom.
IDIOMS **remporter** or **décrocher le ~**○ to come top, to win first prize.

pomponner: **se pomponner** /pɔ̃pɔne/ [1] *v refl* (+ *v être*) to get dolled up.

ponce /pɔ̃s/ *nf* **pierre ~** pumice stone.

poncer /pɔ̃se/ [12] *vtr* **1** (Tech) to sand; **2** to pumice.

ponceuse /pɔ̃søz/ *nf* sander.

ponction /pɔ̃ksjɔ̃/ *nf* **1** (Med) puncture; **2** levy.

ponctionner /pɔ̃ksjɔne/ [1] *vtr* **1** (Med) to puncture; **2** to levy [*sum of money*].

ponctualité /pɔ̃ktɥalite/ *nf* punctuality; **avec ~** punctually.

ponctuation /pɔ̃ktɥasjɔ̃/ *nf* punctuation; **signes de ~** punctuation marks.

ponctuel, **-elle** /pɔ̃ktɥɛl/ *adj* **1** [*person*] punctual; [*payment*] prompt; **2** [*action, operation*] limited; [*problem*] isolated.

ponctuer /pɔ̃ktɥe/ [1] *vtr* to punctuate (**de** with).

pondération /pɔ̃deʀasjɔ̃/ *nf* **1** levelheadedness; **2** balance.

pondéré, **~e** /pɔ̃deʀe/ *adj* **1** [*person*] level-headed; **2** [*factor*] weighted.

pondre /pɔ̃dʀ/ [6] *vtr* **1** to lay [*egg*]; **2**○ to churn out○ [*poetry, articles*].

poney /pɔnɛ/ *nm* pony; **faire du ~** to go pony-riding.

pont /pɔ̃/ **I** *nm* **1** bridge; **2** link, tie; **couper les ~s** to break off all contact; **3** extended weekend (*including day(s) between a public holiday and a weekend*); **faire le ~** to make a long weekend of it; **4** deck; **5** (Sport) crab; **faire le ~** to do the crab.
II ponts *nm pl* **~s (et chaussées)** highways department.
■ **~ aérien** airlift; **~ à péage** toll bridge.
IDIOMS **coucher sous les ~s** to sleep rough, to be a tramp; **il coulera beaucoup d'eau sous les ~s avant que...** it will be a long time before...; **faire un ~ d'or à qn** to offer sb a large sum to accept a job.

ponte[1]○ /pɔ̃t/ *nm* big shot○.

ponte[2] /pɔ̃t/ *nf* laying (*of eggs*).

pontife /pɔ̃tif/ *nm* **1** pontiff; **le souverain ~** the pope; **2**○ pundit○.

pontificat /pɔ̃tifika/ *nm* pontificate.

pontifier /pɔ̃tifje/ [2] *vi* to pontificate.

pont-levis, *pl* **ponts-levis** /pɔ̃ləvi/ *nm* drawbridge.

ponton /pɔ̃tɔ̃/ *nm* **1** landing stage; **2** pontoon; **3** hulk.

pope /pɔp/ *nm* pope, orthodox priest.

popote○ /pɔpɔt/ *nf* cooking.

populace /pɔpylas/ *nf* **la ~** the masses; **une ~** a rabble.

populaire /pɔpylɛʀ/ *adj* **1** [*suburb*] working-class; [*art, novel*] popular; [*edition*] cheap; [*restaurant*] basic; **classe ~** working class; **2** [*tradition*] folk; **culture ~** folklore; **le bon sens ~** popular wisdom; **3** popular (**chez, parmi** with); **4** [*revolt*] popular; [*will*] of the people; **5** [*expression, term*] vulgar; **6 République/Démocratie ~** People's Republic/ Democracy.

populariser /pɔpylaʀize/ [1] *vtr* to popularize.

popularité /pɔpylaʀite/ *nf* popularity (**auprès de** with, among).

population /pɔpylasjɔ̃/ *nf* population; **~ active** working population.

porc /pɔʀ/ *nm* **1** pig, hog (US); **2** pork; **3** pigskin.

porcelaine /pɔʀsəlɛn/ *nf* porcelain, china; **~ de Chine** china.

porcelet /pɔʀsəlɛ/ *nm* piglet.

porc-épic, *pl* **~s** /pɔʀkepik/ *nm* porcupine.

porche /pɔʀʃ/ *nm* porch; **sous le ~** in the porch.

porcherie /pɔʀʃəʀi/ *nf* pigsty.

porcin, **~e** /pɔʀsɛ̃, in/ *adj* **1** [*race*] porcine; **2** [*face, eyes*] piggy, porcine.

pore /pɔʀ/ *nm* pore; **suant la peur par tous les ~s** exuding fear.

poreux, **-euse** /pɔʀø, øz/ *adj* porous.

porno○ /pɔʀno/ *adj, nm* porn○.

pornographique /pɔʀnɔgʀafik/ *adj* pornographic.

port /pɔʀ/ *nm* **1** harbour[GB]; port; **2** haven; **3 le ~ de l'uniforme** wearing uniform; **le ~ du casque est obligatoire** helmets must be worn at all times; **4** carriage; bearing; **5** carriage; postage.
■ **~ d'attache** port of registry; home base; **~ de pêche** fishing harbour[GB]; fishing port; **~ de plaisance** marina.
IDIOMS **arriver à bon ~** to arrive safe and sound.

portable /pɔʀtabl/ *adj* portable; **ordinateur ~** laptop computer.

portail /pɔʀtaj/ *nm* (of park) gate; (of church) great door.

portant, **~e** /pɔʀtɑ̃, ɑ̃t/ *adj* **1** [*wall*] load-bearing; [*wheel*] carrying. **2 bien ~** in good health.

IDIOMS **à bout ~** at point-blank range.

portatif, -ive /pɔRtatif, iv/ *adj* portable.

porte /pɔRt/ *nf* **1** door; gate; **la ~ de derrière** the back door; **devant la ~ de l'hôpital** outside the hospital; **j'ai une gare à ma ~** I have a station on my doorstep; **aux ~s du désert** at the edge of the desert; **ouvrir sa ~ à qn** to let sb in; **c'est la ~ ouverte à la criminalité** it's an open invitation to crime; **mettre à la ~** to expel; to fire; **ce n'est pas la ~ à côté**○ it's quite far; **2** gateway; **la victoire leur ouvre la ~ de la finale** the victory clears the way to the final for them; **3** gate; **~ numéro 10** gate number 10; **4** (in skiing) gate; **5** (car) door; **6** (in electronics) gate.

■ **~ battante** swing door; **~ d'écluse** lock gate; **~ d'entrée** front door; main entrance; **~ de service** service entrance; **~ de sortie** exit; escape route; **~ à tambour** revolving door.

IDIOMS **prendre la ~** to leave; **entrer par la petite/grande ~** to start at the bottom/top; **enfoncer une ~ ouverte** to state the obvious.

porté, ~e[1] /pɔRte/ *adj* **être ~ à se plaindre** to be inclined to complain; **être ~ sur qch** to be keen on sth.

porte-à-faux /pɔRtafo/ *nm inv* **être en ~** [*wall*] to be out of plumb; [*construction*] to be cantilevered; [*person*] to be in an awkward position.

porte-à-porte /pɔRtapɔRt/ *nm inv* **1** door-to-door selling; **2** door-to-door canvassing.

porte-avions /pɔRtavjɔ̃/ *nm inv* aircraft carrier.

porte-bagages /pɔRt(ə)bagaʒ/ *nm inv* carrier; luggage rack; roof rack.

porte-bébé /pɔRt(ə)bebe/ *nm inv* baby carrier.

porte-bonheur /pɔRt(ə)bɔnœR/ *nm inv* lucky charm.

porte-clés, porte-clefs /pɔRt(ə)kle/ *nm inv* key ring.

porte-documents /pɔRt(ə)dɔkymɑ̃/ *nm inv* briefcase, attaché case.

porte-drapeau /pɔRt(ə)dRapo/ *nm inv* standard-bearer.

portée[2] /pɔRte/ I *adj f* ▶ **porté**.

II *nf* **1** range; **arme de longue ~** long-range weapon; **être à ~ de main** or **à la ~ de la main** to be within reach; to be to hand; **2 c'est à la ~ de n'importe qui** anybody can do it; anybody can understand it; anybody can afford it; **se mettre à la ~ de qn** to come down to sb's level; **3** impact; **4** (of kittens) litter; **5** (Mus) staff, stave (GB).

porte-fenêtre, *pl* **portes-fenêtres** /pɔRt(ə)fənɛtR/ *nf* French window.

portefeuille /pɔRt(ə)fœj/ I *adj* **jupe ~** wrap-over skirt.

II *nm* **1** wallet, billfold (US); **2** portfolio.

IDIOMS **faire un lit en ~** to make an apple pie bed.

porte-jarretelles /pɔRt(ə)ʒaRtɛl/ *nm inv* suspender belt (GB), garter belt (US).

portemanteau, *pl* **~x** /pɔRt(ə)mɑ̃to/ *nm* **1** coat rack; **2** coat stand, coat or clothes tree (US); **3** coat hanger.

portemine /pɔRt(ə)min/ *nm* propelling (GB) or mechanical (US) pencil.

porte-monnaie /pɔRt(ə)mɔnɛ/ *nm inv* purse (GB), coin purse (US).

porte-parapluies /pɔRt(ə)paRaplɥi/ *nm inv* umbrella stand.

porte-parole /pɔRt(ə)paRɔl/ *nm inv* **1** spokesperson, spokesman/spokeswoman; **2** mouthpiece.

porter /pɔRte/ [1] I *vtr* **1** to carry; **2 ~ qch quelque part** to take sth somewhere; **~ qch à qn** to take sb sth; **~ des messages** to run messages; **~ une affaire devant les tribunaux** to bring a case to court; **3** [*wall, chair*] to carry, to bear [*weight*]; **4** to wear [*dress, contact lenses*]; to have [*moustache*]; **5** to have [*initials, date, name*]; to bear [*seal*]; **~ la mention 'secret'** to be marked 'secret'; **il porte bien son nom** the name suits him; **bien ~ son âge** to look good for one's age; **6** to bear [*flowers*]; **l'enfant qu'elle porte** the child she is carrying; **7 ~ qch à** [*situation, event*] to bring sth to; [*person, company*] to put sth up to; **cela porte le prix du billet à...** this brings the price of the ticket to...; **~ la température de l'eau à 80°C** to heat the water to 80°C; **8 ~ son regard vers** to look at; **si tu portes la main sur elle** if you lay a finger on her; **~ un jugement sur qch** to pass judgment on sth; **9 ~ qch sur un registre** to enter sth on a register; **être porté disparu** to be reported missing; **se faire ~ malade** to report sick; **~ plainte** to lodge a complaint; **10 ~ qn à être méfiant** to make sb cautious; **tout nous porte à croire que** everything leads us to believe that; **11 ~ bonheur** or **chance** to be lucky.

II **porter sur** *v+prep* **1** [*debate*] to be about; [*measure*] to concern; [*ban*] to apply to; **2** [*structure*] to be resting on.

III *vi* **une voix qui porte** a voice that carries; **le coup a porté** the blow hit home.

IV **se porter** *v refl* (+ *v être*) **1 se ~ bien/mal** [*person*] to be well/ill; [*business*] to be going well/badly; **je ne m'en porte pas plus mal** I'm none the worse for it; **2 se ~ sur** [*suspicion*] to fall on; [*infection*] to spread to.

porte-revues /pɔRt(ə)Rəvy/ *nm inv* magazine rack.

porte-savon /pɔRt(ə)savɔ̃/ *nm inv* soapdish.

porte-serviettes /pɔRt(ə)sɛRvjɛt/ *nm inv* towel rail.

porteur, -euse /pɔRtœR, øz/ I *adj* **1 être ~ d'espoir** to bring hope; **être ~ d'un virus** to carry a virus; **2 mur/essieu ~** load-bearing wall/axle; **3** [*market, sector*] expanding; **4** [*current, wave, frequency*] carrier; **5 être ~ de sens** to have a meaning.

II *nm,f* holder, bearer; **~ d'une carte de crédit** credit-card holder.

III *nm* **1** porter; messenger; **2** (of cheque) bearer; **~ d'actions** shareholder.

■ **~ sain** (Med) symptom-free carrier.

porte-voix /pɔʀt(ə)vwɑ/ *nm inv* megaphone; **les mains en ~** his/her hands cupped around his/her mouth.

portier /pɔʀtje/ *nm* porter.

portière /pɔʀtjɛʀ/ *nf* (of car) door.

portillon /pɔʀtijɔ̃/ *nm* gate.

portion /pɔʀsjɔ̃/ *nf* **1** (Culin) portion; helping; **2** (of inheritance) share; **3** portion; (of road) stretch; (of territory) part.
IDIOMS **réduire qn à la ~ congrue** to give sb the strict minimum.

portique /pɔʀtik/ *nm* **1** portico; **2** frame (in gym); **3** swing frame.

porto /pɔʀto/ *nm* port.

portoricain, **~e** /pɔʀtɔʀikɛ̃, ɛn/ *adj* Puerto Rican.

portrait /pɔʀtʀɛ/ *nm* **1** portrait; **c'est un ~ fidèle** it's a good likeness; **2** description, picture; **faire le ~ de** to paint a picture of; **3 tu es tout le ~ de ton père** you're the spitting image of your father; **4**○ face; **se faire tirer le ~** to have one's photo taken.

portrait-robot, *pl* **portraits-robots** /pɔʀtʀɛʀɔbo/ *nm* photofit®, identikit®.

portuaire /pɔʀtɥɛʀ/ *adj* port.

portugais, **~e** /pɔʀtygɛ, ɛz/ **I** *adj* Portuguese.
II *nm* Portuguese.

Portugal /pɔʀtygal/ *pr nm* Portugal.

pose /poz/ *nf* **1** (of window) putting in, installation; (of cupboard) fitting; (of carpet) laying; (of curtains) hanging; **2** pose; **prendre une ~** to strike a pose; **une séance de ~** a sitting; **3** pretention, affectation; **4** (in photography) exposure.

posé, **~e** /poze/ *adj* [*air, person*] composed; [*gesture, voice*] controlled.

posément /pozemɑ̃/ *adv* calmly, carefully.

poser /poze/ [1] **I** *vtr* **1** to put down [*book, newspaper, glass*]; **~ les yeux sur qn/qch** to look at sb/sth; **2** to put in [*window*]; to install [*radiator*]; to fit [*lock, prosthesis*]; to lay [*tiling, cable*]; to plant [*bomb*]; to put up [*wallpaper, curtains*]; **3** to assert [*theory*]; to lay down [*rules*]; **~ sa candidature à un poste** to apply for a job; **~ une addition** to write a sum down; **~ comme hypothèse que** to put forward the theory that; **4** to ask [*question*]; to set [*riddle*]; **la question reste posée** the question (still) remains; **ça ne pose aucun problème** that's no problem at all; **5** (Mus) to place [*voice*].
II *vi* **1** to pose; **2** to put on airs.
III se poser *v refl* (+ *v être*) **1** [*bird, insect*] to settle, to alight; **2** [*plane*] to land, to touch down; **se ~ en catastrophe** to make an emergency landing; **3** [*eyes*] to fall (**sur** on); **4 se ~ en** to claim to be; to present oneself as; **5 se ~ des questions** to ask oneself questions; **ils vivent sans se ~ de questions** they accept things as they are; **6** [*problem, case*] to arise; **la question ne se pose pas** there's no question of it; it goes without saying.

poseur, **-euse** /pozœʀ, øz/ *nm,f* poser○.
■ **~ d'affiches** billsticker; **~ de bombes** bomber; **~ de moquette** carpet fitter.

positif, **-ive** /pozitif, iv/ *adj* **1** [*reply*] affirmative; **2** [*interview, climate*] constructive; [*outcome*] positive; **3** [*reaction*] favourable[GB]; [*point, image*] positive; **4** [*person, attitude*] positive; **5** [*number, blood group*] positive.

position /pozisjɔ̃/ *nf* **1** position; **la ~ des doigts sur une guitare** the positioning of the fingers on a guitar; **en ~ horizontale** horizontally; **2** position; **placer qn dans une ~ difficile** to put sb in a difficult or an awkward position; **3** position; **sa ~ est très enviée** his/her position is widely envied; **4** (in ranking) place, position; **5** position, stance; **prendre ~ sur un problème** to take a stand on an issue; **camper** or **rester sur ses ~s** to stand one's ground; **6** (bank) balance; **être en ~ créditrice/débitrice** [*account*] to be in credit/debit.

positivement /pozitivmɑ̃/ *adv* [*answer*] positively; [*react, judge*] favourably[GB].

posologie /pozɔlɔʒi/ *nf* dosage.

possédé, **~e** /pɔsede/ *nm,f* **les ~s** the possessed.

posséder /pɔsede/ [14] *vtr* **1** to own, to possess [*property, army*]; to hold [*responsibility*]; **2** to have [*skill, quality*]; **un jardin qui possède un bassin** a garden with a fish pond; **3** to speak [sth] fluently; to have a thorough knowledge of [sth]; **4** [*anger, pain*] to overwhelm; **5**○ **il nous a bien possédés** he really had○ us there.

possesseur /pɔsɛsœʀ/ *nm* (of property) owner; (of diploma) holder; (of secret) keeper; (of passport) bearer.

possessif, **-ive** /pɔsesif, iv/ *adj* possessive.

possession /pɔsesjɔ̃/ *nf* possession; **prendre ~ d'un héritage** to come into one's inheritance.

possibilité /pɔsibilite/ **I** *nf* **1** possibility; **2** opportunity; **~ d'embauche** job opportunity.
II possibilités *nf pl* **1** (of person) abilities; (of appliance, device) potential or possible uses; **avoir de nombreuses ~s** to be versatile; **2** resources.

possible /pɔsibl/ **I** *adj* **1** possible; **dès que ~** as soon as possible; **tout le courage ~** the utmost courage; **tous les cas ~s et imaginables** every conceivable case; **le plus cher ~** [*sell*] at the highest possible price; **le plus de renseignements ~** as much information as possible; **autant que ~** as much as possible; **il n'y a pas d'erreur ~, c'est lui** it's him, without a shadow of a doubt; **tout est ~** anything is possible; **(ce n'est) pas ~**○! I don't believe it!; you're joking!; **'tu vas acheter une voiture?'—'~'** 'are you going to buy a car?'—'maybe'; **2**○ **il a un accent pas ~** he has an atrocious accent; **il a une chance pas ~** he's incredibly lucky.
II *nm* **faire (tout) son ~** to do one's best; **elle est bête au ~**○ she's as stupid as they come.

post(-) /pɔst/ *pref* post(-); **~doctoral** postdoctoral; **~romantique** post-Romantic.

postal, **~e**, *mpl* **-aux** /pɔstal, o/ *adj* [*train,* *boat*] mail; [*van*] post office (GB), mail (US); [*services*] postal.

poste[1] /pɔst/ *nm* **1** position, job; post; **suppression de ~** job cut; **~s vacants** or **à pourvoir** vacancies; **2** (Sport) position; **3** post; **~ (de travail)** work station; **il est toujours fidèle au ~** you can always rely on him; **4 ~ de police** police station; **5 ~ de radio/de télévision** radio/television set; **6** (tele)phone; extension; **7** shift; **8** (in accountancy) item.
■ **~ d'aiguillage** signal box; **~ de douane** customs post; **~ de péage** toll booth; **~ de pilotage** flight deck; **~ de secours** first-aid post (GB) or station.

poste[2] /pɔst/ *nf* post office; **envoyer par la ~** to send [sth] by post (GB), to mail (US).
■ **~ aérienne** airmail; **~ restante** poste restante (GB), general delivery (US).

poster[1] /pɔste/ [1] **I** *vtr* **1** to post (GB), to mail (US); **2** to post, to station [*soldier, guard*]; to put [sb] in place [*spy*].
II se poster *v refl* (+ *v être*) **se ~ devant** to station oneself in front of.

poster[2] /pɔstɛʀ/ *nm* poster.

postérieur, ~e /pɔsteʀjœʀ/ **I** *adj* **1** [*date*] later; [*event*] subsequent; **un écrivain ~ à Flaubert** a writer who came after Flaubert; **2** [*part, section*] posterior; [*legs*] hind.
II° *nm* behind°, posterior.

postérieurement /pɔsteʀjœʀmɑ̃/ *adv* subsequently; **~ à** after.

postérité /pɔsteʀite/ *nf* **1** posterity; **passer à la ~** [*person*] to go down in history; [*work*] to become part of the cultural heritage; **2** descendants.

posthume /pɔstym/ *adj* posthumous.

postiche /pɔstiʃ/ **I** *adj* [*beard*] false; [*emotion*] fake.
II *nm* **1** hairpiece; toupee; wig; **2** false moustache (GB) or mustache (US); **3** false beard.

postier, -ière /pɔstje, ɛʀ/ *nm,f* postal worker.

postillon° /pɔstijɔ̃/ *nm* drop of saliva.

postillonner° /pɔstijɔne/ [1] *vi* to spit (saliva).

postnatal, ~e, *mpl* **~s** /pɔstnatal/ *adj* postnatal; **allocation ~e** maternity allowance.

postopératoire /pɔstɔpeʀatwaʀ/ *adj* postoperative.

post-scriptum /pɔstskʀiptɔm/ *nm inv* postscript.

postsynchroniser /pɔstsɛ̃kʀɔnize/ [1] *vtr* to dub, to add the soundtrack to.

postulant, ~e /pɔstylɑ̃, ɑ̃t/ *nm,f* candidate.

postulat /pɔstyla/ *nm* premise; postulate.

postuler /pɔstyle/ [1] *vi* to apply (**à, pour** for).

posture /pɔstyʀ/ *nf* **1** posture; **2** position.

pot /po/ *nm* **1** container; jar; carton, tub; (earthenware) pot; jug; **plante en ~** potted plant; **un ~ de peinture** a tin of paint; **2** (chamber) pot; potty; **3**° drink; **4**° do° (GB), drinks party; **5**° **avoir du ~** to be lucky.
■ **~ catalytique** catalytic converter; **~ d'échappement** (Aut) silencer (GB), muffler (US); exhaust.
IDIOMS **payer les ~s cassés** to pick up the pieces; **être sourd comme un ~**° to be as deaf as a post; **tourner autour du ~**° to beat about the bush.

potable /pɔtabl/ *adj* **1 eau ~** drinking water; **2**° decent.

potage /pɔtaʒ/ *nm* soup.

potager, -ère /pɔtaʒe, ɛʀ/ **I** *adj* [*plant, herb*] edible; **jardin ~** kitchen garden.
II *nm* kitchen garden.

potasser° /pɔtase/ [1] *vtr* to mug up° (GB), to bone up on° (US).

pot-au-feu /pɔtofø/ *nm inv* **1** boiled beef (*with vegetables*); **2** boiling beef.

pot-de-vin, *pl* **pots-de-vin** /podvɛ̃/ *nm* bribe, backhander° (GB).

pote° /pɔt/ *nm* mate° (GB), pal° (US).

poteau, *pl* **~x** /pɔto/ *nm* post; goalpost; **coiffer qn au ~** to overtake (GB) or pass (US) sb at the finishing line.
■ **~ électrique** electricity pole (*supplying domestic power lines*).

potelé, ~e /pɔtle/ *adj* chubby.

potence /pɔtɑ̃s/ *nf* **1** gallows; **2** (in building) bracket.

potentialité /pɔtɑ̃sjalite/ *nf* **1** potential; **2** potentiality.

potentiel, -ielle /pɔtɑ̃sjɛl/ **I** *adj* potential.
II *nm* potential.

poterie /pɔtʀi/ *nf* **1** pottery; **2** piece of pottery.

potiche /pɔtiʃ/ *nf* **1** vase; **2 être une ~** to look merely decorative.

potier, -ière /pɔtje, ɛʀ/ *nm,f* potter.

potin° /pɔtɛ̃/ *nm* **1** gossip; **2** din°.

potion /posjɔ̃/ *nf* potion.

potiron /pɔtiʀɔ̃/ *nm* pumpkin (GB), winter squash (US).

pot-pourri, *pl* **pots-pourris** /popuʀi/ *nm* **1** (Mus) medley; **2** potpourri.

pou, *pl* **~x** /pu/ *nm* louse.
IDIOMS **chercher des ~x**° to nitpick°; **être laid** or **moche**° **comme un ~**° to be as ugly as sin.

poubelle /pubɛl/ *nf* **1** bin (GB), trash can (US); dustbin (GB), garbage can (US); **2** dumping ground.

pouce /pus/ *nm* **1** thumb; **2** big toe; **3** inch; **ne pas bouger d'un ~** not to budge an inch.
IDIOMS **se tourner** or **rouler les ~s**° to twiddle one's thumbs; **manger sur le ~** to have a quick bite to eat; **donner un coup de ~ à qn/à qch** to help sb/sth get started; to give sb/sth a boost.

poudre /pudʀ/ *nf* (gen) powder; **~ (à canon)** gunpowder; **~ à récurer** scouring powder.
IDIOMS **mettre le feu aux ~s** to bring things to a head; **jeter de la ~ aux yeux** to try to impress; **se répandre comme une traînée de ~** to spread like wildfire.

poudrer /pudʀe/ [1] *vtr* to powder.

poudreux, -euse /pudʀø, øz/ *adj* **1** dusty; **2** [*snow*] powdery.

poudrier /pudʀije/ *nm* powder compact.

poudrière /pudʀijɛʀ/ *nf* **1** powder magazine; **2** (figurative) time bomb.

pouf /puf/ *nm* **1** pouffe; **2 faire ~** to fall with a soft thud.

pouffer /pufe/ [1] *vi* **~ (de rire)** to burst out laughing.

pouilleux, -euse /pujø, øz/ *adj* **1**○ seedy; **2** flea-ridden.

poulailler /pulɑje/ *nm* **1** henhouse; hen run; **2** hens; **3**○ **le ~** the Gods (GB), the gallery.

poulain /pulɛ̃/ *nm* **1** colt; foal; **2** protégé.

poularde /pulaʀd/ *nf* fattened chicken.

poule /pul/ *nf* **1** hen; **2** boiling fowl; **3**○ **ma ~** my pet○, honey○ (US).

■ **~ d'eau** moorhen; **~ faisane** hen pheasant; **~ mouillée**○ wimp○; **~ naine** bantam; **~ pondeuse** laying hen; **~ au pot** boiled chicken.

IDIOMS **quand les ~s auront des dents**○ when pigs fly; **tuer la ~ pour avoir l'œuf, tuer la ~ aux œufs d'or** to kill the goose that lays the golden egg.

poulet /pulɛ/ *nm* **1** chicken; **2**○ **mon ~** my pet○, honey○ (US).

■ **~ d'élevage** ≈ battery chicken; **~ fermier** ≈ free-range chicken.

poulette /pulɛt/ *nf* **1** young hen; pullet; **2**○ bird○ (GB), chick○ (US).

pouliche /puliʃ/ *nf* filly.

poulie /puli/ *nf* pulley.

poulpe /pulp/ *nm* octopus.

pouls /pu/ *nm inv* pulse.

poumon /pumɔ̃/ *nm* lung; **~ d'acier** or **artificiel** iron lung; **à pleins ~s** [*shout*] at the top of one's voice; [*breathe*] deeply.

poupe /pup/ *nf* stern; **avoir le vent en ~** to have the wind in one's sails.

poupée /pupe/ *nf* **1** doll; **jouer à la ~** to play dolls; **2**○ poppet (GB), toots○ (US).

poupin, ~e /pupɛ̃, in/ *adj* chubby.

poupon /pupɔ̃/ *nm* **1** tiny baby; **2** baby doll.

pouponner○ /pupɔne/ [1] *vi* to play the doting father/mother.

pouponnière /pupɔnjɛʀ/ *nf* children's home (*for under-threes*).

pour[1] /puʀ/ *prep* **1** to; **~ faire** to do; in order to do; **pour ne pas faire** so as not to do; **c'était ~ rire** or **plaisanter** it was a joke; **~ que** so that; **~ ainsi dire** so to speak; **2** for; **le train ~ Paris** the train for Paris; the train to Paris; **quelque chose ~ le mal de tête** something for headaches; **ce sera prêt ~ vendredi?** will it be ready for or by Friday?; **~ toujours** forever; **le bébé c'est ~ quand?** when is the baby due?; **je l'ai pris ~ plus bête qu'il n'est** I thought he was more stupid than he really is; **se battre ~ une femme** to fight over a woman; **c'est fait** or **étudié ~**○**!** that's what it's for; **je suis ~**○ I'm in favour[GB]; **3** about; as regards; **se renseigner ~** to find out about; **~ l'argent** as regards the money, as for the money; **c'est bien payé mais ~ la sécurité de l'emploi**... the pay is good but as far as job security goes...; **~ moi, il a tort** as far as I am concerned, he's wrong; **4 elle a ~ ambition d'être pilote** her ambition is to be a pilot; **ils ont ~ habitude de déjeuner tard** they usually have a late lunch; **5 elle avait ~ elle de savoir écouter** she had the merit of being a good listener; **6 ~ riche qu'il soit** no matter how rich he is; **~ autant que je sache** as far as I know; **~ être intelligente, ça elle l'est!** she really is intelligent!; **7 j'ai mis ~ 200 francs d'essence** I've put in 200 francs' worth of petrol (GB) or gas (US); **merci ~ tout** thank you for everything; **je n'y suis ~ rien** I had nothing to do with it; **elle y est ~ beaucoup s'il a réussi** if he has succeeded a lot of the credit should go to her; **je n'en ai pas ~ longtemps** it won't take long; **8 dix ~ cent** ten per cent; **une cuillère de vinaigre ~ quatre d'huile** one spoonful of vinegar to four of oil; **~ une large part** to a large extent.

pour[2] /puʀ/ *nm* **le ~ et le contre** the pros and the cons.

pourboire /puʀbwaʀ/ *nm* tip.

pourcentage /puʀsɑ̃taʒ/ *nm* **1** percentage; **2** commission; **3** cut○ (**sur** of).

pourchasser /puʀʃase/ [1] *vtr* **1** to hunt [*animal, criminal*]; **2** to pursue [*person*].

pourparlers /puʀparle/ *nm pl* talks; **être en ~** [*people*] to be engaged in talks; [*matter*] to be under discussion.

pourpre[1] /puʀpʀ/ *adj, nm* crimson.

pourpre[2] /puʀpʀ/ *nf* **1** Tyrian purple; **2** purple.

pourquoi[1] /puʀkwa/ *adv, conj* why; **~ donc?** but why?; **~ pas** or **non?** why not?; **~ pas un week-end à Paris?** what or how about a weekend in Paris?; **~ s'en priver?** why deny yourself?; **va donc savoir ~!** God knows why!

pourquoi[2] /puʀkwa/ *nm inv* **le ~ et le comment** the why and the wherefore.

pourri, ~e /puʀi/ **I** *pp* ▶ **pourrir**.

II *pp adj* **1** (gen) rotten; [*vegetation*] rotting; **2**○ [*weather, car*] rotten○, lousy○; [*person, mentality*] crooked○, corrupt; [*child*] spoiled.

III *nm* rotten part; **ça sent le ~** it smells rotten.

pourrir /puʀiʀ/ [3] **I** *vtr* **1** to rot [*wood*]; **2** to spoil [*person*]; **3**○ to spoil [sb] rotten○.

II *vi* **1** [*food*] to go bad; **2** [*wood*] to rot; **3** [*person*] to rot; [*situation*] to deteriorate.

pourriture /puʀityʀ/ *nf* **1** rot, decay; **2** corruption, rottenness.

poursuite /puʀsɥit/ *nf* **1** pursuit; **être à la ~ de** to be in pursuit of; **2** chase; **3** continuation (**de** of); **4 ~ (judiciaire)** (judicial) proceedings.

poursuivant, ~e /puʀsɥivɑ̃, ɑ̃t/ *nm,f* **1** pursuer; **2** (Law) plaintiff.

poursuivre /puʀsɥivʀ/ [62] **I** *vtr* **1** to chase; **2** [*person*] to hound; [*nightmare*] to haunt; **~ qn de ses assiduités** to force one's attentions on sb; **cette histoire de vol m'a longtemps poursuivie** that stealing business dogged me for a long time; **3** to seek (after) [*honours, truth*]; to pursue [*goal*]; **4** to continue [*journey, studies*];

to pursue [*talks*]; ~ **une enquête policière** to proceed with a police inquiry; **5** (Law) ~ **qn (en justice** or **devant les tribunaux)** to sue sb.
II *vi* to continue; ~ **sur un sujet** to continue talking on a subject.
III se poursuivre *v refl* (+ *v être*) [*talks, conflict, journey*] to continue.

pourtant /puʀtɑ̃/ *adv* though; **et** ~ and yet; **c'est** ~ **vrai** it's true though; **techniquement** ~, **le film est parfait** technically, however, the film is perfect.

pourtour /puʀtuʀ/ *nm* **1** perimeter; circumference; **2** surrounding area.

pourvoir /puʀvwaʀ/ [40] **I** *vtr* **1** to fill [*post*]; **poste à** ~ vacancy; **2** ~ **qn de** to endow sb with.
II pourvoir à *v+prep* to provide for [*need, safety*]; **j'y pourvoirai** I'll see to it.
III se pourvoir *v refl* (+ *v être*) **se** ~ **de** to provide oneself with [*currency*]; to equip oneself with [*boots*].

pourvoyeur, **-euse** /puʀvwajœʀ, øz/ *nm,f* ~ **de** source of [*jobs, funding*].

pourvu: **pourvu que** /puʀvyk(ə)/ *phr* **1** provided (that), as long as; **2** let's hope; ~ **que ça dure!** let's hope it lasts!

pousse /pus/ *nf* **1** (Bot) shoot; (figurative) offshoot; ~**s de bambou** bamboo shoots; **2** growth; **la** ~ **des ongles** nail growth; **la** ~ **des feuilles** the sprouting of leaves.

poussé, ~**e**[1] /puse/ **I** *pp* ▶ **pousser**.
II *pp adj* **1** [*inquiry*] thorough; [*studies*] advanced; **2 être un peu** ~ [*joke*] to go a bit too far; [*comparison*] to be a bit forced.

pousse-café /puskafe/ *nm inv* (after-dinner) liqueur.

poussée[2] /puse/ *nf* **1** (of water, crowd) pressure; (of wind) force; thrust; **2** attack (**de** of); ~ **de fièvre** sudden high temperature; **3** (in price) (sharp) rise or increase; (in racism, violence) upsurge; ~ **inflationniste** inflationary trend.

pousser /puse/ [1] **I** *vtr* **1** to push [*wheelbarrow, person*]; to move or shift [sth] (out of the way), to push [sth] aside; ~ **une porte** to push a door to; to push a door open; **peux-tu** ~ **ta voiture? elle gêne** can you move your car? it's in the way; ~ **qn du coude** to give sb a dig or to nudge sb with one's elbow; **2 c'est la jalousie qui le pousse** he's driven by jealousy; ~ **qn à faire** to encourage sb to do; to urge sb to do; [*hunger, despair*] to drive sb to do; ~ **à la consommation** to encourage people to buy more; to encourage people to drink more; ~ **qn au suicide** to drive sb to suicide; **3** to push [*pupil*]; to keep [sb] at it [*employee*]; to ride [sth] hard [*horse*]; to drive [sth] hard [*car*]; to flog○ [*engine*]; **4** to push [*product, protégé*]; **5** to pursue [*studies, research*]; **c'est** ~ **un peu loin la plaisanterie** that's taking the joke a bit far; ~ **la bêtise jusqu'à faire** to be stupid enough to do; **6** to let out [*shout*]; to heave [*sigh*]; ~ **un hurlement** to howl.
II *vi* **1** [*child*] to grow; [*plant*] to grow; to sprout; [*tooth*] to come through; [*buildings, towns*] to spring up; **je fais** ~ **des légumes** I grow vegetables; **se laisser** or **se faire** ~ **les cheveux** to grow one's hair; **2** ~ **plus loin/jusqu'à la ville** to go on further/as far as the town; **3**○ to overdo it, to go too far.
III se pousser *v refl* (+ *v être*) to move over.
IDIOMS **à la va comme je te pousse**○ any old how.

poussette /pusɛt/ *nf* pushchair (GB), stroller (US).

poussière /pusjɛʀ/ *nf* **1** dust; **tomber en** ~ to crumble away; to fall to bits; **2** speck of dust.
IDIOMS **10 francs/20 ans et des** ~**s**○ just over 10 francs/20 years.

poussiéreux, **-euse** /pusjeʀø, øz/ *adj* **1** dusty; **2** outdated, fossilized.

poussif, **-ive** /pusif, iv/ *adj* [*person*] wheezy; [*horse*] broken-winded.

poussin /pusɛ̃/ *nm* **1** chick; **2** (Culin) poussin (GB), spring chicken.

poussoir /puswaʀ/ *nm* (push) button.

poutre /putʀ/ *nf* **1** beam; **2** girder.

poutrelle /putʀɛl/ *nf* girder.

pouvoir[1] /puvwaʀ/ [49] **I** *v aux* **1** to be able to; **peux-tu soulever cette boîte?** can you lift this box?; **dès que je pourrai** as soon as I can; **il ne pourra pas venir** he won't be able to come; **il n'a pas pu venir** he wasn't able to come; **je n'en peux plus** I've had it○; I'm full○; **tout peut arriver** anything could happen; **il ne peut pas ne pas gagner** he's bound to win; **on peut toujours espérer** there's no harm in wishing or hoping; **qu'est-ce que cela peut (bien) te faire**○**?** what business is it of yours?; **2** to be allowed to; **est-ce que je peux me servir de ta voiture?** can I use your car?; **puis-je m'asseoir?** may I sit down?; **on peut dire que** it can be said that; **on peut écrire clef ou clé** the word can be written clef or clé; **on peut ne pas faire l'accord** the agreement is optional; **3 pouvez-vous/pourriez-vous me tenir la porte s'il vous plaît?** can you/could you hold the door (open) for me please?; **4 puisse cette nouvelle année exaucer vos vœux les plus chers** may the new year bring you everything you could wish for; **s'il croit que je vais payer il peut toujours attendre** if he thinks I'm going to pay he's got another think coming; **ce qu'il peut être grand!** how tall he is!; **peux-tu être bête!** you can be so silly!
II *vtr* **que puis-je pour vous?** what can I do for you?; **je fais ce que je peux** I'm doing my best.
III *v impers* **il peut faire très froid en janvier** it can get very cold in January; **il pouvait être 10 heures** it was probably about 10 o'clock; **ce qu'il a pu pleuvoir!** you wouldn't believe how much it rained!
IV il se peut *v impers* **il se peut que les prix augmentent en juin** prices may or might rise in June; **se peut-il qu'il m'ait oublié?** can he really have forgotten me?; **cela se pourrait (bien) qu'il soit fâché** he might (well) be angry; **ça ne se peut pas**○ it's impossible.
V on ne peut plus *phr* **il est on ne peut plus timide** he is as shy as can be.

VI **on ne peut mieux** *phr* **c'est on ne peut mieux** it couldn't be better; **ils s'entendent on ne peut mieux** they get on extremely well.

IDIOMS **autant que faire se peut** as far as possible.

pouvoir² /puvwaʀ/ *nm* **1** (gen) power; **~ d'achat** purchasing power; **avoir le ~ de faire** to be able to do, to have the power to do; **le ~ de qn sur qn** sb's power over sb; **je n'ai pas le ~ de décider** it's not up to me to decide; **2** (Pol) power; **après 15 ans au ~** after 15 years in power; **avoir tous ~s** to have or exercise full powers; **le ~ en place** the government in power.

■ **le ~ judiciaire** the judiciary; **~ législatif** legislative power; **~s publics** authorities.

pragmatisme /pʀagmatism/ *nm* pragmatism.

praire /pʀɛʀ/ *nf* clam.

prairie /pʀɛʀi/ *nf* meadow.

praline /pʀalin/ *nf* sugared (GB) or sugar-coated (US) almond.

praliné, **~e** /pʀaline/ I *adj* praline.

II *nm* praline.

praticable /pʀatikabl/ *adj* **1** [*road*] passable; **2** [*sport*] that can be played.

praticien, **-ienne** /pʀatisjɛ̃, ɛn/ *nm,f* **1** general practitioner, GP; **2** practitioner.

pratiquant, **~e** /pʀatikɑ̃, ɑ̃t/ I *adj* practising[GB]; **être très ~** to be very devout.

II *nm,f* practising[GB] Catholic/Muslim/Jew etc.

pratique /pʀatik/ I *adj* practical; [*device*] handy; [*place, route*] convenient; **avoir le sens** or **l'esprit ~** to be practical.

II *nf* **1 la ~ des arts martiaux est très répandue** many people practise[GB] martial arts; **cela nécessite de longues heures de ~** it takes hours of practice; **avoir une bonne ~ de l'anglais** to have a good working knowledge of English; **2** practical experience; **manquer de ~** to lack practical experience; **3** practice; **mettre qch en ~** to put sth into practice; **4** practice; **une ~ courante** a common practice; **les ~s religieuses** religious practices.

pratiquement /pʀatikmɑ̃/ *adv* **1** in practice; **2** practically, virtually; **~ jamais** hardly ever.

pratiquer /pʀatike/ [1] I *vtr* **1** to play [*tennis*]; to do [*yoga*]; to take part in [*activity*]; to practise[GB] [*language*]; **~ l'équitation** to ride; **~ la médecine** to practise[GB] medicine; **il est croyant mais ne pratique pas** he believes in God but doesn't practise[GB] his religion; **2** to use [*method, blackmail*]; to pursue [*policy*]; to charge [*rate of interest*]; **3** to carry out [*examination, graft*]; to administer [*first aid*].

II **se pratiquer** *v refl* (+ *v être*) [*sport*] to be played; [*technique, policy, strategy*] to be used; [*price, tariff*] to be charged; **c'est un sport qui se pratique beaucoup** it's a very popular sport.

pré /pʀe/ *nm* meadow.

pré- /pʀe/ *pref* pre(-); **~industriel** preindustrial; **~-accord** preliminary agreement.

préadolescent, **~e** /pʀeadɔlesɑ̃, ɑ̃t/ *adj, nm,f* pre-teen.

préalable /pʀealabl/ I *adj* [*notice*] prior; [*study*] preliminary.

II *nm* precondition (**à** for, of); preliminary (**à** to).

III **au préalable** *phr* first, beforehand.

préalablement /pʀealabləmɑ̃/ *adv* beforehand.

préambule /pʀeɑ̃byl/ *nm* **1** preamble; **2** forewarning.

préau, *pl* **~x** /pʀeo/ *nm* (of school) covered playground; (of prison) exercise yard; (of hospital) inner courtyard.

préavis /pʀeavi/ *nm inv* notice; **déposer un ~ de grève** to give notice of strike action.

précaire /pʀekɛʀ/ *adj* [*existence*] precarious; [*job*] insecure; [*construction*] flimsy.

précariser /pʀekaʀize/ [1] *vtr* **~ l'emploi** to casualize labour[GB]; **~ la situation de qn** to make sb's position insecure.

précarité /pʀekaʀite/ *nf* precariousness; **la ~ de l'emploi** job insecurity.

précaution /pʀekosjɔ̃/ *nf* **1** precaution; **prendre ses ~s** to take precautions; to go to the toilet just in case; **2** caution; **par ~** as a precaution.

précédemment /pʀesedamɑ̃/ *adv* previously, before.

précédent, **~e** /pʀesedɑ̃, ɑ̃t/ I *adj* previous.

II *nm,f* **le ~**, **la ~e** the previous one.

III *nm* precedent; **sans ~** without precedent.

précéder /pʀesede/ [14] *vtr* **1** [*person*] to go in front of, to precede; [*vehicle*] to be in front of, to precede; **2 il m'avait précédé de cinq minutes** he'd got there five minutes ahead of me; **3** [*paragraph*] to precede; [*event, crisis*] to lead up to, to precede; **la semaine qui a précédé votre départ** the week before you left; **4 Tours précède Grenoble de trois points** Tours is three points ahead of Grenoble.

précepte /pʀesɛpt/ *nm* precept.

précepteur, **-trice** /pʀesɛptœʀ, tʀis/ *nm,f* (private) tutor.

prêcher /pʀeʃe/ [1] I *vtr* **1** to preach; **2** to advocate.

II *vi* to preach.

IDIOMS **~ le faux pour savoir le vrai** to tell a lie in order to get at the truth.

précieusement /pʀesjøzmɑ̃/ *adv* [*keep*] carefully; [*engrave*] minutely.

précieux, **-ieuse** /pʀesjø, øz/ *adj* **1** [*stone, book*] precious; [*piece of furniture*] valuable; **2** [*information*] very useful; [*collaborator*] valued; **3** [*friendship, right*] precious; [*friend*] very dear; **4** [*style, language*] precious.

précipice /pʀesipis/ *nm* precipice; **être au bord du ~** to be on the brink of collapse.

précipitamment /pʀesipitamɑ̃/ *adv* hurriedly.

précipitation /pʀesipitasjɔ̃/ I *nf* haste; **avec ~** hurriedly.

II **précipitations** *nf pl* rainfall, precipitation.

précipité, **~e** /pʀesipite/ *adj* **1** rapid; **2** hasty, precipitate.

précipiter /pʀesipite/ [1] I *vtr* **1 ~ qn dans**

le vide (from roof) to push sb off; (out of window) to push sb out; **~ qn contre** to throw sb against; **2 ~ qn dans le désarroi** to throw sb into confusion; **3** to hasten [*departure, decision*]; to precipitate [*event*]; **~ les choses** to rush things.

II se précipiter *v refl* (+ *v être*) **1 il s'est précipité dans le vide** he jumped off; **2** to rush; **se ~ au secours de qn** to rush to sb's aid; **se ~ sur** to rush at [*person*]; to rush for [*object*]; to pounce on [*idea*]; **3** to rush, to hurry; **4** [*action, event*] to move faster.

précis, **~e** /pʀesi, iz/ **I** *adj* **1** [*programme, criterion*] specific; [*idea, date*] definite; [*moment*] particular; **2** [*person, gesture, answer*] precise; [*figure, data, device*] accurate; [*memory*] clear; [*place, moment*] exact.

II *nm inv* handbook.

précisément /pʀesizemɑ̃/ *adv* precisely.

préciser /pʀesize/ [1] **I** *vtr* **1** to add; **a-t-il précisé** he added; **faut-il le** or **est-il besoin de ~** needless to say; **2** to state; **~ ses intentions** to state one's intentions; **3** to specify [*place, date*]; **pouvez-vous ~?** could you be more specific?; **4** to clarify [*ideas, programme*].

II se préciser *v refl* (+ *v être*) **1** [*danger, future*] to become clearer; [*plan, trip*] to take shape; **2** [*shape, reality*] to become clear.

précision /pʀesizjɔ̃/ *nf* **1** precision; **~ du détail** detailed precision; **2** accuracy; **localiser avec ~** to pinpoint; **instrument de ~** precision instrument; **3** detail; **apporter quelques ~s** to give a few details.

précité, **~e** /pʀesite/ *adj* aforementioned.

précoce /pʀekɔs/ *adj* **1** precocious; **2** [*season*] early; **3** [*senility*] premature.

précocité /pʀekɔsite/ *nf* **1** precociousness; **2 la ~ du dépistage** early detection; **3** (of season) earliness.

préconçu, **~e** /pʀekɔ̃sy/ *adj* preconceived.

préconiser /pʀekɔnize/ [1] *vtr* to recommend; to advocate.

précuit, **~e** /pʀekɥi, it/ *adj* precooked.

précurseur /pʀekyʀsœʀ/ **I** *adj m* precursory; **signes ~s de l'orage** signs that herald a storm.

II *nm* pioneer; **~ de** forerunner of; precursor of.

prédateur, **-trice** /pʀedatœʀ, tʀis/ **I** *adj* predatory.

II *nm* **1** predator; **2** hunter-gatherer.

prédécesseur /pʀedesesœʀ/ *nm* predecessor.

prédestiné, **~e** /pʀedɛstine/ *adj* [*name*] appropriate.

prédestiner /pʀedɛstine/ [1] *vtr* to predestine.

prédicateur, **-trice** /pʀedikatœʀ, tʀis/ *nm,f* preacher.

prédiction /pʀediksjɔ̃/ *nf* prediction.

prédilection /pʀedilɛksjɔ̃/ *nf* predilection, liking; **de ~** favourite[GB].

prédire /pʀediʀ/ [65] *vtr* to predict.

prédisposer /pʀedispoze/ [1] *vtr* to predispose.

prédominant, **~e** /pʀedɔminɑ̃, ɑ̃t/ *adj* predominant.

prédominer /pʀedɔmine/ [1] *vi* to predominate.

prééminent, **~e** /pʀeeminɑ̃, ɑ̃t/ *adj* preeminent.

préencollé, **~e** /pʀeɑ̃kɔle/ *adj* [*envelope*] gummed; [*wallpaper*] prepasted.

préexister /pʀeɛgziste/ [1] *vi* to pre-exist; **~ à qch** to predate sth.

préfabriqué, **~e** /pʀefabʀike/ **I** *adj* prefabricated.

II *nm* **1** prefabricated material; **2** prefab○.

préface /pʀefas/ *nf* preface; **~ d'un livre** preface to a book.

préfectoral, **~e**, *mpl* **-aux** /pʀefɛktɔʀal, o/ *adj* [*level, authorization*] prefectorial; [*administration, building*] prefectural.

préfecture /pʀefɛktyʀ/ *nf* **1** prefecture; **2** *main city of a department*.

■ **~ de police** *police headquarters in some large French cities*.

préférable /pʀefeʀabl/ *adj* preferable.

préféré, **~e** /pʀefeʀe/ *adj, nm,f* favourite[GB].

préférence /pʀefeʀɑ̃s/ *nf* preference; **de ~** preferably; **achète cette marque de ~** if you can, buy this brand.

préférer /pʀefeʀe/ [14] *vtr* to prefer; **(c'est) comme tu préfères** (it's) as you prefer or wish; **j'aurais préféré ne jamais l'apprendre** I wish I'd never heard it.

préfet /pʀefɛ/ *nm* prefect; **~ de police** prefect of police.

préfigurer /pʀefigyʀe/ [1] *vtr* to prefigure.

préfixe /pʀefiks/ *nm* prefix.

préhensile /pʀeɑ̃sil/ *adj* prehensile.

préhistoire /pʀeistwaʀ/ *nf* prehistory.

préjudice /pʀeʒydis/ *nm* harm, damage; **~ matériel** material loss; **~ moral** moral wrong; **porter ~ à qn** to harm sb; **au ~ de qn** to the detriment of sb.

préjugé /pʀeʒyʒe/ *nm* prejudice; **~(s) en faveur de qn** bias in favour[GB] of sb; **avoir un ~ en défaveur de** or **contre qn/qch** to have a prejudice against sb/sth.

préjuger /pʀeʒyʒe/ [13] *vtr*, **préjuger de** *v+prep* to prejudge.

prélasser: **se prélasser** /pʀelase/ [1] *v refl* (+ *v être*) to lounge.

prélat /pʀela/ *nm* prelate.

prélavage /pʀelavaʒ/ *nm* prewash.

prêle /pʀɛl/ *nf* (Bot) horsetail, equisetum.

prélèvement /pʀelɛvmɑ̃/ *nm* **1** sampling; **faire un ~ de sang** to take a blood sample; **2** sample; **3 faire un ~ bancaire de 100 francs** to make a debit of 100 francs.

■ **~ automatique** direct debit; **~ fiscal** deduction of tax; **~ à la source** deduction at source.

prélever /pʀelve/ [16] *vtr* **1** to take a sample of [*blood, water*]; to remove [*organ*]; **2** to debit (**sur** from); **3** to deduct [*tax*] (**sur** from); **4** to take [*percentage*].

préliminaire /pʀelimineʀ/ **I** *adj* preliminary.

II préliminaires *nm pl* preliminaries.

prélude /pʀelyd/ *nm* prelude.

préluder: **préluder à** /pʀelyde/ [1] *v+prep* **~ à** to be a prelude to.

prématuré, **~e** /pʀematyʀe/ **I** *adj* premature.

II *nm,f* premature baby.

préméditation /pʀemeditasjɔ̃/ *nf* premeditation.

préméditer /pʀemedite/ [1] *vtr* to premeditate.

prémices /pʀemis/ *nf pl* (literary) beginnings.

premier, **-ière**[1] /pʀəmje, ɛʀ/ **I** *adj* **1** first; **(dans) les ~s temps tout allait bien** at first, things went well; **2** [*number, word, candidate*] first; **le ~ janvier** the first of January; **Napoléon Ier** Napoleon I, Napoleon the First; **3** [*artist, power*] leading; [*student*] top; **être ~** to be top; to be first; **c'est le ~ prix** it's the cheapest; **4** [*impression*] first, initial; [*appearance*] original; **5** [*quality*] prime; [*objective, consequence*] primary.

II *nm,f* first; **vous êtes le ~ à me le dire** you are the first to tell me; **je préfère le ~** I prefer the first one; **arriver le ~** to come first; **être le ~ de la classe** to be top of the class.

III *nm* **1** first floor (GB), second floor (US); **2** first; **le ~ de l'an** New Year's Day; **3** first arrondissement.

IV en premier *phr* first.

V de première○ *phr* first-rate.

■ **~ âge** [*clothes*] for babies up to six months; **~ de cordée** (Sport) leader; **~ danseur** leading dancer; **~ ministre** prime minister; **le ~ venu** just anybody; **elle s'est jetée dans les bras du ~ venu** she threw herself at the first man to come along; **première nouvelle**○**!** that's the first I've heard about it!; **~s secours** first aid.

première[2] /pʀəmjɛʀ/ **I** ▸ **premier I, II.**

II *nf* **1** first; **~ mondiale** world first; **2** première; **3** (Sch) *sixth year of secondary school, age 16–17*; **4** (Aut) first (gear); **5**○ first class.

premièrement /pʀəmjɛʀmɑ̃/ *adv* **1** firstly, first; **2** for a start, for one thing.

premier-né, **première-née**, *mpl* **premiers-nés**, *fpl* **premières-nées** /pʀəmjene, pʀəmjɛʀne/ *nm,f* **1** first born; **2** first.

prémisse /pʀemis/ *nf* premise, premiss (GB).

prémonition /pʀemɔnisjɔ̃/ *nf* premonition.

prémonitoire /pʀemɔnitwaʀ/ *adj* premonitory.

prémunir /pʀemyniʀ/ [3] **I** *vtr* to protect (**contre** against).

II se prémunir *v refl* (+ *v être*) to protect oneself (**contre** against, from).

prenant, **~e** /pʀənɑ̃, ɑ̃t/ *adj* [*film*] fascinating; [*voice*] captivating; [*work*] absorbing.

prénatal, **~e**, *mpl* **~s** /pʀenatal/ *adj* [*surgery*] prenatal; [*care*] antenatal.

prendre /pʀɑ̃dʀ/ [52]

■ **Note** *Prendre* is very often translated by *to take* but see the entry below for a wide variety of usages.
– For translations of certain fixed phrases such as *prendre froid, prendre soin de, prendre parti* etc, refer to the entries ***froid, soin, parti***.

I *vtr* **1** to take; **~ un vase dans le placard** to take a vase out of the cupboard; **prenez donc une chaise** do have or take a seat; **2 ~ un accent** to pick up an accent; to put on an accent; **~ une habitude** to develop or pick up a habit; **3** to take; **on m'a pris tous mes bijoux** I had all my jewellery (GB) or jewelry (US) stolen; **la guerre leur a pris deux fils** they lost two sons in the war; **4** to bring; **n'oublie pas de ~ des bottes** don't forget to bring a pair of boots; **5** to get [*food, petrol*]; **~ de l'argent au distributeur** to get some money out of the cash dispenser; **6** to have [*drink, meal*]; to take [*medicine*]; **je vais ~ du poisson** I'll have fish; **aller ~ une bière** to go for a beer; **7** to take [*holiday, time off*]; **je vais ~ mon mercredi**○ I'm going to take Wednesday off; **8** to take [*object*]; to choose [*topic, question*]; **~ qn pour époux** to take sb to be one's husband; **9** to charge; **elle prend combien pour une coupe?** how much does she charge for a cut?; **il prend 15% au passage**○ he takes a cut of 15%; **10** to take up [*space, time*]; **11** to take [sb] on; to engage [sb]; **12** to take; **ils ont pris la petite chez eux** they took the little girl in; **ce train ne prend pas de voyageurs** this train doesn't take passengers; **13** to pick [sb/sth] up; **~ les enfants à l'école** to collect the children from school; **14** to catch; **elle s'est fait ~ en train de voler** she got caught stealing; **je vous y prends**○**!** caught you!; **on ne m'y prendra plus**○**!** you won't catch me doing that again!; I won't be taken in○ again!; **15**○ **qu'est-ce qui te prend?** what's the matter with you?; **ça te/leur prend souvent?** are you/they often like this?; **16** to involve [*spectator, reader*]; **être pris par un livre/film** to get involved in a book/film; **17** to get [*slap, sunburn, parking ticket*]; to catch [*cold*]; **18** to take [*bus, taxi, motorway*]; **19** to take; **prenons par exemple Samuel** take Samuel, for example; **à tout ~** all in all; **20** to take; **ne le prends pas mal** don't take it the wrong way; **pour qui me prends-tu?** what do you take me for?; who do you think you're talking to?; **excusez-moi, je vous ai pris pour quelqu'un d'autre** I'm sorry, I thought you were someone else; **21 il est très gentil quand on sait le ~** he's very nice when you know how to handle him; **22** to take [*measurements, temperature, pulse*]; **23** to take [sth] down; **je vais ~ votre adresse** let me just take down your address; **24 ~ que** to get the idea (that); **où a-t-il pris qu'ils allaient divorcer?** where did he get the idea they were going to get divorced?; **25 il faut ~ les gens comme ils sont** you must take people as you find them; **~ les choses comme elles sont** to take things as they come; **26** to take over [*management, power*]; to assume [*control*]; **je prends ça sur moi** I'll see to it; **elle a pris sur elle de leur parler** she took it upon herself to talk to them; **27** to put on [*weight*]; to gain [*lead*]; **28** to take on [*lease*]; to take [*job*]; **29** to take on [*rival*]; **je prends le gagnant** I'll take on the winner; **30** to take, to seize [*town*]; to capture [*ship, tank*]; to take [*chesspiece, card*].

II *vi* **1 ~ à gauche/vers le nord** to go left/north; **~ par le littoral** to follow the coast; **2** [*wood*] to catch; [*fire*] to break out; **3** [*jelly, glue*] to set; [*mayonnaise*] to thicken; **4** [*strike, innovation*] to be a success; [*idea, fashion*] to catch on; [*dye, cutting, graft*] to take; [*lesson*] to sink in; **5 ~ sur son temps libre pour traduire un roman** to translate a novel in one's spare time; **6 ~ sur soi** to take a hold on oneself, to get a grip on oneself; **j'ai pris sur moi pour les écouter** I made myself listen to them; **7**° **ça ne prend pas!** it won't wash° or work!; **8**° **c'est toujours moi qui prends!** I'm always the one who gets it in the neck°!; **il en a pris pour 20 ans** he got 20 years.

III se prendre *v refl* (+ *v être*) **1 en Chine le thé se prend sans sucre** in China they don't put sugar in their tea; **2 les mauvaises habitudes se prennent vite** bad habits are easily picked up; **3 se ~ par la taille** to hold each other around the waist; **4 se ~ les doigts dans la porte** to catch one's fingers in the door; **5**° **il s'est pris une gifle** he got a slap in the face; **6 se ~ à faire** to find oneself doing; **se ~ de sympathie pour qn** to take to sb; **7 pour qui est-ce que tu te prends?** who do you think you are?; **8 s'en ~ à** to attack [*person, press*]; to take it out on [sb]; to go for [sb]; **il ne pourra s'en ~ qu'à lui-même** he will have only himself to blame; **9 savoir s'y ~ avec** to have a way with [*children*]; to know how to handle [*pupils*]; **10 il faut s'y ~ à l'avance pour avoir des places** you have to book ahead to get seats; **tu t'y es pris trop tard** you left it too late; **il s'y est pris à plusieurs fois** he tried several times; **elle s'y prend mal** she goes about it the wrong way.

IDIOMS **c'est à ~ ou à laisser** take it or leave it.

preneur, **-euse** /pʀənœʀ, øz/ *nm,f* taker; **il n'y a pas ~** there are no takers; **trouver ~** to attract a buyer; to find a buyer; **je suis ~** I'll take it.

prénom /pʀenɔ̃/ *nm* first name, forename; **deuxième ~** middle name.

prénommer /pʀenɔme/ [1] I *vtr* to name, to call; **M. Martin, prénommé Henri** Mr Martin, first name Henri.

II se prénommer *v refl* (+ *v être*) to be called.

prénuptial, **~e**, *pl* **-iaux** /pʀenypsjal, o/ *adj* [*agreement*] prenuptial; [*examination*] prior to marriage.

préoccupant, **~e** /pʀeɔkypɑ̃, ɑ̃t/ *adj* worrying.

préoccupation /pʀeɔkypasjɔ̃/ *nf* worry, concern.

préoccuper /pʀeɔkype/ [1] I *vtr* **1** to worry; **ma santé le préoccupe** he's been worried about my health; **avoir l'air préoccupé** to look worried; **2** to preoccupy; **3** to concern; **la question qui nous préoccupe** the question which concerns us.

II se préoccuper *v refl* (+ *v être*) **se ~ de** to be concerned about [*situation*]; to think about [*future*]; **se ~ de sa petite personne** to think only of oneself.

préparatifs /pʀepaʀatif/ *nm pl* preparations.

préparation /pʀepaʀasjɔ̃/ *nf* **1** preparation; **2** training (**à** for).

préparatoire /pʀepaʀatwaʀ/ *adj* preliminary

préparer /pʀepaʀe/ [1] I *vtr* **1** (gen) to prepare; to make [*meal*]; to dress [*wool, fowl*]; to get [sth] ready [*clothes, file*]; to plan [*holidays, future*]; to prepare for [*examination*]; to draw up [*plan*]; to hatch [*plot*]; to lay [*trap*]; **il est en train de ~ le dîner** he's getting dinner ready; **~ le terrain** to prepare the ground (**à qn** for sb); **il prépare un disque pour l'année prochaine** he's working on a record to be released next year; **des plats préparés** ready-to-eat meals; **2 ~ qn à qch** (gen) to prepare sb for sth; to coach sb for sth [*race, examination*]; **essaie de la ~ avant de lui annoncer la nouvelle** try and break the news to her gently.

II se préparer *v refl* (+ *v être*) **1** to get ready; **2** to prepare; **je ne m'étais pas préparé à cette éventualité** I was not prepared for this to happen; **3** [*storm, trouble*] to be brewing; [*changes*] to be in the offing; **un coup d'État se prépare dans le pays** a coup d'état is imminent in the country; **4 se ~ une tasse de thé** to make or fix (US) oneself a cup of tea.

prépondérant, **~e** /pʀepɔ̃deʀɑ̃, ɑ̃t/ *adj* predominant.

préposé, **~e** /pʀepoze/ *nm,f* **1** official; **~ des douanes** customs official; **~ au vestiaire** cloakroom attendant; **2** postman/postwoman.

préposer /pʀepoze/ [1] *vtr* **~ qn à qch/à faire** to assign sb to sth/to do.

préposition /pʀepozisjɔ̃/ *nf* preposition.

prépuce /pʀepys/ *nm* foreskin.

préretraite /pʀeʀətʀɛt/ *nf* **1** early retirement; **2** early retirement pension.

prérogative /pʀeʀɔgativ/ *nf* prerogative (**de faire** to do); **~ de qn/qch sur** primacy of sb/sth over.

près /pʀɛ/ I *adv* **1** close; **ce n'est pas tout ~** it's quite a way; **se raser de ~** to have a close shave; **2 10 kg, à quelques grammes ~** 10 kg, give or take a few grams; **à ceci** or **cela ~ que** except that; **il m'a remboursé au centime ~** he paid me back to the very last penny; **gagner à deux voix ~** to win by two votes; **on n'est pas à cinq minutes ~** five minutes won't make any difference; **précis au millimètre ~** accurate to within a millimetre[GB]; **à une exception ~** with only one exception.

II près de *phr* **1** near; **être ~ du but** to be close to achieving one's goal; **j'aimerais être ~ de toi** I'd like to be with you; **2** near, nearly; **je ne suis pas ~ de recommencer** I'm not about to do that again; **je suis ~ de penser que** I almost think that; **le problème n'est pas ~ d'être résolu** the problem is nowhere near solved; **3** close (**de qn** to sb); **ils sont très ~ l'un de l'autre** they are very close; **4** nearly, almost; **cela coûte ~ de 1000 francs** it costs nearly or almost 1,000 francs.

III de près *phr* closely; **surveiller qn de ~** to keep a close eye on sb; **se suivre de ~** [*competitors*] to be close together; [*siblings*] to be close in age; **voir la mort de ~** to look death in the face.

IV à peu près *phr* **~ vide** practically empty; **~ 200 francs** about 200 francs; **il y a à peu ~ une heure** about an hour ago; **à peu ~ de la même façon** in much the same way.

présage /pʀezaʒ/ *nm* **1** omen (**de** of); **2** harbinger (**de** of); **3** prediction.

présager /pʀezaʒe/ [13] *vtr* [*event*] to presage; [*person*] to predict; **laisser ~** to suggest; **cela ne présage rien de bon** this does not bode well.

presbyte /pʀɛsbit/ *adj* longsighted (GB), farsighted (US).

presbytère /pʀɛsbitɛʀ/ *nm* presbytery.

prescience /pʀesjɑ̃s/ *nf* **1** foresight, prescience; **2** premonition.

prescription /pʀɛskʀipsjɔ̃/ *nf* prescription; **'se conformer aux ~s du médecin'** 'to be taken in accordance with doctor's instructions'.

prescrire /pʀɛskʀiʀ/ [67] *vtr* **1** (Med) to prescribe; **2** to stipulate; **3** [*circumstances*] to call for.

présélectionner /pʀeselɛksjɔne/ [1] *vtr* **1** to shortlist; **2** to preselect [*speed*]; to preset [*channel, station*].

présence /pʀezɑ̃s/ *nf* (gen) presence; (at work) attendance; **il ignore ta ~** he doesn't know you are here; **il fait de la ~, c'est tout** he's present and not much else; **les forces en ~ dans le conflit** the forces involved in the conflict; **il a besoin d'une ~** he needs company; **avoir beaucoup de ~ (sur scène)** to have great stage presence.

■ **~ d'esprit** presence of mind.

présent, **~e**[1] /pʀezɑ̃, ɑ̃t/ **I** *adj* **1** present; **M. Maquanne, ici ~** Mr Maquanne, who is here with us; **j'étais ~ en pensée** I was there in spirit; **avoir qch ~ à l'esprit** to have [sth] in mind [*advice*]; to have [sth] fresh in one's mind [*memory*]; **2** actively involved; **un chanteur très ~ sur scène** a singer with a strong stage presence; **3** present; **par la ~e lettre** by the present (letter).

II *nm,f* **la liste des ~s** the list of those present.

III *nm* **1 le ~** the present; **2** present (tense); **3** gift, present.

IV à présent *phr* at present; now; **à ~ que** now that.

présentable /pʀezɑ̃tabl/ *adj* presentable.

présentateur, **-trice** /pʀezɑ̃tatœʀ, tʀis/ *nm,f* presenter; newsreader (GB), newscaster (US).

présentation /pʀezɑ̃tasjɔ̃/ *nf* **1** introduction; **faire les ~s** to make the introductions; **2** appearance; **3** (of dish, letter) presentation; (of products) display; **4** show, showing; **~ de mode** fashion show; **5** (of programme, news) presentation; **6** (of card, ticket) production; (of cheque) presentation; **sur ~ de** on production of; **7** presentation, exposé.

présente[2] /pʀezɑ̃t/ **I** *adj f* ▶ **présent I**.

II *nf* **1 par la ~** hereby; **joint à la ~** herewith; **2** ▶ **présent II**.

présenter /pʀezɑ̃te/ [1] **I** *vtr* **1** to introduce; to present; **je vous présente mon fils** this is my son, may I introduce my son?; **2** to show [*ticket, card, menu*]; **3** to present [*programme, show, collection*]; to display [*goods*]; **4** to present [*receipt, bill*]; to submit [*estimate, report*]; to table [*motion*]; to introduce [*proposal, bill*]; **~ une liste pour les élections** to put forward a list (of candidates) for the elections; **5** to present [*situation, budget, conclusions*]; to expound, to present [*theory*]; to set out [*objections, point of view*]; **~ qn comme (étant) un monstre** to portray sb as a monster; **être présenté comme un modèle** to be held up as a model; **6** to offer [*condolences*]; **~ des excuses** to apologize; **7** to involve, to present [*risk, difficulty*]; to show [*differences, symptom*]; to offer [*advantage*]; to have [*aspect, feature, flaw*]; **8 ~ son visage au soleil** to turn one's face to the sun.

II *vi* **~ bien** to have a smart appearance.

III se présenter *v refl* (+ *v être*) **1 il faut se ~ à la réception** you must go to reception; **présentez-vous à 10 heures** come at 10 o'clock; **2** to introduce oneself; **3 se ~ à** to take [*examination*]; to stand for [*election*]; **4** [*opportunity*] to arise; [*solution*] to emerge; **lire tout ce qui se présente** to read anything that comes along; **un spectacle étonnant se présenta à mes yeux** an amazing sight met my eyes; **5 se ~ en, se ~ sous forme de** [*product*] to come in the form of; **6 l'affaire se présente bien** things are looking good.

présentoir /pʀezɑ̃twaʀ/ *nm* **1** display stand or unit; **2** display shelf.

préservatif /pʀezɛʀvatif/ *nm* condom.

préservation /pʀezɛʀvasjɔ̃/ *nf* protection; preservation.

préserver /pʀezɛʀve/ [1] **I** *vtr* **1** to preserve; **2** to protect.

II se préserver *v refl* (+ *v être*) **se ~ de** to protect oneself against.

présidence /pʀezidɑ̃s/ *nf* **1** presidency; chairmanship; vice-chancellorship (GB), presidency (US); **2** presidential palace.

président /pʀezidɑ̃/ *nm* president; chairman, chairperson; vice-chancellor (GB), president (US).

■ **~ de la République** President of the Republic.

présidente /pʀezidɑ̃t/ *nf* **1** president; chairwoman, chairperson; chairman; **2** First Lady.

présidentiel, **-ielle**[1] /pʀezidɑ̃sjɛl/ *adj* presidential.

présidentielles[2] /pʀezidɑ̃sjɛl/ *nf pl* presidential election.

présider /pʀezide/ [1] *vtr* **1** to chair; **2** to be the president of; to be the chairman/chairwoman of; to preside over; **~ un dîner** to be the guest of honour[GB] at a dinner.

présomption /pʀezɔ̃psjɔ̃/ *nf* **1** (Law) presumption; **sur de simples ~s** on presumptive grounds alone; **2** assumption; **3** presumption; **plein de ~** presumptuous.

présomptueux, **-euse** /pʀezɔ̃ptɥø, øz/ *adj* arrogant; presumptuous.

presque /pʀɛsk/ *adv* almost, nearly; **il y a trois ans ~ jour pour jour** it's nearly three years to the day; **la même histoire ou ~** the same story or almost the same; **il n'y avait ~ personne** there was hardly anyone there; **c'était le bonheur ou ~** it was as close to happiness as one can get; **il ne reste ~ rien** there's hardly anything left.

presqu'île /pʀɛskil/ *nf* peninsula.

pressant, **~e** /pʀɛsɑ̃, ɑ̃t/ *adj* [*need*] pressing; [*appeal*] urgent; [*salesman*] insistent.

presse /pʀɛs/ *nf* **1** press; newspapers; **avoir bonne ~** to be well thought of; **2** (gen) press; (printing) press; **mettre sous ~** to send [sth] to press; **'sous ~'** 'in preparation'; **3 ~s** (publishing house) press.

pressé, **~e** /pʀese/ *adj* **1** [*person*] in a hurry; [*steps*] hurried; **2 ~ de faire** keen to do; **3** [*business*] urgent; **elle n'a rien eu de plus ~ que de faire** she couldn't wait to do; **aller** or **parer au plus ~** to do the most urgent thing(s) first.

presse-ail /pʀɛsaj/ *nm inv* garlic press.

presse-citron /pʀɛssitʀɔ̃/ *nm inv* lemon squeezer.

pressentiment /pʀesɑ̃timɑ̃/ *nm* premonition; **mes ~s se confirment** it's all turning out as I expected.

pressentir /pʀesɑ̃tiʀ/ [30] *vtr* to have a premonition about.

presse-papiers /pʀɛspapje/ *nm inv* paperweight.

presse-purée /pʀɛspyʀe/ *nm inv* potato masher.

presser /pʀese/ [1] **I** *vtr* **1 ~ qn de faire** to urge sb to do; **2** to press [*debtor, employee*]; to harry [*enemy*]; **~ de questions** to ply [sb] with questions; **3** [*hunger, necessity*] to drive [sb] on; **4** to increase [*rhythm*]; **~ le pas** or **mouvement** to hurry; **5** to press [*button*]; **6** to squeeze [*hand, object*]; **~ qn contre sa poitrine** to clasp sb to one's chest; **7** to squeeze [*orange, sponge*]; to press [*grapes*]; **8** to press [*record*].
II *vi* [*matter*] to be pressing; [*work*] to be urgent; **le temps presse** time is running out.
III se presser *v refl* (+ *v être*) **1 se ~ sur** or **contre** to press oneself against; **se ~ autour de qn/qch** to press around sb/sth; **2** to hurry up; **3** to flock (**à, dans, sur, vers** to).

pressing /pʀesiŋ/ *nm* dry-cleaner's.

pression /pʀɛsjɔ̃/ *nf* **1** (gen) pressure; **hautes/basses ~s** high/low pressure; **~ artérielle** blood pressure; **sous ~** under pressure; pressurized; **faire ~ sur** to press on [*surface*]; to put pressure on [*person*]; **2** snap (fastener).

pressoir /pʀɛswaʀ/ *nm* **1** pressing shed; **2** press; **~ à pommes** cider press.

pressuriser /pʀɛsyʀize/ [1] *vtr* to pressurize.

prestance /pʀɛstɑ̃s/ *nf* **avoir de la ~** to have great presence.

prestataire /pʀɛstatɛʀ/ *nm* **1 ~ de service** (service) contractor, service provider; **2** recipient (*of a state benefit*).

prestation /pʀɛstasjɔ̃/ *nf* **1** benefit; **2** provision; **~ de service** (provision of a) service; **3** service; **4** performance; **~ télévisée** televised appearance.

prestement /pʀɛstəmɑ̃/ *adv* (literary) [*act, reply*] promptly; [*move*] nimbly.

prestidigitateur, **-trice** /pʀɛstidiʒitatœʀ, tʀis/ *nm,f* conjurer.

prestidigitation /pʀɛstidiʒitasjɔ̃/ *nf* conjuring.

prestige /pʀɛstiʒ/ *nm* prestige; **le ~ de l'uniforme** the glamour[GB] of a uniform.

prestigieux, **-ieuse** /pʀɛstiʒjø, øz/ *adj* prestigious.

présumer /pʀezyme/ [1] **I** *vtr* to presume; **le père présumé** the putative father; **le présumé terroriste** the alleged terrorist.
II présumer de *v+prep* **(trop) ~ de ses forces** to overestimate one's strength.

présupposer /pʀesypoze/ [1] *vtr* to presuppose.

prêt, **~e** /pʀɛ, pʀɛt/ **I** *adj* ready (**à qch** for sth; **à faire** to do); **être fin ~** to be all set; **il est ~ à tout pour atteindre son but** he will stop at nothing to get what he wants.
II *nm* **1 le service de ~ de la bibliothèque** the library loans service; **2** loan.

prêt-à-porter /pʀɛtapɔʀte/ *nm* ready-to-wear (clothes).

prétendant, **~e** /pʀetɑ̃dɑ̃, ɑ̃t/ **I** *nm,f* **1** candidate (**à** for); **2** pretender (**à** to).
II *nm* suitor.

prétendre /pʀetɑ̃dʀ/ [6] **I** *vtr* to claim; **à ce qu'il prétend** according to him; **on le prétend très spirituel** he is said to be very witty; **il ne prétend pas rivaliser avec les favoris** he does not expect to keep up with the favourites[GB].
II prétendre à *v+prep* to claim [*damages*]; to aspire to [*job*].
III se prétendre *v refl* (+ *v être*) **il se prétend artiste** he makes out or claims he is an artist.

prétendu, **~e** /pʀetɑ̃dy/ *adj* [*culprit*] alleged; [*doctor*] would-be.

prétendument /pʀetɑ̃dymɑ̃/ *adv* supposedly, allegedly.

prête-nom, *pl* **~s** /pʀɛtnɔ̃/ *nm* frontman, man of straw; **société ~** dummy or fronting (US) company.

prétentieux, **-ieuse** /pʀetɑ̃sjø, øz/ **I** *adj* pretentious.
II *nm,f* pretentious person; **petit ~** pretentious twit.

prétention /pʀetɑ̃sjɔ̃/ **I** *nf* **1** pretentiousness; **être sans ~** to be unpretentious; **2** claim; **avoir des ~s sur** or **à qch** to have a claim to sth; **3 avoir la ~ de faire** to claim to do.
II prétentions *nf pl* **quelles sont vos ~s?** what salary are you asking for?

prêter /pʀete/ [1] **I** *vtr* **1** to lend [*money, object*]; **~ sur gages** to loan against security; **2 ~ son aide à qn** to give sb some help; **~ attention à** to pay attention to; **~ la main à qn** to lend sb a hand; **~ l'oreille** to listen; **~**

serment to take an oath; **3 ~ à qn** to attribute [sth] to sb; **on me prête des propos que je n'ai jamais tenus** I'm credited with remarks I never made.

II **prêter à** *v+prep* to give rise to, to cause [*confusion*]; **son attitude prête à rire** his/her attitude is ridiculous; **tout prête à croire** or **penser que** all the indications would suggest that.

III **se prêter** *v refl* (+ *v être*) **1 se ~ à** to take part in; **2 roman qui se prête à une adaptation cinématographique** novel which lends itself to a film adaptation; **3 se ~ assistance** to assist one another.

prétérit /pʀeteʀit/ *nm* preterite.

prêteur, -euse /pʀɛtœʀ, øz/ I *adj* **il n'est pas ~** he's very possessive about his belongings.

II *nm,f* **~ sur gages** pawnbroker.

prétexte /pʀetɛkst/ *nm* excuse, pretext; **sous ~ de faire** on the pretext of doing; **donner qch comme ~, prendre ~ de qch** to use sth as a pretext or an excuse; **sous aucun ~** on no account.

prétexter /pʀetɛkste/ [1] I *vtr* to use [sth] as an excuse, to plead.

II **prétexter de** *v+prep* **~ de qch pour faire** to use sth as an excuse for doing.

prêtre /pʀɛtʀ/ *nm* priest.

prêtresse /pʀɛtʀɛs/ *nf* priestess.

prêtrise /pʀɛtʀiz/ *nf* priesthood.

preuve /pʀœv/ *nf* **1** proof; **une ~** a piece of evidence; **apporter la ~ de/que** to offer proof of/that; **la meilleure ~ c'est que** the most compelling proof is that; **la ~ est faite de/que** now there is proof of/that; **~ en main** with concrete proof or evidence; **faire ses ~s** to prove oneself; **2** demonstration; **faire ~ de** to show; **~ de bonne volonté** gesture of goodwill.

prévaloir /pʀevalwaʀ/ [45] I *vi* to prevail; **faire ~ son point de vue** to gain acceptance for one's point of view.

II **se prévaloir** *v refl* (+ *v être*) **se ~ d'un règlement** to cite a rule; **se ~ de son ancienneté** to claim seniority.

prévenance /pʀevnɑ̃s/ *nf* consideration.

prévenant, ~e /pʀevnɑ̃, ɑ̃t/ *adj* considerate.

prévenir /pʀevniʀ/ [36] *vtr* **1** to tell; **2** to call [*doctor, police*]; **3** to warn; **4** to prevent [*disaster*]; **5** to anticipate [*wishes*].

IDIOMS **mieux vaut ~ que guérir** (Proverb) prevention is better than cure.

préventif, -ive /pʀevɑ̃tif, iv/ *adj* preventive.

prévention /pʀevɑ̃sjɔ̃/ *nf* **1** prevention; **faire de la ~** to take preventive action; **2** (Law) detention on suspicion.

préventivement /pʀevɑ̃tivmɑ̃/ *adv* **agir ~** to take preventive action.

prévenu, ~e /pʀevny/ *nm,f* (Law) defendant.

prévisible /pʀevizibl/ *adj* predictable.

prévision /pʀevizjɔ̃/ *nf* **1** forecasting; **en ~ de** in anticipation of; **2** prediction; forecast; **~s météorologiques** weather forecast; **faire des ~s** to make forecasts.

prévisionnel, -elle /pʀevizjɔnɛl/ *adj* projected.

prévoir /pʀevwaʀ/ [42] *vtr* **1** to predict [*change*]; to foresee [*event, victory*]; to anticipate [*consequences, reaction*]; to forecast [*result, weather*]; **c'était à ~!** that was predictable!; **2** to plan [*meeting, journey, building*]; to set the date for [*return, move*]; (Law) [*law, legislator*] to make provision for [*case, eventuality*]; **~ de faire** to plan to do; **nous devons ~ une salle de conférence** we must make provision for a conference room; **ce n'était pas prévu!** that wasn't meant to happen!; **remplissez le formulaire prévu à cet effet** fill in the appropriate form; **tout a été prévu** all the arrangements have been made; **3** to make sure one takes [*coat, umbrella*]; **4** to expect [*visitor, shortage, strike*]; **5** to allow [*sum of money, time*].

prévoyance /pʀevwajɑ̃s/ *nf* foresight.

prévoyant, ~e /pʀevwajɑ̃, ɑ̃t/ *adj* far-sighted.

prier /pʀije/ [2] I *vtr* **1 ~ qn de faire** to ask sb to do; **je vous prie d'excuser mon retard** I'm so sorry I'm late; **je vous prie de vous taire** will you kindly be quiet; **vous êtes prié d'assister à l'inauguration** you are invited to attend the opening; **elle ne s'est pas fait ~** she didn't have to be asked twice; **il aime se faire ~** he likes to be coaxed; **2** to pray to [*god*]; **~ que** to pray that.

II *vi* to pray.

prière /pʀijɛʀ/ *nf* **1** prayer; **faire sa ~** or **ses ~s** to say one's prayers; **2** request; plea, entreaty; **~ de ne pas fumer** no smoking please.

prieuré /pʀijœʀe/ *nm* **1** priory; **2** priory church.

primaire /pʀimɛʀ/ I *adj* **1** primary; **2** [*person*] limited; [*reaction*] knee-jerk; [*reasoning*] simplistic.

II *nm* **1** (Sch) **le ~** primary education; **2** (Econ) **le ~** the primary sector; **3 le ~** the palaeozoic era.

primate /pʀimat/ *nm* primate.

primauté /pʀimote/ *nf* primacy.

prime /pʀim/ I *adj* **1 de ~ abord** at first, initially; **la ~ enfance** early childhood; **2 A ~** A prime.

II *nf* **1** bonus; free gift; **2** allowance; **3** subsidy; **4** (in insurance) premium.

■ **~ d'ancienneté** seniority bonus; **~ de licenciement** redundancy payment (GB), severance pay; **~ de risque** danger money.

primer /pʀime/ [1] I *vtr* **1** to take precedence over, to prevail over; **2** to award a prize to; **ce film a été primé** this film won an award.

II **primer sur** *v+prep* (controversial) = **primer** I 1.

III *vi* **pour moi, c'est la qualité qui prime** what counts for me is quality.

primesautier, -ière /pʀimsotje, ɛʀ/ *adj* impulsive.

primeur /pʀimœʀ/ I *nf* **avoir la ~ de l'information** to be the first to hear sth.

II **primeurs** *nf pl* early fruit and vegetables.

primevère /pʀimvɛʀ/ *nf* primrose.

primitif, **-ive** /pʀimitif, iv/ *adj* (gen) primitive; [*budget, difference*] initial; [*project, state*] original; [*reasoning*] crude.

primordial, **~e**, *mpl* **-iaux** /pʀimɔʀdjal, o/ *adj* essential, vital.

prince /pʀɛ̃s/ *nm* prince; **le ~ de la mode** (figurative) the king of fashion.
IDIOMS **être** or **se montrer bon ~** to be magnanimous.

prince-de-galles /pʀɛ̃sdəgal/ *adj inv* prince-of-wales check.

princesse /pʀɛ̃sɛs/ *nf* princess.
IDIOMS **aux frais de la ~**° at the taxpayer's expense; at the company's expense; at sb's expense.

princier, **-ière** /pʀɛ̃sje, ɛʀ/ *adj* [*title, tastes, sum*] princely; [*luxury*] dazzling.

principal, **~e**, *mpl* **-aux** /pʀɛ̃sipal, o/ I *adj* **1** [*factor, concern*] main; [*task, objection*] principal; **2** [*country, role, character*] leading; **3** [*superintendent, inspector*] chief.
II *nm* **1 le ~** the main thing; **2** (Sch) principal.

principauté /pʀɛ̃sipote/ *nf* principality.

principe /pʀɛ̃sip/ I *nm* **1** principle; **par ~** on principle; **pour le ~** as a matter of principle; **accord de ~** provisional agreement; **2** assumption; **3** (concept) principle; **quel est le ~ de la machine à vapeur** how does a steam engine work?.
II **en principe** *phr* **1** as a rule; **2** in theory.

printanier, **-ière** /pʀɛ̃tanje, ɛʀ/ *adj* [*sun*] spring; [*weather*] spring-like.

printemps /pʀɛ̃tɑ̃/ *nm inv* **1** spring; **2**° **mes 60 ~** my 60 summers.

priori ▶ **a priori**.

prioritaire /pʀijɔʀitɛʀ/ *adj* [*file, project*] priority; **être ~** to have priority; (on the road) to have right (GB) or the right (US) of way.

priorité /pʀijɔʀite/ *nf* priority; **en ~** first; **nous nous en occuperons en ~** we'll make it a priority; **avoir la ~** to have right (GB) or the right (US) of way.

pris, **~e**[1] /pʀi, pʀiz/ I *pp* ▶ **prendre**.
II *pp adj* **1** busy; **j'ai les mains ~es** I've got my hands full; **les places sont toutes ~es** all the seats are taken; **2** [*nose*] stuffed up; [*lungs*] congested; **3 ~ de** overcome with; **~ de panique** panic-stricken; **être ~ de nausées** to feel sick (GB) or nauseous.

prise[2] /priz/ *nf* **1** storming; **la ~ de la Bastille** the storming of the Bastille; **2** catching; **une belle ~** a fine catch; **3** (in judo, wrestling) hold; **4 n'offrir aucune ~** to have no handholds; to have no footholds; **avoir ~ sur qn** to have a hold over sb; **donner ~ à** to lay oneself open to; **5** socket (GB), outlet (US); plug; jack; **~ multiple** (multiplug) adaptor; trailing socket.
■ **~ de bec**° row, argument; **~ en charge** (of expenses) payment; **assurer la ~ en charge des frais de qn** to cover sb's expenses; **~ de conscience** realization; **~ de contact** initial contact; **~ de courant** socket (GB), outlet (US); **~ d'eau** water supply point; **~ de sang** blood test; **~ de vue** shooting; shot.
IDIOMS **être aux ~s avec des difficultés** to be grappling with difficulties.

priser /pʀize/ [1] *vtr* **1** to hold [sth] in esteem; **2** to snort [*drug*]; **~ (du tabac)** to take snuff.

prisme /pʀism/ *nm* prism.

prison /pʀizɔ̃/ *nf* prison; **elle a fait de la ~** she has been in prison; **condamné à trois ans de ~** sentenced to three years' imprisonment.

prisonnier, **-ière** /pʀizɔnje, ɛʀ/ I *adj* **il est ~** he is a prisoner; **être ~ de** to be held prisoner by [*person*]; to be a prisoner of [*belief*]; **ma main était prisonnière** my hand was trapped.
II *nm,f* prisoner; **faire qn ~** to take sb prisoner.

privation /pʀivasjɔ̃/ *nf* **1** (of rights) deprivation; **2** want; **s'imposer des ~s** to make sacrifices.

privatiser /pʀivatize/ [1] *vtr* to privatize.

privé, **~e** /pʀive/ I *pp* ▶ **priver**.
II *pp adj* **~ de** deprived of; **un style ~ d'humour** a humourless[GB] style; **tu seras ~ de dessert!** you'll go without dessert!
III *adj* (gen) private; [*interview*] unofficial; **à titre ~** unofficially.
IV *nm* **1** (Econ) private sector; **2** (Sch) **le ~** private schools; **3 en ~** in private; off the record.

priver /pʀive/ [1] I *vtr* **~ qn/qch de** to deprive sb/sth of; **~ qn de sorties** to forbid sb to go out.
II **se priver** *v refl* (+ *v être*) **pourquoi se ~?** why deprive ourselves?; **se ~ de qch/de faire** to go or do without sth/doing; **elle ne s'est pas privée de le leur dire** she didn't hesitate to tell them.

privilège /pʀivilɛʒ/ *nm* privilege.

privilégié, **~e** /pʀivileʒje/ I *pp* ▶ **privilégier**.
II *pp adj* **1** privileged; **2** fortunate; **3** [*moment, links*] special; [*treatment*] preferential; **4** [*expression, target*] preferred.

privilégier /pʀivileʒje/ [2] *vtr* **1** to favour[GB]; **2** to give priority to.

prix /pʀi/ *nm inv* **1** price; **à** or **au ~ coûtant** at cost price; **c'est à quel ~?** how much is it?; **acheter qch à ~ d'or** to pay a small fortune for sth; **si tu veux de la soie, il faut être prêt à y mettre le ~** if you want silk, you have to be prepared to pay for it; **mettre qch à ~ à 50 francs** to start the bidding for sth at 50 francs; **2** (figurative) price; **à tout ~** at all costs; **attacher beaucoup de ~ à** to value [sth] highly [*friendship*]; **3** prize; **~ d'encouragement** incentive prize.

pro(-) /pʀo/ *pref* pro(-); **~-européen** pro-European.

probabilité /pʀɔbabilite/ *nf* **1** probability, likelihood; **2 les ~s** probability theory.

probable /pʀɔbabl/ *adj* probable, likely; **c'est peu ~** it's unlikely.

probablement /pʀɔbabləmɑ̃/ *adv* probably.

probatoire /pRɔbatwaR/ *adj* **examen ~** assessment test; **épreuve ~** aptitude test.

probe /pRɔb/ *adj* upright, honest.

probité /pRɔbite/ *nf* integrity, probity.

problématique /pRɔblematik/ *adj* [*situation*] problematic; [*outcome*] uncertain.

problème /pRɔblɛm/ *nm* problem; **~ moral** moral issue.

procédé /pRɔsede/ *nm* **1** process; **2** practice[GB]; **échange de bons ~s** exchange of courtesies; **3** device.

procéder /pRɔsede/ [14] **I procéder à** *v+prep* **~ à** to carry out [*check, survey*]; to undertake [*reform, job creation*]; **~ à un tirage au sort/un vote** to hold a draw/a vote; **~ à l'arrestation de qn** to arrest sb.

II procéder de *v+prep* to be a product of.

III *vi* to go about things; **~ par élimination** to use a process of elimination.

procédure /pRɔsedyR/ *nf* **1** proceedings; **2** procedure.

procès /pRɔsɛ/ *nm inv* **1** trial; **2** lawsuit, case; **intenter un ~ à qn** to take sb to court, to sue sb; **3** indictment; **faire le ~ de qch/qn** to put sth/sb in the dock.

IDIOMS **sans autre forme de ~** without further ado.

processeur /pRɔsesœR/ *nm* processor.

procession /pRɔsesjɔ̃/ *nf* **1** procession; **2** stream.

processus /pRɔsesys/ *nm inv* **1** process; **2** (Med) evolution.

procès-verbal, *pl* **-aux** /pRɔsɛvɛRbal, o/ *nm* **1** (of meeting) minutes; **2** statement of offence[GB]; **3** (controversial) fine; **avoir un ~** to get a ticket.

prochain, **~e** /pRɔʃɛ̃, ɛn/ **I** *adj* **1** next; **en juin ~** next June; **à la ~e**○**!** see you○!; **2** [*publication*] forthcoming; [*meeting, summit*] coming, forthcoming; [*departure, war*] imminent, impending; **un jour ~** one day soon.

II *nm* fellow man; **aime ton ~** love thy neighbour[GB].

prochainement /pRɔʃɛnmɑ̃/ *adv* soon, shortly.

proche /pRɔʃ/ **I** *adj* **1** nearby; **~ de** close to, near; **le plus ~** the nearest; **2** [*departure*] imminent; **la victoire est ~** victory is at hand; **la fin est ~** the end is (drawing) near; **3** [*event*] recent; [*memory*] real, vivid; **4** similar; **~ de** [*figure, language*] close to; [*theory*] similar to; [*attitude*] verging on; **5** [*people*] close; (on form) **(plus) ~ parent** next of kin.

II de proche en proche *phr* little by little, gradually.

III *nm* **1** close relative; **2** close friend; **3** close associate.

Proche-Orient /pRɔʃɔRjɑ̃/ *pr nm* **le ~** the Near East.

proclamation /pRɔklamasjɔ̃/ *nf* proclamation.

proclamer /pRɔklame/ [1] *vtr* **1** to proclaim; **2** to declare.

procréer /pRɔkRee/ [11] *vi* to procreate.

procuration /pRɔkyRasjɔ̃/ *nf* **1** power of attorney; **2** proxy; proxy form.

procurer /pRɔkyRe/ [1] **I** *vtr* to bring; to give; **~ qch à qn** [*situation*] to give sb sth; [*person*] to get sb sth.

II se procurer *v refl* (+ *v être*) **1** to obtain; **2** to buy.

procureur /pRɔkyRœR/ *nm* prosecutor.

prodigalité /pRɔdigalite/ *nf* **1** extravagance; **2** abundance.

prodige /pRɔdiʒ/ *nm* **1** prodigy; **2** feat; **faire des ~s** to work wonders; **~ technique** technical miracle.

prodigieux, **-ieuse** /pRɔdiʒjø, øz/ *adj* [*quantity*] prodigious; [*person*] wonderful.

prodigue /pRɔdig/ *adj* **1** extravagant; **2 être ~ de** to be lavish with.

prodiguer /pRɔdige/ [1] *vtr* **1** to lavish [*affection*] (**à** on); to give lots of [*advice*] (**à** to); **2** to give [*treatment, first aid*].

producteur, **-trice** /pRɔdyktœR, tRis/ **I** *adj* **pays ~ de pétrole** oil-producing country.

II *nm,f* producer.

productif, **-ive** /pRɔdyktif, iv/ *adj* [*work*] productive; [*investment*] profitable.

production /pRɔdyksjɔ̃/ *nf* **1** (gen) production; (of energy) generation; **2** (gen) products, goods; (agricultural) produce.

■ **~ assistée par ordinateur**, **PAO** computer-aided manufacturing, CAM.

productivité /pRɔdyktivite/ *nf* productivity.

produire /pRɔdɥiR/ [69] **I** *vtr* **1** (gen) to produce; [*manufacturer*] to produce, to make; [*farmer*] to produce, to grow; **cette usine produit peu** this factory has a low output; **un artiste/écrivain qui produit beaucoup** a prolific artist/writer; **2** to bring in [*money, wealth*]; to yield [*interest*]; **3** to produce, to have [*effect, result*]; to produce, to bring about [*change*]; to create, to make [*impression*]; to cause, to create [*sensation, emotion*]; **4** to produce [*identity papers, certificate*].

II se produire *v refl* (+ *v être*) **1** [*event*] to occur, to happen; **2** [*singer*] to perform.

produit /pRɔdɥi/ *nm* **1** product; **des ~s** goods, products; **~s alimentaires** foodstuffs; **~s agricoles** agricultural or farm produce; **2** income; yield, return; profit; **vivre du ~ de sa terre** to live off the land; **le ~ de la vente** the proceeds of the sale; **3** (of research) result; (of activity) product; **c'est le ~ de ton imagination** it's a figment of your imagination.

■ **~ de beauté** beauty product; **~ chimique** chemical; **~ d'entretien** cleaning product, household product.

proéminent, **~e** /pRɔeminɑ̃, ɑ̃t/ *adj* prominent.

profanateur, **-trice** /pRɔfanatœR, tRis/ **I** *adj* sacrilegious.

II *nm,f* profaner.

profanation /pRɔfanasjɔ̃/ *nf* desecration; defilement; debasement.

profane /pRɔfan/ **I** *adj* **1** secular; **2 être ~ en la matière** to know nothing about the subject.

II *nmf* **1** layman/laywoman; **2** nonbeliever.

III *nm* **le ~ et le sacré** the sacred and the profane.

profaner /pRɔfane/ [1] *vtr* to desecrate [*temple*]; to defile [*memory, beauty*]; to debase [*family, institution*].

proférer /pRɔfeRe/ [14] *vtr* to hurl [*insults*]; to make [*threats*]; to utter [*words*].

professer /pRɔfese/ [1] *vtr* to declare, to profess.

professeur /pRɔfesœR/ *nm* (in school) teacher; (in higher education) lecturer (GB), professor (US); (holding university chair) professor.

profession /pRɔfesjɔ̃/ *nf* **1** occupation; profession; **exercer la ~ d'infirmière** to be a nurse by profession; **être sans ~** to have no occupation; **2** declaration, profession; **faire ~ de libéralisme** to profess one's liberalism.
■ **~ libérale** profession.

professionnel, -elle /pRɔfesjɔnɛl/ **I** *adj* **1** [*qualifications, success*] professional; [*life, environment*] working, professional; [*disease*] occupational; [*training*] vocational; [*fair*] trade; **2** [*player, status*] professional.
II *nm,f* professional; **le salon est réservé aux ~s** the fair is restricted to people in the trade; **passer ~** to turn professional.

professionnellement /pRɔfesjɔnɛlmɑ̃/ *adv* professionally.

professoral, ~e, *mpl* **-aux** /pRɔfesɔRal, o/ *adj* professorial; **le corps ~** the teaching profession.

profil /pRɔfil/ *nm* **1** profile; **être de ~** to be in profile; **se mettre de ~** to turn sideways; **2 '~ exigé'** 'qualifications required'.

profiler /pRɔfile/ [1] **I** *vtr* **la tour profile sa silhouette dans le ciel** the tower is silhouetted or outlined against the sky.
II se profiler *v refl* (+ *v être*) [*shape*] to stand out; [*candidate, problem*] to emerge; [*events*] to approach.

profit /pRɔfi/ *nm* **1** benefit, advantage; **au ~ des handicapés** in aid of the handicapped; **espionnage au ~ d'une puissance étrangère** spying for a foreign country; **mettre à ~** to make the most of [*free time, course*]; to turn [sth] to good account [*situation*]; to make good use of [*idea*]; **2** profit; **faire des ~s** to make a profit; **être une source de ~ pour** to be a source of wealth for.

profitable /pRɔfitabl/ *adj* **1** beneficial; **2** profitable (**à** to).

profiter /pRɔfite/ [1] **I profiter à** *v+prep* **~ à qn** to benefit sb; **à qui profite le crime?** who benefits by or from the crime?
II profiter de *v+prep* to use [*advantage*]; to make the most of [*holiday, situation*]; to take advantage of [*visit, weakness, person*]; **profite bien de tes vacances!** have a good holiday!
III○ *vi* [*person, animal*] to grow; [*plant*] to thrive.

profiteur, -euse /pRɔfitœR, øz/ *nm,f* profiteer.

profond, ~e /pRɔfɔ̃, ɔ̃d/ **I** *adj* **1** deep; **peu ~** shallow; **2** [*boredom*] acute; [*sigh*] heavy; [*feeling, sadness, sleep*] deep; [*colour*] deep; **3** [*change, disagreement, ignorance*] profound; [*interest*] keen; **4** [*mind, remark*] profound; [*gaze*] penetrating; **5 la France ~e** provincial France; **l'Amérique ~e** small-town America.
II *adv* deeply, deep down; **creuser ~** to dig deep.

profondément /pRɔfɔ̃demɑ̃/ *adv* **1** [*dig*] deep; **2** [*sleep, breathe, feel, love*] deeply; [*suffer*] greatly; [*affected, bored*] profoundly; [*shocked, moved*] deeply; [*convinced*] utterly; **détester ~** to loathe.

profondeur /pRɔfɔ̃dœR/ *nf* **1** depth; **avoir une ~ de 3 mètres** to be 3 metres[GB] deep; **2** (of feeling) depth; (of remark, work) profundity; **en ~** [*analysis*] in-depth; **travail en ~** thorough work.

profusion /pRɔfyzjɔ̃/ *nf* profusion; abundance; **tout à ~** everything in abundance.

progéniture /pRɔʒenityR/ *nf* progeny.

programmateur, -trice /pRɔgRamatœR, tRis/ **I** *nm,f* programme[GB] planner.
II *nm* timer.

programmation /pRɔgRamasjɔ̃/ *nf* programming.

programme /pRɔgRam/ *nm* **1** programme[GB]; **2** (of action) plan; (of work) programme[GB]; **c'est tout un ~!** (humorous) that'll take some doing!; **3** (Sch) syllabus; **4** (Comput) program.

programmer /pRɔgRame/ [1] *vtr* **1** to schedule [*broadcast*]; to plan [*holiday, work*]; **2** (Comput) to program.

programmeur, -euse /pRɔgRamœR, øz/ *nm,f* (computer) programmer.

progrès /pRɔgRɛ/ *nm inv* **1** progress; **les ~ de la médecine** advances in medicine; **faire des ~** to make progress; **être en ~** [*person*] to be making progress; [*results*] to be improving; **il y a du ~**○**!** things are improving!; **2** increase; **être en ~ de 10%** to be up by 10%; **3** (of illness) progression; (of army) advance.

progresser /pRɔgRese/ [1] *vi* **1** [*rate*] to rise; [*sales*] to increase; **~ de 3%** [*rate*] to rise by 3%; [*party*] to gain 3%; **2** [*politician*] to make gains; [*illness*] to spread; [*ideology*] to gain ground; [*crime*] to be on the increase; **3** [*pupil, inquiry, country*] to make progress; [*relations*] to improve; [*technology*] to progress; **4** [*climber*] to make progress; [*army*] to advance.

progressif, -ive /pRɔgResif, iv/ *adj* progressive.

progression /pRɔgRɛsjɔ̃/ *nf* **1** progress; advance; spread; increase; **être en ~** [*results*] to be up; [*tendency*] to be increasing; **2** (in mathematics, music) progression.

progressiste /pRɔgResist/ *adj, nmf* progressive.

progressivement /pRɔgResivmɑ̃/ *adv* progressively.

prohiber /pRɔibe/ [1] *vtr* to prohibit.

prohibitif, -ive /pRɔibitif, iv/ *adj* **1** [*price*] prohibitive; **2** [*law*] prohibition.

prohibition /pRɔibisjɔ̃/ *nf* prohibition.

proie /pRwɑ/ *nf* prey; **être la ~ des flammes** to be in flames; **être en ~ à l'angoisse** to be racked by anguish; **pays en ~ à la guerre civile** country in the grip of civil war.

projecteur /pʀɔʒɛktœʀ/ *nm* **1** searchlight; floodlight; **être sous les ~s** to be in the spotlight; **2** projector.

projectile /pʀɔʒɛktil/ *nm* missile; projectile.

projection /pʀɔʒɛksjɔ̃/ *nf* **1 l'éruption commença par une ~ de cendres** the eruption began with a discharge of ashes; **2 le cuisinier a reçu des ~s d'huile bouillante** the cook got spattered with scalding oil; **3** projection; showing; **salle de ~** screening room.

projectionniste /pʀɔʒɛksjɔnist/ *nmf* projectionist.

projet /pʀɔʒɛ/ *nm* **1** plan; **mes ~s d'avenir** my plans for the future; **en ~, à l'état de ~** at the planning stage; **2** project; **~ de dictionnaire** dictionary project; **3** (rough) draft; **4** (in architecture) execution plan or drawing.
■ **~ de loi** (government) bill.

projeter /pʀɔʒte/ [20] *vtr* **1** to throw; **le choc l'a projeté par terre** the shock sent him hurtling to the ground; **2** to cast [*shadow*]; **3** to show [*film*]; **4** to plan (**de faire** to do).

prolétaire /pʀɔletɛʀ/ *adj, nmf* proletarian.

prolétariat /pʀɔletaʀja/ *nm* proletariat.

prolétarien, -ienne /pʀɔletaʀjɛ̃, ɛn/ *adj* proletarian.

proliférer /pʀɔlifeʀe/ [14] *vi* to proliferate.

prolifique /pʀɔlifik/ *adj* prolific.

prolixe /pʀɔliks/ *adj* verbose, prolix.

prolo○ /pʀɔlo/ **I** *adj* **ça fait ~** that's a bit common.
II *nmf* pleb○, prole.

prologue /pʀɔlɔg/ *nm* prologue.

prolongation /pʀɔlɔ̃gasjɔ̃/ *nf* continuation; extension; (Sport) extra time.

prolongé, ~e /pʀɔlɔ̃ʒe/ *adj* [*effort*] sustained; [*stop*] lengthy; [*stay*] extended; [*exhibition*] prolonged.

prolongement /pʀɔlɔ̃ʒmɑ̃/ *nm* **1** (of road, stay) extension; **2 la rue Berthollet se trouve dans le ~ de la rue de la Glacière** Rue de la Glacière becomes Rue Berthollet.

prolonger /pʀɔlɔ̃ʒe/ [13] **I** *vtr* **1** to extend [*stay*]; to prolong [*meeting, life*]; to continue [*treatment*]; **2** to extend [*road*].
II se prolonger *v refl* (+ *v être*) **1** to persist; to go on; **2** [*street*] **se ~ jusqu'à** to go as far as.

promenade /pʀɔmnad/ *nf* **1** walk; ride; drive; boat-ride; **2** walkway; promenade.

promener /pʀɔmne/ [16] **I** *vtr* **1** to take [sb] out [*person*]; to take [sth] out for a walk [*animal*]; **nous l'avons promené partout** we took him all over the place; **ça te promènera**○ it'll get you out; **2** to carry [*object*]; **~ son regard sur** to cast an eye over; **3** to show [sb] around.
II se promener *v refl* (+ *v être*) to go for a walk/drive/ride; to go out in a boat; **le dossier s'est promené**○ **dans toute l'usine** the file did the rounds of the factory.

promeneur, -euse /pʀɔmnœʀ, øz/ *nm,f* walker.

promesse /pʀɔmɛs/ *nf* **1** promise; **faire une ~ à qn** to make sb a promise; **avoir la ~ de qn** to have sb's word; **tenir ses ~s** to keep one's promises; **2 ~ de vente** agreement to sell; **honorer ses ~s** to honour[GB] one's commitments.
■ **~ en l'air** or **de Gascon** or **d'ivrogne** empty or idle promise.

prometteur, -euse /pʀɔmɛtœʀ, øz/ *adj* promising.

promettre /pʀɔmɛtʀ/ [60] **I** *vtr* **1 ~ qch à qn** to promise sb sth; **je ne (te) promets rien** I can't promise (anything); **je te promets qu'il le regrettera** he'll regret it, I guarantee you; **2 une soirée qui promet bien des surprises** an evening that holds a few surprises in store; **cette grève nous promet une belle pagaille** this strike is guaranteed to cause chaos.
II *vi* [*pupil*] **1** to show promise; **un film qui promet** a film which sounds interesting; **2**○ **cet enfant promet!** that child is going to be a handful!; **ça promet!** that promises to be fun!
III se promettre *v refl* (+ *v être*) **1** to promise oneself; **2 se ~ de faire** to resolve to do.
IDIOMS **~ monts et merveilles** or **la lune**○ (**à qn**) to promise (sb) the moon.

promiscuité /pʀɔmiskɥite/ *nf* lack of privacy.

promontoire /pʀɔmɔ̃twaʀ/ *nm* promontory.

promoteur, -trice /pʀɔmɔtœʀ, tʀis/ *nm,f* **~ (immobilier)** property developer.

promotion /pʀɔmɔsjɔ̃/ *nf* **1** promotion; **assurer la ~ de** to promote; **2** (special) offer; **en ~** on (special) offer.

promotionnel, -elle /pʀɔmɔsjɔnɛl/ *adj* promotional.

promouvoir /pʀɔmuvwaʀ/ [43] *vtr* to promote.

prompt, ~e /pʀɔ̃, pʀɔ̃t/ *adj* [*reaction*] prompt; [*gesture, glance*] swift; [*return*] sudden; **être ~ à agir** to act swiftly.

promptement /pʀɔ̃tmɑ̃/ *adv* promptly; swiftly; quickly.

promptitude /pʀɔ̃tityd/ *nf* promptness; swiftness; rapidity; suddenness.

promulguer /pʀɔmylge/ [1] *vtr* to promulgate.

prôner /pʀone/ [1] *vtr* to advocate, to extol the virtues of.

pronom /pʀɔnɔ̃/ *nm* pronoun.

pronominal, ~e, *mpl* **-aux** /pʀɔnɔminal, o/ *adj* pronominal.

prononçable /pʀɔnɔ̃sabl/ *adj* pronounceable.

prononcé, ~e /pʀɔnɔ̃se/ *adj* [*accent, taste*] strong; [*wrinkles*] deep; **avoir un goût ~ pour** to be particularly fond of.

prononcer /pʀɔnɔ̃se/ [12] **I** *vtr* **1** to pronounce [*word*]; **2** to mention [*name*]; to say [*phrase*]; **3** to deliver [*speech*]; **4** to pronounce [*death penalty*]; **~ le divorce** to grant a divorce.
II se prononcer *v refl* (+ *v être*) **1** to be pronounced; **2 se ~ contre/en faveur de qch** to declare oneself against/in favour[GB] of sth; **se ~ sur qch** to give one's opinion on sth.

prononciation /pʀɔnɔ̃sjasjɔ̃/ *nf* pronunciation.

pronostic /pʀɔnɔstik/ *nm* **1** forecast; **2** prediction; **3** (medical) prognosis.

propagande /pʀɔpagɑ̃d/ *nf* propaganda; **faire de la ~ pour** to campaign for [*cause*]; to plug, to push [*product*].

propagation /pʀɔpagasjɔ̃/ *nf* spread; propagation.

propager /pʀɔpaʒe/ [13] **I** *vtr* to spread [*rumour, disease*]; to propagate [*species, sound*].
II se propager *v refl* (+ *v être*) to spread; to propagate.

propension /pʀɔpɑ̃sjɔ̃/ *nf* propensity.

prophète /pʀɔfɛt/ *nm* prophet.

prophétesse /pʀɔfetɛs/ *nf* prophetess.

prophétie /pʀɔfesi/ *nf* prophecy.

prophétique /pʀɔfetik/ *adj* prophetic.

propice /pʀɔpis/ *adj* favourable[GB]; **peu ~** rather unfavourable[GB]; **trouver le moment ~** to find the right moment.

proportion /pʀɔpɔʀsjɔ̃/ *nf* proportion; **dans une ~ de cinq contre un** in a ratio of five to one; **en ~, ils sont mieux payés** they are proportionately better paid; **être sans ~ avec** to be out of (all) proportion to; **cela a pris de telles ~s que** it has become so serious that; **toutes ~s gardées** relatively speaking.

proportionnel, -elle[1] /pʀɔpɔʀsjɔnɛl/ *adj* proportional.

proportionnelle[2] /pʀɔpɔʀsjɔnɛl/ *nf* proportional representation.

proportionnellement /pʀɔpɔʀsjɔnɛlmɑ̃/ *adv* proportionately.

proportionner /pʀɔpɔʀsjɔne/ [1] *vtr* **~ qch à qch** to make sth proportional to sth; **proportionné à** proportional to; **bien/mal proportionné** well-/badly-proportioned.

propos /pʀɔpo/ **I** *nm inv* **1 à ~, je...** by the way, I...; **à ~ de** about; **à ~ de qui?** about who?; **à ce ~, je voudrais...** in this connection, I would like...; **2 à ~** at the right moment; **mal à ~** at (just) the wrong moment; **à tout ~** constantly.
II *nm pl* comments; **'~ recueillis par J. Brun'** 'interview by J. Brun'.

proposer /pʀɔpoze/ [1] **I** *vtr* **1** to suggest; **2** to offer [*drink, dish*] (**à qn** to sb); **3** to put forward [*solution*]; to propose [*strategy*]; **~ la candidature de qn** to put sb forward as a candidate.
II se proposer *v refl* (+ *v être*) **1 se ~ pour faire** to offer to do; **2 se ~ de faire** to intend to do.

proposition /pʀɔpozisjɔ̃/ *nf* **1** suggestion; **2** proposal; **faire des ~s à qn** (euphemistic) to proposition sb; **3** clause.
■ **~ de loi** ≈ bill.

propre /pʀɔpʀ/ **I** *adj* **1** clean; **nous voilà ~s!** (figurative) we're in a fine mess now!; **2** tidy, neat; **3** [*person, life*] decent; [*business*] honest; **des affaires pas très ~s** unsavoury[GB] business; **4** own; **ce sont tes ~s paroles** you said so yourself; those were your very words; **5** of one's own; **chaque pays a des lois qui lui sont ~s** each country has its own particular laws; **pour des raisons qui leur sont ~s** for reasons of their own; **6** [*baby*] toilet-trained; [*animal*] housetrained (GB), housebroken (US).
II propre à *phr* **1 ~ à** peculiar to; **2 ~ à faire** likely to do; liable to do; **mesures ~s à limiter le chômage** measures to curb unemployment; **3 ~ à** appropriate for; **produit déclaré ~ à la consommation** product fit for consumption.
III *nm* **1 mettre qch au ~** to make a fair copy of sth; **2 c'est du ~!** (ironic) that's very nice!; **3 le ~ de cette nouvelle technologie est de faire** what is peculiar to this new technology is that it does; **la maison leur appartient en ~** they are the sole owners of the house; **~ à rien** good-for-nothing.

proprement /pʀɔpʀəmɑ̃/ *adv* **1** purely; **à ~ parler** strictly speaking; **quant au procès ~ dit** as for the trial itself; **2** absolutely; **3** really; **4** literally; **l'air est devenu ~ irrespirable** the air has become literally unbreathable; **5** specifically; **6** well and truly; **le professeur l'a ~ remis à sa place** he was well and truly put in his place by the teacher; **7** neatly; **travailler ~** to do a neat job; **mange ~!** don't make a mess when you eat!; **8** [*earn living*] honestly; [*live, behave*] decently.

propreté /pʀɔpʀəte/ *nf* **1** cleanliness; **d'une ~ douteuse** not very clean; **2** honesty.

propriétaire /pʀɔpʀijetɛʀ/ *nmf* **1** owner; home-owner; **un petit ~** a small-scale property owner; **ils sont ~s de leur maison** they own their own house; **faire le tour du ~** to look round (GB) or around the house; **2** landlord/landlady.

propriété /pʀɔpʀijete/ *nf* **1** ownership; **2** property; **~ privée** private property; **3** (of substance) property; **4** (of term) aptness.
■ **~ artistique et littéraire** intellectual property right, copyright; **~ foncière** landed estate; **~ immobilière** real estate.

propulser /pʀɔpylse/ [1] *vtr* to propel.

propulseur /pʀɔpylsœʀ/ **I** *adj m* propellent, propelling.
II *nm* engine; **~ (de fusée)** (rocket) engine.
■ **~ à hélice** propeller; **~ à réaction** jet engine.

propulsion /pʀɔpylsjɔ̃/ *nf* propulsion; **à ~ nucléaire** nuclear-powered.

prorata /pʀɔʀata/ *nm inv* proportion; **au ~ de** in proportion to.

proroger /pʀɔʀɔʒe/ [13] *vtr* **1** to defer [*date*]; to renew [*passport*]; to extend [*deadline*]; **2** to adjourn [*meeting*].

prosaïque /pʀɔzaik/ *adj* prosaic.

prosaïsme /pʀɔzaism/ *nm* mundaneness.

proscrire /pʀɔskʀiʀ/ [67] *vtr* to ban; to banish.

proscrit, ~e /pʀɔskʀi, it/ *nm,f* outcast; **une vie de ~** the life of an outcast.

prose /pʀoz/ *nf* **1** prose; **poème en ~** prose poem; **2** (humorous) distinctive prose; masterpiece.

prosélytisme /pʀɔzelitism/ *nm* proselytizing.

prosodie /pʀɔzɔdi/ *nf* prosody.

prospecter /pʀɔspɛkte/ [1] *vtr* **1** to canvass;

2 to prospect; **~ un sol pour y trouver du pétrole** to prospect for oil in an area of ground.

prospecteur, -trice /pʀɔspɛktœʀ, tʀis/ *nm,f* **1** canvasser; **2** prospector.

prospection /pʀɔspɛksjɔ̃/ *nf* **1** canvassing; **2** prospecting.

prospectus /pʀɔspɛktys/ *nm inv* leaflet.

prospère /pʀɔspɛʀ/ *adj* thriving; prosperous.

prospérer /pʀɔspeʀe/ [14] *vi* to thrive; to prosper.

prospérité /pʀɔspeʀite/ *nf* prosperity.

prostate /pʀɔstat/ *nf* prostate (gland).

prosternation /pʀɔstɛʀnasjɔ̃/ *nf* **1** prostration; **2** (figurative) self-abasement.

prosternement /pʀɔstɛʀnəmɑ̃/ *nm* **1** prostrate position; **2** prostration.

prosterner: se prosterner /pʀɔstɛʀne/ [1] *v refl* (+ *v être*) **1** to prostrate oneself; **prosterné devant l'autel** prostrate before the altar; **2** (figurative) to grovel.

prostitué /pʀɔstitɥe/ *nm* male prostitute (GB), prostitute (US).

prostituée /pʀɔstitɥe/ *nf* prostitute.

prostituer /pʀɔstitɥe/ [1] **I** *vtr* **1** to send [sb] out to work as a prostitute; **2** (figurative) to prostitute [*talent*].

II se prostituer *v refl* (+ *v être*) to prostitute oneself.

prostration /pʀɔstʀasjɔ̃/ *nf* prostration; **un état de ~** a state of shock.

protagoniste /pʀɔtagɔnist/ *nmf* protagonist.

protecteur, -trice /pʀɔtɛktœʀ, tʀis/ **I** *adj* **1** protective; **2** patronizing.

II *nm,f* protector; **~ des arts** patron of the arts.

protection /pʀɔtɛksjɔ̃/ *nf* **1** protection; **assurer la ~ de qn** to protect sb; **être sous haute ~** to be under tight security; **de ~** [*screen, measures*] protective; [*zone, system*] protection; **2** protective device; **3 bénéficier de ~s** to have friends in high places.

■ **~ sociale** social welfare system.

protectionnisme /pʀɔtɛksjɔnism/ *nm* protectionism.

protégé, ~e /pʀɔteʒe/ *nm,f* protégé.

protège-matelas /pʀɔtɛʒmatla/ *nm inv* mattress cover.

protéger /pʀɔteʒe/ [15] **I** *vtr* **1** to protect; **2** to encourage [*art, sport*].

II se protéger *v refl* (+ *v être*) to protect oneself.

protéine /pʀɔtein/ *nf* protein.

protestant, ~e /pʀɔtɛstɑ̃, ɑ̃t/ *adj, nm,f* Protestant.

protestantisme /pʀɔtɛstɑ̃tism/ *nm* Protestantism.

protestataire /pʀɔtɛstatɛʀ/ **I** *adj* [*person*] protesting; [*movement*] protest.

II *nmf* protester.

protestation /pʀɔtɛstasjɔ̃/ *nf* protest; **en signe de ~** as a (mark of) protest.

protester /pʀɔtɛste/ [1] **I protester de** *v+prep* **~ de son innocence** to protest one's innocence.

II *vi* to protest.

prothèse /pʀɔtɛz/ *nf* prosthesis; artificial limb; dentures; **~ auditive** hearing aid; **~ de la hanche** hip replacement.

prothésiste /pʀɔtezist/ *nmf* prosthetist; **~ dentaire** prosthodontist.

protocolaire /pʀɔtɔkɔlɛʀ/ *adj* formal; official; **question ~** question of protocol.

protocole /pʀɔtɔkɔl/ *nm* **1** formalities; protocol; **2 ~ d'accord** draft agreement.

prototype /pʀɔtɔtip/ *nm* prototype.

protubérance /pʀɔtybeʀɑ̃s/ *nf* bump; protuberance.

protubérant, ~e /pʀɔtybeʀɑ̃, ɑ̃t/ *adj* protruding.

prou /pʀu/ *adv* **peu ou ~** more or less.

proue /pʀu/ *nf* prow, bow(s).

prouesse /pʀuɛs/ *nf* feat; (ironic) exploit; **faire une ~** to perform a feat.

prouver /pʀuve/ [1] **I** *vtr* **1** to prove; **il faudrait qu'il accepte, et ça n'est pas prouvé**○ he has to accept and there's no guarantee that he will; **2** to show; **3** to demonstrate.

II se prouver *v refl* (+ *v être*) **1** to prove to oneself; **2 un axiome ne se prouve pas** an axiom cannot be proved; **3 ils se sont prouvé qu'ils s'aimaient** they proved their love for each other.

IDIOMS **n'avoir plus rien à ~** to have proved oneself.

provenance /pʀɔvnɑ̃s/ *nf* origin; **en ~ de** from.

provençal, ~e, *mpl* **-aux** /pʀɔvɑ̃sal, o/ *adj* Provençal; **à la ~e** (Culin) (à la) provençale.

provenir /pʀɔvniʀ/ [36] *vi* **1** to come (**de** from); **provenant de** from; **2** to stem (**de** from).

proverbe /pʀɔvɛʀb/ *nm* proverb; **comme dit le ~** as the saying goes.

proverbial, ~e, *mpl* **-iaux** /pʀɔvɛʀbjal, o/ *adj* proverbial.

providence /pʀɔvidɑ̃s/ **I** *nf* **1** salvation; **2** providence.

II (-)providence (*combining form*) **État(-)~** welfare state.

providentiel, -ielle /pʀɔvidɑ̃sjɛl/ *adj* providential.

province /pʀɔvɛ̃s/ *nf* **1** province; **2 la ~** the provinces; **en ~** in the provinces; **ville de ~** provincial town.

provincial, ~e, *mpl* **-iaux** /pʀɔvɛ̃sjal, o/ *adj, nm,f* provincial.

proviseur /pʀɔvizœʀ/ *nm* headteacher (GB) or principal (US) (*of a lycée*).

provision /pʀɔvizjɔ̃/ **I** *nf* **1** stock; supply; **2** deposit; credit (balance).

II provisions *nf pl* food shopping; **faire ses ~s** to go food shopping.

provisoire /pʀɔvizwaʀ/ **I** *adj* provisional; temporary.

II *nm* **c'est du ~ qui dure** it was supposed to be only temporary.

provisoirement /pʀɔvizwaʀmɑ̃/ *adv* provisionally.

provocant, ~e /pʀɔvɔkɑ̃, ɑ̃t/ *adj* provocative.

provocateur, -trice /pʀɔvɔkatœʀ, tʀis/ **I** *adj* provocative.
II *nm,f* agitator.

provocation /pʀɔvɔkasjɔ̃/ *nf* provocation; **faire de la ~** to be provocative.

provoquer /pʀɔvɔke/ [1] *vtr* **1** to cause [*accident*]; to provoke [*reaction, anger*]; to trigger off [*argument*]; to prompt [*explanations*]; **~ l'accouchement** to induce labour[GB]; **~ une rencontre entre** to set up a meeting between; **2** to provoke; **~ qn en duel** to challenge sb to a duel; **3** (sexually) to arouse.

proxénète /pʀɔksenɛt/ *nm* procurer, pimp.

proxénétisme /pʀɔksenetism/ *nm* procuring.

proximité /pʀɔksimite/ *nf* **1** nearness, proximity; **à ~** nearby; **le commerce de ~** corner shops (GB), convenience stores (US); **à ~ de** near; **2** imminence; **à cause de la ~ de Noël** because it is/was so close to Christmas.

prude /pʀyd/ *adj* prudish.

prudemment /pʀydamɑ̃/ *adv* **1** carefully; **2** cautiously.

prudence /pʀydɑ̃s/ *nf* caution; **donner des conseils de ~** to advise caution; **avec ~** cautiously; with caution; **par ~** as a precaution; **redoubler de ~** to be doubly careful.

prudent, ~e /pʀydɑ̃, ɑ̃t/ *adj* **1** careful; **ce n'est pas ~ de faire** it isn't safe to do; **2** cautious; **3** wise.

prune /pʀyn/ **I** *adj inv* plum-coloured[GB].
II *nf* **1** plum; **2** plum brandy.
IDIOMS **pour des ~s**○ for nothing.

pruneau, *pl* **~x** /pʀyno/ *nm* prune.

prunelle /pʀynɛl/ *nf* **1** sloe; ≈ sloe gin; **2** (of eye) pupil.
IDIOMS **j'y tiens comme à la ~ de mes yeux** it's my pride and joy.

prunier /pʀynje/ *nm* plum tree.

Prusse /pʀys/ *pr nf* Prussia.

PS /peɛs/ *nm* (*abbr* = **post-scriptum**) PS.

psaume /psom/ *nm* psalm.

pseudo- /psødo/ *pref* pseudo; **~-équilibre** so-called balance; **~-savant** self-styled scientist.

pseudonyme /psødɔnim/ *nm* pseudonym.

psychanalyse /psikanaliz/ *nf* psychoanalysis.

psychanalyser /psikanalize/ [1] *vtr* to psychoanalyse[GB].

psychanalyste /psikanalist/ *nmf* psychoanalyst.

psyché /psiʃe/ *nf* **1** cheval glass; **2** psyche.

psychiatre /psikjatʀ/ *nmf* psychiatrist.

psychiatrie /psikjatʀi/ *nf* psychiatry.

psychiatrique /psikjatʀik/ *adj* psychiatric.

psychique /psiʃik/ *adj* mental.

psychisme /psiʃism/ *nm* psyche.

psychologie /psikɔlɔʒi/ *nf* **1** psychology; **2** (psychological) insight.

psychologique /psikɔlɔʒik/ *adj* psychological; **c'est ~!** it's all in the mind!

psychologue /psikɔlɔg/ **I** *adj* **être ~** to understand people very well.
II *nmf* psychologist.

psychopathe /psikɔpat/ *nmf* psychopath.

psychose /psikoz/ *nf* **1** psychosis; **2 ~ de la guerre** obsessive fear of war.

psychosomatique /psikosɔmatik/ *adj* psychosomatic.

psychothérapie /psikoteʀapi/ *nf* psychotherapy.

psychotique /psikɔtik/ *adj, nmf* psychotic.

PTT /petete/ *nf pl* (*abbr* = **Administration des postes et télécommunications et de la télédiffusion**) *former French postal and telecommunications service.*

puant, ~e /pɥɑ̃, ɑ̃t/ *adj* **1** stinking, foul-smelling; smelly; **2**○ **un type ~** an incredibly arrogant guy○.

puanteur /pɥɑ̃tœʀ/ *nf* stench.

pub○ /pyb/ *nf*: *abbr* ▶ **publicité**.

pubère /pybɛʀ/ *adj* pubescent.

puberté /pybɛʀte/ *nf* puberty; **à la ~** at puberty.

pubis /pybis/ *nm inv* pubes; pubis.

public, -ique /pyblik/ **I** *adj* [*place, money*] public; [*education*] state (GB), public (US); [*company*] state-owned; **rendre qch ~** to make sth public; **la dette publique** the national debt; **homme ~** public figure.
II *nm* **1** public; **'interdit au ~'** 'no admittance'; **'avis au ~'** 'public notice'; **2** audience; spectators; **être bon ~** to be a good audience; **tous ~s** for all ages; **3** readership; **4 avoir un ~** to have a following; **5 le ~** the public sector.

publication /pyblikasjɔ̃/ *nf* publication; **la ~ du livre est prévue pour mai** the book is due out in May.
■ **~ assistée par ordinateur, PAO** desktop publishing, DTP.

publicitaire /pyblisitɛʀ/ **I** *adj* [*campaign*] advertising; [*gift*] promotional.
II *nmf* advertising executive; **il est ~** he's in advertising.
III *nm* advertising agency.

publicité /pyblisite/ *nf* **1** advertising; **faire de la ~ pour** to advertise; **2** advertisement, advert (GB), ad○; **passer une ~ à la radio** to run an ad○ on the radio; **3** publicity; **faire de la ~ à qn/qch** to give sb/sth publicity; **faire une mauvaise ~ à qn/qch** to give sb/sth a bad press.
■ **~ comparative** knocking copy○; **~ mensongère** misleading advertising.

publier /pyblije/ [2] *vtr* to publish [*book, author, banns*]; to issue [*statement*].

publiquement /pyblikmɑ̃/ *adv* publicly.

puce /pys/ *nf* **1** flea; **2**○ **ma ~** my pet○; **3 jeu de ~** tiddlywinks; **4** (silicon) chip.
IDIOMS **ça m'a mis la ~ à l'oreille** that set me thinking; **secoue-toi les ~s**○! get a move on○!; **secouer les ~**○ **à qn** to bawl sb out○.

puceau○, *pl* **~x** /pyso/ *adj m* **il est encore ~** he's still a virgin.

pucelle○ /pysɛl/ *adj f* **être ~** to be a virgin.

puceron /pysʀɔ̃/ *nm* aphid.

pudeur /pydœʀ/ *nf* **1** sense of modesty; **sans ~** shamelessly; **2** decency; sense of propriety.

pudibond, **~e** /pydibɔ̃, ɔ̃d/ *adj* prudish.

pudique /pydik/ *adj* **1** modest; **2** discreet.

puer /pɥe/ [1] **I** *vtr* to stink of.
II *vi* to stink; **il puait des pieds** his feet stank.

puéricultrice /pɥeʀikyltʀis/ *nf* pediatric nurse.

puériculture /pɥeʀikyltyʀ/ *nf* childcare.

puéril, **~e** /pɥeʀil/ *adj* childish; puerile.

puis /pɥi/ *adv* **1** then; **des pommes, des poires et ~ des pêches** apples, pears and peaches; **et ~ quoi encore**○! what(ever) next?; **2 et ~ je m'en fiche**○! anyway, I don't care!; **il va être en colère? et ~ (après**○**)?** so what if he's angry!

puisard /pɥizaʀ/ *nm* soakaway (GB), sink hole (US).

puiser /pɥize/ [1] *vtr* **~ qch dans qch** to draw sth from sth; **~ dans ses économies** to draw on one's savings.

puisque (**puisqu'** *before vowel or mute h*) /pɥisk(ə)/ *conj* since; **~ c'est comme ça, je m'en vais** if that's how it is, I'm off.

puissance /pɥisɑ̃s/ *nf* **1** power; **d'une forte ~** very powerful; **la ~ militaire** military strength or might; **il a une ~ de travail remarquable** his capacity for work is remarkable; **un amplificateur d'une ~ de 60 watts** a 60-watt amplifier; **2** (country) power; **une grande ~** a superpower; **3** (of light) intensity; (of sound) volume; **4** (in algebra) power; **dix ~ trois** ten to the power (of) three.

puissant, **~e** /pɥisɑ̃, ɑ̃t/ **I** *adj* powerful; strong.
II puissants *nm pl* **les ~s** the powerful, the mighty.

puits /pɥi/ *nm* **1** well; **~ de pétrole** oil well; **2** shaft.
■ **~ de mine** mine shaft; **~ de science** fount of knowledge.

pull○ /pyl/ *nm* sweater.

pull-over, *pl* **~s** /pylɔvɛʀ/ *nm* sweater.

pulluler /pylyle/ [1] *vi* **1** to proliferate; **2 les touristes pullulent dans la région** the area is swarming with tourists; **les poissons pullulent dans la rivière** the river is teeming with fish.

pulmonaire /pylmɔnɛʀ/ *adj* [*disease*] lung; [*artery*] pulmonary.

pulpe /pylp/ *nf* (of fruit) pulp; (of potato) flesh.

pulpeux, **-euse** /pylpø, øz/ *adj* [*body, lips*] luscious; [*fruit*] fleshy.

pulsation /pylsasjɔ̃/ *nf* beat; **~s cardiaques** heartbeat; heartbeats.

pulsion /pylsjɔ̃/ *nf* impulse, urge; **~ de mort** death wish.

pulvérisateur /pylveʀizatœʀ/ *nm* **1** spray; **2** (in agriculture) sprayer.

pulvériser /pylveʀize/ [1] *vtr* **1** to spray; **2** to pulverize; **3** to shatter○ [*record*].

puma /pyma/ *nm* puma.

punaise /pynɛz/ *nf* **1** drawing pin (GB), thumbtack (US); **2** (Zool) bug.

punch[1] /pɔ̃ʃ/ *nm* (drink) punch.

punch[2] /pœnʃ/ *nm* **1** punch; **avoir du ~** to pack quite a punch; **2** energy; drive; **avoir du ~** [*slogan, speech*] to be punchy○; [*person*] to have drive.

punching-ball, *pl* **~s** /pœnʃiŋbol/ *nm* punchball (GB), punching bag (US).

punir /pyniʀ/ [3] *vtr* to punish.

punitif, **-ive** /pynitif, iv/ *adj* punitive; **expédition punitive** punitive strike.

punition /pynisjɔ̃/ *nf* **1** punishment; **infliger une ~ à qn** to punish sb; **2 il n'a pas fait sa ~** he hasn't done the task he was given as punishment.

pupille[1] /pypij/ *nmf* ward; **~ de l'État** child in care; **~ de la Nation** war orphan.

pupille[2] /pypij/ *nf* (of eye) pupil.

pupitre /pypitʀ/ *nm* **1** control panel; console; **2** music stand; music rest; **qui est au ~?** who's conducting?; **3** desk; **4** lectern.

pur, **~e** /pyʀ/ **I** *adj* **1** (gen) pure; [*diamond*] flawless; [*voice, sky*] clear; **2** [*truth, nastiness*] pure; [*coincidence, pleasure, madness*] sheer; **en ~e perte** to no avail; **~ et simple** outright; **c'est de la paresse ~e et simple** it's laziness, pure and simple; **~ et dur** hardline; **3** [*tradition*] true; **un ~ produit de** a typical product of; **à l'état ~** [*genius, stupidity*] sheer.
II *nm,f* **1** virtuous person; **2 les ~s et durs** the hardliners.

purée /pyʀe/ *nf* purée; **~ (de pommes de terre)** mashed potatoes.
■ **~ de pois** pea souper (GB), fog.

purement /pyʀmɑ̃/ *adv* purely.

pureté /pyʀte/ *nf* purity.

purgatif, **-ive** /pyʀgatif, iv/ **I** *adj* purgative.
II *nm* purgative.

purgatoire /pyʀgatwaʀ/ *nm* **le ~** purgatory.

purge /pyʀʒ/ *nf* **1** purgative; **2** purge.

purger /pyʀʒe/ [13] *vtr* **1** (Med) to purge; **2** to bleed [*radiator*]; to drain [*pipe*]; to purify [*metal*]; **3** (Law) to serve [*sentence*].

purifier /pyʀifje/ [2] **I** *vtr* to purify [*water, air, blood*]; to cleanse [*skin*].
II se purifier *v refl* (+ *v être*) to cleanse oneself.

purin /pyʀɛ̃/ *nm* slurry.

puriste /pyʀist/ *nmf* purist.

puritain, **~e** /pyʀitɛ̃, ɛn/ **I** *adj* puritanical; Puritan.
II *nm,f* puritan; Puritan.

puritanisme /pyʀitanism/ *nm* puritanism.

pur-sang /pyʀsɑ̃/ *nm inv* thoroughbred, purebred.

pus /py/ *nm inv* pus.

pustule /pystyl/ *nf* pustule.

putois /pytwa/ *nm inv* **1** polecat; **2** skunk (fur).
IDIOMS **crier comme un ~**○ to scream one's head off.

putréfaction /pytʀefaksjɔ̃/ *nf* putrefaction; **en état de ~** decomposing.

putréfier: **se putréfier** /pytʀefje/ [2] *v refl* (+ *v être*) [*corpse*] to putrefy; [*meat*] to rot.

putsch /putʃ/ *nm* putsch.

puzzle /pœzl, pyzl/ *nm* **1** jigsaw puzzle; **2** (figurative) jigsaw.

PV○ /peve/ *nm* (*abbr* = **procès-verbal**) fine; parking ticket; speeding ticket.

PVC /pevese/ *nm* (*abbr* = **chlorure de polyvinyle**) PVC.

pygmée /pigme/ *nmf* pygmy.

pyjama /piʒama/ *nm* (pair of) pyjamas (GB), (pair of) pajamas (US).

pylône /pilon/ *nm* pylon; (for radio, TV transmitter) mast; (of bridge) tower.

pyramide /piʀamid/ *nf* pyramid; **~ des âges** age pyramid.

pyrénéen, **-éenne** /piʀeneɛ̃, ɛn/ *adj* Pyrenean.

pyrex® /piʀɛks/ *nm inv* Pyrex®; **en ~** Pyrex.

pyrogravure /piʀogʀavyʀ/ *nf* pokerwork.

pyrolyse /piʀɔliz/ *nf* pyrolysis; **four à ~** self-cleaning oven.

pyromane /piʀɔman/ *nmf* pyromaniac; (Law) arsonist.

pyrotechnie /piʀotɛkni/ *nf* pyrotechnics.

python /pitɔ̃/ *nm* python.

Qq

q, **Q** /ky/ *nm inv* q, Q.

qcm /kyseɛm/ *nm* (*abbr* = **questionnaire à choix multiple**) multiple-choice questionnaire, mcq.

QG /kyʒe/ *nm*: *abbr* ▶ **quartier**.

QI /kyi/ *nm*: *abbr* ▶ **quotient**.

qu' ▶ **que**.

quadragénaire /kwadʀaʒenɛʀ/ **I** *adj* **être ~** to be in one's forties.
II *nmf* forty-year old.

quadriennal, **~e**, *mpl* **-aux** /kwadʀijɛnal, o/ *adj* **1** [*plan*] four-year; **2** quadrennial, four-yearly.

quadrilatère /k(w)adʀilatɛʀ/ *nm* quadrilateral.

quadrillage /kadʀijaʒ/ *nm* **1** cross-ruling; **2 le ~ de la ville par l'armée** the systematic military takeover of the town.

quadrillé, **~e** /kadʀije/ *adj* [*paper*] squared; **une feuille ~e** a sheet of squared paper.

quadriller /kadʀije/ [1] *vtr* **1** [*army*] to take control of; [*police*] to spread one's net over; **2** to cross-rule [*paper*].

quadrimoteur /k(w)adʀimɔtœʀ/ **I** *adj m* four-engined.
II *nm* four-engined plane.

quadrupède /k(w)adʀypɛd/ *adj*, *nm* quadruped.

quadruple /k(w)adʀypl/ **I** *adj* quadruple.
II *nm* **le ~ de cette quantité** four times this amount.

quadruplé, **~e** /k(w)adʀyple/ *nm,f* quadruplet, quad.

quadrupler /k(w)adʀyple/ [1] *vtr*, *vi* to quadruple.

quai /kɛ/ *nm* **1** quay; **le navire est à ~** the ship has docked; **2** (of river) bank; **3** (station) platform.
■ **~ de débarquement** unloading dock; **~ d'embarquement** loading dock; **Quai des Orfèvres** *criminal investigation department of the French police force*; **Quai d'Orsay** French Foreign Office.

qualifiable /kalifjabl/ *adj* able to qualify.

qualificatif, **-ive** /kalifikatif, iv/ **I** *adj* qualifying.
II *nm* **1** (in grammar) qualifier; **2** term, word.

qualification /kalifikasjɔ̃/ *nf* **1** qualification; **2** skills; **sans ~** unskilled; .

qualifié, **~e** /kalifje/ **I** *pp* ▶ **qualifier**.
II *pp adj* **1** [*staff, labour*] skilled; qualified; **2** [*job*] skilled.

qualifier /kalifje/ [2] **I** *vtr* **1** to describe; **2** to qualify.
II se qualifier *v refl* (+ *v être*) (Sport) to qualify.

qualitatif, **-ive** /kalitatif, iv/ *adj* qualitative; **sur le plan ~** in terms of quality.

qualité /kalite/ *nf* **1** quality; **être de ~** to be of good quality; **de première ~** of the highest quality; **2** quality; **avoir beaucoup de ~s** to have many (good) qualities; **ses ~s de gestionnaire** his/her skills as an administrator; **3** status; position; **en (sa) ~ de représentant** in his/her capacity as a representative; **nom, prénom et ~** surname, first name and occupation.

quand /kɑ̃, kɑ̃t/ **I** *conj* **1** when; **~ il arrivera, vous lui annoncerez la nouvelle** when he gets here, you can tell him the news; **tu oses te plaindre ~ des gens meurent de faim!** you dare to complain when there are people starving!; **~ je pense que ma fille va avoir dix ans!** to think that my daughter's almost ten!; **~ je vous le disais!** I told you so!; **2** whenever; **~ il pleut plus de trois jours la cave est inondée** whenever it rains for more than three days, the cellar floods; **3** even if; **~ (bien même) la terre s'écroulerait, il continuerait à dormir** he'd sleep through an earthquake.
II *adv* when; **de ~ date votre dernière réunion?** when was your last meeting?; **c'est pour ~ le bébé?** when is the baby due?; **depuis ~ habitez-vous ici?** how long have you been living here?; **à ~ la semaine de 30 heures○?** when will we get a 30-hour working week?
III quand même *phr* still; **ils ne veulent pas de moi, mais j'irai ~ même!** they don't want me, but I'm still going!; **~ même, tu as vu ça○?** really, did you see that?; **~ même, tu exagères○!** come on, that's going too far!; **tu ne vas pas faire ça ~ même○?** you're not going to do that, are you?

quant: **quant à** /kɑ̃ta/ *phr* **1** as for; **la France, ~ à elle, n'a pas pris position** as for France, it did not take a stand; **~ à dire que** as for saying that; **2** about, concerning.

quantifiable /kɑ̃tifjabl/ *adj* quantifiable.

quantifier /kɑ̃tifje/ [2] *vtr* to quantify.

quantique /kɑ̃tik/ *adj* quantum.

quantitatif, **-ive** /kɑ̃titatif, iv/ *adj* quantitative.

quantité /kɑ̃tite/ *nf* **1** quantity, amount; **faire qch en ~s industrielles** to mass-produce sth; to make vast quantities of sth; **2 des ~s de** scores of [*people*]; a lot of [*things*]; **du pain/vin en ~** plenty of bread/wine.

quarantaine /kaʀɑ̃tɛn/ *nf* **1** about forty; **2 avoir la ~** to be about forty; **3** quarantine; **être en ~** to be in quarantine; to be ostracized.

quarante /kaʀɑ̃t/ *adj inv*, *pron* forty.

quarante-cinq /kaʀɑ̃tsɛ̃k/ *adj inv*, *pron* forty-five.
■ **~ tours** single.

quarantième /kaʀɑ̃tjɛm/ *adj* fortieth.

quart /kaʀ/ *nm* **1** quarter; **un ~ d'heure** a quarter of an hour; **faire passer un mauvais ~ d'heure à qn**○ to give sb a hard time; **les trois ~s du temps**○ most of the time; **2** a quarter-litre[GB] bottle; a quarter-litre[GB] pitcher; **3** beaker (of a quarter-litre[GB] capacity); **4** (Naut) **être de ~** to be on watch.
■ **~ de cercle** quadrant; **~ de tour** 90° or ninety-degree turn; **faire qch au ~ de tour**○ to do sth immediately.

quarté /kaʀte/ *nm*: *betting based on forecasting the first four horses in a race.*

quartier /kaʀtje/ *nm* **1** area, district; **les beaux ~s** fashionable districts; **de ~** [*cinema, grocer*] local; **les gens du ~** the locals; **2** quarter; **un ~ de pommes** a slice of apple; **un ~ d'orange** an orange segment; **3** (of moon) quarter; **4** (Mil) **~s** quarters; **avoir ~ libre** to be off duty; to have time off or free time.
■ **~ général, QG** headquarters, HQ.
IDIOMS **ne pas faire de ~** to show no mercy, to give no quarter.

quart-monde /kaʀmɔ̃d/ *nm inv* underclass.

quartz /kwaʀts/ *nm* quartz; **montre à ~** quartz watch.

quasi /kazi/ **I** *adv* almost.
II quasi- (*combining form*) **~-indifférence** virtual indifference; **la ~-totalité de** almost all of; **à la ~-unanimité** almost unanimously.

quasiment○ /kazimɑ̃/ *adv* practically.

quaternaire /kwatɛʀnɛʀ/ *adj, nm* Quaternary.

quatorze /katɔʀz/ *adj inv, pron* fourteen.
IDIOMS **chercher midi à ~ heures**○ to complicate matters; **c'est reparti comme en 14**○! here we go again!

quatorzième /katɔʀzjɛm/ *adj* fourteenth.

quatrain /katʀɛ̃/ *nm* quatrain.

quatre /katʀ/ *adj inv, pron, nm inv* four.
IDIOMS **dire ses ~ vérités à qn**○ to tell sb a few home truths; **faire les ~ volontés de qn** to give in to sb's every whim; **être tiré à ~ épingles** to be dressed up to the nines○; **manger comme ~** to eat like a horse; **ne pas y aller par ~ chemins** not to beat about the bush; **je vais leur parler entre ~ yeux** or **quat'zyeux**○ I'm going to talk to them face to face; **monter un escalier ~ à ~** to go up the stairs four at a time; **être entre ~ planches**○ to be six feet under.

quatre-cent-vingt-et-un /katsɑ̃vɛ̃teœ̃/ *nm inv*: *game of dice.*

quatre-heures /katʀœʀ/ *nm inv* afternoon snack (*for children*).

quatre-mâts /katʀəmɑ/ *nm inv* four-master.

quatre-quarts /kat(ʀə)kaʀ/ *nm inv* pound cake.

quatre-vingt(s) /katʀəvɛ̃/ *adj, pron* eighty.

quatre-vingt-dix /katʀəvɛ̃dis/ *adj inv, pron* ninety.

quatre-vingt-dixième /katʀəvɛ̃dizjɛm/ *adj* ninetieth.

quatre-vingtième /katʀəvɛ̃tjɛm/ *adj* eightieth.

quatrième /katʀijɛm/ **I** *adj* fourth.
II *nf* **1** (Sch) *third year of secondary school, age 13–14*; **2** (Aut) fourth (gear); **passer en ~** to change or go into fourth gear.
■ **le ~ âge** very old people.
IDIOMS **faire qch en ~ vitesse**○ to do sth in double quick time○.

quatuor /kwatɥɔʀ/ *nm* quartet; **un ~ à cordes** a string quartet.

quat'zyeux○ /katzjø/ ▶ **quatre**.

que (**qu'** *before vowel or mute h*) /kə/ **I** *conj* **1** that; **elle a dit qu'elle le ferait** she said that she would do it; **je pense qu'il a raison** I think he's right; **je veux ~ tu m'accompagne** I want you to come with me; **2** so (that); **approche, ~ je te regarde** come closer so I can look at you; **3** whether; **~ vous le vouliez ou non, ~ cela vous plaise ou non** whether you like it or not; **4 si vous venez et ~ vous ayez le temps** if you come and (if you) have the time; **5 il n'était pas sitôt parti qu'elle appela la police** no sooner had he left than she called the police; **j'avais déjà lu dix pages qu'il n'avait toujours pas commencé** I had already read ten pages while he hadn't even started; **6 ~ tout le monde sorte!** everyone must leave!; **~ ceux qui n'ont pas compris le disent** let anyone who hasn't understood say so; **qu'il crève!**◑ let him rot○!; **~ je leur prête ma voiture!** you expect me to lend them my car!; **7** than; as; **plus gros ~ moi** fatter than me; **aussi grand ~ mon frère** as tall as my brother.
II *pron* what; **~ dire?** what can you or one say?; **~ faire?** what shall I/we do?; what could I/we do?; **je ne sais pas ce qu'il a dit** I don't know what he said; **qu'est-ce que c'est que ça?** what's that?
III *rel pron* that; who(m); which; **je n'aime pas la voiture ~ tu as achetée** I don't like the car (that) you've bought; **c'est la plus belle femme ~ j'aie jamais vue** she's the most beautiful woman (that) I've ever seen.
IV *adv* **~ c'est joli** it's so pretty; **~ de monde** what a lot of people; **'vous ne leur en avez pas parlé?'—'oh ~ si!'** 'haven't you spoken to them about it?'—'yes I have!'

Québec /kebɛk/ **I** *pr nm* **le ~** Quebec.
II *pr n* Quebec.

québécois, ~e /kebekwa, az/ *adj* of Quebec.

Québécois, ~e /kebekwa, az/ *nm,f* Quebecois, Quebecker.

quel, quelle /kɛl/ **I** *det* who; what; which; **~s sont les pays membres de l'UE?** what are the member countries of the EU?; **je me demande quelle est la meilleure solution** I wonder what the best solution is; **de ces deux médicaments, ~ est le plus efficace?** which of these two medicines is more effective?; **de tous les employés, ~ est le plus compétent?** of all the employees, who is the most competent?
II *adj* **1** what; which; **dans ~s pays as-tu vécu?** what countries have you lived in?; **quelle heure est-il?** what time is it?; **dans ~ tiroir l'as-tu mis?** which drawer did you put it

in?; **~ âge as-tu?** how old are you?; **2** what; how; **quelle coïncidence!** what a coincidence!; **quelle horreur!** how dreadful!; **3 quelle que soit la route que l'on prenne** whatever or whichever road we take; **~ que soit le vainqueur** whoever the winner may be; **quelles qu'aient pu être tes raisons** whatever your reasons may have been.

quelconque /kɛlkɔ̃k/ **I** *adj* [*person*] ordinary; ordinary-looking; [*novel, actor*] poor; [*restaurant, product*] second-rate; [*place, decor*] characterless.
II *adj* any; **si pour une raison ~** if for some reason or other; **si le livre avait un intérêt ~** if the book was in any way interesting.

quelle ▸ quel.

quelque /kɛlk/ **I** *quantif* some; a few; any; **depuis ~ temps** for some time; **est-ce qu'il vous reste ~s cartons?** do you have any boxes left?; **je voudrais ajouter ~s mots** I'd like to add a few words; **ça dure trois heures et ~s** it lasts over three hours; **si pour ~ raison que ce soit** if for whatever reason; **~ décision que tu prennes** whatever decision you come to.
II *adv* **1 les ~ deux mille spectateurs** the two thousand odd spectators; **ça lui a coûté ~ 300 francs** it cost him about 300 francs; **2** however; **~ admirable que soit son attitude** however admirable his/her attitude may be.
III quelque chose *pron* something; anything; **il y a ~ chose qui ne va pas** something's wrong; **~ chose de mieux** something better; **si ~ chose leur arrive** if anything should happen to them; **c'est ~ chose d'inimaginable!** it's unbelievable!; **il a ~ chose de son grand-père** he's got a look of his grandfather about him; **ça me dit ~ chose** it rings a bell.
IV quelque part *phr* somewhere; anywhere.
V quelque peu *phr* somewhat.

quelquefois /kɛlkəfwɑ/ *adv* sometimes.

quelques-uns, **quelques-unes** /kɛlkəzœ̃, yn/ *pron* some, a few.

quelqu'un /kɛlkœ̃/ *pron* someone, somebody; anyone, anybody; **~ d'autre** someone else; **il y a ~?** is there anybody here?; **c'est ~ de compétent** he/she is competent

quémander /kemɑ̃de/ [1] *vtr* to beg; **~ qch de qn** to beg sb for sth.

qu'en-dira-t-on /kɑ̃diʀatɔ̃/ *nm inv* gossip.

quenelle /kənɛl/ *nf*: *dumpling made of flour and egg, flavoured*[GB] *with meat or fish*.

quenouille /kənuj/ *nf* distaff.

querelle /kəʀɛl/ *nf* **1** quarrel; **chercher ~ à qn** to pick a quarrel with sb; **~s intestines** internal squabbling; **2** dispute.
■ **~ d'amoureux** lovers' tiff.

quereller: **se quereller** /kəʀele/ [1] *v refl* (+ *v être*) to quarrel.

querelleur, **-euse** /kəʀɛlœʀ, øz/ *adj* quarrelsome.

question /kɛstjɔ̃/ *nf* **1** question; **je ne me suis jamais posé la ~** I've never really thought about it; **pose-leur la ~** ask them; **sans se poser de ~s** unthinkingly; **2** matter, question; issue; **~ d'habitude!** it's a matter of habit; **c'est une ~ de vie ou de mort** it's a matter of life and death; **il en fait une ~ de principe** he's making an issue of it; **en ~** in question; at issue; **(re)mettre en ~** to reappraise; to reassess; **se remettre en ~** to take a new look at oneself; **la ~ n'est pas là** that's not the point; **les ~s à l'ordre du jour** the items on the agenda; **il est ~ d'elle dans l'article** she's mentioned in the article; **il n'est pas ~ que tu partes** you can't possibly leave; **il est hors de ~ d'accepter** to accept is out of the question; **pas ~!** no way○!; **3**○ **~ argent/santé, ça va** where money/health is concerned, things are OK.
IDIOMS **faire les ~s et les réponses** to do all the talking.

questionnaire /kɛstjɔnɛʀ/ *nm* questionnaire.

questionner /kɛstjɔne/ [1] *vtr* to question.

quête /kɛt/ *nf* **1** collection; **faire la ~** to take the collection; to pass the hat round; to collect for charity; **2** search; **être en ~ de qch** to be looking for sth; **la ~ du Graal** the quest for the Holy Grail.

quêter /kete/ [1] **I** *vtr* to look for.
II *vi* to take the collection; **~ pour une œuvre** to collect for a charity.

quetsche /kwɛtʃ/ *nf* (sweet purple) plum.

queue /kø/ *nf* **1** tail; **2** (of flower) stem; (of apple) stalk (GB), stem (US); (of strawberry) hull; **3** (of pot) handle; **4** (Sport) cue; **5** (of procession) tail(-end); (of train) rear, back; **6 ils arrivent en ~ (de peloton) des grandes entreprises** they come at the bottom of the league table of companies; **7** queue (GB), line (US); **faire la ~** to stand in a queue (GB), to stand in line (US); **à la ~!** go to the back of the queue (GB) or line (US).
IDIOMS **une histoire sans ~ ni tête**○ a cock and bull story; **ce film n'a ni ~ ni tête**○ you can't make head or tail of this film; **la ~ basse** with one's tail between one's legs; **il n'y en avait pas la ~ d'un(e)**○ there were none to be seen; **faire une ~ de poisson à qn** to cut in front of sb; **finir en ~ de poisson** to fizzle out.

queue-de-cheval, *pl* **queues-de-cheval** /kødʃəval/ *nf* ponytail.

queue-de-pie○, *pl* **queues-de-pie** /kødpi/ *nf* tails, tailcoat.

queux† /kø/ *nm inv* **maître ~** chef.

qui /ki/ **I** *pron* who; whom; **~ veut-elle voir?** who does she want to speak to?; **à ~ sont ces chaussures?** whose shoes are these?; **de ~ est ce roman?** who is this novel by?
II *rel pron* **1** who; that; which; **est-ce vous ~ venez d'appeler?** was it you who called just now?; **le gouvernement ~ a été formé par** the government (which was) formed by; **ce ~ me plaît chez lui** what I like about him; **2 ~ que vous soyez** whoever you are; **je n'ai jamais frappé ~ que ce soit** I've never hit anybody.

quiche /kiʃ/ *nf* quiche, flan.

quiconque /kikɔ̃k/ I *rel pron* whoever, anyone who.
II *pron* anyone, anybody.

quiétude /kjetyd/ *nf* tranquillity; **travailler en toute ~** to work undisturbed.

quignon /kiɲɔ̃/ *nm* crusty end (of a loaf).

quille /kij/ *nf* **1** skittle; **jouer aux ~s** to play skittles; **2** (Naut) keel.
IDIOMS **être reçu comme un chien dans un jeu de ~s**○ to be given a very unfriendly welcome.

quincaillerie /kɛ̃kajʀi/ *nf* **1** hardware shop (GB) or store (US); **2** hardware; **3** hardware business; **3**○ junk jewellery (GB) or jewelry (US).

quincaillier, -ère /kɛ̃kaje, ɛʀ/ *nm,f* owner of a hardware shop (GB) or store (US).

quinconce /kɛ̃kɔ̃s/ *nm* **en ~** in staggered rows.

quinquagénaire /kɛ̃kaʒenɛʀ/ I *adj* **être ~** to be in one's fifties.
II *nmf* fifty-year old.

quinquennal, ~e, *mpl* **-aux** /kɛ̃kenal, o/ *adj* **1** [*plan*] five-year; **2** five-yearly.

quintal, *pl* **-aux** /kɛ̃tal, o/ *nm* quintal, one hundred kilos.

quinte /kɛ̃t/ *nf* **1** (Mus) fifth; **2 une ~ (de toux)** a coughing fit.

quintessence /kɛ̃tesɑ̃s/ *nf* quintessence.

quintette /kɛ̃tɛt/ *nm* quintet.

quintuple /kɛ̃typl/ I *adj* [*number*] quintuple.
II *nm* **le ~ de cette quantité** five times the amount.

quintuplé, ~e /kɛ̃typle/ *nm,f* quintuplet, quin (GB), quint (US).

quintupler /kɛ̃typle/ [1] *vtr, vi* to quintuple.

quinzaine /kɛ̃zɛn/ *nf* **1** fortnight (GB), two weeks; **la première ~ de mars** the first half of March; **sous ~** within 2 weeks; **2** about fifteen.

quinze /kɛ̃z/ I *adj inv* fifteen; **~ jours** two weeks, a fortnight (GB).
II *pron* fifteen.

quinzième /kɛ̃zjɛm/ *adj* fifteenth.

quiproquo /kipʀɔko/ *nm* **1** case of mistaken identity; **2** misunderstanding.

quittance /kitɑ̃s/ *nf* **1** receipt; **2** bill.

quitte /kit/ I *adj* **1 nous sommes ~s, je suis ~ avec lui** we're quits; **2 en être ~ pour la peur/un rhume** to get off with a fright/a cold.
II **quitte à** *phr* **1 nous voulons un barrage, ~ à inonder quelques fermes** we want a dam even if it means flooding a few farms; **2 ~ à aller à Londres, autant que ce soit pour quelques jours** if you're going to London anyway, you might as well go for a few days.
■ **~ ou double** double or quits.

quitter /kite/ [1] I *vtr* **1** to leave [*place, person, road*]; **il faut ~ la nationale 7 à Valence** you have to come off the nationale 7 at Valence; **2** to leave [*job, organization*]; **~ l'enseignement** to give up teaching; **~ la scène** to give up acting; **il ne l'a pas quittée des yeux de tout le repas** he didn't take his eyes off her throughout the meal; **ne quittez pas** hold the line, please; **3** [*company*] to move from [*street*]; to move out of [*building*]; **4 un grand homme nous a quittés** a great man has passed away; **quand je vous aurai quittés...** when I've gone...; **5** to take off [*garment, hat*].
II **se quitter** *v refl* (+ *v être*) to part; **nous nous sommes quittés bons amis** we parted the best of friends; **ils ne se quittent plus** they're inseparable now.

qui-vive /kiviv/ *nm inv* **être sur le ~** to be on the alert.

quoi /kwa/ I *pron* **1** what; **à ~ penses-tu?** what are you thinking about?; **à ~ bon recommencer?** what's the point of starting again?; **en ~ suis-je responsable?** in what way or how am I responsible?; **~ encore**○**?** what now?; **2 ~ qu'elle puisse en dire** whatever she may say; **si je peux faire ~ que ce soit pour vous aider** if I can do anything to help you; **~ qu'il en soit** be that as it may.
II *rel pron* **il n'y a rien sur ~ vous puissiez fonder vos accusations** there's nothing on which to base your accusations; **il se moque de tout ce en ~ elle croit** he laughs at everything she believes in; **à ~ il a répondu** to which he replied; **après ~ ils sont partis** after which they left; **(il n'y a) pas de ~!** my pleasure, don't mention it; **il n'y a pas de ~ se fâcher** there's no reason to get angry; **il n'a (même) pas de ~ s'acheter un livre** he hasn't (even) got enough money to buy a book; **il a de ~ être satisfait** he's got good reason to feel satisfied.
III *excl* **alors, ~**○**!** really!; **il est prétentieux, stupide, pas du tout intéressant ~**○**!** he's pretentious, stupid, a dead loss○ in fact!

quoique (**quoiqu'** *before vowel or mute h*) /kwak(ə)/ *conj* although, though; **nous sommes mieux ici qu'à Paris, ~** we're better off here than in Paris, but then (again).

quota /kɔta/ *nm* quota (**sur** on).

quote-part, *pl* **quotes-parts** /kɔtpaʀ/ *nf* share.

quotidien, -ienne /kɔtidjɛ̃, ɛn/ I *adj* **1** daily; **2** everyday.
II *nm* **1** daily (paper); **2** everyday life; **vivre la pauvreté au ~** to experience real poverty on a daily basis.

quotidiennement /kɔtidjɛnmɑ̃/ *adv* every day, daily.

quotient /kɔsjɑ̃/ *nm* quotient.
■ **~ intellectuel**, **QI** intelligence quotient, IQ.

r, R /ɛʀ/ *nm inv* r, R; **rouler les ~** to roll one's r's.

rab○ /ʀab/ *nm* **1** extra; **faire du ~** to do extra hours; **2** seconds; **demander du ~** to ask for seconds.

rabâcher /ʀabɑʃe/ [1] **I** *vtr* to keep repeating [*stories, facts*].
II *vi* to keep harping on.

rabais /ʀabɛ/ *nm inv* discount; **acheter qch au ~** to buy sth cheap.

rabaisser /ʀabese/ [1] **I** *vtr* to belittle [*merit, value, person*].
II se rabaisser *v refl* (+ *v être*) to demean oneself.

rabat /ʀaba/ *nm* (of bag, table, pocket) flap.

rabat-joie /ʀabajwɑ/ *adj inv* **être ~** to be a killjoy.

rabattre /ʀabatʀ/ [61] **I** *vtr* **1** [*person*] to shut [*lid*]; to put or fold up [*folding chair, tray*]; **2** to turn [sth] down [*collar, sheet*]; to turn [sth] back [*covers*]; to pull [sth] down [*hat*]; **3** [*player*] to smash [*ball*]; **4** to beat [*game*].
II se rabattre *v refl* (+ *v être*) **1** [*lid*] to shut; [*leaf of table*] to fold up; **2** [*driver, vehicle*] to pull back in; **3 se ~ sur** to make do with.

rabbin /ʀabɛ̃/ *nm* rabbi; **grand ~** chief rabbi.

rabot /ʀabo/ *nm* (tool) plane.

raboter /ʀabɔte/ [1] *vtr* **1** (Tech) to plane; **2** to scrape.

rabougri, ~e /ʀabugʀi/ *adj* [*tree*] stunted; [*fruit*] shrivelled[GB] up.

rabrouer /ʀabʀue/ [1] *vtr* to snub.

racaille /ʀakaj/ *nf* scum.

raccommoder /ʀakɔmɔde/ [1] **I** *vtr* **1** to darn [*socks*]; **2**○ to reconcile [*people*].
II se raccommoder○ *v refl* (+ *v être*) to make it up○.

raccompagner /ʀakɔ̃paɲe/ [1] *vtr* **~ qn chez lui** to walk/to drive sb (back) home.

raccord /ʀakɔʀ/ *nm* **1** (in wallpaper) join; **2** (in painting) touch-up; **3** (in film) link shot.

raccordement /ʀakɔʀdəmɑ̃/ *nm* link road.

raccorder /ʀakɔʀde/ [1] *vtr* **1** (gen) to connect; **2** to link [sth] together [*scenes*].

raccourci /ʀakuʀsi/ *nm* (road) shortcut.

raccourcir /ʀakuʀsiʀ/ [3] **I** *vtr* **1** (gen) to shorten; **2** to cut [*text, speech*].
II *vi* [*days*] to get shorter (**de** by), to draw in.
IDIOMS **tomber sur qn à bras raccourcis**○ to lay into sb.

raccrocher /ʀakʀɔʃe/ [1] **I** *vtr* **1** to hang [sth] back up; **2 ~ le combiné** to put the telephone down.
II *vi* to hang up; **~ au nez de qn**○ to hang up on sb.
III se raccrocher *v refl* (+ *v être*) **se ~ à** to grab hold of [*rail*]; (figurative) to cling to [*person, excuse*]; **il se raccroche à n'importe quoi** he's clutching at straws.

race /ʀas/ *nf* **1** race; **2** (Zool) breed; **chien de ~** pedigree (dog).

racheter /ʀaʃte/ [18] **I** *vtr* **1** to buy [sth] back; **2** to buy some more [*wine*]; **3** to buy new [*sheets*]; **4** to buy out [*company, factory*]; **je rachète votre voiture 5 000 francs** I'll buy your car off you for 5,000 francs; **5** to redeem [*sinner*]; **il n'y en a pas un pour ~ l'autre** they're as bad as each other.
II se racheter *v refl* (+ *v être*) to redeem oneself.

rachitique /ʀaʃitik/ *adj* (Med) rickety; (derogatory) scrawny.

rachitisme /ʀaʃitism/ *nm* rickets.

racial, ~e, *mpl* **-iaux** /ʀasjal, o/ *adj* racial; **émeutes ~es** race riots.

racine /ʀasin/ *nf* root; **prendre le mal à la ~** to strike at the root of the problem.

racisme /ʀasism/ *nm* racism.

raciste /ʀasist/ *adj, nmf* racist.

racket /ʀakɛt/ *nm* **1** extortion racket; **2** racketeering.

raclée○ /ʀɑkle/ *nf* hiding○.

racler /ʀɑkle/ [1] **I** *vtr* **1** to scrape [sth] clean [*plate*]; **2** to scrape off [*rust*]; **3** to scrape against.
II se racler *v refl* (+ *v être*) **se ~ la gorge** to clear one's throat.

raclette /ʀɑklɛt/ *nf* **1** raclette (*Swiss cheese dish*); **2** scraper.

racoler /ʀakɔle/ [1] *vtr* to tout for; [*prostitute*] to solicit.

racontar○ /ʀakɔ̃taʀ/ *nm* piece of idle gossip; **des ~s** idle gossip.

raconter /ʀakɔ̃te/ [1] *vtr* to tell [*story*]; to describe [*incident*]; **on raconte que** they say that.

racornir /ʀakɔʀniʀ/ [3] *vtr*, **se racornir** *v refl* (+ *v être*) **1** to harden; **2** to shrivel (up).

radar /ʀadaʀ/ *nm* radar; **contrôles ~** radar speed checks.

rade /ʀad/ *nf* harbour[GB]; (more technically) roads; **rester en ~**○ [*person*] to be left stranded.

radeau, *pl* **~x** /ʀado/ *nm* raft.

radiateur /ʀadjatœʀ/ *nm* radiator; **~ électrique** electric heater.

radiation /ʀadjasjɔ̃/ *nf* **1** radiation; **2** (of person) (gen) expulsion; (of doctor) striking off from the register (GB), loss of the license to practice medicine (US); (of lawyer) disbarment.

radical, ~e, *mpl* **-aux** /ʀadikal, o/ *adj, nm,f* radical.

radicalement /ʀadikalmɑ̃/ *adv* (gen) radically; [*new*] completely.

radier /ʀadje/ [2] *vtr* **~ qn d'une liste** to

remove sb from a list; **~ un médecin** to strike off a doctor (GB), to take away a doctor's license (US); **~ un avocat** to disbar a lawyer.

radieux, -ieuse /Radjø, øz/ *adj* **1** [*sun*] dazzling; **2** [*weather*] glorious; **3** [*face, smile*] radiant; [*person*] radiant with joy.

radin○, **~e** /Radɛ̃, in/ *adj* stingy○.

radio[1] /Radjo/ **I** *adj inv* [*contact, signal*] radio. **II** *nm* radio operator.

radio[2] /Radjo/ *nf* **1** radio; **un poste de ~** a radio; **2** X-ray.

radioactivité /Radjoaktivite/ *nf* radioactivity.

radiocassette /Radjokasɛt/ *nm* or *f* radio cassette player.

radiodiffuser /Radjodifyze/ [1] *vtr* to broadcast.

radiographie /RadjɔgRafi/ *nf* **1** radiography; **2** X-ray (photograph).

radioguider /Radjogide/ [1] *vtr* to control by radio.

radiologiste /Radjɔlɔʒist/, **radiologue** /Radjɔlɔg/ *nmf* radiologist.

radiophonique /Radjofɔnik/ *adj* [*programme*] radio.

radio-réveil, *pl* **radios-réveils** /Radjo Revɛj/ *nm* clock radio.

radioscopie /Radjɔskɔpi/ *nf* fluoroscopy.

radiothérapie /RadjoteRapi/ *nf* radiotherapy.

radis /Radi/ *nm inv* radish; **je n'ai plus un ~**○ I haven't got a penny.

radoter /Radɔte/ [1] *vi* **1** to talk nonsense; **2** to repeat oneself.

radoteur, -euse /RadɔtœR, øz/ *nm,f* driveller[GB].

radoucir: **se radoucir** /RadusiR/ [3] *v refl* (+ *v être*) [*person*] to soften up; [*weather*] to turn milder.

radoucissement /Radusismɑ̃/ *nm* **la météo annonce un ~** the forecast is for milder weather.

rafale /Rafal/ *nf* **1** (of wind, rain) gust; (of snow) flurry; **2** (of gunfire) burst.

raffermir /RafɛRmiR/ [3] *vtr* **1** to tone [*skin*]; to tone up [*muscles*]; **2** to strengthen [*position*], to steady [*market*].

raffermissement /RafɛRmismɑ̃/ *nm* (of currency) steadying.

raffinage /Rafinaʒ/ *nm* refining; **~ du pétrole** oil refining.

raffiné, ~e /Rafine/ *adj* refined; [*food*] sophisticated.

raffinement /Rafinmɑ̃/ *nm* **1** refinement; **2** elegance.

raffiner /Rafine/ [1] *vtr* to refine.

raffinerie /RafinRi/ *nf* refinery; **~ de pétrole** oil refinery.

raffoler: **raffoler de** /Rafɔle/ [1] *v+prep* to be crazy○ about.

raffut○ /Rafy/ *nm* **1** racket○; **2** stink○, row.

rafiot○ /Rafjo/ *nm* boat, (old) tub○.

rafistoler○ /Rafistɔle/ [1] *vtr* to patch up.

rafle /Rɑfl/ *nf* **1** raid; **2** roundup.

rafler○ /Rɑfle/ [1] *vtr* **1** to make off with, to swipe○; **2** to walk off with [*medal, reward*]; to snap up [*contract*].

rafraîchir /RafRɛʃiR/ [3] **I** *vtr* [*rain*] to cool [*atmosphere*]; **le thé glacé te rafraîchira** the iced tea will cool you down.

II se rafraîchir *v refl* (+ *v être*) [*weather*] to get cooler; [*person*] to refresh oneself.

IDIOMS **~ la mémoire**○ **de qn** to refresh sb's memory.

rafraîchissement /RafRɛʃismɑ̃/ *nm* refreshment.

ragaillardir /RagajaRdiR/ [3] *vtr* to cheer [sb] up.

rage /Raʒ/ *nf* **1** (Med) rabies; **2** rage; **être en ~ contre qn** to be furious with sb; **être fou de ~** to be in a mad rage; **faire ~** [*disease*] to be rife; [*epidemic, fire*] to rage.

■ **~ de dents** raging toothache.

rageant○, **~e** /Raʒɑ̃, ɑ̃t/ *adj* infuriating; **c'est ~** it's infuriating.

rageur, -euse /RaʒœR, øz/ *adj* furious.

ragot○ /Rago/ *nm* malicious gossip.

ragoût /Ragu/ *nm* stew, ragout.

rai /Rɛ/ *nm* **~ de lumière** ray of light.

raid /Rɛd/ *nm* **1** (Mil) raid; **~ aérien** air raid; **2** (Sport) trek.

raide /Rɛd/ *adj* **1** (gen) stiff; [*hair*] straight; [*rope*] taut; **2** steep; **3**○ **je trouve ça un peu ~** that's a bit steep.

IDIOMS **être ~ comme un piquet** to be stiff as a ramrod; **tomber ~** to be flabbergasted; **tomber ~ mort** to drop dead.

raideur /RɛdœR/ *nf* **1** stiffness; **avec ~** stiffly; **2** steepness.

raidir /RɛdiR/ [3] **I** *vtr* to tense [*arm, body*].

II se raidir *v refl* (+ *v être*) **1** [*body*] to tense up; **2** (figurative) **se ~ contre la douleur** to brace oneself against pain.

raie /Rɛ/ *nf* **1** (in hair) parting (GB), part (US); **2** scratch; **3** (Zool) skate.

rail /Rɑj/ *nm* rail, track; **remettre qch sur les ~s** to get sth back on the right track.

■ **~ de sécurité** crash barrier.

railler /Rɑje/ [1] *vtr* to make fun of.

raillerie /RɑjRi/ *nf* mockery.

railleur, -euse /RɑjœR, øz/ *adj* mocking.

rainette /Rɛnɛt/ *nf* tree frog.

rainure /RenyR/ *nf* groove.

raisin /Rɛzɛ̃/ *nm* grapes; **~s de Corinthe** currants; **~s secs** raisins.

raison /Rɛzɔ̃/ *nf* **1** reason; **~ d'agir** reason for action; **~ de plus pour faire** all the more reason to do; **en ~ d'une panne** owing to a breakdown; **à plus forte ~** even more so, especially; **à juste ~** quite rightly; **avec ~** justifiably; **comme de ~** as one might expect; **~ d'espoir** grounds for hope; **2 avoir ~** to be right; **donner ~ à qn** to agree with sb; **3** reason; **se rendre à la ~** to see reason; **faire entendre ~ à qn** to make sb see reason; **ramener qn à la ~** to bring sb to his/her senses; **se faire une ~ de qch** to resign oneself to sth; **plus que de ~** more than is sensible; **avoir ~ de qn/qch** to get the better of sb/sth; **à ~ de** at the rate of.

raisonnable /ʀɛzɔnabl/ *adj* reasonable; moderate; sensible.

raisonnablement /ʀɛzɔnabləmɑ̃/ *adv* reasonably; in moderation; sensibly.

raisonné, ~e /ʀɛzɔne/ **I** *pp* ▶ **raisonner**.
II *pp adj* **1** [*attitude*] cautious; [*decision*] carefully thought out; **2** [*enthusiasm*] measured.

raisonnement /ʀɛzɔnmɑ̃/ *nm* reasoning; **selon le même ~** by the same token; **il tient le ~ suivant** his argument is as follows; **je ne tiens pas le même ~** I look at it differently; **tu ne feras jamais rien avec ce genre de ~** you won't get anywhere with that sort of thinking.

raisonner /ʀɛzɔne/ [1] **I** *vtr* to reason with [*person, child*].
II *vi* to think; **~ à court terme** to think in the short term.
III se raisonner *v refl* (+ *v être*) [*person*] to be more sensible, to pull oneself together.

rajeunir /ʀaʒœniʀ/ [3] **I** *vtr* **1** to make [sb] look/feel younger; **2 ~ qn** to make sb out to be younger; **3** to bring or inject new blood into.
II *vi* **1** to look younger; **2** to feel younger.

rajeunissement /ʀaʒœnismɑ̃/ *nm* **1 nous avons enregistré un ~ de la population** we see that the population is getting younger; **2** modernization; **3** updating; **4** rejuvenation.

rajout /ʀaʒu/ *nm* addition.

rajouter /ʀaʒute/ [1] *vtr* to add; **en ~**° to exaggerate.

rajuster /ʀaʒyste/ [1] *vtr* to straighten [*hat*]; to push [sth] back up [*glasses*].

râle /ʀɑl/ *nm* **1** rale; **2** groan; **3** death rattle.

ralenti, ~e /ʀalɑ̃ti/ **I** *pp* ▶ **ralentir**.
II *pp adj* [*gesture, rhythm, growth*] slower.
III *nm* slow motion; **fonctionner au ~** [*business*] to be just ticking over.

ralentir /ʀalɑ̃tiʀ/ [3] *vtr, vi,* **se ralentir** *v refl* (+ *v être*) to slow down.

ralentissement /ʀalɑ̃tismɑ̃/ *nm* **1** slowing down; **2** tailback.

ralentisseur /ʀalɑ̃tisœʀ/ *nm* sleeping policeman (GB), speed ramp.

râler /ʀɑle/ [1] *vi* **1**° to moan° (**contre** about); **ça me fait ~** it annoys or bugs° me; **2** to groan.

râleur°, **-euse** /ʀɑlœʀ, øz/ *nm,f* moaner°.

ralliement /ʀalimɑ̃/ *nm* rallying.

rallier /ʀalje/ [2] **I** *vtr* **~ qn à sa cause** to win sb over.
II se rallier *v refl* (+ *v être*) **se ~ à** to rally to [*republicans*]; to come round to [*opinion*]; **elle s'est ralliée à notre cause** she was won over.

rallonge /ʀalɔ̃ʒ/ *nf* **1** extension cord, extension lead (GB); **2** (of table) leaf.

rallonger /ʀalɔ̃ʒe/ [13] **I** *vtr* to extend; to lengthen.
II *vi* **les jours rallongent** the days are drawing out.

rallumer: **se rallumer** /ʀalyme/ [1] *v refl* (+ *v être*) [*fire, quarrel*] to flare up again.

rallye /ʀali/ *nm* (car) rally.

ramage /ʀamaʒ/ **I** *nm* (of bird) song.
II ramages *nm pl* foliage pattern; **à ~s** with a foliage pattern.

ramassage /ʀamasaʒ/ *nm* collection; picking up; **car de ~** (for pupils) school bus.

ramassé, ~e /ʀamase/ **I** *pp* ▶ **ramasser**.
II *pp adj* **1** stocky, squat; **2 être ~ sur soi-même** to be hunched up.

ramasser /ʀamase/ [1] **I** *vtr* to collect; to pick up; to dig up [*potatoes*]; **~ à la pelle** to get bucketfuls of [*money*]; **se faire ~ dans une rafle**° to get picked up in a (police) raid.
II se ramasser *v refl* (+ *v être*) **1** to huddle up, to shrink into oneself; **2**° to come a cropper°; **se faire ~ à un examen** to fail or flunk° (US) an exam.

ramassis /ʀamasi/ *nm inv* (derogatory) (of street urchins) bunch; (of ideas, objects) jumble.

rambarde /ʀɑ̃baʀd/ *nf* guardrail.

rame /ʀam/ *nf* **1** oar; **2** (of paper) ream; **3 une ~ de métro** a metro train.

rameau, *pl* **~x** /ʀamo/ *nm* (gen) branch; **~ d'olivier** olive branch.

ramener /ʀamne/ [16] **I** *vtr* **1 ~ l'inflation à 5%** to reduce inflation to 5 per cent; **~ qch à sa juste mesure** to get sth into proportion; **2** to restore [*order*]; **~ qn à la réalité** to bring sb back to reality; **~ qn à de meilleurs sentiments** to put sb into a better frame of mind; **~ qn à la vie** to bring sb round; **~ toujours tout à soi** always to relate everything to oneself; **3** to take [sb/sth] back; **4** to bring back; to return; **5 '~ les genoux vers le menton'** 'draw your knees up to your chin'.
II se ramener *v refl* (+ *v être*) **se ~ à** to come down to, to boil down to.

ramer /ʀame/ [1] *vi* to row.

rameur, -euse /ʀamœʀ, øz/ *nm,f* (gen) rower; (Sport) oarsman/oarswoman.

rameuter /ʀamøte/ [1] *vtr* to round up.

rami /ʀami/ *nm* rummy.

ramier /ʀamje/ *nm* woodpigeon.

ramification /ʀamifikasjɔ̃/ *nf* **1** network; **2** ramification.

ramifier: **se ramifier** /ʀamifje/ [2] *v refl* (+ *v être*) [*stem, nerve*] to branch; [*branch*] to divide.

ramollir /ʀamɔliʀ/ [3] **I** *vtr* **1** to soften; **2** to make [sb] soft.
II se ramollir *v refl* (+ *v être*) **1** to become soft; **2**° [*person*] to get soft.

ramoner /ʀamɔne/ [1] *vtr* to sweep [*chimney*].

ramoneur /ʀamɔnœʀ/ *nm* chimney sweep.

rampe /ʀɑ̃p/ *nf* **1** banister; hand-rail; **2** (in theatre) **la ~** the footlights.
■ **~ d'accès** (for motorway) sliproad (GB), entrance ramp (US); (of building) ramp.

ramper /ʀɑ̃pe/ [1] *vi* **1** to crawl; **2** to creep.

ramure /ʀamyʀ/ *nf* **1** (of tree) branches; **2** antlers.

rancart○ /ʀɑ̃kaʀ/ *nm* **mettre au ~** to scrap; to shunt [sb] aside.

rance /ʀɑ̃s/ *adj* rancid.

rancœur /ʀɑ̃kœʀ/ *nf* resentment.

rançon /ʀɑ̃sɔ̃/ *nf* **1** ransom; **2 la ~ de la gloire** the price of fame.

rançonner /ʀɑ̃sɔne/ [1] *vtr* [*racketeer*] to extort money from.

rancune /ʀɑ̃kyn/ *nf* **1** resentment; **2** grudge; **sans ~!** no hard feelings.

rancunier, **-ière** /ʀɑ̃kynje, ɛʀ/ *adj* **être ~** to be a person who holds grudges.

randonnée /ʀɑ̃dɔne/ *nf* hiking; **la ~ à cheval** pony-trekking.

randonneur, **-euse** /ʀɑ̃dɔnœʀ, øz/ *nm,f* hiker, rambler (GB).

rang /ʀɑ̃/ *nm* **1** row; (in necklace) strand; **se mettre en ~s** [*children*] to get into (a) line; **2** (Mil), (figurative) rank; **sortir du ~** to rise or come up through the ranks; **serrer les ~s** to close ranks; **3** (in a hierarchy) rank; **être au premier ~ mondial** to rank first in the world; **être au 5e ~ mondial des exportateurs** to be the 5th largest exporter in the world; **acteur de second ~** second-rate actor; **des personnes de son ~** people of one's own station.

rangé, **~e**[1] /ʀɑ̃ʒe/ **I** *pp* ▶ **ranger**[1].
II *pp adj* [*life*] orderly; [*person*] well-behaved.

rangée[2] /ʀɑ̃ʒe/ *nf* row.

rangement /ʀɑ̃ʒmɑ̃/ *nm* **1 c'est un maniaque du ~** he's obsessively tidy; **2** storage space.

ranger[1] /ʀɑ̃ʒe/ [13] **I** *vtr* **1** to put away; **où ranges-tu tes verres?** where do you keep the glasses?; **2** to arrange, put into order; **~ un animal dans les mammifères** to class an animal as a mammal; **~ qn de son côté** to win sb over to one's side; **3** to tidy.
II se ranger *v refl* (+ *v être*) **1** to line up; **2** [*vehicle, driver*] to pull over; **3 se ~ à l'avis de qn** to go along with sb; **4** to settle down.

ranger[2] /ʀɑ̃dʒɛʀ/ *nm* **1** ranger; **2** heavy-duty boot.

ranimer /ʀanime/ [1] **I** *vtr* **1** to revive [*person*]; **2** to rekindle [*fire, hope*]; to stir up [*quarrel*]; to liven up [*conversation*].
II se ranimer *v refl* (+ *v être*) [*fire*] to flare up; [*flame, debate*] to be rekindled.

rapace /ʀapas/ **I** *adj* [*person*] rapacious.
II *nm* (Zool) bird of prey.

rapacité /ʀapasite/ *nf* **1** (of animal) ferocity; **2** (of person) greed.

rapatrier /ʀapatʀije/ [2] *vtr* to repatriate.

râpe /ʀɑp/ *nf* (Culin) grater; **~ à fromage** cheese grater.

râper /ʀɑpe/ [1] *vtr* to grate [*cheese, carrot*]; **c'est râpé**○ (figurative) it's off○.

rapetisser /ʀap(ə)tise/ [1] *vi* to shrink.

râpeux, **-euse** /ʀɑpø, øz/ *adj* rough.

raphia /ʀafja/ *nm* raffia.

rapide /ʀapid/ **I** *adj* **1** (gen) quick, rapid; **2** fast; **3** [*reply, decision*] prompt.
II *nm* **1** rapids; **descendre un ~** to shoot the rapids; **2** (train) express.

rapidement /ʀapidmɑ̃/ *adv* quickly; fast.

rapidité /ʀapidite/ *nf* speed.

rapiécer /ʀapjese/ [14] *vtr* to patch.

rappel /ʀapɛl/ *nm* **1** reminder; **~ à l'ordre** call to order; **2 (lettre de) ~** reminder; **'dernier ~'** 'final demand'; **3** back pay; **4** (of ambassador) recall; (of reservists) call-up; (of actors) curtain call; **5** (Med) booster.

rappeler /ʀaple/ [19] **I** *vtr* **1 ~ qch à qn** to remind sb of sth; **rappelons-le** let's not forget; **2** to remind [sb] of; **vous me rappelez votre sœur** you remind me of your sister; **3** (on phone) to call back; **4** to call [sb] back [*person*]; to call back [*actor*]; (Mil) to recall [*reservist*]; **~ qn à l'ordre** to call sb to order.
II se rappeler *v refl* (+ *v être*) to remember.

rappliquer○ /ʀaplike/ [1] *vi* **1** to turn up○; **2** to come back.

rapport /ʀapɔʀ/ **I** *nm* **1** connection, link; **être sans ~ avec**, **n'avoir aucun ~ avec** to have nothing to do with; **un emploi en ~ avec tes goûts** a job suited to your interests; **2 ~s** relations; **avoir** or **entretenir de bons ~s avec qn** to be on good terms with sb; **3 être en ~ avec qn** to be in touch with sb; **nous sommes en ~ avec d'autres entreprises** we have dealings with other companies; **4 sous tous les ~s** in every respect; **5** report; **6** return, yield; **immeuble de ~** block of flats (GB) or apartment block (US) that is rented out; **7** ratio; **bon/mauvais ~ qualité prix** good/poor value for money.
II par rapport à *phr* **1** compared with; **par ~ au dollar** against the dollar; **2 le nombre de voitures par ~ au nombre d'habitants** the number of cars per head of the population; **un changement par ~ à la position habituelle du parti** a departure from the usual party line; **3** with regard to, toward(s); **l'attitude de la population par ~ à l'immigration** people's attitudes to immigration.
■ **~ de force** power struggle; **~s sexuels** sexual relations.

rapporter /ʀapɔʀte/ [1] **I** *vtr* **1** to bring back; to take back (**à** to), to return (**à** to); **2** to bring in [*income*]; **~ 10%** to yield or return 10%; **ça ne rapporte rien** it doesn't pay; **3** to report; to quote [*witticism*]; **on m'a rapporté que** I was told that.
II *vi* **1** to bring in money, to be lucrative; **2**○ to tell tales.
III se rapporter *v refl* (+ *v être*) **1 se ~ à** to relate to, to bear a relation to; **2 s'en ~ à qn/qch** to rely on sb/sth.

rapporteur○, **-euse** /ʀapɔʀtœʀ, øz/ *nm,f* telltale (GB) or tattletale (US).

rapproché, **~e** /ʀapʀɔʃe/ **I** *pp* ▶ **rapprocher**.
II *pp adj* close together; **à intervalles ~s** in quick succession.

rapprochement /ʀapʀɔʃmɑ̃/ *nm* **1** rapprochement; **2** connection.

rapprocher /ʀapʀɔʃe/ [1] **I** *vtr* **1** to move [sth] closer; **2** to bring [sth] forward(s) [*date*]; **3** to bring [sb] (closer) together [*people*]; **4** to

compare; **la situation est à ~ de ce qui s'est passé en 1951** the situation can be compared to that of 1951.
II se rapprocher *v refl* (+ *v être*) to get closer, to get nearer; **leurs peintures se rapprochent des fresques antiques** their paintings are similar to classical frescoes.

rapt /ʀapt/ *nm* kidnapping[GB], abduction.

raquer◐ /ʀake/ [1] *vi* to cough up○, to pay up.

raquette /ʀakɛt/ *nf* **1** (for tennis) racket; (for table-tennis) bat (GB), paddle (US); **2** snowshoe.

rare /ʀɑʀ/ *adj* **1** (not common) (gen) rare; [*job*] unusual; [*intelligence*] exceptional; [*impudence*] singular; **il est ~ qu'il vienne en train** it's unusual for him to come by train; **être d'une bêtise ~** to be singularly stupid; **2** (not numerous) few, rare; [*visits*] infrequent; (not abundant) (gen) scarce; [*hair*] thin; [*vegetation*] sparse; **être l'un des ~s qui** to be one of the few (people) who; **se faire ~** [*product*] to become scarce; **vous vous faites ~ ces temps-ci** you are not around much these days.

raréfaction /ʀɑʀefaksjɔ̃/ *nf* (of gas, air) rarefaction.

raréfier /ʀɑʀefje/ [2] **I** *vtr* **1** to rarefy [*air, gas*]; **2** to make [sth] rare.
II se raréfier *v refl* (+ *v être*) [*air*] to become thinner; [*gas, atmosphere*] to rarefy; [*food, money*] to become scarce; [*species*] to become rare.

rarement /ʀɑʀmɑ̃/ *adv* rarely, seldom.

rareté /ʀɑʀte/ *nf* (of money, foodstuffs) shortage, scarcity; (of edition, event) rarity; (of letters, calls) infrequency.

rarissime /ʀɑʀisim/ *adj* extremely rare.

ras, **~e** /ʀɑ, ʀɑz/ **I** *adj* [*hair*] close-cropped; [*fur*] short; **à poil ~** [*animal*] short-haired; [*carpet*] short-piled; **en ~e campagne** in (the) open country; **une cuillère à café ~e** a level teaspoonful; **à ~ bord** to the brim (**de** with).
II *adv* short; **couper (à) ~** to cut [sth] very short [*hair, lawn*].
III au ras de *phr* **au ~ du sol** at ground level.
IDIOMS **être à ~ du sol** to be rather basic; **faire table ~e de** to make a clean sweep of.

rasade /ʀɑzad/ *nf* **1** glassful; **2** swig○.

rascasse /ʀaskas/ *nf* scorpion fish.

ras-de-cou /ʀɑdku/ *nm inv* **1** crew-neck sweater; **2** choker.

rase-mottes /ʀɑzmɔt/ *nm inv* **faire du ~, voler en ~** to fly low.

raser /ʀɑze/ [1] **I** *vtr* **1** to shave; to shave off; **~ de près** to give [sb] a close shave; **2** to demolish; to raze [sth] to the ground; **3** [*bullet*] to graze; [*plane, bird*] to skim; **4**○ to bore [sb] stiff○.
II se raser *v refl* (+ *v être*) to shave; **se ~ la barbe** to shave off one's beard.
IDIOMS **~ les murs** to hug the walls.

raseur○, **-euse** /ʀɑzœʀ, øz/ *nm,f* bore.

ras-le-bol○ /ʀɑlbɔl/ *nm inv* discontent.

rasoir /ʀɑzwaʀ/ **I**○ *adj inv* boring.
II *nm* **~ mécanique** razor; **~ électrique** electric shaver.

rassasier /ʀasazje/ [2] **I** *vtr* [*food*] to fill [sb] up.
II se rassasier *v refl* (+ *v être*) to eat one's fill.

rassemblement /ʀasɑ̃bləmɑ̃/ *nm* **1** rally; **2** gathering; **3** meeting.

rassembler /ʀasɑ̃ble/ [1] **I** *vtr* to gather [sb/sth] together [*people*]; (Mil) to muster, to assemble [*troops*]; to round up [*sheep, herd*]; to unite [*citizens, nation*]; to gather, to collect [*information, proof*]; **~ ses forces** to summon up one's strength; **~ ses idées** to collect one's thoughts.
II se rassembler *v refl* (+ *v être*) **1** to gather; **2** to assemble.

rasseoir: **se rasseoir** /ʀaswaʀ/ [41] *v refl* (+ *v être*) to sit down (again).

rasséréner /ʀaseʀene/ [14] **I** *vtr* to calm [sb] down [*person*].
II se rasséréner *v refl* (+ *v être*) [*person*] to calm down; [*face*] to clear.

rassis, **~e** /ʀasi, iz/ *adj* [*bread*] stale.

rassurant, **~e** /ʀasyʀɑ̃, ɑ̃t/ *adj* reassuring.

rassurer /ʀasyʀe/ [1] **I** *vtr* to reassure; **~ qn** to reassure sb, to put sb's mind at rest.
II se rassurer *v refl* (+ *v être*) to reassure oneself; **rassure-toi** don't worry; **je suis rassuré** I'm relieved; **je n'étais pas très rassuré** I was quite worried.

rat /ʀa/ *nm* **1** rat; **2** skinflint, cheapskate○.
IDIOMS **on est fait comme des ~s**○ we're caught like rats in a trap.

ratatiner: **se ratatiner** /ʀatatine/ [1] *v refl* (+ *v être*) **1** [*apple*] to shrivel; **2** [*face, person*] to become wizened.

ratatouille /ʀatatuj/ *nf* ratatouille.

rate /ʀat/ *nf* **1** (Zool) female rat; **2** (Anat) spleen.

râteau, *pl* **~x** /ʀɑto/ *nm* rake.

râtelier /ʀɑtəlje/ *nm* hayrack.
IDIOMS **manger à tous les ~s** to run with the hare and hunt with the hounds.

rater /ʀate/ [1] **I** *vtr* **1** to fail, to flunk○ (US) [*exam*]; to spoil [*sauce*]; **j'ai raté ma vie** I wasted my life; **elle a raté son coup**○ she has failed; **2** to miss [*train, target*].
II *vi* [*plan, operation*] to fail, to flop○; **il dit toujours des bêtises, ça ne rate jamais**○ he can always be relied upon to say something stupid.

ratière /ʀatjɛʀ/ *nf* rat trap.

ratifier /ʀatifje/ [2] *vtr* **1** to ratify [*treaty, contract*]; **2** to confirm [*plan, proposal*].

ration /ʀasjɔ̃/ *nf* **1** ration; **2** share.

rationaliser /ʀasjɔnalize/ [1] *vtr* to rationalize.

rationnel, **-elle** /ʀasjɔnɛl/ *adj* rational.

rationnement /ʀasjɔnmɑ̃/ *nm* rationing; **ticket de ~** ration coupon.

rationner /ʀasjɔne/ [1] **I** *vtr* to ration [*petrol*]; to impose rationing on [*population*].
II se rationner *v refl* (+ *v être*) to cut down (**en** on).

ratisser /ʀatise/ [1] *vtr* **1** to rake over; to rake

up; **2** to comb [*area*]; **~ large**○ to cast one's net wide.

raton /ʀatɔ̃/ *nm* young rat.
■ **~ laveur** racoon.

rattachement /ʀataʃmɑ̃/ *nm* **1** (of country) unification (**à** with); **2** (of person) **demander son ~ à** to ask to be posted to.

rattacher /ʀataʃe/ [1] **I** *vtr* **1** to attach [*region*] (**à** to); to link [*currency*] (**à** to); to post [*employee*](**à** to); **2** to associate [*artist, work of* art] (**à** with); **3** to retie; to fasten [sth] again; **4 plus rien ne la rattache à Lyon** she no longer has any ties with Lyons.
II se rattacher *v refl* (+ *v être*) **se ~ à** to be linked to; to relate to.

rattrapage /ʀatʀapaʒ/ *nm* **1** (Econ) adjustment; **2** catching up; **cours de ~** remedial lesson.

rattraper /ʀatʀape/ [1] **I** *vtr* **1** to catch up with [*competitor*]; **2** to catch [*fugitive*]; **3** to make up for [*lost time, deficit*]; to make up [*points, distance*]; **~ son retard** to catch up; **4** to put right [*error*]; to smooth over [*blunder*]; to save [*situation*]; to pick up [*stitch*]; **~ le coup**○ to put things right; **5** to catch [*object*]; **6**○ (Sch) to let [sb] pass [*student, pupil*].
II se rattraper *v refl* (+ *v être*) **1** to redeem oneself (**auprès de qn** with sb); **2** to make up for it; **3** (Sch) to catch up; **4** to make up one's losses (**avec** on); to make up for lost time; **5 se ~ de justesse** to stop oneself just in time; **se ~ à une branche** to save oneself by catching hold of a branch.

rature /ʀatyʀ/ *nf* crossing-out; deletion.

raturer /ʀatyʀe/ [1] *vtr* **1** to cross out; **2** to correct.

rauque /ʀok/ *adj* **1** husky; **2** hoarse.

ravage /ʀavaʒ/ *nm* **les ~s de la guerre** the ravages of war; **faire des ~s** to wreak havoc; [*epidemic*] to take a terrible toll; **tu vas faire des ~s avec ta mini-jupe** (humorous) you'll knock them dead in that mini-skirt.

ravagé○, **~e** /ʀavaʒe/ **I** *pp* ▶ **ravager**.
II *pp adj* crazy.

ravager /ʀavaʒe/ [13] *vtr* **1** [*fire, war*] to devastate, to ravage; **2** [*disease*] to ravage [*face*]; [*grief*] to tear [sb] apart.

ravalement /ʀavalmɑ̃/ *nm* **1** cleaning; **2** refacing; **3** (figurative) facelift.

ravaler /ʀavale/ [1] *vtr* **1** to clean; to reface; to renovate [*building*]; **2** to revamp [*image*]; **3** to suppress [*anger*]; **~ ses larmes** to hold back one's tears; **4 ~ qch au rang de** to reduce sth to the level of.

ravier /ʀavje/ *nm* small dish (*for hors-d'œuvre*).

ravigoter○ /ʀavigɔte/ [1] *vtr* [*fresh air*] to invigorate; [*alcohol*] to perk [sb] up.

ravin /ʀavɛ̃/ *nm* ravine.

raviner /ʀavine/ [1] *vtr* to furrow [*ground, soil*].

ravir /ʀaviʀ/ [3] *vtr* **1** to delight; **ça te va à ~** it really suits you; **2** to steal; **~ qch à qn** to rob sb of sth.

raviser: **se raviser** /ʀavize/ [1] *v refl* (+ *v être*) to change one's mind.

ravissant, **~e** /ʀavisɑ̃, ɑ̃t/ *adj* beautiful, delightful.

ravissement /ʀavismɑ̃/ *nm* **1** rapture; **2** abduction.

ravisseur, **-euse** /ʀavisœʀ, øz/ *nm,f* kidnapper[GB], abductor.

ravitaillement /ʀavitajmɑ̃/ *nm* supplies.

ravitailler /ʀavitaje/ [1] **I** *vtr* **1** to provide [sb] with fresh supplies [*army, town*] (**en qch** of sth); **2** to refuel.
II se ravitailler *v refl* (+ *v être*) to obtain fresh supplies.

raviver /ʀavive/ [1] *vtr* to rekindle; to revive; to bring back [*memory*].

rayé, **~e** /ʀeje/ **I** *pp* ▶ **rayer**.
II *pp adj* **1** [*fabric*] striped; **2** [*record*] scratched.

rayer /ʀeje/ [21] *vtr* **1** to cross [sth] out; **'~ la mention inutile'** 'delete whichever does not apply'; **~ qn d'une liste** to cross sb's name off a list; **2 la ville a été rayée de la carte** the town was wiped off the map; **3** to scratch.

rayon /ʀɛjɔ̃/ *nm* **1** radius; **dans un ~ de 10 km** within a 10 km radius; **~ d'action** range; (figurative) sphere of activity; **2** ray; beam; **~ de soleil** ray of sunshine; **les ~s X** X-rays; **~ laser** laser beam; **être soigné aux ~s** to undergo radiation treatment; **3** (of wheel) spoke; **4** shelf; **~ de bibliothèque** (book)shelf; **5** (in big store) department; (in small shop) section; **le ~ (des) jouets** the toy department; **tous nos modèles sont en ~** all our styles are on display; **6**○ **c'est mon ~** that's my department○; **il en connaît un ~ à ce sujet** he knows a lot about it; **7 ~ (de ruche)** honeycomb.

rayonnage /ʀɛjɔnaʒ/ *nm* shelves.

rayonnant, **~e** /ʀɛjɔnɑ̃, ɑ̃t/ *adj* [*person, face*] radiant (**de** with).

rayonne /ʀɛjɔn/ *nf* rayon.

rayonnement /ʀɛjɔnmɑ̃/ *nm* **1** radiation; **~ radioactif** radiation, radioactivity; **2** radiance; **3** (of country) influence.

rayonner /ʀɛjɔne/ [1] *vi* **1** [*light, heat*] to radiate; **2** [*star*] to shine (forth); **3** [*person*] to glow (**de** with); **4** [*city, country*] to exert its influence, to hold sway; **5** [*soldiers*] to patrol; [*tourists*] to tour around; **6** [*streets*] to radiate.

rayure /ʀɛjyʀ/ *nf* **1** stripe; **2** scratch.

raz-de-marée /ʀadmaʀe/ *nm inv* tidal wave.

razzia /ʀazja/ *nf* raid.

ré /ʀe/ *nm inv* (note) D; (in sol-fa) re.

réacteur /ʀeaktœʀ/ *nm* **1 ~ (nucléaire)** (nuclear) reactor; **2** jet engine.

réaction /ʀeaksjɔ̃/ *nf* **1** reaction; response; **2 avion à ~** jet aircraft.

réactionnaire /ʀeaksjɔnɛʀ/ *adj, nmf* reactionary.

réactiver /ʀeaktive/ [1] *vtr* to rekindle [*fire*]; to relaunch [*negotiations*].

réagir /ʀeaʒiʀ/ [3] *vi* **1** to react; to respond; **2 ~ sur** to have an effect on.

réalisable /ʀealizabl/ *adj* feasible; workable.

réalisateur, **-trice** /ʀealizatœʀ, tʀis/ *nm,f* director.

réalisation /ʀealizasjɔ̃/ *nf* **1** (of dream) fulfilment[GB]; **2** (of study) carrying out; **conception et ~** (of hotel) design and construction; **3** achievement; **4** (of film) production.

réaliser /ʀealize/ [1] **I** *vtr* **1** to fulfil[GB] [*ambition*]; to achieve [*ideal, feat*]; **~ des bénéfices** to make a profit; **2** to make [*model*]; to carry out [*survey, study*]; **3** to direct [*film*]; **4** to realize (**que** that).
II se réaliser *v refl* (+ *v être*) **1** [*dream*] to come true; [*predictions*] to be fulfilled; **2 se ~ (dans qch)** to find fulfilment[GB] (in sth).

réalisme /ʀealism/ *nm* realism.

réaliste /ʀealist/ **I** *adj* (gen) realistic; (in art) realist.
II *nmf* realist.

réalité /ʀealite/ *nf* **la ~** reality; **en ~** in reality; **la ~ du marché** the real nature of the market; **tenir compte des ~s** to take the facts into consideration.

réanimation /ʀeanimasjɔ̃/ *nf* **1** (**service de**) **~** intensive care (unit); **2** resuscitation.

réapparaître /ʀeapaʀɛtʀ/ [73] *vi* [*sun*] to come out again; [*illness*] to recur.

réapparition /ʀeapaʀisjɔ̃/ *nf* **1** recurrence; **2** reappearance.

réapprovisionner /ʀeapʀɔvizjɔne/ [1] **I** *vtr* to restock [*shop*].
II se réapprovisionner *v refl* (+ *v être*) to stock up (**en** on).

réassortir /ʀeasɔʀtiʀ/ [3] *vtr* to replenish [*stock*].

rébarbatif, **-ive** /ʀebaʀbatif, iv/ *adj* off-putting; forbidding.

rebâtir /ʀ(ə)bɑtiʀ/ [3] *vtr* to rebuild.

rebattre /ʀ(ə)batʀ/ [61] *vtr* **~ les oreilles de qn avec une histoire** to go on (and on) about something.

rebattu, **~e** /ʀ(ə)baty/ **I** *pp* ▶ **rebattre**.
II *pp adj* [*joke, story*] hackneyed.

rebelle /ʀəbɛl/ **I** *adj* **1** rebel; **2** rebellious; **3** [*curl, lock of hair*] stray; [*stain*] stubborn.
II *nmf* rebel.

rebeller: **se rebeller** /ʀəbɛle/ [1] *v refl* (+ *v être*) to rebel (**contre** against).

rébellion /ʀebɛljɔ̃/ *nf* rebellion.

rebiffer○: **se rebiffer** /ʀ(ə)bife/ [1] *v refl* (+ *v être*) to rebel (**contre** against).

rebiquer○ /ʀ(ə)bike/ [1] *vi* [*lock of hair, collar*] to stick up.

reboiser /ʀ(ə)bwaze/ [1] *vtr* to reafforest, to reforest.

rebond /ʀ(ə)bɔ̃/ *nm* **1** bounce; **2** recovery; **3** increase.

rebondi, **~e** /ʀ(ə)bɔ̃di/ *adj* **1** [*shape*] round, rounded; [*cheek*] chubby; [*stomach*] fat; [*buttocks*] rounded; **2** (figurative) [*wallet*] bulging.

rebondir /ʀ(ə)bɔ̃diʀ/ [3] *vi* **1** to bounce; **2** [*conversation, controversy*] to start up again; [*plot*] to take a new turn.

rebondissement /ʀ(ə)bɔ̃dismɑ̃/ *nm* (of controversy) sudden revival; (in trial, affair) new development; **les ~s de l'intrigue** the twists and turns of the plot.

rebord /ʀ(ə)bɔʀ/ *nm* **1** ledge; **~ de fenêtre** windowsill; **2** rim; **3** edge.

rebours: **à rebours** /aʀ(ə)buʀ/ *phr* [*count, walk*] backward(s).

rebouteux○, **-euse** /ʀ(ə)butø, øz/ *nm,f* bone-setter.

rebrousse-poil: **à rebrousse-poil** /aʀ(ə)bʀuspwal/ *phr* the wrong way.

rebrousser /ʀ(ə)bʀuse/ [1] *vtr* **1** to brush [sth] the wrong way [*fur*]; **2 ~ chemin** to turn back.

rebuffade /ʀ(ə)byfad/ *nf* rebuff.

rébus /ʀebys/ *nm inv* rebus.

rebut /ʀ(ə)by/ *nm* rubbish; **objets de ~** junk; **mettre au ~** to throw [sth/sb] on the scrapheap.

rebuter /ʀ(ə)byte/ [1] *vtr* **1** to disgust; to repel; **2** to put [sb] off.

récalcitrant, **~e** /ʀekalsitʀɑ̃, ɑ̃t/ *adj* recalcitrant.

recaler○ /ʀ(ə)kale/ [1] *vtr* to fail [*candidate*].

récapitulatif, **-ive** /ʀekapitylatif, iv/ *adj* summary.

récapituler /ʀekapityle/ [1] *vtr* to sum up, to recapitulate.

recaser○ /ʀ(ə)kaze/ [1] **I** *vtr* to find another job for [*person*].
II se recaser *v refl* (+ *v être*) **1** to find another job; **2** to find a new husband/wife.

receler /ʀəs(ə)le, ʀsəle/ [17] *vtr* **1 ~ des marchandises** to possess stolen goods; **2** to contain.

receleur, **-euse** /ʀ(ə)s(ə)lœʀ, ʀsəlœʀ, øz/ *nm,f* possessor of stolen goods.

récemment /ʀesamɑ̃/ *adv* recently; **tout ~** very recently.

recensement /ʀ(ə)sɑ̃smɑ̃/ *nm* **1** census; **2** inventory.

recenser /ʀ(ə)sɑ̃se/ [1] *vtr* **1** to take a census of [*population*]; **2** to list [*objects*].

récent, **~e** /ʀesɑ̃, ɑ̃t/ *adj* [*incident, discovery*] recent; [*house*] new.

récépissé /ʀesepise/ *nm* receipt.

réceptacle /ʀesɛptakl/ *nm* container; **~ à verre** bottle bank.

récepteur /ʀesɛptœʀ/ *nm* (of television, radio) receiver.

réceptif, **-ive** /ʀesɛptif, iv/ *adj* receptive.

réception /ʀesɛpsjɔ̃/ *nf* **1** reception; **2** welcome; **3 s'occuper de la ~ des marchandises** to take delivery of the goods.

réceptionner /ʀesɛpsjɔne/ [1] *vtr* **1** to take delivery of [*goods*]; **2** to catch [*ball*].

réceptionniste /ʀesɛpsjɔnist/ *nmf* receptionist.

récession /ʀesesjɔ̃/ *nf* recession.

recette /ʀ(ə)sɛt/ *nf* **1 ~ (de cuisine)** recipe; **2** formula, recipe; **3** takings; **faire ~** to bring in money; (figurative) to be a success; **les ~s et (les) dépenses** receipts and expenses.

receveur, **-euse** /ʀəs(ə)vœʀ, øz/ *nm,f* (on bus) conductor.
■ **~ des contributions** tax collector; **~ des postes** postmaster.

recevoir /ʀəsvwaʀ, ʀ(ə)səvwaʀ/ [5] **I** *vtr* **1** to receive, to get; **il a reçu une tuile sur la tête** he got hit on the head by a tile; **je n'ai d'ordre à ~ de personne** I don't take orders from anyone; **la mesure a reçu un accueil favorable** the measure met with approval; **2** to welcome, to receive [*guests*]; **être bien reçu** to be well received; to get a good reception; **ils reçoivent beaucoup** they do a lot of entertaining; **Laval reçoit Caen** (Sport) Laval is playing host to Caen; **il va se faire ~**○ he's going to get it○; **3** to see [*patients*]; **4** to receive [*radio signal*]; **5** (Sch) to pass [*candidate*]; **être reçu à un examen** to pass an exam; **être reçu premier** to come first.
II se recevoir *v refl* (+ *v être*) (after jump, fall) to land.

rechange: **de rechange** /dəʀ(ə)ʃɑ̃ʒ/ *phr* [*part*] spare; [*solution*] alternative.

réchapper: **réchapper de** /ʀeʃape/ [1] *v+prep* to come through [*illness, accident*].

recharge /ʀ(ə)ʃaʀʒ/ *nf* refill; reload.

recharger /ʀ(ə)ʃaʀʒe/ [13] *vtr* to reload; to refill; to recharge [*battery*].

réchaud /ʀeʃo/ *nm* stove; **~ électrique** electric ring (GB), hotplate.

réchauffé, **~e** /ʀeʃofe/ **I** *pp* ▶ **réchauffer**.
II *pp adj* [*joke, story*] hackneyed.
III *nm* **ça sent le ~, c'est du ~** there's nothing new about it.

réchauffement /ʀeʃofmɑ̃/ *nm* warming (up).

réchauffer /ʀeʃofe/ [1] **I** *vtr* **1** (Culin) to reheat, to heat [sth] up; **2** to warm up [*person, hands, room*]; **3 ses plaisanteries ont réchauffé l'atmosphère** his/her jokes relaxed or lightened the atmosphere.
II se réchauffer *v refl* (+ *v être*) [*weather*] to warm up.

rêche /ʀɛʃ/ *adj* [*hands, fabric*] rough.

recherche /ʀ(ə)ʃɛʀʃ/ *nf* **1** research; **faire des ~s en biologie** to do research in biology; **2** search; **être à la ~ de** to be looking for, to be in search of; **3 ~ de** pursuit of [*happiness*]; **4 avec ~** with meticulous care; **sans ~** without affectation.
■ **~ d'emploi** job-hunting.

recherché, **~e** /ʀ(ə)ʃɛʀʃe/ **I** *pp* ▶ **rechercher**.
II *pp adj* **1** sought-after; **2** in demand; **3** [*dress*] meticulous; [*style, expression*] original, inventive; **4** [*aim, effect*] intended.

rechercher /ʀ(ə)ʃɛʀʃe/ [1] *vtr* **1** to look for; **~ les causes d'un accident** to look into the causes of an accident; **il est recherché par la police** he's wanted by the police; **'recherchons vendeuse qualifiée'** 'qualified sales assistant (GB) or clerk (US) required'; **2** to seek [*security, allies*]; to fish for [*compliments*].

rechigner /ʀ(ə)ʃiɲe/ [1] **I** *v+prep* **~ à faire** to balk at doing.
II *vi* to grumble; **sans ~** without grumbling or a murmur.

rechute /ʀəʃyt/ *nf* relapse.

récidive /ʀesidiv/ *nf* **1** (Law) second offence[GB]; **2** (figurative) repetition; **3** (Med) recurrence.

récidiver /ʀesidive/ [1] *vi* (Law) to commit subsequent offences[GB].

récidiviste /ʀesidivist/ *nmf* (Law) habitual offender, recidivist.

récif /ʀesif/ *nm* reef.

récipient /ʀesipjɑ̃/ *nm* container.

réciprocité /ʀesipʀɔsite/ *nf* reciprocity; **à titre de ~** in return.

réciproque /ʀesipʀɔk/ **I** *adj* reciprocal, mutual.
II *nf* reverse; **la ~ est vraie** the reverse is true.

récit /ʀesi/ *nm* **1** story; **2** narrative; **3** (in theatre) narrative monologue[GB].

récital /ʀesital/ *nm* recital.

récitation /ʀesitasjɔ̃/ *nf* **apprendre une ~** to learn a text (off) by heart.

réciter /ʀesite/ [1] *vtr* **1** to recite; **2** to trot out○ [*reasons, facts*].

réclamation /ʀeklamasjɔ̃/ *nf* **1** complaint; **2** claim; **sur ~** on request.

réclame /ʀeklam/ *nf* **1** publicity; **2** advertisement; **3 'en ~'** 'on offer' (GB), 'on sale'.

réclamer /ʀeklame/ [1] **I** *vtr* to ask for [*person, thing, money*]; to call for [*reform, inquiry*]; to claim [*compensation*]; to demand [*justice*]; **travail qui réclame de l'attention** work that requires attention.
II se réclamer *v refl* (+ *v être*) **se ~ de** [*party*] to be an expression of [*democracy*]; [*person, group*] to claim to be representative of.

reclasser /ʀəklase/ [1] **I** *vtr* **1** to reclassify [*documents*]; **2** to redeploy.
II se reclasser *v refl* (+ *v être*) to find new employment.

reclus, **~e** /ʀəkly, yz/ *adj* reclusive; **vivre ~** to live as a recluse.

réclusion /ʀeklyzjɔ̃/ *nf* **1** (Law) imprisonment; **2** reclusion.

recoin /ʀəkwɛ̃/ *nm* corner; (figurative) recess.

récolte /ʀekɔlt/ *nf* **1** harvest; **2** crop, harvest.

récolter /ʀekɔlte/ [1] *vtr* **1** to harvest [*corn*]; to dig up [*potatoes*]; **2** [*bee*] to collect [*pollen*]; [*person*] to win [*votes, points*]; to collect [*money, information*]; to reap [*advantage*]; **à les aider, je n'ai récolté que des ennuis**○ I got nothing but trouble in return for helping them.

recommandation /ʀəkɔmɑ̃dasjɔ̃/ *nf* recommendation.

recommandé, **~e** /ʀəkɔmɑ̃de/ **I** *pp* ▶ **recommander**.
II *pp adj* [*letter*] registered; **en ~** by registered post (GB) or mail.

recommander /ʀəkɔmɑ̃de/ [1] **I** *vtr* **1** to advise; **2** to recommend.
II se recommander *v refl* (+ *v être*) **se ~ de qn** to give sb's name as a reference.

recommencement /ʀəkɔmɑ̃smɑ̃/ *nm*

l'histoire est un éternel ~ history is constantly repeating itself.

recommencer /Rəkɔmɑ̃se/ [12] *vtr* **1** to start [sth] again; **2** (gen) to do [sth] again; to repeat [*experience*].

récompense /Rekɔ̃pɑ̃s/ *nf* **1** reward; **2** award; **en ~** as a reward (**de** for).

récompenser /Rekɔ̃pɑ̃se/ [1] *vtr* to reward (**de** for; **par** with).

réconciliation /Rekɔ̃siljasjɔ̃/ *nf* reconciliation.

réconcilier /Rekɔ̃silje/ [2] **I** *vtr* **~ Pierre avec Paul** to bring Pierre and Paul back together; **~ morale et politique** to reconcile morality with politics.

II se réconcilier *v refl* (+ *v être*) [*friends*] to make up; [*nations*] to be reconciled; **se ~ avec soi-même** to learn to live with oneself.

reconduction /R(ə)kɔ̃dyksjɔ̃/ *nf* renewal.

reconduire /R(ə)kɔ̃dɥiR/ [69] *vtr* **1** to see [sb] out; **~ qn chez lui** to take sb home; **2** to extend [*strike, ceasefire*]; to renew [*mandate*]; **~ qn dans ses fonctions** to re-elect sb.

réconfort /Rekɔ̃fɔR/ *nm* comfort.

réconfortant, ~e /Rekɔ̃fɔRtɑ̃, ɑ̃t/ *adj* **1** comforting; **2** cheering; **3** fortifying.

réconforter /Rekɔ̃fɔRte/ [1] **I** *vtr* **1** to comfort; to console; **2 ~ qn** to cheer sb up; **3** to fortify.

II se réconforter *v refl* (+ *v être*) to restore one's strength.

reconnaissable /R(ə)kɔnɛsabl/ *adj* recognizable.

reconnaissance /R(ə)kɔnɛsɑ̃s/ *nf* **1** gratitude; **en ~ de** in appreciation of; **2** recognition; **3** (of wrongs) admission, admitting; (of qualities) recognition, recognizing; **4** (Mil) reconnaissance.

reconnaissant, ~e /R(ə)kɔnɛsɑ̃, ɑ̃t/ *adj* grateful.

reconnaître /R(ə)kɔnɛtR/ [73] **I** *vtr* **1** to recognize; **2** to identify; **je reconnais bien là leur générosité** it's just like them to be so generous; **3** to admit [*facts, errors*]; **il faut ~ que** you have to admit that; **~ qn coupable** to find sb guilty; **4** to recognize [*trade union, regime, qualification*]; **~ un enfant** to recognize a child legally; **5** to acknowledge.

II se reconnaître *v refl* (+ *v être*) **1 se ~ à qch** to be recognizable by sth; **2** to know where one is.

reconnu, ~e /R(ə)kɔny/ **I** *pp* ▶ **reconnaître.**

II *pp adj* [*fact*] recognized; **être ~ fiable** to be known to be reliable.

reconquérir /R(ə)kɔ̃keRiR/ [35] *vtr* to reconquer, to recover [*territory*]; (figurative) to regain [*dignity, esteem*]; to win back [*person, right*].

reconstituer /R(ə)kɔ̃stitɥe/ [1] *vtr* to re-form [*association*]; to reconstruct [*crime*]; to recreate [*era, decor*]; to piece [sth] together again [*broken object*]; to build up again [*reserves, forces*].

reconstruire /R(ə)kɔ̃stRɥiR/ [69] *vtr* **1** to reconstruct; **2** to rebuild.

reconversion /R(ə)kɔ̃vɛRsjɔ̃/ *nf* (of worker) redeployment; (of region) redevelopment; (of economy) restructuring; (of factory) conversion.

reconvertir /R(ə)kɔ̃vɛRtiR/ [3] **I** *vtr* to redeploy [*staff*]; to convert [*factory, building*]; to adapt [*equipment*].

II se reconvertir *v refl* (+ *v être*) [*staff*] to switch to a new type of employment; [*company*] to switch to a new type of production.

recopier /R(ə)kɔpje/ [2] *vtr* **1** to copy out; **2** to write up [*notes*].

record /R(ə)kɔR/ **I** *adj inv* record; **en un temps ~** in record time.

II *nm* (Sport), (figurative) record.

recordman, *pl* **-men** /Rəkɔ̃Rdman, mɛn/ *nm* (men's) record-holder.

recordwoman, *pl* **-men** /RəkɔRdwuman, mɛn/ *nf* (women's) record-holder.

recoudre /R(ə)kudR/ [76] *vtr* **1** to sew [sth] back on [*button*]; **2** (Med) to stitch up [*wound*].

recoupement /R(ə)kupmɑ̃/ *nm* cross-check, cross-checking.

recouper /R(ə)kupe/ [1] **I** *vtr* to cut [sth] again [*hair, hedge*]; to recut [*garment*].

II se recouper *v refl* (+ *v être*) **1** [*versions*] to tally; [*results*] to add up; **2** [*lines*] to intersect.

recourbé, ~e /R(ə)kuRbe/ *adj* (gen) curved; [*nose, beak*] hooked.

recourir: **recourir à** /R(ə)kuRiR/ [26] *v+prep* to use [*remedy*]; to resort to [*strategy*]; to turn to [*friend*].

recours /R(ə)kuR/ *nm inv* **1** recourse; resort; **sans autre ~ que** with no other way out but; **avoir ~ à** to have recourse to [*remedy*]; to resort to [*strategy*]; to turn to [*friend*]; to go to [*expert*]; **en dernier ~** as a last resort; **2** (Law) appeal; **~ en grâce** petition for reprieve.

recouvrement /R(ə)kuvRəmɑ̃/ *nm* **1** collection; **2** recovery.

recouvrer /R(ə)kuvRe/ [1] *vtr* to recover; to collect [*tax*].

recouvrir /R(ə)kuvRiR/ [32] **I** *vtr* **1** to cover; **2** to re-cover; **3** to hide, to conceal.

II se recouvrir *v refl* (+ *v être*) to put one's hat back on.

recracher /R(ə)kRaʃe/ [1] *vtr* to spit out.

récréatif, -ive /RekReatif, iv/ *adj* recreational.

récréation /RekReasjɔ̃/ *nf* **1** playtime (GB), break (GB), recess (US); **2** recreation.

recréer /R(ə)kRee/ [11] *vtr* to recreate.

récrier: **se récrier** /RekRije/ [2] *v refl* (+ *v être*) to exclaim.

récrimination /RekRiminasjɔ̃/ *nf* recrimination.

récriminer /RekRimine/ [1] *vi* to rail (**contre qn/qch** against sb/sth).

recroqueviller: **se recroqueviller** /R(ə)kRɔkvije/ [1] *v refl* (+ *v être*) **1** [*person*] to huddle up; **2** [*leaf, petal*] to shrivel up.

recru, ~e[1] /RəkRy/ *adj* **~ (de fatigue)** exhausted.

recrudescence /R(ə)kRydesɑ̃s/ *nf* (of violence, interest) fresh upsurge; (of bombing, strikes, demands) new wave; (of fire, fighting) renewed outbreak.

recrue[2] /Rəkry/ I *adj f* ▶ **recru**.
II *nf* recruit.

recrutement /R(ə)kRytmɑ̃/ *nm* recruitment.

recruter /R(ə)kRyte/ [1] *vtr* to recruit.

rectal, **~e**, *mpl* **-aux** /Rɛktal, o/ *adj* rectal.

rectangle /Rɛktɑ̃gl/ *nm* rectangle.

rectangulaire /Rɛktɑ̃gylɛR/ *adj* rectangular, oblong.

recteur /RɛktœR/ *nm* (Sch) ≈ chief education officer (GB), ≈ superintendent (of schools) (US).

rectificatif, **-ive** /Rɛktifikatif, iv/ *nm* **1** (in newspaper) correction; **2** (to law) amendment.

rectification /Rɛktifikasjɔ̃/ *nf* correction; rectification; adjustment.

rectifier /Rɛktifje/ [2] *vtr* **1** to correct, to rectify [*error*]; **2** to adjust [*position, figures*]; to rectify [*contract*]; to amend [*document*].

rectiligne /Rɛktiliɲ/ *adj* straight.

rectitude /Rɛktityd/ *nf* rectitude.

recto /Rɛkto/ *nm* front; **~ verso** on both sides.

rectorat /RɛktɔRa/ *nm* ≈ local education authority (GB), ≈ board of education (US).

rectum /Rɛktɔm/ *nm* rectum.

reçu, **~e** /R(ə)sy/ I *pp* ▶ **recevoir**.
II *pp adj* **1** [*candidate*] successful; **2** [*use*] accepted.
III *nm* receipt.

recueil /R(ə)kœj/ *nm* collection; anthology; compendium.

recueillement /Rəkœjmɑ̃/ *nm* **1** contemplation; **2** reverence.

recueilli, **~e** /Rəkœji/ I *pp* ▶ **recueillir**.
II *pp adj* [*air*] rapt; [*person*] rapt in prayer; [*crowd, silence*] reverential.

recueillir /RəkœjiR/ [27] I *vtr* **1** to collect [*donations, signatures, anecdotes*]; to gather, to collect [*evidence, testimonies*]; **2** to get [*votes, news*]; to gain [*consensus*]; to achieve [*unanimity*]; to win [*praise*]; **3** to collect [*water, resin*]; to gather [*honey*]; **4** to take in [*orphan*]; **5** to record [*impressions, opinions*].
II **se recueillir** *v refl* (+ *v être*) to engage in private prayer.

recul /R(ə)kyl/ *nm* **1** detachment; **avec le ~** with hindsight, in retrospect; **manquer de ~** to be incapable of being objective; **prendre du ~** to stand back; **2** (in production) drop, fall; (of doctrine) decline; **3** (of army) pulling or drawing back; (of tide, floodwaters) recession; **avoir un mouvement de ~** to recoil; **feu de ~** reversing light.

reculé, **~e** /Rəkyle/ *adj* remote.

reculer /R(ə)kyle/ [1] I *vtr* **1** to move back [*object*]; **2** (in car) to reverse (GB), to back up; **3** to put off [*event, decision*]; to put back [*date*].
II *vi* **1** [*person*] to move back; to stand back; [*driver, car*] to reverse; **2** [*army*] to pull or draw back; **3** [*forest*] to be gradually disappearing; [*river*] to go down; [*sea*] to recede; **4** [*currency, exports*] to fall; [*doctrine*] to decline; [*politician*] to suffer a drop in popularity; **faire ~ le chômage** to reduce unemployment; **~ de cinq places** [*pupil, athlete*] to fall back five places; **5** to back down; **cela m'a fait ~** it put me off; **~ devant une difficulté** to shrink from a difficulty; **ne ~ devant rien** to stop at nothing.
III **se reculer** *v refl* (+ *v être*) (gen) to move back; to stand back.

reculons: **à reculons** /aR(ə)kylɔ̃/ *phr* **aller à ~** to go backward(s).

récupération /RekypeRasjɔ̃/ *nf* **1** salvage; recycling; **matériaux de ~** salvaged materials; **2** recovery; **3** making up; **4** appropriation.

récupérer /RekypeRe/ [14] I *vtr* **1** to get back, to recover [*money, strength*]; **2** to retrieve; **3** to salvage [*scrap iron*]; to reclaim, to recycle [*rags*]; **4** to save [*boxes*]; **5** to make up [*days*]; **6** to appropriate [*ideas*].
II *vi* to recover.

récurer /RekyRe/ [1] *vtr* to scour [*saucepan*]; to scrub [*sink*].

récurrent, **~e** /RekyRɑ̃, ɑ̃t/ *adj* (gen, Anat, Med) recurrent.

récuser /Rekyze/ [1] I *vtr* to challenge, to object to [*jury, witness*].
II **se récuser** *v refl* (+ *v être*) [*judge*] to decline to act in a case.

recyclage /R(ə)siklaʒ/ *nm* **1** (of material) recycling; **2** (of staff) retraining.

recycler /R(ə)sikle/ [1] I *vtr* **1** to recycle [*material*]; **2 ~ le personnel** to retrain the staff; **3** to recycle [*capital*]; to reinvest [*profits*].
II **se recycler** *v refl* (+ *v être*) **1** to retrain; **2** to change jobs.

rédacteur, **-trice** /RedaktœR, tRis/ *nm,f* **1** author, writer; **2** editor.

rédaction /Redaksjɔ̃/ *nf* **1** writing; **2** editing; **3** editorial offices; **4** editorial staff; **5** (Sch) essay (GB), theme (US).

rédactionnel, **-elle** /Redaksjɔnɛl/ *adj* editorial.

reddition /Rɛdisjɔ̃/ *nf* surrender.

rédemption /Redɑ̃psjɔ̃/ *nf* redemption.

redescendre /Rədɛsɑ̃dR/ [6] I *vtr* (gen) to take [sb/sth] back down; [*person*] to go/come back down [*stairs*].
II *vi* (+ *v être*) (gen) to go (back) down; to go down again; **~ dans les sondages** to drop or to move down in the opinion polls.

redevable /Rədvabl, R(ə)dəvabl/ *adj* **être ~ de qch à qn** to owe sth to sb, to be indebted to sb for sth; **être ~ de l'impôt** to be liable for tax.

redevance /Rədvɑ̃s, R(ə)dəvɑ̃s/ *nf* **1** (gen) charge; (for television) licence (GB) or license (US) fee; (for telephone) rental charge; **2** royalty.

rédhibitoire /RedibitwaR/ *adj* [*cost*] prohibitive; [*obstacle*] insurmountable.

rediffuser /R(ə)difyze/ [1] *vtr* to repeat (GB), to rerun [*programme*].

rédiger /Rediʒe/ [13] *vtr* to write [*article*]; to write up [*notes*]; to draft [*contract*].

redingote /R(ə)dɛ̃gɔt/ *nf* (for man) frock coat; (for woman) fitted coat.

redire /RədiR/ [65] *vtr* to repeat; **~ qch à qn** to

tell sb sth again; **trouver quelque chose à ~ à qch** to find fault with sth.

redite /R(ə)dit/ *nf* (needless) repetition.

redondance /R(ə)dɔ̃dɑ̃s/ *nf* **1** redundancy; **2** superfluous term.

redondant, ~e /R(ə)dɔ̃dɑ̃, ɑ̃t/ *adj* **1** superfluous; **2** redundant.

redonner /R(ə)dɔne/ [1] *vtr* **1 ~ qch à qn** to give sb sth again; **2 ~ courage à qn** to restore sb's courage.

redorer /R(ə)dɔRe/ [1] *vtr* to regild; **~ son blason** [*person*] to restore one's image.

redoublant, ~e /R(ə)dublɑ̃, ɑ̃t/ *nm,f* student repeating a year.

redoublé, ~e /R(ə)duble/ *adj* **frapper qch/qn à coups ~s** to hit sth/sb very hard.

redoublement /R(ə)dubləmɑ̃/ *nm* intensification.

redoubler /R(ə)duble/ [1] **I** *vtr* (Sch) **~ une classe** to repeat a year.
II redoubler de *v+prep* **~ de prudence** to be twice as careful; **~ d'efforts** to redouble one's efforts; **la tempête a redoublé de violence** the storm has become even fiercer.
III *vi* **1** to repeat a year; **2** to intensify.

redoutable /R(ə)dutabl/ *adj* [*weapon, exam*] formidable; [*disease*] dreadful.

redouter /R(ə)dute/ [1] *vtr* **1** to fear [*enemy, death*]; **2** to dread [*future*].

redressement /RədRɛsmɑ̃/ *nm* **1** recovery; **2** re-establishment; **3 maison de ~** reformatory.

redresser /R(ə)dRese/ [1] **I** *vtr* **1** to straighten up [*fence*]; to put [sth] up again [*pole*]; to straighten [sth] out [*bumper*]; to straighten [*tooth*]; **~ la tête** to lift one's head up; **2** to put [sth] back on its feet [*economy*]; to turn [sth] round (GB) or around [*company*]; **3** to aid the recovery of [*currency*]; to improve [*profit margin*]; **4** to straighten up [*glider, steering wheel*]; **~ la barre** to right the helm; (figurative) to put things back on an even keel; **5** to rectify [*error*].
II se redresser *v refl* (+ *v être*) **1** to stand up; to sit up; to stand up straight; to sit up straight; **2** [*economy, plant*] to pick up again, to recover; [*country, company*] to get back on its feet.

redresseur /RədRɛsœR/ *nm* **~ de torts** righter of wrongs.

réduction /Redyksjɔ̃/ *nf* **1** discount, reduction; concession; **~ de 5%** 5% reduction; **~ étudiants** concession for students; **2** cutting, reducing; **~ d'impôts** cutting taxes; **3** reduction, cut; **~s d'effectifs** staff cuts; **4** (of statue, painting) small replica; **5** (of compound, sauce) reduction.

réduire /RedɥiR/ [68] **I** *vtr* **1** to reduce; to cut [*tax*]; to cut down on [*staff, spending*]; **~ l'écart entre** to narrow the gap between; **2** to reduce [*photograph*]; to scale down [*drawing*]; to cut [*text*]; **3 ~ qch en poudre** to crush sth to powder; **être réduit en cendres** [*city*] to be reduced to ashes; [*dreams*] to turn to ashes; **4 ~ à** to reduce to; **voilà à quoi j'en suis réduit!** this is what I've been reduced to!; **5** to subdue [*enemy*]; to silence [*opposition*]; **6** to reduce [*sauce*]; **7** to reduce [*fraction*].
II *vi* [*sauce*] to reduce; [*mushrooms, spinach*] to shrink.
III se réduire *v refl* (+ *v être*) **1** [*costs*] to be reduced; [*imports*] to be cut; **l'écart se réduit** the gap is narrowing; **2 cela se réduit à bien peu de chose** it doesn't amount to very much.

réduit, ~e /Redɥi, it/ **I** *pp* ▶ **réduire**.
II *pp adj* **1** [*rate, speed*] reduced, lower; [*time*] shorter; [*activity*] reduced; [*group*] smaller; **à prix ~** at a reduced price; **visibilité ~e** restricted visibility; **2** [*means, choice*] limited; [*group*] small; **3** [*size*] small; **de taille ~e** small.
III *nm* cubbyhole.

rééditer /Reedite/ [1] *vtr* **1** to reprint [*book*]; **2**○ to repeat [*action, exploit*].

rééducation /Reedykasjɔ̃/ *nf* **1** physiotherapy; **~ de la parole** speech therapy; **2** rehabilitation.

rééduquer /Reedyke/ [1] *vtr* to restore normal functioning to [*limb*]; to rehabilitate.

réel, réelle /Reɛl/ **I** *adj* (gen) real; [*fact*] true.
II *nm* **le ~** the real.

réellement /Reɛlmɑ̃/ *adv* really.

rééquilibrer /ReekilibRe/ [1] *vtr* **1** (Tech) to readjust [*load*]; **2** (Aut) to balance [*wheels*]; **3** to balance [*budget*].

réévaluer /Reevalɥe/ [1] *vtr* **1** to revalue [*currency*]; to revise [*salary, tax*]; **2** to reappraise.

réexpédier /Reɛkspedje/ [2] *vtr* **1** to forward, to redirect; **2** to send [sth] back.

réf (*written abbr* = **référence**) ref.

refaire /RəfɛR/ [10] **I** *vtr* **1** to do [sth] again, to redo [*exercise*]; to make [sth] again [*journey, mistake*]; **~ le même chemin** to go back the same way; **~ un numéro de téléphone** to redial a number; **si c'était à ~** if I had to do it all over again; **2 je vais ~ de la soupe** I'll make some more soup; **3 vouloir ~ le monde** to want to change the world; **se faire ~ le nez** to have one's nose re-modelled[GB]; **~ sa vie (avec quelqu'un d'autre)** to start all over again (with somebody else); **4** to redo [*roof*]; to redecorate [*room*]; to resurface [*road*].
II se refaire *v refl* (+ *v être*) **1 se ~ une santé** to recuperate; **se ~ une beauté** to redo one's make-up; **2 se ~ à** to get used to [sth] again; **3 on ne se refait pas** a person can't change.

réfection /Refɛksjɔ̃/ *nf* repairing.

réfectoire /RefɛktwaR/ *nm* refectory; (Mil) mess.

référence /ReféRɑ̃s/ **I** *nf* **1** reference; **livre de ~** reference book; **en** or **par ~ à** in reference to; **faire ~ à** to refer to; **lui? ce n'est pas une ~!** who, him? well, he's not much of an example!; **2** reference number.
II références *nf pl* references.

référendum /RefeRɛ̃dɔm/ *nm* referendum.

référentiel, -ielle /RefeRɑ̃sjɛl/ *adj* referential.

référer /ʀefeʀe/ [14] **I référer à** *v+prep* **en ~ à** to consult.
II se référer *v refl* (+ *v être*) **se ~ à 1** to refer to; **2** to consult.

refermer /ʀ(ə)fɛʀme/ [1] **I** *vtr* **1** to close; **2** to close [sth] again.
II se refermer *v refl* (+ *v être*) [*door*] to close; [*wound*] to close up.

réfléchi, **~e** /ʀefleʃi/ *adj* **1** [*person*] reflective, thoughtful; [*look*] thoughtful; **2** [*decision*] considered; [*action*] well-considered; **tout bien ~** all things considered; **c'est tout ~** my mind is made up; **3** [*image*] reflected; **4** [*verb*] reflexive.

réfléchir /ʀefleʃiʀ/ [3] **I** *vtr* to reflect [*heat*].
II réfléchir à *v+prep* to think about.
III *vi* to think; **ça fait ~** it makes you think; **si on réfléchit** or **en réfléchissant, on voit bien** if you (stop and) think about it, you realize; **mais réfléchis donc un peu!** use your brain!
IV se réfléchir *v refl* (+ *v être*) [*image*] to be reflected.

réfléchissant, **~e** /ʀefleʃisɑ̃, ɑ̃t/ *adj* reflective.

réflecteur, **-trice** /ʀeflɛktœʀ, tʀis/ **I** *adj* reflecting.
II *nm* reflector.

reflet /ʀ(ə)flɛ/ *nm* **1** reflection; **être le ~ d'une époque** to reflect a period; **2** glint; shimmer; sheen; **cheveux châtains aux ~s roux** brown hair with auburn highlights.

refléter /ʀ(ə)flete/ [14] **I** *vtr* to reflect; **son visage reflétait son émotion** his/her emotion showed in his/her face.
II se refléter *v refl* (+ *v être*) to be reflected.

réflexe /ʀeflɛks/ **I** *adj* reflex.
II *nm* **1** reflex; **2** reaction; **manquer de ~** to be slow to react; **par ~** automatically.
■ **~ conditionné** conditioned reflex.

réflexion /ʀeflɛksjɔ̃/ *nf* **1** thought, reflection; **2** thinking, reflection; **~ faite** or **à la ~, je n'irai pas** on reflection or on second thoughts, I won't go; **à la ~, on s'aperçoit que...** when you really think about it, you realize that...; **donner matière à ~** to be food for thought; **3** remark, comment; **s'attirer des ~s** to attract criticism; **4** study; **document de ~** discussion paper; **5** (of image) reflection.

refluer /ʀ(ə)flɥe/ [1] *vi* [*liquid*] to flow back; [*crowd*] to surge back.

reflux /ʀ(ə)fly/ *nm inv* **1** ebb tide; **2** (of crowd) surging away.

refonte /ʀ(ə)fɔ̃t/ *nf* **1** overhaul; **2** (of contract) rewriting.

reforestation /ʀ(ə)fɔʀɛstasjɔ̃/ *nf* reafforestation.

réformateur, **-trice** /ʀefɔʀmatœʀ, tʀis/ **I** *adj* [*party*] reforming.
II *nm,f* reformer.

réforme /ʀefɔʀm/ *nf* **1** reform; **2** (Mil) discharge; **3 la Réforme** the Reformation.

réformé, **~e** /ʀefɔʀme/ **I** *adj* **1** Reformed; **2** (Mil) [*conscript*] unfit for service; [*soldier*] discharged.
II *nm,f* Calvinist.

reformer /ʀ(ə)fɔʀme/ [1] *vtr* to re-form.

réformer /ʀefɔʀme/ [1] *vtr* **1** to reform; **2** (Mil) to declare [sb] unfit for service [*conscript*]; to discharge [*soldier*].

réformiste /ʀefɔʀmist/ *adj, nmf* reformist.

refoulé, **~e** /ʀ(ə)fule/ *nm,f* repressed or inhibited person.

refoulement /ʀ(ə)fulmɑ̃/ *nm* **1** (of impulse) repression; **2** pushing back; turning back; driving back; forcing back.

refouler /ʀ(ə)fule/ [1] *vtr* **1** to suppress [*memory*]; to repress [*tendency*]; to hold back [*tears*]; to stifle [*sobs*]; **2** to force [sth] back [*liquid*]; to push back [*enemy*]; to turn back [*immigrant*]; to drive back [*crowd*].

réfractaire /ʀefʀaktɛʀ/ *adj* **1 ~ à** resistant to [*influence*]; impervious to [*music*]; **2** refractory.

réfracter /ʀefʀakte/ [1] *vtr* to refract.

réfraction /ʀefʀaksjɔ̃/ *nf* refraction.

refrain /ʀ(ə)fʀɛ̃/ *nm* **1** chorus; **2** (old) refrain.

refréner /ʀ(ə)fʀene/, **réfréner** /ʀefʀene/ [14] *vtr* to curb.

réfrigérant, **~e** /ʀefʀiʒeʀɑ̃, ɑ̃t/ *adj* **1** cooling; **2** (figurative) [*welcome*] frosty.

réfrigérateur /ʀefʀiʒeʀatœʀ/ *nm* refrigerator.

réfrigérer /ʀefʀiʒeʀe/ [14] *vtr* to refrigerate [*food*]; to cool [*place*].

refroidir /ʀəfʀwadiʀ/ [3] **I** *vtr* **1** to cool down; to cool; **2** to dampen [*ardour*]; **~ qn** to dampen sb's spirits
II *vi* **1** to cool down; **2** to get cold.
III se refroidir *v refl* (+ *v être*) [*weather*] to get colder; [*muscle, joint*] to stiffen up; [*person*] to get cold.

refroidissement /ʀəfʀwadismɑ̃/ *nm* **1** drop in temperature; **2** cooling; **liquide de ~** coolant; **3** (Med) chill.

refuge /ʀ(ə)fyʒ/ **I** *nm* **1** refuge; **2** (mountain) refuge; **3** (for animals) sanctuary; **4** traffic island.
II (-)refuge (*combining form*) **investissement ~** safe investment.

réfugié, **~e** /ʀefyʒje/ *nm,f* refugee.

réfugier: **se réfugier** /ʀefyʒje/ [2] *v refl* (+ *v être*) to take refuge.

refus /ʀ(ə)fy/ *nm inv* refusal; **ce n'est pas de ~**○ I wouldn't say no○.
■ **~ d'obtempérer** refusal to comply; **~ de priorité** failure to give way.

refuser /ʀ(ə)fyze/ [1] **I** *vtr* **1** (gen) to refuse; to turn down [*offer*]; **~ de faire** to refuse to do; **il a refusé qu'on vende la maison** he wouldn't allow the house to be sold; **je lui refuse le droit de me juger** he/she has no right to judge me; **2** to reject [*budget, manuscript, racism*]; to refuse to accept [*fact*]; to turn away [*spectator*]; **être refusé à un concours** to fail an examination.
II se refuser *v refl* (+ *v être*) **1 ça ne se refuse pas** it's too good to pass up○ or miss; I wouldn't say no○; **2** to deny oneself [*pleasure*]; **on ne se refuse rien**○**!** you're certainly not

stinting yourself!; **3 se ~ à** to refuse to accept [*evidence*]; to refuse to adopt [*solution*]; **se ~ à faire** to refuse to do.

réfuter /ʀefyte/ [1] *vtr* to refute.

regagner /ʀ(ə)gaɲe/ [1] *vtr* **1** to get back to [*place*]; **2** to regain, to win back [*esteem*]; to pick up [*point*].

regain /ʀ(ə)gɛ̃/ *nm* **~ de** rise in [*inflation*]; revival of [*interest*]; resurgence or renewal of [*violence*]; **connaître un ~ de popularité** to enjoy renewed popularity.

régal /ʀegal/ *nm* **1** culinary delight; **c'est un (vrai) ~**! it's (absolutely) delicious!; **2** (figurative) delight; **un ~ pour les yeux** a feast for the eyes.

régaler /ʀegale/ [1] **I** *vtr* to treat [sb] to a delicious meal.

II se régaler *v refl* (+ *v être*) **1 je me régale** it's delicious; **les enfants se sont régalés avec ton dessert** the children really enjoyed your dessert; **2** (figurative) **se ~ avec** to enjoy [sth] thoroughly [*film*]; **se ~ de** to love [*anecdote*].

regard /ʀ(ə)gaʀ/ **I** *nm* **1** look; **porter son ~ sur qch** to look at sth; **détourner le ~** to look away; **elle attire tous les ~s** everyone looks at her; **j'ai croisé son ~** our eyes met; **à l'abri des ~s indiscrets** far from prying eyes; **soustraire qch aux ~s** to conceal sth from view; **2** expression; **son ~ triste** his/her sad expression; **sous le ~ amusé de qn** under the amused eye of sb; **jeter un ~ noir à qn** to give sb a black look; **3** eye; **le ~ de l'anthropologue** the anthropologist's eye; **le ~ des autres** other people's opinion; **porter un ~ nouveau sur qch** to take a fresh look at sth.

II au regard de *phr* (formal) **au ~ de la loi** in the eyes of the law.

III en regard de *phr* (formal) compared with.

IV en regard *phr* **avec une carte en ~** with a map on the opposite page.

regardant, **~e** /ʀəgaʀdɑ̃, ɑ̃t/ *adj* **ne pas être très ~** not to be very particular or fussy; not to care about what things cost.

regarder /ʀ(ə)gaʀde/ [1] **I** *vtr* **1** to look at [*person, scene, landscape*]; **~ qch méchamment/fixement/longuement** to glare/stare/gaze at sth; **~ rapidement** to have a quick look at; to glance through; **~ qn en face** to look sb in the face; **~ la réalité** or **les choses en face** to face facts; **~ qn de haut** to look down one's nose at sb; **regarde-moi ça!** just look at that!; **2** to watch [*film*]; **regarde bien comment je fais** watch what I do carefully; **3** to look at [*watch, map*]; to have a look at, to check [*tyres, oil*]; **~ dans** to look up [*dictionary*]; **~ si** to have a look to see if; **4** to look at [*situation*]; **~ pourquoi/si/qui** to see why/if/who; **5**○ to concern [*person*]; **ça ne vous regarde pas** it's none of your business; **mêle-toi de ce qui te regarde!** mind your own business○!; **6 elle ne regarde que ses intérêts** she thinks only of her own interests.

II regarder à *v+prep* to think about; **~ à la dépense** to watch what one spends; **ne pas ~ à la dépense** to spare no expense; **à y ~ de plus près** on closer examination; **y ~ à deux fois avant d'acheter** to think twice before buying.

III *vi* to look; **~ en l'air/par terre** to look up/down; **regarde où tu mets les pieds** watch where you put your feet.

IV se regarder *v refl* (+ *v être*) **1** to look at oneself; **2** to look at one another.

régate /ʀegat/ *nf* regatta.

régence /ʀeʒɑ̃s/ **I** *adj inv* [*style*] French Regency.

II *nf* **1** regency; **2 la Régence** the Regency.

régénérer /ʀeʒeneʀe/ [14] **I** *vtr* **1** to regenerate; **2** to reactivate.

II se régénérer *v refl* (+ *v être*) **1** [*cells*] to regenerate; **2** (figurative) to regain one's strength.

régent, **~e** /ʀeʒɑ̃, ɑ̃t/ *nm,f* regent.

régenter /ʀeʒɑ̃te/ [1] *vtr* **1** to rule, to regiment; **2** to regulate.

régie /ʀeʒi/ *nf* **1** state control; local government control; **2 ~ d'État** state-owned company; **3** stage management; production department; central control room.

régime /ʀeʒim/ *nm* **1** diet; **être au ~** to be on a diet; **2** (Pol) system (of government); government; regime; **3** (in administration) system, regime; **~ pénitentiaire** prison system; **~ de faveur** preferential treatment; **~ de retraite** pension scheme; **4** (Law) **~ matrimonial** marriage settlement; **5** (of engine) (running) speed; **bas/haut ~** low/high revs; **tourner à plein ~** [*engine*] to run at top speed; [*factory*] to work at full capacity; **à ce ~** at this rate; **6** (of bananas) bunch.

régiment /ʀeʒimɑ̃/ *nm* **1** regiment; **2**○ military service.

régimentaire /ʀeʒimɑ̃tɛʀ/ *adj* regimental.

région /ʀeʒjɔ̃/ *nf* region; area; **le vin de la ~** the local wine.

régional, **~e**, *mpl* **-aux** /ʀeʒjɔnal, o/ *adj* regional.

régionalisme /ʀeʒjɔnalism/ *nm* regionalism.

régir /ʀeʒiʀ/ [3] *vtr* to govern.

régisseur /ʀeʒisœʀ/ *nm* **1** (of estate) steward, manager; **2** stage manager.

registre /ʀ(ə)ʒistʀ/ *nm* **1** register; **~ d'état civil** register of births, marriages and deaths; **les ~s de la police** police records; **2** (of novel, speech) style; **3** (of language, voice, instrument) register; **cet acteur a un ~ limité** this actor has a limited range.

réglable /ʀeglabl/ *adj* **1** adjustable; **2** payable.

réglage /ʀeglaʒ/ *nm* (of speed) regulating; (of counter, thermostat) setting; (of engine) tuning; (of pressure, volume, seat) adjustment.

règle /ʀɛgl/ **I** *nf* **1** ruler; **2** rule; **~s de sécurité** safety regulations; **respecter les ~s du jeu** to play by the rules; **dans** or **selon les ~s de l'art** by the rule book; **en ~ générale** as a (general) rule.

II règles *nf pl* period.

III en règle *phr* [*request*] formal; [*papers, accounts*] in order; **subir un interrogatoire en ~** to be given a grilling; **bagarre en ~** punch-up○; **pour passer la frontière, il faut**

être en ~ to cross the frontier, your papers must be in order; **se mettre en ~ avec le fisc** to get one's tax affairs properly sorted out.

réglé, ~e /Regle/ *pp adj* **1** ruled, lined; **2** [*life*] well-ordered; [*procession*] well-organized; **3 l'affaire est ~e** the matter is settled; **4** [*adolescent girl*] who has started having periods.

règlement /Rɛgləmɑ̃/ *nm* **1** regulations, rules; **2** payment; **3** settlement.
■ **~ de comptes** settling of scores; **~ interne** rules and regulations.

réglementaire /Rɛgləmɑ̃tɛR/ *adj* [*uniform*] regulation; [*format*] prescribed; [*procedure*] statutory.

réglementation /Rɛgləmɑ̃tasjɔ̃/ *nf* **1** rules, regulations; **2** regulation, control.

réglementer /Rɛgləmɑ̃te/ [1] *vtr* to regulate, to control.

régler /Regle/ [14] *vtr* **1** to settle [*debt*]; to pay [*bill, supplier*]; to pay for [*purchase, work*]; **avoir des comptes à ~ avec qn** (figurative) to have a score to settle with sb; **~ son compte à qn**○ to sort sb out; **2** to settle [*problem*]; **~ ses affaires** to sort out one's affairs; **3** to settle [*details, terms*]; **4** to adjust [*height*]; to regulate [*speed, mechanism*]; to tune [*engine*]; to set [*pressure*]; **5 ~ sa conduite sur celle de qn** to model one's behaviour[GB] on sb's; **~ sa montre sur** to set one's watch by; **6** to rule (lines on) [*paper*].

réglisse /Reglis/ *nf* liquorice (GB), licorice (US).

régnant, ~e /Reɲɑ̃, ɑ̃t/ *adj* [*dynasty*] reigning; [*ideology*] prevailing.

règne /Rɛɲ/ *nm* **1** reign; rule; **2** (figurative) reign; **3** (in biology) kingdom.

régner /Reɲe/ [14] *vi* **1** [*sovereign*] to reign, to rule; **2** [*boss, personality*] to be in control; **~ en maître sur** to reign supreme over; **3** [*confusion, fear, harmony*] to reign; [*smell, atmosphere*] to prevail; **la confiance règne!** (ironic) there's trust for you!; **faire ~** to give rise to [*insecurity*]; to impose [*order*]; **il faisait ~ la terreur dans l'entreprise** he imposed a reign of terror on the company.

regorger /R(ə)gɔRʒe/ [13] *vi* **~ de** [*shop*] to be packed with; [*region*] to have an abundance of; [*speech*] to be crammed with.

régresser /RegRese/ [1] *vi* **1** [*waters*] to recede; [*unemployment*] to go down; **2** [*industry*] to be in decline; [*programme*] to deteriorate; [*politician*] to lose ground; **3** [*epidemic*] to die out.

régressif, -ive /RegResif, iv/ *adj* regressive.

régression /RegResjɔ̃/ *nf* **1** decline; **2** regression.

regret /RəgRɛ/ *nm* regret; **j'apprends avec ~ que** I'm sorry to hear that; **à ~** with regret; **j'ai le** or **je suis au ~ de vous annoncer** I regret to inform you.

regrettable /RəgRɛtabl/ *adj* regrettable.

regretter /RəgRete/ [1] *vtr* **1** to be sorry about, to regret [*situation, action*]; **~ que qn fasse** to be sorry that sb does; **je regrette de ne pas pouvoir t'aider** I'm sorry I can't help you; **'il n'y a pas de dialogue,' regrette un employé** 'there's no dialogue[GB],' complains one employee; **2** to regret [*decision*]; **~ sa peine** to regret having gone to the trouble; **~ d'avoir fait** to regret doing; **je ne regrette rien** I have no regrets; **3** to miss [*person, place*]; **notre regretté collègue** (formal) our late lamented colleague.

regroupement /R(ə)gRupmɑ̃/ *nm* **1** grouping; pooling; bringing together; grouping together; **2** merger; **3** getting [sb/sth] back together; rallying; rounding up.

regrouper /R(ə)gRupe/ [1] **I** *vtr* **1** to group [sth] together [*objects, words, services*]; to bring [sth] together [*people*]; to pool [*interests*]; **~ deux chapitres en un seul** to merge two chapters into one; **2** to reassemble [*pupils*]; to regroup [*party*]; to round up [*animals*].
II se regrouper *v refl* (+ *v être*) **1** [*companies*] to group together; [*malcontents*] to gather (together); **2** [*people*] to regroup; [*runners*] to bunch together again.

régularisation /RegylaRizasjɔ̃/ *nf* **1** sorting out, regularization; **2** (of watercourse) regulation.

régulariser /RegylaRize/ [1] *vtr* **1** to sort out, to regularize [*position, situation*]; to put [sth] in order [*papers*]; **2** to regulate [*flow*]; to stabilize [*price, market*].

régularité /RegylaRite/ *nf* **1** regularity; **2** (of rhythm, production, progress) steadiness; (of features) regularity; (of writing) neatness; (of surface) evenness; (of quantity) consistency; **3** legality.

régulateur, -trice /RegylatœR, tRis/ *adj* regulating.

régulation /Regylasjɔ̃/ *nf* regulation, control; **~ des naissances** birth control.

régulier, -ière /Regylje, ɛR/ *adj* **1** (gen) regular; [*flow, rise, effort*] steady; [*quality*] consistent; [*thickness*] even; [*writing*] neat; [*life*] (well-) ordered; [*façade*] symmetrical; **vol ~** scheduled flight; **2** [*business*] above board; [*person*] honest; [*papers, ballot*] in order; [*government*] legitimate; **3** [*verb*] regular.

régulièrement /RegyljɛRmɑ̃/ *adv* **1** regularly; **2** steadily; **3** evenly; **4** [*elected*] properly, duly; [*carried out*] in the proper manner; **5** normally.

régurgiter /RegyRʒite/ [1] *vtr* to regurgitate.

réhabiliter /Reabilite/ [1] **I** *vtr* **1** to rehabilitate; **2** to renovate.
II se réhabiliter *v refl* (+ *v être*) to redeem oneself.

rehausser /Rəose/ [1] *vtr* **1** to raise; **2** to enhance [*prestige*]; **3** to set off [*pattern*].

réimprimer /Reɛ̃pRime/ [1] *vtr* to reprint.

rein /Rɛ̃/ (Anat) **I** *nm* kidney; **~ artificiel** kidney machine.
II reins *nm pl* **les ~s** the small of the back; **une serviette autour des ~s** a towel around one's waist; **avoir les ~s solides**○ to be strong.

réincarcérer /Reɛ̃kaRseRe/ [14] *vtr* to reimprison.

réincarner: se réincarner /Reɛ̃kaRne/ [1] *v refl* (+ *v être*) to be reincarnated.

reine /Rɛn/ *nf* **1** queen; **2** (figurative) **la ~ du bal**

the belle of the ball; **être la ~ des imbéciles**○ to be a prize idiot.

reine-claude, *pl* **reines-claudes** /ʀɛnklod/ *nf* greengage.

reine-des-prés /ʀɛndepʀe/ *nf inv* (Bot) meadowsweet.

reinette /ʀɛnɛt/ *nf* rennet apple.

réinscrire: **se réinscrire** /ʀeɛ̃skʀiʀ/ [67] *v refl* (+ *v être*) to re-enrol.

réinsérer /ʀeɛ̃seʀe/ [14] *vtr* **1** to reintegrate; **2** to reinsert.

réinstaller /ʀeɛ̃stale/ [1] **I** *vtr* to put [sth] back; **~ qn dans ses fonctions** to reinstate someone.

II se réinstaller *v refl* (+ *v être*) **se ~ dans un fauteuil** to settle (oneself) back into an armchair; **se ~ en banlieue** to move back to the suburbs.

réintégrer /ʀeɛ̃tegʀe/ [14] *vtr* **1** to return to [*place, group, system*]; **2 ~ qn (dans ses fonctions)** to reinstate sb; **~ qn dans la société** to reintegrate sb into society.

réitérer /ʀeiteʀe/ [14] *vtr* to repeat.

rejaillir /ʀ(ə)ʒajiʀ/ [3] *vi* **1** [*liquid*] to splash back; to spurt back; **2 ~ sur qn** [*success*] to reflect on sb; [*scandal*] to affect sb adversely.

rejet /ʀ(ə)ʒɛ/ *nm* **1** (gen) rejection; (of complaint) dismissal; (of motion) defeat; (of request) denial; **2** (of waste) discharge; disposal; **~s** waste; **les ~s en mer (de déchets)** dumping (of waste) at sea; **3 ~ de souche** stump, shoot.

rejeter /ʀəʒte, ʀʒəte/ [20] **I** *vtr* **1** to reject [*advice, candidacy, outsider*]; to turn down [*offer*]; to dismiss [*complaint*]; to defeat [*motion*]; to deny [*request*]; to set aside [*decision*]; **2 ~ qch sur qn** to shift sth onto sb [*blame*]; **3** [*factory*] to discharge [*waste*]; to eject [*smoke*]; **4** [*person, company*] to dispose of [*waste*]; [*fisherman*] to throw [sth] back [*fish*]; [*sea*] to wash up [*body, debris*]; **5 ~ un mot en fin de phrase** to put a word at the end of the sentence; **6** [*army*] to push or drive back [*enemy*]; **7 ~ [qch] en arrière** to throw [sth] back [*head, hair*].

II se rejeter *v refl* (+ *v être*) **1 se ~ en arrière** to throw or fling oneself back; **2 se ~ les torts** or **la faute** to blame each other.

rejeton /ʀəʒ(ə)tɔ̃, ʀʒətɔ̃/ *nm* **1** offshoot; **2**○ offspring.

rejoindre /ʀ(ə)ʒwɛ̃dʀ/ [56] **I** *vtr* **1** to meet up with; **2** to catch up with; **3** to join; to rejoin; **4** to get to; to get back to, to return to; **5 ~ qn sur qch** to concur with sb on sth; **ça rejoint ce qu'il a dit** it ties up with what he said.

II se rejoindre *v refl* (+ *v être*) **1** [*people*] to meet up; [*roads*] to meet; **2** [*people*] to be in agreement; [*tastes*] to be similar.

rejouer /ʀ(ə)ʒwe/ [1] *vtr* (gen) to play [sth] again; to replay [*match, point*]; **~ une pièce** to perform a play again.

réjoui, **~e** /ʀejwi/ *pp adj* cheerful; **tout ~ à l'idée de** delighted at the thought of.

réjouir /ʀeʒwiʀ/ [3] **I** *vtr* **1** to delight [*person*]; to gladden [*heart*]; **2** to amuse.

II se réjouir *v refl* (+ *v être*) to rejoice; **se ~ de qch** to be delighted at [*news*]; to be delighted with [*success*]; **se ~ à l'idée que** to be delighted at the thought that.

réjouissance /ʀeʒwisɑ̃s/ **I** *nf* rejoicing.

II réjouissances *nf pl* celebrations; **quel est le programme des ~s**○**?** what delights are in store for us?

réjouissant, **~e** /ʀeʒwisɑ̃, ɑ̃t/ *adj* **1** heartening, delightful; **la nouvelle n'a rien de bien ~** it's not exactly cheerful news; **2** amusing.

relâche /ʀ(ə)lɑʃ/ *nf* **1** (of theatre, cinema) closure; **faire ~** to be closed; **2** break, rest; **sans ~** relentlessly; **3** port of call.

relâché, **~e** /ʀ(ə)lɑʃe/ *pp adj* [*discipline*] lax, slack; [*style*] slipshod.

relâchement /ʀ(ə)lɑʃmɑ̃/ *nm* **1** (of discipline, effort) slackening; (of morals) loosening; **il y a du ~ dans le travail** the work is slacking off; **2** (of muscle) slackening.

relâcher /ʀ(ə)lɑʃe/ [1] **I** *vtr* **1** to loosen [*hold*]; **2** to release [*captive*]; to let [sth] go [*fish*]; **3** to relax [*discipline*]; **~ son attention** to let one's attention wander; **~ ses efforts** to let up.

II se relâcher *v refl* (+ *v être*) **1** [*hold, tie*] to loosen; [*muscle*] to relax; **2** [*effort*] to slacken; [*zeal*] to flag; [*pupil*] to grow slack.

relais /ʀ(ə)lɛ/ *nm inv* **1** intermediary; **prendre le ~ (de qn/qch)** to take over (from sb/sth); **passer le ~ à** to hand over to; **2** (Sport) relay; **course de ~** relay race; **3** restaurant; hotel; **4** (Tech) relay; **~ hertzien** radio relay station.

relance /ʀ(ə)lɑ̃s/ *nf* (of industry, idea) revival; (of economy) reflation; (of negotiations) reopening; (in terrorism) upsurge; (in inflation) rise; **mesures de ~** reflationary measures; **entraîner la ~ de** to give a boost to [*business*]; to lead to an upsurge of [*terrorism*].

relancer /ʀ(ə)lɑ̃se/ [12] *vtr* **1** to throw [sth] again [*ball*]; to throw [sth] back (again) [*ball*]; **2** to restart [*engine*]; to relaunch [*company, offensive*]; to revive [*idea, tradition*]; to reopen [*debate*]; to boost [*investment*]; to reflate [*economy*]; **3** [*creditor*] to chase [sb] up; [*person*] to pester.

relater /ʀ(ə)late/ [1] *vtr* (formal) to recount.

relatif, **-ive**[1] /ʀ(ə)latif, iv/ **I** *adj* relative; **le risque est très ~** the risk is relatively slight; **un confort très ~** limited comfort.

II *nm* relative (pronoun).

relation /ʀ(ə)lasjɔ̃/ **I** *nf* **1** connection (**avec** with); **2** acquaintance; **~s d'affaires** business acquaintances; **3** connection; **avoir des ~s** to have connections; **4** relationship; **avoir de bonnes ~s avec qn** to have a good relationship with sb; **entrer en ~ avec qn** to get in touch with sb.

II relations *nf pl* relations; **les ~s culturelles** cultural relations.

■ **~s extérieures** foreign affairs; **~s publiques** public relations.

relative[2] /ʀ(ə)lativ/ **I** *adj f* ▶ **relatif I**.

II *nf* relative (clause).

relativement /ʀ(ə)lativmɑ̃/ **I** *adv* relatively.

II relativement à *phr* in relation to, relative to.

relativiser /ʀ(ə)lativize/ [1] *vtr* to put [sth] into perspective.

relativité /ʀ(ə)lativite/ *nf* relativity.

relax○ /ʀəlaks/ *adj inv* [*person*] laid-back○; [*clothes*] casual; [*party*] informal.

relaxant, **~e** /ʀəlaksɑ̃, ɑ̃t/ *adj* relaxing; **médicament ~** relaxant.

relaxation /ʀəlaksasjɔ̃/ *nf* relaxation.

relaxer /ʀəlakse/ [1] **I** *vtr* **1** to discharge [*defendant*]; **2** to relax [*muscle, person*].
II se relaxer *v refl* (+ *v être*) to relax.

relayer /ʀ(ə)leje/ [21] **I** *vtr* **1** to take over from, to relieve; **2** to relay [*broadcast*].
II se relayer *v refl* (+ *v être*) **1** to take turns (**pour faire** doing); **2** to take over from each other.

relecture /ʀ(ə)lɛktyʀ/ *nf* (of book) rereading; (of proofs) proofreading.

reléguer /ʀ(ə)lege/ [14] *vtr* (gen) to relegate (**en, à** to); to consign [*object*] (**à** to); **~ qn/qch au second plan** to push sb/sth into the background.

relent /ʀ(ə)lɑ̃/ *nm* **1** lingering odour[GB]; **2** (figurative) whiff.

relevable /ʀələvabl/ *adj* adjustable.

relève /ʀ(ə)lɛv/ *nf* **1 la ~ s'effectue à 20 heures** the changeover takes place at 8 pm; **la ~ de la garde** the changing of the guard; **prendre** or **assurer la ~** to take over; **2** relief; relief team.

relevé, **~e** /ʀəlve, ʀləve/ **I** *adj* **1** spicy; **2** refined.
II *nm* **1** noting down; **faire le ~ de** to list [*mistakes*]; to make a note of [*expenses*]; to read [*meter*]; **2 ~ bancaire** or **de compte** bank statement; **~ de gaz** gas bill.

relèvement /ʀ(ə)lɛvmɑ̃/ *nm* **1** increasing; **2** increase.

relever /ʀəlve, ʀləve/ [16] **I** *vtr* **1** to pick up [*person, stool*]; to put [sth] back up (again); **2** to raise [*lever*]; **3 ~ la tête** to raise one's head; to look up; (figurative) to refuse to accept defeat; **4** to turn up [*collar*]; to lift [*skirt*]; to wind up [*car window*]; to raise [*sail, blind*]; **~ ses cheveux** to put one's hair up; **5** to note, to notice; to point out; **'il t'a encore critiqué'—'je n'ai pas relevé'** 'he criticized you again'—'I let it go'; **~ la moindre inexactitude** to seize on the slightest inaccuracy; **6** to take down [*date, name*]; to take [*prints*]; **~ le compteur** to read the meter; **7** to take in [*exam papers*]; **8** to react to [*remark*]; **~ le défi/un pari** to take up the challenge/a bet; **9** to rebuild [*wall*]; to put [sth] back on its feet [*country, economy*]; **10** to raise [*standard, price*]; to increase [*productivity*]; **11** to relieve [*team*]; **~ la garde** to change the guard; **12** to spice up [*dish, story*]; **13** (formal) **~ qn de** to release sb from [*vows, obligation*]; **~ qn de ses fonctions** to relieve sb of their duties.
II relever de *v+prep* **1** [*department*] to come under [*Ministry etc*]; [*case*] to come within the competence of [*tribunal*]; **cela ne relève pas de mes fonctions** this doesn't come within my duties; **2 cela relève de la gageure** this comes close to being impossible; **3 ~ de maladie** to recover from an illness.
III se relever *v refl* (+ *v être*) **1** to pick oneself up; to get up again; **2 se ~ automatiquement** to be raised automatically; **3** [*blind*] to be raised; **4 se ~ de** to recover from.

relief /ʀəljɛf/ *nm* **1** relief; (on medal, coin) raised pattern; **en ~** [*globe of the world*] in relief; [*letters*] raised; **cinéma en ~** three-dimensional cinema; **mettre qch en ~** to accentuate sth; **un ~ accidenté** a hilly landscape; **2** depth; **l'effet de ~** the effect of depth; **3 personnage qui manque de ~** one-dimensional or flat character.

relier /ʀəlje/ [2] *vtr* **1** to link; to link up; to link together; to join up; to connect; **2** to bind [*book*]; **relié cuir** leather-bound.

relieur, **-ieuse** /ʀəljœʀ, øz/ *nm,f* (book)binder.

religieuse[1] /ʀəliʒjøz/ **I** *adj f* ▶ **religieux I**.
II *nf* **1** ▶ **religieux II**; **2** (Culin) round éclair, religieuse.

religieusement /ʀəliʒjøzmɑ̃/ *adv* **1** religiously; **2** [*listen*] with rapt attention; **3** [*get married*] in church.

religieux, **-ieuse**[2] /ʀəliʒjø, øz/ **I** *adj* **1** religious; [*school, wedding*] church; [*music*] sacred; **2** (figurative) [*silence*] reverent; **avec un soin ~** most conscientiously.
II *nm,f* monk/nun.

religion /ʀ(ə)liʒjɔ̃/ *nf* **1** religion; **2** faith; **3 se faire une ~ de la ponctualité** to make a fetish of punctuality; **4 entrer en ~** to enter the Church.

reliquaire /ʀ(ə)likɛʀ/ *nm* reliquary.

reliquat /ʀ(ə)lika/ *nm* (of sum) remainder; (of account) balance.

relique /ʀ(ə)lik/ *nf* relic.

relire /ʀ(ə)liʀ/ [66] *vtr* to reread; to read [sth] over.

reliure /ʀəljyʀ/ *nf* **1** binding; **2** bookbinding.

reloger /ʀ(ə)lɔʒe/ [13] *vtr* to rehouse.

reluire /ʀ(ə)lɥiʀ/ [69] *vi* to shine; to glisten; to glitter.
IDIOMS **il sait passer la brosse à ~** he's a real flatterer.

reluisant, **~e** /ʀ(ə)lɥizɑ̃, ɑ̃t/ *adj* shining, shiny; glistening; **peu ~** (figurative) far from brilliant.

remâcher /ʀ(ə)mɑʃe/ [1] *vtr* **1** to chew [sth] again; **2**○ to ruminate over [*problem, past*]; to nurse [*resentment*].

rémanent, **~e** /ʀemanɑ̃, ɑ̃t/ *adj* residual; **image ~e** after-image.

remaniement /ʀ(ə)manimɑ̃/ *nm* modification; revision; reorganization; **~ ministériel** cabinet reshuffle.

remanier /ʀ(ə)manje/ [2] *vtr* to modify; to redraft; to reorganize; to reshuffle.

remarier: **se remarier** /ʀ(ə)maʀje/ [2] *v refl* (+ *v être*) to remarry.

remarquable /ʀ(ə)maʀkabl/ *adj* **1** remarkable; **2** striking; **il est ~ que** it is amazing that; **3** noteworthy.

remarque /ʀ(ə)maʀk/ *nf* **1** remark; **faire des**

~s to comment; **2** comment; **3** critical remark, criticism.

remarqué, **~e** /ʀ(ə)maʀke/ *pp adj* [*initiative*] noteworthy; [*increase*] noticeable.

remarquer /ʀ(ə)maʀke/ [1] **I** *vtr* **1** to point out; **faire ~ à qn que** to point out to sb that; **2** (literary) to observe (**que** that); **3** to notice; **remarque, ce n'est pas très important** mind you, it's not very important; **se faire ~** to draw attention to oneself; **4 ~ un visage dans la foule** to spot a face in the crowd.
II se remarquer *v refl* (+ *v être*) **1** to attract attention; **2** to show.

remballer /ʀɑ̃bale/ [1] *vtr* **1** to pack [sth] up again; **2**○ to send [sb] packing○.

remblai /ʀɑ̃blɛ/ *nm* **1** embankment; **route en ~** raised road; **2** filling in; banking up; **travaux de ~** embankment work; **3** (**terre de**) **~** (for railway, road) ballast; (for ditch) fill; (for excavation) backfill.

remblayer /ʀɑ̃bleje/ [21] *vtr* to fill in [*ditch*]; to bank up [*road*].

rembobiner /ʀɑ̃bɔbine/ [1] *vtr* to rewind.

rembourrer /ʀɑ̃buʀe/ [1] *vtr* to stuff [*chair*]; to pad [*shoulders*].

remboursable /ʀɑ̃buʀsabl/ *adj* **1** repayable; **2** refundable.

remboursement /ʀɑ̃buʀsəmɑ̃/ *nm* **1** repayment; **2** refund; **3** reimbursement.

rembourser /ʀɑ̃buʀse/ [1] *vtr* **1** to pay off, to repay [*loan, debt*]; **2** to give a refund to [*customer*]; to refund the price of [*item*]; **3** to reimburse [*expenses, employee*]; to reimburse or refund the cost of [*medicine*]; **~ un ami** to pay a friend back.

remède /ʀ(ə)mɛd/ *nm* medicine; remedy, cure; **~ universel** cure-all, panacea.
■ **~ de bonne femme** folk remedy; **~ de cheval** strong medicine.
IDIOMS **aux grands maux les grands ~s** desperate times call for desperate measures.

remédier: **remédier à** /ʀ(ə)medje/ [2] *v+prep* to remedy.

remémorer: **se remémorer** /ʀ(ə)memɔʀe/ [1] *v refl* (+ *v être*) to recall, to recollect.

remerciement /ʀ(ə)mɛʀsimɑ̃/ *nm* thanks; **je n'ai pas eu un seul ~** I didn't get a word of thanks; **tous mes ~s** many thanks; **lettre de ~** thank-you letter.

remercier /ʀ(ə)mɛʀsje/ [2] *vtr* **1** to thank (**de qch** for sth; **d'avoir fait** for doing); **je vous remercie** thank you; **2** (ironic) to dismiss, to let [sb] go.

remettre /ʀ(ə)mɛtʀ/ [60] **I** *vtr* **1 ~ qch dans/sur** to put sth back in/on; **~ qch en mémoire à qn** to remind sb of sth; **2 ~ à qn** to hand [sth] over to sb [*keys*]; to hand [sth] in to sb [*letter*]; to present [sth] to sb [*reward*]; **~ qn entre les mains de la justice** to hand sb over to the law; **3 ~ qch droit** or **d'aplomb** to put sth straight again; **4** to postpone, to put off [*visit*]; to defer [*judgment*]; **5** to put [sth] on again [*heating*]; to play [sth] again [*record*]; to switch on again [*wipers*]; **6 ~ une vis** to put a new screw in; **7** to add some more [*salt*]; to add another [*nail*]; **~ de l'argent dans qch** to put some more money in sth; **8** to put [sth] back on [*coat*]; to start wearing [sth] again; **9** (Med) to put [sth] back in place [*joint*]; **10** [*pick-me-up, medicine*] to make [sb] feel better; **11 ~ qn/le visage de qn** to remember sb/sb's face; **12 ~ une peine à qn** to give sb remission; **~ ses péchés à qn** to forgive sb's sins; **13**○ **~ ça** to start again; **on s'est bien amusé, quand est-ce qu'on remet ça?** that was fun, when are we going to do it again?
II se remettre *v refl* (+ *v être*) **1 se ~ à un endroit** to go or get back to a place; **2 se ~ au travail** to go back to work; **se ~ au dessin** to start drawing again; **3 se ~ en jean** to wear jeans again; **4 se ~ de** to recover from [*illness*]; to get over [*shock*]; **remets-toi vite!** get well soon!; **5 s'en ~ à qn** to leave it to sb; **s'en ~ à la décision de qn** to accept sb's decision; **6 se ~ avec qn** to get back together with sb; **7 se ~ qn/le visage de qn** to remember sb/sb's face.

réminiscence /ʀeminisɑ̃s/ *nf* **1** reminiscence; **2** recollection.

remise /ʀ(ə)miz/ *nf* **1 attendre la ~ des clés** to wait for the keys to be handed over; **~ des prix** prizegiving; **~ des médailles** medals ceremony; **2** discount; **3** (from debt, sins) remission; **une ~ de peine** a remission; **4 ~ de fonds** remittance of funds; **5** shed.

rémission /ʀemisjɔ̃/ *nf* remission; **sans ~** [*punish*] mercilessly; [*rain, work*] without stopping.

remodeler /ʀəmɔdle/ [17] *vtr* to restructure; to reshape; to replan.

remontant /ʀ(ə)mɔ̃tɑ̃/ *nm* pick-me-up○, tonic.

remontée /ʀ(ə)mɔ̃te/ *nf* **1** climb up; **la ~ de la Saône en péniche** going up the Saône by barge; **2** (in price) rise; (of politician) recovery; (in violence) increase.
■ **~ mécanique** (Sport) ski lift.

remonte-pente, *pl* **~s** /ʀ(ə)mɔ̃tpɑ̃t/ *nm* ski-tow.

remonter /ʀəmɔ̃te/ [1] **I** *vtr* (+ *v avoir*) **1 ~ qch** to take sth back up/upstairs; to bring sth back up/upstairs; **2** to put [sth] back up; **~ un seau d'un puits** to pull a bucket up from a well; **3** to raise [*shelf, blind*]; to wind [sth] back up [*car window*]; to roll up [*sleeves*]; to hitch up [*trousers*]; to turn up [*collar*]; to pull up [*socks*]; **4** to go/to come back up; to climb back up; to drive back up; **5** to sail up [*river*]; to swim up [*river*]; to go up [*road*]; **~ le flot de voyageurs** to walk against the flow of passengers; **~ une filière** or **piste** to follow a trail; **6** [*cyclist*] to catch up with [*pack*]; **7 ~ qn** or **le moral de qn** to cheer sb up; **8** to put [sth] back together again; to put [sth] back [*wheel*]; **9** to wind [sth] up; **être remonté à bloc**○ to be full of energy; **10** to revive [*play, show*].
II *vi* (+ *v être*) **1** [*person*] to go/to come back up; [*tide*] to come in again; [*price, temperature*] to rise again; **peux-tu ~ chercher mon sac?** can you go back upstairs and get my bag?; **~ sur** to step back onto [*pavement*]; to climb back

onto [*wall*]; **~ à la surface** [*diver*] to surface; [*oil, object*] to rise to the surface; **~ dans les sondages** to move up in the opinion polls; **2 ~ dans le temps** to go back in time; **~ à** [*historian*] to go back to; [*event*] to date back to; [*police*] to follow the trail back to [*person*]; **faire ~** to trace (back) [*origins*]; **3** [*skirt*] to ride up; **4 les odeurs d'égout remontent dans la maison** the smell from the drains reaches our house.

III se remonter *v refl* (+ *v être*) **se ~ le moral** to cheer oneself up; to cheer each other up.

remontoir /ʀ(ə)mɔ̃twaʀ/ *nm* winder.

remontrance /ʀəmɔ̃tʀɑ̃s/ *nf* reprimand.

remords /ʀəmɔʀ/ *nm inv* remorse; **plein de ~** filled with remorse.

remorquage /ʀəmɔʀkaʒ/ *nm* towing.

remorque /ʀəmɔʀk/ *nf* **1** towrope; **prendre en ~** to tow [*car*]; **2** trailer.

remorquer /ʀəmɔʀke/ [1] *vtr* to tow [*vehicle*]; **se faire ~** to be towed.

remorqueur /ʀəmɔʀkœʀ/ *nm* tug.

rémoulade /ʀemulad/ *nf* rémoulade, mayonnaise-type dressing.

remous /ʀ(ə)mu/ *nm inv* **1** eddy; **2** backwash; wash; **3** (of feelings, ideas) turmoil; (in crowd) stir, movement.

rempailler /ʀɑ̃pɑje/ [1] *vtr* to reseat [*chair*].

rempart /ʀɑ̃paʀ/ *nm* **1** rampart; battlements; **les ~s de la ville** the city walls, the ramparts; **2** defence[GB].

remplaçable /ʀɑ̃plasabl/ *adj* replaceable.

remplaçant, ~e /ʀɑ̃plasɑ̃, ɑ̃t/ *nm,f* **1** (gen) substitute, replacement; (at school) supply (GB) or substitute (US) teacher; (actor) stand-in; **2** successor.

remplacement /ʀɑ̃plasmɑ̃/ *nm* **1** (of person) replacement; **faire des ~s** [*teacher*] to do supply (GB) or substitute (US) teaching; [*temp*] to do temporary work; **2** (of thing) replacement; **produit de ~** substitute.

remplacer /ʀɑ̃plase/ [12] *vtr* **1** to stand in for, to cover for [*colleague*]; **2** to replace; **M. Bon remplace Mme Roux à la direction** Mr Bon is replacing or succeeds Mrs Roux as director; **on peut ~ le vinaigre par du jus de citron** you can use lemon juice instead of vinegar.

remplir /ʀɑ̃pliʀ/ [3] *vtr* **1** to fill (up) [*container*]; to fill in or out [*form*]; **~ qch à moitié** to half fill sth; **~ qn de joie** to fill sb with joy; **une vie bien ~e** a full life; **une journée bien ~e** a busy day; **2** to carry out, to perform [*role, mission*]; to fulfil[GB] [*duty, role, function*].

remplissage /ʀɑ̃plisaʒ/ *nm* **1** filling; **2** (derogatory) padding; **faire du ~** to pad out one's work.

remplumer: se remplumer /ʀɑ̃plyme/ [1] *v refl* (+ *v être*) **1**° to get back on one's feet; to put some weight back on; **2** [*bird*] to grow new feathers.

remporter /ʀɑ̃pɔʀte/ [1] *vtr* to win [*seat, title, victory*]; **~ un vif succès** to be a great success.

rempoter /ʀɑ̃pɔte/ [1] *vtr* to repot.

remuant, ~e /ʀ(ə)mɥɑ̃, ɑ̃t/ *adj* **1** rowdy; **2** boisterous; energetic.

remue-ménage /ʀ(ə)mymenaʒ/ *nm inv* **1** commotion; **2** bustle.

remuer /ʀ(ə)mɥe/ [1] **I** *vtr* **1** to move [*hand, head*]; to wiggle [*toe, hips*]; to wag [*tail*]; **2** to shake [*object*]; **3** to move [*object*]; **tout ~ dans le tiroir** to turn the whole drawer upside down; **4** to stir [*soup*]; to toss [*salad*]; **5** to turn over [*earth*]; to poke [*ashes*]; **6** (figurative) to rake up [*past*]; to stir up [*memories*]; **7** to upset [*person*].

II *vi* [*person*] to move; [*leaves*] to flutter; [*boat*] to bob up and down.

III se remuer° *v refl* (+ *v être*) **1** to get a move on°; **2 se ~ pour obtenir** to make an effort to get.

rémunérateur, -trice /ʀemyneʀatœʀ, tʀis/ *adj* lucrative.

rémunération /ʀemyneʀasjɔ̃/ *nf* pay; payment.

rémunérer /ʀemyneʀe/ [14] *vtr* to pay [*person*]; to pay for [*work*].

renâcler /ʀ(ə)nɑkle/ [1] *vi* **1** [*person*] to show reluctance; **~ à qch/à faire** to balk at sth/at doing; **2** [*animal*] to snort.

renaissance /ʀ(ə)nɛsɑ̃s/ *nf* rebirth; (figurative) revival.

Renaissance /ʀ(ə)nɛsɑ̃s/ *nf* Renaissance.

renaître /ʀ(ə)nɛtʀ/ [74] *vi* (+ *v être*) **1** to come back to life; **~ à la vie** to rediscover life; **2** [*hope, desire*] to return; **faire ~ l'espoir** to bring new hope.

rénal, ~e, *mpl* **-aux** /ʀenal, o/ *adj* [*artery*] renal; [*infection*] kidney.

renard /ʀ(ə)naʀ/ *nm* **1** fox; **2** wily old fox, cunning devil.

renarde /ʀ(ə)naʀd/ *nf* vixen.

renardeau, *pl* **~x** /ʀ(ə)naʀdo/ *nm* fox cub.

renchérir /ʀɑ̃ʃeʀiʀ/ [3] *vi* **1** to add; **~ sur ce que dit qn** to add something to what sb says; **2** to go one step further; **3** to raise the bidding.

rencontre /ʀɑ̃kɔ̃tʀ/ *nf* **1** meeting; encounter; **faire la ~ de qn** to meet sb; **aller à la ~ de problèmes** to be heading for trouble; **2** (Sport) match (GB), game (US); **~ d'athlétisme** athletics meeting (GB), track meet (US).

■ **~ au sommet** summit meeting.

rencontrer /ʀɑ̃kɔ̃tʀe/ [1] **I** *vtr* **1** to meet [*person*]; **~ qn sur son chemin** to come across sb; **2** to encounter, to meet with [*problem, opposition*]; **3** to come across [*object, person, word*]; **4** to meet, to play [*player, team*]; to meet (GB), to fight [*boxer*].

II se rencontrer *v refl* (+ *v être*) **1** to meet; **2** [*quality, object, person*] to be found.

rendement /ʀɑ̃dmɑ̃/ *nm* **1** (from land, investment) yield; (of machine, worker) output; **2** (of factory) productivity; (of machine, worker) efficiency; **3** (of sportsman, pupil) performance.

rendez-vous /ʀɑ̃devu/ *nm inv* **1** appointment; date; **sur ~** by appointment; **j'ai ~ avec un ami** I'm meeting a friend; **nous nous sommes donné ~ devant la gare** we arranged to meet outside the station; **le soleil n'était pas au ~** the sun didn't shine; **2** meeting; **3** gathering; meeting place.

rendormir: **se rendormir** /ʀɑ̃dɔʀmiʀ/ [30] *v refl* (+ *v être*) to go back to sleep.

rendre /ʀɑ̃dʀ/ [6] **I** *vtr* **1** (gen) to give back, to return; to repay, pay back [*loan*]; to return [*greeting, invitation, goods*]; **elle ne m'a pas rendu la monnaie** she didn't give me my change; **~ la pareille à qn** to pay sb back; **il la déteste mais elle le lui rend bien** he hates her and she feels the same about him; **2 ~ la santé/vue à qn** to restore sb's health/sight; **3 ~ qn heureux** to make sb happy; **~ qch possible** to make sth possible; **~ qn fou** to drive sb mad; **4** to hand in [*homework*]; **5** [*land*] to yield [*crop, quantity*]; **6** to convey [*atmosphere, nuance*]; **~ l'expression d'un visage** to capture the expression on a face; **un poème chinois merveilleusement rendu en anglais** a Chinese poem beautifully translated into English; **ça ne rendra rien en couleurs** it won't come out in colour[GB]; **7**○ to bring up [*food, bile*]; **8** to pronounce [*judgment, sentence*]; to return [*verdict*]; **9** to give off [*sound*]; **10 les tomates rendent de l'eau (à la cuisson)** tomatoes give out water during cooking.

II *vi* **1 ~ (bien)** [*land*] to be productive; [*plant*] to produce a good crop; [*business*] to be profitable; **2**○ to be sick, to throw up○.

III se rendre *v refl* (+ *v être*) **1 se ~ à Rome/en ville** to go to Rome/to town; **se ~ chez des amis** to go to see friends; **2 se ~ indispensable/malade** to make oneself indispensable/ill; **3** [*criminal*] to give oneself up; [*army, town*] to surrender; **4 se ~ à qch** to bow to [*argument, opinion*].

IDIOMS **~ l'âme** or **l'esprit** to pass away.

rêne /ʀɛn/ *nf* rein; **tenir les ~s** to hold the reins.

renfermé, **~e** /ʀɑ̃fɛʀme/ **I** *pp* ▶ **renfermer**.

II *pp adj* [*person*] withdrawn; [*feeling*] hidden.

III *nm* **odeur de ~** musty smell; **ça sent le ~** it smells musty.

renfermer /ʀɑ̃fɛʀme/ [1] **I** *vtr* to contain.

II se renfermer *v refl* (+ *v être*) to become withdrawn.

renflé, **~e** /ʀɑ̃fle/ *adj* [*vase*] rounded; [*dome*] bulbous; [*stomach*] bulging.

renflement /ʀɑ̃fləmɑ̃/ *nm* bulge.

renflouer /ʀɑ̃flue/ [1] *vtr* **1** to raise [*ship*]; **2** to bail out [*person, company*].

renfoncement /ʀɑ̃fɔ̃smɑ̃/ *nm* recess; **~ de porte** doorway.

renforcer /ʀɑ̃fɔʀse/ [12] **I** *vtr* to reinforce; to strengthen.

II se renforcer *v refl* (+ *v être*) [*power*] to increase; [*control*] to become tighter; [*team, numbers*] to grow; [*country, sector*] to grow stronger.

renfort /ʀɑ̃fɔʀ/ *nm* **1** (Mil) reinforcement; **2** support; **annoncé à grand ~ de publicité** well-publicized, much-publicized; **3** (Sport) substitute.

renfrogner: **se renfrogner** /ʀɑ̃fʀɔɲe/ [1] *v refl* (+ *v être*) to become sullen.

rengaine /ʀɑ̃gɛn/ *nf* corny old song○; **c'est toujours la même ~** (figurative) it's the same old thing every time.

rengainer /ʀɑ̃gɛne/ [1] *vtr* to sheathe [*sword*]; to put [sth] back in its holster [*pistol*].

rengorger: **se rengorger** /ʀɑ̃gɔʀʒe/ [13] *v refl* (+ *v être*) [*bird*] to puff out its breast; [*person*] to swell with conceit.

reniement /ʀ(ə)nimɑ̃/ *nm* disavowal.

renier /ʀənje/ [2] **I** *vtr* to renounce [*religion, opinion*]; to disown [*child, work, friend*]; to disclaim [*obligation*].

II se renier *v refl* (+ *v être*) to go back on what one has said or promised.

reniflement /ʀ(ə)nifləmɑ̃/ *nm* **1** sniffing; **2** sniff.

renifler /ʀ(ə)nifle/ [1] *vtr, vi* to sniff.

renne /ʀɛn/ *nm* reindeer.

renom /ʀənɔ̃/ *nm* **1** fame, renown; **de** or **en ~** famous; **2** reputation.

renommé, **~e**[1] /ʀənɔme/ *adj* famous, renowned.

renommée[2] /ʀənɔme/ *nf* **1** reputation; **2** fame; **de ~ mondiale** world-famous.

renoncement /ʀ(ə)nɔ̃smɑ̃/ *nm* renunciation.

renoncer /ʀ(ə)nɔ̃se/ [12] *v+prep* to give up; **~ à** to give up; to abandon; to renounce; **elle a renoncé à lui** she has finished with him; **~ à faire** to abandon the idea of doing.

renouer /ʀənwe/ [1] **I** *vtr* **1** to retie [*laces*]; **2** to pick up the thread of [*conversation*].

II ~ avec *v+prep* to make up with [*person*]; to get back in touch with [*person*]; to revive [*tradition*]; to go back to [*past*].

renouveau, *pl* **~x** /ʀənuvo/ *nm* revival.

renouvelable /ʀənuvlabl/ *adj* renewable; **non ~** nonrenewable.

renouveler /ʀənuvle/ [19] **I** *vtr* **1** (gen) to renew; to repeat [*suggestion, experience*]; to replace [*equipment, team*]; to change [*water*]; **~ sa confiance en qn** to reaffirm one's faith in sb; **2** to revitalize [*genre, style*].

II se renouveler *v refl* (+ *v être*) **1 une pièce où l'air ne se renouvelle pas** a room which isn't aired; **2** [*artist*] to try out new ideas; **3** [*experience*] to be repeated; **controverse maintes fois renouvelée** recurring controversy.

renouvellement /ʀənuvɛlmɑ̃/ *nm* **1** renewal; **2** replacement; **3** revitalization.

rénovateur, **-trice** /ʀenɔvatœʀ, tʀis/ **I** *adj* reforming.

II *nm,f* reformer.

rénovation /ʀenɔvasjɔ̃/ *nf* renovation.

rénover /ʀenɔve/ [1] *vtr* **1** to renovate [*area, house*]; to restore [*furniture*]; **2** to reform [*institution, policy*]; to revamp [*project*]; to overhaul [*system*].

renseignement /ʀɑ̃sɛɲmɑ̃/ **I** *nm* **1** information; **est-ce que je peux vous demander un ~?** can I ask you something?; **il est allé aux ~s** he went to find out (about it); **~s pris, il**

semblerait que upon investigation, it would appear that; **'pour tous ~s, s'adresser à...'** 'all enquiries to...'; **2** (Mil) intelligence.

II renseignements *nm pl* **1** information; **2** directory enquiries (GB) or assistance (US).

renseigner /ʀɑ̃seɲe/ [1] **I** *vtr* **~ qn** to give information to sb; **être bien renseigné** to be well-informed.

II se renseigner *v refl* (+ *v être*) to find out, to enquire (**sur** about); to make enquiries; **je vais me ~ auprès d'elle** I'll ask her about it.

rentabiliser /ʀɑ̃tabilize/ [1] *vtr* to secure a return on [*investment*]; to make a profit on [*product*]; to make [sth] profitable [*business*].

rentable /ʀɑ̃tabl/ *adj* profitable.

rente /ʀɑ̃t/ *nf* **1** private income; **2** annuity; **~ viagère** life annuity; **3** government stock.

rentier, -ière /ʀɑ̃tje, ɛʀ/ *nm,f* person of independent means.

rentré, ~e[1] /ʀɑ̃tʀe/ *adj* **1** [*anger*] suppressed; **2** [*eyes*] sunken; [*stomach*] held in.

rentrée[2] /ʀɑ̃tʀe/ *nf* **1** (general) return to work (*after the slack period of the summer break, in France*); **~ (des classes** or **scolaire)** start of the (new) school year; beginning of term; **mon livre sera publié à la ~** my book will be published in the autumn (GB) or fall (US); **2** return (to work); **3** comeback; **~ politique** political comeback; **4** receipts; **~ (d'argent)** income; takings; **5** (of spacecraft) re-entry.

■ **~ parlementaire** reassembly of Parliament; **~ universitaire** start of the academic year.

rentrer /ʀɑ̃tʀe/ [1] **I** *vtr* **1** to bring [sth] in; to take [sth] in; **2** to raise [*landing gear*]; to draw in [*claws*]; **rentrez le ventre!** hold your stomach in!; **3** to put [*key*] (**dans** in, into); to tuck [*shirttail*] (**dans** into).

II *vi* (+ *v être*) **1** to go in; to get in; to fit; **~ dans un arbre**○ to hit a tree; **2 ~ dans** to go back into; to come back into; **3 ~ (chez soi)** to get (or go or come) back (home); to return (home); **4 ~ dans ses frais** to recoup one's money; **5** [*money*] to come in; **faire ~ l'argent** to bring money in; **6 faire ~ qch dans la tête de qn** to get sth into sb's head; **7**○ **l'algèbre ça ne rentre pas!** I just can't get my head round○ algebra!

IDIOMS **je vais leur ~ dedans**● I'm going to lay into them○; **il m'est rentré dedans**● he bumped or ran into me; he crashed into me.

renversant, ~e /ʀɑ̃vɛʀsɑ̃, ɑ̃t/ *adj* astounding, astonishing.

renverse /ʀɑ̃vɛʀs/ *nf* **tomber à la ~** to fall flat on one's back.

renversement /ʀɑ̃vɛʀsəmɑ̃/ *nm* **1** reversal; **2** overthrow; removal from office.

renverser /ʀɑ̃vɛʀse/ [1] **I** *vtr* **1** to knock over; to knock down; **2** to spill; **3** to turn [sth] upside down; **4 ~ la tête en arrière** to tip or tilt one's head back; **5** to reverse; **6** to overthrow; to vote [sb/sth] out of office; **7**○ to stagger [*person*].

II se renverser *v refl* (+ *v être*) [*vehicle*] to overturn; [*boat*] to capsize; [*bottle*] to fall over; [*liquid*] to spill.

renvoi /ʀɑ̃vwa/ *nm* **1** expulsion; dismissal; **2** return; **~ d'un colis** return of a parcel; **3** (in tennis) return; (in football) clearance; **4** postponement; **~ de l'affaire devant la Cour d'appel** referral of the case to the court of appeal; **5** cross-reference; **6** belch, burp○.

renvoyer /ʀɑ̃vwaje/ [24] *vtr* **1** to throw [sth] back [*ball*]; to reflect [*light, heat*]; to echo [*sound*]; **2** to return [*mail*]; **3** to send [sb] back; **~ qn chez lui** to send sb home; **4** to expel; to dismiss; **5** to postpone [*debate*]; to adjourn [*case*]; **6 ~ à** to refer to; **l'astérisque renvoie aux notes** the asterisk refers to the notes.

réorganisation /ʀeɔʀganizasjɔ̃/ *nf* reorganization.

réouverture /ʀeuvɛʀtyʀ/ *nf* reopening.

repaire /ʀ(ə)pɛʀ/ *nm* den; hideout.

répandre /ʀepɑ̃dʀ/ [6] **I** *vtr* **1** to spread [*substance*]; to pour [*liquid*]; to spill [*liquid*]; **~ son contenu** to empty its contents; **2** to scatter [*seeds, rubbish*]; **3** to spread [*news, religion*]; to give off [*heat, smoke, smell*].

II se répandre *v refl* (+ *v être*) **1** [*news, religion, smell*] to spread; **2 se ~ en compliments** to be lavish with one's compliments.

répandu, ~e /ʀepɑ̃dy/ *adj* widespread.

réparable /ʀepaʀabl/ *adj* **1** repairable; **2** [*mistake*] which can be put right.

reparaître /ʀ(ə)paʀɛtʀ/ [73] *vi* **1** = **réapparaître**; **2** [*magazine*] to be back in print; [*book*] to be republished.

réparateur, -trice /ʀepaʀatœʀ, tʀis/ **I** *adj* refreshing.

II *nm,f* engineer (GB), fixer (US).

réparation /ʀepaʀasjɔ̃/ *nf* **1** repairing, mending; repair; **être en ~** to be under repair; **2** compensation; **3** redress.

réparer /ʀepaʀe/ [1] *vtr* **1** to repair, to mend, to fix; **2** to put [sth] right [*error*]; to make up for [*oversight*]; **3** to compensate for [*damage*].

reparler: **~ de** /ʀ(ə)paʀle/ [1] *v+prep* to discuss [sth] again.

repartie /ʀepaʀti/ *nf* rejoinder; **elle a de la ~** she always has a ready reply.

repartir /ʀ(ə)paʀtiʀ/ [30] *vi* (+ *v être*) **1** to leave (again); to go back; **2** [*person*] to set off again; [*machine*] to start again; [*sector*] to pick up again; **3 ~ à zéro** to start again from scratch.

répartir /ʀepaʀtiʀ/ [3] **I** *vtr* **1** to share [sth] out; to split [*profits, expenses*]; to distribute [*weight*]; **~ en groupes** to divide into groups; **2** to spread [*payments*].

II se répartir *v refl* (+ *v être*) **1** to share out, to split; **2** [*work, votes*] to be split; **se ~ en** [*people, objects*] to divide (up) into.

répartition /ʀepaʀtisjɔ̃/ *nf* **1** sharing out; dividing up; **2** distribution.

repas /ʀ(ə)pɑ/ *nm inv* meal.

repassage /ʀ(ə)pasaʒ/ *nm* ironing.

repasser /ʀəpase/ [1] **I** *vtr* **1** to iron; **2** to cross [sth] again [*river, border*]; **3** to take [sth] again [*exam*]; **4** to pass [sth] again [*tool, salt*]; to show

[sth] again [*film*]; **je te repasse Jean** (on phone) I'll put you back on to Jean; **5**○ to give [*cold*] (**à qn** to sb).

II *vi* (+ *v être*) **1** to go past again; **si tu repasses à Lyons, viens me voir** if you're ever back in Lyons, come and see me; **je repasserai demain** I'll stop by tomorrow; **2** [*film*] to be showing again; **3 quand elle fait la vaisselle, je dois ~ derrière elle** I always have to do the dishes again after she's done them.

repêchage /R(ə)pɛʃaʒ/ *nm* **1** recovery (*from water*); **2 examen** or **épreuve de ~** resit (GB), retest (US).

repêcher /R(ə)peʃe/ [1] *vtr* **1** to recover; to fish out; **2** to award a discretionary pass to (GB), to raise [sb] to a passing grade (US); (Sport) to allow [sb] to qualify.

repeindre /R(ə)pɛ̃dR/ [55] *vtr* to repaint.

repenser /R(ə)pɑ̃se/ [1] **I** *vtr* to rethink.

II repenser à *v+prep* **~ à** to think back to [*childhood*]; to think again about [*anecdote*].

repenti, **~e** /R(ə)pɑ̃ti/ *adj* repentant.

repentir[1]: **se repentir** /R(ə)pɑ̃tiR/ [30] *v refl* (+ *v être*) **1** to regret; **2** to repent.

repentir[2] /R(ə)pɑ̃tiR/ *nm* repentance.

repérable /R(ə)peRabl/ *adj* that can be spotted.

répercussion /RepɛRkysjɔ̃/ *nf* repercussion.

répercuter /RepɛRkyte/ [1] **I** *vtr* **1** to pass [sth] on [*increase*]; **2** to send back [*sound*].

II se répercuter *v refl* (+ *v être*) **1** [*sound*] to echo; [*increase*] to be reflected (**sur** in); **2** to have repercussions (**sur** on).

repère /R(ə)pɛR/ *nm* **1** marker; (reference) mark; **2** (event) landmark; (date) reference point.

repérer /R(ə)peRe/ [14] **I** *vtr* **1**○ to spot; **~ les lieux** to check out a place; **2** to locate [*target, enemy*].

II se repérer *v refl* (+ *v être*) to get one's bearings.

répertoire /RepɛRtwaR/ *nm* **1** notebook with thumb index; **2 ~ téléphonique** telephone book; **~ d'adresses** address book; **3** repertoire.

répertorier /RepɛRtɔRje/ [2] *vtr* **1** to list; to index; **2** to identify.

répéter /Repete/ [14] **I** *vtr* **1** to repeat; **~ qch à qn** to say sth to sb again; **je ne me le suis pas fait ~ deux fois!** I didn't need to be told twice!; **je te répète que tu as tort** I'm telling you, you're wrong; **2** to rehearse [*play*]; to rehearse for [*concert*]; **~ son rôle** to go over or through one's lines.

II se répéter *v refl* (+ *v être*) **1** to repeat oneself; **2 j'ai beau me ~ que** no matter how often I tell myself that; **3** [*incident*] to be repeated.

répétitif, **-ive** /Repetitif, iv/ *adj* repetitive.

répétition /Repetisjɔ̃/ *nf* **1** repetition; **2** rehearsal; **~ générale** dress rehearsal.

repeuplement /R(ə)pœpləmɑ̃/ *nm* **1** repopulation; **2** reforestation; **3** restocking.

repeupler /R(ə)pœple/ [1] *vtr* **1** to repopulate; **2** to restock; **3** to reforest.

repiquer /R(ə)pike/ [1] *vtr* to transplant [*rice*]; to prick out [*seedlings*].

répit /Repi/ *nm* respite.

replacer /R(ə)plase/ [12] *vtr* to put [sth] back (in its place).

replanter /R(ə)plɑ̃te/ [1] *vtr* **1** to transplant; **2** to replant.

replâtrer /R(ə)plɑtRe/ [1] *vtr* **1** to replaster; **2** to patch up [*group*].

replet, **-ète** /Rəplɛ, ɛt/ *adj* plump, chubby.

repli /R(ə)pli/ *nm* **1** double fold; **2** fold; **les ~s de sa conscience** the recesses of one's conscience; **3** (Mil) (**mouvement de**) **~** withdrawal; **4 ~ sur soi(-même)** withdrawal.

replier /R(ə)plije/ [2] **I** *vtr* **1** to fold up [*map*]; **2** to fold [sth] back [*sheet*]; **3** to fold up [*deck chair, fan*]; to close [*umbrella, penknife*]; **4 elle replia ses jambes** she tucked her legs under her; **~ ses ailes** [*bird*] to fold its wings.

II se replier *v refl* (+ *v être*) **1** [*blade*] to fold up; **2** [*army*] to withdraw; **3 se ~ sur soi-même** [*person*] to become withdrawn.

réplique /Replik/ *nf* **1** retort, rejoinder; **il a la ~ facile** he's always ready with an answer; **2 faire qch sans ~** to do sth without arguing; **pas de ~!** don't answer back!; **3** line; **donner la ~ à qn** to play opposite sb; **manquer sa ~** to miss one's cue; **4** replica; **elle est la ~ de sa mère** she is the image of her mother.

répliquer /Replike/ [1] **I** *vtr* to retort.

II répliquer à *v+prep* to argue with [*person*]; to respond to [*criticism*].

III *vi* **1** to answer back; **2** to retaliate, to respond.

répondant, **~e** /Repɔ̃dɑ̃, ɑ̃t/ *nm,f* referee; (Law) surety, guarantor.

IDIOMS **avoir du ~**○ to have money.

répondeur /Repɔ̃dœR/ *nm* **~ (téléphonique)** (telephone) answering machine.

répondre /Repɔ̃dR/ [6] **I** *vtr* to answer, to reply; **tu réponds n'importe quoi** you just give any answer that comes into your head; **je me suis vu ~ que, il m'a été répondu que** I was told that; **qu'as-tu à ~ (à cela)?** what's your answer (to that)?

II répondre à *v+prep* **1** to reply to, to answer [*person, question, letter*]; to answer [*phone, door*]; to fill in [*questionnaire*]; **2** to talk back to; **3** to answer, to meet [*needs*]; to fulfil[GB] [*wishes*]; to answer, to fit [*description*]; to come up to, to meet [*expectations*]; **4** to respond to [*appeal, criticism*]; to return [*greeting*]; **~ aux critiques de qn par le mépris** to treat sb's criticism with contempt; **~ à un sourire** to smile back; **les freins ne répondent plus** the brakes have failed.

III répondre de *v+prep* **~ de qn** to vouch for sb; **~ de ses actes** to answer for one's actions; **je ne réponds plus de rien** it's out of my hands from now on.

réponse /Repɔ̃s/ *nf* **1** answer, reply; **2** response; **la ~ du public a été favorable** the public has responded favourably[GB].

■ **~ de Normand** noncommittal reply.

report /RəpɔR/ *nm* **1** adjournment; postponement; deferment; **2** transfer; **3** carrying forward.

reportage /R(ə)pɔRtaʒ/ *nm* **1** report; **partir en ~** to go to cover a story; **2** reporting.

reporter[1] /R(ə)pɔRte/ [1] **I** *vtr* **1** to put back [*date*]; to postpone [*event*]; to defer [*judgment*]; **2** to carry forward [*result*]; to copy out [*name*]; **3 ~ un paragraphe en début d'un texte** to move a paragraph to the beginning of a text; **4** to take [sth] back [*goods*]; **5 cela nous reporte longtemps en arrière** that's going back a long time; **6** to transfer [*affection*]; **~ son agressivité sur qn** to take one's aggression out on sb.

II se reporter *v refl* (+ *v être*) **se ~ à** to refer to; to think back to.

reporter[2] /RəpɔRtɛR/ *nm* reporter; **un grand ~** a special correspondent.

repos /Rəpo/ *nm inv* **1** rest; **mon jour de ~** my day off; **ce n'est pas de tout ~** it's no easy task, it's no picnic○; **2** (literary) peace.

reposant, **~e** /Rəpozɑ̃, ɑ̃t/ *adj* peaceful, restful; soothing; relaxing.

reposer /Rəpoze/ [1] **I** *vtr* **1** to rest; **avoir le visage reposé** to look rested; **lire qch à tête reposée** to read sth at one's leisure; **2** to put [sth] down [*phone*]; to put [sth] down again; **3** to ask [sth] again [*question*]; **cela repose le problème du chômage** this raises the problem of unemployment again.

II *vi* **1** to rest; [*wreck*] to lie; **'ici repose le Dr Grunard'** 'here lies Dr Grunard'; **laisser ~ la terre** to rest the land; **'laisser ~ la pâte'** 'let the dough stand'; **2 ~ sur** to be based on; **la poutre repose sur...** the beam is supported by...

III se reposer *v refl* (+ *v être*) **1** to have a rest, to rest; **2 se ~ sur qn** to rely on sb.

repoussant, **~e** /Rəpusɑ̃, ɑ̃t/ *adj* hideous, revolting; **d'une laideur ~e** hideously ugly.

repousser /R(ə)puse/ [1] **I** *vtr* **1** to push [sth] to [*door*]; to push back [*object*]; **2** to push away [*objects*]; to push back [*lock of hair*]; **3** to push or drive back [*crowd, animal*]; (Mil) to repel [*attack*]; **4** to dismiss [*objection*]; to decline [*help*]; to turn down [*request*]; **~ les avances de qn** to spurn sb's advances; **5** to revolt; **6** to postpone [*departure, event*]; to move [sth] back [*date*].

II *vi* to grow again; to grow back; [*tooth*] to come through.

répréhensible /RepReɑ̃sibl/ *adj* reprehensible.

reprendre /R(ə)pRɑ̃dR/ [52] **I** *vtr* **1 ~ du pain/vin** to have some more bread/wine; **j'en ai repris deux fois** I had three helpings; **2** to pick [sth] up again [*object, tool*]; to take [sth] back [*present*]; to go back on [*word*]; to collect [*person, car*]; **tu passes me ~ à quelle heure?** what time will you come back for me?; **3** to take [sb] on again [*employee*]; [*shop*] to take [sth] back [*item*]; **si on me reprend ma vieille voiture** if I can trade in my old car; **4** to resume [*walk, story*]; to take up [sth] again [*studies*]; to revive [*play, tradition*]; **~ le travail** to go back to work; **tu reprends le train à quelle heure?** what time is your train back?; **~ une histoire au début** to go back to the beginning of a story; **~ les arguments un à un** to go over the arguments one by one; **5** to take over [*business, shop*]; **6 on ne me reprendra plus à lui rendre service!** you won't catch me doing him/her any favours[GB] again!; **7 ~ confiance** to regain one's confidence; **~ ses vieilles habitudes** to get back into one's old ways; **8** to alter [*clothes*]; **~ le travail de qn** to correct sb's work; **9** to take up [*idea, thesis, policy*]; **10** to repeat [*argument*]; to take up [*slogan, news*]; **11** to correct [*pupil*]; **12 mon mal de dents m'a repris** my toothache has come back; **voilà que ça le reprend**○! there he goes again!

II *vi* **1** [*business*] to pick up again; [*plant*] to recover, to pick up; **2** to start again; to resume; **3 'c'est bien étrange,' reprit-il** 'it's very strange,' he continued.

III se reprendre *v refl* (+ *v être*) **1** to correct oneself; **2** to pull oneself together; **3 s'y ~ à trois fois pour faire** to make three attempts to do or at doing.

représailles /R(ə)pRezɑj/ *nf pl* reprisals; retaliation.

représentant, **~e** /R(ə)pRezɑ̃tɑ̃, ɑ̃t/ *nm,f* **1** representative; **~ des forces de l'ordre** police officer; **2 ~ (de commerce)** sales representative.

représentatif, **-ive** /RəpRezɑ̃tatif, iv/ *adj* representative.

représentation /RəpRezɑ̃tasjɔ̃/ *nf* **1** representation; **2** performance; **3** commercial travelling[GB]; **~ exclusive** sole agency; **faire de la ~** to be a sales representative.

représenter /RəpRezɑ̃te/ [1] **I** *vtr* **1** [*painting, drawing*] to depict, to show; [*artist*] to depict [*landscape, situation*]; to portray [*person*]; **2** to represent; to mean; **cela représente trop de sacrifices** it means too many sacrifices; **les enfants représentent les deux tiers de la population** children make up two thirds of the population; **3** to represent [*person, organization, company*]; **4** to perform [*play*]; to put on [*show*].

II se représenter *v refl* (+ *v être*) **1** to imagine [*scene*]; **2** [*opportunity*] to arise again; [*problem*] to crop up again; **3 se ~ à un examen** to retake an examination.

répressif, **-ive** /RepResif, iv/ *adj* repressive.

répression /RepResjɔ̃/ *nf* **1** suppression; **2** repression.

réprimande /RepRimɑ̃d/ *nf* reprimand.

réprimander /RepRimɑ̃de/ [1] *vtr* to reprimand.

réprimer /RepRime/ [1] *vtr* to suppress; to repress [*desire*]; to suppress [*uprising*]; to crack down on [*fraud, trafficking*].

repris /R(ə)pRi/ *nm inv* **~ de justice** ex-convict.

reprise /RəpRiz/ *nf* **1** (of work, negotiations) resumption; (of play, film) rerun; (of broadcast) repeat; **à plusieurs** or **maintes ~s** on several occasions, repeatedly; **2** (of demand, production) increase; (of business) revival; (of economy) upturn; **3** (of goods) return, taking back; trade-in, part exchange (GB); (of company) takeover; **4** key money; **5** (Aut) acceleration; **6** mend; darn; **7** (in boxing) round; (in football) start of second half.

repriser /ʀəpʀize/ [1] *vtr* to mend; to darn.

réprobateur, **-trice** /ʀepʀɔbatœʀ, tʀis/ *adj* reproachful, disapproving.

réprobation /ʀepʀɔbasjɔ̃/ *nf* disapproval, reprobation.

reproche /ʀ(ə)pʀɔʃ/ *nm* reproach; **j'ai un ou deux ~s à vous faire** I've one or two criticisms to make; **un ton de ~** a reproachful tone; **sans ~** beyond reproach.

reprocher /ʀəpʀɔʃe/ [1] **I** *vtr* **1 ~ qch à qn** to criticize or reproach sb for sth; **qu'est-ce que tu lui reproches?** what have you got against him/her?; what don't you like about it?; **on ne peut rien lui ~** he's/she's beyond reproach; **elle me reproche de ne jamais lui écrire** she complains that I never write to her; **2 les faits qui lui sont reprochés** the charges against him/her.

II se reprocher *v refl* (+ *v être*) **se ~ qch** to blame or reproach oneself for sth.

reproducteur, **-trice** /ʀəpʀɔdyktœʀ, tʀis/ *adj* **1** reproductive; **2** [*animal*] breeding.

reproduction /ʀ(ə)pʀɔdyksjɔ̃/ *nf* **1** reproduction; **la ~ artificielle** assisted reproduction; **2** reproduction, copy; **droit de ~** copyright.

reproduire /ʀ(ə)pʀɔdɥiʀ/ [69] **I** *vtr* (gen) to reproduce; to repeat [*mistake*]; to recreate [*conditions*].

II se reproduire *v refl* (+ *v être*) **1** [*man, plants*] to reproduce; **2** [*situation*] to recur.

réprouvé, **~e** /ʀepʀuve/ *nm,f* outcast.

réprouver /ʀepʀuve/ [1] *vtr* to condemn.

reptile /ʀɛptil/ *nm* reptile.

républicain, **~e** /ʀepyblikɛ̃, ɛn/ *adj, nm,f* republican.

république /ʀepyblik/ *nf* republic; **on est en ~** it's a free country.

répudier /ʀepydje/ [2] *vtr* **1** to repudiate [*spouse*]; **2** to renounce [*right, faith*].

répugnance /ʀepyɲɑ̃s/ *nf* **1** revulsion; **éprouver de la ~ pour** to find [sth] revolting or disgusting; **2** reluctance; **avec ~** reluctantly.

répugnant, **~e** /ʀepyɲɑ̃, ɑ̃t/ *adj* **1** revolting; **2** disgusting; **3** loathsome.

répugner: **répugner à** /ʀepyɲe/ [1] *v+prep* **1** [*food, person*] to disgust [*person*]; **2** [*person*] to be averse to [*work*]; **~ à faire** to be reluctant to do, to be loath to do.

répulsion /ʀepylsjɔ̃/ *nf* repulsion; **il m'inspire de la ~** I find him repulsive.

réputation /ʀepytasjɔ̃/ *nf* reputation; **se faire une ~** to make a name for oneself; **connaître qn/qch de ~** to know sb/sth by reputation.

réputé, **~e** /ʀepyte/ *adj* **1** [*company*] reputable; [*writer*] of repute; [*product*] well-known; **~ pour qch** renowned for sth; **l'avocat le plus ~ de Paris** the best lawyer in Paris; **2 ~ cher/honnête** reputed to be expensive/honest.

requérir /ʀəkeʀiʀ/ [35] *vtr* **1** to request; **2** to require.

requête /ʀəkɛt/ *nf* **1** request; **2** (Law) petition.

requiem /ʀekwijɛm/ *nm inv* requiem.

requin /ʀ(ə)kɛ̃/ *nm* (Zool), (figurative) shark.

requinquer○ /ʀ(ə)kɛ̃ke/ [1] **I** *vtr* to buck [sb] up○.

II se requinquer *v refl* (+ *v être*) to perk up○.

requis, **~e** /ʀəki, iz/ **I** *pp* ▶ **requérir**.

II *pp adj* [*patience*] necessary; [*diploma, age*] required.

réquisition /ʀekizisjɔ̃/ *nf* requisitioning; conscription.

réquisitionner /ʀekizisjɔne/ [1] *vtr* **1** to requisition; **2** to commandeer [*premises*]; to conscript [*workers*].

réquisitoire /ʀekizitwaʀ/ *nm* **1** closing speech for the prosecution (*requesting a specific sentence*); **2** indictment (**contre** of).

RER /ɛʀəɛʀ/ *nm* (*abbr* = **réseau express régional**) *rapid-transit rail system in the Paris region.*

rescapé, **~e** /ʀɛskape/ **I** *adj* [*person*] surviving.

II *nm,f* survivor (**de** from).

rescousse: **à la rescousse** /alaʀɛskus/ *phr* **aller à la ~ de qn** to go to sb's rescue; **appeler qn à la ~** to call to sb for help.

réseau, *pl* **~x** /ʀezo/ *nm* network; **~ de trafiquants de drogue** drugs ring.

réservation /ʀezɛʀvasjɔ̃/ *nf* reservation, booking (GB).

réserve /ʀezɛʀv/ *nf* **1** reservation (**au sujet de, à l'égard de** about); **sous ~ de changement** subject to alteration; **'sous (toute) ~'** (in a programme) 'to be confirmed'; **je vous le dis sous toutes ~s** I'm telling you for what it's worth; **2** stock; **des ~s de sucre** a stock of sugar; **~(s) d'argent** money in reserve; **3** (Econ) **~s de charbon** coal reserves; **~s d'eau** water supply; **4** (of person, manner) reserve; **5** stockroom; **6** (in museum) storeroom; **7 ~ naturelle/de chasse** nature/game reserve; **8 ~ indienne** Indian reservation; **9** (Mil) **officier de ~** reserve officer.

réservé, **~e** /ʀezɛʀve/ **I** *pp* ▶ **réserver**.

II *pp adj* **1** [*fishing*] private; **2 ~ à la clientèle** for patrons only; **voie ~e aux autobus** bus lane; **'tous droits ~s'** 'all rights reserved'; **3** [*person*] reserved; [*manner*] reticent.

réserver /ʀezɛʀve/ [1] **I** *vtr* **1** to reserve, to book [*seat, ticket*]; **2** to put aside [*goods*] (**pour** for); **~ qch pour les grandes occasions** to keep sth for special occasions; **3** to set aside [*money, time*]; **4 ~ un bon accueil à qn** to give sb a warm welcome; **sans savoir ce que l'avenir nous réserve** without knowing what the future has in store for us; **5 ~ son jugement** to reserve judgment; **~ son diagnostic** to defer diagnosis.

II se réserver *v refl* (+ *v être*) **se ~ les meilleurs morceaux** to save the best bits for oneself; **se ~ le droit de faire** to reserve the right to do; **se ~ pour une meilleure occasion** to wait for a better opportunity; **il se réserve pour la candidature à la présidence** he's saving himself for the presidential race.

réserviste /ʀezɛʀvist/ *nmf* reservist.

réservoir /ʀezɛʀvwaʀ/ *nm* **1** tank; **~ à essence** petrol tank (GB), gas tank (US); **2** reservoir.

résidant, ~e /ʀezidɑ̃, ɑ̃t/ *adj* resident.

résidence /ʀezidɑ̃s/ *nf* **1** residence; **2** place of residence; **en ~ surveillée, assigné à ~** under house arrest.

■ **~ principale/secondaire** main/second home; **~ universitaire** (university) hall of residence (GB), residence hall (US).

résident, ~e /ʀezidɑ̃, ɑ̃t/ *nm,f* resident.

résidentiel, -ielle /ʀezidɑ̃sjɛl/ *adj* residential.

résider /ʀezide/ [1] *vi* **1** to live; **2 ~ dans qch** to lie in sth.

résidu /ʀezidy/ *nm* **1** residue; **2** remnant; **3** waste.

résiduel, -elle /ʀezidɥɛl/ *adj* residual.

résignation /ʀeziɲasjɔ̃/ *nf* resignation (**à** to).

résigner: **se résigner** /ʀeziɲe/ [1] *v refl* (+ *v être*) to resign oneself (**à qch** to sth).

résilier /ʀezilje/ [2] *vtr* to terminate [*contract, lease*].

résine /ʀezin/ *nf* resin.

résineux /ʀezinø/ *nm* conifer.

résistance /ʀezistɑ̃s/ *nf* **1** resistance (**à** to); **opposer une ~ à** to put up resistance to; **manquer de ~** [*person*] to lack stamina; **2** (in electricity) (gen) resistance, resistor; (of household appliance) element.

résistant, ~e /ʀezistɑ̃, ɑ̃t/ **I** *adj* **1** [*person*] tough, resilient; [*plant*] hardy; **2** [*metal*] resistant; [*fabric, garment*] hard-wearing.

II *nm,f* Resistance fighter.

résister: **résister à** /ʀeziste/ [1] *v+prep* (gen) to resist; to stand [*strain*]; to withstand; to get through, to endure [*ordeal*]; **le voleur a tenté de ~** the thief tried to resist arrest; **le mur n'a pas résisté** the wall collapsed or gave; **~ à l'épreuve du temps** to stand the test of time; **théorie qui ne résiste pas à l'analyse** theory that doesn't bear or stand up to analysis; **il ne supporte pas qu'on lui résiste** he doesn't like it when people stand up to him.

résolu, ~e /ʀezɔly/ **I** *pp* ▶ **résoudre**.

II *pp adj* resolute, determined.

résolument /ʀezɔlymɑ̃/ *adv* resolutely; [*confident*] totally; [*believe*] firmly.

résolution /ʀezɔlysjɔ̃/ *nf* **1** (gen, Pol) resolution; **prendre la ~ de faire** to make a resolution to do, to resolve to do; **2** resolve; **3** solution.

résonance /ʀezɔnɑ̃s/ *nf* **1** (gen) resonance; **2** (of poem, music) echo.

résonner /ʀezɔne/ [1] *vi* **1** [*step, laughter*] to ring out; [*alarm*] to resound; [*cymbals*] to clash; **2** [*room*] to echo; **~ de** to resound with.

résorber /ʀezɔʀbe/ [1] **I** *vtr* to absorb [*deficit, surplus*]; to reduce [*inflation*].

II se résorber *v refl* (+ *v être*) **1** [*deficit*] to be reduced; [*inflation*] to be coming down; **2** (Med) to be resorbed.

résorption /ʀezɔʀpsjɔ̃/ *nf* **1** (Med) resorption; **2** (of inflation) reduction.

résoudre /ʀezudʀ/ [75] **I** *vtr* **1** to solve [*equation, problem*]; to resolve [*crisis*]; **2 il résolut d'attendre** he resolved to wait.

II se résoudre *v refl* (+ *v être*) **se ~ à faire** to resolve or make up one's mind to do; **être résolu à faire** to be determined to do **je ne peux pas me ~ à la renvoyer** I can't bring myself to dismiss her.

respect /ʀɛspɛ/ *nm* (gen) respect (**de, pour** for); **manquer de ~ à qn** to be disrespectful to sb; **le ~ de soi** self-respect; **présenter ses ~s à qn** to pay one's respects to sb.

IDIOMS **sauf votre ~** with all due respect; **tenir qn en ~** to keep sb at bay.

respectable /ʀɛspɛktabl/ *adj* respectable.

respecter /ʀɛspɛkte/ [1] **I** *vtr* (gen) to respect; to treat [sth] with respect; to honour[GB] [*commitment*]; **il s'est toujours fait ~ par ses élèves** he has always commanded the respect of his pupils; **faire ~ l'ordre/la loi** to enforce order/ the law.

II se respecter *v refl* (+ *v être*) to respect oneself; **tout homme qui se respecte** any self-respecting man.

respectif, -ive /ʀɛspɛktif, iv/ *adj* respective.

respectueux, -euse /ʀɛspɛktɥø, øz/ *adj* respectful; **~ de la loi** law-abiding; **salutations respectueuses** yours faithfully; yours sincerely.

respiration /ʀɛspiʀasjɔ̃/ *nf* **1** breathing; **avoir une ~ difficile** to have breathing difficulties; **2** breath; **avoir une ~ haletante** to be panting; **retenir sa ~** to hold one's breath.

respiratoire /ʀɛspiʀatwaʀ/ *adj* respiratory.

respirer /ʀɛspiʀe/ [1] **I** *vtr* **1** to breathe in [*air, dust*]; **2** to smell [*perfume*]; **3** [*person, place*] to exude; **il respire la santé** he's a picture of health.

II *vi* **1** to breathe; **2** (figurative) to catch one's breath; **laisse-moi ~** let me get my breath back; **enfin je respire!** at last I can breathe again!

resplendir /ʀɛsplɑ̃diʀ/ [3] *vi* **1** [*light*] to shine brightly; [*snow*] to sparkle; **2 ~ de santé** to be glowing with health.

resplendissant, ~e /ʀɛsplɑ̃disɑ̃, ɑ̃t/ *adj* **1** [*light*] brilliant; **2** [*beauty*] radiant.

responsabiliser /ʀɛspɔ̃sabilize/ [1] *vtr* to give [sb] a sense of responsibility.

responsabilité /ʀɛspɔ̃sabilite/ *nf* (gen) responsibility (**de** for); (Law) liability; **avoir la ~ de** to be responsible for; **sous la ~ de qn** under the supervision of sb; **engageant la ~ de la société** for which the company is liable.

■ **~ civile** (in insurance) personal liability.

responsable /ʀɛspɔ̃sabl/ **I** *adj* **1** [*person, error*] responsible (**de qch** for sth); **2** accountable (**de qch** for sth); (Law) liable (**de qch** for sth); **3 être ~ de qch/qn** to be in charge of sth/sb; **4** [*person, attitude, act*] responsible; **un vote ~** a sensible vote.

II *nmf* **1** (gen) person in charge; (of shop, project) manager; (of party) leader; (of department) head;

2 les ~s de la catastrophe the people responsible or to blame for the catastrophe; **3 le grand ~ c'est le tabac** smoking is the main cause.

■ **~ de classe** (Sch) form representative (*elected by the pupils*).

resquiller○ /ʀɛskije/ [1] *vi* (on train) not to pay the fare; (at show) to sneak in○; (in queue) to queue-jump (GB), to cut in line (US).

resquilleur○, **-euse** /ʀɛskijœʀ, øz/ *nm,f* **1** fare dodger; **2** queue-jumper (GB), person who cuts in line (US).

ressac /ʀəsak/ *nm* backwash.

ressaisir: **se ressaisir** /ʀ(ə)seziʀ/ [3] *v refl* (+ *v être*) to pull oneself together.

ressasser /ʀ(ə)sase/ [1] *vtr* **1** to brood over [*failure*]; to dwell on [*misfortunes*]; **2** to keep trotting out○ [*grievances*].

ressemblance /ʀ(ə)sɑ̃blɑ̃s/ *nf* **1** resemblance, likeness (**avec qn** to sb); **2** (between things) similarity.

ressembler /ʀ(ə)sɑ̃ble/ [1] **I ressembler à** *v+prep* to look like, to resemble; to be like; **cela ne ressemble à rien** it's like nothing on earth.

II se ressembler *v refl* (+ *v être*) **1** to look alike; **2** to be alike.

ressemeler /ʀ(ə)səmle/ [19] *vtr* to resole.

ressentiment /ʀ(ə)sɑ̃timɑ̃/ *nm* resentment; **éprouver du ~** to feel resentful.

ressentir /ʀ(ə)sɑ̃tiʀ/ [30] **I** *vtr* to feel; **ressenti comme une insulte** felt to be an insult.

II se ressentir *v refl* (+ *v être*) **se ~ de** to feel the effects of; to suffer from.

resserrer /ʀ(ə)seʀe/ [1] **I** *vtr* **1** to tighten [*knot, screw, grip*]; **2 resserrez les rangs!** close up a bit!; **3** to tighten up on [*discipline, supervision*].

II se resserrer *v refl* (+ *v être*) **1** [*road*] to narrow; **2** [*friendship*] to become stronger; **3** [*link, knot, grip*] to tighten; **4** [*troops*] to close in; [*gap*] to close; **5** [*group of people*] to draw closer together; **6** [*discipline*] to become stricter.

resservir /ʀ(ə)sɛʀviʀ/ [30] **I** *vtr* **1** to serve [sth] (up) again; **2** to give [sb] another helping; **3**○ to trot○ [sth] out again.

II se resservir *v refl* (+ *v être*) to take another helping.

ressort /ʀ(ə)sɔʀ/ *nm* **1** (Tech) spring; **2 avoir du/manquer de ~** to have/to lack resilience; **3 être du ~ de qn** to be within sb's province; (Law) to fall within the jurisdiction of [*court*]; **en premier/dernier ~** in the first/last resort.

ressortir /ʀ(ə)sɔʀtiʀ/ [30] **I** *vtr* **1** to take [sth] out again; **2** to bring [sth] out again; to dig out○ [*affair, scandal*]; **3**○ **il nous ressort toujours les mêmes histoires** he's always coming out with the same stories.

II *vi* (+ *v être*) **1** [*person*] to go out again; **2** [*bullet*] to come out; **3** to stand out; **voici ce qui ressort de l'étude** the results of the study are as follows; **faire ~** to bring to light [*contradiction*]; [*make-up*] to accentuate [*eyes*]; **faire ~ que** [*study, report*] to bring out the fact that; **4** [*film, record*] to be re-released.

III *v impers* (+ *v être*) **il ressort que** it emerges that.

ressortissant, **~e** /ʀ(ə)sɔʀtisɑ̃, ɑ̃t/ *nm,f* national.

ressouder /ʀ(ə)sude/ [1] **I** *vtr* to solder [sth] again.

II se ressouder *v refl* (+ *v être*) [*bones*] to knit (together); [*fracture*] to mend.

ressource /ʀ(ə)suʀs/ *nf* **1** resource; **les ~s énergétiques** energy resources; **2** option; **en dernière ~** as a last resort; **être à bout de ~** to be at one's wits' end; **3 avoir de la ~**○ to be resourceful; **4 ~s** means; **être sans ~s** to have no means of support.

ressusciter /ʀesysite/ [1] **I** *vtr* **1** to revive [*tradition*]; to resurrect [*past, author*]; **2** to raise [sb] from the dead; (figurative) to bring [sb] back to life.

II *vi* **1** [*dead person*] to rise from the dead; **2** [*nature*] to come back to life.

restant, **~e** /ʀɛstɑ̃, ɑ̃t/ **I** *adj* remaining.

II *nm* **1 le ~** the remainder; the rest; **2 un ~ de poulet** some left-over chicken; **un ~ de clarté** a last glimmer of light.

restaurant /ʀɛstɔʀɑ̃/ *nm* restaurant.

■ **~ d'entreprise** staff canteen; **~ universitaire, RU** university canteen (GB), cafeteria.

restaurateur, **-trice** /ʀɛstɔʀatœʀ, tʀis/ *nm,f* **1** restaurant owner; **2** restorer.

restauration /ʀɛstɔʀasjɔ̃/ *nf* **1** catering; **~ rapide** fast-food industry; **2** restoration.

restaurer /ʀɛstɔʀe/ [1] **I** *vtr* **1** to feed; **2** to restore.

II se restaurer *v refl* (+ *v être*) to have something to eat.

reste /ʀɛst/ **I** *nm* **le ~** the rest; the remainder; **un ~ de tissu** some left-over material; **conserver un ~ de lucidité** to preserve a vestige of lucidity; **je me charge du ~** leave the rest to me; **au ~, du ~** besides.

II restes *nm pl* **1** remains; **2** leftovers.

IDIOMS **elle a encore de beaux ~s**○ (humorous) she's still well preserved; **sans demander son ~** without further ado; **être** or **demeurer en ~ avec qn** to feel indebted to sb; **pour ne pas être en ~** so as not to be outdone.

rester /ʀɛste/ [1] (+ *v être*) **I** *vi* **1** to stay, to remain; **cet enfant ne peut pas ~ en place!** the child can't keep still!; **que ça reste entre nous!** this is strictly between you and me!; **2** to remain; **restez assis!** remain seated!; don't get up!; **~ sans manger** to go without food; **~ paralysé** to be left paralyzed; **~ les bras croisés** (figurative) to stand idly by; **3** to be left, to remain; **le seul ami qui me reste** the only friend I have left; **4** [*memory, work of art*] to live on; **l'habitude lui en est restée** the habit stuck; **5 ~ sur une bonne impression** to be left with a good impression; **leur refus m'est resté sur le cœur** their refusal still rankles; **6 en ~ à** to go no further than; **je compte bien ne pas en ~ là** I won't let the matter rest there; **restons-en là pour le moment** let's leave it at that for now.

II *v impers* **il reste une minute** there is one minute left; **il ne me reste plus que lui** he's all I've got left; **il me reste juste de quoi payer le loyer** I've just got enough left to pay the rent; **il reste que, il n'en reste pas moins que** the fact remains that.

restituer /ʀɛstitɥe/ [1] *vtr* **1** to restore (**à qn** to sb); **2** to reconstruct [*text*]; to reproduce [*sound, picture*]; to recreate [*atmosphere*].

restitution /ʀɛstitysjɔ̃/ *nf* **1** return; restoration; **2** reproduction.

restreindre /ʀɛstʀɛ̃dʀ/ [55] **I** *vtr* to curb, to cut back on; to limit; to restrict.

II **se restreindre** *v refl* (+ *v être*) **1** [*possibilities*] to become restricted; [*influence*] to wane; **2 se ~ (dans ses dépenses)** to cut back (on one's expenses).

restreint, ~e /ʀɛstʀɛ̃, ɛ̃t/ *adj* [*public, vocabulary*] limited; [*team*] small; **cela a été décidé en comité ~** it was decided by just a few people.

restrictif, -ive /ʀɛstʀiktif, iv/ *adj* restrictive.

restriction /ʀɛstʀiksjɔ̃/ *nf* **1** restriction; **~s salariales** wage restraints; **sans ~** freely; **2 apporter une ~ à ce qui est dit** to qualify a statement; **sans ~** [*approve*] without reservations; [*support*] unreservedly.

restructurer /ʀəstʀyktyʀe/ [1] *vtr* to restructure; to redevelop [*area*].

résultat /ʀezylta/ *nm* (gen) result; (of research) results, findings; (of negotiations, inquiry) result, outcome; **sans ~** without success; **avoir pour ~ de faire** to have the effect of doing.

résulter /ʀezylte/ [1] **I résulter de** *v+prep* to be the result of, to result from.

II *v impers* **il résulte de ce que vous venez de dire que** it follows from what you have just said that; **il en résulte que** as a result.

résumé /ʀezyme/ *nm* summary, résumé; **faire le ~ de qch** to summarize sth; **en ~** to sum up; **faire un ~ de qch (à qn)** to give (sb) a rundown of or on sth.

résumer /ʀezyme/ [1] **I** *vtr* **1** to summarize [*text*]; **2** to sum up [*news*].

II **se résumer** *v refl* (+ *v être*) **1** to sum up; **2 se ~ à** to come down to.

resurgir /ʀ(ə)syʀʒiʀ/ [3] *vi* to reappear; [*memory*] to come back.

résurrection /ʀezyʀɛksjɔ̃/ *nf* **1** resurrection; **2** revival; **3** rebirth.

rétablir /ʀetabliʀ/ [3] **I** *vtr* **1** to restore; **~ la situation** to restore normality; **~ la circulation** to get the traffic moving again; **2** to re-establish [*truth, facts*]; **3 ~ qn dans ses fonctions** to reinstate sb in his/her job.

II **se rétablir** *v refl* (+ *v être*) **1** to recover; **2** [*order*] to be restored; [*calm*] to return; [*situation*] to return to normal.

rétablissement /ʀetablismɑ̃/ *nm* **1** restoration; **2** re-establishment; **3** recovery.

rétamer /ʀetame/ [1] **I** *vtr* **1** to re-tin [*saucepan*]; **2**○ to wear [sb] out○; **3** to hammer○.

II **se rétamer**○ *v refl* (+ *v être*) to fall, to come a cropper○.

retaper○ /ʀ(ə)tape/ [1] *vtr* **1** to do up [*house*]; **2** to put [sb] on his/her feet again.

retard /ʀ(ə)taʀ/ *nm* **1** lateness; **2** delay; **un ~ de dix minutes** a ten-minute delay; **avoir du ~** to be late; **nous sommes en ~ sur l'emploi du temps** we're behind schedule; **prendre du ~** to fall or get behind (**dans** with); **avoir du courrier en ~** to have a backlog of mail; **sans ~** without delay; **3** backwardness; **il a deux ans de ~** (Sch) he's two years behind at school; **être en ~ sur son temps** to be behind the times.

retardataire /ʀ(ə)taʀdatɛʀ/ *nmf* latecomer.

retardé, ~e /ʀətaʀde/ *adj* [*person*] backward.

retardement: **à retardement** /aʀ(ə)taʀdəmɑ̃/ *phr* [*mechanism, device*] delayed-action; **bombe à ~** time-bomb; [*act, get angry*] after the event; **il comprend toujours à ~** he's slow on the uptake○.

retarder /ʀ(ə)taʀde/ [1] **I** *vtr* **1** to make [sb] late; **être retardé** [*train*] to be delayed; **2** to hold [sb] up; **3** to put off, to postpone [*departure, operation*]; **4** to put back [*clock*].

II *vi* **1** [*clock*] to be slow; **je retarde de cinq minutes** my watch is five minutes slow; **2 ~ (sur son temps)** to be behind the times; **3**○ to be out of touch.

retenir /ʀət(ə)niʀ, ʀtəniʀ/ [36] **I** *vtr* **1** to keep [*person*]; **je ne vous retiens pas!** don't let me keep you!; **~ qn prisonnier** to hold sb captive; **~ qn à dîner** to ask sb to stay for dinner; **2** to hold [sb] up, to detain [*person*]; **3** to hold [*object, attention*]; to hold back [*hair, dog, crowd*]; to retain [*soil*]; to stop [*person*]; to rein in [*horse*]; **~ sa langue** to hold one's tongue; **~ qn par la manche** to catch hold of sb's sleeve; **votre réclamation a retenu toute notre attention** your complaint is receiving our full attention; **4** to hold back [*tears*]; to hold [*breath*]; to stifle [*scream, yawn*]; to contain, to suppress [*anger*]; **5** to retain [*heat, water, odour*]; **6** to reserve, to book [*table, room*]; to set [*date*]; **7** to deduct [*sum*]; **8** to remember; **cet enfant ne retient rien** that child doesn't take anything in; **toi, je te retiens**○! I won't forget this!; **9** to accept [*argument, plan*]; (Law) to uphold [*charge*]; **votre candidature a été retenue** you're being considered for the post; **10 je pose 5 et je retiens 1** I put down 5 and carry 1.

II **se retenir** *v refl* (+ *v être*) **1** to stop oneself; **se ~ à qch** to hang on to sth; **2 se ~ de pleurer** to hold back the tears; **il n'a pas pu se ~ de rire** he couldn't help laughing; **3**○ to control oneself.

rétention /ʀetɑ̃sjɔ̃/ *nf* **1** (Med) retention; **2** withholding (**de** of).

retentir /ʀ(ə)tɑ̃tiʀ/ [3] *vi* **1** to ring out; to resound; **2 ~ sur** [*fatigue, drug*] to have an impact on; [*event*] to have repercussions on.

retentissant, ~e /ʀ(ə)tɑ̃tisɑ̃, ɑ̃t/ *adj* **1** [*failure*] resounding; [*trial, film*] sensational; **2** [*cry, noise*] ringing; resounding.

retentissement /ʀ(ə)tɑ̃tismɑ̃/ *nm* (gen) effect;

(of book, artist) impact; **avoir un (grand) ~** to cause a (great) sensation.

retenue /Rət(ə)ny/ *nf* **1** restraint; **perdre toute ~** to lose one's inhibitions; **n'avoir aucune ~ dans sa conduite** to behave wildly; **boire sans ~** to drink to excess; **2** deduction (**sur** from); **3** (Sch) detention; **4 tu as oublié la ~ des dizaines** you forgot to carry over from the tens column; **5 ~ (d'eau)** reservoir.

réticence /Retisɑ̃s/ *nf* **1** reluctance; **sans ~** [*talk*] openly; [*accept*] unreservedly; **2 ses ~s en ce qui concerne le passé** his/her reticence about the past.

réticent, ~e /Retisɑ̃, ɑ̃t/ *adj* **1** hesitant; **2** reluctant.

rétif, -ive /Retif, iv/ *adj* [*horse*] restive; [*person*] rebellious.

rétine /Retin/ *nf* retina.

retiré, ~e /RətiRe/ *adj* **1** [*life*] secluded; **2** [*place*] remote.

retirer /RətiRe/ [1] **I** *vtr* **1** to take off [*garment, piece of jewellery*]; **2** to take out, to remove (**de** from); **~ un corps des décombres** to pull a body from or out of the rubble; **~ ses troupes d'un pays** to withdraw one's troops from a country; **3** to withdraw [*foot, hand*]; **retire ta main** move your hand away; **4** to withdraw [*permission, privilege*]; to take away, to remove [*right, property*]; **~ un produit de la vente** to recall a product; **~ une pièce de l'affiche** to close a play; **5** to withdraw [*complaint, offer, support*]; **~ sa candidature** (for a job) to withdraw one's application; (at an election) to stand down; **je retire ce que j'ai dit** I take back what I said; **6** to collect, to pick up [*ticket, luggage*]; to withdraw [*money*]; **7** to get, to derive [*profits*]; **il en retire 10 000 francs par an** he gets 10,000 francs a year out of it; **8** to extract [*mineral, oil*].

II se retirer *v refl* (+ *v être*) **1** to withdraw, to leave; **un homme retiré de la politique** a man retired from political life; **se ~ du combat** to pull out; **2 la mer se retire** the tide is going out.

retombées /Rətɔ̃be/ *nf pl* **1 ~s radioactives** radioactive fallout; **2** effects, consequences; **3** (of invention) spin-offs.

retomber /Rətɔ̃be/ [1] *vi* (+ *v être*) **1** to fall again; **~ dans la misère** to sink back into poverty; **~ en enfance** to regress to childhood; **2** [*person, cat, projectile*] to land; [*ball, curtain*] to come down; [*fog*] to set in again; **ça va te ~ sur le nez**° (figurative) it'll come down on your head; **3** [*anger*] to subside; [*interest*] to wane; **4** [*currency, temperature*] to fall; **5 ~ sur qn** [*responsibility*] to fall on sb; **tu fais des bêtises et c'est sur moi que ça retombe** you behave stupidly, and I'm the one who has to pay for it; **faire ~ la responsabilité sur qn** to pass the buck° to sb.

retordre /R(ə)tɔRdR/ [6] *vtr* **donner du fil à ~ à qn** to give sb a hard time.

rétorquer /RetɔRke/ [1] *vtr* to retort (**que** that).

retors, ~e /RətɔR, ɔRs/ *adj* [*person*] crafty; [*argument*] devious.

rétorsion /RetɔRsjɔ̃/ *nf* retaliation; **mesure de ~** retaliatory measure.

retouche /R(ə)tuʃ/ *nf* alteration; (of photograph, picture) retouching.

retoucher /R(ə)tuʃe/ [1] *vtr* to make alterations to; to touch up.

retour /R(ə)tuR/ *nm* return; **(billet de) ~** return ticket (GB), round trip (ticket) (US); **au ~** on the way back; **être de ~ (à la maison)** to be back (home); **~ à la normale** return to normal; **on attend le ~ au calme** people are waiting for things to calm down; **'~ à la case départ'** 'back to square one'; **il connaît maintenant le succès et c'est un juste ~ des choses** he's successful now, and deservedly so; **faire un ~ en force** [*singer, artist*] to make a big comeback; **elle s'engage, en ~, à payer la facture** she undertakes for her part to pay the bill; **aimer sans ~** to suffer from unrequited love; **'sans ~ ni consigne'** 'no deposit or return'; **par ~ du courrier** by return of post (GB), by the next mail (US).

■ **~ d'âge** change of life; **~ en arrière** flashback; **ce serait un ~ en arrière** it would be a step backward(s); **~ de bâton**° backlash.

IDIOMS **être sur le ~**° to be over the hill°.

retournement /R(ə)tuRnəmɑ̃/ *nm* reversal; **un ~ de l'opinion publique** a turn around in public opinion.

retourner /R(ə)tuRne/ [1] **I** *vtr* (+ *v avoir*) **1** to turn [sth] over; to turn [*mattress*]; **2** to turn [sth] inside out; **3** to turn over [*earth*]; to toss [*salad*]; **~ une idée dans sa tête** to turn an idea over in one's mind; **4** to return [*compliment, criticism*]; **~ la situation** to reverse the situation; **5** to turn [sth] upside down [*room*]; [*news, film*] to shake [*person*]; **je suis encore tout retourné**° I'm still quite shaken; **6** to send [sth] back, to return.

II *vi* (+ *v être*) to go back, to return.

III se retourner *v refl* (+ *v être*) **1** to turn around; **partir sans se ~** to leave without a backward glance; **2** to turn over; **il n'a pas arrêté de se ~ (dans son lit)** he kept tossing and turning; **3**° to get organized; **4 se ~ contre qn** [*person*] to turn against sb; [*arguments*] to backfire on sb; **se ~ contre ses alliés** to turn on one's allies; **5 elle s'est retourné le doigt** she bent back her finger; **6 s'en ~ (chez soi)** to go back (home).

IV *v impers* **j'aime savoir de quoi il retourne** I like to know what's going on.

IDIOMS **~ qn comme une crêpe**° to make sb change their mind completely.

retracer /RətRase/ [12] *vtr* **1** to redraw [*line*]; **2** to recount [*event*].

rétractable /RetRaktabl/ *adj* [*blade*] retractable; [*offer*] revocable.

rétracter /RetRakte/ [1] *vtr*, **se rétracter** *v refl* (+ *v être*) to retract.

retrait /R(ə)tRɛ/ **I** *nm* (gen) withdrawal; (of suitcase, packet) collection; (of defective goods) recall; **~ du permis (de conduire)** disqualification from driving.

II en retrait *phr* **maison (située) en ~ de** house set back from [*road*]; **se tenir en ~** to stand back; **rester en ~** to stay in the background.

retraite /ʀ(ə)tʀɛt/ *nf* **1** retirement; **prendre sa ~** to retire; **~ anticipée** early retirement; **2** pension; **3** (Mil) retreat; **battre en ~** (Mil) to beat a retreat, to retreat; (figurative) to beat a hasty retreat; **4** retreat; (of bandits) hiding place.

retraité, ~e /ʀətʀete/ *nm,f* retired person; **les ~s** retired people.

retraiter /ʀətʀete/ [1] *vtr* to reprocess [*plutonium*].

retranchement /ʀ(ə)tʀɑ̃ʃmɑ̃/ *nm* entrenchment; **pousser qn dans ses derniers ~s** (figurative) to drive sb into a corner.

retrancher /ʀ(ə)tʀɑ̃ʃe/ [1] **I** *vtr* **1** to cut out [*word*]; **2** to subtract [*amount*]; to deduct [*costs*].
II se retrancher *v refl* (+ *v être*) **1** (Mil, gen) to take up position; to entrench oneself; **2 se ~ derrière** to hide behind [*decision, law*].

retransmettre /ʀətʀɑ̃smɛtʀ/ [60] *vtr* **1** to broadcast; **retransmis par satellite** relayed by satellite; **2** to retransmit.

retransmission /ʀətʀɑ̃smisjɔ̃/ *nf* **1** broadcast; **2** relay; **3** retransmission.

rétrécir /ʀetʀesiʀ/ [3] *vi*, **se rétrécir** *v refl* (+ *v être*) **1** to narrow (**en** into); **2** to shrink (**de** by); **3** to contract.

rétrécissement /ʀetʀesismɑ̃/ *nm* **1** shrinkage; **2** narrowing; **3** contraction.

rétribuer /ʀetʀibɥe/ [1] *vtr* to remunerate [*person, work*].

rétribution /ʀetʀibysjɔ̃/ *nf* **1** remuneration; **2** reward (**de** for).

rétro /ʀetʀo/ *nm* **1** nostalgic style; **2** retro fashions.

rétroactif, -ive /ʀetʀoaktif, iv/ *adj* (Law, gen) retroactive.

rétrograde /ʀetʀogʀad/ *adj* **1** [*person*] reactionary; [*policy, measure*] retrograde; **2** [*movement*] retrograde.

rétrograder /ʀetʀogʀade/ [1] **I** *vtr* **1** to demote; **2** (Sport) to relegate.
II *vi* **1** (Aut) to change down (GB), to downshift (US); **2** (in hierarchy) to move down.

rétrospectif, -ive[1] /ʀetʀɔspɛktif, iv/ *adj* retrospective.

rétrospective[2] /ʀetʀɔspɛktiv/ *nf* (gen) retrospective; (of films) festival.

rétrospectivement /ʀetʀɔspɛktivmɑ̃/ *adv* in retrospect; looking back.

retroussé, ~e /ʀ(ə)tʀuse/ *adj* [*nose*] turned up; [*lip*] curling.

retrousser /ʀ(ə)tʀuse/ [1] *vtr* to hitch up (GB), to hike up (US) [*skirt*]; to roll up [*sleeves*].

retrouvailles /ʀətʀuvɑj/ *nf pl* **1** reunion; **2** reconciliation.

retrouver /ʀətʀuve/ [1] **I** *vtr* **1** to find [*lost object*]; **~ son chemin** to find one's way; **2** to find [sth] again [*work, conditions, object*]; **3** to regain, to recover [*strength, health*]; **4** to remember [*name, tune*]; **5** to be back in [*place*]; **6** to recognize [*person, style*]; **je retrouve sa mère en elle** I can see her mother in her; **on le retrouve dans cette œuvre** you can see his hand in this work; **quand tu souris, je te retrouve** that's more like you to be smiling; **7** to join, to meet [*person*]; **je te retrouverai!** I'll get my own back on you!
II se retrouver *v refl* (+ *v être*) **1** to meet (again); **on s'est retrouvé en famille** the family got together; **comme on se retrouve!** fancy seeing you here!; **2 se ~ enceinte** to find oneself pregnant; **se ~ sans argent** to be left penniless; **se ~ au même point** to be back to square one; **3 se** or **s'y ~ dans** to find one's way around in [*place, mess*]; to follow, to understand [*explanation*]; **il y a trop de changements, on ne s'y retrouve plus** there are too many changes, we don't know if we're coming or going; **4**○ **s'y ~** to break even; (making profit) to do well; **5** [*quality*] to be found; [*problem*] to occur; **6 se ~ dans qn/qch** to see or recognize oneself in sb/sth.
IDIOMS **un de perdu, dix de retrouvés** there are plenty more fish in the sea.

rétroviseur /ʀetʀovizœʀ/ *nm* **1** rear-view mirror; **2** wing mirror (GB), outside rear-view mirror (US).

réunification /ʀeynifikasjɔ̃/ *nf* reunification.

réunifier /ʀeynifje/ [2] **I** *vtr* to reunify.
II se réunifier *v refl* (+ *v être*) to be reunified, to reunite.

réunion /ʀeynjɔ̃/ *nf* **1** meeting; **être en ~** [*person*] to be at a meeting; **2** gathering; **3** reunion; **4** (of different talents) combination; (of poems) collection; **5** union (**à** with); (of companies) merger.

réunir /ʀeyniʀ/ [3] **I** *vtr* **1** [*conference*] to bring together [*participants*]; [*organizer*] to get [sb] together [*participants*]; **2** to call [sb] together [*delegates*]; to convene [*assembly*]; **3** to have [sb] round (GB) or over [*friends*]; **4** to join [*edges*]; **~ deux personnes** to bring two people together (again); to reconcile two people; **5** to merge [*companies*]; to unite [*provinces*]; **6 ~ les conditions nécessaires** to fulfil[GB] all the necessary conditions; **7** to raise [*funds*]; **8** to assemble [*elements, evidence*]; to gather [sth] together [*documents*]; **9** [*road, canal*] to connect.
II se réunir *v refl* (+ *v être*) to meet; to get together.

réussir /ʀeysiʀ/ [3] **I** *vtr* to achieve [*unification*]; to carry out [sth] successfully [*operation*]; to make a success of [*life*]; **~ son coup**○ to pull it off○.
II réussir à *v+prep* **1 ~ à faire** to succeed in doing; **~ à un examen** to pass an exam; **2 ~ à qn** [*life, method*] to turn out well for sb; [*rest*] to do sb good; **le vin blanc ne me réussit pas** white wine doesn't agree with me.
III *vi* **1** to succeed; **2** [*attempt*] to be successful; **3** [*person*] to do well.

réussite /ʀeysit/ *nf* **1** (gen) success; **2** (Games) patience (GB), solitaire (US).

revaloir /ʀ(ə)valwaʀ/ [45] *vtr* **je te revaudrai ça** (vengefully) I'll get even with you for that; (in gratitude) I'll return the favour[GB].

revalorisation /ʀ(ə)valɔʀizasjɔ̃/ *nf* **une ~ des salaires de 3%** a 3% wage increase.

revaloriser /ʀ(ə)valɔʀize/ [1] *vtr* **1** to increase [*salary*]; to revalue [*currency*]; **2** to reassert the value of [*manual labour, traditions*]; **3** to renovate [*area*].

revanche /ʀ(ə)vɑ̃ʃ/ **I** *nf* **1** revenge; **2** (Sport) return match (GB) or game (US).
II en revanche *phr* on the other hand.

rêvasser /ʀɛvase/ [1] *vi* to daydream.

rêve /ʀɛv/ *nm* **1** dreaming; **2** dream; **~ éveillé** daydream; **fais de beaux ~s!** sweet dreams!; **en ~** in a dream; **3 ~ de jeunesse** youthful dream; **une maison de ~** a dream house; **3 c'est le ~** this is just perfect.

rêvé, ~e /ʀeve/ *adj* ideal, perfect.

revêche /ʀəvɛʃ/ *adj* [*manner, tone*] sour; [*person*] crabby.

réveil /ʀevɛj/ *nm* **1** waking (up); **au ~, il allume la radio** when he wakes up, he turns on the radio; **2** (after anaesthetic) **j'ai eu des nausées au ~** I felt nauseous when I regained consciousness; **3** (of movement) resurgence; (of pain) return; (of conscience) awakening; (of volcano) return to activity; **4** (Mil) reveille; **5** alarm clock.

réveille-matin /ʀevɛjmatɛ̃/ *nm inv* alarm clock.

réveiller /ʀeveje/ [1] **I** *vtr* **1** to wake [sb] up, to wake; **2** to revive, to bring [sb] round (GB) [*person*]; to whet [*appetite*]; to awaken [*feeling*]; to arouse [*curiosity*]; to stir up [*memory*]; **~ la douleur** to bring back the pain.
II se réveiller *v refl* (+ *v être*) **1** to wake up; to awaken; **2** to regain consciousness; **3** [*nature*] to reawaken; [*volcano*] to become active again; **4** [*pain, appetite*] to come back; [*jealousy, memory*] to be reawakened.

réveillon /ʀevɛjɔ̃/ *nm* **~ du Nouvel An** New Year's Eve party.

réveillonner /ʀevɛjɔne/ [1] *vi* to celebrate Christmas Eve; to see the New Year in.

révélateur, -trice /ʀevelatœʀ, tʀis/ **I** *adj* [*detail, fact*] revealing, telling.
II *nm* **1** (in photography) developer; **2** (of feeling, malaise) sign (**de** to).

révélation /ʀevelasjɔ̃/ *nf* revelation; **être la ~ de l'année** to be the discovery of the year.

révéler /ʀevele/ [14] **I** *vtr* **1** to reveal, to disclose; to give away [*secret*]; **2** to show; **3** to discover, to launch [*author, artist*]; **4** (in photography) to develop.
II se révéler *v refl* (+ *v être*) **se ~ faux** to turn out to be wrong.

revenant, ~e /ʀəv(ə)nɑ̃, ɑ̃t/ *nm,f* ghost; **tiens, une ~e**○! (humorous) long time no see○!

revendeur, -euse /ʀ(ə)vɑ̃dœʀ, øz/ *nm,f* **1** stockist; **2 un ~ de drogue** a drug dealer; **3** seller (of stolen goods).

revendication /ʀ(ə)vɑ̃dikasjɔ̃/ *nf* (of workers) demand; (of country) claim.

revendiquer /ʀ(ə)vɑ̃dike/ [1] *vtr* **1** to demand [*pay rise*]; to claim [*territory*]; **2** to claim responsibility for [*attack*]; **~ la responsabilité de** to take (full) responsibility for; **3** to proclaim [*origins*].

revendre /ʀ(ə)vɑ̃dʀ/ [6] *vtr* **1** to sell [sth] retail, to retail; **2** to resell [*car, house*]; to sell (off) [*shares*]; to sell on [*stolen object*]; **avoir des crayons à ~** to have pencils galore; **avoir de l'énergie à ~** to have energy to spare.

revenir /ʀəvniʀ, ʀvəniʀ/ [36] (+ *v être*) **I** *vi* **1** to come back; to come again; **2** [*person, animal, vehicle*] to come back, to return; **~ sur terre** (figurative) to come down to earth; **~ de loin** to come back from far away; (figurative) to have had a close shave; **mon chèque m'est revenu** my cheque (GB) or check (US) was returned; **3 ~ à** to return to, to come back to [*method, story*]; **~ à ses habitudes** to revert to one's old habits; **n'y reviens pas!** don't let it happen again!; **4** [*appetite, memory, fashion*] to come back; [*sun*] to come out again; [*season*] to return; [*date, holiday*] to come round again (GB), to come again (US); [*idea, theme*] to recur; **le calme est revenu** things have calmed down; **~ à la mémoire** or **l'esprit de qn** to come back to sb; **ça me revient!** now I remember!, now it's coming back!; **5 ~ à 100 francs** to come to 100 francs, to cost 100 francs; **ça revient cher** it works out expensive; **ça revient au même** it amounts or comes to the same thing; **6 ~ sur** to go back over [*question, past*]; to go back on [*decision, promise*]; to retract [*confession*]; **7 ~ de** to get over [*illness, surprise*]; to lose [*illusion*]; to abandon [*theory*]; **la vie à la campagne, j'en suis revenu** as for life in the country, I've seen it for what it is; **être revenu de tout** to be blasé; **je n'en reviens pas**○ **des progrès que tu as faits** I'm amazed at the progress you've made; **8 ~ aux oreilles de qn** [*remark*] to reach sb's ears; **9 ~ à qn** [*property*] to go to sb; [*honour*] to fall to sb; **ça leur revient de droit** it's theirs by right; **les 10% qui me reviennent** the 10% that's coming to me; **la décision revient au rédacteur** it is the editor's decision; **10** (Culin) **faire ~** to brown.
II *v impers* **c'est à vous qu'il revient de trancher** it is for you to decide.
IDIOMS **il a une tête qui ne me revient pas** I don't like the look of him.

revente /ʀ(ə)vɑ̃t/ *nf* **1** (of car, house) resale; **2** (of gold, shares) sale.

revenu /ʀəv(ə)ny, ʀvəny/ *nm* income; (of state) revenue.
■ **~ minimum d'insertion, RMI** *minimum benefit paid to those with no other source of income.*

rêver /ʀeve/ [1] **I** *vtr* **1** to dream (**que** that); **2** to dream of [*success, revenge*].
II *vi* to dream (**de** about); **~ tout éveillé** to be lost in a daydream.

réverbération /ʀevɛʀbeʀasjɔ̃/ *nf* **1** glare; **2** reflection; **3** reverberation.

réverbère /ʀevɛʀbɛʀ/ *nm* street lamp or light.

réverbérer /ʀevɛʀbeʀe/ [14] **I** *vtr* to reflect [*light, heat*].
II se réverbérer *v refl* (+ *v être*) [*light, heat*] to be reflected; [*sound*] to reverberate.

révérence /ʀeveʀɑ̃s/ *nf* **1** curtsey; bow; **2** reverence.
IDIOMS **tirer sa ~**○ to take one's leave (**à qn** of sb).

révérencieux, **-ieuse** /ʀeveʀɑ̃sjø, øz/ *adj* deferential; **peu ~** irreverent.

révérend, **~e** /ʀeveʀɑ̃, ɑ̃d/ *nm,f* **1** Father/Mother Superior; **2** reverend.

révérer /ʀeveʀe/ [14] *vtr* to revere.

rêverie /ʀɛvʀi/ *nf* **1** daydreaming; **2** daydream.

revers /ʀ(ə)vɛʀ/ *nm inv* **1** (of hand) back; (of cloth) wrong side; (of coin) reverse; **le ~ de la médaille** (figurative) the downside○; **2** (on jacket) lapel; (of trousers) turn-up (GB), cuff (US); (of sleeve) cuff; **3** (in tennis) backhand (stroke); **4** setback; **~ de fortune** reversal of fortune.

réversible /ʀevɛʀsibl/ *adj* (gen) reversible; (Law) reversionary.

revêtement /ʀ(ə)vɛtmɑ̃/ *nm* **1** (of road) surface; **2** coating; covering.

revêtir /ʀ(ə)vɛtiʀ/ [33] **I** *vtr* **1** to assume [*gravity, solemnity*]; to have [*disadvantage*] to take on [*aspect, significance*]; to take on [*significance*]; **~ la forme de** to take the form of; **2** to put on [*garment*]; **3 ~ qch de** to cover sth with [*carpet, tiles*].
II se revêtir *v refl* (+ *v être*) **se ~ de** to put on [*cloak*]; to become covered with [*snow*].

rêveur, **-euse** /ʀɛvœʀ, øz/ **I** *adj* dreamy; **cela laisse ~** it makes you wonder.
II *nm,f* dreamer.

revient /ʀ(ə)vjɛ̃/ *nm* **prix de ~** cost price.

revigorer /ʀ(ə)vigɔʀe/ [1] *vtr* **1** [*drink, air*] to revive; **2** to hearten.

revirement /ʀ(ə)viʀmɑ̃/ *nm* turnaround; **~ total** U-turn (GB), flip-flop (US).

réviser /ʀevize/ [1] *vtr* **1** to revise [*position, prices*]; to review [*constitution*]; **2** to overhaul [*car, boiler*]; to revise [*manuscript*]; **3** (Sch) to revise (GB), to review (US).

révision /ʀevizjɔ̃/ *nm* **1** revision; review; **2** (of car) service; (of manuscript) revision; (of accounts) audit; **3** (Sch) revision (GB), review (US).

revitaliser /ʀ(ə)vitalize/ [1] *vtr* to revitalize.

revivre /ʀ(ə)vivʀ/ [63] **I** *vtr* **1** to go over, to relive [*event, past*]; **faire ~ qch à qn** to bring back memories of sth to sb; **2** to live through [sth] again [*war*].
II *vi* **1** to come alive again; **2** to be able to breathe again; **3 faire ~** to revive [*tradition*]; to bring [sth] back to life [*event*].

révocable /ʀevɔkabl/ *adj* [*will*] revocable; [*person*] dismissible (*from office*).

révocation /ʀevɔkasjɔ̃/ *nf* **1** revocation; **2** dismissal.

revoici○ /ʀ(ə)vwasi/ *prep* **~ Marianne!** here's Marianne again!; **nous ~ au point de départ** we are back to square one.

revoilà /ʀ(ə)vwala/ = **revoici**.

revoir[1] /ʀ(ə)vwaʀ/ [46] *vtr* **1** to see [sb/sth] again; **je la revois encore dans sa robe bleue** I can still see her in her blue dress; **2** to go over [*exercise, lesson*]; to review [*method*]; to check through [*accounts*].

revoir[2]: **au revoir** /ɔʀ(ə)vwaʀ/ *phr* goodbye, bye○.

révoltant, **~e** /ʀevɔltɑ̃, ɑ̃t/ *adj* appalling.

révolte /ʀevɔlt/ *nf* **1** revolt; **2** rebellion.

révolter /ʀevɔlte/ [1] **I** *vtr* to appal[GB].
II se révolter *v refl* (+ *v être*) **1** to rebel; **2** to be appalled (**contre, devant** by).

révolu, **~e** /ʀevɔly/ *adj* **1 ce temps est ~** those days are over or past; **2 avoir 12 ans ~s** to be over 12 years of age; **après une année ~e** after a year has gone by.

révolution /ʀevɔlysjɔ̃/ *nf* **1** revolution; **2** turmoil; **3** (of planet) revolution.

révolutionnaire /ʀevɔlysjɔnɛʀ/ *adj, nmf* revolutionary.

révolutionner /ʀevɔlysjɔne/ [1] *vtr* to revolutionize.

revolver /ʀevɔlvɛʀ/ *nm* **1** revolver; **2** handgun; **coup de ~** gunshot.

révoquer /ʀevɔke/ [1] *vtr* **1** to revoke [*will*]; **2** to dismiss [*person*].

revue /ʀ(ə)vy/ *nf* **1** (gen) magazine; (academic) journal; **2** (Mil) parade; **passer en ~** to review [*troops*]; to inspect [*equipment*]; **3** revue; **4** examination; **passer qch en ~** to go over sth.
■ **~ de presse** review of the papers.

révulser /ʀevylse/ [1] **I** *vtr* to appal[GB].
II se révulser *v refl* (+ *v être*) [*eyes*] to roll (upward(s)); [*face*] to contort.

révulsion /ʀevylsjɔ̃/ *nf* (Med, gen) revulsion.

rez-de-chaussée /ʀedʃose/ *nm inv* ground floor (GB), first floor (US).

RF (*written abbr* = **République française**) French Republic.

rhabiller /ʀabije/ [1] *vtr* **~ qn** to dress sb again.

rhapsodie /ʀapsɔdi/ *nf* rhapsody.

rhésus /ʀezys/ *nm inv* **1 facteur ~** rhesus factor; **2** rhesus monkey.

rhétorique /ʀetɔʀik/ **I** *adj* [*effect, device*] rhetorical.
II *nf* rhetoric (**de** of).

Rhin /ʀɛ̃/ *pr nm* **le ~** the Rhine.

rhinocéros /ʀinɔseʀɔs/ *nm inv* rhinoceros.

rhododendron /ʀɔdɔdɛ̃dʀɔ̃/ *nm* rhododendron.

rhubarbe /ʀybaʀb/ *nf* rhubarb; **confiture de ~** rhubarb jam.

rhum /ʀɔm/ *nm* rum.

rhumatisme /ʀymatism/ *nm* rheumatism.

rhume /ʀym/ *nm* cold; **~ des foins** hay fever.

riant, **~e** /ʀijɑ̃, ɑ̃t/ *adj* [*face*] happy; [*landscape*] pleasant.

ribambelle○ /ʀibɑ̃bɛl/ *nf* (of children) flock; (of friends) host; (of names) whole string.

ricanement /ʀikanmɑ̃/ *nm* **1** snigger; **2** giggle.

ricaner /ʀikane/ [1] *vi* **1** to snigger; **2** to giggle.

riche /ʀiʃ/ **I** *adj* (gen) rich; [*person*] rich, wealthy, well-off; [*library*] well-stocked; [*decor*] elaborate; [*novel*] richly textured; **une ~ idée** an excellent idea.

II *nmf* rich man/woman; **les ~s** the rich, the wealthy.

richesse /riʃɛs/ **I** *nf* **1** wealth; **c'est toute notre ~** it's all we have; **2** (of jewellery) magnificence; (of garment) richness; (of furniture) sumptuousness; **3** (of foodstuff) (in fat, fibre) richness; **4** (of fauna, vocabulary, collection) richness; (of documentation) wealth.

II richesses *nf pl* wealth; **~s naturelles** natural resources.

ricin /risɛ̃/ *nf* castor-oil plant; **huile de ~** castor oil.

ricocher /rikɔʃe/ [1] *vi* [*bullet*] to ricochet; [*stone*] (on water) to skim.

ricochet /rikɔʃɛ/ *nm* (of bullet) ricochet; (of stone) bounce; **faire des ~s** to skim stones.

rictus /riktys/ *nm inv* (fixed) grin, rictus.

ride /rid/ *nf* (on face, fruit) wrinkle; (on lake) ripple.

rideau, *pl* **~x** /rido/ *nm* **1** curtain; **2** (of shop) roller shutter; **3** (of flames) wall.

■ **~ de fumée** blanket of smoke; (figurative) smokescreen.

IDIOMS **tirer le ~ sur qch** to draw a veil over sth.

rider /ride/ [1] **I** *vtr* **1** to wrinkle [*face, skin*]; **2** to ripple [*surface, lake*].

II se rider *v refl* (+ *v être*) **1** [*skin*] to wrinkle; **2** [*lake*] to ripple.

ridicule /ridikyl/ **I** *adj* **1** ridiculous; **2** [*wage*] ridiculously low, pathetic.

II *nm* **1** ridicule; **tourner qn en ~** to make sb look ridiculous; **2** (of situation) absurdity.

ridiculiser /ridikylize/ [1] **I** *vtr* to ridicule; to wipe the floor with [*competitor*].

II se ridiculiser *v refl* (+ *v être*) [*person*] to make a fool of oneself.

ridule /ridyl/ *nf* fine wrinkle.

rien[1] /rjɛ̃/ **I** *pron* **1** nothing; **il n'y a plus ~** there's nothing left; **il n'en est ~** it's nothing of the sort; **~ n'y fait!** nothing's any good!; **il n'a ~ d'un intrigant** there's nothing of the schemer about him; **~ d'autre** nothing else; **'pourquoi?'—'pour ~'** 'why?'—'no reason'; **parler pour ~** to waste one's breath; **'merci'—'de ~'** 'thank you'—'you're welcome' or 'not at all'; **en moins de ~** in no time at all; **ça ou ~, c'est pareil** it makes no odds; **c'est trois fois ~**○ it's next to nothing; **2 ~ que la bouteille pèse deux kilos** the bottle alone weighs two kilos; **elle voudrait un bureau ~ qu'à elle**○ she would like an office all to herself; **~ que pour te plaire** just to please you; **~ que ça○?** is that all?; **ils habitent un château, ~ que ça!** (ironic) they live in a castle, no less! or if you please!; **3** anything; **avant de ~ signer** before signing anything; **sans que j'en sache ~** without my knowing anything about it; **4** (Sport, gen) nil; (in tennis) love.

II de rien (du tout) *phr* **fille de ~** worthless girl; **un petit bleu de ~ (du tout)** a tiny bruise.

III un rien○ *phr* a (tiny) bit; **un ~ pédant** a bit pedantic.

IV en rien *phr* at all, in any way.

IDIOMS **~ à faire!** it's no good or use!; **ce n'est pas ~!** (exploit) it's quite something!; (task) it's no joke, it's not exactly a picnic○!; (sum of money) it's not exactly peanuts○!

rien[2] /rjɛ̃/ *nm* **un ~ le fâche** the slightest thing annoys him; **se disputer pour un ~** to quarrel over nothing; **les petits ~s qui rendent la vie agréable** the little things which make life pleasant; **un ~ de cognac** a dash of brandy; **en un ~ de temps** in next to no time; **un/une ~ du tout** a no-good○, a worthless person.

rieur, rieuse /rijœr, øz/ *adj* [*person, tone*] cheerful; [*face, eyes*] laughing.

rigide /riʒid/ *adj* **1** rigid; **2** stiff.

rigidité /riʒidite/ *nf* rigidity.

rigolade○ /rigɔlad/ *nf* **1 quelle ~!** what a laugh○!, what fun!; **2** joke; **3 réparer ça, c'est de la ~!** repairing this is a piece of cake○.

rigole /rigɔl/ *nf* **1** channel; **2** rivulet.

rigoler○ /rigɔle/ [1] *vi* **1** to laugh; **2** to have fun; **3** to joke, to kid○; **il ne faut pas ~ avec la sécurité** you mustn't mess about or fool around with security.

rigolo○, **-ote** /rigɔlo, ɔt/ **I** *adj* **1** funny; **2** odd, funny.

II *nm,f* **1** joker; **2 c'est un petit ~** he's quite a little comedian.

rigoriste /rigɔrist/ *adj* [*attitude*] unbending, rigoristic; [*morals*] strict.

rigoureux, -euse /rigurø, øz/ *adj* **1** [*discipline, regulations, person*] strict; **2** [*climate, working conditions*] harsh, severe; **3** [*research, demonstration*] meticulous; [*analysis, thinking*] rigorous.

rigueur /rigœr/ **I** *nf* **1** strictness; **2** harshness; **3** rigour[GB]; **4** (Econ) austerity.

II de rigueur *phr* obligatory; **visite de ~** obligatory social call.

III à la rigueur *phr* **nous pouvons à la ~ emprunter à mes parents** if we absolutely have to we can borrow from my parents; **à la ~ je peux te prêter 100 francs** at a pinch (GB) or in a pinch (US) I can lend you 100 francs.

IDIOMS **tenir ~ à qn de qch** to bear sb a grudge for sth.

rillettes /rijɛt/ *nf pl* ≈ potted meat.

rime /rim/ *nf* rhyme.

rimer /rime/ [1] *vi* **1** to rhyme; **2 cela ne rime à rien** it makes no sense.

rimmel® /rimɛl/ *nm* mascara.

rinçage /rɛ̃saʒ/ *nm* **1** rinsing; **2** rinse.

rince-doigts /rɛ̃sdwa/ *nm inv* **1** finger bowl; **2** finger wipe.

rincer /rɛ̃se/ [12] **I** *vtr* **1** to rinse; **2** to rinse [sth] out.

II se rincer *v refl* (+ *v être*) **se ~ les mains/les cheveux** to rinse one's hands/hair.

IDIOMS **se ~ l'œil**○ to get an eyeful.

ring /riŋ/ *nm* (boxing) ring.

ringard○, **~e** /rɛ̃gar, ard/ *adj* dated; out of date; behind the times.

ripaille○ /ripɑj/ *nf* blow-out○, feast.

riper /ʀipe/ [1] *vi* [*foot*] to slip; [*bicycle*] to skid.

ripoliner /ʀipɔline/ [1] *vtr* **1** to paint; **2** to give [sth] a face-lift.

riposte /ʀipɔst/ *nf* **1** reply, riposte; **2** response; **3** (Sport) (in fencing) riposte; (in boxing, wrestling) counter.

riposter /ʀipɔste/ [1] **I** *vtr* to retort (**que** that).
II *vi* **1** to retort; **~ à qn/qch par** to counter sb/sth with; **2** to respond; **3** (Mil) to return fire, to shoot back; **4** (in sport) to ripost.

ripou°, *pl* **~x** /ʀipu/ *adj* [*person, policeman*] crooked°, bent°.

riquiqui° /ʀikiki/ *adj inv* [*room, car*] poky°; [*portion*] measly°.

rire[1] /ʀiʀ/ [68] **I** *vi* **1** to laugh; **tu nous feras toujours ~!** you're a real scream°!; **il n'y a pas de quoi ~!** that's not funny!, that's no laughing matter!; **2** to have fun; **il faut bien ~ un peu** you need a bit of fun now and again; **fini de ~** the fun's over; **tu veux ~!** you must be joking or kidding°!; **c'était pour ~** it was a joke; **sans ~**° seriously, honestly; **laisse-moi ~**°, **ne me fais pas ~**° don't make me laugh; **3 ~ de qch/qn** to laugh at sth/sb.
II se rire *v refl* (+ *v être*) **se ~ de qn** (formal) to laugh at sb; **se ~ des difficultés** (formal) to make light of difficulties.
IDIOMS **rira bien qui rira le dernier** (Proverb) he who laughs last laughs longest; **être mort** or **écroulé de ~**° to be doubled up (with laughter).

rire[2] /ʀiʀ/ *nm* laughter; **un ~** a laugh; **il a eu un petit ~** he chuckled; **il éclata d'un gros ~** he let out a guffaw; he gave a hearty laugh.
■ **~s préenregistrés** canned laughter.

ris /ʀi/ *nm inv* **1** (Culin) **~ (de veau)** calf's sweetbread; **2** (Naut) reef.

risée /ʀize/ *nf* **être la ~ de** to be the laughing stock of.

risette° /ʀizɛt/ *nf* smile; **fais ~!** give me a smile!

risible /ʀizibl/ *adj* ridiculous, laughable.

risque /ʀisk/ *nm* risk; **présenter un ~** [*process*] to carry a risk; [*action*] to involve some risk; **c'est sans ~** it's safe; **à ~s** [*group, loan*] high-risk.
■ **les ~s du métier** occupational hazards.

risqué, **~e** /ʀiske/ *adj* **1** risky; [*investment*] high-risk; **2** [*joke*] risqué; [*hypothesis*] daring.

risquer /ʀiske/ [1] **I** *vtr* **1** to face [*accusation, condemnation*]; **~ gros** to face a heavy sentence; **2** to risk [*death, criticism*]; **vas-y, tu ne risques rien** go ahead, you're safe; (figurative) go ahead, you've got nothing to lose; **~ gros** to take a major risk; **3** to risk [*life, reputation, job*]; **~ sa peau**° to risk one's neck°; **4** to venture [*look, question*]; to attempt [*operation*]; **~ un œil** to venture a glance; **~ le coup**° to risk it, to chance it.
II risquer de *v+prep* **1 tu risques de te brûler** you might burn yourself; **ça ne risque pas de m'arriver!** there's no chance of that happening to me!; **2 il ne veut pas ~ de perdre son travail** he doesn't want to risk losing his job.
III se risquer *v refl* (+ *v être*) **1** to venture (**à faire** to do); **je ne m'y risquerais pas!** I wouldn't risk it; **2 se ~ à dire** to dare to say.
IV *v impers* **il risque de pleuvoir** it might rain; **il risque d'y avoir du monde** there may well be a lot of people there.
IDIOMS **qui ne risque rien n'a rien** nothing ventured, nothing gained; **~ le tout pour le tout** to stake or risk one's all.

risque-tout /ʀiskətu/ *adj inv* daredevil.

rissoler /ʀisɔle/ [1] *vtr, vi* (Culin) to brown.

ristourne /ʀistuʀn/ *nf* discount, rebate.

rite /ʀit/ *nm* rite.

rituel, **-elle** /ʀitɥɛl/ *adj, nm* ritual.

rivage /ʀivaʒ/ *nm* shore.

rival, **~e**, *mpl* **-aux** /ʀival, o/ *adj, nm,f* rival.

rivaliser /ʀivalize/ [1] *vi* to compete with; **~ avec qch** to rival sth; **~ d'adresse/d'esprit avec qn** to vie with sb in skill/wit.

rivalité /ʀivalite/ *nf* rivalry.

rive /ʀiv/ *nf* **1** (of river) bank; **2** (of sea, lake) shore.

river /ʀive/ [1] *vtr* to clinch [*nail, rivet*]; **être rivé à qch** (figurative) to be tied to [*one's work*]; **avoir les yeux rivés sur** to have one's eyes riveted on.
IDIOMS **~ son clou à qn**° to leave sb speechless.

riverain, **~e** /ʀivʀɛ̃, ɛn/ *nm,f* (of street) resident; (beside river) riverside resident; (of lake) lakeside resident.

rivet /ʀivɛ/ *nm* rivet.

rivière /ʀivjɛʀ/ *nf* **1** river; **2** (in showjumping) water jump.
■ **~ de diamants** diamond necklace, diamond rivière.

rixe /ʀiks/ *nf* brawl.

riz /ʀi/ *nm* rice.

riziculture /ʀizikyltyʀ/ *nf* rice growing.

rizière /ʀizjɛʀ/ *nf* paddy field.

RMI /ɛʀɛmi/ *nm* (*abbr* = **revenu minimum d'insertion**) *minimum benefit paid to those with no other source of income.*

RMIste /ɛʀɛmist/ *nmf* person receiving minimum benefit payment.

RN /ɛʀɛn/ *nf* (*abbr* = **route nationale**) ≈ A road (GB), highway (US).

robe /ʀɔb/ *nf* **1** (gen) dress; **2** (of lawyer) gown; **3** (of horse) coat; (of wine) colour[GB].
■ **~ de chambre** dressing gown, robe (US).

Robin /ʀɔbɛ̃/ *pr n* Robin; **~ des bois** Robin Hood.

robinet /ʀɔbinɛ/ *nm* (for water) tap (GB), faucet (US); (for gas) tap (GB), valve (US).

robot /ʀɔbo/ *nm* robot; **~ ménager** food processor.

robotique /ʀɔbɔtik/ *nf* robotics.

robotiser /ʀɔbɔtize/ [1] *vtr* to automate, to robotize (US).

robuste /ʀɔbyst/ *adj* robust, sturdy; [*appetite*] healthy; [*faith*] strong.

robustesse /ʀɔbystɛs/ *nf* **1** robustness, sturdiness; **2** soundness.

roc /ʀɔk/ *nm* rock.

rocaille /ʀɔkaj/ *nf* **1** loose stones; **2** rock garden.

rocailleux, **-euse** /ʀɔkajø, øz/ *adj* **1** [*land*] rocky, stony; **2** [*voice*] harsh.

roche /ʀɔʃ/ *nf* rock.

rocher /ʀɔʃe/ [1] *nm* **1** rock; **2** (Culin) praline chocolate.

rocheux, **-euse** /ʀɔʃø, øz/ *adj* rocky; **paroi rocheuse** rock face.

rock /ʀɔk/ *nm* **1** rock (music); **2** jive.

rockeur, **-euse** /ʀɔkœʀ, øz/ *nm,f* **1** rock musician; **2** rock fan.

rococo /ʀɔkoko/ *adj inv* **1** [*art, style*] rococo; **2** old-fashioned.

rodage /ʀɔdaʒ/ *nm* **1** (of vehicle, engine) running in (GB), breaking in (US); **2 le spectacle est encore en ~** (figurative) the show is still getting into its stride.

rodéo /ʀɔdeo/ *nm* rodeo; **~ à la voiture volée** joyriding○.

roder /ʀɔde/ [1] *vtr* **1** to run in (GB), to break in (US) [*vehicle, engine*]; **2** to bring [sth] up to scratch, to polish up [*show, method*]; **être (bien) rodé** [*person*] to have the hang of things; [*department*] to be running smoothly.

rôder /ʀode/ [1] *vi* to prowl; **~ autour de qn** to hang around sb.

rôdeur, **-euse** /ʀodœʀ, øz/ *nm,f* prowler.

rogne○ /ʀɔɲ/ *nf* anger; **se mettre en ~** to get mad○.

rogner /ʀɔɲe/ [1] *vtr* **1** to trim [*angle*]; to clip [*nails, wings*]; **2 ~ sur** to cut down on [*budget*].

rognon /ʀɔɲɔ̃/ *nm* (Culin) kidney.

rognure /ʀɔɲyʀ/ *nf* trimming; clipping.

roi /ʀwa/ *nm* king; **le ~ des imbéciles**○ a complete idiot.

■ **les ~s mages** the (three) wise men.

IDIOMS **tirer les Rois** to eat Twelfth Night cake.

roitelet /ʀwatlɛ/ *nm* **1** goldcrest; **2** kinglet.

rôle /ʀol/ *nm* **1** (for actor) part, role; **premier ~** lead, leading role; **2** (gen) role; (of heart, part of body) function, role; **à tour de ~** in turn.

IDIOMS **avoir le beau ~**○ to have the easy job.

romain, **~e**[1] /ʀɔmɛ̃, ɛn/ *adj* **1** Roman; **2 l'Église ~e** the Roman Catholic Church; **3 caractères ~s** roman typeface.

romaine[2] /ʀɔmɛn/ *nf* cos lettuce, romaine lettuce (US).

roman, **~e** /ʀɔmɑ̃, an/ **I** *adj* **1** [*church, style*] Romanesque; (in England) Norman; **2** [*language*] Romance.

II *nm* **1** novel; **~ courtois** courtly romance; **2** (style) **le ~** the Romanesque.

■ **~ policier** detective story, whodunnit○.

romance /ʀɔmɑ̃s/ *nf* **1** love song; **2** romance.

romancer /ʀɔmɑ̃se/ [12] *vtr* **1** to romanticize; **2** to fictionalize.

romanche /ʀɔmɑ̃ʃ/ *nm, adj* Romans(c)h.

romancier, **-ière** /ʀɔmɑ̃sje, ɛʀ/ *nm,f* novelist.

romand, **~e** /ʀɔmɑ̃, ɑ̃d/ *adj* [*Swiss person*] French-speaking.

romanesque /ʀɔmanɛsk/ **I** *adj* **1** [*person*] romantic; [*situation*] like something out of a novel; **2** [*narrative, story*] fictional.

II *nm* **1 le ~** fiction; **2 le ~ d'une situation** the fantastical aspect of a situation.

roman-feuilleton, *pl* **romans-feuilletons** /ʀɔmɑ̃fœjtɔ̃/ *nm* serial.

roman-fleuve, *pl* **romans-fleuves** /ʀɔmɑ̃ flœv/ *nm* roman-fleuve, saga.

romanichel, **-elle** /ʀɔmaniʃɛl/ *nm,f* (offensive) Romany, gypsy.

roman-photo, *pl* **romans-photos** /ʀɔmɑ̃ foto/ *nm* photo-story.

romantique /ʀɔmɑ̃tik/ *adj, nmf* romantic.

romantisme /ʀɔmɑ̃tism/ *nm* **1** Romanticism; **2** romanticism.

romarin /ʀɔmaʀɛ̃/ *nm* rosemary.

rompre /ʀɔ̃pʀ/ [53] **I** *vtr* (gen) to break, to break off [*relationship*]; to upset [*equilibrium*]; to disrupt [*harmony*]; to end [*isolation*]; to break up [*unity*]; to break through [*dam*].

II *vi* **~ avec** to break with [*habit, tradition*]; to make a break from [*past*]; to break away from [*background*]; to break up with [*fiancé*].

III se rompre *v refl* (+ *v être*) to break.

rompu, **~e** /ʀɔ̃py/ **I** *pp* ▶ **rompre**.

II *pp adj* **1 ~ à** well accustomed to; **2 ~ (de fatigue)** worn-out.

romsteck /ʀɔmstɛk/ *nm* rump steak.

ronce /ʀɔ̃s/ *nf* bramble.

ronchon○, **-onne** /ʀɔ̃ʃɔ̃, ɔn/ *adj* grouchy○, grumpy○

ronchonner○ /ʀɔ̃ʃɔne/ [1] *vi* to grumble, to grouse○.

rond, **~e**[1] /ʀɔ̃, ʀɔ̃d/ **I** *adj* **1** [*object, table, hole*] round; **2** [*writing*] rounded; [*face*] round; [*person*] plump; **3** [*number, figure*] round; **4**○ drunk.

II *nm* circle; **faire des ~s de fumée** to blow smoke rings; **faire des ~s dans l'eau** to make ripples in the water.

■ **~ de serviette** napkin ring.

IDIOMS **ouvrir des yeux ~s** to be wide-eyed with astonishment.

rond-de-cuir, *pl* **ronds-de-cuir** /ʀɔ̃dkɥiʀ/ *nm* penpusher (GB), pencil pusher (US).

ronde[2] /ʀɔ̃d/ **I** *adj f* ▶ **rond I**.

II *nf* **1** round dance; **entrer dans la ~** to join the dance; **2** (of policeman) patrol; (of soldiers) watch; **3** (Mus) semibreve (GB), whole note (US).

III à la ronde *phr* around.

rondelet○, **-ette** /ʀɔ̃dlɛ, ɛt/ *adj* [*person*] plump; [*sum*] tidy○.

rondelle /ʀɔ̃dɛl/ *nf* **1** slice; **2** (Tech) washer.

rondement /ʀɔ̃dmɑ̃/ *adv* promptly.

rondeur /ʀɔ̃dœʀ/ *nf* **1** roundness; **2** curve; **3** openness; **avec ~** frankly.

rondin /ʀɔ̃dɛ̃/ *nm* log; **cabane en ~s** log cabin.

rond-point, *pl* **ronds-points** /Rɔ̃pwɛ̃/ *nm* roundabout (GB), traffic circle (US).

ronéoter○ /Rɔneɔte/, **ronéotyper** /Rɔneɔtipe/ [1] *vtr* to duplicate, to Roneo®.

ronflant, **~e** /Rɔ̃flɑ̃, ɑ̃t/ *adj* **1** [*stove*] roaring; **2** [*style*] high-flown.

ronflement /Rɔ̃fləmɑ̃/ *nm* **1** snore; **2** (of engine) purr.

ronfler /Rɔ̃fle/ [1] *vi* **1** [*sleeper*] to snore; [*engine*] to purr; **2**○ to be fast asleep.

ronger /Rɔ̃ʒe/ [13] **I** *vtr* **1** [*mouse, dog*] to gnaw; [*worms*] to eat into; [*caterpillar*] to eat away; **2** [*water, acid, rust*] to erode; **3** [*disease*] to wear down.

II se ronger *v refl* (+ *v être*) **se ~ les ongles** to bite one's nails.

IDIOMS **se ~ les sangs**○ to worry oneself sick.

rongeur /Rɔ̃ʒœR/ *nm* rodent.

ronron○ /Rɔ̃Rɔ̃/ *nm* (*also onomatopoeic*) **1** (of cat) purr, purring; **2** (of engine) purring.

ronronnement /Rɔ̃Rɔnmɑ̃/ *nm* (of cat, engine) purring.

ronronner /Rɔ̃Rɔne/ [1] *vi* to purr.

roque /Rɔk/ *nm* castling; **grand/petit ~** castling long/short.

roquer /Rɔke/ [1] *vi* **1** (in chess) to castle; **2** (in croquet) to roquet.

roquet /Rɔkɛ/ *nm* **1** yappy little dog; **2**○ bad-tempered little runt○.

roquette /Rɔkɛt/ *nf* (Mil) rocket.

rosace /Rozas/ *nf* **1** rosette; **2** rose window; **3** (decorative motif) rose.

rosaire /RozɛR/ *nm* rosary.

rosbif /Rɔsbif/ *nm* joint of beef (GB), roast of beef (US); (meal) roast beef.

rose[1] /Roz/ *adj* (gen) pink; (with health) [*cheeks*] rosy.

IDIOMS **ce n'est pas (tout) ~** it's not all roses; **la vie n'est pas ~** life isn't a bed of roses.

rose[2] /Roz/ *nf* (Bot) rose; **essence de ~** attar of roses.

■ **~ des sables** gypsum flower; **~ trémière** hollyhock; **~ des vents** compass rose.

IDIOMS **envoyer qn sur les ~s**○ to send sb packing○; **découvrir le pot aux ~s**○ to find out what is going on.

rosé /Roze/ *nm* rosé.

roseau, *pl* **~x** /Rozo/ *nm* (Bot) reed.

rosée /Roze/ *nf* dew.

roseraie /RozRɛ/ *nf* rose garden.

rosier /Rozje/ *nm* (Bot) rosebush, rose.

rosse /Rɔs/ **I**○ *adj* nasty, mean.

II *nf* **1** nag○; **2** meanie○, nasty person.

rossée○ /Rɔse/ *nf* thrashing○.

rosser○ /Rɔse/ [1] *vtr* **1** to give [sb] a good thrashing [*person*]; to beat [*animal*]; **2** to thrash○ [*team, army*].

rossignol /Rɔsiɲɔl/ *nm* **1** nightingale; **2**○ bit of junk.

rot○ /Ro/ *nm* burp○; **faire un ~** to burp○.

rotatif, **-ive**[1] /Rɔtatif, iv/ *adj* rotary.

rotation /Rɔtasjɔ̃/ *nf* **1** (movement) rotation; **2** (Mil) turnaround; **3** (of crops, staff, shift) rotation; **système de ~** rota system.

rotative[2] /Rɔtativ/ **I** *adj f* ▶ **rotatif**.

II *nf* rotary press.

roter○ /Rɔte/ [1] *vtr* to burp○, to belch.

rôti /Rɔti/ *nm* **1** joint; **2** roast.

rôtie /Rɔti/ *nf* piece of toast.

rotin /Rɔtɛ̃/ *nm* rattan; **fauteuil en ~** rattan chair.

rôtir /RɔtiR/ [3] *vtr* to roast [*meat*]; to toast, to grill [*bread*].

IDIOMS **il attend que ça lui tombe tout rôti dans le bec**○ he expects things to fall into his lap.

rôtissoire /RɔtiswaR/ *nf* rotisserie, roasting spit.

rotonde /Rɔtɔ̃d/ *nf* (building) rotunda.

rotule /Rɔtyl/ *nf* **1** (Anat) kneecap; **2** (Tech) ball-and-socket joint.

IDIOMS **être sur les ~s**○ to be on one's last legs.

roturier, **-ière** /RɔtyRje, ɛR/ **I** *adj* [*manners, language*] common, coarse.

II *nm,f* commoner.

rouage /Rwaʒ/ *nm* **1** (of machine) (cog)wheel; **les ~s** the parts or works; **2** (of administration) machinery; **les ~s bureaucratiques** the wheels of bureaucracy.

roublard○, **~e** /RublaR, aRd/ *adj* crafty, cunning.

roucouler /Rukule/ [1] **I** *vtr* to croon [*song*]; to coo [*endearments*].

II *vi* **1** [*bird*] to coo; **2** [*lovers*] to bill and coo.

roue /Ru/ *nf* wheel; **~ dentée** cogwheel.

■ **~ à aube** paddle wheel; **~ motrice** driving wheel; **~ de secours** spare wheel or tyre (GB), spare tire (US).

IDIOMS **être la cinquième ~ du carrosse** to feel unwanted; **pousser qn à la ~** to be behind sb; **faire la ~** [*peacock*] to spread its tail, to display; [*person*] to strut around; (in gymnastics) to do a cartwheel.

roué, **~e** /Rwe/ *nm,f* cunning devil.

rouer /Rwe/ [1] *vtr* **~ qn de coups** to beat sb up.

rouet /Rwɛ/ *nm* spinning wheel.

rouge /Ruʒ/ **I** *adj* **1** (gen) red (**de** with); [*person, face*] flushed; **2** [*beard, hair, fur*] ginger; **3** red-hot.

II *nmf* (communist) Red.

III *nm* **1** red; **le ~ lui monta au visage** he/she went red in the face; **2 ~ à joues** blusher, rouge; **~ à lèvres** lipstick; **3 le feu est au ~** the (traffic) lights are red; **passer au ~** to jump the lights (GB) or a red light; **4**○ red (wine); **gros ~**○ cheap red wine, red plonk○ (GB); **un (petit) coup de ~**○ a glass of red wine; **5 être dans le ~** to be in the red.

IDIOMS **être ~ comme une tomate** or **une écrevisse** (from embarrassment) to be as red as a beetroot (GB) or a beet (US); (from running) to be red in the face.

rougeaud, **~e** /ʀuʒo, od/ *adj* [*person*] ruddy-faced; [*face, complexion*] ruddy.

rouge-gorge, *pl* **rouges-gorges** /ʀuʒgɔʀʒ/ *nm* robin (redbreast).

rougeoiement /ʀuʒwamɑ̃/ *nm* red or reddish glow.

rougeole /ʀuʒɔl/ *nf* measles.

rougeoyant, **~e** /ʀuʒwajɑ̃, ɑ̃t/ *adj* [*glint, glow*] reddish; [*sky*] reddening.

rougeoyer /ʀuʒwaje/ [23] *vi* [*sun*] to glow fiery red; [*fire*] to glow red.

rouget /ʀuʒɛ/ *nm* red mullet, goatfish (US).

rougeur /ʀuʒœʀ/ *nf* **1** redness; **2** redness; flushing; **3** red blotch.

rougir /ʀuʒiʀ/ [3] **I** *vtr* **1** to redden; **2** to make [sth] red hot [*metal*].
II *vi* **1** to blush (**de** with); to flush (**de** with); to go red; **~ jusqu'aux oreilles** to go as red as a beetroot (GB) or a beet (US); **ne ~ de rien** to have no shame; **2** [*fruit, leaves, sky*] to turn red; **3** [*metal*] to become red hot.

rouille /ʀuj/ **I** *adj inv* red-brown, rust(-coloured[GB]).
II *nf* rust.

rouiller /ʀuje/ [1] **I** *vtr* to rust, to make [sth] go rusty.
II *vi* to rust, to go rusty.
III **se rouiller** *v refl* (+ *v être*) [*metal, athlete, memory*] to get rusty.

roulade /ʀulad/ *nf* (Sport) roll.

roulé /ʀule/ *nm* (Culin) roll; **~ au fromage** *puff pastry filled with cheese.*

rouleau, *pl* **~x** /ʀulo/ *nm* **1** roll (**de** of); **2** breaker, roller; **3** (Tech) roller; **4** roller, curler.
■ **~ compresseur** steamroller; **~ à pâtisserie** rolling pin.

roulement /ʀulmɑ̃/ *nm* **1** (of thunder) rumble; (of drum) roll; **2** (of capital) circulation; **3** rotation; **travailler par ~** to work (in) shifts; **faire un ~** to draw up a rota (GB) or schedule; **4** (Tech) **~ à billes** ball bearing.

rouler /ʀule/ [1] **I** *vtr* **1** to roll [*barrel, tyre*]; to wheel [*cart*]; **2** to roll up [*carpet, sleeve, paper*]; to roll [*cigarette*]; **tabac à ~** rolling tobacco; **3** **~ les épaules** to roll one's shoulders; **4**○ **~ qn** to diddle○ (GB) or cheat sb.
II *vi* **1** [*ball, coin, person*] to roll; **faire ~ les dés** to roll the dice; **2** [*vehicle*] to go; **~ à gauche** to drive on the left; **les bus ne roulent pas le dimanche** buses don't run on Sundays.
III **se rouler** *v refl* (+ *v être*) **1** **se ~ dans** to roll in [*grass, mud*]; **2** **se ~ dans** to wrap oneself in [*blanket*].

roulette /ʀulɛt/ *nf* **1** caster; **2** roulette; **3** (dentist's) drill.
IDIOMS **marcher comme sur des ~s**○ to go smoothly or like a dream.

roulis /ʀuli/ *nm* (of boat) rolling; (of car, train) swaying.

roulotte /ʀulɔt/ *nf* (horse-drawn) caravan (GB), trailer (US).

roupie /ʀupi/ *nf* rupee.

roupiller○ /ʀupije/ [1] *vtr* to sleep.

rouquin○, **~e** /ʀukɛ̃, in/ **I** *adj* [*person*] red-haired; [*hair*] red.
II *nm,f* redhead.

rouspéter○ /ʀuspete/ [14] *vi* to grumble (**contre** about; **après** at).

rousse /ʀus/ *adj f* ▶ **roux**.

rousseur /ʀusœʀ/ *nf* (of hair, foliage) redness; (of shade) russet colour[GB].

roussi /ʀusi/ *nm* **ça sent le ~** there's a smell of burning; there's trouble brewing.

roussir /ʀusiʀ/ [3] **I** *vtr* to turn [sth] brown; [*iron*] to scorch.
II *vi* **1** to go brown; **2** (Culin) **faire ~** to brown.

routage /ʀutaʒ/ *nm* sorting and mailing.

route /ʀut/ *nf* **1** road, highway (US); **tenir la ~** [*car*] to hold the road; (figurative)○ [*argument*] to hold water; [*equipment*] to be well-made; **2** road; **il y a six heures de ~** it's a six-hour drive; **faire de la ~**○ to do a lot of mileage; **3** route; **~s maritimes** sea routes; **la ~ est toute tracée désormais** from now on, it's all plain sailing; **4** way; **la ~ sera longue** it will be a long journey; **j'ai changé d'avis en cours de ~** I changed my mind along the way; **être en ~** [*person*] to be on one's way; [*plan*] to be underway; [*dish*] to be cooking; **être en ~ pour** to be en route to; **faire fausse ~** to go off course; to be mistaken; **se mettre en ~** to set off; **en ~!** let's go!; **mettre en ~** to start [*machine, car*]; to get [sth] going [*project, manufacture*].
■ **~ départementale** secondary road; **~ à grande circulation** trunk road (GB), highway (US); **~ nationale** trunk road (GB), ≈ A road (GB), national highway (US).

routier, **-ière** /ʀutje, ɛʀ/ **I** *adj* road.
II *nm* **1** lorry driver (GB), truck driver; **2** transport café (GB), truck stop (US).

routine /ʀutin/ *nf* routine; **tomber dans la ~** to get into a rut.

routinier, **-ière** /ʀutinje, ɛʀ/ *adj* [*person*] set in one's ways; [*method, work, existence*] routine.

rouvrir: **se rouvrir** /ʀuvʀiʀ/ [32] *v refl* (+ *v être*) [*door*] to open (again); [*wound*] to open up (again).

roux, **rousse** /ʀu, ʀus/ **I** *adj* [*leaves*] russet; [*hair*] red; ginger; [*person*] red-haired; [*coat, fur*] ginger.
II *nm,f* red-haired person, redhead.

royal, **~e**, *mpl* **-aux** /ʀwajal, o/ *adj* **1** royal; **2** [*present*] fit for a king; [*tip, salary*] princely; **3** [*indifference*] supreme; [*scorn*] utter; [*peace*] blissful.

royalement /ʀwajalmɑ̃/ *adv* **1** royally; **être payé ~** to be paid handsomely; **2**○ **il se moque ~ de son travail** he really couldn't care less about his work.

royaliste /ʀwajalist/ *adj, nmf* royalist.
IDIOMS **être plus ~ que le roi** to be more Catholic than the pope.

royaume /ʀwajom/ *nm* kingdom.

Royaume-Uni /ʀwajomyni/ *pr nm* **le ~** the United Kingdom.

royauté /ʀwajote/ *nf* **1** kingship; **2** monarchy.

RSVP (*written abbr* = **répondez s'il vous plaît**) RSVP.

ruade /ʀyad/ *nf* **1** (by horse) buck; **2** (by person, party) attack.

ruban /ʀybɑ̃/ *nm* ribbon; **~ adhésif** adhesive tape, sticky tape (GB).

rubéole /ʀybeɔl/ *nf* German measles.

rubis /ʀybi/ *nm inv* **1** ruby; **2** ruby (red); **3** (in watch) jewel.

rubrique /ʀybʀik/ *nf* **1** (of newspaper) section; **~ mondaine** social column; **2** category.

ruche /ʀyʃ/ *nf* **1** beehive; **2** hive of activity.

rude /ʀyd/ *adj* **1** [*job, day*] hard, tough; [*winter*] harsh; [*ordeal*] severe; **2** [*material, beard*] rough; **3** [*features*] coarse; **4 c'est un ~ gaillard** he's a strapping fellow; **5** [*opponent*] tough, formidable.

rudement /ʀydmɑ̃/ *adv* **1** roughly, harshly; **2**○ really.

rudesse /ʀydɛs/ *nf* **1** harshness, severity; **2** coarseness.

rudiment /ʀydimɑ̃/ **I** *nm* (Anat) rudiment; **un ~ de queue** a rudimentary tail.
II rudiments *nm pl* **avoir quelques ~s de** to have a rudimentary knowledge of.

rudimentaire /ʀydimɑ̃tɛʀ/ *adj* **1** basic; **2** (Anat) rudimentary.

rudoyer /ʀydwaje/ [23] *vtr* to bully.

rue /ʀy/ *nf* street; **~ piétonne** pedestrian street.
IDIOMS **ça ne court pas les ~s**○ it's pretty thin on the ground; **mettre qn à la ~** to put sb out on the street; **descendre dans la ~** to take to the street.

ruée /ʀɥe/ *nf* rush; **~ vers l'or** gold rush.

ruelle /ʀɥɛl/ *nf* alleyway, back street.

ruer /ʀɥe/ [1] **I** *vi* [*horse*] to kick.
II se ruer *v refl* (+ *v être*) to rush; **se ~ sur qn/qch** to pounce on sb/sth.
IDIOMS **~ dans les brancards** to kick over the traces, to rebel.

rugby /ʀygbi/ *nm* rugby; **~ à treize** rugby league; **~ à quinze** rugby union.

rugbyman, *pl* **rugbymen** /ʀygbiman, mɛn/ *nm* rugby player.

rugir /ʀyʒiʀ/ [3] **I** *vtr* to bellow (out), to growl.
II *vi* [*animal, engine*] to roar; [*person, wind*] to howl.

rugissement /ʀyʒismɑ̃/ *nm* (of animal, person) roar; (of wind) howling.

rugosité /ʀygozite/ *nf* **1** roughness; **2** rough patch.

rugueux, **-euse** /ʀygø, øz/ *adj* rough.

ruine /ʀɥin/ *nf* **1** (of building, person, reputation, company) ruin; (of civilization) collapse; (of hope) death; **en ~(s)** ruined; **tomber en ~(s)** to fall into ruin; **ce n'est pas la ~**○ it's not that expensive; **2** ruin; **3** wreck.

ruiner /ʀɥine/ [1] **I** *vtr* **1** to ruin [*person, economy*]; **~ qn** to be a drain on sb's resources; **ça ne va pas le ~**○ that's not going to break the bank; **2** to destroy [*health, happiness*]; **3** ruin [*life, reputation*]; to shatter [*hopes*].
II se ruiner *v refl* (+ *v être*) to be ruined, to lose everything; to ruin oneself (**en faisant** doing).

ruineux, **-euse** /ʀɥinø, øz/ *adj* very expensive, extravagant.

ruisseau, *pl* **~x** /ʀɥiso/ *nm* **1** stream, brook; **2 ~ de larmes** stream of tears; **tirer** or **sortir qn du ~** to pull sb out of the gutter.

ruisseler /ʀɥisle/ [19] *vi* **1** [*water*] to stream; [*grease*] to drip; **2** to be streaming (**de** with); **~ de sueur** to be dripping with sweat; **~ de lumière** to be flooded with light.

ruissellement /ʀɥisɛlmɑ̃/ *nm* (of rain) streaming (**sur** down); (of grease) dripping (**sur** down); (of noxious waste) seepage.

rumeur /ʀymœʀ/ *nf* **1** rumour[GB]; **selon certaines ~s, il aurait quitté le pays** rumour[GB] has it that he may have left the country; **2** (of voices, wind) murmur.

ruminant /ʀyminɑ̃/ *nm* ruminant.

ruminer /ʀymine/ [1] **I** *vtr* **1** to ruminate, to chew the cud; **2** to brood on [*misery*]; to chew over○ [*idea, plan*].
II *vi* **1** to ruminate, to chew the cud; **2** [*person*] to brood.

rumsteck /ʀɔmstɛk/ *nm* rump steak.

rupestre /ʀypɛstʀ/ *adj* **1** [*plants*] rock; **2** [*paintings*] cave, rock.

rupture /ʀyptyʀ/ *nf* **1** (of relations) breaking-off; **2** breakdown (**avec** in); **3** break-up; **lettre de ~** letter ending a relationship; **4** (of dam, dyke) breaking; (of pipe) fracture.

rural, **~e**, *mpl* **-aux** /ʀyʀal, o/ *adj* [*exodus, environment*] rural; [*road, life*] country; **l'espace ~** the countryside.

ruse /ʀyz/ *nf* **1** trick, ruse; **~ de guerre** humorous cunning stratagem; **2** cunning, craftiness.

rusé, **~e** /ʀyze/ *adj* cunning, crafty.

ruser /ʀyze/ [1] *vi* **1** to be crafty; **2 ~ avec** to trick [*enemy, police*].

rush, *pl* **rushes** /ʀœʃ/ **I** *nm* **1** (in race) final burst; **2**○ rush; **le ~ sur l'immobilier** the rush to buy property.
II rushes *nm pl* (of film) rushes.

russe /ʀys/ *adj, nm* Russian.

Russie /ʀysi/ *pr nf* Russia.

rustaud, **~e** /ʀysto, od/ *adj* rustic.

rusticité /ʀystisite/ *nf* rustic character.

rustine® /ʀystin/ *nf* (puncture-repair) patch.

rustique /ʀystik/ **I** *adj* rustic, country.
II *nm* **le ~** rustic style.

rustre /ʀystʀ/ **I** *adj* uncouth.
II *nm* lout.

rut /ʀyt/ *nm* rutting season; **être en ~** to be in rut.

rutilant, **~e** /ʀytilɑ̃, ɑ̃t/ *adj* sparkling; gleaming.

rythme /ʀitm/ *nm* **1** rhythm; **marquer le ~** to beat time; **2** (of growth, production) rate; (of life, film) pace.
■ **~ cardiaque** heart rate; **~s scolaires** school timetables.

rythmer /ʀitme/ [1] *vtr* **1** to give rhythm to; **2** to regulate [*life, work*].

rythmique /ʀitmik/ *adj* rhythmic.

Ss

s, **S** /ɛs/ *nm inv* s, S.
s' **1** ▶ **se**; **2** ▶ **si**[1] **III**.
sa ▶ **son**[1].
sabbat /saba/ *nm* **1** Sabbath; **2** witches' Sabbath.
sabbatique /sabatik/ *adj* **1** Sabbatical; **2** **congé ~** sabbatical (leave).
sable /sɑbl/ *nm* sand; **~s mouvants** quicksands.
sablé, **~e** /sable/ **I** *adj* **pâte ~e** shortcrust pastry.
II *nm* shortbread biscuit (GB) or cookie (US).
sabler /sable/ [1] *vtr* **1** to grit [*roadway*]; **2** (Tech) (cleaning) to sandblast.
IDIOMS **~ le champagne** to crack open some champagne.
sablier /sablije/ *nm* hourglass; egg timer.
sablonneux, **-euse** /sablɔnø, øz/ *adj* sandy.
saborder: **se saborder** /sabɔʀde/ [1] *v refl* (+ *v être*) to scuttle one's own ship; (figurative) to sink oneself/itself.
sabot /sabo/ *nm* **1** clog; **2** (Zool) hoof.
sabotage /sabɔtaʒ/ *nm* **1** sabotage; **2** (act of) sabotage.
saboter /sabɔte/ [1] *vtr* to sabotage; **~ un travail**○ to botch○ a job.
saboteur, **-euse** /sabɔtœʀ, øz/ *nm,f* **1** (of equipment) saboteur; **2** (of job) botcher○.
sabre /sɑbʀ/ *nm* **1** sword; **2** sabre[GB].
sabrer /sɑbʀe/ [1] *vtr* **1** (Mil) to cut down; **2**○ to cut chunks out of [*article*]; **3**○ to tear [sb] to pieces [*author*]; to pan○ [*book, film*].
sac /sak/ *nm* **1** (gen) bag; **2** sack; **3** bag(ful), sack(-ful); **4** **mettre à ~** to sack [*city, region*]; to ransack [*shop, house*].
■ **~ de congélation** freezer bag; **~ de couchage** sleeping bag; **~ à dos** rucksack, backpack; **~ à main** handbag, purse (US); **~ postal** mail sack; **~ à provisions** shopping bag, carry-all (US).
IDIOMS **l'affaire est dans le ~**○ it's in the bag○; **avoir plus d'un tour dans son ~** to have more than one trick up one's sleeve; **vider son ~**○ to get it off one's chest; **se faire prendre la main dans le ~** to be caught red-handed; **mettre dans le même ~**○ to lump [sth] together.
saccade /sakad/ *nf* jerk; **avancer par ~s** to jerk along.
saccadé, **~e** /sakade/ *adj* [*movement*] jerky; [*rhythm*] staccato; [*voice*] clipped.
saccage /sakaʒ/ *nm* (of region) devastation; (of building) vandalizing.
saccager /sakaʒe/ [13] *vtr* **1** to wreck, to devastate [*region*]; to vandalize [*building*]; **2** to sack.
saccharine /sakaʀin/ *nf* saccharin.
sacerdoce /sasɛʀdɔs/ *nm* **1** priesthood; **2** (figurative) vocation.
sachet /saʃɛ/ *nm* (of powder) packet; (of herbs, spices) sachet; **~ de thé** tea bag.
sacoche /sakɔʃ/ *nf* **1** bag; **2** (on bicycle) pannier (GB), saddlebag (US).
sacquer○ /sake/ [1] *vtr* **1** to sack○, to fire○; **2** [*teacher*] to mark [sb] strictly; **3** **je ne peux pas le ~** I can't stand the sight of him.
sacraliser /sakʀalize/ [1] *vtr* to make [sth] sacred.
sacre /sakʀ/ *nm* (of king) coronation; (of bishop) consecration.
sacré, **~e** /sakʀe/ *adj* **1** [*art, object, place*] sacred; [*cause*] holy; **2** [*rule, right*] sacred; **3**○ **être un ~ menteur** to be a hell of○ a liar; **il en a pris un ~ coup**○ it was a hell of a blow○ to him; **4**○ **~ Paul, va!** Paul, you old devil!
IDIOMS **avoir le feu ~** to be full of zeal or enthusiasm.
sacrement /sakʀəmɑ̃/ *nm* sacrament; **les derniers ~s** the last rites.
sacrément○ /sakʀemɑ̃/ *adv* incredibly○.
sacrer /sakʀe/ [1] *vtr* to crown [*king*]; to consecrate [*bishop*].
sacrifice /sakʀifis/ *nm* sacrifice; **faire le ~ de qch** to sacrifice sth.
sacrifier /sakʀifje/ [1] **I** *vtr* **1** to sacrifice (**à** to); **2** (figurative) to sacrifice; **~ sa famille à son travail** to put one's work before one's family.
II **sacrifier à** *v+prep* to conform to [*fashion, custom*].
III **se sacrifier** *v refl* (+ *v être*) **1** to sacrifice oneself; **2**○ to make sacrifices.
sacrilège /sakʀilɛʒ/ **I** *adj* sacrilegious.
II *nm* sacrilege; **un ~** an act of sacrilege.
sacristie /sakʀisti/ *nf* (of catholic church) sacristy; (of protestant church) vestry.
sacro-saint, **~e**, *mpl* **~s** /sakʀosɛ̃, ɛ̃t/ *adj* sacrosanct.
sadique /sadik/ **I** *adj* sadistic.
II *nmf* sadist.
sadisme /sadism/ *nm* sadism.
sadomasochisme /sadomazɔʃism/ *nm* sadomasochism.
safari /safaʀi/ *nm* safari.
safran /safʀɑ̃/ *adj inv, nm* saffron.
saga /saga/ *nf* saga.
sagacité /sagasite/ *nf* sagacity, shrewdness.
sagaie /sagɛ/ *nf* assegai.
sage /saʒ/ **I** *adj* **1** wise, sensible; **2** good, well-behaved; **3** [*tastes, fashion*] sober.
II *nm* **1** wise man; (in antiquity) sage; **2** expert.
IDIOMS **être ~ comme une image** to be as good as gold.
sage-femme, *pl* **sages-femmes** /saʒfam/ *nf* midwife.

sagement /saʒmɑ̃/ *adv* **1** wisely; **2** quietly; **3** (gen) properly; [*dress*] soberly.

sagesse /saʒɛs/ *nf* **1** wisdom, common sense; (of advice) soundness; **la voix de la ~** the voice of reason; **2** good behaviour[GB].

Sagittaire /saʒitɛʀ/ *pr nm* Sagittarius.

Sahara /saaʀa/ *pr nm* Sahara.

saharienne /saaʀjɛn/ *nf* safari jacket.

saignant, **~e** /sɛɲɑ̃, ɑ̃t/ *adj* **1** [*meat*] rare; **2**○ (figurative) [*criticism*] savage.

saignée /sɛɲe/ *nf* **1** (Med) bloodletting, bleeding; **faire une ~ à qn** to bleed sb; **2** (in budget) hole; **3** (in tree) cut.

saignement /sɛɲ(ə)mɑ̃/ *nm* bleeding.

saigner /sɛɲe/ [1] **I** *vtr* **1** (Med) to bleed; **2** to kill [*animal*] (*by slitting its throat*); **~ un cochon** to stick a pig.

II *vi* to bleed; **~ du nez** to have a nosebleed.

IDIOMS **~ qn à blanc** to bleed sb dry or white; **se ~ (aux quatre veines) pour qn** to make big sacrifices for sb.

saillant, **~e** /sajɑ̃, ɑ̃t/ *adj* **1** [*jaw*] prominent; [*muscle*] bulging; [*eyes*] protuberant; [*angle*] salient; **2** [*fact, episode*] salient.

saillie /saji/ *nf* **1** projection; **le balcon est en ~** the balcony juts out; **2** (Zool) covering, serving.

saillir /sajiʀ/ [28] *vi* **1** to jut out; **2** [*ribs, muscles*] to bulge.

sain, **~e** /sɛ̃, sɛn/ *adj* (gen) healthy, sound; [*reading*] wholesome; [*wound*] clean; **~ d'esprit** sane; **~ de corps et d'esprit** sound in body and mind; **~ et sauf** [*return*] safe and sound; [*emerge*] unscathed.

saindoux /sɛ̃du/ *nm inv* lard.

sainement /sɛnmɑ̃/ *adv* **1** [*live*] healthily; **2** [*reason*] soundly.

saint, **~e** /sɛ̃, sɛ̃t/ **I** *adj* **1** holy; **vendredi ~** Good Friday; **2 ~ Paul/Thomas d'Aquin** Saint Paul/Thomas Aquinas.

II *nm,f* saint; **se prendre pour un ~/une ~e** to think one is perfect.

■ **~e nitouche** goody-goody○; **la Sainte Vierge** the Virgin Mary.

Saint-Cyr /sɛ̃siʀ/ *pr n*: *French military academy*.

Saint-Esprit /sɛ̃tɛspʀi/ *pr nm* Holy Spirit; **par l'opération du ~**○ by magic.

sainteté /sɛ̃tte/ *nf* saintliness.

IDIOMS **ne pas être en odeur de ~** (**auprès de qn**) to be in sb's bad books.

saint-honoré /sɛ̃tɔnɔʀe/ *nm inv*: *cream-filled tart topped with choux and caramel*.

Saint-Jacques /sɛ̃ʒak/ *pr n* **coquille ~** scallop.

Saint-Jean /sɛ̃ʒɑ̃/ *nf* **la ~** Midsummer Day; **feux de la ~** *bonfires lit on Midsummer Night*.

Saint-Sylvestre /sɛ̃silvɛstʀ/ *nf* **la ~** New Year's Eve.

saisie /sezi/ *nf* **1** (gen, Law) seizure; **2 ~ (informatique)** keyboarding; **~ de données** data capture.

saisir /seziʀ/ [3] **I** *vtr* **1** to grab; to seize; **~ au vol** to catch [*ball*]; **'affaire à ~'** 'amazing bargain'; **2** to understand; **tu saisis**○**?** do you get it○?; **3** to catch [*name, bits of conversation*]; **4** [*emotion, cold*] to grip [*person*]; **saisi de panique** panic-stricken; **5** to strike, to impress [*person*]; **6** (Law) to seize [*property*]; **~ la justice d'une affaire** to refer a matter to a court; **7** (in computing) to capture [*data*]; to key [*text*].

II se saisir *v refl* (+ *v être*) **se ~ de** to catch or grab hold of [*object*].

saisissant, **~e** /sezisɑ̃, ɑ̃t/ *adj* **1** [*cold*] piercing; **2** [*effect, resemblance*] striking.

saison /sɛzɔ̃/ *nf* (gen) season; **en cette ~** at this time of year; **en toute ~** all (the) year round; **à la belle ~** in the summer months; (in tourism, sport) **la haute/morte ~** the high/slack season; **prix hors ~** off-season prices.

saisonnier, **-ière** /sɛzɔnje, ɛʀ/ **I** *adj* seasonal.

II *nm,f* (worker) seasonal worker.

salace /salas/ *adj* salacious.

salade /salad/ *nf* **1** lettuce; **2** salad; **~ verte** green salad; **~ de tomates** tomato salad; **3**○ muddle; **raconter des ~s** to spin yarns○.

saladier /saladje/ *nm* salad bowl.

salaire /salɛʀ/ *nm* salary; wages; **~ brut/net** gross/take-home pay.

■ **~ minimum interprofessionnel de croissance**, **SMIC** guaranteed minimum wage.

salaison /salɛzɔ̃/ *nf* salt meat.

salamandre /salamɑ̃dʀ/ *nf* salamander.

salant /salɑ̃/ *adj m* **marais ~** saltern.

salarial, **~e**, *mpl* **-iaux** /salaʀjal, o/ *adj* **1** [*policy, rise*] wage; **2 cotisation ~e** employee's contribution; **charges ~es** payroll charges.

salarié, **~e** /salaʀje/ **I** *adj* [*worker*] wage-earning; [*job*] salaried.

II *nm,f* **1** wage earner; **2** salaried employee.

salaud◐ /salo/ *nm* (offensive) bastard◐.

sale /sal/ **I** *adj* **1** (*after n*) dirty; **2**○ (*before n*) [*person*] horrible; [*animal, illness, habit*] nasty; [*weather*] foul, horrible; [*work, place*] rotten; **quel ~ gosse**○**!** what a horrible brat○!; **~ menteur!** you dirty liar!; **il a une ~ tête** he looks dreadful; **faire une ~ tête** to look annoyed; **un ~ coup** a very nasty blow; **jouer un ~ tour à qn** to play a dirty trick on sb; **un ~ caractère** a foul temper; **j'ai passé un ~ quart d'heure** I had a pretty grim time (of it).

II *nm* **mettre qch au ~** to put sth in the wash.

salé, **~e** /sale/ *adj* **1** salt, salty; **2** salted; [*snack*] savoury[GB]; **3**○ [*bill*] steep; **4** spicy; **propos ~s** spicy talk.

salement /salmɑ̃/ *adv* **1 manger ~** to be a messy eater; **travailler ~** to do a messy job; **2**○ badly, seriously.

saler /sale/ [1] *vtr* **1** to salt [*food*]; **~ et poivrer** to add salt and pepper; **2**○ to bump up○ [*bill*]; to fleece○ [*customer*]; **3** to grit (GB), to salt (US) [*road*].

saleté /salte/ *nf* **1** dirtiness; dirt; filth; **être d'une ~ repoussante** to be filthy; **ramasser**

les ~s to pick up the rubbish (GB) or trash (US); **faire des ~s** to make a mess; **2**○ **c'est de la ~** (gadget, goods) it's rubbish; **c'est une vraie ~ ce virus!** it's a rotten bug!

salière /saljɛʀ/ *nf* saltcellar, saltshaker (US).

salir /saliʀ/ [3] **I** *vtr* **1** to dirty; to soil; **2** to sully [*reputation*].
II *vi* [*industry, coal*] to pollute.
III se salir *v refl* (+ *v être*) to get dirty, to dirty oneself; **se ~ les mains** to get one's hands dirty.

salissant, ~e /salisɑ̃, ɑ̃t/ *adj* **1** [*colour*] which shows the dirt; **2** [*work*] dirty.

salive /saliv/ *nf* saliva.
IDIOMS **dépenser inutilement sa ~** to waste one's breath.

saliver /salive/ [1] *vi* to salivate; **~ devant qch** to drool over sth.

salle /sal/ *nf* **1** (gen) room; hall; (in restaurant) (dining) room; (in hospital) ward; (in theatre) auditorium; **faire ~ comble** [*show*] to be packed; **en ~** [*sport*] indoor; **2** (figurative) audience.
■ **~ d'attente** waiting room; **~ de bains** bathroom; **~ de cinéma** cinema (GB), movie theater (US); **~ de classe** classroom; **~ de concert** concert hall; **~ d'eau** shower room; **~ d'embarquement** departure lounge; **~ des fêtes** village hall; community centre[GB]; **~ de garde** (in hospital) staff room; **~ de gymnastique** gymnasium; **~ de jeu(x)** (in casino) gaming room; (for children) playroom; **~ à manger** dining room; dining-room suite; **~ d'opération** (Med) operating theatre (GB), operating room (US); **~ de séjour** living room; **~ des ventes** auction room.

salon /salɔ̃/ *nm* **1** (gen) lounge; drawing room; **2** sitting-room suite; **~ de jardin** garden furniture; **3** (trade) show; fair; exhibition; **le ~ de l'auto** the car show; **~ du livre** book fair; **4** (of intellectuals) salon.
■ **~ de beauté** beauty salon; **~ de coiffure** hairdressing salon; **~ d'essayage** fitting room; **~ de thé** tearoom.

saloperie◑ /salɔpʀi/ *nf* **1** muck○; **2** bug○; **3** trash; **cette ~ d'ordinateur** this bloody◑ (GB) or damn○ computer.

salopette /salɔpɛt/ *nf* overalls.

salpêtre /salpɛtʀ/ *nm* saltpetre[GB].

salsifis /salsifi/ *nm inv* salsify.

saltimbanque /saltɛ̃bɑ̃k/ *nmf* **1** street acrobat; **2** entertainer.

salubre /salybʀ/ *adj* [*climate*] healthy; [*lodgings*] salubrious.

salubrité /salybʀite/ *nf* (of air, climate) healthiness; (of accommodation) salubrity.
■ **~ publique** public health.

saluer /salɥe/ [1] *vtr* **1** to greet [*person*]; **~ qn de la tête** to nod to sb; **saluez-la de ma part** say hello to her from me; **2** to say goodbye to [*person*]; **3** (Mil) to salute; **4** to welcome [*decision, news*]; **5** to pay tribute to [*memory*]; **je vous salue Marie** hail Mary.

salut /saly/ *nm* **1** greeting; **~!** hello!, hi!; bye!; **~ de la tête** nod; **2** salute; **3** salvation.

salutaire /salytɛʀ/ *adj* [*experience*] salutary; [*effect*] beneficial; [*air*] healthy; **cela leur a été ~** it did them good.

salutation /salytasjɔ̃/ *nf* (gen) greeting; **sincères ~s** yours sincerely; yours faithfully.

salvateur, -trice /salvatœʀ, tʀis/ *adj* saving.

salve /salv/ *nf* **1** salvo; **tirer une ~ d'honneur** to fire a salute; **2 ~ d'applaudissements** burst of applause; **3 lancer une ~ contre qn** to launch a broadside against sb.

samedi /samdi/ *nm* Saturday.

SAMU /samy/ *nm* (*abbr* = **Service d'assistance médicale d'urgence**) ≈ mobile accident unit (GB), emergency medical service, EMS (US).

sanatorium /sanatɔʀjɔm/ *nm* sanatorium (GB), sanitarium (US).

sanctifier /sɑ̃ktifje/ [1] *vtr* to sanctify.

sanction /sɑ̃ksjɔ̃/ *nf* (Law) penalty, sanction; disciplinary measure; (Sch) punishment; **prendre des ~s contre qn** to discipline sb; to take disciplinary action against sb.

sanctionner /sɑ̃ksjɔne/ [1] *vtr* **1** to punish; **2** to give official recognition to [*training, course of studies*].

sanctuaire /sɑ̃ktɥɛʀ/ *nm* **1** shrine; **2** sanctuary.

sandale /sɑ̃dal/ *nf* sandal.

sandalette /sɑ̃dalɛt/ *nf* light sandal.

sandwich, *pl* **~s** or **~es** /sɑ̃dwitʃ/ *nm* sandwich; **(pris) en ~** sandwiched **(entre** between).

sang /sɑ̃/ *nm* **1** blood; **être en ~** to be covered with blood; **mordre jusqu'au ~** to bite through the skin; **avoir le ~ qui monte au visage** to blush; **se terminer dans le ~** to end in bloodshed; **2 de ~** [*brother, ties*] blood; **être du même ~** to be kin.
IDIOMS **il a ça dans le ~** it's in his blood; **mettre qch à feu et à ~** to put sth to fire and the sword; **mon ~ n'a fait qu'un tour** my heart missed a beat; I saw red; **se faire du mauvais ~**○ to worry; **bon ~ (de bonsoir**○**)!** for God's sake○!

sang-froid /sɑ̃fʀwa/ *nm inv* composure; **garder son ~** to keep one's composure; **garde ton ~!** keep calm!; **de ~** in cold blood.

sanglant, ~e /sɑ̃glɑ̃, ɑ̃t/ *adj* **1** (gen) bloody; **2** [*affront, defeat*] cruel.

sangle /sɑ̃gl/ *nf* **1** (gen) strap; **2** (of saddle) girth; **3** (of seat, bed) webbing.

sangler /sɑ̃gle/ [1] *vtr* to girth [*horse*].

sanglier /sɑ̃glije/ *nm* wild boar.

sanglot /sɑ̃glo/ *nm* sob; **éclater en ~s** to burst out sobbing.

sangloter /sɑ̃glɔte/ [1] *vi* to sob.

sangsue /sɑ̃sy/ *nf* leech.

sanguin, ~e[1] /sɑ̃gɛ̃, in/ *adj* **1** blood; **2** impulsive.

sanguinaire /sɑ̃ginɛʀ/ *adj* [*crime*] bloody; [*person*] bloodthirsty.

sanguine[2] /sɑ̃gin/ **I** *adj f* ▶ **sanguin**.
II *nf* **1** blood orange; **2** red chalk drawing.

sanguinolent, **~e** /sɑ̃ginɔlɑ̃, ɑ̃t/ *adj* [*knife, garment*] blood-stained.

sanisette® /sanizɛt/ *nf* automatic public toilet.

sanitaire /sanitɛʀ/ **I** *adj* [*regulations*] health; [*conditions*] sanitary.
II sanitaires *nm pl* **les ~s** (in house) the bathroom; (in campsite) the toilet block.

sans /sɑ̃/ **I** *adv* without.
II *prep* **1** without; **un couple ~ enfant** a childless couple; **~ cela** otherwise; **lundi ~ faute** Monday without fail; **2 il est resté trois mois ~ téléphoner** he didn't call for three months; **il est poli, ~ plus** he's polite, but that's as far as it goes; **~ plus de commentaires** without any further comment; **3 3500 francs ~ l'hôtel** 3,500 francs not including accommodation.
III sans que *phr* without; **pars ~ qu'on te voie** leave without anyone seeing you.
■ **~ domicile fixe, SDF** of no fixed abode, NFA.

sans-abri /sɑ̃zabʀi/ *nmf inv* **un ~** a homeless person; **les ~** the homeless.

sans-cœur /sɑ̃kœʀ/ *nmf inv* heartless person; **tu es un ~** you're heartless.

sans-emploi /sɑ̃zɑ̃plwa/ *nmf inv* unemployed person.

sans-faute /sɑ̃fot/ *nm inv* faultless performance.

sans-gêne /sɑ̃ʒɛn/ *adj inv* cheeky, bad-mannered.

santal /sɑ̃tal/ *nm* sandalwood.

santé /sɑ̃te/ *nf* health; **avoir la ~** to enjoy good health; **se refaire une ~** to build up one's strength; **avoir une petite ~** to be frail or delicate; **à votre ~!** cheers!; **à la ~ de Janet!** here's to Janet!

santon /sɑ̃tɔ̃/ *nm* Christmas crib figure.

saoul, **~e** = **soûl**.

sape /sap/ *nf* **travail de ~** (Tech) sap digging; (figurative) sabotage.

saper /sape/ [1] **I** *vtr* to undermine.
II se saper° *v refl* (+ *v être*) to dress; **être bien/mal sapé** to be well/badly dressed.

sapeur /sapœʀ/ *nm* sapper.
IDIOMS **fumer comme un ~** to smoke like a chimney.

sapeur-pompier, *pl* **sapeurs-pompiers** /sapœʀpɔ̃pje/ *nm* fireman.

saphir /safiʀ/ *nm* **1** sapphire; **2** (on record player) stylus.

sapin /sapɛ̃/ *nm* **1** fir tree; **~ de Noël** Christmas tree; **2** deal.

sapinière /sapinjɛʀ/ *nf* fir plantation.

saquer° /sake/ [1] *vtr* = **sacquer**.

sarbacane /saʀbakan/ *nf* blowpipe.

sarcasme /saʀkasm/ *nm* **1** sarcasm; **2** sarcastic remark.

sarcastique /saʀkastik/ *adj* sarcastic.

sarcloir /saʀklwaʀ/ *nm* hoe.

sarcophage /saʀkɔfaʒ/ *nm* sarcophagus.

sardine /saʀdin/ *nf* **1** (Zool) sardine; **2**° tent peg.

sardonique /saʀdɔnik/ *adj* sardonic.

sarment /saʀmɑ̃/ *nm* **~ (de vigne)** vine shoot.

sarrasin /saʀazɛ̃/ *nm* (Bot, Culin) buckwheat.

sarrau /saʀo/ *nm* smock.

sas /sɑs/ *nm inv* **1** airlock; **2** (on canal) lock; **3** (in bank) security double door system.

satané°, **~e** /satane/ *adj* damned°.

satanique /satanik/ *adj* **1** [*smile, ruse*] fiendish; **2** [*cult*] Satanic.

satellite /satelit/ *nm* satellite.

satiété /sasjete/ **I** *nf* satiation, satiety.
II à satiété *phr* **1 manger à ~** to eat one's fill; **2** [*say, repeat*] ad nauseam.

satin /satɛ̃/ *nm* satin.

satiné, **~e** /satine/ *adj* [*fabric, cloth*] satiny; [*paint*] satin-finish.

satire /satiʀ/ *nf* satire; **faire la ~ de qch/qn** to satirize sth/sb.

satirique /satiʀik/ *adj* satirical.

satisfaction /satisfaksjɔ̃/ *nf* satisfaction; **motif de ~** reason to feel satisfied; **la ~ de nos besoins** the fulfilment[GB] of our needs; **si le lave-vaisselle ne vous donne pas ~** if you are not entirely satisfied with the dishwasher.

satisfaire /satisfɛʀ/ [10] **I** *vtr* (gen) to satisfy; to fulfil[GB] [*aspiration, requirement*]; **~ l'attente d'un client** to come up to a customer's expectations; **~ un besoin naturel** (euphemistic) to answer a call of nature.
II satisfaire à *v+prep* to fulfil[GB] [*obligation*]; to meet [*norm, standard*].
III se satisfaire *v refl* (+ *v être*) **se ~ de** to be satisfied with [*explanation*]; to be content with [*low salary*].

satisfaisant, **~e** /satisfəzɑ̃, ɑ̃t/ *adj* **1** satisfactory; **2** satisfying.

satisfait, **~e** /satisfɛ, ɛt/ *adj* [*customer, need, smile*] satisfied; [*desire*] gratified; [*person*] happy; **être ~ de soi** to be pleased with oneself.

saturation /satyʀasjɔ̃/ *nf* (of market) saturation; (in trains, hotels) overcrowding; (of network) overloading; **arriver à ~** [*market, network*] to reach saturation point; [*person*] to have had as much as one can take.

saturé, **~e** /satyʀe/ *adj* [*market*] saturated; [*profession*] overcrowded; **le public est ~ de publicité** the public has had its fill of advertising.

saturer /satyʀe/ [1] *vtr* to saturate (**de** with); **on nous sature de feuilletons** we're being inundated with soap operas.

satyre /satiʀ/ *nm* **1** satyr; **2** lecher.

sauce /sos/ *nf* (Culin) sauce; **~ au vin** wine sauce; **plat en ~** dish with sauce; **(r)allonger la ~**° (figurative) to spin things out.
IDIOMS **mettre qch à toutes les ~s** to adapt sth to any purpose.

saucière /sosjɛʀ/ *nf* sauceboat.

saucisse /sosis/ *nf* sausage; **chair à ~** sausage meat.
■ **~ de Francfort** frankfurter.

saucisson /sosisɔ̃/ *nm* (slicing) sausage; **~ à l'ail** garlic sausage; **~ sec** ≈ salami.

sauf[1] /sof/ I *prep* **1** except, but; **2 ~ contrordre** failing an order to the contrary; **~ avis contraire** unless otherwise stated; **~ imprévu** all things being equal; **~ erreur de ma part** if I'm not mistaken.
II **sauf si** *phr* unless.
III **sauf que** *phr* except that.

sauf[2], **sauve** /sof, sov/ *adj* **1** safe; **laisser la vie sauve à qn** to spare sb's life; **2** [*honour, reputation*] intact.

sauf-conduit, *pl* **~s** /sofkɔ̃dɥi/ *nm* safe-conduct.

sauge /soʒ/ *nf* sage.

saugrenu, **~e** /sogʀəny/ *adj* crazy, potty○ (GB).

saule /sol/ *nm* willow; **~ pleureur** weeping willow.

saumâtre /somɑtʀ/ *adj* [*water*] brackish; [*taste*] bitter and salty.

saumon /somɔ̃/ I *adj inv* salmon (pink).
II *nm* salmon; **~ fumé** smoked salmon.

saumure /somyʀ/ *nf* brine; **conserver dans la ~** to pickle in brine.

sauna /sona/ *nm* sauna.

saupoudrer /sopudʀe/ [1] *vtr* **1** to sprinkle; **2** (figurative) to give [sth] sparingly.

saur /sɔʀ/ *adj m* **hareng ~** kipper, kippered herring.

saut /so/ *nm* **1** jump; **faire un petit ~** to skip; **au ~ du lit** first thing in the morning; **2** (Sport) **le ~** jumping; **3**○ **faire un ~ à Paris** to make a flying visit to Paris; **faire un ~ chez qn** to pop in and see sb.
■ **~ de l'ange** swallow dive (GB), swan dive (US); **~ à la corde** skipping;**~ à l'élastique** bungee jumping; **~ en hauteur** high jump; **~ à la perche** pole vault; **~ périlleux** mid-air somersault.

saute /sot/ *nf* **~ de température** sudden change in temperature; **~ d'humeur** mood swing.

sauté, **~e** /sote/ I *adj* (Culin) sautéed.
II *nm* (Culin) **~ d'agneau/de veau** sautéed lamb/veal.

saute-mouton /sotmutɔ̃/ *nm inv* **jouer à ~** to play leapfrog.

sauter /sote/ [1] I *vtr* **1** to jump [*distance, height*]; to jump over [*stream, fence*]; **2** to skip [*meal, paragraph*]; to leave out [*details*]; (Sch) **~ une classe** to skip a year; **3** to miss [*word, line, turn*].
II *vi* **1** to jump; **~ à pieds joints** to jump with one's feet together; **~ à pieds joints dans un piège** (figurative) to fall straight into a trap; **~ à la perche** to pole vault; **~ à la corde** to skip; **faire ~ un enfant sur ses genoux** to dandle a child on one's knee; **~ sur qn** to pounce on sb; **~ sur son téléphone** to grab one's telephone; **~ à la gorge de qn** to go for sb's throat; **~ au cou de qn** to greet sb with a kiss; **2 ~ dans un taxi** to jump or hop into a taxi; **3 ~ d'un sujet à l'autre** to skip from one subject to another; **4**○ **faire ~ une réunion** to cancel a meeting; **le poste va ~** the job is being axed; **faire ~ une contravention** to get out of paying a parking ticket; **5** [*bicycle chain, fan belt*] to come off; **la troisième vitesse saute** the third gear keeps slipping; **6 faire ~ une serrure** to force a lock; **faire ~ les boutons** to burst one's buttons; **faire ~ les barrières** (figurative) to break down the barriers; **7** [*bridge, building*] to be blown up, to go up; **faire ~ les plombs** to blow the fuses; **8** (Culin) **faire ~** to sauté [*onions*]; to toss [*pancake*].
IDIOMS **~ aux yeux** to be blindingly obvious; **et que ça saute**○**!** make it snappy○!; **~ au plafond**○ to jump for joy; to hit the roof○; to be staggered.

sauterelle /sotʀɛl/ *nf* grasshopper.

sauterie /sotʀi/ *nf* party, hop.

sautillant, **~e** /sotijɑ̃, ɑ̃t/ *adj* [*rhythm, gait*] bouncy; [*bird*] hopping.

sautiller /sotije/ [1] *vi* **1** [*bird*] to hop; **2** [*child*] to skip along; to jump up and down.

sautoir /sotwaʀ/ *nm* long necklace.

sauvage /sovaʒ/ I *adj* **1** [*animal, plant*] wild; [*tribe*] primitive; **2** [*behaviour*] savage, wild; [*struggle*] fierce; **3** unsociable; **4** illegal; **urbanisation ~** uncontrolled[GB] growth.
II *nmf* **1** savage; **2** unsociable person, loner.

sauvagement /sovaʒmɑ̃/ *adv* savagely.

sauvageon, **-onne** /sovaʒɔ̃, ɔn/ *nm,f* wild child.

sauvagerie /sovaʒʀi/ *nf* **1** savagery; **2** unsociability.

sauve ▶ **sauf**[2].

sauvegarde /sovgaʀd/ *nf* (of heritage, peace, values) maintenance; (of rights, liberties) protection; **assurer la ~ de** to safeguard.

sauvegarder /sovgaʀde/ [1] *vtr* **1** (gen) to safeguard; **2** (in computing) to save; to back [sth] up [*file*].

sauve-qui-peut /sovkipø/ *nm inv* stampede.

sauver /sove/ [1] I *vtr* **1** (gen) to save; **~ la vie à qn** to save sb's life; **~ qn de la noyade** to save sb from drowning; **elle est sauvée** [*ill person*] she has pulled through○; **2** to salvage [*goods*] (**de** from); **3 ce qui le sauve à mes yeux, c'est sa générosité** his redeeming feature for me is his generosity.
II **se sauver** *v refl* (+ *v être*) **1** to escape; to run away; (from danger) to run; **sauvez-vous!** run (for it)!; **2**○ **il faut que je me sauve** I've got to rush off now.
IDIOMS **~ la situation** to save the day; **sauve qui peut!** run for your life!; (on sinking ship) it's every man for himself.

sauvetage /sovtaʒ/ *nm* rescue; **cours de ~** life-saving training.

sauveteur /sovtœʀ/ *nm* rescuer.

sauvette: **à la sauvette** /alasovɛt/ *phr* **1** [*prepare, sign*] in a rush, hastily; **2** [*film, record*] on the sly; **vendre qch à la ~** to sell sth illegally on the street.

sauveur /sovœʀ/ *nm* saviour[GB].

savamment /savamɑ̃/ *adv* **1** learnedly, eruditely; **2** skilfully[GB].

savane /savan/ *nf* **1** savannah; **2** (in Canada) swamp.

savant, ~e /savɑ̃, ɑ̃t/ **I** *adj* **1** [*person*] learned, erudite; **2** [*edition, study*] scholarly; [*calculation*] complicated, involved; **3** [*manoeuvre*] clever; [*direction, production*] skilful[GB]; **4** [*animal*] performing.
II *nm,f* scholar.
III *nm* scientist.

savate○ /savat/ *nf* **1** old slipper; **2** old shoe.

saveur /savœʀ/ *nf* (of foodstuff, drink) flavour[GB]; **sans ~** tasteless.

savoir[1] /savwaʀ/ [47] **I** *vtr* **1** to know [*truth, answer*]; **vous n'êtes pas sans ~ que** you are no doubt aware that; **~ qch sur qn** to know sth about sb; **va** or **allez ~!** who knows!; **est-ce que je sais, moi!** how should I know!; **elle n'a rien voulu ~** she just didn't want to know; **pour autant que je sache** as far as I know; **comment l'as-tu su ?** how did you find out?; **je l'ai su par elle** she told me about it; **reste à ~ si** it remains to be seen if or whether; **ne ~ que faire pour...** to be at a loss as to how to...; **sachant que** knowing that; given that; **sache que j'avais raison** I'm telling you, I was right; **qui vous savez** you-know-who; **je ne sais qui** somebody or other; **tu en sais des choses!** you really know a thing or two!; **2 ~ faire** to know how to do; **je sais conduire** I can drive; **~ écouter** to be a good listener; **on ne saurait mieux dire** I couldn't have put it better myself; **elle sait y faire avec les hommes** she knows how to handle men.
II se savoir *v refl* (+ *v être*) **ça se saurait** people would know about that; **cela a fini par se ~** word got around.
III à savoir *phr* that is to say.
IDIOMS **ne pas ~ où donner de la tête** not to know whether one is coming or going; **et Dieu sait quoi!** and God knows what else!

savoir[2] /savwaʀ/ *nm* **1** learning; **2** knowledge; **3** body of knowledge.

savoir-faire /savwaʀfɛʀ/ *nm inv* know-how.

savoir-vivre /savwaʀvivʀ/ *nm inv* manners.

savon /savɔ̃/ *nm* **1** soap; **~ de Marseille** household soap; **2** (bar of) soap.
IDIOMS **passer un ~**○ **à qn** to give sb a telling-off.

savonner /savɔne/ [1] *vtr* to soap.

savonnette /savɔnɛt/ *nf* small cake of soap.

savonneux, -euse /savɔnø, øz/ *adj* soapy; **être sur une pente savonneuse** (figurative) to be on the slippery slope.

savourer /savuʀe/ [1] *vtr* to savour[GB] [*success, moment, instant*].

savoureux, -euse /savuʀø, øz/ *adj* [*dish*] tasty; [*anecdote*] juicy.

saxophone /saksɔfɔn/ *nm* **1** saxophone; **2** saxophone player.

saxophoniste /saksɔfɔnist/ *nmf* saxophonist.

scabreux, -euse /skabʀø, øz/ *adj* obscene, gross.

scalp /skalp/ *nm* **1** scalp; **2** scalping.

scalpel /skalpɛl/ *nm* scalpel.

scalper /skalpe/ [1] *vtr* to scalp.

scandale /skɑ̃dal/ *nm* scandal; **faire (un** or **du) ~** (gen) to cause a scandal; [*person*] to cause a fuss; **au grand ~ de** to the great disgust of; **la presse à ~** the gutter press; **c'est un ~!** it's scandalous, it's outrageous!

scandaleux, -euse /skɑ̃dalø, øz/ *adj* scandalous, outrageous.

scandaliser /skɑ̃dalize/ [1] **I** *vtr* to outrage, to scandalize [*person*].
II se scandaliser *v refl* (+ *v être*) to be shocked.

scander /skɑ̃de/ [1] *vtr* **1** to scan; **2** to chant [*slogan, name*].

scandinave /skɑ̃dinav/ *adj* Scandinavian.

scanneur /skanœʀ/ *nm* scanner.

scaphandre /skafɑ̃dʀ/ *nm* **1** deep-sea diving suit; **2** spacesuit.

scaphandrier /skafɑ̃dʀije/ *nm* deep-sea diver.

scarabée /skaʀabe/ *nm* **1** beetle; **2** scarab.

scarifier /skaʀifje/ [1] *vtr* to scarify.

scarlatine /skaʀlatin/ *nf* scarlet fever.

scatologie /skatɔlɔʒi/ *nf* scatology.

sceau, *pl* **~x** /so/ *nm* **1** seal; **sous le ~ du secret** in strictest secrecy; **2** stamp, hallmark.

scélérat, ~e /seleʀa, at/ *nm,f* villain.

scellé /sele/ *nm* seal; **apposer les ~s** to affix seals.

sceller /sele/ [1] *vtr* **1** to seal; **2** to fix [sth] securely [*shelf, bar*].

scénario /senaʀjo/ *nm* **1** screenplay, script; **2** scenario; **~ catastrophe** nightmare or doomsday scenario.

scénariste /senaʀist/ *nmf* scriptwriter.

scène /sɛn/ *nf* **1** stage; **'en ~!'** 'on stage!'; **entrer en ~** to come on; **2** scene; **la ~ se passe à Paris** the scene is set in Paris; **3 quitter la ~** to give up the stage; **musique de ~** music for the theatre[GB]; **mettre en ~** to stage [*play*]; to direct [*film*]; **une excellente mise en ~** an excellent production; **4** scene; **occuper le devant de la ~** (figurative) to be in the news; **5 faire une ~** to throw a fit○; **6** scene; **~s de panique** scenes of panic; **il a assisté à toute la ~** he saw the whole thing.
■ **~ de ménage** domestic dispute.

scepticisme /sɛptisism/ *nm* scepticism (GB), skepticism (US); **envisager qch avec ~** to take a sceptical (GB) or skeptical (US) view of sth.

sceptique /sɛptik/ **I** *adj* sceptical (GB), skeptical (US); **laisser qn ~** to leave sb unconvinced.
II *nmf* sceptic (GB), skeptic (US).

sceptre /sɛptʀ/ *nm* sceptre[GB].

schéma /ʃema/ *nm* **1** diagram; **2** outline; **3** pattern.

schématique /ʃematik/ *adj* **1** [*vision, argument*] simplistic; **2** schematic.

schématiquement /ʃematikmɑ̃/ *adv* [*explain, describe*] in broad outline.

schématiser /ʃematize/ [1] *vtr* **1** to simplify; **2** to oversimplify.

schizophrénie /skizɔfʀeni/ *nf* schizophrenia.

sciatique /sjatik/ **I** *adj* **nerf ~** sciatic nerve.
II *nf* **avoir une ~** to have sciatica.

scie /si/ *nf* saw; **~ sauteuse** jigsaw.

sciemment /sjamɑ̃/ *adv* knowingly.

science /sjɑ̃s/ *nf* **1** science; **2** knowledge, erudition.
■ **~s naturelles** ≈ biology (*sg*); **~s occultes** black arts; **Sciences Po**○ *Institute of Political Science.*

science-fiction /sjɑ̃sfiksjɔ̃/ *nf* science fiction.

scientifique /sjɑ̃tifik/ **I** *adj* scientific.
II *nmf* scientist.

scier /sje/ [2] *vtr* **1** to saw; **2**○ to stun.

scierie /siʀi/ *nf* sawmill.

scinder /sɛ̃de/ [1] **I** *vtr* to split [*group*]; to break down [*question*].
II se scinder *v refl* (+ *v être*) [*organization, party*] to split up.

scintillant, ~e /sɛ̃tijɑ̃, ɑ̃t/ *adj* [*star*] twinkling.

scintillement /sɛ̃tijmɑ̃/ *nm* (of diamond) sparkling; (of stars) twinkling.

scintiller /sɛ̃tije/ [1] *vi* [*diamond*] to sparkle; [*star*] to twinkle; [*water*] to glisten.

scission /sisjɔ̃/ *nf* **1** split, schism; **faire ~** to break away; **2** fission.

sciure /sjyʀ/ *nf* **~ (de bois)** sawdust.

sclérose /skleʀoz/ *nf* **1** (Med) sclerosis; **2** fossilization, ossification.
■ **~ en plaques** multiple sclerosis, MS.

scléroser /skleʀoze/ [1] **I** *vtr* (Med) to sclerose [*veins*].
II se scléroser *v refl* (+ *v être*) **1** (figurative) [*institution, person*] to become fossilized; **2** (Med) [*tissue*] to become hardened.

scolaire /skɔlɛʀ/ *adj* [*holidays, book, syllabus*] school; [*reform, publication*] educational; [*failure, success*] academic; **établissement ~** school.

scolarisation /skɔlaʀizasjɔ̃/ *nf* schooling, education.

scolariser /skɔlaʀize/ [1] *vtr* to send [sb] to school.

scolarité /skɔlaʀite/ *nf* **1** schooling; **durant ma ~** when I was at school; **la ~ obligatoire** compulsory education; **2** (in university) registrar's office.

scoliose /skɔljoz/ *nf* scoliosis; **avoir une ~** to have scoliosis.

scooter /skutœʀ/ *nm* (motor) scooter.

scorbut /skɔʀbyt/ *nm* scurvy.

score /skɔʀ/ *nm* **1** (Sch, Sport) score; **~ nul** draw (GB), tie (US); **2** results.

scorie /skɔʀi/ *nf* **1** scoria; **2** slag.

scorpion /skɔʀpjɔ̃/ *nm* (Zool) scorpion.

Scorpion /skɔʀpjɔ̃/ *pr nm* Scorpio.

scotch, *pl* **~es** /skɔtʃ/ *nm* **1** Scotch (whisky); **2** ®Sellotape® (GB), Scotch® tape (US).

scotcher /skɔtʃe/ [1] *vtr* to Sellotape® (GB), to Scotch-tape® (US).

scout, ~e /skut/ **I** *adj* scout.
II *nm,f* (Catholic) boy scout/(Catholic) girl scout.

scoutisme /skutism/ *nm* scouting; **faire du ~** to be a scout.

scrabble® /skʀabl/ *nm* Scrabble®; **jouer au ~** to play Scrabble®.

scribe /skʀib/ *nm* scribe.

scribouillard○, **~e** /skʀibujaʀ, aʀd/ *nm,f* pen pusher○ (GB), pencil pusher (US).

script /skʀipt/ *nm* **1 écrire en ~** to print; **2** script.

scripte /skʀipt/ *nmf* continuity man/girl.

script-girl, *pl* **~s** /skʀiptgœʀl/ *nf* continuity girl.

scrupule /skʀypyl/ *nm* scruple; **avoir des ~s à faire** to have scruples about doing.

scrupuleusement /skʀypyløzmɑ̃/ *adv* (gen) [*respect, apply*] scrupulously.

scrupuleux, -euse /skʀypylø, øz/ *adj* scrupulous; **peu ~** unscrupulous.

scrutateur, -trice /skʀytatœʀ, tʀis/ *adj* [*look*] searching.

scruter /skʀyte/ [1] *vtr* to scan [*horizon*]; to scrutinize [*object*]; to examine [*ground, person*].

scrutin /skʀytɛ̃/ *nm* **1** ballot; **dépouiller le ~** to count the votes; **2** polls; **jour du ~** polling day; **mode de ~** electoral system.
■ **~ majoritaire** election by majority vote.

sculpter /skylte/ [1] *vtr* to sculpt, to carve.

sculpteur /skyltœʀ/ *nm* sculptor; **~ sur bois** woodcarver.

sculptural, ~e, *mpl* **-aux** /skyltyʀal, o/ *adj* [*art*] sculptural; [*shape, beauty*] statuesque.

sculpture /skyltyʀ/ *nf* sculpture; **la ~ sur bois** woodcarving.

SDF /ɛsdeɛf/ *nmf* (*abbr* = **sans domicile fixe**) of no fixed abode, NFA.

se (**s'** *before vowel or mute h*) /sə, s/ *pron* **1** oneself; himself; herself; itself; **il ~ regarde** he's looking at himself; **~ laver** to wash, to have a wash; **2** each other; **ils ~ regardaient** they were looking at each other; **3 ~ ronger les ongles** to bite one's nails; **il ~ lave les pieds** he's washing his feet; **4 elle ~ comporte honorablement** she behaves honourably[GB]; **l'écart ~ creuse** the gap is widening; **5 les exemples ~ comptent sur les doigts de la main** the examples can be counted on the fingers of your hand; **le médicament ~ vend sans ordonnance** the medicine is sold without a prescription; **6 comment ~ fait-il que...?** how come...?, how is it that...?; **il ~ produit une réaction chimique** there is a chemical reaction.

séance /seɑ̃s/ *nf* **1** (of court, parliament) session; (of committee) meeting; **~ tenante** immediately; **organiser une ~ de travail** to organize a workshop; **2** (in cinema) show; **une ~ privée** a private screening.
■ **~ de spiritisme** séance.

séant /seɑ̃/ *nm* **se mettre sur son ~** to sit up.

seau, *pl* **~x** /so/ *nm* (gen) bucket, pail.

sébile /sebil/ *nf* begging bowl; **tendre la ~** to beg.

sec, sèche[1] /sɛk, sɛʃ/ **I** *adj* **1** [*weather, hair*] dry; [*fruit*] dried; **2** [*wine, cider*] dry; **boire son gin ~** to like one's gin straight; **3** [*person, statement*] terse; [*letter, tone*] curt; [*style*] dry; **4** [*noise*] sharp; **se briser d'un coup ~** to snap.
II *nm* **être à ~** [*river*] to have dried up; (figurative) [*person*] to have no money.
III *adv* **1 se briser ~** to snap; **2**° [*rain, drink*] a lot.
IDIOMS **aussi ~**° immediately; **je l'ai eu ~**° I was pretty choked°.

sécateur /sekatœʀ/ *nm* clippers; **~ à haie** shears.

sécession /sesesjɔ̃/ *nf* secession; **faire ~** to secede.

sèche[2] /sɛʃ/ *adj f* ▶ **sec** I.

sèche-cheveux /sɛʃʃəvø/ *nm inv* hairdrier (GB), blow-dryer.

sèche-linge /sɛʃlɛ̃ʒ/ *nm inv* tumble-drier (GB), tumble-dryer.

sèche-mains /sɛʃmɛ̃/ *nm inv* hand-drier (GB), blower (US).

sèchement /sɛʃmɑ̃/ *adv* drily, coldly; **très ~** curtly.

sécher /seʃe/ [1] **I** *vtr* **1** (gen) to dry; **2**° to skip [*class*].
II *vi* **1** [*hair, clothes*] to dry; [*mud*] to dry up; **fleur/viande séchée** dried flower/meat; **mettre des vêtements à ~** to hang clothes up to dry; **2**° [*person*] to dry up.

sécheresse /seʃʀɛs/ *nf* **1** drought; **2** dryness; **3** curt manner; **la ~ de son ton** his/her curt tone.

séchoir /seʃwaʀ/ *nm* **1** clothes airer, clothes horse; **2** tumble-drier (GB), tumble-dryer.

second, ~e[1] /səgɔ̃, ɔ̃d/ **I** *adj* **1** (in sequence, series) second; **chapitre ~** chapter two; **en ~e lecture** at a second reading; **en ~ lieu** secondly; **dans un ~ temps...** subsequently...; **c'est à prendre au ~ degré** it is not to be taken literally; **2** (in hierarchy) second; **de ~ ordre** second-rate; **politicien de ~ plan** minor politician; **de ~ choix** of inferior quality; **jouer un ~ rôle** (in theatre) to play a supporting role; **jouer les ~ rôles** (figurative) to play second fiddle.
II *nm,f* second one.
III *nm* **1** second-in-command; **2** second floor (GB), third floor (US).
IV en second *phr* [*arrive, leave*] second; **passer en ~** [*friends, work*] to come second.

secondaire /səgɔ̃dɛʀ/ **I** *adj* **1** secondary; **2** minor; **3** (Sch) **école ~** secondary school (GB), high school (US); **4** (gen, Med) **effets ~s** side effects.
II *nm* **1** (Sch) secondary school (GB) or high school (US) education.

secondairement /səgɔ̃dɛʀmɑ̃/ *adv* secondarily.

seconde[2] /səgɔ̃d/ **I** ▶ **second** I, II.
II *nf* **1** ▶ **second** II; **2** second; **en une fraction de ~** in a split second; **3** (Sch) *fifth year of secondary school, age 15–16*; **4 billet de ~** second-class ticket; **5** (Aut) second (gear).

seconder /səgɔ̃de/ [1] *vtr* [*person*] to assist; [*circumstance*] to aid.

secouer /səkwe/ [1] **I** *vtr* **1** to shake [*bottle, branch, person*]; to shake out [*rug, umbrella*]; **~ la tête** to shake one's head; **être un peu secoué** (in car, plane) to have rather a bumpy ride; **2** to shake off [*dust, snow, yoke*]; **3** [*crisis*] to shake [*person, country*]; **être un peu secoué** (by bad news) to be rather shaken up; **4**° to give [sb] a shaking-up° [*person*].
II se secouer *v refl* (+ *v être*) **1** to give oneself a shake; **2** to jump about all over the place; **3**° to pull oneself together; **4**° to wake up, to get moving°.

secourable /səkuʀabl/ *adj* [*person*] helpful.

secourir /səkuʀiʀ/ [26] *vtr* **1** to help; **2** to rescue; **3** to give first aid to; **4** to provide aid for [*refugee*].

secourisme /səkuʀism/ *nm* first aid.

secouriste /səkuʀist/ *nmf* first-aid worker.

secours /səkuʀ/ **I** *nm inv* help; **au ~!** help!; **appeler** or **crier au ~** to shout for help; **être d'un grand ~** to be a great help; **porter ~ à qn** to help sb; **le ~ en mer** sea rescue operations; **de ~** [*wheel*] spare; [*exit*] emergency; [*kit*] first-aid; [*team, operation*] rescue; [*battery, equipment*] back-up.
II *nm pl* **1** rescuers, rescue team; reinforcements; **2** relief supplies; supplies; **premiers ~** first aid.

secousse /səkus/ *nf* jolt; **avancer par ~s** [*car, train*] to jerk forward; **~ (sismique)** (earth) tremor.

secret, -ète /səkʀɛ, ɛt/ **I** *adj* **1** secret; **2** [*person*] secretive.
II *nm* **1** secret; **ne pas avoir de ~s pour qn** to have no secrets from sb; **confier un ~ à qn** to let sb into (GB) or in on a secret; **il n'en fait pas un ~** he makes no secret of it; **2** secrecy; **être tenu au ~** to be sworn to secrecy; **mettre qn dans le ~** to let sb into (GB) or in on the secret; **en ~** in secret; **encore une de ces gaffes dont il a le ~** another of those blunders that only he knows how to make; **3** solitary confinement.
■ **~ de fabrication** industrial secret; **~ de Polichinelle** open secret; **~ professionnel** professional confidentiality.

secrétaire /s(ə)kʀetɛʀ/ **I** *nmf* secretary.
II *nm* (piece of furniture) secretaire (GB), secretary (US).
■ **~ de direction** personal assistant; **~ d'État** (in France) minister; (in Great Britain, America) Secretary of State; **~ de rédaction** subditor (GB), copy-editor.

secrétariat /s(ə)kʀetaʀja/ *nm* **1** secretarial work; **école de ~** secretarial college; **2** secretariat.

secrète ▶ **secret** I.

secrètement /səkʀɛtmɑ̃/ *adv* secretly.

sécréter /sekʀete/ [1] *vtr* **1** to secrete [*sap, bile*]; **2** to exude [*liquid*]; **~ l'ennui** to exude boredom.

sécrétion /sekʀesjɔ̃/ *nf* secretion.

sectaire /sɛktɛʀ/ *adj, nmf* sectarian.

secte /sɛkt/ *nf* sect; faction.

secteur /sɛktœʀ/ *nm* **1** (Econ) sector; **~ primaire/secondaire/tertiaire** primary/manufacturing/service sector; **~ d'activité** sector; **2** area, territory; (Mil) sector; **3**○ neighbourhood[GB]; **4** (electrical) **le ~** the mains; **appareil fonctionnant sur ~** mains-operated appliance; **panne de ~** power failure.

section /sɛksjɔ̃/ *nf* **1** section; (of party, trade union) branch; (of book) part; **2** (Sch) stream (GB), track (US); **choisir une ~ littéraire** to choose a literary option.
■ **~ d'autobus** fare stage.

sectionner /sɛksjɔne/ [1] *vtr* **1** to sever; **2** to divide up [*organization*] (**en** into).

sectoriser /sɛktɔʀize/ [1] *vtr* to divide [sth] into sectors.

séculaire /sekylɛʀ/ *adj* **1** [*tradition*] ancient; **2** [*house, tree*] hundred-year-old.

séculier, -ière /sekylje, ɛʀ/ *adj* [*clergy*] secular.

secundo /səgɔ̃do/ *adv* secondly.

sécuriser /sekyʀize/ [1] *vtr* **1** to reassure; **2** to make [sb] feel secure.

sécurité /sekyʀite/ *nf* **1** security; **~ de l'emploi** job security; **de ~** [*system*] security; [*reasons*] of security; **2** safety; **en toute ~** in complete safety; **se sentir en ~** to feel secure or safe (**auprès de** with).
■ **~ routière** road safety; **~ sociale** *French national health and pensions organization.*

sédatif, -ive /sedatif, iv/ **I** *adj* sedative.
II *nm* sedative.

sédentaire /sedɑ̃tɛʀ/ *adj* sedentary.

sédentariser /sedɑ̃taʀize/ [1] *vtr* to settle.

sédentarité /sedɑ̃taʀite/ *nf* (of population) settled way of life; (of job, situation) sedentary nature.

sédiment /sedimɑ̃/ *nm* sediment.

sédimentation /sedimɑ̃tasjɔ̃/ *nf* sedimentation.

séditieux, -ieuse /sedisjø, øz/ *adj* **1** [*person*] rebellious; **2** [*writing, mind*] seditious.

séducteur, -trice /sedyktœʀ, tʀis/ **I** *adj* seductive, attractive.
II *nm,f* **1** charmer; **2** deceiver/seductress.

séduction /sedyksjɔ̃/ *nf* **1** charm; **2** seduction; **pouvoir de ~** (of person) power of seduction; (of money) lure; (of words) seductive power.

séduire /sedɥiʀ/ [1] *vtr* **1** [*person*] to captivate; **il aime ~** he likes to charm people; **2** to appeal to [*person*]; **3** [*person*] to win over; **4** to seduce.

séduisant, ~e /sedɥizɑ̃, ɑ̃t/ *adj* [*person*] attractive; [*idea*] appealing.

segment /sɛgmɑ̃/ *nm* segment.

segmentation /sɛgmɑ̃tasjɔ̃/ *nf* segmentation.

segmenter /sɛgmɑ̃te/ [1] *vtr*, **se segmenter** *v refl* (+ *v être*) to segment.

ségrégation /segʀegasjɔ̃/ *nf* segregation.

seiche /sɛʃ/ *nf* cuttlefish.

seigle /sɛgl/ *nm* rye; **pain/farine de ~** rye bread/flour.

seigneur /sɛɲœʀ/ *nm* **1** lord; **être grand ~** to be full of largesse; **2** (in industry, high finance) heavyweight.
■ **~ de la guerre** warlord.
IDIOMS **à tout ~ tout honneur** (Proverb) credit where credit is due.

Seigneur /sɛɲœʀ/ *nm* Lord; **~!** Good Lord!

seigneurial, ~e, *mpl* **-iaux** /sɛɲœʀjal, o/ *adj* [*home*] stately; [*manner*] lordly.

sein /sɛ̃/ *nm* **1** (Anat) breast; **les ~s nus** topless; **nourrir (son enfant) au ~** to breast-feed (one's baby); **serrer qn contre son ~** to clasp sb to one's bosom; **2 au ~ de** within.

séisme /seism/ *nm* earthquake, seism; (figurative) upheaval.

seize /sɛz/ *adj inv, pron* sixteen.

seizième /sɛzjɛm/ *adj* sixteenth.
■ **~s de finale** (Sport) *round in competition with thirty-two competitors or teams.*

séjour /seʒuʀ/ *nm* **1** stay; **~s à l'étranger** (on CV) time spent abroad; **2 (salle de) ~** living room; **3 un ~ champêtre** a rural retreat.
■ **~ linguistique** language study holiday (GB) or vacation.

séjourner /seʒuʀne/ [1] *vi* **1** [*person*] to stay; **2** [*liquid*] to remain; [*snow*] to lie.

sel /sɛl/ *nm* **1** salt; **gros ~** coarse salt; **2** (figurative) **la situation ne manque pas de ~** the situation has a certain piquancy.
■ **~s de bain** bath salts.

sélect○**, ~e** /selɛkt/ *adj* [*club, bar*] exclusive; [*clientele*] select.

sélectif, -ive /selɛktif, iv/ *adj* selective.

sélection /selɛksjɔ̃/ *nf* (gen) selection; (for a job) selection process; **~ à l'entrée** selective entry.

sélectionner /selɛksjɔne/ [1] *vtr* to select; **être sélectionné sur dossier** (Sch) to be selected on the basis of one's academic record.

self-service, *pl* **~s** /sɛlfsɛʀvis/ *nm* self-service restaurant.

selle /sɛl/ **I** *nf* **1** saddle; **remis en ~** [*player, regime*] firmly (re)established; **2 aller à la ~** (euphemistic) to have a bowel movement.
II selles *nf pl* (Med) stools.

seller /sele/ [1] *vtr* to saddle.

sellette /selɛt/ *nf* **être sur la ~** to be in the hot seat.

selon /səlɔ̃/ *prep* **1** according to; **~ moi, il va pleuvoir** in my opinion, it's going to rain; **~ les termes du président** in the President's words; **~ la formule** as people or they say; **l'idée ~ laquelle** the idea that; **2** depending on [*time, circumstances*]; **la situation varie ~ les régions** the situation varies from region to region; **c'est ~**○ it all depends; **~ que** depending on whether.

Seltz /sɛlts/ *pr n* **eau de ~** soda water, seltzer water.

semailles /səmɑj/ *nf pl* **1** sowing season; **2** seeds; **3 faire les ~** to sow.

semaine /s(ə)mɛn/ *nf* **1** week; **payer à la ~** to pay by the week; **2** week's wages.

IDIOMS **vivre à la petite ~** to live from day to day.

sémantique /semɑ̃tik/ I *adj* semantic.
II *nf* semantics.

semblable /sɑ̃blabl/ I *adj* **1** similar; **2** identical; **3** such; **~ proposition** such a proposal.
II *nmf* fellow creature; **il n'a pas son ~ pour faire rire les autres** there's nobody funnier; **eux et leurs ~s** they and their kind.

semblant /sɑ̃blɑ̃/ *nm* **un ~ de légalité** a semblance of legality; **faire ~ d'être triste** to pretend to be sad; **elle fait ~ de rien, mais elle t'a vu** she's seen you but she's not letting on○.

sembler /sɑ̃ble/ [1] I *vi* to seem; **tout semble possible** it seems anything is possible.
II *v impers* **il semble bon de faire** it seems appropriate to do; **le problème est réglé à ce qu'il me semble** the problem has been solved, or so it seems to me; **faites comme bon vous semble** do whatever you think best; **il me semble l'avoir déjà rencontrée** I think I've met her before; **elle a, semble-t-il, refusé** apparently, she has refused; **si bon me semble** if I feel like it.

semelle /s(ə)mɛl/ *nf* sole.
■ **~ compensée** wedge heel; **~ intérieure** insole.
IDIOMS **battre la ~** to stamp one's feet; **être dur comme de la ~**○ to be as tough as old boots○ (GB) or leather (US).

semence /s(ə)mɑ̃s/ *nf* seed.

semer /s(ə)me/ [1] *vtr* **1** to sow [*seeds*]; **2** to sow [*discord, doubt*]; to spread [*confusion, panic*]; **3** to scatter [*objects*]; **~ des clous sur la route** to strew the road with nails; **semé de difficultés** plagued with difficulties; **semé de fautes** riddled with errors; **ciel semé d'étoiles** star-spangled sky; **on récolte ce qu'on a semé** as you sow so shall you reap; **4**○ to drop [*purse, keys*]; **5**○ to shake off [*pursuer*]; to leave [sb] behind [*competitor*].

semestre /s(ə)mɛstʀ/ *nm* (Sch) semester.

semestriel, -ielle /səmɛstʀijɛl/ *adj* **1** twice-yearly; half-yearly; **2** (at university) [*exam*] end-of-semester (GB), final (US); [*course, class*] one-semester.

semeur, -euse /səmœʀ, øz/ *nm,f* sower; **~ de troubles** troublemaker.

semi /səmi/ *pref* **~-automatic** semiautomatic; **~-liberté** relative freedom; **~-remorque** articulated lorry (GB), tractor-trailer (US).

sémillant, ~e /semijɑ̃, ɑ̃t/ *adj* spirited; [*mind*] sparkling.

séminaire /seminɛʀ/ *nm* **1** seminar; **2** seminary.

séminariste /seminaʀist/ *nm* seminarist.

semis /s(ə)mi/ *nm inv* **1** sowing; **2** seedling; **3** seedbed.

semoir /səmwaʀ/ *nm* **1** seed drill; **2** seedbag.

semonce /səmɔ̃s/ *nf* reprimand; **coup de ~** warning shot.

semoule /səmul/ *nf* semolina; **sucre ~** caster sugar.

sempiternel, -elle /sɑ̃pitɛʀnɛl/ *adj* perpetual, endless.

sénat /sena/ *nm* senate.

sénateur /senatœʀ/ *nm* senator.

sénile /senil/ *adj* senile.

sénilité /senilite/ *nf* senility; **~ précoce** premature senility.

sens /sɑ̃s/ I *nm inv* **1** direction, way; **dans le ~ de la largeur** widthways, across; **être dans le bon/mauvais ~** to be the right/wrong way up; **retourner un problème dans tous les ~** to consider a problem from every angle; **courir dans tous les ~** to run all over the place; **dans le ~ de la marche** facing the engine; **~ dessus dessous** /sɑ̃d(ə)sydəsu/ upside down; (figurative) very upset; **aller dans le bon ~** [*reforms, measures*] to be a step in the right direction; **le ~ de l'histoire** the tide of history; **nous travaillons dans ce ~** that's what we are working toward(s); **2** meaning; **le ~ figuré d'un mot** the figurative sense of a word; **employer un mot au ~ propre** to use a word literally; **au ~ fort du terme** in the fullest sense of the word; **cela n'a pas de ~** it doesn't make sense; it's absurd; **3** sense; **retrouver l'usage de ses ~** to regain consciousness; **avoir le ~ de l'orientation** to have a good sense of direction; **avoir le ~ pratique** to be practical; **avoir le ~ de l'organisation** to be a good organizer; **ne pas avoir le ~ du ridicule** not to realize when one looks silly; **avoir le ~ des affaires** to have a flair for business; **ne pas avoir le ~ de la langue** to have no feeling for language; **n'avoir aucun ~ des réalités** to live in a dream world.
II *nm pl* senses; **plaisirs des ~** sensual pleasures.
■ **~ giratoire** roundabout (GB), traffic circle (US); **~ interdit** no-entry sign; one-way street; **~ obligatoire** one-way sign; **~ unique** one-way sign; one-way street.

sensation /sɑ̃sasjɔ̃/ *nf* feeling, sensation; **cela ne procure pas les mêmes ~s** it doesn't have the same effect; **aimer les ~s fortes** to like one's thrills; **la décision a fait ~** the decision caused a sensation; **le film a fait ~** the film was a sensation; **un journal à ~** a tabloid.

sensationnel, -elle /sɑ̃sasjɔnɛl/ *adj* **1**○ fantastic○; **2** sensational, astonishing.

sensé, ~e /sɑ̃se/ *adj* sensible.

sensément /sɑ̃semɑ̃/ *adv* sensibly.

sensibilisation /sɑ̃sibilizasjɔ̃/ *nf* **1 campagne de ~** awareness campaign; **2** (Med) sensitizing, sensitization.

sensibiliser /sɑ̃sibilize/ [1] *vtr* **1 ~ le public à un problème** to increase public awareness of an issue; **2** (Med) to sensitize.

sensibilité /sɑ̃sibilite/ *nf* **1** sensibility; **elle est d'une grande ~** she is very sensitive; **2** (in photography) sensitivity.

sensible /sɑ̃sibl/ *adj* **1** (gen) sensitive; **être ~ aux compliments** to like compliments; **être ~ aux charmes de qn** to be susceptible to sb's charms; **je suis ~ au fait que** I am aware that; **être ~ à un argument** to be swayed by an argument; **un être ~** a sentient being; **je suis très ~ au froid** I really feel the cold; **2** [*skin*] sensitive; (because of injury) tender; [*limb*] sore; **j'ai la gorge ~** I often get a sore throat; **j'ai les pieds ~s** my feet are very sensitive; **3** [*rise, difference*] appreciable; [*effort*] real; **la différence est à peine ~** the difference is hardly noticeable.

sensiblement /sɑ̃sibləmɑ̃/ *adv* **1** [*reduce, increase*] appreciably, noticeably; [*different*] perceptibly; **2** [*alike*] roughly.

sensiblerie /sɑ̃sibləʀi/ *nf* sentimentality.

sensitif, -ive /sɑ̃sitif, iv/ *adj* sensory.

sensoriel, -ielle /sɑ̃sɔʀjɛl/ *adj* sensory; **organe ~** sense organ.

sensualité /sɑ̃sɥalite/ *nf* sensuality.

sensuel, -elle /sɑ̃sɥɛl/ *adj* sensual.

sentence /sɑ̃tɑ̃s/ *nf* **1** sentence; **2** maxim.

sentencieux, -ieuse /sɑ̃tɑ̃sjø, øz/ *adj* sententious.

senteur /sɑ̃tœʀ/ *nf* scent.

senti, ~e /sɑ̃ti/ *adj* **bien ~** [*words, remarks*] well-chosen; [*answer, retort*] blunt; [*speech*] forthright.

sentier /sɑ̃tje/ *nm* path, track; **sur le ~ de la guerre** on the warpath; **hors des ~s battus** off the beaten track.

■ **~ de grande randonnée** long-distance footpath.

sentiment /sɑ̃timɑ̃/ *nm* feeling; **il est incapable de ~** he's incapable of emotion; **faire du ~** to sentimentalize; **prendre qn par les ~s** to appeal to sb's better nature; **le ~ de la beauté** a feeling for beauty; **donner le ~ de faire** to give the impression of doing; **les beaux** or **bons ~s** fine sentiments; **être animé de mauvais ~s** to have bad intentions; **~s affectueux** or **amicaux** best wishes.

sentimental, ~e, *mpl* **-aux** /sɑ̃timɑ̃tal, o/ *adj* sentimental; romantic; **vie ~e** lovelife.

sentinelle /sɑ̃tinɛl/ *nf* **1** sentry; **2** (figurative) **faire la ~** to stand guard, to keep watch.

sentir /sɑ̃tiʀ/ [30] **I** *vtr* **1** to smell; **2** to feel; **je ne sens rien** I can't feel anything; **je ne sens plus mes pieds** my feet are numb; **3** to be conscious of [*importance*]; to feel [*beauty, force*]; to appreciate [*difficulties*]; to sense [*danger, disapproval*]; **je sens qu'il est sincère** I feel that he's sincere; **je sens que ce livre te plaira** I have a feeling that you'll like this book; **je te sens inquiet** I can tell you're worried; **se faire ~** [*need, presence*] to be felt.

II *vi* **1** to smell; **tu sens le vin!** you smell of alcohol!; **2 le poisson commence à ~** the fish is beginning to smell; **~ des pieds** to have smelly feet; **3** to smack of; **une fille qui sent la province** rather a provincial girl; **ciel nuageux qui sent l'orage** cloudy sky that heralds a storm.

III se sentir *v refl* (+ *v être*) **1** to feel; **se ~ mieux** to feel better; **ne plus se ~**○ to be overjoyed; to get above oneself; **2** [*phenomenon, improvement, effect*] to be felt.

IDIOMS **je ne peux pas le ~** I can't stand him; **je l'ai senti passer!** it really hurt!; I really got it in the neck!

seoir† /swaʀ/ [41] **I seoir à** *vtr* [*dress*] to suit.

II *v impers* **il sied de faire** it is appropriate to do.

sépale /sepal/ *nm* sepal.

séparable /sepaʀabl/ *adj* separable.

séparation /sepaʀasjɔ̃/ *nf* **1** (gen, Law) separation; **2** (between gardens) boundary; (between rooms) partition; (figurative) boundary, dividing line.

■ **~ de biens** (Law) matrimonial division of property; **~ de corps** (Law) judicial separation.

séparatisme /sepaʀatism/ *nm* separatism.

séparatiste /sepaʀatist/ *adj, nmf* separatist.

séparé, ~e /sepaʀe/ *adj* **1 vivre ~** to live apart; **les deux villages sont ~s de quelques kilomètres** the two villages are a few kilometres[GB] apart; **2** separate.

séparément /sepaʀemɑ̃/ *adv* separately.

séparer /sepaʀe/ [1] **I** *vtr* **1** (gen) to separate (**de** from); to pull [sb] apart [*fighters*]; **c'est un malentendu qui les a séparés** they parted because of a misunderstanding; **2** to distinguish between [*concepts, areas*]; **on ne peut ~ ces deux problèmes** one cannot dissociate these two problems; **3** to divide; **tout les sépare** they are worlds apart; **~ ses cheveux par une raie au milieu** to part one's hair in the middle.

II se séparer *v refl* (+ *v être*) **1** [*guests*] to part, to leave each other; [*partners, lovers*] to split up; to separate; **2 se ~ de** to leave [*friend, group*]; to split up with; (Law) to separate from [*husband, wife*]; **3** [*demonstrators*] to disperse, to split (up); [*assembly*] to break up; **4 se ~ de** to let [sb] go [*employee*]; to part with [*personal possession*]; **5** to divide; **la route se sépare (en deux)** the road forks.

sépia /sepja/ *adj inv* sepia.

sept /sɛt/ *adj inv, pron, nm inv* seven.

■ **les ~ Familles** (Games) Happy Families.

IDIOMS **tourne ~ fois ta langue dans ta bouche avant de parler** think before you speak.

septante /sɛptɑ̃t/ *adj inv, pron* (Belgian Fr, Swiss Fr) seventy.

septembre /sɛptɑ̃bʀ/ *nm* September.

septennat /sɛptena/ *nm* seven-year term (of office).

septentrional, ~e, *mpl* **-aux** /sɛptɑ̃tʀijɔnal, o/ *adj* northern.

septicémie /sɛptisemi/ *nf* blood-poisoning, septicemia.

septième /sɛtjɛm/ **I** *adj* seventh.

II *nf* (Sch) *fifth year of primary school, age 10–11.*

■ **le ~ art** cinematography.

IDIOMS **être au ~ ciel** to be on cloud nine.

septuagénaire /sɛptɥaʒenɛʀ/ **I** *adj* **être ~** to be in one's seventies.

II *nmf* seventy-year old.

septuor /sɛptɥɔʀ/ *nm* septet.

sépulcral, **~e**, *mpl* **-aux** /sepylkʀal, o/ *adj* sepulchral; **silence ~** deathly silence.

sépulcre /sepylkʀ/ *nm* sepulchre[GB].

sépulture /sepyltyʀ/ *nf* **1** grave; **2** burial.

séquelle /sekɛl/ *nf* **1** after-effect; **2** repercussion; **3** consequence.

séquence /sekɑ̃s/ *nf* sequence.

séquestration /sekɛstʀasjɔ̃/ *nf* (gen) confinement; (Law) **~ (arbitraire)** illegal detention.

séquestrer /sekɛstʀe/ [1] *vtr* (gen) to hold [*hostage*]; (Law) to confine [sb] illegally.

sérail /seʀaj/ *nm* **1** seraglio; **2** innermost circle.

serein, **~e** /səʀɛ̃, ɛn/ *adj* [*sky*] clear; [*person, face*] serene; [*judgment*] dispassionate; [*criticism*] objective.

sereinement /səʀɛnmɑ̃/ *adv* [*look*] serenely; [*speak*] calmly; [*envisage future*] with equanimity; [*judge*] dispassionately.

sérénade /seʀenad/ *nf* **1** serenade; **2**° racket°.

sérénité /seʀenite/ *nf* **1** (of face, mind) serenity; (of person) equanimity; **2** (of judge, verdict) impartiality; **3** (of sky, weather) calmness.

serf, **serve** /sɛʀ, sɛʀv/ *nm,f* serf.

sergent /sɛʀʒɑ̃/ *nm* (Mil) (in army) ≈ sergeant.

série /seʀi/ *nf* **1** series; **catastrophes en ~** a series of catastrophes; **2 numéro de ~** serial number; **~ limitée** limited edition; **modèle de ~** (gen) mass-produced model; (car) production model; **voiture hors ~** custom-built car; **numéro hors ~** special issue; **3** set, collection; **4** (on television) series; **5 (film de) ~ B** B movie; **6** (Sport) division.

■ **~ noire** series of disasters; run of bad luck.

sériel, **-ielle** /seʀjɛl/ *adj* serial.

sérieusement /seʀjøzmɑ̃/ *adv* seriously; considerably; **la conférence m'a ~ ennuyé** the lecture bored me stiff°.

sérieux, **-ieuse** /seʀjø, øz/ **I** *adj* **1 être ~ dans son travail** to be serious about one's work; **avoir des lectures sérieuses** to read serious books; **2** [*situation, threat*] serious; [*clue, lead*] important; [*offer*] genuine; **passer aux choses sérieuses** to move on to serious matters; **'pas ~ s'abstenir'** 'genuine enquiries only'; **3** reliable; **4** responsible; **cela ne fait pas très ~** that doesn't make a very good impression; **5** [*effort, need*] real; [*progress*] considerable; [*handicap*] serious.

II *nm* seriousness; **dire qch avec beaucoup de ~** to say sth very seriously; **garder son ~** to keep a straight face; **perdre son ~** to start to laugh; **se prendre au ~** to take oneself seriously.

sérigraphie /seʀigʀafi/ *nf* **1** silkscreen printing; **2** silkscreen print.

serin /səʀɛ̃/ *nm* **1** (Zool) canary; **2 (grand) ~** silly billy°.

seriner° /səʀine/ [1] *vtr* **~ qch à qn** to drum sth into sb.

seringa /səʀɛ̃ga/ *nm* syringa, mock orange.

seringue /səʀɛ̃g/ *nf* syringe.

serment /sɛʀmɑ̃/ *nm* **1** oath; **prêter ~** to take the oath; **2** vow.

■ **un ~ d'ivrogne** an empty promise.

sermon /sɛʀmɔ̃/ *nm* **1** sermon; **2** lecture, talking-to.

sermonner /sɛʀmɔne/ [1] *vtr* to lecture, to give [sb] a talking-to.

séronégatif, **-ive** /seʀonegatif, iv/ *adj* HIV negative.

séropositif, **-ive** /seʀopozitif, iv/ *adj* **1** (gen) seropositive (**à** for); **2** HIV positive.

serpe /sɛʀp/ *nf* billhook; **visage taillé à coups de ~** (figurative) craggy face.

serpent /sɛʀpɑ̃/ *nm* (Zool) snake; **~ à sonnette** rattlesnake.

serpenter /sɛʀpɑ̃te/ [1] *vi* [*road, river*] to wind.

serpentin /sɛʀpɑ̃tɛ̃/ *nm* streamer.

serpette /sɛʀpɛt/ *nf* pruning knife.

serpillière /sɛʀpijɛʀ/ *nf* floorcloth; **passer la ~** to wash the floor.

serre /sɛʀ/ *nf* **1** greenhouse; **2** talon, claw.

serré, **~e** /seʀe/ **I** *adj* **1** [*screw, nut*] tight; [*skirt, trousers*] tight; **robe ~e à la taille** dress fitted at the waist; dress belted at the waist; dress too tight round the waist; **2** [*grass*] thick; [*writing*] cramped; **en rangs ~s** in serried rows; **3** (figurative) [*deadlines, budget*] tight; [*bend*] sharp; [*control*] strict; [*struggle*] hard; [*debate*] heated; [*match*] close; **4** [*coffee*] very strong.

II *adv* [*write*] in a cramped hand; [*knit*] tightly; **il va falloir jouer ~ si**... we can't take any chances if...

serre-livres /sɛʀlivʀ/ *nm inv* book end.

serrer /seʀe/ [1] **I** *vtr* **1** to grip [*steering wheel, rope*]; **~ qn/qch dans ses bras** to hug sb/sth; **~ la main de qn** to shake hands with sb; **~ les poings** to clench one's fists; **la peur me serrait la gorge** my throat was constricted with fear; **ça me serre le cœur de voir ça** it wrings my heart to see that; **2** to tighten [*knot, screw*]; to turn [sth] off tightly [*tap*]; **sans ~** [*attach, screw*] loosely; **trop serré** too tight; **3** [*shoes, clothes*] to be too tight; **4 ~ le trottoir** to hug the kerb (GB) or curb (US); **~ à droite** to get or stay in the right-hand lane; **~ qn de près** to be hot on sb's tail; **5** to push [sth] closer together [*objects, tables*]; to squeeze [*person*] (**dans** in; **contre** against); **être serrés** to be packed together; **~ les rangs** to close ranks; **6** to cut [*expenses, prices*].

II se serrer *v refl* (+ *v être*) **1** to squeeze up; **ils se sont serrés les uns contre les autres** they huddled together; **2 se ~ dans une jupe** to squeeze oneself into a skirt; **nous nous sommes serré la main** we shook hands; **3 avoir le cœur qui se serre** to feel deeply upset; **avoir la gorge qui se serre** to have a lump in one's throat.

serrure /seʀyʀ/ *nf* lock; **trou de ~** keyhole.

serrurerie /seʀyʀʀi/ *nf* **1** locksmith's; **2** locksmith's trade.

serrurier /seʀyʀje/ *nm* locksmith.

sertir /sɛʀtiʀ/ [3] *vtr* to set [*stone*].

sérum /seʀɔm/ *nm* serum; **~ de vérité** truth drug.

servante /sɛʀvɑ̃t/ *nf* maidservant.

serve ▶ **serf**.

serveur, **-euse** /sɛʀvœʀ, øz/ **I** *nm,f* waiter/ waitress.

II *nm* **1** (Sport) server; **2** (in cards) dealer; **3** (Comput) server.

servi, **~e** /sɛʀvi/ **I** *pp* ▶ **servir**.

II *pp adj* **1 'prends de la viande'—'merci je suis déjà ~'** 'have some meat'—'I already have some, thank you'; **2**° **nous voulions du soleil, nous sommes ~s** we wanted some sunshine and we've certainly got it.

serviable /sɛʀvjabl/ *adj* obliging, helpful.

service /sɛʀvis/ **I** *nm* **1** favour[GB]; **rendre un ~ à qn** to do sb a favour[GB]; **elle m'a rendu de nombreux ~s** she's been very helpful; **2** (in transport) service; **~ de bus** bus service; **3 être en ~** [*lift*] to be in working order; [*motorway*] to be open; [*bus*] to be running; **être hors ~** [*lift*] to be out of order; **mettre en ~** to bring [sth] into service [*vehicle*]; to open [*station, motorway*]; **4 rendre ~ à qn** [*machine*] to be a help to sb; [*shop*] to be convenient (for sb); **5** service; **être au ~ de son pays** to serve one's country; **travailler au ~ de la paix** to work for peace; **'à votre ~!'** 'don't mention it!', 'not at all!'; **'que puis-je faire** or **qu'y a-t-il pour votre ~?'** 'may I help you?'; **avoir 20 ans de ~ dans une entreprise** to have been with a firm 20 years; **être de** or **en ~** to be on duty; **état de ~(s)** record of service; **le ~ de nuit** night duty; **pharmacie de ~** duty chemist; **6** (at table) service; **faire le ~** to serve; to act as waiter; **premier ~** first sitting; **7** (domestic) service; **entrer au ~ de qn** to go to work for sb; **prendre qn à son ~** to take sb on, to engage sb; **escalier de ~** backstairs; **8** department; **~ des urgences** casualty department (GB), emergency room (US); **les ~s de sécurité** the security services; **~ de dépannage** breakdown service; **chef de ~** (in administration) section head; (in hospital) senior consultant; **9** (Mil) **~ (militaire)** military or national service; **~ civil** non-military national service; **10** set; **un ~ à thé** a tea set; **~ de table** dinner service; **11** (in church) service; **12** (Sport) service, serve; **être au ~** to serve or be serving.

II services *nm pl* services; **se passer des ~s de qn** to dispense with sb's services.

■ **~ après-vente** after-sales service; **~ minimum** reduced service; **~ d'ordre** stewards; **~ de presse** press office; press and publicity department; **~ public** public service.

serviette /sɛʀvjɛt/ *nf* **1 ~ (de toilette)** towel; **~ (de table)** (table) napkin; **2** briefcase.

■ **~ de bain** bath towel; **~ hygiénique** sanitary towel (GB), sanitary napkin (US).

serviette-éponge, *pl* **serviettes-éponges** /sɛʀvjɛtepɔ̃ʒ/ *nf* terry towel.

servile /sɛʀvil/ *adj* servile; slavish; **travaux ~s** menial tasks.

servilement /sɛʀvilmɑ̃/ *adv* [*obey, imitate*] slavishly; [*flatter*] obsequiously.

servilité /sɛʀvilite/ *nf* servility.

servir /sɛʀviʀ/ [30] **I** *vtr* **1** to serve; **qu'est-ce que je vous sers (à boire)?** what would you like to drink?; **tu es mal servi** you haven't got much; **'Madame est servie'** 'dinner is served, Madam'; **au moment de ~** before serving; **2** [*situation*] to help [*person, cause*]; to serve [*interests*]; [*person*] to further [*ambition, interests*]; **3**° **~ qch comme excuse** to use sth as an excuse; **4** to deal [*cards*].

II servir à *v+prep* **1 ~ à qn** to be used by sb; **~ à qch** to be used for sth; **les exercices m'ont servi à comprendre la règle** the exercises helped me to understand the rule; **2** to come in useful; **cela ne sert à rien** it's useless; it's no good; **cela ne sert à rien de faire** there's no point in doing; **~ à faire** to be used for doing.

III servir de *v+prep* **~ d'intermédiaire à qn** to act as an intermediary for sb; **~ d'arme** to be used as a weapon.

IV *vi* **1** (Mil) **~ dans** to serve in; **2** (Sport) to serve; **à toi de ~** it's your serve or service; **3 il a servi dix ans chez nous** he was in our service for ten years; **~ dans un café** to work as a waiter in a café; to work as a barman; **4** [*object*] to be used.

V se servir *v refl* (+ *v être*) **1** (at table) to help oneself; **se ~ un verre de vin** to pour oneself a glass of wine; **2** (in shop) to serve oneself; **3 se ~ de qch/qn** to use sth/sb; **se ~ d'une situation** to make use of a situation; **4** (Culin) to be served; **ce vin se sert frais** this wine should be served chilled.

VI *v impers* **il ne sert à rien de crier** there's no point in shouting.

serviteur /sɛʀvitœʀ/ *nm* servant.

servitude /sɛʀvityd/ *nf* **1** servitude; **2** (figurative) constraint.

servofrein /sɛʀvofʀɛ̃/ *nm* power(-assisted) brakes.

ses ▶ **son**[1].

sésame /sezam/ *nm* sesame; **un pain au ~** a sesame seed loaf.

session /sɛsjɔ̃/ *nf* **1** session; **2** examination session; **~ de rattrapage** retakes; **3** course.

set /sɛt/ *nm* (Sport) set.

■ **~ de table** place mat.

seuil /sœj/ *nm* **~ (de la porte)** doorstep; doorway, threshold; **au ~ de** (of career) at the beginning of; (of adolescence) on the threshold of.

seul, **~e** /sœl/ *adj* **1** alone, on one's own; **vous êtes ~ dans la vie?** are you single?; **elle veut vous parler ~ à ~** or **~e à ~(e)** she wants to speak to you alone or in private; **parler tout ~** to talk to oneself; **2** by oneself, on one's own; **il a mangé un poulet à lui tout ~** he ate a whole chicken all by himself; **le papier se détache tout ~** the paper comes off easily; **ça va tout ~** it's really easy; things are running smoothly; **3** only; **une ~e femme** only one woman; **la ~e et unique personne** the one and only person; **pas un ~ client** not a single customer; **l'espion et l'ambassadeur sont une ~e et même personne** the spy and the ambassador are one and the same person; **d'une ~e pièce** in one piece; **dans le ~ but de faire** with the sole aim of doing; **à la ~e idée de faire** at the very idea of doing; **ils ont parlé d'une ~e voix** they were unanimous; **4** lonely; **c'est un homme ~** he's a lonely man; **5** only; **elle ~e pourrait vous le dire** only she could tell you; **6 le ~, la ~e** the only one; **les ~s, les ~es** the only ones; **ils sont les ~s à croire que** they're alone in thinking that; **il n'y en a pas un ~ qui se soit levé** not a single person stood up.

seulement /sœlmɑ̃/ *adv* **1** only; **nous étions ~ deux** or **deux ~** there were only the two of us; **'nous étions dix'—'~?'** 'there were ten of us'—'is that all?'; **j'ai compris ~ plus tard** I only realized later; **elle revient ~ demain** she's not coming back until tomorrow; **2** only, but; **c'est possible, ~ je veux y réfléchir** it's possible, only or but I'd like to think about it; **3 si ~** if only.

sève /sɛv/ *nf* **1** sap; **2** (figurative) vigour[GB].

sévère /sevɛʀ/ *adj* [*look, tone, architecture, punishment*] severe; [*person, upbringing*] strict; [*selection*] rigorous; [*judgment*] harsh; [*losses, defeat*] heavy; **la presse est de plus en plus ~** the press is becoming increasingly critical.

sévèrement /sevɛʀmɑ̃/ *adv* severely; harshly; strictly.

sévérité /seveʀite/ *nf* **1** strictness, harshness; **2** sternness, severity.

sévices /sevis/ *nm pl* physical abuse.

sévir /seviʀ/ [3] *vi* **1** to clamp down (**contre** on); **2** [*storm, war*] to rage; [*poverty*] to be rife; **3** (figurative) [*doctrine*] to hold sway; [*phenomenom*] to be rife.

sevrage /səvʀaʒ/ *nm* weaning.

sevrer /səvʀe/ [16] *vtr* to wean.

sexagénaire /sɛksaʒenɛʀ/ **I** *adj* **être ~** to be in one's sixties.

II *nmf* sixty-year old.

sexe /sɛks/ *nm* **1** sex; **indépendamment du ~, de l'ethnie, de l'âge** irrespective of gender, race or age; **un bébé de ~ féminin** a female baby; **2** genitals.

sexiste /sɛksist/ *adj, nmf* sexist.

sexologue /sɛksɔlɔg/ *nmf* sex therapist.

sextuor /sɛkstɥɔʀ/ *nm* sextet.

sextuplé, ~e /sɛkstyple/ *nm,f* sextuplet.

sextupler /sɛkstyple/ [1] *vtr, vi* to increase sixfold.

sexualité /sɛksɥalite/ *nf* sexuality.

sexué, ~e /sɛksɥe/ *adj* [*plant*] sexed; [*reproduction*] sexual.

sexuel, -elle /sɛksɥɛl/ *adj* (gen) sexual; [*education, gland*] sex.

seyant, ~e /sɛjɑ̃, ɑ̃t/ *adj* becoming; **elle a une robe ~e** her dress suits her.

SFP /ɛsɛfpe/ *nf* (*abbr* = **Société française de production et de création audiovisuelles**) *television and video production company*.

shaker /ʃekœʀ/ *nm* cocktail shaker.

shampooing /ʃɑ̃pwɛ̃/ *nm* shampoo.

shampouiner /ʃɑ̃pwine/ [1] *vtr* to shampoo.

shérif /ʃeʀif/ *nm* sheriff.

shetland /ʃɛtlɑ̃d/ *nm* **1** Shetland wool; **2** Shetland pony.

shoot /ʃut/ *nm* **1** (Sport) shot; **2**○ (of drug) fix○.

shooter /ʃute/ [1] **I** *vi* (Sport) to shoot.

II se shooter○ *v refl* (+ *v être*) to shoot up○; **être shooté** to be stoned.

short /ʃɔʀt/ *nm* shorts.

si[1] /si/ **I** *nm inv* if; **des ~ et des mais** ifs and buts.

II *adv* **1** yes; **'tu ne le veux pas?'—'~!'** 'don't you want it?'—'yes I do!'; **il n'ira pas, moi ~** he won't go, but I will; **2** so; **de ~ bon matin** so early in the morning; **c'est un homme ~ agréable** he's such a pleasant man; **~ bien que** so; so much so that; **tant et ~ bien que** so much so that; **rien n'est ~ beau qu'un coucher de soleil** there's nothing so beautiful as a sunset; **est-elle ~ bête qu'on le dit?** is she as stupid as people say (she is)?; **3 ~ loin que vous alliez** ... however far away you go ...

III *conj* (**s'** *before* il *or* ils) **1** if; **~ j'étais riche** if I were rich; **~ j'avais su!** if only I'd known!; **vous pensez ~ j'étais content!** you can imagine how happy I was!; **je me demande s'il viendra** I wonder if or whether he'll come; **~ ce n'est (pas) toi, qui est-ce?** if it wasn't you, who was it?; **il n'a rien pris avec lui ~ ce n'est un livre** he didn't take anything with him apart from a book; **à quoi servent ces réunions ~ ce n'est à nous faire perdre notre temps?** what purpose do these meetings serve other than to waste our time?; **~ tant est qu'une telle distinction ait un sens** if such a distinction makes any sense; **2 ~ tu venais avec moi?** how or what about coming with me?; **et s'il décidait de ne pas venir?** and what if he decided not to come?; **3** whereas.

si[2] /si/ *nm inv* (note) B; (in sol-fa) ti.

siamois, ~e /sjamwa, az/ **I** *adj* **1** [*cat*] Siamese; **2 des frères ~** male Siamese twins.

II *nm inv* **1** Siamese; **2** Siamese cat.

sibylle /sibil/ *nf* sibyl.

sibyllin, ~e /sibilɛ̃, in/ *adj* sibylline.

sicilien, -ienne /sisiljɛ̃, ɛn/ **I** *adj* Sicilian.

II *nm* Sicilian.

sida /sida/ *nm* (*abbr* = **syndrome immunodéficitaire acquis**) Aids.

side-car, *pl* **~s** /sidkaʀ/ *nm* **1** sidecar; **2** motorcycle combination.

sidéral, ~e, *mpl* **-aux** /sideʀal, o/ *adj* sidereal.

sidérer○ /sideʀe/ [14] *vtr* to stagger○, to astonish.

sidérurgie /sideʀyʀʒi/ *nf* steel industry.

sidérurgique /sideʀyʀʒik/ *adj* steel.

siècle /sjɛkl/ *nm* **1** century; **au V**[e] **~ après J.C.** in the 5th century AD; **d'ici la fin du ~** by the turn of the century; **un ~ de photographie** one hundred years of photography; **il y a des ~s**○ **que je ne suis venu ici** I haven't been here for ages; **2** age; **le ~ de Louis XIV** the age of Louis XIV.

sied ▸ **seoir**.

siège /sjɛʒ/ *nm* **1** seat; **~ avant** front seat; **2 ~ (social)** (of company) head office; (of organization) headquarters; (of court) seat; **3** (of MP) seat; **4** (Mil) siege; **5** (Anat) seat; **le bébé se présente par le ~** the baby is in the breech position.

siéger /sjeʒe/ [15] *vi* **1** to sit; **2** to be in session; **3** to have its headquarters.

sien, sienne /sjɛ̃, sjɛn/ **I** *det* **cette maison est sienne à présent** the house is now his/hers.
II le sien, la sienne, les siens, les siennes *pron* his/hers/its; **celui-là, c'est le ~** that's his/hers; **être de retour parmi les ~s** to be back with one's family; to be back among one's own friends; **faire des siennes** [*person*] to be up to mischief; [*computer*] to play up (GB) or act up.

sierra /sjɛʀa/ *nf* sierra.

sieste /sjɛst/ *nf* nap, siesta.

sifflant, ~e /siflɑ̃, ɑ̃t/ *adj* **1** [*sound*] hissing; [*cough*] wheezing; **2** [*consonant*] sibilant.

sifflement /sifləmɑ̃/ *nm* (of person, train) whistle; (of kettle, wind) whistling; (of bird, insect) chirping; (of snake) hissing.

siffler /sifle/ [1] **I** *vtr* **1** to whistle [*tune*]; to whistle for [*dog*]; to whistle at [*person*]; **2** [*referee*] to blow one's whistle for [*foul*]; **3** to hiss, to boo.
II *vi* **1** (gen) to whistle; [*projectile*] to whistle through the air; [*bird*] to chirp; [*snake*] to hiss; **2** to blow one's whistle.

sifflet /siflɛ/ *nm* **1** whistle; **coup de ~** whistle; **2** (of train) whistle; (of kettle) whistling; **3** hiss, boo.
IDIOMS **couper le ~ à qn**○ to shut sb up○; to take the wind out of sb's sails.

sifflotement /siflɔtmɑ̃/ *nm* whistling.

siffloter /siflɔte/ [1] **I** *vtr* to whistle [sth] to oneself [*tune*].
II *vi* to whistle away to oneself.

sigle /sigl/ *nm* acronym.

signal, *pl* **-aux** /siɲal, o/ *nm* signal.
■ **~ d'alarme** alarm signal; **tirer le ~ d'alarme** to pull the alarm; (figurative) to raise the alarm; **~ sonore** (on answerphone) tone.

signalement /siɲalmɑ̃/ *nm* description.

signaler /siɲale/ [1] **I** *vtr* **1 ~ qch à qn** to point sth out to sb; to inform sb of sth; **2 ~ à qn que** to remind sb that; **3** to indicate [*roadworks, danger*]; **un virage mal signalé** a badly signposted bend; **4** to report [*fact*].
II se signaler *v refl* (+ *v être*) **se ~ par qch** to distinguish oneself by sth; **se ~ à l'attention de qn** to get oneself noticed by sb.

signalétique /siɲaletik/ *adj* descriptive; **fiche ~** specification sheet.

signalisation /siɲalizasjɔ̃/ *nf* **1** signalling[GB]; **2** signals.
■ **~ routière** roadsigns and markings.

signaliser /siɲalize/ [1] *vtr* to signpost [*road*]; to put up signals along [*railway line*]; to mark out and light [*runway*].

signataire /siɲatɛʀ/ *nmf* signatory.

signature /siɲatyʀ/ *nf* **1** signature; **2** signing.

signe /siɲ/ *nm* sign; **~ astral** star sign; **~ précurseur** omen; **~ distinctif** or **particulier** distinguishing feature; **c'était un ~ du destin** it was fate; **~s de ponctuation** punctuation marks; **faire ~ à qn** to wave to sb; (figurative) to get in touch with sb; **faire de grands ~s à qn** to gesticulate to sb; **faire ~ à qn de** to motion sb to do; to beckon sb to do; **d'un ~ de la main/tête, elle m'a montré la cuisine** she pointed to/nodded her head in the direction of the kitchen; **faire ~ que oui** to indicate agreement; **faire un ~ de refus** to indicate one's refusal.
IDIOMS **il n'a pas donné ~ de vie depuis six mois** there's been no sign of him for six months.

signer /siɲe/ [1] **I** *vtr* to sign; **il signe son troisième roman** he's written his third novel; **ça, c'est signé ta sœur**○**!** that's your sister all over○!
II se signer *v refl* (+ *v être*) to cross oneself.

signet /siɲɛ/ *nm* bookmark.

signifiant, ~e /siɲifjɑ̃, ɑ̃t/ *adj* significant, meaningful.

significatif, -ive /siɲifikatif, iv/ *adj* significant.

signification /siɲifikasjɔ̃/ *nf* **1** meaning; **2** importance; **avoir une ~ politique** to be politically significant.

signifier /siɲifje/ [1] *vtr* **1** to mean; **2 ~ qch à qn** to inform sb of sth; **~ son congé à qn** to give sb notice.

silence /silɑ̃s/ *nm* **1** silence; **un ~ de mort** a deathly silence; **'un peu de ~ s'il vous plaît'** 'quiet please'; **en ~** in silence; **passer qch sous ~** to say nothing about sth; **2** (Mus) rest.

silencieux, -ieuse /silɑ̃sjø, øz/ **I** *adj* **1** silent; **2** quiet.
II *nm* **1** (on gun) silencer; **2** (on exhaust) silencer (GB), muffler (US).

silex /silɛks/ *nm inv* flint; **en** or **de ~** flint.

silhouette /silwɛt/ *nf* **1** silhouette; outline; **2** figure; shape.

silice /silis/ *nf* silica.

silicium /silisjɔm/ *nm* silicon; **en/au ~** silicon.

silicone /silikon/ *nf* silicone; **~ élastomère** silicone rubber.

sillage /sijaʒ/ *nm* **1** (of ship) wake; (of plane) vapour[GB] trail; slipstream; **2** (of person) wake; (of perfume) trail.

sillon /sijɔ̃/ *nm* **1** furrow; **2** line; **3** fissure; **4** groove.

sillonner /sijɔne/ [1] *vtr* **1** [*roads*] to criss-cross; [*police*] to patrol; **~ la France en voiture** to drive all over France; **2** to furrow; **sillonné de rides** deeply wrinkled.

silo /silo/ *nm* silo.

simagrée /simagʀe/ *nf* play-acting.

simiesque /simjɛsk/ *adj* ape-like.

similaire /similɛʀ/ *adj* similar.

similarité /similaʀite/ *nf* similarity.

similicuir /similikɥiʀ/ *nm* imitation leather, Leatherette®.

similitude /similityd/ *nf* similarity.

simple /sɛ̃pl/ I *adj* **1 c'est (bien) ~, il ne fait plus rien** he simply doesn't do anything any more; **2** [*meal, wedding, life, tastes*] simple; [*decor*] plain; [*person, air*] unaffected; **elle portait une jupe toute ~** she was wearing a very plain skirt; **3** [*origins*] modest; **4** [*worker*] ordinary; **c'est un ~ avertissement** it's just a warning; **pour la ~ raison que** for the simple reason that; **le ~ fait de poser la question** the mere fact of asking the question; **par ~ curiosité** out of pure curiosity; **sur ~ présentation du passeport** on presentation of one's passport; **réduire qch à sa plus ~ expression** to reduce sth to a minimum; **5 il est gentil mais un peu ~** he's nice but a bit simple; **6** [*past, future*] simple; **7** [*ice-cream cone, knot*] single.

II *nm* **1 le prix varie du ~ au double** the price can turn out to be twice as high; **2** (Sport) **~ dames/messieurs** ladies'/men's singles.

■ **~ d'esprit** simple-minded.

simplement /sɛ̃pləmɑ̃/ *adv* **1** simply, merely, just; **vas-y, ~ fais attention** you can go, only be careful; **il faut ~ remplir cette page** you simply have to fill in (GB) or out (US) this page; **2** [*dress, live*] simply; **tout ~** quite simply; **3** easily.

simplet, **-ette** /sɛ̃plɛ, ɛt/ *adj* simple, simple-minded.

simplicité /sɛ̃plisite/ *nf* **1** simplicity; **c'est d'une ~ enfantine** it's so easy a child could do it; **2** (of person) unpretentiousness, lack of pretention; (of thing) simplicity; **avec ~** simply.

simplification /sɛ̃plifikasjɔ̃/ *nf* simplification.

simplifier /sɛ̃plifje/ [2] I *vtr* to simplify.

II **se simplifier** *v refl* (+ *v être*) **se ~ la vie** to make life easier for oneself.

simpliste /sɛ̃plist/ *adj* simplistic.

simulacre /simylakʀ/ *nm* (literary) **1** pretence[GB]; **~ de procès** mock trial; **2** sham; **~ de justice** travesty of justice; **~ de bonheur** illusion of happiness.

simulateur, **-trice** /simylatœʀ, tʀis/ I *nm,f* **1** shammer, faker; **2** malingerer.

II *nm* (Tech) simulator; **~ de vol** flight simulator.

simulation /simylasjɔ̃/ *nf* **1** simulation; **2** malingering.

simuler /simyle/ [1] *vtr* **1** to feign, to simulate; **2** (Tech) to simulate.

simultané, **~e** /simyltane/ *adj* simultaneous.

simultanément /simyltanemɑ̃/ *adv* simultaneously, at the same time.

sincère /sɛ̃sɛʀ/ *adj* (gen) sincere; [*friend*] true; [*emotion, offer, support*] genuine; [*opinion, picture*] honest.

sincèrement /sɛ̃sɛʀmɑ̃/ *adv* **1** [*think*] really; [*regret, thank, speak*] sincerely; **je suis ~ désolé** I'm truly sorry; **2** frankly.

sincérité /sɛ̃seʀite/ *nf* sincerity; honesty; genuineness.

sinécure /sinekyʀ/ *nf* sinecure.

sine qua non /sinekwanɔn/ *phr* **condition ~** sine qua non.

singe /sɛ̃ʒ/ *nm* **1** monkey; ape; **les grands ~s** the apes; **2** mimic; **c'est un vrai ~** he's very agile; **faire le ~** to clown around.

IDIOMS **malin comme un ~** as cunning or sly as a fox.

singer /sɛ̃ʒe/ [13] *vtr* to ape [*person, mannerism*]; to feign, to fake [*attitude*].

singeries /sɛ̃ʒʀi/ *nf pl* antics; **faire des ~** to monkey around; to pull funny faces.

singulariser: **se singulariser** /sɛ̃gylaʀize/ [1] *v refl* (+ *v être*) to draw attention to oneself.

singularité /sɛ̃gylaʀite/ *nf* **1** peculiarity, singularity; **2** uniqueness.

singulier, **-ière** /sɛ̃gylje, ɛʀ/ I *adj* **1** peculiar, unusual; **2 combat ~** single combat.

II *nm* **1** singular; **2** singularity.

singulièrement /sɛ̃gyljɛʀmɑ̃/ *adv* **1** oddly; **2** radically.

sinistre /sinistʀ/ I *adj* **1** [*person, noise, plan*] sinister; [*place, future*] bleak; [*evening, guest*] dreary; **2 de ~s crétins**○ absolute idiots.

II *nm* disaster; accident; blaze.

sinistré, **~e** /sinistʀe/ I *adj* stricken; **région ~e** disaster area.

II *nm,f* disaster victim.

sinon /sinɔ̃/ I *conj* **1** otherwise, or else; **arrête ~ je crie!** stop or (else) I'll scream!; **2** except, apart from; **3** not to say; **c'est devenu difficile ~ impossible** it has become difficult if not impossible.

II **sinon que** *phr* except that, other than that.

sinueux, **-euse** /sinɥø, øz/ *adj* sinuous; winding; tortuous.

sinus /sinys/ *nm inv* **1** sinus; **2** (in mathematics) sine.

sinusite /sinyzit/ *nf* sinusitis.

siphon /sifɔ̃/ *nm* **1** siphon; **2** U-bend; **3** siphon (bottle).

siphonné○, **~e** /sifɔne/ *adj* nuts○, crazy○.

sire /siʀ/ *nm* Sire; **un triste ~** a disreputable character.

sirène /siʀɛn/ *nf* **1** (gen) siren; (of boat) foghorn; **2** mermaid; siren.

■ **~ d'alarme** fire alarm.

sirop /siʀo/ *nm* **1** syrup (GB), sirup (US); cordial; **~ d'orgeat** barley water; **2** (medicine) syrup (GB), sirup (US), mixture; **~ pectoral** cough mixture.

siroter○ /siʀɔte/ [1] *vtr* to sip.

sirupeux, **-euse** /siʀypø, øz/ *adj* syrupy (GB), sirupy (US).

sismique /sismik/ *adj* seismic.

sismographie /sismɔgʀafi/ *nf* seismography.

site /sit/ *nm* **1** area; **~ touristique** or **pittoresque** place of interest; **~ archéologique** archaeological site; **~ classé** conservation area; **2** site.

sitôt /sito/ I *adv* **~ rentré** as soon as he gets back; as soon as he got back; **~ après** immediately after(wards); soon after(wards); **je n'y**

retournerai pas de ~ I won't go back there in a hurry○.

II *conj* **~ que** as soon as.

IDIOMS **~ dit, ~ fait** no sooner said than done.

situ: **in situ** /insity/ *phr* **étudier une plante in ~** to study a plant in its natural habitat.

situation /sitɥasjɔ̃/ *nf* **1** situation; **une population en ~ d'extrême pauvreté** a population suffering from extreme poverty; **2** job, position; **3** location.

■ **~ de famille** marital status; **~ militaire** *status as regards military service.*

situer /sitɥe/ [1] **I** *vtr* **1** (in space and time) to place; **je ne saurais pas ~ cette ville** I couldn't say where the town is; **l'hôtel est bien situé** the hotel is in a good location; **2 ~ une histoire en 2001/à Palerme** to set a story in 2001/in Palermo.

II se situer *v refl* (+ *v être*) **1 se ~ à Paris en 1900** to be set in Paris in 1900; **2 politiquement, je me situe plutôt à gauche** politically I'm more to the left.

six /sis, *but before consonant* si, *and before vowel* siz/ *adj inv, pron, nm inv* six.

sixième /sizjɛm/ **I** *adj* sixth.

II *nf* (Sch) *first year of secondary school, age 11–12.*

skaï® /skaj/ *nm* imitation leather, Leatherette®.

skate-board, *pl* **~s** /skɛtbɔʀd/ *nm* **1** skateboard; **2** skateboarding.

sketch, *pl* **~es** /skɛtʃ/ *nm* sketch.

ski /ski/ *nm* **1** ski; **2 le ~** skiing; **faire du ~** to ski, to go skiing.

■ **~ alpin** Alpine skiing; **~ de fond** cross-country skiing; **~ nautique** water skiing; **~ de piste** downhill skiing.

skier /skje/ [2] *vi* to ski; **~ hors piste** to go off-piste skiing.

skieur, **-ieuse** /skjœʀ, øz/ *nm,f* skier.

slalom /slalɔm/ *nm* slalom; **faire du ~** to slalom.

slalomer /slalɔme/ [1] *vi* **1** (Sport) to slalom; **2** (figurative) to zigzag.

slave /slav/ *adj* Slavonic.

Slave /slav/ *nmf* Slav.

slip /slip/ *nm* **1** underpants; **2** slipway.

slogan /slɔgɑ̃/ *nm* slogan.

slow /slo/ *nm* slow dance.

smala○ /smala/ *nf* tribe○.

smasher /smaʃe/ [1] **I** *vtr* to smash [*ball*].

II *vi* to play a smash.

SMIC /smik/ *nm*: *abbr* ▶ **salaire**.

smocks /smɔk/ *nm pl* smocking; **une robe à ~** a smocked dress.

smoking /smɔkiŋ/ *nm* dinner jacket (GB), tuxedo.

SNCF /ɛsɛnseɛf/ *nf* (*abbr* = **Société nationale des chemins de fer français**) *French national railway company.*

snob /snɔb/ **I** *adj* [*person*] stuck-up○; [*restaurant*] posh.

II *nmf* snob; **c'est un ~** he's a snob.

snober /snɔbe/ [1] *vtr* to snub [*person*].

snobisme /snɔbism/ *nm* snobbery.

sobre /sɔbʀ/ *adj* **1** [*person*] abstemious; sober; temperate; [*life*] simple; **2** [*style*] plain, sober.

sobrement /sɔbʀəmɑ̃/ *adv* soberly; in moderation; [*live*] frugally.

sobriété /sɔbʀijete/ *nf* sobriety, temperance; restraint; moderation.

soc /sɔk/ *nm* ploughshare (GB), plowshare (US).

sociable /sɔsjabl/ *adj* **1** sociable; **2** social.

social, **~e**, *mpl* **-iaux** /sɔsjal, o/ **I** *adj* **1** social; **mesures ~es** social policy measures; **les origines ~es de qn**, **le milieu ~ de qn** sb's social background; **2 conflit ~** industrial or trade dispute.

II *nm* **le ~** social issues.

socialiser /sɔsjalize/ [1] *vtr* **1** to socialize; **2** to collectivize.

socialisme /sɔsjalism/ *nm* socialism.

socialiste /sɔsjalist/ *adj, nmf* socialist.

sociétaire /sɔsjetɛʀ/ *nmf* member.

société /sɔsjete/ *nf* **1** society; **~ de chasse** hunting club; **la haute ~** high society; **2** company; **~ de nettoyage** cleaning company; **3** (formal) **rechercher la ~ de qn** to seek sb's company.

socioculturel, **-elle** /sɔsjokyltyʀɛl/ *adj* sociocultural; **centre/animateur ~** recreation centre[GB]/officer.

socio-démocrate, *pl* **~s** /sɔsjodemɔkʀat/ *adj* social democratic.

sociologie /sɔsjɔlɔʒi/ *nf* sociology.

sociologue /sɔsjɔlɔg/ *nmf* sociologist.

socioprofessionnel, **-elle** /sɔsjopʀɔfɛsjɔnɛl/ *adj* social and occupational.

socle /sɔkl/ *nm* pedestal, plinth; base; stand.

socque /sɔk/ *nm* clog.

socquette /sɔkɛt/ *nf* ankle sock, anklet (US).

soda /sɔda/ *nm* **1** soda water; **2** fizzy drink (GB), soda (US).

sodium /sɔdjɔm/ *nm* sodium.

sodomiser /sɔdɔmize/ [1] *vtr* to sodomize, to bugger.

sœur /sœʀ/ *nf* sister; **~ jumelle** twin sister.

sofa /sɔfa/ *nm* sofa.

soi /swa/ *pron* **1 autour de ~** around one; **apprendre la maîtrise de ~** to learn self-control; **laisser la porte se refermer derrière ~** to let the door shut behind one; **trouver en ~ les ressources nécessaires** to find the necessary inner resources; **garder qch pour ~** to keep sth to oneself; **malgré ~ on est ému** you can't help being moved; **2 la logique n'est pas un objectif en ~** logic is not an end in itself; **cela va de ~** it goes without saying.

soi-disant /swadizɑ̃/ **I** *adj inv* **1** self-styled; **2** (controversial) so-called.

II *adv* supposedly; **elle a ~ la migraine** she has a migraine, or so she says.

soie /swa/ *nf* **1** silk; **2** bristle.

soierie /swaʀi/ *nf* **1** silk; **2** silk industry; **3** silk trade.

soif /swaf/ *nf* **1** thirst; **avoir ~** to be thirsty; **donner ~** to make one thirsty; **2 ~ de** thirst for; hunger for; lust for; **avoir ~ d'affection** to crave affection.

soignant, **~e** /swaɲɑ̃, ɑ̃t/ *adj* medical.

soigné, **~e** /swaɲe/ I *pp* ▸ **soigner**.
II *pp adj* **1** [*nails*] well-manicured; [*hair, clothes*] immaculate; **individu peu ~** unkempt person; **2** [*publication*] carefully produced; [*organization, tactics*] carefully thought out; [*work*] meticulous; **peu ~** [*work*] careless.

soigner /swaɲe/ [1] I *vtr* **1** [*doctor*] to treat; **faire ~ qn** to get sb treatment; **2** to look after [*person, animal, customer*]; **3** to take care over [*appearance*]; to look after [*hands*].
II **se soigner** *v refl* (+ *v être*) **1** to treat oneself; to look after oneself; **2** [*illness*] to be treatable; **3** to take care over one's appearance.

soigneusement /swaɲøzmɑ̃/ *adv* carefully; meticulously; neatly.

soigneux, **-euse** /swaɲø, øz/ *adj* **1** [*work*] conscientious; [*examination*] careful; **2** [*person*] neat, tidy.

soi-même /swamɛm/ *pron* oneself; **être ~** to be oneself.

soin /swɛ̃/ I *nm* **1** care; **prendre ~ de qch** to take care of sth; **prendre ~ de qn/sa santé** to look after sb/one's health; **prendre ~ de sa petite personne** to coddle oneself; **laisser à qn/à d'autres le ~ de faire** to leave it to sb/ to others to do; **2** product; **~ antipelliculaire** dandruff treatment.
II **soins** *nm pl* **1** (Med) treatment; care; **recevoir des ~s** to receive treatment; **~s dentaires** dental care; **les premiers ~s à donner aux brûlés** first-aid treatment for burns; **~s à domicile** homecare; **2** care; **~s corporels** or **du corps** body care; **3 'aux bons ~s de'** 'care of', 'c/o'; **publié par leurs/mes ~s** published by their/my good offices.
IDIOMS **être aux petits ~s pour qn** to attend to sb's every need.

soir /swaʀ/ *nm* **1** evening; night; **le ~ du 3, le 3 au ~** on the evening of the 3rd; **le ~ venu** when evening fell; **il sort tous les samedis ~** he goes out every Saturday night; **6 heures du ~** 6 (o'clock) in the evening; 6 pm; **à ce ~!** see you tonight!; **2** (literary) twilight; **le ~ de la vie** the evening of one's life.

soirée /swaʀe/ *nf* **1** evening; **dans** or **pendant la ~, en ~** in the evening; **la pièce sera jouée en ~** there will be an evening performance of the play; **2** party; **aller dans une** or **en ~** to go to a party; **3** evening performance or show.

soit[1] /swa/ I ▸ **être**[1].
II *conj* **1 ~, ~** either, or; **~ du fromage, ~ un gâteau, ~ des fruits** either cheese, or a cake, or fruit; **c'est ~ l'un ~ l'autre, pas les deux** it's got to be one thing or the other, not both; **2** that is, ie; **toutes mes économies, ~ 200 francs** all my savings, ie or that is, 200 francs; **3** (in mathematics) **~ un triangle ABC** let ABC be a triangle.

soit[2] /swat/ *adv* very well; **je me suis trompé, ~, mais là n'est pas la question** all right, so I was wrong, but that's not the point.

soixantaine /swasɑ̃tɛn/ *nf* **1** about sixty; **2 avoir la ~** to be about sixty.

soixante /swasɑ̃t/ *adj inv, pron* sixty.

soixante-dix /swasɑ̃tdis/ *adj inv, pron* seventy.

soixante-dixième /swasɑ̃tdizjɛm/ *adj* seventieth.

soixantième /swasɑ̃tjɛm/ *adj* sixtieth.

soja /sɔʒa/ *nm* soya bean (GB), soybean (US); **sauce de ~** soy sauce; **salade de (germes** or **pousses de) ~** bean sprout salad.

sol /sɔl/ *nm* **1** ground; floor; **sentir le ~ se dérober sous ses pieds** (figurative) to feel as if one is about to faint; **2** soil; **3** (Mus) (note) G; (in sol-fa) soh.

solaire /sɔlɛʀ/ *adj* [*energy*] solar; [*engine*] solar-powered; [*cream*] sun.

soldat /sɔlda/ *nm* soldier, serviceman.

solde[1] /sɔld/ I *nm* balance; **faire le ~ d'un compte** to settle an account.
II **en solde** *phr* **acheter une veste en ~** to buy a jacket in a sale.
III **soldes** *nm pl* sales; sale; **faire les ~s**○ to go to the sales.

solde[2] /sɔld/ *nf* (Mil) pay; **avoir qn à sa ~** (figurative) to have sb in one's pay.

solder /sɔlde/ [1] I *vtr* **1** to sell off [*merchandise*]; **2** to settle the balance of [*account*].
II **se solder** *v refl* (+ *v être*) **se ~ par qch** to end in sth.

solderie /sɔldəʀi/ *nf* discount shop.

soldeur, **-euse** /sɔldœʀ, øz/ *nm,f* discount trader.

sole /sɔl/ *nf* (Zool) sole.

soleil /sɔlɛj/ *nm* sun; **~ de minuit** midnight sun; **se mettre au ~** to go into the sun; to sit in the sun; **en plein ~** [*sit*] in hot sun; [*leave something*] in direct sunlight; **quand il y a du ~** when it's sunny; **attraper un coup** or **des coups de ~** to get sunburned.

solennel, **-elle** /sɔlanɛl/ *adj* (gen) solemn; [*appeal, declaration*] formal.

solennité /sɔlanite/ *nf* solemnity; **chef d'État reçu avec ~** head of state given a ceremonious reception.

solfège /sɔlfɛʒ/ *nm* **1** music theory; **~ chanté** sol-fa; **2** music theory book.

solfier /sɔlfje/ [2] *vtr* to sing using the tonic sol-fa system.

solidaire /sɔlidɛʀ/ *adj* **1** [*team, group*] united; **être ~ de qn** to be behind sb; **2** (Tech) [*parts*] interdependent.

solidariser: **se solidariser** /sɔlidaʀize/ [1] *v refl* (+ *v être*) **se ~ avec qch/qn** to stand by sth/sb.

solidarité /sɔlidaʀite/ *nf* solidarity.

solide /sɔlid/ I *adj* **1** [*food, matter*] solid; **2** [*house, friendship*] solid; [*shoes, bag*] sturdy; [*link, fastening, blade*] strong; [*position, base*] firm; **la chaise n'est pas très ~** the chair is a bit rickety; **3** [*person, constitution, heart*] strong; **elle a les nerfs ~s** she's got nerves of steel; **avoir la tête ~** (figurative) to have one's head screwed on (right); **4** [*business, knowledge, experience, reasons*] sound; [*guarantees*] firm; [*qualities*] solid; [*partner*] dependable.

II *nm* **1** solid; **manger du ~** to eat solids; **2 ce qu'il te dit, c'est du ~** what he says is sound; **3 les meubles anciens, c'est du ~** antique furniture is solidly built.

solidement /sɔlidmɑ̃/ *adv* **2** [*attach, establish, anchored*] firmly; [*barricaded*] securely; [*armed*] heavily; **un rapport ~ documenté** a soundly-documented report.

solidifier /sɔlidifje/ [2] *vtr*, **se solidifier** *v refl* (+ *v être*) to solidify.

solidité /sɔlidite/ *nf* **1** (of construction) solidity; (of machine) strength; (of link) firmness; (of clothes) hard-wearing quality; **d'une grande ~** well-built; sturdy; strong; hard-wearing; **2** (of argument) soundness.

soliloque /sɔlilɔk/ *nm* soliloquy.

soliloquer /sɔlilɔke/ [1] *vi* to soliloquize.

solipsisme /sɔlipsism/ *nm* solipsism.

soliste /sɔlist/ *nmf* soloist.

solitaire /sɔlitɛʀ/ **I** *adj* **1** [*person, life, walk*] solitary; [*old age, childhood*] lonely; **navigateur ~** single-handed or solo yachtsman; **2** [*house, village*] isolated.

II *nmf* solitary person, loner; **en ~** [*live*] alone; [*sail*] single-handed.

III *nm* **1** (diamond) solitaire; **2** rogue boar; **3** (Games) solitaire.

solitude /sɔlityd/ *nf* **1** solitude; **2** loneliness.

solive /sɔliv/ *nf* joist.

solliciter /sɔlisite/ [1] *vtr* **1** (formal) to seek [*interview, post, advice*]; **son avis est très sollicité** his/her advice is much or highly sought after; **2** to approach, to call on or upon [*person, organization*]; to canvass [*customer, voter*]; **être très sollicité** to be assailed by requests; to be very much in demand; **3** to attract [*attention, looks*]; to call upon [*memory*].

sollicitude /sɔlisityd/ *nf* concern, solicitude (**envers** for).

solstice /sɔlstis/ *nm* solstice.

soluble /sɔlybl/ *adj* **1** [*tablet*] soluble; **2** [*problem*] solvable, soluble.

solution /sɔlysjɔ̃/ *nf* **1** solution, solving; resolution; **2** solution; **tenir la ~ de qch** to have the solution to sth; **une ~ de facilité** an easy way out; **3** (in chemistry) solution.

solvabilité /sɔlvabilite/ *nf* **1** solvency; **2** creditworthiness.

solvant /sɔlvɑ̃/ *nm* solvent.

sombre /sɔ̃bʀ/ *adj* **1** dark; **il fait ~** it's dark; **2** [*thought, future*] dark, black; [*conclusion*] depressing, grim; [*air, person*] solemn, sombre[GB]; **3**○ (*before n*) [*idiot*] absolute; [*affair*] murky.

sombrement /sɔ̃bʀəmɑ̃/ *adv* (literary) [*announce*] in a sombre[GB] tone; [*stare*] gloomily; darkly.

sombrer /sɔ̃bʀe/ [1] *vi* **1** [*ship*] to sink; **2 ~ dans** [*person*] to sink into [*despair, alcoholism*]; **~ dans le ridicule** to become ridiculous.

sommaire /sɔmmɛʀ/ **I** *adj* [*explanation*] cursory; [*description*] rough; [*installation, meal*] rough and ready; [*vision, idea*] shallow; [*execution*] summary.

II *nm* **1** contents; **au ~ de notre numéro de juillet** featured in our July issue; **2**○ **au ~: un débat sur le chômage** a debate on unemployment is on the programme[GB].

sommairement /sɔmmɛʀmɑ̃/ *adv* summarily.

sommation /sɔmmasjɔ̃/ *nf* (from police) warning; (from guard) challenge.

somme¹ /sɔm/ *nm* nap, snooze○.

somme² /sɔm/ *nf* **1** (of money) sum, amount; **2** sum total; **la ~ de nos connaissances** the sum total of our knowledge; **il a fourni une grosse ~ de travail** he did a great deal of work; **en ~, ~ toute** all in all; **3** (in mathematics) sum.

sommeil /sɔmɛj/ *nm* **1** sleep; **avoir ~** to be or feel sleepy; **avoir le ~ agité** to sleep fitfully; **avoir le ~ léger** to be a light sleeper; **tirer qn de son ~** to wake sb up; **2 être en ~** [*project*] to have been put on ice.

IDIOMS **dormir d'un ~ de plomb** to sleep like a log○.

sommeiller /sɔmeje/ [1] *vi* **1** to doze; **2** to lie dormant.

sommelier, -ière /sɔməlje, ɛʀ/ *nm,f* wine waiter, sommelier.

sommer /sɔmme/ [1] *vtr* **~ qn de faire** to command sb to do.

sommet /sɔmmɛ/ *nm* **1** peak; summit; **atteindre le ~ (du mont Blanc)** to reach the summit (of Mont Blanc); **2** (gen) top; (of wave) crest; (of curve, career) peak; **3** (of glory, stupidity) height; **atteindre un ~** or **des ~s** [*prices, sales*] to peak; **4** summit; **conférence au ~** summit meeting; **5** (of triangle, angle) apex; (of cone) vertex.

sommier /sɔmje/ *nm* (bed) base.

sommité /sɔmmite/ *nf* leading expert (**en** in).

somnambule /sɔmnɑ̃byl/ **I** *adj* **être ~** to sleepwalk.

II *nmf* sleepwalker.

somnambulisme /sɔmnɑ̃bylism/ *nm* sleepwalking.

somnifère /sɔmnifɛʀ/ **I** *adj* soporific.

II *nm* **1** soporific; **2** sleeping pill.

somnolence /sɔmnɔlɑ̃s/ *nf* **1** drowsiness; **2** (figurative) lethargy.

somnolent, ~e /sɔmnɔlɑ̃, ɑ̃t/ *adj* **1** drowsy; **2** [*attention*] flagging; [*town*] sleepy; [*industry, country*] lethargic.

somnoler /sɔmnɔle/ [1] *vi* **1** to drowse; **2** [*town*] to be sleepy; [*industry, country*] to be lethargic.

somptueux, -euse /sɔ̃ptɥø, øz/ *adj* sumptuous.

son¹, sa, *pl* **ses** /sɔ̃, sa, sɛ/ *det* his/her/its; **ses enfants** his/her children; **ses pattes** its paws; **un de ses amis** a friend of his/hers; **elle a ~ lundi** she's off on Monday; she gets Mondays off; **~ étourdie de sœur**○ his/her absent-minded sister.

son² /sɔ̃/ *nm* **1** sound; **équipe/ingénieur du ~** sound team/engineer; **2** volume; **baisser le ~** to turn the volume down; **3** bran; **des céréales au ~** cereals with bran; **pain au ~** bran loaf.
IDIOMS **entendre plusieurs ~s de cloche** to hear several different versions (of the same thing).
■ **~ et lumière** son et lumière.

sonar /sɔnaʀ/ *nm* sonar.

sonate /sɔnat/ *nf* sonata.

sondage /sɔ̃daʒ/ *nm* **1** poll; survey; **~ d'opinion** opinion poll; **2** (Med) catheterization; probe; **3** (Naut) sounding.

sonde /sɔ̃d/ *nf* **1** (Med) catheter; probe; **2** sounding lead; sounding line; **3** drill; **4** taster.

sonder /sɔ̃de/ [1] *vtr* **1** to poll; to survey; to sound out; **2** to probe; **3** (Med) to catheterize; to probe; **4** (Naut) to sound; **5** (Tech) to make test drills in.

songe /sɔ̃ʒ/ *nm* (literary) dream.

songer: **songer à** /sɔ̃ʒe/ [13] *v+prep* **~ à qch/à faire** to think of sth/of doing; **tu n'y songes pas!** you can't be serious!; **songez-y** bear it in mind; think about it.

songeur, **-euse** /sɔ̃ʒœʀ, øz/ *adj* pensive; **dit-il, l'air ~** he said pensively.

sonnant, **~e** /sɔnɑ̃, ɑ̃t/ *adj* **à trois heures ~es** on the stroke of three.

sonné, **~e** /sɔne/ **I** *pp* ▶ **sonner**.
II *pp adj* **1** groggy; shattered; **2 il est six heures ~es** it has just struck six o'clock; **elle a quarante ans bien ~s**° she's well into her forties.

sonner /sɔne/ [1] **I** *vtr* **1** to ring [*bell*]; **2** [*clock*] to strike [*hour*]; [*person*] to sound [*retreat, alarm*]; to ring out [*vespers*]; **3** to ring for; **on ne t'a pas sonné**°! did anyone ask you?; **4**° [*blow*] to make [sb] dizzy; [*news*] to stagger; [*alcohol*] to knock [sb] out.
II sonner de *v+prep* to sound [*horn*]; to play [*bagpipes*].
III *vi* **1** [*bell, phone*] to ring; [*hour*] to strike; [*alarm clock*] to go off; [*alarm, trumpet*] to sound; **on a sonné à la porte** the doorbell has just rung; **leur dernière heure a sonné** their hour has come; **2** [*word, expression*] to sound.

sonnerie /sɔnʀi/ *nf* **1** ringing; chimes; **système qui déclenche une ~** system that sets off an alarm; **2** (of horn) sounding.

sonnet /sɔnɛ/ *nm* sonnet.

sonnette /sɔnɛt/ *nf* bell; doorbell; **tirer la ~ d'alarme** to pull the emergency cord; (figurative) to sound the alarm.

sonneur /sɔnœʀ/ *nm* **1** bell-ringer; **2** player.

sonore /sɔnɔʀ/ *adj* **1** [*laugh, kiss, slap*] resounding; [*words*] high-sounding; **2** resonant; echoing; hollow-sounding; **3** [*vibrations*] sound; **le volume ~ est tel que...** the noise level is so high that...; **4 effets ~s** sound effects; **un document ~** a recording; **5** [*consonant*] voiced.

sonorisation /sɔnɔʀizasjɔ̃/ *nf* **1** public address system, PA system; **2 la ~ d'un film** adding the soundtrack to a film.

sonorité /sɔnɔʀite/ *nf* **1** (of instrument, voice) tone; **les ~s de l'italien** the sound of Italian; **2** (of hi-fi) sound quality; **3** resonance.

sophisme /sɔfism/ *nm* sophism.

sophistication /sɔfistikasjɔ̃/ *nf* sophistication.

sophistiqué, **~e** /sɔfistike/ *adj* **1** sophisticated; **2** artificial, mannered.

soporifique /sɔpɔʀifik/ *adj*, *nm* soporific.

soprano /sɔpʀano/ *nmf* (woman) soprano; (child) treble, soprano.

sorbet /sɔʀbɛ/ *nm* sorbet; **~ (au) citron** lemon sorbet.

sorcellerie /sɔʀsɛlʀi/ *nf* witchcraft; sorcery.

sorcier /sɔʀsje/ **I**° *adj m* **ce n'est (pourtant) pas ~!** (but) it's dead° easy!
II *nm* **1** wizard; sorcerer; **2** witch doctor.

sorcière /sɔʀsjɛʀ/ *nf* witch; sorceress.

sordide /sɔʀdid/ *adj* squalid; sordid; [*greed, egoism*] base.

sornettes /sɔʀnɛt/ *nfpl* tall stories.

sort /sɔʀ/ *nm* **1** lot; **être satisfait de son ~** to be satisfied with one's lot; **2** fate; **remettre son ~ entre les mains de qn** to put one's fate in sb's hands; **le ~ est contre moi** I'm ill-fated; **tirer qch au ~** to draw lots for sth; **3** curse, spell; **jeter un ~ à qn** to put a curse or jinx on sb; **le ~ en est jeté** the die is cast.

sortable /sɔʀtabl/ *adj* **mon mari n'est pas ~** I can't take my husband anywhere.

sorte /sɔʀt/ **I** *nf* sort, kind; **d'aucune ~** of any sort or kind or type.
II de la sorte *phr* in this way.
III de sorte que *phr* **1** so that; **2 la toile est peinte de ~ que** the canvas is painted in such a way that; **3 de ~ que je n'ai pas pu venir** with the result that I couldn't come.
IV en quelque sorte *phr* in a way.
V en sorte de *phr* **fais en ~ d'être à l'heure** try to be on time.
VI en sorte que *phr* **1 fais en ~ que tout soit en ordre** make sure everything is tidy; **2** so; **en ~ qu'il n'a rien compris** so he understood nothing.

sortie /sɔʀti/ *nf* **1** exit; **je t'attendrai à la ~** I'll wait for you outside (the building); **prenez la première ~** (on road) take the first exit; **à la ~ de la ville** on the outskirts of the town; on the edge of the town; **2 à ma ~ du tribunal/de l'armée** when I left the court/the army; **se retrouver à la ~ de l'école** to meet after school; **à la ~ de l'hiver** at the end of winter; **3 faire une ~ fracassante** to make a dramatic exit; **~ d'un navire** sailing of a boat; **la ~ de la récession/crise** the end of the recession/crisis; **être interdit de ~ (du territoire)** to be forbidden to leave the country; **4** outing; **faire une ~ avec l'école** to go on a school outing; **ce soir, c'est mon soir de ~** tonight is my night out; **priver qn de ~** to keep sb in; **5** (of new product) launching; (of film) release; (of book) publication; (of fashion collection) showing; **6**° remark; **faire une ~ désagréable** to make a nasty remark; **7** (Tech) output; **faire une ~ sur imprimante**

to print; **~ laser** hardcopy laser output; laser hardcopy.
■ **~ des artistes** stage-door; **~ d'autoroute** exit; **~ de bain** bathrobe.

sortilège /sɔʀtilɛʒ/ *nm* spell.

sortir[1] /sɔʀtiʀ/ [30] **I** *vtr* **1** to take [sb/sth] out [*person, dog*]; **j'y vais moi-même, ça me sortira** I'll go myself, it'll give me a chance to get out; **2** to get [sb/sth] out; **~ l'argenterie** to get out the silverware; **~ qn du lit** to get sb out of bed; **~ les mains de ses poches** to take one's hands out of one's pockets; **~ la poubelle** to put the bin out; **~ sa langue** to stick one's tongue out; **3**° to chuck° [sb] out [*person*]; to send [sb] out [*pupil*]; **se faire ~ en quart de finale** to be knocked out in the quarterfinal; **4 ~ qn de** to get sb out of [*situation*]; **5** to bring out [*book*]; to release [*film*]; to show [*collection*]; **6** to turn out [*book, record, film, product*]; **7** to bring [sth] out [*newspaper*]; **8**° to come out with° [*remarks*]; **~ une blague** to crack a joke.
II *vi* (+ *v être*) **1** to go out; to come out; **~ déjeuner** to go out for lunch; **être sorti** to be out; **~ en courant** to run out; **faire ~ qn** to get sb outside; **laisser ~ qn** to allow sb out; **empêcher de ~** to keep [sb/sth] in; **2** to go out; **~ avec qn** to go out with sb; **inviter qn à sortir** to ask sb out; **3 ~ de** to leave; **~ de chez qn** to leave sb's house; **sortez d'ici!** get out of here!; **~ de son lit** to get out of bed; **~ tout chaud du four** to be hot from the oven; **4 ~ de** to come out of; **~ de chez le médecin** to come out of the doctor's; **5 ~ d'un rêve** to wake up from a dream; **~ de son mutisme** to break one's silence; **~ de la récession** to pull out of the recession; **~ de l'hiver** to reach the end of winter; **6 ~ à peine de l'enfance** to be just emerging from childhood; **~ d'une dépression** to be recovering from a bout of depression; **~ d'une guerre** to emerge from a war; **7** [*water, smoke, cork*] to come out; **faire ~** to squeeze [sth] out [*juice*]; to eject [*cassette*]; **8** [*bud, insect*] to come out; [*tooth*] to come through; **~ de terre** [*plant*] to come through; [*new buildings*] to spring up; **9** to stick out; **il y a un clou qui sort** there's a nail sticking out; **10** [*film, book, new model*] to come out; **~ tous les jours/tous les mois** [*paper*] to be published daily/monthly; **11 sortir de** [*person, product*] to come from; **~ de Berkeley** to have graduated from Berkeley; **d'où sors-tu à cette heure°?** where have you been?; **12 ~ du sujet** [*person*] to wander off the subject; [*remark*] to be beside the point; **cela sort de mes fonctions** that's not within my authority; **13** [*number, subject*] to come up; **14** (Comput) to exit.
III se sortir *v refl* (+ *v être*) **1 se ~ de la pauvreté** to escape from poverty; **s'en ~** to get out of it; to get over it; **s'en ~ vivant** to escape with one's life; **2 s'en ~** to pull through; to cope; to manage; **s'en ~ à peine** to scrape a living.

sortir[2] /sɔʀtiʀ/ *nm* **au ~ de** at the end of.

SOS /ɛsoɛs/ *nm* **1** SOS; **2** emergency service; **~ médecins** emergency medical service; **3** helpline; **~ enfants battus** child abuse helpline.

sosie /sɔzi/ *nm* double; **c'est ton ~!** he/she's the spitting image of you!

sot, sotte /so, sɔt/ **I** *adj* silly.
II *nm,f* silly thing; **petit ~!** you silly thing!

sottement /sɔtmɑ̃/ *adv* foolishly, stupidly.

sottise /sɔtiz/ *nf* **1** silliness, foolishness; **avoir la ~ de faire** to be silly enough to do; **2** silly remark; **dire des ~s** to talk rubbish; **3 c'est une ~ de faire** it's silly to do; **faire des ~s** [*children*] to be naughty.

sou /su/ *nm* **1** penny (GB), cent (US); **il est près de ses ~s** he's a penny-pincher; **c'est une affaire de gros ~s** there's big money involved; **2 il n'a pas un ~ de bon sens** he hasn't got a scrap of common sense; **3** (former unit of French currency) sou.
IDIOMS **s'ennuyer à cent ~s de l'heure** to be bored to death.

soubassement /subɑsmɑ̃/ *nm* **1** (of building, pillar) base; **2** bedrock.

soubresaut /subʀəso/ *nm* start; jolt; **les derniers ~s** the death throes.

soubrette /subʀɛt/ *nf* maid.

souche /suʃ/ *nf* **1** (tree) stump; (vine) stock; **2** stock; **de ~ paysanne** of peasant stock; **3** (of chequebook) stub.
IDIOMS **dormir comme une ~** to sleep like a log.

souci /susi/ *nm* **1 se faire du ~** to worry; **donner (bien) du ~ à qn** to be a (great) worry to sb; **2** problem; **j'ai d'autres ~s (en tête)** I've got other things to worry about; **3** (formal) **avoir le ~ de qch** to care about sth; **avoir le ~ de faire** to be anxious to do; **dans le seul ~ de faire plaisir** with the sole intention of pleasing; **sans ~ de qch/de faire** with no thought for sth/of doing; **4** marigold.

soucier: **se soucier** /susje/ [2] *v refl* (+ *v être*) to care (**de** about); **sans se ~ de qch/faire** without concerning oneself with sth/doing.

soucieux, -ieuse /susjø, øz/ *adj* worried; **être ~ de** to be concerned about; to care about; **être peu ~ de** to care little about.

soucoupe /sukup/ *nf* saucer.
■ **~ volante** flying saucer.

soudain, ~e /sudɛ̃, ɛn/ **I** *adj* sudden, unexpected.
II *adv* suddenly, all of a sudden.

soudainement /sudɛnmɑ̃/ *adv* suddenly.

soude /sud/ *nf* soda; **~ caustique** caustic soda.

souder /sude/ [1] **I** *vtr* **1** to weld; **2** to join [*edges*]; to bind [sb] together [*people*].
II se souder *v refl* (+ *v être*) **1** [*vertebrae*] to fuse; [*bone*] to knit together; **2** [*team*] to become united.

soudoyer /sudwaje/ [23] *vtr* to bribe.

soudure /sudyʀ/ *nf* (Tech) **1** weld, join; **2** solder; **3** welding; soldering.

souffle /sufl/ *nm* **1** breath; **couper le ~ à qn** to wind sb; (figurative) to take sb's breath away;

à couper le ~ [*beauty*] breathtaking; [*beautiful*] breathtakingly; **(en) avoir le ~ coupé** to be winded; (figurative) to be speechless; **être à bout de ~** [*person*] to be out of breath; [*country, economy*] to be running out of steam; **dire qch dans un ~** to say sth in a whisper; **donner un second** or **nouveau ~ à qn/qch** to put new life into sb/sth; **avoir du ~** [*saxophonist*] to have good lungs; [*singer*] to have a powerful voice; [*sportsman*] to be fit; (figurative) [*person*] to have staying power; **2** breathing; **3** breeze; **pas un ~ d'air** not a breath of air; **4** spirit; **~ révolutionnaire** revolutionary spirit; **5** inspiration; **6** touch; **~ de génie** touch of genius; **7** (from fan, explosion) blast; **8** (Med) **~ au cœur** heart murmur.

soufflé, ~e /sufle/ **I** *pp* ▶ **souffler**.
II *pp adj* **1**° flabbergasted; **2** (Culin) souffléed.
III *nm* (Culin) soufflé.

souffler /sufle/ [1] **I** *vtr* **1** to blow out [*candle*]; **2** to blow [*air, smoke, dust*]; **3** to whisper [*words*]; **~ qch à l'oreille de qn** to whisper sth in sb's ear; **~ la réplique à un acteur** to prompt an actor; **4** to suggest [*idea*]; **on lui a soufflé la réponse** he/she was prompted; **5** to blow [*glass*]; to blast [*metal*]; **6** [*explosion*] to blow out [*window*]; to blow up [*building*]; **7**° to flabbergast.
II *vi* **1** [*wind*] to blow; **le vent souffle fort** there's a strong wind; **un vent de folie souffle sur le stade** frenzy is sweeping through the stadium; **2** [*person*] to get one's breath back; [*horse*] to get its wind back; **3** to puff; **suant et soufflant** huffing and puffing; **4** [*person, animal*] to blow; **~ dans une trompette** to blow into a trumpet; **souffle fort!** have a good blow!; **5** to tell sb the answer; **on ne souffle pas!** no prompting!
IDIOMS **~ comme un bœuf** or **un phoque** or **une locomotive** to puff and pant.

soufflerie /sufləʀi/ *nf* **1** wind tunnel; **2** bellows; **3** blower; blower house; **4** glassblower; glassblowing company.

soufflet /suflɛ/ *nm* **1** bellows; **2** gusset.

souffleur, -euse /suflœʀ, øz/ *nm,f* **1** prompter; **2 ~ (de verre)** glassblower.

souffrance /sufʀɑ̃s/ *nf* **1** suffering; **2 en ~** [*parcel*] awaiting delivery; [*file*] pending.

souffrant, ~e /sufʀɑ̃, ɑ̃t/ *adj* unwell.

souffre-douleur /sufʀədulœʀ/ *nm inv* punchbag (GB), punching-bag (US).

souffreteux, -euse /sufʀətø, øz/ *adj* sickly.

souffrir /sufʀiʀ/ [4] **I** *vtr* **1 ~ tout de qn** to put up with anything from sb; **il ne souffre pas la critique** he can't take criticism; **elle ne peut plus le ~** she can't stand him any more; **2 cette affaire ne peut ~ aucun retard** this matter brooks no delay.
II *vi* **1** [*person*] to suffer; **faire ~ qn** to cause sb suffering; **~ de** to suffer from; **ma cheville me fait ~** my ankle hurts; **est-ce qu'il souffre?** is he in pain?; **faire ~** [*person*] to make [sb] suffer; [*situation*] to upset; **~ du racisme** to be a victim of racism; **ils souffrent de ne pas se voir** they find it painful to be separated; **2** [*crops, economy*] to be badly affected; [*country, city*] to suffer.

soufre /sufʀ/ *nm* sulphur[GB].

souhait /swɛ/ *nm* wish; **à ~** [*stupid, beautiful*] incredibly.
IDIOMS **à vos ~s!** bless you!

souhaitable /swɛtabl/ *adj* desirable.

souhaiter /swete/ [1] *vtr* **1** to hope for; **2 ~ qch à qn** to wish sb sth; **~ bonne chance à qn** to wish sb luck; **~ la bienvenue à qn** to welcome sb; **je vous souhaite d'obtenir très bientôt votre diplôme** I hope you get your degree very soon; **3 il souhaite se rendre là-bas en voiture** he would like to go by car.

souiller /suje/ [1] *vtr* **1** to soil, to make [sth] dirty; **être souillé de** to be stained with; **2** (literary) to defile [*place, person*]; to sully [*memory, reputation*].

souillon /sujɔ̃/ *nf* slattern†.

souillure /sujyʀ/ *nf* stain.

souk /suk/ *nm* **1** souk; **2**° mess; racket°.

soûl, ~e /su, sul/ **I** *adj* drunk; **être fin ~**° to be blind drunk.
II tout son soûl *phr* [*drink, eat*] one's fill; **dormir tout son ~** to sleep as much as one wants.

soulagement /sulaʒmɑ̃/ *nm* relief.

soulager /sulaʒe/ [13] **I** *vtr* (gen) to relieve (**de** of); to ease [*conscience*]; **le comprimé m'a soulagé** the tablet made me feel better; **tu m'as soulagé d'un grand poids** you've taken a great weight off my shoulders.
II se soulager *v refl* (+ *v être*) **1**° (euphemistic) to relieve oneself; **2 elle m'a raconté tout cela pour se ~** she told me the whole story to get it off her chest.

soûler /sule/ [1] **I** *vtr* **1** [*person*] to get [sb] drunk; [*alcohol*] to make [sb] drunk; **2** [*perfume*] to intoxicate; **3**° **tu me soûles avec tes histoires** give me a break, my head is spinning!
II se soûler *v refl* (+ *v être*) **1** to get drunk; **2 se ~ de** to become intoxicated with [*words*].

soulèvement /sulɛvmɑ̃/ *nm* uprising.

soulever /sulve/ [16] **I** *vtr* **1** to lift [*object*]; to raise [*dust*]; **~ qn/qch de terre** to pick sb/sth up; **2** to arouse [*enthusiasm, anger*]; to stir up [*crowd*]; to raise [*problems*]; to give rise to [*protest*].
II se soulever *v refl* (+ *v être*) **1** to raise oneself up; **il s'est soulevé sur un coude** he propped himself up on one elbow; **2** to rise up.
IDIOMS **ça me soulève le cœur** it turns my stomach; it makes me sick.

soulier /sulje/ *nm* shoe.
IDIOMS **être dans ses petits ~s** to feel uncomfortable.

souligner /suliɲe/ [1] *vtr* **1** to underline [*word*]; to outline [*eyes*]; **2** to emphasize.

soumettre /sumɛtʀ/ [60] **I** *vtr* **1** to bring [sb/sth] to heel [*person, group, region*]; to subdue [*rebels*]; **2 ~ qn/qch à** to subject sb/sth to; **3** to submit; **~ une proposition à qn** to put forward a proposal to sb; **4 ~ un produit à**

une température élevée to subject a product to a high temperature.
II **se soumettre** *v refl* (+ *v être*) **1** to submit; **2 se ~ à** to accept [*rule*].

soumis, **~e** /sumi, iz/ I *pp* ▶ **soumettre**.
II *pp adj* submissive.

soumission /sumisjɔ̃/ *nf* submission.

soupape /supap/ *nf* valve.

soupçon /supsɔ̃/ *nm* **1** suspicion; **2** (formal) **ne pas avoir ~ de qch** to have no notion of sth; **3**○ (of milk, wine) drop, spot○; (of salt, spice) pinch; (of flavour) hint.

soupçonner /supsɔne/ [1] *vtr* to suspect.

soupçonneux, **-euse** /supsɔnø, øz/ *adj* suspicious, mistrustful.

soupe /sup/ *nf* **1** soup; **~ de légumes** vegetable soup; **à la ~**○**!** (humorous) grub's up○!, come and get it!; **2**○ slush.
■ **~ populaire** soup kitchen.
IDIOMS **être ~ au lait**○ to be quick-tempered; **cracher dans la ~**○ to look a gift horse in the mouth.

soupente /supɑ̃t/ *nf* **1** loft, garret; **2** cupboard under the stairs.

souper[1] /supe/ [1] *vi* to have late dinner.
IDIOMS **en avoir soupé de qch**○ to have had it up to here with sth○.

souper[2] /supe/ *nm* late dinner, supper.

soupeser /supəze/ [16] *vtr* **1** to feel the weight of; **2** to weigh up [*arguments*].

soupière /supjɛʀ/ *nf* soup tureen.

soupir /supiʀ/ *nm* **1** sigh; **2** (Mus) crotchet rest (GB), quarter rest (US).

soupirail, *pl* **-aux** /supiʀaj, o/ *nm* cellar window.

soupirer /supiʀe/ [1] *vi* to sigh; **~ après qch** to yearn for sth.

souple /supl/ *adj* **1** [*body*] supple; [*stalk*] flexible; [*hair*] soft; **2** [*step, style*] flowing; [*shape*] smooth; **3** [*rule*] flexible.

souplesse /suplɛs/ *nf* **1** (of stalk) flexibility; (of hair) softness; (of body) suppleness; **2** (of step) litheness; (of gesture) grace; (of car, drive) smoothness; (of style) fluidity; **en ~** smoothly; **3** (of rule) flexibility.

source /suʀs/ *nf* **1** spring; **2** source; **prendre sa ~ dans** or **à** [*river*] to rise in or at; **citer ses ~s** to give one's sources.
IDIOMS **ça coule de ~** it's obvious; **retour aux ~s** return to basics.

sourcil /suʀsi/ *nm* eyebrow; **~s épais** bushy eyebrows.

sourciller /suʀsije/ [1] *vi* to raise one's eyebrows; **sans ~** without batting an eyelid.

sourd, **~e** /suʀ, suʀd/ I *adj* **1** deaf; **~ à** deaf to [*pleas*]; **2** [*noise*] dull, muffled; [*voice*] muffled; **3** [*pain*] dull; **4** [*struggle, machinations*] secret, hidden; **5** [*consonant*] voiceless, surd.
II *nm,f* deaf person; **les ~s** the deaf.
IDIOMS **faire la ~e oreille** to turn a deaf ear; **comme un ~** [*shout*] at the top of one's voice; **taper comme un ~** to bang (on the door or the wall etc); **ce n'est pas tombé dans l'oreille d'un ~** it didn't go unheard.

sourdine /suʀdin/ *nf* (Mus) mute; (on piano) soft pedal; **écouter la radio en ~** to have the radio on quietly; **mettre une ~ à** to tone down [*criticism*].

sourd-muet, **sourde-muette**, *pl* **sourds-muets**, **sourdes-muettes** /suʀmɥɛ, suʀd mɥɛt/ I *adj* deaf and dumb.
II *nm,f* deaf-mute.

souriant, **~e**, /suʀjɑ̃, ɑ̃t/ *adj* smiling.

souricière /suʀisjɛʀ/ *nf* **1** mousetrap; **2** trap.

sourire[1] /suʀiʀ/ [68] *vi* **1** to smile (**à** at); **~ jusqu'aux oreilles** to grin from ear to ear; **2** (literary) **~ à qn** [*fate, fortune*] to smile on sb; [*idea*] to appeal to sb.
IDIOMS **~ aux anges** to have a silly smile on one's face.

sourire[2] /suʀiʀ/ *nm* smile; **le ~ aux lèvres** with a smile on one's face; **garder le ~** to keep smiling (through).

souris /suʀi/ *nf inv* mouse.

sournois, **~e** /suʀnwa, az/ *adj* [*person, look*] sly; [*behaviour*] underhand; [*pain*] insidious.

sous /su/ *prep* **1** under, underneath; **un journal ~ le bras** a newspaper under one's arm; **~ la pluie** in the rain; **j'aurais voulu rentrer ~ terre** (figurative) I wished the ground would swallow me up; **2** under; **~ le numéro 4757** under number 4757; **3** during; **~ la présidence de Mitterrand** during Mitterrand's presidency; **4** within; **~ peu** before long; **5 ~ traitement** undergoing treatment; **~ antibiotiques** on antibiotics.

sous-alimenté, **~e**, *mpl* **~s** /suzalimɑ̃te/ *adj* undernourished.

sous-bois /subwa/ *nm inv* undergrowth.

sous-catégorie, *pl* **~s** /sukategɔʀi/ *nf* subcategory.

souscripteur, **-trice** /suskʀiptœʀ, tʀis/ *nm,f* subscriber (**de** to).

souscription /suskʀipsjɔ̃/ *nf* **1** subscription; **~ d'actions** application for shares; **2 ~ d'un contrat d'assurances** taking out an insurance policy.

souscrire /suskʀiʀ/ [67] I *vtr* to take out [*insurance*]; to sign [*contract*]; to subscribe [*sum of money*].
II **souscrire à** *v+prep* to subscribe to.

souscrit, **~e** /suskʀi, it/ I *pp* ▶ **souscrire**.
II *pp adj* **1** subscribed; **2** [*letter*] subscript.

sous-cutané, **~e**, *mpl* **~s** /sukytane/ *adj* subcutaneous.

sous-développé, **~e**, *mpl* **~s** /sudevlɔpe/ *adj* underdeveloped.

sous-directeur, **-trice**, *mpl* **~s** /sudiʀɛk tœʀ, tʀis/ *nm,f* assistant manager.

sous-effectif, *pl* **~s** /suzefɛktif/ *nm* understaffing.

sous-entendre /suzɑ̃tɑ̃dʀ/ [6] *vtr* to imply.

sous-entendu, **~e**, *mpl* **~s** /suzɑ̃tɑ̃dy/ I *pp* ▶ **sous-entendre**.
II *pp adj* understood.

III *nm* innuendo; **un sourire plein de ~s** a smile full of innuendo.

sous-estimer /suzestime/ [1] *vtr* to underestimate.

sous-évaluer /suzevalɥe/ [1] *vtr* to underestimate; to undervalue.

sous-fifre°, *pl* **~s** /sufifʀ/ *nm* underling.

sous-jacent, **~e**, *mpl* **~s** /suʒasɑ̃, ɑ̃t/ *adj* **1** [*idea, problem, tension*] underlying; **2** subjacent.

sous-lieutenant, *pl* **~s** /suljøtnɑ̃/ *nm* (in army) ≈ second lieutenant; (in air force) ≈ pilot officer (GB), ≈ second lieutenant (US).

sous-locataire, *pl* **~s** /sulɔkatɛʀ/ *nmf* subtenant.

sous-louer /sulwe/ [1] *vtr* to sublet; to sublease.

sous-main /sumɛ̃/ **I** *nm inv* desk blotter.

II en sous-main *phr* under the table, secretly.

sous-marin, **~e**, *mpl* **~s** /sumaʀɛ̃, in/ **I** *adj* submarine, underwater; deep-sea.

II *nm* **1** submarine; **2**° spy.

sous-officier, *pl* **~s** /suzɔfisje/ *nm* noncommissioned officer.

sous-payer /supeje/ [21] *vtr* to underpay.

sous-préfecture, *pl* **~s** /supʀefɛktyʀ/ *nf*: *administrative subdivision of a department in France.*

sous-préfet, *pl* **~s** /supʀefɛ/ *nm*: *permanent ministerial representative in a department in France.*

sous-produit, *pl* **~s** /supʀɔdɥi/ *nm* **1** by-product; **2** second-rate product.

sous-prolétariat, *pl* **~s** /supʀɔletaʀja/ *nm* underclass.

sous-secrétaire, *pl* **~s** /sus(ə)kʀetɛʀ/ *nmf* **~ d'État** Undersecretary of State.

soussigné, **~e** /susiɲe/ *adj, nm,f* undersigned.

sous-sol, *pl* **~s** /susɔl/ *nm* **1** basement; **2** subsoil.

sous-tasse, *pl* **~s** /sutas/ *nf* saucer.

sous-titre, *pl* **~s** /sutitʀ/ *nm* subtitle.

sous-titrer /sutitʀe/ [1] *vtr* to subtitle.

soustraction /sustʀaksjɔ̃/ *nf* subtraction.

soustraire /sustʀɛʀ/ [58] **I** *vtr* **1** to subtract; **2** to steal; **3** to take away [*person*]; **~ qn/qch à la vue de qn** to hide sb/sth from sb; **4** to shield [*person*]; **~ qn à la mort** to save sb's life.

II se soustraire *v refl* (+ *v être*) **1 se ~ à** to escape from; **se ~ à ses obligations** to shirk one's duties; **2 se ~ à la justice** to escape justice.

sous-traitance, *pl* **~s** /sutʀɛtɑ̃s/ *nf* subcontracting.

sous-verre /suvɛʀ/ *nm inv* **1** clip-frame; **2** coaster.

sous-vêtement, *pl* **~s** /suvɛtmɑ̃/ *nm* underwear.

soutane /sutan/ *nf* cassock; **porter la ~** to be a priest.

soute /sut/ *nf* hold; **~ à bagages** baggage hold.

soutenable /sutnabl/ *adj* **1** bearable; **pas ~** unbearable; **2** tenable.

soutenance /sutnɑ̃s/ *nf* viva voce (GB), orals (US).

soutènement /sutɛnmɑ̃/ *nm* retaining structure; (in mine) props.

souteneur /sutnœʀ/ *nm* pimp°, procurer.

soutenir /sutniʀ/ [36] **I** *vtr* **1** (gen) to support [*person, team, currency*]; **mur soutenu par des étais** wall supported by props; **~ à bout de bras** to keep [sb/sth] afloat [*person, project*]; **~ qn contre qn** to side with sb against sb; **seul l'espoir me soutient** hope alone sustains me; **~ le moral de qn** to keep sb's spirits up; **2** to maintain [*contrary*]; to defend [*paradox*]; to uphold [*opinion*]; **3** to keep [sb] going; **4** to keep [sth] alive [*curiosity, interest*]; to keep [sth] going [*conversation*]; to keep up [*effort, pace*]; **5** to withstand [*shock, attack, stares*]; to bear [*comparison*]; **6 ~ sa thèse** to have one's viva voce (GB) or defense (US).

II se soutenir *v refl* (+ *v être*) to support each other.

soutenu, **~e** /sutny/ **I** *pp* ▶ **soutenir**.

II *pp adj* [*effort, activity*] sustained; [*attention*] close; [*rhythm*] steady.

III *adj* **1** [*market*] firm; [*colour*] deep; [*language*] formal, elevated; **2** (Mus) [*note*] sustained, long-drawn-out.

souterrain, **~e** /sutɛʀɛ̃, ɛn/ **I** *adj* **1** underground; **2** [*agreement*] secret; **économie ~e** black economy.

II *nm* underground passage, tunnel.

soutien /sutjɛ̃/ *nm* support.

soutien-gorge, *pl* **soutiens-gorge** /sutjɛ̃ gɔʀʒ/ *nm* bra.

soutirer /sutiʀe/ [1] *vtr* **~ qch à qn** to squeeze [sth] out of sb [*money*]; to extract [sth] from sb [*confession*].

souvenance /suvnɑ̃s/ *nf* (formal) **avoir ~ de qch** to remember sth.

souvenir[1] /suvniʀ/ [36] **I se souvenir** *v refl* (+ *v être*) **se ~ de qn/qch** to remember sb/sth.

II *v impers* **il me souvient que** (literary) I recollect that.

souvenir[2] /suvniʀ/ *nm* **1** memory; **garder un bon ~ de qch** to have happy memories of sth; **~s d'enfance** childhood memories; **ne pas avoir ~ de** to have no recollection of; **2** memory; **s'effacer du ~ de qn** to fade from sb's memory; **3** souvenir; memento; **en ~** as a souvenir; as a memento; as a keepsake; **boutique de ~s** souvenir shop (GB) or store (US); **4 croyez à mon bon** or **fidèle** or **meilleur ~** (in letter) yours ever; **mon bon ~ à** remember me to.

souvent /suvɑ̃/ *adv* often; **le plus ~** more often than not.

souverain, **~e** /suvʀɛ̃, ɛn/ **I** *adj* **1** [*state*] sovereign; [*authority*] supreme; **2** [*happiness, scorn*] supreme; **3** [*remedy*] sovereign; [*advice, virtue*] sterling; **4** [*person*] haughty.

II *nm,f* sovereign, monarch.

souverainement /suvʀɛnmɑ̃/ *adv* **1** [*judge*] without appeal; **2 votre attitude me déplaît ~** I dislike your attitude intensely.

souveraineté /suvʀɛnte/ *nf* sovereignty.

soviet /sɔvjɛt/ *nm* soviet; **Soviet suprême** Supreme Soviet.

soviétique /sɔvjetik/ *adj* Soviet.

soyeux, -euse /swajø, øz/ *adj* silky.

SPA /ɛspea/ *nf* (*abbr* = **Société protectrice des animaux**) society for the prevention of cruelty to animals.

spacieux, -ieuse /spasjø, øz/ *adj* spacious.

spaghetti /spageti/ *nm inv* **des ~** spaghetti.

sparadrap /spaʀadʀa/ *nm* **1** surgical or adhesive tape; **2** (sticking) plaster (GB), Band-aid®.

spartiate /spaʀsjat/ *adj, nmf* Spartan.

spasme /spasm/ *nm* spasm.

spasmodique /spasmɔdik/ *adj* spasmodic.

spatial, ~e, *mpl* **-iaux** /spasjal, o/ *adj* **1** spatial; **2** space; **vaisseau ~** spaceship.

spatule /spatyl/ *nf* **1** spatula; **2** filling-knife; **3** (on ski) tip.

speaker, speakerine /spikœʀ, spikʀin/ *nm,f* announcer.

spécial, ~e, *mpl* **-iaux** /spesjal, o/ *adj* **1** special; **2** odd.

spécialement /spesjalmɑ̃/ *adv* **1** specially; **2** especially; **pas ~** not especially.

spécialiser: **se spécialiser** /spesjalize/ [1] *v refl* (+ *v être*) to specialize.

spécialiste /spesjalist/ *nmf* specialist.

spécialité /spesjalite/ *nf* speciality (GB), specialty (US).

spécieux, -ieuse /spesjø, øz/ *adj* specious.

spécificité /spesifisite/ *nf* **1** specificity; **2** characteristic; **3** uniqueness.

spécifier /spesifje/ [2] *vtr* to specify; **~ à qn de faire** to tell sb specifically to do.

spécifique /spesifik/ *adj* specific.

spécimen /spesimɛn/ *nm* **1** specimen; **2** (free) sample; **3**○ odd specimen○.

spectacle /spɛktakl/ *nm* **1** sight; **se donner** or **s'offrir en ~** to make an exhibition or a spectacle of oneself; **2** show; **allons au ~** let's go to the theatre[GB]; **~ de danse** dance show; **'~s'** 'entertainment'; **film à grand ~** spectacular; **3** show business.

spectaculaire /spɛktakylɛʀ/ *adj* spectacular.

spectateur, -trice /spɛktatœʀ, tʀis/ *nm,f* **1** member of the audience; **2** spectator.

spectral, ~e, *mpl* **-aux** /spɛktʀal, o/ *adj* **1** spectral; **2** ghostly.

spectre /spɛktʀ/ *nm* **1** ghost; **2** spectre[GB]; **3 ~ lumineux** spectrum of light.

spéculateur, -trice /spekylatœʀ, tʀis/ *nm,f* speculator.

spéculatif, -ive /spekylatif, iv/ *adj* speculative.

spéculer /spekyle/ [1] *vi* to speculate; **~ à la hausse/baisse** to bull/bear.

spéléologie /speleɔlɔʒi/ *nf* **1** caving, potholing (GB), spelunking (US); **2** speleology.

spéléologue /speleɔlɔg/ *nmf* **1** caver, potholer (GB), spelunker (US); **2** speleologist.

spermatozoïde /spɛʀmatɔzɔid/ *nm* **des ~s** spermatozoa.

sperme /spɛʀm/ *nm* sperm.

sphère /sfɛʀ/ *nf* sphere; **les hautes ~s de la finance** the higher echelons of finance.

sphérique /sfeʀik/ *adj* spherical.

sphincter /sfɛ̃ktɛʀ/ *nm* sphincter.

sphinx /sfɛ̃ks/ *nm inv* **1** Sphinx; **2** hawkmoth.

spirale /spiʀal/ *nf* spiral.

spiritisme /spiʀitism/ *nm* spiritualism.

spiritualité /spiʀitɥalite/ *nf* spirituality.

spirituel, -elle /spiʀitɥɛl/ *adj* **1** spiritual; **2** witty.

spiritueux, -euse /spiʀitɥø, øz/ *nm inv* spirit.

spleen /splin/ *nm* spleen; **avoir le ~** to feel despondent.

splendeur /splɑ̃dœʀ/ *nf* (of scenery, site) splendour[GB]; (of era, reign) glory.

splendide /splɑ̃did/ *adj* splendid; magnificent; stunning.

spolier /spɔlje/ [2] *vtr* to despoil.

spongieux, -ieuse /spɔ̃ʒjø, øz/ *adj* spongy.

sponsoriser /spɔ̃sɔʀize/ [1] *vtr* to sponsor.

spontané, ~e /spɔ̃tane/ *adj* spontaneous; **candidature ~e** unsolicited application.

spontanéité /spɔ̃taneite/ *nf* spontaneity.

sporadique /spɔʀadik/ *adj* sporadic.

spore /spɔʀ/ *nf* spore.

sport /spɔʀ/ *nm* sport; sports; **vous faites du ~?** do you do any sports?; **aller aux ~s d'hiver** to go on a winter sports holiday (GB) or vacation (US).

IDIOMS **il va y avoir du ~**○! this is going to be fun or interesting!

sportif, -ive /spɔʀtif, iv/ **I** *adj* **1** [*event*] sports; **je ne suis pas ~** I'm not the sporty type; **2** [*appearance*] athletic, sporty○; **faire preuve d'esprit ~** to be a good sport.

II *nm,f* sportsman/sportswoman; **c'est un ~** he's athletic.

spot /spɔt/ *nm* **1** spotlight; **2 ~ (publicitaire)** commercial.

square /skwaʀ/ *nm* small public garden.

squash /skwaʃ/ *nm* squash.

squatter[1] /skwate/ [1] *vtr* to squat in [*apartment*].

squatter[2] /skwatœʀ/ *nm* squatter.

squelette /skəlɛt/ *nm* **1** skeleton; **2**○ bag of bones○; **3** framework.

squelettique /skəletik/ *adj* [*person, legs*] scrawny; [*tree*] skeletal; [*report*] sketchy.

stabiliser /stabilize/ [1] **I** *vtr* to stabilize; to consolidate.

II se stabiliser *v refl* (+ *v être*) [*unemployment, prices*] to stabilize; [*person*] to become stable.

stabilité /stabilite/ *nf* stability.

stable /stabl/ *adj* stable.

stade /stad/ *nm* **1** (Sport) stadium; **2** stage; **à ce ~** at this stage (**de** of).

stage /staʒ/ *nm* **1** professional training; **2** work experience; **~ pratique** period of work experience; **3** course; **suivre un ~ de formation** to go on a training course.

stagiaire /staʒjɛʀ/ *nmf* **1** trainee; **2** student teacher.

stagnation /stagnasjɔ̃/ *nf* stagnation.

stagner /stagne/ [1] *vi* to stagnate.

stalactite /stalaktit/ *nf* stalactite.

stalagmite /stalagmit/ *nf* stalagmite.

stalle /stal/ *nf* stall.

stand /stɑ̃d/ *nm* stand; stall.
■ **~ de tir** shooting range; shooting gallery.

standard /stɑ̃daʀ/ **I** *adj inv* standard.
II *nm* switchboard.

standardisation /stɑ̃daʀdizasjɔ̃/ *nf* standardization.

standardiste /stɑ̃daʀdist/ *nmf* switchboard operator.

standing /stɑ̃diŋ/ *nm* **1 de ~** [*apartment*] luxury; **2** standard of living.

star /staʀ/ *nf* star.

starlette /staʀlɛt/ *nf* starlet.

starter /staʀtɛʀ/ *nm* choke; **mettre le ~** to pull out the choke.

station /stasjɔ̃/ *nf* **1** station; taxi-rank (GB), taxi stand; **c'est à deux ~s de métro d'ici** it's two tube (GB) or subway (US) stops from here; **2 ~ (de radio)** (radio) station; **3 ~ balnéaire** seaside resort; **~ thermale** spa; **4 ~ météorologique** weather station; **5 ~ debout** or **verticale** upright posture or position; **6** stop, pause.

stationnaire /stasjɔnɛʀ/ *adj* **1** stationary; **2** stable.

stationnement /stasjɔnmɑ̃/ *nm* parking; **~ interdit** no parking.

stationner /stasjɔne/ [1] *vi* to park; **~ en double file** to double-park.

station-service, *pl* **stations-service** /stasjɔ̃sɛʀvis/ *nf* service or filling station.

statique /statik/ *adj* static.

statistique /statistik/ *nf* **1** statistics; **2** statistic.

statue /staty/ *nf* statue; **se changer en ~** to be frozen to the spot.

statuer /statɥe/ [1] *vi* to give a ruling.

statuette /statɥɛt/ *nf* statuette.

statu quo /statykwo/ *nm inv* status quo.

stature /statyʀ/ *nf* **1** stature; **2** height; **3** calibre[GB]; **grande ~** high calibre[GB].

statut /staty/ *nm* **1** statute; **2** status.

statutaire /statytɛʀ/ *adj* statutory.

steak /stɛk/ *nm* steak; **un ~ haché** a hamburger.

sténodactylo /stenodaktilo/ **I** *nmf* shorthand typist (GB), stenographer (US).
II *nf* shorthand typing (GB), stenography (US).

sténographier /stenɔgʀafje/ [2] *vtr* to take [sth] down in shorthand.

stentor /stɑ̃tɔʀ/ *nm* **voix de ~** stentorian voice.

steppe /stɛp/ *nf* steppe.

stère /stɛʀ/ *nm* stere.

stéréo /steʀeo/ *adj inv*, *nf* stereo.

stéréophonie /steʀeɔfɔni/ *nf* stereophony; **en ~** in stereo.

stéréophonique /steʀeɔfɔnik/ *adj* stereophonic.

stéréotype /steʀeɔtip/ *nm* **1** stereotype; **2** cliché.

stérile /steʀil/ *adj* (gen) sterile; [*land*] barren; [*discussion*] fruitless.

stérilet /steʀilɛ/ *nm* coil, IUD, intrauterine device.

stériliser /steʀilize/ [1] *vtr* to sterilize.

stérilité /steʀilite/ *nf* **1** sterility; barrenness; **2** fruitlessness.

sterling /stɛʀliŋ/ *adj inv* sterling; **livre ~** pound sterling.

sternum /stɛʀnɔm/ *nm* breastbone, sternum.

stéthoscope /stetɔskɔp/ *nm* stethoscope.

stigmate /stigmat/ *nm* **1** scar; **2** mark; **3 ~s** stigmata.

stimulant, **~e** /stimylɑ̃, ɑ̃t/ **I** *adj* invigorating; bracing; stimulating.
II *nm* **1** tonic; **2** stimulant; **3** stimulus.

stimuler /stimyle/ [1] **I** *vtr* **1** to stimulate [*organ, function*]; **2** to spur [sb] on.
II *vi* **1** to be bracing; **2**° to act as a spur.

stimulus, *pl* **stimuli** /stimylys, stimyli/ *nm* stimulus.

stipuler /stipyle/ [1] *vtr* to stipulate (**que** that).

stock /stɔk/ *nm* stock; **avoir qch en ~** to have sth in stock.

stockage /stɔkaʒ/ *nm* **1** stocking (**de** of); **2** stockpiling (**de** of); **3** storage (**de** of).

stocker /stɔke/ [1] *vtr* **1** to stock; **2** to stockpile; **3** to store [*data*].

stoïque /stɔik/ *adj* stoical.

stop /stɔp/ *nm* **1** stop sign; **2** brake light; **3**° hitching°; **prendre qn en ~** to give sb a lift (GB) or ride (US).

stopper /stɔpe/ [1] **I** *vtr* **1** to stop; to halt [*development*]; **2** to mend.
II *vi* to stop.

store /stɔʀ/ *nm* **1** blind; **2** awning.

strabisme /stʀabism/ *nm* squint.

strapontin /stʀapɔ̃tɛ̃/ *nm* foldaway seat.

strass /stʀas/ *nm inv* paste; **collier en ~** paste necklace.

stratagème /stʀataʒɛm/ *nm* stratagem.

strate /stʀat/ *nf* stratum.

stratège /stʀatɛʒ/ *nm* strategist.

stratégie /stʀateʒi/ *nf* strategy.

stratégique /stʀateʒik/ *adj* strategic.

stratifié, **~e** /stʀatifje/ **I** *adj* **1** stratified; **2** laminated.
II *nm* **du ~** laminate; **table en ~** laminated table.

stratosphère /stʀatɔsfɛʀ/ *nf* stratosphere.

stress /stʀɛs/ *nm inv* stress.

stressant, **~e** /stʀɛsɑ̃, ɑ̃t/ *adj* stressful; upsetting; worrying.

stresser /stʀese/ [1] *vtr* to put [sb] on edge; to put [sb] under stress.

strict, **~e** /stʀikt/ *adj* **1** [*discipline*] strict; **2 au sens ~** in the strict sense of the word; **c'est la ~e vérité** it's the absolute truth; **3** [*hairstyle, outfit*] severe.

strident, **~e** /stʀidɑ̃, ɑ̃t/ *adj* [*noise*] piercing; [*voice*] strident.

strie /stʀi/ *nf* **1** streak; **2** groove; **3** (in geology) **des ~s** striation.

strier /stʀije/ [2] *vtr* **1** to streak (**de** with); **2** to make grooves in; **3** to striate.

strip-tease /stʀiptiz/ *nm* striptease.

strophe /stʀɔf/ *nf* stanza, verse.

structure /stʀyktyʀ/ *nf* **1** structure; **2** organization; **~ d'accueil** shelter, refuge.

structurer /stʀyktyʀe/ [1] *vtr* to structure.

stuc /styk/ *nm* stucco.

studieux, **-ieuse** /stydjø, øz/ *adj* [*pupil*] studious; [*holiday*] study; [*atmosphere*] industrious.

studio /stydjo/ *nm* **1** studio flat (GB), studio apartment (US); **2** studio.

stupéfaction /stypefaksjɔ̃/ *nf* stupefaction, amazement.

stupéfait, **~e** /stypefɛ, ɛt/ *adj* astounded, dumbfounded.

stupéfiant, **~e** /stypefjɑ̃, ɑ̃t/ **I** *adj* stunning, astounding.
II *nm* drug, narcotic.

stupéfier /stypefje/ [2] *vtr* **1** to astound, to stun; **2** (Med) to stupefy.

stupeur /stypœʀ/ *nf* **1** astonishment; **2** (Med) stupor.

stupide /stypid/ *adj* stupid.

stupidité /stypidite/ *nf* **1** stupidity; **2** stupid remark.

style /stil/ *nm* **1** style; **~ de vie** lifestyle; **c'est bien ton ~ de faire** it's just like you to do; **2 meubles de ~** (reproduction) period furniture; **3** speech form; **~ indirect** indirect or reported speech.

stylé, **~e** /stile/ *adj* well-trained.

styliser /stilize/ [1] *vtr* to stylize.

styliste /stilist/ *nmf* fashion designer.

stylo /stilo/ *nm* (fountain) pen; **~ bille** ballpoint pen; **~ feutre** felt-tip pen.

su /sy/ *nm* **au vu et au ~ de tous** openly, for all to see.

suaire /sɥɛʀ/ *nm* shroud.

suave /sɥav/ *adj* [*perfume, music, smile*] sweet; [*voice*] mellifluous; [*person, manner*] suave.

subalterne /sybaltɛʀn/ **I** *adj* [*post*] junior; [*role*] subordinate; minor.
II *nmf* subordinate; (Mil) low-ranking officer, subaltern.

subconscient /sybkɔ̃sjɑ̃/ *nm* subconscious.

subdiviser /sybdivize/ [1] *vtr* to subdivide (**en** into).

subir /sybiʀ/ [3] *vtr* **1** to be subjected to [*violence, pressure*]; to suffer [*defeat, damage*]; **faire ~ à qn** to subject sb to [*abuse*]; to inflict [sth] on sb [*defeat, losses*]; **2** to take [*examination*]; to have [*operation, test*]; **~ l'influence de qn** to be under sb's influence; **3** to put up with; **4** to undergo.

subit, **~e** /sybi, it/ *adj* sudden.

subitement /sybitmɑ̃/ *adv* suddenly, all of a sudden.

subjectif, **-ive** /sybʒɛktif, iv/ *adj* subjective.

subjectivité /sybʒɛktivite/ *nf* subjectivity.

subjonctif /sybʒɔ̃ktif/ *nm* subjunctive.

subjuguer /sybʒyge/ [1] *vtr* **1** to captivate, to enthral[GB]; **2** to subjugate.

sublime /syblim/ *adj* sublime; **~ de générosité** extraordinarily generous.

sublimer /syblime/ [1] *vtr*, *vi* to sublimate.

submerger /sybmɛʀʒe/ [13] *vtr* **1** to submerge; **2** to flood [*market, switchboard*]; **3** [*crowd, emotion*] to overwhelm; **4 ~ qn de travail** to inundate sb with work; **être submergé d'appels** to be swamped with calls.

submersion /sybmɛʀsjɔ̃/ *nf* (of submarine) submersion; (of ship) sinking.

subordination /sybɔʀdinasjɔ̃/ *nf* subordination.

subordonné, **~e**[1] /sybɔʀdɔne/ *nm,f* subordinate.

subordonnée[2] /sybɔʀdɔne/ *nf* subordinate clause; **~ relative** relative clause.

subordonner /sybɔʀdɔne/ [1] *vtr* **1 être subordonné à qn** to be subordinate to sb; **2 être subordonné à qch** to be subject to or dependent on sth.

suborner /sybɔʀne/ [1] *vtr* to bribe [*witness*].

subreptice /sybʀɛptis/ *adj* surreptitious.

subside /sybsid/ *nm* **1** grant; **2** allowance.

subsidiaire /sybzidjɛʀ/ *adj* subsidiary; **question ~** tiebreaker.

subsistance /sybzistɑ̃s/ *nf* subsistence; (**moyens de**) **~** means of support; **assurer sa propre ~** to support oneself.

subsister /sybziste/ [1] *vi* **1** [*fear, doubt*] to remain; **2** [*custom*] to survive; **3 ça leur suffit à peine pour ~** it's barely enough for them to live on.

substance /sypstɑ̃s/ *nf* substance; **~s toxiques** toxic matter.

substantiel, **-ielle** /sypstɑ̃sjɛl/ *adj* substantial; [*progress*] significant.

substantif /sypstɑ̃tif/ *nm* noun, substantive.

substituer /sypstitɥe/ [1] **I** *vtr* to substitute, to replace.
II se substituer *v refl* (+ *v être*) **se ~ à** to take the place of.

substitut /sypstity/ *nm* **1** deputy public prosecutor; **2** substitute (**de** for).

substitution /sypstitysjɔ̃/ *nf* substitution; **produit de ~ du sucre** sugar substitute.

subterfuge /syptɛʀfyʒ/ *nm* ploy, subterfuge.

subtil, **~e** /syptil/ *adj* subtle; [*manoeuvre*] skilful[GB].

subtiliser /syptilize/ [1] *vtr* **~ qch à qn** to steal sth from sb.

subtilité /syptilite/ *nf* subtlety.

subvenir: **subvenir à** /sybvəniʀ/ [36] *v+prep*

to meet [*expenses, needs*]; **~ aux besoins de sa famille** to provide for one's family.

subvention /sybvɑ̃sjɔ̃/ *nf* **1** grant; **2** subsidy.

subventionner /sybvɑ̃sjɔne/ [1] *vtr* to subsidize.

subversif, -ive /sybvɛʀsif, iv/ *adj* subversive.

subversion /sybvɛʀsjɔ̃/ *nf* subversion.

suc /syk/ *nm* (of fruit) juice; (of plant) sap; **~s digestifs** or **gastriques** gastric juices.

succédané /syksedane/ *nm* substitute, ersatz (**de** for).

succéder /syksede/ [14] **I succéder à** *v+prep* **1** to succeed [*person*]; **2** to follow, to come after.
II se succéder *v refl* (+ *v être*) to succeed or follow one another.

succès /syksɛ/ *nm inv* success; **avoir du ~, être un ~** to be a success (**auprès de** with); [*record*] to be a hit (**auprès de** with); **connaître un grand ~** to be a great success; **à ~** [*actor, film*] successful.

successeur /syksesœʀ/ *nm* successor.

successif, -ive /syksesif, iv/ *adj* successive.

succession /syksesjɔ̃/ *nf* **1** (of people, misfortunes) succession; (of events, numbers) series; **2** succession; **prendre la ~ de** to succeed; **3** (Law) succession; inheritance, estate; **par voie de ~** through inheritance.

succinct, ~e /syksɛ̃, ɛ̃t/ *adj* [*essay*] succinct; [*speech*] brief; [*meal*] frugal.

succion /syksjɔ̃/ *nf* **1** suction; **2** (with mouth) sucking.

succomber /sykɔ̃be/ [1] *vi* **1** to die; **2** to give way, to yield; **~ sous le poids** to collapse under the weight; **~ sous le nombre** to be overwhelmed by numbers; **3 ~ à** to succumb to [*charm, despair*]; to give in to [*temptation*].

succulent, ~e /sykylɑ̃, ɑ̃t/ *adj* **1** delicious; **2 plante ~e** succulent.

succursale /sykyʀsal/ *nf* branch, outlet.

sucer /syse/ [12] *vtr* to suck.

sucette /sysɛt/ *nf* **1** lollipop, lolly°; **2** dummy (GB), pacifier (US).

suçoter /sysɔte/ [1] *vtr* to suck.

sucre /sykʀ/ *nm* **1** sugar; **2** sugar lump
■ **~ cristallisé** granulated sugar; **~ glace** icing sugar (GB), powdered sugar (US); **~ d'orge** stick of barley sugar, ≈ rock; **~ en poudre** caster sugar (GB), superfine sugar (US); **~ roux** brown sugar.
IDIOMS **être tout ~ tout miel** to be all sweetness and light; **casser du ~ sur le dos de qn** to run sb down, to badmouth sb°.

sucré, ~e /sykʀe/ *adj* **1** sweet; sweetened; **2** [*tone*] honeyed.

sucrer /sykʀe/ [1] *vtr* to put sugar in; to sweeten.

sucrerie /sykʀəʀi/ *nf* **1** sugar refinery; **2 ~s** sweets (GB).

sucrier /sykʀije/ *nm* sugar bowl; **~ verseur** sugar shaker.

sud /syd/ **I** *adj inv* south; southern.
II *nm* **1** south; **exposé au ~** south-facing; **le ~ de la France** the south of France; **2 le Sud** the South.

sudation /sydasjɔ̃/ *nf* sweating.

sud-est /sydɛst/ **I** *adj inv* southeast; southeastern.
II *nm* southeast; **le Sud-Est asiatique** South East Asia.

sud-ouest /sydwɛst/ **I** *adj inv* southwest; southwestern.
II *nm* southwest; **le ~ de la France** the southwest of France.

Suède /sɥɛd/ *pr nf* Sweden.

suédois, ~e /sɥedwa, az/ **I** *adj* Swedish.
II *nm* Swedish.

Suédois, ~e /sɥedwa, az/ *nm,f* Swede.

suer /sɥe/ [1] **I** *vtr* **1** to sweat; **~ sang et eau** to sweat blood and tears; **2 une ville qui sue l'ennui** an incredibly boring town.
II *vi* to sweat; **faire ~ qn°** to bore sb stiff°.

sueur /sɥœʀ/ *nf* sweat; **se mettre en ~** to break into a sweat; **j'en avais des ~s froides** I was in a cold sweat about it.

suffire /syfiʀ/ [64] **I** *vi* to be enough; **un rien suffit à le mettre en colère** it only takes the slightest thing to make him lose his temper.
II se suffire *v refl* (+ *v être*) **se ~ (à soi-même)** to be self-sufficient.
III *v impers* **il suffit de me téléphoner** all you have to do is phone me; **il suffit d'une lampe pour éclairer la pièce** one lamp is enough to light the room; **il suffit que je sorte sans parapluie pour qu'il pleuve!** every time I go out without my umbrella, it's guaranteed to rain; **ça suffit (comme ça)!** that's enough!

suffisamment /syfizamɑ̃/ *adv* enough; **~ fort** strong enough.

suffisance /syfizɑ̃s/ *nf* **1** self-importance; **2 avoir qch en ~** to have sufficient quantities of sth.

suffisant, ~e /syfizɑ̃, ɑ̃t/ *adj* **1** sufficient; **2** self-important.

suffixe /syfiks/ *nm* suffix.

suffocant, ~e /syfɔkɑ̃, ɑ̃t/ *adj* **1** suffocating; **2** staggering, astounding.

suffocation /syfɔkasjɔ̃/ *nf* suffocation; choking.

suffoquer /syfɔke/ [1] **I** *vtr* **1** to suffocate; **2° son aplomb m'a suffoqué** I was staggered by his/her cheek°.
II *vi* **1** to suffocate; **2** to choke (**de** with).

suffrage /syfʀaʒ/ *nm* suffrage; **~s exprimés** recorded votes; **recueillir tous les ~s** to meet with universal approval.

suggérer /sygʒeʀe/ [14] *vtr* to suggest.

suggestif, -ive /sygʒɛstif, iv/ *adj* [*music*] evocative; [*pose*] suggestive; [*dress*] provocative.

suggestion /sygʒɛstjɔ̃/ *nf* suggestion.

suicidaire /sɥisidɛʀ/ *adj* suicidal.

suicide /sɥisid/ *nm* suicide.

suicider: se suicider /sɥiside/ [1] *v refl* (+ *v être*) to commit suicide.

suie /sɥi/ *nf* soot.

suinter /sɥɛ̃te/ [1] *vi* **1** [*liquid*] to seep; to ooze; **2** [*walls*] to sweat; [*wound*] to weep.

suisse /sɥis/ I *adj* Swiss.
II *nm* **1** Swiss Guard; **2** verger.

Suisse /sɥis/ *pr nf* Switzerland.

suite /sɥit/ I *nf* **1** rest; **la ~ des événements** what happens next; **2** (of story) continuation; (of series) next instalment[GB]; (of meal) next course; **~ page 10** continued on page 10; **3** sequel; **4** result; **les ~s** (of action) the consequences; (of incident) the repercussions; (of illness) the after-effects; **5 donner ~ à** to follow up [*complaint*]; to deal with [*order*]; **rester sans ~** [*plan*] to be dropped; **6 faire ~ à** to follow upon [*incident*]; **prendre la ~ de qn** to take over from sb; **7 avoir de la ~ dans les idées** to be single-minded; **8** (of incidents) series; (of successes) run; **9** (hotel) suite; **10** (of king) suite; **11** (Mus) suite; **12** (in cards) run.
II **de suite** *phr* in succession, in a row; **et ainsi de ~** and so on.
III **par la suite** *phr* **1** afterward(s); **2** later.
IV **par suite de** *phr* due to.
V **à la suite de** *phr* **1** following; **2** behind.

suivant[1] /sɥivɑ̃/ *prep* **1** along [*dotted line*]; **2** in accordance with [*tradition*]; **~ leur habitude** as they usually do, as is their wont; **3** depending on; **4** according to.

suivant[2], **~e**[1] /sɥivɑ̃, ɑ̃t/ I *adj* **1** following; **2** next.
II *nm,f* **le ~** the following one; the next one.
III **le suivant, la suivante** *phr* as follows.

suivante[2] /sɥivɑ̃t/ *nf* lady's maid.

suivi, **~e** /sɥivi/ I *pp* ▶ **suivre**.
II *pp adj* **1** [*work*] steady; [*effort*] sustained; [*correspondence*] regular; **2 c'est une mode très ~e** it's a fashion which has really caught on; **3** [*argument, policy*] coherent.
III *nm* **1** monitoring; **2** follow-up; **~ des malades** follow-up care for patients.

suivre /sɥivʀ/ [62] I *vtr* **1** to follow [*person, car*]; **ta réputation t'a suivi jusqu'ici** your reputation has preceded you; **suivez le guide!** this way, please!; **2** to follow, to come after [*period, incident*]; **'à ~'** 'to be continued'; **3** to follow [*route, coast*]; [*road*] to run alongside [*railway line*]; **quelle est la marche à ~?** what is the best way to go about it?; **~ le droit chemin** to keep to the straight and narrow; **4** to follow [*example*]; to obey [*impulse*]; **5** to follow [*lesson, match*]; to follow the progress of [*pupil, patient*]; **~ l'actualité** to keep up with the news; **c'est une affaire à ~** it's something worth watching; **6** to do [*course*]; **7** to follow [*explanation, logic*]; **je vous suis** I'm with you; **8** to keep pace with [sb/sth].
II *vi* **1 faire ~ son courrier** to have one's mail forwarded; **faire ~** please forward; **2** (in poker) **je suis** I'm in.
III **se suivre** *v refl* (+ *v être*) **1** [*numbers, pages*] to be in order; [*cards*] to be consecutive; **2** to happen one after the other; **se ~ de près** [*siblings*] to be close in age.
IV *v impers* **comme suit** as follows.

sujet, **-ette** /syʒɛ, ɛt/ I *adj* **être ~ à** to be prone to [*migraine*]; **~ à caution** questionable.
II *nm* **1** subject; **un ~ d'actualité** a topical issue; **c'est à quel ~?** what is it about?; **au ~ de** about; **2** (Sch) question; **~ libre** topic of one's own choice; **hors ~** off the subject; **3** cause; **c'est un ~ d'étonnement** it is amazing; **4 les ~s âgés** the elderly; **c'est un brillant ~** he's a brilliant student; **5** (of kingdom) subject.

sujétion /syʒesjɔ̃/ *nf* **1** subjection; **2** constraint.

sulfate /sylfat/ *nm* sulphate[GB]; **~ de cuivre** copper sulphate[GB].

sulfureux, **-euse** /sylfyʀø, øz/ *adj* [*vapour*] sulphurous[GB]; [*bath*] sulphur[GB].

sultan /syltɑ̃/ *nm* sultan.

sultane /syltan/ *nf* sultana.

summum /sɔm(m)ɔm/ *nm* height.

sumo /sumo, symo/ *nm inv* sumo wrestling.

super[1] /sypɛʀ/ *pref* super.

super[2] /sypɛʀ/ I○ *adj inv* great○.
II *nm* four-star (petrol) (GB), super.
III○ *excl* great○!

superbe /sypɛʀb/ *adj* superb, magnificent; [*person*] superb-looking.

superbement /sypɛʀbəmɑ̃/ *adv* **1** superbly; **2** haughtily.

supercarburant /sypɛʀkaʀbyʀɑ̃/ *nm* four-star petrol (GB), super.

supercherie /sypɛʀʃəʀi/ *nf* **1** deception; **2** hoax.

superficie /sypɛʀfisi/ *nf* area.

superficiel, **-ielle** /sypɛʀfisjɛl/ *adj* (gen) superficial; [*layer*] surface.

superflu, **~e** /sypɛʀfly/ I *adj* **1** superfluous; **2** unnecessary.
II *nm* surplus; **s'offrir le ~** to treat oneself to luxuries.

supérieur, **~e** /sypeʀjœʀ/ I *adj* **1** [*jaw, lip*] upper; [*level, floor*] upper, top; **2** [*ranks, classes*] upper; **3** [*temperature, speed, cost, salary*] higher (**à** than); [*size*] bigger (**à** than); [*length*] longer (**à** than); **4** [*work, quality*] superior (**à** to); **5** [*air, tone*] superior.
II *nm,f* **1** superior; **~ hiérarchique** immediate superior; **2** (in monastery, convent) Superior.
III *nm* higher education.

supériorité /sypeʀjɔʀite/ *nf* superiority.

superlatif, **-ive** /sypɛʀlatif, iv/ *adj, nm* superlative.

supermarché /sypɛʀmaʀʃe/ *nm* supermarket.

superposer /sypɛʀpoze/ [1] *vtr* **1** to stack [sth] (up); **lits superposés** bunk beds; **2** to superimpose [*drawings*].

superposition /sypɛʀpozisjɔ̃/ *nf* superposition.

superproduction /sypɛʀpʀɔdyksjɔ̃/ *nf* blockbuster○.

superpuissance /sypɛʀpɥisɑ̃s/ *nf* superpower.

supersonique /sypɛʀsɔnik/ *adj* supersonic.

superstitieux, -ieuse /sypɛʀstisjø, øz/ *adj* superstitious.

superstition /sypɛʀstisjɔ̃/ *nf* superstition.

superviser /sypɛʀvize/ [1] *vtr* to supervise.

supplanter /syplɑ̃te/ [1] *vtr* to supplant.

suppléance /sypleɑ̃s/ *nf* temporary replacement post; (in school) supply (GB) or substitute (US) post.

suppléant, ~e /sypleɑ̃, ɑ̃t/ *nm,f* replacement; (for judge) deputy; (for teacher) supply (GB) or substitute (US) teacher; (for doctor) locum.

suppléer: **suppléer à** /syplee/ [11] *v+prep* to make up for, to compensate for.

supplément /syplemɑ̃/ *nm* **1** extra or additional charge; supplement; **le vin est en ~** the wine is extra; **2 ~ d'informations** additional information; **3** (newspaper) supplement.

supplémentaire /syplemɑ̃tɛʀ/ *adj* additional, extra; **train ~** relief train.

suppliant, ~e /syplijɑ̃, ɑ̃t/ *adj* [*voice*] pleading; [*look*] imploring.

supplication /syplikasjɔ̃/ *nf* plea.

supplice /syplis/ *nm* torture; **subir un ~** to be tortured; to be in torment; **j'étais au ~** it was agony.

supplicier /syplisje/ [2] *vtr* **1** to torture; **2** to execute.

supplier /syplije/ [2] *vtr* to beg, to beseech.

supplique /syplik/ *nf* petition; **céder aux ~s de qn** to give in to sb's entreaties.

support /sypɔʀ/ *nm* **1** support; **servir de ~ à qch** to serve as a support for sth; **2** (for ornaments) stand; **3** back-up; **~ audiovisuel** audio-visual aid.

supportable /sypɔʀtabl/ *adj* bearable.

supporter[1] /sypɔʀte/ [1] **I** *vtr* **1** to support, to bear the weight of [*structure*]; **2** to bear [*costs*]; **3** to put up with [*misery, behaviour, person*]; to bear, to endure [*suffering, loneliness*], [*plant*] to withstand [*cold*]; **elle ne supporte pas d'attendre** she can't stand waiting; **il a bien supporté son opération** he came through the operation well.

II se supporter *v refl* (+ *v être*) **ils ne peuvent plus se ~** they can't stand each other any more.

supporter[2] /sypɔʀtœʀ/ *nmf* supporter.

supposer /sypoze/ [1] *vtr* **1** to suppose (**que** that); **2** to assume (**que** that); **3** to presuppose (**que** that).

supposition /sypozisjɔ̃/ *nf* supposition, assumption.

suppositoire /sypozitwaʀ/ *nm* suppository.

suppôt /sypo/ *nm* **un ~ de la réaction** a reactionary; **~ de Satan** fiend.

suppression /sypʀesjɔ̃/ *nf* removal; abolition; withdrawal; suppression; elimination; breaking, ending; deletion; **~s d'emplois** job cuts.

supprimer /sypʀime/ [1] **I** *vtr* **1** to cut [*job*]; to stop [*aid, vibration*]; to abolish [*tax, law, censorship, institution*]; to remove [*effect, obstacle*]; to do away with [*examination, class*]; to put an end to [*poverty, discrimination*]; to withdraw [*subsidy, licence*]; to break, to end [*monopoly*]; to eliminate [*nuisance, fault, waste*]; to suppress [*evidence*]; to cut out [*sugar, salt*]; to delete [*word, line*]; **~ un train** to cancel a train; to discontinue a service; **2** to eliminate [*person*].

II se supprimer *v refl* (+ *v être*) to do away with oneself.

suppurer /sypyʀe/ [1] *vi* to suppurate.

supputer /sypyte/ [1] *vtr* to calculate, to work out; **~ ses chances de réussite** to weigh up one's chances of success.

suprématie /sypʀemasi/ *nf* supremacy.

suprême /sypʀɛm/ *adj* supreme.

sur[1] /syʀ/ *prep* **1** on; **~ la table** on the table; **prends un verre ~ la table** take a glass from the table; **appliquer la lotion ~ vos cheveux** apply the lotion to your hair; **la clé est ~ la porte** the key is in the door; **passer la main ~ une étoffe** to run one's hand over a fabric; **écrire ~ du papier** to write on paper; **elle est ~ la photo** she's in the photograph; **dessiner ~ le sable** to draw in the sand; **2** over; **un pont ~ la rivière** a bridge across or over the river; **3 une table d'un mètre ~ deux** a table that measures one metre[GB] by two; **~ 150 hectares** over an area of 150 hectares; **4 se diriger ~ Valence** to head or make for Valence; **5** [*debate, essay, thesis*] on; [*poem*] about; **6 être ~ une affaire** to be involved in a business deal; **7 une personne ~ dix** one person out of or in ten; **une semaine ~ trois** one week in three; **un mardi ~ deux** every other Tuesday; **8 faire proposition ~ proposition** to make one offer after another; **9 ils se sont quittés ~ ces mots** with these words, they parted; **~ le moment** at the time; **~ ce or quoi** upon which, thereupon; **~ ce, je vous laisse** with that, I must leave you.

sur[2], **~e** /syʀ/ *adj* (slightly) sour.

sûr, ~e /syʀ/ **I** *adj* **1** [*information, service, person*] reliable; [*opinion, investment*] sound; **d'une main ~e** with a steady hand; **2** safe; **peu ~** unsafe; **3** certain; **c'est ~ et certain** it's definite; **à coup ~** definitely, for sure; **4** sure; **j'en suis ~ et certain** I'm positive (about it); **il est ~ de lui** he's self-confident, he's sure of himself; **j'en étais ~!** I knew it!

II *adv* **bien ~ (que oui)** of course.

IDIOMS **être ~ de son coup**○ to be confident of success.

surabondance /syʀabɔ̃dɑ̃s/ *nf* overabundance.

surabonder /syʀabɔ̃de/ [1] *vi* to abound (**de, en** in, with).

suraigu, -uë /syʀegy/ *adj* [*sound*] very shrill; [*pain*] very sharp.

suranné, ~e /syʀane/ *adj* [*ideas*] outmoded; [*style*] outdated.

surcharge /syʀʃaʀʒ/ *nf* excess load, overload; **une ~ de travail** extra work.

surcharger /syʀʃaʀʒe/ [13] *vtr* to overload; **~ qn de travail** to overburden sb with work.

surchauffer /syʀʃofe/ [1] *vtr* to overheat.

surclasser /syʀklase/ [1] *vtr* to outclass.

surcroît /syʀkʀwa/ *nm* increase; **un ~ de travail** extra work; **de ~** moreover.

surdité /syʀdite/ *nf* deafness.

surdoué, **~e** /syʀdwe/ *adj* (exceptionally) gifted.

sureau, *pl* **~x** /syʀo/ *nm* elder (tree).

sureffectif /syʀefɛktif/ *nm* excess or surplus staff.

surélever /syʀelve/ [16] *vtr* to raise the height of [*house, road*].

sûrement /syʀmɑ̃/ *adv* **1** most probably; **2 ~ pas** certainly not; **3** safely.

surenchère /syʀɑ̃ʃɛʀ/ *nf* **1** higher bid; **2 une ~ de violence** an escalation of violence; **faire de la ~** to try to go one better.

surenchérir /syʀɑ̃ʃeʀiʀ/ [3] *vi* **1** to make a higher bid; **~ sur une offre** to raise the bidding; **2** to add; to chime in.

surendettement /syʀɑ̃dɛtmɑ̃/ *nm* excessive debt.

surestimer /syʀɛstime/ [1] **I** *vtr* to overvalue [*property*]; to overestimate [*cost*]; to overrate [*qualities*].

II se surestimer *v refl* (+ *v être*) to rate oneself too highly.

sûreté /syʀte/ *nf* **1** (of place, person) safety; (of country) security; **être en ~** to be in a safe place; **2** (of judgment) soundness; (of gesture) steadiness; **3** (on gun) safety catch; (on door) safety lock.

surexciter /syʀɛksite/ [1] *vtr* to overexcite; **foule surexcitée** highly excited crowd.

surf /sœʀf/ *nm* surfing; **faire du ~** to go surfing.

surface /syʀfas/ *nf* **1** surface; **en ~** on the surface; **de ~** [*mail*] surface; [*installations*] above ground; [*friendliness*] superficial; **faire ~** to surface; **2** surface area; **en ~** in area.

surfait, **~e** /syʀfɛ, ɛt/ *adj* [*person, work*] overrated; [*reputation*] inflated.

surfer /sœʀfe/ [1] *vi* to go surfing.

surfiler /syʀfile/ [1] *vtr* to oversew.

surgelé, **~e** /syʀʒəle/ *adj* deep-frozen; **les produits ~s** frozen food.

surgeler /syʀʒəle/ [17] *vtr* to deep-freeze.

surgénérateur /syʀʒeneʀatœʀ/ *nm* fast-breeder reactor.

surgir /syʀʒiʀ/ [3] *vi* [*person*] to appear suddenly; [*difficulty*] to crop up; **faire ~** to spark, to raise [*fears*]; **faire ~ la vérité** to bring the truth to light.

surhomme /syʀɔm/ *nm* superman.

surhumain, **~e** /syʀymɛ̃, ɛn/ *adj* superhuman.

surimposer /syʀɛ̃poze/ [1] *vtr* **1** to surtax; **2** to overtax.

surimpression /syʀɛ̃pʀesjɔ̃/ *nf* double exposure; **en ~** superimposed.

sur-le-champ /syʀləʃɑ̃/ *adv* right away.

surlendemain /syʀlɑ̃d(ə)mɛ̃/ *nm* **le ~** two days later.

surligner /syʀliɲe/ [1] *vtr* to highlight.

surmenage /syʀmənaʒ/ *nm* overwork.

surmener /syʀmene/ [16] **I** *vtr* to overwork.

II se surmener *v refl* (+ *v être*) to push oneself too hard.

surmontable /syʀmɔ̃tabl/ *adj* surmountable.

surmonter /syʀmɔ̃te/ [1] *vtr* **1** to overcome [*obstacle, crisis*]; **2 être surmonté de qch** to be topped or surmounted by sth.

surnaturel, **-elle** /syʀnatyʀɛl/ *adj* **1** supernatural; **2** eerie.

surnom /syʀnɔ̃/ *nm* nickname.

surnombre /syʀnɔ̃bʀ/ *nm* **en ~** [*objects*] surplus; [*employee*] redundant; [*staff*] excess; [*passenger*] extra.

surnommer /syʀnɔme/ [1] *vtr* to nickname.

surpasser /syʀpase/ [1] **I** *vtr* to surpass, to outdo.

II se surpasser *v refl* (+ *v être*) to surpass oneself, to excel oneself.

surpeuplé, **~e** /syʀpœple/ *adj* **1** overpopulated; **2** overcrowded.

surpeuplement /syʀpœpləmɑ̃/ *nm* **1** overpopulation; **2** overcrowding.

surplace /syʀplas/ *nm inv* **faire du ~** (in traffic jam) to be stuck; (in work, inquiry) to be getting nowhere; (in cycling) to do a track stand.

surplomb /syʀplɔ̃/ *nm* overhang; **en ~** overhanging.

surplomber /syʀplɔ̃be/ [1] *vtr* to overhang, to jut out over.

surplus /syʀply/ *nm inv* (of goods) surplus; (of enthusiasm, work) excess; **au ~** moreover.

surpopulation /syʀpɔpylasjɔ̃/ *nf* overpopulation.

surprenant, **~e** /syʀpʀənɑ̃, ɑ̃t/ *adj* surprising; amazing; **n'avoir rien de ~** to be hardly surprising.

surprendre /syʀpʀɑ̃dʀ/ [52] **I** *vtr* **1** to surprise; **il sait ~ son monde** he never fails to surprise; **2** to take [sb] by surprise; **se laisser ~ par la pluie** to get caught in the rain; **3** to catch [*thief*]; **4** to overhear [*conversation*]; to intercept [*smile*].

II *vi* [*behaviour*] to be surprising; [*show*] to surprise; [*person*] to surprise people; **avoir de quoi ~** to be somewhat surprising.

surprise /syʀpʀiz/ *nf* surprise; **créer la ~** to cause a stir; **on veut leur faire une ~** we want it to be a surprise; **il m'a fait la ~ de venir me voir** he came to see me as a surprise; **avoir la bonne ~ d'apprendre que** to be pleasantly surprised to hear that; **voyage sans ~** uneventful trip; **gagner sans ~** to win as expected.

surproduction /syʀpʀɔdyksjɔ̃/ *nf* overproduction.

surréalisme /suʀ(ʀ)ealism/ *nm* surrealism.

surréaliste /suʀ(ʀ)ealist/ **I** *adj* **1** surrealist; **2** [*landscape, vision*] surreal.

II *nmf* surrealist.

sursaut /syʀso/ *nm* **1** start; **en ~** with a start; **2** (of energy, enthusiasm) sudden burst; (of pride, indignation) flash; **dans un dernier ~** in a final spurt of effort.

sursauter /syʀsote/ [1] *vi* to jump, to start.

surseoir /syʀswaʀ/ [41] *vtr* to postpone [*decision*]; to defer [*payment*]; to stay [*judgment, execution*].

sursis /syʀsi/ *nm inv* **1** respite; **2** (Law) suspended sentence; **3** (Mil) deferment of military service.

surtaxe /syʀtaks/ *nf* surcharge.

surtout /syʀtu/ *adv* above all; **~ quand/que** especially when/as; **~ pas!** certainly not!

surveillance /syʀvɛjɑ̃s/ *nf* **1** watch; (police) surveillance; **déjouer la ~ de qn** to escape detection by sb; **2** supervision; **sous ~ médicale** under medical supervision; **3** (Mil) monitoring.

surveillant, **~e** /syʀvɛjɑ̃, ɑ̃t/ *nm,f* **1** (Sch) supervisor; **2 ~ de prison** prison warder (GB) or guard; **3** store detective.

■ **~ de baignade** lifeguard.

surveiller /syʀveje/ [1] **I** *vtr* **1** (gen) to watch, to keep an eye on; to keep watch on [*building*]; **2** to supervise [*work, pupils*]; to monitor [*ceasefire, progress*]; **3 ~ sa santé** to take care of one's health.

II se surveiller *v refl* (+ *v être*) to watch oneself.

survenir /syʀvəniʀ/ [36] *vi* (+ *v être*) [*death, storm*] to occur; [*difficulty, conflict*] to arise.

survêtement /syʀvɛtmɑ̃/ *nm* tracksuit.

survie /syʀvi/ *nf* survival; **~ en mer** survival at sea.

survivance /syʀvivɑ̃s/ *nf* survival.

survivant, **~e** /syʀvivɑ̃, ɑ̃t/ *nm,f* survivor.

survivre /syʀvivʀ/ [63] **I survivre à** *v+prep* [*person*] to survive [*event, injuries*]; to outlive, to survive [*person*]; [*work, influence*] to outlast [*person*].

II *vi* to survive.

survol /syʀvɔl/ *nm* **1** flying over; **2** synopsis (**de** of).

survoler /syʀvɔle/ [1] *vtr* **1** to fly over [*place*]; **2** to skim through [*book*]; to do a quick review of [*problem*].

survolté○, **~e** /syʀvɔlte/ *adj* **1** overexcited; **2** [*circuit*] boosted.

sus: **en sus** /ɑ̃sys/ *phr* **être en ~** to be extra; **en ~ de** on top of; in addition to.

susceptibilité /sysɛptibilite/ *nf* touchiness.

susceptible /sysɛptibl/ *adj* **1** touchy; **2 ~ de faire** likely to do.

susciter /sysite/ [1] *vtr* **1** to spark off [*reaction, debate*]; to create [*problem*]; **2** to arouse [*enthusiasm, interest*]; to give rise to [*fear*].

suspect, **~e** /syspɛ, ɛkt/ **I** *adj* [*death, smell, object*] suspicious; [*information, logic*] dubious; [*foodstuff, honesty, enthusiasm*] suspect; [*person*] suspicious-looking.

II *nm,f* suspect.

suspecter /syspɛkte/ [1] *vtr* to suspect.

suspendre /syspɑ̃dʀ/ [6] **I** *vtr* **1** to hang up; **être suspendu aux lèvres de qn** to be hanging on sb's every word; **2** to suspend [*programme, payment*]; to end [*strike*]; to adjourn [*session, inquiry*]; to stop [*transmission*]; **~ son souffle** to hold one's breath; **3** to suspend [*official, athlete*].

II se suspendre *v refl* (+ *v être*) to hang; **se ~ à une corde** to hang from a rope.

suspens: **en suspens** /ɑ̃syspɑ̃/ *phr* **1 laisser qch en ~** to leave sth unresolved [*question*]; to leave sth unfinished [*work*]; **2 tenir qn en ~** to keep sb in suspense; **3** hanging in the air.

suspense /syspɛns/ *nm* suspense; **film** or **roman à ~** thriller.

suspension /syspɑ̃sjɔ̃/ *nf* **1** (gen, Tech) suspension; **2** (of aid, work) suspension; (of session, trial) adjournment; **être condamné à deux ans de ~ du permis de conduire** to be disqualified (GB) or suspended (US) from driving for two years; **3 en ~** [*particles*] in suspension; **4** pendant, ceiling light.

suspicion /syspisjɔ̃/ *nf* suspicion; **avec ~** suspiciously.

sustenter: **se sustenter** /systɑ̃te/ [1] *v refl* (+ *v être*) to have a little snack.

susurrer /sysyʀe/ [1] *vtr, vi* to whisper.

suture /sytyʀ/ *nf* suture; **point de ~** stitch.

suzerain, **~e** /syzʀɛ̃, ɛn/ *nm,f* suzerain, overlord.

suzeraineté /syzʀɛnte/ *nf* suzerainty.

svelte /svɛlt/ *adj* slender.

sveltesse /svɛltɛs/ *nf* slenderness.

SVP (*written abbr* = **s'il vous plaît**) please.

syllabe /sil(l)ab/ *nf* syllable.

syllabique /sil(l)abik/ *adj* syllabic.

syllogisme /silɔʒism/ *nm* syllogism.

sylviculture /silvikyltyʀ/ *nf* forestry.

symbiose /sɛ̃bjoz/ *nf* symbiosis.

symbole /sɛ̃bɔl/ *nm* **1** symbol; **2** creed.

symbolique /sɛ̃bɔlik/ *adj* **1** [*action, significance*] symbolic; **2** [*gesture, salary*] token; [*price*] nominal.

symboliser /sɛ̃bɔlize/ [1] *vtr* to symbolize.

symétrie /simetʀi/ *nf* symmetry (**par rapport à** in relation to).

symétrique /simetʀik/ *adj* **1** [*design, face*] symmetrical; **2** [*relation*] symmetric.

sympa○ /sɛ̃pa/ *adj inv* nice.

sympathie /sɛ̃pati/ *nf* **1 avoir de la ~ pour qn** to like sb; **montrer de la ~ à qn** to be friendly toward(s) sb; **2** sympathy; **mes ~s vont aux...** my sympathies lie with...; **croyez à toute ma ~** you have my deepest sympathy.

sympathique /sɛ̃patik/ *adj* nice; pleasant.

sympathisant, **~e** /sɛ̃patizɑ̃, ɑ̃t/ *nm,f* sympathizer.

sympathiser /sɛ̃patize/ [1] *vi* to get on well (**avec qn** with sb).

symphonie /sɛ̃fɔni/ *nf* symphony.

symphonique /sɛ̃fɔnik/ *adj* symphonic.

symptomatique /sɛ̃ptɔmatik/ *adj* symptomatic.

symptôme /sɛ̃ptom/ *nm* symptom.

synagogue /sinagɔg/ *nf* synagogue.

synchroniser /sɛ̃kʀɔnize/ [1] *vtr* to synchronize.

syncope /sɛ̃kɔp/ *nf* **1** fainting fit; **tomber en ~** to faint; **2** (Mus) syncopation.

syndic /sɛ̃dik/ *nm* (of building) property manager.

syndical, ~e, *mpl* **-aux** /sɛ̃dikal, o/ *adj* (trade) union.

syndicalisme /sɛ̃dikalism/ *nm* **1** trade unionism; **2** union activities.

syndicaliste /sɛ̃dikalist/ *nmf* union activist.

syndicat /sɛ̃dika/ *nm* **1** trade union; **2** (employers') association.
■ **~ d'initiative** tourist information office.

syndiqué, ~e /sɛ̃dike/ *adj* **être ~** to be a union member.

syndiquer: **se syndiquer**/sɛ̃dike/ [1] *v refl* (+ *v être*) to join a union.

syndrome /sɛ̃dʀom/ *nm* syndrome.
■ **~ immunodéficitaire acquis** acquired immunodeficiency syndrome.

synonyme /sinɔnim/ **I** *adj* synonymous (**de** with).
II *nm* synonym (**de** for, of); **dictionnaire de ~s** ≈ thesaurus.

synovie /sinɔvi/ *nf* **avoir un épanchement de ~** to have water on the knee.

syntaxe /sɛ̃taks/ *nf* syntax.

synthèse /sɛ̃tɛz/ *nf* **1** synthesis; **esprit de ~** ability to synthesize; **2 produit de ~** synthetic product; **3 images de ~** computer-generated images.

synthétique /sɛ̃tetik/ *adj* **1** synthetic; **2** [*vision*] global.

synthétiseur /sɛ̃tetizœʀ/ *nm* synthesizer.

syphilis /sifilis/ *nf inv* syphilis.

systématique /sistematik/ *adj* [*classification, refusal*] systematic.

système /sistɛm/ *nm* **1** system; **~ de canaux** canal system or network; **prenons l'avion, c'est encore le meilleur ~** let's go by plane, it's still the best way; **2 ~ pileux** hair.
■ **le ~ D**○ resourcefulness; **~ monétaire européen, SME** European Monetary System, EMS.
IDIOMS **taper sur le ~ de qn**○ to get on sb's nerves or wick○ (GB).

systémique /sistemik/ *adj* systematic.

Tt

t, **T** /te/ *nm inv* t, T; **en (forme de) T** T-shaped.

t' ▶ **te**.

ta ▶ **ton**[1].

tabac /taba/ *nm* **1** tobacco; **2** tobacconist's (GB), smoke shop (US); **3**○ big hit; **faire un ~** to be a big hit; **4** (Naut) **coup de ~** squall.
■ **~ blond** Virginia tobacco; **~ brun** dark tobacco; **~ à priser** snuff.
IDIOMS **passer qn à ~**○ to beat sb up.

tabagisme /tabaʒism/ *nm* tobacco addiction.

tabasser◑ /tabase/ [1] *vtr* to give [sb] a beating; **se faire ~** to get a beating.

tabatière /tabatjɛʀ/ *nf* **1** snuffbox; **2** skylight.

tabernacle /tabɛʀnakl/ *nm* tabernacle

table /tabl/ *nf* **1** table; **mettre** or **dresser la ~** to set or lay the table; **bien se tenir à ~** to have good table manners; **nous étions toujours à ~ quand**... we were still eating when...; **passer** or **se mettre à ~** to sit down at the table; (figurative)○ to spill the beans○; **2 ~ des négociations** negotiating table; **s'asseoir autour d'une ~** to get round the table; **3 ~ de logarithmes** log table.
■ **~ basse** coffee table; **~ de chevet** bedside table (GB), night stand (US); **~ d'écoute** wiretapping set; **être mis sur ~ d'écoute** to have one's phone tapped; **~ des matières** (table of) contents; **~ de mixage** mixing desk; **~ de nuit** = **~ de chevet**; **~ d'orientation** viewpoint diagram; **~ ronde** round table.
IDIOMS **mettre les pieds sous la ~** to let others wait on you.

tableau, *pl* **~x** /tablo/ *nm* **1** picture; painting; **2** (description) picture; **en plus, il était ivre, tu vois un peu le ~**○! on top of that he was drunk, you can just imagine!; **3** table, chart; **'voir ~'** 'see table'; **4** (Sch) blackboard; **5** (displaying information) (gen) board; (for trains) indicator board; **~ horaire** timetable; **6** (in theatre) short scene.
■ **~ d'affichage** notice board; **~ de bord** (in car) dashboard; (on plane, train) instrument panel; **~ de chasse** (in hunting) total number of kills; (figurative) list of conquests.
IDIOMS **jouer sur les deux ~x** to hedge one's bets.

tabler /table/ [1] *vi* **~ sur** to bank○ on.

tablette /tablɛt/ *nf* **1** (of chocolate) bar; (of chewing-gum) stick; **2** shelf.

tablier /tablije/ *nm* **1** apron; **2** roadway.
IDIOMS **rendre son ~** to give in (GB) or give (US) one's notice.

tabloïd /tablɔid/ *adj, nm* tabloid.

tabou /tabu/ **I** *adj* **1** taboo; **2** [*institution, person*] untouchable, sacred.
II *nm* taboo.

tabouret /tabuʀɛ/ *nm* stool.

tac /tak/ *nm* **répondre du ~ au ~** to answer as quick as a flash.

tache /taʃ/ *nf* **1** stain; **~ d'encre** (gen) ink stain; (on manuscript) ink blot; **~ d'humidité** damp patch; **faire ~** (figurative) to stick out like a sore thumb; **2** (figurative) stain, blot; **sans ~** [*reputation*] spotless; **3** (on fruit) mark; (on skin) blotch, mark; **4** (of colour) spot; patch.
■ **~ de naissance** birthmark; **~s de rousseur** or **son** freckles.
IDIOMS **faire ~ d'huile** to spread like wildfire.

tâche /tɑʃ/ *nf* task, job; **tu ne me facilites pas la ~!** you're not making my job any easier!; **les ~s ménagères** household chores.

tacher /taʃe/ [1] **I** *vtr* **1** [*substance*] to stain; [*person*] to get a stain on [*garment*]; **2** to tarnish, to stain [*reputation*].
II *vi* to stain; **ça ne tache pas** it doesn't stain.

tâcher: **tâcher de** /tɑʃe/ [1] *v+prep* **~ de faire** to try to do.

tacheter /taʃte/ [20] *vtr* to speckle, to spot [*fur*]; to dot [*meadow*].

tacite /tasit/ *adj* tacit.

taciturne /tasityʀn/ *adj* taciturn.

tact /takt/ *nm* tact; **manquer de ~** to be tactless; **avec ~** tactfully.

tactile /taktil/ *adj* [*sense*] tactile.

tactique /taktik/ **I** *adj* (gen, Mil) tactical; **erreur ~** tactical error.
II *nf* **une ~ de vente** a sales tactic; **la ~** tactics.

taie /tɛ/ *nf* **~ (d'oreiller)** pillowcase; **~ (de traversin)** bolstercase.

taillader /tajade/ [1] *vtr* to slash; **~ une table** to make slashes on a table top.

taille /taj/ *nf* **1** waist, waistline; **2** size; **de grande/petite ~** [*animal, company, object*] large/small; **de ~** [*problem, ambition*] considerable; [*event, question*] very important; **être de ~ à faire** to be up to or capable of doing; **3** (of garment) size; **~ 42** size 42; **quelle ~ fais-tu?** what size do you take?; **'~ unique'** 'one size'; **essaie la ~ au-dessus** try the next size up; **avoir la ~ mannequin** to be a standard size; **4** height; **être de grande/petite ~** to be tall/short; **5** (of tree, shrub) pruning; (of hedge) clipping, trimming; (of diamond, glass) cutting; (of wood) carving.

taillé, **~e** /taje/ **I** *pp* ▶ **tailler**.
II *pp adj* **1 ~ en athlète** built like an athlete; **2 être ~ pour faire** to be cut out to do.

taille-crayons /tajkʀɛjɔ̃/ *nm inv* pencil sharpener.

tailler /taje/ [1] **I** *vtr* **1** to cut [*ruby, glass, marble*]; to carve [*wood*]; to sharpen [*pencil*]; to prune [*tree, shrub*]; to cut, to clip [*hedge*]; to trim [*hair, beard*]; **bien taillé** [*moustache, hedge*] neatly trimmed; [*jacket*] well-cut; **2** to cut [*steak*] (**dans** from); to carve [*sculpture*]; to cut out [*garment*]; **taillé sur mesure** [*garment*] made-to-measure (GB), custom-made; (figurative) [*role*] tailor-made.

II *vi* **~ grand/petit** [*garment*] to be cut on the large/small side.

III se tailler *v refl* (+ *v être*) **1** to carve out [sth] for oneself [*career, empire*]; to make [sth] for oneself [*reputation*]; **2**° to beat it°.

tailleur /tajœʀ/ *nm* **1** (woman's) suit; **2** tailor; **s'asseoir en ~** to sit down cross-legged.

■ **~ de pierre** stone-cutter.

taillis /taji/ *nm inv* **1** undergrowth; **2** coppice.

tain /tɛ̃/ *nm* silvering; **glace** or **miroir sans ~** two-way mirror.

taire /tɛʀ/ [59] **I** *vtr* **1** not to reveal [*name, secret*]; to hush up [*truth*]; **2** to keep [sth] to oneself [*sadness, resentment*].

II se taire *v refl* (+ *v être*) **1** [*person*] to be silent, to say nothing; **2** [*person*] to stop talking; [*bird*] to fall silent; [*journalist, opposition*] to fall silent; **faire ~** to make [sb] be quiet [*pupils*]; to silence [*opponent, media*] ; to put a stop to [*rumours, sarcasm*]; **tais-toi!** be quiet!; **3** [*noise, music*] to stop; [*guns, orchestra*] to fall silent.

talc /talk/ *nm* **1** talc, talcum powder; **2** talc(um).

talent /talɑ̃/ *nm* **1** talent; **de ~** talented; **2 un jeune ~** a talented young person.

talentueux, -euse /talɑ̃tɥø, øz/ *adj* talented, gifted.

talisman /talismɑ̃/ *nm* talisman.

talkie-walkie, *pl* **talkies-walkies** /toki woki/ *nm* walkie-talkie.

talon /talɔ̃/ *nm* **1** (of foot, shoe) heel; **2** (of cheque, ticket) stub; **3** (in cards) pile.

■ **~ aiguille** stiletto heel.

IDIOMS **être sur les ~s de qn** to be hard or hot on sb's heels.

talonner /talɔne/ [1] *vtr* **1 ~ qn** to be hot on sb's heels; **2** [*person*] to badger [*person*]; [*hunger, anxiety*] to torment [*person*].

talonnette /talɔnɛt/ *nf* lift (in a shoe).

talquer /talke/ [1] *vtr* to put talcum powder on.

talus /taly/ *nm inv* **1** embankment; **2** bank, slope.

tamanoir /tamanwaʀ/ *nm* anteater.

tambour /tɑ̃buʀ/ *nm* **1** drum; **mener qch ~ battant** (figurative) to deal with sth briskly; **2** (of washing machine, brake) drum.

tambourin /tɑ̃buʀɛ̃/ *nm* tambourine.

tambouriner /tɑ̃buʀine/ [1] *vi* **~ à la porte de qn** to hammer on sb's door.

tamis /tami/ *nm inv* sieve; **passer qch au ~** to sieve, to sift [*flour*].

Tamise /tamiz/ *pr nf* **la ~** the Thames.

tamiser /tamize/ [1] *vtr* to sieve, to sift [*sand, flour*]; to filter [*light, colours*]; **lumières tamisées** subdued lighting.

tampon /tɑ̃pɔ̃/ *nm* **1** (in office) stamp; **~ (encreur)** (ink) pad; **2** (for sponging) (gen) pad; (Med) swab; **~ à récurer** scouring pad; **3 ~ hygiénique** tampon.

IDIOMS **servir de ~** to act as a buffer.

tamponner /tɑ̃pɔne/ [1] *vtr* **1** to swab [*wound, cut*]; to mop [*forehead*]; **2** to stamp [*document*]; **3** to crash into [*vehicle*].

tam-tam, *pl* **~s** /tamtam/ *nm* tomtom.

tandem /tɑ̃dɛm/ *nm* **1** tandem; **2** (figurative) duo.

tandis: **tandis que** /tɑ̃di(s)k(ə)/ *phr* while.

tangent, ~e[1] /tɑ̃ʒɑ̃, ɑ̃t/ *adj* **1** tangent, tangential; **2**° **elle a été reçue, mais c'était ~** she got through, but only by the skin of her teeth°.

tangente[2] /tɑ̃ʒɑ̃t/ *nf* tangent.

IDIOMS **prendre la ~**° to make oneself scarce°.

tangible /tɑ̃ʒibl/ *adj* tangible.

tanguer /tɑ̃ge/ [1] *vi* [*ship, plane*] to pitch.

tanière /tanjɛʀ/ *nf* **1** den; **2** lair.

tank /tɑ̃k/ *nm* tank.

tanker /tɑ̃kœʀ, tɑ̃kɛʀ/ *nm* tanker.

tanner /tane/ [1] *vtr* **1** to tan [*leather, hides*]; **2** [*sun*] to make [sth] leathery [*face, skin*]; **3**° to badger° [*person*] (**avec** with).

IDIOMS **~ le cuir à qn**° to tan sb's hide°.

tannerie /tanʀi/ *nf* **1** tannery; **2** tanning.

tant /tɑ̃/ **I** *adv* **1** (so) much; **il a ~ insisté que** he was so insistent that; **vous m'en direz ~**°**!** you don't say!; **~ il est vrai que**... since it's a well-known fact that...; **le moment ~ attendu** the long-awaited moment; **2 n'aimer rien ~ que**... to like nothing so much as...; **~ bien que mal** [*repair, lead*] after a fashion; [*manage*] more or less; **essayer ~ bien que mal de s'adapter** to be struggling to adapt; **3 ~ que** as long as; **je ne partirai pas ~ qu'il ne m'aura pas accordé un rendez-vous** I won't leave until he's given me an appointment; **~ que tu y es, balaye aussi la cuisine** while you're at it, sweep the kitchen as well; **traite-moi de menteur ~ que tu y es**°**!** go ahead and call me a liar!; **4** (replacing number, figure) **gagner ~ par mois** to earn so much a month; **votre lettre datée du ~** your letter of such-and-such a date.

II tant de *quantif* **Loulou, Grovagnard, Pivachon et ~ d'autres** Loulou, Grovagnard, Pivachon and so many others; **~ de travail** so much work.

III (in phrases) **~ pis** too bad; **~ mieux** so much the better; **~ mieux pour toi** good for you; **~ et plus** a great deal; a great many; **~ et si bien que** so much so that; **s'il avait un ~ soit peu de bon sens** if he had the slightest bit of common sense; **~ qu'à faire, autant repeindre toute la pièce** we may as well repaint the whole room while we're at it; **~ qu'à faire, je préférerais que ce soit lui qui l'achète** since somebody has to buy it, I'd rather it was him; **en ~ que** as; **en ~ que tel** as such; **si ~ est qu'il puisse y aller** that is if he can go at all; **je ne l'aime pas ~ que ça** I don't like him/her all that much.

tante /tɑ̃t/ *nf* aunt; **~ Julie** aunt Julie.

tantôt /tɑ̃to/ *adv* sometimes.

taon /tɑ̃/ *nm* horsefly.

tapage /tapaʒ/ *nm* **1** din, racket○; **faire du ~** to make a racket○; **2** furore (GB), furor (US); **3** hype; **~ médiatique** media hype.
■ **~ nocturne** disturbance of the peace at night.

tapageur, **-euse** /tapaʒœʀ, øz/ *adj* **1** [*person*] rowdy; **2** [*luxury, elegance*] showy; [*campaign*] hyped-up; [*words*] ostentatious.

tapant /tapɑ̃/ *adj f* **à trois heures ~s** at three o'clock sharp or on the dot.

tape /tap/ *nf* pat; slap.

tape-à-l'œil○ /tapalœj/ *adj inv* [*coulour*] loud; [*jewellery, decor*] garish.

taper /tape/ [1] **I** *vtr* **1** to hit [*person, dog*]; **2** to type [*letter*]; **3**○ **je peux te ~ 1 franc?** can I scrounge○ a franc off you?
II taper sur *v+prep* to hit [*nail*]; **~ sur l'épaule de qn** to tap sb on the shoulder.
III *vi* **1 ~ des mains** to clap one's hands; **~ du pied** to tap one's foot; **~ à la porte** to knock at the door; **le soleil tape**○ **aujourd'hui** the sun is beating down today; **2**○ **~ dans ses économies** to dip into one's savings; **3 ~ (à la machine)** to type.
IV se taper *v refl* (+ *v être*) **1**○ **se ~ dessus** to knock each other about; **2 je me suis tapé sur le doigt** I hit myself on the finger; **c'est à se ~ la tête contre les murs** (figurative) it's enough to drive you up the wall; **3**○ to get stuck○ with [*chore, person*].
IDIOMS **elle m'a tapé dans l'œil**○ I thought she was striking.

tapette /tapɛt/ *nf* **1** carpet beater; **2** fly swatter; **3** mousetrap.

tapinois: **en tapinois** /ɑ̃tapinwɑ/ *phr* furtively.

tapioca /tapjɔka/ *nm* tapioca.

tapir[1]: **se tapir** /tapiʀ/ [3] *v refl* (+ *v être*) **1** [*person, animal*] to hide; **2** to crouch.

tapir[2] /tapiʀ/ *nm* (Zool) tapir.

tapis /tapi/ *nm inv* rug; carpet; mat; **mettre qch sur le ~** (figurative) to bring sth up; **mettre** or **envoyer qn au ~** to throw sb.
■ **~ de bain(s)** bathmat; **~ roulant** moving walkway; (for luggage) carousel; (in factory, supermarket) conveyor belt; **~ vert** green baize.

tapisser /tapise/ [1] *vtr* **1** to wallpaper; to decorate [*room*]; to cover [*armchair*]; **2** [*snow*] to carpet [*ground*]; [*residue*] to line [*bottom of container*].

tapisserie /tapisʀi/ *nf* **1** tapestry; **2** wallpaper; **3** tapestry work.
IDIOMS **faire ~** to be a wallflower.

tapissier, **-ière** /tapisje, ɛʀ/ *nm,f* **1** upholsterer; **2** tapestry-maker.

tapoter /tapɔte/ [1] *vtr* to tap [*table, object*]; to pat [*cheeks, back*].

taquin, **~e** /takɛ̃, in/ *adj* [*person*] teasing.

taquiner /takine/ [1] *vtr* [*person*] to tease; ▶ **goujon**.

taquinerie /takinʀi/ *nf* teasing.

tarabiscoté, **~e** /taʀabiskɔte/ *adj* [*design*] over-ornate; [*writing*] over-elaborate; [*reasoning, style*] convoluted.

tarama /taʀama/ *nm* taramasalata.

tard /taʀ/ **I** *adv* late; **plus ~** later; **bien plus ~** much later (on); **au plus ~** at the latest; **~ dans la nuit** in the middle of the night; **pas plus ~ qu'hier** only yesterday.
II sur le tard *phr* [*marry*] late in life.

tarder /taʀde/ [1] **I** *vi* **1 ~ à faire** to take a long time doing; to put off or delay doing; **2** [*reaction, season*] to be a long time coming; **les enfants ne vont pas ~** the children won't be long; **ça n'a pas tardé** it wasn't long coming.
II *v impers* **il me tarde de la revoir** I'm longing to see her again.

tardif, **-ive** /taʀdif, iv/ *adj* [*hour, flowering*] late; [*excuses*] belated.

tardivement /taʀdivmɑ̃/ *adv* [*arrive*] late; [*react*] rather belatedly.

tare /taʀ/ *nf* **1** tare; **2** defect.

taré○, **~e** /taʀe/ *adj* crazy○.

targette /taʀʒɛt/ *nf* bolt.

targuer: **se targuer** /taʀge/ [1] *v refl* (+ *v être*) to claim (**de qch** sth), to boast (**de qch** sth).

tarif /taʀif/ *nm* **1** (gen) rate; (on bus, train) fare; (for consultation) fee; **payer plein ~** to pay full price; to pay full fare; **~ de nuit** night-time rate; **tu connais le ~**○... (figurative) you know the penalty...; **2** price list.
■ **~ douanier** customs tariff.

tarification /taʀifikasjɔ̃/ *nf* **1** price setting; **2** tariff.

tarir /taʀiʀ/ [23] **I** *vtr* to dry up [*source*]; to stem (the tide of) [*resources*]; to sap [*strength*].
II *vi* **ne pas ~ d'éloges sur qch/qn** to be full of praise for sth/sb.
III se tarir *v refl* (+ *v être*) to dry up, to run dry.

tarot /taʀo/ *nm* tarot (*card game*).

tartare /taʀtaʀ/ *adj* **1** Tartar; **2** (Culin) **sauce ~** tartare sauce.

tarte /taʀt/ *nf* **1** (Culin) tart; **~ aux fraises** strawberry tart; **2**○ wallop○.
■ **~ Tatin** apple tart (*with caramel topping*).
IDIOMS **c'est pas de la ~**○ it's no picnic○.

tartelette /taʀtəlɛt/ *nf* (small) tart.

tartine /taʀtin/ *nf* **1** slice of bread and butter; **2**○ **il en a écrit une ~** he wrote reams about it.

tartiner /taʀtine/ [1] *vtr* to spread; **pâte à ~** sandwich spread.

tartre /taʀtʀ/ *nm* (in kettle) scale, fur (GB); (on teeth) tartar.

tas /tɑ/ **I** *nm inv* **1** heap, pile; **en ~** [*put, place*] in a heap or pile; **un ~ de bois** a woodpile; **~ de ferraille** scrap heap; (figurative)○ wreck; **2**○ **un ~, des ~** loads○ (**de** of).
II dans le tas○ *phr* **tirer dans le ~** to fire into the crowd.
III sur le tas *phr* **apprendre sur le ~** to learn on the job; **formation sur le ~** on-the-job training; **grève sur le ~** sit-down strike.

tasse /tɑs/ *nf* cup; **~ à thé** teacup.

IDIOMS **boire la ~**° to swallow a mouthful of water (when swimming).

tassement /tasmɑ̃/ *nm* **~ de vertèbres** compression of the vertebrae.

tasser /tase/ [1] **I** *vtr* to press down [*earth*]; to pack down [*hay*]; to pack [*clothes, people*]; to cram [*luggage*]; **il a la cinquantaine bien ~e**° he's well past fifty.
II se tasser *v refl* (+ *v être*) **1** (with age) to shrink; **2** (in train, car) [*people*] to squash up; **3**° [*story, conflict*] to die down.

tata° /tata/ *nf* auntie.

tâter /tate/ [1] **I** *vtr* to feel; **~ le sol du pied** to test the ground.
II tâter de *v+prep* **~ de tous les métiers** to try one's hand at all kinds of jobs.
III se tâter° *v refl* (+ *v être*) **je me tâte** I'm thinking about it.
IDIOMS **~ le terrain** to put out feelers.

tatillon, -onne /tatijɔ̃, ɔn/ *adj* nit-picking.

tâtonner /tatɔne/ [1] *vi* to grope about or around; **avancer en tâtonnant** to grope one's way along.

tâtons: **à tâtons** /atatɔ̃/ *phr* **avancer à ~** to feel one's way along.

tatouage /tatwaʒ/ *nm* tattoo; **se faire faire un ~** to have a tattoo done.

tatouer /tatwe/ [1] *vtr* to tattoo; **se faire ~** to get tattooed.

taudis /todi/ *nm inv* **1** hovel; **2** pigsty.

taule° /tol/ *nf* prison, nick° (GB); **faire de la ~** to do time°.

taupe /top/ *nf* **1** (Zool) mole; **2** moleskin; **en ~** moleskin.

taupinière /topinjɛʀ/ *nf* **1** molehill; **2** (mole) tunnels.

taureau, *pl* **~x** /tɔʀo/ *nm* (Zool) bull; **~ de combat** fighting bull.
IDIOMS **prendre le ~ par les cornes** to take the bull by the horns.

Taureau /tɔʀo/ *pr nm* Taurus.

tauromachie /tɔʀɔmaʃi/ *nf* bullfighting.

taux /to/ *nm inv* **1** (gen) rate; **~ de chômage** unemployment rate; **2** (Med) (of alcohol, albumen, sugar) level; (of bacteria, sperm) count.

taxation /taksasjɔ̃/ *nf* **1** taxation; **2** assessment.

taxe /taks/ *nf* tax; **boutique hors ~s** duty-free shop (GB) or store (US); **1000 francs toutes ~s comprises** 1,000 francs inclusive of tax.
■ **~ d'habitation** ≈ council tax (*paid by residents to cover local services*).

taxer /takse/ [1] *vtr* **1** (Econ) to tax; **2 ~ qn de laxisme** to accuse sb of being lax.

taxi /taksi/ *nm* taxi, cab (US); **station de ~s** taxi rank (GB), cab stand (US).

taxidermiste /taksidɛʀmist/ *nmf* taxidermist.

Tchad /tʃad/ *pr nm* Chad; **le lac ~** Lake Chad.

tchao° /tʃao/ *excl* bye°!, see you°!

tchèque /tʃɛk/ *adj, nm* Czech.

tchin(-tchin)° /tʃin(tʃin)/ *excl* cheers!

TD° /tede/ *nm pl* (*abbr* = **travaux dirigés**) (Sch) practical.

te (**t'** *before vowel or mute h*) /t(ə)/ *pron* **1** (direct or indirect object) you; **2** (reflexive pronoun) yourself; **va ~ laver les mains** go and wash your hands.

té /te/ *nm* (ruler) T-square; **en ~** T-shaped.

technicien, -ienne /tɛknisjɛ̃, ɛn/ *nm,f* **1** technician; **2** technical expert; **3** engineer.
■ **~ de surface** cleaner.

technique[1] /tɛknik/ **I** *adj* technical.
II *nm* technical subjects.

technique[2] /tɛknik/ *nf* **1** technique; **2** (Econ) technology.

technocrate /tɛknɔkʀat/ *nmf* technocrat.

technologie /tɛknɔlɔʒi/ *nf* technology.

teck /tɛk/ *nm* teak; **en ~** teak.

teckel /tekɛl/ *nm* dachshund.

tee-shirt, *pl* **~s** /tiʃœʀt/ *nm* T-shirt.

teigne /tɛɲ/ *nf* **1** (Med) ringworm; **2** moth; **3**° **être méchant comme une ~** to be a nasty (GB) or real (US) piece of work°.

teigneux°, **-euse** /tɛɲø, øz/ *adj* cantankerous.

teindre /tɛ̃dʀ/ [73] **I** *vtr* to dye [*hair, cloth, leather*]; to stain [*wood*].
II se teindre *v refl* (+ *v être*) [*person*] to dye one's hair.

teint, ~e[1] /tɛ̃, tɛ̃t/ **I** *pp* ▶ **teindre**.
II *pp adj* [*hair, leather, fabric*] dyed; [*wood, piece of furniture*] stained.
III *nm* complexion; **au ~ clair** with a fair complexion; **avoir le ~ rose** or **frais** to have a healthy glow.

teinte[2] /tɛ̃t/ *nf* **1** shade; **2** colour[GB]; **3** (of desire, superiority) **une ~ de** a tinge of.

teinté, ~e /tɛ̃te/ **I** *pp* ▶ **teinter**.
II *pp adj* **1** [*glass*] tinted; [*wood*] stained; **2 ~ de** [*emotion, colour*] tinged with.

teinter /tɛ̃te/ [1] **I** *vtr* **1** to tint [*glass*]; to stain [*wood, piece of furniture*]; to dye [*leather*]; **2 ~ qch de** to tinge sth with.
II se teinter *v refl* (+ *v être*) **se ~ de** to become tinged with.

teinture /tɛ̃tyʀ/ *nf* dye; (for wood) stain; **~ d'iode** tincture of iodine.

teinturerie /tɛ̃tyʀʀi/ *nf* (dry-)cleaner's.

teinturier, -ière /tɛ̃tyʀje, ɛʀ/ *nm,f* **1** dry-cleaner; **2** dyer.

tel, telle /tɛl/ *adj* **1** such; **une telle conduite** such behaviour[GB]; **je n'ai jamais rien vu de ~** I've never seen anything like it; **2** like; **3 telle est la vérité** that is the truth; **comme ~, en tant que ~** as such; **ses affaires étaient restées telles quelles** his/her things were left as they were; **~ que je te connais** if I know you; **4 avec un ~ enthousiasme** with such enthusiasm; **de telle sorte** or **façon** or **manière que** in such a way that; so that; **5 admettons qu'il arrive ~ jour, à telle heure** suppose that he arrives on such and such a day, at such and such a time; **je me moque de ce que pense telle ou telle personne** I don't care what certain people think.

télé° /tele/ *adj inv, nf* TV.

télécommande /telekɔmɑ̃d/ *nf* remote control.

télécommunication /telekɔmynikasjɔ̃/ *nf* telecommunications.

téléconférence /telekɔ̃feʀɑ̃s/ *nf* **1** conference call; **2** teleconference.

télécopieur /telekɔpjœʀ/ *nm* fax machine, fax.

télédiffuser /teledifyze/ [1] *vtr* to broadcast.

télé-enseignement, *pl* **~s** /teleɑ̃sɛɲəmɑ̃/ *nm* distance learning.

téléfilm /telefilm/ *nm* TV film, TV movie.

télégramme /telegʀam/ *nm* telegram, cable (US).

télégraphier /telegʀafje/ [1] *vtr* to telegraph.

télégraphique /telegʀafik/ *adj* [*pole, message*] telegraph; [*style*] telegraphic.

téléguider /telegide/ [1] *vtr* **1** to control [sth] by radio; **2** (figurative) to mastermind.

télématique /telematik/ I *adj* [*service, network*] viewdata (GB), videotex®.
II *nf* telematics.

téléobjectif /teleɔbʒɛktif/ *nm* telephoto lens.

télépathie /telepati/ *nf* telepathy.

téléphérique /telefeʀik/ *nm* cable car, téléphérique.

téléphone /telefɔn/ *nm* phone; **donner un coup de ~** to make a phone call.
■ **~ arabe**○ grapevine, bush telegraph; **~ portable** transmobile phone; **~ portatif** pocket car phone; **~ rose** *erotic chat-line*; **le ~ rouge** the hotline.

téléphoner /telefɔne/ [1] I *vtr* **~ qch à qn** to phone sb with sth.
II *vi* to phone; to make a phone call; **~ à qn** to phone sb.

téléphonique /telefɔnik/ *adj* [*call, box*] (tele)-phone.

télescope /telɛskɔp/ *nm* telescope.

télescoper /telɛskɔpe/ [1] I *vtr* [*truck, juggernaut*] to crush [*car*].
II **se télescoper** *v refl* (+ *v être*) **1** [*vehicles*] to collide; **2** [*notions, tendencies*] to overlap.

télescopique /telɛskɔpik/ *adj* telescopic.

télésiège /telesjɛʒ/ *nm* chair lift.

téléski /teleski/ *nm* ski tow.

téléspectateur, **-trice** /telespɛktatœʀ, tʀis/ *nm,f* viewer.

télésurveillance /telesyʀvɛjɑ̃s/ *nf* electronic surveillance.

téléviseur /televizœʀ/ *nm* television (set); **~ couleur** colour[GB] television.

télévision /televizjɔ̃/ *nf* television, TV; **passer à la ~** to be on television or TV.

télex /telɛks/ *nm inv* telex; **par ~** by telex.

tellement /tɛlmɑ̃/ I *adv* (modifying an adjective or adverb) so; (modifying a verb or comparative) so much; **pas ~** not much; **il n'aime pas ~ lire** he doesn't like reading much; **cela n'a plus ~ d'importance** it doesn't really matter any more; **il y en a ~ qui aimeraient le faire** so many people would like to do it; **j'ai de la peine à suivre ~ c'est compliqué** it's so complicated that I find it hard to follow.
II **tellement de**○ *quantif* **il y a ~ de choses à voir** there's so much to see; **il a eu ~ de chance** he was so lucky; **j'ai vu ~ de monde** I saw so many people.

téméraire /temeʀɛʀ/ *adj* [*person, plan*] reckless; [*judgment*] rash; **courageux mais pas ~** brave but not foolhardy.

témérité /temeʀite/ *nf* (of person, plan) recklessness; (of remarks) rashness.

témoignage /temwaɲaʒ/ *nm* **1** story; **2** account; **~s recueillis auprès de** accounts given by; **3** evidence; testimony; **des ~s contradictoires/qui concordent** conflicting/corroborating evidence; **obtenir le ~ de qn** to get sb's evidence; **4 ~ d'amitié** (gift) token of friendship; **les ~s de sympathie** expressions of sympathy.

témoigner /temwaɲe/ [1] I *vtr* **1** (Law) to testify; **2 ~ de l'affection** to show affection.
II **témoigner de** *v+prep* **1** to show; **2 ~ du courage de qn** to vouch for sb's courage.
III *vi* **1** (Law) to give evidence; **2 'il était toujours poli', témoignent les voisins** neighbours[GB] say he was always polite.

témoin /temwɛ̃/ I *nm* **1** (gen, Law) witness; **~ oculaire** eyewitness; **2** (at duel) second; **3** (of historical event) **avoir été ~ de la naissance du IIIe Reich** to have witnessed the birth of the Third Reich; **4** (Tech) indicator or warning light.
II **(-)témoin** (*combining form*) control; **groupe(-)~** control group.

tempe /tɑ̃p/ *nf* temple.

tempérament /tɑ̃peʀamɑ̃/ *nm* disposition; **avoir du ~** to have a strong character.

tempérance /tɑ̃peʀɑ̃s/ *nf* temperance.

température /tɑ̃peʀatyʀ/ *nf* temperature.

tempéré, **~e** /tɑ̃peʀe/ *adj* [*climate*] temperate.

tempérer /tɑ̃peʀe/ [14] *vtr* to temper; to moderate [*argument*].

tempête /tɑ̃pɛt/ *nf* **1** gale; storm; **2** uproar; **déclencher une ~ de protestations** to trigger a wave of protest.

tempêter /tɑ̃pete/ [1] *vi* to rage (**contre** against).

temple /tɑ̃pl/ *nm* **1** (gen) temple; (protestant) church; **2** (figurative) temple.

tempo /tɛmpo/ *nm* **1** (Mus) tempo; **2** (of novel, film) pace.

temporaire /tɑ̃pɔʀɛʀ/ *adj* temporary; **à titre ~** on a temporary basis.

temporel, **-elle** /tɑ̃pɔʀɛl/ *adj* (gen) temporal; **biens ~s** worldly goods.

temporiser /tɑ̃pɔʀize/ [1] *vi* to stall.

temps /tɑ̃/ *nm inv* **1** weather; **un beau ~** fine weather; **quel beau/sale ~!** what lovely/awful weather!; **le ~ est à la pluie** it looks like rain; **quel ~ fait-il?** what's the weather like?; **par tous les ~** in all weathers; **2** time; **le ~ arrangera les choses** time will take care of everything; **3 peu de ~ avant** shortly before; **en peu de ~** in a short time; **dans peu de ~** shortly; **dans quelque ~** before long; **depuis quelque** or **un certain ~ il est bizarre** he has been behaving oddly for a while now or for some time now; **pendant ce ~(-là)** meanwhile; **qu'as-tu fait tout ce ~(-là)?** what have you been doing all this time?; **en un rien de ~** in no time at all; **les trois quarts du ~** most of the time; **depuis le ~ que j'en parle!** I've been talking about it for long enough!; **le ~ de ranger mes affaires et j'arrive** just let me put my things away and I'll be with you; **on a (tout) le ~** we've got (plenty of) time; **avoir dix** or **cent fois le ~** to have all the time in the world; **laisser à qn le ~ de faire** to give sb time to do; **mettre** or **prendre du ~** to take time; **beaucoup de ~** a long time; **ça a pris** or **mis un ~ fou**○ it took ages○; **tu y as mis le ~!, tu en as mis du ~!** you (certainly) took your time!; **le ~ passe vite** time flies; **faire passer le ~** to while away the time **(en faisant** doing); **avoir du ~ à perdre** to have time on one's hands; **c'est du ~ perdu, c'est une perte de ~** it's a waste of time; **le ~ presse!** time is short! ; **j'ai trouvé le ~ long** (the) time seemed to drag; **nous sommes dans les ~** we've still got time; **finir dans les ~** to finish in time; **4** time; **à ~** [*leave, finish*] in time; **juste à ~** just in time; **de ~ en ~, de ~ à autre** from time to time; **il était ~!** (impatiently) (and) about time too!; (with relief) just in the nick of time!; **en ~ utile** in time; **en ~ voulu** in due course; at the right time; **ne durer qu'un ~** to be short-lived; **5 au** or **du ~ des Grecs** in the time of the Greeks; **au ~ des dinosaures** in the age of the dinosaurs; **au** or **du ~ où** in the days when; **le bon vieux ~** the good old days; **ces derniers ~** recently; **ces ~-ci** lately; **de mon ~** in my day; **dans le ~, on n'avait pas l'électricité** in those days, we didn't have electricity; **il est loin le ~ où** the days are long gone when; **en ~ normal** usually; **en d'autres ~** at any other time; **être de son ~** to move with the times; **6** stage; **dans un premier ~** first; **dans un deuxième ~** subsequently; **dans un dernier ~** finally; **7** (of verb) tense; **8 avoir un travail à ~ partiel/plein** to have a part-/full-time job; **~ de travail quotidien** working day (GB), workday (US); **9** (Sport) time; **il a réalisé le meilleur ~** he got the best time; **améliorer son ~ d'une seconde** to knock a second off one's time; **rester dans les ~** to be inside the time; **10** (of engine) stroke; **11** (Mus) time; **mesure à deux ~** two-four time.

■ **~ d'antenne** airtime; **~ fort** (Mus) forte; (figurative) high point; **~ mort** slack period; **~ universel** Greenwich Mean Time, GMT, universal time.

IDIOMS **au ~ pour moi!** my mistake!; **par les ~ qui courent** with things as they are; **prendre** or **se payer**○ **du bon ~** to have a whale of a time.

tenable /tənabl/ *adj* **1** bearable; **2** (Mil) tenable.

tenace /tənas/ *adj* **1** [*stain, headache*] stubborn; [*perfume*] long-lasting; [*fog, cough, smell*] persistent; [*rumour, memory*] persistent; [*hatred, belief*] entrenched; **2** [*person*] tenacious; persistent; [*will*] tenacious.

ténacité /tenasite/ *nf* **1** tenacity; **2** persistence.

tenaille /tənaj/ *nf* pincers.

tenailler /tənaje/ [1] *vtr* **il était tenaillé par le remords** he was racked with remorse.

tenancier, **-ière** /tənɑ̃sje, ɛʀ/ *nm,f* (of café) landlord/landlady; (of hotel, casino) manager/manageress; **tenancière de maison close** madam.

tenant, **~e** /tənɑ̃, ɑ̃t/ **I** *nm,f* (Sport) **~ du titre** titleholder.

II *nm* **1** advocate; **2 d'un seul ~** all in one piece.

IDIOMS **les ~s et les aboutissants de qch** the ins and outs of sth.

tendance /tɑ̃dɑ̃s/ *nf* **1** tendency; **avoir ~ à faire** to tend to do; **2** (in politics) tendency; **toutes ~s politiques confondues** across party lines; **3** trend.

tendancieux, **-ieuse** /tɑ̃dɑ̃sjø, øz/ *adj* biased[GB], tendentious.

tendeur /tɑ̃dœʀ/ *nm* **1** (of tent) guy rope; **2** (for roof rack) elastic strap.

tendon /tɑ̃dɔ̃/ *nm* tendon; **~ d'Achille** Achilles tendon.

tendre[1] /tɑ̃dʀ/ [6] **I** *vtr* **1** to tighten [*rope, cable*]; to stretch [*elastic, skin*]; to extend [*spring*]; **~ le cou** to crane one's neck; **~ le bras** to reach out; **~ les bras à qn** to greet sb with open arms; **~ la main** to reach out; to hold out one's hand; **~ la main à qn** to hold one's hand out to sb; (figurative) to lend sb a helping hand; **2** to spread [*cloth, sheet*]; **3** to set [*trap*]; to put up [*clothes line*]; **~ un piège à qn** (figurative) to set a trap for sb; **4 ~ qch à qn** to hold sth out to sb.

II tendre à *v+prep* **~ à faire** to tend to do.

III *vi* **1 ~ vers** to strive for; **2 ~ vers** to approach [*value*]; to tend to [*zero*].

IV se tendre *v refl* (+ *v être*) **1** to tighten; **2** to become strained.

tendre[2] /tɑ̃dʀ/ **I** *adj* **1** [*wood, fibre, rock*] soft; [*skin, flesh, vegetables*] tender; **2** [*shoot, grass*] new; **~ enfance** earliest childhood; **3** [*pink, green, blue*] soft; **des chaussettes vert ~** pale green socks; **4** [*person*] loving; [*love, smile, words*] tender; [*temperament*] gentle; **être ~ avec qn** to be loving toward(s) sb; **ne pas être ~ avec qn/qch** to be hard on sb/sth; **5** [*friend, husband, wife*] dear.

II *nmf* soft-hearted person.

tendrement /tɑ̃dʀəmɑ̃/ *adv* tenderly.

tendresse /tɑ̃dʀɛs/ *nf* **1** tenderness; **2** affection.

tendu, **~e** /tɑ̃dy/ **I** *pp* ▶ **tendre[1]**.

II *pp adj* [*rope*] tight.

III *adj* [*person, meeting*] tense; [*market*] nervous.

ténèbres /tenɛbʀ/ *nf pl* **les ~** darkness.

ténébreux, **-euse** /tenebʀø, øz/ *adj* **1** dark; **2** obscure.

teneur /tənœʀ/ *nf* **1** (of solid) content; (of gas, liquid) level; **2** (of report) import.

ténia /tenja/ *nm* tapeworm.

tenir /tənir/ [36] I *vtr* **1** to hold; **~ qn par la main** to hold sb's hand; **tiens!** here you are!; **si je le tenais!** if I could get my hands on him!; **2** to keep [sb] under control; **il nous tient** he's got a hold on us; **3** (Mil) to hold [*hill, bridge, city*]; **4** to hold [*captive, animal*]; **je te tiens!** I've caught or got you!; **5** to have [*information*]; **de qui tenez-vous ce renseignement?** where did you get that information?; **6** to hold [*job*]; to run [*shop, house, business*]; to be in charge of [*switchboard, reception*]; **7** to keep; **'~ hors de portée des enfants'** 'keep out of reach of children'; **8 ~ sa tête droite** to hold one's head upright; **~ les yeux baissés** to keep one's eyes lowered; **9** to hold down [*load, cargo*]; to hold up [*trousers, socks*]; **10** to keep to [*itinerary*]; **11 ~ la mer** [*ship*] to be seaworthy; **~ le coup** to hold out; **~ le choc** [*person*] to stand the strain; **12** to hold [*quantity*]; **13** [*object*] to take up [*room*]; [*person*] to hold [*role, position*]; **14 ~ qn/qch pour responsable** to hold sb/sth responsible; **~ qn pour mort** to give sb up for dead; **~ pour certain que** to regard it as certain that.

II **tenir à** *v+prep* **1** to be fond of, to like; **~ à la vie** to value one's life; **2 j'y tiens** I insist; **~ à ce que qn fasse** to insist that sb should do; **je ne tiens pas à ce qu'elle y aille** I'd rather she didn't go.

III **tenir de** *v+prep* **~ de qn** to take after sb.

IV *vi* **1** [*rope, shelf, dam*] to hold; [*stamp, glue*] to stick (**à** to); [*bandage, structure*] to stay in place; [*hairstyle*] to stay tidy; **2 ~** (**bon**) (gen) to hang on; (Mil) to hold out; **il n'y a pas de télévision qui tienne**○ there's no question of watching television; **3 la neige tient** the snow is settling; **les fleurs n'ont pas tenu** the flowers didn't last long; **4** [*theory*] to hold good; [*alibi*] to stand up; **5** [*people, objects*] to fit; **~ à six dans une voiture** to fit six into a car; **mon article tient en trois pages** my article takes up only three pages; **~ en longueur** to be short enough (**dans** for).

V **se tenir** *v refl* (+ *v être*) **1 se ~ la tête à deux mains** to hold one's head in one's hands; **2 se ~ par le bras** to be arm in arm; **se ~ par la main** to hold hands; **3 se ~ à qch** to hold onto sth; **se ~ par les pieds** to hold on with one's feet; **tiens-toi** or **tenez-vous bien**○ (figurative) prepare yourself for a shock; **4 se ~ accroupi** to be squatting; **se ~ au milieu** to be standing in the middle; **se ~ prêt** to be ready; **se ~ tranquille** to keep still; **5** to behave; **se ~ bien/mal** to behave well/badly; **savoir se ~** to know how to behave; **6 se ~ bien/mal** to have (a) good posture/(a) bad posture; **tiens-toi droit!** stand up straight!; **7** [*demonstration, exhibition*] to be held; **8** [*argument, book*] to hold together; **ça se tient** it makes sense; **9 se ~ pour** to consider oneself to be; **tenez-vous le pour dit**○! I don't want to have to tell you again!; **10 s'en ~ à** to keep to; **s'en ~ aux ordres** to stick to orders; **s'en ~ là** to leave it there; **ne pas savoir à quoi s'en ~** not to know what to make of it.

VI *v impers* **il ne tient qu'à toi de partir** it's up to you to decide whether to leave; **qu'à cela ne tienne!** never mind!

tennis /tenis/ I *nm inv* tennis; **~ de table** table tennis.
II *nm inv* or *nf inv* tennis shoe.

tennisman, *pl* **tennismen** /tenisman, mɛn/ *nm* male tennis player.

ténor /tenɔr/ *nm* **1** tenor; **2** (in sport) star; (in profession, political party) leading light.

tension /tɑ̃sjɔ̃/ *nf* **1** (of cable, rope, muscle) tension; **2** (Med) **~** (**artérielle**) blood pressure; **avoir de la ~** to have high blood pressure; **être sous ~** to be under stress; **3** (in electricity) tension, voltage; **basse ~** low voltage; **sous ~** [*circuit, wire*] live; [*machine*] switched on; **4** (between people, countries) tension.

tentacule /tɑ̃takyl/ *nm* tentacle.

tentation /tɑ̃tasjɔ̃/ *nf* temptation; **la ~ est forte** it's very tempting.

tentative /tɑ̃tativ/ *nf* attempt; **~ de meurtre** (gen) murder attempt; (Law) attempted murder; **faire une ~ auprès de qn pour obtenir qch** to try to obtain sth from sb.

tente /tɑ̃t/ *nf* tent; **dormir sous la ~** to sleep under canvas; to sleep in tents.

tenter /tɑ̃te/ [1] *vtr* **1** to attempt; **~ sa chance** to try one's luck; **je vais ~ l'expérience** I'll have a go; **~ le tout pour le tout** to risk one's all; **2** to tempt; **cela ne la tente guère** that doesn't appeal to her very much; **laisse-toi ~!** be a devil!; **~ le diable** to court disaster.

tenture /tɑ̃tyr/ *nf* **1** curtain; **~s** draperies; **2** fabric wall covering.

tenu, **~e**[1] /təny/ I *pp* ▶ **tenir**.
II *pp adj* **1 bien/mal ~** [*child*] well/badly cared for; [*house*] well/badly kept; **2 ~ de faire** required to do; **~ à** bound by.

tenue[2] /təny/ *nf* **1 ~** (**vestimentaire**) dress, clothes; **~ de ville** smart clothes; **être en ~ légère** to be scantily dressed; **en ~** (Mil) uniformed; **2 avoir de la ~** to have good manners; **un peu de ~!** mind your manners!; **3** posture.

ter /tɛr/ *adv* **1** (in address) ter; cf b; **2** three times.

térébenthine /terebɑ̃tin/ *nf* turpentine; (**essence de**) **~** turpentine.

tergal® /tɛrgal/ *nm* Terylene®; **robe en ~** Terylene dress.

tergiverser /tɛrʒivɛrse/ [1] *vi* **1** to dither; **2** to shilly-shally.

terme /tɛrm/ I *nm* **1** term, word; **c'est en ces ~s que le ministre a décrit la situation** this was how the minister described the situation; **2** end; **mettre un ~ à qch** to put an end to sth; **toucher à son ~** to come to an end; **arriver à ~** [*period, contract*] to expire; **mener à ~** to see [sth] through to completion [*plan, operation*]; **accoucher avant ~** to give birth prematurely; **3 passé ce ~ vous paierez des intérêts** after this date, you will pay interest; **à moyen ~** [*loan, strategy*] medium-term; **4 trouver un moyen ~** to find a compromise.
II **termes** *nm pl* terms; **~s de l'échange** terms of trade; **en bons ~s** on good terms.

terminaison /tɛʀminɛzɔ̃/ *nf* ending.

terminal, **~e**[1], *mpl* **-aux** /tɛʀminal, o/ **I** *adj* [*year*] final; **phase ~e** (of operation) concluding phase; (of illness) terminal phase.
II *nm* terminal.

terminale[2] /tɛʀminal/ *nf* (Sch) final year (*of secondary school*).

terminer /tɛʀmine/ [1] **I** *vtr* **1** to finish; **2** to end.
II *vi* to finish; **en ~ avec** to be through with; **c'est terminé, je n'irai plus jamais!** that's that, I'm never going back!; **pour ~** in conclusion.
III se terminer *v refl* (+ *v être*) **1** to end; **le projet se termine** the project is coming to an end; **être terminé** to be over; **2 se ~ par** [*word, number, object*] to end in.

terminologie /tɛʀminɔlɔʒi/ *nf* terminology.

terminus /tɛʀminys/ *nm inv* (of train) end of the line; (of bus) terminus.

termite /tɛʀmit/ *nm* termite.

terne /tɛʀn/ *adj* [*hair, life*] dull; [*colour*] drab; [*eyes, expression*] lifeless.

ternir /tɛʀniʀ/ [3] **I** *vtr* **1** to tarnish [*metal*]; to fade [*fabric*]; **2** to tarnish [*image, reputation*]; to detract from [*exploit, achievement*].
II se ternir *v refl* (+ *v être*) to tarnish.

terrain /tɛʀɛ̃/ *nm* **1** (gen) ground; (Mil) field; **2** plot of land; **3** land; **4** (for football, rugby, cricket) pitch, field; ground; (for volley-ball, basket-ball, handball, tennis) court; (in golf) course; **5** (figurative) **avancer sur un ~ glissant** to be on slippery ground; **nous ne vous suivrons pas sur ce ~** we won't go along with you there; **un ~ d'entente** common ground; **travailler sur le ~** to do fieldwork; **~ favorable** (Med) predisposing factors; (in sociology) favourable[GB] environment; **être en ~ connu** or **familier** to be on familiar territory; **déblayer le ~** to clear the ground; **préparer le ~** to pave the way; **tâter** or **sonder le ~** to put out feelers.
■ **~ d'atterrissage** landing strip; **~ d'aviation** airfield; **~ de camping** campsite; **~ de jeu(x)** playground; **~ de manœuvre** army training ground; **~ de tir** firing range; **~ de sport(s)** sports ground; **~ vague** wasteland.

terrasse /tɛʀas/ *nf* **1** terrace; **s'installer à la ~ d'un café** to sit at a table outside a café; **2** flat roof; **3** large balcony; **4 culture(s) en ~s** terrace cultivation.

terrasser /tɛʀase/ [1] *vtr* **1** to knock down; **2** [*illness*] to strike down; **terrassé par** (by heat, grief) prostrated by.

terre /tɛʀ/ **I** *nf* **1** ground; **sous ~** underground; **mettre pied à ~** [*horseman*] to dismount; **2** earth; soil; **sortir de ~** [*plant*] to come up; **3** land; **le retour à la ~** the movement back to the land; **4** (as opposed to sea) land; **aller à ~** to go ashore; **s'enfoncer à l'intérieur des ~s** to go deep inland; **5** earth; **il croit que la ~ entière est contre lui** he thinks the whole world is against him; **redescends** or **reviens sur ~!** come back to earth!; **6 de la ~ (glaise)** clay; **un pot de** or **en ~** an earthenware pot; **7** (in electricity) earth (GB), ground (US).
II terre à terre *phr* [*question*] basic; [*conversation, person*] pedestrian.
III par terre *phr* on the ground; on the floor; **c'est à se rouler par ~**○ it's hilarious; **ça a fichu tous nos projets par ~**○ it messed up all our plans○.
■ **~ d'asile** country of refuge; **~ battue** trodden earth; **sur ~ battue** [*tennis*] on a clay court.
IDIOMS **avoir les pieds sur ~**○ to have one's feet firmly planted on the ground; **garder les pieds sur ~**○ to keep one's feet on the ground.

Terre /tɛʀ/ *nf* Earth; **sur la ~** on Earth.

terreau, *pl* **~x** /tɛʀo/ *nm* compost; **~ de feuilles** leaf mould (GB), leaf mold (US).

terre-plein, *pl* **terres-pleins** /tɛʀplɛ̃/ *nm* **1** (in construction) platform; **2** (of road) central reservation (GB), median strip (US).

terrer: **se terrer** /tɛʀe/ [1] *v refl* (+ *v être*) **2** [*rabbit*] to disappear into its burrow; [*fox*] to go to earth; **2** [*fugitive*] to hide.

terrestre /tɛʀɛstʀ/ *adj* **1** (surface, diameter) of the Earth; **2** [*animals*] land; **3** [*war, transport*] land; **la vie/le paradis ~** life/heaven on earth.

terreur /tɛʀœʀ/ *nf* **1** terror; **c'est ma grande ~** it's my greatest fear; **2** (as political weapon) terror.

terreux, **-euse** /tɛʀø, øz/ *adj* earthy.

terrible /tɛʀibl/ *adj* **1** (gen) terrible; [*thirst, desire*] tremendous; **il est ~**○**, il ne veut jamais avoir tort** it's terrible the way he never wants to admit that he's wrong; **2**○ terrific○; **il n'est pas ~ ce film** that's not a great film.

terriblement /tɛʀibləmɑ̃/ *adv* terribly; **~ plus fort** an awful lot stronger.

terrien, **-ienne** /tɛʀjɛ̃, ɛn/ *adj* **propriétaire ~** landowner.

terrier /tɛʀje/ *nm* **1** (gen) hole; **un ~ de renard** a fox's earth; **2** (Zool) terrier.

terrifiant, **~e** /tɛʀifjɑ̃, ɑ̃t/ *adj* **1** terrifying; **2**○ incredible.

terrifier /tɛʀifje/ [2] *vtr* to terrify; **s'enfuir terrifié** to flee in terror.

terrine /tɛʀin/ *nf* (gen) terrine; (round) earthenware bowl.

territoire /tɛʀitwaʀ/ *nm* territory; **sur l'ensemble du ~** throughout the country.
■ **~ d'outre-mer**, **TOM** French overseas (administrative) territory.

territorial, **~e**, *mpl* **-iaux** /tɛʀitɔʀjal, o/ *adj* **1** [*waters, integrity*] territorial; **2** [*administration*] divisional; regional.

terroir /tɛʀwaʀ/ *nm* land; **produits/vin du ~** local products/wine.

terroriser /tɛʀɔʀize/ [1] *vtr* **1** to terrorize; **2** to terrify.

terrorisme /tɛʀɔʀism/ *nm* terrorism.

terroriste /tɛʀɔʀist/ *adj, nmf* terrorist.

tertiaire /tɛʀsjɛʀ/ *adj* **1** (Econ) [*sector, industry*] service; **2** (in geology) Tertiary.

tes ▶ **ton**[1].

tesson /tesɔ̃/ *nm* shard, fragment; **des ~s de bouteille** broken glass.

test /tɛst/ *nm* test; **~ (de dépistage) du sida** Aids test; **faire passer des ~s à qn** (gen) to give sb tests; (Med) to carry out tests on sb.

testament /tɛstamɑ̃/ *nm* (Law) will; (figurative) legacy.

tester /tɛste/ [1] *vtr* to test; **testé en laboratoire** laboratory-tested.

testicule /tɛstikyl/ *nm* testicle.

tétanos /tetanos/ *nm inv* tetanus.

têtard /tɛtaʀ/ *nm* **1** (Zool) tadpole; **2** (tree) pollard.

tête /tɛt/ *nf* **1** head; **en pleine ~** (right) in the head; **garder la ~ haute** to hold one's head high; **~ baissée** [*rush*] headlong; **la ~ en bas** [*hang*] upside down; **se laver la ~** to wash one's hair; **au-dessus de nos ~s** overhead; **donner un coup de ~ à qn** to headbutt sb; **être tombé sur la ~**○ (figurative) to have gone off one's rocker○; **2** face; **une bonne/sale ~** a nice/nasty face; **tu en fais une ~!** what a face!; **quelle ~ va-t-il faire?** how's he going to react?; **il (me) fait la ~** he's sulking; **elle fait sa mauvaise ~** she's being difficult; **il a une ~ à tricher** he looks like a cheat; **tu as une ~ à faire peur, aujourd'hui!** you look dreadful today!; **3 de ~** [*quote, recite*] from memory; [*calculate*] in one's head; **tu n'as pas de ~!** you have a mind like a sieve!; **avoir qch en ~** to have sth in mind; **où avais-je la ~?** whatever was I thinking of?; **ça (ne) va pas, la ~**○**?** are you out of your mind or what?; **n'avoir rien dans la ~** to be empty-headed; **mets-lui ça dans la ~** drum it into him/her; **se mettre dans la** or **en ~ de faire** to take it into one's head to do; **passer par la ~ de qn** [*idea*] to cross sb's mind; **monter la ~ à Pierre contre Paul** to turn Pierre against Paul; **j'ai la ~ qui tourne** my head's spinning; **monter à la ~ de qn, faire tourner la ~ de qn** [*alcohol, success*] to go to sb's head; **il a encore toute sa ~ (à lui)** he's still got all his faculties; **n'en faire qu'à sa ~** to go one's own way; **tenir ~ à qn** to stand up to sb; **sur un coup de ~** on an impulse; **4** (person) **avoir ses ~s** to have one's favourites[GB]; **un dîner en ~ à ~** an intimate dinner for two **par ~** (gen) a head, each; (in statistics) per capita; **5** (measurement) head; **avoir une ~ de plus que qn** to be a head taller than sb; **avoir une ~ d'avance sur qn** to be a short length in front of sb; **6** head; **ma ~ est mise à prix** there's a price on my head; **vouloir la ~ de qn** to want sb's head; to be after sb's head; **risquer sa ~** to risk one's neck○; **des ~s vont tomber** (figurative) heads will roll; **7 le groupe de ~** the leading group; **il a été nommé à la ~ du groupe** he was appointed head of the group; **prendre la ~ des opérations** to take charge of operations; **être à la ~ d'une immense fortune** to be the possessor of a huge fortune; **8** top; **être en ~** (of list, category) to be at the top; (in election, race, survey) to be in the lead; **venir en ~** to come first; **le gouvernement, le premier ministre en ~, a décidé que...** the government, led by the Prime Minister, has decided that...; **en ~ de phrase** at the beginning of a sentence; **9** (of train) front; (of convoy, procession) head; (of tree, mast) top; (of screw, rivet, nail) head; **en ~ de file** first in line; **10** (Sport) (in football) header; **faire une ~** to head the ball; **11** (Mil) (of missile) warhead; **12 ~ de lecture** (in tape recorder, video recorder) head.

■ **~ en l'air** scatterbrain; **~ brûlée** daredevil; **~ à claques**○ pain○; **~ de delco**® distributor cap; **~ de lard**○ grouch; (stubborn person) mule; **~ de linotte** = **~ en l'air**; **~ de mort** skull; death's head; skull and crossbones; **~ de mule**○ mule; **être une vraie ~ de mule**○ to be as stubborn as a mule; **~ de Turc**○ whipping boy.

IDIOMS **j'en mettrais ma ~ à couper** I'd swear to it; **en avoir par-dessus la ~**○ to be fed up to the back teeth○; **se prendre la ~ à deux mains**○ to rack one's brains○; **ça me prend la ~**○ it's a real drag○.

tête-à-tête /tɛtatɛt/ *nm inv* **1** tête-à-tête; **2** private meeting.

tête-bêche /tɛtbɛʃ/ *adv* **1** top-to-tail; **2** head-to-tail.

tétée /tete/ *nf* **1** feeding; **l'heure de la ~** feeding time; **2** feed.

téter /tete/ [14] **I** *vtr* to suck at [*breast*]; to feed from [*bottle*]; to suck [*milk*].

II *vi* to suckle; **donner à ~ à** to feed [*baby*]; [*animal*] to suckle.

tétine /tetin/ *nf* **1** teat (GB), nipple (US); **2** dummy (GB), pacifier (US); **3** (of animal) teat.

têtu, ~e /tety/ *adj* stubborn.

texte /tɛkst/ *nm* **1** text; **'~ intégral'** 'unabridged'; (Comput) full text; **2** (Law) **~ de loi** bill; law.

textile /tɛkstil/ **I** *adj* textile; **fibres ~s** fibres[GB].

II *nm* **1** textile industry; **2 ~s synthétiques** synthetic fibres[GB].

textuellement /tɛkstɥɛlmɑ̃/ *adv* [*recount*] word for word.

texture /tɛkstyʀ/ *nf* **1** (of fabric, material) texture; **2** (of novel) structure.

TGV /teʒeve/ *nm* (*abbr* = **train à grande vitesse**) TGV, high-speed train.

thalassothérapie /talasɔteʀapi/ *nf* thalassotherapy.

thé /te/ *nm* **1** tea; **~ au lait** tea with milk; **2** tea party.

théâtral, ~e, *mpl* **-aux** /teɑtʀal, o/ *adj* **1** [*language*] dramatic; [*performance*] stage; [*season, company*] theatre[GB]; [*production, technique*] theatrical; **l'œuvre ~e de Racine** the plays of Racine; **2** [*gesture*] histrionic; [*tone*] melodramatic.

théâtre /teɑtʀ/ *nm* **1** theatre[GB]; **le ~ antique** Greek classical drama; **de ~** [*actor, director, ticket*] theatre[GB]; [*decor, costume*] stage; **coup de ~** coup de théâtre; (figurative) dramatic turn of events; **2 faire du ~** (as profession) to be an actor; (at school) to do drama; (as amateur) to be involved in amateur dramatics; **3** theatre[GB];

être le ~ d'affrontements (figurative) to be the scene of fighting.
■ **~ de Boulevard** farce.

théière /tejɛʀ/ *nf* teapot.

théine /tein/ *nf* theine.

thème /tɛm/ *nm* **1** (of discussion, programme) topic, subject; (of speech, film) theme; **2** (translation) prose; **3** (Mus) theme.
■ **~ astral** birth chart.

théologie /teɔlɔʒi/ *nf* theology.

théorème /teɔʀɛm/ *nm* theorem.

théorie /teɔʀi/ *nf* theory; **en ~** in theory.

théorique /teɔʀik/ *adj* theoretical.

thérapeute /teʀapøt/ *nmf* therapist.

thérapeutique /teʀapøtik/ **I** *adj* [*effect*] therapeutic; **choix ~** choice of treatment.
II *nf* **1** treatment; **2** therapeutics.

thérapie /teʀapi/ *nf* **1** (Med) treatment; **2** (in psychology) therapy.

thermal, ~e, *mpl* **-aux** /tɛʀmal, o/ *adj* [*spring*] thermal; **station ~e** spa.

thermes /tɛʀm/ *nm pl* **1** (Roman) thermae; **2** thermal baths.

thermique /tɛʀmik/ *adj* thermal.

thermo /tɛʀmo/ *pref* **~chimie** thermochemistry; **~nucléaire** thermonuclear.

thermomètre /tɛʀmɔmɛtʀ/ *nm* thermometer; (figurative) barometer.

thermostat /tɛʀmɔsta/ *nm* thermostat.

thèse /tɛz/ *nf* **1** (for doctorate) thesis (GB), dissertation (US); **2** thesis, argument; **3 avancer la ~ de l'accident** to put forward the theory that it was an accident.

thon /tɔ̃/ *nm* tuna.

thoracique /tɔʀasik/ *adj* thoracic; **cage ~** ribcage.

thorax /tɔʀaks/ *nm inv* thorax.

thym /tɛ̃/ *nm* thyme.

thyroïde /tiʀɔid/ *adj, nf* thyroid.

tibia /tibja/ *nm* shinbone, tibia; **un coup de pied dans les ~s** a kick in the shins.

tic /tik/ *nm* **1** tic; **être plein de ~s** to be constantly twitching; **2** habit; **~ de langage** verbal tic.

ticket /tikɛ/ *nm* (for train, platform) ticket; **~ de caisse** till receipt (GB), sales slip (US).

tic-tac /tiktak/ *nm inv* (*also onomatopoeic*) ticktock; **faire ~** to tick.

tiède /tjɛd/ *adj* **1** [*coffee, soup*] lukewarm; [*bath*] tepid; [*water, air, night*] warm; [*season, temperature*] mild; **2** (figurative) lukewarm.

tièdement /tjɛdmɑ̃/ *adv* (figurative) half-heartedly.

tiédeur /tjedœʀ/ *nf* (of season) mildness; (of air) warmth.

tien, tienne /tjɛ̃, tjɛn/ **le tien, la tienne, les tiens, les tiennes** *pron* yours; **un métie comme le ~** a job like yours; **à la tienne!** cheers!; (ironic) good luck to you!

tiens /tjɛ̃/ ▶ **tenir**.

tierce[1] /tjɛʀs/ **I** *adj f* ▶ **tiers I**.
II *nf* **1** (Games) three card run, tierce; **2** (Mus) third.

tiercé /tjɛʀse/ *nm* (Games) **jouer au ~** to bet on the horses.

tiers, tierce[2] /tjɛʀ, tjɛʀs/ **I** *adj* third; **un pays ~** (gen) another country; a non-member country; **une tierce personne** a third party.
II *nm inv* **1** third; **le ~/les deux ~ du travail** one third/two thirds of the work; **2** (person) outsider; (Law) third party.
■ **le Tiers État** the Third Estate.

tiers-monde /tjɛʀmɔ̃d/ *nm* Third World.

tige /tiʒ/ *nf* **1** (of plant) (gen) stem, stalk; **2** (of feather) shaft.

tigre /tigʀ/ *nm* (Zool) tiger.

tigré, ~e /tigʀe/ *adj* **1** striped; **2** spotted.

tigresse /tigʀɛs/ *nf* (Zool), (figurative) tigress.

tilleul /tijœl/ *nm* **1** limetree; **2** limewood; **3** lime-blossom tea.

tilt○ /tilt/ *nm* **ça a fait ~**○ **(dans mon esprit)** the penny dropped○; **ça a fait ~ entre nous**○ we clicked straight away.

timbale /tɛ̃bal/ *nf* **1** metal (tumbler); **2** (Mus) kettledrum; **~s** timpani; **3** (Culin) timbale.

timbre /tɛ̃bʀ/ *nm* **1** stamp; **2** postmark; **3** (of voice) tone, timbre; **4** (Med) patch.

timbre-poste, *pl* **timbres-poste** /tɛ̃bʀəpɔst/ *nm* postage stamp.

timbrer /tɛ̃bʀe/ [1] *vtr* to stamp, to put a stamp on.

timide /timid/ *adj* [*person*] shy, timid; [*criticism*] timid; [*success*] limited.

timidement /timidmɑ̃/ *adv* **1** shyly; **2** timidly; **3** half-heartedly.

timidité /timidite/ *nf* shyness.

timon /timɔ̃/ *nm* **1** (Naut) tiller; **2** (of harness) shaft.

timonier /timɔnje/ *nm* (Naut) helmsman.

timoré, ~e /timɔʀe/ *adj* timorous.

tintement /tɛ̃tmɑ̃/ *nm* chiming; tinkling.

tinter /tɛ̃te/ [1] *vi* [*bells*] to chime; [*doorbell*] to ring; [*small bell*] to tinkle; [*glass, cutlery, coins*] to clink; [*barrel*] to clang; [*keys*] to jingle; (Mus) [*triangle*] to ring; **faire ~** to ring [*bell*]; to clink [*glass, cutlery, coins*]; to clang [*barrels*].

tipi /tipi/ *nm* te(e)pee.

tique /tik/ *nf* (Zool) tick.

tiquer○ /tike/ [1] *vi* to wince; **sans ~** without batting an eyelid (GB) or eyelash (US).

tir /tiʀ/ *nm* **1** (Mil) fire; **déclencher le ~** to open fire; **2** (Sport) shooting; **3 ~ de grenades** grenade firing; **4** (in games, sports) (with ball) shot; **5** shooting; **~ aux canards** duck shooting; **6 ~ forain** rifle range.

tirade /tiʀad/ *nf* **1** declamation; **2** tirade.

tirage /tiʀaʒ/ *nm* **1 ~ (au sort)** draw; **désigner par ~ (au sort)** to draw [*name, winner*]; **2** impression; **3** edition; **~ limité** limited edition; **4** (of book) run; (of newspaper) circulation; **quotidien à grand ~** mass-circulation daily.

tirailler /tiʀaje/ [1] *vtr* to tug (at), to pull (at) [*rope, sleeve*]; **être tiraillé entre son travail et**

sa famille to be torn between one's work and one's family.

tire-au-flanc○ /tiʀoflɑ̃/ *nm inv* shirker, skiver○ (GB).

tire-bouchon, *pl* **~s** /tiʀbuʃɔ̃/ *nm* corkscrew; **en ~** [*tail*] curly.

tire-d'aile: **à tire-d'aile** /atiʀdɛl/ *phr* in a flurry of wings; (figurative) hurriedly.

tirelire /tiʀliʀ/ *nf* piggy bank.

tirer /tiʀe/ [1] **I** *vtr* **1** to pull [*vehicle*]; to pull up [*chair, armchair*]; to pull away [*rug*]; **2** to pull [*hair*]; to pull on [*rope*]; to tug at [*sleeve*]; **~ qn par le bras** to pull sb's arm; **3 ~ ses cheveux en arrière** to pull back one's hair; **~ ses bas** to pull up one's stockings; **avoir les traits tirés** to look drawn; **4** to draw [*bolt, curtain*]; to pull down [*blind*]; to close [*door, shutter*]; **5** to fire off [*bullet, grenade*]; to fire [*missile*]; to shoot [*arrow*]; **~ un coup de feu** to fire a shot; **6** (Sport) **~ un penalty** to take a penalty; **7 ~ (au sort)** to draw [*card, name, winner*]; to draw for [*partner*]; **8** (in astrology) **~ les cartes à qn** to tell the cards for sb; **se faire ~ les cartes** to have one's fortune told with cards; **9** to draw [*wine*]; to withdraw [*money*]; **~ qch de sa poche** to pull sth out of one's pocket; **10 ~ le pays de la récession** to get the country out of recession; **tire-moi de là!** get me out of this!; **tu l'as tirée de son silence** you drew her out of her silence; **11 ~ [qch] de qn** to get [sth] from sb [*information, confession*]; **~ [qch] de qch** to draw [sth] from sth [*strength, resources*]; to derive [sth] from sth [*pride, satisfaction*]; to make [sth] out of sth [*money*]; **~ le maximum de la situation** to make the most of the situation; **12 ~ de qch** to base [sth] on sth [*story, film*]; to get [sth] from sth [*name*]; **13** to print [*book, negative*]; to run off [*proofs, copies*]; **14** to draw [*line etc*]; **15**○ **plus qu'une semaine à ~** only one more week to go; **16 ~ un chèque** to draw a cheque (GB) or check (US) (**sur** on).

II *vi* **1** to pull; **~ sur qch** to pull on sth; to tug at sth; **2** (with firearm) to shoot; to fire; **3** (in football) to shoot; (in handball, basketball) to take a shot; **4 ~ (au sort)** to draw lots; **5 ~ sur son compte** to draw on one's account; **6 la cheminée tire bien** the chimney draws well; **7 ~ à mille exemplaires** [*periodical*] to have a circulation of one thousand; **8 ~ sur le jaune/l'orangé** [*colour*] to be yellowish/orangy.

III se tirer *v refl* (+ *v être*) **1 se ~ de** to come through [*situation, difficulties*]; **2 se ~ une balle** to shoot oneself; **se ~ dessus** to shoot at one another; **3**○ **s'en ~** to cope; (from accident) to escape; (from illness) to pull through; **s'en ~ à bon prix** to get off lightly.

tiret /tiʀɛ/ *nm* dash.

tirette /tiʀɛt/ *nf* **1** pull tab; cord; **2** (of table) (sliding) support, (sliding) flap.

tireur, **-euse** /tiʀœʀ, øz/ *nm, f* **1** (Mil, Sport) marksman/markswoman; **2** gunman.

tiroir /tiʀwaʀ/ *nm* (in piece of furniture) drawer; **à ~s** (figurative) [*novel, play*] episodic.

IDIOMS **racler les fonds de ~** to scrape some money together.

tiroir-caisse, *pl* **tiroirs-caisses** /tiʀwaʀ kɛs/ *nm* cash register.

tisane /tizan/ *nf* herbal tea, tisane.

tison /tizɔ̃/ *nm* (fire) brand.

tisonnier /tizɔnje/ *nm* poker.

tissage /tisaʒ/ *nm* **1** weaving; **faire du ~** to weave; **2** weave.

tisser /tise/ [1] *vtr* **1** [*person, machine*] to weave; **2** [*spider*] to spin [*web*].

tisserand, **~e** /tisʀɑ̃, ɑ̃d/ *nm,f* weaver.

tissu /tisy/ *nm* **1** material, fabric; **2** (Anat) **le ~ osseux** bone tissue; **3** (of intrigue) web; (of lies) pack, tissue; (of insults) string; **~ social** social fabric.

tissu-éponge, *pl* **tissus-éponges** /tisyepɔ̃ʒ/ *nm* (terry) towelling[GB], terry cloth (US).

titan /titɑ̃/ *nm* titan; **de ~** titanic.

titiller /titije/ [1] *vtr* to titillate.

titre /titʀ/ *nm* **1** (of book, film, chapter) title; (in newspaper) headline; **avoir pour ~** to be entitled; **les ~s de l'actualité** the headlines; **2** title; **~ mondial** world title; **~ nobiliaire** or **de noblesse** title; **le ~ d'ingénieur** the status of qualified engineer; **en ~** [*professor, director*] titular; [*supplier*] appointed; [*mistress, rival*] official; **~s universitaires** university qualifications; **3 à juste ~** quite rightly; **à plus d'un ~** in many respects; **à ~ d'exemple** as an example; **à ~ définitif** on a permanent basis; **à ~ privé** in a private capacity; **à ~ gracieux** free; **à ~ indicatif** as a rough guide; **à quel ~ a-t-il été invité?** why was he invited?; **perçu au ~ de droits d'auteur** received as royalties; **4** (Law) deed; **~ de propriété** title deed; **5** (on stock exchange) security; **6** (Econ) item; **~ budgétaire** budgetary item; **7** (of solution) titre[GB]; (of wines, spirits) strength; (of precious metal) fineness.

■ **~ de gloire** claim to fame; **~ de transport** ticket.

titré, **~e** /titʀe/ *adj* titled; **être ~** to be titled.

titrer /titʀe/ [1] *vtr* (in newspaper) **le journal du dimanche titrait**... the headlines in the Sunday paper read...

titubant, **~e** /titybɑ̃, ɑ̃t/ *adj* [*person, gait*] unsteady.

tituber /titybe/ [1] *vi* to stagger.

titulaire /titylɛʀ/ **I** *adj* (gen) permanent; [*lecturer*] tenured.

II *nmf* **1** (gen) permanent staff member; tenured lecturer (GB) or professor (US); **2** holder; **être ~ de** to hold [*degree, licence, post*]; to have [*bank account, pension*].

titulariser /titylaʀize/ [1] *vtr* to give permanent status to [*agent, staff*]; to grant tenure to [*professor*]; to make [sb] a full member of the team [*player*].

toast /tost/ *nm* **1** toast; **2** toast; **porter un ~ à qch/en l'honneur de qn** to toast sth/sb.

toboggan /tɔbɔgɑ̃/ *nm* **1** slide; **2** ®flyover (GB), overpass (US); **3** (Tech) (for rubble) chute; **4** (Sport) toboggan.

toc /tɔk/ **I**○ *nm* **c'est du ~** it's fake.

II *excl* (*also onomatopoeic*) **~! ~!** knock! knock!

tocsin /tɔksɛ̃/ *nm* alarm (bell), tocsin.

toge /tɔʒ/ *nf* **1** (of academic) gown; (of judge) robe; **2** toga.

toi /twa/ *pron* **1** you; **~, ne dis rien** don't say anything; **elle est plus âgée que ~** she's older than you; **un cadeau pour ~** a present for you; **à ~** (in game) your turn; **c'est à ~** it's yours; **c'est à ~ de choisir** it's your turn to choose; it's up to you to choose; **2** yourself; **reprends-~** pull yourself together.

toile /twal/ *nf* **1** cloth; **~ de lin** linen (cloth); **des vêtements de ~** (heavy) cotton clothes; **de la grosse ~** canvas; **2** (in art) canvas; painting; **~ de maître** master painting; **3** (Naut) canvas.

■ **~ d'araignée** spider's web; cobweb; **~ cirée** oilcloth; **~ goudronnée** tarpaulin; **~ de jute** hessian; **~ de tente** canvas; tent.

toilerie /twalʀi/ *nf* **1** textile manufacture; **2** textile trade.

toilettage /twalɛtaʒ/ *nm* (of animal) grooming.

toilette /twalɛt/ **I** *nf* **1 faire sa ~** [*person*] to have a wash; [*animal*] to wash itself; **faire la ~ d'un mort** to lay out a corpse; **2** outfit; **en grande ~** all dressed up.

II toilettes *nf pl* toilet (GB), bathroom (US); (public) toilets.

toiletter /twalete/ [1] *vtr* to groom [*dog, cat, horse*].

toi-même /twamɛm/ *pron* yourself.

toise /twaz/ *nf* height gauge.

toiser /twaze/ [1] *vtr* to look [sb] up and down [*person*].

toit /twa/ *nm* roof; **habiter sous les ~s** to live in a garret.

■ **le ~ du Monde** the roof of the world; **~ ouvrant** sunroof.

IDIOMS **crier qch sur (tous) les ~s** to shout sth from the rooftops.

toiture /twatyʀ/ *nf* **1** roof; **2** roofing.

tôle /tol/ *nf* **1** sheet metal; **2** metal sheet or plate; **3**° = **taule**.

tolérable /tɔleʀabl/ *adj* [*wait, pain*] bearable; [*attitude*] tolerable, acceptable.

tolérance /tɔleʀɑ̃s/ *nf* **1** tolerance; indulgence; **2 ce n'est pas un droit, c'est une ~** it isn't legal but it is tolerated; **3** (of medicine, noise) tolerance.

tolérant, ~e /tɔleʀɑ̃, ɑ̃t/ *adj* tolerant.

tolérer /tɔleʀe/ [14] *vtr* to tolerate.

tôlerie /tolʀi/ *nf* **1** sheet-metal working; sheet-metal trade; sheet-metal works; **2** metalwork; (of car) bodywork.

tollé /tɔle/ *nm* outcry, hue and cry.

TOM /tɔm/ *nm*: *abbr* ▶ **territoire**.

tomate /tɔmat/ *nf* **1** tomato; **2** tomato plant; **3** *pastis with a dash of grenadine*.

tombal, ~e, *mpl* **-aux** /tɔ̃bal, o/ *adj* **inscription ~e** gravestone inscription.

tombant, ~e /tɔ̃bɑ̃, ɑ̃t/ *adj* [*shoulders*] sloping; [*moustache, eyelids*] drooping; [*ears*] floppy; [*belly*] sagging.

tombe /tɔ̃b/ *nf* **1** grave; **2** gravestone.

tombeau, *pl* **~x** /tɔ̃bo/ *nm* **1** tomb; **mettre qn au ~** to lay sb in their grave; **vivre avec qn jusqu'au ~** to live with sb till the grave; **2 c'est un ~** [*person*] he/she will keep quiet.

IDIOMS **rouler à ~ ouvert**° to drive at breakneck speed.

tombée /tɔ̃be/ *nf* **à la ~ du jour** at close of day; **la ~ de la nuit** nightfall.

tomber[1] /tɔ̃be/ [1] *vi* (+ *v être*) **1** (gen) to fall; [*person, chair*] to fall over; [*tree, wall*] to fall down; (from height) [*person, vase*] to fall off; [*apples, leaves, bombs*] to fall; [*hair, teeth*] to fall out; [*plaster, covering*] to come off; **~ dans un trou** to fall down a hole; **~ du lit/de ma poche** to fall out of bed/out of my pocket; **le vent a fait ~ une tuile du toit** the wind blew a tile off the roof; **se laisser ~ dans un fauteuil** to flop into an armchair; **laisser ~ un gâteau sur le tapis** to drop a cake on the carpet; **2** [*rain, snow*] to fall; [*fog*] to come down; [*ray, light*] to fall; [*theatre curtain*] to fall; **qu'est-ce que ça tombe**°! it's pouring down!; **la foudre est tombée sur un arbre** the lightning struck a tree; **3** [*value, price, temperature*] to fall; [*ardour, anger*] to subside; [*fever*] to come down; [*wind*] to drop; [*day*] to draw to a close; [*conversation*] to die down; **faire ~** to bring down [*price, temperature*]; to dampen [*enthusiasm*]; **il est tombé bien bas dans mon estime** he has gone right down in my esteem; **je tombe de sommeil** I can't keep my eyes open; **4** [*dictator, regime, city*] to fall; [*obstacle, objection*] to vanish; [*opposition*] to subside; [*prejudice*] to die out; **faire ~** to bring down [*regime, dictator*]; (figurative) to break down [*barriers*]; **5** [*belly*] to sag; [*shoulders*] to slope; **6** [*lock of hair*] to fall; **~ bien/mal** [*garment, curtain*] to hang well/badly; **7 ~ dans un piège** (figurative) to fall into a trap; **vous tombez dans le paradoxe** you are being paradoxical; **~ sous le coup d'une loi** to fall within the provisions of a law; **~ aux mains** or **entre les mains de qn** [*document, power*] to fall into sb's hands; **8** to fall; **~ malade/amoureux** to fall ill/in love; **9** [*decision, sentence, verdict*] to be announced; [*news*] to break; [*reply*] to be given; **dès que le journal tombe des presses** as soon as the newspaper comes off the press; **10 ~ sur** to come across [*stranger, detail, object*]; to run into [*friend, acquaintance*]; **~ sur la bonne page/le bon numéro** to hit on the right page/the right number; **si tu prends cette rue, tu tomberas sur la place** if you follow that street, you'll come to the square; **11 c'est tombé juste au bon moment** it came just at the right time; **tu ne pouvais pas mieux ~!** you couldn't have come at a better time!; you couldn't have done better!; **tu tombes mal, j'allais partir** you're unlucky, I was just about to leave; **il faut toujours que ça tombe sur moi**°! (decision, choice) why does it always have to be me?; (misfortune) why does it always have to happen to me?; **12** [*national holiday,* *birthday*] to fall on [*day*]; **13 laisser ~** to give up [*job, activity*]; to drop [*plan, habit*]; **laisse ~!** forget it!; give it a rest○!; **laisser ~ qn** to drop sb; to let sb down; **14 ~ sur qn** [*soldiers, thugs*] to fall on sb, to lay into sb○; [*raiders, police*] to descend on sb; [*critics*] to go for sb.

tomber[2] /tɔ̃be/ *nm* hang; **ce velours a un beau ~** this velvet hangs well.

tombeur○ /tɔ̃bœʀ/ *nm* lady-killer.

tombola /tɔ̃bɔla/ *nf* tombola (GB), lottery.

tome[1] /tom/ *nm* **1** volume; **2** part, book.

tome[2] /tɔm/ *nf* = **tomme**.

tomme /tɔm/ *nf* tomme or tome (cheese).

tommette /tɔmɛt/ *nf* hexagonal floor tile.

ton[1], **ta**, *pl* **tes** /tɔ̃, ta, te/ *det* your; **un de tes amis** a friend of yours.

ton[2] /tɔ̃/ *nm* **1** pitch; tone; **~ grave/aigu** low/high pitch; **d'un ~ dédaigneux** scornfully; **baisser le ~** to lower one's voice; (figurative) to moderate one's tone; **eh bien, si tu le prends sur ce ~** well, if you're going to take it like that; **2** (in linguistics) tone; **langue à ~s** tone language; **3 donner le ~** to set the tone; to set the fashion; **de bon ~** in good taste; **4** (Mus) pitch; key; tone; (instrument) pitch pipe; **5** (of colour) shade, tone; **~ sur ~** in matching tones.

tonalité /tɔnalite/ *nf* **1** (Mus) key; tonality; **2** (of vowel) tone; **3** (of voice) tone; (of novel, film) tone; **4** (of colours) tonality; **5** dialling tone (GB), dial tone (US).

tondeuse /tɔ̃døz/ *nf* **1** (for dog) clippers; (for sheep) shears; **2** (for cutting hair) clippers; **3 ~ (à gazon)** lawnmower.

tondre /tɔ̃dʀ/ [6] *vtr* to shear [*sheep, wool*]; to clip [*dog*]; to mow [*lawn*]; **~ qn** to shave sb's head.

tondu, **~e** /tɔ̃dy/ *adj* **1** [*sheep*] shorn; [*dog*] clipped; **2** [*hair*] shorn; [*head*] shaven (GB), shaved.

tongs /tɔ̃g/ *nf pl* flip-flops, thongs (US).

tonifiant, **~e** /tɔnifjɑ̃, ɑ̃t/ *adj* **1** [*climate, air*] bracing; **2** [*exercise, lotion*] toning.

tonifier /tɔnifje/ [2] *vtr* to tone up [*muscles, skin*].

tonique[1] /tɔnik/ **I** *adj* **1** [*drink, remedy*] tonic; (figurative) [*air, cold*] bracing; [*book, reading*] stimulating; **2 lotion ~** toning lotion; **3** [*accent*] tonic.

II *nm* **1** (Med), (figurative) tonic; **2** toning lotion.

tonique[2] /tɔnik/ *nf* (Mus) tonic.

tonitruant, **~e** /tɔnitʀyɑ̃, ɑ̃t/ *adj* [*laughter, voice*] booming.

tonnage /tɔnaʒ/ *nm* tonnage.

tonne /tɔn/ *nf* (1 000 kg) tonne, metric ton; **des ~s de choses à faire**○ loads○ of things to do.

tonneau, *pl* **~x** /tɔno/ *nm* **1** barrel; **2** (of car) somersault; **3** (of plane) barrel roll; **4** (Naut) ton.

IDIOMS **du même ~**○ of the same kind.

tonnelle /tɔnɛl/ *nf* arbour[GB]; **sous une ~** in an arbour[GB].

tonner /tɔne/ [1] *vi, v impers* to thunder.

tonnerre /tɔnɛʀ/ *nm* **1** thunder; **un coup de ~** a clap of thunder; (figurative) a thunderbolt; **2** (of cannons, artillery) thundering; **un ~ d'applaudissements** thunderous applause; **3**○ **du ~** fabulous; **ça marche du ~** it's going fantastically well.

tonsure /tɔ̃syʀ/ *nf* (of monk) tonsure.

tonte /tɔ̃t/ *nf* **1 ~ (des moutons)** shearing; **2** fleece.

tonton○ /tɔ̃tɔ̃/ *nm* uncle; **~ Pierre** Uncle Pierre.

tonus /tɔnys/ *nm inv* **1** (of person) energy, dynamism; **2** (of muscle) tone, tonus.

top /tɔp/ *nm* pip, beep; **donner le ~ de départ** to give the starting signal.

topaze /tɔpaz/ *nf* topaz.

toper /tɔpe/ [1] *vi* **topons là!** let's shake on it!, done!

topinambour /tɔpinɑ̃buʀ/ *nm* Jerusalem artichoke.

topique /tɔpik/ *adj* **1** [*remark*] apposite; **2** [*drug, ointment*] topical.

topographie /tɔpɔgʀafi/ *nf* topography.

toquade○ /tɔkad/ *nf* **1** (for thing) passion; **2** (on person) crush○.

toque /tɔk/ *nf* **1** (of woman) toque; (of chef) chef's hat; (of judge) hat; **~ en fourrure** fur cap; **2** (of jockey) cap.

toqué○, **~e** /tɔke/ *adj* crazy○.

torche /tɔʀʃ/ *nf* torch; **~ vivante** human torch.

■ **~ électrique** torch (GB), flashlight.

torcher○ /tɔʀʃe/ [1] *vtr* **1** to wipe; **2** to dash off○ [*article, report*]; to cobble [sth] together; **un article bien torché** a well-written article.

torchis /tɔʀʃi/ *nm inv* cob (*for walls*).

torchon /tɔʀʃɔ̃/ *nm* **1** (gen) cloth; (**~ (de cuisine)**) tea towel (GB), dish towel (US); **2** (newspaper) (derogatory) rag○; **3**○ messy piece of work.

IDIOMS **le ~ brûle (entre eux)**○ it's war (between them).

tordant○, **~e** /tɔʀdɑ̃, ɑ̃t/ *adj* hilarious.

tordre /tɔʀdʀ/ [6] **I** *vtr* **1** to twist [*arm, wrist*]; to wring [*neck*]; **2** to bend [*nail, bar, bumper*]; **3** to wring out [*washing*].

II se tordre *v refl* (+ *v être*) **1** [*person*] **se ~ la cheville** to twist one's ankle; **se ~ de douleur** to writhe in pain; **2** [*bumper*] to bend; [*wheel*] to buckle.

tordu, **~e** /tɔʀdy/ *adj* **1** [*nose, legs*] crooked; [*branches, trunk, iron bar*] twisted; **2** (figurative) [*idea*] weird, strange; [*logic, reasoning*] twisted.

tornade /tɔʀnad/ *nf* tornado.

torpeur /tɔʀpœʀ/ *nf* torpor.

torpille /tɔʀpij/ *nf* torpedo.

torpiller /tɔʀpije/ [1] *vtr* to torpedo.

torréfier /tɔʀefje/ [2] *vtr* to roast.

torrent /tɔʀɑ̃/ *nm* torrent; **pleuvoir à ~s** to rain very heavily.

torrentiel, **-ielle** /tɔʀɑ̃sjɛl/ *adj* torrential.

torride /tɔʀid/ *adj* [*climate, region*] torrid; [*sun, summer, heat*] scorching.

tors, **torse**[1] /tɔʀ, tɔʀs/ *adj* (gen) twisted; [*legs*] crooked.

torsade /tɔʀsad/ *nf* **1** twist, coil; **2** cable stitch; **3** (in architecture) cable moulding (GB), cable molding (US).

torsader /tɔʀsade/ [1] *vtr* to twist; **une colonne torsadée** a cable column.

torse[2] /tɔʀs/ *nm* **1** (gen) chest; **se mettre ~ nu** to strip to the waist; **2** (Anat) torso.

torsion /tɔʀsjɔ̃/ *nf* **1** twisting; **2** torsion.

tort /tɔʀ/ **I** *nm* **1 avoir ~** to be wrong; **j'aurais bien ~ de m'inquiéter!** it would be silly of me to worry!; **être en ~, être dans son ~** to be in the wrong; **donner ~ à qn** [*referee, judge*] to blame sb; [*facts*] to prove sb wrong; **2** fault; **les ~s sont partagés** there are faults on both sides; **reconnaître ses ~s** to acknowledge that one has done wrong; **avoir des ~s envers qn** to have wronged sb; **3** mistake; **j'ai eu le ~ de le croire** I made the mistake of believing him; **4** wrong; **faire du ~ à qn/qch** to harm sb/sth.

II à tort *phr* [*accuse*] wrongly; **à ~ ou à raison** rightly or wrongly; **à ~ et à travers** [*spend*] wildly; **parler à ~ et à travers** to talk a lot of nonsense.

torticolis /tɔʀtikɔli/ *nm inv* stiff neck.

tortillard○ /tɔʀtijaʀ/ *nm* small local train.

tortiller /tɔʀtije/ [1] **I** *vtr* to twist [*fibres, strands*]; to twiddle [*handkerchief*].

II se tortiller *v refl* (+ *v être*) to wriggle.

tortionnaire /tɔʀsjɔnɛʀ/ *nmf* torturer.

tortue /tɔʀty/ *nf* **1** (sea) turtle; **2** tortoise, turtle (US); **3** (person) slowcoach○ (GB), slowpoke○ (US); **4** (butterfly) tortoiseshell.

tortueux, -euse /tɔʀtɥø, øz/ *adj* **1** [*road, staircase*] winding; **2** (figurative) [*behaviour*] devious; [*language*] convoluted; [*mind, reasoning*] tortuous.

torture /tɔʀtyʀ/ *nf* torture; **sous la ~** under torture.

torturer /tɔʀtyʀe/ [1] **I** *vtr* **1** to torture [*person*]; **2** [*thought, feeling*] to torment; **3** to distort [*text*]; **style torturé** tortured style.

II se torturer *v refl* (+ *v être*) to torment oneself; **se ~ l'esprit** to rack one's brains.

torve /tɔʀv/ *adj* [*look*] menacing, baleful.

tôt /to/ *adv* **1** [*start*] early; **~ le matin** early in the morning; **2** soon, early; **le plus ~ possible** as soon as possible; **le plus ~ serait le mieux** the sooner the better; **~ ou tard** sooner or later; **tu n'étais pas plus ~ parti qu'il est arrivé** no sooner had you left than he arrived; **on ne m'y reprendra pas de si ~** I won't do that again in a hurry; **tu as fini? ce n'est pas trop ~**○! you've finished? about time too○!

total, ~e, *mpl* **-aux** /tɔtal, o/ **I** *adj* **1** [*contradiction, disappointment*] complete, total; **2** [*price, surface area*] total.

II *nm* total.

III au total *phr* **au ~ cela fait 350 francs** altogether that comes to 350 francs.

totalement /tɔtalmɑ̃/ *adv* totally, completely.

totaliser /tɔtalize/ [1] *vtr* **1** to total [*profits*]; **2** to have a total of [*points, votes*].

totalitaire /tɔtalitɛʀ/ *adj* **1** [*regime, state*] totalitarian; **2** [*doctrine*] all-embracing.

totalitarisme /tɔtalitaʀism/ *nm* totalitarianism.

totalité /tɔtalite/ *nf* **la ~ du personnel** all the staff; **la ~ des dépenses** the total expenditure; **financé en ~ par l'État** entirely state-financed; **nous vous rembourserons en ~** we will refund you in full.

totem /tɔtɛm/ *nm* **1** totem; **2** totem pole.

toucan /tukɑ̃/ *nm* toucan.

touchant, ~e /tuʃɑ̃, ɑ̃t/ *adj* moving; touching.

touche /tuʃ/ *nf* **1** (on keyboard) key; (of washing machine, television set, video) button; (on stringed instrument) fret; **2** (of paintbrush) stroke; (of paint) dash, touch; (of artist) touch; **3** (Sport) (**ligne de**) **~** sideline, touchline; **mettre qn sur la ~** (figurative) to push sb aside; **4** (in fencing) hit; **5** (in fishing) bite.

toucher[1] /tuʃe/ [1] **I** *vtr* **1 ~** (**de la main**) to touch [*object, surface, person*]; **~ du bois** (superstitiously) to touch wood; **~ le front de qn** to feel sb's forehead; **2** to be touching [*wall, ceiling, bottom of sth*]; **~ le sol** [*animal, plane, high jumper*] to land; **3** to hit [*opponent, car, kerb*]; **4** to touch [*person*]; **ça me touche beaucoup** I am very touched; **5** [*event, change, crisis, law*] to affect [*person, sector, country*]; [*storm*] to hit [*region, city*]; **6** [*country, house*] to be next to; **7** [*person*] to get, to receive [*money, allowance*]; to cash [*cheque, postal order*]; to get [*pension*]; **8 ~ trois millions d'auditeurs** to have an audience of three million.

II toucher à *v+prep* **1** to touch [*object*]; **~ à tout** to be into everything; (figurative) to be a jack of all trades; **avec son air de ne pas y ~, c'est un malin**○ he looks as if butter wouldn't melt in his mouth, but he's a sly one; **2** to concern, to relate to [*activity, issue*]; **3** to infringe on [*right, freedom*]; **4** to get on to [*problem*].

III se toucher *v refl* (+ *v être*) [*houses, gardens*] to be next to each other.

toucher[2] /tuʃe/ *nm* **1 le ~** touch, the sense of touch; **2** (of pianist) touch.

touche-touche○: **à touche-touche** /atuʃ tuʃ/ *phr* **être à ~** [*cars*] to be bumper to bumper; [*people, tents*] to be on top of each other○.

touffe /tuf/ *nf* (of hair, grass) tuft; (of trees) clump.

touffu, ~e /tufy/ *adj* **1** [*eyebrows, beard*] bushy; [*vegetation*] dense; [*bush*] thick; [*tree*] leafy; **au poil ~** with thick fur; **2** [*text, style*] dense.

touiller○ /tuje/ [1] *vtr* to stir [*sauce*]; to toss [*salad*].

toujours /tuʒuʀ/ *adv* **1** always; **comme ~** as always; **de ~** [*friend*] very old; [*friendship*] long-standing; **~ plus vite** faster and faster; **des frais ~ plus importants** ever-increasing costs; **2** still; **il n'est ~ pas levé?** is he still not up?; **3** anyway; **on peut ~ essayer** we can always try; **c'est ~ ça de pris** or **de**

gagné that's something at least; **~ est-il que** the fact remains that.

toupet /tupɛ/ *nm* **1**○ cheek○, nerve○; **elle ne manque pas de ~!** she's got a cheek○!; **2** (of hair) tuft; quiff (GB), forelock (US).

toupie /tupi/ *nf* top; **faire tourner une ~** to spin a top.

tour¹ /tuʀ/ *nm* **1** (gen) turn; (around axis) revolution; **donner un ~ de clé** to turn the key; **faire un ~ de manège** to have a go on the merry-go-round; **faire un ~ sur soi-même** [*dance*] to spin around; [*planet*] to rotate; **fermer qch à double ~** to double-lock sth; **à ~ de bras**○ [*hit*] with a vengeance; [*invest, buy up*] left, right and centre[GB]○; **2 faire le ~ de qch** (gen) to go around sth; to drive around sth; **la nouvelle a vite fait le ~ du village** the news spread rapidly through the village; **3** (of pond) edges; (of pipe, tree trunk) circumference; (of head, hips) measurement; (standard measurement) size; **tronc de 15 mètres de ~** trunk 15 metres[GB] in circumference; **4** walk, stroll; (on bicycle) ride; (in car) drive, spin; **je suis allé faire un ~ à Paris** I went to Paris; **je vais faire un ~ chez des amis** I'm just going to go over to some friends; **5** look; **faire le ~ d'un problème** to have a look at a problem; **faire un (rapide) ~ d'horizon** to have a quick overall look; **faire le ~ de ses relations** to go through one's acquaintances; **on en a vite fait le ~**○ there's not much to it/her/them etc; **6** (gen) turn; (in competition, tournament) round; **à qui le ~?** whose turn is it?; **chacun son ~** each one in his turn; **il perd plus souvent qu'à son ~** he loses more often than he would like; he loses more often than he should; **~ à ~** by turns; in turn; **7 ~ de scrutin** ballot, round of voting; **8** trick; **jouer un ~ à qn** to play a trick on sb; **et le ~ est joué** that's done the trick; **ça te jouera des ~s** it's going to get you into trouble one of these days; **9** trick; **~ de cartes** card trick; **~ d'adresse** feat of skill; **~ de main** knack; **en un ~ de main** deftly; in a flash; **10** (in situation, relationship) turn; **donner un ~ nouveau à qch** to give a new twist to sth; **11** (Tech) lathe.

■ **~ de chant** song recital; **~ de garde** turn of duty; **~ de potier** potter's wheel; **~ de rein(s)** back strain.

tour² /tuʀ/ *nf* **1** tower; **2** tower block (GB), high rise (US); **3** (in chess) rook, castle; **4** siege-tower.

tourbe /tuʀb/ *nf* peat.

tourbillon /tuʀbijɔ̃/ *nm* **1** whirlwind; whirlpool; **~ de poussière/feuilles** whirl of dust/leaves; **2** (figurative) (of memories) swirl; (of reforms) whirlwind.

tourbillonner /tuʀbijɔne/ [1] *vi* **1** [*snow, leaves*] to swirl, to whirl; [*dancers*] to twirl; **2** (figurative) [*ideas, memories*] to swirl around.

tourelle /tuʀɛl/ *nf* **1** turret; **2** (of tank) turret; (of submarine) conning tower.

tourisme /tuʀism/ *nm* tourism; **l'industrie du ~** the tourist industry.

touriste /tuʀist/ *nmf* tourist; **il suit les cours en ~** (humorous) he goes to his lessons whenever he feels like it.

touristique /tuʀistik/ *adj* [*brochure, menu, season*] tourist; [*influx*] of tourists; [*town, area*] which attracts tourists.

tourment /tuʀmɑ̃/ *nm* (literary) torment.

tourmenté, ~e /tuʀmɑ̃te/ *adj* **1** [*person, face*] tormented; [*soul*] tortured; **2** [*era, life*] turbulent; **3** [*landscape*] rugged; [*shape*] contorted; **4** [*style*] tortured.

tourmenter /tuʀmɑ̃te/ [1] **I** *vtr* **1** to worry; **2** to torment; **~ qn de reproches** to torment sb with reproaches; **3** [*creditors*] to harass.

II se tourmenter *v refl* (+ *v être*) to worry.

tournage /tuʀnaʒ/ *nm* **1** shooting, filming; **2** film set; **3** (Tech) turning.

tournant, ~e /tuʀnɑ̃, ɑ̃t/ **I** *adj* **1** [*seat, mechanism*] swivel; [*sprinkler*] rotating; [*stage, door*] revolving; **2** [*presidency*] rotating; [*strike*] staggered.

II *nm* **1** (in road) bend; **2** turning point; **3** turn; **au ~ du siècle** at the turn of the century; **4** change of direction; **prendre un ~** to change tack.

tourné, ~e¹ /tuʀne/ *adj* **1 ~ vers** [*eyes, look, person*] turned toward(s); [*activity, policy*] oriented toward(s); **~ vers le passé/l'avenir** backward-/forward-looking; **porte ~e vers la mer** gate facing the sea; **2 bien ~** [*compliment, letter*] nicely phrased; [*person, waist*] shapely; **mal ~** [*sentence*] clumsy; **3** [*milk*] off.

tourne-disque, *pl* **~s** /tuʀnədisk/ *nm* record player.

tournée² /tuʀne/ *nf* **1** (of postman, delivery man) round; **2** (of team, singer, theatre group) tour; **en ~** on tour; **3**○ (of drinks) round.

tournemain: **en un tournemain** /ɑ̃nɛ̃tuʀnəmɛ̃/ *phr* in no time.

tourner /tuʀne/ [1] **I** *vtr* **1** to turn [*steering wheel, key, button*]; **~ la tête vers** to turn to look at; **~ les yeux vers** to look at; **2** to shoot [*film, scene*]; **3** to get around [*difficulty, law*]; **4** to phrase [*letter, compliment, criticism*]; **5** (Tech) to turn [*wood*]; to throw [*pot*]; **6 ~ qn/qch en dérision** or **ridicule** to deride or ridicule sb/sth; **7 ~ et retourner qch dans son esprit** to mull sth over; **8** to stir [*sauce*]; to toss [*salad*].

II *vi* **1** (gen) [*key, record*] to turn; [*wheel*] to turn, to revolve; [*planet, propeller*] to rotate; [*rotating door*] to revolve; [*dancer*] to spin; **faire ~** to turn; to spin; **faire ~ les tables** (in spiritualism) to do table-turning; **2 ~ autour de** (gen) to turn around; [*planet*] to revolve around; [*plane*] to circle; **3 ~ (en rond)** [*person*] to go around and around; [*driver*] to drive around and around; **~ en rond** (figurative) [*discussion*] to go around in circles; **4** to turn; **tournez à gauche** turn left; **5 ~ autour de** [*sum of money*] to be (somewhere) in the region of; **6** [*engine, factory*] to run; **~ rond** [*engine*] to run smoothly; [*business*] to be doing well; **faire ~** to run [*business, company*]; **mon frère ne tourne pas rond**○ **depuis quelque temps** my brother has been acting strangely for some time; **7 les choses ont bien/mal tourné pour lui** things turned out well/badly for him; **~ à l'avantage de qn** to swing in sb's favour[GB];

8 [*director*] to shoot, to film; **~ (dans un film)** [*actor*] to make a film (GB) or movie (US); **9** [*sales representative, show*] to tour; **10** [*milk, meat*] to go off; **11 ~ autour de qn** to hang around sb.

III se tourner *v refl* (+ *v être*) **1 se ~ vers qn/qch** to turn to sb/sth; **2 se ~ vers qn/qch** to turn toward(s) sb/sth; **tous les yeux se sont tournés vers elle** all eyes turned toward(s) her; **3** to turn around; **se ~ et se retourner dans son lit** to toss and turn.

tournesol /turnəsɔl/ *nm* sunflower.

tourneur, -euse /turnœr, øz/ *nm,f* (Tech) turner; lathe operator.

tournevis /turnəvis/ *nm inv* screwdriver.

tourniquet /turnikɛ/ *nm* **1** turnstile; **2** revolving stand; **3** sprinkler.

tournoi /turnwa/ *nm* tournament.

tournoyer /turnwaje/ [23] *vi* **1** [*leaves, papers*] to swirl around; [*vultures*] to wheel; [*flies, moths*] to fly around in circles; **2** [*dancers*] to whirl; **faire ~** to spin [sb] around [*person*]; to twirl [*stick, skirt*].

tournure /turnyr/ *nf* **1** turn; **la ~ des événements** the turn of events; **prendre ~** [*plan*] to take shape; **2 ~ (de phrase)** turn of phrase.

■ **~ d'esprit** frame of mind.

tourte /turt/ *nf* pie; **~ à la viande** meat pie.

tourteau, *pl* **~x** /turto/ *nm* (Culin, Zool) crab.

tourtereau, *pl* **~x** /turtəro/ **I** *nm* (Zool) young turtle dove.

II tourtereaux *nm pl* (humorous) lovebirds.

tourterelle /turtərɛl/ *nf* turtle dove.

tous ▶ tout.

Toussaint /tusɛ̃/ *nf* **la ~** All Saints' Day.

tousser /tuse/ [1] *vi* [*person*] to cough; [*engine*] to splutter.

toussoter /tusɔte/ [1] *vi* [*person*] to have a slight cough; [*engine*] to splutter.

tout /tu/, **~e** /tut/, *mpl* **tous** /tu *adj*, tus *pron*/, *fpl* **toutes** /tut/

■ **Note** You will find translations for expressions such as *à tout hasard*, *tout compte fait*, *tout neuf etc* at the entries ***hasard***, ***compte***, ***neuf*** etc.

I *pron* **1 tout** everything; all; anything; **~ peut arriver** anything can happen; **~ est prétexte à querelle(s)** any pretext will do to start a quarrel; **~ n'est pas perdu** all is not lost; **en ~** in all; in every respect; **en ~ et pour ~** all told; **~ bien compté** or **pesé** or **considéré** all in all; **2 tous** /tus/, **toutes** all; all of them/us/you; **tous ensemble** all together; **est-ce que ça conviendra à tous?** will it suit everybody?

II *adj* **1 bois ~ ton lait** drink all your milk; **~ le reste** everything else; **~ le monde** everybody; **manger ~ un pain** to eat a whole loaf; **il a plu ~e la journée** it rained all day (long); **~ cela ne compte pas** none of that counts; ; **2 c'est ~ un travail** it's quite a job; **3** all; everything; anything; **~ ce qui compte** all that matters; **~ ce qu'il dit n'est pas vrai** not all of what he says is true; **être ~ ce qu'il y a de plus serviable** to be most obliging; **4** any; **à ~ âge** at any age; **à ~ moment** at any time; constantly; **~ autre que lui/toi aurait abandonné** anybody else would have given up; **5 en ~e franchise** in all honesty; **en ~e liberté** with complete freedom; **il aurait ~ intérêt à placer cet argent** it would be in his best interests to invest this money; **6 il a souri pour ~e réponse** his only reply was a smile; **7 tous**, **toutes** all, every; **j'ai ~es les raisons de me plaindre** I have every reason to complain; **nous irons tous les deux** we'll both go; **je les prends tous les trois** I'm taking all three (of them); **8 tous/toutes les** every; **tous les mois/ans** every month/year; **tous les deux jours** every other day; **tous les combien?** how often?

III *adv* **1** very, quite; all; **être ~ étonné** to be very surprised; **c'est ~ naturel** it's quite natural; **~ seul** all by oneself; **~ en haut** right at the top; **la colline est ~ en fleurs** the hill is a mass of flowers; **veste ~ cuir** all leather jacket; **2 ~ prêt** ready-made; **3** while; although; **il lisait ~ en marchant** he was reading as he walked; **elle le défendait ~ en le sachant coupable** she defended him although she knew he was guilty; **4 ~ aussi étrange que cela paraisse** however strange it may seem; **~ malin/roi qu'il est, il**... he may be clever/a king, but he...

IV du tout *phr* **(pas) du ~** not at all.

V *nm* (*pl* **~s**) whole; **le ~** the (whole) lot; the main thing; **former un ~** to make up or form a whole; **le ~ est de réussir** the main thing is to succeed.

VI Tout- (*combining form*) **le Tout-Paris/-Londres** the Paris/London smart set.

■ **~ à coup** suddenly; **~ d'un coup** suddenly; all at once; **~ à fait** quite, absolutely; **être ~ à fait pour/contre** to be totally for/against; **~ à l'heure** in a moment; a little while ago, just now; **à ~ à l'heure!** see you later!; **~ de même** all the same, even so; **~ de même!** really!; **~ de suite** at once.

IDIOMS **être ~ yeux ~ oreilles** to be very attentive.

tout-à-l'égout /tutalegu/ *nm inv* main drainage, main sewer.

toutefois /tutfwa/ *adv* however; **je viendrai demain, si ~ ça ne vous dérange pas** I'll come tomorrow, as long as that doesn't put you out.

toute-puissance /tutpɥisɑ̃s/ *nf* omnipotence; supremacy.

tout-petit, *pl* **~s** /tup(ə)ti/ *nm* **1** baby; **2** toddler.

tout-puissant, toute-puissante, *pl* **~s, toutes-puissantes** /tupɥisɑ̃, tutpɥisɑ̃t/ *adj* all-powerful.

Tout-Puissant /tupɥisɑ̃/ *nm* **le ~** the Almighty, God Almighty.

tout-venant /tuv(ə)nɑ̃/ *nm inv* all and sundry; **il n'a pas choisi, il a pris le ~** he did not choose, he just took whatever there was.

toux /tu/ *nf inv* cough; **avoir une quinte de ~** to have a coughing fit.

toxicité /tɔksisite/ *nf* toxicity.

toxicodépendance /tɔksikodepɑ̃dɑ̃s/ *nf* drug dependency.

toxicodépendant, ~e /tɔksikodepɑ̃dɑ̃, ɑ̃t/ *nm,f* drug addict.

toxicologie /tɔksikɔlɔʒi/ *nf* toxicology.

toxicomane /tɔksikɔman/ *nmf* drug addict.

toxicomanie /tɔksikɔmani/ *nf* drug addiction.

toxine /tɔksin/ *nf* toxin.

toxique /tɔksik/ *adj* toxic, poisonous; **non ~** non toxic.

TP /tepe/ *nm pl*: *abbr* ▶ **travail**.

trac° /tʀak/ *nm* (of actor) stage fright; (before exam, conference) nerves; **avoir le ~** (gen) to feel nervous; [*actor, performer*] to have stage fright.

tracas /tʀaka/ *nm inv* **1** trouble; **donner du ~ à qn** to put sb to a lot of trouble; **2** problems; **~ quotidiens** everyday problems; **3** worries; **se faire du ~ pour qn/qch** to worry about sb/sth.

tracasser /tʀakase/ [1] **I** *vtr* to bother [*person*].
II se tracasser *v refl* (+ *v être*) to worry.

trace /tʀas/ *nf* **1** trail; **perdre la ~ d'un animal** to lose an animal's tracks; **suivre qn à la ~** to track sb; (figurative) to follow sb's trail; **2 ~s** tracks; **~s d'ours/de ski** bear's/ski tracks; **~s de pas** footprints; **un itinéraire touristique sur les ~s de Van Gogh** a tourist route in the footsteps of Van Gogh; **3** (of burn) mark; (of wound) scar; (of paint) mark; (of blood, dampness) trace; **~s de doigts** fingermarks; **~s de coups** bruises; **l'aventure avait laissé des ~s profondes en lui** the experience had marked him deeply; **4** (of activity) sign; (of presence) trace; **des ~s d'effraction** signs of a break-in; **5** trace; **des ~s de mercure** traces of mercury.

tracé /tʀase/ *nm* **1** (of town) layout; (of road) plan; **2** (of road, railway) route; (of river) course; (of border, coast) line; **3** (on graph, in sketch) line.

tracer /tʀase/ [12] *vtr* **1** to draw [*line, map, portrait*]; (on graph) to plot [*curve*]; to write [*word, letters*]; **2 ~ un tableau pessimiste de qch** to paint a pessimistic picture of sth; **à 15 ans son avenir était déjà tout tracé** at 15, his/her future was already mapped out; **3 ~ le chemin à qn** (figurative) to show sb the way.

trachée /tʀaʃe/ *nf* windpipe.

trachéite /tʀakeit/ *nf* tracheitis ¢.

tract /tʀakt/ *nm* pamphlet, tract.

tractation /tʀaktasjɔ̃/ *nf* negotiation.

tracter /tʀakte/ [1] *vtr* [*vehicle*] to tow [*trailer*]; [*cable*] to pull up [*cable car*].

tracteur /tʀaktœʀ/ *nm* tractor.

traction /tʀaksjɔ̃/ *nf* **1** traction; **à ~ mécanique** mechanically drawn; **2** (Sport) **faire des ~s** (using bar) to do pull-ups; (on floor) to do push-ups; **3** (Tech) tension.
■ **~ arrière** (Aut) rear-wheel drive; **~ avant** (Aut) front-wheel drive.

tradition /tʀadisjɔ̃/ *nf* **1** tradition; **2** legend; **la ~ veut que...** legend has it that...

traditionaliste /tʀadisjɔnalist/ *adj, nmf* traditionalist.

traditionnel, -elle /tʀadisjɔnɛl/ *adj* traditional.

traducteur, -trice /tʀadyktœʀ, tʀis/ *nm,f* translator.

traduction /tʀadyksjɔ̃/ *nf* **1** translation; **la ~ en allemand** translating into German; **faire des ~s** to do translation work; **2** (of feelings, ideas) expression.

traduire /tʀadɥiʀ/ [69] **I** *vtr* **1** to translate; **2** [*word, artist, book*] to convey; [*rebellion, violence*] to be the expression of; [*price rise*] to be the result of; **3** (Law) **~ qn en justice** to bring sb to justice.
II se traduire *v refl* (+ *v être*) **1** [*joy, fear*] to show; **2** [*crisis, instability*] to result; [*dissatisfaction*] to find expression; **se ~ par un échec** to result in failure.

traduisible /tʀadɥizibl/ *adj* translatable.

trafic /tʀafik/ *nm* **1** traffic; **~ d'armes** arms dealing; **~ de drogue** drug trafficking; **2 ~ (routier)** traffic; **~ aérien** air traffic.
IDIOMS **qu'est-ce que c'est que ce ~**°? what's going on here?

trafiquant, ~e /tʀafikɑ̃, ɑ̃t/ *nm,f* trafficker, dealer; **~ de drogue** drugs dealer.

trafiquer /tʀafike/ [1] *vtr* **1** to fiddle with [*car, meter*]; **2**° **je me demande ce qu'il trafique** I wonder what he's up to.

tragédie /tʀaʒedi/ *nf* tragedy.

tragique /tʀaʒik/ **I** *adj* tragic; **ce n'est pas ~** it's not the end of the world.
II *nm* tragedy; **prendre qch au ~** to make a drama out of sth.

trahir /tʀaiʀ/ [3] **I** *vtr* **1** to betray [*country, friend, secret*]; to break [*promise*]; **2** [*voice, blush*] to betray [*shame, fear*]; [*writing, words*] to betray [*thoughts*]; **3** [*translator, words*] to misrepresent; **4** [*strength, legs*] to fail [*person*].
II se trahir *v refl* (+ *v être*) to give oneself away, to betray oneself.

trahison /tʀaizɔ̃/ *nf* **1** treachery; **~ de qch/qn** betrayal of sth/sb; **2** treason.

train /tʀɛ̃/ **I** *nm* **1** train; **accompagner qn au ~**° to see sb off at the station; **par le** or **en ~** [*travel, transport*] by train; **2** train; series; **~ de péniches** train of barges; **3** pace; **aller bon** or **grand ~** to walk briskly; **aller bon ~** [*rumours*] to be flying around; [*sales, business*] to be going well; [*conversation*] to flow easily; [*ship, car*] to be going quite fast; **au ~ où vont les choses** (at) the rate things are going; **à fond de ~**° at top speed; **4** (Zool) **~ de derrière** hindquarters; **~ de devant** forequarter.
II en train *phr* **1 être en ~** to be full of energy; **2 mettre en ~** to get [sth] started or going [*process, work*]; **se mettre en ~** to get going; **3 être en ~ de faire** to be (busy) doing; **j'étais en ~ de dormir** I was sleeping.
■ **~ d'atterrissage** undercarriage; **~ électrique** electric train; (toy) train set; **~ de vie** lifestyle.

traînant, ~e /tʀɛnɑ̃, ɑ̃t/ *adj* shuffling; **voix ~e** drawl.

traîne /tʀɛn/ *nf* **1** (of dress) train; **2** seine (net).

IDIOMS **être à la ~** [*person, country*] to lag behind.

traîneau, *pl* **~x** /tʀɛno/ *nm* **1** sleigh; **2** (of vacuum cleaner) cylinder.

traînée /tʀɛne/ *nf* **1** streak; **~ de sang** streak of blood; **2** trail.

traîner /tʀɛne/ [1] **I** *vtr* **1** to drag [sb/sth] (along) [*person, suitcase*]; to drag [sth] across the floor [*chair*]; **2**° to lug° [sth] around [*object*]; to drag [sth] around [*object*]; to drag [sb] along [*person*]; **3 ~ qn chez le médecin** to drag sb off to the doctor's; **4 il traîne un rhume depuis deux semaines** for two weeks now he's had a cold that he can't shake off; **~ les pieds** to drag one's feet.

II *vi* **1 ~ dans les rues** to hang around on the streets; **'qu'est-ce que tu as fait aujourd'hui?'—'j'ai traîné'** 'what did you do today?'—'I loafed around°'; **j'ai traîné au lit** I slept in; **2** to take forever (**pour faire** doing); **ne traîne pas, on doit terminer à 4 heures** get a move on°, we've got to finish at four; **3** to dawdle; **ne traînez pas derrière!** keep up there at the back!; **4** [*building work, illness*] to drag on; [*smell*] to linger; **5 ~ par terre** [*skirt*] to trail on the ground; [*curtains*] to trail on the floor; **6 ~ derrière qch** to be trailing behind sth; **7** [*clothes, toys*] to be lying about or around; **laisser ~ qch** to leave sth lying about or around [*chequebook*].

III se traîner *v refl* (+ *v être*) **1** [*injured person*] **se ~ par terre/jusqu'à la porte** to drag oneself along the ground/to the door; **2 se ~ jusqu'à la cuisine** to drag oneself through to the kitchen; **3** [*car, train*] to crawl along; [*negotiations*] to drag on.

IDIOMS **~ la jambe** or **la patte**° to limp; **~ ses guêtres**° or **ses bottes**° to knock around°.

train(-)train° /tʀɛ̃tʀɛ̃/ *nm inv* (derogatory) daily routine.

traire /tʀɛʀ/ [58] *vtr* to milk [*cow, goat*]; to draw [*milk*].

trait /tʀɛ/ **I** *nm* **1** line; stroke; **souligner un mot d'un ~ rouge** to underline a word in red; **~ pour ~** [*replica*] line for line; [*reproduce*] line by line; **2** (of style, book) feature; (of person) trait; **~ caractéristique** characteristic; **~ de caractère** trait, characteristic; **c'est un ~ commun entre ton fils et le mien** that's something our sons have in common; **3 ~ d'humour** or **d'esprit** witticism; **~ de génie** stroke of genius; **4 avoir ~ à** to relate to; **5 d'un (seul) ~** (gen) at one go; **lire qch d'un ~** to read sth straight through; **6 de ~** [*animal*] draught (GB) or draft (US).

II traits *nm pl* features; **avoir les ~s fatigués** or **tirés** to look drawn.

■ **~ d'union** hyphen; (figurative) link.

IDIOMS **tirer un ~ sur qch** to put sth firmly behind one.

traitant /tʀɛtɑ̃/ *adj m* **médecin ~** doctor, GP.

traite /tʀɛt/ **I** *nf* **1** (Econ) draft, bill; **2 ~ des êtres humains** (Law) prostitution; **la ~ des Blanches** the white slave trade; **3** milking; **la ~ des vaches** milking cows.

II d'une traite *phr* **d'une (seule) ~** [*recite*] in one breath; [*drink*] in one go.

traité /tʀɛte/ *nm* **1** (Law) treaty; **~ commercial** trade agreement; **2** treatise.

traitement /tʀɛtmɑ̃/ *nm* **1** (Med) treatment; **2** salary; **3** handling; **il faut accélérer le ~ des demandes** applications must be dealt with more quickly; **4** (of data) processing; **5** (Tech) (of water, waste) processing; (of wood, textile) treatment.

■ **~ de faveur** preferential treatment; **~ de texte** word-processing; word-processing package.

traiter /tʀɛte/ [1] **I** *vtr* **1** to treat [*person, animal, object*]; **2** (Med) to treat [*sick person, infection*]; **3** to deal with [*question, subject, problem, file, affair*]; **4** to treat [*wood, textile, foodstuff, harvest*]; to process [*waste*]; **non traité** [*wood, foodstuff*] untreated; **5** to process [*data, information*]; **6 ~ qn de qch** to call sb sth.

II traiter de *v+prep* to deal with [*subject, theme*].

III *vi* to negotiate, to do (GB) or make a deal.

IV se traiter *v refl* (+ *v être*) **ils se sont traités de tous les noms** they called each other all sorts of names.

traiteur /tʀɛtœʀ/ *nm* caterer.

traître, traîtresse /tʀɛtʀ, tʀɛtʀɛs/ **I** *adj* treacherous.

II *nm,f* traitor; **prendre qn en ~** to take sb by surprise.

traîtrise /tʀɛtʀiz/ *nf* **1** act of treachery; **2** (of person) treachery.

trajectoire /tʀaʒɛktwaʀ/ *nf* **1** (of bullet, missile) trajectory; **2** (of planet, satellite) path; **3** career, path in life.

trajet /tʀaʒɛ/ *nm* **1** journey, trip; (by sea) crossing; **2** route.

trame /tʀam/ *nf* **1** (of fabric) weft; **2** (of story) framework.

tramer /tʀame/ [1] **I** *vtr* **1** to weave; **2** (figurative) to hatch.

II se tramer *v refl* (+ *v être*) [*plot*] to be hatched.

trampoline /tʀɑ̃pɔlin/ *nm* **1** trampoline; **2** trampolining.

tramway /tʀamwɛ/ *nm* **1** tram (GB), streetcar (US); **2** tramway (GB), streetcar line (US).

tranchant, ~e /tʀɑ̃ʃɑ̃, ɑ̃t/ **I** *adj* **1** sharp; **2** [*person*] forthright; [*tone*] curt.

II *nm* (of blade) sharp edge, cutting edge.

tranche /tʀɑ̃ʃ/ *nf* **1** (of bread, meat, cheese) slice; (of lard, bacon) rasher; **2** (of operation) phase; (in timetable) period, time slot; **3** (of book, coin) edge.

■ **~ d'âge** age bracket; **~ d'imposition** tax bracket.

tranché, ~e[1] /tʀɑ̃ʃe/ **I** *pp* ▶ **trancher**.

II *pp adj* [*salmon*] pre-sliced.

III *adj* **1** [*opinion, position, reply*] cut-and-dried, clear-cut; [*inequalities*] marked; **2** [*colours*] bold, distinct.

tranchée[2] /tʀɑ̃ʃe/ *nf* **1** (Mil) trench; **2** (of road) cutting.

trancher /tʀɑ̃ʃe/ [1] **I** *vtr* **1** to slice, to cut [*bread, meat*]; to cut through [*rope, knot, skin*]; to cut [sth] off [*head, limb*]; to slit [*throat*]; **2** to settle [*litigation*].

II *vi* **1** [*colour, outline*] to stand out; **2** to come to a decision

tranquille /tʀɑ̃kil/ *adj* **1** [*person, life, street, day*] quiet; [*voice, confidence, water, night*] calm; [*holiday*] peaceful; **tiens-toi ~!** keep still!; be quiet!; **il s'est tenu ~ pendant quelques mois** he behaved himself for a few months; **2 être ~** to be or feel easy in one's mind; **sa mère n'est pas ~ quand il sort** his mother worries when he goes out; **3 avoir la conscience ~** to have a clear conscience; **je te laisse ~** I'll leave you in peace.

tranquillement /tʀɑ̃kilmɑ̃/ *adv* **1 elle dort ~** she's sleeping peacefully; **j'aimerais pouvoir travailler ~** I wish I could work in peace; **2** quietly; **3 nous avons marché ~** we walked along at a leisurely pace; **4 nous étions ~ en train de discuter** we were chatting away happily; **expliquer qch ~** to explain sth calmly.

tranquillisant, ~e /tʀɑ̃kilizɑ̃, ɑ̃t/ I *adj* reassuring, comforting.

II *nm* tranquillizer[GB].

tranquilliser /tʀɑ̃kilize/ [1] *vtr* to reassure.

tranquillité /tʀɑ̃kilite/ *nf* **1** (of temperament, person) calmness, serenity; (of moment, place) calm; **2 ~ (d'esprit)** peace of mind; **3 aspirer à la ~** to long for peace and quiet.

transaction /tʀɑ̃zaksjɔ̃/ *nf* transaction.

transalpin, ~e /tʀɑ̃zalpɛ̃, in/ *adj* **1** transalpine; **2** Italian.

transat¹○ /tʀɑ̃zat/ *nm* **1** deckchair; **2** baby chair.

transat² /tʀɑ̃zat/ *nf* (Sport) transatlantic race.

transatlantique /tʀɑ̃zatlɑ̃tik/ *adj* transatlantic.

transcendant, ~e /tʀɑ̃sɑ̃dɑ̃, ɑ̃t/ *adj* **1** (in philosophy) transcendent; **2**○ wonderful; **3** (in mathematics) transcendental.

transcender /tʀɑ̃sɑ̃de/ [1] *vtr* to transcend.

transcription /tʀɑ̃skʀipsjɔ̃/ *nf* transcription.

transcrire /tʀɑ̃skʀiʀ/ [67] *vtr* **1** to transcribe; **2** (figurative) to translate.

transe /tʀɑ̃s/ *nf* trance.

transférer /tʀɑ̃sfeʀe/ [14] *vtr* **1** (gen) to transfer; to relocate [*offices*]; **faire ~** to have [sth] transferred [*contract, phone calls*]; **2** (Law) to transfer, to convey [*property*].

transfert /tʀɑ̃sfɛʀ/ *nm* **1** (of person, data, money) transfer; (of offices) relocation; **2** (of property) transfer, conveyance; **3** (psychological) transference.

transfigurer /tʀɑ̃sfigyʀe/ [1] *vtr* to transform.

transformable /tʀɑ̃sfɔʀmabl/ *adj* convertible.

transformateur /tʀɑ̃sfɔʀmatœʀ/ *nm* transformer.

transformation /tʀɑ̃sfɔʀmasjɔ̃/ *nf* **1** (of person, country) transformation; (of mineral, substance, energy) conversion; **2** (Sport) conversion.

transformer /tʀɑ̃sfɔʀme/ [1] I *vtr* **1** to alter [*garment, façade*]; to change, to alter [*person, attitude, landscape, society*]; **depuis qu'il ne boit plus, il est transformé** since he stopped drinking he's a different person; **2 ~ qn/qch en** (gen) to turn sb/sth into; to transform sb/sth into; **~ un garage en bureau** to convert a garage into an office; **3** (in chemistry) to convert [*substance*]; **4** (Sport) to convert [*try*].

II **se transformer** *v refl* (+ *v être*) **1** [*person*] to transform oneself; to be transformed; **se ~ en** to turn into; to be transformed into; **2** [*embryo, larva, bud*] to turn into.

transfuge /tʀɑ̃sfyʒ/ I *nmf* defector.

II *nm* (Mil) deserter.

transfusé, ~e /tʀɑ̃sfyze/ I *pp* ▸ **transfuser**.

II *pp adj* [*blood*] transfused; [*person*] who has been given a blood transfusion.

transfuser /tʀɑ̃sfyze/ [1] *vtr* to give a blood transfusion to.

transfusion /tʀɑ̃sfyzjɔ̃/ *nf* transfusion.

transgresser /tʀɑ̃sgʀese/ [1] *vtr* to break [*law, rule, taboo*]; to defy [*ban*].

transi, ~e /tʀɑ̃zi/ I *pp* ▸ **transir**.

II *pp adj* chilled; **être ~ jusqu'à la moelle** to be chilled to the marrow; **~ de peur** paralysed[GB] with fear; **un amoureux ~** a bashful lover.

transiger /tʀɑ̃ziʒe/ [13] *vi* to compromise.

transir /tʀɑ̃ziʀ/ [3] *vtr* [*cold*] to chill; [*fear*] to paralyze.

transistor /tʀɑ̃zistɔʀ/ *nm* transistor.

transit /tʀɑ̃zit/ *nm* transit; **en ~** in transit.

transiter /tʀɑ̃zite/ [1] *vi* **~ par** [*goods, passengers*] to pass through, to go via.

transitif, -ive /tʀɑ̃zitif, iv/ *adj* [*verb*] transitive.

transition /tʀɑ̃zisjɔ̃/ *nf* transition; **passer sans ~ à** to move straight on to.

transitoire /tʀɑ̃zitwaʀ/ *adj* transitional.

translucide /tʀɑ̃slysid/ *adj* [*glass, material*] translucent.

transmetteur /tʀɑ̃smɛtœʀ/ *nm* transmitter.

transmettre /tʀɑ̃smɛtʀ/ [60] I *vtr* **1** to pass [sth] on, to convey [*information, greetings, order, news*]; to pass [sth] on [*story, knowledge, discovery*]; to pass [sth] down [*culture, secret, fortune*]; **transmets-leur mes félicitations** give them my congratulations; **2** to transmit [*image, signal, data, sound*]; **3** to broadcast [*news, results, programme*]; **4** to hand [sth] on [*property, land*]; to hand over [*power, leadership*]; **5** (Med) to transmit [*virus, illness*].

II **se transmettre** *v refl* (+ *v être*) **1** to pass [sth] on to each other [*message, data*]; **2** [*signals, data, information*] to be transmitted; **3** [*tradition, secret, culture*] to be handed down; [*story, knowledge*] to be passed on; **4** [*virus, illness*] to be transmitted.

transmissible /tʀɑ̃smisibl/ *adj* transmissible, transmittable.

transmission /tʀɑ̃smisjɔ̃/ *nf* **1** transmission, passing on; **la ~ des connaissances** the communication of knowledge; **2** (of data, signals) transmission; **3** (of programme) broadcasting, transmission; **4** (of tradition, secret, culture) handing down; (of fortune, property) transfer; **5** (Aut) transmission; **6** (Med) transmission.

■ **~ de pensées** thought transference.

transparaître /tʀɑ̃spaʀɛtʀ/ [73] *vi* [*shape, light*] to show through; [*anxiety*] to show; **laisser ~** [*face, words*] to betray; [*person*] to let [sth] show [*emotions*].

transparence /tʀɑ̃spaʀɑ̃s/ *nf* **1** (of glass, fabric, partition) transparency; (of water) clearness; **on voyait ses jambes en ~ (à travers sa jupe)** you could see her legs through her skirt; **2** (of skin, complexion) translucency; (of colour) limpidity; **3** (figurative) (of person, intentions) transparency; (of policy, management) openness.

transparent, **~e** /tʀɑ̃spaʀɑ̃, ɑ̃t/ **I** *adj* **1** [*glass, partition*] transparent; [*water*] clear; **2** [*complexion*] translucent; [*gaze*] limpid; **3** [*person, intentions*] transparent.

II *nm* (for overhead projector) transparency.

transpercer /tʀɑ̃spɛʀse/ [12] *vtr* **1** [*sword, arrow*] to pierce [*body*]; [*bullet*] to go through; **2** [*rain*] to go through; **3** [*pain*] to shoot through; [*cold*] to go right through.

transpiration /tʀɑ̃spiʀasjɔ̃/ *nf* **1** sweating, perspiration; **2** sweat; **3** (Bot) transpiration.

transpirer /tʀɑ̃spiʀe/ [1] *vi* **1** to sweat, to perspire; **2** [*secret*] to leak out.

transplantation /tʀɑ̃splɑ̃tasjɔ̃/ *nf* **1** (of organs) transplant; **2** (of plants) transplantation.

transplanter /tʀɑ̃splɑ̃te/ [1] *vtr* to transplant.

transport /tʀɑ̃spɔʀ/ **I** *nm* transport, transportation (US); **compagnie de ~** (gen) transport company; (by road) haulage company (GB), trucking company (US).

II transports *nm pl* **~s en commun** public transport or transportation (US).

transportable /tʀɑ̃spɔʀtabl/ *adj* transportable; **il n'est pas ~** (injured person) he cannot be moved.

transporter /tʀɑ̃spɔʀte/ [1] *vtr* **1** to carry [*person, object*]; to transport [*passengers, goods*]; **être transporté à l'hôpital** to be taken to hospital; **2** to carry [*pollen, virus, disease*]; **3 être transporté dans un monde féerique** to be transported to a magical world.

transporteur /tʀɑ̃spɔʀtœʀ/ *nm* **1** carrier; **~ aérien** air carrier; **~ routier** road haulier (GB), road haulage contractor (GB), trucking company (US); **2** (machine) conveyor.

transposer /tʀɑ̃spoze/ [1] *vtr* to transpose.

transsexuel, **-elle** /tʀɑ̃ssɛksɥɛl/ *adj, nm,f* transsexual.

transvaser /tʀɑ̃svaze/ [1] *vtr* to decant [*liquid*].

transversal, **~e**, *mpl* **-aux** /tʀɑ̃svɛʀsal, o/ *adj* transverse; **poutre ~e** cross-beam; **rue ~e** side street.

transversalement /tʀɑ̃svɛʀsalmɑ̃/ *adv* **1** (gen) crosswise; **2** (Aut) transversely.

trapèze /tʀapɛz/ *nm* **1** (Sport) trapeze; **2** (in geometry) trapezium (GB), trapezoid (US).

trapéziste /tʀapezist/ *nmf* trapeze artist.

trappe /tʀap/ *nf* **1** (gen) trap door; **2** (in hunting) trap.

trappeur /tʀapœʀ/ *nm* trapper.

trapu, **~e** /tʀapy/ *adj* [*man, outline*] stocky; [*building*] squat.

traquenard /tʀaknaʀ/ *nm* trap.

traquer /tʀake/ [1] *vtr* **1** (gen) to track down, to hunt [sb] down; [*photograph*] to hound [*film star*]; **2** to monitor [*expenses*]; **3** (in hunting) to track down [*animal*].

traumatisant, **~e** /tʀomatizɑ̃, ɑ̃t/ *adj* traumatic.

traumatiser /tʀomatize/ [1] *vtr* to traumatize.

traumatisme /tʀomatism/ *nm* **1** (Med) traumatism; **2** (psychological) trauma.

traumatologie /tʀomatɔlɔʒi/ *nf* traumatology.

travail, *pl* **-aux** /tʀavaj, o/ **I** *nm* **1** work; **se mettre au ~** to get down to work; **2** job; work; **avoir du ~** to have work to do; **j'ai un ~ fou** I'm up to my eyes in work; **les gros travaux** the heavy work; **(félicitations) c'est du beau ~!** you've done a great job on that!; **qu'est-ce que c'est que ce ~?** what do you call this?; **3** (of employee) **ne me téléphone pas à mon ~** don't call me at work; **chercher du/un ~** to look for work/a job; **être sans ~** to be out of work; **le ~ temporaire** temporary work; **un ~ à mi-temps** a part-time job; **le ~ de nuit** nightwork; **4** (Econ) labour[GB]; **entrer dans le monde du ~** to enter the world of work; **5** (of machine) work; **le ~ musculaire** muscular effort; **6 le ~ de** working with or in [*metal, wood, stone*]; **apprendre le ~ du bois** to learn woodwork; **7** workmanship; **un ~ superbe** a superb piece of workmanship; **8** (in physics) work; **9** (of water, erosion) action; (of imagination, unconscious) workings; **10** (of wine) fermentation, working; (of wood) warping; **11** (of woman in childbirth) labour[GB].

II travaux *nm pl* **1** (gen) work; (on road) roadworks (GB), roadwork (US); **travaux de construction** construction work; **faire faire des travaux dans sa maison** to have work done in one's house; **'attention, travaux'** 'caution, work in progress'; (on road) 'caution, road under repair'; **2** (of researcher) work; **3** (of commission) deliberations; **4 les travaux agricoles** agricultural work; **travaux de couture** needlework.

■ **~ à la chaîne** assembly-line work; **~ à domicile** working at or from home; **~ au noir** (gen) *work for which no earnings are declared*; (holding two jobs) moonlighting; **travaux manuels** handicrafts; **travaux pratiques**, **TP** practical work; lab work; **travaux publics**, **TP** civil engineering; civil engineering works.

travaillé, **~e** /tʀavaje/ **I** *pp* ▶ **travailler**.

II *pp adj* [*jewel*] finely-worked; [*carving*] elaborate; [*gold, silver*] wrought; [*metal*] chased; [*drawing*] elaborate; [*language, style*] polished.

travailler /tʀavaje/ [1] **I** *vtr* **1** to work on [*style, school subject, voice, muscles*]; to practise[GB] [*sport, instrument*]; **2** to work [*wood, metal*]; (Culin) to knead [*dough*]; to cultivate [*land*]; **3 ~ qn** [*idea, affair*] to be on sb's mind, to bother sb; [*jealousy, pain*] to plague sb; **un doute me travaillait** I had a nagging doubt.

II travailler à *v+prep* to work on [*project, essay*]; to work toward(s) [*objective*].

III *vi* **1** [*person, machine, muscles*] to work; **~ sur un projet** to work on a project; **faire ~ son cerveau** to apply one's mind; **2** to work; **~ comme secrétaire** to work as a secretary; **~ en équipes** to work shifts; **3** [*shop, hotel, shopkeeper*] to do business; **~ à perte** [*company, business*] to run at a loss; **4 faire ~ son argent** to make one's money work; **5 nous voulons la paix et c'est dans ce sens que nous travaillons** we want peace and we are working toward(s) it; **6** [*athlete*] to train; [*musician, dancer*] to practise[GB]; **7** [*wood*] to warp; [*wine*] to ferment.

travailleur, -euse /tʀavajœʀ, øz/ **I** *adj* **1** [*pupil, employee*] hardworking; **2** [*classes, masses*] working.

II *nm,f* worker.

travailliste /tʀavajist/ **I** *adj* Labour; **être ~** to be a member of the Labour party; to be a Labour party supporter.

II *nmf* Labour MP.

travée /tʀave/ *nf* **1** row; **2** (Tech) span.

travelling /tʀavliŋ/ *nm* (in cinema) tracking; tracking shot.

travers /tʀavɛʀ/ **I** *nm inv* **1** foible, quirk; **2** (Naut) beam; **3** (Culin) **~ de porc** sparerib.

II à travers *phr* **1** [*see, look*] through; **passer à ~ les mailles du filet** to slip through the net; **2** [*travel, walk*] across; **voyager à ~ le monde** to travel all over the world; **3 voyager à ~ le temps** to travel through time; **4** through; **à ~ ces informations** through this information.

III au travers *phr* through; **passer au ~ de** (figurative) to escape [*inspection*].

IV de travers *phr* **1** askew; **ta veste est boutonnée de ~** your jacket is buttoned up wrongly; **il a le nez de ~** he has a twisted nose; **j'ai avalé de ~** it went down the wrong way; **regarder qn de ~** (figurative) to give sb filthy looks; **2** wrong, wrongly; **comprendre de ~** to misunderstand.

V en travers *phr* across; **un bus était en ~ de la route** a bus was stuck across the road; **se mettre en ~ de la route** [*people*] to stand in the middle of the road; **rester en ~ de la gorge de qn**° [*remarks, insults*] to be hard to swallow.

traverse /tʀavɛʀs/ *nf* **1** (on railway line) sleeper (GB), tie (US); **2** (in window, fence, wardrobe) crosspiece, strut; **3** side street.

traversée /tʀavɛʀse/ *nf* **1** crossing; **la ~ du désert** crossing the desert; (figurative) (of company) a difficult period; **2** (of city) **évitez la ~ de Paris** avoid going through Paris.

traverser /tʀavɛʀse/ [1] *vtr* **1** to cross [*road, bridge, border, town, ocean, room*]; to go through, to pass through [*town, country, forest, tunnel*]; to make one's way through [*group, crowd*]; **il traversa le jardin en courant** he ran across the garden (GB) or yard (US); **2** [*river*] to run through [*region, plain*]; [*road, tunnel*] to go through [*town, region, mountain*]; [*bridge, river*] to cross [*railway line, town*]; **3** [*rain*] to soak through [*clothes*]; **la balle lui a traversé le bras** the bullet went right through his/her arm; **4** to go through [*crisis, difficulty*]; to live through [*war, occupation*]; **5** [*pain*] to shoot through; **~ l'esprit de qn** to cross sb's mind.

traversin /tʀavɛʀsɛ̃/ *nm* bolster.

travesti, ~e /tʀavɛsti/ **I** *pp* ▶ **travestir**.

II *pp adj* in disguise; **rôle ~** role played by a member of the opposite sex.

III *nm* **1** transvestite; **2** (actor) actor playing a female role; (in cabaret) drag artist°.

travestir /tʀavɛstiʀ/ [3] **I** *vtr* **1** to dress [sb] up [*person*]; **2** to distort [*truth*].

II se travestir *v refl* (+ *v être*) **1** to dress up; **2** to cross-dress.

trébucher /tʀebyʃe/ [1] *vi* to stumble.

trèfle /tʀɛfl/ *nm* **1** clover; **~ à quatre feuilles** four-leaf clover; **2** (Games) (card) club; (suit) clubs; **3** shamrock.

treillage /tʀɛjaʒ/ *nm* **1** trellis; **2** lattice fence; **3** (for vine) trellis.

treille /tʀɛj/ *nf* **1** (vine) arbour[GB]; **2** climbing vine.

treillis /tʀɛji/ *nm inv* **1** (Mil) fatigues; **2** canvas; **3** trellis; **~ métallique** wire grille.

treize /tʀɛz/ *adj inv, pron* thirteen.

treizième /tʀɛzjɛm/ *adj* thirteenth.

tréma /tʀema/ *nm* diaeresis; **i ~** i diaeresis.

tremblant, ~e /tʀɑ̃blɑ̃, ɑ̃t/ *adj* **1** [*person, animal, hands*] shaking, trembling; **2** [*voice*] trembling; **3** [*image, light*] flickering; [*sound*] tremulous.

tremblement /tʀɑ̃bləmɑ̃/ *nm* **1** (of person, hands) shaking, trembling; (of lips) trembling; **2** (of voice) tremor, trembling; (of sound, note) wavering ₵; [*of light*] flickering; **3** (of leaves) quivering; (of windows) rattling.

■ **~ de terre** earthquake.

trembler /tʀɑ̃ble/ [1] *vi* **1** [*person, hands, legs*] to shake, to tremble; **2** [*voice*] to tremble; to quaver; [*sound, note*] to waver; **3** [*building, floor*] to shake; **4** to tremble; **~ pour qn** to fear for sb; **5** [*light, flame, image*] to flicker; **6** [*leaves*] to quiver.

trembloter /tʀɑ̃blɔte/ [1] *vi* **1** [*person, hands*] to tremble slightly; **2** [*voice*] to tremble; to quaver; **3** [*light, flame*] to flicker.

trémolo /tʀemɔlo/ *nm* **1** (of voice) quaver; **2** (of instrument) tremolo.

trémousser: **se trémousser** /tʀemuse/ [1] *v refl* (+ *v être*) **1** to fidget; **2** to wiggle around.

trempe /tʀɑ̃p/ *nf* **avoir la ~ d'un dirigeant** to have the makings of a leader.

trempé, ~e /tʀɑ̃pe/ **I** *pp* ▶ **tremper**.

II *pp adj* **1** [*person, garments*] soaked (through); [*grass*] sodden; [*washing*] soaking wet; **2** (Tech) [*steel*] tempered; [*glass*] toughened.

tremper /tʀɑ̃pe/ [1] **I** *vtr* **1** [*rain, person*] to soak [*person, garment*]; **2** to dip; **j'ai juste trempé mes lèvres** I just had a sip; **3** to soak [*hands*]; **4** (Tech) to temper.

II *vi* **1** [*clothes, vegetables*] to soak; **faire ~**

qch to soak sth; **2 ~ dans qch** to be mixed up in sth.

III se tremper *v refl* (+ *v être*) to go for a dip; to have a quick bath.

tremplin /tʀɑ̃plɛ̃/ *nm* **1** springboard; **2** ski jump; water-ski jump.

trentaine /tʀɑ̃tɛn/ *nf* **1** about thirty; **2 avoir la ~** to be about thirty.

trente /tʀɑ̃t/ *adj inv, pron* thirty.

trente-et-un /tʀɑ̃teœ̃/ *nm* **être sur son ~**○ to be dressed up to the nines.

trentenaire /tʀɑ̃tənɛʀ/ *adj* [*person*] in his/her thirties; [*tree, building*] around thirty years old.

trente-six /tʀɑ̃tsis/ *adj inv, pron* thirty-six.
IDIOMS **voir ~ chandelles**○ to see stars.

trente-trois /tʀɑ̃ttʀwa/ *adj inv, pron* thirty-three.
■ **~ tours** LP.

trentième /tʀɑ̃tjɛm/ *adj* thirtieth.

trépas† /tʀepɑ/ *nm* demise; **passer de vie à ~** to pass on (GB), to pass away.

trépidant, ~e /tʀepidɑ̃, ɑ̃t/ *adj* **1** [*engine, machine*] vibrating; **2** [*rhythm, speed*] pulsating; [*life*] hectic; [*story*] exciting.

trépied /tʀepje/ *nm* (gen) tripod; (for cauldron) trivet.

trépigner /tʀepiɲe/ [1] *vi* (with anger, impatience) to stamp one's feet; (with joy, excitement) to jump up and down.

très /tʀɛ/ *adv* very; **~ connu** very well-known; **~ disputé** [*match*] closely contested; **être ~ amoureux** to be very much in love; **~ en avance** very early; **~ volontiers** gladly; **à ~ bientôt** see you very soon; **'tu vas bien?'—'non, pas ~'** 'are you well?'—'no, not terribly'; **j'ai ~ soif** I'm very thirsty; **elle a ~ envie de partir** she's dying○ to leave.

trésor /tʀezɔʀ/ *nm* **1** treasure; **chasse** or **course au ~** treasure hunt; **2 ~s archéologiques** archaeological treasures; **3 déployer des ~s d'inventivité** to show infinite inventiveness; **4** (person) treasure; **mon ~** treasure, precious.

trésorerie /tʀezɔʀʀi/ *nf* **1** funds; cash; **avoir des problèmes de ~** to have cash flow problems; **2** (of company) accounts; **3** government finance.

trésorier, -ière /tʀezɔʀje, ɛʀ/ *nm,f* treasurer; (of the Treasury) paymaster.

tressaillement /tʀɛsajmɑ̃/ *nm* **1** (from surprise, fear) start; (of hope, pleasure) quiver; (from pain) wince; **2** (of person, muscle, animal) twitch; (of machine, ground) vibration.

tressaillir /tʀɛsajiʀ/ [28] *vi* **1** (with surprise) to start; (with pleasure) to quiver; (with pain) to wince; **2** [*person, muscle*] to twitch; [*ground, object*] to vibrate.

tresse /tʀɛs/ *nf* **1** plait; **2** (of thread, cloth, leather) braid.

tresser /tʀɛse/ [1] *vtr* to plait [*hair, threads*]; to weave [*straw, string*].

tréteau, *pl* **~x** /tʀeto/ *nm* trestle.

treuil /tʀœj/ *nm* winch.

trêve /tʀɛv/ *nf* **1** (Mil) truce; **2** respite; **sans ~** unceasingly; **~ de plaisanteries/balivernes!** that's enough joking/nonsense!

tri /tʀi/ *nm* **1** sorting; **faire le ~ de** to sort [*mail*]; to sort out [*documents, clothes*]; **2** sorting out; **faire le ~ de** to sort [sth] out [*photographs, information*]; **faire un ~ parmi des choses** to select among things.
■ **~ postal** sorting; **centre de ~ (postal)** sorting office.

triage /tʀijaʒ/ *nm* **gare de ~** marshalling[GB] yard.

triangle /tʀijɑ̃gl/ *nm* triangle.
■ **~ des Bermudes** Bermuda Triangle.

triangulaire /tʀijɑ̃gylɛʀ/ *adj* **1** triangular; **2** [*agreement, partnership*] three-way.

triathlon /tʀiatlɔ̃/ *nm* triathlon.

tribal, ~e, *mpl* **-aux** /tʀibal, o/ *adj* tribal.

tribord /tʀibɔʀ/ *nm* starboard.

tribu /tʀiby/ *nf* tribe.

tribulations /tʀibylasjɔ̃/ *nf pl* tribulations.

tribunal, *pl* **-aux** /tʀibynal, o/ *nm* **1** (Law) court; **traîner qn devant les tribunaux** to take sb to court; **2** (figurative) **le ~ de l'histoire** the judgment of history.

tribune /tʀibyn/ *nf* **1** (in stadium) stand; (in court) gallery; **la ~ officielle** or **d'honneur** the VIP stand; **2** (of speaker) platform, rostrum; **3** (in newspaper) comments column.

tribut /tʀiby/ *nm* tribute.

tributaire /tʀibytɛʀ/ *adj* **être ~ de** [*country, person*] to depend on.

tricentenaire /tʀisɑ̃tnɛʀ/ *adj* three-hundred-year-old.

triche○ /tʀiʃ/ *nf* **c'est de la ~** that's cheating.

tricher /tʀiʃe/ [1] *vi* to cheat; **~ sur son âge** to lie about one's age.

tricherie /tʀiʃʀi/ *nf* **1** cheating; **2 une ~** a trick.

tricheur, -euse /tʀiʃœʀ, øz/ *nm,f* cheat.

tricolore /tʀikɔlɔʀ/ *adj* **1** three-coloured[GB]; **feux ~s** traffic lights; **le drapeau ~** the tricolour[GB], the French flag; **2**○ French; **l'équipe ~** the French team.

tricot /tʀiko/ *nm* **1** knitting; **faire du ~** to knit; **j'ai commencé un ~** I've started knitting something; **2** knitwear; **en ~** knitted.

tricoter /tʀikɔte/ [1] *vtr* to knit; **tricoté (à la) main** handknitted.

tricycle /tʀisikl/ *nm* tricycle.

trident /tʀidɑ̃/ *nm* trident.

tridimensionnel, -elle /tʀidimɑ̃sjɔnɛl/ *adj* three-dimensional.

triennal, ~e, *mpl* **-aux** /tʀijenal, o/ *adj* **1** [*mandate*] three-year; **2** [*exhibition, vote*] three-yearly.

trier /tʀije/ [2] *vtr* **1** to sort [*mail*]; **2** to sort [sth] out [*information*]; to select [*clients*].
IDIOMS **~ sur le volet** to handpick.

trifouiller○ /tʀifuje/ [1] *vi* **~ dans** to rummage through [*cupboard*]; to tinker with [*engine*].

trilingue /tʀilɛ̃g/ *adj* trilingual.

trille /tʀij/ *nm* **1** (Mus) trill; **2 les ~s d'un oiseau** the trilling of a bird.

trilogie /tʀilɔʒi/ *nf* trilogy.

trimbal(l)er° /tʀɛ̃bale/ [1] **I** *vtr* to lug [sth] around; to drag [sb] around.
II se trimbal(l)er *v refl* (+ *v être*) to trail around.

trimer° /tʀime/ [1] *vi* to slave away.

trimestre /tʀimɛstʀ/ *nm* **1** (period) quarter; (Sch) term; **2** quarterly income; quarterly payment.

trimestriel, -ielle /tʀimɛstʀijɛl/ *adj* (gen) quarterly; [*exam*] end-of-term.

trimoteur /tʀimɔtœʀ/ *nm* three-engined plane.

tringle /tʀɛ̃gl/ *nf* **1** (gen) rail; **2** (Tech) rod.

trinité /tʀinite/ *nf* trinity.

trinquer /tʀɛ̃ke/ [1] *vi* **1** to clink glasses; **~ à qch** to drink to sth; **2**° to pay the price; to take the rap°.

trio /tʀi(j)o/ *nm* trio.

triomphal, ~e, *mpl* **-aux** /tʀijɔ̃fal, o/ *adj* triumphant.

triomphant, ~e /tʀijɔ̃fɑ̃, ɑ̃t/ *adj* triumphant.

triomphateur, -trice /tʀijɔ̃fatœʀ, tʀis/ **I** *adj* triumphant.
II *nm,f* triumphant victor.

triomphe /tʀijɔ̃f/ *nm* triumph (**sur** over); **faire un ~ à qn** to give sb a triumphal reception; **avoir le ~ modeste** to be modest about one's success.

triompher /tʀijɔ̃fe/ [1] **I triompher de** *v+prep* to triumph over [*enemy*]; to overcome [*resistance*].
II *vi* **1** [*fighter*] to triumph; [*truth*] to prevail; **2** to be triumphant.

tripatouiller° /tʀipatuje/ [1] *vtr* **1** to fiddle about° with [*text*]; to fiddle° [*results*]; **2** to fiddle with° [*object*]; to paw° [*person*].

triperie /tʀipʀi/ *nf* **1** tripe shop; **2** tripe trade.

tripes /tʀip/ *nf pl* **1** (Culin) tripe; **2**° guts, innards; **rendre ~s et boyaux**° to be as sick as a dog.

triplace /tʀiplas/ *adj* three-seater.

triple /tʀipl/ **I** *adj* triple; **l'avantage est ~** the advantages are threefold; **en ~ exemplaire** in triplicate; **~ idiot**°**!** prize idiot°!
II *nm* **coûter le ~** to cost three times as much.

triplé, ~e /tʀiple/ **I** *nm,f* triplet.
II *nm* (in sport) hat trick.

triplement /tʀipləmɑ̃/ *adv* **1** in three respects; **2** trebly.

tripler /tʀiple/ [1] **I** *vtr* **1** to treble [*quantity, price*]; **2** (Sch) **~ une classe** to repeat a class (GB) or grade (US) a second time.
II *vi* to treble (**de** in).

triplex /tʀiplɛks/ *nm inv* **1** ®safety glass; **2** three-floor maisonette (GB), triplex (apartment) (US).

triporteur /tʀipɔʀtœʀ/ *nm* delivery tricycle.

tripot /tʀipo/ *nm* **1** gambling joint°; **2** dive°.

tripotée° /tʀipɔte/ *nf* **1** (good) hiding°; **2 une ~ de** hordes of.

tripoter° /tʀipɔte/ [1] *vtr* to fiddle with [*object*].

trique /tʀik/ *nf* cudgel; **battre à coups de ~** to cudgel.
IDIOMS **être maigre** or **sec comme un coup de ~** to be as thin as a rake.

trisaïeul, ~e /tʀizajœl/ *nm,f* great-great-grandfather/grandmother; **~s** great-great-grandparents.

trisannuel, -elle /tʀizanɥɛl/ *adj* triennial.

trisomie /tʀizɔmi/ *nf* trisomy; **~ 21** Down's Syndrome.

trisomique /tʀizɔmik/ *adj* **enfant ~** Down's syndrome child.

triste /tʀist/ *adj* **1** (gen) sad; [*town, existence*] dreary; [*weather, day*] gloomy; [*colour*] drab; [*existence*] dreary; **2** [*end, business, reputation*] dreadful; [*consequence*] sad; [*show, state*] sorry; [*character*] unsavoury[GB]; **c'est la ~ vérité** unfortunately, that's the truth of the matter; **faire la ~ expérience de qch** to learn about sth to one's cost; **un ~ imbécile** a despicable character.
IDIOMS **~ comme la pluie** or **à mourir** desperately sad.

tristement /tʀistəmɑ̃/ *adv* sadly; **une vie ~ ordinaire** a drearily ordinary life.

tristesse /tʀistɛs/ *nf* (gen) sadness; (of place, evening) dreariness; (of weather, day) gloominess; **dire avec ~** to say sadly.

triton /tʀitɔ̃/ *nm* (Zool) **1** (mollusc) triton; **2** newt.

triturer /tʀityʀe/ [1] *vtr* to fiddle with [*button*]; to knead [*dough*].
IDIOMS **se ~ la cervelle**° or **les méninges**° to rack one's brains°.

trivial, ~e, *mpl* **-iaux** /tʀivjal, o/ *adj* **1** coarse; **2** ordinary, everyday; [*style*] mundane; **3** [*explanation*] simplistic.

trivialité /tʀivjalite/ *nf* **1** coarseness; **2** triteness, triviality; **3** platitude.

troc /tʀɔk/ *nm* barter; **faire du ~** to barter.

troène /tʀɔɛn/ *nm* privet.

troglodyte /tʀɔglɔdit/ *nm* cave-dweller.

trognon /tʀɔɲɔ̃/ *nm* (of apple) core; (of cabbage) stalk.

trois /tʀwɑ/ *adj inv, pron, nm inv* three.
IDIOMS **être haut comme ~ pommes** to be kneehigh to a grasshopper; **jamais deux sans ~** bad luck comes in threes.

trois-huit /tʀwaɥit/ *nm pl* system of three eight-hour shifts.

troisième /tʀwazjɛm/ **I** *adj* third.
II *nf* **1** (Sch) *fourth year of secondary school, age 14–15*; **2** (Aut) third (gear).
■ **le ~ âge** the elderly.

troisièmement /tʀwazjɛmmɑ̃/ *adv* thirdly.

trois-mâts /tʀwamɑ/ *nm inv* three-master.

trois-quarts /tʀwakaʀ/ **I** *adj inv* [*sleeves*] three-quarter length.
II *nm inv* **1** three-quarter length coat; **2** (rugby player) three-quarter.
III de trois-quarts *phr* [*portrait*] three-quarter length.

trombe /tʀɔ̃b/ *nf* **1** (cyclone) waterspout; **partir en ~** to go hurtling off; **2 ~s d'eau** masses of water; torrential rain.

trombone /tRɔ̃bɔn/ *nm* **1** trombone; **2** trombonist; **3** paperclip.

trompe /tRɔ̃p/ *nf* **1** (Zool) (of elephant) trunk; (of insect) proboscis; **2** (Mus) horn.

trompe-la-mort /tRɔ̃plamɔR/ *nmf inv* daredevil.

trompe-l'œil /tRɔ̃plœj/ *nm inv* **1** (painting) trompe l'oeil; **2** (figurative) smokescreen.

tromper /tRɔ̃pe/ [1] **I** *vtr* **1** (gen) to deceive; to be unfaithful to [*husband, wife*]; **~ les électeurs** to mislead the voters; **2 ~ la vigilance** or **surveillance de qn** to slip past sb's guard; **3** to stave off [*hunger*]; **pour ~ l'attente** to while away the time.
II se tromper *v refl* (+ *v être*) **1** to be mistaken; **se ~ sur qn** to be wrong about sb; **je me suis trompé sur leurs intentions** I misunderstood their intentions; **il ne faut pas s'y ~, qu'on ne s'y trompe pas** make no mistake about it; **2** to make a mistake; **se ~ de bus** to take the wrong bus; **se ~ de date** to get the date wrong.

tromperie /tRɔ̃pRi/ *nf* deceit.

trompette[1] /tRɔ̃pɛt/ *nm* (in orchestra) trumpet (player); (in army) bugler; (in brass band) trumpeter.

trompette[2] /tRɔ̃pɛt/ *nf* trumpet.

trompettiste /tRɔ̃petist/ *nmf* trumpet (player).

trompeur, **-euse** /tRɔ̃pœR, øz/ *adj* [*promise*] misleading; [*appearance*] deceptive.

tronc /tRɔ̃/ *nm* **1** (of tree, body) trunk; (of column) shaft; **2** collection box.
■ **~ commun** (of species) common origin; (of disciplines) (common) core curriculum.

tronçon /tRɔ̃sɔ̃/ *nm* section.

tronçonneuse /tRɔ̃sɔnøz/ *nf* chain saw.

trône /tRon/ *nm* throne; **monter sur le ~** to come to the throne.

trôner /tRone/ [1] *vi* **le professeur trônait au milieu de ses étudiants** the professor was holding court among his students; **~ sur** [*photograph*] to have pride of place on.

tronquer /tRɔ̃ke/ [1] *vtr* to truncate.

trop /tRo/ **I** *adv* too; too much; **beaucoup** or **bien ~ lourd** far or much too heavy; **j'ai ~ mangé** I've had too much to eat; **j'ai ~ dormi** I've slept too long; **ça c'est ~ fort**○! that's too much!; **nous sommes ~ peu nombreux** there are too few of us; **12 francs c'est ~ peu** 12 francs is too little; **ce serait ~ beau!** I/you/we etc should be so lucky!; **c'est ~ bête!** how stupid!; **~ enthousiaste** overenthusiastic; **c'en est ~!** that's the end!; **nous ne serons pas ~ de deux** it'll take at least two of us; **~ c'est ~!** enough is enough!; **c'était ~ drôle** it was so funny.
II trop de *quantif* **~ de pression/meubles** too much pressure/furniture; **~ de livres/monde** too many books/people.
III de trop, **en trop** *phr* **il y a une assiette en ~** there's one plate too many; **si tu as du tissu en ~ tu peux faire un coussin** if you have some material left over, you can make a cushion; **il y a 12 francs de ~** there's 12 francs too much; **ta remarque était de ~** your remark was uncalled for; **se sentir de ~** to feel one is in the way.
IV par trop *phr* = **trop**.

trophée /tRɔfe/ *nm* trophy.

tropical, **~e**, *mpl* **-aux** /tRɔpikal, o/ *adj* tropical.

tropique /tRɔpik/ *nm* tropic; **vivre sous les ~s** to live in the tropics.

trop-plein, *pl* **~s** /tRoplɛ̃/ *nm* **1** (of energy) excess; **2** (Tech) (from bath) overflow.

troquer /tRɔke/ [1] *vtr* (gen) **~ qch contre qch** to swap sth for sth; to barter sth for sth.

trot /tRo/ *nm* trot; **au ~!** (figurative) at the double (GB), on the double (US).

trotte○ /tRɔt/ *nf* **ça fait une ~** it's a fair walk.

trotter /tRɔte/ [1] *vi* **1** [*horse, rider*] to trot; **2** [*person, mouse*] to scurry (about); [*child*] to toddle along; **3** (figurative) **~ dans la tête** [*thought*] to go through one's mind; [*music*] to go through one's head.

trotteuse /tRɔtøz/ *nf* (on watch) second hand.

trottiner /tRɔtine/ [1] *vi* **1** [*horse*] to jog; **2** [*person, mouse*] to scurry along.

trottinette /tRɔtinɛt/ *nf* scooter.

trottoir /tRɔtwaR/ *nm* pavement (GB), sidewalk (US); **le bord du ~** the kerb (GB) or curb (US).
IDIOMS **faire le ~**○ to be a hooker○.

trou /tRu/ *nm* **1** hole; **2** (in timetable) (gen) gap; (Sch) free period; (in budget) deficit; (in savings) hole; **3**○ **~ (perdu)** dump○; **il n'est jamais sorti de son ~** he's never been out of his own backyard.
■ **~ d'aération** airhole; **~ d'air** air pocket; **~ de mémoire** memory lapse; **~ normand** *glass of spirits between courses to aid digestion*; **~ de serrure** keyhole.

troublant, **~e** /tRublɑ̃, ɑ̃t/ *adj* **1** [*problem*] disturbing; [*coincidence, resemblance*] disconcerting; **2** (sexually) unsettling, arousing.

trouble /tRubl/ **I** *adj* **1** [*liquid*] cloudy; [*glasses*] smudgy; **2** [*picture, outline*] blurred; **3** [*feeling*] confused; [*business, milieu*] shady.
II *adv* **je vois ~** my eyes are blurred; I have blurred vision.
III *nm* **1** unrest; **~s ethniques** ethnic unrest; **2** trouble; **jeter le ~** to stir up trouble; **3** confusion; embarrassment; **4** emotion; **ressentir un ~** to feel a thrill of emotion; **5** (Med) **~s** disorders; **~s de la mémoire** memory problems.

trouble-fête /tRubləfɛt/ *nmf inv* spoilsport.

troubler /tRuble/ [1] **I** *vtr* **1** to make [sth] cloudy [*liquid*]; to blur [*sight, picture*]; **2** to disturb [*silence, sleep, person*]; to disrupt [*meeting, plans*]; **en ces temps troublés** in these troubled times; **3** to disconcert [*person*]; **quelque chose me trouble** something's bothering me.
II se troubler *v refl* (+ *v être*) **1** [*person*] to become flustered; **2** [*liquid*] to become cloudy; **ma vue se troubla** my eyes became blurred.

trouée /tRue/ *nf* **1** gap; **2** (Mil) breach.

trouer /tRue/ [1] *vtr* to make a hole (or holes)

in; to wear a hole (or holes) in; **semelle trouée** sole with a hole (or holes) in it.

IDIOMS **~ la peau**○ **à qn** to put a bullet in sb○.

trouillard○, **~e** /tRujaR, aRd/ *nm,f* chicken○, coward.

trouille○ /tRuj/ *nf* fear; **avoir la ~** to be scared.

troupe /tRup/ *nf* **1** (Mil) troops; **2** (of actors) company; (on tour) troupe; **3** (of deer) herd; (of birds) flock; (of tourists) troop; (of children) band.

troupeau, *pl* **~x** /tRupo/ *nm* **1** (of buffalo, cattle) herd; (of sheep) flock; (of geese) gaggle; **2** (of people) herd.

trousse /tRus/ *nf* **1** (little) case; **2** kit.

■ **~ d'écolier** pencil case; **~ de maquillage** make-up bag; **~ de médecin** doctor's bag; **~ de secours** first-aid kit; **~ de toilette** toilet bag.

IDIOMS **être aux ~s de qn** to be hot on sb's heels.

trousseau, *pl* **~x** /tRuso/ *nm* **1** (of keys) bunch; **2** (of bride) trousseau; (of baby) clothes.

trouvaille /tRuvɑj/ *nf* **1** (object) find; **2** bright idea, brainwave.

trouvé, **~e** /tRuve/ **I** *pp* ▶ **trouver**.

II *pp adj* **réplique bien ~e** neat riposte; **tout ~** [*solution*] ready-made; [*culprit*] obvious.

trouver /tRuve/ [1] **I** *vtr* **1** (gen) to find; **on trouve de tout ici** they have everything here; **~ qch par hasard** to come across sth; **~ un intérêt à qch** to find sth interesting; **~ à redire** to find fault; **~ le moyen de faire** to manage to do; **j'ai trouvé!** I've got it!; **tu as trouvé ça tout seul?** (ironic) did you work that out all by yourself?; **si tu continues tu vas me ~**○**!** don't push your luck○!; **il va ~ à qui parler** he's going to be for it○; **~ du plaisir à faire** to get pleasure out of doing; **aller ~ qn** to go and see sb; **2 je trouve ça drôle** I think it's funny, I find it funny; **comment trouves-tu mon ami?** what do you think of my friend?; **j'ai trouvé bon de vous prévenir** I thought it right to warn you; **je me demande ce qu'elle te trouve!** I wonder what she sees in you!; **je te trouve bien calme, qu'est-ce que tu as?** you're very quiet, what's the matter?

II se trouver *v refl* (+ *v être*) **1** to be; **se ~ à Rome** to be in Rome; **se ~ incapable** or **dans l'impossibilité de faire** to be unable to do; **2** to feel; **se ~ mal à l'aise quelque part** to feel uneasy somewhere; **j'ai failli me ~ mal** I nearly passed out; **3 il se ~ beau** he thinks he's good-looking; **4** to find [*excuse*].

III *v impers* **il se trouve que je le connais** I happen to know him; **il se trouve qu'elle ne leur avait rien dit** as it happened, she hadn't told them anything; **si ça se trouve**○ **ça te plaira** you might like it.

truand /tRyɑ̃/ *nm* **1** gangster; **2** crook.

truc /tRyk/ *nm* **1**○ knack; trick; **trouver le ~ pour faire** to find the knack of doing; **avoir un ~ pour gagner de l'argent** to know a good way of making money; **un ~ du métier** a trick of the trade; **2** thing; **il y a un tas de ~s à faire dans la maison** there are loads○ of things to do in the house; **il y a un ~ qui ne va pas** there's something wrong; **le vélo, c'est pas mon ~**○ cycling's not my thing; **3**○ thingummy○, whatsit○; **4** (person) what's-his-name/what's-her-name, thingy○.

trucage /tRykaʒ/ *nm* (in cinema) special effect.

truculent, **~e** /tRykylɑ̃, ɑ̃t/ *adj* earthy.

truelle /tRyɛl/ *nf* trowel.

truffe /tRyf/ *nf* **1** (Culin) truffle; **2** (of dog) nose.

truffer /tRyfe/ [1] *vtr* **il a truffé son discours de citations** he crammed his speech with quotations; **ta lettre est truffée de fautes** your letter is riddled with mistakes.

truie /tRɥi/ *nf* sow.

truite /tRɥit/ *nf* trout.

truquage = **trucage**.

truquer /tRyke/ [1] *vtr* **1** to fiddle○ [*accounts*]; to doctor [*document*]; **2** to mark [*cards*]; **3** to fix, to rig [*elections, match*].

trust /tRœst/ *nm* trust.

tsar /tsaR/ *nm* tsar.

tsé-tsé /tsetse/ *nf inv* (**mouche**) **~** tsetse (fly).

tsigane = **tzigane**.

TTC (*abbr* = **toutes taxes comprises**) inclusive of tax.

tu /ty/ *pron* you.

IDIOMS **être à ~ et à toi avec qn** to be on familiar terms with sb.

tuant○, **~e** /tɥɑ̃, ɑ̃t/ *adj* exhausting.

tuba /tyba/ *nm* **1** (Mus) tuba; **2** (of swimmer) snorkel.

tube /tyb/ **I** *nm* **1** tube; pipe; **2**○ (song) hit.

II à pleins tubes○ *phr* **mettre le son à pleins ~s** to turn the sound right up○.

■ **~ cathodique** cathode ray tube; **~ digestif** digestive tract; **~ à essai** test tube; **~ au néon** fluorescent light; **~ de rouge à lèvres** lipstick.

tubercule /tybɛRkyl/ *nm* **1** (Bot) tuber; **2** (Anat) tuberosity.

tuberculeux, **-euse** /tybɛRkylø, øz/ **I** *adj* tubercular; **être ~** to have TB.

II *nm,f* (Med) TB or tuberculosis sufferer.

tuberculose /tybɛRkyloz/ *nf* tuberculosis, TB.

tubulaire /tybylɛR/ *adj* tubular.

TUC /tyk/ *nm pl* (*abbr* = **travaux d'utilité collective**) paid community service (*for the young unemployed*).

tué /tɥe/ *nm* person killed; **sept ~s** seven people killed.

tuer /tɥe/ [1] **I** *vtr* **1** (gen) to kill; **2**○ to wear [sb] out.

II se tuer *v refl* (+ *v être*) **1** (accidentally) to be killed; **2** to kill oneself; **3 se ~ au travail** to work oneself to death; **je me tue à te le dire** I've told you a thousand times.

IDIOMS **~ le temps** to kill time.

tuerie /tyRi/ *nf* killings.

tue-tête: **à tue-tête** /atytɛt/ *phr* at the top of one's voice.

tueur, **-euse** /tɥœR, øz/ *nm,f* **1** killer; **2** slaughterman/slaughterwoman.

■ **~ à gages** hired or professional killer.

tuile /tɥil/ *nf* **1** tile; **2**○ blow; **quelle ~!** what a blow!; **3** (Culin) *thin almond biscuit*.

tulipe /tylip/ *nf* tulip.

tuméfier /tymefje/ [2] *vtr* to make [sth] swell up.

tumeur /tymœʀ/ *nf* tumour[GB].

tumulte /tymylt/ *nm* **1** uproar; **2** turmoil.

tumultueux, -euse /tymyltɥø, øz/ *adj* [*period*] turbulent; [*life, youth*] tempestuous; [*relationship, interview*] stormy.

tungstène /tœ̃gstɛn/ *nm* tungsten.

tunique /tynik/ *nf* tunic.

tunisien, -ienne /tynizjɛ̃, ɛn/ *adj* Tunisian.

tunnel /tynɛl/ *nm* tunnel; **le ~ sous la Manche** the Channel Tunnel.

IDIOMS **voir le bout du ~** to see light at the end of the tunnel.

turban /tyʀbɑ̃/ *nm* turban.

turbin○ /tyʀbɛ̃/ *nm* daily grind○, work.

turbine /tyʀbin/ *nf* turbine.

turboréacteur /tyʀboʀeaktœʀ/ *nm* turbojet (engine).

turbot /tyʀbo/ *nm* turbot.

turbulence /tyʀbylɑ̃s/ *nf* **1** turbulence; **2** unruliness; **3** unrest.

turbulent, ~e /tyʀbylɑ̃, ɑ̃t/ *adj* [*child*] unruly; [*class*] rowdy; [*life*] tempestuous; [*teenager, country*] rebellious; **être ~ en classe** to be disruptive in class.

turc, turque /tyʀk/ **I** *adj* Turkish.

II *nm* Turkish.

Turc, Turque /tyʀk/ *nm,f* Turk.

turlupiner○ /tyʀlypine/ [1] *vtr* to bother, to bug○.

turque ▶ **turc** I.

Turquie /tyʀki/ *pr nf* Turkey.

turquoise /tyʀkwaz/ *adj inv, nf* turquoise.

tutelle /tytɛl/ *nf* guardianship; **placer qn sous ~** to place sb in the care of a guardian.

tuteur, -trice /tytœʀ, tʀis/ **I** *nm,f* **1** (Law) guardian; **2** tutor.

II *nm* (Bot) stake.

tutoiement /tytwamɑ̃/ *nm* use of the form *'tu'*.

tutoyer /tytwaje/ [23] *vtr* to address [sb] using the 'tu' form.

tutu /tyty/ *nm* tutu.

tuyau, *pl* **~x** /tɥijo/ *nm* **1** (Tech) pipe; **2**○ tip○ (**sur** about).

■ **~ d'arrosage** hose; **~ d'échappement** exhaust.

tuyauterie /tɥijotʀi/ *nf* **1** (Tech) piping; **2** (Mus) pipes.

TVA /tevea/ *nf* (*abbr* = **taxe à la valeur ajoutée**) VAT.

tympan /tɛ̃pɑ̃/ *nm* eardrum.

type /tip/ **I** *nm* **1** type, kind; **plusieurs accidents de ce ~** several accidents of this kind; **il a le ~ nordique** he is the Nordic type; **ce n'est pas mon ~** he's/she's not my type; **2** (classic) example; **elle est le ~ même de la femme d'affaires** she's the classic example of a business woman; **3** (physical) type; **4**○ guy○, chap○; **sale ~!** swine○!; **brave ~** nice chap○; **un pauvre ~** a pathetic individual.

II (-)type (*combining form*) typical, classic; **l'exemple ~** the typical example.

typhoïde /tifɔid/ *adj, nf* typhoid.

typhon /tifɔ̃/ *nm* typhoon.

typique /tipik/ *adj* typical.

typographie /tipɔgʀafi/ *nf* typography.

typographique /tipɔgʀafik/ *adj* typographical.

tyran /tiʀɑ̃/ *nm* tyrant.

tyrannie /tiʀani/ *nf* tyranny.

tyrannique /tiʀanik/ *adj* tyrannical.

tyranniser /tiʀanize/ [1] *vtr* to tyrannize.

tzigane /dzigan, tsigan/ **I** *adj, nmf* gypsy.

II *nm* (language) Romany.

Uu

u, U /y/ *nm inv* u, U; **en (forme de) U** U-shaped.

ubac /ybak/ *nm* north-facing side.

ubiquité /ybikɥite/ *nf* ubiquity ; **je n'ai pas le don d'~!** I can't be everywhere at once!

ubuesque /ybyɛsk/ *adj* grotesque.

ukrainien, -ienne /ykʀɛnjɛ̃, ɛn/ **I** *adj* Ukrainian.
II *nm* Ukrainian.

ulcère /ylsɛʀ/ *nm* ulcer.

ulcérer /ylseʀe/ [14] *vtr* **1** to sicken, to revolt; **2** (Med) to ulcerate.

ulcéreux, -euse /ylseʀø, øz/ *adj* [*wound*] ulcerated.

ULM /yɛlɛm/ *nm inv* (*abbr* = **ultraléger motorisé**) microlight; microlighting; **faire de l'~** to go microlighting.

ultérieur, ~e /ylteʀjœʀ/ *adj* subsequent; **une date ~e** a later date.

ultérieurement /ylteʀjœʀmɑ̃/ *adv* **1** subsequently; **2** later.

ultimatum /yltimatɔm/ *nm* ultimatum.

ultime /yltim/ *adj* **1** final; **2** ultimate.

ultra /yltʀa/ *adj, nmf* extremist.

ultraconfidentiel, -ielle /yltʀakɔ̃fidɑ̃sjɛl/ *adj* top secret.

ultrafin, ~e /yltʀafɛ̃, in/ *adj* [*slice*] wafer-thin; [*stocking*] sheer; [*fibre*] ultra-fine.

ultraléger, -ère /yltʀaleʒe, ɛʀ/ *adj* [*material, cigarette*] ultra light; [*clothing, fabric, equipment*] very light.

ultramoderne /yltʀamɔdɛʀn/ *adj* (gen) ultra modern; [*system, technology*] state-of-the-art.

ultrarapide /yltʀaʀapid/ *adj* high-speed.

ultrasecret, -ète /yltʀasəkʀɛ, ɛt/ *adj* top secret.

ultrasensible /yltʀasɑ̃sibl/ *adj* [*person*] hypersensitive; [*film*] ultrasensitive; [*problem*] highly sensitive.

ultrason /yltʀasɔ̃/ *nm* ultrasound.

ultraviolet, -ette /yltʀavjɔlɛ, ɛt/ **I** *adj* ultraviolet.
II *nm* ultraviolet ray; **séance d'~s** session on a sunbed.

ululer /ylyle/ [1] *vi* to hoot.

un, une[1] /œ̃(n), yn/ **I** *det* (*pl* **des**) **1** a, an; one; **un homme** a man; **une femme** a woman; **avec ~ sang-froid remarquable** with remarkable self-control; **il n'y avait pas ~ arbre** there wasn't a single tree; **~ accident est vite arrivé** accidents soon happen; **2 il y avait des roses et des lis** there were roses and lilies; **il y a des gens qui trichent** there are some people who cheat; **3 il fait ~ froid** or **~ de ces froids!** it's so cold!; **elle m'a donné une de ces gifles!** she gave me such a slap!; **il y a ~ monde aujourd'hui!** there are so many people today!
II *pron* (*pl* **uns, unes**) one; **(l')~ de** or **d'entre nous** one of us; **les ~s pensent que...** some think that...
III *adj* one, a, an; **trente et une personnes** thirty-one people; **~ jour sur deux** every other day.
IV *nm,f* one; **~ par personne** one each; **les deux villes n'en font plus qu'une** the two cities have merged into one; **~ à** or **par ~** one by one.
V *nm* one; **page ~** page one.
IDIOMS **fière comme pas une** extremely proud; **il est menteur comme pas ~** he's the biggest liar; **~ pour tous et tous pour ~** all for one and one for all; ▶ **dix**.

unanime /ynanim/ *adj* unanimous (**à faire** in doing).

unanimement /ynanimmɑ̃/ *adv* **1** [*adopted, elected*] unanimously; **2** (figurative) [*admired*] universally.

unanimité /ynanimite/ *nf* unanimity; **à l'~** [*elected*] unanimously; **à l'~ moins deux voix** with only two votes against; **faire l'~** to have unanimous support or backing.

une[2] /yn/ **I** *det, pron, adj* ▶ **un I, II, III, IV**.
II *nf* **la ~** the front page; **être à la ~** to be in the headlines.

UNESCO /ynɛsko/ *nf* (*abbr* = **United Nations Educational, Scientific and Cultural Organization**) UNESCO.

uni, ~e /yni/ **I** *pp* ▶ **unir**.
II *pp adj* **1** [*family*] close-knit; [*couple*] close; [*people, rebels*] united; **2** [*fabric, colour*] plain; **3** [*surface*] smooth, even.

UNICEF /ynisɛf/ *nm* (*abbr* = **United Nations International Children's Emergency Fund**) UNICEF.

unicité /ynisite/ *nf* uniqueness.

unième /ynjɛm/ *adj* first; **vingt et ~** twenty-first.

unification /ynifikasjɔ̃/ *nf* unification.

unifier /ynifje/ [2] **I** *vtr* **1** to unify [*country, market*]; **2** to standardize [*procedure, system*].
II s'unifier *v refl* (+ *v être*) [*countries, groups*] to unite.

uniforme /ynifɔʀm/ **I** *adj*(gen) uniform; [*buildings, streets, existence*] monotonous; [*regulation*] across-the-board.
II *nm* uniform; **en ~** uniformed.

uniformément /ynifɔʀmemɑ̃/ *adv* uniformly.

uniformiser /ynifɔʀmize/ [1] *vtr* to standardize [*rate*]; to make [sth] uniform [*colour*].

uniformité /ynifɔʀmite/ *nf* (of tastes) uniformity; (of life, buildings) monotony.

unijambiste /yniʒɑ̃bist/ **I** *adj* **être ~** to have only one leg.
II *nmf* one-legged person.

unilatéral, **~e**, *mpl* **-aux** /ynilateʀal, o/ *adj* unilateral; [*parking*] on one side only.

union /ynjɔ̃/ *nf* **1** union; **2** association; **~ de consommateurs** consumers' association; **3** marriage.
■ **~ libre** cohabitation; **~ sportive**, **US** sports club; **Union européenne** European Union.
IDIOMS **l'~ fait la force** (Proverb) united we stand, divided we fall.

unique /ynik/ *adj* **1** only; **il est l'~ témoin** he's the only witness; **être fille** or **fils ~** to be an only child; **2** single; **parti ~** single party; **système à parti ~** one-party system; **'prix ~'** 'all at one price'; **3** unique; **une occasion ~** a unique opportunity; **~ en son genre** [*person, object*] one of a kind; [*event*] one-off (GB), one-shot (US); **4**^O **ce type est ~!** that guy's priceless^O!.

uniquement /ynikmɑ̃/ *adv* (gen) only; **en vente ~ par correspondance** available by mail order only; **c'était ~ pour te taquiner** it was only to tease you; **il pense ~ à s'amuser** all he thinks about is having fun; **~ dans un but commercial** purely for commercial ends.

unir /yniʀ/ [3] **I** *vtr* **1** to unite [*people, country*]; **des hommes unis par les mêmes idées** men brought together by the same ideas; **2** to combine [*qualities, resources*]; **3** to join [sb] in matrimony .
II s'unir *v refl* (+ *v être*) **1** to unite; **2** to marry.

unisexe /yniseks/ *adj* unisex.

unisson /ynisɔ̃/ *nm* unison; **à l'~** (Mus) in unison; (figurative) in accord.

unitaire /ynitɛʀ/ *adj* [*cost*] unit.

unité /ynite/ *nf* **1** unity; **~ d'action** unity of action; **film qui manque d'~** film lacking in cohesion; **il y a ~ de vues entre eux** they share the same viewpoint; **2** unit; **~ monétaire** unit of currency; **20 francs l'~** 20 francs each; **vendre qch à l'~** to sell sth singly.
■ **~ centrale (de traitement)**, (Comput) central processing unit, CPU; **~ de disque** (Comput) disk drive.

univers /ynivɛʀ/ *nm inv* **1** (in astronomy) universe; **2** whole world; **3** world; **l'~ de Kafka** Kafka's world.

universalité /ynivɛʀsalite/ *nf* universality.

universel, **-elle** /ynivɛʀsɛl/ *adj* [*language, theme*] universal; [*history*] world; [*remedy*] all-purpose.

universitaire /ynivɛʀsitɛʀ/ **I** *adj* [*town*] university; [*work*] academic.
II *nmf* academic.

université /ynivɛʀsite/ *nf* university (GB), college (US).
■ **~ d'été** summer school.

uns *pron* ▶ **un** II.

Untel, **Unetelle** /œ̃tɛl, yntɛl/ *nm,f* **Monsieur ~** Mr so-and-so; **Madame Unetelle** Mrs so-and-so.

urbain, **~e** /yʀbɛ̃, ɛn/ *adj* **1** urban; **vie ~e** city life; **2** (formal) urbane.

urbanisation /yʀbanizasjɔ̃/ *nf* urbanization.

urbaniser /yʀbanize/ [1] *vtr* to urbanize [*region*]; **zone urbanisée** built-up area.

urbanisme /yʀbanism/ *nm* town planning (GB), city planning (US).

urbaniste /yʀbanist/ *nmf* town planner (GB), city planner (US).

urée /yʀe/ *nf* urea.

urgence /yʀʒɑ̃s/ *nf* **1** urgency; **il y a ~** it's urgent, it's a matter of urgency; **d'~** [*act*] immediately; [*summon*] urgently; [*measures, treatment*] emergency; **de toute** or **d'extrême ~** as a matter of great urgency; **transporter qn d'~ à l'hôpital** to rush sb to hospital; **en ~** as a matter of urgency; **2** (Med) **une ~** an emergency; **le service des ~s**, **les ~s** the casualty department.

urgent, **~e** /yʀʒɑ̃, ɑ̃t/ *adj* urgent.

Uri /yʀi/ *pr n* **le canton d'~** the canton of Uri.

urinaire /yʀinɛʀ/ *adj* urinary; **appareil ~** urinary tract.

urinal, *pl* **-aux** /yʀinal, o/ *nm* urinal.

urine /yʀin/ *nf* urine.

uriner /yʀine/ [1] *vi* to urinate.

urinoir /yʀinwaʀ/ *nm* urinal.

urne /yʀn/ *nf* **1 ~ (électorale)** ballot box; **se rendre aux ~s** to go to the polls; **2** urn.

urologie /yʀɔlɔʒi/ *nf* urology.

urologue /yʀɔlɔg/ *nmf* urologist.

URSS /yɛʀɛsɛs, yʀs/ *pr nf* Hist (*abbr* = **Union des Républiques socialistes soviétiques**) USSR.

urticaire /yʀtikɛʀ/ *nf* hives.

uruguayen, **-enne** /yʀygwejɛ̃, ɛn/ *adj* Uruguayan.

us /ys/ *nm pl* **les ~ et coutumes** the ways and customs.

US /yɛs/ *nf* (*abbr* = **union sportive**) sports club.

USA /yɛsa/ *nm pl* (*abbr* = **United States of America**) USA.

usage /yzaʒ/ *nm* **1** use; **à l'~**, **par l'~** with use; **en ~** in use; **faire ~ de** to use [*product*]; to exercise [*authority*]; **faire bon/mauvais ~ de qch** to put sth to good/bad use; **faire de l'~** [*garment*] to last; **2** use; **à ~ privé** for private use; **à ~s multiples** [*appliance*] multipurpose; **il a perdu l'~ d'un œil/l'~ de la parole** he's lost the use of one eye/the power of speech; **hors d'~** [*garment*] unwearable; [*machine*] out of order; **3** (referring to language) usage; **en ~** in usage; **4** custom; **l'~ est de faire** the custom is to do; it's usual practice to do; **entrer dans l'~** [*word*] to come into common use; [*behaviour*] to become common practice; [*politeness*] customary; [*precautions*] usual.
■ **~ de faux** (Law) use of false documents; **faux et ~ de faux** forgery and use of false documents.

usagé, **~e** /yzaʒe/ *adj* **1** [*garment*] well-worn; [*tyre*] worn; **2** [*syringe*] used.

usager /yzaʒe/ *nm* (of service) user; (of language) speaker; **~ de la route** road-user.

usant, **~e** /yzɑ̃, ɑ̃t/ *adj* exhausting, wearing.

usé, **~e** /yze/ I *pp* ▶ **user**.
II *pp adj* [*object*] worn; [*person*] worn-down; [*heart, eyes*] worn-out; [*joke*] hackneyed; **~ jusqu'à la corde** [*carpet*] threadbare; [*tyre*] worn down to the tread; (figurative) [*joke*] hackneyed.

user /yze/ [1] I *vtr* to wear out [*shoes*]; to wear down [*person*]; **les piles sont usées** the batteries have run down or out; **~ ses vêtements jusqu'à la corde** to wear one's clothes out; **~ sa santé** to ruin one's health.
II **user de** *v+prep* (gen) to use; to exercise [*right*]; to take [*precautions*]; **~ de diplomatie** to be diplomatic.
III **s'user** *v refl* (+ *v être*) **1** [*shoes*] to wear out; **2** [*person*] **s'~ à la tâche** or **au travail** to wear oneself out with overwork; **s'~ la santé** to ruin one's health.

usine /yzin/ *nf* factory, plant.
■ **~ métallurgique** ironworks; **~ sidérurgique** steelworks.

usiner /yzine/ [1] *vtr* **1** to machine; **2** to manufacture.

usité, **~e** /yzite/ *adj* commonly used.

ustensile /ystɑ̃sil/ *nm* utensil.

usuel, **-elle** /yzɥɛl/ *adj* [*object*] everyday; [*word*] common.

usufruit /yzyfʀɥi/ *nm* (Law) usufruct.

usufruitier, **-ière** /yzyfʀɥitje, ɛʀ/ *nm,f* tenant for life.

usure /yzyʀ/ *nf* **1** (of clothes) wear and tear; (of tyre, machine) wear; **résister à l'~** to wear well; **2** (of energy, enemy) wearing down; **3 ~ du temps** wearing effect of time; **4** usury.

usurier, **-ière** /yzyʀje, ɛʀ/ *nm,f* usurer.

usurpateur, **-trice** /yzyʀpatœʀ, tʀis/ *nm,f* usurper.

usurper /yzyʀpe/ [1] *vtr* to usurp.

ut /yt/ *nm* (Mus) C.

utérus /yteʀys/ *nm inv* womb.

utile /ytil/ I *adj* (gen) useful; **être ~** [*person, book*] to be helpful; [*umbrella*] to come in handy; **il est ~ de signaler** it's worth pointing out; **il n'a pas jugé ~ de me prévenir** he didn't think it necessary to let me know; **en quoi puis-je vous être ~?** how can I help you?
II *nm* **joindre l'~ à l'agréable** to mix business with pleasure.

utilement /ytilmɑ̃/ *adv* [*intervene*] effectively; [*occupy oneself*] usefully.

utilisable /ytilizabl/ *adj* usable.

utilisateur, **-trice** /ytilizatœʀ, tʀis/ *nm,f* user.

utilisation /ytilizasjɔ̃/ *nf* use.

utiliser /ytilize/ [1] *vtr* (gen) to use; to make use of [*resources*].

utilitaire /ytilitɛʀ/ *adj* [*role*] practical; [*object*] functional, utilitarian; [*vehicle*] commercial.

utilité /ytilite/ *nf* **1** usefulness; **d'une grande ~** [*book, machine*] very useful; [*person*] very helpful; **d'aucune ~** of no use; **2** use; **je n'en ai pas l'~** I have no use for it.

utopie /ytɔpi/ *nf* **1** Utopia; **2** wishful thinking.

utopique /ytɔpik/ *adj* utopian.

UV /yve/ *nm pl* (*abbr* = **ultraviolets**) ultraviolet rays; **séance d'~** session on a sunbed.

uvule /yvyl/ *nf* uvula.

v, V /ve/ *nm inv* v, V; **en (forme de) V** V-shaped; **pull en V** V-necked sweater.

va /va/ ▶ **aller**[1].

vacance /vakɑ̃s/ **I** *nf* vacancy.
II vacances *nf pl* holiday (GB), vacation (US); **être en ~s** to be on holiday (GB) or vacation (US); **bonnes ~s!** have a good holiday (GB) or vacation (US)!; **~s d'été, grandes ~s** (Sch) summer holidays (GB), summer or long vacation (US).
■ **~s scolaires** (Sch) school holiday (GB) or vacation (US).

vacancier, -ière /vakɑ̃sje, ɛʀ/ *nm,f* holidaymaker (GB), vacationer (US).

vacant, ~e /vakɑ̃, ɑ̃t/ *adj* vacant.

vacarme /vakaʀm/ *nm* din, racket○.

vacataire /vakatɛʀ/ **I** *adj* [*staff*] temporary.
II *nmf* **1** temporary employee; **2** supply teacher (GB), substitute teacher (US).

vaccin /vaksɛ̃/ *nm* (Med) vaccine.

vaccination /vaksinasjɔ̃/ *nf* vaccination; **~ contre la polio** polio vaccination.

vacciner /vaksine/ [1] *vtr* **1** to vaccinate; **se faire ~** to be or get vaccinated; **2** (humorous) **~ qn contre** to put sb off; **je suis vacciné○!** I've learned my lesson!

vache /vaʃ/ **I**○ *adj* mean, nasty; **faire un coup ~ à qn** to pull a mean trick on sb.
II *nf* **1** cow; **2** cowhide.
■ **~ à eau** water bottle; **~ à lait** (figurative) money-spinner○; **années de ~s maigres** lean years.
IDIOMS **parler français comme une ~ espagnole**○ to speak very bad French.

vachement○ /vaʃmɑ̃/ *adv* really; **il a ~ maigri** he's lost a hell of a lot of weight○.

vacherie○ /vaʃʀi/ *nf* **1** meanness, nastiness; **2** nasty or bitchy○ remark; **3** dirty trick; **4 c'est une vraie ~ ce virus** this virus is a bloody● (GB) or damned○ nuisance.

vachette /vaʃɛt/ *nf* **1** young cow; **2** calfskin.

vaciller /vasije/ [1] *vi* **1** [*person*] to be unsteady on one's legs; [*legs*] to be unsteady; **2** [*person, object*] to sway; [*light, flame*] to flicker; **3** [*health, memory*] to fail; [*power, majority*] to weaken.

vacuité /vakɥite/ *nf* emptiness, vacuity.

vadrouille○ /vadʀuj/ *nf* stroll; **être en ~** to be wandering about.

va-et-vient /vaevjɛ̃/ *nm inv* **1** comings and goings; to-ing and fro-ing; **faire le ~** to go to and fro; to go back and forth; **2** two-way switch.

vagabond, ~e /vagabɔ̃, ɔ̃d/ **I** *adj* [*dog*] stray; [*mood*] ever-changing.
II *nm,f* vagrant.

vagabondage /vagabɔ̃daʒ/ *nm* **1** wandering; **2** (Law) vagrancy.

vagabonder /vagabɔ̃de/ [1] *vi* to wander, to rove, to roam.

vagin /vaʒɛ̃/ *nm* vagina.

vagissement /vaʒismɑ̃/ *nm* wail.

vague[1] /vag/ **I** *adj* vague; **d'un air ~** vaguely; **ce sont de ~s parents** they're distant relatives.
II *nm* **1 il regardait dans le ~** he was staring into space; **2 avoir du ~ à l'âme** to feel melancholic.

vague[2] /vag/ *nf* wave; **faire des ~s** [*wind*] to make ripples; (figurative) [*scandal*] to cause a stir, to make waves.
■ **~ de chaleur** heatwave; **~ de froid** cold spell.
IDIOMS **être au creux de la ~** to be at a low ebb.

vaguement /vagmɑ̃/ *adv* vaguely; **on avait ~ décidé d'y aller** we had sort of decided to go.

vaillant, ~e /vajɑ̃, ɑ̃t/ *adj* **1** courageous; **2** strong.

vain, ~e /vɛ̃, vɛn/ **I** *adj* **1** futile; **mes efforts ont été ~s** my efforts were in vain; **2** [*promises*] empty; [*hopes*] vain; [*pleasure, words*] vain, empty; **3** [*person*] vain.
II en vain *phr* in vain.

vaincre /vɛ̃kʀ/ [57] **I** *vtr* **1** to defeat [*opponent*]; **2** to overcome [*prejudices, complex*]; to beat [*unemployment, illness*].
II *vi* to win.

vaincu, ~e /vɛ̃ky/ **I** *pp* ▶ **vaincre**.
II *pp adj* defeated; **s'avouer ~** to admit defeat.

vainqueur /vɛ̃kœʀ/ **I** *adj m* victorious.
II *nm* victor; winner; prizewinner; conqueror.

vaisseau, *pl* **~x** /vɛso/ *nm* **1** (Anat, Bot) vessel; **2** (Naut) vessel; warship.
■ **~ spatial** spaceship.

vaisselle /vɛsɛl/ *nf* **1** crockery, dishes; **2** dishes; **faire la ~** to do the dishes.

val, *pl* **~s** or **vaux** /val, vo/ *nm* valley.
IDIOMS **être toujours par monts et par vaux** to be always on the move.

valable /valabl/ *adj* **1** [*explanation*] valid; [*solution*] viable; **2** [*document*] valid; **ma proposition reste ~** my offer still holds; **3**○ [*work, project*] worthwhile.

valdinguer○ /valdɛ̃ge/ [1] *vi* [*person, object*] to go flying○.

valet /valɛ/ *nm* **1** manservant; **2** (in cards) jack.
■ **~ de chambre** valet; **~ de ferme** farm hand; **~ de nuit** rack, valet (US).

valeur /valœʀ/ *nf* **1** value; **prendre de la ~** to go up in value; **les objets de ~** valuables; **2** (of person, artist) worth; (of work) value, merit; (of method, discovery) value; **prouver sa ~** to show one's worth; **attacher de la ~ à qch** to value sth; **mettre qch en ~** to emphasize, to highlight [*fact, talent, quality*]; to set off [*eyes, painting*]; **se mettre en ~** to make the best of oneself; to show oneself to best advantage; **3** validity; **4** value; **nous n'avons pas les mêmes ~s** we don't share the same values; **5** (on stock exchange) security; **~s** securities, stock, stocks and shares; **le marché** or **la Bourse des ~s** the stock market.

■ **~ ajoutée** added value; **~ sûre** gilt-edged security (GB), blue chip; (figurative) safe bet; **~s mobilières** securities.

validation /validasjɔ̃/ *nf* **1** validation; **2** stamping.

valide /valid/ *adj* **1** valid; **non ~** invalid; **2** able-bodied; fit.

valider /valide/ [1] *vtr* to stamp [*ticket*]; **faire ~** to have [sth] recognized [*diploma*].

validité /validite/ *nf* validity.

valise /valiz/ *nf* suitcase; **faire ses ~s** to pack.

■ **~ diplomatique** diplomatic bag (GB), diplomatic pouch (US).

IDIOMS **avoir des ~s sous les yeux**○ to have bags under one's eyes.

vallée /vale/ *nf* valley.

vallon /valɔ̃/ *nm* dale, small valley.

vallonné, ~e /valɔne/ *adj* [*landscape*] undulating; [*country*] hilly.

valoir /valwaʀ/ [45] **I** *vtr* **~ qch à qn** to earn sb sth [*praise, criticism*]; to win sb sth [*friendship, admiration*]; to bring sb sth [*problems*].

II *vi* **1 ~ une fortune/cher** to be worth a fortune/a lot; **ça vaut combien?** how much is it worth?, what is it worth?; **~ de l'or** (figurative) to be very valuable; **2 que vaut ce film/vin?** what's that film/wine like?; **il ne vaut pas mieux que son frère** he's no better than his brother; **il ne vaut pas cher** he is a bad lot○; **ne rien ~** to be rubbish, to be no good; to be useless; to be worthless; **la chaleur ne me vaut rien** the heat doesn't suit me; **il ne me dit rien qui vaille** I've got misgivings about him; **ça ne me dit rien qui vaille** I don't like the sound of it; **3** to be as good as; **ton travail vaut bien/largement le leur** your work is just as good/every bit as good as theirs; **rien ne vaut la soie** nothing beats silk; **4** to be worth; **le musée vaut le détour** the museum is worth a detour; **ça en vaut la peine, ça vaut le coup**○ it's worth it; **5** [*rule, criticism*] to apply; **la règle vaut pour tout le monde** the rule applies to everybody; **6 faire ~** to put [sth] to work [*money*]; to point out [*merit, necessity*]; to emphasize, to highlight [*quality, feature*]; to assert [*right*]; **faire ~ que** to point out that; **se faire ~** to push oneself forward, to get oneself noticed (**auprès de qn** by sb).

III se valoir *v refl* (+ *v être*) to be the same.

IV *v impers* **il vaut mieux faire, mieux vaut faire** it's better to do; **il vaut mieux que tu y ailles** you'd better go; **cela vaut mieux**○ it's better like that or that way.

valorisation /valɔʀizasjɔ̃/ *nf* **1** (of product) promotion; **2** (of region, resources) development; **3** (of currency) rise.

valoriser /valɔʀize/ [1] *vtr* **1** to promote [*product*]; to make [sth] attractive [*profession, course*]; **2** to develop [*region, resources*]; to put [sth] to good use [*degree, knowledge*]; **3** to put [sth] to work [*capital*].

valse /vals/ *nf* **1** waltz; **2** (figurative) **~ des ministres** frequent cabinet reshuffles.

valser /valse/ [1] *vi* to waltz; **envoyer ~ qn**○ to send sb flying.

valve /valv/ *nf* valve.

vamp○ /vɑ̃p/ *nf* vamp.

vampire /vɑ̃piʀ/ *nm* **1** vampire; **2** (figurative) bloodsucker; **3** (Zool) vampire bat.

van /vɑ̃/ *nm* **1** horsebox (GB), horse-car (US); **2** van.

vandale /vɑ̃dal/ *nmf* vandal.

vandalisme /vɑ̃dalism/ *nm* vandalism.

vanille /vanij/ *nf* vanilla; **une gousse de ~** a vanilla pod.

vanité /vanite/ *nf* **1** vanity; **tirer ~ de qch** to pride oneself on sth; **2** (of efforts) futility; (of promise) emptiness; (of undertaking) uselessness.

vaniteux, -euse /vanitø, øz/ *adj* vain, conceited.

vanne /van/ *nf* **1** gate; sluice gate; floodgate; **2**○ dig○.

IDIOMS **ouvrir les ~s**○ to make funds available; **fermer les ~s**○ to cut funding.

vanner○ /vane/ [1] *vtr* to tire [sb] out; **je suis vanné!** I'm tired out or whacked○!

vannerie /vanʀi/ *nf* basket-making; **objets en ~** wickerwork.

vantard, ~e /vɑ̃taʀ, aʀd/ *nm,f* boaster, braggart.

vantardise /vɑ̃taʀdiz/ *nf* **1** boastfulness; **2** boast.

vanter /vɑ̃te/ [1] **I** *vtr* to praise, to extol; **tant vanté** much vaunted.

II se vanter *v refl* (+ *v être*) **1** to boast, to brag; **2 se ~ de faire** to pride oneself on doing.

va-nu-pieds /vanypje/ *nmf inv* tramp, bum○.

vapeur /vapœʀ/ **I** *nf* steam; **bateau à ~** steamboat; **renverser la ~** (Naut) to go astern; (figurative) to backpedal; **faire cuire qch à la ~** to steam sth.

II vapeurs *nf pl* fumes.

vaporeux, -euse /vapɔʀø, øz/ *adj* diaphanous.

vaporisateur /vapɔʀizatœʀ/ *nm* spray.

vaporiser /vapɔʀize/ [1] *vtr* **1** to spray; **2** to vaporize.

vaquer: **vaquer à** /vake/ [1] *v+prep* **~ à ses occupations** to attend to one's business.

varappe /vaʀap/ *nf* rock-climbing.

varech /vaʀɛk/ *nm* kelp.

vareuse /vaʀøz/ *nf* **1** jersey; **2** (Mil) uniform jacket.

variable /vaʀjabl/ **I** *adj* **1** variable; **2** [*weather*] changeable; [*mood*] unpredictable.

II *nf* variable.

variante /vaʀjɑ̃t/ *nf* variant.

variation /vaʀjasjɔ̃/ *nf* variation (**de** in); **~s de l'opinion publique** changes in public opinion; **connaître de fortes ~s** [*prices, temperatures*] to fluctuate considerably.

varice /vaʀis/ *nf* varicose vein.

varicelle /vaʀisɛl/ *nf* chicken pox.

varié, ~e /vaʀje/ *adj* **1** varied; **2** various; **'sandwichs ~s'** 'a selection of sandwiches'.

varier /vaʀje/ [2] **I** *vtr* to vary; **pour ~ les plaisirs** just for a (pleasant) change.
II *vi* **1** to vary; **l'inflation varie de 4% à 6%** inflation fluctuates between 4% and 6%; **2 l'accusé ne varie pas** the accused is sticking to his story.

variété /vaʀjete/ **I** *nf* **1** variety; **une grande ~ d'articles** a wide range of items; **2** (Bot) variety; **3** sort; **différentes ~s de céréales** different sorts of cereals.
II variétés *nf pl* **spectacle de ~s** variety show; **les ~s françaises** French popular music.

variole /vaʀjɔl/ *nf* smallpox.

vas /va/ ▶ **aller**.

vase[1] /vɑz/ *nm* vase.
IDIOMS **vivre en ~ clos** to live without any contact with the outside world; **c'est la goutte d'eau qui fait déborder le ~** it's the last straw.

vase[2] /vɑz/ *nf* silt, sludge.

vasectomie /vazɛktɔmi/ *nf* vasectomy.

vaseux, -euse /vazø, øz/ *adj* **1** muddy; **2**○ **je me sens plutôt ~** I'm not really with it○; **3**○ [*speech, explanation*] woolly.

vasistas /vazistas/ *nm inv* louvre[GB] window.

vasque /vask/ *nf* **1** (of fountain) basin; **2** bowl.

vassal, ~e, *mpl* **-aux** /vasal, o/ *nm,f* vassal; (figurative) slave.

vaste /vast/ *adj* **1** [*estate, sector*] vast; [*market*] huge; **la salle n'est pas très ~** the room is not very large; **2** [*audience, choice*] large; **3** [*fraud*] massive; [*campaign*] extensive; [*movement, attack*] large-scale; [*work*] wide-ranging.

va-tout /vatu/ *nm inv* **jouer/tenter son ~** to stake/to risk everything.

vaudeville /vodvil/ *nm* light comedy; **tourner au ~** to turn into a farce.

vaudou /vodu/ *adj inv, nm* voodoo.

vaurien, -ienne /voʀjɛ̃, ɛn/ *nm,f* **1** rascal; **2** lout, yobbo○ (GB), hoodlum○.

vautour /votuʀ/ *nm* vulture.

vautrer: se vautrer /votʀe/ [1] *v refl* (+ *v être*) **1 se ~ sur** to sprawl on; **2 se ~ dans un fauteuil** to loll in an armchair; **3 se ~ dans la boue** to wallow in the mud.

va-vite: à la va-vite /alavavit/ *phr* in a rush.

veau, *pl* **~x** /vo/ *nm* **1** calf; **2** (Culin) veal; **3** calfskin.

vecteur /vɛktœʀ/ *nm* **1** vector; **2** (figurative) vehicle; **3** (of disease) carrier.

vécu, ~e /veky/ **I** *pp* ▶ **vivre**.
II *pp adj* **1** [*drama, story*] real-life; **2** [*time*] subjective.
III *nm* personal experiences; **c'est du ~** it's real life.

vedettariat /vədetaʀja/ *nm* stardom.

vedette /vədɛt/ *nf* **1** star; **avoir la ~** to have top billing; **tenir la ~** to be in the limelight; **se mettre en ~** to push oneself forward; **2** (Naut) launch.

végétal, ~e, *mpl* **-aux** /veʒetal, o/ **I** *adj* vegetable.
II *nm* vegetable.

végétalien, -ienne /veʒetaljɛ̃, ɛn/ *adj, nm,f* vegan.

végétarien, -ienne /veʒetaʀjɛ̃, ɛn/ *adj, nm,f* vegetarian.

végétatif, -ive /veʒetatif, iv/ *adj* vegetative.

végétation /veʒetasjɔ̃/ **I** *nf* vegetation.
II végétations *nf pl* (Med) adenoids.

végéter /veʒete/ [14] *vi* [*person*] to vegetate; [*project*] to stagnate.

véhémence /veemɑ̃s/ *nf* vehemence; **avec ~** vehemently.

véhicule /veikyl/ *nm* vehicle.
▪ **~ de tourisme** private car; **~ utilitaire** commercial vehicle.

véhiculer /veikyle/ [1] *vtr* to carry, to transport [*people, goods*]; to carry [*substance*]; **~ des rumeurs** to circulate rumours[GB]; **~ une image** to promote an image.

veille /vɛj/ *nf* **1 la ~** the day before; **la ~ au soir** the night or evening before; **à la ~ de** on the eve of [*war, elections*]; **être à la ~ de faire** to be on the verge of doing; **2 être en état de ~** to be awake; **3** vigil.

veillée /veje/ *nf* **1** evening; **à la ~** in the evening; **2** vigil; **~ funèbre** wake.

veiller /veje/ [1] **I** *vtr* to watch over [*ill person*]; to keep watch over [*dead person*].
II veiller à *v+prep* to look after [*health*]; **~ à ce que** to see to it that, to make sure that.
III veiller sur *v+prep* to watch over [*child*].
IV *vi* **1** to stay up; **2** to be on watch; **3** to be watchful; **heureusement, la police veille** fortunately, the police are there.
IDIOMS **~ au grain** to be on one's guard.

veilleur, -euse[1] /vɛjœʀ, øz/ *nm,f* look-out; **~ de nuit** night watchman.

veilleuse[2] /vɛjøz/ *nf* **1** night light; **2** pilot light; **3** side light (GB), parking light (US).

veinard○**, ~e** /venaʀ, aʀd/ *nm,f* lucky devil○.

veine /vɛn/ *nf* **1** vein; **2** (in wood) grain; **3** (of coal) seam; **4** inspiration; **de** or **dans la même ~** in the same vein; **être en ~ de générosité** to be in a generous mood; **5**○ luck; **il a de la ~** he's lucky; **c'est bien ma ~!** that's just my luck!

veinure /venyʀ/ *nf* (in wood) grain; (in marble) veining.

vêler /vele/ [1] *vi* [*cow*] to calve.

véliplanchiste /veliplɑ̃ʃist/ *nmf* windsurfer.

velléitaire /velleitɛʀ/ *adj* weak-willed.

velléité /vɛlleite/ *nf* **1** vague desire; **2** vague attempt; **à la moindre ~ de rébellion** at the slightest sign of rebellion.

vélo° /velo/ *nm* bike; **faire du ~** to cycle, to go cycling.
■ **~ d'appartement** exercise bike; **~ tout terrain, VTT** mountain bike.

vélocité /velɔsite/ *nf* (of pianist) nimblefingeredness; (of footballer) speed.

vélo-cross /velokʀɔs/ *nm inv* **1** cyclo-cross; **2** cyclo-cross bike.

vélomoteur /velomɔtœʀ/ *nm* moped.

velours /vəluʀ/ *nm inv* **1** velvet; **2** corduroy, cord.
IDIOMS **une main de fer dans un gant de ~** an iron fist in a velvet glove; **faire patte de ~** to switch on the charm.

velouté, **~e** /vəlute/ I *adj* [*skin, voice*] velvety; [*wine*] smooth.
II *nm* **1** (Culin) **~ de champignons** cream of mushroom soup; **2** softness; smoothness.

velu, **~e** /vəly/ *adj* **1** hairy; **2** (Bot) villous.

venaison /vənɛzɔ̃/ *nf* **1** game; **2** venison.

vénal, **~e**, *mpl* **-aux** /venal, o/ *adj* **1** [*person*] venal; [*behaviour*] mercenary; **2** [*value*] monetary.

vendange /vɑ̃dɑ̃ʒ/ *nf* grape harvest.

vendanger /vɑ̃dɑ̃ʒe/ [13] I *vtr* to harvest [*grapes*]; to pick the grapes from [*vine*].
II *vi* to harvest the grapes.

vendangeur, **-euse** /vɑ̃dɑ̃ʒœʀ, øz/ *nm,f* grape-picker.

vendeur, **-euse** /vɑ̃dœʀ, øz/ *nm,f* **1** shop assistant; **2** salesman/saleswoman.
■ **~ ambulant** pedlar (GB), peddler (US); **~ de journaux** news vendor.

vendre /vɑ̃dʀ/ [6] I *vtr* **1** to sell (**à** to); **~ à crédit** to sell on credit; **~ en gros** to wholesale, to sell [sth] wholesale; **~ au détail** to retail; **~ à la pièce** to sell [sth] singly; **'à ~'** 'for sale'; **2** to betray [*person*] (**à** to); to sell [*secrets, plans*].
II **se vendre** *v refl* (+ *v être*) **1** to be sold; **2 se ~ bien/mal** to sell well/badly; **3** to sell oneself (**à** to); **se ~ à l'ennemi** to sell out to the enemy.

vendredi /vɑ̃dʀədi/ *nm* Friday; **~ saint** Good Friday.

vendu, **~e** /vɑ̃dy/ I *pp* ▶ **vendre**.
II *pp adj* bribed.
III *nm,f* traitor.

vénéneux, **-euse** /venenø, øz/ *adj* poisonous.

vénérable /veneʀabl/ *adj* [*person*] venerable; [*tree, object*] ancient.

vénération /veneʀasjɔ̃/ *nf* veneration.

vénérer /veneʀe/ [14] *vtr* to venerate; to revere.

vénérien, **-ienne** /veneʀjɛ̃, ɛn/ *adj* venereal.

vengeance /vɑ̃ʒɑ̃s/ *nf* revenge; **par ~** out of revenge.

venger /vɑ̃ʒe/ [13] I *vtr* to avenge.
II **se venger** *v refl* (+ *v être*) to get or take one's revenge (**de qn** on sb); **se ~ sur qn/qch** to take it out on sb/sth.

vengeur, **vengeresse** /vɑ̃ʒœʀ, vɑ̃ʒʀɛs/ *adj* [*person, act*] vengeful; [*arm, sword*] avenging; [*letter*] vindictive.

véniel, **-ielle** /venjɛl/ *adj* **1** [*sin*] venial; **2** [*oversight*] excusable.

venimeux, **-euse** /vənimø, øz/ *adj* venomous.

venin /vənɛ̃/ *nm* venom.

venir /vəniʀ/ [36] I *v aux* **1 venir de faire** to have just done; **elle vient de partir** she's just left; **il venait de se marier** he had just got married; **'vient de paraître'** (of book) 'new!'; (of record) 'new release'; **2 ~ aggraver la situation** to make the situation worse; **3 le ballon est venu rouler sous mes pieds** the ball rolled up to my feet; **4 s'il venait à pleuvoir** if it should rain; **il en vint à la détester** he came to hate her.
II *vi* (+ *v être*) **1** to come; **il vient beaucoup de gens le samedi** lots of people come on Saturdays; **~ de** to come from; **~ après/avant** to come after/before; **allez, viens!** come on!; **viens voir** come and see; **viens déjeuner** come for lunch; **j'en viens** I've just been there; **je viens de sa part** he/she sent me to see you; **faire ~ qn** to send for sb; to get sb to come; **faire ~ le médecin** to call the doctor; **ça ne m'est jamais venu à l'idée** or **l'esprit** it never crossed my mind; **dans les jours à ~** in the next few days; **2 en ~ à** to come to; **en ~ aux mains** to come to blows.

vent /vɑ̃/ *nm* **1** wind; **~ d'est/du nord** east/north wind; **~ du large** seaward wind; **grand ~** gale, strong wind; **il fait** or **il y a du ~** it's windy; **le ~ tourne** the wind is turning; **en plein ~** exposed to the wind; in the open; **passer en coup de ~** (figurative) to rush through; **faire du ~** (with fan) to create a breeze; (humorous) to flap around; **2** (Naut) **~ favorable, bon ~** favourable[GB] wind, fair wind; **avoir le ~ en poupe** to sail or run before the wind; (figurative) to have the wind in one's sails; **coup de ~** fresh gale; **3 un ~ de liberté** a wind of freedom; **un ~ de folie soufflait dans le pays** a wave of madness swept through the country; **4** (euphemistic) wind.
IDIOMS **c'est du ~!** it's just hot air!; **du ~°!** get lost°!; **quel bon ~ vous amène?** to what do I or we owe the pleasure (of your visit)?; **être dans le ~** to be trendy; **avoir ~ de qch** to get wind of sth; **contre ~s et marées** come hell or high water; against all odds.

vente /vɑ̃t/ *nf* sale; **en ~ libre** (gen) freely available; [*medicines*] available over the counter; **mettre qch en ~** to put [sth] up for sale [*object*].
■ **~ par correspondance** mail order selling; **~ au détail** retailing; **~ aux enchères** auction (sale); **~ en gros** wholesaling.

ventilateur /vɑ̃tilatœʀ/ *nm* (gen) fan; ventilator.

ventilation /vɑ̃tilasjɔ̃/ *nf* ventilation (system).

ventiler /vɑ̃tile/ [1] *vtr* **1** to ventilate; **2** to break down [*expenses, profits*]; **3** to assign [*staff*]; to allocate [*tasks, equipment*].

ventouse /vɑ̃tuz/ *nf* **1** suction pad (GB), suction cup (US); **faire ~** to stick; **2** plunger; **3** (Med) cupping glass.

ventral, **~e**, *mpl* **-aux** /vɑ̃tʀal, o/ *adj* ventral; **parachute ~** lap-pack parachute.

ventre /vɑ̃tʀ/ *nm* **1** stomach; **avoir mal au ~** to have stomach ache; **ça me donne mal au ~ de voir ça**° (figurative) it makes me sick to see that sort of thing; **avoir le ~ creux** to have an empty stomach; ▶ **affamé**; **2** (of animal) (under-) belly; **3 ne rien avoir dans le ~**° to have no guts°; **avoir la peur au ~** to feel sick with fear; **je ne sais pas ce qu'il a dans le ~**° I don't know what he's made of; **4** (of pot, boat, plane) belly.
IDIOMS **courir ~ à terre** to run flat out.

ventricule /vɑ̃tʀikyl/ *nm* ventricle.

ventriloque /vɑ̃tʀilɔk/ *nmf* ventriloquist.

venu, **~e**[1] /vəny/ **I** *pp* ▶ **venir**.
II *pp adj* **bien ~** apt; **mal ~** badly timed; **il serait mal ~ de le leur dire** it wouldn't be a good idea to tell them.
III *nm,f* **nouveau ~** newcomer.

venue[2] /vəny/ *nf* visit; **lors de votre ~** when you came; **~ au monde** birth.

vêpres /vɛpʀ/ *nf pl* vespers.

ver /vɛʀ/ *nm* worm; woodworm; maggot.
■ **~ à soie** silkworm; **~ solitaire** tapeworm; **~ de terre** earthworm.
IDIOMS **être nu comme un ~** to be stark naked; **tirer les ~s du nez à qn**° to worm information out of sb.

véranda /veʀɑ̃da/ *nf* veranda; **sous la ~** on the veranda.

verbal, **~e**, *mpl* **-aux** /vɛʀbal, o/ *adj* verbal; verb.

verbaliser /vɛʀbalize/ [1] *vi* to record an offence[GB].

verbe /vɛʀb/ *nm* **1** verb; **2** language; **avoir le ~ facile** to be quick to talk; **avoir le ~ haut** to be arrogant in one's speech.

verbiage /vɛʀbjaʒ/ *nm* verbiage, verbosity.

verdâtre /vɛʀdɑtʀ/ *adj* greenish.

verdeur /vɛʀdœʀ/ *nf* sprightliness.

verdict /vɛʀdikt/ *nm* verdict; **rendre un ~** to return a verdict.

verdir /vɛʀdiʀ/ [3] *vi* **1** (gen) to turn green; [*copper*] to tarnish; **2** to turn pale.

verdoyant, **~e** /vɛʀdwajɑ̃, ɑ̃t/ *adj* green, verdant.

verdure /vɛʀdyʀ/ *nf* **1** greenery; **2** green vegetables.

véreux, **-euse** /veʀø, øz/ *adj* **1** [*fruit*] worm-eaten; **2** [*politician, lawyer*] bent°, crooked; [*business*] shady°; [*contract*] dubious.

verge /vɛʀʒ/ *nf* **1** penis; **2** switch, birch.

verger /vɛʀʒe/ *nm* orchard.

verglacé, **~e** /vɛʀglase/ *adj* icy.

verglas /vɛʀgla/ *nm inv* black ice.

vergogne: **sans vergogne** /sɑ̃vɛʀgɔɲ/ *phr* shamelessly.

véridique /veʀidik/ *adj* true.

vérification /veʀifikasjɔ̃/ *nf* (on equipment, identity) check (**de** on); (of alibi, fact) verification; **une ~ d'identité** an identity check.

vérifier /veʀifje/ [2] **I** *vtr* to check; to confirm; to verify.
II se vérifier *v refl* (+ *v être*) [*hypothesis, theory*] to be borne out.

véritable /veʀitabl/ *adj* real; true; genuine.

véritablement /veʀitabləmɑ̃/ *adv* really, actually.

vérité /veʀite/ *nf* **1** truth; **l'épreuve de ~** the acid test; **à la ~** to tell the truth; **2 énoncer des ~s premières** to state the obvious; **toute ~ n'est pas bonne à dire** some things are better left unsaid; **3** sincerity.
IDIOMS **à chacun sa ~** (Proverb) each to his own.

verlan /vɛʀlɑ̃/ *nm*: *French slang formed by inverting the syllables.*

vermeil, **-eille** /vɛʀmɛj/ **I** *adj* **1** bright red; **2** [*wine*] ruby.
II *nm* vermeil.

vermicelle /vɛʀmisɛl/ *nm* **du ~**, **des ~s** vermicelli.

vermifuge /vɛʀmifyʒ/ *nm* wormer.

vermillon /vɛʀmijɔ̃/ *adj inv* bright red, vermilion.

vermine /vɛʀmin/ *nf* **1** vermin; **2** (figurative) scum.

vermoulu, **~e** /vɛʀmuly/ *adj* worm-eaten.

verni, **~e** /vɛʀni/ **I** *pp* ▶ **vernir**.
II *pp adj* [*wood, paintwork*] varnished; [*shoes*] patent-leather; [*pottery*] glazed.
III° *adj* lucky; **il n'est pas ~** he's unlucky.

vernir /vɛʀniʀ/ [3] **I** *vtr* to varnish; to glaze; to apply nail polish to [*nails*].
II se vernir *v refl* (+ *v être*) **se ~ les ongles** to apply nail polish to one's nails.

vernis /vɛʀni/ *nm inv* **1** varnish; glaze; **2** (figurative) veneer; **si on gratte le ~, on voit que...** if you scratch the surface, you'll see that...
■ **~ à ongles** nail varnish (GB) or polish.

vernissage /vɛʀnisaʒ/ *nm* **1** (of art exhibition) preview, private view; **2** varnishing; glazing.

verre /vɛʀ/ *nm* **1** glass; **de** or **en ~** glass; **un ~ à eau/vin** a water/wine glass; **~s et couverts** glassware and cutlery; **lever son ~ à la santé de qn** to raise one's glass to sb; **2** glass, glassful; **un ~ d'eau/de vin** a glass of water/wine; **3** drink; **avoir bu un ~ de trop** to have had one too many; **4** lens; **~s de lunettes** spectacle lenses; **~ grossissant** magnifying glass.
■ **~ de contact** contact lens; **~ gradué** measuring jug; **~ de lampe** lamp chimney; **~ à pied** stemmed glass.

verrerie /vɛʀʀi/ *nf* **1** glassmaking; **2** glassworks, glass factory.

verrier /vɛʀje/ *nm* glassmaker, glass manufacturer.

verrière /vɛʀjɛʀ/ *nf* **1** glass roof; **2** glass wall, glassed-in wall; **3** canopy.

verroterie /vɛʀɔtʀi/ *nf* glass jewellery (GB) or jewelry (US).

verrou /vɛʀu/ *nm* bolt; **mettre le ~** to shoot the bolt.
IDIOMS **être sous les ~s** to be behind bars.

verrouiller /vɛʀuje/ [1] *vtr* to bolt [*window, door*]; to lock [*car door, gun*].

verrue /vεʀy/ *nf* wart; **~ plantaire** verruca.

vers[1] /vεʀ/ *prep*

■ **Note** When *vers* is part of an expression such as *se tourner vers, tendre vers etc*, you will find the translation at the entries ***tourner, tendre***[1] III *etc*.
– See below for other uses of *vers*.

1 toward(s); **il n'a même pas tourné la tête ~ elle** he didn't even look in her direction; **se déplacer de la gauche ~ la droite** to move from left to right; **2** near, around; about; toward(s); **on s'arrêtera ~ Dijon pour déjeuner** we'll stop for lunch near Dijon; **~ cinq heures** at about five o'clock; **~ le soir** toward(s) evening.

vers[2] /vεʀ/ **I** *nm inv* line (of verse).
II *nm pl* poetry.

versant /vεʀsɑ̃/ *nm* side.

versatile /vεʀsatil/ *adj* unpredictable, volatile.

verse: **à verse** /avεʀs/ *phr* **il pleut à ~** it's pouring down.

Verseau /vεʀso/ *pr nm* Aquarius.

versement /vεʀsəmɑ̃/ *nm* **1** payment; **~ comptant** cash payment; **2** instalment[GB]; **3** deposit; **faire un ~ sur son compte** to pay money into one's account.

verser /vεʀse/ [1] **I** *vtr* **1** to pour; **attention, tu verses à côté** careful, you're spilling it; **2** to pay [*sum, pension*]; **on leur verse une commission** they get a commission; **3** to shed [*tear, blood*]; **4 ~ une pièce à un dossier** to add a document to a file.
II *vi* **1** to overturn; **2** to lapse (**dans** into); **3** [*jug*] to pour.

verset /vεʀsε/ *nm* (in Bible, Koran) verse.

version /vεʀsjɔ̃/ *nf* **1** translation (*into one's own language*); **2** version.
■ **~ doublée** dubbed version; **~ originale, vo** original version.

verso /vεʀso/ *nm* back; **voir au ~** see over(-leaf).

vert, ~e /vεʀ, vεʀt/ **I** *adj* **1** green; **être ~ de peur** to be white with fear; **2** [*fruit*] green, unripe; [*wine*] immature; **3** sprightly; **4** (*before n*) [*reprimand*] sharp, stiff.
II *nm* green; **le feu est passé au ~** the light went or turned green.
III verts *nm pl* **les ~s** the Greens, the environmentalists.
IDIOMS **avoir la main ~e** to have green fingers (GB) or a green thumb (US).

vert-de-gris /vεʀdəgʀi/ **I** *adj inv* blue-green.
II *nm inv* verdigris.

vertébral, ~e, *mpl* **-aux** /vεʀtebʀal, o/ *adj* vertebral.

vertèbre /vεʀtεbʀ/ *nf* vertebra; **se déplacer une ~** to slip a disc.

vertébré, ~e /vεʀtebʀe/ **I** *adj* vertebrate.
II *nm* vertebrate.

vertement /vεʀtəmɑ̃/ *adv* sharply.

vertical, ~e[1], *mpl* **-aux** /vεʀtikal, o/ *adj* vertical; upright.

verticale[2] /vεʀtikal/ *nf* vertical; **mettre qch à la ~** to put sth upright.

verticalement /vεʀtikalmɑ̃/ *adv* **1** vertically; **2** (in crossword) down.

vertige /vεʀtiʒ/ *nm* **1** dizziness, giddiness; vertigo; **avoir le ~** to suffer from vertigo; to feel dizzy or giddy; **2 avoir des ~s** to have dizzy or giddy spells.

vertigineux, -euse /vεʀtiʒinø, øz/ *adj* [*height*] dizzy, giddy; [*speed, climb*] breathtaking; [*sum, progress*] staggering.

vertu /vεʀty/ **I** *nf* **1** virtue; **de petite ~** of easy virtue; **2** (of plant, remedy) property.
II en vertu de *phr* by virtue of [*law*]; in accordance with [*agreement*].

vertueux, -euse /vεʀtɥø, øz/ *adj* virtuous.

verve /vεʀv/ *nf* eloquence; **être très en ~** to be in sparkling form.

verveine /vεʀvεn/ *nf* **1** (Bot) verbena; **2** verbena liqueur; **3** verbena tea.

vésicule /vezikyl/ *nf* vesicle; **~ biliaire** gall bladder.

vessie /vesi/ *nf* bladder.
IDIOMS **prendre des ~s pour des lanternes**○ to think the moon is made of green cheese.

veste /vεst/ *nf* jacket; **~ de survêtement** tracksuit top.
IDIOMS **retourner sa ~**○ to change sides, to sell out.

vestiaire /vεstjεʀ/ *nm* **1** (in gym) changing room (GB), locker room; (in theatre) cloakroom; **laisser sa fierté au ~** to forget one's pride; **2** locker.

vestibule /vεstibyl/ *nm* hall; foyer (GB), lobby.

vestige /vεstiʒ/ *nm* **1** relic; **des ~s archéologiques** archaeological remains; **2** vestige.

vestimentaire /vεstimɑ̃tεʀ/ *adj* **tenue ~** way of dressing; **mode ~** fashion.

veston /vεstɔ̃/ *nm* (man's) jacket.

vêtement /vεtmɑ̃/ *nm* **1** piece of clothing; **des ~s** clothes, clothing; **'~s pour hommes'** 'menswear'; **~s de sport** sportswear; **2** clothing trade, garment industry (US).

vétéran /veteʀɑ̃/ *nm* veteran.

vétérinaire /veteʀinεʀ/ **I** *adj* veterinary.
II *nmf* vet, veterinary surgeon (GB), veterinarian (US).

vétille /vetij/ *nf* trifle.

vêtir /vεtiʀ/ [33] **I** *vtr* to dress [*person, doll*] (**de** in).
II se vêtir *v refl* (+ *v être*) to dress (oneself), to get dressed (**de** in).

veto /veto/ *nm* veto; **mettre** or **opposer son ~ à qch** to veto sth.

vêtu, ~e /vεty/ **I** *pp* ▶ **vêtir**.
II *pp adj* dressed; **être ~ de qch** to be dressed or clad in sth, to be wearing sth.

vétuste /vetyst/ *adj* **1** dilapidated; **2** outdated.

veuf, veuve /vœf, vœv/ **I** *adj* widowed.
II *nm,f* widower/widow.
■ **veuve noire** black widow (spider).

veule /vøl/ *adj* weak, spineless.

veuvage /vœvaʒ/ *nm* being a widower, widowhood.

veuve *adj, nf* ▶ **veuf**.

vexant, ~e /vɛksɑ̃, ɑ̃t/ *adj* **1** hurtful; **2** tiresome, vexing.

vexation /vɛksasjɔ̃/ *nf* humiliation.

vexer /vɛkse/ [1] **I** *vtr* **1** to offend, to upset; **2** to annoy.
II se vexer *v refl* (+ *v être*) to take offence[GB], to be upset.

via /vja/ *prep* via; through.

viabilité /vjabilite/ *nf* **1** viability; **2** (of road) suitability for vehicles.

viable /vjabl/ *adj* **1** viable; **2** [*project*] feasible; [*situation*] bearable, tolerable.

viaduc /vjadyk/ *nm* viaduct.

viager /vjaʒe/ *nm* life annuity; **acheter qch en ~** to buy sth by paying a life annuity.

viande /vjɑ̃d/ *nf* meat; **~ de bœuf/mouton** beef/mutton.
■ **~ des Grisons** dried beef; **~ noire** game; **~ rouge** red meat.

vibrant, ~e /vibʀɑ̃, ɑ̃t/ *adj* **1** vibrating; **2** [*voice*] resonant; [*speech*] vibrant; [*praise*] glowing; [*plea*] impassioned; [*crowd*] excited, feverish.

vibration /vibʀasjɔ̃/ *nf* vibration; **ressentir/causer des ~s** to feel/to cause vibrations; **traitement par ~s** vibromassage.

vibrer /vibʀe/ [1] *vi* **1** to vibrate; **2** [*voice*] to quiver (**de** with); [*heart*] to thrill.

vibromasseur /vibʀomasœʀ/ *nm* vibrator.

vicaire /vikɛʀ/ *nm* curate.

vice /vis/ *nm* **1** vice; **vivre dans le ~** to lead a dissolute life; **2** vice; **mon ~, c'est le tabac** my vice is smoking; **3** fault, defect; **~ de fabrication** manufacturing defect.

vice-amiral, *pl* **-aux** /visamiʀal, o/ *nm* ≈ rear-admiral.

vice-présidence, *pl* **~s** /vispʀezidɑ̃s/ *nf* (of State) vice-presidency; (of committee, company) vice-chairmanship, vice-presidency (US).

vice-président, ~e, *mpl* **~s** /vispʀezidɑ̃, ɑ̃t/ *nm,f* (of state) vice-president; (of committee, company) vice-chair(man), vice-president (US).

vice-roi, *pl* **~s** /visʀwa/ *nm* viceroy.

vice(-)versa /visvɛʀsa/ *adv* vice versa.

vichy /viʃi/ *nm* **1** gingham; **2** vichy water.

vicier /visje/ [2] **I** *vtr* to pollute [*air*]; to contaminate [*blood*].
II se vicier *v refl* (+ *v être*) [*air*] to become polluted.

vicieux, -ieuse /visjø, øz/ *adj* **1** lecherous; **il faut être ~ pour aimer ça** you've got to be perverted to like that; **2** [*person*] sly; [*attack*] well-disguised; [*question*] trick; [*argument*] deceitful; **3 un cercle ~** a vicious circle; **4** [*horse*] vicious.

vicissitudes /visisityd/ *nf pl* trials and tribulations, vicissitudes, ups and downs○.

vicomte /vikɔ̃t/ *nm* viscount.

vicomtesse /vikɔ̃tɛs/ *nf* viscountess.

victime /viktim/ *nf* **1** victim, casualty; **être ~ d'un infarctus** to suffer a heart attack; **2** sacrificial victim.

victoire /viktwaʀ/ *nf* (gen) victory; (Sport) win, victory.

victorien, -ienne /viktɔʀjɛ̃, ɛn/ *adj* Victorian.

victorieux, -ieuse /viktɔʀjø, øz/ *adj* [*country, army*] victorious; [*athlete*] winning; [*start, shot*] successful; [*smile*] of victory.

victuailles /viktɥɑj/ *nf pl* provisions, victuals.

vidange /vidɑ̃ʒ/ *nf* **1** emptying; **2** oil change; **huile de ~** waste oil; **3** (of washing machine) waste pipe.

vidanger /vidɑ̃ʒe/ [13] **I** *vtr* **1** to empty, to drain [*tank, ditch*]; **2** to drain off [*liquid*].
II *vi* [*washing machine*] to empty.

vide /vid/ **I** *adj* **1** [*room, box, road, chair*] empty; [*tape, page*] blank; [*flat*] vacant; **tu l'as loué ~ ou meublé?** are you renting it unfurnished or furnished?; **2** [*slogan, mind, day*] empty; [*look*] vacant; **~ de sens** meaningless.
II *nm* **1** space; **sauter** or **se jeter dans le ~** to jump; (figurative) to leap into the unknown; **parler dans le ~** to talk to oneself; to talk at random; **promettre dans le ~** (figurative) to make empty promises; **2** vacuum; void; **emballé sous ~** vacuum packed; **faire le ~ autour de soi** to drive everybody away; **j'ai besoin de faire le ~ dans ma tête** I need to forget about everything; **3** emptiness; **le ~ de l'existence** the emptiness of life; **4** gap; **combler un** or **le ~** to fill in a gap; (figurative) to fill a gap.
III à vide *phr* **1** empty; **2** with no result.

vidéo /video/ **I** *adj inv* video.
II *nf* video; **tourner un film en ~** to make a video.

vidéocassette /videokasɛt/ *nf* videotape, videocassette, video.

vidéoclip /videoklip/ *nm* (music) video.

vidéoclub /videoklœb/ *nm* video store, video shop (GB).

vide-ordures /vidɔʀdyʀ/ *nm inv* rubbish (GB) or garbage (US) chute.

vidéothèque /videɔtɛk/ *nf* **1** video library; **2** video collection.

vide-poches /vidpɔʃ/ *nm inv* tidy.

vider /vide/ [1] **I** *vtr* **1** to empty [*pocket, box, room, glass*]; to drain [*tank, pond, reservoir*]; **~ un coffre fort** to clean out a safe; **2** to empty [sth] (out) [*water, rubbish*]; **3**○ to throw [sb] out○, to kick [sb] out○; **4** (Culin) to gut [*fish*]; to draw [*game*]; **5**○ to wear [sb] out; to drain.
II se vider *v refl* (+ *v être*) to empty; **en été, Paris se vide de ses habitants** in the summer all Parisians leave town.

videur○, **-euse** /vidœʀ, øz/ *nm,f* bouncer.

vie /vi/ *nf* (gen) life; **rendre la ~ à qn** to bring sb back to life; **être en ~** to be alive; **il y a laissé sa ~** that was how he lost his life; **donner la ~ à qn** to bring sb into the world; **ce n'est pas la femme de ma ~** she's not the love of my life; **la ~ est chère** the cost of living is high; **mode de ~** lifestyle; **notre ~ de couple** our relationship; **donner de la ~ à une fête** to liven up a party; **manquant de ~, sans ~** lifeless.

■ **~ active** working life.
IDIOMS **ainsi va la ~** that's the way it goes; **c'est la belle ~!** this is the life!; **avoir la ~ dure** [*prejudices*] to be ingrained; **mener la ~ dure à qn** to make life hard for sb, to give sb a hard time; **faire la ~**○ to have a wild time; to live it up○; **à la ~, à la mort!** till death us do part!

vieil ▶ **vieux**.

vieillard, **~e** /vjɛjaʀ, aʀd/ *nm,f* old man/woman; **les ~s** old people.

vieille ▶ **vieux**.

vieillerie /vjɛjʀi/ *nf* **1** old thing; **2**○ old age.

vieillesse /vjɛjɛs/ *nf* (of person) old age; (of building, tree) great age.

vieilli, **~e** /vjɛji/ **I** *pp* ▶ **vieillir**.
II *pp adj* **1** old-looking; **2** [*equipment*] outdated; [*expression*] dated; **3 vin ~ en fût** wine matured in the cask.

vieillir /vjɛjiʀ/ [3] **I** *vtr* **1** [*hairstyle, dress*] to make [sb] look older; **2 ne me vieillis pas, j'ai 59 ans!** don't make me out to be any older than I am, I'm only 59!; **3** [*illness, poverty*] to age [*person*].
II *vi* **1** to get older; **je vieillis** I'm getting old; **j'ai vieilli** I'm older; I have grown up; **notre population vieillit** we have an ageing population; **je ne veux pas ~ ici** I don't want to be here till I die; **2** [*body, building*] to show signs of age; [*person*] to age; **il vieillit mal** he's losing his looks; **3** [*wine*] to mature, to age; **4** [*work, institution*] to become outdated.
III se vieillir *v refl* (+ *v être*) **1** to make oneself look older; **2** to make oneself out to be older.

vieillissement /vjɛjismɑ̃/ *nm* **1** ageing; **2** stultification.

viennois, **~e** /vjɛnwa, az/ *adj* **1** (in Austria) Viennese; (in France) of Vienne; **2** (Culin) [*chocolate, coffee*] Viennese; **escalope ~e** Wiener schnitzel.

viennoiserie /vjɛnwazʀi/ *nf* Viennese pastry.

vierge /vjɛʀʒ/ **I** *adj* **1** virgin; **2** [*tape, page*] blank; [*notebook, film*] unused; [*police record*] clean; **3** [*wool*] new; [*olive oil*] virgin.
II *nf* virgin.

Vierge /vjɛʀʒ/ **I** *nf* **1 la (Sainte) ~** the (Blessed) Virgin; **2** madonna.
II *pr nf* Virgo.

vieux, (**vieil** *before vowel or mute h*), **vieille**, *mpl* **vieux** /vjø, vjɛj/ **I** *adj* old; **être ~ avant l'âge** to be old before one's time; **une institution vieille de 100 ans** a 100-year-old institution; **le ~ continent** the old world; **au bon ~ temps** in the good old days; **il est très vieille France** he's a gentleman of the old school.
II *nm,f* **1** old person; **un petit ~** a little old man; **les ~** old people; **mes ~**○ my parents; **2**○ **mon pauvre ~** you poor old thing.
III *adv* **vivre ~** to live to a ripe old age; **il s'habille ~** he dresses like an old man.
IV *nm* **le ~** old things; **prendre un coup de ~** to age; **faire du neuf avec du ~** to revamp things.
■ **vieil or** old gold; **vieille fille** old maid; **vieille peau** old bag○; **~ beau** ageing Romeo; **~ garçon** old bachelor; **~ jeu** old-fashioned; **~ rose** dusty pink.
IDIOMS **~ comme le monde**, **~ comme Hérode** as old as the hills.

vif, **vive**[1] /vif, viv/ **I** *adj* **1** [*colour, light*] bright; **2** [*person*] lively, vivacious; [*imagination*] vivid; **3** [*protests*] heated; [*opposition*] fierce; **répondre d'un ton ~** to answer sharply; **sa réaction a été un peu vive** he/she reacted rather strongly; **4** [*contrast*] sharp; [*interest, desire*] keen; [*pain*] acute; [*disappointment*] bitter; [*success*] notable; **5** [*pace, movement*] brisk; **à vive allure** [*drive*] at high speed; **avoir l'esprit ~** to be very quick; **6** [*cold, wind*] biting; [*edge*] sharp; **air ~** fresh air; **cuire à feu ~** to cook over a high heat; **7 de vive voix** in person.
II *nm* **à ~** [*flesh*] bared; [*knee*] raw; [*wire*] exposed; **avoir les nerfs à ~** to be on edge; **la plaie est à ~** it's an open wound; **piquer qn au ~** to cut sb to the quick; **(pris) sur le ~** [*sketch*] thumbnail; [*notes*] taken on the spot.

vigie /viʒi/ *nf* (Naut) **1** lookout; **2** crow's nest.

vigilance /viʒilɑ̃s/ *nf* vigilance; **échapper à la ~ de qn** to escape sb's notice; to escape sb's attention.

vigilant, **~e** /viʒilɑ̃, ɑ̃t/ *adj* [*person*] vigilant; [*eye*] watchful.

vigile /viʒil/ *nm* **1** night watchman; **2** security guard.

vigne /viɲ/ *nf* **1** vine; **2** vineyard; **3** wine growing.
■ **~ mère** stock; **~ vierge** Virginia creeper.

vigneron, **-onne** /viɲ(ə)ʀɔ̃, ɔn/ *nm,f* winegrower.

vignette /viɲɛt/ *nf* **1** *detachable label on medicines for reimbursement by social security*; **2** taxdisc (GB); **3** label; **4** vignette.

vignoble /viɲɔbl/ *nm* vineyard.

vigoureux, **-euse** /viguʀø, øz/ *adj* **1** [*person, handshake*] vigorous; [*athlete, body*] strong; [*plant*] sturdy; **2** [*resistance, style*] vigorous; [*feeling*] strong.

vigueur /vigœʀ/ **I** *nf* **1** vigour[GB]; **avec ~** vigorously; **2** strength.
II en vigueur *phr* [*law, system*] in force; [*regime, conditions*] current; **cesser d'être en ~** to cease to apply; **entrer en ~** to come into force.

VIH /veiaʃ/ *nm* (*abbr* = **virus immunodéficitaire humain**) HIV.

viking /vikiŋ/ *adj* Viking.

vil, **~e** /vil/ *adj* [*person*] base; [*deed*] vile, base.

vilain, **~e** /vilɛ̃, ɛn/ **I** *adj* **1** ugly; **ça fait ~** it doesn't look very nice; **2**○ [*germ, creature*] nasty; [*child*] naughty; **3** [*fault*] bad; [*word*] dirty; **4** [*cough, wound*] nasty.
II *nm* **1** naughty boy/girl; **2** villein.

villa /villa/ *nf* **1** ≈ detached house; **2** villa.

village /vilaʒ/ *nm* village; **~ de vacances** holiday (GB) or vacation (US) village.

villageois, **~e** /vilaʒwa, az/ I *adj* village. II *nm,f* villager.

ville /vil/ *nf* **1** town; city; **la ~ haute** the upper town; **une ~ sainte** a holy city; **aller en ~** to go into town; **2** town or city council.
■ **~ d'eau(x)** spa town; **~ franche** free city; **~ nouvelle** new town.

villégiature /vileʒjatyʀ/ *nf* holiday (GB), vacation (US); **lieu de ~** holiday resort (GB), vacation resort (US).

vin /vɛ̃/ *nm* wine; **~ blanc/rouge** white/red wine; **grand ~** fine wine; **~ de pays** or **de terroir** *quality wine produced in a specific region*; **couper son ~** to add water to one's wine.
■ **~ d'appellation d'origine contrôlée** appellation contrôlée wine (*with a guarantee of origin*); **~ cuit** *wine which has undergone heating during maturation*; **~ d'honneur** reception.
IDIOMS **avoir le ~ gai/triste** to get happy/maudlin after one has had a few drinks; **mettre de l'eau dans son ~** to mellow; **quand le ~ est tiré, il faut le boire** (Proverb) once you have started something, you have to see it through.

vinaigre /vinɛgʀ/ *nm* vinegar; **~ de vin** wine vinegar.
IDIOMS **tourner au ~** to turn sour.

vinaigrette /vinɛgʀɛt/ *nf* vinaigrette, French dressing.

vindicatif, **-ive** /vɛ̃dikatif, iv/ *adj* vindictive.

vingt /vɛ̃, vɛ̃t/ I *adj inv* twenty.
II *pron* twenty; **j'ai eu ~ sur ~ à mon devoir d'histoire** ≈ I got full marks (GB) or full credit (US) for my history paper.

vingtaine /vɛ̃tɛn/ *nf* about twenty.

vingt-deux /vɛ̃tdø/ I *adj inv, pron* twenty-two.
II° *excl* look out!; **~, v'là les flics°**! look out! it's the cops°!

vingtième /vɛ̃tjɛm/ *adj* twentieth.

vinicole /vinikɔl/ *adj* [*sector, region*] wine-producing; [*cellar, trade*] wine.

vinyle /vinil/ *nm* vinyl.

viol /vjɔl/ *nm* **1** rape; **2** (of law, temple) violation.

violacé, **~e** /vjɔlase/ *adj* purplish.

violation /vjɔlasjɔ̃/ *nf* **1** (of law, territory) violation; **2** (of agreement) breach; **~ du secret professionnel** breach of confidentiality.
■ **~ de domicile** forcible entry (*into a person's home*); **~ de sépulture** desecration of a grave.

violemment /vjɔlamɑ̃/ *adv* violently.

violence /vjɔlɑ̃s/ *nf* **1** violence; **~ verbale** verbal abuse; **par la ~** through violence; with violence; **répliquer à la ~ par la ~** to meet violence with violence; **se faire ~** to force oneself; **2** act of violence; **~s à l'enfant** child abuse.

violent, **~e** /vjɔlɑ̃, ɑ̃t/ *adj* [*person, reaction*] violent; [*colour*] harsh.

violenter /vjɔlɑ̃te/ [1] *vtr* **1** to assault sexually; **2** to rape.

violer /vjɔle/ [1] *vtr* **1** to rape; **se faire ~** to be raped; **2** to desecrate [*tomb*]; **~ l'intimité de qn** to invade sb's privacy; **3** to infringe [*law*].

violet, **-ette**[1] /vjɔlɛ, ɛt/ I *adj* purple.
II *nm* purple.

violette[2] /vjɔlɛt/ *nf* violet.

violeur /vjɔlœʀ/ *nm* rapist.

violon /vjɔlɔ̃/ *nm* violin; **jouer du ~** to play the violin.
■ **~ d'Ingres** hobby.
IDIOMS **accorder ses ~s** to agree on the line to take.

violoncelle /vjɔlɔ̃sɛl/ *nm* cello.

violoncelliste /vjɔlɔ̃sɛlist/ *nmf* cellist.

violoniste /vjɔlɔnist/ *nmf* violinist.

vipère /vipɛʀ/ *nf* viper; **avoir une langue de ~** to have a wicked tongue.

virage /viʀaʒ/ *nm* **1** bend; **2** change of direction; **3** (in skiing) turn.
■ **~ à 180 degrés** (figurative) U-turn.

virago /viʀago/ *nf* virago.

viral, **~e**, *mpl* **-aux** /viʀal, o/ *adj* viral.

virement /viʀmɑ̃/ *nm* transfer; **faire un ~** to make a transfer.
■ **~ automatique** standing order; **~ de bord** (Naut) tacking.

virer /viʀe/ [1] I *vtr* **1** to transfer [*money*]; **2°** to fire, to sack° (GB) [*employee*]; **se faire ~** to get fired; **3°** to send [sb] out (of the classroom) [*pupil*]; to expel [*pupil*].
II **virer à** *v+prep* **~ au rouge** to turn red; **~ à l'aigre** to turn sour.
III *vi* **1** [*vehicle*] to turn; **~ de bord** (figurative) to do a U-turn, to do a flip-flop (US); **2** to change colour[GB]; [*colour*] to change.

virevolter /viʀvɔlte/ [1] *vi* to twirl.

virginité /viʀʒinite/ *nf* virginity.

virgule /viʀgyl/ *nf* **1** comma; **à la ~ près** down to the last comma; **2** (decimal) point.

viril, **~e** /viʀil/ *adj* manly, virile; masculine

virilité /viʀilite/ *nf* virility; **manquer de ~** to be rather unmanly.

virtuel, **-elle** /viʀtɥɛl/ *adj* **1** potential; **2** (in science) virtual.

virtuose /viʀtɥoz/ I *adj* virtuoso.
II *nmf* **1** (Mus) virtuoso; **2** master (**de** of).

virtuosité /viʀtɥozite/ *nf* **1** (Mus) virtuosity; **2** brilliance.

virulence /viʀylɑ̃s/ *nf* virulence; **avec ~** virulently.

virulent, **~e** /viʀylɑ̃, ɑ̃t/ *adj* virulent.

virus /viʀys/ *nm inv* **1** virus; **2** bug°, craze.

vis /vis/ *nf inv* screw; **serrer/desserrer une ~** to tighten/loosen a screw.
IDIOMS **serrer la ~ à qn** to tighten the screws on sb.

visa /viza/ *nm* visa; **~ de touriste** tourist visa.
■ **~ de censure** (censor's) certificate.

visage /vizaʒ/ *nm* face; **à deux ~s** two-faced; **à ~ découvert** openly.

vis-à-vis /vizavi/ I *nm inv* **1 avoir la prison pour ~** to live opposite the prison; **maison sans ~** house with an open outlook; **2** (at

table, on train) person opposite; **3 assis en ~** sitting opposite each other; **4** (Sport) opponent; **5** meeting, encounter.
II **vis-à-vis de** *phr* **1 ~ de qch** in relation to sth; **~ de qn** toward(s) sb; **2** beside.
viscéral, ~e, *mpl* **-aux** /viseʀal, o/ *adj* **1** (figurative) deep-rooted; **réaction ~e** gut reaction; **2** visceral.
viscère /visɛʀ/ *nm* **1** internal organ; **2 les ~s** viscera.
viscosité /viskozite/ *nf* viscosity.
visée /vize/ *nf* **1** aim; **2** design; **avoir des ~s sur qn/qch** to have designs on sb/sth; **3** sighting; aiming.
viser /vize/ [1] **I** *vtr* **1** to aim at [*target*]; to aim for [*heart, middle*]; **2** to aim for [*job, results*]; to aim at [*market*]; **3** [*law, campaign*] to be aimed at; [*remark, allusion*] to be meant or intended for; **se sentir visé** to feel one is being got at○.
II **viser à** *v+prep* **~ à qch/à faire** to aim at sth/to do.
III *vi* to aim; **~ (trop) haut** (figurative) to set one's sights (too) high.
viseur /vizœʀ/ *nm* **1** viewfinder; **2** (of gun) sight.
visibilité /vizibilite/ *nf* visibility.
visible /vizibl/ *adj* **1** visible; **2** obvious; **son émotion était ~** he/she was visibly moved.
visière /vizjɛʀ/ *nf* **1** (of cap) peak; **2** eyeshade, visor.
vision /vizjɔ̃/ *nf* **1** eyesight, vision; **2** view; **~ globale** global view; **3** sight; **4 avoir des ~s** to see things, to have visions.
visionnaire /vizjɔnɛʀ/ *adj, nmf* visionary.
visionner /vizjɔne/ [1] *vtr* to view [*film, slides*].
visite /vizit/ *nf* visit; call; **rendre ~ à qn** to pay sb a call or visit; **avoir de la ~** to have visitors; **le médecin fait ses ~s** the doctor is making his (house) calls.
■ **~ de contrôle** (Med) follow-up visit; **~ médicale** medical (examination).
visiter /vizite/ [1] *vtr* **1** to visit, to go round[GB] [*museum, town, country*]; **2** to view [*apartment*]; **3** to visit [*patient, prisoner*].
visiteur, -euse /vizitœʀ, øz/ *nm,f* visitor.
vison /vizɔ̃/ *nm* **1** mink; **2** mink (coat).
visqueux, -euse /viskø, øz/ *adj* **1** viscous, viscid; **2** sticky, gooey○.
visser /vise/ [1] *vtr* **1** to screw [sth] on; **2 être vissé sur sa chaise** to be glued to one's chair.
visualiser /vizɥalize/ [1] *vtr* to visualize.
visuel, -elle /vizɥɛl/ *adj* visual.
vital, ~e, *mpl* **-aux** /vital, o/ *adj* vital.
vitalité /vitalite/ *nf* vitality; energy.
vitamine /vitamin/ *nf* vitamin; **~ A/B** vitamin A/B.
vitaminé, ~e /vitamine/ *adj* with added vitamins.
vite /vit/ *adv* **1** quickly; **~!** quick!; **ça ira ~** it'll soon be over; it won't take long; **on a pris un verre ~ fait**○ we had a quick drink; **2** soon; **c'est une affection bénigne, ça passera ~** it's only a minor trouble, it'll soon get better; **3 j'ai parlé trop ~** I spoke too hastily; I spoke too soon; **c'est ~ dit!** that's easy to say!
vitesse /vitɛs/ *nf* **1** speed; **à grande/petite ~** at high/low speed; **partir à toute ~** to rush away; **à deux ~s** [*system*] two-tier; **faire de la ~** [*driver*] to drive fast; **gagner** or **prendre qn de ~** to outstrip sb; **en ~** quickly; in a rush; **2** gear.
IDIOMS **à la ~ grand V, en quatrième ~** at top speed.
viticole /vitikɔl/ *adj* [*industry, cellar*] wine; [*region*] wine-producing.
viticulture /vitikyltyʀ/ *nf* wine-growing, viticulture.
vitrage /vitʀaʒ/ *nm* windows; **double ~** double glazing.
vitrail, *pl* **-aux** /vitʀaj, o/ *nm* stained glass window.
vitre /vitʀ/ *nf* **1** windowpane; **2** pane of glass; **3** (of car, train) window.
vitreux, -euse /vitʀø, øz/ *adj* **1** [*eyes*] glazed, glassy; **2** vitreous.
vitrier /vitʀije/ *nm* glazier.
vitrifier /vitʀifje/ [2] **I** *vtr* **1** to varnish [*floor*]; **2** (Tech) to vitrify.
II **se vitrifier** *v refl* (+ *v être*) to vitrify.
vitrine /vitʀin/ *nf* **1** (shop or store) window; **en ~** in the window; **faire les ~s** to go window-shopping; **2** display cabinet (GB), curio cabinet (US); **3** (show)case.
vitriol /vitʀijɔl/ *nm* vitriol; **discours au ~** (figurative) vitriolic speech.
vivable /vivabl/ *adj* bearable; **ce n'est pas ~ ici** it is impossible to live here.
vivace /vivas/ *adj* **1 plante ~** perennial; **2** enduring.
vivacité /vivasite/ *nf* **1** (of person) vivacity; (of feeling) intensity; **2** (of intelligence) keenness; (of reaction, movement) swiftness; **avec ~** [*move, react*] swiftly; **3** (of memory, colour, impression) vividness; (in eyes) spark; (of light) brightness.
vivant, ~e /vivɑ̃, ɑ̃t/ **I** *adj* **1** living; **il est ~** he is alive; **un homard ~** a live lobster; **moi ~, jamais il ne l'épousera** he'll marry her over my dead body; **2** [*person, style*] lively; [*description*] vivid; **3 être encore ~** [*custom*] to be still alive.
II *nm* **1** living being; **les ~s** the living; **2 de mon ~** in my lifetime; **du ~ de mon père** while my father was alive.
vive² /viv/ **I** *adj f* ▶ **vif I**.
II *nf* weever.
vivement /vivmɑ̃/ *adv* [*encourage, react*] strongly; [*contrast, speak*] sharply; [*move, feel, regret*] deeply; [*rise*] swiftly.
vivier /vivje/ *nm* **1** fishpond; **2** fish-tank.
vivifier /vivifje/ [2] *vtr* to invigorate.
vivisection /vivisɛksjɔ̃/ *nf* vivisection.
vivoter /vivɔte/ [1] *vi* to struggle along.
vivre /vivʀ/ [63] **I** *vtr* **1** to live through [*era*]; to go through [*difficult times*]; to experience [*love*]; **2** to cope with [*divorce, failure, change*].
II *vi* **1** to live; **~ vieux** to live to a great age;

vive la révolution! long live the revolution!, up the revolution!; **~ à la campagne** to live in the country; **être facile à ~** to be easy to live with; to be easy to get on with; **~ avec son temps** to move with the times; **se laisser ~** to take things easy; **apprendre à ~ à qn**○ to teach sb some manners○; **~ de ses rentes** to have a private income; **~ aux dépens de qn** to live off sb; **2** [*relationship, fashion*] to last; **avoir vécu** [*person*] to have seen a great deal of life; (humorous) [*object, idea*] to have had its day; **3** [*town, street*] to be full of life.

IDIOMS **qui vivra verra** what will be will be.

vivres /vivʀ/ *nm pl* **1** food, supplies; **2 couper les ~ à qn** to cut off sb's allowance.

vizir /viziʀ/ *nm* vizier; **le Grand ~** the Grand Vizier.

vo /veo/ *nf*: *abbr* ▶ **version**.

vocabulaire /vɔkabylɛʀ/ *nm* vocabulary.

vocal, **~e**, *mpl* **-aux** /vɔkal, o/ *adj* vocal.

vocalise /vɔkaliz/ *nf* singing exercise.

vocation /vɔkasjɔ̃/ *nf* **1** vocation, calling; **il n'a pas la ~ de l'enseignement** he's not cut out to be a teacher; **2** purpose; **région à ~ agricole** farming area.

vocifération /vɔsifeʀasjɔ̃/ *nf* clamour[GB].

vociférer /vɔsifeʀe/ [14] *vtr, vi* to shout (**contre** at).

vodka /vɔdka/ *nf* vodka; **~ orange** vodka and orange, screwdriver.

vœu, *pl* **~x** /vø/ *nm* **1** wish; **faire un ~** to make a wish; **2** New Year's greetings; **adresser ses ~x à qn** to wish sb a happy New Year; **3** vow; **~x de pauvreté** vows of poverty; **faire ~ de fidélité** to vow to remain faithful.

■ **~ pieux** wishful thinking.

vogue /vɔg/ *nf* fashion, vogue; **en ~** fashionable; in fashion.

voguer /vɔge/ [1] *vi* [*ship*] to sail.

IDIOMS **et vogue la galère!** come what may!

voici /vwasi/ **I** *prep* here is, this is; here are, these are; **~ mes clés** here are my keys; **'me ~'** 'here I am'; **~ un mois** a month ago; **~ bientôt deux mois qu'elle travaille chez nous** she's been working with us for nearly two months.

II voici que *phr* all of a sudden.

voie /vwa/ *nf* **1** way; **montrer la ~ à qn** to show sb the way; **montrer la ~** to lead the way; **ouvrir la ~ à** to pave the way for; **s'engager dans une ~ dangereuse** to embark on a dangerous course; **être sur la bonne ~** [*person*] to be on the right track; **les travaux sont en bonne ~** the work is progressing; **par ~ de conséquence** consequently; **espèce en ~ de disparition** endangered species; **2** channels; **par des ~ détournées** by roundabout means; **3** lane; **route à trois ~s** three-lane road; **4** (of railway) track; **'défense de traverser les ~s'** 'keep off the tracks'; **le train entre en gare ~ 2** the train is arriving at platform 2; **5 par ~ buccale** or **orale** orally.

■ **~ aérienne** air route; **~ express** expressway; **~ ferrée** railway track (GB), railroad track (US); **~ de garage** siding; **mettre qn sur une ~ de garage** (figurative) to shunt sb onto the sidelines; **Voie lactée** Milky Way; **~ navigable** waterway; **~ privée** private road; **~ publique** public highway; **~ rapide** expressway; **~ sans issue** dead end; no through road; **~s respiratoires** respiratory tract.

voilà /vwala/ **I** *prep* here is, this is; here are, these are; **voici mon fils et ~ ma fille** this is my son and this is my daughter; **me ~!** I'm coming!; here I am!; **le ~ qui se remet à rire!** there he goes again laughing!; **te ~ revenu!** you're back again!; **~ tout** that's all; **~ un mois** a month ago; **~ bientôt deux mois qu'elle travaille chez nous** she's been working with us for nearly two months.

II en voilà *phr* **tu veux des fraises? en ~** you'd like some strawberries? here you are; **en ~ assez!** that's enough!

III voilà que○ *phr* **et ~ qu'une voiture arrive** and the next thing you know, a car pulls up; **~ qu'il se met à rire** all of a sudden he started laughing.

IV *excl* **~! j'arrive!** (I'm) coming!; **(et) ~! il remet ça!** there he goes again!

IDIOMS **il a de l'argent, en veux-tu en ~!** he has as much money as he could wish for!

voilage /vwalaʒ/ *nm* net curtain (GB), sheer curtain (US).

voile[1] /vwal/ *nm* **1** veil; **lever le ~ sur qch** to bring sth out in the open; **2** voile.

■ **~ islamique** yashmak; **~ du palais** soft palate, velum.

voile[2] /vwal/ *nf* (Naut) **1** sail; **faire ~ vers** to sail toward(s); **2** sailing; **cours de ~** sailing lessons.

voilé, **~e** /vwale/ *adj* **1** [*person, object*] veiled; **2** [*sun, sky*] hazy; [*eyes*] misty; [*voice*] with a catch in it; [*photo, film*] fogged; [*moon*] veiled; **3** [*allusion, threat, criticism*] veiled; **4** [*wheel*] buckled; [*panel*] warped.

voiler /vwale/ [1] **I** *vtr* **1** to veil [*landscape, sun*]; [*person, fact*] to conceal [*event, fact*]; **2** to buckle [*wheel*]; **3** to mist [*eyes*]; **4** to cover [*face, nudity*]; to veil [*statue*].

II se voiler *v refl* (+ *v être*) **1** [*sky*] to cloud over; [*sun*] to become hazy; [*eyes*] to become misty; **2** [*person*] to wear a veil; **se ~ le visage** to veil one's face.

IDIOMS **se ~ la face** to look the other way.

voilette /vwalɛt/ *nf* veil.

voilier /vwalje/ *nm* **1** sailing boat (GB), sailboat (US); **2** yacht, sailing ship.

voir /vwaʀ/ [46] **I** *vtr* **1** to see; **faire ~ qch à qn** to show sb sth; **laisser ~ qch** to show sth; **~ qch en rêve** to dream about sth; **~ si/pourquoi** to find out or to see if/why; **on l'a vue entrer** she was seen going in; **je le vois** or **verrais bien enseignant** I can just see him as a teacher; **~ en qn un ami** to see sb as a friend; **aller ~ qn** to go to see sb; **le film est à ~** the film is worth seeing; **~ du pays** to see the world; **je vois ce que tu veux dire** I see what you mean; **on voit bien qu'elle n'a jamais**

travaillé! you can tell she's never worked!; **on n'a jamais vu ça!** it's unheard of!; **2 avoir quelque chose à ~ avec** to have something to do with; **ça n'a rien à ~** that's got nothing to do with it.

II **voir à** *v+prep* to see to; **voyez à ce que tout soit prêt** see to it or make sure that everything is ready.

III *vi* **1 ~, y ~** to be able to see; **je** or **j'y vois à peine** I can hardly see; **~ double** to see double; **2 ~ clair dans qch** to have a clear understanding of sth; **il faut ~** we'll have to see; **3 voyons, sois sage!** come on now, behave yourself!

IV **se voir** *v refl* (+ *v être*) **1** to see oneself; **il s'est vu sombrer dans la folie** he realized he was going mad; **2** [*stain, fault*] to show; **la tour se voit de loin** the tower can be seen from far away; **ça ne s'est jamais vu!** it's unheard of!; **3 se ~ obligé** or **dans l'obligation de faire** to find oneself forced to do; **4** to see each other; **ils ne peuvent pas se ~ (en peinture○)** they can't stand each other.

IDIOMS **ne pas ~ plus loin que le bout de son nez** to see no further than the end of one's nose; **en ~ de toutes les couleurs** to go through some hard times; **j'en ai vu d'autres** I've seen worse; **en faire ~ à qn** to give sb a hard time.

voire /vwaʀ/ *adv* or even, not to say.

voirie /vwaʀi/ *nf* road, rail and waterways network.

voisin, ~e /vwazɛ̃, in/ I *adj* **1** [*house, town*] neighbouring[GB]; [*lake, forest*] nearby; [*room*] next (**de** to); (figurative) [*date, result*] close (**de** to); **les régions ~es de la Manche** the regions bordering the English Channel; **2** [*feelings, ideas*] similar; [*species*] (closely) related; **~ de** [*idea*] akin to; [*species*] related to.

II *nm,f* neighbour[GB]; **ma ~e de palier** the woman across the landing; **mon ~ de table** the man next to me at table; **dire du mal du ~** (figurative) to speak ill of others.

voisinage /vwazinaʒ/ *nm* **1** neighbourhood[GB]; **entretenir des rapports de bon ~** to maintain neighbourly[GB] relations; **des querelles de ~** neighbourhood[GB] disputes; **2** proximity; **vivre dans le ~ d'une usine** to live close to a factory.

voiture /vwatyʀ/ *nf* **1** car, automobile (US); **2** carriage (GB), car (US); **en ~!** all aboard!

■ **~ à bras** hand-drawn cart; **~ de tourisme** saloon (car) (GB), sedan (US).

voiture-balai, *pl* **voitures-balais** /vwatyʀ balɛ/ *nf* support vehicle.

voix /vwa/ *nf inv* **1** (gen) voice; **élever la ~** to raise one's voice; **à ~ haute** out loud; **à ~ basse** in a low voice; **rester sans ~** to remain speechless; **à portée de ~** within earshot; **faire entendre sa ~** (figurative) to make oneself heard; **2** vote; **avoir ~ délibérative** to have the right to vote; **3 à la ~ active/passive** in the active/passive voice.

vol /vɔl/ I *nm* **1** (of bird, plane) flight; **prendre son ~** to fly off; **à ~ d'oiseau** as the crow flies; **le ~ pour Paris** the Paris flight; **il y a trois heures de ~** it's a three-hour flight; **de ~** [*conditions*] flying; [*plan*] flight; **2 un ~ de** a flock of, a flight of [*birds*]; a cloud of [*insects*]; **de haut ~** (figurative) [*diplomat*] high-flying; [*burglar*] big-time; **3** theft, robbery; **c'est du ~ organisé!** (figurative) it's a racket!

II **au vol** *phr* **attraper une balle au ~** to catch a ball in mid-air; **saisir des bribes de conversation au ~** to catch snatches of conversation.

■ **~ à l'arraché** bag snatching; **~ avec effraction** burglary; **~ à l'étalage** shoplifting; **~ libre** hang gliding; **~ à main armée** armed robbery; **~ à la tire** pickpocketing; **~ à voile** gliding.

volage /vɔlaʒ/ *adj* fickle.

volaille /vɔlɑj/ *nf* **1** poultry; **2** fowl.

volant, ~e /vɔlɑ̃, ɑ̃t/ I *adj* flying.

II *nm* **1** steering wheel; **être au ~** to be at the wheel; **un brusque coup de ~** a sharp turn of the wheel; **donner un coup de ~** to turn the wheel sharply; **un as du ~** an ace driver; **la sécurité au ~** safe driving; **2** flounce; **à ~s** flounced; **3** shuttlecock.

volatil, ~e[1] /vɔlatil/ *adj* volatile.

volatile[2] /vɔlatil/ *nm* **1** fowl; **2** bird.

volatiliser: se volatiliser /vɔlatilize/ [1] *v refl* (+ *v être*) **1** to volatilize; **2** (humorous) to vanish into thin air.

volcan /vɔlkɑ̃/ *nm* **1** volcano; **2** (person) spitfire.

volcanique /vɔlkanik/ *adj* **1** [*region*] volcanic; **2** [*temperament*] explosive.

volée /vɔle/ I *nf* **1** (of birds) flock, flight; **2** (of blows, stones) volley (**de** of); **donner une ~ à qn** to give sb a good thrashing; (figurative) to thrash sb; **3** flight (of stairs); **4** (in sport) volley; **saisir la balle à la ~** (figurative) to seize the opportunity.

II **à toute volée** *phr* **les cloches sonnaient à toute ~** the bells were pealing out.

voler /vɔle/ [1] I *vtr* **1 ~ qch à qn** to steal sth from sb; **il s'est fait ~ sa voiture** he's had his car stolen; **tu ne l'as pas volé!** (figurative) it serves you right!; **2 ~ qn** to rob sb; **~ le client** to rip the customer off○; **~ qn sur la quantité** to cheat sb over the quantity.

II *vi* **1** to fly; **~ au secours de qn** to rush to sb's aid; **2 ~ en éclats** [*window*] to shatter; (figurative) [*certainty*] to be shattered.

volet /vɔlɛ/ *nm* **1** shutter; **2** (of leaflet, brochure) (folding) section; (of plan, policy) part, component.

voleter /vɔlte/ [20] *vi* to flutter.

voleur, -euse /vɔlœʀ, øz/ I *adj* **être ~** [*cat*] to be a thief; [*shopkeeper*] to be dishonest.

II *nm,f* thief; swindler.

■ **~ de grand chemin** highwayman.

IDIOMS **être ~ comme une pie** to be a real thieving magpie; **se sauver comme un ~** to slip away like a thief in the night.

volière /vɔljɛʀ/ *nf* aviary.

volley(-ball) /vɔlɛ(bol)/ *nm* volleyball.

volontaire /vɔlɔ̃tɛʀ/ I *adj* **1** [*work*] voluntary;

[*omission*] deliberate; **2** [*person, air*] determined; [*child*] self-willed.

II *nmf* volunteer; **se porter ~** to volunteer.

volontairement /vɔlɔ̃tɛʀmɑ̃/ *adv* [*leave*] voluntarily; [*hurt*] deliberately.

volontariat /vɔlɔ̃taʀja/ *nm* voluntary service.

volonté /vɔlɔ̃te/ **I** *nf* **1** will; **bonne/mauvaise ~** goodwill/ill-will; **aller contre la ~ de qn** to go against sb's wishes; **manifester la ~ de faire** to show one's willingness to do; **2** willpower; **avoir une ~ de fer** to have an iron will.

II à volonté *phr* **1 'vin/pain à ~'** 'unlimited wine/bread'; **2** [*modifiable*] as required.

volontiers /vɔlɔ̃tje/ *adv* **1** gladly; **j'irais ~ à Paris** I'd love to go to Paris; **'tu me le prêtes?'—'~'** 'will you lend it to me?'—'certainly'; **2** [*forget*] easily; [*admit*] readily.

volt /vɔlt/ *nm* volt.

voltage /vɔltaʒ/ *nm* voltage.

volte-face /vɔlt(ə)fas/ *nf inv* **1 faire ~** to turn around; **2** (figurative) volte-face, U-turn.

voltige /vɔltiʒ/ *nf* **1 (haute) ~** acrobatics; **2 ~ (aérienne)** aerobatics.

voltiger /vɔltiʒe/ [13] *vi* **1** to flutter; **2** to go flying.

volubile /vɔlybil/ *adj* (person) voluble.

volume /vɔlym/ *nm* (gen) volume; **donner du ~ à ses cheveux** to give one's hair body; **faire du ~** [*luggage*] to be bulky; **~ sonore** sound level.

volumineux, -euse /vɔlyminø, øz/ *adj* voluminous, bulky.

volupté /vɔlypte/ *nf* voluptuousness.

voluptueux, -euse /vɔlyptɥø, øz/ *adj* voluptuous.

volute /vɔlyt/ *nf* (on pillar, column) volute; (of violin) scroll; (of smoke) curl.

vomir /vɔmiʀ/ [3] **I** *vtr* **1** to bring up [*meal*]; to vomit [*bile*]; **2** to spew out [*lava*]; to belch [*smoke*]; **3** to loathe.

II *vi* [*person*] to be sick; **avoir envie de ~** to feel sick.

vomissement /vɔmismɑ̃/ *nm* vomiting.

vorace /vɔʀas/ *adj* voracious.

voracité /vɔʀasite/ *nf* voracity, voraciousness.

vos ▸ **votre**.

votant, ~e /vɔtɑ̃, ɑ̃t/ *nm,f* voter.

vote /vɔt/ *nm* **1** voting; (of law) passing; **2** vote.

voter /vɔte/ [1] **I** *vtr* to vote [*budget*]; to pass [*parliamentary bill*]; to vote for [*amnesty*]; **~ les pleins pouvoirs à qn** to vote to give sb full powers.

II *vi* to vote; **~ (pour) Durand** to vote for Durand; **~ blanc** to cast a blank vote.

votre, *pl* **vos** /vɔtʀ, vo/ *det* your; **c'est pour ~ bien** it's for your own good; **à ~ arrivée** when you arrive; when you arrived.

vôtre /votʀ/ **I** *det* **mes biens sont ~s** all I have is yours; **'amicalement ~'** 'best wishes'.

II le vôtre, la vôtre, les vôtres *pron* yours; **à la ~**○**!** cheers!

vouer /vwe/ [1] **I** *vtr* **1 ~ une reconnaissance éternelle à qn** to be or feel eternally grateful to sb; **~ un véritable culte à qn** to worship sb; **2** to doom; **film voué à l'échec** film doomed to failure; **3 ~ sa vie à qch** to devote one's life to sth.

II se vouer *v refl* (+ *v être*) **1 se ~ à qch** to devote oneself to sth; **2 ils se vouent une haine féroce** they hate each other intensely.

IDIOMS **je ne sais plus à quel saint me ~** I don't know which way to turn.

vouloir[1] /vulwaʀ/ [48] **I** *vtr* **1** to want; **elle veut que tout soit fini avant 8 heures** she wants everything finished by 8 o'clock; **qu'est-ce qu'ils nous veulent**○ **encore?** what do they want now?; **il en veut 15 000 francs** he wants 15,000 francs for it; **comme le veut la loi** as the law demands; **2 que veux-tu boire?** what do you want to drink?; what would you like to drink?; **comme tu veux** as you wish; **je voudrais un kilo de poires** I'd like a kilo of pears; **je comprends très bien que tu ne veuilles pas répondre** I can quite understand that you may not wish to reply; **il ne suffit pas de ~, il faut encore pouvoir** wishing is not enough; **il suffisait de ~** all you needed was the will to do it; **je ne voudrais pas vous déranger** I don't want to put you out; **sans le ~** [*knock over, reveal*] by accident; [*annoy*] without meaning to; **que tu le veuilles ou non** whether you like it or not; **elle fait ce qu'elle veut de son mari** she twists her husband around her little finger; **je ne vous veux aucun mal** I don't wish you any harm; **tu ne voudrais pas me faire croire que** you're not trying to tell me that; **tu voudrais que je leur fasse confiance?** do you expect me to trust them?; **comment veux-tu que je le sache?** how should I know?; **pourquoi voudrais-tu qu'il refuse?** why should he refuse?; **que veux-tu, on n' y peut rien!** what can you do, it's hopeless!; **j'aurais voulu t'y voir**○**!** I'd like to have seen you in the same position!; **tu l'auras voulu!** it'll be all your own fault!; **3 voulez-vous fermer la fenêtre?** would you mind closing the window?; **voudriez-vous avoir l'obligeance de faire** (formal) would you be so kind as to do; **veuillez patienter** (on phone) please hold the line; **si vous voulez bien me suivre** if you'd like to follow me; **veux-tu te taire!** will you be quiet!; **ils ont bien voulu nous prêter leur voiture** they were kind enough to lend us their car; **elle veut bien prendre ce poste à condition d'être mieux payée** she's happy to take the job on condition that she's paid more; **je veux bien te croire** I'm quite prepared to believe you; **je veux bien qu'il soit malade mais** I know he's ill, but; **'ce n'est pas cher'—'si on veut!'** 'it's not expensive'—'or so you say!'; **4 ~ dire** to mean; **qu'est-ce que ça veut dire?** what does that mean?; what's all this about?; **5 comme le veut la tradition** as tradition has it; **leur théorie veut que** according to their theory.

II en vouloir *v+prep* **1 en ~ à qn** to bear a grudge against sb; **je leur en veux de m'avoir trompé** I hold it against them for not being honest with me; **ne m'en veux pas** please forgive me; **2 en ~ à qch** to be after sth.

III se vouloir *v refl* (+ *v être*) **1** [*person*] to like to think of oneself as; [*book, method*] to be meant to be; **2 se ~ aimable** to try to be friendly; **3 s'en ~** to be cross with oneself; **s'en ~ de** to regret; **je m'en serais voulu de ne pas vous avoir prévenu** I would never have forgiven myself if I hadn't warned you.

IDIOMS **~ c'est pouvoir** (Proverb) where there's a will there's a way.

vouloir[2] /vulwaʀ/ *nm* will; **attendre le bon ~ de qn** to wait on sb's pleasure.

voulu, **~e** /vuly/ *adj* **1** [*skills, money*] required; **on n'obtient jamais les renseignements ~s** you never get the information you want; **en temps ~** in time; **au moment ~** at the right time; **2** [*omission*] deliberate; [*meeting*] planned.

vous /vu/ *pron* **1** you; **je sais que ce n'est pas ~** I know it wasn't you; **c'est ~ qui avez gagné** you have won; **~ aussi, ~ avez l'air malade** you don't look very well either; **ils ~ ont placés ensemble** they have put you together; **à cause de/autour de ~** because of/around you; **ce sont des amis à ~?** are they friends of yours?; **c'est à ~** it's yours, it belongs to you; it's your turn; **à ~** your turn; **à ~ de choisir** it's your turn to choose; it's up to you to choose; **2** yourself; yourselves; **allez ~ laver les mains** go and wash your hands; **prenez soin de ~** look after yourself; **pensez à ~ deux** think of yourselves.

vous-même, *pl* **vous-mêmes** /vumɛm/ *pron* **1** yourself; **vous me l'avez dit ~** you told me yourself; **ne vous repliez pas sur ~** don't turn in on yourself; **2 allez-y ~s** go yourselves; **vous verrez par ~s** you'll see for yourselves.

voûte /vut/ *nf* (gen) vault; (of porch) archway; (of tunnel) roof; (figurative) (of leaves, branches) arch.

■ **la ~ céleste** the sky; (literary) the heavens; **~ crânienne** dome of the skull; **~ du palais** roof of the mouth; **~ plantaire** arch of the foot.

voûté, **~e** /vute/ *adj* **1** [*cellar*] vaulted; **2** [*person*] stooping; [*back*] bent; **il est ~** he has a stoop.

voûter /vute/ [1] **I** *vtr* **1** (in architecture) to vault [*room*]; **2** to give [sb] a stoop.

II se voûter *v refl* (+ *v être*) [*person*] to develop a stoop; [*back*] to become bent.

vouvoiement /vuvwamɑ̃/ *nm* using the 'vous' or polite form.

vouvoyer /vuvwaje/ [23] *vtr* to address [sb] using the 'vous' form.

voyage /vwajaʒ/ *nm* trip; journey; **partir en ~, faire un ~** to go on a trip; **être en ~** to be on a trip; **le ~ aller** the outward journey; **aimer les ~s** to love travelling[GB].

■ **~ d'études** study trip; **~ de noces** honeymoon; **~ organisé** package tour.

voyager /vwajaʒe/ [13] *vi* to travel.

voyageur, **-euse** /vwajaʒœʀ, øz/ *nm,f* **1** passenger; **'réservé aux ~s munis de billets'** 'ticketholders only'; **2** traveller[GB].

■ **~ de commerce** travelling[GB] salesman.

voyance /vwajɑ̃s/ *nf* clairvoyance.

voyant, **~e** /vwajɑ̃, ɑ̃t/ **I** *adj* [*colour*] loud.

II *nm,f* **1** clairvoyant; **2** sighted person.

III *nm* light; **~ d'huile** (Aut) oil warning light.

voyelle /vwajɛl/ *nf* vowel.

voyeurisme /vwajœʀism/ *nm* voyeurism.

voyou /vwaju/ *nm* lout.

vrac: **en vrac** /ɑ̃vʀak/ *phr* **1** loose, unpackaged; **2** in bulk; **3** haphazardly; **jeter ses idées en ~ sur le papier** to jot down one's ideas as they come.

vrai, **~e** /vʀɛ/ **I** *adj* true; real, genuine; **il n'en est pas moins ~ que...** it's nonetheless true that...; **il n'y a rien de ~ dans ses déclarations** there's no truth in his statements; **la ~e raison de mon départ** the real reason for my leaving; **un ~ Rembrandt** a genuine Rembrandt; **une ~e blonde** a natural blonde; **des ~s jumeaux** identical twins; **plus ~ que nature** [*picture, scene*] larger than life.

II *nm* truth; **on ne distingue plus le ~ du faux dans leur histoire** one can't tell fact from fiction in their story; **être dans le ~** to be in the right; **pour de ~** for real; **à ~ dire, à dire ~** to tell the truth.

III *adv* **faire ~** to look real; **son discours sonne ~** his speech has the ring of truth.

vraiment /vʀɛmɑ̃/ *adv* really.

vraisemblable /vʀɛsɑ̃blabl/ *adj* [*excuse*] convincing; [*scenario*] plausible; [*hypothesis*] likely; **il est ~ que** it is likely or probable that.

vraisemblablement /vʀɛsɑ̃blabləmɑ̃/ *adv* probably.

vraisemblance /vʀɛsɑ̃blɑ̃s/ *nf* (of hypothesis) likelihood; (of situation, explanation) plausibility; **selon toute ~** in all likelihood.

vrille /vʀij/ *nf* **1** spiral; (of airplane) tailspin; **descendre en ~** [*airplane*] to go into a spiral dive; **2** (Bot) tendril; **3** (Tech) gimlet.

vrombir /vʀɔ̃biʀ/ [3] *vi* **1** [*engine*] to roar; **faire ~ un moteur** to rev up an engine; **2** [*fly*] to buzz.

VRP /veɛʀpe/ *nm* (*abbr* = **voyageur représentant placier**) representative, rep○.

VTT /vetete/ *nm* (*abbr* = **vélo tout terrain**) mountain bike.

vu, **~e**[1] /vy/ **I** *adj* **1 être bien/mal ~** [*person*] to be/not to be well thought of (**de** by); **c'est bien ~ de faire cela** it's good form to do that; **ce serait plutôt mal ~** it wouldn't go down well; **2 (c'est) bien ~!** good point!; **c'est tout ~** my mind is made up; **3 (c'est bien) ~?** got it○?

II *prep* in view of.

III vu que *phr* in view of the fact that.

IDIOMS **au ~ et au su de tous** openly and publicly.

vue[2] /vy/ *nf* **1** sight; **avoir une bonne ~** to have good eyesight; **don de double ~** gift of second sight; **connaître qn de ~** to know sb by sight; **perdre qn de ~** (figurative) to lose touch with sb; **à ~** [*shoot*] on sight; [*fly plane*] without instruments; [*payable*] on demand; **2** view; **avoir ~ sur le lac** to look out onto the lake; **3** sight; **s'évanouir à la ~ du sang** to faint at the sight of blood; **à ma ~, il s'enfuit** he took to his heels when he saw me; **4** (opinion) view; **~s** views (**sur** on); **~ optimiste des choses** optimistic view of things; **5 avoir des ~s sur qn/qch** to have designs on sb/sth; **6 en ~** in sight; [*person*] prominent; **mettre une photo bien en ~** to display a photo prominently; **c'est quelqu'un de très en ~** he's/she's very much in the public eye; **j'ai un terrain en ~** I have a plot of land in mind; I've got my eye on a piece of land; **en ~ de faire** with a view to doing.

■ **~ d'ensemble** overall view.

IDIOMS **à ~ d'œil** or **de nez**○ at a rough guess; **vouloir en mettre plein la ~ à qn** to try to dazzle sb.

vulgaire /vylgɛʀ/ *adj* **1** vulgar, coarse; **2** common, ordinary; **un ~ chat** a common cat; **c'est un ~ employé** he's just a lowly employee; **la langue ~** the vernacular.

vulgairement /vylgɛʀmɑ̃/ *adv* **1** [*speak*] coarsely; **2** commonly.

vulgarisation /vylgaʀizasjɔ̃/ *nf* popularization; **revue de ~ scientifique** scientific review for the general public.

vulgariser /vylgaʀize/ [1] **I** *vtr* to popularize [*science*]; to bring [sth] into general use [*expression*].

II se vulgariser *v refl* (+ *v être*) [*technology*] to become generally accessible; [*expression*] to come into general use.

vulgarité /vylgaʀite/ *nf* vulgarity, coarseness.

vulnérabilité /vylneʀabilite/ *nf* vulnerability.

vulnérable /vylneʀabl/ *adj* vulnerable (**à** to).

vulve /vylv/ *nf* vulva.

w, **W** /dubləve/ *nm inv* **1** (letter) w, W; **2 W** (*written abbr* = **watt**) **60 W** 60 W.

wagon /vagɔ̃/ *nm* **1** wagon (GB), car (US); (for passengers) carriage (GB), car (US); **2** wagonload (GB), carload (US).
■ **~ à bestiaux** cattle truck (GB), cattle car (US); **~ de marchandises** goods wagon (GB), freight car (US).

wagon-bar, *pl* **wagons-bars** /vagɔ̃baʀ/ *nm* buffet car.

wagon-citerne, *pl* **wagons-citernes** /vagɔ̃ sitɛʀn/ *nm* tanker.

wagon-lit, *pl* **wagons-lits** /vagɔ̃li/ *nm* sleeper, sleeping car (US).

wagonnet /vagɔnɛ/ *nm* trolley (GB), cart (US).

wagon-restaurant, *pl* **wagons-restaurants** /vagɔ̃ʀɛstɔʀɑ̃/ *nm* restaurant car (GB), dining car (US).

wallon, **-onne** /walɔ̃, ɔn/ *adj*, *nm* Walloon.

waters○ /watɛʀ/ *nm pl* toilets.

WC /(dublə)vese/ *nm pl* toilet; **aller aux ~** to go to the toilet.

x, X /iks/ *nm inv* (letter) x, X; **il y a x temps que c'est fini** it's been over for ages; **porter plainte contre X** (Law) to take an action against person or persons unknown; **film classé X** X-rated movie.

xénophobe /gzenɔfɔb/ **I** *adj* xenophobic.
II *nmf* xenophobe.

xénophobie /gzenɔfɔbi/ *nf* xenophobia.

xérès /kseʀɛs/ *nm inv* sherry.

xylophène® /ksilɔfɛn/ *nm* wood preservative.

Yy

y[1], **Y** /igʀɛk/ *nm inv* (letter) y, Y.

y[2] /i/ *pron* **1** it; **tu t'~ attendais?** were you expecting it?; **il n'~ connaît rien** he knows nothing about it; **j'~ pense parfois** I sometimes think about it; **elle n'~ peut rien** there's nothing she can do about it; **j'~ viens** I'm coming to that; **rien n'~ fait** it's no use; **tu n'~ arriveras jamais** you'll never manage; **je n'~ comprends rien** I don't understand a thing; **tu ~ as gagné** you got the best deal; **plus difficile qu'il n'~ paraît** harder than it seems; **2** there; **j'~ ai mangé une fois** I ate there once; **n'~ va pas** don't go; **3 il ~ a** there is/are; **du vin? il n'~ en a plus** wine? there's none left; **il n'~ a qu'à téléphoner** just phone.
IDIOMS **~ mettre du sien** to work at it.

ya(c)k /ˈjak/ *nm* yak.

yaourt /ˈjauʀ(t)/ *nm* yoghurt.

yaourtière /ˈjauʀtjɛʀ/ *nf* yoghurt-maker.

yéménite /ˈjemenit/ *adj* Yemeni.

yeux *nm pl* ▶ **œil**.

yoga /ˈjɔga/ *nm* yoga; **faire du ~** to do yoga.

yole /ˈjɔl/ *nf* skiff.

yougoslave /ˈjugɔslav/ *adj* Yugoslavian.

youyou /ˈjuju/ *nm* **1** ululation; **2** dinghy.

Zz

z, **Z** /zɛd/ *nm inv* z, Z.
zaïrois, **~e** /zaiʀwa, az/ *adj* Zairean.
zambien, **-ienne** /zɑ̃bjɛ̃, ɛn/ *adj* Zambian.
zapper /zape/ [1] *vi* to flick through the TV channels.
zèbre /zɛbʀ/ *nm* **1** zebra; **2**○ (figurative) bloke○ (GB), guy○.
zébré /zebʀe/ *adj* [*fabric*] zebra-striped; **~ de** streaked with.
zébrure /zebʀyʀ/ *nf* stripe.
zébu /zeby/ *nm* zebu.
zèle /zɛl/ *nm* zeal, enthusiasm; **faire du ~** or **de l'excès de ~** to be overzealous.
zélé, **~e** /zele/ *adj* enthusiastic, zealous.
zénith /zenit/ *nm* zenith; **à son ~** [*career*] at its height.
zéro /zeʀo/ **I** *adj* **~ heure** midnight, twenty-four hundred (hours); **il sera exactement ~ heure vingt minutes dix secondes** the time will be twelve twenty and ten seconds; **j'ai eu ~ faute dans ma dictée** I didn't make a single mistake in my dictation; **niveau/croissance ~** zero level/growth.
II *nm* **1** zero, nought (GB); **avoir un ~ en latin** to get zero or nought in Latin; **remettre un compteur à ~** to reset a counter to zero; **avoir le moral à ~** (figurative) to be down in the dumps○; **c'est beau à regarder mais question goût c'est ~**○ it's nice to look at, but no marks for flavour[GB]; **2** (in sport) (gen) nil; (in tennis) love; **trois (buts) à ~** three nil.
■ **~ de conduite** (Sch) bad mark for behaviour[GB].
IDIOMS **partir de ~** to start from scratch; **tout reprendre à ~** to start all over again.
zeste /zɛst/ *nm* **un ~ de citron** the zest of a lemon.
zézayer /zezeje/ [21] *vi* to lisp.
zibeline /ziblin/ *nf* sable.
zigomar○ /zigɔmaʀ/ *nm* (derogatory) guy○.
zigoto○ /zigɔto/ *nm* guy○; **faire le ~** to clown around.
zigue○ /zig/ *nm* guy○.
zigzag /zigzag/ *nm* zigzag; **route en ~** winding road; **faire des ~s** to zigzag (**parmi** through); **partir en ~** to zigzag off.
zinc /zɛ̃g/ *nm* **1** zinc; **toiture de** or **en ~** tin roofing; **2**○ counter, bar.
zingueur /zɛ̃gœʀ/ *nm* roofer.
zinzin○ /zɛ̃zɛ̃/ **I** *adj inv* cracked○.
II *nm* thingamajig○.
zip /zip/ *nm* zip (GB), zipper (US).
zippé, **~e** /zipe/ *adj* zip-up.
zizanie /zizani/ *nf* ill-feeling, discord.
zizi○ /zizi/ *nm* willy○ (GB), penis.
zodiac® /zɔdjak/ *nm* inflatable dinghy.
zodiaque /zɔdjak/ *nm* zodiac.
zona /zona/ *nm* shingles.
zonage /zonaʒ/ *nm* zoning.
zonard○, **~e** /zonaʀ, aʀd/ *nm,f* dropout○.
zone /zon/ *nf* **1** zone, area; **~ interdite** off-limits area; (on signpost) no entry; **2 la ~** the slum belt; **de seconde ~** second-rate.
■ **~ d'activités** business park; **~ artisanale** small industrial estate (GB) or park; **~ bleue** restricted parking zone; **~ industrielle** industrial estate (GB) or park.
zoner○ /zone/ [1] *vi* to hang about○.
zoo /zo/ *nm* zoo.
zoologie /zɔɔlɔʒi/ *nf* zoology.
zoom /zum/ *nm* **1** zoom lens; **2** zoom.
zootechnicien, **-ienne** /zooteknisjɛ̃, ɛn/ *nm,f* animal technician.
zouave /zwav/ *nm* **1**○ clown, comedian; **faire le ~** to clown around○; **2** (soldier) zouave.
zoulou, **~e** /zulu/ *adj* Zulu.
zozoter /zɔzɔte/ [1] *vi* to lisp.
zut○ /zyt/ *excl* damn○!

Éliane Debard
25, rue des Alouettes
38180 Seyssin

Good wishes for the New Year

le 15 décembre 1994

Je vous présente mes meilleurs vœux de bonheur et de réussite pour la nouvelle année. Que 1995 vous apporte tout ce que vous souhaitez, à vous, à votre famille et à tous ceux qui vous sont chers.

Éliane Debard

Accepting an invitation: formal

Troyes, le 17 avril 1995

Chers amis,

Je vous remercie de votre aimable invitation au mariage de votre fille le samedi 12 juin, que j'accepte avec joie. J'arriverai par le train de vendredi soir, puisqu'il n'y a plus de train le samedi.

Dans l'attente du plaisir de vous revoir, je vous adresse mes meilleures salutations.

Thomas Lemaître

Declining an invitation

Londres, le 1er mai 1995

Ma chère Ghislaine

Votre lettre m'a fait grand plaisir, et je tiens à vous remercier d'avoir pensé à moi. Mais je dois hélas refuser votre aimable invitation: je m'étais précédemment engagé à prendre part le même jour à la célébration des noces d'or de tante Agnès et oncle Michel à Nice.

J'espère que nous aurons très bientôt l'occasion de nous revoir. Amicalement à vous.

Marc

Thanking the host family

Nantucket, le 17 septembre 1995

Chers Monsieur et Madame Robin

Je voudrais vous remercier pour les vacances merveilleuses que j'ai passées dans votre propriété de Saint-Malo. Je n'oublierai jamais les repas où il y avait tant de bonnes choses, le bridge et les parties de pêche avec René. J'ai tant de bons souvenirs que je n'arrête pas de parler de la France à tous mes amis. J'espère que j'aurai très bientôt l'occasion de vous revoir tous.

Je vous embrasse affectueusement.

Doug

Arranging an exchange visit

Dublin, le 2 avril 1995

Una et Dan Farrelly
28, Leeson Drive
Artane
Dublin 5
Irlande

Monsieur et Madame Pierre Beaufort
Chalet "Les Edelweiss"
Chemin des Rousses
74400 Chamonix

Chers Danièle et Pierre

Nous serions très heureux d'accueillir votre fils chez nous entre le 10 et le 31 juillet et d'envoyer en échange notre fils Kilian pendant le mois d'août.

Kilian a 16 ans. Il fait du français depuis 4 ans. C'est un garçon sportif: il aime la randonnée, la natation et le tennis.

Merci de nous dire assez rapidement si cette idée vous convient afin que nous puissions réserver les places d'avion.

Croyez en nos sentiments les meilleurs.

U. Farrelly

U. Farrelly

Disputing an invoice: already paid

B. Conrad
Le Manoir aux Emaux
17108 Saintes

Meubles Le Vieux Rustique
Zone artisanale des Fougères
D 939
17030 La Rochelle

le 21 décembre 1995

Monsieur,

Par lettre du 20 décembre, vous me demandez de régler votre facture n° 721 de 47921,37 francs du 11 septembre concernant la livraison de meubles divers. Or cette facture a déjà été payée, par mandat postal daté du 7 octobre. Je vous la renvoie donc, en vous demandant de bien vouloir vérifier vos comptes.

Veuillez agréer, Monsieur, l'expression de mes salutations distinguées.

B Conrad

B.Conrad

P.J.: votre facture

Applying for a job as an au pair

Sally Kendall
5, Tackley Place
Reading RG2 6RN
England

Reading, le 17 avril 1995

Madame, Monsieur,

Vos coordonnées m'ont été communiquées par l'agence "Au Pair International", qui m'a demandé de vous écrire directement. Je suis en effet intéressée par un emploi de jeune fille au pair pour une période de six mois au moins, à partir de l'automne prochain.

J'adore les enfants, quel que soit leur âge, et j'ai une grande expérience du baby-sitting, comme vous pourrez le constater au vu du CV ci-joint.

Dans l'espoir d'une réponse favorable, je vous prie d'agréer, Madame, Monsieur, l'expression de mes respectueuses salutations.

S. Kendall

P.J.: un CV

Replying to a job ad

Jean-Luc Morin
12, Avenue d'Angleterre
62107 Calais

Monsieur le Directeur
Arts et Design Gadgeteria
27, rue Victor Hugo
59001 Lille

Calais, le 14 février 1995

Monsieur,

L'annonce parue en page 2 de l'édition du 12 février du Courrier Picard concernant un poste de concepteur m'a vivement intéressé. Mon contrat à durée déterminée chez Solo and Co. touche à sa fin. Je pense posséder l'expérience et les qualifications requises pour vous donner toute satisfaction dans ce poste, comme vous pourrez le constater au vu de mon CV. Je me tiens à votre disposition pour un entretien éventuel, et vous prie d'agréer, Monsieur, l'expression de mes sentiments distingués.

J.L. Morin

P.J.: un CV avec photo

Enquiry to the tourist office

M. et Mme François Bolard
10, rue Eugène Delacroix
06200 Nice

Nice, le 24 mars 1995

Syndicat d'Initiative
de St-Gervais
74170 Saint-Gervais-les-Bains

Monsieur,

Mon mari et moi envisageons de passer nos vacances d'été à Saint-Gervais. Nous vous serions reconnaissants de bien vouloir nous faire parvenir toute la documentation dont vous disposez sur les hôtels, la station thermale ainsi que sur les activités proposées aux touristes en saison. Vous trouverez ci-joint une enveloppe timbrée pour la réponse.

Dans l'attente de vous lire, je vous prie d'agréer, Monsieur, l'expression de mes sentiments distingués.

Bolard

E. Bolard

Booking a hotel room

Bourguignon, le 22 mars 1995

Madame Solange Vernon
125 bis, Route Nationale
18340 Levet

Maison de Famille Le Repos
Chemin des Lys
06100 Grasse

Monsieur le Directeur,

J'ai bien reçu le dépliant de votre maison, ainsi que les tarifs que je vous avais demandés, et je vous en remercie.

Je souhaite réserver une chambre calme avec bain et wc, en pension complète pour la période du 27 avril au 12 mai. Je vous adresse ci-joint un chèque de 600 francs d'arrhes.

Je vous en souhaite bonne réception, et vous remerciant par avance je vous prie de croire, Monsieur le Directeur, en mes sentiments les meilleurs.

S. Vernon

P.J.: un chèque postal de 600 francs

CV: English graduate

GRANTLEY Paul Alan

Adresse:
26 Countisbury Drive
BRIGHTON BN3 1RG
Grande-Bretagne
Tél.: 01273 53 49 50

Né le 22 mai 1969
Célibataire
Nationalité britannique

FORMATION

1988 - 1991

King's College, Londres: B.Sc. (Licence) en Biochimie (2.1. = mention bien)

1987

A Levels (Deuxième partie du Baccalauréat) options: Biologie, Chimie, Physique et Mathématiques.

1985

O Levels (Première partie du Baccalauréat) options :

Mathématiques, Physique, Biologie, Chimie, Commerce, Anglais, Allemand et Sociologie.

1980 - 1987

Brighton College Boys' School (Lycée)

EXPERIENCE PROFESSIONNELLE

Mars 1989

une semaine comme "double" du Directeur Adjoint du Marketing chez EAA Technology (Sources d'énergie écologiques) à Didcot près d'Oxford.

Juillet 1988

deux semaines chez Alford & Wilston Ltd (Produits chimiques), Warley, Midlands de l'Ouest.

CENTRES D'INTERET

Au Lycée

Capitaine de l'équipe de rugby pendant deux ans.

Membre du club d'échecs.

A l'Université

Membre de l'équipe de rugby.

Organisateur de la Semaine de Charité (1988).

Délégué aux activités sportives dans l'association des étudiants.

DIVERS

Bonne connaissance de l'outil informatique, en particulier sur Macintosh.

Permis de conduire.

Intérêt pour les voyages : tour du monde en 1987-88, entre le Lycée et l'Université.

Immobilier

Locations

Part. à part. ag. s'abst., loue F3, 2ch., sdb, ds immeuble centre Villeurbanne, esp. verts, cave, t.b. état, 2 500F CC, 78 92 13 22 p. 249 hor. bur.

Loue ch. meublée, 18 m² dans tb villa, av. douche, poss. cuis., prise tél. et TV, entrée séparée, lib. imméd., loyer 1 800F cc, tél : 78 49 26 76

URG rech. appart. F3 à louer, env. Saverne, cuis. équip., balc., park., maxi. 3 500F/mois cc, tél. 85 34 37 29

Ventes

VDS mais. F4, tt cft, t. b. état, ch. c., ds résid. stand., px à déb., libre imméd. Tél.HR 72.88.63.29

Échanges vacances

Échange luxueux appt Paris Avenue Foch, 2ch, 2sdb, terrasse, a/c, parking, contre appt similaire centre Londres pour avril mai juin 1996. Tél. 16 (1) 45 27 98 12

Éch. bglw tt cft, 4/5 pers, PALAVAS LES FLOTS, contre logt équiv. Bret. sud, 14 juil/15 août. T. HR 98.72.41.68

House Sale
Apartment/Room Let
Holiday Exchanges

a/c (air conditionné) air conditioning
ag. s'abst. (agences s'abstenir) no agencies (i.e. only private individuals should apply)
appt (appartement) flat
av. (avec) with
balc. (balcon) balcony
bglw (bungalow) holiday chalet
Bret. sud (Bretagne sud) southern Brittany
cc, CC (charges comprises) service charges included (in the rent)
ch. (chambre) bedroom
ch. c. (chauffage central) central heating
cuis. équip. (cuisine équipée) fully fitted kitchen
ds (dans) in
éch. (échange) exchange (offered for)
env. (aux environs de) in the area of, close to
esp. verts (espaces verts) green space (e.g. gardens, parkland)
hor. bur. (horaires de bureau) office hours (between 8 and 12 or between 2 and 5)
HR (heures des repas) meal times (between 12 and 2 or between 7 and 9 p.m.)
imméd. (immédiatement) (available) immediately
lib. (libre) free (from a certain date)
logt équiv. (logement équivalent) equivalent accommodation
m² (mètres carrés) square metres
maxi (maximum) maximum
p. 249 (poste 249) extension 249
park. (parking) parking space
part. à part. (particulier à particulier) private let
pers. (personnes) people
poss. cuis. (possibilité de faire la cuisine) cooking facilities
px à déb. (prix à débattre) price to be discussed
rech. (recherche) is seeking
résid. (résidence) apartment complex
sdb (salle de bains) bathroom
stand. (de bon standing) desirable
T., tél. (téléphone, téléphoner) telephone
tb (très beau/belle) delightful
t.b. état (très bon état) (in) excellent condition
tt cft (tout confort) all mod cons
URG (urgent) urgent(ly)
vds/vd (vends) (I am) selling, for sale

Jobs

Emplois

Jne F., 23 a., diplômée Ec. Sup. Com., bil. fr/angl, tt txte, excel. présent. ch. empl. 1/2 tps, accept. déplcts. Ecr. jrnl Réf. OEZ98

Centre de vac. ch. H à tt faire pr petits trvx, surveill. enfts, sér. réf. exigées, logé, nourri, blanchi + 3 500F/ms. Ecr. jrnl réf. PLM258

Etud. donne crs anglais français ts niveaux tél: 27 42 31 86

Ch. f. de mén. 2x4h/sem., a.m. préfér., sér. réf. exig., Tél Mme PIERRAT 42 59 17 23

Entr. TP ch. VRP multic., départ. 42, 74, 01. Envoy. CV + photo + prétent. à BATIDUR 285 cours Lafayette 69100 Villeurbanne

1/2 tps (mi-temps) half-time
2x4h/sem. (deux fois quatre heures par semaine) 4 hours twice a week
a. (ans) years (old)
accept. déplcts (accepte les déplacements) will travel
angl (anglais) English
a.m. préfér. (l'après-midi de préférence) preferably afternoon
bil. fr/angl (bilingue français/anglais) bilingual French/English
ch. (cherche) seeks
crs (cours) lessons
départ. (départements) departments (French districts)
dispon. (disponible) available
Ec. Sup. Com. (École Supérieure de Commerce) Business School
ecr. (écrire à) (please) write to
empl. (emploi) job
enfts (enfants) children
entr. TP (entreprise de travaux publics) civil engineering firm
envoy. (envoyer) (please) send
étud. (étudiant(e)) student
excel. présent. (excellente présentation) very smart appearance
exig. (exigé) required, essential
f. de mén. (femme de ménage) cleaning lady
fam. (famille) family
F/ms (francs par mois) francs per month
Fr (français) French
H. à tt faire (homme à tout faire) odd-job man
h/sem. (heures par semaine) hours per week
J.F., Jne F (jeune fille/femme) young woman
jrnl (journal) newspaper
juil. (juillet) July
ms (mois) month
nat. (nationalité) nationality
petits trvx (petits travaux) light (manual) work
poss. (possible) possible
pr (pour) for
prétent. (prétentions) salary expectation
réf. (référence) reference (number)
sér. réf. (sérieuses références) excellent references
surveill. enfts (surveillance d'enfants) looking after children
tél. (téléphone) telephone
trav. scol. (travail scolaire) homework
ts (tous) all
tt txte (traitement de texte) word processing
vac. (vacances) holidays
voit. (voiture) car
VRP multic. (voyageur représentant placier multicartes) sales representative for several different companies

English–French Dictionary

a[1], **A** *n* **1** (letter) a, A *m*; **2 to get from A to B** se rendre d'un endroit à un autre.

a[2], **an** *det* un/une.

■ **Note** The determiner or indefinite article *a* or *an* is translated by *un + masculine noun* and by *une + feminine noun*: *a tree* = un arbre; *a chair* = une chaise. There are, however, some cases where the article is not translated:
- with professions and trades: *her mother is a teacher* = sa mère est professeur;
- with other nouns used in apposition: *he's a widower* = il est veuf;
- with *what a*: *what a pretty house* = quelle jolie maison.
– When expressing prices in relation to weight, the definite article *le*/*la* is used in French: *ten francs a kilo* = dix francs le kilo. In other expressions where *a*/*an* means *per* the French translation is *par*: *twice a day* = deux fois par jour; but: *50 kilometres an hour* = 50 kilomètres/heure.

aback *adv* **to be taken ~** être déconcerté (**by** par).

abandon *vtr* abandonner [*person, hope*]; renoncer à [*activity, attempt*].

abandoned *adj* [*person, animal*] abandonné.

abbey *n* abbaye *f*.

abbot *n* (père *m*) abbé *m*.

abbreviation *n* abréviation *f*.

ABC *n* (alphabet) alphabet *m*.

abdomen *n* abdomen *m*.

abduct *vtr* enlever.

abhor *vtr* abhorrer.

abide *vi* **to ~ by** respecter [*rule, decision*].

abilities *n pl* (skills) compétences *fpl*; (Sch) (of pupils) aptitudes *fpl*.

ability *n* **1** (capability) capacité *f*; **to the best of one's ~** de son mieux; **2** (talent) talent *m*.

ablaze *adj* en feu, en flammes.

able *adj*

■ **Note** *to be able to* meaning *can* is usually translated by the verb *pouvoir*: *I was not able to help him* = je ne pouvais pas l'aider.
– When *to be able to* implies the acquiring of a skill, *savoir* is used: *he's nine and he's still not able to read* = il a neuf ans et il ne sait toujours pas lire.

1 (having ability to) **to be ~ to do** pouvoir faire; **he isn't ~ to buy it** il ne peut pas l'acheter; **she was ~ to play the piano at the age of four** elle savait jouer du piano à quatre ans; **2** [*lawyer, teacher*] compétent; [*child*] doué.

abnormal *adj* anormal.

abnormality *n* anomalie *f*.

aboard I *adv* à bord.
II *prep* à bord de [*plane*]; dans [*coach, train*].

abolish *vtr* abolir [*law, right*]; supprimer [*service, allowance*].

abominable *adj* abominable.

Aborigine *n* aborigène *mf* (d'Australie).

abortion *n* avortement *m*; **to have an ~** se faire avorter.

abound *vi* abonder (**in, with** en).

about I *adj* **to be ~ to do** être sur le point de faire; **I'm not ~ to give up** je ne suis pas près d'abandonner.
II *adv* **1** (approximately) environ, à peu près; **it's ~ the same** c'est à peu près pareil; **at ~ 6 pm** vers 18 h; **2** (almost) presque; **that seems ~ right** ça a l'air d'aller; **I've had just ~ enough (of her)!** j'en ai plus qu'assez (d'elle)!; **3** (in circulation) **there was no-one ~** il n'y avait personne; **there is a lot of flu ~** il y a beaucoup de grippes en ce moment; **4** (in the vicinity) **to be somewhere ~** être dans les parages.
III *prep* **1** (concerning) **a book ~ France** un livre sur la France; **what's it ~?** (of book, film) ça parle de quoi?; **may I ask what it's ~?** pourriez-vous me dire de quoi il s'agit?; **it's ~ my son** c'est au sujet de mon fils; **~ your overdraft...** pour ce qui est de votre découvert...; **business is ~ profit** ce qui compte dans les affaires, ce sont les bénéfices; **2 there's something weird ~ him** il a quelque chose de bizarre; **what I like ~ her is her honesty** ce que j'aime chez elle c'est sa franchise; **3 to know what one is ~** savoir ce qu'on fait; **while you're ~ it...** tant que tu y es..., par la même occasion...; **and be quick ~ it!** et fais vite!; **4** (around) **to wander ~ the streets** errer dans les rues; **strewn ~ the floor** éparpillés sur le sol; **5 how** or **what ~ some tea?** et si on prenait un thé?; **how ~ it?** ça te dit?; **6 what ~ the legal costs?** et les frais de justice?; **what ~ you?** et toi?
IDIOMS **it's ~ time (that) somebody made an effort** il serait temps que quelqu'un fasse un effort; **~ time too!** ce n'est pas trop tôt○!

above I *pron* **the ~** (people) les personnes susnommées.
II *prep* **1** au-dessus de; **~ the painting/London** au-dessus du tableau/de Londres; **~ it** au-dessus; **children ~ the age of 12** les enfants âgés de plus de 12 ans; **to rise ~** dépasser [*amount, limit*]; **~ suspicion** au-dessus de tout soupçon; **2** (morally) **he's ~ such petty behaviour** il n'est pas capable d'un comportement aussi mesquin; **they're not ~ cheating** ils sont tout à fait capables de tricher; **3** (in preference to) par-dessus; **~ all others, ~ all else** par-dessus tout; **4 to hear sth ~ the shouting** entendre qch par-dessus les cris.
III *adj* **the ~ items** les articles susmentionnés or figurant ci-dessus.
IV *adv* **1** au-dessus; **a desk with a shelf ~**

un bureau avec une étagère au-dessus; **the apartment ~** l'appartement du dessus; **from ~** d'en haut; **2** (in text) **see ~** voir ci-dessus; **3** (more) plus; **children of 12 and ~** les enfants âgés de 12 ans et plus.
V **above all** *phr* surtout.

above-mentioned *adj* susmentionné.

abreast *adv* **to walk three ~** marcher à trois de front; **to keep ~ of** se tenir au courant de.

abroad *adv* à l'étranger; **from ~** de l'étranger.

abrupt *adj* **1** (sudden, curt) brusque; **2** (steep) abrupt.

abscess *n* abcès *m*.

abseiling ▶ 649 *n* (GB) descente *f* en rappel.

absence *n* absence *f*; **in/during sb's ~** en/pendant l'absence de qn; **in the ~ of** faute de [*alternative, evidence*].

absent *adj* absent (**from** de).

absent-minded *adj* distrait.

absolute *adj* absolu; **~ beginner** débutant complet; **it was ~ chaos** c'était la pagaille○ la plus complète.

absolutely *adv* absolument; **you're ~ right!** tu as entièrement raison; **~ not!** pas du tout!

absorb *vtr* absorber.

absorbed *adj* absorbé (**in** or **by** par); **~ in one's work** plongé dans son travail.

absorbent *n, adj* absorbant (*m*).

absorbing *adj* passionnant.

abstain *vi* s'abstenir (**from** de).

abstract *adj* abstrait.

absurd *adj* absurde, ridicule.

abuse I *n* **1** (maltreatment) mauvais traitement *m*; (sexual) sévices *mpl* (sexuels); **2** (misuse) abus *m*; **alcohol ~** abus d'alcool; **drug ~** usage *m* des stupéfiants; **3** (insults) injures *fpl*.
II *vtr* **1** (hurt) maltraiter; (sexually) abuser de [*woman*]; exercer des sévices sexuels sur [*child*]; **2** abuser de [*position, power, trust*]; **3** (insult) injurier.

abusive *adj* [*person*] grossier/-ière; [*words*] injurieux/-ieuse.

abyss *n* abîme *m*.

academic I *n* universitaire *mf*.
II *adj* **1** [*career, post, book*] universitaire; [*year*] académique; [*achievement, background*] intellectuel/-elle; **2** (theoretical) théorique; **that's ~** ça n'a aucun intérêt pratique.

academy *n* (school) école *f*; (learned society) académie *f*.

Academy Award *n* Oscar *m*.

accelerate *vi* accélérer.

accelerator *n* accélérateur *m*.

accent *n* accent *m*; **in a French ~** avec l'accent français.

accept *vtr* (gen) accepter; (tolerate) admettre.

acceptable *adj* acceptable.

acceptance *n* acceptation *f*.

access I *n* accès *m*; **to gain ~ to sth** accéder à qch; **'No ~'** 'accès interdit'; **open ~** libre accès; **to have ~ to one's children** avoir un droit de visite auprès de ses enfants.
II *vtr* accéder à [*database, information*].

accessible *adj* (gen) accessible (**to** à); (affordable) abordable.

accessory *n* **1** (gen) accessoire *m*; (on car) extra *m*; **2** (Law) complice *mf* (**to** de).

access road *n* (to motorway) bretelle *f* d'accès.

accident *n* **1** (mishap) accident *m* (**with** avec); **by ~** accidentellement; **car/road ~** accident de voiture/de la route; **to have an ~** avoir un accident; **~ and emergency service** service des urgences; **2** (chance) hasard *m*; **by ~** par hasard.

accidental *adj* **1** [*death*] accidentel/-elle; **2** [*meeting, mistake*] fortuit.

accidentally *adv* **1** (by accident) accidentellement; **2** (by chance) par hasard.

accident-prone *adj* sujet/-ette aux accidents.

acclimate (US), **acclimatize** *vtr* acclimater (**to** à); **to get** or **become ~d** s'acclimater.

accommodate *vtr* **1** (put up) loger; **2** (hold, provide space for) contenir; **3** (adapt to) s'adapter à [*change, view*]; **4** (satisfy) satisfaire [*need*].

accommodating *adj* accommodant (**to** envers).

accommodation *n* (also **~s** US) logement *m*; **hotel/student ~** logement en hôtel/pour étudiants; **office ~** bureaux *mpl*.

accompanist *n* accompagnateur/-trice *m/f*.

accompany *vtr* accompagner.

accomplice *n* complice *mf*.

accomplish *vtr* accomplir [*task, mission*]; réaliser [*objective*].

accomplishment *n* réussite *f*.

accord *n* accord *m*; **of my own ~** de moi-même.

accordance: **in accordance with** *phr* [*act*] conformément à [*rules, instructions*]; [*be*] conforme à [*law, agreement*].

according: according to *phr* **1** [*act*] selon [*law, principles*]; **~ to plan** comme prévu; **2** d'après [*newspaper, person*].

accordion ▶ 753 *n* accordéon *m*.

accost *vtr* (approach) aborder; (for sexual purpose) accoster.

account I *n* **1** (in bank, post office, shop) compte *m* (**at, with** à); **in my ~** sur mon compte; **to charge sth to** or **put sth on sb's ~** mettre qch sur le compte de qn; **to settle an ~** régler une note; **2 to take sth into ~, to take ~ of sth** tenir compte de qch; **3** (description) compte-rendu *m*; (if contentious) version *f*; **by all ~s** manifestement; **4** (indicating reason) **on ~ of** à cause de; **on no ~** sous aucun prétexte; **on my ~** à cause de moi.
II **accounts** *n pl* **1** (records) comptabilité *f*, comptes *mpl*; **2** (department) (service *m*) comptabilité *f*.
■ **account for**: **~ for [sth/sb] 1** (explain) expliquer [*events, fact, behaviour*]; justifier [*expense*] (**to sb** auprès de qn); retrouver [*missing people*]; **2** (represent) représenter [*proportion, percentage*].

accountable *adj* responsable (**to** devant; **for** de).

accountancy *n* comptabilité *f*.

accountant ▶805 *n* comptable *mf*.

account: **~ book** *n* livre *m* de comptes; **~ holder** *n* titulaire *mf*; **~ number** *n* numéro *m* de compte.

accumulate I *vtr* accumuler.
II *vi* s'accumuler.

accuracy *n* (of figures, watch) justesse *f*; (of map, aim) précision *f*; (of diagnosis, forecast) exactitude *f*.

accurate *adj* [*figures, watch, information*] juste; [*reports, map, diagnosis, forecast*] exact; [*assessment*] correct.

accurately *adv* [*calculate*] exactement; [*report*] avec exactitude; [*assess*] précisément.

accusation *n* accusation *f* (**of** de; **against** contre; **that** selon laquelle); **to make an ~** porter une accusation.

accuse *vtr* accuser (**of** de); **to ~ sb of doing** (now) accuser qn de faire; (of having done) accuser qn d'avoir fait.

accused *n* **the ~** (one) l'accusé/-e *m/f*; (several) les accusés/-es.

accustomed *adj* **1 to be ~ to sth/to doing** avoir l'habitude de qch/de faire; **to become ~ to sth/to doing** s'habituer à qch/à faire; **2** (usual) habituel/-elle.

ace *n* as *m*.

ache I *n* douleur *f* (**in** à); **~s and pains** douleurs *fpl*.
II *vi* [*person*] avoir mal; [*limb, back*] faire mal; **to ~ all over** avoir mal partout.

achieve *vtr* atteindre [*aim*]; atteindre à [*perfection*]; arriver à [*balance*]; obtenir [*success, result*]; réaliser [*ambition*]; **to ~ nothing** ne rien accomplir.

achievement *n* réussite *f* (**in sth** dans le domaine de qch); **academic ~** le succès universitaire; **the ~ of an ambition** la réalisation d'une ambition; **a sense of ~** un sentiment de satisfaction.

aching *adj* [*body, limbs*] douloureux/-euse.

acid I *n* acide *m*.
II *adj* [*taste, soil*] acide; [*tone*] aigre; [*remark*] caustique.

acid: **~ rain** *n* pluies *fpl* acides; **~ stomach** *n* acidité *f* gastrique.

acknowledge *vtr* admettre [*fact*]; reconnaître [*error, problem, authority*]; répondre à [*applause*]; accuser réception de [*letter*]; citer [*sources*]; **she didn't ~ me** elle a fait semblant de ne pas me voir.

acknowledgement I *n* **1** (of error, guilt) aveu *m*; **2** (confirmation of receipt) accusé *m* de réception.
II **acknowledgements** *n pl* (in book) remerciements *mpl*.

acne ▶686 *n* acné *f*.

acorn *n* gland *m*.

acoustic *adj* acoustique.

acoustic guitar ▶753 *n* guitare *f* sèche.

acoustics *n pl* **the ~ are good** l'acoustique est bonne.

acquaintance *n* connaissance *f* (**with** de); **to make sb's ~** faire la connaissance de qn.

acquainted *adj* **to be ~** se connaître; **to get** or **become ~ with sb** faire la connaissance de qn; **to get** or **become ~ with sth** découvrir qch.

acquire *vtr* acquérir [*expertise*]; obtenir [*information*]; faire l'acquisition de [*possessions*]; acheter [*company*]; **to ~ a taste for sth** prendre goût à qch; **it's an ~d taste** c'est quelque chose qu'il faut apprendre à aimer.

acquit *vtr* (Law) acquitter; **to be ~ted** être disculpé (**of** de).

acre *n* acre *f*, ≈ demi-hectare *m*.

acrobat *n* acrobate *mf*.

acrobatics *n pl* acrobaties *fpl*.

across I *prep* **1** (from one side to the other) **a journey ~ the desert** un voyage à travers le désert; **the bridge ~ the river** le pont qui traverse la rivière; **to go** or **travel ~ sth** traverser qch; **to be lying ~ the bed** être couché en travers du lit; **she leaned ~ the table** elle s'est penchée au-dessus de la table; **2** (on the other side of) de l'autre côté de; **~ the street (from me)** de l'autre côté de la rue; **3** (all over) **~ the world** partout dans le monde, à travers le monde; **~ the country** dans tout le pays.
II *adv* **to help sb ~** aider qn à traverser; **to go ~ to sb** aller vers qn; **to look ~ at sb** regarder vers qn.
III **across from** *phr* en face de.

acrylic *n* acrylique *m*.

act I *n* **1** acte *m*; **an ~ of kindness** un acte de bonté; **2** (Law) loi *f*; **Act of Parliament** loi votée par le Parlement; **3** (in show) numéro *m*; **4 to put on an ~** jouer la comédie.
II *vtr* jouer [*part, role*].
III *vi* **1** (take action) agir; **we must ~ quickly** il faut agir rapidement; **to ~ for sb, to ~ on behalf of sb** agir au nom de or pour le compte de qn; **2** (behave) agir, se comporter; **to ~ aggressively towards sb** se comporter de manière aggressive envers qn; **3** (in films, on stage) jouer, faire du théâtre; **4** (pretend) jouer la comédie, faire semblant; **5** (take effect) [*drug*] agir; **6** (serve) **to ~ as** [*person, object*] servir de.

acting I *n* (performance) jeu *m*, interprétation *f*; (occupation) métier *m* d'acteur; **I've done some ~** j'ai fait du théâtre.
II *adj* [*director, manager*] intérimaire.

action *n* **1** (gen) action *f*; (steps) mesures *fpl*; **to take ~** agir, prendre des mesures (**against** contre); **immediate ~** des mesures immédiates; **to put a plan into ~** mettre un projet à exécution; **2** (deed) acte *m*; **~s speak louder than words** mieux vaut agir que parler; **3** (fighting) action *f*, combat *m*; **killed in ~** tué au combat; **4** (in filming) action *f*; **~!** moteur!

activate *vtr* faire démarrer [*system*]; actionner [*switch*]; déclencher [*alarm*].

active *adj* [*person, life*] actif/-ive; [*volcano*] en activité; **to play an ~ role in sth** jouer un rôle déterminant dans qch; **to take an ~ interest in sth** s'intéresser activement à qch.

activist *n* activiste *mf*.

activity *n* activité *f*.

actor *n* acteur *m*, comédien *m*.

actress *n* actrice *f*, comédienne *f*.

actual *adj* **1** [*circumstances*] réel/réelle; [*words*] exact; **in ~ fact** en fait; **the ~ problem** le problème lui-même; **2** (very) même (*after n*); **the ~ room where Shakespeare worked** la pièce même où Shakespeare travaillait.

actually *adv* **1** (in fact) en fait; **their profits have ~ risen** en fait, leurs bénéfices ont augmenté; **~, I don't feel like it** à vrai dire je n'en ai pas envie; **2** (really) vraiment; **yes, it ~ happened!** mais oui, c'est vraiment arrivé!; **3** (exactly) exactement; **what ~ happened?** qu'est-ce qui s'est passé exactement?; **4** (expressing indignation) carrément; **she ~ accused me of lying!** elle m'a carrément accusé de mentir!; **5** (expressing surprise) **she ~ thanked me** elle est allée jusqu'à me remercier.

acumen *n* sagacité *f*; **business ~** sens *m* des affaires.

acupuncture *n* acupuncture *f*.

acute *adj* **1** [*anxiety, pain*] vif/vive; [*boredom*] profond; [*shortage*] grave; **2** (Med) [*illness*] aigu/aiguë; **3** (keen) [*person, mind*] pénétrant; **4** [*accent, angle*] aigu.

ad *n* (*abbr* = **advertisement**) **1** (also **small ~**) petite annonce *f* (**for** pour); **2** (on radio, TV) pub○ *f* (**for** pour).

AD (*abbr* = **Anno Domini**) ap J.-C.

adamant *adj* catégorique (**about** sur); **he is ~ that** il maintient que.

adapt I *vtr* adapter [*device, system, novel*] (**to** à; **for** pour; **from** de).
II *vi* [*person*] s'adapter (**to** à).

adaptable *adj* souple.

adapter, **adaptor** *n* adaptateur *m*.

add *vtr* **1** ajouter, rajouter (**onto, to** à); **to ~ that...** ajouter que...; **with ~ed vitamins** avec vitamines supplémentaires; **2** (also **~ together**) additionner [*numbers*]; **to ~ sth to** ajouter qch à [*figure, total*].
■ **add up**: ¶ **~ up** [*facts, figures*] s'accorder; **to ~ up to** [*total*] s'élever à [*number*]; ¶ **~ up [sth]** additionner [*cost, numbers*].

adder *n* (snake) vipère *f*.

addict *n* **1** (drug-user) toxicomane *mf*; **2** (of TV, coffee) accro○ *mf* (**of** de).

addicted *adj* **to be/become ~** (to alcohol, drugs) avoir/former une dépendance (**to** à); (to TV, coffee) être/devenir accro○ (**to** de).

addiction *n* dépendance *f* (**to** à).

addition I *n* **1** (to list, house) ajout *m*; (to team, range) adjonction *f*; **2** (in maths) addition *f*.
II **in addition** *phr* en plus.

additional *adj* supplémentaire.

additive *n* additif *m*.

address I *n* **1** adresse *f*; **to change (one's) ~** changer d'adresse; **2 form of ~ (for sb)** formule *f* pour s'adresser à qn.
II *vtr* **1** mettre l'adresse sur [*parcel, letter*]; **to ~ sth to sb** adresser qch à qn; **2** (speak to) s'adresser à [*group*]; **3** (aim) adresser [*remark, complaint*] (**to** à).

address book *n* carnet *m* d'adresses.

adenoids ▶523 *n pl* végétations *fpl* (adénoïdes).

adept *adj* expert.

adequate *adj* **1** (sufficient) [*funds, staff*] suffisant (**for** pour; **to do** pour faire); **2** (satisfactory) [*care, arrangements*] satisfaisant.

adhere *vi* **1** (stick) adhérer (**to** à); **2 to ~ to** adhérer à [*belief*]; observer [*policy, plan, standard*].

adhesive I *n* colle *f*, adhésif *m*.
II *adj* collant; **~ tape** papier *m* collant, Scotch® *m*; **self-~** auto-collant.

adjacent *adj* contigu/-uë; **~ to sth** attenant à qch.

adjective *n* adjectif *m*.

adjourn *vtr* ajourner [*trial*] (**for** pour; **until** à).

adjust I *vtr* régler [*component, level, position, speed*]; ajuster [*price, rate*]; rajuster [*clothing*]; modifier [*figures*].
II *vi* [*person*] s'adapter (**to** à); [*seat*] être réglable.
III **-adjusted** *combining form* **well-~ed** [*person*] équilibré.

adjustable *adj* [*appliance, seat*] réglable; [*rate*] ajustable.

adjustment *n* **1** (of rates, charges) rajustement *m* (**of** de); (of controls, machine) réglage *m* (**of** de); **2** (mental, physical) adaptation *f* (**to** à); **3** (modification) modification *f*; **to make ~s to** apporter des modifications à [*system, machine, lifestyle*]; rajuster [*garment*].

ad-lib *vtr, vi* improviser.

administer *vtr* (also **administrate**) gérer [*company, affairs, estate*]; gouverner [*territory*].

administration *n* **1** (of hospital, school, territory) administration *f*; **2** (of justice) exercice *m*; **3** (paperwork) travail *m* administratif.

administrative *adj* administratif/-ive.

administrator ▶805 *n* administrateur/-trice *m/f*.

admirable *adj* admirable.

admiral *n* amiral *m*.

admiration *n* admiration *f* (**for** pour).

admire *vtr* admirer; **to be ~d by sb** être admiré de qn.

admission *n* **1** (entry) entrée *f*, admission *f* (**to** dans); **'no ~'** 'entrée interdite'; **to refuse sb ~** refuser l'entrée à qn; **2** (fee) (droit *m* d')entrée *f*; **3** (confession) aveu *m*; **an ~ of guilt/weakness** un aveu de culpabilité/faiblesse.

admit *vtr* **1** reconnaître, admettre [*mistake, fact*]; **to ~ that...** reconnaître que...; **to ~ to** reconnaître [*mistake, fact*]; **2** (confess) avouer [*crime*]; reconnaître [*guilt*]; **to ~ to sth/doing** avouer qch/avoir fait; **3** (allow to enter) laisser entrer [*person*] (**into** dans); **to be ~ted to hospital** être hospitalisé; **4** [*club*] admettre [*person*] (**to** à).

admittance *n* accès *m*, entrée *f*; **'no ~'** 'accès interdit au public'.

admittedly *adv* il est vrai, il faut en convenir.

adolescent I *n* adolescent/-e *m/f*.
II *adj* **1** (teenage) [*crisis, rebellion*] d'adolescent; [*problem*] des adolescents; **2** [*humour, behaviour*] puéril.

adopt *vtr* adopter [*child, bill, idea, attitude*]; prendre [*tone, identity*].

adopted *adj* [*child*] adopté; [*son, daughter*] adoptif/-ive.

adoption *n* adoption *f*.

adorable *adj* adorable.

adore *vtr* adorer (**doing** faire).

adrenalin(e) *n* adrénaline *f*.

Adriatic (sea) *pr n* **the ~** la mer *f* Adriatique, l'Adriatique *f*.

adrift *adj, adv* [*person, boat*] à la dérive; **to come ~** se détacher (**of, from** de).

adult I *n* adulte *mf*.
II *adj* [*population, behaviour*] adulte; [*life*] d'adulte; [*film, magazine*] pour adultes.

Adult Education *n* (GB) enseignement *m* pour adultes.

adultery *n* adultère *m* (**with** avec).

advance I *n* **1** (forward movement) avance *f*; (of civilization, in science) progrès *m*; **2** (sum of money) avance *f*, acompte *m* (**on** sur); **3 to make ~s to sb** (sexually) faire des avances à qn.
II *vtr* **1** avancer [*sum of money*]; **2** faire avancer [*career, research*]; servir [*cause, interests*].
III *vi* **1** (move forward) [*person*] avancer, s'avancer (**on, towards** vers); (Mil) [*army*] avancer (**on** sur); **2** (progress) progresser, faire des progrès.
IV in advance *phr* à l'avance; **a month in ~** un mois à l'avance; **here's £30 in ~** voici 30 livres d'avance or d'acompte.

advanced *adj* [*course, class*] supérieur; [*student, stage*] avancé; [*equipment, technology*] de pointe, perfectionné.

advance: **~ payment** *n* avance *f*; **~ warning** *n* préavis *m*.

advantage *n* **1** avantage *m*; **there is an ~ in doing** il y a avantage à faire; **there is no ~ in doing** il n'est pas intéressant de faire; **it is to his/our ~ to do** il est dans son/notre intérêt de faire; **to turn a situation to one's ~** transformer une situation à son avantage; **to show sth to ~** montrer qch sous un jour avantageux; **2** (asset) atout *m*; **their big ~ is to have...** leur grand atout, c'est d'avoir...; **3 to take ~ of** utiliser, profiter de [*situation, offer, service*]; exploiter [*person*].

advantageous *adj* avantageux/-euse; **it would be ~** ce serait une bonne chose.

advent *n* (gen) apparition *f* (**of** de); **Advent** (prior to Christmas) l'Avent *m*.

adventure *n* aventure *f*.

adventurous *adj* aventureux/-euse.

adverb *n* adverbe *m*.

adverse *adj* [*reaction, conditions, publicity*] défavorable; [*effect, consequences*] négatif/-ive.

advert○ *n* (GB) (in newspaper) annonce *f*; (in small ads) petite annonce *f*; (on TV, radio) pub○ *f*, spot *m* publicitaire.

advertise I *vtr* faire de la publicité pour [*product, event, service*]; mettre or passer une annonce pour [*car, house, job*].
II *vi* **1** (for publicity) faire de la publicité; **2** (in small ads) passer une annonce.

advertisement *n* **1** (for product, event) publicité *f* (**for** pour); **a good/bad ~ for** une bonne/mauvaise publicité pour; **2** (to sell house, get job) annonce *f*; (in small ads) petite annonce *f*.

advertising *n* publicité *f*.

advice *n* conseils *mpl* (**on** sur; **about** à propos de); **my ~ is to wait** je vous conseille d'attendre; **a word** or **piece of ~** un conseil; **it was good ~** c'était un bon conseil; **to seek legal/medical ~** consulter un avocat/un médecin.

advisable *adj* **it is ~ to do** il est recommandé de faire.

advise *vtr* **1** (give advice to) conseiller, donner des conseils à (**about** sur); (give information to) renseigner (**about** sur); **to ~ sb to do** conseiller à qn de faire; **to ~ sb against doing sth** déconseiller à qn de faire qch; **2** recommander [*rest, course of action*].

adviser, **advisor** *n* conseiller/-ère *m/f* (**to** auprès de).

Aegean *pr n* **the ~** la mer Égée.

aerial I *n* antenne *f*; **satellite/TV ~** antenne parabolique/de télévision.
II *adj* [*photograph, view, warfare*] aérien/-ienne.

aerobics ▶ 649 *n* aérobic *m*.

aeroplane *n* (GB) avion *m*.

aerosol *n* bombe *f* aérosol.

aesthetic, **esthetic** (US) *adj* **1** [*sense, appeal*] esthétique; **2** [*design*] harmonieux/-ieuse.

affair *n* **1** affaire *f*; **foreign ~s** affaires étrangères; **the Haltrey ~** l'affaire Haltrey; **it's my ~** c'est mon affaire; **state of ~s** situation *f*; **2** (relationship) liaison *f* (**with** avec); (casual) aventure *f*.

affect *vtr* **1** (have effect on) avoir une incidence sur [*price, salary*]; affecter, avoir des conséquences pour [*career, future, environment*]; affecter, toucher [*region, population*]; (influence) influer sur [*decision, outcome*]; **politics ~s all of us** la politique nous concerne tous; **countries ~ed by the famine** les pays touchés par la famine; **2** (emotionally) [*experience, music*] émouvoir; [*news, discovery*] affecter; **3** (Med) atteindre [*person*]; affecter [*health, heart, lungs*].

affection *n* affection *f* (**for sb** pour qn).

affectionate *adj* [*child, animal*] affectueux/-euse; [*memory*] tendre.

affluent *adj* riche.

afford *vtr* **1** (financially) **to be able to ~ sth** avoir les moyens d'acheter qch; **if I can ~ it** si j'ai les moyens; **I can't ~ to pay the rent** je n'ai pas les moyens de payer le loyer; **can we ~ to stay in a hotel?** est-ce qu'on peut se permettre de descendre à l'hôtel?; **2** (spare) **to**

be able to ~ disposer de [*space, time*]; **3** (risk) **to be able to ~ sth/to do** se permettre qch/ de faire; **he can't ~ to wait** il ne peut pas se permettre d'attendre.

affordable *adj* [*price*] abordable; **~ for all** à la portée de toutes les bourses.

afield *adv* **far ~** loin; **further ~** plus loin.

afloat *adj, adv* **to stay ~** [*person, object*] rester à la surface (de l'eau); [*boat*] rester à flot.

afraid *adj* **1** (frightened) **to be ~** avoir peur (**of** de; **to do, of doing** de faire); **don't be ~** n'aie pas peur; **2** (anxious) **to be ~** craindre (**for sb** pour qn); **she was ~ (that) there would be an accident** elle craignait un accident; **I'm ~ it might rain** je crains qu'il (ne) pleuve; **3 I'm ~ I can't come** je suis désolé mais je ne peux pas venir; **'did they win?'—'I'm ~ not'** 'ont-ils gagné?'—'hélas, non'; **I'm ~ the house is in a mess** excusez le désordre dans la maison.

afresh *adv* à nouveau; **to start ~** recommencer; (in life) repartir à zéro.

Africa ▶574 *pr n* Afrique *f*; **to ~** en Afrique.

African I *n* Africain/-e *m/f*.
II *adj* africain; [*elephant*] d'Afrique.

after I *adv* après; **soon** or **not long ~** peu après; **straight ~** (GB), **right ~** (US) tout de suite après; **the year ~** l'année suivante or d'après; **the day ~** le lendemain.
II *prep* **1** après; **shortly ~ the strike** peu après la grève; **~ that date** (in future) au-delà de cette date; (in past) après cette date; **it was ~ six o'clock** il était plus de six heures; **~ that** après (cela); **the day ~ tomorrow** après-demain; **~ all we did!** après tout ce que nous avons fait!; **to tidy up ~ sb** ranger derrière qn; **to ask ~ sb** demander des nouvelles de qn; **~ you!** après vous!; **'~ Rubens'** 'd'après Rubens'; **2** (in pursuit of) **that's the house they're ~** c'est la maison qu'ils veulent acheter; **the police are ~ him** il est recherché par la police; **he'll come ~ me** il va essayer de me retrouver; **3 generation ~ generation** génération après génération; **year ~ year** tous les ans; **it was one disaster ~ another** on a eu catastrophe sur catastrophe; **4** (in honour or memory of) **named ~ James Joyce** [*street, institution*] portant le nom de James Joyce; **we called her Kate ~ my mother** nous l'avons appelée Kate comme ma mère; **5** (US) **it's twenty ~ eleven** il est onze heures vingt.
III *conj* **1** (in sequence of events) après avoir or être (+ *pp*), après que (+ *indic*); **~ we had left we realized that...** après être partis nous nous sommes rendu compte que...; **2 why did he do that ~ we'd warned him?** pourquoi a-t-il fait ça alors que nous l'avions prévenu?
IV after all *phr* après tout.

after: **~birth** *n* placenta *m*; **~-effect** *n* (Med) contrecoup *m*; (figurative) répercussion *f*.

afternoon ▶554 *n* après-midi *m* or *f inv*; **in the ~** (dans) l'après-midi; **at 2.30 in the ~** à 2 h 30 de l'après-midi; **in the early/late ~** en début/en fin d'après-midi; **every Saturday ~** tous les samedis après-midi.

afternoon tea *n* thé *m* (de cinq heures).

after: **~-shave** *n* après-rasage *m*; **~-sun** *adj* [*cream, lotion*] après-soleil *inv*.

afterwards, afterward (US) *adv* **1** (after) après; **not long ~** peu après; **directly/ straight ~** aussitôt/tout de suite après; **2** (later) plus tard; **it was only ~ that I noticed** ce n'est que plus tard que je m'en suis aperçu.

again *adv* encore;

■ **Note** When used with a verb, *again* is often translated by adding the prefix *re* to the verb in French: *to start again* = recommencer; *to marry again* = se remarier; *I'd like to read that book again* = j'aimerais relire ce livre; *she never saw them again* = elle ne les a jamais revus. You can check *re*+ verbs by consulting the French side of the dictionary.
– For other uses of *again*, see below.

---

sing it ~! chante-le encore!; **yet ~ he refused** il a encore refusé; **when you are well ~** quand tu seras rétabli; **I'll never go there ~** je n'y retournerai jamais; **never ~!** jamais plus!; **not ~!** encore!; **~ and ~** à plusieurs reprises; **~, you may think that** et là encore, vous pourriez penser que; **he may go, (and) then ~, he may not** il se peut qu'il y aille, mais il se peut aussi qu'il n'y aille pas.

against *prep*

■ **Note** *against* is translated by *contre* when it means *physically touching* or *in opposition to*: *against the wall* = contre le mur; *he's against independence* = il est contre l'indépendance; *the fight against inflation* = la lutte contre l'inflation.
– For examples and other usages, see the entry below.

---

1 contre; **~ the wall** contre le mur; **I'm ~ it** je suis contre; **I have nothing ~ it** je n'ai rien contre; **20 votes ~** 20 votes contre; **to be ~ the idea** s'opposer à l'idée; **to be ~ doing** être contre l'idée de faire; **the fight ~ inflation** la lutte contre l'inflation; **2 to go** or **be ~** aller à l'encontre de [*tradition, policy*]; [*conditions, decision*] ne pas être favorable à [*person*]; **3** (compared to) **the pound fell ~ the dollar** la livre a baissé par rapport au dollar; **the graph shows age ~ earnings** le graphique représente la courbe des salaires en fonction de l'âge; **4** (in contrast to) sur; **the blue looks pretty ~ the yellow** le bleu est joli sur le jaune; **~ a background of** sur un fond de; **~ the light** à contre-jour; **5** (in exchange for) contre, en échange de.

age ▶492 **I** *n* **1** âge *m*; **she's your ~** elle a ton âge; **to look one's ~** faire son âge; **to be of school ~** être en âge d'aller à l'école; **men of retirement ~** les hommes en âge de la retraite; **to come of ~** atteindre la majorité; **to be under ~** (Law) être mineur/-e; **2** (era) ère *f*, époque *f* (**of** de); **the video ~** l'ère de la vidéo; **in this day and ~** à notre époque; **3**° **it's ~s since I've played golf** ça fait une éternité que je n'ai pas joué au golf; **I've been waiting for ~s** j'attends depuis des heures; **it takes ~s** cela prend un temps fou.
II *vtr, vi* vieillir.

aged *adj* **1 ~ between 20 and 25** âgé/-e de 20

after

As a preposition or an adverb

⇨ I.II

When *after* is used as a preposition or an adverb, it is usually translated by *après:*

*three weeks **after***	= trois semaines **après**
***after** the meal*	= **après** le repas

As a conjunction

Referring to the past

◆ When the two verbs have the same subject, *after* + *verb* is usually translated by ***après*** + *past infinitive* (*past infinitive = auxiliary verb + past participle,* eg avoir mangé, être tombé etc).

For more information on the auxiliary verbs, see the note for **have**.

***after** he had consulted Bill* or ***after** consulting Bill, he left*	= **après** avoir consulté Bill, il est parti
***after** he fell in love with her* or ***after** falling in love with her, he moved to London*	= **après** être tombé amoureux d'elle, il a déménagé à Londres.
***after** she had showered* or ***after** showering, she went out again*	= **après** s'être douchée, elle est ressortie

◆ When the two verbs have different subjects, *after* + *verb* is usually translated by ***après que*** + *indicative* (***après qu'*** before a vowel or mute 'h'):

***after** he phoned us, we went to pick him up*	= **après qu'**il nous eut téléphoné, nous sommes allés le chercher en voiture
*Jane went back to work **after** George had finished his studies*	= Jane a repris le travail **après que** George eut terminé ses études
***after** he had changed, she brought him to the office*	= **après qu'**il se fut changé, elle le conduisit au bureau

◆ When there is a corresponding noun for many of these verbs – *mourir/mort, partir/départ, se marier/mariage, se doucher/douche* etc – the construction ***après*** + *noun* is generally preferred by French native speakers, especially where the subjects differ:

*we went in **after** the film had started*	= nous sommes entrés **après** le début du film
***after** their son was born, they left Paris*	= ils ont quitté Paris **après** la naissance de leur fils
*they gave us the house **after** we married*	= ils nous ont donné la maison **après** notre mariage

Referring to the future

If the English refers to an event in the future, the translation is more likely to be ***quand*** or ***une fois que*** + *indicative* (***une fois qu'*** before a vowel or mute 'h'):

***after** I've finished my book, I'll leave*	= je partirai **quand** j'aurai fini mon livre *or* je partirai **une fois que** j'aurai fini mon livre
*I'll lend it to you **after** Fred has read it*	= je te le prêterai **quand** Fred l'aura lu *or* je te le prêterai **une fois que** Fred l'aura lu

⇨ III

❑ See also the usage note on **The Clock**, ▶ 554

Age

Note that where English says ***to be X years old***, French says ***avoir X ans*** (*to have X years*).

How old?

how old ***are you****?*	= quel âge **as-tu**?
what age ***is she****?*	= quel âge **a-t-elle**?

The word ***ans*** (*years*) is never dropped:

he is forty years old *he is forty* *he is forty years of age*	= il a quarante **ans**
the house is a hundred years old	= la maison a cent **ans**
a man of fifty	= un homme de cinquante **ans**
he looks sixteen	= on lui donnerait seize **ans**

Note the use of ***de*** after ***âgé*** and ***à l'âge***:

a woman aged thirty	= une femme âgée **de** trente ans
at the age of forty	= à l'âge **de** quarante ans

Do not confuse ***que*** and ***de*** used with ***plus*** and ***moins***:

I'm older ***than*** *you*	= je suis plus âgé **que** toi
she's younger ***than*** *him*	= elle est plus jeune **que** lui
Anne's two years ***younger***	= Anne a deux ans **de moins**
Margot's five years ***older than*** *Suzanne*	= Margot a cinq ans **de plus que** Suzanne

X-year-old

a forty-year-old	= quelqu'un de quarante ans
a sixty-year-old woman	= une femme de soixante ans

Approximate ages

Note the various ways of saying these in French:

he is ***about*** *fifty*	= il a **environ** cinquante ans = il **a une cinquantaine d'**années = (*less formally*) il **a dans les** cinquante ans

Other round numbers in ***-aine*** used to express age are ***dizaine*** (10), ***vingtaine*** (20), ***trentaine*** (30), ***quarantaine*** (40), ***soixantaine*** (60) and ***centaine*** (100).

she's just over sixty	= elle vient d'avoir soixante ans
she's just under seventy	= elle aura bientôt soixante-dix ans
she's in her sixties	= elle a entre soixante et soixante-dix ans
she's in her early sixties	= elle a entre soixante et soixante-cinq ans
she's in her late sixties	= elle va avoir soixante-dix ans = (*less formally*) elle va sur ses soixante-dix ans
he's in his mid-forties	= il a environ quarante-cinq ans = (*less formally*) il a dans les quarante-cinq ans
he's ***just*** *ten*	= il a **tout juste** dix ans
games for ***the under*** *twelves*	= jeux pour **les moins de** douze ans
only for ***the over*** *eighties*	= seulement pour **les plus de** quatre-vingts ans

à 25 ans; **a boy ~ 12** un garçon de 12 ans; **2** (old) âgé.

age group *n* tranche *f* d'âge.

agency *n* agence *f*.

agenda *n* **1** (for meeting) ordre *m* du jour; **on the ~** à l'ordre du jour; **2** (list of priorities) programme *m*.

agent *n* agent *m* (**for sb** de qn).

aggression *n* (gen) agression *f*; (of person) agressivité *f*.

aggressive *adj* agressif/-ive.

agile *adj* agile.

agitate *vi* faire campagne (**for** pour).

agitated *adj* agité, inquiet.

agitation *n* agitation *f*.

AGM *n* (*abbr* = **annual general meeting**) assemblée *f* générale annuelle.

agnostic *n, adj* agnostique (*mf*).

ago *adv* **three weeks ~** il y a trois semaines; **some time/long ~** il y a quelque temps/longtemps; **how long ~?** il y a combien de temps?; **not long ~** il y a peu de temps; **as long ~ as 1786** dès 1786, déjà en 1786; **they got married forty years ~ today** cela fait quarante ans aujourd'hui qu'ils sont mariés.

agonize *vi* se tourmenter (**over, about** à propos de).

agony *n* (physical) douleur *f* atroce; (mental) angoisse *f*.

agoraphobia *n* agoraphobie *f*.

agree I *vtr* **1** (concur) être d'accord (**that** sur le fait que); **2** (admit) convenir (**that** que); **I ~ it sounds unlikely** ça a l'air peu probable, j'en conviens; **3** (consent) **to ~ to do** accepter de faire; **she ~d to speak to me** elle a accepté de me parler; **4** (settle on, arrange) se mettre d'accord sur [*date, price*]; **to ~ to do** convenir de faire.

II *vi* **1** (hold same opinion) être d'accord (**with** avec; **about, on** sur; **about doing** pour faire); **'I ~!'** 'je suis bien d'accord!'; **2** (reach mutual understanding) se mettre d'accord, tomber d'accord (**about, on** sur); **3** (consent) accepter; **to ~ to** consentir à [*plan , suggestion, terms*]; **4** (hold with, approve) **to ~ with** approuver [*belief, idea, practice*]; **5** (tally) [*stories, statements, figures*] concorder (**with** avec); **6** (suit) **to ~ with sb** [*climate, weather*] être bon pour qn; [*food*] réussir à qn; **7** (in grammar) s'accorder (**with** avec; **in** en).

III agreed *pp adj* convenu; **is that ~d?** c'est entendu?

agreeable *adj* agréable.

agreement *n* **1** accord *m* (**to do** pour faire); **to come to** or **reach an ~** parvenir à un accord; **to be in ~ with sb** être d'accord avec qn; **2** (undertaking) engagement *m* (**to do** à faire); **3** (contract) contrat *m*; **4** (in grammar) accord *m*.

agricultural *adj* [*land, worker*] agricole; [*expert*] agronome.

agriculture *n* agriculture *f*.

aground *adv* **to run ~** s'échouer.

ahead I *adv* **1** [*run*] en avant; **to send sb on ~** envoyer qn en éclaireur; **to send one's luggage on ~** faire envoyer ses bagages; **a few kilometres ~** à quelques kilomètres; **2** (in time) **in the months ~** pendant les mois à venir; **who knows what lies ~?** qui sait ce que l'avenir nous réserve?; **3** (in leading position) **to be ~ in the polls** être en tête dans les sondages; **to be 30 points ~** avoir 30 points d'avance; **to be 3% ~** avoir une avance de 3%.

II ahead of *phr* **1** (in front of) devant [*person, vehicle*]; **to be three metres/seconds ~ of sb** avoir trois mètres/secondes d'avance sur qn; **~ of time** en avance; **to be ~ of one's time** être en avance sur son temps; **2 to be ~ of sb** (in polls, ratings) avoir un avantage sur qn; **to be (way) ~ of the others** [*pupil*] être (bien) plus avancé que les autres; **to be ~ of the field** [*business*] devancer les autres.

aid I *n* aide *f* (**from** de; **to, for** à); **to come to sb's ~** venir en aide à qn; **in ~ of** au profit de [*charity*].

II *noun modifier* [*programme, organization*] d'entraide.

III *vtr* aider [*person*] (**to do** à faire); faciliter [*digestion, recovery*].

IV *vi* (Law) **charged with ~ing and abetting** accusé de complicité.

aide *n* aide *mf*, assistant/-e *m/f*.

Aids *n* (*abbr* = **Acquired Immune Deficiency Syndrome**) sida *m*.

aim I *n* **1** (purpose) but *m*; **with the ~ of doing** dans le but de faire; **2** (with weapon) **to take ~ at sth/sb** viser qch/qn; **his ~ is bad** il vise mal.

II *vtr* **1 to be ~ed at sb** [*campaign, product, remark*] viser qn; **to be ~ed at doing** [*effort, action*] viser à faire; **2** braquer [*gun*] (**at** sur); lancer [*ball, stone*] (**at** sur); tenter de donner [*blow, kick*] (**at** à); **well-~ed** [*blow, kick*] bien placé.

III *vi* **to ~ for sth, to ~ at sth** viser qch; **to ~ at doing, to ~ to do** (try) s'efforcer de faire; (intend) avoir l'intention de faire.

air I *n* **1** air *m*; **in the open ~** en plein air, au grand air; **I need a change of ~** j'ai besoin de changer d'air; **to let the ~ out of sth** dégonfler qch; **he threw the ball up into the ~** il a jeté le ballon en l'air; **2 by ~** par avion; **Paris (seen) from the ~** Paris vu d'avion; **3** (on radio, TV) **to be/go on the ~** [*broadcaster, interviewee*] être/passer à l'antenne.

II *vtr* **1** (dry) faire sécher [*clothes*]; (freshen) aérer [*garment, room, bed*]; **that shirt hasn't been ~ed** cette chemise n'est pas complètement sèche; **2** (express) exprimer [*opinion, view*]; **to ~ one's grievances** exposer ses griefs.

IDIOMS **to put on ~s** se donner de grands airs; **to vanish into thin ~** se volatiliser.

air: **~ bag** *n* airbag *m*; **~ bed** *n* (GB) matelas *m* pneumatique; **~ brake** *n* frein *m* à air comprimé; **~-conditioned** *adj* climatisé; **~-conditioning** *n* climatisation *f*, air *m* conditionné; **~craft** *n* avion *m*, aéronef *m*; **~crew** *n* équipage *m* (d'un avion); **~fare** *n* tarif *m* d'avion; **~field** *n* aérodrome *m*, terrain *m* d'aviation; **~ force** *n* armée *f* de l'air, forces *fpl* aériennes; **~-freshener** *n* désodorisant *m* d'atmosphère; **~ gun** *n* fusil *m* or carabine *f* à air comprimé; **~ hostess** ▶ 805 *n* hôtesse *f* de l'air; **~line** *n* compagnie *f* aérienne; **~liner** *n* avion *m* de ligne.

airmail I *n* poste *f* aérienne; **by ~** par avion.
II *noun modifier* [*envelope, paper*] par avion.

air: **~plane** *n* (US) avion *m*; **~port** *n* aéroport *m*; **~sickness** *n* mal *m* de l'air; **~ terminal** *n* (at airport) aérogare *f*; (in town: terminus) terminal *m*; **~tight** *adj* étanche à l'air; **~-traffic controller** ▶ 805 *n* contrôleur/-euse *m/f* aérien/-ienne, aiguilleur *m* du ciel.

airy *adj* **1** [*room*] clair/-e et spacieux/-ieuse; **2** (casual) [*manner*] désinvolte, insouciant.

aisle *n* **1** (in church) (side passage) bas-côté *m*; (centre passage) allée *f* centrale; **2** (in train, plane) couloir *m*; (in cinema, shop) allée *f*.

ajar *adj, adv* entrouvert, entrebaillé.

alarm I *n* **1** (fear) frayeur *f*; (concern) inquiétude *f*; **there is no cause for ~** inutile de s'inquiéter; **2** (warning) alarme *f*; **smoke ~** détecteur *m* de fumée; **to raise the ~** donner l'alarme.
II *vtr* inquiéter [*person*].

alarm: **~ bell** *n* sonnette *f* d'alarme; **~ call** *n* réveil *m* par téléphone; **~ clock** *n* réveille-matin *m*, réveil *m*.

alarmed *adj* effrayé; **don't be ~!** rassurez-vous!

Albania ▶ 574 *pr n* Albanie *f*.

album *n* album *m*.

alcohol *n* alcool *m*; **~-free** sans alcool.

alcoholic I *n* alcoolique *mf*.
II *adj* [*drink*] alcoolisé; [*stupor*] alcoolique.

alcove *n* renfoncement *m*.

alder *n* aulne *m*.

ale *n* bière *f*; **brown/light/pale ~** bière brune/légère/blonde.

alert I *n* alerte *f*; **to be on the ~ for** se méfier de [*danger*]; **bomb ~** alerte à la bombe; **security ~** alerte de sécurité.
II *adj* **1** (lively) [*child*] éveillé; [*adult*] alerte; **2** (attentive) vigilant.
III *vtr* **1** alerter [*authorities*]; **2 to ~ sb to** mettre qn en garde contre [*danger*]; attirer l'attention de qn sur [*fact, situation*].

A-levels (GB Sch) *n pl*: *examen de fin de cycle secondaire*, ≈ baccalauréat *m*.

algebra *n* algèbre *f*.

Algeria ▶ 574 *pr n* Algérie *f*.

alibi *n* **1** (Law) alibi *m*; **2** (excuse) excuse *f*.

alien *n* **1** (gen, Law) étranger/-ère *m/f* (**to** à); **2** (from space) extraterrestre *mf*.

alienate *vtr* éloigner [*supporters, colleagues*].

alienation *n* (process) éloignement *m* (**of** de); (state) isolement *m* (**from** de).

alight I *adj* **to be ~** [*building*] être en feu; **to set sth ~** mettre le feu à qch.
II *vi* [*passenger*] descendre (**from** de); [*bird*] se poser (**on** sur).

alike I *adj* (identical) pareil/-eille; (similar) semblable; **to look ~** se ressembler.
II *adv* [*dress, think*] de la même façon; **for young and old ~** pour les jeunes (tout) comme pour les personnes âgées.

alimony *n* pension *f* alimentaire.

alive *adj* **1** vivant, en vie; **to be ~** être vivant; **to be burnt ~** être brûlé/-e vif/vive; **~ and well**, **~ and kicking** bien vivant; **2 to come ~** [*party, place*] s'animer; [*history*] prendre vie; **3 to be ~** [*art, tradition*] être vivant; [*interest, faith*] être vif/vive; **4** (teeming) **~ with** grouillant de [*insects*].

alkaline *adj* alcalin.

all

■ **Note** When *all* is used as a pronoun, it is generally translated by *tout*.
– When *all* is followed by a *that* clause, *all that* is translated by *tout ce que*: *after all (that) we've done* = après tout ce que nous avons fait.
– When referring to a specified group of people or objects, the translation of *all* reflects the number and gender of the people or objects referred to; *tous* is used for a group of people or objects of masculine or mixed or unspecified gender and *toutes* for a group of feminine gender: *we were all delighted* = nous étions tous ravis; *'where are the cups?'—'they're all in the kitchen'* = 'où sont les tasses?'—'elles sont toutes dans la cuisine'. ▶ I
– In French, determiners agree in gender and number with the noun that follows: *all the time* = tout le temps; *all the family* = toute la famille; *all men* = tous les hommes; *all the books* = tous les livres; *all women* = toutes les femmes; *all the chairs* = toutes les chaises. ▶ II
– As an adverb meaning *completely*, *all* is generally translated by *tout*: *he was all alone* = il était tout seul; *the girls were all excited* = les filles étaient tout excitées.
– However, when the adjective that follows is in the feminine and begins with a consonant the translation is *toute/toutes*: *she was all alone* = elle était toute seule; *the girls were all alone* = les filles étaient toutes seules. ▶ III1
– For more examples and particular usages see the entry below.

I *pron* tout; **to risk ~** tout risquer; **that's ~** c'est tout; **500 in ~** 500 en tout; **that's ~ I want** c'est tout ce que je veux; **~ I know is that he's German** tout ce que je sais c'est qu'il est allemand; **I spent it ~**, **I spent ~ of it** j'ai tout dépensé; **we ~ feel that it's unfair** nous pensons tous que c'est injuste; **they've ~ had babies** elles ont toutes eu des enfants; **~ in ~** somme toute.
II *det* (+ *singular noun*) tout/toute; (+ *plural noun*) tous/toutes; **~ those who came** (men, mixed group) tous ceux qui sont venus; (women) toutes celles qui sont venues; **~ his life** toute sa vie; **~ year round** toute l'année; **in ~ honesty** en toute franchise; **beyond ~ expectations** au-delà de toute attente.
III *adv* **1** (emphatic) tout; **~ alone** tout seul; **she's ~ wet** elle est toute mouillée; **~ in white** tout en blanc; **~ along the canal** tout le long du canal; **to be ~ for sth** être tout à fait pour qch; **tell me ~ about it!** raconte-moi tout!; **he's forgotten ~ about us!** il nous a

complètement oubliés!; **2** (Sport) **(they are) six ~** (il y a) six partout.
IV all along *phr* [*know*] depuis le début, toujours.
V all that *phr* **I don't know her ~ that well** je ne la connais pas si bien que ça.
VI all the *phr* **~ the more difficult** d'autant plus difficile; **~ the better!** tant mieux!
VII all too *phr* [*easy, often*] bien trop.
VIII at all *phr* **not at ~!** (acknowledging thanks) de rien!; (answering query) pas du tout!; **it is not at ~ certain** ce n'est pas du tout certain; **if (it is) at ~ possible** si possible; **nothing at ~** rien du tout.
IX of all *phr* **the easiest of ~** le plus facile; **first of ~** pour commencer; **why today of ~ days?** pourquoi justement aujourd'hui?
IDIOMS **he's not ~ there**○ il n'a pas toute sa tête; **it's ~ very well to complain** c'est bien beau de se plaindre.

all clear *n* **to give sb the ~** donner le feu vert à qn (**to do** pour faire).

allegation *n* allégation *f* (**about** sur; **that** selon laquelle).

allege *vtr* **to ~ that** (claim) prétendre que (+ *conditional*); (publicly) déclarer que (+ *conditional*); **it was ~d that** il a été dit que.

allegedly *adv* prétendument.

allegiance *n* allégeance *f*.

allergic *adj* allergique (**to** à).

allergy *n* allergie *f* (**to** à).

alleviate *vtr* soulager [*boredom, pain*]; réduire [*overcrowding, stress*].

alley *n* (walkway) allée *f*; (for vehicles) ruelle *f*.

alliance *n* alliance *f*.

all: **~-inclusive** *adj* [*fee, price*] tout compris; **~-in-one** *adj* [*garment*] d'une seule pièce; **~-night** *adj* [*party, meeting*] qui dure toute la nuit; [*service*] ouvert toute la nuit; [*radio station*] qui émet 24 heures sur 24.

allocate *vtr* affecter [*funds*] (**for, to** à); accorder [*time*] (**to** à); assigner, attribuer [*tasks*] (**to** à).

allot *vtr* attribuer [*money*] (**to** à); assigner [*task*] (**to** à); **in the ~ted time** dans le temps imparti.

allotment *n* (GB) parcelle *f* de terre.

all-out *adj* [*strike*] total; [*attack*] en règle; [*effort*] acharné.

all over I *adj* fini; **when it's ~** quand tout sera fini.
II *adv* (everywhere) partout; **to be trembling ~** trembler de partout.
III *prep* partout dans [*room, town*]; **~ China** partout en Chine; **the news is ~ the village** la nouvelle s'est répandue dans tout le village; **to be ~ sb** être aux petits soins pour qn.

allow *vtr* **1** (authorize) autoriser [*person, organization*] (**to do** à faire); autoriser [*action, change*]; **she isn't ~ed alcohol** l'alcool lui est interdit; **2** (let) laisser; **he ~ed the situation to get worse** il a laissé la situation s'aggraver; **I ~ed myself to be persuaded** je me suis laissé persuader; **3** (enable) **to ~ sb/sth to do** permettre à qn/qch de faire; **it would ~ the company to expand** cela permettrait à la société de s'agrandir; **~ me!** permettez(-moi)!; **4** (allocate) prévoir; **to ~ two days for the job** prévoir deux jours pour faire le travail; **5** [*referee*] accorder [*goal*]; [*insurer*] agréer [*claim*]; [*supplier*] accorder, consentir [*discount*]; **6** [*club*] admettre [*non-member*]; **'no dogs ~ed'** 'interdit aux chiens'; **7** (condone) tolérer [*rudeness, swearing*].
■ **allow for**: **~ for [sth]** tenir compte de [*delays, wastage*].

allowance *n* **1** (gen) allocation *f*; (from employer) indemnité *f*; **2 (tax) ~** abattement *m* fiscal; **3** (spending money) (for child) argent *m* de poche; (for student) argent *m* (pour vivre); (from trust, guardian) rente *f*; **4 your baggage ~ is 40 kgs** vous avez droit à 40 kg de bagages; **5 to make ~(s) for sth** tenir compte de qch; **to make ~(s) for sb** essayer de comprendre qn.

all right, alright I *adj* **1** [*film, garment, place*] pas mal○; **she's ~** (pleasant) elle est plutôt sympa○; (attractive) elle n'est pas mal○; (competent) son travail est correct; **'how did the interview go?'—'~'** 'comment s'est passé ton entretien?'—'pas trop mal', **is my hair ~?** ça va mes cheveux?; **2** (well) **to feel ~** aller bien; **3** (able to manage) **will you be ~?** est-ce que ça va aller?; **to be ~ for** avoir assez de [*money*]; **4** (acceptable) **is it ~ if...?** est-ce que ça va si...?; **would it be ~ to leave early?** est-ce que c'est gênant si on s'en va plus tôt?; **is that ~ with you?** ça ne te dérange pas?; **that's (quite) ~!** ce n'est rien du tout!
II *adv* [*work*] comme il faut; [*see, hear*] bien; **she's doing ~** (doing well) tout va bien pour elle; (managing to cope) elle s'en tire correctement; **she knows ~!** bien sûr qu'elle sait!
III *particle* d'accord.

all-round *adj* [*athlete*] complet/-ète; [*improvement*] général.

all told *adv* en tout.

allusion *n* allusion *f* (**to** à).

ally I *n* allié/-e *m/f*.
II *v refl* **to ~ oneself with** s'allier avec.

almond *n* **1** (nut) amande *f*; **2** (also **~ tree**) amandier *m*.

almost *adv* **1** (practically) presque; **~ any train** presque tous les trains; **we're ~ there** nous sommes presque arrivés; **it's ~ dark** il fait presque nuit; **2** (implying narrow escape) **he ~ died** il a failli mourir; **I ~ forgot** j'ai failli oublier.

alone I *adj* seul; **all ~** tout/-e seul/-e; **to leave sb ~** laisser qn seul; (in peace) laisser qn tranquille; **leave that bike ~!** ne touche pas à ce vélo!; **she is not ~ in thinking that...** elle n'est pas la seule à penser que...; **to stand ~** [*person*] se tenir seul; (figurative) être sans égal.
II *adv* **1** [*work, live, travel*] seul/-e; **2 for this reason ~** rien que pour cette raison; **this figure ~ shows** le chiffre à lui seul montre.
IDIOMS **to go it ~**○ faire cavalier seul.

along

■ **Note** When *along* is used as a preposition meaning *all along* it can usually be translated by *le long*

de: *there were trees along the road* = il y avait des arbres le long de la route. For particular usages see the entry below.
– *along* is often used after verbs of movement. If the addition of *along* does not change the meaning of the verb, *along* will not be translated: *as he walked along* = tout en marchant.

I *adv* **to push/pull sth ~** pousser/tirer qch; **to be walking ~** marcher; **I'll be ~ in a second** j'arrive tout de suite.
II *prep* **1** (all along) le long de; **there were chairs ~ the wall** il y avait des chaises contre le mur; **2 to walk ~ the beach** marcher sur la plage; **to look ~ the shelves** chercher dans les rayons; **somewhere ~ the motorway** quelque part sur l'autoroute; **halfway ~ the path** à mi-chemin.
III **along with** *phr* (accompanied by) accompagné de; (at same time as) en même temps que.

alongside I *prep* **1** (all along) le long de; **2 to draw up ~ sb** [*vehicle*] s'arrêter à la hauteur de qn; **to learn to live ~ each other** [*groups*] apprendre à coexister.
II *adv* à côté.

aloud *adv* [*read*] à haute voix; [*think*] tout haut.

alphabet *n* alphabet *m*.

alphabetically *adv* [*list*] par ordre alphabétique.

alpine *adj* (also **Alpine**) alpin.

Alps *pr n pl* **the ~** les Alpes *fpl*.

already *adv* déjà; **it's 10 o'clock ~** il est déjà 10 heures; **he's ~ left** il est déjà parti.

alright = **all right**.

Alsatian *n* (GB) (dog) berger *m* allemand.

also *adv* **1** aussi; **~ available in red** existe aussi en rouge; **it is ~ worth remembering that**... il serait bon aussi de ne pas oublier que...; **2** (furthermore) **~, he snores** en plus il ronfle.

alter I *vtr* **1** changer [*person*]; (radically) transformer [*person*]; changer [*opinion, rule, timetable*]; modifier [*amount, document*]; affecter [*value, climate*]; **that does not ~ the fact that** cela ne change rien au fait que; **to ~ the appearance of sth** changer l'aspect de qch; **2** retoucher [*dress, shirt*].
II *vi* changer.

alteration I *n* modification *f* (**to, in** de).
II **alterations** *n pl* (building work) travaux *mpl*.

alternate I *adj* **1** (successive) [*chapters, layers*] en alternance; **2** (every other) **on ~ days** un jour sur deux; **3** (US) (other) autre.
II *vtr* **to ~ sth and** or **with sth** alterner qch et qch.
III *vi* [*people*] se relayer; [*colours, patterns, seasons*] alterner (**with** avec); **to ~ between hope and despair** passer de l'espoir au désespoir.

alternately *adv* [*move, bring, ask*] alternativement; **they criticize and praise him ~** tantôt ils le critiquent, tantôt ils le félicitent.

alternative I *n* **1** (specified option) (from two) alternative *f*, autre possibilité *f*; (from several) possibilité *f*; **one ~ is**... une des possibilités serait...; **the ~ is to do** l'autre possibilité serait de faire; **2** (possible option) choix *m*; **to have no ~** ne pas avoir le choix.
II *adj* **1** [*date, flight, method, plan*] autre; [*accommodation, product*] de remplacement; [*solution*] de rechange; **2** (unconventional) alternatif/-ive.

alternatively *adv* sinon; **~, you can book by phone** vous avez aussi la possibilité de réserver par téléphone.

alternative medicine *n* médecines *fpl* parallèles or douces.

although *conj* **1** (in spite of the fact that) bien que (+ *subj*); **~ he is shy** bien qu'il soit timide; **they're generous, ~ poor** ils sont généreux, quoique pauvres; **2** (but, however) mais; **you don't have to attend, ~ we advise it** vous n'êtes pas obligés de venir, mais nous vous le conseillons.

altitude *n* altitude *f*.

alto *n* **1** (voice) (of female) contralto *m*; (of male) haute-contre *f*; **2** (singer) (female) contralto *f*; (male) haute-contre *m*.

altogether *adv* **1** (completely) complètement; **not ~ true** pas complètement vrai; **that's another matter ~** c'est une tout autre histoire; **2** (in total) en tout; **how much is that ~?** ça fait combien en tout?; **3** (all things considered) **~, it was a mistake** tout compte fait, c'était une erreur.

aluminium foil *n* papier *m* aluminium.

always *adv* toujours; **he's ~ complaining** il n'arrête pas de se plaindre.

am ▶ 554 *adv* (*abbr* = **ante meridiem**) **three ~** trois heures (du matin).

amalgamate *vtr*, *vi* fusionner.

amateur I *n* amateur *m*.
II *noun modifier* [*sportsperson, musician, drama*] amateur; [*sport*] en amateur.

amaze *vtr* surprendre; (stronger) stupéfier.

amazed *adj* stupéfait; **I'm ~ (that)** ça m'étonne que (+ *subj*).

amazement *n* stupéfaction *f*; **in ~** avec stupéfaction; **to my ~** à ma grande surprise.

amazing *adj* extraordinaire.

Amazon *pr n* Amazone *m*.

ambassador ▶ 642 *n* ambassadeur *m*.

ambiguous *adj* ambigu/-uë.

ambition *n* ambition *f* (**to do** de faire); **it was her lifelong ~ to visit Japan** son rêve de toujours était de visiter le Japon.

ambitious *adj* ambitieux/-ieuse.

ambulance I *n* ambulance *f*.
II *noun modifier* [*service, station*] d'ambulances; **~ crew** équipe *f* d'ambulanciers/-ières.

ambush I *n* embuscade *f*.
II *vtr* tendre une embuscade à [*soldiers*]; **to be ~ed** être pris en embuscade.

amenable *adj* souple; **~ to** [*person*] sensible à [*reason, advice*].

amend *vtr* amender [*law*]; modifier [*document*].

amendment *n* (to law) amendement *m* (**to** à); (to contract) modification *f* (**to** à).

amends *n pl* **1 to make ~ for** réparer

[*damage, hurt*]; **to make ~ to sb** (financially) dédommager qn; **2 to make ~** (redeem oneself) se racheter.

amenities *n pl* (of hotel) équipements *mpl*; (of house, sports club) installations *fpl*.

America ▶574 *pr n* Amérique *f*.

American ▶712 **I** *n* **1** (person) Américain/-e *m/f*; **2** (also **~ English**) américain *m*.
II *adj* [*people, politics*] américain; [*ambassador, embassy*] des États-Unis.

amiable *adj* [*person*] aimable (**to** or **towards** avec); [*mood*] plaisant.

amiss I *adj* **there is something ~** il y a quelque chose qui ne va pas.
II *adv* **to take sth ~** prendre qch de travers; **a drink wouldn't go ~!** un verre ne serait pas de refus.

ammunition *n* (Mil) munitions *fpl*; (figurative) armes *fpl*.

amnesty *n* amnistie *f*.

among, amongst *prep* **1** (amidst) parmi; **~ the crowd** parmi la foule; **to be ~ friends** être entre amis; **2** (affecting group) chez; **unemployment ~ young people** le chômage chez les jeunes; **3** (one of) **~ the world's poorest countries** un des pays les plus pauvres du monde; **she was ~ those who survived** elle faisait partie des survivants; **to be ~ the first** être dans les premiers; **4** (between) entre; **divided ~ his heirs** partagés entre ses héritiers; **one bottle ~ five** une bouteille pour cinq.

amount *n* **1** (of goods, food) quantité *f*; (of people, objects) nombre *m*; **a considerable/fair ~ of** beaucoup/pas mal de°; **2** (sum of money) somme *f*; (bill) montant *m*; **the full ~** le montant total; **what is the outstanding ~?** combien reste-t-il à payer?
■ **amount to**: **~ to [sth] 1** s'élever à [*total*]; **2** (be equivalent to) revenir à [*confession, betrayal*]; **it ~s to the same thing** cela revient au même; **it ~s to blackmail!** ce n'est rien d'autre que du chantage!

amp *n* **1** (*abbr* = **ampere**) ampère *m*; **2°** (*abbr* = **amplifier**) ampli° *m*.

ample *adj* **1** [*provisions, resources*] largement suffisant (**for** pour); **there's ~ room** il y a largement la place; **he was given ~ warning** il a été largement prévenu; **2** [*proportions, bust*] généreux/-euse.

amplifier *n* amplificateur *m*.

amputate *vtr* amputer; **to ~ sb's leg** amputer qn de la jambe.

amuse I *vtr* **1** (cause laughter) amuser; **to be ~d at** or **by** s'amuser de; **2** (entertain) [*game, story*] distraire; **3** (occupy) [*activity, hobby*] occuper.
II *v refl* **to ~ oneself 1** (entertain) se distraire; **2** (occupy) s'occuper.

amusement *n* **1** (mirth) amusement *m* (**at** face à); **2** (diversion) distraction *f*; **for ~** pour me/se etc distraire.

amusement: **~ arcade** *n* (GB) salle *f* de jeux électroniques; **~ park** *n* parc *m* d'attractions.

amusements *n pl* (at fairground) attractions *fpl*.

amusing *adj* amusant.

an ▶ **a²**.

anachronism *n* anachronisme *m*.

anaesthetic (GB), **anesthetic** (US) *n, adj* anesthésique (*m*); **to be under ~** être sous anesthésie.

analyse (GB), **analyze** (US) *vtr* analyser.

analysis *n* analyse *f*; **in the final** or **last ~** en fin de compte.

analytic(al) *adj* analytique.

anatomy *n* anatomie *f*.

ancestor *n* ancêtre *mf*.

anchor I *n* ancre *f*; **to drop ~** jeter l'ancre.
II *vtr* ancrer [*ship, balloon*]; arrimer [*tent*].

anchovy *n* anchois *m*.

ancient *adj* (dating from BC) antique; (very old) ancien/-ienne; **~ Greek** grec ancien; **~ Greece** la Grèce antique; **~ monument** monument *m* historique.

and *conj* **1** (joining words or clauses) et; **cups ~ plates** des tasses et des assiettes; **he stood up ~ went out** il s'est levé et il est sorti; **~ all that** et tout le reste; **~ so on** et ainsi de suite; **~?** et alors?; **2** (in numbers) **two hundred ~ sixty-two** deux cent soixante-deux; **3** (with repetition) **faster ~ faster** de plus en plus vite; **to talk on ~ on** parler pendant des heures; **4** (in phrases) **it's lovely ~ warm** il fait bon; **come nice ~ early** viens tôt; **summer ~ winter** été comme hiver; **day ~ night** jour et nuit.

Andorra ▶574 *pr n* Andorre *f*.

angel *n* ange *m*.

anger I *n* colère *f* (**at** devant; **towards** contre).
II *vtr* mettre [qn] en colère [*person*].

angle I *n* angle *m*; **camera ~** angle de vue; **to be at an ~ to sth** [*table*] faire un angle avec [*wall*]; [*tower*] pencher par rapport à [*ground*]; **from every ~** sous tous les angles; **at an ~** en biais.
II *vtr* orienter.
III *vi* **1** (fish) pêcher (à la ligne); **2° to ~ for sth** chercher à obtenir qch.

angler *n* pêcheur/-euse *m/f* (à la ligne).

angling ▶649 *n* pêche *f* (à la ligne).

angrily *adv* [*react, speak*] avec colère.

angry *adj* [*person, expression*] furieux/-ieuse; [*outburst, scene, words*] de colère; **to look ~** avoir l'air en colère; **to be ~ at** or **with sb** être en colère contre qn; **I was ~ at having to wait** j'étais en colère d'avoir à attendre; **to get** or **grow ~** se fâcher; **to make sb ~** mettre qn en colère.

animal I *n* animal *m*, bête *f*; **to behave like ~s** [*people*] se conduire comme des brutes.
II *noun modifier* [*welfare, rights*] des animaux; [*behaviour, fat*] animal.

animal: **~ kingdom** *n* règne *m* animal; **~ lover** *n* ami/-e *m/f* des bêtes.

animated *adj* animé.

ankle ▶523 *n* cheville *f*.

ankle sock *n* socquette *f*.

annex I *n* (also **annexe** GB) annexe *f*.
II *vtr* annexer [*territory, land, country*] (**to** à).

annihilate *vtr* anéantir.

anniversary *n* anniversaire *m* (**of** de).

announce I *vtr* annoncer (**that** que).
II *vi* (US) annoncer sa candidature.

announcement *n* **1** (spoken) annonce *f* (**of** de; **that** indiquant que); **2** (written) avis *m*; (of birth, death) faire-part *m inv*.

announcer *n* **1** (on TV) speaker/-erine *m/f*; **radio ~** présentateur/-trice *m/f* de radio; **2** (at rail station) annonceur/-euse *m/f*.

annoy *vtr* [*person*] (by behaviour) agacer; (by opposing wishes) contrarier; [*discomfort, noise*] gêner; **what really ~s me is that** ce qui me contrarie, c'est que; **this man's ~ing me** cet homme m'embête.

annoyance *n* agacement *m* (**at** devant), contrariété *f* (**at** à).

annoyed *adj* contrarié (**at, by** par); (stronger) agacé, fâché (**at, by** par); **~ with sb** fâché contre qn; **she was ~ with him for being late** elle était contrariée parce qu'il était en retard.

annoying *adj* agaçant (**to do** de faire).

annual I *n* **1** (book) album *m* (annuel); **2** (plant) plante *f* annuelle.
II *adj* annuel/-elle.

annually *adv* [*earn, produce*] par an; [*do, inspect*] tous les ans.

anonymous *adj* anonyme; **to remain ~** garder l'anonymat.

anorexia (nervosa) ▶686 *n* anorexie *f* mentale.

another

■ **Note** When *another* is used as a pronoun it is translated by *un autre* or *une autre* according to the gender of the noun it refers to: *that cake was delicious, can I have another?* = ce gâteau était délicieux, est-ce que je peux en prendre un autre?; *I see you like the peaches—have another* = je vois que tu aimes les pêches—prends-en une autre. Note that *en* is always added in French when *un/une autre* are used as pronouns. For more examples and particular usages, see the entry below.

I *det* **1** (an additional) un/-e autre, encore un/-e; **would you like ~ drink?** est-ce que tu veux un autre verre?, encore un verre?; **that will cost you ~ £5** cela vous coûtera 5 livres sterling de plus; **without ~ word** sans rien dire de plus; **in ~ five weeks** dans cinq semaines; **it was ~ ten years before they met again** dix ans se sont écoulés avant qu'ils se rencontrent de nouveau; **and ~ thing,...** et de plus,...; **2** (a different) un/-e autre; **~ time** une autre fois; **he has ~ job now** il a un nouveau travail maintenant.
II *pron* un/-e autre; **can I have ~?** est-ce que je peux en avoir un/-e autre?; **one after ~** l'un/l'une après l'autre; **in one way or ~** d'une façon ou d'une autre.

answer I *n* **1** (reply) réponse *f* (**to** à); **to get/give an ~** obtenir/donner une réponse; **there's no ~** (to door) il n'y a personne; (on phone) ça ne répond pas; **in ~ to sth** en réponse à qch; **I won't take no for an ~!** pas question de refuser!; **2** (to difficulty, puzzle) solution *f* (**to** à); (Sch, Univ) réponse *f* (**to** à); **the right/wrong ~** la bonne/mauvaise réponse.
II *vtr* répondre à; **to ~ that**... répondre que...; **to ~ the door** aller or venir ouvrir la porte; **to ~ the telephone** répondre au téléphone.
III *vi* **1** (respond) répondre; **to ~ to the name of X** répondre au nom de X; **2 to ~ to** répondre or correspondre à [*description*]; **3** (be accountable) **to ~ to sb** être responsable devant qn.
■ **answer back**: ¶ **~ back** répondre; ¶ **~ [sb] back** (GB) répondre.
■ **answer for**: **~ for [sb/sth]** répondre de [*action, person*]; **they have a lot to ~ for!** ils ont beaucoup de comptes à rendre!

answerable *adj* **to be ~ to sb** être responsable devant qn; **to be ~ for** être responsable de [*actions*].

answering machine, **answerphone** *n* répondeur *m* (téléphonique).

ant *n* fourmi *f*.

antagonize *vtr* (annoy) contrarier (**with** avec); (stronger) éveiller l'hostilité de (**by doing** en faisant; **with** avec).

antelope *n* antilope *f*.

antenna *n* antenne *f*.

anti I *prep* contre; **to be ~** être contre.
II **anti(-)** *pref* anti(-).

antibiotic *n* antibiotique *m*; **on ~s** sous antibiotiques.

anticipate *vtr* **1** (expect, foresee) prévoir, s'attendre à [*problem, delay*]; **to ~ that**... prévoir que...; **as ~d** comme prévu; **2** (guess in advance) anticiper [*needs, result*]; **3** (pre-empt) devancer [*person, act*].

anticipation *n* **1** (excitement) excitation *f*; (pleasure in advance) plaisir *m* anticipé; **in ~ of sth** à l'idée de qch; **2** (expectation) prévision *f* (**of** de).

anti: **~climax** *n* déception *f*; **~clockwise** *adj, adv* (GB) dans le sens inverse des aiguilles d'une montre; **~dote** *n* antidote *m* (**to, for** contre, à); **~freeze** *n* antigel *m*; **~histamine** *n* antihistaminique *m*; **~perspirant** *n* produit *m* antitranspiration.

antique I *n* (object) objet *m* ancien or d'époque; (furniture) meuble *m* ancien or d'époque.
II *adj* **1** (old) ancien/-ienne; **2** (old-style) à l'ancienne.

antique shop ▶805 *n* magasin *m* d'antiquités.

antiseptic *n, adj* antiseptique (*m*).

antisocial *adj* **1 ~ behaviour** comportement *m* incorrect; (criminal behaviour) comportement *m* délinquant; **2** (reclusive) sauvage.

antlers *n pl* bois *mpl* de cerf.

anxiety *n* **1** (apprehension) grandes inquiétudes *fpl* (**about** à propos de; **for** pour); **she caused them great ~** elle leur a causé beaucoup de soucis; **to be in a state of ~** être angoissé; **2** (source of worry) souci *m*; **3** (eagerness) désir *m* ardent (**to do** de faire); **4** (in psychology) anxiété *f*.

anxious *adj* **1** (worried) très inquiet/-iète (**about** à propos de; **for** pour); **to be ~ about doing** s'inquiéter de faire; **2** [*moment, time*] angoissant; **3** (eager) très désireux/-euse (**to do** de faire); **I am ~ for him to know** je tiens beaucoup à ce qu'il sache.

anxiously *adv* **1** (worriedly) avec inquiétude; **2** (eagerly) avec impatience.

any

■ **Note** When *any* is used as a determiner in questions and conditional sentences it is translated by *du*, *de l'*, *de la* or *des* according to the gender and number of the noun that follows: *is there any soap?* = y a-t-il du savon?; *is there any flour?* = y a-t-il de la farine?; *are there any questions?* = est-ce qu'il y a des questions?
– In negative sentences *any* is translated by *de* or *d'* (before a vowel or mute 'h'): *we don't have any money* = nous n'avons pas d'argent.
– When *any* is used as a pronoun in negative sentences and in questions it is translated by *en*: *we don't have any* = nous n'en avons pas; *have you got any?* = est-ce que vous en avez?
– For more examples and other uses see the entry below.

I *det* **1** (in questions, conditional sentences) du/de l'/de la/des; **is there ~ tea?** est-ce qu'il y a du thé?; **if you have ~ money** si vous avez de l'argent; **2** (with negative, implied negative) de, d'; **they never receive ~ letters** ils ne reçoivent jamais de lettres; **I don't need ~ advice** je n'ai pas besoin de conseils; **they couldn't get ~ information** ils n'ont pas obtenu la moindre information; **he hasn't got ~ common sense** il n'a aucun bon sens; **3** (no matter which) n'importe quel/quelle, tout; **you can have ~ cup you like** vous pouvez prendre n'importe quelle tasse; **~ information would be very useful** tout renseignement serait très utile; **I'm ready to help in ~ way I can** je suis prêt à faire tout ce que je peux pour aider; **he might return at ~ time** il peut revenir d'un moment à l'autre; **come round and see me ~ time** passe me voir quand tu veux; **I don't buy ~ one brand in particular** je n'achète aucune marque en particulier.
II *pron, quantif* **1** (in questions, conditional sentences) **I'd like some tea, if you have ~** je voudrais du thé, si vous en avez; **have ~ of you got a car?** est-ce que l'un/-e d'entre vous a une voiture?; **are ~ of them blue?** y en a-t-il des bleus?; **2** (with negative, implied negative) en; **he hasn't got ~** il n'en a pas; **there is hardly ~ left** il n'en reste presque pas; **she doesn't like ~ of them** (people) elle n'aime aucun d'entre eux/elles; (things) elle n'en aime aucun/-e; **3** (no matter which) n'importe lequel/laquelle; **'which colour would you like?'—'~'** 'quelle couleur veux-tu?'—'n'importe laquelle'; **~ of those pens** n'importe lequel de ces stylos; **~ of them could do it** n'importe qui d'entre eux/elles pourrait le faire.
III *adv* **is he feeling ~ better?** est-ce qu'il se sent mieux?; **have you got ~ more of these?** est-ce que vous en avez d'autres?; **do you want ~ more wine?** voulez-vous encore du vin?; **I don't know ~ more than that** c'est tout ce que je sais; **he doesn't live here ~ more** il n'habite plus ici; **if we stay here ~ longer** si nous restons plus longtemps; **can't you walk ~ faster?** tu ne peux pas marcher plus vite?; **I can't leave ~ later than 6 o'clock** il faut que je parte à 6 heures au plus tard.

anybody *pron* **1** (in questions, conditional sentences) quelqu'un; **is there ~ in the house?** est-ce qu'il y a quelqu'un dans la maison?; **if ~ asks, tell them I've gone out** si quelqu'un me cherche, dis que je suis sorti; **2** (with negative, implied negative) personne; **there wasn't ~ in the house** il n'y avait personne dans la maison; **without ~ knowing** sans que personne le sache; **I didn't have ~ to talk to** il n'y avait personne avec qui j'aurais pu parler; **3** (no matter who) n'importe qui; **~ could do it** n'importe qui pourrait le faire; **~ but you/his boss would say yes** tout autre que toi/ton patron dirait oui; **'who shall I invite?'—'~ but him'** 'qui vais-je inviter?' 'n'importe qui, sauf lui'; **~ who wants to, can go** tous ceux qui le veulent, peuvent y aller; **~ can make a mistake** ça arrive à tout le monde de faire une erreur; **~ would think you were deaf** c'est à croire que tu es sourd; **we can't ask just ~ to do it** nous ne pouvons pas demander à n'importe qui de le faire.

anyhow *adv* = **anyway** 1.

anyone *pron* = **anybody**.

anything *pron* **1** (in questions, conditional sentences) quelque chose; **if ~ happens to her** s'il lui arrive quoi que ce soit; **is there ~ to be done?** peut-on faire quelque chose?; **is there ~ in the rumour that...?** est-il vrai que...?; **2** (with negative, implied negative) rien; **she didn't say ~** elle n'a rien dit; **he didn't have ~ to do** il n'avait rien à faire; **don't believe ~ he says** ne crois pas un mot de ce qu'il dit; **3** (no matter what) tout; **~ is possible** tout est possible; **I'd give ~ to get that job** je ferais tout pour obtenir cet emploi; **they'd do ~ for you** ils sont toujours prêts à rendre service; **she likes ~ to do with football** elle aime tout ce qui a rapport au football; **he was ~ but happy/a liar** il n'était pas du tout heureux/menteur.
IDIOMS **~ goes** tout est permis; **as easy/funny as ~** facile/drôle comme tout; **to run/laugh/work like ~** courir/rire/travailler comme un fou°.

anytime *adv* (also **any time**) n'importe quand; **~ after 2 pm** n'importe quand à partir de 14 heures; **~ you like** quand tu veux; **if at ~ you feel lonely...** si jamais tu te sens seul...; **at ~ of the day or night** à n'importe quelle heure du jour ou de la nuit; **he could arrive ~ now** il pourrait arriver d'un moment à l'autre.

anyway *adv* **1** (in any case, besides) (also **anyhow**) de toute façon; **2** (nevertheless) quand même; **I don't really like hats, but I'll try it on ~** je n'aime pas vraiment les chapeaux, mais je vais quand même l'essayer; **thanks ~** merci quand même; **3** (at least, at any rate) en tout cas; **we can't go out, not yet ~** nous ne pouvons pas sortir, pas pour l'instant en tout cas; **4** (well) **'~, we arrived at the station...'** 'bon, nous sommes arrivés à la gare...'

anywhere *adv* **1** (in questions, conditional sentences) quelque part; **did you go ~ nice?** est-ce que tu es allé dans un endroit agréable?; **we're going to Spain, if ~** si on va quelque part, ce sera en Espagne; **2** (with negative, implied negative) **you can't go ~** tu ne peux aller nulle part; **there isn't ~ to sit** il n'y a pas de place pour s'asseoir; **you won't get ~ if you don't pass your exams** tu n'arriveras à rien si tu ne réussis pas tes examens; **crying isn't going to get you ~** ça ne t'avancera à rien de pleurer; **3** (no matter where) **~ you like** où tu veux; **~ in England** partout en Angleterre; **~ but Bournemouth** partout sauf à Bournemouth; **~ she goes, he follows her** il la suit partout où elle va.

apart I *adj, adv* **1 trees planted 10 metres ~** des arbres plantés à 10 mètres d'intervalle; **the posts need to be placed further ~** les poteaux doivent être écartés davantage; **2** (separate from each other) séparé; **we hate being ~** nous détestons être séparés; **they need to be kept ~** il faut les garder séparés; **3 dogs ~** à part les chiens; **a world ~** un monde à part.

II apart from *phr* **1** (separate from) à l'écart de; **it stands ~ from the other houses** elle est à l'écart des autres maisons; **he lives ~ from his wife** il vit séparé de sa femme; **2** (leaving aside) en dehors de, à part; **~ from working in an office, he...** en plus de travailler dans un bureau, il...; **~ from being illegal, it's also dangerous** (mis) à part que c'est illégal, c'est aussi dangereux.

apartheid *n* apartheid *m*.

apartment *n* appartement *m*.

apartment: **~ block** *n* immeuble *m*; **~ house** *n* (US) résidence *f*.

apathetic *adj* (by nature) amorphe; (from illness, depression) apathique.

APEX *n* (*abbr* = **Advance Purchase Excursion**) Apex *m*.

apologetic *adj* [*gesture, letter*] d'excuse; **to be ~ (about)** s'excuser (de).

apologize *vi* s'excuser (**to sb** auprès de qn; **for sth** de qch; **for doing** d'avoir fait).

apology *n* excuses *fpl* (**for sth** pour qch; **for doing** pour avoir fait); **to make an ~** s'excuser.

apostrophe *n* apostrophe *f*.

appal (GB), **appall** (US) *vtr* (shock) scandaliser; (horrify, dismay) horrifier.

appalling *adj* **1** [*crime, conditions*] épouvantable; [*injury*] affreux/-euse; **2** [*manners, joke, taste*] exécrable; [*noise, weather*] épouvantable.

apparatus *n* **1** (equipment) équipement *m*; (in lab) instruments *mpl*; (in gym) agrès *mpl*; **2** (for specific purpose) appareil *m*.

apparent *adj* **1** (seeming) [*contradiction, willingness*] apparent; **2** (clear) évident; **for no ~ reason** sans raison apparente.

apparently *adv* apparemment.

appeal I *n* **1** (gen, Law) appel *m* (**for** à; **on behalf of** en faveur de); **2** (attraction) charme *m*; (interest) intérêt *m*.

II *vi* **1** (Law) faire appel (**against** de); **2** (Sport) **to ~ to** demander l'arbitrage de [*referee*]; **to ~ against** contester [*decision*]; **3 to ~ for** lancer un appel à [*order, tolerance*]; faire appel à [*witnesses*]; **to ~ to the public for help** demander de l'aide au public; **4** (attract) **to ~ to sb** [*idea*] tenter qn; [*person*] plaire à qn; [*place*] attirer qn.

appealing *adj* **1** (attractive) [*child, kitten*] attachant; [*plan, theory*] séduisant; [*modesty*] charmant; **2** [*look*] suppliant.

appear *vi* **1** (become visible) apparaître; **2** (turn up) arriver; **3** (seem) **to ~ to be/to do** [*person*] avoir l'air d'être/de faire; **to ~ depressed** avoir l'air déprimé; **it ~s that** il semble que; **4** [*book, article, name*] paraître; **5 to ~ on stage** paraître en scène; **to ~ on TV** passer à la télévision; **6** (Law) **to ~ in court** comparaître devant le tribunal.

appearance *n* **1** (arrival) (of person, vehicle) arrivée *f*; (of development, invention) apparition *f*; **to put in an ~** faire une apparition; **2** (on TV, in play, film) passage *m*; **to make an ~ on television** passer à la télévision; **3** (look) (of person) apparence *f*; (of district, object) aspect *m*; **to judge** or **go by ~s** se fier aux apparences.

appendicitis ▶ 686 *n* appendicite *f*.

appendix *n* appendice *m*; **to have one's ~ removed** se faire opérer de l'appendicite.

appetite *n* appétit *m*; **he has a good/poor ~** il a bon appétit/il n'a pas d'appétit; **it'll spoil your ~** ça va te couper l'appétit.

applaud *vtr, vi* applaudir.

applause *n* applaudissements *mpl*; **there was a burst of ~** les applaudissements ont éclaté.

apple *n* pomme *f*.

apple: **~core** *n* trognon *m* de pomme; **~ tree** *n* pommier *m*.

appliance *n* appareil *m*; **household ~** appareil électroménager.

applicant *n* (for job, membership) candidat/-e *m/f* (**for** à); (for passport, benefit, loan) demandeur/-euse *m/f* (**for** de); (for citizenship) postulant/-e *m/f* (**for** à).

application *n* **1** (for job) candidature *f* (**for** à); (for membership, passport, loan) demande *f* (**for** de); **2** (of ointment, spray) application *f* (**to** à); **3** (implementation) (of law, penalty, rule) application *f*.

application form *n* (for loan, credit card, passport) formulaire *m* de demande; (for job) formulaire *m* de candidature; (for membership) demande *f* d'inscription.

apply I *vtr* appliquer [*rule, standard, term*] (**to** à); appliquer [*paint, bandage*] (**to** sur); exercer [*pressure*] (**to** sur).

II *vi* **1** (request) faire une demande; **to ~ for** demander [*divorce, citizenship*]; faire une demande de [*passport, loan, visa, permit*]; **2** (seek work) poser sa candidature (**for** à); **to ~**

for the job of poser sa candidature au poste de; **3** (to college) faire une demande d'inscription (**to** à); (to club, society) faire une demande d'adhésion (**to** à); **4** (be valid) [*definition, term*] s'appliquer (**to** à); [*ban, rule, penalty*] être en vigueur.
III *v refl* **to ~ oneself** s'appliquer.

appoint *vtr* nommer [*person*] (**to sth** à qch; **to do** pour faire; **as** comme); fixer [*date, place*].

appointment *n* **1** (meeting) rendez-vous *m* (**at** chez; **with** avec; **to do** pour faire); **business ~** rendez-vous *m* d'affaires; **by ~** sur rendez-vous; **to make an ~** prendre rendez-vous; **2** (nomination) nomination *f* (**as** comme; **to sth** à qch).

appraisal *n* évaluation *f*.

appreciate I *vtr* **1** (be grateful for) apprécier [*help, effort*]; être sensible à [*favour*]; être reconnaissant de [*kindness, sympathy*]; **I'd ~ it if you could reply soon** je vous serais reconnaissant de répondre sans tarder; **2** (realize) se rendre (bien) compte de, être conscient de; **as you will ~** comme vous vous en rendrez bien compte; **3** (enjoy) apprécier [*music, art, food*].
II *vi* [*object*] prendre de la valeur; [*value*] monter.

appreciation *n* **1** (gratitude) remerciement *m* (**for** pour); **in ~ of sth** en remerciement de qch; **to show one's ~** manifester sa gratitude; **2** (enjoyment) appréciation *f* (**of** de); **3** (increase) hausse *f* (**of, in** de).

appreciative *adj* **1** (grateful) reconnaissant (**of** de); **2** (admiring) admiratif/-ive.

apprehensive *adj* craintif/-ive; **to feel ~ about sth** (fearful) appréhender qch; (worried) avoir des inquiétudes au sujet de qch.

apprentice I *n* **1** apprenti/-e *m/f* (**to** de).
II *noun modifier* [*baker, mechanic*] apprenti/-e (*before n*).
III *vtr* **to be ~d to sb** être en apprentissage chez qn.

approach I *n* **1** (route of access) (to town, island) voie *f* d'accès; **2** (arrival) (of person, season, old age) approche *f*; **3** (way of handling) approche *f*; **an original ~ to the problem** une façon originale d'aborder le problème; **we need to try a different ~** nous devons essayer une méthode différente; **4** (overture) démarche *f*, proposition *f*; **to make ~s to sb** faire des démarches auprès de qn.
II *vtr* **1** (draw near to) s'approcher de [*person, place*]; (verge on) approcher de; **it was ~ing midnight** il était presque minuit; **2** (deal with) aborder [*problem, subject*]; **3** (make overtures to) s'adresser à; (more formally) faire des démarches auprès de; (with offer of job, remuneration) solliciter (**about** au sujet de); **he has been ~ed by several publishers** il a reçu des propositions de plusieurs maisons d'édition.
III *vi* [*person, car*] (s')approcher; [*event, season*] approcher.

approachable *adj* abordable, d'un abord facile.

appropriate I *adj* **1** [*behaviour, choice, place*] approprié (**for** pour); [*dress, gift*] qui convient (*after n*) (**for** à); [*punishment*] juste (**for** à); [*name*] bien choisi; **~ to** approprié à [*needs, circumstances*]; **2** (relevant) [*authority*] compétent.
II *vtr* s'approprier [*property, document*]; affecter [*funds, land*] (**for** à).

appropriately *adv* **1** [*behave, dress, speak*] avec à-propos; [*dress*] convenablement; **2** [*designed, chosen, sited*] judicieusement.

approval *n* approbation *f* (**of** de; **to do** pour faire); **on ~** à l'essai.

approve I *vtr* approuver [*product, plan*]; accepter [*person*].
II *vi* **to ~ of sth/sb** apprécier qch/qn; (**not**) **to ~ of sb doing** (ne pas) apprécier que qn fasse; **he doesn't ~ of drinking** il est contre l'alcool.

approving *adj* approbateur/-trice.

approximate *adj* approximatif/-ive.

approximately *adv* **1** (about) environ; **at ~ four o'clock** vers quatre heures; **2** [*equal, correct*] à peu près.

approximation *n* approximation *f*.

apricot *n* **1** (fruit) abricot *m*; **2** (tree) abricotier *m*.

April ▶584 *n* avril *m*.

April Fools' Day *n* le premier avril.

apron *n* tablier *m*.

apt *adj* [*choice, description*] heureux/-euse; [*title, style*] approprié (**to, for** à).

aptitude *n* aptitude *f*.

Aquarius *n* Verseau *m*; **I'm ~** je suis Verseau; **what's the horoscope for ~?** que dit l'horoscope pour les Verseaux?

Arab ▶712 I *n* (person) Arabe *mf*.
II *adj* arabe.

Arabic ▶712 I *n* (language) arabe *m*.
II *adj* [*custom, culture*] arabe; [*lesson, teacher*] d'arabe.

arbitrary *adj* arbitraire.

arbitrate *vtr, vi* arbitrer.

arbitration *n* arbitrage *m*; **to go to ~** ≈ aller aux prud'hommes.

arcade *n* arcade *f*; **shopping ~** galerie *f* marchande.

arch I *n* arche *f*.
II *vtr* arquer; **to ~ one's back** [*person*] cambrer le dos; [*cat*] faire le dos rond.
III **arch(-)** *pref* par excellence; **~-enemy** ennemi/-e *m/f* juré/-e; **~-rival** grand rival.

archaeology (GB), **archeology** (US) *n* archéologie *f*.

architect ▶805 *n* architecte *mf*; (figurative) artisan *m* (**of** de).

architecture *n* architecture *f*.

archive *n* archive *f*.

ardent *adj* [*defence, opposition, lover*] passionné; [*supporter*] fervent.

area *n* **1** (region) région *f*; (of city) zone *f*; (district) quartier *m*; **in the London ~** dans la région de Londres; **residential ~** zone *f* résidentielle; **2** (part of building) **dining ~** coin *m* salle-à-manger; **no-smoking ~** zone *f* non-fumeurs;

reception ~ réception *f*; **waiting ~** salle *f* d'attente; **3** (sphere of knowledge) domaine *m*; (part of business, economy) secteur *m*; **~ of interest** domaine d'intérêt; **4** (in geometry) aire *f*; (of land) superficie *f*.

area code *n* indicatif *m* de zone.

arena *n* arène *f*.

arguable *adj* discutable.

argue I *vtr* **1** (debate) discuter (de), débattre (de); **to ~ the case for disarmament** exposer les raisons en faveur du désarmement; **it could be ~d that** on pourrait soutenir que; **well-~d** bien argumenté; **2** (maintain) soutenir.
II *vi* **1** (quarrel) se disputer (**with** avec); **to ~ about** or **over money** se disputer pour des questions d'argent; **don't ~ (with me)!** on ne discute pas!; **2** (debate) discuter; **to ~ about** discuter de; **3** (put one's case) argumenter (**against** contre); **to ~ in favour of/against doing sth** exposer les raisons pour faire/pour ne pas faire qch.

argument *n* **1** (quarrel) dispute *f* (**about** à propos de); **to have an ~** se disputer; **2** (discussion) débat *m*, discussion *f* (**about** à propos de); **there is a lot of ~ about this** c'est un sujet très discuté; **3** (case) argument *m* (**for** en faveur de; **against** contre); (line of reasoning) raisonnement *m*.

Aries *n* Bélier *m*; ▶ **Aquarius**.

arise *vi* **1** [*problem*] survenir (**out of** du fait de); [*question*] se poser; **if the need ~s** si le besoin se fait sentir; **2** (be the result of) résulter (**from** de).

aristocratic *adj* aristocratique.

arithmetic *n* arithmétique *f*.

arm ▶**523** I *n* (Anat) bras *m*; (of chair) accoudoir *m*; **~ in ~** bras dessus bras dessous; **to have sth over/under one's ~** avoir qch sur/sous le bras; **to fold one's ~s** croiser les bras; **within ~'s reach** à portée de la main.
II **arms** *n pl* (weapons) armes *fpl*.
III *vtr* **1** (Mil) armer; **2** (equip) **to ~ sb with sth** munir qn de qch.
IDIOMS **to keep sb at ~'s length** tenir qn à distance.

armaments *n pl* armements *mpl*.

arm: **~band** *n* (for swimmer) bracelet *m* de natation; (for mourner) crêpe *m* de deuil; **~chair** *n* fauteuil *m*.

armed *adj* [*criminal, guard*] armé (**with** de); [*raid, robbery*] à main armée.

armed forces, **armed services** *n pl* forces *fpl* armées.

armistice *n* armistice *m*.

armoured (GB), **armored** (US) *adj* blindé.

armour-plated (GB), **armor-plated** (US) *adj* [*vehicle*] blindé; [*ship*] cuirassé.

armpit *n* aisselle *f*.

army I *n* armée *f*.
II *noun modifier* [*life, uniform*] militaire; [*officer*] de l'armée de terre.

around I *adv* **1** (approximately) environ, à peu près; **at ~ 3 pm** vers 15 heures; **2** (in the vicinity) **to be (somewhere) ~** être dans les parages; **are they ~?** est-ce qu'ils sont là?; **3** (in circulation) **CDs have been ~ for years** ça fait des années que les CD existent; **one of the most gifted musicians ~** un des musiciens les plus doués du moment; **4** (in all directions) **all ~** tout autour; **to go all the way ~** faire tout le tour; **the only garage for miles ~** le seul garage à des kilomètres à la ronde; **5** (in circumference) **three metres ~** de trois mètres de circonférence; **6 a way ~** un chemin pour contourner [*obstacle*]; **there is no way ~ the problem** il n'y a pas moyen de contourner le problème; **to go the long way ~** prendre le chemin le plus long; **to turn sth the other way ~** retourner qch; **I didn't ask her, it was the other way ~** ce n'est pas moi qui lui ai demandé, c'est l'inverse; **the wrong/right way ~** dans le mauvais/bon sens; **to put one's skirt on the wrong way ~** mettre sa jupe à l'envers; **to ask sb (to come) ~** dire à qn de passer.
II *prep* **1** autour de [*fire, table*]; **the villages ~ Dublin** les villages des environs de Dublin; **clothes scattered ~ the room** des vêtements éparpillés partout dans la pièce; **(all) ~ the world** partout dans le monde; **doctors ~ the world** les médecins à travers le monde; **to walk ~ the town** se promener dans la ville; **somewhere ~ the house** quelque part dans la maison; **I like having people ~ the house** j'aime avoir des gens à la maison; **the people ~ here** les gens d'ici; **2** (at) vers; **~ midnight** vers minuit; **3 to go ~** éviter [*town centre*]; contourner [*obstacle*]; **to go ~ the corner** tourner au coin; **to go ~ a bend** prendre un virage.

arouse *vtr* éveiller [*interest, suspicion*]; exciter [*anger, jealousy*]; **to be ~d** [*person*] être excité.

arrange I *vtr* **1** disposer [*chairs, ornaments*]; arranger [*room, hair, clothes*]; arranger, disposer [*flowers*]; **2** (organize) organiser [*party, meeting, holiday*]; fixer [*date, appointment*]; **to ~ to do** s'arranger pour faire; **I'll ~ it** je ferai le nécessaire; **3** convenir de [*loan, mortgage*]; fixer [*price*]; **4** (Mus) arranger, adapter [*piece*].
II *vi* **to ~ for sth** prendre des dispositions pour qch; **to ~ for sb to do** prendre des dispositions pour que qn fasse.

arrangement *n* **1** (of hair) arrangement *m*; (of objects, chairs) disposition *f*; (of flowers) composition *f*; **2** (agreement) entente *f*, accord *m*; **to come to an ~** s'arranger; **3** (plan) dispositions *fpl*; (preparations) préparatifs *mpl*; (measures) mesures *fpl*; **to make ~s to do** s'arranger pour faire.

array *n* gamme *f*.

arrears *n pl* arriéré *m*; **I am in ~ with my payments** j'ai du retard dans mes paiements; **to fall into ~** s'arriérer.

arrest I *n* arrestation *f*; **to be under ~** être en état d'arrestation.
II *vtr* arrêter.

arrival *n* arrivée *f*; **on sb's/sth's ~** à l'arrivée de qn/qch.

arrival: **~ lounge** *n* salon *m* d'arrivée;

~s board *n* tableau *m* d'arrivée; **~ time** *n* heure *f* d'arrivée.

arrive *vi* **1** arriver (**at** à; **from** de); **2 to ~ at** parvenir à [*decision, solution*].

arrogant *adj* arrogant.

arrow *n* flèche *f*.

arson *n* incendie *m* criminel.

art *n* art *m*.

artefact *n* objet *m* (fabriqué).

artery *n* artère *f*.

art exhibition *n* (paintings) exposition *f* de tableaux; (sculpture) exposition *f* de sculpture.

art gallery *n* (museum) musée *m* d'art; (commercial) galerie *f* d'art.

arthritis ▶ **686** *n* arthrite *f*.

artichoke *n* artichaut *m*.

article *n* article *m* (**about, on** sur).

articulate I *adj* [*speaker*] qui s'exprime bien. **II** *vtr* (pronounce) articuler; (express) exprimer. **III** *vi* (pronounce) articuler.

artifice *n* **1** (trick) ruse *f*; **2** (cunning) astuce *f*.

artificial *adj* artificiel/-ielle.

artificial respiration *n* respiration *f* artificielle.

artillery *n* artillerie *f*.

artisan *n* artisan *m*.

artist ▶ **805** *n* artiste *mf*.

artistic *adj* [*talent*] artistique; [*temperament, person*] artiste.

arts *n pl* **1** (culture) **the ~** les arts *mpl*; **2** (Univ) lettres *fpl*; **3 ~ and crafts** artisanat *m*.

art: **~ school** *n* école *f* des beaux-arts; **~s degree** *n* licence *f* ès lettres; **~s student** *n* étudiant/-e *m/f* en lettres; **~ student** *n* étudiant/-e *m/f* des beaux-arts.

as

Note *as* is often translated by *comme*: *as planned* = comme prévu; *as often happens* = comme c'est souvent le cas

– In time expressions where a gradual process is being described, as is translated by *au fur et à mesure que*: *as the day went on, he became more anxious* = au fur et à mesure que la journée avançait il devenait plus inquiet

– As a conjunction meaning *because*, *as* is translated by *comme* or *puisque*: *as he is ill, he can't go out* = comme il est malade or puisqu'il est malade, il ne peut pas sortir

– When used as an adverb in comparisons, *as...as* is translated by *aussi...que*: *he is as intelligent as his brother* = il est aussi intelligent que son frère

– When *as* is used as a preposition to indicate a person's profession or position, it is translated by *comme*: *he works as an engineer* = il travaille comme ingénieur

– Note that the article *a/an* is not translated

– For more examples, particular usages and phrases see the entry below.

I *conj* **1** comme; **~ you know** comme vous le savez; **~ usual** comme d'habitude; **do ~ I say** fais ce que je te dis; **~ I understand it** autant que je puisse en juger; **the street ~ it looked in the 1930s** la rue telle qu'elle était dans les années 30; **leave it ~ it is** laisse-le tel quel; **we're in enough trouble ~ it is** nous avons déjà assez d'ennuis comme ça; **~ she was coming down the stairs** comme elle descendait l'escalier; **~ she grew older** au fur et à mesure qu'elle vieillissait; **~ a child, he...** (quand il était) enfant, il...; **2** (because, since) comme, puisque; **3** (although) **strange ~ it may seem** aussi curieux que cela puisse paraître; **try ~ he might, he could not forget it** il avait beau essayer, il ne pouvait pas oublier; **4 the same...~** le/la même...que; **I've got a jacket the same ~ yours** j'ai la même veste que toi; **the same ~ always** comme d'habitude; **5** (indicating purpose) **so ~ to do** pour faire, afin de faire.

II *prep* comme, en; **dressed ~ a sailor** habillé en marin; **he is portrayed ~ a victim** on le présente comme une victime; **he works ~ a pilot** il travaille comme pilote; **a job ~ a teacher** un poste d'enseignant; **my rights ~ a parent** mes droits en tant que parent; **with Eve Black ~ Vivien** avec Eve Black dans le rôle de Vivien; **to treat sb ~ an equal** traiter qn en égal.

III *adv* **1 he is ~ intelligent ~ you** il est aussi intelligent que toi; **~ fast ~ you can** aussi vite que possible; **he's twice ~ strong ~ me** il est deux fois plus fort que moi; **I have ~ much** or **~ many ~ she has** j'en ai autant qu'elle; **~ much ~ possible** autant que possible; **~ little ~ possible** le moins possible; **~ soon ~ possible** dès que possible; **not ~ often** moins souvent; **she can play the piano ~ well ~ her sister** elle joue du piano aussi bien que sa sœur; **he has a house in Nice ~ well ~ an apartment in Paris** il a une maison à Nice ainsi qu'un appartement à Paris; **2** (expressing similarity) comme; **~ before** comme avant; **I thought ~ much!** c'est ce qu'il me semblait!

IV as against *phr* contre, comparé à.

V as and when *phr* **~ and when the passengers arrive** au fur et à mesure que les voyageurs arrivent.

VI as for *phr* quant à, pour ce qui est de.

VII as from, as of *phr* à partir de.

VIII as if *phr* comme (si); **it's not ~ if she hadn't been warned!** ce n'est pas comme si elle n'avait pas été prévenue!; **it looks ~ if we've lost** on dirait que nous avons perdu; **~ if by magic** comme par magie.

IX as long as *phr* du moment que (+ *indic*), pourvu que (+ *subj*).

X as such *phr* en tant que tel.

asbestos *n* amiante *m*.

ascend *vtr* gravir [*steps, hill*].

ascent *n* ascension *f*.

ascertain *vtr* établir (**that** que).

ash *n* **1** (after burning) cendre *f*; **to be burned to ~es** être réduit en cendres; **2** (also **~ tree**) frêne *m*; **3** (wood) frêne *m*.

ashamed *adj* honteux/-euse; **to be** or **feel ~** avoir honte (**of** de; **to do** de faire); **to be ~ that** avoir honte que (+ *subj*).

ashen *adj* [*complexion*] terreux/-euse.

ashore *adv* **to come/go ~** débarquer; **to swim ~** (in sea) gagner le rivage à la nage; (in river, lake) gagner la rive à la nage; **washed ~** rejeté sur le rivage.

ashtray *n* cendrier *m*.

Asia ▶574| *pr n* Asie *f*.

Asian I *n* (from Far East) Asiatique *mf*; (in UK) *personne originaire du sous-continent indien*.
II *adj* asiatique.

aside I *n* **to say sth in an ~** dire qch en aparté.
II *adv* **to stand** or **step ~** s'écarter; **to set** or **put [sth] ~** (save) mettre [qch] de côté; (in shop) réserver; **to take sb ~** prendre qn à part.
III aside from *phr* à part.

ask I *vtr* **1** demander [*name, reason, permission*]; **to ~ a question** poser une question; **to ~ sb sth** demander qch à qn; **to ~ to do** demander à faire; **to ~ sb to do** demander à qn de faire; **what price is she ~ing for it?** combien elle le vend?; **2** (invite) inviter [*person*] (**to** à); **to ~ sb to dinner** inviter qn à dîner; **to ~ sb in** inviter qn à entrer.
II *vi* **1** (request) demander; **2** (make enquiries) se renseigner; **to ~ about sb** s'informer au sujet de qn.
III *v refl* **to ~ oneself** se demander.
■ **ask after**: **~ after [sb]** demander des nouvelles de [*person*].
■ **ask for**: ¶ **~ for [sth]** demander [*drink, money, help*]; **he ~ed for it**° ! il l'a bien cherché!; ¶ **~ for [sb]** (on telephone) demander à parler à; (from sick bed) demander à voir.

askance *adv* **to look ~ at sb/sth** considérer qn/qch avec méfiance.

askew *adj, adv* de travers.

asleep *adj* **to be ~** dormir; **to fall ~** s'endormir; **to be half ~** être à moitié endormi; **to be sound** or **fast ~** dormir à poings fermés.

asparagus *n* asperge *f*.

aspect *n* **1** (feature) aspect *m*; **2** (angle) point *m* de vue; **3** (of house) (orientation) orientation *f*.

aspen *n* tremble *m*.

asphalt *n* bitume *m*.

aspic *n* aspic *m*.

aspiration *n* aspiration *f* (**to** à).

aspire *vi* [*person*] aspirer (**to** à; **to do** à faire).

aspirin *n* aspirine® *f*; **two ~(s)** deux comprimés d'aspirine.

aspiring *adj* **~ authors** ceux qui aspirent à devenir auteurs.

ass *n* **1** (donkey) âne *m*; **2**° (fool) idiot/-e *m/f*.

assassin *n* assassin *m*.

assassinate *vtr* assassiner.

assassination *n* assassinat *m*.

assault I *n* **1** (Law) agression *f* (**on** sur); **2** (Mil) assaut *m* (**on** de).
II *vtr* **1** (Law) agresser; **to be indecently ~ed** être victime d'une agression sexuelle; **2** (Mil) assaillir.

assemble I *vtr* **1** (gather) rassembler; **2** (construct) assembler; **easy to ~** facile à monter.
II *vi* [*passengers, marchers*] se rassembler; [*parliament, team, family*] se réunir.

assembly *n* **1** (gen) assemblée *f*; **2** (Sch) rassemblement *m*; **3** (of components, machines) assemblage *m*; **~ instructions** instructions *fpl* de montage.

assembly line *n* chaîne *f* de montage.

assent I *n* assentiment *m* (**to** à).
II *vi* donner son assentiment (**to** à).

assert *vtr* **1** (state) affirmer (**that** que); **to ~ one's authority** affirmer son autorité; **to ~ oneself** s'affirmer; **2** revendiquer [*right, claim*].

assertion *n* déclaration *f* (**that** selon laquelle).

assertive *adj* assuré.

assess *vtr* **1** évaluer [*person, problem, result*]; estimer [*damage, value*]; **2** (for taxation) imposer [*person*]; fixer [*tax*]; **3** (Sch) contrôler [*pupil*].

assessment *n* **1** (evaluation) appréciation *f* (**of** de); (of damage, value) estimation *f* (**of** de); **2** (for taxation) imposition *f*; **3** (Sch) contrôle *m*.

asset I *n* atout *m*.
II assets *n pl* (private) avoir *m*; (of company) actif *m*.

assiduous *adj* assidu.

assign *vtr* **1** assigner [*resources*] (**to** à); **2 to ~ a task to sb**, **to ~ sb to a task** affecter qn à une tâche; **3** (attribute) attribuer (**to** à); **4** (appoint) nommer (**to** à).

assignment *n* mission *f*.

assimilate I *vtr* assimiler [*community, information, substance*].
II *vi* [*community, person*] s'assimiler (**into** dans).

assist I *vtr* **1** (help) aider; (in organization) assister (**to do, in doing** à faire); **to ~ one another** s'entraider; **2** (facilitate) faciliter [*development, process*].
II *vi* aider (**in doing** à faire); **to ~ in** prendre part à [*operation, rescue*].

assistance *n* aide *f* (**to** à); (more formal) assistance *f* (**to** à); **with the ~ of** avec l'aide de [*person*]; à l'aide de [*device*].

assistant ▶805| **I** *n* **1** (helper) assistant/-e *m/f*; (in hierarchy) adjoint/-e *m/f*; **2** (GB) (**foreign language**) **~** (in school) assistant/-e *m/f*; (in university) lecteur/-trice *m/f*.
II *noun modifier* [*editor, manager*] adjoint.

associate I *n* associé/-e *m/f*.
II *vtr* **1** associer [*idea, memory*] (**with** à); **2 to be ~d with** [*person*] faire partie de [*movement, group*]; être mêlé à [*shady deal*].
III *vi* **to ~ with sb** fréquenter qn.

association *n* association *f*.

assorted *adj* [*objects, colours*] varié; [*foodstuffs*] assorti.

assortment *n* (of objects, colours) assortiment *m* (**of** de); (of people) mélange *m* (**of** de).

assume *vtr* **1** (suppose) supposer (**that** que); **it is ~d that** on suppose que; **2** prendre [*control, identity, office*]; assumer [*responsibility*]; affecter [*expression, indifference*]; **under an ~d name** sous un nom d'emprunt.

assumption *n* supposition *f*.

assurance *n* assurance *f*.

assure *vtr* assurer; **to ~ sb that** assurer à qn que.

asterisk *n* astérisque *m*.

asthma ▶ 686 *n* asthme *m*.

asthmatic *n, adj* asthmatique (*mf*).

astonish *vtr* surprendre, étonner.

astonished *adj* étonné (**by, at** par; **to do** de faire).

astonishing *adj* [*skill, intelligence*] étonnant; [*beauty, success*] incroyable.

astonishment *n* étonnement *m*.

astound *vtr* stupéfier.

astounding *adj* incroyable.

astray *adv* **1 to go ~** (go missing) se perdre; (go wrong) [*plan*] être contrarié; **2 to lead sb ~** (confuse) induire qn en erreur; (corrupt) détourner qn du droit chemin.

astride I *adv* à califourchon.
II *prep* à califourchon sur.

astrologer, **astrologist** ▶ 805 *n* astrologue *mf*.

astrology *n* astrologie *f*.

astronaut ▶ 805 *n* astronaute *mf*.

astronomer ▶ 805 *n* astronome *mf*.

astronomic, **astronomical** *adj* astronomique.

astronomy *n* astronomie *f*.

astute *adj* astucieux/-ieuse.

asylum *n* asile *m*; **lunatic ~** asile de fous.

at *prep*

■ **Note** *at* is often translated by *à*: *at the airport* = à l'aéroport; *at midnight* = à minuit; *at the age of 50* = à l'âge de 50 ans.
– Remember that *à* + *le always* becomes *au* and *à* + *les always* becomes *aux* (*au bureau, aux bureaux*).
– When *at* means *at the house, shop*, etc *of*, it is translated by *chez*: *at Amanda's* = chez Amanda; *at the hairdresser's* = chez le coiffeur.
– For examples and other usages, see the entry below.

1 à; **~ 4 o'clock** à quatre heures; **~ Oxford** à Oxford; **2** chez; **~ my house** chez moi; **~ home** à la maison, chez soi; **3** (with superlative) **the garden is ~ its prettiest in June** juin est le mois où le jardin est le plus beau; **she was ~ her best at 50** (of musician, artist) à 50 ans elle était au sommet de son art; **4**° (harassing) **he's been (on) ~ me to buy a new car** il n'arrête pas de me casser les pieds pour que j'achète une nouvelle voiture°.
IDIOMS **while we're ~ it**° pendant qu'on y est°; **I've been (hard) ~ it all day** je n'ai pas arrêté de la journée.

atheist *n, adj* athée (*mf*).

Athens ▶ 574 *pr n* Athènes.

athlete *n* athlète *mf*.

athlete's foot ▶ 686 *n* mycose *f*.

athletic *adj* athlétique.

athletics ▶ 649 *n* (GB) athlétisme *m*; (US) sports *mpl*.

Atlantic I *pr n* **the ~** l'Atlantique *m*.
II *adj* [*coast*] atlantique; **~ Ocean** océan *m* Atlantique.

atlas *n* atlas *m*.

atmosphere *n* **1** (air) atmosphère *f*; **2** (mood) ambiance *f*; (bad) atmosphère *f*.

atom *n* atome *m*.

atom bomb *n* bombe *f* atomique.

atomic *adj* [*explosion, power*] nucléaire, atomique.

atomizer *n* atomiseur *m*.

atrocious *adj* (horrifying) atroce; (bad) épouvantable.

atrocity *n* atrocité *f*.

attach *vtr* attacher (**to** à).

attaché *n* attaché/-e *m/f*.

attaché case *n* attaché-case *m*.

attached *adj* **1 to be/grow ~ to** être attaché/s'attacher à; **2** [*document*] ci-joint.

attachment *n* **1** (affection) attachement *m*; **2** (device) accessoire *m*.

attack I *n* **1** (gen, Mil, Sport) attaque *f* (**on** contre); (criminal) agression *f* (**against, on** contre); (terrorist) attentat *m*; **2** (of illness) crise *f* (**of** de); **to have an ~ of flu** attraper la grippe.
II *vtr* **1** (gen, Mil, Sport) attaquer; (criminally) agresser [*victim*]; **2** s'attaquer à [*task, problem*].

attacker *n* (gen) agresseur *m*; (Mil, Sport) attaquant/-e *m/f*.

attempt I *n* **1** tentative *f* (**to do** de faire); **to make an ~ to do** or **at doing** tenter de faire; **in an ~ to do** pour essayer de faire; **he made no ~ to apologize** il n'a même pas tenté de s'excuser; **2 to make an ~ on sb's life** attenter à la vie de qn.
II *vtr* tenter (**to do** de faire); **~ed murder** tentative de meurtre.

attend I *vtr* **1** assister à [*ceremony, meeting*]; aller à [*church, school*]; suivre [*class, course*]; **the event was well ~ed** beaucoup de monde assistait à l'événement; **2** (accompany) accompagner.
II *vi* être présent.
■ **attend to: ~ to [sb/sth]** s'occuper de [*person, problem*].

attendance *n* **1** (at event, meeting, course) présence *f* (**at** à); **to be in ~** être présent; **2** (number of people present) assistance *f*.

attendant ▶ 805 *n* (in cloakroom, museum, car park) gardien/-ienne *m/f*; (at petrol station) pompiste *mf*; (at pool) surveillant/-e *m/f*.

attention *n* **1** (gen) attention *f*; **to attract ~** attirer l'attention; **to draw ~ to sth** attirer l'attention sur qch; **~ to detail** le souci du détail; **for the ~ of** à l'attention de; **2** (Mil) **to stand to** or **at ~** être au garde-à-vous; **~!** garde-à-vous!

attentive *adj* (alert) attentif/-ive; (solicitous) attentionné (**to** à).

attic *n* grenier *m*; **in the ~** au grenier.

attic: **~ room** *n* mansarde *f*; **~ window** *n* lucarne *f*.

attitude *n* attitude *f* (**to, towards** (GB) à l'égard de); **~s are changing** l'attitude des gens commence à changer.

attorney ▶805| *n* (US) avocat *m*; **power of ~** procuration *f*.

attract *vtr* attirer; **he was very ~ed to her** elle l'attirait beaucoup.

attraction *n* **1** (favourable feature) attrait *m* (**of sth** de qch; **of doing** de faire; **for** pour); **2** (entertainment, sight) attraction *f*; **3** (sexual) attirance *f* (**to** pour); **her ~ to him** son attirance pour lui.

attractive *adj* [*person, offer*] séduisant; [*child*] charmant; [*place*] attrayant.

attribute I *n* attribut *m*.
II *vtr* attribuer (**to** à).

aubergine *n* (GB) aubergine *f*.

auburn ▶559| *adj* auburn *inv*.

auction I *n* enchères *fpl*; **to put sth up for ~** mettre qch aux enchères.
II *vtr* (also **~ off**) vendre [qch] aux enchères.

auctioneer ▶805| *n* commissaire-priseur *m*.

audacious *adj* audacieux/-ieuse.

audacity *n* audace *f*.

audible *adj* audible.

audience *n* (in cinema, concert, theatre) public *m*, salle *f*; (of radio programme) auditeurs *mpl*; (of TV programme) téléspectateurs *mpl*.

audio *adj* audio *inv*.

audiovisual, **AV** *adj* audiovisuel/-elle.

audit I *n* audit *m*.
II *vtr* auditer, vérifier.

audition I *n* audition *f* (**for** pour); **to go for an ~** passer une audition.
II *vtr*, *vi* auditionner (**for** pour).

auditor ▶805| *n* **1** commissaire *m* aux comptes; **2** (US) (student) auditeur/-trice *m/f*.

auditorium *n* **1** (in theatre) salle *f*; **2** (US) (for meetings) salle *f* de conférences; (Sch, Univ) amphithéâtre *m*; (concert hall) salle *f* de spectacle; (stadium) stade *m*.

augur *vi* **to ~ well/ill** être de bon/mauvais augure (**for** pour).

August ▶584| *n* août *m*.

aunt *n* tante *f*.

auntie, **aunty**○ *n* tantine○ *f*, tata○ *f*.

au pair *n* (jeune) fille *f* au pair.

aura *n* (of place) atmosphère *f*; (of person) aura *f*.

aural *adj* **1** (gen) auditif/-ive; **2** (Sch) [*comprehension, test*] oral.

auspicious *adj* prometteur/-euse.

austere *adj* austère.

austerity *n* austérité *f*.

Australia ▶574| *pr n* Australie *f*.

Australian ▶712| I *n* Australien/-ienne *m/f*.
II *adj* [*people, politics*] australien/-ienne; [*ambassador, embassy*] d'Australie.

Austria ▶574| *pr n* Autriche *f*.

Austrian ▶712| I *n* Autrichien/-ienne *m/f*.
II *adj* [*culture, people, politics*] autrichien/-ienne; [*ambassador, embassy*] d'Autriche.

authentic *adj* authentique.

author ▶805| *n* auteur *m*.

authoritarian *adj* autoritaire.

authoritative *adj* **1** (forceful) autoritaire; **2** (reliable) [*work*] qui fait autorité; [*source*] bien informé.

authority *n* **1** autorité *f*; **the authorities** les autorités; **the school authorities** la direction de l'école; **2** (permission) autorisation *f*.

authorization *n* autorisation *f*.

authorize *vtr* autoriser (**to do** à faire); **~d** [*signature, version*] autorisé; [*dealer*] agréé.

autistic *adj* [*person*] autiste; [*response*] autistique.

autobiography *n* autobiographie *f*.

autograph I *n* autographe *m*.
II *vtr* dédicacer [*book, record*]; signer [*memento*].

automate *vtr* automatiser [*factory, process*].

automatic I *n* **1** (washing machine) machine *f* à laver automatique; **2** (car) voiture *f* (à changement de vitesse) automatique; **3** (gun) automatique *m*; **4 to be on ~** [*machine*] être en position automatique.
II *adj* automatique.

automatically *adv* automatiquement.

automatic teller machine, **ATM** *n* guichet *m* automatique.

automation *n* automatisation *f*; **office ~** bureautique *f*.

automaton *n* automate *m*.

automobile *n* automobile *f*.

autonomy *n* autonomie *f*.

autopsy *n* autopsie *f*.

autumn *n* automne *m*; **in early/late ~** au début de/à la fin de l'automne; **last ~** l'automne dernier; **every ~** tous les ans en automne; **until ~** jusqu'en automne.

auxiliary I *n* auxiliaire *mf*.
II *adj* [*equipment, staff*] auxiliaire.

avail *n* **to be of no ~** ne servir à rien; **to no ~** en vain.

availability *n* (of option, service) existence *f*; (of drugs) présence *f* (sur le marché); **subject to ~** (of holidays, rooms, theatre seats) dans la limite des places disponibles.

available *adj* disponible (**for** pour; **to** à).

avalanche *n* avalanche *f*.

avant-garde I *n* avant-garde *f*.
II *adj* d'avant-garde.

avarice *n* cupidité *f*.

avenge *vtr* venger.

avenue *n* **1** (street, road) avenue *f*; **2** (path, driveway) allée *f*.

average I *n* moyenne *f* (**of** de); **on (the) ~** en moyenne; **above/below (the) ~** au-dessus de/au-dessous de la moyenne; **the law of ~s** la loi des probabilités.
II *adj* moyen/-enne.
III *vtr* faire en moyenne [*distance, quantity, time*].

averse *adj* opposé (**to** à); **to be ~ to doing** répugner à faire.

aversion *n* aversion *f* (**to** pour).

avert *vtr* éviter; **to ~ one's eyes from sth** détourner les yeux de qch.

aviary *n* volière *f*.

avid *adj* [*collector, reader*] passionné; **to be ~ for sth** être avide de qch.

avocado I *n* **1** (fruit) avocat *m*; **2** (plant) avocatier *m*.
II *noun modifier* [*salad, mousse*] à l'avocat.

avoid *vtr* (gen) éviter; esquiver [*issue, question*]; **to ~ doing** éviter de faire.

await *vtr* attendre; **long-~ed** longuement attendu.

awake I *adj* (not yet asleep) éveillé; (after sleeping) réveillé; **wide ~** bien réveillé; **half ~** mal réveillé; **the noise kept me ~** le bruit m'a empêché de dormir.
II *vtr* réveiller [*person*].
III *vi* [*person*] se réveiller.

awakening *n* (from sleep) réveil *m*; (of emotion, interest) éveil *m* (**of** de).

award I *n* **1** (prize) prix *m* (**for** de); (medal, certificate) distinction *f* honorifique; **2** (grant) bourse *f*.
II *vtr* décerner [*prize*]; attribuer [*grant*]; accorder [*points, penalty*].

award: **~ winner** *n* lauréat/-e *m/f*; **~-winning** *adj* [*book, film, design*] primé; [*writer, architect*] lauréat.

aware *adj* (conscious) conscient (**of** de); (informed) au courant (**of** de); **as far as I'm ~** à ma connaissance; **to be environmentally ~** être au courant des questions d'environnement.

awareness *n* conscience *f* (**of** de; **that** que).

awash *adj* inondé (**with** de).

away

■ **Note** *away* often appears after a verb in English to show that an action is continuous or intense. If *away* does not change the basic meaning of the verb only the verb is translated: *he was snoring away* = il ronflait.

I *adj* (Sport) [*goal, match, win*] à l'extérieur; **the ~ team** les visiteurs *mpl*.
II *adv* **1 to be ~** être absent (**from** de); **to be ~ on business** être en voyage d'affaires; **to be ~ from home** ne pas être chez soi, être absent de chez soi; **she's ~ in Paris** elle est à Paris; **to shuffle/crawl ~** partir en traînant les pieds/en rampant; **3 km ~** à 3 km; **London is two hours ~** Londres est à deux heures d'ici; **my birthday is two months ~** mon anniversaire est dans deux mois; **2** (Sport) [*play*] à l'extérieur.

awe *n* crainte *f* mêlée d'admiration; (less fearful) respect *m*; **to watch/listen in ~** regarder/écouter impressionné; **to be in ~ of sb** avoir peur de qn.

awe-inspiring *adj* impressionnant.

awesome *adj* redoutable.

awful *adj* **1** (in quality) exécrable; (tragic, painful) affreux/-euse, atroce; **2 you look ~** tu n'as pas l'air bien du tout; **I feel ~** (ill) je ne me sens pas bien du tout; (guilty) je culpabilise; **3**○ **an ~ lot** (**of**) énormément (de).

awfully *adv* extrêmement.

awkward *adj* **1** [*tool*] peu commode; [*shape, design*] difficile; **2** (clumsy) [*person, gesture*] maladroit; **3** [*arrangement, issue, choice*] difficile; [*moment, day*] mal choisi; **at an ~ time** au mauvais moment; **to make life ~ for sb** compliquer la vie à qn; **it's a bit ~** c'est difficile; **to feel ~ about doing** se sentir gêné de faire; **4** (embarrassing) [*question*] embarrassant; [*situation*] délicat; [*silence*] gêné; **5** (uncooperative) [*person*] difficile (**about** à propos de).

awning *n* (on shop) banne *f*, auvent *m*; (on tent, house) auvent *m*; (on market stall) bâche *f*.

awry I *adj* de travers *inv*.
II *adv* **to go ~** mal tourner.

axe, ax (US) I *n* hache *f*.
II *vtr* virer○ [*employee*]; supprimer [*jobs*]; abandonner [*plan*].

axis *n* axe *m*.

axle *n* essieu *m*.

azure *adj* [*sea, sky, eyes*] d'azur; [*fabric*] azur *inv*.

Bb

b, **B** *n* b, B *m*.

BA *n* (*abbr* = **Bachelor of Arts**) diplôme *m* universitaire de lettres.

babble *vi* [*baby*] babiller; [*stream*] murmurer.

baby I *n* bébé *m*; (figurative) (of team, group) benjamin/-e *m/f*.
II *noun modifier* [*brother, sister, son*] petit; [*animal*] bébé-; [*vegetable*] nain.

baby: **~ carriage** *n* (US) landau *m*; **~sit** *vi* faire du babysitting; **~sitter** *n* baby-sitter *mf*.

bachelor *n* **1** (single man) célibataire *m*; **2** (Univ) **Bachelor of Arts/Law** ≈ diplôme *m* universitaire de lettres/droit.

back ▶ 523 **I** *n* **1** (of person, animal) dos *m*; **to fall flat on one's ~** tomber sur le dos; **to turn one's ~ on sb/sth** tourner le dos à qn/qch; **to do sth behind sb's ~** faire qch dans le dos de qn; **2** (of page, cheque, hand, fork, envelope, shirt, coat) dos *m*; (of fabric) envers *m*; (of medal, coin) revers *m*; (of vehicle, plane, building, head) arrière *m*; (of electrical appliance) face *f* arrière; (of chair, sofa) dossier *m*; (of cupboard, drawer, fridge, bus, stage) fond *m*; **those at the ~ couldn't see** ceux qui étaient derrière ne pouvaient pas voir; **the steps at the ~ of the building** l'escalier à l'arrière de l'immeuble; **to be out ~**, **to be in the ~** (US) être dans le jardin or la cour; **3** (Sport) arrière *m*; **left ~** arrière gauche; **4** (end) fin *f*; **at the ~ of the book** à la fin du livre.
II *adj* **1** [*leg, paw, edge, wheel*] arrière; [*bedroom*] du fond; [*page*] dernier/-ière (*before n*); [*garden, gate*] de derrière; **2** (in finance) **~ interest/tax** arriérés *mpl* d'intérêts/d'impôts.
III *adv* **1** (after absence) **to be ~** être de retour; **I'll be ~ in five minutes** je reviens dans cinq minutes; **to come ~** rentrer (**from** de); **he's ~ at work** il a repris le travail; **she's ~ in (the) hospital** elle est retournée à l'hôpital; **when is he due ~?** quand doit-il rentrer?; **2** (in return) **to phone ~** rappeler; **I'll write ~ (to him)** je lui répondrai; **to smile ~ at sb** rendre son sourire à qn; **3** (backwards) [*glance, jump, step, lean*] en arrière; **4** (in space) **we overtook him 20 km ~** nous l'avons doublé il y a 20 km; **5** (in time) **~ in 1964/April** en 1964/avril; **~ in the days when** du temps où; **it was obvious as far ~ as last year/1985 that** déjà l'année dernière/en 1985 il était évident que; **6** (referring to location) **to travel to London and ~** faire un aller-retour à Londres; **we walked there and took the train ~** nous y sommes allés à pied et nous avons pris le train pour rentrer; **I'll see you ~ in the office** je te verrai au bureau.
IV *vtr* **1** (support) soutenir [*party, candidate, action, bill*]; appuyer [*application*]; apporter son soutien à [*enterprise, project*]; justifier [*argument, claim*] (**with** à l'aide de); financer [*venture*]; **2** (reverse) **to ~ the car into the garage** rentrer la voiture au garage en marche arrière; **3** (bet on) parier sur [*favourite, winner*].
V back and forth *phr* **to go** or **travel ~ and forth** (commute) [*person, bus*] faire la navette (**between** entre); **to walk** or **go ~ and forth** faire des allées et venues (**between** entre); **to sway ~ and forth** se balancer.
■ **back away** reculer; **to ~ away from** s'éloigner de [*person*]; chercher à éviter [*confrontation*].
■ **back down** céder; **to ~ down over** céder sur [*issue*].
■ **back onto**: **~ onto [sth]** [*house*] donner sur [qch] à l'arrière.
■ **back out**: ¶ **~ out 1** [*car, driver*] sortir en marche arrière; **2** [*person*] se désister; **to ~ out of** annuler [*deal, contract*]; [*competitor*] se retirer de [*event*]; ¶ **~ [sth] out**: **to ~ the car out of the garage** faire sortir la voiture du garage en marche arrière.
■ **back up**: ¶ **~ up 1** (Aut) reculer, faire marche arrière; **2** (US) (block) [*drains*] s'obstruer; [*traffic*] se bloquer; ¶ **~ [sth] up**, **~ up [sth] 1** (support) confirmer [*claims, case, theory*]; ¶ **~ [sb] up** soutenir [*person*].

back: **~ache** *n* mal *m* de dos; **~bencher** *n* (GB) député *m*.

backbone *n* (of person, animal) colonne *f* vertébrale; (of fish) grande arête *f*; (figurative) ossature *f*; **to be the ~ of** [*person, concept*] être le pilier de [*organization, project*].

backdate *vtr* antidater [*cheque, letter*].

back door *n* (of car) portière *f* arrière; (of building) porte de derrière.

backer *n* (supporter) allié/-e *m/f*; (of commercial venture) bailleur *m* de fonds.

backfire *vi* **1** [*scheme, tactics*] avoir l'effet inverse; **to ~ on sb** se retourner contre qn; **2** [*car*] pétarader.

backgammon ▶ 649 *n* jaquet *m*.

background I *n* **1** (of person) (social) milieu *m*; (personal, family) origines *fpl*; (professional) formation *f*; **2** (of events, situation) contexte *m*; **against a ~ of violence** dans un climat de violence; **to remain in the ~** rester au second plan; **voices in the ~** des voix en bruit de fond; **3** (of painting, photo, scene) arrière-plan *m*; **in the ~** à l'arrière-plan.
II *noun modifier* **1** [*information, knowledge*] concernant les origines de la situation; **~ reading** lectures *fpl* complémentaires; **2** [*music, lighting*] d'ambiance; [*noise*] de fond.

backhand *n* (Sport) revers *m*.

backing I *n* **1** (reverse layer) revêtement *m* intérieur; **2** (figurative) (support) soutien *m*.
II *noun modifier* (Mus) [*singer, group*] d'accompagnement.

backlash *n* réaction *f* violente (**against** contre).

backlog *n* retard *m*; **I've got a huge ~ (of work)** j'ai plein de travail en retard.

backpack I *n* sac *m* à dos.
II *vi* **to go ~ing** partir en voyage avec son sac à dos.

back: **~ pay** *n* rappel *m* de salaire; **~ rest** *n* dossier *m*.

back seat *n* siège *m* arrière; **to take a ~** (figurative) s'effacer.

back: **~side**○ *n* derrière *m*; **~stage** *adv* [*work, go*] dans les coulisses.

backstreet I *n* petite rue *f*.
II *noun modifier* [*abortionist*] clandestin.

backstroke *n* dos *m* crawlé.

back to back *adv* **to stand ~** [*two people*] se mettre dos à dos.

back to front *adj, adv* à l'envers.

backtrack *vi* rebrousser chemin; (figurative) faire marche arrière.

backup I *n* (gen) soutien *m*; (Mil) (reinforcements) renforts *mpl*.
II *noun modifier* (replacement) [*plan, system, vehicle*] de secours.

backward I *adj* **1** [*look, step*] en arrière; **2** (retarded) [*nation, society*] arriéré.
II *adv* (US) = **backwards**.

backwards, backward (US) *adv* **1** [*walk, crawl*] à reculons; [*lean, step, fall*] en arrière; **to move ~** reculer; **to walk ~ and forwards** faire des allées et venues; **2** [*count*] à rebours; [*play, wind*] à l'envers.

backyard *n* **1** (GB) (courtyard) arrière-cour *f*; **2** (US) (back garden) jardin *m* de derrière.

bacon *n* bacon *m*, ≈ lard *m*; **~ and egg(s)** des œufs au bacon.

bacteria *n pl* bactéries *fpl*.

bad I *n* **the good and the ~** le bon et le mauvais; **there is good and ~ in everyone** il y a du bon et du mauvais dans chacun.
II *adj* **1** (gen) mauvais (*before n*); [*joke*] stupide; [*language, word*] grossier/-ière; **he has ~ hearing** il n'entend pas très bien; **to be ~ at** être mauvais en [*subject*]; **to be ~ at maths** ne pas être très doué pour les maths; **not ~**○ pas mauvais, pas mal○; **it's ~ enough having to wait, but...** c'est déjà assez pénible de devoir attendre, mais...; **things look ~** cela s'annonce mal; **the exam wasn't ~ at all** l'examen s'est plutôt bien passé; **it's a ~ time to buy a house** ce n'est pas le bon moment pour acheter une maison; **too ~**○**!** (sympathetic) pas de chance!; (hard luck) tant pis!; **~ dog!** vilain!; **it is ~ to tell lies** ce n'est pas bien de mentir; **it will look ~** cela fera mauvais effet; **to feel ~** avoir mauvaise conscience (**about** à propos de); **2** (serious) [*accident, injury, mistake*] grave; **a ~ cold** un gros rhume; **3** (harmful) **~ for** mauvais pour [*person, health*]; **it's ~ for industry** c'est néfaste pour l'industrie; **4** (ill, injured) **to have a ~ back** souffrir du dos; **to have a ~ chest** être malade des poumons; **to be in a ~ way**○ aller très mal; **5** [*loan, debt*] douteux/-euse; **6** (rotten) [*fruit*] pourri; **to go ~** pourrir.

badge *n* (sew-on, pin-on, adhesive) badge *m*; (official) (gen, Mil) insigne *m*.

badly *adv* **1** (not well) [*begin, behave, sleep*] mal; [*educated, fed, made*] mal; **to go ~** [*exam, interview*] mal se passer; **to do ~** [*candidate, company*] obtenir de mauvais résultats; **to take sth ~** mal prendre qch; **2** [*suffer*] beaucoup; [*disrupt, affect*] sérieusement; [*burnt, hurt, damaged*] gravement; **3** (urgently) **to want/need sth ~** avoir très envie de/grand besoin de qch.

badly behaved *adj* désobéissant.

badly off *adj* (poor) pauvre; **to be ~ for** manquer de [*space, clothes*].

bad-mannered *adj* [*person*] mal élevé.

badminton ▶ 649 *n* badminton *m*.

bad-tempered *adj* (temporarily) irrité; (habitually) irritable.

baffle *vtr* rendre [qn] perplexe, confondre.

baffled *adj* perplexe (**by** devant), confondu (**by** par).

bag I *n* (container) sac *m* (**of** de); **20 pence a ~** 20 pence le sac.
II bags *n pl* bagages *mpl*; **to pack one's ~s** faire ses bagages; (figurative) faire ses valises.
IDIOMS **a mixed ~** un mélange hétérogène; **it's in the ~**○ c'est dans la poche○; **to have ~s under one's eyes** avoir des valises sous les yeux○.

baggage *n* bagages *mpl*.

baggage: **~ allowance** *n* franchise *f* de bagages; **~ check** *n* (US) bulletin *m* de consigne; **~ locker** *n* (US) consigne *f* automatique; **~ reclaim** *n* réception *f* des bagages.

Baghdad ▶ 574 *pr n* Bagdad.

bag: **~pipes** ▶ 753 *n* cornemuse *f*; **~ snatcher** *n* voleur/-euse *m/f* de sacs à main.

bail I *n* caution *f*; **to be (out) on ~** être libéré sous caution.
II *vtr* mettre [qn] en liberté provisoire.
■ **bail out**: **~ out [sb/sth], ~ [sb/sth] out** **1** (gen) tirer [qn] d'affaire [*person*]; renflouer [*company*]; **2** (Law) payer la caution pour [*person*].

bait *n* appât *m*.

bake I *vtr* (Culin) faire cuire [qch] au four [*dish, vegetable*]; faire [*bread, cake*].
II *vi* **1** (make bread) faire du pain; (make cakes) faire de la pâtisserie; **2** (cook) [*food*] cuire.
III baked *pp adj* [*salmon, apple*] au four; **~d beans** (Culin) haricots *mpl* blancs à la sauce tomate; **~d potato** pomme *f* de terre en robe des champs (au four).

baker ▶ 805 *n* boulanger/-ère *m/f*.

bakery ▶ 805 *n* boulangerie *f*.

baking: **~ powder** *n* (Culin) levure *f* chimique; **~ soda** *n* (Culin) bicarbonate *m* de soude.

balance I *n* **1** équilibre *m* (**between** entre); **to lose one's ~** perdre l'équilibre; **the ~ of power** (figurative) l'équilibre des forces; **the right ~** le juste milieu; **2** (scales) balance *f*; **to hang in the ~** être en jeu; **3** (in account) solde *m*; **to pay the ~** verser le surplus.
II *vtr* **1** mettre [qch] en équilibre [*ball, plate*]

(**on** sur); **2** (compensate for) (also **~ out**) compenser, équilibrer; **3** (counterbalance) contrebalancer [*weights*]; **4** (adjust) équilibrer [*diet, activity, budget*]; **to ~ the books** dresser le bilan; **5** (weigh up, compare) peser; **to ~ the advantages against the disadvantages** peser le pour et le contre.
III *vi* **1** [*person*] se tenir en équilibre (**on** sur); [*object*] tenir en équilibre (**on** sur); [*two things, persons*] s'équilibrer; **2** [*books, figures, budget*] être en équilibre.
IV balanced *pp adj* [*person, view, diet*] équilibré; [*article, report*] objectif/-ive.

balance sheet *n* bilan *m*.

balcony *n* **1** (in house, hotel) balcon *m*; **2** (of theatre) deuxième balcon *m*.

bald *adj* **1** [*man, head*] chauve; **to go ~** devenir chauve; **2** [*tyre*] lisse.

ball *n* **1** (Sport) (in tennis, golf, cricket) balle *f*; (in football, rugby) ballon *m*; (in billiards) bille *f*; (for gun, machine) balle *f*; **2** (of dough, clay) boule *f* (**of** de); (of wool, string) pelote *f* (**of** de); **3** (dance) bal *m*.

ball cock *n* (Tech) robinet *m* à flotteur.

ballet *n* ballet *m*.

balloon *n* **1** (toy) ballon *m*; **2** (also **hot air ~**) montgolfière *f*.

ballot I *n* **1** scrutin *m*; **the first ~** le premier tour de scrutin; **2** (also **~ paper**) bulletin *m* de vote.
II *vtr* consulter [qn] (par vote) (**on** sur).

ballot box *n* urne *f* (électorale); (figurative) (system) urnes *fpl*; **at the ~** aux urnes.

ball: **~point (pen)** *n* stylo *m* (à) bille; **~room** *n* salle *f* de danse.

Baltic *adj* **the ~ Sea** la mer *f* Baltique.

ban I *n* interdiction *f* (**on sth** de qch; **on doing** de faire).
II *vtr* interdire [*group, activity, book, drug*]; suspendre [*athlete*]; **to ~ sb from** exclure qn de [*sport, event*].

banana I *n* banane *f*.
II *noun modifier* [*yoghurt, ice cream*] à la banane.

band *n* **1** (of people) groupe *m* (**of** de); (of musicians) (rock) groupe (de rock); (municipal) fanfare *f*; **jazz ~** orchestre *m* de jazz; **2** (of light, colour, land) bande *f*; **3** (on radio) bande *f*; **4** (GB) (of age, income tax) tranche *f*; **5** (around arm) brassard *m*; (**hair**) **~** bandeau *m*.
■ **band together** se réunir (**to do** pour faire).

bandage I *n* bandage *m*.
II *vtr* bander [*head, limb, wound*].

bandwagon *n* IDIOMS **to jump** or **climb on the ~** prendre le train en marche.

bang I *n* (of explosion) détonation *f*, boum *m*; (of door, window) claquement *m*.
II○ *adv* **~ in the middle** en plein centre.
III *vtr* **1** taper sur [*drum, saucepan*]; **to ~ sth down on the table** poser bruyamment qch sur la table; **to ~ one's head** se cogner la tête (**on** contre); **to ~ one's fist on the table** taper du poing sur la table; **2** (slam) claquer [*door, window*].
IV *vi* [*door, shutter*] claquer; **to ~ on** cogner à [*wall, door*].
■ **bang into**: **~ into [sb/sth]** heurter.

banish *vtr* bannir (**from** de).

banister(s), **bannister(s)** (GB) *n* (*pl*) rampe *f* (d'escalier).

bank I *n* **1** (institution) banque *f*; **2** (of river, lake) rive *f*; (of major river) bord *m*; (of canal) berge *f*; **3** (mound) talus *m*; (of snow) congère *f*; (mass) (of flowers) massif *m*; (of fog, mist) banc *m*.
II *vi* **to ~ with the National** avoir un compte (bancaire) à la Nationale.
■ **bank on**: **~ on [sb/sth]** compter sur [qn/qch] (**to do** pour faire); **to ~ on doing** escompter faire.

bank: **~ account** *n* compte *m* bancaire; **~ balance** *n* solde *m* bancaire; **~ card** *n* carte *f* bancaire; **~ charges** *n pl* frais *mpl* bancaires; **~ clerk** ▶805 *n* employé/-e *m/f* de banque.

banker ▶805 *n* banquier/-ière *m/f*.

banker: **~'s draft** *n* traite *f* bancaire; **~'s order** *n* virement *m* bancaire.

bank holiday *n* (GB) jour *m* férié; (US) jour *m* de fermeture des banques.

banking I *n* **1** (business) opérations *fpl* bancaires; **2** (profession) la banque.
II *noun modifier* [*group, system, facilities*] bancaire; **~ hours** heures *fpl* d'ouverture des banques.

bank: **~ manager** ▶805 *n* directeur/-trice *m/f* d'agence bancaire; **~note** *n* billet *m* de banque.

bankrupt *adj* [*person*] ruiné; [*economy*] en faillite; **to go ~** faire faillite.

bankruptcy *n* faillite *f*.

bank: **~ statement** *n* relevé *m* de compte; **~ transfer** *n* virement *m* bancaire.

baptize *vtr* baptiser.

bar I *n* **1** (strip of metal, wood) barre *f*; (on cage, window) barreau *m*; **2** (pub) bar *m*; (counter) comptoir *m*; **3 ~ of soap** savonnette *f*; **~ of chocolate** tablette *f* de chocolat; **4** (Law) (profession) **the ~** le barreau; **5** (Sport) barre *f*; **6** (Mus) mesure *f*.
II *prep* sauf; **all ~ one** tous sauf un seul.
III *vtr* **1** barrer [*way, path*]; **to ~ sb's way** barrer le passage à qn; **2** (ban) exclure [*person*] (**from sth** de qch); **to ~ sb from doing** interdire à qn de faire.

barbaric *adj* barbare.

barbecue *n* barbecue *m*.

barbed wire, **barbwire** (US) *n* (fil *m* de fer) barbelé *m*.

barber ▶805 *n* coiffeur *m* (pour hommes).

Barcelona ▶574 *pr n* Barcelone.

bar: **~ chart** *n* histogramme *m*; **~ code** *n* code *m* à barres.

bare I *adj* [*flesh, leg, boards, wall, rock, branch*] nu; [*cupboard, room*] vide; **with one's ~ hands** à mains nues; **the ~ minimum** le strict nécessaire.
II *vtr* **to ~ one's teeth** montrer les dents.

barefoot I *adj* **to be ~** être nu-pieds.
II *adv* [*run, walk*] pieds nus.

barely *adv* à peine.

bargain I *n* **1** (deal) marché *m* (**between** entre); **2** (good buy) affaire *f*; **to get a ~** faire une affaire.
II *noun modifier* [*price*] avantageux/-euse.
III *vi* **1** (for deal) négocier (**with** avec); **2** (over price) marchander (**with** avec).
■ **bargain for, bargain on: ~ for sth, ~ on sth** s'attendre à qch.

bargaining I *n* (over pay) négociations *fpl*.
II *noun modifier* [*position, power, rights*] de négociation.

barge I *n* péniche *f*; (for freight) chaland *m*.
II *vi* **to ~ past sb** passer devant qn en le bousculant.
■ **barge in** (enter noisily) faire irruption; (interrupt) interrompre brutalement.

bark I *n* **1** (of tree) écorce *f*; **2** (of dog) aboiement *m*.
II *vi* [*dog, person*] aboyer (**at sb/sth** après qn/qch).

barking *n* aboiements *mpl*.

barley *n* orge *f*.

bar: **~maid** ▶805 *n* serveuse *f* de bar; **~man** ▶805 *n* barman *m*.

barn *n* (for crops) grange *f*; (for cattle) étable *f*; (for horses) écurie *f*.

baron *n* baron *m*; **drugs ~** baron *m* de la drogue.

barracks *n* caserne *f*.

barrage *n* **1** (dam) barrage *m*; **2** (Mil) tir *m* de barrage; **3** (figurative) (of questions) barrage *m*.

barrel *n* **1** (for beer, wine) tonneau *m*, fût *m*; (for petroleum) baril *m*; **2** (of cannon) tube *m*; (of handgun) canon *m*.

barricade I *n* barricade *f*.
II *vtr* barricader; **to ~ oneself** se barricader (**in, into** dans).

barrier *n* barrière *f*.

barrier cream *n* crème *f* protectrice.

barring *prep* à moins de.

barrister ▶805 *n* (GB) avocat/-e *m/f*.

base I *n* (gen, Mil) base *f*; (of tree, lamp) pied *m*; (of tail) point *m* d'attache; (of statue) socle *m*.
II *adj* [*act, motive, emotion*] ignoble.
III *vtr* fonder [*assumption, decision, character*] (**on** sur); **the film is ~d on a true story** le film est tiré d'une histoire vraie; **to be ~d in Paris** [*person, company*] être basé à Paris.

baseball ▶649 *n* base-ball *m*.

basement *n* sous-sol *m*; **in the ~** au sous-sol.

bashful *adj* timide; **to be ~ about doing** hésiter à faire.

basic *adj* **1** (fundamental) (gen) essentiel/-ielle; [*belief, principle*] fondamental; **2** (elementary) [*education, skill, rule*] élémentaire; [*pay, wage, supplies*] de base; **3** [*accommodation*] rudimentaire (derogatory).

basically *adv* fondamentalement.

basics *n pl* essentiel *m*; **to get down to ~s** aborder l'essentiel.

basil *n* basilic *m*.

basin *n* **1** (bowl) bol *m*; **2** (with taps) lavabo *m*; (for washing up) cuvette *f*.

basis *n* (gen) base *f* (**for, of** de); (of theory) point *m* de départ; (for belief, argument) fondements *mpl* (**for** de); **on the ~ of** sur la base de.

bask *vi* **to ~ in** se prélasser à [*sunshine*]; jouir de [*approval*].

basket *n* panier *m*.

basketball ▶649 *n* (game) basket(-ball) *m*; (ball) ballon *m* de basket.

Basque ▶712 I *n* **1** (person) Basque *mf*; **2** (language) basque *m*.
II *adj* basque.

bass ▶753 *n* basse *f*.

baste *vtr* **1** (Culin) arroser; **2** (in sewing) bâtir, faufiler.

bat *n* **1** (in cricket, baseball) batte *f*; (in table tennis) raquette *f*; **2** (Zool) chauve-souris *f*.
IDIOMS **to be blind as a ~** être myope comme une taupe.

batch *n* (of loaves, cakes) fournée *f*; (of eggs, fish) arrivage *m*; (of books, goods, orders) lot *m*; (of prisoners, students) groupe *m*.

bated *adj* **with ~ breath** en retenant son souffle.

bath I *n* (gen) bain *m*; (GB) (tub) baignoire *f*; **I was in the ~** j'étais dans mon bain.
II **baths** *n pl* **1** (for swimming) piscine *f*; **2** (in spa) thermes *mpl*.
III *vtr* (GB) baigner.

bathe I *vtr* laver [*wound*] (**in** dans; **with** à).
II *vi* **1** (swim) se baigner; **2** (US) (take bath) prendre un bain; **3 to be ~d in** ruisseler de [*sweat*]; être inondé de [*light*].

bathing *n* baignade *f*.

bathing: **~ cap** *n* bonnet *m* de bain; **~ trunks** *n* slip *m* de bain.

bath: **~ mat** *n* tapis *m* de bain; **~ oil** *n* huile *f* de bain; **~robe** *n* sortie *f* de bain.

bathroom *n* **1** salle *f* de bains; **2** (US) (lavatory) (public) toilettes *fpl*.

bathroom: **~ cabinet** *n* armoire *f* de toilette; **~ scales** *n pl* pèse-personne *m*.

bath: **~ salts** *n pl* sels *mpl* de bain; **~ towel** *n* serviette *f* de bain; **~tub** *n* baignoire *f*.

baton *n* (GB) (policeman's) matraque *f*; (used by traffic policeman) bâton *m*; (Mil, Mus) baguette *f*; (Sport) (in relay race) témoin *m*.

batter I *n* (Culin) pâte *f*; (for frying) pâte *f* à frire.
II *vtr* [*person*] battre [*person*]; [*storm, bombs*] ravager; [*waves*] battre.

battered *adj* [*kettle, hat*] cabossé; [*suitcase*] très abîmé; [*wife*] battu.

battery *n* (for camera, radio) pile *f*; (for engine) batterie *f*.

battery: **~ chicken** *n* poulet *m* d'élevage industriel; **~ farming** *n* élevage *m* en batterie.

battle I *n* bataille *f*; (figurative) lutte *f*; **to fight a ~** combattre; **to go into ~** engager le combat.
II *vi* (gen, Mil) combattre (**with sb** contre qn); **to ~ for sth/to do** lutter pour qch/pour faire.

battle: **~field** *n* champ *m* de bataille; **~ship** *n* cuirassé *m*.

bawdy *adj* [*song*] grivois; [*person*] paillard.

bawl *vi* (weep) brailler; (shout) hurler.

bay I *n* **1** (on coast) baie *f*; **2** (Bot) (also **~ tree**) laurier(-sauce) *m*; **3** (parking area) aire *f* de stationnement.
II *vi* [*dog*] aboyer (**at** contre, après).
IDIOMS **to hold [sb/sth] at ~** tenir [qn/qch] à distance [*attacker*]; enrayer [*unemployment*].

bay leaf *n* feuille *f* de laurier.

bayonet *n* baïonnette *f*.

BC (*abbr* = **Before Christ**) av. J.-C.

BCG *n* (Med) BCG *m*.

be

■ **Note** For translations of *there is*, *there are*, *here is* and *here are*, see the entries ***there*** and ***here***.
– This dictionary contains usage notes on topics such as clocktime, age, many of which include translations of particular uses of *to be*. For the index to these notes ▶ 1008.

I *vi* **1** être; **I am tired** je suis fatigué; **she is French** elle est française; **we are late** nous sommes en retard; **he is a doctor/widower** il est médecin/veuf; **he's a good doctor** c'est un bon médecin; **it is Monday** c'est lundi; **it's me!** c'est moi!; **it's yours** c'est à toi; **~ good!** sois sage!; **2** (physical and mental states) avoir; **I am cold/hot** j'ai froid /chaud; **are you hungry/thirsty ?** as-tu faim/soif?; **they are ashamed** ils ont honte; **his hands were cold** il avait froid aux mains; **3** (weather) faire; **it is cold/windy** il fait froid/du vent; **it is 40°** il fait 40°; **4** (health) aller; **how are you?** (polite) comment allez-vous?; (more informally) comment vas-tu?; (very informally) ça va?; **how is your son?** comment va votre fils?; ▶ **well**[1], **fine**, **better**; **5** (visit) **I've never been to Sweden** je ne suis jamais allé en Suède; **have you ever been to Africa?** tu es déjà allé en Afrique?; **has the postman been?** est-ce que le facteur est passé; **6** (age) avoir; **how old are you?** quel âge as-tu?; **I am 23** j'ai 23 ans; **7** (in maths) faire; **2 plus 2 is 4** 2 et 2 font 4; **8** (in probability and supposition) **if Henri were here** si Henri était là; **if I were you** à ta place; **had it not been for Frank, I'd have missed the train** sans Frank, j'aurais raté le train; **9** (phrases) **so ~ it** d'accord; **as it were** pour ainsi dire.
II *v aux* **1** (in passives) être; **the rabbit was killed by a fox** le lapin a été tué par un renard; **the house has been/will be sold** la maison a été/sera vendue; **the doors have been repainted** les portes ont été repeintes, on a repeint les portes; **the road is being resurfaced** on refait or on est en train de refaire la route; **it is said/claimed that...** on dit/prétend que...; **2** (in continuous tenses) **I'm coming/going** j'arrive/j'y vais; **we are going to London tomorrow** nous allons à Londres demain; **it is raining** il pleut; **he is reading** il lit, il est en train de lire; **I've been looking for you** je te cherchais; **we were working** nous travaillions, nous étions en train de travailler; ▶ **for**, **since**; **3** (with infinite) devoir; **you are to do it at once** tu dois le faire tout de suite; **you are not to tell him** il ne faut pas que tu le lui dise; **he was to arrive last Monday** il devait arriver lundi dernier; **she was never to see him again** elle ne devait plus jamais le revoir; **they are to ~ married** ils vont se marier; **it was to ~ expected** il fallait s'y attendre; **it was nowhere to ~ found** il était introuvable; **it was not to ~** le sort en avait décidé autrement; **4** (in tag questions) **it's a lovely house, isn't it?** c'est une très belle maison, n'est-ce pas?; **he was a doctor, wasn't he?** il était médecin, n'est-ce pas?; **they're not in the garden, are they?** ils ne sont pas dans le jardin, par hasard?; **he wasn't serious, was he?** il n'était pas sérieux, si?; **today is Tuesday, isn't it?** c'est bien mardi aujourd'hui?; **5** (in short answers) **'you are not going out'—'yes I am!'** 'tu ne sors pas'—'si!'; **'are you English?'—'yes, I am'** 'vous êtes anglais?'—'oui', 'oui, je suis anglais'; **'was it raining?'—'yes, it was'** 'est-ce qu'il pleuvait?'—'oui'.

beach *n* plage *f*.

beach: **~ ball** *n* ballon *m* de plage; **~wear** *n* tenues *fpl* de plage.

beacon *n* **1** (on runway) balise *f*; **2** (lighthouse) phare *m*; **3** (also **radio ~**) radiobalise *f*.

bead *n* **1** perle *f*; (**string of**) **~s** collier *m*; **2** (of sweat, dew) goutte *f*.

beak *n* bec *m*.

beam I *n* **1** (of light, torch) rayon *m*; (of car lights, lighthouse) faisceau *m*; **2** (piece of wood) poutre *f*; **3** (**radio**) **~** faisceau *m* de guidage.
II *vtr* [*radio, satellite*] transmettre [*programme, signal*].
III *vi* rayonner.

beaming *adj* rayonnant.

bean *n* haricot *m*.

bear I *n* ours *m*.
II *vtr* **1** (carry) (gen) porter; [*person*] apporter [*gift, message*]; **to ~ a resemblance to** ressembler à; **to ~ no relation to** n'avoir aucun rapport avec; **to ~ [sth] in mind** tenir compte de [*suggestion, information*]; **2** (endure) supporter; **I can't ~ to watch** je ne veux pas voir ça; **3** (stand up to) résister à [*scrutiny, inspection*]; **4** (yield) donner [*fruit, blossom, crop*]; [*investment*] rapporter [*interest*].
III *vi* **1 to ~ left/right** [*person*] prendre à gauche/à droite; **2** (weigh) **to ~ heavily on sb** [*tax, price increase*] peser lourdement sur qn; **to bring pressure to ~ on sb** exercer une pression sur qn.
■ **bear away**: **~ [sb/sth] away**, **~ away [sb/sth]** emporter [*person, boat*].
■ **bear out**: ¶ **~ out [sth]** confirmer [*theory, claim, story*]; ¶ **~ [sb] out** appuyer.
■ **bear up** [*person*] tenir le coup; [*structure*] résister.

bearable *adj* supportable.

beard *n* barbe *f*.

bearer *n* (of news, gift, letter) porteur/-euse *m/f*; (of passport) titulaire *mf*.

bearing *n* **1** (of person) allure *f*; **2 to have no/**

little ~ on sth n'avoir aucun rapport/avoir peu de rapport avec qch.

bearings *n pl* **to get one's ~** se repérer.

beast *n* **1** (animal) bête *f*; **2**○ (person) (annoying) chameau○ *m*; (brutal) brute *f*.

beat I *n* **1** (of drum, feet, heart) battement *m*; **to the ~ of the drum** au son du tambour; **2** (Mus) (rhythm) rythme *m*; **3** (of policeman) (area) secteur *m* de surveillance; (route) ronde *f*.
II *vtr* battre; **to ~ sb with a stick** donner des coups de bâton à qn; **to ~ sb at tennis** battre qn au tennis; **to ~ sth into sb** (figurative) inculquer qch à qn; **to ~ time** (Mus) battre la mesure; **to ~ one's way through** se frayer un chemin à travers [*crowd, obstacles*]; **she beat me to it** elle a été plus rapide que moi; **you can't ~ Italian shoes** rien ne vaut les chaussures italiennes.
III *vi* [*waves, rain*] battre (**against** contre); [*person*] cogner (**at, on** à); [*heart, drum, wings*] battre.
■ **beat back**: **~ [sth] back, ~ back [sth]** repousser [*group, flames*].
■ **beat down** [*rain*] tomber à verse (**on** sur); [*sun*] taper (**on** sur).
■ **beat off**: **~ [sb/sth] off, ~ off [sb/sth]** repousser [*attacker*]; chasser [*insects*].
■ **beat up**: **~ [sb] up, ~ up [sb]** tabasser○.

beaten *adj* battu.

beating *n* **1** (punishment) raclée○ *f*, correction *f*; **2** (of drum, heart, wings) battement *m*.

beautiful *adj* beau/belle (*before n*).

■ **Note** the irregular form *bel* of the adjective *beau, belle* is used before masculine nouns beginning with a vowel or a mute 'h'.

---

beautifully *adv* **1** (perfectly) [*play, write*] admirablement; **2** (attractively) [*furnished, situated*] magnifiquement; **~ dressed** habillé avec beaucoup de goût.

beauty I *n* beauté *f*.
II *noun modifier* [*contest, product, treatment*] de beauté.

beauty: **~ parlour** (GB), **~ parlor** (US) ▶805| *n* salon *m* de beauté; **~ queen** *n* reine *f* de beauté; **~ salon** ▶805| *n* salon *m* de beauté.

beauty spot *n* **1** (on skin) grain *m* de beauté; (fake) mouche *f*; **2** (place) beau site *m* or coin *m*.

beaver *n* castor *m*.

because I *conj* parce que.
II **because of** *phr* à cause de.

beckon I *vtr* faire signe à; **to ~ sb in** faire signe à qn d'entrer.
II *vi* faire signe (**to** à).

become I *vi* devenir; **to ~ ill** tomber malade.
II *v impers* **what has ~ of your brother?** qu'est-ce que ton frère est devenu?

becoming *adj* [*behaviour*] convenable; [*garment, haircut*] seyant.

bed *n* **1** lit *m*; **to get into ~** se mettre au lit; **to go to ~** aller au lit; **to put sb to ~** mettre qn au lit; **2** (of flowers) parterre *m*; **3** (of sea) fond *m*; (of river) lit *m*.

bed and breakfast, B and B *n* chambre *f* avec petit déjeuner, ≈ chambre *f* d'hôte; **to stay in a ~** loger chez l'habitant.

bed: **~clothes** *n pl* couvertures *fpl*; **~ linen** *n* draps *mpl*; **~ridden** *adj* alité, cloué au lit.

bedroom I *n* chambre *f* (à coucher).
II *noun modifier* [*carpet, furniture, window*] de chambre.

bedroom slipper *n* pantoufle *f*.

bedside I *n* chevet *m*.
II *noun modifier* [*book, lamp, table*] de chevet.

bed: **~sit**○, **~sitter** *n* (GB) chambre *f* meublée; **~spread** *n* dessus *m* de lit.

bedtime I *n* **it's ~** c'est l'heure d'aller se coucher.
II *noun modifier* [*story, drink*] avant de s'endormir.

bee *n* abeille *f*.

beech *n* **1** (also **~ tree**) hêtre *m*; **2** (also **~ wood**) (bois *m* de) hêtre *m*.

beef *n* bœuf *m*; **roast ~** rôti *m* de bœuf.

beefburger *n* hamburger *m*.

beehive *n* ruche *f*.

beeline *n* IDIOMS **to make a ~ for** se diriger tout droit vers.

beep *n* (of electronic device) bip *m*; (of car) coup *m* de klaxon®.

beer I *n* bière *f*.
II *noun modifier* [*barrel, bottle*] de bière; **~ can** canette *f* de bière.

bee sting *n* piqûre *f* d'abeille.

beet *n* betterave *f*.

beetle *n* (insect) scarabée *m*; (genus) coléoptère *m*.

beetroot *n* (GB) betterave *f*.

before ▶515| I *prep* **1** avant; **the day ~ yesterday** avant-hier; **the day ~ the exam** la veille de l'examen; **I was there the week ~ last** j'y étais il y a deux semaines; **six weeks ~ then** six semaines avant or auparavant; **~ long it will be winter** ce sera bientôt l'hiver; **G comes ~ H in the alphabet** dans l'alphabet le G est avant le H; **for him, work comes ~ everything else** pour lui le travail passe avant tout; **turn left ~ the crossroads** tournez à gauche avant le carrefour; **the page ~ this one** la page précédente; **2** ▶554| (US) (in time expressions) **ten ~ six** six heures moins dix; **3** (in front of) devant; **~ our very eyes** sous nos propres yeux; **to bring a bill ~ parliament** présenter un projet de loi au parlement; **these are the alternatives ~ us** voici les choix qui s'offrent à nous.
II *adj* précédent, d'avant; **the day ~** la veille; **the week ~** la semaine précédente.
III *adv* avant; **long ~** bien avant; **two months ~** deux mois auparavant; **have you been to India ~?** est-ce que tu es déjà allé en Inde?; **I've never been there ~** je n'y suis jamais allé; **I've never seen him ~ in my life** c'est la première fois que je le vois.
IV *conj* **1** (in time) **~ I go, I would like to say that** avant de partir, je voudrais dire que; **~ he goes, I must remind him that** avant qu'il

parte, il faut que je lui rappelle que; **it was some time ~ she was able to walk again** il lui a fallu un certain temps pour pouvoir marcher de nouveau; **oh, ~ I forget**... avant que j'oublie...; **2** (rather than) plutôt que; **he would die ~ betraying that secret** il mourrait plutôt que de révéler ce secret; **3** (or else) **get out of here ~ I call the police!** sortez d'ici ou j'appelle la police!; **4** pour que (+ *subj*); **you have to show your ticket ~ they'll let you in** il faut que tu montres ton ticket pour que tu sois admis.

beforehand *adv* (ahead of time) à l'avance; (earlier) auparavant, avant.

before-tax *adj* [*income*] brut; [*profit*] avant impôts.

beg I *vtr* demander (**from** à); **to ~ sb for sth** demander qch à qn; **I ~ your pardon** je vous demande pardon.
II *vi* [*person*] mendier (**from** à); [*dog*] faire le beau; **to ~ for help** demander de l'aide.

beggar *n* mendiant/-e *m/f*.
IDIOMS **~s can't be choosers** faute de grives on mange des merles (Proverb).

begin I *vtr* commencer [*journey, meeting, meal, game*] (**with** par, avec); provoquer [*debate, dispute*]; lancer [*campaign, trend*]; déclencher [*war*]; marquer le commencement de [*series, collection, festival*]; **to ~ doing** commencer à faire; **he began life as a sailor** il a débuté comme marin.
II *vi* commencer; **to ~ with sth** commencer par qch; **to ~ again** recommencer.
III **to begin with** *phr* (at first) au début, au départ; (firstly) d'abord, premièrement.

beginner *n* débutant/-e *m/f*; **~s' class** cours *m* pour débutants.

beginning *n* début *m*, commencement *m*; **in** or **at the ~** au départ, au début; **at the ~ of September** au début du mois de septembre; **from ~ to end** du début jusqu'à la fin; **to go back to the ~** reprendre au début.

beginnings *n pl* (of person, business) débuts *mpl*; (of movement) origines *fpl*.

behalf: **on ~ of** (GB), **in ~ of** (US) *phr* [*act, speak*] au nom de, pour; [*phone, write*] de la part de; [*negotiate*] pour le compte de.

behave I *vi* se comporter, se conduire (**towards** envers).
II *v refl* **to ~ oneself** bien se comporter; **~ yourself!** tiens-toi bien!

behaviour (GB), **behavior** (US) *n* (gen) comportement *m* (**towards** envers); (Sch) conduite *f*.
IDIOMS **to be on one's best ~** bien se tenir.

behead *vtr* décapiter.

behind I° *n* derrière° *m*.
II *adj* **to be ~ with** avoir du retard dans [*work*]; **to be too far ~** avoir trop de retard.
III *adv* [*follow on*] derrière; [*look, glance*] en arrière; **the car ~** la voiture de derrière.
IV *prep* **1** derrière; **~ my back** derrière le dos; (figurative) derrière mon dos; **he has three years' experience ~ him** il a trois ans d'expérience derrière lui; **I've put all that ~ me now** j'ai oublié tout ça; **the real story ~ the news** la véritable histoire que les médias n'ont pas révélée; **to be ~ the others** [*pupil*] être en retard par rapport aux autres; **2** (motivating) **the reasons ~ his declaration** les raisons qui motivent/motivaient sa déclaration; **who is ~ this proposal?** qui est à l'origine de cette proposition?; **3** (supporting) **to be** (**solidly**) **~ sb** soutenir qn (à fond).

beige ▶559 *n, adj* beige (*m*).

Beijing ▶574 *pr n* Pékin, Bei-jing.

being *n* **1** (**human**) **~** être *m* (humain); **2 to come into ~** prendre naissance.

Beirut ▶574 *pr n* Beyrouth.

Belgian ▶712 I *n* Belge *mf*.
II *adj* [*culture, food, politics*] belge; [*ambassador, embassy*] de Belgique.

Belgium ▶574 *pr n* Belgique *f*.

belief *n* **1** (opinion) conviction *f* (**about** sur, à propos de); **in the ~ that** convaincu que; **2** (confidence) confiance *f*, foi *f* (**in** dans); **3** (religious faith) foi *f*.

believe I *vtr* **1** croire [*evidence, statement, person*]; **~ it or not** croyez-le ou pas; **it has to be seen to be ~d** il faut le voir pour le croire; **I can't ~ (that) he did that** je n'arrive pas à croire qu'il ait fait cela; **I don't ~ you!** ce n'est pas vrai!; **I can well ~ it** je suis prêt à le croire; **2** (think) croire, estimer; **she is ~d to be a spy** on pense que c'est une espionne; **to let sb ~ (that)**... laisser croire à qn que...
II *vi* **to ~ in** croire à [*promises, discipline, ghosts*]; croire en [*God*].

believer *n* (in God) croyant/-e *m/f*; (in progress, liberty) adepte *mf* (**in** de).

bell *n* (in church) cloche *f*; (small) clochette *f*; (on toy, cat) grelot *m*; (on bicycle) sonnette *f*; **door ~** sonnette *f*; **to ring the ~s** faire sonner les cloches.
IDIOMS **that name rings a ~** ce nom me dit quelque chose.

bellow I *vi* [*bull*] mugir (**with** de); [*person*] hurler.
II *vtr* (also **~ out**) brailler [*command*].

bellows *n pl* soufflet *m*.

belly *n* **1**° (stomach) ventre *m*; (paunch) bedaine° *f*; **2** (of animal) ventre *m*.

belong *vi* **to ~ to** [*property*] appartenir à [*person*]; [*person*] faire partie de [*club, society, set*]; **where do these books ~?** où vont ces livres?

belongings *n pl* affaires *fpl*; **personal ~** effets *mpl* personnels.

beloved *adj* bien-aimé.

below I *prep* au-dessous de; **~ the knee** au-dessous du genou; **the apartment ~ mine** l'appartement au-dessous du mien; **~ freezing/sea level** au-dessous de zéro/du niveau de la mer; **the valley ~ there/us** la vallée en contrebas; **~ the surface** sous la surface.
II *adv* **the apartment/tenants ~** l'appartement/les locataires du dessous; **the people (in the street) ~** les gens en bas (dans la rue); **the village ~** le village en contrebas; **100**

before

As a preposition

⇨ I1

When *before* is used as a preposition, it is generally translated by *avant:*

before *the meeting*	= **avant** la réunion
she left ***before*** *me*	= elle est partie **avant** moi

As an adjective

When *before* is used as an adjective after a noun, it is translated by *précédent/-e*, or, less formally, *d'avant*:

the time ***before***	= la fois **précédente**
	= la fois **d'avant**
the month ***before***	= le mois **précédent**
	= le mois **d'avant**

the one before is translated by ***le précédent*** or ***la précédente***: ⇨ II

no, I'm not talking about that meeting but ***the one before***	= non, je ne parle pas de cette réunion-là mais de **la précédente**

As an adverb

◆ When *before* is used as an adverb meaning *beforehand*, it is translated by *avant* in statements about the present or future:

you could have told me ***before***	= tu aurais pu me le dire **avant**
I'll try to talk to her ***before***	= j'essaierai de lui en parler **avant**

◆ When *before* means *previously* in statements about the past, it is translated by *auparavant*:

I had met her two or three times ***before***	= je l'avais rencontrée deux ou trois fois **auparavant**

◆ When *before* means *already*, it is translated by *déjà*:

I've met her ***before***	= je l'ai **déjà** rencontrée
you've asked me that question ***before***	= tu m'as **déjà** posé cette question

◆ In negative sentences, *before* is often used in English simply to reinforce the negative. In such cases it is not translated at all:

I'd never eaten snails ***before***	= je n'avais jamais mangé d'escargots
you've never told me that ***before***	= tu ne m'as jamais dit ça ⇨ III

As a conjunction

◆ When used as a conjunction, *before* + *verb* is translated by *avant de* + *infinitive*, where the two verbs have the same subject:

before *I cook dinner* or ***before*** *cooking dinner I'm going to phone my mother*	= **avant de** préparer le dîner je vais appeler ma mère
she put in her lenses ***before*** *she put on her make-up* or ***before*** *putting on her make-up*	= elle a mis ses lentilles **avant de** se maquiller

◆ When used as a conjunction, *before* + *verb* is translated by *avant que* + *subjunctive*, where the two verbs have different subjects:

Tom wants to see her ***before*** *she leaves*	= Tom veut la voir **avant qu**'elle parte ⇨ IV
I wanted to let you know ***before*** *you make any plans*	= je voulais te prévenir **avant que** tu fasses des projets

metres ~ 100 mètres plus bas; **from ~** d'en bas; **see ~** (on page) voir ci-dessous.

belt I *n* **1** (for person) ceinture *f*; **seat ~** ceinture de sécurité; **2** (on machine) courroie *f*; **3** (area) zone *f*.
II *vtr* **1**° (hit) flanquer une beigne à° [*person*]; **2** (as punishment) donner une correction à.
IDIOMS **to tighten one's ~** se serrer la ceinture.

bench *n* **1** (gen, Sport) (seat) banc *m*; (workbench) établi *m*; **2** (Law) (also **Bench**) (judges collectively) magistrature *f* (assise); (in specific case) Cour *f*.

bend I *n* (in road) tournant *m*, virage *m*; (in river) courbe *f*; **there's a ~ in the road** la route fait un virage.
II *vtr* plier [*arm, leg*]; pencher [*head*]; courber [*back*]; (by mistake) tordre [*pipe, nail*]; **to ~ the rules** contourner la loi (or le règlement); (make exception) faire une exception.
III *vi* **1** [*road, path*] tourner; [*branch*] ployer; **2** [*person*] se pencher; **to ~ forward** se pencher en avant.
■ **bend down, bend over** se pencher.

beneath I *prep* **1** sous; **~ the table** sous la table; **the valley ~ them/you** la vallée en contrebas; **~ the calm exterior** sous des apparences calmes; **2 it is ~ you to do** c'est indigne de toi de faire.
II *adv* en dessous; **the apartment ~** l'appartement en dessous; **the valley ~** la vallée en contrebas.

beneficial *adj* [*effect, influence*] bénéfique; [*change*] salutaire.

benefit I *n* **1** (advantage) avantage *m* (**from** de); **to be to sb's ~** être à l'avantage de qn; **to have the ~ of** bénéficier de [*education*]; **2** (financial aid) allocation *f*; **to be on ~(s)** (GB) toucher les allocations.
II *noun modifier* [*concert, match*] de bienfaisance.
III *vtr* profiter à [*person*]; être avantageux/-euse pour [*group, nation*].
IV *vi* profiter; **to ~ from** tirer profit de; **to ~ from doing** gagner à faire.
IDIOMS **to give sb the ~ of the doubt** accorder à qn le bénéfice du doute.

benevolent *adj* [*person, smile*] bienveillant (**to, towards** envers); [*dictator*] éclairé.

benign *adj* **1** [*person, smile*] bienveillant; **2** (Med) bénin/-igne.

bent *adj* **1** [*nail, wire, stick*] tordu; [*person*] (stooped) courbé; **2 to be ~ on doing sth** vouloir à tout prix faire qch.

bereaved *adj* [*person, family*] endeuillé, en deuil.

berry *n* baie *f*.

berserk *adj* **to go ~** être pris/prise de folie furieuse.

berth I *n* couchette *f*.
II *vtr* faire mouiller; **to be ~ed at** être mouillé à.
IDIOMS **to give sb/sth a wide ~**° éviter qn/qch.

beset *adj* **a country ~ by strikes** un pays en proie aux grèves.

beside *prep* **1** (next to) à côté de; **~ you** à côté de toi; **~ the sea** au bord de la mer; **2** (in comparison with) par rapport à; **my problems seem rather minor ~ yours** mes problèmes semblent assez insignifiants par rapport aux tiens.
IDIOMS **to be ~ oneself (with anger)** être hors de soi; **to be ~ oneself (with excitement)** être surexcité; **to be ~ oneself (with happiness)** être fou/folle de joie.

besides I *adv* **1** (moreover) d'ailleurs; **2** (in addition) en plus, aussi.
II *prep* en plus de; **~ being an artist, she...** en plus d'être une artiste, elle...

besiege *vtr* (Mil) assiéger; (figurative) assaillir.

besotted *adj* follement épris (**with** de).

bespectacled *adj* à lunettes.

best I *n* **1 the ~** le/la meilleur/-e *m/f*; **it's the ~ of his novels** c'est son meilleur roman; **we've had the ~ of the day** le beau temps est fini pour aujourd'hui; **the ~ of its kind** le meilleur du genre; **this play is not her ~** cette pièce n'est pas la meilleure qu'elle ait écrite; **to be the ~ at** être le/la meilleur/-e en [*subject, game*]; **who's the ~ at drawing?** qui dessine le mieux?; **it's for the ~** (of something done) c'est tant mieux; **in the ~ of taste** du meilleur goût; **the ~ of friends** les meilleurs amis du monde; **the ~ we can hope for** le mieux qu'on puisse espérer; **at ~** au mieux; **to make the ~ of sth** s'accommoder de qch; **the city is at its ~ in autumn** c'est en automne que la ville est la plus belle; **to be at one's ~** [*athlete, writer*] être au mieux de sa forme; **to do one's ~ to do** faire de son mieux or faire (tout) son possible pour faire; **is that the ~ you can do?** c'est le mieux que tu puisses faire?; **to get the ~ out of** obtenir le meilleur de [*pupil, worker*]; **2** (good wishes) **all the ~!** (good luck) bonne chance!; (cheers) à ta santé!; **wishing you all the ~ on your retirement** meilleurs vœux de bonheur pour votre retraite.
II *adj* meilleur; **the ~ idea she's had all day** la meilleure idée qu'elle ait eue de la journée; **the ~ thing about sth** (outstanding feature) ce qu'il y a de mieux dans qch; **she looks ~ in black** c'est en noir qu'elle est le mieux; **my ~ dress** ma plus belle robe; **who is the ~ swimmer?** qui nage le mieux?; **the ~ thing to do** la meilleure chose à faire; **the ~ thing would be to refuse** le mieux serait de refuser; **he's the ~ person for the job** c'est la personne qu'il faut pour ce travail.
III *adv* le mieux; **to behave/fit ~** se comporter/aller le mieux; **to like sth ~** aimer qch le mieux or le plus; **~ of all** mieux que tout; **to do ~** réussir le mieux; **you know ~** c'est toi le meilleur juge.

best man *n* témoin *m*.

bestow *vtr* accorder (**on** à); conférer [*title*] (**on** à).

bestseller *n* bestseller *m*.

bet I *n* pari *m*; (in casino) mise *f*; **to place a ~ on** parier sur [*horse, dog*]; miser sur [*number, colour*]; **a safe ~** une valeur sûre.

II *vtr* parier (**on** sur); (in gambling) parier, miser; **I ~ you 100 dollars** je te parie 100 dollars.
III *vi* parier (**on** sur); (in casino) miser; **to ~ on sth happening** parier que qch va se produire; **you can ~ on it** tu peux en être sûr.

Bethlehem ▶574| *pr n* Bethléem.

betray *vtr* trahir [*country, friend, person, trust*]; tromper [*lover*].

betrayal *n* trahison *f*; (of secret, plan) révélation *f*; **~ of trust** abus *m* de confiance.

better

■ **Note** When *better* is used as an adjective, it is translated by *meilleur* or *mieux* depending on the context (see below, and note that *meilleur* is the comparative form of *bon*, *mieux* the comparative form of *bien*). The translation of the construction *to be better than* varies depending on whether *bon* or *bien* works originally with the noun: *their wine is better than our wine* = leur vin est meilleur que le nôtre; *her new apartment is better than her old one* = son nouvel appartement est mieux que l'ancien; *his new film is better than his last one* = son nouveau film est mieux *or* meilleur que le précédent (both *bon* and *bien* work with the noun in this last example). Other constructions may be translated as follows: *this is a better bag/car* = ce sac/cette voiture est mieux; *it is better to do* = il vaut mieux faire *or* il est mieux de faire.
– As an adverb (*to do sth better*), *better* can almost always be translated by *mieux*. For more examples and particular usages, see the entry below.

I *n* **the ~ of the two** le/la meilleur/-e or le/la mieux des deux; **to deserve ~** mériter mieux; **so much the ~** tant mieux.
II *adj* meilleur; **to get ~** [*situation, weather*] s'améliorer; [*ill person*] aller mieux; **things are getting ~** ça va mieux; **that's ~!** voilà qui est mieux!; **to be ~** [*patient, cold*] aller mieux; **to feel all the ~ for** se sentir mieux après [*rest, meal*]; **if it makes you feel any ~** (less sad) si ça peut te consoler; **I sold the car and bought a ~ one** j'ai vendu la voiture et j'en ai acheté une mieux; **to be no ~ than a thief** être un voleur ni plus ni moins; **to be a ~ swimmer than sb** nager mieux que qn; **to be ~ at** être meilleur en [*subject, sport*]; **to be ~ than nothing** être mieux que rien; **the bigger/sooner the ~** le plus grand/vite possible; **the less said about that the ~** mieux vaut ne pas parler de ça.
III *adv* mieux; **to behave ~ than** se comporter mieux que; **~ behaved/educated** plus sage/cultivé; **to do ~** (in career, life) réussir mieux; (in exam, essay) faire mieux; **it couldn't have been ~ timed** ça n'aurait pas pu mieux tomber; **you had ~ do, you'd ~ do** (advising) tu ferais mieux de faire; (warning) tu as intérêt à faire; **we'd ~ leave** on ferait mieux de partir; **'will she come?'—'she'd ~○!'** 'est-ce qu'elle viendra?'—'elle a intérêt!'
IV *vtr* (improve) améliorer [*performance*]; (beat) faire mieux que [*performance*].
IDIOMS **for ~ (or) for worse** advienne que pourra; (in wedding vow) pour le meilleur et pour le pire; **his curiosity got the ~ of him** sa curiosité a pris le dessus; **to go one ~** faire encore mieux (**than** que); **to think ~ of it** changer d'avis.

better off **I** *n* **the better-off** les riches *mpl*.
II *adj* **1** (more wealthy) plus riche (**than** que); **2** (in better situation) mieux.

betting *n* (activity) paris *mpl*; (odds) côte *f*.

betting shop *n* (GB) bureau *m* de PMU.

between

■ **Note** When *between* is used as a preposition expressing physical location (*between the lines*), time (*between 8 am and 11 am*), position in a range (*between 30 and 40 kilometres*), relationship (*link between, difference between*), it is translated by *entre*. For particular usages, see the entry below.

I *prep* **1** entre; **~ you and me, ~ ourselves** entre nous; **~ now and next year** d'ici l'année prochaine; **we mustn't allow this to come ~ us** il ne faut pas que cela crée des problèmes entre nous; **2 the couples have ten children ~ them** à eux tous, les couples ont dix enfants; **they drank the whole bottle ~ (the two of) them** ils ont bu toute la bouteille à eux deux.
II *adv* (also **in ~**) (in space) au milieu, entre les deux; (in time) entre-temps; **the two main roads and the streets (in) ~** les deux rues principales et les petites rues situées entre elles; **neither red nor orange, but somewhere in ~** ni rouge ni orange mais entre les deux.

beverage *n* boisson *f*, breuvage *m*.

bevy *n* (of people) troupeau *m*.

beware **I** *excl* prenez garde!, attention!
II *vi* se méfier (**of** de); **to ~ of doing** faire attention à ne pas faire.

bewildered *adj* [*person*] déconcerté (**at, by** par); [*look*] perplexe.

bewildering *adj* déconcertant.

bewitch *vtr* ensorceler.

beyond **I** *prep* **1** (in space and time) au-delà de; **~ the city walls** au-delà des murs de la ville; **just ~ the lights** juste après les feux; **~ the age of 10** au-delà de l'âge de 10 ans; **~ 1995** au delà de 1995; **2** (outside the range of) **~ one's means** au-dessus de ses moyens; **~ all hope** au-delà de toute espérance; **~ one's control** hors de son contrôle; **he is ~ help** on ne peut rien faire pour lui; **it's ~ me** ça me dépasse; **3** (other than) en dehors de, à part.
II *adv* **1** (in space) **in the room ~** dans la pièce d'à côté; **as far as London and ~** jusqu'à Londres et au-delà; **2** (in time) au-delà.
III *conj* à part (+ *infinitive*); **~ telling him that...** à part lui dire que...
IDIOMS **to be in the back of ~** être au bout du monde.

bias **I** *n* parti *m* pris; **to display ~** faire preuve de parti pris; **an American ~** une tendance pro-américaine.
II *vtr* **to ~ sb against/in favour of** prévenir qn contre/en faveur de.

biased, **biassed** *adj* [*person*] partial; [*report*] manquant d'objectivité; **to be ~** [*person*] avoir des partis pris; **to be ~ against** avoir un préjugé défavorable envers.

Bible *n* Bible *f*.

biblical *adj* biblique.

bibliography *n* bibliographie *f*.

bicentenary, **bicentennial** *n* bicentenaire *m*.

bicker *vi* se chamailler (**about** au sujet de).

bicycle I *n* bicyclette *f*, vélo° *m*; **on a/by ~** à bicyclette; **to ride a ~** faire de la bicyclette.
II *noun modifier* [*pump*] à bicyclette; [*bell, chain, lamp*] de bicyclette; [*hire, repair*] de bicyclettes; [*race*] cycliste.

bicycle: **~ clip** *n* pince *f* à vélo; **~ lane** *n* piste *f* cyclable; **~ rack** *n* (in yard) parc *m* à bicyclettes; (on car) galerie *f*.

bid I *n* **1** (at auction) enchère *f* (**for** sur; **of** de); **2** (for contract) soumission *f*; **3** (attempt) tentative *f* (**to do** pour faire).
II *vtr* **1** offrir [*money*] (**for** pour); **2** (say) **to ~ sb good morning** dire bonjour à qn.
III *vi* (at auction) enchérir (**for** sur); (for contract) soumissionner (**for** pour); **to ~ against sb** (at auction) renchérir sur qn.

bidder *n* **1** (at auction) enchérisseur/-euse *m/f* (**for** pour); **to go to the highest ~** être adjugé au plus offrant; **2** (for contract) soumissionnaire *m* (**for** pour).

bidding *n* (at auction) enchères *fpl*.

bide *vi* IDIOMS **to ~ one's time** attendre le bon moment.

biennial *adj* [*plant*] bisannuel/-elle; [*event*] biennal.

bifocals *n pl* verres *mpl* à double foyer.

big *adj* (gen) grand (*before n*); [*animal, car, boat, parcel, box, organization*] gros/grosse (*before n*), grand (*before n*); [*meal*] copieux/-ieuse; **to get ~(ger)** (taller) grandir; (fatter) grossir; **a ~ book** (thick) un gros livre; (large-format) un grand livre; **his ~ brother** son grand frère, son frère aîné; **a ~ mistake** une grave erreur; **to be in ~ trouble** être dans le pétrin°; **he fell for her in a ~ way** il est tombé follement amoureux d'elle; **to have ~ ideas**, **to think ~** voir grand.

bigamy *n* bigamie *f*.

big business *n* **1** les grandes entreprises *fpl*; **2 to be ~** rapporter gros.

big: **~ cat** *n* grand félin *m*; **~ dipper** *n* (GB) (at fair) montagnes *fpl* russes; **~ game** *n* gros gibier *m*; **~headed**° *adj* prétentieux/-ieuse.

bigmouth° *n* **he's such a ~°!** il ne sait pas tenir sa langue!

big name *n* **to be a ~** être connu (**in** dans le monde de).

bigoted *adj* intolérant, sectaire.

big: **~ screen** *n* grand écran *m*; **~ shot**° *n* gros bonnet° *m*; **~ toe** *n* gros orteil *m*; **~ top** *n* (tent) grand chapiteau *m*.

bike *n* (cycle) vélo *m*; (motorbike) moto *f*.

biker° *n* motard° *m*; **~('s) jacket** veste *f* de moto.

bikini *n* bikini® *m*.

bilateral *adj* bilatéral.

bilingual *adj* bilingue.

bilious *adj* **~ attack** crise *f* de foie.

bill I *n* **1** (in restaurant) addition *f*; (for services, electricity) facture *f*; (from hotel, doctor, dentist) note *f*; **2** (proposed law) (also **Bill**) projet *m* de loi; **3** (poster) affiche *f*; **to top the ~** être en tête d'affiche; **4** (US) (banknote) **dollar ~** billet *m* d'un dollar.
II *vtr* **to ~ sb for sth** facturer qch à qn.
IDIOMS **to fit** or **fill the ~** faire l'affaire.

billboard *n* panneau *m* d'affichage.

billet *vtr* cantonner [*soldier, refugee*] (**on, with** chez).

billiards ▶ 649 *n* billard *m*.

billion *n* (a thousand million) milliard *m*; (GB) (a million million) billion *m*.

billionaire *n* milliardaire *mf*.

bill of sale *n* acte *m* de vente.

billow *vi* [*clouds, smoke*] s'élever en tourbillons.
■ **billow out** [*skirt, sail*] se gonfler; [*steam*] s'élever.

billy goat *n* bouc *m*.

bin *n* (GB) (for rubbish) poubelle *f*.

binary *adj* binaire.

bind *vtr* **1** (tie up) attacher (**to** à); **2 to be bound by** être tenu par [*law, oath*]; **3** (also **~ together**) unir [*people, community*].
■ **bind over**: **~ [sb] over** (Law) relâcher [qn] sous condition.
■ **bind up**: **~ up [sth]**, **~ [sth] up** bander [*wound*].

binder *n* (for papers, lecture notes) classeur *m*.

binding I *n* reliure *f*.
II *adj* [*agreement, contract*] qui engage.

binge° *n* **to go on a ~** faire la noce.

bingo ▶ 649 *n* bingo *m*.

bin liner *n* (GB) sac *m* poubelle.

binoculars *n pl* jumelles *fpl*.

biochemistry *n* biochimie *f*.

biodegradable *adj* biodégradable.

biographer ▶ 805 *n* biographe *mf*.

biographical *adj* biographique.

biography *n* biographie *f*.

biological *adj* biologique.

biology *n* biologie *f*.

biopsy *n* biopsie *f*.

birch *n* **1** (also **~ tree**) bouleau *m*; **2** (whip) fouet *m*.

bird *n* **1** (Zool) oiseau *m*; **2**° (GB) (girl) nana° *f*.
IDIOMS **to kill two ~s with one stone** faire d'une pierre deux coups.

bird: **~ of prey** *n* oiseau *m* de proie; **~ sanctuary** *n* réserve *f* ornithologique; **~'s eye view** *n* vue *f* d'ensemble; **~song** *n* chant *m* des oiseaux.

bird-watching *n* **to go ~** observer les oiseaux.

biro® *n* (GB) stylo-bille *m*, bic®.

birth *n* naissance *f* (**of** de); **to give ~ to** [*woman*] accoucher de; [*animal*] mettre bas.

birth: **~ certificate** *n* certificat *m* de naissance; **~ control** *n* (in society) contrôle *m* des naissances; (by couple) contraception *f*.

birthday I *n* anniversaire *m*.
II *noun modifier* [*cake, card, present*] d'anniversaire.

birthday party *n* (for child) goûter d'anniversaire; (for adult) soirée *f* d'anniversaire.

birth: **~mark** *n* tache *f* de naissance; **~place** *n* lieu *m* de naissance; **~rate** *n* taux *m* de natalité.

biscuit *n* **1** (GB) biscuit *m*, petit gâteau *m*; **2** (US) pain *m* au lait.
IDIOMS **that takes the ~**○**!** ça, c'est le pompon!

biscuit barrel, **biscuit tin** *n* boîte *f* à biscuits.

bisect *vtr* diviser [qch] en deux parties égales.

bisexual *n, adj* bisexuel/-elle (*m/f*).

bishop *n* **1** (religious leader) évêque *m*; **2** (in chess) fou *m*.

bit I *n* **1** (of food, substance, wood) morceau *m* (**of** de); (of paper, string, land) bout *m* (**of** de), **2**○ (small amount) **a ~ of** un peu de [*time, butter, money*]; **a ~ of advice** un petit conseil; **with a ~ of luck** avec un peu de chance; **wait a ~!** attends un peu!; **a good ~ bigger** bien plus grand; **3**○ (section) (of book, film) passage *m*; **4** (of horse) mors *m*.
II **a bit**○ *phr* un peu; **a ~ early** un peu trop tôt; **she isn't a ~ like me** elle ne me ressemble pas du tout; **it's a ~ of a surprise** c'est un peu surprenant.
IDIOMS **~ by ~** petit à petit; **~s and pieces** (fragments) morceaux *mpl*; (belongings) affaires *fpl*; **every ~ as good** tout aussi bon; **to do one's ~** faire sa part (de boulot○).

bitch *n* **1** (dog) chienne *f*; **2**○ (derogatory) garce○ *f*.

bite I *n* **1** (mouthful) bouchée *f*; **to take a ~ of sth** prendre une bouchée de qch; **2** (from insect) piqûre *f*; (from dog, snake) morsure *f*.
II *vtr* [*animal, person*] mordre; [*insect*] piquer; **to ~ one's nails** se ronger les ongles.
III *vi* [*fish*] mordre.

biting *adj* **1** [*wind*] cinglant; **2** [*comment*] mordant.

bitter *adj* [*person, taste, fruit, tone, memory*] amer/-ère; [*hatred*] profond; [*feud*] âpre; [*wind*] glacial; [*disappointment, truth*] cruel/-elle.
IDIOMS **to the ~ end** jusqu'au bout.

bitterly *adv* [*complain, speak*] amèrement; [*regret*] profondément.

bitterness *n* amertume *f*.

bizarre *adj* bizarre.

black ▶559 **I** *n* **1** (colour) noir *m*; **he sees everything in ~ and white** (figurative) pour lui c'est tout noir ou tout blanc; **2** (also **Black**) (person) Noir/-e *m/f*; **3 to be in the ~** être créditeur/-trice.
II *adj* **1** [*object, paint, hair, garment*] noir; [*night*] obscur; **to paint sth ~** peindre qch en noir; **to turn ~** noircir; **2** (also **Black**) [*community, culture*] noir; **3** [*coffee*] noir; [*tea*] nature; **4** [*mood, picture*] noir; [*despair*] profond; [*day*] mauvais; **5** (angry) [*look*] meurtrier/-ière; [*mood*] massacrant; **6** (evil) [*magic*] noir.
■ **black out**: ¶ **~ out** [*person*] s'évanouir; ¶ **~ [sth] out, ~ out [sth] 1** (darken) faire l'obscurité sur [*stage*]; **2** (cut power) couper le courant dans [*area*].

black: **~ American** *n* noir/-e *m/f* américain/-e; **~ belt** *n* ceinture *f* noire (**in** de); **~berry** *n* mûre *f*; **~bird** *n* merle *m*; **~board** *n* tableau *m* (noir); **~ box** *n* (in plane, computer) boîte *f* noire; **~currant** *n* cassis *m*.

blacken *vtr* [*actor*] se noircir [*face*]; [*smoke*] noircir [*brick, wood*].

black: **~ eye** *n* œil *m* poché, œil *m* au beurre noir○; **~head** *n* point *m* noir; **~ ice** *n* verglas *m*.

blacklist I *n* liste *f* noire.
II *vtr* mettre [qn] à l'index.

blackmail I *n* chantage *m*.
II *vtr* faire chanter [*victim*].

black: **~mailer** *n* maître-chanteur *m*; **~ mark** *n* (figurative) mauvais point *m*.

black market *n* **on the ~** au marché noir.

blackout *n* **1** (power cut) panne *f* de courant; (in wartime) black-out *m*; **2** (faint) étourdissement *m*.

black: **~ pepper** *n* poivre *m* noir; **~ pudding** *n* (GB) boudin *m* noir; **Black Sea** *pr n* mer *f* Noire; **~ sheep** *n* (figurative) brebis *f* galeuse; **~smith** ▶805 *n* forgeron *m*.

bladder *n* vessie *f*.

blade *n* (of knife, sword, axe) lame *f*; (of fan, propeller, oar) pale *f*; (of grass) brin *m*.

blame I *n* responsabilité *f* (**for** de); **to lay the ~ for sth on sb** attribuer la responsabilité de qch à qn.
II *vtr* en vouloir à [*person, group*]; **to ~ sb for sth** reprocher qch à qn; **to ~ sth on sb** tenir qn responsable de qch; **to be to ~ for sth** être responsable de qch.
III *v refl* **to ~ oneself for sth** se sentir responsable de qch.

blameless *adj* irréprochable.

blancmange *n* blanc-manger *m*.

bland *adj* [*food, flavour*] fade; [*person*] terne.

blank I *n* **1** (empty space) blanc *m*; **my mind's a ~** j'ai la tête vide; **2** (cartridge) cartouche *f* à blanc.
II *adj* **1** [*paper, page*] blanc/blanche; [*screen*] vide; [*cassette, disk*] vierge; **2** [*expression*] ébahi; **to look ~** avoir l'air ébahi; **my mind went ~** j'ai eu un trou de mémoire.
IDIOMS **to draw a ~** faire chou blanc.

blank cheque (GB), **blank check** (US) *n* **1** chèque *m* en blanc; **2** (figurative) carte *f* blanche.

blanket I *n* **1** couverture *f*; **2** (of snow, ash) couche *f*; (of cloud, fog) nappe *f*.
II *adj* (wholescale) global.

blasphemous *adj* [*person*] blasphémateur/-trice; [*statement*] blasphématoire.

blasphemy *n* blasphème *m*.

blast I *n* **1** (explosion) explosion *f*; **2** (of air)

souffle *m*; **3 at full ~** [*play music*] à plein volume.
II *vtr* [*frost, disease*] détruire [*crop*].
III *vi* [*miner*] utiliser des explosifs.
■ **blast off** [*rocket*] décoller.

blasting *n* travail *m* à l'explosif.

blast-off *n* lancement *m*.

blatant *adj* [*lie, bias, disregard*] éhonté; [*example, abuse*] flagrant.

blatantly *adv* ouvertement; **to be ~ obvious** sauter aux yeux.

blaze I *n* **1** (fire) (in hearth) feu *m*, flambée *f*; (accidental) incendie *m*; **2** (sudden burst) (of flames) embrasement *m*; **in a ~ of publicity** sous les feux des médias.
II *vtr* **to ~ a trail** faire œuvre de pionnier.
III *vi* (also **~ away**) **1** (burn) [*fire, house*] brûler; **2** [*lights*] briller.
IV blazing *pres p adj* [*fire*] (in hearth) ronflant; [*building*] embrasé; [*sunshine*] plein (*before n*).

blazer *n* blazer *m*.

bleach I *n* **1** (disinfectant) eau *f* de javel; **2** (for hair) décolorant *m*.
II *vtr* décolorer [*hair*]; blanchir [*linen*].

bleak *adj* [*landscape*] désolé; [*weather*] maussade; [*outlook, future*] sombre.

bleary *adj* [*eyes*] bouffi; **to be ~-eyed** avoir les yeux bouffis.

bleat *vi* [*sheep, goat*] bêler.

bleed I *vtr* **to ~ sb dry** saigner qn à blanc.
II *vi* **1** saigner; **my finger's ~ing** j'ai le doigt qui saigne; **2** [*colour, dye*] déteindre.

bleeding I *n* saignement *m*; (heavy) hémorragie *f*.
II *adj* [*wound*] saignant; [*hand, leg*] qui saigne.

bleep I *n* bip *m*, bip-bip *m*.
II *vtr* (GB) **to ~ sb** appeler qn (au bip), biper qn.
III *vi* émettre un signal sonore or des signaux sonores.

blemish *n* (gen) imperfection *f*; (on fruit) tache *f*; (pimple) bouton *m*.

blend I *n* mélange *m* (**of** de).
II *vtr* mélanger [*ingredients, colours, styles*].
III *vi* **to ~ (together)** [*colours, tastes, styles*] se fondre; **to ~ with** [*colours, tastes, sounds*] se marier à; [*smells*] se mêler à.
■ **blend in**: ¶ **~ in** s'harmoniser (**with** avec); ¶ **~ in [sth], ~ [sth] in** incorporer [*ingredient*].

blender *n* mixeur *m*, mixer *m*.

bless *vtr* bénir; **~ you!** (after sneeze) à vos souhaits!; **to be ~ed with** jouir de [*health, beauty*].

blessed *adj* [*place*] béni; [*saint*] bienheureux/-euse.

blessing *n* **1** (asset, favour) bienfait *m*; **a ~ in disguise** un bienfait caché; **2** (ritual) bénédiction *f*; **with sb's ~** avec la bénédiction de qn.

blight *n* (on society) plaie *f* (**on** de); **urban ~** délabrement *m* urbain.

blind I *n* **1 the ~** les aveugles *mpl*; **2** (on window) store *m*.
II *adj* [*person*] aveugle; **to go ~** perdre la vue; **~ in one eye** borgne.
III *vtr* **1** [*injury, accident*] rendre aveugle; **2** [*sun, light*] éblouir; **3** [*pride, love*] aveugler.
IDIOMS **to turn a ~ eye** fermer les yeux (**to** sur).

blind alley *n* voie *f* sans issue.

blindfold I *n* bandeau *m*.
II *adj* (also **~ed**) aux yeux bandés.
III *vtr* bander les yeux à [*person*].

blindly *adv* [*obey, follow*] aveuglément.

blindness *n* **1** (handicap) cécité *f*; **2** (figurative) aveuglement *m*.

blind spot *n* **1** (in eye) point *m* aveugle; **2** (in car, on hill) angle *m* mort; **3** (figurative) **to have a ~ about sth** avoir un bandeau sur les yeux quand il s'agit de qch.

blink *vi* [*person*] cligner des yeux.
IDIOMS **on the ~**○ [*television, microwave*] détraqué○.

blinker *n* (Aut) clignotant *m*; (US) (at crossing) (feu *m*) clignotant *m*.

blinkered *adj* [*attitude, approach*] borné.

blip *n* **1** (on screen) spot *m*; (on graph, line) accident *m* (d'une courbe); **2** (sound) bip *m*; **3** (hitch) contretemps *m*.

bliss *n* (figurative) bonheur *m* parfait.

blissfully *adv* **~ happy** au comble du bonheur; **~ ignorant** dans la plus parfaite ignorance.

blister I *n* (on skin) ampoule *f*.
II *vi* [*skin, paint*] cloquer.

blithely *adv* (nonchalantly) avec insouciance; (cheerfully) allègrement.

blitz I *n* bombardement *m* aérien; **the Blitz** (GB) le Blitz.
II *vtr* bombarder.

blizzard *n* tempête *f* de neige; (in Arctic regions) blizzard *m*.

bloated *adj* [*face, body*] bouffi; [*stomach*] ballonné.

blob *n* **1** (drop) grosse goutte *f*; **2** (shape) forme *f* floue.

block I *n* **1** (slab) bloc *m*; **2** (building) **~ of flats** immeuble *m* (d'habitation); **office ~** immeuble de bureaux; **3** (group of buildings) pâté *m* de maisons; **4** (for butcher, executioner) billot *m*.
II *vtr* bloquer [*exit, road*]; boucher [*drain, hole, artery*]; gêner [*traffic*]; faire obstacle à [*advance, progress*]; **to ~ sb's way** or **path** barrer le passage à qn.
■ **block off**: **~ [sth] off, ~ off [sth]** (seal off) barrer [*road, path*].
■ **block out**: **~ out [sth], ~ [sth] out** cacher [*light*]; refouler [*memory, problem*].
■ **block up**: **~ up [sth], ~ [sth] up** boucher.

blockade (Mil) **I** *n* blocus *m*.
II *vtr* bloquer, faire le blocus de [*port*].

blockage *n* (in artery) obstruction *f*; (in pipe, drain) blocage *m*.

blockbuster○ *n* **1** (book) livre *m* à succès, bestseller *m*; **2** (film) superproduction *f*.

block capitals, block letters *n pl* **in ~** (on

form) en caractères *mpl* or capitales *fpl* d'imprimerie.

blonde ▶ 559 I *n* blonde *f*.
II *adj* blond.

blood *n* sang *m*.
IDIOMS **to kill sb in cold ~** tuer qn de sang-froid; **it's like getting ~ out of a stone** autant essayer de faire parler un muet.

blood: **~ bank** *n* banque *f* du sang; **~bath** *n* bain *m* de sang; **~ cell** *n* globule *m* (du sang); **~curdling** *adj* à vous figer le sang dans les veines; **~ donor** *n* donneur/-euse *m/f* de sang; **~ group** *n* groupe *m* sanguin.

bloodless *adj* [*revolution, coup*] sans effusion de sang.

blood pressure *n* (Med) tension *f* artérielle; **high ~** hypertension *f*.

blood: **~shed** *n* effusion *f* de sang; **~shot** *adj* injecté de sang; **~ sport** *n* sport *m* sanguinaire; **~stained** *adj* taché de sang; **~stream** *n* courant *m* sanguin; **~ test** *n* analyse *f* de sang; **~thirsty** *adj* sanguinaire; **~ transfusion** *n* transfusion *f* sanguine; **~ type** *n* groupe *m* sanguin.

bloody I *adj* **1** [*hand, body*] ensanglanté; [*battle*] sanglant; **2 ~ fool**○! (GB) espèce d'idiot○!
II● *adv* (GB) [*dangerous, expensive, well*] sacrément○.

bloom I *n* **1** (flower) fleur *f*; **in ~** en fleur; **2** (on skin, fruit) velouté *m*.
II *vi* (be in flower) être fleuri; (come into flower) fleurir.

blossom I *n* (flower) fleur *f*; (flowers) fleurs *fpl*; **in ~** en fleur(s).
II *vi* fleurir; **to ~ (out)** (figurative) s'épanouir.

blot I *n* (gen) tache *f*; (of ink) pâté *m*; (figurative) ombre *f*; **to be a ~ on the landscape** gâter le paysage.
II *vtr* **1** (dry) sécher [qch] au buvard [*ink*]; **2** (stain) tacher.
■ **blot out**: **~ out [sth]** [*person*] effacer; [*mist, rain*] masquer.

blotch *n* (on skin) plaque *f* rouge; (of ink, colour) tache *f*.

blouse *n* (woman's) chemisier *m*.

blow I *n* coup *m*; **to come to ~s** en venir aux mains; **to be a ~** (figurative) être un coup terrible (**to sth** porté à qch; **to sb** pour qn).
II *vtr* **1 the wind blew the door shut** un coup de vent a fermé la porte; **to be blown off course** [*ship*] être dévié par le vent; **2** [*person*] faire [*bubble, smoke ring*]; souffler [*glass*]; **to ~ one's nose** se moucher; **to ~ one's whistle** donner un coup de sifflet; **3** [*explosion*] faire [*hole*] (**in** dans); **to be blown to pieces** or **bits by** être réduit en poussière par; **4** faire sauter [*fuse*]; griller [*light bulb*].
III *vi* **1** [*wind*] souffler; [*person*] souffler (**into** dans; **on** sur); **2 to ~ in the wind** [*flag, clothes*] voler au vent; **3** [*fuse*] sauter; [*bulb*] griller; [*tyre*] éclater.
■ **blow down**: ¶ **~ down** [*tree, fence*] tomber (à cause du vent); ¶ **~ [sth] down, ~ down [sth]** [*wind*] faire tomber [*tree*].
■ **blow off**: ¶ **~ off** [*hat*] s'envoler; ¶ **~ [sth] off, ~ off [sth]** [*wind*] emporter [*hat*]; [*explosion*] emporter [*roof*]; **to ~ the leaves off the trees** [*wind*] faire tomber les feuilles des arbres.
■ **blow out**: **~ [sth] out, ~ out [sth]** souffler [*candle*]; éteindre [*flames*].
■ **blow over** [*storm*] s'apaiser; [*affair*] être oublié.
■ **blow up**: ¶ **~ up** [*building*] sauter; [*bomb*] exploser; ¶ **~ [sth/sb] up, ~ up [sb/sth]** faire sauter [*building, person*]; faire exploser [*bomb*]; ¶ **~ [sth] up, ~ up [sth] 1** gonfler [*tyre*]; **2** agrandir [*photograph*].

blow-dry I *n* brushing *m*.
II *vtr* **to ~ sb's hair** faire un brushing à qn.

bludgeon *vtr* **to ~ sb to death** tuer qn à coups de matraque.

blue ▶ 559 I *n* bleu *m*; **to go** or **turn ~** devenir bleu.
II *adj* **1** (in colour) bleu; **2**○ (smutty) [*movie*] porno○; [*joke*] cochon/-onne○.
IDIOMS **to appear/happen out of the ~** apparaître/se passer à l'improviste; **to vanish into the ~** s'évanouir dans la nature; **black and ~** couvert de bleus.

blue: **~bell** *n* jacinthe *f* des bois; **~berry** *n* (US) myrtille *f*; **~-blooded** *adj* de sang bleu or noble; **~ cheese** *n* (fromage *m*) bleu *m*; **~ chip** *adj* [*company, investment*] de premier ordre.

blue collar worker *n* ouvrier *m*, col *m* bleu.

blue: **~-eyed** *adj* aux yeux bleus; **~ jeans** *n pl* jean *m*; **~print** *n* bleu *m*; (figurative) projet *m* (**for** pour; **for doing** pour faire).

blues *n pl* **1** (Mus) **the ~** le blues *m*; **2**○ (depression) **to have the ~** avoir le cafard○.

bluff I *vtr* bluffer○; **to ~ one's way out of a situation** se tirer d'une situation en bluffant.
II *vi* bluffer○.
IDIOMS **to call sb's ~** prendre qn au mot (*sachant qu'il bluffe*).

blunder I *n* bourde *f*.
II *vi* **1** (make mistake) faire une bourde; **2** (move clumsily) **to ~ into sth** se cogner à qch.

blunt I *adj* **1** [*knife, scissors*] émoussé; [*pencil*] mal taillé; [*instrument*] contondant; **2** [*person, manner*] abrupt; [*criticism*] direct.
II *vtr* émousser [*knife*].

bluntly *adv* franchement.

blur I *n* image *f* floue.
II *vtr* brouiller.

blurb *n* (on book cover) texte *m* de présentation; (derogatory) baratin *m*.

blurred *adj* indistinct; [*image, idea*] flou; [*memory*] confus; **to have ~ vision** avoir des troubles de la vue.

blurt *v*
■ **blurt out**: **~ [sth] out, ~ out [sth]** laisser échapper [*truth, secret*].

blush *vi* rougir (**at** devant; **with** de); **to ~ for sb** avoir honte pour qn.

blusher *n* fard *m* à joues.

blustery *adj* **~ wind** bourrasque *f*.

B movie *n* film *m* de série B.

BO° *n* (*abbr* = **body odour**) odeur *f* corporelle; **he's got ~** il sent mauvais.

boar *n* (also **wild ~**) sanglier *m*.

board I *n* **1** (plank) planche *f*; **bare ~s** plancher nu; **2** (committee) conseil *m*; **~ of directors** conseil d'administration; **3** (for chess, draughts) tableau *m*; **4** (in classroom) tableau *m* (noir); **5** (notice board) panneau *m* d'affichage; (to advertise) panneau *m*; **6** (Comput) plaquette *f*; **7** (accommodation) **full ~** pension *f* complète; **half ~** demi-pension *f*; **~ and lodging** le gîte et le couvert.
II *vtr* monter à bord de [*plane, ship*]; monter dans [*bus, train*]; [*pirates*] aborder [*vessel*].
III **on board** *phr* **to be on ~** être à bord; **to go on ~** monter à bord.
IDIOMS **above ~** légal; **across the ~** à tous les niveaux.
■ **board up**: **~ [sth] up, ~ up [sth]** boucher [qch] avec des planches [*window*]; barricader [qch] avec des planches [*house*].

boarder *n* **1** (lodger) pensionnaire *m*; **2** (school pupil) interne *mf*.

board game *n* jeu *m* de société (à damier).

boarding *n* (at port, airport) embarquement *m*.

boarding: **~ card** *n* carte *f* d'embarquement; **~ school** *n* école *f* privée avec internat.

boardroom *n* salle *f* du conseil.

boast I *vtr* [*town*] s'enorgueillir de [*cathedral, monument*].
II *vi* se vanter (**about** de).

boastful *adj* [*person*] vantard; **without being ~** sans se vanter.

boat *n* bateau *m*; (sailing) voilier *m*; (rowing) barque *f*; (liner) paquebot *m*.
IDIOMS **to be in the same ~**° être tous dans la même galère.

boathouse *n* abri *m* à bateaux.

boating *n* (in pleasure craft) navigation *f* de plaisance; (rowing) canotage *m*.

bob I *vi* [*boat, float*] danser; **to ~ up and down** [*heads*] apparaître et disparaître.
II **bobbed** *pp adj* [*hair*] coupé court.

bobsled, bobsleigh ▶ 649 *n* bobsleigh *m*.

bode *vi* **to ~ well/ill** être de bon/mauvais augure.

bodice *n* (of dress) corsage *m*.

bodily *adj* [*function*] physiologique; [*fluid*] organique.

body *n* **1** (of person, animal) corps *m*; **~ and soul** corps et âme; **2** (corpse) corps *m*, cadavre *m*; **3** (of car) carrosserie *f*; **4** (quantity) (of water) étendue *f*; (of laws) recueil *m*; **5** (organization) organisme *m*; **6** (of wine) corps *m*; (of hair) volume *m*.

body: **~-building** *n* culturisme *m*; **~guard** *n* garde *m* du corps; **~ odour** (GB), **~ odor** (US) *n* odeur *f* corporelle; **~ weight** *n* poids *m*; **~work** *n* carrosserie *f*.

bog *n* **1** (marshy ground) marais *m*; **2** (also **peat ~**) tourbière *f*.
IDIOMS **to get ~ged down in sth** s'enliser dans qch.

boggle *vi* **the mind ~s!** c'est époustouflant!

bogus *adj* [*doctor, document*] faux/fausse (*before n*); [*claim*] bidon; [*company*] factice.

bohemian *adj* [*lifestyle*] de bohème; [*person*] bohème *inv*.

boil I *n* **1 to bring sth to the ~** porter qch à ébullition; **2** (on skin) furoncle *m*.
II *vtr* faire bouillir; **to ~ an egg** faire cuire un œuf.
III *vi* bouillir; **the kettle is ~ing** l'eau bout (dans la bouilloire); **to make sb's blood ~** faire sortir qn de ses gonds.
IV **boiled** *pp adj* **~ed egg** œuf *m* à la coque.
■ **boil down to** (figurative) se ramener à.

boiler *n* chaudière *f*; (for storing water) chauffe-eau *m inv*.

boiler suit *n* (GB) (workman's) bleu *m* de travail.

boiling *adj* [*liquid*] bouillant; **it's ~**°! il fait une chaleur infernale!

boiling point *n* point *m* d'ébullition; (figurative) point *m* limite.

boisterous *adj* [*adult, game*] bruyant; [*child*] turbulent.

bold *adj* **1** (daring) [*person*] intrépide; [*attempt, plan*] audacieux/-ieuse; **2** (cheeky) [*person*] effronté; **3** [*colour*] vif/vive; [*design*] voyant.

boldly *adv* **1** (daringly) hardiment; (cheekily) avec effronterie; **2** [*outlined*] nettement.

bollard *n* balise *f*.

bolster I *n* traversin *m*.
II *vtr* (also **~ up**) soutenir.

bolt I *n* **1** (lock) verrou *m*; **2 ~ of lightning** coup *m* de foudre.
II *vtr* **1** (lock) verrouiller; **2** (also **~ down**) (swallow) engloutir [*food*].
III *vi* [*horse*] s'emballer; [*person*] détaler°.
IV **bolt upright** *phr* droit comme un i.
IDIOMS **a ~ out of the blue** un coup de tonnerre.

bomb I *n* bombe *f*.
II *vtr* bombarder [*town, house*].

bombard *vtr* bombarder (**with** de).

bombardment *n* bombardement *m*.

bomb: **~ disposal** *n* déminage *m*; **~ disposal expert** ▶ 805 *n* démineur *m*.

bomber *n* **1** (plane) bombardier *m*; **2** (terrorist) poseur/-euse *m/f* de bombes.

bomber jacket *n* blouson *m* d'aviateur.

bombing *n* bombardement *m*; (by terrorists) attentat *m* à la bombe.

bomb: **~shell** *n* obus *m*; (figurative) bombe *f*; **~site** *n* zone *f* touchée par une explosion.

bona fide *adj* [*attempt*] sincère; [*member*] vrai (*before n*); [*contract*] de bonne foi.

bonanza *n* (source of wealth) mine *f* d'or; (wave of prosperity) boom *m*; (windfall) manne *f*; **oil/tax ~** manne pétrolière/fiscale; **jobs ~** boom dans l'emploi; **to enjoy a ~** [*bargain-hunters*] faire d'excellentes affaires.

bond I *n* **1** (link) lien(s) *m(pl)* (**of** de; **between** entre); **to feel a strong ~ with sb** se sentir

The Human Body

When it is clear who owns the part of the body mentioned, French tends to use the definite article, where English uses a possessive adjective:

*he raised **his** hand*	= il a levé **la** main
*she closed **her** eyes*	= elle a fermé **les** yeux

Note, for instance, the use of ***la*** and ***mon*** here:

*she ran **her** hand over **my** forehead*	= elle a passé **la** main sur **mon** front

For expressions such as *he hurt his foot* or *she brushed her teeth*, where the action involves more than the simple movement of a body part, use a reflexive verb in French:

*she **has broken** her leg*	= elle **s'est cassé** la jambe
*he **was rubbing** his hands*	= il **se frottait** les mains
*she **was holding** her head*	= elle **se tenait** la tête

Note also the following:

*she broke **his** leg*	= elle **lui** a cassé **la** jambe (*literally* she broke to him the leg)
*the stone split **his** lip*	= le caillou **lui** a fendu **la** lèvre (*literally* the stone split to him the lip)

Describing people

❑ For ways of saying how tall someone is or of stating someone's weight, ▶ 738, and of talking about the colour of hair and eyes, ▶ 559.

Here are some ways of describing people in French:

his hair is long	= il a les cheveux longs
he has long hair	= il a les cheveux longs
a boy with long hair	= un garçon aux cheveux longs
a long-haired boy	= un garçon aux cheveux longs
the boy with long hair	= le garçon aux cheveux longs
her eyes are blue	= elle a les yeux bleus
she has blue eyes	= elle a les yeux bleus
she is blue-eyed	= elle a les yeux bleus
the girl with blue eyes	= la fille aux yeux bleus
a blue-eyed girl	= une fille aux yeux bleus
his nose is red	= il a le nez rouge
he has a red nose	= il a le nez rouge
a man with a red nose	= un homme au nez rouge
a red-nosed man	= un homme au nez rouge

When referring to a temporary state, the following phrases are useful:

his leg is broken	= il a la jambe cassée
the man with the broken leg	= l'homme à la jambe cassée

but note

a man with a broken leg	= un homme avec une jambe cassée

❑ For other expressions with terms relating to parts of the body, ▶ 686.

très proche de qn; **2** (in finance) obligation *f*; **savings ~** bon *m* d'épargne.
II *vi* **1** s'attacher (**with** à); **2** [*materials*] adhérer (**with** à).

bonding *n* **1** (between mother and baby) formation *f* des liens maternels; **2** (between people) formation *f* du lien affectif (**between** entre).

bone I *n* os *m*; (of fish) arête *f*.
II bones *n pl* (animal skeleton) ossements *mpl*; (human) (in archaeology) ossements *mpl* humains.
III *vtr* désosser [*joint, chicken*]; enlever les arêtes de [*fish*].
IDIOMS **~ of contention** sujet *m* de dispute; **to have a ~ to pick with sb** avoir un compte à régler avec qn.

bone dry *adj* complètement sec/sèche.

bonfire *n* (of rubbish) feu *m* de jardin; (for celebration) feu *m* de joie.

bonnet *n* (GB Aut) capot *m*.

bonus *n* **1** (payment) prime *f*; **2** (advantage) avantage *m* (**of being** d'être).

bony *adj* [*person, body*] anguleux/-euse; [*finger, arm*] osseux/-euse.

boo I *n* huée *f*.
II *excl* (to give sb a fright) hou!; (to jeer) hou! hou!
III *vtr* huer [*actor, speaker*].

booby trap *n* **1** mécanisme *m* piégé; **2** (joke) traquenard *m*.

booing *n* huées *fpl*.

book I *n* **1** livre *m* (**about** sur; **of** de); **history ~** livre d'histoire; **to go by the ~** (figurative) suivre le règlement; **2** (exercise book) cahier *m*; **3** (of cheques, tickets, vouchers, stamps) carnet *m*; **~ of matches** pochette *f* d'allumettes.
II books *n pl* **1** (accounts) comptabilité *f*; **to keep the ~s** tenir les comptes; **2** (records of firm, business) registre *m*.
III *vtr* **1** réserver [*table, room, taxi, ticket*]; faire les réservations pour [*holiday*]; engager [*babysitter, entertainer*]; **to be fully ~ed** être complet/-ète; **2** (charge) [*policeman*] dresser un procès-verbal or un P.V.○ à [*motorist, offender*]; (US) (arrest) arrêter [*suspect*]; **3** [*referee*] donner un carton jaune à [*player*].
IV *vi* réserver.
IDIOMS **to be in sb's good ~s** être dans les petits papiers de qn○; **to be in sb's bad ~s** ne pas avoir la cote avec qn.
■ **book in**: ¶ **~ in** (GB) (check in) se présenter à la réception; ¶ **~ [sb] in** réserver une chambre pour.
■ **book up**: **to be ~ed up** être complet/-ète.

book: **~case** *n* bibliothèque *f*; **~ club** *n* club *m* du livre.

booking *n* **1** (GB) (reservation) réservation *f*; **2** (of performer) engagement *m*.

booking: **~ clerk** ▶805 *n* (GB) préposé/-e *m/f* aux réservations; **~ office** *n* (GB) bureau *m* de location.

bookkeeping *n* comptabilité *f*.

booklet *n* brochure *f*.

book: **~maker** ▶805 *n* bookmaker *m*; **~seller** ▶805 *n* (person) libraire *mf*; **~shelf** *n* (single) étagère *f*; (in bookcase) rayon *m*; **~shop**, **~ store** (US) ▶805 *n* librairie *f*; **~ token** *n* (GB) chèque-livre *m*.

boom I *n* **1** (of cannon, thunder) grondement *m*; (of drum) boum *m*; (of explosion) détonation *f*; **~!** badaboum!; **2** (Econ) boom *m*; (in prices, sales) explosion *f* (**in** de); **property ~** boom immobilier.
II *vi* **1** [*cannon, thunder*] gronder; [*bell, voice*] retentir; **2** [*economy*] prospérer; [*exports, sales*] monter en flèche; **business is ~ing** les affaires vont bien.

boomerang *n* boomerang *m*.

booming *adj* **1** [*sound*] retentissant; [*voice*] tonitruant; **2** (flourishing) [*economy*] en plein essor; [*exports, sales*] en forte progression.

boon *n* **1** (asset) aide *f* précieuse (**to** à); **to be a great ~ to sb** apporter une aide précieuse à qn; **2** (stroke of luck) aubaine *f* (**for** pour).

boorish *adj* grossier/-ière.

boost I *n* coup *m* de fouet (**to** à); **to give sth a ~** stimuler qch.
II *vtr* **1** (stimulate) stimuler [*economy, sales*]; encourager [*investment*]; augmenter [*pay, profit*]; **to ~ sb's confidence** redonner confiance à qn; **to ~ morale** remonter le moral; **2** (enhance) améliorer [*image, performance*].

booster *n* (Med) vaccin *m* de rappel.

boot *n* **1** (footwear) botte *f*; (of climber, hiker) chaussure *f*; (for workman, soldier) brodequin *m*; **football ~** (GB) chaussure *f* de football; **to put the ~ in** y aller fort; **2** (GB) (of car) coffre *m*.

bootee *n* chausson *m*.

booth *n* (in language lab) cabine *f*; (in restaurant) alcôve *f*; (at fair) baraque *f*; **polling ~** isoloir *m*; **telephone ~** cabine *f* (téléphonique).

bootlace *n* lacet *m* (de chaussure).

border I *n* **1** (frontier) frontière *f*; **to cross the ~** passer la frontière; **2** (edge) (of forest) lisière *f*; (of estate, lake, road) bord *m*; **3** (flowerbed) platebande *f*.
II *noun modifier* [*control*] aux frontières; [*crossing, patrol, state*] frontalier/-ière; [*town*] frontière *inv* (*after n*); [*police*] des frontières.
III *vtr* **1** [*road, land*] longer [*lake, forest*]; [*country*] border [*ocean*]; avoir une frontière commune avec [*country*]; **2** (surround) border; **to be ~ed by trees** être bordé d'arbres.
■ **border on**: **~ on [sth] 1** [*country*] être limitrophe de; [*garden, land*] toucher; **2** (verge on) friser [*rudeness, madness*].

borderline *n* frontière *f*, limite *f* (**between** entre); **a ~ case** un cas limite.

bore I *n* **1** (person) raseur○/-euse *m/f*; **2** (situation) **what a ~!** quelle barbe!; **3** (of gun barrel, pipe) calibre *m*; **12-~ shotgun** fusil *m* de calibre 12.
II *vtr* **1** ennuyer [*person*]; **2** (drill) percer [*hole*]; creuser [*well, tunnel*].

bored *adj* [*person*] qui s'ennuie; [*expression, voice*] ennuyé; **to get ~** s'ennuyer (**with** de).
IDIOMS **to be ~ stiff** or **~ to tears** s'ennuyer à mourir.

boredom *n* ennui *m*.

boring *adj* ennuyeux/-euse.

born *adj* [*person, animal*] né (**of** de; **to do** pour faire); **to be ~** naître; **she was ~ in May** elle est née en mai; **to be ~ blind** être aveugle de naissance; **to be a ~ leader** être un chef né.

born-again *adj* [*Christian*] régénéré.

borough *n* arrondissement *m* urbain.

borrow I *vtr* emprunter [*money, car, books*] (**from** à).
II *vi* [*person*] faire un emprunt (**from** à).

borrower *n* emprunteur/-euse *m/f*.

borrowing *n* emprunt(s) *m(pl)*.

Bosnia ▶574 *pr n* Bosnie *f*.

bosom *n* poitrine *f*; **in the ~ of one's family** au sein de sa famille.

boss○ *n* (person in charge) patron/-onne *m/f*; (in politics, underworld) chef *m*.
■ **boss about**○, **boss around**○: **~ [sb] about** mener [qn] par le bout du nez.

bossy○ *adj* autoritaire.

botanic(al) *adj* botanique; **~ gardens** jardin *m* botanique.

botanist ▶805 *n* botaniste *mf*.

botany *n* botanique *f*.

botch○ *vtr* bâcler.

both I *det* **~ sides of the road** les deux côtés de la rue; **~ children came** les enfants sont venus tous les deux; **~ her parents** ses deux parents.
II *conj* **~ here and abroad** ici comme à l'étranger; **~ Paris and London have their advantages** aussi bien Paris que Londres a ses avantages.
III *pron, quantif* (of things) les deux; (of people) tous les deux; **'which do you want?'—'~'** 'lequel/laquelle veux-tu?'—'les deux'; **let's do ~** faisons les deux; **they are ~ young** ils sont jeunes tous les deux; **let's take ~ of them** prenons les deux; **~ of you are wrong** vous avez tort tous les deux.

bother I *n* **1** (inconvenience) ennui *m*, embêtement○ *m*; **without any ~** sans aucune difficulté; **he's no ~** il ne dérange pas du tout; **2**○ (GB) (trouble) ennuis *mpl*; **to be in a spot of ~** avoir des ennuis.
II *vtr* **1** (worry) tracasser; **don't let it ~ you** ne te tracasse pas avec ça; **it ~s me that** ça me tracasse que (+ *subj*); **2** (inconvenience) déranger; **I'm sorry to ~ you** je suis désolé de vous déranger.
III *vi* **1** (take trouble) **please don't ~** s'il te plaît, ne te dérange pas; **don't** or **you needn't ~ doing** ce n'est pas la peine de faire; **2** (worry) **to ~ about** se soucier de; **it's not worth ~ing about** ça ne vaut pas la peine qu'on s'en occupe.

bottle I *n* (for drinks) bouteille *f*; (for perfume, medicine) flacon *m*; (for baby) biberon *m*.
II *vtr* **1** embouteiller [*milk, wine*]; **2** (GB) mettre [qch] en conserve [*fruit*].
III **bottled** *pp adj* [*beer, gas*] en bouteille; **~d water** eau *f* minérale.
■ **bottle up**: **~ [sth] up**, **~ up [sth]** étouffer [*anger, grief*].

bottle: **~ bank** *n* réceptacle *m* à verre; **~ feed** *vtr* nourrir [qn] au biberon.

bottleneck *n* **1** (traffic jam) embouteillage *m*; **2** (narrow part of road) rétrécissement *m* de la chaussée.

bottle-opener *n* décapsuleur *m*.

bottom I *n* **1** (of hill, steps, wall) pied *m*; (of page, list) bas *m*; (of bag, bottle, hole, river, sea, garden, field) fond *m*; (of boat) carène *f*; (of vase, box) dessous *m*; (of league) dernière place *f*; **at the ~ of the pile** sous le tas; **to be ~ of the class** être dernier/-ière de la classe; **2** (buttocks) derrière○ *m*.
II *adj* [*layer, shelf*] du bas; [*sheet*] de dessous; [*bunk*] inférieur; [*division, half, place, team*] dernier/-ière; **~ of the range** bas de gamme.
IDIOMS **to get to the ~ of a matter** découvrir le fin fond d'une affaire.

bottom: **~ gear** *n* (GB) première *f*; **~less** *adj* sans fond.

boulder *n* rocher *m*.

bounce I *n* **1** (of ball) rebond *m*; **2** (of mattress, material) élasticité *f*; (of hair) souplesse *f*.
II *vtr* **1** faire rebondir [*ball*]; **2**○ **to ~ a cheque** [*bank*] (GB) refuser d'honorer un chèque; [*person*] (US) faire un chèque sans provision.
III *vi* **1** [*ball, object*] rebondir (**off** sur; **over** au dessus de); **to ~ up and down on sth** [*person*] sauter sur qch; **2**○ [*cheque*] être sans provision.
■ **bounce back** (after illness) se remettre; (in career) faire un retour en force.

bouncer○ *n* videur *m*.

bound I *n* bond *m*; **in a ~, with one ~** d'un bond.
II **bounds** *n pl* limites *fpl*; **to be out of ~s** [*place*] être interdit d'accès; (Sport) être hors du terrain.
III *adj* **1 to be ~ to do sth** aller sûrement faire qch; **it was ~ to happen** cela devait arriver; **2** (obliged) (by promise, rules, terms) tenu (**by** par; **to do** de faire); **3** [*book*] relié; **leather-~** relié en cuir; **4 ~ for** [*person, bus, train*] en route pour; [*aeroplane*] à destination de.
IV *vi* bondir; **to ~ into the room** entrer dans la pièce en coup de vent.

boundary *n* (gen) limite *f* (**between** entre); (of sports field) limites *fpl* du terrain; **national ~** frontières *fpl* du pays.

bounty *n* **1** (generosity) générosité *f*; **2** (gift) don *m*; **3** (reward) prime *f*.

bouquet *n* bouquet *m*.

bourgeois *adj* bourgeois.

bout *n* **1** (of fever, malaria) accès *m*; (of insomnia) crise *f*; **drinking ~** soûlerie *f*; **2** (in boxing) combat *m*; **3** (period of activity) période *f*.

boutique ▶805 *n* boutique *f*.

bow[1] *n* **1** (weapon) arc *m*; **2** (for violin) archet *m*; **3** (knot) nœud *m*.

bow[2] I *n* **1** (movement) salut *m*; **to take a ~** saluer; **2** (of ship) avant *m*, proue *f*.
II *vtr* baisser [*head*]; courber [*branch*]; incliner [*tree*].
III *vi* saluer; **to ~ to sb** saluer qn; **to ~ to**

s'incliner devant [*wisdom, necessity*]; **to ~ to pressure** céder à la pression.
IV **bowed** *pp adj* [*head*] penché; [*back*] courbé.

bowel *n* intestin *m*; **the ~s of the earth** les entrailles *fpl* de la terre.

bowl I *n* **1** (for food) bol *m*; (large) saladier *m*; (for soup) assiette *f* creuse; (for washing) cuvette *f*; (of lavatory) cuvette *f*; **a ~ of milk** un bol de lait; **2** (ball) boule *f* (en bois).
II *vtr* **1** (roll) faire rouler [*hoop, ball*]; **2** (throw) lancer [*ball*].
III *vi* **1** lancer; **to ~ to sb** lancer la balle à qn; **2** (US) (go bowling) aller au bowling.
■ **bowl over**: **~ [sb] over 1** (knock down) renverser [*person*]; **2 to be ~ed over** (by news) être stupéfait; (by beauty, generosity) être bouleversé.

bowlegged *adj* [*person*] aux jambes arquées.

bowler *n* **1** (in cricket) lanceur *m*; (in bowls) joueur/-euse *m/f* de boules (*sur gazon*); **2** (also **~ hat**) chapeau *m* melon.

bowling ▶649 *n* (also **tenpin ~**) bowling *m*.

bowling: **~ alley** *n* bowling *m*; **~ green** *n* terrain *m* de boules (*sur gazon*).

bowls ▶649 *n* jeu *m* de boules (*sur gazon*).

bow: **~ tie** *n* nœud-papillon *m*; **~ window** *n* fenêtre *f* en saillie.

box I *n* **1** (cardboard) boîte *f*; (crate) caisse *f*; **~ of matches** boîte d'allumettes; **2** (on page, application form) case *f*; **3** (seating area) (in theatre) loge *f*; (in stadium) tribune *f*; **4** (in stable) box *m*; **5** (also **PO Box**) boîte *f* postale.
II *vtr* **1** (pack) mettre [qch] en caisse; **2 to ~ sb's ears** gifler qn.
III *vi* (Sport) boxer.

boxer ▶805 *n* **1** (fighter) boxeur *m*; **2** (dog) boxer *m*.

boxer shorts *n pl* caleçon *m* (court).

boxing ▶649 I *n* boxe *f*.
II *noun modifier* [*glove, match*] de boxe; **~ ring** ring *m*.

Boxing Day *n* (GB) lendemain *m* de Noël.

box office *n* guichet *m*; **to do well at the ~** faire recette.

boy *n* garçon *m*.

boycott I *n* boycottage *m* (**against, of, on** de).
II *vtr* boycotter.

boyfriend *n* (petit) copain *m* or ami *m*.

boyish *adj* [*looks*] d'adolescent; [*grin, charm*] enfantin.

bra *n* soutien-gorge *m*.

brace I *n* **1** (for teeth) appareil *m* dentaire; **2** (for broken limb) attelle *f*.
II **braces** *n pl* (GB) bretelles *fpl*.
III *vtr* [*person*] arc-bouter [*body, back*] (**against** contre).
IV *v refl* **to ~ oneself** (physically) s'arc-bouter; (mentally) se préparer (**for** à; **to do** à faire).

bracelet *n* bracelet *m*.

bracing *adj* vivifiant, tonifiant.

bracken *n* fougère *f*.

bracket I *n* **1** (round) parenthèse *f*; (square) crochet *m*; **in ~s** entre parenthèses or crochets; **2** (for shelf) équerre *f*; (for lamp) applique *f*; **3** (category) **age ~** tranche d'âge.
II *vtr* **1** (put in brackets) (round) mettre [qch] entre parenthèses; (square) mettre [qch] entre crochets; **2** (also **~ together**) mettre [qn] dans le même groupe [*people*].

brag I *n* (boast) fanfaronnade *f*.
II *vi* se vanter (**to** auprès de; **about** de).

bragging *n* fanfaronnade *f* (**about** au sujet de).

braid *n* **1** (of hair) tresse *f*, natte *f*; **2** (trimming) galon *m*.

brain I *n* **1** (organ) cerveau *m*; **2** (substance) **~s** cervelle *f*; **to blow one's ~s out**○ se faire sauter la cervelle○; **he's the ~s of the family** c'est lui le cerveau de la famille; **to use one's ~s** faire marcher ses cellules grises.
II *noun modifier* [*cell, haemorrhage*] cérébral; [*tumour*] au cerveau.

brain: **~child** *n* grande idée *f*; **~ damage** *n* lésions *fpl* cérébrales; **~ dead** *adj* dans un coma dépassé; **~ drain** *n* fuite *f* des cerveaux; **~less** *adj* idiot; **~storming** *n* remue-méninges *m inv*; **~ surgeon** ▶805 *n* neurochirurgien/-ienne *m/f*; **~ surgery** *n* neurochirurgie *f*; **~wash** *vtr* faire subir un lavage de cerveau à; **~washing** *n* (of prisoners) lavage *m* de cerveau; (of public) bourrage○ *m* de crâne; **~wave** *n* idée *f* géniale, illumination *f*.

braise *vtr* braiser.

brake I *n* frein *m*; **to apply the ~(s)** freiner.
II *vi* freiner.

bramble *n* **1** (plant) ronce *f*; **2** (GB) (berry) mûre *f*.

bran *n* son *m*.

branch *n* **1** (of tree) branche *f*; (of road, railway) embranchement *m*; (of river) bras *m*; (of candlestick) branche *f*; (of antlers) ramure *f*; (of family, language) rameau *m*; (of subject) domaine *m*; **2** (of shop) succursale *f*; (of bank) agence *f*; (of company) filiale *f*.
■ **branch off** [*road, river, railway*] bifurquer; **to ~ off from** se séparer de.
■ **branch out** [*business*] se diversifier; **to ~ out into** se lancer dans.

brand I *n* marque *f*.
II *vtr* **1** marquer (au fer) [*animal*]; **2** (label) marquer [*person*]; **to ~ sb as sth** désigner qn comme qch.

brandish *vtr* brandir.

brand: **~ name** *n* marque *f* déposée; **~-new** *adj* tout neuf/toute neuve.

brandy *n* (gen) eau-de-vie *f*; (from Cognac region) cognac *m*.

brash *adj* [*person, manner*] bravache; [*colour, decor*] tape-à-l'œil (*inv*).

brass I *n* **1** (metal) laiton *m*, cuivre *m* jaune; **2** (fittings, objects) cuivres *mpl*; **3** (Mus) (also **~ section**) cuivres *mpl*.
II *noun modifier* [*button, plaque*] en cuivre jaune.

brass: **~ band** *n* orchestre *m* de cuivres, fanfare *f*; **~ instrument** ▶753 *n* cuivre *m*.

bravado *n* bravade *f*.

brave I *n* **1** (Indian) brave *m*; **2 the ~** les courageux *mpl*.
II *adj* [*person, effort, gesture, decision*] courageux/-euse; [*smile*] brave; **to put on a ~ face** faire bonne contenance.
III *vtr* braver.

bravely *adv* courageusement.

bravery *n* courage *m*, bravoure *f*.

bravura *n* bravoure *f*.

brawl I *n* bagarre *f*.
II *vi* se bagarrer (**with** avec).

bray *vi* [*donkey*] braire; [*person*] brailler.

brazen *adj* éhonté.
■ **brazen out**: **~ it out** payer d'audace.

Brazil ▶ 574 *pr n* Brésil *m*.

breach I *n* **1** (of rule) infraction *f* (**of** à); (of discipline, duty) manquement *m* (**of** à); (of copyright) violation *f*; **~ of security** (of official secret) atteinte *f* à la sûreté nationale; **~ of contract** rupture *f* de contrat; **to be in ~ of** enfreindre [*law*]; violer [*agreement*]; **2** (gap) brèche *f*.
II *vtr* faire une brèche dans [*defence*]; ne pas respecter [*rule*].

bread *n* pain *m*.

bread: **~ and butter** *n* tartine *f* de pain beurré; (figurative) gagne-pain *m*; **~bin** *n* (GB) boîte *f* or huche *f* à pain; **~board** *n* planche *f* à pain.

breadcrumb *n* miette *f* de pain; **~s** chapelure *f*.

breadline *n* **to be on the ~** être au seuil de l'indigence.

bread roll *n* petit pain *m*.

breadth ▶ 738 *n* largeur *f*; (figurative) (of experience, knowledge) étendue *f*.

breadwinner *n* soutien *m* de famille.

break I *n* **1** (in bone) fracture *f*; **2** (gap) (in wall) brèche *f*; (in row, line) espace *m*; (in circuit) rupture *f*; (in match) pause *f*; (in performance) entracte *m*; **3** (also **commercial ~**) page *f* de publicité; **4** (pause) (gen) pause *f*; (at school) récréation *f*; **to take a ~** faire une pause; **5** (holiday) **the Christmas ~** les vacances de Noël; **6** rupture *f* (**with** avec); **a ~ with tradition** une rupture avec la tradition; **7** (dawn) **at the ~ of day** au lever du jour, à l'aube *f*.
II *vtr* **1** casser [*chair, toy, egg, window, machine*]; briser [*seal*]; rompre [*silence, monotony, spell, links*]; briser [*rebellion, will*]; **to ~ a tooth** se casser une dent; **to ~ one's leg** se casser la jambe; **to ~ one's neck** avoir une rupture des vertèbres cervicales; (figurative) se casser la figure; **to ~ a habit** se défaire d'une habitude; **to ~ sb's spirit** briser la volonté de qn; **the river broke its banks** la rivière a débordé; **2** (disobey) enfreindre [*law, rule*]; ne pas respecter [*embargo, terms*]; briser [*strike*]; rompre [*vow*]; **to ~ one's promise** manquer à sa promesse; **3** (exceed, surpass) dépasser [*speed limit, bounds*]; battre [*record*]; **4** [*branches*] freiner [*fall*]; [*hay*] amortir [*fall*]; **5** (tame) débourrer [*young horse*]; **6** (in tennis) **to ~ sb's serve** faire le break; **7** (announce) annoncer [*news*]; **to ~ the news to sb** apprendre la nouvelle à qn.
III *vi* **1** [*branch, chair, egg, tooth, plate, toy*] se casser; [*arm, bone, leg*] se fracturer; [*bag*] se déchirer; **to ~ in two** se casser en deux; **the sound of ~ing glass** le bruit de verre brisé; **2** (separate) [*clouds*] se disperser; [*waves*] se briser; **3** (change) [*good weather*] se gâter; [*heatwave*] cesser; **4** (begin) [*day*] se lever; [*storm, scandal, story*] éclater; **5 to ~ with sb** rompre les relations avec qn; **to ~ with tradition** rompre avec la tradition; **6** [*boy's voice*] muer.
■ **break away 1** se détacher (**from** de); **to ~ away from** se détacher de [*herd*]; rompre [*moorings*]; **2** (escape) échapper (**from** à); **3** [*runner, cyclist*] se détacher (**from** de).
■ **break down**: ¶ **~ down 1** [*car, lift, machine*] tomber en panne; [*negotiations*] échouer; [*law and order*] se dégrader; [*system*] s'effondrer; **2** [*person*] s'effondrer, craquer°; **to ~ down in tears** fondre en larmes; ¶ **~ [sth] down, ~ down [sth] 1** enfoncer [*door*]; (figurative) faire tomber [*barriers*]; vaincre [*resistance*]; **2** (analyse) ventiler [*cost, statistics*]; décomposer [*data, findings*] (**into** par).
■ **break even** rentrer dans ses frais.
■ **break free** [*prisoner*] s'évader.
■ **break in**: ¶ **~ in 1** [*thief*] entrer (par effraction); [*police*] entrer de force; **2** (interrupt) interrompre; ¶ **~ [sth] in** débourrer [*young horse*]; assouplir [*shoe*].
■ **break into**: **~ into [sth] 1** entrer dans [qch] (par effraction) [*building*]; forcer [*safe*]; **her car was broken into** sa voiture a été cambriolée; **2** (start to use) entamer [*new packet, savings*]; **3 to ~ into song/into a run** se mettre à chanter/courir; **4** [*company*] s'implanter sur [*market*].
■ **break off**: ¶ **~ off 1** [*end*] se casser; [*handle, piece*] se détacher; **2** [*speaker*] s'interrompre; ¶ **~ off [sth], ~ [sth] off** casser [*branch, piece*]; (figurative) rompre [*engagement, negotiations*]; interrompre [*conversation*].
■ **break out 1** [*epidemic, fire*] se déclarer; [*fight, riot, storm*] éclater; [*rash*] apparaître; **to ~ out in a rash** [*person*] avoir une éruption de boutons; **2** (escape) [*prisoner*] s'évader; **to ~ out of** s'échapper de [*prison*].
■ **break through**: ¶ **~ through** [*army*] faire une percée; ¶ **~ through [sth]** percer [*defences, reserve*]; franchir [*barrier*]; [*sun*] percer [*clouds*].
■ **break up**: ¶ **~ up 1** [*empire*] s'effondrer; [*alliance*] éclater; [*family, couple*] se séparer; **2** (disperse) [*crowd, cloud*] se disperser; [*meeting*] se terminer; **3** (GB Sch) **schools ~ up on Friday** les cours finissent vendredi; ¶ **~ [sth] up** démanteler [*drugs ring*]; séparer [*team, couple*]; désunir [*family*]; briser [*alliance, marriage*]; démembrer [*empire*]; mettre fin à [*demonstration*].

breakable *adj* fragile.

breakage *n* (damage) casse *f*; (broken item) article *m* cassé.

breakaway *adj* [*faction, group, state*] séparatiste.

breakdown I *n* **1** (of vehicle, machine) panne *f*

(**in, of** de); **2** (collapse) (of communications, negotiations) rupture *f*; (of discipline, order) effondrement *m*; **3** dépression *f*; **to have a (nervous) ~** faire une dépression (nerveuse); **4** (of figures, statistics) ventilation *f*.
II *noun modifier* [*vehicle, truck*] de dépannage.

breaker *n* brisant *m*.

breaker's yard *n* casse *f*.

breakfast *n* petit déjeuner *m*.

break: **~-in** *n* cambriolage *m*; **~neck** *adj* [*pace, speed*] fou/folle, insensé; **~-out** *n* évasion *f*; **~through** *n* (in science, medicine, career, battle) percée *f*; (in negotiations, investigation) progrès *m*; **~-up** *n* (of empire) démembrement *m*; (of alliance, relationship) rupture *f*; (of family, group) éclatement *m*; (of marriage) échec *m*; **~water** *n* brise-lames *m inv*.

breast *n* **1** (woman's) sein *m*; (chest) poitrine *f*; **2** (Culin) (of poultry) blanc *m*, filet *m*; (of lamb) poitrine *f*; (of veal) tendron *m*; (of duck, pigeon) filet *m*, magret *m*.

breast: **~-feed** *vtr, vi* allaiter; **~ pocket** *n* poche *f* de poitrine; **~ stroke** *n* brasse *f*.

breath *n* **1** souffle *m*; **to get one's ~ back** reprendre son souffle; **out of ~** à bout de souffle; **to be short of ~** avoir le souffle court; **to hold one's ~** retenir sa respiration; (figurative) retenir son souffle; **to take a deep ~** respirer profondément; **to go out for a ~ of (fresh) air** sortir prendre l'air; **2** (from mouth) haleine *f*; (visible) respiration *f*; **to have bad ~** avoir (une) mauvaise haleine.
IDIOMS **to take sb's ~ away** couper le souffle à qn.

breathalyse (GB), **breathalyze** (US) *vtr* faire subir un alcootest à [*driver*].

Breathalyzer® *n* alcootest *m*.

breathe I *vtr* **1** (inhale) respirer [*air, oxygen*]; **2** (exhale) souffler [*air, smoke, germs*] (**on** sur); cracher [*fire*]; **3** (figurative) **don't ~ a word!** pas un mot!
II *vi* **1** [*person, animal*] respirer; **to ~ heavily** souffler fort, haleter; **2** [*wine*]) s'aérer.
■ **breathe in**: ¶ **~ in** inspirer; ¶ **~ in [sth]**, **~ [sth] in** inhaler.
■ **breathe out**: ¶ **~ out** expirer; ¶ **~ out [sth]**, **~ [sth] out** exhaler.

breathing *n* respiration *f*.

breathing space *n* **1** (respite) répit *m*; **2** (postponement) délai *m*.

breathless *adj* [*runner*] hors d'haleine; [*asthmatic*] haletant; **to leave sb ~** essouffler qn.

breathtaking *adj* [*feat, skill*] stupéfiant; [*scenery*] à vous couper le souffle.

breeches *n pl* culotte *f*.

breed I *n* (of animal) race *f*; (of person, thing) type *m*, espèce *f*.
II *vtr* élever [*animals*]; produire [*plants, children*]; engendrer [*disease, unrest*].
III *vi* [*animals*] se reproduire; [*organisms*] se multiplier.
IV **bred** *pp adj* **ill-/well-~** mal/bien élevé.

breeder *n* (of animals) éleveur *m*.

breeding *n* **1** (of animals) reproduction *f*; **2** (good manners) bonnes manières *fpl*.

breeze I *n* brise *f*; **sea ~** brise de mer; **in the ~** dans la brise.
II *vi* **to ~ in/out** entrer/sortir d'un air dégagé; **to ~ through an exam** réussir un examen sans difficulté.

brevity *n* (of event) brièveté *f*; (of speech) concision *f*.

brew I *n* **1** (beer) bière *f*; **2** (tea) thé *m*, infusion *f*; **3** (figurative) mixture *f*.
II *vtr* brasser [*beer*]; préparer [*tea*]; **freshly ~ed coffee** café fraîchement passé.
III *vi* **1** [*beer*] fermenter; [*tea*] infuser; **2** [*storm, crisis*] se préparer; **there's trouble ~ing** il y a de l'orage dans l'air.

brewer ▶805 *n* brasseur *m*.

brewery *n* brasserie *f*.

bribe I *n* pot-de-vin *m*.
II *vtr* soudoyer [*police*]; suborner [*witness*]; acheter [*servant, voter*].

bribery *n* corruption *f*.

brick I *n* **1** (for building) brique *f*; **2** (GB) (child's toy) cube *m*.
II *noun modifier* [*wall*] de briques; [*building*] en briques.

bricklayer ▶805 *n* maçon *m*.

bridal *adj* [*dress*] de mariée; [*car*] des mariés; [*suite*] nuptial.

bride *n* (jeune) mariée *f*; **the ~ and groom** les (jeunes) mariés *mpl*.

bride: **~groom** *n* jeune marié *m*; **~smaid** *n* demoiselle *f* d'honneur.

bridge I *n* **1** pont *m* (**over** sur; **across** au-dessus de); (figurative) (link) rapprochement *m*; **2** (on ship) passerelle *f*; **3** (of nose) arête *f*; (of spectacles) arcade *f*; **4** (on guitar, violin) chevalet *m*; **5** (for teeth) bridge *m*; **6** ▶649 (Games) bridge *m*.
II *vtr* **1 to ~ a gap in [sth]** combler un vide dans [*conversation*]; combler un trou dans [*budget*]; **2** (span) enjamber [*two eras*].

bridle I *n* bride *f*.
II *vtr* brider [*temper*]; brider [*horse*].
III *vi* se cabrer (**at** contre; **with** sous l'effet de).

brief I *n* **1** (GB) (remit) attributions *fpl*; (role) tâche *f*; **2** (Law) dossier *m*.
II **briefs** *n pl* slip *m*.
III *adj* [*event, summary, speech*] bref/brève; [*reply*] laconique; **in ~** en bref.
IV *vtr* informer [*politician, worker*] (**on** de); donner des instructions à [*police, troops*] (**on** sur); **to be well-~ed** être bien au courant.

briefcase *n* serviette *f*; (without handle) porte-documents *m inv*.

briefing *n* briefing *m* (**on** sur), réunion *f* d'information (**on** sur).

briefly *adv* **1** (gen) brièvement; [*look, pause*] un bref instant; **2** (in short) en bref.

brigade *n* brigade *f*.

bright *adj* **1** (vivid) [*colour*] vif/vive; [*garment, carpet*] aux couleurs vives; **2** (clear) [*sunshine*] éclatant; [*room, day*] clair; [*sky*] lumineux/-euse; **~ spell** éclaircie *f*; **3** (shiny) [*star, eye, metal*] brillant; **4** (clever) intelligent; **a ~ idea** une idée lumineuse; **5** [*smile, face*] radieux/

-ieuse; **to look on the ~ side** voir le bon côté des choses.

brighten *v* ■ **brighten up**: ¶ **~ up 1** [*person, mood*] s'égayer (**at** à); [*face*] s'éclairer (**at** à); **2** (improve) [*weather, sky*] s'éclaircir; ¶ **~ up [sth], ~ [sth] up 1** (cheer up) égayer [*room, decor*]; **2** (illuminate) éclairer.

brightly *adv* **1** [*dressed*] de couleurs vives; **2** [*shine, burn*] d'un vif éclat.

brightness *n* **1** (of colour, light, smile) éclat *m*; **2** (of room) clarté *f*.

bright spark○ *n* (GB) petit/-e futé/-e○ *m/f*.

brilliance *n* (of light, music) éclat *m*; (of person) génie *m*.

brilliant I *adj* **1** (successful) [*student, career, success*] brillant; **2** (bright) éclatant; **3** (GB)○ (fantastic) génial○; **to be ~ at sth** être doué en qch; **to be ~ at doing** avoir le don de faire.
II *excl* super○!

brilliantly *adv* **1** (very well) brillamment; **2** (particularly) [*witty, clever*] extrêmement.

brim *n* bord *m*; **filled to the ~ with** rempli jusqu'au bord de [*liquid, objects*].

brine *n* **1** (sea water) eau *f* de mer; **2** (for pickling) saumure *f*.

bring I *vtr* **1** apporter [*present, object, supplies, message*]; amener [*person, animal, car*]; **to ~ sth with one** apporter qch; **to ~ sb to** amener qn à [*party, office*]; **to ~ sb flowers** apporter des fleurs à qn; **to ~ sth/sb into the room** faire entrer qch/qn dans la pièce; **to ~ sth upstairs/downstairs** monter/descendre qch; **to ~ sb upstairs/downstairs** faire monter/descendre qn; **to ~ drugs into a country** faire entrer or introduire de la drogue dans un pays; **to ~ sb home** (transport) ramener qn; (to meet the family) amener qn à la maison; **2** apporter [*happiness, rain, change, hope*]; **to ~ sb wealth/fame** rendre qn riche/célèbre; **to ~ prosperity to a region** rendre une région prospère; **to ~ a smile to sb's face** faire sourire qn; **to ~ the conversation around to** amener la conversation à; **you brought it on yourself** tu l'as cherché; **that ~s the total to 100** cela fait un total de 100; **3** (lead, draw) **the path ~s you to the church** le chemin te conduit jusqu'à l'église; **the noise brought them to the window** le bruit les a attirés à la fenêtre.
II *v refl* **to ~ oneself to do** se décider à faire; **I couldn't ~ myself to tell him** je n'ai pas pu le lui dire.
■ **bring about**: **~ about [sth]** provoquer [*change, disaster*]; amener [*settlement*]; entraîner [*success, defeat*].
■ **bring along**: ¶ **~ [sth] along** apporter [*object*]; ¶ **~ [sb] along** amener, venir avec [*friend, partner*].
■ **bring back**: **~ back [sth], ~ [sth] back 1** rapporter [*souvenir*] (**from** de); **to ~ sth back for sb** rapporter qch à qn; **to ~ back memories** ranimer des souvenirs; **2** (reintroduce) rétablir [*custom*]; restaurer [*monarchy*].
■ **bring down**: **~ down [sth], ~ [sth] down 1** renverser [*government*]; **2** réduire [*inflation, expenditure*]; faire baisser [*rate, price, temperature*]; **3** (shoot down) abattre.
■ **bring forward**: **~ [sth] forward** avancer [*wedding, meeting*] (**by** de).
■ **bring in**: ¶ **~ in [sth]** rapporter [*money, interest*]; ¶ **~ in [sth], ~ [sth] in 1** (introduce) introduire [*legislation, measure*]; **2** rentrer [*harvest*]; ¶ **~ in [sb], ~ [sb] in** faire appel à [*expert, army*].
■ **bring off**: **~ off [sth], ~ [sth] off** réussir [*feat*]; conclure [*deal*].
■ **bring on**: ¶ **~ on [sth], ~ [sth] on** provoquer [*attack, migraine, labour*]; ¶ **~ on [sb], ~ [sb] on** faire entrer [*dancer, substitute player*].
■ **bring out**: **~ out [sth], ~ [sth] out 1** sortir [*edition, new model*]; **2** (highlight) faire ressortir [*flavour, meaning*].
■ **bring round**: **~ [sb] round 1** (revive) faire revenir [qn] à soi; **2** (convince) convaincre.
■ **bring together**: **~ together [sth/sb], ~ [sth/sb] together 1** (assemble) réunir; **2** (create bond between) rapprocher.
■ **bring up**: ¶ **~ [sth] up 1** (mention) aborder, parler de; **2** (vomit) vomir, rendre; ¶ **~ [sb] up, ~ up [sb]** élever; **to ~ sb up to do** apprendre à [qn] à faire; **well brought up** bien élevé.

brink *n* bord *m*; **on the ~ of doing** sur le point de faire.

brisk *adj* **1** (efficient) [*manner, tone*] vif/vive; [*person*] efficace; **2** (energetic) [*pace, trot*] rapide; **at a ~ pace** à vive allure; **3** (good) [*business, trade*] florissant; **business was ~** les affaires marchaient bien; **4** [*air*] vivifiant; [*wind*] vif/vive.

briskly *adv* **1** [*say*] vivement; [*work*] rapidement; **2** (quickly) [*walk*] d'un bon pas; [*sell*] très vite.

bristle I *n* (on brush, chin, animal) poil *m*; (on pig) soie *f*.
II *vi* **1** [*hairs*] se dresser; **2** [*person*] se hérisser (**at** à; **with** de).
■ **bristle with**: **~ with [sth]** grouiller de [*police, soldiers*].

bristly *adj* [*beard, fibres*] dru; [*surface*] couvert de poils durs.

Britain *pr n* (also **Great ~**) Grande-Bretagne *f*.

British ▶712 I *n pl* **the ~** les Britanniques *mpl*.
II *adj* britannique; **the ~ embassy** l'ambassade *f* de Grande-Bretagne.

Briton *n* Britannique *mf*.

Brittany *pr n* Bretagne *f*.

brittle *adj* [*twig*] cassant; [*nails, hair*] fragile; [*tone, laughter*] cassant.

broach *vtr* aborder [*subject*]; entamer [*bottle*].

broad ▶738 *adj* **1** (wide) large; **to have ~ shoulders** être large d'épaules; **2** (wide-ranging) [*choice, range*] grand (*before n*); [*meaning, term*] large; (general) [*outline, principle, consensus*] général; **3** [*accent*] fort (*before n*); **in ~ daylight** en plein jour.

broad bean *n* fève *f*.

broadcast I *n* émission *f*.
II *vtr* **1** diffuser [*programme*] (**to** à); **2** (tell) raconter.
III *vi* **1** [*station, channel*] émettre (**on** sur); **2** [*person*] faire une émission.

broadcaster ▶805| *n* animateur/-trice *m/f*; **news ~** journaliste *mf* de radio or télévision.

broadcasting *n* (field) communication *f* audiovisuelle; (action) diffusion *f*.

broadcasting ban *n* interdiction *f* d'antenne.

broad-chested *adj* de forte carrure.

broaden I *vtr* étendre [*appeal, scope*]; élargir [*horizons, knowledge*]; **travel ~s the mind** les voyages ouvrent l'esprit.
II *vi* [*appeal, horizons, scope*] s'élargir.

broadly *adv* [*agree, correspond*] en gros; [*similar, true*] globalement.

broadminded *adj* [*person*] large d'esprit; [*attitude*] libéral.

brocade *n* brocart *m*.

broccoli *n* (Bot) brocoli *m*; (Culin) brocolis *mpl*.

brochure *n* (booklet) brochure *f*; (larger) catalogue *m*; (leaflet) dépliant *m*; (for hotel) prospectus *m*.

broil *vtr* (US) faire griller [*meat*].

broke *adj* [*person*] fauché○; **to go ~** [*company*] faire faillite.

broken *adj* **1** (damaged) [*glass, window*] brisé; [*tooth, bone, leg, bottle, chair, toy*] cassé; [*radio, machine*] détraqué; **2** [*voice*] brisé; [*coastline*] découpé; **3** (depressed) [*man, woman*] brisé; **4** [*engagement, promise*] rompu; **5** (flawed) [*French*] mauvais (*before n*); [*sentence*] maladroit.

broken-hearted *adj* **to be ~** avoir le cœur brisé.

broken: **~ home** *n* famille *f* désunie; **~ marriage** *n* foyer *m* désuni.

broker ▶805| *n* courtier *m*; **insurance ~** courtier *m* d'assurance.

brokerage *n* (fee, business) courtage *m*.

broking (GB), **brokering** (US) *n* courtage *m*.

bronchitis ▶686| *n* bronchite *f*; **to have ~** avoir une bronchite.

bronze ▶559| I *n* **1** (colour) (couleur *f* de) bronze *m*; **2** (statue, metal) bronze *m*.
II *noun modifier* [*coin, ornament*] en bronze; [*medal*] de bronze.

brooch *n* broche *f*.

brood I *n* **1** (of birds) couvée *f*; (of mammals) nichée *f*; **2** (of children) nichée *f*.
II *vi* **1** (ponder) broyer du noir; **to ~ about** ressasser, ruminer [*problem*]; **2** [*bird*] couver.

brook *n* ruisseau *m*.

broom *n* **1** (for sweeping) balai *m*; **2** (plant) genêt *m*.

broth *n* bouillon *m*.
IDIOMS **too many cooks spoil the ~** on n'arrive à rien quand tout le monde s'en mêle.

brothel *n* maison *f* close.

brother *n* frère *m*.

brother-in-law *n* beau-frère *m*.

brotherly *adj* fraternel/-elle.

brow *n* **1** (forehead) front *m*; (eyebrow) sourcil *m*; **2** (of hill) sommet *m*.

browbeat *vtr* intimider; **to ~ sb into doing** forcer qn à faire.

brown ▶559| I *n* (colour) (of object) marron *m*; (of hair, skin, eyes) brun *m*.
II *adj* **1** (in colour) [*shoes, leaves, paint, eyes*] marron *inv*; [*hair*] châtain *inv*; **light/dark ~** marron clair/foncé; **2** (tanned) bronzé; **to go ~** bronzer.
III *vtr* faire roussir [*sauce*]; faire dorer [*meat, onions*].
IV *vi* [*meat, potatoes*] dorer.

brown: **~ ale** *n* (GB) bière *f* brune; **~ bear** *n* ours *m* brun; **~ bread** *n* pain *m* complet; **~ envelope** *n* enveloppe *f* kraft; **~ paper** *n* papier *m* kraft; **~ rice** *n* riz *m* complet; **~ sugar** *n* sucre *m* brun, cassonade *f*.

browse *vi* **1** (look at objects in shop) regarder; **2** (graze) brouter.
■ **browse through**: **~ through [sth]** feuilleter [*book*]; faire [*shops*].

bruise I *n* (on skin) bleu *m*; (more technically) ecchymose *f* (**on** sur); (on fruit) tache *f* (**on** sur).
II *vtr* meurtrir [*person*]; taler, abîmer [*fruit*]; **to ~ one's arm** se meurtrir le bras.
III *vi* **to ~ easily** [*fruit*] s'abîmer facilement; [*person*] se faire facilement des bleus.

brunch *n* brunch *m*.

brunette *n* brune *f*.

brunt *n* **to bear the ~ of** être le plus touché par [*disaster, unemployment*]; subir tout le poids de [*anger*].

brush I *n* **1** (for hair, clothes, shoes) brosse *f*; (small, for sweeping up) balayette *f*; (broom) balai *m*; (for paint) pinceau *m*; **2** (act of brushing) coup *m* de brosse; **to give one's teeth a quick ~** se brosser rapidement les dents; **3 to have a ~ with death** frôler la mort; **to have a ~ with the law** avoir des démêlés avec la justice; **4** (fox's tail) queue *f* de renard.
II *vtr* brosser [*carpet, clothes*]; **to ~ one's hair/teeth** se brosser les cheveux/les dents.
III *vi* **to ~ against** frôler; **to ~ past sb** frôler qn en passant.
IV **brushed** *pp adj* [*fabric*] gratté.
■ **brush aside**: **~ [sb/sth] aside** repousser [*idea, criticism, person*].
■ **brush away**: **~ away [sth]**, **~ [sth] away** enlever [*crumbs*]; essuyer [*tear*].
■ **brush back**: **~ back [sth]**, **~ [sth] back** brosser [qch] en arrière [*hair*].
■ **brush up (on)**: **~ up (on) [sth]**, **~ [sth] up** se remettre à [*skill, subject*].

brush-off○ *n* **to give sb the ~** rembarrer○ qn.

brushwood *n* (firewood) brindilles *fpl*; (brush) broussailles *fpl*.

brusque *adj* brusque (**with** avec).

Brussels ▶574| *pr n* Bruxelles.

Brussels sprout *n* chou *m* de Bruxelles.

brutal *adj* (gen) brutal; [*murderer, régime*] cruel/-elle; [*attack*] sauvage.

brutality *n* brutalité *f* (**of** de).

brutalize *vtr* **1** (make brutal) rendre [qn] brutal; **2** (treat brutally) brutaliser.

brutally *adv* [*murder, treat*] sauvagement; **~ honest** d'une franchise brutale.

brute I *n* **1** (man) brute *f*; **2** (animal) bête *f*.
II *adj* [*strength*] simple (*before n*); **by ~ force** par la force.

B side *n* face *f* B.

bubble I *n* bulle *f* (**in** dans); **to blow ~s** faire des bulles.
II *vi* [*person*] faire des bulles; [*fizzy drink*] pétiller; [*boiling liquid*] bouillonner; **to ~ (over) with** déborder de [*enthusiasm, ideas*].

bubble bath *n* bain *m* moussant.

bubbling I *n* (sound) glouglou *m*, gargouillis *m*.
II *adj* bouillonnant.

Bucharest ▶574 *pr n* Bucarest.

buck I *n* **1** (US)° dollar *m*; **2**° (money) fric° *m*; **3** (male animal) mâle *m*.
II *vtr* (also **~ off**) [*horse*] désarçonner [*rider*].
III *vi* [*horse*] ruer.
IDIOMS **to pass the ~** refiler° la responsabilité à quelqu'un d'autre.

bucket *n* seau *m* (**of** de).

buckle I *n* **1** (clasp) boucle *f*; **2** (dent) (in metal) gondolage *m*.
II *vtr* **1** attacher, boucler [*belt, shoe, strap*]; **~d** bien attaché; **2** (damage) gondoler [*material, surface*].
III *vi* **1** [*metal, surface*] se gondoler; [*wheel*] se voiler; **2** [*belt, shoe, strap*] s'attacher, se boucler.
■ **buckle down** se mettre au boulot°.

bud I *n* (of leaf) bourgeon *m*; (of flower) bouton *m*.
II *vi* **1** (develop leaf buds) bourgeonner; (develop flower buds) boutonner; **2** [*flower, breast*] pointer.

Buddha *pr n* Bouddha *m*.

Buddhism *n* bouddhisme *m*.

budding *adj* **1** (into leaf) bourgeonnant; (into flower) boutonnant; **2** [*athlete, champion*] en herbe; [*talent, career, romance*] naissant.

buddy° *n* copain *m*, pote° *m*.

budge I *vtr* **1** (move) bouger; **2** (persuade) faire changer d'avis à.
II *vi* **1** (move) bouger (**from, off** de); **2** (give way) changer d'avis (**on** sur).

budgerigar *n* perruche *f*.

budget I *n* budget *m* (**for** pour).
II *noun modifier* [*cut, deficit*] budgétaire; [*holiday, price*] pour petits budgets; **a low-~ film** un film à petit budget.
III *vtr* budgétiser [*money*].
IV *vi* **to ~ for** budgétiser ses dépenses en fonction de [*increase, needs*].

budgetary *adj* budgétaire.

buff I *n* **1**° (enthusiast) mordu/-e *m/f*; **2** (colour) chamois *m*; **3** (leather) peau *m* de buffle.
II *adj* (also **~-coloured**) (couleur) chamois.

buffalo *n* (GB) buffle *m*; (US) bison *m*.

buffer *n* **1** (protection) tampon *m*; **~ state** État *m* tampon; **2** (for polishing) polissoir *m*.

buffet[1] *n* buffet *m*.

buffet[2] *vtr* [*wind*] ballotter [*ship*]; battre [*coast*].

buffoon *n* bouffon/-onne *m/f*.

bug I *n* **1**° (insect) (gen) bestiole *f*; (bedbug) punaise *f*; **2**° (also **stomach ~**) ennuis *mpl* gastriques; **3** (germ) microbe *m*; **4** (fault) (gen) défaut *m*; (Comput) bogue *f*, bug *m*; **5** (hidden microphone) micro *m* caché.
II *vtr* **1** poser des micros dans [*room, building*]; **the room is ~ged** il y a un micro (caché) dans la pièce; **2**° (annoy) embêter° [*person*].

bugging device *n* micro *m* d'écoute.

buggy *n* **1** (GB) (pushchair) poussette *f*; **2** (US) (pram) landau *m*; **3** (carriage) boghei *m*.

bugle ▶753 *n* clairon *m*.

build I *n* (of person) carrure *f*.
II *vtr* construire [*house, wall, factory, railway*]; édifier [*church, monument*]; bâtir [*career, future*]; fonder [*empire*]; **to be well built** [*person*] être bien bâti.
III *vi* construire; **to ~ on** tirer parti de [*popularity, success*].
■ **build up**: ¶ **~ up** [*gas, deposits*] s'accumuler; [*traffic*] s'intensifier; [*business, trade*] se développer; [*tension, excitement*] monter; ¶ **~ up [sth], ~ [sth] up 1** (accumulate) accumuler [*wealth*]; **2** (boost) établir [*trust*]; gonfler [*morale*]; **3** (establish) constituer [*collection*]; créer [*business*]; établir [*picture, profile*]; se faire [*reputation*]; ¶ **~ [sth/sb] up, ~ up [sth/sb]** (strengthen) affermir [*muscles*]; **to ~ oneself up, to ~ up one's strength** prendre des forces.

builder ▶805 *n* (contractor) entrepreneur *m* en bâtiment; (worker) ouvrier/-ière *m/f* du bâtiment.

building *n* **1** bâtiment *m*; (with offices, apartments) immeuble *m*; (palace, church) édifice *m*; **2** (action) construction *f*.

building: **~ site** *n* chantier *m* (de construction); **~ society** *n* (GB) société *f* d'investissement et de crédit immobilier.

build-up *n* **1** (in traffic, pressure) intensification *f* (**of** de); (in weapons, stocks) accumulation *f* (**of** de); (in tension) accroissement *m* (**of** de); **2** (publicity) **the ~ to sth** les préparatifs de qch; **to give sth a good ~** faire du battage° autour de qch.

built-in *adj* **1** [*wardrobe*] encastré; **2** [*guarantee*] intégré.

built-up *adj* [*region*] urbanisé; **~ area** agglomération *f*.

bulb *n* **1** (electric) ampoule *f* (électrique); **2** (of plant) bulbe *m*.

bulbous *adj* bulbeux/-euse; **a ~ nose** un gros nez.

Bulgaria ▶574 *n* Bulgarie *f*.

Bulgarian ▶712 **I** *n* **1** (person) Bulgare *mf*; **2** (language) bulgare *m*.
II *adj* [*culture, food, politics*] bulgare; [*teacher, lesson*] de bulgare; [*ambassador, embassy*] de Bulgarie.

bulge I *n* (in clothing, carpet) bosse *f*; (in pipe, tube) renflement *m*; (in tyre) hernie *f*; (in wall) bombement *m*; (in plaster) boursouflure *f*; (in cheek) gonflement *m*.

II *vi* [*bag, pocket, cheeks*] être gonflé; [*wallet*] être bourré; [*surface*] se boursoufler; [*stomach*] ballonner; **his eyes were bulging** les yeux lui sortaient de la tête.

bulging *adj* [*eye*] exorbité; [*stomach, vein*] gonflé; [*muscle*] saillant.

bulimia (nervosa) ▶686 *n* boulimie *f*.

bulk *n* (of package, correspondence) volume *m*; (of building, vehicle) masse *f*; **in ~** [*buy, sell*] en gros; [*transport*] en vrac.

bulk: **~-buying** *n* achat *m* en gros; **~head** *n* (of ship, plane) cloison *f*.

bulky *adj* [*person*] corpulent; [*package*] volumineux/-euse; [*book*] épais/-aisse.

bull I *n* taureau *m*.
II *noun modifier* [*elephant, whale*] mâle *m*.

bulldog *n* bouledogue *m*.

bulldoze *vtr* **1** détruire [qch] au bulldozer [*building*]; nettoyer [qch] au bulldozer [*site*]; **2** (force) forcer (**into doing** à faire).

bulldozer *n* bulldozer *m*, bouteur *m*.

bullet *n* balle *f*.

bulletin *n* bulletin *m*; **news ~** bulletin d'informations.

bulletin board *n* (gen) tableau *m* d'affichage; (Comput) messagerie *f*.

bulletproof *adj* [*glass, vehicle, door*] blindé; **~ vest** gilet *m* pare-balles *inv*.

bull: **~fight** *n* corrida *f*; **~fighter** ▶805 *n* torero *m*; **~fighting** *n* (gen) corridas *fpl*; (art) tauromachie *f*; **~frog** *n* grenouille *f* taureau.

bullion *n* lingots *mpl*.

bullish *adj* [*market, shares, stocks*] en hausse, haussier/-ière.

bullock *n* (young) bouvillon *m*; (mature) bœuf *m*.

bullring *n* (arena) arène *f*; (building) arènes *fpl*.

bull's-eye *n* (on a target) mille *m*.

bully I *n* (child) petite brute *f*; (adult) tyran *m*; **the class ~** la terreur de la classe.
II *vtr* [*person, child*] maltraiter; [*country*] intimider; **to ~ sb into doing sth** forcer qn à faire qch.

bullying *n* (of person, child) mauvais traitements *mpl*; (of country) intimidation *f*.

bulrush *n* jonc *m* (des chaisiers).

bum○ *n* **1** (GB) (buttocks) derrière *m*; **2** (US) (vagrant) clochard *m*.
■ **bum around 1** (travel aimlessly) vadrouiller○; **2** (be lazy) traînasser.

bumble *vi* (also **~ on**) (mumble) marmonner.

bumblebee *n* bourdon *m*.

bump I *n* **1** (lump) (on body) bosse *f* (**on** à); (on road surface) bosse *f* (**on, in** sur); **2** (jolt) secousse *f*; **3** (sound of fall) bruit *m* sourd.
II *vtr* cogner (**against, on** contre); **to ~ one's head** se cogner la tête.
III *vi* **1** (knock) **to ~ against** buter contre; **2** (move jerkily) **to ~ along** [*vehicle*] brinquebaler sur [*road*]; **to ~ over** [*vehicle*] cahoter sur [*road*].
■ **bump into**: ¶ **~ into [sb/sth]** (collide) rentrer dans [*person, object*]; ¶ **~ into [sb]**○ (meet) tomber sur○ qn.

bumper I *n* **1** (of car) pare-chocs *m*; **2** (US) (of train) butoir *m*.
II *adj* [*crop, sales, year*] record *inv* (*after n*); [*edition*] exceptionnel/-elle.

bumper car *n* auto *f* tamponneuse.

bumpkin○ *n* (also **country ~**) péquenaud/-e○ *m/f*.

bumpy *adj* [*road surface*] accidenté; [*wall*] irrégulier/-ière; [*landing*] agité.

bun *n* **1** (roll) petit pain *m*; (cake) petit cake *m*; **2** (hairstyle) chignon *m*.

bunch *n* (of flowers) bouquet *m*; (of vegetables) botte *f*; (of bananas) régime *m*; (of keys) trousseau *m*; (of feathers) touffe *f*; (of people) groupe *m*; **a mixed ~** un groupe hétéroclite; **a ~ of idiots** une bande d'imbéciles; **the best of the ~** le meilleur du lot.

bundle I *n* (of wool, clothes) (tied-up) ballot *m*; (loose) pile *f*; (of papers, banknotes) liasse *f*; (of books) paquet *m*; (of straw) botte *f*; **~ of sticks** fagot *m* de bois; **~ of nerves** boule *f* de nerfs.
II○ *vtr* **to ~ sb/sth into** fourrer○ qn/qch dans.

bungalow *n* pavillon *m* (sans étage).

bungle I *n* gaffe *f*.
II *vtr* rater○ [*attempt, burglary*].

bungling *adj* maladroit.

bunion *n* oignon *m*.

bunk *n* **1** (on ship, train) couchette *f*; **2** (also **~ bed**) (whole unit) lits *mpl* superposés; **the top/lower ~** le lit du haut/du bas.

bunker *n* **1** (for commander) bunker *m*; (for gun) blockhaus *m*; (beneath building) abri *m*; **2** (in golf) bunker *m*; **3** (container) soute *f*.

bunny *n* **1** (also **~ rabbit**) (Jeannot) lapin *m*; **2** (also **~ girl**) hôtesse *f*.

Bunsen (burner) *n* (bec *m*) Bunsen *m*.

bunting *n* guirlandes *fpl*.

buoy I *n* (gen) bouée *f*; (for marking) balise *f* (flottante).
II *vtr* (also **~ up**) **1** revigorer [*person, morale*] (**by** par); **2** (keep up) stimuler [*share prices*] (**by** par); **3** (keep afloat) maintenir à flot.

buoyancy *n* (of floating object) flottabilité *f*; (of water) poussée *f*.

buoyant *adj* **1** [*object*] qui flotte; **2** (cheerful) [*person*] vif/vive; [*mood, spirits*] enjoué; [*step*] allègre; **3** [*market, prices*] ferme; [*economy*] en expansion.

burbling *adj* [*stream, voice*] qui gargouille.

burden I *n* fardeau *m* (**to sb** pour qn); **the ~ of guilt/of taxation** le poids de la culpabilité/de l'impôt.
II *vtr* **1** (also **~ down**) encombrer (**with** de); **2** (figurative) (with work, taxes) accabler (**with** de); **I don't want to ~ you with my problems** je ne veux pas vous ennuyer avec mes problèmes.

bureau *n* **1** (agency) agence *f*; (office) bureau *m*; **2** (US) (government department) service *m*; **3** (GB) (writing desk) secrétaire *m*; **4** (US) (chest of drawers) commode *f*.

bureaucracy *n* bureaucratie *f*.

bureaucrat *n* bureaucrate *mf*.

bureaucratic *adj* bureaucratique.

burgeoning *adj* (growing) croissant; (thriving) florissant.

burger *n* hamburger *m*.

burglar *n* cambrioleur/-euse *m/f*.

burglar alarm *n* sonnerie *f* d'alarme.

burglary *n* (gen) cambriolage *m*; (Law) vol *m* avec effraction.

burgle *vtr* cambrioler.

burgundy ▶559 I **Burgundy** *pr n* Bourgogne *f*; **in ~** en Bourgogne.
II *n* **1** (also **Burgundy**) (wine) bourgogne *m*; **2** (colour) (couleur *f*) bordeaux *m*.

burial *n* **1** (ceremony) enterrement *m*; **2** (of body) inhumation *f*; (of object, waste) ensevelissement *m*.

burlesque I *n* (piece of writing) parodie *f*; (genre) (genre *m*) burlesque *m*.
II *adj* **1** [*style, show*] burlesque; **2** (sham) caricatural.

burly *adj* [*person*] solidement charpenté; [*build*] imposant.

Burma ▶574 *pr n* Birmanie *f*.

burn I *n* brûlure *f*.
II *vtr* **1** brûler [*papers, skin, surface, grass*]; incendier, faire brûler [*building*]; laisser brûler [*food*]; [*acid*] ronger, brûler; **to be ~ed to ashes** être réduit en cendres; **to be ~ed alive** être brûlé vif; **to ~ one's finger** se brûler le doigt; **2** (use) **to ~ coal/gas** [*boiler*] marcher au charbon/au gaz.
III *vi* **1** [*wood, fuel, toast, meat*] brûler; **2** [*light*] être allumé; **3** [*blister, wound*] cuire; (from sun) brûler; **he ~s easily** il attrape facilement des coups de soleil.
IV *v refl* **to ~ oneself** se brûler.
■ **burn down**: ¶ **~ down 1** [*house*] être détruit par le feu; **2** [*candle, fire*] baisser; ¶ **~ down [sth], ~ [sth] down** réduire [qch] en cendres [*house*].
■ **burn out**: ¶ **~ out** [*candle, fire*] s'éteindre; [*light bulb*] griller; [*fuse*] sauter; [*person*] (through overwork) s'user; ¶ **~ out [sth], ~ [sth] out** incendier [*building, vehicle*].
■ **burn up**: **~ up [sth], ~ [sth] up** brûler [*calories, fuel, waste*]; dépenser [*energy*].

burner *n* (on gas cooker) brûleur *m*; (of lamp) bec *m* (de gaz).

burning I *n* **1 there's a smell of ~** ça sent le brûlé; **2** (setting on fire) incendie *m*.
II *adj* **1** (on fire) en flammes, en feu; (alight) [*candle, lamp, fire*] allumé; [*ember, coal*] embrasé; (very hot) brûlant; **a ~ sensation** une sensation de brûlure; **2** (intense) [*fever, desire*] brûlant; [*passion*] ardent.

burnt *adj* [*food, papers, earth*] brûlé; [*smell, taste*] de brûlé, de roussi.

burnt-out *adj* [*building, car*] calciné; [*person*] usé (par le travail).

burp○ I *n* rot○ *m*, renvoi *m*.
II *vi* [*person*] roter○; [*baby*] faire son rot○.

burrow I *n* terrier *m*.
II *vtr* [*animal*] creuser [*hole, tunnel*].
III *vi* [*animal*] creuser un terrier; **to ~ into/under sth** creuser dans/sous qch.

burst I *n* (of flame) jaillissement *m*; (of gunfire) rafale *f*; (of activity, enthusiasm) accès *m*; **a ~ of laughter** un éclat de rire; **a ~ of applause** un tonnerre d'applaudissements.
II *vtr* crever [*balloon, bubble, tyre*]; rompre [*blood vessel*]; **to ~ its banks** déborder; **a burst pipe** un tuyau éclaté.
III *vi* [*balloon, bubble, tyre*] crever; [*pipe, boiler*] éclater; [*dam*] rompre; **to be ~ing with health/pride** déborder de santé/fierté.
■ **burst into**: **~ into [sth] 1** faire irruption dans [*room, meeting*]; **2 to ~ into flames** s'enflammer; **to ~ into tears** fondre en larmes.
■ **burst out 1 to ~ out of a room** sortir en trombe d'une pièce; **2** (start) **to ~ out laughing** éclater de rire; **to ~ out crying** fondre en larmes.
■ **burst through**: **~ through [sth]** rompre [*barricade*]; **to ~ through the door** entrer violemment.

bury *vtr* enterrer [*dead person, animal*]; enterrer, enfouir [*treasure, bone*]; [*avalanche*] ensevelir [*person, town*]; enterrer [*differences, memories*]; **to ~ one's face in one's hands** se cacher le visage dans ses mains; **to be buried in** être plongé dans [*book, work*].

bus I *n* (vehicle) autobus *m*, bus *m*; (long-distance) autocar *m*, car *m*; **by ~** [*come, go, travel*] en (auto)bus, par le bus; **on the ~** dans le bus.
II *noun modifier* [*depot, service, stop, ticket*] d'autobus.

bus: **~ conductor** ▶805 *n* receveur *m* d'autobus; **~ driver** ▶805 *n* conducteur/-trice *m/f* d'autobus.

bush *n* **1** (shrub) buisson *m*; **2** (in Australia, Africa) **the ~** la brousse *f*.
IDIOMS **don't beat about the ~** cessez de tourner autour du pot.

bushel *n* boisseau *m*.

bushfire *n* feu *m* de brousse.

bushy *adj* [*hair, tail*] touffu; [*beard*] épais/-aisse; [*eyebrows*] broussailleux/-euse.

business I *n* **1** (commerce) affaires *fpl*; **to be in ~** être dans les affaires; **to go into ~** se lancer dans les affaires; **to do ~ with sb** faire des affaires avec qn; **she's gone to Brussels on ~** elle est allée à Bruxelles en voyage d'affaires; **the recession has put them out of ~** la récession les a obligés à cesser leurs activités; **it's good for ~** ça fait marcher les affaires; **to mix ~ with pleasure** joindre l'utile à l'agréable; **it is/it was ~ as usual** c'est/c'était comme à l'habitude; **2** (custom, trade) **to lose ~** perdre de la clientèle; **~ is slow at the moment** les affaires marchent au ralenti en ce moment; **we are doing twice as much ~ as last summer** notre chiffre d'affaires a doublé par rapport à l'été dernier; **3** (trade, profession) métier *m*; **he's in the insurance ~** il travaille dans les assurances; **4** (company, firm) affaire *f*, entreprise *f*; (shop) commerce *m*, boutique *f*; **small ~es** les petites entreprises; **5** (important matters) questions *fpl* importantes; (duties, tasks) occupations *fpl*; **let's get down to ~** passons aux choses sérieuses; **to go about one's ~** vaquer à ses occupations; **6** (concern) **that's her ~** ça la regarde; **it's none of your ~!** ça ne

te regardé pas!; **mind your own ~**○! occupe-toi de tes affaires○!
II *noun modifier* [*address, letter, transaction*] commercial; [*meeting*] d'affaires; **~ people** hommes *mpl* d'affaires.

business: **~ associate** *n* associé/-e *m/f*; **~ card** *n* carte *f* de visite; **~ class** *n* (on plane) classe *f* affaires; **~ deal** *n* affaire *f*; **~ expenses** *n pl* frais *mpl* professionnels; **~ hours** *n pl* (in office) heures *fpl* de bureau; (of shop) heures *fpl* d'ouverture; **~like** *adj* sérieux/-ieuse; **~man** ▶805 *n* homme *m* d'affaires; **~ park** *n* parc *m* d'affaires or d'activités; **~ reply envelope** *n* enveloppe *f* pré-affranchie; **~ school** *n* école *f* de commerce; **~ studies** *n pl* études *fpl* de commerce; **~ trip** *n* voyage *m* d'affaires; **~woman** *n* femme *f* d'affaires.

busk *vi* (GB) [*musician*] jouer dans la rue; [*singer*] chanter dans la rue.

busker *n* (GB) musicien/-ienne *m/f* ambulant/-e.

bus: **~ lane** *n* couloir *m* d'autobus; **~ pass** *n* carte *f* de bus; **~ route** *n* ligne *f* d'autobus; **~ shelter** *n* abribus® *m*; **~ station** *n* gare *f* routière.

bust I *n* **1** (breasts) poitrine *f*; **2** (statue) buste *m*.
II *noun modifier* **~ size, ~ measurement** tour *m* de poitrine.
III○ *adj* **1** (broken) fichu○; **2** (bankrupt) **to go ~** faire faillite.
IV○ *vtr* [*police*] (raid) faire une descente dans [*premises*]; (arrest) épingler○ [*suspect*].

bus terminus *n* (GB) terminus *m* des bus.

bustle I *n* (activity) affairement *m* (**of** de); **hustle and ~** grande animation *f*.
II *vi* [*person, crowd*] s'affairer; **to ~ in/out** entrer/sortir d'un air affairé.

bustling *adj* [*street, shop, town*] animé; [*person*] affairé.

busy I *adj* **1** [*person*] occupé (**with** avec; **doing** à faire); **to keep sb ~** trouver de quoi occuper qn; **2** [*shop*] où il y a beaucoup de monde; [*junction, airport*] où le trafic est intense; [*road*] très fréquenté; [*street, town*] animé; [*day, week*] chargé; **3** (engaged) [*line*] occupé.
II *v refl* **to ~ oneself doing** s'occuper à faire.

busybody○ *n* **he's a real ~** il se mêle de tout.

but I *adv* **I can ~ try** je peux toujours essayer; **one can't help ~ admire her** on ne peut pas s'empêcher de l'admirer.
II *prep* sauf; **anything ~ that** tout, sauf ça; **anybody ~ him** n'importe qui sauf lui; **everybody ~ Paul** tout le monde sauf Paul; **nobody ~ me knows how to do it** il n'y a que moi qui sache le faire; **he's nothing ~ a coward** ce n'est qu'un lâche; **to do nothing ~ disturb people** ne rien faire d'autre que déranger les gens; **there's nothing for it ~ to leave** il n'y a plus qu'une solution, c'est de partir; **the last ~ one** l'avant-dernier.
III *conj* mais; **cheap ~ nourishing** bon marché mais nourrissant.
IV **but for** *phr* **~ for you, I would have died** sans toi je serais mort; **he would have gone ~ for me** si je n'avais pas été là il serait parti.

butane *n* butane *m*.

butcher ▶805 I *n* boucher *m*; **~'s (shop)** boucherie *f*.
II *vtr* abattre [*animal*]; massacrer [*people*].

butler ▶805 *n* maître *m* d'hôtel, majordome *m*.

butt I *n* **1** (of rifle) crosse *f*; (of cigarette) mégot○ *m*; **2**○ (US) (buttocks) derrière○ *m*; **3** (barrel) (gros) tonneau *m*; **4 to be the ~ of sb's jokes** être la cible des blagues de qn.
II *vtr* [*person*] donner un coup de tête à; [*animal*] donner un coup de corne à.
■ **butt in** interrompre.

butter I *n* beurre *m*.
II *vtr* beurrer [*bread*].
IDIOMS **it's her bread and ~** c'est son gagne-pain; **~ wouldn't melt in her mouth** on lui donnerait le bon Dieu sans confession.

buttercup *n* bouton d'or *m*.

butterfly *n* papillon *m*.
IDIOMS **to have butterflies (in one's stomach)** avoir le trac○.

butterfly stroke *n* brasse *f* papillon.

butter: **~ knife** *n* couteau *m* à beurre; **~milk** *n* babeurre *m*; **~scotch** *n* (sweet) caramel *m* dur; (flavour) caramel *m*.

buttock *n* fesse *f*.

button I *n* **1** (on coat, switch) bouton *m*; **2** (US) (badge) insigne *m*, badge *m*.
II *vi* [*dress*] se boutonner.
■ **button up**: **~ [sth] up** boutonner [*garment*].

buttonhole I *n* **1** (on garment) boutonnière *f*; **2** (GB) (flower) fleur *f* (*portée à la boutonnière*).
II○ *vtr* accrocher○ [*person*].

buttress *n* **1** (gen) contrefort *m*; (figurative) soutien *m*; **2** (also **flying ~**) arc-boutant *m*.

buxom *adj* [*woman*] à la poitrine généreuse.

buy I *n* **1** (bargain) **a good/bad ~** une bonne/mauvaise affaire; **2** (purchase) acquisition *f*.
II *vtr* acheter (**from sb** à qn); **to ~ sth from the supermarket/from the baker's** acheter qch au supermarché/chez le boulanger; **to ~ sb sth** acheter qch à qn; **to ~ some time** gagner du temps.
III *v refl* **to ~ oneself sth** s'acheter qch.
■ **buy into**: **~ into [sth]** acheter or acquérir une part dans [*company*].
■ **buy off**: **~ [sb] off, ~ off [sb]** acheter [*person, witness*].
■ **buy out**: **~ [sb] out, ~ out [sb]** racheter la part de [*co-owner*].
■ **buy up**: **~ up [sth], ~ [sth] up** acheter systématiquement [*shares, property*].

buyer ▶805 *n* acheteur/-euse *m/f*; **~'s market** marché *m* d'acheteurs, marché *m* où la demande est faible.

buying *n* achat *m*.

buyout *n* rachat *m* d'entreprise.

buzz I *n* (of insect, conversation) bourdonnement *m*.
II *vtr* **1** (call) **to ~ sb** appeler qn au bip, biper;

2 [*plane*] raser [*crowd, building*]; frôler [*other plane*].

III *vi* [*bee, fly*] bourdonner; [*buzzer*] sonner.

buzzard *n* buse *f*.

buzzer *n* (gen) sonnerie *f*; (on pocket) bip *m*.

buzzing *n* (of insects) bourdonnement *m*; (of buzzer) vibration *f*.

by I *prep* **1** (with passive verbs) par; **he was bitten ~ a snake** il a été mordu par un serpent; **forbidden ~ law** interdit par la loi; **we were overwhelmed ~ the news** nous avons été bouleversés par la nouvelle; **2** (with present participle) en; **~ working extra hours** en faisant des heures supplémentaires; **to learn French ~ listening to the radio** apprendre le français en écoutant la radio; **to begin ~ saying** commencer par dire; **3** (by means of) par; **to pay ~ cheque** payer par chèque; **I took him ~ the hand** je l'ai pris par la main; **~ mistake/accident** par erreur/accident; **~ telephone** par téléphone; **~ the back door** par la porte de derrière; **to travel to Rome ~ Venice** aller à Rome en passant par Venise; **to travel ~ bus/train** voyager en bus/train; **~ bicycle** à bicyclette, en vélo; **~ candlelight** [*dine*] aux chandelles; [*read*] à la bougie; **an architect ~ trade** architecte de son métier; **~ birth** de naissance; **4** (from) à; **I could tell ~ the look on her face that** rien qu'à la regarder je savais que; **I knew him ~ his walk** je l'ai reconnu à sa démarche; **5** (near) à côté de, près de; **~ the window** à côté de la fenêtre; **~ the sea** au bord de la mer; **6** (showing authorship) de; **a film ~ Claude Chabrol** un film de Claude Chabrol; **who is it ~?** c'est de qui?; **7** (in time expressions) avant; **~ midnight/next Thursday** avant minuit/jeudi prochain; **~ this time next week** d'ici la semaine prochaine; **~ the time she had got downstairs he was gone** le temps qu'elle descende, il était parti; **he should be here ~ now** il devrait être déjà là; **~ day and ~ night** de jour comme de nuit; **8** (according to) selon; **to play ~ the rules** jouer selon les règles; **~ western standards** selon or d'après les critères occidentaux; **~ my watch** à ma montre; **9** (showing amount) de; **prices have risen ~ 20%** les prix ont augmenté de 20%; **he's taller than me ~ two centimetres** il fait deux centimètres de plus que moi; **10** (in measurements) sur; **20 metres ~ 10 metres** 20 mètres sur 10; **11** (showing rate, quantity) à; **paid ~ the hour** payé à l'heure; **~ the dozen** à la douzaine; **12 little ~ little** peu à peu; **day ~ day** jour après jour; **one ~ one** un par un, une par une; **13 ~ oneself** tout/-e seul/-e; **14 to go** or **pass ~ sb/sth** passer devant qn/qch; **15** (in compass directions) quart; **south ~ south-west** sud quart sud-ouest.

II *adv* **1** (past) **to go ~** passer; **the people walking ~** les gens qui passent/passaient, les passants; **let us get ~** laissez-nous passer; **a lot of time has gone ~ since then** il s'est écoulé beaucoup de temps depuis lors; **as time goes ~** avec le temps; **2** (near) près; **he lives close ~** il habite tout près; **3** (aside) **to put money ~** mettre de l'argent de côté.

IDIOMS **~ and ~** bientôt; **~ the ~** à propos; **but that's ~ the ~** mais ça c'est un détail or autre chose.

bye° *excl* (also **~-bye**) au revoir!; **~ for now!** à bientôt!

by(e)-election *n* (GB) élection *f* partielle.

bygone *adj* [*days, years, scene*] d'antan; **a ~ era** une époque révolue.

IDIOMS **to let ~s be ~s** enterrer le passé.

by(e)law *n* arrêté *m* municipal.

bypass I *n* **1** (road) rocade *f*; **2** (pipe, channel) by-pass *m inv*; **3** (in electricity) dérivation *f*; **4** (Med) (also **~ operation**) pontage *m*.

II *vtr* contourner [*town, city*]; éviter [*question*]; éviter de passer par [*manager*].

by: **~-product** *n* dérivé *m*; (figurative) effet *m* secondaire; **~road** *n* petite route *f*, petit chemin *m*; **~stander** *n* spectateur/-trice *m/f*.

byte *n* (Comput) octet *m*.

Cc

c, C *n* **1** (letter) c, C *m*; **2** (*written abbr* = **century**) **c19th, C19th** XIXᵉ siècle
cab *n* **1** (taxi) taxi *m*; **2** (for driver) cabine *f*.
cabbage *n* chou *m*.
cabin *n* **1** (hut) cabane *f*; (in holiday camp) chalet *m*; **2** (in boat) cabine *f*; **3** (in plane) (for passengers) cabine *f*; (cockpit) cabine *f* de pilotage.
cabin: **~ crew** *n* personnel *m* de bord; **~ cruiser** *n* cruiser *m*.
cabinet *n* **1** (cupboard) petit placard *m*; (glass-fronted) vitrine *f*; (decorative, on legs) cabinet *m*; **2** (GB) cabinet *m*; ≈ Conseil *m* des ministres.
cabinet minister *n* (GB) ministre *m*.
cable *n* câble *m*.
cable: **~ car** *n* téléphérique *m*; **~ railway** *n* funiculaire *m*; **~ TV** *n* télévision *f* par câble.
cab-rank, cab stand *n* station *f* de taxis.
cackle *vi* [*hen*] caqueter; [*person*] (talk) caqueter; (laugh) ricaner.
caddy *n* **1** (US) (shopping trolley) chariot *m*, caddie *m*; **2** (Sport) caddie *m*.
cadet *n* (Mil) élève *mf* officier; (in police force) élève *mf* agent de police.
café *n* **1** ≈ snack-bar *m*; **pavement ~, sidewalk ~** café *m*; **2** (US) bistro *m*.
cafeteria *n* (gen) cafétéria *f*; (Sch) cantine *f*; (Univ) restaurant *m* universitaire.
caffein(e) *n* caféine *f*; **~-free** décaféiné.
cage **I** *n* cage *f*.
II *vtr* mettre [qch] en cage [*animal*]; **a ~d animal** un animal en cage.
cagoule *n* (GB) K-way® *m*.
Cairo ▶ 574 *pr n* Le Caire.
cake *n* **1** (Culin) gâteau *m*; (sponge) génoise *f*; **2** (of soap, wax) pain *m*; **3** (of fish, potato) croquette *f*.
IDIOMS **it's a piece of ~**° c'est du gâteau°.
cake: **~ shop** *n* ≈ pâtisserie *f*; **~ tin** *n* moule *m* à gâteaux.
calamine lotion *n* lotion *f* calmante à la calamine.
calculate *vtr* **1** (work out) calculer [*cost, distance, price*]; **2** (estimate) évaluer [*effect, probability*]; **3** (intend) **to be ~d to do** avoir été conçu pour faire.
calculating *adj* [*manner, person*] calculateur/-trice.
calculation *n* **1** (sums) calcul *m*; **2** (scheming) préméditation *f*.
calculator *n* calculatrice *f*, calculette *f*.
calendar *n* calendrier *m*.
calendar: **~ month** *n* mois *m* calendaire; **~ year** *n* année *f* civile.
calf *n* **1** (Zool) veau *m*; **2** (leather) vachette *f*; **3** (part of leg) mollet *m*.
calibre (GB), **caliber** (US) *n* calibre *m*.
call **I** *n* **1** (also **phone ~**) appel *m* (téléphonique) (**from** de); **to make a ~** appeler, téléphoner; **to make a ~ to Italy** appeler l'Italie, téléphoner en Italie; **to return sb's ~** rappeler qn; **2** (cry) (human) appel *m* (**for** à); (animal) cri *m*; **3** (summons) appel *m*; **to put out a ~ for sb** (over public address) faire appeler qn; **4** (visit) visite *f*; **to make** or **pay a ~** rendre visite (**on** à); **5** (demand) demande *f* (**for** de); **there were ~s for his resignation** sa démission a été réclamée; **to have first ~ on sth** avoir la priorité sur qch; **6** (need) **there's no ~ for sth/to do** il n'y a pas de raison pour qch/de faire; **7** (Sport) décision *f*; **8** (duty) **to be on ~** [*doctor*] être de garde; [*engineer*] être de service.
II *vtr* **1** (also **~ out**) appeler [*name, number*]; crier [*answer, instructions*]; annoncer [*result, flight*]; **2** (summon) appeler [*lift*]; (by shouting) appeler [*person, animal*]; (by phone) appeler; (by letter) convoquer; **the boss ~ed me into his office** le chef m'a fait venir dans son bureau; **the police were ~ed to the scene** la police a été appelée sur les lieux; **3** (telephone) appeler (**at** à; **from** de); **4** (give a name) appeler [*person, animal, place, product*] (**by** par) ; intituler [*book, film, play*]; **5** (arrange) organiser [*strike*]; convoquer [*meeting, rehearsal*]; fixer [*election*]; **6** (waken) réveiller [*person*]; **7** (describe as) **to ~ sb stupid** traiter qn d'imbécile; **I wouldn't ~ it spacious** je ne dirais pas que c'est spacieux; **it's not what you'd ~ an exciting film** on ne peut pas dire que ce film soit passionnant; **8** (Sport) [*referee*] déclarer; **9** (Comput) appeler [*file*].
III *vi* **1** (also **~ out**) [*person, animal*] appeler; (louder) crier; [*bird*] crier; **London ~ing** (on radio) ici Londres; **2** (telephone) appeler; **thank you for ~ing** merci d'avoir appelé; **who's ~ing?** qui est à l'appareil?; **3** (visit) passer; **to ~ at** passer chez [*person, shop*]; passer à [*bank, library*]; [*train*] s'arrêter à [*town, station*]; [*ship*] faire escale à [*port*].
IV *v refl* **to ~ oneself** se faire appeler [*Smith*]; (claim to be) se dire [*poet*].
■ **call away**: **~ [sb] away** appeler; **to be ~ed away** être obligé de s'absenter.
■ **call back**: ¶ **~ back 1** (on phone) rappeler; **2** (return) repasser; ¶ **~ [sb] back** rappeler [*person*].
■ **call for**: **~ for [sth] 1** (shout) appeler à [*help*]; appeler [*ambulance, doctor*]; **2** (demand) demander [*food, equipment*]; réclamer [*changes*]; **3** (require) exiger [*treatment, skill*]; nécessiter [*change*]; **this ~s for a celebration!** ça se fête!
■ **call in**: ¶ **~ in 1** (visit) passer; **2** (telephone) appeler; **to ~ in sick** [*employee*] appeler pour dire qu'on est malade; ¶ **~ in [sb], ~ [sb] in**

faire entrer [*client, patient*]; faire appel à [*expert*].

■ **call off**: **~ off** [**sth**], **~** [**sth**] **off 1** rappeler [*dog*]; **2** abandonner [*investigation*]; annuler [*deal, wedding*]; rompre [*engagement*].

■ **call on**: **~ on** [**sb/sth**] **1** (visit) rendre visite à [*relative, friend*]; visiter [*patient, client*]; **2** (invite) demander à [*speaker*] (**to do** de faire); **3** (urge) demander à (**to do** de faire).

■ **call out**: ¶ **~ out** appeler; (louder) crier; ¶ **~ out** [**sb**], **~** [**sb**] **out 1** (summon outside) appeler; **2** (send for) appeler [*doctor, troops*]; **3** [*union*] lancer un ordre de grève à [*members*]; ¶ **~** [**sth**] **out**, **~ out** [**sth**] appeler [*name, number*].

■ **call up**: ¶ **~ up** appeler; ¶ **~ up** [**sb/sth**], **~** [**sb/sth**] **up 1** (on phone) appeler; **2** (Mil) appeler [qn] sous les drapeaux [*soldier*]; **3** (evoke) rappeler [*memory*]; **4** (Comput) appeler (à l'écran), afficher [*file*]; **5** (Sport) sélectionner [*player*].

call: **~back facility** *n* (on phone) rappel *m* automatique; **~ box** *n* (GB) cabine *f* téléphonique; (US) poste *m* téléphonique.

caller *n* **1** (on phone line) personne *f* qui appelle; **2** (visitor) visiteur/-euse *m/f*.

callous *adj* inhumain.

call: **~-out** *n* dépannage *m*; **~-out charge** *n* frais *mpl* de déplacement; **~-up** *n* (Mil) appel *m*; (of reservists) rappel *m*.

calm I *n* calme *m*; (in adversity) sang-froid *m*.
II *adj* calme; **keep ~!** du calme!
III *vtr* calmer.

■ **calm down**: ¶ **~ down** se calmer; ¶ **~** [**sth/sb**] **down**, **~ down** [**sth/sb**] calmer.

calmly *adv* [*act, speak*] calmement; [*sleep, smoke*] tranquillement.

Calor gas® *n* (GB) butane *m*.

calorie *n* calorie *f*; **low-~ diet/drink** régime/boisson à basses calories.

camcorder *n* caméscope® *m*.

camel ▶559| *n* **1** (Zool) chameau *m*; (female) chamelle *f*; **2** (colour) couleur *f* caramel.

camera *n* **1** (for photos) appareil *m* photo; (for filming) caméra *f*; **2** (Law) **in ~** à huis clos.

camera: **~ crew** *n* équipe *f* de télévision; **~man** ▶805| *n* cadreur *m*, cameraman *m*; **~work** *n* prise *f* de vues.

camisole *n* caraco *m*.

camouflage I *n* camouflage *m*.
II *vtr* camoufler (**with** avec).

camp I *n* **1** (of tents) camp *m*; (of nomads) campement *m*; **2** (group) camp *m*; **to go over to the other ~** changer de camp.
II *adj* **1** (exaggerated) [*person*] cabotin○; [*performance*] théâtral; **2** (effeminate) efféminé.
III *vi* camper; **to go ~ing** faire du camping.
IDIOMS **to ~ it up**○ (overact) cabotiner○; (act effeminately) forcer dans le genre efféminé.

campaign I *n* campagne *f*.
II *vi* faire campagne (**for** pour; **against** contre).

campaigner *n* militant/-e *m/f* (**for** pour; **against** contre); (in election) candidat/-e *m/f* en campagne (électorale).

campaign worker *n* (GB) (for politician) membre *m* de l'état-major.

camp: **~ bed** *n* lit *m* de camp; **~ chair** *n* (US) chaise *f* pliante.

camper *n* **1** (person) campeur/-euse *m/f*; **2** (also **~ van**) camping-car *m*; **3** (US) (folding caravan) caravane *f* pliante.

camping *n* camping *m*.

camping: **~ equipment** *n* matériel *m* de camping; **~ gas** *n* camping-gaz® *m*; **~ holiday** *n* vacances *fpl* sous la tente; **~ stove** *n* réchaud *m*.

camp: **~site** *n* terrain *m* de camping, camping *m*; **~ stool** *n* pliant *m*.

campus *n* campus *m*.

can[1] *modal aux* **1** (expressing possibility) **~ you come?** est-ce que tu peux venir?, peux-tu venir?; **where ~ I buy stamps?** où est-ce que je peux acheter des timbres?; **we ~ bring you home** nous pouvons te déposer chez toi; **I can't afford to fly** je ne peux pas me permettre de prendre l'avion; **'~ I pay later?'—'you ~'** 'est-ce que je peux payer plus tard?'—'bien sûr'; **he ~ be quite nice** il peut être charmant; **we will do all we ~** nous ferons tout ce que nous pouvons or tout notre possible; **2** (expressing permission) **you can't turn right** vous ne pouvez pas or vous n'avez pas le droit de tourner à droite; **'~ I smoke here?'—'you ~'** 'est-ce que je peux or j'ai le droit de fumer ici?'—'oui'; **3** (in requests, offers, suggestions) **~ you do me a favour?** peux-tu or est-ce que tu peux me rendre un service?; **~ I give you a hand?** est-ce que je peux te donner un coup de main?; **~ I take a message?** est-ce que je peux prendre un message?; **you ~ phone again later if you like** si vous voulez, vous pouvez rappeler plus tard; **can't we take the train?** pourquoi ne pas prendre le train?; **4** (expressing ability, skill) **she ~ swim** elle sait nager; **I can't drive** je ne sais pas conduire; **~ he type?** est-ce qu'il sait taper à la machine?; **she ~ play the piano** elle joue du piano; **I ~ speak French** je parle français; **5** (with verbs of perception) **~ they see us?** est-ce qu'ils nous voient?; **I can't feel a thing** je ne sens rien; **she can't understand English** elle ne comprend pas l'anglais; **I ~ hear you better now** je t'entends mieux maintenant; **6** (in expressions) **~ you believe it!** tu te rends compte?; **you cannot be serious!** tu veux rire!; **what ~ she want from me?** qu'est-ce qu'elle peut bien me vouloir?; **this can't be right** il doit y avoir une erreur; **you ~ get lost!** va te faire voir!

can[2] I *n* (of food) boîte *f*; (aerosol) bombe *f*; (for petrol) bidon *m*; (of drink) cannette *f*.
II *vtr* mettre [qch] en conserve; **~ned vegetables** légumes en conserve.
IDIOMS **to carry the ~ for sb**○ porter le chapeau à la place de qn○.

Canada ▶574| *pr n* Canada *m*.

Canadian ▶712| **I** *n* Canadien/-ienne.
II *adj* [*people, culture, politics*] canadien/-ienne; [*ambassador, embassy*] du Canada; **to speak ~ French** parler le français du Canada.

canal *n* **1** (waterway) canal *m*; **2** (in ear) conduit *m*.

canal boat, canal barge *n* péniche *f*.

Canaries *pr n pl* (also **Canary Islands**) **the ~** les Canaries *fpl*.

cancel I *vtr* **1** (call off) annuler; **2** (make invalid) résilier [*contract*]; annuler [*debt*]; mettre une opposition à [*cheque*].
II *vi* (from meal, function, meeting) se décommander; (after booking) annuler.
■ **cancel out**: **~ out [sth]** neutraliser [*emotion, effect*].

cancellation *n* (of event, booking, flight, debt) annulation *f*; (of contract, policy) résiliation *f*; (of order, decree) levée *f*.

cancer ▶686| *n* cancer *m*; **to have ~** avoir un cancer; **lung ~** cancer du poumon.

Cancer *n* Cancer *m*; ▶ **Aquarius**.

candid *adj* franc/franche.

candidate *n* **1** (in election, for exam) candidat/-e *m/f*; **the ~ for mayor** le candidat à la mairie; **to stand as a ~ (in an election)** se porter candidat (à une élection); **2** (for job) candidat/-e *m/f*, postulant/-e *m/f*; **the successful ~** (in ad) le candidat retenu.

candle *n* bougie *f*; (in church) cierge *m*.

candle: **~light** *n* lueur *f* de bougie; **~stick** *n* bougeoir *m*; (ornate) chandelier *m*.

candy *n* (US) **1** (sweets) bonbons *mpl*; **2** (sweet) bonbon *m*.

cane *n* **1** (material) rotin *m*; **~ furniture** meubles en rotin; **2** (of sugar, bamboo) canne *f*; **3** (for walking) canne *f*; (for plant) tuteur *m*; (GB) (for punishment) badine *f*.

canine *n* canine *f*.

canoe ▶649| **I** *n* (gen) canoë *m*; (African) pirogue *f*; (Sport) canoë-kayac *m*.
II *vi* faire du canoë; **they ~d down the river** ils ont descendu la rivière en canoë.

canoeing ▶649| *n* **to go ~** faire du canoë-kayac.

can-opener *n* ouvre-boîtes *m inv*.

cant *n* (false words) paroles *fpl* creuses; (ideas) notions *fpl* creuses.

canteen *n* **1** (GB) (dining room) cantine *f*; **in the ~** à la cantine; **2** (Mil) (flask) bidon *m*; (mess tin) gamelle *f*; **3 a ~ of cutlery** une ménagère.

canter *vi* [*rider*] faire un petit galop; [*horse*] galoper.

canvas I *n* **1** (fabric, for picture) toile *f*; (for tapestry) canevas *m*; **2** (in boxing) tapis *m*.
II *noun modifier* [*shoes, bag, chair*] en toile.

canvass I *vtr* **1** (prior to election) **to ~ voters** faire du démarchage électoral auprès des électeurs; **to ~ people for their votes** solliciter les voix des électeurs; **2** (in survey) sonder [*public*]; **to ~ opinion on sth** sonder l'opinion au sujet de qch; **3** (for business) prospecter [*area*].
II *vi* **1** (for election) faire du démarchage électoral (**for** pour); **2** (for business) faire du démarchage (**for** pour).

cap I *n* **1** (headgear) (peaked) casquette *f*; **baseball ~** casquette de baseball; **2** (GB Sport) **he's got his Scottish ~** il a été selectionné pour l'équipe écossaise; **3** (of pen, valve) capuchon *m*; (of bottle) capsule *f*; **4** (for tooth) couronne *f*.
II *vtr* **1** (limit) imposer une limite budgétaire à [*local authority*]; plafonner [*budget*]; **2** [*dentist*] couronner [*tooth*]; **3** (GB Sport) sélectionner [qn] pour l'équipe nationale; **4** (cover) couronner (**with** de).
IDIOMS **to ~ it all** pour couronner le tout.

capability *n* **1** (of intellect, machine, system) capacité *f* (**to do** de faire); **2** (aptitude) aptitude *f* (**for** à); **outside my capabilities** au-delà de mes compétences.

capable *adj* **1** (competent) compétent; **2** (able) capable (**of** de); **to be ~ of doing** (have potential to) être capable de faire; (be in danger of) risquer de faire.

capacity *n* **1** (ability to hold) (of box, bottle) contenance *f*; (of building) capacité *f* d'accueil; (of road) capacité *f*; **seating/storage ~** capacité d'accueil/de stockage; **full to ~** comble; **2** (of factory) capacité *f* de production; **to operate at full ~** opérer au maximum de ses capacités; **3** (role) **in my ~ as a doctor** en ma qualité de médecin; **4** (ability) **to have a ~ for** avoir de la facilité pour [*learning, maths*]; **a ~ for doing** une aptitude à faire; **a great ~ for hard work** une grande capacité de travail; **to have the ~ to do** avoir les moyens de faire.

cape *n* **1** (for rainwear, fashion) cape *f*; (for child, policeman) pèlerine *f*; **2** (on coast) promontoire *m*, cap *m*.

caper I *n* **1** (Culin) (berry) câpre *f*; **2**○ (funny film) comédie *f*.
II capers *n pl* aventures *fpl*.

Cape Town ▶574| *pr n* Le Cap.

capital I *n* **1** (letter) majuscule *f*; **2** (also **~ city**) capitale *f*; **3** (in financial sense) capital *m*; **to make ~ out of** tirer parti de [*situation, event*].
II *noun modifier* [*loss, outlay, turnover*] de capital.
III *adj* **1** [*letter*] majuscule; **~ A** A majuscule; **2** (Law) [*offence*] capital.

capital: **~ account** *n* compte *m* capital; **~ assets** *n pl* actif *m* immobilisé; **~ cost** *n* coût *m* d'investissement; **~ gains tax** *n* impôt *m* sur les plus-values des capitaux; **~ goods** *n pl* biens *mpl* d'équipement; **~ investment** *n* dépenses *fpl* d'investissement.

capitalist *n, adj* capitaliste (*m*).

capitalize I *vtr* **1** capitaliser [*assets*]; **2** écrire [qch] en majuscules.
II *vi* **to ~ on** tirer parti de [*situation, advantage*].

capital sum *n* (gen) capital *m*; (of loan) principal *m*.

capitulate *vi* capituler (**to** devant).

Capricorn *n* Capricorne *m*; ▶ **Aquarius**.

capsize *vi* chavirer.

captain I *n* capitaine *m*.
II *vtr* être le capitaine de [*team*]; commander [*ship, platoon*].

caption *n* **1** (under photo) légende *f*; **2** (subtitle) sous-titre *m*.

captive *n* captif/-ive *m/f*; **to hold sb ~** garder qn en captivité; **to take sb ~** faire qn prisonnier.

capture I *n* (of person, animal) capture *f*; (of stronghold) prise *f*.
II *vtr* **1** capturer [*person, animal*]; prendre [*stronghold*]; s'emparer de [*market*]; **2** saisir [*moment, likeness*]; rendre [*feeling, beauty*].

car I *n* **1** (Aut) voiture *f*; **2** (on train) wagon *m*, voiture *f*; **restaurant ~** wagon-restaurant *m*; **3** (US) (also **street~**) tramway *m*.
II *noun modifier* [*industry, insurance*] automobile; [*journey, chase*] en voiture; [*accident*] de voiture; **~ allowance** indemnité *f* de déplacement.

caravan I *n* (for holiday) caravane *f*; (for circus, gypsies) roulotte *f*.
II *noun modifier* (GB) [*holiday*] en caravane; [*site, park*] pour caravanes.
III *vi* **to go ~ning** (GB) faire du caravanage.

carbohydrate *n* hydrate *m* de carbone.

car bomb *n* bombe *f* dissimulée dans une voiture.

carbon: **~ copy** *n* copie *f* carbone; (replica) réplique *f* exacte; **~ dioxide** *n* dioxyde *m* de carbone.

carburettor (GB), **carburetor** (US) *n* carburateur *m*.

card *n* **1** (for correspondence, greetings) carte *f*; (for indexing) fiche *f*; **2** (Games) carte *f* (à jouer); **to play ~s** jouer aux cartes.
IDIOMS **to play one's ~s right** bien jouer son jeu○.

cardboard *n* carton *m*; **~ box** (boîte *f* en) carton *m*.

card: **~ catalogue**, **~ catalog** (US) *n* fichier *m*; **~ game** *n* partie *f* de cartes.

cardiac *adj* cardiaque; **~ arrest** arrêt *m* du cœur.

card: **~ key** *n* carte *f* magnétique; **~phone** *n* téléphone *m* à carte.

care I *n* **1** (attention) attention *f*, soin *m*; **to take ~ to do** prendre soin de faire; **to take ~ not to do** faire attention de ne pas faire; **to take ~ when doing** faire attention en faisant; **to take ~ in doing sth** faire qch avec soin; **'take ~!'** 'fais attention!'; (expression of farewell) 'à bientôt!'; **'handle with ~'** 'fragile'; **2** (looking after) (of person, animal) soins *mpl*; (of car, plant, clothes) entretien *m* **(of** de); **to take ~ of** (deal with) s'occuper de [*child, client*]; soigner [*patient*]; (be responsible for) s'occuper de [*garden, details*]; (be careful with) prendre soin de [*machine, car*]; (keep in good condition) entretenir [*car, teeth*]; (look after) garder [*shop, watch*]; **to take good ~ of sb/sth** prendre soin de qn/qch; **customer ~** service *m* auprès des clients; **to leave sb/sth in sb's ~** confier qn/qch à qn; **in his/your ~** à sa/ta garde; **~ of** (on letter) chez *or* aux bons soins de; **to take ~ of oneself** (look after oneself) prendre soin de soi; (cope) se débrouiller tout/-e seul/-e; (defend oneself) se défendre; **that takes ~ of that** c'est réglé; **3** (Med) soins *mpl*; **~ in the community** soins en dehors du milieu hospitalier; **4** (GB) **to be in ~** [*child*] être (placé) en garde; **5** (worry) souci *m*.
II *vtr* **would you ~ to sit down?** voulez-vous vous asseoir?
III *vi* **1** (feel concerned) **she really ~s** elle prend ça à cœur; **to ~ about** s'intéresser à [*art, environment*]; se soucier du bien-être de [*pupils, the elderly*]; **I don't ~!** ça m'est égal!; **he couldn't ~ less!** ça lui est complètement égal!; **she couldn't ~ less about**... elle se moque *or* se fiche○ complètement de...; **I couldn't ~ less who wins** je me moque *or* me fiche○ de savoir qui va gagner; **I'm past caring** je m'en moque; **who ~s?** qu'est-ce que ça peut faire?; **2** (love) **to ~ about sb** aimer qn.
■ **care for**: ¶ **~ for [sth] 1** (like) aimer; **would you ~ for a drink?** voulez-vous boire quelque chose?; **2** (maintain) entretenir [*car, garden*]; prendre soin de [*skin, plant*]; ¶ **~ for [sb/sth]** s'occuper de [*child, animal*]; soigner [*patient*].

career I *n* carrière *f*; **a ~ in television** une carrière à la télévision; **a ~ as a journalist** une carrière de journaliste; **school ~** scolarité *f*.
II *vi* **to ~ off the road** quitter la route.

career: **~ break** *n* interruption *f* de carrière; **~s guidance** *n* orientation *f* professionnelle.

carefree *adj* insouciant.

careful *adj* [*person, driving*] prudent; [*planning, preparation*] minutieux/-ieuse; [*research, monitoring, examination*] méticuleux/-euse; **to be ~ to do** *or* **about doing** prendre soin de faire; **to be ~ that** faire attention que (+ *subj*); **to be ~ with sth** faire attention à qch; **to be ~ (when) doing** faire attention en faisant; **be ~!** (fais) attention!

carefully *adv* [*go, walk*] prudemment; [*say*] avec circonspection; [*open, remove, handle*] prudemment, avec précaution; [*write, organize, wash*] soigneusement; [*listen, read, look*] attentivement; **drive ~!** soyez prudent!; **listen ~!** écoutez bien!

careless *adj* [*person*] négligent, imprudent; [*work*] bâclé; [*writing*] négligé; [*driving, handling*] négligent; [*talk*] imprudent; **~ mistake** faute d'étourderie; **it was ~ of me to do** ça a été de la négligence de ma part de faire; **to be ~ about sth/about doing** négliger qch/de faire; **to be ~ with** ne pas prendre soin de [*books, clothes*].

carelessly *adv* [*do, act*] avec négligence; [*repair, write*] sans soin; [*drive*] avec imprudence; [*break, lose*] par manque d'attention.

carelessness *n* négligence *f*.

caress *vtr* caresser.

caretaker ▶ 805 *n* concierge *mf*.

car ferry *n* ferry *m*.

cargo *n* chargement *m*.

cargo ship *n* cargo *m*.

car hire *n* location *f* de voitures.

caring *adj* **1** (loving) [*parent*] affectueux/-euse;

[*environment*] chaleureux/-euse; **2** (compassionate) [*person, attitude*] compréhensif/-ive; [*society*] humain.

carnation *n* œillet *m*.

carnival *n* **1** (GB) (procession) carnaval *m*; **2** (US) (funfair) fête *f* foraine.

carousel *n* **1** (merry-go-round) manège *m*; **2** (for luggage, slides) carrousel *m*.

car park *n* (GB) parc *m* de stationnement.

carpenter ▶ 805 *n* menuisier *m*.

carpentry *n* menuiserie *f*.

carpet *n* (fitted) moquette *f*; (loose) tapis *m*; **~ tile** dalle *f* de moquette.

IDIOMS **to brush** or **sweep sth under the ~** enterrer or étouffer qch.

car: **~ phone** *n* téléphone *m* de voiture; **~ radio** *n* autoradio *m*.

carriage *n* **1** (ceremonial) carrosse *m*; **2** (of train) wagon *m*, voiture *f*; **3** (of goods) transport *m*; **~ free/paid** port *m* gratuit/payé; **4** (of typewriter) chariot *m*.

carrier *n* **1** (transport company) transporteur *m*; (airline) compagnie *f* aérienne; **2** (of disease) porteur/-euse *m/f*; **3** (GB) (also **~ bag**) sac *m* (en plastique).

carrot *n* carotte *f*.

carry **I** *vtr* **1** (in hands) porter [*bag, paper*] (**in** dans; **on** sur); **to ~ sth up/down** porter qch en haut/en bas; **to ~ sth in/out** apporter/emporter qch; **to ~ cash** avoir de l'argent liquide sur soi; **to ~ [sth] too far** pousser [qch] trop loin [*joke*]; **2** [*vehicle, pipe, vein*] transporter; [*tide, current*] emporter; **to be carried on the wind** être porté par le vent; **3** (feature) comporter [*warning, guarantee, report*]; porter [*symbol, label*]; publier [*advert*]; **4** (entail) comporter [*risk*]; être passible de [*penalty*]; **to ~ conviction** être convaincant; **5** (bear, support) [*bridge, road*] supporter [*load, traffic*]; **6** (win) l'emporter dans [*state, constituency*]; remporter [*battle, match*]; **the motion was carried by 20 votes to 13** la motion l'a emporté par 20 votes contre 13; **7** (Med) être porteur/-euse de [*disease, virus*]; **8** (be pregnant with) [*woman*] être enceinte de; [*animal*] porter; **9** (stock, sell) faire [*item, brand*]; **we ~ a wide range of** nous offrons un grand choix de; **10** (hold, bear) porter [*head*].

II *vi* [*sound, voice*] porter; **to ~ well** porter bien.

IDIOMS **to get carried away**° s'emballer°, se laisser emporter.

■ **carry forward**: **~ forward [sth]**, **~ [sth] forward** reporter [*balance, total*].

■ **carry off**: **~ off [sth]** emporter [*goods*]; remporter [*prize*]; **to ~ it off**° réussir, y arriver.

■ **carry on**: ¶ **~ on 1** (continue) continuer (**doing** à faire); **to ~ on down the road** (in car) continuer la route; (on foot) poursuivre son chemin; **2**° (behave) se conduire; **3**° (have affair) avoir une liaison; ¶ **~ on [sth]** maintenir [*tradition*]; poursuivre [*activity, discussion*].

■ **carry out**: **~ out [sth]**, **~ [sth] out** réaliser [*study*]; effectuer [*experiment, reform, attack, repairs*]; exécuter [*plan, orders*]; mener [*investigation, campaign*]; accomplir [*mission*]; remplir [*duties*]; mettre [qch] à exécution [*threat*]; tenir [*promise*].

■ **carry through**: ¶ **~ through [sth]**, **~ [sth] through** mener [qch] à bien [*reform, policy, task*]; ¶ **~ [sb] through** [*humour*] soutenir [*person*].

carry: **~all** *n* (US) fourre-tout *m inv*; **~cot** *n* (GB) porte-bébé *m*.

car seat *n* siège-auto *m*.

carsick *adj* **to be ~** avoir le mal de la route.

cart **I** *n* (for goods) charrette *f*; (for passengers) carriole *f*.

II° *vtr* (also **~ around**, **~ about**)° trimballer° [*bags*].

cartel *n* cartel *m*; **drug ~** cartel *m* de la drogue.

carton *n* (small) boîte *f*; (of yoghurt, cream) pot *m*; (of juice, milk, ice cream) carton *m*, brique *f*; (of cigarettes) cartouche *f*; (US) (for house removals) carton *m*.

cartoon *n* **1** (film) dessin *m* animé; **2** (drawing) dessin *m* humoristique; (in comic) bande *f* dessinée.

cartridge *n* (for pen, gun, video) cartouche *f*; (for camera) chargeur *m*.

carve **I** *vtr* **1** (sculpt) tailler, sculpter; **2** (inscribe) graver; **3** (Culin) découper.

II *vi* (Culin) découper.

■ **carve out**: **~ out [sth]**, **~ [sth] out 1** se faire [*niche, name*]; se tailler [*reputation, market*]; se construire [*career*]; **2** creuser [*gorge, channel*].

carving *n* **1** (sculpture) sculpture *f*; **2** (of object) sculpture *f*; (of motif) gravure *f*.

carving knife *n* couteau *m* à découper.

car: **~ wash** *n* lavage *m* automatique; **~ worker** ▶ 805 *n* ouvrier/-ière *m/f* de l'industrie automobile.

case[1] **I** *n* **1** (instance) cas *m*; **on a ~ by ~ basis** au cas par cas; **in which ~**, **in that ~** en ce cas, dans ce cas-là; **in 7 out of 10 ~s** 7 fois sur 10, dans 7 cas sur 10; **a ~ in point** un cas d'espèce, un exemple typique; **2** (situation) cas *m*; **this being the ~** en ce cas, dans ce cas-là; **is it the ~ that...?** est-il vrai que...?; **as** or **whatever the ~ may be** selon le(s) cas; **3** (Law) **the ~ for the Crown** (GB), **the ~ for the State** (US) l'accusation *f*; **the ~ for the defence** la défense; **to state the ~** exposer les faits; **the ~ against Foster** les faits qui sont reprochés à Foster; **the ~ is closed** l'affaire or la cause est entendue; **4** (argument) arguments *mpl*; **to make a good ~ for sth** donner des arguments convaincants en faveur de qch; **there's a strong ~ for/against doing** il y a de bonnes raisons pour/pour ne pas faire; **5** (trial) affaire *f*, procès *m*; **his ~ comes up next week** il passe en jugement la semaine prochaine; **6** (Med) (instance of disease) cas *m*; (patient) malade *mf*; **7**° **a hopeless ~** un cas désespéré; **8** (in grammar) cas *m*.

II **in any case** *phr* **1** (besides, anyway) de toute façon; **2** (at any rate) en tout cas.

III in case *phr* au cas où (+ *conditional*); **just in ~** au cas où.
IV in case of *phr* en cas de [*fire, accident*].

case² *n* **1** (suitcase) valise *f*; (crate, chest) caisse *f*; **2** (display cabinet) vitrine *f*; **3** (for spectacles, binoculars, weapon) étui *m*; (of camera, watch) boîtier *m*.

case: **~ history** *n* (Med) antécédents *mpl*; **~ notes** *n pl* dossier *m*.

cash I *n* **1** (notes and coin) espèces *fpl*, argent *m* liquide; **£3,000 (in) ~** 3 000 livres sterling en espèces; **I haven't got any ~ on me** je n'ai pas d'argent liquide; **2** (money in general) argent *m*; **3** (payment) comptant *m*; **discount for ~** remise *f* pour paiement comptant; **£50 ~ in hand** 50 livres en liquide.
II *noun modifier* [*offer, discount*] au comptant; [*deposit, refund, prize*] en espèces.
III *vtr* encaisser [*cheque*].
■ **cash in**: ¶ **~ in** en profiter; **to ~ in on** tirer profit de, profiter de; ¶ **~ in [sth], ~ [sth] in** se faire rembourser, réaliser [*bond, policy*]; (US) encaisser [*check*].

cash: **~-and-carry** *n* libre-service *m* de vente en gros; **~ card** *n* carte *f* de retrait; **~ desk** *n* caisse *f*; **~ dispenser** *n* distributeur *m* automatique de billets de banque, billetterie *f*; **~ flow** *n* marge *f* brute d'auto-financement, MBA *f*.

cashier ▶805 *n* caissier/-ière *m/f*.

cashmere *n* (lainage *m* en) cachemire *m*.

cash: **~ on delivery, COD** *n* envoi *m* contre remboursement; **~point** *n* = **cash dispenser**; **~ register** *n* caisse *f* enregistreuse.

casserole *n* **1** (container) daubière *f*, cocotte *f*; **2** (GB) (food) ragoût *m* cuit au four.

cassette *n* cassette *f*.

cassette: **~ deck** *n* platine *f* à cassettes; **~ player** *n* lecteur *m* de cassettes; **~ recorder** *n* magnétophone *m* à cassettes; **~ tape** *n* cassette *f* audio.

cast I *n* **1** (list of actors) distribution *f*; (actors) acteurs *mpl*; **~ of characters** (in play, novel) liste *f* des personnages; **2** (Med) (also **plaster ~**) plâtre *m*.
II *vtr* **1** (throw) jeter, lancer [*stone, fishing line*]; projeter [*light, shadow*]; **to ~ doubt on** émettre des doutes sur; **to ~ light on** éclairer; **to ~ a spell on** jeter un sort à; **2** (direct) jeter [*glance*] (**at** sur); **if you ~ your mind back to last week** si tu te rappelles ce qui s'est passé la semaine dernière; **3** distribuer les rôles de [*play, film*]; **she was cast as Blanche** elle a joué Blanche; **4** couler [*plaster, metal*]; **5 to ~ one's vote** voter.

caster sugar *n* (GB) sucre *m* en poudre.

casting *n* distribution *f*.

casting: **~ director** ▶805 *n* directeur/-trice *m/f* de la distribution; **~ vote** *n* voix *f* prépondérante.

cast iron *n* fonte *f*; **a ~ alibi** un alibi en béton°.

castle *n* **1** château *m*; **2** (in chess) tour *f*.

cast-offs *n pl* vêtements *mpl* dont on n'a plus besoin, vieux vêtements.

casual *adj* **1** (informal) décontracté; **to have a ~ chat** bavarder; **2** [*acquaintance, relationship*] de passage; **~ sex** relations *fpl* sexuelles non suivies; **3** [*attitude, remark*] désinvolte; [*cruelty, violence*] ordinaire; **4** [*glance*] superficiel/-ielle; **5** [*worker, labour*] (temporary) temporaire; (occasional) occasionnel/-elle.

casually *adv* **1** [*enquire, remark*] d'un air détaché; **2** [*dressed*] simplement; **3** [*employed*] temporairement.

casuals *n pl* vêtements *mpl* sport.

casualty I *n* **1** (person) victime *f*; **2** (hospital ward) urgences *fpl*; **in ~** aux urgences.
II casualties *n pl* (soldiers) pertes *fpl*; (civilians) victimes *fpl*.

cat *n* (domestic) chat *m*; (female) chatte *f*; **the big ~s** les grands félins *mpl*.
IDIOMS **to let the ~ out of the bag** vendre la mèche; **to rain ~s and dogs** pleuvoir des cordes.

catalogue, catalog (US) *n* **1** (of goods, books) catalogue *m*; **2** (series) série (**of** de); **3** (US Univ) brochure *f* (universitaire).

catalytic *adj* catalytique; **~ converter** pot *m* catalytique.

catastrophe *n* catastrophe *f*.

catch I *n* **1** (on purse, door) fermeture *f*; **2** (drawback) piège *m*; **3** (act of catching) prise *f*; **to take a ~** (GB), **to make a ~** (US) (Sport) prendre la balle; **to play ~** jouer à la balle; **4** (haul) pêche *f*; (one fish) prise *f*.
II *vtr* **1** [*person*] attraper [*ball, fish*]; [*container*] recueillir [*water, dust*]; (by running) [*person*] attraper [*person*]; **2** (take by surprise) prendre, attraper; **to ~ sb doing** surprendre qn en train de faire; **to be** or **get caught** se faire prendre; **to ~ sb in the act, to ~ sb at it**° prendre qn sur le fait; **we got caught in the rain** nous avons été surpris par la pluie; **3** prendre [*bus, plane*]; **to ~ the last post** (GB) avoir la dernière levée; **4** (see) voir [*programme*]; aller voir [*show*]; **5** (grasp) prendre [*hand, arm*]; agripper [*branch, rope*]; captiver, éveiller [*interest*]; **to ~ hold of sth** attraper qch; **to ~ sb's attention** or **eye** attirer l'attention de qn; **6** (hear) saisir°, comprendre; **7** (perceive) surprendre [*look*]; **to ~ sight of sb/sth** surprendre qn/qch; **8** (get stuck) **to ~ one's fingers in** se prendre les doigts dans [*drawer, door*]; **to get one's shirt caught on** accrocher sa chemise à [*nail*]; **to get caught in** se prendre dans [*barbed wire, thorns*]; **9** (Med) attraper [*disease, flu*]; **10** [*wind*] emporter [*paper, bag*]; **to ~ one's breath** retenir son souffle; **11** (be affected by) **you've caught the sun** on voit bien que tu es resté au soleil; **to ~ fire** prendre feu, s'enflammer; **to ~ the light** refléter la lumière; **12** (convey) rendre [*atmosphere*].
III *vi* **1 to ~ on** [*shirt*] s'accrocher à [*nail*]; [*wheel*] frotter contre [*frame*]; **2** [*wood, fire*] prendre.
■ **catch on 1** (become popular) devenir populaire (**with** auprès de); **2** (understand)

comprendre, saisir; **to ~ on to sth** comprendre or saisir qch.

■ **catch out**: **~ [sb] out 1** (take by surprise) prendre [qn] de court; (doing something wrong) prendre [qn] sur le fait; **2** (trick) attraper, jouer un tour à.

■ **catch up**: ¶ **~ up** (in race) regagner du terrain; (in work) rattraper son retard; **to ~ up with sb** rattraper qn; **to ~ up on** rattraper [*work, sleep*]; se remettre au courant de [*news*]; ¶ **~ [sb/sth] up 1** (reach) rattraper; **2 to get caught up in** se laisser entraîner par [*excitement*]; se trouver pris dans [*traffic*]; se trouver mêlé à [*scandal, argument*].

catch: **~-22 situation** *n* situation *f* inextricable; **~-all** *adj* [*term*] passe-partout *inv*; [*clause*] couvrant tous les cas de figure; **~phrase** *n* formule *f* favorite, rengaine *f*; **~word** *n* mot *m* d'ordre.

catchy *adj* [*tune*] entraînant; [*slogan*] accrocheur/-euse.

categorical *adj* catégorique.

categorize *vtr* classer (**by** d'après).

category *n* catégorie *f*.

cater *vi* **1** [*caterer*] organiser des réceptions; **2 to ~ for** (GB) or **to** (US) accueillir [*children, guests*]; pourvoir à [*needs*]; [*programme*] s'adresser à.

caterer ▶ 805 *n* traiteur *m*.

catering *n* (provision) approvisionnement *m*; (trade, industry, career) restauration *f*.

catering course *n* études *fpl* spécialisées dans la restauration.

caterpillar *n* chenille *f*; **~ track** (Tech) chenille *f*.

cat: **~flap** *n* chattière *f*; **~ food** *n* aliments *mpl* pour chats.

cathedral *n* cathédrale *f*.

Catholic *n, adj* catholique (*mf*).

cattle I *n* bovins *mpl*.
II *noun modifier* [*breeder, raising*] de bétail.

catwalk *n* podium *m*; **~ show** défilé *m* de mode.

cauliflower *n* chou-fleur *m*; **~ cheese** gratin *m* de chou-fleur.

cause I *n* **1** (reason) cause *f*, raison *f* (**of** de); **there is ~ for concern/optimism** il y a des raisons de s'inquiéter/d'être optimiste; **to have ~ to do** avoir des raisons de faire; **to give ~ for concern** susciter des inquiétudes; **with good ~** à juste titre; **without good ~** sans motif valable; **2** (objective) cause *f*; **all in a good ~** pour la bonne cause; **in the ~ of equality** pour la cause de l'égalité.
II *vtr* causer, occasionner [*damage, grief, problem*]; provoquer [*chaos, disease, controversy*]; susciter [*surprise*]; entraîner [*suffering*]; amener [*confusion*]; **to ~ sb problems** causer des problèmes à qn; **to ~ trouble** créer des problèmes.

caustic *adj* caustique; **~ soda** soude *f* caustique.

caution I *n* **1** (care) prudence *f*; **to err on the side of ~** pécher par excès de prudence; **2** (wariness) circonspection *f*; **3** (warning) avertissement *m*; **a word of ~** un petit conseil; **'Caution! Drive slowly!'** 'Attention! Conduire lentement!'; **4** (Law) avertissement *m*.
II *vtr* **1** (warn) avertir (**that** que); **to ~ sb against doing** avertir qn de ne pas faire; **2** (Sport) donner un avertissement à [*player*].
IDIOMS **to throw** or **cast ~ to the wind (s)** oublier toute prudence.

cautious *adj* **1** (careful) prudent; **2** (wary) [*person, reception, response*] réservé; [*optimism*] prudent; **to be ~ about doing** ne pas aimer faire.

cautiously *adv* **1** (carefully) prudemment; **2** (warily) [*react*] avec circonspection.

cave *n* grotte *f*.
■ **cave in 1** [*tunnel, roof, building*] s'effondrer; **2** [*person*] céder.

cave painting *n* peinture *f* rupestre.

caver *n* spéléologue *mf*.

caving *n* spéléologie *f*; **to go ~** faire de la spéléologie.

cavity *n* cavité *f*.

caw *vi* croasser.

cc *n* (*abbr* = **cubic centimetre**) cm^3.

CD *n* (*abbr* = **compact disc**) (disque *m*) compact *m*, CD *m*; **on ~** sur (disque) compact.

CD player, **CD system** *n* platine *f* laser.

CD-ROM *n* disque *m* optique compact, CD-ROM *m*.

cease-fire I *n* cessez-le-feu *m inv*.
II *noun modifier* [*agreement*] de cessez-le-feu; [*call*] au cessez-le-feu.

cedilla *n* cédille *f*.

ceiling *n* plafond *m*.
IDIOMS **to hit the ~** sortir de ses gonds.

celebrate I *vtr* fêter; (more formally) célébrer.
II *vi* faire la fête; **let's ~!** il faut fêter ça!

celebrated *adj* célèbre (**for** pour).

celebration *n* **1** (action of celebrating) célébration *f*; **2** (party) fête *f*; **to have a ~** faire une fête; **3** (public festivities) **~s** cérémonies *fpl*; **4** (tribute) hommage *m* (**of** à).

celebrity *n* célébrité *f*.

celeriac *n* céleri-rave *m*.

celery *n* céleri *m*; **a stick/head of ~** une côte/un pied de céleri.

cell *n* **1** (in prison) cellule *f*; **2** (in biology) cellule *f*; **3** (in electricity) élément *m*.

cellar *n* cave *f*.

cello ▶ 753 *n* violoncelle *m*.

cellphone, **cellular phone** *n* radiotéléphone *m*.

Celsius *adj* Celsius *inv*.

cement *n* **1** (for building) ciment *m*; (for tiles) mastic *m*; **2** (in dentistry) amalgame *m*.

cement mixer *n* bétonnière *f*.

cemetery *n* cimetière *m*.

censor I *n* censeur *mf*.
II *vtr* censurer.

censorship *n* censure *f* (**of** de).

census *n* recensement *m*; **traffic ~** étude *f* chiffrée de la circulation.

cent ▶748| *n* cent *m*; **I haven't got a ~** je n'ai pas un sou.

centenary *n* centenaire *m*.

center *n* (US) = **centre**.

centigrade *adj* [*thermometer*] Celsius *inv*; **in degrees ~** en degrés Celsius.

centimetre (GB), **centimeter** (US) ▶738| *n* centimètre *m*.

central *adj* **1** (in the middle) central; **~ London** le centre de Londres; **2** (in the town centre) situé en centre-ville; **3** (key) principal; **~ to** essentiel à.

central heating *n* chauffage *m* central.

centralize *vtr* centraliser.

central: **~ locking** *n* (Aut) verrouillage *m* central or centralisé; **~ reservation** *n* (GB) terre-plein *m* central.

centre (GB), **center** (US) **I** *n* **1** (middle) centre *m*; **in the ~** au centre; **town ~**, **city ~** centre-ville *m*; **2** (focus) centre *m*; **at the ~ of a row** au centre d'une dispute; **the ~ of attention** le centre de l'attention; **the ~ of power** le siège du pouvoir; **3** (area) centre *m*; **business ~** quartier *m* des affaires; **shopping/sports ~** centre *m* commercial/sportif; **4** (in politics) centre *m*; **to be left of ~** être à gauche du centre; **5** (Sport) centre *m*.

II *vtr*, *vi* (Comput, Sport, Tech) centrer.

■ **centre around**, **centre on**: **~ around [sth]** [*activities, person*] se concentrer sur; [*people, industry*] se situer autour de [*town*]; [*life, thoughts*] être centré sur [*person, work*]; [*demands*] viser [*pay*].

centre: **~-forward** *n* (Sport) avant-centre *m*; **~-half** *n* (Sport) demi-centre *m*; **~piece** (GB), **centerpiece** (US) *n* (of table) décoration *f* centrale; (of exhibition) clou *m*.

centre stage (GB), **center stage** (US) *n* centre *m* de la scène; **to take ~** devenir le point de mire.

century ▶915| *n* siècle *m*; **in the 20th ~** au XXe siècle; **at the turn of the ~** au début du siècle.

ceramic *adj* [*tile, pot*] en céramique; [*hob*] en vitro-céramique.

ceramics *n* **1** (study) céramique *f*; **2** (artefacts) céramiques *fpl*.

cereal *n* céréale *f*; **breakfast ~** céréales *fpl* pour le petit déjeuner.

cerebral palsy ▶686| *n* paralysie *f* motrice centrale.

ceremonial *adj* **1** [*dress*] de cérémonie; **2** (ritual) cérémoniel/-ielle; (solemn) solennel/-elle; (official) officiel/-ielle.

ceremony *n* cérémonie *f*; **to stand on ~** faire des cérémonies.

certain *adj* **1** (sure, definite) certain, sûr (**about, of** de); **I'm ~ of it** or **that** j'en suis certain or sûr; **absolutely ~** sûr et certain; **I'm ~ that I checked** je suis sûr d'avoir vérifié; **I'm ~ that he refused** je suis sûr qu'il a refusé; **to make ~ that** (ascertain) vérifier que; (ensure) faire en sorte que (+ *subj*); **the strike seems ~ to continue** il est presque certain que la grève continuera; **I know for ~ that** je sais de façon sûre que; **nobody knows for ~** personne ne sait au juste; **I can't say for ~** je ne sais pas au juste; **2** (assured, guaranteed) [*death, defeat*] certain; **to be ~ of doing** être sûr or certain de faire; **3** [*amount, number*] certain (*before n*); **~ people** certains *mpl*; **4** [*shyness, difficulty*] certain (*before n*); **to a ~ extent** dans une certaine mesure; **a ~ amount of time** un certain temps.

certainly *adv* (without doubt) certainement; (indicating assent) certainement, bien sûr; **~ not!** certainement pas!; **it's ~ possible that there will be redundancies** il est tout à fait possible qu'il y ait des licenciements; **we shall ~ attend the meeting** nous serons à la réunion sans faute; **'are you annoyed?'—'I most ~ am!'** 'tu es fâché?'—'ah! ça, oui alors!'

certainty *n* certitude *f*; **it's by no means a ~** ce n'est pas du tout sûr (**that** que + *subj*); **this candidate is a ~ for election** ce candidat est sûr d'être élu; **we have no ~ of success** nous ne sommes pas certains de réussir.

certificate *n* **1** (academic) certificat *m*; (more advanced) diplôme *m*; **2** (for electrician, instructor, first-aider) brevet *m*; **3** (of child's proficiency in sth) brevet *m*; **4** (of safety, building standards) certificat *m*; **test ~**, **MOT ~** (GB) certificat *m* de contrôle technique; **5** (of birth, death, marriage) acte *m*; **6** (of authenticity, quality) certificat *m*; **7 18-~ film** film interdit aux moins de 18 ans.

certify *vtr* **1** (confirm) certifier, constater [*death*]; **to ~ sth a true copy** certifier qch copie conforme; **2** (authenticate) authentifier; **3** garantir [*goods*]; **to send by certified mail** (US) envoyer en recommandé.

cervical: **~ cancer** *n* ▶686| cancer *m* du col de l'utérus; **~ smear** *n* frottis *m* vaginal.

CFC *n* (*abbr* = **chlorofluorocarbon**) CFC *m*; **'contains no ~s'** 'sans CFC'.

chafe *vi* frotter (**on, against** sur).

chain I *n* **1** (metal links) chaîne *f*; **2** (on lavatory) chasse *f* (d'eau); **3** (on door) chaîne *f* de sûreté; **4** (in retail trade) chaîne *f* (**of** de); **supermarket ~** chaîne *f* de supermarchés; **5** (of events) série *f*; (of ideas) enchaînement *m*; **a link in the ~** un maillon de la chaîne; **to form a (human) ~** faire la chaîne.

II *vtr* enchaîner [*person*]; **to ~ a bicycle to sth** attacher une bicyclette à qch avec une chaîne; **to be ~ed to one's desk** être esclave de son travail.

chain: **~ reaction** *n* réaction *f* en chaîne; **~ saw** *n* tronçonneuse *f*; **~-smoker** *n* gros fumeur/grosse fumeuse *m/f*; **~ store** *n* (single shop) magasin *m* faisant partie d'une chaîne; (retail group) magasin *m* à succursales multiples.

chair I *n* **1** (seat) chaise *f*; (upholstered) fauteuil *m*; **to take a ~** s'asseoir; **2** (chairperson) président/-e *m/f*; **to be in the ~** présider; **3** (Univ) chaire *f* (**of, in** de).

II *vtr* présider [*meeting*].

chair lift *n* télésiège *m*.

chairman ▶642| *n* président/-e *m/f*; **Mr**

Chairman monsieur le Président; **Madam Chairman** madame la Présidente.

chairperson *n* président/-e *m/f*.

chalet *n* (mountain) chalet *m*; (in holiday camp) bungalow *m*.

chalk *n* craie *f*; **a piece of ~** un bâton de craie.

challenge **I** *n* **1** (provocation) défi *m*; **to put out a ~** lancer un défi; **to take up a ~** relever un défi; **2** (situation or opportunity) (stimulating) challenge *m*; (considered difficult) épreuve *f*; **to present a ~** représenter un challenge; **to rise to the ~** relever le challenge; **to face a ~** affronter une épreuve; **3** (contest) **to make a ~ for** essayer de s'emparer de [*title, leadership*]; entrer dans la course à [*presidency*]; **4** (of claim, authority) contestation *f* (**to** de); **5** (Sport) attaque *f*.

II *vtr* **1** (invite to justify) défier [*person*] (**to** à; **to do** de faire); **2** (question) débattre [*ideas*]; contester [*statement, authority*]; **3** (test) mettre à l'épreuve [*skill, person*].

chamber **I** *n* **1** (gen, Tech) chambre *f*; **council ~** (GB) salle *f* de réunion; **2** (GB) **the upper/lower ~** la Chambre des lords/des communes.

II chambers *n pl* (Law) cabinet *m*; **in ~s** en cabinet.

chamber: **~maid** ▶805 *n* femme *f* de chambre; **~ music** *n* musique *f* de chambre; **~ orchestra** *n* orchestre *m* de chambre.

champagne *n, adj* champagne (*m*) *inv*.

champion **I** *n* champion/-ionne *m/f*; **world ~** champion/-ionne *m/f* du monde.

II *vtr* se faire le champion de [*cause*]; prendre fait et cause pour [*person*].

championship *n* championnat *m*.

chance **I** *n* **1** (opportunity) occasion *f*; **to have** or **get the ~ to do** avoir l'occasion de faire; **give me a ~ to explain** laisse-moi t'expliquer; **to take one's ~** saisir l'occasion; **you've missed your ~** tu as laissé passer l'occasion; **now's your ~!** c'est l'occasion ou jamais!; **I haven't had a ~ yet** je n'en ai pas encore eu l'occasion; **if you get a ~** si tu en as la possibilité; **when you get a** or **the ~, can you...?** quand tu auras le temps est-ce que tu pourras...?; **2** (likelihood) chance *f*; **there's little ~ of him coming back** il y a peu de chances qu'il revienne; **there is a ~ that she'll get a job in Paris** il y a des chances qu'elle trouve un travail à Paris; **the ~s are that** il y a de grandes chances que (+ *subj*); **she has a good ~** elle a de bonnes chances; **what are his ~s of recovery?** a-t-il des chances de s'en tirer?; **3** (luck) hasard *m*; **by ~** par hasard; **4** (risk) risque *m*; **to take a ~** prendre un risque; **5** (possibility) chance *f*; **not to stand a ~** n'avoir aucune chance; **do you have his address by any ~?** auriez-vous, par hasard, son adresse?

II *vtr* **to ~ doing** courir le risque de faire; **to ~ one's arm, to ~ it** tenter sa chance; **I wouldn't ~ it** je ne risquerais pas le coup.

IDIOMS **no ~**○! pas question○!

chancellor *n* (head of government) chancelier *m*.

Chancellor of the Exchequer *n* (GB) Chancelier *m* de l'Échiquier.

chandelier *n* lustre *m*.

change **I** *n* **1** (by replacement) changement *m*; (by adjustment) modification *f*; **the ~ in the schedule** la modification du programme; **~ of plan** changement de programme; **a ~ of clothes** des vêtements de rechange; **a ~ for the better/worse** un changement en mieux/pire; **to make ~s in** apporter des changements à [*text*]; faire des changements dans [*room, company*]; **social ~** changements sociaux; **2** (different experience) changement *m*; **it makes a ~ from television/from staying at home** cela change un peu de la télévision/de rester chez soi; **that makes a nice ~** ça change agréablement; **she needs a ~** elle a besoin de se changer les idées; **to need a ~ of air** avoir besoin de changer d'air; **for a ~** pour changer; **3** (cash) monnaie *f*; **small ~** petite monnaie; **she gave me 10 francs ~** elle m'a rendu 10 francs; **have you got ~ for 50 francs?** pouvez-vous me changer un billet de 50 francs?

II *vtr* **1** (alter) (completely) changer; (in part) modifier; **to ~ X into Y** transformer X en Y; **to ~ one's mind** changer d'avis (**about** à propos de); **to ~ one's mind about doing** abandonner l'idée de faire; **to ~ sb's mind** faire changer qn d'avis; **to ~ one's ways** changer de mode de vie; **to ~ colour** changer de couleur; **that won't ~ anything** ça n'y changera rien; **2** (exchange) changer de [*clothes, name, car*]; (in shop) échanger [*item*] (**for** pour); **can I ~ it for a size 12?** est-ce que je peux l'échanger contre une taille 12?; **3** (replace) changer [*battery, tyre*]; **to ~ a bed** changer les draps; **4** (exchange with sb) échanger [*clothes, seats*]; **to ~ places** (seats) changer de place (**with** avec); (roles) intervertir les rôles; **5** (actively switch) changer de [*job, TV channel, doctor*]; **to ~ hands** [*property*] changer de propriétaire; **6** (convert) changer [*cheque, currency*] (**into, for** en).

III *vi* **1** [*situation, person*] changer; [*wind*] tourner; **to ~ from gas to electricity** passer du gaz à l'électricité; **the lights ~d from red to orange** les feux sont passés du rouge à l'orange; **2** (into different clothes) se changer; **to ~ into** passer [*garment*]; **to ~ out of** ôter, enlever [*garment*]; **3** (from bus, train) changer.

■ **change down** (GB Aut) rétrograder.

■ **change over** [*drivers*] changer.

■ **change round**: ¶ **~ round** (GB) changer de place; ¶ **~ [sth/sb] round** déplacer [*large objects*]; changer [qn/qch] de place [*workers, objects, words*].

■ **change up** (GB Aut) passer à une vitesse supérieure.

changeable *adj* [*condition, weather*] changeant; [*price*] variable.

change: **~ machine** *n* distributeur *m* de monnaie; **~ of address** *n* changement *m* d'adresse; **~ of life** *n* retour *m* d'âge.

changeover *n* **1** (time period) phase *f* de changement; **2** (transition) passage *m* (**to** à); **3** (of employees, guards) relève *f*; **4** (Sport) (in relay) passage *m* du témoin.

changing *adj* [*colours, environment*] changeant; [*attitude, world*] en évolution.

changing room *n* (at sports centre) vestiaire *m*; (US) (in shop) cabine *f* d'essayage.

channel I *n* **1** (TV station) chaîne *f*; (radio band) canal *m*; **to change ~s** changer de chaîne; **2** (groove) rainure *f*; (canal) canal *m*; (navigable water) chenal *m*; **3** (means) **to do sth through the proper** or **usual ~s** faire qch par la voie normale; **to go through official ~s** passer par la voie officielle.
II *vtr* **1** acheminer, canaliser [*liquid*] (**to, into** dans); **2** concentrer, canaliser [*efforts*] (**into** dans; **into doing** pour faire); affecter [*funds*] (**into** à).

Channel *pr n* **the** (**English**) **~** la Manche.

channel: **~ ferry** *n* ferry *m* trans-Manche; **Channel Islands** *pr n pl* îles *fpl* Anglo-Normandes; **Channel Tunnel** *pr n* tunnel *m* sous la Manche.

chant I *n* **1** (of crowd) chant *m* scandé; **2** (of devotees) mélopée *f*.
II *vi* [*crowd*] scander des slogans; [*choir, monks*] psalmodier.

chaos *n* (gen) pagaille○ *f*; (political) confusion *f*, désordre *m*; (economic, cosmic) chaos *m*; **in a state of ~** [*house*] sens dessus dessous; [*country*] en plein chaos.

chaotic *adj* désordonné; **it's absolutely ~**○ c'est la pagaille○.

chap I○ *n* (GB) (man) type○ *m*; (boy) garçon *m*; (young man) gars○ *m*.
II *vtr* gercer; **~ped lips** lèvres gercées.

chapel *n* chapelle *f*.

chapter *n* chapitre *m*; **in ~ 3** au chapitre 3.

character *n* **1** (personality) caractère *m*; **to have a pleasant ~** être d'un caractère agréable; **to act in/out of ~** agir de façon habituelle/surprenante; **his remarks are totally out of ~** ces remarques me surprennent de sa part; **2** (in book, play, film) personnage *m* (**from** de); **3** (person) individu *m*; **a real ~** un sacré numéro○; **a local ~** une figure locale; **4** (letter, number) caractère *m*.

characteristic I *n* (of person) trait *m* de caractère; (of place, work) caractéristique *f*.
II *adj* caractéristique (**of** de).

characterize *vtr* **1** (depict) dépeindre (**as** comme); **2** (typify) caractériser; **to be ~d by** se caractériser par; **3** représenter [*era, place*]; faire le portrait de [*person*].

charade *n* **1** (Games) **to play ~s** jouer aux charades; **2** (pretence) comédie *f*.

charcoal ▶559 I *n* **1** (fuel) charbon *m* de bois; **2** (for drawing) fusain *m*.
II *adj* (also **~ grey**) (gris) anthracite *inv*.

charge I *n* **1** (fee) frais *mpl*; **delivery/handling ~** frais de livraison/manutention; **additional** or **extra ~** supplément *m*; **there's a ~ of £2 for postage** il y a 2 livres de frais de port; **there's no ~ for installation** l'installation est gratuite; **2** (accusation) accusation *f* (**of** de); (official) inculpation *f*; **murder ~** inculpation d'assassinat; **criminal ~s** poursuites *fpl* criminelles; **to press ~s against sth** engager des poursuites contre qch; **3** (attack) charge *f* (**against** contre); **4** (control) **to be in ~** (gen) être responsable (**of** de); (Mil) commander; **the person in ~** le/la responsable; **the pupils in my ~** les élèves à ma charge; **to take ~** prendre les choses en main; **5** (child) enfant *mf* dont on s'occupe; (pupil) élève *mf*; (patient) malade *mf*; **6** (explosive) charge *f*; **7** (electrical) charge *f*.
II *vtr* **1** prélever [*commission*]; percevoir [*interest*] (**on** sur); **to ~ sb for sth** faire payer qch à qn; **how much do you ~?** vous prenez combien?; **I ~ £20 an hour** je prends 20 livres de l'heure; **2 to ~ sth to** mettre qch sur [*account*]; **3** (accuse) [*police*] inculper [*suspect*] (**with** de); **4** (rush at) charger [*enemy*]; [*bull*] foncer sur [*person*]; **5** charger [*battery*].
III *vi* **1** (demand payment) **to ~ for** faire payer [*delivery, admission*]; **2** (rush at) **to ~ at** charger [*enemy*]; [*bull*] foncer sur [*person*]; **~!** à l'attaque!; **3** (run) **to ~ into/out of** se précipiter dans/de [*house, classroom*]; **to ~ through** traverser [qch] à toute vitesse [*room*]; **to ~ up/down** monter/descendre [qch] à toute vitesse [*stairs*].

charge: **~ account** *n* (US) compte-client *m*; **~ card** *n* (credit card) carte *f* de crédit; (store card) carte *f* d'achat.

charged *adj* **1** [*battery*] chargé; **2** [*atmosphere*] très tendu; **emotionally ~** chargé d'émotion.

char-grilled *adj* [*steak*] grillé au charbon de bois.

charisma *n* charisme *m*.

charismatic *adj* charismatique.

charitable *adj* charitable (**to** envers).

charity *n* **1** (virtue) charité *f*; **out of ~** par charité; **2** (aid, aid organizations) **to give to/collect money for ~** donner à/collecter des fonds pour des œuvres de bienfaisance; **to accept ~** accepter l'aumône *f*; **3** (charitable organization) organisation *f* caritative.

charity work *n* travail *m* bénévole.

charm *n* **1** (quality) charme *m*; **to turn on the ~** se mettre à faire du charme; **2** (jewellery) amulette *f*; **~ bracelet** bracelet *m* à breloques; **lucky ~** porte-bonheur *m inv*.

charming *adj* [*person, place*] charmant; [*child, animal*] adorable.

charred *adj* carbonisé.

chart I *n* **1** (graph) graphique *m*; **temperature ~** feuille *f* de température; **2** (table) tableau *m*; **3** (map) carte *f*; **weather ~** carte du temps; **4** (in pop music) **the ~s** le hit-parade.
II *vtr* **1** (on map) tracer [*route*]; **2** (record) enregistrer [*changes, progress*].

charter I *n* **1** (for citizens) charte *f*; (for company) acte *m* constitutif; **the ~ of human rights** la charte des droits de l'homme; **2** affrètement *m*; **on ~ to** sous contrat d'affrètement avec.
II *vtr* affréter [*plane*].
III **chartered** *pp adj* [*professional*] agréé; [*corporation*] à charte.

charter: **~ed accountant, CA** ▶805 *n*

(GB) = expert-comptable *m*; **~ flight** *n* (GB) vol *m* charter.

chase I *n* poursuite *f* (**after** de); **car/police ~** poursuite *f* en voiture/par la police.
II *vtr* **1** (also **~ after**) pourchasser [*person, animal*]; courir après [*contract, job*]; **to ~ sb/sth up** or **down the street** courir après qn/qch dans la rue; **2** (also **~ after**) courir après [*woman, man*]; **3**° viser [*title*].
■ **chase away**: **~ [sb/sth] away, ~ away [sb/sth]** chasser.
■ **chase down** (US) = **chase up**.
■ **chase up** (GB): ¶ **~ up [sth]** retrouver; ¶ **~ [sb] up, ~ up [sb]** activer.

chassis *n* (Aut) châssis *m*.

chastity *n* chasteté *f*.

chat I *n* conversation *f*; **to have a ~** bavarder (**with** avec; **about** sur).
II *vi* bavarder (**with, to** avec).
■ **chat up**°: **~ up [sb], ~ [sb] up** (GB) (flirtatiously) draguer°.

chat show *n* (GB) talk-show *m*.

chattel *n* bien *m*, possession *f*; **goods and ~s** biens et effets.

chatter I *n* (of person) bavardage *m*; (of crowd) bourdonnement *m*; (of birds) gazouillis *m*.
II *vi* [*person*] bavarder; [*birds*] gazouiller; **her teeth were ~ing** elle claquait des dents.

chatty *adj* [*person*] ouvert; [*letter, style*] vivant.

chauffeur ▶805 **I** *n* chauffeur *m*; **a ~-driven car** une voiture avec chauffeur.
II *vtr* conduire.

chauvinism *n* **1** (gen) chauvinisme *m*; **2** (also **male ~**) machisme *m*.

chauvinist *n, adj* **1** (gen) chauvin/-e (*m/f*); **2** (also **male ~**) macho° (*m*).

cheap I *adj* **1** bon marché *inv*; **to be ~** être bon marché, ne pas coûter cher *inv*; **it's ~ to produce** cela ne revient pas cher de le/la produire; **it works out ~er to take the train** cela revient moins cher de prendre le train; **the ~ seats** les places moins chères; **2** (shoddy) de mauvaise qualité; **it's ~ and nasty** c'est de la camelote; **3** [*joke*] facile; **4** [*trick, liar*] sale (*before n*).
II on the cheap *phr* [*buy, sell*] au rabais; **to do things on the ~** y aller à l'économie°.

cheapen *vtr* rendre [qch] moins cher [*process*]; dévaloriser [*life, liberty*].

cheaply *adv* [*produce, sell*] à bas prix; **to eat ~** manger pour pas cher.

cheap rate *adj, adv* à tarif réduit.

cheat I *n* tricheur/-euse *m/f*.
II *vtr* tromper; **to feel ~ed** se sentir lésé; **to ~ sb (out) of** dépouiller qn de.
III *vi* tricher (**in** à); **to ~ at cards** tricher aux cartes; **to ~ on sb** tromper qn.

check I *n* **1** (for quality, security) contrôle *m* (**on** sur); **to carry out ~s** exercer des contrôles; **to keep a (close) ~ on sb/sth** surveiller qn/qch (de près); **2** (medical) examen *m*; **to have an eye ~** se faire faire un examen des yeux; **3** (restraint) frein *m* (**on** à); **4** (in chess) **~!** échec au roi!; **in ~** en échec; **your king is in ~** échec au roi; **5** (also **~ fabric**) tissu *m* à carreaux; (also **~ pattern**) carreaux *mpl*; **6** (US) (cheque) chèque *m*; **7** (US) (bill) addition *f*; **to pick up the ~** payer l'addition; **8** (US) (receipt) ticket *m*; **9** (US) (tick) croix *f*.
II *vtr* **1** (examine) vérifier [*vehicle, banknote, signature, spelling, details*]; contrôler [*product, ticket, area, work*]; prendre [*temperature, blood pressure*]; tester [*reflexes*]; examiner [*eyesight, watch, map, pocket*]; **to ~ that/whether** vérifier que/si; **to ~ sth for defects** contrôler la qualité de qch; **to ~ sth against** vérifier qch par rapport à [*data, inventory*]; comparer qch avec [*signature*]; **2** (curb) contrôler [*price rises, inflation*]; freiner [*increase, growth*]; réduire [*emigration, influence*]; démentir [*rumour*]; maîtriser [*emotions*]; **3** (stop) arrêter [*person, rebellion*]; **4** (in chess) faire échec à; **5** (US) (also **~ in**) mettre [qch] au vestiaire [*coat*]; mettre [qch] à la consigne [*baggage*]; **6** (US) (register) enregistrer [*baggage*]; **7** (US) (tick) cocher.
III *vi* **1** (verify) vérifier; **to ~ with sb** demander à qn; **2** (examine) **to ~ for** dépister [*problems, disease*]; chercher [*leaks, flaws*]; **3** (register) **to ~ into** arriver à [*hotel*].
■ **check in**: ¶ **~ in** (at airport) enregistrer; (at hotel) remplir la fiche (**at** à); (US) (clock in) pointer (à l'entrée); ¶ **~ [sb/sth] in, ~ in [sb/sth]** enregistrer [*baggage, passengers*]; accueillir [*hotel guest*].
■ **check off**: **~ off [sth], ~ [sth] off** cocher [*items*].
■ **check on**: **~ on [sb/sth]** surveiller [*person*]; **to ~ on sb's progress** vérifier les progrès de qn.
■ **check out**: ¶ **~ out 1** (leave) partir; **to ~ out of** quitter [*hotel*]; **2** (US) (clock out) pointer (à la sortie); ¶ **~ out [sth], ~ [sth] out 1** (investigate) vérifier [*information*]; examiner [*package, building*]; se renseigner sur [*club, scheme*]; **2** (US) (remove) (from library) emprunter; (from cloakroom, left luggage) retirer; ¶ **~ [sb] out, ~ out [sb]** faire une enquête sur [*person*].
■ **check through**: **~ [sth] through** (US) enregistrer [*baggage*] (**to** pour).
■ **check up on** (observe) surveiller [*person*]; (investigate) faire une enquête sur [*person*]; vérifier [*story, details*].

checkbook *n* (US) carnet *m* de chèques, chéquier *m*.

checker ▶805 *n* **1** (employee) vérificateur/-trice *m/f*; **2** (US) (cashier) caissier/-ière *m/f*; **3** (US) (in fabric) carreau *m*; **4** (US Games) (piece) pion *m*.

checkered *adj* (US) = **chequered**.

checkers ▶649 *n* (US) jeu *m* de dames; **to play ~** jouer aux dames.

check-in *n* **1** (also **~ desk**) enregistrement *m*; **2** (procedure) enregistrement *m*.

checking *n* vérification *f*.

checking account *n* (US) compte *m* courant.

check: **~list** *n* liste *f* de contrôle; **~mate** *n* (Games) échec *m* et mat.

checkout *n* caisse *f*; **on the ~** à la caisse.

checkout operator ▶805 *n* (GB) caissier/-ière *m/f*.

check: **~point** *n* poste *m* de contrôle; **~room** *n* (US) (cloakroom) vestiaire *m*; (for baggage) consigne *f*.

checkup *n* **1** (at doctor's) examen *m* médical, bilan *m* de santé; **to have a ~** se faire faire un examen médical; **2** (at dentist's) visite *f* de routine.

cheek *n* **1** (of face) joue *f*; **~ to ~** joue contre joue; **2** culot○ *m*; **what a ~!** quel culot!

cheekbone *n* pommette *f*.

cheeky *adj* [*person*] effronté, insolent; [*question*] impoli; [*grin*] espiègle, coquin.

cheer I *n* acclamation *f*; **to give a ~** pousser une acclamation or un hourra; **to get a ~** être acclamé; **to give three ~s for** faire un ban à; **three ~s!** un ban!, hourra!

II **cheers** *excl* **1** (toast) à la vôtre○!; (to close friend) à la tienne○!; **2**○ (GB) (thanks) merci!; **3**○ (GB) (goodbye) salut!

III *vtr*, *vi* applaudir.

■ **cheer up**: ¶ **~ up** reprendre courage; **~ up!** courage!; ¶ **~ [sb] up** remonter le moral à [*person*]; ¶ **~ [sth] up** égayer [*room*].

cheerful *adj* [*person, mood, music*] joyeux/-euse; [*news*] réjouissant; [*remark, tone*] enjoué; [*colour*] gai; [*optimism*] inébranlable.

cheerleader *n* majorette *f*.

cheese *n* fromage *m*; **~ sandwich** sandwich au fromage.

cheese: **~board** *n* (object) plateau *m* à fromage; (selection) plateau *m* de fromages; **~cake** *n* cheesecake *m*; **~cloth** *n* étamine *f*; **~ counter** *n* fromagerie *f*.

cheetah *n* guépard *m*.

chef ▶ 805 *n* chef *m* cuisinier.

chemical I *n* produit *m* chimique.

II *adj* [*reaction, industry, warfare, waste*] chimique; [*equipment*] de chimie.

chemist ▶ 805, 805 *n* **1** (GB) (person) pharmacien/-ienne *m/f*; **~'s (shop)** pharmacie *f*; **2** (scientist) chimiste *mf*.

chemistry *n* **1** (science, subject) chimie *f*; **2** (rapport) affinités *fpl*.

cheque (GB), **check** (US) *n* chèque *m*; **by ~** par chèque; **to make out** or **write a ~ for £20** faire un chèque de 20 livres sterling.

cheque: **~book** (GB), **checkbook** (US) *n* chéquier *m*, carnet *m* de chèques; **~ card** *n* (GB) carte *f* de garantie bancaire.

chequered (GB), **checkered** (US) *adj* **1** [*cloth*] à damiers; **2** [*career, history*] en dents de scie.

chequers ▶ 649 *n* (GB) ▶ **checkers**.

cherish *vtr* caresser [*ambition*]; chérir [*memory, person*].

cherry ▶ 559 I *n* **1** (fruit) cerise *f*; **2** (also **~ tree**) cerisier *m*; **3** (also **~wood**) cerisier *m*.

II *adj* (also **~-red**) rouge cerise *inv*.

chervil *n* cerfeuil *m*.

chess ▶ 649 *n* échecs *mpl*; **a game of ~** une partie d'échecs.

chess: **~board** *n* échiquier *m*; **~ set** *n* jeu *m* d'échecs.

chest I *n* **1** (of person) poitrine *f*; **~ measurement** tour *m* de poitrine; **2** (furniture) coffre *m*; **~ of drawers** commode *f*; **3** (crate) caisse *f*.

II *noun modifier* [*pains*] de poitrine; [*infection*] des voies respiratoires; [*X-ray*] des poumons.

IDIOMS **to get something off one's ~**○ vider son sac○.

chestnut I *n* **1** (nut) marron *m*, châtaigne *f*; **2** (also **~ tree**) (horse) marronnier *m* (d'Inde); (sweet) châtaignier *m*; **3** (wood) châtaignier *m*.

II *adj* [*hair*] châtain; **a ~ horse** un (cheval) alezan.

chew *vtr* **1** [*person*] mâcher [*food, gum*]; mordiller [*pencil*]; ronger [*bone*]; **to ~ one's nails** se ronger les ongles; **2** [*animal*] ronger [*bone*]; mordiller [*carpet*].

chewing gum *n* chewing-gum *m*.

chick *n* (fledgling) oisillon *m*; (of fowl) poussin *m*.

chicken I *n* **1** (fowl) poulet *m*, poule *f*; **2** (meat) poulet *m*; **3**○ (coward) poule *f* mouillée.

II *noun modifier* [*wing, stock*] de poulet; [*sandwich, soup*] au poulet.

chicken: **~ breast** *n* filet *m* de poulet; **~ curry** *n* poulet *m* au curry; **~ drumstick** *n* pilon *m*; **~ pox** ▶ 686 *n* varicelle *f*; **~ wire** *n* grillage *m* (à mailles fines).

chickpea *n* pois *m* chiche.

chicory *n* **1** (vegetable) endive *f*; **2** (in coffee) chicorée *f*.

chief I *n* chef *m*; **defence ~s** responsables *mpl* de la défense.

II *adj* **1** [*reason*] principal; **2** [*editor*] en chef.

chief executive *n* **1** (in organization) directeur *m* général; **2** (US) (President) Chef *m* de l'Exécutif (*le Président*).

chief: **Chief of Staff** *n* (Mil) chef *m* d'état-major; (of White House) secrétaire *m* général; **~ of state** *n* (US) chef *m* d'État.

chiffon *n* mousseline *f*.

chilblain *n* engelure *f*.

child *n* enfant *mf*; **when I was a ~** quand j'étais enfant; **~ prodigy** enfant *mf* prodige.

childbirth *n* accouchement *m*; **in ~** en couches.

childcare facilities *n pl* crèche *f*.

childhood I *n* enfance *f*; **in (his) early ~** dans sa prime enfance.

II *noun modifier* [*friend, memory*] d'enfance; [*illness*] infantile.

childish *adj* [*person, behaviour*] puéril.

childishness *n* puérilité *f*.

childlike *adj* enfantin.

child: **~minder** ▶ 805 *n* (GB) nourrice *f*; **~-proof** *adj* [*container, lock*] de sécurité.

chill I *n* **1** (coldness) fraîcheur *f*; **there is a ~ in the air** le fond de l'air est frais; **to send a ~ down sb's spine** donner des frissons à qn; **2** (illness) coup *m* de froid.

II *adj* **1** [*wind*] frais/fraîche; **2** [*reminder, words*] brutal.

III *vtr* **1** (make cool) mettre [qch] à refroidir [*dessert, soup*]; rafraîchir [*wine*]; **2** (make cold) faire frissonner [*person*]; **to ~ sb's** or **the blood** glacer le sang à qn.

IV *vi* [*dessert*] refroidir; [*wine*] rafraîchir.

chilli, **chili** *n* **1** (also **~ pepper**) piment *m* rouge; **2** (also **~ powder**) chili *m*; **3** (also **~ con carne**) chili *m* con carne.
chilly *adj* froid; **it's ~** il fait froid.
chime *n* carillon *m*.
chimney *n* cheminée *f*.
chimney sweep ▶805 *n* ramoneur *m*.
chimpanzee *n* chimpanzé *m*.
chin *n* menton *m*.
china I *n* porcelaine *f*; **a piece of ~** une porcelaine.
II *noun modifier* [*cup, plate*] en porcelaine.
China ▶574 *pr n* Chine *f*.
Chinese ▶712 I *n* **1** (person) Chinois/-oise *m/f*; **2** (language) chinois *m*.
II *adj* [*culture, food, politics*] chinois/-oise; [*ambassador, embassy*] de Chine; [*teacher, lesson*] de chinois; **to eat ~** manger chinois.
chink *n* **1** (in wall) fente *f*; (in curtain) entrebâillement *m*; **2** (sound) tintement *m*.
chip I *n* **1** (fragment) fragment *m* (**of** de); (of wood) copeau *m*; (of glass) éclat *m*; **2** (in wood, china) ébréchure *f*; **3** (microchip) puce *f* (électronique).
II **chips** *n pl* **1** (GB) (fried potatoes) frites *fpl*; **2** (US) (crisps) chips *fpl*.
III *vtr* ébrécher [*glass, plate*]; écorner [*precious stone*]; écailler [*paint*]; **to ~ a tooth** se casser une dent.
IV *vi* [*plate, glass*] s'ébrécher; [*paint*] s'écailler; [*tooth*] se casser; [*gem*] s'écorner.
IDIOMS **to have a ~ on one's shoulder** être amer/-ère.
■ **chip away**: ¶ **~ away** [*paint, plaster*] s'écailler; **to ~ away at** tailler [*stone*]; affaiblir [qch] progressivement [*authority*]; miner [*confidence*]; ¶ **~ away [sth], ~ [sth] away** enlever [qch] petit à petit [*plaster*].
■ **chip in** (GB)○ (financially) donner un peu d'argent.
chipboard *n* aggloméré *m*.
chiropodist ▶805 *n* pédicure *mf*.
chiropractor ▶805 *n* chiropraticien/-ienne *m/f*, chiropracteur *m*.
chirp *vi* [*bird*] pépier.
chisel I *n* ciseau *m*.
II *vtr* tailler au ciseau; (finely) ciseler; **finely ~led** finement ciselé.
chitchat○ *n* bavardage *m*.
chive *n* ciboulette *f*.
chlorine *n* chlore *m*.
chloroform *n* chloroforme *m*.
choc-ice *n* (GB) esquimau *m*.
chock-a-block *adj* plein à craquer.
chocolate I *n* chocolat *m*; **cooking ~** chocolat *m* de ménage; **hot ~** chocolat *m* chaud; **a bar of ~** une tablette de chocolat; **a box of ~s** une boite de chocolats.
II *noun modifier* [*eggs, sweets*] en chocolat; [*biscuit, cake, ice cream*] au chocolat.
choice *n* choix *m* (**between, of** entre); **to make a ~** faire un choix, choisir; **it was my ~ to do** c'est moi qui ai choisi de faire; **it's your ~** c'est à toi de choisir; **to have the ~** avoir le choix; **to have a free ~** être libre de choisir; **you have a ~ of three colours** tu as le choix entre trois couleurs; **a wide ~** un grand choix; **a narrow ~** un choix limité; **to be spoilt for ~** avoir l'embarras du choix; **a car of my ~** une voiture de mon choix; **out of** or **from ~** par choix.
choir *n* (of church, school) chorale *f*; (professional) chœur *m*; (of boys at cathedral) maîtrise *f*; **to be** or **sing in the ~** faire partie de la chorale.
choir: **~boy** *n* petit chanteur *m*, jeune choriste *m*; **~girl** *n* jeune choriste *f*.
choke I *n* (Aut) starter *m*; **to use the ~** mettre le starter.
II *vtr* **1** (throttle) étrangler [*person*]; **2** [*fumes, smoke*] étouffer.
III *vi* s'étouffer; **to ~ on a drink** s'étouffer en buvant; **to ~ to death** mourir étouffé.
■ **choke back** étouffer [*cough, sob*]; **to ~ back one's tears** retenir ses larmes.
■ **choke up**: **~ [sth] up** boucher [*drain*]; **~d up with traffic** embouteillé.
cholera ▶686 *n* choléra *m*.
cholesterol *n* cholestérol *m*.
choose I *vtr* **1** (select) choisir [*book, person, option*] (**from** parmi); **to ~ sb as** choisir qn comme [*adviser, friend*]; élire qn [*leader*]; **2** (decide) décider (**to do** de faire).
II *vi* **1** (select) choisir (**between** entre); **there are many models to ~ from** il y a un grand choix de modèles; **there's not much to ~ from** il y a très peu de choix; **2** (prefer) vouloir; **to ~ to do** préférer faire.
choosy *adj* difficile (**about** en ce qui concerne).
chop I *n* (Culin) côtelette *f*; **pork ~** côtelette *f* de porc.
II *vtr* **1** (also **~ up**) couper [*wood*]; couper, émincer [*vegetable, meat*]; hacher [*parsley, onion*]; **to ~ sth into cubes** couper qch en cubes; **to ~ sth finely** hacher qch; **2** réduire [*service, deficit*]; **3** couper [*quote, footage*].
IDIOMS **to ~ and change** [*person*] changer d'avis comme de chemise; **to get the ~**○ (GB) [*person*] se faire sacquer○; [*scheme, service*] être supprimé.
■ **chop down**: **~ [sth] down** abattre.
■ **chop off**: **~ [sth] off** couper [*branch, end*]; trancher [*head, hand, finger*].
chopping: **~ board** *n* planche *f* à découper; **~ knife** *n* couteau *m* de cuisine.
choppy *adj* [*sea, water*] agité; [*wind*] instable.
chopstick *n* baguette *f* (chinoise).
chord *n* accord *m*; **to strike the right ~** toucher la corde sensible.
chore *n* tâche *f*; **to do the ~s** faire le ménage; **what a ~!** quelle corvée!
choreographer ▶805 *n* chorégraphe *mf*.
choreography *n* chorégraphie *f*.
chorus *n* **1** (singers) chœur *m*; **2** (piece of music) chœur *m*; **3** (refrain) refrain *m*; (in jazz) chorus *m*; **4** (of bird song) concert *m*; **a ~ of protest** une tempête de protestations.
choux pastry *n* pâte *f* à choux.
Christ *pr n* le Christ, Jésus-Christ.

christen *vtr* baptiser; **I was ~ed John** mon nom de baptême est John.

christening *n* baptême *m*.

Christian I *n* chrétien/-ienne *m/f*; **to become a ~** se faire chrétien.
II *adj* [*faith, art*] chrétien/-ienne; [*attitude*] charitable; **a ~ burial** un enterrement convenable.

Christianity *n* christianisme *m*.

Christian name *n* nom *m* de baptême.

Christmas I *n* **~ (day)** (jour *m* de) Noël; **at ~** à Noël; **over ~** pendant la période de Noël; **Merry ~!, Happy ~!** Joyeux Noël!
II *noun modifier* [*cake, card, present*] de Noël.

Christmas: **~ carol** *n* chant *m* de Noël; **~ cracker** *n* (GB) diablotin *m*; **~ dinner** *n* repas *m* de Noël; **~ eve** *n* veille *f* de Noël; **~ tree** *n* sapin *m* de Noël.

chrome I *n* chrome *m*.
II *noun modifier* [*article*] chromé, en chrome.

chromosome *n* chromosome *m*.

chronic *adj* **1** [*illness*] chronique; **2** [*liar*] invétéré; [*problem, shortage*] chronique.

chronological *adj* chronologique.

chubby *adj* [*child, finger*] potelé; [*cheek*] rebondi; [*face*] joufflu; [*adult*] rondelet/-ette.

chuck I *n* (also **~ steak**) macreuse *f*.
II○ *vtr* **1** (throw) balancer○, jeter; **2** larguer○ [*boyfriend, girlfriend*].

chuckle *vi* glousser, rire; **to ~ at** or **over sth** rire de qch; **to ~ to oneself** rire sous cape.

chuffed○ *adj* (GB) vachement○ content (**about, at, with** de).

chum○ *n* copain/copine○ *m/f*, pote○ *m*.

chummy○ *adj* sociable; **they're very ~** ils sont très copains○.

chunk *n* **1** (of meat, fruit) morceau *m*; (of wood) tronçon *m*; (of bread) quignon *m*; **pineapple ~s** ananas *m* en morceaux; **2** (of population, text, day) partie *f* (**of** de).

chunky *adj* [*sweater, jewellery*] gros/grosse; [*person*] costaud○, trapu.

Chunnel○ *n* (GB) tunnel *m* sous la Manche.

church I *n* (Catholic, Anglican) église *f*; (Protestant) temple *m*.
II *noun modifier* [*bell, choir, steeple*] d'église; [*fête*] paroissial; [*wedding*] religieux/-ieuse.

church: **~goer** *n* pratiquant/-e *m/f*; **~ hall** *n* salle *f* paroissiale; **~ school** *n* école *f* religieuse; **~ service** *n* office *m*; (Catholic) messe *f*; **~yard** *n* cimetière *m*.

churn I *n* **1** (for butter) baratte *f*; **2** (GB) (for milk) bidon *m*.
II *vtr* **to ~ butter** baratter.
III *vi* **my stomach was ~ing** (nauseous) mon cœur se soulevait; (with nerves) j'avais l'estomac noué.
■ **churn out**: **~ [sth] out, ~ out [sth]** pondre [qch] en série [*novels*]; produire [qch] en série [*goods*].
■ **churn up**: **~ [sth] up, ~ up [sth]** faire des remous dans [*water*].

chute *n* **1** (slide) toboggan *m*; **2** (for rubbish) vide-ordures *m inv*; **3** (for toboggan) piste *f* de toboggan; **4**○ (parachute) parachute *m*.

cicada *n* cigale *f*.

cider *n* cidre *m*; **dry/sweet ~** cidre brut/doux.

cigar I *n* cigare *m*.
II *noun modifier* [*box, case*] à cigares; [*smoker*] de cigares.

cigarette *n* cigarette *f*.

cigarette: **~ butt** *n* mégot *m*; **~ lighter** *n* briquet *m*; (in car) allume-cigares *m inv*.

cinder *n* (glowing) braise *f*; (ash) cendre *f*; **to burn sth to a ~** réduire qch en cendres; **~ track** (piste *f*) cendrée *f*.

Cinderella *pr n* Cendrillon.

cine: **~camera** *n* caméra *f* (d'amateur); **~ film** *n* pellicule *f* cinématographique.

cinema *n* cinéma *m*.

cinema: **~ complex** *n* complexe *m* multisalles; **~goer** *n* cinéphile *mf*.

cinnamon ▶559 I *n* **1** (spice) cannelle *f*; **2** (tree) cannelier *m*.
II *adj* **1** [*cake, cookie*] à la cannelle; [*stick*] de cannelle; **2** (colour) cannelle *inv*.

circle I *n* **1** (shape) cercle *m*; (of spectators, trees, chairs) cercle *m*; (of fabric, paper, colour) rond *m*; **to form a ~** [*objects*] former un cercle; [*people*] faire un cercle; **to sit in a ~** s'asseoir en cercle; **to go round in ~s** tourner en rond; **to have ~s under one's eyes** avoir les yeux cernés; **2** (group) cercle *m*, groupe *m*; **his ~ of friends** le cercle de ses amis; **in business ~s** dans les milieux d'affaires; **3** (in theatre) balcon *m*; **in the ~** au balcon.
II *vtr* **1** (move round) [*plane*] tourner autour de [*airport*]; [*satellite*] graviter autour de [*planet*]; [*person, animal, vehicle*] faire le tour de [*building*]; tourner autour de [*person, animal*]; **2** (surround) encercler.
III *vi* tourner en rond (**around** autour de).
IDIOMS **to come full ~** [*person*] boucler la boucle.

circuit *n* **1** (track) (for vehicles) circuit *m*; (for athletes) piste *f*; **2** (lap) tour *m*; **to do 15 ~s of the track** faire 15 tours de circuit; **3** (regular round) circuit *m*; **the tennis ~** le circuit du tennis; **4** (round trip) circuit *m*; **5** (electrical) circuit *m*.

circular I *n* (newsletter) circulaire *f*; (advertisement) prospectus *m*.
II *adj* [*object*] rond; [*argument*] circulaire.

circulate I *vtr* **1** (to limited circle) faire circuler; (widely) diffuser (**to** entre); **2** faire circuler [*blood, water*].
II *vi* circuler; **let's ~** (at party) on va aller faire connaissance.

circulation *n* **1** (of blood, air, water, fuel) circulation *f*; **2** (distribution) (of newspaper) tirage *m*; **a ~ of 2 million** un tirage de 2 millions d'exemplaires; **3** (of coins, books) circulation *f*; **4** (of document, information) circulation *f*; (to wide public) diffusion *f*.

circumcise *vtr* circoncire [*boy*]; exciser [*girl*].

circumcision *n* (of boy) circoncision *f*; (of girl) excision *f*.

circumference *n* circonférence *f*.

circumflex *n* accent *m* circonflexe (**on, over** sur).

circumstance I *n* circonstance *f*.
II circumstances *n pl* **1** (state of affairs) circonstances *fpl*; **in** or **under the ~s** dans ces circonstances; **under no ~s** en aucun cas; **2** (conditions of life) situation *f*.

circumstantial *adj* [*evidence*] indirect.

circus *n* cirque *m*.

cirrhosis ▶686 *n* cirrhose *f*.

CIS *pr n* (*abbr* = **Commonwealth of Independent States**) CEI *f*.

cistern *n* (of lavatory) réservoir *m* de chasse d'eau; (in loft or underground) citerne *f*.

citizen *n* **1** (of state) citoyen/-enne *m/f*; (when abroad) ressortissant/-e *m/f*; **2** (of town) habitant/-e *m/f*.

citizen: **~'s arrest** *n* arrestation *f* par un particulier; **~ship** *n* nationalité *f*.

citrus *n* (tree) citrus *m*; (fruit) agrume *m*.

citrus fruit *n* (individual) agrume *m*; (collectively) agrumes *mpl*.

city *n* (grande) ville *f*; **~ life** la vie citadine; **the City** (GB) la City.

city: **~ centre** (GB), **~ center** (US) *n* centre-ville *m*; **~ council** *n* conseil *m* municipal.

city hall *n* (US) **1** (building) (in large town) hôtel *m* de ville; (in small town) mairie *f*; **2** (municipal government) administration *f* municipale.

civic *adj* [*administration, official*] municipal; [*pride, responsibility*] civique.

civic centre (GB), **civic center** (US) *n* centre *m* municipal (culturel et administratif).

civil *adj* **1** [*case, court, offence*] civil; [*claim*] au civil; **2** (polite) courtois.

civil: **~ engineer** ▶805 *n* ingénieur *m* des travaux publics; **~ engineering** *n* génie *m* civil.

civilian *n* civil/-e *m/f*.

civilization *n* civilisation *f*.

civilized *adj* civilisé; **to become ~** se civiliser.

civil: **~ law** *n* droit *m* civil; **~ liability** *n* (Law) responsabilité *f* civile; **~ liberty** *n* libertés *fpl* individuelles; **~ rights** *n pl* droits *mpl* civils; **~ servant** ▶805 *n* fonctionnaire *mf*; **~ service** *n* fonction *f* publique; **~ war** *n* guerre *f* civile; **~ wedding** *n* mariage *m* civil.

claim I *n* **1** (demand) revendication *f*; **to lay ~ to** prétendre à [*throne*]; revendiquer [*right, land, title*]; **2** (in insurance) (against a person) réclamation *f*; (for fire, theft) demande *f* d'indemnisation; **to make** or **put in a ~** faire une demande d'indemnisation; **3** (for welfare benefit) demande *f* d'allocation; **4** (refund request) demande *f* de remboursement; **travel ~** demande *f* de remboursement des frais de déplacement; **5** (assertion) affirmation *f* (**about** au sujet de; **by** de la part de; **of** de); **his ~ that he is innocent** ses protestations d'innocence; **my ~ to fame** ma prétention à la gloire.
II *vtr* **1** (assert) **to ~ to be able to do** prétendre pouvoir faire; **to ~ to be innocent** prétendre être innocent; **to ~ responsibility for an attack** revendiquer un attentat; **2** revendiquer [*money, property*]; **to ~ the right to sth** revendiquer le droit à qch; **3** faire une demande de [*benefit*]; faire une demande de remboursement de [*expenses*].
III *vi* **1 to ~ for damages** faire une demande pour dommages et intérêts; **2** (apply for benefit) faire une demande d'allocation.

claimant *n* **1** (for benefit, grant, compensation) demandeur/-euse *m/f* (**to** à); **2** (to title, estate) prétendant/-e *m/f* (**to** à).

claim form *n* déclaration *f* de sinistre.

clairvoyant *n* voyant/-e *m/f*, extralucide *mf*.

clam *n* palourde *f*.
■ **clam up** ne plus piper mot (**on sb** à qn).

clammy *adj* [*skin, hand*] moite (**with** de); [*surface*] collant; [*weather*] moite.

clamour (GB), **clamor** (US) **I** *n* **1** (loud shouting) clameur *f*; **2** (demands) réclamations *fpl*.
II *vi* **1** (demand) **to ~ for sth** réclamer qch; **to ~ for sb to do** réclamer à qn de faire; **2** (rush, fight) se bousculer (**for** pour avoir; **to do** pour faire).

clamp I *n* **1** (on bench) valet *m*; (unattached) presse *f*; **2** (also **wheel~**) sabot *m* de Denver.
II *vtr* **1** cramponner [*two parts*]; (at bench) fixer [qch] à l'aide d'un valet (**onto** à); **2** (clench) serrer [*jaw, teeth*]; **3** (also **wheel~**) mettre un sabot de Denver à [*car*].
■ **clamp down** prendre des mesures; **to ~ down on** faire de la répression contre [*crime*]; mettre un frein à [*extravagance*].

clampdown *n* mesures *fpl* de répression (**on sb** contre qn; **on sth** de qch).

clan *n* clan *m*.

clandestine *adj* clandestin.

clang I *n* fracas *m*, bruit *m* métallique.
II *vi* [*gate*] claquer avec un son métallique; [*bell*] retentir.

clap I *n* **to give sb a ~** applaudir qn; **a ~ of thunder** un coup de tonnerre.
II *vtr* **1 to ~ one's hands** battre or taper des mains, frapper dans ses mains; **to ~ one's hand over sb's mouth** mettre or plaquer la main sur la bouche de qn; **to ~ sb on the back** taper qn dans le dos; **2** (applaud) applaudir.
III *vi* applaudir.

clapping *n* applaudissements *mpl*.

claret ▶559 *n* **1** (wine) bordeaux *m* (rouge); **2** (colour) bordeaux *m*.

clarification *n* éclaircissement *m*, clarification *f*.

clarify *vtr* éclaircir, clarifier [*point*].

clarinet ▶753 *n* clarinette *f*.

clarity *n* clarté *f*.

clash I *n* **1** (confrontation) affrontement *m*; (disagreement) querelle *f*; **2** (contradiction) conflit *m*, incompatibilité *f*; **a ~ of cultures** un conflit de cultures; **a personality ~** un conflit de personnalités; **3** (inconvenient coincidence) **there's a ~ of meetings** les réunions ont lieu en

même temps; **4** (noise) **a ~ of cymbals** un coup de cymbales.
II *vtr* entrechoquer [*bin lids*]; frapper [*cymbals*].
III *vi* **1** (meet and fight) [*armies, groups*] s'affronter; (disagree) s'affronter; **to ~ with sb** (fight) se heurter à qn; (disagree) se quereller avec qn (**on, over** au sujet de); **2** (be in conflict) [*interests, beliefs*] être incompatibles; **3** (coincide) [*meetings*] avoir lieu en même temps (**with** que); **4** (not match) [*colours*] jurer.

clasp *n* (on bracelet, bag, purse) fermoir *m*; (on belt) boucle *f*.

class I *n* **1** (social group) classe *f*; **2** (group of students) classe *f*; (lesson) cours *m* (**in** de); **in ~** en cours or classe; **to give a ~** assurer un cours; **to take a ~** (GB) assurer un cours; (US) suivre un cours; **3** (year group) promotion *f*, classe *f*; **4** (category) classe *f*; **to be in a ~ of one's own** être hors catégorie; **5**○ (elegance) classe *f*; **to have ~** avoir de la classe; **6** (in transport) classe *f*; **to travel first/second ~** voyager en première/deuxième classe; **7** (GB Univ) ≈ mention *f*; **a first-/second-~ degree** ≈ licence avec mention très bien/bien.
II *vtr* classer; **to ~ sb/sth as** assimiler qn/qch à.

classic *n, adj* classique (*m*).

classical *adj* classique; **~ scholar** philologue *mf*.

classics *n* lettres *fpl* classiques.

classification *n* **1** (category) classification *f*, catégorie *f*; **2** (categorization) classement *m*.

classified I *n* (also **~ ad**) petite annonce *f*.
II *adj* **1** (categorized) classifié; **2** (secret) confidentiel/-ielle.

classify *vtr* **1** (file) classer; **2** (declare secret) classer [qch] confidentiel/-ielle.

class: **~mate** *n* camarade *mf* de classe; **~room** *n* salle *f* de classe; **~ system** *n* système *m* de classes.

classy○ *adj* [*hotel*] de luxe; [*actor*] de grande classe; **she's ~** elle a de la classe.

clatter I *n* cliquetis *m*; (loud) fracas *m*.
II *vi* [*typewriter*] cliqueter; [*dishes*] s'entrechoquer.

clause *n* **1** (in grammar) proposition *f*; **2** (in contract, treaty) clause *f*; (in will, act of Parliament) disposition *f*.

claustrophobia *n* claustrophobie *f*.

claustrophobic *adj* claustrophobe; **it's ~ in here** il y a une atmosphère oppressante ici; **to get ~** avoir une sensation de claustrophobie.

claw *n* **1** (of animal) griffe *f*; (of bird of prey) serre *f*; (of crab, lobster) pince *f*; **2** (on hammer) arrache-clou *m*, pied-de-biche *m*.

clay *n* **1** (for sculpture) argile *f*, terre *f* glaise; **2** (soil) argile *f*; **3** (in tennis) terre *f* battue.

clean I *adj* **1** [*clothes, dishes, floor*] propre; [*air, water*] pur; [*syringe*] désinfecté; **she keeps her house ~** elle tient sa maison propre; **my hands are ~** j'ai les mains propres; **~ and tidy** d'une propreté irréprochable; **a ~ sheet of paper** une feuille blanche; **keep your shoes ~** ne salis pas tes chaussures; **2** [*joke*] anodin; **3** [*reputation*] sans tache; [*record, licence*] vierge; **4** (Sport) [*tackle*] sans faute; [*hit*] précis; **5** (neat) [*lines, profile*] pur; **~ break** (Med) fracture *f* simple.
II *adv* **the bullet went ~ through his shoulder** la balle lui a littéralement traversé l'épaule; **to jump ~ over the wall** sauter par-dessus le mur sans le toucher; **we're ~ out of bread** on n'a plus de pain.
III *vtr* nettoyer [*room, shoes*]; effacer [*blackboard*]; vider [*fish*]; **to ~ sth from** or **off** enlever qch de [*hands, car*]; **to have sth ~ed** donner qch à nettoyer; **to ~ one's teeth** se brosser les dents; **to ~ itself** [*animal*] faire sa toilette.
■ **clean out**: **~ [sth] out, ~ out [sth]** nettoyer [qch] à fond; [*thief*] mettre [qch] à sac [*house*].
■ **clean up**: ¶ **~ up 1** (remove dirt) tout nettoyer; **2** (tidy) tout remettre en ordre (**after sb** derrière qn); **3** (wash oneself) se débarbouiller; **4**○ (make profit) [*dealer*] faire son beurre○ (**on** avec); [*gambler*] rafler la mise○; ¶ **~ [sb] up** faire la toilette de [*patient*]; ¶ **~ [sth] up, ~ up [sth]** nettoyer.

cleaner ▶ 805 *n* **1** (person) (in workplace) agent *m* de nettoyage; (in home) (woman) femme *f* de ménage; (man) agent *m* de nettoyage; **2** (machine) **carpet ~** shampouineuse *f* (de tapis); **3** (detergent) **suede ~** produit *m* pour nettoyer le daim; **4** (shop) **cleaner's** pressing *m*.

cleaning *n* (domestic) ménage *m*; (commercial) nettoyage *m*, entretien *m*.

cleaning: **~ lady** ▶ 805 *n* femme *f* de ménage; **~ product** *n* produit *m* d'entretien.

cleanliness *n* propreté *f*.

cleanly *adv* [*cut*] bien, franchement; **to break off ~** se casser net.

cleanse *vtr* nettoyer [*skin, wound*].

cleanser *n* **1** (for face) démaquillant *m*; **2** (household) produit *m* d'entretien.

clean-shaven *adj* **he's ~** il n'a ni barbe ni moustache.

clear I *adj* **1** (transparent) [*glass, liquid*] transparent; [*blue*] limpide; [*lens, varnish*] incolore; [*honey*] liquide; **~ soup** consommé *m*; **2** (distinct) [*image, outline*] net/nette; [*writing*] lisible; [*sound, voice*] clair; **3** (comprehensible) [*description, instruction*] clair; **to make sth ~ to sb** faire comprendre qch à qn; **I wish to make it ~ that** je tiens à préciser que; **is that ~?** est-ce que c'est clair?; **4** (obvious) [*need, sign*] évident; [*advantage*] net/nette (*before n*); [*majority*] large (*before n*); **it is ~ that** il est clair que; **5** (not confused) [*idea, memory*] clair; [*plan*] précis; **to keep a ~ head** garder les idées claires; **6** (empty) [*view*] dégagé; [*table*] débarrassé; [*space*] libre; **7** [*conscience*] tranquille; **8** [*skin*] net/nette; [*X-ray, scan*] normal; [*sky*] sans nuage; [*day, night*] clair; **on a ~ day** par temps clair; **9** (exempt from) **to be ~ of** être libre de [*debt*]; être exempt de [*blame*]; être lavé de [*suspicion*]; **10** (free) [*day*] libre; **keep Monday ~** ne prévois rien d'autre lundi.
II *adv* **to jump ~ of sth** éviter qch en sautant sur le côté; **to pull sb ~ of** extraire qn de

[*wreckage*]; **to steer ~ of** éviter [*town centre, troublemakers*].

III *vtr* **1** (remove) abattre [*trees*]; arracher [*weeds*]; enlever [*debris, papers, mines*]; dégager [*snow*] (**from, off** de); **2** (free from obstruction, empty) déboucher [*drains*]; débarrasser [*table, room*]; vider [*desk*]; évacuer [*area, building*]; effacer [*screen*]; déblayer [*site*]; défricher [*land*]; dégager [*nose*]; **to ~ the road of obstacles** dégager les obstacles de la route; **to ~ sth out of the way** (from table) enlever qch; (from floor) enlever qch du passage; **to ~ the way for** libérer le passage pour [*person, vehicle*]; ouvrir la voie pour [*developments*]; laisser la place à [*successor*]; **to ~ the air** aérer; (in tense situation) apaiser les tensions; **to ~ one's throat** se racler la gorge; **3** (create) **to ~ a space** faire de la place; **to ~ a path through sth** se frayer un chemin à travers qch; **4** (disperse) dissiper [*fog, smoke*]; disperser [*crowd*]; **5** (eliminate) faire disparaître [*dandruff, spots*]; **6** (dispose of) liquider [*stock*]; **'reduced to ~'** 'solde'; **7** (pay off) s'acquitter de [*debt*]; **8** [*bank*] compenser [*cheque*]; **9** (free from blame) innocenter [*accused*] (**of** de); **to be ~ed of suspicion** être lavé de tout soupçon; **to ~ one's name** blanchir son nom; **10** mener une enquête administrative sur [*employee*]; approuver [*request*]; **to ~ sth with sb** obtenir l'accord de qn pour qch; **11** (jump over) franchir [*hurdle, wall*]; **12** (pass through) passer sous [*bridge*]; **to ~ customs** passer à la douane.

IV *vi* **1** [*liquid, sky*] s'éclaircir; **2** [*smoke, fog, cloud*] se dissiper; **3** [*air*] se purifier; **4** (go away) [*rash*] disparaître; **5** [*cheque*] être compensé.

■ **clear away**: ¶ **~ away** débarrasser; ¶ **~ [sth] away, ~ away [sth]** balayer [*leaves*]; enlever [*rubbish*]; ranger [*papers, toys*].

■ **clear up**: ¶ **~ up 1** (tidy up) faire du rangement; **2** (improve) [*weather*] s'éclaircir; [*infection*] disparaître; ¶ **~ up [sth], ~ [sth] up 1** (tidy) ranger [*mess, room, toys*]; ramasser [*litter*]; **2** (resolve) résoudre [*problem*]; dissiper [*misunderstanding*].

clearance *n* **1** (permission) autorisation *f*; **security ~** habilitation *f* sécuritaire; **to have ~ to do** être autorisé à faire; **2** (customs certificate) déclaration *f* en douane; **3** (also **~ sale**) liquidation *f*; **4** (of cheque) compensation *f*.

clear-cut *adj* [*plan, division*] précis; [*difference*] net/nette (*before n*); [*problem, rule*] clair; **the matter is not so ~** l'affaire n'est pas si simple.

clear-headed *adj* lucide.

clearing *n* **1** (glade) clairière *f*; **2** (removal) (of obstacles) enlèvement *m*; (of road, debris) déblaiement *m*; **3** (levelling) (of forest) abattage *m*; (of land) défrichage *m*.

clearly *adv* **1** (distinctly) [*speak, hear, write*] clairement; [*see*] bien; [*audible*] nettement; [*visible*] bien; [*labelled*] clairement; **2** (intelligibly) [*describe*] clairement; **3** (lucidly) [*think*] clairement; **4** (obviously) manifestement.

clearness *n* (of air) pureté *f*; (of note, voice) clarté *f*; (of image, writing) netteté *f*.

cleavage *n* décolleté *m*.

cleaver *n* fendoir *m*.

clef *n* clef *f*; **in the treble ~** en clef de fa.

cleft *adj* [*chin*] marqué d'un sillon; [*palate*] fendu.

clench *vtr* serrer; **to ~ one's fist** serrer le poing; **to ~ one's teeth** serrer les dents.

clergy *n* clergé *m*.

clerical *adj* **1** (of clergy) [*matters*] clérical; [*control*] du clergé; **2** [*staff*] de bureau; **~ work** travail *m* de bureau.

clerical assistant ▶ **805** *n* commis *m*.

clerk ▶ **805** *n* **1** (in office, bank) employé/-e *m/f*; **booking ~** employé/-e *m/f* aux réservations; **2** (GB) (to lawyer) ≈ clerc *m*; (in court) greffier/-ière *m/f*; **3** (US) (in hotel) réceptionniste *mf*; (in shop) vendeur/-euse *m/f*.

clever *adj* **1** (intelligent) intelligent; **to be ~ at sth/at doing** être doué pour qch/pour faire; **2** (ingenious) [*solution, gadget, person*] astucieux/-ieuse, futé; **3** (skilful) habile, adroit; **to be ~ at doing** être habile pour faire; **he's ~ with his hands** il est adroit de ses mains; **4** [*argument, advertisement*] astucieux/-ieuse; [*lawyer, salesperson*] malin/-igne; **to be too ~ for sb** être trop malin/-igne pour qn.

cleverness *n* (intelligence) intelligence *f*; (ingenuity) ingéniosité *f*; (dexterity) adresse *f*, habileté *f*.

cliché *n* cliché *m*, lieu *m* commun.

click I *n* (of machine) déclic *m*; (of fingers, heels, tongue) claquement *m*.

II *vtr* **to ~ one's fingers** faire claquer ses doigts; **to ~ one's heels** claquer des talons.

III *vi* [*camera, lock*] faire un déclic; [*door*] faire un petit bruit sec.

client *n* client/-e *m/f*.

clientele *n* clientèle *f*.

cliff *n* (by sea) falaise *f*; (inland) escarpement *m*.

cliffhanger° *n* (film) film *m* à suspense; (story) récit *m* à suspense.

climate *n* climat *m*.

climax *n* (of war, conflict) paroxysme *m*; (of plot, speech, play) point *m* culminant; (of career) apogée *m*; **to reach its ~** [*battle*] atteindre son paroxysme; [*contest, performance*] atteindre son point culminant.

climb I *n* **1** (of hill) escalade *f* (**up** de; **to** jusqu'à); (of tower) montée *f* (**up** de; **to** jusqu'à); (of mountain, rock face) ascension *f* (**up** de; **to** jusqu'à); **2** (of aeroplane) montée *f*; **3** (rise) ascension *f*.

II *vtr* [*car, person*] grimper [*hill*]; faire l'ascension de [*cliff, mountain*]; escalader [*lamppost, wall*]; grimper à [*ladder, tree*]; monter [*staircase*].

III *vi* **1** (scale) grimper (**to** jusqu'à); **to go ~ing** faire de l'escalade; **to ~ down** descendre [*rock face*]; **to ~ over** enjamber [*stile*]; passer par-dessus [*fence, wall*]; escalader [*debris, rocks*]; **to ~ up** grimper à [*ladder, tree*]; monter [*steps*]; **2** (rise) [*aircraft*] monter; **3** (slope up) [*road*] monter; **4** (increase) monter.

■ **climb down** revenir sur sa décision.

climber *n* grimpeur/-euse *m/f*, alpiniste *mf*.

climbing ▶ 649 *n* escalade *f*.

clinch *vtr* **1** (secure) décrocher [*victory, order*]; **to ~ a deal** (in business) conclure une affaire; (in politics) conclure un accord; **2** (resolve) décider de [*argument*]; **what ~ed it was...** ce qui a été décisif c'est...

cling *vi* **1 to ~ (on) to sb/sth** se cramponner à qn/qch; **to ~ together** se cramponner l'un à l'autre; **2** [*smell*] résister.

clingfilm *n* (GB) scellofrais® *m*.

clinic *n* **1** (treatment centre) centre *m* médical; **Dr X's ~** le service du Dr X; **2** (GB) (nursing-home) clinique *f*; **3** (advice or teaching session) clinique *f*.

clinical *adj* **1** [*medicine*] clinique; [*approach*] objectif/-ive; **2** (unfeeling) froid.

clink I *vtr* faire tinter [*glass, keys*]; **to ~ glasses with** trinquer avec.
II *vi* [*glass, keys*] tinter.

clip I *n* **1** (on earring) clip *m*; (for hair) barrette *f*; **2** (from film) extrait *m*.
II *vtr* **1** tailler [*hedge*]; couper [*nails, moustache*]; tondre [*dog, sheep*]; **2** (attach) accrocher [*microphone*] (**to** à); fixer [*brooch*] (**to** à); **3** heurter [*cyclist*].
III *vi* (by hooking) s'accrocher (**to** à); (by fastening) se fixer (**to à**).
IDIOMS **to ~ sb' s wings** rogner les ailes à qn.

clip: **~board** *n* (gen) porte-bloc *m inv* à pince; (Comput) presse-papiers *m inv*; **~ frame** *n* sous-verre *m inv*.

clip-ons *n pl* clips *mpl*.

clipped *adj* [*speech*] haché.

clippers *n pl* (for nails) coupe-ongles *m inv*; (for hair, hedge) tondeuse *f*.

clipping I *n* coupure *f* de presse.
II **clippings** *n pl* (hair) cheveux *mpl* coupés; (nails) bouts *mpl* d'ongles.

clique *n* clique *f*, bande *f*.

cloak I *n* cape *f*; (long, worn by men) houppelande *f*.
II *vtr* **1** (surround) **~ed in** enveloppé dans [*darkness*]; enveloppé de [*ambiguity, secrecy*]; **2** (disguise) masquer.

cloakroom *n* **1** (for coats) vestiaire *m*; **2** (GB) (lavatory) toilettes *fpl*.

clock ▶ 554 *n* **1** (timepiece) (large) horloge *f*; (small) pendule *f*; (Sport) chronomètre *m*; **to set a ~** mettre une pendule à l'heure; **to put the ~s forward/back one hour** avancer/reculer les pendules d'une heure; **to work around the ~** travailler 24 heures sur 24; **2** (timer) (in computer) horloge *f* (interne); (for central heating system) horloge *f* (incorporée).
■ **clock off** (GB) pointer (à la sortie).
■ **clock on** (GB) pointer.

clock: **~ face** *n* cadran *m*; **~maker** ▶ 805 *n* horloger/-ère *m/f*; **~ radio** *n* radio-réveil *m*; **~ tower** *n* beffroi *m*; **~wise** *adj*, *adv* dans le sens des aiguilles d'une montre.

clockwork I *n* (in clock) mécanisme *m* or mouvement *m* d'horloge; (in toy) mécanisme *m*.
II *adj* [*toy*] mécanique.
IDIOMS **to go like ~** aller comme sur des roulettes.

clog *n* sabot *m*.

cloister *n* cloître *m*.

clone *n* clone *m*.

close[1] I *adj* **1** (near) proche (**to** de), voisin (**to** de); **2** [*relative, friend*] proche; [*resemblance*] frappant; **to bear a ~ resemblance to** ressembler beaucoup à; **~ links with** liens étroits avec [*country*]; liens d'amitié avec [*group*]; **in ~ contact with** en contact permanent avec; **3** [*contest, result*] serré; **'is it the same?'—'no but it's ~'** 'c'est le même?'—'non mais c'est proche'; **4** [*scrutiny*] minutieux/-ieuse; [*supervision*] étroit; **to pay ~ attention to sth** faire une attention toute particulière à qch; **to keep a ~ watch** or **eye on sb/sth** surveiller étroitement qn/qch; **5** (compact) [*print, formation*] serré; **6** [*weather*] lourd; **it 's ~** il fait lourd.
II *adv* **1** (nearby) **to live quite ~ (by)** habiter tout près; **how ~ is the town?** est-ce que la ville est loin?; **the closer he came** plus il approchait; **to bring sth closer** approcher qch; **to follow ~ behind** suivre de près; **to hold sb ~** serrer qn; **~ together** serrés les uns contre les autres; **2** (in time) **the time is ~ when** dans peu de temps; **how ~ are they in age?** combien ont-ils de différence d'âge?; **Christmas is ~** Noël approche; **3** (almost) **that's closer to the truth** ça c'est plus proche de la vérité.
III **close enough** *phr* **that's ~ enough** (no nearer) tu es assez près; (acceptable) ça ira.
IV **close to** *phr* **1** (near) près de [*place, person, object*]; **how ~ are we to...?** à quelle distance sommes-nous de...?; **2** (on point of) au bord de [*tears, hysteria*]; **to be ~ to doing** être sur le point de faire; **3** (almost at) **closer to 30 than 40** plus proche or plus près de 40 ans que de 30; **to come closest to** s'approcher le plus de [*ideal, conception*]; **to come ~ to doing** faillir faire; **how ~ are you to completing...?** est-ce que vous êtes sur le point de finir...?; **~ to the time when** à peu près au moment où; **4** (approximately) près de, presque.
V **close by** *phr* près de [*wall, bridge*]; **the ambulance is ~ by** l'ambulance n'est pas loin.
IDIOMS **(from) ~ up** de près; **it was a ~ call**○ or **shave**○ or **thing** je l'ai/tu l'as etc échappé belle.

close[2] I *n* fin *f*; **to draw to a ~** tirer à sa fin; **~ of trading** clôture *f*.
II *vtr* **1** (shut) fermer [*door, book*]; **2** (block) fermer [*border, port*]; boucher [*pipe*]; barrer [*road*]; interdire l'accès à [*area*]; **3** (bring to an end) mettre fin à [*meeting*]; fermer [*account*]; **4 to ~ the gap** réduire l'écart; **5** (agree) conclure [*deal*].
III *vi* **1** (shut) [*airport, polls, shop*] fermer; [*door, container, eyes, mouth*] se fermer; **2** (cease to operate) fermer définitivement; **3** (end) [*meeting, play*] prendre fin; **to ~ with** se terminer par [*song*]; **4** [*currency, index*] clôturer (**at** à);

The Clock

What time is it?

what time is it?	= quelle heure est-il?
could you tell me the time?	= pouvez-vous me donner l'heure?
it's exactly four o'clock	= il est exactement quatre heures

It is . . .	*Il est . . .*	*say . . .*
4 o'clock	4 heures	
	4 h	quatre heures
4 o'clock in the morning / 4 am	4 h 00	quatre heures du matin
4 o'clock in the afternoon / 4 pm	16 h 00	quatre heures de l'après-midi
		seize heures*
4.10 / ten past four	4 h 10	quatre heures dix
4.15	4 h 15	quatre heures quinze
a quarter past four	4 h 15	quatre heures et quart
4.20	4 h 20	quatre heures vingt
4.25	4 h 25	quatre heures vingt-cinq
4.30	4 h 30	quatre heures trente
half past four	4 h 30	quatre heures et demie†
4.35	4 h 35	quatre heures trente-cinq
twenty-five to five	4 h 35	cinq heures moins vingt-cinq
4.40	4 h 40	quatre heures quarante
twenty to five	4 h 40	cinq heures moins vingt
4.45 / a quarter to five	4 h 45	cinq heures moins le quart
4.50	4 h 50	quatre heures cinquante
ten to five	4 h 50	cinq heures moins dix
4.55	4 h 55	quatre heures cinquante-cinq
five to five	4 h 55	cinq heures moins cinq
5 o'clock	5 h	cinq heures
16.15	16 h 15	seize heures quinze
8 o'clock in the evening	8 h du soir	huit heures du soir
8 pm	20 h 00	vingt heures
12.00	12 h 00	douze heures
noon / 12 noon	12 h 00	midi
midnight / 12 midnight	24 h 00	minuit

* In timetables etc, the twenty-four hour clock is used, so that ***4 pm*** is ***seize heures***. In ordinary usage, one says ***quatre heures*** (***de l'après-midi***).

† ***Demi*** agrees when it follows its noun, but not when it comes before the noun to which it is hyphenated, eg ***quatre heures et demie*** but ***les demi-heures*** etc. Note that ***midi*** and ***minuit*** are masculine, so ***midi et demi*** and ***minuit et demi***.

When?

French never drops the word ***heures***: ***at five*** is ***à cinq heures*** and so on.

French always uses ***à***, whether or not English includes the word ***at***. The only exception is when there is another preposition present, as in ***vers cinq heures*** (*about five o'clock*), ***avant cinq heures*** (*before five o'clock*) etc:

what *time did it happen?*	= **à quelle** heure cela s'est-il passé?
what *time will he come* ***at****?*	= **à quelle** heure va-t-il venir?
it happened ***at*** *two o'clock*	= c'est arrivé **à** deux heures
he'll come ***at*** *four*	= il viendra **à** quatre heures
at about *five*	= **vers** cinq heures / **à** cinq heures **environ**
it must be ready ***by*** *ten*	= il faut que ce soit prêt **avant** dix heures
closed ***from*** *1* ***to*** *2 pm*	= fermé **de** treize **à** quatorze heures
every hour ***on*** *the hour*	= toutes les heures **à** l'heure juste

the market ~d down/up le marché a clôturé en baisse/en hausse; **5** [*gap*] se réduire.

IV closed *pp adj* fermé; **'~d'** (sign in shop) 'fermé'; (in theatre) 'relâche'; **'~d for lunch/for repairs'** 'fermé pour le déjeuner/pour cause de réparations'; **behind ~d doors** à huis clos; **to have a ~d mind** avoir l'esprit fermé.

■ **close down**: ¶ **~ down** [*shop, business*] fermer définitivement; ¶ **~ down [sth], ~ [sth] down** fermer [qch] définitivement [*business, factory*].

■ **close in** [*pursuers*] se rapprocher (**on** de); [*winter*] approcher.

■ **close off**: **~ off [sth], ~ [sth] off** fermer [qch] au public.

■ **close up**: ¶ **~ up 1** [*flower, wound*] se refermer; [*group*] se serrer; **2** [*shopkeeper*] fermer; ¶ **~ up [sth], ~ [sth] up 1** fermer [*shop*]; **2** boucher [*hole*].

closed-circuit television *n* télévision *f* en circuit fermé.

close: **~-fitting** *adj* [*garment*] ajusté, près du corps; **~-knit** *adj* [*family, group*] très uni.

closely *adv* [*follow, study, monitor*] de près; [*resemble*] beaucoup; [*coordinated*] bien; **to work ~ together** travailler en étroite collaboration; **to be ~ related** [*ideas*] être étroitement lié (**to** à); [*people*] être proches parents.

closeness *n* **1** (emotionally) intimité *f*; **2** (rapport) rapport *m* (**to** à); **3** (of place) proximité *f*; (of event) approche *f*; **4** (of atmosphere) (inside) manque *m* d'air; **the ~ of the weather** le temps lourd.

closet I *n* (US) (cupboard) placard *m*; (for clothes) penderie *f*; **linen ~** placard *m* à linge.

II *noun modifier* [*alcoholic, fascist*] inavoué, qui s'en cache.

close-up I *n* gros plan *m*; **in ~** en gros plan.

II close up *adv* (**from**) **~** de près.

closing I *n* fermeture *f*; **Sunday ~** fermeture *f* dominicale (des magasins).

II *adj* [*minutes, words*] dernier/-ière (*before n*); [*scene, stage*] final; [*speech*] de clôture.

closing: **~ date** *n* date *f* limite (**for** de); **~-down sale, ~-out sale** (US) *n* liquidation *f*; **~ time** *n* heure *f* de fermeture.

closure *n* fermeture *f*.

clot I *n* caillot *m*; **~ on the brain** embolie *f* cérébrale.

II *vtr, vi* coaguler, cailler.

cloth *n* **1** (fabric) tissu *m*; **wool ~** tissu *m* de laine; **2** (for polishing, dusting) chiffon *m*; (for floor) serpillière *f*; (for drying dishes) torchon *m*; (for table) nappe *f*.

clothes I *n pl* **1** (garments) vêtements *mpl*; **to put on/take off one's ~** s'habiller/se déshabiller; **without any ~ on** tout nu; **2** (washing) linge *m*.

II *noun modifier* [*basket, line, peg*] à linge.

clothes: **~ brush** *n* brosse *f* à habits; **~ drier** *n* (machine) sèche-linge *m inv*; (airer) séchoir *m* à linge; **~hanger** *n* cintre *m*; **~ shop** *n* (GB) magasin *m* de vêtements.

clothing *n* vêtements *mpl*; **an item** or **article of ~** un vêtement.

cloud I *n* nuage *m*; **there's a lot of ~ about** il fait un temps très nuageux; **to cast a ~ over sth** jeter une ombre sur qch.

II *vtr* **1** (blur) [*steam, breath*] embuer [*mirror*]; [*tears*] brouiller [*vision*]; **2** (confuse) obscurcir [*judgment*]; brouiller [*memory*]; **to ~ the issue** brouiller les cartes.

IDIOMS **to be living in ~-cuckoo-land** croire au père Noël.

■ **cloud over** [*sky*] se couvrir (de nuages); [*face*] s'assombrir.

cloudy *adj* [*weather*] couvert; **it's ~** le temps est couvert.

clout *n* **1** (blow) claque *f*, coup *m*; **2** (influence) influence *f* (**with** auprès de, sur); **to have** or **carry a great deal of ~** avoir beaucoup d'influence, avoir du poids.

clove *n* **1** (spice) clou *m* de girofle; **oil of ~s** essence *f* de girofle; **2** (of garlic) gousse *f*.

clover *n* trèfle *m*.

clown *n* **1** (in circus) clown *m*; **2** (fool) clown *m*, pitre *m*.

■ **clown around** (GB) faire le clown or le pitre.

club *n* ▶ 649 **1** (association) club *m*; **tennis/book ~** club *m* de tennis/de livres; **to be in a ~** faire partie d'un club; **2**○ (nightclub) boîte *f* de nuit○; **3** (for golf) club *m*; **4** (in cards) trèfle *m*.

■ **club together** cotiser (**for** pour; **to do** pour faire).

club: **~ car** *n* (US) wagon-bar *m* de première classe; **~ class** *n* classe *f* club or affaires.

club foot *n* pied *m* bot; **to have a ~** être pied-bot.

cluck *vi* [*hen*] glousser.

clue *n* indication *f* (**to, as to** quant à); (in police investigation) indice *m* (**to** quant à); (in crossword) définition *f*; **I'll give you a ~** je vais vous mettre sur la piste; **give me a ~** aide-moi; **I haven't (got) a ~**○ je n'ai aucune idée.

clump *n* (of flowers, grass) touffe *f*; (of trees) massif *m*; (of earth) motte *f*.

clumsiness *n* (carelessness) maladresse *f*; (awkwardness) gaucherie *f*.

clumsy *adj* [*person, attempt*] maladroit; [*object*] grossier/-ière; [*animal*] pataud; [*tool*] peu maniable; [*style*] lourd; **to be ~ with one's hands** ne pas être très adroit de ses mains.

cluster I *n* (of flowers, berries) grappe *f*; (of people, islands, trees) groupe *m*; (of houses) ensemble *m*; (of diamonds) entourage *m*; (of stars) amas *m*.

II *vi* [*people*] se rassembler (**around** autour de).

clutch I *n* **1** (Aut) embrayage *m*; **to let in the ~** débrayer; **to let out the ~** embrayer; **2** (of eggs, chicks) couvée *f*; (of books, awards) ensemble *m*; (of people) groupe *m*.

II *vtr* tenir fermement [*object, child*]; **to ~ sb/sth to** serrer qn/qch contre [*chest*].

■ **clutch at**: **~ at [sth/sb]** tenter d'attraper [*branch, rail, person*]; saisir [*arm*].

clutch bag *n* pochette *f*.

clutches *n pl* **to fall into the ~ of** tomber sous les griffes or la patte○ de.

clutter *v* ■ **clutter up**: **~ up** [**sth**], **~** [**sth**] **up** encombrer.

cluttered *adj* encombré (**with** de).

c/o *prep* (*abbr* = **care of**) chez.

coach I *n* **1** (bus) (auto)car *m*; **by ~** en (auto)-car; **2** (GB) (of train) wagon *m*; **3** (Sport) entraîneur/-euse *m/f*; **4** (for drama, voice) répétiteur/-trice *m/f*.
II *vtr* **1** (Sport) entraîner [*team*]; **2** (teach) **to ~ sb** donner des leçons particulières à qn (**in** en); **to ~ sb for an exam** préparer qn à un examen.

coach: **~ party** *n* (GB) groupe *m* voyageant en autocar; **~ station** *n* (GB) gare *f* routière; **~ trip** *n* excursion *f* en autocar.

coal I *n* charbon *m*; **hot** or **live ~s** charbons *mpl* ardents.
II *noun modifier* [*cellar, shed, shovel*] à charbon.
IDIOMS **to haul sb over the ~s**○ passer un savon à qn○.

coal: **~face** *n* front *m* de taille or d'abattage; **~field** *n* bassin *m* houiller; **~ fire** *n* (GB) cheminée *f*; **~ industry** *n* industrie *f* minière.

coalition *n* coalition *f* (**between** entre; **with** avec).

coal: **~ merchant** ▶ 805 *n* charbonnier *m*, marchand *m* de charbon; **~mine** *n* mine *f* de charbon; **~miner** ▶ 805 *n* mineur *m*; **~mining** *adj* [*family, region*] de mineurs; **~ scuttle** *n* seau *m* à charbon.

coarse *adj* **1** [*texture*] grossier/-ière; [*skin*] épais/-aisse; [*sand, salt*] gros/grosse (*before n*); **2** (not refined) [*laugh, manners*] grossier/-ière; [*accent*] vulgaire; **3** [*language, joke*] cru.

coast I *n* côte *f*; **off the ~** près de la côte; **from ~ to ~** dans tout le pays.
II *noun modifier* [*road, path*] côtier/-ière.

coaster *n* **1** (mat) dessous-de-verre *m inv*; **2** (boat) caboteur *m*.

coastguard ▶ 805 *n* (person) garde-côte *m*.

coastguard: **~ station** *n* poste *m* de la gendarmerie maritime; **~ vessel** *n* (vedette *f*) garde-côte *m*.

coastline *n* littoral *m*.

coat I *n* **1** (garment) manteau *m*; (for men) pardessus *m*; (jacket) veste *f*; **2** (of dog) poil *m*, pelage *m*; (of cat) fourrure *f*, pelage *m*; (of horse, leopard) robe *f*; **3** (layer) couche *f*.
II *vtr* **1** (cover) **to ~ sth with** enduire qch de [*paint, adhesive*]; revêtir qch de [*rubber*]; couvrir qch de [*dust, oil*]; **2** (Culin) **to ~ sth in** or **with** enrober qch de [*breadcrumbs, chocolate, sauce*]; dorer qch à [*egg*]; **~ed with sugar** [*sweet*] glacé.

coated *adj* [*tongue*] chargé.

coat: **~ hanger** *n* cintre *m*; **~ of arms** *n* blason *m*, armoiries *fpl*; **~rack** *n* portemanteau *m*; **~room** *n* (US) vestiaire *m*; **~ tree** *n* (US) portemanteau *m*.

coax *vtr* cajoler; **to ~ sb into doing sth** persuader qn (gentiment) de faire qch.

cobbler ▶ 805 *n* cordonnier *m*.

cobblestones *n pl* pavés *mpl*.

cobweb *n* toile *f* d'araignée.
IDIOMS **that will blow away the ~s** ça me/te etc rafraîchira les idées.

cocaine *n* cocaïne *f*.

cochairman *n* coprésident *m*.

cock I *n* **1** (rooster) coq *m*; **2** (male bird) (oiseau *m*) mâle *m*; **3** (of hay, straw) meulon *m*; **4** (weathervane) girouette *f*.
II *vtr* **1** (raise) **to ~ an eyebrow** hausser les sourcils; **to ~ a leg** [*dog*] lever la patte; **to keep an ear ~ed** dresser l'oreille; **2** (tilt) pencher; **3** (Mil) armer [*gun*].

cock-and-bull story *n* histoire *f* abracadabrante or à dormir debout.

cockatoo *n* cacatoès *m*.

cockcrow *n* **at ~** au chant du coq.

cockerel *n* jeune coq *m*.

cockle *n* coque *f*.

cock: **~pit** *n* cockpit *m*, poste *m* de pilotage; **~roach** *n* cafard *m*.

cocktail *n* **1** (drink) cocktail *m*; **gin ~** cocktail à base de gin; **to have ~s** prendre l'apéritif; **2** (Culin) **fruit ~** salade *f* de fruits; **seafood ~** cocktail *m* de fruits de mer.

cocktail: **~ bar**, **~ lounge** *n* bar *m*; **~ dress** *n* robe *f* de cocktail; **~ party** *n* cocktail *m*; **~ shaker** *n* shaker *m*; **~ stick** *n* pique *f* (à apéritif).

cocky *adj* impudent.

cocoa *n* **1** (substance) cacao *m*; **2** (drink) chocolat *m*.

coconut I *n* noix *f* de coco.
II *noun modifier* [*milk, oil, butter*] de coco; **~ palm** cocotier *m*.

cocoon *n* cocon *m*.

cod *n* **1** (also **~fish**) morue *f*; **2** (Culin) cabillaud *m*.

COD *n* (*abbr* = **cash on delivery**) envoi *m* contre remboursement.

code I *n* **1** code *m*; **safety ~** règlement *m* de sécurité; **~ of practice** (in medicine) déontologie *f* (médicale); (in advertising) code *m* de bonne conduite; **~ of ethics** moralité *f*; **~ of conduct/honour** code *m* de conduite/d'honneur; **2** (cipher) code *m*; **in ~** en code; **3** (also **dialling ~**) indicatif *m*; **4** (Comput) code *m*.
II *vtr* coder.

codeine *n* codéine *f*.

code: **~ name** *n* nom *m* de code; **~word** *n* (name) nom *m* de code; (password) mot *m* de passe.

co-driver *n* copilote *mf*.

coeducational *adj* (also **coed**) mixte.

coerce *vtr* exercer des pressions sur; **to ~ sb into doing** contraindre qn à faire.

coercion *n* coercition *f*.

coexist *vi* coexister (**with** avec).

C of E *n*, *adj* (GB) (*abbr* = **Church of England**) Église *f* d'Angleterre.

coffee I *n* café *m*; **a cup of ~** une tasse de café; **a black/white ~** un café (noir)/au lait.
II *noun modifier* [*cake*] au café; [*cup, filter, grinder, spoon*] à café.

coffee bean *n* grain *m* de café; **a kilo of ~s** un kilo de café en grains.

coffee: **~ break** *n* pause(-)café *f*; **~-coloured** (GB), **~-colored** (US) *adj* café-au-lait *inv*; **~ grounds** *n* marc *m* de café; **~ machine** *n* (in café) percolateur *m*; (domestic) cafetière *f* électrique; (vending machine) machine *f* à café; **~ maker**, **~ percolator** *n* (electric) cafetière *f* électrique; (on stove) cafetière *f*; **~ pot** *n* cafetière *f*; **~ shop** ▶805 *n* café *m*; **~ table** *n* table *f* basse.

coffin *n* cercueil *m*.

cog *n* (tooth) dent *f* d'engrenage; (wheel) pignon *m*.

cohabit *vi* cohabiter (**with** avec).

coherence *n* (of thought) cohérence *f*; **to give ~ to sth** apporter une cohérence à qch.

coherent *adj* cohérent; **he was barely ~** on avait peine à le comprendre.

coil I *n* **1** (of rope, barbed wire) rouleau *m*; (of electric wire) bobine *f*; (of smoke) volute *f*; (of hair) boucle *f*; (of snake) anneau *m*; **2** (contraceptive) stérilet *m*.
II *vtr* (also **~ up**) enrouler [*hair, rope, wire*].

coin I *n* pièce *f* (de monnaie); **a pound ~** une pièce d'une livre.
II *vtr* forger [*term*]; **to ~ a phrase** comme on dit.

coin box *n* **1** (pay phone) cabine *f* (téléphonique) à pièces; **2** (on pay phone, in laundromat) caisse *f*.

coincide *vi* coïncider (**with** avec).

coincidence *n* coïncidence *f*, hasard *m*; **it is a ~ that** c'est par coïncidence que; **a happy ~** un heureux hasard; **by ~** par hasard.

coincidentally *adv* tout à fait par hasard.

coke *n* **1** (fuel) coke *m*; **2**○ (cocaine) coke◑ *f*, cocaïne *f*.

Coke® *n* coca *m*.

cola *n* (drink) coca *m*.

colander *n* passoire *f*.

cold I *n* **1** (chilliness) froid *m*; **to feel the ~** être sensible au froid, être frileux/-euse; **to come in from** or **out of the ~** se mettre à l'abri du froid; **2** (Med) rhume *m*; **to have a ~** être enrhumé, avoir un rhume; **a bad ~** un gros rhume.
II *adj* **1** (chilly) froid; **to be** or **feel ~** [*person*] avoir froid; **the room was ~** il faisait froid dans la pièce; **it's** or **the weather's ~** il fait froid; **to go ~** [*food, water*] se refroidir; **don't let the baby get ~** ne laisse pas le bébé prendre froid; **to keep sth ~** tenir [qch] au frais [*food*]; **2** [*manner*] froid; **to be ~ to** or **towards sb** être froid avec qn; **3** (unconscious) **to be out ~** être sans connaissance.
IDIOMS **in ~ blood** de sang-froid; **to pour ~ water on sth** descendre qch en flammes○.

cold: **~ calling** *n* démarchage *m* par téléphone; **~ comfort** *n* piètre consolation *f* (**for** pour); **~ cuts** *n pl* assiette *f* anglaise.

coldness *n* froideur *f*.

cold shoulder *n* **to give sb the ~** snober qn, battre froid à qn.

cold: **~ snap** *n* brève vague *f* de froid; **~ sore** *n* bouton *m* de fièvre.

cold sweat *n* **to bring sb out in a ~** donner des sueurs froides à qn.

coleslaw *n* salade *f* à base de chou cru.

colic *n* coliques *fpl*.

collaboration *n* collaboration *f* (**between** entre; **with** avec; **in** à).

collaborator *n* collaborateur/-trice *m/f*.

collage *n* **1** (picture) collage *m*; **2** (film) montage *m*.

collapse I *n* **1** (of regime, economy, hopes) effondrement *m* (**of, in** de); **2** (of deals, talks) échec *m*; **3** (of company) faillite *f* (**of** de); **4** (of person) (physical) écroulement *m*; (mental) effondrement *m*; **to be close to ~** être sur le point de s'écrouler; **5** (of building, bridge) effondrement *m*; (of tunnel, wall) écroulement *m*; **6** (Med) (of lung) collapsus *m*.
II *vi* **1** (founder) [*regime, economy, hopes*] s'effondrer; [*case, deal, talks*] échouer; **2** [*company*] faire faillite; **3** (slump) [*person*] s'écrouler; **to ~ and die** mourir subitement; **4** (fall down) [*building, bridge*] s'effondrer; [*tunnel, wall*] s'écrouler; [*chair*] s'affaisser (**under** sous); **5** (Med) [*lung*] se dégonfler; **6** (fold) [*bike, pushchair*] se plier.

collapsible *adj* pliant.

collar *n* **1** (on garment) col *m*; **2** (for animal) collier *m*.
IDIOMS **to get hot under the ~** se mettre en rogne○.

collar: **~bone** *n* clavicule *f*; **~ size** *n* encolure *f*.

colleague *n* collègue *mf*.

collect I *adv* (US) **to call sb ~** appeler qn en PCV.
II *vtr* **1** (gather) ramasser [*wood, litter*]; rassembler [*information*]; recueillir [*signatures*]; **2** (as hobby) collectionner, faire collection de [*stamps, coins*]; **3** (attract) [*objects*] prendre, ramasser [*dust*]; **4** (obtain) percevoir [*rent*]; encaisser [*fares, money*]; recouvrer [*debt*]; toucher [*pension*]; percevoir [*tax, fine*]; remporter [*prize*]; **5** (take away) ramasser [*rubbish*]; faire la levée de [*mail, post*]; **6** (pick up) aller chercher [*person*]; récupérer [*keys, book*].
III *vi* **to ~ for charity** faire la quête pour des bonnes œuvres.

collect call *n* (US) appel *m* en PCV.

collection *n* **1** (of objects) ramassage *m*; (of old clothes, newspapers) collecte *f*; (of information, facts) rassemblement *m*; (of rent) encaissement *m*; (of debt) recouvrement *m*; (of tax) perception *f*; (of mail) levée *f*; **your suit is ready for ~** votre costume est prêt; **2** (of coins, records) collection *f*; (anthology) recueil *m*; **art ~** collection *f* (de tableaux); **3** (money collected) collecte *f* (**for** pour); (in church) quête *f*.

collective *adj* collectif/-ive.

collective: **~ noun** *n* (nom *m*) collectif *m*; **~ ownership** *n* copropriété *f*.

collector *n* **1** (of coins, stamps) collectionneur/-euse *m/f*; **2** (official) (of taxes) percepteur *m*; (of rent, debts) encaisseur *m*.

college *n* (place of third-level education) établissement *m* d'enseignement supérieur; (school, part of university) collège *m*; (US Univ) faculté *f*; **to go to ~, to be at** or **in** (US) **~** faire des études supérieures.

college of education *n* (GB) ≈ École *f* normale.

collide *vi* [*vehicle, plane*] entrer en collision (**with** avec).

collie *n* colley *m*.

colliery *n* houillère *f*.

collision *n* **1** (crash) collision *f*; **2** (clash) affrontement *m* (**between** entre).

colloquial *adj* familier/-ière; **~ English** anglais parlé.

cologne *n* eau *f* de Cologne.

colon *n* **1** (Anat) côlon *m*; **2** (in punctuation) deux points *mpl*.

colonel *n* colonel *m*.

colonialist *n, adj* colonialiste (*mf*).

colonize *vtr* coloniser.

colony *n* colonie *f*.

colour (GB), **color** (US) ▶ 559 **I** *n* **1** (hue) couleur *f*; **what ~ is it?** de quelle couleur est-il/elle?; **the sky was the ~ of lead** le ciel était couleur de plomb; **in ~** en couleur; **to give ~ to sth** colorer qch; **2** (dye) (for food) colorant *m*; (for hair) teinture *f*; **3** (make-up) **eye ~** fard *m* à paupières; **lip ~** rouge *m* à lèvres; **4** (pigmentation) couleur *f* de peau; **people of all races and ~s** des gens de toutes races et de toutes couleurs; **5** (complexion) couleur *f*; **to lose (one's) ~** perdre ses couleurs; **to put ~ into sb's cheeks** redonner des couleurs à qn; **he's getting his ~ back** il reprend des couleurs.

II *noun modifier* [*photography*] (en) couleur; **~ film** (for camera) pellicule *f* couleur.

III *vtr* **1** (with paints, crayons) colorier; (with commercial paints) peindre; (with food dye) colorer; (with hair dye) teindre; **to ~ sth blue** colorier or teindre qch en bleu; **2** (prejudice) fausser [*judgment*].

IDIOMS **to show one's true ~s** se montrer sous son vrai jour.

colour: **~ blind** *adj* daltonien/-ienne; **~ code** *vtr* classer [qch] par couleurs.

coloured (GB), **colored** (US) *adj* [*pen, paper, bead*] de couleur; [*picture*] en couleur; [*light, glass*] coloré.

colour: **~-fast** *adj* grand teint *inv*; **~ filter** *n* filtre *m* coloré.

colourful (GB), **colorful** (US) *adj* **1** [*dress, shirt*] aux couleurs vives; **2** [*story, life*] haut en couleur; [*character*] pittoresque.

colouring (GB), **coloring** (US) *n* **1** (of plant, animal) couleurs *fpl*; **2** (complexion) teint *m*; **3** (decoration) coloriage *m*; **~ book** album *m* à colorier; **4** (for food) colorant *m*.

colour: **~ scheme** *n* couleurs *fpl*, coloris *m*; **~ supplement** *n* supplément *m* illustré; **~ television** *n* télévision *f* (en) couleur.

colt *n* poulain *m*.

column *n* **1** (pillar) colonne *f*; **2** (on page, list) colonne *f*; **3** (newspaper article) rubrique *f*; **sports ~** rubrique sportive; **letters ~** courrier *m* des lecteurs.

columnist *n* journaliste *mf*.

coma *n* coma *m*; **in a ~** dans le coma; **to go into a ~** entrer dans le coma.

comb I *n* peigne *m*.

II *vtr* **to ~ sb's hair** peigner qn; **to ~ one's hair** se peigner.

combat I *n* combat *m*; **in ~** au combat; **close ~** combat rapproché.

II *vtr* lutter contre, combattre.

combat jacket *n* veste *f* de treillis.

combination *n* **1** (mixture) combinaison *f* (**of** de); (of factors) conjonction *f*; **2** (mixing) mélange *m* (**of** de); **3** (of numbers) combinaison *f*; **~ lock** serrure *f* à combinaison.

combine I *vtr* **1** (link) combiner [*activities, colours, items*] (**with** avec); associer [*ideas, aims*] (**with** à); **to ~ two companies** regrouper deux sociétés; **to ~ forces** (merge) s'allier; (cooperate) collaborer; **2** (Culin) (mix) mélanger (**with** avec).

II *vi* **1** (go together) [*activities, colours, elements*] se combiner (**to do** pour faire); **2** (join) [*people, groups*] s'associer; [*institutions, firms*] fusionner (**into** en).

combined *adj* **1** (joint) **a ~ effort** une collaboration; **2** [*salary, age*] total; **3** [*effects*] combiné; [*forces*] conjoint; **~ with** combiné avec.

combined pill *n* pilule *f* combinée.

combine harvester *n* moissonneuse-batteuse *f*.

combustion *n* combustion *f*; **internal ~ engine** moteur *m* à combustion interne.

come I *vtr* **to ~ 100 km to see sb/sth** faire 100 km pour voir qn/qch.

II *vi* **1** (arrive) [*person, day, fame*] venir; [*bus, news, winter, war*] arriver; **to ~ after sb** poursuivre qn; **to ~ by taxi** prendre un taxi; **I came on foot/by bike** je suis venu à pied/à bicyclette; **to ~ down** descendre [*stairs, street*]; **to ~ up** monter [*stairs, street*]; **to ~ from** venir de [*airport, hospital*]; **to ~ into** entrer dans [*house, room*]; **to ~ through** [*person*] passer par [*town centre, tunnel*]; [*water, object*] traverser [*window*]; **to ~ to** venir à [*school, telephone*]; **to ~ to the door** venir ouvrir; **to ~ running** arriver en courant; **when the time ~s** lorsque le moment sera venu; **the time has come to do** le moment est venu de faire; **(I'm) coming!** j'arrive!; **to ~ and go** aller et venir; **you can ~ and go as you please** tu es libre de tes mouvements; **there's still the speech to ~** il y a encore le discours; **2** (approach) s'approcher; **to ~ and help sb** venir aider qn; **to ~ to sb for** venir demander [qch] à qn [*money, advice*]; **don't ~ any closer** ne vous approchez pas (plus); **3** (call, visit) [*dustman, postman*] passer; [*cleaner*] venir;

Colours

Not all English colour terms have a single exact equivalent in French: eg in some cases ***brown*** is ***marron***, in others ***brun***. If in doubt, look the word up in the dictionary.

Colour terms

what colour *is it?*	= il / elle est **de quelle couleur**?
	= (*more formally*) **de quelle couleur** est-il / est-elle?
it's green	= il est vert / elle est verte
to paint something green	= peindre quelque chose en vert
dressed in green	= habillé en vert
green suits her	= le vert lui va bien

Most adjectives of colour agree with the noun they modify:

a blue coat / dress	= un manteau **bleu** / une robe **bleue**

But some words that translate English adjectives are really nouns in French, and so don't show agreement:

brown shoes / eyes	= des chaussures *fpl* / les yeux *mpl* **marron**
orange tablecloths	= des nappes *fpl* **orange**

Shades of colour

Expressions like ***pale blue***, ***dark green*** or ***light yellow*** are also invariable in French and show no agreement:

a ***blue*** */* ***pale blue*** *shirt*	= une chemise **bleue** / **bleu pâle**
green */* ***dark green*** *blankets*	= des couvertures *fpl* **vertes** / **vert foncé**

In the following examples, ***blue*** stands for most basic colour terms:

pale */* ***light*** */* ***bright*** *blue*	= bleu **pâle** / **clair** / **vif**
a ***navy-blue*** *jacket*	= une veste **bleu marine**

For colour terms with the ending ***-ish***, to show that something is approximately a certain colour, the French equivalent is ***-âtre***:

bluish	= bleuâtre

Note that these words are often rather negative in French. It is better not to use them if you want to be complimentary. Use instead ***tirant sur le rouge*** / ***jaune*** etc.

English colour compounds consisting of a *noun* + *-coloured* are translated as follows:

a ***chocolate-coloured*** *skirt*	= une jupe **couleur chocolat**

Colour verbs

to blacken / redden / whiten	= noircir / rougir / blanchir

Other French colour terms that behave like this are: ***bleu*** (*bleuir*), ***jaune*** (*jaunir*), ***rose*** (*rosir*) and ***vert*** (*verdir*). It is always safe, however, to use ***devenir***, thus:

to ***turn*** *purple*	= **devenir** violet

Describing people

Note the use of the definite article in the following:

to have ***blue eyes***	= avoir **les yeux bleus**

Note the use of ***à*** in the following:

a girl ***with*** *blue eyes*	= une jeune fille **aux** yeux bleus

Note these nouns in French:

a fair-haired man / woman	= un blond / une blonde
a dark-haired man / woman	= un brun / une brune

I've come to repair the radiator je viens réparer le radiateur; **my brother is coming for me at 10 am** mon frère passe me prendre à 10 heures; **4** (attend) venir; **to ~ to** venir à [*meeting, party*]; **5** (reach) **to ~ up/down to** [*water*] venir jusqu'à; [*dress, curtain*] arriver à; **6** (happen) **how ~?** comment ça se fait?; **to take things as they ~** prendre les choses comme elles viennent; **~ to think of it** en fait; **7** (begin) **to ~ to hate** finir par détester; **8** (originate) **to ~ from** [*person*] être originaire de, venir de [*city, country*]; [*word, legend*] venir de [*country, language*]; [*substance*] provenir de [*raw material*]; [*coins, stamps, painting*] provenir de [*place*]; [*smell, sound*] venir de [*place*]; **9** (be available) **to ~ in** exister en [*sizes, colours*]; **10** (tackle) **to ~ to** aborder [*problem, subject*]; **I'll ~ to that in a moment** je reviendrai sur ce point dans un moment; **11** (develop) **it ~s with practice** cela s'apprend avec la pratique; **wisdom ~ s with age** la sagesse vient en vieillissant; **12** (be situated) venir; **to ~ after** suivre, venir après; **to ~ before** (in time, list, queue) précéder; (in importance) passer avant; **to ~ first/last** (in race) arriver premier/dernier; **my family ~s first** ma famille passe avant tout; **don't let this ~ between us** on ne va pas se fâcher pour ça; **to ~ between two people** s'interposer entre deux personnes; **13 when it ~s to sth/to doing** lorsqu'il s'agit de qch/de faire.

IDIOMS **I don't know if I'm coming or going** je ne sais plus où j'en suis.

■ **come across**: ¶ **~ across** [*meaning, message*] passer; [*feelings*] transparaître; **she ~s across well on TV** elle passe bien à la télé; **~ across as** donner l'impression d'être [*liar, expert*]; paraître [*honest*]; ¶ **~ across [sth]** tomber sur [*article*].

■ **come along 1** [*bus, person*] arriver; [*opportunity*] se présenter; **2** (hurry up) **~ along!** dépêche-toi!; **3** (attend) venir (**to** à); **4** (make progress) [*pupil*] faire des progrès; [*book, work, project*] avancer; [*painting, tennis*] progresser; [*seedling*] pousser.

■ **come apart 1** (accidentally) [*book, box*] se déchirer; [*toy, camera*] se casser; **2** (intentionally) [*components*] se séparer; [*machine*] se démonter.

■ **come around** (US) = **come round**.

■ **come away** partir; **to ~ away from** quitter [*cinema, match*]; sortir de [*meeting*]; **to ~ away with the feeling that** rester sur l'impression que.

■ **come back 1** (return) revenir (**from** de; **to** à); (to one's house) rentrer; **to ~ running back** revenir en courant; **to ~ back to** revenir à [*topic, problem*]; **to ~ back with sb** raccompagner qn; **to ~ back with** revenir avec [*present, idea, flu*]; (reply) répondre par [*offer, suggestion*]; **can I ~ back to you on that?** est-ce que nous pourrions en reparler?; **2** [*law, system*] être rétabli; [*trend*] revenir à la mode.

■ **come down 1** (move lower) [*person, lift, blind*] descendre; [*curtain*] tomber; **2** (drop) [*price, inflation, temperature*] baisser (**from** de; **to** à); [*cost*] diminuer; **3** (in showers) [*snow, rain*] tomber; **4** (crash) [*plane*] s'écraser; **5** (fall) [*ceiling, wall*] s'écrouler; [*hem*] se défaire; **6** (catch) **to ~ down with** attraper [*flu*].

■ **come forward 1** (step forward) s'avancer; **2** (volunteer) se présenter.

■ **come in 1** (enter) entrer (**through** par); **2** (return) rentrer (**from** de); **3** (come inland) [*tide*] monter; **4** (arrive) arriver; **5** (become current) [*trend, invention*] faire son apparition; **6** (serve purpose) **to ~ in useful** être utile; **7** (receive) **to ~ in for criticism** [*person*] être critiqué; [*plan*] faire l'objet de nombreuses critiques.

■ **come into**: **~ into [sth]**: **to ~ into it** [*age, experience*] entrer en ligne de compte, jouer; **luck doesn't ~ into it** ce n'est pas une question de hasard.

■ **come off 1** (become detached) [*button, handle*] se détacher; [*lid*] s'enlever; [*paint*] s'écailler; **2** (wash, rub off) [*ink*] s'effacer; [*stain*] partir; **3** (succeed) [*plan, trick*] réussir.

■ **come on 1** (exhortation) **~ on!** allez!; **2** (make progress) [*person, patient*] faire des progrès; [*bridge, novel*] avancer; [*plant*] pousser; **3** (start to work) [*light*] s'allumer; [*heating, fan*] se mettre en route; **4** (appear) [*actor*] entrer en scène.

■ **come out 1** (emerge) [*person, animal, vehicle*] sortir (**of** de); [*star*] apparaître; [*sun, moon*] se montrer; **2** (originate) **to ~ out of** [*news report*] provenir de; **the money will have to ~ out of your savings** il faudra prendre l'argent sur tes économies; **3** (strike) faire la grève; **to ~ out on strike** faire la grève; **4** (fall out) [*contact lens, tooth*] tomber; [*contents*] sortir; [*cork*] s'enlever; **5** (be emitted) [*water, smoke*] sortir (**through** par); **6** (wash out) [*stain*] s'en aller, partir; **7** [*magazine, novel*] paraître; [*album, film, product*] sortir; **8** [*feelings*] se manifester; [*details, facts*] être révélé; [*results*] être connu; **9** [*photo, photocopy*] être réussi; **10** (say) **to ~ out with** sortir [*excuse*]; raconter [*nonsense*]; **to ~ straight out with it** le dire franchement.

■ **come over**: ¶ **~ over 1** (drop in) venir (**to** do faire); **~ over for a drink** venez prendre un verre; **2** (travel) venir; **3** (convey impression) [*message*] passer; [*feelings*] transparaître; **to ~ over very well** [*person*] donner une très bonne impression; ¶ **~ over [sb]** [*feeling*] envahir; **what's come over you?** qu'est-ce qui te prend?

■ **come round** (GB), **come around** (US) **1** (regain consciousness) reprendre connaissance; **2** (circulate) [*waitress*] passer; **3** (visit) venir; **4** (change mind) changer d'avis; **to ~ round to my way of thinking** se rallier à mon point de vue.

■ **come through**: ¶ **~ through 1** (survive) s'en tirer; **2** (penetrate) [*heat, ink*] traverser; [*light*] passer; **3** (emerge) apparaître; ¶ **~ through [sth]** se tirer de [*crisis*]; se sortir de [*recession*]; survivre à [*operation, ordeal*].

■ **come to**: ¶ **~ to** reprendre connaissance; ¶ **~ to [sth]** [*shopping*] revenir à; [*bill, total*] s'élever à; **that ~s to £40** cela fait 40 livres sterling; **it may not ~ to that** nous n'en arriverons peut-être pas là.

■ **come under 1** (be subjected to) **to ~ under**

scrutiny faire l'objet d'un examen minutieux; **to ~ under suspicion/threat** être soupçonné/menacé; **2** (be classified under) être classé dans le rayon [*reference, history*].

■ **come up 1** [*problem, issue*] être soulevé; [*name*] être mentionné; **2** (be due) **my salary ~s up for review in April** mon salaire sera révisé en avril; **3** (occur) [*opportunity*] se présenter; **something urgent has come up** j'ai quelque chose d'urgent à faire; **a vacancy has come up** une place s'est libérée; **4** (rise) [*sun, moon*] sortir; [*tide*] monter; [*daffodils*] sortir; **5** [*case*] passer au tribunal; **6 to ~ up against** se heurter à [*problem*]; **7** (find) **to ~ up with** trouver.

comeback *n* **1** (of musician, actor, boxer) comeback *m*; **to make a ~** [*person*] faire un comeback; **2** (redress) recours *m*.

comedian ▶805 *n* (male) comique *m*; (also **comedienne**) actrice *f* comique.

comedy *n* comédie *f*; **black ~** comédie *f* macabre.

comet *n* comète *f*.

comfort I *n* **1** (well-being) confort *m*; (wealth) aisance *f*; **to live in ~** vivre dans l'aisance; **2** (amenity) confort *m*; **every modern ~** tout le confort moderne; **home ~s** le confort du foyer; **3** (consolation) réconfort *m*, consolation *f*; (relief from pain) soulagement *m*.

II *vtr* consoler; (stronger) réconforter.

comfortable *adj* **1** [*chair, clothes, journey*] confortable; [*temperature*] agréable; **2** (relaxed) [*person*] à l'aise; **to make sb feel ~** mettre qn à l'aise; **3** (financially) [*person*] aisé; **4** [*idea, thought*] sécurisant.

comfortably *adv* **1** (physically, financially) confortablement; **2** (easily) facilement, aisément.

comforting *adj* réconfortant.

comical *adj* cocasse, comique.

comic strip *n* bande *f* dessinée.

coming I *n* **1** (arrival) arrivée *f*; **~ and going** va-et-vient *m inv*; **~s and goings** allées et venues *fpl*; **2** (of winter, old age) approche *f*; (of new era, event) arrivée *f*.

II *adj* [*election, event*] prochain (*before n*); [*months, weeks*] à venir.

comma *n* virgule *f*.

command I *n* **1** (order) ordre *m*; **to carry out a ~** exécuter un ordre; **2** (military control) commandement *m*; **to be in ~** commander; **to be under the ~ of sb** être sous les ordres de qn; **~ of the air** maîtrise *f* du ciel; **3** (mastery) maîtrise *f*; **an excellent ~ of Russian** une excellente maîtrise du russe; **to be in ~ of the situation** avoir la situation en main; **4** (Comput) commande *f*.

II *vtr* **1** ordonner à [*person*] (**to do** de faire); **2** inspirer [*affection, respect*]; **to ~ a good price** se vendre cher; **3** (Mil) commander [*regiment*]; maîtriser [*air, sea*].

commandant *n* (Mil) commandant *m*.

commander *n* (gen) chef *m*; (Mil) commandant *m*.

commanding *adj* [*manner, voice*] impérieux/-ieuse; [*presence*] imposant.

commandment *n* **1** (order) injonction *f*; **2** (in religion) commandement *m*.

commando *n* commando *m*.

commemorate *vtr* commémorer.

commend *vtr* louer (**on** pour); **to have much to ~ it** avoir de grandes qualités.

commendable *adj* louable; **highly ~** très louable.

comment I *n* **1** (public) commentaire *m* (**on** sur); (in conversation) remarque *f* (**on** sur); (written) annotation *f*; **2** (discussion) commentaires *mpl* (**about** portant sur); **'no ~'** 'je n'ai pas de déclaration à faire'; **3** (reflection) **to be a ~ on** en dire long sur.

II *vi* **1** (remark) faire des commentaires *mpl* (**on** sur); **2** (discuss) **to ~ on** commenter [*text*].

commentary *n* commentaire *m* (**on** de).

commentate *vi* faire le commentaire; **to ~ on** commenter [*sporting event*].

commentator ▶805 *n* (sports) commentateur/-trice *m/f*; (current affairs) journaliste *mf*.

commerce *n* commerce *m*; **in ~** dans les affaires.

commercial I *n* annonce *f* publicitaire, publicité *f*; **TV ~** annonce publicitaire à la télé.

II *adj* [*airline, sector, radio, product*] commercial.

commercial: **~ artist** *n* graphiste *mf*; **~ break** *n* publicité *f*; **~ law** *n* droit *m* commercial; **~ traveller** (GB), **~ traveler** (US) ▶805 *n* voyageur *m* de commerce; **~ vehicle** *n* véhicule *m* utilitaire.

commiserate *vi* compatir (**with** avec; **about, over** à propos de).

commission I *n* **1** (for goods sold) commission *f*; **to get a 5% ~** recevoir une commission de 5%; **to work on ~** travailler à la commission; **2** (fee) commission *f*; **to charge 1% ~ on** prendre 1% de commission sur; **3** (order) commande *f* (**for** de); **to give sb a ~** passer une commande à qn; **4** (committee) commission *f* (**on** sur).

II *vtr* **1** (order) commander (**from** à); **a ~ed portrait** un portrait sur commande; **2** (instruct) **to ~ sb to do** charger qn de faire; **3** (Mil) **to be ~ed (as) an officer** être nommé officier.

commissioner *n* **1** (gen) membre *m* d'une commission; **2** (GB) (in police) = préfet *m* de police; **3** (in the EC) membre *m* de la Commission européenne.

commit *vtr* **1** (perpetrate) commettre [*crime, error*]; **to ~ adultery** commettre un adultère; **2 to ~ oneself** s'engager (**to** à); **I can't ~ myself** je ne peux rien promettre; **3** (Law) **to ~ sb for trial** mettre qn en accusation.

commitment *n* **1** (obligation) engagement *m* (**to do** à faire); **to meet one's ~s** honorer ses engagements; **family ~s** obligations *fpl* familiales; **2** (sense of duty) attachement *m* (**to** à).

committed *adj* **1** (devoted) [*parent, teacher*] dévoué; [*Christian, Socialist*] fervent; **to be ~ to/to doing** se consacrer à/à faire; **to be politically ~** être engagé politiquement; **2** (by obligations) pris (**to doing** pour faire); **I am heavily**

~ (timewise) je suis très pris; (financially) j'ai de lourds engagements.

committee *n* comité *m*; (to investigate, report) commission *f*.

commodity *n* **1** (commercial item) article *m*; (food) denrée *f*; **2** (on stock market) matière *f* première.

common I *n* terrain *m* communal.
II **commons** *n pl* (also **Commons**) **the ~s** les Communes *fpl*.
III *adj* **1** (frequent) courant, fréquent; **in ~ use** d'un usage courant; **2** (shared) commun (**to** à); **in ~** en commun; **it is ~ property** c'est la propriété de tous; **it is ~ knowledge** c'est de notoriété publique; **3** (ordinary) [*man*] du peuple; **the ~ people** le peuple; **a ~ criminal** un criminel ordinaire; **4** (low-class) commun; **it looks/sounds ~** ça fait commun.

common: **~ cold** ▶686| *n* rhume *m* de cerveau; **~ ground** *n* terrain *m* d'entente; **~-law husband** *n* concubin *m*; **~-law wife** *n* concubine *f*.

commonly *adv* communément; **~ known as** communément appelé.

common: **Common Market** *n* Marché *m* commun; **~ noun** *n* nom *m* commun; **~ room** *n* salle *f* de détente; **~ sense** *n* bon sens *m*, sens *m* commun.

commotion *n* **1** (noise) vacarme *m*, brouhaha *m*; **to make a ~** faire du vacarme; **2** (disturbance) émoi *m*, agitation *f*; **to cause a ~** causer un grand émoi.

communal *adj* [*property, area, showers*] commun; [*garden, facilities*] collectif/-ive; [*life*] communautaire; **~ ownership** copropriété *f*.

commune *n* communauté *f*; **to live in a ~** vivre en communauté.

communicate I *vtr* communiquer [*ideas, feelings*] (**to** à); transmettre [*information*] (**to** à).
II *vi* communiquer (**by** par; **through** au moyen de; **with** avec).

communication I *n* **1** (of information) transmission *f*; (of ideas, feelings) communication *f*; **2** (contact) communication *f*; **the lines of ~** les voies *fpl* de communication; **to be in ~ with sb** être en communication or en contact avec qn; **3** (message) communication *f*.
II **communications** *n pl* communications *fpl*, liaison *f*.

communication: **~ cord** *n* (GB) sonnette *f* d'alarme; **~s link** *n* liaison *f*; **~s satellite** *n* satellite *m* de communication.

communicator *n* **to be a good ~** avoir le sens de la communication.

Communion *n* (sainte) communion *f*, Eucharistie *f*; **to make one's First ~** faire sa première communion.

Communist, **communist** *n, adj* communiste (*mf*).

community I *n* communauté *f*; **the Italian ~** la communauté italienne; **the business ~** le monde des affaires; **relations between the police and the ~** les relations entre la police et le public.
II **Community** *pr n* **the (European) Community** la Communauté (Européenne).

community: **~ care** *n* soins *mpl* en dehors du milieu hospitalier; **~ centre** (GB), **~ center** (US) *n* maison *f* de quartier; **~ health centre** (GB), **~ health center** (US) *n* centre *m* médico-social; **~ life** *n* vie *f* associative; **~ policing** *n* ≈ îlotage *m*; **~ service** *n* travail *m* d'intérêt public; **~ spirit** *n* esprit *m* communautaire; **~ worker** *n* animateur/-trice *m/f* socio-culturel/-elle.

commute *vi* **to ~ between Oxford and London** faire le trajet entre Oxford et Londres tous les jours; **she ~s to Glasgow** elle se rend à Glasgow tous les jours.

commuter *n* navetteur/-euse *m/f*, migrant/-e *m/f* journalier/-ière.

commuter: **~ belt** *n* grande banlieue *f*; **~ train** *n* train *m* de banlieue.

compact I *n* poudrier *m*.
II *adj* **1** [*snow*] compact, dense; **2** (neat) compact.

companion *n* **1** (friend) compagnon/compagne *m/f*; **2** (object) pendant *m* (**to** de).

company I *n* **1** (enterprise) société *f*; **airline ~** compagnie *f* aérienne; **2** (artistic) troupe *f*, compagnie *f*; **theatre ~** troupe *f* de théâtre, compagnie *f* théâtrale; **3** (Mil) compagnie *f*; **4** (companionship) compagnie *f*; **to keep sb ~** tenir compagnie à qn; **to be good ~** être d'une compagnie agréable; **to keep bad ~** avoir de mauvaises fréquentations; **to be fit ~ for sb** être une fréquentation pour qn; **5** (visitors) visiteurs *mpl*; **to have ~** avoir du monde; **6** (society) **in ~** en société; **Lisa and ~** Lisa et compagnie○.
II *noun modifier* [*law, profits*] des sociétés; [*headquarters*] de la société.

company: **~ car** *n* voiture *f* de fonction; **~ director** ▶805| *n* directeur/-trice *m/f* général/-e; **~ name** *n* (Law) raison *f* sociale; **~ pension scheme** *n* régime *m* de retraite de l'entreprise; **~ policy** *n* politique *f* de l'entreprise; **~ secretary** ▶805| *n* secrétaire *mf* général/-e; **~ tax** *n* impôt *m* sur les sociétés.

comparable *adj* comparable (**to, with** à).

comparative I *n* (in grammar) comparatif *m*.
II *adj* **1** (in grammar) comparatif/-ive; **2** (relative) relatif/-ive; **in ~ terms** en termes relatifs; **3** [*study*] comparatif/-ive; [*literature*] comparé.

compare I *vtr* comparer; **to ~ sb/sth with** or **to** comparer qn/qch à or avec; **to ~ oneself with** or **to** se comparer à; **~d with sb/sth** par rapport à qn/qch; **to ~ notes with sb** échanger ses impressions avec qn.
II *vi* être comparable (**with** à); **to ~ favourably with** soutenir la comparaison avec; **how does this job ~ with your last one?** comment trouvez-vous cet emploi par rapport au précédent?

comparison *n* comparaison *f*; **in** or **by ~ with** par rapport à.

compartment *n* compartiment *m*.

compass *n* boussole *f*; (also **ship's ~**)

compas *m*; **the points of the ~** les points *mpl* cardinaux.

compassion *n* compassion *f* (**for** pour).

compassionate *adj* compatissant; **on ~ grounds** pour raisons *fpl* personnelles; **~ leave** (Mil) permission *f* exceptionnelle.

compatible *adj* compatible (**with** avec); **X-~** (Comput) compatible X.

compel *vtr* contraindre (**to do** à faire), obliger (**to do** de faire).

compelling *adj* [*reason, argument*] convaincant; [*speaker*] fascinant.

compensate I *vtr* dédommager, indemniser [*person*]; **to ~ sb for loss of earnings** dédommager qn d'un manque à gagner.
II *vi* compenser; **to ~ for** compenser [*loss, difficulty*].

compensation *n* **1** (gen) compensation *f* (**for** de); **2** (Law) indemnisation *f*.

compete *vi* **1** (for prominence, job, prize) rivaliser; **to ~ against** or **with** rivaliser avec (**for** pour obtenir); **to ~ for the same job** se disputer le même emploi; **I just can't ~ (with her)** je ne peux pas lui faire concurrence; **2** (commercially) [*companies*] se faire concurrence; **to ~ with** faire concurrence à (**for** pour obtenir); **3** (Sport) être en compétition (**against, with** avec); **to ~ in** participer à [*Olympics, race*].

competence *n* **1** (ability) compétence *f*; **to have the ~ to do** avoir la compétence voulue pour faire; **2** (skill) compétences *fpl*; **~ in word-processing** connaissances *fpl* en traitement de texte.

competent *adj* **1** (capable) compétent, capable; (trained) qualifié; **2** (adequate) [*performance*] honorable; [*knowledge*] suffisant; [*answer*] satisfaisant.

competition *n* **1** (rivalry) concurrence *f*, compétition *f* (**between** entre); **in ~ with** en concurrence or compétition avec (**for** pour); **2** (for prize, award, job) concours *m*; (race) compétition *f*; **3** (competitors) concurrence *f*, compétition *f*.

competitive *adj* **1** [*person*] qui a l'esprit de compétition; [*environment*] compétitif/-ive; **2** [*price, product*] compétitif/-ive; **~ edge** avantage *m* concurrentiel; **~ tender** appel *m* d'offres; **3** [*sport*] de compétition; **by ~ examination** sur concours.

competitor *n* concurrent/-e *m/f*.

compile *vtr* **1** (gen) dresser [*list, catalogue*]; établir [*report*]; **2** (Comput) compiler.

compiler *n* compilateur/-trice *m/f*.

complacent *adj* suffisant; **to be ~ about** être trop confiant de [*success, future*].

complain *vi* se plaindre (**to** à; **about** de; **of** de); (officially) se plaindre (**to** auprès de); **I can't ~** je n'ai pas à me plaindre.

complaint *n* plainte *f* (**about** concernant, au sujet de); (official) réclamation *f* (**about** concernant, au sujet de); **there have been ~s about the noise** on s'est plaint du bruit; **to have grounds** or **cause for ~** avoir lieu de se plaindre; **to file a ~ against sb** déposer une plainte or porter plainte contre qn.

complement *vtr* compléter; **to ~ one another** se compléter.

complete I *adj* **1** (total, utter) complet/-ète, total; **he's a ~ fool** il est complètement idiot; **it's the ~ opposite** c'est tout à fait le contraire; **with ~ confidence** avec une confiance totale; **2** (finished) achevé; **3** (entire, full) [*collection, works, set*] complet/-ète.
II *vtr* **1** (finish) terminer [*building, course, exercise*]; achever [*task, journey*]; **half ~d** inachevé; **2** (make whole) compléter [*collection, phrase*]; **3** (fill in) remplir [*form*].

completely *adv* complètement.

completion *n* **1** (of task) achèvement *m* (**of** de); **2** (of house sale) signature *f* de la vente.

complex I *n* **1** (development) complexe *m*; **sports/housing ~** complexe sportif/résidentiel; **2** (problem) complexe *m*; **he's got a ~ about his weight** son poids lui donne un complexe.
II *adj* complexe.

complexion *n* teint *m*; **to have a fair/dark ~** avoir un teint clair/mat.

complexity *n* complexité *f*.

complicate *vtr* compliquer; **to ~ matters** compliquer les choses.

complication *n* **1** (problem) inconvénient *m*, problème *m*; **2** (Med) complication *f*.

compliment I *n* compliment *m*; **to pay sb a ~** faire un compliment à qn.
II compliments *n pl* **1** (in expressions of praise) compliments *mpl* (**to** à); **to give sb one's ~s** faire ses compliments à qn; **2** (in expressions, greetings) **'with ~s'** (on slip) 'avec tous nos compliments'; **'with the ~s of the season'** 'meilleurs vœux'.
III *vtr* complimenter, faire des compliments à.

comply *vi* **to ~ with** se conformer à [*orders*]; respecter, observer [*rules*].

component *n* (gen) composante *f*; (in car, machine) pièce *f*; (electrical) composant *m*.

compose *vtr* **1** (gen, Mus) composer; **2** (arrange) composer [*painting*]; **3** (order) composer [*features*]; rassembler [*thoughts*]; **4** (constitute) **~d of** composé de.

composed *adj* calme.

composer ▶ 805 *n* compositeur/-trice *m/f* (**of** de).

composition *n* **1** (make-up) composition *f* (**of** de); **2** (Mus) composition *f* (**of** de); **3** (essay) rédaction *f* (**about, on** sur); **4** (of picture) composition *f*.

compost *n* compost *m*.

composure *n* calme *m*; **to regain one's ~** retrouver son calme.

compound I *n* **1** (enclosure) enceinte *f*; **prison ~** enceinte *f* de prison; **workers' ~** quartier *m* de travailleurs; **2** (in chemistry) composé *m* (**of** de); **3** (word) mot *m* composé.
II *adj* **1** (in science) composé; **2** [*tense, noun*] composé; [*sentence*] complexe; **3** (Med) [*fracture*] multiple; **4** [*interest*] composé.

comprehension *n* (Sch, Univ) exercice *m* de compréhension.

comprehensive I *n* (GB Sch) école *f* (publique) secondaire.
II *adj* [*report, list*] complet/-ète, détaillé; [*knowledge*] étendu; [*planning*] global; [*training*] complet/-ète; **~ insurance policy** assurance *f* tous risques.

compromise I *n* compromis *m*; **to reach a ~** arriver or aboutir à un compromis.
II *vtr* compromettre [*person, principles, chances*]; **to ~ oneself** se compromettre.
III *vi* transiger, arriver à un compromis; **to ~ on sth** trouver un compromis sur qch.

compulsive *adj* **1** (inveterate) invétéré; (psychologically) compulsif/-ive; **~ eater** boulimique *mf*; **2** (fascinating) fascinant; **to be ~ viewing** être fascinant.

compulsory *adj* obligatoire.

computer *n* ordinateur *m*; **to have sth on ~** avoir qch sur ordinateur; **the ~ is up/down** l'ordinateur fonctionne/est en panne.

computer: **~-aided design**, **CAD** *n* conception *f* assistée par ordinateur, CAO *f*; **~-aided language learning**, **CALL** *n* apprentissage *m* des langues assisté par ordinateur; **~ dating service** *n* club *m* de rencontres (*utilisant un ordinateur*); **~ engineer** ▶805 *n* technicien/-ienne *m/f* en informatique; **~ game** *n* jeu *m* informatique; **~ graphics** *n* infographie *f*; **~ hacker** *n* pirate *m* informatique.

computerize *vtr* mettre [qch] sur ordinateur [*accounts*]; informatiser [*list*].

computer: **~ keyboard** *n* clavier *m* d'ordinateur; **~ language** *n* langage *m* de programmation; **~-literate** *adj* ayant des notions d'informatique; **~ operator** ▶805 *n* opérateur/-trice *m/f* sur ordinateur; **~ program** *n* programme *m* informatique; **~ programmer** ▶805 *n* programmeur/-euse *m/f*; **~ programming** *n* programmation *f*; **~ science** *n* informatique *f*; **~ scientist** ▶805 *n* informaticien/-ienne *m/f*; **~ studies** *n* informatique *f*; **~ virus** *n* virus *m* informatique.

computing *n* informatique *f*.

comradeship *n* camaraderie *f*.

con *n* escroquerie *f*, arnaque◑ *f*.

conceal I *vtr* dissimuler (**from** à).
II **concealed** *pp adj* caché.

concede *vtr* **1** (admit) concéder [*point*]; **to ~ that** reconnaître que; **2** (surrender) accorder [*right*] (**to** à); céder [*territory*] (**to** à); **3** (Sport) concéder [*point, goal*]; **4** (in politics) **to ~ an election** concéder la victoire électorale (**to** à).

conceit *n* suffisance *f*.

conceited *adj* [*person*] vaniteux/-euse; [*remark*] suffisant.

conceive *vi* concevoir, devenir enceinte.

concentrate I *n* concentré *m*; **tomato ~** concentré de tomates.
II *vtr* concentrer [*effort*] (**on** sur; **on doing** pour faire); employer [*resources*] (**on** sur; **on doing** à faire); centrer [*attention*] (**on** sur).
III *vi* **1** (pay attention) [*person*] se concentrer (**on** sur); **to ~ on doing** s'appliquer à faire; **2** (focus) **to ~ on** [*film, journalist*] s'intéresser surtout à.

concentration *n* concentration *f* (**on** sur); **my powers of ~** mon pouvoir de concentration; **to lose one's ~** se déconcentrer.

concept *n* concept *m*.

conception *n* (Med) conception *f* (**of** de).

concern I *n* **1** (worry) inquiétude *f* (**about** à propos de); **to cause ~** être inquiétant; **there is no cause for ~** il n'y a pas lieu d'être inquiet; **he expressed ~ at my results** il m'a fait part de son inquiétude quant à mes résultats; **2** (preoccupation) préoccupation *f*; **environmental ~s** des préoccupations écologiques; **3** (care) (for person) prévenance *f*; **I did it out of ~ for him** je l'ai fait par égard pour lui; **4** (company) entreprise *f*; **a going ~** une affaire rentable.
II *vtr* **1** (worry) inquiéter; **2** (affect, interest) concerner, intéresser; **to whom it may ~** à qui de droit; (in letter) Monsieur; **as far as the pay is ~ed** en ce qui concerne le salaire; **3** (involve) **to be ~ed with** s'occuper de [*security, publicity*]; **4** (be about) [*book, programme*] traiter de; [*fax, letter*] concerner.

concerned *adj* **1** (anxious) inquiet/-ète (**about** à propos de); **to be ~ at the news** trouver la nouvelle inquiétante; **to be ~ that sb might be upset** être inquiet/-iète à l'idée que qn soit vexé; **to be ~ for sb** se faire du souci pour qn; **2** (involved) concerné; **all (those) ~** toutes les personnes concernées.

concerning *prep* concernant.

concert I *n* concert *m*; **in ~ at/with** en concert à/avec.
II *noun modifier* [*music, ticket, pianist*] de concert.

concert: **~goer** *n* habitué/-e *m/f* des concerts; **~ hall** *n* salle *f* de concert; **~ performer** *n* concertiste *mf*; **~ tour** *n* tournée *f*.

concession *n* **1** (compromise) concession *f* (**on** sur; **to** à); **as a ~** à titre de concession; **2** (discount) réduction *f*; **'~s'** 'tarif réduit'.

concessionaire *n* concessionnaire *mf*.

conciliation *n* conciliation *f*; **~ service** commission *f* de conciliation.

conciliatory *adj* [*gesture, terms*] conciliant; [*measures*] conciliatoire.

concise *adj* concis.

conclude I *vtr* **1** (finish) conclure, terminer; **2** (deduce) conclure (**from** de).
II *vi* [*story, event*] se terminer (**with** par, sur); [*speaker*] conclure (**with** par).

conclusion *n* **1** (end) fin *f*; **in ~** en conclusion, pour terminer; **2** (opinion, resolution) conclusion *f*; **to come to a ~** arriver à une conclusion; **to draw a ~ from sth** tirer une conclusion de qch; **don't jump to ~s!** ne tire pas de conclusions hâtives!

conclusive *adj* concluant.

concrete I *n* béton *m*.
II *adj* **1** [*block*] de béton; [*base*] en béton; **2** (real) concret/-ète.

concuss *vtr* **to be ~ed** être commotionné.

concussion *n* commotion *f* cérébrale.

condemn *vtr* **1** (censure) condamner (**for doing** pour avoir fait); **to ~ sth as pointless** condamner la futilité de qch; **to ~ sb as an opportunist** dénoncer l'opportunisme de qn; **2** (sentence) **to ~ sb to death/life imprisonment** condamner qn à mort/à perpétuité; **3** (doom) **to be ~ed to do** être condamné à faire; **4** (declare unsafe) déclarer [qch] inhabitable [*building*].

condemnation *n* **1** (censure) condamnation *f*; **2** (indictment) **to be a ~ of sb/sth** remettre qn/qch en question.

condensation *n* (on walls) condensation *f*; (on windows) buée *f*.

condensed milk *n* lait *m* concentré sucré or condensé.

condescending *adj* condescendant.

condition I *n* **1** (stipulation) condition *f*; **to meet** or **satisfy the ~s** remplir les conditions; **on ~ that you come** à condition que tu viennes; **2** (state) état *m*, condition *f*; **to be in good/bad ~** [*house, car*] être en bon/mauvais état; **to be in a critical ~** être dans un état critique; **3** (disease) maladie *f*; **a heart/skin ~** une maladie cardiaque/de la peau.
II conditions *n pl* conditions *fpl*; **housing/living ~s** conditions de logement/de vie; **weather ~s** conditions météorologiques.

conditional *n* conditionnel *m*; **in the ~** au conditionnel.

conditioner *n* après-shampooing *m*, démêlant *m*.

conditioning *n* **1** (of person) conditionnement *m*; **2** (of hair) traitement *m*.

condolence *n* **letter of ~** lettre *f* de condoléance.

condolences *n pl* condoléances *fpl*.

condom *n* préservatif *m*.

condominium *n* (US) (also **~ unit**) appartement *m* (dans une copropriété).

condone *vtr* tolérer.

conduct I *n* conduite *f* (**towards** envers).
II *vtr* **1** (manage) mener [*life, business*]; **2** mener [*experiment, inquiry*]; célébrer [*ceremony*]; **3** (Mus) diriger [*orchestra*]; **4** conduire [*electricity, heat*].

conductor ▶805 *n* **1** (Mus) chef *m* d'orchestre; **2** (on bus) receveur *m*; (on train) chef *m* de train.

conductress ▶805 *n* receveuse *f*.

cone *n* **1** (shape) cône *m*; **paper ~** cornet *m* (en papier); **2** (also **ice-cream ~**) cornet *m*; **3** (for traffic) balise *f*.

confectioner ▶805 *n* (of sweets) confiseur/-euse *m/f*; (of cakes) pâtissier-confiseur *m*; **~'s custard** crème *f* pâtissière; **~'s (shop)** pâtisserie-confiserie *f*.

confectionery *n* (sweets) sucreries *fpl*; (high quality) confiserie *f*; (cakes) pâtisserie *f*.

conference I *n* (academic, business) conférence *f*; (political) congrès *m*.
II *noun modifier* [*room, centre*] de conférences; **~ member** participant/-e *m/f*.

confess I *vtr* **1** avouer (**that** que); **2** confesser [*sins*].
II *vi* avouer; **to ~ to a crime** avouer (avoir commis) un crime.

confession *n* **1** (gen, Law) aveu *m* (**of** de); **to make a full ~** faire des aveux complets; **2** (in religion) confession *f*; **to go to ~** se confesser.

confetti *n* confettis *mpl*.

confide *vi* **to ~ in** se confier à [*person*].

confidence *n* **1** (faith) confiance *f* (**in** en); **to have (every) ~ in sb/sth** avoir (pleine) confiance en qn/qch; **2** (in politics) **vote of ~** vote *m* de confiance; **motion of no ~** motion *f* de censure; **3** (self-assurance) assurance *f*, confiance *f* en soi; **4** (certainty) assurance *f*; **I can say with ~ that** je suis sûr que; **5** (confidentiality) **to tell sb sth in ~** dire qch à qn confidentiellement.

confidence: **~ trick** *n* escroquerie *f*; **~ trickster** *n* (GB) escroc *m*.

confident *adj* **1** (sure) sûr, confiant; **to be ~ that** être sûr or persuadé que; **to feel ~ about the future** avoir confiance en l'avenir; **2** (self-assured) assuré, sûr de soi.

confidential *adj* confidentiel/-ielle *m/f*.

confidentiality *n* confidentialité *f*.

confine *vtr* confiner [*person*] (**in, to** dans); enfermer [*animal*] (**in** dans); **to be ~d to bed** être alité; **to be ~d to the house** être obligé de rester à la maison.

confinement *n* (in cell) détention *f* (**in, to** dans); (Law) réclusion *f*.

confirm *vtr* confirmer; **two people were ~ed dead** on a confirmé que deux personnes ont trouvé la mort; **to ~ receipt of sth** accuser réception de qch.

confirmation *n* confirmation *f*.

confiscate *vtr* confisquer (**from** à).

conflict I *n* conflit *m*; **to cause ~** provoquer des conflits; **to be in/come into ~** être/entrer en conflit (**with** avec); **~ of interests** conflit d'intérêts.
II *vi* être en contradiction (**with** avec).

conflicting *adj* [*views, feelings*] contradictoire.

conform I *vtr* conformer (**to** à).
II *vi* [*person*] se conformer (**with, to** à); [*model*] être conforme (**to** à).

confront *vtr* affronter [*danger, enemy*]; faire face à [*problem*]; **to ~ the truth** voir la réalité en face; **to be ~ed by sth** être confronté à qch; **to be ~ed by the police** se retrouver face à la police.

confrontation *n* affrontement *m*.

confuse *vtr* **1** (bewilder) troubler [*person*]; **2** (fail to distinguish) confondre (**with** avec); **3** (complicate) compliquer [*argument*]; **to ~ the issue** compliquer les choses.

confused *adj* **1** [*person*] troublé; [*thoughts, mind*] confus; **to get ~** s'embrouiller; **he was ~ about the instructions** il ne comprenait pas bien le mode d'emploi; **I'm ~ about what to do** je ne sais pas trop ce que je dois faire; **2** (muddled) [*account, memories*] confus; [*voices*] indistinct; [*impression*] vague.

confusing *adj* déroutant, peu clair.

confusion *n* confusion *f*; **to create ~** jeter la confusion (dans les esprits); **to avoid ~** pour éviter toute confusion.

congeal *vi* [*fat*] se figer; [*blood*] se coaguler.

congested *adj* **1** [*road*] embouteillé; [*district*] surpeuplé; **2** [*lungs*] congestionné; [*nose*] bouché.

congestion *n* **1** (of district) surpeuplement *m*; (of road) encombrement *m*; **traffic ~** embouteillages *mpl*; **2** (of lungs) congestion *f*.

congratulate *vtr* féliciter (**on** de; **on doing** d'avoir fait); **to ~ oneself** se féliciter (**on** de).

congratulations *n pl* félicitations *fpl*; **~ on your success/on the birth of your new baby** (toutes mes or nos) félicitations pour votre succès/à l'occasion de la naissance de votre bébé; **to offer one's ~ to sb** adresser ses félicitations à qn.

congregate *vi* se rassembler (**around** autour de).

congregation *n* assemblée *f* des fidèles.

congress *n* congrès *m* (**on** sur).

Congress *n* (US) Congrès *m*.

congress: **~man** *n* (US) (also **Congressman**) membre *m* du Congrès; **~woman** *n* (US) (also **Congresswoman**) membre *m* du Congrès.

conifer *n* conifère *m*.

conjugal *adj* conjugal.

conjunctivitis ▶ 686 *n* conjonctivite *f*.

conjurer *n* prestidigitateur/-trice *m/f*.

con man *n* arnaqueur◐ *m*, escroc *m*.

connect *vtr* **1** (attach) raccorder [*end, hose*] (**to** à); accrocher [*coach*] (**to** à); **2** (link) [*road, railway*] relier [*place, road*] (**to, with** à); **3** (to mains) brancher [*appliance*] (**to** à); brancher [qch] sur le secteur [*household*]; **4** raccorder [*phone, subscriber*]

■ **connect up**: **~ up [sth], ~ [sth] up** faire les branchements de [*video, computer*]; **to ~ sth up to** brancher qch sur; **to ~ two machines up** connecter deux machines.

connected *adj* **1** (related) [*idea, event*] lié (**to, with** à); **everything ~ with music** tout ce qui se rapporte à la musique; **2** (in family) apparenté (**to** à); **to be well ~** (through family) être de bonne famille; (having influence) avoir des relations.

connecting *adj* **1** [*flight*] de correspondance; **2** [*room*] attenant.

connection *n* **1** (link) (between events) rapport *m*; (of person) lien *m* (**between** entre; **with** avec); **to have no ~ with** n'avoir aucun rapport or n'avoir rien à voir avec; **to make the ~** faire le rapprochement; **in ~ with** au sujet de, à propos de; **2** (contact) relation *f*; **to have useful ~s** avoir des relations; **3** (to mains) branchement *m*; (of pipes, tubes) raccord *m*; (of wires) câblage *m*; **4** (to telephone network) raccordement *m*; (to number) mise *f* en communication (**to** avec); **bad ~** mauvaise communication *f*; **5** (in travel) correspondance *f*.

connive *vi* **to ~ at** contribuer délibérément à; **to ~ (with sb) to do sth** être de connivence or de mèche○ (avec qn) pour faire qch.

connoisseur *n* connaisseur/-euse *m/f*.

connotation *n* connotation *f* (**of** de).

conquer *vtr* conquérir [*territory, people*]; vaincre [*enemy, unemployment*].

conqueror *n* conquérant/-e *m/f*.

conquest *n* conquête *f*.

conscience *n* conscience *f*; **they have no ~** ils n'ont aucun sens moral; **to have a guilty ~** avoir mauvaise conscience; **to have a clear ~** avoir la conscience tranquille.

conscientious *adj* consciencieux/-ieuse.

conscientious objector *n* objecteur *m* de conscience.

conscious *adj* **1** (aware) conscient (**of** de; **that** du fait que); **politically ~** politisé; **to be environmentally ~** avoir une conscience écologique; **2** (deliberate) [*decision*] réfléchi; [*effort*] consciencieux; **3** (awake) réveillé.

consciousness *n* **to lose/regain ~** perdre/reprendre connaissance.

conscript *n* appelé *m*.

consecrate *vtr* consacrer.

consecutive *adj* consécutif/-ive.

consensus *n* consensus *m* (**among** au sein de; **about** quant à; **on** sur).

consent **I** *n* **1** (by person in authority) consentement *m*; (other) accord *m*; **age of ~** âge *m* légal; **2** (agreement) **by common** or **mutual ~** d'un commun accord.

II *vtr* **to ~ to do** consentir à faire.

III *vi* consentir (**to** à); **to ~ to sb doing** consentir à ce que qn fasse.

consequence *n* conséquence *f*; **as a ~ of** du fait de [*change, process*]; à la suite de [*event*]; **to face/suffer the ~s** accepter/subir les conséquences.

consequently *adv* par conséquent.

conservation **I** *n* **1** (of nature) protection *f* (**of** de); **energy ~** maîtrise *f* de l'énergie; **2** (of heritage) conservation *f*.

II *noun modifier* [*group, measure*] de protection; **~ area** zone *f* protégée.

conservationist *n* défenseur *m* des ressources naturelles.

conservative **I** *n* conservateur/-trice *m/f*.

II *adj* **1** [*party*] conservateur/-trice; **2** [*taste, style*] classique.

Conservative Party *n* (GB) parti *m* conservateur.

conservatory *n* **1** (for plants) jardin *m* d'hiver; **2** (academy) conservatoire *m*.

conserve *vtr* **1** (protect) protéger [*forest*]; sauvegarder [*wildlife*]; conserver [*remains, ruins*]; **2** (save up) économiser [*resources*]; ménager [*energy*].

consider *vtr* **1** (give thought to) considérer [*options, facts*]; examiner [*evidence, problem*]; étudier [*offer*]; **to ~ whether** décider si; **the jury is ~ing its verdict** le jury délibère; **2** (take into account) prendre [qch] en considération [*risk, cost*]; songer à [*person*]; faire attention à [*person's feelings*]; **when you ~ that** quand on songe que; **3** (envisage) **to ~ doing** envisager de faire; **to ~ sb/sth as sth** penser à qn/qch comme qch; **4** (regard) **to ~ that** considérer or estimer que; **to ~ oneself (to be) a genius** se considérer comme un génie.

considerable *adj* considérable; **to a ~ degree** or **extent** dans une large mesure.

considerate *adj* [*person*] attentionné; [*behaviour*] courtois; **to be ~ towards sb** avoir des égards pour qn.

consideration *n* **1** (thought) considération *f*, réflexion *f*; **to give sth careful ~** réfléchir longuement à qch; **to take sth into ~** prendre qch en considération; **2** (thoughtfulness) considération *f* (**for** envers); **out of ~** par considération; **3** (fee) **for a ~** moyennant finance.

considering *prep, conj* étant donné, compte tenu de; **~ (that) he was tired** étant donné sa fatigue.

consign *vtr* expédier [*goods*] (**to** à).

consignment *n* (sending) expédition *f*; (goods) lot *m*, livraison *f*; **for ~** à expédier.

consist *vi* **to ~ of** se composer de; **to ~ in** résider dans; **to ~ in doing** consister à faire.

consistency *n* **1** (texture) consistance *f*; **2** (of view, policy) cohérence *f*.

consistent *adj* **1** [*growth, level, quality*] régulier/-ière; [*kindness, help*] constant; [*sportsman*] régulier/-ière; **2** [*attempts, demands*] répété; **3** [*argument*] cohérent; **~ with** en accord avec [*account, belief*].

consistently *adv* (invariably) systématiquement, invariablement; (repeatedly) à maintes reprises.

consolation *n* consolation *f* (**to** à); **~ prize** prix *m* de consolation.

console I *n* **1** (control panel) console *f*; **2** (for hi-fi) meuble *m* hi-fi; (for video) meuble *m* vidéo.
II *vtr* consoler (**for, on** de; **with** avec); **to ~ oneself** se consoler.

consolidate *vtr* **1** consolider [*position*]; **2** réunir [*resources*]; fusionner [*companies*].

consolidation *n* **1** (of position) consolidation *f*; **2** (of companies) fusion *f*.

consonant *n* consonne *f*.

consortium *n* consortium *m*.

conspicuous *adj* [*feature, sign*] visible; [*garment*] voyant; **to be ~** se remarquer (**for** à cause de); **I feel ~** j'ai l'impression que tout le monde me regarde; **in a ~ position** bien en évidence.

conspiracy *n* conspiration *f* (**against** contre; **to do** en vue de faire).

conspirator *n* conspirateur/-trice *m/f*.

conspire *vi* conspirer; **to ~ to do** [*people*] conspirer en vue de faire.

constant *adj* [*problem, reminder, threat*] permanent; [*care, temperature*] constant; [*disputes, questions*] incessant; [*attempts*] répété; [*companion*] éternel/-elle.

constantly *adv* constamment.

constellation *n* constellation *f*.

constipated *adj* constipé.

constipation ▶686 *n* constipation *f*; **to have ~** être constipé.

constituency *n* (district) circonscription *f* électorale; (voters) électeurs *mpl*.

constitution *n* constitution *f*.

constitutional *adj* constitutionnel/-elle.

constraint *n* contrainte *f*; **to put a ~ on** imposer une contrainte à.

constrict I *vtr* comprimer [*flow, blood vessel*]; gêner [*breathing, movement*].
II **constricted** *pp adj* [*breathing*] gêné; [*space*] restreint.

construct *vtr* construire (**of** avec; **in** en).

construction *n* (building) construction *f*; **under ~** en construction.

construction worker ▶805 *n* ouvrier/-ière *m/f* du bâtiment.

constructive *n* constructif/-ive.

consul *n* consul *m*; **the French ~** le consul de France.

consulate *n* consulat *m*.

consult I *vtr* consulter (**about** sur).
II *vi* (also **~ together**) s'entretenir (**about** sur).

consultancy *n* **1** (also **~ firm**) cabinet-conseil *m*; **2** (advice) conseils *mpl*; **to work in ~** travailler comme consultant; **3** (GB) (job) poste *m* de spécialiste (*dans un hôpital*).

consultant ▶805 *n* **1** (expert) consultant/-e *m/f*, conseiller/-ère *m/f* (**on, in** en); **beauty ~** esthéticienne-conseil *f*; **2** (GB) (doctor) spécialiste *mf* (*attaché à un hôpital*).

consultation *n* **1** (meeting) (for advice) consultation *f* (**about** sur); (for discussion) entretien *m* (**about** sur); **to have ~s with sb** (for advice) conférer avec qn; (for discussion) s'entretenir avec qn; **2** (process) consultation *f*.

consume *vtr* **1** manger [*food*]; boire [*drink*]; **2** (use up) consommer [*fuel, food, drink*]; absorber [*time*]; **3** (destroy) [*flames*] consumer; **4** (overwhelm) **to be ~d by** or **with** être dévoré par [*envy*]; brûler de [*desire*]; être rongé par [*guilt*].

consumer *n* consommateur/-trice *m/f*; (of electricity, gas) abonné/-e *m/f*.

consumer: **~ advice** *n* conseils *mpl* au consommateurs; **~ durables** *n pl* biens *mpl* durables; **~ goods** *n pl* biens *mpl* de consommation; **~ products** *n pl* produits *mpl* de consommation; **~ protection** *n* défense *f* du consommateur; **~ society** *n* société *f* de consommation.

consummate *vtr* consommer [*marriage*].

consumption *n* consommation *f*; **electricity ~** la consommation d'électricité; **unfit for human ~** impropre à la consommation.

contact I *n* **1** (touch) contact *m* (**between** entre; **with** avec); **to be in/make ~** être en/se mettre en contact; **to maintain/lose ~** garder/perdre contact; **to be in constant ~** être en rapports constants; **2** (by radar, radio, electrical) contact *m*; **3** (acquaintance) connaissance *f*; (professional) contact *m*; (for drugs, spy) contact *m*; **sporting ~s** relations *fpl* sportives.
II *vtr* contacter, se mettre en rapport avec.

contactable *adj* joignable; **she is not ~** on ne peut pas la joindre.

contact lens *n* lentille *f* or verre *m* de contact.

contagious *adj* contagieux/-ieuse.

contain *vtr* **1** (hold) contenir [*amount, ingredients*]; contenir, comporter [*information, mistakes*]; **2** (curb) maîtriser [*blaze*]; enrayer [*epidemic*]; limiter [*costs, problem*]; canaliser [*strike*]; retenir [*flood*].

container *n* (for food, liquids) récipient *m*; (for plants) bac *m*; (for waste, for transporting) conteneur *m*.

container: **~ ship** *n* porte-conteneurs *m inv*; **~ truck** *n* porte-conteneur *m*.

contaminate *vtr* contaminer.

contamination *n* contamination *f*.

contemplate *vtr* envisager (**doing** de faire).

contemporary **I** *n* contemporain/-e *m/f*; **our contemporaries** les gens de notre âge.
II *adj* (present-day) contemporain; (up-to-date) moderne; (of same period) de l'époque.

contempt *n* mépris *m* (**for** de); **to feel ~ for sb/sth** mépriser qn/qch; **to be beneath ~** être en-dessous de tout; **~ of court** outrage *m* à magistrat.

contemptible *adj* méprisable.

contend **I** *vtr* soutenir (**that** que).
II *vi* **to ~ with** affronter; **he's got a lot to ~ with** il a beaucoup de problèmes.

contender *n* **1** (in competition) concurrent/-e *m/f*; **2** (for post) candidat/-e *m/f* (**for** à).

content **I** *n* **1** (relative quantity) teneur *f*; **the fat ~** la teneur en matières grasses; **low/high lead ~** faible/forte teneur en plomb; **to have a low/high fat ~** être pauvre/riche en matières grasses; **2** (meaning) fond *m*; **form and ~** le fond et la forme.
II *adj* satisfait (**with** de); **to be ~ to do** se contenter de faire; **not ~ with doing** non content de faire; **he's ~ with what he has** il se contente de ce qu'il a.
III *v refl* **to ~ oneself with sth/with doing** se contenter de qch/de faire.

contented *adj* [*person*] content (**with** de); [*feeling*] de bien-être; **a ~ child** un enfant heureux.

contention *n* assertion *f*; **it is my ~ that** je soutiens que.

contentious *adj* [*issue*] controversé; [*view*] discutable.

contentment *n* contentement *m*; **with ~** [*sigh*] de bien-être.

contents *n pl* (gen) contenu *m*; (of house, for insurance) biens *mpl* mobiliers; **list** or **table of ~** table *f* des matières.

contest **I** *n* concours *m*; **fishing ~** concours *m* de pêche; **sports ~** rencontre *f* sportive.
II *vtr* **1** (object to) contester; **2** (compete for) disputer [*match*].

contestant *n* (in competition, game) concurrent/-e *m/f*; (in fight) adversaire *mf*; (for job, in election) candidat/-e *m/f*.

context *n* contexte *m*; **in ~** dans son contexte; **out of ~** hors contexte; **to put sth into ~** replacer qch dans son contexte.

continent *n* **1** continent *m*; **2 the Continent** (GB) l'Europe *f* continentale; **on the Continent** (GB) en Europe continentale.

continental **I** *n* (GB) Européen/-éenne *m/f* du continent.
II *noun modifier* **1** [*climate*] continental; **2** (GB) [*holiday*] en Europe continentale.

continental quilt (GB) *n* couette *f*.

contingency *n* imprévu *m*; **to provide for all contingencies** parer à toute éventualité.

contingency: **~ fund** *n* fonds *m* de secours; **~ plan** *n* plan *m* de réserve.

continual *adj* continuel/-elle.

continuation *n* **1** (of situation, process) continuation *f*; **2** (resumption) continuation *f*, reprise *f*; **3** (in book) suite *f*; (of route) prolongement *m*.

continue **I** *vtr* **1** (carry on) continuer, poursuivre [*career, inquiry, journey*]; **2** (resume) continuer; **'to be ~d'** (in film) 'à suivre'; **'~d overleaf'** 'suite page suivante'.
II *vi* [*person*] continuer (**doing, to do** à or de faire); [*noise, debate, strike*] se poursuivre; **he ~d down the street** il a continué de descendre la rue; **she will ~ as minister** elle restera ministre; **to ~ with** continuer, poursuivre [*task, treatment*].
III continuing *pres p adj* continuel/-elle.

continuity *n* continuité *f*.

continuous *adj* **1** [*growth, decline, noise*] continu; [*care*] constant; [*line*] ininterrompu; **~ assessment** (GB) contrôle *m* continu; **2** [*tense*] progressif/-ive.

continuously *adv* (without a break) sans interruption; (repeatedly) continuellement.

contour *n* **1** contour *m*; **2** (also **~ line**) courbe *f* hypsométrique or de niveau.

contraband *n* contrebande *f*.

contraception *n* contraception *f*.

contraceptive **I** *n* contraceptif *m*.
II *adj* [*method*] contraceptif/-ive; **~ device** contraceptif *m*.

contract **I** *n* **1** (agreement) contrat *m* (**for** pour; **with** avec); **employment ~, ~ of employment** contrat *m* de travail; **to enter into a ~ with** passer un contrat avec; **to be on a ~** être sous contrat; **2** (tender) contrat *m*; **to win/lose a ~** remporter/perdre un contrat; **to place a ~ for sth with** octroyer un contrat pour qch à; **to put work out to ~** donner un travail en sous-traitance.
II *noun modifier* [*labour*] contractuel/-elle.
III *vtr* **1** contracter [*disease*] (**from** par le contact avec); **2** contracter [*debt, loan*]; **to be ~ed to do** être tenu par contrat de faire.
IV *vi* **1** (undertake) **to ~ to do** s'engager par contrat à faire; **2** (shrink) [*metal*] se contracter; [*market*] diminuer; **3** [*muscle*] se contracter.

contraction *n* contraction *f*.

contractor ▶ 805 *n* **1** (business) entrepreneur/-euse *m/f*; **2** (worker) contractuel/-elle *m/f*.

contradict *vtr, vi* contredire.

contradiction *n* contradiction *f*; **a ~ in terms** une contradiction criante.

contradictory *adj* contradictoire (**to** à).

contraflow *n* (GB) circulation *f* à sens alterné.

contrary I *n* contraire *m*; **quite the ~** bien au contraire; **on the ~** (bien) au contraire; **despite claims to the ~** contrairement à ce que certains disent; **evidence to the ~** une preuve du contraire; **unless you hear anything to the ~** sauf contrordre.
II *adj* **1** [*idea, view*] contraire; **to be ~ to** être contraire à; **2** [*person*] contrariant.
III **contrary to** *phr* contrairement à; **~ to popular belief** contrairement à ce que l'on peut croire; **~ to expectations** contre toute attente.

contrast I *n* **1** (difference) contraste *m*; **in ~ to sth, by ~ with sth** par contraste avec qch; **in ~ to sb** à la différence de qn; **to be a ~ to** or **with** présenter un contraste avec; **by** or **in ~** par contre; **2** (on photo, TV) contraste *m*.
II *vtr* **to ~ X with Y** faire ressortir le contraste (qui existe) entre X et Y.
III *vi* contraster (**with** avec).
IV **contrasting** *adj* [*examples*] opposé; [*colour, material*] contrasté.

contribute I *vtr* **1** verser [*sum*] (**to** à); financer [*costs*]; **2** (to gift, charity) donner (**to** à; **towards** pour); **3** (put up) contribuer; **to ~ £5m** contribuer pour 5 millions de livres; **4** apporter [*ideas*] (**to** à); écrire [*article*] (**to** pour).
II *vi* **1 to ~ to** or **towards** contribuer à [*change, awareness, decline*]; **2** (to community life, research) participer (**to** à); **3 to ~ to** cotiser à [*pension fund*]; **4** (to charity) donner (de l'argent) (**to** à); (to programme, magazine) collaborer (**to** à).

contribution *n* **1** (to tax, pension, profits, cost) contribution *f* (**towards** à); **2** (to charity, campaign) don *m*; **to make a ~** faire un don (**to** à); **3** (role played) **sb's ~ to** le rôle que qn a joué dans [*success, undertaking*]; ce que qn a apporté à [*science, sport*]; **4** (to programme) participation *f*; (to magazine) article *m*.

contributor *n* (to charity) donateur/-trice *m/f*; (in discussion) participant/-e *m/f*; (to magazine, book) collaborateur/-trice *m/f*.

contrived *adj* **1** [*incident, meeting*] non fortuit; **2** [*plot*] tiré par les cheveux; [*style, effect*] étudié.

control I *n* **1** (of animals, crowd, organization) contrôle *m* (**of** de); (of operation, project) direction *f* (**of** de); (of life, fate) maîtrise *f* (**of, over** de); (of disease, social problem) lutte *f* (**of** contre); **to be in ~ of** contrôler [*territory*]; diriger [*operation, organization*]; maîtriser [*problem*]; **to have ~ over** maîtriser [*fate, life*]; **to take ~ of** prendre le contrôle de [*territory*]; prendre la direction de [*organization, project*]; prendre [qch] en main [*situation*]; **to be under ~** [*fire, riot*] être maîtrisé; **everything's under ~** tout va bien; **to bring** or **keep [sth] under ~** maîtriser; **to be out of ~** [*crowd, riot*] être déchaîné; [*fire*] ne plus être maîtrisable; **the situation is out of ~** la situation est devenue incontrôlable; **to lose ~ of sth** perdre le contrôle de qch; **to be beyond sb's ~** échapper au contrôle de qn; **2** (of self, emotion) maîtrise *f*; **to have ~ over sth** maîtriser qch; **to be in ~ (of oneself)** se maîtriser; **to lose ~ (of oneself)** perdre le contrôle (de soi); **3** (of vehicle, machine, ball) contrôle *m*; (of body, process, system) maîtrise *f*; **to be in ~ of** avoir le contrôle de; **to keep/lose ~ of a car** garder/perdre le contrôle d'une voiture; **4** (on vehicle, equipment) commande *f*; (on TV) bouton *m* de réglage; **to be at the ~s** être aux commandes; **5** (regulation) contrôle *m* (**on** de); **price ~s** contrôles des prix.
II *vtr* **1** (dominate) dominer [*market, situation*]; contrôler [*territory*]; diriger [*traffic, project*]; être majoritaire dans [*company*]; **2** (discipline) maîtriser [*person, animal, inflation, fire*]; endiguer [*epidemic*]; dominer [*emotion*]; retenir [*laughter*]; commander à [*limbs*]; **to ~ oneself** se contrôler; **3** (operate) commander [*machine, process*]; manœuvrer [*boat, vehicle*]; piloter [*plane*]; contrôler [*ball*]; **4** (regulate) régler [*speed, temperature*]; contrôler [*immigration, prices*].

controlled *adj* [*explosion, landing*] contrôlé; [*person*] calme; [*economy*] dirigé; **electronically ~** contrôlé électroniquement.

controller *n* **1** (boss) directeur/-trice *m/f*; **2** (of accounts) planificateur/-trice *m/f*.

controlling *adj* [*group*] de contrôle; **~ interest** majorité *f* de contrôle.

control: **~ panel** *n* (on plane) tableau *m* de bord; (on machine) tableau *m* de contrôle; (on TV) (panneau *m* de) commandes *fpl*; **~ tower** *n* tour *f* de contrôle.

controversial *adj* **1** (criticized) controversé; (open to criticism) qui prête à controverse; **2** (much discussed) controversé; (dubious) douteux/-euse.

controversy *n* controverse *f*.

conundrum *n* énigme *f*.

convalesce *vi* se remettre; **he's convalescing** il est en convalescence.

convene *vtr* organiser [*meeting*]; convoquer [*group*].

convenience *n* avantage *m* (**of doing** de faire); **the ~ of** les avantages de [*practice, method*]; la commodité de [*instant food, device, shop*]; **for (the sake of) ~** pour raisons de commodité; **for our ~** pour notre convenance; **at your ~** quand cela vous conviendra; **at your earliest ~** dès que cela vous sera possible.

convenient *adj* **1** (suitable) [*place, time*] commode; **it isn't very ~ at the moment** ce n'est pas vraiment le moment maintenant; **to be ~ for sb** convenir à qn; **2** (useful, practical) pratique, commode (**that** que + *subj*; **to do** de faire); **3** (near) [*shops*] situé tout près; [*chair*] à portée de main; **to be ~ for** (GB) or **to** (US) ne pas être loin de [*station*]; **4** [*excuse*] commode; **it's ~ for them** ça les arrange.

conveniently *adv* **~ situated, ~ located** bien situé, bien placé.

convent *n* couvent *m*.

convention *n* **1** (of party, profession) convention

f, congrès *m*; (of society, fans) assemblée *f*; **2** (social norms) convenances *fpl*, conventions *fpl*; **to flout ~** braver les convenances; **3** (usual practice) convention *f*.

conventional *adj* **1** [*person*] conformiste; [*idea, role*] conventionnel/-elle; **2** [*approach, method*] conventionnel/-elle; [*medicine*] traditionnel/-elle; **3** [*weapons*] conventionnel/-elle.

conversation *n* conversation *f*; **to have** or **hold a ~** avoir une conversation; **to make ~** faire la conversation.

conversational *adj* [*ability, skill*] de conversation.

converse *vi* converser (**with** avec; **in** en).

conversion *n* **1** (transformation) transformation *f* (**from** de; **to, into** en); **2** (of currency, measurement) conversion *f* (**from** de; **into** en); **3** (of building) aménagement *m* (**to, into** en); **4** (to new beliefs) conversion *f* (**from** de; **to** à); **5** (in rugby) transformation *f*.

convert I *n* converti/-e *m/f* (**to** à).
II *vtr* **1** (change into sth else) transformer; (modify) adapter; **2** convertir [*currency, measurement*] (**from** de; **to, into** en); **3** aménager [*building, loft*] (**to, into** en); **4** (to new beliefs) convertir (**to** à; **from** de); **5** (in rugby) transformer [*try*].
III *vi* **1** [*sofa, device*] être convertible (**into** en); **2** [*person*] se convertir (**to** à; **from** de).

convertible I *n* (car) décapotable *f*.
II *adj* [*currency*] convertible; [*car*] décapotable.

convex *adj* convexe.

convey *vtr* **1** [*person*] transmettre [*information*] (**to** à); exprimer [*condolences, feeling, idea*] (**to** à); **to ~ to sb that** faire savoir à qn que; **2** [*words, images*] traduire [*mood, impression*]; **3** [*vehicle*] transporter; [*pipes, network*] amener.

conveyance *n* (of goods, passengers) transport *m*, acheminement *m*.

conveyancing *n* rédaction *f* des actes de propriété.

conveyor *n* **1** (also **~ belt**) (in factory) transporteur *m* à bande or à courroie; (for luggage) tapis *m* roulant; **2** (of goods, persons) transporteur *m*.

convict I *n* (imprisoned criminal) détenu/-e *m/f*; (deported criminal) bagnard *m*.
II *vtr* reconnaître or déclarer [qn] coupable (**of** de; **of doing** d'avoir fait).

conviction *n* **1** (Law) condamnation *f* (**for** pour); **2** (belief) conviction *f* (**that** que).

convince *vtr* convaincre [*person, jury, reader*] (**of** de; **that** que; **about** au sujet de); persuader [*voter, consumer*] (**to do** de faire).

convincing *adj* [*account, evidence*] convaincant; [*victory, lead*] indiscutable.

convivial *adj* [*atmosphere, evening*] cordial; [*person*] chaleureux/-euse.

convoy *n* convoi *m*; **in ~** en convoi.

convulsion *n* convulsion *f*.

cook ▶805 I *n* cuisinier/-ière *m/f*; **he's a good ~** c'est un bon cuisinier.
II *vtr* faire cuire [*vegetables, pasta, eggs*]; préparer [*meal*] (**for** pour).
III *vi* [*person*] cuisiner, faire la cuisine; [*vegetable, meat, meal*] cuire.
IV **cooked** *pp adj* cuit; **lightly ~ed** à peine cuit.

cooker *n* (GB) cuisinière *f*.

cookery book *n* (GB) livre de cuisine.

cookie *n* gâteau *m* sec, biscuit *m* (sec).

cooking *n* cuisine *f*; **to do the ~** faire la cuisine; **Chinese ~** cuisine chinoise.

cooking: **~ apple** *n* pomme *f* à cuire; **~ chocolate** *n* chocolat *m* pâtissier.

cool I *n* **1** (coldness) fraîcheur *f*; **2**○ (calm) sang-froid *m*; **to keep one's ~** (not get angry) ne pas s'énerver; (stay calm) garder son sang-froid; **to lose one's ~** (get angry) s'énerver; (panic) perdre son sang-froid.
II *adj* **1** [*day, drink, water, weather*] frais/fraîche; [*dress*] léger/-ère; [*colour*] froid; **it's ~ today** il fait frais aujourd'hui; **2** (calm) [*approach, handling*] calme; **to stay ~** garder son sang-froid; **keep ~!** reste calme; **3** (unemotional) [*manner*] détaché; [*logic*] froid; **4** (unfriendly) froid; **to be ~ with sb** être froid avec qn; **5** (casual) décontracté, cool○; **6**○ (sophisticated) branché○.
III *vtr* **1** refroidir [*soup*]; rafraîchir [*wine, room*]; **2** calmer [*anger, ardour*].
IV *vi* **1** (get colder) refroidir; **2** (subside) [*enthusiasm*] faiblir; [*friendship*] se dégrader.
■ **cool down**: ¶ **~ down** [*engine, water*] refroidir; [*person, situation*] se calmer; ¶ **~ [sth] down** refroidir [*mixture*]; rafraîchir [*wine*].
■ **cool off** **1** (get colder) se rafraîchir; **2** calm down) se calmer.

coolly *adv* **1** [*greet, say*] froidement; **2** (calmly) calmement.

coolness *n* **1** (coldness) fraîcheur *f*; **2** (unfriendliness) froideur *f*.

cooperate *vi* coopérer (**with** avec; **in** à; **in doing** pour faire).

cooperation *n* coopération *f* (**on** à); **in (close) ~** en (étroite) coopération.

cooperative I *n* **1** (organization) coopérative *f*; **2** (US) (apartment house) immeuble *m* en copropriété.
II *adj* **1** (joint) conjoint; **2** (helpful) coopératif/-ive; **3** [*movement, society*] coopératif/-ive; **4** (US) [*apartment, building*] en copropriété.

coordinate *vtr* coordonner (**with** avec).

coordinated *adj* coordonné.

coordinates *n pl* (clothes) ensemble *m*.

coordination *n* coordination *f*.

co-owner *n* copropriétaire *mf*.

cope *vi* **1** (practically) [*person*] s'en sortir○, se débrouiller; [*police, system*] faire face; **to ~ with** [*person*] s'occuper de [*person, work*]; [*police, system*] faire face à [*demand, disaster, enquiries*]; **it's more than I can ~ with** je ne m'en sors plus○; **2** (financially) s'en sortir○; **3** (emotionally) **to ~ with** supporter [*death, depression, difficult person*].

Copenhagen ▶574 *pr n* Copenhague.

copper ▶559 I *n* **1** (metal) cuivre *m*; **2**○ (GB)

(coin) petite monnaie *f*; **a few ~s** quelques sous; **3** (colour) couleur *f* cuivre.

II *noun modifier* [*bracelet, coin, pipe*] de or en cuivre; [*kettle, pan*] en cuivre.

copy I *n* **1** (reproduction, imitation) copie *f*; **certified ~** copie *f* certifiée conforme; **2** (of book, newspaper, report) exemplaire *m*; **3** (journalist's, advertiser's text) copie *f*; **to be** or **make good ~** être un bon sujet d'article.

II *vtr* **1** (imitate) copier [*person, design*] (**from** sur); **2** (duplicate) copier [*document, disk*]; **to ~ sth onto a disk** copier qch sur disquette; **to have sth copied** faire faire une copie de qch.

III *vi* copier (**from** sur); **to ~ in a test** copier à un examen.

■ **copy down**: **~ down [sth], ~ [sth] down** recopier.

■ **copy out**: **~ out [sth], ~ [sth] out** recopier.

copyright *n* copyright *m*, droit *m* d'auteur; **to have** or **hold the ~** détenir le copyright or les droits.

coral *n* corail *m*.

cord I *n* **1** (of dressing gown, curtains) cordon *m*; **2** (wire) fil *m*, cordon *m*.

II *n pl* **cords**○ (also **corduroys**) pantalon *m* en velours (côtelé).

cordial I *n* **1** (fruit drink) sirop *m* de fruits; **2** (US) (liqueur) liqueur *m*.

II *adj* cordial (**to, with** avec).

cordless *adj* [*telephone, kettle*] sans fil.

cordon *n* cordon *m*; **police ~** cordon *m* de police.

■ **cordon off**: **~ off [sth], ~ [sth] off** boucler [*street, area*]; contenir [*crowd*].

corduroy *n* velours *m* côtelé.

core *n* **1** (of apple) trognon *m*; **2** (of problem) cœur *m*; **3** (inner being) **rotten to the ~** pourri jusqu'à l'os; **English to the ~** anglais jusqu'au bout des ongles; **4** (of nuclear reactor) cœur *m*; **5** (small group) noyau *m*; **hard ~** noyau dur.

Corfu *pr n* Corfou *f*.

cork I *n* **1** (substance) liège *m*; **2** (object) bouchon *m*.

II *vtr* boucher [*bottle*].

corkscrew *n* tire-bouchon *m*.

corn *n* **1** (GB) (wheat, barley) blé *m*; **2** (US) (maize) maïs *m*; **3** (on foot) cor *m*.

cornea *n* cornée *f*.

corner I *n* **1** (in geometry) angle *m*; (of street, building) angle *m*, coin *m*; (of table, field, room) coin *m*; (bend) virage *m*; **the house on the ~** la maison qui fait l'angle; **at the ~ of the street** au coin de la rue; **to go round the ~** tourner au coin de la rue; **just around the ~** (nearby) tout près; (around the bend) juste après le coin; **spring is just around the ~** le printemps approche; **2** (of eye, mouth) coin *m*; **out of the ~ of one's eye** du coin de l'œil; **3** (place) coin *m*; **a remote ~ of India** une région reculée de l'Inde; **to search every ~ of the house** chercher partout dans la maison; **4** (in boxing) coin *m* (de repos); (in football, hockey) corner *m*; **to take a ~** tirer un corner.

II *vtr* **1** acculer [*animal, enemy*]; coincer○ [*person*]; **2** accaparer [*market*].

IDIOMS **in a tight ~** dans une impasse; **to cut ~s** (financially) faire des économies.

corner: **~ shop** *n* petite épicerie *f*; **~stone** *n* pierre *f* angulaire.

corn: **~field** *n* champ *m* de blé; (sweetcorn) champ *m* de maïs; **~flour** *n* farine *f* de maïs; **~flower** *n* bleuet *m*, barbeau *m*; **~ oil** *n* huile *f* de maïs; **~ on the cob** *n* maïs *m* en épi; **~ plaster** *n* pansement *m* pour cors; **~ starch** *n* (US) = **cornflour**.

Cornwall *pr n* (comté *m* de) Cornouailles *f*.

corny○ *adj* [*joke*] (old) éculé; (feeble) faiblard○; [*film, story*] à la guimauve.

coronary *n* infarctus *m*.

coronation *n* couronnement *m*.

coroner *n* coroner *m*.

corporal punishment *n* châtiment *m* corporel.

corporate *adj* **1** [*accounts, funds*] appartenant à une société; [*clients, employees*] d'une société (or de sociétés); **2** [*action*] commun; [*decision*] collectif/-ive.

corporate: **~ identity, ~ image** *n* image *f* de marque (d'une société); **~ law** *n* (US) droit *m* des sociétés; **~ lawyer** *n* (US) (in a firm) avocat/-e *m/f* d'entreprise; (business law expert) juriste *mf* d'entreprise.

corporation *n* (grande) société *f*.

corporation tax *n* (GB) impôt *m* sur les sociétés.

corpse *n* cadavre *m*.

corpuscle *n* (**blood**) **~** globule *m* sanguin; **red/white (blood) ~** globule *m* rouge/blanc.

correct I *adj* **1** [*amount, answer, decision*] correct; [*figure*] exact; **that is ~** c'est exact; **the ~ time** l'heure exacte; **2** [*behaviour*] correct, convenable.

II *vtr* corriger; **~ me if I'm wrong** arrêtez-moi si je me trompe; **I stand ~ed** je reconnais mon erreur; **to ~ oneself** se reprendre.

correcting fluid *n* liquide *m* correcteur.

correction *n* correction *f*.

correlate *vi* être en corrélation (**with** avec).

correspond *vi* **1** (match) concorder, correspondre (**with** à); **2** (be equivalent) être équivalent (**to** à); **3** (exchange letters) correspondre (**with** avec; **about** au sujet de).

correspondence *n* correspondance *f*; **to be in ~ with** correspondre avec.

correspondence course *n* cours *m* par correspondance.

correspondent ▶ 805 *n* **1** (journalist) journaliste *mf*; (abroad) correspondant/-e *m/f*; **political ~** commentateur/-trice *m/f* politique; **2** (letter writer) correspondant/-e *m/f*.

corridor *n* couloir *m*; **the ~s of power** les hautes sphères *fpl* du pouvoir.

corroborate *vtr* corroborer.

corrode I *vtr* corroder.

II *vi* se corroder.

corrosion *n* corrosion *f*.

corrugated: **~ cardboard** *n* carton *m* ondulé; **~ iron** *n* tôle *f* ondulée.

corrupt I *adj* corrompu.
II *vtr* corrompre.

corruption *n* corruption *f*.

Corsica *pr n* Corse *f*.

cosh *n* (GB) matraque *f*.

cos lettuce *n* (salade *f*) romaine *f*.

cosmetic *n* produit *m* de beauté.

cosmetic surgery *n* chirurgie *f* esthétique.

cosmic *adj* [*ray*] cosmique; [*dust*] interstellaire; [*struggle*] prodigieux/-ieuse.

cosmonaut ▶805 *n* cosmonaute *mf*.

cosmopolitan *n*, *adj* cosmopolite (*mf*).

cost I *n* **1** (price) coût *m*, prix *m* (**of** de); (expense incurred) frais *mpl*; **at a ~ of £100** au prix de 100 livres; **at ~** au prix coûtant; **you'll bear the ~** les frais seront à votre charge; **at no extra ~** sans frais supplémentaires; **at great ~** à grands frais; **2** (figurative) prix *m*; **at all ~s** à tout prix; **he knows to his ~ that** il a appris à ses dépens que; **whatever the ~** quoi qu'il en coûte.
II **costs** *n pl* **1** (Law) **to pay ~s** être condamné aux dépens; **2** (gen) frais *mpl*; **transport ~s** frais de transport; **to cut ~s** réduire les coûts.
III *vtr* **1** coûter; **how much does it ~?** combien ça coûte?; **the TV will ~ £100 to repair** la réparation de la télé coûtera 100 livres; **to ~ money** coûter cher; **that decision cost him his job** cette décision lui a coûté son travail; **2** (estimate price of) calculer le prix de revient de [*product*]; calculer le coût de [*project, work*].

cost: **~-effective** *adj* rentable; **~-effectiveness** *n* rentabilité *f*.

costing *n* **1** (discipline) comptabilité *f* analytique or d'exploitation; **2** (for project) établissement *m* des coûts; (for product) établissement *m* des coûts de production.

cost: **~ of living** *n* coût *m* de la vie; **~ price** *n* (for producer) prix *m* de revient; (for consumer) prix *m* coûtant.

costume *n* **1** (clothes) costume *m*; **2** (GB) (also **swimming ~**) maillot *m* de bain.

costume jewellery (GB), **costume jewelry** (US) *n* bijoux *mpl* fantaisie.

cosy (GB), **cozy** (US) *adj* douillet/-ette; **it's ~ here** on est bien ici.

cot *n* **1** (GB) (for baby) lit *m* de bébé; **2** (US) (bed) lit *m* de camp.

cot death *n* (GB) mort *f* subite du nourrisson.

cottage *n* maisonnette *f*; (thatched) chaumière *f*.

cottage cheese *n* fromage *m* blanc à gros grains.

cotton *n* **1** (plant, material) coton *m*; **2** (thread) fil *m* de coton.

cotton wool *n* ouate *f* (de coton).

couch *n* **1** (sofa) canapé *m*; **2** (doctor's) lit *m*; (psychoanalyst's) divan *m*.

cough I *n* toux *f*; **to have a ~** tousser.
II *vi* tousser.
■ **cough up**: **~ up [sth]** cracher [*blood*].

coughing *n* toux *f*; **~ fit** accès *m* de toux.

could *modal aux* **1** (expressing ability, willingness) **I couldn't move** je ne pouvais pas bouger; **she couldn't come yesterday** elle n'a pas pu venir hier; **he couldn't sleep for weeks** il n'a pas pu dormir pendant des semaines; **they did all they ~** ils ont fait tout leur possible or tout ce qu'ils pouvaient; **he ~ be quite nice** il pouvait être charmant; **2** (expressing ability, skill) **he couldn't swim** il ne savait pas nager; **I couldn't read or write** je ne savais ni lire ni écrire; **she ~ play the guitar** elle jouait de la guitare; **he ~ speak four languages** il parlait quatre langues; **3** (with verbs of perception) **they couldn't understand me** ils ne me comprenaient pas; **we ~ hear them laughing** on les entendait rire; **I couldn't see a thing** je n'y voyais rien; **I ~ feel my heart beating** je sentais battre mon cœur; **4** (expressing possibility) **a bike ~ be useful** un vélo pourrait être utile; **it ~ have something to do with the delay** cela pourrait avoir un rapport avec le retard; **I ~ be wrong** je me trompe peut-être; **you ~ have died** tu aurais pu mourir; **if only we ~ start again** si seulement nous pouvions tout recommencer; **I wish I ~ go to Japan** j'aimerais (pouvoir) aller au Japon; **who ~ that be?** qui cela peut-il bien être?; **5** (expressing permission) **we ~ work at home** on pouvait or on avait le droit de travailler chez soi; **people couldn't smoke in cinemas** on ne pouvait pas fumer or on n'avait pas le droit de fumer dans les salles de cinema; **6** (in requests, suggestions) **~ I speak to Annie?** pourrais-je or est-ce que je pourrais parler à Annie?; **~ you take a message?** pourriez-vous or est-ce que vous pourriez prendre un message?; **we ~ ask Gary** on pourrait demander à Gary; **you ~ try calling her at home** vous pourriez essayer de lui téléphoner chez elle; **couldn't we write them a letter?** est-ce qu'on ne pourrait pas leur écrire?; **~ I interrupt?** puis-je vous interrompre?; **7** (expressing annoyance) **they ~ have warned us!** ils auraient pu nous prévenir!; **I was so mad I ~ have screamed** j'aurais hurlé tellement j'étais en colère; **you ~ at least say sorry!** tu pourrais au moins t'excuser!; **how ~ you!** comment as-tu pu faire une chose pareille!

council *n* conseil *m*; **the town ~** le conseil municipal; **the Council of Europe** le Conseil de l'Europe.

council house *n* habitation *f* à loyer modéré.

councillor, **councilor** (US) *n* conseiller/-ère *m/f*.

council tax *n* (GB) ≈ impôts *mpl* locaux.

counsel I *n* avocat/-e *m/f*; **~ for the defence** avocat/-e *m/f* de la défense; **~ for the prosecution** procureur *m*.
II *vtr* conseiller [*person*] (**about, on** sur).

counselling, **counseling** (US) *n* **1** (psychological advice) aide *f* psychosociale; **2** (practical advice) assistance *f*; **careers ~** orientation *f* professionnelle.

counsellor, **counselor** (US) ▶805 *n* **1** (adviser) conseiller/-ère *m/f*; **2** (US) (in holiday camp) moniteur/-trice *m/f*.

count I *n* **1** (numerical record) décompte *m*; (at election) dépouillement *m*; **at the last ~** au dernier décompte; **to lose ~** ne plus savoir où on en est dans ses calculs; **to be out for the ~**° être KO°; **2** (level) taux *m*; **cholesterol ~** taux de cholestérol; **3** (figure) chiffre *m*; **4** (Law) chef *m* d'accusation; **on three ~s** pour trois chefs d'accusation; **5** (nobleman) comte *m*.
II *vtr* **1** compter [*points, people, objects*]; énumérer [*reasons, causes*]; **~ing the children** en comptant les enfants; **not ~ing my sister** sans compter ma sœur; **2** (consider) **to ~ sb as sth** considérer qn comme qch.
III *vi* **1** (enumerate) compter; **2** (matter) compter; **to ~ for little** compter peu; **it's the thought that ~s** c'est l'intention qui compte.
▪ **count against**: **~ against** [**sb**] jouer contre.
▪ **count on**: **~ on** [**sb/sth**] compter sur; **don't ~ on it!** ne comptez pas dessus!
▪ **count up**: **~ up** [**sth**] calculer [*cost, hours*]; compter [*money, boxes*].

countdown *n* compte *m* à rebours (**to** avant).

counter I *n* **1** (in shop, snack bar) comptoir *m*; (in bank, post office) guichet *m*; (in pub, bar) bar *m*; **the girl behind the ~** (in shop) la vendeuse; (in bank, post office) la caissière; **available over the ~** [*medicine*] vendu sans ordonnance; **under the ~** en sous-main; **2** (section of a shop) rayon *m*; **perfume ~** rayon parfumerie; **cheese ~** fromagerie *f*, rayon *m* fromagerie; **3** (token) jeton *m*.
II *vtr* répondre à [*threat*]; neutraliser [*effet*]; parer [*blow*]; enrayer [*inflation*].
III *vi* riposter (**with sth** par qch).
IV counter to *phr* [*be, go, run*] à l'encontre de; [*act, behave*] contrairement à.

counter: **~act** *vtr* contrebalancer [*influence*]; contrecarrer [*negative effects*]; **~-attack** *n* contre-attaque *f* (**against** sur); **~balance** *vtr* contrebalancer; **~-bid** *n* contre-offre *f*; **~-clockwise** *adj, adv* (US) dans le sens inverse des aiguilles d'une montre; **~-espionage** *n* contre-espionnage *m*.

counterfeit I *adj* [*signature, note*] contrefait; **~ money** fausse monnaie *f*.
II *vtr* contrefaire.

counter: **~foil** *n* talon *m*, souche *f*; **~-inflationary** *adj* anti-inflationniste; **~part** *n* (of person) homologue *mf*; (of company, institution) équivalent *m*; **~-productive** *adj* contre-productif/-ive; **~sign** *vtr* contresigner; **~ staff** *n* caissiers/-ières *mpl/fpl*.

countess *n* (also **Countess**) comtesse *f*.

counting *n* calcul *m*; **the ~ of votes** le dépouillement du scrutin.

countless *adj* **~ letters** un nombre incalculable de lettres; **on ~ occasions** je ne sais combien de fois.

country ▶**574** **I** *n* **1** (nation, people) pays *m*; **developing/third world ~** pays en voie de développement/du tiers monde; **the old ~** le pays natal; **2** (also **~side**) campagne *f*; **in the ~** à la campagne; **open ~** rase campagne; **across ~** à travers la campagne.
II *adj* [*road*] de campagne; [*scene*] campagnard; **~ life** la vie à la campagne.

country: **~ and western** *n* musique *f* country et western; **~ dancing** *n* danse *f* folklorique; **~ house** *n* manoir *m*; **~man** *n* (also **fellow ~**) compatriote *m*; **~ music** *n* country music *f*; **~side** *n* campagne *f*; **~wide** *adj, adv* dans tout le pays.

county *n* comté *m*.

county council *n* (GB) ≈ conseil *m* régional.

coup *n* (also **~ d'état**) coup *m* d'État; **to pull off a ~** réussir un beau coup.

couple *n* **1** couple *m*; **2 a ~ of** (two) deux; (a few) deux ou trois; **a ~ of times** deux ou trois fois.

coupon *n* **1** (for goods) bon *m*; **petrol ~** (GB) bon d'essence; **2** (in ad) coupon *m*; **reply ~** coupon-réponse *m*.

courage *n* courage *m*; **to pluck up the ~ to do** trouver le courage de faire.

courageous *adj* courageux/-euse.

courier ▶**805** *n* **1** (also **travel ~**) accompagnateur/-trice *m/f*; **2** (for parcels, documents) coursier *m*; (for drugs) transporteur *m*.

course I *n* **1** (of time, event, history) cours *m* (**of** de); **in the ~ of** au cours de; **in (the) ~ of time** avec le temps; **to run** or **take its ~** suivre son cours; **in due ~** en temps utile; **2** (route) cours *m*; (of boat, plane) cap *m*; **to be on ~** [*boat, plane*] tenir le cap; **to go off ~** [*ship*] dévier de son cap; **to change ~** (gen) changer de direction; [*boat, plane*] changer de cap; **to take a ~ of action** adopter une certaine conduite; **3** (classes) cours *m* (**in** en; **of** de); **French ~** cours *m* de français; **beginners' ~** cours *m* pour débutants; **to go on** or **be on a ~** (aller) suivre un cours; **4** (Med) **a ~ of treatment** un traitement; **5** (Sport) (in golf, athletics) parcours *m*; (in racing) cours *m*; **6** (part of meal) plat *m*; **the main ~** le plat principal; **five-~ meal** repas *m* de cinq plats.
II of course *phr* bien sûr, évidemment; **of ~ I do!** (confirming suggestion) bien sûr que oui!; (refuting allegation) bien sûr que si!; **of ~ he doesn't!** bien sûr que non!

court I *n* **1** (Law) cour *f*, tribunal *m*; **to go to ~** aller devant les tribunaux (**over** pour); **to take sb to ~** poursuivre qn en justice; **2** (for tennis, squash) court *m*; (for basketball) terrain *m*; **3** (of sovereign) cour *f*.
II *vtr* courtiser [*woman, voters*].

court case *n* procès *m*, affaire *f*.

courteous *adj* courtois (**to** envers).

courtesy *n* courtoisie *f*; **it is only common ~** c'est la moindre des politesses.

court: **~house** *n* (Law) palais *m* de justice; **~-martial** *vtr* faire passer [qn] en cour martiale; **~ of law** *n* cour *f* de justice; **~ order** *n* décision *f* judiciaire; **~room** *n* salle *f* d'audience; **~yard** *n* cour *f*.

cousin *n* cousin/-e *m/f*.

cover I *n* **1** (protective lid, sheath) couverture *f*; (for duvet, typewriter, cushion, furniture) housse *f*;

Countries, Cities, and Continents

Countries and continents

Most countries and all continents are used with the definite article in French:

I like France / Canada	= j'aime **la** France / **le** Canada
to visit the United States	= visiter **les** États-Unis

A very few countries are not:

to visit Israel	= visiter Israël

All the continent names are feminine in French. Most names of countries are feminine eg ***la France***, but some are masculine eg ***le Canada***.

Most names of countries are singular in French, but some are plural eg ***les États-Unis mpl***. Note the plural verb:

*the United States **is** a rich country*	= les États-Unis **sont** un pays riche

In, to, and from somewhere

With continent names, feminine singular names of countries and masculine singular names of countries beginning with a vowel, for ***in*** and ***to*** use ***en***, and for ***from*** use ***de*** (or ***d'*** before a vowel or mute 'h'):

*to go **to** Europe / **to** France / **to** Iraq*	= aller **en** Europe / **en** France / **en** Irak
*to come **from** France*	= venir **de** France

With masculine countries beginning with a consonant, use ***au*** for ***in*** and ***to***, and ***du*** for ***from***. With plurals, use ***aux*** for ***in*** and ***to***, and ***des*** for ***from***:

*to live **in** Canada / **in** the United States*	= vivre **au** Canada / **aux** États-Unis
*to come **from the** United States*	= venir **des** États-Unis

Adjective uses: français *or* de France*?*

Taking the word ***French*** as an example, the translation ***français*** is usually safe.

Some nouns, however, occur more commonly with ***de France***:

*the Ambassador **of France*** *the **French** Ambassador*	= l'ambassadeur **de France**

Towns and cities

For ***in*** and ***to*** with the name of a town, use ***à*** in French; if the French name includes the definite article, ***à*** will become ***au***, ***à la***, ***à l'*** or ***aux***.

*to live **in** Toulouse / **in** le Havre/* ***in** la Rochelle*	= vivre **à** Toulouse / **au** Havre/ **à la** Rochelle

Similarly, ***from*** is ***de***, becoming ***du***, ***de la***, ***de l'*** or ***des*** when it combines with the definite article in town names:

*to come **from** Toulouse /* ***from** le Havre / **from** les Arcs*	= venir **de** Toulouse / **du** Havre / **des** Arcs

Most towns in French-speaking countries have a corresponding adjective and noun. The noun forms, spelt with a capital letter, mean *a person from X*:

*the inhabitants **of Bordeaux***	= les **Bordelais** *mpl*

The adjective forms, spelt with a small letter, are often used where in English the town name is used as an adjective:

***Paris** shops*	= les magasins **parisiens**

However, some of these French words are fairly rare and it is always safe to say ***les habitants de X*** or, for the adjective, simply ***de X***:

*a **Bordeaux** accent*	= l'accent **de Bordeaux**

2 (blanket) couverture *f*; **3** (of book, magazine) couverture *f*; (of record) pochette *f*; **on the ~** (of book) sur la couverture; (of magazine) en couverture; **from ~ to ~** de la première à la dernière page; **4** (shelter) abri *m*; **take ~!** aux abris!; **5** (for spy, crime) couverture *f* (**for** pour); **6** (Mil) couverture *f*; **air ~** couverture aérienne; **7** (for teacher, doctor) remplacement *m*; **to provide emergency ~** offrir un service d'urgence; **8** (insurance) assurance *f* (**for** pour; **against** contre); **to provide ~ against** garantir contre.
II *vtr* **1** (conceal or protect) couvrir (**with** avec); recouvrir [*cushion, sofa*] (**with** de); **2** (coat) recouvrir [*surface, person, cake*] (**with** de); **3** (be all over) [*litter, bruises*] couvrir; **~ed in spots** couvert de boutons; **4** (travel over) parcourir [*distance, area*]; (extend over) s'étendre sur [*area*]; **to ~ a lot of miles** faire beaucoup de kilomètres; **5** (deal with, include) [*article, speaker*] traiter; [*term*] englober; [*teacher*] faire; [*rule, law*] s'appliquer à; [*department*] s'occuper de; [*rep*] couvrir; **6** (report on) [*journalist*] couvrir; **~ed live on BBC1** diffusé en direct par BBC1; **7** (pay for) couvrir [*costs*]; combler [*loss*]; **to ~ one's costs** rentrer dans ses frais; **8** (insure) assurer, couvrir (**for, against** contre; **for doing** pour faire); **9** (Mil, Sport) couvrir; **10** (conceal) cacher [*ignorance*]; masquer [*smell*].
■ **cover for**: **~ for [sb]** remplacer [*employee*].
■ **cover over**: **~ over [sth], ~ [sth] over** couvrir [*yard, pool*] (**with** avec); recouvrir [*mark*] (**with** de).
■ **cover up**: ¶ **~ up 1** (put clothes on) se couvrir (**with** de); **2 to ~ up for** couvrir [*friend*]; **they're ~ing up for each other** ils se couvrent l'un l'autre; ¶ **~ up [sth], ~ [sth] up** recouvrir [*object*]; dissimuler [*mistake, truth*]; étouffer [*scandal*].

coverage *n* couverture *f*; **newspaper ~** couverture par les journaux; **live ~** reportage *m* en direct.

covering *n* **1** (for wall, floor) revêtement *m*; **2** (layer of snow, moss) couche *f*.

covering letter *n* lettre *f* d'accompagnement.

covert *adj* [*operation*] secret/-ète; [*glance*] furtif/-ive; [*threat*] voilé.

cover: **~-up** *n* opération *f* de camouflage; **~ version** *n* version *f*.

cow *n* vache *f*.

coward *n* lâche *mf*.

cowardice *n* lâcheté *f*.

cowboy ▶805 *n* **1** (US) cowboy *m*; **2** (incompetent worker) fumiste *m*.

cowl neck *n* col *m* boule.

coy *adj* **1** [*smile, look*] de fausse modestie; **2** (reticent) réservé (**about** à propos de).

cozy (US) = **cosy**.

crab *n* crabe *m*.

crack I *n* **1** (in varnish, ground) craquelure *f* (**in** dans); (in wall, cup, bone) fêlure *f* (**in** dans); **2** (in door) entrebâillement *m*; (in curtains) fente *f*; (in rock) fissure *f*; **3** (also **~ cocaine**) crack *m*; **4** (noise) craquement *m*; **5**○ (attempt) essai *m*, tentative *f*; **to have a ~ at doing** essayer de faire; **6** plaisanterie *f* (**about** à propos de); **a cheap ~** une plaisanterie facile.
II *adj* [*player*] de première; [*troops, shot*] d'élite.
III *vtr* **1** (make a crack in) fêler [*bone, wall, cup*]; fendiller, faire craqueler [*varnish*]; **2** (break) casser [*nut, egg*]; faire craquer [*defences*]; **to ~ a safe** fracturer un coffre-fort; **to ~ sth open** ouvrir qch; **to ~ one's head open** se fendre le crâne; **3** (solve) résoudre [*problem*]; déchiffrer [*code*]; **4** faire claquer [*whip*]; faire craquer [*knuckles, joints*].
IV *vi* **1** [*bone, cup, wall, ice*] se fêler; [*varnish*] se craqueler; [*skin*] se crevasser; [*ground*] se fendre; **2** [*person*] craquer; **to ~ under pressure** ne pas tenir le coup; **3** [*knuckles, twig*] craquer; [*whip*] claquer; **4** [*voice*] se casser.
■ **crack down** prendre des mesures énergiques, sévir (**on** contre).

cracker *n* **1** (biscuit) cracker *m*, biscuit *m* salé; **2** (for Christmas) diablotin *m*.

crackle I *n* crépitement *m*.
II *vi* [*twig, fire, radio*] crépiter; [*hot fat*] grésiller.

cradle *n* berceau *m*.

craft I *n* artisanat *m*; **arts and ~s** artisanat (d'art).
II *noun modifier* [*exhibition, guild*] artisanal.

craftsman *n* (skilled manually) artisan *m*; (skilled artistically) artiste *m*.

crafty *adj* astucieux/-ieuse.

cram I *vtr* **to ~ sth into** enfoncer or fourrer○ qch dans [*bag, car*]; **to ~ sb into** entasser qn dans [*room*]; **~med full** plein à craquer.
II *vi* [*student*] bachoter (**for** pour).

cramp *n* crampe *f*; **to have ~** (GB) or **a ~** (US) avoir une crampe; **a ~ in one's foot/leg** une crampe dans le pied/à la jambe; **stomach ~s** crampes d'estomac.

cramped *adj* [*house, office*] exigu/-uë; **~ conditions** conditions d'exiguïté.

cranberry *n* canneberge *f*; **~ sauce** sauce *f* à la canneberge.

crane *n* grue *f*.

cranium *n* crâne *m*, boîte *f* crânienne.

crank *n* **1**○ (freak) fanatique *mf*, fana○ *mf*; **2** (handle) manivelle *f*.

crash I *n* **1** (noise) fracas *m*; **2** (accident) accident *m*; **car ~** accident de voiture; **train ~** catastrophe *f* ferroviaire; **3** (of stock market) krach *m*.
II *vtr* **to ~ one's car into a bus** rentrer dans or percuter un bus.
III *vi* **1** [*car, plane*] s'écraser; [*vehicles, planes*] se rentrer dedans, se percuter; **to ~ into sth** rentrer dans or percuter qch; **2** [*share prices*] s'effondrer.

crash: **~ barrier** *n* glissière *f* de sécurité; **~ course** *n* cours *m* intensif; **~ diet** *n* régime *m* d'amaigrissement intensif; **~ helmet** *n* casque *m*; **~-land** *vi* atterrir en catastrophe; **~ landing** *n* atterrissage *m* en catastrophe.

crate *n* (for bottles, china) caisse *f*; (for fruit, vegetables) cageot *m*.

crater *n* (of volcano) cratère *m*; (caused by explosion) entonnoir *m*.

crave *vtr* (also **~ for**) avoir un besoin maladif de [*drug*]; avoir soif de [*affection*]; avoir envie de [*food*].

craving *n* (for drug) besoin *m* maladif (**for** de); (for affection) soif *f* (**for** de); (for food) envie *f* (**for** de).

crawl I *n* **1** (in swimming) crawl *m*; **2 at a ~** au pas; **to go at a ~** [*vehicle*] rouler au pas.
II *vi* **1** [*insect, snake, person*] ramper; **to ~ in/out** entrer/sortir en rampant; **2** [*baby*] marcher à quatre pattes; **3** [*vehicle*] rouler au pas; **to ~ up sth** monter lentement qch; **4** [*time*] se traîner; **5 to be ~ing with** fourmiller de [*insects, tourists*]; **6**° (flatter) faire du lèche-bottes° (**to** à).

crayfish *n* **1** (freshwater) écrevisse *f*; **2** (spiny lobster) langouste *f*.

crayon *n* (wax) craie *f* grasse; (pencil) crayon *m* de couleur.

craze *n* vogue *f*; **it's just a ~** c'est une toquade; **to be the latest ~** faire fureur.

crazy° *adj* **1** [*person, price, speed*] fou/folle; [*behaviour, idea*] insensé; **to go ~** devenir fou/folle; **2** (infatuated) **~ about** fou/folle de [*person*]; passionné de [*activity*].

crazy golf ▶ 649 *n* (GB) mini-golf *m*.

creak I *n* (of hinge) grincement *m*; (of floorboard) craquement *m*.
II *vi* [*hinge*] grincer; [*floorboard*] craquer.

creaky *adj* [*door, hinge*] grinçant; [*joint, floorboard*] qui craque.

cream ▶ 559 **I** *n* crème *f*; **strawberries and ~** fraises à la crème; **shoe ~** crème à chaussures.
II *noun modifier* [*cake, bun*] à la crème.
III *adj* (couleur) crème *inv*.
IV *vtr* **~ed potatoes** purée *f* de pommes de terre.

cream: **~ cheese** *n* fromage *m* à tartiner; **~ soda** *n* soda *m* parfumé à la vanille.

creamy *adj* [*texture*] crémeux/-euse; [*complexion*] laiteux/-euse.

crease I *n* (intentional) pli *m*; (accidental) faux pli *m*.
II *vtr* froisser [*paper, cloth*].
III *vi* [*cloth*] se froisser.

create *vtr* créer [*product, job, work of art*]; lancer [*fashion*]; provoquer [*interest, repercussion*]; poser [*problem*]; faire [*good impression*].

creation *n* création *f*; **job ~** création d'emplois.

creative *adj* **1** [*person*] créatif/-ive; **2** [*process, imagination*] créateur/-trice.

creativity *n* créativité *f*.

creator *n* créateur/-trice *m/f* (**of** de).

creature *n* **1** (living being) créature *f*; **poor ~!** le/la pauvre!; **2** (animal) animal *m*.

creature comforts *n pl* confort *m* matériel; **to like one's ~** aimer son confort.

crèche *n* (GB) (nursery) crèche *f*; (in shopping centre) halte-garderie *f*.

credentials *n pl* **1** (reputation) qualifications *fpl*; **2** (reference) pièce *f* d'identité.

credibility *n* crédibilité *f*.

credible *adj* crédible.

credit I *n* **1** (merit) mérite *m* (**for** de); **to get/take the ~** se voir attribuer/s'attribuer le mérite (**for** de); **to be a ~ to sb/sth** faire honneur à qn/qch; **it does you ~** c'est tout à votre honneur; **he is more intelligent than he is given ~ for** il est plus intelligent qu'on ne le croit généralement; **~ where ~ is due** il faut en convenir; **2** (in business) crédit *m*; **on ~** à crédit; **to live on ~** vivre de crédits; **to give sb ~** faire crédit à qn.
II *vtr* **1 to ~ sb with** attribuer à qn [*achievement*]; **2** créditer [*account*] (**with** de); **to ~ sth to an account** porter qch sur un compte

credit: **~ account** *n* compte *m* personnel; **~ balance** *n* solde *m* créditeur; **~ card** *n* carte *f* de crédit; **~ control** *n* encadrement *m* du crédit; **~ facilities** *n pl* facilités *fpl* de crédit; **~ limit** *n* limite *f* de crédit.

creditor *n* créancier/-ière *m/f*.

credits *n pl* générique *m*.

creed *n* (religious persuasion) croyance *f*; (opinions) principes *mpl*, credo *m*.

creek *n* **1** (GB) (coastal) bras *m* de mer; (from river) bras *m* mort; **2** (stream) ruisseau *m*.

creep *vi* **1 to ~ in/out** [*person*] entrer/sortir à pas de loup; **to ~ under sth** se glisser sous qch; **to ~ along** [*vehicle*] avancer lentement; [*insect, cat*] ramper; **2** [*plant*] (horizontally) ramper; (climb) grimper.

creeper *n* (in jungle) liane *f*; (climbing plant) plante *f* grimpante.

cremate *vtr* incinérer.

cremation *n* **1** (ceremony) crémation *f*; **2** (practice) incinération *f*.

crematorium (GB) *n* crématorium *m*.

crepe, crêpe *n* crêpe *m*.

crescendo *n* **to reach a ~** [*campaign*] atteindre son apogée; [*noise, protest*] atteindre son paroxysme.

crescent moon *n* croissant *m* de (la) lune.

cress *n* cresson *m*.

crest *n* **1** (ridge) crête *f*; **2** (coat of arms) armoiries *fpl*.

Crete *pr n* Crète *f*.

crevice *n* fissure *f*.

crew *n* **1** (staff) équipage *m*; **2** (rowing, filming) équipe *f*; **3**° (gang) bande *f*.

crewcut *n* coupe *f* (de cheveux) en brosse.

crew neck sweater *n* pull *m* ras du cou.

crib I *n* **1** (cot) lit *m* d'enfant; **2** (GB) (Nativity) crèche *f*; **3** (translation) traduction *f*.
II *vi* copier (**from** sur).

crick *n* **a ~ in one's back** un tour de reins; **a ~ in one's neck** un torticolis.

cricket ▶ 649 *n* **1** (insect) grillon *m*; **2** (game) cricket *m*
IDIOMS **it's not ~** ce n'est pas franc-jeu.

crime I *n* **1** (minor) délit *m*; (serious) crime *m* (**against** contre); **2** (phenomenon) criminalité *f*.
II *noun modifier* [*fiction, novel, writing*] policier/-ière; [*wave, rate*] de criminalité.

crime prevention *n* lutte *f* contre le crime.

criminal I *n* criminel/-elle *m/f*.
II *adj* **1** criminel/-elle; **2 it's ~!** c'est un crime!

criminal charges *n pl* charges *fpl*; **to face ~** être sous le coup d'une inculpation.

criminal: **~ offence** (GB), **~ offense** (US) *n* délit *m*; **~ proceedings** *n pl* poursuites *fpl* judiciaires.

criminal record *n* casier *m* judiciaire; **to have a/no ~** avoir un casier judiciaire chargé/vierge.

crimson ▶559 I *n* cramoisi *m*.
II *adj* pourpre; **to go ~** devenir cramoisi.

cringe *vi* **1** (physically) avoir un mouvement de recul; **2** (with embarrassment) avoir envie de rentrer sous terre.

cripple I *n* impotent/-e *m/f*; **emotional ~** personne *f* bloquée sur le plan émotionnel.
II *vtr* **1** estropier; **~d for life** infirme à vie; **2** paralyser [*country, industry*].

crippled *adj* **1** (physically) impotent; **to be ~ with sth** être perclus de qch; **2** (by debt) [*person*] écrasé (**by** par); [*country, industry*] paralysé (**by** par).

crippling *adj* [*disease*] invalidant; [*taxes, debts*] écrasant; [*strike, effect*] paralysant.

crisis *n* crise *f* (**in** dans; **over** à cause de); **cabinet ~** crise au sein du gouvernement; **midlife ~** crise des cinquante ans; **to be in ~** [*people*] être en crise.

crisp *adj* [*biscuit*] croustillant; [*fruit*] croquant; [*garment*] frais/fraîche; [*banknote, snow*] craquant; [*air*] vif/vive; [*manner*] brusque.
IDIOMS **to be burnt to a ~**○ être carbonisé.

crispbread *n* (GB) pain *m* grillé suédois.

crisps *n pl* (also **potato ~**) chips *fpl*.

crispy *adj* croustillant.

crisscross *adj* [*pattern*] en croisillons.

criterion *n* critère *m* (**for** de).

critic ▶805 *n* **1** (reviewer) critique *m*; **2** (opponent) détracteur/-trice *m/f*.

critical *adj* [*point, condition, remark*] critique; [*stage*] crucial; [*moment*] décisif/-ive; **to be ~ of sb/sth** critiquer qn/qch.

critically *adv* **1** [*compare, examine*] d'un œil critique; **2** [*view*] sévèrement; [*speak*] avec animosité (**of, about** de); **3** [*ill*] très gravement.

criticism *n* critique *f*.

criticize *vtr* critiquer; **to ~ sb for sth** reprocher qch à qn; **to ~ sb for doing** reprocher à qn de faire.

croak *vi* **1** (frog) coasser; **2**◐ (die) crever◐.

Croatia ▶574 *pr n* Croatie *f*.

crochet I *n* crochet *m*.
II *vtr* faire [qch] au crochet; **a ~(ed) sweater** un pull au crochet.

crockery *n* vaisselle *f*.

crocodile *n* **1** (animal, leather) crocodile *m*; **2** (GB) (line) rang *m* par deux.
IDIOMS **to shed ~ tears** verser des larmes de crocodile.

crony *n* (petit/-e) copain/copine *m/f*.

crook○ *n* escroc *m*.
IDIOMS **by hook or by ~** coûte que coûte.

crooked *adj* **1** [*line*] brisé; **a ~ smile** un sourire en coin; **2** (off-centre) [*frame, beam*] de travers; [*house*] de guingois *inv*; **3**○ (dishonest) malhonnête.

crop *n* **1** (produce) culture *f*; (harvest) récolte *f*; **2** (of medals) moisson *f*; (of students, films) cuvée *f*; (of weeds) paquet○ *m*; **3** (haircut) coupe *f* courte; **4** (whip) cravache *f*.
■ **crop up** [*matter, problem*] surgir; [*name*] être mentionné; [*opportunity*] se présenter.

croquet ▶649 *n* croquet *m*.

cross I *n* **1** (shape) croix *f*; **to put a ~ against** cocher [*name, item*]; **2** (hybrid) croisement *m*; (mixture of two things) mélange *m*.
II *adj* **1** (angry) fâché (**with** contre); **to be ~ about sth** être agacé par qch; **to get ~** se fâcher (**with** contre); **to make sb ~** fâcher qn, agacer qn; **2** [*breeze*] contraire.
III *vtr* **1** [*person*] traverser [*road*]; traverser, passer [*river*]; franchir [*border, line*]; [*bridge*] franchir, enjamber; [*road, railway line*] traverser; [*person*] dépasser [*limit, boundary*]; **it ~ed his mind that** il lui est venu à l'esprit or l'idée que; **2** (intersect with) couper; **3 to ~ one's legs** croiser les jambes; **4** croiser [*breed, species*] (**with** avec); **5** contrarier [*person*]; **6** barrer [*cheque*].
IV *vi* **1** (also **~ over**) **to ~ to North America** aller en Amérique; **to ~ into Italy** passer en Italie; **2** (intersect) se croiser; **3** [*letters*] se croiser.
V **crossed** *pp adj* [*line*] brouillé.
■ **cross off**: **~ [sth/sb] off, ~ off [sth/sb]** barrer, rayer [*name, item*].
■ **cross out**: **~ out [sth], ~ [sth] out** rayer, barrer.

cross: **~breed** *vtr* croiser [*animals*]; hybrider [*plants*]; **~-Channel** *adj* trans-Manche; **~-check** *vtr, vi* revérifier.

cross-country I ▶649 *n* **1** (running) cross *m*; **2** (skiing) ski *m* de fond.
II *adj* **1** [*runner*] de fond; [*race, champion*] de cross; **2** [*skiing, skier*] de fond.

cross: **~-court** *adj* [*volley*] droit croisé; **~-examination** *n* contre-interrogatoire *m*; **~-examine** *vtr* interroger; (in courtroom) faire subir un contre-interrogatoire à [*person*].

cross-eyed *adj* [*person*] atteint de strabisme; **to be ~** loucher, avoir un strabisme.

crossfire *n* feux *mpl* croisés; **to get caught in the ~** être pris entre deux feux.

crossing *n* **1** (journey) traversée *f*; **2** (area of road) passage *m* (pour) piétons, passage *m* clouté; (level crossing) passage *m* à niveau.

crossing-out *n* rature *f*.

cross-legged *adv* [*sit*] en tailleur.

cross-purposes *n pl* **we are at ~** il y a un malentendu; (disagreement) nous sommes en désaccord.

cross: **~-question** *vtr* faire subir un interrogatoire à [*person*]; **~-reference** *n* renvoi *m* (**to** à); **~roads** *n* carrefour *m*; **~-section** *n* échantillon *m* (**of** de); **~word** *n* (also **~ puzzle**) mots *mpl* croisés.

crotch *n* **1** (of body) entrecuisse *m*; **2** (in trousers) entrejambe *m*.

crotchet *n* (GB) noire *f*.

crouch *vi* (also **~ down**) [*person*] s'accroupir; [*animal*] (to spring) se ramasser.

croupier ▶ 805 *n* croupier *m*.

crow I *n* corbeau *m*.
II *vi* **1** (exult) exulter; **2** [*baby*] gazouiller; **3** [*cock*] chanter.
IDIOMS **as the ~ flies** à vol d'oiseau.

crowbar *n* pince-monseigneur *f*.

crowd I *n* **1** (mass of people) foule *f*; (watching sport, play) spectateurs *mpl*; **~s of people** une foule de gens; **a ~ gathered at the scene** un attroupement s'est formé sur les lieux; **2**○ (group) bande *f*.
II *vtr* **1** (squash) entasser [*people, furniture*] (**into** dans); **to ~ as much as possible into a visit** voir le plus de choses possible; **2** (fill to excess) encombrer [*room, house*] (**with** de); **3**○ (put pressure on) harceler.
III *vi* **to ~ into** s'entasser dans [*room, lift, vehicle*]; **to ~ onto** s'entasser dans [*bus, train*]; **to ~ (up) against** se presser contre [*barrier*].

crowded *adj* **1** [*place*] plein de monde; (jam-packed) bondé; **to be ~ with** être plein de [*people, cars*]; **2** (busy) [*schedule*] chargé.

crown I *n* **1** (of monarch) couronne *f*; **2** (top) (of hill) crête *f*; (of hat) fond *m*; (of head) crâne *m*; **3** (on tooth) couronne *f*.
II *vtr* **1** couronner; **to ~ it all** pour couronner le tout; **2** couronner [*tooth*].

crown: **~ jewels** *n pl* joyaux *mpl* de la Couronne; **~ prince** *n* prince *m* héritier.

crow: **~'s feet** *n pl* pattes-d'oie *fpl*; **~'s nest** *n* nid *m* de pie.

crucial *adj* crucial.

crucify○ *vtr* démolir○.

crude *adj* **1** [*method*] rudimentaire; [*estimate*] approximatif/-ive; **2** [*joke*] grossier/-ière; [*person*] vulgaire; **3** (unprocessed) brut; **~ oil** pétrole *m* brut.

crudely *adv* **1 ~ speaking,...** grosso modo...; **2** [*painted, made*] grossièrement.

cruel *adj* cruel/-elle; [*winter, climate*] rigoureux/-euse; **a ~ blow** un coup très dur.

cruelty *n* cruauté *f* (**to** envers).

cruise I *n* croisière *f*; **to go on a ~** faire une croisière.
II *vtr* [*driver, taxi*] parcourir [*street, city*].
III *vi* **1** [*liner, tourist*] faire une croisière (**in** en; **along** le long de; **around** aux abords de); **2 to ~ at 10,000 metres** [*plane*] voler à une altitude de croisière de 10 000 mètres; **3**○ **to ~ to victory** triompher sans peine.

cruiser *n* petit bateau *m* de croisière.

crumb *n* **1** (of food) miette *f*; **2** (tiny amount) **a ~ of** une bribe de [*information, conversation*]; **a ~ of comfort** une maigre consolation.

crumble I *vtr* (also **~ up**) émietter [*bread*].
II *vi* **1** [*rock*] s'effriter; [*building*] se délabrer; **2** [*relationship, economy*] se désagréger; [*opposition*] s'effondrer.

crumbling *adj* **1** [*building, façade*] délabré; **2** [*economy, empire*] prêt à s'effondrer.

crummy○ *adj* minable○.

crumple *vtr* (also **~ up**) froisser [*paper*]; **to ~ sth into a ball** rouler qch en boule.

crunch *vtr* croquer [*apple, biscuit*].
IDIOMS **when** or **if it comes to the ~** au moment crucial; **the ~ came when** le moment critique est arrivé lorsque.

crunchy *adj* croquant.

crusade *n* croisade *f*.

crush I *n* bousculade *f*.
II *vtr* **1** écraser [*enemy, uprising*]; étouffer [*protest*]; **to be ~ed by** être accablé par [*defeat*]; **2** (squash) écraser [*can, person, vehicle*] (**against** contre); broyer [*arm, leg*]; **to be ~ed to death** (by vehicle) se faire écraser; (by masonry) être écrasé sous les décombres; **3** (crease) chiffonner [*garment, fabric*].

crush: **~ barrier** *n* (GB) barrière *f* de sécurité; **~ed velvet** *n* velours *m* frappé.

crushing *adj* [*defeat, weight*] écrasant; [*blow*] percutant; [*setback*] cuisant.

crust *n* croûte *f*; **the earth's ~** l'écorce *f* terrestre.

crusty *adj* **1** [*bread*] croustillant; **2**○ (irritable) grincheux/-euse.

crutch *n* béquille *f*; **to be on ~es** marcher avec des béquilles.

crux *n* **the ~ of the matter** le point crucial.

cry I *n* cri *m*; **a ~ for help** (figurative) un appel à l'aide.
II *vi* pleurer (**about** à cause de; **with** de); **to ~ with laughter** rire aux larmes.
IDIOMS **to ~ one's eyes out** pleurer à chaudes larmes.
■ **cry off**○ (GB) se décommander.
■ **cry out 1** (with pain, grief) pousser un cri or des cris; **2** (call) crier, s'écrier.

crying I *n* pleurs *mpl*.
II *adj* [*need*] urgent; **it's a ~ shame!** c'est une honte!

crypt *n* crypte *f*.

crystal *n* **1** (glassware) cristal *m*; **2** (on watch-face) verre *m*.

crystal clear *adj* **1** [*water*] cristallin; **2** [*explanation*] clair comme de l'eau de roche.

crystallized *adj* [*fruit, ginger*] confit.

CS gas *n* (GB) gaz *m* lacrymogène.

cub *n* (Zool) petit *m*.

Cuba ▶ 574 *pr n* Cuba *f*; **to go to ~** aller à Cuba.

cubby-hole○ *n* **1** (cramped space) réduit *m*; **2** (storage space) cagibi○ *m*.

cube I *n* cube *m*; **ice ~** glaçon *m*.
II *vtr* couper [qch] en cubes [*meat*].

cubic *adj* **1** (form) cubique; **2** (measurement) [*metre, centimetre*] cube *inv*.

cubicle *n* (in changing room) cabine *f*; (in public toilets) cabinet *m*.

cuckoo *n* coucou *m*.

cucumber *n* concombre *m*.
IDIOMS **to be as cool as a ~** être d'un calme absolu.

cuddle I *n* câlin *m*; **to give sb a ~** faire un câlin à qn.
II *vtr* câliner.

cuddly *adj* (sweet) adorable; (soft) doux/douce.

cue *n* **1** (line) réplique *f* précédente; (action) signal *m*; **on ~** (figurative) à point nommé; **2** (Sport) queue *f* de billard.

cuff *n* **1** (at wrist) poignet *m*; (on shirt) manchette *f*; **2** (US) (on trousers) revers *m*.
IDIOMS **to speak off the ~** faire un discours au pied levé.

cuff link *n* bouton *m* de manchette.

cuisine *n* cuisine *f*; **haute ~** la grande cuisine.

cul-de-sac *n* impasse *f*, cul-de-sac *m*.

culminate *vtr* aboutir (**in** à).

culottes *n pl* jupe-culotte *f*.

culprit *n* coupable *mf*.

cult I *n* culte *m*; (contemporary religion) secte *f*.
II *noun modifier* **a ~ film** un film-culte; **to be a ~ figure** faire l'objet d'un culte.

cultivate *vtr* cultiver.

cultural *adj* culturel/-elle.

cultural attaché ▶ 805 *n* attaché/-e *m/f* culturel/-elle.

culture *n* culture *f*; **drug ~** l'univers *m* de la drogue.

culture: **~-bound** *adj* culturel/-elle; **~ shock** *n* choc *m* culturel.

culvert *n* conduite *f* souterraine.

-cum- *combining form* **garage~workshop** garage-atelier *m*.

cumbersome *adj* [*luggage, furniture*] encombrant.

cumulative *adj* cumulatif/-ive.

cunning I *n* **1** (of person) ruse *f*; (nastier) fourberie *f*.
II *adj* **1** [*person*] rusé; (nastier) fourbe; **2** [*trick*] habile; [*device*] astucieux/-ieuse.

cup I *n* **1** (object, contents) tasse *f*; **2** (trophy) coupe *f*.
II *vtr* **to ~ one's hands around** mettre ses mains en paravent autour de [*flame*].

cupboard *n* placard *m*.
IDIOMS **the ~ is bare** les caisses sont vides.

cup tie *n* (GB) match *m* de coupe.

curable *adj* guérissable.

curate *n* vicaire *m*.

curator ▶ 805 *n* conservateur/-trice *m/f*.

curb I *n* **1** (control) restriction *f* (**on** à); **2** (US) (sidewalk) bord *m* du trottoir.
II *vtr* refréner [*desires*]; limiter [*powers*]; juguler [*spending*]; restreindre [*consumption*].

curdle *vi* [*milk*] se cailler; [*sauce*] tourner.

cure I *n* (remedy) remède *m* (**for** à); (for illness) traitement *m* (**for** pour).
II *vtr* **1** guérir [*disease, patient*] (**of** de); **2** guérir [*bad habit, person*] (**of** de).

cure-all *n* panacée *f* (**for** contre).

curfew *n* couvre-feu *m*; **ten o'clock ~** couvre-feu à partir de dix heures.

curio *n* curiosité *f*, objet *m* rare.

curiosity *n* curiosité *f* (**about** sur, au sujet de); **out of ~** par curiosité.
IDIOMS **~ killed the cat** la curiosité est un vilain défaut.

curious *adj* curieux/-ieuse; **I'm just ~!** j'aurais aimé savoir, c'est tout!

curiously *adv* [*silent, detached*] étrangement; **~ enough** chose assez curieuse.

curl I *n* boucle *f*.
II *vtr* friser [*hair*].
III *vi* **1** [*hair*] friser; **2** (also **~ up**) [*paper*] (se) gondoler; [*edges, leaf*] se racornir.
■ **curl up** [*person*] se pelotonner; [*cat*] se mettre en rond; **to ~ up in bed** se blottir dans son lit; **to ~ up into a ball** [*hedgehog*] se mettre en boule.

curler *n* bigoudi *m*.

curly *adj* [*hair*] (tight curls) frisé; (loose curls) bouclé; [*tail, eyelashes*] recourbé.

currant *n* raisin *m* de Corinthe.

currency ▶ 748 *n* monnaie *f*, devise *f*; **to buy foreign ~** acheter des devises étrangères; **~ market** marché *m* monétaire.

current I *n* (of electricity, water) courant *m*; (of air) flux *m*; (trend) tendance *f*.
II *adj* [*leader, situation, policy*] actuel/-elle; [*year, research*] en cours.

current: **~ account** *n* (GB) compte *m* courant; **~ affairs** *n* actualité *f*.

currently *adv* actuellement, en ce moment.

curriculum *n* programme *m*; **in the ~** au programme.

curry *n* curry *m*; **chicken ~** curry de poulet.
IDIOMS **to ~ favour** chercher à se faire bien voir (**with sb** de qn).

curse I *n* **1** (scourge) fléau *m*; **2** (swearword) juron *m*; **3** (spell) malédiction *f*.
II *vtr* maudire.
III *vi* jurer (**at** après); **to ~ and swear** jurer comme un charretier.

cursor *n* curseur *m*.

curt *adj* sec/sèche.

curtain *n* rideau *m*; **after the final ~** après la chute du rideau.

curtain call *n* rappel *m*.

curve I *n* courbe *f*.
II *vi* [*line, wall*] s'incurver; [*road, railway*] faire une courbe.

curved *adj* courbe; [*staircase, blade*] incurvé; [*edge*] arrondi; [*arch*] cintré.

cushion *n* **1** coussin *m*; **2** (protection, reserve) garantie *f*.

custard *n* (GB) (creamy) ≈ crème *f* anglaise; (set, baked) flan *m*.

custodian ▶805 *n* (of collection) gardien/-ienne *m/f*; (in museum) conservateur/-trice *m/f*.

custody *n* **1** (detention) détention *f*; **in ~** en détention; **to take sb into ~** arrêter qn; **2** (of child) garde *f*; **to award ~** accorder la garde.

custom *n* **1** (personal habit) coutume *f*, habitude *f*; **2** (convention) coutume *f*, usage *m*; **3** (patronage) clientèle *f*; **to lose ~** perdre des clients.

customary *adj* habituel/-elle; (more formal) coutumier/-ière; **as is/was ~** comme de coutume.

custom-built *adj* [*house*] fait sur plans.

customer *n* **1** client/-e *m/f*; **'~ services'** 'service *m* clientèle'; **2**° (person) type° *m*.

custom-made *adj* fait sur mesure.

customs *n* douane *f*; **to go through ~** passer à la douane.

customs: **Customs and Excise** *n* (GB) douane *f* (britannique); **~ declaration** *n* déclaration *f* en douane; **~ duties** *n pl* droits *mpl* de douane; **~ hall** *n* douane *f*; **~ officer**, **~ official** ▶805 *n* douanier/-ière *m/f*.

cut I *n* **1** (incision) entaille *f*; (in surgery) incision *f*; **2** (wound) coupure *f*; **3** (hairstyle) coupe *f*; **4**° (share) part *f*; **5** (reduction) réduction *f* (**in** de); **job ~s** suppression *f* d'emplois; **a ~ in salary** une baisse de salaire.

II *vtr* **1** (with knife, scissors) couper [*bread, fabric, wood*]; faire [*hole, slit*]; **to ~ sth out of** couper qch dans [*fabric*]; découper qch dans [*magazine*]; **2** (sever) couper [*rope, corn, flower*]; rompre [*ties*]; **3** (draw blood) [*knife*] couper; [*remark*] blesser; **to ~ oneself** se couper; **to ~ one's finger** se couper le doigt; **4** (trim) couper [*grass, hair*]; tailler [*hedge*]; **to have one's hair cut** se faire couper les cheveux; **5** (shape, fashion) tailler [*gem, suit, marble*]; [*locksmith*] faire [*key*]; **6** (liberate) **to ~ sb from sth** dégager qn de [*wreckage*]; **to ~ sb free** or **loose** libérer qn (**from** de); **7** (edit) couper [*article, film*]; supprimer [*scene*]; **8** (reduce) réduire; **9** (grow) **to ~ a tooth** percer une dent; **to ~ one's teeth** faire ses dents; **10** (record) faire, graver [*album*]; **11** (Comput) couper [*paragraph*]; **12**° sécher° [*class*]; **13** (snub) ignorer, snober; **to ~ sb dead** ignorer complètement qn.

III *vi* **1** (with knife, scissors) couper; **to ~ into** entamer [*cake*]; couper [*fabric, paper*]; inciser [*flesh*]; **2 to ~ down a sidestreet** couper par une petite rue; **to ~ in front of sb** (in a queue) passer devant qn; (in a car) faire une queue de poisson à qn; **3 to ~ into** empiéter sur [*leisure time*].

IV cut *pp adj* **1** (sliced, sawn) coupé; **2** [*gem, stone*] taillé; **3** (bleeding) **to have a cut finger** avoir une coupure au doigt; **4** [*hay*] fauché; [*grass, flowers*] coupé.

IDIOMS **to have one's work cut out** avoir du travail en perspective.

■ **cut back**: ¶ **~ back** faire des économies; ¶ **~ back [sth]**, **~ [sth] back 1** (reduce) réduire [*production, spending*] (**to** à); **2** (prune) tailler.

■ **cut down**: ¶ **~ down** réduire sa consommation; **to ~ down on smoking** fumer moins; ¶ **~ down [sth]**, **~ [sth] down 1** (chop down) abattre; **2** (reduce) réduire.

■ **cut off**: ¶ **~ off [sth]**, **~ [sth] off 1** (remove) couper [*hair, piece, corner*]; enlever [*excess, crusts*]; **2** (reduce) **to ~ 20 minutes off the journey** raccourcir le trajet de 20 minutes; **3** (disconnect) couper [*mains service*]; ¶ **~ off [sth]** suspendre [*aid*]; **to ~ off sb's allowance** couper les vivres à qn; ¶ **~ [sb] off 1** (on phone) couper qn; **2** (isolate) **to feel cut off** se sentir isolé; **to ~ oneself off** s'isoler.

■ **cut out**: ¶ **~ out** [*engine, fan*] s'arrêter; ¶ **~ out [sth]** (eliminate) supprimer; ¶ **~ [sth] out**, **~ out [sth] 1** (snip out) découper (**from** dans); **2** supprimer [*scene, chapter*]; éliminer [*draught*]; **to ~ sb out of one's will** déshériter qn; **3**° (stop) **~ it out!** ça suffit!; **4 to be cut out for teaching** être fait pour être professeur.

■ **cut short**: **~ short [sth]**, **~ [sth] short** abréger [*holiday, discussion*].

■ **cut up**: **~ [sth] up**, **~ up [sth]** couper [*food*] (**into** en).

cutback *n* réduction *f*; **~s in** réductions dans le budget de [*health, education*].

cute° *adj* **1** (sweet, attractive) mignon/-onne; (sickly sweet) mièvre; **2** (clever) (US) malin/-igne; **to get ~** faire le malin.

cutlery *n* couverts *mpl*; **a set of ~** (for one) un couvert.

cutlet *n* côtelette *f*.

cut: **~-off date** *n* date-limite *f*; **~-off point** *n* limite *f*; **~-price** (GB), **~-rate** (US) *adj* à prix réduit.

cut-throat *adj* [*competition*] acharné; **a ~ business** un milieu très dur.

cutting I *n* **1** (from newspaper) coupure *f* (**from** de); **2** (in film-making) montage *m*.

II *adj* [*tone*] cassant; [*remark*] désobligeant.

cutting edge *n* **to be at the ~ of** être à l'avant-garde de.

cutting room *n* salle *f* de montage.

CV, **cv** *n* (*abbr* = **curriculum vitae**) cv, CV *m*, curriculum vitae *m*.

cyanide *n* cyanure *m*.

cycle I *n* **1** (series) cycle *m*; **wash ~** cycle *m* de lavage; **2** (bicycle) vélo *m*.

II *vi* aller à vélo; **to go cycling** faire du vélo.

cycle: **~ clip** *n* pince *f* à vélo; **~ lane** *n* piste *f* cyclable; **~ race** *n* course *f* cycliste; **~ rack** *n* parking *m* à vélos; **~ track** *n* piste *f* cyclable.

cycling ▶649 *n* cyclisme *m*; **to do a lot of ~** faire beaucoup de vélo.

cycling: **~ holiday** *n* (GB) vacances *fpl* à vélo; **~ shorts** *n pl* cuissard *m*.

cyclist *n* (gen) cycliste *mf*; (Sport) coureur/-euse *m/f* cycliste.

cygnet *n* jeune cygne *m*.

cylinder *n* **1** (in engine) cylindre *m*; **four-~** à quatre cylindres; **2** (of gas) bouteille *f*; **3** (GB) (also **hot water ~**) ballon *m* d'eau chaude.

cynic *n* cynique *mf*.

cynical *adj* cynique (**about** en ce qui concerne).

cynicism *n* cynisme *m*.

Cyprus ▶574 *pr n* Chypre *f*.

cyst *n* kyste *m*.

Czech ▶712 **I** *n* **1** (person) Tchèque *mf*; **2** (language) tchèque *m*.
II *adj* [*culture, politics*] tchèque; [*ambassador, embassy*] de la République tchèque; [*teacher, lesson*] de tchèque.

Czech Republic ▶574 *pr n* République *f* tchèque.

Dd

d, D *n* d, D *m*.
dab I *n* (of paint) touche *f*; (of butter) petit morceau *m*.
II *vtr* tamponner [*stain*] (**with** de); **to ~ one's eyes** se tamponner les yeux.
dabble *v* ■ **dabble in**: **~ in [sth]** faire [qch] en amateur [*painting, politics*].
dachshund *n* teckel *m*.
dad○, **Dad**○ *n* (child speaker) papa○ *m*; (adult speaker) père *m*.
daddy○, **Daddy**○ *n* papa○ *m*.
daffodil *n* jonquille *f*.
dagger *n* poignard *m*.
IDIOMS **to look ~s at sb** fusiller qn du regard.
daily I *n* **1** (newspaper) **the national dailies** les grands quotidiens; **2**○ (GB) (also **~ help, ~ maid**) femme *f* de ménage.
II *adj* **1** [*visit, routine*] quotidien/-ienne; **on a ~ basis** tous les jours; **2** [*wage, rate, intake*] journalier/-ière.
dainty *adj* [*porcelain, handkerchief*] délicat; [*shoe, hand, foot*] mignon/-onne.
dairy I *n* **1** (on farm) laiterie *f*; (shop) crémerie *f*; **2** (company) société *f* laitière.
II *noun modifier* [*butter*] fermier/-ière; [*cow, farm, product, cream*] laitier/-ière.
daisy *n* (common) pâquerette *f*; (garden) marguerite *f*.
IDIOMS **to be as fresh as a ~** être frais/fraîche comme une rose.
dam I *n* (construction) barrage *m*; (to prevent flooding) digue *f*.
II *vtr* construire un barrage sur [*river*]; (to prevent flooding) endiguer [*river*].
damage I *n* **1** (gen) dégâts *mpl* (**to** causés à); **2** (Med) **brain ~** lésions *fpl* cérébrales; **3 to do ~ to** porter atteinte à [*reputation*]; **the ~ is done** le mal est fait.
II *vtr* **1** endommager [*building*]; nuire à [*environment, health*]; **to ~ one's eyesight** s'abîmer les yeux; **2** porter atteinte à [*reputation*].
damages *n pl* dommages-interêts *mpl*.
damaging *adj* **1** (to career) préjudiciable (**to** à, pour); **2** (to health) nuisible (**to** pour).
damn○ **I** *n* **not to give a ~ about sb/sth** se ficher○ de qn/qch.
II *adj* (also **damned**) [*key, car*] fichu○ (*before n*).
III *excl* merde○!, zut○!
damning *adj* accablant.
damp I *n* humidité *f*.
II *adj* [*clothes, house*] humide; [*skin*] moite.
■ **damp down**: **~ [sth] down, ~ down [sth]** couvrir [*fire*]; étouffer [*flames*].
dampen *vtr* **1** humecter [*cloth*]; **2** refroidir [*enthusiasm*].
damson *n* prune *f* de Damas.
dance I *n* (activity) danse *f*; (social occasion) soirée *f* dansante.
II *vi* [*person*] danser (**with** avec); [*eyes*] briller (**with** de).
■ **~ about, ~ up and down** sautiller sur place.
dancer *n* danseur/-euse *m/f*.
dancing I *n* danse *f*.
II *noun modifier* [*class, school*] de danse.
D and C *n* (Med) (*abbr* = **dilation and curettage**) curetage *m*.
dandruff *n* pellicules *fpl*.
Dane ▶ 712 *n* Danois/-e *m/f*.
danger *n* danger *m* (**of** de; **to** pour); **to be in ~** être en danger; **to be in ~ of doing** risquer de faire; **there is a ~ that** il y a un risque que (+ *subj*).
dangerous *adj* dangereux/-euse (**for** pour; **to do** de faire).
IDIOMS **to be on ~ ground** être sur un terrain miné.
dangerously *adv* (gen) dangereusement; [*ill*] gravement; **~ high blood pressure** une tension artérielle dangereusement élevée; **to live ~** prendre des risques.
danger signal *n* signal *m* de danger.
dangle I *vtr* balancer [*puppet, keys*]; laisser pendre [*legs*].
II *vi* [*puppet, keys*] se balancer (**from** à); [*earrings*] pendiller.
Danish ▶ 712 **I** *n* (language) danois *m*.
II *adj* [*culture, food, politics*] danois; [*ambassador, embassy*] du Danemark; [*teacher, lesson*] de danois.
dare I *n* défi *m*; **to do sth for a ~** faire qch pour répondre à un défi.
II *modal aux* **1** (to have the courage to) oser; **to ~ to do sth** avoir le courage de faire qch; **they don't ~** or **daren't** (GB) ils n'osent pas; **2** (expressing anger) oser (**do** faire); **don't (you) ~ speak to me like that!** je t'interdis de me parler sur ce ton!; **don't you ~!** ne t'avise pas de faire ça!
III *vtr* **to ~ sb to do** défier qn de faire; **I ~ you!** chiche que tu ne le fais pas○!
daredevil *n, adj* casse-cou (*mf*) *inv*.
daring *adj* **1** (courageous, novel) audacieux/-ieuse; **2** [*suggestion, dress*] osé.
dark I *n* **in the ~** dans le noir or l'obscurité; **before/until ~** avant/jusqu'à la (tombée de la) nuit; **after ~** après la tombée de la nuit.
II *adj* **1** (lacking in light) sombre; **it is getting ~** il commence à faire noir or nuit; **it's ~** il fait noir or nuit; **2** [*colour, suit*] sombre; **a ~ blue dress** une robe bleu foncé; **3** [*hair, person*] brun; **4** [*secret, thought*] noir (*before n*); [*threat*] sombre.
IDIOMS **to be in the ~** être dans le noir; **to**

leave sb in the ~ laisser qn dans l'ignorance; **to keep sb in the ~ about sth** cacher qch à qn.

darken I *vtr* **1** obscurcir [*sky, landscape*]; assombrir [*house*]; **2** foncer [*colour*].
II *vi* **1** (lose light) s'obscurcir; **2** (in colour) foncer; [*skin*] brunir.

dark: **~-eyed** *adj* [*person*] aux yeux noirs; **~ glasses** *n pl* lunettes *fpl* noires.

darkness *n* obscurité *f*; **in ~** dans l'obscurité; **as ~ fell** à la tombée de la nuit.

dark: **~room** *n* chambre *f* noire; **~-skinned** *adj* basané.

darling *n* **1** (term of address) (to loved one) chéri/-e *m/f*; (to child) mon chou°; (to acquaintance) mon cher/ma chère *m/f*; **2** (kind, lovable person) amour *m*, ange *m*.

darn *vtr* repriser.

dart ▶649| *n* fléchette *f*; **to play ~s** jouer aux fléchettes.

dartboard *n* cible *f*.

dash I *n* **1** (rush) course *f* folle; **it has been a mad ~** on a dû se presser; **to make a ~ for the train** courir pour attraper le train; **2** (small amount) (of liquid) goutte *f*; (of powder) pincée *f*; (of colour) touche *f*; **3** (punctuation) tiret *m*.
II *vtr* **1 to ~ sb/sth against** projeter qn/qch contre [*rocks*]; **2** anéantir [*hope*].
III *vi* se précipiter (**into** dans); **to ~ out of** sortir en courant de [*shop, room*].
■ **dash off**: ¶ **~ off** se sauver; ¶ **~ off [sth], ~ [sth] off** écrire [qch] en vitesse.

dashboard *n* tableau *m* de bord.

data *n pl* données *fpl*.

data: **~ analysis** *n* analyse *f* de données; **~base** *n* base *f* de données; **~ capture** *n* saisie *f* de données; **~ entry** *n* introduction *f* de données; **~ file** *n* fichier *m* de données; **~ handling** *n* manipulation *f* de données; **~ input** *n* introduction *f* de données; **~ item** *n* donnée *f* élémentaire; **~ processing** *n* (procedure) traitement *m* des données; (career) informatique *f*; (department) service *m* informatique; **~ protection** *n* protection *f* de l'information; **~ retrieval** *n* extraction *f* de données; **~ security** *n* sécurité *f* des données; **~ storage** *n* (process) stockage *m* des données; (medium) support *m* d'information.

date ▶584| I *n* **1** (day of the month) date *f*; **~ of birth** date de naissance; **what ~ is your birthday?** quelle est la date de ton anniversaire?; **what's the ~ today?** on est le combien aujourd'hui?; **at a later ~, at some future ~** plus tard; **2** (year) (of event) date *f*; (on coin) millésime *m*; **3** (meeting) rendez-vous *m*; **to have a lunch ~** être pris à déjeuner; **to make a ~ for Monday** prendre rendez-vous pour lundi; **4 who's your ~ for tonight?** avec qui sors-tu ce soir?; **5** (fruit) datte *f*.
II *vtr* **1** [*person*] dater; [*machine*] imprimer la date sur; **~d March 21st** daté du 21 mars; **2** dater [*building, object*]; **3** sortir avec [*person*].
III *vi* **to ~ from** or **back to** [*building*] dater de; [*problem, friendship*] remonter à.
IV **to date** *phr* à ce jour, jusqu'ici.

dated *adj* [*clothes, style*] démodé; [*idea, custom*] dépassé; [*language*] vieilli; **the film seems ~ now** le film a mal vieilli.

daughter *n* fille *f*.

daughter-in-law *n* belle-fille *f*, bru *f*.

daunting *adj* [*task, prospect*] décourageant; [*person*] intimidant.

dawdle *vi* flâner, traînasser°.

dawn I *n* aube *f*; **at ~** à l'aube; **before** or **by ~** avant l'aube; **at the crack of ~** à l'aube; **from ~ till dusk** du matin au soir.
II *vi* **1** [*day*] se lever; **2** (become apparent) **it ~ed on me that** je me suis rendu compte que; **it suddenly ~ed on him why** il a compris soudain pourquoi.

day ▶915| *n* **1** jour *m*; **one summer's ~** un jour d'été; **what ~ is it today?** quel jour sommes-nous aujourd'hui? **~ after ~, ~ in ~ out** jour après jour; **every ~** tous les jours; **every other ~** tous les deux jours; **from ~ to ~** [*live*] au jour le jour; [*change*] d'un jour à l'autre; **from one ~ to the next** d'un jour à l'autre; **one ~, some ~** un jour; **the ~ when** or **that** le jour où; **to come on the wrong ~** se tromper de jour; **the ~ after** le lendemain; **the ~ before** la veille; **the ~ before yesterday** avant-hier; **the ~ after tomorrow** après-demain; **two ~s after/two ~s before the wedding** le surlendemain/l'avant-veille du mariage; **from that ~ onwards** dès lors; **2** (until evening) journée *f*; **all ~** toute la journée; **all that ~** tout au long de cette journée; **during/for the ~** pendant/pour la journée; **we haven't got all ~!** nous n'avons pas la journée devant nous!; **it was a hot ~** il faisait chaud; **have a nice ~!** bonne journée!; **3** (daylight) jour *m*; **it's almost ~** il fait presque jour; **by ~** de jour; **4** (historical period) époque *f*; **in those ~s** à cette époque; **in my ~** (at that time) de mon temps; (at height of success, vitality) dans le temps; **these ~s** ces temps-ci.
IDIOMS **it's not your ~ is it?** décidément c'est ton jour!; **it's one of those ~s!** il y a des jours comme ça!; **those were the ~s** c'était le bon temps; **that'll be the ~!** je voudrais voir ça!; **to call it a ~** s'arrêter là; **to have an off ~** ne pas être dans son assiette; **to save the ~** sauver la situation.

day: **~boy** *n* (GB Sch) externe *m*; **~break** *n* aube *f*.

daydream I *n* rêves *mpl*.
II *vi* rêver (**about** de); **stop ~ing!** arrête de rêvasser!

daylight *n* **1** (light) jour *m*, lumière *f* du jour; **it was still ~** il faisait encore jour; **in (the) ~** (in natural light) à la lumière du jour; **2** (dawn) lever *m* du jour, point *m* du jour.

daylight saving time, DST *n* heure *f* d'été.

day: **~ nursery** *n* garderie *f*; **~ release** *n* formation *f* permanente; **~ return (-ticket)** *n* (GB) aller-retour *m* valable une journée; **~ school** *n* externat *m*; **~time** *n* journée *f*; **~-to-day** *adj* quotidien/-ienne; **~-trip** *n*

Dates, Days, and Months

The days of the week

Note that the French uses lower-case letters for the names of days.
Write the names of days in full; do not abbreviate as in English (*Tues*, *Sat* and so on).

Monday	= lundi	*Friday*	= vendredi
Tuesday	= mardi	*Saturday*	= samedi
Wednesday	= mercredi	*Sunday*	= dimanche
Thursday	= jeudi		

lundi in the notes below stands for any day; they all work the same way.
Note the use of ***le*** for regular occurrences, and no article for single ones. (*Remember*: do not translate ***on***.)

on Monday	= lundi
on Mondays	= le lundi
what day is it?	= quel jour sommes-nous? / on est quel jour?
Monday afternoon	= lundi après-midi
last Monday night	= la nuit de lundi dernier (*if evening*) lundi dernier dans la soirée
early on Monday	= lundi matin de bonne heure
late on Monday	= lundi soir tard
last / next Monday	= lundi dernier / prochain
the Monday before last	= l'autre lundi
a month from Monday	= dans un mois lundi
from Monday on	= à partir de lundi

The months of the year

As with the days of the week, do not use capitals to spell the names of the months in French, and do not abbreviate as in English (*Jan*, *Feb* and so on).

January	= janvier	*May*	= mai	*September*	= septembre
February	= février	*June*	= juin	*October*	= octobre
March	= mars	*July*	= juillet	*November*	= novembre
April	= avril	*August*	= août	*December*	= décembre

May in the notes below stands for any month; they all work the same way.

in May	= en mai / au mois de mai
next May	= en mai prochain
last May	= l'année dernière en mai
in early / late May	= début / fin mai

Dates

French has only one generally accepted way of writing dates: ***le 10 mai*** (*say* ***le dix mai***).
If the day of the week is included, put it after the ***le***:

Monday, May 1st 1901	= le lundi 1er mai 1901
what's the date?	= quel jour sommes-nous?
it's the tenth of May	= nous sommes / on est le dix mai
in 1968	= en 1968
in the year 2000	= en l'an deux mille
in the seventeenth century	= au dix-septième siècle

	Write	***Say***
May 1	le 1er mai	le premier mai
May 2	le 2 mai	le deux mai
from 4th to 16th May	du 4 au 16 mai	du quatre au seize mai
May 6 1968	le 6 mai 1968	le six mai mille neuf cent soixante-huit
in the 1980s	dans les années 80	dans les années quatre-vingt
the 16th century	le XVIe siècle	le seizième siècle

excursion *f* pour la journée; **~-tripper** *n* excursionniste *mf*.

dazed *adj* (by news) ahuri; (by blow) étourdi.

dazzle *vtr* éblouir; **to ~ sb with** éblouir qn par [*beauty, knowledge*].

dazzling *adj* éblouissant.

D-day *n* (figurative) jour *m* J.

dead I *n* **1 the ~** (people) les morts *mpl*; **2** (depths) **at ~ of night** en pleine nuit; **in the ~ of winter** en plein hiver.
II *adj* **1** (no longer living) mort; **the ~ man/woman** le mort/la morte; **a ~ body** un cadavre; **to drop (down) ~** tomber raide mort; **to shoot sb ~** abattre qn; **to give sb up for ~** tenir qn pour mort; **2** (extinct) [*language*] mort; **3** (dull, not lively) [*place*] mort; [*audience*] apathique; **the ~ season** la morte-saison; **4 the phone went ~** la ligne a été coupée; **5** [*limb*] engourdi; **6** (absolute) **~ silence** un silence de mort.
III *adv* (GB) [*certain, straight*] absolument; **~ on time** pile○ à l'heure; **~ easy**○ simple comme bonjour○; **they were ~ lucky**○! ils ont eu du pot○!; **~ tired**○ crevé○, claqué○; **you're ~ right**○! tu as parfaitement raison!; **'~ slow'** (Aut) 'roulez au pas'; **to be ~ set on doing** être tout à fait décidé à faire; **to stop ~** s'arrêter net.
IDIOMS **to be ~ to the world** dormir comme une souche.

deaden *vtr* calmer [*pain*]; amortir [*blow*]; assourdir [*sound*].

dead end I *n* impasse *f*.
II **dead-end** *noun modifier* [*job*] sans perspectives.

dead heat *n* (in athletics) arrivée *f* ex-aequo; (in horseracing) dead-heat *m inv*.

deadline *n* date *f* or heure *f* limite, délai *m*; **to meet a ~** respecter un délai; **the ~ for applications is the 15th** les candidatures doivent être déposées avant le 15.

deadlock *n* impasse *f*; **to reach (a) ~** aboutir à une impasse.

dead loss○ *n* **to be a ~** être nul/nulle○.

deadly I *adj* **1** [*poison, enemy*] mortel/-elle; **2 in ~ earnest** avec le plus grand sérieux.
II *adv* [*dull, boring*] terriblement.

deadpan *adj* [*humour*] pince-sans-rire *inv*.

dead ringer○ *n* **to be a ~ for sb** être le sosie de qn.

deaf I *n* **the ~** les sourds *mpl*, les malentendants *mpl*.
II *adj* **1** sourd; **to go ~** devenir sourd; **to be ~ in one ear** être sourd d'une oreille; **2 to turn a ~ ear to** faire la sourde oreille à, rester sourd à.
IDIOMS **to be as ~ as a post**○ être sourd comme un pot○.

deaf: **~ aid** *n* (GB) prothèse *f* auditive; **~ and dumb, ~ without speech** *adj* sourd-muet/sourde-muette.

deafening *adj* assourdissant.

deafness *n* surdité *f*.

deal I *n* **1** (agreement) accord *m*; (in commerce, finance) affaire *f*; (with friend, criminal) marché *m*; **it's a ~!** marché conclu!; **the ~'s off** le marché ne tient pas; **2** (sale) vente *f*; **3** (amount) **a great** or **good ~** beaucoup (**of** de); **she means a great ~ to me** je tiens beaucoup à elle; **it means a great ~ to me** cela compte beaucoup pour moi.
II *vtr* **1** porter [*blow*] (**to** à); **2** distribuer [*cards*]; donner [*hand*].
III *vi* **to ~ in** être dans le commerce de [*commodity, shares*].
IDIOMS **big ~**○! la belle affaire!; **it's no big ~**○ (not hard) ce n'est rien du tout.
■ **deal with**: **~ with [sth] 1** s'occuper de [*problem, request*]; **2** traiter de [*topic*].

dealer ▶ 805 *n* **1** (in business) marchand/-e *m/f*; (large-scale) négociant/-e *m/f*; (for specific product) concessionnaire *m*; **2** (on stock exchange) opérateur/-trice *m/f*; **3** (in drugs) revendeur/-euse *m/f* de drogue, dealer○ *m*.

dealing I *n* vente *f*; **foreign exchange ~** opérations *fpl* de change.
II **dealings** *n pl* relations *fpl* (**with** avec); **business ~s** relations *fpl* commerciales.

dear I *n* mon chéri/ma chérie *m/f*; (more formal) mon cher/ma chère *m/f*.
II *adj* **1** [*friend, mother*] cher/chère; **he's my ~est friend** c'est mon meilleur ami; **the project is ~ to his heart** le projet lui tient vraiment à cœur; **her ~est wish** son vœu le plus cher; **2** (expressing admiration) **a ~ little house** une jolie petite maison; **a ~ old lady** une vieille dame adorable; **3** (in letter) cher/chère; **Dear Sir/Madam** Monsieur, Madame; **Dear Sirs** Messieurs; **Dear Mr Jones** Cher Monsieur; **Dear Mr and Mrs Jones** Cher Monsieur, Chère Madame; **Dear Anne and Paul** Chers Anne et Paul; **4** (expensive) cher/chère; **to get ~er** augmenter.
III *excl* **oh ~!** (dismay, surprise) oh mon Dieu!; (less serious) aïe!, oh là là!

dearly *adv* **to love sb ~** aimer tendrement qn; **they would ~ love to see you fail** ils seraient ravis de te voir échouer.

death *n* (of person) mort *f*, décès *m*; (of hopes, democracy) anéantissement *m*; **at (the time of) his ~** à sa mort; **a ~ in the family** un décès dans la famille; **to drink/work oneself to ~** se tuer en buvant/au travail; **she fell to her ~** elle s'est tuée en tombant; **to die a violent ~** mourir de mort violente; **'Deaths'** 'Nécrologie'.
IDIOMS **he'll be the ~ of me!** il me tuera!; **to look like ~ warmed up** avoir une mine de déterré; **to be at ~'s door** être à l'article de la mort; **to frighten sb to ~** faire une peur bleue à qn○; **to be bored to ~**○ s'ennuyer à mourir; **I'm sick to ~**○ **of this!** j'en ai par-dessus la tête!; **you'll catch your ~ (of cold)**○ tu vas attraper la crève○.

death: **~ penalty** *n* peine *f* de mort; **~ sentence** *n* condamnation *f* à mort; **~ toll** *n* nombre *m* de morts; **~ warrant** *n* ordre *m* d'exécution.

debar *vtr* **to be ~red from doing** ne pas avoir le droit de faire.

debatable *adj* discutable; **that's ~!** cela se discute!

debate *n* (formal, about an issue) débat *m* (**on, about** sur); (informal discussion) discussion *f* (**about** à propos de); **to hold a ~ on** débattre de [*issue*].

debauchery *n* débauche *f*.

debilitating *adj* [*disease*] débilitant.

debit I *n* débit *m*.
II *noun modifier* [*account, balance*] débiteur/-trice.
III *vtr* débiter [*account*] (**with** de).

debrief *vtr* interroger; **to be ~ed** [*diplomat, agent*] rendre compte (oralement) d'une mission; [*defector, freed hostage*] être interrogé.

debris *n* (of plane) débris *mpl*; (of building) décombres *mpl*; (rubbish) déchets *mpl*.

debt *n* dette *f* (**to** envers); **bad ~s** créances *fpl* douteuses; **to get into ~** s'endetter.

debt collector *n* agent *m* de recouvrement.

debtor *n* débiteur/-trice *m/f*.

debug *vtr* déboguer [*computer*].

debut *n* (artistic, sporting) débuts *mpl*; **to make one's ~ as** faire ses débuts comme [*director, musician*]; débuter dans le rôle de [*Hamlet*].

decade *n* décennie *f*.

decaffeinated *adj* décaféiné.

decalitre (GB), **decaliter** (US) *n* décalitre *m*.

decanter *n* (for wine, port) carafe *f* (à décanter); (for whisky) flacon *m* à whisky.

decay I *n* **1** (of timber, vegetation) pourriture *f*; **to fall into ~** [*building*] se délabrer; **2** (dental) carie *f*; **tooth ~** carie dentaire.
II *vi* **1** [*timber, vegetation*] pourrir; [*tooth*] se carier; **2** [*building*] se détériorer.

deceased I *n* **the ~** (individual) le défunt/la défunte; (several) les défunts *mpl*.
II *adj* décédé, défunt.

deceit *n* malhonnêteté *f*.

deceitful *adj* malhonnête.

deceive I *vtr* **1** tromper, duper [*friend*]; **to be ~d** être dupe; **2** tromper [*spouse, lover*].
II *v refl* **to ~ oneself** se faire des illusions.

December ▶ **584** *n* décembre *m*.

decency *n* **1 common ~** la simple politesse; **2** (propriety) convenances *fpl*; (in sexual matters) décence *f*.

decent *adj* **1** (respectable) [*family, man, woman*] comme il faut, bien° *inv*; **no ~ person would do a thing like that** quelqu'un de normal ne ferait jamais ça; **a ~ burial** un enterrement convenable; **to do the ~ thing** faire la seule chose convenable; **2** (pleasant) sympathique, bien° *inv*; **it's ~ of him** c'est très gentil à lui; **3** (adequate) convenable; **4** (not shabby) [*garment*] correct; **I've nothing ~ to wear** je n'ai rien de mettable; **5** (good) [*camera, education, result*] bon/bonne (*before n*); [*profit*] appréciable; **to make a ~ living** bien gagner sa vie; **a ~ night's sleep** une bonne nuit de sommeil.

deception *n* duplicité *f*.

deceptive *adj* [*appearance*] trompeur/-euse.

deceptively *adv* **it looks ~ simple** c'est plus difficile qu'il n'y paraît.

decide I *vtr* **1 to ~ to do** (take a decision) décider de faire; (after much hesitation) se décider à faire; **I ~d to do it** j'ai décidé de le faire; **I finally ~d to do it** je me suis décidé à le faire; **2** (settle) régler [*matter*]; décider de [*fate, outcome*]; **3** (influence) **to ~ sb to do** décider qn à faire.
II *vi* décider; **let her ~** laisse-la décider or prendre la décision; **I can't ~** je n'arrive pas à me décider; **have you ~d?** as-tu pris une décision?; **to ~ against** écarter [*plan, idea*]; **to ~ between** choisir, faire un choix entre [*applicants, books*].
■ **decide on**: **~ on [sth] 1** se décider pour [*hat, wallpaper*]; fixer [*date*]; **2** décider de [*course of action, size, budget*].

decided *adj* **1** [*increase, tendency*] net/nette; **2** [*tone*] décidé, résolu.

decider *n* (point) point *m* décisif; (goal) but *m* décisif; **the ~** (game) la belle.

decilitre (GB), **deciliter** (US) *n* décilitre *m*.

decimal *adj* [*system, currency*] décimal; **~ point** virgule *f*.

decision *n* décision *f*; **to make** or **take a ~** prendre une décision.

decision-making I *n* **to be good/bad at ~** savoir/ne pas savoir prendre des décisions.
II *noun modifier* **~ skills** compétences *fpl* en matière de décision.

decisive *adj* **1** (firm) [*manner, tone*] ferme; **2** (conclusive) [*battle, factor*] décisif/-ive; [*argument*] concluant.

deck *n* **1** (on ship) pont *m*; **car ~** pont des voitures; **on ~** sur le pont; **below ~(s)** sur le pont inférieur; **2** (US) (terrace) terrasse *f*; **3 ~ of cards** jeu *m* de cartes.
IDIOMS **to clear the ~s** déblayer le terrain; **to hit the ~**° tomber par terre.

deckchair *n* chaise *f* longue.

declaration *n* déclaration *f*; **a customs ~** une déclaration en douane.

declare *vtr* **1** (state firmly) déclarer (**that** que); (state openly) annoncer [*intention, support*]; **2** (proclaim) déclarer [*war*] (**on** à); proclamer [*independence*]; **3** (officially) déclarer [*income*].

declassify *vtr* rendre [qch] accessible [*document, information*].

decline I *n* **1** (waning) déclin *m* (**of** de); **2** (drop) baisse *f* (**in, of** de); **to be on the** or **in ~** être en baisse.
II *vi* **1** (drop) [*demand, quality*] baisser (**by** de); [*support*] être en baisse; **2** (wane) être sur le déclin; **3** (refuse) refuser.
III **declining** *pres p adj* **1** (diminishing) [*birthrate*] en baisse; **declining sales** la baisse des ventes; **2** (in decline) [*industry, influence*] en déclin.

decode *vtr* décoder [*code, message, signal*].

decoder *n* décodeur *m*.

decompose *vi* se décomposer.

decor *n* (style) décoration *f*, décor *m*; (of house) décoration *f*; (on stage) décor *m*.

decorate I *vtr* **1** décorer [*cake, tree*] (**with** de, avec); **2 to ~ a room** (paint) peindre une pièce; (paper) tapisser une pièce.
II *vi* faire des travaux de décoration.

decoration *n* **1** (object) décoration *f*; **to put up/take down ~s** mettre/enlever les décorations; **2** (for festivities) décoration *f*; **3** (by painter) travaux *mpl* de décoration.

decorative *adj* [*border, frill*] décoratif/-ive; [*sculpture, design*] ornemental.

decorator *n* peintre *m*, décorateur/-trice *m/f*.

decrease I *n* diminution *f* (**in** de); (in price) baisse *f* (**in** de).
II *vi* [*population*] diminuer; [*price, popularity, rate*] baisser, diminuer.

decreasing *adj* [*population, proportion*] décroissant.

decree *n* **1** (order) décret *m*; **2** (judgment) jugement *m*, arrêt *m*; **~ absolute/nisi** (in divorce) jugement définitif/provisoire (de divorce).

decrepit *adj* [*building*] délabré; [*horse, old person*] décrépit.

dedicate *vtr* dédier [*book*] (**to** à); consacrer [*life*] (**to** à).

dedicated *adj* [*teacher, mother, fan*] dévoué; [*worker*] zélé; **we only want people who are really ~** nous ne voulons que des gens sérieux.

dedication *n* **1** (devoted attitude) dévouement *m* (**to** à); **~ to duty** dévouement; **2** (in a book, on music programme) dédicace *f*.

deduce *vtr* déduire (**that** que).

deduct *vtr* prélever [*subscription, tax*] (**from** sur); déduire [*sum*] (**from** de).

deduction *n* **1** (on wages) retenue *f* (**from** sur); (of tax) prélèvement *m*; **after ~s** une fois les retenues effectuées; **2** (conclusion) déduction *f*, conclusion *f*.

deed *n* **1** (action) action *f*; **to do one's good ~ for the day** faire sa bonne action or sa B.A.○; **2** (for property) acte *m* de propriété.

deep ▶738 I *adj* **1** (from top to bottom) [*hole, water, wound, sigh*] profond; [*snow, carpet*] épais/épaisse; **a ~-pile carpet** une moquette de haute laine; **how ~ is the lake?** quelle est la profondeur du lac?; **the lake is 13 m ~** le lac fait 13 m de profondeur; **a hole 5 cm ~** un trou de 5 cm de profondeur; **2** (from front to back) [*shelf, alcove, stage*] profond; **a shelf 30 cm ~** une étagère de 30 cm de profondeur; **3** (intense) [*admiration, sorrow*] profond; [*desire, need*] grand (*before n*); **4** (impenetrable) [*jungle, mystery*] profond; [*secret*] grand (*before n*); [*person*] réservé; **5** (profound) [*meaning*] profond; [*knowledge*] approfondi; **6** (dark) [*colour*] intense; [*tan*] prononcé; **~ blue eyes** des yeux d'un bleu profond; **7** (low) [*voice*] profond; **8** (absorbed) plongé dans [*book, conversation*]; **to be ~ in thought** être plongé dans ses pensées.
II *adv* **1** (a long way down) [*dig, bury, cut*] profondément; **~ beneath the earth's surface** à une grande profondeur sous la surface de la terre; **to dig ~er into an affair** creuser (plus loin) une affaire; **2** (a long way in) **~ in** or **into** au cœur de [*region*]; **~ into the night** jusque tard dans la nuit; **3** (emotionally, in psyche) **~ down** or **inside** dans mon/ton etc for intérieur; **to go ~** [*faith, loyalty*] être profond; **it goes ~er than that** c'est plus sérieux que ça; **to run ~** [*belief, feeling*] être bien enraciné.

deepen I *vtr* **1** (make deeper) creuser [*channel*]; **2** (intensify) augmenter [*admiration, concern, love*]; **3** rendre [qch] plus grave [*voice, tone*]; **4** foncer [*colour*].
II *vi* **1** (intensify) [*admiration, concern, love*] augmenter; [*knowledge*] s'approfondir; [*crisis*] s'aggraver; [*mystery*] s'épaissir; [*silence*] se faire plus profond; **2** (grow lower) [*voice, pitch, tone*] devenir plus grave; **3** (grow darker) [*colour*] foncer.

deep end *n* grand bassin *m*.
IDIOMS **to go off the ~**○ sortir de ses gonds○; **to jump in at the ~** prendre le taureau par les cornes; **to throw sb in at the ~** forcer qn à prendre le taureau par les cornes.

deep: **~-freeze** *n* congélateur *m*; **~-fried** *adj* frit; **~-frozen** *adj* congelé; **~-fry** *vtr* faire frire.

deeply *adv* [*felt, moved*] profondément; [*involved*] à fond; [*breathe, sigh, sleep*] profondément.

deep: **~-rooted** *adj* [*anxiety, prejudice*] profondément enraciné; **~-sea** *adj* [*diver, diving*] sous-marin/-e; [*fisherman, fishing*] hauturier/-ière.

deer *n* (female) biche *f*; (red) cerf *m*; (roe) chevreuil *m*; (fallow) daim *m*.

deface *vtr* abîmer [*wall*]; dégrader, couvrir [qch] d'inscriptions [*monument*].

default I *vi* ne pas régler ses échéances; **to ~ on payments** or **on a loan** ne pas régler les échéances d'un emprunt.
II **by default** *phr* par défaut; **to win by ~** gagner par forfait.

defeat I *n* **1** défaite *f*; **to suffer a ~** essuyer une défaite; **2** (of proposal, bill) rejet *m* (**of** de); **3** (personal failure) échec *m*; **an admission of ~** un aveu d'échec.
II *vtr* **1** (beat) vaincre [*enemy*]; battre [*team, opposition, candidate*]; faire subir une défaite à [*government*]; **the government was ~ed** le gouvernement a été mis en échec; **2** (overthrow) rejeter [*bill, proposal*].

defect I *n* **1** (flaw) défaut *m*; (minor) imperfection *f*; **mechanical ~** faute *f* mécanique; **structural ~** vice *m* de construction; **2** (disability) **a speech ~** un défaut d'élocution.
II *vi* faire défection; **to ~ to the West** passer à l'Ouest.

defective *adj* [*part, method*] défectueux/-euse; [*sight, hearing*] déficient.

defector *n* transfuge *mf* (**from** de).

defence (GB), **defense** (US) I *n* **1** défense *f*; **to put up a spirited ~** se défendre vaillamment; **2** (in court) **the ~** la défense; **the case for the ~** la défense; **in her ~** à sa décharge;

3 (in sport) défense *f*; **to play in ~** jouer en défense; **4** (Univ) soutenance *f* (de thèse).
II **defences** *n pl* défenses *fpl*.
III *noun modifier* **1** [*budget, industry*] de la défense; [*policy, forces*] de défense; [*cuts*] dans la défense; **2** [*lawyer*] pour la défense; [*witness*] à décharge.

defenceless (GB), **defenseless** (US) *adj* [*person, animal*] sans défense; [*town, country*] sans défenses.

defend *vtr* défendre [*fort, freedom, interests, title*]; justifier [*behaviour, decision*]; **to ~ a thesis** soutenir une thèse.

defendant *n* accusé/-e *m/f*.

defender *n* défenseur *m*.

defensive *adj* [*reaction, behaviour*] de défense; **to be (very) ~** être sur la défensive.

defer I *vtr* reporter [*meeting, decision*] (**until** à); remettre [qch] à plus tard [*departure*]; différer [*payment*].
II *vi* **to ~ to sb** s'incliner devant qn.
III **deferred** *pp adj* [*departure, payment*] différé; [*sale*] à tempérament, à crédit.

deference *n* déférence *f*; **in ~ to** par déférence pour.

defiance *n* attitude *f* de défi.

defiant *adj* [*person*] rebelle; [*behaviour*] provocant.

deficiency *n* **1** (shortage) insuffisance *f* (**of, in** de); (of vitamins) carence *f* (**of** en); **2** (Med) (weakness) défaut *m*; **hearing ~** défaut de l'ouïe.

deficient *adj* (faulty, flawed) déficient (**in** en).

deficit *n* déficit *m*; **in ~** en déficit.

define *vtr* définir [*term, limits, responsibilities*].

definite *adj* **1** (not vague) [*plan, amount*] précis; [*feeling*] net/nette; **a ~ answer** une réponse claire et nette; **~ evidence** preuves *fpl* formelles; **nothing is ~ yet** rien n'est encore sûr; **2** (firm) [*decision, agreement*] ferme; [*refusal*] catégorique; **3** (obvious) [*change, improvement, increase, smell*] net/nette (*before n*); [*advantage*] certain, évident; **4 to be ~** [*person*] (sure) être certain (**about** de); (unyielding) être formel/-elle (**about** sur).

definitely *adv* sans aucun doute; **he ~ said he wasn't coming** il a bien dit qu'il ne viendrait pas; **I'm ~ not going** c'est décidé, je n'y vais pas; **it's ~ colder today** il fait nettement plus froid aujourd'hui; **this one is ~ the best** celui-ci est sans conteste le meilleur; **'~!'** 'absolument!'

definition *n* définition *f*.

deflect *vtr* **1** défléchir, dévier [*missile*]; **2** détourner [*blame, criticism, attention*].

deformed *adj* déformé; (from birth) difforme.

defraud *vtr* escroquer [*client, employer*]; frauder [*tax office*].

defrost I *vtr* décongeler [*food*]; dégivrer [*refrigerator*].
II *vi* [*refrigerator*] dégivrer; [*food*] décongeler.

deft *adj* adroit de ses mains, habile.

defunct *adj* défunt.

defuse *vtr* désamorcer.

defy *vtr* **1** (disobey) défier [*authority, person*]; **2** (challenge) **to ~ sb to do** mettre qn au défi de faire; **3** (elude, resist) défier [*description*].

degrade *vtr* humilier [*person*].

degrading *adj* [*conditions, film*] dégradant; [*job*] avilissant; [*treatment*] humiliant.

degree *n* **1** (unit of measurement) degré *m*; **ten ~s of latitude/longitude** 10 degrés de latitude/longitude; **30 ~s centigrade** 30 degrés centigrades; **a temperature of 104 ~s** 39 de fièvre; **2** (from university) diplôme *m* universitaire; **first** or **bachelor's ~** ≈ licence *f*; **to have a ~** être diplômé; **3** (amount) degré *m*; **a high ~ of efficiency** beaucoup de compétence; **to such a ~ that** à un tel point que; **to a ~, to some ~** dans une certaine mesure; **by ~s** petit à petit; **4** (US) **first ~ murder** homicide *m* volontaire avec préméditation.

dehydrated *adj* déshydraté; [*milk*] en poudre; **to become ~** se déshydrater.

de-icer *n* dégivrant *m*.

dejected *adj* découragé.

delay I *n* **1** (of train, plane, post) retard *m* (**of** de; **to, on** sur); **a few minutes' ~** un délai de quelques minutes; **2** (slowness) **without (further) ~** sans (plus) tarder; **3** (time lapse) délai *m* (**of** de; **between** entre).
II *vtr* **1** (postpone) différer [*decision, publication*]; **to ~ doing** attendre pour faire; **2** (hold up) retarder [*train, arrival, post*].

delegate I *n* délégué/-e *m/f*.
II *vtr* déléguer [*responsibility, task*] (**to** à).

delete *vtr* supprimer (**from** de); (with pen) barrer; (on computer) effacer.

deliberate *adj* **1** (intentional) délibéré; **it was ~** il/elle l'a fait etc exprès; **2** (measured) mesuré.

deliberately *adv* [*do, say*] exprès; [*sarcastic, provocative*] délibérément.

delicacy *n* **1** (of object, situation) délicatesse *f*; **2** (of mechanism) sensibilité *f*; **3** (edible) (savoury) mets *m* raffiné; (sweet) friandise *f*.

delicate *adj* [*fabric, health, mechanism, situation*] délicat; [*features*] fin.

delicatessen *n* **1** (shop) épicerie *f* fine; **2** (US) (eating-place) restaurant-traiteur *m*.

delicious *adj* délicieux/-ieuse.

delight I *n* joie *f*, plaisir *m*; **to take ~ in sth/in doing** prendre plaisir à qch/à faire.
II *vtr* ravir [*person*] (**with** par).

delighted *adj* ravi (**at, by, with** de; **to do** de faire); **~ to meet you** enchanté.

delinquency *n* délinquance *f*.

delinquent *n* délinquant/-e *m/f*.

delirious *adj* **to be ~** délirer.

delirium *n* délire *m*.

deliver I *vtr* **1** (hand over) livrer [*goods, groceries*] (**to** à); distribuer ([*mail*] (**to** à); remettre [*note*] (**to** à); **2** (assist at birth) mettre au monde [*baby*]; délivrer [*baby animal*]; **to be ~ed** [*baby*] être né; **3** faire [*speech*]; donner [*ultimatum*]; rendre [*verdict*].
II *vi* [*tradesman*] livrer; [*postman*] distribuer le courrier.

delivery I *n* (of goods, milk) livraison *f*; (of mail) distribution *f*; **on ~** à la livraison.
II *noun modifier* [*date, order, service, vehicle*] de livraison.

delivery: **~ man** *n* livreur *m*; **~ room** *n* salle *f* d'accouchement.

deluge I *n* déluge *m*.
II *vtr* submerger (**with** de).

de luxe *adj* [*model, version, edition*] de luxe; [*accommodation*] luxueux/-euse.

demand I *n* **1** (request) demande *f*; **on ~** [*divorce*] à la demande; [*payable*] à vue; **2** (pressure) exigence *f*; **3** (Econ) demande *f* (**for** de); **4 to be in ~** être très demandé.
II *vtr* **1** (request) demander [*reform*]; (forcefully) exiger [*ransom*]; réclamer [*inquiry*]; **2** (require) demander [*skill*] (**of sb** de qn); (more imperatively) exiger.

demanding *adj* **1** [*person*] exigeant; **2** [*work, course*] ardu; [*schedule*] chargé.

demented *adj* fou/folle.

demerara (sugar) *n* sucre *m* roux cristallisé.

demerger *n* scission *f*.

demister *n* (GB) dispositif *m* antibuée.

demo○ *n* **1** (protest) manif○ *f*; **2** (car) modèle *m* de démonstration.

democracy *n* démocratie *f*.

democratic *adj* démocratique.

demolish *vtr* démolir [*building, argument, person*].

demolition *n* démolition *f*.

demonstrate I *vtr* **1** (illustrate, prove) démontrer [*theory, truth*]; **2** (show, reveal) manifester [*concern, support*]; montrer [*skill*]; **3** (display) faire la démonstration de [*machine, product*]; **to ~ how to do** montrer comment faire.
II *vi* manifester (**for** en faveur de; **against** contre).

demonstration *n* **1** (march) manifestation *f* (**against** contre; **for** en faveur de); **2** (of support) manifestation *f*; **3** (of machine, theory) démonstration *f*.

demonstrative *adj* [*person*] démonstratif/-ive.

demonstrator *n* manifestant/-e *m/f*.

demoralize *vtr* démoraliser.

demote *vtr* rétrograder.

den *n* **1** (of lion) antre *m*; (of fox) tanière *f*; **2** (room) tanière *f*.

denationalize *vtr* dénationaliser.

denial *n* (of accusation, rumour) démenti *m*; (of guilt, rights, freedom) négation *f*.

denim I *n* jean *m*; **~s** jean *m*.
II *noun modifier* [*jacket, skirt*] en jean; **~ jeans** jean *m*.

Denmark **▶574** *pr n* Danemark *m*.

denounce *vtr* **1** (inform on, criticize) dénoncer; **2** (accuse) accuser.

dense *adj* dense.

dent I *n* (in metal) bosse *f*.
II *vtr* cabosser [*car*].

dental *adj* [*decay, hygiene*] dentaire.

dental: **~ clinic** *n* centre *m* de soins dentaires; **~ floss** *n* fil *m* dentaire; **~ surgeon** **▶805** *n* chirurgien-dentiste *m*; **~ surgery** *n* (GB) (premises) cabinet *m* dentaire; (treatment) chirurgie *f* dentaire.

dentist **▶805** *n* dentiste *mf*.

dentistry *n* médecine *f* dentaire.

dentures *n pl* dentier *m*.

deny *vtr* **1** démentir [*rumour*]; nier [*accusation*]; **to ~ doing** or **having done** nier avoir fait; **he denies that this is true** il nie que cela soit vrai; **2** (refuse) **to ~ sb sth** refuser qch à qn.

deodorant *n* (personal) déodorant *m*; (for room) déodorisant *m*.

depart *vi* **1** partir (**from** de; **for** pour); **the train now ~ing from platform one** le train au départ du quai numéro un; **2** (deviate) **to ~ from** s'éloigner de [*position*].

department *n* **1** (section of large firm) service *m*; **2** (governmental) ministère *m*; (administrative) service *m*; **social services ~** services sociaux; **3** (in store) rayon *m*; **toy ~** rayon jouets; **4** (in hospital) service *m*; **5** (in university) département *m*; **6** (in school) section *f*.

departmental *adj* **1** (in government circles) [*meeting*] de ministère; **2** (elsewhere) [*head, meeting*] de service, de département.

department head *n* **1** (in company) chef *m* de service, directeur/-trice *m/f* du service; **2** (in a university) directeur/-trice *m/f* de département.

department store *n* grand magasin *m*.

departure *n* (of person, train) départ *m*; (from truth, regulation) entorse *f* (**from** à); (from policy, tradition) rupture *f* (**from** par rapport à).

departure: **~ gate** *n* porte *f* de départ; **~s board** *n* tableau *m* des départs.

depend *vi* **to ~ on** dépendre de, compter sur (**for** pour); **to ~ on sb/sth to do** compter sur qn/qch pour faire; **~ing on the season** suivant la saison.

dependable *adj* [*person*] digne de confiance; [*machine*] fiable.

dependant *n* personne *f* à charge.

dependence, dependance (US) *n* **1** (reliance) dépendance *f* (**on** vis-à-vis de); **2** (addiction) dépendance *f* (**on** à).

dependent *adj* [*relative*] à charge; **to be ~ (up)on sb** vivre à la charge de qn.

depict *vtr* (visually) représenter; (in writing) dépeindre (**as** comme).

depilatory *n, adj* dépilatoire (*m*).

deplore *vtr* déplorer.

deploy *vtr* déployer.

depopulate *vtr* dépeupler.

deport *vtr* expulser (**to** vers).

deportation *n* expulsion *f*.

deportee *n* déporté/-e *m/f*.

depose *vtr* déposer.

deposit I *n* **1** (to bank account) dépôt *m*; **on ~** en dépôt; **2** (part payment) (on house, hire purchase goods) versement *m* initial (**on** sur); (on holiday, goods) acompte *m*, arrhes *fpl* (**on** sur); **3** (against damage, breakages) caution *f*; **4** (on bottle)

consigne *f*; **5** (of silt, mud) dépôt *m*; (of coal, mineral) gisement *m*.
II *vtr* déposer [*money*]; **to ~ sth with sb** confier qch à qn.

deposit account *n* (GB) compte *m* de dépôt.

depot *n* **1** (for storage) dépôt *m*; **2** (terminus, garage) **bus ~** dépôt *m* d'autobus; **3** (US) (station) (bus) gare *f* routière; (rail) gare *f* ferroviaire.

depreciate *vi* se déprécier (**against** par rapport à).

depress *vtr* **1** déprimer [*person*]; **2** faire baisser [*prices*]; affaiblir [*trading*].

depressed *adj* **1** [*person*] déprimé; **I got ~ about it** cela m'a déprimé; **2** [*region, market, industry*] en déclin; [*sales, prices*] très bas/basse.

depressing *adj* déprimant.

depression *n* dépression *f*; **to suffer from ~** être dépressif/-ive.

deprivation *n* (material) privations *fpl*; (emotional) carence *f* affective.

deprive *vtr* priver (**of** de).

deprived *adj* [*area, family*] démuni; [*childhood*] malheureux/-euse.

depth ▶ 738 *n* **1** (of hole, water) profondeur *f*; (of layer) épaisseur *f*; **at a ~ of 30 m** à 30 m de profondeur; **to be out of one's ~** (in water) ne plus avoir pied; (in situation) être complètement perdu; **2** (of colour, emotion) intensité *f*; (of crisis) gravité *f*; **to be in the ~s of despair** toucher le fond du désespoir; **3** (of knowledge) étendue *f*; (of analysis, novel) profondeur *f*; **to examine sth in ~** examiner qch en détail.

deputize *vi* **to ~ for sb** remplacer qn.

deputy I *n* **1** (aide) adjoint/-e *m/f*; (replacement) remplaçant/-e *m/f*; **2** (politician) député *m*.
II *noun modifier* [*director, editor, head, manager, mayor*] adjoint.

deputy: **~ chairman** *n* vice-président *m*; **~ leader** *n* (GB) vice-président *m*; **~ premier**, **~ prime minister** *n* vice-premier ministre *m*.

derail *vtr* faire dérailler.

deregulate *vtr* libérer [*prices*]; déréguler [*market*].

derelict *adj* [*building*] délabré.

derision *n* moqueries *fpl*.

dermatitis ▶ 686 *n* dermatite *f*.

derogatory *adj* désobligeant (**about** envers); [*term*] péjoratif/-ive.

descend I *vtr* descendre [*steps, slope, path*].
II *vi* **1** (go down) [*person, plane*] descendre (**from** de); **2** (fall) [*rain, darkness, mist*] tomber (**on, over** sur); **3** (arrive) **to ~ on sb** débarquer° chez qn; **4** (be related to) **to be ~ed from** descendre de.

descendant *n* descendant/-e *m/f* (**of** de).

descent *n* **1** descente *f* (**on, upon** sur); **to make one's ~** faire sa descente; **2** (extraction) descendance *f*; **a British citizen by ~** un citoyen britannique par filiation.

describe *vtr* **1** décrire [*person, event, object*]; **2** (characterize) qualifier; **to ~ sb as an idiot** qualifier qn d'idiot; **he's ~d as generous** on dit de lui qu'il est généreux.

description *n* description *f* (**of** de); (for police) signalement *m* (**of** de).

descriptive *adj* descriptif/-ive.

desegregate *vtr* **to ~ a school** abolir la ségrégation dans une école.

desensitize *vtr* désensibiliser (**to** à).

desert I *n* désert *m*.
II *vtr* abandonner [*person*] (**for** pour); déserter [*cause*]; abandonner [*post*].
III *vi* [*soldier*] déserter; [*politician*] faire défection.

desert boot *n* pataugas® *m*.

deserted *adj* **1** (empty) désert; **2** [*person*] abandonné.

deserter *n* déserteur *m* (**from** de).

desert island *n* île *f* déserte.

deserve *vtr* mériter (**to do** de faire).

deservedly *adv* à juste titre.

deserving *adj* [*winner*] méritant; [*cause*] louable.

design I *n* **1** (idea, conception) conception *f*; **2** (planning, development) (of object, appliance) conception *f*; (of building, room) agencement *m*; (of clothing) création *f*; **3** (drawing, plan) (detailed) plan *m* (**for** de); (sketch) croquis *m* (**for** de); **4** (model) modèle *m*; **5** (art of designing) design *m*; (fashion) stylisme *m*; **6** (decorative pattern) motif *m*; **a leaf ~** un motif de feuilles; **7** (subject of study) arts *mpl* appliqués.
II *vtr* **1** (conceive) concevoir [*building, appliance, course*]; **2** (intend) **to be ~ed for sth/ to do** (destined for) être destiné à qch/à faire; (made for) être conçu pour qch/pour faire; **3** (draw plan for) [*draughtsman*] dessiner le patron de [*garment*]; [*designer*] créer [*costume, garment*]; dessiner [*building, appliance*].

designate I *adj* [*president, director*] en titre.
II *vtr* **to ~ sb (as) sth** désigner qn (comme) qch; **to ~ sth (as) sth** classer qch (comme) qch; **to ~ sth for** destiner qch à.

design consultant ▶ 805 *n* conseiller/-ère *m/f* en aménagement.

designer ▶ 805 **I** *n* concepteur/-trice *m/f*; (of furniture, in fashion) créateur/-trice *m/f*; (of sets) décorateur/-trice *m/f*; **costume ~** costumier/-ière *m/f*.
II *noun modifier* **~ clothes, ~ labels** vêtements *mpl* griffés; **~ label** griffe *f*.

design: **~ fault** *n* faute *f* de conception; **~ feature** *n* caractéristique *f* (nominale).

desirable *adj* **1** [*outcome, solution*] souhaitable; [*area, position*] convoité; [*job, gift*] séduisant; **~ residence** (in ad) maison *f* de standing; **2** (sexually) désirable.

desire I *n* désir *m* (**for** de); **to have no ~ to do** n'avoir aucune envie de faire.
II *vtr* désirer; **it leaves a lot to be ~d** cela laisse beaucoup à désirer.

desk *n* **1** (furniture) bureau *m*; (Mus) pupitre *m*; **writing ~** secrétaire *m*; **2** (Sch) (pupil's) table *f*; (teacher's) bureau *m*; **3** (in public building) **recep-**

tion ~ réception *f*; **information ~** bureau *m* de renseignements; **cash ~** caisse *f*.

desk clerk *n* (US) réceptionniste *mf*.

desktop *n* (also **~ computer**) ordinateur *m* de bureau.

desktop publishing *n* micro-édition *f*, PAO *f*.

despair I *n* désespoir *m*; **to do sth in** or **out of ~** faire qch par désespoir.
II *vi* désespérer (**of** de; **of doing** de faire).

desperate *adj* **1** [*person, plea, situation*] désespéré; [*criminal*] prêt à tout; **to be ~ to do** avoir très envie de faire; **to be ~ for** avoir désespérément besoin de [*affection, help*]; attendre désespérément [*news*]; **2**○ (terrible) affreux/-euse.

desperately *adv* **1** [*plead, look, fight*] désespérément; **to need sth ~** avoir très besoin de qch; **2** [*poor*] terriblement; [*ill*] très gravement.

desperation *n* désespoir *m*.

despicable *adj* méprisable.

despise *vtr* mépriser.

dessert *n* dessert *m*.

dessert: **~spoon** *n* cuillère *f* à dessert; **~ wine** *n* vin *m* doux.

destination *n* destination *f*.

destiny *n* destin *m*, destinée *f*.

destitute *adj* [*person*] sans ressources; **to leave sb ~** laisser qn dans le dénuement.

destroy *vtr* **1** détruire [*building, evidence*]; briser [*career, person*]; **2** (kill) abattre [*animal*]; détruire, anéantir [*population, enemy*].

destruction *n* (of building, evidence) destruction *f*; (of reputation) ruine *f*.

destructive *adj* **1** (causing destruction) destructeur/-trice; **2** [*weapon, capacity*] destructif/-ive; [*emotion, criticism*] destructeur/-trice.

detach *vtr* détacher (**from** de).

detachable *adj* [*coupon, strap*] détachable; [*collar*] amovible; [*lens*] mobile.

detached *adj* **1** (separate) détaché; **2** (objective) [*person, view*] détaché; [*observer*] indépendant.

detached: **~ house** *n* maison *f* (individuelle); **~ retina** *n* rétine *f* décollée.

detachment *n* **1** (objectivity) détachement *m*; **2** (of soldiers) détachement *m*.

detail I *n* détail *m*; **in (more) ~** (plus) en détail; **to go into ~s** entrer dans les détails; **to have an eye for ~** prêter attention aux détails; **for further ~s, contact**... pour de plus amples renseignements, adressez-vous à...
II *vtr* exposer [qch] en détail [*plans*]; énumérer [*items*].

detain *vtr* **1** (delay) retenir; **2** (keep in custody) placer [qn] en détention; **to be ~ed for questioning** être placé en garde à vue pour être interrogé.

detainee *n* (general) détenu/-e *m/f*; (political) prisonnier/-ière *m/f* (politique).

detect *vtr* déceler [*error, traces*]; détecter [*crime, leak, sound*]; sentir [*mood*].

detectable *adj* discernable.

detection *n* (of disease, error) détection *f*; **crime ~** la lutte contre la criminalité; **to escape ~** [*criminal*] ne pas être découvert; [*error*] ne pas être décelé.

detective *n* ≈ inspecteur/-trice *m/f* (de police); **private ~** détective *m*.

detective: **~ story** *n* roman *m* policier, polar○ *m*; **~ work** *n* enquêtes *fpl*.

detention *n* **1** (confinement) détention *f*; **2** (prison sentence) détention *f* criminelle; (awaiting trial) détention *f* provisoire; **3** (in school) retenue *f*, colle○ *f*.

deter *vtr* **1** (dissuade) dissuader; **2** (prevent) empêcher (**from doing** de faire).

detergent *n* détergent *m*.

deteriorate *vi* [*weather, health, situation*] se détériorer; [*economy, sales*] décliner; [*work, building*] se dégrader; **to ~ into** [*discussion*] dégénérer en.

deterioration *n* (in weather, of building) dégradation *f* (**in** de); (in health, situation) détérioration *f* (**in** de); (in work) baisse *f* de qualité (**in** de).

determination *n* détermination *f*.

determine *vtr* déterminer; **to ~ how** établir comment.

determined *adj* [*person*] fermement décidé (**to do** à faire); [*air*] résolu.

deterrent I *n* (gen) moyen *m* de dissuasion; (Mil) force *f* de dissuasion; **to be a ~ to** dissuader.
II *adj* [*effect*] dissuasif/-ive; [*measure*] de dissuasion.

detest *vtr* détester (**doing** faire).

detonate *vtr* faire exploser [*bomb*].

detour *n* détour *m*.

detract *vi* **to ~ from** porter atteinte à [*success, value*]; nuire à [*image*].

detrimental *adj* nuisible (**to** à).

deuce *n* **1** (Sport) **~!** égalité!; **2** (in cards) deux *m*.

devaluation *n* (of currency) dévaluation *f*.

devalue I *vtr* **1** [*currency*] dévaluer; **~d by 6%** dévalué de 6%; **2** dévaloriser [*person*].
II *vi* [*currency*] être dévalué (**against** par rapport à); [*property*] baisser.

develop I *vtr* **1** (acquire) acquérir [*knowledge*]; attraper [*illness*]; prendre [*habit*]; présenter [*symptom*]; **to ~ an awareness of** prendre conscience de; **to ~ cancer** avoir un cancer; **2** (evolve) élaborer [*plan*]; mettre au point [*technique*]; exposer [*theory*]; développer [*argument*]; **3** (create) créer [*market*]; établir [*links*]; **4** (expand, build up) développer [*mind, business, market*]; **5** (improve) mettre en valeur [*land, site*]; aménager [*city centre*]; **6** (in photography) développer.
II *vi* **1** (evolve) [*child, society, country, plot*] se développer; [*skills*] s'améliorer; **to ~ into** devenir; **2** (come into being) [*friendship, difficulty*] naître; [*crack*] se former; [*illness*] se déclarer; **3** (progress, advance) [*friendship*] se développer; [*difficulty, illness*] s'aggraver; [*crack, fault*] s'accentuer; [*game, story*] se dérouler; **4** (in size) [*town, business*] se développer.

developer *n* **1** (also **property ~**) promoteur *m* (immobilier); **2** (in photography) révélateur *m*; **3** (Sch) **early ~** enfant *m* précoce.

developing country *n* pays *m* en voie de développement.

development I *n* **1** (creation) (of product) mise *f* au point; (of housing, industry) création *f*; **2** (evolution, growth, fostering) développement *m*; **3** (of land) mise *f* en valeur; (of site, city centre) aménagement *m*; **housing ~** ensemble *m* d'habitation; **commercial ~** (ensemble de) commerces et bureaux à bâtir; **4** (innovation) progrès *m*; **major ~s** des découvertes *fpl* majeures (**in** dans le domaine de); **5** (event) changement *m*; **recent ~s in Europe** les derniers événements en Europe.
II *noun modifier* [*area, planning*] d'aménagement; [*costs, bank*] de développement.

development company *n* groupe *m* immobilier.

deviate *vi* **1** (from norm) s'écarter (**from** de); **2** (from course) dévier (**from** de).

device *n* **1** (household) appareil *m*; **labour-saving ~** appareil *m* électroménager; **2** (Tech) dispositif *m*; **security ~** système *m* de sécurité; **3** (also **explosive ~**, **incendiary ~**) engin *m* explosif; **4** (means) moyen *m* (**for doing, to do** de or pour faire).
IDIOMS **to be left to one's own ~s** être laissé à soi-même.

devil *n* **1** (also **Devil**) **the ~** le Diable; **2** (evil spirit) démon *m*; **3**○ (for emphasis) **we'll have a ~ of a job doing** ça va être sacrément○ dur de faire.
IDIOMS **speak of the ~!** quand on parle du loup (on en voit la queue)○!

devious *adj* [*person, mind, plan*] retors; [*method*] détourné.

devise *vtr* concevoir [*scheme, course*]; inventer [*product, machine*].

devolution *n* **1** (of powers) transfert *m* (**from** de; **to** à); **2** (policy) régionalisation *f*.

devote *vtr* consacrer (**to** à; **to doing** à faire); **to ~ oneself** se consacrer (**to** à).

devoted *adj* [*person, animal*] dévoué (**to** à); [*service*] loyal; [*fan*] fervent.

devotion *n* (to person, work, homeland) dévouement *m* (**to** à); (to doctrine, cause) attachement *m* (**to** à); (to God) dévotion *f* (**to** à).

devout *adj* [*Catholic, prayer*] fervent; [*person*] pieux/pieuse.

dew *n* rosée *f*.

diabetic *n, adj* diabétique (*mf*).

diagnose *vtr* diagnostiquer.

diagnosis *n* diagnostic *m*.

diagonal I *n* diagonale *f*.
II *adj* [*line*] diagonal; **our street is ~ to the main road** notre rue part en biais de la rue principale.

diagram *n* schéma *m*; (in mathematics) figure *f*.

dial I *n* cadran *m*.
II *vtr* faire, composer [*number*]; appeler [*person*]; **to ~ 999** (for police, ambulance) ≈ appeler police secours; (for fire brigade) ≈ appeler les pompiers.

dialect *n* dialecte *m*.

dialling (GB), **dialing** (US) *n* **direct ~** appel *m* direct.

dialling: **~ code** *n* (GB) indicatif *m*; **~ tone** (GB), **dial tone** (US) *n* tonalité *f*.

diameter *n* diamètre *m*; **to be 2 m in ~** avoir 2 m de diamètre.

diamond ▶649 *n* **1** (gem) diamant *m*; **2** (shape) losange *m*; **3** (in cards) carreau *m*.

diamond: **~ jubilee** *n* soixantième anniversaire *m*; **~ wedding (anniversary)** *n* noces *fpl* de diamant.

diaper (US) **I** *n* couche *f* (de bébé).
II *vtr* changer la couche de [*baby*].

diaphragm *n* diaphragme *m*.

diarrhoea (GB), **diarrhea** (US) *n* diarrhée *f*.

diary *n* **1** (for appointments) agenda *m*; **to put sth in one's ~** noter qch dans son agenda; **2** (journal) journal *m* intime; **3** (in newspaper) chronique *f*.

dice I *n* (object) dé *m*; (game) dés *mpl*; **no ~**○! (refusal) pas question!
II *vtr* couper [qch] en cubes [*vegetable, meat*].

dictate I *vtr* **1** (out loud) dicter; **2** (prescribe) imposer [*terms*] (**to** à); déterminer [*outcome*]; régenter [*policy*]; **to ~ how** prescrire comment.
II *vi* **1** (out loud) **to ~ to one's secretary** dicter une lettre (or un texte) à sa secrétaire; **2 to ~ to sb** imposer sa volonté à qn.

dictation *n* dictée *f*.

dictator *n* (ruler) dictateur *m*; (domineering person) tyran *m*.

diction *n* diction *f*.

dictionary *n* dictionnaire *m*.

die I *vtr* **to ~ a violent death** mourir de mort violente.
II *vi* **1** (expire) mourir; **to be dying** être mourant, se mourir; **to be dying of cancer** être atteint d'un cancer incurable; **she ~d** elle est morte; **to be left to ~** être abandonné à la mort; **when I ~** quand je mourrai; **to ~ of** or **from** mourir de [*starvation, disease*]; **2** (be killed) mourir (**doing** en faisant); **to ~ for** mourir pour [*beliefs*]; **3** (of boredom) mourir (**of** de); **4**○ (long) **to be dying to do** mourir d'envie de faire; **to be dying for** avoir une envie folle de.
■ **die down** [*emotion, row*] s'apaiser; [*scandal, opposition, shock*] disparaître; [*fighting*] s'achever; [*storm*] se calmer; [*laughter*] diminuer; [*applause*] se calmer.
■ **die out** [*species*] disparaître.

diesel *n* **1** (also **~ fuel**, **~ oil**) gazole *m*; **2** (also **~ car**) diesel *m*.

diesel train *n* train *m* Diesel.

diet *n* **1** (normal food) (of person) alimentation *f* (**of** à base de); (of animal) nourriture *f* (**of** à base de); **2** (slimming food) régime *m*; **to go on a ~** se mettre au régime.

dietary *adj* [*habit*] alimentaire.

dietary fibre (GB), **dietary fiber** (US) *n* fibres *fpl* alimentaires.

differ *vi* **1** (be different) différer (**from** de; **in** par); **to ~ widely** être complètement différent; **2** (disagree) différer (d'opinion) (**on** sur; **from sb** de qn).

difference *n* **1** (dissimilarity) différence *f* (**in, of** de); **what's the ~ between...?** quelle est la différence entre...?; **to tell the ~ between** faire la différence entre; **it won't make any ~** ça ne changera rien; **what ~ does it make if...?** qu'est-ce que ça change si...?; **it makes no ~ to me** cela m'est égal; **2** (disagreement) différend *m* (**over** à propos de; **with** avec); **a ~ of opinion** une divergence d'opinion.

different *adj* **1** (dissimilar) différent (**from, to** (GB), **than** (US) de); **they are ~ in this respect** ils diffèrent à cet égard; **2** (other) autre; **to be a ~ person** être une tout autre personne; **that's ~** c'est autre chose; **3** (distinct, unusual) différent; **he has to be ~** il faut qu'il se distingue.

differentiate *vi* **1** (tell the difference) faire la différence (**between** entre); **2** (show the difference) faire la distinction (**between** entre).

differently *adv* **1** (in another way) autrement (**from** que); **I'd have done it ~** je l'aurais fait autrement; **2** (in different ways) différemment (**from** de); **it affects men and women ~** cela touche les hommes et les femmes différemment.

difficult *adj* **1** (not easy) difficile; **Russian is ~ to learn** le russe est difficile à apprendre; **it will be ~ (for me) to decide** il (me) sera difficile de décider; **to find it ~ to do** avoir du mal à faire; **2** [*age, position*] difficile; **to be ~ to get on with** être difficile à vivre.

difficulty *n* **1** (of task, situation, puzzle) difficulté *f*; **to have ~ (in) doing** avoir du mal à faire; **2** (problem) difficulté *f*, problème *m*; **3** (trouble) **in ~** en difficulté.

diffidence *n* manque *m* d'assurance.

diffident *adj* [*person*] qui manque d'assurance; [*smile, gesture*] timide.

dig I *n* **1** (with elbow) coup *m* de coude (**in** dans); **2**○ (jibe) **to take a ~ at sb** lancer une pique○ à qn; **3** (in archaeology) fouilles *fpl*; **to go on a ~** aller faire des fouilles.
II **digs** *n pl* (GB) chambre *f* (meublée).
III *vtr* **1** (excavate) creuser (**in** dans); **2** bêcher [*garden, plot*]; fouiller [*site*]; **3** (extract) arracher [*root crops*]; extraire [*coal*] (**out of** de).
IV *vi* [*miner*] creuser; [*archaeologist*] fouiller; [*gardener*] bêcher.
■ **dig in**: ¶ **~ in** se retrancher; ¶ **~ in [sth]**, **~ [sth] in** enterrer [*compost*].
■ **dig up**: **~ up [sth]**, **~ [sth] up 1** déterrer [*body, treasure, scandal*]; arracher [*roots, weeds*]; excaver [*road*]; dénicher○ [*information*]; **2** bêcher [*garden*].

digest *vtr* digérer [*food*]; assimiler [*facts*].

digestion *n* digestion *f*.

digger *n* excavateur *m*.

digging *n* **1** (in garden) **to do some ~** bêcher; **2** (in construction) creusement *m*.

digital *adj* [*display, recording*] numérique; [*watch*] à affichage numérique.

digital: **~ computer** *n* calculateur *m* numérique; **~ lock** *n* digicode® *m*.

dignified *adj* [*person*] digne; [*manner*] empreint de dignité.

dignity *n* dignité *f*; **to stand on one's ~** prendre de grands airs.

digression *n* digression *f*.

dilapidated *adj* délabré.

dilate I *vtr* dilater; **to be 5 cm ~d** [*cervix*] être dilaté de 5 cm.
II *vi* se dilater.

dilemma *n* dilemme *m* (**about** à propos de); **to be in a ~** être pris dans un dilemme.

dill *n* aneth *m*.

dilute *vtr* diluer [*liquid*] (**with** avec); éclaircir [*colour*].

dim I *adj* **1** [*room*] sombre; **2** [*light*] faible; **to grow ~** baisser; **3** [*outline*] vague; **4** [*memory*] vague (*before n*); **5**○ (stupid) bouché○.
II *vtr* baisser [*light, headlights*]; mettre [qch] en veilleuse [*lamp*].
IDIOMS **to take a ~ view of sth** n'apprécier guère qch.

dime *n* (US) (pièce *f* de) dix cents *mpl*.
IDIOMS **they're a ~ a dozen**○ on en trouve à la pelle○.

dimension *n* **1** (aspect) dimension *f*; **2** (scope) **~s** étendue *f* (**of** de); **3** (measurement) dimension *f*; (in architecture) cote *f*.

-dimensional *combining form* **three~** à trois dimensions.

dime store *n* (US) bazar *m*.

diminish *vi* **1** [*resources, numbers*] diminuer; **2** [*influence*] s'amoindrir.

dimple *n* fossette *f*.

diner *n* **1** (person) dîneur/-euse *m/f*; **2** (US) (restaurant) café-restaurant *m*.

dinghy *n* **1** (also **sailing ~**) dériveur *m*; **2** (inflatable) canot *m*.

dining: **~ car** *n* wagon-restaurant *m*; **~ hall** *n* réfectoire *m*; **~ room** *n* (in house) salle *f* à manger; (in hotel) salle *f* de restaurant.

dinner *n* **1** (meal) (evening) dîner *m*; (midday) déjeuner *m*; **at ~** au dîner or déjeuner; **to go out to ~** dîner dehors; **to have ~** dîner; **to give the dog its ~** donner à manger au chien; **2** (banquet) dîner *m* (**for** en l'honneur de).

dinner: **~ jacket**, **DJ** *n* smoking *m*; **~ party** *n* dîner *m*; **~ plate** *n* grande assiette *f*; **~time** *n* heure *f* du dîner.

dip I *n* **1** (in ground, road) creux *m*; **2** (bathe) baignade *f*; **3** (in prices, rate, sales) (mouvement *m* de) baisse *f* (**in** dans); **4** (Culin) sauce *f* froide (*pour crudités*).
II *vtr* **1** (put partially) tremper (**in, into** dans); **2** (immerse) plonger [*garment*]; tremper [*food*]; **3** (GB Aut) baisser [*headlights*]; **~ped headlights** codes *mpl*.
III *vi* **1** (move downwards) piquer; **2** (slope downwards) être en pente; **3** (decrease) [*value, rate*] descendre; **4 to ~ into** puiser dans [*savings*]; parcourir [*novel*].

diploma *n* diplôme *m* (**in** en).

diplomacy *n* diplomatie *f*.

diplomat ▶ 805 *n* diplomate *mf*.

diplomatic *adj* diplomatique; **to be ~** avoir du tact.

dipstick *n* (Aut) jauge *f* de niveau d'huile.

direct I *adj* **1** (without intermediary, detour) direct; **in ~ contact with** (touching) en contact direct avec; (communicating) directement en contact avec; **2** (clear) [*cause, influence, reference*] direct; [*contrast, evidence*] flagrant; **3** (frank) [*answer*] direct; [*person*] franc/franche.
II *adv* **1** [*contact, dial*] directement; **2** (without detour) directement (**from** de).
III *vtr* **1** (address, aim) adresser [*appeal, criticism*] (**at** à; **against** contre); cibler [*campaign*] (**at** sur); orienter [*effort, resource*] (**to, towards** vers); **2** (control) diriger [*company, project*]; régler [*traffic*]; **3** diriger [*attack, light*] (**at** vers); **4** réaliser [*film, programme*]; mettre [qch] en scène [*play*]; diriger [*actor, opera*]; **5** (show route) **to ~ sb to sth** indiquer le chemin de qch à qn.
IV *vi* (in cinema, radio, TV) faire de la réalisation; (in theatre) faire de la mise en scène.

direct: **~ access** *n* (Comput) accès *m* direct; **~ debit** *n* prélèvement *m* automatique.

direction I *n* **1** (left, right, north, south) direction *f*; **in the right/wrong ~** dans la bonne/mauvaise direction; **to go in the opposite ~** aller en sens inverse; **from all ~s** de tous les côtés; **2** (taken by company, government) orientation *f*; **the right/wrong ~ for sb** la bonne/mauvaise option pour qn; **3** (in cinema, radio, TV) réalisation *f*; (in theatre) mise *f* en scène; (of orchestra) direction *f*; **4** (control) direction *f*; (guidance) conseils *mpl*.
II directions *n pl* **1** (for route) indications *fpl*; **to ask for ~s** demander son chemin (**from** à); **2** (for use) instructions *fpl* (**as to, about** sur); **~s for use** mode *m* d'emploi.

directly *adv* **1** [*connect, challenge, go*] directement; [*point*] droit; [*above*] juste; **2** (at once) **~ after** aussitôt après; **~ before** juste avant; **3** (very soon) d'ici peu; **4** (frankly) [*speak*] franchement.

direct object *n* objet *m* direct.

director *n* **1** (of company, programme) (sole) directeur/-trice *m/f*; (on board) administrateur/-trice *m/f*; **2** (of project, investigation) responsable *mf*; **3** (of play, film) metteur *m* en scène; (of orchestra) chef *m* d'orchestre; (of choir) chef *m* des chœurs; **4** (Sch, Univ) **~ of studies** directeur/-trice *m/f* des études.

directory *n* **1** (also **telephone ~**) annuaire *m*; **2** (for business use) répertoire *m* d'adresses; **street ~** répertoire *m* des rues; **3** (Comput) répertoire *m*.

directory assistance *n* (US), **directory enquiries** *n pl* (GB) (service *m* des) renseignements *mpl*.

direct: **~ speech** *n* style *m* direct; **~ transfer** *n* virement *m* automatique.

dirt *n* **1** (mess) (on clothing, in room) saleté *f*; (on body, cooker) crasse *f*; (in carpet, engine, filter) saletés *fpl*; **to show the ~** être salissant; **2** (soil) terre *f*; (mud) boue *f*.

dirt track *n* **1** (Sport) cendrée *f*; **2** (road) chemin *m* de terre battue.

dirty I *adj* **1** [*face, clothing, street*] sale; [*work*] salissant; **to get ~** se salir; **to get** or **make sth ~** salir qch; **2** [*needle*] qui a déjà servi; [*wound*] infecté; **3**○ [*book, joke*] cochon/-onne○; [*mind*] mal tourné; **4**○ [*fighter*] déloyal; [*trick*] sale (*before n*).
II *vtr* salir; **to ~ one's hands** se salir les mains (**doing** en faisant).
IDIOMS **to give sb a ~ look**○ regarder qn d'un sale œil.

dirty: **~ tricks** *n pl* diffamation *f*; **~ weekend**○ *n* week-end *m* de débauche.

disability I *n* infirmité *f*; **physical ~** handicap *m* physique.
II *noun modifier* [*benefit, pension*] d'invalidité.

disable *vtr* **1** [*accident*] rendre [qn] infirme; **to be ~d by arthritis** être handicapé par l'arthrite; **2** immobiliser [*machine*]; **3** (Comput) désactiver.

disabled I *n* **the ~** les handicapés *mpl*.
II *adj* handicapé.

disabled: **~ access** *n* voie *f* d'accès pour handicapés; **~ person** *n* invalide *mf*.

disadvantage *n* **1** (drawback) inconvénient *m*; **the ~ is that**... l'inconvénient, c'est que...; **2** (position of weakness) **to be at a ~** être désavantagé; **to get sb at a ~** avoir l'avantage sur qn.

disadvantaged *adj* défavorisé.

disagree *vi* **1** (differ) ne pas être d'accord (**with** avec; **on, about** sur); **we often ~** nous avons souvent des avis différents; **2** (oppose) **to ~ with** s'opposer à [*plan*]; **3** (conflict) être en désaccord (**with** avec); **4 to ~ with sb** [*food*] ne pas réussir à qn.

disagreement *n* **1** (difference of opinion) désaccord *m* (**about, on** sur); **there is some ~ as to our aims** les avis divergent quant à nos objectifs; **2** (argument) différend *m* (**about, over** sur); **3** (inconsistency) divergence *f* (**between** entre).

disallow *vtr* **1** (Sport) refuser [*goal*]; **2** (gen, Law) rejeter [*claim, decision*].

disappear *vi* disparaître.

disappearance *n* disparition *f* (**of** de).

disappoint *vtr* décevoir.

disappointed *adj* **1** (let down) déçu (**about, with sth** par qch); **I am ~ that he failed** je suis déçu qu'il ait échoué; **I am ~ in you** tu me déçois; **2** (unfulfilled) déçu.

disappointing *adj* décevant; **it's ~ that** c'est décevant que (+ *subj*).

disappointment *n* **1** (feeling) déception *f*; **2 to be a ~ to sb** décevoir qn.

disapproval *n* désapprobation *f* (**of** de).

disapprove *vi* **to ~ of** désapprouver [*person, lifestyle*]; être contre [*smoking*].

disarm *vtr*, *vi* désarmer.

disarmament *n* désarmement *m*.

disaster *n* catastrophe *f*; (long-term) désastre *m*; **~ struck** le malheur a frappé.

disaster: **~ area** *n* région *f* sinistrée; (figurative) catastrophe *f*; **~ fund** *n* fonds *m* de soutien; **~ victim** *n* sinistré/-e *m/f*.

disastrous *adj* désastreux/-euse.

disbelief *n* incrédulité *f*.

disc, disk (US) *n* **1** (gen, Mus) disque *m*; **2** (Anat) disque *m* (intervertébral); **a slipped ~** une hernie discale; **3** (gen, Mil) **identity ~** plaque *f* d'identité; **4** (Aut) **tax ~** vignette *f* (automobile).

discard *vtr* **1** (get rid of) se débarrasser de [*possessions*]; mettre [qch] au rebut [*furniture*]; **2** (drop) abandonner [*plan, policy*]; laisser tomber [*person*].

discerning *adj* perspicace.

discharge I *n* **1** (of patient) renvoi *m* au foyer; **2** (of gas) émission *f*; (of liquid) écoulement *m*; (of pus) suppuration *f*; (of blood) perte *f*; **3** (emptying out) (of waste) déversement *m*; **4** (waste) déchets *mpl*; (from eye, wound) sécrétions *fpl*.
II *vtr* **1** (release) renvoyer [*patient*]; décharger [*accused*]; **to be ~d from hospital** être autorisé à quitter l'hôpital; **to be ~d from the army** être libéré de l'armée; **2** (dismiss) renvoyer [*employee*]; **to ~ sb from his duties** démettre qn de ses fonctions; **3** (give off) émettre [*gas*]; déverser [*sewage*]; **4** (Med) **to ~ pus** suppurer.

discipline I *n* discipline *f*.
II *vtr* **1** (control) discipliner; **2** (punish) punir.

disclaim *vtr* nier.

disclose *vtr* révéler [*information*].

disclosure *n* révélation *f* (**of** de).

disco *n* **1** (event) soirée *f* disco; **2** (club) discothèque *f*.

discomfort *n* **1** (physical) sensation *f* pénible; **to be in ~, to suffer ~** avoir mal; **2** (embarrassment) sentiment *m* de gêne.

disconcerting *adj* (worrying) troublant; (unnerving) déconcertant.

disconnect *vtr* débrancher [*pipe, fridge*]; couper [*telephone*]; décrocher [*carriage*].

discontent *n* mécontentement *m*.

discontinue *vtr* supprimer [*service*]; arrêter [*production*]; cesser [*visits*].

discount I *n* remise *f* (**on** sur); (on minor purchase) rabais *m* (**on** sur); **a 10% ~** une remise de 10%; **to give sb a ~** faire une remise à qn; **~ for cash** escompte *m* de caisse (pour paiement au comptant); **at a ~** [*sell, purchase*] à prix réduit.
II *vtr* écarter [*idea, possibility*]; ne pas tenir compte de [*advice, report*].

discourage *vtr* **1** (dishearten) décourager; **2** (deter) décourager (**from doing** de faire).

discover *vtr* découvrir (**that** que).

discovery *n* découverte *f*; **a voyage of ~** un voyage d'exploration.

discredit *vtr* discréditer [*person, organization*]; mettre en doute [*report, theory*].

discreet *adj* discret/-ète.

discrepancy *n* divergence *f*.

discretion *n* discrétion *f*; **to use one's ~** agir à sa discrétion.

discriminate *vi* **1** (act with bias) établir une discrimination (**against** envers; **in favour of** en faveur de); **2** (distinguish) **to ~ between** faire une or la distinction entre.

discrimination *n* discrimination *f*.

discuss *vtr* (talk about) discuter de; (in writing) examiner.

discussion *n* discussion *f*; (in public) débat *m*; (in text) analyse *f*; **under ~** en discussion; **to be open to ~** être à discuter.

disease *n* **1** (specific illness) maladie *f*; **2** (range of infections) maladies *fpl*.

diseased *adj* malade.

disembark *vtr, vi* débarquer.

disenchanted *adj* désabusé; **to become ~ with sth** perdre ses illusions sur qch.

disengage *vtr* dégager (**from** de).

disfigure *vtr* défigurer.

disgrace I *n* honte *f*; **to be in ~** (officially) être en disgrâce.
II *vtr* déshonorer [*team, family*]; **he ~d himself** il s'est mal conduit.

disgraceful *adj* [*conduct*] scandaleux/-euse; **it's ~!** c'est une honte!

disguise I *n* déguisement *m*; **in ~** déguisé.
II *vtr* déguiser [*person, voice*]; camoufler [*blemish*]; cacher [*emotion, fact*].

disgust I *n* (physical) dégoût *m*; (moral) écœurement *m* (**at** devant); **in ~** dégoûté, écœuré.
II *vtr* (physically) dégoûter; (morally) écœurer.

disgusting *adj* (physically) répugnant; (morally) écœurant.

dish I *n* **1** (plate) (for eating) assiette *f*; (for serving) plat *m*; **2** (food) plat *m*; **3** (also **satellite ~**) antenne *f* parabolique.
II dishes *n pl* vaisselle *f*; **to do the ~es** faire la vaisselle.
■ **dish out**: **~ out [sth]** distribuer [*advice, compliments, money*]; servir [*food*].
■ **dish up**: **~ up [sth]** servir [*meal*].

dishcloth *n* (for washing) lavette *f*; (for drying) torchon *m* (à vaisselle).

dishevelled *adj* [*person*] débraillé; [*hair*] décoiffé; [*clothes*] en désordre.

dishonest *adj* malhonnête.

dishonesty *n* (financial) malhonnêteté *f*; (moral) mauvaise foi *f*.

dish: **~pan** *n* (US) cuvette *f*; **~rag** *n* (US) lavette *f*; **~towel** *n* torchon *m*; **~washer** *n* (machine) lave-vaisselle *m inv*; (person) plongeur/-euse *m/f*.

disillusioned *adj* désabusé; **to be ~ with** perdre ses illusions sur.

disinfect *vtr* désinfecter.

disinfectant *n* désinfectant *m*.

disintegrate *vi* [*wood, mind*] se désagréger; [*aircraft*] se désintégrer.

disinterested *adj* [*observer, party, stance, advice*] impartial.

disk *n* **1** (Comput) disque *m*; **on ~** sur disque; **2** (US) = **disc**.

disk: **~ directory** *n* répertoire *m* disques; **~ drive (unit)** *n* unité *f* de disques; **~ management** *n* gestion *f* disques; **~**

operating system, DOS *n* système *m* d'exploitation à disques, DOS *m*.
dislike I *n* aversion *f* (**for** pour); **to take a ~ to sb** prendre qn en aversion.
II *vtr* ne pas aimer (**doing** faire); **I have always ~d him** il m'a toujours été antipathique; **I don't ~ city life** je n'ai rien contre la vie urbaine.
dislocate *vtr* **to ~ one's shoulder** se démettre l'épaule.
dislocation *n* (of hip, knee) luxation *f*.
dislodge *vtr* déplacer [*rock, tile, obstacle*]; déloger [*foreign body, sniper*].
disloyal *adj* déloyal (**to** envers).
dismal *adj* **1** [*place, sight*] lugubre; **2**○ [*failure, attempt*] lamentable.
dismantle *vtr* **1** démonter [*construction*]; **2** démanteler [*organization*].
dismay *n* consternation *f* (**at** devant).
dismiss *vtr* **1** (reject) écarter [*idea, suggestion*]; exclure [*possibility*]; **to ~ sth as insignificant** faire peu de cas de qch; **2** (put out of mind) chasser [*thought, worry*]; **3** (sack) licencier [*employee*]; révoquer [*civil servant*]; démettre [qn] de ses fonctions [*director, official*]; **4** (end interview with) congédier [*person*]; (send out) [*teacher*] laisser sortir [*class*]; **5** (Law) **the case was ~ed** il y a eu non-lieu.
dismissal *n* (of employee) licenciement *m*; (of civil servant) révocation *f*; (of manager, minister) destitution *f*; **unfair ~** licenciement abusif.
dismissive *adj* [*attitude, person*] dédaigneux/-euse.
disobedient *adj* [*child*] désobéissant.
disobey I *vtr* désobéir à [*person*]; enfreindre [*law*].
II *vi* [*person*] désobéir.
disorder *n* **1** (lack of order) désordre *m*; **2** (disturbances) émeutes *fpl*; **3** (Med) (malfunction) troubles *mpl*; (disease) maladie *f*.
disorganized *adj* désorganisé.
disorientate *vtr* désorienter.
disown *vtr* renier [*person*]; désavouer [*document*].
dispatch I *n* **1** (report) dépêche *f*; **2** (sending) expédition *f*: **date of ~** date d'expédition.
II *vtr* envoyer [*person*] (**to** à); expédier [*letter, parcel*] (**to** à).
dispel *vtr* dissiper [*doubt, fear, myth*].
dispensary *n* (GB) (in hospital) pharmacie *f*; (in chemist's) officine *f*.
dispense *vtr* **1** [*machine*] distribuer [*drinks, money*]; **2** [*chemist*] préparer [*medicine, prescription*]; **3** (exempt) dispenser (**from sth** de qch; **from doing** de faire).
■ **dispense with 1** (manage without) se passer de [*services, formalities*]; **2** (get rid of) abandonner [*policy*]; **3** (make unnecessary) rendre inutile [*resource*].
dispenser *n* distributeur *m*.
disperse I *vtr* disperser [*crowd, fumes*].
II *vi* **1** [*crowd*] se disperser; **2** [*mist*] se dissiper.
displaced person *n* personne *f* déplacée.
display I *n* **1** (for sale) étalage *m*; (of larger objects) exposition *f*; **window ~** vitrine *f*; **to be on ~** être exposé; **to put sth on ~** exposer qch; **2** (demonstration) (of art, craft) démonstration *f*; (of dance, sport) exhibition *f*; **air ~** fête *f* aéronautique; **3** (of emotion, failing, quality) démonstration *f*; (of strength) déploiement *m*; (of wealth) étalage *m*; **4** (Aut, Comput) écran *m*.
II *vtr* **1** (show, set out) afficher [*information, poster*]; exposer [*object*]; **2** (reveal) faire preuve de [*intelligence, interest, skill*]; révéler [*emotion, vice, virtue*]; **3** (flaunt) faire étalage de [*beauty, knowledge, wealth*]; exhiber [*legs, chest*].
display: **~ advertisement** *n* grande annonce *f*; **~ cabinet, ~ case** *n* (in museum) vitrine *f* d'exposition; **~ panel** *n* écran *m* d'affichage; **~ rack** *n* présentoir *m*.
displeased *adj* mécontent (**with, at** de).
disposable *adj* **1** (throwaway) jetable; **2** (available) disponible.
disposal *n* **1** (of waste product) élimination *f*; **for ~** à jeter; **2** (of company, property) vente *f*; **3** (for use, access) **to be at sb's ~** être à la disposition de qn.
dispose *v* ■ **dispose of**: **~ of [sth/sb] 1** se débarrasser de [*body, rubbish*]; détruire [*evidence*]; désarmer [*bomb*]; **2** écouler [*stock*]; vendre [*car, shares*].
disproportionate *adj* disproportionné (**to** par rapport à).
disprove *vtr* réfuter.
dispute I *n* **1** (quarrel) (between individuals) dispute *f*; (between groups) conflit *m* (**over, about** à propos de); **to have a ~ with** se disputer avec; **2** (controversy) controverse *f* (**over, about** sur); **to be in ~** [*fact*] être controversé; **to be open to ~** être contestable.
II *vtr* **1** contester [*claim, figures*]; **2** se disputer [*property, title*].
disqualification *n* **1** (from post) exclusion *f* (**from** de); **2** (Sport) disqualification *f*; **3** (also **driving ~**) retrait *m* du permis de conduire.
disqualify *vtr* **1** (from post, career) exclure; **to ~ sb from doing** interdire à qn de faire; **2** (Sport) [*regulation*] disqualifier; [*physical condition*] empêcher (**from doing** de faire); **3** (GB Aut) **to ~ sb from driving** retirer le permis de conduire à qn.
disregard I *n* (for problem, person) indifférence *f* (**for sth** à qch; **for sb** envers qn); (for danger, convention, life, law, right) mépris *m* (**for** de).
II *vtr* **1** ne pas tenir compte de [*problem, evidence, remark*]; fermer les yeux sur [*fault*]; mépriser [*danger*]; **2** ne pas respecter [*law, instruction*].
disrepair *n* délabrement *m*; **to fall into ~** se délabrer.
disreputable *adj* [*person*] peu recommandable; [*place*] mal famé.
disrespect *n* manque *m* de respect (**for** envers).
disrespectful *adj* [*person*] irrespectueux/-euse (**to, towards** envers).
disrupt *vtr* perturber [*traffic, trade, meeting*];

bouleverser [*lifestyle, schedule, routine*]; interrompre [*power supply*].

disruption *n* **1** (disorder) perturbations *fpl* (**in** dans); **2** (of service, meeting) perturbation *f*; (of schedule) bouleversement *m*; (of power supply) interruption *f*.

disruptive *adj* perturbateur/-trice.

dissatisfaction *n* mécontentement *m*.

dissatisfied *adj* mécontent (**with** de).

dissect *vtr* **1** disséquer [*cadaver*]; **2** disséquer [*relationship*]; éplucher [*book*].

dissident *n, adj* dissident/-e (*m/f*).

dissolve I *vtr* **1** [*acid, water*] dissoudre [*solid, grease*]; **2** faire dissoudre [*tablet, powder*] (**in** dans); **3** (break up) dissoudre [*assembly, parliament, partnership*].
II *vi* **1** [*tablet*] se dissoudre (**in** dans; **into** en); **2** [*hope, feeling, opposition*] s'évanouir; [*outline, image*] disparaître; **3 to ~ into tears** fondre en larmes.

distance ▶738 I *n* distance *f* (**between** entre; **from** de; **to** à); **a short ~ away** pas loin; **to keep sb at a ~** tenir qn à distance; **to keep one's ~** garder ses distances (**from** avec); **from a/in the ~** de/au loin; **it's within walking ~** on peut y aller à pied.
II *v refl* **to ~ oneself** (dissociate oneself) se distancier; (stand back) prendre du recul (**from** par rapport à).

distant *adj* **1** (remote) éloigné; **the ~ sound of sth** le bruit de qch dans le lointain; **2** (faint) [*memory, prospect*] lointain; **3** (cool) [*person*] distant.

distinct *adj* **1** [*image*] (not blurred) net/nette; (easily visible) distinct; **2** (definite) [*resemblance, preference, progress*] net/nette (*before n*); [*advantage*] indéniable; **3** (separable) distinct (**from** de); **4** (different) différent (**from** de); **as ~ from** par opposition à.

distinction *n* **1** (differentiation) distinction *f*; **2** (difference) différence *f* (**between** entre); **3** (preeminence) mérite *m*; **to have the ~ of doing** (have honour) avoir le mérite de faire; (be the only one) avoir la particularité de faire; **4** (elegance) distinction *f*; **5** (specific honour) distinction *f*; **6** (Univ) (mark) mention *f* très bien.

distinctive *adj* caractéristique (**of** de).

distinctly *adv* **1** [*speak, hear, see*] distinctement; [*remember*] nettement; [*say, tell*] explicitement; **2** [*possible, odd*] vraiment.

distinguish I *vtr* distinguer (**from** de); **to be ~ed by** se caractériser par.
II **distinguishing** *pres p adj* [*feature, factor*] distinctif/-ive.

distinguished *adj* **1** (elegant) distingué; **2** (famous) éminent.

distort *vtr* **1** dénaturer [*statement, fact*]; déformer [*truth*]; **2** déformer [*features, sound, metal*].

distortion *n* (of truth) déformation *f*; (of metal) déformation *f*; (of sound, features, figures) distorsion *f*.

distract *vtr* distraire; **to ~ sb from doing** empêcher qn de faire; **to ~ attention** détourner l'attention (**from** de).

distraction *n* **1** (from concentration) distraction *f*; **a moment's ~** un moment d'inattention; **2** (diversion) diversion *f*; **to be a ~ from** détourner l'attention de [*problem, priority*].

distress I *n* **1** (emotional) désarroi *m*; **to cause sb ~** faire de la peine à qn; **2** (physical) souffrance(s) *f(pl)*; **foetal ~** (Med) souffrance *f* fœtale; **3** [*ship*] **in ~** en détresse.
II *noun modifier* [*call, rocket, signal*] de détresse.
III *vtr* faire de la peine à [*person*]; (stronger) bouleverser [*person*] (**to do** de faire).

distressed *adj* (upset) peiné (**at, by** par); (stronger) bouleversé (**at, by** par).

distressing *adj* [*case, event, idea*] pénible; [*news*] navrant; [*sight*] affligeant.

distribute *vtr* **1** (share out) distribuer [*information, films, supplies, money*] (**to** à; **among** entre); **2** (spread out) répartir [*weight, load, tax burden*].

distribution *n* distribution *f*.

distributor *n* distributeur *m* (**for sth** de qch).

district *n* (in country) région *f*; (in city) quartier *m*; (administrative) district *m*.

district attorney *n* (US) représentant *m* du ministère public.

disturb *vtr* **1** (interrupt) déranger [*person, work*]; troubler [*silence, sleep*]; **2** (upset) troubler [*person*]; (concern) inquiéter [*person*].

disturbance *n* **1** (interruption, inconvenience) dérangement *m*; **2** (riot) troubles *mpl*; (fight) altercation *f*.

disturbed *adj* **1** [*sleep*] agité; **2** [*child*] perturbé.

disturbing *adj* **1** (unsettling) [*portrayal*] troublant; [*book, film*] perturbant; **2** (worrying) [*report, increase*] inquiétant; (stronger) alarmant.

disused *adj* abandonné, désaffecté.

ditch I *n* fossé *m*.
II○ *vtr* **1** (get rid of) laisser tomber [*friend, ally*]; abandonner [*system, agreement*]; plaquer○ [*girlfriend, boyfriend*]; **2 to ~ a plane** faire un amerrissage forcé.

dither *vi* tergiverser (**about, over** sur).

dive I *n* **1** (by swimmer) plongeon *m*; **2** (of plane, bird) piqué *m*; **3** (lunge) **to make a ~ for sth** foncer vers qch.
II *vi* **1** [*person*] plonger (**off, from** de; **down to** jusqu'à); **2** (as hobby) faire de la plongée; **3** (rush) **to ~ into** s'engouffrer dans [*bar, shop*].
■ **dive for**: **~ for [sth] 1** [*diver*] pêcher [*pearls*]; **2** [*player*] plonger sur [*ball*]; **3** [*person*] foncer vers [*exit*]; **to ~ for cover** foncer à l'abri.

diverge *vi* [*interests, opinions*] diverger; **to ~ from** s'écarter de [*truth, norm*].

diversion *n* (of river, money) détournement *m*; (of traffic) déviation *f*.

divert *vtr* **1** (redirect) détourner [*water, flow*]; dévier [*traffic*] (**onto** vers; **through** par); dérouter [*flight, plane*] (**to** sur); détourner [*resources, funds, manpower*] (**to** au profit de); **2** (distract) détourner [*attention, conversation*].

divide I *n* division *f* (**between** entre); **the North-South ~** l'opposition *f* Nord-Sud.
II *vtr* **1** (also **~ up**) partager [*food, money, time, work*]; **they ~d the profits among themselves** ils se sont partagé les bénéfices; **2** (separate) séparer (**from** de); **3** (split) diviser [*friends, management, group*].
III *vi* [*road*] bifurquer; [*river, train*] se séparer en deux; [*group*] (into two) se séparer en deux; [*cell, organism*] se diviser.

divided skirt *n* jupe-culotte *f*.

dividend *n* dividende *m*.

dividing *adj* [*wall, fence*] mitoyen/-enne.

dividing line *n* ligne *f* de démarcation.

diving *n* (from board) plongeon *m*; (under sea) plongée *f* sous-marine.

diving: **~ board** *n* plongeoir *m*; **~ suit** *n* scaphandre *m*.

division *n* **1** (splitting) division *f* (**into** en); **2** (sharing) (of one thing) répartition *f*; (of several things) distribution *f*; **3** (military unit) division *f*; (administrative unit) circonscription *f*; **4** (in company) (branch, sector) division *f*; (department, team) service *m*; **5** (in container) compartiment *m*; **6** (in football league) division *f*.

divisive *adj* [*policy*] qui sème la discorde.

divorce I *n* divorce *m* (**from** avec; **between** entre); **to file for ~** intenter une action en divorce.
II *vtr* **to ~ sb** divorcer de *or* d'avec qn; **she ~d him** elle a divorcé.

DIY *n* (GB) (*abbr* = **do-it-yourself**) bricolage *m*.

dizzy *adj* **to make sb ~** donner le vertige à qn; **to feel ~** avoir la tête qui tourne.

DJ *n* (*abbr* = **disc jockey**) DJ *mf*.

DNA *n* (*abbr* = **deoxyribonucleic acid**) ADN *m*.

do I *v aux* ▶ 599 **J own up, did you or didn't you take my pen?** avoue, est-ce que c'est toi qui as pris mon stylo ou pas?; **didn't he look wonderful!** il était beau, hein?; **don't ~ that!** ne fais pas ça!; **so you ~ want to go after all!** alors tu veux vraiment y aller finalement! ; **he said he'd tell her and he did** il a dit qu'il le lui dirait et il l'a fait; **'I love peaches'—'so ~ I'** 'j'adore les pêches'—'moi aussi'; **~ shut up!** tais-toi veux-tu!; **don't you tell me what to do!** je n'ai pas de leçons à recevoir de toi!; **'who wrote it?'—'I did'** 'qui l'a écrit?'—'moi'; **'shall I tell him?'—'no don't'** 'est-ce que je le lui dis?'—'non'; **he lives in London, doesn't he?** il habite à Londres, n'est-ce pas?; **'he knows the President'—'does he?'** 'il connaît le Président'—'vraiment?'; **so/neither does he** lui aussi/non plus.
II *vtr* **1** (accomplish) faire [*washing up, ironing, duty*]; **to ~ one's homework** faire ses devoirs; **to ~ sth again** refaire qch; **she's ~ing too much** elle en fait trop; **will you ~ something for me?** peux-tu me rendre un service?; **2** (make smart) **to ~ sb's hair** coiffer qn; **to ~ one's teeth** se brosser les dents; **3** (complete, finish) faire [*military service, period of time*]; **have you done**° **complaining?** tu as fini de te plaindre?; **tell him now and have done with it** dis-le-lui maintenant, ce sera fait; **it's as good as done** c'est comme si c'était fait; **4** (complete through study) faire [*subject, degree, homework*]; **5** (write) faire [*translation, essay*]; **6** (effect change) faire; **what have you done to your hair?** qu'est-ce que vous avez fait à vos cheveux?; **what has he done with the newspaper?** qu'est-ce qu'il a fait du journal?; **I haven't done anything with your pen!** je n'ai pas touché à ton stylo!; **7** (hurt) faire; **to ~ something to one's arm** se faire mal au bras; **8**° (deal with) **they don't ~ theatre tickets** ils ne vendent pas de billets de théâtre; **to ~ breakfasts** servir le petit déjeuner; **9** (cook) faire [*sausages, spaghetti*]; **well done** [*meat*] bien cuit; **10** (prepare) préparer [*vegetables*]; **11** (produce) monter [*play*]; faire [*film, programme*] (**on** sur); **12** (travel at) faire; **to ~ 60** faire du 60 à l'heure; **13** (cover distance of) faire [*30 km*]; **14**° (satisfy needs of) **will this ~ you?** ça vous ira?; **15**° (cheat) **we've been done** on s'est fait avoir; **to ~ sb out of £5** refaire° qn de 5 livres sterling; **16**° (rob) **to ~ a bank** faire un casse° dans une banque.
III *vi* **1** (behave) faire; **~ as you're told** (by me) fais ce que je te dis; (by others) fais ce qu'on te dit; **2** (serve purpose) **that box will ~** cette boite fera l'affaire; **3** (be acceptable) **this really won't ~!** [*situation, attitude*] ça ne peut pas continuer comme ça!; [*work*] c'est franchement mauvais!; **4** (be sufficient) [*amount of money*] suffire; **5** (in competitive situation) [*person*] s'en sortir; [*business*] marcher; **6** (in health) **mother and baby are both ~ing well** la mère et l'enfant se portent bien; **the patient is ~ing well** le malade est en bonne voie.
IDIOMS **it doesn't ~ to be** ce n'est pas une bonne chose d'être; **it was all I could ~ not to laugh** je me suis retenu pour ne pas rire; **nothing ~ing!** pas question!; **well done!** bravo!; **what are you ~ing with yourself these days?** qu'est-ce que tu deviens?; **what are you going to ~ for money?** où vas-tu trouver l'argent?
■ **do away with**: **~ away with [sth]** se débarrasser de [*procedure, custom, rule, feature*]; supprimer [*bus service*]; démolir [*building*].
■ **do up**: ¶ **~ up** [*dress, coat*] se fermer; ¶ **~ [sth] up, ~ up [sth] 1** (fasten) nouer [*laces*]; remonter [*zip*]; **~ up your buttons** boutonne-toi; **2** (wrap) faire [*parcel*]; **3** (renovate) restaurer [*house, furniture*]; ¶ **~ oneself up** se faire beau/belle.
■ **do with**: **~ with [sth/sb] 1** (involve) **it has something to ~ with** ça a quelque chose à voir avec; **what's it (got) to ~ with you?** en quoi est-ce que ça te regarde?; **it has nothing to ~ with you** cela ne vous concerne pas; **2** (tolerate) supporter; **3** (need) **I could ~ with a holiday** j'aurais bien besoin de partir en vacances; **4** (finish) **it's all over and done with** c'est bien fini.
■ **do without**: **~ without [sb/sth]** se passer de [*person, advice*].

do

The French equivalent of the verb ***to do*** in *subject + to do + object* sentences is ***faire***:

*she's **doing** her homework* = elle **fait** ses devoirs
*what **has** he **done** with the newspaper?* = qu'est-ce qu'il **a fait** du journal?

Grammatical functions of *do*, auxiliary verb

In questions

In French there is no auxiliary verb in questions equivalent to ***do*** in English.

When the subject is a pronoun, use either of these structures: *verb + hyphen + subject* or, less formally, ***est-ce que*** *+ subject + verb*:

***do** you like Mozart?* = aimes-tu Mozart?
= **est-ce que** tu aimes Mozart?

When the subject is a noun, there are again two possibilities:

***did** your sister ring?* = **est-ce que** ta sœur a téléphoné?
= ta sœur a-t-elle téléphoné?

In negatives

Equally, auxiliaries are not used in negatives in French:

*I **don't** like Mozart* = je n'aime pas Mozart

In emphatic uses

There is no verbal equivalent for the use of ***do*** in such expressions as *I do like your dress.* In emphatic uses, French may use an intensifying adverb (***beaucoup, vraiment***):

*I **do** like your dress* = j'aime **beaucoup** ta robe
*I **do** think you should go* = je crois **vraiment** que tu devrais y aller

When referring back to another verb

In this case the verb ***to do*** is not translated at all:

*I live in Oxford and so **does** Lily* = j'habite à Oxford et Lily aussi
*she gets paid more than I **do*** = elle est payée plus que moi
*'I don't like carrots' – 'Neither **do** I'* = 'je n'aime pas les carottes' – 'moi non plus'

In polite requests

In polite requests the phrase ***je vous en prie*** or ***je t'en prie*** is useful:

***do** sit down* = asseyez-vous, je **vous en prie**

In imperatives

In French there is no use of an auxiliary verb in imperatives:

***don't** shut the door* = ne ferme pas la porte
***do** be quiet!* = tais-toi!

In tag questions

With tag questions like ***doesn't he?*** or ***didn't it?***, there is a general tag question ***n'est-ce pas?*** which will work in many cases:

*you like fish, **don't you**?* = tu aimes le poisson, **n'est-ce pas**?

With positive tag questions ***par hasard*** can often be useful as a translation:

*Lola didn't phone, **did she**?* = Lola n'a pas téléphoné **par hasard**?

In short answers

Where the answer ***yes*** is used to contradict a negative question or statement, ***si*** is often employed:

*'Marion didn't say that' – '**yes she did**'* = 'Marion n'a pas dit ça' – '**si**'

In response to a standard enquiry, the tag will not be translated:

*'do you like strawberries?' – '**yes I do**'* = 'aimez-vous les fraises?' – '**oui**'

For more examples, see the entry **do I**.

dock I *n* **1** (in port) dock *m*; (for repairing ship) cale *f*; **2** (US) (wharf) appontement *m*; **3** (GB Law) banc *m* des accusés.
II *vi* (come into port) arriver au port; (moor) accoster.

dock: **~worker** ▶805 *n* docker *m*; **~yard** *n* chantier *m* naval.

doctor ▶805, 642 I *n* **1** (Med) médecin *m*, docteur *m*; **2** (Univ) docteur *m*.
II *vtr* frelater [*food, wine*]; falsifier [*figures*]; altérer [*document*].

document *n* (gen) document *m*; (Law) acte *m*; **travel/insurance ~s** papiers *mpl* de voyage/ d'assurance; **policy ~** déclaration *f* de politique générale.

documentary I *n* documentaire *m* (**about, on** sur).
II *adj* **~ evidence** (Law) preuves *fpl* écrites; (historical) documents *mpl* de l'époque.

documentation *n* documentation *f*; (in business) documents *mpl*.

dodge I *n* **1** (movement) mouvement *m* de côté; (Sport) esquive *f*; **2**○ (GB) (trick) combine○ *f*.
II *vtr* esquiver [*bullet, blow, question*]; se dérober à [*confrontation, accusation*]; éviter de payer [*tax*]; éviter [*person*]; **to ~ the issue** éluder la question.

dodgem (car) *n* (GB) auto *f* tamponneuse.

dog I *n* **1** chien *m*; (female) chienne *f*; **2** (male fox, wolf) mâle *m*.
II *noun modifier* [*biscuit, basket*] pour chien; [*food*] pour chiens.
IDIOMS **it's ~ eat ~** c'est chacun pour soi; **to go to the ~s**○ [*company, country*] aller à vau-l'eau.

dog: **~ collar** *n* collier *m* de chien; **~-eared** *adj* écorné.

dogged *adj* [*attempt*] obstiné; [*person, refusal*] tenace; [*resistance*] opiniâtre.

doghouse *n* (US) niche *f* (à chien).

dogmatic *adj* dogmatique (**about** sur).

do-gooder○ *n* bonne âme *f*.

dog: **~ paddle** *n* nage *f* à la manière d'un chien; **~sbody**○ *n* (GB) bonne *f* à tout faire.

doh *n* (Mus) do *m*, ut *m*.

doing *n* **this is her ~** c'est son ouvrage; **it takes some ~**! ce n'est pas facile du tout!

dole○ *n* (GB) allocation *f* de chômage; **on the ~** au chômage.
■ **dole out**○: **~ out [sth], ~ [sth] out** distribuer.

doll *n* poupée *f*; **to play with one's ~s** jouer à la poupée.
■ **doll up**: **to be all ~ed up** être sur son trente et un○.

dollar ▶748 *n* dollar *m*.

dollar bill *n* billet *m* d'un dollar.

dolphin *n* dauphin *m*.

domain *n* domaine *m* (**of** de).

dome *n* (of building) coupole *f*.

domestic *adj* **1** [*market, flight*] intérieur; [*crisis, issue*] de politique intérieure; **2** [*life, harmony*] familial; [*dispute*] conjugal; [*violence*] dans la famille.

domestic appliance *n* appareil *m* électroménager.

domesticate *vtr* domestiquer; **to be ~d** [*person*] savoir tenir une maison.

domestic: **~ help** *n* aide *f* ménagère; **~ science** *n* (GB) arts *mpl* ménagers.

dominance *n* domination *f* (**of** de); (in animal kingdom) dominance *f*.

dominant *adj* dominant.

dominate I *vtr* dominer [*person, region, market*].
II *vi* [*person*] dominer; [*issue*] prédominer.

domineering *adj* autoritaire.

domino ▶649 *n* domino *m*; **to play ~es** jouer aux dominos.

donation *n* don *m* (**of** de; **à** to).

done *excl* marché conclu!
IDIOMS **it's not the ~ thing** ça ne se fait pas.

donkey *n* âne *m*.
IDIOMS **she could talk the hind leg off a ~!** c'est un vrai moulin à paroles○!

donkey work *n* travail *m* pénible.

donor *n* (of organ) donneur/-euse *m/f*; (of money) donateur/-trice *m/f*.

doom *n* **1** (death) mort *f*; **2** (downfall) (of person) perte *f*; (of country) catastrophe *f*.

door *n* **1** (in building) porte *f* (**to** de); (in car, train) porte *f*, portière *f*; **a few ~s down** quelques maisons plus loin; **behind closed ~s** à huis clos; **2** (entrance) entrée *f*.
IDIOMS **to get a foot in the ~** mettre un pied dans la place.

door: **~ bell** *n* sonnette *f*; **~man** *n* (at hotel) portier *m*; (at cinema) contrôleur *m*; **~mat** *n* paillasson *m*.

doorstep *n* **1** (step) pas *m* de porte; **2** (threshold) seuil *m*; **on one's ~** (nearby) tout près; (unpleasantly close) juste à côté.

doorstop *n* butoir *m* (de porte).

door to door *adv* **to sell ~** faire du porte à porte; **it's 90 minutes ~** le trajet prend 90 minutes de porte à porte.

doorway *n* **1** (frame) embrasure *f*; **2** (entrance) porte *f*, entrée *f*.

dope I○ *n* **1** cannabis *m*; **2** (fool) imbécile○ *mf*.
II *vtr* **1** (Sport) doper [*horse, athlete*]; (gen) droguer [*person*]; **2** mettre un somnifère dans [*food, drink*].

dope test *n* (Sport) contrôle *m* antidopage.

dormant *adj* **1** [*emotion, talent*] latent; **to lie ~** sommeiller; **2** [*volcano*] en repos.

dormitory I *n* **1** (GB) dortoir *m*; **2** (US Univ) résidence *f*, foyer *m*.
II *noun modifier* [*suburb, town*] dortoir *inv*.

dormouse *n* muscardin *m*.

dosage *n* posologie *f*.

dose I *n* dose *f* (**of** de); **a ~ of flu** une bonne grippe.
II *vtr* **to ~ sb with medicine** bourrer○ qn de médicaments.

IDIOMS **he's all right in small ~s** il est supportable à doses homéopathiques.

dot *n* (on page, screen) point *m*; (on fabric, wallpaper) pois *m*.
IDIOMS **since the year ~**○ depuis toujours; **at ten on the ~** à dix heures pile.

dote *vi* **to ~ on sb/sth** adorer qn/qch.

dotted line *n* pointillé *m*; **'tear along ~'** 'découpez suivant le pointillé'.

double I *n* **1** (measure of alcohol) **a ~ please** un double, s'il vous plaît; **2** (of person) sosie *m*; (in film, play) doublure *f*.
II doubles *n pl* double *m*; **mixed ~s** double mixte.
III *adj* **1** [*portion, dose*] double (*before n*); **2 with a ~ 'n'** avec deux 'n'; **two ~ four (244)** deux cent quarante-quatre; **3** (dual) double; **with a ~ meaning** à double sens; **4** [*sheet, garage*] double; [*ticket, invitation*] pour deux.
IV *adv* **1** (twice) **to take ~ the time** prendre deux fois plus de temps; **2 to see ~** voir double.
V *vtr* **1** doubler [*amount, dose*]; multiplier [qch] par deux [*number*]; **2** (also **~ over**) plier [qch] en deux [*blanket*]; **3** (in spelling) doubler [*letter*].
VI *vi* **1** [*sales, prices, salaries*] doubler; **2 to ~ for sb** (actor) doubler qn; **3 the sofa ~s as a bed** le canapé fait aussi lit.
IDIOMS **on** or **at the ~** au plus vite.
■ **double back** rebrousser chemin.
■ **double up 1** se plier en deux; **to ~ up with laughter** être plié en deux de rire; **2** (share bedroom) partager la même chambre.

double: **~ act** *n* duo *m*; **~-barrelled name** (GB) ≈ nom à particule; **~ bass** ▶ **753** *n* contrebasse *f*; **~ bed** *n* lit *m* double, grand lit; **~ boiler** *n* (US) ≈ bain-marie *m inv*.

double-book *vtr* **to ~ a room/seat** réserver la même chambre/place pour deux personnes; **to ~ a flight** (deliberately) surbooker un vol.

double: **~-breasted** *adj* [*jacket*] croisé; **~-check** *vtr* vérifier [qch] à nouveau [*detail*]; **~ chin** *n* double menton *m*; **~ cream** *n* (GB) ≈ crème *f* fraîche; **~-cross**○ *vtr* doubler, trahir [*person*]; **~-dealing** *n* fourberie *f*; **~-decker** *n* (GB) (bus) autobus *m* à impériale or à deux étages; (sandwich) sandwich *m* double; **~ door(s)** *n (pl)* porte *f* à deux battants; **~ Dutch**○ *n* baragouinage○ *m*; **~-edged** *adj* [*sword*] à double tranchant; **~ entendre** *n* sous-entendu *m* (grivois); **~ fault** *n* double faute *f*; **~ feature** *n* séance *f* avec deux films à la suite.

double figures *n pl* **to go into ~** [*inflation*] passer la barre des 10%.

double: **~ glazing** *n* double vitrage *m*; **~-park** *vi* se garer en double file.

double-quick *adj* **in ~ time** en un rien de temps.

double: **~ room** *n* chambre *f* pour deux personnes; **~ saucepan** *n* (GB) ≈ bain-marie *m inv*; **~ spacing** *n* double interligne *m*.

double standard *n* **to have ~s** faire deux poids deux mesures.

double time *n* **to be paid ~** être payé double.

double vision *n* **to have ~** voir double.

doubt I *n* doute *m*; **there is no ~ (that)** il ne fait aucun doute que; **there is little ~ (that)** il est presque certain que; **to have no ~ (that)** être certain que; **to have one's ~s about doing** hésiter à faire; **to be in ~** [*outcome, project*] être incertain; [*honesty, innocence*] être douteux/-euse; (on particular occasion) être mis en doute; **if** or **when in ~** dans le doute; **without (a) ~** sans aucun doute.
II *vtr* douter de [*fact, ability, honesty, person*]; **I ~ it!** j'en doute!; **I ~ if he'll come** je doute qu'il vienne.

doubtful *adj* **1** (unsure) incertain; **it is ~ if** or **whether he will come** il n'est pas certain qu'il vienne; **to be ~ about** être peu convaincu par [*idea, plan*]; avoir des doutes sur [*job, purchase*]; **2** [*character, activity, taste*] douteux/-euse.

doubtfully *adv* **1** (hesitantly) d'un air or d'un ton hésitant; **2** (with disbelief) d'un air or d'un ton sceptique.

dough *n* (Culin) pâte *f*.

doughnut, **donut** (US) *n* beignet *m*; **jam ~** beignet à la confiture.

dour *adj* [*person*] renfrogné; [*landscape*] morne.

douse, **dowse** *vtr* **to ~ sb/sth with petrol** arroser qn/qch d'essence.

dove *n* colombe *f*.

Dover ▶ **574** *pr n* Douvres; **the Straits of ~** le Pas de Calais.

dowdy *adj* [*woman*] mal fagoté; [*clothes*] sans chic.

down[1]

■ **Note** When used to indicate vague direction, *down* often has no explicit translation in French: *to go down to London* = aller à Londres; *down in Brighton* = à Brighton.
– For examples and further usages, see the entry below.

I *adv* **1 to go** or **come ~** descendre; **to fall ~** tomber; **to sit ~ on the floor** s'asseoir par terre; **to pull ~ a blind** baisser un store; **~!** (to dog) couché!; **'~'** (in crossword) 'verticalement'; **~ below** en bas; **two floors ~** deux étages plus bas; **it's on the second shelf ~** c'est au deuxième rayon en partant du haut; **~ at the bottom of the lake** tout au fond du lac; **the telephone lines are ~** les lignes téléphoniques sont coupées; **face ~** [*fall*] face contre terre; [*lie*] à plat ventre; (in water) le visage dans l'eau; **they've gone ~ to the country** ils sont allés à la campagne; **they moved ~ here from Scotland** ils ont quitté l'Écosse pour venir s'installer ici; **they live ~ south**○ ils habitent dans le sud; **2** (in a range, scale, hierarchy) **children from the age of 10 ~** les enfants de moins de dix ans; **everybody from the Prime Minister ~ (to the secretary)** tout le monde depuis le Premier Ministre

(jusqu'au secrétaire); **3** (lower) **bookings are ~ by a half** les réservations ont baissé de moitié; **profits are well ~ on last year's** les bénéfices sont nettement inférieurs à ceux de l'année dernière; **to get one's weight ~** maigrir; **I'm ~ to my last cigarette** il ne me reste plus qu'une cigarette; **4** (on list, schedule) **you're ~ to speak next** c'est toi qui es le prochain à intervenir; **I've got you ~ for next Thursday** (in appointment book) vous avez rendez-vous jeudi prochain; **5 to be ~ with the flu** avoir la grippe; **6** (Sport) (behind) **to be two sets ~** [*tennis player*] perdre par deux sets; **7** (as deposit) **to pay £40 ~** payer 40 livres sterling comptant.
II *prep* **to run ~ the hill** descendre la colline en courant; **to go ~ town** aller en ville; **they live ~ the road** ils habitent un peu plus loin dans la rue; **a few miles ~ the river from here** à quelques kilomètres en aval; **to go ~ the street** descendre la rue; **with buttons all ~ the front** boutonné sur le devant; **he looked ~ her throat** il a regardé au fond de sa gorge; (throughout) **~ the ages** or **centuries** à travers les siècles.
III *adj* **1**○ **to feel ~** être déprimé; **2** [*escalator*] qui descend; **3** [*computer*] en panne.
IDIOMS **to have a ~ on sb** en vouloir à qn; **it's ~ to you to do it** c'est à toi de le faire; **~ with tyrants!** à bas les tyrans!

down² *n* duvet *m*.

down-and-out *n* clochard/-e *m/f*.

downfall *n* chute *f*; **drink proved to be his ~** c'est la boisson qui a causé sa perte.

down: **~grade** *vtr* rétrograder [*employee*]; dévaloriser [*task*]; **~hearted** *adj* abattu.

downhill *adv* **to go ~** [*person, vehicle*] descendre; **he's going ~** (declining) il est sur le déclin; **from now on it's ~ all the way** (easy) à partir de maintenant il ne devrait plus y avoir de problèmes; (disastrous) à partir de maintenant c'est le déclin.

downhill skiing *n* ski *m* de descente.

down: **~market** *adj* [*products, hotel*] bas de gamme *inv*; [*area*] populaire; [*newspaper*] grand public *inv*; **~ payment** *n* acompte *m*; **~pour** *n* averse *f*.

downright **I** *adj* [*insult*] véritable (*before n*); [*refusal*] catégorique; [*liar*] fieffé (*before n*).
II *adv* [*stupid, rude*] carrément.

Down's syndrome *n* trisomie *f* 21.

downstairs **I** *n* rez-de-chaussée *m inv*.
II *adj* [*room*] en bas; (on ground-floor) du rez-de-chaussée; **the ~ flat** (GB) or **apartment** (US) l'appartement du rez-de-chaussée.
III *adv* en bas; **to go** or **come ~** descendre (l'escalier).

downstream *adj, adv* en aval (**of** de); **to go ~** descendre le courant.

down-to-earth *adj* pratique; **she's very ~** (practical) elle a les pieds sur terre; (unpretentious) elle est très simple.

downtown *adj* (US) [*store, hotel*] du centre ville.

down: **~trodden** *adj* tyrannisé; **~turn** *n* (in economy) ralentissement *m* (**in** de); (in profits, spending) baisse *f* (**in** de); **~ under**○ *adv* en Australie.

downward *adj* [*movement*] vers le bas; **~ trend** (Econ) tendance *f* à la baisse.

downwards *adv* [*look*] vers le bas; **to slope ~** descendre en pente (**to** vers).

doze *vi* somnoler.
■ **doze off** (momentarily) s'assoupir; (to sleep) s'endormir.

dozen ▶813 *n* **1** (twelve) douzaine *f*; **a ~ eggs** une douzaine d'œufs; **by the ~** à la douzaine; **2** (several) **~s of** des dizaines de [*people, things, times*].

drab *adj* [*colour, life*] terne; [*building*] triste.

draft **I** *n* **1** (of letter, speech) brouillon *m*; (of novel, play) ébauche *f*; (of contract, law) avant-projet *m*; **2** (on bank) traite *f* (**on** sur); **3** (US) (conscription) service *m* militaire; **4** (US) = **draught 1**, **2**, **3**, **4**.
II *noun modifier* [*version*] préliminaire; **~ legislation** avant-projet *m* de loi.
III *vtr* **1** faire le brouillon de [*letter*]; rédiger [*contract, law*]; **2** (US) (conscript) incorporer (**into** dans); **3** (GB) (transfer) détacher (**to** auprès de; **from** de).
■ **draft in** (GB): **~ in [sb]**, **~ [sb] in** faire venir, amener (**to do** pour faire).

draftsman (US) = **draughtsman**.

drag **I** *n* **1**○ **what a ~!** quelle barbe○!; **2** [*person*] **in ~** en travesti.
II *noun modifier* **1** [*artist*] de spectacle de travestis; **2** [*racing*] de dragsters.
III *vtr* **1** (pull) tirer (**to, up to** jusqu'à; **towards** vers); **to ~ sth along the ground** traîner qch par terre; **to ~ sb from** arracher qn de [*chair, bed*]; **to ~ sb to** traîner qn à [*place*]; traîner qn chez [*person*]; **don't ~ my mother into this** ne mêle pas ma mère à ça; **2** draguer [*river, lake*]; **3** (trail) traîner; **to ~ one's feet** traîner les pieds; (as delaying tactic) faire preuve de mauvaise volonté (**on** quant à).
IV *vi* **1** [*hours, days*] traîner; [*story, plot*] traîner en longueur; **2** (trail) **to ~ in** [*hem, belt*] traîner dans [*mud*]; **3 to ~ on** tirer une bouffée de [*cigarette*].
■ **drag along**: **~ [sth] along** traîner.
■ **drag away**: ¶ **~ [sb] away** emmener [qn] de force; **to ~ sb away from** arracher qn à; ¶ **~ [oneself] away from [sth]** partir à regret de.
■ **drag on** traîner en longueur.

drain **I** *n* **1** (in street) canalisation *f*; (in building) canalisation *f* d'évacuation; (pipe) descente *f* d'eau; (ditch) fossé *m* d'écoulement; **2** (of people, skills, money) hémorragie *f*; **to be a ~ on sb's resources** épuiser les ressources de qn.
II *vtr* **1** drainer [*land*]; purger [*radiator*]; **2** épuiser [*resources*]; **3** vider [*glass*].
III *vi* **1** [*liquid*] s'écouler (**out of, from** de); [*bath, sink*] se vider; **to ~ into** s'écouler dans [*sea, gutter*]; s'infiltrer dans [*soil*]; **2** [*dishes, food*] s'égoutter.
IDIOMS **that's £100 down the ~**○ ça fait 100 livres sterling de fichues en l'air○.

■ **drain off, drain out**: **~ [sth] off, ~ off [sth]** vider [*fluid, water*].

drainage *n* (of land) drainage *m*; (system) tout-à-l'égout *m inv*.

draining board *n* égouttoir *m*.

drainpipe *n* descente *f*.

drake *n* canard *m* (mâle).

drama I *n* (genre) théâtre *m*; (as opposed to documentary programmes) fiction *f*; (acting, directing) art *m* dramatique; (play, dramatic event) drame *m*; **TV/radio ~** dramatique *f*; **to make a ~ out of sth** faire tout un drame de qch.
II *noun modifier* [*school*] d'art dramatique; **~ critic** critique *m* dramatique.

dramatic *adj* [*art, effect, event*] dramatique; [*change, landscape*] spectaculaire.

dramatics *n pl* **1** (drama) art *m* dramatique; **2** (histrionics) cinéma○ *m*.

dramatize *vtr* **1** (adapt) (for stage) adapter [qch] pour la scène; (for screen) adapter [qch] pour l'écran; (for radio) adapter [qch] pour la radio; **2** (make dramatic) donner un caractère dramatique à; (excessively) dramatiser.

drape I *n* (US) rideau *m*.
II *vtr* draper (**with** de); **~d in sth** enveloppé dans qch.

drastic *adj* [*policy, measure*] draconien/-ienne; [*reduction, remedy*] drastique; [*effect*] catastrophique; [*change*] radical.

draught (GB), **draft** (US) *n* **1** (cold air) courant *m* d'air; **2** (in fireplace) tirage *m*; **3 on ~** [*beer*] à la pression; **4** (of liquid, air) trait *m*; **5** (GB Games) pion *m* (de jeu de dames).

draughtproof (GB), **draftproof** (US) *adj* calfeutré.

draughts ▶649 *n* (GB) jeu *m* de dames; **to play ~** jouer aux dames.

draughtsman (GB), **draftsman** (US) *n* dessinateur/-trice *m/f*.

draw I *n* **1** (in lottery) tirage *m* (au sort); **2** (Sport) match *m* nul; **it was a ~** (in race) ils sont arrivés ex aequo.
II *vtr* **1** faire [*picture, plan*]; dessiner [*person, object*]; tracer [*line*]; **2** dépeindre [*character, picture*]; faire [*comparison*]; **3** (pull) [*animal, engine*] tirer; [*machine*] (by suction) aspirer; **to ~ blood** provoquer un saignement; **4** (derive) tirer [*conclusion*] (**from** de); **I drew comfort from the fact that** cela m'a un peu réconforté de savoir que; **5** (cause to talk, react) faire parler [*person*] (**about, on** de); **to ~ sth from** arracher qch à qn [*truth, smile*]; **6** (attract) attirer [*crowd*] (**to** vers); susciter [*reaction*]; **to ~ sb into** mêler qn à [*conversation*]; entraîner qn dans [*argument, battle*]; **they were drawn together by their love of art** leur amour de l'art les a rapprochés; **7** (withdraw, receive) retirer [*money*] (**from** de); tirer [*cheque*] (**on** sur); toucher [*wages, pension*]; **8** (in lottery) tirer [qch] au sort [*ticket*]; **9** (remove) retirer [*cork*] (**from** de); sortir [*sword, knife*]; tirer [*card*].
III *vi* **1** (make picture) dessiner; **2** (move) **to ~ ahead (of sth/sb)** (in race) gagner du terrain (sur qch/qn); (in contest, election) prendre de l'avance (sur qch/qn); **to ~ alongside** [*boat*] accoster; **to ~ near** [*time*] approcher; **to ~ level** se retrouver au même niveau; **to ~ over** [*vehicle*] (stop) se ranger; (still moving) se rabattre vers le bas-côté; **3** (in match) faire match nul; **4** (choose at random) **to ~ for sth** tirer qch (au sort); **5** [*tea*] infuser.
IDIOMS **to ~ the line** fixer des limites; **to ~ the line at doing** se refuser à faire.

■ **draw aside**: **~ [sb] aside** prendre [qn] à part.

■ **draw away**: ¶ **~ away** (move off) s'éloigner (**from** de); (move ahead) prendre de l'avance (**from** sur); ¶ **~ [sb] away** éloigner [*person, object*].

■ **draw back**: ¶ **~ back** reculer; ¶ **~ [sth] back, ~ back [sth]** ouvrir [*curtains*]; retirer [*hand, foot*]; ¶ **~ [sb] back, ~ back [sb]** faire revenir [*person*].

■ **draw in**: ¶ **~ in 1** [*days, nights*] raccourcir; **2** (arrive) [*bus*] arriver; [*train*] entrer en gare; ¶ **~ [sth] in, ~ in [sth] 1** (in picture) ajouter; **2** rentrer [*stomach, claws*]; **to ~ in one's breath** inspirer; **3** (attract) attirer.

■ **draw on**: **~ on [sth]** exploiter [*skills, reserves*]; s'inspirer de [*memories*]; **to ~ on one's experience** faire appel à son expérience.

■ **draw out**: ¶ **~ out** [*train, bus*] partir; **the train drew out of the station** le train a quitté la gare; ¶ **~ [sth] out, ~ out [sth] 1** (remove) tirer [*purse, knife*] (**of** de); retirer [*nail, cork*] (**of** de); **2** (withdraw) retirer [*money*]; **3** (prolong) faire durer; (unnecessarily) faire traîner; **4** obtenir [*information*]; (using force) soutirer; ¶ **~ [sb] out** faire sortir [qn] de sa coquille.

■ **draw up**: **~ up [sth], ~ [sth] up 1** établir [*contract*]; dresser, établir [*list, report*]; **2** (pull) hisser [*bucket*]; approcher [*chair*] (**to** de).

drawback *n* inconvénient *m*.

drawer *n* tiroir *m*.

drawing I *n* dessin *m*.
II *noun modifier* [*class, teacher, tools*] de dessin; [*paper, pen*] à dessin.

drawing: **~ board** *n* planche *f* à dessin; **~ pin** *n* punaise *f*; **~ room** *n* salon *m*.

drawl *n* voix *f* traînante.

drawn *adj* **1 to look ~** avoir les traits tirés; **2** [*game, match*] nul/nulle.

dread *vtr* appréhender; (stronger) redouter; **I ~ to think!** je préfère ne pas y penser!

dreadful *adj* épouvantable, affreux/-euse; **to feel ~** ne pas se sentir bien du tout; **I feel ~ about it** j'en suis malade.

dreadfully *adv* [*disappointed*] terriblement; [*suffer*] affreusement; [*behave*] abominablement; **I'm ~ sorry** je suis navré.

dream I *n* rêve *m*; **to have a ~ about sth** rêver de qch; **to be in a ~** être dans les nuages; **to make sb's ~ come true** faire que le rêve de qn devienne réalité.
II *noun modifier* [*house, car, vacation*] de rêve.
III *vtr* rêver (**that** que); **I never dreamt (that)** je n'aurais jamais pensé que.
IV *vi* rêver; **he dreamt about** or **of sth/doing** il a rêvé de qch/qu'il faisait; **you must be ~ing if you think...** tu te fais des illusions si tu crois que...; **I wouldn't ~ of selling the**

house il ne me viendrait jamais à l'esprit de vendre la maison.

■ **dream up**: **~ up [sth]** concevoir [*idea*]; imaginer [*character, plot*].

dreamer *n* **1** (inattentive person) rêveur/-euse *m/f*; **2** (idealist) idéaliste *mf*.

dreary *adj* [*weather, landscape, life*] morne; [*person*] ennuyeux/-euse.

dredge *vtr* **1** draguer [*river*]; **2** (Culin) saupoudrer (**with** de).

dregs *n pl* (of wine) lie *f*; (of coffee) marc *m*.

drench *vtr* (in rain, sweat) tremper (**in** de); **~ed to the skin** trempé jusqu'aux os.

dress I *n* **1** (garment) robe *f*; **2** (way of dressing) tenue *f*.

II *vtr* **1** habiller [*person*]; **to get ~ed** s'habiller; **to be ~ed in** être vêtu de; **to ~ oneself** s'habiller; **2** assaisonner [*salad*]; préparer [*meat, fish*]; **3** panser [*wound*].

■ **dress up**: ¶ **~ up** (smartly) s'habiller; (in fancy dress) se déguiser (**as** en); ¶ **~ [sb] up, ~ up [sb]** déguiser.

dress: **~ circle** *n* premier balcon *m*; **~ designer** ▶ 805 *n* modéliste *mf*.

dresser *n* **1 to be a stylish ~** s'habiller avec chic; **2** (for dishes) buffet *m*; **3** (US) (for clothes) commode-coiffeuse *f*.

dressing *n* **1** (Med) pansement *m*; **2** (sauce) assaisonnement *m*; **3** (US) (stuffing) farce *f*.

dressing: **~ gown** *n* robe *f* de chambre; **~ room** *n* loge *f*; **~ table** *n* coiffeuse *f*.

dress: **~maker** ▶ 805 *n* couturière *f*; **~ rehearsal** *n* (répétition *f*) générale *f*.

dress sense *n* **to have ~** s'habiller avec goût.

dress suit *n* queue-de-pie *f*.

dribble I *n* **1** (of liquid) filet *m*; (of saliva) bave *f*; **2** (Sport) drible *m*.

II *vi* **1** [*liquid*] dégouliner (**on, onto** sur; **from** de); [*person*] baver; **2** (Sport) dribler.

dried *adj* [*fruit, herb*] sec/sèche; [*flower, vegetable*] séché; [*milk, egg*] en poudre.

drier *n* (for clothes, hair) séchoir *m*; (helmet type) casque *m*.

drift I *n* **1** (flow, movement) **the ~ of the current** le sens du courant; **the slow ~ of strikers back to work** le lent retour des grévistes au travail; **2** (of snow) congère *f*; (of leaves, sand) tas *m*; (of smoke, mist) nuage *m*; **3** (meaning) sens *m* (général); **to catch the ~ of sb's argument** comprendre où quelqu'un veut en venir.

II *vi* **1** (be carried by current) dériver; (by wind) [*balloon*] voler à la dérive; [*smoke, fog*] flotter; **2** (pile up) [*snow*] former des congères *fpl*; [*leaves*] s'amonceler; **3 to ~ along** se laisser aller; **to ~ from job to job** passer d'un emploi à un autre.

■ **drift apart** [*friends*] se perdre de vue; [*lovers*] se détacher progressivement l'un de l'autre.

drill I *n* **1** (for wood, masonry) perceuse *f*; (for oil) trépan *m*; (for mining) foreuse *f*; (for teeth) roulette *f*; **2** (Mil) exercice *m*; **3 fire ~** exercice *m* d'évacuation en cas d'incendie.

II *vtr* **1** percer [*hole, metal*]; passer la roulette à [*tooth*]; **2** (Mil) entraîner [*soldiers*].

III *vi* **1** (in wood, masonry) percer un trou (**into** dans); **to ~ for sth** faire des forages pour trouver qch; **2** (Mil) [*soldiers*] faire de l'exercice.

drilling *n* (for oil, gas) forage *m* (**for** pour trouver); (in wood, masonry) perçage *m*.

drink I *n* boisson *f*; **to have a ~** boire quelque chose; (with alcohol) prendre un verre.

II *vtr* boire (**from sth** dans qch).

III *vi* boire (**from** dans); **don't ~ and drive** ne conduisez pas si vous avez bu.

■ **drink up**: ¶ **~ up** finir son verre; ¶ **~ up [sth], ~ [sth] up** finir.

drink-driving *n* (GB) conduite *f* en état d'ivresse.

drinking *n* consommation *f* d'alcool; **~ and driving** l'alcool au volant.

drinking water *n* eau *f* potable.

drink: **~s cupboard** *n* (GB) bar *m*; **~s dispenser** *n* (GB) distributeur *m* de boissons; **~s party** *n* (GB) cocktail *m*.

drip I *n* **1** (drop) goutte *f* (qui tombe); **2** (GB Med) **to be on a ~** être sous perfusion.

II *vi* **1** [*liquid*] tomber goutte à goutte; **to ~ from** or **off** dégouliner de; **2** [*tap, branches*] goutter; [*washing*] s'égoutter; [*engine*] fuir; **to be ~ping with** dégouliner de [*liquid*]; ruisseler de [*sweat*].

drip-dry *adj* [*garment*] qui se lave et s'étend sans essorage.

dripping I *n* (Culin) graisse *f* de rôti.

II *adj* [*tap*] qui goutte; [*washing*] trempé; **~ wet** trempé.

drive I *n* **1** (in car) **to go for a ~** aller faire un tour (en voiture); **it's a 40 km ~** il y a 40 km de route; **2** (campaign) campagne *f* (**against** contre; **for, towards** pour; **to do** pour faire); **3** (motivation) dynamisme *m*; **4** (Comput) entraînement *m* de disques; **5** (Aut) transmission *f*; **6** (path) allée *f*; **7** (Sport) drive *m*.

II *vtr* **1** (Aut) conduire [*vehicle, passenger*]; piloter [*racing car*]; **I ~ 15 km every day** je fais 15 km en voiture chaque jour; **to ~ sth into** rentrer qch dans [*garage, space*]; **2** (compel) pousser (**to do** à faire); **to be driven out of business** être conduit à la faillite; **he was driven out of the country** il a été chassé du pays; **3** (power, propel) actionner; **to be driven by steam** fonctionner à la vapeur; **4** (force, push) pousser [*boat, person*]; **to ~ a nail through sth** enfoncer un clou dans qch; **5** (in golf) envoyer [*ball*].

III *vi* **1** (Aut) conduire; **to ~ along** rouler; **to ~ to work** aller au travail en voiture; **to ~ into** entrer dans [*car park*]; rentrer dans [*tree*]; **to ~ up a hill** monter une côte; **to ~ past** passer; **2** (Sport) (in golf) driver; (in tennis) faire un drive.

■ **drive away**: ¶ **~ away** démarrer; ¶ **~ away [sth/sb], ~ [sth/sb] away** chasser.

■ **drive back**: ¶ **~ back** rentrer; **to ~ there and back** faire l'aller-retour; ¶ **~ back [sth/sb], ~ [sth/sb] back 1** repousser [*people, animals*]; **2** ramener [*passenger*].

■ **drive off** (Aut) démarrer.

■ **drive on**: **~** [sb] **on** pousser.
■ **drive out**: **~ out** [sth/sb], **~** [sth/sb] **out** chasser.

driven *adj* passionné, motivé.

driver *n* conducteur/-trice *m/f*; **~s** (motorists) automobilistes *mfpl*.

driver's licence *n* (US) permis *m* de conduire.

driving I *n* conduite *f*; **his ~ has improved** il conduit mieux qu'avant.
II *adj* [*rain*] battant; [*wind, hail*] cinglant.

driving ~ force *n* (person) force *f* agissante (**behind** de); (money, ambition) moteur *m* (**behind** de); **~ instructor** ▶805 *n* moniteur/-trice *m/f* d'auto-école; **~ lesson** *n* leçon *f* de conduite; **~ licence** *n* (GB) permis *m* de conduire; **~ mirror** *n* rétroviseur *m*; **~ school** *n* auto-école *f*; **~ seat** *n* place *f* du conducteur.

drizzle *vi* bruiner.

drone *n* (of engine) ronronnement *m*; (of insects) bourdonnement *m*.
■ **drone on** faire de longs discours rasants○.

drool *vi* baver; **to ~ over sth/sb** s'extasier sur qch/qn.

droop *vi* [*eyelids, head, shoulders*] tomber; [*plant*] commencer à se faner.

drop I *n* **1** (gen, Med) goutte *f*; **2** (decrease) (in prices, inflation, temperature) baisse *f* (**in** de); (in blood pressure) chute *f* (**in** de); **a 5% ~ in sth** une baisse de 5% de qch; **3** (fall) **there's a ~ of 100 m** il y a un dénivelé de 100 m; **a steep ~ on either side** une pente abrupte de chaque côté; **a sheer ~** un à-pic; **4** (delivery) (from aircraft) largage *m*; (from lorry, van) livraison *f*; (parachute jump) saut *m* en parachute.
II *vtr* **1** (by accident) laisser tomber; (on purpose) mettre, lâcher; **2** (deliver) [*aircraft*] parachuter [*person, supplies*]; larguer [*bomb*]; **3** (also **~ off**) déposer [*person, object*]; **4** (lower) baisser [*level, price*]; **5 to ~ a hint about sth** faire allusion à qch; **to ~ sb a line** envoyer un mot à qn; **6** (deliberately) supprimer [*article, episode*]; écarter [*player*]; (by mistake) omettre [*figure, letter*]; **7** (abandon) laisser tomber [*friend, school subject*]; renoncer à [*habit, idea*]; retirer [*accusation*]; **to ~ everything** tout laisser tomber; **8** (lose) perdre [*point*].
III *vi* **1** (fall) [*object*] tomber; [*person*] (deliberately) se laisser tomber; (by accident) tomber; **the plane ~ped to an altitude of 1,000 m** l'avion est descendu à une altitude de 1000 m; **2** (fall away) **the cliff ~s into the sea** la falaise tombe dans la mer; **3** (decrease) baisser; **to ~ (from sth) to sth** tomber (de qch) à qch; **she ~ped to third place** elle est descendue à la troisième place.
IDIOMS **a ~ in the ocean** une goutte d'eau dans la mer.
■ **drop back** (deliberately) rester en arrière; (unable to keep up) prendre du retard.
■ **drop by** passer.
■ **drop in**: **~ in** passer; **I'll ~ it in (to you)** je passerai te le donner.
■ **drop off 1** [*object*] tomber; **2 ~ off (to sleep)** s'endormir; **3** (decrease) diminuer.
■ **drop out 1** (fall out) tomber (**of** de); **2** (from race) se désister; (from project) se retirer; (from school, university) abandonner ses études; (from society) se marginaliser.

drop: **~ handlebars** *n pl* guidon *m* de course; **~out** *n* marginal/-e *m/f*.

droppings *n pl* (of mouse, sheep) crottes *fpl*; (of horse) crottin *m*; (of bird) fiente *f*.

drop shot *n* (Sport) amorti *m*.

drought *n* sécheresse *f*.

droves *n pl* **in ~** [*come, leave*] en masse; **~ of people** des foules *fpl* de gens.

drown I *vtr* noyer [*person, animal*]; couvrir [*sound*].
II *vi* se noyer.
IDIOMS **to ~ one's sorrows** noyer son chagrin dans l'alcool.
■ **drown out**: ¶ **~** [sth] **out**, **~ out** [sth] couvrir [*sound*]; ¶ **~** [sb] **out** couvrir la voix de [*person*].

drowning *n* noyade *f*.

drowsiness *n* somnolence *f*.

drowsy *adj* à moitié endormi; **to feel ~** avoir envie de dormir.

drug I *n* **1** (Med) médicament *m*; **to be on ~s** prendre des médicaments; **2** (narcotic) drogue *f*; **to be on** or **to take ~s** [*person*] se droguer; [*athlete*] se doper.
II *noun modifier* **1** [*problem*] de drogue; **~ trafficking** trafic *m* de drogue; **2** (Med) [*company, industry*] pharmaceutique.
III *vtr* **1** (sedate) [*kidnapper*] administrer des somnifères à [*victim*]; [*vet*] endormir [*animal*]; **2** (dope) mettre un somnifère dans [*drink*]; doper [*horse*].

drug: **~ abuse** *n* consommation *f* de stupéfiants; **~ addict** *n* toxicomane *mf*; **~ addiction** *n* toxicomanie *f*; **Drug Squad** *n* (GB) brigade *f* des stupéfiants; **~store** *n* (US) drugstore *m*; **~ test** *n* (Sport) contrôle *m* antidopage; **~ user** *n* toxicomane *mf*.

drum I *n* ▶753 **1** (Mus) tambour *m*; **2** (for industrial use) bidon *m*; (larger) baril *m*; **3** (Aut) tambour *m*.
II drums *n pl* batterie *f*; **to play ~s** jouer de la batterie.
III *vtr* **to ~ one's fingers** tambouriner des doigts (**on** sur); **to ~ sth into sb** enfoncer qch dans le crâne de qn○.
■ **drum up**: ¶ **~ up** [sth] trouver [*business*]; ¶ **~ up** [sb] racoler [*customers*].

drummer ▶805, 753 *n* (in army) tambour *m*; (jazz or pop) batteur *m*; (classical) percussionniste *mf*.

drumstick *n* **1** (Mus) baguette *f* de tambour; **2** (of chicken, turkey) pilon *m*.

drunk I *n* (also **drunkard**) ivrogne/-esse *m/f*.
II *adj* ivre; **to get ~** s'enivrer (**on** de); **to get sb ~** faire boire qn.

drunken *adj* [*person*] ivre; [*party*] bien arrosé; [*sleep*] éthylique; [*state*] d'ivresse.

dry I *adj* **1** sec/sèche; **to run ~** se tarir; **to keep sth ~** tenir qch au sec; **to get sth ~** (faire) sécher qch; **on ~ land** sur la terre ferme; **a ~ day** un jour sans pluie; **2** [*wit,*

person, remark] pince-sans-rire *inv*; [*book*] aride.
II *vtr* faire sécher [*clothes, washing*]; sécher [*meat, produce*]; **to ~ the dishes** essuyer la vaisselle; **to ~ oneself** se sécher: **to ~ one's hands** se sécher les mains.
III *vi* [*clothes, washing*] sécher.
■ **dry off**: ¶ **~ off** [*material, object*] sécher; [*person*] se sécher; ¶ **~ off [sb/sth]**, **~ [sb/sth] off** sécher [*person, object*].
■ **dry out 1** [*cloth*] sécher; [*plant*] se dessécher; **2**° [*alcoholic*] se faire désintoxiquer.
■ **dry up**: ¶ **~ up 1** [*river, well*] s'assécher; **2** (run out) se tarir; **3** (wipe crockery) essuyer la vaisselle; ¶ **~ up [sth]**, **~ [sth] up** assécher [*river*]; essuyer [*crockery*].

dry-clean *vtr* **to have sth ~ed** faire nettoyer qch (chez le teinturier).

dry: **~-cleaner's** ▶ 805 *n* teinturerie *f*; **~-cleaning** *n* nettoyage *m* à sec.

dryer *n* (for clothes, hair) séchoir *m*; (helmet type) casque *m*.

drying-up *n* (GB) **to do the ~** essuyer la vaisselle.

dry martini *n* martini-dry *m*.

DTP *n* (*abbr* = **desktop publishing**) PAO *f*.

dual *adj* double.

dual: **~ carriageway** *n* (GB) route *f* à quatre voies; **~ nationality** *n* double nationalité.

dub *vtr* (into foreign language) doubler (**into** en); **~bed film** film doublé.

dubbing *n* doublage *m*.

dubious *adj* [*reputation, answer*] douteux/-euse; [*claim*] suspect; [*distinction*] discutable; **to be ~ (about sth)** avoir des doutes (en ce qui concerne qch).

duchess ▶ 642 *n* duchesse *f*.

duck I *n* (Zool, Culin) (male, species) canard *m*; (female) cane *f*.
II *vtr* **1 to ~ one's head** baisser vivement la tête; **2** (dodge) esquiver.
III *vi* baisser vivement la tête; [*boxer*] esquiver un coup; **to ~ behind** se cacher derrière.
IDIOMS **it's like water off a ~'s back** ça ne le/la etc touche absolument pas.

duct *n* **1** (for air, water) conduit *m*; (for wiring) canalisation *f*; **2** (Anat, Med) conduit *m*.

dud° *adj* [*banknote*] faux/fausse; [*cheque*] en bois°; [*book, movie*] nul/nulle°.

due I *n* dû *m*; **I must give her her ~, she**... il faut lui rendre cette justice, elle...
II *adj* **1** (payable) **to be/fall ~** arriver/venir à échéance; **when ~** à l'échéance; **the rent is ~ on the 6th** le loyer doit être payé le 6; **the balance ~** le solde dû; **2** (owed) **the respect ~ to him** le respect auquel il a droit, le respect qu'on lui doit; **3** (about to be paid, given) **I'm ~ some back pay** on me doit des arriérés; **we are ~ (for) a wage increase soon** nos salaires doivent bientôt être augmentés; **4** (appropriate) **after ~ consideration** après mûre réflexion; **in ~ course** (at the proper time) en temps voulu; (later) plus tard; **5 to be ~ to do** devoir faire; **to be ~ (in)** [*train, bus*] être attendu; [*person*] devoir arriver.
III *adv* **to face ~ north** [*building*] être orienté plein nord.
IV **due to** *phr* en raison de; **to be ~ to** [*delay, cancellation*] être dû/due à; **~ to unforeseen circumstances** pour des raisons indépendantes de notre volonté.

dues *n pl* (for membership) cotisation *f*; (for import, taxes) droits *mpl*.

duet *n* duo *m*.

duke ▶ 642 *n* duc *m*.

dull I *adj* **1** [*person, book*] ennuyeux/-euse; [*life, journey*] monotone; [*appearance*] triste; [*weather*] maussade; **2** [*eye, colour, complexion*] terne.
II *vtr* ternir [*shine*]; émousser [*blade, pain*].

dullness *n* (of life) ennui *m*; (of routine) monotonie *f*.

duly *adv* (in proper fashion) dûment; (as expected, as arranged) comme prévu.

dumb *adj* **1** (speech-impaired) muet/muette; **to be struck ~** rester muet/muette (**with** de); **2**° (stupid) [*person*] bête; [*question, idea*] idiot.

dumbfounded *adj* abasourdi.

dummy *n* **1** (model) mannequin *m*; **2** (GB) (for baby) tétine *f*.

dump I *n* **1** (public) décharge *f* publique; (rubbish heap) tas *m* d'ordures; **2** (Mil) **arms ~** dépôt *m* d'armes; **3**° (town, village) trou° *m*; (house) baraque° *f* minable.
II *vtr* jeter [*refuse*]; ensevelir [*nuclear waste*]; déverser [*sewage*].
IDIOMS **to be down in the ~s**° avoir le cafard°.

dumper *n* **1** (small) motobasculeur *m*; **2** (large truck) tombereau *m*.

dunce *n* cancre *m* (**at, in** en).

dune *n* dune *f*.

dung *n* excrément *m*; (for manure) fumier *m*.

dungarees *n pl* (fashionwear) salopette *f*; (workwear) bleu *m* de travail.

Dunkirk ▶ 574 *pr n* Dunkerque.

duo *n* duo *m*.

duplicate I *n* (of document) double *m* (**of** de); (of painting, cassette) copie *f*.
II *adj* **1** [*cheque, receipt*] en duplicata; **a ~ key** un double de clé; **2** (in two parts) [*form, invoice*] en deux exemplaires.
III *vtr* **1** (copy) faire un double de [*document*]; copier [*painting, cassette*]; **2** (photocopy) photocopier; **3** (repeat) refaire [qch] inutilement [*work*].

durable *adj* [*material*] résistant; [*equipment*] solide; [*friendship, tradition*] durable.

during *prep* pendant, au cours de.

dusk *n* nuit *f* tombante, crépuscule *m*; **at ~** à la nuit tombante.

dust I *n* poussière *f*; **to allow the ~ to settle** (figurative) laisser les choses se calmer.
II *vtr* épousseter [*furniture*]; saupoudrer [*cake*] (**with** de, avec).
IDIOMS **to bite the ~** [*person*] mordre la poussière; [*plan, idea*] tomber à l'eau.
■ **dust down**: **~ [sth] down**, **~ down [sth]** épousseter.

dust: **~bin** *n* (GB) poubelle *f*; **~bin man** *n*

(GB) éboueur *m*; **~ cover** *n* (on book) jaquette *f*; (on furniture) housse *f* (de protection).

duster *n* chiffon *m* (à poussière).

dusting *n* époussetage *m*; **to do the ~** épousseter.

dust: **~man** *n* (GB) éboueur *m*; **~pan** *n* pelle *f* (à poussière).

dusty *adj* [*house, table, road*] poussiéreux/-euse.

Dutch ▶712 **I** *n* **1** (language) néerlandais *m*; **2** (people) **the ~** les Néerlandais *mpl*.
II *adj* [*culture, food, politics*] néerlandais; [*teacher, lesson*] de néerlandais; [*ambassador, embassy*] des Pays-Bas.
IDIOMS **to go ~**° payer chacun sa part; **to go ~ with sb**° faire fifty-fifty avec qn°.

Dutch: **~man** *n* Néerlandais *m*; **~woman** *n* Néerlandaise *f*.

duty *n* **1** (obligation) devoir *m* (**to** envers); **in the course of ~** (Mil) en service; (gen) dans l'exercice de ses fonctions; **to feel ~ bound to do** se sentir tenu de faire; **2** (task) fonction *f*; **to take up one's duties** prendre ses fonctions; **3** (work) service *m*; **to be on/off ~** (Mil, Med) être/ne pas être de service; (Sch) être/ne pas être de surveillance; **to go on/off ~** commencer/finir son service; **4** (tax) taxe *f*; **customs duties** droits *mpl* de douane; **to pay ~ on sth** payer des droits de douane sur qch.

duty: **~ chemist** *n* pharmacien/-ienne *m/f* de garde; **~-free** *adj, adv* hors taxes *inv*.

duvet *n* (GB) couette *f*; **~ cover** housse *f* de couette.

dwarf *n, adj* nain/naine (*m/f*).

dwell *v* ■ **dwell on**: **~ on** [**sth**] (talk) s'étendre sur; (think) s'attarder sur.

dwindle *vi* [*numbers, resources*] diminuer; [*interest*] tomber.

dye I *n* teinture *f*; **vegetable ~** colorant *m* végétal.
II *vtr* teindre; **to ~ sth red** teindre qch en rouge; **to ~ one's hair** se teindre les cheveux.
III dyed *pp adj* [*hair, fabric*] teint.

dying I *n* **the ~** les agonisants *mpl*.
II *adj* **1** mourant; **2** [*art*] en voie de disparition; [*community*] moribond.

dyke *n* **1** (on coast) digue *f*; (beside ditch) remblai *m*; **2** (GB) (ditch) fossé *m*.

dynamic *adj* dynamique.

dynamics *n pl* dynamique *f*.

dynamite *n* dynamite *f*; **political ~** une bombe politique.

dynamo *n* **1** (for power) dynamo *f*; **2**° **he's a real ~** il déborde d'énergie.

dysentery ▶686 *n* dysenterie *f*.

dyslexic *n, adj* dyslexique (*mf*).

Ee

e, E *n* e, E *m*.

each I *det* [*person, group, object*] chaque *inv*; **~ time I see him** chaque fois que je le vois; **~ morning** chaque matin, tous les matins; **~ person will receive a ticket** chaque personne or tout le monde recevra un billet; **~ and every day** tous les jours sans exception.

II *pron* chacun/-e *m/f*; **~ will receive** chacun recevra; **we ~ want something different** chacun de nous veut une chose différente; **~ of you** chacun/-e de vous, chacun/-e d'entre vous; **three bundles of ten notes ~** trois liasses de dix billets chacune; **I'll try a little of ~** je prendrais bien un peu de chaque; **oranges at 30p ~** des oranges à 30 pence pièce.

each other *pron*

■ **Note** *each other* is very often translated by using a reflexive pronoun (*nous, vous, se, s'*).

(also **one another**) **they know ~** ils se connaissent; **to help ~** s'entraider; **they wear ~'s clothes** ils se prêtent leurs vêtements; **to worry about ~** s'inquiéter l'un pour l'autre; **kept apart from ~** séparés l'un de l'autre.

eager *adj* [*person, acceptance*] enthousiaste; [*face*] où se lit l'enthousiasme; [*student*] plein d'enthousiasme; **~ to do** (keen) désireux/-euse de faire; (impatient) pressé de faire; **~ for sth** avide de qch; **to be ~ to please** chercher à faire plaisir; **to be ~ for sb to do** tenir vraiment à ce que qn fasse.

eagle *n* aigle *m*.

ear ▶523 *n* **1** oreille *f*; **to play (music) by ~** jouer de la musique à l'oreille; **2** (of wheat, corn) épi *m*.

IDIOMS **to play it by ~** improviser.

earache *n* **to have ~** (GB) or **an ~** avoir une otite.

eardrum *n* tympan *m*.

earl *n* comte *m*.

earlobe *n* lobe *m* de l'oreille.

early I *adj* **1** (one of the first) [*years, novels*] premier/-ière; **~ man** les premiers hommes; **2** [*delivery*] rapide; [*vegetable, fruit*] précoce; **to have an ~ lunch/night** déjeuner/se coucher tôt; **to take ~ retirement** partir en préretraite; **at the earliest possible opportunity** le plus tôt possible; **3 in ~ childhood** dans la petite or première enfance; **at an ~ age** à un très jeune âge; **to be in one's ~ thirties** avoir entre 30 et 35 ans; **to make an ~ start** partir tôt; **to take the ~ train** prendre le premier train; **at the earliest** au plus tôt; **the earliest I can manage is Monday** je ne peux rien faire avant lundi; **in the ~ hours** au petit matin; **in the ~ spring** au début du printemps; **in the ~ afternoon** en début d'après-midi.

II *adv* **1** tôt; **to get up ~** se lever tôt or de bonne heure; **it's too ~** il est trop tôt; **can you make it earlier?** pouvez-vous plus tôt?; **as ~ as 1983** dès 1983; **~ next year** au début de l'année prochaine; **~ in the afternoon** en début d'après-midi; **(very) ~ on** dès le début; **as I said earlier** comme je l'ai déjà dit; **2** en avance; **I'm a bit ~** je suis un peu en avance; **to do sth three weeks ~** faire qch avec trois semaines d'avance.

IDIOMS **it's ~ days yet** ce n'est que le début; **it's the ~ bird that catches the worm** l'avenir appartient à ceux qui se lèvent tôt.

earn *vtr* **1** [*person*] gagner [*money*]; toucher [*salary*]; [*investment*] rapporter [*interest*]; **to ~ a** or **one's living** gagner sa vie; **2 to ~ sb's respect** se faire respecter de qn; **well-~ed** bien mérité.

earnest I *n* **in ~** [*speak*] sérieusement; [*begin*] vraiment, pour de bon; **he was in ~** il était sérieux.

II *adj* [*person*] sérieux/-ieuse; [*wish*] sincère.

earning power *n* capacité *f* de gain.

earnings *n pl* (of person) salaire *m*, revenu *m* (**from** de); (of company) gains *mpl* (**from** de); (from shares) (taux *m* de) rendement *m*.

ear: **~phones** *n pl* (over ears) casque *m*; (in ears) écouteurs *mpl*; **~ring** *n* boucle *f* d'oreille.

earth I *n* **1** terre *f*; **the ~'s atmosphere** l'atmosphère terrestre; **to come down to ~** revenir sur terre; **2**° **how/where/who on ~...?** comment/où/qui donc or diable°...?; **nothing on ~ would persuade me to come** pour rien au monde je ne viendrais.

II *vtr* (GB) mettre [qch] à la terre.

earthenware *n* faïence *f*.

earth: **~quake** *n* tremblement *m* de terre; **~ tremor** *n* secousse *f* sismique.

ear: **~wax** *n* cérumen *m*; **~wig** *n* perce-oreille *m*.

ease I *n* **1** (lack of difficulty) facilité *f*; **2 to feel/be at ~** se sentir/être à l'aise; **to put sb at their ~** mettre qn à son aise; **to put sb's mind at ~** rassurer qn (**about** à propos de).

II *vtr* **1** atténuer [*pain, tension, pressure*]; réduire [*congestion*]; diminuer [*burden*]; **2** faciliter [*communication, transition*]; **3 to ~ sth into** introduire qch délicatement dans; **to ~ sth out of** sortir qch délicatement de.

III *vi* [*tension, pain, pressure*] s'atténuer; [*rain*] diminuer.

■ **ease off**: ¶ **~ off** [*business*] se ralentir; [*demand*] se réduire; [*traffic, rain*] diminuer; [*person*] relâcher son effort; ¶ **~ [sth] off, ~ off [sth]** ôter délicatement.

■ **ease up** [*tense person, storm*] se calmer; [*worker*] relâcher ses efforts; [*authorities*] relâcher la discipline; **to ~ up on sb/on sth** être moins sévère envers qn/pour qch.

easel *n* chevalet *m*.

easily *adv* facilement; **it's ~ the best** c'est de loin le meilleur; **she could ~ die** elle pourrait bien mourir.

easiness *n* (of question, exam) simplicité *f*; (of task, climb) facilité *f*.

east I *n* **1** (compass direction) est *m*; **2 the East** (Orient) l'Orient *m*; (of country) l'Est *m*.
II *adj* (gen) est *inv*; [*wind*] d'est.
III *adv* [*move*] vers l'est; [*live, lie*] à l'est (**of** de).

Easter I *n* Pâques *m*; **at ~** à Pâques; **Happy ~** Joyeuses Pâques.
II *noun modifier* [*Sunday, egg*] de Pâques.

eastern *adj* **1** [*coast*] est; [*town, accent*] de l'est; [*Europe, United States*] de l'Est; **~ France** l'est de la France; **2** (also **Eastern**) (oriental) oriental.

easy I *adj* **1** [*job, question, life, victim*] facile; **that's ~ to fix** c'est facile à réparer; **it's not ~ to talk to him** ce n'est pas facile de lui parler; **within ~ reach** tout près (**of** de); **to make it** or **things easier** faciliter les choses (**for** pour); **2** (relaxed) [*smile, grace*] décontracté; [*style*] plein d'aisance; **at an ~ pace** d'un pas tranquille; **3**° **I'm ~** ça m'est égal.
II *adv* **1 to take it** or **things ~** ne pas s'en faire; **2**° **to go ~ on** or **with** y aller doucement avec.
IDIOMS **~ come, ~ go** ça se remplace facilement.

easygoing *adj* [*person*] accommodant; [*manner, attitude*] souple.

eat I *vtr* manger [*food*]; prendre [*meal*]; **to ~ (one's) lunch/dinner** déjeuner/dîner; **to ~ one's words** ravaler ses paroles.
II *vi* manger; **to ~ from** or **out of** manger dans; **we ~ at six** nous dînons à 18 heures.
■ **eat out** aller au restaurant.

eavesdrop *vi* écouter aux portes.

ebb I *n* reflux *m*.
II *vi* [*tide*] descendre; [*enthusiasm*] décliner; **to ~ and flow** monter et descendre.

ebony *n* **1** (wood) ébène *f*; **2** ▶**559** (colour) noir *m* d'ébène.

EC I *n* (*abbr* = **European Community**) communauté *f* européenne;
II *noun phrase* [*policy, directive*] de la communauté européenne.

eccentric *n, adj* excentrique (*mf*).

eccentricity *n* excentricité *f*.

echo I *n* écho *m*.
II *vtr* répercuter [*sound*].
III *vi* retentir, résonner (**to, with** de; **around** dans).

eclipse I *n* éclipse *f* (**of** de).
II *vtr* éclipser.

ecological *adj* écologique.

ecologist *n, adj* écologiste (*mf*).

ecology *n* écologie *f*.

economic *adj* **1** (financial) économique; **2** (profitable) [*business*] rentable.

economical *adj* [*person*] économe; [*machine, method*] économique; **to be ~ on petrol** consommer peu d'essence.

economic and monetary union, EMU *n* Union *f* économique et monétaire.

economics I *n* (science) économie *f*; (subject of study) sciences *fpl* économiques; (financial aspects) aspects *mpl* économiques (**of** de).
II *noun modifier* [*degree, textbook, faculty*] de sciences économiques; [*editor, expert*] en économie.

economist ▶**805** *n* économiste *mf*.

economize *vtr, vi* économiser.

economy *n* économie *f*; **the ~** l'économie du pays.

economy: **~ class** *n* classe *f* économique; **~ pack, ~ size** *n* paquet *m* économique.

ecstasy *n* **1** extase *f*; **2** (drug) ecstasy *m*.

ecu, ECU ▶**748** *n* (*abbr* = **European Currency Unit**) écu *m*, ÉCU *m*.

eczema ▶**686** *n* eczéma *m*.

Eden *pr n* Éden *m*, paradis *m* terrestre.

edge I *n* **1** (outer limit) bord *m*; (of wood, clearing) lisière *f*; **on the ~ of the city** en bordure de la ville; **the film had us on the ~ of our seats** le film nous a tenus en haleine; **2** (of blade) tranchant *m*; **with a sharp ~** bien aiguisé; **3** (of book, plank) tranche *f*; **4 to give an ~ to** aiguiser [*appetite*]; **to take the ~ off** gâter [*pleasure*]; calmer [*anger, appetite*]; **there was an ~ to his voice** sa voix avait quelque chose de tendu; **5 to be on ~** [*person*] être énervé.
II *vtr* **1 to ~ one's way along** longer la bordure de [*cliff, parapet*]; **2** (trim) border.
III *vi* **to ~ forward** avancer doucement; **to ~ towards** s'approcher à petits pas de.

edgeways, edgewise *adv* [*move*] latéralement; [*lay, put*] sur le côté.
IDIOMS **I can't get a word in ~** je n'arrive pas à placer un mot.

edgy *adj* énervé, anxieux/-ieuse.

edible *adj* [*fruit, plant, mushroom, snail*] comestible; [*meal*] mangeable.

Edinburgh ▶**574** *pr n* Édimbourg.

edit *vtr* **1** (in publishing) éditer; **2** (cut) couper [*text, version*]; **3** monter [*film, programme*].

editing *n* **1** édition *f*; **2** (of film) montage *m*; **3** (of newspaper) rédaction *f*.

edition *n* (gen) édition *f*; (of documentary) émission *f*.

editor ▶**805** *n* (of newspaper) rédacteur/-trice *m/f* en chef (**of** de); (of book, manuscript) correcteur/-trice *m/f*; (of writer, works, anthology) éditeur/-trice *m/f*; (of film) monteur/-euse *m/f*.

editorial I *n* éditorial *m* (**on** sur).
II *adj* **1** (in journalism) de la rédaction; **2** (in publishing) éditorial.

educate *vtr* **1** [*teacher*] instruire; **2** [*parent*] assurer l'instruction de; **to ~ one's children privately** mettre ses enfants dans une école privée; **to be ~d in Paris** faire ses études à Paris; **3** (inform) informer [*public*] (**about, in** sur).

educated *adj* [*person*] (having an education) instruit; (cultivated) cultivé; [*accent*] élégant; [*classes*] instruit.

IDIOMS **~ guess** opinion fondée (sur l'expérience).

education I *n* **1** éducation *f*, instruction *f*; **health ~** hygiène *f*; **2** (formal schooling) études *fpl*; **to have had a university** or **college ~** avoir fait des études supérieures; **3** (national system) enseignement *m*.
II *noun modifier* [*budget*] de l'enseignement; [*Minister, Ministry*] de l'éducation; **the ~ system** le système éducatif.

educational *adj* **1** [*establishment*] d'enseignement; **2** [*game, programme, value*] éducatif/-ive; [*talk*] instructif/-ive.

EEC *n* (*abbr* = **European Economic Community**) CEE *f*.

eel *n* anguille *f*.

eerie *adj* [*silence, place*] étrange et inquiétant.

effect I *n* **1** effet *m* (**of** de; **on** sur); **the film had quite an ~ on me** ce film m'a fait forte impression; **to use sth to good ~** employer qch avec succès; **to take ~** [*price increases*] prendre effet; [*pills, anaesthetic*] commencer à agir; **to come into ~** [*law, rate*] entrer en vigueur; **with ~ from January 1** à dater du 1er janvier; **a remark to that ~** une remarque en ce sens; **or words to that ~** ou quelque chose de ce genre; **the overall ~** l'effet d'ensemble; **he paused for ~** il a fait une pause théâtrale; **she dresses like that for ~** elle s'habille comme ça pour faire de l'effet; **2** (repercussions) répercussions *fpl* (**of** de; **on** sur).
II **effects** *n pl* effets *mpl*.
III *vtr* effectuer [*repair, sale, change*].
IV **in effect** *phr* en fait, en réalité.

effective *adj* efficace (**against** contre; **in doing** pour faire).

effectively *adv* **1** (efficiently) efficacement; **2** (in effect) en fait, en réalité.

effectiveness *n* efficacité *f* (**of** de).

effeminate *adj* efféminé.

efficiency *n* (of person, method, organization) efficacité *f* (**in doing** à faire); (of machine) rendement *m*.

efficient *adj* **1** [*person, management*] efficace (**at doing** pour ce qui est de faire); **2** [*machine*] économique.

effort *n* **1** (energy) efforts *mpl*; **to put a lot of ~ into sth/into doing** se donner beaucoup de peine pour qch/pour faire; **to spare no ~** ne pas ménager ses efforts; **it's a waste of ~** c'est du travail pour rien; **to be worth the ~** en valoir la peine; **2** (difficulty) effort *m*; **it is an ~ to do** il est pénible de faire; **3** (attempt) **to make the ~** faire l'effort; **he made no ~ to apologize** il n'a fait aucun effort pour s'excuser; **his ~s at doing** ses tentatives pour faire; **to make every ~** faire tout son possible; **not a bad ~** pas mal; **4** (initiative) initiative *f*; **joint ~** initiative *f* commune; **war ~** effort *m* de guerre.

EFL *n* (*abbr* = **English as a Foreign Language**) anglais *m* langue étrangère.

eg (*abbr* = **exempli gratia**) par ex.

egg *n* œuf *m*.
■ **egg on**: **~ [sb] on** pousser.

egg: **~ box** *n* boîte *f* à œufs; **~cup** *n* coquetier *m*; **~plant** *n* (US) aubergine *f*; **~shell** *n* coquille *f* d'œuf; **~ white** *n* blanc *m* d'œuf; **~ yolk** *n* jaune *m* d'œuf.

ego *n* **1** moi *m*, ego *m*; **2**° amour-propre *m*.

egoism *n* égoïsme *m*.

egoist *n* égoïste *mf*.

egotism *n* égotisme *m*.

egotist *n* égotiste *mf*.

Egypt ▶ 574 *pr n* Égypte *f*.

eiderdown *n* édredon *m*.

eight ▶ 492, 554 I *n, pron* huit (*m*) *inv*.
II *det* huit *inv*; **~-hour day** journée *f* de huit heures.

eighteen ▶ 492, 554 *n, pron, det* dix-huit (*m*) *inv*.

eighteenth ▶ 584, 642 I *n* **1** (in order) dix-huitième *mf*; **2** (of month) dix-huit *m inv*.
II *adj, adv* dix-huitième.

eighth ▶ 584, 642 I *n* (in order) huitième *mf*; (of month) huit *m inv*; (fraction) huitième *m*.
II *adj, adv* huitième.

eighties ▶ 584, 492 *n pl* **1** (era) **the ~** les années *fpl* quatre-vingt; **2** (age) **to be in one's ~** avoir entre quatre-vingts et quatre-vingt-dix ans.

eightieth I *n* (in order, sequence) quatre-vingtième *mf*.
II *adj, adv* quatre-vingtième.

eighty ▶ 492 *n, pron, det* quatre-vingts (*m*).

eighty-one *n, pron, det* quatre-vingt-un (*m*).

Éire ▶ 574 *pr n* Éire *f*, République *f* d'Irlande.

either I *pron, quantif* **1** (one or other) l'un/-e ou l'autre; **take ~ (of them)** prends l'un/-e ou l'autre; **I don't like ~ (of them)** je n'aime ni l'un/-e ni l'autre; **without ~ (of them)** sans l'un/-e ni l'autre; **'which book do you want?'—'~'** 'quel livre veux-tu?'—'n'importe'; **2** (both) **~ of the two is possible** les deux sont possibles; **~ of us could win** nous avons tous les deux les mêmes chances de gagner.
II *det* **1** (one or the other) n'importe lequel/laquelle; **take ~ road** prenez n'importe laquelle des deux routes; **I can't see ~ child** je ne vois aucun des deux enfants; **2** (both) **~ one of the solutions is acceptable** les deux solutions sont acceptables; **in ~ case** dans les deux cas; **~ way, it will be difficult** de toute manière, ce sera difficile.
III *adv* non plus; **I can't do it ~** je ne peux pas le faire non plus.
IV *conj* **1** (as alternatives) **~...or...** soit...soit..., (ou)...ou...; **I was expecting him ~ Tuesday or Wednesday** je l'attendais soit mardi, soit mercredi, je l'attendais (ou) mardi ou mercredi; **~ you finish your work or you will be punished!** ou tu finis ton travail ou je te punis!; **it's ~ him or me** c'est lui ou moi; **2** (in the negative) **I wouldn't believe ~ Patrick or Emily** je ne croirais ni Patrick ni Emily.

ejaculation *n* éjaculation *f*.

eject I *vtr* **1** [*machine, system*] rejeter [*waste*]; [*volcano*] cracher [*lava*]; **2** faire sortir [*cassette*]; **3** expulser [*troublemaker*].

II *vi* [*pilot*] s'éjecter.

eke *v* ■ **eke out**: **~ out [sth], ~ [sth] out** faire durer [*income, supplies*] (**by** à force de; **by doing** en faisant); **to ~ out a living** or **an existence** essayer de joindre les deux bouts.

elaborate I *adj* [*excuse*] compliqué; [*network, plan*] complexe; [*design*] travaillé; [*painting, sculpture*] ouvragé; [*costume*] recherché; [*preparation*] minutieux/-ieuse.
II *vtr* élaborer [*theory, scheme*]; développer [*point, statement, idea*].
III *vi* entrer dans les détails; **to ~ on** s'étendre sur [*proposal*]; développer [*remark*].

elapse *vi* s'écouler.

elastic *n, adj* élastique (*m*).

elasticated *adj* [*waistband, bandage*] élastique.

elastic band *n* élastique *m*.

elated *adj* transporté de joie.

elbow I *n* coude *m*; **to lean on one's ~s** être accoudé.
II *vtr* **to ~ sb aside** écarter qn du coude; **to ~ one's way through a crowd** se frayer un passage à travers la foule (en jouant des coudes).

elbowroom *n* (room to move) espace *m* vital; (figurative) marge *f* de manœuvre.

elder I *n* **1** (older person) aîné/-e *m/f*; (of tribe, group) ancien *m*; **2** (plant) sureau *m*.
II *adj* aîné; **the ~ girl** l'aînée *f*, la fille aînée.

elderberry *n* baie *f* de sureau.

elderly I *n* **the ~** les personnes *fpl* âgées.
II *adj* [*person, population*] âgé.

eldest I *n* aîné/-e *m/f*; **my ~** mon aîné/-e.
II *adj* aîné; **the ~ child** l'aîné/-e.

elect *vtr* **1** (by vote) élire (**from, from among** parmi); **to ~ sb (as) president** élire qn président; **2** (choose) choisir (**to do** de faire).

election I *n* élection *f*, scrutin *m*; **in** or **at the ~** aux élections; **to win/lose an ~** gagner/perdre aux élections; **to stand for ~** se porter candidat aux élections.
II *noun modifier* [*manifesto*] électoral; [*day, results*] du scrutin.

elector *n* **1** (voter) électeur/-trice *m/f*; **2** (US) membre *m* du collège électoral.

electoral *adj* électoral; **~ register** or **roll** listes *fpl* électorales.

electorate *n* électorat *m*, électeurs *mpl*.

electric *adj* électrique.

electrical *adj* électrique.

electrician ▶**805** *n* électricien/-ienne *m/f*.

electricity I *n* électricité *f*; **to turn off/on the ~** couper/rétablir le courant (électrique).
II *noun modifier* [*generator, cable*] électrique; [*bill, charges*] d'électricité.

electric shock *n* décharge *f* électrique; **to get an ~** recevoir une décharge.

electrify *vtr* **1** électrifier [*railway*]; **2** électriser [*audience*].

electrocute *vtr* électrocuter; **to be ~d** (accidentally) s'électrocuter.

electronic *adj* électronique.

electronics *n* électronique *f*.

elegance *n* élégance *f*.

elegant *adj* [*person, clothes, gesture*] élégant; [*manners*] distingué; [*restaurant*] chic (*inv*).

element *n* **1** élément *m*; **the time ~** le facteur temps; **an ~ of luck/risk** une part de chance/risque; **2** (in heater, kettle) résistance *f*.

elementary *adj* **1** (basic) élémentaire; **2** [*school*] primaire; [*teacher*] de primaire.

elephant *n* éléphant *m*; **baby ~** éléphanteau *m*.

elevate *vtr* élever (**to** au rang de).

elevated *adj* [*language, rank, site*] élevé; [*railway, canal*] surélevé.

elevator *n* **1** (US) (lift) ascenseur *m*; **2** (hoist) élévateur *m*.

eleven ▶**492**, **554** I *n* onze *m inv*; **a football ~** une équipe de football.
II *pron, det* onze *inv*.

eleventh ▶**584**, **642** I *n* **1** (in order) onzième *mf*; **2** (of month) onze *m inv*.
II *adj, adv* onzième.

elf *n* lutin *m*.

eligible *adj* **to be ~ for** avoir droit à [*allowance, benefit, membership*]; **to be ~ to do** être en droit de faire.

eliminate *vtr* (gen) éliminer; écarter [*suspect*].

elimination *n* élimination *f*; **by a process of ~** en procédant par élimination.

élite I *n* élite *f*.
II *adj* [*group, minority*] élitaire; [*restaurant, club*] réservé à l'élite; [*troop, team, squad*] d'élite.

elm *n* **1** (also **~ tree**) orme *m*; **2** (also **~wood**) (bois *m* d')orme *m*.

elongated *adj* allongé.

elope *vi* [*couple*] s'enfuir ensemble; [*man, woman*] s'enfuir (**with** avec).

eloquent *adj* éloquent.

else I *adv* d'autre; **somebody/nothing ~** quelqu'un/rien d'autre; **something ~** autre chose; **somewhere** or **someplace** (US) **~** ailleurs; **how ~ can we do it?** comment le faire autrement?; **what ~ would you like?** qu'est-ce que tu voudrais d'autre?; **there's not much ~ to do** il n'y a pas grand-chose d'autre à faire; **he talks of little ~** il ne parle presque que de ça; **everyone ~ but me went to the football match** tout le monde est allé voir le match de football sauf moi; **was anyone ~ there?** y avait-il quelqu'un d'autre?; **he didn't see anybody ~** il n'a vu personne d'autre.
II **or else** *phr* sinon.

elsewhere *adv* ailleurs.

elusive *adj* [*person, animal, happiness*] insaisissable; [*prize, victory*] hors d'atteinte; [*scent, memory*] fugace.

emaciated *adj* [*person, feature*] émacié; [*limb, body*] décharné; [*animal*] étique.

E-mail *n* (*abbr* = **electronic mail**) courrier *m* or messagerie *f* électronique.

emancipate *vtr* émanciper; **to become ~d** [*woman*] s'émanciper.

embalm *vtr* embaumer.

embankment *n* **1** (for railway, road) remblai *m*; **2** (by river) quai *m*, digue *f*.

embargo *n* embargo *m* (**on** sur; **against** contre); **trade ~** embargo commercial.

embark *vi* **1** (on ship) s'embarquer (**for** pour); **2 to ~ on** entreprendre [*journey*]; se lancer dans [*career, process, project*].

embarrass *vtr* plonger [qn] dans l'embarras; **to be/feel ~ed** être/se sentir gêné.

embarrassing *adj* embarrassant; **my uncle is ~** mon oncle me fait honte; **to put sb in an ~ position** mettre qn dans l'embarras.

embarrassment *n* confusion *f*, gêne *f* (**about, at** devant); **to my ~** à ma grande confusion; **to be an ~ to sb** [*person*] faire honte à qn.

embassy *n* ambassade *f*.

embers *n pl* braises *fpl*.

embezzle *vtr* détourner [*funds*] (**from** de).

emblem *n* emblème *m*.

embrace I *n* étreinte *f*.
II *vtr* **1** (hug) étreindre; **2** (include) comprendre.
III *vi* s'étreindre.

embroider I *vtr* **1** broder (**with** de); **2** embellir [*story, truth*].
II *vi* broder, faire de la broderie.

embroidery *n* broderie *f*.

embryo *n* embryon *m*.

emerald I *n* **1** (stone) émeraude *f*; **2** ▶559 (colour) émeraude *m*.
II *adj* **1** [*ring, necklace*] d'émeraudes; **2** (colour) émeraude *inv*.

emerge I *vi* **1** [*person, animal*] sortir (**from** de); **2** [*problem, result*] se faire jour; [*pattern*] se dégager; [*truth*] apparaître; [*evidence*] ressortir.
II emerging *pres p adj* [*market*] naissant; [*democracy*] qui émerge; [*artist*] qui devient connu.

emergency I *n* (gen) cas *m* d'urgence; (Med) urgence *f*; **in an ~, in case of ~** en cas d'urgence; **it's an ~** c'est urgent; **state of ~** état *m* d'urgence.
II *noun modifier* [*plan, repairs, call, stop*] d'urgence; [*meeting*] extraordinaire; [*brakes, vehicle*] de secours.

emergency: **~ exit** *n* sortie *f* de secours; **~ landing** *n* atterrissage *m* d'urgence; **~ number** *n* numéro *m* des urgences; **~ room** *n* (US) = **emergency ward**; **~ services** *n pl* (police) police *f* secours; (ambulance) service *m* d'aide médicale d'urgence; (fire brigade) (sapeurs-) pompiers *mpl*; **~ ward** *n* salle *f* des urgences.

emigrant *n* (about to leave) émigrant/-e *m/f*; (settled elsewhere) émigré/-e *m/f*.

emigrate *vi* émigrer.

emission *n* émission *f* (**from** provenant de).

emit *vtr* émettre [*gas, heat, sound, signal*]; dégager [*smell, vapour*].

emotion *n* émotion *f*.

emotional *adj* [*problem*] émotif/-ive; [*reaction, state*] émotionnel/-elle; [*tie, response*] affectif/-ive; [*film, occasion*] émouvant; [*speech*] passionné; **to feel ~** se sentir ému (**about** par); **she's rather ~** elle est facilement émue.

emperor *n* empereur *m*.

emphasis *n* accent *m*; **to put special ~ on sth** insister sur l'importance de qch.

emphasize *vtr* mettre l'accent sur [*policy, need*]; mettre [qch] en valeur [*eyes*]; **to ~ that** insister sur le fait que; **to ~ the importance of sth** insister sur l'importance de qch.

emphatic *adj* [*statement*] catégorique; [*voice, manner*] énergique; **to be ~ about/that** insister sur/pour que.

empire *n* empire *m*.

employ *vtr* **1** employer [*person, company*] (**as** en qualité de); **2** (use) utiliser [*machine, tool*]; employer [*tactics, technique*]; recourir à [*measures*].

employable *adj* [*person*] capable de faire un travail.

employed I *n* **the ~** les actifs *mpl*.
II *adj* [*person*] qui a un emploi.

employee *n* salarié/-e *m/f*.

employer *n* employeur/-euse *m/f*.

employment *n* travail *m*, emploi *m*; **to seek/find ~** chercher/trouver du travail; **to be in ~** avoir un emploi; **place of ~** lieu *m* de travail.

employment: **~ agency** *n* bureau *m* de recrutement; **Employment Minister, Employment Secretary** *n* ministre *m* du Travail.

empress *n* impératrice *f*.

emptiness *n* vide *m*.

empty I *adj* **1** [*street*] désert; [*desk*] libre; [*container*] vide; [*page*] vierge; **to stand ~** être inoccupé; **2** [*promise, threat*] en l'air; [*gesture*] vide de sens; [*life*] vide.
II *vtr, vi* = **empty out**.
■ **empty out**: ¶ **~ out** [*building, container*] se vider; [*contents*] se répandre; ¶ **~ [sth] out, ~ out [sth]** vider [*container, drawer*]; verser [*liquid*].

emulsion *n* émulsion *f*.

enable *vtr* **1 to ~ sb to do** permettre à qn de faire; **2** (facilitate) faciliter [*growth*]; favoriser [*learning*].

enamel *n* émail *m*.

enchant *vtr* enchanter.

enchanting *adj* [*vision*] enchanteur/-eresse; [*smile*] ravissant.

encircle *vtr* [*troops, police*] encercler; [*fence, wall*] entourer; [*belt, bracelet*] enserrer.

enclose *vtr* **1** (gen) entourer (**with, by** de); (with fence, wall) clôturer (**with, by** avec); (in outer casing) enfermer (**in** dans); **2** (in letter) joindre (**with, in** à); **please find ~d a cheque for £10** veuillez trouver ci-joint un chèque de dix livres.

enclosure *n* **1** (for animals) enclos *m*; (for racehorses) paddock *m*; (for officials) enceinte *f*; **2** (fence) clôture *f*.

encompass *vtr* inclure, comprendre.

encore I *n* bis *m*; **to give** or **play an ~** jouer un bis; **to get an ~** être bissé.
II *excl* **~!** bis!

encounter I *n* (gen) rencontre *f* (**with** avec); (Mil) affrontement *m*.
II *vtr* rencontrer [*opponent, resistance, problem*]; essuyer [*setback*]; croiser [*person*].

encourage *vtr* **1** encourager (**to do** à faire); **2** stimuler [*investment*]; favoriser [*rise, growth*].

encouragement *n* encouragement *m* (**to** pour).

encouraging *adj* encourageant.

encroach *vi* **to ~ on** [*sea, vegetation*] gagner du terrain sur [*land*]; [*person*] empiéter sur; **to ~ on sb's privacy** violer l'intimité de qn.

encyclop(a)edia *n* encyclopédie *f*.

end I *n* **1** (final part) fin *f*; **'The End'** 'Fin'; **at the ~ of** à la fin de [*year, story*]; **at the ~ of May** fin mai; **by the ~ of** à la fin de [*year, journey, game*]; **to put an ~ to sth, to bring sth to an ~** mettre fin à qch; **to come to an ~** se terminer; **in the ~ I went home** finalement je suis rentré chez moi; **for days on ~** pendant des jours et des jours; **there is no ~ to his talent** son talent n'a pas de limites; **2** (extremity) bout *m*, extrémité *f*; **at the ~ of, on the ~ of** au bout de; **at the ~ of the garden** au fond du jardin; **from one ~ to another** d'un bout à l'autre; **from ~ to ~** de bout en bout; **the third from the ~** le/la troisième avant la fin; **to stand sth on (its) ~** mettre qch debout; **3 things are fine at my** or **this ~** de mon côté tout va bien; **to keep one's ~ up** tenir bon; **4** (of scale) extrémité *f*; **at the lower ~ of the scale** au plus bas de l'échelle; **5** (aim) but *m*; **to this** or **that ~** dans ce but; **a means to an ~** un moyen d'arriver à ses fins; **6** (Sport) **to change ~s** changer de côté; **7 to meet one's ~** trouver la mort.
II *vtr* mettre fin à [*strike, friendship, debate*]; rompre [*marriage*]; **to ~ sth with** terminer qch par; **to ~ it all** en finir avec la vie; **the sale to ~ all sales** ce qu'il y a de mieux comme soldes.
III *vi* [*day, book*] se terminer (**in, with** par); [*contract, agreement*] expirer.
■ **end up**: finir par devenir [*president*]; finir par être [*rich*]; **to ~ up (by) doing** finir par faire; **to ~ up in Paris** se retrouver à Paris.

endanger *vtr* mettre [qch] en danger [*health, life*]; compromettre [*career, prospects*]; constituer une menace pour [*species*]; **~ed species** espèce *f* menacée.

endearing *adj* [*person, habit*] attachant; [*smile*] engageant.

endeavour, endeavor (US) I *n* **1** (attempt) tentative *f* (**to do** de faire); **2** (industriousness) effort *m*.
II *vtr* **to ~ to do** (do one's best) faire tout son possible pour faire; (find a means) trouver un moyen de faire.

ending *n* fin *f*, dénouement *m*.

endive *n* (GB) chicorée *f*; (US) endive *f*.

endless *adj* [*patience, choice*] infini; [*supply*] inépuisable; [*list, search, meeting*] interminable.

endorse *vtr* **1** donner son aval à [*policy*]; appuyer [*decision*]; approuver [*product*]; endosser [*cheque*]; **2** (GB) **to have one's licence ~d** ≈ perdre des points sur son permis de conduire.

endow *vtr* doter [*hospital, charity, person*] (**with** de); **~ed with** doté de.

endurance *n* (physical) endurance *f*; (moral) courage *m*.

endure I *vtr* endurer [*hardship*]; supporter [*behaviour, person*]; subir [*attack, defeat*].
II *vi* durer.

enema *n* lavement *m*.

enemy I *n* ennemi/-e *m/f*; **to make enemies** se faire des ennemis; **to be one's own worst ~** être son pire ennemi.
II *noun modifier* [*forces, aircraft, territory*] ennemi; [*agent*] de l'ennemi.

energetic *adj* (gen) énergique; [*exercise*] vigoureux/-euse.

energy *n* énergie *f*.

enforce *vtr* appliquer [*rule, policy*]; faire respecter [*law, court order*]; imposer [*silence, discipline*]; exiger [*payment*].

engage I *vtr* **1 to be ~d in** se livrer à [*activity*]; **to be ~d in discussions/negotiations** être en discussion/négociations; **to ~ sb in conversation** engager la conversation avec qn; **to be otherwise ~d** être pris ailleurs; **2** passer [*gear*]; **to ~ the clutch** embrayer.
II *vi* **to ~ in** se livrer à [*activity*]; se lancer dans [*research*].

engaged *adj* **1 to be ~** être fiancé (**to** à); **to get ~** se fiancer (**to** à); **2** [*WC, phone*] occupé.

engaged tone *n* (GB) tonalité *f* 'occupé'.

engagement *n* **1** (appointment) rendez-vous *m inv*; (for performer, artist) engagement *m*; **2** (before marriage) fiançailles *fpl*.

engagement ring *n* bague *f* de fiançailles.

engine *n* **1** (gen) moteur *m*; (in ship) machines *fpl*; **jet ~** moteur à réaction; **2** locomotive *f*; **diesel/steam ~** locomotive diesel/à vapeur.

engine driver ▶ 805 *n* mécanicien *m*.

engineer ▶ 805 I *n* (graduate) ingénieur *m*; (in factory) mécanicien *m* monteur; (repairer) technicien *m*; (on ship) mécanicien *m*.
II *vtr* **1** (plot) manigancer; **2** (build) construire.

engineering *n* **1** (subject, science) ingénierie *f*; **civil ~** génie *m* civil; **2** (industry) industrie *f* mécanique; **light ~** génie *m* léger.

England ▶ 574 *pr n* Angleterre *f*.

English ▶ 712 I *n* **1** (language) anglais *m*; **2** (people) **the ~** les Anglais.
II *adj* [*language, food*] anglais; [*lesson, teacher*] d'anglais; [*ambassador, embassy*] d'Angleterre.

English Channel *n* **the ~** la Manche.

English: **~ Language Teaching, ELT** *n* enseignement *m* de l'anglais; **~man** *n* Anglais *m*; **~ speaker** *n* anglophone *mf*; **~-speaking** *adj* anglophone; **~woman** *n* Anglaise *f*.

engrave *vtr* graver.

engraving *n* gravure *f*.

engrossed *adj* **to be ~ in** être absorbé or plongé dans.

engulf *vtr* engloutir.

enhance *vtr* améliorer [*prospects, status*]; mettre [qch] en valeur [*appearance, qualities*]; majorer [*pension, salary*].

enigma *n* énigme *f*.

enigmatic *adj* énigmatique.

enjoy I *vtr* **1** aimer; **I ~ looking after Paul** j'aime bien m'occuper de Paul; **he knows how to ~ life** il sait vivre; **I ~ed my day in London** j'ai passé une bonne journée à Londres; **I didn't ~ the party** je ne me suis pas bien amusé à la soirée; **2** (have) jouir de [*good health, popularity*].
II *v refl* **to ~ oneself** s'amuser (**doing** à faire).

enjoyable *adj* agréable.

enjoyment *n* plaisir *m*.

enlarge I *vtr* agrandir.
II *vi* **1** [*pupil, pores*] se dilater; [*tonsils*] enfler; **2 to ~ on** s'étendre sur [*subject*]; développer [*idea*].

enlighten *vtr* éclairer (**on** sur).

enlightened *adj* éclairé.

enlightening *adj* instructif/-ive.

enlightenment *n* (edification) instruction *f*; (clarification) éclaircissement *m*; **the (Age of) Enlightenment** le Siècle des lumières.

enlist I *vtr* recruter; **to ~ sb's help** s'assurer l'aide de qn.
II *vi* s'enrôler, s'engager.

enmity *n* inimitié *f* (**towards** envers).

enormity *n* énormité *f*.

enormous *adj* (gen) énorme; [*effort*] prodigieux/-ieuse; **an ~ amount of** énormément de; **an ~ number of people** un monde fou.

enough

■ **Note** When *enough* is used as a pronoun and if the sentence does not specify what it is enough of, the pronoun *en*, meaning *of it/of them*, must be added before the verb in French: *will there be enough?* = est-ce qu'il y en aura assez?

I *pron, quantif* assez; **have you had ~ to eat?** avez-vous assez mangé?; **there's more than ~ for everybody** il y a largement assez pour tout le monde; **is that ~?** ça suffit?; **I've had ~ of him** j'en ai assez de lui; **I've got ~ to worry about** j'ai assez de soucis (comme ça); **that's ~ (from you)!** ça suffit!; **~ said!** j'ai compris!
II *adv* assez; **big ~ for us** assez grand pour nous; **big ~ to hold 50 people** assez grand pour contenir 50 personnes; **you're not trying hard ~** tu ne fais pas assez d'efforts; **is he old ~ to vote?** a-t-il l'âge de voter?; **curiously ~,...** aussi bizarre que cela puisse paraître...
III *det* assez de; **have you got ~ money/chairs?** avez-vous assez d'argent/de chaises?; **we haven't bought ~ wine** nous n'avons pas acheté assez de vin.

enquire I *vtr* demander.
II *vi* se renseigner (**about** sur); **to ~ after sb** demander des nouvelles de qn.

enquiring *adj* [*look, voice*] interrogateur/-trice; [*mind*] curieux/-ieuse.

enquiry *n* demande *f* de renseignements; **to make enquiries** demander des renseignements (**about** sur); ▶ **inquiry**.

enrage *vtr* mettre [qn] en rage, rendre [qn] furieux/-ieuse.

enrich *vtr* enrichir.

enrol, **enroll** (US) I *vtr* (gen) inscrire; (Mil) enrôler.
II *vi* (gen) s'inscrire (**in, on** à); (Mil) s'engager (**in** dans).

enrolment, **enrollment** (US) *n* (gen) inscription *f* (**in, on** à); (Mil) enrôlement *m*.

en suite *adj* attenant.

ensure *vtr* garantir; **to ~ that...** s'assurer que...

entail *vtr* impliquer [*travel, work*]; entraîner [*expense*]; nécessiter [*effort*].

enter I *vtr* **1** entrer dans, pénétrer dans [*room, house*]; entrer dans [*phase, period*]; entamer [*new term, final year*]; entrer dans [*profession, army*]; participer à [*race, competition*]; entrer à [*parliament*]; **to ~ sb's mind** or **head** venir à l'idée or à l'esprit de qn; **2** inscrire [*competitor, candidate*] (**for** à); engager [*horse*] (**for** dans); présenter [*poem, picture*] (**for** à); **3** inscrire [*figure, fact*] (**in** dans); (in diary) noter [*appointment*] (**in** dans); (in computer) entrer [*data*].
II *vi* **1** (come in) entrer; **2 to ~ for** s'inscrire à [*exam*]; s'inscrire pour [*race*].
■ **enter into**: **~ into [sth] 1** entrer en [*correspondence, conversation*]; entamer [*negotiations*]; se lancer dans [*explanations*]; passer [*contract*]; **2** faire partie de [*plans*]; **that doesn't ~ into it** c'est sans rapport.

enterprise *n* **1** entreprise *f*; **business ~** affaire *f* commerciale; **2** (initiative) esprit *m* d'initiative.

enterprising *adj* [*person*] entreprenant; [*plan*] audacieux/-ieuse.

entertain I *vtr* **1** (keep amused) divertir; (make laugh) amuser; (keep occupied) distraire, occuper; **2** (play host to) recevoir; **3** entretenir [*idea*]; nourrir [*doubt, ambition, illusion*].
II *vi* recevoir.

entertainer ▶ **805** *n* (comic) comique *mf*; (performer, raconteur) amuseur/-euse *m/f*.

entertaining I *adj* divertissant.
II *n* art *m* de recevoir; **they do a lot of ~** ils reçoivent beaucoup.

entertainment I *n* **1** divertissement *m*, distractions *fpl*; **the world of ~** le monde du spectacle; **2** (event) spectacle *m*.
II *noun modifier* [*allowance, expenses*] de représentation; [*industry*] du spectacle.

enthusiasm *n* enthousiasme *m* (**for** pour).

enthusiast *n* (for sport, DIY) passionné/-e *m/f*; (for music, composer) fervent/-e *m/f*.

enthusiastic *adj* [*crowd, response*] enthousiaste; [*discussion*] exalté; [*worker, gardener*] passionné; [*member*] fervent; **to be ~ about sth** (present or future event) être enthousiasmé par qch; (past event) parler de qch avec enthousiasme; **he's not very ~ about his work** il ne montre pas beaucoup d'enthousiasme pour son travail.

entice *vtr* (with offer, charms, prospects) attirer; (with food, money) appâter.

entire *adj* entier/-ière; **the ~ family** toute la famille, la famille (tout) entière; **throughout her ~ career** pendant toute sa carrière; **the ~ length of the street** toute la longueur de la rue; **the ~ 50,000 dollars** les 50 000 dollars dans leur totalité.

entirely *adv* [*destroy, escape*] entièrement; [*different, unnecessary*] complètement; **that changes things ~** ça change tout.

entirety *n* ensemble *m*, totalité *f*; **in its ~** dans son ensemble.

entitle *vtr* **to ~ sb to sth** donner droit à qch à qn; **to ~ sb to do** autoriser qn à faire; **to be ~d to sth** avoir droit à qch; **to be ~d to do** avoir le droit de faire; **everyone's ~d to their own opinion** à chacun ses opinions.

entitlement *n* droit *m* (**to sth** à qch; **to do** de faire).

entity *n* entité *f*.

entrance I *n* **1** (door, act of entering) entrée *f*; **to make an ~** faire son entrée; **2** (admission) admission *f*.
II *vtr* transporter, ravir.

entrance: **~ examination** *n* (GB Sch, Univ) examen *m* d'entrée; (for civil service) concours *m* d'entrée; **~ fee** *n* droit *m* d'entrée; **~ hall** *n* (in house) vestibule *m*; (in public building) hall *m*; **~ requirements** *n pl* diplômes *mpl* requis.

entreat *vtr* implorer, supplier (**to do** de faire).

entreaty *n* prière *f*, supplication *f*.

entrée *n* (GB) entrée *f*; (US) plat *m* principal.

entrepreneur *n* entrepreneur/-euse *m/f*.

entrepreneurial *adj* **to have ~ spirit/skills** avoir le sens/le don des affaires.

entrust *vtr* confier; **to ~ sb with sth**, **to ~ sth to sb** confier qch à qn.

entry *n* **1** (door, act of entering) entrée *f*; **to gain ~ to** or **into** s'introduire dans [*building*]; accéder à [*computer file*]; **to force ~ to** or **into** s'introduire de force dans; **2** (admission) admission *f*; (to country) entrée *f*; **'no ~'** (on door) 'défense d'entrer'; (in one way street) 'sens interdit'; **3** (in dictionary) entrée *f*; (in encyclopedia) article *m*; (in diary) note *f*; (in register) inscription *f*; (in ledger) écriture *f*; **4** (for competition) œuvre *f* présentée à un concours; (for song contest) titre *m*.

entry: **~ form** *n* fiche *f* d'inscription; **~ permit** *n* visa *m* d'entrée; **~ phone** *n* interphone *m*.

envelope *n* enveloppe *f*; **to put sth in an ~** mettre qch sous enveloppe.

envious *adj* [*person*] envieux/-ieuse; [*look*] d'envie, envieux/-ieuse; **to be ~ of sb/sth** envier qn/qch; **to make sb ~** rendre qn jaloux/-ouse.

environment *n* (physical, cultural) environnement *m*; (social) milieu *m*; **working ~** conditions *fpl* de travail.

environmental *adj* [*conditions, changes*] du milieu; [*concern, issue*] lié à l'environnement, écologique; [*damage, protection, pollution*] de l'environnement.

environmental health *n* hygiène *f* publique.

environmentalist *n* écologiste *mf*.

environmentally *adv* **~ safe**, **~ sound** qui ne nuit pas à l'environnement; **~ friendly product** produit qui respecte l'environnement.

envisage *vtr* (anticipate) prévoir (**doing** de faire); (visualize) envisager (**doing** de faire).

envoy *n* envoyé/-e *m/f*.

envy I *n* envie *f*; (long-term) jalousie *f*; **out of ~** par jalousie; **in ~** par envie.
II *vtr* envier; **to ~ sb sth** envier qch à qn.

enzyme *n* enzyme *f*.

epic I *n* (gen) épopée *f*; (film) film *m* à grand spectacle; (novel) roman-fleuve *m*.
II *adj* épique.

epicentre (GB), **epicenter** (US) *n* épicentre *m*.

epidemic I *n* épidémie *f*.
II *adj* épidémique.

epilepsy ▶ 686 *n* épilepsie *f*.

epileptic *n*, *adj* épileptique (*mf*).

episode *n* épisode *m*.

epitome *n* épitomé *m*; **the ~ of kindness** la bonté incarnée.

epitomize *vtr* personnifier, incarner.

epoch *n* époque *f*.

equal I *n* égal/-e *m/f*.
II *adj* **1** égal (**to** à); **~ opportunities/rights** égalité *f* des chances/des droits; **they're about ~** [*candidates*] ils se valent à peu près; **2 to be/feel ~ to** être/se sentir à la hauteur de; **to feel ~ to doing** se sentir à même de faire.
III *adv* [*finish*] à égalité.
IV *vtr* égaler.
IDIOMS **all things being ~** sauf imprévu.

equality *n* égalité *f*; **sexual ~** égalité des sexes.

equally *adv* [*divide, share*] en parts égales; **~ difficult** tout aussi difficile; **~, we might say that...** de même, on pourrait dire que...

equals sign (GB), **equal sign** (US) *n* signe *m* égal.

equate *vtr* (identify) assimiler (**with, to** à); (compare) comparer (**with, to** à).

equation *n* équation *f*.

equator *n* équateur *m*.

equilibrium *n* équilibre *m*; **in ~** en équilibre.

equinox *n* équinoxe *m*.

equip *vtr* équiper (**for** pour); **fully ~ped kitchen** cuisine équipée.

equipment *n* (gen) équipement *m*; (office, electrical, photographic) matériel *m*; **a piece** or **item of ~** un article.

equities *n pl* actions *fpl* ordinaires.

equity *n* (fairness) équité *f*.

equivalent *n*, *adj* équivalent (*m*).

era *n* (in history, geology) ère *f*; (in politics, fashion) époque *f*.

eradicate *vtr* éliminer [*poverty, crime*]; éradiquer [*disease*].

erase *vtr* effacer.

eraser *n* (rubber) gomme *f*; (for blackboard) brosse *f* feutrée.

erect I *adj* [*posture*] droit; [*tail, ears*] dressé.
II *vtr* ériger [*building*]; monter [*scaffolding, tent, screen*].

erection *n* **1** (gen) érection *f*; (of building, bridge) construction *f*; **2** (edifice) édifice *m*.

ermine *n* hermine *f*.

erode *vtr* éroder [*rock, metal*]; saper [*confidence*].

erosion *n* érosion *f*.

erotic *adj* érotique.

err *vi* **1** (make mistake) faire erreur; **to ~ in one's judgment** faire une erreur de jugement; **2** (stray) pécher; **to ~ on the side of caution** pécher par excès de prudence.

errand *n* commission *f*, course *f*; **to go on** or **to run an ~ for sb** aller faire une commission pour qn.

erratic *adj* [*behaviour, person, driver*] imprévisible; [*performance*] inégal; [*moods*] changeant; [*movements*] désordonné.

erroneous *adj* erroné, faux/fausse.

error *n* (in spelling, grammar, typing) faute *f*; (in calculation, on computer) erreur *f*; **margin of ~** marge *f* d'erreur.

ersatz *n* ersatz *m*, succédané *m*.

erudite *adj* [*person*] érudit; [*book, discussion*] savant.

erupt *vi* **1** [*volcano*] entrer en éruption; [*rash*] apparaître; **2** [*violence*] éclater.

eruption *n* (of volcano, rash) éruption *f*; (of violence, anger) explosion *f*.

escalate I *vtr* intensifier [*war, problem, efforts*]; aggraver [*inflation*].
II *vi* [*conflict, violence*] s'intensifier; [*prices*] monter en flèche; [*unemployment*] augmenter rapidement.

escalator *n* escalier *m* mécanique, escalator® *m*.

escapade *n* frasque *f*.

escape I *n* fuite *f* (**from** de; **to** vers); **to make an** or **one's ~** s'évader; **to have a narrow** or **lucky ~** l'échapper belle.
II *vtr* **1 to ~ death/danger** échapper à la mort/au danger; **to ~ defeat** éviter la défaite; **to ~ detection** [*person*] échapper aux recherches (de la police); [*fault*] ne pas être détecté; **we cannot ~ the fact that** on ne peut pas ignorer le fait que; **2** [*name, fact*] échapper à [*person*].
III *vi* **1** [*person*] s'enfuir, s'évader; [*animal*] s'échapper (**from** de); (figurative) s'évader; **to ~ with one's life** s'en sortir vivant; **2** (leak) fuir.

escapism *n* (in literature, cinema) évasion *f* (du réel); (of person) refus *m* d'affronter la réalité.

escort I *n* **1** escorte *f*; **police ~** escorte de police; **armed ~** escorte de soldats; **to put under ~** placer sous escorte; **2** (companion) compagnon/compagne *m/f*.
II *vtr* **1** escorter; **to ~ sb in/out** faire entrer/sortir qn sous escorte; **2** (to a function) accompagner; (home) raccompagner.

especially *adv* **1** (above all) surtout, en particulier; **him ~** lui en particulier; **~ as it's so hot** d'autant plus qu'il fait si chaud; **2** (on purpose) exprès, spécialement; **3** (unusually) particulièrement.

espresso *n* express *m inv*.

essay *n* **1** (Sch) rédaction *f* (**on, about** sur); (extended) dissertation *f* (**on** sur); **2** (literary) essai *m* (**on** sur).

essence *n* essence *f*.

essential I *n* **a car is not an ~** une auto n'est pas indispensable; **the ~s** l'essentiel *m*.
II *adj* [*role, feature, element*] essentiel/-ielle; [*ingredient, reading*] indispensable; [*difference*] fondamental; **it is ~ to arrive on time** il est indispensable d'arriver à l'heure; **it is ~ for us to agree** or **that we agree** il est indispensable que nous soyons d'accord.

essentially *adv* essentiellement.

establish *vtr* (gen) établir; fonder [*company*]; **to ~ that** montrer que; **to ~ oneself as a market leader** s'imposer comme leader du marché.

establishment *n* **1** (process) instauration *f*; **2** (institution, organization) établissement *m*; **3** (shop, business) maison *f*.

estate *n* **1** (stately home and park) domaine *m*, propriété *f*; **2** = **housing estate**; **3** (assets) biens *mpl*; **4** (GB) (also **~ car**) break *m*.

estate: **~ agency** *n* (GB) agence *f* immobilière; **~ agent** *n* (GB) agent *m* immobilier.

esteem *n* **to go up/down in sb's ~** remonter/baisser dans l'estime de qn.

estimate I *n* **1** estimation *f*; **at a rough ~** très approximativement; **2** (quote for client) devis *m*.
II *vtr* évaluer [*value, size, distance*]; **to ~ that** estimer que.
III estimated *pp adj* [*cost, figure*] approximatif/-ive; **an ~d 300 people** environ 300 personnes.

estimated: **~ time of arrival, ETA** *n* heure *f* d'arrivée prévue; **~ time of departure, ETD** *n* heure *f* de départ prévue.

Estonia ▶ 574 *pr n* Estonie *f*.

estranged *adj* **~ from sb** séparé de qn; **her ~ husband** son mari dont elle est/était séparée.

estrogen *n* (US) = **oestrogen**.

etc *adv* (*written abbr* = **et cetera**) etc.

etching *n* eau-forte *f*.

eternal *adj* [*life*] éternel/-elle; [*chatter, optimist*] perpétuel/-elle.

ethical *adj* moral.

ethics *n* (code) moralité *f*; **professional ~** déontologie *f*; **medical ~** déontologie *f* médicale.

ethnic *adj* ethnique.

etiquette *n* **1** (social) bienséance *f*, étiquette *f*; **2** (professional, diplomatic) protocole *m*.

etymology *n* étymologie *f*.

eurocheque *n* Eurochèque *m*; **~ card** carte *f* Eurochèque.

Euro-MP *n* député *m* européen.

Europe ▶574 *pr n* (continent) Europe *f*; (EEC) le Marché commun.

European I *n* Européen/-éenne *m/f*.
II *adj* européen/-éenne.

European: **~ Commission** *n* Commission *f* européenne; **~ Monetary System, EMS** système *m* monétaire européen, SME *m*; **~ Union, EU** Union *f* européenne, UE *f*.

euthanasia *n* euthanasie *f*.

evacuate *vtr* évacuer.

evade *vtr* esquiver [*blow*]; éluder [*question, problem*].

evaluate *vtr* évaluer [*situation, ability, results*]; mesurer [*progress*].

evaporate *vi* [*liquid*] s'évaporer.

evaporated milk *n* lait *m* condensé non sucré.

evasion *n* (of responsibility) dérobade *f* (**of** à); **tax ~** évasion *f* fiscale.

evasive *adj* [*answer*] évasif/-ive; [*look*] fuyant.

eve *n* veille *f*; **on the ~ of** à la veille de.

even[1] **I** *adv* **1** (showing surprise) même; **he didn't ~ try** il n'a même pas essayé; **without ~ apologizing** sans même s'excuser; **2** (emphasizing point) même; **I can't ~ swim, never mind dive** je ne sais même pas nager, encore moins plonger; **don't tell anyone, not ~ Bob** ne dis rien à personne, pas même à Bob; **~ if/when** même si/quand; **3** (with comparative) encore; **~ colder** encore plus froid.
II even so *phr* quand même; **it was interesting ~ so** c'était quand même intéressant.
III even then *phr* (at that time) même à ce moment-là; (all the same) de toute façon.
IV even though *phr* bien que (+ *subj*).

even[2] *adj* [*surface, voice, temper*] égal; [*teeth, hemline*] régulier/-ière; [*temperature*] constant; [*number*] pair; **we're ~** nous sommes quittes; **to get ~ with sb** rendre à qn la monnaie de sa pièce; **to be ~** [*competitors*] être à égalité.

evening ▶554 **I** *n* soir *m*; (with emphasis on duration) soirée *f*; **in the ~** le soir; **during the ~** pendant la soirée; **6 o'clock in the ~** six heures du soir; **this ~** ce soir; **later this ~** plus tard dans la soirée; **tomorrow/yesterday ~** demain/hier soir; **on the ~ of the 14th** le 14 au soir; **on Friday ~** vendredi soir; **on the following** or **next ~** le lendemain soir; **the previous ~, the ~ before** la veille au soir; **every ~** tous les soirs; **every Thursday ~** tous les jeudis soir; **all ~** toute la soirée.
II *noun modifier* [*bag, shoe*] habillé; [*meal, newspaper, walk*] du soir.

evening: **~ class** *n* cours *m* du soir; **~ dress** *n* (formal clothes) tenue *f* de soirée.

event *n* **1** événement *m*; **2** (eventuality) cas *m*; **in the ~ of a fire** en cas d'incendie; **in any ~** de toute façon; **it was quite an ~** c'était un événement; **3** (in athletics) épreuve *f*; **field/track ~** épreuve *f* d'athlétisme/de vitesse.

eventful *adj* mouvementé.

eventually *adv* finalement; **to do sth ~** finir par faire qch.

ever I *adv* **1** (at any time) **nothing was ~ said** rien n'a jamais été dit; **no-one will ~ forget** personne n'oubliera jamais; **hardly ~** rarement, presque jamais; **has he ~ lived abroad?** est-ce qu'il a déjà vécu à l'étranger?; **have you ~ seen anything like it?** as-tu jamais vu rien de pareil?; **do you ~ make mistakes?** est-ce qu'il t'arrive de te tromper?; **he's happier than he's ~ been** il n'a jamais été aussi heureux; **the worst mistake I ~ made** la pire erreur que j'aie jamais faite; **the first ~** le tout premier; **2** (when making comparisons) **more beautiful than ~** plus beau/belle que jamais; **it's windier than ~ today** il y a encore plus de vent aujourd'hui; **3** (always) toujours; **as cheerful as ~** toujours aussi gai; **the same as ~** toujours le même; **they lived happily ~ after** ils vécurent toujours heureux; **4** (expressing irritation) **don't (you) ~ do that again!** ne refais jamais ça!; **that's all he ~ does!** c'est tout ce qu'il sait faire!
II ever since *phr* depuis; **~ since we arrived** depuis notre arrivée.

evergreen *n* arbre *m* à feuilles persistantes.

every I *det* **1** (each) **~ house in the street** toutes les maisons de la rue; **I've read ~ one of her books** j'ai lu tous ses livres; **~ time I go there** chaque fois que j'y vais; **I enjoyed ~ (single) minute of it** chaque minute a été un plaisir; **~ second day** tous les deux jours; **in ~ way** (from every point of view) à tous les égards; (using every method) par tous les moyens; **2** (emphatic) **there is ~ chance that you'll have a place** il y a toutes les chances que tu aies une place; **to have ~ right to complain** avoir tous les droits de se plaindre; **I wish you ~ success** je vous souhaite beaucoup de succès; **3** (indicating frequency) **~ Thursday** tous les jeudis; **once ~ few days** tous les deux ou trois jours; **~ 20 kilometres** tous les 20 kilomètres.
II every other *phr* **~ other day** tous les deux jours; **~ other Sunday** un dimanche sur deux.
IDIOMS **~ now and then, ~ so often, ~ once in a while** de temps en temps.

everybody *pron* (also **everyone**) tout le monde; **~ else** tous les autres; **~ knows that** tout le monde le sait.

everyday *adj* [*life*] quotidien/-ienne; [*clothes*] de tous les jours; **in ~ use** d'usage courant.

everyone *pron* = **everybody**.

everything *pron* tout; **is ~ all right?** est-ce que tout va bien?; **don't believe ~ you hear** il ne faut pas croire tout ce que tu entends; **~ else is hers** tout le reste est à elle; **he's got ~ going for him** il a tout pour lui.

everywhere *adv* partout; **~ else** partout ailleurs; **~ I go** partout où je vais; **she's been ~** elle a voyagé partout.

evict *vtr* expulser (**from** de).

eviction *n* expulsion *f* (**from** de).

evidence *n* **1** (proof) preuves *fpl* (**that** que; **of,**

for de; **against** contre); **a piece of ~** une preuve; **2** (testimony) témoignage *m* (**from** de); **to be used in ~ against sb** servir de témoignage contre qn; **to give ~** témoigner, déposer (**for sb** en faveur de qn; **against sb** contre qn); **3** (trace) trace *f* (**of** de).

evident *adj* [*anger, relief*] manifeste.

evidently *adv* **1** (apparently) apparemment; **2** (patently) manifestement.

evil I *n* **1 ~** le mal; **2** (bad thing) mal *m*; **the ~s of racism** les maux du racisme.
II *adj* [*person, forces*] malfaisant; [*act*] diabolique; [*spirit*] maléfique; [*smell*] nauséabond.
IDIOMS **the lesser of two ~s** le moindre mal.

evolution *n* évolution *f* (**from** à partir de).

ewe *n* brebis *f*.

ex- *pref* ex-, ancien/-ienne (*before n*).

exact *adj* exact; **it's the ~ opposite** c'est exactement le contraire; **it was in the summer, July to be ~** c'était en été, plus précisément en juillet.

exactly *adv* exactement; **what ~ were you doing?** que faisais-tu au juste?

exaggerate I *vtr* (gen) exagérer; (in one's own mind) s'exagérer [*problem, effect*].
II *vi* exagérer.

exaggeration *n* exagération *f*

exam *n* examen.

examination *n* examen *m* (**in** de); **French ~** examen *m* de français; **to take/pass an ~** passer/réussir un examen; **to have an ~** (Med) passer un examen médical.

examine *vtr* examiner.

example *n* exemple *m*; **for ~** par exemple; **to set a good ~** donner l'exemple; **you're setting a bad ~** tu ne donnes pas le bon exemple; **to make an ~ of sb** punir qn pour l'exemple.

excavate I *vtr* fouiller [*site*]; creuser [*tunnel*].
II *vi* faire des fouilles.

excavation *n* excavation *f*; **~s** (archaeological) fouilles *fpl*.

exceed *vtr* dépasser [*speed limit, credit limit*] (**by** de).

excel *vi* exceller (**at, in** en; **at** or **in doing** à faire).

excellent *adj* excellent.

except

■ **Note** There are three frequently used translations for *except*. By far the most frequent of these is *sauf*; the others are *excepté* and *à l'exception de*. Note, however, that in *what/where/who* questions, *except* is translated by *sinon*.

I *prep* **everybody ~ Lisa** tout le monde sauf Lisa, tout le monde à l'exception de or excepté Lisa; **~ if/when** sauf si/quand; **~ that** sauf que, si ce n'est que; **nothing ~ the car** rien d'autre que la voiture; **nobody ~ me** personne d'autre que moi; **who could have done it ~ him?** qui aurait pu le faire sinon lui?
II except for *phr* à part, à l'exception de.

exception *n* exception *f* (**for** pour); **with the ~ of** à l'exception de; **with some ~s** à quelques exceptions près.

exceptional *adj* exceptionnel/-elle.

excess I *n* excès *m* (**of** de).
II *adj* **~ weight** excès *m* de poids; **~ baggage** excédent *m* de bagages.

excessive *adj* excessif/-ive.

exchange I *n* **1** échange *m*; **in ~** en échange (**for** de); **~ visit** voyage *m* d'échange; **2** (in banking) change *m*; **the rate of ~, the ~ rate** le taux de change; **3** (also **telephone ~**) central *m* (téléphonique).
II *vtr* échanger (**for** contre; **with** avec).

Exchange Rate Mechanism, **ERM** *n* système *m* monétaire européen.

Exchequer *pr n* (GB) **the ~** l'Échiquier *m*, le ministère des finances.

excite *vtr* (thrill) exciter; (fire with enthusiasm) enthousiasmer.

excited *adj* [*person, crowd, animal*] excité; [*voice, conversation*] animé; **to be ~ about sth** (enthusiastic) s'enthousiasmer pour qch; (in anticipation) être emballé° à l'idée de qch; **to get ~** s'exciter.

excitement *n* excitation *f*; **in the ~** dans l'agitation générale.

exciting *adj* passionnant.

exclaim *vtr* s'exclamer.

exclamation mark, **exclamation point** (US) *n* point *m* d'exclamation.

exclude *vtr* exclure [*person, group*] (**from** de); ne pas inclure [*name*] (**from** dans); exclure [*issue, possibility*] (**from** de).

excluding *prep* à l'exclusion de; **~ VAT** TVA non compris.

exclusion *n* exclusion *f* (**from** de).

exclusive I *n* (report) exclusivité *f*.
II *adj* **1** [*club, social circle*] fermé; [*hotel*] de luxe; [*school, district*] huppé; **2** [*story, coverage, rights*] exclusif/-ive; [*interview*] en exclusivité; **~ to Harrods** une exclusivité de Harrods; **~ of meals** les repas non compris.

excruciating *adj* **1** [*pain*] atroce; **2°** (awful) exécrable.

excursion *n* (organized) excursion *f*; (casual) promenade *f*.

excuse I *n* excuse *f*; (**for sth** à qch; **for doing** pour faire; **to do** pour faire); **to make ~s** trouver des excuses; **to be an ~ to do** or **for doing** servir de prétexte pour faire; **I have a good ~** j'ai une bonne excuse; **an ~ to leave early** un bon prétexte pour partir tôt; **there's no ~ for such behaviour** ce genre de conduite est inexcusable; **that's no ~** ce n'est pas une excuse or une raison.
II *vtr* **1** excuser [*person*] (**for doing** de faire, d'avoir fait); **~ me!** (bumping into sb) excusez-moi!, pardon!; (beginning an enquiry, making polite correction) excusez-moi; (making angry correction) je regrette, mais; (not hearing properly) pardon?; **2** (exempt) dispenser (**from sth** de qch; **from doing** de faire).

ex-directory *adj* (GB) [*telephone number*] sur la liste rouge.

execute *vtr* exécuter.

execution *n* exécution *f*.

executioner *n* bourreau *m*.

executive I *n* **1** cadre *m*; **top ~** cadre *m* supérieur; **2** (committee) exécutif *m*, comité *m* exécutif; **party ~** bureau *m* du parti.
II *adj* [*power*] exécutif/-ive; [*status, post*] de cadre.

exemplary *adj* [*behaviour, life*] exemplaire; [*student*] modèle (*after n*).

exemplify *vtr* illustrer, exemplifier.

exemption *n* exemption *f* (**from** de); **tax ~** dégrèvement *m* d'impôts.

exercise I *n* **1** exercice *m*; **physical/maths ~** exercice physique/de maths; **2 public relations ~** campagne *f* de relations publiques.
II *vtr* **1** exercer [*body*]; faire travailler [*limb, muscles*]; **2** faire preuve de [*control, restraint*]; exercer [*power, right*].
III *vi* faire de l'exercice.

exercise: **~ bicycle** *n* vélo *m* d'entraînement; **~ book** *n* cahier *m*.

exert *vtr* exercer [*pressure, influence*] (**on** sur); **to ~ oneself** se fatiguer.

exhale *vi* [*person*] expirer.

exhaust I *n* **1** (also **~ pipe**) pot *m* d'échappement; **2** (also **~ fumes**) gaz *mpl* d'échappement.
II *vtr* épuiser; **to ~ oneself** s'épuiser; **~ed** épuisé.

exhaustion *n* épuisement *m*.

exhibit I *n* **1** œuvre *f* exposée; **2** (US) (exhibition) exposition *f*.
II *vtr* exposer [*work of art*]; manifester [*preference, sign*].

exhibition *n* exposition *f*; **art ~** exposition; **the Picasso ~** l'exposition Picasso; **to make an ~ of oneself** se donner en spectacle.

exhibition centre (GB), **exhibition center** (US) *n* palais *m* des expositions.

exhibitor *n* exposant/-e *m/f*.

exhilarate *vtr* **to feel ~d** être tout joyeux/toute joyeuse.

exhilarating *adj* [*game*] stimulant; [*experience*] exaltant; [*music*] grisant; [*speed*] enivrant.

ex-husband *n* ex-mari *m*.

exile I *n* **1** (person) exilé/-e *m/f*; **2** (expulsion) exil *m* (**from** de); **in ~** en exil.
II *vtr* exiler (**de** from).

exist *vi* **1** (be) exister; **2** (live) vivre; **to ~ on a diet of potatoes** ne vivre que de pommes de terre.

existence *n* existence *f* (**of** de).

existing *adj* [*laws, order*] existant; [*policy, management*] actuel/-elle.

exit I *n* sortie *f*; **'no ~'** 'interdit'.
II *vi* sortir.

exodus *n* exode *m*.

exotic *adj* exotique.

expand I *vtr* développer [*business, network, range*]; élargir [*horizon, knowledge*]; accroître [*production, workforce*]; étendre [*empire*]; gonfler [*lungs*].
II *vi* [*business, sector, town*] se développer; [*population, production*] s'accroître; [*market, economy*] être en expansion; [*metal*] se dilater; [*institution*] s'agrandir.

expanding *adj* [*population, sector*] en expansion.

expanse *n* (of land, water) étendue *f*; (of flesh) étalage *m*.

expatriate *n*, *adj* expatrié/-e (*m/f*).

expect I *vtr* **1** s'attendre à [*event, victory, defeat, trouble*]; **to ~ the worst** s'attendre au pire; **to ~ sb to do** s'attendre à ce que qn fasse; **she is ~ed to win** on s'attend à ce qu'elle gagne; **he is ~ed to arrive at six** on l'attend pour six heures; **to ~ that** s'attendre à ce que (+ *subj*); **I ~ (that) I'll lose** je m'attends à perdre; **more/worse than ~ed** plus/pire que prévu; **2** s'attendre à [*sympathy, help*] (**from** de la part de); **3** attendre [*baby, guest, company*]; **4** (require) demander, attendre [*commitment, hard work*] (**from** de); **I ~ you to be punctual** je vous demande d'être ponctuel; **it's too much to ~** c'est trop demander; **5** (GB) (suppose) **I ~ so** je pense que oui; **I ~ he's tired** il doit être fatigué.
II *vi* **1 to ~ to do** s'attendre à faire; **2** (require) **I ~ to see you there** je compte bien vous y voir; **3** (be pregnant) **to be ~ing** attendre un enfant.

expectant *adj* **1** [*look*] plein d'attente; **2** [*mother*] futur (*before n*).

expectation *n* **1** (prediction) prévision *f*; **against all ~(s)** à l'encontre des prévisions générales; **2** (hope) aspiration *f*, attente *f*; **to live up to sb's ~s** répondre à l'attente de qn; **I don't want to raise their ~s** je ne veux pas trop leur promettre.

expedient *adj* **1** (appropriate) opportun; **2** (advantageous) politique.

expedition *n* expédition *f*; **to go on an ~** partir en expédition.

expel *vtr* **1** expulser [*alien, diplomat*]; renvoyer [*pupil*]; **2** expulser [*air*].

expenditure *n* **1** (amount spent) dépenses *fpl*; **public ~** la dépense publique; **2** (of energy, time, money) dépense *f*.

expense I *n* **1** frais *mpl*; dépense *f*; **at one's own ~** à ses propres frais; **to go to great ~** dépenser beaucoup d'argent (**to do** pour faire); **to spare no ~** ne pas regarder à la dépense; **a wedding is a big ~** un mariage revient cher; **2 at the ~ of** au détriment de [*health, public, safety*]; **at sb's ~** [*laugh, joke*] aux dépens de qn.
II **expenses** *n pl* frais *mpl*.

expensive *adj* [*area, house, car, garment*] cher/chère; [*holiday, mistake*] coûteux/-euse; [*taste*] de luxe.

experience I *n* expérience *f*; **management ~** expérience *f* de la gestion; **from my own ~** d'après mon expérience; **to know from ~** savoir d'expérience; **the ~ of a lifetime** une expérience unique.
II *vtr* connaître [*loss, problem*]; éprouver [*emotion*].

experienced *adj* (gen) expérimenté; [*eye*] entraîné.

experiment I *n* expérience *f* (**in** en; **on** sur); **to carry out an ~** faire une expérience.
II *vi* expérimenter, faire des essais.

experimental *adj* expérimental.

expert I *n* spécialiste *mf* (**in** en, de), expert *m* (**in** en); **computer ~** spécialiste *mf* en informatique.
II *adj* [*knowledge*] spécialisé; [*opinion, advice*] autorisé; [*witness*] expert; [*eye*] exercé; **an ~ cook** un cordon bleu.

expertise *n* compétences *fpl*; (very specialized) expertise *f* (**in** dans le domaine de).

expiration date *n* (US) = **expiry date**.

expire *vi* [*deadline, offer*] expirer; [*period*] arriver à terme; **my passport has ~d** mon passeport est périmé.

expiry date *n* (GB) (of credit card, permit) date *f* d'expiration; (of contract) terme *m*.

explain *vtr* expliquer (**that** que; **to** à); **I can't ~** je ne peux pas dire pourquoi.

explanation *n* explication *f* (**of** de; **for** à).

explanatory *adj* explicatif/-ive.

explicit *adj* (gen) explicite; [*declaration, denial*] formel/-elle; [*aim*] avoué.

explode I *vtr* **1** faire exploser [*bomb*]; **2** pulvériser [*theory, rumour, myth*].
II *vi* (gen) exploser; [*boiler, building, ship*] sauter.

exploit I *n* exploit *m*.
II *vtr* exploiter.

exploitation *n* exploitation *f*.

explore I *vtr* explorer.
II *vi* **to go exploring** partir en exploration.

explorer *n* explorateur/-trice *m/f*.

explosion *n* explosion *f*; **to hear an ~** entendre une détonation.

explosive I *n* explosif *m*.
II *adj* [*device, force*] explosif/-ive; [*substance*] explosible.

export I *n* (process) exportation *f* (**of** de); (product) produit *m* d'exportation.
II *vtr* exporter; **to ~ sth to France/Japan** exporter qch en France/au Japon.
III *vi* exporter (**to** vers).

exporter *n* exportateur/-trice *m/f* (**of** de).

expose I *vtr* **1** exposer (**to** à); **2** (make public) révéler [*identity*]; dénoncer [*injustice, person, scandal*].
II *v refl* **to ~ oneself** commettre un outrage à la pudeur.

exposure *n* **1** (of secret, crime) révélation *f*; **to fear ~** craindre d'être démasqué; **2** (to light, sun, radiation) exposition *f* (**to** à); **3 to die of ~** mourir de froid; **4** (also **~ time**) temps *m* de pose; **5** (picture) pose *f*; **a 24 ~ film** une pellicule de 24 poses.

express I *n* rapide *m*.
II *adj* [*letter, parcel*] exprès; [*delivery, train*] rapide.
III *adv* **to send sth ~** envoyer qch en exprès.
IV *vtr* exprimer; **to ~ oneself** s'exprimer (**in** en; **through** à travers).

expression *n* expression *f*; **as an ~ of** en témoignage de.

expressionless *adj* [*eyes, face*] inexpressif/-ive; [*voice*] monocorde; [*playing*] plat.

expressive *adj* expressif/-ive.

exquisite *adj* exquis.

extend I *vtr* **1** agrandir [*house*]; prolonger [*runway*]; élargir [*range*]; **2** prolonger [*visit, visa, show*]; proroger [*loan*]; **3** étendre [*arm, leg*]; tendre [*hand*].
II *vi* s'étendre (**as far as** jusqu'à; **beyond** au-delà de; **from** de).

extension *n* **1** (on cable, table) rallonge *f*; (of road) prolongement *m*; (to house) addition *f*; **2** (phone) poste *m* supplémentaire; **~ (number)** (numéro *m* de) poste *m*; **3** (of deadline) délai *m* supplémentaire.

extension: **~ ladder** *n* échelle *f* coulissante; **~ lead** *n* rallonge *f*.

extensive *adj* **1** [*network, programme*] vaste (*before n*); [*list*] long/longue (*before n*); [*tests*] approfondi; [*changes*] important; [*training*] complet; **2** [*investment*] considérable; [*damage, loss*] grave, considérable; [*burns*] grave.

extent *n* **1** étendue *f*; (of damage) ampleur *f*; **2** mesure *f*; **to what ~...?** dans quelle mesure...?; **to a certain/great ~** dans une certaine/large mesure; **to the ~ that** dans la mesure où.

exterior I *n* extérieur *m* (**of** de); **on the ~** à l'extérieur.
II *adj* extérieur (**to** à).

exterminate *vtr* éliminer [*vermin*]; exterminer [*people, race*].

external *adj* (gen) extérieur (**to** à); [*surface, injury, examiner*] externe; **'for ~ use only'** 'usage externe'.

extinct *adj* [*species*] disparu; [*volcano*] éteint; **to become ~** [*species, animal, plant*] disparaître; [*volcano*] s'éteindre.

extinction *n* extinction *f*.

extinguish *vtr* éteindre [*fire, cigarette*]; anéantir [*hope*].

extinguisher *n* extincteur *m*.

extra I *n* **1** (charge) supplément *m*; **there are no hidden ~s** il n'y a pas de faux frais *mpl*; **2** (feature) option *f*; **the sunroof is an ~** le toit ouvrant est en option; **3** (actor) figurant/-e *m/f*.
II *adj* supplémentaire; **an ~ £1,000** 1 000 livres de plus; **postage is ~** les frais de port sont en supplément or en sus.
III *adv* **~ careful** encore plus prudent (que d'habitude); **you have to pay ~** il faut payer un supplément; **that model costs ~** ce modèle coûte plus cher.

extra charge *n* supplément *m*; **at no ~** sans supplément.

extract I *n* extrait *m* (**from** de).
II *vtr* **1** extraire (**from** de); **2** arracher [*promise*] (**from** à).

extraordinary *adj* extraordinaire; **to go to ~ lengths to do sth** se donner un mal extraordinaire pour faire qch; **there's nothing ~ about it** cela n'a rien d'extraordinaire; **I**

find it ~ that so few people replied je trouve extraordinaire que si peu de gens aient répondu.

extra: **~-special** *adj* exceptionnel/-elle; **~-strong** *adj* [*coffee*] très serré.

extra time *n* (Sport) prolongation *f*; **to go into** or **play ~** jouer les prolongations.

extravagance *n* **1** (trait) prodigalité *f*; **2** (luxury) luxe *m*.

extravagant *adj* **1** [*person*] dépensier/-ière; [*way of life*] dispendieux/-ieuse; **to be ~ with sth** gaspiller qch; **2** (luxurious) luxueux/-euse.

extreme I *n* extrême *m*; **to go from one ~ to the other** passer d'un extrême à l'autre; **to take/carry sth to ~s** pousser/porter qch à l'extrême; **to go to ~s** pousser les choses à l'extrême.

II *adj* (gen) extrême; [*view, measure, reaction*] extrémiste; **on the ~ right/left** à l'extrême droite/gauche.

extremely *adv* extrêmement; **he did ~ well** il s'est vraiment bien débrouillé.

extrovert *n, adj* extraverti/-e (*m/f*).

ex-wife *n* ex-femme *f*.

eye ▶ 523 **I** *n* **1** œil *m*; **with blue ~s** aux yeux bleus; **to open/close one's ~s** ouvrir/fermer les yeux; **in front of** or **before your (very) ~s** sous vos yeux; **to see sth with one's own ~s** voir qch de ses propres yeux; **to keep an ~ on sth/sb** surveiller qch/qn; **to have one's ~ on** (watch) surveiller [*person, property*]; (want) avoir envie de [*house*]; viser [*job*]; **to catch sb's ~** attirer l'attention de qn; **as far as the ~ can see** à perte de vue; **she couldn't take her ~s off him** elle ne le quittait pas des yeux; **in the ~s of the law** aux yeux de la loi; **in his ~s...** à ses yeux...; **to have an ~ for** avoir le sens de [*detail, colour*]; **2** (of needle) chas *m*.

II *vtr* regarder.

IDIOMS **an ~ for an ~** œil pour œil; **to make ~s at sb** faire les yeux doux à qn; **to see ~ to ~ with sb (about sth)** partager le point de vue de qn (au sujet de qch).

■ **eye up**°: **~ [sb] up** lorgner°, reluquer°.

eyeball *n* globe *m* oculaire.

eyebrow *n* sourcil *m*; **to raise one's** or **an ~** (in surprise) hausser les sourcils; (in disapproval) froncer les sourcils.

eye: **~brow pencil** *n* crayon *m* à sourcils; **~-catching** *adj* [*design, poster*] attrayant; [*advertisement, headline*] accrocheur/-euse.

eye contact *n* échange *m* de regards; **to make ~ with sb** croiser le regard de qn.

eye: **~drops** *n pl* gouttes *fpl* pour les yeux; **~glasses** *n pl* (US) lunettes *fpl* (de vue); **~lash** *n* cil *m*; **~lid** *n* paupière *f*; **~ make-up** *n* maquillage *m* pour les yeux; **~shade** *n* visière *f*; **~ shadow** *n* fard *m* à paupières; **~sight** *n* vue *f*; **~ strain** *n* fatigue *f* oculaire; **~ test** *n* examen *m* de la vue; **~witness** *n* témoin *m* oculaire.

f, **F** *n* f, F *m*.

fa *n* (Mus) fa *m*.

fable *n* fable *f*.

fabric *n* **1** (cloth) tissu *m*; **2** (of building) structure *f*; (basis) **the ~ of society** le tissu social.

fabricate *vtr* **1** inventer [qch] de toutes pièces [*story, evidence*]; **2** fabriquer [*document*].

fabulous **I** *adj* **1** fabuleux/-euse; **2**° (wonderful) sensationnel/-elle°.
II° *excl* génial!

façade, **facade** *n* façade *f* (**of** de).

face **I** *n* **1** (of person) visage *m*, figure *f*; (of animal) face *f*; **to slam the door/laugh in sb's ~** claquer la porte/rire au nez de qn; **to be ~ up/down** [*person*] être sur le dos/ventre; **to pull** or **make a ~** faire une grimace; (in disgust) faire la grimace; **2** (outward appearance) **to change the ~ of** changer le visage de [*industry*]; **the changing ~ of Europe** la face changeante de l'Europe; **3** **to lose ~** perdre la face; **to save ~** sauver la face; **4** (of clock, watch) cadran *m*; (of coin) côté *m*; (of planet) surface *f*; (of cliff, mountain) face *f*; (of playing card) face *f*; **~ up/down** à l'endroit/l'envers.
II *vtr* **1** (look towards) [*person*] faire face à; [*building, room*] donner sur; [*photo, diagram*] être face à [*page*]; **to ~ north/south** [*person*] regarder au nord/sud; [*building*] être orienté au nord/sud; **2** se trouver face à [*challenge, crisis*]; se voir contraint de payer [*fine*]; se trouver menacé de [*defeat, redundancy*]; être contraint de faire [*choice*]; affronter [*rival, team*]; **he could ~ a fine/prison** il risque une amende/la prison; **to be ~d with** se trouver confronté à [*problem, decision*]; **3** (acknowledge) **~ the facts, you're finished!** regarde la réalité en face, tu es fini!; **let's ~ it, nobody's perfect** admettons-le, personne n'est parfait; **4** (tolerate prospect) **I can't ~ doing** je n'ai pas le courage de faire; **he couldn't ~ the thought of eating** l'idée de manger lui était insupportable; **5** revêtir [*façade, wall*] (**with** de).
III *vi* **to ~ towards** [*person, chair*] être tourné vers; [*building, house*] être en face de; **to ~ forward** regarder devant soi; **to ~ backwards** [*person*] tourner le dos; **to be facing forward** [*person*] être de face.
IV in the face of *phr* **1** en dépit de [*difficulties*]; **2** face à, devant [*opposition, enemy, danger*].
■ **face up to**: ¶ **~ up to [sth]** faire face à [*problem, responsibilities*]; ¶ **~ up to [sb]** affronter.

face-lift *n* lifting *m*; **to have a ~** se faire faire un lifting; **to give [sth] a ~** rénover [*building*]; réaménager [*town centre*].

facetious *adj* [*remark*] facétieux/-ieuse; [*person*] farceur/-euse.

face to face *adv* [*be seated*] face à face; **to come ~ with** se retrouver face à; **to meet sb ~** rencontrer qn en face-à-face; **to talk to sb ~** parler à qn en personne.

face value *n* (of coin) valeur *f* nominale; **to take [sth] at ~** prendre [qch] au pied de la lettre [*claim*]; prendre [qch] pour argent comptant [*compliment*]; **to take sb at ~** juger qn sur les apparences.

facial **I** *n* soin *m* (complet) du visage.
II *adj* [*hair*] du visage; [*muscle*] facial; **~ expression** expression *f*.

facile *adj* [*assumption, suggestion*] spécieux/-ieuse, facile.

facilitate *vtr* faciliter [*progress, talks*]; favoriser [*development*].

facility **I** *n* **1** (building) complexe *m*, installation *f*; **2** (ease) facilité *f*; **3** (ability) talent *m*; **4** (feature) fonction *f*; **a pause ~** une fonction pause.
II facilities *n pl* (equipment) équipement *m*; (infrastructure) infrastructure *f*; **facilities for the disabled** installations *fpl* pour les handicapés; **to have cooking and washing facilities** être équipé d'une cuisine et d'une laverie; **parking facilities** parking *m*.

facsimile *n* (gen) fac-similé *m*; (sculpture) reproduction *f*.

fact *n* fait *m*; **~s and figures** les faits et les chiffres; **to know for a ~ that** savoir de source sûre que; **owing** or **due to the ~ that** étant donné que; **in ~, as a matter of ~** en fait; **the ~ remains (that)** toujours est-il que; **the story was presented as ~** l'histoire a été présentée comme véridique; **to be based on ~** être fondé sur des faits réels.
IDIOMS **to know the ~s of life** savoir comment les enfants viennent au monde; **the (hard) ~s of life** les réalités de la vie.

fact-finding *adj* [*mission, tour, trip*] d'information.

faction *n* faction *f*.

factor *n* facteur *m*; **common ~** point *m* commun; (in mathematics) facteur commun; **protection ~** indice *m* de protection.

factory *n* usine *f*.

factory worker ▶ 805 *n* ouvrier/-ière *m/f* (d'usine).

fact sheet *n* bulletin *m* d'informations.

factual *adj* [*evidence*] factuel/-elle; [*account, description*] basé sur les faits.

faculty *n* **1** (ability) faculté *f* (**of** de; **for** de; **for doing** de faire); **2** (GB Univ) faculté *f*; **3** (US Univ, Sch) (staff) corps *m* enseignant.

fad *n* **1** (craze) engouement *m* (**for** pour); **2** (whim) (petite) manie *f*.

fade **I** *vtr* décolorer [*curtains*].
II *vi* [*fabric*] se décolorer, se défraîchir;

[*colour*] passer; [*lettering*] s'effacer; [*flowers*] se faner; [*image*] s'estomper; [*sound*] s'affaiblir; [*smile, memory*] s'effacer; [*interest, excitement*] s'évanouir; [*hearing, light*] baisser; **to ~ in the wash** [*garment*] se décolorer au lavage; [*colour*] passer au lavage.

■ **fade away** [*sound*] s'éteindre; [*sick person*] dépérir.

faded *adj* [*clothing*] décoloré; [*colour, glory*] passé; [*jeans*] délavé; [*image*] estompé; [*photo*] jauni; [*flower, beauty*] fané; [*lettering*] à demi effacé.

faeces, feces (US) *n pl* matières *fpl* fécales.

fail I *n* (in exam) échec *m*.
II *vtr* **1** échouer à [*exam, driving test*]; échouer en [*subject*]; coller○ [*candidate, pupil*]; **2** (omit) **to ~ to do** manquer de faire; **to ~ to mention that**... omettre de signaler que...; **3** (be unable) **to ~ to do** ne pas réussir à faire; **4** [*person*] laisser tomber [*friend*]; [*courage*] manquer à [*person*]; [*memory*] faire défaut à [*person*].
III *vi* **1** [*exam candidate, attempt, plan*] échouer; [*crop*] être mauvais; **if all else ~s** en dernier recours; **2** [*eyesight, hearing, light*] baisser; [*health*] décliner; **3** [*brakes*] lâcher; [*power*] être coupé; [*heart*] lâcher.
IV **without fail** *phr* [*arrive, do*] sans faute; [*happen*] à coup sûr.

failing I *n* défaut *m*.
II *prep* **~ that, ~ this** sinon.

fail-safe *adj* [*device, system*] à sécurité intégrée.

failure *n* **1** (lack of success) échec *m* (**in** à); (of business) faillite *f*; **his ~ to understand the problem** son incapacité *f* à comprendre le problème; **2** (person) raté/-e○ *m/f*; (venture or event) échec *m*; **he was a ~ as a teacher** comme professeur il ne valait rien; **3** (of engine, machine) panne *f*; (of liver, kidney) défaillance *f*; **power ~** panne de courant; **4** (omission) **~ to comply with the rules** non-respect *m* de la réglementation; **~ to pay** non-paiement *m*.

faint I *n* évanouissement *m*.
II *adj* **1** [*smell, accent, breeze*] léger/-ère; [*sound, voice, protest*] faible; [*markings*] à peine visible; [*recollection*] vague; **I haven't the ~est idea** je n'en ai pas la moindre idée; **2** (dizzy) **to feel ~** se sentir mal, défaillir.
III *vi* s'évanouir (**from** sous l'effet de).

fair I *n* (funfair, market) foire *f*; (for charity) kermesse *f*; **trade ~** foire commerciale.
II *adj* **1** (just, reasonable) [*arrangement, person, trial, wage*] équitable (**to** envers); [*comment, decision, point*] juste; **it's only ~ that she should be first** ce n'est que justice qu'elle soit la première; **to be ~, he did try to pay** il faut dire à sa décharge qu'il a essayé de payer; **it isn't ~** ce n'est pas juste; **2** (moderately good) [*chance, condition, performance*] assez bon/bonne; **3 a ~ number of** un bon nombre de; **the house was a ~ size** la maison était de bonne taille; **4** [*weather*] beau/belle (*before n*); [*wind*] favorable; **5** [*hair*] blond; [*complexion*] clair; **6 with her own ~ hands** de ses belles mains; **the ~ sex** le beau sexe.
III *adv* [*play*] franc jeu.
IDIOMS **to win ~ and square** remporter une victoire indiscutable.

fair: **~ground** *n* champ *m* de foire; **~-haired** *adj* blond.

fairly *adv* **1** (quite, rather) assez; [*sure*] pratiquement; **2** (justly) [*obtain, win*] honnêtement.

fair-minded *adj* impartial.

fairness *n* **1** (of person) équité *f*; (of judgment) impartialité *f*; **in all ~** en toute justice; **2** (of complexion) blancheur *f*; (of hair) blondeur *f*.

fair trade *n* **1** commerce *m* loyal; **2** (US) régime *m* des prix imposés.

fairy *n* fée *f*.

fairy story, fairy tale *n* conte *m* de fées.

faith *n* **1** (confidence) confiance *f*; **I have no ~ in her** elle ne m'inspire pas confiance; **in good ~** en toute bonne foi; **2** (belief) foi *f* (**in** en); **the Muslim ~** la foi musulmane.

faithful I *n* **the ~** les fidèles *mpl*.
II *adj* fidèle (**to** à).

faithfully *adv* fidèlement; **yours ~** veuillez agréer, Monsieur/Madame, mes/nos salutations distinguées.

faithfulness *n* fidélité *f*.

fake I *n* **1** (jewel, work of art, note) faux *m*; **2** (person) imposteur *m*.
II *adj* [*fur, gem, passport*] faux/fausse (*before n*); [*smile*] feint; **it's ~ wood** c'est de l'imitation bois.
III *vtr* contrefaire [*signature, document*]; falsifier [*results*]; feindre [*emotion, illness*].

falcon *n* faucon *m*.

fall I *n* **1** (gen) chute *f* (**from** de); (in wrestling) tombé *m*; (of axe, hammer, dice) coup *m*; **a heavy ~ of rain** une grosse averse; **to have a ~** faire une chute, tomber; **2** (decrease) baisse *f* (**in** de); (more drastic) chute *f* (**in** de); **a ~ in value** une dépréciation; **3** (in pitch) descente *f*; **4** (of government) chute *f*; (of monarchy) renversement *m*; **5** (US) (autumn) automne *m*.
II **falls** *n pl* chutes *fpl*.
III *vi* **1** tomber; **to ~ 10 metres** tomber de 10 mètres; **to ~ from** or **out of** tomber de [*boat, nest, bag, hands*]; **to ~ off** or **from** tomber de [*chair, table, roof, bike, wall*]; **to ~ on** tomber sur [*person*]; **to ~ in** or **into** tomber dans [*bath, river*]; **to ~ down** tomber dans [*hole, stairs*]; **to ~ under** tomber sous [*table*]; passer sous [*bus, train*]; **to ~ through** passer à travers [*ceiling, hole*]; **to ~ on** or **to the floor** or **the ground** tomber par terre; **to ~ into bed** se laisser tomber sur son lit; **to ~ at sb's feet** se jeter aux pieds de qn; **to ~ from power** tomber; **to ~ to** tomber aux mains de [*enemy*]; **the seat fell to Labour** le siège a été perdu au profit des travaillistes; **2** [*quality, standard, level*] diminuer; [*temperature, price, production, number*] baisser (**by** de); **to ~ to** descendre à; **to ~ from** descendre de; **to ~ below zero/5%** descendre au-dessous de zéro/5%; **3** [*night, gaze*] tomber (**on** sur); [*blame*] retomber (**on** sur); [*shadow*] se projeter (**over** sur); **suspicion fell on her husband** les soupçons se sont portés sur son mari; **4** (occur)

[*stress*] tomber (**on** sur); **Christmas ~s on a Monday** Noël tombe un lundi.
■ **fall apart** [*bike, table*] être délabré; [*shoes*] être usé; [*car, house*] tomber en ruine.
■ **fall back** reculer.
■ **fall back on**: **~ back on [sth]** avoir recours à [*savings, parents*]; **to have something to ~ back on** avoir quelque chose sur quoi se rabattre.
■ **fall behind**: **~ behind** prendre du retard; **to ~ behind with** (GB) or **in** (US) prendre du retard dans [*work, project*]; être en retard pour [*payments, rent*].
■ **fall down 1** [*person, poster*] tomber; [*tent, scaffolding*] s'effondrer; **2** (GB) [*argument, comparison*] faiblir; **to ~ down on** échouer à cause de [*detail*].
■ **fall for**: ¶ **~ for [sth]** se laisser prendre à [*trick, story*]; ¶ **~ for [sb]** tomber amoureux/-euse de.
■ **fall in 1** [*walls, roof*] s'écrouler, s'effondrer; **2** [*soldier*] rentrer dans les rangs; [*soldiers*] former les rangs.
■ **fall in with**: **~ in with [sth/sb] 1** faire la connaissance de [*group*]; **2** se conformer à [*plans, action*].
■ **fall off 1** [*person, hat, label*] tomber; **2** [*attendance, sales, output*] diminuer; [*quality*] baisser; [*support*] retomber.
■ **fall on**: ¶ **~ on [sth]** se jeter sur [*food, treasure*]; ¶ **~ on [sb]** tomber sur [*person*].
■ **fall open** [*book*] tomber ouvert; [*robe*] s'entrebâiller.
■ **fall out 1** tomber; **his hair is ~ing out** il perd ses cheveux; **2**○ (quarrel) se brouiller (**over** à propos de; **with** avec).
■ **fall over**: ¶ **~ over** [*person*] tomber (par terre); [*object*] se renverser; ¶ **~ over [sth]** trébucher sur [*object*].
■ **fall through** [*plans, deal*] échouer.

fallacy *n* (belief) erreur *f*; (argument) faux raisonnement *m*.

fallible *adj* faillible.

false *adj* faux/fausse; **a ~ alarm** une fausse alerte.

false: **~ alarm** *n* fausse alerte *f*; **~ bottom** *n* (in bag, box) double fond *m*.

falsely *adv* **1** (wrongly) faussement; (mistakenly) à tort; **2** [*smile, laugh*] avec affectation.

false teeth *n pl* dentier *m*.

falsify *vtr* falsifier [*documents, accounts*]; déformer [*facts*].

falsity *n* fausseté *f*.

falter *vi* **1** [*economy*] fléchir; [*person, courage*] faiblir; **2** (when speaking) [*person*] bafouiller; [*voice*] trembloter; **3** (when walking) [*person*] chanceler; [*footstep*] hésiter.

fame *n* renommée *f* (**as** en tant que); **~ and fortune** la gloire et la fortune.

familiar *adj* (gen) familier/-ière (**to** à); (customary) habituel; **her face looked ~ to me** son visage m'était familier; **that name sounds ~** ce nom me dit quelque chose; **it's a ~ story** c'est un scénario connu; **to be ~ with sth** connaître qch; **to be too ~ with sb** être trop familier avec qn.

familiarity *n* (gen) familiarité *f* (**with** avec); (of surroundings, place) caractère *m* familier.

familiarize I *vtr* **to ~ sb with** familiariser qn avec [*job, procedure*]; habituer qn à [*environment, person*].
II *v refl* **to ~ oneself with** se familiariser avec [*system, work*]; s'habituer à [*person, place*].

family *n* famille *f*; **to run in the ~** tenir de famille; **to be one of the ~** faire partie de la famille; **to start a ~** avoir un (premier) enfant.

family: **~ man** *n* bon père *m* de famille; **~ name** *n* nom *m* de famille; **~ planning** *n* planning *m* familial; **~ tree** *n* arbre *m* généalogique.

famine *n* famine *f*.

famous *adj* (gen) célèbre (**for** pour); [*school, university*] réputé (**for** pour).

fan I *n* **1** (of jazz) mordu/-e○ *m/f*; (of star, actor) fan○ *mf*; (Sport) supporter *m*; **2** (for cooling) (mechanical) ventilateur *m*; (hand-held) éventail *m*.
II *vtr* **to ~ one's face** s'éventer le visage.
■ **fan out**: ¶ **~ out** [*police, troops*] se déployer (en éventail); ¶ **~ [sth] out**, **~ out [sth]** ouvrir [qch] en éventail [*cards, papers*].

fanatic *n* fanatique *mf*.

fanatical *adj* fanatique.

fanaticism *n* fanatisme *m*.

fan belt *n* courroie *f* de ventilateur.

fancy I *n* **1** (liking) **to catch** or **take sb's ~** [*object*] faire envie à qn; **to take a ~ to sb** s'attacher à qn; (sexually) (GB) s'enticher de qn; **2** (whim) caprice *m*; **as/when the ~ takes me** comme/quand ça me prend; **3** (fantasy) imagination *f*; **a flight of ~** une lubie.
II *adj* [*equipment*] sophistiqué; [*food, hotel, restaurant*] de luxe; [*paper, box*] fantaisie *inv*; [*clothes*] chic.
III *vtr* **1**○ (want) avoir (bien) envie de [*food, drink, object*]; **what do you ~ for lunch?** qu'est-ce qui te plairait pour le déjeuner?; **I don't ~ the idea of sharing a flat** l'idée de partager un appartement ne me dit rien; **2**○ (GB) **she fancies him** elle s'est entichée de lui; **3 ~ seeing you here**○! tiens donc, toi ici?; **4** (Sport) voir [qn/qch] gagnant [*athlete, horse*].
IV○ *v refl* **he fancies himself** il ne se prend pas pour rien; **he fancies himself as James Bond** il se prend pour James Bond.

fancy dress I *n* (GB) déguisement *m*; **in ~** déguisé.
II (also **fancy-dress**) *noun modifier* [*party*] costumé; [*competition*] de déguisement.

fang *n* (of dog, wolf) croc *m*; (of snake) crochet *m* (à venin).

fan: **~ heater** *n* radiateur *m* soufflant; **~ mail** *n* lettres *fpl* envoyées par des admirateurs.

fantasize I *vtr* **to ~ that** rêver que.
II *vi* fantasmer (**about** sur); **to ~ about doing** rêver de faire.

fantastic *adj* **1**○ (wonderful) merveilleux, super○; **2** (unrealistic) [*story*] invraisemblable; **3**○

(huge) [*profit*] fabuleux/-euse; [*speed, increase*] vertigineux/-euse; **4** (magical) fantastique.

fantasy *n* **1** rêve *m*; (in psychology) fantasme *m*; **2** (genre) fantastique *m*.

far I *adv* **1** (in space) loin; **have you come ~?** est-ce que vous venez de loin?; **is it ~ to York?** est-ce que York est loin d'ici?; **~ off, ~ away** au loin; **how ~ is it to Leeds?** combien y a-t-il (de kilomètres) jusqu'à Leeds?; **how ~ is Glasgow from London?** Glasgow est à quelle distance de Londres?; **as ~ as** jusqu'à; **2** (in time) **as ~ back as 1965** déjà en 1965; **as ~ back as he can remember** d'aussi loin qu'il s'en souvienne; **the holidays are not ~ off** c'est bientôt les vacances; **he's not ~ off 70** il n'a pas loin de 70 ans; **3** (very much) bien; **~ better** bien mieux; **~ too fast** bien trop vite; **~ too much money** bien trop d'argent; **~ more** bien plus; **~ above the average** bien au-dessus de la moyenne; **4 how ~ have they got?** où en sont-ils?; **as** or **so ~ as we can, as** or **so ~ as possible** autant que possible, dans la mesure du possible; **as** or **so ~ as we know** pour autant que nous le sachions; **as** or **so ~ as I am concerned** quant à moi; **5 to go too ~** aller trop loin; **she carried the joke too ~** elle a poussé la plaisanterie un peu loin; **to push sb too ~** pousser qn à bout.
II *adj* **1** (remote) **the ~ north/south (of)** l'extrême nord/sud (de); **the ~ east/west (of)** tout à fait à l'est/l'ouest (de); **2** (further away, other) autre; **at the ~ end of the room** à l'autre bout de la pièce; **on the ~ side of the wall** de l'autre côté du mur; **3** (of political spectrum) **the ~ right/left** l'extrême droite/gauche.
III **by far** *phr* de loin.
IV **far and away** *phr* de loin.
V **far from** *phr* loin de; **~ from satisfied** loin d'être satisfait.
VI **so far** *phr* **1** (up till now) jusqu'ici, jusqu'à présent; **so ~, so good** pour l'instant tout va bien; **2** (up to a point) **they will only compromise so ~** ils sont prêts à transiger jusqu'à un certain point seulement; **you can only trust him so ~** tu ne peux pas lui faire entièrement confiance.
IDIOMS **not to be ~ off** or **out** or **wrong** ne pas être loin du compte; **~ and wide** partout; **~ be it from me to do** loin de moi l'idée de faire; **to be a ~ cry from** être bien loin de; **she will go ~** elle ira loin; **this wine/food won't go very ~** on ne va pas aller loin avec ce vin/ce qu'on a à manger.

faraway *adj* lointain.

farce *n* farce *f*.

fare *n* **1** (on bus, underground) prix *m* du ticket; (on train, plane) prix du billet; **taxi ~** prix *m* de la course; **child/adult ~** tarif *m* enfants/adultes; **half/full ~** demi-/plein tarif *m*; **return ~** prix *m* d'un aller-retour; **~s are going up** les tarifs augmentent; **2** (taxi passenger) client/-e *m/f* (d'un taxi).

far: **Far East** *pr n* Extrême-Orient *m*; **Far Eastern** *adj* de l'Extrême-Orient.

farewell *n* adieu *m*.

farewell speech *n* discours *m* d'adieu.

far-fetched *adj* tiré par les cheveux°.

farm I *n* ferme *f*; **chicken/pig ~** élevage *m* de poulets/de porcs.
II *noun modifier* [*building, animal*] de ferme.
III *vtr* cultiver, exploiter [*land*].

farmer ▶805 *n* (gen) fermier *m*; (in official terminology) agriculteur *m*; (arable) cultivateur *m*; **pig ~** éleveur *m* de porcs; **~'s wife** fermière *f*.

farming I *n* (profession) agriculture *f*; (of land) exploitation *f*; **sheep ~** élevage *m* de moutons.
II *noun modifier* [*community*] rural; [*method*] de culture; [*subsidy*] à l'agriculture.

far-off *adj* lointain.

far-sighted *adj* **1** (prudent) [*person, policy*] prévoyant; **2** (US) [*person*] presbyte.

farther I *adv* ▶ **further** I 1, 2.
II *adj* ▶ **further** II 2.

farthest *adj, adv* = **furthest**.

fascinate *vtr* (interest) passionner; (stronger) fasciner.

fascinated *adj* (by spectacle) captivé; (by person) fasciné; (by subject) passionné.

fascinating *adj* [*book, discussion*] passionnant; [*person*] fascinant.

fascination *n* **1** (interest) passion *f* (**with, for** pour); **in ~** captivé; (stronger) fasciné; **2** (power) (pouvoir *m* de) fascination *f*.

fascism *n* fascisme *m*.

fascist *n, adj* fasciste (*mf*).

fashion I *n* **1** mode *f* (**for** de); **in ~** à la mode; **out of ~** démodé; **the latest ~** la dernière mode; **to go out of ~** se démoder, passer de mode; **to be all the ~** faire fureur; **2** (manner) façon *f*, manière *f*; **in my own ~** à ma manière; **after a ~** plus ou moins bien.
II *noun modifier* [*accessory, magazine*] de mode.
III **fashions** *n pl* **ladies' ~s** vêtements *mpl* pour femmes; **Paris ~s** la mode parisienne.
IV *vtr* façonner [*clay, wood*] (**into** en); fabriquer [*object*] (**out of, from** de).

fashionable *adj* [*clothes*] à la mode (**among, with** parmi); [*resort, restaurant*] chic *inv* (**among, with** parmi); **it's no longer ~ to smoke** cela ne se fait plus de fumer.

fashion: **~ model** ▶805 *n* mannequin *m*; **~ show** *n* présentation *f* de collection.

fast I *n* jeûne *m*.
II *adj* **1** (speedy) rapide; **a ~ car** une voiture rapide; **a ~ train** un express; **to be a ~ reader/runner** lire/courir vite; **2** (Sport) [*court, pitch, track*] rapide; **a ~ time** un bon temps; **3** (ahead of time) **my watch is ~** ma montre avance; **you're five minutes ~** ta montre avance de cinq minutes; **4 ~ dye** grand teint *m*.
III *adv* **1** vite, rapidement; **how ~ can you type?** tu tapes combien de mots à la minute?; **how ~ can you run?** est-ce que tu cours vite?; **I need help ~** j'ai besoin d'aide tout de suite; **2** [*hold*] ferme; [*stuck*] bel et bien; [*shut*] bien; **to be ~ asleep** dormir à poings fermés.

fasten I *vtr* **1** fermer [*lid, case*]; attacher [*belt, necklace*]; boutonner [*coat*]; boucler [*buckle*]; **2** fixer [*notice, shelf*] (**to** à; **onto** sur); attacher [*lead, rope*] (**to** à).
II *vi* [*box*] se fermer; [*necklace, skirt*] s'attacher.
■ **fasten on**: ¶ **~ on** [*lid, handle*] s'attacher; ¶ **~ [sth] on** attacher [*lid, handle*].

fastener *n* (gen) attache *f*; (hook) agrafe *f*; (clasp) fermoir *m*.

fast food I *n* nourriture *f* de fast-food.
II *noun modifier* [*chain*] de restauration rapide or de fast-food; **a ~ restaurant** un fast-food.

fast-forward I *n* avance *f* rapide.
II *vtr* faire avancer rapidement [*tape*].

fast lane *n* voie *f* de dépassement.

fat I *n* **1** (in diet) matières *fpl* grasses; **animal ~s** graisses *fpl* animales; **2** (on meat) gras *m*; **you can leave the ~** tu peux laisser le gras; **3** (for cooking) (gen) matière *f* grasse; (from meat) graisse *f*; **4** (in body) graisse *f*.
II *adj* **1** [*person, animal, body, bottom*] gros/grosse (*before n*); **to get ~** grossir; **2** [*wallet, envelope*] rebondi; [*file, magazine*] épais/épaisse; **3** [*profit, cheque*] gros/grosse (*before n*).

fatal *adj* [*accident, injury, blow*] mortel/-elle (**to** pour); [*flaw, mistake*] fatal; [*decision*] funeste; [*day, hour*] fatidique; **to be a ~ blow to sb/sth** porter un coup fatal à qn/qch.

fatalist *n* fataliste *mf*.

fatalistic *adj* fataliste.

fatality *n* mort *m*; **road fatalities** accidents *mpl* mortels de la route.

fatally *adv* **1** [*injured, wounded*] mortellement; **2** [*flawed, compromised*] irrémédiablement.

fate *n* sort *m*.

fateful *adj* [*decision*] fatal; [*day*] fatidique.

fat-free *adj* sans matières grasses.

father I *n* père *m*; **like ~ like son** tel père tel fils; **the Our Father** le Notre Père.
II *vtr* engendrer [*child*].

father: **Father Christmas** (GB) *n* le père Noël; **~ figure** *n* image *f* du père; **~hood** *n* paternité *f*; **~-in-law** *n* beau-père *m*.

fatherly *adj* paternel/-elle.

fathom I *n* brasse *f* anglaise (= *1,83 m*).
II *vtr* (also **~ out** GB) comprendre.

fatigue I *n* **1** (of person) épuisement *m*; **2 metal ~** fatigue *f* du métal; **3** (US Mil) corvée *f*.
II **fatigues** *n pl* **1** (uniform) treillis *m*; **2** (duties) corvée *f*.

fatness *n* corpulence *f*.

fatten I *vtr* (also **~ up**) engraisser [*animal*]; faire grossir [*person*].
II *vi* [*animal*] engraisser.

fattening *adj* [*food, drink*] qui fait grossir.

fatty *adj* [*tissue, deposit*] graisseux/-euse; [*food, meat*] gras/grasse.

fatuous *adj* [*comment, smile*] stupide; [*activity*] futile.

faucet *n* (US) robinet *m*.

fault I *n* **1** (flaw) défaut *m* (**in** dans); **structural ~** défaut structurel; **he's always finding ~** il trouve toujours quelque chose à redire; **2** (responsibility) faute *f*; **to be sb's ~**, **to be the ~ of sb** être (de) la faute de qn; **it's his ~ that** c'est sa faute si; **it's my own ~** c'est de ma faute; **whose ~ was it?** à qui la faute?; **3** (in tennis) **~!** faute!; **to serve a ~** faire une faute au service; **4** (in earth) faille *f*.
II *vtr* prendre [qch/qn] en défaut; **it cannot be ~ed** c'est irréprochable.

faulty *adj* [*wiring, machine*] défectueux/-euse; [*logic, argument*] erroné.

faun *n* faune *m*.

fauna *n* faune *f*.

faux pas *n* impair *m*.

favour (GB), **favor** (US) I *n* **1** (kindness) service *m*; **to do sb a ~** rendre service à qn; **as a (special) ~** à titre de service exceptionnel; **to ask a ~ of sb**, **to ask sb a ~** demander un service à qn; **to return a** or **the ~** rendre la pareille (**by doing** en faisant); **2 to be in sb's ~** [*situation*] être avantageux pour qn; [*financial rates, wind*] être favorable à qn; **to have sth in one's ~** avoir qch pour soi; **the plan has a lot in its ~** le projet présente beaucoup d'avantages; **3 to win/lose ~ with sb** s'attirer/perdre les bonnes grâces de qn; **to fall** or **go out of ~** [*idea, method*] passer de mode.
II *vtr* **1** (prefer) être pour [*method, solution*]; être partisan de [*political party, course of action*]; **to ~ sb** montrer une préférence pour qn; (unfairly) accorder un traitement de faveur à qn; **2** (benefit) [*circumstances*] favoriser [*person*]; [*law*] privilégier [*person*].
III **in favour of** *phr* **1** (on the side of) en faveur de; **to be in ~ of sb/sth** être pour qn/qch; **2** (to the advantage of) **to work in sb's ~** avantager qn; **to decide in sb's ~** (gen) donner raison à qn; (Law) donner gain de cause à qn; **3** (out of preference for) [*reject*] au profit de.

favourable (GB), **favorable** (US) *adj* [*conditions, impression, reply*] favorable (**to** à); [*result, sign*] bon/bonne (*before n*).

favourite (GB), **favorite** (US) I *n* **1** (gen) préféré/-e *m/f*; **to be a great ~ with sb** avoir beaucoup de succès auprès de qn; **2** (Sport) favori/-ite *m/f*.
II *adj* préféré, favori/-ite.

favouritism (GB), **favoritism** (US) *n* favoritisme *m*.

fax I *n* **1** (also **~ message**) télécopie *f*, fax *m*; **2** (also **~ machine**) télécopieur *m*, fax *m*.
II *vtr* télécopier, faxer [*document*]; envoyer une télécopie or un fax à [*person*].

fax number *n* numéro *m* de télécopie or de fax.

fear I *n* **1** (fright) peur *f*; **he accepted out of ~** c'est la peur qui l'a fait accepter; **to live** or **go in ~ of one's life** craindre pour sa vie; **2** (apprehension) crainte *f* (**for** pour); **my ~s proved groundless** mes craintes se sont révélées injustifiées; **3** (possibility) **there's no ~ of him** or **his being late** il n'y a pas de danger qu'il soit en retard.
II *vtr* craindre; **it is ~ed (that)** on craint que (+ *subj*); **to ~ the worst** craindre le pire, s'attendre au pire.

III *vi* **to ~ for sth/sb** craindre pour qch/qn.

feasibility *n* **1** (of idea, plan, proposal) faisabilité *f* (**of** de); **the ~ of doing** la possibilité de faire; **2** (of claim, story) vraisemblance *f* (**of** de).

feasible *adj* **1** (possible) [*project*] réalisable; **it is ~ that** il est possible que (+ *subj*); **2** [*excuse, explanation*] plausible.

feast I *n* (sumptuous meal) festin *m*; (religious) fête *f*.
II *vi* se régaler (**on** de).

feat *n* exploit *m*; **it was no mean ~** cela n'a pas été une mince affaire; **a ~ of engineering** une prouesse technologique.

feather *n* plume *f*.

feature I *n* **1** (distinctive characteristic) trait *m*, caractéristique *f*; **a ~ of those times** une caractéristique de cette époque; **2** (aspect) aspect *m*, côté *m*; **to have no redeeming ~s** n'avoir rien pour soi; **3** (of face) trait *m*; **with sharp ~s** aux traits anguleux; **4** (of car, computer, product) accessoire *m*; **built-in safety ~s** équipement *m* de sécurité intégré; **5** (report) (in paper) article *m* de fond (**on** sur); (on TV, radio) reportage *m* (**on** sur).
II *vtr* [*film, magazine*] présenter [*story, photo, star*]; [*advert, poster*] représenter [*person, scene*]; **to be ~d in** figurer dans.
III *vi* **1** (figure) figurer; **2** [*performer*] jouer (**in** dans).

February ▶ **584** *n* février *m*.

federal I Federal *pr n* (US) (historically) (supporter) Fédéraliste *mf*; (soldier) nordiste *m*.
II *adj* [*court, judge, police*] fédéral; **the ~ government** (US) le gouvernement fédéral.

federalist *n, adj* fédéraliste (*mf*).

federally *adv* **1** [*elect, govern*] à un niveau fédéral; **2** (US) [*funded, built*] par le gouvernement fédéral.

federate *vi* se fédérer.

federation *n* fédération *f*.

fed up° *adj* **to be ~** en avoir marre° (**of** de).

fee *n* **1** (for service) honoraires *mpl*; **school ~s** frais *mpl* de scolarité; **2** (for admission) droit *m* d'entrée; (for membership) cotisation *f*.

feeble *adj* (gen) faible; [*argument, excuse*] peu convaincant; [*joke, attempt*] médiocre.

feed I *n* (for animals) ration *f* de nourriture; (for baby) (breast) tétée *f*; (bottle) biberon *m*.
II *vtr* **1** nourrir [*animal, plant, person*] (**on** de); donner à manger à [*pet*]; ravitailler [*army*]; **to ~ a baby** (on breast) donner le sein à un bébé; (on bottle) donner le biberon à un bébé; **2** (supply) alimenter [*machine*]; mettre des pièces dans [*meter*]; fournir [*information*] (**to** à); faire passer [*ball*] (**to** à); **to ~ sth into** mettre or introduire qch dans.
■ **feed up** (GB): **~ [sth/sb] up** bien nourrir [*child, invalid*]; engraisser [*animal*].

feedback *n* **1** (from people) remarques *fpl* (**on** sur; **from** de la part de); **I'd like some ~** j'aimerais avoir vos impressions; **we haven't had any ~** il n'y a pas eu de réactions; **2** (on hi-fi) réaction *f* parasite.

feel I *n* **1** (atmosphere, impression created) atmosphère *f*; **there was a relaxed ~ about it** il régnait une atmosphère détendue; **it has the ~ of a country cottage** cela a l'allure d'une maison de campagne; **2** (sensation to the touch) sensation *f*; **to have an oily ~** être huileux au toucher; **I like the ~ of leather** j'aime le contact du cuir; **3 to have a ~ of sth** tâter qch; **4 to get the ~ of** se faire à [*controls, system*]; **to get the ~ of doing** s'habituer à faire; **5** (flair) don *m* (**for** pour); **to have a ~ for language** bien savoir manier la langue.
II *vtr* **1** éprouver [*affection, desire, pride*]; ressentir [*hostility, obligation, effects*]; **I no longer ~ anything for her** je n'éprouve plus rien pour elle; **the effects will be felt throughout the country** les effets se feront sentir dans tout le pays; **2** (believe) **to ~ (that)** estimer que; **I ~ he's hiding something** j'ai l'impression qu'il cache quelque chose; **3** (physically) sentir [*blow, draught, heat*]; ressentir [*ache, stiffness, effects*]; **she ~s/doesn't ~ the cold** elle est/n'est pas frileuse; **4** (touch) tâter [*washing, cloth*]; palper [*patient, shoulder, parcel*]; **to ~ the weight of sth** soupeser qch; **to ~ one's way** avancer à tâtons; (figurative) tâter le terrain; **5** avoir conscience de [*presence, tension, seriousness*].
III *vi* **1** se sentir [*sad, happy, nervous, safe*]; être [*sure, surprised*]; avoir l'impression d'être [*trapped, betrayed*]; **to ~ afraid/ashamed** avoir peur/honte; **to ~ as if** or **as though** avoir l'impression que; **how do you ~?** que ressens-tu?; **how do you ~ about marriage?** qu'est-ce que tu penses du mariage?; **how does it ~** or **what does it ~ like to be a dad?** qu'est-ce que ça fait d'être papa?; **2** se sentir [*ill, better, tired*]; **to ~ hot/thirsty** avoir chaud/soif; **it felt as if I was floating** j'avais l'impression de flotter; **she isn't ~ing herself today** elle n'est pas dans son assiette aujourd'hui°; **3** (create sensation) être [*cold, smooth*]; avoir l'air [*eerie*]; **the house ~s empty** la maison fait vide; **something doesn't ~ right** il y a quelque chose qui ne va pas; **it ~s like (a) Sunday** on se croirait un dimanche; **4** (want) **to ~ like sth** avoir envie de qch; **I ~ like a drink** je prendrais bien un verre; **I don't ~ like it** je n'en ai pas envie; **5 to ~ (around** or **about) in** fouiller dans [*bag, pocket, drawer*]; **to ~ along** tâtonner le long de [*edge, wall*].
■ **feel for**: ¶ **~ (around) for [sth]** chercher [qch] à tâtons; ¶ **~ for [sb]** plaindre.
■ **feel out**: **~ [sb] out, ~ out [sb]** tester [*person*].
■ **feel up to**: **~ up to (doing) sth** se sentir d'attaque° or assez bien pour (faire) qch.

feeling *n* **1** (emotion) sentiment *m*; **to put one's ~s into words** trouver les mots pour dire ce que l'on ressent; **to spare sb's ~s** ménager qn; **to hurt sb's ~s** blesser qn; **2** (opinion, belief) sentiment *m*; **I have strong ~s about it** c'est quelque chose qui me tient à cœur; **~s are running high** les esprits s'échauffent; **3** (sensitivity) sensibilité *f*; **to speak with great ~** parler avec beaucoup de passion; **4** (impression) impression *f*; **I had a ~ you'd say that** je sentais que tu allais dire ça; **I've got a bad**

~ about this j'ai le pressentiment que cela va mal se passer; **5** (physical sensation) sensation *f*; **a dizzy ~** une sensation de vertige; **6** (instinct) don *m* (**for** pour).

feign *vtr* feindre [*innocence, surprise*]; simuler [*illness, sleep*].

feline *n, adj* félin (*m*).

fell I *n* montagne *f*.
II *vtr* abattre [*tree*]; assommer [*person*].
IDIOMS **in one ~ swoop** d'un seul coup.

fellow I *n* **1**○ (man) type○ *m*, homme *m*; **2** (of society, association) membre *m* (**of** de); **3** (GB) (lecturer) membre *m* (du corps enseignant) d'un collège universitaire; **4** (US) (researcher) universitaire *mf* titulaire d'une bourse de recherche.
II *noun modifier* **her ~ lawyers/teachers** ses collègues avocats/professeurs.

fellowship *n* **1** (companionship) camaraderie *f*; **2** (association) association *f*.

felony *n* crime *m*.

felt *n* (cloth) feutre *m*; (thinner) feutrine *f*.

felt-tip (pen) *n* feutre *m*.

female I *n* **1** (Bot, Zool) femelle *f*; **2** (woman) femme *f*.
II *adj* **1** (Bot, Zool) femelle; **~ rabbit** lapine *f*; **2** (relating to women) [*population, role, trait*] féminin; [*voice*] de femme; **~ student** étudiante *f*; **3** [*plug, socket*] femelle.

feminine *n, adj* féminin (*m*).

femininity *n* féminité *f*.

feminist *n, adj* féministe (*mf*).

fence I *n* **1** clôture *f*; **2** (in showjumping) obstacle *m*; (in horseracing) haie *f*.
II *vtr* clôturer [*area, garden*].
III *vi* **1** (Sport) faire de l'escrime; **2** (be evasive) se dérober.
IDIOMS **to sit on the ~** ne pas prendre position.

fencing ▶ 649 *n* escrime *f*.

fend *vi* **to ~ for oneself** se débrouiller (tout/-e seul/-e).
■ **fend off**: **~ [sb/sth] off, ~ off [sb/sth]** repousser [*attacker*]; parer [*blow*]; écarter [*question*].

fender *n* **1** (for fire) garde-cendre *m*; **2** (US Aut) aile *f*.

fennel *n* fenouil *m*.

fern *n* fougère *f*.

ferocious *adj* [*animal*] féroce; [*attack*] sauvage; [*heat*] accablant.

ferocity *n* férocité *f*.

ferret *n* furet *m*.

ferry I *n* (long-distance) ferry *m*; (over short distances) bac *m*.
II *vtr* transporter [*passenger, goods*].

fertile *adj* [*land, imagination*] fertile; [*human, animal, egg*] fécond.

fertility *n* fertilité *f*, fécondité *f*.

fertilize *vtr* fertiliser [*land*]; féconder [*animal, plant, egg*].

fertilizer *n* engrais *m*.

fervent *adj* [*admirer*] fervent; [*support*] inconditionnel.

fester *vi* [*wound, sore*] suppurer; [*situation*] pourrir; [*feeling*] s'envenimer.

festival *n* (gen) fête *f*; (arts event) festival *m*.

festivity *n* réjouissance *f*.

fetch *vtr* **1** aller chercher; **to ~ sth for sb** aller chercher qch pour qn; **~ him a chair please** apporte-lui une chaise s'il te plait; **~!** (to dog) rapporte!; **2** (bring financially) [*goods*] rapporter; **to ~ a good price** rapporter un bon prix; **these vases can ~ up to £600** le prix de ces vases peut atteindre 600 livres.

fete *n* (church, village) kermesse *f* (paroissiale); **charity ~** fête *f* de bienfaisance.

fetus (US) = **foetus**.

feud I *n* querelle *f* (**with** avec; **between** entre).
II *vi* se quereller (**with** avec; **about** au sujet de).

feudal *adj* féodal.

fever *n* fièvre *f*; **to have a ~** avoir de la fièvre; **gold ~** la fièvre de l'or.

feverish *adj* [*person, eyes*] fiévreux/-euse; [*dreams*] délirant; [*excitement, activity*] fébrile.

few

■ **Note** When *a few* is used as a pronoun and if the sentence does not specify what it refers to, the pronoun *en* (= *of them*) must be added before the verb in French: *there were only a few* = il n'y en avait que quelques-uns/quelques-unes.

I *det* **1** (not many) peu de; **~ visitors/letters** peu de visiteurs/lettres; **one of my ~ pleasures** un de mes rares plaisirs; **the ~ people who knew her** le peu de gens qui la connaissaient; **too ~ women** trop peu de femmes; **with ~ exceptions** à quelques exceptions près; **2** (couple of) **every ~ days** tous les deux ou trois jours; **over the next ~ weeks** (in future) dans les semaines à venir; **these past ~ days** ces derniers jours; **the first ~ weeks** les premières semaines.
II **a few** *det, quantif, pron* **1** (as determiner, quantifier) quelques; **a ~ people/houses** quelques personnes/maisons; **quite a ~ people** pas mal○ de gens, un bon nombre de personnes; **a ~ of the soldiers/countries** quelques soldats/pays; **a ~ of us** un certain nombre d'entre nous; **2** (as pronoun) quelques-uns/quelques-unes; **I would like a ~ more** j'en voudrais quelques-uns/quelques-unes de plus; **I only need a ~** il ne m'en faut que quelques-uns/quelques-unes.
III *pron, quantif* peu; **~ of us succeeded** peu d'entre nous ont réussi; **there are so ~ of them that** il y en a tellement peu que; **the ~ who voted for him** les rares personnes qui ont voté pour lui.
IDIOMS **they are ~ and far between** ils sont rarissimes.

fewer I *det* moins de; **~ and ~ pupils** de moins en moins d'élèves.
II *pron* moins; **~ than 50 people** moins de 50 personnes; **no ~ than** pas moins de; **they were ~ than before** ils étaient moins nombreux qu'avant.

fewest I *det* le moins de.
II *pron* le moins.

fiancé *n* fiancé *m*.

fiancée *n* fiancée *f*.

fibre (GB), **fiber** (US) *n* **1** (strand) (of thread, wood) fibre *f*; **2** (material) fibre *f*; **3** (in diet) fibres *fpl*; **a high ~ diet** une alimentation riche en fibres.

fibreglass (GB), **fiberglass** (US) *n* fibres *fpl* de verre.

fickle *adj* [*lover, friend*] inconstant; [*fate, public opinion*] changeant; [*weather*] capricieux/-ieuse.

fiction *n* **1** (genre) le roman; (books) romans *mpl*; **2** (invention) fiction *f*; **they keep up the ~ that** ils font croire à tout le monde que.

fictional *adj* [*character, event*] imaginaire.

fictionalize *vtr* romancer.

fictitious *adj* **1** (false) [*name, address*] fictif/-ive; [*report*] fallacieux/-ieuse; **2** (imaginary) imaginaire.

fiddle I *n* ▶ 753 violon *m*.
II○ *vtr* falsifier [*tax return, figures*].
III *vi* **1** (fidget) **to ~ with sth** tripoter qch; **2** (adjust) **to ~ with** tourner [*knobs, controls*].

fidelity *n* fidélité *f* (**of** de; **to** à).

fidget I *n* **they're real ~s** ils n'arrêtent pas de gigoter○.
II *vi* ne pas tenir en place.

field I *n* **1** (land) champ *m* (**of** de); (sports ground) terrain *m*; **football ~** terrain de football; **2** (area of knowledge) domaine *m* (**of** de); **3** (range) champ *m*; **force ~** champ de force; **~ of fire** (Mil) secteur *m* de tir.
II *noun modifier* **1** [*hospital*] de campagne; **2** [*test, study*] sur le terrain; [*work*] de terrain.
III *vtr* **1** (Sport) réceptionner [*ball*]; **2** faire jouer [*team, player*]; présenter [*candidate*]; **3** répondre à [*questions*].

field day *n* **1** (school trip) sortie *f* (éducative); **2** (US) (sports day) journée *f* sportive.
IDIOMS **to have a ~** [*press, critics*] jubiler; (make money) [*shopkeepers*] faire d'excellentes affaires; **to have a ~ with sth** exploiter qch à fond.

fielder *n* (Sport) homme *m* de champ, défenseur *m*.

field sports *n pl* sports *mpl* de plein air.

fierce *adj* [*animal, expression, person*] féroce; [*battle, storm, hatred*] violent; [*determination, loyalty*] farouche; [*supporter*] fervent; [*criticism, speech*] virulent; [*competition*] acharné; [*flames, heat*] intense.

fiesta *n* fête *f*.

fifteen ▶ 492, 554 *n, pron, det* quinze (*m*) *inv*.

fifteenth ▶ 584, 642 I *n* **1** (in order) quinzième *mf*; **2** (of month) quinze *m inv*.
II *adj, adv* quinzième.

fifth ▶ 584, 642 I *n* **1** (in order) cinquième *mf*; **2** (of month) cinq *m*; **3** (fraction) cinquième *m*; **4** (also **~ gear**) (Aut) cinquième *f*.
II *adj, adv* cinquième.

Fifth Amendment *n* (US Law) cinquième amendement *m*.

fifties ▶ 584, 492 *n pl* **1** (era) **the ~** les années *fpl* cinquante; **2** (age) **to be in one's ~** avoir entre cinquante et soixante ans.

fiftieth I *n* (in order, sequence) cinquantième *mf*.
II *adj, adv* cinquantième.

fifty ▶ 492, 554 *n, pron, det* cinquante (*m*) *inv*.

fifty-fifty I *adj* **to have a ~ chance** avoir une chance sur deux (**of doing** de faire).
II *adv* **to split** or **share sth ~** partager qch moitié-moitié; **to go ~** faire moitié-moitié.

fig *n* figue *f*.

fight I *n* **1** (gen) bagarre *f* (**between** entre; **over** pour); (Mil) bataille *f* (**between** entre; **for** pour); (in boxing) combat *m* (**between** entre); **to get into** or **have a ~ with sb** se bagarrer contre or avec qn; **2** (struggle) lutte *f* (**against** contre; **for** pour; **to do** pour faire); **the ~ for equality/against inflation** la lutte pour l'égalité/contre l'inflation; **3** (argument) dispute *f* (**over** au sujet de; **with** avec); **to have a ~ with sb** se disputer avec qn.
II *vtr* **1** se battre contre [*person*]; **2** lutter contre [*disease, opponent, emotion, proposal*]; combattre [*fire*]; mener [*campaign, war*] (**against** contre); **to ~ one's way through** se frayer un passage dans [*crowd*]; **3** [*candidate*] disputer [*seat, election*]; **4** (Law) défendre [*case, cause*].
III *vi* **1** se battre; **2** (campaign) lutter; **3** (squabble) se quereller (**over** à propos de).
■ **fight back**: ¶ **~ back** se défendre (**against** contre); (emotionally) ne pas se laisser faire; ¶ **~ back [sth]** refréner [*tears, fear, anger*].
■ **fight off**: ¶ **~ off [sb/sth], ~ [sb/sth] off** se libérer de [*attacker*]; vaincre [*troops*]; repousser [*attack*]; ¶ **~ off [sth]** lutter contre [*illness, despair*].

fighter *n* **1** (Sport) boxeur *m*; **2** (determined person) lutteur/-euse *m/f*; **3** (also **~ plane**) avion *m* de chasse.

fighting I *n* (gen) bagarre *f*; (Mil) combat *m*; **~ has broken out** la bataille a éclaté.
II *adj* **1** [*unit, force*] de combat; **2** [*talk*] agressif/-ive.

figment *n* **a ~ of the/of your imagination** un produit de l'imagination/de ton imagination.

fig tree *n* figuier *m*.

figurative *adj* figuré.

figure I *n* **1** chiffre *m*; **a four-/six-~ number** un nombre de quatre/six chiffres; **in double ~s** à deux chiffres; **to have a head for ~s, to be good with ~s** être doué pour le calcul; **2** (person) personnage *m*; **a familiar ~** un personnage familier; **well-known ~** personnalité *f* célèbre; **reclining ~** (in art) figure *f* allongée; **3 father ~** image *f* du père; **authority ~** symbole *m* de l'autorité; **4** (body shape) ligne *f*; **to lose one's ~** prendre de l'embonpoint; **5** (diagram, shape) figure *f*.
II *vi* (appear) figurer (**in** dans).
■ **figure out**: **~ [sth] out** trouver [*answer, reason*]; **to ~ out who/why** arriver à comprendre qui/pourquoi.

figure: **~head** *n* (symbolic leader) représentant/-e *m/f* nominal/-e; (of ship) figure *f* de proue; **~ of speech** *n* figure *f* de rhétorique.

file I *n* **1** (for papers) (gen) dossier *m*; (cardboard) chemise *f*; (ring binder) classeur *m*; (card tray) fichier *m*; **2** (record) dossier *m* (**on** sur); **to be on ~** être classé; **3** (Comput) fichier *m*; **4** (tool) lime *f*; **5 in single ~** en file indienne.
II *vtr* **1** classer [*invoice, letter, record*] (**under** sous); **2** déposer [*application, complaint*] (**with** auprès de); **to ~ a lawsuit (against sb)** intenter or faire un procès (à qn); **3** limer [*wood, metal*]; **to ~ one's nails** se limer les ongles.
III *vi* **they ~d into/out of the classroom** ils sont entrés dans/sortis de la salle l'un après l'autre.

file cabinet (US), **filing cabinet** *n* classeur *m* à tiroirs.

fill I *n* **to eat/drink one's ~** manger/boire tout son content; **to have had one's ~** en avoir assez (**of** de).
II *vtr* **1** remplir [*container, page*] (**with** de); garnir [*cushion, pie, sandwich*] (**with** de); [*dentist*] plomber [*tooth, cavity*]; **tears ~ed his eyes** ses yeux se sont remplis de larmes; **2** (occupy) [*crowd, sound*] remplir [*room, street*]; [*smoke, gas, light, protesters*] envahir [*building, room*]; occuper [*time, day, hours*]; [*emotion, thought*] remplir [*mind, person*] (**with** de); **3** (plug) boucher [*crack, hole, void*] (**with** avec); **4** (fulfil) répondre à [*need*]; **5** (appoint for) [*company, university*] pourvoir [*post, vacancy*]; **6** (perform duties of) [*applicant*] occuper [*post, vacancy*]; **7** [*wind*] gonfler [*sail*].
III *vi* se remplir (**with** de).
IV **-filled** *combining form* rempli de; **smoke-~ed room** pièce remplie de fumée.
■ **fill in**: ¶ **~ in** [*person*] faire un remplacement; **to ~ in for sb** remplacer qn; ¶ **~ in [sth]** passer [*time, hour*]; ¶ **~ in [sth/sb]**, **~ [sth/sb] in 1** remplir [*form, section*]; **2** boucher [*hole, crack*] (**with** avec); **3** donner [*detail, name, date*]; **4** (inform) mettre [qn] au courant (**on** de); **5** (colour in) remplir [*shape, panel*].
■ **fill out**: ¶ **~ out** [*person*] prendre du poids; [*face*] s'arrondir; ¶ **~ out [sth]**, **~ [sth] out** remplir [*form, application*]; faire [*certificate, prescription*].
■ **fill up**: ¶ **~ up** [*bath, theatre, bus*] se remplir (**with** de); **to ~ up on sth** [*person*] se bourrer° de [*bread, sweets*]; ¶ **~ up [sth]**, **~ [sth] up** remplir [*kettle, box, room*] (**with** de); ¶ **~ [sb] up** bourrer° qn (**with** de).

fillet I *n* filet *m*; **~ steak** filet *m* de bœuf.
II *vtr* enlever les arêtes de, fileter [*fish*].

filling I *n* **1** (of sandwich, baked potato) garniture *f*; (for peppers, meat) farce *f*; **2** (for tooth) plombage *m*.
II *adj* [*food, dish*] bourratif/-ive°.

filling station *n* station-service *f*.

film I *n* **1** (movie) film *m*; **to be** or **work in ~s** travailler dans le cinéma; **2** (for snapshots) pellicule *f*; (for movies) film *m*; **3** (layer) pellicule *f*.
II *vtr* [*person*] filmer [*event, programme*]; enregistrer [*action, scene*].
III *vi* [*camera man, crew*] tourner.

filming *n* tournage *m*.

filter I *n* filtre *m*; **sun ~** filtre solaire.
II *vtr* filtrer [*liquid, gas*]; faire passer [*coffee*].
III *vi* **to ~ into** [*light, sound, water*] pénétrer dans [*area*].

filth *n* **1** (dirt) crasse *f*; **2** (vulgarity) obscénités *fpl*; (swearing) grossièretés *fpl*.

filthy *adj* **1** (dirty) crasseux/-euse; (revolting) répugnant; **2** (vulgar) [*language*] ordurier/-ière; [*mind*] mal tourné; **3** (GB) [*look*] noir.

fin *n* (of fish, seal) nageoire *f*; (of shark) aileron *m*.

final I *n* (Sport) finale *f*.
II *adj* **1** (last) dernier/-ière; **2** (definitive) [*decision, invoice*] définitif/-ive; [*result*] final; [*judgment*] irrévocable.

finale *n* finale *f*.

finalist *n* finaliste *mf*.

finalize *vtr* conclure [*contract*]; arrêter [*plan, details*]; faire la dernière mise au point de [*article*]; fixer [*timetable, route*].

finally *adv* **1** (eventually) [*decide, accept, arrive, happen*] finalement, enfin; **2** (lastly) finalement, pour finir; **3** (definitively) [*settle, decide*] définitivement.

finals *n pl* **1** (GB Univ) examens *mpl* de fin d'études; (US Univ) examens *mpl* de fin de semestre; **2** (Sport) (last few games) phase *f* finale; (last game) finale *f*.

finance I *n* **1** (banking, money systems) finance *f*; **2** (funds) fonds *mpl* (**for** pour; **from** auprès de); **3** (credit) crédit *m*.
II *noun modifier* [*minister, ministry*] des Finances; [*committee, director*] financier/-ière.
III *vtr* financer [*project*].

finance company, **finance house** *n* société *f* de financement.

finances *n pl* situation *f* financière.

financial *adj* financier/-ière.

financially *adv* financièrement.

financial year *n* (GB) exercice *m*, année *f* budgétaire.

financier *n* financier *m*.

financing *n* financement *m*.

find I *n* (gen) découverte *f*; (lucky purchase) trouvaille *f*.
II *vtr* **1** trouver; **I can't ~ my keys** je ne trouve pas mes clés; **to ~ one's place (in a book)** retrouver sa page; **to ~ sb doing** trouver qn en train de faire; **to ~ one's way** or **the way** trouver or retrouver son chemin; **to ~ one's way out of** arriver à sortir de [*building, forest, city*]; **to ~ sth for sb, to ~ sb sth** trouver qch pour qn; **I couldn't ~ the time** je n'ai pas eu le temps; **to ~ sb a bore** trouver qn ennuyeux; **to ~ sth easy to do** trouver qch facile à faire; **to ~ it easy to do** trouver facile de faire; **2** (experience) éprouver [*pleasure, satisfaction*] (**in** dans); **3** (reach) **to ~ its mark/its target** toucher son but/sa cible; **to ~ its way to** or **into** arriver dans [*bin, pocket, area*]; **4** (Law) **to ~ that** conclure que; **to ~ sb guilty** déclarer qn coupable; **5** (Comput) rechercher.
III *v refl* **to ~ oneself 1** (discover suddenly) se

retrouver; **to ~ oneself unable to do** se sentir incapable de faire; **to ~ oneself doing** se surprendre à faire; **2** (discover one's vocation) se découvrir.

IDIOMS **to ~ one's feet** [*person*] prendre ses marques; [*company*] prendre pied; **to take sb as one ~s him/her** prendre qn comme il/elle est.

■ **find out**: ¶ **~ out** se renseigner; **if he ever ~s out** si jamais il l'apprend; ¶ **~ out [sth], ~ [sth] out** découvrir [*fact, answer, name, cause, truth*]; ¶ **~ out who/why/where** trouver qui/pourquoi/où; ¶ **~ out that** découvrir or apprendre que; ¶ **~ [sb] out** découvrir [*person*]; ¶ **~ out about [sth] 1** (learn by chance) découvrir [*plan, affair, breakage*]; **2** (research) faire des recherches sur [*subject*].

findings *n pl* conclusions *fpl*.

fine I *n* (penalty) amende *f*; (for traffic offence) contravention *f* (**for** pour).
II *adj* **1** (very good) [*performance, writer, example, quality*] excellent; **2** (satisfactory) [*holiday, meal, arrangement*] bon/bonne; **that's ~** très bien; **'~, thanks'** 'très bien, merci'; **'we'll go now'—'~'** 'on y va maintenant'—'d'accord'; **that's ~ by** or **with me** je n'y vois pas d'inconvénient; **3** (nice) [*weather, morning, day*] beau/belle (*before n*); **it's** or **the weather's ~** il fait beau; **4** (delicate) [*hair, line, features, mist, powder*] fin; [*sieve, net*] à mailles fines; [*china, lace, linen, wine*] fin; **5** (subtle) [*adjustment, detail, distinction*] subtil; **6** (refined) [*lady, clothes*] beau/belle (*before n*); **7** (commendable) [*person*] merveilleux/-euse.
III *adv* [*get along, come along, do*] très bien.
IV *vtr* (penalize) condamner [qn] à une amende [*offender*] (**for** pour; **for doing** pour avoir fait); (for traffic offence) donner une contravention à [*offender*].

fine art *n* beaux-arts *mpl*.
IDIOMS **she's got cheating down to a ~** elle est passée maître dans l'art de tricher.

finely *adv* **1** [*chopped, grated*] finement; **2** [*balanced*] soigneusement.

fine print *n* petits caractères *mpl*.

fine-tooth(ed) comb *n* peigne *m* fin.
IDIOMS **to go over** or **through sth with a ~** passer qch au peigne fin.

fine: **~-tune** *vtr* ajuster; **~ tuning** *n* ajustement *m*.

finger I *n* ▶ **523** doigt *m*; **to point one's ~ at sb/sth** montrer qn/qch du doigt.
II *vtr* toucher [*fruit, goods*]; tripoter○ [*necklace*].
IDIOMS **to keep one's ~s crossed** croiser les doigts (**for sb** pour qn); **to point the ~ at sb** accuser qn; **to slip through sb's ~s** [*opportunity*] passer sous le nez de qn; [*wanted man*] filer entre les doigts de qn.

finger: **~-nail** *n* ongle *m*; **~print** *n* empreinte *f* digitale; **~tip** *n* bout *m* du doigt.

finicky *adj* [*person*] difficile (**about** pour); [*job, task*] minutieux/-ieuse.

finish I *n* **1** (end) fin *f*; **from start to ~** du début (jusqu')à la fin; **2** (Sport) arrivée *f*; **3** (of clothing, wood, car) finition *f*; (of fabric, leather) apprêt *m*; **paint with a matt ~** peinture mate.
II *vtr* **1** finir, terminer [*chapter, sentence, task*]; terminer, achever [*building, novel, sculpture, opera*]; **to ~ doing** finir de faire; **2** (leave) finir [*work, school*]; **3** (consume) finir [*cigarette, drink, meal*]; **4** (put an end to) briser [*career*].
III *vi* **1** (gen) finir; [*speaker*] finir de parler; [*conference, programme, term*] finir, se terminer; [*holidays*] se terminer; **the film ~es on Thursday** le film ne passe plus à partir de jeudi; **I'll see you when the concert ~es** je te verrai à la fin du concert; **2** (reach end of race) arriver; **the horse failed to ~** le cheval n'a pas fini la course.
IV **finished** *pp adj* **1 beautifully ~ed** avec des finitions soignées; **the ~ed product** le produit fini; **2** (accomplished) [*performance*] accompli; **3** (ruined) [*person, career*] fini, fichu○.
■ **finish off**: ¶ **~ [sth] off, ~ off [sth]** finir, terminer [*letter, meal, task*]; ¶ **~ [sb] off 1** (exhaust, demoralize) achever○ [*person*]; **2** (kill) achever [*person, animal*].
■ **finish up**: ¶ **~ up** finir; ¶ **~ [sth] up, ~ up [sth]** finir [*milk, paint, cake*].
■ **finish with**: ¶ **~ with [sth]** finir avec [*book, tool, pen*]; **I'm ~ed with politics!** j'en ai assez de la politique!; ¶ **~ with [sb]** (split up) rompre avec [*girlfriend, boyfriend*].

finish: **~ing line** (GB), **~ line** (US) *n* ligne *f* d'arrivée; **~ing post** *n* (Sport) poteau *m* d'arrivée.

finishing touch *n* **to put the ~(es) to sth** mettre la dernière main à qch.

finite *adj* (gen) fini; [*resources*] limité.

Finland ▶ **574** *pr n* Finlande *f*.

Finn ▶ **712** *n* **1** (citizen) Finlandais/-e *m/f*; **2** (speaker) Finnois/-e *m/f*.

Finnish ▶ **712** I *n* (language) finnois *m*.
II *adj* [*culture, food, politics*] finlandais; [*teacher, lesson*] de finnois; [*ambassador, embassy*] de Finlande.

fir *n* (also **~ tree**) sapin *m*.

fire I *n* **1** feu *m*; **to set ~ to sth** mettre le feu à qch; **to be on ~** être en feu; **to catch ~** prendre feu; **to sit by the ~** s'asseoir près du feu or au coin du feu; **2** (blaze) incendie *m*; **to start a ~** provoquer un incendie; **3 to open ~ on sb** ouvrir le feu sur qn; **the police came under ~** on a tiré sur la police.
II *excl* **1** (raising alarm) au feu!; **2** (Mil) feu!
III *vtr* **1** décharger [*gun, weapon*]; tirer [*shot*]; lancer [*arrow, missile*]; **to ~ questions at sb** bombarder qn de questions; **to ~ sb's imagination** enflammer l'imagination de qn; **2** (dismiss) renvoyer, virer○ [*person*].
IV *vi* tirer (**at, on** sur).

fire: **~ alarm** *n* alarme *f* incendie; **~arm** *n* arme *f* à feu; **~ bell** *n* sonnerie *f* d'alarme.

firebomb I *n* bombe *f* incendiaire.
II *vtr* incendier [*building*].

fire: **~ brigade** *n* pompiers *mpl*; **~ door** *n* porte *f* coupe-feu; **~ drill** *n* exercice *m* d'évacuation en cas d'incendie; **~-eater** *n* cracheur/-euse *m/f* de feu; **~ engine** *n* voiture *f* de pompiers; **~ escape** *n* escalier *m* de secours; **~ exit** *n* sortie *f* de secours; **~ extinguisher** *n* extincteur *m*; **~guard** *n* pare-étincelles *m inv*; **~man** ▶ 805 *n* pompier *m*; **~place** *n* cheminée *f*; **~proof** *adj* [*door, clothing*] ignifugé; **~ station** *n* caserne *f* de pompiers; **~wood** *n* bois *m* à brûler.

firework *n* feu *m* d'artifice.

fireworks display *n* feu *m* d'artifice.

firing *n* (of guns) tir *m*.

firing squad *n* peloton *m* d'exécution; **to face the ~** être fusillé.

firm I *n* entreprise *f*, société *f*.
II *adj* **1** [*mattress, fruit, handshake*] ferme; **2** [*basis, grasp*] solide; **3** [*offer, intention, refusal*] ferme; [*evidence*] concret/-ète; **4** [*person, leadership*] ferme (**with sb** avec qn); **he needs a ~ hand** il a besoin qu'on soit ferme avec lui.
III *adv* **to stand ~** tenir bon (**against** contre).

firmly *adv* **1** [*say*] d'un ton ferme; **2** [*believe, deny*] fermement; **3** [*hold, press*] fermement; [*attach*] solidement.

firmness *n* fermeté *f*.

first ▶ 584, 642 **I** *n* **1** (in order) premier/-ière *m/f*; **2** (of month) premier *m inv*; **the ~ of May** le premier mai; **3** (also **~ gear**) (Aut) première *f*; **4** (GB Univ) (also **~-class honours degree**) ≈ licence *f* avec mention très bien.
II *pron* premier/-ière *m/f* (**to do** à faire); **that's the ~ I've heard of it!** première nouvelle!
III *adj* premier/-ière (*before n*); **the ~ three pages** les trois premières pages; **at ~ glance** or **sight** à première vue; **I'll ring ~ thing in the morning** je vous appellerai en tout début de matinée; **I'll do it ~ thing** je le ferai dès que possible.
IV *adv* **1** [*arrive, leave*] le premier/la première; **women and children ~** les femmes et les enfants d'abord; **to come ~** [*contestant*] terminer premier/première (**in** à); [*career, family*] passer avant tout; **2** (to begin with) d'abord; **~ of all** tout d'abord; **when he ~ arrived** quand il est arrivé; **3** (for the first time) pour la première fois; **I ~ met him in Paris** je l'ai rencontré pour la première fois à Paris.
V at first *phr* au début.
IDIOMS **~ come ~ served** les premiers arrivés sont les premiers servis; **~ things ~** chaque chose en son temps.

first aid *n* **1** (treatment) premiers soins *mpl*; **2** (as skill) secourisme *m*.

first-aid: **~ kit** *n* trousse *f* de secours; **~ officer** *n* secouriste *mf*.

first class I *adj* **1** [*compartment, hotel, ticket*] de première (classe); **2** [*stamp, mail*] (au) tarif rapide; **3** (GB) [*degree*] avec mention très bien; **4** (excellent) excellent.
II *adv* **1** [*travel*] en première (classe); **2** [*post*] au tarif rapide.

first: **~ cousin** *n* (male) cousin *m* germain; (female) cousine *f* germaine; **~ floor** *n* (GB) premier étage *m*; (US) rez-de-chaussée *m*; **~ form** *n* (GB Sch) (classe *f* de) sixième *f*; **~ grade** *n* (US Sch) cours *m* préparatoire.

firstly *adv* premièrement.

first: **~ name** *n* prénom *m*; **~-rate** *adj* excellent; **~ year** *n* (Sch, Univ) (group) première année *f*; (pupil) élève *mf* de première année; (student) étudiant/-e *m/f* de première année.

fiscal *adj* fiscal.

fiscal year *n* exercice *m* budgétaire or fiscal.

fish I *n* poisson *m*.
II *vi* pêcher; **to ~ for trout** pêcher la truite; **to ~ for compliments** rechercher les compliments.
IDIOMS **to be like a ~ out of water** ne pas se sentir dans son élément; **to have other ~ to fry** avoir d'autres chats à fouetter.

fish: **~ and chips** *n* poisson *m* frit avec des frites; **~ and chip shop** ▶ 805 *n* (GB) friterie *f*; **~bowl** *n* bocal *m* (à poissons).

fisherman ▶ 805 *n* pêcheur *m*.

fishing I *n* pêche *f*; **to go ~** aller à la pêche.
II *noun modifier* [*boat, port, line, net*] de pêche.

fishing rod *n* canne *f* à pêche.

fish market *n* halle *f* aux poissons.

fishmonger ▶ 805 *n* (GB) poissonnier/-ière *m/f*; **~'s (shop)** poissonnerie *f*.

fish: **~net** *adj* [*stockings*] à résille; **~ shop** (GB), **~ store** (US) ▶ 805 *n* poissonnerie *f*; **~ tank** *n* aquarium *m*.

fishy *adj* **1** [*smell, taste*] de poisson; **2**° (suspect) louche°.

fission *n* (also **nuclear ~**) fission *f*.

fist *n* poing *m*; **to shake one's ~ at sb** menacer qn du poing.

fit I *n* **1** (Med) crise *f*, attaque *f*; **to have a ~** avoir une attaque or une crise; **2** (of rage, passion, panic) accès *m*; **~ of coughing** quinte *f* de toux; **to have sb in ~s**° donner le fou rire à qn.
II *adj* **1** [*person*] (in trim) en forme; (not ill) en bonne santé; **to get ~** retrouver la forme; **2 to be ~ for** (worthy of) être digne de [*person, hero, king*]; (capable of) être capable de faire [*job*]; **not ~ for human consumption** impropre à la consommation; **to be ~ to drive** être en état de conduire; **~ to live in** habitable; **I'm not ~ to be seen!** je ne suis pas présentable!; **to see** or **think ~ to do** juger bon de faire; **to be in no ~ state to do** ne pas être en état de faire.
III *vtr* **1** [*garment*] être à la taille de; [*shoe*] être à la pointure de; [*key*] aller dans [*lock*]; aller dans [*envelope, space*]; **2 to ~ sth in** or **into** trouver de la place pour qch dans [*room, house, car*]; **3** (install) mettre [qch] en place [*lock, door, kitchen, shower*]; **4** correspondre à [*description, requirements*].
IV *vi* **1** [*garment*] être à ma/ta/sa taille, aller; [*shoes*] être à ma/ta/sa pointure, aller; [*key, lid, sheet*] aller; **2** [*toys, books*] tenir (**into** dans); **will the table ~ in that corner?** y a-t-il de la place pour la table dans ce coin?; **to ~ into place** [*part, handle*] bien aller; [*cupboard, brick*] bien rentrer; **3 something doesn't**

quite ~ here il y a quelque chose qui ne va pas ici; **to ~ with** correspondre à [*story, facts*].

IDIOMS **in ~s and starts** par à-coups.

■ **fit in**: ¶ **~ in 1** [*key, object*] aller; **will you all ~ in?** (into car, room) est-ce qu'il y a de la place pour vous tous?; **2** (figurative) [*person*] s'intégrer (**with** à); **I'll ~ in with your plans** j'accorderai mes projets avec les vôtres; ¶ **~ [sth/sb] in, ~ in [sth/sb]** caser [*books, objects*]; faire entrer [*key*]; caser [*game, meeting*]; trouver le temps pour voir [*patient, colleague*].

■ **fit out**: **~ [sth] out, ~ out [sth]** équiper (**with** de).

fitness I *n* (physical) forme *f*.

II *noun modifier* [*club, room*] de culture physique.

fitted *adj* [*wardrobe*] encastré; [*kitchen*] intégré.

fitted: **~ carpet** *n* moquette *f*; **~ sheet** *n* drap-housse *m*.

fitting I *n* **1** (of bathroom) installation *f*; **2** (for clothes, hearing aid) essayage *m*.

II *adj* [*description*] adéquat; [*memorial, testament*] qui convient.

fitting room *n* salon *m* d'essayage.

five ▶ 492, 554 *n, pron, det* cinq (*m*) *inv*.

fix I *n* **to be in a ~**○ être dans le pétrin○.

II *vtr* **1** fixer [*date, venue, price, limit*]; déterminer [*position*]; **to ~ tax at 20%** établir un impôt de 20%; **2** arranger [*meeting, visit*]; préparer [*drink, meal*]; **to ~ one's hair** se donner un coup de peigne; **how are we ~ed for time/money?** qu'est- ce qu'on a comme temps/argent○?; **3** (mend) réparer [*article, equipment*]; **4** fixer [*handle, shelf*] (**on** sur; **to** à); **5** fixer [*attention*] (**on** sur); placer [*hopes*] (**on** dans); tourner [*thoughts*] (**on** vers); **6**○ truquer [*contest, election*].

III **fixed** *pp adj* [*gaze, income, price*] fixe; [*intervals*] régulier/-ière; [*aim*] arrêté; [*proportion*] constant; [*expression*] figé; [*menu*] à prix fixe.

■ **fix up**: **~ up [sth], ~ [sth] up** organiser [*holiday, meeting*]; décider de [*date*].

fixed assets *n pl* immobilisations *fpl*, actif *m* immobilisé.

fixture *n* **1** installation *f*; **~s and fittings** équipements *mpl*; **2** (Sport) rencontre *f*.

fizzy *adj* gazeux/-euse.

flabby *adj* [*skin, muscle*] flasque; [*person*] aux chairs flasques.

flag I *n* drapeau *m*; (as signal) (on ship) pavillon *m*; (on railways) drapeau *m*.

II *vi* [*interest*] faiblir; [*strength*] baisser; [*conversation*] languir; [*athlete*] flancher○.

■ **flag down**: **~ [sth] down, ~ down [sth]** faire signe de s'arrêter à [*train*]; héler [*taxi*].

flagpole *n* mât *m*.

flagship I *n* vaisseau *m* amiral.

II *noun modifier* [*company, product*] vedette.

flag: **~stone** *n* dalle *f*; **~ stop** *n* (US) arrêt *m* facultatif.

flail *v* ■ **flail about, flail around**: ¶ **~ around** [*person*] se débattre; [*arms, legs*] s'agiter; ¶ **~ [sth] around** agiter [*arms, legs*].

flair *n* **1** (talent) don; **to have a ~ for** être doué pour [*languages*]; **2** (style) classe *f*.

flake I *n* (of snow) flocon *m*.

II *vi* (also **~ off**) [*paint, varnish*] s'écailler; [*plaster, stone*] s'effriter; [*skin*] peler.

flaky *adj* [*paint*] qui s'écaille; [*skin*] qui pèle.

flamboyant *adj* [*person*] haut en couleur; [*lifestyle*] exubérant; [*colour, clothes*] voyant; [*gesture*] extravagant.

flame *n* flamme *f*; **in ~s** en flammes; **to go up in ~s** s'enflammer; **to burst into ~s** s'embraser.

flamingo *n* flamant *m* (rose).

flammable *adj* inflammable.

flan *n* (savoury) quiche *f*, tarte *f*; (sweet) tarte *f*.

flank I *n* **1** flanc *m*; **2** (in politics, sports) aile *f*; **3** (Culin) flanchet *m*.

II *vtr* **to be ~ed by** [*person*] être flanqué par; [*place*] être bordé par.

flannel *n* **1** (wool) flanelle *f*; (cotton) pilou *m*; **2** (GB) (also **face ~**) ≈ gant *m* de toilette.

flannels *n pl* pantalon *m* de flanelle.

flap I *n* **1** (on pocket, envelope, tent) rabat *m*; (on table) abattant *m*; **2** (of wings) battement *m* (**of** de); (of sail) claquement *m* (**of** de).

II *vtr* **the bird ~ped its wings** l'oiseau battait des ailes.

III *vi* [*wing*] battre; [*sail, flag*] claquer; [*clothes*] voleter.

flare I *n* **1** (on runway) balise *f* lumineuse; (distress signal) fusée *f* (de détresse); (Mil) (on target) fusée *f* éclairante; **2** (of match, lighter) lueur *f*.

II **flares** *n pl* pantalon *m* à pattes d'éléphant.

III *vi* **1** [*firework, match*] jeter une brève lueur; **2** [*violence*] éclater; **3** [*skirt*] s'évaser; [*nostrils*] se dilater.

■ **flare up 1** [*fire*] s'embraser; **2** [*violence*] éclater; [*person*] s'emporter; **3** [*illness*] réapparaître; [*pain*] se réveiller.

flared *adj* [*skirt*] évasé; [*trousers*] à pattes d'éléphant.

flash I *n* **1** (of torch, headlights) lueur *f* soudaine; (of jewels, metal) éclat *m*; **a ~ of lightning** un éclair; **2 a ~ of inspiration** un éclair d'inspiration; **in** or **like a ~** en un clin d'œil; **3** (on camera) flash *m*.

II *vtr* **1**○ (show) [*person*] montrer [qch] rapidement [*card, money*]; **2** (also **~ about, ~ around**) exhiber [*credit card*]; étaler [*money*]; **3 to ~ one's headlights (at)** faire un appel de phares (à); **4** lancer [*look, smile*] (**at** à); **5** (transmit) faire apparaître [*message*].

III *vi* [*light*] clignoter; [*jewels*] étinceler; [*eyes*] lancer des éclairs; **to ~ on and off** clignoter.

IDIOMS **to be a ~ in the pan** être un feu de paille.

■ **flash by, flash past** [*person, bird*] passer comme un éclair; [*landscape*] défiler.

flashback *n* **1** (in film) flash-back *m* (**to** à); **2** (memory) souvenir *m*.

flashing *adj* [*light, sign*] clignotant.

flash light *n* lampe *f* de poche.

flashy○ *adj* [*car, dress, tie*] tape-à-l'œil *inv*; [*jewellery*] clinquant.

flask *n* thermos® *f* or *m inv*; (**hip**) ~ flasque *f*.

flat I *n* **1** (GB) appartement *m*; **one-bedroom ~** deux pièces *m inv*; **2 the ~ of** le plat de [*hand, sword*].
II *adj* **1** (gen) plat; [*nose, face*] aplati; **2** [*tyre, ball*] dégonflé; **to have a ~ tyre** avoir un pneu à plat; **3** [*shoes, heels*] plat; **4** [*refusal, denial*] catégorique; **5** [*fare, fee*] forfaitaire; [*charge, rate*] fixe; **6** [*voice, tone*] plat, monocorde; [*performance, style*] plat; **7** [*beer*] éventé; **8** (GB) [*car battery*] à plat; [*battery*] usé; **9** (Mus) [*note*] bémol *inv*; [*voice, instrument*] faux/fausse.
III *adv* **1** [*lay, lie*] à plat; [*fall*] de tout son long; **to knock sb ~** terrasser qn; **to lie ~** [*person*] s'étendre; **~ on one's back** sur le dos; **2** (exactly) **in 10 minutes ~** en 10 minutes pile; **3** [*sing*] faux.
IDIOMS **to fall ~** [*joke*] tomber à plat; [*party*] tourner court; [*plan*] tomber à l'eau.

flat-bottomed *adj* [*boat*] à fond plat.

flat-footed *adj* **to be ~** avoir les pieds plats.

flat-hunting *n* (GB) **to go ~** chercher un appartement.

flatmate *n* (GB) colocataire *mf*.

flat out○ *adv* [*drive*] à fond de train; [*work*] d'arrache-pied.

flatten I *vtr* **1** [*rain*] coucher [*crops, grass*]; abattre [*fence*]; [*bombing*] raser [*building*]; **2** (smooth out) aplanir [*surface*]; aplatir [*metal*]; **3** (crush) écraser [*animal, fruit, object*].
II *v refl* **to ~ oneself** s'aplatir (**against** contre).

flatter I *vtr* flatter (**on** sur).
II *v refl* **to ~ oneself** se flatter (**on being** d'être).

flatterer *n* flatteur/-euse *m/f*.

flattering *adj* flatteur/-euse.

flattery *n* flatterie *f*.

flaunt *vtr* étaler [*wealth*]; faire étalage de [*charms, knowledge*].

flavour (GB), **flavor** (US) **I** *n* goût *m*; (subtler) saveur *f*; **full of ~** savoureux/-euse.
II *vtr* (improve taste) donner du goût à; (add specific taste) parfumer (**with** à).

flavouring (GB), **flavoring** (US) *n* (for sweet taste) parfum *m*; (for meat, fish) assaisonnement *m*.

flaw *n* défaut *m*.

flawed *adj* défectueux/-euse.

flea I *n* puce *f*.
II *noun modifier* [*collar*] antipuce; [*powder*] antiparasitaire.

flea market *n* marché *m* aux puces.

fleck I *n* (of colour, light) tache *f*; (of foam) flocon *m*; (of blood, paint) petite tache *f*; (of dust) particule *f*.
II *vtr* **~ed with** [*fabric*] moucheté de [*colour*]; [*eye*] piqueté de [*colour*]; tacheté de [*paint, light*].

fledg(e)ling *n* oisillon *m*.

flee *vtr, vi* fuir.

fleece *n* (on animal) toison *f*; **~-lined** fourré.

fleet *n* **1** (of ships) flotte *f*; (of small vessels) flottille *f*; **2** (of vehicles) (on road) convoi *m*.

fleeting *adj* [*memory, pleasure*] fugace; [*moment*] bref/brève (*before n*); [*glance*] rapide.

Flemish ▶ 712 **I** *n* **1** (language) flamand *m*; **2 the ~** les Flamands *mpl*.
II *adj* flamand.

flesh *n* chair *f*; **I'm only ~ and blood** je ne suis qu'un être humain; **one's own ~ and blood** la chair de sa chair; **in the ~** en chair et en os.

fleshy *adj* [*arm, fruit, leaf*] charnu.

flex I *n* (GB) fil *m*.
II *vtr* faire jouer [*muscle*]; fléchir [*limb*]; plier [*finger*].

flexibility *n* souplesse *f*, flexibilité *f*.

flexible *adj* **1** [*arrangement, plan*] flexible; **2** [*person*] souple (**about** en ce qui concerne).

flexitime *n* horaire *m* flexible or souple.

flick I *n* (with finger) chiquenaude *f*; (with whip, cloth) petit coup *m*.
II *vtr* **1** (with finger) donner une chiquenaude à; (with tail, cloth) donner un petit coup à; **he ~ed his ash on the floor** il a fait tomber sa cendre par terre; **2** appuyer sur [*switch*].

flicker I *n* **1 the ~ of a candle** la flamme vacillante d'une bougie; **2** (of interest, hope, anger) lueur *f* (**of** de).
II *vi* [*fire, light*] vaciller, trembloter; [*image*] clignoter; [*eye, eyelid*] cligner.
III **flickering** *pres p adj* [*light, flame*] vacillant; [*image*] tremblant.

flick knife *n* (GB) couteau *m* à cran d'arrêt.

flight *n* **1** vol *m* (**to** vers; **from** de); **the ~ from Dublin to London** le vol Dublin-Londres; **we took the next ~ (out)** nous avons pris l'avion suivant; **2** (of bird, insect) vol *m*; (of missile, bullet) trajectoire *f*; **3** (escape) fuite *f* (**from** devant); **to take ~** prendre la fuite; **4 a ~ of steps** une volée de marches; **six ~s (of stairs)** six étages; **5 a ~ of fancy** une invention.

flight attendant ▶ 805 *n* (male) steward *m*; (female) hôtesse *f* de l'air.

flimsy *adj* [*fabric*] léger/-ère; [*structure*] peu solide; [*excuse*] piètre (*before n*); [*evidence*] mince.

flinch *vi* tressaillir; **without ~ing** sans broncher; **to ~ from doing** hésiter à faire; **to ~ at** tiquer sur [*criticism, insult*].

fling I *n* **1**○ (spree) bon temps *m*; **to have a ~** se payer du bon temps; **2**○ (affair) aventure *f*.
II *vtr* lancer [*ball, grenade*] (**onto** sur; **into** dans); lancer [*insult*] (**at** à); **to ~ sb to the ground** [*person*] jeter qn à terre; [*blast*] projeter qn à terre.
■ **fling open**: **~ [sth] open, ~ open [sth]** ouvrir [qch] brusquement [*door*]; ouvrir [qch] tout grand [*window*].

flint *n* **1** (rock) silex *m*; **2** (in lighter) pierre *f* à briquet.

flip I *n* (somersault) tour *m*.
II *vtr* **1** lancer [*coin*]; faire sauter [*pancake*]; **let's ~ a coin to decide** décidons à pile ou face; **2** basculer [*switch*].
■ **flip through**: **~ through [sth]** feuilleter [*book*].

flip-flop *n* **1** (sandal) tong *f*; **2** (Comput) bascule *f*; **3** (US) (about-face) volte-face *f inv*.

flippant *adj* [*remark, person*] désinvolte; [*tone, attitude*] cavalier/-ière.

flipper *n* **1** (Zool) nageoire *f*; **2** (for swimmer) palme *f*.

flirt I *n* flirteur/-euse *m/f*, dragueur/-euse° *m/f* (derogatory).
II *vi* flirter; **to ~ with** flirter avec [*person*]; jouer avec [*danger*]; caresser [*idea*].

flirtatious *adj* [*person, glance*] charmeur/-euse, dragueur/-euse° (derogatory).

flit *vi* **1** (also **~ about**) [*bird, moth*] voleter; [*person*] aller d'un pas léger; **2 a look of panic ~ted across his face** une expression de panique lui traversa le visage.

float I *n* **1** (on net) flotteur *m*; (on line) bouchon *m*; **2** (GB) (swimmer's aid) planche *f*; (US) (life jacket) gilet *m* de sauvetage; **3** (carnival vehicle) char *m*.
II *vtr* **1** [*person*] faire flotter [*boat, logs*]; [*tide*] mettre à flot [*ship*]; **2** émettre [*shares, securities, loan*]; lancer [qch] en Bourse [*company*]; laisser flotter [*currency*].
III *vi* **1** flotter; **to ~ on one's back** [*swimmer*] faire la planche; **the boat was ~ing out to sea** le bateau voguait vers le large; **to ~ up into the air** s'envoler; **2** [*currency*] flotter.
■ **float off** [*boat*] dériver; [*balloon*] s'envoler; [*person*] partir d'un pas léger.

floating *adj* **1** [*bridge*] flottant; **2** [*population*] instable.

floating: **~ assets** *n pl* actif *m* circulant; **~ capital** *n* capital *m* disponible; **~ exchange rate** *n* taux *m* de change flottant; **~ voter** *n* électeur *m* indécis.

flock I *n* (of sheep, goats) troupeau *m*; (of birds) volée *f*.
II *vi* [*animals, people*] affluer (**around** autour de; **into** dans); **to ~ together** [*people*] s'assembler; [*animals*] se rassembler.

flog *vtr* flageller.

flood I *n* **1** inondation *f*; **2 a ~ of** un flot de [*people, memories*]; un déluge de [*letters, complaints*]; **to be in ~s of tears** verser des torrents de larmes.
II *vtr* **1** inonder [*area*]; faire déborder [*river*]; **2** [*light*] inonder; **3** inonder [*shops*] (**with** de); **4** (Aut) noyer [*engine*].
III *vi* **1** [*river*] déborder; **2 to ~ into sth** [*light*] inonder qch; [*people*] envahir qch; **to ~ over sb** [*emotion*] envahir qn.
■ **flood back** [*memories*] remonter à la surface.
■ **flood in** [*light*] entrer à flots; [*people, money*] affluer.

floodgate *n* vanne *f*.

floodlight I *n* projecteur *m*; **under ~s** (Sport) en nocturne.
II *vtr* illuminer [*building*]; éclairer [*stage*].

floor I *n* **1** (of room) (wooden) plancher *m*, parquet *m*; (stone) sol *m*; (of car, lift) plancher *m*; **dance ~** piste *f* de danse; **on the ~** par terre; **2** (of stock exchange) parquet *m*; (of debating chamber) auditoire *m*; (of factory) atelier *m*; **3** (storey) étage *m*; **on the first ~** (GB) au premier étage; (US) au rez-de-chaussée.
II *vtr* **1** terrasser [*attacker, boxer*]; **2** (silence) réduire [qn] au silence [*person, critic*]; (stump) [*question*] décontenancer [*candidate*].
IDIOMS **to wipe the ~ with sb** battre qn à plates coutures.

floor: **~board** *n* latte *f*, planche *f*; **~ cloth** *n* serpillière *f*; **~ lamp** *n* (US) lampadaire *m*.

flop I° *n* fiasco° *m*.
II *vi* **1 to ~ down** s'effondrer; **to ~ down on** s'affaler sur [*bed, sofa*]; **2**° [*play, film*] faire un four°; [*project, venture*] être un fiasco°.

floppy *adj* [*ears*] pendant; [*hat*] à bords tombants.

floppy disk *n* disquette *f*.

flora *n* flore *f*.

floral *adj* [*design, fabric*] à fleurs; [*arrangement*] floral.

Florida *pr n* Floride *f*.

florist ▶ 805 *n* (person) fleuriste *mf*; (shop) fleuriste *m*.

floss *n* fil *m* dentaire.

flotation *n* (of company, loan) lancement *m*; (of shares) émission *f*; (of currency) flottement *m*.

flounce I *n* (frill) volant *m*.
II *vi* **to ~ in/off** entrer/partir dans un mouvement d'indignation.

flounder *vi* **1** [*animal, person*] se débattre (**in** dans); **2** (falter) [*speaker*] bredouiller; [*economy*] stagner; [*career, company*] piétiner.

flour *n* farine *f*.

flourish I *n* **1** (gesture) geste *m* théâtral; **with a ~** [*do*] de façon théâtrale; **2** (in style) fioriture *f*.
II *vtr* brandir [*ticket, document*].
III *vi* [*plant, bacteria*] prospérer; [*child*] s'épanouir; [*firm, democracy*] prospérer.

flourishing *adj* [*garden, industry*] florissant; [*business, town*] prospère.

flout *vtr* se moquer de [*convention, rules*].

flow I *n* **1** (of liquid) écoulement *m*; (of blood, electricity) circulation *f*; (of refugees, words) flot *m*; (of information) circulation *f*; **in full ~** [*speaker*] en plein discours; **traffic ~** circulation *f*; **2** (of tide) flux *m*.
II *vi* **1** [*liquid*] couler (**into** dans); **to ~ past sth** passer devant qch; **the river ~s into the sea** le fleuve se jette dans la mer; **2** [*conversation, words*] couler; [*wine, beer*] couler à flots; **3** (circulate) [*blood, electricity*] circuler (**through, round** dans); **4** [*hair, dress*] flotter.

flowchart *n* organigramme *m*.

flower I *n* **1** fleur *f*; **to be in ~** être en fleur; **2 the ~ of** la fine fleur de [*age, era, group*]; **in the ~ of her youth** dans la fleur de l'âge.
II *vi* **1** [*flower, tree*] fleurir; **2** [*love, person*] s'épanouir.

flower arranging *n* décoration *f* florale.

flowering I *n* floraison *f* (**of** de).
II *adj* [*shrub, tree*] (producing blooms) à fleurs; (in bloom) en fleurs.

flowing *adj* [*style, movement*] coulant; [*rhythm*] berceur/-euse; [*hair, clothes*] flottant.

flu ▶686 I *n* grippe *f*; **to come down with ~** attraper une grippe.
II *noun modifier* [*virus*] de la grippe; [*epidemic*] de grippe; [*vaccine*] contre la grippe.

fluctuate *vi* fluctuer (**between** entre).

flue *n* (of chimney) conduit *m*; (of stove, boiler) tuyau *m*.

fluency *n* aisance *f*.

fluent *adj* **1 her French is ~** elle parle couramment le français; **a ~ Greek speaker** une personne qui parle grec couramment; **in ~ English** dans un anglais parfait; **2** [*speech*] éloquent; [*style*] coulant.

fluently *adv* couramment.

fluff I *n* (on clothes) peluche *f*; (on carpet) poussière *f*; (under furniture) mouton *m*, flocon *m* de poussière.
II *vtr* **1** (also **~ up**) hérisser [*feathers*]; faire bouffer [*hair*]; **2**° rater [*cue, exam*].

fluffy *adj* **1** [*toy*] en peluche; [*hair*] bouffant; **2** (light) [*mixture*] léger/-ère; [*egg white, rice*] moelleux/-euse.

fluid I *n* fluide *m*.
II *adj* fluide.

fluid ounce *n* once *f* liquide.

fluke *n* coup *m* de veine°; **by a (sheer) ~** (tout à fait) par hasard.

fluorescent *adj* fluorescent.

fluoride *n* fluorure *m*.

flush I *n* **1** (blush) rougeur *f*; **2** (surge) **a ~ of** un élan de [*pleasure, pride*]; un accès de [*anger, shame*]; **3** (of toilet) chasse *f* d'eau.
II *vtr* **1 to ~ the toilet** tirer la chasse (d'eau); **2 to ~ sb's cheeks** empourprer les joues de qn.
III *vi* **1** (redden) rougir (**with** de); **2 the toilet doesn't ~** la chasse d'eau ne fonctionne pas.
■ **flush away**: **~ [sth] away, ~ away [sth]** faire partir [*waste*].
■ **flush out**: **~ out [sb/sth]** débusquer [*sniper, spy*]; **to ~ sb/sth out of** faire sortir qn/qch de [*shelter*].

flushed *adj* **1** [*cheeks*] rouge (**with** de); **to be ~** avoir les joues rouges; **2 ~ with** rayonnant de [*pride*].

fluster I *n* agitation *f*.
II *vtr* énerver; **to look ~ed** avoir l'air énervé.

flute ▶753 *n* flûte *f*.

flutter I *n* (of wings, lashes) battement *m*.
II *vtr* **1 the bird ~ed its wings** l'oiseau battait des ailes; **2** agiter [*fan, handkerchief*]; **to ~ one's eyelashes** battre des cils.
III *vi* **1 the bird's wings ~ed** l'oiseau battit des ailes; **2** [*flag*] flotter; [*clothes, curtains*] s'agiter; [*eyelids, lashes*] battre; **3** (also **~ down**) [*leaves*] tomber en voltigeant; **4** [*heart*] palpiter (**with** de); [*pulse*] battre faiblement.

flux *n* **in (a state of) ~** dans un état de perpétuel changement.

fly I *n* mouche *f*.
II **flies** *n pl* (of trousers) braguette *f*.
III *vtr* **1** piloter [*aircraft, balloon*]; faire voler [*kite*]; **the pilot flew the plane to...** le pilote a emmené l'avion jusqu'à...; **2** (transport) emmener [qn] par avion [*person*]; **3** [*bird, aircraft*] parcourir [*distance*]; **I ~ over 10,000 km a year** [*passenger*] je vole plus de 10 000 km par an; **4** [*ship*] arborer [*flag*]; **the embassy was ~ing the German flag** le drapeau allemand flottait sur l'ambassade.
IV *vi* **1** [*bird, insect, aircraft, kite*] voler (**from** de; **to** à); **to ~ over** or **across sth** survoler qch; **to ~ over(head)** passer dans le ciel; **2** [*passenger*] voyager en avion, prendre l'avion; [*pilot*] piloter, voler; **to ~ from Orly** partir d'Orly; **to ~ from Rome to Athens** aller de Rome à Athènes en avion; **3** [*bullet, glass, sparks, insults*] voler; **to ~ open** s'ouvrir brusquement; **to go ~ing**° [*person*] faire un vol plané; [*object*] valdinguer°; **to ~ into a rage** se mettre en colère; **4** (also **~ past, ~ by**) [*time, holidays*] passer très vite, filer°; **5** [*flag, scarf, hair*] flotter; **to ~ in the wind** flotter au vent.
■ **fly away** s'envoler.

flying I *n* **to be afraid of ~** avoir peur de l'avion.
II *noun modifier* [*lesson, instructor, school*] de pilotage; [*helmet, jacket*] d'aviateur; [*suit*] de vol.
III *adj* **1** [*insect, machine*] volant; [*object, broken glass*] qui vole; **to take a ~ leap** sauter avec élan; **2** [*visit*] éclair *inv*.
IDIOMS **with ~ colours** [*pass*] haut la main.

flying start *n* **to get off to a ~** prendre un très bon départ.

flyover *n* **1** (GB) pont *m* routier; **2** (US) (aerial display) défilé *m* aérien.

fly sheet *n* **1** (of tent) double-toit *m*; **2** (handbill) prospectus *m*.

fly: **~ spray** *n* bombe *f* insecticide; **~ swatter** *n* tapette *f* à mouches.

FM *n* (*abbr* = **frequency modulation**) FM *f*.

foal *n* poulain *m*.

foam I *n* **1** (on sea) écume *f*; (on drinks, bath) mousse *f*; **2** (on animal) sueur *f*; (from mouth) écume *f*; **3** (chemical) mousse *f*; **4** (made of rubber, plastic) mousse *f*.
II *noun modifier* [*bath*] moussant; [*rubber, mattress*] mousse.
III *vi* **1** (also **~ up**) [*beer*] mousser; [*sea*] se couvrir d'écume; **to ~ at the mouth** écumer; (figurative) écumer de rage; **2** [*horse*] suer.

fob *n* (pocket) gousset *m*; (chain) chaîne *f*.
■ **fob off**: ¶ **~ [sb] off, ~ off [sb]** se débarrasser de [*enquirer, customer*]; ¶ **~ off [sth]** rejeter [*enquiry*].

focal point *n* **1** (in optics) foyer *m*; **2** (of village, building) point *m* de convergence (**of** de; **for** pour); **3** (main concern) point *m* central.

focus I *n* **1** (focal point) foyer *m*; **in ~** au point; **to go out of ~** [*device*] se dérégler; [*image*] devenir flou; **2** (device on lens) mise *f* au point; **3** (of attention, interest) centre *m*; **4** (emphasis) accent *m*.
II *vtr* **1** concentrer [*ray*] (**on** sur); fixer [*eyes*]

(**on** sur); **2** mettre [qch] au point, régler [*lens, camera*].
III *vi* **1** **to ~ on** [*photographer*] cadrer sur; [*eyes, attention*] se fixer sur; **2** (concentrate) **to ~ on** [*report*] se concentrer sur.

fodder *n* fourrage *m*.

foe *n* ennemi/-e *m/f*.

foetus, **fetus** (US) *n* fœtus *m*.

fog **I** *n* **1** brouillard *m*; **2** **a ~ of** un nuage épais de [*cigarette smoke*].
II *vtr* (also **~ up**) [*steam*] embuer [*glass*]; [*light*] voiler [*film*].

foggy *adj* [*day, weather*] brumeux/-euse; **it will be ~ tomorrow** il y a aura du brouillard demain.

foghorn *n* corne *f* de brume.

foil **I** *n* papier *m* d'aluminium; **silver ~** papier argenté.
II *vtr* contrecarrer [*person*]; déjouer [*attempt*].

foist *vtr* **to ~ sth on sb** repasser qch à qn.

fold **I** *n* **1** (in fabric, paper, skin) pli *m*; **2** (for sheep) parc *m*.
II **-fold** *combining form* **to increase twofold/threefold** doubler/tripler.
III *vtr* **1** plier [*paper, shirt, chair, umbrella*]; replier [*wings*]; **2** croiser [*arms*]; joindre [*hands*]; **he ~ed his arms** il a croisé les bras.
IV *vi* **1** [*chair*] se plier; **2** (fail) [*play*] quitter l'affiche; [*company*] fermer.
IDIOMS **to return to the ~** rentrer au bercail.
■ **fold back**: **~ back [sth]**, **~ [sth] back** rabattre [*shutters, sheet, sleeve*].
■ **fold down**: **~ [sth] down**, **~ down [sth]** replier [*collar, flap, sheets*]; rabattre [*seat*].
■ **fold in**: **~ in [sth]**, **~ [sth] in** incorporer [*sugar, flour*]; **to ~ [sth] into** incorporer [qch] à.
■ **fold up**: **~ [sth] up**, **~ up [sth]** plier [*newspaper, chair, umbrella*].

folder *n* **1** (for papers) chemise *f*; **2** (for artwork) carton *m*.

folding *adj* [*bed, table, umbrella*] pliant; [*door*] en accordéon.

folding: **~ seat** *n* strapontin *m*; **~ stool** *n* (siège *m*) pliant *m*.

foliage *n* feuillage *m*.

folk **I** *n* **1** (people) gens *mpl*; **2** (Mus) folk *m*.
II *noun modifier* **1** (traditional) [*tale, song*] folklorique; **2** (modern) [*music*] folk *inv*; [*group*] de musique folk; **3** [*hero*] populaire.

folklore *n* folklore *m*.

follow **I** *vtr* **1** suivre [*person, car*] (**into** dans); succéder à [*monarch, leader*]; **~ed by** suivi de; **to ~ sb in** entrer derrière qn; **she ~ed her father into politics** elle est entrée dans la politique comme son père; **2** suivre [*path, fashion, instinct, instructions*]; **3** suivre [*teachings, example*]; adhérer à [*faith*]; être le disciple de [*leader*]; **4** suivre [*serial, trial, team, explanation, plot*]; **5** **it ~s that** il s'ensuit que; **it doesn't necessarily ~ that** ça ne veut pas forcément dire que.
II *vi* **1** suivre; **to ~ in sb's footsteps** suivre les traces de qn; **there's ice cream to ~** ensuite il y a de la glace; **the results were as ~s** les résultats ont été les suivants; **2** (understand) suivre; **I don't ~** je ne suis pas.
■ **follow up**: **~ up [sth]**, **~ [sth] up** confirmer [*victory, success*] (**with** par); consolider [*good start*] (**with** par); donner suite à [*letter, threat, offer*] (**with** par); suivre [*story, lead*].

follower *n* **1** (of thinker, artist) disciple *m*; (of political leader) partisan/-e *m/f*; (of teachings, tradition) adepte *mf*; **2** (of team) supporter *m*.

following **I** *n* **1** (of religion, cult) adeptes *mfpl*; (of party, political figure) partisans/-anes *mpl/fpl*; (of soap opera, show) public *m*; (of sports team) supporters *mpl*; **2** **you will need the ~** vous aurez besoin des choses suivantes; **the ~ is a guide to**... ce qui suit est un guide sur...
II *adj* [*year, article, remark*] suivant.
III *prep* suite à, à la suite de [*incident, allegation*].

folly *n* folie *f*.

fond *adj* **1** [*embrace, farewell*] affectueux/-euse; [*eyes, smile*] tendre; **~ memories** de très bons souvenirs; **2** (heartfelt) [*wish, ambition*] cher/chère; **3** **to be ~ of sb** aimer beaucoup qn; **to be ~ of sth** aimer qch; **4** (irritatingly prone) **to be ~ of doing** aimer bien faire.

fondle *vtr* caresser.

fondness *n* (for person) affection *f* (**for** pour); (for thing, activity) passion *f* (**for** pour).

food **I** *n* nourriture *f*, alimentation *f*; **frozen ~** aliments surgelés; **Chinese ~** la cuisine chinoise; **that's ~ for thought** ça donne à réfléchir.
II *noun modifier* [*industry, product*] alimentaire; [*shop*] d'alimentation.

food: **~ parcel** *n* colis *m* de vivres; **~ poisoning** *n* intoxication *f* alimentaire; **~ processor** *n* robot *m* ménager; **~stuff** *n* denrée *f* alimentaire.

fool **I** *n* **1** idiot/-e *m/f* (**to do** de faire); **you stupid ~**○! espèce d'idiot/-e!; **to make sb look a ~** faire passer qn pour un/-e idiot/-e; **to act the ~** faire l'imbécile; **2** (jester) fou *m*.
II *vtr* tromper, duper; **you don't ~ me for a minute** je ne te crois pas un seul instant; **to ~ sb into believing that**... faire croire à qn que...
■ **fool about**○ (GB), **fool around**○ (GB) (waste time) perdre son temps; (act stupidly) faire l'imbécile.

foolhardy *adj* téméraire.

foolish *adj* **1** [*person*] bête (**to do** de faire); **2** [*grin, expression*] stupide; **to feel ~** se sentir ridicule; **to make sb look ~** ridiculiser qn; **3** [*decision, question, remark*] idiot.

foolproof *adj* **1** [*method, plan*] infaillible; **2** [*machine*] d'utilisation très simple.

foolscap *n* (GB) papier *m* ministre.

foot ▶523|, 738| **I** *n* **1** (of person, horse) pied *m*; (of rabbit, cat, dog, cow) patte *f*; (of sock, chair) pied *m*; **on ~** à pied; **from head to ~** de la tête aux pieds; **to help sb to their feet** aider qn à se lever; **to wait on sb hand and ~** faire tout pour qn; **to put one's ~ down** faire acte d'autorité; (Aut) accélérer; **2** (measure-

ment) pied *m* (anglais) (= *0,3048 m*); **3** (of mountain) pied *m* (**of** de); **at the ~ of** au pied de [*bed*]; à la fin de [*list, letter*]; en bas de [*page, stairs*].
II *vtr* **to ~ the bill** payer la facture (**for** pour).
IDIOMS **not to put a ~ wrong** ne pas commettre la moindre erreur; **to be under sb's feet** être dans les jambes de qn; **rushed off one's feet** débordé; **to fall on one's feet** retomber sur ses pieds; **to keep one's feet on the ground** avoir les pieds sur terre; **to put one's ~ in it**° faire une gaffe; **to put one's feet up** se reposer; **to stand on one's own (two) feet** se débrouiller tout/-e seul/-e.

footage *n* film *m*, pellicule *f*; **some ~ of** des images de.

foot and mouth (disease) *n* fièvre *f* aphteuse.

football ▶ 649 *n* **1** (game) (GB) football *m*; (US) football *m* américain; **2** (ball) ballon *m* de football.

footballer ▶ 805 *n* (GB) joueur/-euse *m/f* de football.

foot: **~ brake** *n* (Aut) frein *m* (à pied); **~bridge** *n* passerelle *f*.

foothold *n* prise *f* (de pied); **to gain a ~** [*company*] prendre pied; [*ideology*] s'imposer.

footing *n* **1** (basis) **on a firm ~** sur une base solide; **to be on an equal** or **even ~ with sb** être sur un pied d'égalité avec qn; **2 to lose one's ~** perdre pied.

footlights *n pl* rampe *f*.

footloose *adj* libre comme l'air.
IDIOMS **~ and fancy free** sans attache.

foot: **~note** *n* note *f* de bas de page; **~ passenger** *n* passager *m* sans véhicule; **~path** *n* (in countryside) sentier *m*; (in town) trottoir *m*; **~print** *n* empreinte *f* (de pied); **~rest** *n* repose-pied *m*.

footstep *n* pas *m*.
IDIOMS **to follow in sb's ~s** suivre les traces de qn.

foot: **~stool** *n* repose-pied *m*; **~wear** *n* chaussures *fpl*.

for *prep* ▶ 639 **1** pour; **to do sth ~ sb** faire qch pour qn; **he cooked dinner ~ us** il nous a préparé à manger; **what's it ~?** c'est pour quoi faire?, ça sert à quoi?; **it's not ~ cleaning windows** ce n'est pas fait pour nettoyer les vitres; **to go ~ a swim** aller nager; **a ticket ~ Dublin** un billet pour Dublin; **to leave ~ work** partir travailler; **I sent it away ~ cleaning** je l'ai renvoyé pour qu'il soit nettoyé; **that's ~ us to decide** c'est à nous de décider; **she's the person ~ the job** elle est la personne qu'il faut pour le travail; **the best thing would be ~ them to leave** le mieux serait qu'ils s'en aillent; **the reason ~ doing** la raison pour laquelle on fait; **she's been criticized ~ her views** on lui a reproché ses opinions; **if it weren't ~ her...** sans elle...; **to be mature ~ one's age** être mûr pour son âge; **2** (as member, employee of) [*work, play*] pour; (as representative) [*MP*] de; **the minister ~ education** le ministre de l'éducation; **3** (on behalf of) pour; **to be pleased ~ sb** être content pour qn; **say hello to him ~ me** dis-lui bonjour de ma part; **I can't do it ~ you** je ne peux pas le faire à ta place; **I speak ~ everyone here** je parle au nom de toutes les personnes ici présentes; **4** (in time expressions) **the best show I've seen ~ years** le meilleur spectacle que j'aie vu depuis des années; **we've been together ~ two years** ça fait deux ans que nous sommes ensemble; **she's off to Paris ~ the weekend** elle va à Paris pour le week-end; **to stay ~ a year** rester un an; **to be away ~ a year** être absent pendant un an; **I was in Paris ~ two weeks** j'ai passé deux semaines à Paris; **the car won't be ready ~ another six weeks** la voiture ne sera pas prête avant six semaines; **it's time ~ bed** c'est l'heure d'aller au lit; **5** (indicating distance) pendant; **to drive ~ miles** rouler pendant des kilomètres; **the last shop ~ 30 miles** le dernier magasin avant 50 kilomètres; **6** (indicating cost, value) pour; **it was sold ~ £100** ça s'est vendu (pour) 100 livres sterling; **I'll let you have it ~ £20** je vous le laisse à 20 livres sterling; **a cheque ~ £20** un chèque de 20 livres sterling; **7** (in favour of) **to be ~** être pour [*peace, divorce*]; **the argument ~ recycling** l'argument en faveur du recyclage; **8 T ~ Tom** T comme Tom; **what's the French ~ 'boot'?** comment dit-on 'boot' en français?; **9** (in explanations) **~ one thing... and ~ another...** premièrement... et deuxièmement...; **I, ~ one, agree with her** en tout cas moi, je suis d'accord avec elle.

forbid *vtr* **1** (disallow) défendre, interdire; **to ~ sb to do** défendre or interdire à qn de faire; **to ~ sb sth** défendre or interdire qch à qn; **2** (prevent, preclude) interdire; **God ~!** Dieu m'en/l'en etc garde!

forbidden *adj* [*subject, fruit*] défendu; [*place*] interdit; **smoking is ~** il est interdit de fumer.

forbidding *adj* [*edifice*] intimidant; [*landscape*] inhospitalier/-ière; [*expression*] rébarbatif/-ive.

force I *n* force *f*; **by ~** par la force; **from ~ of habit** par la force de l'habitude; **a ~ for good** une force agissant pour le bien; **expeditionary ~** forces expéditionnaires; **the police ~** la police; **~ of gravity** pesanteur *f*; **a ~ 10 gale** un vent de force 10.
II forces *n pl* (also **armed ~s**) **the ~s** les forces *fpl* armées.
III *vtr* **1** forcer [*person*] (**to do** à faire); **to be ~d to do** or **into doing** être forcé de faire; **to ~ one's way through** se frayer un chemin à travers or dans [*crowd, jungle*]; **2** forcer [*door, window, safe*]; forcer sur [*screw*]; **to ~ an entry** (Law) entrer par effraction.
IV *v refl* **to ~ oneself** se forcer (**to do** à faire).
V in force *phr* **1** (in large numbers, strength) en force; **2** [*law, prices, ban*] en vigueur.
■ **force down**: **~ [sth] down**, **~ down [sth]** **1** se forcer à avaler [*food*]; **2** diminuer [qch] (de force) [*prices, wages*]; réduire [qch] (de force) [*value, profits, inflation*].

for

Some general uses

◆ *for* is generally translated by ***pour***:

***for** my sister*	= **pour** ma sœur
***for** me*	= **pour** moi

◆ When *for* is used as a preposition indicating purpose followed by a verb, it is translated by ***pour*** + *infinitive*:

***for** cleaning windows*	= **pour** nettoyer les vitres

◆ When *for* is used in the construction ***it is/was*** etc + *adjective* + ***for*** + *pronoun* + *infinitive,* the translation in French is as follows:

*it's impossible **for** me to stay*	= il m'est impossible de rester;
*it was hard **for** him to understand that . . .*	= il lui était difficile de comprendre que . . .

For examples and particular usages, see the entry **for**.

In time expressions

◆ When *for* is used to express the time period of something that started in the past and is still going on, French uses *present tense* + ***depuis***:

*I have been waiting **for** three hours* (and I am still waiting)	= j'attends **depuis** trois heures
*we've been together **for** two years* (and we're still together)	= nous sommes ensemble **depuis** deux ans

◆ When *for* is used after a verb in the past perfect tense, French uses *imperfect* + ***depuis***:

*I had been waiting **for** two hours* (and was still waiting)	= j'attendais **depuis** deux heures

◆ When *for* is used in negative sentences with the present perfect tense to express the time that has elapsed since something has happened, French uses the same tense as English, *perfect* + ***depuis***:

*I haven't seen him **for** ten years* (and I still haven't seen him)	= je ne l'ai pas vu **depuis** dix ans

In spoken French, there are two ways of expressing this:

= ça fait dix ans que je ne l'ai pas vu
= il y a dix ans que je ne l'ai pas vu

◆ When *for* is used in negative sentences after a verb in the past perfect tense, French uses *past perfect* + ***depuis***:

*I hadn't seen him **for** ten years*	= je ne l'avais pas vu **depuis** dix ans

◆ When *for* is used after the preterite to express the time period of something that happened in the past and is no longer going on, French uses *present perfect* + ***pendant***:

*last Sunday I gardened **for** two hours*	= dimanche dernier j'ai jardiné **pendant** deux heures

◆ When *for* is used after the present progressive or the future tense to express an anticipated time period in the future, French uses *present* or *future* + ***pour***:

*I'm going to Rome **for** six weeks*	= je vais à Rome **pour** six semaines
*I will go to Rome **for** six weeks*	= j'irai à Rome **pour** six semaines

◆ When the verb ***to be*** is used in the future with *for* to emphasize the period of time, French uses *future* + ***pendant***:

*I will be in Rome **for** six weeks*	= je serai à Rome **pendant** six semaines

■ **force on**: **~ [sth] on sb** imposer [qch] à qn, forcer qn à accepter [qch]; **the decision was ~d on him** il a été forcé de prendre cette décision.
■ **force open**: **~ [sth] open, ~ open [sth]** forcer [*door, window, box, safe*].
■ **force out**: **~ [sth] out, ~ out [sth]** faire sortir [qch] par la force [*enemy, object*]; enlever [qch] de force [*cork*]; **to ~ sth out of sb** arracher qch à qn [*information, apology, confession*].
■ **force through**: **~ [sth] through, ~ through [sth]** faire adopter [*legislation, measures*].

force-feed *vtr* gaver [*animal, bird*] (**on, with** de); alimenter [qn] de force [*person*].

force field *n* champ *m* de force.

forceful *adj* [*person, behaviour*] énergique; [*attack, speech*] vigoureux/-euse.

ford I *n* gué *m*.
II *vtr* **to ~ a river** passer une rivière à gué.

fore I *n* **to the ~** en vue, en avant; **to come to the ~** [*person, issue*] s'imposer à l'attention; [*quality*] ressortir.
II *excl* (in golf) gare!

forearm *n* avant-bras *m inv*.

foreboding *n* pressentiment *m*; **to have ~s about** avoir de sombres pressentiments quant à.

forecast I *n* **1** (also **weather ~**) météo° *f*, bulletin *m* météorologique; **2** (outlook) (gen) pronostics *mpl*; (Econ) prévisions *fpl*.
II *vtr* prévoir (**that** que); **sunshine is forecast for tomorrow** on prévoit du soleil pour demain.

forecaster *n* **1** (of weather) spécialiste *mf* de la météorologie; **2** (economic) conjoncturiste *mf*; **3** (gen, Sport) pronostiqueur/-euse *m/f*.

forefinger *n* index *m*.

forefront *n* **at** or **in the ~ of** à la pointe de [*change, research, debate*]; au premier plan de [*campaign, struggle*]; **it's in the ~ of my mind** c'est ma première préoccupation.

foregone *adj* **it is/was a ~ conclusion** c'est/c'était couru d'avance.

fore: **~ground** *n* premier plan *m*; **~hand** *n* (Sport) coup *m* droit; **~head** *n* front *m*.

foreign *adj* **1** [*country, imports, policy*] étranger/-ère; [*market*] extérieur; [*trade, travel*] à l'étranger; **2** (alien) [*concept*] étranger/-ère (**to** à).

foreign: **~ affairs** *n pl* affaires *fpl* étrangères; **~ body** *n* corps *m* étranger; **~ correspondent** ▶**805** *n* correspondant/-e *m/f* à l'étranger.

foreigner *n* étranger/-ère *m/f*.

foreign: **~ exchange** *n* devises *fpl*; **~ legion** *n* légion *f* étrangère; **~ minister, ~ secretary** (GB) *n* ministre *m* des Affaires étrangères; **Foreign Office, FO** *n* (GB) ministère *m* des Affaires étrangères.

foreman ▶**805** *n* **1** (supervisor) contremaître *m*; **2** (Law) président *m* (d'un jury).

foremost I *adj* premier/-ière, plus grand.
II *adv* **first and ~** avant tout.

forename *n* prénom *m*.

forensic *adj* **~ tests** expertises *fpl* médico-légales; **~ evidence** résultats *mpl* des expertises médico-légales.

forensics *n pl* (US) (public speaking) art *m* oratoire.

forensic: **~ science** *n* médecine *f* légale; **~ scientist** ▶**805** *n* médecin *m* légiste.

forerunner *n* **1** (person) précurseur *m*; (institution, invention, model) ancêtre *m*; **2** (sign) signe *m* avant-coureur.

foresee *vtr* prévoir.

foreseeable *adj* prévisible (**that** que).

foresight *n* prévoyance *f* (**to do** de faire).

foreskin *n* prépuce *m*.

forest *n* forêt *f*.

forester *n* forestier/-ière *m/f*.

forest: **~ fire** *n* incendie *m* de forêt; **~ ranger** *n* (US) forestier *m*.

forestry *n* (science) sylviculture *f*; (industry) exploitation *f* des forêts.

foretaste *n* avant-goût *m* (**of** de).

foretell *vtr* prédire.

forever *adv* pour toujours; **it can't go on ~** ça ne peut pas toujours durer; **~ after(wards)** pour toujours; **to go on ~** [*pain, noise, journey*] durer une éternité; **the desert seemed to go on ~** le désert semblait ne pas avoir de limites; **she is ~ complaining** elle est toujours en train de se plaindre.

forevermore *adv* pour toujours.

foreword *n* avant-propos *m inv*.

forfeit I *n* **1** (sum, token) gage *m*; **2** (Law) (fine) amende *f*.
II *vtr* **1** perdre [*right, liberty*]; (voluntarily) renoncer à [*right*]; **2** (Law) verser [*sum*].

forge I *n* forge *f*.
II *vtr* **1** forger [*metal*]; **2** contrefaire [*banknotes, signature*]; **a ~d passport** un faux passeport; **3** forger [*alliance*]; établir [*identity, link*].
III *vi* **to ~ ahead** accélérer; **to ~ ahead with** aller de l'avant dans [*plan*].

forger *n* (of documents) faussaire *m*; (of artefacts) contrefacteur/-trice *m/f*; (of money) faux-monnayeur *m*.

forgery *n* contrefaçon *f*.

forget I *vtr* oublier (**that** que; **to do** de faire; **how** comment).
II *vi* [*person*] oublier.
■ **forget about**: **~ about [sth/sb]** oublier.

forgetful *adj* distrait; **to become ~** perdre un peu la mémoire.

forgetfulness *n* **1** distraction *f*, perte *f* de mémoire; **2** (carelessness) étourderie *f*.

forget-me-not *n* myosotis *m*.

forgive *vtr* pardonner à [*person*]; pardonner [*act, remark*]; **to ~ sb sth** pardonner qch à qn; **to ~ sb for doing** pardonner à qn d'avoir fait.

forgiveness *n* pardon *m*; **to be full of ~** être très indulgent.

fork I *n* **1** (for eating) fourchette *f*; **2** (tool) four-

che *f*; **3** (in river, on bicycle) fourche *f*; (in railway) embranchement *m*; (in road) bifurcation *f*.
II *vtr* fourcher.
III *vi* (also **~ off**) bifurquer.
■ **fork out**○ casquer○ (**for** pour).

forked lightning *n* éclair *m* en zigzag.

forklift truck *n* (GB) (also **forklift** US) chariot *m* élévateur à fourche.

form **I** *n* **1** (of exercise, transport, government, protest) forme *f*; (of entertainment, taxation, disease) sorte *f*; **in the ~ of** sous forme de; **he won't touch alcohol in any ~** il évite l'alcool sous toutes ses formes; **2** (document) formulaire *m*; **blank ~** formulaire vierge; **3** (shape, structure) forme *f*; **4** (of athlete, horse, performer) forme *f*; **to be in good ~** être en bonne or pleine forme; **5** (etiquette) **it is bad ~** cela ne se fait pas (**to do** de faire); **purely as a matter of ~** purement par politesse or pour la forme; **6** (GB Sch) classe *f*; **in the first ~** ≈ en sixième.
II *vtr* **1** former [*queue, circle, barrier, band*] (**from** avec); nouer [*friendship, relationship*]; **how are stalactites ~ed?** comment se forment les stalactites?; **to ~ part of** faire partie de; **2** se faire [*impression, opinion*]; **3** former [*personality, tastes, ideas, attitudes*].
III *vi* se former.

formal *adj* **1** (official) [*agreement, complaint, invitation, reception*] officiel/-ielle; **2** (not casual) [*language*] soutenu; [*occasion*] solennel/-elle; [*manner*] cérémonieux/-ieuse; [*clothing*] habillé; **3** (in recognized institution) [*training*] professionnel/-elle; [*qualification*] reconnu.

formal dress *n* tenue *f* de soirée.

formality *n* **1** (legal or social convention) formalité *f*; **2** (of occasion, manner) solennité *f*; (of language) caractère *m* soutenu.

formally *adv* **1** (officially) officiellement; **2** (not casually) cérémonieusement.

format **I** *n* format *m*.
II *vtr* (Comput) formater.

formation *n* formation *f*.

former **I** *n* **the ~** (singular noun) celui-là/celle-là *m/f*; (plural noun) ceux-là/celles-là *mpl/fpl*.
II *adj* **1** (earlier) [*era, life*] antérieur; [*size, state*] initial, original; **he's a shadow of his ~ self** il n'est plus que l'ombre de lui-même; **2** [*leader, husband, champion*] ancien/-ienne (*before n*); **3** (first of two) premier/-ière (*before n*).
III **-former** *combining form* (GB Sch) **fourth-~** ≈ élève *mf* de troisième.

formerly *adv* autrefois.

formidable *adj* **1** (intimidating) redoutable; **2** (awe-inspiring) impressionnant.

formula *n* **1** formule *f* (**for** de; **for doing** pour faire); **2** (US) lait *m* en poudre; (also **~ milk**) lait *m* reconstitué.

fort *n* fort *m*.

forte *n* **to be sb's ~** être le fort de qn.

forth *adv* **from this day ~** à partir d'aujourd'hui; **from that day ~** à dater de ce jour; ▶ **back, so**.

forthcoming *adj* **1** [*event, book*] prochain (*before n*); **2 she wasn't very ~ about it** elle était peu disposée à en parler.

forthright *adj* direct.

forties ▶ 584, 492 *n pl* **1** (era) **the ~** les années *fpl* quarante; **2** (age) **to be in one's ~** avoir entre quarante et cinquante ans.

fortieth **I** *n* (in order) quarantième *mf*.
II *adj, adv* quarantième.

fortified *adj* **~ wine** vin *m* doux; **~ with vitamins** vitaminé.

fortnight ▶ 915 *n* (GB) quinze jours *mpl*; **the first ~ in August** la première quinzaine d'août.

fortunate *adj* heureux/-euse; **it was ~ for him that you arrived** heureusement pour lui que tu es arrivé.

fortunately *adv* heureusement.

fortune *n* **1** fortune *f*; **to make a ~** faire fortune; **to seek fame and ~** chercher fortune; **2 to have the good ~ to do** avoir la chance or le bonheur de faire; **3 to tell sb's ~** dire la bonne aventure à qn.

fortune-teller *n* diseur/-euse *m/f* de bonne aventure.

forty ▶ 492, 554 *n, pron, det* quarante (*m*) *inv*.

forward **I** *n* (Sport) avant *m*.
II *adj* **1** (bold) effronté; **2** (at the front) [*movement*] en avant; **to be too far ~** [*seat*] être trop en avant; **3** (advanced) avancé; **he's no further ~** il n'est pas plus avancé.
III *adv* (also **forwards**) **to step ~** faire un pas en avant; **to fall ~** tomber en avant; **to go** or **walk ~** avancer; **to move sth ~** avancer qch; **a way ~** une solution.
IV *vtr* **1** expédier [*goods*]; envoyer [*catalogue, parcel*]; **2** (send on) faire suivre, réexpédier [*mail*].

forwarding: **~ address** *n* nouvelle adresse *f* (pour faire suivre le courrier); **~ agent** *n* transitaire *m*.

forward planning *n* planification *f* à long terme.

forwards *adv* = **forward** III; ▶ **backwards**.

fossil *n* fossile *m*.

foster **I** *adj* [*child, parent*] adoptif/-ive (*dans une famille de placement*).
II *vtr* **1** (encourage) encourager [*attitude*]; promouvoir [*activity*]; **2** (act as parent to) prendre [qn] en placement [*child*].

foster: **~ family** *n* famille *f* de placement; **~ home** *n* foyer *m* de placement.

foul **I** *n* (Sport) faute *f* (**by** de; **on** sur).
II *adj* **1** (putrid) [*smell, air*] fétide; [*taste*] infect; **2** (grim) épouvantable; **to be in a ~ mood** être d'une humeur massacrante○; **to have a ~ temper** avoir un sale caractère; **3** [*language*] ordurier/-ière.
III *adv* **to taste ~** avoir un goût infect.
IV *vtr* **1** polluer [*environment*]; souiller [*pavement*]; **2** (Sport) commettre une faute contre [*player*].

foul-mouthed *adj* grossier/-ière.

found *vtr* fonder (**on** sur).

foundation *n* **1** (founding) fondation *f*; **2 ~s**

Forms of Address

Only those forms of address in frequent use are included here; for letter formulae (openings and closings), see the *French correspondence* section.

Speaking to someone

Where English puts the surname after the title, French normally uses the title alone (note that in written conversations French does not use a capital letter for ***monsieur***, ***madame*** and ***mademoiselle***, unlike English ***Mr*** etc, nor for titles such as ***docteur***).

good morning, Mr Johnson = bonjour, monsieur

good evening, Mrs Jones = bonsoir, madame

The French ***monsieur*** and ***madame*** tend to be used more often than the English ***Mr X*** or ***Mrs Y***. Also, in English, people often say simply ***good morning*** or ***excuse me***; in the equivalent situation in French, they might say ***bonjour, monsieur*** or ***pardon, madame***. In both languages, other titles are also used:

hallo, Dr. Brown
hallo, Doctor = bonjour, docteur

In some cases where titles are not used in English, they are used in French, eg ***bonjour, Monsieur le directeur*** or ***bonjour, Madame la directrice*** to a head teacher, or ***bonjour, maître*** to a lawyer of either sex. Other titles, such as ***professeur*** (in the sense of ***professor***), are used much less than their English equivalents in direct address. Where in English one might say ***good morning, Professor***, in French one would probably say ***bonjour, monsieur*** or ***bonjour, madame***.

Titles of important positions are used in direct forms of address, preceded by ***Monsieur le*** or ***Madame la*** or ***Madame le***, as in:

yes, Chair = oui, **Monsieur le** président
= (*to a woman*) oui, **Madame la** présidente

yes, Minister = oui, Monsieur le ministre
= (*to a woman*) oui, **Madame le** ministre

Note the use of ***Madame le*** when the noun in question, like ***ministre*** here, or ***professeur*** and other titles, has no feminine form.

Speaking about someone

Mr Smith is here = monsieur Smith est là

Mrs Jones phoned = madame Jones a téléphoné

Miss Black has arrived = mademoiselle Black est arrivée
(*French has no equivalent of Ms.*)

When the title accompanies someone's name, the definite article must be used in French:

Dr Blake has arrived = **le** docteur Blake est arrivé

Professor Jones spoke = **le** professeur Jones a parlé

This is true of all titles:

Prince Charles = **le** prince Charles

Princess Marie = **la** princesse Marie

Note that with royal etc titles, only ***Ier*** is spoken as an ordinal number (***premier***) in French; unlike English, all the others are spoken as cardinal numbers (***deux***, ***trois***, and so on):

King Richard I = le roi Richard **Ier** (*say* Richard **premier**)

Queen Elizabeth II = la reine Elizabeth **II** (*say* Elizabeth **deux**)

Pope John XXIII = le pape Jean **XXIII** (*say* Jean **vingt-trois**)

(of building) fondations *fpl*; **3** (also **~ cream**) fond *m* de teint.

founder *n* fondateur/-trice *m/f*.

founder member *n* (GB) membre *m* fondateur.

foundry *n* fonderie *f*.

fountain *n* fontaine *f*.

fountain pen *n* stylo *m* (à encre).

four ▶ 492, 554 *n, pron, det* quatre (*m*) *inv*.
IDIOMS **on all ~s** à quatre pattes.

four: **~-door** *adj* (Aut) [*car*] quatre portes; **~-letter word** *n* mot *m* grossier.

four-star I *n* (GB) (also **~ petrol**) super(-carburant) *m*.
II *adj* [*hotel, restaurant*] quatre étoiles.

fourteen ▶ 492, 554 *n, pron, det* quatorze (*m*) *inv*.

fourteenth ▶ 584, 642 I *n* **1** (in order) quatorzième *mf*; **2** (of month) quatorze *m inv*.
II *adj, adv* quatorzième.

fourth ▶ 584, 642 I *n* **1** (in order) quatrième *mf*; **2** (of month) quatre *m inv*; **3** (fraction) quatrième *m*; **4** (also **~ gear**) (Aut) quatrième *f*.
II *adj, adv* quatrième.

four-wheel drive (**vehicle**) *n* quatre-quatre *m inv*, 4 x 4 *m inv*.

fowl *n* volaille *f*.

fox *n* renard *m*.

fox hunting *n* chasse *f* au renard.

fraction *n* fraction *f* (**of** de); **a ~ more** un petit peu plus.

fracture I *n* fracture *f*.
II *vtr* fracturer [*bone, rock*].
III *vi* [*bone*] se fracturer; [*pipe, masonry*] se fissurer.

fragile *adj* fragile.

fragment *n* (of rock, manuscript) fragment *m*; (of glass, china) morceau *m*; **~s of conversation** bribes *fpl* de conversation.

fragrance *n* parfum *m*.

fragrant *adj* odorant.

frail *adj* [*person*] frêle; [*health, hope*] précaire.

frame I *n* **1** (of building, boat, roof) charpente *f*; (of car) châssis *m*; (of bicycle, racquet) cadre *m*; (of bed) sommier *m*; (of tent) armature *f*; **2** (of picture, window) cadre *m*; (of door) encadrement *m*; **3** (body) corps *m*; **4** (in snooker) (triangle) triangle *m*; (game) manche *f*; **5** (Comput) bloc *m*.
II **frames** *n pl* (of spectacles) monture *f*.
III *vtr* **1** encadrer [*picture, face, view*]; **2** (formulate) formuler [*question*].

frame of mind *n* état *m* d'esprit; **to be in the right/wrong ~ for sth** être/ne pas être d'humeur pour qch.

framework *n* **1** (structure) structure *f*; **2** (of society) cadre *m*; (of novel, play) structure *f*; **a ~ for sth** un cadre pour qch.

franc ▶ 748 *n* franc *m*.

France ▶ 574 *pr n* France *f*.

franchise I *n* **1** **universal ~** suffrage *m* universel; **2** (commercial) franchise *f*.
II *noun modifier* [*business, chain*] franchisé; [*holder*] de franchise.

frank *adj* franc/franche (**about** en ce qui concerne).

Frankfurt ▶ 574 *pr n* Francfort.

frankly *adv* franchement.

frankness *n* franchise *f*.

frantic *adj* **1** [*activity*] frénétique; **2** [*effort, search*] désespéré; **to be ~ with worry** être fou/folle d'inquiétude.

fraternal *adj* fraternel/-elle.

fraud *n* fraude *f*.

fraudulent *adj* [*practice, use*] frauduleux/-euse; [*signature, cheque*] falsifié; [*earnings*] illicite.

fray *vi* [*material, rope*] s'effilocher; [*nerves*] craquer○.

freak I *n* **1** (strange person) original/-e *m/f*; **2** (at circus) phénomène *m*; **~ show** exhibition *f* de monstres; **3** (unusual occurrence) aberration *f*; **a ~ of nature** une bizarrerie de la nature; **4**○ (enthusiast) mordu/-e○ *m/f*, fana○ *mf*.
II *adj* [*accident, storm*] exceptionnel/-elle.

freckle *n* tache *f* de rousseur.

free I *adj* **1** [*person, country, press*] libre (*after n*); [*access, choice*] libre (*before n*); **to be ~ to do** être libre de faire; **to leave sb ~ to do** laisser qn libre de faire; **to feel ~ to do** ne pas hésiter à faire; **to be allowed ~ expression** pouvoir s'exprimer librement; **2** (not captive) [*person, limb*] libre; [*animal, bird*] en liberté; **to set [sb/sth] ~** libérer [*person*]; rendre la liberté à [*animal*]; **to pull sth ~** dégager qch; **they had to cut the driver ~ (from his car)** on a dû couper la tôle de la voiture pour dégager le chauffeur; **the boat broke ~ from its moorings** le bateau a rompu ses amarres; **3** (devoid) **to be ~ of sb** être libéré de qn; **~ from** or **of pollution** dépourvu de pollution; **a day ~ from** or **of interruptions** une journée sans interruptions; **4** (also **~ of charge**) gratuit; **'admission ~'** 'entrée gratuite'; **5** (not occupied) libre; **are you ~ for lunch on Monday?** es-tu libre lundi pour déjeuner?; **is this seat ~?** cette place est-elle libre?; **6** être prodigue de [*advice*]; **to be very ~ with money** dépenser sans compter.
II *adv* **1** [*run, roam*] librement, en toute liberté; **to go ~** [*hostage*] être libéré; [*criminal*] circuler en toute liberté; **2** (without payment) gratuitement; **children are admitted ~** l'entrée est gratuite pour les enfants.
III *vtr* **1** (gen) libérer; (from wreckage) dégager; **2** débloquer [*money, resources*].
IV **-free** *combining form* **smoke/sugar-~** sans fumée/sucre; **interest-~** sans intérêt.
V **for free** *phr* gratuitement.
IDIOMS **to have a ~ hand** avoir carte blanche (**in** pour).

free agent *n* **to be a ~** pouvoir agir à sa guise.

free and easy *adj* (easygoing) décontracté; (too casual) désinvolte.

freedom *n* liberté *f* (**to do** de faire); **~ of the press** liberté de la presse; **~ of information**

libre accès *m* à l'information; **they gave us the ~ of their house** ils nous ont laissé le plein usage de leur maison; **to have** or **enjoy ~ from** être à l'abri de [*hunger, fear, war*].

free: **~ enterprise** *n* libre entreprise *f*; **~fall** *n* chute *f* libre; **Freefone®** *n* ≈ numéro *m* vert®; **~-for-all** *n* mêlée *f* générale; **~ gift** *n* cadeau *m*; **~hold** *n* pleine propriété *f*, propriété *f* foncière perpétuelle et libre; **~ kick** *n* coup *m* franc.

freelance I *n* (also **freelancer**) free-lance *mf*.
II *adv* [*work*] en free-lance.

freely *adv* **1** [*travel, speak, sell*] librement; [*breathe*] aisément; (figurative) librement; [*spend, give*] sans compter; **to move ~** (around building, country) se déplacer librement; **2** [*admit*] volontiers; **3** [*translate, adapt*] librement.

free: **~ market** *n* (also **~ economy**) économie *f* de marché; **Freephone®** *n* = **Freefone®**; **~post** *n* (GB) port *m* payé; **~-range** *adj* [*chicken*] élevé en plein air; **~-range eggs** *n pl* œufs *mpl* de poules élevées en plein air; **~style** *n* (in swimming) nage *f* libre; (in skiing) figures *fpl* libres; (in wrestling) lutte *f* libre; **~ trade** *n* libre-échange *m*; **~way** *n* (US) autoroute *f*.

free will *n* libre arbitre *m*; **to do sth of one's (own) ~** faire qch de son plein gré.

freeze I *n* **1** (in weather) gelées *fpl*; **2** (Econ) gel *m* (**on** de).
II *vtr* **1** congeler [*food*]; [*cold weather*] geler [*liquid, pipes*]; **2** (Econ) bloquer, geler [*price, wages, assets*]; **3** (anaesthetize) insensibiliser [*gum, skin*]; **4** (Comput) figer [*window*].
III *vi* **1** [*water, pipes*] geler; [*food*] se congeler; **2** (feel cold) geler; **to be freezing to death** mourir de froid.
IV *v impers* geler.

freeze: **~-dried** *adj* lyophilisé; **~ frame** *n* arrêt *m* sur image.

freezer *n* congélateur *m*.

freezer compartment *n* freezer *m*.

freezing I *n* zéro *m*; **below ~** en-dessous de zéro.
II *adj* **I'm ~** je suis gelé; **it's ~ in here** on gèle ici.

freezing: **~ cold** *adj* [*room, wind*] glacial; [*water*] glacé; **~ fog** *n* brouillard *m* givrant.

freight I *n* **1** (goods) fret *m*, marchandises *fpl*; **2** (transport system) transport *m*; **3** (cost) (frais *mpl* de) port *m*.
II *noun modifier* [*company, service*] de transport; [*train*] de marchandises.

freighter *n* **1** (ship) cargo *m*; **2** (plane) avion-cargo *m*.

French ▶**712** **I** *n* **1** (language) français *m*; **2** (people) **the ~** les Français *mpl*.
II *adj* [*culture, food, politics*] français; [*teacher, lesson*] de français; [*ambassador, embassy*] de France.
IDIOMS **to take ~ leave** filer à l'anglaise.

French: **~ bean** *n* haricot *m* vert; **~ Canadian** ▶**712** *n* (person) Canadien/-ienne *m/f* francophone; **~ doors** *n pl* (US) porte-fenêtre *f*; **~ dressing** *n* (GB) vinaigrette *f*; (US) sauce *f* mayonnaise; **~ fries** *n pl* frites *fpl*; **~man** *n* Français *m*; **~ mustard** *n* moutarde *f* douce; **~ Riviera** *n* Côte *f* d'Azur; **~-speaking** *adj* francophone; **~ toast** *n* pain *m* perdu; **~ window** *n* porte-fenêtre *f*; **~woman** *n* Française *f*.

frenetic *adj* [*activity*] frénétique; [*lifestyle*] trépidant.

frenzied *adj* [*activity*] frénétique; [*attempt*] désespéré.

frenzy *n* frénésie *f*, délire *m*; **to be in a (state of) ~** être exalté; **there was a ~ of activity** ça grouillait d'activité.

frequency *n* fréquence *f* (**of** de).

frequent *adj* **1** (common, usual) [*expression, use*] courant; **2** (happening often) fréquent; **to make ~ use of sth** se servir souvent or fréquemment de qch.

frequently *adv* souvent, fréquemment.

fresco *n* fresque *f*.

fresh *adj* **1** frais/fraîche; **to feel ~** [*foodstuff*] être frais au toucher; **to taste/smell ~** avoir un goût frais/une odeur fraîche; **bread ~ from the oven** du pain frais sorti du four; **~ orange juice** jus d'orange pressée; **while it is still ~ in your mind** tant que tu l'as tout frais à l'esprit; **2** [*evidence, attempt*] nouveau/-elle (*before n*); [*linen*] propre; **to make a ~ start** prendre un nouveau départ; **3** [*approach, outlook*] (tout) nouveau/(toute) nouvelle (*before n*); **4 to feel** or **be ~** [*person*] être plein d'entrain; **5**° impertinent; **to be ~ with sb** être un peu familier/-ière avec qn.

fresh air *n* air *m* frais; **to get some ~** prendre l'air, s'oxygéner.

freshen *v* ■ **freshen up** faire un brin de toilette.

freshness *n* fraîcheur *f*.

fresh water *n* eau *f* douce.

fret *vi* **1** (be anxious) s'inquiéter (**over, about** pour, au sujet de); **2** [*child*] pleurer, pleurnicher.

Freudian slip *n* lapsus *m*.

friction *n* **1** (rubbing) frottement *m*; **2** (conflict) conflits *mpl* (**between** entre); **to cause ~** être cause de friction.

Friday ▶**584** *n* vendredi *m*.

fridge *n* (GB) frigo° *m*, réfrigérateur *m*.

fridge-freezer *n* réfrigérateur *m* avec congélateur.

friend *n* ami/-e *m/f* (**of** de); **to make ~s** se faire des amis; **to make ~s with sb** devenir ami/-e *m/f* avec qn; **Maura is a ~ of mine** Maura est une de mes amies; **to have ~s in high places** avoir des amis influents.

friendliness *n* gentillesse *f* (**of** de).

friendly I *n* (Sport) match *m* amical.
II *adj* [*person*] amical, sympathique; [*animal*] affectueux/-euse; [*attitude, argument, match*] amical; [*smile*] (polite) aimable; (warm) amical; [*government, nation*] ami *inv* (*after n*); **to be ~ with sb** être ami/-e *m/f* avec qn; **to get** or **become ~ with sb** se lier d'amitié avec qn; **to be on ~ terms with sb** être en bons

termes avec qn; **the people round here are very ~** les gens par ici sont très gentils.
III **-friendly** *combining form* **environment-~** qui ne nuit pas à l'environnement; **user-~** d'utilisation facile, convivial.

friendship *n* amitié *f*.

fries○ *n pl* (US) frites *fpl*.

fright *n* peur *f*; **to take ~** prendre peur, s'effrayer; **to have** or **get a ~** avoir peur; **to give sb a ~** faire peur à qn, effrayer qn.

frighten *vtr* faire peur à, effrayer; **to ~ sb into doing** faire tellement peur à qn qu'il/elle finit par faire.
■ **frighten off**: **~ off [sb]** chasser [*intruder*]; effaroucher [*rival, buyer*].

frightened *adj* **to be ~** avoir peur (**of** de; **to do** de faire); **to be ~ that** craindre que (+ *subj*), avoir peur que (+ *subj*); **I was ~ that they'd hurt him** j'avais peur qu'ils lui fassent mal.

frightening *adj* effrayant.

frill *n* (on dress) volant *m*; (on shirt) jabot *m*.

fringe *n* **1** frange *f*; **on the ~s of society** en marge de la societé; **2** (in theatre) **the ~** théâtre *m* alternatif.

fringe benefits *n pl* avantages *mpl* sociaux or en nature.

frisk *vtr* fouiller [*person*].

fritter *n* beignet *m*.

frivolous *adj* frivole.

frizzy *adj* [*hair*] crépu.

frog *n* grenouille *f*.
IDIOMS **to have a ~ in one's throat** avoir un chat dans la gorge.

frog: **~man** *n* homme-grenouille *m*; **~s' legs** *n pl* cuisses *fpl* de grenouille.

from *prep*

■ **Note** *from* is often translated by *de*: *from Rome* = de Rome; *from the sea* = de la mer.
– Remember that *de* + *le* always becomes *du* (*from the office* = du bureau), and *de* + *les* always becomes *des* (*from the United States* = des États-Unis).
– For examples and particular usages, see the entry below.

1 de; **where is he ~?** d'où est-il?, d'où vient-il?; **she comes ~ Oxford** elle vient d'Oxford; **paper ~ Denmark** du papier provenant du Danemark; **a flight ~ Nice** un vol en provenance de Nice; **a friend ~ Chicago** un ami (qui vient) de Chicago; **a colleague ~ Japan** un collègue japonais; **people ~ Spain** les Espagnols; **a man ~ the council** un homme qui travaille pour le conseil municipal; **a rep ~ McCann & Co.** un représentant de chez McCann et Cie; **a letter ~ Tim** une lettre (de la part) de Tim; **who is it ~?** c'est de la part de qui?; **best wishes ~ my mother** vous avez le bonjour de ma mère; (more formal) vous avez le bonjour de la part de ma mère; **alcohol can be made ~ a wide range of products** on peut faire de l'alcool à partir de produits très variés; **noises ~ upstairs** du bruit venant d'en haut; **10 km ~ the sea** à 10 km de la mer; **15 years ~ now** dans 15 ans, d'ici 15 ans; **2 ~ ... to...** de ... à ...; **the journey ~ A to B** le voyage de A à B; **the road ~ A to B** la route qui va de A à B; **open ~ 2 pm to 5 pm** ouvert de 14 à 17 heures; **~ June to August** du mois de juin au mois d'août; **to rise ~ 10 to 17%** passer de 10 à 17%; **~ start to finish** du début à la fin; **everything ~ paperclips to wigs** tout, des trombones aux perruques; **~ day to day** de jour en jour; **3** à partir de; **~ today/May** à partir d'aujourd'hui/du mois de mai; **wine ~ £5 a bottle** du vin à partir de 5 livres la bouteille; **~ then on** dès lors; **~ the age of 8** depuis l'âge de 8 ans; **4** (based on) **~ a short story** d'après un conte; **to speak ~ experience** parler d'expérience; **5** (among) **to choose** or **pick ~** choisir parmi; **6** (in maths) **10 ~ 27 leaves 17** 27 moins 10 égale 17; **7** (because of) **I know ~ speaking to her that** j'ai appris en lui parlant que; **I know her ~ work** je la connais car on travaille ensemble; **~ what I saw/he said** d'après ce que j'ai vu/ce qu'il a dit.

front I *n* **1** (of house) façade *f*; (of shop) devanture *f*; (of cupboard, box, sweater, building) devant *m*; (of book) couverture *f*; (of card, coin, banknote) recto *m*; (of car, boat) avant *m*; (of fabric) endroit *m*; **to button at the ~** se boutonner sur le devant; **on the ~ of the envelope** au recto de l'enveloppe; **2** (of train, queue) tête *f*; (of auditorium) premier rang *m*; **at the ~ of the line** en tête de la file; **to sit at the ~ of the class** s'asseoir au premier rang de la classe; **I'll sit in the ~** je vais m'asseoir devant; **at the ~ of the coach** à l'avant du car; **3** (GB) (promenade) front *m* de mer, bord *m* de mer; **on the sea ~** au bord de la mer; **4** (area of activity) côté *m*; **changes on the domestic** or **home ~** des changements côté politique intérieure; **5** (outer appearance) façade *f*; **it's just a ~** ce n'est qu'une façade.
II *adj* [*entrance*] côté rue; [*garden, window*] de devant; [*bedroom*] qui donne sur la rue; [*wheel*] avant; [*seat*] (in cinema) au premier rang; (in vehicle) de devant; [*leg, paw, tooth*] de devant; [*carriage*] de tête; [*page*] premier/-ière (*before n*); [*view*] de face.
III *vtr* **1**○ être à la tête de [*band*]; **2** présenter [*TV show*].
IV *vi* **to ~ onto** (GB) or **on** (US) donner sur.
V **in front** *phr* **who's in ~?** qui gagne?; **I'm 30 points in ~** j'ai 30 points d'avance.
VI **in front of** *phr* devant.

front bench *n* (GB) (also **frontbenchers**○ *n pl*) députés *mpl* membres du gouvernement.

front: **~ cover** *n* couverture *f*; **~ door** *n* porte *f* d'entrée.

frontier I *n* frontière *f*.
II *noun modifier* [*town, zone*] frontière *inv* (*after n*), frontalier/-ière.

front line *n* **1** (Mil) front *m*; **2 to be in** (GB) or **on** (US) **the ~** être en première ligne; **3** (in rugby) **the ~** les avants *mpl* première ligne.

front page I *n* première page *f*.
II **front-page** *noun modifier* [*picture, story*] à

la une○; **the ~ headlines** les gros titres, la manchette.

front-wheel drive *n* traction *f* avant.

frost *n* gel *m*.
■ **frost over, frost up** se couvrir de givre.

frost: **~bite** *n* gelures *fpl*; **~bitten** *adj* gelé.

frosty *adj* **1** [*morning*] glacial; [*windscreen*] couvert de givre; **it was a ~ night** il gelait cette nuit-là; **2** (unfriendly) [*reception*] glacial.

froth *n* (on beer, champagne) mousse *f*; (on water) écume *f*; (around mouth) écume *f*.

frown *vi* froncer les sourcils; **to ~ at sb** regarder qn en fronçant les sourcils.
■ **frown on, frown upon**: **~ on** or **upon [sth]** désapprouver, critiquer; **to be ~ed upon** être mal vu.

frozen *adj* **1** (of food) (bought) surgelé; (home-prepared) congelé; **2** gelé; **I'm ~** je suis gelé; **to be ~ stiff** être transi de froid; **to be ~ with fear** être paralysé par la peur; **to be ~ to the spot** être cloué sur place.

fruit *n* fruit *m*; **a piece of ~** un fruit.

fruit: **~ cake** *n* cake *m*; **~ machine** *n* machine *f* à sous; **~ salad** *n* salade *f* de fruits; **~ tree** *n* arbre *m* fruitier.

fruity *adj* [*wine, fragrance*] fruité.

frustrate *vtr* frustrer [*person*]; réduire [qch] à néant [*effort*]; contrarier [*plan*]; entraver [*attempt*].

frustrated *adj* frustré.

frustrating *adj* **1** (irritating) énervant; **2** (unsatisfactory) frustrant.

frustration *n* frustration *f* (**at, with** quant à).

fry I *n* **1** (fish) fretin *m*; **2 small ~** (children) petits *mpl*, mioches○ *mpl*; (unimportant people) menu fretin *m*.
II *vtr* faire frire.
III **fried** *pp adj* **fried fish** poisson *m* frit; **fried food** friture *f*; **fried eggs** œufs *mpl* au plat; **fried potatoes** pommes *fpl* de terre sautées.

frying pan (GB) *n* poêle *f* (à frire).

fuel I *n* (for heating) combustible *m*; (for car, plane) carburant *m*.
II *vtr* **1** alimenter [*engine*]; **to be ~led by gas** marcher au gaz; **2** ravitailler [*plane*]; **3** aggraver [*tension*]; attiser [*hatred*].

fuel tank *n* (of car) réservoir *m*.

fugitive *n* fugitif/-ive *m/f*, fuyard/-e *m/f*.

fulfil (GB), **fulfill** (US) *vtr* **1** réaliser [*ambition*]; répondre à [*desire, need*]; **to ~ one's potential** se réaliser; **to feel ~led** se sentir comblé; **2** remplir [*duty, conditions, contract*].

fulfilment (GB), **fulfillment** (US) *n* **1** (satisfaction) épanouissement *m*; **personal ~** accomplissement *m* de soi; **2 the ~ of** la réalisation de [*ambition, need*].

full I *adj* **1** (gen) plein (**of** de); [*hotel, flight, car park*] complet/-ète; [*theatre*] comble; **a ~ bottle of whisky** une pleine bouteille de whisky; **~ to overflowing** [*bucket*] plein à déborder; [*suitcase*] plein à craquer○; **I've got my hands ~** j'ai les mains pleines; (busy) je suis débordé; **I'm ~ (up)** je n'en peux plus; **2** (busy) [*day, week*] chargé, bien rempli; **a very ~ life** une vie très remplie; **3** (complete) [*name, breakfast, story*] complet/-ète; [*price, control*] total; [*responsibility*] entier/-ière; [*support*] inconditionnel/-elle; [*inquiry*] approfondi; **the ~ extent of the damage** l'ampleur des dégâts; **4** (officially recognized) [*member*] à part entière; [*right*] plein (*before n*); **5** (maximum) [*employment, bloom*] plein (*before n*); **at ~ volume** à plein volume; **at ~ speed** à toute vitesse; **to make ~ use of sth** profiter pleinement de qch; **to get ~ marks** (GB) obtenir la note maximale; **6** (for emphasis) [*hour, kilo, month*] bon/bonne (*before n*); **7** (rounded) [*cheeks*] rond; [*figure*] fort; [*skirt, sleeve*] ample; **8 there's a ~ moon** c'est la pleine lune.
II *adv* **to hit sb ~ in the face** frapper qn en plein visage; **to know ~ well that** savoir fort bien que; **with the heating up ~** avec le chauffage à fond.
III **in full** *phr* [*pay*] intégralement; **to write sth in full** écrire qch en toutes lettres.

full: **~-back** *n* (Sport) arrière *m*; **~ beam** *n* (Aut) pleins phares *mpl*.

full-blown *adj* **1** [*disease*] déclaré; [*epidemic*] extensif/-ive; **to have ~ Aids** être atteint d'un sida avéré; **2** [*crisis, war*] à grande échelle.

full: **~ board** *n* (in hotel) pension *f* complète; **~-bodied** *adj* [*wine*] corsé; **~-cream milk** *n* (GB) lait *m* entier.

full-length *adj* [*coat, curtain*] long/longue; [*mirror*] en pied; **a ~ film** un long métrage.

full: **~ name** *n* nom *m* et prénom *m*; **~-page** *adj* [*advertisement*] pleine page; **~ price** *adj, adv* au prix fort.

full-scale *adj* **1** [*drawing*] grandeur *f* nature; **2** [*investigation*] approfondi; **3** [*alert*] général; [*crisis*] généralisé.

full: **~-size(d)** *adj* grand format *inv*; **~ stop** *n* (GB) point *m*.

full time I *n* (Sport) fin *m* du match.
II **full-time** *noun modifier* **1** (Sport) [*score*] final; **2** [*job, student*] à plein temps.
III *adv* [*study, work*] à plein temps.

fully *adv* **1** [*understand*] très bien; [*recover*] tout à fait; [*dressed*] entièrement; [*awake, developed*] complètement; [*aware*] parfaitement; **to be ~ qualified** avoir obtenu tous ses diplômes; **2** [*open*] à fond; **~ booked** complet/-ète.

fume *vi* **1** [*chemical, mixture*] fumer; **2**○ **to be fuming** être furibond○.

fumes *n pl* émanations *fpl*; **petrol ~** (GB), **gas ~** (US) vapeurs *fpl* d'essence.

fun *n* plaisir *m*, amusement *m*; **to have ~** s'amuser (**doing** en faisant; **with** avec); **we had great ~** nous nous sommes beaucoup amusés; **windsurfing is ~** c'est amusant de faire de la planche à voile; **to do sth for ~** faire qch pour s'amuser; **it's not much ~** ce n'est pas très amusant (**for** pour); **to spoil sb's ~** gâcher le plaisir de qn; **she is great ~ to be with** on s'amuse beaucoup avec elle.
IDIOMS **to make ~ of** or **poke ~ at sb/sth** se moquer de qn/qch.

function I *n* **1** fonction *f*; **2** (reception) réception *f*; (ceremony) cérémonie *f* (officielle).

II *vi* **1** (work properly) fonctionner; **2 to ~ as** [*object*] faire fonction de, servir de; [*person*] jouer le rôle de.

functional *adj* (in working order) opérationnel/-elle.

fund I *n* fonds *m*; **relief ~** caisse *f* de secours; **disaster ~** collecte *f* en faveur des sinistrés.
II *vtr* financer [*company, project*].

fundamental *adj* [*issue, meaning*] fondamental (**to** pour); [*error, importance*] capital; [*concern*] principal; **to be ~ to** être essentiel à.

fundamentals *n pl* **the ~** les règles *fpl* de base.

funding *n* financement *m*; **to receive ~ from** être financé par.

fund: **~-raiser** *n* collecteur/-trice *m/f* de fonds; **~-raising** *n* collecte *f* de fonds.

funds *n pl* fonds *mpl*, capitaux *mpl*; **to be in ~** avoir de l'argent.

funeral *n* enterrement *m*, obsèques *fpl* (formal).

funeral: **~ director** ▶805 *n* entrepreneur *m* de pompes funèbres; **~ home** (US), **~ parlour** *n* chambre *f* mortuaire (*chez un entrepreneur de pompes funèbres*).

fun fair *n* fête *f* foraine.

fungus *n* **1** (mushroom) champignon *m*; **2** (mould) moisissure *f*.

funnel *n* **1** (for liquids) entonnoir *m*; **2** (on ship) cheminée *f*.

funny *adj* (amusing) drôle, amusant; (odd) bizarre; **it's ~ that she hasn't phoned** c'est drôle or bizarre qu'elle n'ait pas appelé; **there's something ~ going on** il se passe des choses bizarres; **to feel ~**○ se sentir tout/-e chose○.
IDIOMS **~ peculiar or ~ ha-ha?** drôle-bizarre ou drôle-amusant?

fur I *n* (of animal) poils *mpl*; (for garment) fourrure *f*.
II *noun modifier* [*collar, coat*] de fourrure.

furious *adj* **1** furieux/-ieuse (**with, at** contre); **he's ~ about it** cela l'a rendu furieux; **I was ~ with her for coming** or **that she had come** j'étais furieux qu'elle soit venue; **2** [*debate, struggle*] acharné; [*storm*] déchaîné; **at a ~ rate** à un rythme effréné.

furnace *n* (boiler) chaudière *f*; (in foundry) fourneau *m*; (for forging) four *m*.

furnish *vtr* meubler [*room, apartment*] (**with** avec).

furnishings *n pl* ameublement *m*.

furniture *n* mobilier *m*, meubles *mpl*; **a piece of ~** un meuble.

furniture: **~ polish** *n* encaustique *f*; **~ remover** ▶805 *n* (GB) déménageur *m*; **~ van** *n* camion *m* de déménagement.

furry *adj* [*toy*] en peluche; [*kitten*] au poil touffu.

further I *adv* **1** (also **farther**) plus loin (**than** que); **how much ~ is it?** c'est encore loin?; **to get ~ and ~ away** s'éloigner de plus en plus; **~ back/forward** plus en arrière/en avant; **~ away** or **off** plus loin; **~ on** encore plus loin; **2** (in time) (also **farther**) **~ back than 1964** avant 1964; **we must look ~ ahead** nous devons regarder plus vers l'avenir; **I haven't read ~ than page twenty** je n'ai pas lu au-delà de la page vingt; **3 prices fell (even) ~** les prix ont baissé encore plus.
II *adj* **1** (additional) **a ~ 500 people** 500 personnes de plus; **~ changes** d'autres changements; **there have been ~ allegations that** il y a eu de nouvelles allégations selon lesquelles; **~ details can be obtained by writing to the manager** pour plus de renseignements, adressez-vous à la direction; **without ~ delay** sans plus attendre; **2** (also **farther**) [*side, end*] autre.
III *vtr* augmenter [*chances*]; faire avancer [*career, plan*]; servir [*cause*].

further education *n* (GB Univ) ≈ enseignement *m* professionnel.

furthest I *adj* le plus éloigné.
II *adv* **1** (also **the ~**) le plus loin; **this plan goes ~ towards solving the problem** c'est ce projet qui s'approche le plus de la solution du problème; **2** (in time) **the ~ back I can remember is 1970** je ne me rappelle rien avant 1970; **the ~ ahead we can look is next week** nous ne pouvons rien prévoir au-delà de la semaine prochaine.

furtive *adj* [*glance, movement*] furtif/-ive; [*behaviour*] suspect.

fury *n* fureur *f*; **to be in a ~** être en fureur.

fuse, **fuze** (US) **I** *n* fusible *m*; **to blow a ~** faire sauter un fusible; (get angry) piquer une crise○.
II *vtr* munir [qch] d'un fusible [*plug*].

fuse: **~ box** *n* boîte *f* à fusibles; **~ wire** *n* fusible *m*.

fuss I *n* **1** (agitation) remue-ménage *m inv*; (verbal) histoires *fpl*; **to make a ~** faire des histoires; **to make a ~ about sth** faire toute une histoire à propos de qch; **to make a (big) ~ about nothing** faire un tas○ d'histoires pour rien; **2 to kick up a ~ about sth**○ piquer une crise○ à propos de qch; **3** (attention) **to make a ~ of** être aux petits soins avec or pour [*person*]; caresser [*animal*].
II *vi* **1** (worry) se faire du souci (**about** pour); **he's always ~ing over** or **about his appearance** il est obsédé par son apparence; **2** (show attention) **to ~ over sb**○ être aux petits soins avec or pour qn.

fussy *adj* **to be ~ about one's food/about details** être difficile sur la nourriture/maniaque sur les détails.

future I *n* **1** avenir *m*; **in the ~** dans l'avenir; **in the near** or **not too distant ~** dans un proche avenir; **in ~** à l'avenir; **2** (also **~ tense**) futur *m*; **in the ~** au futur.
II *adj* [*generation, developments, investment, earnings*] futur; [*prospects*] d'avenir; [*queen, king*] futur (*before n*); **at some ~ date** à une date ultérieure.

futures *n pl* (on stock exchange) contrats *mpl* à terme.

fuze (US) = **fuse**.

fuzzy *adj* **1** [*hair, beard*] (curly) crépu; (downy) duveteux/-euse; **2** [*image*] flou; [*idea, mind*] confus.

g, G *n* **1** (letter) g, G *m*; **2 g** (*written abbr* = **gram(s)**) g.

gadget *n* gadget *m*.

gaffe *n* bévue *f*.

gag I *n* **1** (on hostage, media) bâillon *m*; **2**○ (joke) blague○ *f*.
II *vtr* bâillonner [*hostage, media*].
III *vi* avoir un haut-le-cœur.

gage (US) = **gauge**.

gain I *n* **1** (financial) gain *m*, profit *m*; **2** (increase) augmentation *f* (**in** de); **3** (advantage) gain *m*; (advances) progrès *m* (**in** de).
II *vtr* **1** acquérir [*experience*] (**from** de); obtenir [*advantage*] (**from** grâce à); gagner [*respect, support, time*]; conquérir [*freedom*]; **to ~ popularity** gagner en popularité; **we have nothing to ~** nous n'avons rien à gagner; **to ~ control of sth** prendre le contrôle de qch; **to ~ possession of sth** s'assurer la possession de qch; **to ~ ground** gagner du terrain (**on** sur); **2 to ~ speed** prendre de la vitesse or de l'élan; **to ~ weight** prendre du poids; **to ~ 3 minutes** prendre 3 minutes d'avance; **3** (win) gagner [*points*]; **they ~ed four seats from the Democrats** ils ont pris quatre sièges aux Démocrates.
III *vi* **1** (increase) **to ~ in popularity** gagner en popularité; **to ~ in value** prendre de la valeur; **2** (profit) **she hasn't ~ed by it** cela ne lui a rien rapporté.
■ **gain on**: **~ on [sb/sth]** rattraper [*person, vehicle*].

galaxy *n* galaxie *f*.

gale *n* vent *m* violent; **a force 9 ~** un vent force 9.

gallery *n* **1** (**art**) ~ musée *m* (d'art); **2** galerie *f*; **press/public ~** galerie de la presse/du public; **3** (in theatre) dernier balcon *m*.

Gallic *adj* **1** (French) français; **2** (of Gaul) gaulois.

gallon *n* gallon *m* ((GB) = *4.546 litres*; (US) = *3.785 litres*).

gallop I *n* galop *m*.
II *vi* galoper.

gambit *n* **1** tactique *f*; **2** (in chess) gambit *m*.

gamble I *n* pari *m*.
II *vtr* **1** jouer [*money*]; **2** (figurative) miser (**on** sur).
III *vi* (at cards, on shares) jouer; (on horses) parier.

gambling *n* jeu *m* (d'argent).

game I *n* **1** jeu *m*; **to play a ~** jouer à un jeu; **to have a ~ of** faire une partie de; **2** (match) match *m* (**of** de); (part of match) (in tennis) jeu *m*; (in bridge) manche *f*; **we're two ~s all** nous sommes à deux jeux partout; **3** (Culin) gibier *m*.
II games *n pl* **1** (GB Sch) sport *m*; **2** (also **Games**) (sporting event) Jeux *mpl*.
IDIOMS **that's the name of the ~** c'est la règle du jeu; **the ~'s up** tout est fichu○; **to give the ~ away** vendre la mèche; **two can play at that ~** à bon chat, bon rat (Proverb).

game: **~ point** *n* (in tennis) balle *f* de jeu; **~ show** *n* jeu *m* télévisé.

gammon *n* jambon *m*.

gang *n* **1** (of criminals) gang *m*; (of youths, friends) bande *f*; **2** (of workmen, prisoners) équipe *f*.

Ganges *pr n* Gange *m*.

gangster *n* gangster *m*.

gangway *n* **1** (to ship) passerelle *f*; **2** (GB) (in bus, cinema) allée *f*.

gap *n* **1** (gen) trou *m* (**in** dans); (between planks, curtains) interstice *m* (**in** entre); (between buildings, cars) espace *m* (**in** entre); (in cloud) trouée *f* (**in** dans); **to fill a ~** combler un vide; **2** (of time) intervalle *m*; (in conversation) silence *m*; **3** (discrepancy) (in age, scores) différence *f*; (between opinions) divergence *f*; **a 15-year age ~** une différence d'âge de 15 ans; **to close the ~** supprimer l'écart; **4** (in knowledge) lacune *f* (**in** dans); **5** (in market) créneau *m*; **to fill a ~ in the market** répondre à un besoin réel du marché; **6** (in finance) déficit *m*; **trade ~** déficit commercial.

gape *vi* **1** (stare) rester bouche bée; **to ~ at sth/sb** regarder qn/qch bouche bée; **2 to ~ open** [*chasm*] s'ouvrir tout grand; [*wound*] être béant; [*garment*] bâiller.

gaping *adj* [*person*] bouche bée; [*wound, hole*] béant.

garage *n* garage *m*.

garage mechanic ▶**805** *n* mécanicien *m*.

garbage *n* **1** (US) (refuse) ordures *fpl*; **2** (nonsense) âneries *fpl*, bêtises *fpl*.

garbage: **~ can** *n* (US) poubelle *f*; **~ chute** *n* (US) vide-ordures *m inv*; **~ truck** *n* (US) camion *m* des éboueurs.

garden I *n* **1** (GB) jardin *m*; **front/back ~** jardin situé devant/derrière la maison; **2** (US) (flowerbed) platebande *f*; (vegetable garden) potager *m*.
II gardens *n pl* jardin *m* public.
III *noun modifier* [*furniture*] de jardin; [*wall, fence, shed*] du jardin.
IV *vi* jardiner, faire du jardinage.

garden centre (GB), **garden center** (US) *n* jardinerie *f*.

gardener ▶**805** *n* jardinier/-ière *m/f*.

gardening *n* jardinage *m*.

gargle *vi* se gargariser (**with** avec).

garlic I *n* ail *m*.
II *noun modifier* [*sausage, mushrooms*] à l'ail; [*sauce*] aillé; [*salt*] d'ail; **~ butter** beurre *m* d'ail.

garment *n* vêtement *m*.

Games and Sports

With or without the definite article?

French normally uses the definite article with names of games and sports:

football	= **le** football
bridge	= **le** bridge
chess	= **les** échecs *mpl*
to play football	= jouer **au** football
to play bridge	= jouer **au** bridge
to play chess	= jouer **aux** échecs
to like football	= aimer **le** football

But most compound nouns (eg ***saute-mouton***, ***colin-maillard***) work like this:

hide-and-seek	= cache-cache *m*
to play at hide-and-seek	= jouer à cache-cache
to like hide-and-seek	= aimer jouer à cache-cache

Names of other 'official' games and sports follow the same pattern as ***bridge*** in the following phrases:

to play bridge with X against Y	= jouer au bridge avec X contre Y
to beat sb at bridge	= battre qn au bridge
to win at bridge	= gagner au bridge
to lose at bridge	= perdre au bridge
she's good at bridge	= elle joue bien au bridge

Players and events

a bridge player	= un joueur de bridge

but

I'm not a bridge player	= je ne joue pas au bridge
he's a good bridge player	= il joue bien au bridge
a game of bridge	= une partie de bridge
a bridge champion	= un champion de bridge
the French bridge champion	= le champion de France de bridge
a bridge championship	= un championnat de bridge
the rules of bridge	= les règles du bridge

Playing cards

The names of the four suits work like ***clubs*** here:

clubs	= les trèfles *mpl*
to play a club	= jouer un trèfle
the eight of clubs	= le huit de trèfle
the ace of clubs	= l'as de trèfle
I've no clubs left	= je n'ai plus de trèfle
have you any clubs?	= as-tu du trèfle?
clubs are trumps	= l'atout est trèfle
to call two clubs	= demander deux trèfles

Other games vocabulary can be found in the dictionary at *game*, *trick* etc.

garnish *vtr* garnir (**with** de).

garter belt *n* (US) porte-jarretelles *m inv*.

gas I *n* **1** (fuel) gaz *m*; **to cook with ~** cuisiner au gaz; **2** (anaesthetic) anesthésie *f*; **3** (US) (petrol) essence *f*; **4**○ (US) (also **~ pedal**) accélérateur *m*.
II *vtr* gazer; **to ~ oneself** se suicider au gaz.
IDIOMS **to step on the ~** appuyer sur le champignon○.

gas: **~ cooker** *n* cuisinière *f* à gaz; **~ fire** *n* (GB) (appareil *m* de) chauffage *m* à gaz; **~ heater** *n* (for room) (appareil *m* de) chauffage *m* à gaz; (for water) chauffe-eau *m inv*; **~ main** *n* canalisation *f* de gaz; **~ meter** *n* compteur *m* à gaz.

gasoline *n* (US) essence *f*.

gas oven *n* four *m* à gaz.

gasp I *n* halètement *m*; **to give a ~** avoir le souffle coupé.
II *vi* **1** (for air) haleter; **2 to ~ in** or **with amazement** avoir le souffle coupé par la surprise.

gas: **~ pedal** *n* (US) accélérateur *m*; **~ ring** *n* (GB) (fixed) brûleur *m* à gaz; (portable) réchaud *m* à gaz; **~ station** *n* (US) station-service *f*; **~ stove** *n* cuisinière *f* à gaz.

gastric *adj* gastrique.

gastric flu ▶ 686 *n* grippe *f* intestinale.

gate *n* (of field, level crossing) barrière *f*; (in underground) portillon *m* automatique; (in town, prison, airport, garden) porte *f*; (of courtyard, palace) portail *m*; **at the ~** à l'entrée.

gather I *n* (in garment) fronce *f*.
II *vtr* **1** cueillir [*fruit, flowers*]; ramasser [*fallen fruit, wood*]; recueillir [*information*]; rassembler [*courage*]; **to ~ one's strength** rassembler ses forces; **the movement is ~ing strength** le mouvement devient plus puissant; **to ~ momentum** gagner du terrain; **to ~ speed** prendre de la vitesse; **2 to ~ that...** déduire que...; **I ~ (that) he was there** d'après ce que j'ai compris il était là; **I ~ from her (that) he was there** d'après ce qu'elle m'a dit il était là; **as far as I can ~** autant que je sache; **3** (in sewing) faire des fronces à; **~ed at the waist** froncé à la taille.
III *vi* [*people, crowd*] se rassembler; [*family*] se réunir; [*clouds*] s'amonceler.
■ **gather in**: **~ [sth] in**, **~ in [sth]** ramasser [*papers, crop*]; recueillir [*money, contributions*].
■ **gather round**: ¶ **~ round** se rassembler; **~ round!** approchez-vous!; ¶ **~ round [sth/sb]** se rassembler autour de.
■ **gather together**: ¶ **~ together** se réunir; ¶ **~ [sth] together**, **~ together [sth]** rassembler [*belongings, notes, followers*]; recueillir [*information*].
■ **gather up**: **~ [sth] up**, **~ up [sth]** ramasser [*belongings, objects*].

gathering *n* réunion *f*; **social/family ~** réunion entre amis/de famille.

gauge, gage (US) **I** *n* **1** (of gun, screw) calibre *m*; (of metal, wire) épaisseur *f*; **2** (of railway) écartement *m* (des voies); **3** (measuring instrument) jauge *f*; **fuel ~** jauge d'essence; **4** (way of judging) moyen *m* de jauger.
II *vtr* **1** mesurer [*diameter*]; jauger [*distance, quantity*]; calibrer [*gun*]; **2** évaluer [*mood, reaction*].

gauze *n* (fabric) gaze *f*; (wire) grillage *m*.

gay I *n* homosexuel/-elle *m/f*, gay *mf*.
II *adj* **1** homosexuel/-elle; **2** (happy) gai; [*laughter*] joyeux/-euse.

gaze I *n* regard *m*.
II *vi* **to ~ at sb/sth** regarder qn/qch; (in wonder) contempler qn/qch.
■ **gaze about**, **gaze around** regarder autour de soi.

GB *n* (*abbr* = **Great Britain**) G.-B.

GCSE *n* (*abbr* = **General Certificate of Secondary Education**) certificat *m* d'études secondaires.

gear I *n* **1** (equipment) matériel *m*; **climbing ~** matériel d'alpinisme; **2**○ (possessions) affaires *fpl*; **3** (clothes) fringues○ *fpl*; **football ~** tenue *f* de football; **4** (Aut) vitesse *f*; **to be in third ~** être en troisième; **to put a car in ~** passer la vitesse; **you're not in ~** tu es au point mort.
II gears *n pl* (Aut) changement *m* de vitesse.
III *noun modifier* [*stick*] de vitesses; **~box** boîte *f* de vitesses; **~ wheel** (on bicycle) pignon *m*.

gel I *n* gel *m*.
II *vi* **1** (Culin) prendre; **2** (figurative) prendre forme.

Gemini *n* Gémeaux *mpl*; ▶ **Aquarius**.

gender *n* **1** (of word) genre *m*; **2** (of person, animal) sexe *m*.

general I *n* général *m*.
II *adj* général; **as a ~ rule** normalement, en règle générale; **to be a ~ favourite** être apprécié de tous; **in ~ use** [*word, term*] d'usage courant; [*equipment*] d'utilisation courante; **a ~ discussion** une discussion d'ensemble; **~ assistant** employé/-e *m/f* de bureau.
III in general *phr* (usually or non-specifically) en général; (overall, mostly) dans l'ensemble; **things in ~** tout.

general: **~ election** *n* élections *fpl* législatives; **~ headquarters** *n* quartier *m* général.

generalization *n* généralisation *f* (**about** sur).

generalize *vtr, vi* généraliser (**about** à propos de).

general knowledge *n* culture *f* générale.

generally *adv* **1** (widely, usually) en général, généralement; **~ available** disponible pour le grand public; **~ (speaking)...** en règle générale...; **2** (overall) **the industry ~ will be affected** l'ensemble de l'industrie sera touché; **the quality is ~ good** dans l'ensemble la qualité est bonne; **3** [*talk*] d'une manière générale.

general: **~ manager** ▶ 805 *n* directeur/-trice *m/f* général/-e; **~ meeting** *n* assemblée *f* générale.

general practice *n* **1** (field of doctor's work) médecine *f* générale; **2** (health centre) cabinet *m* de médecine générale.

general: **~ practitioner**, **GP** ▶805 *n* (médecin *m*) généraliste *mf*; **~ public** *n* (grand) public *m*; **~-purpose** *adj* à usages multiples; **~ secretary** *n* secrétaire *m* général; **~ strike** *n* grève *f* générale.

generate *vtr* produire [*power, heat, income, waste*]; créer [*employment*]; susciter [*interest, tension, ideas*]; entraîner [*profit, publicity*].

generation *n* **1** génération *f*; **the younger/older ~** la jeune/l'ancienne génération; **second ~ robots** des robots de la deuxième génération; **2** (of electricity, data) production *f*.

generation gap *n* fossé *m* des générations.

generator *n* (of electricity) générateur *m*; (in hospital, on farm) groupe *m* électrogène.

generic *adj* générique.

generosity *n* générosité *f* (**to, towards** envers).

generous *adj* **1** généreux/-euse; **to be ~ with** ne pas être avare de [*praise, time*]; **2** [*quantity, supply*] généreux/-euse; [*size*] grand (*before n*); [*hem*] bon/bonne (*before n*); **3** (magnanimous) magnanime.

genetics *n* génétique *f*.

Geneva ▶574 *pr n* Genève; **Lake ~** le lac Léman or de Genève.

genial *adj* cordial.

genius *n* génie *m*; **a mathematical ~** un mathématicien de génie; **a mechanical ~** un génie de la mécanique.

gentle *adj* **1** [*person, animal, voice, music, heat*] doux/douce; [*dentist, nurse*] qui a la main douce; [*hint, reminder*] discret/-ète; [*teasing*] anodin; **be ~ with her, she's tired** ne la brusque pas, elle est fatiguée; **2** [*slope, curve*] doux/douce; [*stop*] en douceur; **3** [*pressure, touch, breeze*] léger/-ère; [*exercise*] modéré; [*massage*] en douceur.

gentleman *n* **1** (man) monsieur *m*; **2** (well-bred) gentleman *m*.

gentlemanly *adj* courtois.

gentleness *n* douceur *f*.

gently *adv* **1** [*rock, blow, stir*] doucement; [*comb, treat, cleanse*] avec douceur; [*cook*] à feu doux; **2** (kindly) gentiment; **treat her ~** soyez gentil avec elle; **to break the news ~** annoncer la nouvelle avec ménagement; **3** (lightly) [*exercise*] sans forcer; **he kissed her ~ on the cheek** il lui posa un léger baiser sur la joue; **4 to slope ~ up/down** monter/descendre en pente douce.

gents *n pl* (toilets) toilettes *fpl*; (on sign) 'Messieurs'.

genuine *adj* **1** (real) [*reason, motive*] vrai; **in case of ~ emergency** s'il y a vraiment urgence; **2** (authentic) [*work of art*] authentique; [*jewel, substance*] véritable; **3** (sincere) [*person, effort, interest*] sincère; [*simplicity*] vrai; [*buyer*] sérieux/-ieuse.

genuinely *adv* (really and truly) vraiment; (in reality) réellement.

geographic(al) *adj* géographique.

geography *n* géographie *f*.

geology *n* géologie *f*.

geometry *n* géométrie *f*.

geriatric *adj* [*hospital, ward*] gériatrique; **~ care** soins *mpl* aux vieillards.

germ *n* **1** (microbe) microbe *m*; **2** (seed) germe *m* (**of** de).

German ▶712 **I** *n* **1** (person) Allemand/-e *m/f*; **2** (language) allemand *m*.
II *adj* [*custom, food*] allemand; [*ambassador, embassy*] d'Allemagne; [*teacher, course*] d'allemand.

German: **~ measles** ▶686 *n* rubéole *f*; **~ shepherd** *n* (US) berger *m* allemand.

Germany ▶574 *pr n* Allemagne *f*.

germinate **I** *vtr* faire germer.
II *vi* germer.

gesture **I** *n* geste *m* (**of** de); **a nice ~** un beau geste.
II *vi* faire un geste; **to ~ at** or **towards sth** désigner qch d'un geste; **to ~ to sb** faire signe à qn.

get

■ **Note** This much-used verb has no multi-purpose equivalent in French and therefore is very often translated by choosing a synonym: *to get lunch* = *to prepare lunch* = préparer le déjeuner.

– When *get* is used to express the idea that a job is done not by you but by somebody else (*to get a room painted*), *faire* is used in French followed by an infinitive (*faire repeindre une pièce*).

– When *get* has the meaning of *become* and is followed by an adjective (*to get rich*), *devenir* is sometimes useful but check the appropriate entry (***rich***) as a single verb often suffices (*s'enrichir*).

– The phrasal verbs (*get around, get down, get on* etc) are listed separately at the end of the entry ***get***.

– For examples and further uses of *get* see the entry below .

I *vtr* **1** (receive) recevoir [*letter, grant*]; recevoir, percevoir [*salary, pension*]; capter [*channel*]; **what did you ~ for your car?** combien as-tu revendu ta voiture?; **we ~ a lot of rain** il pleut beaucoup ici; **our garden ~s a lot of sun** notre jardin est bien ensoleillé; **we ~ a lot of tourists** nous avons beaucoup de touristes; **you ~ what you pay for** si on veut de la qualité il faut y mettre le prix; **2** (inherit) **to ~ sth from sb** hériter qch de qn [*article, money*]; tenir qch de qn [*trait*]; **3** (obtain) (by applying) obtenir [*permission, divorce*]; trouver [*job*]; (by contacting) trouver [*plumber*]; appeler [*taxi*]; (by buying) acheter [*item*] (**from** chez); avoir [*ticket*]; **to ~ sb sth, to ~ sth for sb** (as gift) acheter qch à qn; **I'll ~ sth to eat at the airport** je mangerai qch à l'aéroport; **4** (subscribe to) acheter [*newspaper*]; **5** (acquire) se faire [*reputation*]; **6** (achieve) obtenir [*grade, answer*]; **he got it right** (of calculation) il a obtenu le bon résultat; (of answer) il a répondu juste; **7** (fetch) chercher [*person, help*]; **go and ~ a chair** va chercher une chaise; **to ~ sb sth, to ~ sth for sb** aller chercher qch pour qn; **8** (move) **to ~ sb/sth downstairs** faire descendre qn/qch; **I'll ~ them there somehow** je les ferai parvenir d'une façon ou d'une autre; **9** (help progress)

is this discussion ~ting us anywhere? est-ce que cette discussion est bien utile?; **10** (contact) **did you ~ Harry on the phone?** tu as réussi à avoir Harry au téléphone?; **11** (deal with) **I'll ~ it** (of phone) je réponds; (of doorbell) j'y vais; **12** (prepare) préparer [*breakfast, lunch*]; **13** (take hold of) attraper [*person*] (**by** par); **I've got you, don't worry** je te tiens, ne t'inquiète pas; **to ~ sth from** or **off** prendre qch sur [*shelf, table*]; **to ~ sth from** or **out of** prendre qch dans [*drawer, cupboard*]; **14**○ (oblige to give) **to ~ sth from** or **out of sb** faire sortir qch à qn [*money*]; obtenir qch de qn [*truth*]; **15**○ (catch) arrêter [*escapee*]; **got you!** je t'ai eu!; (caught in act) vu!; **16** (contract) attraper [*disease*]; **he got measles from his sister** sa sœur lui a passé la rougeole; **17** (use as transport) prendre [*bus, train*]; **18** (have) **to have got** avoir [*object, money, friend*]; **I've got a headache** j'ai mal à la tête; **19** (start to have) **to ~ (hold of) the idea that** se mettre dans la tête que; **20** (suffer) **to ~ a surprise** être surpris; **to ~ a shock** avoir un choc; **to ~ a bang on the head** recevoir un coup sur la tête; **21** (as punishment) prendre [*five years*]; avoir [*fine*]; **22** (hit) **to ~ sb/sth with** toucher qn/qch avec [*stone*]; **23** (understand, hear) comprendre; **now let me ~ this right...** alors si je comprends bien...; **24**○ (annoy) **what ~s me is...** ce qui m'agace c'est que...; **25** (learn, learn of) **to ~ to like sb** finir par apprécier qn; **how did you ~ to hear of...?** comment avez-vous entendu parler de...?; **we got to know them last year** on a fait leur connaissance l'année dernière; **26** (have opportunity) **to ~ to do** avoir l'occasion de faire, pouvoir faire; **27** (start) **to ~ (to be)** commencer à devenir; **we'll have to ~ going** il va falloir y aller; **28** (must) **to have got to do** devoir faire [*homework, chore*]; **it's got to be done** il faut le faire; **you've got to realize that...** il faut que tu te rendes compte que...; **there's got to be a reason** il doit y avoir une raison; **29** (persuade) **to ~ sb to do** demander à qn de faire; **I got her to talk** j'ai réussi à la faire parler; **30 to ~ sth done** faire faire qch; **to ~ the car repaired** faire réparer la voiture; **to ~ one's hair cut** se faire couper les cheveux; **how do you ever ~ anything done?** comment est-ce que tu arrives à travailler?; **31** (cause) **to ~ the car going** faire démarrer la voiture; **to ~ one's socks wet** mouiller ses chaussettes; **to ~ one's finger trapped** se coincer le doigt.

II *vi* **1** (become) devenir [*suspicious, old*]; **it's ~ting late** il se fait tard; **2** (forming passive) **to ~ (oneself) killed** se faire tuer; **to ~ hurt** être blessé; **3** (become involved in) **to ~ into**○ se mettre à [*archaeology*]; commencer dans [*publishing*]; **to ~ into a fight** se battre; **4** (arrive) **to ~ there** arriver; **to ~ to the airport** arriver à l'aéroport; **how did your coat ~ here?** comment est-ce que ton manteau est arrivé là?; **how did you ~ here?** (by what means) comment est-ce que tu es venu?; **where did you ~ to?** où est-ce que tu étais passé?; **5** (progress) **I'm ~ting nowhere with this essay** je n'avance pas dans cette dissertation; **now we're ~ting somewhere** il y a du progrès; **I'm ~ting there** je progresse; **6** (put on) **to ~ into** mettre, enfiler○ [*pyjamas*].

IDIOMS **I'll ~ you**○ **for that** je vais te le faire payer○; **he's got it bad**○ il est vraiment mordu; **I've got it** j'ai compris; **to ~ it together**○ se ressaisir; **to tell sb where to ~ off** envoyer promener qn; **what's got into her?** qu'est-ce qui lui a pris?; **you've got me there!** alors là tu me poses une colle○!

■ **get about 1** (move) se déplacer; **2** (travel) voyager.

■ **get across**: ¶ **~ across 1** (cross river, road) traverser; **2** [*message*] passer; ¶ **~ across [sth]** traverser [*river, road*]; ¶ **~ [sth] across 1** (transport) **how will we ~ it across?** comment est-ce qu'on le/la fera passer de l'autre côté?; **2** faire passer [*message*] (**to** à).

■ **get ahead 1** (make progress) progresser; **to ~ ahead of** prendre de l'avance sur [*competitor*]; **2** (go too fast) **let's not ~ ahead of ourselves** n'anticipons pas.

■ **get along 1 how are you ~ting along?** (in job, school) comment ça se passe?; (to sick or old person) comment ça va?; **2** [*people*] bien s'entendre (**with** avec).

■ **get around**: ¶ **~ around 1** = **get about**; **2** (manage to do) **she'll ~ around to visiting us eventually** elle va bien finir par venir nous voir; **I haven't got around to it yet** je n'ai pas encore eu le temps de m'en occuper; ¶ **~ around [sth]** contourner [*problem, law*]; **there's no ~ting around it** il n'y a rien à faire.

■ **get at**○: **~ at [sb/sth] 1** (reach) atteindre [*object*]; arriver jusqu'à [*person*]; découvrir [*truth*]; **2** (spoil) **the ants have got at the sugar** les fourmis ont attaqué le sucre; **3** (criticize) être après [*person*]; **4** (insinuate) **what are you ~ting at?** où est-ce que tu veux en venir?

■ **get away**: **~ away 1** (leave) partir; **2** (escape) s'échapper; **3 to ~ away with a crime** échapper à la justice; **you'll never ~ away with it!** tu ne vas pas t'en tirer comme ça!

■ **get away from**: ¶ **~ away from [sth] 1** (leave) quitter; **I must ~ away from here!** il faut que je parte d'ici!; **2 there's no ~ting away from it** on ne peut pas le nier; **3** abandonner [*practice*]; ¶ **~ away from [sb]** échapper à.

■ **get back**: ¶ **~ back 1** (return) rentrer; (after short time) revenir; **2** (move backwards) reculer; ¶ **~ back to [sth] 1** (return to) rentrer à [*house, city*]; revenir à [*office, point*]; **when we ~ back to London** à notre retour à Londres; **2** (return to former condition) revenir à [*job*]; **to ~ back to sleep** se rendormir; **to ~ back to normal** redevenir normal; **3** (return to earlier stage) revenir à [*main topic, former point*]; ¶ **~ back to [sb]** revenir à; **I'll ~ right back to you** (on phone) je vous rappelle tout de suite; ¶ **~ [sth] back 1** (return) (personally) ramener; (by post) renvoyer; **2** (regain) récupérer [*lost object*]; reprendre [*strength*]; **she got her money back** elle a été remboursée.

■ **get behind**: ¶ **~ behind** prendre du

retard; ¶ ~ **behind [sth]** se mettre derrière [*door*].

■ **get by 1** (pass) passer; **2** (survive) s'en sortir (**on, with** avec).

■ **get down**: ¶ ~ **down 1** (descend) descendre (**from, out of** de); **2** (on floor) se coucher; (crouch) se baisser; **to ~ down on one's knees** s'agenouiller; **to ~ down to** arriver à [*lower level*]; se mettre à [*work*]; **to ~ down to sb's level** se mettre à la portée de qn; **to ~ down to doing** se mettre à faire; ¶ ~ **down [sth]** descendre [*slope*]; ¶ ~ **[sth] down, ~ down [sth] 1** (from height) descendre; **2** (record) noter; ¶ ~ **[sb] down 1** (from height) faire descendre; **2**○ (depress) déprimer.

■ **get in**: ¶ ~ **in 1** (to building) entrer; (to vehicle) monter; **2 to ~ in on** réussir à s'introduire dans [*project, scheme*]; **3** (return home) rentrer; **4** (arrive) arriver; **5** (penetrate) pénétrer; **6** [*party*] passer; [*candidate*] être élu; **7** (Sch, Univ) [*applicant*] être admis; ¶ ~ **[sth] in, ~ in [sth] 1** (buy) acheter; **2 I can't ~ the drawer in** je n'arrive pas à faire rentrer le tiroir; **3** (hand in) rendre [*essay*]; ¶ ~ **[sb] in** faire entrer.

■ **get into**: ¶ ~ **into [sth] 1** (enter) entrer dans [*building*]; monter dans [*vehicle*]; **2** (as member) devenir membre de; (as student) être admis à; **3** (squeeze into) rentrer dans [*garment, size*]; ¶ ~ **[sb/sth] into** faire entrer [qn/qch] dans.

■ **get off**: ¶ ~ **off 1** (from bus) descendre (**at** à); **2** (start on journey) partir; **3** (leave work) finir; **4**○ (escape punishment) s'en tirer (**with** avec); **5 to ~ off to** partir pour [*destination*]; **to ~ off to a good start** prendre un bon départ; **to ~ off to sleep** s'endormir; ¶ ~ **off [sth] 1** descendre de [*wall, bus*]; **2** s'écarter de [*subject*]; ¶ ~ **[sb/sth] off 1** descendre [*object*]; **2** envoyer [*letter, person*]; **3** enlever [*stain*].

■ **get on**: ¶ ~ **on 1** (climb aboard) monter; **2** (GB) (like each other) bien s'entendre; **3** (fare) **how did you ~ on?** comment est-ce que ça s'est passé?; **how are you ~ting on?** comment est-ce que tu t'en sors?; **4** (GB) (approach) **he's ~ting on for 40** il approche des quarante ans; **it's ~ting on for midnight** il est presque minuit; ¶ ~ **on [sth]** monter dans [*vehicle*]; ¶ ~ **[sth] on, ~ on [sth]** mettre [*garment, lid*]; monter [*tyre*].

■ **get onto**: ~ **onto [sth] 1** monter dans [*vehicle*]; **2** être nommé à [*committee*]; **3** (GB) contacter [*person, organization*].

■ **get on with**: ¶ ~ **on with [sth]**: **to ~ on with one's work** continuer à travailler; ¶ ~ **on with [sb]** (GB) s'entendre avec [*person*].

■ **get out**: ¶ ~ **out 1** (exit) sortir (**through, by** par); ~ **out!** va-t'en!; **2** (socially) sortir; **3** (resign) partir; **4** (alight) descendre; **5** [*prisoner*] être libéré; ¶ ~ **[sth] out, ~ out [sth] 1** (bring out) sortir; **2** retirer [*cork*]; **3** enlever [*stain*]; **4** emprunter [*library book*]; ¶ ~ **[sb] out** faire libérer [*prisoner*]; **to ~ sth out of sth** sortir qch de qch; **I can't ~ it out of my mind** je ne peux pas l'effacer de mon esprit.

■ **get out of**: ~ **out of [sth] 1** sortir de [*building, meeting*]; descendre de [*vehicle*]; être libéré de [*prison*]; quitter [*organization, profession*]; **2 to ~ out of doing** s'arranger pour ne pas faire; **I'll try to ~ out of it** j'essaierai de me libérer; **3** perdre [*habit*]; **4 what do you ~ out of your job?** qu'est-ce que ton travail t'apporte?; **what will you ~ out of it?** qu'est-ce que vous en retirerez?

■ **get over**: ¶ ~ **over** passer; ¶ ~ **over [sth] 1** (cross) traverser; **2** se remettre de [*illness, shock*]; **I can't ~ over it** (amazed) je n'en reviens pas; **3** surmonter [*problem*]; **to ~ sth over with** en finir avec qch; ¶ ~ **[sth] over** faire passer [qch] au-dessus de [*bridge, wall*].

■ **get round** (GB): ¶ ~ **round** = **get around**; ¶ ~ **round [sth]** = **get around [sth]**; ¶ ~ **round**○ **[sb]** persuader [qn].

■ **get through**: ¶ ~ **through 1** (squeeze through) passer; **2** (on phone) **to ~ through to sb** avoir qn au téléphone; **3** (communicate with) **to ~ through to sb** communiquer avec qn; **4** [*news, supplies*] arriver; **5** [*examinee*] réussir; ¶ ~ **through [sth] 1** traverser [*checkpoint*]; terminer [*book*]; finir [*meal, task*]; réussir à [*exam*]; **2** (use) manger [*food*]; boire [*drink*]; dépenser [*money*]; ¶ ~ **[sb/sth] through 1** faire passer [*person, goods*]; **2** (help to endure) aider qn à tenir le coup○; **3** (Sch, Univ) (help to pass) permettre à [qn] de réussir; **4** faire passer [*bill*].

■ **get together**: ¶ ~ **together** se réunir (**about, over** pour discuter de); ¶ ~ **[sb/sth] together, ~ together [sb/sth]** réunir [*people*]; former [*company*].

■ **get under**: ¶ ~ **under** passer en-dessous; ¶ ~ **under [sth]** passer sous.

■ **get up**: ¶ ~ **up 1** (from bed, chair) se lever (**from** de); **2** (on ledge, wall) monter; **3** [*storm*] se préparer; [*wind*] se lever; **4 what did you ~ up to?** (enjoyment) qu'est-ce que tu as fait de beau?; (mischief) qu'est-ce que tu as fabriqué○?; ¶ ~ **up [sth] 1** arriver en haut de [*hill, ladder*]; **2** augmenter [*speed*].

get: **~-together** *n* réunion *f* (entre amis); **~ well** *adj* [*card, wishes*] de prompt rétablissement.

ghastly *adj* horrible.

ghost *n* fantôme *m*.

giant *n, adj* géant (*m*).

giddy *adj* **1** (dizzy) **to feel ~** avoir la tête qui tourne; **2** [*height, speed*] vertigineux/-euse; [*success*] enivrant; **3** (frivolous) [*person*] écervelé; [*behaviour*] irréfléchi.

gift *n* **1** (present) cadeau *m* (**to** à); **to give a ~ to sb, to give sb a ~** faire or offrir un cadeau à qn; **2** (donation) don *m*; **3** (talent) don *m*; **to have a ~ for doing** avoir le don de faire.

gifted *adj* doué.

gift: **~ shop** *n* magasin *m* de cadeaux; **~ token, ~ voucher** *n* (GB) chèque-cadeau *m*; **~ wrap** *n* papier *m* cadeau.

giggle I *n* (silly) petit rire *m* bête; (nervous) petit rire *m* nerveux; **to get the ~s** attraper un fou rire.

II *vi* (stupidly) rire bêtement; (nervously) rire nerveusement.

gimmick *n* (scheme) truc○ *m*; (object) gadget *m*.

gin *n* gin *m*; **~ and tonic** gin tonic *m*.

ginger *n* **1** (Bot, Culin) gingembre *m*; **2** (hair or fur colour) roux *m*.

girl *n* **1** (child) fille *f*; (teenager) jeune fille *f*; **baby ~** petite fille *f*, bébé *m*; **little ~** petite fille *f*, fillette *f*; **2** (daughter) fille *f*.

girlfriend *n* (female friend) amie *f*; (sweetheart) (petite) amie *f*.

giro I *n* (GB) (system) système *m* de virement bancaire; (cheque) mandat *m*.
II *noun modifier* **~ payment, ~ transfer** (at bank) virement *m* bancaire; (at post office) virement *m* postal.

gist *n* essentiel *m* (**of** de).

give I *n* élasticité *f*.
II *vtr* donner (**to** à); transmettre [*message*] (**to** à); transmettre, passer [*illness*] (**to** à); laisser [*seat*] (**to** à); accorder [*grant*] (**to** à); faire [*injection, massage*] (**to** à); **to ~ sb sth** donner qch à qn; (politely, as a gift) offrir qch à qn; **to ~ sb pleasure** faire plaisir à qn; **~ him my best (wishes)** transmets-lui mes amitiés; **she gave him a drink** elle lui a donné à boire; **to ~ sb enough room** laisser suffisamment de place à qn.
III *vi* [*mattress, sofa*] s'affaisser; [*shelf, floorboard*] fléchir; [*branch*] ployer.
IDIOMS **~ or take an inch (or two)** à quelques centimètres près; **to ~ and take** faire des concessions; **to ~ as good as one gets** rendre coup pour coup; **to ~ it all one's got**○ (y) mettre le paquet.
■ **give away**: ¶ **~ away [sth], ~ [sth] away 1** donner [*item, sample*]; **2** révéler [*secret*]; **3** laisser échapper [*match, goal, advantage*] (**to** au bénéfice de); ¶ **~ [sb] away, ~ away [sb] 1** (betray) [*expression, fingerprints*] trahir; [*person*] dénoncer (**to** à); **to ~ oneself away** se trahir; **2** (in marriage) conduire [qn] à l'autel.
■ **give back**: **~ [sth] back, ~ back [sth]** rendre (**to** à); **...or we'll ~ you your money back** ...ou vous serez remboursé.
■ **give in**: ¶ **~ in 1** (yield) céder (**to** à); **2** (stop trying) abandonner; **I ~ in—tell me!** je donne ma langue au chat○—dis-le-moi!; ¶ **~ in [sth], ~ [sth] in** rendre [*written work*]; remettre [*ticket, key*].
■ **give off**: **~ off [sth]** émettre [*signal, scent, radiation, light*]; dégager [*heat, fumes, oxygen*].
■ **give onto**: **~ onto [sth]** donner sur [*street, yard*].
■ **give out**: ¶ **~ out** [*strength*] s'épuiser; [*engine*] tomber en panne; ¶ **~ out [sth], ~ [sth] out 1** (distribute) distribuer (**to** à); **2** (emit) = **give off**.
■ **give up**: ¶ **~ up** abandonner; **to ~ up on** laisser tomber [*diet, crossword, pupil, patient*]; ne plus compter sur [*friend, partner*]; ¶ **~ up [sth], ~ [sth] up 1** renoncer à [*habit, title, claim*]; sacrifier [*free time*]; quitter [*job*]; **to ~ up smoking/drinking** cesser de fumer/de boire; **2** abandonner [*search, hope, struggle*]; renoncer à [*idea*]; **to ~ up trying** abandonner; **3** céder [*seat, territory*]; ¶ **~ up [sb], ~ [sb] up 1** (hand over) livrer (**to** à); **to ~ oneself up** se livrer (**to** à); **2** laisser tomber [*lover*]; délaisser [*friend*].
■ **give way 1** (collapse) s'effondrer; [*fence, cable*] céder; **his legs gave way** ses jambes se sont dérobées sous lui; **2** (GB) (when driving) céder le passage (**to** à); **3** (yield) céder; **to ~ way to** faire place à.

give-and-take *n* concessions *fpl* mutuelles.

giveaway *n* **to be a ~** [*fact, remark*] être révélateur/-trice.

given I *adj* **1** [*point, level, number*] donné; [*volume, length*] déterminé; **the ~ date** la date convenue; **at any ~ moment** à n'importe quel moment; **2 to be ~ to sth/to doing** avoir tendance à qch/à faire; **I am not ~ to doing** je n'ai pas l'habitude de faire.
II *prep* **1** (in view of) **~ (the fact) that** étant donné que; **2** (with) avec [*training, proper care*]; **~ the right conditions** dans de bonnes conditions.

given name *n* prénom *m*.

give way sign *n* (GB) panneau *m* 'cédez le passage'.

glad *adj* content, heureux/-euse (**about** de; **that** que; **to do** de faire); **I am ~ (that) you are able to come** je suis content que vous puissiez venir; **he was only too ~ to help me** il ne demandait qu'à m'aider.

gladly *adv* (willingly) volontiers; (with pleasure) avec plaisir.

glamorize *vtr* peindre [qn/qch] sous de belles couleurs.

glamorous *adj* [*person, image, look*] séduisant; [*older person*] élégant; [*dress*] splendide; [*occasion*] brillant; [*job*] prestigieux/-ieuse.

glamour, glamor (US) *n* (of person) séduction *f*; (of job) prestige *m*; (of travel, cars) fascination *f*.

glance I *n* coup *m* d'œil.
II *vi* **to ~ at** jeter un coup d'œil à; **to ~ out of the window** jeter un coup d'œil par la fenêtre; **to ~ around the room** parcourir la pièce du regard.
■ **glance off**: **~ off [sth]** [*bullet, stone*] ricocher sur *or* contre.

glancing *adj* [*blow, kick*] oblique.

gland *n* glande *f*; **to have swollen ~s** avoir des ganglions.

glare I *n* **1** (angry look) regard *m* furieux; **2** (from lights) lumière *f* éblouissante.
II *vi* [*person*] lancer un regard furieux (**at** à).

glaring *adj* [*mistake, injustice*] flagrant.

glass I *n* **1** verre *m*; **wine ~** verre à vin; **a ~ of wine** un verre de vin; **2** (mirror) miroir *m*.
II *noun modifier* [*bottle, shelf*] en verre.
III glasses *n pl* lunettes *fpl*; **a pair of ~es** une paire de lunettes; **he wears reading ~es** il doit porter des lunettes quand il lit.

glassy-eyed *adj* (from drink, illness) aux yeux vitreux; (hostile) au regard glacial.

glazed *adj* [*door, window*] vitré; [*ceramics*] vernissé; [*paper*] glacé; [*meat, ham*] glacé; **to have a ~ look in one's eyes** avoir les yeux vitreux.

gleam I *n* (of light) lueur *f*; (of sunshine) rayon *m*; (of gold, polished surface) reflet *m*.
II *vi* [*light*] luire; [*knife, leather, surface*] reluire; [*eyes*] briller.

gleaming *adj* **1** [*eyes, light*] brillant; [*leather, surface*] reluisant; **2** (clean) étincelant (de propreté).

glide *vi* [*skater, boat*] glisser (**on, over** sur); (in air) planer.

glider *n* planeur *m*.

gliding ▶ 649 *n* vol *m* à voile.

glimpse I *n* **1** vision *f* fugitive (**of** de); **to catch a ~ of sth** entrevoir qch; **2** (insight) aperçu *m* (**of, at** de).
II *vtr* entrevoir.

glitter I *n* **1** (substance) paillettes *fpl*; **2** (sparkle) éclat *m*.
II *vi* scintiller.

gloat *vi* jubiler (**at, over** à l'idée de).

global *adj* **1** (world-wide) mondial; **2** (comprehensive) global.

global warming *n* réchauffement *m* de l'atmosphère.

globe *n* **1 the ~** le globe; **2** (model) globe *m* terrestre.

globe artichoke *n* artichaut *m*.

gloom *n* **1** (darkness) obscurité *f*; **2** (despondency) morosité *f* (**about, over** à propos de).

gloomily *adv* [*say, do*] d'un air lugubre.

gloomy *adj* **1** (dark) sombre; **2** [*expression, person, voice*] lugubre; [*weather*] morose; [*news, outlook*] déprimant; **to be ~ about sth** être pessimiste à propos de qch.

glorious *adj* **1** [*view, weather*] magnifique; [*holiday*] merveilleux/-euse; **2** (illustrious) glorieux/-ieuse.

glory I *n* **1** gloire *f*; **2** (splendour) splendeur *f*; **the glories of nature** les splendeurs de la nature.
II *vi* **to ~ in** être très fier/fière de.

gloss I *n* **1** (shine) lustre *m*; **2** (explanation) glose *f*; **3** (paint) laque *f* (brillante).
II *vtr* gloser [*word, text*].
■ **gloss over**: **~ over [sth]** (pass rapidly over) glisser sur; (hide) dissimuler.

gloss paint *n* laque *f* (brillante).

glossy *adj* **1** [*hair, material*] luisant; [*photograph*] brillant; [*brochure*] luxueux/-euse; **2** (derogatory) [*production, film, interior*] qui a un éclat plutôt superficiel.

glossy magazine *n* magazine *m* illustré (de luxe).

glove *n* gant *m*.

glow I *n* **1** (from fire) rougeoiement *m*; (of candle) lueur *f*; **2** (of complexion) éclat *m*; **3** (feeling) douce sensation *f*; **it gives you a warm ~** ça fait chaud au cœur.
II *vi* **1** [*metal, embers*] rougeoyer; [*lamp, cigarette*] luire; **2 her skin ~ed** elle avait un teint éblouissant; **to ~ with health** resplendir de santé; **to ~ with pride** rayonner de fierté.

glowing *adj* **1** [*ember*] rougeoyant; [*face, cheeks*] (from exercise) rouge; (from pleasure) radieux/-ieuse; **2** [*account, terms*] élogieux/-ieuse.

glue I *n* colle *f*.
II *vtr* coller; **to ~ sth on** or **down** coller qch.
III **glued**○ *pp adj* **to have one's eyes ~d to sb/sth** avoir les yeux fixés sur qn/qch; **to be ~d to the TV** être collé○ devant la télé; **to be ~d to the spot** être cloué sur place.

glut I *n* surabondance *f*, excès *m*.
II *vtr* inonder [*economy, market*].

glutton *n* glouton/-onne *m/f*.

glycerin(e) *n* glycérine *f*.

GMT *n* (*abbr* = **Greenwich Mean Time**) TU.

gnash *vtr* **to ~ one's teeth** grincer des dents.

gnaw I *vtr* ronger [*bone, wood*].
II *vi* **1 to ~ at** or **on sth** ronger qch; **2 to ~ at sb** [*hunger, remorse, pain*] tenailler qn.

go

■ **Note**

As an intransitive verb

– *go* as a simple intransitive verb is translated by *aller*: *we're going to Paris* = nous allons à Paris; *where are you going?* = où vas-tu?; *Sasha went to London last week* = Sasha est allée à Londres la semaine dernière.

– Note that *aller* conjugates with *être* in compound tenses. For the conjugation of *aller*, see the French verb tables.

– The verb *go* produces a great many phrasal verbs (*go up, go down, go out, go back* etc). Many of these are translated by a single verb in French (*monter, descendre, sortir, retourner* etc). The phrasal verbs are listed separately at the end of the entry *go*.

As an auxiliary verb

– When *go* is used as an auxiliary to show intention, it is also translated by *aller*: *I'm going to buy a car tomorrow* = je vais acheter une voiture demain; *I was going to talk to you about it* = j'allais t'en parler; *he's not going to ask for a rise* = il ne va pas demander d'augmentation.

– For translations of *go* used with destinations, consult the Usage Note on ***Countries, Cities, and Continents*** ▶ 574.

– For examples and particular usages, see the entry below.

I *vi* **1** aller (**from** de; **to** à, en); **to ~ to Paris/to California** aller à Paris/en Californie; **to ~ to town/to the country** aller en ville/à la campagne; **they went home** ils sont rentrés chez eux; **to ~ up/down/across** monter/descendre/traverser; **I went into the room** je suis entré dans la pièce; **to ~ by bus/train** voyager en bus/train; **to ~ shopping** aller faire des courses; **to ~ on holiday** partir en vacances; **to ~ for a drink** aller prendre un verre; **~ and ask her** va lui demander; **to ~ to school/work** aller à l'école/au travail; **to ~ to the doctor's** aller chez le médecin; **to ~ to war** [*country*] entrer en guerre; **that car's going very fast!** cette voiture roule très vite!; **there he goes again!** (that's him again) le revoilà!; (he's starting again) le voilà qui recommence!; **2** (be spent) partir; **the money**

goes on school fees l'argent part en frais de scolarité; **the money will ~ towards a new car** l'argent servira à payer une nouvelle voiture; **a hundred pounds doesn't ~ far these days** on ne va pas loin avec cent livres sterling de nos jours; **3** (become) **to ~ red** rougir; **to ~ white** blanchir; **to ~ mad** devenir fou/folle; **4** (be, remain) **we went for two days without food** nous avons passé deux jours sans rien manger; **to ~ unnoticed** passer inaperçu; **the question went unanswered** la question est restée sans réponse; **he was allowed to ~ free** il a été libéré; **it wasn't a bad party, as parties ~** c'était une soirée plutôt réussie par rapport à la moyenne; **5** (become impaired) **his memory is going** il perd la mémoire; **my voice is going** je n'ai plus de voix; **the battery is going** la batterie est presque à plat; **6** (of time) **there are only three days to ~ before Christmas** il ne reste plus que trois jours avant Noël; **it's just gone seven o'clock** il est sept heures passées; **7** (be got rid of) **he'll have to ~!** il va falloir qu'on se débarrasse de lui!; **either she goes or I do!** c'est elle ou moi!; **8** (operate, function) [*vehicle, machine, clock*] marcher, fonctionner; **to set [sth] going** mettre [qch] en marche; **to get going** [*engine, machine*] se mettre en marche; [*business*] démarrer; **to keep going** [*business*] se maintenir; [*machine*] continuer à marcher; **9** (start) **let's get going!** allons-y!; **to get things going** mettre les choses en train; **here goes!**, **here we ~!** c'est parti!; **10** (belong, be placed) aller; **where do these plates ~?** où vont ces assiettes?; **the suitcases will have to ~ in the back** il va falloir mettre les valises derrière; **it won't ~ into the box** ça ne rentre pas dans la boîte; **five into four won't ~** quatre n'est pas divisible par cinq; **11** (be about to) **to be going to do** aller faire; **it's going to snow** il va neiger; **12** (happen) **the party went very well** la soirée s'est très bien passée; **the way things are going** si ça continue comme ça; **how's it going**°**?** comment ça va°?; **13** (be given) [*award*] aller (**to** à); **the job went to a local man** le poste a été donné à un homme de la région; **14** (emphatic use) **why did he ~ and spoil it?** pourquoi est-il allé tout gâcher?; **you've really gone and done it now!** tu peux être fier de toi!; **15** (make sound, perform action or movement) (gen) faire; [*bell, alarm*] sonner; **she went like this with her fingers** elle a fait comme ça avec ses doigts; **16** (take one's turn) **you ~ next** c'est ton tour après, c'est à toi après; **you ~ first** après vous; **17** (of colours, furnishings) **those two colours don't ~ together** ces deux couleurs ne vont pas ensemble; **18** (other uses) **it goes without saying that** il va sans dire que; **as the saying goes** comme dit le proverbe; **how does the song ~?** quel est l'air de la chanson?; **anything goes** tout est permis.

II *vtr* faire [*distance, number of miles*].

III *n* **1** (GB) (turn) tour *m*; (try) essai *m*; **whose ~ is it?** à qui le tour?; (in game) à qui de jouer?; **2**° (energy) **to be full of ~, to be all ~** être très dynamique.

IDIOMS **to make a ~ of sth** réussir qch; **she's always on the ~** elle n'arrête jamais; **we have several different projects on the ~** nous avons plusieurs projets différents en chantier; **in one ~** d'un seul coup.

■ **go about**: **~ about [sth]** s'attaquer à [*task*]; **he knows how to ~ about it** il sait s'y prendre; **to ~ about one's business** vaquer à ses occupations.

■ **go across**: **~ across [sth]** traverser.

■ **go after**: **~ after [sb]** poursuivre.

■ **go against**: **~ against [sb/sth] 1** être contraire à [*rules, principles*]; **to ~ against the trend** aller à l'encontre de la tendance; **the vote went against them** le vote leur a été défavorable; **2** (resist, oppose) s'opposer à.

■ **go ahead** [*event*] avoir lieu; **~ ahead and shoot!** vas-y, tire!; **they are going ahead with the project** ils ont décidé de mettre le projet en route.

■ **go along** aller; **to make sth up as one goes along** inventer qch au fur et à mesure.

■ **go along with**: **~ along with [sb/sth]** être d'accord avec, accepter.

■ **go around**: ¶ **~ around 1** se promener, circuler; **she goes around on a bicycle** elle circule à bicyclette; **they ~ around everywhere together** ils vont partout ensemble; **2** [*rumour*] courir; ¶ **~ around [sth]** faire le tour de [*house, shops*].

■ **go away** [*person*] partir; **~ away and leave me alone!** va-t-en et laisse-moi tranquille!

■ **go back 1** (return) retourner; (turn back) rebrousser chemin; (resume work) reprendre le travail; (resume classes) reprendre les cours; **let's ~ back to France** retournons en France; **to ~ back to sleep** se rendormir; **to ~ back to work** se remettre au travail; **2** (in time) remonter; **3** (revert) revenir (**to** à).

■ **go back on**: **~ back on [sth]** revenir sur [*promise, decision*].

■ **go before**: ¶ **~ before** (go in front) aller au devant; (in time) se passer avant; ¶ **~ before [sb /sth]** comparaître devant [*court*].

■ **go by**: ¶ **~ by** [*person*] passer; **as time goes by** avec le temps; ¶ **~ by [sth] 1** (judge by) juger d'après [*appearances*]; **2 to ~ by the rules** suivre le règlement.

■ **go down**: ¶ **~ down 1** (descend) (gen) descendre; [*sun*] se coucher; **to ~ down on one's knees** se mettre à genoux; **2** [*person, aircraft*] tomber; [*ship*] couler; **3** (be received) **to ~ down well/badly** être bien/mal reçu; **4** [*price, temperature, standard*] baisser; [*tide*] descendre; [*storm, wind*] se calmer; **5** [*swelling*] désenfler; [*tyre*] se dégonfler; **6** (gen, Sport) (be defeated) perdre; (be downgraded) redescendre; **7** (be remembered) **he will ~ down as a great statesman** on se souviendra de lui comme d'un grand homme d'État; **8 to ~ down with flu** attraper la grippe; **9** (Comput) tomber en panne; ¶ **~ down [sth]** descendre [*hill*].

■ **go for**: ¶ **~ for [sb/sth] 1**° (be keen on) aimer; **2** (apply to) **the same goes for him!** c'est valable pour lui aussi!; ¶ **~ for [sb] 1** (attack) attaquer; **2 he has a lot going for him** il a beaucoup de choses pour lui; ¶ **~ for [sth] 1** essayer d'obtenir [*honour, victory*]; **she's going for the world record** elle vise le record mondial; **~ for it**○! vas-y, fonce○!; **2** (choose) choisir, prendre.

■ **go in 1** (enter) entrer; (go back in) rentrer; **2** [*troops*] attaquer; **3** [*sun*] se cacher.

■ **go in for**: **~ in for [sth] 1** (be keen on) aimer; **2** s'inscrire à [*exam, competition*].

■ **go into**: **~ into [sth] 1** (enter) entrer dans [*building*]; se lancer dans [*business, profession*]; **2** (examine) étudier [*question*]; **let's not ~ into that now** laissons cela de côté pour l'instant; **3 a lot of work went into this project** beaucoup de travail a été investi dans ce projet.

■ **go off**: ¶ **~ off 1** [*bomb*] exploser; **2** [*alarm clock*] sonner; [*fire alarm*] se déclencher; **3** [*person*] partir, s'en aller; **4** (GB) [*milk, cream*] tourner; [*meat*] s'avarier; [*butter*] rancir; [*performer, athlete*] perdre sa forme; **5** [*lights, heating*] s'éteindre; **6** (happen, take place) **the concert went off very well** le concert s'est très bien passé; ¶ **~ off [sb/sth]** (GB) **I've gone off whisky** je n'aime plus tellement le whisky; **I think she's gone off the idea** je crois qu'elle a renoncé à l'idée.

■ **go off with**: **~ off with [sb/sth]** partir avec.

■ **go on**: ¶ **~ on 1** (happen) se passer; **how long has this been going on?** depuis combien de temps est-ce que ça dure?; **a lot of stealing goes on** il y a beaucoup de vols; **2** (continue on one's way) poursuivre son chemin; **3** (continue) continuer; **the meeting went on into the afternoon** la réunion s'est prolongée jusque dans l'après-midi; **the list goes on and on** la liste est infinie; **4** (of time) (elapse) **as time went on, they...** avec le temps, ils...; **as the evening went on** au fur et à mesure que la soirée avançait; **5 to ~ on about sth** ne pas arrêter de parler de qch; **6** (proceed) passer; **let's ~ on to the next item** passons au point suivant; **he went on to say that...** puis il a dit que...; **7** [*heating, lights*] s'allumer; **8** [*actor*] entrer en scène; ¶ **~ on [sth]** se fonder sur [*evidence, information*]; **that's all we've got to ~ on** c'est tout ce que nous savons avec certitude.

■ **go on at**: **~ on at [sb]** s'en prendre à.

■ **go out 1** (leave, depart) sortir; **to ~ out walking** aller se promener; **to ~ out for a drink** aller prendre un verre; **2** (have relationship) **to ~ out with sb** sortir avec qn; **3** [*tide*] descendre; **4** [*fire, light*] s'éteindre; **5** [*invitation, summons*] être envoyé; [*programme*] être diffusé; **6** (be eliminated) (gen, Sport) être éliminé.

■ **go over**: ¶ **~ over 1** (cross over) aller (**to** vers); **2** [*speech, performance*] être reçu; **to ~ over well** être bien reçu; **3** (switch to other side) passer (**to** à); **to ~ over to the other side** (figurative) passer dans l'autre camp; ¶ **~ over [sth] 1** passer [qch] en revue [*details, facts*]; vérifier [*accounts, figures*]; relire [*article*]; **2** (exceed) dépasser [*limit, sum*].

■ **go round** (GB): ¶ **~ round 1** [*wheel*] tourner; **2 to ~ round to see sb** aller voir qn; **3** [*rumour*] circuler; **4** (make detour) faire un détour; **we had to ~ the long way round** il a fallu qu'on prenne un chemin plus long; ¶ **~ round [sth]** faire le tour de [*shops, house, museum*].

■ **go through**: ¶ **~ through** [*law*] passer; [*divorce*] être prononcé; [*business deal*] être conclu; ¶ **~ through [sth] 1** endurer, subir [*experience*]; passer par [*stage, phase*]; traverser [*crisis*]; **she's gone through a lot** elle a beaucoup souffert; **you have to ~ through the switchboard** il faut passer par le standard; **2** (check) examiner; (rapidly) parcourir [*documents, list*]; **3** (search) fouiller [*belongings*]; **4** (perform) répéter [*scene*]; expliquer [*procedure*]; remplir [*formalities*]; **5** (use up) dépenser [*money*]; consommer [*food, drink*].

■ **go through with**: **~ through with [sth]** réaliser [*plan*]; **I can't ~ through with it** je ne peux pas le faire.

■ **go together 1** (harmonize) aller ensemble; **2** (entail each other) aller de pair.

■ **go under** [*ship, drowning person*] couler; (figurative) [*person*] succomber.

■ **go up**: ¶ **~ up 1** (ascend) monter; **to ~ up to bed** monter se coucher; **2** (rise) [*price, temperature*] monter; [*figures*] augmenter; [*curtain*] se lever (**on** sur); **3** (be upgraded) **the team has gone up to the first division** l'équipe est passée en première division; **4** (continue) **the book goes up to 1990** le livre va jusqu'en 1990; ¶ **~ up [sth] 1** monter, gravir [*hill*]; **2 to ~ up a class** (Sch) passer dans une classe supérieure.

■ **go with**: **~ with [sth] 1** (match, suit) aller avec; **2 the car goes with the job** la voiture va de pair avec le poste.

■ **go without**: ¶ **~ without** s'en passer; ¶ **~ without [sth]** se passer de.

go-ahead○ *n* **to give sb the ~** donner le feu vert à qn; **to get the ~** recevoir le feu vert.

goal *n* but *m*.

goal: **~keeper** *n* gardien *m* de but; **~post** *n* poteau *m* de but.

goat *n* chèvre *f*.

gobble I *vtr* (also **~ down**) engloutir [*food*]. **II** *vi* [*turkey*] glouglouter.

■ **gobble up**: **~ [sth] up, ~ up [sth]** engloutir.

go-between *n* intermédiaire *mf*.

god *n* dieu *m*; **God** Dieu *m*.

god: **~child** *n* filleul/-e *m/f*; **~daughter** *n* filleule *f*.

goddess *n* déesse *f*.

god: **~father** *n* parrain *m*; **~-fearing** *adj* pieux/pieuse; **~mother** *n* marraine *f*; **~parent** *n* parrain/marraine *m/f*; **~send** *n* aubaine *f*; **~son** *n* filleul *m*.

go-getter○ *n* fonceur/-euse○ *m/f*.

goggles *n pl* (cyclist's, worker's) lunettes *fpl* protectrices; (skier's) lunettes *fpl* de ski; (for swimming) lunettes *fpl* de plongée.

going I *n* **1** (departure) départ *m*; **2** (progress) **that's not bad ~!, that's good ~!** c'est rapide!; **it was slow ~, the ~ was slow** (on journey) ça a été long; (at work) ça n'avançait pas vite; **to be heavy ~** [*book*] être difficile à lire;

[*work, conversation*] être laborieux/-ieuse; **3 when the ~ gets tough** quand les choses vont mal; **she finds her new job hard ~** elle trouve que son nouveau travail est difficile; **they got out while the ~ was good** ils s'en sont tirés○ avant qu'il ne soit trop tard.
II *adj* **1** [*price*] actuel, en cours; **the ~ rate** le tarif en vigueur; **2 ~ concern** affaire *f* qui marche; **they bought the business as a ~ concern** quand ils ont acheté l'entreprise elle était déjà montée; **3 it's the best model ~** c'est le meilleur modèle sur le marché.

go-karting *n* karting *m*; **to go ~** faire du karting.

gold I *n* **1** (metal) or *m*; **2** = **gold medal**.
II *noun modifier* [*jewellery, tooth*] en or; [*coin, ingot, ore, wire*] d'or.
IDIOMS **as good as ~** sage comme une image; **to be worth one's weight in ~** valoir son pesant d'or.

golden *adj* **1** (made of gold) en or, d'or; **2** (gold coloured) doré, d'or; **~ hair** cheveux *mpl* blonds dorés; **3** [*age, days*] d'or; **a ~ opportunity** une occasion en or.

golden: **~-brown** ▶ **559** *n, adj* mordoré (*m*); **~ rule** *n* règle *f* d'or; **~ wedding** *n* noces *fpl* d'or.

gold: **~fish** *n* poisson *m* rouge; **~ medal** *n* médaille *f* d'or; **~ mine** *n* mine *f* d'or; **~-plated** *adj* plaqué or *inv*; **~ rush** *n* ruée *f* vers l'or; **~smith** ▶ **805** *n* orfèvre *m*.

golf ▶ **649** *n* golf *m*; **to play ~** faire du golf.

golf: **~ club** *n* (place) club *m* de golf; (stick) crosse *f* de golf; **~ course**, **~ links** *n* (terrain *m* de) golf *m*.

gondola *n* **1** (Venetian) gondole *f*; **2** (under airship, balloon) nacelle *f*.

gong *n* gong *m*.

gonorrh(o)ea ▶ **686** *n* blennorragie *f*.

good I *n* **1** (virtue) bien *m*; **~ and evil** le bien et le mal; **to be up to no ~**○ mijoter qch○; **to come to no ~** mal tourner; **2** (benefit) bien *m*; **for all the ~ it did me** pour le peu de bien que ça m'a fait; **for the ~ of his health** pour sa santé; **it didn't do my migraine any ~** ça n'a pas arrangé ma migraine; **no ~ will come of waiting** il vaut mieux agir tout de suite; **3** (use) **it's no ~ crying** ça ne sert à rien de pleurer; **what ~ would it do me?** à quoi cela me servirait-il?
II *adj* **1** bon/bonne; **it's a ~ film** c'est un bon film; **it was a ~ party** c'était une soirée réussie; **the ~ weather** le beau temps; **to have a ~ time** bien s'amuser; **have a ~ day!** bonne journée!; **it's ~ to see you again** je suis content de vous revoir; **to feel ~ about** être content de; **I didn't feel very ~ about lying to him** je n'étais pas très fier de lui avoir menti; **be ~!** sois sage!; **you don't look too ~** tu as mauvaise mine; **I don't feel too ~** je ne me sens pas très bien; **the ~ thing is that**... ce qui est bien c'est que...; **to taste ~** avoir bon goût; **to smell ~** sentir bon; **to look ~** [*food*] avoir l'air bon; **it looks ~ on a CV** (GB) or **résumé** (US) ça fait bien sur un CV; **we had a ~ laugh** on a bien ri; **to wait/walk for a ~ hour** attendre/marcher une bonne heure; **2** (high quality) [*hotel*] bon/bonne (*before n*); [*coat, china*] beau/belle (*before n*); [*degree*] avec mention; **3** (attractive) **to look ~ with** [*garment, accessories*] aller bien avec; **she looks ~ in blue** le bleu lui va bien; **4** (kind) [*person*] gentil/-ille; (virtuous) [*man, life*] vertueux/-euse; **a ~ deed** une bonne action, une BA○; **to do sb a ~ turn** rendre service à qn; **would you be ~ enough to do** auriez-vous la gentillesse de faire; **5** (competent) bon/bonne; **she's a ~ swimmer** elle nage bien; **he speaks ~ Spanish** il parle bien espagnol; **to be ~ at** être bon en [*Latin, physics*]; être bon à [*badminton, chess*]; **to be no ~ at** être nul/nulle en [*tennis, chemistry*]; être nul/nulle à [*chess, cards*]; **to be ~ with** savoir comment s'y prendre avec [*children, animals*]; aimer [*figures*]; **to be ~ with one's hands** être habile de ses mains; **to be ~ with words** savoir manier la langue; **6** (beneficial) **to be ~ for** faire du bien à [*person, plant*]; être bon pour [*health, business, morale*]; **exercise is ~ for you** ça fait du bien de faire de l'exercice; **7** (fortunate) **it's a ~ job** or **thing (that)** heureusement que; **it's a ~ job** or **thing too!** tant mieux!; **it's too ~ to be true** c'est trop beau pour être vrai; ▶ **better**, **best**.
III *excl* (expressing pleasure, satisfaction) c'est bien!; (with relief) tant mieux!; (to encourage, approve) très bien!
IV as good as *phr* **1** (virtually) quasiment; **to be as ~ as new** être comme neuf/neuve; **2 it's as ~ as saying yes** c'est comme si tu disais oui; **he as ~ as called me a liar** il m'a plus ou moins traité de menteur.
V for good *phr* pour toujours.
IDIOMS **~ for you!** bravo!; **you can have too much of a ~ thing** il ne faut pas abuser des bonnes choses.

good: **~ afternoon** *phr* (in greeting) bonjour; (in farewell) au revoir; **~bye** *phr* au revoir; **~ evening** *phr* bonsoir; **~-for-nothing** *n* bon/bonne *m/f* à rien.

good-humoured (GB), **good-humored** (US) *adj* [*crowd, discussion*] détendu; [*rivalry*] amical; [*remark, smile*] plaisant; **to be ~** avoir bon caractère.

good: **~-looking** *adj* beau/belle (*before n*); **~ looks** *n pl* beauté *f*; **~ morning** *phr* (in greeting) bonjour; (in farewell) au revoir; **~-natured** *adj* [*person*] agréable; [*animal*] placide.

goodness I *n* **1** (quality, virtue) bonté *f*; **2** (nourishment) **to be full of ~** être plein de bonnes choses.
II *excl* (also **~ gracious!**) mon Dieu!
IDIOMS **for ~' sake!** pour l'amour de Dieu!

goodnight *phr* bonne nuit.

goods I *n pl* **1** (for sale) articles *mpl*, marchandise *f*; **stolen ~** marchandise volée; **electrical ~** appareils *mpl* électroménagers; **2** (property) affaires *fpl*, biens *mpl*.
II *noun modifier* (GB) [*train, wagon*] de marchandises.

goodwill *n* **1 to show ~ to sb** faire preuve de bienveillance à l'égard de qn; **in a spirit of ~** en toute amitié; **2** (of business) clientèle *f*.

goose *n* oie *f*.

gooseberry *n* groseille *f* à maquereau.
IDIOMS **to be a** or **play ~** tenir la chandelle.

goose pimples *n pl* chair *f* de poule; **to get ~** avoir la chair de poule.

goose-step I *n* pas *m* de l'oie.
II *vi* défiler au pas de l'oie.

gorge I *n* gorge *f*.
II *v refl* **to ~ oneself** se gaver (**on** de).

gorgeous *adj* **1**° [*food, scenery*] formidable°; [*kitten, baby*] adorable; [*weather, day, person*] splendide; **2** (sumptuous) somptueux/-euse.

gorilla *n* gorille *m*.

gorse *n* ajoncs *mpl*.

gory *adj* sanglant.

gosh° *excl* ça alors°!

gospel I *n* Évangile *m*.
II *noun modifier* **~ music** gospel *m*; **~ singer** chanteur/-euse *m/f* de gospel.

gossip I *n* **1** (malicious) commérages *mpl* (**about** sur); (not malicious) nouvelles *fpl* (**about** sur); **2** (person) **he's/she's a real ~** c'est une vraie commère.
II *vi* bavarder; (more maliciously) faire des commérages (**about** sur).

gossip: **~ column** *n* échos *mpl*; **~ columnist** *n* échotier/-ière *m/f*.

got: **to have got** *phr* **1 to have ~** avoir; **2 I've ~ to go** il faut que j'y aille; **you've ~ to meet Sue** il faut absolument que tu fasses la connaissance de Sue.
IDIOMS **to feel ~ at**° se sentir persécuté.

gothic, Gothic I *n* gothique *m*.
II *adj* [*cathedral, art, script*] gothique; [*gloom, horror*] noir.

gouge *v* ■ **gouge out**: **~ [sth] out, ~ out [sth]** creuser [*pattern*]; **to ~ sb's eyes out** arracher les yeux de qn.

gourd *n* **1** (container) gourde *f*; **2** (fruit) calebasse *f*.

gout ▶ **686** *n* goutte *f*.

govern I *vtr* **1** gouverner [*country, state, city*]; administrer [*colony, province*]; **2** (control) régir [*use, conduct, treatment*]; **3** (determine) déterminer [*decision, development*]; régler [*flow, input, speed*].
II *vi* [*parliament, president*] gouverner; [*administrator, governor*] administrer.

governess *n* gouvernante *f*.

government I *n* (system, body) gouvernement *m*; (the State) l'État *m*.
II *noun modifier* [*minister*] du gouvernement; [*department, policy*] gouvernemental; [*expenditure, borrowing*] de l'État; [*loan, funds*] public/-ique.

governmental *adj* gouvernemental.

governor *n* (of state, colony, bank) gouverneur *m*; (of prison) directeur *m*; (of school) membre *m* du conseil d'établissement.

gown *n* (of judge, academic) toge *f*; (of surgeon) blouse *f*; (of patient) chemise *f* (d'hôpital).

GP ▶ **805** *n* (*abbr* = **general practitioner**) (médecin *m*) généraliste *mf*.

grab I *n* **to make a ~ at** or **for sth** essayer d'attraper qch.
II *vtr* empoigner [*money, object*]; saisir [*arm, person, opportunity*]; **to ~ sth from sb** arracher qch à qn; **to ~ hold of** se saisir de.

grace *n* **1** grâce *f*; **to do sth with (a) good/bad ~** faire qch de bonne/mauvaise grâce; **sb's saving ~** ce qui sauve qn; **2 to give sb two days' ~** accorder un délai de deux jours à qn; **3** (prayer) (before meal) bénédicité *m*; (after meal) grâces *fpl*.
IDIOMS **to be full of airs and ~s** prendre des airs.

graceful *adj* [*dancer, movement*] gracieux/-ieuse; [*person*] élégant.

gracefully *adv* [*move*] avec grâce; [*concede*] gracieusement.

grade I *n* **1** qualité *f*; **high-/low-~** de qualité supérieure/inférieure; **2** (mark) note *f* (**in** en); **to get good ~s** avoir de bonnes notes; **3** (rank, of salary) échelon *m*; **4** (US) (class) classe *f*; **eighth ~** ≈ (classe de) quatrième.
II *vtr* (by quality) classer (**according to** selon); (by size) calibrer (**according to** selon).
IDIOMS **to make the ~** se montrer à la hauteur.

grade school *n* (US) école *f* primaire.

gradient *n* pente *f*, inclinaison *f*; **a ~ of 1 in 4** or **25%** une pente de 25%.

gradual *adj* **1** [*change, increase*] progressif/-ive; **2** [*slope*] doux/douce.

gradually *adv* (slowly) peu à peu; (by degrees) progressivement.

graduate I *n* diplômé/-e *m/f* (**in** en; **of, from** de); **arts ~** diplômé/-e *m/f* en lettres.
II *vi* **1** terminer ses études (**at** or **from** à); (US Sch) ≈ finir le lycée; **2** (progress) **to ~ (from sth) to** passer (de qch) à.

graduate school *n* (US) ≈ troisième cycle *m*.

graduation *n* **1** (also **~ ceremony**) (cérémonie *f* de) remise *f* des diplômes; **2** (end of course) obtention *f* d'un diplôme.

graffiti *n* graffiti *mpl*.

graffiti artist *n* tagger *m*.

graft I *n* greffe *f*; **skin ~** greffe de la peau.
II *vtr* greffer (**onto** sur).

grain *n* **1** (commodity) céréales *fpl*; **2** (seed) (of rice, wheat) grain *m*; **long ~ rice** riz *m* long; **3** (of sand, salt) grain *m*; **4** (figurative) (of truth, comfort) brin *m*; **5** (in wood, stone) veines *fpl*; (in leather, paper, fabric) grain *m*.
IDIOMS **it goes against the ~** c'est contre tous mes/nos/leurs principes.

gram(me) ▶ **738** *n* gramme *m*.

grammar *n* grammaire *f*.

grammar school *n* (GB) ≈ lycée *m* (à recrutement sélectif).

grammatical *adj* **1** [*error*] de grammaire; **2** (correct) grammaticalement correct.

granary I *n* grenier *m*.
II *noun modifier* (GB) [*bread*] complet/-ète.

grand *adj* [*building, ceremony*] grandiose;

[*park*] magnifique; **in ~ style** en grande pompe; **on a ~ scale** sur un grand pied; **the Grand Canyon** le Grand Cañon *m*; **to play the ~ lady** jouer à la grande dame.

grandchild *n* (girl) petite-fille *f*; (boy) petit-fils *m*; **his grandchildren** ses petits-enfants *mpl*.

grand: **~dad**○ *n* pépé○ *m*, papy○ *m*, papi *m*; **~daughter** *n* petite-fille *f*.

grandee *n* grand personnage *m*.

grandeur *n* (of scenery) majesté *f*; (of building) caractère *m* grandiose.

grand: **~father** *n* grand-père *m*; **~father clock** *n* horloge *f* comtoise; **~ finale** *n* finale *m*; **~ma**○ *n* mémé○ *f*, mamy○ *f*, mamie○ *f*; **~ master** *n* grand maître *m*; **~mother** *n* grand-mère *f*; **~pa**○ *n* pépé○ *m*, papy○ *m*, papi○ *m*; **~parents** *n pl* grands-parents *mpl*; **~ piano** ▶753 *n* piano *m* à queue; **~son** *n* petit-fils *m*; **~stand** *n* tribune *f*.

grand total *n* total *m*; **the ~ for the repairs came to £3,000** en tout, les travaux sont revenus à 3 000 livres sterling.

granite *n* granit(e) *m*.

granny○ *n* mémé○ *f*.

grant I *n* (from government, local authority) subvention *f* (**for** pour; **to do** pour faire); (for study) bourse *f*; **research ~** subvention *f* de recherche.
II *vtr* **1** accorder [*permission*]; accéder à [*request*]; **2 to ~ sb [sth], to ~ [sth] to sb** accorder [qch] à qn [*interview, leave, visa*]; concéder [qch] à qn [*citizenship*]; **3 to ~ that** reconnaître que.
IDIOMS **to take sth for ~ed** considérer qch comme allant de soi; **he takes his mother for ~ed** il croit que sa mère est à son service; **~ed, it's magnificent** c'est magnifique, soit.

granulated *adj* [*sugar*] cristallisé.

granule *n* (of sugar, salt) grain *m*; (of coffee) granulé *m*.

grape *n* grain *m* de raisin; **a bunch of ~s** une grappe de raisin; **I love ~s** j'adore le raisin; **to harvest the ~s** vendanger.

grapefruit *n* pamplemousse *m*.

grapevine *n* (in vineyard) pied *m* de vigne; (in greenhouse, garden) vigne *f*.
IDIOMS **to hear sth on the ~** apprendre qch par le téléphone arabe.

graph *n* graphique *m*.

graphic *adj* [*account*] (pleasantly described) vivant; (gory) cru.

graphic design *n* graphisme *m*.

graphics *n pl* **1** (on screen) visualisation *f* graphique; **2 computer ~** infographie *f*; **3** (in film, TV) images *fpl*; (in book) illustrations *fpl*.

graph paper *n* papier *m* millimétré.

grasp I *n* **1** (hold, grip) prise *f*; (stronger) poigne *f*; **to take a firm ~ of sth** empoigner fermement qch; **2** (understanding) maîtrise *f*.
II *vtr* **1** empoigner [*rope, hand*]; saisir [*opportunity*]; **2** (comprehend) saisir, comprendre [*concept, subject*]; suivre [*argument*].
III *vi* **1 to ~ at** tenter de saisir; **2** saisir [*excuse*].

grasping *adj* cupide.

grass I *n* herbe *f*; (lawn) pelouse *f*.
II *noun modifier* [*slope, verge*] gazonné.
IDIOMS **the ~ is greener (on the other side of the fence)** on croit toujours que c'est mieux ailleurs.

grass: **~ court** *n* court *m* en gazon; **~ cuttings** *n pl* herbe *f* coupée; **~hopper** *n* sauterelle *f*.

grassroots I *n pl* **the ~** le peuple.
II *adj* [*movement*] populaire; [*support*] de base.

grassy *adj* herbeux/-euse.

grate I *n* (fire-basket) grille *f* de foyer; (hearth) âtre *m*.
II *vtr* râper [*carrot, cheese*].
III *vi* **1** [*metal object*] grincer (**on** sur); **2** (annoy) agacer; **that ~s** ça m'agace.

grateful *adj* reconnaissant (**to** à; **for** de); **to be ~ that** être heureux/-euse que (+ *subj*); **I would be ~ if you could reply** je vous serais reconnaissant de bien vouloir répondre.

grater *n* râpe *f*.

gratify *vtr* satisfaire [*desire*].

grating I *n* **1** (bars) grille *f*; **2** (noise) grincement *m*.
II *adj* [*noise*] grinçant; [*voice*] désagréable.

gratitude *n* reconnaissance *f* (**to, towards** envers; **for** de).

grave I *n* tombe *f*; **beyond the ~** après la mort.
II *adj* **1** [*illness*] grave; [*risk*] sérieux/-ieuse; [*danger*] grand (*before n*); **2** (solemn) sérieux/-ieuse.

gravel *n* (coarse) graviers *mpl*; (fine) gravillons *mpl*.

graveside *n* **at the ~** autour de la tombe.

grave: **~stone** *n* pierre *f* tombale; **~yard** *n* cimetière *m*.

gravitate *vi* **to ~ to(wards)** graviter vers.

gravity *n* **1** pesanteur *f*; **centre of ~** centre *m* de gravité; **the pull of the earth's ~** l'attraction *f* terrestre; **2** (of situation) gravité *f*.

gravy *n* sauce *f* (au jus de rôti).

gravy boat *n* saucière *f*.

graze I *n* écorchure *f*.
II *vtr* **1 to ~ one's knee** s'écorcher le genou (**on, against** sur); **2** (touch lightly) frôler.
III *vi* [*sheep*] brouter; [*cow*] paître.

grease I *n* graisse *f*.
II *vtr* graisser.

greasy *adj* [*hair, skin, food*] gras/grasse; [*overalls*] graisseux/-euse.

great I *n* **the ~** les grands *mpl*.
II *adj* **1** grand (*before n*); [*number, increase*] important; [*heat*] fort (*before n*); **a ~ deal (of)** beaucoup (de); **a ~ many people** beaucoup de personnes, un grand nombre de personnes; **~ difficulty** beaucoup de mal; **in ~ detail** [*explain*] dans les moindres détails; **the map was a ~ help** la carte a été très utile; **2**○ [*book, party, weather*] génial○, formidable○; [*opportunity*] formidable○; **to feel ~** se sentir en pleine forme; **to have a ~ time** bien s'amuser.

III○ *adv* **I'm doing ~** ça marche très bien pour moi○.

great: **~ big** *adj* (très) grand (*before n*), énorme; **Great Britain** ▶574| *pr n* Grande-Bretagne *f*; **~ grandchild** *n* (girl) arrière-petite-fille *f*; (garçon) arrière-petit-fils *m*; **~ grandfather** *n* arrière-grand-père *m*; **~ grandmother** *n* arrière-grand-mère *f*; **~-great grandchild** *n* (girl) arrière-arrière-petite-fille *f*; (boy) arrière-arrière-petit-fils *m*.

greatly *adv* [*admire, regret*] beaucoup, énormément; [*surprised, distressed*] très, extrêmement; [*improved, changed*] considérablement.

greatness *n* (of achievement) importance *f*; (of person) grandeur *f*.

Great Power *n* grande puissance *f*.

Grecian *adj* grec/grecque.

Greece ▶574| *pr n* Grèce *f*.

greed *n* **1** (for money, power) avidité *f* (**for** de); **2** (also **greediness**) (for food) gourmandise *f*.

greedy *adj* **1** [*person*] (for food) gourmand; (stronger) goulu; [*look*] avide; **a ~ pig**○ un goinfre○; **2** (for money, power) avide (**for** de).

Greek ▶712| I *n* **1** (person) Grec/Grecque *m/f*; **2** (language) grec *m*.
II *adj* [*government, island*] grec/grecque; [*teacher, lesson*] de grec; [*ambassador, embassy*] de Grèce.
IDIOMS **it's all ~ to me** c'est du chinois pour moi.

green ▶559| I *n* **1** (colour) vert *m*; **2** (in village) terrain *m* communal; **3** (in bowling) boulingrin *m*; (in golf) green *m*; **4** (person) écologiste *mf*; **the Greens** les Verts.
II **greens** *n pl* (GB) légumes *mpl* verts.
III *adj* **1** vert; **to go** or **turn ~** [*traffic lights*] passer au vert; [*person*] verdir, devenir vert; **2** [*countryside*] verdoyant; **3**○ (naïve) naïf/naïve; **4** (inexperienced) novice; **5** [*policies, candidate, issues*] écologiste; [*product*] écologique.

green card *n* **1** (driving insurance) carte *f* verte (internationale); **2** (US) (residence and work permit) carte *f* de séjour.

greenery *n* verdure *f*.

green: **~grocer** ▶805| *n* marchand *m* de fruits et légumes; **~house** *n* serre *f*; **~house effect** *n* effet *m* de serre.

greenish ▶559| *adj* tirant sur le vert; (unpleasantly) verdâtre.

greenness *n* **1** verdeur *f*; (of countryside) verdure *f*; **2** (inexperience) inexpérience *f*.

Greenwich Mean Time, GMT *n* temps *m* universel, TU.

greet *vtr* **1** saluer; **to ~ sb in the street** dire bonjour à qn dans la rue; **2 to be ~ed with** or **by** provoquer [*dismay, amusement*]; **3** [*sight*] s'offrir à [*person*].

greeting I *n* salutation *f*.
II **greetings** *n pl* **Christmas ~s** vœux *mpl* de Noël; **Season's ~s** meilleurs vœux.

greetings card (GB), **greeting card** (US) *n* carte *f* de vœux.

grey (GB), **gray** (US) ▶559| I *n* gris *m*.
II *adj* **1** (in colour) gris; **2** (grey-haired) aux cheveux gris, grisonnant; **to go** or **turn ~** grisonner; **3** (dull, boring) [*existence, day*] morne; [*person, town*] terne.
III *vi* grisonner; **to be ~ing at the temples** avoir les tempes grisonnantes.

greyhound *n* lévrier *m*.

grid *n* **1** grille *f*; **2** (GB) (network) réseau *m*.

gridlock *n* embouteillage *m*, bouchon *m*.

grief *n* chagrin *m*.
IDIOMS **to come to ~** [*person*] (have an accident) avoir un accident; (fail) échouer; [*business*] péricliter.

grievance *n* griefs *mpl* (**against** contre).

grieve *vi* **to ~ for** or **over** pleurer [*person*].

grievous bodily harm, GBH *n* (Law) coups *mpl* et blessures *fpl*.

grill I *n* gril *m*.
II *vtr* **1** faire griller [*meat, fish*]; **2**○ (interrogate) mettre [qn] sur la sellette○.
III *vi* [*steak, fish*] griller.

grille *n* grille *f*; (on car) calandre *f*.

grim *adj* **1** [*news, town*] sinistre; [*sight, conditions*] effroyable; [*reality*] dur; **her future looks ~** son avenir a l'air sombre; **2** [*struggle*] acharné; [*resolve*] terrible; **3** [*face*] grave; **4**○ [*accommodation, food*] très mauvais.

grimace I *n* grimace *f* (**of** de).
II *vi* (involuntary) faire une grimace (**with, in** de); (pull a face) faire la grimace.

grime *n* (of city) saleté *f*; (on object, person) crasse *f*.

grimy *adj* [*city*] noir; [*hands, window*] crasseux/-euse.

grin I *n* sourire *m*.
II *vi* sourire (**at** à; **with** de).
IDIOMS **to ~ and bear it** souffrir en silence.

grind I○ *n* boulot○ *m* or travail *m* monotone; **the daily ~** le boulot○ or le train-train○ quotidien.
II *vtr* moudre [*corn, coffee beans*]; écraser [*grain*]; hacher [*meat*]; **to ~ one's teeth** grincer des dents.
III *vi* [*machine*] grincer; **to ~ to a halt** [*machine*] s'arrêter; [*vehicle*] s'arrêter avec un grincement de freins; [*factory, production*] s'immobiliser.

grinder *n* (industrial) broyeur *m*; (domestic) moulin *m*.

grinding I *n* grincement *m*.
II *adj* [*noise*] grinçant; **~ poverty** misère *f* noire.

grindstone *n* meule *f* or pierre *f* à aiguiser.
IDIOMS **to keep** or **have one's nose to the ~** travailler sans relâche.

grip I *n* **1** prise *f* (**on** sur); **2 to lose one's ~ on reality** perdre contact avec la réalité; **to come to ~s with sth** en venir aux prises avec qch; **get a ~ on yourself!** ressaisis-toi!; **3** (of tyre) adhérence *f*.
II *vtr* **1** (grab) agripper; (hold) serrer; **2** [*tyres*] adhérer à [*road*]; [*shoes*] accrocher à [*ground*]; **3** (captivate) captiver.

gripping *adj* captivant.

grisly *adj* [*story, sight*] horrible; [*remains*] macabre.

grist *n* IDIOMS **it's all ~ to the mill** tout sert.

gristle *n* cartilage *m*.

grit I *n* **1** (on lens) grains *mpl* de poussière; (sandy dirt) grains *mpl* de sable; **2** (GB) (for roads) sable *m*.
II *vtr* (GB) sabler [*road*].
IDIOMS **to ~ one's teeth** serrer les dents.

grizzly *n* (also **~ bear**) grizzli *m*.

groan I *n* (of pain, despair) gémissement *m*; (of disgust, protest) grognement *m*.
II *vi* (in pain) gémir; (in disgust, protest) grogner.

grocer ▶805 *n* (person) épicier/-ière *m/f*; **~'s (shop)** épicerie *f*.

groceries *n pl* provisions *fpl*.

grocery ▶805 *n* (also **~ shop** (GB), **~ store**) épicerie *f*.

groggy *adj* groggy; **to feel ~** avoir les jambes en coton°.

groin ▶523 *n* aine *f*.

groom I *n* **1** (bridegroom) **the ~** le jeune marié; **2** (for horse) palefrenier/-ière *m/f*.
II *vtr* **1** panser [*horse*]; **2 to ~ sb for** préparer qn [*exam, career*].

groove *n* (on record) sillon *m*; (for sliding door) coulisse *f*; (on screw) fente *f*.

grope I *vtr* **1 he ~d his way past the furniture** il contourna les meubles à tâtons; **2**° (sexually) tripoter°.
II *vi* **to ~ for sth** chercher qch à tâtons.

gross I *n* grosse *f*.
II *adj* **1** [*income, profit*] brut; **2** [*error, exaggeration*] grossier/-ière; [*ignorance*] crasse; [*abuse, inequality*] choquant; [*injustice*] flagrant; **3** [*behaviour*] vulgaire; [*language*] cru; **4**° (revolting) dégoûtant; **5**° (obese) obèse.
III *vtr* [*business, company*] faire un bénéfice brut de.

grotesque *n, adj* grotesque (*m*).

grotto *n* grotte *f*.

ground I *n* **1** sol *m*, terre *f*; **to throw sth on the ~** jeter qch par terre; **to sit on the ~** s'asseoir par terre; **to fall to the ~** tomber (par terre); **to get off the ~** [*plane*] décoller; [*idea*] prendre; **2** (area, territory) terrain *m*; **to break new ~** innover; **on neutral ~** en terrain neutre; **to gain ~** gagner du terrain (**on, over** sur); **to hold one's ~** tenir bon; **3** (sportsground) terrain *m*.
II **grounds** *n pl* **1** (garden) parc *m* (**of** de); **2** (reasons) **~s for** motifs *mpl* de [*divorce, criticism, hope*]; **to have ~s for complaint** avoir des motifs de se plaindre; **~s for doing** motifs pour faire; **on (the) ~s of** en raison de [*cost, public interest*]; pour cause de [*adultery, negligence*]; **on (the) ~s of ill-health** pour raisons de santé; **on the ~s that** en raison du fait que.
III **ground** *pp adj* [*coffee, pepper*] moulu.
IV *vtr* **1** immobiliser [*aircraft*]; **2** [*ship*] **to be ~ed** s'échouer.
IDIOMS **to be thin on the ~** ne pas être légion *inv*; **to go to ~** se terrer; **that suits me down to the ~** ça me convient parfaitement.

ground floor *n* rez-de-chaussée *m inv*; **on the ~** au rez-de-chaussée.

grounding *n* bases *fpl* (**in** en, de); **to have a good ~ in sth** avoir de bonnes bases en qch.

groundwork *n* travail *m* préparatoire (**for** à).

group I *n* groupe *m*; **in ~s** en groupes.
II *vtr* (also **~ together**) grouper [*people, objects*].
III *vi* **~ together** [*people*] se grouper (**around** autour de).

grouse *n* tétras *m*.

grove *n* bosquet *m*; **lemon ~** verger *m* de citronniers.

grovel *vi* ramper (**to, before** devant).

grovelling, **groveling** (US) *adj* obséquieux/-ieuse.

grow I *vtr* **1** cultiver [*plant, crop*]; **2** laisser pousser [*beard, nails*]; **to ~ 5 cm** [*person*] grandir de 5 cm; [*plant*] pousser de 5 cm.
II *vi* **1** [*person*] grandir (**by** de); [*plant, hair*] pousser (**by** de); [*tumour*] se développer; **2** [*population, tension*] augmenter (**by** de); [*company, economy*] être en expansion; [*movement, opposition, support, problem*] devenir plus important; [*poverty, crisis*] s'aggraver; **3** devenir [*hotter, stronger*]; **to ~ old** vieillir; **to ~ more and more impatient** s'impatienter de plus en plus; **I soon grew to like him** j'ai vite fini par l'aimer.
■ **grow apart** s'éloigner l'un de l'autre.
■ **grow on**: **~ on [sb]** [*habit*] s'imposer; **it ~s on you** on finit par l'aimer.
■ **grow out of**: **~ out of [sth]**: **he's grown out of his suit** son costume est devenu trop petit pour lui.
■ **grow up 1** [*child*] grandir; **2** (become adult, mature) devenir adulte; **when I ~ up** quand je serai grand.

grower *n* (of fruit) producteur/-trice *m/f*; (of flowers) horticulteur/-trice *m/f*.

growing I *n* culture *f*.
II *adj* **1** [*child*] en pleine croissance; [*business*] en expansion; **2** [*number, demand*] croissant; [*pressure, optimism, opposition*] grandissant.

growl I *n* grondement *m*.
II *vi* [*dog*] gronder.

grown-up I *n* adulte *mf*, grande personne *f*.
II *adj* adulte.

growth *n* **1** (of person, plant) croissance *f*; (of hair, nails) pousse *f*; **2** (of population, movement, idea) croissance *f* (**in, of** de); (of economy) expansion *f* (**in, of** de); (in numbers, productivity) augmentation *f* (**in** de); **3** (tumour) grosseur *f*, tumeur *f*.

grudge I *n* **to bear sb a ~** en vouloir à qn.
II *vtr* **to ~ sb their success** en vouloir à qn de sa réussite; **to ~ doing** rechigner à faire.

gruelling, **grueling** (US) *adj* exténuant.

gruesome *adj* (gory) horrible; (horrifying) épouvantable.

gruff *adj* bourru.

grumble *vi* [*person*] ronchonner (**at sb** après qn; **to** auprès de); **to ~ about** se plaindre de.

grumpy *adj* grincheux/-euse, grognon.

grunt I *n* grognement *m*.
II *vi* [*pig*] grogner; [*person*] grogner (**with, in** de).

guarantee I *n* garantie *f* (**against** contre); **there is a ~ on the vehicle** le véhicule est sous garantie; **there is no ~ that** il n'est pas certain que.
II *vtr* **1** garantir (**against** contre); **it's ~d** il est garanti; **2** (assure) garantir, assurer; **I can ~ that...** je peux vous garantir que...; **3 to ~ a loan** se porter garant d'un emprunt; **to ~ a cheque** garantir un chèque.

guard I *n* **1** (for person) surveillant/-e *m/f*; (for place, object, at prison) gardien/-ienne *m/f*; (soldier) garde *m*; **under armed ~** sous escorte armée; **2** (military duty) garde *f*, surveillance *f*; **to be on ~** être de garde; **to stand ~** monter la garde (**over** auprès de); **the changing of the ~** (GB) la relève de la garde; **3 to catch sb off ~** prendre qn au dépourvu; **to be on one's ~** se méfier (**against** de); **4** (GB) (on train) chef *m* de train.
II *vtr* **1** (protect) surveiller [*place, object*]; protéger [*person*]; **heavily ~ed** sous haute surveillance; **2** surveiller [*hostage, prisoner*]; **3** garder [*secret*].
■ **guard against**: **~ against [sth]** se prémunir contre; **to ~ against doing** prendre garde à ne pas faire.

guard dog *n* chien *m* de garde.

guarded *adj* circonspect (**about** à propos de).

guardian *n* **1** (gen) gardien/-ienne *m/f* (**of** de); **2** (Law) (of child) tuteur/-trice *m/f*.

guardian angel *n* ange *m* gardien.

Guernsey *pr n* Guernesey *f*.

guerrilla *n* guérillero *m*.

guerrilla war *n* guérilla *f*.

guess I *n* supposition *f*, conjecture *f*; **at a (rough) ~ I would say that...** au hasard je dirais que...; **that was a good ~!** tu as deviné juste!; **your ~ is as good as mine** je n'en sais pas plus que toi; **it's anybody's ~!** les paris sont ouverts!
II *vtr* **1** deviner; **to ~ that** supposer que; **I ~ed as much!** je m'en doutais!; **~ what!** tu sais quoi°!; **~ who!** devine qui c'est!; **2** (US) (suppose) supposer; (believe, think) penser, croire.
III *vi* deviner; **to ~ right** deviner juste; **to ~ wrong** se tromper; **to keep sb ~ing** ne pas satisfaire la curiosité de qn.

guesswork *n* conjecture *f*.

guest I *n* (in one's home) invité/-e *m/f*; (at hotel) client/-e *m/f*; **be my ~!** je vous en prie!
II *noun modifier* [*speaker*] invité; **~ book** livre *m* d'or.

guest: **~house** *n* pension *f* de famille; **~ room** *n* chambre *f* d'amis.

guidance *n* conseils *mpl* (**from** de).

guide I *n* **1** (person) guide *m*; **tour ~** guide (touristique); **to act as a ~** servir de guide; **2** (estimate, idea) indication *f*; **as a rough ~** à titre d'indication; **3** (book) guide *m* (**to** de); **4** (also **Girl Guide**) guide *f*.
II *vtr* guider (**to** vers).

guide: **~ book** *n* guide *m*; **~ dog** *n* chien *m* d'aveugle; **~d tour** *n* visite *f* guidée.

guideline *n* indication *f*; (in political context) directive *f*; **pay ~s** base *f* des négociations salariales.

guiding *adj* **~ force** moteur *m*; **~ principle** principe *m* directeur.

guild *n* (medieval) guilde *f*; (modern) association *f*.

guillotine *n* **1** guillotine *f*; **2** (for paper) massicot *m*.

guilt *n* **1** (blame) culpabilité *f*; **2** (feeling) sentiment *m* de culpabilité (**about sb** envers qn; **about** or **over sth** pour qch).

guilty *adj* **1** (culpable) coupable; **the ~ party** le/la coupable *m/f*; **2** [*expression*] de culpabilité; [*look*] coupable; **to feel ~** culpabiliser; **to make sb feel ~** culpabiliser qn; **to feel ~ about** se sentir coupable vis-à-vis de.

guinea-pig *n* **1** (Zool) cochon *m* d'Inde; **2** (in experiment, trial) cobaye *m*.

guitar ▶753 I *n* guitare *f*; **on the ~** à la guitare.
II *noun modifier* [*lesson, player, string, teacher*] de guitare.

guitarist ▶805, 753 *n* guitariste *mf*.

gulch *n* (US) ravin *m*.

gulf *n* **1** golfe *m*; **the Gulf** la région *f* du Golfe; **2** (figurative) fossé *m* (**between** qui sépare).

gull *n* mouette *f*.

gullibility *n* crédulité *f*.

gullible *adj* crédule.

gully *n* ravin *m*.

gulp I *n* **1** (of liquid) gorgée *f*; (of air) bouffée *f*, goulée *f*; **she drained her glass in one ~** elle a vidé son verre d'un trait; **2** (nervous) serrement *m* de gorge; (tearful) hoquet *m*.
II *vi* avoir la gorge serrée.

gum *n* **1** (in mouth) gencive *f*; **2** (also **chewing ~**) chewing-gum *m*; **a piece of ~** un chewing-gum; **3** (adhesive) colle *f*; **4** (resin) gomme *f*.

gun *n* (weapon) arme *f* à feu; (revolver) revolver *m*; (rifle) fusil *m*; (cannon) canon *m*; **to fire a ~** tirer.
IDIOMS **to jump the ~** agir prématurément; **to stick to one's ~s°** s'accrocher°.
■ **gun down**: **~ [sb] down, ~ down [sb]** abattre, descendre.

gun: **~dog** *n* chien *m* de chasse; **~fire** *n* (from hand-held gun) coups *mpl* de feu; (from artillery) fusillade *f*; **~ laws** *n pl* législation *f* sur les armes à feu; **~man** *n* homme *m* armé.

gunpoint *n* **to hold sb up at ~** tenir qn sous la menace d'une arme.

gun: **~powder** *n* poudre *f*; **~running** *n* trafic *m* d'armes; **~shot** *n* coup *m* de feu; **~shot wound** *n* blessure *f* par balle.

gurgle I *n* (of water) gargouillement *m*; (of baby) gazouillis *m*.
II *vi* [*water*] gargouiller; [*baby*] gazouiller.

guru *n* gourou *m*.

gush *vi* jaillir.

gushing *adj* [*person*] hyperexpansif/-ive°; [*letter, style*] dithyrambique°.

gust *n* (of wind, rain, snow) rafale *f*; **a ~ of hot air** une bouffée d'air chaud.

gusto *n* **with ~** avec enthousiasme.

gut I° *n* bide° *m*.
II *noun modifier* [*feeling, reaction*] viscéral, instinctif/-ive.
III *vtr* [*fire*] ravager [*buildings*].

guts° *n pl* **1** (insides) (of human) tripes° *fpl*; (of animal) entrailles *fpl*; **2** (courage) cran° *m*.

gutter *n* (on roof) gouttière *f*; (in street) caniveau *m*.

guttering *n* gouttières *fpl*.

gutter: **~ press** *n* presse *f* à sensation; **~snipe** *n* gosse *mf* des rues.

guy° *n* type° *m*; **a good/bad ~** (in films) un bon/méchant.

guzzle° *vtr* engloutir.

gym ▶ 649 *n* **1** (*abbr* = **gymnasium**) salle *f* de gym°, gymnase *m*; **2** (*abbr* = **gymnastics**) gym° *f*.

gymnasium *n* gymnase *m*.

gymnast *n* gymnaste *mf*.

gymnastics ▶ 649 *n pl* gymnastique *f*.

gym shoe *n* tennis *f*.

gynaecologist (GB), **gynecologist** (US) ▶ 805 *n* gynécologue *mf*.

gypsy I *n* bohémien/-ienne *m/f*; (Central European) tzigane *mf*; (Spanish) gitan/-e *m/f*.
II *noun modifier* [*camp*] de bohémiens; [*music*] tzigane.

h, H *n* h, H *m*.

habit *n* **1** habitude *f*; **to have a ~ of doing** avoir l'habitude de faire; **to get into/out of the ~ of doing sth** prendre/perdre l'habitude de faire qch; **to do sth out of ~** faire qch par habitude; **2** (addiction) accoutumance *f*; **3** (of monk, nun) habit *m*.

habitable *adj* habitable.

habitat *n* habitat *m*.

habitation *n* habitation *f*; **unfit for human ~** insalubre.

habitual *adj* [*behaviour, reaction*] habituel/-elle; [*drinker, smoker, liar*] invétéré.

hack **I** *n* **1**° (writer) écrivaillon *m*; (journalist) journaliste *m/f* qui fait la rubrique des chiens écrasés; **2** (Comput) = **computer hacker**.
II *vtr* **1** taillader [*branch, object*] (**with** avec, à coups de); tailler dans [*bushes*] (**with** à coups de); **to ~ sth/sb to pieces** tailler qch/qn en pièces; **to ~ a path through sth** se tailler un chemin à travers qch; **2** (Comput) s'introduire dans [*database*].
III *vi* **1** (chop) taillader (**with** à coups de); **to ~ through sth** tailler dans qch; **2**° (Comput) pirater°; **to ~ into** s'introduire dans [*system*].

hackles *n pl* (on cockerel) camail *m*; (on dog) poils *mpl* du cou; **the dog's ~ began to rise** le chien se hérissait.

hackneyed *adj* [*joke*] éculé; [*subject*] rebattu; **~ phrase** cliché *m*.

haddock *n* églefin *m*.

haemoglobin (GB), **hemoglobin** (US) *n* hémoglobine *f*.

haemophilia (GB), **hemophilia** (US) ▶686 *n* hémophilie *f*.

haemorrhage (GB), **hemorrhage** (US) **I** *n* hémorragie *f*.
II *vi* faire une hémorragie.

haemorrhoids (GB), **hemorrhoids** (US) *n pl* hémorroïdes *fpl*.

haggard *adj* [*appearance, person*] exténué; [*face, expression*] défait.

haggle *vi* marchander; **to ~ over sth** discuter du prix de qch.

Hague ▶574 *pr n* **The ~** La Haye.

hail **I** *n* **1** grêle *f*; **2** (of bullets, insults) grêle *f* (**of** de).
II *vtr* **1** héler [*person, taxi, ship*]; **2** (praise) **to ~ sb as** acclamer qn comme; **to ~ sth as sth/as being** saluer qch comme qch/comme étant.
III *v impers* grêler.

hail: **~stone** *n* grêlon *m*; **~storm** *n* averse *f* de grêle.

hair *n* **1** (on head) cheveux *mpl*; (on body) poils *mpl*; (of animal) poil *m*; **to have one's ~ done** se faire coiffer; **long/short-~ed** [*person*] aux cheveux longs/courts; [*animal*] à poil long/court; **2** (individually) (on head) cheveu *m*; (on body) poil *m*; (animal) poil *m*.
IDIOMS **to split ~s** couper les cheveux en quatre.

hair: **~band** *n* bandeau *m*; **~brush** *n* brosse *f* à cheveux; **~cut** *n* coupe *f* (de cheveux); **~do**° *n* coiffure *f*; **~dresser** ▶805, 805 *n* coiffeur/-euse *m/f*; **~drier** *n* (hand-held) sèche-cheveux *m inv*; (hood) casque *m*; **~ gel** *n* gel *m* coiffant; **~grip** *n* (GB) pince *f* à cheveux; **~net** *n* filet *m* à cheveux; **~pin bend** *n* virage *m* en épingle à cheveux; **~-raising** *adj* [*adventure, tale*] à vous faire dresser les cheveux sur la tête; **~ remover** *n* crème *f* dépilatoire; **~-slide** *n* (GB) barrette *f*; **~spray** *n* laque *f*; **~style** *n* coiffure *f*.

hairy *adj* [*coat, dog, chest*] poilu; [*stem*] villeux/-euse.

halal *adj* [*meat*] hallal *inv*.

half ▶554 **I** *n* **1** moitié *f*; **to cut sth in ~** couper qch en deux; **2** (fraction) demi *m*; **four and a ~** quatre et demi; **3** (Sport) (time period) mi-temps *f*; (pitch area) moitié *f* de terrain; **4**° (GB) (half pint) demi-pinte *f*.
II *adj* **a ~ circle** un demi-cercle; **a ~-litre, ~ a litre** un demi-litre; **two and a ~ cups** deux tasses et demie.
III *pron* **1** moitié *f*; **~ of the students** la moitié des étudiants; **to cut sth by ~** réduire qch de moitié; **2** (in time) demi/-e *m/f*; **an hour and a ~** une heure et demie; **~ past two/six** (GB), **~ two/six** deux/six heures et demie; **she is ten and a ~** elle a dix ans et demi.
IV *adv* à moitié; **to ~ close sth** fermer qch à moitié; **it's ~ the price** c'est moitié moins cher; **~ as much money/as many people** moitié moins d'argent/de personnes; **~ as big** moitié moins grand; **he's ~ Spanish ~ Irish** il est mi-espagnol mi-irlandais; **he was only ~ serious** il n'était qu'à moitié sérieux; **~ disappointed ~ relieved** mi-déçu mi-soulagé; **I was ~ hoping that...** j'espérais à moitié que...; **I ~ expected it** je m'y attendais plus ou moins.
IDIOMS **to go halves with sb** se mettre de moitié avec qn.

half: **~back** *n* (Sport) demi *m*; **~ century** *n* demi-siècle *m*; **~ day** *n* demi-journée *f*; **~-dozen** *n, pron, adj* demi-douzaine (*f*); **~ fare** *n* demi-tarif *m*; **~-hearted** *adj* [*attempt, smile*] peu enthousiaste; **~-heartedly** *adv* sans conviction.

half hour ▶915 *n* demi-heure *f*; **on the ~** à la demie.

half-mast *n* **at ~** en berne.

half-moon *n* **1** demi-lune *f*; **2** (of fingernail) lunule *f*.

half: **~ price** *adv, adj* à moitié prix; **~**

term (GB Sch) *n* vacances *fpl* de la mi-trimestre.

half-time *n* (Sport) mi-temps *f*; **at ~** à la mi-temps.

halfway *adv* **1** à mi-chemin (**between** entre; **to** de); **~ up** or **down** à mi-hauteur de [*stairs, tree*]; **~ down the page** à mi-page; **to be ~ through doing sth** avoir à moitié fini de faire qch; **2 to go ~ to** or **towards** (GB) **sth/doing** être à mi-chemin de qch/de faire; **I met him ~** j'ai fait un compromis avec lui.

half-yearly *adj* [*meeting, payment*] semestriel/-ielle.

hall *n* **1** (in house) entrée *f*; (corridor) couloir *m*; (in hotel, airport) hall *m*; (for public events) (grande) salle *f*; **2** (Univ) (residence) résidence *f* universitaire; **3** (country house) manoir *m*.

hallelujah *excl* alléluia!

hallmark I *n* **1** (GB) (on metal) poinçon *m*; **2** (typical feature) caractéristique *f*.

II *vtr* poinçonner; **to be ~ed** porter un poinçon.

Halloween *n*: *la veille de la Toussaint*.

hallucination *n* hallucination *f*.

hallway *n* entrée *f*.

halo *n* **1** (around head) auréole *f*; **2** (in astronomy) halo *m*.

halogen lamp *n* lampe *f* halogène.

halt I *n* **1** (stop) arrêt *m*; **to call a ~ to sth** mettre fin à qch; **2** (temporary) (in activity) suspension *f* (**in** dans); (in proceedings) pause *f* (**in** au cours de).

II *vtr* arrêter, mettre fin à.

halve I *vtr* réduire [qch] de moitié [*number, rate*]; couper [qch] en deux [*carrot, cake*].

II *vi* [*number, rate, time*] diminuer de moitié.

ham *n* jambon *m*.

hamburger *n* **1** (patty) hamburger *m*; **2** (US) (ground beef) pâté *m* de viande.

hammer I *n* **1** marteau *m*; **2** (Sport) (event) **the ~** le lancer de marteau.

II *vtr* **1** marteler [*metal, table, keys*]; **to ~ sth into** enfoncer qch dans [*wall, fence*]; **2 to ~ sth into sb** faire entrer qch dans la tête de qn; **to ~ home a message** bien faire comprendre un message.

III *vi* **1** (use hammer) frapper à coups de marteau; **2** (pound) tambouriner (**on, at** contre).

hamper I *n* panier *m* à pique-nique.

II *vtr* entraver [*movement, career, progress*]; handicaper [*person*].

hamster *n* hamster *m*.

hamstring *n* (of human) tendon *m* du jarret; (of horse) corde *f* du jarret.

hand ▶523 **I** *n* **1** main *f*; **he had a pencil/an umbrella in his ~** il avait un crayon/un parapluie à la main; **to get** or **lay one's ~s on sth** mettre la main sur qch; **to hold sb's ~** tenir qn par la main; (give support) tenir la main à qn; **to do** or **make sth by ~** faire qch à la main; **the letter was delivered by ~** la lettre a été remise en mains propres; **to have one's ~s full** avoir les mains pleines; (figurative) avoir assez à faire; **to give sb a (helping) ~** donner un coup de main à qn; **to be on one's ~s and knees** être à quatre pattes; **to change ~s** changer de mains; **to be in good** or **safe ~s** [*child, money*] être en bonnes mains; **to have sth to ~** avoir qch sous la main; **to be on ~** [*person*] être disponible; **to get out of ~** [*inflation*] déraper; [*children, crowd*] devenir incontrôlable; **to take sth/sb in ~** prendre qch/qn en main [*situation, person*]; **2** (Games) (cards dealt) jeu *m*; (game) partie *f*; **to show one's ~** montrer son jeu; **3** (worker) ouvrier/-ière *m/f*; (crew member) membre *m* de l'équipage; **4** (skill) **to try one's ~ at sth** s'essayer à; **5** (on clock, dial) aiguille *f*; **6** (aspect, side) **on the one ~..., on the other ~...** d'une part..., d'autre part...; **on the other ~** (conversely) par contre.

II *vtr* **to ~ sb sth, to ~ sth to sb** donner qch à qn.

III in hand *phr* [*job*] en cours; **the preparations are well in ~** les préparatifs sont bien avancés.

IV out of hand *phr* [*reject*] d'emblée.

IDIOMS to have a ~ in sth prendre part à qch; **to know sth like the back of one's ~** connaître qch comme sa poche; **you've got to ~ it to her/them...** il faut lui/leur faire cette justice...

■ **hand down**: **~ [sth] down, ~ down [sth]** passer [*object, clothes*] (**to sb** à qn); transmettre [*property, skill*].

■ **hand in**: **~ [sth] in, ~ in [sth]** remettre [*form, petition*] (**to** à); rendre [*homework, keys*].

■ **hand out**: **~ [sth] out, ~ out [sth]** distribuer.

■ **hand over**: ¶ **~ over to [sb]** passer l'antenne à [*reporter*]; passer la main à [*deputy, successor*]; ¶ **~ over [sth], ~ [sth] over** rendre [*weapon*]; céder [*territory, business*]; remettre [*keys, money*]; ¶ **~ [sb] over, ~ over [sb] 1** (transfer) livrer [*prisoner*]; confier [*child, patient*]; **2** (on phone) **I'll just ~ you over to Martine** je te passe Martine.

■ **hand round**: **~ [sth] round, ~ round [sth]** faire circuler [*leaflets, drinks, sandwiches*].

hand: **~bag** *n* sac *m* à main; **~ baggage** *n* bagages *mpl* à main; **~ball** ▶649 *n* (Sport) handball *m*; **~book** *n* manuel *m*; (technical) livret *m* technique; **~brake** *n* frein *m* à main.

handcuff *vtr* passer les menottes à [*person*].

handcuffs *n pl* menottes *fpl*.

handful *n* **1** (fistful) poignée *f*; **2** (of people) poignée *f*; (of buildings, objects) petit nombre *m*; **3**○ **to be a ~** être épuisant.

handicap I *n* handicap *m*.

II *vtr* handicaper.

handicapped *adj* [*person*] handicapé; **mentally/physically ~ children** des enfants handicapés mentaux/physiques.

handicraft *n* **'~s'** (on sign) 'artisanat' *m*.

hand in hand *adv* [*run, walk*] la main dans la main; **to go ~** aller de pair (**with** avec).

handiwork *n* ouvrage *m*; (when viewed negatively) œuvre *f*.

handkerchief *n* mouchoir *m*.

handle I *n* (on door, drawer, bag) poignée *f*; (on

bucket, cup, basket) anse *f*; (on frying pan) queue *f*; (on saucepan, cutlery, hammer, spade) manche *m*; (on wheelbarrow, pump) bras *m*.

II *vtr* **1** manipuler [*explosives, samples, food*]; manier [*gun, tool*]; **to ~ sb gently** traiter qn gentiment; **'~ with care'** 'fragile'; **2** (manage) manier [*horse*]; manœuvrer [*car*]; **to know how to ~ children** savoir s'y prendre avec les enfants; **3** (deal with) faire face à [*crisis*]; supporter [*stress*]; [*person*] manier [*information*]; [*department, official, lawyer*] s'occuper de [*enquiries, case*].

handlebars *n pl* guidon *m*.

handling *n* (of food, waste) manipulation *f*; (of tool, weapon) maniement *m*; **her ~ of the theme** sa façon de traiter le thème.

handling charge *n* **1** (commercial) frais *mpl* de manutention; **2** (administrative) frais *mpl* administratifs.

hand: **~ lotion** *n* lotion *f* pour les mains; **~ luggage** *n* bagages *mpl* à main; **~made** *adj* fait à la main.

handout *n* **1** (payment) (welfare) allocation *f*; (subsidy) subvention *f*; (charitable) don *m*; **2** (document) document *m*; (leaflet) prospectus *m*.

hand: **~over** *n* (of property, power) transfert *m*; (of prisoner, ransom) remise *f*; **~pick** *vtr* cueillir [qch] à la main [*grapes*]; trier [qn] sur le volet [*staff*]; **~shake** *n* poignée *f* de main; **~ signal** *n* (gen, Aut) signal *m* de la main.

handsome *adj* [*person, building, sum*] beau/belle (*before n*).

hand: **~stand** *n* (Sport) équilibre *m*; **~writing** *n* écriture *f*; **~written** *adj* manuscrit.

handy *adj* [*book, skill*] utile; [*tool, pocket, format, size*] pratique; **to keep/have [sth] ~** garder/avoir [qch] sous la main [*keys, passport*].

handyman *n* bricoleur *m*.

hang I *n* **to get the ~ of sth**○ piger○ qch.

II *vtr* **1** (suspend) (from hook, coat-hanger) accrocher (**from** à; **by** par; **on** à); (from string, rope) suspendre (**from** à); (drape over) étendre (**over** sur); (peg up) étendre [*washing*] (**on** sur); **2** (also **~ down**) (let dangle) suspendre [*rope, line*] (**out of** par); laisser pendre [*arm, leg*]; **3** poser [*wallpaper*]; **to be hung with** être orné de [*flags, tapestries*]; **4** pendre [*criminal, victim*].

III *vi* **1** (on hook) être accroché; (from height) être suspendu; (on washing line) être étendu; [*arm, leg*] pendre; **2** (drape) [*curtain, garment*] tomber; **3** (float) [*fog, cloud, smoke*] flotter; **4** (die) être pendu (**for** pour).

IV *v refl* **to ~ oneself** se pendre (**from** à).

■ **hang around**○ **1** (also **~ about**) (wait) attendre; (aimlessly) traîner; **2 to ~ around with sb** passer son temps avec qn.

■ **hang back** (in fear) rester derrière; (figurative) être réticent.

■ **hang down** (gen) pendre; [*hem*] être défait.

■ **hang on**: ¶ **~ on 1**○ (wait) attendre; **2**○ (survive) tenir○; **~ on in there**○! tiens bon!; ¶ **~ on [sth]** (depend on) dépendre de.

■ **hang on to**: **~ on to [sth/sb]** s'agripper à [*object, person*]; s'accrocher à○ [*possession, power*].

■ **hang out**: ¶ **~ out** [*handkerchief, shirt*] pendre; ¶ **~ out [sth]**, **~ [sth] out** étendre [*washing*]; sortir [*flag*].

■ **hang over**: **~ over [sb/sth]** [*threat, suspicion*] planer sur [*person, project*].

■ **hang up**: ¶ **~ up** (on phone) raccrocher; **to ~ up on sb** raccrocher au nez de qn; ¶ **~ up [sth]**, **~ [sth] up** (on hook) accrocher; (on hanger) suspendre; (on line) étendre.

hangar *n* hangar *m*.

hang: **~-glider** *n* (craft) deltaplane *m*; (pilot) deltaplaniste *mf*; **~-gliding** **▶649** *n* deltaplane *m*.

hanging *n* **1** (of person) pendaison *f*; **2** (curtain) rideau *m*; (on wall) tenture *f*.

hangman *n* **1** (at gallows) bourreau *m*; **2** **▶649** (game) potence *f*.

hangover *n* **1** (from drink) gueule *f* de bois○; **2** (legacy) héritage *m* (**from** de).

hang-up○ *n* complexe *m*, problème *m*.

hankering *n* grande envie *f* (**for**).

haphazard *adj* peu méthodique.

happen *vi* **1** (occur) arriver, se passer, se produire; **what's ~ing?** qu'est-ce qui se passe?; **the accident ~ed yesterday** l'accident est arrivé or s'est produit hier; **to ~ again** se reproduire; **whatever ~s** quoi qu'il arrive; **it was bound to ~** (GB) ça devait arriver; **what will ~ to the children?** que deviendront les enfants?; **2** (befall) **to ~ to sb** arriver à qn; **if anything ~s to her**... s'il lui arrive quoi que ce soit...; **3** (occur by chance) **there ~s to be a free parking space** il se trouve qu'il y a une place libre; **as it ~ed, the weather that day was bad** il s'est trouvé qu'il faisait mauvais ce jour-là; **I ~ to think that**... je pense que...

happily *adv* **1** [*laugh, chat, play, say*] joyeusement; **a ~ married man** un mari heureux; **they all lived ~ ever after** ils vécurent heureux jusqu'à la fin de leurs jours; **2** (willingly) [*admit, agree, leave*] volontiers.

happiness *n* bonheur *m*.

happy *adj* **1** (content) heureux/-euse (**about** de; **that** que + *subj*); **to be ~ doing** bien aimer faire; **to be ~ with sth** être satisfait de qch; **to keep a child ~** amuser un enfant; **2** (willing) **to be ~ to do** être heureux/-euse de faire; **3** (in greetings) **Happy Birthday!** Bon anniversaire!; **Happy Christmas!** Joyeux Noël!; **Happy New Year!** Bonne année!

happy: **~ ending** *n* heureux dénouement *m*; **~ medium** *n* juste milieu *m*.

harangue I *n* (political) harangue *f*; (moral) sermon *m*.

II *vtr* (about politics) haranguer; (moralize) sermonner.

harass *vtr* harceler.

harassed *adj* excédé.

harassment *n* harcèlement *m*; **racial ~** persécution *f* raciste.

harbour (GB), **harbor** (US) **I** *n* port *m*.

II *vtr* nourrir [*suspicion, illusion*]; receler [*criminal*].

hard I *adj* **1** (firm) dur; **to go ~** durcir; **2** (difficult) [*problem, question, task*] dur, difficile; [*choice, decision*] difficile; [*negotiations, fight*] dur, serré; **I've had a ~ day** j'ai eu une dure journée; **it's ~ to do/to understand** c'est dur or difficile à faire/à comprendre; **to find it ~ to do sth** avoir du mal à faire qch; **it's ~ to believe that...** on a du mal à croire que...; **it was ~ work** ça a été dur or difficile; **to be a ~ worker** être travailleur/-euse; **to learn sth the ~ way** apprendre qch à ses dépens; **3** (harsh) [*life, year*] difficile; [*blow*] dur, terrible; [*winter*] rude; **to be ~ on sb** [*person*] être dur envers qn; **this tax is very ~ on the unemployed** cet impôt frappe durement les chômeurs ; **~ luck!** pas de chance!; **to take a ~ line** adopter une attitude ferme (**on sth** à propos de qch; **with sb** envers qn); **no ~ feelings!** sans rancune!; **to fall on ~ times** connaitre des temps difficiles; **he's having a ~ time (of it)** il traverse une période difficile; **4** [*person, look, words*] dur, sévère; **5** [*evidence, fact*] solide; **6** (strong) [*liquor*] fort; [*drug*] dur; **7** [*water*] dur, calcaire; **8** [*consonant*] dur; **9** [*currency*] fort.

II *adv* [*push, hit, cry*] fort; [*work*] dur; [*study, think*] sérieusement; [*look, listen*] attentivement; **to be ~ hit** être durement frappé (**by** par); **to try ~** (intellectually) faire beaucoup d'efforts; (physically) essayer de toutes ses forces; **no matter how ~ I try, I...** j'ai beau essayer, je...; **to be ~ at work** être en plein travail.

hardback *n* livre *m* relié; **in ~** en édition reliée.

hard: **~board** *n* aggloméré *m*; **~-boiled** *adj* [*egg*] dur; [*person*] endurci; **~-core** *adj* [*opponent*] irréductible; [*pornography*] hard○ *inv*; **~ court** *n* court *m* en dur; **~-earned** *adj* [*cash*] durement gagné.

harden I *vtr* **1** (faire) durcir [*glue, wax*]; **2** endurcir [*person*] (**to** à); durcir [*attitude*]; **to ~ one's heart** s'endurcir (**to** à).

II *vi* **1** [*glue, wax, skin*] durcir; **2** [*voice, stance*] se durcir.

hardened *adj* [*criminal*] endurci; [*drinker*] invétéré.

hard: **~ hat** *n* (helmet) casque *m*; (for riding) bombe *f*; **~-hearted** *adj* insensible; **~-hitting** *adj* [*speech, criticism*] musclé; [*report*] très critique; **~ labour** (GB), **~ labor** *n* (US) travaux *mpl* forcés; **~line** *adj* [*communist, conservative*] intransigeant; **~liner** *n* jusqu'au-boutiste *mf*; (political) partisan/-e *m/f* de la ligne dure.

hardly *adv* **1** (barely) [*begin, know, see*] à peine; **~ had they set off when** à peine étaient-ils partis que; **2** (not really) **one can ~ expect/hope that** on ne peut guère s'attendre à ce que/espérer que; **it's ~ likely** c'est peu probable; **it's ~ surprising** ce n'est guère étonnant; **I can ~ believe it!** j'ai peine à le croire!; **3 ~ any/ever/anybody** presque pas/jamais/personne.

hardness *n* dureté *f*.

hardship *n* **1** (difficulty) détresse *f*; (poverty) privations *fpl*; **2** (ordeal) épreuve *f*.

hard: **~ up**○ *adj* fauché○; **~ware** *n* (gen) articles *mpl* de quincaillerie; (Comput) matériel *m* (informatique); (Mil) équipement *m*; **~ware shop**, **~ware store** ▶ **805** *n* quincaillerie *f*; **~-working** *adj* travailleur/-euse.

hardy *adj* [*person*] robuste; [*plant*] résistant.

hare *n* lièvre *m*.

haricot *n* (GB) (also **~ bean**) (dried) haricot *m* blanc; (fresh) haricot *m* vert.

harm I *n* mal *m*; **I meant no ~ (by it)** je n'ai pas dit ça méchamment; **it would do no ~ to do** tu ferais or on ferait mieux de faire; **out of ~'s way** en sûreté.

II *vtr* faire du mal à [*person*]; endommager [*crops, lungs*]; nuire à [*population*].

harmful *adj* [*chemical, ray*] nocif/-ive; [*behaviour, gossip*] nuisible (**to** pour).

harmless *adj* **1** [*chemical, virus*] inoffensif/-ive (**to** pour); [*growth, cyst*] bénin/bénigne; [*rash, bite*] sans danger; **2** [*person*] inoffensif/-ive; [*fun, joke*] innocent

harmonica ▶ **753** *n* harmonica *m*.

harmonious *adj* harmonieux/-ieuse.

harmonize I *vtr* harmoniser.

II *vi* [*musician, instrument*] jouer en harmonie (**with** avec).

harmony *n* harmonie *f*.

harness I *n* harnais *m*.

II *vtr* **1** harnacher [*horse*]; **2** (attach) atteler [*animal*] (**to** à); **3** exploiter [*power, energy*].

harp ▶ **753** *n* harpe *f*.

harpoon *n* harpon *m*.

harrowing *adj* [*experience, ordeal*] atroce; [*film, image*] déchirant.

harsh *adj* **1** [*punishment, measures*] sévère; [*tone, regime, person*] dur; [*conditions*] difficile; **2** [*light, colour*] cru; [*sound*] rude, dur à l'oreille; [*chemical*] corrosif/-ive.

harshness *n* (of punishment, measures, law, regime) sévérité *f*; (of criticism, tone) dureté *f*; (of climate) rigueur *f*; (of sound) rudesse *f*.

harvest I *n* (of wheat, fruit) récolte *f*; (of grapes) vendange *f*.

II *vtr* moissonner [*corn*]; récolter [*vegetables*]; cueillir [*fruit*].

III *vi* (of wheat, fruit) faire la récolte; (of grapes) faire la vendange.

hassle○ I *n* complications *fpl*; **to cause (sb) ~** créer des complications (à qn).

II *vtr* talonner (**about** à propos de).

hassled *adj* stressé.

haste *n* hâte *f*; **to act in ~** agir à la hâte.

hasten I *vtr* accélérer [*destruction*]; précipiter [*departure, death, decline*].

II *vi* se hâter; **to ~ to do** s'empresser de faire.

hasty *adj* [*talks, marriage, departure*] précipité; [*meal*] rapide; [*note*] écrit à la hâte; [*decision*] inconsidéré; [*conclusion*] hâtif/-ive.

hat *n* chapeau *m*.

hatch I *n* **1** (on aircraft) panneau *m* mobile; (in boat) écoutille *f*; (in car) portière *f*; **2** (also **serving ~**) passe-plats *m inv*.

II *vtr* **1** faire éclore [*eggs*]; **2** tramer [*plot, scheme*].
III *vi* [*chicks, fish eggs*] éclore.

hatchback *n* (car) voiture *f* avec hayon.

hatchet *n* hachette *f*.
IDIOMS **to bury the ~** faire la paix.

hate I *n* haine *f*.
II *vtr* **1** (dislike) détester; (violently) haïr; **to ~ sb for sth/for doing** en vouloir à qn de qch/d'avoir fait; **2** (not enjoy) avoir horreur de [*sport, food, activity*]; **3** (in apology) **to ~ to do, to ~ doing** être désolé de faire.

hatred *n* haine *f* (**of** de; **for** pour); (less violent) aversion *f* (**of** pour).

haughty *adj* [*person*] hautain; [*manner*] altier/-ière.

haul I *n* **1** (taken by criminals) butin *m*; **2** (found by police, customs) saisie *f*; **arms ~** saisie d'armes; **3** (in transportation) courrier *m*; **long/short ~** long/court courrier; **4** (of fish) pêche *f*.
II *vtr* **1** (drag) tirer; **to ~ oneself up on the roof** se hisser sur le toit; **2** (by lorry) transporter.

haulage *n* **1** (transport) transport *m* routier; **2** (cost) frais *mpl* de transport.

haunch *n* hanche *f*.

haunt I *n* lieu *m* de prédilection.
II *vtr* hanter; **he is ~ed by the fear of dying** il a la hantise de la mort.

haunted *adj* [*house*] hanté; [*face, look*] tourmenté.

haunting *adj* [*film, book, image, music, beauty, doubt*] lancinant; [*memory*] obsédant.

Havana ▶ 574 *pr n* La Havane *f*.

have ▶ 671 I *vtr* (*uses not covered in note*) **1** (possess) avoir; **she has (got) a dog** elle a un chien; **2** (consume) **to ~ a sandwich** manger un sandwich; **to ~ a whisky** boire un whisky; **to ~ a cigarette** fumer une cigarette; **to ~ breakfast** prendre le petit déjeuner; **to ~ lunch** déjeuner; **I had some more cake** j'ai repris du gâteau; **3** (want) vouloir, prendre; **what will you ~?** qu'est-ce que vous prendrez or voulez?; **she won't ~ him back** elle ne veut plus de lui; **4** (receive, get) recevoir [*letter, information*]; **I've had no news from him** je n'ai pas eu de nouvelles de lui; **I must ~ the money soon** il me faut l'argent bientôt; **to let sb ~ sth** donner qch à qn; **5** (hold) faire [*party*]; tenir [*meeting*]; organiser [*competition, exhibition*]; avoir [*conversation*]; **6** (exert, exhibit) avoir [*effect, influence*]; avoir [*courage, courtesy*] (**to do** de faire); **7** (spend) passer; **to ~ a nice day** passer une journée agréable; **to ~ a good time** bien s'amuser; **to ~ a hard time** traverser une période difficile; **to ~ a good holiday** (GB) or **vacation** (US) passer de bonnes vacances; **8** (also **~ got**) **to ~ sth to do** avoir qch à faire; **I've got letters to write** j'ai du courrier à faire; **I've got a lot of work to do** j'ai beaucoup de travail; **9** (undergo, suffer) avoir; **to ~ (the) flu/a heart attack** avoir la grippe/une crise cardiaque; **to ~ toothache** avoir mal aux dents; **he had his car stolen** il s'est fait voler sa voiture; **she has had her windows broken** on lui a cassé ses vitres; **to ~ an interview** avoir or passer un entretien; **10 to ~ sth done** faire faire qch; **to ~ the house painted** faire peindre la maison; **to ~ one's hair cut** se faire couper les cheveux; **to ~ an injection** se faire faire une piqûre ; **they would ~ us believe that...** ils voudraient nous faire croire que...; **I would ~ you know that...** je voudrais que vous sachiez que...; **11** (cause to become) **we'll soon ~ everything ready** nous aurons bientôt fini de tout préparer; **she had them completely baffled** elle les a complètement déroutés; **I had it finished by 5 o'clock** je l'avais fini avant 5 heures; **12** (allow) tolérer; **I won't ~ this kind of behaviour!** je ne tolérerai pas ce comportement!; **I won't ~ it!** ça ne va pas se passer comme ça!; **13** (physically hold) tenir; **she had the glass in her hand** elle avait le verre à la main; **she had him by the throat** elle le tenait à la gorge; **14** (give birth to) [*woman*] avoir [*child*]; [*animal*] mettre bas, avoir [*young*]; **she's having a baby (in May)** elle va avoir un enfant (en mai); **15** (as impersonal verb) **over here, we ~ a painting by Picasso** ici vous avez un tableau de Picasso.
II *modal aux* (must) (*see note*) **something has (got) to be done** il faut faire quelque chose; **you don't ~ to leave so early** tu n'as pas besoin de or tu n'es pas obligé de partir si tôt; **why did this ~ to happen?** pourquoi fallait-il que ça arrive?; **this has (got) to be the most difficult decision I've ever made** c'est sans doute la décision la plus difficile que j'aie jamais eu à prendre.
III *v aux* **1** avoir; (with movement and reflexive verbs) être; **she has lost her bag** elle a perdu son sac; **she has already left** elle est déjà partie; **he has hurt himself** il s'est blessé; **2** (in tags, short answers) **you've seen the film, haven't you?** tu as vu le film, n'est-ce pas?; **you haven't seen the film, ~ you?** tu n'as pas vu le film?; **you haven't seen my bag, ~ you?** tu n'as pas vu mon sac, par hasard?; **'you've never met him'—'yes I ~!'** 'tu ne l'as jamais rencontré'—'mais si!'
IV **having** *v aux* **1** (in time clauses) **having finished his breakfast, he went out** après avoir fini son petit déjeuner, il est sorti; **2** (because, since) **having already won twice, he...** comme il a déjà gagné deux fois, il...
IDIOMS **I've had it (up to here) with...**○ j'en ai marre de...○; **to ~ it in for sb**○ avoir qn dans le collimateur○; **she doesn't ~ it in her to do** elle est incapable de faire; **to ~ it out with sb** s'expliquer avec qn; **the ~s and the ~-nots** les riches et les pauvres.

■ **have back**: **~ [sth] back**: **you can ~ it back tomorrow** je te le rendrai demain; **when can I ~ my car back?** quand est-ce que tu me rends ma voiture?

■ **have on**: ¶ **~ [sth] on, ~ on [sth]** porter [*coat, skirt*]; **he had (got) nothing on** il n'avait rien sur lui; ¶ **~ [sth] on** (be busy) avoir [qch] de prévu; ¶ **~ [sb] on**○ faire marcher○.

■ **have over, have round**: **~** **[sb] over** inviter [*person*].

haven *n* **1** (safe place) refuge *m* (**for** pour); **2** (harbour) port *m*.

havoc *n* dévastation *f*; **to wreak ~ on** dévaster [*building, landscape*]; **to cause ~** provoquer des dégâts; (figurative) tout mettre sens dessus dessous.

Hawaii *pr n* Hawaï *m*.

hawk *n* faucon *m*.

hawthorn *n* aubépine *f*.

hay *n* foin *m*; **to make ~** faire les foins.

hay fever ▶686 *n* rhume *m* des foins.

haystack *n* meule *f* de foin.
IDIOMS **it is/was like looking for a needle in a ~** autant chercher une aiguille dans une botte de foin.

hazard I *n* **1** (risk) risque *m* (**to** pour); **the ~s of doing** les risques qu'il y a à faire; **to be a health ~** constituer un risque pour la santé; **fire ~** risque d'incendie; **2** (chance) hasard *m*.
II *vtr* hasarder [*opinion, explanation*]; **to ~ a guess** (theory) hasarder une hypothèse; (quantity, price) hasarder un chiffre.

haze *n* (mist) brume *f*; (of smoke, dust) nuage *m*.

hazel I *n* noisetier *m*.
II ▶559 *adj* [*eyes*] (couleur de) noisette *inv*.

hazelnut *n* noisette *f*.

hazy *adj* [*weather, morning*] brumeux/-euse; [*sunshine*] voilé.

he *pron* il.

■ **Note** *he* is almost always translated by *il*: *he closed the door* = il a fermé la porte. The emphatic form is *lui*.

~'s seen us il nous a vus; **here ~ is** le voici; **there ~ is** le voilà; **HE didn't take it** ce n'est pas lui qui l'a pris; **she lives in Oxford but ~ doesn't** elle habite Oxford mais lui non; **~'s a genius** c'est un génie; **~ and I** lui et moi.

head ▶523 **I** *n* **1** tête *f*; **from ~ to foot** or **toe** de la tête aux pieds; **to stand on one's ~** faire le poirier; **to hold a gun to sb's ~** (figurative) tenir le couteau sous la gorge de qn; **£10 a ~** or **per ~** 10 livres sterling par personne; **2** (mind) tête *f*; **I can't get it into her ~ that** je n'arrive pas à lui enfoncer dans la tête que; **he has got it into his ~ that** il s'est mis dans la tête que; **to be over sb's ~** (too difficult) passer par-dessus la tête de qn; **her success has turned her ~** son succès lui a tourné la tête; **to have a (good) ~ for figures** être doué pour le calcul; **to have no ~ for heights** avoir le vertige; **3** (of family, church, agency) chef *m*; (of social service, organization) responsable *mf*, directeur/-trice *m/f*; **at the ~ of** à la tête de; **~ of State** chef d'État; **4** (of nail, hammer, golf club) tête *f*; (of axe, spear, arrow) fer *m*; (of tennis racquet) tamis *m*; (of stick) pommeau *m*; (of cabbage, lettuce) pomme *f*; (of garlic) tête *f*; **5** (of tape recorder, computer, video) tête *f*; **6** (of bed) tête *f*; (of table) (haut) bout *m*; (of procession) tête *f*; (of pier, river, valley) extrémité *f*; **7** (on boil, spot) tête *f*; **to come to a ~** [*boil*] mûrir; [*crisis*] arriver au point critique.
II heads *n pl* (tossing coin) face *f*; **'~s or tails?'** 'pile ou face?'
III *noun modifier* **1** [*injury*] à la tête; **2** (chief) [*cashier, cook, gardener*] en chef.
IV *vtr* **1** être en tête de [*list, queue*]; être à la tête de [*firm, team*]; mener [*expedition, inquiry*]; **2** (entitle) intituler [*chapter*]; **~ed writing paper** papier *m* à lettres à en-tête; **3** (steer) diriger [*vehicle*] (**towards** vers); **4** (Sport) **to ~ the ball** faire une tête.
V *vi* **where was the train ~ed** or **~ing?** où allait le train?; **to ~ home** rentrer; **he's ~ing this way!** il vient par ici!
IDIOMS **to go to sb's ~** monter à la tête de qn; **to keep/lose one's ~** garder/perdre son sang-froid; **off the top of one's ~** [*say, answer*] sans réfléchir.
■ **head for**: **~ for [sth]** se diriger vers; **to ~ for home** prendre le chemin du retour.
■ **head off**: ¶ **~ off** partir (**for, towards** vers); ¶ **~ [sth] off, ~ off [sth]** éviter [*quarrel, question*].

headache ▶686 *n* mal *m* de tête; **to have a ~** avoir mal à la tête.

head: **~ cold** ▶686 *n* rhume *m* de cerveau; **~dress** *n* (of feathers) coiffure *f*; (of lace) coiffe *f*; **~first** *adv* [*fall, plunge*] la tête la première; [*rush into*] tête baissée; **~-hunt** *vtr* (chercher à) recruter.

heading *n* (of article) titre *m*; (in library catalogue) rubrique *f*; (on notepaper, letter) en-tête *m*.

headlamp, headlight *n* (of car) phare *m*; (of train) fanal *m*.

headline *n* (in press) gros titre *m*; (on radio, TV) titre *m*; **to hit the ~s** faire la une°; **the front-page ~** la manchette; **the news ~s** les grands titres (de l'actualité).

headlong I *adj* **a ~ dash** une ruée.
II *adv* [*fall*] la tête la première; [*run*] à toute vitesse.

head: **~ office** *n* siège *m* social; **~-on** *adj* [*crash, collision*] de front.

headphones *n pl* casque *m*; **a pair of ~** un casque.

head: **~quarters** *n pl* (gen) siège *m* social; (Mil) quartier *m* général; **~ rest** *n* (gen) appui-tête *m*; (Aut) repose-tête *m inv*.

head start *n* **to have a ~** avoir une longueur d'avance (**over** sur).

head: **~stone** *n* pierre *f* tombale; **~strong** *adj* [*person*] têtu; [*attitude*] obstiné; **~ teacher** ▶805 *n* directeur/-trice *m/f*.

headway *n* **to make ~** avancer, faire des progrès.

heady *adj* [*wine, mixture*] capiteux/-euse; [*perfume*] entêtant; [*experience*] grisant.

heal I *vtr* guérir [*person, injury*].
II *vi* [*wound, cut*] se cicatriser; **the fracture has ~ed** l'os s'est ressoudé.

healer *n* guérisseur/-euse *m/f*.

healing I *n* guérison *f*.
II *adj* [*power*] curatif/-ive; [*effect*] salutaire; **the ~ process** le rétablissement.

have

As a transitive verb

◆ When ***have*** or ***have got*** is used as a straightforward transitive verb meaning ***possess***, it can generally be translated by ***avoir***:

*I **have (got)** a car*	= j'**ai** une voiture
*she **has (got)** a good memory*	= elle **a** une bonne mémoire
*they **have (got)** problems*	= ils **ont** des problèmes

For examples and particular usages see the entry **have**; see also the entry **got**.

◆ ***have*** is also used with certain noun objects where the whole expression is equivalent to a verb: *to have dinner* = to dine; *to have a walk* = to walk.

In such cases, the phrase is very often translated by the equivalent verb in French (*dîner*, *se promener*). For translations, consult the appropriate noun entry (*dinner*, *walk*).

As an auxiliary verb

◆ When used as an auxiliary in present perfect, future perfect and past perfect tenses, ***have*** is normally translated by ***avoir***:

*I **have** seen*	= j'**ai** vu
*I **had** seen*	= j'**avais** vu

◆ However, some verbs in French, especially verbs of movement and change of state (*aller*, *venir*, *descendre*, *mourir*), always take ***être*** in these tenses:

*he **has** left*	= il **est** parti

In this case, remember the past participle agrees with the subject of the verb:

*she **has** gone*	= elle **est** allée
*they **had** come back*	= ils **étaient** revenus
*we **had** stayed at home*	= nous **étions** restés chez nous

If you are in doubt as to whether a verb conjugates with ***être*** or ***avoir***, consult the French entry, where verbs taking ***être*** will be indicated like this: (*+v être*).

◆ Reflexive verbs (*se lever*, *se coucher*) always conjugate with ***être***:

*she **has** fainted*	= elle s'**est** évanouie
*he **had** fallen asleep*	= il s'**était** endormi

In this case, the past participle agrees with the reflexive pronoun only when the pronoun is a direct object. Otherwise there is no agreement:

*she **has** hurt herself*	= elle s'est fait mal
***I've** washed my hair*	= je me suis lavé les cheveux

to have (got) to

◆ ***to have (got) to*** meaning *must* is translated by either ***devoir*** or the impersonal construction ***il faut que*** + *subjunctive*:

*I **have to** leave now*	= **il faut que** je parte maintenant
	= je **dois** partir maintenant

◆ In negative sentences, ***not to have to*** is usually translated by ***ne pas être obligé de***:

*you **don't have to** go*	= tu **n'es pas obligé d**'y aller

Conditional

◆ ***had*** is used in English at the beginning of a clause to replace an expression with ***if***. Such expressions are generally translated by ***si*** + *past perfect tense*:

***had I taken** the train, this would never have happened*	= **si j'avais pris** le train, cela ne serait jamais arrivé

❑ For ***have*** used with illnesses, see usage note **Illnesses, Aches, and Pains**, ▶ 686.

health *n* santé *f*; **in good/bad ~** en bonne/mauvaise santé; **here's (to your) ~!** à votre santé!

health insurance *n* assurance *f* maladie.

Health Service *n* **1** (GB) (for public) services *mpl* de santé; **2** (US Univ) infirmerie *f*.

healthy *adj* [*person, dog*] en bonne santé; [*livestock, plant, lifestyle, diet*] sain; [*air*] salutaire; [*appetite*] robuste; [*crop*] abondant; [*economy*] sain.

heap *n* tas *m*; **to lie in a ~** [*person*] être affalé; [*objects, bodies*] être entassés.

■ **heap up**: **~ [sth] up, ~ up [sth]** entasser [*leaves*]; empiler [*food*].

heaped *adj* **a ~ spoonful** une bonne cuillerée.

hear I *vtr* **1** entendre; **we haven't heard the last of it** on n'a pas fini d'en entendre parler; **to make oneself heard** se faire entendre; (figurative) faire entendre sa voix; **2** (learn) apprendre [*news, rumour*]; **to ~ (tell) of sth** entendre parler de qch; **I've heard so much about you** on m'a tant parlé de vous; **so I ~, so I've heard** c'est ce que j'ai entendu dire; **did you ~ whether/why/how?** sais-tu si/pourquoi/comment?; **3** (listen to) écouter [*lecture, broadcast*]; [*judge*] entendre [*case, evidence*].

II *vi* entendre; **to ~ about** entendre parler de.

IDIOMS **~! ~!** bravo!

■ **hear from**: **~ from [sb] 1** (get news) avoir des nouvelles de; **2** (on TV, radio) entendre le point de vue de [*expert*]; écouter le récit de [*witness*].

■ **hear of**: **~ of [sb/sth]** entendre parler de; **I won't ~ of it!** il n'en est pas question!

■ **hear out**: **~ [sb] out, ~ out [sb]** écouter [qn] jusqu'au bout.

hearing I *n* **1** (sense) ouïe *f*, audition *f*; **his ~ is not very good** il n'a pas l'oreille très fine; **2** (before court) audience *f*; **3 to get a ~** se faire entendre.

II *noun modifier* [*test*] d'audition.

hearing: **~ aid** *n* prothèse *f* auditive; **~-impaired** *adj* malentendant.

hearsay *n* ouï-dire *m inv*, on-dit *m inv*; **based on ~** fondé sur des ouï-dire or on-dit.

hearse *n* corbillard *m*.

heart ▶ 649 | **I** *n* **1** cœur *m*; **to break sb's ~** briser le cœur de qn; **by ~** [*learn, know*] par cœur; **my ~ goes out to you/them** je te/les plains de tout mon cœur; **from the bottom of one's ~, from the ~** du fond du cœur; **to take sth to ~** prendre qch à cœur; **I wish with all my ~ that** je souhaite de tout cœur que (+ *subj*); **in my ~ (of ~s)** au fond de moi-même; **I have your interests at ~** je ne pense qu'à ton bien; **he's a child at ~** au fond, c'est toujours un enfant; **I didn't have the ~ to refuse** je n'ai pas eu le cœur de refuser; **2** (courage) courage *m*; **to take/lose ~** prendre/perdre courage; **3** (centre) (of district) cœur *m*; **right in the ~ of London** en plein cœur de Londres; **the ~ of the matter** le fond du problème; **4** (in cards) cœur *m*; **5** (of vegetable) cœur *m*.

II *noun modifier* [*patient, specialist*] du cœur; [*muscle, valve*] cardiaque; **to have a ~ condition** être cardiaque.

IDIOMS **to have one's ~ set on sth** vouloir qch à tout prix.

heart: **~ache** *n* chagrin *m*; **~ attack** *n* crise *f* cardiaque, infarctus *m*; **~beat** *n* battement *m* de cœur; **~breaking** *adj* [*sight, story*] navrant; [*cry, appeal*] déchirant.

heartbroken *adj* **to be ~** avoir le cœur brisé.

heart: **~burn** *n* brûlures *fpl* d'estomac; **~ disease** *n* maladies *fpl* cardiaques.

heartening *adj* encourageant.

heart: **~ failure** *n* arrêt *m* du cœur; **~felt** *adj* sincère.

hearth *n* foyer *m*; **~ rug** petit tapis *m*.

heartily *adv* [*greet*] chaleureusement; [*agree*] tout à fait; [*laugh, eat*] de bon cœur; [*glad*] vraiment.

heartless *adj* [*person*] sans cœur; [*attitude, treatment*] cruel.

heart-to-heart *adj, adv* à cœur ouvert.

heart: **~ transplant** *n* greffe *f* du cœur; (more technically) transplantation *f* cardiaque; **~ trouble** *n* problèmes *mpl* cardiaques.

hearty *adj* [*welcome*] cordial; [*person*] jovial; [*laugh*] franc/franche; [*appetite*] solide; [*approval*] chaleureux/-euse.

heat I *n* **1** chaleur *f*; **in this ~** par cette chaleur; **in the ~ of the moment** dans le feu de l'action; **2** (of hotplate, gas ring) feu *m*; (of oven) température *f*; **cook at a low ~** (on ring) faire cuire à feu doux; (in oven) faire cuire à basse température; **3** (Sport) (round) épreuve *f* éliminatoire; (in athletics) série *f*; **4** (Zool) **to be on** or **in ~** être en chaleur.

II *vtr* chauffer [*house, pool*]; faire chauffer [*food, oven*].

III *vi* [*oven, food, water*] chauffer.

■ **heat up**: ¶ **~ up** [*food, drink*] chauffer; ¶ **~ [sth] up** faire chauffer [*food*]; (reheat) faire réchauffer.

heated *adj* **1** [*water, pool*] chauffé; **2** [*debate, argument*] animé.

heater *n* appareil *m* de chauffage.

heathen *n, adj* (irreligious) païen/-ïenne (*m/f*); (uncivilized) barbare (*mf*).

heather *n* bruyère *f*.

heating *n* chauffage *m*.

heatwave *n* vague *f* de chaleur.

heave I *vtr* (lift) hisser; (pull) traîner péniblement; (throw) lancer (**at** sur); **to ~ a sigh** pousser un soupir.

II *vi* **1** [*sea, ground*] se soulever et s'abaisser; **2** (pull) tirer de toutes ses forces; **3** (retch) avoir un haut-le-cœur; (vomit) vomir.

heaven *n* ciel *m*, paradis *m*; **~ and earth** ciel et terre; **~ and hell** l'enfer et le paradis; **thank ~(s)!** Dieu soit loué!

heavenly *adj* **1** [*choir, body*] céleste; [*peace*] divin; **2**° (wonderful) divin.

heavily *adv* **1** [*lean, fall, weigh*] lourdement; [*sleep, sigh*] profondément; [*breathe*] (noisily) bruyamment; (with difficulty) péniblement; **~ built** solidement bâti; **~ underlined** souligné d'un gros trait; **2** (abundantly) [*rain*] très fort; [*snow, invest, smoke, drink, rely*] beaucoup; [*bleed*] abondamment; [*taxed, armed*] fortement; **~ made-up** très maquillé.

heavy ▶**738** *adj* [*person, load, fabric, food, defeat, debt, humour, responsibility*] lourd; [*shoes, frame*] gros/grosse (*before n*); [*line, features*] épais/épaisse; [*blow*] violent; [*rain, frost, perfume, accent*] fort; [*snow*] abondant; [*traffic*] dense; [*gunfire*] nourri; [*bleeding*] abondant; [*sentence, fine*] sévère; [*criticism*] fort (*before n*); [*cold*] gros/grosse (*before n*); **with a ~ heart** le cœur gros; **to be a ~ sleeper** avoir le sommeil lourd; **to be a ~ drinker** boire beaucoup; **~ fighting** de violents combats; **in ~ seas** par grosse mer.

heavy: **~-handed** *adj* maladroit; **~ industry** *n* industrie *f* lourde; **~ metal** *n* hard rock *m*; **~weight** *n* (boxer) poids *m* lourd; (intellectual)○ grosse tête○ *f*.

Hebrew ▶**712** I *n* (language) hébreu *m*.
II *adj* [*calendar, alphabet*] hébraïque; [*lesson*] d'hébreu.

heckle I *vtr* (barrack) interpeller; (interrupt) interrompre grossièrement.
II *vi* chahuter.

heckler *n* chahuteur/-euse *m/f*.

hectare *n* hectare *m*.

hectic *adj* [*period*] mouvementé, agité; [*day, life, schedule*] mouvementé.

hedge I *n* haie *f*.
II *vi* se dérober.
IDIOMS **to ~ one's bets** se couvrir.

hedge: **~hog** *n* hérisson *m*; **~row** *n* haie *f*.

hedonism *n* hédonisme *m*.

heed I *n* **to pay ~ to** or **take ~ of sb** tenir compte de ce que dit qn; **to pay ~ to** or **take ~ of sth** tenir compte de qch.
II *vtr* tenir compte de [*warning, advice*].

heedless *adj* irréfléchi.

heel *n* (of foot, shoe, sock) talon *m*; **to turn on one's ~** tourner les talons; **to bring a dog to ~** rappeler un chien.
IDIOMS **to fall head over ~s in love with sb** tomber éperdument amoureux de qn; **to be hot on sb's ~s** talonner qn.

hefty *adj* [*person*] costaud○; [*portion*] imposant; [*sum*] considérable.

heifer *n* génisse *f*.

height ▶**738** *n* **1** (of person) taille *f*; (of table, tower, tree) hauteur *f*; **2** (of mountain, plane) altitude *f*; **at a ~ of 200 metres** à 200 mètres d'altitude; **from a great ~** de très haut; **to be scared of ~s** avoir le vertige; **3** (peak) **at the ~ of the season** en pleine saison; **at the ~ of** au plus fort de [*storm, crisis*]; **to be at the ~ of one's powers** être au sommet de son talent; **the ~ of** le comble de [*luxury, stupidity, cheek*]; **to be the ~ of fashion** être le dernier cri.

heighten I *vtr* intensifier [*emotion*]; augmenter [*tension, suspense*]; accentuer [*effect*].
II *vi* [*tension*] monter.

heir *n* héritier/-ière *m/f* (**to** de).

heiress *n* héritière *f*.

heirloom *n* héritage *m*; **a family ~** un objet de famille.

helicopter *n* hélicoptère *m*.

heliport *n* héliport *m*.

helium *n* hélium *m*.

hell *n* **1** enfer *m*; **in ~** en enfer; **to make sb's life ~** rendre la vie infernale à qn; **2**○ (as intensifier) **a ~ of a shock** un choc terrible; **a ~ of a lot worse** nettement pire; **oh, what the ~!** (too bad) tant pis!; **to ~ with it!** je laisse tomber○!
IDIOMS **all ~**○ **broke loose** le raffut a éclaté; **to do sth for the ~ of it**○ faire qch pour le plaisir; **to raise ~**○ faire une scène (**with sb** à qn).

hello *excl* **1** (greeting) bonjour!; (receiving a phone call) allô!; **2** (in surprise) tiens!

helm *n* barre *f*; **at the ~** à la barre.

helmet *n* casque *m*.

help I *n* **1** aide *f*; (in emergency) secours *m*; **with the ~ of** à l'aide de [*stick, knife*]; avec l'aide de [*person*]; **to cry for ~** appeler au secours; **2** (also **daily ~**) femme *f* de ménage.
II *excl* au secours!
III *vtr* **1** aider (**to do** à faire); (more urgently) secourir; **to ~ each other** s'entraider; **can I ~ you?** je peux vous aider?; (in shop) vous désirez?; **to ~ sb across/down** aider qn à traverser/descendre; **I ~ed him to his feet** je l'ai aidé à se lever; **2** (serve) **to ~ sb to** servir [qch] à qn [*food, wine*]; **to ~ oneself** se servir; **~ yourselves to coffee** prenez du café; **3** (prevent) **it can't be ~ed!** on n'y peut rien!; **he can't ~ being stupid!** ce n'est pas de sa faute s'il est stupide!; **you can't ~ but pity him** on ne peut pas s'empêcher d'avoir pitié de lui.
IV *vi* aider; **he never ~s with the housework** il n'aide jamais à faire le ménage; **this map doesn't ~ much** cette carte n'est pas d'un grand secours.
■ **help out**: ¶ **~ out** aider, donner un coup de main○; ¶ **~ [sb] out** aider, donner un coup de main○ à; (financially) dépanner○.

helper *n* aide *mf*, assistant/-e *m/f*; (for handicapped person) aide *f* sociale.

helpful *adj* [*tool, machine*] utile; [*person*] serviable; [*advice, suggestion*] utile.

helping *n* portion *f*.

helping hand *n* **to give** or **lend sb a ~** donner un coup de main à qn.

helpless *adj* **1** (powerless) [*person*] impuissant; (because of infirmity, disability) impotent; **2** (defenceless) [*person*] sans défense; [*victim*] malheureux/-euse (*before n*).

helplessly *adv* [*watch*] sans pouvoir rien faire.

helplessness *n* impuissance *f*; (due to disability) impotence *f*; (of baby) vulnérabilité *f*.

helter-skelter *adv* **to run ~** courir comme un dératé○ (or des dératés○).

hem *n* ourlet *m*.

■ **hem in**: **~** [sb/sth] **in**, **~ in** [sb/sth] cerner.

hemisphere *n* hémisphère *m*.

hemp *n* chanvre *m*.

hen *n* poule *f*; (female bird) femelle *f*.

hence *adv* (*before n*) d'où; (*before adj*) donc; **there's a strike, ~ the delay** il y a une grève, d'où le retard; **she was more active and ~ slimmer** elle était plus active et donc plus mince.

henchman *n* acolyte *m*.

hen-pecked *adj* **~ husband** mari *m* mené par le bout du nez.

hepatitis ▶686 *n* hépatite *f*.

her ▶675 I *pron* (direct object) la, l'; (indirect object) lui; **I saw ~** je l'ai vue; **he gave ~ the book** il lui a donné le livre.
II *det* son/sa/ses.

herald I *n* héraut *m*.
II *vtr* (also **~ in**) annoncer.

heraldry *n* héraldique *f*.

herb *n* herbe *f*; **mixed ~s** ≈ herbes de Provence.

herbal *adj* [*remedy*] à base de plantes.

herbal tea *n* tisane *f*, infusion *f*.

herd I *n* (of sheep, cattle, goats) troupeau *m*; (of reindeer) harde *f*; (of people) troupeau *m*.
II *vtr* rassembler; **to ~ people into a room** conduire des gens dans une pièce.
IDIOMS **to follow the ~** être un mouton de Panurge.
■ **herd together** se rassembler; (closely) se masser.

here *adv*

■ **Note** When *here* is used to indicate the location of an object, a point etc close to the speaker, it is generally translated by *ici*: *come and sit here* = viens t'asseoir ici.
– When the location is not so clearly defined, *là* is the usual translation: *he's not here at the moment* = il n'est pas là pour l'instant.
– *voici* is used to translate *here is* and *here are* when the speaker is drawing attention to an object, a place, a person etc physically close to him or her.
– For examples and particular usages, see the entry below.

1 ici; **near ~** près d'ici; **two kilometres from ~** à deux kilomètres d'ici; **come over ~** venez par ici; **up to ~, down to ~** jusqu'ici; **I'm up ~** je suis là-haut; **~ and there** par endroits; **~ they are/she comes!** les/la voici!; **~ is my key/are my keys** voici ma clé/mes clés; **~ comes the bus** voilà le bus; **~ you are** tiens, tenez; **~'s what you do** voilà ce qu'il faut faire; **2** (indicating presence, arrival) **she's not ~ right now** elle n'est pas là pour le moment; **~ we are at last** nous voilà enfin; **we get off ~** c'est là qu'on descend; **now that summer's ~** maintenant que c'est l'été; **~'s our chance** voilà notre chance.
IDIOMS **~'s to our success!** à notre succès!; **~'s to you!** à la tienne!; **it's neither ~ nor there** c'est sans importance.

hereabout (US), **hereabouts** (GB) *adv* par ici.

hereafter I *n* **the ~** l'au-delà *m*.
II *adv* (Law) ci-après.

here and now I *n* **the ~** (present) le présent.
II *adv* immédiatement.

hereby *adv* **I ~ declare that** (in document) je déclare par la présente que.

hereditary *adj* héréditaire.

heredity *n* hérédité *f*.

heresy *n* hérésie *f*.

heretic *n* hérétique *mf*.

heritage *n* patrimoine *m*.

hermit *n* ermite *m*.

hernia *n* hernie *f*.

hero *n* héros *m*.

heroic *adj* héroïque.

heroin *n* héroïne *f*.

heroin addict *n* héroïnomane *mf*.

heroine *n* héroïne *f*.

heroism *n* héroïsme *m*.

heron *n* héron *m*.

hero-worship I *n* culte *m* du héros, adulation *f*.
II *vtr* aduler.

herpes ▶686 *n* herpès *m*.

herring *n* hareng *m*.

hers *pron*

■ **Note** In French, possessive pronouns reflect the gender and number of the noun they are standing for; *hers* is translated by *le sien*, *la sienne*, *les siens*, *les siennes*, according to what is being referred to.

my car is red but ~ is blue ma voiture est rouge mais la sienne est bleue; **the green pen is ~** le stylo vert est à elle; **which house is ~?** sa maison c'est laquelle?; **I'm a friend of ~** c'est une amie à moi; **it's not ~** ce n'est pas à elle; **the money wasn't ~ to give away** elle n'avait pas à donner cet argent.

herself *pron*

■ **Note** When used as a reflexive pronoun, direct and indirect, *herself* is translated by *se* (*s'* before a vowel or mute 'h'): *she's enjoying herself* = elle s'amuse bien; *she's cut herself* = elle s'est coupée.
– When used for emphasis, the translation is *elle-même*: *she herself didn't know* = elle ne le savait pas elle-même.
– After a preposition, the translation is *elle* or *elle-même*: *she can be proud of herself* = elle peut être fière d'elle *or* d'elle-même.

1 (reflexive) se, s'; **she's hurt ~** elle s'est blessée; **2** (after preposition) elle, elle-même; **for ~** pour elle, pour elle-même; **(all) by ~** toute seule; **she's not ~ today** elle n'est pas dans son assiette aujourd'hui.

hesitant *adj* hésitant; **to be ~ about doing** hésiter à faire.

hesitate *vi* hésiter (**over** sur; **to do** à faire).

hesitation *n* hésitation *f*; **to have no ~ in doing** n'avoir aucune hésitation à faire.

her

As a pronoun

◆ When used as a direct object pronoun, ***her*** is translated by ***la*** (***l'*** before a vowel or mute 'h'). Note that the object pronoun normally comes before the verb in French and that, in compound tenses like the perfect and past perfect, the past participle agrees with the pronoun:

*I know **her*** = je **la** connais
*I've already seen **her*** = je l'ai déjà vue
*I'll try to contact **her*** = je vais essayer de **la** contacter

In imperatives, the direct object pronoun is translated by ***la*** and comes after the verb:

*catch **her**!* = attrape-**la**!*

In negative commands, however, ***la*** comes before the verb:

*don't hit **her**!* = ne **la** frappe pas!

◆ When used as an indirect object pronoun, ***her*** is translated by ***lui***:

*I've given **her** the book* = je **lui** ai donné le livre
*I've given it to **her*** = je le **lui** ai donné
*I'm going to write to **her*** = je vais **lui** écrire

In imperatives, the indirect object pronoun is translated by ***lui*** and comes after the verb:

*phone **her*** = téléphone-**lui***
*give them to **her*** = donne-les-**lui***

In negative commands, however, ***lui*** comes before the verb:

*don't tell **her** the truth* = ne **lui** dis pas la vérité

After prepositions and after the verb ***to be***, the translation is ***elle***:

*he did it for **her*** = il l'a fait pour **elle**
*it's **her*** = c'est **elle**

* Note the hyphen(s).

As a determiner

◆ When translating ***her*** as a determiner (***her house*** etc), remember that in French determiners agree in gender and number with the noun that follows; ***her*** is translated by ***son*** + *masculine singular noun*:

***her** dog* = **son** chien

sa + *feminine singular noun* beginning with a consonant:

***her** house* = **sa** maison

son + *feminine singular noun* beginning with a vowel or mute 'h':

***her** plate* = **son** assiette

ses + *plural noun*:

***her** children* = **ses** enfants

When ***her*** is stressed, ***à elle*** is added after the noun:

__her__ house = **sa maison à elle**
__her__ books = **ses livres à elle**

❑ For ***her*** used with parts of the body, see the usage note **The Human Body** ▶ 523.

heterosexual *n, adj* hétérosexuel/-elle (*m/f*).
hexagon *n* hexagone *m*.
hey○ *excl* (call for attention) hé!, eh!; (in protest) dis donc!
heyday *n* (of movement) âge *m* d'or; (of person) beaux jours *mpl*; **in her ~** quand elle était au sommet de sa gloire.
HGV *n* (GB) (*abbr* = **heavy goods vehicle**) PL *m*, poids *m* lourd.
hi○ *excl* salut○!
hibernate *vi* hiberner.
hiccup, **hiccough** *n* **1** (physical) hoquet *m*; **to have (the) ~s** avoir le hoquet; **2** (setback) anicroche *f*.
hidden *adj* caché; **~ from view** caché, invisible.
hide I *n* (skin) peau *f*; (leather) cuir *m*.
II *vtr* cacher [*object, person*] (**from** à); dissimuler [*feeling*] (**from** à); **to ~ oneself** se cacher.
III *vi* se cacher.
hide: **~ and seek** (GB), **~-and-go-seek** (US) ▶649 *n* cache-cache *m inv*; **~away** *n* retraite *f*.
hideous *adj* [*person, monster, object*] hideux/-euse; [*noise*] affreux/-euse.
hiding *n* **1 to go into ~** se cacher; **to come out of ~** sortir de sa cachette; **2** (beating) correction *f*.
hiding place *n* cachette *f*.
hierarchy *n* hiérarchie *f*.
hieroglyph, **hieroglyphic** *n* hiéroglyphe *m*.
hi-fi *n* **1** (set of equipment) chaîne *f* hi-fi *inv*; **2** (*abbr* = **high fidelity**) hi-fi *f inv*.
high ▶738 I *n* **1 to reach a new ~** atteindre son niveau le plus élevé; **2**○ **to be on a ~** être en pleine euphorie.
II *adj* **1** [*building, table, forehead, collar*] haut; **~ cheekbones** pommettes *fpl* saillantes; **how ~ is the cliff?** quelle est la hauteur de la falaise?; **it is 50 m ~** ça fait 50 m de haut; **how ~ (up) are we?** (on top of building) on est à combien de mètres au-dessus du sol?; (on mountain) à quelle altitude sommes-nous?; **2** [*number, ratio, price, frequency, volume*] élevé; [*wind*] violent; [*hope, expectation*] grand (*before n*); **at ~ speed** à grande vitesse; **to have a ~ temperature** avoir de la fièvre; **~ in** riche en [*fat, iron*]; **on a ~ heat** à feu vif; **to have a ~ colour** avoir le teint rougeaud; **3** (important) [*quality, standard, rank*] supérieur; **friends in ~ places** des amis haut placés; **4** [*ideal, principle*] noble; **5** (acute) [*pitch, sound, voice*] aigu/-uë; [*note*] haut; **6**○ (on drug) défoncé○; (happy) ivre de joie.
III *adv* **1** haut; **~er up** plus haut; **don't go any ~er than £5,000** ne dépasse pas 5000 livres sterling; **2** (at a high level, pitch) [*set, turn on*] fort; [*sing, play*] haut.
high: **~ beam** *n* (US) pleins phares *mpl*; **~brow** *n, adj* intellectuel/-elle (*m/f*); **~ chair** *n* chaise *f* de bébé; **~-class** *adj* [*hotel, shop, car*] de luxe; [*goods*] de première qualité; [*area*] de grand standing; **~ commissioner** ▶805 *n* haut-commissaire *m*; **~ court** *n* cour *f* suprême; **~-definition** *adj* (à) haute définition *inv*; **~er education** *n* enseignement *m* supérieur; **~-fibre** (GB), **~-fiber** (US) *adj* riche en fibres; **~ finance** *n* haute finance *f*; **~-flier** *n* (ambitious person) jeune loup *m*, ambitieux/-ieuse *m/f*; (gifted pupil) élève *mf* doué/-e; **~-frequency** *adj* (à) haute fréquence; **~-handed** *adj* despotique; **~ heels** *n pl* hauts talons *mpl*; **~ jump** ▶649 *n* (Sport) saut *m* en hauteur.
Highlands *pr n pl* Highlands *mpl*, Hautes-Terres *fpl* (d'Écosse).
high: **~-level** *adj* [*talks*] à haut niveau; **~ life** *n* grande vie *f*.
highlight I *n* **1** (in hair) (natural) reflet *m*; (artificial) mèche *f*; **2** (of exhibition) clou *m*; (of match) point *m* culminant; (of year) point *m* fort.
II **highlights** *n pl* (on radio, TV) résumé *m*.
III *vtr* **1** (with pen) surligner; **2** (emphasize) mettre l'accent sur.
highly *adv* [*dangerous, intelligent*] extrêmement; **~ unlikely** fort peu probable; **to think ~ of sb** penser beaucoup de bien de qn.
highly: **~-charged** *adj* [*atmosphere*] très tendu; **~-paid** *adj* très bien payé; **~-strung** *adj* très tendu.
high-necked *adj* à col montant.
Highness ▶642 *n* **His** or **Her (Royal) ~** Son Altesse *f*.
high: **~-pitched** *adj* [*voice, sound*] aigu/-uë; **~ point** *n* point *m* culminant; **~-powered** *adj* [*car, engine*] de grande puissance; [*person*] dynamique; [*job*] de haute responsabilité; **~ pressure** *n* (in weather) hautes pressions *fpl*; **~-profile** *adj* [*politician, group*] bien en vue; **~-ranking** *adj* de haut rang; **~ rise (building)** *n* tour *f* (d'habitation); **~-risk** *adj* à haut risque; **~ school** *n* (US Sch) ≈ lycée *m*; (GB Sch) établissement *m* secondaire.
high sea *n* **on the ~s** en haute mer.
high: **~ season** *n* haute saison *f*; **~-speed** *adj* [*train*] à grande vitesse.
high spirits *n pl* entrain *m*; **to be in ~** être plein d'entrain.
high street (GB) (also **High Street**) *n* (in town) rue *f* principale; (in village) grand-rue *f*.
high: **~-tech** *adj* [*industry*] de pointe; [*equipment, car*] ultramoderne; **~ tide** *n* marée *f* haute; **~ voltage** *n* haute tension *f*.
highway *n* (GB) route *f* nationale; (US) autoroute *f*.
highway: **Highway Code** *n* (GB) Code *m* de la Route; **~ patrol** *n* (US) police *f* de la route.
hijack *vtr* détourner [*plane*]; récupérer [*event, demonstration*].
hijacker *n* (of plane) pirate *m* (de l'air); (of bus, truck) pirate *m* (de la route).
hijacking *n* détournement *m*.
hike I *n* randonnée *f*; **to go on a ~** faire une randonnée.
II *vtr* (also **~ up**) augmenter [*rate, price*].
hiker *n* randonneur/-euse *m/f*.
hiking ▶649 *n* randonnée *f*.
hilarious *adj* désopilant, hilarant.

hill *n* colline *f*; (hillside) coteau *m*; (incline) pente *f*, côte *f*.

hillside *n* **on the ~** à flanc de coteau.

hilltop *n* sommet *m* de colline.

hilly *adj* vallonné.

him *pron*

■ **Note** When used as a direct object pronoun, *him* is translated by *le* (*l'* before a vowel or mute 'h'). Note that the object pronoun normally comes before the verb in French: *I know him* = je le connais; *I've already seen him* = je l'ai déjà vu.
– In imperatives, the direct object pronoun is translated by *le* and comes after the verb: *catch him!* = attrape-le! (note the hyphen).
– When used as an indirect object pronoun, *him* is translated by *lui*: *I've given him the book* = je lui ai donné le livre; *I've given it to him* = je le lui ai donné.
– In imperatives, the indirect object pronoun is translated by *lui* and comes after the verb: *phone him!* = téléphone-lui!; *give it to him* = donne-le-lui (note the hyphens).
– After prepositions and after the verb *to be*, the translation is *lui*: *she did it for him* = elle l'a fait pour lui; *it's him* = c'est lui.

Himalayas *pr n pl* (montagnes *fpl* de) l'Himalaya *m*.

himself *pron*

■ **Note** When used as a reflexive pronoun, direct and indirect, *himself* is translated by *se* (*s'* before a vowel or mute 'h'): *he's enjoying himself* = il s'amuse bien; *he's cut himself* = il s'est coupé.
– When used for emphasis, the translation is *lui-même*: *he himself didn't know* = il ne le savait pas lui-même.
– After a preposition, the translation is *lui* or *lui-même*: *he can be proud of himself* = il peut être fier de lui *or* de lui-même.

1 (reflexive) se, s'; **he's hurt ~** il s'est blessé; **2** (after preposition) lui, lui-même; **for ~** pour lui, pour lui-même; **(all) by ~** tout seul; **he's not ~ today** il n'est pas dans son assiette aujourd'hui.

hinder *vtr* (hamper) entraver [*development, career*]; (delay) freiner [*progress, efforts*]; retarder [*plan*].

hind legs *n pl* pattes *fpl* de derrière.

hindquarters *n pl* arrière-train *m*.

hindsight *n* **with (the benefit of) ~** avec du recul, rétrospectivement.

Hindu *adj* hindou.

hinge **I** *n* charnière *f*; (lift-off) gond *m*.
II *vi* **to ~ on** dépendre de.

hint **I** *n* **1** (remark) allusion *f* (**about** à); **to drop ~s** faire des allusions; **all right, I can take a ~** c'est bon, j'ai compris; **2** (clue) indication *f*; (piece of advice) conseil *m*; **3** (of spice, accent) pointe *f*; (of colour) touche *f*; (of smile) ébauche *f*; (of irony) soupçon *m*.
II *vtr* **to ~ that** laisser entendre que (**to** à).

hip **I** *n* ▶ **523** hanche *f*; **to break one's ~** se casser le col du fémur.
II *excl* **~ ~ hurrah!** hip hip hip hourra!

hip measurement, **hip size** *n* tour *m* de hanches.

hippie, **hippy** *n*, *adj* hippie (*mf*), hippy (*mf*).

hippopotamus, **hippo** *n* hippopotame *m*.

hire **I** *n* location *f*; **car ~** location de voitures; **for ~** [*boat, skis*] à louer; [*taxi*] libre.
II *vtr* louer [*equipment*]; engager [*person*].

hire purchase, **HP** *n* achat *m* à crédit; **on ~** à crédit.

his

■ **Note** In French determiners agree in gender and number with the noun that follows. So *his*, when used as a determiner, is translated by *son* + masculine singular noun (son chien), by *sa* + feminine singular noun (sa maison) BUT by *son* + feminine noun beginning with a vowel or mute 'h' (son assiette) and by *ses* + plural noun (ses enfants).
– When *his* is stressed, *à lui* is added after the noun: HIS *house* = sa maison à lui.
– For *his* used with parts of the body ▶ **523**.
– In French possessive pronouns reflect the gender and number of the noun they are standing for. When used as a possessive pronoun, *his* is translated by *le sien*, *la sienne*, *les siens* or *les siennes* according to what is being referred to.

I *det* son/sa/ses.
II *pron* **all the drawings were good but ~ was the best** tous les dessins étaient bons mais le sien était le meilleur; **the blue car is ~** la voiture bleue est à lui; **it's not ~** ce n'est pas à lui; **which house is ~?** sa maison c'est laquelle?; **the money was not ~ to give away** il n'avait pas à donner cet argent; **I'm a colleague of ~** je suis un/-e de ses collègues.

Hispanic *adj* (Spanish) hispanique; (Latin American) latino-américain.

hiss **I** *n* sifflement *m*.
II *vi* [*person, steam, snake*] siffler; [*cat*] cracher; [*fat*] grésiller.

historian ▶ **805** *n* historien/-ienne *m/f*.

historic(al) *adj* historique.

history **I** *n* **1** histoire *f*; **French ~** histoire de France; **~ of art** histoire de l'art; **to make ~** entrer dans l'histoire; **2** (past experience) antécédents *mpl*; **to have a ~ of heart trouble** avoir des antécédents cardiaques; **to have a ~ of violence** avoir un passé violent.
II *noun modifier* [*book, teacher*] d'histoire.

hit **I** *n* **1** (blow, stroke in sport) coup *m*; (in fencing) touche *f*; **to score a ~** marquer un point; **2** (success) (play, film) succès *m*; (record) tube° *m*; **to be a big ~** avoir un succès fou.
II *vtr* **1** (strike) frapper [*person, ball*]; [*head, arm*] cogner contre [*wall*]; **to ~ one's head on sth** se cogner la tête contre qch; **2** atteindre [*target, enemy*]; **3** (collide with) heurter [*wall*]; (more violently) percuter [*wall*]; [*vehicle*] renverser [*person*]; **4** (affect adversely) affecter, toucher; **5** (reach) arriver à [*motorway*]; rencontrer [*traffic, bad weather*]; [*figures, weight*] atteindre [*level*].
IDIOMS **to ~ it off with sb** bien s'entendre avec qn.
■ **hit back**: ¶ **~ back** riposter; ¶ **~ [sb]**

back rendre un coup à; ¶ **~ [sth] back** renvoyer [*ball*].
■ **hit upon**, **hit on**: **~ (up)on [sth]** découvrir [*solution*]; tomber sur [*problem*].

hit-and-run *adj* [*accident*] où le chauffeur a pris la fuite.

hitch I *n* problème *m*, pépin○ *m*.
II *vtr* **1** attacher [*trailer*] (**to** à); **2**○ **to ~ a lift** faire du stop○.
III○ *vi* faire du stop○.

hitchhike *vi* faire du stop○ *m*; **to ~ to Paris** aller à Paris en stop○.

hitch: **~hiker** *n* auto-stoppeur/-euse *m/f*; **~hiking** *n* auto-stop *m*.

hit: **~ list** *n* liste *f* noire; **~ parade** *m* palmarès *m*, hit-parade *m*.

HIV *n* (*abbr* = **human immunodeficiency virus**) (virus *m*) VIH *m*.

hive I *n* ruche *f*; **a ~ of activity** une vraie ruche.
II **hives** *n pl* ▶ 686 urticaire *f*.

HIV positive *adj* séropositif/-ive (au virus VIH).

hoard I *n* (of treasure) trésor *m*; (of provisions) provisions *fpl*; (of miser) magot○ *m*.
II *vtr* amasser [*objects, money, food*].

hoarding *n* (GB) **1** (billboard) panneau *m* publicitaire; **2** (fence) palissade *f*.

hoarse *adj* [*voice*] rauque; **to be ~** être enroué.

hoax I *n* canular *m*.
II *noun modifier* [*call, warning*] bidon○ *inv*.

hob *n* (on cooker) table *f* de cuisson.

hobble *vi* boitiller.

hobby *n* passe-temps *m inv*; **hobbies and interests** (on CV) centres *mpl* d'intérêt.

hobnail *n* **~(ed) boots** souliers *mpl* ferrés or à clous.

hockey ▶ 649 *n* (GB) hockey *m*; (US) hockey *m* sur glace; **~ stick** crosse *f* de hockey.

hoe I *n* houe *f*, binette *f*.
II *vtr* biner [*ground*]; sarcler [*flowerbeds*].

hog I *n* **1** (GB) (castrated pig) porc *m* châtré; **2** (US) (pig) porc *m*, verrat *m*.
II○ *vtr* monopoliser.
IDIOMS **to go the whole ~**○ (be extravagant) faire les choses en grand; (go to extremes) aller jusqu'au bout.

hoist *vtr* hisser [*flag, sail, heavy object*].

hold I *n* **1** (grasp) prise *f*; **to get ~ of** attraper [*rope, ball*]; **2** (possession) **to get ~ of** se procurer [*book, ticket*]; découvrir [*information*]; **3 to get ~ of sb** (contact) joindre qn; (find) trouver qn; **4** (control) emprise *f* (**on, over** sur); **to have a ~ on** or **over sb** avoir de l'emprise sur qn; **to get a ~ of oneself** se reprendre; **5 to put a call on ~** mettre un appel en attente; **6** (in plane) soute *f*; (on boat) cale *f*.
II *vtr* **1** tenir; **to ~ sth in one's hand** tenir qch à la main [*brush, pencil*]; (enclosed) tenir qch dans la main [*coin, sweet*]; **to ~ sb (in one's arms)** serrer qn dans ses bras; **to ~ each other tightly** s'étreindre; **to ~ oneself well** se tenir bien; **to ~ sth in place** maintenir qch en place; **2** (arrange) organiser [*meeting, competition, reception*]; célébrer [*church service*]; mener [*inquiry*]; faire passer [*interview*]; **to be held** avoir lieu; **3** (contain) [*drawer, box, case*] contenir [*objects, possessions*]; **to ~ a maximum of 300** [*hall*] pouvoir accueillir 300 personnes au maximum; **4** avoir [*opinion, belief*]; **5** (keep against will) détenir [*person*]; **to ~ sb hostage** garder qn en otage; **6** (possess) détenir, avoir [*shares, power, record*]; être titulaire de [*degree*]; occuper [*job*]; avoir [*passport, licence*]; porter [*title*]; **7** garder [*place, ticket*]; faire attendre [*train, flight*]; **to ~ sb's attention** retenir l'attention de qn; **to ~ sb responsible** tenir qn pour responsable; **8** (defend successfully) tenir [*territory, city*]; conserver [*title, seat*]; **to ~ one's own** bien se défendre; **9** (on phone) **can you ~ the line please?** ne quittez pas s'il vous plaît.
III *vi* **1** (remain intact) tenir; **2** (continue) [*weather*] se maintenir; [*luck*] durer; **3** (wait on phone) patienter
■ **hold against**: **to ~ sth against sb** reprocher qch à qn; **it could be held against you** [*age, sex*] ça pourrait jouer en ta défaveur.
■ **hold back**: ¶ **~ back** se retenir (**from doing** de faire); ¶ **~ [sb/sth] back**, **~ back [sb/sth] 1** contenir [*water, crowd, anger*]; retenir [*tears, person*]; **2** entraver [*development*].
■ **hold down**: **~ [sb/sth] down**, **~ down [sb/sth] 1** tenir, maîtriser [*person*]; **2** garder [*job*].
■ **hold on 1** (wait) attendre; **'~ on...'** (on telephone) 'ne quittez pas...'; **2 '~ on (tight)!'** 'tiens-toi (bien)!'
■ **hold on to**: **~ on to [sb/sth] 1** (grip) s'agripper à; (to prevent from falling) retenir [*person*]; serrer [*object, purse*]; **2** conserver [*power*]; garder [*shares, car*].
■ **hold out**: ¶ **~ out** tenir bon; **to ~ out against** tenir bon devant [*threat, changes*]; ¶ **~ [sth] out, ~out [sth]** tendre [*hand*] (**to** à).
■ **hold to**: **~ sb to [sth]** faire tenir [qch] à qn [*promise*].
■ **hold together**: **~ [sth] together** faire tenir [*machine, chair*]; assurer la cohésion de [*party, government*].
■ **hold up**: **~ [sb/sth] up**, **~ up [sb/sth] 1** soutenir [*shelf*]; tenir [*trousers*]; **2** (raise) lever; **to ~ one's hand up** lever la main; **3** (delay) retarder [*person, flight*]; ralentir [*production, traffic*]; **4** (rob) attaquer.

holdall *n* fourre-tout *m*, sac *m*.

holder *n* (of passport, degree, post) titulaire *mf*; (of ticket, record) détenteur/-trice *m/f*; (of title) tenant/-e *m/f*; **account ~** titulaire d'un compte.

hold-up *n* **1** (delay) retard *m*; (on road) embouteillage *m*, bouchon *m*; **2** (robbery) hold-up *m*, attaque *f* à main armée.

hole *n* **1** (in clothing, hedge) trou *m*; **2** (GB) (in tooth) cavité *f*; **3** (pothole) nid *m* de poule; **4** (flaw) **to pick ~s in an argument** repérer les failles d'un raisonnement; **5** (of mouse) trou *m*; (of fox, rabbit) terrier *m*.

holiday *n* **1** (GB) (vacation) vacances *fpl*; **on ~**

en vacances; **the school/summer ~s** les vacances scolaires/d'été; **half-term ~** petites vacances; **2** (GB) (time off work) congé *m*; **3** (public, bank) jour *m* férié.

holiday: **~ home** *n* (GB) résidence *f* secondaire; **~ job** *n* (GB) (in summer) job○ *m* d'été; **~maker** *n* (GB) vacancier/-ière *m/f*; (summer visitor) estivant/-e *m/f*; **~ resort** *n* lieu *m* de villégiature.

Holland ▶**574** *pr n* Hollande *f*, Pays-Bas *mpl*.

hollow **I** *n* **1** (in tree, of hand, back) creux *m*; **2** (small valley) cuvette *f*.

II *adj* [*object, cheeks*] creux/creuse; [*words*] faux/fausse, vain; **a ~ laugh** un rire forcé; **to sound ~** sonner faux.

holly *n* houx *m*.

holocaust *n* holocauste *m*; **the Holocaust** l'Holocauste *m*.

hologram *n* hologramme *m*.

holster *n* étui *m* de revolver.

holy *adj* [*place, day, city, person*] saint; [*water*] bénit; **~ picture** image *f* pieuse.

holy: **Holy Bible** *n* Sainte Bible *f*; **Holy Communion** *n* sainte communion *f*; **Holy Land** *pr n* Terre *f* Sainte; **Holy Spirit** *n* Saint-Esprit *m*; **Holy Trinity** *n* sainte Trinité *f*; **Holy Week** *n* semaine *f* sainte.

homage *n* hommage *m*; **to pay ~ to** rendre hommage à.

home **I** *n* **1** (dwelling) logement *m*; (house) maison *f*; (country) pays *m* natal; **to be far from ~** être loin de chez soi; **make yourself at ~** fais comme chez toi; **to work from ~** travailler à domicile; **broken ~** foyer désuni; **to leave ~** quitter la maison; **2** (institution) maison *f*; **to put sb in a ~** mettre qn dans un établissement spécialisé; **3** (source) **~ of** pays *m* de [*speciality*]; **4** (Sport) **to play at ~** jouer à domicile.

II *noun modifier* **1** (family) [*life*] de famille; [*comforts*] du foyer; **2** (national) [*market, affairs*] intérieur; [*news*] national; **3** (Sport) [*match, win*] à domicile; [*team*] qui reçoit.

III *adv* **1** [*come, go, arrive*] (to house) à la maison, chez soi; (to country) dans son pays; **on the way ~** en rentrant chez moi/nous etc; (by boat, plane) pendant le voyage de retour; **to take sb ~** raccompagner qn à la maison; **to be ~** (around) être à la maison; (from work) être rentré; **2 to bring sth ~ to sb** faire comprendre or voir qch à qn; **to strike ~** toucher juste.

■ **home in on**: **~ in on [sth]** se diriger sur [*target*].

home: **~ address** *n* (on form) domicile *m*; (personal) adresse *f* personnelle; **~ birth** *n* accouchement *m* à domicile; **~ cooking** *n* bonne cuisine *f* familiale.

home ground *n* (figurative) terrain *m* familier; **on one's ~** (Sport) à domicile.

home help *n* (GB) aide *f* familiale.

homeless *n* **the ~** les sans-abri *mpl inv*.

homeloving *adj* casanier/-ière.

homely *adj* **1** (GB) (cosy, welcoming) accueillant; **2** (GB) (unpretentious) simple; **3** (US) (plain) [*person*] sans attraits.

home: **~made** *adj* fait maison, maison *inv*; **~ movie** *n* film *m* d'amateur; **Home Office** *n* ministère *m* de l'Intérieur.

homeopathic *adj* [*medicine*] homéopathique.

home: **~ owner** *n* propriétaire *mf*; **Home Secretary** *n* Ministre *m* de l'Intérieur.

homesick *adj* **to be ~** (for country) avoir le mal du pays; [*child*] s'ennuyer de ses parents.

home: **~sickness** *n* mal *m* du pays; **~spun** *adj* [*cloth*] artisanal; **~ town** *n* ville *f* natale; **~ video** *n* vidéo *f* d'amateur; **~ visit** *n* (Med) visite *f* à domicile.

homeward *adv* **to travel ~(s)** rentrer; **to be ~ bound** être sur le chemin de retour.

homework *n* **1** (Sch) devoirs *mpl*; **2** (research) **to do some ~ on** faire quelques recherches au sujet de.

homeworker *n* travailleur/-euse *m/f* à domicile.

homicidal *adj* homicide.

homicide *n* **1** (murder) homicide *m*; **~ bureau** (US) brigade *f* criminelle; **2** (person) meurtrier/-ière *m/f*.

homing *adj* [*system*] d'autoguidage; **~ pigeon** pigeon *m* voyageur.

homogenous *adj* homogène.

homosexual *n*, *adj* homosexuel/-elle (*m/f*).

honest *adj* [*person*] (truthful) honnête; (sincere) franc/franche; [*answer, account*] sincère; **to be ~ about** être honnête au sujet de; **to be ~ with sb** être franc avec qn; **to be ~ with oneself** être honnête avec soi-même; **to be ~, I don't care** à dire vrai, ça m'est égal.

honestly *adv* honnêtement; (sincerely) [*believe*] sincèrement; [*say*] franchement.

honesty *n* honnêteté *f*.

honey *n* **1** (food) miel *m*; **clear ~** miel liquide; **2**○ (term of endearment) chéri/-e *m/f*.

honey: **~bee** *n* abeille *f*; **~comb** *n* (in hive) rayon *m* de miel; (for sale) gâteau *m* de miel.

honeymoon *n* **1** (wedding trip) voyage *m* de noces; **~ couple** couple *m* en voyage de noces; **2** (also **~ period**) lune *f* de miel.

honeysuckle *n* chèvrefeuille *m*.

Hong Kong ▶**574** *pr n* Hongkong *m*.

honk *vtr* **to ~ one's horn** donner un coup de klaxon®.

honor (US) = **honour**.

honorable (US) = **honourable**.

honorary *adj* [*doctorate*] honorifique, honoris causa *inv*; [*member*] honoraire.

honor: **~ roll** *n* (US Sch, Sport) tableau *m* d'honneur; **~ system** *n* (US Sch) système *m* de l'autodiscipline.

honour (GB), **honor** (US) **I** *n* **1** honneur *m*; **in ~ of** en l'honneur de; **to give one's word of ~** donner sa parole d'honneur; **2** (in titles) **Your Honour** Votre Honneur.

II *vtr* honorer [*person, cheque, contract*]; tenir [*promise, commitment*].

IDIOMS **to do the ~s** (serve food, drinks) faire les honneurs; (introduce guests) faire les présentations.

honourable (GB), **honorable** (US) *adj* **1** [*profession, tradition, victory, settlement*] honorable; [*person, intention*] honnête; **2** ▶ 642 (in titles) **the Honourable Mr Justice Jones** le Juge Jones.

honours *n pl* (GB) **first/second class ~s** ≈ mention très bien/bien.

honours degree *n* (GB) *licence réservée aux meilleurs étudiants.*

hood *n* **1** (head gear) (attached) capuchon *m*; (detached) capuche *f*; (balaclava) cagoule *f*; **2** (on cooker) hotte *f*; **3** (GB) (on car, pram) capote *f*; **4** (US Aut) (bonnet) capot *m*.

hoof *n* sabot *m*; **bought on the ~** acheté sur pied.

hook I *n* **1** (for clothing, picture) crochet *m*; **2** (on fishing line) hameçon *m*; **3** (fastener) agrafe *f*; **~s and eyes** agrafes *fpl*; **4 to take the phone off the ~** décrocher le téléphone.
II *vtr* accrocher (**on, onto** à).
IDIOMS **to get sb off the ~** tirer qn d'affaire.
■ **hook up**: ¶ **~ up** [*garment*] s'agrafer; ¶ **~ up [sth], ~ [sth] up** agrafer [*garment*]; connecter [*appliance*].

hooked *adj* **1** [*nose, beak*] crochu; **2 to be ~ on** se camer○ à [*drugs*]; être mordu○ de [*films, computer games*].

hooligan *n* vandale *m*, voyou *m*; **soccer ~** hooligan *m*.

hoop *n* (ring) cerceau *m*; (in croquet) arceau *m*.

hooray *excl* hourra!

hoot I *n* (of owl) (h)ululement *m*; (of siren) mugissement *m*; (of car) coup *m* de klaxon®.
II *vtr* **to ~ one's horn** donner un coup de klaxon®.
III *vi* [*owl*] (h)ululer; [*siren*] mugir; [*car*] klaxonner; [*person, crowd*] (derisively) huer; **to ~ with laughter** éclater de rire.

hoover *vtr* (GB) **to ~ a room** passer l'aspirateur dans une pièce.

Hoover® *n* (GB) aspirateur *m*.

hop I *n* (of frog, rabbit, child) bond *m*; (of bird) sautillement *m*.
II hops *n pl* houblon *m*.
III *vi* [*person*] sauter; (on one leg) sauter à cloche-pied; [*bird*] sautiller; **to ~ into bed/off a bus** sauter dans son lit/d'un bus.

hope I *n* **1** espoir *m* (**of** de); **in the ~ of sth** dans l'espoir de qch; **to have high ~s of sb/sth** fonder de grands espoirs sur qn/qch; **there is no ~ left for them** il n'y a plus d'espoir pour eux; **to raise sb's ~s** faire naître l'espoir chez qn; **to give up ~** abandonner tout espoir; **2** (chance) chance *f*, espoir *m*; **to have no ~ of sth** n'avoir aucune chance de qch; **there is no ~ of an improvement** on ne peut pas s'attendre à une amélioration; **my last ~** mon dernier espoir.
II *vtr* espérer (**that** que); **to ~ to do** espérer faire; **we cannot ~ to compete** nous n'avons aucune chance de leur/lui faire concurrence; **I (do) ~ so/not** j'espère (bien) que oui/que non; **hoping to hear from you** dans l'espoir d'avoir de vos nouvelles.
III *vi* espérer; **to ~ for a reward** espérer avoir une récompense; **let's ~ for the best** espérons que tout se passera bien.

hopeful *adj* [*person, expression*] plein d'espoir; [*attitude, mood*] optimiste; [*sign, situation*] encourageant.

hopefully *adv* **1** (with luck) avec un peu de chance; **'will he pay?'—'~'** 'c'est lui qui paiera?'—'je l'espère'; **2** (with hope) [*say*] avec optimisme.

hopeless *adj* **1** [*attempt, case, struggle*] désespéré; **it's ~!** inutile!; **2**○ (incompetent) nul/nulle○; **to be ~ at doing** être incapable de faire.

hopelessness *n* **1** (despair) désespoir *m*; **2** (futility) futilité *f* (**of doing** de faire).

hopscotch ▶ 649 *n* marelle *f*.

horizon *n* horizon *m*; **on the ~** (visible) à l'horizon; (imminent) en vue; **to broaden one's ~s** élargir ses horizons.

horizontal *adj* horizontal; **~ bar** barre *f* fixe.

hormone *n* hormone *f*.

hormone: **~ replacement therapy, HRT** *n* hormonothérapie *f* substitutive; **~ treatment** *n* traitement *m* hormonal.

horn *n* **1** (of animal, snail) corne *f*; **2** (Mus) ▶ 753 cor *m*; **3** (of car) klaxon® *m*; (of ship) sirène *f*.

hornet *n* frelon *m*.

horn: **~pipe** *n* matelote *f*; **~-rimmed** *adj* [*spectacles*] à monture d'écaille.

horoscope *n* horoscope *m*.

horrendous *adj* [*crime, accident*] épouvantable; [*noise*] effroyable.

horrible *adj* **1** (unpleasant) [*place, clothes, smell*] affreux/-euse; [*weather, food, person*] épouvantable; **to be ~ to sb** être méchant avec qn; **2** (shocking) horrible.

horrid *adj* affreux/-euse.

horrific *adj* atroce.

horrified *adj* horrifié (**at, by** par; **that** que + *subj*).

horrifying *adj* [*experience, sight*] horrifiant; [*behaviour*] effroyable.

horror *n* horreur *f* (**at** devant); **to have a ~ of sth/of doing** avoir horreur de qch/de faire.

horror film *n* film *m* d'épouvante.

horse *n* **1** cheval *m*; **2** (in gym) cheval *m* de saut; (pommel) cheval *m* d'arçons.
IDIOMS **from the ~'s mouth** de source sûre.
■ **horse about, horse around** chahuter.

horse: **~back riding** ▶ 649 *n* (US) équitation *f*; **~box** *n* van *m*; **~ chestnut** *n* (tree) marronnier *m* (d'Inde); (fruit) marron *m* (d'Inde); **~fly** *n* taon *m*.

horsepower *n* puissance *f* (en chevaux); **a 90 ~ engine** un moteur de 90 chevaux.

horse: **~racing** *n* courses *fpl* de chevaux, courses *fpl* hippiques; **~radish sauce** *n* sauce *f* au raifort; **~riding** ▶ 649 *n* équitation *f*; **~shoe** *n* fer *m* à cheval; **~show** *n* concours *m* hippique.

horticulture *n* horticulture *f*.

hose *n* **1** (for garden) tuyau *m* d'arrosage; **2** (Aut) (in engine) tuyau *m*; **3** (tubing) tuyau *m*.

hosepipe (GB) *n* **1** (for garden) tuyau *m* d'arrosage; **2** (fire brigade's) lance *f* à incendie.

hospice *n* établissement *m* de soins palliatifs.

hospitable *adj* [*person, country*] hospitalier/-ière (**to** envers).

hospital I *n* hôpital *m*; **to/from ~** (GB) or **the ~** (US) à/de l'hôpital.
II *noun modifier* [*staff, treatment, ward*] hospitalier/-ière; **~ beds** lits *mpl* d'hôpital; **~ patient** patient/-e *m/f*.

hospitality *n* hospitalité *f*.

hospitalize *vtr* hospitaliser.

host I *n* **1** (to guests, visitors) hôte *m*; **to play ~ to sb** recevoir qn; **2** (Zool) (to parasite) hôte *m*; **3** (on radio, TV) animateur/-trice *m/f*; **4** (multitude) foule *f* (**of** de).
II *vtr* organiser [*function*]; animer [*TV programme, radio programme*].

hostage *n* otage *m*; **to hold sb ~** garder qn en otage.

hostel *n* (for workers, refugees) foyer *m*; **(youth) ~** auberge *f* de jeunesse.

hostess *n* **1** (to guests) hôtesse *f*, maîtresse *f* de maison; (on plane) hôtesse *f*; **2** (on radio, TV) animatrice *f*.

hostile *adj* hostile (**to** à).

hostility *n* hostilité *f* (**towards sb/sth** à l'égard de qn/à qch).

hot *adj* **1** chaud; **it's ~ here** il fait chaud ici; **it was a ~ day** il faisait chaud ce jour-là; **to be** or **feel ~** [*person*] avoir chaud; **to get ~** [*person*] commencer à avoir trop chaud; [*engine, oven*] chauffer; [*weather*] se réchauffer; **your forehead feels ~** tu as le front chaud; **when the sun is at its ~test** quand le soleil chauffe le plus; **to be ~ from the oven** sortir du four; **to go ~ and cold** (with fever) être fiévreux/-euse; (with fear) avoir des sueurs froides; **to have a ~ temper** s'emporter facilement; **2** (Culin) [*mustard, spice*] fort; [*sauce, dish*] épicé; **3** (close) **to be ~ on the trail of sth** être sur la piste de qch; **to set off in ~ pursuit of sb** se lancer à la poursuite de qn.

hot: **~ air balloon** *n* montgolfière *f*; **~ dog** *n* hot dog *m*.

hotel I *n* hôtel *m*.
II *noun modifier* [*room, manager*] d'hôtel; [*price*] hôtelier/-ière; [*work*] dans l'hôtellerie.

hotelier, hotelkeeper ▶805 *n* (GB) hôtelier/-ière *m/f*.

hot: **~plate** *n* plaque *f* de cuisson; **~pot** *n* (GB) ragoût *m*; **~ spot**○ *n* (trouble spot) point *m* chaud; (sunny country) pays *m* du soleil; **~ spring** *n* source *f* chaude; **~-tempered** *adj* colérique; **~ water bottle** *n* bouillotte *f*.

hound I *n* chien *m* de chasse.
II *vtr* harceler, traquer [*person*].
■ **hound out**: **~ [sb] out** chasser (**of** de).

hour ▶915, 554 I *n* heure *f*; **an ~ ago** il y a une heure; **it's an ~ (away) from London** c'est à une heure de Londres; **twice an ~** deux fois par heure; **£10 per ~** 10 livres sterling (de) l'heure; **to be paid by the ~** être payé à l'heure; **the bus leaves on the ~** le bus part à l'heure juste; **in the early ~s** au petit matin; **at this ~?** à l'heure qu'il est?; **her finest ~** son heure de gloire.
II **hours** *n pl* heures *fpl*; **opening ~s** heures *fpl* d'ouverture; **office ~s** heures *fpl* de permanence.

hourly I *adj* [*rate*] horaire; **the buses are ~** les bus partent toutes les heures; **on an ~ basis** à l'heure.
II *adv* [*arrive, phone*] toutes les heures.

house I *n* **1** (home) maison *f*; **at my/his ~** chez moi/lui; **to go to sb's ~** aller chez qn; **to keep ~** tenir la maison (**for** de); **2** (also **House**) (parliament) Chambre *f*; **3** (business) maison *f*; **on the ~** aux frais de la maison; **4** (in theatre) (audience) assistance *f*; (auditorium) salle *f*; (performance) séance *f*; **'~ full'** 'complet'; **5** (music) house music *f*.
II *vtr* (permanently) loger; (temporarily) héberger; **badly** or **poorly ~d** mal logé.

house: **~ arrest** *n* résidence *f* surveillée; **~boat** *n* (barge) péniche *f* aménagée; **~fly** *n* mouche *f* domestique.

household I *n* maison *f*; (in census) ménage *m*; **head of the ~** chef *m* de famille.
II *noun modifier* [*accounts, bill*] du ménage; [*chore, item*] ménager/-ère.

household appliance *n* appareil *m* électroménager.

householder *n* (occupier) occupant/-e *m/f*; (owner) propriétaire *mf*; (tenant) locataire *mf*.

house-hunting *n* **to go ~** se lancer à la recherche d'une maison (à acheter).

house: **~keeper** ▶805 *n* gouvernante *f*; **~keeping** *n* (money) argent *m* du ménage; (managing of money) gestion *f* de l'argent du ménage; **House of Commons** *n* Chambre *f* des communes; **House of Lords** *n* (GB) Chambre *f* des lords, Chambre *f* haute; **House of Representatives** *n* (US) Chambre *f* des représentants; **~ painter** ▶805 *n* peintre *m* en bâtiment; **~plant** *n* plante *f* d'intérieur; **~ prices** *n pl* prix *mpl* du marché immobilier; **~-proud** *adj* qui est toujours en train d'astiquer; **Houses of Congress** *n pl* (US) *le Sénat et la Chambre des représentants*; **Houses of Parliament** *n pl* (GB) Parlement *m* Britannique; **~-trained** *adj* (GB) propre; **~-warming (party)** *n* pendaison *f* de crémaillère; **~wife** *n* femme *f* au foyer; (with emphasis on domestic labour) ménagère *f*; **~ wine** *n* cuvée *f* maison or du patron.

housework *n* travaux *mpl* ménagers; **to do the ~** s'occuper de la maison; (clean) faire le ménage.

housing I *n* logements *mpl*.
II *noun modifier* [*crisis, problem*] du logement; [*conditions*] de logement.

housing: **~ benefit** *n* (GB) ≈ allocation *f* logement; **~ estate** *n* (GB) (large) cité *f*; (small) lotissement *m*; (council-run) ≈ cité *f* or lotissement *m* HLM; **~ project** (US) *n* ≈ cité *f* or lotissement *m* HLM.

hover *vi* [*eagle*] planer; [*helicopter*] faire du surplace; **to ~ around sb/sth** tourner autour de qn/qch.

hovercraft *n* aéroglisseur *m*.

how

■ **Note** When *how* is used as an adverb (*how did you get here?*), it is almost always translated by *comment*: comment es-tu arrivé ici?
– When *how* is used as a conjunction meaning *the way in which*, it is often translated by *comment*: *I don't know how they did it* = je ne sais pas comment ils ont fait.

I *adv* **1** (in what way) comment; **to know ~ to do** savoir faire; **I learned ~ to do it** j'ai appris à le faire; **2** (when enquiring) **~ are you?** comment allez-vous?; **~'s your foot?** comment va ton pied?; **~'s your brother?** comment va ton frère?; **~ are things?** comment ça va?; **~ do you do!** enchanté!; **3** (in number, quantity questions) **~ much is this?** combien ça coûte?; **~ much do you weigh?** combien pèses-tu?; **~ many people?** combien de personnes?; **~ many times have you been to France?** combien de fois es-tu allé en France?; **~ long will it take?** combien de temps cela va-t-il prendre?; **~ tall are you?** combien mesures-tu?; **~ far is it?** c'est à quelle distance?; **~ old is she?** quel âge a-t-elle?; **~ soon can you get here?** dans combien de temps peux-tu être ici?; **4** (in exclamations) **~ wonderful/awful!** c'est fantastique/affreux!; **~ clever of you!** comme c'est intelligent de ta part!
II *conj* **1** (that) que; **you know ~ he always arrives late** tu sais qu'il arrive toujours en retard; **2** (in whichever way) comme; **I'll dress ~ I like!** je m'habille comme je veux!
III○ **how come** *phr* **~ come?** pourquoi?; **~ come you always get the best place?** comment ça se fait que tu aies toujours la meilleure place?

however I *conj* toutefois, cependant; **~, the recession is not over yet** toutefois, la récession n'est pas encore terminée; **they can, ~, explain why** ils peuvent, cependant, expliquer pourquoi.
II *adv* **~ hard I try, I can't** j'ai beau essayer de toutes mes forces, je n'y arrive pas; **~ difficult the task is, we can't give up** si difficile que soit la tâche, nous ne pouvons pas abandonner; **~ small she may be** si petite soit-elle; **everyone, ~ poor** chacun, si pauvre soit-il; **~ much it costs** quel qu'en soit le prix; **~ long it takes** quel que soit le temps que ça prendra; **~ you like** comme tu veux.

howl I *n* hurlement *m*; **~s of protest** des protestations *fpl* bruyantes.
II *vi* [*child*] hurler, pousser des hurlements; [*dog, wind*] hurler.

HQ *n* (Mil) (*abbr* = **headquarters**) QG *m*.

hubcap *n* (Aut) enjoliveur *m*.

huddle I *n* (of people) petit groupe *m*; (of buildings) entassement *m*.
II *vi* **he was huddling in a corner** il était blotti dans un coin.

hue and cry *n* tollé *m*.

huff○ *n* **in a ~** vexé; **to go into a ~** prendre la mouche.

hug I *n* étreinte *f*; **to give sb a ~** serrer qn dans ses bras.
II *vtr* **1** (embrace) serrer [qn] dans ses bras; **2** **to ~ the coast** serrer la côte.

huge *adj* [*object, garden, city, country*] immense; [*person, animal*] gigantesque; [*appetite, success*] énorme; [*debts, sum*] gros/grosse (*before n*).

hull *n* (of ship, plane) coque *f*; (of tank) carcasse *f*.

hum I *n* (of insect, traffic, voices) bourdonnement *m*; (of machinery) ronronnement *m*.
II *vi* [*person*] fredonner; [*insect, aircraft*] bourdonner; [*machine*] ronronner.

human I *n* humain *m*; **fellow ~** semblable *mf*.
II *adj* [*body, behaviour*] humain; [*characteristic, rights*] de l'homme.

human being *n* être *m* humain.

humane *adj* [*person*] humain; [*act*] d'humanité.

humanist *n, adj* humaniste (*mf*).

humanitarian *adj* humanitaire.

humanities *n pl* (Univ) humanités *fpl*.

humanity *n* humanité *f*.

human nature *n* nature *f* humaine; **it's ~ to...** il est humain de...

human resources *n pl* ressources *fpl* humaines.

humble *adj* [*origin, position, dwelling*] modeste; [*person*] humble.

humid *adj* [*climate*] humide; [*weather*] lourd.

humidity *n* humidité *f*.

humiliate *vtr* humilier.

humiliating *adj* humiliant.

humorous *adj* **1** (amusing) humoristique; **2** (amused) plein d'humour.

humour (GB), **humor** (US) I *n* **1** (wit) humour *m*; **a good sense of ~** le sens de l'humour; **2** (mood) humeur *f*; **to be in good/bad ~** être de bonne/mauvaise humeur.
II *vtr* amadouer [*person*].

humourless (GB), **humorless** (US) *adj* [*person*] qui manque d'humour.

hump *n* bosse *f*.

hunch I *n* intuition *f*; **to have a ~ that** avoir l'intuition que.
II *vi* **to ~ over one's desk** se tenir penché à son bureau.

hunched *adj* [*back*] voûté; [*shoulders*] rentré.

hundred ▶ 492 I *n* cent *m*; **two ~** deux cents; **two ~ and one** deux cent un; **sold by the ~** vendu par centaines; **in nineteen ~** en mille neuf cents; **in nineteen ~ and three** en mille neuf cent trois; **~s of times** des centaines de fois.
II *pron, det* cent; **two ~ francs** deux cents francs; **two ~ and five francs** deux cent cinq francs; **about a ~ people** une centaine de personnes.

hundredth I *n* (in order, sequence) centième *mf*.
II *adj, adv* centième.

hundredweight ▶738 *n* (GB) = *50,80 kg;* (US) = *45,36 kg.*

Hungarian ▶712 **I** *n* **1** (person) Hongrois/-e *m/f*; **2** (language) hongrois *m*.
II *adj* [*culture, food, politics*] hongrois; [*teacher, lesson*] d'hongrois; [*ambassador, embassy*] de Hongrie.

Hungary ▶574 *pr n* Hongrie *f*.

hunger *n* (physical) faim *f*; (emotional, spiritual) désir *m* ardent (**for** de).

hunger strike *n* grève *f* de la faim.

hungry *adj* **to be ~** avoir faim; **to make sb ~** donner faim à qn; **to go ~** souffrir de la faim; **~ for** assoiffé de [*success, power*].

hung-up° *adj* **1** (tense) complexé; **2** (obsessed with) **to be ~ on sb/sth** être dingue° de qn/qch.

hunk *n* **1** (of bread) gros morceau *m*; **2**° (man) beau mec° *m*.

hunt I *n* chasse *f* (**for** à); (in fox-hunting) chasse *f* à courre; **treasure ~** chasse au trésor.
II *vtr* rechercher [*person*]; chasser [*animal*].
III *vi* **1** (for prey) chasser; **2** (search) **to ~ for sth** chercher [qch] partout [*object, person*]; être à la recherche de [*truth, cure*].

hunted *adj* traqué.

hunter *n* (person) chasseur/-euse *m/f*; (in fox-hunting) chasseur/-euse *m/f* à courre.

hunting *n* chasse *f* (**of** à); **to go ~** aller à la chasse.

hurdle *n* ▶649 **1** (Sport) haie *f*; **to clear a ~** franchir une haie; **2** (obstacle) obstacle *m*.

hurl *vtr* **1** (throw) lancer (**at** sur); **to be ~ed to the ground** être projeté au sol; **2** (shout) **to ~ insults at sb** accabler qn d'injures.

hurrah, hurray *n, excl* hourra (*m*); **~ for Laurence!** vive Laurence!

hurricane *n* ouragan *m*; **~ force wind** vent *m* soufflant en ouragan.

hurry I *n* hâte *f*, empressement *m*; **to be in a ~** être pressé (**to do** de faire); **there's no ~** ça ne presse pas; **to do sth in a ~** faire qch à la hâte.
II *vtr* terminer [qch] à la hâte [*meal, task*]; bousculer [*person*].
III *vi* se dépêcher (**over doing** de faire); **to ~ out** sortir précipitamment.
■ **hurry back** (to any place) se dépêcher de retourner (**to** à); (to one's home) se dépêcher de rentrer (chez soi).
■ **hurry up** se dépêcher; **~ up!** dépêche-toi!

hurt I *adj* peiné, blessé; **to look/feel ~** avoir l'air/être peiné.
II *vtr* **1** (injure) **to ~ oneself** se blesser, se faire mal; **to ~ one's back** se blesser or se faire mal au dos; **was anybody hurt?** y a-t-il eu des blessés?; **somebody's going to get hurt** quelqu'un va se faire mal; **2** (cause pain to) faire mal à; **you're ~ing my arm** vous me faites mal au bras; **3** (emotionally) blesser; (offend) froisser; **to ~ sb's feelings** blesser quelqu'un; **she's afraid of getting hurt** elle a peur de souffrir.
III *vi* **1** (be painful) faire mal; **my throat ~s** j'ai mal à la gorge; **where does it ~?** où est-ce que vous avez mal?; **it ~s when I laugh** j'ai mal quand je ris; **2** (emotionally) blesser.

hurtful *adj* blessant.

hurtle *vi* **to ~ down sth** dévaler qch; **to ~ along a road** foncer sur une route.

husband *n* mari *m*; (on form) époux *m*.

hush *n* silence *m*.
■ **hush up**: ¶ **~ up [sth], ~ [sth] up** étouffer [*affair*]; ¶ **~ up [sb], ~ [sb] up** faire taire [*person*].

hushed *adj* **in ~ tones** à voix basse.

hustle I *n* **~ (and bustle)** (lively) effervescence *f*; (tiring) agitation *f*.
II *vtr* pousser, bousculer [*person*]; **~ sb (into doing)** pousser qn (à faire).

hut *n* (native type) hutte *f*; (on building site) baraque *f* (de chantier); (on beach) cabine *f* (de plage).

hutch *n* clapier *m*.

hydrant *n* **1** (gen) prise *f* d'eau; **2** (also **fire ~**) bouche *f* d'incendie.

hydraulic ramp *n* (Aut) pont-élévateur *m*.

hydroelectric *adj* hydroélectrique.

hydrofoil *n* **1** (craft) hydroptère *m*; **2** (foil) aile *f* portante.

hydrogen *n* hydrogène *m*.

hydrolysis *n* hydrolyse *f*.

hyena *n* hyène *f*.

hygiene *n* hygiène *f*; **food ~** hygiène alimentaire.

hygienic *adj* hygiénique.

hymn *n* cantique *m*.

hype° *n* battage *m* publicitaire.
■ **hype up**: **~ up [sth]** faire du battage pour [*film, star, book*]; gonfler [*story*].

hyperactive *adj* hyperactif/-ive.

hypermarket *n* (GB) hypermarché *m*.

hyperventilate *vi* être en hyperventilation.

hyphen *n* trait *m* d'union.

hypnosis *n* hypnose *f*; **under ~** sous hypnose.

hypnotherapy *n* hypnothérapie *f*.

hypnotist *n* hypnotiseur *m*.

hypnotize *vtr* hypnotiser.

hypocrisy *n* hypocrisie *f*.

hypocrite *n* hypocrite *mf*.

hypocritical *adj* hypocrite.

hypodermic *adj* hypodermique.

hypothermia *n* hypothermie *f*.

hysteria *n* hystérie *f*.

hysterical *adj* [*person, behaviour*] hystérique; [*speech*] délirant.

hysterics *n* **1** (fit) crise *f* de nerfs; **to have ~** avoir une crise de nerfs; **2** (laughter) **to be in ~** rire aux larmes.

Ii

i, I *n* i, I *m*.
I *pron* je, j'.

■ **Note** *I* is almost always translated by *je* which becomes *j'* before a vowel or mute 'h': *I closed the door* = j'ai fermé la porte. The emphatic form is *moi*.

I am called Frances je m'appelle Frances; **he's a student but I'm not** il est étudiant mais moi pas; **he and I went to the cinema** lui et moi sommes allés au cinéma.

ice I *n* glace *f*; (on roads) verglas *m*; (in drinks) glaçons *mpl*.
II *vtr* glacer [*cake*].
III **iced** *pp adj* [*water*] avec des glaçons; [*tea*] glacé; [*coffee*] frappé.
IDIOMS **to break the ~** rompre la glace.
■ **ice over** [*windscreen, river*] se couvrir de glace.

iceberg *n* iceberg *m*.
IDIOMS **the tip of the ~** la partie visible de l'iceberg.

icebox *n* **1** (GB) (freezer compartment) freezer *m*; **2** (US) (fridge) réfrigérateur *m*.

ice: **~-cold** *adj* glacé; **~ cream** *n* glace *f*; **~-cube** *n* glaçon *m*; **~ hockey** ▶**649** *n* hockey *m* sur glace.

Iceland ▶**574** *pr n* Islande *f*.

Icelandic ▶**712** I *n* (language) islandais.
II *adj* [*people, customs*] islandais.

ice rink *n* patinoire *f*.

ice-skate ▶**649** I *n* patin *m* à glace.
II *vi* **to go ice-skating** faire du patin *m* à glace.

ice-skating ▶**649** *n* patinage *m* sur glace.

icicle *n* stalactite *f* (de glace).

icing *n* glaçage *m*.

icing sugar *n* (GB) sucre *m* glace.

icon *n* icône *f*.

icy *adj* **1** [*road*] verglacé; **~ patches** plaques *fpl* de verglas; **2** [*wind*] glacial; [*hands*] glacé; **3** [*look, reception*] glacial.

ID *n* pièce *f* d'identité; **~ card** carte *f* d'identité.

idea *n* idée *f* (**about, on** sur); **he came up with the ~ of buying a farm** l'idée lui est venue d'acheter une ferme; **to be full of ~s** avoir plein d'idées; **to have no ~ why/how** ne pas savoir pourquoi/comment; **I've an ~ that he might be lying** j'ai dans l'idée qu'il ment.

ideal *n, adj* idéal (*m*).

idealism *n* idéalisme *m*.

idealist *n* idéaliste *mf*.

idealistic *adj* idéaliste.

idealize *vtr* idéaliser.

identical *adj* identique (**to, with** à).

identical twin *n* vrai jumeau/vraie jumelle *m/f*.

identification *n* **1** identification *f* (**with** à); **2** (proof of identity) pièce *f* d'identité.

identify I *vtr* identifier (**as** comme étant; **to** à); (pick out) distinguer; **to ~ sb/sth with sb/sth** identifier qn/qch à qn/qch; **to ~ oneself** donner son identité.
II *vi* **to ~ with** s'identifier à.

identity *n* identité *f*; **have you any proof of ~?** avez-vous une pièce d'identité?; **it is a case of mistaken ~** il y a eu erreur sur la personne.

identity: **~ card** *n* carte *f* d'identité; **~ parade** *n* (GB) séance *f* d'identification.

ideological *adj* idéologique.

ideology *n* idéologie *f*.

idiom *n* **1** (phrase) idiome *m*; **2** (language) (of speakers) parler *m*; (of theatre, sport) langue *f*; (of music) style *m*.

idiomatic *adj* idiomatique.

idiosyncrasy *n* particularité *f*.

idiosyncratic *adj* particulier/-ière.

idiot *n* idiot/-e *m/f*.

idiotic *adj* bête.

idle I *adj* **1** (lazy) [*person*] paresseux/-euse, fainéant; **2** [*boast, threat*] vain; [*curiosity*] oiseux/-euse; [*chatter*] inutile; **3** (without occupation) [*person*] oisif/-ive; [*day, hour, moment*] de loisir; **4** [*port, dock, mine*] à l'arrêt; [*machine*] arrêté; **to lie** or **stand ~** [*machine, factory*] être à l'arrêt.
II *vi* [*engine*] tourner au ralenti.
■ **idle away**: **~ away [sth], ~ [sth] away** passer [qch] à ne rien faire [*day, time*].

idleness *n* (inaction) inactivité *f*; (laziness) paresse *f*.

idly *adv* **1** (lazily) paresseusement; **2** [*chat*] pour passer le temps.

idol *n* idole *f*.

idolize *vtr* adorer [*friend, parent*]; idolâtrer [*star*].

idyll *n* idylle *f*.

idyllic *adj* idyllique.

ie (*abbr* = **that is**) c-à-d.

if I *conj* **1** si; **~ you like** si tu veux; **~ it rains, we won't go** s'il pleut, nous n'irons pas; **~ I won a lot of money, I would travel** si je gagnais beaucoup d'argent, je voyagerais; **~ I had known, I would have told you** si j'avais su, je te l'aurais dit; **~ I were you, I...** (moi) à ta place, je...; **~ it were not for the baby** s'il n'y avait pas le bébé; **~ so** si c'est le cas; **~ not** sinon; **tomorrow, ~ not sooner** demain au plus tard, demain ou même avant; **~ you mention his name, she cries** il suffit de prononcer son nom pour qu'elle pleure; **I wonder ~ they will come** je me demande s'ils vont venir; **do you mind ~ I smoke?** cela vous dérange si je fume?; **~ you would**

follow me please si vous voulez bien me suivre; **what ~ he died?** et s'il mourait?; **what ~ I say no?** et si je dis non?; **2** (although) si; **we'll go even ~ it's dangerous** nous irons même si c'est dangereux; **it's a good shop, ~ a little expensive** c'est un bon magasin, bien qu'un peu cher.
II if only *phr* **~ only because (of)** ne serait-ce qu'à cause de; **~ only for a moment** ne serait-ce que pour un instant; **~ only I had known!** si (seulement) j'avais su!

igloo *n* igloo *m*, iglou *m*.

ignite I *vtr* faire exploser [*fuel*]; enflammer [*material*].
II *vi* [*petrol, gas*] s'enflammer; [*rubbish, timber*] prendre feu.

ignition *n* (Aut, Tech) **1** (system) allumage *m*; **2** (also **~ switch**) contact *m*.

ignorance *n* ignorance *f*; **to be in ~ of sth** ignorer qch.

ignorant *adj* (of a subject) ignorant; (uneducated) inculte; **to be ~ about** tout ignorer de [*subject*]; **to be ~ of** ignorer [*possibilities*].

ignore *vtr* ignorer [*person*]; ne pas relever [*mistake, remark*]; ne pas tenir compte de [*feeling, fact*]; ne pas respecter [*rule*]; ne pas suivre [*advice*]; se désintéresser complètement de [*problem*]; **to ~ sb's very existence** faire comme si qn n'existait pas.

ill I *n* mal *m*; **to wish sb ~** souhaiter du mal à qn; **economic ~s** les maux de l'économie.
II *adj* malade; **I feel ill** je ne me sens pas bien; **to be taken ~, to fall ~** tomber malade.
III *adv* **1 he is ~ suited to the post** il n'est guère fait pour ce poste; **to speak ~ of sb** dire du mal de qn; **2 it ~ becomes you to criticize** il ne vous sied guère de critiquer.

ill: **~-advised** *adj* malavisé; **~ at ease** *adj* gêné, mal à l'aise; **~ effect** *n* conséquence *f* néfaste.

illegal I *n* (US) immigrant/-e *m/f* clandestin/-e.
II *adj* (gen) illégal; [*parking*] illicite; [*immigrant*] clandestin; (Sport) irrégulier/-ière.

illegality *n* illégalité *f*.

illegible *adj* illisible.

illegitimate *adj* illégitime.

illicit *adj* illicite.

illiterate *n*, *adj* analphabète (*mf*).

illness ▶ 686 *n* maladie *f*.

illogical *adj* illogique.

illuminate *vtr* éclairer; (light for effect) illuminer; **~d** [*sign*] lumineux/-euse.

illumination *n* **1** (of building, sign) éclairage *m*; (for effect) illumination *f*; **2** (enlightenment) illumination *f*.

illusion *n* illusion *f*; **to have no ~s about sth** ne pas se faire d'illusions sur qch; **to be** or **to labour under the ~ that** s'imaginer que.

illusionist *n* illusionniste *mf*.

illusive, **illusory** *adj* (misleading) trompeur/-euse; (apparent) illusoire.

illustrate *vtr* illustrer; **~d** [*book, poem*] illustré; [*lecture*] avec support visuel.

illustration *n* illustration *f*.

illustrator ▶ 805 *n* illustrateur/-trice *m/f*.

ill will *n* rancune *f*.

image *n* (gen) image *f*; (of company, personality) image *f* de marque; **he is the (spitting) ~ of you** c'est toi tout craché.

imagery *n* images *fpl*.

imaginable *adj* imaginable; **the funniest thing ~** la chose la plus amusante qu'on puisse imaginer.

imaginary *adj* imaginaire.

imagination *n* imagination *f*; **to show ~** faire preuve d'imagination; **not by any stretch of the ~ could you say that...** même en faisant un grand effort d'imagination on ne pourrait pas dire que...

imaginative *adj* [*person, performance*] plein d'imagination; [*mind*] imaginatif/-ive; [*solution, device*] ingénieux/-ieuse.

imagine *vtr* **1** (visualize, picture) (s')imaginer; **to ~ being rich/king** s'imaginer riche/roi; **you must have ~d it** ce doit être un effet de ton imagination; **2** (suppose) supposer, imaginer (**that** que).

imbalance *n* déséquilibre *m*.

imbecile *n*, *adj* imbécile (*mf*).

IMF *n* (*abbr* = **International Monetary Fund**) FMI *m*.

imitate *vtr* imiter.

imitation I *n* **1** imitation *f*; **2** (fake) contrefaçon *f*.
II *adj* [*snow*] artificiel/-ielle; **~ fur** imitation *f* de fourrure; **~ jewel** faux bijou *m*; **~ leather** similicuir *m*.

imitator *n* imitateur/-trice *m/f*.

immaculate *adj* [*dress, manners*] impeccable; [*performance*] parfait.

immaterial *adj* **1** (unimportant) sans importance; **2** (intangible) immatériel/-ielle.

immature *adj* **1** [*plant*] qui n'est pas arrivé à maturité; **2** (childish) immature; **don't be so ~!** ne te conduis pas comme un enfant!

immaturity *n* (childishness) manque *m* de maturité.

immediacy *n* immédiateté *f*.

immediate *adj* **1** [*effect, reaction*] immédiat; [*thought*] premier/-ière (*before n*); **2** [*concern, goal*] premier/-ière (*before n*); [*problem, crisis*] urgent; **3** [*vicinity*] immédiat; **his ~ family** ses proches; **in the ~ future** dans l'avenir proche; **on my ~ left** juste à ma gauche.

immediately *adv* immédiatement; **~ after/before** juste avant/après.

immense *adj* immense.

immerse *vtr* plonger (**in** dans).

immigrant *n*, *adj* (recent) immigrant/-e (*m/f*); (established) immigré/-e (*m/f*).

immigrate *vi* immigrer (**to** à, en).

immigration *n* immigration *f*.

imminent *adj* imminent; **rain is ~** la pluie menace.

immobile *adj* immobile.

immobilize *vtr* paralyser [*traffic, organization*]; immobiliser [*engine, patient, limb*].

Illnesses, Aches, and Pains

Where does it hurt?

where does it hurt?	= où est-ce que ça vous fait mal?
his leg hurts	= sa jambe lui fait mal

(Do not confuse ***faire mal à qn*** with ***faire du mal à qn***, which means ***to harm sb.***)

he has a pain in his leg	= il a mal à la jambe

Note that with ***avoir mal à*** French uses the definite article (***le, la, les,*** or ***l'***) with the part of the body, where English has a possessive, hence:

***his head** was aching*	= il avait mal à **la tête**

Accidents

*she broke **her** leg*	= elle s'est cassé **la** jambe
*they burned **their** hands*	= ils se sont brûlé **les** mains

Chronic conditions

French often uses ***fragile*** (***weak***) to express a chronic condition:

*he has a **weak** heart*	= il a le cœur **fragile**

Note that French uses the definite article here.

Being ill

French mostly uses the definite article with the name of an illness:

to have flu / measles	= avoir **la** grippe / **la** rougeole

This applies to most infectious diseases. However, note the exceptions ending in ***-ite*** (eg ***une hépatite, une bronchite***) below.

When the illness affects a specific part of the body, French uses the indefinite article:

to have cancer / pneumonia	= avoir **un** cancer / **une** pneumonie
to have a stomach ulcer	= avoir **un** ulcère à l'estomac

Most English words in ***-itis*** (French ***-ite***) work like this:

to have bronchitis / hepatitis	= avoir **une** bronchite / **une** hépatite

When the illness is a generalized condition, French tends to use ***du, de la*** or ***des***:

to have rheumatism	= avoir **des** rhumatismes
to have asthma / arthritis	= avoir **de l'**asthme / **de l'**arthrite

One exception here is:

to have hay fever	= avoir le rhume des foins

When there is an adjective for such conditions, this is often preferred in French:

to have asthma / epilepsy	= être asthmatique / épileptique

Falling ill

The above guidelines on the use of the definite and indefinite articles in French hold good for talking about the onset of illnesses.

French has no general equivalent of ***to get***. However, where English can use ***catch***, French can use ***attraper***:

*to **catch** malaria*	= **attraper** la malaria
*to **catch** a cold / bronchitis*	= **attraper** un rhume / une bronchite

For attacks of chronic illnesses, French uses ***faire une crise de***:

to have an** asthma / epileptic **attack	= **faire une crise** d'asthme / d'épilepsie

Treatment

*to be treated **for** polio*	= se faire soigner **contre** la polio
*to take sth **for** hay fever*	= prendre qch **contre** le rhume des foins
*to be operated on **for** cancer*	= être opéré **d'**un cancer
*to operate on sb **for** appendicitis*	= opérer qn **de** l'appendicite

immoral *adj* immoral.
immortal *n, adj* immortel/-elle (*m/f*).
immortality *n* immortalité *f*.
immovable *adj* **1** (immobile) fixe; **2** (unchanging) [*opinion*] inébranlable; [*person*] immuable.
immune *adj* **1** (Med) [*person*] immunisé (**to** contre); [*reaction, system*] immunitaire; **2** (oblivious) **~ to** insensible à; **3 to be ~ from** être à l'abri de [*attack, arrest*]; être exempté de [*tax*].
immunity *n* **1** immunité *f* (**to, against** contre); **2** (to criticism) impassibilité *f* (**to** devant).
immunize *vtr* immuniser.
impact *n* **1** (effect) impact *m* (**on** sur); **to make an ~** faire de l'effet; **2** (violent contact) (of hammer, vehicle) choc *m*; (of bomb, bullet) impact *m*; **on ~** au moment de l'impact.
impair *vtr* affecter [*performance*]; diminuer [*ability*]; affaiblir [*hearing, vision*]; détériorer [*health*].
impaired *adj* [*hearing, vision*] affaibli; [*mobility*] réduit; **his speech is ~** il a des problèmes d'élocution.
impart *vtr* **1** transmettre [*knowledge, enthusiasm*] (**to** à); communiquer [*information*] (**to** à); **2** donner [*atmosphere*].
impartial *adj* [*advice, judge*] impartial; [*account*] objectif/-ive.
impassable *adj* [*obstacle*] infranchissable; [*road*] impraticable.
impasse *n* impasse *f*.
impassioned *adj* [*debate*] passionné; [*plea*] véhément.
impassive *adj* (expressionless) impassible; (unruffled) imperturbable.
impatience *n* **1** (eagerness) impatience *f* (**to do** de faire); **2** (irritation) agacement *m* (**with** à l'égard de; **at** devant); **my worst fault is ~** mon plus grand défaut est mon manque de patience.
impatient *adj* **1** (eager) [*person*] impatient; [*gesture, tone*] d'impatience; **to be ~ to do** être impatient or avoir hâte de faire; **2** (irritable) agacé (**at** par); **to be/get ~ with sb** s'impatienter contre qn.
impatiently *adv* [*wait*] impatiemment; [*say*] d'un ton agacé.
impeccable *adj* [*behaviour*] irréprochable; [*appearance*] impeccable.
impede *vtr* entraver.
impediment *n* (obstacle) obstacle *m* (**to** à).
impending *adj* imminent.
impenetrable *adj* impénétrable.
imperative **I** *n* impératif *m*.
II *adj* [*need*] urgent; [*tone*] impérieux/-ieuse.
imperceptible *adj* imperceptible.
imperfect **I** *n* imparfait *m*.
II *adj* [*goods*] défectueux/-euse; [*logic, knowledge*] imparfait; **the ~ tense** l'imparfait *m*.
imperfection *n* (in object, in person) défaut *m*; (state) imperfection *f*.
imperial *adj* **1** impérial; **2** (GB) [*measure*] conforme aux normes britanniques.
imperious *adj* impérieux/-ieuse.
impersonal *adj* impersonnel/-elle.
impersonate *vtr* (imitate) imiter; (pretend to be) se faire passer pour [*police officer*].
impersonator *n* imitateur/-trice *m/f*.
impertinent *adj* impertinent (**to** envers).
impervious *adj* **1** (to water, gas) imperméable (**to** à); **2** (to charm, suffering) indifférent (**to** à); (to demands) imperméable (**to** à).
impetuous *adj* [*person*] impétueux/-euse; [*action*] impulsif/-ive.
impetus *n* **1** impulsion *f*; **2** (momentum) élan *m*; **to gain/lose ~** prendre/perdre de l'élan.
impinge *vi* **to ~ on** (restrict) empiéter sur; (affect) affecter.
implacable *adj* implacable.
implant **I** *n* implant *m*.
II *vtr* implanter.
implement **I** *n* (gen) instrument *m*; (tool) outil *m*; **farm ~s** outillage *m* agricole.
II *vtr* **1** exécuter [*contract, idea*]; mettre [qch] en application [*law*]; **2** implanter [*software*]; implémenter [*system*].
implicate *vtr* impliquer (**in** dans).
implication *n* (possible consequence) implication *f*; (suggestion) insinuation *f*.
implicit *adj* **1** (implied) implicite (**in** dans); **2** [*faith, trust*] absolu.
implied *adj* implicite.
imply *vtr* **1** [*person*] (insinuate) insinuer (**that** que); (make known) laisser entendre (**that** que); **2** (mean) [*argument*] impliquer; [*term, word*] laisser supposer (**that** que).
impolite *adj* impoli (**to** envers).
import **I** *n* **1** (Econ) importation *f*; **2** (importance) importance *f*; **of no (great) ~** de peu d'importance.
II *vtr* importer (**from** de; **to** en).
importance *n* importance *f*; **it is of great ~ that** il est essentiel que (+ *subj*); **an event of great political ~** un événement d'une grande portée politique; **it is a matter of the utmost ~** c'est une question de la plus haute importance.
important *adj* important; **it is ~ that** il est important que (+ *subj*); **his children are very ~ to him** ses enfants comptent beaucoup pour lui; **he's an ~ social figure** c'est une personne en vue.
importer *n* importateur/-trice *m/f*.
impose **I** *vtr* imposer [*embargo, rule*] (**on sb** à qn; **on sth** sur qch); infliger [*sanction*] (**on** à); **to ~ a fine on sb** frapper qn d'une amende; **to ~ a tax on tobacco** imposer le tabac.
II *vi* s'imposer; **to ~ on sb's kindness** abuser de la bonté de qn.
imposing *adj* [*person*] imposant; [*sight*] impressionnant.
impossibility *n* impossibilité *f*.
impossible **I** *n* **the ~** l'impossible *m*.

II *adj* impossible; **to make it ~ for sb to do sth** mettre qn dans l'impossibilité de faire qch.

impotent *adj* impuissant.

impound *vtr* emmener [qch] à la fourrière [*vehicle*]; confisquer [*goods*].

impractical *adj* (unworkable) irréalisable; (unrealistic) peu réaliste; **to be ~** [*person*] manquer d'esprit pratique.

imprecise *adj* imprécis.

impress I *vtr* **1** impressionner [*person*] (**with** par; **by doing** en faisant); **to be easily ~ed** se laisser facilement impressionner; **they were (favourably) ~ed** ça leur a fait bonne impression; **2 to ~ sth (up)on sb** faire bien comprendre qch à qn.
II *vi* faire bonne impression.

impression *n* impression *f*; **to be under** or **have the ~ that** avoir l'impression que; **to make a good/bad ~** faire bonne/mauvaise impression (**on** sur); **an artist's ~ of the building** le bâtiment vu par un artiste.

impressionable *adj* [*child, mind*] influençable.

impressionistic *adj* impressionniste.

impressive *adj* [*achievement, display, result*] impressionnant; [*building, sight*] imposant; **she is very ~** elle en impose.

imprint I *n* empreinte *f*.
II *vtr* **1** (fix) graver (**on** dans); **2** (print) imprimer (**on** sur).

imprison *vtr* emprisonner.

improbability *n* improbabilité *f*; (of something being true) invraisemblance *f*.

improbable *adj* improbable; (unlikely to be true) invraisemblable.

impromptu *n, adj* impromptu (*m*).

improper *adj* (unseemly) malséant; (dishonest) irrégulier/-ière; (indecent) indécent; (incorrect) impropre, abusif/-ive.

improve I *vtr* **1** améliorer; **to ~ one's Italian** se perfectionner en italien; **the new arrangements did not ~ matters** les nouveaux accords n'ont pas arrangé les choses; **to ~ one's mind** se cultiver (l'esprit); **2** augmenter [*wages, chances*]; accroître [*productivity*].
II *vi* **1** s'améliorer; **2 to ~ on** améliorer [*score*]; renchérir sur [*offer*]; **3** [*productivity*] augmenter.

improvement *n* **1** (change for the better) amélioration *f* (**in, of, to** de); **an ~ on last year's performance** une amélioration par rapport aux résultats de l'an dernier; **the new edition is an ~ on the old one** la nouvelle édition est bien meilleure que l'ancienne; **2** (progress) progrès *mpl*; **there is room for ~** on pourrait encore faire mieux; **3** (alteration) aménagement *m*; **home ~s** aménagements *mpl* du domicile.

improvisation *n* improvisation *f*.

improvise I *vtr* improviser; **an ~d table** une table de fortune.
II *vi* improviser.

impudent *adj* insolent, impudent.

impulse *n* impulsion *f*; **to have a sudden ~ to do** avoir une envie soudaine de faire; **on (an) ~** sur un coup de tête; **a generous ~** un élan de générosité.

impulsion *n* envie *f* irrésistible.

impulsive *adj* (spontaneous) spontané; (rash) impulsif/-ive.

impure *adj* impur.

in

■ **Note** For translations of *in* with geographical place names (*in Europe, in Greece, in Rome*), see the usage note for ***Countries, Cities, and Continents*** ▶ 574.

I *prep* **1** (inside) dans; **~ the box** dans la boîte; **~ the newspaper** dans le journal; **~ the school/town** dans l'école/la ville; **~ school/town** à l'école/en ville; **~ the country(side)** à la campagne; **there are seven days ~ a week** il y a sept jours dans la semaine; **there's something ~ it** il y a quelque chose dedans or à l'intérieur; **there's something ~ what he says** il y a du vrai dans ce qu'il dit; **~ the photo** sur la photo; **chicken ~ a white wine sauce** du poulet à la sauce au vin blanc; ▶ **bath**; **2** (showing occupation, activity) dans; **~ insurance** dans les assurances; **to be ~ politics** faire de la politique; **to be ~ the team** faire partie de l'équipe; **3** (present in) chez; **symbolism ~ Mallarmé** le symbolisme chez Mallarmé; **it's rare ~ cats** c'est rare chez les chats; **he hasn't got it ~ him to succeed** il n'est pas fait pour réussir; **4** (showing manner, medium) en; **~ Greek** en grec; **~ B flat** en si bémol; **~ a skirt** en jupe; **dressed ~ black** habillé en noir; **~ pencil/ink** au crayon/à l'encre; **to speak ~ a whisper** chuchoter; **available ~ several colours** disponible en plusieurs couleurs; **~ that size we only have it ~ blue** dans cette taille nous ne l'avons qu'en bleu; **~ pairs** par deux; **~ a circle** en cercle; **~ the rain** sous la pluie; **5** (as regards) **rich ~ minerals** riche en minéraux; **deaf ~ one ear** sourd d'une oreille; **10 cm ~ length** 10 cm de long; **6** (because of) dans; **~ his hurry** dans sa précipitation; **~ the confusion** dans la mêlée; **7** (with reflexive pronoun) **it's no bad thing ~ itself** ce n'est pas une mauvaise chose en soi; **how do you feel ~ yourself?** est-ce que tu as le moral?; **8** (with present participle) en; **~ accepting** en acceptant; **~ doing so** en faisant cela; **9** (with superlatives) de; **the tallest tower ~ the world** la plus grande tour du monde; **10** (in ratios) **a gradient of 1 ~ 4** une pente de 25%; **a tax of 20 pence ~ the pound** une taxe de 20 pence par livre sterling; **to have a one ~ five chance** avoir une chance sur cinq; **11** (with numbers) **she's ~ her twenties** elle a entre vingt et trente ans; **they came ~ their thousands** ils sont venus par milliers; **to cut sth ~ three** couper qch en trois; **the temperature was ~ the thirties** il faisait dans les trente degrés; **12** (during) **~ May** en mai; **~ 1963** en 1963; **~ the night** pendant la nuit; **~ the morning(s)** le matin; **at four ~ the morning** à quatre heures du matin; **~ the twenties** dans les années 20; **13** (within) **to do sth ~ ten minutes** faire qch en dix minutes; **I'll be back ~ half an hour** je serai de retour dans une demi-heure; **14** (for) depuis; **it hasn't rained ~ weeks** il n'a pas plu depuis des semaines, ça fait des semaines qu'il n'a pas plu.

II *adv* **1** (indoors) **to come ~** entrer; **to run ~** entrer en courant; **to ask** or **invite sb ~** faire entrer qn; **2** (at home) **to be ~** être là; **to be ~ by midnight** être rentré avant minuit; ▶ **keep, stay**; **3** (in prison, in hospital) **he's ~ for murder** il a été emprisonné pour meurtre; **she's ~ for a biopsy** elle est entrée à l'hôpital pour une biopsie; **4** (arrived) **the train is ~** le train est en gare; **the ferry is ~** le ferry est à quai; **the sea** or **tide is ~** c'est marée haute; ▶ **come, get**; **5** (Sport) **the ball is ~** la balle est bonne; **6** (gathered) **the harvest is ~** la moisson est rentrée; **7** (in supply) **we don't have any ~** nous n'en avons pas en stock; **we've got some new titles ~** on a reçu quelques nouveaux titres; **to get some beer ~** aller chercher de la bière; **8** (submitted) **applications must be ~ by the 23rd** les candidatures doivent être déposées avant le 23; **the homework has to be ~ tomorrow** le devoir doit être rendu demain.

III○ *adj* **to be ~, to be the ~ thing** être à la mode.

IV **in and out** *phr* **to come ~ and out** entrer et sortir; **to weave ~ and out of** se faufiler entre [*traffic, tables*].

V **in that** *phr* dans la mesure où.

IDIOMS **to have it ~ for sb**○ avoir qn dans le collimateur○; **he's ~ for a shock/surprise** il va avoir un choc/être surpris.

inability *n* (to drive, pay) incapacité *f* (**to do** de faire); (to help) impuissance *f* (**to do** à faire).

inaccessible *adj* (out of reach) inaccessible; (hard to understand) peu accessible (**to** à).

inaccurate *adj* inexact.

inactivity *n* inactivité *f*.

inadequate *adj* [*funding, measures, knowledge*] insuffisant (**for** pour); [*system, facilities*] inadéquat; **to feel ~** être complexé.

inadvisable *adj* inopportun, à déconseiller.

inane *adj* [*person, conversation*] idiot; [*programme*] débile○.

inanimate *adj* inanimé.

inappropriate *adj* **1** [*behaviour*] inconvenant, peu convenable; [*remark*] inopportun; **2** [*advice, word*] qui n'est pas approprié.

inarticulate *adj* **1 to be ~** ne pas savoir s'exprimer; **2** [*mumble*] inarticulé; [*speech*] inintelligible.

inasmuch: **inasmuch as** *phr* (insofar as) dans la mesure où; (seeing as) vu que.

inaudible *adj* [*sound*] inaudible; **he was almost ~** on l'entendait à peine.

inaugurate *vtr* inaugurer [*exhibition*]; investir [qn] de ses fonctions [*president, official*].

inauguration *n* (of exhibition) inauguration *f*; (of president) investiture *f*.

in-between *adj* intermédiaire.

inbuilt *adj* intrinsèque.

incapability *n* incapacité *f* (**to do** de faire).

incapable *adj* incapable (**of doing** de faire).

incapacitate *vtr* [*accident, illness*] immobiliser.

incense *n* encens *m*.

incensed *adj* outré (**at** de; **by** par).

incentive *n* **1 to give sb the ~ to do** donner envie à qn de faire; **there is no ~ for people to save** rien n'incite les gens à faire des économies; **2** (**cash**) **~** prime *f*.

incessant *adj* incessant.

incessantly *adv* sans cesse.

incest *n* inceste *m*.

incestuous *adj* incestueux/-euse.

inch ▶ 738 *n* **1** pouce *m* (= *2,54 cm*); **2 ~ by ~** petit à petit; **to come within an ~ of winning** passer à deux doigts de la victoire; **she won't give** or **budge an ~** elle ne veut pas bouger d'un pouce.

incident *n* incident *m*.

incidental *adj* [*detail, remark*] secondaire; [*error*] mineur; **to be ~ to** accompagner [*activity, job*].

incidentally *adv* (by the way) à propos; (by chance) par la même occasion.

incinerate *vtr* incinérer.

incite *vtr* **to ~ violence** inciter à la violence; **to ~ sb to do** pousser or inciter qn à faire.

incl I *adj* (*written abbr* = **inclusive**) TTC; **£110 ~** 110 livres sterling TTC.

II *prep* (*written abbr* = **including**) compris; **£20,000 ~ bonuses** 20 000 livres, primes comprises.

inclination *n* tendance *f*, inclination *f*; (**to, towards** à); **by ~** par nature.

incline I *vtr* **1** incliner [*head*]; **2 to be ~d to do** avoir tendance à faire; **if you feel so ~d** si l'envie vous en prend.

II *vi* **1** (tend) **to ~ to** or **towards** tendre vers; **2** (lean) s'incliner.

include *vtr* inclure, comprendre; **all the ministers, Blanc ~d** tous les ministres, Blanc inclu; **breakfast is ~d in the price** le petit déjeuner est compris; **your duties ~ answering the phone** répondre au téléphone fait partie de vos fonctions.

including *prep* (y) compris; **£50 ~ VAT** 50 livres sterling TVA comprise; **~ service** service compris; **~ July** y compris juillet; **not ~ July** sans compter juillet; **up to and ~ Monday** jusqu'à lundi inclus.

inclusive *adj* [*charge*] inclus; [*price*] forfaitaire; **those aged 17–24 ~** les personnes âgées de 17 à 24 ans inclus; **£50 all-~** 50 livres sterling tout compris; **all-~ holiday** séjour tout compris.

incognito I *adj* **to be/remain ~** rester dans/garder l'incognito.

II *adv* [*travel*] incognito.

incoherent *adj* incohérent.

income *n* revenus *mpl*, revenu *m*.

income tax *n* impôt *m* sur le revenu.

incomparable *adj* sans pareil/-eille.

incompatible *adj* [*person, computer, drug*] incompatible; [*idea, activity*] inconciliable.

incompetent I *n* incapable *mf*.
II *adj* [*doctor, government*] incompétent; [*work, performance*] mauvais.

incomplete *adj* **1** [*work, building*] inachevé; **2** [*set*] incomplet/-ète.

incomprehensible *adj* [*reason*] incompréhensible; [*speech*] inintelligible.

inconceivable *adj* inconcevable.

incongruous *adj* [*sight*] déconcertant; [*appearance*] surprenant.

inconsiderate *adj* [*person*] peu attentif/-ive à autrui; [*remark*] maladroit; **to be ~ towards sb** manquer d'égards envers qn.

inconsistency *n* incohérence *f*.

inconsistent *adj* [*work*] inégal; [*behaviour*] changeant; [*argument*] incohérent; [*attitude*] inconsistant.

inconspicuous *adj* [*person*] qui passe inaperçu, qui ne se fait pas remarquer; [*place, clothing*] discret/-ète.

incontinent *adj* incontinent.

inconvenience I *n* **1** (trouble) dérangement *m*; **to put sb to great ~** causer beaucoup de dérangement à qn; **2** (disadvantage) inconvénient *m*.
II *vtr* déranger.

inconvenient *adj* [*location, arrangement, device*] incommode; [*time*] inopportun; **if it's not ~** si cela ne vous/les etc dérange pas.

incorporate *vtr* **1** (make part of) incorporer (**into** dans); **2** (contain) comporter; **3 Smith and Brown Incorporated** Smith et Brown SA.

incorrect *adj* incorrect (**to do** de faire).

incorrigible *adj* incorrigible.

increase I *n* **1** (in amount) augmentation *f* (**in, of** de); **price ~** augmentation de prix; **a 5% ~** une augmentation de 5%; **2** (in degree) accroissement *m*; **to be on the ~** être en progression.
II *vtr* augmenter (**by** de; **to** jusqu'à); **I ~d my offer to $100** je suis monté à 100 dollars.
III *vi* [*output, sales, volume*] augmenter (**by** de); [*appetite*] grandir; [*workload*] s'accroître; [*wind*] redoubler; **to ~ in number/value** augmenter en nombre/valeur; **to ~ in volume** augmenter de volume; **to ~ in size** s'agrandir.
IV **increasing** *pres p adj* [*number*] croissant.
V **increased** *pp adj* [*demand, risk*] accru; [*attacks*] plus fréquent.

increasingly *adv* de plus en plus.

incredible *adj* incroyable.

incredibly *adv* (astonishingly) incroyablement; (extremely) extrêmement.

incredulous *adj* incrédule.

incriminate *vtr* incriminer; **to ~ sb in** impliquer qn dans [*crime, activity*].

incriminating *adj* [*statement, document*] compromettant; [*evidence*] incriminant.

incubator *n* (for child) couveuse *f*; (for eggs, bacteria) incubateur *m*.

incumbent I *n* (person in post) personne *f* exerçant une charge; (minister) ministre *m*.
II *adj* **1 to be ~ on** or **upon sb to do** incomber à qn de faire; **2** (in office) en exercice.

incur *vtr* contracter [*debts*]; subir [*loss*]; encourir [*expense, risk, wrath*].

incurable *adj* [*disease*] incurable; [*optimist, romantic*] incorrigible.

incursion *n* (gen) intrusion *f*; (Mil) incursion *f*.

indebted *adj* **to be ~ to sb** (under an obligation) être redevable à qn; (grateful) être reconnaissant à qn.

indecent *adj* **1** (sexually) indécent; **2** (unseemly) malséant.

indecent: **~ assault** *n* attentat *m* à la pudeur (**on** contre); **~ exposure** *n* outrage *m* public à la pudeur.

indecision *n* indécision *f* (**about** quant à).

indecisive *adj* [*person, reply, result*] indécis (**about** quant à); [*battle, election*] peu concluant.

indeed *adv* **1** (certainly) en effet, effectivement; **'~ I am!'** 'bien sûr que oui!'; **'~ you can'** 'bien sûr que oui'; **2** (in fact) en fait; **she is polite, ~ charming** elle est polie et même charmante; **if ~ that is what consumers want** si c'est vraiment ce que veulent les consommateurs; **3** (for emphasis) vraiment; **that was praise ~** c'était vraiment un compliment; **thank you very much ~** merci mille fois.

indefinite *adj* **1** (vague) vague; **2** [*period, delay*] illimité; [*number*] indéterminé; [*ban*] pour une durée indéterminée; **3 the ~ article** l'article *m* indéfini.

indefinitely *adv* [*continue, stay*] indéfiniment; [*postpone, ban*] pour une durée indéterminée.

indelible *adj* [*ink, mark*] indélébile; [*impression*] ineffaçable.

indelicate *adj* (tactless) indélicat; (coarse) grossier/-ière.

indemnity *n* **1** (protection) assurance *f*; **2** (payment) indemnité *f*; **3** (exemption) décharge *f*.

independence *n* indépendance *f*.

Independence Day *n* (US) fête *f* de l'Indépendance.

independent *adj* indépendant; **~ means, an ~ income** des revenus personnels.

in-depth I *adj* [*analysis, study, knowledge*] approfondi, détaillé; [*guide*] détaillé; [*interview*] en profondeur.
II **in depth** *phr* [*examine, study*] en détail.

indescribable *adj* [*chaos, noise, smell*] indescriptible; [*pleasure, beauty*] inexprimable.

indestructible *adj* indestructible.

index I *n* **1** (of book) index *m inv*; **thumb ~** index à onglets; **2** (catalogue) catalogue *m*; **card ~** fichier *m*; **3** (Econ) indice *m*; **cost-of-living ~** (GB), **consumer price ~** (US) indice des prix à la consommation; **share ~, stock ~** indice boursier.
II *vtr* **1** munir [qch] d'un index [*book*]; indexer [*word*]; **2** (catalogue) classer, cataloguer (**under** sous, à); **3** (Econ) indexer (**to** sur).

index: **~ card** *n* fiche *f*; **~ finger** *n* index *m inv*; **~-linked** *adj* indexé.

India ▶574 *pr n* Inde *f*.

Indian ▶712 I *n* **1** (from India) Indien/-ienne *m/f*; **2** (Native American) Indien/-ienne *m/f* d'Amérique.
II *adj* **1** (of India) [*people, culture*] indien/-ienne; [*ambassador, embassy*] de l'Inde; [*Empire*] des Indes; **2** (Native American) indien/-ienne, amérindien/-ienne.

Indian Ocean *pr n* **the ~** l'océan *m* Indien.

Indian summer *n* été *m* de la Saint Martin.

indicate I *vtr* indiquer (**that** que; **with** de).
II *vi* [*driver*] mettre son clignotant; [*cyclist*] faire signe.

indication *n* indication *f*, indice *m*; **to be an ~ of** indiquer; **it is an ~ that** c'est signe que; **to give no ~ that** [*person*] ne pas laisser entrevoir que; **all the ~s are that** tout porte à croire que.

indicative I *n* indicatif *m*; **in the ~** à l'indicatif.
II *adj* **1 to be ~ of** montrer; **2** (in grammar) indicatif/-ive.

indicator *n* **1** (pointer) aiguille *f*; (in chemistry) indicateur *m*; **2** (board) tableau *m*; **arrivals ~** tableau des arrivées; **3** (on car) clignotant *m*.

indict *vtr* inculper.

indictment *n* **1** (Law) acte *m* d'accusation; **under ~ for murder** inculpé/-e de meurtre; **2** (criticism) mise *f* en accusation.

indifference *n* indifférence *f* (**to, towards** envers).

indifferent *adj* **1** (uninterested) indifférent (**to, as to** à); (to charms) insensible (**to** à); **2** (mediocre) médiocre.

indigenous *adj* indigène (**to** à).

indigestion *n* indigestion *f*; **to have ~** avoir des brûlures d'estomac.

indignant *adj* indigné (**at** de; **about, over** par); **to become** or **get ~** s'indigner (**at, about** de).

indignity *n* indignité *f*.

indigo ▶559 *n, adj* indigo (*m*) *inv*.

indirect *adj* indirect.

indirectly *adv* indirectement.

indiscreet *adj* indiscret/-ète.

indiscriminate *adj* (general) sans distinction; (not fussy) sans discernement.

indispensable *adj* indispensable.

indisputable *adj* [*champion*] indiscuté; [*fact*] indiscutable.

indistinct *adj* [*sound, markings*] indistinct; [*memory*] confus; [*photograph*] flou.

individual I *n* individu *m*.
II *adj* **1** [*effort, freedom, portion*] individuel/-elle; [*comfort, attitude*] personnel/-elle; [*tuition*] particulier/-ière; **2** (separately) **each ~ article** chaque article (individuellement); **3** (idiosyncratic) particulier/-ière.

individuality *n* individualité *f*.

individually *adv* (personally, in person) individuellement; (one at a time) séparément.

indivisible *adj* indivisible; **~ from** inséparable de.

indoctrinate *vtr* endoctriner.

indoctrination *n* endoctrinement *m*.

indoor *adj* [*pool, court*] couvert; [*lavatory*] à l'intérieur; [*photography, shoes*] d'intérieur.

indoors *adv* à l'intérieur, dans la maison; **~ and outdoors** dedans et dehors; **to go ~** rentrer.

induce *vtr* **1** (persuade) persuader (**to do** de faire); (stronger) inciter (**to** à; **to do** à faire); **2** (bring about) provoquer [*emotion, response*]; **drug-/stress-~d** provoqué par la drogue/le stress; **to ~ labour** provoquer l'accouchement.

inducement *n* **1** (reward) récompense *f*; (bribe) pot-de-vin *m*; **2** (incentive) motivation *f* (**to do** pour faire).

indulge I *vtr* **1** céder à [*whim, desire*]; **2** gâter [*child*]; céder à [*adult*].
II *vi* se laisser tenter; (drink) boire de l'alcool; **to ~ in** se livrer à [*speculation*]; se complaire dans [*nostalgia*]; se laisser tenter par [*food*].
III *v refl* **to ~ oneself** se faire plaisir.

indulgence *n* **1** (tolerance) indulgence *f* (**towards** envers; **for** pour); **2 ~ in food** gourmandise *f*; **it's my one ~** c'est mon péché mignon.

indulgent *adj* indulgent (**to, towards** pour, envers).

industrial *adj* [*city, area, sector, park, machinery*] industriel/-ielle; [*accident*] du travail; [*tool*] à usage industriel; [*worker*] de l'industrie.

industrialize *vtr* industrialiser.

industrious *adj* diligent.

industry *n* **1** industrie *f*; **the oil ~** l'industrie du pétrole; **2** (diligence) zèle *m* (au travail).

inebriated *adj* ivre.

inedible *adj* [*meal*] immangeable; [*plants*] non comestible.

ineffective *adj* inefficace.

ineffectual *adj* [*person*] incapable; [*policy*] inefficace; [*attempt*] infructueux/-euse; [*gesture*] sans effet.

inefficiency *n* (lack of organization) manque *m* d'organisation; (incompetence) incompétence *f*; (of machine, method) inefficacité *f*.

inefficient *adj* (disorganized) mal organisé; (incompetent) incompétent; (not effective) inefficace.

ineligible *adj* **to be ~** (for job) ne pas remplir les conditions pour poser sa candidature (**for** à); (for election) être inéligible; (for pension, benefit) ne pas avoir droit (**for** à).

inept *adj* incompétent.

inequality *n* inégalité *f*.

inert *adj* inerte; **~ gas** gaz *m* rare.

inertia *n* inertie *f*.

inevitable *adj* inévitable (**that** que + *subj*).

inevitably *adv* inévitablement.

inexact *adj* inexact.

inexcusable *adj* inexcusable (**that** que + *subj*).

inexpensive *adj* pas cher.

inexperience *n* inexpérience *f*.

inexperienced *adj* inexpérimenté.

inexplicable *adj* inexplicable.

infallible *adj* infaillible.

infamous *adj* [*person*] tristement célèbre; [*crime*] infâme.
infancy *n* **1** petite enfance *f*; **2** (figurative) débuts *mpl*; **in its ~** à ses débuts.
infant *n* (baby) bébé *m*; (child) petit/-e enfant *m/f*.
infantry *n* infanterie *f*, fantassins *mpl*.
infant school *n* ≈ école *f* maternelle.
infatuate *vtr* **~d with** entiché de; **to become ~d with** s'éprendre de [*person*]; s'engouer de or pour [*idea, object*].
infatuation *n* engouement *m* (**with** pour).
infect *vtr* contaminer [*person, blood, food*]; infecter [*wound*].
infection *n* infection *f*; **to be exposed to ~** [*person*] être exposé à la contagion.
infectious *adj* **1** [*disease*] infectieux/-ieuse; [*person*] contagieux/-ieuse; **2** [*laughter*] communicatif/-ive.
infer *vtr* déduire.
inferior I *n* inférieur/-e *m/f*.
II *adj* **1** [*goods, work*] de qualité inférieure; **2** [*position*] inférieur; **to make sb feel ~** donner un sentiment d'infériorité à qn.
inferiority *n* infériorité *f* (**to** vis-à-vis de); **~ complex** complexe *m* d'infériorité.
inferno *n* **1** (raging fire) brasier *m*; **2** (hell) enfer *m*.
infertile *adj* [*land*] infertile, stérile; [*person*] stérile.
infest *vtr* infester (**with** de).
infidelity *n* infidélité *f*.
infighting *n* conflits *mpl* internes.
infiltrate *vtr* infiltrer [*organization, group*].
infinite *adj* infini.
infinitely *adv* infiniment.
infinitesimal *adj* infinitésimal.
infinitive *n* infinitif *m*; **in the ~** à l'infinitif.
infinity *n* infini *m*; **to ~** à l'infini.
infirmary *n* hôpital *m*; (in school, prison) infirmerie *f*.
inflame *vtr* **1** enflammer [*imagination, crowd*]; exacerber [*passion*]; aggraver [*situation*]; **2** (Med) irriter.
inflammable *adj* inflammable.
inflammation *n* inflammation *f*.
inflatable *adj* [*mattress, dinghy*] pneumatique; [*toy*] gonflable.
inflate I *vtr* gonfler [*mattress, dinghy*].
II *vi* [*mattress, dinghy*] se gonfler.
inflation *n* inflation *f*.
inflexible *adj* **1** [*person, attitude, will*] inflexible; [*system*] rigide; **2** [*material*] rigide.
inflict *vtr* infliger [*pain, presence, defeat*] (**on** à); causer [*damage*] (**on** à); **to ~ a wound on sb** blesser qn.
in-flight *adj* en vol.
influence I *n* influence *f*; **to be** or **have an ~ on** avoir une influence sur; **to drive while under the ~ of alcohol** conduire en état d'ébriété.
II *vtr* influencer [*person*] (**in** dans); influer sur [*decision, choice, result*]; **to be ~d by sb/sth** se laisser influencer par qn/qch.
influential *adj* [*person, newspaper, work*] influent; **he's ~** il a de l'influence; **~ friends** des amis importants or en place; **to be ~ on** [*factor*] influer sur [*decision*].
influenza ▶ 686 *n* grippe *f*.
influx *n* **1** (of people, money) afflux *m*; **2** (of liquid) arrivée *f*.
info° *n* renseignements *mpl*, tuyaux° *mpl*.
inform I *vtr* informer, avertir (**of, about** de; **that** du fait que); **to keep sb ~ed** tenir qn informé or au courant (**of, as to** de).
II *vi* **to ~ on** or **against** dénoncer.
informal *adj* **1** [*person*] sans façons; [*manner, style*] simple; **2** [*language*] familier/-ière; **~ clothes** vêtements *mpl* de tous les jours; **3** [*mood*] décontracté; [*group*] informel/-elle; **4** [*announcement*] officieux/-ieuse; [*visit*] privé; [*invitation*] verbal; [*discussion, interview*] informel/-elle.
informally *adv* **1** [*dress*] en tenue décontractée; [*dine*] en toute simplicité; **2** [*act, discuss*] officieusement.
information *n* **1** renseignements *mpl*, informations *fpl* (**on, about** sur); **a piece of ~** un renseignement, une information; **2** (US) (service *m* des) renseignements *mpl*.
information: **~ desk**, **information office** *n* bureau *m* des renseignements; **~ technology**, **IT** *n* informatique *f*.
informative *adj* [*lecture, book, day*] instructif/-ive; [*guide*] savant.
informer *n* indicateur/-trice *m/f*.
infrared *adj* infrarouge.
infrastructure *n* infrastructure *f*.
infringe I *vtr* enfreindre [*rule*]; ne pas respecter [*rights*].
II *vi* **to ~ on** or **upon** empiéter sur [*rights*].
infringement *n* (of rule) infraction *f* (**of** à); (of rights) violation *f*.
infuriating *adj* exaspérant.
ingenious *adj* ingénieux/-ieuse, astucieux/-ieuse.
ingenuity *n* ingéniosité *f*.
ingenuous *adj* ingénu, candide.
ingot *n* lingot *m*.
ingrained *adj* [*dirt*] bien incrusté; [*habit, hatred*] enraciné.
ingratiate *v refl* **to ~ oneself** se faire bien voir (**with** de).
ingratitude *n* ingratitude *f*.
ingredient *n* (Culin) ingrédient *m*; (figurative) élément *m* (**of** de).
ingrowing toenail, **ingrown toenail** *n* ongle *m* de pied incarné.
inhabit *vtr* **1** habiter [*house, region, planet*]; **2** vivre dans [*fantasy world*].
inhabitant *n* habitant/-e *m/f*.
inhale I *vtr* aspirer, inhaler [*fumes*]; avaler [*smoke*]; humer, respirer [*scent*].
II *vi* (breathe in) inspirer; (smoke) avaler la fumée.

inhaler *n* inhalateur *m*.
inherent *adj* **~ in** inhérent or propre à.
inherit *vtr* hériter de [*money, property, title*]; **to ~ sth from sb** hériter qch de qn.
inheritance *n* **1** héritage *m*; **to come into an ~** faire un héritage; **2** (succession) succession *f*; **by** or **through ~** par voie de succession.
inheritance tax *n* (US) droits *mpl* de succession.
inhibit *vtr* inhiber [*person, reaction*]; entraver [*activity, progress*].
inhibited *adj* inhibé, refoulé; **~ by** handicapé par.
inhibition *n* inhibition *f*.
inhospitable *adj* inhospitalier/-ière.
in-house *adj* interne.
inhuman *adj* inhumain.
inhumanity *n* inhumanité *f* (**to** envers).
initial I *n* initiale *f*.
II *adj* initial; **~ letter** initiale *f*; **in the ~ stages** au début.
III *vtr* parapher, parafer.
initially *adv* au départ.
initiate I *n* initié/-e *m/f*.
II *vtr* **1** mettre en œuvre [*project, reform*]; amorcer [*talks*]; entamer, engager [*proceedings*]; **2 to ~ sb into** admettre qn au sein de [*secret society*]; initier qn à [*astrology*].
initiation *n* **1** (into sect) admission *f* (**into** au sein de); (into knowledge) initiation *f* (**into** à); **2 ~ (ceremony)** cérémonie *f* d'initiation.
initiative *n* initiative *f*; **to have** or **show ~** faire preuve d'initiative; **on one's own ~** de son propre chef.
inject *vtr* injecter [*vaccine*] (**into** dans); **to ~ sb (with sth)** faire une injection or une piqûre (de qch) à qn.
injection *n* **1** (Med) piqûre *f*; **2** (Tech) injection *f*.
injure *vtr* **1** blesser [*person*]; **to ~ one's hand** se blesser la main; **2** nuire à, compromettre [*health, reputation*].
injured I *n* **the ~** les blessés *mpl*.
II *adj* **1** (gen) blessé; **2** (Law) **the ~ party** la partie lésée.
injury *n* blessure *f*; **head injuries** blessures à la tête.
injury time *n* (Sport) arrêts *mpl* de jeu.
injustice *n* injustice *f*.
ink *n* encre *f*; **in ~** à l'encre.
inkling *n* petite idée *f*; **to have an ~ that** avoir idée que.
inland I *adj* intérieur.
II *adv* [*travel, lie*] à l'intérieur des terres.
Inland Revenue *n* (GB) service *m* des impôts britannique.
in-laws *n pl* (parents) beaux-parents *mpl*; (other relatives) belle-famille *f*, parents *mpl* par alliance.
inmate *n* (of mental hospital) interné/-e *m/f*; (of prison) détenu/-e *m/f*.
inn *n* **1** (hotel) (small) auberge *f*; (larger) hôtellerie *f*; **2** (pub) pub *m*.
inner *adj* intérieur.
inner ear *n* oreille *f* interne.
innermost *adj* **sb's ~ thoughts** les pensées les plus intimes de qn.
innocence *n* innocence *f*.
innocent I *n* innocent/-e *m/f*.
II *adj* innocent.
innovation *n* innovation *f*.
innovative *adj* innovateur/-trice.
innuendo *n* (veiled slights) insinuations *fpl*; (sexual references) allusions *fpl* grivoises.
inoculation *n* vaccination *f*, inoculation *f*.
inoffensive *adj* inoffensif/-ive.
in-patient *n* malade *mf* hospitalisé/-e.
input *n* **1** (of money) apport *m*; (of energy) alimentation *f* (**of** en); **2** (contribution) contribution *f*; **3** (Comput) (data) données *fpl* d'entrée or à traiter.
inquest *n* enquête *f* (**on, into** sur); **to hold an ~** mener or conduire une enquête.
inquire = **enquire**.
inquiry *n* enquête *f* (**into** sur); **murder ~** enquête criminelle; ▶ **enquiry**.
inquisitive *adj* curieux/-ieuse.
insane *adj* (gen) fou/folle; (Law) aliéné; **to go ~** perdre la raison.
insanity *n* (gen) folie *f*; (Law) aliénation *f* mentale.
insatiable *adj* insatiable.
inscription *n* inscription *f*.
insect *n* insecte *m*; **~ bite** piqûre *f* d'insecte
insecticide *n, adj* insecticide (*m*).
insect repellent *n* insectifuge *m*, produit *m* anti-insecte.
insecure *adj* **1** [*person*] qui manque d'assurance; **to be ~** manquer d'assurance; **2** [*job*] précaire; [*investment*] risqué.
insecurity *n* **1** (psychological) manque *m* d'assurance; **2** (of position, situation) insécurité *f*; (of income) précarité *f*.
insensitive *adj* [*person*] (tactless) sans tact; (unfeeling) insensible (**to** à); [*remark*] indélicat.
insensitivity *n* insensibilité *f* (**to** à).
inseparable *adj* inséparable (**from** de).
insert *vtr* insérer (**in** dans).
inside I *n* intérieur *m*; **to be on the ~** [*runner*] être dans le couloir intérieur or à la corde; [*horse*] tenir la corde; **to overtake on the ~** (in Europe, US) doubler à droite; (in GB, Australia) doubler à gauche; **people on the ~** les gens qui sont dans la place.
II *prep* (also US **~ of**) **1** à l'intérieur de; **~ the box** à l'intérieur de or dans la boîte; **to be ~ (the house)** être à l'intérieur (de la maison); **2** (under) **~ (of) an hour** en moins d'une heure; **to be ~ the world record** battre le record mondial; **~ the permitted time** dans les limites du temps imparti.
III *adj* **1** [*cover, pocket*] intérieur; [*toilet*] à l'intérieur; **2** [*information*] de première main; **the ~ story** la vérité; **an ~ source** un informateur dans la place; **an ~ job** un coup monté de l'intérieur or par quelqu'un de la maison; **3 the ~ lane** (of road) (in Europe, US)

la voie de droite; (in GB, Australia) la voie de gauche; (of athletics track) le couloir intérieur.
IV *adv* (indoors) à l'intérieur; (in a container) à l'intérieur, dedans; **she's ~** elle est à l'intérieur; **to look ~** regarder à l'intérieur or dedans; **to go** or **come** or **step ~** entrer; **to bring sth ~** rentrer [*chairs*].
V inside out *phr* à l'envers; **to turn sth ~ out** retourner qch; **to know sb/sth ~ out** connaître qn/qch à fond.

inside: **~ leg** *n* entrejambes *m inv*; **~ leg measurement** *n* hauteur *f* de l'entrejambes.

insider *n* initié/-e *m/f*.

insides° *n pl* (of human) intestin *m*, estomac *m*, boyaux° *mpl*.

insight *n* **1** (glimpse, understanding) aperçu *m*, idée *f*; **to give an ~ into sth** donner une idée de qch; **2** (intuition) perspicacité *f*, intuition *f*.

insignificance *n* insignifiance *f*; **to pale** or **fade into ~** devenir dérisoire.

insignificant *adj* [*cost, difference*] négligeable; [*person, detail*] insignifiant.

insincere *adj* peu sincère; **to be ~** manquer de sincérité.

insincerity *n* (of person) manque *m* de sincérité; (of smile, remark, compliment) hypocrisie *f*.

insinuate *vtr* insinuer (**that** que).

insinuation *n* insinuation *f*; **he made all sorts of ~s about me** il a insinué toutes sortes de choses à mon propos.

insipid *adj* fade.

insist I *vtr* **1** (demand) insister (**that** pour que); **2** (maintain) affirmer (**that** que).
II *vi* insister; **if you ~** puisque tu insistes; **to ~ on** exiger [*punctuality, silence*]; **to ~ on doing** vouloir à tout prix faire, tenir à faire; **to ~ on sb doing** insister pour que qn fasse.

insistent *adj* **to be ~** insister (**about** sur; **that** pour que + *subj*).

insofar: **insofar as** *phr* **~ as** dans la mesure où.

insole *n* semelle *f* (intérieure).

insolent *adj* insolent.

insolvent *adj* insolvable.

insomnia *n* insomnie *f*.

insomniac *n* insomniaque *mf*.

inspect *vtr* examiner [qch] de près [*document, product*]; contrôler, vérifier [*accounts*]; inspecter [*school, factory, pitch, wiring*]; contrôler [*passport, ticket, baggage*].

inspection *n* (of document, picture) examen *m*, inspection *f*; (of school, machinery, wiring) inspection *f*; (of ticket, passport) contrôle *m*; **to make an ~** procéder à une inspection; **on closer ~** en y regardant de plus près.

inspector *n* **1** (gen) inspecteur/-trice *m/f*; **2** (GB) **police ~** inspecteur *m* de police; **3** (GB) (on bus) contrôleur/-euse *m/f*.

inspiration *n* **1** inspiration *f* (**for** pour); **to draw one's ~ from sth** s'inspirer de qch; **2** (person, thing that inspires) source *f* d'inspiration.

inspire *vtr* inspirer; **to be ~d by sth** s'inspirer de qch.

inspiring *adj* [*person, speech*] enthousiasmant; [*thought, music*] exaltant.

instability *n* instabilité *f*.

instal(l) *vtr* **1** installer [*equipment*]; poser [*windows*]; **2 to ~ sb in office** installer qn.

installation *n* installation *f*.

instalment (GB), **installment** (US) *n* versement *m* partiel; **monthly ~** mensualité *f*, versement *m* mensuel; **in ~s** en plusieurs versements.

instance *n* exemple *m*; **for ~** par exemple.

instant I *n* instant *m*; **come here this ~!** viens ici tout de suite!
II *adj* **1** [*access, effect, rapport, success*] immédiat; [*solution*] instantané; **~ camera** polaroïd® *m*; **2** [*coffee, soup*] instantané.

instantly *adv* immédiatement.

instead I *adv* **we didn't go home—we went to the park ~** au lieu de rentrer nous sommes allés au parc; **let's take a taxi ~** prenons plutôt un taxi; **I was going to phone but wrote ~** j'allais téléphoner mais finalement j'ai écrit; **her son went ~** son fils y est allé à sa place.
II instead of *phr* **~ of doing** au lieu de faire; **~ of sth** au lieu de qch; **use oil ~ of butter** utilisez de l'huile à la place du beurre; **~ of sb** à la place de qn.

instep *n* cou-de-pied *m*; **to have a high ~** avoir le pied cambré.

instigate *vtr* lancer [*attack*]; engager [*proceedings*].

instil (GB), **instill** (US) *vtr* inculquer [*attitude*] (**in** à); donner [*confidence*] (**in** à).

instinct *n* instinct *m* (**for** de); **the ~ to do** l'instinct qui pousse à faire.

instinctive *adj* instinctif/-ive.

institute I *n* institut *m*.
II *vtr* instituer, instaurer [*custom*]; engager [*proceedings*].

institution *n* **1** institution *f*; **financial ~** organisme *m* financier; **2** (home, hospital) établissement *m* spécialisé; (old people's home) asile *m* de vieillards; (mental hospital) hôpital *m* psychiatrique.

institutional *adj* [*structure, reform*] institutionnel/-elle; [*food*] de collectivité; **to be put in ~ care** [*child*] être placé dans un établissement spécialisé.

institutionalize *vtr* (place in care) placer [qn] dans un établissement spécialisé; (in mental hospital) interner.

instruct *vtr* **1 to ~ sb to do** donner l'ordre à qn de faire; **to be ~ed to do** recevoir l'ordre de faire; **2** (teach) instruire; **to ~ sb in** enseigner [qch] à qn [*subject*].

instruction *n* instruction *f*; **~s for use** mode *m* d'emploi.

instruction: **~ book** *n* livret *m* de l'utilisateur; **~ manual** *n* manuel *m* d'utilisation.

instructor ▶ 805 *n* **1** (in sports, driving, flying) moniteur/-trice *m/f* (**in** de); (military) instructeur *m*; **2** (US) (gen) professeur *m*; (in university) ≈ assistant/-e *m/f*.

instrument ▶753| *n* instrument *m*; **to play an ~** jouer d'un instrument.

instrument panel *n* tableau *m* de bord.

insufferable *adj* [*heat, conditions*] insupportable; [*rudeness*] intolérable.

insufficient *adj* **there are ~ copies** il n'y a pas assez d'exemplaires (**to do** pour faire); **to be ~ for** être insuffisant pour.

insulate *vtr* isoler [*roof, room, wire*]; calorifuger [*tank*].

insulation *n* isolation *f*.

insulin *n* insuline *f*.

insult I *n* insulte *f*.
II *vtr* insulter.

insulting *adj* insultant.

insurance *n* assurance *f* (**against** contre; **for** pour); **to take out ~ against sth** s'assurer contre qch; **accident/fire ~** assurance contre les accidents/l'incendie; **travel ~** assurance voyage.

insurance: **~ claim** *n* demande *f* d'indemnité; **~ company** *n* compagnie *f* d'assurances; **~ policy** *n* (police *f* d')assurance *f*.

insure *vtr* **1** assurer (**against** contre); **to ~ oneself** prendre une assurance-vie; **2 to ~ against delay** se garantir contre les retards.

insured party *n* assuré/-e *m/f*.

insurer *n* assureur *m*.

intact *adj* intact.

intake *n* **1** (consumption) consommation *f*; **2** (Sch, Univ) (admissions) admissions *fpl*; **3 an ~ of breath** une inspiration *f*.

intangible *adj* insaisissable.

integral *adj* **1** [*part, feature*] intégrant; **~ to** intrinsèque à; **2** [*lighting, component*] incorporé; [*garage*] intégré.

integrate I *vtr* **1** (incorporate, absorb) intégrer (**into** dans; **with** à); **2** (combine) combiner [*systems*].
II *vi* [*person*] s'intégrer (**with** à; **into** dans).

integration *n* intégration *f* (**with** à).

integrity *n* intégrité *f*; **a man of ~** un homme intègre.

intellect *n* **1** (mental capacity) intelligence *f*; **2** (person) esprit *m*.

intellectual *n, adj* intellectuel/-elle (*m/f*).

intelligence *n* **1** intelligence *f* (**to do** de faire); **2** (gen, Mil) (information) renseignements *mpl*; **latest ~** informations *fpl* de dernière minute; **3** (Mil) (secret service) services *mpl* de renseignements.

intelligent *adj* intelligent.

intelligible *adj* intelligible (**to** à).

intend *vtr* vouloir [*outcome*]; **as I ~ed** comme je le voulais; **sooner than I had ~ed** plus tôt que je ne voulais; **to ~ to do, to ~ doing** avoir l'intention de faire; **to ~ sth as a joke** dire qch pour plaisanter; **to be ~ed for** être destiné à [*person*]; être prévu pour [*purpose*]; **the law is ~ed to prevent drug trafficking** la loi vise à empêcher le trafic de drogue.

intense *adj* **1** [*activity, feeling, colour, pressure*] intense; [*interest, satisfaction*] vif/vive (*before n*); **2** [*person*] sérieux/-ieuse.

intensify I *vtr* intensifier.
II *vi* s'intensifier.

intensity *n* intensité *f* (**of** de).

intensive *adj* intensif/-ive.

intensive care *n* **in ~** en réanimation.

intensive care unit *n* service *m* de soins intensifs.

intent *adj* **~ on doing** résolu à faire.
IDIOMS **to all ~s and purposes** quasiment, en fait.

intention *n* intention *f* (**to do, of doing** de faire); **our ~ is to do** nous avons l'intention de faire.

intentional *adj* intentionnel.

interact *vi* [*two factors, phenomena*] agir l'un sur l'autre, s'influencer mutuellement; [*people*] communiquer; (Comput) dialoguer.

interactive *adj* interactif/-ive.

intercept *vtr* intercepter.

interchange I *n* **1** (road junction) échangeur *m*; **2** (exchange) échange *m*
II *vtr* (exchange) échanger; (change places of) permuter.

interchangeable *adj* interchangeable.

intercom *n* interphone® *m*; **over** or **on the ~** par l'interphone®.

intercourse *n* rapports *mpl* (sexuels).

interdependence *n* interdépendance *f*.

interest I *n* **1** (enthusiasm) intérêt *m* (**in** pour); **of no ~ to me/us** sans intérêt pour moi/nous; **to hold sb's ~** retenir l'attention de qn; **just for ~** pour le plaisir; **as a matter of ~**... juste pour savoir...; **2** (hobby) centre *m* d'intérêt; **he has wide ~s** il s'intéresse à énormément de choses; **3** (benefit) intérêt *m*; **in the ~(s) of** dans l'intérêt de [*peace, freedom, person*]; (out of concern for) par souci de [*hygiene, justice*]; **it's in your (own) ~(s) to do** il est dans ton intérêt de faire; **to have sb's best ~s at heart** vouloir le bien de qn; **4** (concern) intérêt *m*; (financial) participation *f*; **5** (on loan, from investment) intérêts *mpl* (**on** de).
II *vtr* intéresser (**in** à).

interested *adj* [*expression, onlooker*] intéressé; **to be ~ in** s'intéresser à [*subject, activity*]; **I am ~ in doing** ça m'intéresse de faire.

interesting *adj* intéressant.

interest rate *n* taux *m* d'intérêt.

interfere *vi* **1 to ~ in** se mêler de [*affairs*]; **she never ~s** elle ne se mêle jamais de ce qui ne la regarde pas; **2** (intervene) intervenir; **to ~ in** s'ingérer dans [*private life*]; **3 to ~ with** toucher, traficoter○ [*machine*]; **4** [*activity*] **to ~ with** empiéter sur [*family life*].

interference *n* **1** (by government, boss) ingérence *f* (**in** dans); (by family) immixtion *f* (**in** dans); **2** (on radio) parasites *mpl*.

interfering *adj* [*person*] envahissant.

interim I *n* **in the ~** entre-temps.
II *adj* [*arrangement, government*] provisoire; [*interest, payment*] intermédiaire; [*post, employee*] intérimaire.

interior I *n* **1** intérieur *m*; **2 Secretary/Department of the Interior** (US) ministre *m*/ministère *m* de l'Intérieur.
II *adj* intérieur.

interior decorator ▶805 *n* décorateur/-trice *m/f*.

interlink *vtr* **to be ~ed** être lié (**with** à).

interlock *vi* [*pipes*] s'emboîter; [*mechanisms*] s'enclencher; [*fingers*] s'entrelacer.

interlude *n* (interval) intervalle *m*; (during play, concert) entracte *m*.

intermediary *n*, *adj* intermédiaire (*mf*).

intermediate I *n* **1** intermédiaire *mf*; **2** (US Aut) automobile *f* de taille moyenne.
II *adj* **1** [*stage*] intermédiaire; **2** (Sch) [*exam*] de difficulté moyenne; [*course*] de niveau moyen; [*level*] moyen/-enne.

intermission *n* entracte *m*.

intern I *n* (US) **1** (Med) interne *mf*; **2** (gen) stagiaire *mf*.
II *vtr* (Mil) interner.

internal *adj* [*mechanism, organ, problem, call*] interne; [*flight, trade*] intérieur; **~ injuries** lésions *fpl* internes; **~ examination** toucher *m* vaginal.

international *adj* international.

internationally *adv* [*known, respected*] dans le monde entier.

international: **International Monetary Fund, IMF** *n* Fonds *m* monétaire international, FMI *m*; **~ money order** *n* mandat-poste *m* international; **~ reply coupon** *n* coupon-réponse *m* international.

interplay *n* interaction *f* (**of** de).

interpret I *vtr* interpréter (**as** comme).
II *vi* faire l'interprète.

interpretation *n* interprétation *f* (**by** par; **of** de).

interpreter *n* interprète *mf*.

interpreting *n* interprétariat *m*.

interrogate *vtr* interroger.

interrogation *n* interrogatoire *m*.

interrogative *n* interrogatif *m*; **in the ~** à la forme interrogative.

interrogator *n* interrogateur/-trice *m/f*.

interrupt *vtr*, *vi* interrompre.

interruption *n* interruption *f*.

intersect I *vtr* croiser.
II *vi* [*roads*] se croiser; **to ~ with** croiser.

intersection *n* intersection *f*.

interstate (US) I *n* (also **~ highway**) autoroute *f* (inter-États).
II *adj* [*commerce, links*] entre États.

interval *n* **1** intervalle *m*; **at regular ~s** à intervalles réguliers; **at four-hourly ~s** toutes les quatre heures; **at 100 metre ~s** à 100 mètres d'intervalle; **2** (GB) (in theatre) entracte *m*.

intervene *vi* intervenir (**on behalf of** en faveur de).

intervening *adj* **in the ~ period** entre-temps.

intervention *n* intervention *f* (**on behalf of** en faveur de).

interview I *n* **1** (also **job ~**) entretien *m*; **2** (in newspaper) interview *f*.
II *vtr* **1** faire passer un entretien à [*candidate*]; **2** [*journalist*] interviewer [*celebrity*]; [*police*] interroger [*suspect*].

interviewee *n* **1** (for job, place) candidat/-e *m/f*; **2** (on TV, radio) personne *f* interviewée.

interviewer *n* **1** (for job, course) personne *f* faisant passer l'entretien; **2** (on radio, TV, in press) intervieweur/-euse *m/f*.

intestine *n* intestin *m*.

intimacy *n* intimité *f*.

intimate *adj* [*detail, secret, relationship, atmosphere*] intime; [*belief, friendship*] profond; **to be on ~ terms with sb** être intime avec qn.

intimidate *vtr* intimider.

intimidating *adj* [*behaviour, experience, person*] intimidant; [*obstacle, sight, size*] impressionnant; [*prospect*] redoutable.

intimidation *n* intimidation *f* (**by** de la part de).

into *prep* **1** [*put, go, disappear*] dans [*place*]; **to speak ~ the microphone** parler dans le microphone; **pour the mixture ~ it** versez-y le mélange; **to run ~ a wall** rentrer dans un mur; **to bang ~ sb/sth** heurter qn/qch; **to move sth ~ the shade** mettre qch à l'ombre; **to go ~ town/~ the office** aller en ville/au bureau; **to get ~ a car** monter dans une voiture; **to get ~ bed** se mettre au lit; **2** [*transform*] en; **to change dollars ~ francs** changer des dollars en francs; **to translate sth ~ French** traduire qch en français; **3 to continue ~ the 18th century** continuer jusqu'au XVIIIe siècle; **well ~ the afternoon** jusque tard dans l'après-midi; **we were well ~ 1988 when...** l'année 1988 était bien entamée quand...; **well ~ the second half** bien après le début de la deuxième mi-temps; **to be (well) ~ one's thirties** avoir une bonne trentaine d'années; **4**° **to be ~** être fana° de [*jazz*]; **to be ~ drugs** se droguer; **5** (in division) **8 ~ 24 goes 3 times** or **is 3** 24 divisé par 8 égale 3.

intolerable *adj* intolérable, insupportable.

intolerance *n* intolérance *f* (**of, towards** vis-à-vis de; **to** à).

intolerant *adj* intolérant (**of, towards** vis-à-vis de; **with** envers).

intoxicated *adj* ivre.

intoxicating *adj* [*drink*] alcoolisé; [*effect, substance*] toxique.

intransigence *n* intransigeance *f* (**about, over** sur; **towards** envers).

intransitive *adj* intransitif/-ive.

intravenous: **~ drip** *n* perfusion *f* intraveineuse; **~ injection** *n* (piqûre *f*) intraveineuse *f*.

in-tray *n* corbeille *f* arrivée.

intrepid *adj* intrépide.

intricacy *n* complexité *f*.

intricate *adj* [*mechanism, plot, task*] compliqué; [*problem*] complexe.

intrigue *n* intrigue *f*; **political ~** les intrigues politiques.

intriguing *adj* [*person, smile*] fascinant; [*story*] curieux/-ieuse, intéressant.

introduce *vtr* **1** présenter [*person*] (**as** comme; **to** à); **may I ~ my son?** je vous présente mon fils; **have you been ~d?** on vous a présentés?; **to ~ sb to** initier qn à [*painting, drugs*]; **2** introduire [*law, reform, word, product, change*] (**in, into** dans); **3** (on TV, radio) présenter [*programme*]; **4** présenter [*proposal*].

introduction *n* **1** (of person) présentation *f*; **letter of ~** lettre de recommandation; **2** (of liquid, system, law) introduction *f* (**into** dans); **3** (to speech, book) introduction *f*.

introductory *adj* **1** [*speech, paragraph*] préliminaire; [*course*] d'initiation; **2** [*offer*] de lancement.

introvert *n* introverti/-e *m/f*.

intrude *vi* **1 to ~ in(to)** s'immiscer dans [*affairs, conversation*]; **2 to ~ (on sb's privacy)** être importun.

intruder *n* intrus/-e *m/f*.

intuition *n* intuition *f* (**about** concernant).

intuitive *adj* intuitif/-ive.

inundate *vtr* inonder [*land*]; submerger [*organization, market*].

invade *vtr* envahir.

invalid I *n* (sick person) malade *mf*; (disabled person) infirme *mf*.

II *adj* [*claim, passport*] pas valable; [*contract, marriage*] nul/nulle.

invalidate *vtr* annuler [*claim*]; vicier [*contract*]; rendre [qch] nul et sans effet [*will*].

invaluable *adj* [*assistance, experience*] inestimable; [*person, service*] précieux/-ieuse.

invasion *n* invasion *f*; **~ of (sb's) privacy** atteinte *f* à la vie privée (de qn).

invent *vtr* inventer.

invention *n* invention *f*.

inventive *adj* inventif/-ive.

inventor *n* inventeur/-trice *m/f*.

inventory *n* **1** inventaire *m*; **2** (US) stock *m*.

inverted commas *n pl* (GB) guillemets *mpl*; **in ~** entre guillemets.

invest I *vtr* investir, placer [*money*]; consacrer [*time, energy*] (**in** à).

II *vi* **1** investir; **to ~ in shares** placer son argent en valeurs; **2** (buy) **to ~ in** investir dans [*equipment*]; **I ~ed in a carpet** je me suis acheté un tapis.

investigate *vtr* **1** enquêter sur [*crime, case*]; faire une enquête sur [*person*]; vérifier [*allegation*]; **2** (study) examiner [*question, possibility, report*]; sonder [*market, sector*]; **3** (try out) essayer [*restaurant, club*].

investigation *n* **1** enquête *f* (**of, into** sur); **he is under ~** il fait l'objet d'une enquête; **2** (of accounts, reports) vérification *f*.

investigative *adj* [*committee, journalist*] d'investigation.

investigator *n* enquêteur/-trice *m/f*.

investment *n* **1** investissement *m*, placement *m*; **2 a huge emotional ~** un énorme engagement personnel.

investor *n* investisseur/-euse *m/f* (**in** dans); (in shares) actionnaire *mf*.

invisible *adj* invisible.

invisible ink *n* encre *f* sympathique.

invitation *n* invitation *f*; **an ~ to dinner** une invitation à dîner; **an ~ to bid** or **tender** un appel d'offres; **an open ~ to burglars** une incitation manifeste pour les cambrioleurs.

invitation card *n* carton *m* (d'invitation).

invite *vtr* inviter [*person*]; **to ~ sb for a drink** inviter qn à prendre un verre; **to ~ sb out/in** inviter qn à sortir avec soi/à entrer; **to ~ sb over** or **round (to one's house)** inviter qn chez soi; **to ~ sb for (an) interview** convoquer qn pour un entretien.

inviting *adj* [*room*] accueillant; [*meal*] appétissant; [*prospect*] alléchant.

invoice I *n* facture *f*.

II *vtr* envoyer une facture à; **to ~ sb for sth** facturer qch à qn.

invoicing *n* facturation *f*.

involve *vtr* **1** (entail) impliquer, nécessiter [*effort, travel*]; entraîner [*problems*]; **there is a lot of work/effort ~d** cela implique beaucoup de travail/d'efforts; **there is some travelling ~d** cela nécessite des déplacements; **2** (cause to participate) faire participer [*person*] (**in** à); **to be ~d in** (positive) participer à, être engagé dans [*business, project*]; (negative) être mêlé à [*scandal, robbery*]; **3** (affect) concerner, impliquer [*person, animal, vehicle*]; **their safety is ~d** leur sécurité est en jeu; **4** (engross) [*film, book*] faire participer, prendre [*person*]; **to get ~d in** se laisser prendre par, se plonger dans [*film, book, work*]; **5 to get ~d with sb** avoir une liaison avec qn; **to be (too) ~d in** prendre [qch] à cœur [*problem*].

involved *adj* **1** (complicated) [*explanation*] compliqué; **2** [*person, group*] (implicated) impliqué; (affected) concerné; **3** (necessary) [*effort*] à fournir; **because of the expense ~** à cause de la dépense que cela entraîne.

involvement *n* **1** (in activity, task) participation *f* (**in** à); (in enterprise, politics) engagement *m* (**in** dans); **2** (with group) liens *mpl*; (with person) relations *fpl*.

inward I *adj* [*satisfaction*] personnel/-elle; [*relief, calm*] intérieur.

II *adv* = **inwards**.

inwards *adv* (also **inward**) [*open, move, grow*] vers l'intérieur.

iodine *n* (element) iode *m*; (antiseptic) teinture *f* d'iode.

IOU *n* reconnaissance *f* de dette.

IQ *n* (*abbr* = **intelligence quotient**) QI *m*.

Iraq ▶574 *pr n* Iraq *m*.

irate *adj* furieux/-ieuse (**about** au sujet de).

Ireland ▶574 *pr n* Irlande *f*; **the Republic of ~** la République d'Irlande.

Irish ▶712 I *n* **1** (language) irlandais *m*; **2** (people) **the ~** les Irlandais *mpl*.
II *adj* [*culture, people, politics*] irlandais; [*ambassador, embassy*] d'Irlande; [*teacher, lesson*] d'irlandais.

Irish: **~man** *n* Irlandais *m*; **~ Republic** ▶574 *n* République *f* d'Irlande; **~ sea** *n* mer *f* d'Irlande; **~woman** *n* Irlandaise *f*.

iron I *n* **1** (metal) fer *m*; **old** or **scrap ~** ferraille *f*; **2** (for clothes) fer *m* (à repasser); **with a cool ~** à fer doux; **to give sth an ~** donner un coup de fer à qch.
II *vtr* repasser [*clothes*].
■ **iron out**: **~ out [sth]** faire partir [qch] au fer [*creases*]; aplanir [*difficulty*].

ironic(al) *adj* ironique.

ironically *adv* ironiquement; **~, she...** l'ironie, c'est qu'elle...

ironing *n* repassage *m*.

ironing board *n* planche *f* à repasser.

ironmonger ▶805 *n* quincaillier/-ière *m/f*; **~'s (shop)** quincaillerie *f*.

irony *n* ironie *f*.

irrational *adj* [*behaviour*] irrationnel/-elle; [*fear, hostility*] sans fondement; **he's rather ~** il n'est pas très raisonnable.

irrecoverable *adj* [*loss*] irréparable; [*debt*] irrécouvrable.

irredeemable *adj* **1** [*loss*] irrémédiable; **2** [*shares*] irremboursable; [*loan*] non amortissable.

irregular *adj* **1** irrégulier/-ière; **2** (US) [*merchandise*] de second choix.

irregularity *n* irrégularité *f*.

irrelevance *n* manque *m* d'à-propos.

irrelevant *adj* **1** [*remark*] hors de propos; [*fact*] qui n'est pas pertinent; [*question*] sans rapport avec le sujet; **to be ~ to sth** n'avoir aucun rapport avec qch; **2** (unimportant) **the money's ~** ce n'est pas l'argent qui compte.

irreligious *adj* irréligieux/-ieuse.

irreparable *adj* irréparable.

irreplaceable *adj* irremplaçable.

irrepressible *adj* [*high spirits*] irrépressible; [*person*] infatigable.

irresistible *adj* irrésistible.

irrespective: **irrespective of** *phr* sans tenir compte de [*age, class*]; sans distinction de [*race*]; **everyone, ~ of who they are** tous, sans exception.

irresponsible *adj* irresponsable.

irritable *adj* irritable.

irritate *vtr* irriter.

irritating *adj* irritant.

-ish *combining form* ▶559 **greenish** tirant sur le vert; (unpleasantly) verdâtre; **darkish** plutôt sombre; **earlyish** assez tôt; **at fourish** vers quatre heures.

Islam *n* Islam *m*.

Islamic *adj* islamique.

island *n* **1** île *f*; (small) îlot *m*; **2** (also **traffic ~**) refuge *m*.

islander *n* insulaire *mf*, habitant/-e *m/f* d'une île (or de l'île).

Isle of Man *pr n* île *f* de Man.

isolate *vtr* isoler (**from** de).

isolation *n* isolement *m*.

Israel ▶574 *pr n* Israël (*never with article*); **in ~** en Israël.

Israeli ▶712 I *n* Israélien/-ienne *m/f*.
II *adj* [*people, culture, politics*] israélien/-ienne; [*ambassador, embassy*] d'Israël.

issue I *n* **1** problème *m*, question *f*; **to make an ~ (out) of** faire une histoire de; **her beliefs are not at ~** ses croyances ne sont pas en question; **I must take ~ with you on that** je dois vous signifier mon désaccord sur ce point; **2** (of stamps, shares) émission *f*; (of book) publication *f*; **3** (journal, magazine) numéro *m*; **back ~** vieux numéro *m*.
II *vtr* **1** (allocate) distribuer; **to ~ sb with sth** fournir qch à qn; **to be ~d with** recevoir; **2** délivrer [*declaration*]; émettre [*order, warning*]; **3** émettre [*stamps, shares*]; **4** (publish) publier.

it ▶699 *pron* (in questions) **who is ~?** qui est-ce?, qui c'est°?; **~'s me** c'est moi; **where is ~?** (of object) où est-il/elle?; (of place) où est-ce?, où est-ce que c'est?, c'est où°?; **what is ~?** (of object, noise) qu'est-ce que c'est?, c'est quoi°?; (what's happening?) qu'est-ce qui se passe?; (what is the matter?) qu'est-ce qu'il y a?; **how was ~?** comment cela s'est-il passé?, ça s'est passé comment°?
IDIOMS **I've had ~ (with this job)!** j'en ai ras le bol° (de ce travail)!

IT *n* (*abbr* = **information technology**) informatique *f*.

Italian ▶712 I *n* **1** (person) Italien/-ienne *m/f*; **2** (language) italien *m*.
II *adj* [*culture, food, politics*] italien/-ienne; [*teacher, lesson*] d'italien; [*ambassador, embassy*] d'Italie.

italics *n pl* italique *m*; **in ~** en italique.

Italy ▶574 *pr n* Italie *f*.

itch I *n* démangeaison *f*.
II *vi* avoir des démangeaisons; **my back is ~ing** j'ai le dos qui me démange; **these socks make me ~** ces chaussettes me grattent.

itchy° *adj* **I feel ~ all over** ça me gratte partout.
IDIOMS **to have ~ feet**° avoir la bougeotte°.

item *n* **1** article *m*; **luxury ~** produit *m* de luxe; **an ~ of furniture** un meuble; **~s of clothing** vêtements *mpl*; **news ~** article *m*; **2** (on agenda) point *m*.

itinerary *n* itinéraire *m*.

its *det* son/sa/ses.

■ **Note** In French determiners agree in number and gender with the noun that follows. *its* is translated by *son + masculine noun*: *its nose* = son nez; by *sa + feminine noun*: *its tail* = sa queue; BUT by *son + feminine noun beginning with a vowel or mute 'h'*: *its ear* = son oreille; and by *ses + plural noun*: *its ears* = ses oreilles.

---

it

Pronoun uses

- When *it* is used as a subject pronoun to stand for a specific object (or animal), ***il*** or ***elle*** is used in French according to the gender of the object referred to:

  'where is the book / chair?'– 'it's in the kitchen' = 'où est le livre / la chaise?'– '**il / elle** est dans la cuisine'

  However, if the object referred to is named in the same sentence, *it* is translated by ***ce*** (*c'* before a vowel):

  it's a good film = **c'**est un bon film.

- When *it* is used as an object pronoun, it is translated by ***le*** or ***la*** (***l'*** before a vowel or mute 'h') according to the gender of the object referred to:

  *it's my book / my chair and I want **it*** = c'est mon livre / ma chaise et je **le / la** veux

  Note that the object pronoun normally comes before the verb in French and that in tenses like the perfect and the past perfect, the past participle agrees with it:

  *I liked his shirt, did you notice **it**?* = sa chemise m'a plu, est-ce que tu **l'**as remarquée? *or* **l'**as-tu remarquée?

  In imperatives the pronoun comes after the verb:

  it's my book, give it to me = c'est mon livre, donne-**le**-moi*

  * Note the hyphens.

  However, in negative commands, the pronoun comes before the verb:

  *it's my book, don't give **it** to him!* = c'est mon livre, ne **le** lui donne pas!

- When *it* is used after a preposition in English, the two words (*preposition* + ***it***) are often translated by one word in French. If the preposition would normally be translated by ***de*** in French (***of***, ***about***, ***from*** etc), the preposition + ***it*** = ***en***:

  *I've heard **about it*** = j'**en** ai entendu parler

  If the preposition would normally be translated by ***à*** in French (***to***, ***in***, ***at*** etc), the preposition + ***it*** = ***y***:

  *they went **to it*** = ils **y** sont allés

  For translations of *it* following prepositions not normally translated by ***de*** or ***à*** (*above, under, over* etc), consult the entry for the preposition.

Impersonal uses of pronoun

- When *it* refers back to something that has already been mentioned, French will use either ***ce*** (***c'*** before a vowel) + *être*:

  *they like English because **it's** easy to learn* = ils aiment l'anglais parce que **c'**est facile à apprendre

  or ***ça*** (***cela***) + *other French verbs*:

  *'I'm sorry' – '**it** doesn't matter'* = 'je suis désolé' – '**ça** ne fait rien.'

- When *it* introduces an idea or information, French will use either ***il*** + *être*:

  ***it** is easy to learn English* = **il** est facile d'apprendre l'anglais

  or ***ça*** (***cela***) + *other French verbs*:

  ***it** upset me to see that . . .* = **ça** m'a fait de la peine de voir que . . .

- When *it* is used in expressions like *it's raining, it will snow* etc, the translation will always be ***il***: ***il** pleut*, ***il** va neiger*.

  See the entry for the verb in question.

❑ For translations of *it's Friday*, *it's five o'clock* etc, consult the usage notes on **Dates, Days, and Months**, ▶ 584 and **The Clock**, ▶ 554.

For other uses, see the entry **it**.

itself *pron*

■ **Note** When used as a reflexive pronoun, direct and indirect, *itself* is translated by *se* (*s'* before a vowel or mute 'h'): *a problem presented itself* = un problème s'est présenté.
– When used for emphasis, *itself* is translated by *lui-même* when standing for a masculine noun and *elle-même* when standing for a feminine noun: *the car itself was not damaged* = la voiture elle-même n'était pas endommagée.
– For uses with prepositions (*by itself etc*), see 3 below.

1 (reflexive) se, s'; **the cat hurt ~** le chat s'est fait mal; **2** (emphatic) lui-même/elle-même; **the house ~ was pretty** la maison elle-même était jolie; **he was kindness ~** c'était la bonté même or personnifiée; **3** (after prepositions) **the heating comes on by ~** le chauffage se met en marche tout seul; **the house stands by ~** la maison est toute seule; **learning French is not difficult in ~** l'apprentissage du français n'est pas difficile en soi.

IUD *n* (*abbr* = **intrauterine device**) stérilet *m*.

ivory *n, adj* ivoire (*m*).

ivy *n* lierre *m*.

Ivy League *adj* (US) ≈ bon chic bon genre; **the ~ colleges** *les huit universités prestigieuses de la côte est américaine.*

Jj

j, J *n* j, J *m*.
jab I *n* **1** (GB) (vaccination) vaccin *m*; (injection) piqûre *f*; **2** (in boxing) direct *m*.
II *vtr* **to ~ sth into sth** planter qch dans qch.
jabber *vi* (chatter) jacasser; (in foreign language) baragouiner.
jack *n* **1** (for car) cric *m*; **2** (in cards) valet *m* **(of** de); **3** (in bowls) cochonnet *m*.
IDIOMS **to be a ~ of all trades** être un/-e touche-à-tout *inv*.
jackal *n* chacal *m*.
jackdaw *n* choucas *m*.
jacket *n* **1** (garment) veste *f*; (man's) veste *f*, veston *m*; **2** (also **dust ~**) jaquette *f*; **3** (US) (of record) pochette *f*.
jacket potato *n* pomme *f* de terre en robe des champs (au four).
jack-in-the-box *n* diable *m* à ressort.
jackknife *vi* [*lorry*] se mettre en portefeuille.
jackpot *n*
IDIOMS **to hit the ~** (win prize) gagner le gros lot; (have great success) faire un tabac°.
jade *n* **1** (stone) jade *m*; **2** ▶559 (also **~ green**) vert *m* jade.
jaded *adj* **1** (exhausted) fatigué; **2** (bored) [*person, palate*] blasé.
jagged *adj* [*rock, cliff*] déchiqueté; [*tooth, blade*] ébréché; [*knife, saw*] dentelé.
jail I *n* prison *f*.
II *vtr* mettre [qn] en prison.
jam I *n* **1** confiture *f*; **apricot ~** confiture d'abricots; **2** (of people) foule *f*; (of traffic) embouteillage *m*; **3** (of machine, system, department) blocage *m*; **4**° (difficulty) pétrin° *m*; **to be in a ~** être dans le pétrin°; **5** (also **~ session**) bœuf° *m*, jam-session *f*.
II *vtr* **1 to ~ one's foot on the brake** freiner à bloc; **2** (wedge) coincer; **the key's ~med** la clé s'est coincée; **3** (also **~ up**) (crowd) encombrer; **cars ~med (up) the roads** les routes étaient embouteillées; **4** (block) enrayer [*mechanism*]; coincer [*lock, door, system*]; **5** (cause interference in) brouiller [*frequency*].
III *vi* **1** [*mechanism*] s'enrayer; [*lock, door*] se coincer; **2** (Mus) improviser.
Jamaica ▶574 *pr n* Jamaïque *f*.
jam-packed *adj* bondé; **to be ~ with sth** être bourré de qch.
jangle I *n* (of bells, pots) tintement *m*; (of keys) cliquetis *m*.
II *vi* [*bells*] tinter; [*bangles*] cliqueter.
janitor *n* (US) gardien *m*.
January ▶584 *n* janvier *m*.
Japan ▶574 *pr n* Japon *m*.
Japanese ▶712 **I** *n* **1** (person) Japonais/-e *m/f*; **2** (language) japonais *m*.
II *adj* [*culture, food, politics*] japonais; [*teacher, lesson*] de japonais; [*ambassador, embassy*] du Japon.
jar I *n* **1** pot *m*; (large) bocal *m*; (earthenware) jarre *f*; **2** (jolt) secousse *f*, choc *m*.
II *vtr* **1** ébranler, secouer; **to ~ one's shoulder** se cogner l'épaule; **2** (US) **to ~ sb into action** pousser qn à agir.
III *vi* **1** [*music, voice*] rendre un son discordant; **to ~ on sb's nerves** agacer qn; **2** (clash) [*colours*] jurer; [*note*] sonner faux.
jargon *n* jargon *m*.
jasmine *n* jasmin *m*.
jaundice ▶686 *n* jaunisse *f*.
javelin ▶649 *n* javelot *m*.
jaw ▶523 *n* mâchoire *f*.
jaw: **~bone** *n* mâchoire *f*; **~line** *n* menton *m*.
jay *n* geai *m*.
jazz I *n* jazz *m*.
II *noun modifier* [*musician, singer*] de jazz; **~ band** jazz-band *m*.
IDIOMS **and all that ~**° et tout le bataclan°.
■ **jazz up**°: **~ up [sth], ~ [sth] up** rajeunir [*dress*]; égayer [*room*].
jazzy *adj* **1** [*colour*] voyant; [*pattern, dress*] bariolé; **2** [*music*] jazzy *inv*.
jealous *adj* jaloux/-ouse **(of** de); **to make sb ~** rendre qn jaloux.
jealousy *n* jalousie *f*.
jeans *n pl* jean *m*; **a pair of ~** un jean.
jeer I *n* (from crowd) huée *f*; (from person) raillerie *f*.
II *vtr* huer.
III *vi* se moquer; **to ~ at sb** [*crowd*] huer qn; [*individual*] railler qn.
jeering *n* huées *fpl*.
jellied *adj* en aspic; **~ eels** anguilles *fpl* en gelée.
Jell-o® *n* (US) gelée *f* de fruits.
jelly *n* **1** (savoury) gelée *f*; (sweet) gelée *f* de fruits; **2** (jam) confiture *f*.
jellyfish *n* méduse *f*.
jeopardize *vtr* compromettre [*career, plans*]; mettre [qch] en péril [*lives, troops*].
jeopardy *n* **in ~** en péril, menacé.
jerk I *n* (of vehicle) secousse *f*; (of muscle, limb) tressaillement *m*, (petit) mouvement *m* brusque; **with a ~ of his head** d'un brusque mouvement de la tête.
II *vtr* tirer brusquement [*object*].
III *vi* **to ~ to a halt** [*vehicle*] s'arrêter avec un soubresaut.
jerky I *n* (US) (also **beef ~**) bœuf *m* séché.
II *adj* [*movement*] saccadé; [*style, phrase*] haché.
jersey *n* **1** (sweater) pull-over *m*; **2** (for sports) maillot *m*; **3** (fabric) jersey *m*.
Jersey *pr n* Jersey *f*.

Jerusalem ▶574 *pr n* Jérusalem.

jest *n* plaisanterie *f*; **in ~** pour plaisanter.

jester *n* bouffon *m*.

Jesuit *n, adj* jésuite (*m*).

Jesus *pr n* Jésus; **~ Christ** Jésus-Christ.

jet I *n* **1** (also **~ plane**) jet *m*, avion *m* à réaction; **2** (of water, flame) jet *m*; **3** (on hob) brûleur *m*; (of engine) gicleur *m*; **4** (stone) jais *m*.
II *vi* **to ~ off to** s'envoler pour.

jet: **~ engine** *n* moteur *m* à réaction, réacteur *m*; **~lag** *n* décalage *m* horaire.

jet setter *n* **to be a ~** faire partie du jet-set.

jettison *vtr* (from ship) jeter [qch] par-dessus bord; (from plane) larguer.

jetty *n* (of stone) jetée *f*; (of wood) appontement *m*.

Jew *n* juif/juive *m/f*.

jewel *n* **1** (gem) pierre *f* précieuse, (piece of jewellery) bijou *m*; (in watch) rubis *m*; **2** (person) perle *f*; (town, object) joyau *m*.

jeweller (GB), **jeweler** (US) ▶805 *n* (person) bijoutier/-ière *m/f*; **~'s (shop)** bijouterie *f*.

jewellery (GB), **jewelry** (US) *n* (gen) bijoux *mpl*; (in shop, workshop) bijouterie *f*; **a piece of ~** un bijou.

Jewish *adj* juif/juive.

jib *n* **1** (sail) foc *m*; **2** (of crane) flèche *f*.

jibe *n* moquerie *f*.

Jiffy bag® *n* enveloppe *f* matelassée.

jig *n* gigue *f*.

jiggle I *vtr* agiter.
II *vi* (also **~ about**, **~ around**) gigoter; (impatiently) se trémousser.

jigsaw *n* **1** (also **~ puzzle**) puzzle *m*; **2** (saw) scie *f* sauteuse.

jingle I *n* **1** (of bells) tintement *m*; (of keys) cliquetis *m*; **2** (verse) ritournelle *f*; (for advert) refrain *m* publicitaire, sonal *m*.
II *vi* [*keys, coins*] cliqueter.

jingoist *n, adj* chauvin/-e (*m/f*).

jinx *n* **1** (curse) sort *m*; **to put a ~ on** jeter un sort à; **there's a ~ on me** j'ai la poisse○; **2** (unlucky person, object) porte-malheur *m inv*.

jitters *n pl* **to have the ~** [*person, stock market*] être nerveux/-euse; [*actor*] avoir le trac.

job I *n* **1** (employment) emploi *m*; (post) poste *m*; **to get a ~** trouver un emploi; **a teaching ~** un poste d'enseignant; **what's her ~?** qu'est-ce qu'elle fait (comme travail)?; **to have a ~ as a secretary** être employé comme secrétaire; **out of a ~** sans emploi; **2** (role) fonction *f*; **it's my ~ to do** c'est à moi de faire; **3** (duty) travail *m*; **she's only doing her ~** elle fait son travail; **4** (task) travail *m*; **to find a ~ for sb to do** trouver du travail pour qn; **5** (assignment) tâche *f*; **6** (result of work) **a poor ~** du mauvais travail; **to make a good ~ of sth** faire du bon travail avec qch; **7**○ (difficult activity) **a real ~**, **quite a ~** toute une affaire○ (**to do, doing** de faire).
II *noun modifier* [*advert, offer*] d'emploi; [*analysis*] de poste; [*pages*] des emplois.
IDIOMS **to learn on the ~** apprendre sur le tas○; **that'll do the ~** ça fera l'affaire.

job: **~-hunting** *n* chasse *f* à l'emploi; **~ sharing** *n* partage *m* de poste.

jockey *n* jockey *m*.

jockey shorts *n pl* (US) slip *m* (d'homme).

jockstrap○ *n* suspensoir *m*.

jodhpurs *n pl* jodhpurs *mpl*.

jog I *n* **1** (with elbow) coup *m* de coude; **2 at a ~** au petit trot○; **3** (Sport) **to go for a ~** aller faire un jogging; **4** (US) (in road) coude *m*.
II *vtr* (with elbow) donner un coup de coude à; **to ~ sb's memory** rafraîchir la mémoire de qn.
III *vi* **to go ~ging** faire du jogging.

jogger *n* joggeur/-euse *m/f*.

jogging ▶649 *n* jogging *m*.

join I *n* raccord *m*.
II *vtr* **1** (meet up with) rejoindre [*person*]; **may I ~ you?** (sit down) puis-je me joindre à vous?; **2** se mettre dans [*queue*]; **3** devenir membre de [*organization, team*]; adhérer à [*club*]; s'inscrire à [*library*]; entrer dans [*firm*]; s'engager dans [*army*]; **to ~ a union** se syndiquer; **4** (associate with) se joindre à [*person*] (**to do, in doing** pour faire); s'associer à [*colleague*] (**to do, in doing** pour faire); **5** (connect) réunir, joindre [*ends, pieces*]; assembler [*parts*]; relier [*points, towns*] (**to** à); **6** (merge with) [*road*] rejoindre [*motorway*]; [*river*] se jeter dans [*sea*].
III *vi* **1** (become member) (of party, club) adhérer; (of group, class) s'inscrire; **2** [*pieces*] se joindre; [*wires*] se raccorder; [*roads*] se rejoindre.
■ **join in**: ¶ **~ in** participer; ¶ **~ in [sth]** participer à [*talks, game*]; prendre part à [*strike, demonstration, bidding*]; **to ~ in the fun** se joindre à la fête.
■ **join up**: ¶ **~ up 1** (enlist) s'engager; **2** (meet up) [*people*] se retrouver; [*roads, tracks*] se rejoindre; ¶ **~ up [sth]**, **~ [sth] up** relier [*characters, dots*].

joiner ▶805 *n* menuisier/-ière *m/f*.

joint I *n* **1** (Anat) articulation *f*; **to be out of ~** [*shoulder*] être déboîté; **aching ~s** douleurs *fpl* articulaires; **2** (in carpentry) assemblage *m*; (in metalwork) joint *m*; **3** (of meat) rôti *m*; **4**○ (place) endroit *m*; (café) boui-boui○ *m*; **5**○ (cannabis) joint○ *m*.
II *adj* [*action*] collectif/-ive; [*programme, session*] mixte; [*measures, procedure*] commun; [*winner*] ex aequo *inv*; [*talks*] multilatéral.

joint: **~ account** *n* compte *m* joint; **~ effort** *n* collaboration *f*.

jointly *adv* [*manage*] conjointement; **to be ~ owned by** être la copropriété de.

joint-stock company *n* société *f* par actions.

joint venture *n* **1** (Econ) coentreprise *f*; **2** (gen) projet *m* en commun.

joke I *n* **1** (amusing story) plaisanterie *f*, blague○ *f* (**about** sur); **to have a ~ about sth** plaisanter sur qch; **can't you take a ~?** tu ne supportes pas la plaisanterie?; **it's no ~ doing** ce n'est pas facile de faire; **2** (person) guignol *m*; (event, situation) farce *f*.
II *vi* plaisanter, blaguer○; **you must be joking!** tu veux rire!

joker *n* **1** (who plays tricks) farceur/-euse *m/f*; **2** (in cards) joker *m*.

jolly I *adj* [*person*] enjoué; [*tune*] joyeux/-euse.
II *vtr* **to ~ sb along** amadouer qn.

jolt I *n* **1** (jerk) secousse *f*; **2** (shock) choc *m*.
II *vtr* secouer [*passenger*].
III *vi* [*vehicle*] cahoter.

jostle *vi* se bousculer (**for** pour; **to do** pour faire).

jot *v* ■ **jot down**: **~ [sth] down, ~ down [sth]** noter [*ideas, names*].

journal *n* **1** (diary) journal *m*; **2** (periodical) revue *f*; (newspaper) journal *m*.

journalism *n* journalisme *m*.

journalist *n* journaliste *mf*.

journey *n* (long) voyage *m*; (short or habitual) trajet *m*; **bus ~** trajet en bus; **to go on a ~** partir en voyage; **to break a ~** faire étape.

jowl *n* (jaw) mâchoire *f*; (fleshy fold) bajoue *f*.

joy *n* **1** (delight) joie *f* (**at** devant); **2** (pleasure) plaisir *m*; **the ~ of doing** le plaisir de faire.
IDIOMS **to be full of the ~s of spring** être en pleine forme.

joy: **~rider** *n* jeune chauffard *m* en voiture volée; **~riding** *n* rodéo *m* à la voiture volée; **~stick** *n* (in plane) manche *m* à balai; (for video game) manette *f*.

jubilant *adj* [*person*] exultant; [*crowd*] en liesse; [*expression, mood*] réjoui.

jubilee *n* jubilé *m*.

Judaism *n* judaïsme *m*.

judge I *n* **1** ▶ 642 (in court) juge *m*; **2** (at competition) (gen) membre *m* du jury; (Sport) juge *m*; **3 to be a good ~ of character** savoir juger les gens.
II *vtr* **1** juger [*person*]; **2** faire partie du jury de [*show, competition*]; **3** estimer [*distance, age*]; prévoir [*outcome, reaction*]; **4** (consider) juger, estimer.
III *vi* juger; **judging by** or **from**... à en juger par, d'après...

judgment, **judgement** *n* **1** jugement *m*; **to pass ~** prononcer un jugement; **to sit in ~ on** or **over sb** juger qn; **2** (opinion) avis *m*, opinion *f*; **3** (discernment) jugement *m*; **use your own ~** (in assessing) c'est à vous de juger; (in acting) faites comme bon vous semblera.

judgmental, **judgemental** *adj* **don't be so ~**! ne juge pas tant les autres!

judicial *adj* [*inquiry, process*] judiciaire; [*decision*] jurisprudentiel/-ielle.

judiciary *n* **1** (system of courts) système *m* judiciaire; **2** (judges) magistrature *f*.

judo ▶ 649 *n* judo *m*.

jug *n* **1** (GB) (earthenware) pichet *m*; (pot-bellied) cruche *f*; (glass) carafe *f*; (for cream, milk, water) pot *m*; **2** (US) (flagon) cruche *f*.

juggernaut *n* (GB) poids *m* lourd.

juggle *vi* jongler (**with** avec).

juggler *n* jongleur/-euse *m/f*.

jugular *n, adj* jugulaire (*f*).

juice *n* **1** (from fruit, meat) jus *m*; **fruit ~** jus de fruit; **2** (sap) suc *m*; **3 gastric ~s** sucs digestifs or gastriques.

juicy *adj* **1** [*fruit*] juteux/-euse; **2**° [*story*] croustillant.

jukebox *n* juke-box *m*.

July ▶ 584 *n* juillet *m*.

jumble *n* **1** (of papers, objects) tas *m*; (of ideas) fouillis *m*; (of words) fatras *m*; **2** (GB) (items for sale) bric-à-brac *m*, vieux objets *mpl*.
■ **jumble up**: **~ [sth] up, ~ up [sth]** mélanger [*letters, shapes*].

jumble sale *n* (GB) vente *f* de charité.

jumbo *n* (also **~ jet**) gros-porteur *m*.

jump I *n* **1** (leap) saut *m*, bond *m*; **parachute ~** saut en parachute; **2** (in horse race) obstacle *m*; **water ~** rivière; **3** (in price, wages) bond *m* (**in** dans).
II *vtr* **1** sauter [*obstacle, ditch*]; **2 to ~ the lights** griller° le feu (rouge); **to ~ the queue** passer devant tout le monde; **3 to ~ ship** ne pas rejoindre son bâtiment.
III *vi* **1** (leap) sauter; **to ~ across** or **over sth** franchir qch d'un bond; **to ~ up and down** sautiller; (in anger) trépigner de colère; **2** (start in surprise) sursauter; **3** [*prices, rate*] monter en flèche; **4 to ~ at** sauter sur [*opportunity*]; accepter [qch] avec enthousiasme [*offer*].
■ **jump back** [*person*] faire un bond en arrière; [*lever*] lâcher brusquement.
■ **jump down** [*person*] sauter (**from** de).
■ **jump on**: ¶ **~ on [sth]** sauter dans [*bus, train*]; sauter sur [*bicycle, horse*]; ¶ **~ on [sb]** sauter sur qn.
■ **jump out** [*person*] sauter; **to ~ out of** sauter par [*window*]; sauter de [*bed, train*].
■ **jump up** [*person*] se lever d'un bond.

jumper *n* **1** (GB) (sweater) pull *m*, pull-over *m*; **2** (US) (pinafore) robe *f* chasuble.

jumper cables *n pl* (US Aut) câbles *mpl* de démarrage.

jump: **~-jet** *n* avion *m* à décollage vertical; **~ leads** *n pl* (Aut) câbles *mpl* de démarrage; **~-start** *vtr* faire démarrer [qch] avec des câbles [*car*]; **~ suit** *n* combinaison *f*.

jumpy° *adj* [*person*] nerveux/-euse; [*market*] instable.

junction *n* **1** (of two roads) carrefour *m*; (on motorway) échangeur *m*; **2** (of railway lines) nœud *m* ferroviaire; (station) gare *f* de jonction.

June ▶ 584 *n* juin *m*.

jungle *n* jungle *f*.

junior I *n* **1** (younger person) cadet/-ette *m/f*; **2** (low-ranking worker) subalterne *mf*; **3** (GB Sch) élève *mf* du primaire; **4** (US Univ) ≈ étudiant/-e *m/f* de premier cycle; (in high school) ≈ élève *mf* de première.
II *adj* **1** [*colleague, rank, position*] subalterne; **2** (Sport) [*race, team*] des cadets; [*player*] jeune; **3** (also **Junior**) **Mortimer ~** Mortimer fils or junior.

junior: **~ high school** *n* (US) ≈ collège *m*; **~ minister** *n* secrétaire *m* d'État; **~ school** *n* (GB) école *f* (primaire).

junk *n* **1** (rubbish) camelote° *f*; **2** (second-hand) bric-à-brac *m*; **3** (boat) jonque *f*.

junk: **~ food** *n* nourriture *f* industrielle; **~ mail** *n* prospectus *mpl*; **~ shop** *n* boutique *f* de bric-à-brac; **~yard** *n* (for scrap) dépotoir *m*; (for old cars) cimetière *f* de voitures.

junta *n* junte *f*.

Jupiter *pr n* Jupiter *f*.

jurisdiction *n* **1** (gen) compétence *f* (**over** sur); **2** (Law) juridiction *f* (**over** sur); **3** (US) (court) juridiction *f*.

juror *n* juré *m*.

jury *n* jury *m*.

jury: **~ box** *n* banc *m* des jurés; **~ duty** *n* (US) = **jury service**.

jury service *n* (GB) **to do ~** faire partie d'un jury.

just[1] I *adv* **1** (very recently) **to have ~ done** venir (juste) de faire; **he had only ~ left** il venait tout juste de partir; **2** (immediately) juste; **~ before** juste avant; **it's ~ after 10 am** il est tout juste un peu plus de 10 heures; **3** (slightly) **~ over/under 20 kg** un peu plus/ moins de 20 kg; **~ after the station** juste après la gare; **4** (only, merely) juste; **~ for fun** juste pour rire; **~ two days ago** il y a juste deux jours; **~ last week** pas plus tard que la semaine dernière; **he's ~ a child** ce n'est qu'un enfant; **5** (purposely) exprès; **he did it ~ to annoy us** il l'a fait exprès pour nous embêter; **6** (barely) tout juste; **~ on time** tout juste à l'heure; **he's ~ 20** il a tout juste 20 ans; **I (only) ~ caught the train** j'ai eu le train de justesse; **7** (simply) tout simplement; **~ tell the truth** dis la vérité, tout simplement; **she ~ won't listen** elle ne veut tout simplement pas écouter; **'~ a moment'** 'un instant'; **8** (exactly) exactement; **that's ~ what I suggested** c'est exactement ce que j'ai suggéré; **it's ~ right** c'est parfait; **she looks ~ like her father** c'est son père tout craché○; **it's ~ like him to forget** c'est bien de lui d'oublier; **9** (possibly) **it might** or **could ~ be true** il se peut que ce soit vrai; **10** (at this or that very moment) **to be ~ doing** être en train de faire; **to be ~ about to do** être sur le point de faire; **he was ~ leaving** il partait; **11** (positively, totally) vraiment; **12** (easily) **I can ~ imagine her as president** je n'ai aucun mal à l'imaginer présidente; **I can ~ smell the pineforests** je sens déjà l'odeur des pins; **13** (in requests) **if I could ~ interrupt you** si je peux me permettre de vous interrompre; **14** (equally) **~ as big as**... (tout) aussi grand que...
II just about *phr* [*cooked*] presque; **I can ~ about see it** je peux tout juste le voir.
III just as *phr* **~ as he came** juste au moment où il est arrivé.
IV just now *phr* en ce moment; **I saw him ~ now** je viens juste de le voir.

just[2] *adj* [*person, decision*] juste; [*demand*] justifié; [*claim, criticism*] légitime.

justice *n* **1** (fairness) justice *f*; **the portrait doesn't do her ~** le portrait ne l'avantage pas; **2** (the law) justice *f*; **to bring sb to ~** traduire qn en justice.

justice: **Justice Department** *n* (US) ministère *m* de la justice; **Justice of the Peace** *n* juge *m* de paix.

justifiable *adj* (that is justified) légitime; (that can be justified) justifiable.

justification *n* raison *f*; **to have some ~ for doing** avoir des raisons de faire.

justified *adj* justifié; **to feel ~ in doing** se sentir en droit de faire.

justify *vtr* justifier.

jut *vi* (also **~ out**) [*cape*] s'avancer en saillie (**into** dans); [*balcony*] faire saillie (**over** sur).

juvenile *n* (gen) jeune *mf*; (Law) mineur/-e *m/f*.

juvenile: **~ delinquent** *n* jeune délinquant/ -e *m/f*; **~ offender** *n* délinquant/-e *m/f* mineur/-e.

juxtapose *vtr* juxtaposer (**with** à).

k, K *n* k, K *m*.
kale *n* (also **curly ~**) chou *m* frisé.
kaleidoscope *n* kaléidoscope *m*.
kangaroo *n* kangourou *m*.
karaoke *n* karaoké *m*.
karate ▶649 *n* karaté *m*; **~ chop** coup de karaté.
kayak *n* kayak *m*.
kebab *n* (also **shish ~**) chiche-kebab *m*.
kedgeree *n* (GB) pilaf *m* de poisson.
keel *n* quille *f*.
■ **keel over** [*boat*] chavirer; [*person*] s'écrouler; [*tree*] s'abattre.
keen *adj* **1** (eager) [*artist, footballer, supporter*] enthousiaste; [*student*] assidu; [*admirer*] fervent; **to be ~ on** tenir à [*plan, project*]; être chaud° pour [*idea*]; être passionné de [*activity*]; avoir une passion pour [*animals*]; **to be ~ on doing** or **to do** tenir à faire; **to be ~ for sb to do** or **that sb should do** tenir à ce que qn fasse; **to be ~ on sb°** en pincer° pour qn; **2** [*appetite, interest*] vif/vive; [*admiration, sense of loss*] intense; [*eye, intelligence*] vif/vive; [*sight*] perçant; [*hearing, sense of smell*] fin; **3** [*competition*] intense; [*demand*] fort (*before n*); [*debate*] animé.
keep I *n* **1** pension *f*; **to pay for one's ~** payer une pension; **2** (tower) donjon *m*.
II *vtr* **1** (cause to remain) **to ~ sb in hospital** [*person*] garder qn à l'hôpital; [*illness*] retenir qn à l'hôpital; **to ~ sth/sb clean** garder qch/qn propre; **to ~ sth warm** garder qch au chaud; **to ~ sb warm** protéger qn du froid; **to be kept clean/locked** rester propre/fermé (à clé); **to ~ sb waiting** faire attendre qn; **to ~ sb talking** retenir qn; **to ~ an engine running** laisser un moteur en marche; **2** (detain) retenir; **I won't ~ you a minute** je n'en ai pas pour longtemps; **3** (retain) garder [*receipt, money, letter, seat*]; **4** tenir [*shop*]; élever [*chickens*]; **5** (sustain) **to ~ [sth] going** entretenir [*conversation, fire*]; maintenir [*tradition*]; **I'll make you a sandwich to ~ you going** je te ferai un sandwich pour que tu tiennes le coup; **6** (store) mettre, ranger; **where do you ~ your cups?** où rangez-vous vos tasses?; **7** (stock) vendre, avoir [*brand, product*]; **8** (support) faire vivre, entretenir [*family*]; **9** tenir [*accounts, diary*]; **10 to ~ sth from sb** taire or cacher qch à qn; **to ~ sth to oneself** garder qch pour soi; **11** (prevent) **to ~ sb from doing** empêcher qn de faire; **12** (observe) tenir [*promise*]; garder [*secret*]; se rendre à [*appointment*]; **13** (Mus) **to ~ time** battre la mesure; **14** entretenir [*house*].
III *vi* **1** (continue) **to ~ doing** continuer à or de faire, ne pas arrêter de faire; **to ~ going** [*person*] continuer; **~ at it!** persévérez!; **~ straight on** continuez tout droit; **2** (remain) **to ~ indoors** rester à l'intérieur; **to ~ out of the rain** se protéger de la pluie; **to ~ warm** se protéger du froid; **to ~ calm** rester calme; **to ~ silent** garder le silence; **3** [*food*] se conserver, se garder; **4** [*news, business*] attendre; **5 'how are you ~ing?'** 'comment allez-vous?'; **she's ~ing well** elle va bien.
IV *v refl* **to ~ oneself to oneself** ne pas être sociable.
V for keeps *phr* pour de bon, pour toujours.
IDIOMS **to ~ in with sb** rester en bons termes avec qn.
■ **keep away**: ¶ **~ away** ne pas s'approcher (**from** de); ¶ **~ [sth/sb] away** empêcher [qch/qn] de s'approcher; **to ~ sb away from** empêcher qn de s'approcher de [*person, fire*]; tenir qn éloigné de [*family*].
■ **keep back**: ¶ **~ back** ne pas s'approcher (**from** de); ¶ **~ [sth/sb] back, ~ back [sth/sb] 1** empêcher [qn] de s'approcher [*crowd*] (**from** de); faire redoubler [*student*]; [*dam*] retenir [*water*]; **2** (retain) garder [*money*]; conserver [*food*].
■ **keep down**: **~ [sth] down, ~ down [sth]** limiter [*number, speed*]; empêcher [qch] d'augmenter [*prices, unemployment*]; maîtriser [*inflation*]; **~ your voice down!** baisse la voix!
■ **keep in**: **~ [sb/sth] in 1** empêcher [qn/qch] de sortir [*person, animal*]; garder [*contact lenses*]; **they're ~ing her in** (in hospital) ils la gardent; **2** rentrer [*stomach*].
■ **keep off**: ¶ **~ off [sth] 1** ne pas marcher sur [*grass*]; **2** éviter [*alcohol*]; s'abstenir de parler de [*subject*]; ¶ **~ [sth] off, ~ off [sth]** éloigner [*insects*]; **this plastic sheet will ~ the rain off** cette housse en plastique protège de la pluie.
■ **keep on**: ¶ **~ on doing** continuer à faire; **to ~ on about** ne pas arrêter de parler de; **to ~ on at sb** harceler qn (**to do** pour qu'il fasse); ¶ **~ [sb] on** garder.
■ **keep out**: ¶ **~ out of [sth] 1** ne pas entrer dans [*house*]; **'~ out!'** 'défense d'entrer'; **2** rester à l'abri de [*sun, danger*]; **3** ne pas se mêler de [*argument*]; **to ~ out of sb's way** (not hinder) ne pas gêner qn; (avoid seeing) éviter qn; ¶ **~ [sb/sth] out, ~ out [sb/sth]** ne pas laisser entrer [*person, animal*]; **to ~ the rain out** empêcher la pluie d'entrer.
■ **keep to**: **~ to [sth]** ne pas s'écarter de [*road*]; respecter, s'en tenir à [*facts*].
■ **keep up**: ¶ **~ up** [*car, runner, person*] suivre; [*competitors*] rester à la hauteur; ¶ **~ [sth] up, ~ up [sth] 1** tenir [*trousers*]; **2** continuer [*attack, studies*]; entretenir [*correspondence, friendship*]; maintenir [*membership, tradition, pace*]; **to ~ up the pressure** continuer à faire pression (**for** pour obtenir; **on** sur); **to ~**

up one's spirits garder le moral; ¶ **~ [sb] up** [*noise*] empêcher [qn] de dormir.

■ **keep up with**: **~ up with [sb/sth] 1** aller aussi vite que [*person*]; suivre [*class*]; [*wages*] suivre [*inflation*]; faire face à [*demand*]; **2** suivre [*fashion, developments*].

keeper *n* (curator) conservateur/-trice *m/f*; (guard) gardien/-ienne *m/f*.

keep fit *n* gymnastique *f* d'entretien.

keeping *n* **1** (custody) **in sb's ~** à la garde de qn; **to put sb/sth in sb's ~** confier qn/qch à qn; **2** (conformity) **in ~ with** conforme à [*law, tradition*]; **to be in ~ with** correspondre à [*image, character*]; s'harmoniser avec [*surroundings*].

keg *n* (for liquid) fût *m*; (for gunpowder) baril *m*.

kennel *n* **1** (GB) (for dog) niche *f*; **2** (establishment) chenil *m*.

kerb *n* (GB) bord *m* du trottoir.

kerb crawling *n* (GB) drague○ *f* au volant.

kernel *n* (of nut, fruitstone) amande *f*; (whole seed) grain *m*.

kerosene, kerosine *n* **1** (US) (paraffin) pétrole *m* (lampant); **2** (fuel) kérosène *m*.

kestrel *n* (faucon *m*) crécerelle *f*.

kettle *n* bouilloire *f*; **to put the ~ on** mettre l'eau à chauffer.

kettledrum ▶ 753 *n* timbale *f*.

key I *n* **1** clé *f*; **a front-door ~** une clé de maison; **a set** or **bunch of ~s** un jeu de clés; **under lock and ~** sous clé; **radiator ~** clavette *f* à radiateur; **2** (on computer, piano) touche *f*; (on oboe, flute) clé *f*; **3** (vital clue) clé *f*, secret *m* (**to** de); **to hold the ~ to the mystery** [*person*] détenir la clé du mystère; **4** (on map) légende *f*; (to abbreviations, symbols) liste *f*; (for code) clé *f*; **5** (to test, riddle) solutions *fpl*; (Sch) corrigé *m*; **6** (Mus) ton *m*, tonalité *f*; **in a major ~** en majeur; **to sing in/off ~** chanter juste/faux.

II *noun modifier* [*figure, role*] clé *inv*; [*point*] capital.

III *vtr* **1** (also **~ in**) saisir [*data*]; **2** (adapt) adapter (**to** à).

keyboard ▶ 753 **I** *n* clavier *m*.

II keyboards *n pl* synthétiseur *m*.

keyed-up *adj* (excited) excité; (tense) tendu.

keyhole *n* trou *m* de serrure.

keynote *n* thème *m* principal.

keynote: **~ speaker** *n* intervenant/-e *m/f* principal/-e; **~ speech** *n* discours *m* programme.

key: **~-ring** *n* porte-clés *m inv*; **~word** *n* mot *m* clé.

khaki *adj* kaki *inv*.

kibbutz *n* kibboutz *m*.

kick I *n* **1** (of person, horse) coup *m* de pied; (of donkey, cow) coup *m* de sabot; (of swimmer) battement *m* de pieds; (of footballer) tir *m*; **2**○ (thrill) **to get a ~ from doing** prendre plaisir à faire; **3** (of firearm) recul *m*.

II *vtr* (once) [*person*] donner un coup de pied à [*person*]; donner un coup de pied dans [*door, ball, tin can*]; [*horse*] botter [*person*]; [*donkey, cow*] donner un coup de sabot à [*person*]; (repeatedly) [*person*] donner des coups de pied à [*person*]; donner des coups de pieds dans [*object*]; **to ~ sb on the leg** [*person, horse*] donner à qn un coup de pied à la jambe; [*donkey, cow*] donner à qn un coup de sabot dans la jambe; **to ~ sth away** éloigner qch d'un coup de pied; **to ~ one's legs** [*baby*] pédaler.

III *vi* [*person*] (once) donner un coup de pied; (repeatedly) donner des coups de pied; [*swimmer*] faire des battements de pieds; [*cow*] ruer; [*horse*] botter.

IDIOMS **to ~ the habit**○ (of drug addiction) décrocher○; (of smoking) arrêter de fumer; **I could have ~ed myself** je me serais donné des claques○.

■ **kick around, kick about**: **~ [sth] around 1** donner des coups de pied dans, s'amuser avec [*ball, object*]; **2**○ discuter de, explorer [*idea*].

■ **kick against**: **~ against [sth]** regimber contre [*system*].

■ **kick down**: **~ [sth] down, ~ down [sth]** [*person*] enfoncer [qch] d'un coup de pied or à coups de pied [*door*]; [*horse*] renverser [*fence*].

■ **kick off 1** (Sport) donner le coup d'envoi; **2**○ (start) commencer.

■ **kick out**: ¶ **~ out** [*animal*] ruer; [*person*] lancer des coups de pied; **to ~ out at sb** [*person*] lancer des coups de pied à qn; ¶ **~ [sb] out, ~ out [sb]**○ virer○.

■ **kick up**: **~ [sth] up, ~ up [sth]** soulever [*dust*]; **to ~ up a fuss**○ faire des histoires○ (**about** à propos de).

kick: **~back** *n* pot-de-vin *m*; **~-off** *n* (Sport) coup *m* d'envoi.

kick-start I *n* (also **~-starter**) kick *m*.

II *vtr* **1** faire démarrer [qch] au pied [*motorbike*]; **2** relancer [*economy*].

kid I *n* **1**○ (child) enfant *mf*, gosse○ *mf*; (youth) gamin/-e○ *m/f*; **2** (young goat) chevreau/-ette *m/f*; **3** (goatskin) chevreau *m*.

II○ *vtr* charrier○ (**about** à propos de).

III○ *vi* (tease) rigoler○; **no ~ding!** sans blague○!

IV○ *v refl* **to ~ oneself** se faire des illusions.

kidnap *vtr* enlever.

kidnapper *n* ravisseur/-euse *m/f*.

kidnapping *n* enlèvement *m*.

kidney *n* **1** (Anat) rein *m*; **2** (Culin) rognon *m*.

kidney: **~ bean** *n* haricot *m* rouge; **~ failure** *n* défaillance *f* rénale.

kidney machine *n* rein *m* artificiel; **to be on a ~** être en dialyse.

kill I *n* **1** (in hunting) mise *f* à mort; **2** (prey) proie *f*.

II *vtr* **1** tuer [*person, animal*]; **they ~ed each other** ils se sont entre-tués; **~ed in action** or **battle** tombé au champ d'honneur; **even if it ~s me**○! même si je dois y laisser ma peau○!; **2**○ (hurt) **it wouldn't ~ you to turn up on time** tu pourrais faire l'effort d'arriver à l'heure; **my feet are ~ing me** j'ai mal aux pieds; **3** (end, stop) mettre fin à, étouffer

[*rumour*]; [*editor*] supprimer [*story*]; faire échouer [*idea*]; **that remark ~ed the conversation dead** cette remarque a jeté un froid dans la conversation; **4** (deaden) tuer [*smell, flavour*]; faire disparaître [*pain*]; ôter [*appetite*]; **5** (spend) **to ~ time** tuer le temps (**by doing** en faisant).
III *vi* [*person, animal, drug*] tuer.
IV *v refl* **to ~ oneself** se suicider; **to ~ oneself doing** se tuer à faire.

killer *n* (person) meurtrier *m*; (animal) tueur/-euse *m/f*; **heroin is a ~** l'héroïne tue.

killing *n* (of individual) meurtre *m* (**of** de); (of animal) mise *f* à mort (**of** de).

kiln *n* four *m*.

kilo ▶ 738 *n* kilo *m*.

kilobyte, KB *n* kilo-octet *m*, Ko *m*.

kilogram(me) ▶ 738 *n* kilogramme *m*.

kilometre (GB), **kilometer** (US) ▶ 738 *n* kilomètre *m*.

kilowatt *n* kilowatt *m*.

kind I *n* **1** (sort, type) sorte *f*, genre *m*, type *m*; **this ~ of person** ce genre de personne; **all ~s of people** toutes sortes de personnes; **what ~ of dog is it?** qu'est-ce que c'est comme chien?; **what ~ of person is she?** comment est-elle?, quel genre de personne est-ce?; **what ~ of person does he think I am?** pour qui me prend-il?; **what ~ of (a) person would do a thing like that?** qui pourrait faire une chose pareille?; **what ~ of an answer is that?** qu'est-ce que c'est que cette réponse?; **what ~ of talk is that?** en voilà des façons de parler!; **this is the only one of its ~, this is one of a ~** c'est unique en son genre; **they found a fossil of some ~** ils ont trouvé une sorte de fossile; **it's some ~ of cleaning device** ce doit être un système de nettoyage; **books, toys, that ~ of thing** des livres, des jouets, ce genre de choses; **that's the ~ of person she is** elle est comme ça; **I'm not that ~ of person** ce n'est pas mon genre; **2** (in vague descriptions) **a ~ of** une sorte de; **a ~ of soup** une sorte de soupe; **I heard a ~ of rattling noise** j'ai entendu comme un cliquetis; **3** (classified type) espèce *f*, genre *m*; **one's own ~** les gens de son espèce.
II *adj* [*person*] gentil/-ille; [*act*] bon/bonne (*before n*); [*gesture, words*] gentil/-ille; **to be ~ to sb** être gentil avec qn; **to be ~ to animals** bien traiter les animaux; **that's very ~ of you** c'est très gentil or aimable de votre part; **would you be ~ enough to pass me the salt?** auriez-vous l'amabilité de me passer le sel?
III **in kind** *phr* [*pay*] en nature; **to repay sb in ~** rendre la pareille à qn.
IV **kind of**° *phr* **he's ~ of cute** il est plutôt mignon; **I ~ of like him** en fait, je l'aime bien; **'is it interesting?'—'~ of'** 'est-ce que c'est intéressant?'—'assez'.

kindergarten *n* jardin *m* d'enfants.

kind-hearted *adj* [*person*] de cœur.

kindly I *adj* [*person*] gentil/-ille; [*smile*] bienveillant.
II *adv* **1** (in a kind way) avec gentillesse; **to speak ~ of sb** dire du bien de qn; **2** (obligingly) gentiment; **would you ~ do/refrain from doing** auriez-vous l'amabilité de faire/de ne pas faire; **3** (favourably) **to take ~ to** apprécier.

kindness *n* gentillesse *f*, bonté *f*; **to show ~ to(wards) sb** témoigner de la gentillesse à l'égard de or envers qn; **an act of ~** un acte de bonté; **out of ~** par gentillesse.

kindred spirit *n* âme *f* sœur.

kinetics *n* cinétique *f*.

king ▶ 642 *n* **1** (monarch) roi *m*; **King Charles** le roi Charles; **the ~ of comedy** le roi de la comédie; **2** (in chess, cards) roi *m*; (in draughts, checkers) dame *f*.

kingdom *n* **1** (country) royaume *m*; **2** (Bot, Zool) règne *m*; **the animal ~** le règne animal.

kingfisher *n* martin-pêcheur *m*.

king-size(d) *adj* [*cigarette*] extra-longue; [*packet*] géant; [*portion, garden*] énorme; **~ bed** grand lit *m*.

kink *n* (in rope, tube) nœud *m*; **the hosepipe has a ~ in it** le tuyau d'arrosage est tordu; **your hair has a ~** vos cheveux frisent légèrement.

kiosk *n* **1** (stand) kiosque *m*; **2** (GB) (phone box) cabine *f*.

kipper *n* (GB) hareng *m* fumé et salé, kipper *m*.

kiss I *n* baiser *m*; **to give sb a ~** embrasser qn, donner un baiser à qn.
II *vtr* embrasser, donner un baiser à [*person*]; **to ~ sb on** embrasser qn sur [*cheek, lips*]; **we ~ed each other** nous nous sommes embrassés.
III *vi* s'embrasser.

kiss of life *n* (GB) bouche-à-bouche *m inv*; **to give sb the ~** faire le bouche à bouche à qn.

kit *n* **1** (implements) trousse *f*; **2** (gear, clothes) affaires *fpl*; **football ~** affaires de football; **3** (for assembly) kit *m*; **4** (Mil) paquetage *m*.
■ **kit out** (GB): **~ out [sb/sth], ~ [sb/sth] out** équiper (**with** de).

kitbag *n* (for sport) sac *m* de sport; (for travel) sac *m* de voyage; (Mil) sac *m* de soldat.

kitchen *n* cuisine *f*.

kitchenette *n* kitchenette *f*.

kitchen: **~ foil** *n* papier *m* d'aluminium; **~ garden** *n* jardin *m* potager; **~ roll** *n* essuie-tout *m inv*.

kite *n* cerf-volant *m*; **to fly a ~** faire voler un cerf-volant.

kitten *n* chaton *m*.

kitty *n* cagnotte *f*.

kiwi fruit *n* kiwi *m*.

kleptomaniac *n, adj* kleptomane (*mf*).

knack *n* **1** (dexterity) tour *m* de main (**of doing** pour faire); **to get the ~** attraper le tour de main; **to lose the ~** perdre la main; **2** (talent) don *m* (**for doing** de faire).

knapsack *n* sac *m* à dos.

knave *n* (Games) valet *m*.

knead *vtr* pétrir [*dough*]; masser [*flesh*].

knee I ▶523 *n* genou *m*; **on (one's) hands and ~s** à quatre pattes.
II *vtr* donner un coup de genou à [*person*].
IDIOMS **to go weak at the ~s** avoir les jambes qui flageolent.

kneecap *n* rotule *f*.

knee-deep *adj* **the water was ~** l'eau arrivait aux genoux.

kneel *vi* (also **~ down**) se mettre à genoux; (in prayer) s'agenouiller; **~ing** à genoux; (in prayer) agenouillé.

knee-length *adj* [*skirt*] qui s'arrête au genou; [*boots*] haut; [*socks*] long/longue.

knickers *n pl* (GB) petite culotte *f*.

knick-knack *n* bibelot *m*.

knife I *n* couteau *m*.
II *vtr* donner un coup de couteau à; **to be ~d** recevoir un coup de couteau.

knife-edge *n* **to be on a ~** [*negotiations*] ne tenir qu'à un fil; **to be (living) on a ~** marcher au bord du précipice.

knife-point *n* **at ~** sous la menace d'un couteau.

knight I *n* (gen) chevalier *m*; (Games) cavalier *m*.
II *vtr* (GB) anoblir [*person*] (**for** pour).

knighthood *n* titre *m* de chevalier.

knit I *n* tricot *m*; **cotton ~** tricot en coton.
II *vtr* tricoter [*sweater, hat*]; **~ted** en tricot.
III *vi* **1** (with wool) tricoter; **2** [*broken bones*] se souder.

knitting *n* tricot *m*.

knob *n* **1** (of door) bouton *m*; (on bannister) boule *f*; **2** (control button) bouton *m*.

knobbly (GB), **knobby** (US) *adj* [*fingers*] noueux/-euse; [*knees*] saillant.

knock I *n* **1** (blow) coup *m* (**on** sur; **with** de); **a ~ at the door** un coup à la porte; **~! ~!** toc! toc!; **2** (setback) coup *m*; **to take a ~** en prendre un coup.
II *vtr* **1** (strike) cogner [*object*]; **to ~ one's head on sth** se cogner la tête contre qch; **to ~ sth against** projeter qch contre; **to ~ sb unconscious** assommer qn; **to ~ sth off** or **out of sth** faire tomber qch de qch; **to ~ a nail into sth** enfoncer un clou dans qch; **to ~ sb off his feet** [*blast*] projeter qn à terre; **2**° (criticize) dénigrer.
III *vi* **1** [*branch, engine, object*] cogner (**on, against** contre); [*person*] frapper (**at, on** à); **2** (collide) **to ~ into** or **against sth** heurter qch.
■ **knock about**°, **knock around**°: ¶ **~ about** traîner; **to ~ about with sb**° fréquenter qn; ¶ **~ about [sth]** [*object*] traîner dans [*house*].
■ **knock back**: ¶ **~ back [sth], ~ [sth] back 1** [*player*] renvoyer [*ball*]; **2**° (swallow) descendre° [*drink*]; ¶ **~ [sb] back** [*news*] secouer [*person*].
■ **knock down**: **~ [sb/sth] down, ~ down [sb/sth] 1** (deliberately) jeter [qn] à terre [*person*]; défoncer [*door*]; démolir [*building*]; (accidentally) renverser [*person, object*]; abattre [*fence*]; **2** [*buyer*] faire baisser [*price*]; [*seller*] baisser [*price*].
■ **knock off**: ¶ **~ off**° arrêter de travailler; ¶ **~ [sb/sth] off, ~ off [sb/sth] 1** (cause to fall) faire tomber [*person, object*]; **2**° (reduce) **to ~ £10 off the price/value of sth** réduire le prix/la valeur de qch de 10 livres; **3**° subtiliser [*car, object*]; **4**° **~ it off!** ça suffit!
■ **knock out**: ¶ **~ [sb/sth] out, ~ out [sb/sth] 1** (dislodge) casser [*tooth*]; arracher [*nail, support*]; **2** (make unconscious) [*person, blow*] assommer; [*drug*] endormir; [*boxer*] mettre [qn] au tapis [*opponent*]; **3** (Sport) éliminer [*opponent, team*]; **4** redresser [*dent, metal*]; **5**° (overwhelm) émerveiller [*person*]; ¶ **~ oneself out** s'assommer.
■ **knock over**: **~ [sb/sth] over, ~ over [sb/sth]** renverser.
■ **knock together**: ¶ **~ together** [*knees, objects*] s'entrechoquer; ¶ **~ [sth] together, ~ together [sth]**° bricoler [*furniture*]; confectionner [*meal*].
■ **knock up**: **~ [sth] up, ~ up [sth] 1**° bricoler [*furniture*]; confectionner [*meal, outfit*]; **2**° (Sport) totaliser [*points*]; réaliser [*score*].

knockabout *n* (Sport) échange *m* de balles.

knocker *n* heurtoir *m*.

knocking *n* (at door) coups *mpl*; (in engine) cognement *m*.

knock: **~-kneed** *adj* cagneux/-euse; **~-on effect** *n* implications *fpl*.

knock-out I *n* (in boxing) knock-out *m*.
II *adj* **1** (Sport) [*competition*] avec tours éliminatoires; **2**° [*pills*] sédatif/-ive.

knot I *n* **1** nœud *m*; **to tie sth in a ~** nouer qch; **to comb the ~s out of one's hair** se démêler les cheveux avec un peigne; **to have a ~ in one's stomach** avoir l'estomac noué; **2** (in wood) nœud *m*; **3** (group) petit groupe *m* (**of** de).
II *vtr* nouer (**together** ensemble).
IDIOMS **to get tied up in ~s** s'embrouiller.

know I *vtr* (be acquainted or familiar with) connaître [*place, person, system, way*]; (experience) connaître [*poverty, hunger, happiness*]; (in one's mind, through learning) savoir [*lesson*]; **to ~ why/how** savoir pourquoi/comment; **to ~ how to do** savoir faire; **to ~ sb by name** connaître qn de nom; **he ~s everything** il sait tout; **to ~ sth by heart** savoir or connaître qch par cœur; **to ~ that...** savoir que...; **to ~ for certain** or **for sure that** savoir de façon certaine que; **I wasn't to ~ that...** je ne pouvais pas savoir que...; **you ~ what children are** tu sais comment sont les enfants; **to let it be known that** faire savoir que; **it has been known to snow here** il est arrivé qu'il neige ici; **if I ~ him** tel que je le connais; **he is known to the police** il est connu de la police; **there's no ~ing whether** on ne peut pas savoir si; **I ~ that for a fact** j'en suis absolument sûr; **I ~ what!** j'ai une idée!; **he ~s all about it** il est au courant; **I knew it!** j'en étais sûr!; **to be known for sth/for doing** être connu pour qch/pour faire; **the most dangerous substance known to man** la substance la plus dangereuse que l'homme connaisse.
II *vi* savoir; **as you ~** comme vous le savez;

I wouldn't ~ je ne saurais dire; **to ~ about** (have information) être au courant de [*event*]; (have skill) s'y connaître en [*computing, engines*]; **to ~ of** (from experience) connaître; (from information) avoir entendu parler de; **not that I ~ of** pas que je sache; **to let sb ~ of** or **about** tenir qn au courant de; **we'll let you ~** nous vous le ferons savoir; **how should I ~**○! comment veux-tu que je sache!; **you ~ better than to argue with him** (it's futile) tu as mieux à faire que de te disputer avec lui; (it's unwise) tu sais qu'il vaut mieux ne pas se disputer avec lui; **you should have known better** tu n'aurais pas dû; **'he won't win'—'oh I don't ~'** 'il ne va pas gagner'—'oh je n'en suis pas si sûr'; **I don't ~ about you but**... je ne sais ce que tu en penses, mais...

IDIOMS **not to ~ what to do with oneself** ne pas savoir quoi faire de son temps; **not to ~ where** or **which way to turn** ne pas savoir à quel saint se vouer; **to be in the ~**○ être bien informé.

know: **~-all**○ *n* (GB) je-sais-tout *mf inv*; **~-how**○ *n* savoir-faire *m inv*.

knowing *adj* [*look, smile*] entendu.

knowledge *n* **1** (awareness) connaissance *f*; **to bring sth to sb's ~** porter qch à la connaissance de qn; **to my ~** à ma connaissance; **with the full ~ of sb** au vu et au su de qn; **he has no ~ of what happened** il ne sait pas ce qui s'est passé; **without sb's ~** à l'insu de qn; **2** (factual wisdom) connaissances *fpl*; (of specific field) connaissance *f*; **technical ~** connaissances techniques.

knowledgeable *adj* [*person*] savant; **to be ~ about** s'y connaître en [*subject*].

known *adj* [*authority, danger*] reconnu; [*cure*] connu; [*quantity*] défini.

knuckle *n* **1** (of person) jointure *f*, articulation *f*; **to crack one's ~s** faire craquer ses doigts; **to rap sb on the ~s** taper sur les doigts de qn; **2** (on animal) jarret *m*; **3** (Culin) (of lamb, mutton) manche *m* de gigot; (of pork, veal) jarret *m*.

■ **knuckle down**○ s'y mettre (sérieusement).

knuckle: **~bone** *n* articulation *f*, jointure *f*; **~-duster** *n* coup-de-poing *m* américain.

koala (bear) *n* koala *m*.

Koran *n* Coran *m*.

Korea ▶ 574 *pr n* Corée *f*.

kosher *adj* **1** [*food, restaurant*] casher; **2**○ (not illegal) **it's ~** c'est réglo○.

kudos○ *n* prestige *m*.

l, L *n* **1** (letter) l, L *m*; **2 L** (US) **the L** le métro aérien.

lab *n* labo○ *m*.

lab coat *n* blouse *f* blanche.

label I *n* **1** (on clothing, jar) étiquette *f*; **2** (also **record ~**) label *m*; **3** (Comput) label *m*.
II *vtr* **1** étiqueter [*clothing, jar*]; **2** classer, étiqueter (derogatory) (**as** comme).

labia *n pl* lèvres *fpl* (de la vulve).

labor (US) = **labour**.

laboratory *n* laboratoire *m*.

laboratory: **~ assistant** *n* laborantin/-e *m/f*; **~ technician** *n* technicien/-ienne *m/f* de laboratoire.

labor: **Labor Day** *n* (US) fête *f* du travail; **Labor Department** *n* (US) ministère *m* du travail.

laborer (US) = **labourer**.

labor union *n* (US) syndicat *m*.

labour (GB), **labor** (US) **I** *n* **1** (work) travail *m*; **to withdraw one's ~** se mettre en grève; **2** (also **~ force**) main-d'œuvre *f*; **3** (Med) accouchement *m*; **to be in ~** être en train d'accoucher; **~ pains** douleurs *fpl* de l'accouchement.
II *noun modifier* [*dispute, relations*] ouvriers-patronat *inv*; [*market*] du travail.
III *vi* travailler (dur) (**at** à; **on** sur; **to do** pour faire)
IDIOMS **to ~ the point** insister lourdement.

Labour *n* (GB) parti *m* travailliste.

labour camp *n* camp *m* de travaux forcés, bagne *m*.

labourer (GB), **laborer** (US) ▶ 805 *n* ouvrier/-ière *m/f* du bâtiment.

labour: **~ law** *n* législation *f* or droit *m* du travail; **Labour Party** *n* (GB) parti *m* travailliste; **~-saving device** *n* appareil *m* ménager; **~ ward** *n* salles *fpl* d'accouchement.

lace I *n* **1** (fabric) dentelle *f*; **2** (on shoe, boot, dress) lacet *m*; (on tent) cordon *m*.
II *vtr* **1** (tie) lacer [*shoes*]; **2 to ~ a drink with sth** mettre qch dans une boisson.

laceration *n* (gen, Med) lacération *f*.

lace-up (shoe) *n* chaussure *f* à lacet.

lack I *n* manque *m* (**of** de); **through ~ of** par manque de [*funds, confidence*].
II *vtr* manquer de [*confidence, humour, funds*].

lacklustre (GB), **lackluster** (US) *adj* [*person, performance, style*] terne.

lacquer *n* **1** (for hair) laque *f*; **2** (varnish) laque *f*; **3** (ware) laques *mpl*.

lad○ *n* **1** (boy) garçon *m*; **2** (in racing stables) lad *m*; (in riding stables) palefrenier *m*.

ladder I *n* **1** (for climbing) échelle *f*; **2** (GB) (in stockings) échelle *f*, maille *f* filée.
II *vtr* filer [*stocking*].

ladle *n* (Culin) louche *f*.

lady I *n* **1** (woman) dame *f*; **ladies and gentlemen** mesdames et messieurs; **a little old ~** une petite vieille; **she's a real ~** elle est très distinguée; **the ~ of the house** la maîtresse de maison; **2** ▶ 642 (in titles) **Lady Churchill** Lady Churchill.
II ladies *n pl* toilettes *fpl*; (on sign) 'Dames'.

lady: **~bird** *n* coccinelle *f*; **~ friend** *n* amie *f*; **~like** *adj* [*behaviour*] distingué.

lag I *n* (also **time ~**) décalage *m*.
II *vtr* calorifuger [*pipe, tank*]; isoler [*roof*].
■ **lag behind**: ¶ **~ behind** [*person, prices*] être à la traîne; ¶ **~ behind [sb/sth]** traîner derrière [*person*]; être en retard sur [*rival, product*].

lager *n* bière *f* blonde.

lagoon *n* lagune *f*.

lah, la *n* (Mus) la *m*.

laidback○ *adj* décontracté.

laid up *adj* **to be ~** être alité.

lake *n* lac *m*.
IDIOMS **go and jump in the ~**○! va te faire voir ailleurs○!

lamb *n* agneau *m*; **leg of ~** gigot *m* d'agneau.

lambing *n* agnelage *m*.

lamb: **~skin** *n* peau *f* d'agneau; **~'s wool** *n* laine *f* d'agneau, lambswool *m*.

lame *adj* [*person, animal, excuse*] boiteux/-euse; **to be ~** [*person, animal*] boiter.

lament *vtr* se lamenter sur [*fate, misfortune*].

laminated *adj* [*plastic*] stratifié; [*wood*] contreplaqué; [*card*] plastifié.

lamp *n* lampe *f*.

lamp: **~ bracket** *n* applique *f*; **~post** *n* réverbère *m*; **~shade** *n* abat-jour *m*.

lance *vtr* percer [*boil, abscess*].

land I *n* **1** (terrain, property) terrain *m*; (very large) terres *fpl*; **private ~** propriété *f* privée; **2** (farmland) terre *f*; **to work the ~** travailler la terre; **3** (countryside) campagne *f*; **to leave the ~** quitter la campagne; **4** (country) pays *m*; **5** (not sea) terre *f*; **to reach ~** toucher terre; **by ~** par voie de terre.
II *noun modifier* [*prices*] du terrain; [*purchase, sale*] de terrain; [*tax*] foncier/-ière.
III *vtr* **1** [*pilot*] poser [*aircraft*]; faire atterrir [*space capsule*]; **2** prendre [*fish*]; **3**○ décrocher○ [*job, contract, prize*]; **4**○ **to be ~ed with sb/sth** se retrouver avec qn/qch sur les bras.
IV *vi* **1** [*aircraft, passenger*] atterrir; **2** [*passenger*] débarquer; [*ship*] accoster; **3** [*person, animal, object*] atterrir; [*ball*] toucher le sol; **most of the paint ~ed on me** presque toute la peinture m'est tombée dessus.
IDIOMS **to find out how the ~ lies** savoir de quoi il retourne.

land agent ▶805 *n* (on estate) régisseur *m*; (broker) expert *m* foncier.

landing *n* **1** (at turn of stairs) palier *m*; (storey) étage *m*; **2** (from boat) (of people) débarquement *m*; (of cargo) déchargement *m*; **3** (by plane) atterrissage *m* (**on** sur).

landing: **~ beacon** *n* balise *f* d'atterrissage; **~ card** *n* carte *f* de débarquement; **~ gear** *n* train *m* d'atterrissage; **~ lights** *n pl* (on plane) phares *mpl* d'atterrissage; (on airfield) balises *fpl* d'atterrissage.

land: **~lady** *n* (owner) propriétaire *f*; (live-in) logeuse *f*; (of pub) patronne *f*; **~lord** *n* (owner) propriétaire *m*; (live-in) logeur *m*; (of pub) patron *m*; **~mark** *n* (for bearings) point *m* de repère; (major step) étape *f* importante; **~ mine** *n* mine *f* terrestre; **~owner** *n* propriétaire *mf* foncier/-ière; **Land Rover®** *n* Land Rover® *f*.

landscape *n* paysage *m*.

landscape gardener ▶805 *n* jardinier/-ière *m/f* paysagiste.

landscaping *n* aménagement *m* paysager.

landslide *n* **1** glissement *m* de terrain; **2** (also **~ victory**) victoire *f* écrasante.

land: **~ surveyor** ▶805 *n* géomètre *m*; **~ yacht** *n* char *m* à voile.

lane *n* **1** (in country) chemin *m*, petite route *f*; (in town) ruelle *f*; **2** (of road) voie *f*, file *f*; (air, sea) couloir *m*; (Sport) couloir *m*; **to keep in ~** (GB) rester sur la même voie; **to be in the wrong ~** être dans la mauvaise file.

language ▶712 *n* **1** (system in general) langage *m*; **2** (of a particular nation) langue *f*; **the French ~** la langue française; **3** (of a particular group, style) langage *m*; **legal ~** langage juridique; **spoken ~** langue parlée; **bad** or **foul ~** langage grossier; **mind your ~!** reste poli!; **4** (Comput) langage *m*.

language laboratory, **language lab** *n* laboratoire *m* de langues.

lanolin *n* lanoline *f*.

lantern *n* lanterne *f*.

lap *n* **1** (area of body) genoux *mpl*; **in one's ~** sur les genoux; **2** (Sport) (of track) tour *m* de piste; (of racecourse) tour *m* de circuit; **to be on the last ~** faire le dernier tour; (figurative) en être à la dernière étape; **3** (part of journey) étape *f*.

IDIOMS **in the ~ of luxury** dans le plus grand luxe.

■ **lap up**: **~ [sth] up, ~ up [sth] 1** laper [*milk, water*]; **2** boire [qch] comme du petit lait [*compliment, flattery*].

lapel *n* revers *m*.

lapse I *n* **1** (slip) défaillance *f*; **a ~ of memory** un trou de mémoire; **a ~ in concentration** un relâchement de l'attention; **2** (interval) intervalle *m*, laps *m* de temps.

II *vi* **to ~ into** se mettre à parler [*jargon, German*]; tomber dans [*coma*].

laptop *n* (also **~ computer**) portable *m*.

larceny *n* vol *m*.

lard *n* saindoux *m*.

larder *n* garde-manger *m inv*.

large I *adj* **1** (big) [*area, car, feet, house, size*] grand (*before n*); [*appetite, piece, nose*] gros/grosse (*before n*); **2** (substantial) [*amount*] important, gros/grosse (*before n*); [*part*] gros/grosse (*before n*); [*number, quantity, range*] grand (*before n*); [*population*] fort (*before n*), important; [*crowd, family*] nombreux/-euse; **3** (fat) [*person*] gros/grosse (*before n*).

II at large *phr* **1** [*prisoner, criminal*] en liberté; **2** [*society, population*] en général, dans son ensemble.

IDIOMS **by and ~** en général; **larger than life** exubérant.

large: **~ intestine** *n* gros intestin *m*; **~-scale** *adj* à grande échelle.

lark *n* **1** (Zool) alouette *f*; **2**° (fun) **to do sth for a ~** faire qch pour rigoler°.

larva *n* larve *f*.

laryngitis ▶686 *n* laryngite *f*.

larynx *n* larynx *m*.

lasagne *n* lasagnes *fpl*.

laser I *n* laser *m*.

II *noun modifier* [*beam, disc*] laser *inv*; [*printer*] à laser; [*treatment*] au laser.

lash I *n* **1** (eyelash) cil *m*; **2** (whipstroke) coup *m* de fouet.

II *vtr* fouetter [*person, animal*]; [*rain*] cingler [*windows*]; [*waves*] fouetter [*shore*].

■ **lash out** [*person*] devenir violent, se démener; **to ~ out at sb** (physically) frapper qn; (verbally) invectiver qn.

last ▶915 **I** *pron* **the ~** le dernier/la dernière *m/f* (**to do** à faire); **the ~ of the guests** les derniers invités; **that was the ~ I saw of her** c'est la dernière fois que je l'ai vue; **you haven't heard the ~ of this!** l'affaire n'en restera pas là!; **the night before ~** (evening) avant-hier soir; (night) la nuit d'avant-hier; **the week before ~** il y a deux semaines.

II *adj* **1** (final) [*hope, novel, time*] dernier/-ière (*before n*); **the ~ person to arrive** la dernière personne à arriver; **for the ~ time, will you be quiet!** c'est la dernière fois que je vous le dis, taisez-vous!; **your ~ name please?** votre nom de famille s'il vous plaît?; **in my ~ job** là où je travaillais avant; **the ~ few children** les deux ou trois derniers enfants; **2** (describing past time) dernier/-ière; **~ week/year** la semaine/l'année dernière; **~ Christmas** à Noël l'an dernier; **in** or **over the ~ ten years** durant ces dix dernières années; **she's been in Cambridge for the ~ eight months** elle est à Cambridge depuis huit mois; **~ night** (evening) hier soir; (night-time) la nuit dernière; **3** (most unlikely) dernier/-ière; **he's the ~ person I'd ask!** c'est la dernière personne à qui je m'adresserais!; **the ~ thing they want is publicity!** la publicité, c'est vraiment ce qu'ils souhaitent le moins!

III *adv* **1** (in final position) **to come in ~** [*runner, racing car*] arriver en dernier; **to be placed ~** être classé dernier/-ière; **the girls left ~** les filles sont parties les dernières; **to leave sth till ~** s'occuper de qch en dernier (lieu); **~ of all** en dernier lieu; **2 she was ~**

Languages and Nationalities

Languages

Note that names of languages in French are always written with a small letter, not a capital as in English; also, French almost always uses the definite article with languages, while English does not. In the examples below, the name of any language may be substituted for ***French*** and ***français***:

to learn French	= apprendre le français

However, the article is never used after ***en***:

*say it **in** French*	= dis-le **en** français
*to translate sth **into** French*	= traduire qch **en** français

and it may be omitted with ***parler***:

to speak French	= parler français / parler le français

but

the lecturer spoke in French	= le conférencier a parlé en français

When ***French*** means *in French* or *of the French*, it is translated by ***français***:

*the **French** language*	= la langue **française**
*a **French** word*	= un mot **français**

If you want to make it clear you mean *in French* and not *from France*, use ***en français***:

*a **French** book*	= un livre **en français**
*a **French** broadcast*	= une émission **en français**

When ***French*** means *relating to French* or *about French*, it is translated by ***de français***:

*a **French** class*	= une classe **de français**
*a **French** dictionary*	= un dictionnaire **de français**

but

*a **French-English** dictionary*	= un dictionnaire **français-anglais**

See the dictionary entry for **speaking** and **speaker** for expressions like *French-speaking* or *French speaker*. French has special words for some of these expressions:

English-speaking	= anglophone
a French speaker	= un / une francophone

Nationalities

Note again the different use of capital letters in English and French; adjectives never have capitals in French:

a French student	= un étudiant français / une étudiante française

Nouns have capitals in French when they mean a person of a specific nationality:

a Frenchman	= un Français
a Frenchwoman	= une Française
French people or *the French*	= les Français *mpl*

English sometimes has a special word for a person of a specific nationality; in French, the same word is almost always either an adjective (no capitals) or a noun (with capitals):

Danish	= danois
a Dane	= un Danois / une Danoise
the Danes	= les Danois *mpl*

Note the alternatives using either adjective (***il/elle est . . .*** etc) or noun (***c'est un/une, ce sont des . . .*** etc) in French:

***he is** French*	= **il est** français / **c'est un** Français

When the subject is a noun, the adjective construction is normally used in French:

*the teacher **is** French*	= le professeur **est** français

here in 1976 la dernière fois qu'elle est venue ici, c'était en 1976.
IV *vi* **1** (extend in time) durer; **it's too good to ~!** c'est trop beau pour que ça dure!; **he won't ~ long here** il ne tiendra pas longtemps ici; **2** [*fabric*] faire de l'usage; [*perishables*] se conserver.

lasting *adj* [*effect, impression*] durable; [*relationship*] sérieux/-ieuse.

lastly *adv* enfin, finalement.

last: **~-minute** *adj* de dernière minute; **~ rites** *n pl* derniers sacrements *mpl*.

latch *n* (fastening) loquet *m*; (spring lock) serrure *f* (de sûreté); **to put the door on the ~** bloquer le verrou en position ouverte.
■ **latch on**○: **~ on to [sth/sb]** s'accrocher à [*object, person*]; exploiter [*idea*].

latchkey *n* clé *f* plate.

late I *adj* **1** [*arrival, publication*] tardif/-ive; **in case of ~ delivery** en cas de retard de livraison; **to be ~ (for sth)** être en retard (pour qch); **to make sb ~** retarder qn; **to be ~ with the rent** payer son loyer avec du retard; **dinner will be a bit ~** le dîner sera retardé; **2** [*hour, supper, date, pregnancy*] tardif/-ive; **to have a ~ night** (aller) se coucher tard; **to be in one's ~ fifties** approcher de la soixantaine; **at this ~ stage** à ce stade avancé; **in ~ January** (à la) fin janvier; **in the ~ 50s** à la fin des années 50; **3** (deceased) **my ~ husband** mon pauvre mari.
II *adv* **1** [*arrive, start, finish*] en retard; **to be running ~** [*person*] être en retard; [*train, bus*] avoir du retard; **to start three months ~** commencer avec trois mois de retard; **2** [*get up, open, close*] tard; [*marry*] sur le tard; **~ last night/in the evening** tard hier soir/dans la soirée; **too ~!** trop tard!; **don't leave it too ~!** n'attendez pas trop (longtemps)!

latecomer *n* retardataire *mf*.

lately *adv* ces derniers temps.

later *adv* plus tard; **~ on** plus tard; **six months ~** six mois après; **to leave no ~ than 6 am** partir au plus tard à 6 heures; **see you ~!** à tout à l'heure!

latest I *adj* dernier/-ière (*before n*).
II *pron* **1** (news) **have you heard the ~?** est-ce que tu connais la dernière○?; **what's the ~ on her condition?** quoi de neuf sur son état de santé?; **2** (most recent) **the ~ in children's fashion** le dernier cri en matière de mode enfantine.
III **at the latest** *phr* au plus tard.

lathe *n* tour *m*.

lather *n* mousse *f*.

Latin ▶712 I *n* **1** (language) latin *m*; **2** (Hispanic) Latin/-e *m/f*.
II *adj* [*grammar, poetry*] latin; [*teacher, lesson*] de latin.

Latin: **~ America** *pr n* Amérique *f* latine; **~ American** *adj* latino-américain.

Latino *n* (US) Latino-Américain/-e *m/f*.

latitude *n* latitude *f*.

latrine *n* latrines *fpl*.

latter *n* **the ~** (singular noun) ce dernier/cette dernière *m/f*; (plural noun) ces derniers/ces dernières *mpl/fpl*.

lattice window *n* fenêtre *f* à croisillons de plomb.

Latvia ▶574 *pr n* Lettonie *f*.

laugh I *n* **1** (amused noise) rire *m*; **she gave a loud ~** elle a ri bruyamment; **with a ~** en riant; **to like a good ~** aimer bien rire; **to get a ~** faire rire; **2**○ (source of amusement) **to do sth for a ~** faire qch pour rigoler○; **their brother is a real ~** leur frère est très drôle or marrant○; **it will be a ~**○ on va bien s'amuser.
II *vi* rire (**about, over** de); **to make sb ~** faire rire qn; **to ~ out loud** rire aux éclats, rire tout haut; **to ~ to oneself** rire en soi-même, rire tout bas; **to ~ at sb/sth** rire de qn/qch; **the children ~ed at the clown** le clown a fait rire les enfants; **he's afraid of being ~ed at** il a peur qu'on se moque de lui.
IDIOMS **you'll be ~ing on the other side of your face** ça va t'ôter l'envie de rire; **to ~ in sb's face** rire au nez de qn; **to ~ oneself sick** se tordre de rire.
■ **laugh off**: **~ [sth] off, ~ off [sth]** choisir de rire de [*criticism, insult*].

laughable *adj* ridicule.

laughing stock *n* risée *f*; **the ~ of Europe** la risée de toute l'Europe.

laughter *n* rires *mpl*; **to roar with ~** hurler de rire; **a fit of ~** un fou rire.

launch I *n* **1** (for patrolling) vedette *f*; (for pleasure) bateau *m* de plaisance; **2** (of new boat, rocket) lancement *m*; (of lifeboat) mise *f* à l'eau; (of campaign, product) lancement *m*.
II *vtr* **1** mettre [qch] à l'eau [*dinghy, lifeboat*]; lancer [*new ship, missile, rocket*]; **2** (start) lancer [*campaign, career, product*]; ouvrir [*investigation*].

launch pad, **launching pad** *n* aire *f* de lancement.

launderette (GB), **laundromat** (US) *n* laverie *f* automatique.

laundering *n* blanchissage *m*.

laundry *n* **1** (commercial) blanchisserie *f*; (in hotel, house) laverie *f*; **2** (linen) linge *m*; **to do the ~** faire la lessive.

laurel *n* laurier *m*.

lava *n* lave *f*.

lavatory *n* toilettes *fpl*.

lavender ▶559 *n* lavande *f*.

lavender blue ▶559 *n, adj* bleu (*m*) lavande *inv*.

lavish *adj* [*party, lifestyle*] somptueux/-euse.

law *n* **1** (body of rules) loi *f*; **to obey/break the ~** respecter/enfreindre la loi; **to be against the ~** être interdit; **under Italian ~** d'après la loi italienne; **by ~** conformément à la loi; **court of ~** cour *f* de justice; **to take the ~ into one's own hands** faire justice soi-même; **2** (rule) loi *f*; **a ~ against vagrancy** une loi interdisant le vagabondage; **the ~s on drink-driving** les lois sur la conduite en état d'ivresse; **3**○ (police) police *f*; **4** (Univ) droit *m*; **to study ~** faire son droit.

IDIOMS **to lay down the ~** dicter or imposer sa loi.

law: **~-abiding** *adj* respectueux/-euse des lois; **~ and order** *n* ordre *m* public; **~-breaking** *n* violation(s) *f(pl)* de la loi; **~ court** *n* tribunal *m*; **~ faculty** *n* faculté *f* de droit.

lawful *adj* [*owner, strike*] légal; [*conduct*] licite; [*wife, husband*] légitime.

lawless *adj* [*period, society*] anarchique; [*area*] tombé dans l'anarchie.

lawn *n* pelouse *f*.

lawnmower *n* tondeuse *f* (à gazon).

law: **~ school** *n* faculté *f* de droit; **~suit** *n* procès *m*.

lawyer ▶805 *n* (who practises law) avocat/-e *m/f*; (expert in law) juriste *mf*.

lax *adj* [*government*] laxiste; [*security*] relâché.

laxative *n* laxatif *m*.

lay **I** *adj* **1** (non-specialist) **~ person** profane *mf*; **2** [*preacher, member*] laïque.

II *vtr* **1** (place) poser [*object, card*] (**in** dans; **on** sur); (spread out) étaler [*rug, newspaper*] (**on** sur); (arrange) disposer (**on** sur); déposer [*wreath*]; **to ~ hands on sth** (find) mettre la main sur qch; **2** (set for meal) **to ~ the table** (**for**) mettre la table (pour); **to ~ an extra place** ajouter un couvert; **3** (prepare) préparer [*plan, trail*]; poser [*basis, foundation*]; tendre [*trap*]; **4** (fix in place) poser [*carpet, tiles, cable, mine*]; construire [*railway, road, sewer*]; **5** (Zool) pondre [*egg*].

III *vi* [*bird*] pondre.

IDIOMS **to ~ it on a bit thick**○ forcer un peu la dose○.

■ **lay down**: **~ down [sth]**, **~ [sth] down** **1** coucher [*baby, patient*]; étaler [*rug, cards*]; poser [*book, implement*]; déposer [*weapon*]; **2** (give) **to ~ down one's life for** sacrifier sa vie pour; **3** établir [*rule*]; poser [*condition*].

■ **lay off**: **~ off [sb]**, **lay [sb] off** (temporarily) mettre [qn] en chômage technique; (permanently) licencier.

■ **lay on**: **~ on [sth]**, **~ [sth] on** prévoir [*meal, transport*]; organiser [*trip*].

■ **lay out**: ¶ **~ [sth] out**, **~ out [sth]** **1** disposer [*goods, food*]; étaler [*map, garment, fabric*]; **2** concevoir [*building, advert*]; mettre [qch] en page [*letter*]; monter [*page*]; dessiner [*town, garden*]; **3** exposer [*reasons, facts*]; ¶ **~ [sb] out** faire la toilette mortuaire de [*person*].

lay: **~about**○ *n* fainéant/-e○ *m/f*; **~-by** *n* (GB) aire *f* de repos.

layer **I** *n* couche *f*.

II *vtr* **1** couper [qch] en dégradé [*hair*]; **2** disposer [qch] en couches [*cheese, potatoes*].

layman *n* profane *m*.

lay-off *n* (permanent) licenciement *m*; (temporary) mise *f* en chômage technique.

layout *n* (of page, book, computer screen) mise *f* en page; (of advert, article) présentation *f*; (of building) agencement *m*; (of town) plan *m*; (of garden) dessin *m*.

layout artist ▶805 *n* maquettiste *mf*.

laze *vi* (also **~ about**, **~ around**) paresser; **to ~ in bed** traîner○ au lit.

laziness *n* paresse *f*.

lazy *adj* [*person*] paresseux/-euse; [*day, holiday*] paisible; [*movement, pace*] lent.

LCD *n* (*abbr* = **liquid crystal display**) affichage *m* à cristaux liquides.

lead[1] **I** *n* **1** (in contest) **to be in the ~** être en tête; **to go into the ~** passer en tête; **to have a ~ of three points** avoir trois points d'avance; **to increase one's ~** creuser l'écart (**by** de); **2** (initiative) **to take the ~** prendre l'initiative; **to take the ~ in doing** être le premier/la première à faire; **to follow sb's ~** suivre l'exemple de qn; **3** (clue) piste *f*; **4** (role) rôle *m* principal; **5** (wire) fil *m*; **6** (GB) (for dog) laisse *f*.

II *noun modifier* [*guitarist*] premier/-ière (*before n*); [*role, singer*] principal.

III *vtr* **1** (guide, escort) mener, conduire [*person*] (**to sth** à qch; **to sb** auprès de qn; **out of** hors de; **through** à travers); **to ~ sb away** éloigner qn (**from** de); **to ~ sb across the road** faire traverser la rue à qn; **2** (bring) [*path, sign, smell*] mener (**to** à); **to ~ sb to do** amener qn à faire; **to be easily led** être très influençable; **3** mener [*army, team, attack, strike*]; diriger [*orchestra, research*]; **4** (be ahead of) avoir une avance sur [*rival, team*]; **to ~ the world** être au premier rang mondial; **to ~ the field** (in commerce, research) être le plus avancé; (in race) mener, être en tête; **5** (conduct, have) mener [*active life*]; **to ~ a life of luxury** vivre dans le luxe.

IV *vi* **1 to ~ to** [*path*] mener à; [*door*] s'ouvrir sur; [*exit, trapdoor*] donner accès à; **2** (result in) **to ~ to** entraîner [*complication, discovery, accident*]; **it was bound to ~ to trouble** ça devait mal finir; **3** [*runner, car, company*] être en tête; [*team, side*] mener; **to ~ by 15 seconds** avoir 15 secondes d'avance; **4** (in walk) aller devant; (in action, discussion) prendre l'initiative; (in dancing) conduire.

■ **lead on**: **~ [sb] on** **1** mener [qn] en bateau○ [*investor*]; **2** (sexually) provoquer.

■ **lead up to**: **~ up to [sth]** **1** précéder [*event*]; **2** se terminer par [*argument*]; **3** amener [*topic*].

lead[2] *n* **1** plomb *m*; **2** (in pencil) mine *f*; **3** (of window) (baguette *f* de) plomb *m*.

IDIOMS **to get the ~ out**○ (US) (stop loafing) se bouger; (speed up) se grouiller○.

leaded petrol (GB), **leaded gasoline** (US) *n* essence *f* au plomb.

leader *n* **1** (of nation) chef *m* d'État, dirigeant/-e *m/f*; (of gang) chef *m*; (of association) président/-e *m/f*; (of party) leader *m*; (of trade union) secrétaire *mf*; (of strike, movement) meneur/-euse *m/f*; (of project) directeur/-trice *m/f*; **2** (in competition) premier/-ière *m/f*; (horse) cheval *m* de tête; (in market, field) leader *m*.

leadership *n* dirigeants *mpl*, direction *f*; **under the ~ of** sous la direction de.

leadership qualities *n pl* qualités *fpl* de leader.

lead-free *adj* sans plomb.

leading *adj* **1** [*lawyer, politician*] éminent, important; [*company, bank*] important; [*brand*] dominant; [*position*] de premier plan; **2** [*role*] (main) majeur; (in theatre) principal; **3** (Sport) [*driver, car*] en tête de course; [*team*] en tête du classement.

leading edge *n* **at the ~ of** à la pointe de [*technology*].

leading: **~ lady** *n* actrice *f* principale; **~ man** *n* acteur *m* principal.

lead: **~ pencil** *n* crayon *m* à papier; **~ poisoning** *n* intoxication *f* par le plomb.

lead story *n* histoire *f* à la une○.

leaf *n* **1** (of plant) feuille *f*; **2** (of paper) feuille *f*; (of book) page *f*.
IDIOMS **to turn over a new ~** tourner la page.
■ **leaf through**: **~ through [sth]** feuilleter [*pages, papers, book*].

leaflet *n* dépliant *m*; **advertising ~** prospectus *m*.

league *n* **1** (alliance) ligue *f*; **to be in ~ with sb** être de mèche○ avec qn; **2** (GB Sport) (competition) championnat *m*; (association) ligue *f*; **3 they're not in the same ~** ils ne sont pas comparables.

league: **~ championship** *n* championnat *m* de ligue; **~ standings** (US) *n pl*, **~ table** (GB) *n* classement *m*.

leak I *n* **1** (crack) (in container, roof) fuite *f*; (in ship) voie *f* d'eau; **to spring a ~** se mettre à fuir; **2** (of liquid, gas) fuite *f*; **3** (disclosure) fuite *f* (**about** au sujet de).
II *vtr* divulguer [*information, document*].
III *vi* **1** [*container, roof*] fuir; [*boat*] faire eau; **2** [*liquid, gas*] s'échapper (**from** de).

lean I *adj* [*body, face*] mince; [*meat*] maigre.
II *vtr* appuyer (**against** contre); **to ~ one's elbows on sth** s'accouder à qch.
III *vi* [*wall, building*] pencher; **to ~ against sth** [*bicycle, ladder*] être appuyé contre qch; [*person*] s'appuyer à qch; (with back) s'adosser à qch; **to ~ out of the window** se pencher par la fenêtre.
■ **lean back** se pencher en arrière.
■ **lean forward** se pencher en avant.
■ **lean on**: ¶ **~ on [sth]** s'appuyer sur [*stick*]; s'accouder à [*windowsill*]; ¶ **~ on [sb] 1** (as support) s'appuyer sur [*person*]; **2** (depend on) compter sur [*person*]; **3** (pressurize) faire pression sur [*person*].

leap I *n* **1** (gen) saut *m*, bond *m*; (Sport) saut *m*; **in one ~** d'un bond; **2** (step in process) bond *m* (en avant); **a ~ of the imagination** un grand effort d'imagination; **3** (in price) bond *m* (**in** dans).
II *vi* **1** [*person, animal*] bondir, sauter; **to ~ to one's feet, to ~ up** se lever d'un bond; **to ~ across** or **over sth** franchir qch d'un bond; **to ~ out of bed** sauter du lit; **2** [*heart*] bondir (**with** de); **to ~ to sb's defence** bondir au secours de qn; **3** (also **~ up**) [*price, profit*] grimper (**by** de).
■ **leap at**: **~ at [sth]** sauter sur [*chance, offer*].
■ **leap out**: ¶ **~ out** surgir (**from behind** de derrière); ¶ **~ out at [sb]** surgir devant [*passerby*].

leap: **~frog** *n* saute-mouton *m*; **~ year** *n* année *f* bissextile.

learn I *vtr* **1** apprendre [*language, facts, trade*]; acquérir [*skills*] (**from** de); **to ~ (how) to windsurf** apprendre à faire de la planche à voile; **to ~ to live with sth** finir par se faire à qch; **2 to ~ that** apprendre que.
II *vi* apprendre; **to ~ about sth** apprendre qch; **to ~ from one's mistakes** tirer la leçon de ses erreurs.

learned *adj* [*person, book*] érudit; [*journal*] spécialisé; [*society*] savant.

learner *n* apprenant/-e *m/f*; **to be a quick/slow ~** apprendre/ne pas apprendre vite.

learning difficulties *n pl* difficultés *fpl* scolaires.

lease I *n* bail *m*.
II *vtr* louer [qch] à bail [*house*]; louer [*car*].
IDIOMS **to give sb a new ~ of** (GB) or **on life** [*drug*] redonner vie à qn; [*experience*] redonner des forces à qn.

leaseholder *n* locataire *mf* à bail.

leash *n* laisse *f*.

leasing *n* (by company) crédit-bail *m*; (by individual) location *f* avec option d'achat.

least

■ **Note** When *the least* followed by a noun is used to mean *the smallest quantity of*, it is translated by *le moins de*: *to have the least food* = avoir le moins de nourriture.
– When *the least* is used to mean *the slightest*, it is translated by *le* or *la moindre*: *I haven't the least idea* = je n'en ai pas la moindre idée.
– For further examples and particular usages, see the entry below.

I *det* (**the**) **~** (le) moins de; (in negative constructions) (le or la) moindre; **they have the ~ money** ce sont eux qui ont le moins d'argent; **they haven't the ~ chance of winning** ils n'ont pas la moindre chance de gagner; **the ~ thing annoys him** la moindre chose l'agace.
II *pron* le moins; **we have the ~** c'est nous qui en avons le moins; **it was the ~ I could do!** c'est la moindre des choses!; **that's the ~ of our problems!** c'est le cadet de nos soucis!
III *adv* **1** (with adjective or noun) **the ~** le/la moins; (with plural noun) les moins; **they were the ~ affected** c'étaient eux les moins affectés; **the ~ wealthy families** les familles les moins riches; **2** (with verbs) le moins *inv*; **I like that one (the) ~** c'est celui-là que j'aime le moins; **nobody liked it, ~ of all John** personne ne l'aimait, John encore moins que les autres.
IV at least *phr* (at the minimum) au moins; (qualifying statement) du moins; **she's at ~ 40** elle a au moins 40 ans; **they could at ~ have phoned!** ils auraient au moins pu téléphoner!; **he's gone to bed—at ~ I think so** il est allé se coucher—du moins, je pense.
V in the least *phr* **I'm not in the ~ (bit) worried** je ne suis pas inquiet du tout.

IDIOMS **last but not ~, last but by no means ~** enfin et surtout.

leather I *n* **1** (material) cuir *m*; **2** (also **wash ~**) peau *f* de chamois.
II *noun modifier* [*garment, object*] de cuir, en cuir.

leave I *n* **1** (also **~ of absence**) congé *m*; **three days' ~** trois jours de congé; **2** (permission) autorisation *f*; **to give sb ~ to do** donner à qn l'autorisation de faire.
II *vtr* **1** (depart from) partir de; (more permanently) quitter; (by going out) sortir de; **he left home early** il est parti tôt de chez lui; **to ~ school** quitter l'école; **to ~ the road** quitter la route; **to ~ the track** [*train*] dérailler; **to ~ the ground** [*plane*] décoller; **to ~ one's seat** se lever; **2** (forgetfully) oublier [*child, object*]; (deliberately) quitter [*partner*]; laisser [*key, instructions, tip*] (**for** pour; **with** à); (permanently) abandonner [*animal, family*]; **to ~ sb sth** laisser qch à qn; **to ~ sb/sth in sb's care** confier qn/qch à qn; **3** laisser [*food, drink, gap*]; **to ~ sth lying around** laisser traîner qch; **to ~ sth tidy** laisser qch en ordre; **we have five minutes left** il nous reste cinq minutes; **the accident left him a cripple** l'accident a fait de lui un invalide; **4** (allow to do) **to ~ sth to sb** laisser [qch] à qn [*job, task*]; **to ~ it (up) to sb to do** laisser à qn le soin de faire; **to ~ the decision (up) to sb** laisser à qn le soin de décider; **to ~ sb to it** laisser qn se débrouiller; **~ it to** or **with me** je m'en occupe; **to ~ it at that** en rester là; **5** [*oil, wine*] faire [*stain*]; [*cup, plate*] laisser [*stain, mark*]; faire [*hole, dent*]; **6** (postpone) laisser [*task, homework*]; **~ it till tomorrow** laisse ça pour demain; **7** (bequeath) léguer (**to sb** à qn).
III *vi* partir (**for** pour).

■ **leave around**: **~ [sth] around** laisser traîner [*books, toys*].

■ **leave aside**: **~ [sth] aside, ~ aside [sth]** laisser [qch] de côté; **leaving aside the question of...** sans parler du problème de...

■ **leave behind**: **~ [sb/sth] behind 1** (go faster than) distancer [*person, competitor*]; **to be** or **get left behind** (physically) se faire distancer; (intellectually) ne pas suivre, être largué°; (in business) [*country, company*] se laisser distancer; **2** [*traveller*] laisser [qch] derrière soi [*town, country*]; [*person*] quitter [*family, husband*]; en finir avec [*past*]; **3** (forget) oublier, laisser [*object, child, animal*]; **4** [*person*] laisser [*chaos, problems*]; [*earthquake, storm*] faire [*damage*].

■ **leave off**: **~ [sth] off 1** ne pas mettre [*coat, lid, blanket*]; (not put back on) ne pas remettre [*coat, lid, blanket*]; **2** ne pas allumer [*light, TV*]; ne pas brancher [*iron*]; (leave switched off) laisser [qch] éteint [*light, TV*]; laisser [qch] débranché [*iron*].

■ **leave on**: **~ [sth] on 1** garder [*coat, hat*]; laisser [*lid, blanket, bandage*]; **2** laisser [qch] allumé [*light, TV*]; laisser [qch] branché [*iron*]; laisser [qch] ouvert [*gas, tap*].

■ **leave out**: **~ [sb/ sth] out, ~ out [sb/ sth] 1** (accidentally) oublier [*word, ingredient, person*]; (deliberately) omettre [*name, fact*]; ne pas mettre [*ingredient, object*]; tenir [qn] à l'écart [*person*]; **to feel left out** se sentir tenu à l'écart; **to ~ sb out of** exclure qn de [*group*]; **2** (let remain outdoors) laisser [qch] dehors.

■ **leave over**: **~ [sth] over** laisser [*food, drink*].

Lebanon ▶574 *pr n* (also **the ~**) (le) Liban *m*.

lecherous *adj* lubrique.

lecture I *n* (public talk) conférence *f* (**on** sur); (GB Univ) cours *m* magistral (**on** sur); **to give a ~** (public talk) donner une conférence (**to** à); (GB Univ) faire un cours (**to** à).
II *vtr* **1** (GB Univ) donner des cours à [*class*]; **2** (scold) faire la leçon à [*person*].
III *vi* **1** (GB Univ) **she ~s in mathematics** elle enseigne les mathématiques (à l'université); **2** (give public talk) donner une conférence (**on** sur).

lecture: **~ hall** *n* (US) amphithéâtre *m*; **~ notes** *n pl* (GB Univ) notes *fpl* de cours.

lecturer ▶805 *n* **1** (speaker) conférencier/-ière *m/f*; **2** (GB Univ) enseignant/-e *m/f* (du supérieur); **3** (US Univ) ≈ chargé *m* de cours.

lecture theatre *n* (GB) amphithéâtre *m*.

ledge *n* **1** (shelf) rebord *m*; **2** (on mountain) saillie *f* (rocheuse); (in climbing) vire *f*.

ledger *n* registre *m* de comptabilité, grand livre *m*.

leech *n* sangsue *f*.

leek *n* poireau *m*.

leer *vi* **to ~ at sb/sth** lorgner° qn/qch.

left I *n* gauche *f*; **to the ~** vers la gauche; **on the ~** sur la gauche; (politically) à gauche.
II *adj* gauche.
III *adv* à gauche.

left: **~-hand drive** *adj* [*car*] avec la conduite à gauche; **~-handed** *adj* gaucher/-ère; **~-luggage (office)** *n* (GB) consigne *f*; **~overs** *n pl* restes *mpl*.

left wing I *n* **the ~** la gauche *f*.
II **left-wing** *adj* [*attitude*] de gauche; **they are very ~** ils sont très à gauche.

leg I *n* **1** ▶523 (of person, horse) jambe *f*; (of other animal) patte *f*; **2** (of furniture) pied *m*; **3** (Culin) (of lamb) gigot *m*; (of veal) cuisseau *m*; (of poultry, pork, frog) cuisse *f*; (of venison) cuissot *m*; **4** (of trousers) jambe *f*; **5** (of journey, race) étape *f*.
II° *vtr* **to ~ it** (walk) marcher, aller à pied; (run away) cavaler°.
IDIOMS **to cost an arm and a ~** coûter les yeux de la tête; **to pull sb's ~** faire marcher qn.

legacy *n* legs *m*; **the ~ of** l'héritage *m* de [*era, artist*]; les séquelles *fpl* de [*war*].

legal *adj* **1** [*document, system*] juridique; [*costs*] de justice; **to take ~ advice** consulter un avocat; **2** [*heir, right, separation*] légal; [*owner, claim*] légitime.

legal action *n* **to take ~ against sb** intenter un procès à qn.

legal: **~ aid** *n* aide *f* juridique; **~ holiday** *n* (US) jour *m* férié.

legalize *vtr* légaliser.

legally *adv* **1** [*liable, valid, void*] juridiquement; **2** [*act*] légalement.

legal: **~ practitioner** *n* juriste *mf*; **~ proceedings** *n pl* poursuites *fpl* judiciaires; **~ tender** *n* monnaie *f* légale.

legend *n* légende *f* (**of** de); **~ has it that...** selon la légende...

leggings *n pl* (for baby) collant *m*; (for woman) caleçon *m*.

legible *adj* lisible.

legionnaire's disease ▶686| *n* maladie *f* du légionnaire.

legislation *n* législation *f*; **a piece of ~** une loi.

legitimacy *n* légitimité *f*.

legitimate *adj* **1** (justifiable) [*action, question, request*] légitime; [*excuse*] valable; **2** (lawful) [*organization*] régulier/-ière; [*child, heir, owner*] légitime.

leisure I *n* loisirs *mpl*; **to do sth at (one's) ~** prendre son temps pour faire qch.
II *noun modifier* [*centre, facilities*] de loisirs; **~ industry** industrie *f* des loisirs.

leisure: **~ time** *n* loisirs *mpl*, temps *m* libre; **~ wear** *n* vêtements *mpl* de sport.

lemon ▶559| *n* **1** (fruit) citron *m*; **2**° (fool) **to look a ~** avoir l'air tout bête.

lemonade *n* (fizzy) limonade *f*; (still) citronnade *f*; (US) (fresh) citron *m* pressé.

lemon: **~ cheese**, **~ curd** *n* (GB) crème *f* au citron; **~ juice** *n* jus *m* de citron; (GB) (drink) citron *m* pressé; **~ sole** *n* (GB) limande-sole *f*; **~ tea** *n* thé *m* au citron; **~ tree** *n* citronnier *m*; **~ yellow** ▶559| *n, adj* jaune (*m*) citron *inv*.

lend *vtr* prêter [*object, money*]; conférer [*quality, credibility*] (**to** à); prêter [*support*]; **to ~ sb sth, to ~ sth to sb** prêter qch à qn; **to ~ a hand** donner un coup de main; **to ~ one's name to** prêter son nom à; **to ~ weight to sth** donner du poids à qch.

length ▶738| **I** *n* **1** longueur *f*; **what ~ is the plank?** de quelle longueur est la planche?; **to be 50 cm in ~** faire 50 cm de long; **to cycle the ~ of Italy** faire l'Italie d'un bout à l'autre à bicyclette; **2** (of book, film, list) longueur *f*; (of event, prison sentence) durée *f*; **he can't concentrate for any ~ of time** il n'arrive pas à se concentrer pendant (très) longtemps; **3** (of string, carpet, wood) morceau *m*; (of fabric) ≈ métrage *m*; (of pipe, track) tronçon *m*; **dress ~** hauteur *f* de robe; **4** (Sport) longueur *f*.
II at length *phr* longuement.

lengthen I *vtr* rallonger [*garment*] (**by** de, par); prolonger [*shelf*] (**by** de, par); prolonger [*stay*].
II *vi* [*queue, list*] s'allonger; [*skirts*] devenir plus long; [*days*] rallonger.

lengths *n pl* **to go to great ~ to do** se donner beaucoup de mal pour faire

lengthy *adj* long/longue.

lenient *adj* [*person*] indulgent (**with** pour); [*punishment*] léger/-ère.

lens *n* (in optical instruments) lentille *f*; (in spectacles) verre *m*; (in camera) objectif *m*; (contact) lentille *f*; **hard/soft ~es** lentilles *fpl* rigides/souples.

lens: **~ cap** *n* bouchon *m* d'objectif; **~ hood** *n* parasoleil *m*.

lentil *n* lentille *f*.

Leo *pr n* Lion *m*; ▶ **Aquarius**.

leopard *n* léopard *m*.

leotard *n* justaucorps *m inv*.

leprosy *n* lèpre *f*.

lesbian *n* lesbienne *f*.

less

■ **Note** When used as a determiner to indicate a smaller amount of something, *less* is often translated by *moins de*: *less traffic* = moins de circulation. – When used to modify an adjective or adverb, *less* is translated by *moins*: *less interesting* = moins intéressant; *less often* = moins souvent.

I *det* moins de; **~ beer** moins de bière; **I have ~ money than him** j'ai moins d'argent que lui.
II *pron* moins; **I have ~ than you** j'en ai moins que toi; **even ~** encore moins; **they let me have it for ~** ils me l'ont laissé pour moins; **she's nothing ~ than a liar** elle n'est rien de moins qu'une menteuse; **he's ~ of a fool than you think** il est moins bête que tu ne le penses; **the ~ said about it the better** moins on en parle, mieux ça vaut.
III *adv* moins; **I read ~ these days** je lis moins à présent; **it matters ~ than it did before** cela a moins d'importance qu'avant; **she is no ~ qualified than you** elle n'est pas moins qualifiée que toi; **the more I see him, the ~ I like him** plus je le vois, moins je l'aime.
IV *prep* moins; **~ 15% discount** moins 15% de remise; **~ tax** avant impôts.
V less and less *phr* de moins en moins.
VI less than *phr* **1** (smaller amount) moins de; **~ than half** moins de la moitié; **in ~ than three hours** en moins de trois heures; **a sum of not ~ than £1,000** une somme qui s'élève au moins à 1 000 livres sterling; **2** (not very) **he was ~ than helpful** il était loin d'être serviable.

lessen *vtr* diminuer [*influence*]; réduire [*cost*]; atténuer [*impact, pain*].

lesser I *adj* moindre; **to a ~ extent** à un moindre degré; **~ being** être inférieur.
II *adv* moins; **~ known** moins connu.

lesson *n* cours *m*, leçon *f*; **Spanish ~** cours d'espagnol; **driving ~** leçon de conduite; **to give ~s** donner des cours (**in** de); **to take ~s** prendre des cours (**in** de); **I'm going to teach him a ~!** je vais lui donner une bonne leçon!

let[1]

■ **Note** When *let* is used with another verb to make a suggestion (*let's do it at once*), the first person plural of the appropriate verb can generally be used to express this in French: *faisons-le tout de suite*. (Note that the verb alone translates *let us do* and no pronoun appears in French.)

– In the spoken language, however, French speakers will use the much more colloquial *on* + *present tense* or *si on* + *imperfect tense*:
– *let's go!* = allons-y *or* on y va!; *let's go to the cinema tonight* = si on allait au cinéma ce soir?
– These translations can also be used for suggestions in the negative:
– *let's not take* or *don't let's take the bus—let's walk* = on ne prend pas le bus, on y va à pied *or* ne prenons pas le bus, allons-y à pied.
– When *let* is used to mean *allow*, it is generally translated by the verb *laisser*. For more examples and particular usages, see the entry below.

I *vtr* **1** (in suggestions, commands) **~'s get out of here!** sortons d'ici!; **~'s not** or **don't ~'s** (GB) **talk about that!** n'en parlons pas!; **~'s pretend that...** faisons comme si...; **~ me see, ~'s see...** voyons...; **~ me think about it** laisse-moi réfléchir; **never ~ it be said that** qu'il ne soit pas dit que; **just ~ him try it!** qu'il essaie!; **2** (allow) **to ~ sb do sth** laisser qn faire qch; **~ me explain** laisse-moi t'expliquer; **she let herself be intimidated** elle s'est laissée intimider; **don't ~ it get you down** ne te laisse pas abattre; **she wanted to go but they wouldn't ~ her** elle voulait y aller mais ils ne l'ont pas laissée faire; **I won't ~ them talk to me like that!** je ne permets pas qu'on me parle sur ce ton!; **~ me see, ~ me have a look** fais voir, fais-moi voir; **to ~ sth fall** laisser tomber qch; **to ~ one's hair grow** se laisser pousser les cheveux; **can you ~ me off here?** pouvez-vous me déposer ici?
II **let alone** *phr* à plus forte raison.
■ **let away**○: **~ [sb] away with doing sth** laisser qn faire qch.
■ **let down**: ¶ **~ [sb] down 1** (disappoint) laisser tomber [qn]; **it has never let me down** [*technique* , *machine*] ça a toujours marché; **to feel let down** être déçu; **2** (embarrass) faire honte à [qn]; ¶ **~ [sth] down, ~ down [sth] 1** (GB) dégonfler [*tyre*]; **2** rallonger [*garment*].
■ **let go**: ¶ **~ go** lâcher prise; **to ~ go of sb/sth** lâcher qn/qch; ¶ **~ [sb] go, ~ go [sb] 1** relâcher [*prisoner*]; **2** lâcher [*person, arm*]; **3** licencier [*employee*]; **4 to ~ oneself go** se laisser aller; ¶ **~ [sth] go, ~ go [sth]** lâcher [*rope, bar*].
■ **let in**: ¶ **~ in [sth], ~ [sth] in** [*roof, window*] laisser passer [*rain*]; [*shoes*] prendre [*water*]; [*curtains*] laisser passer [*light*]; ¶ **~ [sb] in, ~ in [sb] 1** (show in) faire entrer; (admit) laisser entrer; **I let myself in** je suis entré avec ma clé; **2 to ~ oneself in for** aller au devant de [*trouble*].
■ **let off**: ¶ **~ off [sth]** tirer [*fireworks*]; faire exploser [*bomb*]; faire partir [*gun*]; ¶ **~ [sb] off 1** (GB Sch) laisser sortir [*pupils*]; **2** (excuse) **to ~ sb off** dispenser qn de [*homework*]; **3** (leave unpunished) ne pas punir [*culprit*]; **to ~ sb off lightly** laisser qn s'en tirer à bon compte.
■ **let on 1** (GB) **to ~ on that** faire croire que; **2** (reveal) dire (**to sb** à qn).
■ **let out**: ¶ **~ out** (US) [*school*] finir (**at** à); ¶ **~ out [sth] 1** laisser échapper [*cry*]; **to ~ out a roar** beugler; **2** (GB) (reveal) révéler (**that** que); ¶ **~ [sth] out, ~ out [sth] 1** faire sortir [*animal*]; donner libre cours à [*anger*]; **2** élargir [*waistband*]; rallonger [*skirt*]; ¶ **~ [sb] out** laisser sortir [*prisoner*] (**of** de); faire sortir [*pupils, employees*] (**of** de).
■ **let through**: ¶ **~ [sb] through, ~ through [sb] 1** (in crowd) laisser passer; **2** (Sch, Univ) accorder un examen à; ¶ **~ [sth] through, ~ through [sth]** laisser passer [*error*].
■ **let up** [*rain, wind*] se calmer; [*pressure*] s'arrêter; [*heat*] diminuer.

let[2] *vtr* (also **~ out** GB) louer (**to** à); **'to ~'** 'à louer'.

letdown *n* déception *f*.

lethal *adj* [*substance, gas, dose*] mortel/-elle; [*weapon*] meurtrier/-ière.

letter *n* **1** lettre *f* (**to** pour; **from** de); **he receives a lot of ~s** il reçoit beaucoup de courrier; **2** (of alphabet) lettre *f*; **3** (character) caractère *m*.

letter: **~ bomb** *n* lettre *f* piégée; **~ box** *n* boîte *f* à lettres; **~head** *n* en-tête *m*; **~ post** *n* tarif *m* lettre; **~ rack** *n* porte-lettres *m inv*; **~s page** *n* courrier *m* des lecteurs.

letting *n* (GB) location *f*.

lettuce *n* salade *f*, laitue *f*.

leuk(a)emia ▶ 686 *n* leucémie *f*; **to have ~** être atteint de leucémie.

level I *n* **1** (gen, Sch) niveau *m*; **to be on the same ~ as sb** être du même niveau que qn; **at street ~** au niveau de la rue; **on a purely practical ~** sur un plan strictement pratique; **2** (standard) qualité *f*; **the ~ of training** la qualité de la formation; **3** (of pollution, noise) niveau *m*; (of unemployment, illiteracy) taux *m*; (of spending) montant *m*; (of satisfaction, anxiety) degré *m*; **4** (in hierarchy) échelon *m*; **at local ~** à l'échelon local; **5** (tool) niveau *m*.
II *adj* **1** [*shelf, floor*] droit; [*surface*] plan; [*table*] horizontal; **2** [*ground, surface, land*] plat; **3** (Culin) [*teaspoonful*] ras; **4 to be ~** [*shoulders, windows*] être à la même hauteur; [*floor, building*] être au même niveau; **~ with the ground** au ras du sol; **5 to remain ~** [*figures*] rester stable.
III *adv* **to draw ~** arriver à la même hauteur (**with** que).
IV *vtr* **1** raser [*village*]; **2** lancer [*accusation*] (**at** contre); adresser [*criticism*] (**at** à).
IDIOMS **to be ~-pegging** être à égalité; **to keep a ~ head** garder son sang-froid.
■ **level off** [*path*] continuer sur terrain plat; [*prices, curve*] se stabiliser.

level: **~ crossing** *n* passage *m* à niveau; **~-headed** *adj* sensé.

lever *n* (Aut, Tech) levier *m*; (small) manette *f*.

levy *n* taxe *f*, impôt *m*; **import ~** taxe à l'importation.

lewd *adj* [*joke, gesture, remark*] obscène; [*person*] lubrique.

liability I *n* **1** (Law) responsabilité *f*; **2** (drawback) handicap *m*.
II **liabilities** *n pl* passif *m*, dettes *fpl*.

liable *adj* **1** (likely) **to be ~ to do** risquer de faire; **it's ~ to rain** il risque de pleuvoir, il se peut qu'il pleuve; **2** (legally subject) **to be ~ to** être passible de [*fine*]; **to be ~ for tax** [*person, company*] être imposable; [*goods*] être soumis à l'impôt; **~ for military service** astreint au service militaire.

liaise *vi* travailler en liaison (**with** avec).

liaison *n* liaison *f*.

liaison officer *n* (Mil) officier *m* de liaison; (gen) responsable *mf* de la communication.

liar *n* menteur/-euse *m/f*.

libel I *n* **1** (crime) diffamation *f*; **to sue sb for ~** intenter un procès en diffamation à qn; **2** (article, statement) écrit *m* diffamatoire; **3** (slander) calomnie *f*.
II *vtr* diffamer.

liberal I *n* **1** libéral/-e *m/f*; **2** (derogatory) gauchisant/-e *m/f*.
II *adj* **1** (politically) libéral; **2** [*amount*] généreux/-euse; [*person*] prodigue (**with** de).

Liberal *n* libéral/-e *m/f*; **~ Democrat** (GB) libéral-démocrate *mf*.

liberalize *vtr* libéraliser.

liberated *adj* [*lifestyle, woman*] libéré.

liberation *n* libération *f* (**from** de); **women's ~** libération de la femme.

liberty *n* liberté *f*; **to take the ~ of doing** prendre la liberté de faire.

Libra *n* Balance *f*; ▶ **Aquarius**.

librarian ▶ 805 *n* bibliothécaire *mf*.

library I *n* bibliothèque *f*; **public ~** bibliothèque municipale; **mobile ~** (GB) bibliobus *m*.
II *noun modifier* [*book, card, ticket*] de bibliothèque.

lice *n pl* poux *mpl*.

licence (GB), **license** (US) *n* **1** (for trading) licence *f*; **2** (to drive, fish) permis *m*; (for TV) redevance *f*; **to lose one's (driving) ~** se faire retirer son permis (de conduire); **to be married by special ~** se marier avec dispense; **artistic ~** liberté *f* de l'artiste.

licence: **~ number** *n* (of car) numéro *m* minéralogique or d'immatriculation; **~ plate** *n* plaque *f* minéralogique or d'immatriculation.

license I *n* (US) = **licence**.
II *vtr* **1** (authorize) autoriser (**to do** à faire); **2** faire immatriculer [*vehicle*].

licensed *adj* **1** [*restaurant*] qui a une licence de débit de boissons; **2** [*dealer, firm, taxi*] agréé; [*pilot*] breveté; [*vehicle*] en règle.

licensing laws *n pl* (GB) lois *fpl* réglementant la vente des boissons alcoolisées.

lick *vtr* **1** lécher; **the cat was ~ing its paws** le chat se léchait les pattes; **to ~ one's lips** (at prospect) se délecter (**at** à); **to ~ sb's boots**○ lécher les bottes○ de qn; **2**○ écraser [*team, opponent*]; **to get ~ed** se faire écraser.
IDIOMS **to ~ one's wounds** panser ses blessures.

licorice (US) = **liquorice**.

lid *n* **1** (cover) couvercle *m*; **2** (eyelid) paupière *f*.
IDIOMS **to blow the ~ off sth**○ lever le voile sur qch; **to flip one's ~**○ éclater.

lie I *n* mensonge *m*; **to tell a ~** mentir; **to give the ~ to sth/sb** démentir qch/qn.
II *vi* **1** (tell falsehood) mentir (**to sb** à qn; **about** à propos de); **he ~d about her** il a menti à son propos; **2** [*person, animal*] (action) s'allonger; (state) être allongé; [*objects*] être couché; **he was lying on the bed** il était allongé sur le lit; **to ~ on one's back** être allongé or s'allonger sur le dos; **~ still** ne bougez pas; **he lay dead** il gisait mort; **here ~s John Brown** ci-gît John Brown; **3** (be situated) être; (remain) rester; **that's where our future ~s** c'est là qu'est notre avenir; **to ~ before sb** [*life, career*] s'ouvrir devant qn; **what ~s ahead?** qu'est-ce qui nous attend?; **the house lay empty for years** la maison est restée vide pendant des années; **4** (can be found) résider; **their interests ~ elsewhere** leurs intérêts résident ailleurs; **to ~ in** [*cause, secret, talent*] résider dans; [*popularity, strength, fault*] venir de; **the responsibility ~s with them** ce sont eux qui sont responsables.
IDIOMS **to ~ low** garder un profil bas; **to take it lying down**○ se laisser faire.
■ **lie around** traîner; **to leave sth lying around** laisser traîner qch.
■ **lie down** (briefly) s'allonger; (for longer period) se coucher.

lie-in *n* **to have a ~** faire la grasse matinée.

life *n* **1** (as concept) vie *f*; **a matter of ~ and death** une question de vie ou de mort; **to bring sb back to ~** (Med) ranimer qn; **to take ~ as it comes** prendre la vie comme elle vient; **to make ~ difficult for sb** compliquer la vie à qn; **~ must go on** la vie continue; **that's ~!** c'est la vie!; **run for your ~!** sauve qui peut!; **2** (period from birth to death) vie *f*; **the first time in my ~** la première fois de ma vie; **a job for ~** un emploi à vie; **a friend for ~** un ami pour la vie; **to spend one's ~ doing** passer sa vie à faire; **early in ~** très tôt; **for the rest of one' s ~** pour le restant de ses jours; **3** (animation) vie *f*, vitalité *f*; **full of ~** plein de vie; **to come to ~** [*shy person*] sortir de sa réserve; [*fictional character*] prendre vie; [*party*] s'animer; **4** (lifestyle) vie *f*; **private ~** vie privée; **his way of ~** son mode de vie; **a ~ of crime** une vie de criminel; **a sheltered ~** une vie protégée; **it's no ~ for a child** ce n'est pas une vie pour un enfant; **5** (of machine, product) durée *f*; **6** (Law) **to serve ~** être emprisonné à vie; **to sentence sb to ~** condamner qn à perpétuité.
IDIOMS **to have the time of one's ~** s'amuser comme un fou/une folle.

life: **~belt** *n* bouée *f* de sauvetage; **~boat** *n* canot *m* de sauvetage; **~buoy** *n* bouée *f* de sauvetage; **~ drawing** *n* dessin *m* d'après modèle; **~guard** ▶ 805 *n* surveillant/-e *m/f* de baignade; **~ imprisonment** *n* réclusion *f* à perpétuité; **~ insurance** *n* assurance-vie *f*; **~jacket** *n* gilet *m* de sauvetage.

lifeless *adj* [*body, object*] inanimé; [*performance*] peu vivant; [*voice*] éteint.

life: **~like** *adj* très ressemblant; **~line** *n* (on boat) bouée *f* de sauvetage; (in climbing) assurance *f*; **~saving** *n* (gen) sauvetage *m*; (Med) secourisme *m*; **~ sentence** *n* condamnation *f* à perpétuité; **~-size** *adj* grandeur nature *inv*; **~ span** *n* durée *f* de vie; **~ story** *n* vie *f*; **~style** *n* style *m* de vie.

life-support machine *n* **to be on a ~** être sous assistance respiratoire.

lifetime *n* vie *f*; **the chance of a ~** une chance unique.

lift I *n* **1** (GB) (elevator) (for people) ascenseur *m*; (for goods) monte-charge *m inv*; **2** (ride) **she asked me for a ~** elle m'a demandé de la conduire; **can I give you a ~?** je peux te déposer quelque part?; **3**° (boost) **to give sb a ~** remonter le moral à qn.
II *vtr* **1** (raise) soulever [*object, person*]; lever [*ban, sanctions*]; **to ~ one's arm** lever le bras; **to ~ sth out of the box** sortir qch de la boîte; **to ~ sth over the wall** faire passer qch pardessus le mur; **2** (boost) **to ~ sb's spirits** remonter le moral à qn; **3**° (steal) piquer° (**from** dans).
III *vi* [*bad mood, headache*] disparaître; [*fog*] se dissiper.
■ **lift off**: ¶ **~ off** [*rocket*] décoller; [*top, cover*] s'enlever; ¶ **~ [sth] off, ~ off [sth]** enlever [*cover, lid*].
■ **lift up**: **~ [sb/sth] up, ~ up [sb/sth]** soulever [*book, suitcase, lid*]; lever [*head, veil, eyes*]; relever [*jumper, coat*].

lift-off *n* lancement *m*.

ligament *n* ligament *m*.

light I *n* **1** (brightness) lumière *f*; **by the ~ of** à la lumière de [*torch*]; à la clarté de [*moon*]; **to hold sth up to the ~** tenir qch à la lumière; **against the ~** à contre-jour; **2** (in building, machine) lumière *f*; (in street) réverbère *m*; (on ship) feu *m*; **to turn a ~ on/off** allumer/éteindre une lumière; **a ~ came on** une lumière s'est allumée; **3** (part of gauge, dashboard) voyant *m* (lumineux); **4** (Aut) (headlight) phare *m*; (rearlight) feu *m* arrière; (inside car) veilleuse *f*; **to put one's ~s on** allumer ses phares; **5** (flame) **to set ~ to** mettre le feu à; **have you got a ~?** tu as du feu?; **6** (aspect) jour *m*; **to see sth in a different ~** voir qch sous un jour différent; **to appear in a bad ~** apparaître sous un jour défavorable; **7** (exposure) **to come to** or **be brought to ~** être découvert.
II **lights** *n pl* (**traffic**) **~s** feu *m*, feux *mpl*; **the ~s are red** le feu est au rouge.
III *adj* **1** (bright) **to get** or **grow ~er** [*sky*] s'éclaircir; **while it's still ~** pendant qu'il fait encore jour; **2** [*colour, wood, skin*] clair; **~ blue** bleu clair *inv*; **3** [*material, wind, clothing, meal*] léger/-ère; [*rain*] fin; [*drinker*] modéré; **to be a ~ sleeper** avoir le sommeil léger; **she is 2 kg ~er** elle pèse 2 kg de moins; **4** [*knock, footsteps*] léger/-ère; **5** [*work*] peu fatigant; [*exercise*] léger/-ère; **6** [*music*] léger/-ère; **a bit of ~ relief** un peu de divertissement; **some ~ reading** quelque chose de facile à lire.
IV *vtr* **1** allumer [*oven, cigarette*]; enflammer [*paper*]; craquer [*match*]; **to ~ a fire** faire un or du feu; **to ~ the fire** allumer le feu; **2** [*torch, lamp*] éclairer.
IDIOMS **to go out like a ~** s'endormir tout de suite.
■ **light up** [*lamp*] s'allumer; [*face*] s'éclairer; [*eyes*] briller de joie.

light bulb *n* ampoule *f*.

lighten I *vtr* éclaircir [*colour, hair, skin*]; détendre [*atmosphere*].
II *vi* [*sky, hair*] s'éclaircir; [*atmosphere*] se détendre.

light entertainment *n* variétés *fpl*.

lighter *n* (for smokers) briquet *m*; (for gas cooker) allume-gaz *m inv*.

light: **~-hearted** *adj* humoristique; **~house** *n* phare *m*; **~ industry** *n* industrie *f* légère.

lighting *n* éclairage *m*.

lightly *adv* **1** [*touch, kiss, season*] légèrement; **2** [*undertake, dismiss*] à la légère; **3 to get off ~** s'en tirer à bon compte.

lightning *n* éclairs *mpl*; **struck by ~** frappé par la foudre.

light: **~ opera** *n* opérette *f*; **~ railway** *n* transport *m* urbain sur rail; **~-sensitive** *adj* photosensible; **~ switch** *n* interrupteur *m*; **~weight** *adj* [*garment*] léger/-ère; [*champion*] des poids légers; **~ year** *n* année-lumière *f*.

like[1]

■ **Note** When *like* is used as a preposition (*like a child, do it like this*), it can generally be translated by *comme*.

I *prep* **1** (in the same manner as) comme; **to act ~ a professional** agir comme un professionnel or en professionnel; **I'm sorry to disturb you ~ this** je suis désolé de vous déranger comme ça; **stop behaving ~ an idiot!** arrête de faire l'idiot!; **2** (similar to, resembling) comme; **to be ~ sb/sth** être comme qn/qch; **to look ~** ressembler à; **big cities ~ London** les grandes villes comme Londres or telles que Londres; **you know what she's ~!** tu sais comment elle est!; **it was just ~ a fairytale!** on aurait dit un conte de fée!; **what's it ~?** c'est comment?; **there's nothing ~ a nice warm bath!** rien ne vaut un bon bain chaud!; **I've never seen anything ~ it!** je n'ai jamais rien vu de pareil!; **what was the weather ~?** quel temps faisait-il?; **3** (typical of) **it's not ~ her to be late** ça ne lui ressemble pas or ce n'est pas son genre d'être en retard; **4** (expressing probability) **it looks ~ rain** on dirait qu'il va pleuvoir; **you seem ~ an intelligent man** tu as l'air intelligent; **5** (close to) **it cost something ~ £20** cela a coûté environ 20 livres.
II *conj* **1** (in the same way as) comme; **~ they used to** comme ils le faisaient autrefois; **2**° (as if) comme si; **he acts ~ he owns the place** il se conduit comme s'il était chez lui.
III *n* **fires, floods and the ~** les incendies, les inondations et autres catastrophes de ce genre; **she won't speak to the ~s of us**°**!** elle refuse de parler à des gens comme nous!

like[2] *vtr* **1** aimer bien [*person*]; aimer (bien) [*artist, food, music, style*]; **to ~ A best** préférer A; **to be well ~d** être apprécié; **to want**

to be ~d vouloir plaire; **what I ~ about him/this car is**... ce que j'aime (bien) chez lui/dans cette voiture, c'est...; **I don't ~ the look/sound of that** ça ne me dit rien qui vaille; **if you ~ that sort of thing** à condition d'aimer ce genre de choses; **I ~ swimming, I ~ to swim** j'aime (bien) nager; **how do you ~ living in London?** ça te plaît de vivre à Londres?; **I ~ it!** ça me plaît!; **she doesn't ~ to be kept waiting** elle n'aime pas qu'on la fasse attendre; **2** (wish) vouloir, aimer; **I would ~ a ticket** je voudrais un billet; **I would** or **should ~ to do** je voudrais or j'aimerais faire; **would you ~ to come to dinner?** voudriez-vous venir dîner?; **we'd ~ her to come** nous voudrions or aimerions qu'elle vienne; **would you ~ me to come?** voulez-vous que je vienne?; **if you ~** si tu veux; **you can do what you ~** tu peux faire ce que tu veux.

likeable *adj* [*person*] sympathique; [*novel, music*] agréable.

likelihood *n* probabilité *f*, chances *fpl*; **in all ~** selon toute probabilité.

likely *adj* **1** (probable) probable; [*explanation*] plausible; **prices are ~ to rise** les prix risquent d'augmenter; **to be ~ to become president** avoir de fortes chances de devenir président; **it is** or **seems ~ that she'll come** il est probable qu'elle viendra; **it is hardly ~ that she'll come** il y a peu de chances qu'elle vienne; **a ~ story!** à d'autres○!; **2** (promising) [*candidate*] prometteur/-euse; **3** (potential) [*client*] potentiel/-ielle.

likeness *n* **family ~** air *m* de famille; **to be a good ~** être ressemblant.

likewise *adv* (similarly) également, de même; (also) aussi, de même.

liking *n* **to take a ~ to sb** se prendre d'affection pour qn.

lilac ▶ 559 *n, adj* lilas (*m*) *inv*.

lily *n* lys *m inv*.

lily: **~ of the valley** *n* muguet *m*; **~ pond** *n* bassin *m* planté de nénuphars.

limb *n* **1** (arm, leg) membre *m*; **2** (of tree) branche *f* (maîtresse).

lime *n* **1** (calcium) chaux *f*; **2** (fruit) citron *m* vert; **3** (also **~ tree**) tilleul *m*.

lime: **~ green** ▶ 559 *n, adj* citron (*m*) vert *inv*; **~ juice** *n* jus *m* de citron vert.

limelight *n* vedette *f*; **to be in the ~** tenir la vedette.

limestone *n* calcaire *m*.

limit I *n* **1** (boundary) limite *f*; **within the ~s of what we can do** dans la limite de ce que l'on peut faire; **to push sb to the ~** pousser qn à bout; **2** limitation *f* (**on** sur); **speed ~** limitation de vitesse; **to be over the ~** avoir trop d'alcool dans le sang.
II *vtr* limiter (**to** à); **to ~ oneself to** se limiter à.

limitation *n* **1** (restriction) restriction *f* (**on** à); **2** (shortcoming) limite *f*; **to know one's (own) ~s** connaître ses propres limites.

limited *adj* [*resources, intelligence*] limité.

limited company *n* (GB) société *f* anonyme.

limousine *n* limousine *f*.

limp I *n* **to have a ~** boiter.
II *adj* [*material, handshake*] mou/molle.
III *vi* **to ~ along** boiter; **to ~ in/away** entrer/s'éloigner en boitant.

line I *n* **1** (gen, Sport) ligne *f*; (shorter, thicker) trait *m*; (in drawing) trait *m*; **a straight ~** une ligne droite; **2** (of people, cars) file *f*; (of trees) rangée *f*; **3 to be in ~ for promotion** avoir des chances d'être promu; **you're next in ~** ça va être ton tour; **in ~ for** bien placé pour obtenir; **4** (queue) file *f*; **to stand in** or **wait in ~** faire la queue; **5** (on face) ride *f*; **6** (rope) corde *f*; (for fishing) ligne *f*; **to put the washing on the ~** étendre le linge; **7** (electric cable) ligne *f* (électrique); **8** (phone connection) ligne *f*; **at the other end of the ~** au bout du fil; **the ~ went dead** la ligne a été coupée; **9** (rail route) ligne *f* (**between** entre); (rails) voie *f*; **10** (shipping company, airline) compagnie *f*; **11** (in genealogy) lignée *f*; **she is second in ~ to the throne** elle est la deuxième dans l'ordre de succession au trône; **12** (in prose) ligne *f*; (in poetry) vers *m*; (of music) ligne *f*; **to start a new ~** aller à la ligne; **a ~ from** une citation de [*poem*]; **to learn one's ~s** [*actor*] apprendre son texte; **13** (conformity) **to fall into ~ with** s'aligner sur; **to bring sb into ~** ramener qn dans le rang; **to keep sb in ~** tenir qn en main; **our prices are out of ~ with theirs** nos prix ne s'accordent pas avec les leurs; **14** (stance) **the official ~** la position officielle; **to take a firm ~ with sb** se montrer ferme avec qn; **I don't know what ~ to take** je ne sais pas quelle ligne de conduite adopter; **15** (type of product) gamme *f*; **16** (Mil) **enemy ~s** lignes *fpl* ennemies.
II *vtr* doubler [*garment*] (**with** avec); tapisser [*shelf*] (**with** de); border [*route*].
III in line with *phr* en accord avec [*policy, trend*]; **to increase in ~ with** augmenter proportionnellement à.
IDIOMS **somewhere along the ~** (in time) à un certain moment; (at stage) quelque part.
■ **line up**: ¶ **~ up** (side by side) se mettre en rang; (one behind the other) se mettre en file; ¶ **~ [sth] up, ~ up [sth] 1** (align) aligner (**with** sur); **2** sélectionner [*team*].

lined *adj* [*face*] ridé; [*paper*] ligné; [*curtains*] doublé.

line management *n* direction *f* hiérarchique.

linen I *n* **1** (fabric) lin *m*; **2** (household) linge *m* de maison; (underwear) linge *m* de corps.
II *noun modifier* [*jacket, sheet*] en lin, de lin.

linen: **~ basket** *n* panier *m* à linge sale; **~ cupboard** (GB), **~ closet** (US) *n* armoire *f* à linge.

line: **~ of enquiry** *n* piste *f*; **~ of fire** *n* ligne *f* de tir; **~ of work** *n* métier *m*.

liner *n* paquebot *m* de grande ligne.

linesman *n* (GB) (in tennis) juge *m* de ligne; (in football, hockey) juge *m* de touche.

line: **~-spacing** *n* interlignage *m*; **~-up** *n* (Sport) équipe *f*; (personnel, pop group) groupe *m*.

linger *vi* **1** [*person*] s'attarder; [*gaze*] s'attarder (**on** sur); **2** [*memory, smell*] persister; **3** [*doubt, suspicion*] subsister.

lingerie *n* lingerie *f*.

linguist *n* linguiste *mf*.

linguistic *adj* linguistique.

linguistics *n* linguistique *f*.

lining *n* doublure *f*.

link I *n* **1** (in chain) maillon *m*; **the weak ~** le point faible; **2** (connection by rail, road) liaison *f*; **3** (between facts, events) rapport *m* (**between** entre); (between people) lien *m* (**with** avec); **4** (tie) relation *f*, lien *m* (**with** avec; **between** entre); **5** (in TV, radio, computing) liaison *f*.
II *vtr* **1** [*road, cable*] relier [*places, objects*]; **to ~ A to B** or **A and B** relier A à B; **to ~ arms** [*people*] se donner le bras; **to ~ arms with sb** donner le bras à qn; **2 to ~ sth to** or **with** lier qch à [*inflation*]; établir un lien entre qch et [*fact, crime, illness*]; **his name has been ~ed with** son nom a été associé à [*deed, name*]; **3** connecter [*terminals*]; **4** (in TV, radio) établir une liaison entre [*places*] (**by** par).
III linked *pp adj* [*issues, problems*] liés.
■ **link up** [*firms*] s'associer; **to ~ up with** s'associer avec [*college, firm*].

link: **~ road** *n* (GB) route *f* de raccordement; **~-up** *n* (on TV, radio) liaison *f*.

lino *n* lino *m*.

lint *n* tissu *m* ouaté.

lion *n* lion *m*; **the ~'s den** l'antre du lion.
IDIOMS **to take the ~'s share** se tailler la part du lion.

lion cub *n* lionceau *m*.

lioness *n* lionne *f*.

lip *n* **1** lèvre *f*; **my ~s are sealed!** bouche cousue○!; **2** (of jug) bec *m*.
IDIOMS **to keep a stiff upper ~** rester impassible.

lip: **~ gloss** *n* brillant *m* à lèvres; **~ pencil** *n* crayon *m* à lèvres; **~-read** *vi* lire sur les lèvres de quelqu'un; **~salve** *n* baume *m* pour les lèvres; **~stick** *n* rouge *m* à lèvres.

liqueur *n* liqueur *f*.

liqueur glass *n* verre *m* à liqueur.

liquid *n*, *adj* liquide (*m*).

liquidate *vtr* liquider.

liquidation *n* liquidation *f*.

liquid diet *n* diète *f* hydrique.

liquidizer *n* (GB Culin) mixeur *m*.

liquor *n* alcool *m*.

liquorice, licorice (US) *n* **1** (plant) réglisse *f*; **2** (substance) réglisse *m*.

liquor store *n* (US) magasin *m* de vins et spiritueux.

Lisbon ▶ 574 *pr n* Lisbonne.

lisp *n* zézaiement *m*; **to have a ~** zézayer.

list I *n* liste *f* (**of** de); **to be at the top of the ~** arriver en tête de liste; (a priority) être en tête des priorités.
II *vtr* **1** (gen) faire la liste de [*objects, people*]; **to be ~ed under** figurer sous; **to be ~ed in a directory** être repris dans un répertoire; **2** (Comput) lister.
III *vi* [*vessel*] donner de la bande.
IV listed *pp adj* (GB) [*building*] classé.

listen *vi* **1** écouter; **to ~ to sb/sth** écouter qn/qch; **to ~ at the door** écouter à la porte; **2** (pay heed) écouter; **to ~ to reason** écouter la voix de la raison; **3 to ~ (out) for** guetter [*sound*].
■ **listen in** écouter (indiscrètement).

listener *n* **1 to be a good ~** savoir écouter; **2** (to radio) auditeur/-trice *m/f*.

listeria *n* ▶ 686 listériose *f*.

listing I *n* (gen) inscription *f* (**in** dans); (Comput) listing *m*.
II listings *n pl* pages *fpl* d'informations.

listless *adj* [*person*] apathique.

literal *adj* **1** [*meaning*] littéral; **2** [*translation*] mot à mot.

literally *adv* [*mean*] littéralement; [*translate*] mot à mot; **to take sth ~** prendre qch au pied de la lettre; (**quite**) **~** bel et bien.

literary *adj* littéraire.

literary: **~ critic** *n* critique *m* littéraire; **~ criticism** *n* critique *f* littéraire.

literate *adj* **to be ~** savoir lire et écrire.

literature *n* **1** (literary writings) littérature *f*; **a work of ~** une œuvre littéraire; **2** (pamphlets, brochures) documentation *f*.

lithograph *n* lithographie *f*.

Lithuania ▶ 574 *pr n* Lituanie *f*.

litmus: **~ paper** *n* papier *m* de tournesol; **~ test** *n* (figurative) test *m* décisif.

litre, liter (US) *n* litre *m*.

litter I *n* **1** (rubbish) détritus *mpl*; (substantial) ordures *fpl*; (paper) papiers *mpl*; **2** (of young) portée *f*; **to have a ~** mettre bas; **3** (for pet tray) litière *f*.
II *vtr* **to be ~ed with** [*ground*] être jonché de.

litter: **~ bin** *n* poubelle *f*; **~ tray** *n* bac *m* à litière.

little[1]

■ **Note** When *a little* is used as a pronoun and if the sentence does not specify what it refers to, the pronoun *en* (= *of it*) must be added before the verb: *I have a little left* = il m'en reste un peu.

I *det* peu de; **~ chance** peu de chances; **very ~ damage** très peu de dégâts; **there's so ~ time** il y a si peu de temps; **too ~ money** trop peu or pas assez d'argent; **~ or no influence** presque pas d'influence.
II *pron* **a ~** un peu; **save a ~ for me** gardes-en un peu pour moi; **I only ate a ~** je n'en ai mangé qu'un peu; **I did what ~ I could** j'ai fait le peu que j'ai pu; **he remembers very ~** il ne se souvient pas bien; **there's ~ I can do** je ne peux pas faire grand-chose; **age has ~ to do with it** l'âge n'a pas grand-chose à voir là-dedans; **to do as ~ as possible** en faire le moins possible; **~ or nothing** quasiment rien.
III *adv* **1** (not much) peu; **I go there very ~** j'y vais très peu; **the next results were ~ better**

les résultats suivants étaient à peine meilleurs; **~ more than an hour ago** il y a à peine plus d'une heure; **a ~-known novel** un roman peu connu; **2** (not at all) **~ did they know that** ils étaient bien loin de se douter que.
IV a little (bit) *phr* un peu; **a ~ (bit) anxious** un peu inquiet; **a ~ less/more** un peu moins/plus; **stay a ~ longer** reste encore un peu.
V as little as *phr* **for as ~ as 10 dollars a day** pour seulement 10 dollars par jour; **as ~ as £60** juste 60 livres sterling.

little² *adj* **1** (small) [*house, smile, voice*] petit (*before n*); **poor ~ thing** pauvre petit/-e *m/f*; **2** (young) [*sister, boy*] petit (*before n*); **when I was ~** quand j'étais petit; **3** (in a small way) [*farmer, businessman*] petit (*before n*); **4** (expressing scorn) **a nasty ~ boy** un méchant petit garçon; **5** (short) [*snooze*] petit (*before n*); **a ~ holiday** quelques jours de vacances; **a ~ break** une petite pause.
IDIOMS **~ by ~** petit à petit.

little finger *n* petit doigt *m*, auriculaire *m*.
IDIOMS **to wrap** or **twist sb around one's ~** mener qn par le bout du nez.

live¹ *vi* **1** (dwell) [*animal*] vivre; [*person*] vivre, habiter (**with** avec); **they ~ at number 7** ils habitent au numéro 7; **to ~ in** vivre dans, habiter [*house, apartment*]; **not fit to ~ in** insalubre; **easy to ~ with** facile à vivre; **Paris is a nice place to ~** Paris est une ville agréable; **have you found anywhere to ~ yet?** avez-vous trouvé à vous loger?; **2** (exist) vivre; **to ~ for** ne vivre que pour [*sport, work*]; **nothing left to ~ for** plus de raison de vivre; **3** (remain alive) vivre; (survive) survivre; **to ~ to be eighty** vivre jusqu'à l'âge de quatre-vingts ans; **as long as I ~...** tant que je vivrai...; **he won't ~ through the night** il ne passera pas la nuit; **to ~ to regret sth** en venir à regretter qch; **long ~ democracy!** vive la démocratie!; **4** (subsist) vivre; **to ~ by one's wits** vivre d'expédients; **to ~ on** or **off** vivre de [*fruit, charity*]; vivre sur [*wage, capital*]; **that's not enough to ~ on** ça ne suffit pas pour vivre; **to ~ on junk food** ne manger que des cochonneries°; **5** (put up with) **to ~ with** accepter [*situation*]; supporter [*decor*].
IDIOMS **to ~ it up**° mener la grande vie; **to ~ sth down** faire oublier qch.
■ **live in** [*maid*] être logé et nourri.
■ **live on** [*reputation, tradition*] se perpétuer.
■ **live up to** [*person*] répondre à [*expectations*]; être à la hauteur de [*reputation*].

live² **I** *adj* **1** (alive) vivant; **2** [*broadcast*] en direct; [*performance*] sur scène; [*album*] enregistré en public; **before a ~ audience** devant un public; **3** [*cable*] sous tension.
II *adv* [*appear, broadcast*] en direct.

livelihood *n* gagne-pain *m*; **to lose one's ~** perdre ses moyens d'existence.

lively *adj* **1** [*person*] plein d'entrain; [*place, atmosphere, conversation*] animé; [*account*] vivant; [*mind*] vif/vive; **2** (fast) [*pace*] vif/vive; [*music, dance*] entraînant.

liven *v* ■ **liven up**: ¶ **~ up** s'animer; ¶ **~ up [sth], ~ [sth] up** animer [*event*].

liver *n* foie *m*.

liver: **~ salts** *n pl* sels *mpl* pour le foie; **~ spot** *n* tache *f* de vieillesse.

live: **~stock** *n* bétail *m*; **~ wire** *n* (person) boute-en-train *m inv*.

livid *adj* furieux/-ieuse; **~ with rage** blême de rage.

living **I** *n* **1** vie *f*; **to work for a ~** travailler pour gagner sa vie; **what do you do for a ~?** qu'est-ce que vous faites dans la vie?; **2** (lifestyle) vie *f*; **easy ~** une vie facile.
II *adj* vivant; **within ~ memory** de mémoire d'homme.

living: **~ conditions** *n pl* conditions *fpl* de vie; **~ quarters** *n pl* quartiers *mpl*; **~ room** *n* salle *f* de séjour, salon *m*; **~ standards** *n pl* niveau *m* de vie.

lizard *n* lézard *m*.

llama *n* lama *m*.

load **I** *n* **1** (sth carried) charge *f*; (on vehicle, animal) chargement *m*; (on ship, plane) cargaison *f*; (figurative) fardeau *m*; **three (lorry-)~s of sand** trois camions de sable; **2** (Tech) (weight) charge *f* (**on** sur); **3**° (a lot) **a (whole) ~ of people** des tas° de gens; **that's a ~ of nonsense**° c'est vraiment n'importe quoi°.
II loads° *n pl* **~s of** (+ plural nouns) des tas° de; **~s of times** plein de or des tas° de fois; **we've got ~s of time** nous avons tout notre temps; **~s of work** un travail fou°.
III *vtr* **1** (gen) charger [*vehicle, gun*] (**with** de); mettre un film dans [*camera*]; **2** (Comput) charger [*program*]; **3 to ~ sb with** combler qn de [*presents, honours*].
IDIOMS **the dice are ~ed against him** tout est contre lui.
■ **load down**: **~ [sb] down** charger qn (**with** de); **to be ~ed down with sth** plier sous le poids de qch.

loaded *adj* **1** [*tray, lorry, gun*] chargé (**with** de); **2**° (rich) bourré de fric°; **3** [*question*] tendancieux/-ieuse.

loading *n* (of vehicle) chargement *m*.

loaf *n* pain *m*; **a ~ of bread** un pain.
■ **loaf about, loaf around** traînasser.

loafer *n* **1** (shoe) mocassin *m*; **2** (idler) flemmard/-e° *m/f*.

loan **I** *n* (when borrowing) emprunt *m*; (when lending) prêt *m*; **to be on ~** [*museum object*] être prêté (**to** à); **the book is already on ~** le livre a déjà été emprunté.
II *vtr* (also **~ out**) prêter [*object, money*] (**to** à).

loan: **~ agreement** *n* contrat *m* de prêt; **~ shark**° *n* usurier/-ière *m/f*.

loathe *vtr* détester (**doing** faire).

lobby **I** *n* **1** (of hotel) hall *m*; (of theatre) lobby *m*; **2** (also **~ group**) lobby *m*.
II *vi* faire pression (**for** pour obtenir).

lobe *n* (Anat, Bot) lobe *m*.

lobotomy *n* lobotomie *f*.

lobster **I** *n* homard *m*.

II *noun modifier* [*salad, soup*] au homard.
lobster pot *n* casier *m* à homards.
local I *n* **1 the ~s** les gens *mpl* du coin; **2** (pub) pub *m* du coin.
II *adj* **1** (of district) [*library, shop*] du quartier; [*newspaper*] local; [*radio, news*] régional; [*speciality*] du pays; [*tradition*] local; **2** (of country) [*currency, time*] local.
local: **~ anaesthetic** *n* anesthésique *m* local; **~ authority** *n* (GB) autorités *fpl* locales; **~ call** *n* communication *f* téléphonique locale; **~ election** *n* élection *f* locale; **~ government** *n* administration *f* locale.
locality *n* **1** (neighbourhood) voisinage *m*; **2** (place) endroit *m*.
localized *adj* localisé.
locate *vtr* **1** (find) retrouver [*object*]; localiser [*fault*]; **2** (position) situer [*site*].
location *n* endroit *m*; **on ~** [*filmed*] en extérieur.
lock I *n* **1** (with key) serrure *f*; (with bolt) verrou *m*; **under ~ and key** sous clé; **2** (of hair) mèche *f*; **3** (on canal) écluse *f*; **4** (Comput) verrouillage *m*.
II *vtr* (with key) fermer [qch] à clé; (with bolt) verrouiller.
III *vi* **1** [*door, drawer*] fermer à clé; **2** [*steering wheel*] se bloquer.
■ **lock away**: **~ [sth] away** mettre [qch] sous clé.
■ **lock in**: **~ [sb] in** enfermer [*person*]; **to ~ oneself in** s'enfermer.
■ **lock out**: **~ [sb] out** (on purpose) fermer la porte à clé pour empêcher qn d'entrer; (by mistake) laisser qn dehors sans clé.
■ **lock together** [*components, pieces*] s'emboîter.
■ **lock up**: ¶ **~ up** fermer; ¶ **~ [sth] up, ~ up [sth]** fermer [qch] à clé [*house*]; ¶ **~ [sb] up, ~ up [sb]** enfermer [*hostage*]; mettre [qn] sous les verrous [*killer*].
locker *n* casier *m*, vestiaire *m*.
locker room *n* vestiaire *m*.
locket *n* médaillon *m*.
lock: **~ gate** *n* porte *f* d'écluse; **~ keeper** *n* éclusier/-ière *m/f*; **~-out** *n* lock-out *m inv*, grève *f* patronale; **~smith** *n* serrurier *m*.
locomotive *n* locomotive *f*.
lodge I *n* (small house) pavillon *m*; (for gatekeeper) loge *f* (du gardien).
II *vtr* **1** (house) loger [*person*]; **2** (Law) **to ~ an appeal** faire appel; **to ~ a complaint** porter plainte; **to ~ a protest** protester.
III *vi* **1** [*person*] loger (**with** chez); **2** [*bullet*] se loger; [*small object*] se coincer.
lodger *n* (room only) locataire *mf*; (with meals) pensionnaire *mf*.
lodgings *n pl* logement *m*.
loft *n* **1** (attic) grenier *m*; **2** (US) (apartment) loft *m*.
log I *n* **1** (of wood) rondin *m*; (for burning) bûche *f*; **2** (written record) registre *m*; **3** (of ship) journal *m* de bord; (of plane) carnet *m* de vol.
II *vtr* **1** (record) noter; **2** (also **~ up**) avoir à son actif [*miles*].
IDIOMS **to sleep like a ~** dormir comme une souche.
■ **log in, log on** (Comput) ouvrir une session, se connecter.
■ **log off, log out** (Comput) clore une session, se déconnecter.
log: **~ cabin** *n* cabane *f* en rondins; **~ fire** *n* feu *m* de bois.
loggerheads *n pl* **to be at ~** être en désaccord (**with** avec).
logic *n* logique *f*.
logical *adj* logique.
logo *n* logo *m*.
loin *n* (Culin) (GB) ≈ côtes *fpl* premières; (US) ≈ filet *m*.
loiter *vi* (idly) traîner; (pleasurably) flâner; (suspiciously) rôder.
lollipop *n* sucette *f*.
London ▶ 574 *pr n* Londres.
loneliness *n* (of person) solitude *f*; (of position) isolement *m*.
lonely *adj* [*person*] seul; [*life*] solitaire; [*place*] isolé.
lonely hearts' club *n* club *m* de rencontres.
loner *n* solitaire *mf*.
lonesome *adj* (US) solitaire.
long ▶ 738 I *adj* **1** [*process, wait, journey*] long/longue; [*delay*] important; **to be 20 minutes ~** durer 20 minutes; **how ~ is the interval?** combien de temps dure l'entracte?; **is an hour ~ enough?** est-ce qu'une heure suffira?; **it's been a ~ day** la journée a été longue; **to get ~er** [*days*] s'allonger; **to work ~ hours** faire de longues journées; **2** (in expressions of time) **she's been away a ~ time** elle est restée longtemps absente; **it's been a ~ time since**... ça fait longtemps que...; **that's a ~ time** c'est long; **she hasn't been well for a ~ time** ça fait longtemps qu'elle est malade; **to take a ~ time** [*person*] être lent; [*task*] prendre longtemps; **3** [*dress, hair, queue*] long/longue; [*grass*] haut; [*detour*] grand (*before n*); **a 20 m-~ rope** une corde de 20 m de long; **to be 20 m ~** avoir or faire 20 m de long; **to get ~** [*grass, hair*] pousser; [*list, queue*] s'allonger; **4** (in expressions of distance) **a ~ way off** loin; **we've come a ~ way** nous avons fait beaucoup de chemin; **to go a ~ way towards doing** contribuer largement à faire; **by a ~ way** de loin.
II *adv* **1** (a long time) longtemps; **I won't be ~** je n'en ai pas pour longtemps; **how ~ will you be?** tu en as pour combien de temps?; **don't be ~** dépêche-toi; **I've been here ~er than you** je suis ici depuis plus longtemps que toi; **(for) as ~ as you like** aussi longtemps que tu veux; **the ~er we stayed the hotter it grew** plus le temps passait et plus il faisait chaud; **it 's been so ~ since**... ça fait si longtemps que...; **has he been gone ~?** est-ce qu'il y a longtemps qu'il est parti?; **I haven't got ~** je n'ai pas beaucoup de temps; **~ enough** assez longtemps; **just ~ enough to**... juste le temps de...; **this won't take ~** ça ne prendra pas longtemps; **~er than expected**

plus longtemps que prévu; **how ~ did it take him?** il lui a fallu combien de temps?; **~er than he thought** plus de temps qu'il ne pensait; **before ~** (in past) peu après; (in future) dans peu de temps; **not for ~** pas longtemps; **~ after** longtemps après; **not ~ after** peu après; **it's ~ past your bedtime** tu devrais être couché depuis longtemps; **~ ago** il y a longtemps; **~ before** bien avant; **~ since** depuis longtemps; **he's no ~er head** il n'est plus chef; **2** (for a long time) depuis longtemps; **those days are ~ gone** ce temps-là n'est plus.
III *vi* **to ~ for sth** avoir très envie de qch; **to ~ to do** rêver de faire.
IV **as long as** *phr* (provided) du moment que (+ *indic*), pourvu que (+ *subj*).
IDIOMS **~ time no see**○! ça fait une paye○ qu'on ne s'est pas vus!; **so ~**○! salut!.

long-distance *adj* [*runner*] de fond; [*telephone call*] (within the country) interurbain; (abroad) international; **~ lorry driver** (GB) routier *m*.

long-haul *adj* [*flight, aircraft*] long-courrier *inv*.

longing *n* grand désir *m* (**for** de; **to do** de faire); (nostalgic) nostalgie *f* (**for** de).

longitude *n* longitude *f*; **at a ~ of 52°** par 52° de longitude.

long: **~ jump** ▶649 *n* (GB) saut *m* en longueur; **~-life** *adj* [*milk*] longue conservation *inv*; [*battery*] longue durée *inv*; **~-range** *adj* [*missile*] (à) longue portée; [*forecast*] à long terme; **~-sighted** *adj* presbyte; **~-standing** *adj* de longue date; **~-wave** *n* grandes ondes *fpl*; **~-winded** *adj* verbeux/-euse.

loo○ *n* (GB) vécés○ *mpl*, toilettes *fpl*.

look I *n* **1** (glance) coup *m* d'œil; **to have** or **take a ~ at sth** jeter un coup d'œil à or sur qch; **to have** or **take a good ~ at** regarder [qch] de près; **to have a ~ inside/behind sth** regarder à l'intérieur de/derrière qch; **to have a ~ round** faire un tour dans [*park, town*]; **to have a ~ round the shops** faire les magasins; **to have a ~ through** chercher dans [*archives, files*]; parcourir [*essay, report*]; **to take a long hard ~ at sth** étudier sérieusement qch; **2** (search) **to have a (good) ~** (bien) chercher; **3** (expression) regard *m*; **a ~ of sadness** un regard triste; **from the ~ on his face...** à son expression...; **4** (appearance) (of person) air *m*; (of building, scenery) aspect *m*; **I like the ~ of it** ça a l'air bien; **I like the ~ of him** il a l'air sympa○; **I don't like the ~ of him** il ne m'inspire pas confiance.
II **looks** *n pl* **~s aren't everything** il n'y a pas que la beauté qui compte; **he's losing his ~s** il n'est pas aussi beau qu'autrefois.
III *vtr* **1** (gaze, stare) regarder; **to ~ sb in the eye** regarder qn dans les yeux; **~ who it is!** regarde qui voilà!; **2** (appear) **to ~ one's age** faire son âge; **she's 40 but she doesn't ~ it** elle a 40 ans mais elle ne les fait pas; **to ~ one's best** être à son avantage; **she still ~s the same** elle n'a pas changé; **it won't ~ good** ça sera mal vu.
IV *vi* **1** regarder (**into** dans; **over** par-dessus); **to ~ away** détourner le regard or les yeux; **to ~ out of the window** regarder par la fenêtre; **to ~ the other way** (figurative) fermer les yeux; **2** (search) chercher, regarder; **3** (appear, seem) avoir l'air, paraître; **you ~ cold** tu as l'air d'avoir froid; **he ~s young for his age** il fait jeune pour son âge; **that makes you ~ younger** ça te rajeunit; **how do I ~?** comment me trouves-tu?; **you ~ well** (healthy) tu as bonne mine; **the picture will ~ good in the study** le tableau ira bien dans le bureau; **it doesn't ~ right** ça ne va pas; **how does it ~ to you?** qu'est-ce que tu en penses?; **things are ~ing good** les choses se présentent bien; **it ~s to me as if...** j'ai l'impression que...; **it ~s likely that** il semble probable que (+ *subj*); **to ~ like sb/sth** ressembler à qn/qch; **what does the house ~ like?** comment est la maison?; **it ~s like rain** on dirait qu'il va pleuvoir; **it certainly ~s like it** ça en a tout l' air; **4 ~ here** écoute-moi bien.
IDIOMS **if ~s could kill (I'd be dead by now)** il/elle etc m'a fusillé du regard.

■ **look after**: ¶ **~ after [sb/sth]** soigner [*patient*]; garder [*child*]; s'occuper de [*customer, plant, finances, shop*]; surveiller [*class, luggage*]; entretenir [*car*]; ¶ **~ after oneself** (care) se soigner; (cope) se débrouiller tout/-e seul/-e; **~ after yourself!** fais bien attention à toi!

■ **look around**: ¶ **~ around 1** (glance) regarder autour de soi; **2 to ~ around for sb/sth** chercher qn/qch; **3** (in town) faire un tour; ¶ **~ around [sth]** visiter [*church, town*].

■ **look at**: **~ at [sth] 1** regarder; (briefly) jeter un coup d'œil sur; **~ at (the state of) you!** regarde un peu de quoi tu as l'air!; **2** (examine) vérifier [*equipment*]; examiner [*patient*]; jeter un coup d'œil à [*car, plumbing*]; étudier [*problem, options*]; **3** (see, view) voir [*life, situation*]; envisager [*problem*].

■ **look back**: **~ back 1** (turn around) se retourner (**at** pour regarder); **2 to ~ back on** se tourner sur [*past*]; repenser à [*experience*]; **~ing back on it** rétrospectivement.

■ **look down**: ¶ **~ down** (from a height) regarder en bas; ¶ **~ down on [sb/sth] 1** regarder [qch] d'en haut; **2** (condescendingly) mépriser.

■ **look for**: ¶ **~ for [sb/sth]** chercher [*person, object*]; ¶ **~ for [sth]** attendre [*commitment, result, reward*] (**from** de).

■ **look forward**: **to ~ forward to [sth]** attendre [qch] avec impatience; **she's ~ing forward to going on holiday** elle a hâte de partir en vacances; **I ~ forward to hearing from you** (in letter) j'espère avoir bientôt de tes nouvelles; (formal) dans l'attente de votre réponse, je vous prie d'agréer mes sincères salutations.

■ **look into**: **~ into [sth]** examiner [*matter*]; enquêter sur [*death*].

■ **look on**: ¶ **~ on** (watch) regarder; (be present) assister à; ¶ **~ on [sb/sth]** considérer [*person, event*] (**as** comme; **with** avec).

■ **look onto**: **~ onto [sth]** [*house*] donner sur [*street*].

■ **look out**: ¶ **~ out** (take care) faire attention

(**for** à); (be wary) se méfier (**for** de); **~ out!** attention!; ¶ **~ out for [sb/ sth]** guetter [*person*]; être à l'affût de [*bargain, new talent*]; guetter l'apparition de [*symptoms*].

■ **look over**: ¶ **~ [sb] over** passer [qn] en revue [*troops*]; ¶ **~ [sth] over** examiner [*car, animal*]; ¶ **~ over [sth]** examiner [*document*]; (rapidly) parcourir [*document*].

■ **look round** ¶ (look behind) se retourner; (look about) regarder autour de soi; ¶ **~ round [sth]** visiter [*town*]; **to ~ round the shops** faire les magasins.

■ **look through**: ¶ **~ through [sth] 1** parcourir [*report*]; feuilleter [*magazine*]; **2** fouiller dans [*belongings*]; ¶ **~ through [sb]** faire semblant de ne pas voir.

■ **look to**: ¶ **~ to [sb/sth] 1** (rely on) compter sur [qn/qch]; **2** (turn to) se tourner vers [*future, friends*]; ¶ **~ to [sth]** veiller à [*interests*].

■ **look up**: ¶ **~ up** (raise eyes) lever les yeux (**from** de); (raise head) lever la tête; **to ~ up at the clouds** regarder les nuages; **things are ~ing up for us** les choses s'arrangent pour nous; ¶ **~ [sb/sth] up, ~ up [sb/sth] 1** chercher [*phone number, price*] (**in** dans); **2** passer voir [*acquaintance*]; ¶ **~ up to [sb]** admirer [*person*].

look-in *n* (GB) **to get a ~** avoir sa chance; **to give sb a ~** donner sa chance à qn.

look-out *n* **1 to be on the ~ for** rechercher [*stolen vehicle*]; être à l'affût de [*bargain, new talent*]; guetter [*visitor*]; **2** (place) poste *m* d'observation.

loom I *n* métier *m* à tisser.

II *vi* **1** (also **~ up**) surgir (**out of** de; **over** au-dessus de); **2** [*war, crisis*] menacer; [*exam, interview*] être imminent; **to ~ large** [*issue*] peser lourd.

loop I *n* **1** boucle *f*; **2 to ~ the ~** [*plane*] faire un looping; **3** (Comput) boucle *f*.

II *vtr* nouer.

III *vi* [*road, path*] faire une boucle.

loophole *n* (figurative) lacune *f*.

loose I *n* **he is still on the ~** il est toujours en liberté.

II *adj* **1** [*knot, screw*] desserré; [*handle, tooth*] branlant; [*button*] qui se découd; [*thread*] décousu; **to come ~** [*knot, screw*] se desserrer; [*handle, tooth*] être branlant; **to hang ~** [*hair*] être dénoué; **~ connection** faux contact; **2** (free) **to break ~** [*animal*] s'échapper (**from** de); **to cut sb ~** détacher qn; **to let ~** libérer [*animal, prisoner*]; **3** [*page*] détaché; **to come ~** [*pages*] se détacher; **~ change** petite monnaie; **'~ chippings'** (GB), **'~ gravel'** (US) 'attention gravillons'; **4** [*jacket, trousers*] ample; [*collar*] lâche; **5** [*link, weave*] lâche; **6** [*translation, interpretation*] assez libre; [*wording*] imprécis; [*connection, guideline*] vague; [*style*] relâché; **7** [*morals*] dissolu.

IDIOMS **to be at a ~ end** (GB), **to be at ~ ends** (US) ne pas trop savoir quoi faire.

loose: **~ cover** *n* (GB) housse *f* (de fauteuil); **~-fitting** *adj* ample.

loosely *adv* **1** [*wrap*] sans serrer; **his clothes hung ~ on him** il flottait dans ses vêtements; **2** [*connected*] de façon souple; [*structured*] assez librement; **3** [*translate*] assez librement; **to be ~ based on** être une adaptation assez libre de.

loosen *vtr* **1** desserrer [*belt, strap, collar*]; dégager [*nail, post*]; relâcher [*grip, rope, control*]; dénouer [*hair*]; **2 to ~ the bowels** avoir une action laxative.

loot I *vtr* piller [*shops*].

II *vi* [*person*] se livrer au pillage.

lopsided *adj* [*object, smile*] de travers; [*argument, view*] irrationnel/-elle.

lord ▶642 *n* **1** (ruler) seigneur *m* (**of** de); **2** (peer) lord *m*; **the (House of) Lords** la Chambre des Lords; **my Lord** (to noble) Monsieur le comte/duc etc.

IDIOMS **to ~ it over sb**° regarder qn de haut.

Lord *n* **1** (in prayers) Seigneur *m*; **2**° (in exclamations) **good ~!** grand Dieu!.

Lord Mayor ▶642 *n* lord-maire *m*.

lordship ▶642 *n* (also **Lordship**) **your/his ~** (of noble) Monsieur; (of judge) Monsieur le Juge.

lorry *n* (GB) camion *m*; **heavy ~** poids *m* lourd.

lorry driver ▶805 *n* (GB) routier *m*, chauffeur *m* de poids lourd.

lose I *vtr* **1** perdre [*object, person*]; **to ~ one's way** se perdre; (figurative) s'égarer; **to ~ interest in sth** se désintéresser de qch; **to ~ touch** perdre contact; **to ~ the use of** perdre l'usage de [*limb, muscle*]; **200 jobs will be lost** 200 emplois vont être supprimés; **to ~ one's figure** s'épaissir; **he's losing his looks** il n'est plus aussi beau qu'autrefois; **nothing to ~** rien à perdre; **2** (miss, waste) manquer [*chance*]; perdre [*time*]; **there's no time to ~** il n'y a pas de temps à perdre; **3** perdre [*war, race, bet, election*]; avoir le dessous dans [*argument*]; perdre en [*appeal*]; **4** (lose sight of) perdre [qch] de vue [*moving object*]; **you've lost me there**°! je ne vous suis plus!; **5** (get rid of) se débarrasser de [*habit*]; **6** [*clock*] retarder de [*minutes, seconds*]; **7 to ~ sb [sth]** faire perdre [qch] à qn [*votes*].

II *vi* **1** (be defeated) se faire battre (**to** par); **2** (deteriorate) perdre.

■ **lose out** être perdant; **to ~ out on** perdre dans [*deal*].

loser *n* (gen, Sport) perdant/-e *m/f*; **to be a good/bad ~** être bon/mauvais perdant.

losing *adj* **1** (gen, Sport) [*team*] perdant; **2** [*business concern*] déficitaire.

loss *n* perte *f* (**of** de); **there was heavy ~ of life** il y a eu de nombreuses victimes; **~ of income** manque *m* à gagner; **~ of sound/vision** (on TV) interruption *f* du son/de l'image; **the ~ of 300 jobs** la suppression de 300 emplois; **it's their ~** tant pis pour eux; **to be at a ~** (puzzled) être perplexe; (helpless) être perdu; **to be at a ~ as to what to do** ne pas savoir du tout quoi faire.

lost *adj* **1** [*person, animal*] perdu; **to get ~** [*person, animal*] se perdre; [*object*] s'égarer; **get**

~○! fiche le camp○!; **2** [*opportunity*] manqué; [*cause*] perdu; [*civilization*] disparu; **to be ~ on sb** passer au-dessus de la tête de qn; **to be ~ for words** être interloqué; **to be ~ in** être plongé dans [*book, thought*].

lost: **~ and found** *n* objets *mpl* trouvés; **~ property** (GB) *n* objets *mpl* trouvés.

lot[1] **I** *pron* **1** (great deal) **a ~** beaucoup; **he spent a ~** il a beaucoup dépensé, il a dépensé beaucoup d'argent; **to get a ~ out of** tirer beaucoup de [*book*]; **we don't have a ~** nous n'avons pas grand-chose; **he knows a ~ about sport** il s'y connaît beaucoup en sport; **it says a ~ about her** ça en dit long sur elle; **that has a ~ to do with it** c'est très lié; **to mean quite a ~ to sb** avoir beaucoup d'importance pour qn; **2**○ **the ~** (le) tout; **the nicest dress of the ~** la plus belle robe de toutes; **she's the nicest of the ~** c'est la plus gentille (de tous/toutes); **they're not a bad ~** ils ne sont pas méchants; **the best of a bad ~**○ le moins pire○.

II *quantif* **a ~ of money/time** beaucoup d'argent/ de temps; **I see a ~ of him** je le vois beaucoup; **quite a ~ of** beaucoup or pas mal○ de; **I'd sack the ~ of them!** je les mettrais tous à la porte!

III lots○ *quantif, pron* **~s (and ~s) of** des tas○ de (+ *plural*), beaucoup de; **~s of things** des tas○ de choses.

IV a lot *phr* beaucoup; **he's a ~ better/ worse** il va beaucoup mieux/plus mal; **this happens quite a ~** cela arrive très souvent.

lot[2] *n* **1** (destiny) sort *m*; (quality of life) condition *f*; **2** (US) parcelle *f* (de terrain); **vacant ~** terrain *m* vague; **3** (at auction) lot *m*; **4 to draw ~s** tirer au sort; **5** (batch) fournée *f*.

lotion *n* lotion *f*.

lottery *n* loterie *f*.

loud I *adj* **1** [*music, voice*] fort; [*noise, scream*] grand (*before n*); [*comment, laugh*] bruyant; [*applause*] vif/vive; **2** [*colour*] criard; [*person, behaviour*] exubérant.

II *adv* fort; **out ~** à voix haute; **~ and clear** clairement.

loudly *adv* [*knock, talk*] bruyamment; [*scream*] fort; [*protest*] vivement.

loud: **~mouth**○ *n* grande gueule○ *f*; **~speaker** *n* (for announcements) haut-parleur *m*; (for hi-fi) enceinte *f*.

Louisiana *pr n* Louisiane *f*.

lounge *n* **1** (in house, hotel) salon *m*; **2** (in airport) **departure ~** salle *f* d'embarquement; **3** (US) (also **cocktail ~**) bar *m*.

■ **lounge about, lounge around** paresser (derogatory).

lousy *adj* minable○; **a ~ trick** un sale tour.

louvred (GB), **louvered** (US) *adj* [*doors*] à lamelles.

lovable *adj* [*person*] sympathique; [*child*] adorable.

love I *n* **1** amour *m*; **to be/fall in ~** être/ tomber amoureux/-euse (**with** de); **to make ~** faire l'amour; **for the ~ of God!** pour l'amour de Dieu!; **Andy sends his ~** Andy t'embrasse; **with ~ from Bob, ~ Bob** affectueusement, Bob; **2** (GB) (term of affection) mon chéri/ma chérie *m/f*; **3** (in tennis) zéro *m*.

II *noun modifier* [*letter, song, nest, story*] d'amour.

III *vtr* **1** aimer; **to ~ each other** s'aimer; **2** (appreciate) aimer beaucoup (**to do** faire) ; **'I'd ~ to!'** 'avec plaisir!'.

IDIOMS **~ at first sight** le coup de foudre; **there's no ~ lost between them** ils/elles se détestent cordialement.

love: **~ affair** *n* liaison *f* (**with** avec; **between** entre); **~less** *adj* [*marriage*] sans amour; **~-life** *n* vie *f* amoureuse.

lovely *adj* **1** (beautiful) [*colour, garden, woman*] beau/belle (*before n*), joli (*before n*); **to look ~** [*child, dress*] être ravissant; **2** (pleasant) [*letter, person*] charmant; [*meal, smell*] délicieux/-ieuse; [*idea, surprise*] bon/bonne (*before n*); [*present, weather*] magnifique; **it's ~ to do** c'est tellement agréable de faire; **to smell ~** sentir bon; **~ and hot/fresh** bien chaud/frais.

love: **~making** *n* rapports *mpl* (sexuels); **~ match** *n* union *f* parfaite.

lover *n* **1** (male) amant *m*; (female) maîtresse *f*; **they are ~s** ils sont amants; **2** (person in love) amoureux/-euse *m/f*; **3 jazz ~** amateur de jazz.

loving *adj* [*mother, husband, look, smile*] tendre; [*care*] affectueux/-euse; **your ~ son** (in letter) ton fils qui t'aime.

low I *n* **1** (in weather) dépression *f*; **2 to be at** or **have hit an all-time ~** être au plus bas.

II *adj* **1** [*branch, building, chair, cloud*] bas/ basse; **on ~ ground** [*flood*] dans les basses terres; **2** [*reservoir, stocks, level*] bas/basse; [*battery*] presque à plat *inv*; **to be ~ on staff** manquer de personnel; **to be ~ in sugar** contenir peu de sucre; **3** [*price, wage, pressure*] bas/basse; [*speed*] réduit; [*number, rate*] faible; **on a ~ heat** à feu doux; **4** [*mark, quality*] mauvais; **5** (depressed) déprimé; **6** (deep) [*tone, voice*] bas/basse; **in a ~ voice** tout bas; **7** [*behaviour*] ignoble.

III *adv* **1** [*aim*] bas; [*bend*] très bas; [*fly*] à basse altitude; **2** (in importance) **it's very ~ (down) on the list** c'est tout à fait secondaire; **3** [*speak, sing*] bas; **to turn [sth] down ~** baisser [*heating, light*]; **to rate sb pretty ~** ne pas tenir qn en grande estime.

IV *vi* [*cow*] meugler.

IDIOMS **to be the ~est of the ~** être le dernier des derniers.

low: **~-alcohol** *adj* peu alcoolisé; **~brow** *adj* [*person*] peu intellectuel/-elle; **~-budget** *adj* à petit budget; **~-calorie** *adj* [*diet*] hypocalorique; [*food*] à faible teneur en calories; **Low Countries** *pr n pl* Pays-Bas *mpl*; **~-cut** *adj* décolleté.

lower I *adj* inférieur; **in the ~ back** au bas du dos.

II *vtr* **1** baisser [*barrier, curtain, flag*]; abaisser [*ceiling*]; **to ~ sb/sth** descendre qn/qch (**into** dans; **onto** sur); **2** (reduce) baisser [*prices, standards*]; réduire [*pressure, temperature*]; abaisser [*age limit*]; **to ~ one's voice** baisser la voix; **3** affaler [*sail*]; mettre [qch] à la mer [*lifeboat*].

III *v refl* **to ~ oneself 1** s'abaisser; **2 to ~ oneself into** s'asseoir précautionneusement dans [*bath, armchair*].

lower case *n* bas *m* de casse, minuscules *fpl*.

lower class *n* **the ~(es)** la classe ouvrière.

lowering *n* (of prices, standards) baisse *f*; (of age limit) abaissement *m*; (of trade barriers) abolition *f*.

lower middle class I *n* **the ~(es)** la petite bourgeoisie.

II *adj* petit-bourgeois/petite-bourgeoise.

lowest common denominator *n* plus petit dénominateur *m* commun.

low: **~-fat** *adj* [*diet*] sans matières grasses; [*cheese*] allégé; [*milk*] écrémé; **~-flying** *adj* volant à faible altitude; **~-frequency** *adj* [*sound*] (à) basse fréquence; **~-income** *adj* [*family*] à faible revenu; [*bracket*] des bas salaires; **~-key** *adj* [*approach*] discret/-ète; [*meeting, talks*] informel/-elle; **~lands** *n pl* basses-terres *fpl*; **~-level** *adj* [*bombing*] à basse altitude; [*talks*] informel/-elle; [*radiation*] faible; **~-life** *n* ○(person) crapule *f*; **~-lying** *adj* à basse altitude; **~-necked** *adj* décolleté; **~-paid** *adj* [*job*] faiblement rémunéré; [*worker*] peu rémunéré; **~-priced** *adj* à bas prix; **~-profile** *adj* discret/-ète; **~-quality** *adj* de qualité inférieure; **~ season** *n* basse saison *f*; **~-tar** *adj* à faible teneur en goudrons; **~ tide** *n* marée *f* basse; **~-voltage** *adj* de basse tension.

loyal *adj* [*friend*] loyal (**to** envers); [*customer*] fidèle (**to** à).

loyalist *n*, *adj* loyaliste (*mf*).

loyalty *n* loyauté *f* (**to, towards** envers).

lozenge *n* pastille *f*.

LP *n* (disque *m*) 33 tours *m*.

L-plate *n* (GB Aut) plaque *f* d'élève conducteur débutant accompagné.

lubricant *n* lubrifiant *m*.

lucid *adj* **1** (clear) clair; **2** (sane) [*person*] lucide; [*moment*] de lucidité.

luck *n* **1** (fortune) **good ~** chance *f*; **bad ~** malchance *f*; **to bring sb good/bad ~** porter bonheur/malheur à qn; **it's good ~** ça porte bonheur; **it is bad ~ that** ce n'est pas de chance que (+ *subj*); **to try one's ~** tenter sa chance; **bad** or **hard ~!** pas de chance!; **just my ~!** c'est bien ma chance!; **good ~!** bonne chance!; **better ~ next time!** tu auras plus de chance la prochaine fois!; **2** (good luck) chance *f*; **our ~ ran out** notre chance a tourné; **to wear sth for ~** porter qch comme porte-bonheur; **by a stroke of ~** par un coup de chance; **to be in/out of ~** avoir de la/ne pas avoir de chance.

IDIOMS **it's the ~ of the draw** c'est une question de chance; **my ~'s in!** c'est mon jour de chance!; **no such ~!** hélas non!

luckily *adv* heureusement (**for** pour).

lucky *adj* **1** (fortunate) **to be ~ (enough) to do/to be** avoir la chance de faire/d'être; **~ you**○! veinard/-e○ *m/f*!; **you should count yourself ~** estime-toi heureux/-euse; **to have a ~ escape** l'échapper belle; **2** [*charm, colour, number*] porte-bonheur *inv*; **it's my ~ day!** c'est mon jour de chance!

IDIOMS **to strike it ~** décrocher le gros lot○.

lucrative *adj* lucratif/-ive.

ludicrous *adj* grotesque.

ludo ▶ 649 *n* (GB) jeu *m* des petits chevaux.

luggage *n* bagages *mpl*.

luggage: **~ rack** *n* porte-bagages *m inv*; **~ van** *n* (GB) fourgon *m* à bagages.

lukewarm *adj* tiède.

lull I *n* (in storm, fighting) accalmie *f*; (in conversation) pause *f*.

II *vtr* **to ~ sb into thinking that...** faire croire à qn que...; **to be ~ed into a false sense of security** se laisser aller à un sentiment de sécurité trompeur.

lullaby *n* berceuse *f*.

lumber I *n* (US) bois *m* de construction.

II *vtr* ○(GB) **to get** or **be ~ed with sb/sth** se retrouver avec qn/qch sur les bras.

III *vi* (also **~ along**) avancer d'un pas lourd; [*vehicle*] avancer péniblement.

lumberjack ▶ 805 *n* bûcheron/-onne *m/f*.

luminous *adj* lumineux/-euse.

lump I *n* **1** morceau *m*; (of soil, clay) motte *f*; (in sauce) grumeau *m*; **2** (on body) (from knock) bosse *f* (**on** sur); **3** (tumour) grosseur *f* (**in, on** à).

II *vtr* **to ~ X together with Y** mettre X et Y dans le même panier○.

IDIOMS **to have a ~ in one's throat** avoir la gorge serrée.

lump sum *n* (complete payment) versement *m* unique.

lumpy *adj* [*sauce*] grumeleux/-euse; [*mattress, pillow, soil*] défoncé.

lunar *adj* [*landscape*] lunaire; [*eclipse*] de lune; [*landing*] sur la lune.

lunatic *n* fou/folle *m/f*.

lunch *n* déjeuner *m*; **to have ~** déjeuner; **to take sb out for ~** emmener qn déjeuner au restaurant; **she's gone to ~** elle est partie déjeuner; **to close for ~** fermer le midi.

lunch: **~box** *n* boite *f* à sandwichs; **~break** *n* pause-déjeuner *f*.

luncheon voucher, **LV** *n* ticket-repas *m*, ticket-restaurant® *m*.

lunch: **~ hour** *n* heure *f* du déjeuner; **~time** *n* heure *f* du déjeuner.

lung I *n* poumon *m*.

II *noun modifier* [*disease*] pulmonaire; [*transplant, cancer*] du poumon.

lunge *vi* bondir (**forward** en avant).

lurch I *n* **to give a ~** [*vehicle*] faire une embardée.

II *vi* [*person, vehicle*] tanguer; **to ~ forward** [*car*] faire un bond en avant.

IDIOMS **to leave sb in the ~** abandonner qn.

lure I *n* **1** (attraction) attrait *m* (**of** de); **2** (in hunting) leurre *m*.

II *vtr* attirer (**into** dans; **with** avec); **they ~d him out of his house** ils ont réussi à le faire sortir de chez lui par la ruse.

lurk *vi* **he was ~ing in the bushes** il était

tapi dans les buissons; **to ~ in the garden** rôder dans le jardin.

luscious *adj* [*food*] succulent.

lush *adj* [*vegetation*] luxuriant; [*surroundings*] luxueux/-euse.

lust **I** *n* **1** désir *m*; (deadly sin) luxure *f*; **2** (for power, blood) soif *f* (**for** de).
II *vi* **to ~ for** or **after sb/sth** convoiter qn/qch.

lute ▶ 753 | *n* luth *m*.

Luxembourg ▶ 574 | *pr n* Luxembourg *m*.

luxurious *adj* [*apartment, lifestyle*] de luxe; **his apartment is ~** son appartement est luxueux.

luxury **I** *n* luxe *m*; **to live a life of ~** vivre dans le luxe.
II *noun modifier* [*hotel, product, holiday*] de luxe.

lychee *n* litchi *m*.

lying *n* mensonges *mpl*.

lymph node *n* ganglion *m* lymphatique.

lynch *vtr* lyncher.

lynch mob *n* lyncheurs *mpl*.

Lyons ▶ 574 | *pr n* Lyon.

lyrical *adj* lyrique; **to wax ~ (about sth)** disserter avec lyrisme (sur qch).

lyrics *n pl* paroles *fpl*.

Mm

m, M *n* m, M *m*.
MA *n* (*abbr* = **Master of Arts**) diplôme *m* supérieur de lettres.
macabre *adj* macabre.
macaroni *n* macaronis *mpl*.
mace *n* **1** (spice) macis *m*; **2** (ceremonial staff) masse *f*.
machete *n* machette *f*.
machination *n* machination *f*.
machine *n* machine *f*; **sewing ~** machine à coudre; **by ~** à la machine.
machine gun *n* mitrailleuse *f*.
machinery *n* **1** (equipment) machines *fpl*; (working parts) mécanisme *m*, rouages *mpl*; **a piece of ~** une machine; **heavy ~** machines *fpl* lourdes; **2** (figurative) (apparatus) dispositifs *mpl*; **the ~ of justice** les rouages de la justice.
mackerel *n* maquereau *m*.
mackintosh, macintosh *n* imperméable *m*.
mad *adj* **1** [*person*] fou/folle (**with** de); [*dog*] enragé; [*idea, scheme*] insensé; **to go ~** devenir fou/folle; **2**○ (angry) furieux/-ieuse; **to be ~ at** or **with sb** être très en colère contre qn; **to go ~** se mettre dans une colère folle; **to drive sb ~** rendre qn fou; **3**○ (enthusiastic) **~ about** or **on** fou de○ [*person, hobby*]; **4** [*panic*] infernal; **the audience went ~** le public s'est déchaîné.
IDIOMS **to work like ~** travailler comme un fou/une folle.
madam ▶642 *n* madame *f*; **Dear Madam** (in letter) Madame.
maddening *adj* [*person*] énervant; [*delay, situation*] exaspérant.
made *adj* **to be ~** avoir réussi; **a ~ man** un homme qui a réussi.
IDIOMS **he's got it ~**○ (sure to succeed) sa réussite est assurée; (has succeeded) il n'a plus à s'en faire.
Madeira *pr n* Madère.
made-to-measure *adj* [*garment*] fait sur mesure.
made-up *adj* **1** (wearing make-up) maquillé; **2** [*story*] fabriqué.
madly *adv* **1** (frantically) frénétiquement; **2** [*jealous*] follement; **~ in love (with sb)** follement or éperdument amoureux (de qn).
madman○ *n* fou○ *m*, malade○ *m*.
madness *n* folie *f*; **it is ~ to do** c'est de la folie de faire.
mafia *n* **the Mafia** la Mafia; **the ~** (figurative) la mafia.
magazine *n* **1** revue *f*; (mainly photos) magazine *m*; **fashion ~** magazine de mode; **women's ~** journal *m* féminin; **2** (on radio, TV) magazine *m*; **3** (of gun, camera) magasin *m*.
maggot *n* (in fruit) ver *m*; (for fishing) asticot *m*.
magic I *n* magie *f*; **as if by ~** comme par enchantement.
II *adj* magique.
magical *adj* magique.
magic carpet *n* tapis *m* volant.
magician *n* (wizard) magicien *m*; (entertainer) illusionniste *m*.
magistrate ▶805 *n* magistrat *m* (*non professionnel*).
magnanimous *adj* magnanime.
magnate *n* magnat *m*; **oil ~** magnat du pétrole.
magnesium *n* magnésium *m*.
magnet *n* aimant *m*; (figurative) pôle *m* d'attraction (**for** pour).
magnetic *adj* **1** [*rod*] aimanté; [*field, force, storm*] magnétique; **2** [*appeal*] irrésistible; **to have a ~ personality** avoir du charisme.
magnetism *n* magnétisme *m*.
magnificent *adj* magnifique.
magnify *vtr* grossir.
magnifying glass *n* loupe *f*.
magnitude *n* ampleur *f* (**of** de).
magnolia ▶559 *n* **1** (also **~ tree**) magnolia *m*; **2** (colour) crème *m*.
magpie *n* pie *f*.
mahogany ▶559 I *n* **1** (wood, colour) acajou *m*; **2** (also **~ tree**) acajou *m*.
II *noun modifier* [*table*] en acajou, d'acajou.
maid *n* (in house) bonne *f*; (in hotel) femme *f* de chambre.
maiden I *n* jeune fille *f*.
II *adj* [*flight, voyage, speech*] inaugural.
maiden name *n* nom *m* de jeune fille.
mail I *n* **1** (postal service) poste *f*; **by ~** par la poste; **2** (letters) courrier *m*.
II *vtr* envoyer, expédier [*letter, parcel*] (**to** à).
mailbox *n* (for posting) boîte *f* aux lettres; (for delivery) boîte *f* à lettres.
mailman ▶805 *n* (US) facteur *m*.
mail order I *n* **to buy (by) ~** acheter par correspondance.
II *noun modifier* [*business, goods*] de vente *f* par correspondance.
maim *vtr* estropier.
main I *n* **1** (pipe) canalisation *f*; (for sewage) égout *m* (collecteur); **2 the ~s** (of water, gas, electricity) le réseau de distribution; (of sewage) le réseau d'évacuation; **to turn sth off at the ~s** couper qch (au compteur); **to work off the ~s** fonctionner sur secteur.
II *adj* principal.
main: **~ course** *n* plat *m* principal; **~frame** *n* (also **~ computer**) ordinateur *m* central.

mainland *n* territoire *m* continental; **on the ~** sur le continent.

mainly *adv* surtout, essentiellement.

main road *n* (in country) route *f* principale; (in town) grande rue *f*.

mainstream I *n* courant *m* dominant.
II *adj* **1** (conventional) traditionnel/-elle; **2 ~ jazz** jazz mainstream.

maintain *vtr* **1** maintenir [*temperature, standards*]; **2** subvenir aux besoins de [*family*]; entretenir [*army, house, property*]; **3** continuer à affirmer [*innocence*]; **to ~ that** soutenir que.

maintenance I *n* **1** (upkeep) entretien *m* (**of** de); **2** (GB Law) (alimony) pension *f* alimentaire.
II *noun modifier* [*crew, fees*] d'entretien; **~ man** ouvrier *m* chargé de l'entretien.

maisonette *n* duplex *m*.

maize *n* maïs *m*.

majestic *adj* majestueux/-euse.

majesty *n* **1** (grandeur) majesté *f*; **2 His/Her ~** sa Majesté.

major I *n* **1** (Mil) commandant *m*; **2** (US Univ) matière *f* principale; **3** (Mus) ton *m* majeur.
II *adj* **1** [*event*] important; [*role*] majeur; [*significance*] capital; **a ~ operation, ~ surgery** une grosse opération; **2** (main) principal; **3** (Mus) majeur; **in a ~ key** en majeur.
III *vi* (US Univ) **to ~ in** se spécialiser en.

Majorca *pr n* Majorque *f*; **in ~** à Majorque.

majority I *n* majorité *f* (**of** de); **to be in a** or **the ~** être en majorité.
II *noun modifier* [*government*] majoritaire; [*decision*] pris à la majorité.

make I *n* marque *f*.
II *vtr* **1** faire; **to ~ the bed** faire le lit; **to ~ a rule** établir une règle; **to ~ room/the time (for sth)** trouver de la place/du temps (pour qch); **to ~ friends/enemies** se faire des amis/des ennemis; **to ~ oneself understood** se faire comprendre; **it's made (out) of gold** c'est en or; **made in France** fabriqué en France; **he was made treasurer** on l'a fait trésorier; **to ~ a habit/an issue of sth** faire de qch une habitude/une affaire; **it's been made into a film** on en a fait or tiré un film; **three and three ~ six** trois et trois font six; **2** (with adjective) **to ~ sb happy/ill** rendre qn heureux/malade; **to ~ sb hungry** donner faim à qn; **to ~ sth better/bigger/worse** améliorer/agrandir/aggraver qch; **3** (with infinitive) **to ~ sb cry** faire pleurer qn; **I made her smile** je l'ai fait sourire; **to ~ sb do sth** faire faire qch à qn; (force) obliger or forcer qn à faire qch; **to ~ sb wait** faire attendre qn; **they made me do it** ils m'ont obligé or forcé; **to ~ sth happen** faire que qch se produise; **it ~s her voice sound funny** ça lui donne une drôle de voix; **4** (earn) gagner [*salary*]; **to ~ a living** gagner sa vie; **to ~ a profit** réaliser des bénéfices; **to ~ a loss** subir des pertes; **5** (reach) arriver jusqu'à [*place, position*]; atteindre [*ranking, level*]; **we'll never ~ it** nous n'y arriverons jamais; **to ~ the front page** faire la une; **6** (estimate, say) **what time do you ~ it?** quelle heure as-tu?; **I ~ it five o'clock** il est cinq heures à ma montre; **let's ~ it five dollars** disons cinq dollars; **can we ~ it a bit later?** peut-on dire un peu plus tard?; **what do you ~ of it?** qu'en dis-tu?; **7** (cause success of) assurer la réussite de [*holiday, meal*]; **it really made my day** ça m'a rendu heureux pour la journée.
IDIOMS **to be on the ~**○ (out of self-interest) être intéressé; (for profit) se remplir les poches; **to ~ it**○ (in career, life) y arriver; (to party, meeting) réussir à venir; **I can't ~ it** je ne peux pas venir.
■ **make do** faire avec; **to ~ do with** se contenter de qch.
■ **make for**: **~ for [sth] 1** (head for) se diriger vers; **2** (help create) permettre, assurer.
■ **make good**: ¶ **~ good** réussir; ¶ **~ good [sth] 1** réparer [*damage, omission*]; rattraper [*lost time*]; combler [*deficit*]; **2** tenir [*promise*].
■ **make out**: ¶ **~ out** affirmer, prétendre (**that** que); ¶ **~ out [sth/sb], ~ [sth/sb] out 1** (see, distinguish) distinguer; **2** (claim) **to ~ sth out to be** prétendre que qch est; **3** (understand) comprendre (**if** si); **I can't ~ him out** je n'arrive pas à le comprendre; **4** (write out) faire, rédiger; **to ~ out a cheque to sb** faire un chèque à qn; **it is made out to X** il est à l'ordre de X.
■ **make up**: ¶ **~ up 1** (after quarrel) se réconcilier (**with** avec); **2 to ~ up for** rattraper [*lost time, lost sleep*]; compenser [*personal loss*]; ¶ **~ up [sth], ~ [sth] up 1** inventer [*story, excuse*]; **2** (prepare) faire [*parcel, garment, bed*]; préparer [*prescription*]; **3** (constitute) faire; **to be made up of** être fait or composé de; **4** (compensate for) rattraper [*loss, time*]; combler [*deficit*].

make-believe *n* fantaisie *f*; **it's only ~** ce n'est qu'une histoire imaginaire.

maker *n* (of clothes, food, appliance) fabricant *m*; (of cars, aircraft) constructeur *m*; ▶ **coffee maker**.

makeshift *adj* improvisé.

make-up *n* **1** maquillage *m*; **to wear ~** se maquiller; **to put on one's ~** se maquiller; **2** (character) **to be part of sb's ~** faire partie du caractère de qn.

make-up remover *n* démaquillant *m*.

making *n* (of film, programme) réalisation *f*; (of product) fabrication *f*; (of clothes) confection *f*; **his problems are of his own ~** ses ennuis sont de sa faute; **a disaster is in the ~** une catastrophe se prépare.
IDIOMS **to have all the ~s of** avoir tout pour faire.

malaria ▶ **686** *n* paludisme *m*.

Malaysia ▶ **574** *pr n* Malaisie *f*.

male I *n* **1** (animal) mâle *m*; **2** (man) homme *m*.
II *adj* **1** [*plant, animal*] mâle; **2** [*population, role, trait*] masculin; [*company*] des hommes; **a ~ voice** une voix d'homme; **the ~ body** le corps de l'homme; **~ singer** chanteur *m*; **~ student** étudiant *m*; **3** [*plug, socket*] mâle.

male: **~ chauvinist** *n* phallocrate *m*;

~ model *n* mannequin *m* homme; **~ voice choir** *n* chœur *m* d'hommes.

malevolent *adj* malveillant.

malfunction **I** *n* **1** (poor operation) mauvais fonctionnement *m*; **2** (breakdown) défaillance *f*; **a computer ~** une défaillance de l'ordinateur.
II *vi* mal fonctionner.

malice *n* méchanceté *f* (**towards** à).

malicious *adj* [*comment, person*] malveillant; [*act*] méchant; [*lie*] calomnieux/-ieuse.

malign *vtr* calomnier; **much-~ed** tant décrié.

malignant *adj* **1** (gen) [*look*] malveillant; [*person*] malfaisant; **2** (Med) malin/-igne.

mall *n* **1** (shopping arcade) (in town) galerie *f* marchande; (in suburbs) (US) centre *m* commercial; **2** (US) (street) rue *f* piétonne.

mallet *n* maillet *m*.

malpractice *n* **1** (gen, Law) malversations *fpl*; **2** (US Med) erreur *f* médicale.

malt *n* **1** (grain) malt *m*; **2** (whisky) whisky *m* pur malt; **3** (US) (malted milk) lait *m* malté.

Malta *pr n* Malte *f*.

Maltese **▶712** **I** *n* **1** (person) Maltais/-e *m/f*; **2** (language) maltais *m*.
II *adj* [*people, customs, politics*] maltais.

mammal *n* mammifère *m*.

mammoth **I** *n* mammouth *m*.
II *adj* [*task*] gigantesque; [*organization*] géant.

man **I** *n* **1** homme *m*; **middle-aged ~** homme d'âge mûr; **a blind ~** un aveugle; **an old ~** un vieillard; **a single ~** un célibataire; **a ladies' ~** un homme à femmes; **~ to ~** d'homme à homme; **~ of the match** héros *m* du match; **~ and wife** mari et femme; **2** (mankind) (also **Man**) l'humanité *f*; **3** (in chess) pièce *f*; (in draughts) pion *m*.
II *vtr* **1** tenir [*switchboard, desk*]; **2** armer [qch] en hommes [*ship*]; assigner des hommes à [*gun*].
IDIOMS **every ~ for himself** chacun pour soi; **to a ~** sans exception.

manage **I** *vtr* **1** **to ~ to do** réussir à faire, se débrouiller° pour faire; **she ~d a smile** elle a réussi à sourire; **2** diriger [*project, finances, organization*]; gérer [*business, shop, hotel, estate*]; gérer [*money, time*]; **3** (handle) savoir s'y prendre avec [*person, animal*]; manier [*tool, boat*].
II *vi* se débrouiller°; **can you ~?** tu y arrives?

manageable *adj* [*size, car*] maniable; [*problem*] maîtrisable; [*person, animal*] docile.

management **I** *n* **1** (system, field) gestion *f*; **bad ~** mauvaise gestion; **2** (managers) direction *f*; **top ~** la haute direction.
II *noun modifier* [*committee, studies*] de gestion; [*job*] de cadre; **the ~ team** l'équipe dirigeante.

management: **~ buyout**, **MBO** *n* rachat *m* d'une entreprise par ses cadres; **~ consultant** **▶805** *n* conseiller *m* en gestion or en management.

manager *n* (of firm, bank) directeur/-trice *m/f*; (of shop) gérant/-e *m/f*; (of farm) exploitant/-e *m/f*; (of project) chef *m*, directeur/-trice *m/f*; (in show business) directeur/-trice *m/f* artistique; (Sport) manager *m*.

manageress *n* (of firm, bank) directrice *f*; (of shop, hotel) gérante *f*; (of project) chef *m*, directrice *f*; (in show business) directrice *f* artistique.

managing director, **MD** *n* directeur/-trice *m/f* général/-e.

mandarin *n* **1** (fruit) mandarine *f*; (tree) mandarinier *m*; **2** (person) mandarin *m*.

mane *n* crinière *f*.

manger *n* mangeoire *f*.

mangle **I** *n* essoreuse *f* à rouleaux.
II *vtr* mutiler [*body*]; broyer [*vehicle*].

mango *n* **1** (fruit) mangue *f*; **2** (also **~ tree**) manguier *m*.

mangrove *n* palétuvier *m*, manglier *m*.

mangy *adj* [*dog*] galeux/-euse.

manhandle *vtr* malmener, maltraiter.

man: **~hole** *n* regard *m*; **~hood** *n* âge *m* d'homme; (masculinity) masculinité *f*.

mania *n* manie *f*.

maniac *n* **1**° (reckless, crazy person) fou/folle *m/f*; **2** (in psychology) maniaque *mf*.

manic *adj* **1** (manic-depressive) maniaco-dépressif/-ive; (obsessive) obsessionnel/-elle; **2** (figurative) [*activity, behaviour*] frénétique.

manic depression **▶686** *n* psychose *f* maniaco-dépressive.

manicure **I** *n* manucure *f*; **to give sb a ~** manucurer qn.
II *vtr* **to ~ one's nails** se faire les ongles.

manifest **I** *adj* manifeste, évident.
II *vtr* manifester; **to ~ itself** se manifester.

manifestation *n* manifestation *f*.

manifesto *n* manifeste *m*, programme *m*.

manifold **I** *n* (Aut) collecteur *m*.
II *adj* multiple, nombreux/-euse.

manipulate *vtr* manipuler.

manipulative *adj* manipulateur/-trice.

mankind *n* humanité *f*.

manly *adj* viril.

man-made *adj* [*fibre, fabric*] synthétique; [*lake*] artificiel/-ielle; [*tools*] fait à la main.

manna *n* manne *f*.

manner **I** *n* **1** (way, method) manière *f*, façon *f*; **in this ~** de cette manière or façon; **in a ~ of speaking** pour ainsi dire; **2** (way of behaving) attitude *f*; **she has an aggressive ~** elle a une attitude agressive; **something in his ~ disturbed her** quelque chose dans son comportement la troublait; **3** (sort, kind) sorte *f*, genre *m* (**of** de).
II **manners** *n pl* **1** manières *fpl*; **to have good/bad ~s** avoir de bonnes/mauvaises manières; **it's bad ~s to do** il est mal élevé de faire; **he has no ~s** il n'a aucun savoir-vivre; (of a child) il ne sait pas se tenir; **2** (customs) mœurs *fpl*; **comedy of ~s** comédie *f* de mœurs.
III **-mannered** *combining form* **ill/well-~ed** mal/bien élevé.

mannerism *n* (habit) particularité *f*; (quirk) manie *f*.

manoeuvre (GB), **maneuver** (US) **I** *n* manœuvre *f*; **some room for ~** une marge de manœuvre.
II *vtr* **1** manœuvrer [*vehicle, object*]; **to ~ sth into position** manœuvrer qch pour le/la mettre en position; **2** (figurative) manœuvrer [*person*]; faire dévier [*discussion*] (**to** vers).
III *vi* manœuvrer.

manor *n* (also **~ house**) manoir *m*.

manpower *n* main-d'œuvre *f*.

mansion *n* (in countryside) demeure *f*; (in town) hôtel *m* particulier.

manslaughter *n* homicide *m* involontaire.

mantelpiece *n* (manteau *m* de) cheminée *f*.

manual I *n* manuel *m*.
II *adj* [*labour, worker*] manuel/-elle; [*gearbox, typewriter*] mécanique.

manufacture I *n* (of materials, textiles, tools, electrical goods) fabrication *f*; (of clothes) confection *f*; **car ~** construction *f* automobile.
II *vtr* fabriquer.
III manufactured *pp adj* **~d goods** produits manufacturés.

manufacturer *n* fabricant *m* (**of** de).

manufacturing *n* (of materials, textiles, tools, electrical goods) fabrication *f*; (of cars, heavy machinery) construction *f*.

manure *n* fumier *m*; **horse ~** crottin *m* de cheval.

manuscript *n* manuscrit *m*.

many I *det* beaucoup de, un grand nombre de; **~ people** beaucoup de gens, un grand nombre de personnes; **~ times** de nombreuses fois, bien des fois; **for ~ years** pendant de nombreuses années; **his ~ friends** ses nombreux amis; **how ~ people/times?** combien de personnes/fois?; **there are too ~ people** il y a trop de monde; **in ~ ways** à bien des égards; **like so ~ other women** comme tant d'autres femmes; **I have as ~ books as you (do)** j'ai autant de livres que toi.
II *pron, quantif* beaucoup; **not ~** pas beaucoup; **too ~** trop; **how ~?** combien?; **as ~ as you like** autant que tu veux; **I didn't know there were so ~** je ne savais pas qu'il y en avait autant; **we don't need ~ more** il ne nous en faut pas beaucoup plus; **~ (of them) were killed** beaucoup d'entre eux ont été tués; **there were too ~ of them** ils étaient trop nombreux; **you've set one place too ~** tu as mis un couvert de trop; **to have had one too ~**○ avoir bu un coup de trop○.

map *n* carte *f* (**of** de); (of town, underground) plan *m* (**of** de); **street ~** plan des rues.
■ **map out**: **~ out [sth], ~ [sth] out** élaborer, mettre [qch] au point [*plans, strategy*]; tracer [*future*].

maple *n* **1** (also **~ tree**) érable *m*; **2** (wood) bois *m* d'érable.

mar *vtr* gâcher.

marathon I *n* marathon *m*.
II *noun modifier* **1** (Sport) **~ runner** marathonien/-ienne *m/f*; **2** (massive) -marathon *inv*; **a ~ session** une séance-marathon.

marble *n* **1** (stone) marbre *m*; **2** (Games) bille *f*; **to play ~s** jouer aux billes.
IDIOMS **to lose one's ~s**○ perdre la boule○.

march I *n* marche *f*; **peace ~** marche *f* pacifiste.
II *vtr* **she ~ed him into the office** elle l'a emmené d'autorité dans le bureau.
III *vi* **1** (Mil) marcher au pas; **to ~ (for) 40 km** faire une marche de 40 km; **forward ~!** en avant, marche!; **2** (in protest) manifester (**against** contre; **for** pour); **3 to ~ along** (walk briskly) marcher d'un pas vif; **to ~ in** (angrily) entrer l'air furieux; **she ~ed up to his desk** elle s'est dirigée droit sur son bureau.

March ▶584 *n* mars *m*.

mare *n* (horse) jument *f*; (donkey) ânesse *f*.

margarine *n* margarine *f*.

margin *n* marge *f*; **by a narrow ~** de justesse, de peu; **~ of** or **for error** marge d'erreur; **safety ~** marge de sécurité; **profit ~** marge *f* bénéficiaire.

marginal *adj* marginal.

marginalize *vtr* marginaliser.

marigold *n* souci *m*.

marijuana *n* marijuana *f*.

marinade *vtr* (also **marinate**) faire mariner (**in** dans).

marine I *n* **1** (soldier) fusilier *m* marin; **the Marines** les marines *mpl*; **2** (navy) **the merchant ~** la marine marchande.
II *adj* [*mammal, biology*] marin; [*explorer, life*] sous-marin; [*insurance, law*] maritime.

marital *adj* conjugal; **~ status** situation *f* de famille.

marjoram *n* marjolaine *f*.

mark I *n* **1** marque *f*; (stain, animal marking) tache *f*; **2 as a ~ of** en signe de [*esteem, respect*]; **3** (Sch, Univ) note *f*; **he gets no ~s for effort** (figurative) pour l'effort, il mérite zéro; **4 the high-tide ~** le maximum de la marée haute; **at gas ~ 7** à thermostat 7; **5** (Sport) **on your ~s!** à vos marques!; **6** ▶748 (also **Deutschmark**) deutschmark *m*.
II *vtr* **1** marquer; (stain) tacher; **to ~ sb for life** (psychologically) marquer qn à vie; **2** [*arrow, sign, label*] indiquer [*position, road*]; **3** (Sch, Univ) corriger; **to ~ sb absent** noter qn absent; **4** (Sport) marquer.
III *vi* **1** [*teacher*] faire des corrections; **2** (stain) se tacher; **3** (Sport) marquer.
IDIOMS **~ my words** crois-moi; **to ~ time** (Mil) marquer le pas; (figurative) (wait) attendre; (wait for right moment) attendre le bon moment; **he's very quick/a bit slow off the ~** il a l'esprit vif/un peu lent; **to be wide of the ~** être à côté de la plaque○.
■ **mark out**: **~ [sb] out, ~ out [sb] 1** (distinguish) distinguer (**from** de); **2** (select) désigner (**for** pour).

marked *adj* **1** [*increase, contrast*] marqué, net/nette (*before n*); [*accent*] prononcé; **2 he's a ~ man** on en veut à sa vie.

marker *n* **1** (pen) marqueur *m*; **2** (tag) repère *m*.

market I *n* **1** (gen, Econ) marché *m*; **domestic/French ~** marché intérieur/français; **to go to ~** aller au marché; **fish ~** halle *f* aux poissons; **2** (stock market) Bourse *f*; **to play the ~** spéculer.
II *vtr* **1** (sell) commercialiser, vendre; **2** (promote) lancer or mettre [qch] sur le marché.

market: **~ day** *n* jour *m* du marché; **~ gardening** *n* culture *f* maraîchère.

marketing *n* **1** (field) marketing *m*, mercatique *f*; **2** (department) service *m* de marketing.

market: **~place** *n* place *f* du marché; **~ price** *n* prix *m* du marché; **~ research** *n* étude *f* de marché; **~ researcher** ▶805 *n* chargé/-e *m/f* d'études de marketing; **~ town** *n* bourg *m*.

marking *n* (on animal) tache *f*; (on aircraft) marque *f*; **road ~s** signalisation *f* horizontale.

marksman *n* tireur *m* d'élite.

marmalade *n* confiture *f* or marmelade *f* d'oranges.

maroon ▶559 I *n* bordeaux *m*.
II *vtr* **to be ~ed on an island** être bloqué sur une île; **the ~ed sailors** les naufragés.

marquee *n* **1** (GB) (tent) grande tente *f*; (of circus) chapiteau *m*; **2** (US) (canopy) (grand) auvent *m*.

marquetry *n* marqueterie *f*.

marriage I *n* mariage *m* (**to** avec).
II *noun modifier* [*guidance*] conjugal; [*vows*] de mariage; [*ceremony*] nuptial.

marriage certificate *n* extrait *m* d'acte de mariage.

married *adj* [*person*] marié (**to** à); [*life*] conjugal; **~ couple** couple *m*.

marrow *n* **1** (in bone) moelle *f*; **2** (GB) (vegetable) courge *f*; **baby ~** (GB) courgette *f*.

marrowbone *n* os *m* à moelle.

marry I *vtr* [*priest*] marier [*couple*]; se marier avec, épouser [*fiancé(e)*]; **to get married** se marier (**to** avec); **will you ~ me?** veux-tu m'épouser?
II *vi* se marier; **to ~ beneath oneself** se mésallier.

Mars *pr n* Mars *f*.

Marseilles ▶574 *pr n* Marseille.

marsh *n* (also **marshland**) (terrain) marécage *m*; (region) marais *m*.

marshal I *n* **1** (Mil) maréchal *m*; **2** (at rally, ceremony) membre *m* du service d'ordre; **3** (US) (in fire service) capitaine *m* des pompiers.
II *vtr* rassembler.

martial *adj* [*art, law*] martial; [*spirit*] guerrier/-ière.

martyr I *n* martyr/-e *m/f*.
II *vtr* martyriser.

martyrdom *n* martyre *m*.

marvel I *n* merveille *f*.
II *vi* s'étonner (**at** de), être émerveillé (**at** par).

marvellous (GB), **marvelous** (US) *adj* merveilleux/-euse; **that's ~!** c'est formidable!

marvellously (GB), **marvelously** (US) *adv* [*sing, get on*] à merveille; [*clever*] extraordinairement.

marzipan *n* pâte *f* d'amandes.

mascot *n* mascotte *f*; **lucky ~** porte-bonheur *m inv*.

masculine *n, adj* masculin (*m*).

masculinity *n* masculinité *f*.

mash I *n* (for animals) pâtée *f*.
II *vtr* (also **~ up**) écraser [*fruit*]; **~ed potatoes** purée de pommes de terre.

mask I *n* **1** (for face) masque *m*; (for eyes only) loup *m*; **2** (Comput) masque *m*.
II *vtr* masquer.

mask: **~ed ball** *n* bal *m* masqué; **~ing tape** *n* ruban *m* adhésif.

masochist *n, adj* masochiste (*mf*).

mason ▶805 *n* **1** (in building) maçon *m*; **2 Mason** (also **Free~**) franc-maçon *m*.

masonic *adj* maçonnique.

masonry *n* maçonnerie *f*.

masquerade I *n* bal *m* masqué; (figurative) mascarade *f*.
II *vi* **to ~ as sb/sth** se faire passer pour qn/qch.

mass I *n* **1** masse *f* (**of** de); (of people) foule *f* (**of** de); (of details) quantité *f* (**of** de); **2** (in church) messe *f*.
II **masses** *n pl* **1 the ~es** les masses *fpl*; **2**° (GB) **~es of work** beaucoup or plein° de travail; **~es of people** des tas° de gens.
III *noun modifier* [*audience, movement, tourism*] de masse; [*exodus, protest, unemployment*] massif/-ive; **~ meeting** rassemblement *m* de masse; **~ hysteria** hystérie *f* collective.
IV *vi* [*troops*] se regrouper; [*bees*] se masser; [*clouds*] s'amonceler.

massacre I *n* massacre *m*.
II *vtr* massacrer.

massage I *n* massage *m*.
II *vtr* **1** masser [*person*]; **2** (figurative) tricher sur [*figures*]; flatter [*ego*].

massive *adj* [*object, amount, debt, error*] énorme; [*majority*] écrasant; [*increase, cut*] massif/-ive; [*haemorrhage*] grave.

mass: **~ media** *n* (mass) médias *mpl*; **~-produce** *vtr* fabriquer [qch] en série; **~ production** *n* fabrication *f* en série.

mast *n* (on ship, for flags) mât *m*; (for aerial) pylône *m*.

master I *n* **1** maître *m*; **to be ~ in one's own house** être maître chez soi; **2** (Sch) (primary) maître *m*, instituteur *m*; (secondary) professeur *m*; (GB Univ) (of college) principal *m*; **3** (also **~ copy**) original *m*.
II *noun modifier* [*chef*] maître (*before n*); [*spy*] professionnel/-elle.
III *vtr* **1** maîtriser [*subject*]; posséder [*art, skill*]; **2** dominer [*feelings*]; surmonter [*phobia*].

master: **~ bedroom** *n* chambre *f* principale; **~ key** *n* passe-partout *m inv*.

masterly *adj* magistral.

mastermind I *n* cerveau *m* (**of, behind** de).

II *vtr* organiser [*robbery, event*].

master: **Master of Arts** *n* diplôme *m* supérieur de lettres; **~ of ceremonies** *n* (in cabaret) animateur/-trice *m/f*; (at banquet) maître *m* des cérémonies; **Master of Science** *n* diplôme *m* supérieur en sciences; **~piece** *n* chef-d'œuvre *m*; **~ plan** *n* plan *m* d'ensemble; **~'s (degree)** *n* ≈ maîtrise (**in** de); **~stroke** *n* (piece of skill) coup *m* de maître; (idea) idée *f* de génie; **~ tape** *n* bande *f* mère.

mastery *n* maîtrise *f* (**of** de).

mat I *n* **1** (on floor) (petit) tapis *m*; (for wiping feet) paillasson *m*; **exercise ~** tapis; **2** (on table) (heatproof) dessous-de-plat *m inv*; (ornamental) napperon *m*; **place ~** set *m* de table.
II *vi* [*hair*] s'emmêler; [*wool*] se feutrer; [*fibres*] s'enchevêtrer.

match I *n* **1** (Sport) match *m*; **2** (matchstick) allumette *f*; **3** (equal) **to be a ~ for sb** être un adversaire à la mesure de qn; **to be no ~ for sb** être trop faible pour qn.
II *vtr* **1** [*colour, bag*] être assorti à; [*blood type*] correspondre à; [*word*] correspondre à [*definition*]; **to ~ (up) the names to the photos** trouver les noms qui correspondent aux photos; **2** (equal) égaler [*record, achievements*].
III *vi* [*colours, clothes, curtains*] être assortis/-ies; [*components*] aller ensemble; **with gloves to ~** avec des gants assortis.

match: **~box** *n* boîte *f* d'allumettes; **~maker** *n* marieur/-euse *m/f*.

match point *n* balle *f* de match; **at ~** à la balle de match.

matchstick *n* (bois *m* d')allumette *f*.

mate I *n* **1**○ (GB) (friend) copain○ *m*; (at work, school) camarade *mf*; **2** (Zool) (male) mâle *m*; (female) femelle *f*; **3** (assistant) aide *mf*; **builder's ~** aide-maçon *m*; **4** (in navy) second *m*.
II *vtr* **1** accoupler [*animal*] (**with** à or avec); **2** (in chess) faire mat.
III *vi* [*animal*] s'accoupler (**with** à, avec).

material I *n* **1** (substance) (gen) matière *f*, substance *f*; (Tech) matériau *m*; **waste ~** déchets *mpl*; **2** (fabric) tissu *m*, étoffe *f*; **3** (written matter) documentation *f*; **teaching ~** matériel *m* pédagogique; **reading ~** lecture *f*; **4** (potential) étoffe *f*; **she is star ~** elle a l'étoffe d'une vedette.
II **materials** *n pl* (equipment) matériel *m*; **cleaning ~s** produits *mpl* d'entretien; **building ~s** matériaux de construction.
III *adj* matériel/-ielle.

materialistic *adj* matérialiste.

materialize *vi* **1** [*hope, offer, plan, threat*] se concrétiser; [*event, situation*] se réaliser; [*idea*] prendre forme; **2** (appear) [*person, object*] surgir; [*spirit*] se matérialiser.

maternal *adj* maternel/-elle (**towards** avec).

maternity I *n* maternité *f*.
II *noun modifier* [*clothes*] de grossesse; [*leave, benefit*] de maternité; **~ ward** maternité *f*.

math○ *n* (US) math○ *fpl*.

mathematical *adj* mathématique.

mathematician ▶**805** *n* mathématicien/-ienne *m/f*.

mathematics *n* mathématiques *fpl*.

maths○ (GB) *n* maths○ *fpl*.

matinée I *n* matinée *f*.
II *noun modifier* [*performance*] en matinée.

mating: **~ call** *n* chant *m* nuptial; **~ season** *n* saison *f* des amours.

matriculate I *vtr* inscrire [*student*].
II *vi* [*student*] s'inscrire.

matrimony *n* mariage *m*.

matrix *n* matrice *f*.

matron *n* **1** (GB) (in hospital) infirmière *f* en chef; (in school) infirmière *f*; **2** (of nursing home) directrice *f*; **3** (US) (warder) gardienne *f*.

matt (GB), **matte** (US) *adj* [*paint*] mat; [*photograph*] sur papier mat.

matter I *n* **1** (affair) affaire *f*; (requiring solution) problème *m*; (on agenda) point *m*; **business ~s** affaires *fpl*; **it will be no easy ~** cela ne sera pas (une affaire) facile; **important ~s to discuss** des choses importantes à discuter; **private ~** affaire privée; **a ~ for the police** un problème qui relève de la police; **that's another ~** c'est une autre histoire; **to take the ~ further** aller plus loin; **the fact of the ~ is that** la vérité est que; **2** (question) question *f*; **it's a ~ of urgency** c'est urgent; **a ~ of life and death** une question de vie ou de mort; **it will just be a ~ of months** ce ne sera qu'une question de mois; **a ~ of a few days** l'affaire de quelques jours; **it's only a ~ of time before they separate** ils vont se séparer, ce n'est plus qu'une question de temps; **3** (trouble) **is anything the ~?** y a-t-il un problème?; **what's the ~?** qu'est-ce qu'il y a?; **what's the ~ with Louise?** qu'est-ce qu'elle a, Louise?; **4** (substance) matière *f*; **vegetable ~** matière végétale; **5** (on paper) **printed ~** imprimés *mpl*; **advertising ~** publicité *f*; **reading ~** lecture *f*; **6** (of book, speech) **subject ~** contenu *m*; **7** (Med) (pus) pus *m*.
II *vi* être important; **it doesn't ~** ça ne fait rien; **it doesn't ~ whether he comes or not** peu importe qu'il vienne ou pas.
IDIOMS **as a ~ of course** automatiquement; **as a ~ of fact** en fait; **for that ~** d'ailleurs; **no ~ how late it is** peu importe l'heure; **no ~ what (happens)** quoi qu'il arrive; **and to make ~s worse** et pour ne rien arranger; **to take ~s into one's own hands** prendre les choses en main.

matter-of-fact *adj* [*voice, tone*] détaché; [*person*] terre à terre.

mattress *n* matelas *m*.

mature I *adj* **1** [*plant, animal*] adulte; **2** (psychologically) [*person*] mûr; [*attitude, reader*] adulte; **3** [*hard cheese*] fort; [*soft cheese*] affiné; [*whisky*] vieux.
II *vi* **1** (physically) [*person, animal*] devenir adulte; **2** (psychologically) [*person*] mûrir; **3** [*idea*] mûrir; **4** [*wine*] vieillir; [*cheese*] s'affiner; **5** [*policy*] arriver à échéance.

maturity *n* maturité *f*; **to reach ~** [*person*] atteindre l'âge adulte; [*tree*] arriver à maturité.

maudlin *adj* [*song*] larmoyant; [*person*] mélancolique.

maul *vtr* [*animal*] lacérer.

mausoleum *n* mausolée *m*.

mauve ▶ 559 *n, adj* mauve (*m*).

maverick *n, adj* nonconformiste (*mf*).

maxim *n* maxime *f*.

maximize *vtr* maximiser [*profit, sales*].

maximum **I** *n* maximum *m*; **to hold a ~ of 300** contenir 300 personnes au maximum.
II *adj* [*price*] maximum; [*temperature*] maximal; [*speed*] maximum, maximal; [*load*] limite.

may *modal aux* **1** (expressing possibility) **it ~ rain** il pleuvra peut-être; **she ~ not have seen him** elle ne l'a peut-être pas vu; **'are you going to accept?'—'I ~'** 'tu vas accepter'—'peut-être'; **you ~ think I'm crazy but...** tu penses peut-être que je suis fou mais...; **even if I invite him he ~ not come** même si je l'invite il risque de ne pas venir; **be that as it ~** quoi qu'il en soi; **2** (expressing permission) **you ~ sit down** vous pouvez vous asseoir; **~ I come in?** puis-je entrer?; **you ~** oui bien-sûr; **I'll sit down, if I ~** je vais m'asseoir si vous le permettez; **if I ~ say so** si je puis me permettre.

May ▶ 584 *n* mai *m*.

maybe *adv* peut-être; **~ they'll arrive early** peut-être qu'ils arriveront tôt; **~ three weeks ago** il y a peut-être trois semaines.

May Day *n* premier mai *m*, fête *f* du travail.

mayhem *n* (chaos) désordre *m*; (violence) grabuge° *m*.

mayor ▶ 642 *n* maire *m*.

mayoress ▶ 642 *n* (wife of mayor) femme *f* du maire; (lady mayor) mairesse *f*.

maze *n* (puzzle, in gardens) labyrinthe *m*; (of streets, corridors) dédale *m*.

MC *n* (*abbr* = **Master of Ceremonies**) (in cabaret) animateur/-trice *m/f*; (at banquet) maître *m* des cérémonies.

me[1] *pron* me, m'.

Note When used as a direct or indirect object pronoun, *me* is translated by *me* (or *m'* before a vowel or mute 'h'): *she knows me* = elle me connaît; *he loves me* = il m'aime.
– Note that the object pronoun normally comes before the verb in French and that in compound tenses like the present perfect and past perfect, the past participle of the verb agrees with the direct object pronoun: *he's seen me* (female speaker) = il m'a vue.
– In imperatives, the translation for both the direct and the indirect object pronoun is *moi* and comes after the verb: *kiss me!* = embrasse-moi!; *give it to me!* = donne-le-moi! (note the hyphens).
– After prepositions and the verb *to be*, the translation is *moi*: *she did it for me* = elle l'a fait pour moi; *it's me* = c'est moi.

---

it's for ~ c'est pour moi.

me[2] *n* (Mus) mi *m*.

mead *n* hydromel *m*.

meadow *n* **1** (field) pré *m*; **2** (also **~land**) prés *mpl*, prairies *fpl*; **3** (also **water ~**) prairie *f* inondable.

meagre (GB), **meager** (US) *adj* [*income, sum, portion*] maigre (*before n*); [*response, returns*] piètre (*before n*).

meal *n* **1** repas *m*; **to go out for a ~** aller (manger) au restaurant; **2** (from grain) farine *f*.

mean **I** *n* moyenne *f*.
II *adj* **1** [*person*] avare, radin°; [*attitude, nature*] mesquin; **he's ~ with money** il est près de ses sous; **2** (unkind, vicious) méchant (**to** avec); **a ~ trick** un sale tour; **3** (average) [*weight, age*] moyen/-enne; **4 that's no ~ feat!** ce n'est pas un mince exploit!
III *vtr* **1** [*word, phrase, symbol*] signifier, vouloir dire; [*sign*] vouloir dire; **the term ~s nothing to him** le terme ne lui dit rien; **2** (intend) **to ~ to do** avoir l'intention de faire; **to ~ sb to do** (GB), **to ~ for sb to do** (US) vouloir que qn fasse; **to be meant for sb** être destiné à qn; **I meant it as a joke** c'était une blague de ma part; **she meant no offence** elle n'y entendait pas malice; **he doesn't ~ you any harm** il ne te veut aucun mal; **to ~ well** avoir de bonnes intentions; **he ~s what he says** (he is sincere) il est sérieux; (he is menacing) il ne plaisante pas; **without ~ing to** par inadvertance; **3** (entail) [*strike, law*] entraîner [*shortages, changes*]; **4** (intend to say) vouloir dire; **what do you ~ by that remark?** qu'est-ce que tu veux dire par là?; **do you ~ me?** c'est de moi que tu parles?; **I know what you ~** je comprends; **5** (be of value) **a promise ~s nothing** une promesse ne veut pas dire grand-chose; **money ~s a lot to him** l'argent compte beaucoup pour lui; **your friendship ~s a lot to me** ton amitié est très importante pour moi; **6** (be destined) **to be meant to do** être destiné à faire; **it was meant to be** or **happen** cela devait arriver; **they were meant for each other** ils étaient faits l'un pour l'autre; **7** (be supposed to be) **he's meant to be/to be doing** il est censé être/faire.

meander *vi* [*river, road*] serpenter; **~ing path** sentier sinueux.

meaning *n* (of word, remark, action, life) sens *m*; (of symbol, film, dream) signification *f*.

meaningful *adj* **1** (significant) [*word, statement, result*] significatif/-ive; **2** (profound) [*relationship, comment, lyrics*] sérieux/-ieuse; [*experience*] riche; [*insight*] poussé; **3** (eloquent) [*look, smile*] entendu; [*gesture*] significatif/-ive.

meaningless *adj* **1** [*claim, phrase*] dépourvu de sens; [*figure*] incompréhensible; **2** (worthless) [*role, title*] insignifiant; [*action, remark*] sans importance; [*effort*] inutile; **3** (pointless) [*act, sacrifice*] futile, vain; [*violence*] insensé; **my life is ~** ma vie n'a pas de sens.

means **I** *n* moyen *m* (**of doing** de faire); **by whatever ~ possible** pour tous les moyens; **a ~ of** un moyen de [*communication, transport*]; **by ~ of** au moyen de; **yes, by all ~** oui, certainement; **it is by no ~ certain** c'est loin d'être sûr.
II *n pl* moyens *mpl*, revenus *mpl*; **to live within one's ~** vivre selon ses moyens.

means test *n* enquête *f* sur les ressources.

meantime *adv* **(in the) ~** pendant ce temps; **for the ~** pour le moment.

meanwhile *adv* **1** (during this time) pendant ce temps; **2** (until then) en attendant; **3** (since then) entre-temps.

measles ▶ 686 *n* rougeole *f*.

measure ▶ 738 I *n* **1** (action, step) mesure; **to take ~s** prendre des mesures; **safety ~** mesure de sécurité; **as a precautionary ~** par mesure de précaution; **as a temporary ~** provisoirement; **2** (unit) unité *f* de mesure; **weights and ~s** les poids et mesures *mpl*; **it's made to ~** (garment) c'est fait sur mesure; **3** (of alcohol) mesure *f*; **4** (device for measuring) instrument *m* de mesure; **5 beyond ~** [*change*] énormément; [*beautiful*] extrêmement; **to take the ~ of sb** jauger qn.
II *vtr* **1** mesurer; **to ~ four by five metres** mesurer quatre mètres sur cinq; **a tremor measuring 5.2 on the Richter scale** une secousse de 5,2 sur l'échelle de Richter; **2** (compare) **to ~ sth against** comparer qch à [*achievement*].
IDIOMS **for good ~** pour faire bonne mesure.
■ **measure out**: **~ out [sth]** mesurer [*land, flour, liquid*]; doser [*medicine*].
■ **measure up** [*person*] avoir les qualités requises; **to ~ up to** être à la hauteur de [*expectations*]; soutenir la comparaison avec [*achievement*].

measurement ▶ 738 *n* **1** (of room, object) dimension *f*; **2** (of person) **to take sb's ~s** prendre les mensurations de qn; **chest ~** tour *m* de poitrine; **leg ~** longueur *f* de jambe.

measuring: **~ jug** *n* verre *m* gradué; **~ spoon** *n* cuillère-mesure *f*.

meat *n* viande *f*; **red ~** viande rouge; **crab ~** chair *f* de crabe.

meaty *adj* **1** [*stew, sauce*] riche en viande; [*flavour, smell*] de viande; **2** [*role*] étoffé; [*work*] riche; [*article*] substantiel.

Mecca ▶ 574 *pr n* La Mecque.

mechanic ▶ 805 *n* mécanicien/-ienne *m/f*.

mechanical *adj* mécanique.

mechanics *n pl* **1** (field) mécanique *f*; **2** (workings) mécanisme *m*; **the ~ of** le mécanisme de [*engine*]; les mécanismes de [*management, law*].

mechanism *n* mécanisme *m* **(of** de).

mechanization *n* mécanisation *f*.

medal *n* médaille *f*; **gold/silver ~** médaille d'or/d'argent.

medallion *n* médaillon *m*.

medallist (GB), **medalist** (US) *n* médaillé/-e *m/f*; **gold/silver ~** médaillé/-e *m/f* d'or/d'argent.

meddle *vi* **to ~ in** s'immiscer dans [*affairs*]; **to ~ with** toucher à [*property*].

media I *n* **the ~** les médias *pl*; **news ~** presse *f* d'information; **in the ~** dans les médias.
II *noun modifier* [*advertising*] dans les médias; [*interest*] des médias; [*coverage, image*] médiatique; [*consultant*] de médias; [*sales*] par les médias.

median (strip) *n* (US) terre-plein *m* central.

media studies *n pl* communication *f* et journalisme *m*.

mediate I *vtr* négocier [*settlement, peace*].
II *vi* [*person*] arbitrer; **to ~ in/between** servir de médiateur dans/entre.

mediator *n* médiateur/-trice *m/f*.

medical I *n* visite *f* médicale; (private) examen *m* médical.
II *adj* médical; **on ~ grounds** pour raisons de santé.

medicated *adj* [*bandage*] médical; [*shampoo*] traitant.

medication *n* médicament *m*; **to be on ~** prendre des médicaments.

medicinal *adj* [*property, use*] thérapeutique; [*herb*] médicinal.

medicine *n* **1** (field) médecine *f*; **to study ~** étudier la médecine; **2** (drug) médicament *m* **(for** pour).

medicine: **~ cabinet**, **~ cupboard** *n* armoire *f* à pharmacie; **~ man** *n* sorcier *m* guérisseur.

medieval *adj* médiéval.

mediocre *adj* médiocre.

mediocrity *n* **1** (state) médiocrité *f*; **2** (person) médiocre *mf*.

meditate *vtr*, *vi* méditer.

Mediterranean I *pr n* **1** (also **~ sea**) **the ~** la (mer) Méditerranée; **2** (region) **the ~** les pays méditerranéens.
II *adj* méditerranéen/-éenne.

medium I *n* **1** (means) moyen *m*; **2 to find** or **strike a happy ~** trouver le juste milieu; **3** (spiritualist) médium *m*.
II *adj* **1** [*size, temperature*] moyen/-enne; **in the ~ term** à moyen terme; **2** [*wave*] moyen/-enne; **on ~ wave** sur les ondes moyennes.

medium: **~-dry** *adj* [*drink*] demi-sec; **~-rare** *adj* [*meat*] à point; **~-sized** *adj* de taille moyenne.

medley *n* **1** (Mus) pot-pourri *m* **(of** de); **2** (mixture) mélange *m*.

meek *adj* docile.

meet I *n* **1** (Sport) rencontre *f* (sportive); **track ~** (US) rencontre *f* d'athlétisme; **2** (GB) (in hunting) rendez-vous *m* de chasseurs.
II *vtr* **1** rencontrer [*person, team, enemy*]; **2** (make acquaintance of) faire la connaissance de [*person*]; **Paul, ~ Natalie** Paul, je vous présente Natalie; **have you met each other?** vous vous connaissez?; **3** (await) attendre; (fetch) chercher; **she went to ~ them** elle est allée les attendre or chercher; **to ~ sb off** (GB) or **at** (US) **the plane** attendre qn à l'aéroport; **4** répondre à, satisfaire à [*criteria, standards, needs*]; payer [*bills, costs*]; couvrir [*debts, overheads*]; faire face à [*obligations, commitments*]; remplir [*conditions*]; **5** se montrer à la hauteur de [*challenge*].
III *vi* **1** [*people, teams*] se rencontrer; [*committee, parliament*] se réunir; **to ~ again** [*people*] se revoir; **2** (make acquaintance) [*people*] faire

Length and Weight Measurements

Note that French has a comma where English has a decimal point:

1 in	= 2,54 cm (centimètres)	*1 yd*	= 91,44 cm
1 ft	= 30,48 cm	*1 ml*	= 1,61 km (kilomètres)

Length

	how long is the rope?	= quelle est la longueur de la corde?
	it's ten metres long	= elle fait dix mètres (de† long)
	it's three metres too short / long	= il est trop court / long de trois mètres

Height

People	*how tall is he?*	= quelle est sa taille? combien est-ce qu'il mesure?
	he's six feet tall	= il fait / il mesure un mètre quatre-vingts
	Tom is taller / smaller than Jane	= Tom est plus grand / plus petit que Jane
Things	*how high is the tower?*	= quelle est la hauteur de la tour?
	it's 100 metres high	= elle fait cent mètres de† haut / de hauteur
	at a height of two metres	= à deux mètres de† hauteur
	A is higher / lower than B	= A est plus haut / moins haut que B

Distance

	what's the distance from Paris to Nice?	= quelle distance y a-t-il entre Paris et Nice?
	how far is it from Paris to Nice?	= combien y a-t-il de kilomètres de Paris à Nice?
	it's about 800 kilometres	= il y a environ 800 kilomètres
	at a distance of five kilometres	= à une distance de cinq kilomètres

Width / breadth

	how wide is it?	= combien fait-elle de† large?
	it's seven metres wide	= elle fait sept mètres de† large / de† largeur

Depth

	how deep is it?	= combien fait-elle de† profondeur?
	it's four metres deep	= elle fait quatre mètres de† profondeur
	at a depth of ten metres	= à une profondeur de dix mètres

Note the French construction with ***de***, coming after the noun it describes:

	an avenue four kilometres long	= une avenue **de** quatre kilomètres de† long
	a 100-metre-high tower	= une tour **de** 100 mètres de† haut
	a ten-kilometre walk	= une promenade **de** dix kilomètres
	a river 50 metres wide	= une rivière **de** 50 mètres de† largeur

Weight measurement

Again, note that French has a comma where English has a decimal point:

1 oz	= 28,35 g (grammes)	*1 st*	= 6,35 kg (kilos)
*1 lb**	= 453,60 g	*1 ton*	= 1 014,60 kg

* ***a pound*** is translated by ***une livre*** in French, but the French *livre* = 500 grams (half a kilo).

People	*how much does he weigh?*	= combien pèse-t-il?
	he weighs 10 st / 140 lbs	= il pèse 63 kg 500 (soixante-trois kilos et demi)
Things	*what does the parcel weigh?*	= combien pèse le colis?
	how heavy is it?	= quel poids fait-il?
	it weighs ten kilos	= il pèse dix kilos
	it was 2 kilos overweight	= il pesait deux kilos **de** trop
	A weighs more than B	= A pèse plus lourd que B
	a parcel 3 kilos in weight	= un colis de† trois kilos
	sold by the kilo	= vendu au kilo

† The use of ***de*** is obligatory in these constructions.

connaissance; **3** [*lips, roads*] se rencontrer; **their eyes met** leurs regards se croisèrent.

IDIOMS **to make ends ~** joindre les deux bouts.

■ **meet up**○ se retrouver; **to ~ up with**○ retrouver [*friend*].

■ **meet with**: ¶ **~ with** [sb] rencontrer [*person, delegation*]; ¶ **~ with** [sth] rencontrer [*opposition, success, suspicion*]; être accueilli avec [*approval*]; subir [*failure*]; **he met with an accident** il lui est arrivé un accident; **to be met with** être accueilli par [*silence, shouts*]; se heurter à [*disapproval*]; susciter [*anger*].

meeting *n* réunion *f*; **to call a ~** convoquer une réunion; **in a ~** en réunion; **athletics ~** rencontre *f* d'athlétisme.

meeting: **~-place** *n* (lieu *m* de) rendez-vous *m*; **~ point** *n* point *m* de rencontre.

megabyte, MB *n* mégaoctet *m*, Mo *m*.

megalomaniac *n, adj* mégalomane (*mf*).

megaphone *n* porte-voix *m inv*.

melancholy I *n* mélancolie *f*.

II *adj* [*person*] mélancolique; [*music, occasion*] triste.

mellow I *adj* **1** [*wine*] moelleux/-euse; [*flavour*] suave; [*tone*] mélodieux/-ieuse; **2** (weathered) [*stone*] patiné par l'âge; **3** (calm) **to get** or **grow ~ with age** s'assagir avec l'âge; **4** (relaxed) [*person*] détendu; [*atmosphere*] serein.

II *vtr* [*experience*] assagir [*person*]; [*music, wine*] détendre [*person*].

III *vi* **1** [*person, behaviour*] s'assagir; [*attitude*] s'adoucir; **2** [*taste*] prendre du moelleux.

melodic *adj* (gen) mélodieux/-ieuse; (Mus) mélodique.

melodrama *n* mélodrame *m*.

melodramatic *adj* mélodramatique; **you're being ~**! tu dramatises les choses!

melody *n* mélodie *f*.

melon *n* melon *m*.

melt I *vtr* **1** faire fondre [*snow, plastic, butter*]; **2** attendrir [*heart*].

II *vi* **1** fondre; **to ~ in your mouth** fondre dans la bouche; **2 to ~ into** se fondre dans [*crowd*].

■ **melt away 1** [*snow, ice*] fondre complètement; **2** [*fear, confidence*] se dissiper; [*crowd, people*] se disperser; [*money*] fondre.

meltdown *n* fusion *f* du cœur d'un réacteur.

melting point *n* point *m* de fusion.

melting pot *n* (of people, nationalities) melting-pot *m*.

IDIOMS **to be in the ~** être remis en question.

member I *n* **1** membre *m*; **to be a ~ of** faire partie de [*group*]; être membre de [*club, committee*]; **~ of staff** (gen) employé/-e *m/f*; (Sch, Univ) enseignant/-e *m/f*; **~ of the opposite sex** personne *f* de l'autre sexe; **~ of the public** (in street) passant/-e *m/f*; (in theatre, cinema) spectateur/-trice *m/f*; **an ordinary ~ of the public** un simple citoyen; **2** (also **Member**) (of parliament) député *m*; **3** (limb) membre *m*.

II *noun modifier* **~ nation** or **state** pays *m* membre.

Member of Congress, MC *n* (US) membre *m* du Congrès.

Member of Parliament, MP ▶ 642 *n* (GB) député *m* (**for** de).

Member of the European Parliament, MEP *n* (GB) député *m* au Parlement européen.

membership *n* **1** adhésion *f* (**of** à); **EC ~** adhésion à la CEE; **to take out joint ~** adhérer en couple; **2** (fee) cotisation *f*; **3** (people belonging) membres *mpl*; **it has a ~ of 200** il y a 200 membres.

membrane *n* membrane *f*.

memento *n* souvenir *m* (**of** de); **as a ~** en souvenir.

memo *n* note *f* de service.

memoirs *n pl* mémoires *mpl*.

memorabilia *n pl* souvenirs *mpl*.

memorable *adj* [*event*] mémorable; [*person, quality*] inoubliable.

memorandum *n* **1** mémorandum *m*; **2** (memo) note *f* de service.

memorial I *n* mémorial *m* (**to** à).

II *adj* commémoratif/-ive; **~ service** messe *f* commémorative.

memorize *vtr* apprendre [qch] par cœur.

memory *n* **1** mémoire *f*; **to have a good ~** avoir bonne mémoire; **to have a bad ~** ne pas avoir de mémoire; **from ~** de mémoire; **to have a good ~ for faces** être physionomiste; **in (loving) ~ of** à la mémoire de; **in living** or **recent ~** de mémoire d'homme; **2** (recollection) souvenir *m*; **childhood memories** souvenirs d'enfance; **to keep sb's ~ alive** maintenir le souvenir de qn en vie.

memory: **~ bank** *n* bloc *m* mémoire; **~ span** *n* empan *m* mnémonique.

menace I *n* menace *f*.

II *vtr* menacer (**with** de, avec).

menacing *adj* menaçant.

mend I *n* **1** (in fabric) (stitched) raccommodage *m*; (darned) reprise *f*; (patched) rapiéçage *m*; **2 to be on the ~** [*person*] être en voie de guérison; [*economy*] reprendre.

II *vtr* réparer [*object, road*]; (stitch) raccommoder; (darn) repriser; (add patch) rapiécer; **to ~ relations with** améliorer les relations avec; **that won't ~ matters** ça n'arrangera pas les choses.

III *vi* [*injury*] guérir; [*person*] se rétablir.

IDIOMS **to ~ one's ways** s'amender.

menial *adj* [*job*] subalterne; [*attitude*] servile; **~ tasks** basses besognes.

meningitis ▶ 686 *n* méningite *f*.

menopause *n* ménopause *f*.

men's room *n* (US) toilettes *fpl* pour hommes.

menstruate *vi* avoir ses règles.

menswear *n* prêt-à-porter *m* pour hommes.

mental *adj* [*state, illness, handicap*] mental; [*ability, effort, energy*] intellectuel/-elle; [*hospital, institution*] psychiatrique; [*calculation, image*] mental.

mentality *n* mentalité *f*.

mentally *adv* **1 ~ handicapped** handicapé

mental; **the ~ ill** les malades mentaux; **2 ~ exhausted** surmené intellectuellement; **3** [*resolve*] dans son for intérieur; [*calculate*] mentalement.

mentholated *adj* au menthol.

mention I *n* mention *f* (**of** de); **to make no ~ of** [*report, person*] ne pas faire mention de; **it got a ~ on the radio** on en a parlé à la radio.
II *vtr* **1** (allude to) faire mention de [*person, topic, fact*]; **please don't ~ my name** ne mentionnez pas mon nom; **she never ~s her work** elle ne parle jamais de son travail; **to ~ sb/sth to sb** parler de qn/qch à qn; **to ~ that...** dire (en passant) que...; **not to ~** sans parler de; **without ~ing any names** sans nommer personne; **don't ~ it!** je vous en prie!, je t'en prie!; **2** (acknowledge) citer [*name*].

menu *n* menu *m*.

MEP *n* (GB) (*abbr* = **Member of the European Parliament**) député *m* au Parlement européen.

mercenary *n* mercenaire *mf*.

merchandise *n* marchandise(s) *f(pl)*.

merchant *n* (selling in bulk) négociant *m*; (selling small quantities) marchand *m*.

merchant: **~ bank** *n* (GB) banque *f* d'affaires; **~ navy** (GB), **~ marine** (US) *n* marine *f* marchande.

merciful *adj* **1** [*person, sentence*] clément (**to, towards** envers); [*act*] charitable; [*God*] miséricordieux/-ieuse; **2** [*occurrence*] heureux/-euse; **a ~ release** une délivrance.

merciless *adj* [*ruler, criticism*] impitoyable (**to, towards** envers); [*heat*] implacable.

mercury I *n* mercure *m*.
II Mercury *pr n* Mercure *f*.

mercy *n* clémence *f*; **to have ~ on sb** avoir pitié de qn; **to beg for ~** demander grâce; **an act of ~** un acte de compassion; **a mission of ~** une mission humanitaire; **at the ~ of** à la merci de; **to throw oneself on sb's ~** s'en remettre au bon vouloir de qn.

mere *adj* **1** [*coincidence, nonsense*] pur (*before n*); [*formality*] simple (*before n*); **he's a ~ child** ce n'est qu'un enfant; **the beach is a ~ 2 km from here** la plage n'est qu'à 2 km d'ici; **to last a ~ 20 minutes** durer tout juste 20 minutes; **2** (very) [*sight, idea*] simple (*before n*); **the ~ sight of her** sa seule vue; **the ~ presence of asbestos**... le seul fait qu'il y ait de l'amiante...

merely *adv* simplement, seulement.

merge I *vtr* **1 to ~ sth with** fusionner qch avec [*company, group*]; **2** mélanger [*colours, designs*].
II *vi* **1** (also **~ together**) [*companies, departments*] fusionner; [*roads, rivers*] se rejoindre; **to ~ with** fusionner avec [*company, department*]; rejoindre [*river, road*]; **2** [*colours, sounds*] se confondre; **to ~ into** se fondre avec [*colour, trees*].

merger *n* fusion *f*.

meringue *n* meringue *f*.

merit I *n* mérite *m*; **a work of ~** une œuvre de valeur; **to judge sb on their own ~s/sth on its own ~s** juger qn selon son mérite/qch selon ses qualités propres.
II *vtr* mériter.

mermaid *n* sirène *f*.

merrily *adv* **1** (happily) joyeusement; **2** (unconcernedly) avec insouciance.

merriment *n* (fun) joie *f*; (laughter) hilarité *f*.

merry *adj* **1** (happy) joyeux/-euse, gai; **Merry Christmas!** joyeux Noël!; **2**° (tipsy) éméché.

merry-go-round *n* manège *m*.

mesh I *n* **1** (of string) filet *m*; (of metal) grillage *m*; **2** (net) mailles *fpl*.
II *vi* **1** (also **~ together**) [*branches*] s'enchevêtrer; [*ideas*] concorder; **2** (Tech) [*cogs*] s'engrener; **to ~ with** s'emboiter dans.

mesmerize I *vtr* hypnotiser.
II mesmerized *pp adj* fasciné, médusé.

mess I *n* **1** désordre *m*; **what a ~!** quel désordre!, quelle pagaille°!; **to make a ~** [*person*] mettre du désordre; **in a ~** en désordre; **to tidy** or **clear up the ~** mettre de l'ordre; **this report is a ~!** ce rapport est fait n'importe comment!; **my hair is a ~** je suis complètement décoiffée; **to make a ~ on the carpet** salir la moquette; **to make a ~ of the job** massacrer° le travail; **2 to make a ~** [*dog*] faire ses saletés; **3** (Mil) cantine *f*; **officers' ~** (in the army) mess *m*; (in the navy) carré *m* des officiers.
II° *vi* **1 to ~ with** toucher à [*drugs*]; **2 don't ~ with him** évite-le; **don't ~ with me** ne me cherche pas.
■ **mess about**°, **mess around**°: ¶ **~ around 1** faire l'imbécile; **to ~ around with** jouer avec [*chemicals, matches*]; toucher à [*drugs*]; **2** (potter) **to ~ around in the garden** bricoler dans le jardin; ¶ **~ [sb] around**° traiter qn par-dessus la jambe°, prendre qn pour un imbécile.
■ **mess up**°: ¶ **~ up** (US) faire l'imbécile; ¶ **~ [sth] up**, **~ up [sth] 1** semer la pagaille dans [*papers*]; mettre du désordre dans [*kitchen*]; **2** (ruin) louper° [*exam*]; gâcher [*chances, life*]; ¶ **~ [sb] up** [*drugs, alcohol*] détruire [*person*]; [*experience*] faire perdre les pédales° à qn.

message *n* message *m* (**about** au sujet de); **a telephone ~** un message téléphonique; **to get one's ~ across** (be understood) se faire comprendre; (convince people) faire passer son message.

messenger *n* messager/-ère *m/f*; (for hotel, company) garçon *m* de courses, coursier/-ière *m/f*.

messy *adj* **1** [*house*] en désordre; [*appearance*] négligé; [*handwriting*] peu soigné; **2** [*activity*] salissant; **he's a ~ eater** il mange comme un cochon; **3** [*lawsuit*] compliqué; **a ~ business** une sale affaire.

metabolism *n* métabolisme *m*.

metal *n* métal *m*.

metallic *adj* [*substance*] métallique; [*paint, finish*] métallisé; [*taste*] de métal.

metamorphosis *n* métamorphose *f* (**into** en).

metaphor *n* métaphore *f*.

metaphoric(al) *adj* métaphorique.

metaphorically *adv* métaphoriquement; **~ speaking** pour employer une métaphore.

mete *v* ■ **mete out**: **~ [sth] out, ~ out [sth]** infliger [*punishment*]; rendre [*justice*].

meteor *n* météore *m*.

meteoric *adj* **1** météorique; **2** (figurative) [*rise*] fulgurant.

meteorite *n* météorite *f*.

meteorology *n* météorologie *f*.

meter I *n* **1** compteur *m*; **gas ~** compteur de gaz; **to read the ~** relever le compteur; **2** (also **parking ~**) parcmètre *m*; **3** (US) = **metre**.

II *vtr* mesurer la consommation de [*electricity, gas*].

meter reader *n* releveur *m* de compteur.

method *n* **1** (of teaching, contraception, training) méthode *f* (**for doing** pour faire); (of payment, treatment) mode *m* (**of** de); **production ~s** modes de production; **2** (orderliness) méthode *f*; **a man of ~** un homme méthodique.

methodical *adj* méthodique.

Methodist *n, adj* méthodiste (*mf*).

methylated spirit(s) *n* alcool *m* à brûler.

meticulous *adj* méticuleux/-euse; **~ about** méticuleux/-euse dans [*work*]; **to be ~ about one's appearance** être toujours impeccable.

metre (GB), **meter** (US) ▶ 738 *n* mètre *m*.

metric *adj* métrique; **to go ~**○ adopter le système métrique.

metropolitan *adj* **1** [*area, population*] urbain; **~ New York** l'agglomération de New York; **2** métropolitain; **~ France** la France métropolitaine.

mettle *n* courage *m*; **to be on one's ~** être sur la sellette; **to put sb on his ~** amener qn à montrer de quoi il est capable.

Mexico ▶ 574 *pr n* Mexique *m*.

mi *n* (Mus) mi *m*.

miaow I *n* miaou *m*.

II *vi* miauler.

micro+ *pref* micro-.

microbe *n* microbe *m*.

micro: **~biology** *n* microbiologie *f*; **~chip** *n* puce *f*, circuit *m* intégré; **~cosm** *n* microcosme *m*; **~film** *n* microfilm *m*; **~lighting** ▶ 649 *n* ULM *m*, ultra léger *m* motorisé; **~phone** *n* microphone *m*.

microscope *n* microscope *m*; **under the ~** au microscope.

microwave I *n* **~ (oven)** four *m* à micro-ondes.

II *vtr* passer [qch] au four à micro-ondes.

mid- *pref* **in the ~20th century** au milieu du vingtième siècle; **~afternoon** milieu *m* de l'après-midi; **(in) ~May** (à la) mi-mai; **he's in his ~forties** il a environ quarante-cinq ans.

midair I *adj* [*collision*] en plein vol.

II **in midair** *phr* (in mid-flight) en plein vol; (in the air) en l'air; **to leave sth in ~** (figurative) laisser qch en suspens.

midday ▶ 554 *n* midi *m*.

middle I *n* milieu *m*; **in the ~ of** au milieu de; **I was in the ~ of a book when...** j'étais plongé dans un livre quand...; **in the ~ of May** à la mi-mai; **right in the ~ of** en plein milieu de; **to be in the ~ of doing** être en train de faire; **to split [sth] down the ~** partager [qch] en deux [*bill, work*]; diviser [qch] en deux [*group, opinion*]; **in the ~ of nowhere** en pleine brousse○.

II *adj* [*door, shelf*] du milieu; [*price*] modéré; [*size, difficulty*] moyen/-enne; **there must be a ~ course** or **way** il doit y avoir une solution intermédiaire.

middle: **~ age** *n* âge *m* mûr; **~-aged** *adj* [*person*] d'âge mûr; [*outlook, view*] vieux jeu *inv*.

Middle Ages *n pl* **the ~** le Moyen Âge.

middle class I *n* classe *f* moyenne.

II **middle-class** *adj* [*person*] de la classe moyenne; [*attitude, view*] bourgeois.

middle distance I *n* **in the ~** au loin; **to gaze into the ~** regarder dans le vague.

II **middle-distance** *adj* (Sport) [*event, athlete*] de demi-fond.

Middle East *pr n* Moyen-Orient *m*.

middle: **~man** *n* intermédiaire *m*; **~weight** *n* poids *m* moyen.

middling *adj* moyen/-enne.

IDIOMS **fair to ~** pas trop mal.

midfield *n* milieu *m* du terrain.

mid-flight I *adj* en plein vol.

II **in mid-flight** *phr* en plein vol.

midge *n* moucheron *m*.

midget *n* nain/-e *m/f*.

midnight ▶ 554 *n* minuit *m*.

midst *n* **in the ~ of** au beau milieu de; **in the ~ of change/war** en plein changement/pleine guerre; **in our ~** parmi nous.

midsummer *n* milieu *m* de l'été; (solstice) solstice *m* d'été.

Midsummer('s) Day *n* la Saint-Jean.

midtown *n* (US) centre-ville *m*.

midway I *n* (US) attractions *fpl* foraines.

II *adj* [*post, position*] de mi-course; [*stage, point*] de mi-parcours.

III *adv* **~ between/along** à mi-chemin entre/le long de; **~ through** au milieu de.

midweek I *adj* de milieu de semaine.

II *adv* en milieu de semaine.

midwife ▶ 805 *n* sage-femme *f*; **male ~** homme *m* sage-femme.

midwinter *n* milieu *m* de l'hiver; (solstice) solstice *m* d'hiver.

might[1] ▶ 743 *modal aux* **1 'will you come?'—'I ~'** 'tu viendras?'—'peut-être'; **he ~ be very brilliant but he's not a politician** il est peut-être très brillant mais ce n'est pas un homme politique; **she ~ not have heard the news** elle n'a peut-être pas entendu la nouvelle; **I ~ lose my job** je risque de perdre mon travail; **however unlikely that ~ be** si improbable que cela puisse paraître; **2 you ~ have been killed!** tu aurais pu te faire tuer!; **I ~ have known!** j'aurais dû m'en douter!; **3 I thought it ~ rain** j'ai pensé qu'il risquait de pleuvoir; **I thought you ~ say that** je m'attendais à ce que tu dises ça; **4 you ~ try leaving a message** vous devriez laisser un message; **~ I make a suggestion?** puis-je me permettre de faire une suggestion?

might² *n* **1** (power) puissance *f*; **2** (physical strength) force *f*; **with all his ~** de toutes ses forces.

mighty **I** *n* **the ~** les puissants.
II *adj* puissant.

migrant **I** *n* (person) migrant/-e *m/f*; (bird) oiseau *m* migrateur; (animal) animal *m* migrateur.
II *adj* [*labour*] saisonnier/-ière; [*bird, animal*] migrateur/-trice.

migrate *vi* **1** [*person*] émigrer; **2** [*bird, animal*] migrer.

migration *n* migration *f*.

mike○ *n* micro○ *m*.

mild *adj* **1** [*surprise*] léger/-ère; [*interest, irritation*] modéré; **2** [*weather, winter*] doux/douce; [*climate*] tempéré; **3** [*beer, taste, tobacco*] léger/-ère; [*cheese*] doux/douce; [*curry*] peu épicé; **4** [*soap, detergent, cream*] doux/douce; **5** [*infection*] bénin/-igne; [*attack, sedative*] léger/-ère; **a ~ heart attack** une petite crise cardiaque; **6** [*person, voice*] doux/douce.

mildew *n* **1** (on plant) mildiou *m*; **2** (mould) moisissure *f*.

mildly *adv* [*speak*] avec douceur; **to put it ~** pour dire les choses avec modération; **that's putting it ~** c'est un euphémisme.

mile ▶ **738**, **813** *n* **1** mile *m* (= *1609 mètres*); **it's 50 ~s away** ≈ c'est à 80 kilomètres d'ici; **2 to walk for ~s** marcher pendant des kilomètres; **it's ~s away!** c'est au bout du monde; **to be ~s away** (daydreaming) être complètement ailleurs; **~s from anywhere** loin de tout; **you could smell it a ~ off** on pouvait le sentir à cent lieues à la ronde; **to stand out a ~** sauter aux yeux.

mileage *n* **1** nombre *m* de miles; **what's the ~ for the trip?** ≈ combien de kilomètres fait l'ensemble du voyage?; **2** (done by car) kilométrage *m*; **3** (miles per gallon) consommation *f*.

milestone *n* borne *f* (milliaire); (figurative) étape *f* importante.

militant **I** *n* agitateur/-trice *m/f*.
II *adj* militant.

military **I** *n* **the ~** (army) l'armée *f*; (soldiers) les militaires *mpl*.
II *adj* militaire.

military service *n* service *m* militaire.

milk **I** *n* lait *m*; **condensed ~** lait concentré sucré; **powdered/evaporated ~** lait en poudre/concentré; **full cream ~** lait entier; **skimmed ~** lait écrémé.
II *vtr* **1** traire [*cow*]; **2** (exploit) exploiter [*situation, system*]; **to ~ sb for money** soutirer de l'argent à qn; **to ~ sb dry** saigner qn à blanc.
III *vi* [*cow, goat*] donner du lait; [*farmer*] faire la traite.

milk: **~ chocolate** *n* chocolat *m* au lait; **~man** ▶ **805** *n* laitier *m*.

milky *adj* **1** [*drink*] au lait; [*diet*] lacté; **2** [*skin, liquid, colour*] laiteux/-euse.

Milky Way *pr n* Voie *f* lactée.

mill **I** *n* **1** moulin *m*; **water/pepper ~** moulin à eau/à poivre; **2** (factory) fabrique *f*; **steel ~** aciérie *f*.
II *vtr* moudre [*flour, pepper*].

millennium *n* **1** (cycle, anniversary) millénaire *m*; **2 the ~** le millénium.

milligram(me) ▶ **738** *n* milligramme *m*.

millimetre (GB), **millimeter** (US) ▶ **738** *n* millimètre *m*.

million **I** *n* million *m*; **~s of** des millions de.
II *adj* **a ~ people/pounds** un million de personnes/de livres.

millionaire *n* millionnaire *mf*.

millipede *n* mille-pattes *m inv*.

milometer *n* (GB) ≈ compteur *m* kilométrique.

mime **I** *n* mime *m*; **~ show** pantomime *f*.
II *vtr, vi* mimer.

mime artist ▶ **805** *n* mime *mf*.

mimic **I** *n* imitateur/-trice *m/f*.
II *vtr* imiter.

mimicry *n* imitation *f*.

mince **I** *n* (GB) viande *f* hachée; **beef ~** bœuf *m* haché.
II *vtr* hacher [*meat*].

mind **I** *n* **1** esprit *m*; **peace of ~** tranquillité d'esprit; **it's all in the ~** c'est tout dans la tête○; **to cross sb's ~** venir à l'esprit de qn; **at the back of my ~ I had my doubts** au fond de moi j'avais des doutes; **that's a load** or **weight off my ~** ça me soulage beaucoup; **to have something on one's ~** être préoccupé; **to set sb's ~ at rest** rassurer qn; **nothing could be further from my ~** loin de moi cette pensée; **it's a case of ~ over matter** c'est la victoire de l'esprit sur la matière; **to have a logical ~** avoir l'esprit logique; **to take sb's ~ off sth** distraire qn de qch; **my ~'s a blank** j'ai un trou de mémoire; **I can't get him out of my ~** je n'arrive pas à l'oublier; **2** (brain) intelligence *f*; **with the ~ of a two-year-old** avec l'intelligence d'un enfant de deux ans; **3** (opinion) avis *m*; **to my ~** à mon avis; **to make up one's ~ about/to do** se décider à propos de/à faire; **my ~'s made up** je suis décidé; **to change one's ~ about sth** changer d'avis sur qch; **to keep an open ~ about sth** réserver son jugement sur qch; **to know one's own ~** avoir des idées bien à soi; **to speak one's ~** dire ce qu'on a à dire; **4 his ~ is going** il perd la tête; **are you out of your ~**○**?** tu es fou/folle○?
II *vtr* **1** surveiller [*manners, language*]; faire attention à [*hazard*]; **2 I don't ~** ça m'est égal, ça ne me dérange pas; **I don't ~ the cold** le froid ne me dérange pas; **I don't ~ cats, but I prefer dogs** je n'ai rien contre les chats, mais je préfère les chiens; **will they ~ us being late?** est-ce qu'ils seront fâchés si

might[1]

◆ ***might***, when it means that something is possible, is translated using the adverb ***peut-être*** with the appropriate verb:

*it **might** be true*	= c'est **peut-être** vrai
*she **might** be right*	= elle a **peut-être** raison
*they **might** not or **might**n't go*	= **peut-être** qu'ils n'iront pas
*she **might** have got lost*	= elle s'est **peut-être** perdue
*they **might** have to go away*	= il va **peut-être** falloir qu'ils partent ⇨ **1**

Sometimes it is possible to translate ***might*** by using the construction ***risquer de*** + *infinitive,* in contexts where the speaker views the outcome as undesirable:

*you **might** miss the plane if you leave later*	= tu **risques de** rater l'avion si tu pars plus tard
*they **might** lose a lot of money*	= ils **risquent de** perdre beaucoup d'argent

◆ ***might***, when it refers to something which could have happened (but didn't), is usually translated by the past conditional of the verb *pouvoir* in French:

it might have been serious	= ça aurait pu être grave
more might have been done to improve standards	= on aurait pu faire plus pour améliorer le niveau
he was thinking about what might have been	= il pensait à ce qui aurait pu se passer

It can also express annoyance:

you might have warned me!	= tu aurais pu me prévenir!
they might at least have apologized	= ils auraient au moins pu s'excuser
I might have guessed	= j'aurais dû m'en douter ⇨ **2**

◆ ***might***, when it occurs in indirect statements, indicates possibility and *conditional* + ***peut-être*** is useful as a translation:

he said you might be hurt	= il a dit que tu serais peut-être blessé
I thought you might like to see the film	= j'ai pensé que tu aimerais peut-être voir le film
they said they might go into town	= ils ont dit qu'ils iraient peut-être en ville ⇨ **3**

◆ ***might*** can be used to make polite suggestions and French often uses the conditional of the verb:

it might be better to wait	= ce serait peut-être mieux d'attendre
it might be a good idea to phone her	= ce serait peut-être une bonne idée de lui téléphoner
you might try making some more enquiries	= vous devriez essayer d'obtenir plus d'informations ⇨ **4**

nous sommes en retard?; **would you ~ keeping my seat for me?** est-ce que ça vous ennuierait de garder ma place?; **I wouldn't ~ a glass of wine** je prendrais volontiers un verre de vin; **if you don't ~** si cela ne vous fait rien; **3 never ~** (don't worry) ne t'en fais pas; (it doesn't matter) peu importe; **he can't afford an apartment, never ~ a big house** il ne peut pas se permettre un appartement encore moins une grande maison; **4** s'occuper de [*animal, children*]; tenir [*shop*].

III in mind *phr* **I bought it with you in ~** je l'ai acheté en pensant à toi; **I have something in ~ for this evening** j'ai une idée pour ce soir; **with the future in ~** en prévision de l'avenir; **with this in ~,...** avec cette idée en tête,...; **to put sb in ~ of sb/sth** rappeler qn/qch à qn.

IDIOMS **to read sb's ~** lire dans les pensées de qn; **to see sth in one's ~'s eye** imaginer qch; **to have a ~ of one's own** savoir ce qu'on veut.

minded *combining form* **1 to be mechanically-/business-~** avoir le sens de la mécanique/des affaires; **2 to be small-/open-~** avoir l'esprit étroit/ouvert.

mindless *adj* [*person, programme*] bête; [*work*] abrutissant; [*vandalism*] gratuit; [*task*] machinal.

mine[1] *pron*

Note In French, possessive pronouns reflect the gender and number of the noun they are standing for. So *mine* is translated by *le mien, la mienne, les miens, les miennes*, according to what is being referred to.

his car is red but ~ is blue sa voiture est rouge mais la mienne est bleue; **which (glass) is ~?** lequel (de ces verres) est le mien or est à moi?; **his children are older than ~** ses enfants sont plus âgés que les miens; **the blue car is ~** la voiture bleue est à moi; **she's a friend of ~** c'est une amie à moi; **it's not ~** ce n'est pas à moi.

mine[2] I *n* mine *f*.

II *vtr* **1** extraire [*gems, mineral*]; exploiter [*area*]; **2** (Mil) miner [*area*].

III *vi* exploiter un gisement; **to ~ for** extraire [*gems, mineral*].

minefield *n* champ *m* de mines; (figurative) terrain *m* miné.

miner ▶805 *n* mineur *m*.

mineral I *n* (substance, class) minéral *m*; (for extraction) minerai *m*.

II *adj* minéral; **~ ore** minerai *m*.

mineral water *n* eau *f* minérale.

mingle *vi* **1 to ~ with** se mêler à [*crowd, guests*]; fréquenter [*social group*]; **2** [*sounds*] se confondre (**with** à); [*smells, feelings*] se mêler (**with** à).

miniature I *n* miniature *f*.

II *adj* [*camera, railway, version, village*] miniature; [*breed, dog, horse*] nain.

minicab *n* (GB) taxi *m* (non agréé).

minim *n* (GB Mus) blanche *f*.

minimum I *n* minimum *m* (**of** de); **the bare** or **absolute ~** le strict minimum.

II *adj* minimum, minimal.

mining I *n* exploitation *f* minière.

II *noun modifier* [*industry, town*] minier/-ière; [*accident*] de mine.

mini-skirt *n* mini-jupe *f*.

minister I *n* **1** (GB) ministre *m*; **~ of** or **for Defence, Defence ~** ministre de la Défense; **2** (clergyman) ministre *m* du culte.

II *vi* **to ~ to** donner des soins à [*person*]; **to ~ to sb's needs** pourvoir aux besoins de qn.

minister of state *n* (GB) ministre *m* délégué; **Minister of State for Education** ministre délégué auprès du ministre de l'Éducation.

ministry *n* (GB) ministère *m*; **Ministry of Transport** ministère des Transports.

mink *n* vison *m*.

minor I *n* (Law) mineur/-e *m/f*.

II *adj* **1** [*change, defect, operation, role*] mineur; [*injury, burn*] léger/ère; **~ road** route secondaire; **2** (Mus) mineur; **in a ~ key** en mineur.

minority I *n* **1** minorité *f* (**of** de); **to be in a** or **the ~** être en minorité; **2** (US) opposition *f*.

II *noun modifier* minoritaire.

minstrel *n* ménestrel *m*.

mint I *n* **1** (herb) menthe *f*; **2** (sweet) bonbon *m* à la menthe; **3** (for coins) hôtel *m* des Monnaies.

II *noun modifier* [*sauce, tea*] à la menthe; [*essence, leaf*] de menthe.

III *adj* **in ~ condition** à l'état neuf.

IV *vtr* **1** frapper [*coin*]; **2** forger [*word, expression*].

minuet *n* menuet *m*.

minus I *n* **1** (in mathematics) moins *m*; **2** (drawback) inconvénient *m*.

II *adj* **1** [*symbol, button*] moins; [*number, quantity, value*] négatif/-ive; **~ sign** signe moins; **2** [*factor, point*] négatif/-ive; **on the ~ side...** pour ce qui est des inconvénients...

III *prep* **1** moins; **what is 20 ~ 8?** combien font 20 moins 8?; **it is ~ 15 (degrees)** il fait moins 15 (degrés); **2** (without) sans; **he woke up ~ his passport** quand il s'est réveillé il n'avait plus son passeport.

minuscule *n, adj* minuscule (*f*).

minute[1] ▶915, 554 **I** *n* **1** minute *f*; **five ~s past ten** dix heures cinq; **it's five ~s' walk away** c'est à cinq minutes à pied; **2 the ~ I heard the news** dès que j'ai appris la nouvelle; **any ~ now** d'une minute à l'autre; **at the last ~** à la dernière minute.

II minutes *n pl* compte-rendu *m*; **to take the ~s** rédiger le compte-rendu.

minute[2] *adj* [*particle*] minuscule; [*quantity*] infime; [*risk, variation*] minime.

minute hand *n* aiguille *f* des minutes.

miracle I *n* miracle *m*; **to work** or **perform ~s** faire des miracles.

II *noun modifier* [*cure, drug*] miracle; [*recovery*] miraculeux.

miraculous *adj* **1** [*cure, escape, recovery*] miraculeux/-euse; **2** [*speed, strength*] prodigieux/-ieuse.

mirror I *n* **1** (gen) miroir *m*, glace *f*; (Aut) rétroviseur *m*; **2** (figurative) reflet *m*.
II *vtr* refléter; **to be ~ed in** se refléter dans.

mirth *n* (laughter) hilarité *f*; (joy) joie *f*.

misadventure *n* mésaventure *f*; **verdict of death by ~** (GB) verdict de mort accidentelle.

misapprehension *n* malentendu *m*, erreur *f*; **to be (labouring) under a ~** se tromper.

misappropriate *vtr* détourner [*funds*].

misbehave *vi* [*child*] se tenir mal; [*adult*] se conduire mal.

miscalculation *n* erreur *f* de calcul; (figurative) mauvais calcul *m*.

miscarriage *n* **1** (Med) fausse couche *f*; **to have a ~** faire une fausse couche; **2** (Law) **a ~ of justice** une grave erreur judiciaire.

miscarry *vi* [*woman*] faire une fausse couche; [*animal*] avorter.

miscellaneous *adj* divers.

mischief *n* espièglerie *f*; **to get into** or **make ~** faire des bêtises; **he's up to ~** il prépare quelque chose; **to be full of ~** être espiègle; **it keeps them out of ~** ça les occupe.

mischievous *adj* [*child, comedy, humour*] espiègle; [*smile, eyes*] malicieux/-ieuse.

mischievousness *n* espièglerie *f*.

misconception *n* idée *f* fausse; **it is a popular ~ that** on croit souvent à tort que.

misconduct *n* (moral) inconduite *f*; **professional ~** faute professionnelle.

misconstrue *vtr* mal interpréter.

misdemeanour, misdemeanor (US) *n* délit *m*.

miser *n* avare *mf*.

miserable *adj* **1** [*person, event, expression*] malheureux/-euse; [*thoughts*] noir; [*weather*] sale (*before n*); **to feel ~** avoir le cafard; **2** [*amount*] misérable; [*wage, life*] de misère; [*attempt, failure, performance, result*] lamentable.

miserably *adv* **1** [*speak*] d'un ton malheureux; [*stare*] d'un air malheureux; **he was ~ cold** il avait horriblement froid; **2** [*fail, perform*] lamentablement.

miserly *adj* [*person*] avare; [*habits*] mesquin; [*allowance, amount*] maigre.

misery *n* **1** (unhappiness) souffrance *f*; (gloom) abattement *m*; **to make sb's life a ~** faire de la vie de qn un enfer; **2** (misfortune) **the miseries of unemployment** le chômage et son cortège de misères; **3**○ (GB) (child) pleurnicheur/-euse *m/f*; (adult) rabat-joie *m inv*.

misfire *vi* **1** [*gun, rocket*] faire long feu; [*engine*] avoir des ratés; **2** [*plan, joke*] tomber à plat.

misfit *n* marginal/-e *m/f*; **social ~** inadapté/-e *m/f* social/-e.

misfortune *n* (unfortunate event) malheur *m*; (bad luck) malchance *f*; **to have the ~ to do** avoir la malchance de faire.

misgiving *n* crainte *f*; **to have ~s about sth** avoir des craintes quant à qch; **to have ~s about sb** avoir des doutes au sujet de qn.

misguided *adj* [*strategy, attempt*] peu judicieux/-ieuse; [*politician, teacher*] malavisé.

mishandle *vtr* **1** mal conduire [*operation, meeting*]; mal s'y prendre avec [*person*]; **2** (roughly) manier [qch] sans précaution [*object*]; malmener [*person, animal*].

mishap *n* incident *m*.

mishear *vtr* mal entendre.

misinform *vtr* mal renseigner.

misinterpret *vtr* mal interpréter.

misjudge *vtr* mal évaluer [*speed, distance, public opinion*]; mal calculer [*shot*]; mal juger [*person, character*].

mislay *vtr* égarer.

mislead *vtr* (deliberately) tromper; (unintentionally) induire [qn] en erreur.

misleading *adj* [*impression, title, information*] trompeur/-euse; [*claim, statement, advertising*] mensonger/-ère.

mismanage *vtr* mal diriger [*firm, project*]; mal gérer [*finances*].

misogynist *n* misogyne *mf*.

misplace I *vtr* **1** (mislay) égarer; **2** (put in wrong place) mal ranger.
II misplaced *pp adj* [*criticism*] déplacé; [*trust*] mal placé; [*fears*] sans fondement.

misprint *n* coquille *f*, faute *f* typographique.

mispronounce *vtr* mal prononcer.

misrepresent *vtr* présenter [qn] sous un faux jour [*person*]; déformer [*views, facts*].

miss I *n* **1** (in game) coup *m* manqué or raté; **2 to give [sth] a ~**○ ne pas aller à [*film, lecture*]; se passer de [*dish, drink, meal*].
II Miss ▶ 642 Mademoiselle *f*; (written abbreviation) Mlle.
III *vtr* **1** manquer [*target*]; **the stone just ~ed my head** la pierre m'a frôlé la tête; **he just ~ed a pedestrian** il a failli renverser un piéton; **2** rater [*bus, plane, event, meeting*]; laisser passer [*chance, opportunity*]; **I ~ed the train by five minutes** j'ai raté le train de cinq minutes; **3** (fail to see) rater; **the shop's easy to ~** la boutique est facile à louper○; **4** ne pas saisir [*joke, remark*]; **he doesn't ~ a thing** rien ne lui échappe; **you've ~ed the whole point!** tu n'as rien compris!; **5** sauter [*line, class*]; manquer [*school*]; **6** (avoid) échapper à [*death, injury*]; éviter [*traffic, bad weather, rush hour*]; **he just ~ed being caught** il a failli être pris; **7** (notice absence of) remarquer la disparition de; **oh, is it mine? I hadn't ~ed it** c'est le mien? je n'avais pas remarqué qu'il avait disparu; **keep it, I won't ~ it** garde-le, je n'en aurai pas besoin; **8 I ~ you** tu me manques; **he ~ed Paris** Paris lui manquait; **I'll ~ coming to the office** le bureau va me manquer; **she'll be greatly** or **sadly ~ed** on va beaucoup la regretter; **he won't be ~ed**○! bon débarras!
IV *vi* **1** (Games, Sport, Mil) rater son coup; **~ed!** raté!; **2** [*engine*] avoir des ratés.

■ **miss out**: ¶ **~ out** être lésé; ¶ **~ out on [sth]** laisser passer, louper○; ¶ **~ out [sb/sth], ~ [sb/sth] out** sauter [*line, verse*]; omettre [*fact, point, person*].

misshapen *adj* [*leg*] difforme; [*object*] déformé.

missile *n* **1** (Mil) missile *m*; **2** (rock, bottle) projectile *m*.

missing *adj* **the ~ jewels/child** les bijoux disparus/l'enfant disparu; **there are two books ~** il manque deux livres; **the ~ link** le chaînon manquant; **to be ~** manquer; **to go ~** [*person, object*] disparaître; **to report sb ~** signaler la disparition de qn.

mission *n* mission *f*.

missionary ▶ 805 *n* missionnaire *mf*.

misspent *adj* **a ~ youth** une folle jeunesse.

mist I *n* (thin fog) brume *f*; (from breath, on window) buée *f*; (from spray) brume *f*.
II *vtr* vaporiser [*plant*].
■ **mist over**, **mist up** [*lens, window*] s'embuer.

mistake I *n* erreur *f*; (in text, spelling, typing) faute *f*; **to make a ~** se tromper; **by ~** par erreur; **there must be some ~** il doit y avoir erreur; **to learn by one's ~s** tirer la leçon de ses erreurs.
II *vtr* **1 to ~ sth for sth else** prendre qch pour qch d'autre; **to ~ sb for sb else** confondre qn avec qn d'autre; **there's no mistaking that voice** il est impossible de ne pas reconnaître cette voix; **2** mal interpréter [*meaning*].

mistaken *adj* **1 to be ~** avoir tort; **he was ~ in thinking it was over** il avait tort de croire que c'était fini; **unless I'm very much ~** si je ne me trompe; **it's a case of ~ identity** il y a erreur sur la personne; **2** [*enthusiasm, generosity*] mal placé.

mistletoe *n* gui *m*.

mistranslation *n* erreur *f* de traduction.

mistreat *vtr* maltraiter.

mistress *n* maîtresse *f*.

mistrust I *n* méfiance *f* (**of, towards** à l'égard de).
II *vtr* se méfier de.

misty *adj* [*conditions, morning*] brumeux/-euse; [*lens, window*] embué; [*photo*] flou; **it's ~** il y a de la brume.

misunderstand I *vtr* mal comprendre; (completely) ne pas comprendre.
II **misunderstood** *pp adj* **to feel misunderstood** se sentir incompris.

misunderstanding *n* malentendu *m*.

misuse I *n* (of equipment) mauvais usage *m*; (of word) usage *m* impropre; (of power, authority) abus *m*.
II *vtr* faire mauvais usage de [*equipment*]; mal employer [*word, resources*]; abuser de [*authority*].

mitigate *vtr* atténuer [*effects, distress, sentence*]; réduire [*risks*]; minimiser [*loss*]; **mitigating circumstances** circonstances *fpl* atténuantes.

mitre (GB), **miter** (US) *n* mitre *f*.

mitten *n* moufle *f*.

mix I *n* **1** mélange *m*; **a cake ~** une préparation pour gâteau; **2** (Mus) mixage *m*, mix *m*.
II *vtr* **1** mélanger [*colours, ingredients*] (**with** avec; **and** à); **to ~ sth into** incorporer qch à; **to ~ and match** assortir [*colours, styles, garments*]; **2** préparer [*drink*]; malaxer [*cement, paste*]; **3** (Mus) mixer.
III *vi* **1** (also **~ together**) se mélanger (**with** avec, à); **2** (socialize) être sociable; **to ~ with** fréquenter.
■ **mix up**: **~ [sth/sb] up**, **~up [sth/sb] 1** confondre; **to get two things/people ~ed up** confondre deux choses/personnes; **2** (jumble up) mélanger, mêler [*papers, photos*]; **3 to ~ sb up in** impliquer qn dans; **to get ~ed up in** se trouver mêlé à.

mixed *adj* **1** [*collection, programme, diet*] varié; [*nuts, sweets*] assorti; [*salad*] composé; [*group, community*] (socially, in age) mélangé; (racially) d'origines diverses; **of ~ blood** de sang mêlé; **2** (for both sexes) [*school, team, sauna*] mixte; **3** [*reaction, feelings, reception*] mitigé; **to be a ~ blessing** avoir ses avantages et ses inconvénients.

mixer *n* **1** (Culin) batteur *m* électrique; **2** (drink) boisson *f* nonalcoolisée; **3** (Mus) (engineer) ingénieur *m* du son; (device) mélangeur *m* de son.

mixture *n* mélange *m* (**of** de).

mix-up *n* confusion *f* (**over** sur).

moan I *n* **1** (noise) gémissement *m*; **2**° (complaint) plainte *f* (**about** au sujet de).
II *vi* **1** (groan) gémir (**with** de); **2**° (complain) râler° (**about** contre).

moat *n* douve *f*.

mob I *n* foule *f* (**of** de).
II *vtr* assaillir [*person*]; envahir [*place*].

mobile I *n* mobile *m*.
II *adj* **1** [*object, population*] mobile; [*canteen*] ambulant; **2 to be ~** (able to walk) pouvoir marcher; (able to travel) pouvoir se déplacer.

mobile phone *n* téléphone *m* sans fil.

mocha *n* **1** (coffee) moka *m*; **2** (flavour) arôme *m* de café et de chocolat.

mock I *n* (GB Sch) examen *m* blanc.
II *adj* **1** [*suede, ivory*] faux/fausse (*before n*); **~ leather** similicuir *m*; **2** (feigned) simulé; **in ~ terror** en feignant la terreur.
III *vtr* se moquer de [*person, efforts, beliefs*].
IV *vi* [*person*] se moquer.

mockery *n* moquerie *f*; **to make a ~ of** tourner [qn/qch] en dérision [*person, process, report, work*]; bafouer [*law, rule*].

mocking *adj* moqueur/-euse.

mod con *n* (GB) confort *m* (moderne).

mode *n* **1** mode *m*; **2 ~ of production** méthode *f* de production.

model I *n* **1** (of car, appliance, garment) modèle *m*; **2** (person) (artist's) modèle *m*; (fashion) mannequin *m*; **3** (scale model) maquette *f*; **4** (perfect example) modèle *m* (**of** de).
II *adj* **1** [*railway, soldier, village*] miniature; [*aeroplane, boat, car*] modèle réduit; **2** [*husband, student, hospital, prison*] modèle.
III *vtr* **1** modeler [*clay, wax*]; **2** [*fashion model*] présenter [*garment*].
IV *vi* **1** [*artist's model*] poser; **2** [*fashion model*]

travailler comme mannequin; **3 to ~ in** modeler en [*clay, wax*].

moderate I *adj* **1** (not extreme) modéré (**in** dans); **2** [*success, income*] moyen/-enne.
II *vtr* modérer.
III *vi* se modérer.

moderation *n* modération *f* (**in** dans); **in ~** avec modération.

modern I *n* moderne *mf*.
II *adj* moderne; **the ~ world** le monde contemporain.

modernize *vtr* moderniser.

modern languages *n pl* langues *fpl* vivantes.

modest *adj* **1** modeste (**about** au sujet de); **he's just being ~!** il fait le modeste!; **2** [*gift, aim*] modeste; [*sum, salary*] modique.

modesty *n* modestie *f*.

modify *vtr* modifier.

mogul *n* magnat *m*.

Mohammed, Mahomet *pr n* Mahomet.

moist *adj* [*soil*] humide; [*cake*] moelleux/-euse; [*hands*] moite; [*skin*] bien hydraté.

moisten *vtr* humecter; (in cooking) mouiller légèrement.

moisture *n* (of soil, in walls) humidité *f*; (on glass) buée *f*; (in skin) hydratation *f*.

moisturizer *n* (lotion) lait *m* hydratant; (cream) crème *f* hydratante.

molar *n, adj* molaire (*f*).

mold (US) = **mould**.

mole *n* **1** (Zool) taupe *f*; **2** (on skin) grain *m* de beauté.

molecule *n* molécule *f*.

molehill *n* taupinière *f*.
IDIOMS **to make a mountain out of a ~** faire une montagne d'une taupinière.

molest *vtr* agresser [qn] sexuellement.

mollycoddle *vtr* dorloter.

molt (US) = **moult**.

molten *adj* en fusion.

moment *n* **1** (instant) instant *m*; **in a ~** dans un instant; **at any ~** à tout instant; **2** (point in time) moment *m*; **at the ~** en ce moment; **at the right ~** au bon moment; **3 he has his ~s** il a ses bons côtés.

momentarily *adv* **1** (for an instant) momentanément; **2** (US) (very soon) dans un instant; (at any moment) d'un moment à l'autre.

momentary *adj* passager/-ère.

momentous *adj* capital.

momentum *n* élan *m*; (in physics) vitesse *f*.

Mona Lisa *pr n* **the ~** la Joconde.

monarchy *n* monarchie *f*.

monastery *n* monastère *m*.

Monday ▶584 *n* lundi *m*.

money ▶748 *n* argent *m*; **to make ~** [*person*] gagner de l'argent; [*business, project*] rapporter de l'argent; **to get one's ~ back** (in shop) être remboursé; (after risky venture, with difficulty) récupérer son argent.
IDIOMS **to be in the ~** être en fonds; **to be made of ~** être cousu d'or; **to get one's ~'s worth, to get a good run for one's ~** en avoir pour son argent; **your ~ or your life!** la bourse ou la vie!

money: **~ belt** *n* ceinture *f* porte-monnaie; **~box** *n* tirelire *f*; **~making** *adj* [*scheme*] qui rapporte; **~ order, MO** *n* mandat *m* postal.

mongrel *n* (chien *m*) bâtard *m*.

monitor I *n* (Comput, Med) moniteur *m*.
II *vtr* **1** surveiller [*results, patient, breathing*]; **2** être à l'écoute de [*broadcast*].

monk *n* moine *m*.

monkey *n* **1** (Zool) singe *m*; **2**○ (rascal) galopin○ *m*.

monochrome *adj* [*film*] en noir et blanc; [*colour scheme*] monochrome.

monogamy *n* monogamie *f*.

monologue, monolog (US) *n* monologue *m*.

monoplane *n* monoplan *m*.

monopolize *vtr* détenir le monopole de [*market, supply*]; (figurative) monopoliser.

monopoly *n* monopole *m*.

monosyllable *n* monosyllabe *m*.

monotonous *adj* monotone.

monotony *n* monotonie *f*.

monsoon *n* mousson *f*.

monster *n* monstre *m*; **sea ~** monstre marin.

monstrous *adj* **1** (ugly) monstrueux/-euse; [*building*] hideux/-euse; **2** (huge) énorme.

month ▶915 *n* mois *m*; **in two ~s, in two ~s' time** dans deux mois; **every other ~** tous les deux mois; **in the ~ of June** au mois de juin; **at the end of the ~** à la fin du mois; (in business) fin courant; **a ~'s rent** un mois de loyer; **six ~s' pay** six mois de salaire.

monthly I *n* (journal) mensuel *m*.
II *adj* mensuel/-elle; **~ instalment** mensualité *f*.
III *adv* [*pay, earn*] au mois; [*happen, visit, publish*] tous les mois.

Montreal ▶574 *pr n* Montréal.

monument *n* monument *m*.

moo *vi* meugler.

mood *n* **1** (humour) humeur *f*; **in a good/bad ~** de bonne/mauvaise humeur; **to be in the ~ for doing** avoir envie de faire; **to be in no ~ for doing** ne pas être d'humeur à faire; **when he's in the ~** quand l'envie l'en prend; **when** or **as the ~ takes him** selon son humeur; **I'm not in the ~** ça ne me dit rien; **2** (bad temper) saute *f* d'humeur; **to be in a ~** être de mauvaise humeur.

moody *adj* **1** (unpredictable) d'humeur changeante, lunatique; **2** (sulky) de mauvaise humeur.

moon *n* lune *f*; **there will be a ~ tonight** il y aura clair de lune cette nuit.
IDIOMS **to be over the ~** être aux anges; **once in a blue ~** tous les trente-six du mois○; **the man in the ~** le visage de la Lune.

moonlight I *n* clair *m* de lune.
II *vi* travailler au noir.

Currencies and Money

French money

write	say
25 c	vingt-cinq centimes
1 F	un franc
1,50 F†	un franc cinquante
	un franc cinquante centimes
2 F	deux francs
2,75 F†	deux francs soixante-quinze
20 F	vingt francs
100 F	cent francs
1 000 F	mille francs
1 000 000 F	un million de francs

† French uses a comma to separate units (***2,75 F***), where English normally has a full stop or period (***£5.50***).

British money

write	say
1p	un penny
25p	vingt-cinq pence
50p	cinquante pence
£1	une livre
£1.50	une livre cinquante
	une livre cinquante pence
£2.00	deux livres

American money

write	say
12c	douze cents
$1	un dollar
$1.50	un dollar cinquante
	un dollar cinquante cents

a dollar bill = un billet d'un dollar
a dollar coin = une pièce d'un dollar

How much?

how much is it / does it cost? = combien est-ce que cela coûte?
it's / it costs 15 francs = cela coûte 15 francs
it costs 100 francs a metre = cela coûte 100 francs le mètre

Note the use of ***à*** in French to introduce the amount that something costs:

a five-franc stamp = un timbre **à** cinq francs
a £10 meal = un repas **à** 10 livres

and the use of ***de*** to introduce the amount that something consists of:

a £500 cheque = un chèque **de** 500 livres
a ten-franc coin = une pièce **de** dix francs
a 50-centime piece = une pièce **de** cinquante centimes
a five-pound note = un billet **de** cinq livres

Handling money

500 francs in cash = 500 francs en liquide
there are 6 francs to the dollar = le dollar vaut 6 francs

moonlit *adj* éclairé par la lune; **a ~ night** une nuit de lune.

moor I *n* lande *f*; **on the ~s** sur la lande.
II *vtr* amarrer [*boat*].
III *vi* [*boat*] mouiller.

moorings *n pl* amarres *fpl*; **a boat at its ~** un bateau amarré.

moorland *n* lande *f*.

moose *n* (Canadian) orignal *m*; (European) élan *m*.

mop I *n* **1** (of cotton) balai *m* à franges; (of sponge) balai *m* éponge; **2 ~ of hair** crinière○ *f*.
II *vtr* **1** laver [qch] à grande eau [*floor*]; **2 to ~ one's face/brow** s'éponger le visage/le front.
■ **mop up**: **~ up [sth], ~ [sth] up** éponger [*milk, wine*].

mope *vi* se morfondre.
■ **mope about, mope around** traîner (comme une âme en peine).

moped *n* vélomoteur *m*.

moral I *n* morale *f*; **to draw a ~ from sth** tirer une leçon de qch.
II morals *n pl* moralité *f*; **to have no ~s** être sans moralité.
III *adj* moral.

morale *n* moral *m*; **to boost ~** remonter le moral à qn.

moral fibre (GB), **moral fiber** (US) *n* force *f* morale.

moralistic *adj* moralisateur/-trice.

morality *n* moralité *f*.

morally *adv* moralement; **~ wrong** contraire à la morale.

morbid *adj* morbide.

more

■ **Note** When used to form the comparative, *more* is very often translated by *plus*: *more expensive* = plus cher/chère; *more easily* = plus facilement.
– When used as a determiner to indicate a greater amount or quantity of something, *more* is very often translated by *plus de*: *more jobs/people* = plus d'emplois/de gens.

I *adv* **1** (comparative) **it's ~ serious than we thought** c'est plus grave que nous ne pensions; **2** (to a greater extent) plus, davantage; **you must rest ~** il faut que tu te reposes davantage; **the ~ you think about it, the harder it will seem** plus tu y penseras, plus ça te paraîtra dur; **3** (longer) **I don't work there any ~** je n'y travaille plus; **4** (again) **once ~** une fois de plus; **5** (rather) **~ surprised than angry** plus étonné que fâché; **6** (else) **nothing ~** rien de plus; **something ~** autre chose.
II *det* plus de; **I have ~ money than him** j'ai plus d'argent que lui; **~ cars than people** plus de voitures que de gens; **some ~ books** quelques livres de plus; **there's no ~ bread** il n'y a plus de pain; **have some ~ beer!** reprenez de la bière; **have you any ~ questions?** avez-vous d'autres questions?
III *pron, quantif* **1** (larger amount or number) plus; **it costs ~** il/elle coûte plus cher (**than** que); **he eats ~ than you** il mange plus que toi; **the children take up ~ of my time** les enfants prennent une plus grande partie de mon temps; **2** (additional amount) davantage; (additional number) plus; **I need ~ of them** il m'en faut plus; **I need ~ of it** il m'en faut davantage; **I can't tell you any ~** je ne peux pas t'en dire plus; **I have nothing ~ to say** je n'ai rien à ajouter; **we'll say no ~ about it** n'en parlons plus.
IV more and more *phr* de plus en plus; **~ and ~ work** de plus en plus de travail.
V more or less *phr* plus ou moins.
VI more so *phr* encore plus; **even ~ so in Oxford** encore plus à Oxford; **just as clever, if not ~ so** tout aussi intelligent, si ce n'est plus.
VII more than *phr* **1** (greater amount or number) plus de; **~ than 20 people** plus de 20 personnes; **~ than half** plus de la moitié; **~ than enough** plus qu'assez; **2** (extremely) **~ than generous** plus que généreux; **the cheque ~ than covered the cost** le chèque a amplement couvert les frais.
IDIOMS **he's no ~ than a servant** ce n'est qu'un serviteur.

moreish○ *adj* (GB) **to be ~** avoir un petit goût de revenez-y.

moreover *adv* de plus, qui plus est.

morning ▶554 **I** *n* matin *m*; (with emphasis on duration) matinée *f*; **in the ~** le matin; **at 3 o'clock in the ~** à 3 heures du matin; **on Monday ~s** le lundi matin; **(on) Monday ~** lundi matin; **later this ~** plus tard dans la matinée; **yesterday/tomorrow ~** hier/demain matin; **the previous ~** la veille au matin; **the following ~, the ~ after, the next ~** le lendemain matin.
II *excl* **(good) ~!** bonjour!
IDIOMS **the ~ after the night before** un lendemain de cuite○.

Morocco ▶574 *pr n* Maroc *m*.

Morse (code) *n* morse *m*; **in ~** en morse.

morsel *n* morceau *m*; **a tasty ~** un morceau de choix.

mortal *adj* [*life, danger, sin*] mortel/-elle; [*injury, blow*] fatal.

mortality *n* mortalité *f*.

mortgage I *n* emprunt-logement *m* (**on** pour).
II *noun modifier* [*agreement, deed*] hypothécaire.

mortuary *n* morgue *f*.

mosaic I *n* mosaïque *f*.
II *noun modifier* [*floor, pattern*] en mosaïque.

Moscow ▶574 *pr n* Moscou.

Moses *pr n* Moïse; **Holy ~**○**!** grand Dieu!

Moslem ▶ **Muslim**.

mosque *n* mosquée *f*.

mosquito *n* moustique *m*; **~ repellent** anti-moustique *m*.

moss *n* mousse *f*.

most

■ **Note** When used to form the superlative of adjectives, *most* is translated by *le plus* or *la plus* depending on the gender of the noun and by *les* *plus* with plural noun: *the most beautiful woman in the room* = la plus belle femme de la pièce; *the most expensive hotel in Paris* = l'hôtel le plus cher de Paris; *the most difficult problems* = les problèmes les plus difficiles. For examples and further uses, see the entry below.

I *det* **1** (the majority of) la plupart de; **~ people** la plupart des gens; **2** (in superlatives) le plus de; **she got the ~ votes** c'est elle qui a obtenu le plus de voix.
II *pron* **1** (the greatest number) la plupart (**of** de); (the largest part) la plus grande partie (**of** de); **~ of the time** la plupart du temps; **~ of us** la plupart d'entre nous; **for ~ of the day** pendant la plus grande partie de la journée; **~ of the bread** presque tout le pain; **2** (all) **the ~ you can expect is...** tout ce que tu peux espérer c'est...; **3** (in superlatives) le plus; **John has got the ~** c'est John qui en a le plus.
III *adv* **1** (in superlatives) **the ~ beautiful château in France** le plus beau château de France; **~ easily** le plus facilement; **2** (very) très, extrêmement; **~ encouraging** très or extrêmement encourageant; **~ probably** très vraisemblablement; **3** (more than all the rest) le plus; **what annoyed him ~ (of all) was** ce qui l'ennuyait le plus c'était que.
IV **at (the) most** *phr* au maximum, au plus.
V **for the most part** *phr* (most of them) pour la plupart; (most of the time) la plupart du temps; (chiefly) surtout, essentiellement.
VI **most of all** *phr* par-dessus tout.
IDIOMS **to make the ~ of** tirer le meilleur parti de [*situation, resources, abilities*]; profiter de [*opportunity, good weather*].

mostly *adv* **1** (chiefly) surtout, essentiellement; (most of them) pour la plupart; **he composes ~ for the piano** il compose surtout pour le piano; **200 people, ~ Belgians** 200 personnes, des Belges pour la plupart; **2** (most of the time) la plupart du temps.

MOT (GB) I *n* (also **~ test**) contrôle *m* technique des véhicules; **to pass the ~** obtenir le certificat de contrôle.
II *vtr* effectuer le contrôle technique de [*car*].

moth *n* papillon *m* de nuit; (in clothes) mite *f*.

mother I *n* mère *f*.
II *vtr* (coddle) dorloter.

motherhood *n* maternité *f*.

mother-in-law *n* belle-mère *f*.

motherly *adj* maternel/-elle.

mother-of-pearl *n* nacre *f*.

mother: **~'s boy** *n* fils *m* à maman°; **Mother's Day** *n* fête *f* des Mères; **~ tongue** *n* langue *f* maternelle.

motion I *n* **1** mouvement *m*; **to set [sth] in ~** mettre [qch] en marche [*machine*]; mettre [qch] en route [*plan*]; déclencher [*chain of events*]; **to set the wheels in ~** (figurative) mettre les choses en route; **2** (gesture) (of hands) geste *m*; **3** (proposal) motion *f*.
II *vi* **to ~ to sb (to do)** faire signe à qn (de faire).
IDIOMS **to go through the ~s** agir machinalement.

motionless *adj* [*cloud*] immobile; [*stand*] sans bouger.

motion picture *n* film *m*.

motivate *vtr* motiver [*person*]; **to ~ sb to do** inciter or pousser qn à faire.

motivated *adj* **1** [*person, pupil*] motivé; **2 politically/racially ~** [*act*] politique/raciste.

motivation *n* motivation *f* (**for** de; **for doing, to do** pour faire).

motive *n* motif *m* (**for, behind** de); (for crime) mobile *m* (**for** de).

motley *adj* [*crowd, gathering*] bigarré; [*collection*] hétéroclite.

motor I *n* moteur *m*.
II *noun modifier* **1** [*vehicle*] automobile; [*show*] de l'automobile; **2** [*mower*] à moteur.

motor: **~bike** *n* moto *f*; **~boat** *n* canot *m* automobile; **~cycle** *n* motocyclette *f*; **~cyclist** *n* motocycliste *mf*; **~ home** *n* auto-caravane *f*.

motorist *n* automobiliste *mf*.

motor: **~ racing** ▶ 649 *n* course *f* automobile; **~way** *n* (GB) autoroute *f*.

mottled *adj* [*skin, paper*] marbré; [*hands*] tacheté.

motto *n* devise *f*.

mould (GB), **mold** (US) I *n* **1** (Culin, figurative) moule *m*; **2** (fungi) moisissure *f*.
II *vtr* modeler [*plastic, clay, shape*]; façonner [*character, opinions*] (**into** pour en faire); **to be ~ed to sb's body** [*dress*] mouler (le corps de) qn.

mouldy (GB), **moldy** (US) *adj* moisi; **to go ~** moisir.

moult (GB), **molt** (US) *vi* [*cat, dog*] perdre ses poils; [*bird*] muer.

mound *n* (hillock) tertre *m*; (heap) monceau *m* (**of** de).

mount I *vtr* monter sur [*platform, horse*]; monter [*jewel, picture, exhibit, campaign*]; organiser [*demonstration*].
II *vi* **1** [*person, staircase*] monter (**to** jusqu'à); **2** [*number, toll*] augmenter; [*concern*] grandir; **3** (on horse) se mettre en selle.
III **mounting** *pres p adj* croissant.

mountain *n* montagne *f*; **in the ~s** à la montagne; **meat/butter ~** excédents *mpl* de viande/de beurre.

mountain: **~ bike** *n* vélo *m* tout-terrain, VTT *m*; **~ climbing** ▶ 649 *n* alpinisme *m*.

mountaineer ▶ 805 *n* alpiniste *mf*.

mountaineering ▶ 649 *n* alpinisme *m*.

mountainous *adj* montagneux/-euse; (figurative) gigantesque.

mountain: **~ range** *n* chaîne *f* de montagnes; **~ top** *n* cime *f*.

mounted police *n* police *f* montée.

mourn I *vtr* pleurer [*person, death*].
II *vi* [*person*] porter le deuil; **to ~ for sth/sb** pleurer qch/qn.

mourning *n* deuil *m*.

mouse *n* souris *f*.

mousey *adj* **1** [*hair*] châtain terne *inv*; **2** (timid) effacé.

moustache, mustache (US) *n* moustache *f*.

mouth I *n* **1** (of human, horse) bouche *f*; (of other animal) gueule *f*; **2** (of cave, tunnel) entrée *f*; (of river) embouchure *f*; (of geyser, volcano) bouche *f*.
II *vtr* articuler silencieusement [*words, answer*].
IDIOMS **by word of ~** de bouche à oreille; **his heart was in his ~** son cœur battait la chamade; **to take the words right out of sb's ~** ôter les mots de la bouche de qn.

mouthful *n* **1** (of food) bouchée *f*; (of liquid) gorgée *f*; **2**° (word) mot *m* long d'un kilomètre°; (name) nom *m* à coucher dehors°.

mouth: **~ organ** ▶ 753 *n* harmonica *m*; **~-to-mouth resuscitation** *n* bouche-à-bouche *m inv*; **~wash** *n* eau *f* dentifrice; **~-watering** *adj* appétissant.

move I *n* **1** (movement) mouvement *m*; (gesture) geste *m*; **2** (of residence) déménagement *m*; (of company) transfert *m*; **3** (in game) coup *m*; **it's your ~** c'est ton tour; **4** (step, act) manœuvre *f*; **a good/bad ~** une bonne/mauvaise idée; **to make the first ~** faire le premier pas.
II *vtr* **1** déplacer [*game piece, cursor, car, furniture*]; transporter [*patient, army*]; **to ~ sth (out of the way)** enlever qch; **to ~ sth further away/closer** éloigner/rapprocher qch; **2** [*person*] bouger [*limb, head*], [*wind, mechanism*] faire bouger [*leaf, wheel*]; **3** (relocate) muter [*staff*]; transférer [*office*]; **to ~ house** déménager; **4** (affect) émouvoir; **to be deeply ~d** être très ému.
III *vi* **1** (stir) bouger; [*lips*] remuer; **will you please ~!** veux-tu te pousser?; **2** (travel) [*vehicle*] rouler; [*person*] avancer; [*procession, army*] être en marche; **things are starting to ~ on the job front** les choses commencent à avancer côté travail; **go on, get moving!** allez, avance!; **to ~ back** reculer; **to ~ forward** s'avancer; **to ~ away** s'éloigner; **3** (change home, location) déménager; **to ~ to the countryside/ to Japan** s'installer à la campagne/au Japon; **4** (change job) être muté; **5** (act) agir.
IV **on the move** *phr* **on the ~** [*army*] en mouvement; **to be always on the ~** [*diplomat, family*] être tout le temps en train de déménager; [*nomad, traveller*] être toujours sur les routes.
■ **move about, move around**: ¶ **~ about** [*person*] remuer; [*object*] bouger; ¶ **~ [sb/sth] about** déplacer.
■ **move along**: ¶ **~ along** (stop loitering) circuler; (proceed) avancer; (squeeze up) se pousser; ¶ **~ [sb/sth] along** faire circuler [*onlookers, crowd*].
■ **move away** s'éloigner; (move house) déménager.
■ **move in 1** (to house) emménager; **to ~ in with** s'installer avec [*friend, relative*]; aller vivre avec [*lover*]; **2** (advance, attack) s'avancer (**on** sur).
■ **move on** [*person, traveller*] se mettre en route; [*vehicle*] repartir; **to ~ on to** passer à [*next item*].
■ **move out** (of house) déménager; **to ~ out of** quitter.
■ **move over 1** (make room) se pousser; **2** (figurative) céder la place (**for sb** à qn).
■ **move up 1** (make room) se pousser; **2** (be promoted) être promu; **to ~ up to the first division** passer en première division.

movement *n* mouvement *m*; (of hand, arm) geste *m*; **to watch sb's ~s** surveiller les faits et gestes de qn.

movie I *n* film *m*.
II **movies** *n pl* **the ~s** le cinéma.

movie: **~goer** *n* spectateur/-trice *m/f* de cinéma; **~ star** *n* vedette *f* de cinéma; **~ theater** *n* cinéma *m*.

moving *adj* **1** [*vehicle*] en marche; [*parts, target*] mobile; [*staircase, walkway*] roulant; **2** [*scene, speech*] émouvant.

mow *vtr* tondre [*grass, lawn*].

mower *n* tondeuse *f* à gazon.

MP *n* (GB) (*abbr* = **Member of Parliament**) député *m* (**for** de).

mpg *n pl* (*written abbr* = **miles per gallon**) miles *mpl* au gallon; (GB) **35 ~** 8 litres aux cent; (US) **30 ~** 8 litres aux cent.

mph *n* (*abbr* = **miles per hour**) miles *mpl* à l'heure.

Mr ▶ 642 *n* M., Monsieur.

Mrs ▶ 642 *n* Mme, Madame.

Ms ▶ 642 *n* ≈ Mme.

MSc *n* (*abbr* = **Master of Science**) diplôme *m* supérieur en sciences.

much

■ **Note** When *much* is used as an adverb, it is translated by *beaucoup*: *it's much longer* = c'est beaucoup plus long; *she doesn't talk much* = elle ne parle pas beaucoup.
– For particular usages, see I below.
– When *much* is used as a pronoun, it is usually translated by *beaucoup*: *there is much to learn* = il y a beaucoup à apprendre. However, in negative sentences *grand-chose* is also used: *I didn't learn much* = je n'ai pas beaucoup appris *or* je n'ai pas appris grand-chose.
– When *much* is used as a determiner, it is translated by *beaucoup de*: *they don't have much money* = ils n'ont pas beaucoup d'argent.
– For particular usages see III below.

I *adv* **1** (to a considerable degree) beaucoup; **~ more/less** beaucoup plus/moins; **~ smaller** beaucoup plus petit; **it's ~ better organized** c'est beaucoup mieux organisé; **I don't read ~** je ne lis pas beaucoup; **we'd ~ rather stay here** nous préférerions de beaucoup rester ici; **he's not ~ good at doing** il n'est pas très doué pour faire; **does it hurt ~?** est-ce que ça fait très mal?; **~ to my surprise** à ma grande surprise; **2** (often) beaucoup, souvent; **we don't go out ~** nous ne sortons pas beaucoup; **3** (nearly) plus ou moins, à peu près; **it's ~ the same** c'est à peu près pareil (**as** que); **it's pretty ~ like driving a car** c'est plus ou moins la même chose que de conduire une voiture; **in ~ the same way** à peu près de la

même façon (**as** que); **4** (specifying degree to which something is true) **too ~** trop; **very ~** (a lot) beaucoup; (absolutely) tout à fait; **he misses you very ~** tu lui manques beaucoup; **it's very ~ the norm** c'est tout à fait la norme; **so ~** tellement; **as ~** autant (**as** que); **they hated each other as ~ as ever** ils se détestaient toujours autant; **I thought as ~** ça ne m'étonne pas, je m'en doutais.
II *pron, quantif* **1** (a great deal) beaucoup; (in negative sentences) grand-chose; **do you have ~ left?** est-ce qu'il vous en reste beaucoup?; **we didn't eat ~** nous n'avons pas mangé grand-chose; **I don't see ~ of them now** je ne les vois plus beaucoup maintenant; **2** (expressing a relative amount, degree) **so ~** tellement, tant; **we'd eaten so ~ that** nous avions tellement mangé que; **too ~** trop; **it costs too ~** c'est trop cher; **it's too ~!** c'est trop!; (in protest) c'en est trop!; **the job is too ~ for me** (hard) le travail est trop difficile pour moi; **the heat was too ~ for them** ils n'ont pas pu supporter la chaleur; **twice as ~** deux fois plus; **as ~ as possible** autant que possible; **as ~ as to say...** d'un air de dire...; **how ~?** combien?; **3** (focusing on inadequacy) **it's not** or **nothing ~** ce n'est pas grand-chose; **it's not up to ~** (GB) ça ne vaut pas grand-chose; **he's not ~ to look at** il n'est pas très beau.
III *det* beaucoup de; **I haven't got ~ time** je n'ai pas beaucoup de temps; **she didn't speak ~ English** elle ne connaissait que quelques mots d'anglais; **too ~ money** trop d'argent; **don't use so ~ salt** ne mets pas tant de sel; **we paid twice as ~** nous avons payé deux fois plus; **how ~ time have we got left?** combien de temps nous reste-t-il?
IV **much–** *pref* **~loved** très apprécié; **~needed** indispensable.
V **much as** *phr* bien que (+ *subj*); **~ as we regret our decision** bien qu'il nous en déplaise d'avoir eu à prendre cette décision.
VI **much less** *phr* encore moins.
VII **so much as** *phr* **without so ~ as an apology** sans même s'excuser; **if you so ~ as move** si tu fais le moindre mouvement.
IDIOMS **she's late again? that's a bit ~!** elle est encore en retard? elle exagère!

mud *n* boue *f*.

muddle *n* **1** (mess) pagaille○; **2** (mix-up) malentendu *m* (**over** à propos de); **3 to get into a ~** [*person*] s'embrouiller.
■ **muddle up**: ¶ **~ [sth] up, ~ up [sth]** (disorder) semer la pagaille○ dans; ¶ **~ [sb] up** embrouiller les idées de; **to get [sth] ~d up** s'embrouiller dans [*dates, names*].

muddled *adj* confus.

muddy *adj* [*hand*] couvert de boue; [*shoe, garment*] crotté; [*road, water*] boueux/-euse; [*green, yellow*] terne.

mudguard *n* garde-boue *m inv*.

muffle *vtr* **1** (wrap up) emmitoufler (**in** dans); **2** assourdir [*bell, drum*].

muffler *n* **1** (garment) cache-nez *m inv*; **2** (US) (silencer) silencieux *m*.

mug I *n* **1** grande tasse *f*; **2** (GB) (fool) poire○ *f*; **it's a ~'s game** c'est un attrape-nigaud.
II *vtr* agresser; **to be ~ged** se faire agresser.

mugger *n* agresseur *m*.

muggy *adj* [*room, day*] étouffant; [*weather*] lourd.

Muhammad *pr n* Mahomet.

mule *n* mulet *m*, mule *f*.
IDIOMS **as stubborn as a ~** têtu comme une mule.

mull *v* ■ **mull over**: **~ over [sth], ~ [sth] over** retourner [qch] dans sa tête.

mulled wine *n* vin *m* chaud.

multinational *adj* multinational.

multiple *n, adj* multiple (*m*).

multiple sclerosis, MS ▶ 686 *n* sclérose *f* en plaques.

multiply I *vtr* multiplier (**by** par).
II *vi* se multiplier.

multipurpose *adj* [*tool*] à usages multiples; [*area, organization*] polyvalent.

multistorey *adj* (GB) [*car park*] à niveaux multiples; [*building*] à étages.

multitude *n* multitude *f*.

mum○, **Mum**○ *n* (GB) maman *f*.
IDIOMS **~'s the word** motus et bouche cousue; **to keep ~** ne pas piper mot.

mumble *vtr, vi* marmonner.

mumbo jumbo○ *n* charabia○ *m*.

mummy *n* **1**○ (also **Mummy**) maman *f*; **2** (embalmed body) momie *f*.

mumps ▶ 686 *n* oreillons *mpl*.

munch *vtr* [*person*] mâcher; [*animal*] mâchonner.

mundane *adj* terre-à-terre, quelconque.

municipal *adj* municipal.

mural *n* (wall painting) peinture *f* murale; (in cave) peinture *f* rupestre.

murder I *n* meurtre *m*.
II *noun modifier* [*investigation*] sur un or le meurtre; [*scene, weapon*] du crime; [*trial*] criminel/-elle; [*story*] policier/-ière; **~ hunt** chasse *f* à l'assassin; **~ suspect** meurtrier/-ière *m/f* présumé/-e; **~ victim** victime *f*.
III *vtr* assassiner.
IDIOMS **to get away with ~** exercer ses talents en toute impunité.

murderer *n* assassin *m*, meurtrier *m*.

murderess *n* meurtrière *f*.

murderous *adj* [*look*] assassin; [*deeds, thoughts*] meurtrier/-ière.

murky *adj* **1** [*light, water, colour*] glauque; [*weather*] maussade; **2** [*past*] trouble.

murmur I *n* murmure *m* (**of** de).
II *vtr, vi* murmurer.

muscle *n* muscle *m*.
■ **muscle in**○ s'imposer (**on** dans).

muscular *adj* [*disease, tissue*] musculaire; [*body, limbs*] musclé; **to have a ~ build** être tout en muscles.

museum *n* musée *m*.

Musical Instruments

Playing an instrument

Note the use of ***de*** with ***jouer***:

to play the piano	= jouer **du** piano
to play the violin	= jouer **du** violon
to play the clarinet	= jouer **de la** clarinette
to play the flute	= jouer **de la** flûte

but

to learn the piano	= apprendre **le** piano
to learn the guitar	= apprendre **la** guitare

Players

English ***-ist*** is often French ***-iste***; the gender reflects the sex of the player:

a violinist	= un violoniste / une violoniste
a pianist	= un pianiste / une pianiste
a flautist	= un flûtiste / une flûtiste
a cellist	= un violoncelliste / une violoncelliste

A phrase with ***joueur / joueuse de X*** is usually safe:

a piccolo player	= un joueur de piccolo / une joueuse de piccolo
a horn player	= un joueur de cor / une joueuse de cor

But note the French when these words are used with *good* and *bad* like this:

he's a good pianist	= il joue bien du piano
he's not a good pianist	= il ne joue pas bien du piano
he's a bad pianist	= il joue mal du piano

As in English, the name of the instrument is often used to refer to its player:

she's a first violin	= elle est premier violon

Music

a piano piece	= un morceau pour piano
a piano arrangement	= un arrangement pour piano
a piano sonata	= une sonate pour piano
a concerto for piano and orchestra	= un concerto pour piano et orchestre
the piano part	= la partie pour piano
a piano trio	= un trio pour piano

Use with another noun

de is usually correct:

to take piano lessons	= prendre des leçons **de** piano
a violin maker	= un fabricant **de** violons
a violin solo	= un solo **de** violon
a piano teacher	= un professeur **de** piano
a piano tuner	= un accordeur **de** pianos

but note the ***à*** here:

a violin case	= un étui **à** violon

mushroom ▶559| *n* **1** (Bot, Culin) champignon *m*; **2** (colour) beige *m* rosé.

music *n* **1** musique *f*; **to set sth to ~** mettre qch en musique; **2** (printed) partition *f*.
IDIOMS **to face the ~** affronter l'orage.

musical I *n* comédie *f* musicale.
II *adj* **1** [*person*] (gifted) musicien/-ienne; (interested) mélomane; **2** [*voice, laughter*] mélodieux/-ieuse; [*score*] musical.

musical: **~ box** *n* (GB) boîte *f* à musique; **~ instrument** ▶753| *n* instrument *m* de musique.

musician ▶805| *n* musicien/-ienne *m/f*.

musk *n* musc *m*.

musketeer *n* mousquetaire *m*.

Muslim I *n* Musulman/-e *m/f*.
II *adj* musulman.

mussel *n* moule *f*.

must I *modal aux* **1** (expressing obligation) **I ~ go** je dois partir, il faut que je parte; **he ~ sit the exam in June** il faut qu'il passe l'examen au mois de juin; **you ~ check your rear-view mirror first** il faut regarder dans le rétroviseur d'abord; **2** (stressing a point) **I ~ ask you not to smoke** je dois vous demander de ne pas fumer; **I ~ say I was impressed** je dois dire que j'ai été impressionné; **you ~ warn her** il faut que tu la préviennes, tu dois la prévenir; **we mustn't tell anyone** il ne faut en parler à personne, nous ne devons en parler à personne; **3** (making assumptions) **they ~ really detest each other** ils doivent vraiment se détester; **it ~ be pleasant living there** ça doit être agréable de vivre là-bas; **that ~ be Marie-Hélène's tea** ça doit être le thé de Marie-Hélène; **there ~ be a mistake** il doit y avoir une erreur; **it mustn't have been very difficult** ça n'a pas dû être très difficile; **4** (expressing annoyance) **why ~ you always be so critical?** pourquoi faut-il toujours que tu sois si critique?; **you ~ be mad!** tu es fou!
II *n* **it's a ~** c'est indispensable; **this film is a ~** ce film est à voir or à ne pas rater; **a visit to the Louvre is a ~** une visite au Louvre s'impose.

mustache (US) = **moustache**.

mustard ▶559| *n* **1** (condiment, plant) moutarde *f*; **2** (colour) (jaune *m*) moutarde *m*.

muster *vtr* (also **~ up**) rassembler [*troops*]; rallier [*support*]; préparer [*argument*]; trouver [*energy, enthusiasm*].
IDIOMS **to pass ~** être acceptable.

musty *adj* **to smell ~** sentir le moisi or le renfermé.

mute *adj* muet/-ette.

mutilate *vtr* mutiler.

mutiny *n* mutinerie *f*.

mutter *vtr*, *vi* marmonner.

mutton *n* mouton *m*.
IDIOMS **(it's) ~ dressed as lamb** elle s'habille trop jeune pour son âge.

mutual *adj* **1** (reciprocal) réciproque; **the feeling is ~** c'est réciproque; **2** [*friend, interests*] commun; [*consent*] mutuel/-elle; **by ~ agreement** d'un commun accord.

my

■ Note In French, determiners agree in gender and number with the noun that follows. So *my* is translated by *mon* + masculine singular noun (mon chien), *ma* + feminine singular noun (ma maison) BUT by *mon* + feminine noun beginning with a vowel or mute 'h' (mon assiette) and by *mes* + plural noun (mes enfants).
– When *my* is stressed, *à moi* is added after the noun: MY *house* = ma maison à moi.
– For *my* used with parts of the body, see the Usage Note ▶523|.

I *det* mon/ma/mes.
II *excl* **~ ~!** ça alors!

myself *pron*

■ Note When used as a reflexive pronoun, direct and indirect, *myself* is translated by *me* (or *m'* before a vowel or mute 'h') which is always placed before the verb: *I've hurt myself* = je me suis fait mal.
– When used for emphasis, the translation is *moi-même*: *I did it myself* = je l'ai fait moi-même.
– When used after a preposition, *myself* is translated by *moi* or *moi-même*: *I did it for myself* = je l'ai fait pour moi *or* moi-même.

---

1 (reflexive) me, m'; **2** (emphatic) moi-même; **I saw it ~** je l'ai vu moi-même; **(all) by ~** tout/-e seul/-e; **3** (after prepositions) moi, moi-même; **I feel proud of ~** je suis fier de moi; **4** (expressions) **I'm not much of a dog-lover ~** personnellement je n'aime pas trop les chiens; **I'm not ~ today** je ne suis pas dans mon assiette aujourd'hui.

mysterious *adj* mystérieux/-ieuse.

mystery I *n* **1** mystère *m*; **it's a ~ how** on ne sait pas comment; **2** (book) roman *m* policier.
II *noun modifier* [*death, illness, voice*] mystérieux/-ieuse; **~ guest** invité/-e *m/f* mystère; **~ tour** visite *f* surprise.

mystify *vtr* laisser [qn] perplexe.

myth *n* mythe *m*.

mythology *n* mythologie *f*.

Nn

n, N *n* n, N *m*.

nadir *n* nadir *m*; (figurative) point *m* le plus bas.

nag I *vtr* enquiquiner○ (**about** au sujet de).
II nagging *pres p adj* **1 his ~ging wife** sa mégère de femme (derogatory); **2** [*pain, doubt*] tenace.

nail I *n* **1** (on finger, toe) ongle *m*; **2** (Tech) clou *m*.
II *vtr* clouer.
IDIOMS **to hit the ~ on the head** mettre le doigt dessus.
■ **nail down**: ¶ **~ down [sth], ~ [sth] down** clouer; ¶ **~ [sb] down** coincer○ [*person*]; **to ~ sb down to a date/price** obtenir de qn qu'il fixe (*subj*) une date/un prix.

nail: **~brush** *n* brosse *f* à ongles; **~ file** *n* lime *f* à ongles; **~ scissors** *n pl* ciseaux *mpl* à ongles; **~ varnish** *n* vernis *m* à ongles; **~ varnish remover** *n* dissolvant *m*.

naïve *adj* naïf/-ïve.

naked *adj* **1** nu; **~ to the waist** torse nu; **2** [*flame, light bulb*] nu; [*truth*] tout nu; **to the ~ eye** à l'œil nu.

name I *n* **1** (gen) nom *m*; (of book, film) titre *m*; **first ~** prénom *m*; **my ~ is Louis** je m'appelle Louis; **2** (reputation) réputation *f*; **3** (insult) **to call sb ~s** injurier qn.
II *vtr* **1** (call) appeler [*person, area*]; baptiser [*boat*]; **they ~d her after** (GB) or **for** (US) **her mother** ils l'ont appelée comme sa mère; **a boy ~d Pascal** un garçon nommé Pascal; **2** (cite) citer; **~ three American States** citez trois États américains; **3** révéler [*sources*]; révéler l'identité de [*suspect*]; **to ~ ~s** donner des noms; **4** (state) indiquer [*place, time*]; fixer [*price, terms*].

name-drop *vi* citer des gens célèbres (*qu'on prétend connaître*).

namely *adv* à savoir.

namesake *n* homonyme *m*.

nanny *n* (GB) bonne *f* d'enfants.

nanny goat *n* chèvre *f*.

nap I *n* petit somme *m*; **afternoon ~** sieste *f*.
II *vi* sommeiller.
IDIOMS **to catch sb ~ping**○ prendre qn au dépourvu.

nape *n* nuque *f*; **the ~ of the neck** la nuque.

napkin *n* serviette *f* (de table); **~ ring** rond *m* de serviette.

nappy *n* (GB) couche *f* (de bébé).

narcotic I *n* (soporific) narcotique *m*; (illegal drug) stupéfiant *m*.
II *adj* narcotique.

narration *n* récit *m*, narration *f*.

narrative I *n* (account) récit *m*; (storytelling) narration *f*.
II *noun modifier* [*prose, poem*] narratif/-ive; [*skill, talent*] de conteur.

narrator *n* narrateur/-trice *m/f*.

narrow ▶ 738 **I** *adj* [*street, room, shoe, jacket*] étroit; [*range*] restreint; [*sense, definition*] étroit; [*interests*] limité; [*views*] étriqué; [*majority, margin*] faible (*before n*); **to have a ~ lead** avoir une légère avance; **to have a ~ escape** l'échapper belle.
II *vtr* **1** (gen) limiter (**to** à); restreindre [*sense, definition*] (**to** à); **to ~ the gap** (in race, poll) réduire l'écart; **2** rétrécir [*road, path, arteries*].
III *vi* (gen) se rétrécir; [*valley*] se resserrer; [*gap, margin*] se réduire (**to** à).
■ **narrow down**: **~ [sth] down, ~ down [sth]** réduire [*numbers, list, choice*] (**to** à); limiter [*investigation, research*] (**to** à).

narrowly *adv* (barely) de justesse; (strictly) strictement.

narrow-minded *adj* borné.

nasal *adj* [*vowel*] nasal; [*accent, voice*] nasillard.

nasal spray *n* nébuliseur *m* (*pour le nez*).

nastiness *n* (of person, remark) méchanceté *f*; (of food, medicine) mauvais goût *m*.

nasty *adj* **1** [*person, expression, remark*] méchant; [*experience, surprise, feeling, task*] désagréable; [*habit, smell, taste*] mauvais; [*trick*] sale (*before n*); [*cut, bruise*] vilain (*before n*); [*accident*] grave; **to turn ~** [*person, dog*] devenir méchant; [*situation*] mal tourner; [*weather*] se gâter; **2** (ugly) affreux/-euse.

nation *n* (entity) nation *f*; (people) peuple *m*.

national I *n* ressortissant/-e *m/f*.
II *adj* national; **the ~ press** (GB) les grands quotidiens *mpl*.

national: **~ anthem** *n* hymne *m* national; **~ debt** *n* dette *f* publique; **National Health Service, NHS** *n* (GB) services *mpl* de santé britanniques, ≈ Sécurité *f* Sociale; **National Insurance, NI** *n* (GB) securité *f* sociale britannique.

nationalism *n* nationalisme *m*.

nationality *n* nationalité *f*.

nationalize *vtr* nationaliser [*industry*].

national monument *n* monument *m* historique.

nationwide *adj* [*campaign*] national; [*survey, poll*] à l'échelle nationale.

native I *n* (person) autochtone *mf*; (flora, fauna) espèce *f* indigène; **to be a ~ of** être originaire de.
II *adj* **1** [*land*] natal; [*tongue*] maternel/-elle; **~ German speaker** personne *f* de langue maternelle allemande; **2** [*flora, fauna*] indigène.

Native American *n, adj* amérindien/-ienne (*m/f*).

Nativity *n* nativité *f*.

NATO *n* (*abbr* = **North Atlantic Treaty Organization**) OTAN *f*.

natural *adj* **1** (gen) naturel/-elle; **it's only ~**

c'est tout à fait naturel; **it's ~ to do/to be** c'est normal de faire/d'être; **to die of ~ causes** mourir de mort naturelle; **2** (unaffected) simple, naturel/-elle.

naturalist *n, adj* naturaliste (*mf*).

naturalization *n* **1** (gen) naturalisation *f*; **2** (Bot, Zool) acclimatation *f*.

naturalize *vtr* **1** (gen) naturaliser [*person*]; **to be ~d** se faire naturaliser; **2** (Bot, Zool) acclimater.

naturally *adv* **1** (obviously, of course) naturellement; **2** (by nature) de nature; **politeness comes ~ to him** il est d'un naturel poli; **3** [*behave, smile*] avec naturel.

nature *n* **1** (the natural world) nature *f*; **let ~ take its course** laissez faire la nature; **2** (character) nature *f*; **it's not in her ~ to be aggressive** elle n'est pas agressive de nature; **matters of a medical ~** des choses d'ordre médical; **it is in the ~ of things** il est dans l'ordre des choses.

nature: **~ reserve** *n* réserve *f* naturelle; **~ trail** *n* sentier *m* écologique.

naughty *adj* **1** [*child*] vilain; **a ~ word** un gros mot; **2** (suggestive) coquin.

nausea *n* nausée *f*.

nauseating *adj* écœurant.

nauseous *adj* [*taste, smell*] écœurant; **to feel ~** avoir la nausée.

nautical *adj* nautique.

naval *adj* [*battle, forces, base*] naval; [*officer, recruit, uniform, affairs*] de la marine.

nave *n* nef *f*.

navel *n* nombril *m*.

navigate I *vtr* **1** parcourir [*seas*]; **2** (guide) piloter [*plane, ship*]; **3** (steer) gouverner [*ship*].
II *vi* (in vessel, plane) naviguer; (in rally) faire le copilote; (on journey) tenir la carte.

navigation *n* navigation *f*.

navigator *n* (in vessel, plane) navigateur/-trice *m/f*; (in car) copilote *mf*.

navy I *n* **1** (fleet) flotte *f*; (fighting force) marine *f*; **2** (also **~ blue**) bleu *m* marine.
II *adj* ▶ 559 (also **~ blue**) bleu marine *inv*.

Nazi *n, adj* nazi/-e (*m/f*).

near I *adv* **1** **to live quite ~** habiter tout près; **to move ~er** s'approcher davantage (**to** de); **to bring sth ~er** approcher qch; **autumn is drawing ~** l'automne approche; **2** (nearly) **as ~ perfect as it could be** aussi proche de la perfection que possible; **nowhere ~ finished** loin d'être fini.
II *prep* **1** près de; **~ here** près d'ici; **~ the beginning of the article** presque au début de l'article; **he's no ~er (making) a decision** il n'est pas plus décidé; **2** (in time) **~er the time** quand la date approchera; **it's getting ~ Christmas** Noël approche.
III *adj* proche; **in the ~ future** dans un avenir proche; **the ~est shops** les magasins les plus proches.
IV *vtr* approcher de; **to ~ completion** toucher à sa fin.
V near enough *phr* à peu près.
VI near to *phr* **1** (in space) près de; **~ to where** près de l'endroit où; **how ~ are we to Dijon?** à quelle distance sommes-nous de Dijon?; **2** (on point of) au bord de [*tears, collapse*]; **3** (in degree) **to come ~est to** s'approcher le plus de; **to come ~ to doing** faillir faire.

nearby I *adj* [*person*] qui se trouve/trouvait etc à proximité; [*town, village*] d'à côté.
II *adv* à proximité; **~, there's a village** tout près il y a un village.

nearly *adv* presque; **I very ~ gave up** j'ai bien failli abandonner; **not ~ as talented as** loin d'être aussi doué que.

nearness *n* (in space) proximité *f*; (in time) approche *f*.

neat I *adj* **1** (tidy) [*person*] (in habits) ordonné; (in appearance) soigné; [*room, house, desk*] bien rangé; [*garden, handwriting*] soigné; **2** [*explanation, solution*] habile; **3** (trim) [*figure*] bien fait; [*features*] régulier/-ière; **4** [*alcohol, spirits*] sans eau.
II *adv* [*drink whisky*] sec, sans eau.

neatly *adv* **1** (tidily) [*dress, fold, arrange*] avec soin; [*write*] proprement; **2** (perfectly) [*illustrate, summarize*] parfaitement; [*link*] habilement.

neatness *n* (of person, garden) aspect *m* soigné; (of room, house) propreté *f*; (of handwriting) netteté *f*.

necessarily *adv* (definitely) forcément; (of necessity) nécessairement.

necessary *adj* (gen) nécessaire; [*qualification*] requis; **if ~, as ~** si besoin est; **to find it ~ to do** éprouver le besoin de faire; **it is ~ for him to do** il faut qu'il fasse.

necessitate *vtr* nécessiter.

necessity *n* **1** (need) nécessité *f*; **from ~** par nécessité; **the ~ for** le besoin de; **2** (essential item) **to be an absolute ~** être indispensable; **the necessities of life** les produits *mpl* de première nécessité.

neck *n* ▶ 523 **1** (of person) cou *m*; (of horse, donkey) encolure *f*; **2** (collar) col *m*; (neckline) encolure *f*; **with a high ~** à or avec un col montant; **3** (of bottle, vase, womb) col *m*.
IDIOMS **to be ~ and ~** être à égalité; **to stick one's ~ out**° prendre des risques.

neck: **~lace** *n* collier *m*; **~line** *n* encolure *f*; **~tie** *n* (US) cravate *f*.

nectar *n* nectar *m*.

nectarine *n* nectarine *f*, brugnon *m*.

need

■ **Note** When *need* is used as a verb meaning *to require* or *to want*, it is generally translated by *avoir besoin de* in French: *I need help* = j'ai besoin d'aide.
– When *need* is used as a verb to mean *have to*, it can generally be translated by *devoir + infinitive* or by *il faut que + subjunctive*: *I need to leave* = je dois partir, il faut que je parte.

I *modal aux* **you needn't finish it today** tu n'es pas obligé de le finir aujourd'hui; **~ he reply?** est-ce qu'il faut qu'il réponde?, est-ce qu'il doit répondre?; **I needn't have hurried** ce

n'était pas la peine de me dépêcher, ce n'était pas la peine que je me dépêche; **~ I say more?** tu vois ce que je veux dire?; **nothing more ~ be said** on n'en parlera plus; **nobody ~ know** que cela reste entre nous.
II *vtr* **1** (require) **to ~ sth** avoir besoin de qch; **more money is ~ed** nous avons besoin de plus d'argent; **everything you ~** tout ce qu'il vous faut; **to raise the money ~ed for the deposit** réunir l'argent nécessaire pour la caution; **you don't ~ me to tell you that...** vous n'êtes pas sans savoir que...; **everything you ~ to know about computers** tout ce que vous devez savoir sur les ordinateurs; **that's all I ~!** il ne me manquait plus que ça!; **2** (have to) **you'll ~ to work hard** il va falloir que tu travailles dur; **he didn't ~ to ask permission** il n'était pas obligé de demander la permission; **something ~ed to be done** il fallait faire quelque chose.
III *n* **1** (necessity) nécessité *f* (**for** de); **I can't see the ~ for it** je n'en vois pas la nécessité; **to feel the ~ to do** éprouver le besoin de faire; **there's no ~ to wait** inutile d'attendre; **there's no ~ to worry** ce n'est pas la peine de s'inquiéter; **there's no ~, I've done it** inutile, c'est fait; **2** (requirement) besoin *m* (**for** de); **to meet sb's ~s** répondre aux besoins de qn; **energy ~s** besoins *mpl* en énergie; **3** (poverty) **to be in ~** être dans le besoin.

needle I *n* aiguille *f*.
II *vtr* harceler.
IDIOMS **to have pins and ~s** avoir des fourmis.

needless *adj* [*anxiety, suffering*] inutile; [*intrusion, intervention*] inopportun.

needlework *n* couture *f*.

needy *adj* [*person*] nécessiteux/-euse; [*sector, area*] sans ressources.

negative I *n* **1 to answer in the ~** répondre par la négative; **2** (of photo) négatif *m*; **3** (in grammar) négation *f*; **in the ~** à la forme négative.
II *adj* **1** (gen) négatif/-ive; [*effect, influence*] néfaste; **2** (in photography) en négatif.

neglect I *n* **1** (of person) négligence *f*; (of building, garden) manque *m* d'entretien; (of health, appearance) manque *m* de soin; **2** (lack of interest) indifférence *f* (**of** à l'égard de).
II *vtr* **1** ne pas s'occuper de [*person, dog, plant*]; ne pas entretenir [*garden, house*]; négliger [*health, friend, work*]; **2** (fail) **to ~ to do** négliger de faire.

neglected *adj* (gen) négligé; [*garden, building*] mal entretenu; **to feel ~** se sentir délaissé.

negligence *n* négligence *f*.

negligent *adj* [*person, procedure*] négligent; [*air, manner*] nonchalant.

negligible *adj* négligeable.

negotiable *adj* **1** [*price, salary, securities*] négociable; **2** [*road*] praticable.

negotiate I *vtr* **1** (in business, diplomacy) négocier; **2** négocier [*bend*]; franchir [*obstacle*].
II *vi* négocier (**with** avec; **for** pour obtenir).

negotiating *adj* [*team*] qui conduit les négociations; [*table*] des négociations.

negotiation *n* négociation *f*; **to be under ~** être en cours de négociations.

negotiator *n* négociateur/-trice *m/f*.

neigh *vi* hennir.

neighbour (GB), **neighbor** (US) *n* voisin/-e *m/f*.

neighbourhood (GB), **neighborhood** (US) *n* **1** (district) quartier *m*; **2** (vicinity) **in the ~** dans le voisinage.

neighbouring (GB), **neighboring** (US) *adj* voisin.

neighbourly (GB), **neighborly** (US) *adj* [*person*] gentil/-ille; [*relations*] de bon voisinage.

neither

■ **Note** When used as conjunctions, *neither...nor* are translated by *ni...ni*: *she speaks neither English nor French* = elle ne parle ni anglais ni français; *neither tea, nor milk* = ni (le) thé, ni (le) lait. Note that the preceding verb is negated by *ne*.
– When used as a conjunction to show agreement or similarity with a negative statement, *neither* is translated by *non plus*: *'I don't like him'—'neither do I'* = 'je ne l'aime pas'—'moi non plus'; *'he's not Spanish'—'neither is John'* = 'il n'est pas espagnol'—'John non plus'.

I *conj* **I have ~ the time nor the money** je n'ai ni le temps ni l'argent; **'I can't sleep'—'neither can I'** 'je n'arrive pas à dormir'—'moi non plus'.
II *det* aucun/-e des deux; **~ book is suitable** aucun des deux livres ne convient; **~ girl replied** aucune des deux filles n'a répondu.
III *pron, quantif* ni l'un/-e, ni l'autre *m/f*; **~ of them came** ni l'un ni l'autre n'est venu.

neologism *n* néologisme *m*.

neon I *n* néon *m*.
II *noun modifier* [*light, lighting, sign*] au néon; [*atom*] de néon.

nephew *n* neveu *m*.

Neptune *pr n* Neptune *m*.

nerve I *n* **1** (Anat) nerf *m*; (Bot) nervure *f*; **2 to lose one's ~** perdre son courage; **3 you've got a ~**○! tu as un sacré culot○!
II **nerves** *n pl* (nervousness) nerfs *mpl*; (stage fright) trac○ *m*; **to have an attack of ~s** faire une crise de nerfs.

nerve racking, **nerve wracking** *adj* angoissant.

nervous *adj* **1** [*person*] (fearful) timide; (anxious) angoissé; (highly strung) nerveux/-euse; [*smile, laugh, habit*] nerveux/-euse; **to be ~ about doing** avoir peur de faire; **to feel ~** (apprehensive) être angoissé; (before performance) avoir le trac○; (afraid) avoir peur; (ill at ease) se sentir mal à l'aise; **2** (Anat, Med) nerveux/-euse.

nervous breakdown *n* dépression *f* nerveuse.

nervously *adv* nerveusement.

nervous: **~ system** *n* système *m* nerveux; **~ wreck**○ *n* boule *f* de nerfs○.

nest I *n* **1** (of bird, animal) nid *m*; (group of baby

birds, mice) nichée *f* (**of** de); **2 ~ of tables** tables *fpl* gigognes.
II *vi* [*bird*] faire son nid.

nest egg *n* magot○ *m*.

nestle *vi* **1** [*person, animal*] se blottir (**against** contre; **under** sous); **2** [*village, house*] être niché.

net I *n* (gen) filet *m*; (in football) filets *mpl*; **to slip through the ~** passer à travers les mailles du filet.
II *adj* (also **nett**) [*profit, income, increase*] net/nette; [*loss*] sec/sèche.
III *vtr* **1** (catch) prendre [qch] au filet [*fish*]; **2** (financially) [*person*] faire un bénéfice de; [*sale, export, deal*] rapporter; **3** (in football) marquer [*goal*].

net curtain *n* voilage *m*.

Netherlands ▷574 *pr n* **the ~** les Pays-Bas *mpl*, la Hollande.

netting *n* (of rope) filet *m*; (of metal, plastic) grillage *m*; (fabric) voile *m*.

nettle *n* (also **stinging ~**) ortie *f*.

network *n* réseau *m* (**of** de).

network television *n* (US) chaîne *f* nationale.

neuralgia ▷686 *n* névralgie *f*.

neurologist ▷805 *n* neurologue *mf*.

neurosis *n* névrose *f*.

neurosurgeon ▷805 *n* neurochirurgien *m*.

neurotic I *n* névrosé/-e *m/f*.
II *adj* névrosé.

neuter I *n* neutre *m*.
II *adj* neutre.
III *vtr* châtrer [*animal*].

neutral I *n* **1** (politically) neutre *mf*; **2** (Aut) **in/into ~** au point mort.
II *adj* neutre (**about** en ce qui concerne).

neutrality *n* neutralité *f*.

neutralize *vtr* neutraliser.

neutron I *n* neutron *m*.
II *noun modifier* [*bomb, star*] à neutrons.

never *adv*

■ **Note** When *never* is used to modify a verb (*she never wears a hat, I've never seen him*), it is translated *ne...jamais* in French; *ne* comes before the verb, and before the auxiliary in compound tenses, and *jamais* comes after the verb or auxiliary: *elle ne porte jamais de chapeau, je ne l'ai jamais vu.*

1 (not ever) **I ~ go to London** je ne vais jamais à Londres; **she ~ says anything** elle ne dit jamais rien; **~ have I seen such poverty** je n'ai jamais vu une telle pauvreté; **it's now or ~** c'est le moment ou jamais; **~ again** plus jamais; **~ ever lie to me again!** ne me mens plus jamais!; **2** (emphatic negative) **he ~ said a word** il n'a rien dit; **I ~ knew that** je ne le savais pas; **he ~ so much as apologized** il ne s'est même pas excusé.

nevertheless *adv* **1** (all the same) quand même; **thanks ~** merci quand même; **2** (nonetheless) pourtant, néanmoins.

new *adj* nouveau/-elle (*before n*); (brand new) neuf/neuve; **I bought a ~ computer** (to replace old one) j'ai acheté un nouvel ordinateur; (a brand new model) j'ai acheté un ordinateur neuf; **as good as ~** comme neuf; **someone/something ~** quelqu'un/quelque chose d'autre; **to be ~ to** ne pas être habitué à [*job, way of life*]; **we're ~ to the area** nous sommes nouveaux venus dans la région; **the subject is ~ to me** je ne connais rien au sujet.

newborn *adj* nouveau-né/-née; **~ baby** nouveau-né/-née *m/f*.

new: **~comer** *n* (in place, job, club) nouveau venu/nouvelle venue *m/f*; (in sport, theatre, cinema) nouveau/-elle *m/f*; **~found** *adj* tout nouveau/toute nouvelle.

newly *adv* **1** (recently) [*arrived, built, formed, qualified*] nouvellement; [*washed*] fraîchement; **2** (differently) différemment.

newlyweds *n pl* jeunes mariés *mpl*.

news *n* **1** nouvelle(s) *f(pl)*; **a piece of ~** une nouvelle; (in newspaper) une information; **have you heard the ~?** tu connais la nouvelle?; **the latest ~ is that all is quiet** aux dernières nouvelles tout était calme; **the ~ that she had resigned** la nouvelle selon laquelle elle aurait démissionné; **to be in the ~** défrayer la chronique; **2** (on radio, TV) **the ~** les informations *fpl*, le journal *m*; **to see sth/sb on the ~** voir qch/qn aux informations.

news: **~ agency** *n* agence *f* de presse; **~agent's** *n* (GB) magasin *m* de journaux; **~ bulletin** (GB), **~cast** (US) *n* bulletin *m* d'information; **~caster** ▷805 *n* présentateur/-trice *m/f* des informations; **~dealer** ▷805 *n* (US) marchand *m* de journaux; **~ desk** *n* (at newspaper) (salle *f* de) rédaction *f*; **~ headlines** *n pl* (on TV) titres *mpl* de l'actualité; **~letter** *n* bulletin *m*.

newspaper I *n* (item) journal *m*; (substance) papier *m* journal.
II *noun modifier* [*article, cutting*] de presse; [*archives*] du journal.

news: **~print** *n* (paper) papier *m* journal; (ink) encre *f* d'imprimerie; **~reader** ▷805 *n* (GB) présentateur/-trice *m/f* des informations; **~reel** *n* actualités *fpl*; **~stand** *n* kiosque *m* à journaux.

new wave *n, adj* nouvelle vague (*f*).

New Year *n* le nouvel an *m*; **to see in the ~** fêter la Saint-Sylvestre; **Happy ~!** bonne année!

New Year: **~'s day** (GB), **~'s** (US) *n* le jour *m* de l'an; **~'s Eve** *n* la Saint-Sylvestre.

New Zealand ▷574 *pr n* Nouvelle-Zélande *f*.

next

■ **Note** When *next* is used as an adjective, it is generally translated by *prochain* when referring to something which is still to come or happen and by *suivant* when it generally means *following: I'll be 40 next year* = j'aurai 40 ans l'année prochaine; *the next year, he went to Spain* = l'année suivante il est allé en Espagne.
– For examples and further usages see the entry below.

I *pron* **after this train the ~ is at noon** après ce train, le suivant est à midi; **I hope my ~ will be a boy** j'espère que mon prochain enfant sera un garçon; **from one minute to the ~** d'un instant à l'autre; **the ~ to speak was Emily** ensuite, c'est Emily qui a parlé; **the week after ~** dans deux semaines.
II *adj* **1** prochain, suivant; **get the ~ train** prenez le prochain train; **he got on the ~ train** il a pris le train suivant; **'~!'** 'au suivant!'; **'who's ~?'** 'c'est à qui le tour?'; **'you're ~'** 'c'est à vous'; **the ~ size (up)** la taille au-dessus; **~ Thursday** jeudi prochain; **he's due to arrive in the ~ 10 minutes** il devrait arriver d'ici 10 minutes; **this time ~ week** dans une semaine; **the ~ week she was late** la semaine suivante elle était en retard; **the ~ day** le lendemain; **2** [*room, street*] voisin; [*building, house*] voisin, d'à côté.
III *adv* **1** (afterwards) ensuite, après; **what happened ~?** que s'est-il passé ensuite?; **2** (now) **~, I'd like to say...** je voudrais dire maintenant...; **what shall we do ~?** qu'est-ce qu'on fait maintenant?; **3** (on a future occasion) **when I ~ go there** la prochaine fois que j'irai; **they ~ met in 1981** ils se sont ensuite revus en 1981; **4** (nearest in order) **the ~ tallest is Patrick** ensuite c'est Patrick qui est le plus grand; **the ~ best thing would be to...** à défaut, le mieux serait de...
IV next to *phr* (almost) presque; **~ to impossible** presque impossible; **to get sth for ~ to nothing** avoir qch pour quasiment rien; **in ~ to no time it was over** en un rien de temps c'était fini.
V next to *phr* (beside, close to) à côté de; **two seats ~ to each other** deux sièges l'un à côté de l'autre; **to wear silk ~ to the skin** porter de la soie à même la peau.

next door I *adj* (also **next-door**) d'à côté.
II *adv* [*live, move in*] à côté.

next of kin *n* **to be sb's ~** être le parent le plus proche de qn.

nib *n* plume *f*.

nibble *vi* [*animal*] mordiller; [*person*] grignoter; **to ~ at** (gen) grignoter; [*fish*] mordre à [*bait*].

nice *adj* **1** (enjoyable) agréable; **did you have a ~ time?** tu t'es bien amusé?; **~ to have met you** ravi d'avoir fait votre connaissance; **have a ~ day!** bonne journée!; **2** (attractive) (gen) beau/belle (*before n*); [*place*] agréable; **you look very ~** tu es très chic; **3** (tasty) bon/bonne (*before n*); **to taste ~** avoir bon goût; **4** (kind) sympathique; **to be ~ to sb** être gentil avec qn; **5** [*neighbourhood, school*] comme il faut *inv*; **it is not ~ to tell lies** ce n'est pas bien de mentir.

nice-looking *adj* beau/belle (*before n*).

nicely *adv* **1** (kindly) gentiment; **2** (attractively) agréablement; **3** (politely) [*speak*] convenablement; [*ask*] poliment.

niceness *n* (kindness) gentillesse *f*; (subtlety) subtilité *f*.

nicety *n* subtilité *f*; **social niceties** raffinements *mpl* mondains.

niche *n* **1** (role) place *f*; (recess) niche *f*; **2** (in market) créneau *m*.

nick I *n* encoche *f* (**in** dans).
II *vtr* **1** (cut) faire une entaille dans; **2**° (GB) (steal) piquer°; (arrest) pincer°.

nickel *n* **1** (US) (coin) pièce *f* de cinq cents; **2** (metal) nickel *m*.

nickname I *n* surnom *m*.
II *vtr* surnommer.

nicotine *n* nicotine *f*.

niece *n* nièce *f*.

niggling *adj* [*person*] tatillon/-onne; [*doubt, worry*] insidieux/-ieuse.

night ▶ 915 *n* nuit *f*; (before going to bed) soir *m*; **at ~** la nuit; **all ~ long** toute la nuit; **late at ~** tard le soir; **he arrived last ~** il est arrivé hier soir; **I slept badly last ~** j'ai mal dormi cette nuit or la nuit dernière; **the ~ before last** avant-hier soir; **on Tuesday ~s** le mardi soir; **to get an early ~** se coucher tôt; **to stay out all ~** ne pas rentrer de la nuit; **it's my ~ off** ce soir je suis libre; **a ~ at the opera** une soirée à l'opéra.

night: **~club** *n* boîte *f* de nuit°; **~dress** *n* chemise *f* de nuit.

nightingale *n* rossignol *m*.

nightlife *n* vie *f* nocturne.

nightmare *n* cauchemar *m*; **to have a ~** faire un cauchemar.

night: **~ nurse** *n* infirmier/-ière *m/f* de nuit; **~ porter** *n* portier *m* de nuit; **~ school** *n* cours *mpl* du soir; **~ shelter** *n* asile *m* de nuit; **~shirt** *n* chemise *f* de nuit (d'homme); **~stand** (US), **~ table** *n* table *f* de nuit.

night-time I *n* nuit *f*; **at ~** la nuit.
II *noun modifier* nocturne.

night: **~ vision** *n* vision *f* nocturne; **~ watchman** ▶ 805 *n* veilleur *m* de nuit.

nil *n* **1** (Sport) zéro *m*; **2** (on forms) néant *m*.

Nile *pr n* Nil *m*.

nimble *adj* [*person*] agile (**at doing** pour faire; **with** de); [*fingers*] habile.

nine ▶ 492, 554 *n, pron, det* neuf (*m*) *inv*.

nineteen ▶ 492, 554 *n, pron, det* dix-neuf (*m*) *inv*.

nineteenth ▶ 584, 642 **I** *n* **1** (in order) dix-neuvième *mf*; **2** (of month) dix-neuf *m inv*.
II *adj, adv* dix-neuvième.

nineties ▶ 584, 492 *n pl* **1** (era) **the ~** les années *fpl* quatre-vingt-dix; **2** (age) **to be in one's ~** avoir entre quatre-vingt-dix et cent ans.

ninetieth I *n* (in order, sequence) quatre-vingt-dixième *mf*.
II *adj, adv* quatre-vingt-dixième.

nine-to-five *adj* [*job, routine*] de bureau.

ninety ▶ 492 *n, pron, det* quatre-vingt-dix (*m*) *inv*.

ninth ▶ 584, 642 **I** *n* **1** (in order) neuvième *mf*; **2** (of month) neuf *m inv*; **3** (fraction) neuvième *m*; **4** (Mus) neuvième *f*.
II *adj, adv* neuvième.

nip I *n* (pinch) pincement *m*; (bite) morsure *f*; **there's a ~ in the air** il fait frisquet°.
II *vtr* (pinch) pincer; (bite) donner un petit coup de dent à; (playfully) mordiller.
III *vi* (bite) mordre; (playfully) mordiller.
IDIOMS **to ~ sth in the bud** étouffer qch dans l'œuf.

nipple *n* mamelon *m*.

nit *n* (egg) lente *f*; (larva) larve *f* de pou.

nitrate *n* **1** (chemical) nitrate *m*; **2** (fertilizer) engrais *m* azoté.

nitrogen *n* azote *m*.

nitty-gritty° *n* **to get down to the ~** passer aux choses sérieuses.

no I *particle* non; **~ thanks** non merci.
II *det* **1** (none, not any) **to have ~ money** ne pas avoir d'argent; **~ two people would agree on this** il n'y a pas deux personnes qui seraient d'accord là-dessus; **of ~ interest** sans intérêt; **2** (prohibiting) **~ smoking** défense de fumer; **~ parking** stationnement interdit; **~ talking!** silence!; **3** (for emphasis) **he's ~ expert** ce n'est certes pas un expert; **this is ~ time to cry** ce n'est pas le moment de pleurer; **4** (hardly any) **in ~ time** en un rien de temps.
III *adv* **it's ~ further than** ce n'est pas plus loin que; **I ~ longer work there** je n'y travaille plus; **~ later than Wednesday** pas plus tard que mercredi.

no., No. (*written abbr* = **number**) n°.

Noah *pr n* Noé; **~'s Ark** l'arche *f* de Noé.

nobility *n* noblesse *f*.

noble *n, adj* noble (*m*).

nobody I *pron* (also **no-one**) personne; **~ saw her** personne ne l'a vue; **there was ~ in the car** il n'y avait personne dans la voiture; **I heard ~** je n'ai entendu personne; **~ but me** personne sauf moi.
II *n* **to be a ~** être insignifiant.

nocturnal *adj* nocturne.

nod I *n* **she gave him a ~** elle lui a fait un signe de (la) tête; (as greeting) elle l'a salué d'un signe de tête; (indicating assent) elle a fait oui de la tête.
II *vtr* **to ~ one's head** faire un signe de tête; (to indicate assent) hocher la tête.
III *vi* faire un signe de tête (**to** à); (in assent) faire oui de la tête.

noise *n* bruit *m*; (shouting) tapage *m*; **to make a ~** faire du bruit.

noise: **~ level** *n* niveau *m* sonore; **~ pollution** *n* nuisances *fpl* sonores.

noisily *adv* bruyamment.

noisy *adj* [*person, place*] bruyant; [*meeting, protest*] tumultueux/-euse.

nomad *n* nomade *mf*.

nominal *adj* (gen) nominal; [*fee, sum*] minimal; [*fine*] symbolique.

nominate *vtr* **1** (propose) proposer; **to ~ sb for a prize** sélectionner qn pour un prix; **2** (appoint) nommer; **to ~ sb to do** désigner qn pour faire.

nomination *n* **1** (for award) sélection *f*; **2** (appointment) nomination *f* (**to** à).

nominative *n, adj* nominatif (*m*).

nonalcoholic *adj* non alcoolisé.

nonchalant *adj* nonchalant.

noncommittal *adj* [*person, reply*] évasif/-ive (**about** au sujet de).

nonconformist *adj* non conformiste.

nondenominational *adj* [*church*] œcuménique; [*school*] laïque.

nondescript *adj* [*person, clothes*] insignifiant; [*building*] quelconque.

none *pron* **1** (not any) aucun/-e *m/f*; **~ of them** aucun d'entre eux; **'have you any pens?'—'~ at all'** 'as-tu des stylos?'—'pas un seul'; **three dogs, ~ of which had a tail** trois chiens, dont aucun n'avait de queue; **~ of the wine was French** il n'y avait aucun vin français; **~ of the milk had been drunk** on n'avait pas touché au lait; **~ of the bread was fresh** tout le pain était rassis; **'is there any money left?'—'~ at all'** 'est-ce qu'il reste de l'argent?'—'pas du tout'; **we have ~** nous n'en avons pas; **there's ~ left** il n'y en a plus; **~ of it was true** il n'y avait rien de vrai; **2** (nobody) personne; **~ but him** personne sauf lui; **it was ~ other than** ce n'était autre que.

nonentity *n* (person) personne *f* insignifiante.

nonessentials *n pl* (objects) accessoires *mpl*; (details) accessoire *m*.

nonetheless *adv* ▶ **nevertheless 2**.

nonexistent *adj* inexistant.

nonfiction *n* œuvres *fpl* non fictionnelles.

non-infectious *adj* intransmissible.

non-profitmaking *adj* [*organization*] à but non lucratif.

nonreligious *adj* laïque.

nonresident I *n* non-résident/-e *m/f*.
II *adj* **1** [*student, visitor*] non résident; [*caretaker*] de jour; **2** (also **non-residential**) [*job, course*] sans hébergement.

nonsense *n* (foolishness) absurdités *fpl*; **what's all this ~ about leaving work?** qu'est-ce que c'est que ces histoires de quitter le travail?

nonsmoker *n* non-fumeur/-euse *m/f*.

nonstick *adj* antiadhésif/-ive.

nonstop I *adj* [*journey*] sans arrêt; [*train, flight*] direct; [*noise*] incessant.
II *adv* [*work, talk, drive, argue*] sans arrêt; [*fly*] sans escale.

non-taxable *adj* non imposable.

noodles *n pl* nouilles *fpl*.

nook *n* coin *m*; **every ~ and cranny** tous les coins et recoins.

noon *n* midi *m*; **at 12 ~** à midi; **at high ~** en plein midi.

no-one *pron* = **nobody I**.

noose *n* (loop) nœud *m* coulant; (for hanging) corde *f*.

nor *conj*

Note If you want to know how to translate *nor* when used in combination with *neither*, look at the entry *neither*.
– When used as a conjunction to show agreement or similarity with a negative statement, *nor* is very

often translated by *non plus*: *'I don't like him'—'nor do I'* = 'je ne l'aime pas'—'moi non plus'; *'I can't sleep'—'nor can I'* = 'je n'arrive pas à dormir'—'moi non plus'.

he was not a cruel man, ~ a mean one il n'était ni cruel, ni méchant; **she hasn't written, ~ has she telephoned** elle n'a pas écrit, et elle n'a pas téléphoné non plus.

norm *n* norme *f* (**for** pour; **to do** de faire).

normal I *n* normale *f*; **above/below ~** au-dessus/en dessous de la norme.
II *adj* (gen) normal; [*place, time*] habituel/-elle; **in ~ circumstances** en temps normal.

normality *n* normalité *f*.

normally *adv* normalement.

Norman I *n* **1** (person) Normand/-e *m*/*f*; **2** (also **~ French**) normand *m*.
II *adj* **1** (from Normandy) normand; **2** (in architecture) roman.

Normandy *pr n* Normandie *f*.

north I *n* **1** (compass direction) nord *m*; **2 the North** (part of world, country) le Nord.
II *adj* (gen) nord *inv*; [*wind*] du nord; **in ~ London** dans le nord de Londres.
III *adv* [*move*] vers le nord; [*lie, live*] au nord (**of** de).

north: **North Africa** ▶ 574 *pr n* Afrique *f* du Nord; **North America** ▶ 574 *pr n* Amérique *f* du Nord.

northeast I *n* nord-est *m*.
II *adj* [*coast, side*] nord-est *inv*; [*wind*] de nord-est.
III *adv* [*move*] vers le nord-est; [*lie, live*] au nord-est.

northern *adj* [*coast*] nord *inv*; [*town, accent*] du nord; [*hemisphere*] Nord *inv*; **~ England** le nord de l'Angleterre.

Northern Ireland ▶ 574 *pr n* Irlande *f* du Nord.

North Pole *pr n* pôle *m* Nord.

North Sea *pr n* **the ~** la mer du Nord.

northwest I *n* nord-ouest *m*.
II *adj* [*coast*] nord-ouest *inv*; [*wind*] de nord-ouest.
III *adv* [*move*] vers le nord-ouest; [*lie, live*] au nord-ouest.

Norway ▶ 574 *pr n* Norvège *f*.

Norwegian ▶ 712 I *n* **1** (person) Norvégien/-ienne *m*/*f*; **2** (language) norvégien *m*.
II *adj* [*culture, food, politics*] norvégien/-ienne; [*teacher, lesson*] de norvégien; [*ambassador, embassy*] de Norvège.

nose *n* **1** (Anat) nez *m*; **2** (of plane, boat) nez *m*; (of car) avant *m*.
IDIOMS **to look down one's ~ at sb/sth** prendre qn/qch de haut; **to turn one's ~ up at sth** faire le dégoûté/la dégoûtée devant qch.
■ **nose about**, **nose around** fouiner (**in** dans).

nosebleed *n* saignement *m* de nez.

nose-dive *n* piqué *m*; **to go into a ~** faire un piqué; (figurative) chuter.

nostalgia *n* nostalgie *f*.

nostalgic *adj* nostalgique; **to feel ~ for** avoir la nostalgie de.

nostril *n* (of person) narine *f*; (of horse) naseau *m*.

nosy° *adj* fouineur/-euse°.

not ▶ 762 I *adv* ne...pas; **she isn't at home** elle n'est pas chez elle; **we won't need a car** nous n'aurons pas besoin d'une voiture; **has he ~ seen it?** il ne l'a pas vu alors?; **I hope ~** j'espère que non; **certainly ~** sûrement pas; **~ only** or **just** non seulement; **whether it rains or ~** qu'il pleuve ou non; **why ~?** pourquoi pas?; **he's ~ so much aggressive as assertive** il est plutôt sûr de lui qu'agressif; **~ everyone likes it** ça ne plaît pas à tout le monde; **it's ~ every day that** ce n'est pas tous les jours que; **~ a sound was heard** on n'entendait pas un bruit.
II **not at all** *phr* (in no way) pas du tout; (responding to thanks) de rien.
III **not that** *phr* **~ that I know of** pas (autant) que je sache; **if she refuses, ~ that she will...** si elle refuse, je ne dis pas qu'elle le fera...

notable *adj* [*person*] remarquable; [*event, success, difference*] notable.

notably *adv* (in particular) notamment; (markedly) remarquablement.

notation *n* notation *f*.

notch I *n* (in plank) entaille *f*; (in lid, as record) encoche *f*.
II *vtr* encocher [*stick*].
■ **notch up**°: **~ up [sth]** remporter [*point, prize*].

note I *n* **1** (gen) note *f*; (short letter) mot *m*; **to take ~ of** prendre note de; **2** (Mus) (sound, symbol) note *f*; (piano key) touche *f*; **3** (**bank**) **~** billet *m*.
II *vtr* noter.
III **noted** *pp adj* [*intellectual, criminal*] célèbre; **to be ~d for** être réputé pour.
IV **of note** *phr* [*person*] éminent, réputé; [*development*] digne d'intérêt.
IDIOMS **to compare ~s** échanger ses impressions (**with** avec).
■ **note down**: **~ down [sth]**, **~ [sth] down** noter.

note: **~book** *n* carnet *m*; **~pad** *n* bloc-notes *m*; **~paper** *n* papier *m* à lettres; **~worthy** *adj* remarquable.

nothing

■ **Note** When *nothing* is used alone as a reply to a question in English, it is translated by *rien*: *'what are you doing?'—'nothing'* = 'que fais-tu?'—'rien'.
– *nothing* as a pronoun, when it is the subject of a verb, is translated by *rien ne* (+ verb or, in compound tenses, + auxiliary verb): *nothing changes* = rien ne change; *nothing has changed* = rien n'a changé.
– *nothing* as a pronoun, when it is the object of a verb, is translated by *ne...rien*; *ne* comes before the verb, and before the auxiliary in compound tenses, and *rien* comes after the verb or auxiliary: *I see nothing* = je ne vois rien; *I saw nothing* = je n'ai rien vu.

not

Used without a verb

When ***not*** is used without a verb before an adjective, a noun, an adverb, a verb or a pronoun it is translated by ***pas***:

***not** at all*	= **pas** du tout
***not** bad*	= **pas** mal
*it's a cat **not** a dog*	= c'est un chat **pas** un chien
*they're children **not** adults*	= ce sont des enfants **pas** des adultes
*you should walk, **not** run*	= il faut marcher, **pas** courir
*she should apologise, **not** me*	= c'est elle qui devrait s'excuser, **pas** moi

Used with a verb

◆ When ***not*** is used with the verbs *be, do, have, will* and *would*, the translation is ***ne . . . pas*** (***n'*** before a vowel or mute 'h'): ***ne*** comes before the verb or the auxiliary, and ***pas*** comes after the verb or auxiliary:

*it's **not** a cat*	= ce **n'**est **pas** un chat
*he does**n't** like oranges*	= il **n'**aime **pas** les oranges
*I have**n't** seen him*	= je **ne** l'ai **pas** vu
*she has**n't** arrived yet*	= elle **n'**est **pas** encore arrivée
*they will **not** agree to the reforms*	= ils **n'**accepteront **pas** les réformes
*she wo**n't** come by car*	= elle **ne** viendra **pas** en voiture
*it would**n't** matter*	= ce **ne** serait **pas** grave

◆ When used with a verb in the infinitive, ***ne*** and ***pas*** are placed together before the verb:

*he decided **not** to go*	= il a décidé de **ne pas** y aller
*you were wrong **not** to tell her*	= tu as eu tort de **ne pas** le lui dire
*it's difficult **not** to take things to heart*	= il est difficile de **ne pas** prendre les choses à cœur

Used in question tags

When ***not*** is used in question tags, the whole tag can usually be translated by the French ***n'est-ce pas***:

*she bought it, **didn't she**?*	= elle l'a acheté, **n'est-ce pas**?
*you were there too, **weren't you**?*	= tu y étais aussi, **n'est-ce pas**?
*they're living in Germany, **aren't they**?*	= ils habitent en Allemagne, **n'est-ce pas**?
*he likes fish, **doesn't he**?*	= il aime le poisson, **n'est-ce pas**?
*he's got a lot of money, **hasn't he**?*	= il a beaucoup d'argent, **n'est-ce pas**?
*you'll come too, **won't you**?*	= vous viendrez vous aussi, **n'est-ce pas**?
*she's English, **isn't she**?*	= elle est anglaise, **n'est-ce pas**?
*we should let them know, **shouldn't we**?*	= nous devrions les prévenir, **n'est-ce pas**?

For examples and particular usages, see the entry **not**.

– When *ne rien* is used with an infinitive, the two words are not separated: *I prefer to say nothing* = je préfère ne rien dire.
– For more examples and particular usages, see the entry below.

I *pron* **I knew ~ about it** je n'en savais rien; **we can do ~ (about it)** nous n'y pouvons rien; **~ much** pas grand-chose; **~ more** rien de plus; **is there ~ more you can do?** vous ne pouvez rien faire de plus?; **~ else** rien d'autre; **I had ~ to do with it!** je n'y étais pour rien!; **it's ~ to do with us** ça ne nous regarde pas; **to stop at ~** ne reculer devant rien (**to do** pour faire); **he means ~ to me** il n'est rien pour moi; **it meant ~ to him** ça lui était complètement égal (**that, whether** que + *subj*); **the names meant ~ to him** les noms ne lui disaient rien; **for ~** (for free) gratuitement; (pointlessly) pour rien; **there's ~ like it!** il n'y a rien de tel or de mieux!; **I can think of ~ worse than** je ne peux rien imaginer de pire que; **to say ~ of** sans parler de; **you get ~ out of it** ça ne rapporte rien; **there's ~ in it for me** ça n'a aucun intérêt pour moi.
II *adv* **it is ~ like as difficult as** c'est loin d'être aussi difficile que; **she is** or **looks ~ like her sister** elle ne ressemble pas du tout à sa sœur.
III *adj* **to be ~ without sb/sth** ne rien être sans qn/qch.
IV **nothing but** *phr* **he's ~ but a coward** ce n'est qu'un lâche; **they've done ~ but moan**○ ils n'ont fait que râler○; **it's caused me ~ but trouble** ça ne m'a valu que des ennuis.
V **nothing less than** *phr* **it's ~ less than a betrayal** c'est une véritable trahison; **~ less than real saffron will do** il n'y a que du vrai safran qui fera l'affaire.
VI **nothing more than** *phr* **it's ~ more than a strategy to do** ce n'est qu'une stratégie pour faire; **the stories are ~ more than gossip** ces histoires ne sont rien d'autre que des ragots.

notice I *n* **1** (written sign) pancarte *f*; (advertisement) annonce *f*; (announcing birth, marriage, death) avis *m*; (review of a play) compte-rendu *m*; **2** (attention) attention *f*; **to take ~** faire attention (**of** à); **3** (notification) préavis *m*; **one month's ~** un mois de préavis; **until further ~** jusqu'à nouvel ordre; **to be invited/cancelled at short ~** être invité/annulé à la dernière minute; **I'm sorry it's such short ~** je suis désolé de vous prévenir si tard; **to give in one's ~** donner sa démission.
II *vtr* remarquer [*absence, mark*]; **to get oneself ~d** se faire remarquer.

noticeable *adj* visible.

noticeboard *n* panneau *m* d'affichage.

notification *n* notification *f*; (in newspaper) avis *m*.

notify *vtr* **1** (GB) (give notice of) notifier; **to ~ sb of** or **about** aviser qn de [*result, incident*]; avertir qn de [*intention*]; **2 to ~ sb of** informer qn de [*birth, death*].

notion *n* **1** (idea) idée *f*; **2** (understanding) notion *f*.

notoriety *n* notoriété *f* (**for** pour).

notorious *adj* [*criminal, organization*] notoire; [*district*] mal famé; [*case*] tristement célèbre.

notwithstanding I *adv* néanmoins.
II *prep* (in spite of) en dépit de; (excepted) exception faite de.

nought *n* zéro *m*.

noun *n* nom *m*, substantif *m*.

nourish *vtr* nourrir (**with** avec; **on** de).

nourishment *n* nourriture *f*.

novel I *n* roman *m*.
II *adj* original.

novelist ▶ 805 *n* romancier/-ière *m/f*.

novelty *n* nouveauté *f* (**of doing** de faire).

November ▶ 584 *n* novembre *m*.

novice *n* débutant/-e *m/f*; (in religious order) novice *mf*.

now I *conj* **~ (that)** maintenant que.
II *adv* **1** maintenant; **do it ~** fais-le maintenant; **I'm doing it ~** je suis en train de le faire; **~ is the best time to do** c'est le meilleur moment pour faire; **right ~** tout de suite; **it's a week ~ since she left** cela fait une semaine (maintenant) qu'elle est partie; **any time ~** d'un moment à l'autre; **(every) ~ and then** or **again** de temps en temps; **2** (with preposition) **you should have phoned him before ~** tu aurais dû lui téléphoner avant; **before** or **until ~** jusqu'à présent; **he should be finished by ~** il devrait avoir déjà fini; **between ~ and next Friday** d'ici vendredi prochain; **between ~ and then** d'ici là; **from ~ on(wards)** dorénavant; **3** (in the past) **it was ~ 4 pm** il était alors 16 heures; **by ~ it was too late** à ce moment-là, il était trop tard; **4 ~ there's a man I can trust!** ah! voilà un homme en qui on peut avoir confiance!; **careful ~!** attention!; **~ then, let's get back to work** bon, reprenons le travail.

nowadays *adv* (these days) de nos jours; (now) actuellement.

nowhere I *adv* nulle part; **I've got ~ else to go** je n'ai nulle part où aller; **there's ~ to sit down** il n'y a pas d'endroit pour s'asseoir; **all this talk is getting us ~** tout ce bavardage ne nous avance à rien; **flattery will get you ~!** tu n'arriveras à rien en me flattant.
II **nowhere near** *phr* loin de; **~ near sufficient** loin d'être suffisant.

noxious *adj* nocif/-ive.

nozzle *n* (of hose, pipe) ajutage *m*; (of hoover) suceur *m*; (for icing) douille *f*.

nuance *n* nuance *f*.

nuclear *adj* nucléaire.

nuclear: **~ bomb** *n* bombe *f* atomique; **~ deterrent** *n* force *f* de dissuasion nucléaire; **~ energy**, **~ power** *n* énergie *f* nucléaire or atomique; **~ power station** *n* centrale *f* nucléaire; **~ scientist** *n* chercheur/-euse *m/f* en physique nucléaire; **~ shelter** *n* abri *m* antiatomique.

nucleus *n* noyau *m*.

nude I *n* nu/-e *m/f*; **in the ~** nu.
II *adj [person]* nu.
nudge *vtr* (push) pousser du coude; (accidentally) heurter; (brush against) frôler.
nudist *n, adj* nudiste (*mf*).
nudity *n* nudité *f*.
nugget *n* pépite *f*.
nuisance *n* (gen) embêtement *m*; (Law) nuisance *f*; **what a ~!** que c'est agaçant!
null *adj* (Law) **~ and void** nul et non avenu.
numb I *adj* **1** *[limb, face]* (due to cold) engourdi (**with** par); (due to anaesthetic) insensible; **to go ~** s'engourdir; **2** (figurative) *[person]* hébété (**with** par).
II *vtr [cold]* engourdir; (Med) insensibiliser; **to ~ the pain** endormir la douleur.
number I *n* **1** (gen) nombre *m*; (written figure) chiffre *m*; **a three-figure ~** un nombre à trois chiffres; **2** (of bus, house, page, telephone) numéro *m*; **a wrong ~** un faux numéro; **3** (quantity, series) nombre *m*; **a ~ of** un certain nombre de; **for a ~ of reasons** pour plusieurs raisons; **in equal ~s** en nombre égal; **4** (by performer) (act) numéro *m*; (song) chanson *f*.
II numbers *n pl* (in company, school) effectifs *mpl*; (of crowd, army) nombre *m*.
III *vtr* **1** (allocate number to) numéroter; **2** (amount to, include) compter.
IDIOMS **his days are ~ed** ses jours sont comptés.
numberplate *n* (GB) plaque *f* minéralogique or d'immatriculation.
numeral *n* chiffre *m*.
numerical *adj* numérique.
numerous *adj* nombreux/-euse.
nun *n* religieuse *f*, bonne sœur *f*.
nurse ▶805 **I** *n* **1** (Med) infirmier/-ière *m/f*; **male ~** infirmier *m*; **2** = **nursemaid**.
II *vtr* **1** (Med) soigner *[person, cold]*; **2** (suckle) allaiter *[baby]*; **3** nourrir *[grievance, hope]*.
nursemaid *n* nurse *f*, bonne *f* d'enfants.
nursery *n* **1** (also **day ~**) crèche *f*; (in hotel, shop) garderie *f*; **2** (room) chambre *f* d'enfants; **3** (for plants) pépinière *f*.
nursery: **~ rhyme** *n* comptine *f*; **~ school** *n* école *f* maternelle.
nursing ▶805 **I** *n* **1** (profession) profession *f* d'infirmier/-ière; **2** (care) soins *mpl*.
II *adj [mother]* qui allaite.
nursing home *n* **1** (old people's) maison *f* de retraite; (convalescent) maison *f* de repos; **2** (GB) (hospital) clinique *f*; (maternity) clinique *f* obstétrique.
nurture *vtr* **1** élever *[child]*; soigner *[plant]*; **2** nourrir *[hope, feeling, talent]*.
nut *n* **1** (walnut) noix *f*; (hazel) noisette *f*; (almond) amande *f*; (peanut) cacahuète *f*; **2** (Tech) écrou *m*.
nut: **~cracker(s)** *n (pl)* casse-noisettes *m inv*; **~meg** *n* noix *f* de muscade.
nutrient *n* substance *f* nutritive.
nutrition *n* (process) nutrition *f*, alimentation *f*; (science) diététique *f*.
nutritional *adj [value]* nutritif/-ive; *[composition]* nutritionnel/-elle.
nutshell *n* **1** coquille *f* de noix or noisette; **2** (figurative) **in a ~** en un mot.
nuzzle *vtr* frotter son nez contre.
■ **nuzzle up**: **to ~ up against** or **to sb** se blottir contre qn.
nylon *n* nylon® *m*.
nymph *n* nymphe *f*.

Oo

o, O *n* **1** (letter) o, O *m*; **2 O** (spoken number) zéro.

oaf *n* (clumsy) balourd/-e *m/f*; (loutish) mufle *m*.

oak I *n* **1** (also **~ tree**) chêne *m*; **2** (wood) chêne *m*.
II *noun modifier* [*table*] de or en chêne.

oar *n* rame *f*.

oasis *n* (in desert) oasis *f*; (figurative) (of peace) havre *m*.

oath *n* **1** serment *m*; **under ~, on ~** (GB) sous serment; **to take the ~** prêter serment; **2** (swearword) juron *m*.

oatmeal *n* **1** (cereal) farine *f* d'avoine; **2** (US) (porridge) bouillie *f* d'avoine.

oats *n pl* avoine *f*.

obedience *n* obéissance *f* (**to** à).

obedient *adj* obéissant.

obediently *adv* docilement.

obese *adj* obèse.

obey I *vtr* obéir à [*person, instinct*]; se conformer à [*instructions, law*].
II *vi* [*person*] obéir.

obituary *n* (also **~ notice**) nécrologie *f*.

object I *n* **1** (item) objet *m*; **2** (goal) but *m* (**of** de); **3** (focus) **to be the ~ of** être l'objet de.
II *vtr* objecter (**that** que).
III *vi* soulever des objections; **to ~ to** protester contre [*attitude, comment*]; **I ~ to their behaviour** je trouve leur comportement inadmissible.

objection *n* objection *f* (**to** à; **from** de la part de); **I've no ~(s)** je n'y vois pas d'inconvénient.

objectionable *adj* [*remark*] désobligeant; [*behaviour*] choquant.

objective I *n* objectif *m*.
II *adj* objectif/-ive, impartial (**about** en ce qui concerne).

objectively *adv* objectivement.

obligation *n* **1** (duty) devoir *m* (**towards, to** envers); **to be under (an) ~ to do** être obligé de faire; **2** (commitment) (contractual) obligation *f* (**to** envers; **to do** de faire); (personal) engagement *m* (**to** envers); **3** (debt) (financial) dette *f*; (of gratitude) dette *f* de reconnaissance.

obligatory *adj* (compulsory) obligatoire (**to do** de faire); (customary) de rigueur.

oblige *vtr* **1** (compel) obliger (**to do** à faire); **2** (be helpful) rendre service à; **3 to be ~d to sb** être reconnaissant à qn (**for** de; **for doing** d'avoir fait).

obliging *adj* serviable.

obliterate *vtr* effacer [*trace, word, memory*]; anéantir [*landmark, city*].

oblivion *n* **1** (obscurity) oubli *m*; **2** (unconsciousness) néant *m*.

oblivious *adj* (unaware) inconscient; **to be ~ of** or **to** ne pas être conscient de.

oblong I *n* rectangle *m*.
II *adj* [*table, building*] oblong/oblongue, rectangulaire.

obnoxious *adj* [*person, behaviour*] odieux/-ieuse, exécrable.

obscene *adj* [*film, remark*] obscène; [*wealth*] indécent; [*war*] monstrueux/-euse.

obscure I *adj* obscur; (indistinct) vague.
II *vtr* obscurcir [*truth*]; cacher [*view*]; **to ~ the issue** embrouiller la question.

obsequious *adj* obséquieux/-ieuse.

observant *adj* observateur/-trice.

observation *n* observation *f* (**of** de); **to keep sb/sth under ~** surveiller qn/qch.

observe *vtr* **1** (see, notice) observer (**that** que); **2** [*doctor, police*] surveiller; **3** (remark) faire observer (**that** que); **4** observer [*law, custom*].

observer *n* observateur/-trice *m/f* (**of** de).

obsess *vtr* obséder.

obsessed *adj* obsédé; **~ by** or **with** obsédé par.

obsession *n* obsession *f*; **an ~ with tidiness** la manie de l'ordre.

obsessive *adj* [*person*] maniaque; [*neurosis*] obsessionnel/-elle; [*thought*] obsédant.

obsolete *adj* [*technology*] dépassé; [*custom, idea*] démodé; [*word*] désuet.

obstacle *n* obstacle *m*; **to be an ~** faire obstacle (**to** à).

obstacle race *n* course *f* d'obstacles.

obstinacy *n* entêtement *m* (**in doing** à faire).

obstinate *adj* [*person*] têtu (**about** en ce qui concerne); [*behaviour, silence, effort*] obstiné; [*resistance*] acharné; [*cough*] persistant; [*stain*] rebelle.

obstreperous *adj* (boisterous) tapageur/-euse; (defiant) récalcitrant.

obstruct *vtr* **1** (block) cacher [*view*]; bloquer [*road*]; **2** (impede) gêner [*traffic, person, progress*]; faire obstruction à [*player*]; entraver le cours de [*justice*].

obstruction *n* **1** (blockage) (to traffic, progress) obstacle *m*; (in pipe) bouchon *m*; **2** (in sport) obstruction *f*.

obstructive *adj* [*policy, tactics, attitude*] obstructionniste; [*behaviour*] récalcitrant.

obtain *vtr* obtenir [*information, permission, degree, visa, prize*]; (for oneself) se procurer [*money, goods*]; acquérir [*experience*].

obtrusive *adj* [*noise*] gênant; [*person, behaviour*] importun.

obtuse *adj* [*person*] obtus; [*remark*] stupide.

obvious I *n* **to state the ~** enfoncer les portes ouvertes.
II *adj* évident (**to** pour); **the ~ thing to do** la chose à faire.

obviously I *adv* manifestement; **she ~**

needs help il est évident qu'elle a besoin d'aide; **he's ~ lying** il est clair qu'il ment.
II *excl* bien sûr!, évidemment!

occasion *n* occasion *f*; **on one ~** une fois; **on the ~ of** à l'occasion de; **to rise to the ~** se montrer à la hauteur des circonstances; **on special ~s** dans les grandes occasions.

occasional *adj* [*event*] qui a lieu de temps en temps; **the ~ letter** une lettre de temps en temps.

occasionally *adv* de temps à autre; **very ~** très rarement.

occupancy *n* occupation *f*.

occupant *n* **1** (of building, bed) occupant/-e *m/f*; **2** (car passenger) passager/-ère *m/f*.

occupation *n* **1** (of house) **ready for ~** prêt à être habité; **2** (Mil) occupation *f* (**de** of); **3** (trade) métier *m*; (profession) profession *f*; **4** (activity) occupation *f*.

occupational hazard *n* risque *m* du métier.

occupier *n* occupant/-e *m/f*.

occupy *vtr* occuper; **to keep oneself occupied** s'occuper (**by doing** en faisant).

occur *vi* **1** [*event, change, error, disease*] se produire; [*epidemic*] se déclarer; [*symptom*] apparaître; [*opportunity*] se présenter; [*species, misprint*] se trouver; **2 the idea ~red to me that**... l'idée m'est venue à l'esprit que...; **it didn't ~ to me** ça ne m'est pas venu à l'idée.

occurrence *n* **1** (event) fait *m*; **to be a rare ~** se produire rarement; **2** (instance) occurrence *f*; **3** (of disease, phenomenon) cas *m*.

ocean I *n* océan *m*.
II *noun modifier* [*voyage*] océanique; **~ bed** fond *m* de l'océan.

o'clock ▶ 554 *adv* **at one ~** à une heure; **it's two ~** il est deux heures.

octagon *n* octogone *m*.

octave *n* octave *f*.

October ▶ 584 *n* octobre *m*.

octopus *n* (Zool) pieuvre *f*; (on menu) poulpe *m*.

odd I *adj* **1** (strange, unusual) [*person, object, occurrence*] bizarre; **2** [*socks, gloves*] dépareillés; **3** (miscellaneous) **some ~ bits of cloth** quelques bouts de tissu; **4** [*number*] impair; **5 to be the ~ one out** (person, animal, plant) être l'exception *f*; (drawing, word) être l'intrus *m*; (when selecting team) [*person*] être sans partenaire.
II -odd *combining form* **sixty-~ people/companies** une soixantaine de personnes/d'entreprises.

oddity *n* (odd thing) bizarrerie *f*; (person) excentrique *mf*.

odd job *n* (for money) petit boulot *m*; **~s** (in house, garden) petits travaux *mpl*.

odd-job man *n* homme *m* à tout faire.

odds *n pl* **1** (in betting) cote *f* (**on** sur); **2** (chance, likelihood) chances *fpl*; **the ~ are against his winning** il y a peu de chances qu'il gagne (*subj*); **to win against the ~** gagner contre toute attente.
IDIOMS **at ~** (in dispute) être en conflit; (inconsistent) en contradiction (**with** avec).

odds and ends (GB) *n pl* bricoles° *fpl*.

odour (GB), **odor** (US) *n* odeur *f*.

odourless (GB), **odorless** (US) *adj* [*gas*] inodore; [*cosmetic*] non parfumé.

odyssey *n* odyssée *f*; **the Odyssey** l'Odyssée *f*.

oestrogen (GB), **estrogen** (US) *n* œstrogène *m*.

of *prep*

Note In almost all its uses, the preposition *of* is translated by *de*. For exceptions, see the entry below.
– Remember that *de + le* always becomes *du* and that *de + les* always becomes *des*.
– When *of it* or *of them* are used for something already referred to, they are translated by *en*: *there's a lot of it* = il y en a beaucoup; *there are several of them* = il y en a plusieurs.
– Note, however, the following expressions used when referring to people: *there are six of them* = ils sont six; *there were several of them* = ils étaient plusieurs.
– For particular usages see the entry below.
– This dictionary contains usage notes on such topics as ***age***, ***dates***, ***illnesses***, and ***quantities***. For the index to these notes ▶ 1008.

---

1 (in most uses) de; **the leg ~ the table** le pied de la table; **2** (made of) **a ring (made) ~ gold** une bague en or; **a will ~ iron** une volonté de fer; **3 a friend ~ mine** un ami à moi; **that's kind ~ you** c'est très gentil de votre part or à vous; **some ~ us/them** quelques-uns d'entre nous/d'entre eux.

off I *adv* **1** (leaving) **to be ~** partir, s'en aller; **it's time you were ~** il est temps que tu partes; **I'm ~** je m'en vais; **to be ~ to a good start** avoir pris un bon départ; **2** (at a distance) **to be 30 metres ~** être à 30 mètres; **some way ~** assez loin; **3** (ahead in time) **Easter is a month ~** Pâques est dans un mois; **the exam is still several months ~** l'examen n'aura pas lieu avant plusieurs mois.
II *adj* **1** (free) **Tuesday's my day ~** je ne travaille pas le mardi; **to have the morning ~** avoir la matinée libre; **2** (turned off) **to be ~** [*water, gas*] être coupé; [*tap*] être fermé; [*light, TV*] être éteint; **3** (cancelled) [*match, party*] annulé; **our engagement's ~** nous avons rompu nos fiançailles; **the 'coq au vin' is ~** il n'y a plus de 'coq au vin'; **4** (removed) **the lid is ~** il n'y a pas de couvercle; **with her make-up ~** sans maquillage; **25% ~** (in sales) 25% de remise; **5**° (bad) **to be ~** [*food*] être avarié; [*milk*] avoir tourné.
III *prep* **1** (also **just ~**) juste à côté de [*kitchen*]; **~ the west coast** au large de la côte ouest; **just ~ the path** tout près du sentier; **2 to be a long way ~ doing** être encore loin de faire; **it is ~ the point** là n'est pas la question; **to be ~ centre** être mal centré; **3**° **to be ~ one's food** ne pas avoir d'appétit.
IDIOMS **to feel a bit ~°(-colour)** (GB) ne pas être dans son assiette°; **to have an ~ day** ne pas être dans un de ses bons jours.

off: **~beat** *adj* [*humour*] cocasse; **~-centre** (GB), **~-center** (US) *adj* décentré.

off-chance *n* **just on the ~** au cas où.

offence (GB), **offense** (US) *n* **1** (crime) délit *m*; **2** (insult) **to cause ~ to sb** offenser qn; **to take ~ (at)** s'offenser (de); **3** (Mil) offensive *f*.

offend I *vtr* blesser [*person*].
II *vi* commettre une infraction (**against** à); **to ~ again** récidiver.
III **offending** *pres p adj* [*object*] en cause; [*person*] responsable.

offender *n* (against the law) délinquant/-e *m/f*; **the worst ~** le/la plus à blâmer.

offensive I *n* **1** (Mil, Sport) offensive *f* (**against** contre); **2** (campaign) campagne *f*.
II *adj* [*remark*] injurieux/-ieuse (**to** pour); [*behaviour*] insultant; [*language*] grossier/-ière.

offer I *n* **1** (proposition) offre *f* (**to do** de faire); **job ~** offre d'emploi; **2** (of goods) **to be on special ~** être en promotion.
II *vtr* offrir [*cigarette, job, reward, support, advantages*]; donner [*advice, explanation, information*]; émettre [*opinion*]; proposer [*service*]; **to ~ to do** se proposer pour faire; **to ~ sth for sale** mettre qch en vente.
III *vi* [*volunteer*] se proposer.

offering *n* (gift) cadeau *m*; (sacrifice) offrande *f*.

offhand I *adj* désinvolte.
II *adv* **~, I don't know** comme ça au pied levé je ne sais pas.

office *n* **1** (place) bureau *m*; **lawyer's ~** cabinet *m* d'avocat; **2** (position) fonction *f*, charge *f*; **public ~** fonctions *fpl* officielles; **to hold ~** [*president, mayor*] être en fonction; [*political party*] être au pouvoir.

office block, **office building** *n* (GB) immeuble *m* de bureaux.

officer *n* **1** (in army, navy) officier *m*; **2** (also **police ~**) policier *m*.

office worker ▶805| *n* employé/-e *m/f* de bureau.

official I *n* fonctionnaire *mf*; (of party, union) officiel/-ielle *m/f*; (at town hall) employé/-e *m/f*.
II *adj* [*statement, document, visit, strike*] officiel/-ielle; [*biography*] autorisé.

officiate *vi* [*official*] présider.

officious *adj* trop empressé, zélé.

offing: **in the offing** *phr* [*deal, wedding*] en perspective.

off: **~-licence** *n* (GB) magasin *m* de vins et de spiritueux; **~-limits** *adj* interdit; **~-peak** *adj* [*electricity*] au tarif de nuit; [*travel*] en période creuse; [*call*] au tarif réduit.

off-putting *adj* (GB) [*manner*] peu engageant; **it was very ~** c'était déroutant.

off-season *adj* [*cruise, holiday*] hors saison.

offset *vtr* compenser (**by** par); **to ~ sth against sth** mettre qch et qch en balance.

offshore *adj* [*waters*] du large; [*fishing*] au large; **~ oil rig** plate-forme *f* pétrolière offshore.

offside I *n* (GB) côté *m* conducteur.
II *adj* **1** (GB) [*lane*] (in France) de gauche; (in UK) de droite; **2** (in soccer) [*position*] hors jeu.

off: **~spring** *n* progéniture *f*; **~stage** *adj, adv* dans les coulisses; **~-the-cuff** *adj* [*remark, speech*] impromptu; **~-the-peg** *adj* [*garment*] de prêt-à-porter; **~-white** *adj* blanc cassé *inv*.

often *adv* souvent; **as ~ as not**, **more ~ than not** le plus souvent; **how ~ do you meet?** vous vous voyez tous les combien?; **once too ~** une fois de trop; **every so ~** de temps en temps.

oh *excl* oh!; **~ dear!** (sympathetic) oh là là!; (dismayed, cross) mon Dieu!; **~ (really)?** (interested) ah bon?; (sceptical) tiens donc!

oil I *n* **1** (for fuel) pétrole *m*; (for lubrication) huile *f*; **crude ~** pétrole brut; **engine ~** huile de moteur; **heating ~** fioul *m*; **to check the ~** vérifier le niveau d'huile; **2** (for cooking) huile *f*; **3** (in art) huile *f*; **to work in ~s** peindre à l'huile; **4** (medicinal, beauty) huile *f*.
II *noun modifier* [*producer*] de pétrole; [*prices*] du pétrole; [*company, crisis, industry*] pétrolier/-ière.
III *vtr* huiler.

oil: **~ change** *n* vidange *f*; **~cloth** *n* toile *f* cirée; **~ field** *n* champ *m* pétrolifère; **~-fired** *adj* [*furnace, heating*] au fuel or fioul; **~ gauge** *n* jauge *f* de niveau d'huile; **~ painting** *n* peinture *f* à l'huile; **~ refinery** *n* raffinerie *f* de pétrole; **~ rig** *n* (offshore) plate-forme *f* pétrolière offshore; (on land) tour *f* de forage; **~skins** (GB) *n pl* ciré *m*; **~ slick** *n* marée *f* noire; **~ well** *n* puits *m* de pétrole.

oily *adj* [*cloth, food, hair*] gras/grasse; [*dressing, substance*] huileux/-euse.

ointment *n* pommade *f*.

okay, **OK**○ I *n* **to give sth the ~** donner le feu vert à qch.
II *adj* **it's ~ by me** ça ne me dérange pas; **is it ~ if...?** est-ce que ça va si...?; **he's ~** (nice) il est sympa○; **to feel ~** aller bien; **that's ~ for men, but...** les hommes peuvent se le permettre, mais...; **it's ~ to ask** on peut demander.
III *adv* [*cope, work out*] (assez) bien.
IV *particle* **1** (giving agreement) d'accord; **2** (introducing topic) bien.

old ▶492| *adj* **1** [*person*] vieux/vieille (*before n*), âgé; [*object, tradition, song*] vieux/vieille (*before n*); **an ~ man** un vieil homme, un vieillard; **an ~ woman** une vieille femme, une vieille; **~ people** les vieux; **to get ~** vieillir; **2** (of a particular age) **how ~ are you?** quel âge as-tu?; **a six-year-~ boy** un garçon (âgé) de six ans; **a week ~** [*bread*] vieux d'une semaine; **to be as ~ as sb** avoir le même âge que qn; **she is 10 years ~er than him** elle a 10 ans de plus que lui; **my ~er brother** mon frère aîné; **I'm the ~est** c'est moi l'aîné/-e; **to be ~ enough to do** être en âge de faire; **you're ~ enough to know better** à ton âge tu devrais avoir plus de bon sens; **3** (former, previous) [*address, school, job, system*] ancien/-ienne (*before n*); **in the ~ days** autrefois; **just like ~ times** comme au bon vieux temps.

■ **Note** The irregular form *vieil* of the adjective vieux/vieille is used before masculine nouns beginning with a vowel or a mute 'h'.

old age *n* vieillesse *f*.

old: **~-age pension** *n* (GB) pension *f* de retraite; **~-age pensioner, OAP** *n* (GB) retraité/-e *m/f*.

old-fashioned *adj* [*person, ways*] vieux jeu *inv*; [*idea, attitude, garment, machine*] démodé.

old: **~ master** *n* (artist) maître *m* ancien; (work) tableau *m* de maître ancien; **~ people's home** *n* maison *f* de retraite; **~ wives' tale** *n* conte *m* de bonne femme.

olive I *n* **1** (fruit) olive *f*; **2** (also **~ tree**) olivier *m*.
II *adj* [*dress, eyes*] vert olive *inv*; [*complexion*] olivâtre.

olive: **~ green** ▷ 559 *n, adj* vert (*m*) olive *inv*; **~ oil** *n* huile *f* d'olive.

Olympics *n pl* (also **Olympic Games**) jeux *mpl* Olympiques.

ombudsman *n* médiateur *m*.

omelette *n* omelette *f*.

omen *n* présage *m*.

ominous *adj* [*cloud*] menaçant; [*news*] inquiétant; [*sign*] de mauvais augure.

omission *n* omission *f*.

omit *vtr* omettre (**from** de; **to do** de faire).

omnipotent *adj* omnipotent.

omnipresent *adj* omniprésent.

on I *prep* **1** (position) sur [*table, coast, motorway*]; **~ the beach** sur la plage; **~ top of the piano** sur le piano; **~ the floor** par terre; **there's a stain ~ it** il y a une tache dessus; **to live ~ Park Avenue** habiter Park Avenue; **a studio ~ Avenue Montaigne** un studio Avenue Montaigne; **the paintings ~ the wall** les tableaux qui sont au mur; **I've got no small change ~ me** je n'ai pas de monnaie sur moi; **to have a smile ~ one's face** sourire; **2** (indicating attachment) **to hang sth ~ a nail** accrocher qch à un clou; **~ a string** au bout d'une ficelle; **3** (about, on the subject of) sur; **~ Africa** sur l'Afrique; **4 to be ~** faire partie de [*team*]; être membre de [*committee*]; **a job ~ the railways** un travail dans les chemins de fer; **there's a bouncer ~ the door** il y a un videur à la porte; **5** (in expressions of time) **~ 22 February** le 22 février; **~ Friday** vendredi; **~ Saturdays** le samedi; **~ my birthday** le jour de mon anniversaire; **~ sunny days** quand il fait beau; **6** (immediately after) **~ his arrival** à son arrivée; **~ hearing the truth she...** quand elle a appris la vérité, elle...; **7** (taking) **to be ~ steroids** prendre des stéroïdes; **to be ~ drugs** se droguer; **8** (powered by) **to run ~ batteries** fonctionner sur piles; **to run ~ electricity** marcher à l'électricité; **9** (indicating a medium) **~ TV** à la télé; **~ the news** aux informations; **~ video** en vidéo; **~ drums** à la batterie; **10** (earning) **to be ~ £20,000 a year** gagner 20 000 livres sterling par an; **to be ~ a low income** avoir un bas salaire; **11** (paid for by) **it's ~ me** je t'invite; **12** (indicating transport) **to travel ~ the bus** voyager en bus; **~ the plane** dans l'avion; **to be ~ one's bike** être à vélo; **to leave ~ the first train** prendre le premier train.
II *adj* **1 while the meeting is ~** pendant la réunion; **I've got a lot ~** je suis très occupé; **the news is ~ in 10 minutes** les informations sont dans 10 minutes; **what's ~?** (on TV) qu'est-ce qu'il y a à la télé?; (at the cinema, theatre) qu'est-ce qu'on joue?; **there's nothing ~** il n'y a rien de bien; **2 to be ~** [*TV, oven, light*] être allumé; [*dishwasher, radio*] marcher; [*tap*] être ouvert; **the power is ~** il y a du courant; **the power is back ~** le courant est rétabli; **3 to be ~** [*lid*] être mis.
III *adv* **1 to have nothing ~** être nu; **to have make-up ~** être maquillé; **with slippers ~** en pantoufles; **2 from that day ~** à partir de ce jour-là; **20 years ~** 20 ans plus tard; **to walk ~** continuer à marcher; **to go to Paris then ~ to Marseilles** aller à Paris et de là à Marseille; **a little further ~** un peu plus loin.
IV on and off *phr* (also **off and on**) **to see sb ~ and off** voir qn de temps en temps.
V on and on *phr* **to go ~ and ~** [*speaker*] parler pendant des heures; [*speech*] durer des heures; **to go ~ and ~ about** ne pas arrêter de parler de.
IDIOMS **it's just** or **simply not ~** (GB) (out of the question) c'est hors de question; (not the done thing) ça ne se fait pas; (unacceptable) c'est inadmissible.

once I *n* **just this ~** pour cette fois; **for ~** pour une fois.
II *adv* **1** (one time) une fois; **~ and for all** une bonne fois pour toutes; **~ too often** une fois de trop; **~ a day** une fois par jour; **2** (formerly) autrefois; **~ upon a time there was a king** il était une fois un roi.
III *conj* une fois que, dès que.
IV at once *phr* **1** (immediately) tout de suite; **2** (simultaneously) à la fois.

oncoming *adj* [*car, vehicle*] venant en sens inverse.

one ▷ 492, 554

■ **Note** When *one* is used as a personal pronoun, it is translated by *on* when it is the subject of the verb: *one never knows* = on ne sait jamais. When *one* is the object of the verb or comes after a preposition, it is usually translated by *vous*: *it can make one ill* = cela peut vous rendre malade.
– For more examples and all other uses, see the entry below.

I *det* **1** (single) un/une; **~ car** une voiture; **~ dog** un chien; **to raise ~ hand** lever la main; **2** (unique, sole) seul; **the ~ and only Edith Piaf** l'incomparable Edith Piaf; **3** (same) même; **at ~ and the same time** en même temps.
II *pron* **1** (indefinite) un/une *m/f*; **can you lend me ~?** tu peux m'en prêter un/une?; **she's ~ of us** elle est des nôtres; **2** (impersonal) (as subject) on; (as object) vous; **~ would like to think that** on aimerait penser que; **3 I'm not ~ for doing** ce n'est pas mon genre de faire; **she's a clever ~** elle est intelligente; **I for ~ think that** pour ma part je crois que; **4** (demonstrative) **the grey ~** le gris/la grise; **this ~** celui-ci/celle-ci; **which ~?** lequel/laquelle?; **that's the ~** c'est celui-là/celle-là; **he's/she's**

the ~ who c'est lui/elle qui; **5 ~-fifty** (in sterling) une livre cinquante.

III *n* **1** (number) un *m*; (referring to feminine) une *f*; **~ o'clock** une heure; **in ~s and twos** par petits groupes; **2 the little ~s** les petits.

IV one by one *phr* [*pick up*] un par un/une par une.

IDIOMS **to be ~ up on sb**○ avoir un avantage sur qn; **to go ~ better than sb** faire mieux que qn; **a thousand and ~ things to do** un tas de choses à faire.

one another *pron*

■ Note *one another* is very often translated by using a reflexive pronoun (*nous, vous, se, s'*).

(also **each other**) **they love ~** ils s'aiment; **to help ~** s'entraider; **we often use ~'s cars** souvent nous échangeons nos voitures; **to worry about ~** s'inquiéter l'un pour l'autre; **kept apart from ~** séparés l'un de l'autre.

one: **~-eyed** *adj* borgne; **~-legged** *adj* unijambiste; **~-man show** *n* one-man show *m*, spectacle *m* solo; **~-off** *adj* (GB) [*experiment*] unique; [*event, payment*] exceptionnel/-elle; **~-parent family** *n* famille *f* monoparentale.

one-piece *adj* **~ swimsuit** maillot *m* de bain une pièce.

one's *det* son/sa/ses.

■ Note In French determiners agree in gender and number with the noun that follows. So when *one's* is used as a determiner, it is translated by *son* + masculine singular noun (*son argent*), by *sa* + feminine noun (*sa voiture*) BUT by *son* + feminine noun beginning with a vowel or mute 'h' (*son assiette*) and by *ses* + plural noun (*ses enfants*).
– When *one's* is used as a reflexive pronoun, it is translated by *se* (or *s'* before a vowel or mute 'h'): *to brush one's teeth* = se brosser les dents; ▶ 523.

~ books/friends ses livres/amis; **to wash ~ hands** se laver les mains; **to do ~ best** faire de son mieux; **a house of ~ own** une maison à soi.

oneself *pron*

■ Note When used as a reflexive pronoun, direct and indirect, *oneself* is translated by *se* (or *s'* before a vowel or mute 'h'): *to hurt oneself* = se blesser; *to enjoy oneself* = s'amuser.
– When used for emphasis, the translation is *soi-même*: *to do something oneself* = faire quelque chose soi-même.
– After a preposition, the translation is *soi*.

1 (reflexive) se, s'; **to wash/cut ~** se laver/couper; **2** (for emphasis) soi-même; **3** (after prepositions) soi; **sure of ~** sûr de soi; **to have the house all to ~** (for evening, day) être seul à la maison; **to talk to ~** parler tout seul/toute seule; **(all) by ~** tout seul/toute seule.

one: **~-sided** *adj* [*account*] partial; [*contest*] inégal; [*deal*] inéquitable; **~-to-one tuition** *n* cours *mpl* particuliers; **~-upmanship** *n* art *m* de paraître supérieur aux autres.

one-way *adj* **1** [*traffic*] à sens unique; **~ street** sens *m* unique; **2 ~ ticket** aller *m* simple.

ongoing *adj* [*process*] continu; [*battle, story*] continuel/-elle.

onion *n* oignon *m*.

onlooker *n* spectateur/-trice *m/f*.

only I *conj* mais, seulement; **I'd go ~ I'm too old** j'irais bien mais je suis trop vieux.

II *adj* seul; **~ child** enfant unique.

III *adv* **1** (exclusively) **~ in Italy can one...** il n'y a qu'en Italie que l'on peut...; **~ time will tell** seul l'avenir nous le dira; **'men ~'** 'réservé aux hommes'; **2** (in expressions of time) **~ yesterday** pas plus tard qu'hier; **it seems like ~ yesterday** j'ai l'impression que c'était hier; **3** (merely) **you ~ had to ask** tu n'avais qu'à demander; **it's ~ fair** ce n'est que justice; **he ~ grazed his knees** il s'est juste égratigné les genoux; **~ half the money** juste la moitié de l'argent.

IV only just *phr* **1** (very recently) **to have ~ just done** venir juste de faire; **2** (barely) **~ just wide enough** juste assez large; **~ just** (narrowly) de justesse.

V only too *phr* **~ too well** trop bien; **~ too pleased** trop content.

onset *n* début *m* (**of** de).

onslaught *n* attaque *f* (**on** contre).

on-the-job *adj* [*training*] sur le lieu de travail.

on-the-spot I *adj* [*investigation*] sur les lieux; [*advice*] immédiat.

II on the spot *phr* [*decide*] sur-le-champ; [*killed*] sur le coup.

onto *prep* (also **on to**) sur.

IDIOMS **to be ~ something**○ être sur une piste.

onus *n* obligation *f*; **the ~ is on sb to do sth** il incombe à qn de faire qch.

onward I *adj* **~ flight** correspondance *f* (**to** à destination de).

II *adv* = **onwards**.

onwards *adv* **from now ~** à partir d'aujourd'hui; **from that day ~** à dater de ce jour.

ooze *vtr* **the wound ~d blood** du sang suintait de la blessure; **oozing butter** dégoulinant de beurre.

opal *n* opale *f*.

opaque *adj* opaque.

open I *n* (outside) **in the ~** dehors, en plein air; **to bring sth out into the ~** (secret, plot) mettre qch au grand jour.

II *adj* **1** [*shop, door, box, eyes, wound, shirt*] ouvert; [*arms*] écartés; **to be half ~** [*door*] être entrouvert; **the ~ air** le plein air; **in ~ country** en rase campagne; **on ~ ground** sur un terrain découvert; **the ~ road** la grand-route; **the ~ sea** la haute mer; **2** (not covered) [*car, carriage*] découvert, décapoté; [*sewer*] à ciel ouvert; **an ~ fire** un feu (de cheminée); **3 ~ to** exposé à [*air, wind, elements*]; **~ to attack** exposé à l'attaque; **~ to offers** ouvert à toute proposition; **to lay oneself ~ to criticism** s'exposer (ouvertement) à la critique; **4** [*access, competition*] ouvert à tous; [*meeting, session*] public/-ique; **5**

(candid) [*person*] franc/franche (**about** à propos de); **6** (blatant) [*hostility, contempt*] non dissimulé; [*disagreement*] manifeste; **7** (undecided) **to leave the date ~** laisser la date en suspens; **to keep an ~ mind** réserver son jugement.
III *vtr* ouvrir [*shop, door, letter, box, shirt*]; entamer [*discussions*]; **to ~ fire** ouvrir le feu.
IV *vi* **1** [*door, flower, curtain*] s'ouvrir; **to ~ onto sth** [*door, window*] donner sur qch; **2** [*shop, bar*] ouvrir; [*meeting, play*] commencer (**with** par); **3** (have first performance) [*film*] sortir (sur les écrans); [*exhibition*] ouvrir.
■ **open up**: ¶ **~ up 1** [*shop, branch*] ouvrir; **2** (appear) [*gap*] se creuser; [*market*] s'ouvrir; **3** (figurative) [*person*] se confier; ¶ **~ [sth] up, ~ up [sth]** ouvrir [*parcel, building, area, road, shop*].

open: **~-air** *adj* [*pool, stage*] en plein air; **~ day** *n* journée *f* portes ouvertes.

opener *n* (for bottles) décapsuleur *m*; (for cans) ouvre-boîte *m*.

opening I *n* **1** (of book, film, piece of music) début *m*; **2** (of exhibition, shop) ouverture *f*; (of play, film) première *f*; **3** (gap) trouée *f*; **4** (opportunity) occasion *f* (**to do** de faire); (in market) débouché *m* (**for** pour).
II *adj* [*scene, move*] premier/-ière (*before n*); [*remarks*] préliminaire; [*ceremony*] d'inauguration; **~ hours** heures *fpl* d'ouverture.

open-minded *adj* **to be ~** avoir l'esprit ouvert.

open: **~-mouthed** *adj* bouche bée *inv*; **~-necked** *n* [*shirt*] à col ouvert; **~-plan** *adj* [*office*] paysagé; **~ secret** *n* secret *m* de Polichinelle.

opera *n* opéra *m*.

opera: **~ glasses** *n* jumelles *fpl* de théâtre; **~ house** *n* opéra *m*.

operate ▶686 I *vtr* **1** faire marcher [*appliance, vehicle*]; **2** pratiquer [*policy, system*]; **3** (manage) gérer [*radio station*].
II *vi* **1** (do business) opérer; **2** (function) marcher; **3** (run) [*service*] fonctionner; **4** (Med) opérer; **to ~ on** opérer [*person*]; **to ~ on sb's leg** opérer qn à la jambe.

operating *adj* [*costs*] d'exploitation.

operating: **~ instructions** *n pl* mode *m* d'emploi; **~ room** (US), **~ theatre** (GB) *n* salle *f* d'opération.

operation *n* **1** (surgical) opération *f*; **to have a heart ~** se faire opérer du cœur; **2** (use) **to be in ~** [*plan*] être en vigueur; [*machine*] fonctionner; **3** (undertaking, venture) opération *f*.

operative I *n* (worker) employé/-e *m/f*.
II *adj* **1** [*system*] en vigueur; **2 the ~ word** le mot qui compte.

operator ▶805 *n* **1** (on telephone) standardiste *mf*; **2** (of radio, computer) opérateur *m*; **3 he's a smooth ~** il sait s'y prendre.

opinion *n* (estimation) opinion *f* (**about** de); (view) avis *m* (**about, on** sur); **to have a high/low ~ of sb/sth** avoir une bonne/mauvaise opinion de qn/qch; **in my ~** à mon avis; **~ is divided** les avis sont partagés.

opinionated *adj* **to be ~** avoir des avis sur tout.

opinion poll *n* sondage *m* d'opinion.

opponent *n* (in contest) adversaire *mf*; (of regime) opposant/-e *m/f* (**of** à).

opportunity *n* occasion *f* (**for** de); **to take the ~ to do** profiter de l'occasion pour faire; **training opportunities** possibilités de formation.

oppose I *vtr* s'opposer à [*plan, bill*]; **to be ~d to sth/to doing** être contre qch/contre l'idée de faire.
II **opposing** *pres p adj* [*party, team*] adverse; [*army*] ennemi; [*view, style*] opposé.
III **as opposed to** *phr* par opposition à.

opposite I *n* contraire *m* (**to, of** de); **the exact ~** l'inverse.
II *adj* [*direction, side, attitude, viewpoint, sex*] opposé; [*building*] d'en face; [*page*] ci-contre; [*effect*] inverse; **at ~ ends of** aux deux bouts de [*table, street*].
III *adv* [*live, stand*] en face; **directly ~** juste en face.
IV *prep* en face de [*building, park, person*].

opposite number *n* (gen) homologue *m*; (Sport) adversaire *mf*.

opposition *n* opposition *f* (**to** à); **the Opposition** (in politics) l'opposition *f*.

oppress *vtr* opprimer [*people, nation*].

oppressive *adj* **1** [*law*] oppressif/-ive; **2** [*heat, atmosphere*] oppressant.

opt *vi* **to ~ for sth** opter pour qch; **to ~ to do** choisir de faire.
■ **opt out** décider de ne pas participer (**of** à).

optical *adj* optique.

optical illusion *n* illusion *f* d'optique.

optician ▶805 *n* (selling glasses) opticien/-ienne *m/f*; (eye specialist) (GB) optométriste *mf*.

optimism *n* optimisme *m*.

optimist *n* optimiste *mf*.

optimistic *adj* optimiste (**about** quant à); **to be ~ that** avoir bon espoir que.

option *n* **1** option *f* (**to do** de faire); **to have first ~** avoir priorité d'option; **safe ~** solution *f* la plus sûre; **to have the ~ of doing sth** pouvoir choisir de faire qch; **I didn't have much ~** je n'avais guère le choix; **2** (course of study) option *f*.

optional *adj* [*activity, subject*] facultatif/-ive; **~ extras** accessoires *mpl* en option.

opulent *adj* [*lifestyle*] opulent; [*hotel, furnishings*] somptueux/-euse.

or *conj*

■ **Note** In most cases *or* is translated by *ou*. There are two exceptions to this:
– When used to link alternatives after a negative verb (*I can't come today or tomorrow*), the structure *ne...ni...ni* can be used: *je ne peux venir ni aujourd'hui ni demain*. For translations, see 2 below.
– When used to mean *otherwise* (*it can't be serious or she'd have called us*), the translation is

sinon: ça ne peut pas être grave sinon elle nous aurait appelés.

---

1 ou; **black ~ white?** noir ou blanc?; **any brothers ~ sisters?** tu as des frères et sœurs?; **either here ~ at Dave's** soit ici soit chez Dave; **whether he likes it ~ not** que cela lui plaise ou non; **once ~ twice** une ou deux fois; **in a week ~ so** dans huit jours environ; **~ should I say** ou bien devrais-je dire; **2** (linking alternatives in the negative) **not today ~ tomorrow** ni aujourd'hui ni demain; **don't tell Mum ~ Dad!** ne le dis ni à Maman ni à Papa!; **she doesn't drink ~ smoke** elle ne boit pas et ne fume pas non plus, elle ne boit ni ne fume; **3** (otherwise) sinon, autrement; **be careful ~ you'll cut yourself** fais attention sinon tu vas te couper; **do as you're told—~ else**○! fais ce qu'on te dit—sinon (gare○ à toi)!

oral I *n* oral *m*.
II *adj* [*examination, communication*] oral; [*contraceptive, medicine*] par voie orale.

orange ▶559| **I** *n* **1** (fruit) orange *f*; **2** (colour) orange *m*.
II *noun modifier* [*drink, pudding, sauce*] à l'orange.
III *adj* orange *inv*.

orange: **~ juice** *n* jus *m* d'orange; **~ tree** *n* oranger *m*.

orbit I *n* orbite *f*.
II *vtr* décrire une orbite autour de [*sun, planet*].

orchard *n* verger *m*.

orchestra *n* orchestre *m*.

orchestral *adj* [*concert, music*] orchestral; [*instrument*] d'orchestre.

orchid *n* orchidée *f*.

ordeal *n* épreuve *f*.

order I *n* **1** ordre *m*; **in alphabetical ~** dans l'ordre alphabétique; **in the right/wrong ~** dans le bon/mauvais ordre; **to restore ~** rétablir l'ordre; **2** (command) ordre *m* (**to do** de faire); **to be under ~s to do** avoir (l')ordre de faire; **I'm not taking ~s from you** je ne suis pas à vos ordres; **3** (in shop, restaurant) commande *f*; **4** (operational state) **in working ~** en état de marche; **to be out of ~** [*phone line*] être en dérangement; [*lift, machine*] être en panne; **5** (all right) **in ~** [*documents*] en règle; **that remark was way out of ~** cette remarque était tout à fait déplacée; **6** (also **religious ~**) ordre *m*.
II *vtr* **1** (command) ordonner [*inquiry, retrial*]; **to ~ sb to do** ordonner à qn de faire; **2** commander [*goods, meal*]; réserver [*taxi*] (**for** pour).
III *vi* [*diner, customer*] commander.
IV in order that *phr* (with the same subject) afin de (+ *infinitive*), pour (+ *infinitive*); (when subject of verb changes) afin que (+ *subj*), pour que (+ *subj*).
V in order to *phr* **in ~ to talk to him** pour lui parler, afin de lui parler.
■ **order about, order around**: **to ~ people around** donner des ordres.

order form *n* bon *m* or bulletin *m* de commande.

orderly I *n* (medical) aide-soignant/-e *m/f*.
II *adj* [*queue, line*] ordonné; [*pattern, row, rank*] régulier/-ière; [*mind, system*] méthodique; [*lifestyle*] bien réglé; [*crowd, demonstration*] calme.

ordinary I *n* **to be out of the ~** sortir de l'ordinaire.
II *adj* **1** (normal) [*family, life, person*] ordinaire; [*clothes*] de tous les jours; **2** (average) [*consumer, family*] moyen/-enne; **3** (uninspiring) quelconque (derogatory).

ore *n* minerai *m*; **iron ~** minerai de fer.

organ ▶753| **I** *n* **1** (Anat) organe *m*; **2** (Mus) orgue *m*; **on the ~** à l'orgue; **3** (organization, publication) organe *m*.
II *noun modifier* [*music, composition*] pour orgue.

organic *adj* [*substance, development*] organique; [*produce, farming*] biologique.

organism *n* organisme *m*.

organization *n* **1** (group) organisation *f*; (bureaucratic) organisme *m*; (voluntary) association *f*; **2** (arrangement) organisation *f* (**of** de).

organize *vtr* organiser [*event, time, life*]; ranger [*books, papers*]; **to get (oneself) ~d** s'organiser.

organized: **~ crime** *n* le grand banditisme *m*; **~ labour** (GB), **~ labor** (US) *n* main-d'œuvre *f* syndiquée.

organizer *n* organisateur/-trice *m/f* (**of** de); ▶ **personal organizer**.

orgy *n* orgie *f*.

orient I *n* **the Orient** l'Orient *m*.
II *vtr* (also **orientate**) orienter [*measure, policy, scheme*] (**towards** vers); **child-~ed** adapté aux besoins des enfants.

oriental *adj* (gen) oriental; [*appearance, eyes*] d'Oriental; [*carpet*] d'Orient.

-oriented *combining form* **family~** orienté vers la famille.

orienteering ▶649| *n* course *f* d'orientation.

origin *n* **1** (of person, custom, idea) origine *f*; **2** (of goods) provenance *f*.

original I *n* **to read sth in the ~** lire qch dans le texte original.
II *adj* **1** (initial) [*inhabitant, owner*] premier/-ière (*before n*); [*question, site, strategy*] originel/-elle; **2** [*manuscript, painting, version*] original; **3** (innovative) [*design, suggestion, film*] original.

originality *n* originalité *f*.

originally *adv* **1** (initially) au départ; **2** (in the first place) à l'origine.

originate *vi* [*custom, style, tradition*] voir le jour; [*fire*] se déclarer; **to ~ from** [*goods*] provenir de.

Orkney *pr n pl* (also **~ Islands**) (îles *fpl*) Orcades.

ornament *n* **1** (trinket) bibelot *m*; **2** (ornamentation) ornement *m*.

ornamental *adj* [*plant*] ornemental; [*lake*] d'agrément; [*motif*] décoratif/-ive.

ornate *adj* [*room, furniture*] richement orné; [*style*] très fleuri.

ornithology *n* ornithologie *f*.

orphan **I** *n* orphelin/-e *m/f*.
II *adj* orphelin.

orphanage *n* orphelinat *m*.

orthodox *adj* orthodoxe.

orthopaedic (GB), **orthopedic** (US) *adj* orthopédique.

orthopaedic surgeon ▶ 805 *n* chirugien *m* orthopédiste.

ostensible *adj* apparent.

ostensibly *adv* (supposedly) soi-disant.

ostentatious *adj* [*decor*] tape-à-l'œil○; [*wealth*] ostentatoire.

osteopath ▶ 805 *n* ostéopathe *mf*.

ostracize *vtr* ostraciser.

ostrich *n* autruche *f*.

other **I** *adj* **1** autre; **the ~ one** l'autre; **the ~ 25** les 25 autres; **2** (alternative, additional) autre; **I only have one ~ shirt** je n'ai qu'une seule autre chemise; **~ people** les autres; **some ~ time perhaps** une autre fois peut-être; **he was going the ~ way** il allait dans la direction opposée; **the ~ day** l'autre jour; **she will visit Japan, among ~ places** entre autres, elle ira au Japon; **3** (alternate) **every ~ year** tous les deux ans; **every ~ Saturday** un samedi sur deux.
II *pron* **the ~s** les autres; **~s** (as subject) d'autres; (as object) les autres; **one after the ~** l'un après l'autre; **someone or ~** quelqu'un; **some book or ~** un livre, je ne sais plus lequel; **somehow or ~** d'une manière ou d'une autre.
III other than *phr* **~ than that** à part ça; **there's nobody here ~ than Carole** il n'y a personne ici à part Carole.

otherwise **I** *adv* **1** (differently, in other ways) **to do ~** faire autrement; **no woman, married or ~** aucune femme, mariée ou non; **2** (in other respects) à part cela, par ailleurs.
II *conj* sinon; **it's quite safe, ~ I wouldn't do it** ce n'est pas dangereux du tout, sinon je ne le ferais pas.

otter *n* loutre *f*.

ouch *excl* aïe!

ought *modal aux* **1** (expressing expectation) **that ~ to fix it** ça devrait arranger les choses; **2** (making firm suggestion) **oughtn't we to ask?** ne croyez-vous pas que nous devrions demander?; **we ~ to say something** nous devrions dire quelque chose; **3** (indicating moral obligation) **someone ~ to have accompanied her** quelqu'un aurait dû l'accompagner.

ounce ▶ 738 *n* **1** (weight) once *f* (= *28,35 g*); **2** (GB) (fluid) = *0,028 l*; (US) = *0,035 l*; **3** (figurative) once *f*.

our *det* notre/nos.

■ **Note** In French, determiners agree in gender and number with the noun that follows. So *our* is translated by *notre* + masculine or feminine singular noun (notre chien, notre maison) and *nos* + plural noun (nos enfants).
– When *our* is stressed, *à nous* is added after the noun: OUR house = notre maison à nous.
– For *our* used with parts of the body ▶ 523.

ours *pron*

■ **Note** In French, possessive pronouns reflect the number and gender of the noun they are standing for. Thus *ours* is translated by *le nôtre, la nôtre* or *les nôtres* according to what is being referred to.

their children are older than ~ leurs enfants sont plus âgés que les nôtres; **which tickets are ~?** lesquels de ces billets sont les nôtres or à nous?; **a friend of ~** un ami à nous; **the blue car is ~** la voiture bleue est à nous; **it's not ~** ce n'est pas à nous.

ourselves *pron*

■ **Note** When used as a reflexive pronoun, direct and indirect, *ourselves* is translated by *nous* in standard French: *we've hurt ourselves* = nous nous sommes fait mal. However, if the more informal *on* is used to translate *we*, the translation of ourselves will be *se* (or *s'* before a vowel or mute 'h'): on s'est fait mal.
– When used for emphasis, the translation is *nous-mêmes*: *we did it ourselves* = nous l'avons fait nous-mêmes.
– When used after a preposition, *ourselves* is translated by *nous* or *nous-mêmes*.

1 (reflexive) nous; (more informally) se, s'; **2** (emphatic) nous-mêmes; **3** (after prepositions) **for ~** pour nous, pour nous-mêmes; **(all) by ~** tout seuls/toutes seules.

out

■ **Note** When *out* is used as an adverb meaning *outside*, it often adds little to the sense of the phrase: *they're out in the garden = they're in the garden*. In such cases *out* will not usually be translated: *ils sont dans le jardin*.

I *adv* **1** (outside) dehors; **to stay ~ in the rain** rester (dehors) sous la pluie; **~ there** dehors; **2 to go** or **walk ~** sortir; **I couldn't find my way ~** je ne trouvais pas la sortie; **two days ~ from port** à deux jours du port; **when the tide is ~** à marée basse; **further ~** plus loin; **to invite sb ~ to dinner** inviter qn au restaurant; **3** (absent) **to be ~** être sorti; **4 to be ~** [*book, exam results*] être publié; **5 to be ~** [*sun, moon, stars*] briller; **6 to be ~** [*fire, light*] être éteint; **7** (Sport) **to be ~** [*player*] être éliminé; **'~!'** (of ball) 'out!'; **8** (over) **before the week is ~** avant la fin de la semaine; **9**○ **to be ~ to do sth** être bien décidé à faire qch; **he's just ~ for what he can get** c'est l'intérêt qui le guide; **he's ~ to get you** il t'en veut à mort.
II out of *phr* **1 to go** or **walk** or **come ~** sortir de; **to jump ~ of the window** sauter par la fenêtre; **to take sth ~ of one's bag** prendre qch dans son sac; **taken ~ of a book** tiré d'un livre; **2** (expressing ratio) sur; **two ~ of every three** deux sur trois; **3** hors de [*reach, sight*]; en dehors de [*city*]; à l'abri de [*sun*]; **4 to be (right) ~ of** ne plus avoir de [*item*].
IDIOMS **to be ~ of it**○ être dans les vapes○.

outback *n* **the ~** la brousse (australienne).

outbid *vtr* surenchérir sur.
outbreak *n* (of war) début *m*; (of violence, spots) éruption *f*; (of disease) déclaration *f*.
outbuilding *n* dépendance *f*.
outburst *n* accès *m*.
outcast *n* exclu/-e *m/f*.
outcome *n* résultat *m*.
outcry *n* tollé *m* (**about, against** contre).
outdated *adj* [*idea, practice, theory*] dépassé; [*clothing*] démodé.
outdo *vtr* surpasser.
outdoor *adj* [*life, activity, sport*] de plein air; [*restaurant*] en plein air.
outdoors *adv* [*sit, work, play*] dehors; [*live*] en plein air.
outer *adj* **1** (furthest) [*limit*] extrême; **2** (outside) extérieur.
outer: **~ space** *n* espace *m* (extra-atmosphérique); **~ suburbs** *n pl* grande banlieue *f*.
outfit *n* tenue *f*.
outflow *n* (of money) sortie *f*.
outgoing *adj* **1** (sociable) ouvert et sociable; **2** [*government*] sortant.
outgoings *n pl* (GB) sorties *fpl* (de fonds).
outgrow *vtr* **1** (grow too big for) devenir trop grand pour; **2** (grow too old for) se lasser de [qch] avec le temps; **he'll ~ it** ça lui passera
outlast *vtr* durer plus longtemps que.
outlaw I *n* hors-la-loi *m inv*.
II *vtr* déclarer illégal [*practice, organization*].
outlay *n* dépenses *fpl* (**on** en); **initial ~** mise *f* de fonds initiale.
outlet *n* **1** (for gas, air, water) tuyau *m* de sortie; **2 retail ~** point *m* de vente; **3** (for emotion, talent) exutoire *m*; **4** (US) (socket) prise *f* de courant.
outline I *n* **1** (of object) contour *m*; **2** (of plan, policy) grandes lignes *fpl*; (of essay) plan *m*.
II *vtr* exposer brièvement [*aims, plan, reasons*].
outlive *vtr* survivre à [*person*]; **it has ~d its usefulness** il a fait son temps.
outlook *n* **1** (attitude) vue *f*; **2** (prospects) perspectives *fpl*.
outnumber *vtr* être plus nombreux que.
out-of-date *adj* [*ticket, passport*] périmé; [*concept*] dépassé.
outpatient *n* malade *mf* externe; **~s' department** service *m* de consultation.
outpost *n* (Mil, gen) avant-poste *m*; **the last ~** le dernier bastion (**of** de).
output *n* (yield) rendement *m*; (of factory) production *f*.
outrage I *n* **1** (anger) indignation *f* (**at** devant); **2** (atrocity) atrocité *f*; **3** (scandal) scandale *m*.
II *vtr* scandaliser [*public*].
outrageous *adj* [*attitude, behaviour*] scandaleux/-euse; [*remark*] outrancier/-ière.
outright I *adj* [*control, majority*] absolu; [*ban*] catégorique; [*victory, winner*] incontesté; [*hostility*] pur et simple.
II *adv* (gen) catégoriquement; [*killed*] sur le coup.
outside I *n* **1** extérieur *m*; **on the ~** à l'extérieur; **on the ~ of** sur l'extérieur de [*box, file*]; **2** (maximum) **at the ~** au maximum.
II *adj* extérieur; **~ lane** (in GB) voie *f* de droite; (in US, Europe) voie *f* de gauche; (on athletics track) couloir *m* extérieur; **an ~ chance** une faible chance.
III *adv* dehors.
IV *prep* (also **~ of**) **1** en dehors de [*city*]; de l'autre côté de [*boundary*]; à l'extérieur de [*prison*]; **2** (in front of) devant [*house*].
outsider *n* **1** (in community) étranger/-ère *m/f*; **2** (Sport) outsider *m*.
outsize *adj* (in clothes sizes) grande taille *inv*.
outskirts *n pl* périphérie *f*.
outspoken *adj* **to be ~** parler sans détour.
outstanding *adj* **1** (praiseworthy) remarquable; **2** (striking) frappant; **3** [*interest*] échu; **~ debts** créances *fpl* à recouvrer.
outstay *vtr* **to ~ one's welcome** s'éterniser.
outstretched *adj* [*hand, arm, fingers*] tendu; [*wings*] déployé; [*legs*] allongé.
outstrip *vtr* dépasser [*person*]; excéder [*production, demand*].
outward I *adj* [*appearance, sign*] extérieur; [*calm*] apparent; **~ journey** aller *m*.
II *adv* = **outwards**.
outwardly *adv* (apparently) en apparence.
outwards *adv* (also **outward**) [*open, turn*] vers l'extérieur.
outweigh *vtr* l'emporter sur.
outwit *vtr* être plus futé que [*person*]; déjouer les manœuvres de [*opponent*].
oval *n, adj* ovale (*m*).
ovary *n* ovaire *m*.
ovation *n* ovation *f*; **to give sb a standing ~** se lever pour ovationner qn.
oven *n* four *m*.
oven: **~ cleaner** *n* nettoyant *m* pour four; **~proof** *adj* qui va au four; **~-ready** *adj* prêt à cuire.

over

■ **Note** *over* is often used with another preposition in English (*to, in, on*) without altering the meaning. In this case *over* is usually not translated in French: *to be over in France* = être en France; *to swim over to sb* = nager vers qn.

I *prep* **1** par-dessus; **he jumped ~ it** il a sauté par-dessus; **to wear a sweater ~ one's shirt** porter un pull par-dessus sa chemise; **a bridge ~ the Thames** un pont sur la Tamise; **2** (across) **it's just ~ the road** c'est juste de l'autre côté de la rue; **~ here/there** par ici/là; **come ~ here!** viens (par) ici!; **3** (above) au-dessus de; **they live ~ the shop** ils habitent au-dessus de la boutique; **children ~ six** les enfants de plus de six ans; **temperatures ~ 40°** des températures supérieures à or au-dessus de 40°; **4** (in the course of) **~ the weekend** pendant le week-end; **~ a period of** sur une période de; **~ the last few days** au cours de ces derniers jours; **~ the years** avec le temps; **~ Christmas** à Noël; **to stay with sb ~ Easter** passer les vacances de Pâques chez qn;

5 to be ~ s'être remis de [*illness, operation*]; **to be ~ the worst** avoir passé le pire; **6** (by means of) **~ the phone** par téléphone; **~ the radio** à la radio; **7** (everywhere) **all ~ the house** partout dans la maison.
II *adj, adv* **1** (finished) **to be ~** [*term, meeting*] être terminé; [*war*] être fini; **2** (more) **children of six and ~** les enfants de plus de six ans; **3 to invite** or **ask sb ~** inviter qn; **we had them ~ on Sunday** ils sont venus dimanche; **4** (on radio, TV) **~ to you** à vous; **now ~ to our Paris studios** nous passons l'antenne à nos studios de Paris; **5** (showing repetition) **five times ~** cinq fois de suite; **to start all ~ again** recommencer à zéro; **I had to do it ~** (US) j'ai dû recommencer; **I've told you ~ and ~ (again)**... je t'ai dit je ne sais combien de fois...; **6** (GB) **I'm not ~ keen** je ne suis pas très enthousiaste.
III over and above *phr* **~ and above that** en plus de cela; **~ and above the minimum requirement** au-delà du minimum requis.

overact *vi* en faire trop.

overall I *n* (GB) (coat-type) blouse *f*; (child's) tablier *m*.
II overalls *n pl* (GB) combinaison *f*; (US) salopette *f*.
III *adj* [*cost*] global; [*improvement*] général; [*effect*] d'ensemble; [*majority*] absolu.
IV *adv* **1** (in total) en tout; **2** (in general) dans l'ensemble.

overawe *vtr* intimider.

overboard *adv* à l'eau; **to go ~**° (figurative) aller trop loin.

overbook *vtr, vi* surréserver.

overcast *adj* [*sky*] couvert.

overcharge *vtr* faire payer trop cher à; **they ~d him by £10** ils lui ont fait payer 10 livres de trop.

overcoat *n* pardessus *m*.

overcome I *vtr* battre [*opponent*]; vaincre [*enemy*]; surmonter [*dislike, fear*]; **to be overcome with despair** succomber au désespoir.
II *vi* triompher.

overcook *vtr* trop cuire.

overcrowded *adj* [*train, room*] bondé (**with** de); [*city*] surpeuplé (**with** de); [*class*] surchargé.

overcrowding *n* (in city) surpeuplement *m*; (in transport) surencombrement *m*.

overdo *vtr* **to ~ it** (when describing) exagérer; (when performing) forcer la note°; (when working) en faire trop°.

overdone *adj* **1** (exaggerated) exagéré; **2** (overcooked) trop cuit.

overdose *n* surdose *f*; **to take an ~** absorber une dose excessive de médicaments.

overdraft *n* découvert *m*; **to have an ~** être à découvert.

overdraw I *vtr* **my account is ~n** mon compte est à découvert.
II *vi* être à découvert.

overdue *adj* [*baby, work*] en retard (**by** de); [*bill*] impayé; **this measure is long ~** cette mesure aurait dû être prise il y a longtemps.

overeat *vi* manger à l'excès.

overestimate *vtr* surestimer.

overexposure *n* (in photography) surexposition *f*.

overflow I *vtr* [*river*] inonder [*banks*].
II *vi* déborder (**into** dans; **with** de).

overgrown *adj* [*garden*] envahi par la végétation.

overhanging *adj* [*ledge, cliff*] en surplomb; [*tree, branch*] qui surplombe.

overhaul I *n* (of machine) révision *f*; (of system) restructuration *f*.
II *vtr* réviser [*car, machine*]; restructurer [*system*].

overhead I *adj* [*cable, railway*] aérien/-ienne.
II *adv* **1** (in sky) dans le ciel; **2** (above sb's head) au-dessus de ma/sa etc tête.

overhead projector *n* rétroprojecteur *m*.

overheads *n pl* frais *mpl* généraux.

overhear *vtr* entendre par hasard.

overheat I *vtr* (Culin) faire trop chauffer.
II *vi* [*car, equipment*] chauffer; [*oven*] chauffer trop.

overindulge *vi* faire des excès.

overland I *adj* [*route*] terrestre; [*journey*] par route.
II *adv* par route.

overlap I *n* chevauchement *m* (**between** de); (undesirable) empiétement *m*.
II *vi* **1** [*theories*] se chevaucher; [*duties*] se recouvrir partiellement; [*visits, holidays*] coïncider en partie; **2** [*materials, edges*] se recouvrir partiellement.

overload *vtr* surcharger (**with** de).

overlook *vtr* **1** [*building, window*] donner sur; **2** (miss) ne pas voir [*detail, error*]; **to ~ the fact that** négliger le fait que; **3** (ignore) ignorer [*effect, need*].

overnight I *adj* **1** [*journey, train*] de nuit; [*stop*] pour une nuit; **2** [*success*] immédiat.
II *adv* **1 to stay ~** passer la nuit; **2** [*change, disappear, transform*] du jour au lendemain.

overpopulated *adj* surpeuplé.

overpower *vtr* **1** maîtriser [*thief*]; vaincre [*army*]; **2** [*smell, smoke*] accabler.

overpowering *adj* [*person*] intimidant; [*desire, urge*] irrésistible; [*heat*] accablant; [*smell*] irrespirable.

overqualified *adj* surqualifié.

overrate *vtr* surestimer.

overrated *adj* [*person, work*] surfait; **his films are ~** ses films sont loin d'être aussi bien qu'on le dit.

overreact *vi* réagir de façon excessive.

overrule *vtr* **to be ~d** [*decision*] être annulé.

overrun *vtr* **1** (invade) envahir [*country, site*]; **2** (exceed) dépasser [*time, budget*].

overseas I *adj* **1** [*student, investor*] étranger/-ère; **2** [*trade, market*] extérieur.
II *adv* [*work, retire*] (abroad) à l'étranger; (across the sea) outre-mer.

overshadow *vtr* éclipser [*achievement*].

oversight *n* erreur *f*; **due to an ~** par inadvertance.

oversleep *vi* se réveiller trop tard; **I overslept** je ne me suis pas réveillé.

overspending *n* (personal) dépense *f* excessive; (organizational) dépassement *m* budgétaire.

overstaffed *adj* **to be ~** avoir du personnel en surnombre.

overstate *vtr* exagérer.

overstatement *n* exagération *f*.

overstep *vtr* dépasser [*bounds*]; **to ~ the mark** aller trop loin.

overt *adj* évident, manifeste.

overtake I *vtr* dépasser [*vehicle*].
II *vi* (GB) [*driver, vehicle*] dépasser.

overtax I *vtr* **1 to ~ one's brain** se surmener; **2** surimposer [*taxpayer*].
II *v refl* **to ~ oneself** se surmener.

overthrow *vtr* renverser [*government, system*].

overtime I *n* heures *fpl* supplémentaires.
II *adv* **to work ~** [*person*] faire des heures supplémentaires.

overtly *adv* ouvertement.

overtone *n* sous-entendu *m*, connotation *f*.

overture *n* (gen, Mus) ouverture *f*; (in business) proposition *f*.

overturn I *vtr* **1** renverser [*car, chair*]; faire chavirer [*boat*]; **2** faire annuler [*decision, sentence*].
II *vi* [*car, chair*] se renverser; [*boat*] chavirer.

overweight *adj* **1** [*person*] trop gros/grosse; **2 to be ~** [*suitcase*] être trop lourd.

overwhelm I *vtr* **1** [*wave, avalanche*] submerger; [*enemy*] écraser; **2** [*shame, grief*] accabler.
II **overwhelmed** *pp adj* (with letters, offers, kindness) submergé (**with, by** de); (with shame, work) accablé (**with, by** de); (by sight, experience) ébloui (**by** par).

overwhelming *adj* [*defeat, victory, majority*] écrasant; [*desire*] irrésistible; [*heat, sorrow*] accablant; [*support*] massif/-ive.

overwhelmingly *adv* [*vote, reject*] à une écrasante majorité.

overwork *vi* se surmener.

overworked *adj* [*employee*] surmené; [*excuse, word*] éculé.

overwrought *adj* à bout de nerfs.

owe *vtr* devoir; **to ~ sth to sb** devoir qch à qn; **he ~s me a favour** il me doit bien ça; **I ~ you an apology** je te dois des excuses.

owing I *adj* à payer, dû (**for** pour).
II **owing to** *phr* en raison de.

owl *n* hibou *m*; (with tufted ears) chouette *f*.

own I *adj* propre; **her ~ car** sa propre voiture.
II *pron* **my ~** le mien, la mienne; **his/her ~** le sien, la sienne; **he has a room of his ~** il a sa propre chambre or une chambre à lui; **a house of our (very) ~** une maison (bien) à nous.
III *vtr* avoir [*car, house, dog*]; **she ~s three shops** elle est propriétaire de trois magasins; **who ~s that house?** à qui est cette maison?; **he walks around as if he ~s the place** il se conduit comme s'il était chez lui.
IDIOMS **to get one's ~ back** se venger (**on sb** de qn); **on one's ~** tout/-e seul/-e.
■ **own up** avouer.

owner *n* propriétaire *mf*; **car ~** automobiliste *mf*; **home ~** propriétaire *mf*.

ownership *n* propriété *f*; (of land) possession *f*; **joint ~** copropriété *f*.

ox *n* bœuf *m*.

oxygen I *n* oxygène *m*.
II *noun modifier* [*supply, tank*] d'oxygène; [*mask, tent*] à oxygène.

oyster *n* huître *f*.

oyster: **~ bed** *n* banc *m* d'huîtres; **~ farm** *n* parc *m* à huîtres.

ozone *n* **1** ozone *m*; **2**° (sea air) air *m* pur marin.

ozone layer *n* couche *f* d'ozone.

p, P *n* p, P *m*.

p.a. *adv* (*written abbr* = **per annum**) par an.

PA ▶805| *n* (*abbr* = **personal assistant**) secrétaire *mf* de direction.

pace I *n* (short stride, unit of measurement) pas *m*; (of person walking, of life) rythme *m*; **at a fast/slow ~** vite/lentement; **to keep ~ with developments** rester à la page; **I can't stand the ~** je n'arrive pas à suivre.
II *vi* **to ~ up and down** faire les cent pas; **to ~ up and down** arpenter [*cage, room*].
IDIOMS **to put sb through their ~s** mettre qn à l'épreuve.

pacemaker *n* **1** (Med) stimulateur *m* cardiaque; **2** (athlete) lièvre *m*.

Pacific *pr n* **the ~** le Pacifique; **the ~ Ocean** l'océan Pacifique.

pacifist *n, adj* pacifiste (*mf*).

pacify *vtr* apaiser [*person*].

pack I *n* **1** (US) (box) paquet *m*; (large box) boîte *f*; (bag) sachet *m*; **2** (group) bande *f*; (of hounds) meute *f*; (of scouts) section *f*; **a ~ of lies** un tissu de mensonges; **3** (in rugby) pack *m*; **4** (of cards) jeu *m* de cartes; **5** (backpack) sac *m* à dos.
II *vtr* **1** (in suitcase) mettre [qch] dans une valise [*clothes*]; (in box, crate) emballer [*ornaments, books*]; **2** emballer [*box, crate*]; **to ~ one's suitcase** faire sa valise; **3** conditionner [*fruit, meat, goods*]; **4** [*crowd*] remplir complètement [*church, theatre*]; **to be ~ed with** être bondé de [*people*]; être plein de [*ideas*]; **5** tasser [*snow, earth*].
III *vi* **1** [*person*] faire ses valises; **2 to ~ into** [*crowd*] s'entasser dans [*place*].
■ **pack off**: **~ [sb] off, ~ off [sb]** expédier.
■ **pack up**: ¶ **~ up 1** [*person*] faire ses valises; **2**○ (break down) [*TV, machine*] se détraquer○; [*car*] tomber en panne; [*heart, liver*] lâcher○; ¶ **~ [sth] up, ~ up [sth]** (in boxes, crates) emballer [*books, objects*].

package I *n* **1** (parcel) paquet *m*, colis *m*; **2** (series, range) ensemble *m* (**of** de); **3** (Comput) progiciel *m*.
II *vtr* **1** emballer [*goods*]; **2** concevoir un conditionnement pour [*product*]; présenter [*policy*].

package: **~ deal** *n* offre *f* globale; **~ holiday** (GB), **~ tour** *n* voyage *m* organisé.

packaging *n* **1** (materials) emballage *m*; **2** (promotion) (of product) conditionnement *m*; (of policy, film, singer) image *f* publique.

packed *adj* comble; **~ with** plein de.

packed lunch *n* panier-repas *m*.

packet *n* (box) paquet *m*; (bag) sachet *m*; (parcel) paquet *m*.

packing *n* **1** (packaging) emballage *m*; **2 to do one's ~** faire ses valises.

pact *n* pacte *m*; **to make a ~ to do** se mettre d'accord pour faire.

pad I *n* **1** (of paper) bloc *m*; **2** (to prevent chafing) protection *f*; (for leg) jambière *f*; (to absorb liquid) tampon *m*; (to give shape) rembourrage *m*; **3** (sticky part on object, plant) ventouse *f*; **4** (of paw) coussinet *m*; (of finger) pulpe *f*; **5** (sanitary towel) serviette *f* hygiénique; **6** (also **launch ~**) rampe *f* de lancement.
II *vtr* rembourrer [*chair, shoulders, jacket*] (**with** avec); capitonner [*walls*].
III *vi* **to ~ along/around** avancer/aller et venir à pas feutrés.
■ **pad out**: **~ out [sth], ~ [sth] out** étoffer, délayer [*essay, speech*].

padded: **~ cell** *n* cellule *f* capitonnée; **~ envelope** *n* enveloppe *f* matelassée.

padding *n* (stuffing) rembourrage *m*; (on large surface) capitonnage *m*.

paddle I *n* **1** (oar) pagaie *f*; **2 to go for a ~** faire trempette *f*.
II *vi* **1** (row) pagayer; **2** (wade) patauger; **3** [*duck, swan*] barboter.

paddling pool *n* (public) pataugeoire *f*; (inflatable) piscine *f* gonflable.

padlock I *n* (on door) cadenas *m*; (for bicycle) antivol *m*.
II *vtr* cadenasser [*door, gate*]; mettre un antivol à [*bicycle*].

paediatrician (GB), **pediatrician** (US) ▶805| *n* pédiatre *mf*.

pagan *n, adj* païen/païenne (*m/f*).

page I *n* **1** (in book) page *f*; **on ~ two** à la page deux; **2** (Comput) page-écran *f*; **3** (attendant) groom *m*; (US) coursier *m*.
II *vtr* (on pager) rechercher; (over loudspeaker) faire appeler.

pageant *n* (play) reconstitution *f* historique; (carnival) fête *f* à thème historique.

pageboy *n* (at wedding) garçon *m* d'honneur.

pager *n* récepteur *m* d'appel.

paid *adj* [*job*] rémunéré; [*holiday*] payé; **~ assassin** tueur *m* à gages.

paid-up member *n* (GB) adhérent/-e *m/f*.

pain I *n* **1** douleur *f*; **to feel ~, to be in ~** souffrir; **period ~s** règles *fpl* douloureuses; **where is the ~?** où avez-vous mal?; **2**○ (annoying person, thing) **he's/it's a ~** il est/c'est enquiquinant○; **he's a ~ in the neck**○ il est casse-pieds○; **3 on ~ of death** sous peine de mort.
II pains *n pl* **to be at ~s to do sth** prendre grand soin de faire qch; **to take great ~s over** or **with sth** se donner beaucoup de mal pour faire qch.

painful *adj* **1** [*injury, treatment*] douloureux/-euse; [*lesson, memory, task*] pénible; [*blow*] dur; **2**○ (bad) lamentable.

painfully *adv* **to be ~ shy** être d'une timidité maladive; **I am ~ aware of that** je n'en ai que trop conscience.

painkiller *n* analgésique *m*.

painless *adj* **1** (pain-free) indolore; **2** (trouble-free) sans peine.

painstaking *adj* minutieux/-ieuse.

paint I *n* peinture *f*.
II **paints** *n pl* couleurs *fpl*.
III *vtr* **1** peindre [*wall, subject*]; peindre le portrait de [*person*]; **to ~ one's nails** se vernir les ongles; **2** (depict) dépeindre; **3** (Med) badigeonner [*cut, wound*] (**with** de).
IV *vi* peindre.

paint: **~box** *n* boîte *f* de couleurs; **~brush** *n* pinceau *m*.

painter ▶805 *n* peintre *m*.

painting *n* **1** (activity, art form) peinture *f*; **2** (work of art) tableau *m*; (unframed) toile *f*; (of person) portrait *m*; **3** (decorating) peintures *fpl*.

paint: **~pot** *n* pot *m* de peinture; **~ stripper** *n* (chemical) décapant *m*; (tool) racloir *m*; **~work** *n* (in house) peintures *fpl*; (on car) peinture *f*.

pair I *n* **1** (two matching items) paire *f*; **to be one of a ~** faire partie d'une paire; **2** (two people, animals) paire *f*; (sexually involved) couple *m*; **in ~s** [*work*] en groupes de deux; **3 a ~ of scissors** une paire de ciseaux; **a ~ of trousers** un pantalon.
II *vtr* ranger par deux [*gloves, socks*]; **to ~ Paul with Julie** mettre Paul avec Julie.
■ **pair off** [*couple*] se mettre ensemble; (for temporary purposes) se mettre par deux.
■ **pair up** [*dancers, lovers*] former un couple; [*competitors*] faire équipe.

paisley *n* tissu *m* à motifs cachemire.

pajamas (US) = **pyjamas**.

Pakistan ▶574 *pr n* Pakistan *m*.

Pakistani ▶712 I *n* Pakistanais/-e *m/f*.
II *adj* [*culture, people, politics*] pakistanais; [*ambassador, embassy*] du Pakistan.

palace *n* (of monarch) palais *m*; (of bishop) évêché *m*.

palatable *n* [*food*] savoureux; [*solution, law*] acceptable.

palate *n* palais *m*; **too sweet for my ~** trop sucré à mon goût.

pale I *adj* [*colour, complexion*] pâle; [*light, dawn*] blafard; **to turn** or **go ~** pâlir.
II *vi* pâlir; **to ~ into insignificance** devenir dérisoire.
IDIOMS **to be beyond the ~** [*remark, behaviour*] être inadmissible; [*person*] être infréquentable.

Palestine ▶574 *pr n* Palestine *f*.

Palestinian ▶712 I *n* Palestinien/-ienne *m/f*.
II *adj* palestinien/-ienne.

palette *n* palette *f*.

palette knife *n* **1** (for artist) couteau *m* à palette; **2** (Culin) palette *f*.

pall *n* **1** (coffin-cloth) drap *m* mortuaire; (coffin) cercueil *m*; **2** (of smoke, dust) nuage *m*; (of gloom, silence) manteau *m*.

pallet *n* (for loading) palette *f*.

pallid *adj* [*skin, light*] blafard.

palm *n* **1** paume *f*; **in the ~ of one's hand** dans le creux de la main; **he read my ~** il m'a lu les lignes de la main; **2** (also **~ tree**) palmier *m*; (branch) branche *f* de palmier; **3** (also **~ leaf**) palme *f*.
■ **palm off**°: **~ [sth] off, ~ off [sth]** faire passer qch (as pour); **to ~ sth off on sb, to ~ sb off with sth** refiler° qch à qn.

Palm Sunday *n* dimanche *m* des Rameaux.

palpable *adj* [*fear, tension*] palpable; [*lie, error, nonsense*] manifeste.

palpitate *vi* palpiter (**with** de).

paltry *adj* [*sum*] dérisoire; [*excuse*] piètre (*before n*).

pamper *vtr* choyer [*person, pet*]; **to ~ oneself** se bichonner°.

pamphlet *n* brochure *f*; (political) tract *m*; (satirical) pamphlet *m*.

pan I *n* **1** (saucepan) casserole *f*; **2** (on scales) plateau *m*; **3** (in lavatory) cuvette *f*.
II *vtr* **1**° (criticize) éreinter; **2** (in photography) faire un panoramique de
■ **pan out** (turn out) marcher; (turn out well) s'arranger.

pancake *n* crêpe *f*.
IDIOMS **as flat as a ~**° plat comme une galette.

pancake day *n* mardi *m* gras.

pandemonium *n* tohu-bohu *m*.

pander *vi* **to ~ to** céder aux exigences de [*person*]; flatter [*whim*].

pane *n* vitre *f*, carreau *m*; **a ~ of glass** une vitre, un carreau.

panel *n* **1** (of experts, judges) commission *f*; (on discussion programme) invités *mpl*; (on quiz show) jury *m*; **2** (section of wall) panneau *m*; **3** (Aut, Tech) (section) panneau *m*; (of instruments, switches) tableau *m*.

panel: **~ beater** ▶805 *n* tôlier *m*; **~ game** *n* (radio) jeu *m* radiophonique; (TV) jeu *m* télévisé.

panelled, **paneled** (US) *adj* [*fencing*] en panneaux; [*wall, ceiling*] lambrissé; [*door*] à panneaux; [*bath*] cloisonné.

panellist, **panelist** (US) *n* (radio) invité/-e *m/f*.

pang *n* **1** (emotional) serrement *m* de cœur; **a ~ of jealousy** une pointe de jalousie; **~s of conscience** or **guilt** remords *mpl* de conscience; **2 ~s of hunger** crampes *fpl* d'estomac; **birth ~s** (figurative) difficultés *fpl* initiales.

panhandler° *n* (US) mendiant/-e *m/f*.

panic I *n* affolement *m*; **to get into a ~** s'affoler; **to throw sb into a ~** affoler qn.
II *vtr* affoler [*person, animal*]; semer la panique dans [*crowd*].
III *vi* s'affoler.

panic buying *n* achats *mpl* par crainte de la pénurie.

pannier *n* (on bike) sacoche *f*; (on mule) panier *m* de bât.

pansy *n* pensée *f*.

pant *vi* haleter; **to be ~ing for breath** être tout essoufflé.

panther *n* **1** (leopard) panthère *f*; **2** (US) (puma) puma *m*.

pantomime *n* (GB) spectacle *m* pour enfants.

pantry *n* garde-manger *m inv*.

pants *n pl* **1** (US) (trousers) pantalon *m*; **2** (GB) (underwear) slip *m*.

pantsuit *n* (US) tailleur-pantalon *m*.

panty: **~ hose** *n* (US) collant *m*; **~-liner** *n* protège-slip *m*.

papal *adj* papal, pontifical.

paper I *n* **1** (for writing, drawing) papier *m*; **a piece of ~** (scrap) un bout de papier; (clean sheet) une feuille (de papier); (for wrapping) un morceau de papier; **writing/tissue ~** papier à lettres/de soie; **to get** or **put sth down on ~** mettre qch par écrit; **2** (also **wall~**) papier *m* peint; **3** (newspaper) journal *m*; **4** (scholarly article) article *m* (**on** sur); (lecture) communication *f* (**on** sur); (report) exposé *m* (**on** sur); **5** (examination) épreuve *f* (**on** de); **6** (government publication) livre *m*.
II **papers** *n pl* (for administrative purposes) papiers *mpl*.
III *noun modifier* [*bag, hat, handkerchief, napkin*] en papier; [*plate, cup*] en carton; [*industry*] du papier; [*manufacture*] de papier.
IV *vtr* tapisser [*room, wall*].

paper: **~back** *n* livre *m* de poche; **~ bank** *n* conteneur *m* de récupération de vieux papiers; **~ boy** *n* livreur *m* de journaux; **~ chain** *n* guirlande *f* de papier; **~clip** *n* trombone *m*; **~ knife** *n* coupe-papier *m inv*; **~ mill** *n* papeterie *f*, fabrique *f* de papier; **~ shop** *n* marchand *m* de journaux; **~ towel** *n* essuie-tout *m inv*; **~weight** *n* presse-papier *m inv*; **~work** *n* (administration) travail *m* administratif; (documentation) documents *mpl*.

par *n* **1 to be on a ~ with** [*performance*] être comparable à; [*person*] être l'égal de; **to be up to ~** être à la hauteur; **to be below** or **under ~** [*performance*] être en dessous de la moyenne; [*person*] ne pas se sentir en forme; **2** (in golf) par *m*.

parachute I *n* parachute *m*.
II *vtr* parachuter.
III *vi* **to go parachuting** faire du parachutisme.

parachute: **~ drop** *n* parachutage *m*; **~ jump** *n* saut *m* en parachute.

parachuting ▶ 649 *n* parachutisme *m*.

parade I *n* **1** (procession) parade *f*; **2** (Mil) (march) défilé *m*; (review) prise *f* d'armes; (in barracks) appel *m*; **to be on ~** être à l'exercice.
II *vtr* **1** (display) faire étalage de; **2** (claim) **to ~ sth as sth** présenter qch comme qch.
III *vi* défiler (**through** dans); **to ~ up and down** [*soldier, model*] défiler; [*child*] parader.

parade ground *n* champ *m* de manœuvres.

paradise *n* paradis *m*; **in ~** au paradis.

paradox *n* paradoxe *m*.

paradoxical *adj* paradoxal.

paraffin I *n* **1** (GB) (fuel) pétrole *m*; **2** (also **~ wax**) paraffine *f*.
II *noun modifier* (GB) [*lamp, heater*] à pétrole.

paragliding ▶ 649 *n* parapente *m*.

paragon *n* modèle *m* (**of** de).

paragraph *n* **1** (section) paragraphe *m*; **2** (in newspaper) entrefilet *m*.

parallel I *n* **1** (in mathematics) parallèle *f*; **2** (comparison) parallèle *m*; **on a ~ with** comparable à.
II *adj* **1** parallèle; **2** (similar) analogue (**to, with** à); **3** (simultaneous) parallèle.
III *adv* **~ to, ~ with** parallèlement à.
IV *vtr* (equal) égaler; (find a comparison) trouver un équivalent à.

paralyse (GB), **paralyze** (US) *vtr* paralyser.

paralysed (GB), **paralyzed** (US) *adj* paralysé; **to be ~ from the waist down** être paraplégique.

paralysis *n* paralysie *f*.

paramedic ▶ 805 *n* auxiliaire *mf* médical/-e.

parameter *n* paramètre *m*; **within the ~s of** dans les limites de.

paramilitary *n* membre *m* d'une organisation paramilitaire.

paramount *adj* **to be ~, to be of ~ importance** être d'une importance capitale.

paranoid I *n* paranoïaque *mf*.
II *adj* (Med) paranoïde; (gen) paranoïaque (**about** au sujet de).

parapet *n* parapet *m*.

paraphernalia *n* (articles) attirail *m*.

paraphrase *vtr* paraphraser.

paraplegic *n* paraplégique *mf*.

parasite *n* parasite *m*.

paratrooper *n* parachutiste *m*.

parboil *vtr* faire cuire [qch] à demi [*vegetables*].

parcel *n* **1** (package) paquet *m*, colis *m*; **2**° (of people, problems) tas° *m*.
IDIOMS **to be part and ~ of** faire partie intégrante de.

parcel: **~ bomb** *n* colis *m* piégé; **~ post** *n* service *m* de colis postaux.

parched *adj* **1** [*earth*] desséché; **2 to be ~**° mourir de soif.

parchment *n* (document) parchemin *m*; (paper) papier-parchemin *m*.

pardon I *n* **1** (gen) pardon *m*; **2** (Law) (also **free ~**) grâce *f*.
II *excl* (what?) pardon?; (sorry!) pardon!
III *vtr* (gen) pardonner; (Law) grâcier [*criminal*].

pare *vtr* peler [*apple*].

pared-down *adj* [*budget*] réduit; [*version*] abrégé; [*prose, plot*] dépouillé.

parent *n* parent *m*.

parental *adj* [*role, authority*] des parents, parental (formal).

parent company *n* maison *f* mère.

parenthood *n* (fatherhood) paternité *f*; (motherhood) maternité *f*.

parenting *n* éducation *f* des enfants.

parings *n pl* **1** (of fruit) épluchures *fpl*; **2** (of nails) rognures *fpl*.

Paris ▶ 574 *pr n* Paris.

parish *n* **1** paroisse *f*; **2** (GB) (administrative) commune *f*.

Parisian I *n* Parisien/-ienne *m/f*.
II *adj* parisien/-ienne.

parity *n* parité *f* (**with** avec).

park I *n* **1** (public garden) jardin *m* public; **2** (estate) parc *m*; **3** (GB) (pitch) terrain *m*; (US) (stadium) stade *m*; **4** (on automatic gearbox) position *f* parking.
II *vtr* garer [*car*].
III *vi* [*driver*] se garer.

parking I *n* **1** (action) stationnement *m*; **'No ~'** 'stationnement interdit'; **2** (space for cars) place *f* de stationnement.
II *noun modifier* [*area, permit, restrictions*] de stationnement.

parking: **~ light** *n* (Aut) feu *m* de position; **~ lot** *n* (US) parking *m*; **~ meter** *n* parcmètre *m*; **~ offence** (GB), **~ offense** (US) *n* infraction *f* aux règles de stationnement; **~ place**, **~ space** *n* place *f*; **~ ticket** *n* (fine) contravention *f*, PV° *m*.

park warden ▶**805** *n* (on estate) garde *m* forestier; (in reserve) garde-chasse *m*.

parliament I *n* parlement *m*.
II **Parliament** *pr n* (GB) **1** (institution) Parlement *m*; **to get into Parliament** être élu député; **2** (parliamentary session) session *f* parlementaire.

parliamentary *adj* parlementaire.

parliamentary election *n* élections *fpl* législatives.

parlour (GB), **parlor** (US) *n* **1**† (in house) petit salon *m*; **2** (in convent) parloir *m*.

parochial *adj* [*view*] borné; **~ attitude(s)** esprit *m* de clocher.

parody I *n* parodie *f*.
II *vtr* parodier [*person, style*].

parole *n* liberté *f* conditionnelle; **on ~** en liberté conditionnelle.

paroxysm *n* crise *f* (**of** de).

parquet *n* **1** (floor) parquet *m*; **2** (US) (in theatre) parterre *m*.

parrot *n* perroquet *m*.

parry *vtr* **1** (Sport) parer; **2** éluder [*question*].

parsley *n* persil *m*.

parsnip *n* panais *m*.

part I *n* **1** (of whole) partie *f*; (of country) région *f*; **in** or **around these ~s** dans la région; **to be (a) ~ of** faire partie de; **the early ~ of my life** ma jeunesse; **that's the best/hardest ~** c'est ça le meilleur/le plus dur; **that's the ~ I don't understand** voilà ce que je ne comprends pas; **to be good in ~s** (GB) avoir de bons passages; **for the most ~** dans l'ensemble; **2** (Tech) (component) pièce *f*; **spare ~s** pièces détachées; **3** (of programme) partie *f*; (of serial) épisode *m*; **a two-~ documentary** un documentaire en deux parties; **4** (share, involvement) rôle *m* (**in** dans); **I want no ~ in it** je ne veux pas m'en mêler; **to take ~** participer (**in** à); **5** (actor's role) rôle *n* (**of** de); **6** (equal measure) mesure *f*; **mix X and Y in equal ~s** mélangez une quantité égale de X et Y; **7** (Mus) (for instrument, voice) partie *f*; (score) partition *f*; **8** (behalf) **on the ~ of** de la part de; **9** (US) (in hair) raie *f*.
II *adv* **~ French, ~ Chinese** moitié français, moitié Chinois.
III *vtr* séparer [*two people*]; écarter [*legs*]; entrouvrir [*lips, curtains*]; **to ~ one's hair** se faire une raie.
IV *vi* **1** (split up) se séparer; **to ~ from sb** quitter qn; **2** [*crowd, clouds*] s'ouvrir.
IDIOMS **to look the ~** avoir la tête de l'emploi.
■ **part with**: **~ with [sth]** se séparer de [*object*]; **to ~ with money** débourser.

part exchange *n* (GB) reprise *f*; **to take sth in ~** reprendre qch.

partial *adj* **1** (not complete) partiel/-ielle; **2** (biased) partial; **3** (fond) **to be ~ to** avoir un faible pour.

partially *adv* **1** (incompletely) partiellement; **2** (with bias) avec partialité.

partially sighted *adj* malvoyant.

participant *n* participant/-e *m/f* (**in** à).

participate *vi* participer (**in** à).

participation *n* participation *f* (**in** à).

participle *n* participe *m*.

particle *n* particule *f*.

particular I *adj* **1** (specific) particulier/-ière; **is there any ~ colour you would prefer?** est-ce que vous désirez une couleur en particulier?; **2** (special, exceptional) particulier/-ière; **to take ~ care over sth** faire qch avec un soin tout particulier; **3** (fussy) méticuleux/-euse; **to be ~ about** être exigeant sur [*cleanliness, punctuality*]; prendre grand soin de [*appearance*]; être difficile pour [*food*];
II **in particular** *phr* en particulier.

particularly *adv* **1** (in particular) en particulier; **2** (especially) spécialement.

particulars *n pl* (information) détails *mpl*; (name, address) coordonnées *fpl*; (for missing person, suspect) signalement *m*; (for vehicle, stolen goods) description *f*.

parting I *n* **1** (division) séparation *f*; **2** (GB) (in hair) raie *f*.
II *adj* [*gift, words*] d'adieu; **~ shot** flèche *f* du Parthe.

partisan *n* (gen, Mil) partisan *m*.

partition I *n* **1** (in room, house) cloison *f*; **2** (of country) partition *f*.
II *vtr* **1** cloisonner [*area, room*]; **2** diviser [*country*].

partly *adv* en partie.

partner *n* **1** (professional) associé/-e *m/f* (**in** dans); **business ~** associé/-e *m/f*; **general ~** commandité/-e *m/f*; **limited ~** commanditaire *mf*; **2** (economic, political, sporting) partenaire *m*; **3** (married) époux/-se *m/f*; (unmarried) partenaire *mf*.

partnership *n* **1** (Law) association *f*; **to go into ~ with** s'associer à; **2** (alliance) partenariat *m*; **3** (pairing) association *f*; **a working ~** une équipe.

part: **~ of speech** *n* partie *f* du discours; **~ owner** *n* copropriétaire *mf*; **~ payment** *n* règlement *m* partiel; **~-time** *adj, adv* [*work, worker*] à temps partiel.

party I *n* **1** (social event) fête *f*; (in evening) soirée *f*; (formal) réception *f*; **birthday ~** (fête d')anniversaire *m*; **children's ~** goûter *m* d'enfants; **leaving ~** pot *m* de départ; **2** (group) groupe *m*; (Mil) détachement *m*; **rescue ~** équipe *f* de secouristes; **3** (in politics) parti *m*; **4** (Law) partie *f*; **5 to be a ~ to** être complice de [*crime*].
II *noun modifier* **1** [*spirit*] de fête; **2** [*member, policy*] du parti.

party: **~ game** *n* jeu *m* de société; **~goer** *n* fêtard/-e° *m/f*; **~ hat** *n* chapeau *m* en papier.

party line *n* **1 the ~** la ligne du parti; **2** (phone line) ligne *f* commune.

pass I *n* **1** (to enter, leave) laisser-passer *m inv*; (for journalists) coupe-file *m inv*; (to be absent) permission *f*; **2** (travel document) carte *f* d'abonnement; **3** (Sch, Univ) (success) moyenne *f* (**in** en); **to get a ~** être reçu; **4** (Sport) (in ball games) passe *f*; (in fencing) botte *f*; **5** (in mountains) col *m*.
II *vtr* **1** passer [*checkpoint, customs*]; passer devant [*building, area*]; dépasser [*vehicle, level, expectation*]; **to ~ sb in the street** croiser qn dans la rue; **2** (hand over) (directly) passer; (indirectly) faire passer; **~ me your plate** passe-moi ton assiette; **3** (move) passer [*ball*]; **~ the rope through the ring** passez la corde dans l'anneau; **4** (spend) passer [*time*] (**doing** à faire); **5** (succeed in) [*person*] réussir; [*car, machine*] passer [qch] (avec succès); **6** admettre [*candidate*]; approuver [*invoice*]; **7** adopter [*bill, motion*]; **8** prononcer [*sentence*]; **to ~ a remark about sb/sth** faire une remarque sur qn/qch; **9** (Med) **to ~ blood** avoir du sang dans les urines.
III *vi* **1** [*person, car, time, crisis*] passer; [*property*] passer (**to** à); **let me ~** laissez-moi passer; **to ~ unnoticed** passer inaperçu; **he'd ~ for an Italian** il pourrait passer pour un Italien; **she ~es for 40** on lui donnerait 40 ans; **2** (in exam) réussir.
IDIOMS **to make a ~ at sb** faire du plat° à qn; **to ~ the word** passer la consigne.
■ **pass around, pass round**: **~ [sth] around, ~ around [sth]** faire circuler [*document, photos*]; faire passer [*food, plates*].
■ **pass away** décéder.
■ **pass by** [*procession*] défiler; [*person*] passer.
■ **pass down**: **~ [sth] down, ~ down [sth]** transmettre (**from** de; **to** à).
■ **pass off**: ¶ **~ off** [*demonstration*] se dérouler; ¶ **~ [sb/sth] off, ~ off [sb/sth]** faire passer (**as** pour).
■ **pass on**: **~ [sth] on, ~ on [sth]** transmettre [*condolences, message*]; passer [*clothes, cold*] (**to** à).
■ **pass out 1** (faint) perdre connaissance; (fall drunk) tomber ivre mort; **2** (Mil) sortir avec ses diplômes (**of, from** de).
■ **pass over**: ¶ **~ [sb] over** délaisser; ¶ **~ over [sth]** ne pas tenir compte de.
■ **pass through**: **~ through [sth]** traverser.

passable *adj* **1** [*standard, quality*] passable; [*knowledge, performance*] assez bon/bonne; **2** [*road*] praticable; [*river*] franchissable.

passage *n* **1** (also **~way**) (indoors) corridor *m*; (outdoors) passage *m*; **2** (Anat) conduit *m*; **nasal ~s** fosses *fpl* nasales; **3** (in book) passage *m*; **4** (movement) passage *m*; **5** (journey) traversée *f*.

passenger *n* (in car, plane, ship) passager/-ère *m/f*; (in train, bus, on underground) voyageur/-euse *m/f*.

passerby *n* passant/-e *m/f*.

passing *adj* **1** [*motorist, policeman*] qui passe/qui passait; **2** [*whim*] passager/-ère; **3** [*reference*] en passant *inv*; **4** [*resemblance*] vague (*before n*).

passion *n* **1** (love, feeling) passion *f*; **2** (anger) colère *f*.

passionate *adj* [*kiss, person, speech, plea*] passionné; [*advocate*] ardent; **to have a ~ belief in** croire passionnément à.

passionately *adv* [*love, kiss, believe*] passionnément; [*write*] avec passion; [*defend, want*] ardemment; [*oppose*] farouchement.

passive I *n* **the ~** le passif, la voix passive.
II *adj* passif/-ive.

pass: **~key** *n* passe *m*; **~ mark** *n* (Sch, Univ) moyenne *f*.

Passover *n* Pâque *f* juive.

pass: **~port** *n* passeport *m*; **~word** *n* mot *m* de passe.

past

■ **Note** For a full set of translations for *past* used in clocktime, consult the Usage Note ▶ 554.

I *n* **1** passé *m*; **in the ~** dans le passé; **she has a ~** elle a un passé chargé; **2** (also **~ tense**) passé *m*; **in the ~** au passé.
II *adj* **1** (preceding) [*weeks, months*] dernier/-ière (*before n*); **during the ~ few days** ces derniers jours; **2** (former) [*times, problems, experience*] passé; [*president*] ancien/-ienne (*before n*); [*government*] précédent; **in times ~** autrefois, jadis; **3 summer is ~** l'été est fini; **that's all ~** c'est du passé.
III *prep* **1 to walk** or **go ~ sb/sth** passer devant qn/qch; **to drive ~ sth** passer devant qch (en voiture); **2** (in time) **it's ~ 6** il est 6 heures passées; **twenty ~ two** deux heures vingt; **half ~ two** deux heures et demie; **he is ~ 70** il a 70 ans passés; **3** (beyond) après; **~ the church** après l'église; **he didn't get ~ the first chapter** il n'est pas allé plus loin que le premier chapitre; **he didn't get ~ the first interview** il n'a pas passé la barrière du premier entretien; **to be ~ caring** ne plus s'en faire.
IV *adv* **to go** or **walk ~** passer.
IDIOMS **to be ~ it**° avoir passé l'âge; **to be ~ its best** [*food*] être un peu avancé; [*wine*] être un peu éventé; **I wouldn't put it ~ him (to do)** ça ne m'étonnerait pas de lui (qu'il fasse).

pasta *n* pâtes *fpl* (alimentaires).

paste I *n* **1** (glue) colle *f*; **2** (mixture) pâte *f*; **3** (Culin) (fish, meat) pâté *m*; (vegetable) purée *f*.

II *vtr* coller (**onto** sur; **into** dans; **together** ensemble).

pastel I *n* **1** (artistic medium, stick) pastel *m*; **2** (also **~ drawing**) dessin *m* au pastel.
II *noun modifier* [*colour, pink, shade*] pastel.

pasteurize *vtr* pasteuriser.

past historic *n* passé *m* simple.

pastime *n* passe-temps *m inv*.

pastor ▶805| *n* pasteur *m*.

pastoral *adj* **1** (in art, literature) pastoral; **2** (GB) [*role, work*] de conseiller/-ère.

past perfect *n* plus-que-parfait *m*.

pastrami *n* bœuf *m* fumé.

pastry *n* **1** (mixture) pâte *f*; **2** (cake) pâtisserie *f*.

past tense *n* passé *m*.

pasture *n* (land) pré *m*, pâturage *m*; (grass) herbe *f*.

pat I *n* **1** (gentle tap) petite tape *f*; **2** (of butter) noix *f*; (larger) morceau *m*.
II *vtr* tapoter [*hand*]; caresser [*dog*]; **to ~ one's hair into place** arranger ses cheveux.
IDIOMS **to have sth off** (GB) or **down ~** connaître qch par cœur.

patch I *n* **1** (in clothes) pièce *f*; (on tyre, airbed) rustine® *f*; (on eye) bandeau *m*; **2** (of snow, ice) plaque *f*; (of damp, rust, sunlight) tache *f*; (of fog) nappe *f*; (of oil) flaque *f*; (of blue sky) coin *m*; **3** (area of ground) zone *f*; (for planting) carré *m*; **a ~ of grass** un coin d'herbe; **4**° (GB) (territory) territoire *m*; **5**° (period) période *f*.
II *vtr* rapiécer [*hole, trousers*]; réparer [*tyre*].
■ **patch up**: ¶ **~ up [sth]**, **~ [sth] up** soigner [*person*]; rapiécer [*hole, trousers*]; réparer [*tyre*]; rafistoler° [*marriage*]; ¶ **~ up [sth]** résoudre [*differences*].

patchy *adj* [*essay, quality*] inégal; [*knowledge*] incomplet/-ète.

patent I *n* (document) brevet *m* (**for, on** pour).
II *adj* **1** (obvious) manifeste; **2** (licensed) breveté.
III *vtr* faire breveter.

patent leather *n* (cuir *m*) verni *m*.

patently *adv* manifestement.

paternal *adj* paternel/-elle.

paternity *n* paternité *f*.

paternity suit *n* action *f* en recherche de paternité.

path *n* **1** (track) (also **~way**) chemin *m*; (narrower) sentier *m*; (in garden) allée *f*; **2** (course) (of projectile, vehicle, sun) trajectoire *f*; (of river) cours *m*; (of hurricane) itinéraire *m*; **destroying everything in its ~** détruisant tout sur son passage; **3** (option) voie *f*; **4** (means) (difficult) chemin *m* (**to** de); (easy) route *f* (**to** de).

pathetic *adj* **1** (moving) pathétique; **2** (inadequate) misérable; **3**° lamentable.

pathological *adj* [*fear, hatred*] pathologique; [*jealousy*] maladif/ive.

pathologist ▶805| *n* (doing post-mortems) médecin *m* légiste; (specialist in pathology) pathologiste *mf*.

pathology *n* pathologie *f*.

patience ▶649| *n* **1** (virtue) patience *f* (**with** avec); **2** (game) réussite *f*.

patient I *n* patient/-e *m/f*; **heart ~** patient souffrant d'une maladie cardiaque.
II *adj* patient (**with** avec).

patiently *adv* avec patience, patiemment.

patio *n* **1** (terrace) terrasse *f*; **2** (courtyard) patio *m*.

patriotic *adj* [*mood, song*] patriotique; [*person*] patriote.

patriotism *n* patriotisme *m*.

patrol I *n* patrouille *f*; **to carry out a ~** faire une ronde.
II *vtr, vi* patrouiller.

patrol: **~ boat**, **~ vessel** *n* patrouilleur *m*; **~ car** *n* voiture *f* de police.

patron *n* **1** (of artist) mécène *m*; (of person) protecteur/-trice *m/f*; (of charity) bienfaiteur/-trice *m/f*; **to be ~ of an organization** parrainer une organisation; **2** (client) client/-e *m/f* (**of** de).

patronize *vtr* **1** traiter [qn] avec condescendance; **don't ~ me!** ne prends pas cet air supérieur avec moi!; **2** fréquenter [*restaurant, cinema*]; se fournir chez [*grocer's*]; **3** protéger [*charity, the arts*].

patronizing *adj* condescendant.

patron saint *n* saint/-e *m/f* patron/-onne (**of** de).

patter I *n* (of rain) crépitement *m*; **~ of footsteps** bruit *m* de pas rapides et légers.
II *vi* [*child, mouse*] trottiner; [*rain, hailstones*] crépiter.

pattern *n* **1** (design) dessin *m*, motif *m*; **2** (regular way of happening) **behaviour ~** mode *m* de comportement; **the current ~ of events** la situation actuelle; **to follow a set ~** se dérouler toujours de la même façon; **weather ~s** tendances *fpl* climatiques; **3** (in dressmaking) patron *m*; (in knitting) modèle *m*; **4** (sample) échantillon *m*.

patterned *adj* [*fabric*] à motifs.

patty *n* **1** (US) (in hamburger) steak *m* haché; **2** (pie) petit feuilleté *m*.

pauper *n* indigent/-e *m/f*.

pause I *n* **1** (silence) silence *m*; **2** (break) pause *f*; **3** (stoppage) interruption *f*.
II *vi* **1** (stop speaking) marquer une pause; **2** (stop) s'arrêter; **to ~ in** interrompre [*activity*]; **to ~ for thought** faire une pause pour réfléchir; **3** (hesitate) hésiter.

pave *vtr* paver (**with** de).
IDIOMS **to ~ the way for sth** ouvrir la voie à qch.

pavement *n* **1** (GB) (footpath) trottoir *m*; **2** (US) (roadway) chaussée *f*; (road surface) revêtement *m* (de la chaussée); **3** (US) (material) dallage *m*.

pavilion *n* pavillon *m*.

paving slab, **paving stone** *n* dalle *f*.

paw I *n* patte *f*.
II *vtr* **to ~ the ground** [*horse*] piaffer; [*bull*] frapper le sol du sabot.

pawn I *n* pion *m*.
II *vtr* mettre [qch] au mont-de-piété.

pawn: **~broker** ▶805| *n* prêteur/-euse *m/f* sur gages; **~shop** *n* mont-de-piété *m*.

pay I *n* salaire *m*; (on forms) traitement *m*; (to soldier) solde *f*; **back ~** rappel *m* de salaire.
II *noun modifier* [*claim, deal*] salarial; [*rise, cut*] de salaire; [*freeze*] des salaires.
III *vtr* **1** (for goods, services) payer; **to ~ cash** payer comptant; **to ~ sth into** verser qch sur [*account*]; **all expenses paid** tous frais payés; **2** rapporter [*interest*]; **to ~ dividends** (figurative) porter ses fruits; **3** (give) **to ~ attention to** faire attention à; **to ~ a tribute to sb** rendre hommage à qn; **to ~ sb a compliment** faire des compliments à qn; **to ~ sb a visit** rendre visite à qn; **4** (benefit) **it would ~ him to do** il y gagnerait à faire; **it doesn't ~ to do** cela ne sert à rien de faire.
IV *vi* **1** [*person*] payer; **to ~ for sth** payer qch; **they're paying for him to go to college** ils lui paient ses études; **you have to ~ to get in** l'entrée est payante; **to ~ one's own way** payer sa part; **the work doesn't ~ very well** le travail est mal payé; **2** [*business*] rapporter; [*activity*] payer; **to ~ for itself** [*business, purchase*] s'amortir.
■ **pay back**: **~ [sb/sth] back** rembourser.
■ **pay down**: **~ [sth] down** verser un acompte de.
■ **pay in** (GB): **~ [sth] in**, **~ in [sth]** déposer.
■ **pay off**: ¶ **~ off** être payant; ¶ **~ [sb] off**, **~ off [sb]** (dismiss) congédier [*worker*]; ¶ **~ off [sth]**, **~ [sth] off** rembourser.
■ **pay out**: **~ out [sth]** débourser (**in** pour).
■ **pay up**○ payer.

payable *adj* **1** (which will be paid) à payer; **to make a cheque ~ to** faire un chèque à l'ordre de; **2 to be ~** être payable; **~ on demand** payable à vue.

pay-as-you-earn, **PAYE** *n* (GB) (tax) prélèvement *m* de l'impôt à la source.

pay: **~ cheque** (GB), **~ check** (US) *n* chèque *m* de paie; **~day** *n* (for wages) jour *m* de paie; (in stock exchange) séance *f* de liquidation; **~desk** *n* caisse *f*.

payee *n* bénéficiaire *mf*.

paying guest *n* hôte *m* payant.

payment *n* paiement *m*; (in settlement) règlement *m*; (into account, of instalments) versement *m*; (to creditor) remboursement *m*; **cash ~** (not credit) paiement comptant; (not cheque) paiement en liquide; **monthly ~** mensualité.

pay: **~ phone** *n* téléphone *m* public; **~roll** *n* (list) fichier *m* des salaires; (sum of money) paie *f* (de tous les employés); (employees collectively) ensemble *m* du personnel; **~slip** *n* bulletin *m* de salaire.

pc, **PC** *n* (*abbr* = **personal computer**) ordinateur *m* (personnel).

PE *n* (*abbr* = **physical education**) éducation *f* physique.

pea *n* **1** (plant) pois *m*; **2** (Culin) (also **green ~**) petit pois *m*.

peace I *n* paix *f*; **to be at ~** (free from war) être en paix; (dead) avoir trouvé la paix; **to keep the ~** (between countries, individuals) maintenir la paix; (in town) [*police*] maintenir l'ordre public; [*citizen*] ne pas troubler l'ordre public; **I need a bit of ~ and quiet** j'ai besoin d'un peu de calme; **to find ~ of mind** trouver la paix.
II *noun modifier* [*plan, talks*] de paix; [*campaign, march*] pour la paix.

peace envoy *n* négociateur/-trice *m/f* de paix.

peaceful *adj* **1** (tranquil) paisible; **2** (without conflict) pacifique.

peacefully *adv* **1** [*sleep*] paisiblement; **2** (without violence) pacifiquement.

peace: **~keeping** *adj* [*force, troops*] de maintien de la paix; **~-loving** *adj* pacifique; **~maker** *n* (in diplomacy) artisan *m* de la paix; (in family) conciliateur *m*; **~ offering** *n* gage *m* de réconciliation.

peach *n* **1** (fruit, colour) pêche *f*; **2** (also **~ tree**) pêcher *m*.

peacock *n* paon *m*.

peak I *n* **1** (of mountain) pic *m* (**of** de); **2** (of cap) visière *f*; **3** (of inflation, demand, price) maximum *m* (**in** dans; **of** de); (on a graph) sommet *m*; **4** (of career, empire, creativity) apogée *m* (**of** de); (of fitness, form) meilleur *m* (**of** de); **in the ~ of condition** en excellente santé; **to be past its** or **one's ~** avoir fait son temps.
II *noun modifier* [*figure, level, price*] maximum; [*fitness*] meilleur.
III *vi* culminer (**at** à); **to ~ too early** [*runner*] se lancer à fond trop tôt; [*prodigy*] s'épanouir trop tôt; (in career) réussir trop tôt.

peaked *adj* **1** [*cap, hat*] à visière; [*roof*] pointu; **2** (US) pâlot/otte.

peak: **~ period** *n* période *f* de pointe; **~ rate** *n* (for phone calls) tarif *m* rouge; **~ time** *n* (on TV) heures *fpl* de grande écoute; (for switchboard, traffic) heures *fpl* de pointe.

peaky○ *adj* pâlot/-otte.

peal *n* (of bells) carillonnement *m*; (of doorbell) sonnerie *f*; **~s of laughter** éclats *mpl* de rire.

peanut *n* (nut) cacahuète *f*; (plant) arachide *f*.

pear *n* **1** (fruit) poire *f*; **2** (also **~ tree**) poirier *m*.

pearl ▶ 559 I *n* **1** (gem) perle *f* (**of** de); **2** (person, object) perle *f*; (city, building) joyau *m*; **~s of wisdom** trésors *mpl* de sagesse; **3** (colour) (couleur *f*) perle *f*.
II *noun modifier* [*necklace, brooch*] de perles; [*button*] en nacre.

peasant *n* paysan/-anne *m/f*.

peat *n* tourbe *f*.

pebble *n* caillou *m*; (on beach) galet *m*.

pecan *n* **1** (nut) noix *f* de pecan; **2** (tree) pacanier *m*.

peck I *vtr* [*bird*] picorer [*food*]; donner un coup de bec à [*person, animal*].
II *vi* **1** [*bird*] **to ~ at** picorer [*food*]; donner des coups de bec contre [*window, tree*]; **2**○ **to ~ at one's food** [*person*] chipoter.

pecking order *n* ordre *m* hiérarchique.

pectorals *n pl* (also **pecs**○) pectoraux *mpl*.

peculiar *adj* **1** (odd) bizarre; **to feel ~** se sentir bizarre; **2** [*situation*] particulier/-ière; **3 to be ~ to** être particulier/-ière à or propre à.

peculiarity *n* **1** (feature) particularité *f*; **2** (strangeness) bizarrerie *f*.
pedagogic(al) *adj* pédagogique.
pedal I *n* pédale *f*.
II *vi* pédaler; **to ~ hard** pédaler dur.
pedal: **~ bin** *n* (GB) poubelle *f* à pédale; **~ boat** *n* pédalo® *m*.
pedantic *adj* pédant.
peddle *vtr* colporter [*wares, ideas*]; **to ~ drugs** revendre de la drogue.
peddler *n* **1** (in street) colporteur *m*; **2 drug ~** revendeur/-euse *m/f* de drogue.
pedestal *n* (of statue, ornament) socle *m*, piédestal *m*; (of washbasin) colonne *f*.
IDIOMS **to put sb on a ~** mettre qn sur un piédestal.
pedestrian *n* piéton *m*.
pedestrian: **~ crossing** *n* passage *m* pour piétons, passage *m* clouté; **~ precinct** *n* (GB) zone *f* piétonne; **~ street** *n* rue *f* piétonne.
pediatrician (US) ▶ **paediatrician**.
pedicure *n* **to have a ~** se faire soigner les pieds.
pedigree I *n* **1** (ancestry) (of animal) pedigree *m*; (of person, family) (line) ascendance *f*; (tree, chart) arbre *m* généalogique; **2** (purebred animal) animal *m* avec pedigree.
II *noun modifier* [*animal*] de pure race.
pee° *n* pipi° *m*; **to have** or **do a ~** faire pipi°.
peek *n* **to have a ~ at** jeter un coup d'œil furtif à.
peel I *n* peau *f*; (of citrus) écorce *f*; (of onion) pelure *f*; (peelings) épluchures *fpl*.
II *vtr* éplucher [*vegetable, fruit*]; décortiquer [*prawn*]; écorcer [*stick*].
III *vi* [*skin*] peler; [*fruit, vegetable*] s'éplucher.
■ **peel off**: ¶ **~ off** [*label*] se détacher (**from** de); [*paint*] s'écailler; [*paper*] se décoller; ¶ **~ off [sth]**, **~ [sth] off** enlever [*clothing, label, leaves*].
peelings *n pl* épluchures *fpl*.
peep I *n* **1 to have a ~ at sth** jeter un coup d'œil à qch; (furtively) regarder qch à la dérobée; **2** (of chick) pépiement *m*.
II *vi* **1** jeter un coup d'œil (**over** par-dessus; **through** par); **to ~ at sth/sb** jeter un coup d'œil à qch/qn; (furtively) regarder qch/qn furtivement; **2** [*chick*] pépier.
peephole *n* (in fence) trou *m*; (in door) judas *m*.
peer I *n* **1** (equal) (in status) pair *m*; (in profession) collègue *m/f*; **2** (contemporary) (adult) personne *f* de la même génération; (teenager) adolescent/-e *m/f* du même âge; (child) enfant *mf* du même âge; **3** (person of equal merit) égal/-e *m/f*; **4** (GB) pair *m*.
II *vi* **to ~ at** scruter, regarder attentivement.
peer group *n* **1** (of same status) pairs *mpl*; **2** (contemporaries) (adults) personnes *fpl* de la même génération; (children) enfants *mpl* du même âge.
peevish *adj* grognon.
peg I *n* **1** (to hang garment) patère *f*; **2** (GB) (also **clothes ~**) pince *f* à linge; **3** (to mark place) piquet *m*; **4** (in carpentry, music) cheville *f*; **5** (Econ) indice *m*; **6** (barrel stop) fausset *m*.
II *vtr* **1 to ~ sth on** or **onto a line** accrocher qch à une corde avec des pinces; **to ~ sth down** or **in place** fixer qch avec des piquets; **2** (fasten wood) cheviller (**to** à; **together** ensemble); **3** (Econ) indexer (**to** sur).
pejorative *adj* péjoratif/-ive.
Peking ▶ 574 *pr n* Pékin.
pelican *n* pélican *m*.
pellet *n* **1** (of paper, wax, mud) boulette *f*; **2** (of shot) plomb *m*.
pelmet *n* cantonnière *f*.
pelt I *n* (fur) fourrure *f*; (hide) peau *f*.
II *vtr* bombarder (**with sth** de qch).
III *vi* (also **~ down**) tomber à verse.
pelvis ▶ 523 *n* bassin *m*, pelvis *m*.
pen I *n* **1** (for writing) stylo *m*; **to put ~ to paper** (write) écrire, prendre la plume; **2** (for animals) parc *m*, enclos *m*; **3** (Zool) cygne *m* femelle.
II *vtr* **1** (write) écrire; **2** (also **~ in**) enfermer, parquer.
penal *n* [*reform, law, code, system*] pénal; [*colony, institution*] pénitentiaire.
penalize *vtr* pénaliser.
penalty *n* **1** (punishment) peine *f*, pénalité *f*; (fine) amende *f*; **on ~ of** sous peine de; **2** (figurative) prix *m* (**for** de); **3** (in soccer) penalty *m*; (in rugby) pénalité *f*.
penance *n* pénitence *f*.
pencil I *n* crayon *m*; **in ~** au crayon.
II *vtr* écrire [qch] au crayon.
pencil: **~ case** *n* trousse *f* (à crayons); **~ sharpener** *n* taille-crayon *m*.
pendant *n* **1** (necklace) pendentif *m*; **2** (on chandelier) pendeloque *f*.
pending I *adj* **1** [*case, charge*] en instance; [*matter*] en souffrance; **patent ~** brevet en instance d'homologation; **2** (imminent) imminent.
II *prep* en attendant.
pendulum *n* pendule *m*, balancier *m*.
penetrate I *vtr* **1** pénétrer [*protective layer, territory*]; percer [*cloud, silence, defences*]; traverser [*wall*]; **2** pénétrer [*market, mind, ideas*]; infiltrer [*organization*].
II *vi* **1** (enter) pénétrer (**into** dans; **as far as** jusqu'à); **2** [*sound*] parvenir (**to** à).
penetrating *adj* [*cold, eyes, question*] pénétrant; [*sound, voice*] perçant.
penetration *n* (entering) pénétration *f*; (by spies) infiltration *f*.
pen friend *n* correspondant/-e *m/f*.
penguin *n* pingouin *m*, manchot *m*.
penicillin *n* pénicilline *f*.
peninsula *n* péninsule *f*.
penis *n* pénis *m*.
penitent *n, adj* pénitent/-e (*m/f*).
penitentiary *n* (US) prison *f*.
pen: **~knife** *n* canif *m*; **~ name** *n* pseudonyme *m*, nom *m* de plume.
pennant *n* **1** (flag) (on boat) flamme *f*; (in competition, procession, on car) fanion *m*; **2** (US Sport) championnat *m*.

penny *n* **1** (small amount of money) ≈ centime *m*; **not to have a ~ to one's name** être sans le sou; **2** (GB) (unit of currency) penny *m*; **a five pence** or **five p piece** une pièce de cinq pence; **a 25p stamp** un timbre-poste à 25 pence; **3** (US) cent *m*.
IDIOMS **the ~ dropped**○ ça a fait tilt○.

penny-pinching *adj* grippe-sou *inv*.

pension *n* **1** (from state) pension *f*; **to be** or **live on a ~** être pensionné; **2** (from employer) retraite *f*; **company ~** retraite *f* de société; **3** (hotel) pension *f*.

pensionable *adj* [*post, service*] donnant droit à une retraite; [*employee*] ayant droit à la retraite; **to be of ~ age** avoir l'âge de la retraite.

pensioner *n* retraité/-e *m/f*.

pension: **~ fund** *n* fonds *m* d'assurance-vieillesse; **~ plan**, **~ scheme** *n* plan *m* de retraite.

pentagon *n* **1** (in mathematics) pentagone *m*; **2 the Pentagon** (US) le Pentagone *m*.

pentathlon *n* pentathlon *m*.

Pentecost *n* Pentecôte *f*.

penthouse *n* **1** (flat) appartement *m* de grand standing; **2** (roof) auvent *m*.

pent-up *adj* [*energy, frustration*] contenu; [*feelings*] réprimé.

peony *n* pivoine *f*.

people I *n* (nation) peuple *m*; **the English-speaking ~s** les anglophones *mpl*.
II *n pl* **1** (in general) gens *mpl*; (specified or counted) personnes *fpl*; **old ~** les personnes âgées; **they're nice ~** ce sont des gens sympathiques; **there were a lot of ~** il y avait beaucoup de monde; **other ~'s property** le bien des autres; **~ in general** la plupart des gens; **2** (of a town) habitants *mpl*; (of a country) peuple *m*; **3** (citizens, subjects) **the ~** le peuple; **a man of the ~** un homme du peuple; **4**○ (relations) famille *f*; (parents) parents *mpl*.

■ **Note** *gens* is masculine plural and never countable. When counting people, you must use *personnes* rather than *gens*: *three people* = trois personnes.
– When used with *gens*, some adjectives such as *vieux, bon, mauvais, petit, vilain* placed before *gens* take the feminine form: *les vieilles gens*.

pep *v* ■ **pep up**: **~ [sb] up**, **~ up [sb]** remettre [qn] d'aplomb.

pepper I *n* **1** (spice) poivre *m*; **black/white ~** poivre noir/blanc; **2** (vegetable) poivron *m*.
II *vtr* **1** poivrer [*food*]; **2 to be ~ed with** être parsemé de [*swearwords, criticisms*].

pepper: **~corn** *n* grain *m* de poivre; **~ mill** *n* moulin *m* à poivre; **~ pot**, **~ shaker** *n* poivrier *m*.

pep: **~ pill**○ *n* excitant *m*; **~ talk**○ *n* laïus○ *m* d'encouragement.

peptic ulcer *n* ulcère *m* de l'estomac.

per *prep* **1** par; **~ head** par tête or personne; **80 km ~ hour** 80 km à l'heure; **£5 ~ hour** 5 livres (de) l'heure; **2 as ~ invoice** suivant facture; **as ~ your instructions** conformément à vos instructions.

per capita *adj, adv* par personne.

perceive *vtr* percevoir; **to ~ oneself as (being) sth** se percevoir comme qch.

per cent, pc I *n* pour cent *m*.
II *adj, adv* pour cent.

percentage I *n* pourcentage *m*; **to get a ~ on** toucher un pourcentage sur [*sale*].
II *noun modifier* [*increase, decrease, change*] en pourcentage.

perceptible *adj* perceptible (**to** à).

perception *n* **1** perception *f*; **2** (view) **my ~ of him** l'idée que je me fais de lui; **the popular ~ of** l'idée que les gens se font de.

perceptive *adj* [*person*] perspicace; [*analysis*] fin; [*article*] intelligent.

perceptiveness *n* (of person) perspicacité *f*; (of essay, novel) finesse *f*.

perch I *n* **1** (for bird) perchoir *m*; **2** (seat) perchoir *m*; **3** (fish) perche *f*.
II *vi* se percher (**on** sur).

percolate I *vtr* passer [*coffee*]; **~d coffee** café fait dans une cafetière à pression.
II *vi* (also **~ through**) [*coffee, water*] passer; [*information*] filtrer (**into, to** jusqu'à).

percolator *n* cafetière *f* à pression.

percussion instrument *n* instrument *m* à percussion.

percussionist *n* percussionniste *mf*.

percussion section *n* percussions *fpl*.

perennial *adj* **1** (recurring) perpétuel/-elle; **2** [*plant*] vivace.

perfect I *n* parfait *m*; **in the ~** au parfait.
II *adj* **1** (gen) parfait (**for** pour); [*moment, name, place, partner, solution*] idéal (**for** pour); [*hostess*] exemplaire; **that screw will be ~ for the job** cette vis fera parfaitement l'affaire; **that jacket is a ~ fit** cette veste va parfaitement; **2** [*stranger, fool*] parfait (*before n*); [*pest*] véritable (*before n*); **3 the ~ tense** le parfait.
III *vtr* perfectionner.

perfection *n* perfection *f* (**of** de); **to ~** à la perfection.

perfectionist *n, adj* perfectionniste (*mf*).

perfectly *adv* **1** (totally) tout à fait; **to be ~ entitled to do** avoir parfaitement le droit de faire; **2** (very well) [*fit, illustrate*] parfaitement.

perforate *vtr* perforer.

perforated ulcer ▶ 686 *n* perforation *f* ulcéreuse.

perform I *vtr* **1** exécuter [*task*]; accomplir [*duties*]; procéder à [*operation*]; **2** jouer [*play*]; chanter [*song*]; exécuter [*dance, trick*]; **3** célébrer [*ceremony*].
II *vi* **1** [*actor, musician*] jouer; **2 to ~ well/badly** [*team*] bien/mal jouer; [*interviewee*] faire bonne/mauvaise impression; [*exam candidate, company, department*] avoir de bons/de mauvais résultats.

performance *n* **1** (rendition) interprétation *f* (**of** de); **2** (concert, show, play) représentation *f* (**of** de); **to put on a ~ of Hamlet** donner une représentation d'Hamlet; **3** (of team, sportsman) performance *f* (**in** à); **4** (economic, political record) performances *fpl*; **5** (of duties) exercice *m* (**of** de); (of rite) célébration *f* (**of** de); (of task) exécution *f* (**of** de); **6** (Aut) (of car, engine) performances *fpl*.

performer *n* artiste *mf*.

performing arts *n pl* arts *mpl* scéniques.

perfume I *n* parfum *m*.
II *vtr* parfumer.

perhaps *adv* peut-être; **~ she's forgotten** elle a peut-être oublié.

peril *n* péril *m*, danger *m*.

perimeter *n* périmètre *m*; **on the ~ of** aux abords de [*park, site*].

period I *n* **1** (in time) période *f*; (longer) époque *f*; **trial ~** période d'essai; **spread over a two-year ~** échelonné sur deux ans; **Picasso's blue ~** la période bleue de Picasso; **2** (US) (full stop) point *m*; **3** (menstruation) règles *fpl*; **4** (Sch) (lesson) cours *m*, leçon *f*.
II *noun modifier* (of a certain era) [*costume, furniture*] d'époque; (reproduction) [*costume*] caractéristique de l'époque; [*furniture*] de style (ancien).

periodical *n, adj* périodique (*m*).

periodic table *n* tableau *m* de classification périodique des éléments.

period: **~ of office** *n* mandat *m*; **~ pains** *n pl* règles *fpl* douloureuses.

peripheral *adj* [*vision, suburb*] périphérique; [*issue, investment*] annexe.

periphery *n* **1** (edge) périphérie *f*; **2** (fringes) **to be on the ~ of** être dans la mouvance de [*party*]; **to remain on the ~ of** rester à l'écart de [*event, movement*].

periscope *n* périscope *m*.

perish *vi* **1** (die) périr (**from** de); **2** [*food*] se gâter; [*rubber*] se détériorer.

perishables *n pl* denrées *fpl* périssables.

periwinkle *n* **1** (flower) pervenche *f*; **2** (shellfish) bigorneau *m*; **3** ▶559 (also **~ blue**) bleu *m* pervenche.

perjure *v refl* **to ~ oneself** faire un faux témoignage.

perjury *n* faux témoignage *m*.

perk○ *n* (advantage) avantage *m*; (benefit in kind) avantage *m* en nature.
■ **perk up** [*person*] se ragaillardir; [*business, life, plant*] reprendre.

perky *adj* guilleret/-ette.

perm *n* permanente *f*; **to have a ~** se faire faire une permanente.

permanence *n* permanence *f*.

permanent I *n* (US) permanente *f*.
II *adj* [*job, disability, exhibition, address*] permanent; [*premises, closure*] définitif/-ive; [*contract*] à durée indéterminée; [*staff*] ayant un contrat à durée indéterminée.

permanently *adv* [*happy, tired*] en permanence; [*employed, disabled*] de façon permanente; [*appointed*] à titre définitif; [*close, emigrate, settle*] définitivement.

permeate *vtr* **1** [*liquid, gas*] s'infiltrer dans; [*odour*] pénétrer dans; **2** [*ideas*] imprégner.

permissible *adj* [*level, conduct*] admissible; [*error*] acceptable.

permission *n* permission *f*; (official) autorisation *f*; **to get ~ to do** obtenir la permission or l'autorisation de faire.

permissive *adj* **1** (morally lax) permissif/-ive; **2** (liberal) [*view, law*] libéral.

permissiveness *n* permissivité *f*.

permit I *n* **1** (document) permis *m*; (official permission) autorisation *f*; **work ~** permis *m* de travail: **2** (US Aut) permis *m* (de conduire).
II *vtr* **1** (allow) permettre [*action, measure*]; **smoking is not ~ted** il est interdit de fumer; **to ~ sb to do** permettre à qn de faire; **2** (allow formally, officially) autoriser.
III *vi* permettre; **weather ~ting** si le temps le permet; **time ~ting** à condition d'en avoir le temps.

permutation *n* permutation *f*.

peroxide *n* **1** (chemical) peroxyde *m*; **2** (also **hydrogen ~**) eau *f* oxygénée.

perpendicular *adj* [*line*] perpendiculaire; **a ~ cliff face** un à-pic.

perpetrator *n* auteur *m* (**of** de).

perpetual *adj* [*meetings, longing, turmoil*] perpétuel/-elle; [*darkness, stench*] permanent.

perpetuate *vtr* perpétuer.

perplexed *adj* perplexe; **to be ~ as to why/how** se demander pourquoi/comment.

persecute *vtr* persécuter.

persecution *n* persécution *f*.

perseverance *n* persévérance *f*.

persevere *vi* persévérer (**with, at** dans).

persist *vi* persister (**in** dans; **in doing** à faire).

persistence *n* persévérance *f*; (extreme) persistance *f* (**in** dans; **in doing** à faire).

persistent *adj* **1** (persevering) persévérant; (obstinate) obstiné (**in** dans); **2** [*rain, denial*] persistant; [*enquiries, noise, pressure*] continuel/-elle; [*illness, fears, idea*] tenace.

persistent offender *n* récidiviste *mf*.

person *n* **1** personne *f*; **to do sth in ~** faire qch en personne; **he's not the kind of ~ who would do such a thing** ce n'est pas le genre à faire ça; **single ~** célibataire *mf*; **what's she like as a ~?** en tant que femme, elle est comment?; **2** (in grammar) personne *f*; **the first ~ singular** la première personne du singulier.

personable *adj* [*person*] qui présente bien.

personal I *n* (US) petite annonce *f* personnelle.
II *adj* [*opinion, life, call, matter*] personnel/-elle; [*safety, choice, income, insurance*] individuel/-elle; [*service*] personnalisé; **don't be so ~!** ne fais pas d'allusions personnelles!; **the discussion became rather ~** la discussion a pris un ton personnel; **on** or **at a ~ level** sur le plan personnel; **to make a ~ appearance** venir en personne (**at** à); **~ belongings** or **effects** effets *mpl* personnels; **~ hygiene** hygiène *f* intime; **as a ~ favour to you** pour te faire plaisir.

personal: **~ ad** *n* petite annonce *f* personnelle; **~ column** *n* petites annonces *fpl* personnelles; **~ details** *n pl* renseignements *mpl* d'ordre personnel; (more intimate) détails *mpl* intimes; (on application form) état civil *m* et coordonnées *fpl*.

personality *n* **1** (character) personnalité *f*; **2** (person) personnalité *f*.

personalize *vtr* **1** personnaliser [*stationery, clothing*]; **2** ramener [qch] à un plan personnel [*issue, dispute*].

personally *adv* personnellement; **to take sth ~** se sentir visé personnellement par qch.

personal: **~ organizer** *n* ≈ agenda *m*; **~ property** *n* biens *mpl* personnels.

personification *n* (of ideal) incarnation *f* (**of** de).

personnel *n* **1** (staff, troops) personnel *m*; **2** (also **Personnel**) service *m* du personnel.

personnel: **~ department** *n* service *m* du personnel; **~ manager** ▶805 *n* directeur/-trice *m/f* du personnel; **~ officer** ▶805 *n* responsable *m/f* du personnel.

perspective *n* perspective *f*; **to keep things in ~** garder un sens de la mesure; **to put things into ~** relativiser les choses.

perspex® *n* plexiglas® *m*.

perspiration *n* **1** (sweat) sueur *f*; **2** (sweating) transpiration *f*.

perspire *vi* transpirer.

persuade *vtr* **1** (influence) persuader; **to ~ sb to do** persuader qn de faire; **2** (convince) convaincre (**of** de); **to ~ oneself** réussir à se convaincre (**that** que).

persuasion *n* **1** (persuading) persuasion *f*; **to be open to ~** être prêt à se laisser convaincre; **2** (religion) confession *f*; **3** (political views) conviction *f*.

persuasive *adj* [*person*] persuasif/-ive; [*argument, evidence*] convaincant.

pert *adj* [*person, manner*] espiègle; [*hat, nose*] coquin.

pertain *vi* **to ~ to** (Law) dépendre de; (gen) se rapporter à.

pertinent *adj* [*question, point*] pertinent; **to be ~ to** avoir rapport à.

perturb *vtr* perturber; **to be ~ed by** être troublé par; (more deeply) être alarmé par.

pervade *vtr* imprégner.

pervasive *adj* [*smell*] pénétrant; [*feeling*] envahissant.

perverse *adj* **1** (twisted) [*person*] retors; [*desire*] pervers; **2** (contrary) [*refusal, attempt, attitude*] illogique; **to take a ~ pleasure in doing** prendre un malin plaisir à faire.

perversion *n* **1** (deviation) perversion *f* (**of** de); **2** (of facts, justice) travestissement *m* (**of** de).

perversity *n* (of person) mauvais esprit *m*; (of action) malignité *f*.

pervert I *n* pervers/-e *m/f*.
II *vtr* **1** (corrupt) corrompre; **2** (misrepresent) travestir [*truth*]; dénaturer [*meaning*]; fausser [*values*]; **to ~ the course of justice** entraver l'action de la justice.

pessimist *n* pessimiste *mf*.

pessimistic *adj* pessimiste.

pest *n* **1** (animal) animal *m* nuisible; (insect) insecte *m* nuisible; **2**○ (person) enquiquineur/-euse○ *m/f*; (little boy) garnement *m*; (little girl) chipie○ *f*.

pester *vtr* harceler; **stop ~ing me!** fiche-moi la paix○!

pet I *n* **1** (animal) animal *m* de compagnie; **'no ~s'** 'les animaux domestiques ne sont pas acceptés'; **2** (favourite) chouchou/chouchoute○ *m/f*; **3** (person) chou○ *m*; **yes ~** oui mon chou.
II *adj* [*charity, theory*] favori/-ite; **~ dog** chien.

petal *n* pétale *m*.

peter *v* ■ **peter out** [*conversation*] tarir; [*supplies*] s'épuiser.

pet: **~ food** *n* aliments *mpl* pour chiens et chats; **~ hate** (GB) *n* bête *f* noire.

petition I *n* **1** (document) pétition *f* (**to** à; **calling for** réclamant); **2** (formal request) pétition *f*.
II *vtr* adresser une pétition à [*person, body*].
III *vi* **to ~ for divorce** demander le divorce.

pet: **~ name** *n* petit nom *m*; **~ project** *n* enfant *m* chéri.

petrified *adj* pétrifié.

petrochemicals *n pl* produits *mpl* pétrochimiques.

petrol (GB) *n* essence *f*; **to fill up with ~** faire le plein (d'essence); **to run out of ~** [*car*] tomber en panne d'essence; [*garage*] ne plus avoir d'essence.

petrol: **~ bomb** *n* (GB) cocktail *m* Molotov; **~ can** *n* (GB) bidon *m* à essence.

petroleum I *n* pétrole *m*.
II *noun modifier* [*product, industry, engineer*] pétrolier/-ière.

petrol: **~ gauge** *n* (GB) jauge *f* d'essence; **~ pump** *n* (GB) (at garage, in engine) pompe *f* à essence; **~ station** *n* (GB) station *f* d'essence; **~ tanker** *n* (GB) camion-citerne *m*.

pet: **~ shop** (GB), **~ store** (US) *n* animalerie *f*; **~ subject** *n* sujet *m* favori, dada *m*.

petticoat *n* (full slip) combinaison *m*; (half slip) jupon *m*.

pettiness *n* mesquinerie *f*.

petty *adj* [*person, squabble*] mesquin; [*detail*] insignifiant.

petty: **~ cash** *n* petite caisse *f*; **~-minded** *adj* mesquin; **~ officer** *n* ≈ maître *m*.

pew *n* banc *m* (d'église).

pewter *n* étain *m*.

pharmaceutical *adj* pharmaceutique.

pharmaceuticals I *n pl* produits *mpl* pharmaceutiques.
II *noun modifier* [*industry, factory*] pharmaceutique.

pharmacist ▶805, 805 *n* pharmacien/-ienne *m/f*.

pharmacology *n* pharmacologie *f*.

pharmacy ▶805 *n* **1** (shop) pharmacie *f*; **2** (also **pharmaceutics**) pharmaceutique *f*.

phase I *n* phase *f*; **it's just a ~ (he's/they're going through)** ça lui/leur passera.
II *vtr* échelonner [*changes*] (**over** sur).

■ **phase out**: ~ **out [sth]** supprimer [qch] peu à peu.

PhD *n* (*abbr* = **Doctor of Philosophy**) doctorat *m*.

pheasant *n* faisan/-e *m/f*.

phenomenal *adj* phénoménal.

phenomenally *adv* [*stupid, successful*] extraordinairement.

phenomenon *n* phénomène *m*.

phew *excl* (in relief) ouf!; (when too hot) pff!

philanderer *n* coureur *m* de jupons○.

philanthropist *n* philanthrope *mf*.

philharmonic *adj* philharmonique.

philistine *n* béotien/-ienne *m/f*.

Phillips screwdriver *n* tournevis *m* cruciforme.

philology *n* philologie *f*.

philosopher ▶ 805 *n* philosophe *mf*.

philosophic(al) *adj* **1** [*knowledge, question*] philosophique; **2** (calm, stoical) philosophe (**about** à propos de).

philosophy *n* philosophie *f*.

phobia *n* phobie *f*.

phone I *n* téléphone *m*; **to be on the ~** (be talking) être au téléphone (**to sb** avec qn); (be subscriber) avoir le téléphone.
II *vtr* passer un coup de fil à○, téléphoner à [*person, company*].
III *vi* téléphoner; **to ~ for a taxi** appeler un taxi.
■ **phone in** téléphoner; **she ~d in sick** elle a téléphoné au bureau pour dire qu'elle était malade.

phone: ~ **book** *n* annuaire *m* (du téléphone); ~ **booth**, ~ **box** (GB) *n* cabine *f* téléphonique; ~ **call** *n* coup *m* de fil○; (more formal) communication *f* (téléphonique); ~ **card** *n* (GB) télécarte *f*; **~-in** *n* émission *f* à ligne ouverte; ~ **number** *n* numéro *m* de téléphone; ~ **tapping** *n* écoutes *fpl* téléphoniques.

phoney○ I *n* **1** (affected person) poseur/-euse *m/f*; **2** (impostor) charlatan *m*.
II *adj* [*address, accent*] faux/fausse (*before n*); [*company, excuse*] bidon○; [*emotion*] simulé.

phosphates *n pl* phosphates *mpl*, engrais *mpl* phosphatés.

photo *n* photo *f*; ▶ **photograph** I.

photo: ~ **album** *n* album *m* de photos; ~ **booth** *n* photomaton® *m*; **~call** *n* (GB) séance *f* de photos.

photocopier *n* photocopieuse *f*.

photocopy I *n* photocopie *f*.
II *vtr* photocopier.

photo: ~ **finish** *n* arrivée *f* départagée au photo-finish; **~genic** *adj* photogénique.

photograph I *n* photo *f*; **in the ~** sur la photo; **to take a ~ of sb/sth** prendre qn/qch en photo.
II *vtr* photographier, prendre [qn/qch] en photo.

photographer ▶ 805 *n* photographe *mf*.

photographic *adj* [*image, reproduction, equipment*] photographique; [*studio*] de photo; [*shop, agency, exhibition*] de photos; **to have a ~ memory** avoir une mémoire visuelle exceptionnelle.

photography *n* photographie *f*.

photo: **~journalist** ▶ 805 *n* photojournaliste *mf*; ~ **opportunity** *n* séance *f* de photos; **~sensitive** *adj* photosensible; ~ **session** *n* séance *f* de photos.

phrase I *n* expression *f*.
II *vtr* formuler [*question, speech*].

phrasebook *n* manuel *m* de conversation.

physical I○ *n* bilan *m* de santé; **to have a ~** se faire faire un bilan de santé.
II *adj* **1** [*strength, pain*] physique; ~ **abuse** sévices *mpl*; **2** [*chemistry, science, property*] physique.

physical: ~ **fitness** *n* forme *f* physique; ~ **geography** *n* géographie *f* physique.

physically handicapped *adj* **to be ~** être handicapé/-e *m/f* physique.

physical: ~ **sciences** *n pl* sciences *fpl* physiques; ~ **therapist** ▶ 805 *n* (US) kinésithérapeute *mf*; ~ **therapy** *n* (US) kinésithérapie *f*.

physicist ▶ 805 *n* physicien/-ienne *m/f*.

physics *n* physique *f*.

physiological *adj* physiologique.

physiologist ▶ 805 *n* physiologiste *mf*.

physiology *n* physiologie *f*.

physiotherapist ▶ 805 *n* kinésithérapeute *mf*.

physiotherapy *n* kinésithérapie *f*.

physique *n* physique *m*.

pianist ▶ 805, 753 *n* pianiste *mf*.

piano ▶ 753 I *n* piano *m*.
II *noun modifier* [*lesson, teacher*] de piano; [*concerto, music*] pour piano.

piazza *n* **1** (public square) place *f*; **2** (US) (veranda) véranda *f*.

pick I *n* **1** (tool) pioche *f*, pic *m*; (of climber) piolet *m*; **2** (choice) choix *m*; **to have one's ~ of** avoir le choix parmi; **take your ~** choisis; **3 the ~ of the bunch** (singular) le/la meilleur/-e du lot; (plural) les meilleurs/-es du lot.
II *vtr* **1** (choose, select) choisir (**from** parmi); (in sport) sélectionner [*player*] (**from** parmi); former [*team*]; **to ~ the wrong person** choisir la mauvaise personne; **to ~ a fight** chercher à se bagarrer○ (**with** avec); (quarrel) chercher querelle (**with** à); **2** (navigate) **to ~ one's way through** avancer avec précaution parmi [*rubble, litter*]; **3** cueillir [*fruit, flowers*]; **4** (poke at) gratter [*spot, scab*]; **to ~ sth off** enlever qch de; **to ~ one's teeth/nose** se curer les dents/le nez.
III *vi* choisir; **he can ~ and choose** il peut se permettre d'être exigeant.
■ **pick at**: ~ **at [sth] 1** [*person*] manger [qch] du bout des dents [*food*]; gratter [*spot, scab*]; **2** [*bird*] picorer [*crumbs*].
■ **pick off**: ~ **[sth] off sth** cueillir [qch] sur qch [*apple, cherry*].
■ **pick on**: ~ **on [sb]** harceler, s'en prendre à.

■ **pick out**: **~ [sb/sth] out, ~ out [sb/sth] 1** (select) choisir; (single out) repérer; **2** distinguer [*landmark*]; reconnaitre [*person in photo*]; repérer [*person in crowd*].

■ **pick up**: ¶ **~ up** [*trade, market*] reprendre; [*weather, performance, health*] s'améliorer; [*ill person*] se rétablir; ¶ **~ [sb/sth] up, ~ up [sb/sth] 1** (to tidy) ramasser; (to examine) prendre; (after fall) relever; (for cuddle) prendre [qn] dans ses bras; **to ~ up the receiver** décrocher le téléphone; **to ~ oneself up** se relever; **2** prendre [*passenger, cargo*]; passer prendre [*ticket, keys*]; **could you ~ me up?** est-ce que tu peux venir me chercher?; ¶ **~ [sth] up, ~ up [sth] 1** prendre, acheter [*milk, paper*]; **2** apprendre [*language*]; prendre [*habit, accent*]; développer [*skill*]; **you'll soon ~ it up** tu t'y mettras vite; **3** attraper [*illness*]; **4** repérer [*error*]; **5** (detect) trouver [*trail, scent*]; [*radar*] détecter la présence de [*aircraft, person, object*]; [*radio receiver*] capter [*signal*]; **6** gagner [*point, size*]; acquérir [*reputation*]; **to ~ up speed** prendre de la vitesse; **7** (resume) reprendre [*conversation, career*]; ¶ **~ [sb] up, ~ up [sb] 1** ramasser [*partner, prostitute*]; **2** (fault) faire des remarques à [*person*] (**on** sur).

pickaxe (GB), **pickax** (US) *n* pioche *f*.

picket I *n* (group) piquet *m* (de grève); (one person) gréviste *mf*.
II *vtr* (to stop work) installer un piquet de grève aux portes de [*factory*]; (to protest) former un cordon de protestation devant [*meeting place, embassy*].

picket: **~ fence** *n* palissade *f*; **~ line** *n* (cordon *m* de) piquet *m* de grève.

pickle I *n* **1** (preserves) conserves *fpl* au vinaigre; **2** (gherkin) cornichon *m*.
II *vtr* (in vinegar) conserver [qch] dans du vinaigre.
IDIOMS **to be in a ~** être dans le pétrin°.

pick: **~-me-up** *n* remontant *m*; **~pocket** *n* voleur *m* à la tire.

pickup *n* **1** (also **~ arm**) lecteur *m*; **2** (on electric guitar) capteur *m*; **3** (in business, economy) reprise *f* (**in** de).

pickup: **~ point** *n* point *m* de ramassage; **~ truck** *n* (GB) pick-up *m inv*.

picky° *adj* difficile (**about** pour ce qui est de).

picnic *n* pique-nique *m*.

pictorial *adj* [*record, information*] graphique; [*technique*] artistique.

picture I *n* **1** (painting) peinture *f*, tableau *m*; (drawing) dessin *m*; (in book) illustration *f*; (in child's book) image *f*; (in mind) image *f*; **to paint a ~ of sb/sth** peindre qn/qch; **to paint sb's ~** faire le portrait de qn; **2** (description) description *f*; **to present a clear ~ of sth** décrire or dépeindre qch avec clarté; **3** (snapshot) photo *f*, photographie *f*; **4** (overview) situation *f*; **I get the ~** je vois; **to be in the ~** être au courant; **5** (film) film *m*; **6** (on TV screen) image *f*.
II pictures° *n pl* **the ~s** le cinéma.
III *vtr* s'imaginer.
IDIOMS **her face was a ~!** j'aurais voulu que tu voies sa tête!

picture: **~ frame** *n* cadre *m*; **~ postcard** *n* carte *f* postale.

picturesque *adj* pittoresque.

piddle° *vi* faire pipi°.

pie *n* **1** (savoury) tourte *f*; **meat ~** tourte à la viande; **pork ~** pâté *m* de porc en croûte; **2** (sweet) tarte *f* (*recouverte de pâte*).
IDIOMS **it's all ~ in the sky** c'est de l'utopie; **as easy as ~** simple comme bonjour; **to have a finger in every ~** être mêlé à tout.

piece *n* **1** (gen) morceau *m*; (of string, ribbon) bout *m*; **2** (unit) **a ~ of furniture** un meuble; **a ~ of luggage** une valise; **a ~ of advice** un conseil; **a ~ of information** un renseignement; **a ~ of legislation** une loi; **a ~ of work** un travail; (referring to book) une œuvre; **a ~ of luck** un coup de chance; **£20 a~** 20 livres pièce; **3** (of jigsaw, machine, model) pièce *f*; **in ~s** en pièces (détachées); **to come in ~s** [*furniture*] être livré en kit; **to take sth to ~s** démonter qch; **4** (broken fragment) morceau *m*; **to fall to ~s** [*object*] tomber en morceaux; [*argument*] s'effondrer; **to go to ~s** (from shock) s'effondrer; (emotionally) craquer°; (in interview) paniquer complètement; **5** (of music) morceau *m*; (article) article *m* (**on** sur); **6** (instance) **a ~ of** un exemple de [*propaganda*]; **a wonderful ~ of running/acting** une très belle course/interprétation; **7** (coin) **a 50p ~** une pièce de 50 pence; **8** (in chess) pièce *f*.
IDIOMS **to give sb a ~ of one's mind** dire ses quatre vérités à qn.

piecemeal *adj* (random) fragmentaire; (at different times) irrégulier/-ière.

pier *n* (at seaside) jetée *f* (sur pilotis); (landing stage) embarcadère *f*.

pierce *vtr* (make hole in) percer; (penetrate) transpercer [*armour, skin*].

piercing *adj* [*noise*] perçant; [*light*] intense; [*wind*] glacial, pénétrant.

pig *n* **1** (animal) porc *m*, cochon *m*; **2**° (greedy) goinfre° *m*; (dirty) cochon/-onne° *m/f*; (nasty) sale type° *m*; **to make a ~ of oneself** manger comme un goinfre°.
IDIOMS **~s might fly!** le jour où les poules auront des dents!
■ **pig out**° se goinfrer°, s'empiffrer° (**on** de).

pigeon *n* pigeon *m*.
IDIOMS **to set the cat among the ~s** jeter or lancer un pavé dans la mare.

pigeonhole (GB) **I** *n* casier *m*.
II *vtr* étiqueter, cataloguer.

pigeon-toed *adj* **to be ~** marcher les pieds en dedans.

piggyback (**ride**) *n* **to give sb a ~** porter qn sur son dos or sur ses épaules.

piggy bank *n* tirelire *f*.

pigheaded *adj* entêté, obstiné.

pigmentation *n* pigmentation *f*.

pig: **~pen** *n* (US) = **pigsty**; **~skin** *n* peau *f* de porc; **~sty** *n* porcherie *f*; **~tail** *n* natte *f*.

pile I *n* **1** (heap) tas *m* (**of** de); (stack) pile *f* (**of** de); **in a ~** en tas or en pile; **2** (of fabric, carpet) poil *m*; **3**° **~s of** des tas° de [*books, letters*];

un tas de [*work*]; **~s of money** plein d'argent○.
II piles ▶ **686** *n pl* hémorroïdes *fpl*.
III *vtr* entasser (**on** sur; **into** dans).
■ **pile up** [*debts, problems, work*] s'accumuler.

pileup *n* carambolage *m*.

pilfering *n* vol *m*.

pilgrim *n* pèlerin *m* (**to** de).

pilgrimage *n* pèlerinage *m*.

pill *n* comprimé *m*, cachet *m*; **to be on the ~** prendre la pilule.
IDIOMS **to sweeten the ~** dorer la pilule○.

pillar *n* (in building) pilier *m*; (of smoke, fire) colonne *f*.
IDIOMS **to rush about from ~ to post**○ courir à droite et à gauche.

pillar box *n* (GB) boîte *f* aux lettres.

pillion I *n* (also **~ seat**) siège *m* de passager.
II *adv* **to ride ~** monter en croupe.

pillow *n* oreiller *m*.

pilot ▶ **805** **I** *n* pilote *m*.
II *vtr* piloter.

pilot: **~ light** *n* veilleuse *f*; (electric) voyant *m* lumineux; **~ scheme** *n* projet-pilote *m*; **~'s licence** (GB), **~'s license** (US) *n* brevet *m* de pilote.

pimple *n* bouton *m*.

pin I *n* **1** (for cloth, paper) épingle *f*; **2** **three-~ plug** prise *f* à trois fiches; **3** (for wood, metal) goujon *m*; **4** (Med) broche *f*; **5** (brooch) barrette *f*.
II *vtr* **1** épingler [*dress, hem, curtain*] (**to** à); **to ~ sth with** attacher qch avec [*brooch, pin*]; **2** (trap) **to ~ sb to** coincer qn contre [*wall, floor*]; **3**○ **to ~ [sth] on sb** mettre [qch] sur le dos de qn [*theft*].
IDIOMS **you could have heard a ~ drop** on aurait entendu voler une mouche.
■ **pin down**: ¶ **~ down [sb], ~ [sb] down** **1** (physically) immobiliser (**to** à); **2** (figurative) coincer; **to ~ sb down to a definite date** arriver à soutirer une date fixe à qn; ¶ **~ down [sth], ~ [sth] down** identifier [*concept, feeling*].
■ **pin up**: **~ up [sth], ~ [sth] up** accrocher [*poster, notice*] (**on** à).

PIN (number) *n* (*abbr* = **personal identification number**) code *m* confidentiel (pour carte bancaire).

pinball ▶ **649** *n* flipper *m*.

pincers *n pl* tenailles *fpl*.

pinch I *n* **1** pincement *m*; **to give sb a ~** pincer qn; **2** (of salt, spice) pincée *f*.
II *vtr* **1** (on arm, leg) pincer; **2** [*shoe*] serrer; **3**○ (steal) faucher○ (**from** à).
III *vi* [*shoe*] serrer.
IDIOMS **to feel the ~** avoir de la peine à joindre les deux bouts.

pine I *n* **1** (also **~ tree**) pin *m*; **2** (wood) pin *m*; **stripped ~** pin décapé.
II *noun modifier* [*furniture*] en pin.
III *vi* [*person*] languir (**for** après); [*animal*] s'ennuyer (**for** de).

pine: **~apple** *n* ananas *m*; **~cone** *n* pomme *f* de pin; **~-needle** *n* aiguille *f* de pin.

ping-pong® ▶ **649** *n* ping-pong® *m*.

pink ▶ **559** **I** *n* **1** (colour) rose *m*; **2** (flower) œillet *m* mignardise.
II *adj* rose; **to go** or **turn ~** rosir; (blush) rougir (**with** de).

pinking shears, **pinking scissors** *n pl* ciseaux *mpl* cranteurs.

pin money *n* argent *m* de poche.

pinnacle *n* (of rock) cime *f* (**of** de); (of career) apogée *m* (**of** de).

pinpoint *vtr* indiquer [*problem, causes, location, site*]; déterminer [*time*].

pinstripe(d) *adj* [*fabric, suit*] à fines rayures.

pint *n* **1** pinte *f* ((GB) = *0.57 l*, (US) = *0.47 l*); **a ~ of milk** ≈ un demi-litre de lait; **2**○ (GB) **to go for a ~** aller boire une bière.

pinup *n* **1** (woman) pin-up○ *f inv*; **2** (poster of star) affiche *f* de vedette.

pioneer I *n* pionnier *m* (**of, in** de).
II *vtr* **to ~ the use of** être le premier à utiliser.
III pioneering *pres p adj* [*scientist, scheme*] innovateur/-trice.

pip *n* **1** (seed) pépin *m*; **2** (on radio) top *m*.
IDIOMS **to be ~ped at** or **to the post** se faire souffler la victoire.

pipe ▶ **753** **I** *n* **1** (for gas, water) tuyau *m*; (underground) conduite *f*; **2** (smoker's) pipe *f*.
II pipes *n pl* cornemuse *f*.
III *vtr* **1** (carry) **water is ~d across/to** l'eau est acheminée par canalisation à travers/ jusqu'à; **2** (in cooking) **to ~ icing onto a cake** décorer un gâteau.
■ **pipe down**○ faire moins de bruit.

pipe: **~d music** *n* musique *f* d'ambiance; **~-dream** *n* chimère *f*.

pipeline *n* oléoduc *m*; **to be in the ~** être prévu.

piper ▶ **805**, **753** *n* joueur/-euse *m/f* de cornemuse.
IDIOMS **he who pays the ~ calls the tune** l'argent c'est le pouvoir.

piping hot *adj* fumant.

pique *n* dépit *m*; **in a fit of ~** dans un accès de dépit.

piracy *n* **1** (at sea) piraterie *f*; **2** (of tapes, software) duplication *f* pirate (**of** de).

pirate I *n* pirate *m*.
II *noun modifier* [*video, tape, radio*] pirate (*after n*); [*ship*] de pirates.
III *vtr* pirater [*tape, video, software*].

pirouette *n* pirouette *f*.

Pisa ▶ **574** *pr n* Pise.

Pisces *n* Poissons *mpl*; ▶ **Aquarius**.

pit I *n* **1** (in ground, in garage) fosse *f*; (trap) trappe *f*; (at racetrack) stand *m*; **gravel ~** carrière *f* de gravier; **2** (mine) mine *f*; **to go down the ~** aller travailler à la mine; **3** (in theatre) parterre *m*; **4** (US) (in peach, olive) noyau *m*.
II *vtr* **to ~ one's wits against sb** se mesurer à qn.
IDIOMS **it's the ~s**○! c'est l'horreur!

pitch I *n* **1** (sportsground) terrain *m*; **football ~** terrain de foot(ball); **2** (of note, voice) hauteur *f*; (in music) ton *m*; **absolute ~, perfect ~** oreille *f* absolue; **3** (highest point) comble *m*; **4** (sales talk) boniment *m*; **5** (for street trader) emplacement *m*.
II *vtr* **1** jeter [*object*] (**into** dans); (in sport) lancer; **2** adapter [*campaign, speech*] (**at** à); **3** [*singer*] trouver [*note*]; **4** planter [*tent*]; **to ~ camp** établir un camp.
III *vi* **1 to ~ and toss** tanguer; **2** (US) (in baseball) lancer (la balle).
■ **pitch in**○ (eat) attaquer○; (help) donner un coup de main○.

pitch: **~-and-putt** *n* mini-golf *m*; **~-black, ~ dark** *adj* tout noir.

pitcher *n* **1** (jug) cruche *f*; **2** (US Sport) lanceur *m*.

pitchfork *n* fourche *f*.

pitfall *n* écueil *m* (**of** de).

pithy *adj* (concise) concis; (incisive) piquant.

pitiful *adj* [*cry, sight*] pitoyable; [*state*] lamentable; [*amount*] ridicule.

pittance *n* **to live on/earn a ~** vivre avec/ gagner trois fois rien.

pitted *adj* **1** [*surface*] rongé; [*face, skin*] grêlé (**with** de); **2** [*olive*] dénoyauté.

pity I *n* **1** (compassion) pitié *f* (**for** pour); **out of ~** par pitié; **to feel ~** avoir de la pitié; **2** (shame) dommage *m*; **what a ~!** quel dommage!
II *vtr* plaindre.

pivot I *vtr* faire pivoter [*lever*]; orienter [*lamp*].
II *vi* [*lamp, device*] pivoter (**on** sur).

pizza *n* pizza *f*.

pizza parlour (GB), **pizza parlor** (US) *n* pizzeria *f*.

placard *n* (at protest march) pancarte *f*; (on wall) affiche *f*.

place I *n* **1** (location, position) endroit *m*; **from ~ to ~** d'un endroit à l'autre; **in ~s** [*hilly, damaged, worn*] par endroits; **in several ~s** (in region) dans plusieurs endroits; (on body) à plusieurs endroits; **~ of birth/work** lieu *m* de naissance/travail; **~ of residence** domicile *m*; **to be in the right ~ at the right time** être là où il faut quand il le faut; **in Oxford, of all ~s!** à Oxford, figure-toi!; **to lose/find one's ~** (in book) perdre/retrouver sa page; (in paragraph, speech) perdre/retrouver le fil; **some ~**○ quelque part; **2** (town, hotel) endroit *m*; **a good ~ to eat** une bonne adresse (pour manger); **a little ~ called...** un petit village du nom de...; **all over the ~** (everywhere) partout; **3** (home) **at Isabelle's ~** chez Isabelle; **your ~ or mine?** chez toi ou chez moi?; **4** (on bus, at table, in queue) place *f*; (setting) couvert *m*; **please take your ~s** veuillez prendre place; **5** (on team, with firm) place *f* (**on** dans, **as** comme); **6** (GB) (for academic study) place *f* (**at** à); **to get a ~ on** obtenir une place dans [*course*]; **7** (in competition, race) place *f*; **to finish in first ~** terminer premier/-ière or à la première place; **to take second ~** (in importance) passer au deuxième plan; **in the first ~** (firstly, when listing) premièrement; (most importantly, most notably) tout d'abord, pour commencer; **8** (correct position) **everything is in its ~** tout est bien à sa place; **to hold sth in ~** maintenir qch en place; **in ~** [*law, system, scheme*] en place; **to put sb in his/her ~** remettre qn à sa place; **9** (personal level or position) **it's not my ~ to do** ce n'est pas à moi de faire; **in his ~** à sa place; **to change ~s with sb** changer de place avec qn; **10** (moment) moment *m*; **in ~s** [*funny, boring, silly*] par moments.
II *vtr* **1** (put) placer, mettre [*object*]; mettre [*advertisement*]; passer [*order*]; **2** (in competition, exam) classer; **to be ~d third** [*horse, athlete*] arriver troisième; **3** (identify) situer [*person*]; reconnaître [*accent*]; **4** placer [*student, child*].
III **out of place** *phr* déplacé; **to look out of ~** [*building, person*] détonner.
IDIOMS **to have friends in high ~s** avoir des amis haut placés.

placement *n* **1** (GB) (also **work ~**) stage *m*; **2** (of child, unemployed person) placement *m* (**in** dans).

place-name *n* nom *m* de lieu.

placid *adj* placide.

plague I *n* **1** (bubonic) peste *f*; **2** (epidemic) épidémie *f*; **3** (of ants, locusts) invasion *f*.
II *vtr* **1 to be ~d by** être en proie à [*doubts, difficulties*]; **2** (harass) harceler.
IDIOMS **to avoid sb/sth like the ~** fuir qn/ qch comme la peste.

plaice *n* plie *f*, carrelet *m*.

plaid *adj* [*scarf, shirt, design, fabric*] écossais.

plain I *n* plaine *f*.
II *adj* **1** [*dress, food, language*] simple; [*building, furniture*] sobre; **a ~ man** un homme simple; **2** [*background, fabric*] uni; [*envelope*] sans inscription; **3** [*woman*] quelconque; **she's rather ~** elle n'a rien d'une beauté; **4** (obvious) évident, clair; **it's ~ to see** ça saute aux yeux; **to make it ~ to sb that** faire comprendre clairement à qn que; **5 in ~ English** en clair; **6** [*common sense*] simple (*before n*); [*ignorance*] pur et simple (*after n*); **7** [*yoghurt, rice*] nature *inv*.

plain clothes *adj* [*policeman*] en civil.

plainly *adv* **1** (obviously) manifestement; **2** [*see, remember*] clairement; **3** [*speak*] franchement; **4** [*dress, eat*] simplement; [*furnished*] sobrement.

plait *n* natte *f*; **to wear ~s** avoir des nattes.

plan I *n* **1** (scheme) plan *m*; **the ~ is to leave very early** nous avons prévu de partir très tôt; **to go according to ~** se passer comme prévu; **2** (definite aim) projet *m* (**for** de; **to do** pour faire); **to have a ~ to do** projeter de faire; **3** (outline, map) plan *m*.
II **plans** *n pl* **1** (arrangements) projets *mpl*; **I have no particular ~s** (for tonight) je n'ai rien de prévu; (for the future) je n'ai pas de projets bien déterminés; **2** (of building) **the ~s** les plans *mpl*.
III *vtr* **1** (prepare, organize) planifier [*future, economy*]; organiser, préparer [*timetable, meeting, expedition*]; préparer [*retirement*]; organiser

[*day*]; faire un plan de [*career*]; faire le plan de [*essay, book*]; préméditer [*crime*]; **2** (intend, propose) projeter [*visit, trip*]; prévoir [*new development, factory*]; **to ~ to do** projeter de faire; **3** (design) concevoir [*kitchen, garden, city centre*].
IV *vi* prévoir; **to ~ on doing** (intend) compter faire.
■ **plan ahead** (vaguely) faire des projets; (look, think ahead) prévoir.

plane I *n* **1** (aircraft) avion *m*; **2** (in geometry) plan *m*; **3** (tool) rabot *m*; **4** (also **~ tree**) platane *m*.
II *vtr* raboter [*wood, edge*]; **to ~ sth smooth** lisser qch au rabot.

planet *n* planète *f*.

plank *n* **1** (beam) planche *f*; **2** (of policy, argument) point *m*.

planner *n* planificateur/-trice *m/f*; (in town planning) urbaniste *mf*.

planning *n* **1** (of industry, economy, work) planification *f*; (of holiday, party) organisation *f*; **2** (in town) urbanisme *m*; (out of town) aménagement *m* du territoire.

planning: **~ application** *n* demande *f* de permis de construire; **~ department** *n* service *m* d'urbanisme; **~ permission** *n* permis *m* de construire.

plant I *n* **1** (Bot) plante *f*; **2** (factory) usine *f*; (power station) centrale *f*; **3** (buildings and machinery) installations *fpl* industrielles et commerciales.
II *vtr* **1** planter [*seed, bulb, tree*]; **2** placer [*bomb, spy*]; **to ~ drugs on sb** cacher de la drogue sur qn pour l'incriminer.
III *v refl* **to ~ oneself between/ in front of** se planter entre/devant.

plantation *n* plantation *f*.

plaque *n* (on wall, monument) plaque *f*.

plaster I *n* **1** (material) plâtre *m*; **2** (GB) (also **sticking ~**) sparadrap *m*.
II *vtr* **1** faire les plâtres de [*house*]; **2** (with posters) couvrir (**with** de).

plasterer ▶ 805 *n* plâtrier *m*.

plastic I *n* plastique *m*.
II *adj* [*bag, toys, container*] en plastique.

plastic: **~ arts** *n pl* arts *mpl* plastiques; **~ bomb** *n* bombe *f* au plastic; **~ surgeon** ▶ 805 *n* chirurgien *m* esthétique; **~ surgery** *n* chirurgie *f* plastique.

plate *n* **1** (dish) (for eating) assiette *f*; (for serving) plat *m*; **to hand sth to sb on a ~** (GB) (figurative) apporter or présenter qch à qn sur un plateau; **2** (dishful) assiette *f*; **3** (sheet of metal) plaque *f*, tôle *f*; **4** (numberplate) plaque *f* minéralogique; **5** (illustration) planche *f*; **6** (in dentistry) dentier *m*; **7** (in earth's crust) plaque *f*.
IDIOMS **to have a lot on one's ~** avoir du pain sur la planche.

plate glass *n* verre *m* à vitre.

platform *n* **1** (for performance) estrade *f*; (at public meeting) tribune *f*; **2** (in oil industry, in scaffolding) plate-forme *f*; **3** (pre-election) plateforme *f* électorale; **4** (at station) quai *m*.

platinum I *n* platine *m*.
II *noun modifier* [*ring*] de or en platine.

platonic *adj* [*love, relationship*] platonique.

platoon *n* (of soldiers, police, firemen) section *f*; (in cavalry) peloton *m*.

platter *n* **1** (dish) plat *m*; **2** (Culin) **seafood ~** assiette *f* de fruits de mer.

plausible *adj* [*story, plot, alibi*] plausible, vraisemblable; [*person*] convaincant.

play ▶ 649, 753 **I** *n* **1** (in theatre) pièce *f* (**about** sur); **2** (recreation) **to learn through ~** apprendre par le jeu; **3** (in sport) (specific game) partie *f*; **~ starts at 11** la partie commence à 11 heures; **out of ~/in ~** [*ball*] hors jeu/en jeu; **4** (movement, interaction) jeu *m*; **to come into ~** entrer en jeu; **a ~ on words** un jeu de mots.
II *vtr* **1** (Games, Sport) jouer à [*game, match, cards*]; jouer [*card*]; **to ~ hide and seek** jouer à cache-cache; **to ~ a joke on sb** jouer un tour à qn; **2** (in music) jouer de [*instrument*]; jouer [*tune, symphony, chord*]; jouer à [*venue*]; **3** (in theatre) interpréter, jouer [*role*]; **4** mettre [*tape, video, CD*]; **~ me the record** mets-moi le disque.
III *vi* **1** [*children*] jouer (**with** avec); **2** (figurative) **to ~ at being an artist** jouer à l'artiste; **what does he think he's ~ing at**○**?** (GB) qu'est-ce qu'il fabrique○?; **3** (in sport, game) jouer; **do you ~?** est-ce que tu sais jouer?; **to ~ fair** jouer franc-jeu; **4** [*musician, band, orchestra*] jouer; **to ~ to large audiences** jouer devant un grand public; **5** [*play*] se jouer; [*film*] passer; [*actor*] jouer; **6** (Mus) [*record*] jouer.
IDIOMS **to ~ for time** essayer de gagner du temps.
■ **play along**: **to ~ along with sb** entrer dans le jeu de qn.
■ **play around**○ (be silly) faire l'imbécile; (be unfaithful) coucher à droite et à gauche.
■ **play back**: **~ [sth] back, ~ back [sth]** repasser [*song, film, video*].
■ **play down**: **~ down [sth]** minimiser.
■ **play off**: **to ~ sb off against sb** monter qn contre qn (pour en tirer avantage).
■ **play on**: **~ on [sth]** exploiter [*fears, prejudices*].
■ **play up**○ [*computer, person*] faire des siennes○.

play: **~-acting** *n* comédie *f*, simagrées *fpl*; **~ area** *n* (outside) aire *f* de jeu; (inside) coin-jeu *m*; **~boy** *n* playboy *m*.

player *n* (in sport, music) joueur/-euse *m/f*; (actor) comédien/-ienne *m/f*; (in negotiations, crisis) protagoniste *mf*; **tennis ~** joueur/-euse *m/f* de tennis.

playful *adj* [*remark*] taquin; [*child, kitten*] joueur/-euse.

play: **~ground** *n* cour *f* de récréation; **~group** *n* ≈ halte-garderie *f*; **~house** *n* théâtre *m*; **~-off** *n* (GB) prolongation *f*; (US) match *m* crucial; **~room** *n* salle *f* de jeux; **~thing** *n* jouet *m*; **~wright** *n* auteur *m* dramatique.

plaza *n* **1** (square) place *f*; **shopping ~** centre *m* commercial; **2** (US) péage *m*.

plc, **PLC** *n* (GB) (*abbr* = **public limited company**) SA.

plea *n* (for tolerance, mercy) appel *m* (**for** à); (for money, food) demande *f* (**for** de); **a ~ for aid** un appel à l'aide; **to enter a ~ of guilty/not guilty** plaider coupable/non coupable.

plead I *vtr* **to ~ ignorance/sb's case** plaider l'ignorance/la cause de qn.
II *vi* **1 to ~ with sb** supplier qn; (more fervently) implorer qn; **2** (Law) plaider.

pleasant *adj* agréable; **it makes a ~ change from work!** ça change du travail!

pleasantly *adv* [*say, smile*] aimablement; **~ surprised** agréablement surpris.

please I *adv* s'il vous plaît; (informally) s'il te plaît; **'~ do not smoke'** 'prière de ne pas fumer'; **~, come in** entrez, je vous en prie; **'may I?'—'~ do'** 'je peux?'—'oui, je vous en prie'; **~ tell me if** n'hésitez pas à me dire si.
II *vtr* faire plaisir à [*person*]; **she is hard to ~** elle est difficile (à contenter); **there's no pleasing him** il n'est jamais satisfait.
III *vi* plaire; **do as you ~** fais comme il te plaira, fais comme tu veux.

pleased *adj* content (**that** que + *subj*; **about, at** de; **with** de); **to look ~ with oneself** avoir l'air content de soi; **I am ~ to announce that...** j'ai le plaisir d'annoncer que...; **~ to meet you** enchanté.

pleasing *adj* [*appearance, colour, voice*] agréable; [*manner, personality*] avenant; [*effect, result*] heureux/-euse.

pleasure *n* **1** (enjoyment) plaisir *m* (**of** de; **of doing** de faire); **to do sth for ~** faire qch par plaisir; **to take ~ in doing** prendre plaisir à faire; **2** (enjoyable activity, experience) plaisir *m* (**of** de); **it was a ~ to do** c'était agréable de faire; **to mix business and ~** joindre l'utile à l'agréable; **are you in Paris for business or ~?** êtes-vous à Paris pour affaires ou pour le plaisir?; **3** (in polite formulae) **it gives me great ~ to do** c'est avec plaisir que je fais; **my ~** (replying to request for help) avec plaisir; (replying to thanks) je vous en prie; **what an unexpected ~!** quelle excellente surprise!

pleasure: **~ boat** *n* bateau *m* de plaisance; **~ craft** *n* bateaux *mpl* de plaisance.

pleat *n* pli *m*.

pleated *adj* [*skirt*] plissé; [*trousers*] à plis (*after n*).

pledge I *n* **1** (promise) promesse *f*; **to give** or **make a ~ to do** prendre l'engagement de faire; **2** (money promised to charity) promesse *f* de don.
II *vtr* promettre [*allegiance, aid, support*] (**to** à); **to ~ one's word** donner sa parole.

plentiful *adj* [*diet, food, harvest*] abondant; **a ~ supply of** une abondance de.

plenty *quantif, pron* **to have ~ of** avoir beaucoup de [*time, money, friends*]; **there is ~ of time** on a tout le temps qu'il faut; **that's ~** ça suffit largement.

pliable *adj* [*twig, plastic*] flexible.

pliers *n pl* pinces *fpl*; **a pair of ~s** des pinces.

plight *n* **1** (dilemma) situation *f* désespérée; **2** (suffering) détresse *f*.

plimsoll *n* (GB) chaussure *f* de tennis.

plod *v* ■ **plod along** avancer d'un pas lent.
■ **plod away** travailler ferme, bosser○.
■ **plod on** continuer à marcher; (figurative) persévérer.

plodder *n* bûcheur/-euse○ *m/f*.

plonk I *n* **1** (sound) plouf○ *m*, son *m* creux; **2**○ (wine) vin *m* ordinaire, pinard◐ *m*.
II○ *vtr* (also **~ down**) planter [*plate, bottle, box*] (**on** sur).

plot I *n* **1** (conspiracy) complot *m*; **2** (of novel, film, play) intrigue *f*; **the ~ thickens** l'histoire se corse; **3 ~ of land** parcelle *f* de terre; **a vegetable ~** un carré de légumes; **4** (site) terrain *m* à bâtir.
II *vtr* **1** (plan) comploter [*murder, attack, return*]; fomenter [*revolution*]; **2** (chart) relever [qch] sur une carte [*course*]; tracer [qch] sur une carte [*progress*]; **3** (on graph) tracer [qch] point par point [*curve, graph*]; **to ~ the progress of sth** tracer la courbe de progression de qch.
III *vi* (conspire) conspirer (**against** contre).

plough (GB), **plow** (US) I *n* charrue *f*; **the ~** le Grand Chariot *m*.
II *vtr* **1** labourer [*land, field*]; creuser [*furrow*]; **2** (invest) **to ~ money into** investir beaucoup d'argent dans [*project, company*].
■ **plough back**: **~ [sth] back, ~ back [sth]** réinvestir [*profits*] (**into** dans).
■ **plough into**: **~ into [sth]** [*vehicle*] percuter [*tree, wall*]; foncer dans [*crowd*].
■ **plough through**: **~ through [sth]** avancer péniblement dans [*mud, snow*]; ramer○ sur [*book*].

ploughing (GB), **plowing** (US) *n* labourage *m*.

ploy *n* stratagème *m* (**to do** pour faire).

pluck I *n* courage *m*, cran○ *m*.
II *vtr* **1** cueillir [*flower, fruit*]; **2** plumer [*chicken*]; **3** (in music) pincer [*strings*]; pincer les cordes de [*guitar*]; **4 to ~ one's eyebrows** s'épiler les sourcils.
IDIOMS **to ~ up one's courage** prendre son courage à deux mains.

plucky *adj* courageux/-euse.

plug I *n* **1** (on appliance) prise *f* (de courant); (on computer, for phone) fiche *f*; **to pull out the ~** débrancher la prise; **2** (stopper) bonde *f*; **to pull out the ~** retirer la bonde; **3** (also **spark ~**) bougie *f*; **4** (in advertising) **to give sth a ~** faire de la publicité pour qch.
II *vtr* **1** boucher [*hole*] (**with** avec); **2**○ (promote) faire de la publicité pour [*book, show, product*]; **3 to ~ sth into** brancher qch à.
■ **plug in**: ¶ **~ in** se brancher; ¶ **~ [sth] in, ~ in [sth]** brancher [*appliance*].

plughole *n* (GB) bonde *f*; **to go down the ~** [*ring*] tomber dans le trou de l'évier; (figurative)○ s'en aller à vau-l'eau.

plug-in *adj* [*appliance*] enfichable.

plum ▶559 I *n* **1** (fruit) prune *f*; **2** (also **~ tree**) prunier *m*.

II *noun modifier* [*tart*] aux prunes; [*jam*] de prunes.
III *adj* **1** (colour) prune *inv*; **2**○ **to get a ~ job** décrocher un boulot en or○.

plumb I *adv* **1**○ (US) [*crazy*] complètement; **2**○ **~ in the middle** en plein milieu.
II *vtr* sonder [*depths*]; **to ~ the depths of** toucher le fond de [*despair, misery*].

plumber *n* plombier *m*.

plumbing *n* plomberie *f*.

plummet *vi* chuter, dégringoler○.

plump *adj* [*person, arm, leg*] potelé; [*cheek, face*] rond, plein.

plunge I *vtr* plonger (**into** dans); **to be ~d into** être plongé dans [*darkness, crisis*]; être submergé de [*debt*].
II *vi* [*road, cliff, waterfall*] plonger; [*bird, plane*] piquer; [*person*] (dive) plonger; (fall) tomber (**from** de); [*rate, value*] chuter.
IDIOMS **to take the ~** se jeter à l'eau.

plunger *n* ventouse *f*.

plural I *n* pluriel *m*; **in the ~** au pluriel.
II *adj* [*noun, adjective*] au pluriel; [*form, ending*] du pluriel.

plus I *n* avantage *m*.
II *adj* positif/-ive; **~ factor, ~ point** (figurative) atout *m*; **the ~ side** le côté positif; **the 65-~ age group** les personnes qui ont 65 ans et plus.
III *prep* plus; **15 ~ 12** 15 plus 12.
IV *conj* et; **bedroom ~ bathroom** chambre et salle de bains.

plus: **~-fours** *n pl* culotte *f* de golf; **~ sign** *n* signe *m* plus.

Pluto *pr n* Pluton *f*.

ply *vtr* **1** vendre [*wares*]; **to ~ one's trade** exercer son métier; **2 to ~ sb with food/drink** ne cesser de remplir l'assiette/le verre de qn.

plywood *n* contreplaqué *m*.

pm ▶554 *adv* (*abbr* = **post meridiem**) **two ~** deux heures de l'après-midi; **nine ~** neuf heures du soir.

PMT *n* (*abbr* = **premenstrual tension**) SPM *m*, syndrome *m* prémenstruel.

pneumatic drill *n* marteau *m* piqueur.

pneumonia ▶686 *n* pneumonie *f*.

poach I *vtr* **1** chasser [qch] illégalement [*game*]; **2** (cook in water) faire pocher.
II *vi* braconner.

poacher *n* braconnier *m*.

pocket I *n* **1** (in garment) poche *f*; **2** (in billiards) bourse *f*.
II *noun modifier* [*diary, dictionary, edition*] de poche.
III *vtr* empocher.
IDIOMS **to be in ~** (GB) être en fonds; **to be out of ~** (GB) en être de sa poche.

pocket: **~book** *n* (US) (wallet) portefeuille *m*; (handbag) sac *m* à main; **~knife** *n* couteau *m* de poche; **~ money** *n* argent *m* de poche.

pod *n* (of peas, beans) (intact) gousse *f*; (empty) cosse *f*; (of vanilla) gousse *f*.

podium *n* (for speaker, conductor) estrade *f*; (for winner) podium *m*.

poem *n* poème *m*.

poet *n* poète *m*.

poetic *adj* poétique.

poetry *n* poésie *f*; **to write/read ~** écrire/lire des poèmes.

poignant *adj* poignant.

point I *n* **1** (of knife, needle, pencil) pointe *f*; **2** (location, position on scale) point *m*; (less specific) endroit *m*; **~ of entry** (into country) point d'arrivée; **~ of no return** point de non-retour; **3** (extent, degree) point *m*; **up to a ~** jusqu'à un certain point; **4** (moment) (precise) moment *m*; (stage) stade *m*; **to be on the ~ of doing** être sur le point de faire; **at this ~ in her career** à ce stade(-là) de sa carrière; **at some ~ in the future** plus tard; **at one ~** à un moment donné; **5** (question, idea) point *m*; **to take up** or **return to sb's ~** revenir sur un point soulevé par qn; **this proves my ~** cela confirme ce que je viens de dire; **a three-~ plan** un plan en trois points; **~ by ~** point par point; **to make the ~ that** faire remarquer que; **you've made your ~** vous vous êtes exprimé; **to make a ~ of doing sth** (as matter of pride) mettre un point d'honneur à faire qch; (do deliberately) faire qch exprès; **to raise a ~ about sth** soulever la question de qch; **that's a good ~** c'est une remarque judicieuse; **I take your ~** (agreeing) je suis d'accord avec vous; **I take your ~, but** je vois bien où vous voulez en venir, mais; **good ~!** très juste!; **6** (central idea) point *m* essentiel; **to come straight to the ~** aller droit au fait; **to keep** or **stick to the ~** rester dans le sujet; **to miss the ~** ne pas comprendre; **that's beside the ~** là n'est pas la question; **to get the ~** comprendre; **that's not the ~** il ne s'agit pas de cela; **7** (purpose) objet *m*; **what's the ~ of doing...?** à quoi bon faire...?; **there's no ~ in doing** ça ne sert à rien de faire; **I don't see the ~ of doing** je ne vois pas l'intérêt de faire; **8** (feature, characteristic) point *m*, côté *m*; **her strong ~** son point fort; **9** (in scoring) point *m*; **to win by 4 ~s** l'emporter de 4 points; **match ~** (in tennis) balle *f* de match; **10** (decimal point) virgule *f*; **11** (headland) pointe *f*.
II *vtr* **1** (aim, direct) **to ~ sth at sb** braquer qch sur qn [*camera, gun*]; **to ~ one's finger at sb** montrer qn du doigt; **to ~ sb in the right direction** mettre qn sur la bonne route; **2** (show) **to ~ the way to** indiquer la direction de; **3** (in ballet, gym) **to ~ one's toes** faire des pointes.
III *vi* **1** (indicate) indiquer or montrer (du doigt); **to ~ at sb/sth** montrer qn/qch du doigt; **2** [*signpost, arrow, compass*] indiquer; **to be ~ing at sb** or **in sb's direction** [*gun, camera*] être braqué sur qn.
■ **point out**: ¶ **~ out [sth/sb]**, **~ [sth/sb] out** montrer (**to** à); ¶ **~ out [sth]** faire remarquer [*fact, discrepancy*]; **as he ~ed out** comme il l'a fait remarquer.

point-blank *adv* **1** [*shoot*] à bout portant; **2** [*refuse, deny*] catégoriquement.

pointed *adj* **1** [*hat, stick, chin*] pointu; [*window*] en pointe; [*arch*] en ogive; **2** [*remark*] qui vise quelqu'un.

pointing *n* jointoiement *m*.

pointless *adj* [*request, activity*] absurde; **it's ~ to do/for me to do** ça ne sert à rien de faire/que je fasse.

point: **~ of reference** *n* point *m* de repère; **~ of sale** *n* point *m* de vente; **~ of view** *n* point *m* de vue; **~ system** *n* système *m* de points.

poise *n* **1** (confidence) assurance *f*; **2** (physical elegance) aisance *f*.

poised *adj* **1** (self-possessed) plein d'assurance; **2** (elegant) plein d'aisance; **3** (on the point of) **to be ~ to do** être sur le point de faire.

poison I *n* poison *m*.
II *vtr* empoisonner [*person, environment, relationship*]; [*fumes*] intoxiquer [*person*].

poisoning *n* empoisonnement *m*.

poisonous *adj* **1** [*chemicals, gas*] toxique; [*mushroom, berry*] vénéneux/-euse; [*snake, insect, bite*] venimeux/-euse; **2** [*rumour, propaganda*] pernicieux/-ieuse.

poke *vtr* **1** (jab, prod) pousser [qn] du bout du doigt [*person*]; donner un coup dans [*pile, substance*]; tisonner [*fire*]; **2** (push, put) **to ~ sth into** enfoncer qch dans [*hole, pot*]; **to ~ one's head out of the window** passer la tête par la fenêtre.
IDIOMS **it's better than a ~ in the eye (with a burnt stick)** c'est mieux que rien.
■ **poke around**, **poke about** farfouiller (**in** dans).

poker *n* **1** (for fire) tisonnier *m*; **2** ▶649 (cardgame) poker *m*.
IDIOMS **(as) stiff as a ~** raide comme la justice.

poker-faced *adj* [*person*] impassible.

Poland ▶574 *pr n* Pologne *f*.

polar *adj* [*lights, bear, region*] polaire.

polarize *vtr* diviser [*opinion*].

pole *n* **1** (stick) perche *f*; (for tent, flag) mât *m*; (for skiing) bâton *m*; (piste marker) piquet *m*; **2** (of earth's axis) pôle *m*; **3** (in fishing) canne *f* à pêche.
IDIOMS **to be ~s apart** [*people*] être complètement différents; [*theories, methods, opinions*] être diamétralement opposés.

Pole ▶712 *n* Polonais/-e *m/f*.

pole: **~ star** *n* étoile *f* polaire; **~ vault** *n* saut *m* à la perche.

police I *n* **1** (official body) **the ~** la police; **2** (individuals) policiers *mpl*.
II *vtr* **1** (keep order) maintenir l'ordre dans [*area*]; **2** (patrol) surveiller [*area, frontier*]; organiser le service d'ordre pour [*demonstration, match*].

police: **~ constable**, **PC** *n* agent *m* de police; **~ custody** *n* garde *f* à vue; **Police Department**, **PD** *n* (US) services *mpl* de police (d'une ville); **~ escort** *n* escorte *f* policière; **~ force** *n* police *f*; **~ headquarters** *n pl* administration *f* centrale de la police; **~man** *n* agent *m* de police; **~ officer** *n* policier *m*; **~ state** *n* État *m* policier; **~ station** *n* poste *m* de police; (larger) commissariat *m*; **~ van** *n* fourgon *m* cellulaire; **~woman** *n* femme *f* policier.

policy I *n* **1** (plan, rule) politique *f* (**on** sur); **to have** or **follow a ~ of doing** avoir pour politique de faire; **2** (in insurance) (cover) contrat *m*; (document) police *f*.
II *noun modifier* [*decision*] de principe; [*paper*] de politique générale.

polio(myelitis) ▶686 *n* poliomyélite *f*.

polish I *n* **1** (for wood, floor) cire *f*; (for shoes) cirage *m*; (for brass, silver) pâte *f* à polir; (for car) lustre *m*; **2** (shiny surface) éclat *m*; **3** (of manner, performance) élégance *f*.
II *vtr* **1** cirer [*shoes, furniture*]; astiquer [*leather, car, glass, brass*]; polir [*stone*]; **2** (refine) soigner [*performance, image*]; affiner [*style*].
■ **polish off**○: **~ off [sth]**, **~ [sth] off** expédier○ [*food, job*].

Polish ▶712 **I** *n* (language) polonais *m*.
II *adj* [*culture, food, politics*] polonais; [*teacher, lesson*] de polonais; [*ambassador, embassy*] de Pologne.

polished *adj* **1** [*surface, wood*] poli; [*floor, shoes*] ciré; **2** [*manner*] raffiné; **3** [*performance*] (bien) rodé.

polite *adj* poli (**to** avec); **to be ~ about sth** se montrer diplomate dans ses commentaires sur qch; **to make ~ conversation** échanger des politesses.

politeness *n* politesse *f*.

political *adj* politique.

political analyst ▶805 *n* commentateur/-trice *m/f* politique.

politically correct, **PC** *adj* politiquement correct.

political: **~ prisoner** *n* prisonnier/-ière *m/f* politique; **~ science** *n* sciences *fpl* politiques.

politician ▶805 *n* homme/femme *m/f* politique.

politics *n* **1** (political life) politique *f*; **2** (subject) sciences *fpl* politiques; **3** (views) opinions *fpl* politiques.

poll I *n* **1** (vote casting) scrutin *m*, vote *m*; (election) élections *fpl*; (number of votes cast) voix *fpl*; **the result of the ~** les résultats du scrutin; **to go to the ~s** se rendre aux urnes; **2** (survey) sondage *m* (**on** sur).
II *vtr* **1** (obtain in election) obtenir [*votes*]; **2** (canvass) interroger [*group*].

pollen count *n* taux *m* de pollen dans l'atmosphère.

polling: **~ booth** *n* isoloir *m*; **~ day** *n* jour *m* des élections; **~ station** *n* bureau *m* de vote.

poll tax *n* (GB) ≈ impôts *mpl* locaux.

pollute *vtr* polluer [*environment*].

pollution *n* pollution *f*.

polo ▶649 *n* polo *m*.

polo neck *n* (GB) col *m* roulé.

poltergeist *n* esprit *m* frappeur.

poly I° *n* (GB) *abbr* ▶ **polytechnic.**
II **poly+** *pref* poly-.

polyglot *n, adj* polyglotte (*mf*).

polyp *n* polype *m*.

polytechnic *n* (GB) établissement *m* d'enseignement supérieur.

polythene *n* (GB) polyéthylène *m*.

polyunsaturates *n pl* acides *mpl* gras polyinsaturés.

pomegranate *n* (fruit) grenade *f*; (tree) grenadier *m*.

pomp *n* pompe *f*; **~ and circumstance** grand apparat.

pompom, pompon *n* pompon *m*.

pompous *adj* [*person*] plein de suffisance; [*air, speech, style*] pompeux/-euse.

pond *n* (large) étang *m*; (smaller) mare *f*; (in garden) bassin *m*.

ponder *vi* réfléchir (**on** à); (more deeply) méditer (**on** sur).

pong° *n* (GB) puanteur *f*; **what a ~!** ça pue°!

pontiff *n* pontife *m*.

pontoon *n* **1** (pier) ponton *m*; **2** ▶ 649 (GB Games) vingt-et-un *m*.

pony *n* poney *m*.

ponytail *n* queue *f* de cheval.

poodle *n* caniche *m*.

pool I *n* **1** (pond) étang *m*; (artificial) bassin *m*; (underground: of oil, gas) nappe *f*; **2** (also **swimming ~**) piscine *f*; **3** (of water, light) flaque *f*; **a ~ of blood** une mare de sang; **4** (kitty) cagnotte *f*; (in cards) mises *fpl*; **5** (of money, resources) pool *m*; (of ideas, experience) réservoir *m*; (of labour) réserve *f*; (of teachers, players, candidates) liste *f*; **6** (billiards) billard *m* américain.
II **pools** *n pl* (GB) (also **football ~s**) ≈ loto *m* sportif.
III *vtr* mettre [qch] en commun [*money, resources, information*].

poor *adj* **1** [*person, country*] pauvre (**in** en); **to become** or **get ~er** s'appauvrir; **2** (inferior) [*quality, result, work, education, planning, weather, visibility*] mauvais (*before n*); [*school work*] faible; [*soil*] pauvre; [*attendance*] faible; **to be ~ at** être faible en [*mathematics, French*]; **3** (deserving pity) pauvre (*before n*); **~ you!** mon/ma pauvre!; **4** [*attempt, excuse*] piètre (*before n*).

poorly *adv* **1** [*live, dress, dressed*] pauvrement; **2** [*written, lit, paid*] mal.

poor relation *n* parent *m* pauvre.

pop I *n* **1** (sound) pan *m*; **to go ~** faire pan; **2**° (drink) soda *m*; **3** (music) musique *f* pop.
II *noun modifier* [*concert, group, music, song*] pop; [*record, singer*] de pop.
III *vtr* **1**° (burst) faire éclater [*balloon, bubble*]; **2** (remove) faire sauter [*cork*]; **3**° (put) **to ~ sth in(to)** mettre qch dans [*oven, cupboard, mouth*].
IV *vi* **1** [*balloon*] éclater; [*cork, buttons*] sauter; **2** [*ears*] se déboucher brusquement; **her eyes were ~ping out of her head** les yeux lui sortaient de la tête; **3**° (GB) (go) **to ~ into town/the bank** faire un saut° en ville/à la banque.
■ **pop in**° (GB) passer.
■ **pop out** (GB) sortir.

pope *n* pape *m*; **Pope Paul VI** le Pape Paul VI.

poplar *n* peuplier *m*.

poppy *n* pavot *m*; **wild ~** coquelicot *m*.

pop sock *n* mi-bas *m*.

popular *adj* **1** [*actor, politician*] populaire (**with, among** parmi); [*profession, hobby, sport*] répandu (**with, among** chez); [*food, dish*] prisé (**with, among** par); [*product, resort, colour, design*] en vogue (**with, among** chez); **John is very ~** John a beaucoup d'amis; **she's ~ with the boys** elle a du succès auprès des garçons; **I'm not very ~ at the moment** je n'ai pas tellement la cote° en ce moment; **2** (of or for the people) [*music, movement, press*] populaire; [*entertainment*] grand public *inv*; [*science, history*] de vulgarisation; [*enthusiasm, interest, support*] du public; [*discontent*] du peuple; **by ~ demand** à la demande générale.

popularity *n* popularité *f* (**of** de; **with** auprès de).

popularize *vtr* **1** (make fashionable) généraliser; **2** (make accessible) vulgariser.

populate *vtr* peupler (**with** de).

population I *n* population *f*.
II *noun modifier* [*increase, decrease, explosion, figure*] démographique.

porcelain *n* porcelaine *f*.

porch *n* **1** (of house, church) porche *m*; **2** (US) (veranda) véranda *f*.

porcupine *n* porc-épic *m*.

pore *n* pore *m*.
■ **pore over**: **~ over [sth]** être plongé dans [*book*]; étudier soigneusement [*map*].

pork *n* (viande *f* de) porc *m*; **a leg of ~** un jambon.

pork: **~ butcher** *n* charcutier/-ière *m/f*; **~ chop** *n* côte *f* de porc.

pornographic *adj* pornographique.

pornography *n* pornographie *f*.

porpoise *n* marsouin *m*.

port I *n* **1** (harbour) port *m*; **in ~** au port; **the ship left ~** le bateau a appareillé; **~ of call** escale *f*; (figurative) arrêt *m*; **2** (drink) porto *m*.
II *noun modifier* [*area, authorities, facilities, security*] portuaire.

portable *adj* portable.

porter ▶ 805 *n* **1** (in station, airport, hotel) porteur *m*; (in hospital) brancardier *m*; (in market) débardeur *m*; **2** (GB) (of hotel) portier *m*; (of apartment block) gardien/-ienne *m/f*; (of school) concierge *mf*; **3** (US) (steward) employé *m* des wagons-lits.

portfolio *n* **1** (case) porte-documents *m inv*; (for drawings) carton *m* (à dessins); **2** (sample) portfolio *m*; **3** (ministerial post) portefeuille *m* (ministériel).

porthole *n* hublot *m*.

portion *n* **1** (of house, machine, document, country) partie *f* (**of** de); **2** (share) (of money, food) part *f* (**of** de); (of responsibility, blame) part *f* (**of** de); **3** (at meal) portion *f*.

portrait *n* portrait *m*.

portray *vtr* **1** (depict) décrire [*place, era, event*]; présenter [*person, situation*]; **2** [*actor*] interpréter [*character*]; **3** [*artist*] peindre [*person*]; [*picture, artist*] représenter [*scene*].

portrayal *n* **1** (by actor) interprétation *f* (**of** de); **2** (by author, director) portrait *m*.

Portugal ▶574 *pr n* Portugal *m*.

Portuguese ▶712 **I** *n* **1** (person) Portugais/-e *m/f*; **2** (language) portugais *m*.
II *adj* [*culture, food, politics*] portugais; [*teacher, lesson*] de portugais; [*ambassador, embassy*] du Portugal.

pose I *vtr* poser [*problem*] (**for** pour); présenter [*challenge*] (**to** à); représenter [*threat, risk*] (**to** pour); soulever [*question*] (**about** de).
II *vi* **1** [*artist's model*] poser; [*performer*] prendre des poses; **2 to ~ as** se faire passer pour; **3** (posture) frimer○.

poser○ *n* **1** (person) frimeur/-euse○ *m/f*; **2** (puzzle) colle○ *f*.

posh○ *adj* [*person*] huppé○; [*house, area, clothes, car*] chic *inv*; [*voice*] distingué.

position I *n* **1** (situation, state) situation *f*; **in a strong ~** en position de force; **to be in a ~ to do** être en mesure de faire; **to be in a good/in no ~ to do** être bien/mal placé pour faire; **if I were in your ~** si j'étais à ta place; **2** (attitude, stance) position *f*; **the official ~** la position officielle; **3** (place, location) position *f*; **to be in ~** (in place) être en place; (ready) être prêt; **the house is in a good ~** la maison est bien située; **4** (posture) position *f*; **to be in a sitting ~** être assis; **5** (of lever, switch) position *f*; **6** (ranking) place *f*, rang *m*; (in sport, competition) position *f*; **7** (Sport) poste *m*; **what ~ does he play?** quel est son poste?; **8** (job) poste *m*; **to hold** or **occupy a senior ~** occuper un poste responsable; **9** (place in society, army) position *f*.
II *vtr* poster [*policemen, soldiers*]; disposer [*object*].

positive *adj* **1** (affirmative) [*answer, reaction, result*] positif/-ive; **2** (optimistic) [*message, person, feeling, tone*] positif/-ive; **to be ~ about** être enthousiaste à propos de [*idea, proposal*]; **to think ~** voir les choses de façon positive; **3** (constructive) [*contribution, effect, progress*] positif/-ive; [*advantage, good*] réel/réelle; **4** (sure) [*identification, proof*] formel/-elle; [*fact*] indéniable; **to be ~** être sûr (**about** de; **that** que); **5** (forceful) [*action, measure*] catégorique; **6** (in mathematics, science) positif/-ive; **7** (extreme) [*pleasure*] pur (*before n*); [*disgrace, outrage, genius*] véritable (*before n*).

positively *adv* **1** [*contribute, criticize*] de façon constructive; **2** [*react, speak*] favorablement; **3** [*participate, promote*] activement; **4** [*identify, prove*] formellement; **5** [*disgraceful, dangerous*] vraiment; [*refuse, forbid*] catégoriquement.

possess *vtr* **1** posséder [*property, weapon, proof, charm*]; avoir [*power, advantage*]; (illegally) détenir [*arms, drugs*]; **2** (take control of) [*anger, fury*] s'emparer de [*person*]; [*devil*] posséder [*person*]; **what ~ed you to do that?** qu'est-ce qui t'a pris de faire ça?

possession I *n* **1** (gen) possession *f*; **to be in ~ of** être en possession de; **to have ~ of sth** posséder qch; **2** (Law) (illegal) détention *f* (**of** de); **3** (Law) (of property) jouissance *f* (**of** de); **to take ~ of** prendre possession de [*premises, property*].
II possessions *n pl* biens *mpl*.

possessive I *n* (in grammar) possessif *m*.
II *adj* possessif/-ive (**towards** à l'égard de; **with** avec).

possibility *n* **1** (chance, prospect) possibilité *f*; **there is a definite ~ that he'll come** il y a de très grandes chances qu'il vienne; **there is no ~ of changing the text** il est impossible de changer le texte; **2** (eventuality) éventualité *f*; **the ~ of a refusal** l'éventualité d'un refus.

possible I *n* (for job) candidat *m* possible; (for team) joueur/-euse *m/f* possible.
II *adj* possible; **he did as much as ~** il a fait tout son possible; **as far as ~** dans la mesure du possible; **as quickly as ~** le plus vite possible.

possibly *adv* **1** (maybe) peut-être; **2** (for emphasis) **how could they ~ understand?** comment donc pourraient-ils comprendre?; **we can't ~ afford it** nous n'en avons absolument pas les moyens.

post I *n* **1** (job) poste *m* (**as, of** de); **to hold a ~** occuper un poste; **2** (GB) (postal system) poste *f*; (letters) courrier *m*; (delivery) distribution *f*; **by return of ~** par retour du courrier; **it was lost in the ~** cela s'est égaré dans le courrier; **3** (duty, station) poste *m*; **at one's ~** à son poste; **4** (pole) poteau *m*; **to be the first past the ~** (Sport) être le premier à l'arrivée; (in election) obtenir la majorité.
II post- *pref* post-; **in ~-1992 Europe** dans l'Europe d'après 1992.
III *vtr* **1** (GB) (send by post) poster, expédier [qch] (par la poste); (put in letterbox) mettre [qch] à la poste; **2** (stick up) afficher [*notice, poster*]; annoncer [*details, results*]; **3** (gen, Mil) (send abroad) affecter (**to** à); **4** (station) poster [*guard, sentry*].

postage *n* affranchissement *m*; **including ~ and packing** frais *mpl* d'expédition inclus; **~ free** franc de port.

postal *adj* [*charges, district*] postal; [*application*] par la poste.

postal: **~ order**, **PO** *n* (GB) mandat *m* (**for** de); **~ vote** *n* (process) vote *m* par correspondance.

post: **~bag** *n* (GB) (postman's) sac *m* postal; (mail) courrier *m*; **~box** *n* (GB) boîte *f* aux lettres; **~card** *n* carte *f* postale; **~ code** *n* (GB) code *m* postal; **~date** *vtr* postdater.

poster *n* (for information) affiche *f*; (decorative) poster *m*.

posterity *n* postérité *f*.

poster paint *n* gouache *f*.

postgraduate I *n* ≈ étudiant/-e *m/f* de troisième cycle.
II *adj* ≈ de troisième cycle.

posthumous *adj* posthume.

post: **~man** ▶805| *n* facteur *m*; **~mark** *n* cachet *m* de la poste.

post-mortem *n* autopsie *f*.

post-natal *adj* post-natal.

post office, PO *n* poste *f*.

postpone *vtr* reporter, remettre (**until** à; **for** de).

postponement *n* report *m*, renvoi *m* (**until** à).

postscript *n* (in letter) post-scriptum *m inv* (**to** à); (to book) postface *f* (**to** à).

posture I *n* **1** (pose) posture *f*; (figurative) (stance) position *f*; **2** (bearing) maintien *m*; **to have good/bad ~** se tenir bien/mal.
II *vi* poser, prendre des poses.

postwar *adj* d'après-guerre.

pot I *n* **1** (container) pot *m*; **a ~ of tea for two** deux thés; **to make a ~ of tea/coffee** faire du thé/du café; **~s and pans** casseroles *fpl*; **2** (piece of pottery) poterie *f*.
II *vtr* **1** mettre [qch] en pot [*jam*]; **2** (in billiards) blouser [*ball*]; **3** (also **~ up**) mettre [qch] en pot [*plant*].
III potted *pp adj* **1** (GB Culin) **~ted meat** terrine *f* de viande; **2** [*palm, plant*] en pot; **3** [*biography, history*] bref/brève.
IDIOMS **to go to ~**○ (person) se laisser aller; (thing) aller à vau-l'eau; **to take ~ luck** (for meal) (GB) manger à la fortune du pot.

potassium *n* potassium *m*.

potato *n* pomme *f* de terre.

potato: **~ chips** (US), **~ crisps** (GB) *n pl* chips *fpl*; **~ peeler** *n* épluche-légumes *m inv*.

pot belly *n* bedaine *f*.

potency *n* **1** (of drug, image) puissance *f*; (of drink) force *f*; **2** (sexual) virilité *f*.

potent *adj* **1** [*symbol, drug*] puissant; [*drink*] fort; **2** (sexually) viril.

potential I *n* potentiel *m* (**as** en tant que; **for** de); **the ~ to do** les qualités *fpl* nécessaires pour faire; **to fulfil one's ~** montrer de quoi on est capable.
II *adj* [*buyer, danger, energy, market, victim*] potentiel/-ielle; [*champion, rival*] en puissance; [*investor*] éventuel/-elle.

pot: **~hole** *n* fondrière *f*, nid *m* de poule; **~holing** ▶649| *n* (GB) spéléologie *f*; **~ plant** *n* plante *f* d'appartement.

potter ▶805| *n* potier *m*.
■ **potter about, potter around** (GB) (do odd jobs) bricoler○; (go about daily chores) suivre son petit train-train○; (pass time idly) traîner.

pottery *n* **1** (craft) poterie *f*; **2** (ware) poteries *fpl*; **3** (place) poterie *f*.

potty○ **I** *n* pot *m* (d'enfant).
II *adj* (GB) [*person*] dingue○; [*idea*] farfelu○; **to be ~ about** être toqué○ de.

potty-train *vtr* **to ~ a child** apprendre à un enfant à aller sur le pot.

pouch *n* **1** (bag) petit sac *m*; (for tobacco) blague *f* (à tabac); (for ammunition) étui *m* (à munitions); **2** (of marsupials) poche *f* ventrale; (of rodents) abajoue *f*.

poultry *n* (birds) volailles *fpl*; (meat) volaille *f*.

pounce *vi* bondir; **to ~ on** [*animal*] bondir sur [*prey, object*]; [*person*] se jeter sur [*victim*].

pound I *n* **1** ▶738| (weight measurement) livre *f* (*de 453,6g*); **two ~s of apples** ≈ un kilo de pommes; **pears are 80 pence a** or **per ~** ≈ les poires sont à 80 pence la livre; **2** ▶748| (unit of currency) livre *f*; **3** (for dogs, cars) fourrière *f*.
II *vtr* **1** (Culin) piler [*spices, grain*]; aplatir [*meat*]; **to ~ sth to** réduire qch en [*powder, paste*]; **2** (beat) [*waves*] battre [*shore*]; **3** [*artillery*] pilonner [*city*].
III *vi* **1 to ~ on** marteler [*door, wall*]; **2** [*heart*] battre; **to ~ on** [*waves*] battre contre [*beach, rocks*]; **3 to ~ up/down the stairs** monter/descendre l'escalier d'un pas lourd; **4 my head is ~ing** j'ai l'impression que ma tête va éclater.

pour I *vtr* **1** verser [*liquid*]; couler [*cement, metal, wax*]; **2** (also **~ out**) servir [*drink*]; **can I ~ you some more coffee?** puis-je vous resservir du café?; **to ~ oneself a drink** se servir un verre; **3 to ~ money into** investir des sommes énormes dans.
II *vi* **1** [*liquid*] couler (à flots); **to ~ into** [*water, liquid*] couler dans; [*smoke, fumes*] se répandre dans; [*light*] inonder [*room*]; **to ~ out of** or **from** [*smoke, fumes*] s'échapper de; [*water*] ruisseler de; **tears ~ed down her face** les larmes ruisselaient sur son visage; **2 to ~ into** [*people*] affluer dans; **to ~ from** or **out of** [*people, cars*] sortir en grand nombre de; [*supplies, money*] sortir en masse de.
III *v impers* **it's ~ing (with rain)** il pleut à verse.
■ **pour away**: **~ away [sth]**, **~ [sth] away** vider.
■ **pour down** pleuvoir à verse.
■ **pour in** [*people*] affluer; [*letters, money*] pleuvoir; [*water*] entrer à flots.
■ **pour out**: ¶ **~ out** [*liquid, smoke, crowd*] se déverser; [*people*] sortir en grand nombre; ¶ **~ out [sth]**, **~ [sth] out 1** verser, servir [*coffee, wine*]; **2** rejeter [*fumes, sewage*]; **to ~ out one's troubles** or **heart to sb** s'épancher auprès de qn.

pout *vi* faire la moue.

poverty *n* pauvreté *f*; (more severe) misère *f*.

poverty: **~ line** *n* seuil *m* de pauvreté; **~-stricken** *adj* dans la misère.

powder I *n* **1** (substance) poudre *f*; **in ~ form** en poudre; **2** (snow) poudreuse *f*.
II *vtr* **to ~ one's face** se poudrer le visage.
III powdered *pp adj* [*egg, milk, coffee*] en poudre.

powdery *adj* [*snow*] poudreux/-euse; [*stone*] friable.

power I *n* **1** (control) pouvoir *m*; **to be in/come to ~** être/accéder au pouvoir; **to be in sb's ~** être à la merci de qn; **2** (influence) influence *f* (**over** sur); **3** (capability) pouvoir *m*; **to do everything in one's ~** faire tout ce qui est en son pouvoir (**to do** pour faire); **to be at the height of one's ~s** avoir atteint la plénitude de ses moyens; [*artist*] être au sommet de son art; **4** (also **~s**) (authority) attributions *fpl*;

police ~s les attributions de la police; **5** (physical force) (of person, explosion) force *f*; (of storm) violence *f*; **6** (Tech) énergie *f*; (current) courant *m*; **to switch on the ~** mettre le courant; **7** (of vehicle, plane) puissance *f*; **to be running at full/half ~** fonctionner à plein/mi-régime; **8** (in mathematics) **6 to the ~ of 3** 6 puissance 3; **9** (country) puissance *f*.
II *noun modifier* [*drill, cable*] électrique; [*steering, brakes*] assisté.
III *vtr* faire marcher [*engine*]; propulser [*plane, boat*]; **~ed by** propulsé par [*engine*]; alimenté par [*electricity, gas, generator*].
IDIOMS **to do sb a ~ of good** faire à qn un bien fou; **the ~s that be** les autorités.

power: **~boat** *n* hors-bord *m inv*; **~ cut** *n* coupure *f* de courant.

powerful *adj* [*person, engine, computer*] puissant; [*smell, emotion, voice, government*] fort; [*argument*] solide.

powerless *adj* impuissant (**against** face à); **to be ~ to do** ne pas pouvoir faire.

power: **~ line** *n* ligne *f* à haute tension; **~ plant** (US) = **power station**; **~ sharing** *n* partage *m* du pouvoir; **~ station** *n* centrale *f* (électrique).

pp 1 (on document) (*abbr* = **per procurationem**) po; **2** (*abbr* = **pages**) pp.

PR *n* **1** (*abbr* = **public relations**) relations *fpl* publiques; **2** *abbr* ▶ **proportional representation**.

practical I *n* (exam) épreuve *f* pratique; (lesson) travaux *mpl* pratiques.
II *adj* **1** (concrete) pratique; **in ~ terms** en pratique; **2** [*person*] (sensible) pratique; (with hands) adroit; **3** (functional) [*clothes, furniture*] pratique; **4** (practicable) [*plan*] réalisable.

practicalities *n pl* détails *mpl* pratiques.

practicality *n* **1** (of person) esprit *m* pratique; (of equipment) facilité *f* d'utilisation; **2** (of scheme, idea, project) aspect *m* pratique.

practical joke *n* farce *f*.

practically *adv* **1** (almost) pratiquement; **2** (in practical way) d'une manière pratique.

practice I *n* **1** (exercises) exercices *mpl*; (experience) entraînement *m*; **to have had ~ in** or **at sth/in** or **at doing sth** avoir déjà fait qch; **to be out of ~** être rouillé○; **2** (for sport) entraînement *m*; (for music, drama) répétition *f*; **3** (procedure) pratique *f*, usage *m*; **it's standard ~ to do** il est d'usage de faire; **business ~** usage en affaires; **4** (habit) habitude *f*; **5** (custom) coutume *f*; **6** (business of doctor, lawyer) cabinet *m*; **7** (not theory) pratique *f*; **in ~** en pratique.
II *noun modifier* [*game, match*] d'essai; [*flight*] d'entraînement.
III *vtr*, *vi* (US) = **practise**.
IDIOMS **~ makes perfect** c'est en forgeant qu'on devient forgeron (Proverb).

practise (GB), **practice** (US) **I** *vtr* **1** travailler [*song, speech, French*]; s'exercer à [*movement, shot*]; réviser [*technique*]; répéter [*play*]; **to ~ the piano** travailler le piano; **to ~ doing** or **how to do** s'entraîner à faire; **2** (use) pratiquer [*restraint, kindness*]; utiliser [*method*]; **3** (work) exercer; **4** (observe) pratiquer [*custom, religion*].
II *vi* **1** (train) (at piano, violin) s'exercer; (for sports) s'entraîner; (for play, concert) répéter; **2** (work) exercer; **to ~ as** exercer la profession de [*doctor, lawyer*].

pragmatic *adj* pragmatique.

pragmatics *n* (of scheme, situation) détails *mpl* pratiques.

prairie *n* plaine *f* (herbeuse).

praise I *n* éloges *mpl*, louanges *fpl*.
II *vtr* **1** faire l'éloge de [*person, book, achievement*] (**as** en tant que); **to ~ sb for sth/for doing** féliciter qn de qch/d'avoir fait; **2** louer [*God*] (**for** pour).

praiseworthy *adj* digne d'éloges.

pram *n* (GB) landau *m*.

prance *vi* [*horse*] caracoler; [*person*] sautiller; **to ~ in/out** [*person*] entrer/sortir allègrement.

prattle *vi* bavarder; [*children*] babiller; **to ~ on about sth** parler de qch à n'en plus finir.

prawn *n* crevette *f* rose, bouquet *m*.

pray *vi* prier (**for** pour).

prayer *n* prière *f*; (hope) souhait *m*; **to say one's ~s** faire sa prière.

prayer book *n* livre *m* de prières.

preach I *vtr* prêcher (**to** à); (figurative) prêcher, prôner [*tolerance, virtue, pacifism*].
II *vi* prêcher (**to** à); (figurative) sermonner.
IDIOMS **to practise what one ~es** prêcher d'exemple.

preacher *n* prédicateur *m*; (clergyman) pasteur *m*.

prearrange *vtr* fixer [qch] à l'avance.

precarious *adj* précaire.

precaution *n* précaution *f* (**against** contre).

precautionary *adj* préventif/-ive.

precede *vtr* précéder.

precedence *n* **1** (in importance) priorité *f* (**over** sur); **2** (in rank) préséance *f* (**over** sur).

precedent *n* précédent *m*; **to set a ~** créer un précédent.

preceding *adj* précédent.

precinct *n* **1** (GB) (also **shopping ~**) quartier *m* commerçant; **2** (GB) (also **pedestrian ~**) zone *f* piétonne; **3** (US) (administrative district) circonscription *f*.

precious *adj* **1** (valuable) précieux/-ieuse; **2** (held dear) [*person*] cher/chère (**to** à); **3** (affected) [*person, style*] précieux/-ieuse, affecté.

precipice *n* précipice *m*.

précis *n* résumé *m*.

precise *adj* **1** [*measurement*] précis; **2** [*person, mind*] méticuleux/-euse.

precisely *adv* **1** (exactly) exactement, précisément; **at ten o'clock ~** à dix heures précises; **2** (accurately) [*describe, record*] avec précision.

precision *n* précision *f*.

preclude *vtr* exclure [*possibility*]; empêcher [*action*].

precocious *adj* précoce.

preconceived *adj* préconçu.

precondition *n* condition *f* requise.

precook *vtr* précuire.

precursor *n* (person) précurseur *m*; (sign) signe *m* avant-coureur.

predate *vtr* **1** antidater [*cheque*]; **2** [*discovery, building*] être antérieur à.

predator *n* prédateur *m*.

predatory *adj* prédateur/-trice.

predecessor *n* prédécesseur *m*.

predicament *n* situation *f* difficile.

predict *vtr* prédire.

predictable *adj* prévisible.

predictably *adv* [*boring, late*] comme prévu; **~**,... comme on pouvait s'y attendre,...

prediction *n* prédiction *f* (**that** selon laquelle).

predispose *vtr* prédisposer.

predominance *n* prédominance *f* (**of** de; **over** sur).

predominant *adj* prédominant.

predominantly *adv* [*feature*] principalement; [*Muslim*] essentiellement.

pre-eminence *n* (gen) suprématie *f*; (Sport) supériorité *f*.

pre-eminent *adj* [*celebrity, scientist*] éminent.

pre-empt *vtr* **1** (anticipate) anticiper [*question, decision, move*]; devancer [*person*]; **2** (thwart) contrecarrer [*action, plan*].

pre-emptive *adj* [*strike, move, attack*] préventif/-ive.

preen *v refl* **to ~ oneself** [*bird*] se lisser les plumes; [*person*] se pomponner.

pre-exist I *vtr* préexister à.
II **pre-existing** *pres p adj* préexistant.

prefab *n* (bâtiment *m*) préfabriqué *m*.

preface I *n* (to book) préface *f*; (to speech) préambule *m*.
II *vtr* préfacer [*livre*]; **to ~ sth with sth** faire précéder qch de qch.

prefect *n* (GB Sch) élève *m/f* chargé/-e de la surveillance.

prefecture *n* préfecture *f*.

prefer I *vtr* **1** (like better) préférer, aimer mieux; **I ~ painting to drawing** je préfère la peinture au dessin; **to ~ it if** aimer mieux que (+ *subj*); **2** (Law) **to ~ charges** [*police*] déférer [qn] au parquet.
II **preferred** *pp adj* [*method, option*] préféré; [*creditor, candidate*] prioritaire.

preferable *adj* préférable (**to** à).

preferably *adv* de préférence.

preference *n* préférence *f* (**for** pour); **in ~ to** de préférence à; **in ~ to doing** plutôt que de faire.

preferential *adj* préférentiel/-ielle.

prefix *n* préfixe *m*.

pregnancy *n* (gen) grossesse *f*; (Zool) gestation *f*.

pregnant *n* (gen) enceinte; (Zool) pleine; **to get sb ~**° faire un enfant à qn°.

preheat *vtr* préchauffer [*oven*].

prehistoric *adj* préhistorique.

prejudice I *n* préjugé *m*; **racial/political ~** préjugés raciaux/en matière de politique.
II *vtr* **1** (bias) influencer; **to ~ sb against/in favour of** prévenir qn contre/en faveur de; **2** porter préjudice à [*claim, case*]; léser [*person*]; compromettre [*chances*].

prejudiced *adj* [*person*] plein de préjugés; [*account*] partial; [*opinion*] préconçu.

preliminary I *n* **1** (gen) **as a ~ to** en prélude à; **2** (Sport) épreuve *f* éliminatoire.
II **preliminaries** *n pl* préliminaires *mpl* (**to** à).
III *adj* [*inquiry, ruling, comment, data, test*] préliminaire; [*round*] éliminatoire.

prelude *n* prélude *m* (**to** à).

premature *adj* [*baby, action*] prématuré; [*ejaculation, menopause*] précoce.

premedication *n* (also **premed**) (Med) prémédication *f*.

premeditate *vtr* préméditer.

premier I *n* **1** (prime minister) premier ministre *m*; **2** (head of government) chef *m* du gouvernement.
II *adj* premier/-ière.

première I *n* première *f*.
II *vtr* donner [qch] en première [*film, play*].

premises *n pl* locaux *mpl*; **on the ~** sur place; **off the ~** à l'extérieur; **to leave the ~** quitter les lieux.

premium *n* **1** (extra payment) supplément *m*; **2** (on stock exchange) prime *f* d'émission; **3** (in insurance) prime *f* (d'assurance); **4** (payment for lease) reprise *f*; **5 to be at a ~** valoir de l'or; **to set a (high) ~ on sth** mettre qch au (tout) premier plan.

premium bond (GB) *n* obligation *f* à lots.

premonition *n* prémonition *f*.

prenatal *adj* prénatal.

preoccupation *n* préoccupation *f*; **his ~ with** son obsession pour.

preoccupied *adj* préoccupé.

prepaid *adj* payé d'avance; **~ envelope** enveloppe *f* affranchie pour la réponse.

preparation *n* **1** (of meal, report, lecture, event) préparation *f*; **~s** préparatifs *mpl*; **in ~ for sth** en vue de qch; **2** (physical, psychological) préparation *f* (**for** pour); (sporting) entraînement (**for** pour); **3** (substance) préparation *f*.

preparatory *adj* [*training, course, drawing*] préparatoire; [*meeting, report, investigations*] préliminaire; **~ to sth/to doing** en vue de qch/de faire.

preparatory school *n* **1** (GB) école *f* primaire privée; **2** (US) lycée *m* privé.

prepare I *vtr* préparer [*food, room, class, report, surprise*]; **to ~ to do** se préparer à faire; **to ~ sb for** préparer qn à [*situation, shock*].
II *vi* **to ~ for** se préparer à [*trip, talks, exam, war*]; se préparer pour [*party, ceremony, game*]; **to ~ oneself** se préparer.

prepared *adj* **1** (willing) **to be ~ to do** être prêt à faire; **2** (ready) **to be ~ for** être prêt pour [*event*]; **to be well-/ill-~** (with materials) être bien/mal équipé; **to come ~** venir bien préparé; **to be ~ for the worst** s'attendre au pire.

preposition *n* préposition *f*.

preposterous *adj* grotesque.

prerequisite *n* **1** (gen) préalable *m* (**of** de; **for** à); **2** (US Univ) unité *f* de valeur.

prerogative *n* (official) prérogative *f*; (personal) droit *m*.

preschool I *n* (US) école *f* maternelle; **in ~** à l'école maternelle.
II *adj* [*child*] d'âge préscolaire *inv*; [*years*] préscolaire.

prescribe I *vtr* **1** (Med, figurative) prescrire (**for sb** à qn; **for sth** pour qch); **2** imposer [*rule*].
II **prescribed** *pp adj* **1** [*remedy*] prescrit; **2** [*rule*] imposé; [*text*] inscrit au programme.

prescription *n* ordonnance *f*; **on ~** sur ordonnance.

presence *n* présence *f*; **a heavy police ~** (in streets) une forte présence policière; (at match, demonstration) un important service d'ordre.

presence of mind *n* présence *f* d'esprit.

present I *n* **1** (gift) cadeau *m*; **to give sb a ~** offrir un cadeau à qn; **2 the ~** le présent; **for the ~** pour le moment, pour l'instant; **3** (also **~ tense**) présent *m*.
II *adj* **1** (attending) présent; **to be ~ at** assister à; **2** (current) actuel/-elle; **up to the ~ day** jusqu'à ce jour; **at the ~ time** or **moment** actuellement; **3** [*tense*] présent.
III *vtr* **1** présenter [*problem, challenge, risk*]; offrir [*chance, opportunity*]; **2** présenter [*tickets*]; **to be ~ed with a choice** se trouver face à un choix; **to be ~ed with a huge bill** se retrouver avec une énorme facture; **3** présenter [*plan, figures, petition*]; fournir [*evidence*]; **4** remettre [*prize, certificate*] (**to** à); **5** présenter [*person, situation*] (**as** comme étant); **may I ~ my son Piers?** permettez-moi de vous présenter mon fils Piers; **6** présenter [*programme, show*]; donner [*production, play*].
IV *vi* (Med) [*patient, baby*] se présenter; [*symptom, condition*] apparaître.
V *v refl* **to ~ oneself** se présenter; **to ~ itself** [*opportunity, thought*] se présenter.
VI **at present** *phr* (at this moment) en ce moment; (nowadays) actuellement.

presentable *adj* présentable.

presentation *n* **1** (of plan, report, idea, person) présentation *f*; **2** (by salesman, colleague) exposé *m*; **3** (of gift, award) remise *f* (**of** de); **4** (portrayal) représentation *f*; **5** (of baby) présentation *f*.

presenter ▶ **805** *n* présentateur/-trice *m*/*f*.

presently *adv* (currently) à présent; (soon, in future) bientôt.

present perfect *n* passé *m* composé.

preservation *n* (of building, wildlife, peace) préservation *f* (**of** de); (of food) conservation *f* (**of** de); (of life) protection *f* (**of** de).

preservative *n* (for food) agent *m* de conservation; (for wood) revêtement *m* (protecteur).

preserve I *n* **1** (Culin) (jam) confiture *f*; (pickle) conserve *f*; **2** (territory) chasse *f* gardée (**of** de).
II *vtr* **1** (save) préserver [*land, building, tradition*] (**for** pour); entretenir [*wood, leather, painting*]; **2** (maintain) préserver [*peace, standards, rights*]; maintenir [*order*]; **3** (keep, hold onto) garder [*humour, dignity, health*]; **4** conserver [*food*].

preset *vtr* régler (à l'avance) [*timer, cooker*]; programmer [*video*].

preside *vi* présider; **to ~ at sth** présider qch; **to ~ over** présider [*committee*].

presidency *n* présidence *f*.

president ▶ **642** *n* **1** président/-e *m*/*f*; **to run for ~** être candidat/-e à la présidence; **2** (US) (managing director) président-directeur *m* général.

presidential *adj* [*election, government, term*] présidentiel/-ielle.

press I *n* **1** (medium) **the ~**, **the Press** la presse *f*; **to get a good/bad ~** avoir bonne/mauvaise presse; **2** (also **printing ~**) presse *f*; **to go to ~** être mis sous presse; **3** (publishing house) maison *f* d'éditon; (print works) imprimerie *f*; **4** (device for flattening) presse *f*; **5** (with iron) repassage *m*; **to give sth a ~** repasser qch.
II *noun modifier* [*photographer*] de presse; [*announcement*] par voie de presse.
III *vtr* **1** (push) appuyer sur; **to ~ sth in** enfoncer qch; **to ~ sth into** enfoncer qch dans [*mud, ground, pillow*]; **to ~ sth into sb's hand** glisser qch dans la main de qn; **2** (apply) **to ~ one's nose against sth** coller son nez contre qch; **to ~ one's hands to one's ears** se plaquer les mains contre les oreilles; **to ~ one's knees together** serrer les genoux; **3** (squeeze) presser [*fruit, flower*]; serrer [*arm, hand, person*]; **4** (iron) repasser [*clothes*]; **5** (urge) faire pression sur [*person*]; mettre [qch] en avant [*issue*]; défendre [qch] avec insistance [*case*]; **to ~ sb to do** presser qn de faire; **to ~ sb into doing** forcer qn à faire; **to ~ a point** insister; **6** (Tech) former [*shape, object*]; presser [*record, CD*]; emboutir [*metal, car body*].
IV *vi* **1 to ~ down** appuyer; **2** [*crowd, person*] se presser (**forward** vers l'avant).
V *v refl* **to ~ oneself against** se plaquer contre [*wall*]; se presser contre [*person*].
■ **press ahead** aller de l'avant; **to ~ ahead with [sth]** faire avancer [*reform, plan*].
■ **press for**: **~ for [sth]** faire pression pour obtenir [*change, support, release*]; **to be ~ed for** ne pas avoir beaucoup de [*time, cash*].
■ **press on** continuer; **to ~ on with** faire avancer [*reform, plan*].

press: **~ agency** *n* agence *f* de presse; **~ conference** *n* conférence *f* de presse; **~ cutting** *n* coupure *f* de presse.

pressing *adj* **1** (urgent) urgent; **2** [*invitation*] pressant.

press: **~ release** *n* communiqué *m* de presse; **~ story**, **~ report** *n* reportage *m*; **~-stud** *n* (GB) (bouton-)pression *m*; **~-up** *n* pompe° *f*.

pressure *n* **1** pression *f*; **to put ~ on sb** faire pression sur qn; **to do sth under ~** faire qch sous la contrainte; **financial ~s** contraintes financières; **the ~s of modern**

life le stress de la vie moderne; **2** (of traffic, tourists) flux *m*.

pressure: **~ cooker** *n* cocotte-minute® *f*; **~ group** *n* groupe *m* de pression.

pressurize *vtr* **1** pressuriser [*cabin, suit, gas*]; **2** faire pression sur [*person*]; **he was ~d into going** on a fait pression sur lui pour qu'il y aille.

prestige *n* prestige *m*.

prestigious *adj* prestigieux/-ieuse.

presumably *adv* sans doute.

presume I *vtr* **1** (suppose) supposer, présumer; **I ~d him to be honest** je le croyais honnête; **2** (presuppose) présupposer; **3** (dare) **to ~ to do** se permettre de faire.
II *vi* **to ~ upon** abuser de [*person, kindness*].

presumption *n* supposition *f* (**that** que); **to make a ~** supposer.

presumptuous *adj* présomptueux/-euse, arrogant.

presuppose *vtr* présupposer (**that** que).

pretence (GB), **pretense** (US) *n* **1** (false show) faux-semblant *m*; **to make a ~ of sth** feindre qch; **to make a ~ of doing** faire semblant de faire; **to make no ~ of sth** ne pas se donner la peine de feindre qch; **on** or **under the ~ of doing** sous prétexte de faire; **2** (sham) simulacre *m* (**of** de); (of illness) simulation *f* (**of** de).

pretend I *vtr* **1** (feign) simuler; **to ~ that all is well** faire comme si tout allait bien; **to ~ to do** faire semblant de faire; **2** (claim) **to ~ to be** prétendre être.
II *vi* **1** (feign) faire semblant; **2** (maintain deception) jouer la comédie; **I was only ~ing** c'était pour rire.

pretender *n* prétendant/-e *m/f* (**to** à).

pretension *n* prétention *f*; **to have ~s to sth** prétendre à qch.

pretentious *adj* prétentieux/-ieuse.

preterite *n* prétérit.

pretext *n* prétexte *m*.

pretty I *adj* joli; **it was not a ~ sight** ce n'était pas beau à voir.
II° *adv* (very) vraiment; (fairly) assez; **~ good** pas mal du tout.
IDIOMS **~ as a picture** ravissant; **to be sitting ~**° avoir une bonne situation, se la couler douce°.

prevail *v* ■ **prevail upon**: **~ upon** [**sb**] persuader.

prevailing *adj* [*attitude, style*] qui prévaut; [*rate*] en vigueur; [*wind*] dominant.

prevalence *n* **1** (frequency) fréquence *f*; **2** (superior position) prédominance *f*.

prevalent *adj* **1** (widespread) répandu; **2** (ruling) qui prévaut.

prevent *vtr* prévenir [*fire, illness, violence*]; éviter [*conflict, disaster, damage*]; faire obstacle à [*marriage*]; **to ~ sb from doing** empêcher qn de faire.

prevention *n* prévention *f*; **crime ~** lutte *f* contre la délinquance.

preventive *adj* préventif/-ive.

preview *n* (of film, play) avant-première *f*; (of exhibition) vernissage *m*; (of match, programme) présentation *f* (**of** de).

previous *adj* [*day, meeting, manager*] précédent; (further back in time) antérieur; **on ~ occasions** à plusieurs reprises; **he has no ~ convictions** il a un casier judiciaire vierge; **to have a ~ engagement** être déjà pris.

previously *adv* (before) auparavant, avant; (already) déjà.

prewar *adj* d'avant-guerre *inv*.

prey *n* proie *f*.
■ **prey on**: ¶ **~ on** [**sth**] **1** (hunt) chasser; **2** (worry) **to ~ on sb's mind** préoccuper qn; ¶ **~ on** [**sb**] [*con man*] choisir ses victimes parmi; [*rapist*] s'attaquer à.

price I *n* **1** (cost) prix *m*; **the ~ per kilo** le prix du kilo; **to go up in ~** augmenter; **to pay a high ~ for sth** payer qch cher; **2** (value) valeur *f*; **to put a ~ on** évaluer [*object, antique*]; **to put** or **set a high ~ on** attacher beaucoup de prix à [*loyalty, hard work*].
II *vtr* **1** fixer le prix de (**at** à); **a dress ~d at £30** une robe à 30 livres; **a moderately-~d hotel** un hôtel aux tarifs raisonnables; **2** (with price tag) marquer le prix de.

price: **~ bracket** *n* = **price range**; **~ cutting** *n* baisse *f* des prix.

priceless *adj* **1** (extremely valuable) inestimable; **2**° (amusing) impayable°.

price: **~ list** *n* (in shop, catalogue) liste *f* des prix; (in bar, restaurant) tarif *m*; **~ range** *n* fourchette *f*; **~ tag** *n* (label) étiquette *f*; (cost) coût *m*; **~ ticket** *n* étiquette *f*; **~ war** *n* guerre *f* des prix.

prick I *n* (of needle) (feeling) piqûre *f*; (hole) trou *m* (d'épingle).
II *vtr* **1** piquer; **to ~ one's finger** se piquer le doigt; **2** percer [*paper, plastic*]; crever [*balloon*]; piquer [*potato*].
III *vi* **1** [*eyes*] piquer; [*skin*] picoter; **2** [*thorn*] piquer.
■ **prick up**: **~ up** [*dog's ears*] se dresser; **to ~ up one's ears** [*person*] dresser l'oreille; **the dog ~ed up its ears** le chien a dressé les oreilles.

prickle I *n* (of hedgehog, plant) piquant *m*.
II *vi* [*hairs*] se hérisser (**with** de).

prickly *adj* **1** [*bush, leaf*] épineux/-euse; [*animal*] armé de piquants; [*thorn*] piquant; **2** (itchy) qui gratte; **3**° (touchy) irritable (**about** à propos de).

pride I *n* **1** fierté *f* (**in being** d'être; **in sth** qu'on tire de qch); **to take ~ in** être fier/fière de [*ability, achievement*]; soigner [*appearance, work*]; **to be sb's ~ and joy** être la (grande) fierté de qn; **2** (self-respect) amour-propre *m*; (excessive) orgueil *m*; **family ~** honneur *m* familial; **national ~** sentiment *m* de fierté nationale; **3** (of lions) troupe *f*.
II *v refl* **to ~ oneself on sth/on doing** être fier/fière de qch/de faire.
IDIOMS **to have ~ of place** occuper la place d'honneur.

priest *n* prêtre *m*; **parish ~** curé *m*.

priesthood *n* (calling) prêtrise *f*; **to enter the ~** entrer dans les ordres.
prig *n* bégueule *mf*.
prim *adj* (also **~ and proper**) [*person, manner, appearance*] guindé; [*expression*] pincé; [*voice*] affecté; [*clothing*] très convenable.
prima ballerina *n* danseuse *f* étoile.
primarily *adv* (chiefly) essentiellement; (originally) à l'origine.
primary I *n* **1** (US) (also **~ election**) primaire *f*; **2** (Sch) ▶ **primary school**.
II *adj* **1** (main) principal; [*sense, meaning, stage*] premier/-ière; **of ~ importance** de première importance; **2** (Sch) [*teaching, education*] primaire; **3** [*industry, products*] de base.
primary: **~ colour** (GB), **~ color** (US) *n* couleur *f* primaire; **~ school** *n* école *f* primaire; **~ sector** *n* secteur *m* primaire; **~ (school) teacher** ▶ 805 *n* (GB) instituteur/-trice *m/f*.
primate *n* **1** (mammal) primate *m*; **2** (also **Primate**) primat *m* (**of** de).
prime I *n* **in one's ~** (professionally) à son apogée; (physically) dans la fleur de l'âge; **in its ~** à son apogée; **to be past its ~** avoir connu des jours meilleurs.
II *adj* **1** (chief) principal; [*importance*] primordial; **2** (good quality) [*site*] de premier ordre ; [*meat, cuts*] de premier choix; [*foodstuffs*] d'une parfaite fraîcheur; **in ~ condition** [*machine*] en parfait état; [*livestock*] en parfaite condition; **of ~ quality** de première qualité; **3** (classic) [*example*] excellent (before n).
III *vtr* **1** (brief) préparer; **to ~ sb about** mettre qn au courant de; **to ~ sb to say** souffler à qn de dire; **2** (Mil, Tech) amorcer.
prime: **~ minister**, **PM** ▶ 642 *n* Premier ministre *m*; **~ number** *n* nombre *m* premier; **~ time** *n* heures *fpl* de grande écoute *m*.
primeval *adj* primitif/-ive.
primitive I *n* primitif *m*.
II *adj* primitif/-ive.
primrose *n* primevère *f* (jaune).
prince ▶ 642 *n* prince *m*.
princess ▶ 642 *n* princesse *f*.
principal I *n* **1** ▶ 642 (of senior school) proviseur *m*; (of junior school, college) directeur/-trice *m/f*; **2** (actor, actress) acteur/-trice *m/f* principal/-e; **3** (Mus) chef *m* de pupitre; **4** (interest-bearing sum) capital *m*; (debt before interest) principal *m*.
II *adj* **1** (main) principal; **2** [*violin, clarinet*] premier/-ière (*before n*); [*dancer*] étoile.
principality *n* principauté *f*.
principle *n* principe *m*; **to have high ~s** avoir beaucoup de principes; **in ~** en principe; **on ~** par principe; **to make it a ~ to do** avoir pour principe de faire.
print I *n* **1** (typeface) caractères *mpl*; **the small** or **fine ~** (figurative) les détails; **2** (published form) **in ~** disponible en librairie; **out of ~** épuisé; **to put** or **get sth into ~** publier qch; **3** (etching) estampe *f*; (engraving) gravure *f*; **4** (of photo) épreuve *f*; **5** (of film) copie *f*; **6** (of finger, hand, foot) empreinte *f*; (of tyre) trace *f*; **7** (fabric) tissu *m* imprimé; **8** (handwriting) script *m*.
II *vtr* **1** imprimer [*book, banknote, pattern, design*]; **2** (publish) publier; **3** tirer [*copy*]; faire développer [*photos*]; **4** (write) écrire [qch] en script.
III *vi* **1** (write) écrire en script; **2** (on press) imprimer.
■ **print off**: **~ off [sth]**, **~ [sth] off** tirer [*copies*].
■ **print out**: **~ out [sth]**, **~ [sth] out** imprimer.
printer *n* (person, firm) imprimeur *m*; (machine) imprimante *f*.
printing: **~ business**, **~ house**, **~ industry** *n* imprimerie *f*; **~ press** *n* presse *f* (typographique); **~ run** *n* tirage *m*; **~ works** *n* imprimerie *f*.
prior I *adj* **1** (previous) préalable; **~ notice** préavis *m*; **2** (more important) prioritaire.
II **prior to** *phr* avant.
priority *n* priorité *f*; **the main ~** la priorité absolue; **to get one's priorities right/wrong** définir correctement/mal définir l'ordre de ses priorités.
priory *n* prieuré *m*.
prise *v* ■ **prise apart**: **~ [sb/sth] apart** séparer [*layers, people*].
■ **prise off**: **~ [sth] off** enlever [qch] en forçant.
■ **prise open**: **~ [sth] open**, **~ open [sth]** ouvrir [qch] en forçant.
prism *n* prisme *m*.
prison I *n* prison *f*; **to put sb in ~** emprisonner qn.
II *noun modifier* [*administration, authorities, regulation*] pénitentiaire; [*population, reform*] pénal; [*cell, governor, visitor, guard, yard*] de prison.
prison camp *n* camp *m* de prisonniers.
prisoner *n* prisonnier/-ière *m/f*; (in jail) détenu/-e *m/f*; **they took me ~** ils m'ont fait prisonnier; **~ of conscience** prisonnier/-ière *m/f* d'opinion.
prison sentence, **prison term** *n* peine *f* de prison.
prissy *adj* [*person*] collet monté *inv*; [*style*] surchargé.
privacy *n* vie *f* privée; **to invade sb's ~** s'immiscer dans la vie privée de qn.
private I *n* simple soldat *m*.
II *adj* **1** [*property, vehicle, meeting, life*] privé; [*letter, phone call*] personnel/-elle; [*sale*] de particulier à particulier; [*place*] tranquille; **room with ~ bath** chambre avec salle de bains particulière; **to keep one's family life ~** préserver son intimité; **a ~ joke** une plaisanterie pour initiés; **2** [*sector, education, school, hospital*] privé; [*accommodation, lesson*] particulier/-ière; **~ industry** le (secteur) privé.
III **in private** *phr* en privé.
privately *adv* (in private) en privé; (out of public sector) dans le privé.
private: **~ parts** *n pl* parties *fpl* génitales; **~ secretary** *n* secrétaire *mf* particulier/-ière; (politician) conseiller/-ère *mf* particulier/-ière.

privatization *n* privatisation *f*.

privatize *vtr* privatiser.

privilege *n* **1** (honour, advantage) privilège *m*; **tax ~s** avantages *mpl* fiscaux; **2** (prerogative) apanage *m*; **3** (US) (in finance) option *f*.

privileged *adj* [*minority, life*] privilégié; [*information*] confidentiel/-ielle.

prize I *n* **1** (award) prix *m*; (in lottery) lot *m*; **first ~** premier prix; (in lottery) gros lot; **2** (valued object) trésor *m*; (reward for effort) récompense *f*.
II *noun modifier* **1** [*vegetable, bull*] (for competitions) de concours; (also **~-winning**) primé; [*pupil*] hors-pair *inv*; **2** [*possession*] précieux/-ieuse.
III **prized** *pp adj* [*possession, asset*] précieux/-ieuse.

prize: **~ draw** *n* (for charity) tombola *f*; (for advertising) tirage *m* au sort; **~-giving** *n* remise *f* des prix; **~ money** *n* (for one prize) argent *m* du prix; **~winner** *n* (in lottery) gagnant/-e *m/f*; (of literary award) lauréat/-e *m/f*.

pro I *n* **1**° (professional) pro° *mf*; **2** (advantage) **the ~s and cons** le pour et le contre; **the ~s and cons of sth** les avantages et les inconvénients de qch.
II° *prep* (in favour of) pour.
III **pro-** *pref* **to be ~-democracy** être pour la démocratie.

probability *n* (of desirable event) chances *fpl*; (of unwelcome event) risques *mpl*.

probable *adj* probable.

probably *adv* probablement.

probation *n* **1** (for adult) sursis *m* avec mise à l'épreuve; (for juvenile) mise *f* en liberté surveillée; **2** (trial period) période *f* d'essai; **on ~** à l'essai.

probation officer ▶805 *n* (for juveniles) délégué/-e *m/f* à la liberté surveillée; (for adults) agent *m* de probation.

probe I *n* **1** (investigation) enquête *f*; **2** (instrument) sonde *f*; (operation) sondage *m*; **3** (in space) sonde *f*.
II *vtr* **1** enquêter sur [*affair, mystery*]; **2** [*dentist*] examiner [qch] avec une sonde [*tooth*]; **3** (Med, Tech) sonder [*ground, wound*] (**with** avec); **4** explorer [*space*].

probing *adj* [*look*] inquisiteur/-trice; [*question*] pénétrant; [*study*] très poussé.

problem I *n* problème *m*; **to cause** or **present a ~** poser un problème.
II *noun modifier* [*child*] difficile; [*family*] à problèmes.

problematic(al) *adj* problématique.

problem: **~ case** *n* cas *m* social; **~ page** *n* courrier *m* du cœur.

procedure *n* procédure *f*.

proceed *vi* **1** (set about) procéder; (continue) poursuivre; **to ~ with** poursuivre [*idea, plan, sale*]; procéder à [*election*]; **to ~ to** passer à [*item, problem*]; **2** (be in progress) [*project, work*] avancer; [*interview, talks, trial*] se poursuivre; (take place) [*work, interview, talks*] se dérouler; **3** [*person, road*] continuer; [*vehicle*] avancer.

proceedings *n pl* **1** (meeting) réunion *f*; (ceremony) cérémonie *f*; (discussion) débats *mpl*; **to direct ~** diriger les opérations; **2** (Law) poursuites *fpl*; **to take** or **institute ~** engager des poursuites; **to start divorce ~** intenter un procès en divorce; **3** (report) rapport *m*; (of conference, society) actes *mpl*.

proceeds *n pl* (of deal) produit *m*; (of event) recette *f*.

process I *n* **1** processus *m* (**of** de); **the ~ of doing** le processus consistant à faire; **to begin the ~ of doing** entreprendre de faire; **to be in the ~ of doing** être en train de faire; **in the ~** en même temps; **2** (method) procédé *m*.
II *vtr* **1** traiter [*applications, data*]; **2** traiter [*raw materials, chemical, waste*]; **3** développer [*film*]; **4** (Culin) (mix) mixer; (chop) hacher.
III **processed** *pp adj* [*food*] qui a subi un traitement; [*meat, peas*] en conserve; [*steel*] traité.

processing *n* **1** (of applications, data) traitement *m*; **2** (of raw material, food product, chemical waste) traitement *m*; **the food ~ industry** l'industrie alimentaire.

procession *n* (of demonstration, carnival) défilé *m*; (formal) cortège *m*; (religious) procession *f*.

proclaim *vtr* proclamer (**that** que).

proclamation *n* proclamation *f*.

procrastinate *vi* atermoyer.

procure *vtr* **1** (obtain) procurer; **to ~ sth for sb** (directly) procurer qch à qn; (indirectly) faire obtenir qch à qn; **2** (Law) procurer [*prostitutes*].

procurer *n* (gen) acheteur/-euse *m/f*; (Law) proxénète *m*.

prod I *n* **1** (poke) petit coup *m*; **2**° (reminder) **to give sb a ~** secouer° qn.
II *vtr* **1** (also **~ at**) (with foot, instrument, stick) donner des petits coups à; (with finger) toucher; (with fork) piquer; **2**° **to ~ sb into doing** pousser qn à faire.

prodding *n* **1 after a bit of ~ he agreed** il a fallu insister pour qu'il donne son accord; **2** (interrogation) questions *fpl*.

prodigy *n* prodige *m*.

produce I *n* produits *mpl*.
II *vtr* **1** (cause) produire [*result, effect, plant*]; provoquer [*reaction, change*]; **2** [*region, farmer, company*] produire (**from** à partir de); [*worker, machine*] fabriquer; **3** (generate) produire [*heat, sound, energy*]; rapporter [*gains, profits, returns*]; **4** (present) produire [*passport, report*]; fournir [*evidence, argument, example*]; **to ~ sth from** sortir qch de [*pocket, bag*]; **5** produire [*show, film*]; (GB) mettre [qch] en scène [*play*]; **well-~d** bien réalisé; **6** (put together) préparer [*meal*]; mettre au point [*argument, timetable, package, solution*]; éditer [*brochure, guide*].

producer ▶805 *n* **1** (of produce, food) producteur *m*; (of machinery, goods) fabricant *m*; **2** (of programme, film) producteur/-trice *m/f*; (GB) (of play) metteur *m* en scène.

producing *adj* producteur/-trice; **oil-~ countries** pays producteurs de pétrole.

product I *n* produit *m*; **consumer ~s** produits de consommation.
II *noun modifier* [*design, launch, development,*

testing] d'un produit; **~ range** gamme *f* de produits; **~ designer** créateur/-trice *m/f* de produits.

production I *n* **1** (of crop, foodstuffs, metal) production *f* (**of** de); (of machinery, furniture, cars) fabrication (**of** de); **to be in full ~** tourner à plein rendement; **2** (output) production *f*; **3** (presentation) (of document, ticket) présentation *f* (**of** de); (of evidence) production *f*; **4** (of film, opera) production *f* (**of** de); (of play) mise *f* en scène (**of** de).
II *noun modifier* [*costs, levels, methods, company, quota*] de production; [*department, manager*] de la production; **~ line** chaîne *f* de fabrication.

productive *adj* **1** [*factory, land*] productif/-ive; [*system, method, use*] efficace; **2** [*discussion*] fructueux/-euse; [*day, phase, period*] productif/-ive.

productivity *n* productivité *f*.

profane *adj* **1** (blasphemous) impie; **2** (secular) profane.

profess *vtr* **1** (claim) prétendre (**to do** de faire; **that** que); **2** (declare openly) faire profession de [*opinion, religion*].

profession *n* **1** (occupation, group) profession *f*; **by ~** de profession; **the ~s** les professions libérales; **the legal ~** le corps judiciaire; **2** (statement) déclaration *f*.

professional I *n* **1** (not amateur) professionnel/-elle *m/f*; **2** (in small ad) salarié/-e *m/f*.
II *adj* professionnel/-elle; **~ soldier** soldat *m* de carrière; **~ career** carrière *f*; **he needs ~ help** il devrait consulter un spécialiste; **they are ~ people** ils exercent une profession libérale; **to turn ~** [*actor, singer*] devenir professionnel/-elle; [*footballer, athlete*] passer professionnel/-elle.

professionalism *n* (of person, organization, sportsman) professionnalisme *m*; (of performance, piece of work) (haute) qualité *f*.

professionally *adv* **1** (expertly) [*designed*] par un professionnel; **he is ~ trained** il a reçu une formation professionnelle; **2** (from an expert standpoint) d'un point de vue professionnel; **3** (in work situation) dans un cadre professionnel; **4** [*play sport*] en professionnel/-elle; **5** (to a high standard) de manière professionnelle.

professor **▶ 642** *n* (Univ) (chair holder) professeur *m* d'Université; (US Univ) (teacher) professeur *m*.

proficiency *n* (practical) compétence *f* (**in, at** en; **in doing** à faire); (academic) niveau *m* (**in** en).

proficient *adj* compétent.

profile I *n* **1** (of face) profil *m*; (of body) silhouette *f*; **in ~** de profil; **to have/maintain a high ~** occuper/rester sur le devant de la scène; **2** (by journalist) portrait *m* (**of** de).
II *vtr* [*journalist*] dresser le portrait de [*person*].

profit I *n* **1** bénéfice *m*, profit *m*; **gross/net ~** bénéfice brut/net; **to operate at a ~** être rentable; **2** (figurative) profit *m*.
II *vtr* profiter à [*person, group*].
III *vi* **to ~ by** or **from sth** tirer profit de qch.

profitability *n* rentabilité *f*.

profitable *adj* rentable; (figurative) fructueux/-euse; **to make ~ use of sth** mettre qch à profit; **it's very ~** [*business, trade*] cela rapporte gros.

profiteer I *n* profiteur/-euse *m/f*.
II *vi* faire des bénéfices excessifs.

profit: **~ margin** *n* marge *f* bénéficiaire; **~ sharing** *n* intéressement *m* des salariés aux bénéfices.

profound *adj* profond.

profusely *adv* [*sweat, bleed*] abondamment; **to apologize ~** se confondre en excuses.

progesterone *n* progestérone *f*.

prognosis *n* **1** (Med) pronostic *m* (**on, about** sur); **2** (prediction) pronostics *mpl*.

program I *n* **1** (Comput) programme *m*; **to run a ~** lancer un programme; **2** (US) (on radio, TV) émission *f*.
II *vtr, vi* programmer (**to do** pour faire).

programme (GB), **program** (US) I *n* **1** (single broadcast) émission *f* (**about** sur); (schedule of broadcasting) programme *m*; **2** (schedule) programme *m*; **3** (for play, opera) programme *m*.
II *vtr* programmer [*machine*] (**to do** pour faire).

programmer **▶ 805** *n* programmeur/-euse *m/f*.

progress I *n* **1** (advances) progrès *m*; **to make ~** [*person*] faire des progrès; **the patient is making ~** l'état de santé du malade s'améliore; **2** (of person, inquiry) progression *f*; (of talks, disease, career) évolution *f*; **to make steady ~** progresser régulièrement; **to be in ~** [*discussions, exam*] être en cours.
II *vi* [*person, vehicle, discussion, studies*] progresser.

progression *n* **1** (evolution) évolution *f*; (improvement) progression *f*; **2** (series) suite *f*.

progressive *adj* **1** [*increase, change*] progressif/-ive; [*illness*] évolutif/-ive; **2** [*person, policy*] progressiste; [*school*] parallèle; [*age, period*] progressif/-ive; **3** [*tense*] progressif/-ive.

progress report *n* (on construction work) rapport *m* sur l'état des travaux; (on project) rapport *m* sur l'état du projet; (on patient) bulletin *m* de santé; (on pupil) bulletin *m* scolaire.

prohibit *vtr* interdire; **to ~ sb from doing** interdire à qn de faire.

prohibition *n* interdiction *f* (**on, against** de).

prohibitive *adj* [*cost, price*] prohibitif/-ive.

project I *n* **1** (scheme) projet *m* (**to do** pour faire); **2** (Sch) dossier *m* (**on** sur); (Univ) mémoire *m* (**on** sur); **research ~** programme *m* de recherches; **3** (US) (state housing) (large) ≈ cité *f* HLM; (small) ≈ lotissement *m* HLM.
II *vtr* **1** envoyer [*missile*]; faire porter [*voice*]; **to ~ oneself** faire impression; **to ~ oneself as being** donner l'impression d'être; **2** projeter [*guilt, anxiety*] (**onto** sur); **3** (estimate) prévoir; **4** projeter [*image, slides*].
III **projected** *pp adj* [*figure, deficit*] prévu.

projecting *adj* saillant.

Shops, Trades, and Professions

Shops

In English you can say *at the baker's* or *at the baker's shop*; in French the construction with ***chez*** (*at the house* or *premises of*. . .) is common but you can also use the name of the particular shop:

***at** the baker's*	= **à** la boulangerie
	= **chez** le boulanger
*I'm going **to** the grocer's*	= je vais **à** l'épicerie
	= je vais **chez** l'épicier
*I bought it **at** the fishmonger's*	= je l'ai acheté **à** la poissonnerie
	= je l'ai acheté **chez** le poissonnier
go to the chemist's	= va **à** la pharmacie
	= va **chez** le pharmacien
*to work **in** a butcher's*	= travailler **dans** une boucherie

chez is also used with the names of professions:

***at** / **to** the doctor's*	= **chez** le médecin
***at** / **to** the lawyer's*	= **chez** le notaire
***at** / **to** the dentist's*	= **chez** le dentiste

Note that there are specific names for the place of work of some professions:

*the lawyer's **office***	= l'**étude** *f* du notaire
*the doctor's **surgery*** (GB) / ***office*** (US)	= le **cabinet** du médecin

cabinet is also used for architects and dentists. If in doubt, check in the dictionary.

People

Talking of someone's profession, we could say *he is a dentist*. In French this would be either *il est dentiste* or *c'est un dentiste*. Only when the sentence begins with ***c'est*** can the indefinite article (*un* or *une*) be used:

Paul is a dentist	= Paul est dentiste
she's a geography teacher	= elle est professeur de géographie
	= c'est un professeur de géographie

With adjectives, only the ***c'est*** construction is possible:

she is a good dentist	= c'est une bonne dentiste

In the plural, if the construction begins with ***ce sont*** then you need to use ***des*** (or ***de*** before an adjective):

they are mechanics	= ils sont mécaniciens
	= ce sont **des** mécaniciens
they are good mechanics	= ce sont **de** bons mécaniciens

Trades and professions

what does he do?	= qu'est-ce qu'il fait?
what's your job?	= qu'est-ce que vous faites dans la vie?
I'm a teacher	= je suis professeur
to work as a dentist	= travailler comme dentiste
to work for an electrician	= travailler pour un électricien
he wants to be a baker	= il veut devenir boulanger

projection *n* **1** (of emotions, images) projection *f*; **2** (estimate) prévision *f*.

projection room *n* cabine *f* de projection.

projector *n* projecteur *m*.

proliferate *vi* proliférer.

prolific *adj* [*writer, plant, parent*] prolifique; [*decade*] fécond; [*growth*] rapide.

prologue *n* prologue *m* (**to** de); (figurative) prélude *m* (**to** à).

prolong *vtr* prolonger.

promenade *n* (path) promenade *f*; (by sea) front *m* de mer.

prominence *n* (of person, issue) importance *f*; (of object, feature) proéminence *f*.

prominent *adj* **1** [*figure, campaigner*] très en vue; [*artist*] éminent; **to play a ~ part in sth** jouer un rôle de premier plan dans qch; **2** [*place, feature*] proéminent; [*ridge, cheekbone*] saillant; [*eye*] exorbité.

promiscuity *n* vagabondage *m* sexuel.

promiscuous *adj* [*person*] aux mœurs légères.

promise I *n* **1** promesse *f*; **to break one's ~** manquer à sa promesse; **2 the ~ of** l'espoir *m* de [*peace, happiness*]; **3 she shows great ~** elle promet beaucoup.
II *vtr* **to ~ sb sth** promettre qch à qn; **as ~d** comme promis.
III *vi* promettre; **do you ~?** c'est promis?

promising *adj* [*situation, result, future*] prometteur/-euse; [*artist, candidate*] qui promet; **the future looks more ~** l'avenir s'annonce meilleur.

promote *vtr* **1** (in rank) promouvoir (**to** à); **2** (advertise) faire de la publicité pour; (market) promouvoir; **3** (encourage) promouvoir; **4** (GB) (in football) **to be ~d from the fourth to the third division** passer de quatrième en troisième division.

promoter *n* promoteur/-trice *m/f*.

promotion *n* **1** (of employee) promotion *f*; **to be in line for ~** avoir des chances d'être promu; **2** (of product) promotion *f* (**of** de).

promotional *adj* promotionnel/-elle.

promotional video *n* (for product) vidéo *f* publicitaire; (for artiste) vidéo *f* de présentation.

prompt I *adj* rapide; **to be ~ to do** être prompt à faire.
II *vtr* **1** provoquer [*reaction, decision*]; susciter [*concern, comment*]; **to ~ sb to do sth** inciter qn à faire qch; **2** (remind) souffler à [*person, actor*].

prompter *n* **1** (in theatre) souffleur/-euse *m/f*; **2** (US) (teleprompter) téléprompteur *m*.

promptly *adv* **1** (immediately) immédiatement; **2** (without delay) rapidement; **3** (punctually) à l'heure; **~ at six o'clock** à six heures précises.

promptness *n* (speed) rapidité *f* (**in doing** à faire); (punctuality) ponctualité *f*.

prone *adj* **1 to be ~ to** être sujet/-ette à [*colds*]; être enclin à [*depression*]; **2 to lie ~** être allongé sur le ventre; (injured) être allongé face contre terre.

-pronged *combining form* **two/three~ attack** attaque *f* sur deux/trois fronts.

pronoun *n* pronom *m*.

pronounce I *vtr* **1** prononcer [*letter, word*]; **2** prononcer [*judgment, sentence*]; rendre [*verdict*]; **to ~ sb dead** déclarer qn mort.
II *vi* (Law) prononcer; **to ~ against sb** rendre un jugement défavorable à qn.
■ **pronounce on**: **~ on [sth]** se prononcer sur [*case, matter*].

pronounced *adj* [*accent, tendency*] prononcé; [*change, increase*] marqué.

pronunciation *n* prononciation *f*.

proof I *n* **1** (evidence) preuve *f*; **to have ~ that** pouvoir prouver que; **there is no ~ that** rien ne prouve que; **~ of identity** pièce *f* d'identité; **2** (in printing, photography) épreuve *f*; **3** (of alcohol) **to be 70° or 70% ~** ≈ titrer 40° d'alcool.
II *adj* **to be ~ against** être à l'épreuve de [*heat, infection*].

proof: **~ of purchase** *n* justificatif *m* d'achat; **~read** *vtr* (check copy) corriger; (check proofs) corriger les épreuves de; **~reader** ▶805 *n* correcteur/-trice *m/f*; **~reading** *n* correction *f* d'épreuves.

prop I *n* étai *m*.
II **props** *n pl* (also **properties**) accessoires *mpl*.
III *vtr* **1** (also **~ up**) étayer; **2 to ~ sb/sth against sth** appuyer qn/qch contre qch.

propaganda *n* propagande *f*.

propagate *vi* se propager.

propel *vtr* **1** propulser [*vehicle, ship*]; **2** (violently) propulser [*person*].

propeller *n* hélice *f*.

proper *adj* **1** (right) [*term, spelling*] correct; [*order, tool, response*] bon/bonne (*before n*); [*sense*] propre; [*precautions*] nécessaire; [*clothing*] qu'il faut; **everything is in the ~ place** tout est à sa place; **2** (adequate) [*funding, recognition, facilities*] convenable; [*education, training*] bon/bonne (*before n*); [*care, control*] requis; **3** (respectable) [*person*] correct; [*upbringing*] convenable; **4** (real, full) [*doctor, holiday, job*] vrai (*before n*); **5** (actual) **in the village ~** dans le village même.

properly *adv* **1** (correctly) correctement; **behave ~!** tiens-toi comme il faut!; **2** (fully) complètement; **I didn't have time to thank you ~** je n'ai pas eu le temps de vous remercier; **3** (adequately) convenablement; **4** [*dressed*] correctement.

proper name, **proper noun** *n* nom *m* propre.

property I *n* **1** (belongings) propriété *f*, bien(s) *m(pl)*; **that is not your ~** cela ne vous appartient pas; **2** (real estate) biens *mpl* immobiliers; **to invest in ~** investir dans l'immobilier; **~ was damaged** il y a eu des dégâts matériels; **3** (house) propriété *f*.
II *noun modifier* [*company, law*] immobilier/-ière; [*market, prices*] de l'immobilier.

property: **~ dealer** *n* marchand *m* de biens; **~ developer** *n* promoteur *m* immobilier;

~ owner *n* propriétaire *mf*; **~ tax** *n* impôt *m* foncier.

prophecy *n* prophétie *f*.

prophet *n* prophète *m*.

proportion I *n* **1** (of group, population) proportion *f* (**of** de); (of income, profit, work) part *f* (**of** de); **2** (ratio) proportion *f*; **the ~ of pupils to teachers** le rapport élèves-enseignants; **tax should be in ~ to income** l'impôt devrait être proportionnel au revenu; **3** (harmony) **out of/in ~** hors de/en proportion; **4** (perspective) **to get sth out of all ~** faire tout un drame de qch; **to be out of all ~** être tout à fait disproportionné (**to** par rapport à).
II **proportions** *n pl* dimensions *fpl*.

proportional *adj* proportionnel/-elle.

proportional representation, PR *n* représentation *f* proportionnelle.

proportionate *adj* proportionnel/-elle.

proposal *n* **1** (suggestion) proposition *f*; **2** (of marriage) demande *f* en mariage.

propose I *vtr* proposer [*course of action, solution*]; présenter [*motion*].
II *vi* faire sa demande en mariage (**to** à).
III **proposed** *pp adj* [*action, reform*] envisagé.

proposition I *n* **1** (suggestion) proposition *f*; **2** (assertion) assertion *f*.
II *vtr* faire une proposition à [*person*].

proprietary *adj* [*rights, duties*] du propriétaire; [*attitude*] de propriétaire.

proprietor *n* propriétaire *mf* (**of** de).

propriety *n* **1** (politeness) correction *f*; **2** (morality) décence *f*.

propulsion *n* propulsion *f*.

prosaic *adj* prosaïque.

proscribe *vtr* proscrire.

prose *n* **1** (not verse) prose *f*; **2** (GB) (translation) thème *m*.

prosecute I *vtr* poursuivre [qn] en justice; **to ~ sb for doing** poursuivre qn pour avoir fait.
II *vi* engager des poursuites.

prosecution *n* (Law) **1** (accusation) poursuites *fpl* (judiciaires); **2 the ~** (private individual) le/les plaignant/-s; (state, Crown) le ministère public.

prosecutor *n* (Law) **1** (in court) procureur *m*; **2** (US) (also **prosecuting attorney**) avocat/-e *m/f* de la partie civile; (public official) procureur *m*.

prospect I *n* **1** (of change) espoir *m*; (of success) chance *f*; **2** (outlook) perspective *f*.
II **prospects** *n pl* (in career) perspectives *fpl*; **to have no ~s** [*person*] ne pas avoir d'avenir; [*job*] être sans avenir.

prospective *adj* [*buyer, candidate*] potentiel/-ielle; [*husband*] futur.

prospectus *n* brochure *f*; **university ~** ≈ livret *m* de l'étudiant.

prosperity *n* prospérité *f*.

prosperous *adj* [*person, farm, country*] prospère; [*appearance*] de prospérité.

prostate *n* (also **~ gland**) prostate *f*.

prostitute I *n* prostituée *f*; **male ~** prostitué *m*.
II *vtr* prostituer [*person, talent*].

prostitution *n* prostitution *f*.

prostrate *adj* **to lie ~** être allongé de tout son long; **~ with grief** accablé de chagrin.

protagonist *n* (in drama) protagoniste *mf*.

protect I *vtr* protéger [*person, property, environment, economy, data*]; défendre [*consumer, interests*] (**against** contre); préserver [*privacy*].
II *v refl* **to ~ oneself** (against threat) se protéger; (against attack) se défendre.

protection *n* **1** (safeguard) protection *f*; **for his own ~** (moral) pour son bien; (physical) pour le protéger; **2** (also **trade ~**) protectionnisme *m*; **3** (extortion) **to pay sb ~** payer un impôt à qn.

protection factor *n* indice *m* de protection.

protectionist *n, adj* protectionniste (*mf*).

protective *adj* **1** [*clothing*] protecteur/-trice; [*measure*] de protection; **2** (caring) protecteur/-trice; **to be ~ of** veiller jalousement sur [*possessions*].

protector *n* protecteur/-trice *m/f*; (of rights) défenseur *m*.

protein *n* protéine *f*; **high-~** riche en protéines.

protest I *n* **1** (disapproval) protestation *f*; **in ~** en signe de protestation; **2** (complaint) réclamation *f*; **as a ~ against sth** pour protester contre qch; **3** (demonstration) manifestation *f*.
II *vtr* **1 to ~ that** protester que; **to ~ one's innocence** protester de son innocence; **2** (US) (complain about) protester contre (**to** auprès de).
III *vi* **1** (complain) protester; **2** (demonstrate) manifester (**against** contre).

Protestant I *n* protestant/-e *m/f*.
II *adj* protestant.

protester *n* manifestant/-e *m/f*.

protocol *n* protocole *m*.

prototype *n* prototype *m* (**of** de).

protruding *adj* [*rock*] en saillie; [*nail*] qui dépasse; [*eyes*] globuleux/-euse; [*ears*] décollé; [*ribs*] saillant; [*chin*] en avant.

proud *adj* **1** fier/fière; [*owner*] heureux/-euse (*before n*); **2** [*day, moment*] grand (*before n*).

proudly *adv* [*display, show*] avec fierté; [*move, speak*] fièrement.

prove I *vtr* prouver; (by demonstration) démontrer; **to ~ a point** montrer qu'on a raison.
II *vi* s'avérer; **it ~d otherwise** il en est allé autrement.
III *v refl* **to ~ oneself** faire ses preuves; **to ~ oneself (to be)** se révéler.

proverb *n* proverbe *m*.

provide *vtr* **1** (supply) fournir [*opportunity, evidence, jobs, meals*] (**for** à); apporter [*answer, support*] (**for** à); assurer [*service, access, training, shelter*] (**for** à); **please use the bin ~d** veuillez utiliser la poubelle mise à votre disposition; **2** [*clause, law*] prévoir (**that** que).
■ **provide for**: ¶ **~ for [sth] 1** (account for) envisager; **2** (Law) prévoir; ¶ **~ for [sb]** subvenir aux besoins de [*family*]; **to be well ~d for** être à l'abri du besoin.

provided, providing *conj* (also **~ that**) à condition que (+ *subj*).

providence *n* providence *f*.

provident *adj* prévoyant.

province *n* province *f*; **in the ~s** en province.

provincial *adj* **1** [*newspaper, capital*] de province; [*life*] provincial; **2** (narrow) provincial.

provision I *n* **1** (of goods, equipment) fourniture *f* (**of** de; **to** à); (of service) prestation *f*; **~ of food/supplies** approvisionnement *m* (**to** de); **2** (for future) dispositions *fpl*; **3** (of agreement) clause *f*; (of bill, act) disposition *f*; **under the ~s of** aux termes de.
II provisions *n pl* (food) provisions *fpl*.

provisional *adj* provisoire.

provocation *n* provocation *f*.

provocative *adj* **1** [*dress, remark*] provocant; **2** [*book*] qui fait réfléchir.

provoke *vtr* **1** (annoy) provoquer; **2** (cause) susciter [*anger, complaints*]; provoquer [*laughter, reaction*].

provost *n* **1** (GB Sch, Univ) principal *m*; **2** (US Univ) doyen *m*; **3** (in Scotland) maire *m*.

prowess *n* **1** (skill) prouesses *fpl*; **2** (bravery) vaillance *f*.

prowl *vi* (also **~ around, ~ about** (GB)) [*animal, person*] rôder.

proximity *n* proximité *f*.

proxy *n* **1** (person) mandataire *mf*; **2** procuration *f*; **by ~** [*vote*] par procuration.

prudent *adj* prudent.

prudish *adj* pudibond, prude.

prune I *n* (Culin) pruneau *m*.
II *vtr* (also **~ back**) (cut back) tailler; (thin out) élaguer.

pry *vi* **to ~ into** mettre son nez dans [*private affairs*].

PS *n* (*abbr* = **postscriptum**) PS *m*.

psalm *n* psaume *m*.

pseudonym *n* pseudonyme *m*.

psychiatric *adj* [*hospital, care, nurse, help*] psychiatrique; [*illness*] mental.

psychiatrist ▶**805** *n* psychiatre *mf*.

psychiatry *n* psychiatrie *f*.

psychic *n* médium *m*, voyant/-e *m/f*.

psychoanalysis *n* psychanalyse *f*.

psychological *adj* psychologique.

psychologist ▶**805** *n* psychologue *mf*.

psychology *n* psychologie *f*.

psychopath *n* psychopathe *mf*.

psychotherapist ▶**805** *n* psychothérapeute *mf*.

PTO (*abbr* = **please turn over**) TSVP.

pub *n* (GB) pub *m*; **to go to the ~** aller au pub.

puberty *n* puberté *f*.

public I *n* **the ~** le public.
II *adj* [*health, property, park, inquiry*] public/-ique; [*enthusiasm, support*] général; [*library, amenity*] municipal; [*duty, spirit*] civique; **to be in the ~ eye** occuper le devant de la scène; **at ~ expense** aux frais du contribuable.
III in public *phr* en public.

public address (system) *n* (système *m* de) sonorisation *f*.

public assistance *n* (US) aide *f* sociale.

publication *n* publication *f*; **on the day of ~** le jour de la sortie.

public: **~ convenience** *n* (GB) toilettes *fpl*; **~ examination** *n* examen *m* ouvert à tous; **~ holiday** *n* (GB) jour *m* férié.

publicist *n* (also **publicity agent**) attaché/-e *m/f* de presse.

publicity *n* **1 to attract ~** attirer l'attention des médias; **to receive bad ~** faire l'objet de critiques dans les médias; **2** (advertising) publicité *f*; **advance ~** promotion *f*; **3** (brochures) brochures *fpl* publicitaires; (posters) affiches *fpl* publicitaires; (films) films *mpl* publicitaires.

publicity stunt *n* coup *m* publicitaire.

publicize *vtr* **1** attirer l'attention du public sur [*issue, problem*]; **2** (make public) rendre [qch] public [*information, facts*]; **3** (advertise) faire de la publicité pour [*show*].

publicly *adv* publiquement.

public: **~ opinion** *n* opinion *f* publique; **~ prosecutor** *n* procureur *m* général; **Public Records Office** *n* Archives *fpl* nationales; **~ relations, PR** *n* relations *fpl* publiques; **~ relations officer, PRO** *n* responsable *mf* des relations publiques; **~ school** *n* (GB) école *f* privée; (US) école *f* publique; **~ sector** *n* secteur *m* public; **~ servant** *n* fonctionnaire *mf*; **~ service** *n* (transport, education) service *m* public; (civil service) fonction *f* publique; **~ transport** *n* transports *mpl* en commun; **~ utilities** *n pl* équipements *mpl* collectifs; **~ utility** *n* service *m* public.

publish *vtr* publier [*book, letter, guide*]; éditer [*newspaper, magazine*].

publisher ▶**805** *n* (person) éditeur/-trice *m/f*; (also **publishing house**) maison *f* d'édition; **newspaper ~** (person) patron *m* de presse; (company) maison *f* de presse.

publishing *n* édition *f*.

pudding *n* **1** (GB) (dessert) dessert *m*; **2** (cooked dish) pudding *m*; **3** (GB) (sausage) **black/white ~** boudin *m* noir/blanc.

puddle *n* flaque *f*.

puff I *n* **1** (of air, smoke, steam) bouffée *f*; (of breath) souffle *m*; **2** (Culin) feuilleté *m*.
II *vtr* tirer sur [*pipe*].
III *vi* **1** souffler; **to ~ (away) at** tirer des bouffées de [*cigarette*]; **to ~ along** [*train*] avancer en lançant des bouffées de fumée; **2** (pant) souffler.
■ **puff out**: **~ out [sth], ~ [sth] out 1** gonfler [*sails*]; [*bird*] hérisser [*feathers*]; **2 to ~ out smoke** lancer des bouffées de fumée.
■ **puff up**: ¶ **~ up** [*feathers*] se hérisser; [*eyes*] bouffir; [*rice*] gonfler; ¶ **~ up [sth], ~ [sth] up** hérisser [*feathers, fur*]; **~ed up with pride** rempli d'orgueil.

puff pastry *n* pâte *f* feuilletée.

puffy *adj* bouffi.

pugnacious *adj* combatif/-ive.

pull I *n* **1** (tug) coup *m*; **to give sth a ~** tirer sur qch; **2** (attraction) force *f*; (figurative) attrait *m* (**of** de); **3**° (influence) influence *f* (**over, with** sur).
II *vtr* **1** (tug) tirer [*chain, curtain, hair, tail*]; tirer sur [*cord, rope*]; **2** (tug, move) (towards oneself) tirer (**towards** vers); (by dragging) traîner (**along** le long de); (to show sth) entraîner [qn] par le bras [*person*]; **to ~ sb/sth through** faire passer qn/qch par [*hole, window*]; **3** (draw) [*horse, person*] tirer; [*vehicle*] tracter; **4** (remove) **to ~ sth out of** tirer qch de [*pocket, drawer*]; **to ~ sb out of** retirer qn de [*wreckage*]; sortir qn de [*river*]; **5**° sortir [*gun , knife*]; **to ~ a gun on sb** menacer qn avec un pistolet; **6** appuyer sur [*trigger*]; tirer [*lever*]; **7** (Med) se faire une élongation à [*muscle*]; **8**° (GB) tirer [*pint of beer*]; **9 to ~ a face** faire la grimace.
III *vi* tirer (**at , on** sur); **to ~ at sb's sleeve** tirer qn par la manche.
■ **pull apart**: **~ [sth] apart 1** (dismantle) démonter; **2** (destroy) [*child*] mettre en pièces; [*animal*] déchiqueter.
■ **pull away**: ¶ **~ away** [*car*] démarrer; [*person*] s'écarter; ¶ **~ [sb/sth] away** éloigner [*person*]; retirer [*hand*]; **to ~ sth away from sb** arracher qch à qn; **to ~ sb/sth away from** écarter qn/qch de [*window, wall*].
■ **pull back 1** [*troops*] se retirer (**from** de); **2** [*car, person*] reculer.
■ **pull down**: **~ [sth] down, ~ down [sth]** démolir [*building*]; baisser [*blind, trousers*].
■ **pull in**: ¶ **~ in** [*car, bus, driver*] s'arrêter; ¶ **~ [sb] in, ~ in [sb]** [*exhibition, show*] attirer [*crowds, tourists*].
■ **pull off**: ¶ **~ off [sth]** quitter [*road*]; ¶ **~ off [sth], ~ [sth] off 1** ôter [*coat, sweater*]; enlever [*shoes, lid, sticker*]; **2** conclure [*deal*]; réaliser [*feat*].
■ **pull out**: ¶ **~ out 1** [*car, truck*] déboîter; **to ~ out of sth** quitter qch [*station, drive*]; **2** [*troops, participants*] se retirer (**of** de); ¶ **~ [sth] out, ~ out [sth] 1** extraire [*tooth*]; enlever [*splinter*]; arracher [*weeds*]; **2** (from pocket) sortir.
■ **pull over**: ¶ **~ over** [*motorist, car*] s'arrêter (sur le côté); ¶ **~ [sb/sth] over** [*police*] forcer [qn/qch] à se ranger sur le côté.
■ **pull through** [*accident victim*] s'en tirer.
■ **pull together**: ¶ **~ together** faire un effort; ¶ **~ oneself together** se ressaisir.
■ **pull up**: ¶ **~ up** s'arrêter; ¶ **~ up [sth], ~ [sth] up 1** (uproot) arracher; **2** lever [*anchor*]; remonter [*trousers, socks*]; prendre [*chair*]; ¶ **~ [sb] up 1** (lift) hisser; **2** (reprimand) réprimander; **3** arrêter [*driver*].

pulley *n* poulie *f*.

pullover *n* pull-over *m*.

pulmonary *adj* pulmonaire.

pulp I *n* (soft centre) pulpe *f*; (crushed mass) pâte *f*.
II *vtr* écraser [*fruit, vegetable*]; réduire [qch] en pâte [*wood, cloth*]; mettre [qch] au pilon [*newspapers, books*].

pulp fiction *n* littérature *f* de gare.

pulpit *n* chaire *f*.

pulse *n* (Med) pouls *m*; **to take/feel sb's ~** prendre/tâter le pouls de qn.

pulse rate *n* pouls *m*.

pulverize *vtr* pulvériser.

pump I *n* **1** (for air) pompe *f*; **bicycle ~** pompe à bicyclette; **2** (plimsoll) chaussure *f* de sport; (GB) (flat shoe) ballerine *f*; (US) (shoe with heel) chaussure *f* à talon.
II *vtr* **1** pomper [*air, gas, water*] (**out of** de); **the boiler ~s water to the radiators** la chaudière distribue l'eau dans les radiateurs; **2**° (question) cuisiner° [*person*]; **3** (Med) **to ~ sb's stomach** faire un lavage d'estomac à qn.
III *vi* **1** (flow) gicler (**from, out of** de); **2** (beat) battre violemment.
■ **pump out**: **~ out [sth], ~ [sth] out** débiter [*music, propaganda*]; cracher [*fumes*]; déverser [*sewage*].
■ **pump up**: **~ up [sth], ~ [sth] up** gonfler [*tyre, air bed*].

pumpkin *n* citrouille *f*.

pun *n* jeu *m* de mots, calembour *m*.

punch I *n* **1** (blow) coup *m* de poing; **2** (forcefulness) (of person) punch° *m*; (of style, performance) énergie *f*; **3** (drink) punch *m*.
II *vtr* **1** (hit) **to ~ sb in the face** donner un coup de poing dans la figure de qn; **2** perforer [*cards, tape*]; appuyer sur [*key*]; **3** (make hole in) (manually) poinçonner [*ticket*]; (in machine) composter [*ticket*].
III *vi* cogner, donner des coups de poing.
IDIOMS **to pull no ~es** ne pas y aller de main morte.

Punch-and-Judy show *n* ≈ (spectacle *m* de) guignol *m*.

punch: **~bag** *n* (GB) sac *m* de sable; **~ card** *n* carte *f* perforée; **~ line** *n* chute *f*.

punctual *adj* ponctuel/-elle.

punctuality *n* ponctualité *f*.

punctually *adv* [*start, arrive, leave*] à l'heure.

punctuation *n* ponctuation *f*.

punctuation mark *n* signe *m* de ponctuation.

puncture I *n* crevaison *f*; **we had a ~ on the way** on a crevé en chemin.
II *vtr* crever [*tyre, balloon, air bed*]; **to ~ a lung** se perforer un poumon.

puncture (repair) kit *n* boîte *f* de rustines®.

pungent *adj* [*flavour*] relevé; [*smell*] fort; [*gas, smoke*] âcre; [*satire*] mordant.

punish *vtr* punir.

punishment *n* punition *f*; (stronger) châtiment *m*; **as ~ for** en punition de.

punnet *n* (GB) barquette *f*.

punt *n* **1** (boat) barque *f* (*à fond plat*); **2** (Irish pound) livre *f* irlandaise.

puny *adj* [*person, body*] chétif/-ive.

pup *n* (also **puppy**) chiot *m*; (seal, otter) petit *m*.

pupil *n* **1** (Sch) élève *mf*; **2** (in eye) pupille *f*.

puppet *n* marionnette *f*.

purchase I *n* achat *m*.
II *vtr* acheter.

pure *adj* pur; **~ new wool** laine *f* vierge.

puree *n* purée *f*.

purely *adv* purement; **~ to be polite** uniquement pour être poli.

purge I *n* purge *f*.
II *vtr* purger [*party, system*] (**of** de); expier [*sin*].

purify *vtr* épurer [*water, chemical*]; purifier [*air*].

purist *n, adj* puriste (*mf*).

purity *n* pureté *f*.

purple ▶ 559 I *n* violet *m*.
II *adj* (bluish) violet/-ette; (reddish) pourpre.

purpose I *n* **1** (aim) but *m*; **for the ~ of doing** dans le but de faire; **for cooking ~s** pour la cuisine; **for all practical ~s** en pratique; **2** (also **strength of ~**) résolution *f*.
II **on ~** *phr* exprès.

purpose-built *adj* (GB) [*premises, stadium*] construit spécialement; **a ~ apartment** ≈ un appartement indépendant.

purposely *adv* exprès, intentionnellement.

purr I *n* (of cat, engine) ronronnement *m*.
II *vi* [*cat, engine*] ronronner.

purse *n* (for money) porte-monnaie *m inv*; (US) (handbag) sac *m* à main.
IDIOMS **to hold the ~-strings** tenir les cordons de la bourse.

purser ▶ 805 *n* commissaire *m* de bord.

pursue *vtr* poursuivre [*person, aim, ambition, studies*]; mener [*policy*]; se livrer à [*occupation, interest*]; **to ~ a career** faire carrière (**in** dans).

pursuer *n* poursuivant/-e *m/f*.

pursuit *n* **1** poursuite *f*; **in ~ of** à la poursuite de; **in hot ~** à vos/ses etc trousses; **2 artistic ~s** activités *fpl* artistiques.

push I *n* poussée *f*; **to give sb/sth a ~** pousser qn/qch.
II *vtr* **1** pousser [*person, car, pram*]; appuyer sur [*button, switch*]; **to ~ sb/sth away** repousser qn/qch; **she ~ed him down the stairs** elle l'a poussé dans l'escalier; **to ~ sb/sth out of the way** écarter qn/qch; **to ~ sb aside** écarter qn; **to ~ one's way through sth** se frayer un chemin à travers qch; **to ~ the door open** pousser la porte; **to ~ sb too far** pousser qn à bout; **2**○ (promote) promouvoir [*policy, theory*]; **3**○ (sell) vendre [*drugs*].
III *vi* pousser; **to ~ past sb** bousculer qn.
IDIOMS **at a ~**○ (GB) s'il le faut; **to ~ one's luck** aller un peu trop loin.

■ **push around**○: **~ [sb] around** bousculer.

■ **push back**: **~ [sth] back, ~ back [sth]** repousser [*frontier, date, enemy*].

■ **push down**: ¶ **~ [sth] down, ~ down [sth]** faire chuter; ¶ **~ down [sb], ~ [sb] down** faire tomber.

■ **push for**: **~ for [sth]** faire pression en faveur de [*reform*].

■ **push forward**: ¶ **~ forward** (with plans) persévérer (**with** dans); (on journey) continuer; ¶ **~ oneself forward** se mettre en avant.

■ **push in**: **~ [sth] in, ~ in [sth]** enfoncer [*button, door, window*].

■ **push over**: ¶ **~ over**○**!** pousse-toi!; ¶ **~ over [sth/sb], ~ [sth/sb] over** renverser [*person, table, car*].

■ **push through**: **~ [sth] through, ~ through [sth]** faire voter [*bill, legislation*]; faire passer [*deal*].

■ **push up**: **~ up [sth], ~ [sth] up** faire monter [*prices, unemployment*].

push: **~-button** *adj* [*telephone*] à touches; **~cart** *n* charrette *f* à bras; **~chair** *n* (GB) poussette *f*.

pusher *n* ○(also **drug ~**) revendeur/-euse *m/f* de drogue.

push: **~pin** *n* (US) punaise *f*; **~-start** *vtr* pousser [qch] pour le/la faire démarrer [*vehicle*]; **~-up** *n* (Sport) pompe○ *f*.

put *vtr* **1** (place) mettre [*object, person*] (**in** dans; **on** sur); **to ~ more sugar in one's tea** ajouter du sucre dans son thé; **to ~ more soap in the bathroom** remettre du savon dans la salle de bains; **2 to ~ sth through** glisser qch dans [*letterbox*]; **to ~ one's head through the window** mettre le nez à la fenêtre; **to ~ sb through** envoyer qn à [*university*]; faire passer qn par [*ordeal*]; faire passer [qch] à qn [*test*]; **to ~ one's hand to** porter la main à [*mouth*]; **3** (devote, invest) **to ~ money/energy into sth** investir de l'argent/son énergie dans qch; **to ~ a lot into** s'engager à fond pour [*work, project*]; sacrifier beaucoup à [*marriage*]; **4 to ~ money towards** (contribute) donner de l'argent pour [*gift*]; **~ it towards some new clothes** sers-t'en pour acheter des vêtements; **to ~ tax on sth** taxer qch; **5** (express) **to ~ it bluntly** pour parler franchement; **let me ~ it another way** laissez-moi m'exprimer différemment; **6** présenter [*point of view, proposal*]; **to ~ sth to the vote** mettre qch au vote.
IDIOMS **I wouldn't ~ it past him!** ça ne m'étonnerait pas de lui!

■ **put across**: **~ across [sth], ~ [sth] across** communiquer [*idea, case*]; **to ~ oneself across** se mettre en valeur.

■ **put away**: **~ away [sth], ~ [sth] away** **1** (tidy away) ranger; **2** (save) mettre [qch] de côté; **3**○ avaler [*food*]; descendre○ [*drink*].

■ **put back**: **~ back [sth], ~ [sth] back 1** (return) remettre; **to ~ sth back where it belongs** remettre qch à sa place; **2** remettre [*meeting*] (**to** à; **until** jusqu'à); repousser [*date*]; **3** retarder [*clock, watch*]; **4** (delay) retarder (**by** de).

■ **put down**: ¶ **~ [sth] down, ~ down [sth] 1** poser [*object*]; **2** réprimer [*rebellion*]; **3** (write down) mettre (par écrit); **4** (ascribe) **to ~ sth down to** mettre qch sur le compte de; **to ~ sth down to the fact that** imputer qch au fait que; **5** (by injection) piquer [*animal*]; (by other method) abattre [*animal*]; **6 to ~ down a deposit** verser des arrhes; **to ~ £50 down on sth** verser 50 livres d'arrhes sur qch; ¶ **~ [sb] down 1** déposer [*passenger*]; **2**○ (humiliate) rabaisser.

■ **put forward**: ¶ **~ forward [sth], ~ [sth]**

forward 1 (propose) avancer [*theory, name*]; soumettre [*plan*]; émettre [*opinion*]; **2** (in time) avancer [*meeting, date, clock*] (**by** de; **to** à); ¶ **~ [sb] forward, ~ forward [sb]** présenter la candidature de.

■ **put in**: ¶ **~ in 1** [*ship*] faire escale (**at** à; **to** dans; **for** pour); **2 to ~ in for** postuler pour [*job, promotion, rise*]; demander [*transfer*]; ¶ **~ in [sth], ~ [sth] in 1** installer [*heating, units*]; **2** (make) faire [*request, claim*]; **to ~ in an appearance** faire une apparition; **3** passer [*time*]; **4** (insert) mettre [*word, reference*].

■ **put off**: ¶ **~ off [sth], ~ [sth] off 1** (delay, defer) remettre [qch] (à plus tard); **2** (turn off) éteindre [*light, radio*]; ¶ **~ off [sb], ~ [sb] off 1** décommander [*guest*]; dissuader [*person*]; **to be easily put off** se décourager facilement; **2** (repel) [*appearance, smell*] dégoûter; [*manner, person*] déconcerter.

■ **put on**: ¶ **~ on [sth], ~ [sth] on 1** mettre [*garment, make-up*]; **2** allumer [*light, heating*]; mettre [*record, music*]; **to ~ the kettle on** mettre de l'eau à chauffer; **3** prendre [*weight, kilo*]; **4** (produce) monter [*play, exhibition*]; **5** (adopt) prendre [*accent, expression*]; **he 's ~ting it on** il fait semblant; **6** ajouter [*train, bus service*]; ¶ **~ [sb] on** passer [*caller*]; **I'll ~ him on** je vous le passe.

■ **put out**: ¶ **~ out [sth], ~ [sth] out 1** (extend) tendre [*hand*]; **to ~ out one's tongue** tirer la langue; **2** éteindre [*fire, cigarette*]; **3** sortir [*bin, garbage*]; faire sortir [*cat*]; **4** diffuser [*warning, statement*]; **5** mettre [*food, towels*]; **6** [*plant*] déployer [*buds, shoots*]; **7** (dislocate) se démettre [*shoulder*]; ¶ **~ [sb] out 1** (inconvenience) déranger; **2** (annoy) contrarier.

■ **put through**: **~ [sth/sb] through, ~ through [sth/sb] 1** (implement) faire passer [*bill, reform*]; **2** passer [*caller*] (**to** à).

■ **put together**: **~ [sb/sth] together, ~ together [sb/sth] 1** (assemble) assembler [*pieces, parts*]; **to ~ sth back together** reconstituer qch; **2** (place together) mettre ensemble; **3** établir [*list*]; faire [*film, programme*]; **4** construire [*argument*].

■ **put up**: ¶ **~ up [sth]** opposer [*resistance*]; **to ~ up a fight** combattre; ¶ **~ [sth] up, ~ up [sth] 1** hisser [*flag, sail*]; relever [*hair*]; **to ~ up one's hand** lever la main; **2** mettre [*sign, plaque*]; afficher [*list*]; **3** (erect) dresser [*fence, tent*]; **4** augmenter [*rent, prices, tax*]; faire monter [*temperature*]; **5** (provide) fournir [*money*]; ¶ **~ [sb] up, ~ up [sb] 1** (lodge) héberger; **2** (incite) **to ~ sb up to sth** pousser qn à qch.

■ **put upon**: **to be put upon** se faire marcher sur les pieds.

■ **put up with** supporter [*person, situation*].

put-down *n* remarque *f* humiliante.

putty *n* mastic *m*.

puzzle I *n* **1** (mystery) mystère *m*; **2** (Games) casse-tête *m inv*.

II *vtr* [*question, attitude*] déconcerter [*person*].

puzzle book *n* livre *m* de jeux.

puzzled *adj* [*person, smile*] perplexe; **to be ~ as to why** se demander pourquoi.

PVC *n* (*abbr* = **polyvinyl chloride**) PVC *m*.

pygmy *n* pygmée *mf*.

pyjamas (GB), **pajamas** (US) *n pl* pyjama *m*; **a pair of ~** un pyjama.

pylon *n* pylône *m*.

pyramid *n* pyramide *f*.

Qq

q, Q *n* q, Q *m*.
QED (*abbr* = **quod erat demonstrandum**) CQFD.
quack **I** *n* **1** (impostor) charlatan *m*; **2**○ (GB) (doctor) toubib○ *m*; **3** (of duck) coin-coin *m inv*.
II *vi* cancaner.
quadrangle *n* **1** (shape) quadrilatère *m*; **2** (in architecture) cour *f* carrée.
quadruple **I** *n*, *adj* quadruple (*m*).
II *vtr*, *vi* quadrupler.
quadruplet *n* quadruplé/-e *m/f*.
quagmire *n* bourbier *m*.
quail **I** *n* caille *f*; **~'s egg** œuf *m* de caille.
II *vi* trembler.
quaint *adj* **1** (pretty) pittoresque; **2** (old-world) au charme vieillot; **3** (odd) bizarre.
quake *vi* trembler.
qualification *n* **1** (diploma, degree) diplôme *m* (**in** en); (experience, skills) qualification *f*; **2** (restriction) restriction *f*; **without ~** sans réserves.
qualified *adj* **1** (for job) (having diploma) diplômé; (having experience, skills) qualifié; **to be ~ for sth** (on paper) avoir les titres requis pour qch; (by experience, skills) être qualifié pour qch; **2** (competent) (having authority) qualifié; (having knowledge) compétent; **3** (modified) nuancé, mitigé.
qualifier *n* **1** (Sport) (contestant) qualifié/-e *m/f*; (match) éliminatoire *m*; **2** (in grammar) qualificatif *m*.
qualify **I** *vtr* **1 to ~ sb for a job** [*degree, diploma*] habiliter qn à exercer un emploi; [*experience, skills*] rendre qn apte à exercer un emploi; **2 to ~ sb for membership/benefits** donner le droit à qn d'être membre/de recevoir des allocations; **3** (give authority to) **to ~ sb to do** autoriser qn à faire; **4** (modify) nuancer [*approval, opinion*]; préciser [*statement, remark*]; **5** (in grammar) qualifier.
II *vi* **1** (obtain diploma, degree) obtenir son diplôme (**as** de, en); **2** (be eligible) remplir les conditions (requises); **to ~ for** avoir droit à [*membership, legal aid*]; **to ~ to do** avoir le droit de faire; **3** (meet standard) **he hardly qualifies as a poet** ce n'est pas vraiment ce que l'on peut appeler un poète; **4** (Sport) se qualifier.
qualifying *adj* **1** [*match, exam*] de qualification; **2** [*adjective*] qualificatif/-ive.
quality **I** *n* qualité *f*.
II *noun modifier* [*car, press*] de qualité.
quality control *n* contrôle *m* de qualité.
qualm *n* scrupule *m*; **to have no ~s about doing** ne pas avoir le moindre scrupule à faire.
quandary *n* embarras *m*; (serious) dilemme *m*.
quantify *vtr* évaluer [qch] avec précision; (scientifically) quantifier.
quantity ▶**813** *n* quantité *f*; **in ~** en grande quantité; **unknown ~** inconnue *f*.
quantity: **~ surveying** *n* métrage *m*; **~ surveyor** ▶**805** *n* métreur *m*.
quantum leap *n* saut *m* quantique; (figurative) bond *m* prodigieux.
quarantine **I** *n* quarantaine *f*; **in ~** en quarantaine.
II *vtr* mettre [qn/qch] en quarantaine.
quarrel **I** *n* **1** (argument) dispute *f* (**between** entre; **over** au sujet de); **to have a ~** se disputer; **2** (feud) brouille *f* (**about, over** au sujet de).
II *vi* **1** (argue) se disputer; **2** (sever relations) se brouiller; **3 to ~ with** contester [*claim, idea*]; se plaindre de [*price, verdict*].
quarrelling, quarreling (US) *n* disputes *fpl*.
quarry **I** *n* **1** (in ground) carrière *f*; **2** (prey) proie *f*; (in hunting) gibier *m*.
II *vtr* (also **~ out**) extraire [*stone*].
quart *n* ≈ litre *m* ((GB) = *1.136 litres*, (US) = *0.946 litres*).
quarter ▶**554**, **748**, **738** **I** *n* **1** (one fourth) quart *m*; **~ of an hour** quart *m* d'heure; **2** (three months) trimestre *m*; **3** (district) quartier *m*; **4** (group) milieu *m*; **don't expect help from that ~** n'attends aucune aide de ce côté-là.
II quarters *n pl* (Mil) quartiers *mpl*; (gen) logement *m*.
III *pron* **1** (25%) quart *m*; **only a ~ passed** seul le quart a réussi; **2** (in time phrases) **at (a) ~ to 11** (GB), **at a ~ of 11** (US) à onze heures moins le quart; **an hour and a ~** une heure et quart; **3** (in age) **she's ten and a ~** elle a dix ans et trois mois.
IV *adj* **a ~ century** un quart de siècle.
V *adv* **a ~ full** au quart plein; **a ~ as big** quatre fois moins grand; **~ the price** quatre fois moins cher.
VI *vtr* couper [qch] en quatre [*cake, apple*].
VII at close quarters *phr* de près.
quarterfinal *n* quart *m* de finale.
quarterly **I** *adj* trimestriel/-ielle.
II *adv* tous les trois mois.
quartet *n* quatuor *m*; **jazz ~** quartette *m*.
quartz **I** *n* quartz *m*.
II *noun modifier* [*crystal*] de quartz; [*clock*] à quartz.
quash *vtr* rejeter [*proposal*]; réprimer [*rebellion*].
quasi(-) *pref* quasi (+ *adj*), quasi- (+ *noun*).
quaver **I** *n* **1** (GB Mus) croche *f*; **2** (trembling) tremblement *m* (**in** dans).
II *vi* trembloter.
quay *n* quai *m*; **on the ~** sur le quai.
queasiness *n* nausée *f*.
queasy *adj* **to be** or **feel ~** avoir mal au cœur.

Quantities

Note the use of ***en*** (*of it* or *of them*) in the following examples. This word must be included when the thing you are talking about is not expressed. However, ***en*** is not needed when the commodity is specified (*there is a lot of butter = il y a beaucoup de beurre*):

how much is there?	= combien y **en** a-t-il?
there's a lot	= il y **en** a beaucoup
there's not much	= il n'y **en** a pas beaucoup
there's two kilos	= il y **en** a deux kilos
how much sugar have you?	= combien de sucre as-tu?
I've got a lot	= j'en ai beaucoup
I haven't got (very) much	= je n'**en** ai pas beaucoup
I've got two kilos	= j'**en** ai deux kilos
how many are there?	= combien y **en** a-t-il?
there are a lot	= il y **en** a beaucoup
there aren't many	= il n'y **en** a pas beaucoup
there are twenty	= il y **en** a vingt
how many apples have you?	= combien de pommes as-tu? tu as combien de pommes?
I've got a lot	= j'**en** ai beaucoup
I haven't got many	= je n'**en** ai pas beaucoup
I've got twenty	= j'**en** ai vingt
Tim has got more than Tom	= Tim **en** a plus que Tom
Tim has got more money than Tom	= Tim a plus d'argent que Tom
much more than	= beaucoup plus que
a little more than	= un peu plus que
Tim has got more apples than Tom	= Tim a plus de pommes que Tom
many more apples than Tom	= beaucoup plus de pommes que Tom
a few more apples than Tom	= quelques pommes de plus que Tom
a few more people than yesterday	= quelques personnes de plus qu'hier
Tom has got less than Tim	= Tom **en** a moins que Tim
Tom has got less money than Tim	= Tom a moins d'argent que Tim
much less than	= beaucoup moins que
a little less than	= un peu moins que
Tom has got fewer than Tim	= Tom **en** a moins que Tim
Tom has got fewer apples than Tim	= Tom a moins de pommes que Tim
many fewer than	= beaucoup moins que

Relative quantities

how many are there to the kilo?	= combien y **en** a-t-il au kilo?
there are ten to the kilo	= il y **en** a dix au kilo
how many do you get for ten francs?	= combien peut-on **en** avoir pour dix francs?
you get five for ten francs	= il y **en** a cinq pour dix francs
how much does it cost a litre?	= combien coûte le litre?
it costs £5 a litre	= ça coûte cinq livres le litre
how much do apples cost a kilo?	= combien coûte le kilo de pommes?
apples cost ten francs a kilo	= les pommes coûtent dix francs le kilo
how many glasses do you get to the bottle?	= combien y a-t-il de verres par bouteille?
you get six glasses to the bottle	= il y a six verres par bouteille

Quebec ▶574| *pr n* Québec *m*; **in ~** (city) à Québec; (province) au Québec.

queen ▶642| *n* **1** (monarch) reine *f*; **2** (Zool) reine *f*; **3** (Games) (in chess) reine *f*; (in cards) dame *f*.
IDIOMS **to ~ it over sb** prendre de grands airs avec qn.

queen: **~ bee** *n* reine *f* des abeilles; **~ mother** *n* Reine mère *f*; **Queen's Counsel, QC** *n* (GB Law) avocat *m* éminent (*qui tient son titre de la Reine*).

Queen's English *n* **to speak the ~** parler un anglais correct.

queer *adj* **1** (strange) étrange, bizarre; **2** (suspicious) louche, suspect.

quell *vtr* étouffer [*anger, anxiety, revolt*].

quench *vtr* étancher [*thirst*]; étouffer [*desire*].

querulous *adj* grincheux/-euse.

query I *n* question *f* (**about** au sujet de); **a ~ from sb** une question venant de qn; **queries from customers** demandes *fpl* de renseignement venant des clients.
II *vtr* mettre en doute; **to ~ whether** demander si; **to ~ sb's ability** mettre en doute les capacités de qn.

quest *n* quête *f*; **the ~ for sb/sth** la recherche de qn/qch.

question I *n* **1** (request for information) question *f* (**about** sur); (in exam) question *f*; **to ask sb a ~** poser une question à qn; **what a ~!** en voilà une question!; **a ~ from the floor** (in parliament) une question provenant de l'assemblée; **2** (practical issue) problème *m*; (ethical issue) question *f*; **the Palestinian ~** la question palestinienne; **the ~ of pollution** le problème de la pollution; **it's a ~ of doing** il s'agit de faire; **the ~ of where to live** le problème de savoir où habiter; **that's another ~** c'est une autre affaire; **the ~ is whether** il s'agit ici de savoir si; **there was never any ~ of you paying** il n'a jamais été question que tu paies; **the person in ~** la personne en question; **it's out of the ~ for him to leave** il est hors de question qu'il parte; **3** doute *m*; **to call sth into ~** mettre qch en doute; **it's open to ~** cela se discute.
II *vtr* **1** (interrogate) questionner [*suspect, politician*]; **2** (cast doubt upon) (on one occasion) mettre en doute [*tactics, methods*]; (over longer period) douter de [*tactics, methods*]; **to ~ whether** douter que (+ *subj*).

questionable *adj* [*motive, decision*] discutable; [*taste*] douteux/-euse; **it is ~ whether** il est douteux que (+ *subj*).

questioner *n* interrogateur/-trice *m/f*.

questioning I *n* **1** (of person) interrogation *f*; (relentless) interrogatoire *m*; **they brought him in for ~** ils l'ont fait venir pour l'interroger; **a line of ~** une série de questions; **2** (of criteria) remise *f* en question (**of** de).
II *adj* **1** [*look, tone*] interrogateur/-trice; **2** [*techniques*] d'interrogation.

question mark *n* **1** (in punctuation) point *m* d'interrogation; **2** (doubt) **there is a ~ hanging over his future** l'incertitude plane sur son avenir.

questionnaire *n* questionnaire *m* (**on** sur; **to do** pour faire).

queue I *n* (GB) (of people) queue *f*, file *f* (d'attente); (of vehicles) file *f*; **to stand in a ~** faire la queue; **to join the ~** [*person*] se mettre à la queue; [*car*] se mettre dans la file; **to jump the ~**○ passer avant son tour.
II *vi* (also **~ up**) [*people*] faire la queue (**for** pour); [*taxis*] attendre en ligne.

quibble *vi* chicaner (**about, over** sur).

quick I *n* **to bite one's nails to the ~** se ronger les ongles jusqu'au sang.
II *adj* **1** (speedy) [*pace, reply, profit, meal*] rapide; [*storm, shower*] bref/brève (*before n*); **to have a ~ coffee** prendre un café en vitesse; **to have a ~ wash** faire une toilette rapide; **she's a ~ worker** elle travaille vite; **the ~est way to do** le meilleur moyen de faire; **to make a ~ recovery** se rétablir vite; **to pay a ~ visit to sb** faire une petite visite à qn; **be ~ (about it)!** dépêche-toi!; **2** (clever) [*child, student*] vif/vive d'esprit; **to be ~ at** être bon/bonne en [*arithmetic*]; **3** (prompt) [*reaction*] vif/vive; **to be a ~ learner** apprendre vite; **to be (too) ~ to condemn** condamner (trop) facilement; **she was ~ to see the advantages** elle a tout de suite vu les avantages; **4** (lively) **to have a ~ temper** s'emporter facilement.
III *adv* **~!** vite!; **~ as a flash** avec la rapidité de l'éclair.
IDIOMS **to cut** or **sting sb to the ~** piquer qn au vif.

quicken I *vtr* accélérer [*pace*]; stimuler [*interest*].
II *vi* [*pace*] s'accélérer; [*anger*] s'intensifier.

quicklime *n* chaux *f* vive.

quickly *adv* [*arrive, resolve*] (rapidly) vite, rapidement; (without delay) sans tarder; **(come) ~!** (viens) vite!

quick march *n* (Mil) ≈ pas *m* cadencé; **~!** ≈ pas cadencé marche!

quickness *n* **1** (speed) (of person, movement) rapidité *f*; **~ to react** promptitude *f* à réagir; **2** (liveliness of mind) vivacité *f* d'esprit.

quick: **~sand** *n* sables *mpl* mouvants; (figurative) bourbier *m*; **~silver** *n* mercure *m*; **~-tempered** *adj* coléreux/-euse; **~ time** *n* (US) marche *f* rapide.

quiet I *n* **1** (silence) silence *m*; **~ please!** silence, s'il vous plaît!; **2** (peace) tranquillité *f*; **3**○ (secret) **to do sth on the ~** faire qch discrètement.
II *adj* **1** (silent) [*church, person, room*] silencieux/-ieuse; **to keep ~** garder le silence; **to go ~** [*person, assembly*] se taire; **to keep sb ~** faire taire [*dog, child*]; **be ~** (stop talking) tais-toi; (make no noise) ne fais pas de bruit; **2** (not noisy) [*voice*] bas/basse; [*engine*] silencieux/-ieuse; [*music*] doux/douce; [*cough*] discret/-ète; **in a ~ voice** à voix basse; **to keep the children ~** [*activity*] tenir les enfants tranquilles; **3** (discreet) discret/-ète; **to have a ~ word with sb** prendre qn à part

pour lui parler; **4** (calm) [*village, holiday, night, life*] tranquille; **5** [*meal*] intime; [*wedding*] célébré dans l'intimité; **6** (secret) **to keep [sth] ~** ne pas divulguer [*plans*]; garder [qch] secret/-ète [*engagement*].

quieten *vtr* **1** (calm) calmer [*person, animal*]; **2** (silence) faire taire [*critics, children*].
■ **quieten down**: ¶ **~ down 1** (become calm) [*person, activity*] se calmer; **2** (fall silent) se taire; ¶ **~ down [sb/sth], ~ [sb/sth] down 1** (calm) calmer; **2** (silence) faire taire.

quietly *adv* **1** (not noisily) [*move*] sans bruit; [*cough, speak*] doucement; **2** (silently) [*play, read, sit*] en silence; **3** (discreetly) [*live*] simplement; **to get married ~** se marier dans l'intimité; **to be ~ confident that** avoir l'intime conviction que; **4** (calmly) calmement.

quietness *n* **1** (silence) silence *m*; **2** (of voice) faiblesse *f*; **3** (of place) tranquillité *f*.

quiff *n* (GB) (on forehead) toupet *m*; (on top of head) houppe *f*.

quill *n* **1** (feather) penne *f*; (stem of feather) tuyau *m* de plume; **2** (on porcupine) piquant *m*; **3** (also **~ pen**) plume *f* d'oie.

quilt I *n* **1** (GB) (duvet) couette *f*; **2** (bed cover) dessus *m* de lit.
II *vtr* matelasser.

quinine *n* quinine *f*.

quintessential *adj* [*quality*] fondamental; **the ~ star** la vedette par excellence.

quintuple I *adj* quintuple.
II *vtr* quintupler.

quintuplet *n* quintuplé/-e *m/f*.

quirk *n* (of person) excentricité *f*; (of fate, nature) caprice *m*.

quit I *vtr* démissionner de [*job*]; quitter [*place, person, profession*].
II *vi* **1** (give up) arrêter (**doing** de faire); **2** (resign) démissionner.

quite *adv* **1** (completely) [*new, ready, understand*] tout à fait; [*alone, empty, exhausted*] complètement; [*impossible*] totalement; [*extraordinary*] vraiment; **I ~ agree** je suis tout à fait d'accord; **you're ~ right** vous avez entièrement raison; **it's ~ all right** c'est sans importance; **are you ~ sure?** en êtes-vous certain?; **~ clearly** [*see*] très clairement; **and ~ right too!** à juste titre!; **that's ~ enough!** ça suffit!; **2** (exactly) **not ~** pas exactement; **not ~ so much** un petit peu moins; **not ~ as many** pas tout à fait autant; **I don't ~ know** je ne sais pas du tout; **that's not ~ all** (when giving account) et ce n'est pas tout; **3** (definitely) **it was ~ the best answer** c'était de loin la meilleure réponse; **~ simply** tout simplement; **4** (rather) [*big, easily, often*] assez; **it's ~ small** ce n'est pas très grand; **it's ~ warm today** il fait bon aujourd'hui; **it's ~ likely that** il est très probable que; **I ~ like Chinese food** j'aime assez la cuisine chinoise; **~ a few** un bon nombre de [*people, examples*]; **~ a lot of money** pas mal d'argent; **I've thought about it ~ a bit** j'y ai pas mal réfléchi; **5** (as intensifier) **~ a difference** une différence considérable; **that will be ~ a change for you** ce sera un grand changement pour toi; **she's ~ a woman!** quelle femme!; **6** (expressing agreement) **~ (so)** c'est sûr.

quits○ *adj* **to be ~** être quitte (**with sb** envers qn).

quiver I *n* **1** tremblement *m*; **2** (for arrows) carquois *m*.
II *vi* [*voice, lip, animal*] trembler (**with** de); [*leaves*] frémir; [*flame*] vaciller.

quiz I *n* **1** (game) jeu *m* de questions-réponses, quiz *m*; (written, in magazine) questionnaire *m* (**about** sur); **2** (US Sch) interrogation *f*.
II *vtr* questionner (**about** au sujet de).

quiz game, **quiz show** *n* jeu *m* de questions-réponses.

quizzical *adj* interrogateur/-trice.

quota *n* **1** (prescribed number, amount) quota *m* (**of, for** de); **2** (share) part *f* (**of** de); (officially allocated) quote-part *f*.

quotation *n* **1** citation *f*; **2** (estimate) devis *m*; **3** (on stock exchange) cours *m*, cote *f*.

quotation marks *n pl* guillemets *mpl*; **in ~** entre guillemets.

quote I *n* **1** (quotation) citation *f* (**from** de); **2** (statement to journalist) déclaration *f*; **3** (estimate) devis *m*; **4** (on stock exchange) cote *f*.
II **quotes** *n pl* = **quotation marks**.
III *vtr* **1** citer [*person, passage, proverb*]; rapporter [*words*]; rappeler [*reference number*]; **she was ~d as saying that...** elle aurait dit que...; **2** (state) indiquer [*price, figure*]; **they ~d us £200** dans leur devis, ils ont demandé £200; **3** (on stock exchange) coter [*share, price*] (**at** à); **4** (in betting) **to be ~d 6 to 1** être coté entre 6 et 1.
IV *vi* (from text, author) faire des citations; **to ~ from Keats** citer Keats.

r, R *n* r, R *m*.
rabbi ▶805 *n* rabbin *m*.
rabbit *n* lapin *m*.
rabid *adj* **1** (with rabies) enragé; **2** (fanatical) fanatique.
rabies ▶686 *n* rage *f*.
race I *n* **1** (gen, Sport) course *f*; **to have a ~** faire la course; **2** (ethnic group) race *f*.
II *vtr* faire la course avec [*person, car, horse*] (**to** jusqu'à).
III *vi* **1** (gen, Sport) courir (**at** à; **to** vers; **for** pour atteindre); **to ~ in/away** entrer/partir en courant; **2** (hurry) se dépêcher (**to do** de faire).
race: **~goer** *n* turfiste *mf*; **~horse** *n* cheval *m* de course.
racer *n* (bike) vélo *m* de course; (car) voiture *f* de course.
racetrack *n* (for horses) champ *m* de courses; (for cars) circuit *m*; (for dogs, cycles) piste *f*.
racial *adj* racial.
racing I *n* courses *fpl*.
II *noun modifier* [*car, yacht*] de course; [*fan, commentator*] de courses.
racing driver *n* coureur/-euse *m/f* automobile.
racist *n, adj* raciste (*mf*).
rack I *n* **1** (for plates) égouttoir *m*; (for clothes) portant *m*; (for bottles) casier *m*; ▶ **roof rack**; **2** (torture) chevalet *m*; **3 ~ of lamb** carré *m* d'agneau.
II *vtr* **~ed with** torturé par [*guilt*].
IDIOMS **to ~ one's brains** se creuser la cervelle°.
racket *n* **1** (also **racquet**) raquette *f*; **2**° (noise) vacarme *m*; **3** (swindle) escroquerie *f*.
racketeering *n* racket *m*.
racquetball ▶649 *n* (US) ≈ squash *m*.
racy *adj* [*account, style*] plein de verve; (risqué) osé.
radar *n* radar *m*.
radiance *n* éclat *m*.
radiant *adj* radieux/-ieuse.
radiate *vtr* **1** rayonner de [*happiness*]; déborder de [*confidence*]; **2** émettre [*heat*].
radiation I *n* (medical, nuclear) radiation *f*; (rays) radiations *fpl*.
II *noun modifier* [*levels*] de radiation; [*leak*] de radiations.
radiation: **~ sickness** *n* maladie *f* des rayons; **~ therapy** *n* radiothérapie *f*.
radiator *n* radiateur *m*.
radical *n, adj* radical/-e (*m/f*).
radio I *n* radio *f*; **on the ~** à la radio.
II *noun modifier* [*contact, signal*] radio *inv*; [*programme*] de radio.
III *vtr* **to ~ sth (to sb)** communiquer qch par radio (à qn).
IV *vi* **to ~ for help** appeler au secours par radio.
radio: **~active** *adj* radioactif/-ive; **~ announcer** *n* speaker/-erine *m/f*; **~ broadcast** *n* émission *f* radiophonique; **~ cassette (recorder)** *n* radiocassette *f*.
radiographer ▶805 *n* manipulateur/-trice *m/f* radiographe.
radiologist ▶805 *n* radiologue *mf*.
radio: **~ station** *n* (channel) station *f* de radio; (installation) station *f* émettrice; **~therapy** *n* radiothérapie *f*.
radish *n* radis *m*.
radius *n* rayon *m*; **within a 10 km ~ of here** dans un rayon de 10 km.
raffle *n* tombola *f*.
raft *n* radeau *m*.
rafter *n* chevron *m*.
rag *n* **1** (cloth) chiffon *m*; **in ~s** [*person*] en haillons; [*clothes*] en loques; **2**° (newspaper) torchon° *m* (derogatory).
ragbag *n* (figurative) ramassis *m*.
rage I *n* **1** rage *f*, colère *f*; **to fly into a ~** entrer dans une colère noire; **2**° **to be (all) the ~** faire fureur.
II *vi* **1** [*storm, battle*] faire rage; **2** [*person*] tempêter (**at, against** contre).
ragged *adj* [*garment*] en loques; [*cuff, collar*] effiloché; [*person*] dépenaillé.
raging *adj* **1** [*passion, argument*] violent; [*thirst, pain*] atroce; **a ~ toothache** une rage de dents; **2** [*blizzard, sea*] déchaîné.
raid I *n* raid *m* (**on** sur); (on bank) hold-up *m* (**on** de); (by police, customs) rafle *f* (**on** dans).
II *vtr* [*military*] faire un raid sur; [*police*] faire une rafle dans; [*criminals*] attaquer [*bank*].
raider *n* **1** (thief) pillard *m*; **2** (also **corporate ~**) raider *m*.
rail I *n* **1** (in fence) barreau *m*; (on balcony) balustrade *f*; (on tower) garde-fou *m*; (handrail) rampe *f*; **2** (for curtains) tringle *f*; **3** (for train) rail *m*; **by ~** par chemin de fer; **to go off the ~s** [*train*] dérailler.
II *noun modifier* [*network*] ferroviaire; **~ strike** grève *f* des cheminots.
railing *n* (also **~s**) grille *f*.
railroad *n* (US) **1** (network) chemin *m* de fer; **2** (also **~ track**) voie *f* ferrée.
railroad car *n* (US) wagon *m*.
railway (GB) **I** *n* **1** (network) chemin *m* de fer; **2** (also **~ line**) ligne *f* de chemin de fer; **3** (also **~ track**) voie *f* ferrée.
II *noun modifier* [*bridge*] de chemin de fer; [*link, tunnel, accident*] ferroviaire.
railway: **~ carriage** *n* (GB) wagon *m*; **~ station** *n* (GB) gare *f*.

rain I *n* pluie *f*; **the ~ stopped** il s'est arrêté de pleuvoir; **in the ~** sous la pluie.
II *v impers* pleuvoir; **it's ~ing (hard)** il pleut (à verse).

rain: **~bow** *n* arc-en-ciel *m*; **~coat** *n* imperméable *m*; **~drop** *n* goutte *f* de pluie; **~fall** *n* niveau *m* de précipitations; **~ forest** *n* forêt *f* tropicale; **~storm** *n* pluie *f* torrentielle.

rainy *adj* [*afternoon, climate*] pluvieux/-ieuse; **~ season** saison *f* des pluies.

raise I *n* (US) (pay rise) augmentation *f*.
II *vtr* **1** (lift) lever [*baton, barrier, curtain*]; hisser [*flag*]; soulever [*lid*]; renflouer [*sunken ship*]; **to ~ one's hand/head** lever la main/tête; **he ~d the glass to his lips** il a porté le verre à ses lèvres; **2** (increase) augmenter [*price, offer, salary*] (**from** de; **to** à); élever [*standard*]; reculer [*age limit*]; **to ~ one's voice** (to be heard) parler plus fort; (in anger) hausser le ton; **3** (cause) faire naître [*fears*]; soulever [*dust*]; **4** (mention) soulever [*issue, objection*]; **5** (bring up) élever [*child, family*]; **6** (breed) élever [*livestock*]; **7** (find) trouver [*capital*]; **8** (collect) lever [*tax*]; [*person*] collecter [*money*]; **9** (end) lever [*ban*]; **10** (give) **to ~ the alarm** donner l'alarme; **11** (improve) **to ~ the tone** hausser le ton; **to ~ sb's spirits** remonter le moral à qn; **12 to ~ the bidding** (in gambling) monter la mise; (at auction) monter l'enchère.

raised *adj* [*platform, jetty*] surélevé; **~ voices** des éclats de voix.

raisin *n* raisin *m* sec.

rake I *n* râteau *m*.
II *vtr* ratisser [*grass, leaves*].

rally I *n* **1** (meeting) rassemblement *m*; **2** (race) rallye *m*; **3** (in tennis) échange *m*.
II *vtr* rassembler [*support, troops*].
III *vi* **1** [*people*] se rallier (**to** à); **2** (recover) [*patient*] se rétablir.
■ **rally round, rally around**: ¶ **~ round** [*supporters*] se rallier; ¶ **~ round [sb]** soutenir [*person*].

ram I *n* bélier *m*.
II *vtr* **1** (crash into) rentrer dans, heurter; **2** (push) enfoncer [*fist, object*].
■ **ram home**: **~ [sth] home, ~ home [sth]** faire clairement comprendre [*message*].

RAM *n* (Comput) (*abbr* = **random access memory**) RAM *f*.

ramble *n* randonnée *f*, balade *f*.
■ **ramble on** discourir (**about** sur).

rambler *n* randonneur/-euse *m/f*.

rambling I *n* randonnée *f*.
II *adj* **1** [*house*] plein de coins et de recoins; **2** [*talk, article*] décousu.

ramification *n* ramification *f*.

ramp *n* rampe *f*; (GB) (in roadworks) dénivellation *f*; (for car repairs) pont *m* de graissage; (up to plane) passerelle *f*; (US) (slip road) bretelle *f*.

rampage *n* **to be** or **go on the ~** tout saccager.

rampant *adj* [*crime, disease*] endémique.

rampart *n* rempart *m*.

ramshackle *adj* délabré.

ranch *n* ranch *m*.

rancid *adj* rance; **to go ~** rancir.

random *adj* (fait) au hasard.

range I *n* **1** (of prices, products) gamme *f*; (of activities, options) éventail *m*, choix *m*; (of influence, knowledge) étendue *f*; (of research) domaine *m*; (of radar, weapon) portée *f* (**of** de); **age ~** tranche *f* d'âge; **2** (US) (prairie) prairie *f*; **3** (of mountains) chaîne *f*; **4** (stove) (wood) fourneau *m*; **5** (also **shooting ~**) champ *m* de tir.
II *vi* aller (**from** de; **to** à); (vary) varier; **to ~ over sth** couvrir qch.

ranger *n* **1** (in forest) garde-forestier *m*; **2** (US) ranger *m*.

rank I *n* **1** (in military, police) grade *m*; (in company, politics) rang *m*; (social status) rang *m*; **to break ~s** [*soldiers*] rompre les rangs; (figurative) [*politician*] se rebeller; **to close ~s** serrer les rangs; **to rise through the ~s** sortir du rang; **2 taxi ~** station de taxis.
II *adj* **1** [*outsider, beginner*] complet/-ète; **2** [*odour*] fétide.
III *vtr* [*person*] classer [*player, novel, restaurant*] (**among** parmi).
IV *vi* se classer (**among** parmi).

rank and file *n* **the ~** la base *f*.

rankle *vi* **it still ~s** je ne l'ai pas encore digéré○.

ransack *vtr* fouiller [*drawer*] (**for** pour trouver); mettre [qch] à sac [*house*].

ransom *n* rançon *f*; **to hold sb to** (GB) or **for** (US) **~** garder qn en otage.

rant *vi* déclamer; **to ~ and rave** tempêter (**at** contre).

rap I *n* **1** (tap) coup *m* sec; **2** (music) rap *m*.
II *vtr* frapper sur [*table, door*].

rape I *n* **1** (attack) viol *m*; **2** (plant) colza *m*.
II *vtr* violer.

rapid *adj* rapide; **in ~ succession** coup sur coup.

rapidly *adv* rapidement.

rapids *n pl* rapides *mpl*.

rapist *n* violeur *m*.

rapport *n* **to have a good ~ with sb** s'entendre bien avec qn.

rapt *adj* absorbé; [*smile*] extasié.

rapture *n* ravissement *m*; **to go into ~s about sth** s'extasier sur qch.

rapturous *adj* [*delight*] extasié; [*applause*] frénétique.

rare *adj* **1** (uncommon) rare; **2** [*steak*] saignant.

rarely *adv* rarement.

rarity *n* **to be a ~** [*occurrence*] être rare; [*plant*] être une plante rare; [*collector's item*] être une pièce rare.

rascal *n* coquin/-e *m/f*.

rash I *n* **1** (on skin) rougeurs *fpl*; **2** (figurative) vague *f* (**of** de).
II *adj* [*person, decision*] irréfléchi; **it was ~ to do** il n'était pas raisonnable de faire.

rasher *n* tranche *f*.

rasp I *vtr* râper.

II rasping *pres p adj* [*voice, sound*] râpeux/-euse.

raspberry I *n* framboise *f*.
II *noun modifier* [*ice cream, tart*] à la framboise; [*jam*] de framboise.

rat *n* rat *m*.
IDIOMS **to smell a ~** flairer quelque chose de louche.

rate I *n* **1** (speed) rythme *m*; **at this ~** (figurative) à ce train-là; **2** (level) taux *m*; **the interest ~** le taux d'intérêt; **3** (charge, fee) tarif *m*; **4** (in foreign exchange) cours *m*.
II rates *n pl* (GB) impôts *mpl* locaux; **business ~s** ≈ taxe *f* professionnelle.
III *vtr* **1** (classify) **to ~ sb as sth** considérer qn comme qch; **to ~ sb among** classer qn parmi; **highly ~d** très coté; **2** estimer [*honesty, friendship, person*].
IDIOMS **at any ~** en tout cas.

rather *adv* **1** plutôt; **I ~ like him** je le trouve plutôt sympathique; **it's ~ like an apple** ça ressemble un peu à une pomme; **it's ~ more difficult** c'est un peu plus difficile; **practical ~ than decorative** pratique plutôt que décoratif; **2** (preferably) **I would (much) ~ do** je préférerais (de loin) faire (**than do** que faire); **I'd ~ die!** plutôt mourir!; **I'd ~ not** j'aimerais mieux pas.

ratify *vtr* ratifier.

rating I *n* (score) cote *f*.
II ratings *n pl* (of TV audience) indice *m* d'écoute, audimat® *m*.

ratio *n* proportion *f*, rapport *m*; **in** or **by a ~ of 60:40** dans une proportion de 60 à 40.

ration I *n* ration *f*.
II *vtr* rationner [*food*] (**to** à); limiter la ration de [*person*] (**to** à).

rational *adj* [*approach, argument*] rationnel/-elle; [*person*] sensé.

rationale *n* **1** (reasons) raisons *fpl* (**for** pour; **for doing** de faire); **2** (logic) logique *f* (**behind** de).

rationalization *n* **1** justification *f* (**for** de); **2** (GB) (streamlining) rationalisation *f*.

rationalize *vtr* **1** (justify) justifier; **2** (GB) (streamline) rationaliser.

rationing *n* rationnement *m*.

rat: **~ poison** *n* mort-aux-rats *f inv*; **~ race** *n* foire *f* d'empoigne.

rattle I *n* **1** (noise) (of bottles, cutlery, chains) cliquetis *m*; (of window, engine) vibrations *fpl*; **2** (baby's) hochet *m*.
II *vtr* [*wind*] faire vibrer [*window*]; [*person*] s'acharner sur [*handle*].
III *vi* [*bottles, cutlery, chains*] s'entrechoquer; [*window*] vibrer.

rattlesnake *n* serpent *m* à sonnette, crotale *m*.

raucous *adj* [*laugh*] éraillé; [*person*] bruyant.

raunchy○ *adj* **1** (earthy) [*performer, voice, song*] torride; **2** (US) (bawdy) paillard.

ravage *vtr* ravager.

ravages *n pl* ravages *mpl* (**of** de).

rave I○ *n* (GB) (party) bringue○ *f* (branchée○).
II○ *adj* **a ~ review** une critique dithyrambique.
III *vi* (enthusiastically) parler avec enthousiasme (**about** de); (when fevered) délirer.

ravenous *adj* [*animal*] vorace; **to be ~** avoir une faim de loup.

ravine *n* ravin *m*.

raving *adj* (fanatical) enragé; **a ~ lunatic** un fou furieux/une folle furieuse.

ravings *n pl* divagations *fpl*.

ravishing *adj* ravissant.

raw *adj* **1** [*food*] cru; [*rubber, sugar, data*] brut; [*sewage*] non traité; **2** (without skin) [*patch*] à vif; **3** (cold) [*weather*] froid et humide; [*air*] cru; [*wind*] pénétrant; **4** (inexperienced) inexpérimenté; **5** [*emotion*] à l'état brut; [*energy*] sauvage.
IDIOMS **to give sb a ~ deal**○ traiter qn de façon injuste.

raw: **~hide** *n* cuir *m* brut; **~ material** *n* matière *f* première.

ray *n* rayon *m*; **a ~ of** une lueur de [*hope*].

raze *vtr* raser.

razor *n* rasoir *m*.

razor blade *n* lame *f* de rasoir.

razzmatazz○ *n* folklore○ *m*, cirque○ *m*.

RC *n, adj* (*abbr* = **Roman Catholic**) catholique (*mf*).

re[1] *n* (Mus) ré *m*.

re[2] *prep* (*abbr* = **with reference to**) (in letterhead) 'objet'; (about) au sujet de.

reach I *n* portée *f*; **out of ~** hors de portée; **within (arm's) ~** à portée de (la) main; **within ~** à la portée (**of** de).
II *vtr* **1** atteindre [*place, person, object, switch*]; [*sound, news, letter*] parvenir à [*person, place*]; **2** (come to) arriver à [*decision, understanding*]; **to ~ a verdict** (Law) rendre un verdict; **3** toucher [*audience, market*]; **4** (in height, length) arriver à [*floor, ceiling*].
III *vi* **1 to ~ up/down** lever/baisser le bras; **to ~ across** tendre le bras; **2** (extend) **to ~ (up/down) to** arriver jusqu'à.
■ **reach out** tendre le bras.

reaches *n pl* **the upper/lower ~** (of river) la partie supérieure/inférieure.

react *vi* réagir (**to** à; **against** contre; **with** avec; **on** sur).

reaction *n* réaction *f*.

reactionary *n, adj* réactionnaire (*mf*).

reactor *n* réacteur *m*.

read I *vtr* **1** lire [*text, music, handwriting*]; (figurative) reconnaître [*signs*]; **to ~ sb's mind** lire dans les pensées de qn; **2** (at university) faire des études de [*history, French*]; **3** relever [*meter*]; lire [*dial*].
II *vi* lire (**to sb** à qn); **it ~s well** ça se lit bien.
IDIOMS **to take sth as read** être sûr de qch.
■ **read out**: **~ [sth] out, ~ out [sth]** lire [qch] à haute voix.
■ **read over, read through**: **~ over** or **through [sth], ~ [sth] over** or **through** lire; (reread) relire.

readable *adj* [*handwriting, letters*] lisible.

reader *n* lecteur/-trice *m/f*; **he's a slow ~** il lit lentement.

readily *adv* **1** (willingly) [*accept, reply, give*] sans hésiter; **2** (easily) facilement.

readiness *n* **in ~ for sth** en prévision de qch.

reading *n* **1** lecture *f*; **2** (on meter) relevé *m* (**on** de); (on instrument) indication *f* (**on** de); **3** (interpretation) interprétation *f* (**of** de).

reading: **~ glasses** *n pl* lunettes *fpl* (pour lire); **~ lamp** *n* (by bed) lampe *f* de chevet; (on desk) lampe *f* de bureau.

readjust I *vtr* régler [qch] de nouveau [*TV, lens*].
II *vi* [*person*] se réadapter (**to** à).

ready *adj* **1** (prepared) prêt (**for** pour); **to get ~** se préparer; **to get sth ~** préparer qch; **~, steady, go** à vos marques, prêts, partez!; **2** (willing) prêt (**to do** à faire); **to be ~ for** avoir besoin de [*meal, vacation*]; **3** (quick) [*answer*] tout prêt; [*wit*] vif/vive.

ready: **~-made** *adj* [*clothes*] de confection; [*curtains*] prêt à poser; **~-to-wear** *adj* [*garment*] prêt-à-porter.

real *adj* **1** (not imaginary) véritable, réel/réelle; **in ~ life** dans la réalité; **2** (not artificial) [*diamond, flower, leather*] vrai (*before n*), authentique; **3** (true, proper) [*holiday, rest*] véritable, vrai (*before n*); **4** (for emphasis) [*charmer, pleasure*] vrai (*before n*); **it's a ~ shame** c'est vraiment dommage.

real estate *n* **1** (property) biens *mpl* immobiliers; **2** (US) (profession) immobilier *m*.

realign I *vtr* (figurative) redéfinir [*views*].
II *vi* former de nouvelles alliances; **to ~ with** se réaligner sur.

realism *n* réalisme *m*.

realistic *adj* réaliste.

reality *n* réalité *f* (**of** de).

realization *n* prise *f* de conscience (**of** de; **that** du fait que).

realize *vtr* **1** (know) se rendre compte de [*error, significance, fact*]; **more than people ~** plus que les gens n'en ont conscience; **to make sb ~ sth** faire comprendre qch à qn; **2** réaliser [*idea, dream, goal*]; **to ~ one's potential** développer ses capacités.

reallocate *vtr* réattribuer.

really I *adv* vraiment; **what I ~ mean is that...** en fait, ce que je veux dire c'est que...; **I'll tell you what ~ happened** je vais te dire ce qui s'est réellement passé; **~?** (expressing disbelief) c'est vrai?
II *excl* (also **well ~**) franchement!

reap *vtr* **1** moissonner [*corn*]; **2** récolter [*benefits*]; **to ~ the rewards of one's efforts** recueillir le fruit de ses efforts.

reappear *vi* reparaître.

reappearance *n* réapparition *f*.

reapply *vi* reposer sa candidature (**for** à).

rear I *n* **1** (of building, car, room) arrière *m*; (of procession, train) queue *f*; **at the ~ of the house** derrière la maison; **2** (of person) derrière° *m*.
II *adj* **1** [*door, garden*] de derrière; **2** (of car) [*light, seat, wheel*] arrière *inv*.
III *vtr* élever [*child, animals*]; cultiver [*plants*].
IV *vi* (also **~ up**) [*horse*] se cabrer.

rear end *n* **1** (of vehicle) arrière *m*; **2** (of person) derrière *m*.

rearguard action *n* combat *m* d'arrière-garde.

rearmament *n* réarmement *m*.

rearrange *vtr* réaménager [*room*]; modifier [*plans*]; changer [*appointment*].

rear-view mirror *n* rétroviseur *m*.

reason I *n* **1** (cause) raison *f* (**for, behind** de); **for no (good) ~** sans raison valable; **I have ~ to believe that...** j'ai des raisons de croire que...; **the ~ why...** la raison pour laquelle...; **I'll tell you the ~ why** je vais te or vous dire pourquoi; **to have every ~ to do** avoir tout lieu de faire; **with good ~** à juste titre; **2** (common sense) raison *f*; **to listen to** or **see ~** entendre raison; **it stands to ~ that** il va sans dire que; **within ~** dans la limite du raisonnable.
II *vtr* soutenir.
III *vi* **to ~ with sb** raisonner qn.

reasonable *adj* **1** (sensible) raisonnable; **2** (justified) légitime; **beyond ~ doubt** sans aucun doute possible; **3** (moderately good) convenable.

reasonably *adv* **1** (sensibly) raisonnablement; **2** (rather) assez.

reasoning *n* raisonnement *m*.

reassemble *vtr* remonter [*unit, engine*].

reassert *vtr* réaffirmer [*authority, claim*].

reassess *vtr* réexaminer, reconsidérer [*problem, situation*].

reassurance *n* **1** (comfort) réconfort *m*; **2** (official guarantee) garantie *f*.

reassure *vtr* rassurer [*person*] (**about** sur).

reassuring *adj* rassurant.

reawaken *vtr* faire renaître [*enthusiasm*].

rebate *n* remboursement *m*.

rebel I *n, noun modifier* rebelle (*mf*).
II se rebeller.

rebellion *n* rébellion *f*, révolte *f*.

rebellious *adj* [*nation, child*] rebelle, insoumis.

rebirth *n* renaissance *f*.

reborn *adj* **to be ~** renaître.

rebuff I *n* rebuffade *f*.
II *vtr* rabrouer [*person*]; repousser [*suggestion, advances*].

rebuild *vtr* reconstruire.

rebuilding *n* reconstruction *f*.

rebuke I *n* réprimande *f*.
II *vtr* réprimander (**for** pour).

rebut *vtr* réfuter.

recall *vtr* **1** (remember) se souvenir de; **2** (remind of) rappeler; **3** (summon back) rappeler [*troops, witness, faulty product*]; convoquer [*parliament*].

recapitulate *vtr, vi* récapituler.

recapitulation *n* récapitulation *f*.

recapture *vtr* recapturer [*prisoner*]; reprendre [*town*]; retrouver [*feeling*].

recede I *vi* s'éloigner; (figurative) [*hope, prospect*] s'estomper; [*threat*] s'éloigner.
II **receding** *pres p adj* [*chin*] fuyant; **he has a receding hairline** son front se dégarnit.

receipt I *n* **1** reçu *m*, récépissé *m* (**for** pour); (from till) ticket *m* de caisse; (on delivery of letter) accusé *m* de réception (**for** pour); **2** (act of receiving) réception *f*.
II **receipts** *n pl* (takings) recette *f* (**from** de).

receive I *vtr* **1** recevoir [*letter, money, advice, training, TV channel*]; receler [*stolen goods*]; **'~d with thanks'** 'pour acquit'; **2** (meet) accueillir, recevoir [*visitor, proposal, play*] (**with** avec); **to be well ~d** être bien reçu.
II **received** *pp adj* [*ideas, opinions*] reçu.

receiver *n* **1** (telephone) combiné *m*; **2** (radio or TV) (poste *m*) récepteur *m*.

receivership *n* (GB) **to go into ~** être placé sous administration judiciaire.

recent *adj* [*event, change, arrival, film*] récent; [*acquaintance, development*] nouveau/-elle (*before n*); **in ~ years** au cours des dernières années.

recently *adv* récemment; **as ~ as Monday** pas plus tard que lundi; **until ~** jusqu'à ces derniers temps.

reception *n* **1** (also **~ desk**) réception *f*; **2** (gathering) réception *f* (**for sb** en l'honneur de qn; **for sth** à l'occasion de qch); **3** (public response) accueil *m* (**for** de); **4** (of TV picture) réception *f*; **5** (in house) ▶ **reception room**.

receptionist ▶ 805 *n* réceptionniste *mf*.

reception room *n* (in house) salon *m*; (in public building) salle *f* de réception.

receptive *adj* réceptif/-ive (**to** à).

recess *n* **1** (in parliament) (holiday) vacances *fpl*; **2** (US) (break) (in school) récréation *f*; (during meeting) pause *f*; **3** (for door, window) embrasure *f*; (alcove) alcôve *f*, recoin *m*.

recession *n* récession *f*.

recharge *vtr* recharger.

recipe *n* recette *f* (**for** de); **~ book** livre *m* de recettes.

recipient *n* (of benefits, aid, cheque) bénéficiaire *mf*; (of prize, award) lauréat/-e *m/f*.

reciprocal *adj* réciproque.

reciprocate I *vtr* retourner [*compliment*]; payer [qch] de retour [*love*]; rendre [*affection*].
II *vi* rendre la pareille.

recital *n* (of music, poetry) récital *m*; (narration) récit *m*.

recite *vtr*, *vi* réciter.

reckless *adj* [*person, driving*] imprudent; **~ behaviour** inconscience *f*.

reckon *vtr* **1** (judge) considérer (**that** que); **2**○ (think) **to ~ (that)** croire que; **3** calculer [*amount*].
■ **reckon on**○: ¶ **~ on [sb/sth]** compter sur; ¶ **~ on doing** compter faire.
■ **reckon with**: **~ with [sb/sth]** compter avec.

reckoning *n* (estimation) estimation *f*; (accurate calculation) calculs *mpl*.
IDIOMS **day of ~** jour *m* du Jugement.

reclaim *vtr* **1** reconquérir [*coastal land*]; assécher [*marsh*]; défricher [*forest*]; récupérer [*glass, metal*]; **2** récupérer [*deposit, money*].

recline *vi* [*person*] s'allonger; [*seat*] s'incliner.

reclining *adj* **1** [*figure*] allongé; **2** [*seat*] inclinable.

recluse *n* reclus/-e *m/f*.

recognition *n* reconnaissance *f*; **to win ~ for** être reconnu pour [*talent, work*]; **in ~ of** en reconnaissance de.

recognizable *adj* reconnaissable.

recognize I *vtr* reconnaître (**by** à; **as** comme étant); identifier [*symptom*].
II **recognized** *pp adj* [*expert, organization*] reconnu; **~d dealer** concessionnaire *m* attitré.

recoil *vi* [*person*] (physically) avoir un mouvement de recul (**from, at** devant); (mentally) reculer (**from** devant).

recollect I *vtr* se souvenir de, se rappeler.
II *vi* [*person*] se souvenir.

recollection *n* souvenir *m*.

recommend *vtr* **1** (commend) recommander; **2** (advise) conseiller, recommander.

recommendation *n* recommandation *f* (**to** à; **on** sur).

recompense *n* récompense *f* (**for** de).

reconcile *vtr* **1** (after quarrel) réconcilier [*people*]; **to be ~d** se réconcilier; **2** concilier [*attitudes, views*]; **3 to become ~d to sth** se résigner à qch.

reconciliation *n* réconciliation *f*.

reconnaissance *n* reconnaissance *f*.

reconnoitre (GB), **reconnoiter** (US) *vtr* (Mil) reconnaître.

reconsider *vtr* réexaminer.

reconstruction *n* **1** (of building) reconstruction *f*; **2** (of crime) reconstitution *f*.

record I *n* **1** (of events) compte-rendu *m*; (of official proceedings) procès-verbal *m*; **to keep a ~ of sth** noter qch; **the hottest summer on ~** l'été le plus chaud qu'on ait jamais enregistré; **to say sth off the ~** dire qch en privé; **I'd like to set the ~ straight** je voudrais mettre les choses au clair; **2** (data) **~s** (historical, public) archives *fpl*; (personal, administrative) dossier *m*; **3** (history) (of individual) passé *m*; (of organization, group) réputation *f*; **4** (also **criminal ~**) casier *m* judiciaire; **5** (Mus) disque *m*; **6** (of athlete) record *m* (**for, in** de); **world ~** record *m* mondial.
II *noun modifier* **1** [*company, label*] de disques; **2** (best) [*sales, time*] record *inv* (*after n*); **to be at a ~ high/low** être à son niveau le plus haut/bas.
III *vtr* **1** (note) noter [*detail, idea, opinion*]; [*diary, report*] rapporter; **2** (on disc, tape) enregistrer; **3** [*instrument*] enregistrer [*temperature, rainfall*].

recorded *adj* **1** (on tape, record) enregistré; **2** (documented) [*case, sighting*] connu.

record-holder *n* recordman/recordwoman *m/f*.
recording *n* enregistrement *m*.
record: **~ library** *n* discothèque *f* de prêt; **~ player** *n* tourne-disque *m*.
recourse *n* recours *m* (**to** à).
recover **I** *vtr* **1** retrouver, récupérer [*money, vehicle*]; récupérer [*territory*]; (from water) repêcher, retrouver [*body, wreck*]; **to ~ one's strength** reprendre des forces; **2** (recoup) réparer, compenser [*losses*].
II *vi* (from illness) se remettre (**from** de); (from defeat) se ressaisir (**from** après).
recovery *n* **1** (getting better) rétablissement *m*, guérison *f*; **to be on the road to ~** être sur la voie de la guérison; **2** (of economy, company, market) reprise *f*; **3** (getting back) (of vehicle) rapatriement *m*; (of money) récupération *f*.
recovery: **~ service** *n* service *m* de dépannage; **~ truck** *n* camion *m* de dépannage.
recreate *vtr* recréer.
recreation **I** *n* **1** (leisure) loisirs *mpl*; **2** (playtime) récréation *f*.
II *noun modifier* [*facilities, centre*] de loisirs.
recrimination *n* récrimination *f*.
recruit **I** *n* recrue *f*.
II *vtr* recruter (**from** dans).
recruitment *n* recrutement *m*.
rectangular *adj* rectangulaire.
rectify *vtr* rectifier.
rector *n* pasteur *m*.
recuperate *vi* se rétablir (**from** de), récupérer.
recur *vi* [*event, error*] se reproduire; [*illness*] réapparaître; [*theme*] revenir.
recurrence *n* (of illness) récurrence *f*; (of symptom) réapparition *f*.
recurrent *adj* récurrent.
recycle *vtr* recycler [*paper, waste*].
red ▷**559** **I** *n* **1** (colour) rouge *m*; **in ~** en rouge; **2**° (also **Red**) (communist) rouge *mf*; **3 to be in the ~** [*person, account*] être à découvert; [*company*] être en déficit.
II *adj* (in colour) rouge (**with** de); [*hair*] roux/rousse; **to go** or **turn ~** rougir.
red: **~ alert** *n* alerte *f* rouge; **~ blood cell** *n* globule *m* rouge; **~ carpet** *n* tapis *m* rouge; **Red Cross** *n* Croix-Rouge *f*.
redden *vtr, vi* rougir.
redecorate *vtr* repeindre et retapisser, refaire.
redeem *vtr* **1** retirer [*pawned goods*]; rembourser [*debt*]; **2 her one ~ing feature is...** ce qui la rachète, c'est...; **3** racheter [*sinner*].
redemption *n* (religious) rédemption *f*.
redeploy *vtr* redéployer [*troops*]; réaffecter [*staff*].
redesign *vtr* transformer [*area, building*]; **to ~ the book jacket** refaire la jaquette.
redevelop *vtr* réaménager [*site, town*].
redevelopment *n* réaménagement *m*.
red: **~-haired** *adj* roux/rousse; **~head** *n* roux/rousse *m/f*; **~ herring** *n* faux problème *m*; **~-hot** *adj* [*metal, coal*] chauffé au rouge; [*passion*] ardent.
redial **I** *vtr* refaire [*number*].
II *vi* recomposer le numéro.
redirect *vtr* canaliser [*resources*]; dévier [*traffic*]; réexpédier [*mail*].
rediscover *vtr* redécouvrir.
redness *n* rougeur *f*.
redo *vtr* refaire.
red pepper *n* poivron *m* rouge.
redraft *vtr* rédiger [qch] à nouveau.
redress *vtr* **to ~ the balance** rétablir l'équilibre.
red tape *n* paperasserie *f*.
reduce **I** *vtr* **1** réduire [*inflation, number, pressure, sentence*] (**by** de); baisser [*prices, temperature*]; **to ~ speed** ralentir; **to ~ sb to tears** faire pleurer qn; **to be ~d to begging** en être réduit à la mendicité; **2** (in cooking) faire réduire [*sauce, stock*].
II reduced *pp adj* réduit; **~d goods** marchandises en solde.
reduction *n* **1** (in inflation, pressure, number) réduction *f* (**in** de); (of weight, size) diminution *f* (**in** de); **2** (discount) réduction *f*, rabais *m*.
redundancy *n* **1** (unemployment) chômage *m*; **2** (dismissal) licenciement *m*.
redundant *adj* **1** (GB) (dismissed) licencié; (out of work) au chômage; **to be made ~** être licencié; **2** (not needed) superflu; **to feel ~** se sentir de trop.
red: **~ wine** *n* vin *m* rouge; **~ wine vinegar** *n* vinaigre *m* de vin rouge.
reed *n* **1** (plant) roseau *m*; **2** (Mus) anche *f*.
re-educate *vtr* rééduquer.
reef *n* récif *m*, écueil *m*.
reek *vi* **to ~ of sth** puer qch; (figurative) avoir des relents de qch.
reel **I** *n* bobine *f*; (for fishing) moulinet *m*.
II *vi* (sway) [*person*] tituber; **the blow sent him ~ing** le coup l'a projeté en arrière.
▪ **reel off**: **~ off [sth]** débiter [*list, names*].
re-election *n* réélection *f*; **to run for ~** se représenter (aux élections).
re-enact *vtr* reconstituer [*crime*].
re-enter *vtr* entrer à nouveau dans.
re-entry *n* rentrée *f*; (figurative) retour *m*.
re-examine *vtr* réexaminer [*issue, problem*]; interroger à nouveau [*witness*].
refectory *n* réfectoire *m*.
refer **I** *vtr* **1** renvoyer [*task, problem, enquiry*] (**to** à); **to ~ sb to** [*person*] envoyer qn à [*department*]; [*critic, text*] renvoyer qn à [*article, footnote*]; **2** (in law) déférer [*case*] (**to** à).
II *vi* **1** (allude to) **to ~ to** parler de, faire allusion à [*person, topic, event*]; **she ~s to him as Bob** elle l'appelle Bob; **2** (relate, apply) **to ~ to** [*number, date, term*] se rapporter à; **3** (consult) **to ~ to** consulter [*notes, article*].
referee **I** *n* **1** arbitre *m*; **2** (GB) (giving job reference) personne *f* pouvant fournir des références.
II *vtr, vi* arbitrer.

reference I *n* **1** (allusion) référence *f* (**to** à), allusion *f* (**to** à); **2** (consultation) **without ~ to sb/sth** sans consulter qn/qch; **for future ~** pour information; **3** (in commercial correspondence) référence *f*; **4** (testimonial) références *fpl*.
II **with reference to** *phr* **with ~ to your letter** suite à votre lettre.

reference: **~ book** *n* ouvrage *m* de référence; **~ number** *n* numéro *m* de référence.

referendum *n* référendum *m*.

refill I *n* (for ballpoint, lighter, perfume) recharge *f*.
II *vtr* recharger [*pen, lighter*]; remplir [qch] à nouveau [*glass, bottle*].

refine *vtr* **1** raffiner [*oil, sugar*]; **2** (improve) peaufiner [*theory*].

refined *adj* **1** [*oil, sugar*] raffiné; [*metal*] affiné; **2** (cultured) raffiné.

refinement *n* (elegance) raffinement *m*.

refinery *n* raffinerie *f*.

refit *vtr* rééquiper [*shop, factory*]; réarmer [*ship*].

reflect I *vtr* **1** (visually) refléter; **to be ~ed in sth** se refléter dans qch; **2** (throw back) renvoyer, réfléchir [*light, heat*]; **3** (think) se dire, penser.
II *vi* **1** (think) réfléchir (**on, upon** à); **2 to ~ well/badly on sb** faire honneur/du tort à qn.

reflection *n* **1** (image) reflet *m* (**of** de), image *f* (**of** de); **2** (thought) réflexion *f*; **on ~** à la réflexion.

reflector *n* (on vehicle) catadioptre *m*.

reflex I *n* réflexe *m*.
II *adj* réflexe; **a ~ action** un réflexe.

reflexive verb *n* verbe *m* pronominal réfléchi.

refloat *vtr* renflouer [*ship, economy*].

reform I *n* réforme *f*.
II *vtr* réformer.
III **reformed** *pp adj* [*state, system*] réformé; [*criminal, drinker*] repenti.

reformation *n* réforme *f*; **the Reformation** la Réforme.

reformer *n* réformateur/-trice *m/f*.

refrain I *n* refrain *m*.
II *vi* se retenir; **to ~ from doing** s'abstenir de faire.

refresh *vtr* [*bath, drink*] rafraîchir; [*rest*] reposer.

refresher course *n* cours *m* de recyclage.

refreshing *adj* [*drink, shower*] rafraîchissant; [*rest*] réparateur/-trice.

refreshment *n* (food, drink) restauration *f*; **~s** (drinks) rafraîchissements *mpl*; **light ~s** repas *m* léger.

refrigerate I *vtr* frigorifier; **'keep ~d'** 'conserver au réfrigérateur'.
II **refrigerated** *pp adj* [*product*] frigorifié; [*transport*] frigorifique.

refrigerator *n* réfrigérateur *m*, frigidaire® *m*.

refuel *vi* se ravitailler en carburant.

refuge *n* **1** (shelter, protection) refuge *m* (**from** contre); **to take ~ from** s'abriter de [*storm*]; **2** (hostel) foyer *m*.

refugee I *n* réfugié/-e *m/f*.
II *noun modifier* [*camp*] de réfugiés; [*status*] de réfugié.

refund I *n* remboursement *m*.
II *vtr* rembourser.

refurbish *vtr* rénover.

refusal *n* refus *m* (**to do** de faire); (to application) réponse *f* négative.

refuse[1] I *vtr* refuser (**to do** de faire).
II *vi* refuser.

refuse[2] *n* (GB) (household) ordures *fpl*; (industrial) déchets *mpl*; (garden) déchets *mpl* de jardinage.

refuse: **~ collector** ▶805 *n* (GB) éboueur *m*; **~ disposal** *n* (GB) traitement *m* des ordures.

refute *vtr* réfuter.

regain *vtr* retrouver [*health, strength, sight, composure*]; reconquérir [*power, seat*]; reprendre [*lead, control*]; **to ~ consciousness** reprendre connaissance.

regal *adj* royal.

regale *vtr* régaler (**with** de).

regalia *n pl* insignes *mpl*; **in full ~** en grande tenue.

regard I *n* **1** (consideration) égard *m*; **out of ~ for** par égard pour; **2** (esteem) estime *f* (**for** pour); **to hold sb/sth in high ~** avoir beaucoup d'estime pour qn/qch; **3 with** or **in ~ to** en ce qui concerne; **in this ~** à cet égard.
II *vtr* (consider) considérer; **highly ~ed** très apprécié.

regarding *prep* concernant.

regardless I *prep* **~ of** sans tenir compte de.
II *adv* malgré tout.

regards *n pl* amitiés *fpl*; **give them my ~** transmettez-leur mes amitiés.

regatta *n* régate *f*.

regenerate *vtr* régénérer.

regent *n* régent/-e *m/f*.

reggae *n* reggae *m*.

regime, **régime** *n* régime *m*.

regiment *n* régiment *m*.

region *n* région *f*; (**somewhere**) **in the ~ of £300** environ 300 livres sterling.

regional *adj* régional; **~ development** aménagement *m* du territoire.

register I *n* registre *m*; (at school) cahier *m* des absences.
II *vtr* **1** [*member of the public*] déclarer [*birth, death*]; faire immatriculer [*vehicle*]; faire enregistrer [*luggage, company*]; déposer [*trademark, complaint*]; [*official*] enregistrer [*birth, death, company*]; immatriculer [*vehicle*]; **2** [*instrument*] indiquer [*speed, temperature*]; [*person*] exprimer [*anger, disapproval*]; **3** (mentally) (notice) remarquer; (realize) se rendre compte; **4** envoyer [qch] en recommandé [*letter*].
III *vi* (for course, school, to vote) s'inscrire; (at hotel) se présenter; (with police) se faire recenser (**for** pour).

registered *adj* **1** [*voter*] inscrit; [*vehicle,*

student] immatriculé; [*charity*] ≈ agréé; **2** [*letter*] recommandé; **by ~ post** en recommandé.

registered trademark *n* marque *m* déposée.

registrar ▶805| *n* **1** (GB) (gen) officier *m* d'état civil; (medical) adjoint *m*; **2** (academic) responsable *mf* du bureau de la scolarité.

registration *n* (of person) (for course) inscription *f*; (of trademark, patent) dépôt *m*; (of birth, death, marriage) déclaration *f*.

registration: **~ number** *n* numéro *m* d'immatriculation; **~ plate** *n* plaque *f* d'immatriculation.

registry office *n* (GB) bureau *m* de l'état civil; **to get married in a ~** se marier civilement.

regression *n* régression *f*.

regret I *n* regret *m* (**about** à propos de); **to have no ~s about doing** ne pas regretter d'avoir fait; **to my great ~** à mon grand regret.

II *vtr* regretter (**that** que + *subj*); **to ~ doing** regretter d'avoir fait; **I ~ to inform you that** j'ai le regret de vous informer que.

regretfully *adv* à regret.

regrettable *adj* regrettable (**that** que + *subj*).

regrettably *adv* **1** (sadly) malheureusement; **2** [*lax, inattentive*] fâcheusement.

regular I *n* **1** (habitual client, visitor) habitué/-e *m/f*; **2** (US) (petrol) ordinaire *m*.

II *adj* **1** [*habit, job, income, interval, features*] régulier/-ière; **to take ~ exercise** faire de l'exercice régulièrement; **2** (usual) [*activity, customer, visitor*] habituel/-elle; [*viewer, listener*] fidèle; **3** [*army, soldier*] de métier.

regularity *n* régularité *f*.

regularly *adv* régulièrement.

regulate *vtr* **1** (gen, Econ) réguler; **2** (adjust) régler [*mechanism*].

regulation I *n* (for safety, fire) consigne *f*; (for discipline) règlement *m*; (legal) disposition *f* réglementaire; **under the (new) ~s** selon la (nouvelle) réglementation; **against the ~s** contraire au règlement or aux normes.

II *noun modifier* [*width, length, uniform*] réglementaire.

regurgitate *vtr* régurgiter; (figurative) ressortir.

rehabilitate *vtr* réinsérer [*handicapped person, ex-prisoner*]; réhabiliter [*addict, area*].

rehabilitation *n* **1** (social) réinsertion *f*; **2** (of area, addict) réhabilitation *f*.

rehearsal *n* répétition *f* (**of** de); (figurative) préparation *f* (**of** de).

rehearse I *vtr* répéter [*scene*]; préparer [*speech, excuse*].

II *vi* répéter (**for** pour).

reheat *vtr* réchauffer.

reign I *n* règne *m*; **in the ~ of** sous le règne de.

II *vi* régner (**over** sur).

reimburse *vtr* rembourser.

rein *n* rêne *f*; **to keep sb on a tight ~** tenir qn de près.

reincarnation *n* réincarnation *f*.

reindeer *n* renne *m*.

reinforce *vtr* renforcer; **~d concrete** béton *m* armé.

reinforcement *n* (support) renfort *m*; **~s** (Mil) renforts.

reinstate *vtr* réintégrer [*employee*].

reissue *vtr* rééditer [*book, record*]; ressortir [*film*].

reject I *n* marchandise *f* de deuxième choix.

II *vtr* rejeter [*advice, application, person, transplant*]; refuser [*candidate, manuscript*]; démentir [*claim, suggestion*].

rejection *n* rejet *m*; (of candidate, manuscript) refus *m*.

rejoice *vi* se réjouir (**at, over** de).

rejuvenate *vtr* rajeunir.

rekindle *vtr* ranimer.

relapse I *n* rechute *f*.

II *vi* (gen) **to ~ into** retomber dans; (Med) rechuter.

relate I *vtr* **1** (connect) faire le rapprochement entre; **2** raconter [*story*] (**to** à).

II *vi* **to ~ to** (have connection) se rapporter à; (communicate) s'entendre avec.

related *adj* **1** [*person, language*] apparenté (**by, through** par; **to** à); **to be ~ by marriage** être parents par alliance; **2** (connected) [*subject*] connexe (**to** à); [*area, idea, incident*] lié (**to** à); [*species*] similaire (**to** à); **drug-~** lié à la drogue.

relation I *n* **1** (relative) parent/-e *m/f*; **my ~s** ma famille; **2** (connection) rapport *m*; **in ~ to** par rapport à.

II **relations** *n pl* (dealings) relations *fpl* (**with** avec).

relationship *n* **1** (between people) relation(s) *f(pl)*; (with colleagues) rapport(s) *m(pl)*; **to form ~s** se lier; **to have a good ~ with** s'entendre bien avec; **sexual ~** relation sexuelle; **2** (connection) rapport *m* (**to, with** avec).

relative I *n* parent/-e *m/f*; **my ~s** ma famille.

II *adj* **1** [*comfort, happiness, frequency*] relatif/-ive; **2** (respective) respectif/-ive; **3** (in grammar) [*pronoun*] relatif/-ive.

relatively *adv* relativement; **~ speaking** toutes proportions gardées.

relativity *n* relativité *f* (**of** de).

relax I *vtr* décontracter [*muscle*]; assouplir [*restrictions*]; détendre [*body*]; relâcher [*efforts, grip, concentration*].

II *vi* **1** [*person*] se détendre; **2** [*grip*] se relâcher; [*jaw, muscle*] se décontracter.

relaxation *n* **1** (recreation) détente *f*; **2** (of grip, concentration) relâchement *m*; (of restrictions, discipline) assouplissement *m* (**in** de); (of body) détente *f*.

relaxed *adj* détendu, décontracté.

relaxing *adj* [*atmosphere, activity*] délassant; [*vacation*] reposant.

relay I *n* **1** (of workers) équipe *f* (de relais); **2** (also **~ race**) course *f* de relais.

II *vtr* transmettre [*message*] (**to** à).

release I *n* **1** (liberation) libération *f*; **2** (relief)

soulagement *m*; **his death was a ~** sa mort a été une délivrance; **3** (for press) communiqué *m*; **4** (of film) sortie *f*; **the film is now on general ~** le film passe maintenant dans toutes les grandes salles de cinéma; **5** (film, video, record) (also **new ~**) nouveauté *f*; **6** (discharge form) décharge *f*.
II *vtr* **1** libérer [*prisoner*]; dégager [*accident victim*]; relâcher [*animal*]; **to ~ sb from** dégager qn de [*promise*]; **2** faire jouer [*catch, clasp*]; déclencher [*shutter*]; desserrer [*handbrake*]; larguer [*bomb*]; **3** (let go) lâcher [*object* , *arm, hand*]; **4** faire sortir [*film, record*].

relegate *vtr* **1** reléguer [*person, object*] (**to** à); **2** (GB Sport) reléguer (**to** en).

relent *vi* [*person, government*] céder.

relentless *adj* [*ambition*] implacable; [*noise, activity*] incessant; [*attack*] acharné.

relevance *n* pertinence *f* (**to** pour), intérêt *m* (**to** pour).

relevant *adj* **1** [*issue, facts, point*] pertinent; [*information*] utile; **to be ~ to** avoir rapport à; **2** (appropriate) [*chapter*] correspondant; [*period*] en question.

reliability *n* (of employee, firm) sérieux *m*; (of car, machine) fiabilité *f*.

reliable *adj* [*friend, witness*] digne de confiance, fiable; [*employee, firm*] sérieux/-ieuse; [*car, memory, account*] fiable; [*information, source*] sûr.

reliance *n* dépendance *f* (**on** vis-à-vis de).

reliant *adj* **to be ~ on** être dépendant de.

relic *n* (religious) relique *f*; (figurative) vestige *m* (**of** de).

relief I *n* **1** (from pain, distress) soulagement *m*; **2** (help) aide *f*, secours *m*; **famine ~** aide aux victimes de la famine; **3** (diversion) divertissement *m*; **4** (of garrison, troops) délivrance *f*; **5** (in sculpture, geography) relief *m*; **in ~** en relief.
II *noun modifier* [*operation*] de secours; [*programme, effort*] d'aide.

relief map *n* carte *f* en relief.

relieve *vtr* **1** soulager [*pain, suffering, tension*]; dissiper [*boredom*]; remédier à [*poverty, famine*]; **to be ~d that** être soulagé que (+ *subj*); **2 to ~ sb of** débarrasser qn de [*plate, coat, bag*]; soulager qn de [*burden*]; **3** (help) secourir [*troops, population*]; **4** relever [*worker, sentry*]; **to ~ the guard** relever la garde.

religion *n* religion *f*.

religious *adj* [*faith, art, music*] religieux/-ieuse; [*person*] croyant; [*war*] de religion.

religious education, **RE** *n* éducation *f* religieuse.

relinquish *vtr* renoncer à [*claim, right, privilege*] (**to** en faveur de); céder [*task, power*] (**to** à); abandonner [*responsibility*].

relish I *n* **1 with ~** [*eat, drink*] avec un plaisir évident; **2** (Culin) condiment *m*.
II *vtr* savourer [*food*]; se réjouir de [*prospect*].

relocate I *vtr* muter [*employee*].
II *vi* [*company*] déménager; [*employee*] être muté.

relocation *n* (of company) déménagement *m*; (of employee) mutation *f* (**to** à, en).

reluctance *n* réticence *f* (**to do** à faire).

reluctant *adj* [*person*] peu enthousiaste; [*consent, promise*] accordé à contrecœur; **to be ~ to do** être peu disposé à faire.

reluctantly *adv* à contrecœur.

rely *vi* **1** (be dependent) **to ~ on** dépendre de [*person, aid, industry*]; reposer sur [*method, technology, exports*]; **2** (count) **to ~ on sb/sth** compter sur qn/qch (**to do** pour faire).

remain *vi* (gen) rester; [*problem, doubt*] subsister; **it ~s to be seen whether** il reste à voir si; **to ~ silent** garder le silence.

remainder *n* reste *m* (**of** de).

remainders *n pl* invendus *mpl* soldés.

remains *n pl* restes *mpl*.

remand I *n* **on ~** (in custody) en détention provisoire; (on bail) en liberté sous caution.
II *vtr* renvoyer [*case, accused*]; **to be ~ed on bail** être mis en liberté sous caution.

remark I *n* remarque *f* (**about** à propos de, sur), réflexion *f* (**about** à propos de, sur).
II *vtr* **1** (comment) faire remarquer (**that** que; **to** à); **2** (notice) remarquer (**that** que).

remarkable *adj* remarquable (**that** que + *subj*).

remarkably *adv* remarquablement.

remarry *vi* se remarier.

remedial *adj* **1** (Sch) [*class*] de rattrapage; **2** (Med) curatif/-ive.

remedy I *n* remède *m* (**for** à, contre).
II *vtr* remédier à.

remember I *vtr* **1** (recall) se souvenir de, se rappeler [*fact, name, place, event*]; se souvenir de [*person*]; **to ~ doing** se rappeler avoir fait, se souvenir d'avoir fait; **I don't ~ anything about it** je n'en ai aucun souvenir; **2** (not forget) **to ~ to do** penser à faire, ne pas oublier de faire; **did you ~ to feed the cat?** tu as pensé à donner à manger au chat?; **3** (commemorate) commémorer [*battle, dead*].
II *vi* se souvenir; **as far as I can ~** pour autant que je me souvienne.

remind *vtr* rappeler; **to ~ sb of sth/sb** rappeler qch/qn à qn; **to ~ sb to do** rappeler à qn de faire; **that ~s me** à propos.

reminder *n* rappel *m* (**of** de; **that** du fait que).

reminisce *vi* évoquer ses souvenirs (**about** de).

reminiscence *n* (recalling) réminiscence *f*; (memory) souvenir *m*.

reminiscent *adj* **to be ~ of sb/sth** faire penser à qn/qch.

remiss *adj* négligent; **it was ~ of him** c'était négligent de sa part.

remission *n* **1** (of sentence, debt) remise *f*; **2** (Med) rémission *f*.

remit *n* attributions *fpl*; **it's outside my ~** ce n'est pas dans mes attributions.

remnant *n* (gen) reste *m*; (of building, past) vestige *m*; (of fabric) coupon *m*.

remorse *n* remords *m* (**for** de).

remorseless *adj* **1** (brutal) impitoyable; **2** [*ambition*] implacable.
remote *adj* **1** [*area, village*] isolé; [*era*] lointain; [*ancestor, country*] éloigné; **in the ~st corner of Asia** au fin fond de l'Asie; **2** (aloof) [*person*] distant; **3** (slight) [*chance*] vague, infime; **there is only a ~ possibility that** il est très peu probable que (+ *subj*).
remote: **~ control** *n* télécommande *f*; **~-controlled** *adj* télécommandé.
remotely *adv* **1** [*situated*] à l'écart de tout; **2** (slightly) [*resemble*] vaguement.
remoteness *n* isolement *m*; (in time) éloignement *m* (dans le temps).
removable *adj* amovible.
removal I *n* **1** (of tax, barrier, threat) suppression *f*; (of doubt, worry) disparition *f*; (of demonstrators) expulsion *f*; (of troops) retrait *m*; (Med) ablation *f*; **stain ~** détachage *m*; **2** (change of home) déménagement *m* (**from** de; **to** à); **3** (of employee) renvoi *m*; (of leader) déposition *f*.
II *noun modifier* [*costs, firm, van*] de déménagement; **~ man** déménageur *m*.
remove I *n* **to be at one ~ from** être tout proche de.
II *vtr* **1** (gen, Med) enlever (**from** de); enlever, ôter [*clothes, shoes*]; supprimer [*tax, subsidy, threat*]; chasser [*doubt*]; **cousin once ~d** cousin au deuxième degré; **2 to ~ sb from office** démettre qn de ses fonctions.
remuneration *n* rémunération *f*.
Renaissance *n* **the ~** la Renaissance.
render *vtr* **1** rendre; **to ~ sth impossible** rendre qch impossible; **2** traduire [*text*] (**into** en).
rendezvous I *n* rendez-vous *m inv*.
II *vi* **to ~ with sb** rejoindre qn.
renegade *n* (abandoning beliefs) renégat/-e *m/f*; (rebel) rebelle *mf*.
renew I *vtr* renouveler [*efforts, contract, passport*]; renouer [*acquaintance*]; reprendre [*negotiations*].
II renewed *pp adj* [*interest, optimism*] accru; [*attack, call*] renouvelé.
renewal *n* (of contract, passport) renouvellement *m*; (of hostilities) reprise *f*; (of interest) regain *m*.
renounce *vtr* renoncer à [*claim, nationality, strategy*]; renier [*faith, friend*]; dénoncer [*agreement, treaty*].
renovate *vtr* rénover [*building*].
renovation *n* rénovation *f*; **~s** travaux *mpl* de rénovation.
renowned *adj* célèbre (**for** pour).
rent I *n* loyer *m*; **for ~** à louer.
II *vtr* **1** (hire) louer [*house*]; **2** (let) = **rent out**.
III *vi* [*tenant*] être locataire.
■ **rent out**: **~ [sth] out, ~ out [sth]** louer (**to** à).
rental *n* (of car, premises, equipment) location *f*; (of phone line) abonnement *m*; **car ~** location de voitures.
renunciation *n* (of right, nationality) renonciation *f* (**of** à); (of faith, friend) reniement *m* (**of** de).
reopen *vtr, vi* rouvrir.
reopening *n* réouverture *f*.
reorganize *vtr* réorganiser.
rep ▶ **805** *n* représentant/-e *m/f* (de commerce).
repair I *n* **1** réparation *f*; **under ~** [*building*] en réparation; **to be (damaged) beyond ~** ne pas être réparable; **2 to be in good/bad ~** être en bon/mauvais état.
II *vtr* réparer.
repair: **~ kit** *n* trousse *f* de réparation; **~man** *n* réparateur *m*.
reparation *n* réparation *f*; (war) **~s** indemnités *fpl* de guerre.
repatriate *vtr* rapatrier.
repatriation *n* rapatriement *m*.
repay *vtr* rembourser [*person, sum*]; rendre [*hospitality, favour*].
repayment *n* remboursement *m* (**on** de).
repeal I *n* abrogation *f* (**of** de).
II *vtr* abroger.
repeat I *n* (gen) répétition *f*; (on radio, TV) rediffusion *f*; (Mus) reprise *f*.
II *vtr* (gen) répéter; (Sch) redoubler [*year*]; rediffuser [*programme*]; (Mus) reprendre [*theme*]; **to ~ oneself** se répéter.
repeated *adj* [*warnings, requests, attempts*] répété; [*setbacks*] successif/-ive.
repeatedly *adv* plusieurs fois, à plusieurs reprises.
repel *vtr* repousser.
repellent *adj* repoussant.
repent *vi* se repentir.
repentance *n* repentir *m*.
repentant *adj* repentant (formal).
repercussion *n* répercussion *f*.
repertoire *n* répertoire *m*.
repetition *n* répétition *f*.
repetitive *adj* répétitif/-ive.
replace *vtr* **1** (put back) remettre [*lid, cork*]; remettre [qch] à sa place [*book, ornament*]; **2** remplacer [*goods*] (**with** par); (in job) remplacer [*person*].
replacement *n* **1** (person) remplaçant/-e *m/f* (**for** de); **2** (act) remplacement *m*; **3** (spare part) pièce *f* de rechange.
replay I *n* **1** (Sport) match *m* rejoué; **2** (figurative) répétition *f*.
II *vtr* rejouer [*piece of music*]; écouter [qch] à nouveau [*record*]; (Sport) rejouer.
replenish *vtr* reconstituer [*stocks*].
replete *adj* (with food) rassasié (**with** de).
replica *n* réplique *f*, copie *f* (**of** de).
reply I *n* réponse *f*.
II *vtr, vi* répondre.
report I *n* **1** (written account) rapport *m* (**on** sur); (verbal account, minutes) compte-rendu *m*; (in media) communiqué *m*; (longer) reportage *m*; **we are getting ~s of heavy fighting** des combats intensifs auraient lieu; **according to ~s** selon certaines sources; **2** (GB Sch) (also **school ~**) bulletin *m* scolaire; (US Sch) (review) critique *f*; **3** (noise) détonation *f*.
II *vtr* **1** signaler [*fact, event, theft, accident*]; [*re-*

porter] faire le compte rendu de [*debate*]; **to ~ sth to sb** transmettre qch à qn [*result, decision, news*]; **he is ~ed to have said that**... il aurait dit que...; **2** (make complaint about) signaler [*person*]; se plaindre de [*noise*].
III *vi* **1** (give account) **to ~ on** faire un compte-rendu sur [*talks, progress*]; [*reporter*] faire un reportage sur [*events*]; **2** (present findings) [*committee, group*] faire son rapport (**on** sur); **3** (present oneself) (at reception) se présenter; **to ~ for duty** prendre son service; **4 to ~ to** être sous les ordres (directs) de [*manager, superior*].
■ **report back 1** [*employee*] se présenter; **2** (present findings) présenter un rapport.

report card *n* (US) bulletin *m* scolaire.

reporter ▶ 805 *n* journaliste *mf*, reporter *mf*.

reporting *n* reportages *mpl*.

repose *n* repos *m*; **in ~** au repos.

repository *n* **1** (of secret, authority) dépositaire *mf*; **2** (place) dépôt *m* (**of, for** de).

repossess *vtr* [*bank*] saisir [*house*]; [*creditor*] reprendre possession de [*property*].

repossession *n* saisie *f* immobilière.

reprehensible *adj* répréhensible.

represent *vtr* **1** (act on behalf of) représenter [*person*]; **2** (present) présenter [*person, event*] (**as** comme); **3** [*painting, sculpture, symbol*] représenter.

representation *n* **1** (of person, group) représentation *f* (**of** de; **by** par); **2 to make ~s to sb** faire des démarches *fpl* auprès de qn.

representative I ▶ 805 *n* **1** représentant/-e *m/f*; (in sales) représentant/-e *m/f*, agent *m* (commercial); **2** (US) (politician) député *m*.
II *adj* représentatif/-ive (**of** de), typique (**of** de).

repress *vtr* réprimer [*reaction, smile*]; refouler [*feelings*].

repression *n* répression *f*; (in psychology) refoulement *m*.

repressive *adj* répressif/-ive.

reprieve I *n* **1** (Law) remise *f* de peine; **2** (delay) sursis *m*; **3** (respite) répit *m*.
II *vtr* accorder une remise de peine à [*prisoner*].

reprimand I *n* réprimande *f*.
II *vtr* réprimander.

reprisal *n* représailles *fpl*; **in ~ for sth** en représailles de qch.

reproach I *n* reproche *m*; **beyond ~** irréprochable.
II *vtr* reprocher à [*person*]; **to ~ sb with** or **for sth** reprocher qch à qn.

reproachful *adj* [*person, remark, look*] réprobateur/-trice; [*letter, word*] de reproche.

reprocess *vtr* retraiter.

reprocessing plant *n* (also **nuclear ~**) usine *f* de retraitement (des déchets nucléaires).

reproduce I *vtr* reproduire.
II *vi* se reproduire.

reproduction *n* reproduction *f*.

reproductive *adj* reproducteur/-trice.

reproof *n* réprimande *f*.

reprove *vtr* réprimander (**for doing** de faire).

reptile *n* reptile *m*.

republic *n* république *f*.

republican I *n* républicain/-e *m/f*; **Republican** (US) Républicain/-e *m/f*.
II *adj* (also **Republican**) républicain.

repudiate *vtr* rejeter [*findings, decision, argument, movement, authority*]; abandonner [*violence, aim*].

repugnant *adj* répugnant; **to be ~ to sb** répugner à qn.

repulse *vtr* repousser.

repulsion *n* répulsion *f*.

repulsive *adj* repoussant.

reputable *adj* de bonne réputation.

reputation *n* réputation *f* (**as** de); **to have a good/bad ~** avoir bonne/mauvaise réputation; **he has a ~ for honesty** il a la réputation d'être honnête.

repute *n* **of ~** réputé.

reputed *adj* (gen) réputé; (Law) putatif/-ive; **he is ~ to be very rich** à ce que l'on dit il serait très riche.

request I *n* **1** demande *f* (**for** de; **to** à), requête *f* (**for** de; **to** à); **on ~** sur demande; **2** (on radio) dédicace *f*; **to play a ~ for sb** passer un disque à la demande de qn.
II *vtr* demander (**from** à); **to ~ sb to do** demander à qn de faire; **to ~ that** demander que (+ *subj*); **as ~ed** (in correspondence) conformément à votre demande.

requiem *n* requiem *m*; **~ mass** messe *f* de requiem.

require I *vtr* **1** (need) avoir besoin de [*help, money, staff*]; **2** (necessitate) [*job, situation*] exiger [*funds, qualifications*]; **to be ~d to do** être tenu de faire.
II **required** *pp adj* [*amount, size*] exigé; **by the ~d date** en temps voulu.

requirement *n* **1** (need) besoin *m*; **2** (condition) condition *f*; **to meet the ~s** remplir les conditions; **3** (obligation) obligation *f* (**to do** de faire); **4** (US Univ) matière *f* obligatoire.

requisite I *n* **1** condition *f* (**for** pour); **2 ~s** fournitures *fpl*; **toilet ~s** articles *mpl* de toilette.
II *adj* exigé, requis.

requisition *vtr* réquisitionner.

reroute *vtr* changer l'itinéraire de [*flight*]; dévier [*traffic*].

reschedule *vtr* (change time) changer l'heure de; (change date) changer la date de.

rescue I *n* **1** (aid) secours *m*; **to come/go to sb's ~** venir/aller au secours de qn; **to come to the ~** venir à la rescousse; **2** (operation) sauvetage *m* (**of** de).
II *noun modifier* [*bid, mission*] de sauvetage; **~ party** équipe *f* de secours.
III *vtr* (save) sauver [*person*]; (aid) porter secours à [*person, company*]; (release) libérer.

rescue worker *n* secouriste *mf*.

research I *n* recherche *f* (**into, on** sur).
II *noun modifier* [*grant, project*] de recherche; [*student*] qui fait de la recherche; **~ work** recherche *f*; **~ scientist** chercheur/-euse *m/f*.

III *vtr* faire des recherches sur [*topic*]; préparer [*book, article*]; **well ~ed** bien documenté.

research and development, R&D *n* recherche-développement *f*, recherche *f* et développement *m*.

researcher ▶805 *n* chercheur/-euse *m/f*; (in TV) documentaliste *mf*.

resell *vtr* revendre.

resemblance *n* ressemblance *f* (**between** entre; **to** avec); **to bear a close ~ to** ressembler fort à; **family ~** air *m* de famille.

resemble *vtr* ressembler à; **to ~ each other** se ressembler.

resent *vtr* en vouloir à [*person*] (**for doing** d'avoir fait); ne pas aimer [*tone*]; **to ~ the fact that** ne pas supporter le fait que (+ *subj*).

resentful *adj* plein de ressentiment (**of sb** envers qn).

resentment *n* ressentiment *m* (**about** au sujet de; **against** envers; **at** à l'égard de).

reservation *n* **1** (doubt) réserve *f*; **without ~** sans réserve; **to have ~s about sth** avoir des doutes sur qch; **2** (booking) réservation *f*; **3** (US) (**Indian**) **~** réserve *f* (indienne).

reservation desk *n* bureau *m* des réservations.

reserve I *n* **1** (resource, stock) réserve *f*; **oil ~s** réserves de pétrole; **to keep sth in ~** tenir qch en réserve; **2** (reticence) réserve *f*; **to lose one's ~** sortir de sa réserve; **3** (Mil) **the ~(s)** la réserve; **4** (Sport) remplaçant/-e *m/f*; **5** réserve *f*; **wildlife ~** réserve naturelle.

II *vtr* **1** réserver; **to ~ the right to do sth** se réserver le droit de faire qch; **2** (book) réserver [*room, seat*].

reserved *adj* réservé; **to be ~ about sth** rester réservé sur qch.

reservoir *n* réservoir *m*.

reset *vtr* régler [*machine*]; remettre [qch] à l'heure [*clock*].

reshuffle *n* remaniement *m*; **cabinet ~** remaniement ministériel.

reside *vi* résider, habiter (**with** avec).

residence *n* **1** (house) maison *f*, demeure *f*; **2** résidence *f*; **place of ~** lieu de résidence; **to take up ~** élire domicile; **3** (US Univ) (also **~ hall**) résidence *f* universitaire.

residence permit *n* permis *m* de séjour.

resident I *n* (of city, region) résident/-e *m/f*; (of street) riverain/-e *m/f*; (of hostel) résident/-e *m/f*; (of guest house) pensionnaire *mf*; **~s association** association *f* de quartier.

II *adj* [*population*] local; [*staff, tutor*] à demeure; [*band*] permanent.

residential *adj* [*area*] résidentiel/-ielle; [*staff*] à demeure; [*course*] en internat; **to be in ~ care** être pris en charge par une institution.

residue *n* résidu *m* (**of** de); (figurative) reste *m* (**of** de).

resign I *vtr* démissionner de [*post, job*].

II *vi* démissionner (**as** du poste de; **from** de; **over** à cause de).

III *v refl* **to ~ oneself** se résigner (**to** à).

resignation *n* **1** (from post) démission *f* (**from** de; **as** du poste de); **2** (patience) résignation *f*.

resigned *adj* résigné (**to** à).

resilience *n* (of person) (mental) détermination *f*; (physical) résistance *f* physique.

resilient *adj* (morally) déterminé; (physically) résistant.

resin *n* résine *f*.

resist I *vtr* résister à [*attack, suggestion, offer, damage*]; s'opposer à [*attempt, reform*].

II *vi* résister.

resistance *n* résistance *f* (**to** à); **to meet with ~** se heurter à une résistance.

IDIOMS **to take the line of least ~** choisir la voie de la facilité.

Resistance *n* **the ~** la Résistance.

resistant *adj* **1 heat-~** résistant à la chaleur; **water-~** imperméable; **2** (opposed) **~ to** réfractaire à.

resit *vtr* (GB) repasser [*exam, test*].

resolute *adj* [*person*] résolu.

resolution *n* résolution *f*; **to make a ~ to do** prendre la résolution de faire.

resolve I *n* détermination *f*; **to strengthen sb's ~** rendre qn plus décidé.

II *vtr* **1** résoudre [*dispute*]; dissiper [*doubts*]; **2 to ~ that** décider que; **to ~ to do** résoudre de faire.

resonant *adj* [*voice*] sonore.

resort I *n* **1** recours *m*; **as a last ~** en dernier recours; **2** (place) lieu *m* de villégiature; **seaside ~** station *f* balnéaire; **ski ~** station *f* de ski.

II *vi* **to ~ to** recourir à.

resound *vi* **1** [*noise*] retentir (**through** dans); **2** [*place*] retentir (**with** de).

resounding *adj* [*cheers*] retentissant; [*success*] éclatant.

resource *n* ressource *f*; **natural/energy ~s** ressources naturelles/énergétiques.

resourceful *adj* [*person*] plein de ressources, débrouillard○.

resourcefulness *n* ressource *f*, débrouillardise○ *f*.

respect I *n* **1** (esteem) respect *m*, estime *f*; **to win sb's ~** gagner l'estime de qn; **2** (for human rights, privacy) respect *m* (**for** de); **out of ~** par respect (**for** pour); **with (all due) ~** sauf votre respect; **with ~ to** par rapport à; **3** (aspect) égard *m*; **in many ~s** à bien des égards.

II **respects** *n pl* respects *mpl*; **to pay one's ~s to sb** présenter ses respects à qn.

III *vtr* respecter.

respectability *n* respectabilité *f*.

respectable *adj* **1** [*person, family*] respectable; **in ~ society** entre gens convenables; **2** (adequate) [*amount*] respectable; [*performance*] honorable.

respectful *adj* respectueux/-euse (**to, towards** envers).

respective *adj* respectif/-ive.

respiration *n* respiration *f*.

respirator *n* respirateur *m*; **to be on a ~** être sous respirateur.

respiratory *adj* respiratoire.

respite *n* répit *m* (**from** dans); **a brief ~** un court répit.

respond *vi* **1** (answer) répondre (**to** à; **with** par); **2** (react) réagir (**to** à); [*car*] répondre.

respondent *n* **1** (to questionnaire) personne *f* interrogée; **2** (Law) défendeur/-eresse *m/f*.

response *n* **1** (answer) réponse *f* (**to** à); **in ~ to** en réponse à; **2** (reaction) réaction *f* (**to** à; **from** de); **to meet with a favourable ~** être bien reçu.

responsibility *n* responsabilité *f* (**for** de); **to take ~ for sth** prendre la responsabilité de qch; **it's your ~** c'est à vous de vous en occuper; **to claim ~ for an attack** revendiquer une attaque.

responsible *adj* **1** (to blame) **~ for killing ten people** responsable de la mort de dix personnes; **2** (in charge) **~ for producing/organizing sth** chargé de produire/d'organiser qch; **3 to be ~ to sb** être responsable devant qn; **4** (trustworthy) responsable; **5** [*job*] à responsabilités.

responsive *adj* réceptif/-ive.

respray *vtr* repeindre [*vehicle*].

rest I *n* **1** (remainder) **the ~** (of food, day, story) le reste (**of** de); **for the ~ of my life** pour le restant de mes jours; **2** (other people) **he is no different from the ~** (**of them**) il n'est pas différent des autres; **and what about the ~ of us?** et nous alors?; **3** (repose) repos *m*; (break) pause *f*; **to have a ~** se reposer.
II *vtr* **1** (lean) **to ~ sth on** appuyer qch sur; **2** reposer [*legs*]; ne pas utiliser [*injured limb*]; **3** (Law) **to ~ one's case** conclure sa plaidoirie; **I ~ my case** je n'ai rien à ajouter.
III *vi* **1** se reposer; **to ~ easy** être tranquille; **to let the matter ~** en rester là; **2** (be supported) **to ~ on** reposer sur; **3 to ~ in peace** reposer en paix.
■ **rest on**: **~ on [sb/sth] 1** [*eyes*] s'arrêter sur; **2** [*decision*] reposer sur [*assumption*].
■ **rest with**: **~ with [sb/sth]** être entre les mains de.

restart *vtr* **1** reprendre [*talks*]; **2** remettre [qch] en marche [*engine*].

restaurant *n* restaurant *m*.

restaurant car *n* (GB) wagon-restaurant *m*.

restitution *n* (gen, Law) restitution *f*.

restless *adj* [*person*] nerveux/-euse; [*patient, sleep*] agité; **to grow ~** [*audience*] commencer à s'impatienter; [*populace*] commencer à s'agiter.

restlessness *n* **1** (physical) agitation *f*; **2** (of character) instabilité *f*.

restoration *n* **1** (of territory) restitution *f* (**to** à); **2** (of monarchy, painting) restauration *f*; (of democracy) rétablissement *m*.

restore *vtr* **1** restituer [*property*] (**to** à); **2** rétablir [*health, peace, monarchy*]; rendre [*faculty*]; **to ~ sb to power** ramener qn au pouvoir; **3** (repair) restaurer.

restrain I *vtr* retenir [*person*]; contenir [*crowd*]; maîtriser [*animal*].
II *v refl* **to ~ oneself** se retenir.

restrained *adj* [*manner*] calme; [*reaction*] modéré; [*person*] posé.

restraint *n* **1** (moderation) modération *f*; (of furnishing, style) sobriété *f*; **2** (restriction) restriction *f*; **wage ~** contrôle *m* des salaires; **3** (constraint) contrainte *f*.

restrict *vtr* limiter [*activity, choice, growth*] (**to** à); restreindre [*freedom*]; réserver [*access, membership*] (**to** à).

restriction *n* limitation *f*; **~s on arms sales** limitations *fpl* de ventes d'armes; **price ~s** contrôle *m* des prix; **there are ~s on advertising** la publicité est réglementée.

restrictive *adj* restrictif/-ive.

re-string *vtr* changer les cordes de [*guitar*]; recorder [*racket*]; renfiler [*necklace*].

rest room *n* (US) toilettes *fpl*.

result I *n* résultat *m* (**of** de); **exam(ination) ~s** les résultats des examens; **as a ~ of** à la suite de; **as a ~** en conséquence.
II *vi* résulter; **to ~ in** avoir pour résultat.

resume I *vtr* reprendre [*talks*]; regagner [*seat*]; renouer [*relations*].
II *vi* reprendre.

résumé *n* **1** (summary) résumé *m*; **2** (US) (CV) curriculum vitae *m inv*.

resumption *n* reprise *f* (**of** de).

resurface I *vtr* refaire (la surface de).
II *vi* [*submarine*] faire surface; [*person*] refaire surface.

resurgence *n* (of party, danger, tradition) résurgence *f*; (of interest) regain *m*; (of economy) reprise *f*.

resurrect *vtr* ressusciter.

resurrection *n* résurrection *f*; **the Resurrection** la Résurrection.

resuscitate *vtr* (Med) réanimer.

resuscitation *n* réanimation *f*.

retail I *n* vente *f* au détail.
II *noun modifier* [*business, sector*] de détail.
III *adv* au détail.
IV *vi* **to ~ at** se vendre au détail à.

retailer *n* détaillant *m*.

retail: **~ price** *n* prix *m* de détail; **~ price index, RPI** *n* indice *m* des prix à la consommation.

retain *vtr* garder [*control, identity*]; conserver [*heat, title*]; retenir [*water, fact*].

retaliate *vi* réagir.

retaliation *n* représailles *fpl* (**for** de; **against** contre).

retarded *adj* retardé.

retch *vi* avoir des haut-le-cœur.

rethink *n* **to have a ~** y repenser.

reticence *n* réticence *f* (**on, about** à propos de).

reticent *adj* réticent; **to be ~ about sth** être discret sur qch.

retina *n* rétine *f*.

retinue *n* escorte *f*.

retire I *vi* **1** (from work) prendre sa retraite; **2** (withdraw) se retirer (**from** de); **3** (Sport) abandonner; **to ~ from sth** se retirer de qch.
II **retired** *pp adj* retraité.
III **retiring** *adj* **1** (leaving job) qui prend sa retraite; **2** (shy) réservé.

retirement *n* retraite *f*; **to take early ~** partir en retraite anticipée.

retort I *n* riposte *f*.
II *vtr* rétorquer (**that** que).

retrace *vtr* **to ~ one's steps** revenir sur ses pas.

retract I *vtr* rétracter [*statement, claws*]; escamoter [*landing gear*].
II *vi* [*landing gear*] s'escamoter.

retractable *adj* [*landing gear*] escamotable; [*pen*] à pointe rétractable.

retrain I *vtr* recycler [*staff*].
II *vi* [*person*] se recycler.

retraining *n* recyclage *m*.

retreat I *n* retraite *f*; **to beat a hasty ~** décamper.
II *vi* [*person*] se retirer (**into** dans; **from** de); [*army*] se replier (**to** sur); [*flood water*] reculer; **to ~ into a dream world** se réfugier dans un monde imaginaire.

retrial *n* nouveau procès *m*.

retribution *n* châtiment *m*.

retrieve *vtr* récupérer [*object*]; redresser [*situation*]; extraire [*data*].

retrograde *adj* rétrograde.

retrospect: **in retrospect** *phr* rétrospectivement.

retrospective I *n* (also **~ exhibition** or **~ show**) rétrospective *f*.
II *adj* **1** (gen) rétrospectif/-ive; **2** (Law) rétroactif/-ive.

retrospectively *adv* **1** (gen) rétrospectivement; **2** (Law) rétroactivement.

return I *n* **1** (going back) retour *m* (**to** à; **from** de); **2** (of law, practice, symptom) retour *m* (**of** de); (of money, object) restitution *f* (**of** de); **3** (of letter, goods) renvoi *m* (**of** de); **by ~ of post** par retour du courrier; **4** (yield on investment) rendement *m* (**on** de); (on capital) rémunération *f*.
II *vtr* **1** (give back) rendre; (pay back) rembourser; **I'll ~ the favour** je te revaudrai ça; **to ~ sb's call** rappeler qn; **2** (bring back) rapporter (**to** à); **3** (put back) remettre; **4** (send back) renvoyer; **'~ to sender'** 'retour à l'expéditeur'; **5** (reciprocate) répondre à [*love*]; **6** (Mil) riposter à [*fire*]; **7** (Law) prononcer [*verdict*]; **8** rapporter [*profit*]; **9** élire [*candidate*].
III *vi* **1** (come back) revenir (**from** de); retourner (**to** à); (get back from abroad) rentrer (**from** de); (get back home) rentrer chez soi; **2** (resume) **to ~ to** reprendre [*activity*]; **to ~ to power** revenir au pouvoir; **3** (recur) [*symptom, doubt*] réapparaître.
IV **in return** *phr* en échange (**for** de).
IDIOMS **many happy ~s!** bon anniversaire!

return: **~ fare** *n* prix *m* d'un billet aller-retour; **~ ticket** *n* billet *m* aller-retour; **~ trip** *n* retour *m*.

reunification *n* réunification *f*.

reunion *n* réunion *f*.

reunite *vtr* réunir [*family*]; réunifier [*party*].

rev○ *vtr* (also **~ up**) monter le régime de [*engine*].

revalue *vtr* réévaluer.

revamp *vtr* rajeunir [*image*]; réorganiser [*company*]; retaper○ [*building*].

reveal *vtr* dévoiler [*truth*]; révéler [*secret*]; découvrir [*view*]; **to ~ sth to sb** révéler qch à qn.

revealing *adj* **1** [*remark*] révélateur/-trice; **2** [*blouse*] décolleté.

revel *vi* **to ~ in sth/in doing** se délecter de qch/à faire.

revelation *n* révélation *f*.

reveller, **reveler** (US) *n* fêtard/-e○ *m/f*.

revenge *n* **1** vengeance *f*; **to get one's ~** se venger (**for** de; **on** sur); **2** (getting even) revanche *f*.

revenue *n* revenus *mpl*; **oil ~s** revenus *mpl* pétroliers.

reverberate *vi* [*hills, room*] résonner (**with** de); [*shock*] se propager.

revere *vtr* révérer.

reverence *n* profond respect *m*.

Reverend ▶ 642 *n* **1** (Protestant) pasteur *m*; **2** (as title) **the ~ Jones** le révérend Jones; **~ Mother** Révérende Mère.

reverent *adj* [*hush*] religieux/-ieuse; [*expression*] de respect.

reverie *n* rêverie *f*.

reversal *n* (of policy, roles) renversement *m*; (of order, trend) inversion *f*; (of fortune) revers *m*.

reverse I *n* **1** (opposite) **the ~** le contraire; **2** (back) **the ~** (of coin) le revers; (of banknote) le verso; (of fabric) l'envers *m*; **3** (Aut) (also **~ gear**) marche *f* arrière.
II *adj* **1** [*effect*] contraire; **in ~ order** [*answer question*] en commençant par le dernier; [*list*] en commençant par la fin; **2** (Aut) **~ gear** marche *f* arrière.
III *vtr* inverser [*trend, process*]; renverser [*roles*]; faire rouler [qch] en marche arrière [*car*]; **to ~ the charges** appeler en PCV.
IV *vi* [*driver*] faire marche arrière; **to ~ into a parking space** se garer en marche arrière.
V **in reverse** *phr* en sens inverse.

reverse charge call *n* appel *m* en PCV.

reversible *adj* réversible.

reversing light *n* (Aut) feu *m* de recul.

reversion *n* retour *m* (**to** à).

revert *vi* **to ~ to** reprendre [*habit, name*]; redevenir [*wilderness*]; **to ~ to normal** redevenir normal.

review I *n* **1** (reconsideration) révision *f* (**of** de); (report) rapport *m* (**of** sur); **to come under ~** être réexaminé; **2** (of book, film) critique *f* (**of** de); **3** (magazine) revue *f*; **4** (Mil) revue *f*; **5** (US Sch, Univ) révision *f*.
II *vtr* **1** (re-examine) reconsidérer [*situation*]; réviser [*attitude, policy*]; passer [qch] en revue [*troops*]; **2** faire la critique de [*book, film*]; **3** (US Sch, Univ) réviser.

reviewer *n* critique *m*.

revise I *vtr* **1** (alter) réviser [*estimate, figures*]; changer [*attitude*]; **~d upwards/downwards** [*figures, profits*] révisé à la hausse/à la baisse; **2** (GB) (for exam) réviser [*subject*]; **3** (correct) réviser [*text*].
II *vi* (GB) [*student*] réviser.

revision *n* révision *f*.

revisit *vtr* revisiter [*museum*]; retourner voir [*person, home*]; (figurative) revoir.

revitalize *vtr* revitaliser.

revival *n* **1** (of economy) reprise *f*; (of interest) regain *m*; (of custom, language) renouveau *m*; (of law) remise *f* en vigueur; **2** (of play) reprise *f*.

revive I *vtr* **1** (from coma, faint) ranimer [*person*]; **2** raviver [*custom*]; ranimer [*interest, hopes*]; relancer [*movement, fashion*]; reprendre [*play*]; revigorer [*economy*].
II *vi* **1** [*person*] (from coma, faint) reprendre connaissance; **2** [*economy*] reprendre.

revoke *vtr* révoquer [*will*]; annuler [*decision, order*].

revolt I *n* révolte *f* (**against** contre); (verbal) rébellion *f* (**over** contre); **to be in ~** être en révolte or en rébellion; **to rise in ~** se soulever.
II *vtr* dégoûter, révolter.
III *vi* se révolter (**against** contre); (verbally) se rebeller (**against, over** contre).

revolting *adj* **1** (physically) répugnant; (morally) révoltant; **2**° [*food*] infect; [*person*] affreux/-euse.

revolution *n* **1** révolution *f* (**in** dans); **2** (Aut, Tech) tour *m*.

revolutionary *n, adj* révolutionnaire (*mf*).

revolutionize *vtr* révolutionner.

revolve *vi* **1** (turn) tourner; **2 to ~ around** (be focused on) être axé sur.

revolving *adj* [*chair*] pivotant; [*stage*] tournant; **~ door** porte *f* à tambour *m*.

revue *n* revue *f*.

revulsion *n* dégoût *m* (**against** pour).

reward I *n* récompense *f*; **a £50 ~** 50 livres sterling de récompense.
II *vtr* récompenser (**for** de, pour).

rewarding *adj* [*experience*] enrichissant; [*job*] gratifiant; **financially ~** rémunérateur/-trice.

rewind *vtr* rembobiner [*tape, film*].

rewire *vtr* refaire l'installation électrique de [*building*].

reword *vtr* reformuler.

rewrite *vtr* ré(é)crire [*story, history*].

rhapsodize *vi* **to ~ about** or **over sth** s'extasier sur qch.

rhapsody *n* rhapsodie *f*.

rhetoric *n* rhétorique *f*.

rhetorical *adj* rhétorique.

rheumatic *adj* [*joint*] rhumatisant; [*pain*] rhumatismal.

rheumatism ▶ 686 *n* rhumatisme *m*.

Rhine *pr n* Rhin *m*.

rhinoceros *n* rhinocéros *m*.

rhubarb *n* rhubarbe *f*.

rhyme I *n* **1** rime *f*; **2** (poem) vers *mpl*; (children's) comptine *f*.
II *vi* rimer (**with** avec).
IDIOMS **without ~ or reason** sans rime ni raison.

rhythm *n* rythme *m*.

rhythmic(al) *adj* rythmique.

rib *n* **1** (Anat, Culin) côte *f*; **2** (in umbrella) baleine *f*; (in plane, building) nervure *f*.

ribbon *n* ruban *m*; **in ~s** en lambeaux *mpl*.

rib cage *n* cage *f* thoracique.

rice *n* riz *m*.

rice: **~field** *n* rizière *f*; **~ paper** *n* feuille *f* de pain azyme; (artist's) papier *m* de riz.

rich I *n* **the ~** les riches *mpl*.
II *adj* riche; **to grow** or **get ~** s'enrichir; **to make sb ~** enrichir qn; **~ in** riche en [*vitamins*].

riches *n pl* richesses *fpl*.

richly *adv* [*decorated, coloured*] richement; **~ deserved** amplement mérité.

richness *n* richesse *f*.

Richter scale *n* échelle *f* de Richter; **on the ~** sur l'échelle de Richter.

rickety *adj* [*chair, coalition*] branlant; [*house*] délabré.

rickshaw *n* pousse-pousse *m inv*.

ricochet *vi* ricocher (**off** sur).

rid I *vtr* **to ~ sb/sth of** débarrasser qn/qch de.
II *pp adj* **to get ~ of** se débarrasser de [*old car, guests*]; éliminer [*poverty*].

riddance *n* IDIOMS **good ~ (to bad rubbish)!** bon débarras°!

riddle I *n* **1** (puzzle) devinette *f*; **2** (mystery) énigme *f*.
II *vtr* **to be ~d with** être criblé de [*bullets*]; être rongé par [*disease, guilt*].

ride I *n* **1** (in vehicle, on bike) trajet *m* (**in, on** en, à); (for pleasure) tour *m*, promenade *f*; **to go for a ~** aller faire un tour; **to give sb a ~** (US) emmener qn (en voiture); **2** (on horse) promenade *f* à cheval.
II *vtr* **1** monter [*animal*]; rouler à [*bike*]; **to ~ a horse** monter à cheval; **can you ~ a bike?** sais-tu faire du vélo?; **2** (US) prendre [*bus, subway*]; parcourir [*range*]; **3** chevaucher [*wave*].
III *vi* (go horse-riding) faire du cheval; **we rode for three hours** nous avons fait trois heures de cheval; **she was riding on a camel** elle était sur un chameau; **to ~ across** traverser; **to ~ in** or **on** prendre [*bus*]; **to ~ on** [*surfer*] être porté par [*wave*].
IDIOMS **to take sb for a ~**° rouler qn°.
■ **ride out**: **~ [sth] out, ~ out [sth]** surmonter [*crisis*]; survivre à [*recession*]; **to ~ out the storm** surmonter la crise.
■ **ride up 1** [*rider*] s'approcher (**to** de); **2** [*skirt*] remonter.

rider *n* **1** (on horse) cavalier/-ière *m/f*; (on motorbike) motocycliste *mf*; (on bike) cycliste *mf*; (in bike race) coureur/-euse *m/f*; (in horse race) jockey *m*; **2** (as proviso) correctif *m*; (to document) annexe *f*.

ridge *n* **1** (along mountain top) arête *f*, crête *f*; (on hillside) corniche *f*; **2** (on rock, metal surface) strie *f*; (in ploughed land) crête *f*; **3** (on roof) faîte *m*, faîtage *m*; **4 ~ of high pressure** ligne *f* de hautes pressions.

ridicule I *n* ridicule *m*.
II *vtr* tourner [qn/qch] en ridicule.

ridiculous *adj* ridicule.

riding ▶649 I *n* équitation *f*; **to go ~** faire de l'équitation.
II *noun modifier* [*boots, lesson*] d'équitation; **~ school** centre *m* équestre.

rife *adj* **to be ~** être répandu.

riffraff *n* populace *f*.

rifle I *n* (firearm) fusil *m*; (at fairground) carabine *f*.
II *vtr* vider [*wallet, safe*].
■ **rifle through**: **~ through** [**sth**] fouiller dans.

rift *n* **1** (disagreement) désaccord *m*; (permanent) rupture *f*; **2** (split) (in rock) fissure *f*; (in clouds) trouée *f*.

rig I *n* (for oil) (on land) tour *f* de forage; (offshore) plate-forme *f* pétrolière offshore.
II *vtr* truquer [*election, result*].
■ **rig out**○: **he was ~ged out in his best clothes** il portait ses plus beaux habits.
■ **rig up**: **~ up** [**sth**] installer [*equipment*]; improviser [*clothes line, shelter*].

rigging *n* **1** (on ship) gréement *m*; **2** (of election, competition, result) truquage *m*.

right I *n* **1** (side, direction) droite *f*; **on** or **to your ~** à votre droite; **2** (in politics) (also **Right**) **the ~** la droite; **3** (morally) bien *m*; **~ and wrong** le bien et le mal; **4** (just claim) droit *m*; **to have a ~ to sth** avoir droit à qch; **the ~ to work/to strike** le droit au travail/de grève; **civil ~s** droits civils.
II **rights** *n pl* **1** (legal) droits *mpl*; **film ~s** droits d'adaptation cinématographique; **2** (moral) **the ~s and wrongs of a matter** les aspects *mpl* moraux d'une question.
III *adj* **1** (as opposed to left) droit, de droite; **on my ~ hand** (position) sur ma droite; **2** (morally) bien; (fair) juste; **it's not ~ to steal** ce n'est pas bien de voler; **I thought it ~ to tell him** j'ai jugé bon de lui dire; **it is only ~ and proper** ce n'est que justice; **to do the ~ thing** faire ce qu'il faut; **3** (correct) [*choice, direction, size, answer*] bon/bonne (*before n*); [*word*] juste; [*time*] exact; **to be ~** [*person*] avoir raison; [*answer*] être juste; **that's ~** c'est ça; **what's the ~ time?** quelle est l'heure exacte?; **is this the ~ train for Dublin?** c'est bien le train pour Dublin?; **is this the ~ way to the station?** est-ce que c'est la bonne direction pour aller à la gare?; **4** (suitable clothes, equipment) qui convient; **the ~ person for the job** la personne qu'il faut pour le poste; **when the time is ~** quand le moment sera venu; **to be in the ~ place at the ~ time** être là où il faut au bon moment; **5** (in good order) **the engine isn't quite ~** le moteur ne fonctionne pas très bien; **I don't feel quite ~ these days** je ne me sens pas très bien ces jours-ci; **things were not quite ~** il y avait quelque chose qui n'allait pas; **6 to put** or **set ~** corriger [*mistake*]; réparer [*injustice*]; arranger [*situation*]; réparer [*machine*]; **set one's watch ~** remettre sa montre à l'heure; **to put** or **set sb ~** détromper qn; **7** [*angle*] droit; **at ~ angles to** à angle droit avec, perpendiculaire à.
IV *adv* **1** (of direction) à droite; **to turn/look ~** tourner/regarder à droite; **2** (directly) droit, directement; **it's ~ in front of you** c'est droit or juste devant toi; **I'll be ~ back** je reviens tout de suite; **to walk ~ up to sb** marcher droit vers qn; **3** (exactly) **~ in the middle of the room** en plein milieu de la pièce; **~ now** (immediately) tout de suite; (US) (at this point in time) en ce moment; **I'm staying ~ here** je ne bougerai pas d'ici; **~ there** juste là; **4** (correctly) juste, comme il faut; **you're not doing it ~** tu ne fais pas ça comme il faut; **to guess ~** deviner juste; **5** (completely) tout; **go ~ back to the beginning** revenez tout au début; **~ at the bottom** tout au fond; **to turn the central heating ~ up** mettre le chauffage central à fond; **~ up until the 1950s** jusque dans les années 50; **6** (very well) bon; **~, let's have a look** bon, voyons ça.
V *vtr* redresser [*vehicle, ship*]; **to ~ a wrong** redresser un tort.
IDIOMS **by ~s** normalement, en principe.

right: **~ angle** *n* angle *m* droit; **~ away** *adv* tout de suite.

righteous *adj* vertueux/-euse.

rightful *adj* légitime.

right-hand *adj* du côté droit; **on the ~ side** sur la droite.

right: **~-hand drive** *n* conduite *f* à droite; **~-handed** *adv* [*person*] droitier/-ière; [*blow*] du droit; **~-hand man** *n* bras *m* droit.

rightly *adv* **1** (accurately) correctement; **if I remember ~** si je me souviens bien; **2** (justifiably) à juste titre; **~ or wrongly** à tort ou à raison; **3** (with certainty) au juste; **I don't ~ know** je ne sais pas au juste.

right off *adv* tout de suite.

right of way *n* **1** (Aut) priorité *f*; **2** (over land) droit *m* de passage; **'no ~'** 'entrée *f* interdite'.

right wing I *n* **the ~** la droite.
II **right-wing** *adj* [*attitude*] de droite; **they are very ~** ils sont très à droite.

rigid *adj* [*rules, person, material*] rigide; [*controls, timetable*] strict.

rigidity *n* rigidité *f*.

rigor mortis *n* rigidité *f* cadavérique.

rigorous *adj* rigoureux/-euse.

rigorously *adv* rigoureusement.

rigour (GB), **rigor** (US) *n* rigueur *f*.

rim I *n* bord *m*; (on wheel) jante *f*.
II **-rimmed** *combining form* **gold-~med spectacles** lunettes *fpl* à monture dorée.

rind *n* **1** (on cheese) croûte *f*; (on bacon) couenne *f*; **2** (on fruit) peau *f*.

ring I *n* **1** anneau *m*; (with stone) bague *f*; **a diamond ~** une bague de diamants; **a wedding ~** une alliance; **2** (circle) cercle *m*; **to have ~s under one's eyes** avoir les yeux cernés; **3** (sound) (at door) coup *m* de sonnette;

(of phone) sonnerie *f*; **4** (in circus) piste *f*; (in boxing) ring *m*; **5** (of smugglers, spies) réseau *m*; **6** (on cooker) (electric) plaque *f*; (gas) brûleur *m*.
II *vtr* **1** sonner [*church bells*]; **to ~ the doorbell** or **bell** sonner; **2** (GB) (also **~ up**) appeler.
III *vi* **1** [*bell, telephone, person*] sonner; **the doorbell rang** on a sonné à la porte; **2** [*footsteps, laughter, words*] résonner; **to ~ true** sonner vrai; **3** (GB) (phone) téléphoner; **to ~ for** appeler [*taxi*].
■ **ring off** (GB) raccrocher.
■ **ring out** [*voice, cry*] retentir; [*bells*] sonner.

ring binder *n* classeur *m* à anneaux.

ringing *n* **1** (noise of bell, alarm) sonnerie *f*; **2** (in ears) bourdonnement *m*.

ring: **~leader** *n* meneur/-euse *m/f*; **~let** *n* anglaise *f*; **~road** *n* (GB) périphérique *m*.

rinse I *n* rinçage *m*.
II *vtr* rincer; (wash) laver.

riot I *n* **1** émeute *f*, révolte *f*; **prison ~** mutinerie *f*; **2 a ~ of** une profusion de [*colours*].
II *vi* [*crowd, demonstrators*] se soulever; [*prisoner*] se mutiner.
IDIOMS **to run ~** [*crowd*] se déchaîner; [*imagination*] se débrider; [*plant*] proliférer.

rioter *n* émeutier/-ière *m/f*; (in prison) mutin *m*.

riot gear *n* tenue *f* antiémeutes.

rioting *n* émeutes *fpl*, bagarres *fpl*.

riot: **~ police** *n* forces *fpl* antiémeutes; **~ shield** *n* bouclier *m* antiémeutes.

rip I *vtr* déchirer; **to ~ a hole in sth** faire un trou dans qch; **to ~ sth out** arracher qch.
II *vi* [*fabric*] se déchirer.

RIP *abbr* qu'il/elle repose en paix or qu'ils/elles reposent en paix.

ripe *adj* [*fruit*] mûr; [*cheese*] fait.

ripen I *vtr* mûrir [*fruit*]; affiner [*cheese*].
II *vi* [*fruit*] mûrir; [*cheese*] se faire.

ripeness *n* maturité *f*.

ripple I *n* (in water, corn, hair) ondulation *f*; **~ of applause** cascade *f* d'applaudissements.
II *vi* **1** [*water*] se rider; (making noise) clapoter; **2** [*hair, corn*] onduler; [*muscles*] saillir.

rise I *n* **1** (in amount, inflation, rates) augmentation *f* (**in** de); (in prices, pressure) hausse *f* (**in** de); (in temperature) élévation *f* (**in** de); **2** (of person) ascension *f*; (of empire) essor *m*; **3** (slope) montée *f*; (hill) butte *f*.
II *vi* **1** [*water, tension*] monter; [*price, temperature*] augmenter; [*voice*] devenir plus fort; [*frustration, hopes*] grandir; **to ~ above** dépasser [*level*]; **2** (get up) [*person*] se lever; (after falling) se relever; **to ~ from the dead** ressusciter; **to ~ to the occasion** se montrer à la hauteur; **to ~ through the ranks** gravir tous les échelons; **3** [*road*] monter; [*cliff*] s'élever; **4** [*sun, moon*] se lever; **5** [*dough*] lever.
IDIOMS **to give ~ to** donner lieu à [*rumours*]; causer [*problem*].
■ **rise above**: **~ above [sth]** surmonter.
■ **rise up 1** [*bird, plane*] s'élever; [*smoke*] monter; **2** (rebel) se soulever.

riser *n* **to be an early ~** être un/une lève-tôt.

rising I *n* soulèvement *m*.
II *adj* [*costs, unemployment, temperature*] en hausse; [*tension*] grandissant; [*sun, moon*] levant.

risk I *n* risque *m*; **there is no ~ to consumers** il n'y a aucun danger pour le consommateur; **to run a ~** courir un risque; **to take ~s** prendre des risques; **at ~** menacé.
II *vtr* risquer; **to ~ one's life/neck** risquer sa vie/peau; **to ~ doing** courir le risque de faire.

risky *adj* [*decision, undertaking*] risqué; [*share, investment*] à risques.

risqué *adj* osé.

rite *n* rite *m*; **~ of passage** rite de passage.

ritual I *n* rituel *m*, rites *mpl*.
II *adj* [*dance, murder*] rituel/-elle; [*visit*] traditionnel/-elle.

rival I *n* (person) rival/-e *m/f*; (company) concurrent/-e *m/f*.
II *adj* [*team, business*] rival; [*claim*] opposé.
III *vtr* **1** (equal) égaler (**in** en); **2** (compete favourably) rivaliser avec (**in** de).

rivalry *n* rivalité *f* (**between** entre).

river *n* (flowing into sea) fleuve *m*; (tributary) rivière *f*.

riverbank *n* berge *f*; **along the ~** le long de la rivière.

riverside I *n* berges *fpl*.
II *adj* [*pub*] au bord de la rivière.

rivet I *n* rivet *m*.
II *vtr* **to be ~ed** être captivé; **to be ~ed to the spot** être cloué sur place.

riveting *adj* fascinant.

Riviera *n* **the Italian ~** la Riviera; **the French ~** la Côte d'Azur.

road I *n* **1** route *f*; **the ~ to Leeds** la route de Leeds; **to take (to) the ~** prendre la route; **2** (street) rue *f*; **3** (figurative) (way) voie *f* (**to** de); **to be on the right ~** être sur la bonne voie.
II *noun modifier* [*map, safety*] routier/-ière; [*accident*] de la route.

roadblock *n* barrage *m* routier; **police ~** barrage de police.

road: **~ haulage** *n* transports *mpl* routiers; **~ hog**° *n* chauffard° *m*.

roadside *n* bord *m* de la route; **by the ~** au bord de la route.

road: **~sign** *n* panneau *m* de signalisation; **~works** *n pl* travaux *mpl* (routiers).

roam I *vtr* parcourir [*countryside*]; faire le tour de [*shops*]; traîner dans [*streets*].
II *vi* **to ~ through** parcourir [*countryside*]; faire le tour de [*building*].
■ **roam around** [*person*] vadrouiller°.

roar I *n* (of lion) rugissement *m*; (of person) hurlement *m*; (of engine) vrombissement *m*; (of traffic) grondement *m*; **a ~ of laughter** un éclat de rire.
II *vi* [*lion*] rugir; [*person*] hurler; [*sea, wind*] mugir; [*fire*] ronfler; [*engine*] vrombir.

roaring I *n* (of lion) rugissement *m*; (of crowd) clameur *f*.
II *adj* **1** [*engine, traffic*] grondant; **a ~ fire** une belle flambée; **2** [*success*] fou/folle.

roast I *n* (Culin) rôti *m*; (US) barbecue *m*.

II *adj* [*meat, potatoes*] rôti; **~ beef** rôti *m* de bœuf, rosbif *m*.
III *vtr* rôtir [*meat, potatoes*]; (faire) griller [*chestnuts*]; torréfier [*coffee beans*].
IV *vi* [*meat*] rôtir; **I'm ~ing**○! je crève de chaud○!

rob *vtr* [*thief*] voler [*person*]; dévaliser [*bank, train*]; **to ~ sb of sth** voler qch à qn; (figurative) priver qn de qch.

robber *n* voleur/-euse *m/f*.

robbery *n* vol *m*.

robe *n* robe *f*; **ceremonial ~s** vêtements *mpl* de cérémonie.

robin *n* **1** (also **~ redbreast**) rouge-gorge *m*; **2** (US) merle *m* migrateur.

Robin Hood *pr n* Robin des bois.

robot *n* robot *m*.

robotize *vtr* robotiser.

robust *adj* [*health, furniture, toy*] robuste; [*economy, appetite*] solide; [*wine*] corsé.

rock I *n* **1** (substance) roche *f*; **solid ~** roche dure; **2** (boulder) rocher *m*; **3** (also **~ music**) rock *m*.
II *noun modifier* [*band, concert*] rock; [*industry*] du rock.
III *vtr* **1** balancer [*cradle*]; bercer [*baby, boat*]; **2** [*tremor*] secouer [*town*]; [*scandal*] ébranler [*government*].
IV *vi* **1** [*person*] se balancer; **to ~ back and forth** se balancer d'avant en arrière; **2** (shake) trembler.
IDIOMS **to be on the ~s** [*marriage*] aller à vau-l'eau.

rock and roll *n* (also **rock'n'roll**) rock and roll *m*.

rock bottom *n* **to be at ~** être au plus bas; **to hit ~** toucher le fond.

rock climber *n* varappeur/-euse *m/f*.

rock climbing ▶649 *n* varappe *f*; **to go ~** faire de la varappe.

rocker *n* **1** (US) (chair) fauteuil *m* à bascule; **2** (on cradle, chair) bascule *f*.

rockery *n* (GB) rocaille *f*.

rocket I *n* **1** (gen, Mil) fusée *f*; **2** (salad) roquette *f*.
II *vi* [*price, profit*] monter en flèche.

rocket launcher *n* lance-fusées *m inv*.

rock face *n* paroi *f* rocheuse.

rocking *n* (gentle) balancement *m*; (vigorous) ballottement *m*.

rocking: **~ chair** *n* fauteuil *m* à bascule; **~ horse** *n* cheval *m* à bascule.

rock star *n* rock-star *f*.

rocky *adj* **1** [*beach, path, road*] rocailleux/-euse; [*coast*] rocheux/-euse; **a ~ road** (figurative) un chemin difficile; **2** [*relationship, period*] difficile; [*business*] précaire.

Rocky Mountains *pr n pl* (also **Rockies**) **the ~** les montagnes *fpl* Rocheuses.

rod *n* **1** (gen, Tech) tige *f*; **curtain/stair ~** tringle à rideaux/de marche; **2** (for punishment) baguette *f*; **3** (for fishing) canne *f* à pêche.

rodent *n* rongeur *m*.

rodeo *n* rodéo *m*.

roe *n* **1** (eggs) œufs *mpl* (de poisson); **2** (milt) laitance *f*.

roe deer *n* (male) chevreuil *m*; (female) chevrette *f*.

rogue *n* **1** (rascal) coquin *m*; **2** (animal) solitaire *m*.

roguish *adj* espiègle, coquin.

role *n* rôle *m* (**of** de); **title ~** rôle-titre *m*; **vital** or **key ~** rôle primordial.

role: **~ model** *n* modèle *m*; **~-play** *n* psychodrame *m*; (Sch) jeu *m* de rôle.

roll I *n* **1** (of paper, cloth) rouleau *m*; (of banknotes) liasse *f*; (of flesh) bourrelet *m*; **a ~ of film** une pellicule; **2** (bread) petit pain *m*; **cheese ~** sandwich *m* au fromage; **3** (movement) (of ship, train) roulis *m*; **4** (of dice) lancer *m*; **5** (register) liste *f*; **electoral ~** listes électorales; **to call the ~** faire l'appel.
II *vtr* **1** rouler [*ball, log*]; faire rouler [*dice*]; **to ~ one's eyes** rouler les yeux; **to ~ sth into a ball** faire une boulette de [*paper*]; faire une boule de [*clay, dough*]; **2** étendre [*dough*]; rouler [*lawn*]; laminer [*metal*]; **3** faire tourner [*camera, presses*]; **4 to ~ one's 'r's** rouler les 'r's.
III *vi* **1** [*person, animal*] rouler (**onto** sur); [*car, plane*] faire un tonneau; [*ship*] tanguer; **to ~ down** [*car, rock*] dévaler [*hill*]; **2** [*thunder*] gronder; [*drum*] rouler; **3** [*camera, press*] tourner.
■ **roll about** (GB), **roll around** [*animal, person*] se rouler; [*marbles, tins*] rouler.
■ **roll back**: **~ [sth] back**, **~ back [sth] 1** rouler [*carpet*]; **2** faire reculer [*years*].
■ **roll down**: **~ [sth] down**, **~ down [sth]** baisser [*blind, sleeve*].
■ **roll in 1** [*tourists, money*] affluer; **2** [*tanks, trucks*] entrer.
■ **roll off**: **~ off [sth]** sortir de [*production line*].
■ **roll on** [*time*] passer.
■ **roll over** se retourner; **to ~ over on one's stomach** rouler sur le ventre.
■ **roll up**: **~ up [sth]**, **~ [sth] up** enrouler [*rug, poster*]; **to ~ up one's sleeves** retrousser ses manches.

roller *n* **1** rouleau *m*; **paint ~** rouleau de peintre; **2** (curler) bigoudi *m*.

roller: **~ blind** *n* store *m*; **~ coaster** *n* montagnes *fpl* russes; **~-skate** *n* patin *m* à roulettes.

roller-skating ▶649 *n* patinage *m* à roulettes; **to go ~** faire du patin à roulettes.

rolling: **~ pin** *n* rouleau *m* à pâtisserie; **~ stock** *n* matériel *m* roulant; **~ stone** *n* vagabond/-e *m/f*.

rollneck *n* col *m* roulé.

roll-on roll-off *adj* **~ ferry** navire *m* roulier.

roman *n, adj* (print) romain (*m*).

Roman I *n* Romain/-e *m/f*.
II *adj* [*empire, calendar, alphabet*] romain; **~ numerals** chiffres *mpl* romains.

Roman: **~ Catholic** *n, adj* catholique (*mf*); **~ Catholicism** *n* catholicisme *m*.

romance *n* **1** (of era, place) charme *m*; (of travel) côté *m* romantique; **2** (love affair) histoire *f* d'amour; (love) amour *m*; (passing affair) aventure *f*; **3** (novel) roman *m* d'amour; (film) film *m* d'amour.

Romance *adj* [*language*] roman.

Romanesque *adj* roman.

Romania ▶574 *pr n* Roumanie *f*.

Romanian ▶712 **I** *n* **1** (person) Roumain/-e *m/f*; **2** (language) roumain *m*.
II *adj* [*culture, food, politics*] roumain; [*teacher, lesson*] de roumain; [*ambassador, embassy*] de Roumanie.

romantic I *n* romantique *mf*; **the Romantics** les romantiques *mpl*.
II *adj* **1** [*setting, story, person*] romantique; **2** [*attachment*] sentimental; **3** [*novel, film*] d'amour.

romanticism *n* romantisme *m*.

romanticize *vtr* idéaliser.

Romany *n* Tzigane *mf*, Romani *mf*.

Romeo *pr n* **1** (character) Roméo *m*; **2** (figurative) don Juan *m*.

romp I *n* **1** (frolic) ébats *mpl*; **2** (easy victory) victoire *f* facile.
II *vi* s'ébattre; **to ~ home** l'emporter facilement.

rompers *n pl* (also **romper suit**) barboteuse *f*.

roof *n* **1** (on building) toit *m*; **2** (Anat) **the ~ of the mouth** la voûte du palais.

roofing *n* **1** (material) toiture *f*, couverture *f*; **2** (process) pose *f* de la toiture.

roof rack *n* galerie *f*.

rooftop *n* toit *m*; **to shout sth from the ~s** crier qch sur tous les toits.

rook *n* **1** (bird) (corbeau *m*) freux *m*; **2** (in chess) tour *f*.

rookery *n* colonie *f* de freux.

room I *n* **1** pièce *f*; (for sleeping) chambre *f*; (for working) bureau *m*; (for meetings, teaching, operating) salle *f*; **2** (space) place *f*; **to make ~** faire de la place; **3** (opportunity) **~ for improvement** possibilité *f* d'amélioration; **~ for manoeuvre** marge *f* de manœuvre.
II *vi* (US) loger (**with** chez).

roommate *n* **1** (in same room) camarade *mf* de chambre; **2** (US) (flatmate) compagnon/compagne *m/f* d'appartement.

room service *n* service *m* de chambre.

room temperature *n* température *f* ambiante; **at ~** [*wine*] chambré.

roomy *adj* [*car, house*] spacieux/-ieuse; [*garment*] ample; [*bag, cupboard*] grand.

roost I *n* perchoir *m*.
II *vi* (in trees) percher (pour la nuit); (in attic) se nicher.
IDIOMS **to rule the ~** faire la loi.

rooster *n* coq *m*.

root I *n* **1** racine *f*; **to take ~** [*plant*] prendre racine; [*idea, value*] s'établir; [*industry*] s'implanter; **to pull sth up by the ~s** déraciner qch; **2** (of problem) fond *m*; (of evil) origine *f*; **at the ~ of** à l'origine de.
II *noun modifier* [*cause, issue*] fondamental.
III *vtr* **to be ~ed in** être ancré dans; **deeply-~ed** bien enraciné; **~ed to the spot** figé sur place.
■ **root around**, **root about** fouiller (**in** dans).
■ **root out**: ¶ **~ out [sth]**, **~ [sth] out** traquer [*corruption*]; ¶ **~ out [sb]**, **~ [sb] out** déloger [*person*].

root ginger *n* gingembre *m* frais.

rootless *adj* sans racines.

rope I *n* (gen, Sport) corde *f*; (of pearls) rang *m*.
II *vtr* attacher [*victim, animal*] (**to** à); encorder [*climber*].
IDIOMS **to know the ~s** connaître les ficelles°.

rope ladder *n* échelle *f* de corde.

rosary *n* (prayer) rosaire *m*; (beads) chapelet *m*.

rose *n* **1** (flower) rose *f*; (shrub) rosier *m*; **2** (on watering can) pomme *f*.

rose: **~bed** *n* parterre *m* de roses; **~bud** *n* bouton *m* de rose; **~ bush** *n* rosier *m*.

rosemary *n* romarin *m*.

rose-tinted *adj* IDIOMS **to see the world through ~ spectacles** voir la vie en rose.

rosette *n* **1** (for winner) cocarde *f*; (on horse) flot *m*; (on gift) nœud *m*; **2** (Bot) rosette *f*.

roster *n* (also **duty ~**) tableau *m* de service.

rostrum *n* estrade *f*.

rosy *adj* [*cheek, light*] rose; **to paint a ~ picture** peindre un tableau favorable.

rot I *n* pourriture *f*; (figurative) mal *m*; **the ~ has set in** ça commençe à se gâter.
II *vtr* pourrir.
III *vi* (also **~ away**) pourrir; (figurative) [*person*] moisir°.

rota *n* (GB) tableau *m* de service; **on a ~ basis** à tour de rôle.

rotary *adj* rotatif/-ive.

rotate I *vtr* **1** faire tourner [*blade*]; **2** faire [qch] à tour de rôle [*job*]; alterner [*roles*].
II *vi* [*blade, handle, wings*] tourner.

rotating *adj* **1** [*blade, globe*] tournant; **2** [*post, presidency*] tournant.

rotation *n* rotation *f*; **to work in ~** travailler par roulement or à tour de rôle.

rote *n* **by ~** par cœur.

rotor *n* rotor *m*.

rotten *adj* **1** [*produce*] pourri; [*teeth*] gâté; [*smell*] de pourriture; **2** (corrupt) pourri°; **3**° (bad) [*weather*] pourri; [*food*] infect; [*cook, driver*] exécrable.

rotund *adj* [*person*] rondelet/-ette°; [*stomach*] rebondi.

rouble ▶748 *n* rouble *m*.

rough I *adj* **1** [*material*] rêche; [*hand, skin, surface, rock*] rugueux/-euse; [*terrain*] cahoteux/-euse; **2** [*person, behaviour, sport*] brutal, violent; [*landing*] brutal; [*area*] dur; **3** [*description, map*] sommaire; [*figure, idea, estimate*] approximatif/-ive; **~ justice** justice *f*

sommaire; **4** (difficult) dur, difficile; **a ~ time** une période difficile; **to give sb a ~ ride** rendre la vie dure à qn; **5** (crude) grossier/-ière; **6** (harsh) [*voice, taste, wine*] âpre; **7** (stormy) [*sea, crossing*] agité; **in ~ weather** par gros temps.
II *adv* **to sleep ~** dormir à la dure.
IDIOMS **to ~ it** vivre à la dure.

roughage *n* fibres *fpl.*

rough: **~-and-ready** *adj* [*person, manner*] fruste; [*conditions*] rudimentaire; [*method, system*] sommaire; **~-and-tumble** *n* chahut *m*; (figurative) mêlée *f* (**of** de); **~ diamond** *n* (gem) diamant *m* brut; (GB) (man) brave homme *m*.

roughen *vtr* rendre [qch] rêche or rugueux.

rough-hewn *adj* [*wood*] équarri.

roughly *adv* **1** [*calculate*] grossièrement; **~ speaking** en gros; **~ 10%** à peu près 10%; **2** [*treat, hit*] brutalement; **3** [*make*] grossièrement.

roughness *n* **1** (of skin, surface, material) rugosité *f*; (of terrain) inégalité *f*; **2** (violence) brutalité *f*; **3** (lack of sophistication) (of person) rudesse *f*.

rough paper *n* feuille *f* de brouillon.

roulette *n* roulette *f*.

round I *adv* (GB) **1 all ~** tout autour; **whisky all ~!** du whisky pour tout le monde!; **to go all the way ~** faire tout le tour; **to go ~ and ~** tourner en rond; **2** (to place, home) **to go ~ to the office/to sb's house** passer au bureau/chez qn; **to ask sb ~** dire à qn de passer à la maison; **to invite sb ~ for lunch** inviter qn à déjeuner (chez soi); **I'll be ~ in a minute** j'arrive (dans un instant); **3 all year ~** toute l'année; **this time ~** cette fois-ci.
II *prep* (GB) **1** autour de [*table*]; **to sit ~ the fire** s'asseoir au coin du feu; **the wall goes right ~ the house** le mur fait le tour de la maison; **what do you measure ~ the waist?** combien fais-tu de tour de taille?; **2 to go ~ the corner** tourner au coin de la rue; **just ~ the corner** tout près; **to go ~ a bend** prendre un virage; **to go ~ an obstacle** contourner un obstacle; **3 her sister took us ~ Oxford** sa sœur nous a fait visiter Oxford; **to go ~ the shops** faire les magasins.
III *n* **1** (of competition) manche *f*; (of golf, cards) partie *f*; (in boxing) round *m*; (in showjumping) parcours *m*; (in election) tour *m*; (of talks) série *f*; **a ~ of drinks** une tournée; **a ~ of ammunition** une cartouche; **a ~ of applause** une salve d'applaudissements; **to get a ~ of applause** être applaudi; **a ~ of toast** un toast; **the daily ~ of activities** le train-train quotidien; **2 to do one's ~s** [*postman, milkman*] faire sa tournée; [*doctor*] visiter ses malades; [*guard*] faire sa ronde; **to go** or **do the ~s** [*rumour, flu*] circuler; **3** (shape) rondelle *f*.
IV *adj* rond; **~-faced** au visage rond; **her eyes grew ~** elle a ouvert des yeux ronds; **to have ~ shoulders** avoir le dos voûté; **in ~ figures, that's £100** ça fait 100 livres sterling en arrondissant; **a ~ dozen** une douzaine exactement; **a nice ~ sum** une somme rondelette○.
V *vtr* contourner [*headland*]; **to ~ the corner** tourner au coin; **to ~ a bend** prendre un virage.
VI **round about** *phr* **1** (approximately) à peu près, environ; **it happened ~ about here** ça s'est passé par ici; **2** (vicinity) **the people ~ about** les gens des environs.
■ **round down**: **~ [sth] down, ~ down [sth]** arrondir [qch] au chiffre inférieur.
■ **round off**: **~ off [sth], ~ [sth] off 1** finir [*meal, evening*] (**with** par); conclure [*speech*]; **2** arrondir [*corner, figure*].
■ **round on** (GB): **~ on [sb]** attaquer violemment; **she ~ed on me** elle m'est tombée dessus○.
■ **round up**: **~ up [sb/sth], ~ [sb/sth] up 1** regrouper [*people*]; rassembler [*livestock*]; **2** arrondir [qch] au chiffre supérieur [*figure*].

roundabout I *n* (GB) (in fairground) manège *m*; (in playground) tourniquet *m*; (for traffic) rond-point *m*.
II *adj* **to come by a ~ way** faire un détour; **by ~ means** par des moyens détournés; **a ~ way of saying** une façon détournée or alambiquée○ de dire.

rounded *adj* **1** [*shape, edge*] arrondi; **2** [*phrase*] bien tourné.

rounders *n* (GB) ≈ baseball *m*.

roundness *n* rondeur *f*.

round: **~-the-world** *adj* autour du monde; **~ trip** *n* aller-retour *m*.

roundup *n* **1** (herding) rassemblement *m* (**of** de); **2** (by police) rafle *f*.

roundworm *n* ascaris *m*.

rouse *vtr* réveiller [*person*]; susciter [*anger, interest*].

rousing *adj* [*speech*] galvanisant; [*music*] exaltant.

rout I *n* déroute *f*, défaite *f*.
II *vtr* (Mil) mettre en déroute; (figurative) battre à plates coutures.

route I *n* chemin *m*, itinéraire *m*; (official) parcours *m*; (in shipping) route *f*; (in aviation) ligne *f*; (figurative) (to power) voie *f* (**to** de); **bus ~** ligne d'autobus.
II *vtr* expédier, acheminer [*goods*].

routine I *n* **1** routine *f*; **office ~** travail *m* de routine; **2** (act) numéro *m*.
II *adj* **1** [*enquiry, matter*] de routine; **2** (uninspiring) routinier/-ière.

roving *adj* [*ambassador*] itinérant; [*life*] de nomade.

row[1] **▶ 649** I *n* **1** (of people, plants, stitches) rang *m* (**of** de); (of houses, seats, books) rangée *f* (**of** de); **2** (succession) **six times in a ~** six fois de suite; **the third week in a ~** la troisième semaine d'affilée.
II *vtr* **to ~ a boat up the river** remonter la rivière à la rame.
III *vi* (gen) ramer; (Sport) faire de l'aviron; **to ~ across** traverser [qch] à la rame [*lake*].

row[2] I *n* **1** (public) querelle *f*; (private) dispute *f* (**about** à propos de); **to have a ~ with** se disputer avec; **2** (noise) tapage *m*.
II *vi* se disputer (**with** avec; **about, over** à propos de).

rowdy *adj* (noisy) tapageur/-euse; (violent) bagarreur/-euse; (in class) chahuteur/-euse.

rower *n* rameur/-euse *m/f*.

rowing ▶649 *n* aviron *m*.

rowing: **~ boat** *n* (GB) bateau *m* à rames; **~ machine** *n* rameur *m*.

royal *adj* royal; **to give sb a ~ welcome** faire un accueil royal à qn.

royal blue ▶559 *n, adj* bleu (*m*) roi *inv*.

Royal Highness ▶642 *n* **His ~** Son Altesse *f* royale; **Your ~** Votre Altesse *f*.

royalty *n* **1** (persons) membres *mpl* d'une famille royale; **2** (to author, musician) droits *mpl* d'auteur; (on patent) royalties *fpl*.

rub I *n* **1** (massage) friction *f*; **2** (polish) coup *m* de chiffon; **to give [sth] a ~** donner un coup de chiffon à [*table*]; frotter [*stain*].
II *vtr* se frotter [*chin, eyes*]; frotter [*stain, surface*]; frictionner [*sb's back*]; **to ~ sth into the skin** faire pénétrer qch dans la peau.
III *vi* frotter; **to ~ against** frotter contre [*mudguard*].
IDIOMS **to ~ sb up the wrong way** prendre qn à rebrousse-poil○.
■ **rub down**: ¶ **~ [sb] down, ~ down [sb]** frictionner [*athlete*]; ¶ **~ [sth] down, ~ down [sth]** **1** bouchonner [*horse*]; **2** poncer [*plaster, wood*].
■ **rub off**: ¶ **~ off** [*dye, ink*] déteindre; ¶ **~ [sth] off, ~ off [sth]** faire disparaître [*stain*].
■ **rub out**: ¶ **~ out** s'effacer; ¶ **~ [sth] out, ~ out [sth]** effacer.

rubber I *n* **1** (substance) caoutchouc *m*; **2** (GB) (eraser) gomme *f*.
II *noun modifier* [*ball, sole*] de or en caoutchouc.

rubber: **~ band** *n* élastique *m*; **~ plant** *n* caoutchouc *m*; **~ stamp** *n* tampon *m*; **~ tree** *n* hévéa *m*.

rubbish I *n* **1** (refuse) déchets *mpl*; (domestic) ordures *fpl*; (on site) gravats *mpl*; **2** (inferior goods) camelote○ *f*; (discarded objects) saletés○ *fpl*; **3** (nonsense) bêtises *fpl*; **this book is ~**○! ce livre est nul○!
II *vtr* (GB) descendre [qn/qch] en flammes.

rubbish: **~ bin** *n* (GB) poubelle *f*; **~ heap** *n* tas *m* d'ordures.

rubble *n* (after explosion) décombres *mpl*; (on site) gravats *mpl*.

ruby ▶559 I *n* **1** (gem) rubis *m*; **2** (also **~ red**) rouge *m* rubis.
II *noun modifier* [*bracelet, necklace*] de rubis.
III *adj* [*liquid, lips*] vermeil/-eille; **~ wedding** noces *fpl* de vermeil.

rucksack *n* sac *m* à dos.

rudder *n* (on boat) gouvernail *m*; (on plane) gouverne *f*.

ruddy *adj* [*cheeks*] coloré.

rude *adj* **1** (impolite) [*comment*] impoli; [*person*] mal élevé; **to be ~ to sb** être impoli envers qn; **2** (indecent) [*joke*] grossier/-ière; [*book*] osé; **a ~ word** un gros mot.

rudely *adv* (impolitely) de façon impolie; (abruptly) brutalement.

rudeness *n* manque *m* de correction.

rudimentary *adj* rudimentaire.

rudiments *n pl* rudiments *mpl* (**of** de).

rueful *adj* [*smile, thought*] triste.

ruff *n* (of lace) fraise *f*; (of fur, feathers) collier *m*.

ruffle I *n* (at sleeve) manchette *f*; (at neck) ruche *f*; (on shirt front) jabot *m*.
II *vtr* **1** ébouriffer [*hair, fur*]; hérisser [*feathers*]; rider [*water*]; **2** (disconcert) énerver; (upset) froisser.

rug *n* **1** tapis *m*; (by bed) descente *f* de lit; **2** (GB) (blanket) couverture *f*.

rugby ▶649 *n* rugby *m*.

rugged *adj* **1** [*landscape*] accidenté; [*coastline*] déchiqueté; **2** [*man, features*] rude.

ruin I *n* **1** (physical, financial) ruine *f*; (moral) perte *f*; **in ~s** en ruines; **2** (building) ruine *f*.
II *vtr* **1** ruiner [*economy, career*]; **to ~ one's health** se ruiner la santé; **to ~ one's eyesight** s'abîmer la vue; **2** gâcher [*holiday, meal*]; abîmer [*clothes*].
IDIOMS **to go to rack and ~** se délabrer.

ruination *n* ruine *f*.

rule I *n* **1** (of game, language) règle *f*; (of school, organization) règlement *m*; **the ~s of the game** les règles or la règle du jeu; **against the ~s** contraire aux règles or au règlement (**to do** de faire); **~s and regulations** réglementation *f*; **as a ~** généralement; **2** (authority) domination *f*, gouvernement *m*; **majority ~** gouvernement majoritaire; **3** (for measuring) règle *f*.
II *vtr* **1** [*ruler, law*] gouverner; [*monarch*] régner sur; [*party*] diriger; [*army*] commander; **2** [*factor*] dicter [*strategy*]; **to be ~d by** [*person*] être mené par [*passions, spouse*]; **3** (draw) faire, tirer [*line*]; **~d paper** papier réglé; **4** [*court, umpire*] **to ~ that** décréter que.
III *vi* **1** [*monarch, anarchy*] régner; **2** [*court, umpire*] statuer.
■ **rule out**: **~ out [sth], ~ [sth] out** **1** exclure [*possibility, candidate*] (**of** de); **to ~ out doing** exclure de faire; **2** interdire [*activity*].

ruler *n* **1** (leader) dirigeant/-e *m/f*; **2** (measure) règle *f*.

ruling I *n* décision *f* (**against** à l'encontre de; **by** de; **on** sur).
II *adj* **1** (in power) dirigeant; **2** (dominant) dominant.

rum *n* rhum *m*.

rumble I *n* (of thunder, artillery, trucks) grondement *m*; (of stomach) gargouillement *m*.
II *vi* [*thunder, artillery*] gronder; [*stomach*] gargouiller.

ruminate *vi* **1** (think) **to ~ on** or **about** ruminer sur; **2** (Zool) ruminer.

rummage *vi* fouiller (**through** dans; **for** à la recherche de).

rummy ▶649 *n* rami *m*.

rumour (GB), **rumor** (US) *n* rumeur *f*, bruit *m* (**about** sur); **~ has it that** le bruit court que.

rumoured (GB), **rumored** (US) *adj* **it is ~ that** il paraît que, on dit que.

rump *n* **1** (also **~ steak**) rumsteck *m*; **2** (of animal) croupe *f*.

rumple *vtr* ébouriffer [*hair*]; froisser [*clothes, sheets, papers*].

run I *n* **1** course *f*; **a two-mile ~** une course de deux miles; **to go for a ~** aller courir; **to break into a ~** se mettre à courir; **2** (flight) **on the ~** en fuite; **to be on the ~ from sb/sth** fuir qn/qch; **to make a ~ for it** fuir, s'enfuir; **3** (series) (of successes, failures) série *f*; (in printing) tirage *m*; **to have a ~ of luck** être en veine; **4** (in theatre) série *f* de représentations; **to have a six-month ~** tenir l'affiche pendant six mois; **5** (on stock exchange) ruée *f* (**on** sur); **6** (trip, route) trajet *m*; **7** (in cricket, baseball) point *m*; **8** (for rabbit, chickens) enclos *m*; **9** (in tights, material) échelle *f*; **10** (for skiing) piste *f*; **11** (in cards) suite *f*.
II *vtr* **1** courir [*distance, marathon*]; **to ~ a race** faire une course; **2** (drive) **to ~ sb to the station** conduire qn à la gare; **3** (pass, move) **to ~ one's hand over** passer la main sur; **to ~ one's eye(s) over** parcourir rapidement; **4** (manage) diriger; **a well-/badly-run organization** une organisation bien/mal dirigée; **5** (operate) faire fonctionner [*machine*]; faire tourner [*motor*]; exécuter [*program*]; entretenir [*car*]; **to ~ tests on** effectuer des tests sur; **6** (organize, offer) organiser [*competition, course*]; mettre [qch] en place [*bus service*]; **7** faire couler [*bath*]; ouvrir [*tap*]; **8** (publish) publier [*article*]; **9** (enter) faire courir [*horse*]; présenter [*candidate*].
III *vi* **1** [*person, animal*] courir; **to ~ across/down sth** traverser/descendre qch en courant; **to ~ for the bus** courir pour attraper le bus; **to come ~ning** accourir (**towards** vers); **2** (flee) fuir, s'enfuir; **to ~ for one's life** s'enfuir pour sauver sa peau°; **3**° (rush off) filer°; **4** (function) [*machine*] marcher; **to leave the engine ~ning** laisser tourner le moteur; **to ~ on** marcher à [*diesel, unleaded petrol*]; **5** (continue, last) [*contract, lease*] être valide; **to ~ from... to...** [*school year, season*] aller de... à...; **6** [*play, musical*] tenir l'affiche (**for** pendant); **7** (pass) **to ~ past/through** [*frontier, path*] passer/traverser; **to ~ (from) east to west** aller d'est en ouest; **to ~ parallel to** être parallèle à; **8** (move) [*sledge*] glisser; [*curtain*] coulisser; **a wave of excitement ran through the crowd** un frisson d'excitation a parcouru la foule; **9** (operate regularly) [*bus, train*] circuler; **10** (flow) couler; **tears ran down his face** les larmes coulaient sur son visage; **11** [*dye, garment*] déteindre; [*make-up*] couler; **12** (as candidate) se présenter; **to ~ for president** être candidat/-e à la présidence.
IDIOMS **in the long ~** à long terme; **in the short ~** à brève échéance.
■ **run about, run around** courir.
■ **run across**°: **~ across [sth/sb]** tomber sur°.
■ **run at**: **~ at [sth]** se précipiter sur.
■ **run away**: ¶ **~ away** s'enfuir; **to ~ away from home** [*child*] faire une fugue; ¶ **~ away with [sth/sb] 1** (flee) partir avec; **2** rafler° [*prize, title*].
■ **run down**: ¶ **~ down** [*battery*] se décharger; [*watch*] retarder; ¶ **~ down [sth/sb], ~ [sth/sb] down 1** (in vehicle) renverser; **2** réduire [*production, defences*]; user [*battery*]; **3** (disparage) dénigrer.
■ **run into**: **~ into [sth/sb] 1** heurter, rentrer dans° [*car, wall*]; **2** (encounter) rencontrer [*person, difficulty*]; **3** (amount to) s'élever à [*hundreds, millions*].
■ **run off 1** (leave) partir en courant; **to ~ off with** partir avec; **2** [*liquid*] couler.
■ **run out** ¶ **1** [*supplies, oil*] s'épuiser; **time is ~ning out** le temps manque; **2** [*pen, machine*] être vide; **3** [*contract, passport*] expirer; ¶ **~ out of** ne plus avoir de [*petrol, time, money, ideas*]; **to be ~ning out of** n'avoir presque plus de [*petrol, time, money, ideas*].
■ **run over**: ¶ **~ over 1** [*meeting, programme*] se prolonger; **2** (overflow) déborder; ¶ **~ over [sth]** (go through) passer [qch] en revue [*arrangements*]; ¶ **~ over [sth/sb], ~ [sth/sb] over** (injure) renverser; (kill) écraser.
■ **run through**: ¶ **~ through [sth] 1** (be present in) se retrouver dans [*work*]; **2** (look through) parcourir [*list, article*]; (discuss) passer [qch] en revue; ¶ **~ through [sth], ~ [sth] through** répéter [*scene, speech*].
■ **run up**: **~ up [sth]** accumuler [*debt*].
■ **run up against**: **~ up against [sth]** se heurter à [*difficulty*].

runaway *adj* [*teenager*] fugueur/-euse; [*slave*] fugitif/-ive; [*horse*] emballé.

rundown *n* récapitulatif *m* (**on** de).

run-down *adj* **1** (exhausted) fatigué, à plat°; **2** (shabby) décrépit.

rung *n* **1** (of ladder) barreau *m*; **2** (in hierarchy) échelon *m*.

runner *n* **1** (person, animal) coureur *m*; **2** (horse) partant/-e *m/f*; **3** (messenger) estafette *f*; **4** (for door, seat) glissière *f*; (for drawer) coulisseau *m*; (for curtain) chariot *m*; (on sled) patin *m*; **5** (in hall) chemin *m* de couloir; (on stairs) chemin *m* d'escalier.

runner: **~ bean** *n* (GB) haricot *m* d'Espagne; **~ up** *n* second/-e *m/f* (**to** après).

running ▶ 649 **I** *n* **1** (sport, exercise) course *f* à pied; **2** (management) direction *f* (**of** de).
II *adj* **1** [*water*] courant; [*tap*] ouvert; **2 five days ~** cinq jours de suite.
IDIOMS **to be in/out of the ~** être/ne plus être dans la course (**for** pour).

running: **~ commentary** *n* commentaire *m* ininterrompu; **~ costs** *n* (of car) frais *mpl* d'entretien.

runny *adj* [*jam, sauce*] liquide; [*butter*] fondu; [*omelette*] baveux/-euse; **to have a ~ nose** avoir le nez qui coule.

run-of-the-mill *adj* ordinaire, banal.

runt *n* **1** (of litter) le plus faible *m* de la portée; **2** (weakling) avorton *m* (derogatory).

run-up *n* **1** (Sport) course *f* d'élan; **2 the ~ to** la dernière ligne droite avant.

runway *n* piste *f* d'aviation.

rupee ▶ 748 *n* roupie *f*.

rupture I *n* **1** (hernia) hernie *f*; (of blood vessel, kidney) rupture *f*; **2** (in relations) rupture *f*.
II *vi* **1** [*appendix*] se rompre; **2** [*container*] éclater.

rural *adj* (country) rural; (pastoral) champêtre.

ruse *n* stratagème *m*.

rush I *n* **1** (of crowd) ruée *f* (**to do** pour faire); **to make a ~ for sth** [*crowd*] se ruer vers qch; [*individual*] se précipiter vers qch; **2** (hurry) **to be in a ~** être pressé (**to do** de faire); **in a ~** en vitesse; **3** (of liquid, adrenalin) montée *f*; (of air) bouffée *f*; **4** (plant) jonc *m*.
II *vtr* **1 to ~ sth to** envoyer qch d'urgence à; **to be ~ed to the hospital** être emmené d'urgence à l'hôpital; **2** expédier [*task, speech*]; **3** (pressurize, hurry) bousculer [*person*]; **4** (charge at) sauter sur [*person*]; prendre d'assaut [*building*].
III *vi* [*person*] (make haste) se dépêcher (**to do** de faire); (rush forward) se précipiter (**to do** pour faire); **to ~ out of the room** se précipiter hors de la pièce; **to ~ down the stairs/past** descendre l'escalier/passer à toute vitesse; **to ~ along** filer.
■ **rush into**: ¶ **to ~ into marriage/a purchase** se marier/acheter sans prendre le temps de réfléchir; ¶ **~ [sb] into doing** bousculer [qn] pour qu'il/elle fasse.
■ **rush through**: ¶ **~ through [sth]** expédier [*task*]; ¶ **~ [sth] through, ~ through [sth]** adopter en vitesse [*legislation*]; traiter en priorité [*order, application*].

rushed *adj* [*attempt, letter*] expédié.

rush hour *n* heures *fpl* de pointe.

rusk *n* biscuit *m* pour bébés.

russet *adj* roussâtre.

Russia ▶ 574 *pr n* Russie *f*.

Russian ▶ 712 **I** *n* **1** (person) Russe *mf*; **2** (language) russe *m*.
II *adj* [*culture, food, politics*] russe; [*teacher, lesson*] de russe; [*ambassador, embassy*] de Russie.

rust I *n* rouille *f*.
II *vtr* rouiller [*metal*].
III *vi* [*metal*] se rouiller.

rustic *adj* [*furniture*] rustique; [*charm*] champêtre; [*accent*] rustique.

rustle I *n* (of paper, dry leaves) froissement *m*; (of leaves, silk) bruissement *m*.
II *vtr* froisser [*papers*].

rust-proof *adj* [*material*] inoxydable; [*paint, coating*] antirouille.

rusty *adj* rouillé.

rut *n* **1** (in ground) ornière *f*; **2** (routine) **be in a ~** être enlisé dans la routine; **3** (Zool) **the ~** le rut.

ruthless *adj* impitoyable (**in** dans).

RV *n* (US) (*abbr* = **recreational vehicle**) camping-car *m*, autocaravane *f*.

rye *n* **1** (cereal) seigle *m*; **2** (US) (also **~ whiskey**) whisky *m* à base de seigle.

rye bread *n* pain *m* de seigle.

Ss

s, S *n* s, S *m*.
sabbath *n* (also **Sabbath**) (Jewish) sabbat *m*; (Christian) jour *m* du seigneur.
sabotage I *n* sabotage *m*.
II *vtr* saboter [*equipment, campaign, discussion*]; saper [*economy*].
saboteur *n* saboteur/-euse *m/f*.
sabre, saber (US) *n* sabre *m*.
sachet *n* sachet *m*.
sack I *n* **1** sac *m*; **2 to get the ~**○ se faire mettre à la porte○.
II *vtr* **1**○ mettre [qn] à la porte○ [*employee*]; **2** mettre [qch] à sac [*town*].
sacrament *n* sacrement *m*.
sacred *adj* sacré (**to** pour); **to hold sth ~** tenir qch pour sacré.
sacrifice I *n* sacrifice *m* (**to** à; **of** de).
II *vtr* **1** sacrifier (**to** à); **2** (to the gods) offrir [qch] en sacrifice (**to** à).
III *v refl* **to ~ oneself** se sacrifier (**for** pour).
sacrilege *n* sacrilège *m*.
sacrosanct *adj* sacro-saint.
sad *adj* triste; **it makes me ~** cela me rend triste; **to be ~ that** [*person*] être triste que (+ *subj*); **it's ~ that** c'est triste que (+ *subj*); **it was a ~ sight** c'était triste à voir.
sadden *vtr* attrister; **it ~s me that** cela m'attriste que (+ *subj*).
saddle I *n* selle *f*.
II *vtr* **1** seller [*horse*]; **2 to ~ sb with** mettre [qch] sur les bras de qn [*responsibility, task*].
saddle bag *n* sacoche *f*.
sadism *n* sadisme *m*.
sadist *n* sadique *mf*.
sadistic *adj* sadique.
sadness *n* tristesse *f*.
sae *n*: *abbr* ▶**stamped addressed envelope**.
safari *n* safari *m*; **to go on ~** aller faire un safari.
safari park *n* parc *m* (zoologique).
safe I *n* coffre-fort *m*.
II *adj* **1** (after ordeal, risk) [*person*] sain et sauf; [*object*] intact; **we know they are ~** nous les savons hors de danger; **~ and sound** sain et sauf; **2** (free from threat, harm) **to be ~** [*person*] être en sécurité; [*document, valuables*] être en lieu sûr; [*company, job, reputation*] ne pas être menacé; **to feel ~** se sentir en sécurité; **is the bike ~ here?** est-ce qu'on peut laisser le vélo ici sans risque?; **have a ~ journey!** bon voyage!; **the money is ~ with him** avec lui l'argent ne risque rien; **3** (risk-free) [*toy, level, method*] sans danger; [*place, environment, vehicle, route*] sûr; [*structure, building*] solide; **the ~st way to do** la façon la plus sûre de faire; **to watch from a ~ distance** observer à distance respectueuse; **it's not ~** c'est dangereux; **the toy/park is not ~ for children** le jouet/parc est dangereux pour les enfants; **the meat is ~ to eat** on peut manger la viande sans danger; **that car is not ~ to drive** cette voiture est dangereuse; **4** (prudent) [*investment*] sûr; [*choice*] prudent; [*topic*] anodin; **5** (reliable) **to be in ~ hands** être en bonnes mains.
IDIOMS **better ~ than sorry!** mieux vaut prévenir que guérir!; **just to be on the ~ side** simplement par précaution; **to play (it) ~** être prudent.
safe bet *n* **it's a ~** c'est quelque chose de sûr; **it's a ~ that** il est certain que.
safe-deposit box *n* coffre *m* (à la banque).
safeguard I *n* garantie *f* (**for** pour; **against** contre).
II *vtr* protéger (**against, from** contre).
safe house *n* refuge *m*.
safekeeping *n* **in sb's ~** à la garde de qn.
safely *adv* **1** [*come back*] (of person) sans encombre; (of parcel, goods) sans dommage; (of plane) [*land, take off*] sans problème; **I arrived ~** je suis bien arrivé; **2 we can ~ assume that...** nous pouvons être certains que...; **3** [*locked, hidden*] bien; **he's ~ behind bars** heureusement il est sous les verrous.
safety I *n* sécurité *f*; **there are fears for her ~** on est inquiet sur son sort; **in ~** en (toute) sécurité; **to reach ~** parvenir en lieu sûr; **road ~** sécurité routière.
II *noun modifier* [*regulations*] de sécurité; [*bolt, blade, strap*] de sûreté.
IDIOMS **there's ~ in numbers** plus on est nombreux, moins on court de risques.
safety: **~ belt** *n* ceinture *f* de sécurité; **~ net** *n* filet *m* (de protection); (figurative) filet *m* de sécurité; **~ pin** *n* épingle *f* de sûreté.
sag *vi* **1** [*beam, mattress*] s'affaisser; [*tent, rope*] ne pas être bien tendu; **2** [*breasts*] pendre; [*flesh*] être flasque.
sage *n* **1** (herb) sauge *f*; **2** (wise person) sage *m*.
Sagittarius *n* Sagittaire *m*; ▶**Aquarius**.
Sahara *pr n* Sahara *m*; **the ~ desert** le désert du Sahara.
sail I *n* **1** voile *f*; **to set ~** prendre la mer; **to set ~ from/for** partir en bateau de/pour; **a ship in full ~** un navire toutes voiles dehors; **2** (of windmill) aile *f*.
II *vtr* **1** piloter [*ship, yacht*]; **2** traverser [qch] en bateau [*ocean, channel*].
III *vi* **1** [*person*] voyager en bateau; **to ~ around the world** faire le tour du monde en bateau; **2** [*ship*] **to ~ across** traverser [*ocean*]; **to ~ into** entrer dans [*port*]; **the boat ~s at 10 am** le bateau part à 10 h; **3** (as hobby) **to go ~ing** faire de la voile.
■ **sail through**: **~ through [sth]** gagner [qch] facilement [*match*]; **to ~ through an**

exam réussir un examen les doigts dans le nez○.

sailboat *n* (US) bateau *m* à voiles.

sailing ▶649| *n* voile *f*.

sailing: **~ boat** *n* bateau *m* à voiles; **~ ship** *n* voilier *m*.

sailor *n* marin *m*.

saint *n* saint/-e *m/f*; **Saint Mark** saint Marc.

sake *n* **1 for the ~ of clarity** pour la clarté; **for the ~ of argument** à titre d'exemple; **to kill for the ~ of killing** tuer pour le plaisir de tuer; **for old times' ~** en souvenir du bon vieux temps; **2** (benefit) **for the ~ of sb, for sb's ~** par égard pour qn; **for God's/heaven's ~!** pour l'amour de Dieu/du ciel!

salad *n* salade *f*; **ham ~** salade au jambon.

salad: **~ bowl** *n* saladier *m*; **~ dressing** *n* sauce *f* pour salade.

salami *n* saucisson *m* sec.

salary *n* salaire *m*.

sale *n* **I 1** vente *f* (**of** de; **to** à); **for ~** à vendre; **to put sth up for ~** mettre qch en vente; **on ~** (GB) en vente; **2** (in shop) solde *f*; **the January sales** les soldes de janvier; **in the ~(s)** (GB), **on ~** (US) en solde.

II sales *n pl* **1** (career) commerce *m*; **2** (department) service *m* des ventes.

sale: **~s assistant** ▶805| *n* (GB) vendeur/-euse *m/f*; **~sgirl** ▶805| *n* vendeuse *f*.

salesman ▶805| *n* **1** (rep) représentant *m*; **insurance ~** représentant d'assurances; **2** (in shop) vendeur *m*.

sale: **~s patter**○ *n* baratin○ *m*; **~s rep, sales representative** ▶805| *n* représentant/-e *m/f*; **~swoman** ▶805| *n* (rep) représentante *f*; (in shop) vendeuse *f*.

saliva *n* salive *f*.

salivate *vi* saliver.

sallow *adj* cireux/-euse.

salmon *n* saumon *m*

salmonella *n* salmonelle *f*.

salmonella poisoning ▶686| *n* salmonellose *f*.

salon *n* salon *m*; **hairdressing/beauty ~** salon de coiffure/de beauté.

saloon *n* **1** (GB) (also **~ car**) berline *f*; **2** (US) saloon *m*, bar *m*; **3** (on boat) salon *m*.

salt I *n* sel *m*; **to put ~ on** saler [*food*].

II *vtr* saler [*meat, fish, road, path*].

saltcellar *n* salière *f*.

salty *adj* [*water, food, flavour*] salé.

salutary *adj* salutaire.

salute I *n* **1** salut *m*; **to give a ~** faire un salut; **2 a 21-gun ~** une salve de 21 coups de canon.

II *vtr* saluer.

salvage I *n* **1** (rescue) sauvetage *m* (**of** de); **2** (goods rescued) biens *mpl* récupérés.

II *noun modifier* [*operation, team, equipment*] de sauvetage.

III *vtr* **1** sauver [*cargo, materials, belongings*] (**from** de); effectuer le sauvetage de [*ship*]; **2** sauver [*marriage, reputation, game*]; **3** (for recycling) récupérer [*metal, paper*].

salvation *n* salut *m*.

Salvation Army *n* Armée *f* du Salut.

salve I *n* baume *m*.

II *vtr* **to ~ one's conscience** soulager sa conscience.

Samaritan *n* **the Good ~** le bon Samaritain; **the ~s** les Samaritains *mpl*.

same I *adj* même (**as** que); **to be the ~** être le/la même; **the ~ one** le/la même; **it is the ~ for** c'est la même chose pour; **it is the ~ with** il en est de même pour; **to look the ~** être pareil; **to be the ~ as sth** être comme qch; **the ~ time next week** la semaine prochaine à la même heure; **the ~ time last year** l'année dernière à lá même époque; **~ time ~ place** même heure même endroit; **in the ~ way** (in a similar manner) de la même manière (**as** que); (likewise) de même; **it amounts** or **comes to the ~ thing** cela revient au même; **it's all the ~ to me** ça m'est complètement égal; **if it's all the ~ to you** si ça ne te fait rien; **at the ~ time** en même temps; **the very ~ day that** le jour même où; **things are just the ~ as before** rien n'a changé; **it's/he's the ~ as ever** c'est/il est toujours pareil; **to remain** or **stay the ~** ne pas changer; **it's not the ~ without you** ce n'est pas pareil sans toi; **the ~ old routine/excuse** toujours la même routine/la vieille excuse.

II the same *pron* la même chose (**as** que); **I'll have the ~** je prendrai la même chose; **the ~ goes for** il en va de même pour; **to do the ~ as sb** faire comme qn; **the ~ to you!** (in greeting) à toi aussi, à toi de même!; (of insult) et toi-même○!; **(the) ~ again please!** la même chose s'il vous plaît!

III the same *phr* de la même façon; **to feel the ~ as sb** penser comme qn; **to feel the ~ about** avoir les mêmes sentiments à l'égard de.

IDIOMS **all the ~..., just the ~,...** tout de même,...; **thanks all the ~** merci quand même.

sample I *n* **1** (of product, fabric) échantillon *m*; **2** (for analysis) prélèvement *m*; **to take a blood ~** faire une prise de sang.

II *noun modifier* **1 ~ bottle/packet** échantillon *m*; **2** [*question*] type; **~ prices** prix *mpl* donnés à titre d'exemple.

III *vtr* **1** (taste) goûter (à) [*food, wine*]; **2** (test) essayer [*products*]; sonder [*opinion, market*].

sanatorium (GB), **sanitarium** (US) *n* (GB) sanatorium *m*.

sanctify *vtr* sanctifier.

sanctimonious *adj* supérieur.

sanction I *n* sanction *f*; **to impose ~s** prendre des sanctions.

II *vtr* (give permission for) autoriser; (give approval to) sanctionner.

sanctity *n* **1** (of law) inviolabilité *f*; **2** (of person) sainteté *f*; (of place) caractère *m* sacré.

sanctuary *n* **1** (safe place) refuge *m*; **2** (holy place) sanctuaire *m*; **3** (for wildlife) réserve *f*; (for mistreated pets) refuge *m*.

sand I *n* sable *m*.
II *vtr* **1** (also **~ down**) poncer [*floor*]; frotter [qch] au papier de verre [*woodwork*]; **2** sabler [*icy road*].
IDIOMS **to bury one's head in the ~** pratiquer la politique de l'autruche.

sandal *n* sandale *f*.

sand: **~bag** *n* sac *m* de sable; **~bank** *n* banc *m* de sable; **~ castle** *n* château *m* de sable; **~ dune** *n* dune *f*.

sandpaper I *n* papier *m* de verre.
II *vtr* poncer [*plaster, wood*]; polir [*glass, metal*].

sand: **~pit** *n* (quarry) sablière *f*; (for children) bac *m* à sable; **~stone** *n* grès *m*; **~storm** *n* tempête *f* de sable.

sandwich I *n* sandwich *m*; **cucumber ~** sandwich au concombre.
II *vtr* **to be ~ed between** [*car, building, person*] être pris en sandwich entre.

sandy *adj* **1** [*beach*] de sable; [*path, soil*] sablonneux/-euse; **2** [*hair*] blond roux *inv*; [*colour*] sable *inv* (*after n*).

sane *adj* **1** [*person*] sain d'esprit; **2** [*policy, judgment*] sensé.

sanitarium (US) = **sanatorium**.

sanitary *adj* **1** [*engineer, facilities, installations*] sanitaire; **2** (hygienic) hygiénique; (clean) propre.

sanitary towel (GB), **sanitary napkin** (US) *n* serviette *f* hygiénique or périodique.

sanitize *vtr* **1** (tone down) aseptiser [*art, politics*]; expurger [*document*]; rendre [qch] plus acceptable [*violence*]; **2** (sterilize) désinfecter.

sanity *n* équilibre *m* mental; **to keep one's ~** rester sain d'esprit.

Sanskrit ▶712 *n* sanscrit *m*.

Santa (Claus) *pr n* le père Noël.

sap I *n* sève *f*.
II *vtr* saper [*strength, courage, confidence*].

sapling *n* jeune arbre *m*.

sapphire ▶559 I *n* **1** (stone) saphir *m*; **2** (colour) bleu *m* saphir.
II *adj* bleu saphir *inv*.

sarcasm *n* sarcasme *m*.

sarcastic *adj* sarcastique.

sardine *n* sardine *f*.

Sardinia *pr n* Sardaigne *f*.

sardonic *adj* [*laugh, look*] sardonique; [*person, remark*] acerbe.

sari *n* sari *m*.

sash *n* **1** (round waist) large ceinture *f*; (ceremonial) écharpe *f*; **2** (window frame) châssis *m* d'une fenêtre à guillotine.

sash window *n* fenêtre *f* à guillotine.

Satan *pr n* Satan.

satanic *adj* [*rites*] satanique; [*pride, smile*] démoniaque.

satchel *n* cartable *m* (à bandoulière).

sated *adj* [*desire*] assouvi; [*person*] rassasié; [*appetite*] satisfait.

satellite I *n* satellite *m*.
II *noun modifier* [*broadcasting, link*] par satellite; [*town, photograph*] satellite.

satellite: **~ dish** *n* antenne *f* parabolique; **~ TV** *n* télévision *f* par satellite.

satin I *n* satin *m*.
II *noun modifier* [*garment, shoe*] de satin; **with a ~ finish** satiné.

satire *n* satire *f* (**on** sur).

satiric(al) *adj* satirique.

satirist *n* satiriste *mf*.

satirize *vtr* faire la satire de; **to be ~d by** faire l'objet de la satire de.

satisfaction *n* satisfaction *f*; **to get ~ from sth** retirer des satisfactions de qch; **to get ~ from doing sth** éprouver du plaisir à faire qch.

satisfactory *adj* satisfaisant; **to be ~ to sb** convenir à qn; **his work is far from ~** son travail laisse fort à désirer; **her condition was said to be ~** son état a été déclaré satisfaisant.

satisfied *adj* **1** (pleased) satisfait (**with, about** de); **not ~ with this, they...** non contents de cela, ils...; **2** (convinced) convaincu (**by** par; **that** que).

satisfy *vtr* **1** satisfaire [*person, need, desires, curiosity*]; assouvir [*hunger*]; **2** (persuade) convaincre [*person, public opinion*] (**that** que); **3** (meet) satisfaire à [*demand, requirements, conditions*].

satisfying *adj* **1** [*meal*] substantiel/-ielle; **2** [*job*] qui apporte de la satisfaction; [*relationship*] heureux/-euse; **3** [*result, progress*] satisfaisant.

saturate *vtr* saturer (**with** de).

saturated *adj* **1** (wet) [*person, clothes*] trempé; [*ground*] détrempé; **2** [*market*] saturé (**with** de); **3** [*fats*] saturé.

saturation *n* saturation *f*.

saturation point *n* point *m* de saturation; **to reach ~** arriver à saturation.

Saturday ▶584 *n* samedi *m*.

Saturn *pr n* Saturne *f*.

sauce *n* sauce *f*; **orange ~** sauce à l'orange; **tomato ~** sauce tomate.

saucepan *n* casserole *f*.

saucer *n* soucoupe *f*.

Saudi Arabia ▶574 *pr n* Arabie *f* saoudite.

sauerkraut *n* choucroute *f*.

sauna *n* sauna *m*.

saunter *vi* (also **~ along**) marcher d'un pas nonchalant; **to ~ off** s'éloigner d'un pas nonchalant.

sausage *n* (for cooking) saucisse *f*; (ready to eat) saucisson *m*.

savage I *n* sauvage *mf*.
II *adj* **1** [*blow, beating*] violent; [*attack*] sauvage; **2** [*mood, satire*] féroce; [*criticism*] virulent; **a ~ temper** un caractère violent.
III *vtr* [*dog*] attaquer [qn/qch] sauvagement; [*lion*] déchiqueter.

save I *n* (Sport) arrêt *m* de but.
II *vtr* **1** (rescue) sauver (**from** de); **to ~ sb's**

life sauver la vie à qn; **to ~ the day** sauver la situation; **2** (put by, keep) mettre [qch] de côté [*money, food*] (**to do** pour faire); garder [*goods, documents*] (**for** pour); sauvegarder [*data, file*]; **to have money ~d** avoir de l'argent de côté; **to ~ sth for sb, to ~ sb sth** garder qch pour qn; **3** (economize on) économiser [*money, energy*] (**by doing** en faisant); gagner [*time, space*] (**by doing** en faisant); **to ~ one's energy** ménager ses forces; **you'll ~ money/£20** vous ferez des économies/une économie de 20 livres; **it'll ~ us time** cela nous fera gagner du temps; **to ~ sb/sth (from) having to do** éviter à qn/qch de faire; **4** (Sport) arrêter [*penalty*].

III *vi* **1** (put by funds) = **save up**; **2** (economize) économiser, faire des économies; **to ~ on** faire des économies de [*energy, paper*].

■ **save up** faire des économies; **to ~ up for** mettre de l'argent de côté pour s'acheter [*car, house*]; mettre de l'argent de côté pour s'offrir [*holiday*].

saving I *n* économie *f* (**in** de; **on** sur).
II savings *n pl* économies *fpl*; **to live off one's ~s** vivre de ses économies.

saving grace *n* bon côté *m*; **it's his ~** c'est ce qui le sauve.

saving: **~s account** *n* (GB) compte *m* d'épargne; (US) compte *m* rémunéré; **~s bank** *n* caisse *f* d'épargne.

saviour (GB), **savior** (US) *n* sauveur *m*.

savor (US) = **savour**.

savory (US) = **savoury**.

savour (GB), **savor** (US) **I** *n* **1** (flavour) saveur *f*; **2** (figurative) goût *m*.
II *vtr* savourer.

savoury (GB), **savory** (US) *adj* (not sweet) salé; (appetizing) appétissant.

saw I *n* scie *f*; **electric/power ~** scie électrique/mécanique.
II *vtr* scier; **to ~ through/down/off** scier.

sawdust *n* sciure *f* (de bois).

sawn-off shotgun *n* (GB) fusil *m* à canon scié.

saxophone ▶ 753 *n* saxophone *m*.

saxophonist ▶ 805, 753 *n* saxophoniste *mf*.

say I *n* **to have one's ~** dire ce qu'on a à dire (**on** sur); **to have a ~/no ~ in sth** avoir/ne pas avoir son mot à dire sur qch; **to have no ~ in the matter** ne pas avoir voix au chapitre.

II *vtr* **1** [*person*] dire [*words, prayer, hello, no*] (**to** à); **'hello,' he said** 'bonjour,' dit-il; **~ after me...** répète après moi...; **to ~ (that)** dire que; **she said we were to wait** elle a dit que nous devions attendre; **he said to wait here** il a dit d'attendre ici; **as they ~** comme on dit; **I don't care what anyone ~s** je me moque du qu'en-dira-t-on; **they ~ she's very rich, she is said to be very rich** on dit qu'elle est très riche; **to ~ sth about sth/sb** dire qch au sujet de qch/qn; **to ~ sth to oneself** se dire qch; **to ~ whether/who** dire si/qui; **let's ~ no more about it** n'en parlons plus; **it goes without ~ing that** il va sans dire que; **that is to ~** c'est-à-dire; **let's ~ there are 20** mettons or supposons qu'il y en ait 20; **2** [*writer, book, letter, report, map*] dire; [*sign, clock, dial, gauge*] indiquer; **she wrote ~ing she couldn't come** elle a écrit pour dire qu'elle ne pouvait pas venir; **it ~s on the radio/in the rules that** la radio/le règlement dit que; **it ~s here that** il est dit ici que; **3** (guess) dire (**that** que); **that's impossible to ~** c'est impossible à dire; **how high would you ~ it is?** à ton avis, quelle en est la hauteur?; **I'd ~ she was about 25** je lui donnerais environ 25 ans.

III *vi* **stop when I ~** arrête quand je te le dirai; **he wouldn't ~** il n'a pas voulu le dire.

IDIOMS **it doesn't ~ much for their marriage** cela en dit long sur leur mariage; **it ~s a lot for sb/sth** c'est tout à l'honneur de qn/qch; **there's a lot to be said for that method** cette méthode est très intéressante à bien des égards; **when all is said and done** tout compte fait, en fin de compte.

saying *n* dicton *m*; **as the ~ goes** comme on dit.

scab *n* croûte *f*.

scaffolding *n* échafaudage *m*.

scald *vtr* ébouillanter.

scale I *n* **1** (extent) (of disaster, success, violence) étendue *f* (**of** de); (of defeat, recession, task) ampleur *f* (**of** de); (of activity, operation) envergure *f* (**of** de); (of support, change) degré *m* (**of** de); **2** échelle *f*; **pay ~, salary ~** échelle des salaires; **on a ~ of 1 to 10** sur une échelle allant de 1 à 10; **3** (on map, diagram) échelle *f*; **on a large ~** [*map*] à grande échelle; (figurative) sur une grande échelle; **4** (on ruler, gauge) graduation *f*; **5** (for weighing) balance *f*; **6** (Mus) gamme *f*; **7** (on fish, insect) écaille *f*; **8** (deposit) (in kettle, pipes) (dépôt *m*) calcaire *m*; (on teeth) tartre *m*.
II scales *n pl* balance *f*.
III *vtr* **1** escalader [*wall, mountain*]; **2** écailler [*fish*].

scale: **~d-down** *adj* réduit; **~ drawing** *n* dessin *m* à l'échelle; **~ model** *n* maquette *f* à l'échelle.

scallop, **scollop** *n* **1** (Zool) pecten *m*; **2** (Culin) coquille *f* Saint-Jacques.

scalp I *n* cuir *m* chevelu.
II *vtr* scalper.

scamper *vi* **to ~ about** or **around** [*child, dog*] gambader; [*mouse*] trottiner; **to ~ away** or **off** détaler.

scan *vtr* **1** lire rapidement [*page, newspaper*]; **2** (examine) scruter [*face, horizon*]; **3** [*beam of light, radar*] balayer; **4** (Med) faire un scanner de [*organ*].

scandal *n* scandale *m*; **the Grunard ~** l'affaire *f* Grunard.

scandalize *vtr* scandaliser.

scandalous *adj* scandaleux/-euse.

Scandinavia *pr n* Scandinavie *f*.

scanty *adj* [*meal, supply*] maigre (*before n*); [*information*] sommaire; [*knowledge*] rudimentaire; [*swimsuit*] minuscule; [*report*] succinct.

scapegoat *n* bouc *m* émissaire (**for** de).

scar I *n* cicatrice *f*; (on face from knife) balafre *f*.
II *vtr* marquer; (on face with knife) balafrer; **to ~ sb for life** laisser à qn une cicatrice permanente; (figurative) marquer qn pour la vie.

scarce *adj* rare; **to become ~** se faire rare.

scarcely *adv* à peine; **~ anybody believes it** presque personne ne le croit.

scarcity *n* **1** (dearth) pénurie *f* (**of** de); **2** (rarity) rareté *f* (**of** de).

scare I *n* **1** peur *f*; **to give sb a ~** faire peur à qn; **2** (alert) alerte *f*; **bomb ~** alerte à la bombe.
II *vtr* faire peur à.
■ **scare away, scare off**: **~ away [sth/sb], ~ [sth/sb] away** faire fuir [*animal, attacker*]; (figurative) dissuader.

scarecrow *n* épouvantail *m*.

scared *adj* [*animal, person*] effrayé; [*look*] apeuré; **to be** or **feel ~** avoir peur; **to be ~ about sth** craindre qch; **to be ~ stiff**○ avoir une peur bleue○.

scarf *n* (long) écharpe *f*; (square) foulard *m*.

scarlet ▶559| *n, adj* écarlate (*f*).

scarlet fever ▶686| *n* scarlatine *f*.

scathing *adj* [*remark, report, tone, wit*] cinglant; [*criticism*] virulent.

scatter I *vtr* **1** (also **~ around, ~ about**) répandre [*seeds, earth*]; éparpiller [*books, papers, clothes*]; disperser [*debris*]; **to be ~ed around** être éparpillé; **2** disperser [*crowd, herd*].
II *vi* [*people, animals, birds*] se disperser.

scatter-brained *adj* [*person*] étourdi; [*idea*] farfelu○.

scattered *adj* [*houses, trees, population, clouds*] épars; [*books, litter*] éparpillé; [*support, resistance*] clairsemé; **~ showers** averses *fpl* intermittentes.

scavenge I *vtr* récupérer (**from** dans).
II *vi* **to ~ for food** [*bird, animal*] chercher de la nourriture.

scavenger *n* **1** (animal) charognard *m*; **2** (person) (for food) faiseur *m* de poubelles; (for objects) récupérateur *m*.

scenario *n* scénario *m*; (figurative) cas *m* de figure.

scene *n* **1** scène *f*; **behind the ~s** dans les coulisses *fpl*; **you need a change of ~** tu as besoin de changer de décor; **the jazz ~** le monde du jazz; **there were ~s of violence after the match** il y a eu des incidents violents après le match; **2** (of crime, accident) lieu *m*; **at** or **on the ~** sur les lieux; **3** (image, sight) image *f*; **4** (view) vue *f*.

scenery *n* **1** (landscape) paysage *m*; **2** (in theatre) décors *mpl*.

scenic *adj* [*drive, route, walk*] panoramique; [*location*] pittoresque.

scent I *n* **1** (smell) odeur *f*; **2** (perfume) parfum *m*; **3** (body smell) (of animal) fumet *m*; (in hunting) piste *f*.
II *vtr* **1** flairer [*prey, animal*]; **2** pressentir [*danger, trouble*]; **3** (perfume) parfumer [*air*].

scented *adj* parfumé (**with** de).

sceptic (GB), **skeptic** (US) *n* sceptique *mf*.

sceptical (GB), **skeptical** (US) *adj* sceptique (**about, of** en ce qui concerne).

scepticism (GB), **skepticism** (US) *n* scepticisme *m*.

schedule I *n* **1** programme *m*; (timetable) horaire *m*; **to be ahead of/behind ~** être en avance/en retard; (with work) avoir de l'avance/être en retard dans son travail; [*project*] être en avance/en retard sur les prévisions; **to be on ~** progresser comme prévu; **to fit sb/sth into one's ~** intégrer qn/qch dans son programme; **2 to arrive on/ahead of ~** arriver à l'heure/en avance; **3** (of prices, charges) barème *m*.
II *vtr* (plan) prévoir; (arrange) programmer; **the plane is ~d to arrive at 2.00** l'avion est attendu à 2 heures.

scheduled flight *n* vol *m* régulier.

scheme I *n* **1** projet *m*, plan *m* (**to do, for doing** pour faire); **insurance/pension ~** régime *m* d'assurances/de retraite; **2** (plot) combine *f* (**to do** pour faire).
II *vi* comploter (**to do** pour faire; **against sb** contre qn).

scheming I *n* machinations *fpl*.
II *adj* [*person*] intrigant.

scholar *n* érudit/-e *m/f*; **Hebrew ~** spécialiste *mf* de l'hébreu.

scholarship *n* bourse *f* (**to** pour).

school I *n* **1** école *f*; **at ~** à l'école; **to go to medical/law ~** faire des études de médecine/droit; **2** (US) (university) université *f*; **3** (of fish) banc *m*.
II *noun modifier* [*holiday, outing, uniform, year*] scolaire.

school: **~boy** *n* (pupil) élève *m*; (primary) écolier *m*; (secondary) collégien *m*; **~ bus** *n* car *m* scolaire; **~child** *n* écolier/-ière *m/f*; **~ fees** *n pl* frais *mpl* de scolarité; **~friend** *n* camarade *mf* de classe; **~girl** *n* (pupil) élève *f*; (primary) écolière *f*; (secondary) collégienne *f*; **~ inspector** ▶805| *n* inspecteur/-trice *m/f*; **~-leaver** *n* (GB) jeune *mf* ayant fini sa scolarité; **~ leaving age** *n* âge *m* de fin de scolarité; **~ report** (GB), **~ report card** (US) *n* bulletin *m* scolaire; **~room** *n* salle *f* de classe; **~teacher** ▶805| *n* enseignant/-e *m/f*; (primary) instituteur/-trice *m/f*; (secondary) professeur *m*; **~work** *n* travail *m* de classe.

science I *n* science *f*; **to study ~** étudier les sciences.
II *noun modifier* [*exam*] scientifique; [*department*] des sciences; [*teacher, textbook*] de sciences.

science fiction *n* science-fiction *f*.

scientific *adj* scientifique.

scientist ▶805| *n* scientifique *mf*; (eminent) savant *m*.

scissors *n pl* ciseaux *mpl*.

scoff I○ *vtr* (GB) engloutir○, bouffer○.
II *vi* se moquer (**at** de).

scold I *vtr* gronder (**for doing** pour avoir fait).
II *vi* râler○.

scoop I *n* **1** (for measuring) mesure *f*; **2** (of ice cream) boule *f*; **3** (in journalism) exclusivité *f*.
II○ *vtr* décrocher○ [*prize, sum of money, story*].
■ **scoop out**: **~ out [sth], ~ [sth] out** creuser; **to ~ the flesh out of a tomato** évider une tomate.

scooter *n* **1** (child's) trottinette *f*; **2** (motorized) scooter *m*.

scope *n* **1** (opportunity) possibilité *f* (**for** de); **there is ~ for sb to do** il y a des possibilités pour qn de faire; **2** (of inquiry, report, book) portée *f*; (of plan) envergure *f*; **the research is broad in ~** le champ de la recherche est large; **3** (of person) compétences *fpl*.

scorch I *n* (also **~ mark**) légère brûlure *f*.
II *vtr* [*fire*] brûler; [*sun*] dessécher [*grass, trees*]; griller [*lawn*]; [*iron*] roussir [*fabric*].

score I *n* **1** (Sport) score *m*; (in cards) marque *f*; **to keep (the) ~** marquer les points; (in cards) tenir la marque; **2** (in exam, test) note *f*, résultat *m*; **3** (Mus) (written music) partition *f*; (for ballet) musique *f* (du ballet); (for film) musique *f* (du film); **4** (twenty) **a ~** vingt *m*, une vingtaine *f*; **by the ~** à la pelle; **5 on this** or **that ~** à ce sujet.
II *vtr* **1** marquer [*goal, point*]; remporter [*victory, success*]; **to ~ 9 out of 10** avoir 9 sur 10; **2** (cut) entailler.
III *vi* (gain point) marquer un point; (obtain goal) marquer un but.
IDIOMS **to settle a ~** régler ses comptes.
■ **score off**: **~ off [sth], ~ [sth] off** rayer.

scoreboard *n* tableau *m* d'affichage.

scorn *n* mépris *m* (**for** pour); **to pour** or **heap ~ on** accabler [qn] de mépris [*person*]; dénigrer [*attempt, argument*].

scornful *adj* méprisant; **to be ~ of** manifester du mépris pour.

Scorpio *n* Scorpion *m*; ▶ **Aquarius**.

Scot ▶ 712 *n* Écossais/-e *m/f*.

Scotch I *n* (also **~ whisky**) whisky *m*, scotch *m*.
II *adj* écossais.

Scotch tape® *n* (US) scotch® *m*.

Scotland ▶ 574 *pr n* Écosse *f*.

Scottish ▶ 712 *adj* écossais.

scour *vtr* **1** (scrub) récurer; **2** (search) parcourir [*area, list*] (**for** à la recherche de); **to ~ the shops for sth** faire le tour des magasins à la recherche de qch.

scourge *n* fléau *m*.

scout *n* **1** (also **boy ~**) scout *m*; **2** (Mil) éclaireur *m*; **3** (also **talent ~**) découvreur/-euse *m/f* de nouveaux talents.
■ **scout around** explorer; **to ~ around for sth** rechercher qch.

scowl I *n* air *m* renfrogné; **with a ~** d'un air renfrogné.
II *vi* prendre un air renfrogné.

scramble I *n* **1** (rush) course *f* (**for** pour; **to do** pour faire); **2** (climb) escalade *f*.
II *vtr* **to ~ eggs** faire des œufs brouillés.
III *vi* **1 to ~ up** escalader; **to ~ down** dégringoler.

scrambled egg *n* (also **~s** *n pl*) œufs *mpl* brouillés.

scrap I *n* **1** (of paper, cloth) petit morceau *m*; (cutting) coupure *f*; **there wasn't a ~ of evidence** il n'y avait pas la moindre preuve; **2** (old iron) ferraille *f*; **to sell sth for ~** vendre qch à la ferraille.
II **scraps** *n pl* (of food) restes *mpl*; (from butcher's) déchets *mpl*.
III *vtr* **1**○ abandonner [*idea, plan, system*]; **2** détruire [*aircraft, equipment*].

scrap: **~book** *n* album *m*; **~ dealer** *n* = **scrap metal dealer**.

scrape I *n* **to get into a ~**○ s'attirer des ennuis.
II *vtr* **1** gratter [*vegetables, shoes*]; **to ~ sth clean** nettoyer qch en le grattant; **2** érafler [*car, paintwork, furniture*]; **3 to ~ one's knees** s'écorcher les genoux.
III *vi* **1 to ~ against sth** (rub) frotter contre qch; (scratch) érafler qch; **2** (economize) économiser le moindre sou.
IDIOMS **to ~ the bottom of the barrel** être à court d'idées (or d'imagination or de personnes qualifiées etc).
■ **scrape by** (financially) s'en sortir à peine; (in situation) s'en tirer de justesse.
■ **scrape off**: **~ off [sth], ~ [sth] off** enlever [qch] en grattant.
■ **scrape through**: ¶ **~ through** s'en tirer de justesse; ¶ **~ through sth** réussir de justesse à qch [*exam, test*].

scrap: **~ iron, ~ metal** *n* ferraille *f*; **~ metal dealer** ▶ 805 *n* ferrailleur *m*; **~ paper** *n* papier *m* brouillon; **~ yard** *n* chantier *m* de ferraille, casse *f*.

scratch I *n* **1** (on skin) égratignure *f*; (from a claw, fingernail) griffure *f*; **2** (on metal, furniture) éraflure *f*; (on record, glass) rayure *f*; **3** (sound) grattement *m*; **4**○ **he/his work is not up to ~** il/son travail n'est pas à la hauteur; **5 to start from ~** partir de zéro.
II *vtr* **1 to ~ one's initials on sth** graver ses initiales sur qch; **2** [*cat, person*] griffer; [*thorns, rose bush*] égratigner; **to ~ sb's eyes out** arracher les yeux à quelqu'un; **3 to ~ sb's back** gratter le dos de qn; **to ~ an itch** se gratter; **to ~ one's head** se gratter la tête; (figurative) être perplexe; **4** érafler [*car, wood*]; rayer [*record*]; [*cat*] se faire les griffes sur [*furniture*].
III *vi* se gratter.

scrawl I *n* gribouillage *m*.
II *vtr, vi* gribouiller.

scrawny *adj* [*person, animal*] décharné; [*vegetation*] maigre.

scream I *n* **1** (of person, animal) cri *m* (perçant); (stronger) hurlement *m*; **~s of laughter** éclats *mpl* de rire; **2** (of brakes) grincement *m*; (of tyres) crissement *m*.
II *vtr* crier.
III *vi* crier; (stronger) hurler; **to ~ at sb** crier après qn○; **to ~ with** hurler de [*fear, pain, rage*]; pousser des cris de [*pleasure*].

screech I *n* (of person, animal) cri *m* strident; (of tyres) crissement *m*.
II *vtr* hurler.
III *vi* [*person, animal*] pousser un cri strident; [*tyres*] crisser.

screen I *n* **1** (on TV, VDU, at cinema) écran *m*; **2** (furniture) paravent *m*; (partition) cloison *f* mobile; **3** (US) (in door) grille *f*.
II *vtr* **1** (at cinema) projeter; (on TV) diffuser; **2** (conceal) cacher; (protect) protéger (**from** de); **3** (test) examiner le cas de [*applicants, candidates*]; contrôler [*baggage*]; **4 to ~ sb for cancer** faire passer à qn des tests de dépistage du cancer.
▪ **screen off**: **~ off [sth], ~ [sth] off** isoler [*part of room, garden*].

screenplay *n* scénario *m*.

screw I *n* vis *f*.
II *vtr* visser (**into** dans); **to ~ sth onto** or **to a door** visser qch sur une porte.
▪ **screw down**: **~ [sth] down, ~ down [sth]** visser (à fond).
▪ **screw on**: **~ [sth] on, ~ on [sth]** visser.
▪ **screw together**: **~ [sth] together, ~ together [sth]** assembler [qch] avec des vis.
▪ **screw up**: ¶ **~ [sth] up, ~ up [sth] 1** froisser [*piece of paper, material*]; **to ~ up one's eyes** plisser les yeux; **to ~ up one's face** faire la grimace; **2**° faire foirer° [*plan, task*]; **3 to ~ up the courage to do** trouver le courage de faire; ¶ **~ [sb] up**° perturber° [*person*]; **~ed up**° perturbé°.

screwdriver *n* **1** (tool) tournevis *m*; **2** (cocktail) vodka-orange *f*.

screw-in *adj* [*light bulb*] à vis.

scribble *vtr, vi* griffonner, gribouiller.
▪ **scribble down**: **~ [sth] down, ~ down [sth]** griffonner.

scrimp *vi* économiser; **to ~ and save** se priver de tout.

script *n* **1** (for film, radio, TV) script *m*; (for play) texte *m*; **2** (GB Sch, Univ) copie *f* (d'examen).

scripture *n* (also **Holy Scripture, Holy Scriptures**) (Christian) Écritures *fpl*; (other) textes *mpl* sacrés.

scriptwriter ▶ 805 *n* scénariste *mf*.

scroll *n* rouleau *m*.

scrub I *n* **1** (clean) **to give sth a (good) ~** (bien) nettoyer qch; **2** (Bot) broussailles *fpl*.
II *vtr* frotter [*back, clothes*]; récurer [*pan, floor*]; nettoyer [*vegetable*]; **to ~ one's nails/hands** se brosser les ongles/les mains.
▪ **scrub up** [*doctor*] se stériliser les mains.

scrubbing brush, scrub brush (US) *n* brosse *f* de ménage.

scruff *n* **by the ~ of the neck** par la peau du cou.

scruffy *adj* [*clothes, person*] dépenaillé; [*flat, town*] délabré.

scrum, scrummage *n* (in rugby) mêlée *f*.

scruple *n* scrupule *m* (**about** vis-à-vis de).

scrupulous *adj* scrupuleux/-euse.

scrutinize *vtr* scruter [*face, motives*]; examiner [qch] minutieusement [*document, plan*]; vérifier [*accounts, votes*]; surveiller [*activity, election*].

scrutiny *n* examen *m*; **close ~** examen approfondi; **to come under ~** être examiné.

scuba diving ▶ 649 *n* plongée *f* sous-marine.

scuff I *n* (also **~ mark**) (on floor, furniture) rayure *f*; (on leather) éraflure *f*.
II *vtr* érafler [*shoes*]; rayer [*floor, furniture*].

scuffle *n* bagarre *f*.

scullery *n* (GB) arrière-cuisine *f*.

sculpt *vtr, vi* sculpter.

sculptor ▶ 805 *n* sculpteur *m*.

sculpture *n* sculpture *f*.

scum *n* **1** (on pond) écume *f*; **2** (on liquid) mousse *f*; **3 they're the ~ of the earth** c'est de la racaille.

scuttle I *vtr* **1** saborder [*ship*]; **2** faire échouer [*talks, project*].
II *vi* **to ~ away** or **off** filer; **to ~ across sth** traverser qch à toute vitesse.

scythe *n* faux *f inv*.

sea I *n* mer *f*; **beside** or **by the ~** au bord de la mer; **the open ~** le large; **to be at ~** être en mer; **to put (out) to ~, to go to ~** prendre la mer; **a long way out to ~** très loin de la côte; **by ~** [*travel*] en bateau; [*send*] par bateau.
II *noun modifier* [*air, breeze*] marin; [*bird, water*] de mer; [*crossing, voyage*] par mer; [*battle*] naval; [*power*] maritime.

sea: **~ anemone** *n* anémone *f* de mer; **~bed** *n* fonds *mpl* marins; **~food** *n* fruits *mpl* de mer; **~front** *n* front *m* de mer; **~gull** *n* mouette *f*; **~ horse** *n* hippocampe *m*.

seal I *n* **1** (Zool) phoque *m*; **2** (stamp) sceau *m*; **to give sth one's ~ of approval** approuver qch; **3** (on container) plomb *m*; (on package, letter) cachet *m*; (on door) scellés *mpl*.
II *vtr* **1** cacheter [*document*]; **~ed with wax** cacheté à la cire; **2** fermer, cacheter [*envelope*]; **3** fermer [qch] hermétiquement [*jar, tin*]; rendre [qch] étanche [*window frame*]; **4** sceller [*alliance, friendship*] (**with** par); conclure [*deal*] (**with** par); **to ~ sb's fate** décider du sort de qn.
▪ **seal off**: **~ [sth] off, ~ off [sth]** isoler [*corridor, ward*]; boucler [*area, building*]; barrer [*street*].

sea: **~ level** *n* niveau *m* de la mer; **~ lion** *n* lion *m* de mer.

seam *n* couture *f*; **to be bursting at the ~s** [*suitcase*] être plein à craquer; **to come apart at the ~** [*garment, marriage*] craquer.

seaplane *n* hydravion *m*.

search I *n* **1** (for person, object) recherches *fpl* (**for sb/sth** pour retrouver qn/qch); **in ~ of** à la recherche de; **2** (of place) fouille *f* (**of** de); **to carry out a ~ of sth** fouiller qch; **3** (Comput) recherche *f*.
II *vtr* **1** fouiller [*area, building*]; fouiller dans [*cupboard, drawer, memory*]; **2** examiner (attentivement) [*page, map, records*].
III *vi* **1** chercher; **to ~ for** or **after sb/sth**

chercher qn/qch; **to ~ through** fouiller dans [*cupboard, bag*]; examiner [*records, file*]; **2** (Comput) **to ~ for** rechercher [*data, file*].

searching *adj* [*look, question*] pénétrant.

search: **~light** *n* projecteur *m*; **~ party** *n* équipe *f* de secours; **~ warrant** *n* mandat *m* de perquisition.

sea: **~ salt** *n* sel *m* de mer; **~shell** *n* coquillage *m*; **~shore** *n* (part of coast) littoral *m*; (beach) plage *f*.

seasick *adj* **to be** or **get** or **feel ~** avoir le mal de mer.

seasickness *n* mal *m* de mer.

seaside I *n* **the ~** le bord de la mer.
II *noun modifier* [*hotel*] en bord de mer; [*town*] maritime; **~ resort** station *f* balnéaire.

season I *n* saison *f*; **strawberries are in/out of ~** c'est/ce n'est pas la saison des fraises; **out of ~** hors saison; **the holiday ~** la période des vacances; **Season's greetings!** Joyeuses fêtes!
II *vtr* **1** (with spices) relever; (with condiments) assaisonner; **~ with salt and pepper** salez et poivrez; **2** sécher [*timber*].

seasonal *adj* [*work, change*] saisonnier/-ière; [*fruit, produce*] de saison.

seasoned *adj* **1** [*timber*] bien séché; **2** [*soldier*] aguerri; [*politician, leader*] chevronné; [*campaigner, performer*] expérimenté; **3** [*dish*] assaisonné; **highly ~** relevé, épicé.

seasoning *n* assaisonnement *m*.

season ticket *n* (for travel) carte *f* d'abonnement; (for theatre, matches) abonnement *m*.

seat I *n* **1** siège *m*; (bench-type) banquette *f*; **the back ~** la banquette arrière; **2** (place) place *f*; **take** or **have a ~** asseyez-vous; **to book a ~** réserver une place; **a ~ next to the window** (on plane) une place côté hublot; **3** (GB) (in politics) siège *m*; **to have a ~ on the council** siéger au conseil; **4** (centre) siège *m*; **~ of government** siège du gouvernement; **5** (of trousers) fond *m*.
II *vtr* **1** placer [*person*]; **2 the car ~s five** c'est une voiture à cinq places; **the table ~s six** c'est une table de six couverts; **the room ~s 30 people** la salle peut accueillir 30 personnes.

seatbelt *n* ceinture *f* (de sécurité).

-seater *combining form* **a two~** (plane) un avion *m* à deux places; (car) un coupé; (sofa) un (canapé) deux places; **all~ stadium** (GB) stade *m* sans places debout.

seating *n* **1** (chairs) sièges *mpl*; (places) places *fpl* assises; **2** (arrangement) **I'll organize the ~** je placerai les gens.

sea: **~ urchin** *n* oursin *m*; **~weed** *n* algue *f* marine.

secateurs *n pl* (GB) sécateur *m*.

secluded *adj* retiré.

seclusion *n* isolement *m* (**from** à l'écart de).

second ▶554, 584, 642 I *n* **1** (in order) deuxième *mf*, second/-e *m/f*; **2** (unit of time) seconde *f*; (instant) instant *m*; **they should arrive any ~ now** ils devraient arriver d'un instant à l'autre; **3** (of month) deux *m inv*; **the ~ of May** le deux mai; **4** (also **~ gear**) (Aut) deuxième *f*, seconde *f*; **5** (defective article) article *m* qui a un défaut; **6** (also **~-class honours degree**) (GB Univ) ≈ licence *f* avec mention bien.
II *adj* deuxième, second; **the ~ teeth** les dents définitives; **every ~ Monday** un lundi sur deux; **to have a ~ helping (of sth)** reprendre (de qch); **to have a ~ chance to do sth** avoir une nouvelle chance de faire; **to ask for a ~ opinion** (from doctor) demander l'opinion d'un autre médecin.
III *adv* **1** (in second place) deuxième; **to come** or **finish ~** arriver deuxième; **I agreed to speak ~** j'ai accepté de parler le deuxième; **the ~ biggest building** le deuxième bâtiment de par sa grandeur; **2** (also **secondly**) deuxièmement.
IV *vtr* (in debate) appuyer [*proposal*].
IDIOMS **to be ~ nature** être automatique; **to be ~ to none** être sans pareil; **on ~ thoughts** à la réflexion; **to have ~ thoughts** avoir quelques hésitations or doutes.

secondary *adj* secondaire.

secondary school *n* ≈ école *f* secondaire.

second best *n* **to settle for ~** se contenter de pis-aller.

second class I **second-class** *adj* **1** [*post, stamp*] au tarif lent; **2** [*carriage, ticket*] de deuxième classe; **3** (second-rate) de qualité inférieure; **~ citizen** citoyen/-enne *m/f* de seconde zone.
II *adv* [*travel*] en deuxième classe; [*send*] au tarif lent.

second hand I *n* (on watch, clock) trotteuse *f*.
II **second-hand** *adj* [*clothes, car*] d'occasion; [*news, information*] de seconde main; **~ dealer** vendeur/-euse *m/f* d'objets d'occasion; **~ car dealer** vendeur/-euse *m/f* de voitures d'occasion.
III *adv* [*buy*] d'occasion; [*find out, hear*] indirectement.

second in command *n* **1** (Mil) commandant *m* en second; **2** (deputy) second *m*, adjoint *m*.

secondly *adv* deuxièmement.

second: **~ name** *n* (surname) nom *m* de famille; **~-rate** *adj* [*actor, novel*] de second ordre.

secrecy *n* secret *m*; **she's been sworn to ~** on lui a fait jurer le secret.

secret I *n* secret *m*; **to tell sb a ~** confier un secret à qn; **to let sb in on a ~** mettre qn dans le secret.
II *adj* [*passage, ingredient, admiration*] secret/-ète; **to keep sth ~ from sb** cacher qch à qn.
III **in secret** *phr* en secret.

secretarial *adj* [*course, skills, work*] de secrétaire; [*college*] de secrétariat; **~ staff** personnel *m* de secrétariat.

secretary ▶805 *n* **1** (assistant) secrétaire *mf* (**to sb** de qn); **2** (GB) **Foreign/Home Secretary** ministre *m* des Affaires étrangères/de l'Intérieur; **Secretary of State for the Environment** ministre *m* de l'Environnement; **3** (US) **Defense Secretary** ministre *m* de la Défense;

Secretary of State ministre *m* des Affaires étrangères.

secretive *adj* [*person, organization*] secret/-ète; **to be ~ about sth** faire un mystère de qch.

secret: **~ police** *n* police *f* secrète; **~ service** *n* services *mpl* secrets.

sect *n* secte *f*.

sectarian *n, adj* sectaire (*mf*).

section *n* **1** (of train, aircraft, town, forest) partie *f*; (of pipe, tunnel, road) tronçon *m*; (of object, kit) élément *m*; (of fruit) quartier *m*; (of population) tranche *f*; **2** (of company, department) service *m*; (of library, shop) rayon *m*; **3** (of act, bill, report) article *m*; (of newspaper) rubrique *f*; **under ~ 24** aux termes de l'article 24; **4** (of book) passage *m* (**on** sur); (larger) partie *f* (**on** qui traite de).

sector *n* secteur *m*.

secular *adj* [*politics, society, education*] laïque; [*belief, music*] profane.

secure I *adj* **1** [*job, marriage, income*] stable; [*basis, base*] solide; **2** [*hiding place*] sûr; **3** [*padlock, knot*] solide; [*structure, ladder*] stable; [*rope*] bien attaché; [*door, window*] bien fermé; **4** [*family, background*] sécurisant; **to feel ~** se sentir en sécurité.

II *vtr* **1** obtenir [*promise, release, right, victory*]; **2** bien attacher [*rope*]; bien fermer [*door, window*]; fixer [*wheel*]; stabiliser [*ladder*]; **3** protéger [*house*]; assurer [*position, future*]; **4** garantir [*loan, debt*] (**against, on** sur).

securities *n pl* titres *mpl*.

security I *n* **1** sécurité *f*; **~ of employment, job ~** sécurité de l'emploi; **state** or **national ~** sûreté *f* de l'État; **2** (department) service *m* de sécurité; **3** (guarantee) garantie *f* (**on** sur); **to stand ~ for sb** se porter garant de qn.

II *noun modifier* [*camera, check, measures*] de sécurité; [*firm, staff*] de surveillance.

security: **~ guard** ▶805 *n* garde *m* sécurité, vigile *m*; **~ van** *n* (GB) fourgon *m* blindé.

sedate I *adj* [*person*] posé; [*lifestyle, pace*] tranquille.

II *vtr* mettre [qn] sous calmants [*patient*].

sedation *n* sédation *f*; **under ~** sous calmants.

sedative *n* sédatif *m*, calmant *m*.

seduce *vtr* séduire.

seductive *adj* [*person*] séduisant; [*smile*] aguicheur/-euse.

see I *vtr* **1** voir; **can you see him?** est-ce que tu le vois?; **I can't ~ him** je ne le vois pas; **I could ~ she'd been crying** je voyais bien qu'elle avait pleuré; **I don't know what you ~ in him**○ je ne sais pas ce que tu lui trouves○; **I must be ~ing things!** j'ai des visions!; **I'm ~ing a psychiatrist** je vais chez un psychiatre; **to ~ the sights** faire du tourisme; **they ~ a lot of each other** ils se voient souvent; **~ you next week!** à la semaine prochaine!; **do you ~ what I mean?** tu vois ce que je veux dire?; **to ~ sb as** considérer qn comme [*friend, hero*]; **it remains to be seen whether** or **if** reste à voir si; **I can't ~ the situation changing/him agreeing** je ne pense pas que la situation puisse changer/qu'il soit d'accord; **2** (make sure) **to ~ (to it) that** veiller à ce que (+ *subj*); **~ (to it) that the children are in bed by nine** veillez à ce que les enfants soient couchés à neuf heures; **3** (accompany) **to ~ sb to the station** accompagner qn à la gare; **to ~ sb home** raccompagner qn chez lui/elle.

II *vi* **1** voir; **I can't ~** je ne vois rien; **so I ~** c'est ce que je vois; **you can ~ for miles** on y voit à des kilomètres; **2 I'll go and ~** je vais voir; **we'll just have to wait and ~** il ne nous reste plus qu'à attendre; **let's ~, let me ~** voyons (un peu).

■ **see off**: **~ [sb] off, ~ [off] sb** dire au revoir à qn.

■ **see out**: **~ [sb] out** raccompagner [qn] à la porte; **I'll ~ myself out** je m'en vais mais ne vous dérangez pas.

■ **see through**: ¶ **~ through [sth]** déceler [*deception, lie*]; ¶ **~ through [sb]** percer [qn] à jour; ¶ **~ [sth] through** mener [qch] à bonne fin.

■ **see to**: **~ to [sth]** s'occuper de.

seed *n* **1** (of plant) graine *f*; (fruit pip) pépin *m*; **2** (for sowing) semences *fpl*; (Culin) graines *fpl*; **to go to ~** [*plant*] monter en graine; [*person*] se ramollir; [*organization, country*] être en déclin; **3** (Sport) tête *f* de série; **the top ~** la tête de série numéro un.

seedless *adj* sans pépins.

seedling *n* plant *m*.

seedy *adj* [*person*] louche; [*area, club*] mal famé.

seek *vtr* **1** chercher [*agreement, refuge, solution*]; demander [*advice, help, permission*]; **to ~ revenge** chercher à se venger; **2** [*police, employer*] rechercher [*person*].

■ **seek out**: **~ out [sth/sb], ~ [sth/sb] out** aller chercher, dénicher.

seem *vi* sembler; **it ~s that** il semble que (+ *subj*); **it ~s to me that** il me semble que (+ *indic*); **he ~s happy/disappointed** il a l'air heureux/déçu; **it ~s odd (to me)** ça (me) paraît bizarre; **he ~s to be looking for someone** on dirait qu'il cherche quelqu'un; **things are not always what they ~** les apparences sont souvent trompeuses; **it ~ed like a good idea at the time** cela avait l'air d'une bonne idée; **what ~s to be the problem?** quel est le problème?; **he can't ~ to relax** on dirait qu'il n'arrive pas à se détendre.

seep *vi* suinter; **to ~ away** s'écouler; **to ~ through sth** [*water, gas*] s'infiltrer à travers qch; [*light*] filtrer à travers qch.

seesaw *n* tapecul *m*.

seethe *vi* **1 to ~ with rage** [*person*] bouillir de colère; **he was seething** il était furibond; **2** (teem) grouiller; **the streets were seething with tourists** les rues grouillaient de touristes.

see-through *adj* transparent.

segment *n* **1** segment *m*; **2** (of orange) quartier *m*.

segregate *vtr* **1** (separate) séparer (**from** de); **2** (isolate) isoler (**from** de).

segregated *adj* [*education, society*] ségrégationniste; [*area, school*] où la ségrégation raciale (or religieuse) est en vigueur; [*facilities*] séparé.

segregation *n* ségrégation *f* (**from** de); (of prisoners) isolement *m*.

seize *vtr* **1** saisir; **to ~ hold of** se saisir de [*person*]; s'emparer de [*object*]; **2** s'emparer de [*territory, prisoner, power*]; prendre [*control*].
■ **seize up** [*engine*] se gripper; [*limb*] se bloquer.

seizure *n* **1** (of territory, power) prise *f*; (of arms, drugs, property) saisie *f*; **2** (Med) attaque *f*.

seldom *adv* rarement; **~ if ever** rarement, pour ne pas dire jamais.

select I *adj* [*group*] privilégié; [*hotel*] chic *inv*, sélect; [*area*] chic *inv*, cossu.
II *vtr* sélectionner (**from, from among** parmi).
III **selected** *pp adj* [*ingredients*] de premier choix; **in ~ed stores** dans certains magasins.

selection *n* sélection *f*.

selective *adj* **1** [*memory, recruitment*] sélectif/-ive; [*education*] élitiste, basé sur la sélection; **2** [*account*] tendancieux/-ieuse.

self *n* moi *m*; **he's back to his old ~ again** il est redevenu lui-même.

self: **~-addressed envelope**, **SAE** *n* enveloppe *f* à mon/votre etc adresse; **~-adhesive** *adj* autocollant; **~-analysis** *n* auto-analyse *f*; **~-assembly** *adj* en kit.

self-assured *adj* plein d'assurance; **to be very ~** avoir beaucoup d'assurance.

self-awareness *n* conscience *f* de soi/de lui-même etc.

self-catering *adj* (GB) [*flat*] meublé; **~ holiday** vacances *fpl* en location.

self: **~-centred** (GB), **~-centered** (US) *adj* égocentrique; **~-confessed** *adj* avoué; **~-confidence** *n* assurance *f*; **~-confident** *adj* [*person*] sûr de soi/de lui etc; [*attitude*] plein d'assurance.

self-conscious *adj* **1** (shy) timide; **to be ~ about sth/about doing** être gêné par qch/de faire; **2** [*style*] conscient; **3** (aware) conscient de ma/sa etc personne.

self: **~-control** *n* sang-froid *m*; **~-defence** (GB), **~-defense** (US) *n* (gen) autodéfense *f*; (Law) légitime défense *f*; **~-destruct** *vi* s'autodétruire; **~-destructive** *adj* autodestructeur/-trice; **~-disciplined** *adj* autodiscipliné; **~-effacing** *adj* effacé.

self-employed I *n* **the ~** les travailleurs *mpl* indépendants.
II *adj* indépendant; **to be ~** travailler à son compte.

self: **~-esteem** *n* amour-propre *m*; **~-evident** *adj* évident; **~-explanatory** *adj* explicite; **~-important** *adj* suffisant; **~-imposed** *adj* auto-imposé; **~-indulgence** *n* complaisance *f*; **~-indulgent** *adj* complaisant; **~-interest** *n* intérêt *m* personnel; **~-interested** *adj* intéressé.

selfish *adj* égoïste (**to do** de faire); **it was ~ of him** c'était égoïste de sa part.

selfishness *n* égoïsme *m*.

self: **~-pity** *n* apitoiement *m* sur soi-même; **~-portrait** *n* autoportrait *m*; **~-preservation** *n* autoconservation *f*; **~-raising flour** (GB), **~-rising flour** (US) *n* farine *f* à gâteau; **~-reliant** *adj* autosuffisant; **~-respect** *n* respect *m* de soi/de lui-même etc; **~-respecting** *adj* [*teacher, journalist, comedian*] qui se respecte; **~-righteous** *adj* satisfait de soi/de lui-même etc; **~-rule** *n* autonomie *f*; **~-sacrifice** *n* abnégation *f*; **~-satisfied** *adj* satisfait de soi/de lui-même etc.

self-service I *n* libre-service *m*.
II *adj* [*cafeteria*] en libre-service.

self: **~-sufficient** *adj* autosuffisant (**in** en matière de); **~-taught** *adj* autodidacte.

sell I *vtr* **1** vendre; **to ~ sth to sb**, **to ~ sb sth** vendre qch à qn; **to ~ sth at** or **for £5 each** vendre qch 5 livres sterling pièce; **the novel has sold millions (of copies)** le roman s'est vendu à des millions d'exemplaires; **2** (promote sale of) faire vendre; **her name will help to ~ the film** son nom aidera à promouvoir le film; **3** faire accepter [*idea, image, policy, party*].
II *vi* **1** [*person, shop, dealer*] vendre (**to sb** à qn); **2** [*goods, product, house, book*] se vendre; **the new model is/isn't ~ing (well)** le nouveau modèle se vend bien/mal.
III *v refl* **to ~ oneself** se vendre.
■ **sell out 1** [*merchandise*] se vendre; **we've sold out of tickets** tous les billets ont été vendus; **sorry, we've sold out** désolé, mais nous avons tout vendu; **2** (in theatre, cinema) **the play has sold out** la pièce affiche complet; **3**° (betray one's principles) retourner sa veste°.

sell-by date *n* date *f* limite de vente.

selling I *n* vente *f*; **telephone ~** vente par téléphone.
II *noun modifier* [*price*] de vente.

Sellotape® I *n* scotch® *m*.
II **sellotape** *vtr* scotcher.

sellout *n* **the show was a ~** le spectacle affichait complet; **the product has been a ~** le produit s'est très bien vendu.

selvage, **selvedge** *n* lisière *f*.

semen *n* sperme *m*.

semester *n* (US) semestre *m*.

semi: **~automatic** *n, adj* semi-automatique (*m*); **~breve** *n* (GB Mus) ronde *f*; **~circle** *n* demi-cercle *m*; **~colon** *n* point-virgule *m*; **~conscious** *adj* à peine conscient; **~darkness** *n* pénombre *f*, demi-jour *m*; **~-detached (house)** *n* maison *f* jumelée; **~final** *n* demi-finale *f*; **~finalist** *n* demi-finaliste *mf*.

seminar *n* séminaire *m* (**on** sur).

semi: **~quaver** *n* (GB Mus) double croche *f*; **~-skilled** *adj* [*worker*] spécialisé; **~-skimmed** *adj* [*milk*] demi-écrémé.

senate *n* sénat *m*.

senator ▶ 642 *n* sénateur *m* (**for** de).

send *vtr* **1** envoyer; **to ~ help** envoyer des secours; **to ~ sth to sb**, **to ~ sb sth**

envoyer qch à qn; **to ~ sth to the cleaner's** faire nettoyer qch; **to ~ sb home** (from school, work) renvoyer qn chez lui/elle; **to ~ sb to prison** mettre qn en prison; **~ her my love!** embrasse-la de ma part; **~ them my regards** transmettez-leur mes amitiés; **2 the noise sent people running** le bruit a fait courir les gens; **to ~ share prices soaring** faire monter le cours des actions; **to ~ shivers down sb's spine** donner froid dans le dos à qn; **3 to ~ sb mad** rendre qn fou; **to ~ sb into a rage** mettre qn dans une rage folle; **to ~ sb to sleep** endormir qn; **to ~ sb into fits of laughter** faire éclater de rire qn.

IDIOMS **to ~ sb packing**○, **to ~ sb about her/his business**○ envoyer balader qn○.

■ **send away**: ¶ **~ away for [sth]** commander [qch] par correspondance; ¶ **~ [sb/sth] away** faire partir; ¶ **to ~ an appliance away to be mended** envoyer un appareil chez le fabricant pour le faire réparer.

■ **send for**: **~ for [sb/sth]** appeler [*doctor, plumber*]; demander [*reinforcements*].

■ **send in**: **~ [sb/sth] in, ~ in [sb/sth]** envoyer [*letter, form, troops*]; faire entrer [*visitor*]; **to ~ in one's application** poser sa candidature.

■ **send off**: ¶ **~ off for [sth]** commander [qch] par correspondance; ¶ **~ [sth] off, ~ off [sth]** envoyer, expédier [*letter*]; ¶ **~ [sb] off, ~ off [sb]** (Sport) expulser; ¶ **~ [sb] off to** envoyer [qn] à; **to ~ [sb] off to do** envoyer [qn] faire.

■ **send on**: **~ [sth] on, ~ on [sth]** expédier [qch] à l'avance [*baggage*]; faire suivre [*letter, parcel*].

■ **send out**: ¶ **~ [sth] out, ~ out [sth]** émettre [*light, heat*]; ¶ **~ [sb] out** faire sortir [*pupil*]; **to ~ sb out for some milk** envoyer qn chercher du lait.

■ **send up**: **~ [sb/sth] up**○ (GB) parodier.

sender *n* expéditeur/-trice *m/f*.

send: **~-off** *n* adieux *mpl*; **~-up**○ *n* (GB) parodie *f*.

senile dementia *n* démence *f* sénile.

senior I *n* aîné/-e *m/f*; **to be sb's ~** être plus âgé que qn.

II *adj* **1** (older) [*person*] plus âgé; **2** [*civil servant*] haut (*before n*); [*partner*] principal; [*colleague*] plus ancien/-ienne; [*figure, member*] prédominant; [*officer, job, post*] supérieur; **to be ~ to sb** être le supérieur de qn.

senior: **~ citizen** *n* personne *f* du troisième âge; **~ executive** *n* cadre *m* supérieur; **~ high school** *n* (US Sch) ≈ lycée *m*.

seniority *n* (in years) âge *m*; (in rank) statut *m* supérieur; (in years of service) ancienneté *f*.

senior: **~ management** *n* direction *f*; **~ manager** *n* cadre *m* supérieur; **~ officer** *n* (police) officier *m* de police supérieur; (in administration) haut/-e fonctionnaire *m/f*; **~ partner** *n* associé/-e *m/f* principal/-e; **~ school** *n* (GB) (secondary school) lycée *m*; (older pupils) grandes classes *fpl*.

sensation *n* sensation *f*; **to cause** or **create a ~** faire sensation.

sensational *adj* sensationnel/-elle.

sensationalist *adj* [*headline, story, writer*] à sensation.

sensationalize *vtr* faire un reportage à sensation sur [*event, story*].

sense I *n* **1** (faculty, ability) sens *m*; **~ of hearing** ouïe *f*; **~ of sight** vue *f*; **~ of smell** odorat *m*; **~ of taste** goût *m*; **~ of touch** toucher *m*; **to lose all ~ of time** perdre toute notion du temps; **2** (feeling) **a ~ of identity** un sentiment d'identité; **a ~ of purpose** le sentiment d'avoir un but; **3 (common) ~** bon sens *m*; **to have the ~ to go home** avoir le bon sens de rentrer; **to have more ~ than to do** avoir suffisamment de bon sens pour ne pas faire; **4** (reason) **there's no ~ in complaining** cela ne sert à rien de se plaindre; **to make ~ of sth** comprendre qch; **I can't make ~ of this article** je ne comprends rien à cet article; **it makes ~ to do** c'est une bonne idée de faire; **to make ~** [*sentence, film*] avoir un sens; **what he said didn't make much ~ to me** ce qu'il a dit ne m'a pas semblé très logique; **5** (meaning) sens *m*; **in every ~ of the word** dans tous les sens du mot.

II senses *n pl* **to bring sb to their ~s** ramener qn à la raison; **to take leave of one's ~s** perdre la raison.

III *vtr* **1** deviner (**that** que); **to ~ danger** sentir un danger; **2** [*machine*] détecter.

IDIOMS **to see ~** entendre raison; **to talk ~** dire des choses sensées.

senseless *adj* **1** [*violence*] gratuit; [*discussion*] absurde; [*act, waste*] insensé; **2 to knock sb ~** faire perdre connaissance à qn.

sensible *adj* [*person, attitude*] raisonnable; [*decision, solution*] judicieux/-ieuse; [*garment*] pratique; [*diet*] intelligent.

sensitive *adj* **1** [*person*] sensible (**to** à); **2** [*situation*] délicat; [*issue*] difficile; [*information*] confidentiel/-ielle.

sensitivity *n* sensibilité *f* (**to** à).

sensual *adj* sensuel/-elle.

sentence I *n* **1** (Law) peine *f*; **to serve a ~** purger une peine; **2** (in grammar) phrase *f*.

II *vtr* condamner (**to** à; **to do** à faire; **for** pour).

sentiment *n* **1** sentiment *m* (**for** pour, **towards** envers); **public ~** le sentiment général; **2** (opinion) opinion *f*; **my ~s exactly!** c'est bien mon avis!

sentimental *adj* sentimental; **too ~** trop mélo○; **to be ~ about** faire du sentiment pour [*children, animals*]; évoquer [qch] avec émotion [*childhood, past*].

sentry *n* sentinelle *f*.

separate I *adj* **1** (with singular noun) [*section, organization*] à part; [*issue, occasion*] autre (*before n*); **she has a ~ room** elle a une chambre à part; **the flat is ~ from the rest of the house** l'appartement est indépendant du reste de la maison; **a ~ appointment for each child** un rendez-vous pour chaque enfant; **2** (with plural noun) [*sections, problems*] différent; [*organizations, agreements*] distinct; **they have ~ rooms** ils ont chacun leur chambre; **they**

asked for ~ bills (in restaurant) ils ont demandé chacun leur addition.
II *adv* **keep the knives ~** rangez les couteaux séparément; **keep the knives ~ from the forks** séparez les couteaux des fourchettes.
III *vtr* **1** séparer; **the child became ~d from his mother** l'enfant s'est retrouvé séparé de sa mère; **2** (sort out) répartir [*people*]; trier [*objects, produce*].
IV *vi* se séparer (**from** de).

separately *adv* séparément.

separates *n pl* (garments) coordonnés *mpl*.

separation *n* séparation *f* (**from** de).

September ▶ 584 *n* septembre *m*.

septic *adj* infecté; **to go** or **turn ~** s'infecter.

septic tank *n* fosse *f* septique.

sequel *n* suite *f* (**to** à).

sequence *n* **1** série *f*; **~ of tenses** (in grammar) concordance *f* des temps; **2** (order) ordre *m*; **in ~** dans l'ordre; **3** (in film) séquence *f*; **the dream ~** la scène du rêve.

Serbia ▶ 574 *pr n* Serbie *f*.

Serbo-Croat *n, adj* serbo-croate (*m*).

serene *adj* serein.

sergeant *n* **1** (GB Mil) sergent *m*; **2** (US Mil) caporal-chef *m*; **3** (in police) ≈ brigadier *m*.

serial *n* feuilleton *m*; **TV ~** feuilleton télévisé.

serialize *vtr* adapter [qch] en feuilleton.

serial: **~ killer** *n* auteur *m* d'une série de meutres; **~ number** *n* numéro *m* de série.

series *n* série *f*; **a drama ~** une série de fiction.

serious *adj* **1** [*person, expression, discussion, offer*] sérieux/-ieuse; [*work, literature, actor*] de qualité; [*attempt, concern*] réel/réelle; [*intention*] ferme; **to be ~ about sth** prendre qch au sérieux; **to be ~ about doing** avoir vraiment l'intention de faire; **2** [*accident, crime, crisis, problem*] grave; **this is a very ~ matter** l'affaire est très grave.

seriously *adv* **1** [*speak, think*] sérieusement; **to take sb/sth ~** prendre qn/qch au sérieux; **he takes himself too ~** il se prend trop au sérieux; **2** [*ill, injured*] gravement; [*underestimate*] vraiment.

seriousness *n* **1** (of person, film, study) sérieux *m*; (of tone, occasion, reply) gravité *f*; **in all ~** sérieusement; **2** (of illness, problem, situation) gravité *f*.

sermon *n* sermon *m*.

serrated *adj* dentelé; **~ knife** couteau-scie *m*.

serum *n* sérum *m*.

servant *n* ▶ 805 domestique *mf*.

serve I *n* (Sport) service *m*; **it's my ~** à moi de servir.
II *vtr* **1** servir [*country, cause, public*]; travailler au service de [*employer, family*]; **2** servir [*customer, guest, meal, dish*]; **are you being ~ed?** on vous sert?; **to ~ sb with sth** servir qch à qn; **3** (provide facility) [*power station, reservoir*] alimenter; [*public transport, library, hospital*] desservir; **4** (satisfy) servir [*interests*]; satisfaire [*needs*]; **5** (function) être utile à; **this old pen has ~d me well** ce vieux stylo m'a été très utile; **to ~ a purpose** être utile; **to ~ no useful purpose** ne servir à rien; **to ~ the** or **sb's purpose** faire l'affaire; **6** purger [*prison sentence*]; **to ~ one's time** (in army) faire son temps de service; (in prison) purger sa peine; **7** (Law) délivrer [*injunction*] (**on sb** à qn); **to ~ a summons on sb** citer qn à comparaître; **8** (Sport) servir.
III *vi* **1** (in shop) servir; (at table) faire le service; **2 to ~ on** être membre de [*committee, jury*]; **3** (Mil) servir (**as** comme; **under** sous); **4 to ~ as sth** servir de qch; **this should ~ as a warning** cela devrait nous servir d'avertissement; **5** (Sport) servir (**for** pour); **Bruno to ~** au service, Bruno.
IDIOMS **it ~s you right!** ça t'apprendra!

server *n* **1** (Sport) serveur *m*; **2** (Culin) couvert *m* de service.

service I *n* **1** service *m*; **(accident and) emergency ~** service des urgences; **for ~s rendered** pour services rendus; **I'm at your ~** je suis à votre service; **to get good/bad ~** être bien/mal servi; **15% for ~** 15% pour le service; **'out of ~'** (on machine) 'en panne'; **an hourly bus/train ~** un autobus/train toutes les heures; **2** (overhaul) révision *f*; **the photocopier is due for a ~** la photocopieuse a besoin d'être révisée; **3** (ceremony) office *m*; **Sunday ~** office du dimanche; **marriage ~** cérémonie *f* nuptiale.
II **services** *n pl* **1** (also **~ area**) aire *m* de services; **2** (Mil) **the Services** les armées.
III *vtr* faire la révision de [*vehicle*]; entretenir [*machine, boiler*]; **to have one's car ~d** faire réviser sa voiture.

service charge *n* **1** (in restaurant) service *m*; **what is the ~?** le service est de combien?; **2** (in banking) frais *mpl* de gestion de compte.

service station *n* station-service *f*.

serving *n* portion *f*.

serving: **~ dish** *n* plat *m* (de service); **~ spoon** *n* cuillère *f* de service.

session *n* **1** (of parliament) session *f*; **2** (sitting) séance *f*; **emergency ~** séance exceptionnelle; **the court is in ~** le tribunal tient séance; **3** (GB Sch) (year) année *f* scolaire; (US) (term) trimestre *m*; (period of lessons) cours *mpl*.

set I *n* **1** (of keys, tools) jeu *m*; (of golf clubs, chairs) série *f*; (of cutlery) service *m*; (of rules, instructions, tests) série *f*; **a new ~ of clothes** des vêtements neufs; **they're sold in ~s of 10** ils sont vendus par lots *mpl* de 10; **a ~ of fingerprints** des empreintes digitales; **a ~ of traffic lights** des feux *mpl* (de signalisation); **2 a chess ~** un jeu d'échecs; **a magic ~** une mallette de magie; **3 a ~ of footprints** l'empreinte des deux pieds; **a ~ of false teeth** un dentier; **both ~s of parents agreed with us** les parents des deux côtés étaient d'accord avec nous; **4** (Sport) (in tennis) set *m*; **5 TV** or **television ~** poste *m* de télévision; **6** (group) (social) monde *m*; (sporting) milieu *m*; **the smart ~** les gens *mpl* à la mode; **he's not part of our ~** il ne fait pas partie de notre groupe *m*; **7** (scenery) (for play) décor *m*; (for film) plateau *m*; **8** (GB Sch) groupe *m*; **9** (hair-do) mise *f* en plis; **to**

have a shampoo and ~ se faire faire un shampooing et une mise en plis.
II *adj* **1** [*pattern, procedure, rule, task*] bien déterminé; [*time, price*] fixe; [*menu*] à prix fixe; **~ phrase** expression *f* consacrée; **to be ~ in one's ideas** or **opinions** avoir des idées bien arrêtées; **to be ~ in one's ways** avoir ses habitudes; **2** [*expression, smile*] figé; **3** (Sch, Univ) [*text*] au programme; **4** (ready) prêt (**for** pour); **to be (all) ~ to leave/start** être prêt à partir/commencer; **5 to be (dead) ~ against sth/doing** être tout à fait contre qch/l'idée de faire; **to be ~ on doing** tenir absolument à faire; **6** [*jam, jelly, honey*] épais/épaisse; [*cement*] dur; [*yoghurt*] ferme.
III *vtr* **1** (place) placer [*object*] (**on** sur); monter [*gem*] (**in** dans); **a house set among the trees** une maison située au milieu des arbres; **to ~ the record straight** mettre les choses au point; **his eyes are set very close together** ses yeux sont très rapprochés; **2** mettre [*table*]; tendre [*trap*]; **3** fixer [*date, deadline, price, target*]; lancer [*fashion, trend*]; donner [*tone*]; établir [*precedent, record*]; **to ~ a good/bad example to sb** montrer le bon/mauvais exemple à qn; **to ~ one's sights on** viser; **4** mettre [qch] à l'heure [*clock*]; mettre [*alarm clock, burglar alarm*]; **to ~ the video to record the film** programmer le magnétoscope pour enregistrer le film; **~ your watch by mine** règle ta montre sur la mienne; **5** (start) **to ~ sth going** mettre qch en marche [*machine*]; **to ~ sb laughing/thinking** faire rire/réfléchir qn; **6** donner [*homework, essay*]; **to ~ an exam** préparer les sujets d'examen; **to ~ sb the task of doing** charger qn de faire; **7** (in fiction, film) situer; **to ~ a book in 1960/New York** situer un roman en 1960/ à New York; **the film is set in Munich** le film se passe à Munich; **8 to ~ sth to music** mettre qch en musique; **9** (Med) immobiliser [*broken bone*]; **10 to ~ sb's hair** faire une mise en plis à qn; **to have one's hair set** se faire faire une mise en plis.
IV *vi* **1** [*sun*] se coucher; **2** [*jam, concrete*] prendre; [*glue*] sécher; **3** (Med) [*fracture*] se ressouder.
■ **set about** se mettre à [*work*]; **to ~ about (the job** or **task of) doing** commencer à faire; **I don't know how to ~ about it** je ne sais pas comment m'y prendre.
■ **set apart**: **~ [sb/sth] apart** distinguer (**from** de).
■ **set aside**: **~ [sth] aside, ~ aside [sth]** réserver [*area, room, time*] (**for** pour); mettre [qch] de côté [*money, stock*].
■ **set in** [*infection*] se déclarer; [*winter*] arriver; [*depression, resentment*] s'installer; **the rain has set in for the afternoon** la pluie va durer toute l'après-midi.
■ **set off**: ¶ **~ off** partir (**for** pour); **to ~ off on a journey** partir en voyage; **to ~ off to do** partir faire; ¶ **~ [off] sth, ~ [sth] off 1** faire partir [*firework*]; faire exploser [*bomb*]; déclencher [*riot, panic, alarm*]; **2** (enhance) mettre [qch] en valeur [*garment*]; **3 to ~ sth off against profits/debts** déduire qch des bénéfices/des dettes; ¶ **~ [sb] off** faire pleurer [*baby*]; **she laughed and that set me off** elle a ri et ça m'a fait rire à mon tour.
■ **set on**: ¶ **~ on [sb]** attaquer qn; ¶ **~ [sth] on sb** lâcher [qch] contre qn [*dog*].
■ **set out**: ¶ **~ out** se mettre en route (**for** pour; **to do** pour faire); **we set out from Paris at 9 am** nous avons quitté Paris à 9 heures; **to ~ out to do** [*person*] entreprendre de faire; ¶ **~ [sth] out, ~ out [sth] 1** disposer [*goods, chairs, food*]; préparer [*board game*]; organiser [*information*]; **2** présenter [*ideas, proposals*]; formuler [*objections, terms*].
■ **set up**: ¶ **~ up**: **to ~ up on one's own** s'établir à son compte; **to ~ up in business** monter une affaire; ¶ **~ [sth] up, ~ up [sth] 1** monter [*stand, stall*]; assembler [*equipment, easel*]; déplier [*deckchair*]; ériger [*roadblock*]; **to ~ up home** s'installer; **2** préparer [*experiment*]; (Sport) préparer [*goal, try*]; **3** créer [*business, company*]; implanter [*factory*]; former [*support group, charity*]; constituer [*committee*]; ouvrir [*fund*]; lancer [*scheme*]; **4** organiser [*conference, meeting*]; mettre [qch] en place [*procedures*]; ¶ **~ [sb] up**: **1 she set her son up (in business) as a gardener** elle a aidé son fils à s'installer comme jardinier; **2 that deal has set her up for life** grâce à ce contrat elle n'aura plus à se soucier de rien; **3°** (GB) [*police*] tendre un piège à [*criminal*]; [*colleague, friend*] monter un coup contre [*person*].

setback *n* revers *m* (**for** pour); **to suffer a ~** essuyer un revers.

settee *n* canapé *m*.

setting *n* **1** cadre *m*; **a house in a riverside ~** une maison au bord d'une rivière; **Milan will be the ~ for the film** le film va se passer à Milan; **2** (in jewellery) monture *f*; **3** (position on dial) position *f* (de réglage); **speed ~** vitesse *f*; **put the iron on the highest ~** mets le fer à repasser au maximum.

settle I *vtr* **1** installer [*person, animal*]; **to ~ a child on one's lap** asseoir un enfant sur ses genoux; **2** calmer [*stomach, nerves*]; **3** régler [*matter, business, dispute*]; mettre fin à [*conflict, strike*]; régler, résoudre [*problem*]; décider [*match*]; **~ it among yourselves** réglez ça entre vous; **that's ~d** voilà qui est réglé; **4** fixer [*arrangements, price*]; **nothing is ~d yet** rien n'est encore fixé; **5 to ~ one's affairs** mettre de l'ordre dans ses affaires; **6** régler [*bill, debt, claim*].
II *vi* **1** [*dust*] se déposer; [*bird, insect*] se poser; **let the wine ~** laisse le vin décanter; **to let the dust ~** (after row) attendre que les choses se calment; **2** (in new home) s'installer; (more permanently) se fixer; **3** [*contents, ground*] se tasser; **4** [*weather*] se mettre au beau fixe; **to be settling** [*snow*] tenir; [*mist*] persister; **5** (Law) régler; **to ~ out of court** parvenir à un règlement à l'amiable.
■ **settle down 1** (get comfortable) s'installer (**on** sur; **in** dans); **2** (calm down) [*person*] se calmer; [*situation*] s'arranger; **to ~ down to work** se concentrer sur son travail; **3** (marry) se ranger.
■ **settle for**: **~ for sth** se contenter de qch;

why ~ for less? pourquoi se contenter de moins?

■ **settle in 1** (move in) s'installer; **2** (become acclimatized) s'adapter.

■ **settle up 1** (pay) payer; **to ~ up with** régler [*waiter, tradesman*]; **2** (sort out who owes what) faire les comptes.

settlement *n* **1** (agreement) accord *m*; **2** (Law) règlement *m*; **3** (dwellings) village *m*; (colonial) territoire *m*.

settler *n* colon *m*.

seven ▶ 492, 554 *n, pron, det* sept (*m*) *inv*.

seventeen ▶ 492, 554 *n, pron, det* dix-sept (*m*) *inv*.

seventeenth ▶ 584, 642 I *n* **1** (in order) dix-septième *mf*; **2** (of month) dix-sept *m inv*.
II *adj, adv* dix-septième.

seventh ▶ 584, 642 I *n* **1** (in order) septième *mf*; **2** (of month) sept *m inv*.
II *adj, adv* septième.

seventies ▶ 584, 492 *n pl* **1** (era) **the ~** les années *fpl* soixante-dix; **2** (age) **to be in one's ~** avoir plus de soixante-dix ans.

seventieth I *n* (in order, sequence) soixante-dixième *mf*.
II *adj, adv* soixante-dixième.

seventy ▶ 492 *n, pron, det* soixante-dix (*m*) *inv*.

seventy-eight *n* **a ~ (record** or **disc)** un soixante-dix-huit tours *m inv*.

sever *vtr* **1** sectionner [*limb, artery*]; couper [*rope, branch*]; **2** rompre [*link, relations*]; couper [*communications*].

several I *quantif* **~ of you/us** plusieurs d'entre vous/d'entre nous; **~ of our group** plusieurs membres de notre groupe.
II *det* plusieurs; **~ books** plusieurs livres.

severance *n* licenciement *m*; **~ pay** indemnités *fpl* de licenciement.

severe *adj* **1** [*problem, damage, shortage, injury, depression, shock*] grave; [*weather, cold, winter*] rigoureux/-euse; [*headache*] violent; [*loss*] lourd; **2** (harsh) sévère (**with sb** avec qn); **3** [*haircut, clothes*] austère.

severity *n* (of problem, illness) gravité *f*; (of punishment, treatment) sévérité *f*; (of climate) rigueur *f*.

sew I *vtr* coudre; **he ~ed the button back on** il a recousu le bouton.
II *vi* coudre, faire de la couture.

■ **sew up**: **~ [sth] up, ~ up [sth]** recoudre [*hole, tear*]; faire [*seam*]; (re)coudre [*wound*].

sewage *n* eaux *fpl* usées.

sewer *n* égout *m*.

sewing *n* (activity) couture *f*; (piece of work) ouvrage *m*.

sewing machine *n* machine *f* à coudre.

sex I *n* **1** (gender) sexe *m*; **the opposite ~** le sexe opposé; **2** (intercourse) (one act) rapport *m* sexuel; (repeated) rapports *mpl* sexuels.
II *noun modifier* sexuel/-elle.

sexist *n, adj* sexiste (*mf*).

sexual *adj* sexuel/-elle.

sexuality *n* sexualité *f*.

sexy○ *adj* [*person, clothing*] sexy○ *inv*; [*book*] érotique.

shabby *adj* [*person*] habillé de façon miteuse; [*room, furnishings, clothing*] miteux/-euse; [*treatment*] mesquin.

shack *n* cabane *f*.

shade I *n* **1** (shadow) ombre *f*; **in the ~** à l'ombre (**of** de); **2** (of colour) ton *m*; **an attractive ~ of blue** un beau bleu; **3** (also **lamp ~**) abat-jour *m inv*; **4** (US) (also **window ~**) store *m*.
II *vtr* donner de l'ombre à; **the garden was ~d by trees** le jardin était ombragé par des arbres; **to ~ one's eyes (with one's hand)** s'abriter les yeux de la main.
III *vi* se fondre (**into** en).
IDIOMS **to put sb in the ~** éclipser qn; **to put sth in the ~** surpasser or surclasser qch.

shadow I *n* ombre *f*; **to have ~s under one's eyes** avoir les yeux cernés; **without** or **beyond the ~ of a doubt** sans l'ombre d'un doute.
II *vtr* filer [*person*].

shadow cabinet *n* (GB) cabinet *m* fantôme.

shadowy *adj* **1** (dark) sombre; **2** (indistinct) [*image, outline*] flou; [*form*] indistinct; **3** (mysterious) mystérieux/-ieuse.

shady *adj* **1** [*place*] ombragé; **2** [*deal, businessman*] véreux/-euse.

shaft *n* **1** (of tool) manche *m*; (of arrow) tige *f*; (in machine) axe *m*; **2** (passage, vent) puits *m*; **3 ~ of light** rai *m*; **~ of lightning** éclair *m*.

shaggy *adj* [*hair, beard, eyebrows*] en broussailles; [*animal*] poilu.

shake I *n* **1 to give sb/sth a ~** secouer qn/qch; **2** (also **milk-~**) milk-shake *m*.
II *vtr* **1** secouer; **to ~ one's head** (in dismay) hocher la tête; (to say no) faire non de la tête; **to ~ hands with sb, to ~ sb's hand** serrer la main de qn, donner une poignée de main à qn; **2** ébranler [*confidence, faith, resolve*]; [*event, disaster*] secouer [*person*]; **it really shook me to find out that she had lied** cela m'a vraiment donné un choc de découvrir qu'elle avait menti.
III *vi* **1** trembler; **to ~ with** trembler de [*fear, cold, emotion*]; se tordre de [*laughter*]; **2** (shake hands) **'let's ~ on it!'** 'serrons-nous la main!'

■ **shake off**: **~ [sb/sth] off, ~ off [sb/sth]** se débarrasser de [*cold, depression, habit, person*]; se défaire de [*feeling*].

■ **shake up**: ¶ **~ up [sth], ~ [sth] up** agiter [*bottle, mixture*]; ¶ **~ [sb] up, ~ up [sb]** [*experience, news*] secouer.

shaken *adj* (shocked) choqué; (upset) bouleversé.

shaker *n* (for cocktails) shaker *m*; (for dice) gobelet *m* à dés; (for salt) salière *f*; (for pepper) poivrière *f*; (for salad) saladier *m*.

shaky *adj* **1** [*chair, ladder*] branlant; **I feel a bit ~** je me sens un peu flageolant; **2** [*relationship, position*] instable; [*evidence, argument*] peu solide; [*knowledge, memory, prospects*] peu sûr; [*regime*] chancelant; **3 we got off to a rather ~ start** au début cela a été difficile pour nous;

my French is a bit ~ mon français est un peu hésitant.

shall *modal aux* **1** (in future tense) **I ~** or **I'll see you tomorrow** je vous verrai demain; **we ~ not** or **shan't have a reply before Friday** nous n'aurons pas de réponse avant vendredi; **2** (in suggestions) **~ I set the table?** est-ce que je mets la table?; **~ we go to the cinema tonight?** et si on allait au cinéma ce soir?; **let's buy some peaches, ~ we?** et si on achetait des pêches?

shallot *n* **1** (GB) échalote *f*; **2** (US) cive *f*.

shallow ▶ 738 *adj* [*container, water, grave*] peu profond; [*stairs*] aux marches basses; [*breathing, character, response*] superficiel/-ielle; [*conversation*] plat; **the ~ end of the pool** l'extrémité la moins profonde de la piscine.

shallows *n pl* bas-fonds *mpl*.

sham I *n* **1** (person) imposteur *m*; **2 it's (all) a ~** c'est de la comédie.
II *adj* [*event*] prétendu (*before n*); [*object, building, idea*] factice; [*activity, emotion*] feint; [*organization*] fantoche.
III *vi* faire semblant.

shambles○ *n* pagaille○ *f*.

shame I *n* **1** honte *f*; **he has no (sense of) ~** il n'a honte de rien; **to bring ~ on** être or faire la honte de; **~ on you!** tu devrais avoir honte!; **2 it's a (real) shame** c'est (vraiment) dommage; **it was a ~ (that) she lost** c'est dommage qu'elle ait perdu.
II *vtr* **1** (embarrass) faire honte à; **he was ~d into a confession** il a eu tellement honte qu'il a avoué; **2** (disgrace) déshonorer (**by doing** en faisant).

shamefaced *adj* [*person, look*] penaud.

shameful *adj* [*conduct, waste*] honteux/-euse; **it is ~ that** c'est une honte que (+ *subj*).

shameless *adj* [*person*] éhonté; [*attitude*] effronté; [*negligence*] scandaleux/-euse.

shampoo I *n* shampooing *m*.
II *vtr* faire un shampooing à; **to ~ one's hair** se faire un shampooing.

shamrock *n* trèfle *m*.

shandy, shandygaff (US) *n* panaché *m*.

shape I *n* **1** forme *f*; **a square ~** une forme carrée; **what ~ is it?** de quelle forme est-ce?; **to be an odd ~** avoir une drôle de forme; **in the ~ of** en forme de; **to take ~** [*sculpture, building*] prendre forme; **to lose its ~** [*garment*] se déformer; **to bend sth out of ~** gauchir qch; **in all ~s and sizes** de toutes les formes et de toutes les tailles; **2 to be in/out of ~** être/ne pas être en forme; **to get in ~** se mettre en forme; **to knock sth into ~** mettre qch au point [*project, idea, essay*]; **the ~ of things to come** ce que sera l'avenir.
II *vtr* **1** modeler [*clay*]; sculpter [*wood*]; **he ~d my hair into a bob** il m'a coupé les cheveux au carré; **~ the dough into balls** faites des boules avec la pâte; **2** [*person, event*] influencer; (stronger) déterminer [*future, idea*]; modeler [*character*]; [*person*] formuler [*policy, project*].

shaped I *adj* **to be ~ like sth** avoir la forme de qch; **a teapot ~ like a house** une théière en forme de maison.
II **-shaped** *combining form* **star-/V-~** en forme d'étoile/de V.

shapeless *adj* sans forme, informe.

shapely *adj* [*woman*] bien fait; [*ankle*] fin; [*leg*] bien galbé.

share I *n* **1** part *f* (**of** de); **to have more than one's fair ~ of** avoir plus que sa part de [*bad luck*]; **to do one's ~ of sth** faire sa part de qch; **to pay one's (fair) ~** payer sa part; **2** (in stock market) action *f*.
II *vtr* partager [*money, house, opinion*] (**with** avec); se partager [*chore*]; **we ~ an interest in animals** nous aimons tous les deux les animaux.
III *vi* **to ~ in** prendre part à [*success, happiness, benefits*].
■ **share out**: **~ [sth] out, ~ out [sth]** (amongst selves) partager [*food*]; (amongst others) répartir [*food*] (**among, between** entre).

shareholder *n* actionnaire *mf*.

shark *n* requin *m*.

sharp I *adj* **1** [*razor*] tranchant; [*edge*] coupant; [*blade, scissors, knife*] bien aiguisé; [*saw*] bien affûté; **2** [*tooth, fingernail, end, needle*] pointu; [*pencil*] bien taillé; [*features*] anguleux/-euse; [*nose*] pointu; **3** [*angle*] aigu/-uë; [*bend*] brusque; [*drop, incline*] fort; [*fall, rise*] brusque, brutal; **4** [*taste, smell*] âcre; [*fruit*] acide; **5** [*pain, cold*] vif/vive; [*cry*] aigu/-uë; [*blow*] sévère; [*frost*] fort, intense; **6** [*tongue*] acéré; [*tone*] acerbe; **7** [*person, mind*] vif/ vive; [*eyesight*] perçant; [*hearing*] fin; **8** [*businessman*] malin/-igne; **~ operator** filou *m*; **9** [*image*] net/nette; [*contrast*] prononcé; **10** (Mus) [*note*] dièse *inv*; (too high) aigu/-uë.
II *adv* **1** [*stop*] net; **to turn ~ left** tourner brusquement vers la gauche; **2**○ **at 9 o'clock ~** à neuf heures pile○; **3** (Mus) [*sing, play*] trop haut.

sharpen *vtr* **1** aiguiser, affûter [*blade, scissors*]; tailler [*pencil*]; **2** rendre [qch] plus net [*contrast*]; affiner [*focus*]; régler [*image*].

sharpener *n* taille-crayon *m*.

sharply *adv* **1** [*turn, change, rise, fall*] brusquement, brutalement; [*stop*] net; **2** [*speak*] d'un ton brusque; [*criticize*] vivement, sévèrement.

sharpness *n* **1** (of blade, scissors) tranchant *m* (**of** de); **2** (of image, sound) netteté *f* (**of** de); **3** (of voice, tone) brusquerie *f* (**of** de); **4** (of fruit, drink) acidité *f*.

shatter I *vtr* fracasser [*window, glass*]; rompre [*peace, silence*]; briser [*life, hope*]; démolir [*nerves*].
II *vi* [*window, glass*] voler en éclats.

shattered *adj* **1** [*dream*] brisé; [*life, confidence*] anéanti; **2** [*person*] (devastated) effondré; (tired)○ crevé○, épuisé.

shave I *n* **to have a ~** se raser; **to give sb a ~** raser qn.
II *vtr* [*barber*] raser [*person*]; **to ~ one's beard off** se raser la barbe; **to ~ one's legs** se raser les jambes.
III *vi* se raser.

IDIOMS **that was a close ~!** je l'ai/il l'a etc échappé belle!

shaver *n* (also **electric ~**) rasoir *m* électrique.

shaving I *n* **1** (action) rasage *m*; **2 ~s** (of wood, metal) copeaux *mpl*.
II *noun modifier* [*cream, foam*] à raser; [*kit*] de rasage.

shaving: **~ brush** *n* blaireau *m*; **~ mirror** *n* petit miroir *m*.

shawl *n* châle *m*.

she

■ **Note** *she* is translated by *elle*: *she closed the door* = elle a fermé la porte.

pron elle; **~'s not at home** elle n'est pas chez elle; **here ~ is** la voici; **there ~ is** la voilà; SHE **didn't take it** ce n'est pas elle qui l'a pris; **he lives in Dublin but ~ doesn't** il habite Dublin mais elle non; **~'s a genius** c'est un génie; **~'s a lovely boat** c'est un beau bateau.

shear *vtr* tondre [*grass, sheep*].

shears *n pl* **1** (for garden) cisaille *f*; **2** (for sheep) tondeuse *f*.

shed I *n* (in garden) remise *f*, abri *m*; (at factory site, port) hangar *m*.
II *vtr* **1** verser [*tears*]; perdre [*leaves, weight, antlers*]; [*lorry*] déverser [*load*]; **to ~ skin** muer; **to ~ blood** (one's own) perdre du sang; **too much blood has been shed** trop de sang a coulé; **2** répandre [*light, happiness*].

sheep *n* mouton *m*; (ewe) brebis *f*; **black/lost ~** brebis *f* galeuse/égarée.

sheep dog *n* chien *m* de berger.

sheepish *adj* penaud.

sheepskin *n* peau *f* de mouton.

sheer *adj* **1** [*boredom, hypocrisy, stupidity*] pur; **out of ~ malice** par pure méchanceté; **2** [*cliff*] à pic; **3** [*fabric*] léger/-ère, fin; [*stockings*] extra-fin.

sheet *n* **1** (of paper, stamps) feuille *f*; (of metal, glass) plaque *f*; **2** (for bed) drap *m*; **dust ~** housse *f*; **3 fact ~** bulletin *m* d'informations; **4** (of ice) couche *f*; (of flame) rideau *m*; **in ~s** [*rain*] à torrents.
IDIOMS **to be as white as a ~** être blanc comme un linge.

sheet lightning *n* éclair *m* en nappe.

sheik *n* cheik *m*.

shelf *n* **1** étagère *f*; (in oven) plaque *f*; (in shop, fridge) rayon *m*; **(a set of) shelves** une étagère; **2** (in rock, ice) corniche *f*.

shell I *n* **1** (of egg, nut, snail) coquille *f*; (of crab, tortoise, shrimp) carapace *f*; **sea ~** coquillage *m*; **to come out of one's ~** sortir de sa coquille; **2** (bomb) obus *m*; (cartridge) cartouche *f*; **3** (remains) (of building) carcasse *f*.
II *vtr* **1** (Mil) pilonner [*town, installation*]; **2** (Culin) écosser [*peas*]; décortiquer [*prawn, nut*]; écailler [*oyster*].

shellfish *n pl* **1** (Zool) crustacés *mpl*; (mussels, oysters) coquillages *mpl*; **2** (Culin) fruits *mpl* de mer.

shelter I *n* **1** abri *m*; **in the ~ of** à l'abri de; **to take ~ from** s'abriter de [*weather*]; **to give sb ~** [*person*] donner un abri à qn; [*hut, tree*] offrir un abri à qn; [*country*] donner asile à qn; **2** (for homeless) refuge *m* (**for** pour); (for refugee) asile *m*.
II *vtr* **1** (against weather) abriter (**from, against** de); (from truth) protéger (**from** de); **2** donner refuge or asile à [*refugee, criminal*].
III *vi* se mettre à l'abri; **to ~ from the storm** s'abriter de l'orage.

shepherd ▶ 805 *n* berger *m*.

sheriff ▶ 805 *n* shérif *m*.

sherry *n* xérès *m*, sherry *m*.

Shetland I *pr n* (also **~ Islands** *pr n pl*) îles *fpl* Shetland.
II *noun modifier* (also **~ wool**) [*scarf, sweater, gloves*] en shetland.

shield I *n* **1** (Mil) bouclier *m*; **2** (on machine) écran *m* de protection; (around gun) pare-balles *m inv*; **3** (US) (policeman's badge) insigne *m*.
II *vtr* protéger; **to ~ one's eyes** se protéger les yeux.

shift I *n* **1** (change) changement *m* (**in** de), modification *f* (**in** de); **a sudden ~ in public opinion** un retournement de l'opinion publique; **2** (at work) période *f* de travail; (group of workers) équipe *f*; **to be on night ~s** être (d'équipe) de nuit; **to work an eight-hour ~** faire les trois-huit.
II *vtr* **1** déplacer [*furniture, vehicle*]; bouger, remuer [*arm*]; changer [*theatre scenery*]; **2** faire partir, enlever [*stain, dirt*]; **3** rejeter [*blame, responsibility*] (**onto** sur); **to ~ attention away from a problem** détourner l'attention d'un problème; **4** (US Aut) **to ~ gear** changer de vitesse.
III *vi* (also **~ about**) [*load*] bouger; **to ~ from one foot to the other** se dandiner d'un pied sur l'autre.

shift key *n* touche *f* de majuscule.

shiftless *adj* paresseux/-euse, apathique.

shift work *n* travail *m* posté; **to be on ~** faire un travail posté.

shifty *adj* [*person, manner*] louche, sournois.

shimmer *vi* **1** [*jewels, water*] scintiller; [*silk*] chatoyer; **2** (in heat) [*landscape*] vibrer.

shin, shinbone *n* tibia *m*.

shine I *n* lustre *m*.
II *vtr* **1** braquer [*headlights, spotlight, torch*] (**on** sur); **2** faire reluire [*silver*]; cirer [*shoes*].
III *vi* **1** [*hair, light, sun*] briller; [*brass, floor*] reluire; **the light is shining in my eyes** j'ai la lumière dans les yeux; **2** [*eyes*] briller (**with** de); [*face*] rayonner (**with** de); **3** (excel) briller; **to ~ at** être brillant en [*science, languages*].
IDIOMS **to take a ~ to sb**° s'enticher° de qn.

shingle I *n* **1** (on beach) galets *mpl*; **2** (on roof) bardeau *m*.
II **shingles** ▶ 686 *n pl* (Med) zona *m*.

shinguard *n* jambière *f*.

shining *adj* **1** [*hair, metal*] brillant; [*floor*] reluisant; **2** [*eyes*] brillant; [*face*] radieux/-ieuse; **3** [*example*] parfait (**of** de).

shiny *adj* **1** [*metal, surface, hair*] brillant; **2** [*shoes, wood*] bien ciré.

ship I *n* navire *m*; (smaller) bateau *m*; **passenger ~** paquebot *m*.
II *vtr* transporter [qch] par mer.

ship: **~building** *n* construction *f* navale; **~ment** *n* cargaison *f*; **~ owner** *n* armateur *m*; **~ping** *n* navigation *f*, trafic *m* maritime.

shipwreck I *n* (event) naufrage *m*; (ship) épave *f*.
II *vtr* **to be ~ed** faire naufrage; **a ~ed sailor** un marin naufragé.

shirk *vtr* esquiver [*task, duty*]; fuir [*responsibility*]; éluder [*problem*]; **to ~ doing sth** éviter de faire qch.

shirt *n* (man's) chemise *f*; (woman's) chemisier *m*; (for sport) maillot *m*.

shirt-sleeve *n* manche *f* de chemise; **in one's ~s** en manches de chemise; **to roll up one's ~s** remonter ses manches (de chemise).

shit◐ *excl* merde◐!

shiver I *n* frisson *m*; **to give sb the ~s** donner froid dans le dos à qn.
II *vi* (with cold) grelotter (**with** de); (with fear) frémir (**with** de); (with disgust) frissonner (**with** de).

shoal *n* (of fish) banc *m*.

shock I *n* **1** choc *m*; **to get** or **have a ~** avoir un choc; **to give sb a ~** faire un choc à qn; **it came as a bit of a ~** cela m'a fait comme un choc; **her death came as a ~ to us** sa mort a été un choc pour nous; **2** (Med) **to be in (a state of) ~** être en état de choc; **3** (electrical) décharge *f*; **to get a ~** prendre une décharge; **to give sb a ~** donner une décharge à qn; **4** (of collision) choc *m*; (of earthquake) secousse *f*; (of explosion) souffle *m*; **5 a ~ of red hair** une tignasse rousse.
II *vtr* (distress) consterner; (scandalize) choquer.

shock absorber *n* amortisseur *m*.

shocking *adj* [*sight*] consternant; [*news*] choquant.

shock wave *n* onde *f* de choc; (figurative) remous *mpl*.

shoddy *adj* [*product*] de mauvaise qualité; [*work*] mal fait.

shoe I *n* chaussure *f*; (for horse) fer *m*.
II *vtr* ferrer [*horse*].

shoe: **~horn** *n* chausse-pied *m*; **~lace** *n* lacet *m* de chaussure; **~ polish** *n* cirage *m*; **~ repair shop** ▶805 *n* cordonnier *m*; **~ shop** ▶805 *n* magasin *m* de chaussures; **~ size** *n* pointure *f*; **~string** *n* (US) lacet *m* de chaussure.

shoo *vtr* (also **~ away**) chasser.

shoot I *n* (Bot) pousse *f*.
II *vtr* **1** (fire) tirer [*bullet, arrow*] (**at** sur); lancer [*missile*] (**at** sur); **2** tirer sur [*person, animal*]; (kill) abattre [*person, animal*]; **she shot him in the leg** elle lui a tiré dans la jambe; **to be shot in the back** recevoir une balle dans le dos; **to ~ sb dead** abattre qn; **to ~ oneself** se tirer une balle; **3 to ~ questions at sb** bombarder qn de questions; **4** (film) tourner [*film, scene*]; prendre [qch] (en photo) [*subject*]; **5** mettre [*bolt*]; **6 to ~ the rapids** franchir les rapides; **7** (US) jouer à [*pool*].
III *vi* **1** tirer (**at** sur); **to ~ to kill** tirer pour tuer; **2 to ~ forward** s'élancer à toute vitesse; **the car shot past** la voiture est passée en trombe; **to ~ to fame** percer, devenir célèbre subitement; **3** (Sport) [*player*] tirer, shooter.
■ **shoot down**: **~ down [sb/sth], ~ [sb/sth] down** abattre, descendre○ [*plane, pilot*]; **to ~ [sb/sth] down in flames** descendre [qn/qch] en flammes.
■ **shoot out** [*flame, water*] jaillir; [*car*] sortir en trombe.
■ **shoot up**: ¶ **~ up** [*flames, spray*] jaillir; [*prices, profits*] monter en flèche; ¶ **~ up [sth], ~ [sth] up** se shooter à○ [*heroin*].

shooting I *n* **1** (killing) meurtre *m* (par arme à feu); **2** (shots) coups *mpl* de feu, fusillade *f*.
II *adj* [*pain*] lancinant.

shooting: **~ party** *n* groupe *m* de chasseurs; **~ range** *n* stand *m* de tir; **~ star** *n* étoile *f* filante; **~ stick** *n* canne-siège *f*.

shop I *n* **1** magasin *m*; (small, fashionable) boutique *f*; **to go to the ~s** aller faire les courses; **2** (US) (in department store) rayon *m*; **3** (workshop) atelier *m*.
II *vi* **to go ~ping** (spend money) aller faire des courses; (browse) aller faire les magasins.
IDIOMS **to talk ~** parler boutique.

shop: **~ assistant** ▶805 *n* (GB) vendeur/-euse *m/f*; **~ front** *n* devanture *f*; **~keeper** ▶805 *n* commerçant/-e *m/f*; **~lifter** *n* voleur/-euse *m/f* à l'étalage.

shopping *n* courses *fpl*.

shopping: **~ bag** *n* sac *m* à provisions; **~ centre** (GB), **~ mall** (US) *n* centre *m* commercial; **~ trolley** *n* caddie® *m*.

shop: **~-soiled** *adj* [*garment*] sali; **~ window** *n* vitrine *f*.

shore *n* **1** (of sea) côte *f*, rivage *m*; (of lake) rive *f*; (of island) côte *f*; **2** (dry land) terre *f*; **on ~** à terre.

short ▶738 I *n* **1** (drink) alcool *m* fort; **2** (film) court métrage *m*.
II **shorts** *n pl* short *m*; (underwear) caleçon *m*.
III *adj* **1** [*stay, memory, period*] court (*before n*); [*course*] de courte durée; [*conversation, speech, chapter*] bref/brève; [*walk*] petit (*before n*); **a ~ time ago** il y a peu de temps; **the days are getting ~er** les jours diminuent or raccourcissent; **2** [*hair, dress, distance, stick*] court (*before n*); **to have one's hair cut ~** se faire couper les cheveux court; **3** [*person*] petit; **4 to be in ~ supply** être difficile à trouver; **time is getting ~** le temps presse; **5** [*rations*] insuffisant; **he gave me a ~ measure** (in shop) il a triché sur le poids; **6** (lacking) **he is ~ of sth** il lui manque qch; **to be ~ on** [*person*] manquer de [*talent, tact*]; **to run ~ of** manquer de [*clothes, money, food*]; **7 Tom is ~ for Thomas** Tom est le diminutif de Thomas; **this is Nicholas, Nick for ~!** je te présente Nicholas, mais on l'appelle Nick; **8** (abrupt) **to be ~ with sb** être brusque avec qn; **9** [*pastry*] brisé.
IV *adv* [*stop*] net; **to stop ~ of doing** se retenir pour ne pas faire.

V **in short** *phr* bref.
VI **short of** *phr* **1** (just before) un peu avant; **2** (just less than) pas loin de; **a little ~ of £1,000** pas loin de 1 000 livres sterling; **3** (unless) **~ of doing** à moins de faire.
IDIOMS **~ and sweet** bref/brève; **to pull sb up ~** couper qn dans son élan; **to sell oneself ~** se sous-estimer; **to make ~ work of sth/sb** expédier qch/qn.

shortage *n* pénurie *f*, manque *m* (**of** de); **housing ~** crise *f* du logement; **there is no ~ of applicants** les candidats ne manquent pas.

short: **~bread**, **~cake** *n* sablé *m*; **~-change** *vtr* ne pas rendre toute sa monnaie à.

short circuit I *n* court-circuit *m*.
II **short-circuit** *vtr* court-circuiter.
III **short-circuit** *vi* faire court-circuit.

short: **~comings** *n pl* points *mpl* faibles; **~crust pastry** *n* pâte *f* brisée; **~cut** *n* raccourci *m*.

shorten I *vtr* abréger [*visit, life*]; raccourcir [*garment, talk*]; réduire [*time, list*].
II *vi* [*days*] diminuer.

shortening *n* (Culin) matière *f* grasse.

shortfall *n* (in budget, accounts) déficit *m*; (in earnings, exports) manque *m*.

shorthand *n* sténographie *f*, sténo° *f*; **in ~** en sténo°.

shorthand-typist ▶ 805 *n* sténo-dactylo *f*.

short-haul *adj* [*aircraft, flight*] court-courrier.

shortlist I *n* liste *f* des candidats sélectionnés.
II *vtr* sélectionner [*applicant*] (**for** pour).

short-lived *adj* **to be ~** ne pas durer longtemps.

shortly *adv* **1** [*return*] bientôt; [*be published*] prochainement; **2 ~ after(wards)/before** peu (de temps) après/avant; **3** (crossly) sèchement.

shortsighted *adj* **1** myope; **2** (figurative) [*person*] peu clairvoyant; [*policy, decision*] à courte vue.

shortsightedness *n* myopie *f*.

short-sleeved *adj* [*blouse, dress*] à manches courtes.

short-staffed *adj* **to be ~** manquer de personnel.

short story *n* nouvelle *f*.

short term I *n* **in the ~** dans l'immédiat.
II **short-term** *adj* à court terme.

shortwave *n* ondes *fpl* courtes; **broadcast on ~** diffusé sur ondes courtes.

shot I *n* **1** (from gun) coup *m* (de feu); **to fire a ~ at sb/sth** tirer sur qn/qch; **2** (Sport) (in tennis, golf, cricket) coup *m*; (in football) tir *m*; **to take a ~ at goal** tirer au but; **3** (snapshot) photo *f* (**of** de); **4** (in film-making) plan *m* (**of** de); **action ~** scène *f* d'action; **5** (injection) piqûre *f* (**of** de) ; **to give sb a ~** faire une piqûre à qn; **6 to have a ~ at doing** essayer de faire qch; **7** (in shotputting) poids *m*; **8** (person) **a good ~** un bon tireur.
II *adj* [*silk*] changeant.
IDIOMS **to call the ~s** dicter la loi; **to be ~ of** être débarrassé de.

shot: **~gun** *n* fusil *m*; **~ put** *n* (Sport) lancer *m* de poids.

should ▶ 857 *modal aux* **1 ~ I call the doctor?** est-ce que je devrais faire venir le médecin?; **why shouldn't I do it?** pourquoi est-ce que je ne le ferais pas?; **2 you ~ find it interesting** ça devrait t'intéresser; **it shouldn't be difficult** ça ne devrait pas être difficile; **she ~ have been here hours ago** elle aurait dû arriver il y a plusieurs heures déjà; **3 I shouldn't worry if I were you** à votre place, je ne m'inquièterais pas; **I ~ like a drink** je prendrais volontiers un verre; **I ~ think she's about 40** à mon avis, elle doit avoir à peu près 40 ans; **4 if you ~ change your mind** si vous changez d'avis; **~ you require any further information, please contact...** si vous souhaitez plus de renseignements, adressez-vous à...; **5 I ~ think so!** je l'espère!; **I ~ think not!** j'espère bien que non!; **how ~ I know?** comment veux-tu que je le sache?; **flowers? you shouldn't have!** des fleurs? il ne fallait pas!

shoulder I *n* épaule *f*; **on** or **over one's ~** [*rifle*] à l'épaule; **on** or **over one's ~s** [*shawl*] sur les épaules; **to have round ~s** avoir le dos rond.
II *vtr* se charger de [*burden, expense, task*]; endosser [*responsibility*].
IDIOMS **to rub ~s with sb** côtoyer qn.

shoulder: **~ bag** *n* sac *m* à bandoulière; **~ blade** *n* omoplate *f*; **~-length** *adj* [*hair*] mi-long; **~ pad** *n* épaulette *f*.

shout I *n* cri *m* (**of** de).
II *vtr* crier; (stronger) hurler.
III *vi* crier; **to ~ at sb** crier après qn; **to ~ at** or **to sb to come back** crier à qn de revenir; **to ~ for help** crier pour demander de l'aide.
■ **shout out**: ¶ **~ out** pousser un cri; ¶ **~ out [sth]** lancer [qch] à haute voix.

shouting *n* cris *mpl*.

shove° I *n* **to give sb/sth a ~** pousser qn/qch.
II *vtr* **1** (push) pousser (**against** contre; **towards** vers); **to ~ sb/sth aside** écarter qn/qch en le poussant; **to ~ sth into sth** fourrer qch dans qch; **2** (jostle) bousculer [*person*].
III *vi* pousser.
IDIOMS **if push comes to ~** au pire.

shovel I *n* pelle *f*.
II *vtr* enlever [qch] à la pelle [*dirt, leaves, snow*] (**off** de); **to ~ sth into sth** verser qch dans qch à l'aide d'une pelle.

show I *n* **1** spectacle *m*; (particular performance) représentation *f*; (in cinema) séance *f*; (on radio, TV) émission *f*; (of slides) projection *f*; **family ~** spectacle pour tous; **2** (exhibition) exposition *f*; (of cars, boats) salon *m*; (of fashion) défilé *m*; **flower/dog ~** exposition florale/canine; **to be on ~** être exposé; **3** (of feelings) semblant *m* (**of** de); (of strength) démonstration *f* (**of** de); (of wealth) étalage *m* (**of** de); **he made a ~ of concern** il a affiché sa sollicitude; **to be just for ~** être de l'esbroufe°; **4** (performance) **the team put up a good ~** l'equipe s'est bien défendue; **5 she runs the whole ~** c'est elle qui fait marcher l'affaire.

should

◆ ***should***, when it implies an *obligation* (= ***ought to***), is translated by the present conditional of ***devoir***:

*she **should** learn to drive* = elle **devrait** apprendre à conduire

*we **should** leave now* = nous **devrions** partir maintenant

***shouldn't** you be at school?* = est-ce que tu ne **devrais** pas être à l'école?

*he **shouldn't** smoke so much* = il ne **devrait** pas tant fumer

*I **should** explain that she's shortsighted* = je **devrais** peut-être expliquer qu'elle est myope

To translate ***should have*** (= ***ought to have***), use the past conditional of ***devoir***:

*we **should have** had a party* = nous **aurions dû** faire une fête

*you **should have** told me before* = tu **aurais dû** me le dire avant

*you **shouldn't** have said that* = tu n'**aurais** pas **dû** dire ça ⇨ **1**

◆ ***should*** can also mean that something is *probable*: use the present conditional of ***devoir***:

*dinner **should** be ready soon* = le dîner **devrait** être bientôt prêt

*it **should**n't be difficult to convince her* = ça ne **devrait** pas être trop difficile de la convaincre

*we **should** be there by six o'clock* = nous **devrions** arriver vers six heures

The past tense ***should have*** (***done/said*** etc) is translated by the past conditional of ***devoir*** and implies that what was *probable* did not occur:

*the letter **should have** arrived yesterday* = la lettre **aurait dû** arriver hier

*the ticket **should**n't have cost so much* = le billet n'**aurait** pas **dû** coûter si cher

***should**n't they have consulted you first?* = est-ce qu'ils n'**auraient** pas **dû** te consulter avant? ⇨ **2**

◆ ***should***, as a more formal version of ***would***, is translated by the conditional of the appropriate verb:

*I **should like** to go to Paris* = j'**aimerais** aller à Paris

*I **shouldn't be** surprised* = cela ne m'**étonnerait** pas

*I **should have thought** he'd be delighted* = j'**aurais pensé** qu'il serait ravi ⇨ **3**

◆ In formal uses, ***should*** can refer to a future possibility, and the structure ***si*** + *present tense* is often used:

***should** the opportunity arise* = **si** l'occasion se présente

***if** you **should** change your mind, don't hesitate to contact me* = **si** vous changez d'avis, n'hésitez pas à me contacter

***should** you be interested, I should be happy to provide further details* = **si** vous désirez obtenir des renseignements supplémentaires, je reste à votre disposition 

For translations of some idiomatic expressions using ***should***, see the entry **should**. ⇨ **5**

II *vtr* **1** montrer [*person, object, photo, feelings*] (**to** à); présenter [*ticket*] (**to** à); [*TV channel, cinema*] passer [*film*]; [*garment*] laisser voir [*underclothes, dirt, stain*]; indiquer [*time, direction, area*]; **to ~ sb sth** montrer qch à qn; **2** (exhibit) présenter [*animal*]; exposer [*flower, vegetables*]; **3** [*reply*] témoigner de [*wit, intelligence*]; **to ~ consideration/favouritism towards sb, to ~ sb consideration/favouritism** être gentil avec/favoriser qn; **to ~ one's age** accuser son âge; **as shown in diagram 12** comme on le voit figure 12; **4** (prove) démontrer [*truth, validity, guilt*]; **to ~ that** [*document*] prouver que; [*findings*] démontrer que; [*facial expression*] montrer que; **5 to ~ sb to their seat** placer qn; **to ~ sb to their room** accompagner qn à sa chambre; **to ~ sb to the door** reconduire qn.

III *vi* **1** [*stain, label*] se voir; [*emotion*] se voir; (in eyes) se lire; **2** (be exhibited) [*artist*] exposer; [*film*] passer.

IDIOMS **to have nothing to ~ for sth** ne rien avoir tiré de qch; **to steal the ~** être l'attraction.

▪ **show in**: **~ [sb] in** faire entrer.

▪ **show off**: ¶ **~ off**○ faire le fier/la fière; ¶ **~ [sb/sth] off, ~ off [sb/sth]** mettre [qch] en valeur [*special feature*]; faire admirer [*skill*]; exhiber [*baby, car*].

▪ **show out**: **~ [sb] out** accompagner [qn] à la porte.

▪ **show round**: **~ [sb] round** faire visiter.

▪ **show up**: ¶ **~ up** ○(arrive) se montrer○; ¶ **~ up [sth]** révéler [*fault, mark*]; ¶ **~ [sb] up**: **to ~ sb up for what he/she is** montrer la vraie nature de qn.

show: **~ business** *n* industrie *f* du spectacle; **~down** *n* confrontation *f*.

shower I *n* **1** douche *f*; **to have a ~** prendre une douche; **2** (of rain) averse *f*; **light/heavy ~** petite/grosse averse.

II *vtr* **1 to ~ sb with sth** couvrir qn de [*gifts, compliments, praise*].

III *vi* [*person*] prendre une douche.

show: **~ jumping** *n* saut *m* d'obstacles; **~room** *n* exposition *f*.

shrapnel *n* éclats *mpl* d'obus.

shred I *n* **1** (of paper, fabric) lambeau *m*; **2** (of evidence, truth) parcelle *f*.

II *vtr* déchiqueter [*paper*]; râper [*vegetables*].

shrewd *adj* [*person*] habile; [*face*] plein d'astuce; [*move, investment*] astucieux/-ieuse; **to make a ~ guess** deviner juste.

shriek I *n* **1** (of pain, fear) cri *m* perçant, hurlement *m*; (of delight) cri *m*; **~s of laughter** éclats *mpl* de rire; **2** (of bird) cri *m*.

II *vi* crier, hurler (**in, with** de).

shrill *adj* [*voice, cry, laugh*] perçant; [*whistle, tone*] strident.

shrimp *n* crevette *f* grise.

shrine *n* **1** (place) lieu *m* de pèlerinage; **2** (building) chapelle *f*; **3** (tomb) tombeau *m*.

shrink I *vtr* faire rétrécir [*fabric*]; contracter [*wood*].

II *vi* **1** [*fabric*] rétrécir; [*timber*] se contracter; [*dough, meat*] réduire; [*forest, area*] reculer; [*sales*] être en recul; [*resources*] s'amenuiser; [*old person, body*] se tasser; **2 to ~ from** se dérober devant [*conflict, responsibility*]; **to ~ from doing** hésiter à faire.

shrinkage *n* (of fabric) rétrécissement *m*; (of timber) contraction *f*.

shrinking *adj* [*population, market*] en baisse.

shrivel I *vtr* [*sun, heat*] flétrir [*skin*]; dessécher [*plant, leaf*].

II *vi* (also **~ up**) [*fruit, vegetable*] se ratatiner; [*skin*] se flétrir; [*plant, meat*] se dessécher.

shroud I *n* linceul *m*.

II *vtr* envelopper (**in** dans).

Shrove Tuesday *n* mardi *m* gras.

shrub *n* arbuste *m*.

shrubbery *n* massif *m* d'arbustes.

shrug I *n* haussement *m* d'épaules.

II *vtr* **to ~ one's shoulders** hausser les épaules.

▪ **shrug off**: **~ off [sth], ~ [sth] off** ignorer [*problem, rumour*].

shudder I *n* **1** (of person) frisson *m* (**of** de); **2** (of vehicle) secousse *f*.

II *vi* **1** [*person*] frissonner (**with** de); **2** [*vehicle*] **to ~ to a halt** avoir quelques soubresauts et s'arrêter.

shuffle I *vtr* **1** battre [*cards*]; **2** brasser [*papers*].

II *vi* **to ~ along** marcher en traînant les pieds.

shun *vtr* fuir [*people, publicity, temptation*]; dédaigner [*work*].

shunt I *vtr* aiguiller [*wagon, engine*] (**into** sur).

II *vi* [*train*] changer de voie; **to ~ back and forth** manœuvrer.

shut I *adj* fermé; **her eyes were ~** elle avait les yeux fermés; **to slam the door ~** claquer la porte (pour bien la fermer); **to keep one's mouth**○ **~** se taire.

II *vtr* fermer.

III *vi* **1** [*door, book, box, mouth*] se fermer; **2** [*office, factory*] fermer.

▪ **shut down**: ¶ **~ down** [*business*] fermer; [*machinery*] s'arrêter; ¶ **~ [sth] down, ~ down [sth]** fermer [*business*]; arrêter [*machinery*].

▪ **shut off**: ¶ **~ [sth] off, ~ off [sth]** couper [*supply, motor*]; arrêter [*oven, fan*]; fermer [*access, valve*]; ¶ **~ [sb/sth] off** isoler (**from** de).

▪ **shut out**: **~ out [sb/sth], ~ [sb/sth] out** **1** laisser [qn/qch] dehors [*animal, person*]; éliminer [*noise*]; **to be shut out** être à la porte; **2** empêcher [qch] d'entrer [*light*]; bloquer [*view*].

▪ **shut up**: ¶ **~ up**○ se taire (**about** au sujet de); ¶ **~ [sb] up, ~ up [sb] 1**○ (silence) faire taire [*person*]; **2** (confine) enfermer [*person, animal*] (**in** dans); **3** fermer [*house*]; **to ~ up shop**○ fermer boutique○.

shutdown *n* (of factory) fermeture *f*; (of reactor) arrêt *m* (du réacteur).

shutter *n* **1** (wooden, metal) volet *m*; (on shop front) store *m*; **2** (on camera) obturateur *m*.

shuttle I *n* **1** navette *f*; **2** (also **~cock**) volant *m*.
II *vtr* transporter [*passengers*].
III *vi* **to ~ between** faire la navette entre [*terminals*].

shy I *adj* [*person*] timide (**with, of** avec); [*animal*] farouche (**with, of** avec).
II *vi* [*horse*] faire un écart (**at** devant).

shyness *n* timidité *f*.

sibling *n* frère/sœur *m/f*.

Sicily *pr n* Sicile *f*.

sick *adj* **1** (ill) malade; **worried ~** malade d'inquiétude; **2** (nauseous) **to be ~** vomir; **to feel ~** avoir mal au cœur; **rhubarb makes him ~** il ne supporte pas la rhubarbe; **you'll make yourself ~** tu vas te rendre malade; **3** [*joke, mind*] malsain; **4** (disgusted) écœuré, dégoûté; **it's enough to make you ~** c'est écœurant; **5**○ **to be ~ of sb/sth**○ en avoir assez or marre○ de qn/qch; **to be ~ and tired of sth/sb**○ en avoir ras le bol○ de qch/qn.

sick bay *n* infirmerie *f*.

sicken I *vtr* (disgust) écœurer.
II *vi* **to be ~ing for sth** couver qch.

sick leave *n* congé *m* de maladie.

sickly *adj* **1** [*person, plant*] chétif/-ive; [*complexion*] blafard; **2** [*smell, taste*] écœurant; [*colour*] fadasse; **~ sweet** douceâtre.

sickness *n* **1** (illness) maladie *f*; **2** (nausea) **bouts of ~** vomissements *mpl*.

sick: **~pay** *n* indemnité *f* de maladie; **~room** *n* infirmerie *f*.

side I *n* **1** côté *m*; (of animal's body, hill, boat) flanc *m*; (of lake, road) bord *m*; **on my left/right ~** à ma gauche/droite; **on one's/its ~** sur le côté; **~ by ~** côte à côte; **on the hill ~** à flanc de coteau; **the north ~ of town** le nord de la ville; **the right ~** (of cloth) l'endroit *m*; (of paper) le recto; **the wrong ~** (of cloth) l'envers *m*; (of paper) le verso; **at** or **by the ~ of** au bord de [*lake, road*]; à côté de [*building*]; **to take ~s** prendre position; **2** (Sport) (team) équipe *f*.
II *noun modifier* [*door, window, entrance, view*] latéral.
III **on the side** *phr* **with salad on the ~** avec de la salade; **to do sth on the ~** (in addition) faire qch à côté; (illegally) faire qch au noir.
■ **side with** se mettre du côté de [*person*].

side: **~board** *n* buffet *m*; **~boards** (GB), **~burns** *n pl* pattes *fpl*; **~ dish** *n* plat *m* d'accompagnement; **~ effect** *n* (of drug) effet *m* secondaire; (of action) répercussion *f*; **~light** *n* feu *m* de position.

sideline *n* **1 as a ~** comme à-côté; **2** (Sport) ligne *f* de touche; **over the ~** en touche; **on the ~s** sur la touche.

side: **~long** *adj* [*look*] oblique; **~ plate** *n* petite assiette *f*; **~ road** *n* petite route *f*; **~ saddle** *adv* en amazone; **~ show** *n* attraction *f*; **~step** *vtr* éviter [*opponent*]; éluder [*issue*]; **~ street** *n* petite rue *f*; **~ stroke** *n* brasse *f* indienne.

sidetrack *vtr* fourvoyer [*person*]; **to get ~ed** se fourvoyer.

sidewalk *n* (US) trottoir *m*.

sideways I *adj* [*look, glance*] de travers.
II *adv* [*move*] latéralement; [*look at*] de travers.

siding *n* voie *f* de garage.

siege *n* siège *m*; **to lay ~ to sth** assiéger qch.

siesta *n* sieste *f*; **to have a ~** faire la sieste.

sieve I *n* (for draining) passoire *f*; (for sifting) tamis *m*.
II *vtr* tamiser [*flour*].

sift *vtr* **1** tamiser, passer [qch] au tamis [*flour*]; **2** passer [qch] au crible [*data, evidence, information*].
■ **sift through**: **~ through [sth]** trier [*applications*]; fouiller (dans) [*ashes*].

sigh I *n* soupir *m*.
II *vi* soupirer, pousser un soupir; **to ~ with relief** pousser un soupir de soulagement.

sight I *n* **1** vue *f*; **to have good/poor ~** avoir une bonne/mauvaise vue; **at first ~** à première vue; **at the ~ of blood** à la vue du sang; **to catch ~ of sb/sth** apercevoir qn/qch; **to lose ~ of sb/sth** perdre qn/qch de vue; **to know sb by ~** connaître qn de vue; **I can't stand the ~ of him!** je ne peux pas le voir○ (en peinture)!; **to be in ~** [*land, border*] être en vue; [*peace, freedom*] être proche; **to come into ~** apparaître; **to be out of ~** être caché; **to stay out of ~** rester caché; **don't let her out of your ~!** ne la quitte pas des yeux!; **2** (scene) spectacle *m*; **it was not a pretty ~!** ce n'était pas beau à voir!
II **sights** *n pl* **1** attractions *fpl* touristiques (**of** de); **to see the ~s** faire du tourisme; **2** (on rifle, telescope) viseur *m*; **3 to set one's ~s on sth** viser qch.

sightseeing *n* tourisme *m*; **to go ~** faire du tourisme.

sightseer *n* touriste *mf*.

sign I *n* **1** signe *m*; **the ~ of the cross** le signe de la croix; **the pound ~** le symbole de la livre sterling; **2** (road sign, billboard) panneau *m* (**for** pour); (smaller) pancarte *f*; (outside shop) enseigne *f*.
II *vtr* signer.
III *vi* **1** signer; **~ for** signer un reçu pour; **2** (Sport) signer son contrat (**with** avec; **for** pour); **3** (in sign language) communiquer en langage des sourds-muets.
■ **sign on**: ¶ **~ on 1** (GB) (for benefit) pointer au chômage; **2** (to course of study) s'inscrire (**for** à, dans); ¶ **~ on [sb]** engager.
■ **sign up 1** (in forces) s'engager; **2** (for course) s'inscrire (**for** à, dans).

signal I *n* signal *m* (**for** de).
II *vtr* **to ~ (to sb) that** faire signe (à qn) que.
III *vi* **1** (gesture) faire des signes; **2** (in car) mettre son clignotant.

signature *n* signature *f*.

signature tune *n* indicatif *m*.

significance *n* **1** (importance) importance *f*; **not of any ~, of no ~** sans aucune importance; **2** (meaning) signification *f*.

significant *adj* [*amount, impact*] considérable; [*event, role*] important; [*gesture*] éloquent; [*name, figure*] significatif/-ive.

signify *vtr* indiquer.
sign language *n* code *m* or langage *m* gestuel.
signpost I *n* panneau *m* indicateur.
II *vtr* indiquer [*place, direction*]; **to be ~ed** être indiqué.
silence I *n* silence *m*; **in ~** en silence.
II *vtr* faire taire.
silencer *n* silencieux *m*.
silent *adj* **1** silencieux/-ieuse; **to be ~** se taire; **to remain ~** rester silencieux; **to fall ~** se taire; **2** [*disapproval, prayer*] muet/muette; **3** [*film*] muet/muette.
silent partner *n* commanditaire *m*.
silhouette *n* silhouette *f*.
silicon chip *n* puce *f* électronique.
silk *n* soie *f*.
silky *adj* soyeux/-euse.
silly I *adj* [*person*] idiot; [*question, game*] stupide; [*behaviour, clothes*] ridicule; **to make sb look ~** faire passer qn pour un/-e idiot/-e.
II *adv* **to drink oneself ~** s'abrutir d'alcool; **to bore sb ~** assommer qn.
silo *n* silo *m*.
silt *n* limon *m*, vase *f*.
silver ▶559 I *n* **1** (metal, colour) argent *m*; **2** (silverware) argenterie *f*; (cutlery) couverts *mpl* en argent; (coins) monnaie *f*; **3** (medal) médaille *f* d'argent.
II *adj* [*ring, coin*] en argent; [*hair, moon*] argenté; [*paint*] gris métallisé *inv*.
silver: **~ birch** *n* bouleau *m* argenté; **~ foil** *n* (GB) papier *m* d'aluminium; **~ plated** *adj* plaqué argent; **~smith** ▶805 *n* orfèvre *mf*; **~ware** *n* argenterie *f*.
similar *adj* similaire, analogue; **something ~** quelque chose de similaire; **~ to** analogue à, comparable à; **~ in price** comparable pour ce qui est du prix; **~ in colour** dans les mêmes tons.
similarity *n* ressemblance *f* (**to, with** avec).
similarly *adv* [*behave, dressed*] de la même façon; **and ~,...** et de même,...
simmer *vi* **1** [*soup*] cuire à feu doux, mijoter; [*water*] frémir; **2** [*person*] bouillonner (**with** de); [*revolt, violence*] couver.
simple *adj* **1** simple; [*dress, furniture, style*] sobre; **2** (dimwitted) simplet/-ette°, simple d'esprit.
simplicity *n* simplicité *f*.
simplify *vtr* simplifier.
simplistic *adj* simpliste.
simultaneous *adj* simultané; **to be ~** avoir lieu en même temps (**with** que).
sin I *n* péché *m*, crime *m*.
II *vi* pécher (**against** contre).
since ▶861 I *prep* depuis; **I haven't seen him ~ then** je ne l'ai pas vu depuis; **I haven't been feeling well ~ Monday** je ne me sens pas bien depuis lundi.
II *conj* **1** (from the time when) depuis que; **~ he's been away** depuis qu' il est absent; **ever ~ I married him** depuis que nous nous sommes mariés, depuis notre mariage; **I've known him ~ I was 12** je le connais depuis que j'ai 12 ans or depuis l'age de 12 ans; **it's 10 years ~ we last met** cela fait 10 ans que nous ne nous sommes pas revus; **2** (because) comme; **~ she was ill, she couldn't go** comme elle était malade, elle ne pouvait pas y aller; **~ you're so clever, do it yourself!** puisque tu es tellement malin, fais-le toi-même!
III *adv* **she has ~ qualified** depuis elle a obtenu son diplôme; **I haven't phoned her ~** je ne lui ai pas téléphoné depuis.
sincere *adj* sincère.
sincerely *adv* sincèrement; **Yours ~**, **Sincerely yours** (US) Veuillez agréer, Monsieur/Madame, l'expression de mes sentiments les meilleurs; (less formally) Cordialement (vôtre).
sincerity *n* sincérité *f*.
sinew *n* tendon *m*.
sinewy *adj* **1** [*person, animal*] (mince et) musclé; **2** [*meat*] tendineux/-euse.
sing I *vtr* chanter; **to ~ sb's praises** chanter les louanges de qn.
II *vi* chanter; **to ~ in/out of tune** chanter juste/faux.
Singapore ▶574 *pr n* Singapour *f*; **in/to ~** à Singapour.
singe *vtr* brûler [qch] légèrement [*hair, clothing*]; (with iron) roussir [*clothes*].
singer ▶805 *n* chanteur/-euse *m/f*.
singing I *n* chant *m*; **to hear ~** entendre chanter.
II *noun modifier* [*lesson*] de chant; [*career*] dans la chanson.
singing voice *n* voix *f*.
single I *n* **1** (also **~ ticket**) aller *m* simple; **2** (also **~ room**) chambre *f* à une personne; **3** (record) 45 tours *m*.
II *adj* **1** (sole) seul; **a ~ rose** une seule rose; **in a ~ day** en une seule journée; **2** (not double) [*sink*] à un bac; [*sheet, duvet*] pour une personne; **inflation is in ~ figures** l'inflation est inférieure à 10%; **3** (for one) [*bed, tariff, portion*] pour une personne; **4** (unmarried) célibataire; **5 every ~ day** tous les jours sans exception; **every ~ one of those people** chacune de ces personnes; **not a ~ thing was left** il ne restait pas la moindre chose; **6 the ~ most important factor** le facteur principal; **the ~ most important reason** la cause majeure.
■ **single out**: **~ [sb/sth] out**, **~ out [sb/sth]** choisir; **to be ~d out for** faire l'objet de [*praise, criticism*]; être l'objet de [*attention*].
single: **~-breasted** *adj* [*jacket*] droit; **~ cream** *n* ≈ crème *f* fraîche liquide; **~ file** *adv* en file indienne; **~-handed(ly)** *adv* tout/-e seul/-e; **~-lens reflex**, **SLR** *n* reflex *m* à un objectif; **~ market** *n* marché *m* unique; **~-minded** *adj* tenace, résolu; **~ mother** *n* mère *f* qui élève ses enfants seule; **~-parent** *adj* [*family*] monoparental.
singles *n pl* (Sport) **the women's/men's ~** le simple dames/messieurs.

since

As a preposition

◆ ***since*** is used in English to indicate the point when an event that is still going on started. To express this, French uses *present* + ***depuis***:

I've been waiting ***since*** *Saturday* = j'attends **depuis** samedi
I've lived in Rome ***since*** *1988* = je vis à Rome **depuis** 1988
he's been in France ***since*** *March* = il est en France **depuis** le mois de mars

◆ When ***since*** places the event further back in the past, French uses *imperfect* + ***depuis***:

I had been waiting ***since*** *9 o'clock* = j'attendais **depuis** 9 heures
she had been a teacher ***since*** *1965* = elle était professeur **depuis** 1965
they had been living there ***since*** *1960* = ils habitaient là **depuis** 1960

◆ In negative sentences, ***since*** is again translated by ***depuis***, but the tenses used are generally the same in both languages:

I haven't seen him ***since*** *Monday* = je ne l'ai pas vu **depuis** lundi
we haven't heard from them ***since*** *June* = nous n'avons pas eu de leurs nouvelles depuis le mois de juin
I hadn't seen him ***since*** *1978* = je ne l'avais pas vu **depuis** 1978
he hadn't been back to Poland ***since*** *the end of the war* = il n'était pas retourné en Pologne **depuis** la fin de la guerre ⇨ **I**

As a conjunction

◆ When ***since*** is used as a conjunction in time expressions, it is usually translated by ***depuis que*** and the tenses used are the same as those used with the preposition ***depuis***:

since *she's been living in Oxford* = **depuis qu'**elle habite à Oxford
since *I'd been in Paris* = **depuis que** j'étais à Paris
since *we've been working here* = **depuis que** nous travaillons ici ⇨ **II1**

◆ Note that in time expressions with ***since***, where English uses a verb (*arrive* = arriver; *leave* = partir; *die* = mourir etc), French native speakers will generally prefer to use the corresponding noun (*arrival* = arrivée; *departure* = départ; *death* = mort etc):

I haven't seen him ***since he left*** = je ne l'ai pas vu **depuis son départ**
she's been living in Nice ***since she got married*** = elle habite à Nice **depuis son mariage**
we've known each other ***since we were 12 years old*** = nous nous connaissons **depuis l'âge de 12 ans**

◆ When ***since*** is used as a conjunction to mean *because* it is translated by ***comme***:

since *it was raining, we stayed at home* = **comme** il pleuvait, nous sommes restés à la maison
since *I haven't got her address, I can't write to her* = **comme** je n'ai pas son adresse, je ne peux pas lui écrire ⇨ **II2**

As an adverb

◆ When ***since*** is used as an adverb, it is translated by ***depuis***:

he hasn't been seen ***since*** = on ne l'a pas vu **depuis**
we've kept in touch ever ***since*** = nous sommes restés en contact **depuis** ⇨ **III**

singlet *n* (GB) **1** (Sport) maillot *m*; **2** (vest) maillot *m* de corps.

singular *n* singulier *m*; **in the ~** au singulier.

sinister *adj* sinistre.

sink I *n* (in kitchen) évier *m*; (in bathroom) lavabo *m*; **double ~** évier à deux bacs.
II *vtr* **1** couler [*ship*]; **2** forer [*oil well, shaft*]; creuser [*foundations*]; enfoncer [*post, pillar*] (**into** dans); **the dog sank its teeth into my arm** le chien a planté ses crocs dans mon bras.
III *vi* **1** [*ship, object, person*] couler; **2** [*sun, water level, pressure*] baisser; [*cake*] redescendre; **to ~ to the floor** s'effondrer; **to ~ into a chair** s'affaler dans un fauteuil; **to ~ into a deep sleep** sombrer dans un profond sommeil; **3** (fall) baisser; **he has sunk in my estimation** il a baissé dans mon estime; **4** [*building, wall*] s'effondrer; **to ~ into** s'enfoncer dans [*mud*]; sombrer dans [*anarchy, obscurity*].
■ **sink in** [*news, announcement*] faire son chemin; **it took several minutes for the truth to ~ in** il m'a fallu plusieurs minutes pour accepter la vérité.

sinus *n* sinus *m inv*.

sinusitis ▶ 686 *n* sinusite *f*.

sip I *n* petite gorgée *f*.
II *vtr* boire [qch] à petites gorgées.

siphon I *n* siphon *m*.
II *vtr* (also **~ off**) siphonner [*petrol, water*].

sir ▶ 642 *n* Monsieur; **yes ~** (in general) oui, Monsieur; (to president) oui, Monsieur le président; (to headmaster) oui, Monsieur le directeur; **Dear Sir** Monsieur.

siren *n* sirène *f*.

sirloin *n* aloyau *m*.

sister *n* **1** (sibling) sœur *f*; **older** or **elder/younger ~** sœur aînée/cadette; **2** (GB) (nurse) infirmière *f* chef.

sister-in-law *n* belle-sœur *f*.

sit I *vtr* **1 to ~ sb in/near** asseoir qn dans/près de; **2** (GB) se présenter à, passer [*exam*].
II *vi* **1** s'asseoir (**at** à; **in** dans; **on** sur); **to ~/be sitting on the floor** s'asseoir/être assis par terre; **to ~ for two hours** rester assis pendant deux heures; **to ~ quietly** être tranquillement assis; **to ~ still** se tenir tranquille; **2** [*committee, court*] siéger; **3 to ~ on** faire partie de [*committee, jury*]; **4 the books were still ~ting on the desk** les livres étaient toujours sur le bureau; **the car is ~ting there rusting** la voiture reste là à rouiller; **5** [*hen*] **to ~ on** couver [*eggs*].
■ **sit about, sit around** rester assis à ne rien faire.
■ **sit down** s'asseoir (**at** à; **in** dans; **on** sur); **to ~ down to dinner** se mettre à table.
■ **sit in** [*observer*] assister (**on** à).
■ **sit up** se redresser; **to be ~ing up** être assis; **~ up straight!** tiens-toi droit!

sitcom○ *n* sitcom *m*.

site *n* **1** (also **building ~**) (before building) terrain *m*; (during building) chantier *m*; **2** (for tent) emplacement *m*; **caravan ~** (GB) terrain *m* de caravaning; **3** (archaeological) site *m*.

sitting *n* **1** (session) séance *f*; **I read it at one ~** je l'ai lu d'un seul trait; **2** (in canteen) service *m*.

sitting: **~ room** *n* salon *m*; **~ target** *n* cible *f* facile.

situate *vtr* situer; **to be ~d** être situé, se trouver.

situation *n* situation *f*; **'~s vacant'** 'offres *fpl* d'emploi'; **'~s wanted'** 'demandes *fpl* d'emploi'.

sit-ups *n pl* abdominaux *mpl*.

six ▶ 492, 554 *n, pron, det* six (*m*) *inv*.
IDIOMS **it's ~ of one and half a dozen of the other** c'est bonnet blanc et blanc bonnet, c'est du pareil au même○.

sixteen ▶ 492, 554 *n, pron, det* seize (*m*) *inv*.

sixteenth ▶ 584, 642 **I** *n* **1** (in order) seizième *mf*; **2** (of month) seize *m inv*.
II *adj, adv* seizième.

sixth ▶ 584, 642 **I** *n* **1** (in order) sixième *mf*; **2** (of month) six *m inv*; **3** (fraction) sixième *m*.
II *adj, adv* sixième.

sixth form (GB Sch) *n* (lower) ≈ classes *fpl* de première; (upper) ≈ classes *fpl* de terminale; **in the ~** ≈ en première or en terminale.

sixth sense *n* sixième sens *m*.

sixties ▶ 492, 584 *n pl* **1 the ~** les années *fpl* soixante; **2 to be in one's ~** avoir entre soixante et soixante-dix ans.

sixtieth I *n* (in order, sequence) soixantième *mf*.
II *adj, adv* soixantième.

sixty ▶ 492 *n, pron, det* soixante (*m*) *inv*.

size *n* **1** taille *f*; (of container, room, building, region) grandeur *f*; (of apple, egg, book, parcel) grosseur *f*; (of carpet, bed, machine) dimensions *fpl*; **it's about the ~ of an egg/of this room** c'est à peu près de la grosseur d'un œuf/de la grandeur de cette pièce; **he's about your ~** il est à peu près de ta taille; **2** (of population, audience) importance *f*; (of class, school, company) effectif *m*; **3** (of garment) taille *f*; (of shirt collar) encolure *f*; (of shoes, gloves) pointure *f*; **a pair of shoes ~ 39** une paire de chaussures pointure 39; **have you got this in a smaller/larger ~?** avez-vous ce modèle en plus petit/plus grand?; **what ~ do you take?, what ~ are you?** (in clothes) quelle taille faites-vous?; (in shoes) quelle pointure faites-vous?, vous chaussez du combien?; **to take ~ X** (in clothes) faire du X; (in shoes) chausser or faire du X.
IDIOMS **to cut sb down to ~** remettre qn à sa place, rabattre le caquet à qn○.
■ **size up**: **~ up [sb/sth], ~ [sb/sth] up** se faire une opinion de [*person*]; évaluer [qch] du regard [*surroundings*]; évaluer [*situation*]; mesurer [*problem*].

sizeable *adj* [*proportion*] non négligeable; [*amount*] assez important; [*house, field, town*] assez grand.

sizzle *vi* grésiller.

skate I *n* **1** (ice) patin *m* à glace; (roller) patin *m* à roulettes; **2** (fish) raie *f*.

II *vi* patiner (**on, along** sur); **to ~ across** or **over** traverser [qch] en patins [*lake*].

skate: **~board** *n* skateboard *m*, planche *f* à roulettes; **~boarding** ▶649 *n* skateboard *m*, planche *f* à roulettes.

skater *n* patineur/-euse *m/f*.

skating ▶649 *n* patinage *m*.

skating: **~ boots** *n pl* (GB) patins *mpl* à glace; **~ rink** *n* (ice) patinoire *f*; (roller-skating) piste *f* de patins à roulettes.

skeleton *n* squelette *m*.

skeleton key *n* passe-partout *m inv*.

skeptic (US) = **sceptic**.

skeptical (US) = **sceptical**.

skepticism (US) = **scepticism**.

sketch **I** *n* **1** (drawing, draft) esquisse *f*; (hasty outline) croquis *m*; **rough ~** ébauche *f*; **2** (comic scene) sketch *m*.
II *vtr* faire une esquisse de; (hastily) faire un croquis de.

sketch: **~book** *n* carnet *m* à croquis; **~pad** *n* bloc *m* à dessin.

sketchy *adj* [*information, details*] sommaire; [*memory*] vague; [*work*] rapide.

skewer **I** *n* (for kebab) brochette *f*; (for joint) broche *f*.
II *vtr* embrocher [*joint*]; mettre [qch] en brochette [*chicken pieces*].

ski **I** *n* ski *m*.
II *vi* faire du ski; **to ~ down a slope** descendre une pente à skis; **to go ~ing** faire du ski.

skibob ▶649 *vi* faire du ski-bob.

skid **I** *n* dérapage *m*.
II *vi* déraper (**on** sur).

skier *n* skieur/-ieuse *m/f*.

skiing ▶649 *n* ski *m*; **cross country ~** ski *m* de fond; **downhill ~** ski *m* alpin.

skilful (GB), **skillful** (US) *adj* **1** [*person*] habile, adroit; [*portrayal*] excellent; **2** [*operation*] délicat.

ski lift *n* remontée *f* mécanique.

skill **I** *n* **1** (intellectual) habileté *f*, adresse *f*; (physical) dextérité *f*; **~ at** habileté or adresse à; **2** (special ability) (acquired) compétence *f*, capacités *fpl*; (innate) aptitude *f*; (practical) technique *f*; (gift) talent *m*; **your ~(s) as** vos talents de [*linguist, politician, mechanic*]; **~ at** or **in sth** compétence en qch.
II skills *n pl* (training) connaissances *fpl*.

skilled *adj* **1** (trained) [*labour, work*] qualifié; **semi-~** spécialisé; **2** (talented) [*actress, negotiator*] consommé.

skim **I** *vtr* **1** (remove cream) écrémer; (remove scum) écumer; (remove fat) dégraisser; **2** [*plane, bird*] raser, frôler [*surface, treetops*]; **3 to ~ stones** faire des ricochets avec des cailloux.
II *vi* **to ~ through** or **over** parcourir [*book, article*]; **to ~ over** passer rapidement sur [*event, facts*].

skim milk, **skimmed milk** *n* lait *m* écrémé.

skimp *vi* **to ~ on** lésiner sur [*expense, food, materials*]; économiser [*effort*].

skimpy *adj* [*garment*] minuscule; [*portion, allowance, income*] maigre (*before n*).

skin **I** *n* peau *f*; (of onion) pelure *f*.
II *vtr* **1** dépecer [*animal*]; **2 to ~ one's knee** s'écorcher le genou.
IDIOMS **to have a thick ~** être insensible; **to be** or **get soaked to the ~** être trempé jusqu'aux os○; **by the ~ of one's teeth** [*manage, pass, survive*] de justesse.

skin diving ▶649 *n* plongée *f* sous-marine.

skinny○ *adj* maigre.

skintight *adj* moulant.

skip **I** *n* **1** (jump) petit bond *m*; **2** (GB) (container) benne *f*.
II *vtr* **1** sauter [*meeting, lunch, school*]; **2** (leave out) sauter [*pages, chapter*]; **to ~ the formalities** sauter les formalités.
III *vi* **1** (once) bondir; (several times) sautiller; **2** (with rope) sauter à la corde.

ski: **~ pants** *n* fuseau *m* (de ski); **~ pass** *n* forfait-skieur *m*; **~ pole** *n* bâton *m* de ski.

skipper *n* (of ship) capitaine *m*; (of fishing boat) patron *m*; (of yacht) skipper *m*.

skipping rope *n* corde *f* à sauter.

skirt **I** *n* jupe *f*.
II *vtr* **1** contourner [*wood, village, city*]; **2** esquiver [*problem*].

skirting board *n* plinthe *f*.

ski: **~ slope** *n* piste *f*; **~ tow** *n* téléski *m*.

skittle ▶649 **I** *n* quille *f*.
II skittles *n pl* (jeu *m* de) quilles *fpl*.

skulk *vi* rôder; **to ~ out/off** sortir/s'éloigner furtivement.

skull *n* crâne *m*.

skull and crossbones *n* (emblem) tête *f* de mort; (flag) pavillon *m* à tête de mort.

skunk *n* moufette *f*.

sky *n* ciel *m*; **clear ~** ciel dégagé; **in(to) the ~** dans le ciel.

sky: **~-blue** ▶559 *n, adj* bleu (*m*) ciel *inv*; **~diving** ▶649 *n* parachutisme *m* (en chute libre).

sky-high *adv* **to rise ~** monter en flèche; **to blow sth ~** faire voler qch en éclats.

sky: **~light** *n* fenêtre *f* à tabatière; **~scraper** *n* gratte-ciel *m inv*.

slab *n* (of stone, wood, concrete) dalle *f*; (of meat, cheese, cake) pavé *m*; (of chocolate) tablette *f*; **fishmonger's ~** étal *m* de poissonnier.

slack **I** *n* (in rope, cable) mou *m*; **to take up the ~ in a rope** tendre une corde.
II *adj* **1** [*worker*] peu consciencieux/-ieuse; [*management*] négligent; [*student*] peu appliqué; [*work*] peu soigné; **to be ~ about doing** négliger de faire; **2** [*period*] creux/creuse (*after n*); [*demand, sales*] faible; **business is ~** les affaires tournent au ralenti; **3** [*cable, rope, body*] détendu.
III *vi* [*worker*] se relâcher dans son travail.

slacken **I** *vtr* **1** donner du mou à [*rope*]; lâcher [*reins*]; **2** réduire [*pace*].

II *vi* **1** [*rope*] se relâcher; **2** [*activity, pace, speed, business*] ralentir.
■ **slacken off** [*business, demand*] diminuer; [*gale, rain*] se calmer.

slacks *n pl* pantalon *m*; **a pair of ~** un pantalon.

slag *n* (from coal) (GB) stériles *mpl*; (from metal) scories *fpl*.

slag heap *n* terril *m*.

slalom ▶ 649 *n* slalom *m*.

slam I *n* **1** (of door) claquement *m*; **2** (in games) chelem *m*.
II *vtr* **1** [*person*] claquer [*door*]; [*wind*] faire claquer [*door*]; **to ~ the door behind one** sortir en claquant la porte derrière soi; **to ~ the door in sb's face** claquer la porte au nez de qn; **to ~ one's fist on the table** taper du poing sur la table; **to ~ the ball into the net** renvoyer brutalement la balle dans le filet; **2**○ (criticize) critiquer [qn] violemment (**for** pour; **for doing** pour avoir fait).
III *vi* [*door*] claquer (**against** contre); **to ~ shut** se refermer en claquant.
■ **slam down**: **~ down [sth], ~ [sth] down** raccrocher violemment [*phone*]; refermer violemment [*lid, car bonnet*]; jeter brutalement [*object*] (**on, onto** sur).

slander *n* (gen) calomnie *f* (**on** sur); (Law) diffamation *f* orale.

slanderous *adj* (gen) calomnieux/-ieuse; (Law) diffamatoire.

slang *n* argot *m*.

slant I *n* **1** (perspective) point *m* de vue (**on** sur); **with a European ~** d'un point de vue européen; **2** (bias) tendance *f*; **3** (slope) pente *f*; **the floor has a ~** le plancher est en pente.
II *vi* [*floor, ground*] être en pente; [*handwriting*] pencher (**to** vers); [*painting*] être de travers.
III **slanting** *pres p adj* [*roof*] en pente; **~ing eyes** yeux *mpl* bridés.

slanted *adj* **1** (biased) orienté (**to, towards** vers); **2** (sloping) en pente.

slap I *n* **1** tape *f* (**on** sur); (stronger) claque *f* (**on** sur); **a ~ on the face** une gifle; **to give sb a ~ on the back** (in congratulation) féliciter qn; **2** (sound) (bruit *m* d'une) claque *f*.
II *vtr* donner une tape à [*person, animal*]; **to ~ sb in** or **across the face** gifler qn.

slap bang○ *adv* **he ran ~ into the wall** il s'est cogné en plein dans le mur en courant; **~ in the middle (of)** au beau milieu (de).

slapdash○ *adj* [*person*] brouillon/-onne○; **in a ~ way** à la va-vite.

slash I *n* **1** (wound) balafre *f* (**on** à); **2** (cut) (in fabric, seat, tyre) lacération *f*; (in painting) entaille *f*; (in skirt) fente *f*; **3** (in printing) barre *f* oblique.
II *vtr* **1** balafrer [*cheek*]; faire une balafre à [*person*]; couper [*throat*]; [*knife*] entailler [*face*]; **to ~ one's wrists** se tailler les veines; **2** taillader [*painting, fabric, tyres*]; trancher [*cord*]; **3** (reduce) réduire [qch] (considérablement) [*amount, spending*]; sacrifier [*price*].

slat *n* (of shutter, blind) lamelle *f*; (of table, bench, bed) lame *f*.

slate I *n* ardoise *f*; **a roof ~** une ardoise.
II *vtr* **1** couvrir [qch] d'ardoises [*roof*]; **2**○ (GB) (criticize) [*press, critic*] taper sur○ [*film, politician, policy*] (**for** pour).
IDIOMS **to wipe the ~ clean** faire table rase.

slaughter I *n* **1** (in butchery) abattage *m*; **to go to ~** aller à l'abattoir; **2** (massacre) massacre *m*, boucherie○ *f*.
II *vtr* **1** abattre [*animal*]; **2** massacrer [*people*]; **3**○ (defeat) écraser.

slaughterhouse *n* abattoir *m*.

Slav I *n* Slave *mf*.
II *adj* slave.

slave I *n* esclave *mf*.
II *vi* (also **~ away**) travailler comme un forçat, trimer○.

slaver *vi* [*person, animal*] baver.

slavery *n* esclavage *m*.

slave trade *n* commerce *m* des esclaves; **the African ~** la traite des Noirs.

slaw (US) = **coleslaw**.

slay *vtr* faire périr [*enemy*]; pourfendre [*dragon*].

sleazy○ *adj* [*club, area, character*] louche; [*story, aspect*] scabreux/-euse; [*café, hotel*] borgne.

sled, **sledge** (GB) I *n* luge *f*; (sleigh) traineau *m*.
II *vi* faire de la luge; **to go sledging** faire de la luge.

sledgehammer *n* masse *f*.

sleek *adj* **1** [*hair*] lisse et brillant; [*animal*] au poil lisse et brillant; **2** [*shape*] élégant; [*figure*] mince et harmonieux/-ieuse.

sleep I *n* sommeil *m*; **to go** or **get to ~** s'endormir; **to go back to ~** se rendormir; **to send** or **put sb to ~** endormir qn; **to get some ~** or **to have a ~** dormir; **my leg has gone to ~**○ j'ai la jambe engourdie; **I didn't get any ~** or **a wink of ~ last night** j'ai passé une nuit blanche, je n'ai pas fermé l'œil de la nuit; **to put an animal to ~** faire piquer un animal.
II *vi* dormir; **to ~ soundly** (deeply) dormir profondément, dormir à poings fermés; (without worry) dormir tranquille; **~ tight!** dors bien!; **to ~ at a friend's house** coucher chez un ami.
IDIOMS **to ~ like a log** or **top** dormir comme une souche or un loir.
■ **sleep in** **1** (US) (lie in) faire la grasse matinée; **2** (live in) être logé sur place.
■ **sleep on**: **~ on [sth]**: **to ~ on a decision** attendre le lendemain pour prendre une décision.

sleeping *adj* [*person, animal*] qui dort, endormi.
IDIOMS **let ~ dogs lie** il ne faut pas réveiller le chat qui dort.

sleeping: **~ bag** *n* sac *m* de couchage; **~ car** *n* voiture-lit *f*, wagon-lit *m*; **~ pill** *n* somnifère *m*.

sleepless *adj* **to pass a ~ night** passer une nuit blanche.

sleep: **~walk** *vi* marcher en dormant, être somnambule; **~walking** *n* somnambulisme *m*.

sleepy *adj* [*voice, village*] endormi, somnolent; **to feel** or **be ~** avoir envie de dormir, avoir sommeil; **to make sb ~** [*fresh air*] donner envie de dormir à qn; [*wine*] endormir qn, assoupir qn.

sleet *n* neige *f* fondue.

sleeve *n* **1** (of garment) manche *f*; **to roll up one's ~s** retrousser ses manches; **2** (of record) pochette *f*; (of CD) boîtier *m*; **3** (Tech) (inner) chemise *f*; (outer) gaine *f*.
IDIOMS **to laugh up one's ~** rire sous cape; **to have something up one's ~** avoir quelque chose en réserve; **to have a few tricks up one's ~** avoir plus d'un tour dans son sac.

sleeveless *adj* sans manches.

sleigh *n* traîneau *m*.

sleight of hand *n* **1** (dexterity) dextérité *f*; **2** (trick) tour *m* de passe-passe.

slender *adj* **1** [*person*] mince; [*waist*] fin; [*finger*] effilé; [*neck*] gracile; [*stem, arch*] élancé; **2** [*income, means*] modeste, maigre (*before n*).

sleuth *n* limier *m*, détective *m*.

slew *vi* [*vehicle*] déraper; [*mast*] pivoter.

slice I *n* **1** (of bread, meat, fish) tranche *f*; (of cheese) morceau *m*; (of pie, tart) part *m*; (of lemon, cucumber, sausage) rondelle *f*; **2** (of profits) part *f*; (of territory, population) partie *f*; **3** (utensil) spatule *f*; **4** (Sport) slice *m*; **forehand ~** coup *m* droit; **back-hand ~** revers *m* slicé.
II *vtr* **1** couper [qch] (en tranches) [*loaf, roast*]; couper [qch] en rondelles [*lemon, cucumber*]; **2** fendre [*air*]; **3** (Sport) slicer, couper [*ball*].
III *vi* **to ~ through** fendre [*water, air*]; trancher [*timber, rope, meat*].

sliced bread *n* pain *m* en tranches.

slick I *n* (also **oil ~**) (on water) nappe *f* de pétrole; (on shore) marée *f* noire.
II *adj* **1** [*production, campaign*] habile; [*operation, deal*] mené rondement; **2** (superficial) [*programme, publication*] qui a un éclat plutôt superficiel; **3** [*person*] roublard°; [*answer*] astucieux/-ieuse; [*excuse*] facile; **4** (US) (slippery) [*road, surface*] glissant; [*hair*] lissé.

slide I *n* **1** (in playground) toboggan *m*; **2** (photographic) diapositive *f*; **lecture with ~s** conférence avec projections; **3** (microscope plate) lame *f* porte-objet; **4** (GB) (also **hair ~**) barrette *f*; **5** (decline) baisse *f* (**in** de).
II *vtr* faire glisser.
III *vi* **1** [*car, person*] glisser, partir en glissade (**into** dans; **on** sur); **to ~ off** glisser de [*roof, table, deck*]; sortir de [*road*]; **2 to ~ down** dévaler [*slope*]; glisser le long de [*bannisters*]; **to ~ in and out** [*drawer, component*] coulisser; **3** [*prices, shares*] baisser; **to let sth ~** laisser qch aller à la dérive.

slide: **~ guitar** ▶753 *n* bottleneck *m*; **~ projector** *n* projecteur *m* de diapositives; **~ rule** (GB), **~ ruler** (US) *n* règle *f* à calcul; **~ show** *n* (at exhibition) diaporama *m*; (at lecture, at home) séance *f* de projection.

sliding *adj* [*door*] coulissant; [*roof*] ouvrant.

sliding scale *n* échelle *f* mobile.

slight I *n* affront *m* (**on** à; **from** de la part de).
II *adj* **1** [*change, delay, exaggeration, movement, rise*] léger/-ère (*before n*); [*risk, danger*] faible (*before n*); [*pause, hesitation*] petit (*before n*); **the chances of it happening are ~** il y a peu de chances que cela arrive; **not to have the ~est difficulty** ne pas avoir la moindre difficulté; **2** (in build) mince.
III *vtr* **1** (offend) humilier [*person*]; **2** (US) (underestimate) sous-estimer.

slightly *adv* [*fall, change*] légèrement; [*embarrassed, uneasy, different, more, less*] un peu; **~ built** mince.

slim I *adj* [*person, figure*] mince; [*ankle, leg*] fin, mince; [*watch, calculator*] plat.
II *vi* (GB) maigrir; **I'm ~ming** je fais un régime amaigrissant.

slime *n* dépôt *m* gluant or visqueux; (on riverbed) vase *f*; (of slug, snail) bave *f*.

slimline *adj* [*garment*] amincissant; [*drink*] diététique.

slimy *adj* [*weed, mould*] visqueux/-euse; [*plate*] gluant; [*wall*] suintant.

sling I *n* **1** (weapon) fronde *f*; (smaller) lance-pierres *m inv*; **2** (Med) écharpe *f*; **3** (for carrying baby) porte-bébé *m*; (for carrying load) élingue *f*.
II *vtr* lancer [*object, insult*] (**at** à); **to ~ a bag over one's shoulder** mettre son sac sur son épaule; **to be slung over sth** être jeté par-dessus qch.

slink *vi* **to ~ in** entrer furtivement; **to ~ off** [*person*] s'éloigner furtivement; [*dog*] s'en aller la queue basse.

slip I *n* **1** (error) erreur *f*; **~ of the tongue** lapsus *m*; **2** (receipt) reçu *m*; (for salary) bulletin *m*; **~ of paper** bout *m* de papier; **3** (stumble) faux pas *m*; **4** (petticoat) (full) combinaison *f*; (half) jupon *m*.
II *vtr* **1 to ~ [sth] into sth** glisser [qch] dans qch [*note, coin, joke*]; **she ~ped the shirt over her head** (put on) elle a enfilé sa chemise; (take off) elle a retiré sa chemise; **2**° **to ~ sb sth, to ~ sth to sb** glisser qch à qn; **3** [*dog*] se dégager de [*leash*]; [*boat*] filer [*moorings*]; **it ~ped my notice** or **attention that** je ne me suis pas aperçu que; **it had ~ped my mind (that)** j'avais complètement oublié (que); **to let ~ an opportunity** or **a chance (to do)** laisser échapper une occasion (de faire); **to let ~ a remark** laisser échapper une remarque; **4** (in knitting) **to ~ a stitch** glisser une maille; **5** (Med) **to ~ a disc** avoir une hernie discale; **6** (Aut) **to ~ the clutch** faire patiner l'embrayage.
III *vi* **1 ~ into** passer [*dress, costume*]; tomber dans [*coma*]; **2 to ~ into/out of** se glisser dans/hors de [*room, building*]; **3** [*person, vehicle*] glisser (**on** sur; **off** de); [*knife, razor, pen*] glisser, déraper; **the glass ~ped out of his hand** le verre lui a échappé des mains; **to ~ through sb's fingers** [*money, opportunity*] filer entre les doigts de qn; **4** (Aut) [*clutch*] patiner.

■ **slip away** partir discrètement.

■ **slip by** [*life, weeks, months*] s'écouler; [*time*] passer.

■ **slip out 1** [*person*] sortir discrètement; **2 it just ~ped out!** ça m'a échappé!

slip: **~knot** *n* nœud *m* coulant; **~-on (shoe)** *n* mocassin *m*.

slipped disc *n* hernie *f* discale.

slipper *n* pantoufle *f*.

slippery *adj* **1** [*road, fish, surface*] glissant; **2 a ~ customer**° un personnage suspect.

slip: **~ road** *n* bretelle *f* d'accès; **~shod** *adj* [*person*] négligent; [*appearance, work*] négligé, peu soigné; **~stream** *n* sillage *m*; **~-up**° *n* bourde° *f*; **~way** *n* cale *f* de construction.

slit I *n* fente *f* (**in** dans).
II *adj* [*eyes*] bridé; [*skirt*] fendu.
III *vtr* (on purpose) faire une fente dans; (by accident) déchirer; **to ~ sb's throat** égorger qn; **to ~ one's wrists** s'ouvrir les veines.

slither *vi* glisser.

sliver *n* (of glass) éclat *m*; (of food) mince tranche *f*.

slog° I *n* **a hard ~** un travail dur; **it's a long, hard ~ to the village** il faut un long effort pour atteindre le village.
II *vtr* taper de toutes ses forces dans [*ball*].
III *vi* (also **~ away**) travailler dur, bosser°.

slop I *vtr* renverser [*liquid*] (**onto** sur; **into** dans).
II *vi* (also **~ over**) [*liquid*] déborder (**into** dans).

slope I *n* **1** (incline) pente *f*; (of writing) inclinaison *f*; **2** (hillside) flanc *m*; **uphill ~** montée *f*; **downhill ~** descente *f*; **upper ~s** sommet *m* de la montagne.
II *vi* être en pente (**towards** vers); [*writing*] pencher (**to** vers).

sloppy *adj* **1**° [*personal appearance*] débraillé; [*work*] peu soigné; [*method, thinking*] qui manque de rigueur; **to be a ~ eater** manger comme un cochon; **2**° (over-emotional) sentimental; **3** (GB) (baggy) ample.

slops *n pl* (food) aliment *m* liquide; (dirty water) eaux *fpl* sales.

slot I *n* **1** (for coin, ticket) fente *f*; (for letters) ouverture *f*; (groove) rainure *f*; **2** (in timetable, schedule) créneau *m*; **a prime-time ~** une tranche horaire de grande écoute.
II *vtr* **to ~ sth into a machine** insérer qch dans une machine.
III *vi* **to ~ into sth** [*coin, piece*] s'insérer dans; **to ~ into place** or **position** s'encastrer.
■ **slot in**: ¶ **~ in** se mettre en place; ¶ **~ [sth] in, ~ in [sth]** insérer [*coin, piece*]; placer [*person*].

sloth *n* (Zool) paresseux *m*.

slot machine *n* (Games) machine *f* à sous; (vending machine) distributeur *m* automatique.

slouch *vi* **1** être avachi; **2** (also **~ around**) traînasser.

Slovak ▸**712** I *n* **1** (person) Slovaque *mf*; **2** (language) slovaque *m*.
II *adj* slovaque.

Slovakia ▸**574** *pr n* Slovaquie *f*.

Slovak Republic ▸**574** *pr n* République *f* slovaque.

Slovenia ▸**574** *pr n* Slovénie *f*.

slovenly *adj* [*person, dress, style*] négligé; [*habits*] malpropre; [*work*] bâclé.

slow I *adj* **1** lent; **he's a ~ worker** il est lent au travail; **to make ~ progress/a ~ recovery** avancer/se remettre lentement; **to be ~ to do** tarder à faire; **to be ~ in doing** être lent à faire; **2** (slack) [*business, trade, market*] stagnant; [*economic growth*] lent; **3** (dull-witted) lent (d'esprit); **4 to be ~** [*clock, watch*] retarder; **to be 10 minutes ~** retarder de 10 minutes; **5** [*pitch, court*] lourd.
II *adv* lentement.
III *vtr, vi* ▸ **slow down**.
■ **slow down**: ¶ **~ down** ralentir; ¶ **~ down [sth/sb], ~ [sth/sb] down** ralentir.

slowly *adv* lentement.

slow motion *n* ralenti *m*; **in ~** au ralenti.

slowness *n* lenteur *f*.

sludge *n* **1** (also **sewage ~**) eaux *fpl* usées; **2** (mud) vase *f*.

slug *n* limace *f*.

sluggish *adj* **1** [*person, animal*] léthargique; [*circulation, reaction*] lent; [*river*] stagnant; **2** [*market, trade, economy*] qui stagne.

sluice *n* **1** (also **~ gate**) vanne *f*; **2** (also **~way**) canal *m*.

slum *n* **1** (area) quartier *m* pauvre; **2** (dwelling) taudis *m*.

slumber I *n* sommeil *m*.
II *vi* sommeiller.

slump I *n* (in trade, prices, market) effondrement *m* (**in** de).
II *vi* **1** [*demand, trade, value, price*] chuter (**from** de; **to** à; **by** de); [*economy, market*] s'effondrer; [*support, popularity*] être en forte baisse; **2** [*person, body*] s'affaler°.

slur I *n* **1** (in speech) marmonnement *m*; **2** (Mus) liaison *f*; **3** (aspersion) calomnie *f*; **to cast a ~ on sb/sth** répandre des calomnies sur qn/qch; **to be a ~ on sb/sth** porter atteinte à qn/qch.
II *vtr* **1 to ~ one's speech** or **words** manger ses mots; **2** (Mus) lier.
III **slurred** *pp adj* [*voice, words, speech*] inarticulé.

slush *n* neige *f* fondue.

slush fund *n* caisse *f* noire.

sly *adj* [*person, animal*] rusé; [*remark, smile*] entendu.
IDIOMS **on the ~** en douce°, en cachette.

smack I *n* claque *f*; (on face) gifle *f*.
II° *adv* (also **~ bang, ~ dab** US) en plein°; **~ in the middle of** en plein milieu de.
III *vtr* (on face) gifler [*person*]; taper [*object*] (**on** sur; **against** contre); **she ~ed him (on the bottom)** or **she ~ed his bottom** elle lui a donné une claque sur les fesses.
IV *vi* **to ~ of** sentir; **it ~s of incompetence** ça sent l'incompétence.

small I *n* **the ~ of the back** le creux du dos.
II *adj* **1** [*country, house, car, animal, book, job, mistake, sum*] petit (*before n*); [*increase, proportion, quantity, amount*] faible (*before n*); **the dress is too ~ for her** la robe est trop petite pour elle; **a ~ sweatshirt** un sweatshirt de petite taille; **it's a ~ world!** que le monde est

petit!; [*crowd*] peu nombreux/-euse; **2** (petty) [*person, act*] mesquin; **3 to feel** or **look ~** être dans ses petits souliers○; **to make sb feel** or **look ~** humilier qn.
III *adv* [*write*] petit.

small: **~ ad** *n* (GB) petite annonce *f*; **~ change** *n* petite monnaie *f*.

smallness *n* (of object, person group) petite taille *f*; (of sum) modicité *f*.

small talk *n* banalités *fpl*; **to make ~** faire la conversation.

smart I *adj* **1** (elegant) [*person, clothes*] élégant; [*restaurant, hotel, street*] chic *inv*; **2** (clever) [*child, decision*] malin; [*politician, journalist*] habile; **3** [*blow*] vif/vive; [*rebuke*] cinglant; **to walk at a ~ pace** marcher à vive allure; **4** (Comput) intelligent.
II *vi* [*cut, cheeks*] brûler; **his eyes were ~ing from the smoke** la fumée lui brûlait les yeux.

smarten *v* ■ **smarten up**: **~ [sth/sb] up, ~ up [sth/sb]** embellir.

smash I *n* **1**○ (also **~-up**) (accident) collision *f*; **2**○ (also **~ hit**) tube○ *m*; **to be a ~** faire un tabac○; **3** (in tennis) smash *m*.
II *vtr* **1** briser [*glass, door, car*]; (more violently) fracasser; **2** écraser [*opponent*]; démanteler [*drugs ring, gang*]; **3** (Sport) pulvériser○ [*record*]; **to ~ the ball** faire un smash.
III *vi* se briser, se fracasser (**on** sur, **against** contre).
■ **smash up**: **~ [sth] up, ~ up [sth]** démolir.

smashing○ *adj* (GB) formidable○.

smattering *n* notions *fpl* (**of** de); **to have a ~ of Russian** avoir quelques connaissances en russe.

smear I *n* **1** (spot) tache *f*; (streak) traînée *f*; **2** (defamation) propos *m* diffamatoire; **a ~ on sb's character** une tache sur la réputation de qn; **3** (Med) = **smear test**.
II *vtr* **1** faire des taches sur [*glass, window*]; **her face was ~ed with jam** elle avait le visage barbouillé de confiture; **2** étaler [*butter, paint*]; appliquer [*sun oil, lotion*] (**on** sur); **3** (slander) salir [*person*].
III *vi* [*ink, paint*] s'étaler; [*lipstick, make-up*] couler.

smear: **~ campaign** *n* campagne *f* de diffamation (**against** contre); **~ test** *n* (Med) frottis *m*.

smell I *n* **1** odeur *f*; **a ~ of burning** une odeur de brûlé; **2** (sense) odorat *m*; **sense of ~** odorat *m*.
II *vtr* **1** [*person*] sentir; [*animal*] renifler, sentir; **I can ~ burning** ça sent le brûlé; **2** flairer [*danger*].
III *vi* sentir; **that ~s nice/horrible** ça sent bon/très mauvais; **to ~ of roses** sentir la rose.

smelling salts *n pl* sels *mpl*.

smelly *adj* [*animal, person, clothing*] qui sent mauvais.

smelt *vtr* extraire [qch] par fusion [*metal*]; fondre [*ore*].

smile I *n* sourire *m*; **to give sb a ~** adresser un sourire à qn; **with a ~** en souriant.
II *vi* sourire (**at sb** à qn; **with** de); **we ~d at the idea** cette idée nous a fait sourire; **to ~ to oneself** sourire intérieurement.

smirk I *n* (self-satisfied) petit sourire *m* satisfait; (knowing) sourire *m* en coin.
II *vi* (in a self-satisfied way) avoir un petit sourire satisfait; (knowingly) avoir un sourire en coin.

smithereens *n pl* **in ~** en mille morceaux; **to smash sth to ~** faire voler qch en éclats.

smock *n* blouse *f*, sarrau *m*.

smog *n* smog *m*.

smoke I *n* fumée *f*.
II *vtr* fumer.
III *vi* fumer.
IV smoked *pp adj* fumé.

smokeless *adj* [*fuel*] non polluant; [*zone*] où l'utilisation de combustibles polluants est interdite.

smoker *n* fumeur/-euse *m/f*; **a light ~** une personne qui fume peu.

smoke screen *n* **1** (Mil) écran *m* de fumée; **2** (figurative) diversion *f*; **to create** or **throw up a ~** faire diversion.

smoking I *n* **~ and drinking** le tabac et l'alcool; **~ damages your health** le tabac nuit à la santé; **to give up ~** arrêter de fumer; **'no ~'** 'défense de fumer'.
II *adj* [*compartment, section*] fumeurs (*after n*).

smoky *adj* [*atmosphere, room*] enfumé; [*fire*] qui fume; [*cheese, bacon, glass*] fumé.

smooth I *adj* **1** [*stone, sea, surface, skin, fabric*] lisse; [*road*] plan; [*curve, line, breathing*] régulier/-ière; [*sauce, paste*] homogène; [*crossing, flight*] sans heurts; [*movement*] aisé; [*rhythm, playing*] fluide; **2** [*taste, wine, whisky*] moelleux/-euse; **3** (suave) [*person*] mielleux/-euse; [*manners, appearance*] onctueux/-euse; **to be a ~ talker** être enjôleur/-euse.
II *vtr* **1** (flatten out) lisser; (get creases out) défroisser; **2** faciliter [*transition, path*].

smother *vtr* étouffer.

smoulder (GB), **smolder** (US) *vi* **1** [*cigarette, fire*] se consumer; **2** [*hatred, jealousy*] couver; **to ~ with** être consumé/-e de [*resentment, jealousy*].

smudge I *n* trace *f*.
II *vtr* étaler [*make-up, print, ink, paint*]; faire des traces sur [*paper, paintwork*].
III *vi* [*make-up, print, ink, paint*] s'étaler.

smug *adj* suffisant; **to be ~ about winning** être fier d'avoir gagné.

smuggle I *vtr* faire passer [qch] clandestinement [*message, food*] (**into** dans); faire du trafic de [*arms, drugs*]; faire passer [qch] en contrebande [*watches, alcohol, cigarettes*]; **to ~ sth/sb in** faire entrer qch/qn clandestinement; **to ~ sth through** or **past customs** faire passer qch en fraude.
II *vi* faire de la contrebande.

smuggler *n* contrebandier/-ière *m/f*; **drug/arms ~** passeur/-euse *m/f* de drogue/d'armes.

smuggling *n* contrebande *f*; **drug/arms ~** trafic *m* de drogue/d'armes.

smutty *adj* **1** (crude) grivois; **2** (dirty) [*face*] noir; [*mark*] noirâtre.

snack *n* **1** (small meal) repas *m* léger; (instead of meal) casse-croûte *m inv*; **to have a ~** manger quelque chose; **2** (crisps, peanuts) **~s** amuse-gueule *m inv*.

snag *n* **1** (hitch) inconvénient *m* (**in** de); **there's just one ~** il y a un problème; **2** (tear) accroc *m* (**in** à).

snail *n* escargot *m*.

snake I *n* **1** (Zool) serpent *m*; **2** (person) **~ (in the grass)** traître/traîtresse *m/f*.
II *vi* [*road*] serpenter (**through** à travers).

snake: **~bite** *n* morsure *f* de serpent; **~ charmer** *n* charmeur/-euse *m/f* de serpents.

snap ▶649 I *n* **1** (of branch) craquement *m*; (of fingers, lid, elastic) claquement *m*; **2** (of jaws) claquement *m*; **3**○ (photograph) photo *f*; **4** (Games) ≈ bataille *f*.
II *adj* [*decision, judgment, vote*] rapide.
III *vtr* **1** faire claquer [*fingers, jaws, elastic*]; **2** (break) (faire) casser net; **3** (say crossly) dire [qch] hargneusement.
IV *excl* **1** (Games) ≈ bataille!; **2**○ **~! we're wearing the same tie!** coïncidence! nous portons la même cravate!
V *vi* **1** (break) se casser; **2** (speak sharply) parler hargneusement.
■ **snap at**: **~ at [sth/sb] 1** (speak sharply) parler sèchement à; **2** [*dog*] essayer de mordre.
■ **snap up**: **~ up [sth]** sauter sur [*bargain, opportunity*].

snappy *adj* **1** (bad-tempered) sec/sèche; **2** (lively) [*rhythm, reply, item*] rapide; (punchy) [*advertisement, feature*] percutant; **3**○ (smart) [*clothing*] chic *inv*.

snapshot *n* photo *f*.

snare I *n* piège *m*.
II *vtr* prendre [qn/qch] au piège [*animal, person*].

snarl *vi* [*animal*] gronder férocement; [*person*] grogner; **the dog ~ed at me** le chien m'a montré les dents.

snatch I *n* **1** (of conversation) bribe *f*; (of poem, poet) quelques vers *mpl*; (of tune) quelques notes *fpl*; **2** (theft) vol *m*.
II *vtr* **1** (grab) attraper [*book, key*]; saisir [*opportunity*]; arracher [*victory*]; **to ~ sth from sb** arracher qch à qn; **2**○ (steal) voler [*handbag, jewellery, kiss*] (**from** à); kidnapper [*baby*].

sneak *vi* **to ~ away** s'éclipser discrètement; **to ~ around** rôder; **to ~ in/out** entrer/sortir furtivement; **to ~ up on sb/sth** s'approcher sans bruit de qn/qch.

sneaker *n* (US) basket *f*, (chaussure *f* de) tennis *f*.

sneak preview *n* avant-première *f*.

sneaky *adj* [*behaviour, person*] sournois; [*method, plan*] rusé; **to have a ~ look at sth** regarder qch en cachette.

sneer I *n* sourire *m* méprisant.
II *vi* sourire avec mépris.

sneeze I *n* éternuement *m*.
II *vi* éternuer.

snide *adj* sournois.

sniff I *n* reniflement *m*.
II *vtr* [*dog*] flairer; [*person*] humer [*air*]; sentir [*perfume, food*]; inhaler [*glue, cocaine*].
III *vi* renifler; **to ~ at sth** renifler qch [*food, drink*]; **a free car is not to be ~ed at** une voiture gratuite, ça ne se refuse pas.

snigger I *n* ricanement *m*.
II *vi* ricaner; **to ~ at [sb/sth]** se moquer de [*person*]; ricaner en voyant [*appearance, action*].

snip I *n* **1** petit coup *m* (de ciseaux); **2** (piece of fabric) échantillon *m*.
II *vtr* découper (à petits coups de ciseaux) [*fabric, paper*]; tailler [*hedge*].
■ **snip off**: **~ [sth] off, ~ off [sth]** couper.

snipe *vi* **to ~ at** (shoot) tirer sur; (criticize) envoyer des piques à.

sniper *n* tireur *m* embusqué.

snippet *n* (of conversation, information) bribes *f*; (of text, fabric, music) fragment *m*.

snivel *vi* pleurnicher.

snob I *n* snob *mf*.
II *noun modifier* [*value, appeal*] pour les snobs.

snobbery *n* snobisme *m*.

snobbish *adj* snob *inv*.

snooker ▶649 I *n* **1** (game) snooker *m*; **2** (shot) coup *m* fumant.
II *vtr* **1** (Sport) (figurative) coincer [*player, person*]; **2** (US) (deceive) avoir○ [*person*].

snoop○ I *n* fouineur/-euse *m/f*.
II *vi* espionner.
■ **snoop around**○ fouiner, fureter.

snooze○ I *n* petit somme *m*.
II *vi* sommeiller.

snore I *n* ronflement *m*.
II *vi* ronfler.

snorkel I *n* **1** (for swimmer) tuba *m*; **2** (on submarine) schnorchel *m*.
II *vi* faire de la plongée avec tuba.

snorkelling ▶649 *n* plongée *f* avec tuba.

snort *vi* [*person, pig*] grogner; [*horse, bull*] s'ébrouer.

snout *n* museau *m*; (of pig) groin *m*.

snow I *n* neige *f*.
II *v impers* neiger; **it's ~ing** il neige.

snowball I *n* boule *f* de neige.
II *vi* [*profits, problem, plan, support*] faire boule de neige.

snow: **~drift** *n* congère *f*; **~drop** *n* perce-neige *m inv*; **~flake** *n* flocon *m* de neige; **~man** *n* bonhomme *m* de neige; **~ plough** (GB), **~ plow** (US) *n* chasse-neige *m inv*; **~ shoe** *n* raquette *f*; **~storm** *n* tempête *f* de neige.

snub I *n* rebuffade *f*.
II *vtr* rembarrer; **to be ~bed** essuyer une rebuffade (**by** de la part de).

snub-nosed *adj* au nez retroussé.

snuff *n* tabac *m* à priser.

snug *adj* [*bed, room*] douillet/-ette; [*coat*] chaud.

snuggle *vi* se blottir (**into** dans; **against** contre).
■ **snuggle up** se blottir (**against, beside** contre).

so I *adv* **1** (to such an extent) si, tellement; **~ happy/quickly** si or tellement heureux/vite; **what's ~ funny?** qu'est-ce qu'il y a de si drôle?; **~ much noise/many things** tant de bruit/de choses; **~ much of her life** une si grande partie de sa vie; **~ many of her friends** un si grand nombre de ses amis; **we can only work ~ fast and no faster** nous ne pouvons vraiment pas travailler plus vite; **2** (in such a way) **~ arranged/worded that** organisé/rédigé d'une telle façon que; **and ~ on and ~ forth** et ainsi de suite; **~ be it!** soit!; **3** (thus) ainsi; (therefore) donc; **~ it was that** c'est ainsi que; **she was young and ~ lacked experience** elle était jeune et donc sans expérience; **~ there you are** te voilà donc; **~ that's the reason** voilà donc pourquoi; **~ you're going are you?** alors tu y vas?; **4** (true) **is that ~?** c'est vrai?; **if (that's) ~** si c'est vrai; **5** (also) aussi; **~ is she** elle aussi; **if they accept, ~ do I** s'ils acceptent, j'accepte aussi; **6**○ (thereabouts) environ; **20 or ~** environ 20; **7** (other uses) **I believe ~** je crois; **~ I believe** c'est ce que je crois; **I'm afraid ~** j'ai bien peur que oui or si; **~ it would appear** c'est ce qu'il semble; **~ to speak** si je puis dire; **I told you ~** je te l'avais bien dit; **~ I see** je le vois bien; **who says ~?** qui dit ça?; **only more ~** mais encore plus; **he dived and as he did ~...** il a plongé et en le faisant...; **'it's broken'—'~ it is'** 'c'est cassé'—'je le vois bien!'; **'I'm sorry'—'~ you should be'** 'je suis désolé'—'j'espère bien'; **it just ~ happens that** il se trouve justement que; **~ what's the problem?** et alors, où est le problème?; **~ (what)?** et alors?

II so (that) *phr* **1** (in such a way that) de façon à ce que (+ *subj*); **2** (in order that) pour que (+ *subj*); **be quiet ~ I can work** tais-toi que je puisse travailler.

III so as *phr* pour; **~ as to attract attention** pour attirer l'attention.

IV so much *phr* (see also I, 1) **1** tellement; **she worries ~ much** elle s'inquiète tellement; **she taught me ~ much** elle m'a tant appris; **~ much worse** tellement pire; **~ much ~ that** à un tel point que; **thank you ~ much** merci beaucoup; **2 not ~ much unpleasant as boring** moins désagréable qu'ennuyeux.

V so much for *phr* **~ much for that problem, now for...** assez parlé de ce problème, parlons maintenant de...; **~ much for equality!** bonjour○ l'égalité!

IDIOMS **~ much the better** tant mieux; **~ ~** comme ci comme ça.

soak I *vtr* **1** [*rain*] tremper [*person, clothes*]; **to get ~ed** se faire tremper; **2** [*person*] faire tremper [*clothes, foods*].

II *vi* **1** [*clothes, foods*] tremper; **to leave sth to ~** mettre qch à tremper; **2** [*liquid*] **to ~ into** être absorbé par; **to ~ through** traverser.

III soaked *pp adj* trempé; **to be ~ed through** or **~ed to the skin** être trempé jusqu'aux os.

■ **soak in** [*news*] pénétrer.

■ **soak up**: **~ [sth] up, ~ up [sth]** absorber.

soap *n* savon *m*; **a bar of ~** un savon.

soap: **~ opera** *n* feuilleton *m*; **~ powder** *n* lessive *f* (en poudre).

soapy *adj* [*water*] savonneux/-euse; [*hands, face*] plein de savon.

soar *vi* **1** [*ball*] filer; [*bird, plane*] prendre son essor; [*price, temperature, costs*] monter en flèche; [*hopes, spirits*] s'accroître considérablement; **2** (glide) planer; **3** [*tower, cliffs*] se dresser.

sob I *n* sanglot *m*.

II *vi* sangloter.

sober I *adj* **1 I'm ~** (not drunk) je n'ai pas bu d'alcool; (in protest) je ne suis pas ivre; **2** (no longer drunk) dessoûlé; **3** (serious) [*person*] sérieux/-ieuse; [*mood*] grave; **4** [*colour, style*] sobre; [*tie, suit*] sobre, discret/-ète.

II *vtr* [*news, reprimand*] calmer.

■ **sober up**: ¶ **~ up** dessoûler; ¶ **~ [sb] up** dégriser.

soccer ▶ 649 *n* football *m*.

sociable *adj* [*person*] sociable; [*evening*] agréable.

social I *n* (party) soirée *f*; (gathering) réunion *f*.

II *adj* **1** [*background, class, function, problem*] social; **2** [*call, visit*] amical; **he's a ~ drinker** il boit de l'alcool en société; **he's a ~ smoker** c'est un fumeur occasionnel.

socialism *n* socialisme *m*.

socialist *n, adj* (also **Socialist**) socialiste (*mf*).

socialite *n* mondain/-e *m/f*.

socialize *vi* rencontrer des gens; **to ~ with sb** fréquenter qn.

socializing *n* **we don't do much ~** on ne sort pas beaucoup.

social life *n* (of person) vie *f* sociale; (of town) vie *f* culturelle.

social security *n* aide *f* sociale; **to be on ~** recevoir l'aide sociale.

social: **Social Services** *n pl* (GB) services *mpl* sociaux; **~ work** *n* travail *m* social; **~ worker** ▶ 805 *n* travailleur/-euse *m/f* social/-e.

society *n* **1** société *f*; **a multicultural ~** une société multiculturelle; **2** (club) société *f*; (for social contact) association *f*; **3** (also **high ~**) haute société *f*.

sociologist ▶ 805 *n* sociologue *mf*.

sociology *n* sociologie *f*.

sock *n* chaussette *f*.

socket *n* **1** (for plug) prise *f* (de courant); (for bulb) douille *f*; **2** (of joint) cavité *f* articulaire; (of eye) orbite *f*.

soda *n* **1** (chemical) soude *f*; **2** (also **washing ~**) soude *f* ménagère; **3** (also **~ water**) eau *f* de seltz; **whisky and ~** whisky *m* soda; **4** (also **~ pop**) (US) soda *m*.

sodden *adj* [*towel, clothing*] trempé; [*ground*] détrempé.

sofa *n* canapé *m*.

sofa bed *n* canapé-lit *m*.

soft *adj* **1** [*fabric, fur, pencil, skin, hand, cheek*] doux/douce; [*ground, soil*] meuble; [*rock, metal*] tendre; [*bed, cushion*] moelleux/-euse; [*brush, hair*] souple; [*dough, butter*] mou/molle; **~ to the touch** doux au toucher; **2** [*colour, sound*] doux/douce; [*step*] feutré; **~ lighting** éclairage *m* tamisé; **3** [*rain, water, breeze, look, words*] doux/douce; [*impact, touch*] léger/-ère; [*eyes, heart*] tendre; **4** [*outline, shape*] flou; [*fold*] souple; **5** (lenient) [*parent, teacher*] (trop) indulgent; **6**○ **to be ~ on sb** en pincer○ pour qn; **to be ~ in the head** être ramolli du cerveau○.

soft: **~-boiled** *adj* [*egg*] à la coque; **~ drink** *n* boisson *f* non alcoolisée.

soften I *vtr* **1** adoucir [*skin, water, sound, light, outline, refusal*]; amollir [*ground, metal*]; ramollir [*butter*]; **2** atténuer [*blow, shock, pain*].
II *vi* **1** [*light, outline, music, colour*] s'adoucir; [*skin*] devenir plus doux; [*substance, ground*] se ramollir; **2** [*person*] s'assouplir (**towards sb** vis-à-vis de qn).
■ **soften up**: ¶ **~ up** amollir; ¶ **~ up [sb]**, **~ [sb] up** affaiblir [*enemy, opponent*]; attendrir [*customer*].

softener *n* **1** (also **fabric ~**) (produit *m*) assouplissant *m*; **2** (also **water ~**) adoucisseur *m*.

softly *adv* [*speak, touch, blow*] doucement; [*fall*] en douceur.

softness *n* (of texture, skin, colour, light, sound) douceur *f*; (of substance) consistance *f* molle.

soft option *n* facilité *f*; **to take the ~** choisir la facilité.

soft spot○ *n* **to have a ~ for sb** avoir un faible○ pour qn.

soft: **~-top** *n* décapotable *f*; **~ touch**○ *n* poire○ *f*; **~ toy** *n* peluche *f*; **~ware** *n* logiciel *m*.

soggy *adj* [*ground*] détrempé; [*food*] ramolli.

soh *n* (Mus) sol *m*.

soil I *n* sol *m*, terre *f*.
II *vtr* salir.

soiled *adj* **1** (dirty) sali; **2** (also **shop-~**) vendu avec défaut.

solace I *n* (feeling of comfort) consolation *f*; (source of comfort) réconfort *m*.
II *vtr* consoler (**for** de).

solar *adj* solaire.

solder *vtr, vi* souder (**onto, to** à).

soldier ▶ **805** *n* soldat *m*.
■ **soldier on** persévérer contre vents et marées.

sole I *n* **1** (fish) sole *f*; **2** (of foot) plante *f*; (of shoe, sock) semelle *f*.
II *adj* **1** (single) seul, unique; **for the ~ purpose of doing** uniquement pour faire; **2** [*agent, right*] exclusif/-ive; [*trader*] indépendant.

solemn *adj* [*occasion, person, voice*] solennel/-elle; [*duty, warning*] formel/-elle.

solemnity *n* solennité *f*.

sol-fa *n* solfège *m*.

solicit I *vtr* **1** solliciter [*information, help, money, votes*]; rechercher [*business, investment, orders*]; **2** [*prostitute*] racoler.
II *vi* **1** [*prostitute*] racoler; **2 to ~ for** solliciter [*votes, support*]; rechercher [*orders*].

solicitor ▶ **805** *n* **1** (GB) (for documents, oaths) ≈ notaire *m*; (for court and police work) ≈ avocat/-e *m/f*; **2** (US) démarcheur/-euse *m/f*; **telephone ~** télévendeur/-euse *m/f*.

solid I *n* solide *m*.
II solids *n pl* (food) aliments *mpl* solides.
III *adj* **1** [*substance, structure, foundation, evidence*] solide; **to go** or **become ~** se solidifier; **to be on ~ ground** (figurative) être en terrain sûr; **2** [*gold, marble*] massif/-ive; **the gate was made of ~ steel** le portail était tout en acier; **cut through ~ rock** taillé dans la roche; **3** [*crowd*] compact; [*line*] continu; **five ~ days, five days ~** cinq jours entiers; **4** [*advice, worker, work*] sérieux/-ieuse; [*investment*] sûr; **5** [*punch*] fort; **6** (*after n*) [*citizen*] modèle.
IV *adv* [*freeze*] complètement; **to be packed ~** [*hall*] être bondé; **the play is booked ~** la pièce affiche complet.

solidarity *n* solidarité *f*; **to feel ~ with sb** se sentir solidaire de qn.

solidify I *vtr* solidifier.
II *vi* [*liquid*] se solidifier; [*honey, oil*] se figer.

solitary *adj* **1** (unaccompanied) [*occupation, walker*] solitaire; **2** (lonely) [*person*] très seul; [*farm, village*] isolé; **3** (single) seul; **a ~ case of** un cas unique de.

solitary confinement *n* isolement *m* cellulaire.

solo I *n* solo *m*.
II *adj* [*album, appearance, flight, pilot*] en solo.
III *adv* [*dance, fly, perform, play*] en solo.

soloist *n* soliste *mf*.

solstice *n* solstice *m*; **the summer/winter ~** le solstice d'été/d'hiver.

soluble *adj* soluble; **water-~** soluble dans l'eau.

solution *n* solution *f*.

solve *vtr* résoudre [*equation, problem*]; élucider [*crime*]; trouver la solution de [*mystery*]; trouver la solution à [*clue, crossword*]; trouver une solution à [*crisis, poverty, unemployment*].

solvency *n* solvabilité *f*.

solvent I *n* solvant *m*.
II *adj* (in funds) solvable.

sombre (GB), **somber** (US) *adj* sombre.

some

■ **Note** When *some* is used to mean an unspecified amount of something, it is translated by *du*, *de l'* (before a vowel or mute 'h'), *de la* or *des* according to the gender and number of the noun that follows: *I'd like some bread* = je voudrais du pain; *have some water* = prenez de l'eau; *we've bought some beer* = nous avons acheté de la bière; *they've bought some peaches* = ils ont acheté des pêches.
– But note that when a plural noun is preceded by an adjective in French, *some* is translated by *de* alone: *some pretty dresses* = de jolies robes.

– When *some* is used as a pronoun, it is translated by *en* which is placed before the verb in French: *would you like some?* = est-ce que vous en voulez?; *I've got some* = j'en ai.
– For further examples, see the entry below.

I *det* **1** (an unspecified amount or number) du/de l'/de la/des; **~ old socks** de vieilles chaussettes; **~ red socks** des chaussettes rouges; **I need ~ help** j'ai besoin d'aide; **2** (certain) certain (*before n*); **~ people say that** certaines personnes disent que; **in ~ ways, I agree** d'une certaine façon, je suis d'accord; **3** (a considerable amount or number) **he has ~ cause for complaint** il a des raisons de se plaindre; **his suggestion was greeted with ~ hostility** sa suggestion a été accueillie avec hostilité; **it will take ~ doing** ça ne va pas être facile à faire; **we stayed there for ~ time** nous sommes restés là assez longtemps; **4** (a little, a slight) **the meeting did have ~ effect** la réunion a eu un certain effet; **there must be ~ reason for it** il doit y avoir une raison; **you must have ~ idea where the house is** tu dois avoir une idée de l'endroit où se trouve la maison; **to ~ extent** dans une certaine mesure; **5** (an unknown) **~ man came here** un homme est venu ici; **he's doing ~ course** il suit des cours; **a car of ~ sort, ~ sort of car** une voiture quelconque; **6**° **that was ~ film!** ça c'était un film!; **~ help you are!** c'est ça que tu appelles aider!
II *pron, quantif* **1** (an unspecified amount or number) en; **he took ~ of it/of them** il en a pris un peu/quelques-uns; **(do) have ~!** servez-vous!; **2** (certain ones) certain; **~ (of them) are blue** certains sont bleus; **~ say that**... certaines personnes disent que...; **~ (of them) arrived early** certains d'entre eux sont arrivés tôt.
III *adv* **1** (approximately) environ; **~ 20 people** environ 20 personnes; **2**° (US) un peu.

somebody *pron* **1** (also **someone**) quelqu'un; **~ famous** quelqu'un de célèbre; **2 Janet Somebody** Janet Machin; **3 he (really) thinks he's ~** il ne se prend pas pour n'importe qui.

somehow *adv* **1** (also **~ or other**) (of future action) d'une manière ou d'une autre; (of past action) je ne sais comment; **we'll get there ~** on y arrivera d'une manière ou d'une autre; **we managed it ~** nous avons réussi je ne sais comment; **2** (for some reason) **~ it doesn't seem very important** en fait, ça ne semble pas très important.

someone *pron* = **somebody 1**.

somersault I *n* (of gymnast) roulade *f*; (of child) galipette *f*; (of diver) saut *m* périlleux; (accidental) culbute *f*.
II *vi* [*gymnast*] faire une roulade; [*diver*] faire un saut périlleux; [*vehicle*] faire un tonneau.

something I *pron* **1** quelque chose; **~ new/interesting** quelque chose de nouveau/d'intéressant; **~ to do** quelque chose à faire; **there's ~ wrong** il y a un problème; **there's ~ odd about her** elle a quelque chose de bizarre; **~ or other** quelque chose; **to make ~ of oneself** or **one's life** réussir sa vie; **he got ~ out of it** il en a tiré quelque chose; **he is quite** or **really ~!** c'est vraiment un numéro!; **that house is quite** or **really ~!** cette maison c'est quelque chose!; **there's ~ in what he says** il y a du vrai dans ce qu'il dit; **he has a certain ~** il a un petit quelque chose; **2 his name's Andy ~** il s'appelle Andy quelque chose; **in nineteen-sixty-~** en mille neuf cent soixante et quelques; **she's gone shopping or ~** elle est allée faire les courses ou quelque chose comme ça.
II **something of** *phr* **she is ~ of an expert on**... elle est assez experte en...; **it was ~ of a surprise/of a disaster** c'était assez étonnant/plutôt désastreux.

sometime *adv* **we'll have to do it ~** il va falloir qu'on le fasse un jour ou l'autre; **I'll tell you about it ~** je te raconterai ça un de ces jours; **I'll phone you ~ next week** je te téléphonerai dans le courant de la semaine prochaine.

sometimes *adv* parfois, quelquefois; **~ angry, ~ depressed** tantôt en colère, tantôt déprimé.

somewhat *adv* (with adjective) plutôt; (with verb, adverb) un peu; **things have changed ~** les choses ont un peu changé; **~ surprisingly** de façon quelque peu surprenante.

somewhere *adv* **1** (some place) quelque part; **she's ~ about** elle est quelque part par là, elle est dans les parages; **~ hot** un endroit chaud; **he needs ~ to sleep** il a besoin d'un endroit pour dormir; **~ or other** je ne sais où; **~ (or other) in Asia** quelque part en Asie; **they live in Manchester or ~**° ils habitent à Manchester ou quelque chose comme ça; **2 ~ between 50 and 100 people** entre 50 et 100 personnes; **~ around 10 o'clock** vers 10 heures.

son *n* fils *m*.

sonata *n* sonate *f*; **violin ~** sonate pour violon.

song *n* **1** chanson *f*; **to burst into ~** se mettre à chanter; **2** (of bird) chant *m* (**of** de).

sonic *adj* sonore.

sonic boom *n* bang *m*.

son-in-law *n* gendre *m*.

sonnet *n* sonnet *m*.

soon *adv* **1** (in a short time) bientôt; **see you ~!** à bientôt!; **2** (quickly) vite; **it ~ became clear that** il est vite devenu évident que; **3** (early) tôt; **the ~er the better** le plus tôt sera le mieux; **as ~ as possible** dès que possible; **I spoke too ~!** j'ai parlé trop vite!; **as ~ as he arrives** dès qu'il arrivera; **as ~ as you can** dès que tu pourras; **as ~ as he has finished** dès qu'il aura fini; **~er or later** tôt ou tard; **4** (not long) **they left ~ after us** ils sont partis peu après nous; **~ afterwards** peu après; **no ~er had I finished than**... j'avais à peine fini que...; **5** (rather) **I would just as ~ go to Spain as go to Italy** j'aime autant aller en Espagne qu'aller en Italie; **I would ~er not do** j'aime autant ne pas faire.

soot *n* suie *f*.

soothe *vtr* calmer [*pain, nerves, fear, person*]; apaiser [*sunburn*].

soothing *adj* [*music, person, voice*] apaisant; [*cream, effect*] calmant; [*words*] rassurant.

sophisticated *adj* **1** [*person*] (cultured) raffiné; (affectedly) sophistiqué; (elegant) chic *inv*; [*clothes*] recherché; [*restaurant*] chic *inv*; **2** [*taste*] raffiné; [*audience*] averti; [*civilization*] évolué; **3** [*equipment, technology*] sophistiqué.

soporific *adj* **1** (sleep-inducing) soporifique; **2** (sleepy) somnolent.

soprano *n* **1** (person) soprano *mf*; **2** (voice, instrument) soprano *m*.

sorcerer *n* sorcier *m*.

sordid *adj* sordide.

sore I *n* plaie *f*.
II *adj* **1** [*eyes, gums*] irrité; [*muscle, arm, foot*] endolori; **to have a ~ throat** avoir mal à la gorge; **to be** or **feel ~ (all over)** avoir mal (partout); **2** [*subject, point*] délicat.
IDIOMS **it is a sight for ~ eyes** ça réjouit le cœur de voir cela.

sorrow *n* chagrin *m*.

sorrowful *adj* [*look*] affligé; [*voice*] triste.

sorry I *adj* **1** désolé; (stronger) navré; **I'm terribly ~** je suis vraiment désolé, je suis navré; **I'm ~ I'm late** je suis désolé d'être en retard; **to be ~ about** s'excuser de [*behaviour, mistake, change*]; **to say ~** s'excuser; **2 to be ~ to hear of sth/to hear that** être désolé d'apprendre qch/d'apprendre que; **3** (regretful) **to be ~ to do** regretter de faire; **will you be ~ to go back?** est-ce que tu auras des regrets en rentrant?; **no-one will be ~ to see him go!** personne ne regrettera son départ!; **4** (pitying) **to be** or **feel ~ for sb** plaindre qn; **to feel ~ for oneself** s'apitoyer sur soi-même; **5** [*state, sight, business*] triste; [*person*] minable; **this is a ~ state of affairs!** c'est vraiment lamentable!
II *excl* **1** (apologizing) pardon!, désolé!; **2** (pardon) **~?** pardon?

sort I *n* sorte *f*, genre *m*; **books, records—that ~ of thing** des livres, des disques, ce genre de choses; **I'm not that ~ of person** ce n'est pas mon genre; **some ~ of computer** une sorte d'ordinateur; **any ~ of knife will do** n'importe quel couteau fera l'affaire.
II *vtr* **1** classer [*data, files, stamps*]; trier [*letters, apples, potatoes*]; **to ~ books into piles** ranger des livres en piles; **2** (separate) séparer; **to ~ the old stock from the new** séparer les vieux stocks des nouveaux.
III of sorts, of a sort *phr* **a duck of ~s** or **of a ~** une sorte de canard; **progress of ~s** un semblant de progrès.
IV° **sort of** *phr* **1 ~ of cute** plutôt mignon/-onne; **I ~ of understand** je comprends plus ou moins; **2 ~ of blue-green** dans les bleu-vert; **it just ~ of happened** c'est arrivé comme ça; **he was just ~ of lying there** il était étendu par terre comme ça.
IDIOMS **to be** or **feel out of ~s** (ill) ne pas être dans son assiette; (grumpy) être de mauvais poil°; **it takes all ~s (to make a world)** il faut de tout pour faire un monde.
■ **sort out**: ¶ **~ [sth] out, ~ out [sth] 1** régler [*problem, matter*]; **2** s'occuper de [*details, arrangements*]; **I'll ~ it out** je m'en occuperai; **3** ranger [*cupboard, desk*]; classer [*files, documents*]; mettre de l'ordre dans [*finances, affairs*]; clarifier [*ideas*]; **4** trier [*photos, clothes*]; ¶ **~ out [sth]: to ~ out the clean socks from the dirty** séparer les chaussettes propres des chaussettes sales; ¶ **~ [sb] out**° **1** (punish) régler son compte à qn°; **2** (help) aider; **the doctor will soon ~ you out** le médecin te remettra sur pied; ¶ **~ [oneself] out** (get organized) s'organiser; (in one's personal life) résoudre ses problèmes; **things will ~ themselves out** les choses vont s'arranger d'elles-mêmes; **the problem ~ed itself out** le problème s'est résolu de lui-même.
■ **sort through**: **~ through [sth]** regarder.

SOS *n* SOS *m*.

so-so° I *adj* moyen/-enne.
II *adv* comme ci comme ça°.

sought-after *adj* [*person, skill*] demandé, recherché; [*job, brand, area*] prisé.

soul *n* **1** âme *f*; **to throw oneself into sth heart and ~** se donner corps et âme à qch; **you mustn't tell a ~!** ne le dis à personne!; **2** (also **~ music**) soul *m*.

soulful *adj* mélancolique.

soul: **~ mate** *n* âme *f* sœur; **~-searching** *n* débat *m* intérieur.

sound I *n* **1** son *m*; **to fly at the speed of ~** voler à la vitesse du son; **to turn the ~ up/down** augmenter/baisser le volume; **2** (noise) bruit *m* (**of** de); (of bell, instrument, voice) son *m* (**of** de); **the ~ of voices** un bruit de voix; **a grating** or **rasping ~** un grincement; **without a ~** sans bruit; **3** (figurative) **by the ~ of it, we're in for a rough crossing** d'après ce qu'on a dit, la traversée va être mauvaise; **he was in a bad temper that day, by the ~ of it** il semble que ce jour-là il ait été de mauvaise humeur; **4** (Med) sonde *f*; **5** (strait) détroit *m*.
II *adj* **1** [*foundations, heart, constitution*] solide; [*health, physique*] bon/bonne (*before n*); **to be of ~ mind** être sain d'esprit; **2** [*basis, argument, knowledge*] solide; [*judgment, management*] sain; [*investment*] bon/bonne (*before n*), sûr; **some ~ advice** un bon conseil; **our products are ecologically ~** nos produits ne nuisent pas à l'environnement; **she's politically ~, her ideas are politically ~** elle a des idées politiques de bon ton.
III *vtr* faire retentir [*siren, foghorn*]; sonner [*trumpet*]; **to ~ one's horn** klaxonner; **to ~ the alarm** sonner l'alarme.
IV *vi* **1** (seem) sembler; **it ~s as if he's really in trouble** il semble qu'il ait vraiment des ennuis; **it ~s like it might be dangerous** ça a l'air dangereux; **it doesn't ~ to me as if she's interested** je ne pense pas qu'elle soit intéressée; **2 to ~ boring** paraître ennuyeux; **you make it ~ interesting** à t'écouter ça a l'air intéressant; **it ~s like a flute** on dirait une flûte; **she calls herself Geraldine—it ~s**

more sophisticated elle se fait appeler Géraldine—ça fait plus sophistiqué; **3** [*alarm, buzzer, bugle*] sonner; [*siren*] hurler.
V *adv* **to be ~ asleep** dormir à poings fermés.
▪ **sound out**: **~ out [sb], ~ [sb] out** sonder, interroger.

sound: **~ barrier** *n* mur *m* du son; **~ effect** *n* effet *m* sonore.

soundproof I *adj* [*wall, room*] insonorisé; [*material*] insonorisant.
II *vtr* insonoriser [*room*].

soundtrack *n* (of film) bande *f* sonore; (on record) bande *f* originale.

soup *n* soupe *f*, potage *m*.

soupspoon *n* cuillère *f* à soupe.

sour I *adj* **1** aigre; **to go ~** [*milk*] tourner; **2** (bad-tempered) revêche.
II *vtr* gâter [*relations, atmosphere*].
III *vi* [*attitude*] s'aigrir; [*relationship*] se dégrader.

source *n* source *f*; **~ of income** source de revenu; **at ~** à la source; **~ of** source *f* de [*anxiety, resentment, satisfaction*]; cause *f* de [*problem, error, infection, pollution*]; origine *f* de [*rumour*].

sourdough *n* (US) levain *m*.

south I *n* **1** (compass direction) sud *m*; **2** (part of world, country) **the South** le Sud.
II *adj* (gen) sud *inv*; [*wind*] du sud; **in ~ London** dans le sud de Londres.
III *adv* [*move*] vers le sud; [*lie, live*] au sud (**of** de).

south: **South Africa** ▶574 *pr n* Afrique *f* du Sud; **South America** ▶574 *pr n* Amérique *f* du Sud.

southeast I *n* sud-est *m*.
II *adj* [*coast, side*] sud-est *inv*; [*wind*] de sud-est.
III *adv* [*move*] vers le sud-est; [*lie, live*] au sud-est.

southern *adj* [*coast*] sud *inv*; [*town, accent*] du sud; [*hemisphere*] Sud *inv*; **~ England** le sud de l'Angleterre.

South Pole *pr n* pôle *m* Sud.

southwest I *n* sud-ouest *m*.
II *adj* [*coast*] sud-ouest *inv*; [*wind*] de sud-ouest.
III *adv* [*move*] vers le sud-ouest; [*lie, live*] au sud-ouest.

souvenir *n* souvenir *m*.

souvenir shop *n* magasin *m* de souvenirs.

sovereign I *n* **1** (monarch) souverain/-e *m/f*; **2** (coin) souverain *m*.
II *adj* [*power, state*] souverain (*after n*); [*rights*] de souveraineté.

sovereignty *n* souveraineté *f*.

Soviet Union *pr n* Union *f* soviétique.

sow[1] *n* truie *f*.

sow[2] *vtr* **1** semer [*seeds, corn*]; **2** ensemencer [*field, garden*] (**with** de); **3** (figurative) semer [*discord*]; **to ~ the seeds of doubt** semer le doute (**in sb** dans l'esprit de qn).

soya *n* soja *m*.

soya sauce, soy sauce *n* sauce *f* soja.

spa *n* **1** (town) station *f* thermale; **2** (US) (health club) club *m* de remise en forme.

space I *n* **1** (also **outer ~**) espace *m*; **2** (room) place *f*, espace *m*; **to take up a lot of ~** prendre beaucoup de place; **to make ~ for sb/sth** faire de la place pour qn/qch; **3** (gap) espace *m* (**between** entre); **in the ~ provided** (on form) dans la case prévue à cet effet; **4** (interval of time) intervalle *m*; **in the ~ of five minutes** en l'espace de cinq minutes; **in a short ~ of time** en très peu de temps; **5** (area of land) espace *m*; **open ~** espaces libres.
II *noun modifier* [*research, programme, rocket*] spatial.
III *vtr* espacer.
▪ **space out**: **to ~ out [sth], ~ [sth] out** espacer [*words, objects*]; échelonner [*payments*].

space: **~ship** *n* vaisseau *m* spatial; **~ station** *n* station *f* orbitale; **~suit** *n* combinaison *f* spatiale.

spacious *adj* spacieux/-ieuse.

spade ▶649 *n* **1** (implement) bêche *f*, pelle *f*; **2** (in cards) pique *m*.
IDIOMS **to call a ~ a ~** appeler un chat un chat.

Spain ▶574 *pr n* Espagne *f*.

span I *n* **1** (of time) durée *f*; **2** (of bridge) travée *f*; **(wing)~** envergure *f*.
II *vtr* **1** [*bridge, arch*] enjamber; **2** (figurative) s'étendre sur.

Spaniard ▶712 *n* Espagnol/-e *m/f*.

spaniel *n* épagneul *m*.

Spanish ▶712 **I** *n* **1** (people) **the ~** les Espagnols *mpl*; **2** (language) espagnol *m*.
II *adj* [*culture, food, politics*] espagnol; [*teacher, lesson*] d'espagnol; [*ambassador, embassy*] d'Espagne.

spank *vtr* donner une fessée à.

spanner *n* (GB) clé *f* (de serrage); **adjustable ~** clé à molette.

spar *vi* [*boxers*] échanger des coups; [*debaters*] se livrer à des joutes oratoires.

spare I *n* (part) pièce *f* de rechange; (wheel) roue *f* de secours.
II *adj* **1** [*cash*] restant; [*seat*] disponible; [*copy*] en plus; **I've got a ~ ticket** j'ai un ticket en trop; **a ~ moment** un moment de libre; **2** [*part*] de rechange; [*wheel*] de secours; **3** [*person, build*] élancé.
III *vtr* **1 to have sth to ~** avoir qch de disponible; **to catch the train with five minutes to ~** prendre le train avec cinq minutes d'avance; **2** (treat leniently) épargner; **to ~ sb sth** épargner qch à qn; **3 can you ~ a minute?** as-tu un moment?; **to ~ a thought for** penser à; **4** (manage without) se passer de [*person*].
IDIOMS **to ~ no effort** faire tout son possible.

spare: **~ part** *n* pièce *f* de rechange; **~ room** *n* chambre *f* d'amis; **~ time** *n* loisirs *mpl*.

sparingly *adv* [*use, add*] en petite quantité.

spark I *n* **1** (from fire, firework) étincelle *f*; **2** (of originality) éclair *m*; (of enthusiasm) étincelle *f*; (of intelligence) lueur *f*.

II *vtr* = **spark off**.
■ **spark off**: **~ off [sth]** provoquer [*controversy, reaction, panic*]; être à l'origine de [*friendship, affair*].

sparkle I *n* scintillement *m*; (in eye) éclair *m*; **she's lost her ~** elle a perdu sa joie de vivre.
II *vi* [*flame, light*] étinceler; [*jewel, frost, metal, water*] scintiller; [*eyes*] briller; [*drink*] pétiller.

sparkler *n* cierge *m* magique.

sparkling *adj* **1** [*light, flame*] étincelant; [*jewel, metal, water*] scintillant; [*eyes*] brillant (**with** de); **2** [*conversation, wit*] plein de brio; **3** [*drink*] pétillant.

sparrow *n* moineau *m*.

sparse *adj* [*population, vegetation, hair*] clairsemé; [*resources*] maigre; [*information*] épars.

sparsely *adv* peu; **~ wooded/attended** peu boisé/fréquenté; **~ furnished** sommairement meublé; **~ populated** à faible population.

spartan *adj* [*lifestyle, tastes*] spartiate.

spasm *n* (of pain) spasme *m* (**of** de); (of panic, rage) accès *m* (**of** de).

spasmodic *adj* [*activity*] intermittent; [*coughing, cramp*] spasmodique.

spate *n* **1 in full ~** (GB) (river) en pleine crue; (person) en plein discours; **2 a ~ of** une série de [*incidents*].

spatial *adj* spatial.

spatula *n* spatule *f*.

speak I *vtr* **1** parler [*language*]; **can you ~ English?** parlez-vous (l')anglais?; **2** dire [*truth*]; prononcer [*word, name*]; **to ~ one's mind** dire ce qu'on pense.
II *vi* parler (**to, with** à; **about, of** de); **to ~ in a whisper** parler tout bas; **who's ~ing?** (on phone) qui est à l'appareil?; (**this is**) **Eileen ~ing** c'est Eileen; **'is that Miss Durham?'—'~ing!'** 'Mademoiselle Durham?' —'c'est moi!'; **he spoke very highly of her** il a parlé d'elle en termes très élogieux; **personally ~ing** personnellement; **generally ~ing** en règle générale; **roughly ~ing** en gros; **strictly ~ing** à proprement parler.
■ **speak up 1** (louder) parler plus fort; **2** (dare to speak) intervenir.

speaker *n* **1** (person talking) personne *f* qui parle; (orator, public speaker) orateur/-trice *m/f*; (invited lecturer) conférencier/-ière *m/f*; **2 a French ~** un/-e francophone *mf*; **a Russian ~** quelqu'un qui parle le russe; **3** (on stereo system) haut-parleur *m*.

speaking *combining form* **English-/French-~** anglophone/francophone; **Welsh-~** [*person*] qui parle le gallois; [*area*] de langue galloise.

speaking terms *n pl* **we're not on ~** nous ne nous adressons pas la parole.

spear *n* **1** (weapon) lance *f*; **2** (of asparagus) pointe *f*.

spearmint *n* menthe *f* verte.

special *adj* spécial; [*affection, interest*] tout/-e particulier/-ière; [*case, reason, significance, treatment*] particulier/-ière; [*friend*] très cher/chère; **to make a ~ effort** faire un effort.

special: **~ agent** *n* agent *m* secret; **~ delivery** *n* service *m* exprès; **~ effect** *n* effet *m* spécial.

specialist ▶ 805 *n* spécialiste *mf* (**in** de); **heart ~** cardiologue *m*.

speciality (GB), **specialty** (US) *n* spécialité *f*.

specialize *vi* se spécialiser; **we ~ in repairing computers** nous sommes spécialisés dans la réparation des ordinateurs.

specially *adv* **1** (specifically) spécialement; **I made it ~ for you** je l'ai fait exprès pour toi; **2** (particularly) particulièrement; [*like, enjoy*] surtout.

species *n* espèce *f*.

specific *adj* précis.

specifically *adv* **1** (specially) spécialement (**for** pour); **2** (explicitly) explicitement; **3** (in particular) en particulier; **more ~** plus particulièrement.

specification I *n* **1** (also **specifications** *n pl*) (of design, building) spécification *f* (**for, of** de); **2** (stipulation) stipulation *f* (**that** que).
II **specifications** *n pl* (features of car, computer) caractéristiques *fpl*.

specify *vtr* stipuler; [*person*] préciser (**that** que; **where** où; **who** qui).

specimen I *n* (of rock, urine, handwriting) échantillon *m* (**of** de); (of blood, tissue) prélèvement (**of** de); (of species, plant) spécimen *m* (**of** de).
II *noun modifier* [*page, copy, signature*] spécimen *inv*.

speck *n* (of dust, soot) grain *m*; (of dirt, mud, blood) petite tache *f* (**of** de); (of light) point *m* (**of** de).

speckled *adj* [*hen*] au plumage tacheté; [*egg*] moucheté.

spectacle I *n* spectacle *m*.
II **spectacles** *n pl* lunettes *fpl*.

spectacular I *n* superproduction *f*.
II *adj* spectaculaire.

spectator *n* spectateur/-trice *m/f*.

spectre (GB), **specter** (US) *n* spectre *m*.

spectrum *n* **1** (of colours) spectre *m*; **2** (range) gamme *f*; **people across the political ~** des gens de toutes les tendances politiques.

speculate I *vtr* **to ~ that** supposer que; **it has been widely ~d that he will resign** la rumeur court qu'il va démissionner.
II *vi* spéculer (**on** sur; **about** à propos de).

speculation *n* **1** (conjecture) spéculations *fpl*; **2** (financial) spéculation *f* (**in** sur).

speech *n* **1** discours *m* (**on** sur; **about** à propos de); **to give a ~** faire un discours; **2** (faculty) parole *f*; **3** (language) langage *m*.

speech impediment *n* défaut *m* d'élocution.

speechless *adj* muet/-ette; **to be ~ with** rester muet de; **I'm ~**○! je suis soufflé○!

speech therapist ▶ 805 *n* orthophoniste *mf*.

speed I *n* **1** vitesse *f*; (of response, reaction) rapidité *f*; **at (a) great ~** or **top ~** à toute vitesse; **what ~ were you doing?** à quelle

vitesse est-ce que tu roulais?; **2** (of film) sensibilité *f*; (of shutter) vitesse *f* d'obturation; **3**° (drug) amphétamines *fpl*.
II *vtr* hâter [*process, recovery*].
III *vi* **1 to ~ along** [*driver, car*] rouler à toute allure; **to ~ away** s'eloigner à toute allure; **2** (drive too fast) conduire trop vite; **he was caught ~ing** il a eu une contravention (pour excès) de vitesse.
■ **speed up**: ¶ **~ up** [*walker, train*] aller plus vite; [*athlete, driver, car*] accélérer; [*worker*] travailler plus vite; ¶ **~ up [sth], ~ [sth] up** accélérer.

speed: **~boat** *n* hors-bord *m*; **~ hump** *n* ralentisseur *m*.

speeding *n* excès *m* de vitesse.

speed limit *n* limitation *f* de vitesse.

speedometer *n* compteur *m* (de vitesse).

spell I *n* **1** (period) moment *m*, période *f*; **for a ~** pendant un certain temps; **a ~ in hospital** un séjour à l'hôpital; **a warm ~** une période de beau temps; **sunny ~** éclaircie *f*; **2** (magic words) formule *f* magique; **evil ~** maléfice *m*; **to be under a ~** être envoûté; **to cast** or **put a ~ on sb** jeter un sort à qn; **to be under sb's ~** être sous le charme de qn.
II *vtr* **1** (aloud) épeler; (on paper) écrire; **the word is spelt like this** le mot s'écrit comme ça; **she ~s her name with an e** son nom s'écrit avec un e; **to ~ sth properly** orthographier qch correctement; **C-A-T ~s cat** les lettres C-A-T forment le mot cat; **2** signifier [*danger, disaster, ruin*]; sonner [*end*].
III *vi* **he can't/can ~** il a une mauvaise/bonne orthographe.
■ **spell out**: **~ out [sth], ~ [sth] out 1** épeler [*word*]; **2** expliquer [qch] clairement.

spellbound *adj* envoûté (**by** par).

spelling *n* orthographe *f*.

spend I *vtr* **1** dépenser [*money, salary*] (**on** en); **2** passer [*time*].
II *vi* [*person, organization*] dépenser.

spending *n* dépenses *fpl*; **credit-card ~** achats *mpl* sur carte de crédit; **defence ~** dépense *f* en matière de défense; **government ~, public ~** dépense *f* publique.

spendthrift I *n* **to be a ~** être dépensier/-ière.
II *adj* [*person*] dépensier/-ière; [*habit, policy*] dispendieux/-ieuse.

sperm *n* **1** (cell) spermatozoïde *m*; **2** (semen) sperme *m*.

spew *vtr* vomir.

sphere *n* **1** (shape) sphère *f*; **2** (planet) sphère *f* céleste; **3** (field) domaine *m* (**of** de); **~ of influence** sphère *f* d'influence; **4** (social circle) milieu *m*.

spherical *adj* sphérique.

spice *n* (Culin) épice *f*; (figurative) piment *m*.
IDIOMS **variety is the ~ of life** la diversité est le sel de la vie.

spick-and-span *adj* impeccable.

spicy *adj* **1** [*food*] épicé; **2** [*detail*] croustillant.

spider *n* araignée *f*.

spiderweb *n* (US) toile *f* d'araignée.

spike I *n* pointe *f*.
II spikes *n pl* chaussures *fpl* à pointes.
III° *vtr* corser [*drink*] (**with** de).

spiky *adj* [*hair*] en brosse *inv*; [*branch*] piquant; [*object*] acéré.

spill I *n* **1** (of oil) déversement *m* accidentel; **2** (for lighting candles) allume-feu *m inv*.
II *vtr* **1** renverser [*drink*] (**on, over** sur); **2** déverser [*oil, rubbish, chemicals*] (**into** dans; **on(to)** sur).
III *vi* se répandre (**onto** sur; **into** dans); **to ~ (out) into** or **onto the street** [*crowds, people*] se répandre dans la rue.

spillage *n* déversement *m* accidentel; **oil ~** déversement *m* accidentel d'hydrocarbures.

spin I *n* **1** (of wheel) tour *m*; (of dancer, skate) pirouette *f*; **to give sth a ~** faire tourner qch; **2 to go into a ~** [*plane*] descendre en vrille; **3 to go for a ~** (in car) aller faire un tour.
II *vtr* **1** lancer [*top*]; faire tourner [*globe, wheel*]; **2** filer [*wool, thread*]; **3** [*spider*] tisser [*web*].
III *vi* [*wheel*] tourner; [*weathercock, top*] tournoyer; [*dancer*] pirouetter; **my head is ~ning** j'ai la tête qui tourne; **the room was ~ning** les murs de la pièce tournaient.
■ **spin out**: **~ [sth] out, ~ out [sth]** prolonger [*visit*]; faire traîner [qch] en longueur [*speech*]; faire durer [*work, money*].
■ **spin round**: ¶ **~ round** [*person*] se retourner rapidement; [*dancer, skater*] pirouetter; [*car*] faire un tête-à-queue; ¶ **~ [sb/sth] round** faire tourner [*wheel*].

spinach *n* **1** (plant) épinard *m*; **2** (Culin) épinards *mpl*.

spinal *adj* [*injury, damage*] de la colonne vertébrale.

spinal cord *n* moelle *f* épinière.

spindly *adj* grêle.

spin: **~-drier, ~ dryer** *n* essoreuse *f*; **~-dry** *vtr* essorer [qch] (à la machine).

spine *n* **1** (Anat) colonne *f* vertébrale; **2** (on hedgehog, cactus) piquant *m*; **3** (of book) dos *m*.

spineless *adj* mou/molle.

spin-off *n* **1** (incidental benefit) retombée *f* favorable; **2** (by-product) sous-produit *m* (**of, from** de); **3 TV ~ from the film** adaptation télévisée du film.

spinster *n* célibataire *f*; (derogatory) vieille fille *f*.

spiral I *n* spirale *f*.
II *noun modifier* [*structure*] en spirale.
III *vi* [*prices, costs*] monter en flèche.

spiral staircase *n* escalier *m* en colimaçon.

spire *n* flèche *f*.

spirit I *n* **1** esprit *m*; **to enter into the ~ of things** se mettre dans l'ambiance; **2** (courage, determination) courage *m*; **to show ~** se montrer courageux/-euse; **to break sb's ~** briser la résistance de qn; **3** (drink) **wines and ~s** vins et spiritueux *mpl*.
II spirits *n pl* **to be in good ~s** être de bonne humeur; **to be in high ~s** être d'excel-

lente humeur; **to keep one's ~s up** garder le moral.
III *noun modifier* [*lamp, stove*] à alcool.
spirited *adj* [*horse, debate, reply*] fougueux/-euse; [*attack, defence*] vif/vive.
spiritual I *n* spiritual *m*.
II *adj* spirituel/-elle.
spiritualism *n* spiritisme *m*.
spit I *n* **1** (saliva) salive *f*; **2** (for cooking) broche *f*; **rotating ~** tournebroche *m*.
II *vtr* [*person*] cracher; [*pan*] projeter [*oil*].
III *vi* [*cat, person*] cracher (**at, on** sur; **into** dans; **out of** de); [*oil, sausage*] grésiller; [*logs, fire*] crépiter.
IV *v impers* **it's ~ting (with rain)** il bruine.
IDIOMS **to be the ~ting image of sb** être le portrait tout craché de qn.
spite I *n* (malice) méchanceté *f*; (vindictiveness) rancune *f*.
II *vtr* faire du mal à; (less strong) embêter.
III **in spite of** *phr* malgré; **in ~ of the fact that** bien que.
IDIOMS **to cut off one's nose to ~ one's face** scier la branche sur laquelle on est assis.
spiteful *adj* [*person*] (malicious) méchant; (vindictive) rancunier/-ière; [*remark*] méchant; **~ gossip** commérages *mpl*.
splash I *n* **1** (sound) plouf *m*; **2** (of mud) tache *f*; (of water, oil) éclaboussure *f*; (of colour) touche *f*; (of tonic, soda) goutte *f*.
II *vtr* éclabousser; **to ~ sth over sb/sth** éclabousser qn/qch de qch; **to ~ water on to one's face** s'asperger le visage d'eau; **the news was ~ed across the front page** la nouvelle s'étalait à la une des journaux.
III *vi* faire des éclaboussures.
■ **splash out**○ faire des folies; **to ~ out on sth** faire la folie de s'offrir qch.
splatter I *vtr* **to ~ sb/sth with sth** éclabousser qn/qch de qch.
II *vi* **to ~ onto** or **over sth** [*ink, paint, mud*] gicler sur qch.
splay *vtr* écarter [*feet, fingers*].
spleen *n* (Anat) rate *f*.
splendid *adj* [*building, scenery, collection*] splendide; [*idea, performance*] merveilleux/-euse; **~!** (c'est) formidable○!
splendour (GB), **splendor** (US) *n* splendeur *f*.
splice *vtr* coller [*tape, film*]; épisser [*ends of rope*].
splint *n* (for injury) attelle *f*.
splinter I *n* (of glass, metal, wood) éclat *m*; **to get a ~ in one's finger** s'enfoncer une écharde dans le doigt.
II *vi* [*glass, windscreen*] se briser; [*wood*] se fendre; [*alliance*] se scinder.
splinter group *n* groupe *m* dissident.
split I *n* **1** (in fabric) déchirure *f*; (in rock, wood) fissure *f*; **2** (in party, alliance) scission *f* (**in** de); (stronger) rupture *f* (**in, into** dans); **3** (dessert) ≈ coupe *f* glacée.
II **splits** *n pl* **to do the ~s** faire le grand écart.
III *adj* [*fabric*] déchiré; [*seam*] défait; [*log, lip*] fendu.
IV *vtr* **1** (cut, slit) fendre [*log, rock*] (**in, into** en); déchirer [*fabric, garment*]; **2** diviser [*party*]; **3** (share) partager (**between** entre); **to ~ sth three ways** partager qch en trois.
V *vi* **1** [*wood, log, rock*] se fendre (**in , into** en); [*fabric, garment*] se déchirer; **2** [*party, alliance*] se diviser; (stronger) se scinder.
IDIOMS **to ~ the difference** couper la poire en deux.
■ **split off**: ¶ **~ off** [*branch, piece*] se détacher (**from** de); [*political group*] faire scission; [*company*] se séparer (**from** de); ¶ **~ [sth] off** détacher [*branch, piece*].
■ **split up**: ¶ **~ up** [*couple, band*] se séparer; [*alliance*] éclater; **to ~ up with** quitter [*husband*]; ¶ **~ [sth] up, ~ up [sth]** diviser [*area, group*] (**into** en).
split: **~ level** *adj* [*room, apartment*] sur deux niveaux; **~ personality** *n* double personnalité *f*; **~ second** *n* fraction *f* de seconde.
splitting *adj* **to have a ~ headache** avoir horriblement mal à la tête.
splutter *vi* [*fire, candle, match*] grésiller.
spoil I *vtr* **1** (mar) gâcher (**by doing** en faisant); gâter [*place, taste, effect*]; **to ~ sth for sb** gâcher qch à qn; **2** (ruin) abîmer; **3** (pamper) gâter [*child, pet*] (**by doing** en faisant).
II *vi* [*product, foodstuff*] s'abîmer.
III *v refl* **to ~ oneself** se faire un petit plaisir.
spoiled, spoilt (GB) *adj* **1** [*child, dog*] gâté; **a ~ brat**○ un gamin pourri○; **2** [*ballot paper*] nul/nulle.
spoils *n pl* (of war) butin *m* (**of** de).
spoilsport○ *n* **to be a ~** être un rabat-joie.
spoke *n* (in wheel) rayon *m*; (on ladder) barreau *m*.
spoken *adj* [*word, dialogue, language*] parlé.
spokesman *n* porte-parole *m inv*.
spokeswoman *n* porte-parole *m inv*.
sponge I *n* **1** éponge *f*; **2** (also **~ cake**) génoise *f*.
II *vtr* éponger [*material, stain, face*].
III○ *vi* **to ~ off** or **on** vivre sur le dos de [*family, state*].
sponge bag *n* (GB) trousse *f* de toilette.
spongy *adj* [*ground, moss*] spongieux/-ieuse; [*material, texture*] moelleux/-euse.
sponsor I *n* **1** (advertiser, backer) sponsor *m*; **2** (patron) mécène *m*; **3** (when immigrating) garant/-e *m/f*; **4** (of political bill) initiateur/-trice *m/f*.
II *vtr* **1** (fund) sponsoriser [*event, team*]; financer [*student, course*]; parrainer [*child*]; **2** présenter [*bill*].
sponsorship *n* **1** (corporate funding) parrainage *m*, sponsorat *m* (**from** de); **2** (backing) (financial) sponsorat *m*; (cultural) patronage *m*.
spontaneity *n* spontanéité *f*.
spontaneous *adj* spontané.
spontaneously *adv* spontanément.
spoof○ *n* **1** (parody) parodie *f* (**on** de); **2** (trick) blague○ *f*.
spooky○ *adj* [*house, atmosphere*] sinistre; [*story*] qui fait froid dans le dos.

spool *n* bobine *f*.

spoon *n* cuillère *f*; (teaspoon) petite cuillère *f*.

spoon-feed *vtr* nourrir [qn] à la cuillère; (figurative) [*teacher*] mâcher la besogne à [*pupils*].

spoonful *n* cuillerée *f*, cuillère *f*.

sporadic *adj* sporadique.

sport ▶**649** *n* **1** sport *m*; **to be good at ~s** être bon en sport; **2 he's a good ~** (good loser) il est beau joueur; (when teased) il prend bien la plaisanterie.

sporting *adj* **1** [*fixture, event*] sportif/-ive; **2** (fair, generous) [*gesture*] généreux/-euse.

sport: **~s car** *n* voiture *f* de sport; **~scast** *n* (US) émission *f* sportive; **~s centre** (GB), **~s center** (US) *n* centre *m* sportif; **~s club** *n* club *m* sportif; **~s day** *n* (GB) fête *f* des sports; **~s ground** *n* (large) stade *m*; (in school, club) terrain *m* de sports; **~s jacket** *n* (GB) veste *f* en tweed; **~sman** *n* sportif *m*; **~smanship** *n* (skill in sports) sportivité *f*; (generous behaviour) fair-play *m*; **~s page** *n* page *f* sport; **~swoman** *n* sportive *f*.

spot I *n* **1** (on animal) tache *f*; (on fabric) pois *m*; (on dice, domino) point *m*; **2** (stain) tache *f*; **3** (pimple) bouton *m*; **to come out in ~s** être couvert de boutons; **4** (place) endroit *m*; **on the ~** (at place) sur place; (forthwith) sur-le-champ; **5**○ (small amount) **a ~ of** un peu de; **6**○ **to be in a (tight) ~** être dans une situation embêtante.
II *vtr* **1** (see) apercevoir [*person*]; (recognize) repérer [*difference, mistake*]; **well ~ted!** bien vu!; **2** (stain) tacher.

spot check *n* (unannounced) contrôle *m* surprise (**on** sur); (random) contrôle *m* fait au hasard (**on** sur).

spotless *adj* impeccable.

spotlight *n* (in theatre, film set) projecteur *m*; (in home) spot *m*.

spot-on *adj* (GB) exact; **he was absolutely ~** il a mis dans le mille.

spotted *adj* [*fabric*] à pois (*after n*); [*fur, dog*] tacheté.

spotty *adj* [*adolescent, skin*] boutonneux/-euse.

spout I *n* (of kettle, teapot) bec *m* verseur; (of gutter) gargouille *f*.
II *vtr* **1** (spurt) faire jaillir [*water*]; **2** (recite) débiter [*poetry, statistics*].
III *vi* [*liquid*] jaillir (**from, out of** de).

sprain I *n* entorse *f*; (less severe) foulure *f*.
II *vtr* **to ~ one's ankle** se faire une entorse à la cheville; (less severely) se fouler la cheville.

sprawl I *n* (of suburbs, buildings) étendue *f*.
II *vi* s'étaler; **she lay ~ed across the sofa** elle était étalée sur le canapé.

sprawling *adj* [*suburb, city*] tentaculaire.

spray I *n* **1** (seawater) embruns *mpl*; (other) nuages *mpl* de (fines) gouttelettes; **2** (container) (for perfume) vaporisateur *m*; (can) bombe *f*; (for inhalant, throat, nose) pulvérisateur *m*; **3** (of flowers) (bunch) gerbe *f*; (single branch) rameau *m*.
II *noun modifier* [*deodorant*] en spray; [*paint, starch*] en atomiseur.
III *vtr* **1** vaporiser [*liquid*]; asperger [*person*] (**with** de); arroser [*demonstrators*] (**with** de); **to ~ sth onto sth** (onto fire) projeter qch sur qch [*foam, water*]; (onto surface, flowers) vaporiser qch sur qch [*paint, water*].

spread I *n* **1** (of disease, drugs) propagation *f*; (of news, information) diffusion *f*; (of democracy) progression *f*; **2** (in newspaper) **double-page ~** page *f* double; **3** (Culin) pâte *f* à tartiner.
II *vtr* **1** (unfold) étaler, étendre [*cloth, newspaper, map*] (**on, over** sur); [*bird*] déployer [*wings*]; **2** étaler [*butter, jam, glue*] (**on, over** sur); **3** (distribute) disperser [*troops*]; répartir [*workload, responsibility*]; **4** (also **~ out**) étaler, échelonner [*payments, meetings*] (**over** sur); **5** propager [*disease, fire*]; semer [*confusion, panic*]; faire circuler [*rumour, story*]; **to ~ the word that** dire à tout le monde que.
III *vi* **1** [*butter, jam, glue*] s'étaler; **2** (extend, proliferate) [*forest, drought*] s'étendre (**over** sur); [*disease, fear, fire*] se propager; [*rumour, story*] circuler; [*stain, damp*] s'étaler; **to ~ to** [*fire, disease, riots*] s'étendre à, gagner [*building, region*]; [*rain*] s'étendre (**to** à).
■ **spread out**: ¶ **~ out** [*group*] se disperser (**over** sur); [*wings, tail*] se déployer; ¶ **~ [sth] out, ~ out [sth] 1** étaler, étendre [*cloth, map, rug*] (**on, over** sur); **the town lay spread out below them** la ville s'étendait à leurs pieds; **2** disperser [*forces, troops*].

spread: **~-eagled** *adj* bras et jambes écartés; **~sheet** *n* tableur *m*.

spree *n* **to go on a ~** (drinking) faire la bringue○; **to go on a shopping ~** aller faire des folies dans les magasins.

sprig *n* (of holly) petite branche *f*; (of parsley) brin *m*.

sprightly *adj* alerte, gaillard.

spring I *n* **1** (season) printemps *m*; **in ~** au printemps; ▶ **autumn**; **2** (of wire) ressort *m*; **3** (leap) bond *m*; **to have a ~ in one's step** marcher d'un pas allègre; **4** (water source) source *f*.
II *vtr* **1** (set off) déclencher [*trap, lock*]; **2 to ~ a leak** [*tank, barrel*] commencer à fuir; **3 to ~ [sth] on sb** annoncer [qch] de but en blanc à qn [*news, plan*].
III *vi* **1** (jump) bondir (**onto** sur); **to ~ to one's feet** se lever d'un bond; **2 to ~ open** [*door, panel*] s'ouvrir brusquement; **to ~ into action** [*team, troops*] passer à l'action; **3** (originate) **to ~ from** venir de [*jealousy, fear, prejudice*].
■ **spring up** [*new building*] apparaître.

spring: **~-clean** *vtr* nettoyer [qch] de fond en comble [*house*]; **~-cleaning** *n* grand nettoyage *m* de printemps; **~ tide** *n* grande marée *f*.

springy *adj* [*mattress, seat*] élastique.

sprinkle *vtr* **to ~ sth with** saupoudrer qch de [*salt, sugar*]; parsemer qch de [*herbs*]; **to ~ sth with water** humecter qch.

sprinkler *n* **1** (for lawn) arroseur *m*; (for field) (large, rotating) canon *m* arroseur; **2** (to extinguish fires) diffuseur *m*.

sprinkling *n* (of salt, sugar) petite pincée *f*; (of snow) fine couche *f*.

sprint I *n* (race) sprint *m*, course *f* de vitesse.
II *vi* (in athletics) sprinter; (to catch bus) courir (à toute vitesse).

sprout I *n* (also **Brussels ~**) chou *m* de Bruxelles.
II *vi* [*seed, shoot*] germer; [*grass, weeds*] pousser.
■ **sprout up** [*buildings, suburbs*] pousser comme des champignons.

spruce I *n* (also **~ tree**) épicéa *m*.
II *adj* [*person*] soigné; [*house, garden*] bien tenu.
■ **spruce up**: **~ up [sth], ~ [sth] up** astiquer [*house*]; nettoyer [*garden*]; **to ~ oneself up** se faire beau/belle.

spry *adj* alerte, leste.

spun *adj* [*glass, gold, sugar*] filé.

spur I *n* **1** (for horse) éperon *m*; (figurative) aiguillon *m*; **2** (of rock) contrefort *m*.
II *vtr* (also **~ on**) éperonner [*horse*]; aiguillonner [*person*]; **to ~ sb to do** inciter qn à faire.
IDIOMS **on the ~ of the moment** sur une impulsion.

spurious *adj* faux/fausse.

spurn *vtr* refuser [qch] (avec mépris) [*advice, offer, gift*]; éconduire [*suitor*].

spurt I *n* **1** (gush) (of water, oil, blood) giclée *f*; (of flame) jaillissement *m*; (of steam) jet *m*; **2** (of activity) regain *m*; (of energy) sursaut *m*; (in growth) poussée *f*; **to put on a ~** [*runner, cyclist*] pousser une pointe de vitesse.
II *vi* (also **~ out**) jaillir (**from, out of** de).

spy I *n* (political, industrial) espion/-ionne *m/f*; (for police) indicateur/-trice *m/f*.
II *noun modifier* [*film, novel, scandal*] d'espionnage.
III *vtr* remarquer, discerner [*figure, object*].
IV *vi* **to ~ on sth/sb** espionner qch/qn.

spying *n* espionnage *m*.

squabble *vi* se disputer, se chamailler○ (**over, about** à propos de).

squabbling *n* chamailleries○ *fpl*, disputes *fpl*.

squad *n* (Mil) escouade *f*; (sports team) sélection *f*.

squad car *n* voiture *f* de police.

squadron *n* **1** (in army) escadron *m*; **2** (in other services) escadrille *f*.

squalid *adj* [*house, street, affair*] sordide; [*furnishings*] minable.

squall *n* (wind) bourrasque *f*, rafale *f* (**of** de); (at sea) grain *m*.

squalor *n* (filth) saleté *f* repoussante; (wretchedness) misère *f* (noire); **in ~** dans des conditions sordides.

squander *vtr* gaspiller [*talents, opportunities, resources*]; gâcher [*youth, health*].

square I *n* **1** (geometrical shape) carré *m*; **2** (in town) place *f*; (in barracks) cour *f*; **3** (in board game, crossword) case *f*; (of glass, linoleum) carreau *m*; **4**○ (person) ringard/-e○ *m/f*.
II *adj* **1** (right-angled) [*shape, building, box, jaw, shoulders*] carré; (correctly aligned) bien droit; **2 four ~ metres** quatre mètres carrés; **an area four metres ~** une surface de quatre mètres sur quatre; **3** (figurative) (quits) **to be ~** [*people*] être quitte; **4** (honest) [*person, transaction*] honnête (**with** avec).
III *vtr* **1 to ~ one's shoulders** redresser les épaules; **2** (settle) régler [*account, debt*].
IDIOMS **to go back to ~ one** retourner à la case départ.
■ **square up 1** (figurative) faire face (**to** à); **2** (settle accounts) régler ses comptes.
■ **square with** correspondre à, cadrer avec [*evidence, fact*].

squash I *n* **1** ▶ 649 (also **~ rackets**) squash *m*; **2** (drink) sirop *m*; **3** (vegetable) courge *f*.
II *vtr* **1** (crush) écraser; **2** (force) **to ~ sth/sb into sth** caser qch/qn dans qch.
■ **squash in**○: ¶ **~ in** (into lift, taxi) s'entasser; ¶ **~ in [sth/sb], ~ [sth/sb] in** trouver de la place pour.

squat I○ *n* squat○ *m*.
II *adj* [*person, structure, object*] trapu.
III *vi* **1** (crouch) s'accroupir; **2 to ~ in** squatter [*building*].

squawk I *n* (of hen) gloussement *m*; (of duck, parrot) cri *m* rauque.
II *vi* [*hen*] pousser des gloussements; [*duck, parrot*] pousser des cris rauques.

squeak I *n* (noise) (of door, wheel, chalk) grincement *m*; (of mouse, soft toy) couinement *m*; (of furniture, shoes) craquement *m*.
II *vi* [*door, wheel, chalk*] grincer; [*mouse, soft toy*] couiner; [*shoes, furniture*] craquer (**on** sur).

squeaky *adj* [*voice*] aigu/-uë; [*gate, hinge, wheel*] grinçant.

squeal I *n* (of animal, person) cri *m* aigu.
II *vi* **1** [*person, animal*] pousser des cris aigus (**in, with** de); **2**○ (inform) vendre la mèche○; **to ~ on sb** balancer○ qn.

squeamish *adj* impressionnable, sensible.

squeeze I *n* **1** (on credit, finances) resserrement *m* (**on** de); **2**○ (crush) **it will be a tight ~** ce sera un peu juste.
II *vtr* **1** presser [*lemon, bottle, tube*]; serrer [*arm, hand*]; appuyer sur [*trigger*]; percer [*spot*]; **to ~ water out of** essorer, tordre [*cloth*]; **2** (figurative) réussir à obtenir [*money*] (**out of** de); **to ~ the truth out of sb** arracher la vérité à qn; **3** (fit) **we can ~ a few more people in** on a encore de la place pour quelques personnes; **I can just ~ into that dress** je rentre tout juste dans cette robe; **to ~ behind/under sth** se glisser derrière/sous qch; **4** (in finance) resserrer [*profit, margins*].

squelch *vi* [*water, mud*] glouglouter; **to ~ along** avancer en pataugeant.

squib *n* pétard *m*.

squid *n* calmar *m*, encornet *m*.

squiggle *n* gribouillis *m*.

squint I *n* strabisme *m*; **to have a ~** loucher.
II *vi* **1** (look narrowly) plisser les yeux; **2** (have eye condition) loucher.

squire *n* ≈ châtelain *m*.

squirm *vi* [*person, snake*] se tortiller; [*fish*] frétiller; [*kitten*] remuer; [*person*] (in pain) se tordre; (with embarrassment) être très mal à l'aise.

squirrel *n* écureuil *m*.

squirt I *n* **1** (small amount) goutte *f*; **2**○ **a little ~** un petit morveux○.
II *vtr* faire gicler [*liquid*]; **to ~ water at sb** asperger qn d'eau.
III *vi* [*liquid*] jaillir (**from, out of** de).

stab I *n* **1** (act) coup *m* de couteau; **a ~ in the back** (figurative) un coup en traître; **2** (of pain) élancement *m* (**of** de).
II *vtr* poignarder [*person*]; **to ~ sb to death** tuer qn à coups de couteau; **to ~ sb in the back** poignarder qn dans le dos.

stabbing I *n* agression *f* au couteau.
II *adj* [*pain*] lancinant.

stability *n* stabilité *f*.

stabilize I *vtr* stabiliser.
II *vi* se stabiliser.
III **stabilizing** *pres p adj* [*effect, influence*] stabilisateur/-trice.

stable I *n* écurie *f*; **riding ~s** manège *m*.
II *adj* **1** (steady) stable; **2** (psychologically) [*person, temperament*] équilibré.
IDIOMS **to shut the ~ door after the horse has bolted** fermer la cage quand les oiseaux se sont envolés.

stack I *n* (pile) pile *f*; (of hay, straw) meule *f*.
II **stacks** *n pl* **1** (in library) rayons *mpl*; **2**○ **~s of** plein de○ [*food, work*].
III *vtr* **1** (also **~ up**) (pile) empiler; **2** (fill) remplir [*shelves*]; **3** mettre [qch] en attente [*planes, calls*].

stadium *n* stade *m*.

staff *n* **1** (employees) (of company) personnel *m*; (of a school, college) (also **teaching ~**) personnel *m* enseignant; (of household) (also **domestic ~**) domestiques *mpl*; **2** (military) état-major *m*.

staff room *n* salle *f* des professeurs.

stag *n* cerf *m*.

stage I *n* **1** (phase) (of illness, career, life) stade *m* (**of, in** de); (of project, process, plan) phase *f* (**of, in** de); (of journey, negotiations) étape *f* (**of, in** de); **at this ~** (at this point) à ce stade; (yet, for the time being) pour l'instant; **at every ~** à chaque étape; **in ~s** en plusieurs étapes; **2** (raised platform) estrade *f*; (in theatre) scène *f*; **to go on the ~** (figurative) faire du théâtre.
II *noun modifier* [*play, lighting*] de théâtre; [*production*] théâtral.
III *vtr* **1** (organize) organiser [*event, rebellion, strike*]; **2** (fake) simuler [*quarrel, scene*]; **3** (in theatre) monter [*play*].

stage: **~coach** *n* diligence *f*; **~ direction** *n* indication *f* scénique; **~ door** *n* entrée *f* des artistes; **~ fright** *n* trac *m*; **~hand** ▶805 *n* machiniste *m*; **~-manage** *vtr* orchestrer; **~ name** *n* nom *m* de théâtre; **~-struck** *adj* qui rêve de faire du théâtre.

stagger I *vtr* **1** (astonish) stupéfier, abasourdir; **2** échelonner [*holidays, payments*].
II *vi* [*person*] (from weakness) chanceler; (drunkenly) tituber; [*animal*] vaciller; **to ~ in/out** entrer/sortir en chancelant.

staggering *adj* [*amount, increase, loss*] prodigieux/-ieuse; [*news, revelation*] renversant; [*event*] bouleversant; [*achievement*] stupéfiant.

staging *n* (of play) mise *f* en scène.

stagnant *adj* stagnant.

stagnate *vi* [*person, economy, society*] stagner.

stag night, **stag party** *n* soirée *f* pour enterrer une vie de garçon.

stagy *adj* théâtral.

staid *adj* guindé.

stain I *n* **1** (mark) tache *f*; **it will leave a ~** ça fera une tache; **2** (dye) (for wood) teinture *f*.
II *vtr* **1** (soil) tacher [*clothes, carpet, table*]; **2** teindre [*wood*].
III *vi* [*fabric*] se tacher.

stained: **~ glass** *n* verre *m* coloré; **~ glass window** *n* vitrail *m*.

stainless steel *n* acier *m* inoxydable.

stain remover *n* détachant *m*.

stair I *n* (step) marche *f* (d'escalier).
II **stairs** *n pl* **the ~s** l'escalier; **to fall down the ~s** tomber dans l'escalier.

stair: **~case**, **~way** *n* escalier *m*; **~well** *n* cage *f* d'escalier.

stake I *n* **1** (amount risked) enjeu *m*; **to raise the ~s** monter la mise; (figurative) fair monter les enchères; **to be at ~** être en jeu; **2** (investment) participation *f* (**in** dans); **3** (post) pieu *m*; (thicker) poteau *m*; (marker) piquet *m*.
II **stakes** *n pl* **1** (prize money) montant *m* du prix; **2** (name of race) course *f*.
III *vtr* **1** (gamble) miser [*money, property*]; risquer [*reputation*]; **I would ~ my life on it** j'en mettrais ma tête à couper○; **2** (support) mettre un tuteur à [*plant, tree*].
IDIOMS **to ~ one's claim to** exposer ses revendications sur.

stale *adj* [*bread, cake*] rassis; [*beer*] éventé; [*smell*] de renfermé; [*jokes, ideas*] éculé; **to go ~** [*bread*] se rassir.

stalemate *n* **1** (in chess) pat *m*; **2** (deadlock) impasse *f*.

stalk I *n* (on plant, flower) tige *f*; (of leaf, apple) queue *f*; (of mushroom) pied *m*; (of cabbage) trognon *m*.
II *vtr* **1** [*hunter, murderer*] traquer [*prey, victim*]; [*animal*] chasser [*prey*]; **2** [*fear, danger*] régner sur [*town, region*].

stall I *n* **1** (at market, fair) stand *m*; **2** (in stable) stalle *f*.
II **stalls** *n pl* (GB) orchestre *m*; **in the ~s** à l'orchestre.
III *vtr* **1** caler [*engine, car*]; **2** (hold up) bloquer [*talks, action, process*].
IV *vi* **1** [*car*] caler; **2** [*plane engine*] décrocher; **3** (play for time) temporiser.

stallion *n* étalon *m*.

stalwart *adj* [*defender, member, supporter*] loyal.

stamina *n* résistance *f*, endurance *f*.

stammer I *n* bégaiement *m*.
II *vi* bégayer.

stamp I *n* **1** (for envelope) timbre *m*; **a three-franc ~** un timbre à trois francs; **2** (towards bill, TV licence) timbre *m*; **3** (on passport, document) cachet *m*; **4** (marker) (rubber) tampon *m*; (metal) cachet *m*; **date ~** timbre *m* dateur; **5** (figurative) (hallmark) marque *f*, empreinte *f*.
II *vtr* **1** (mark) apposer [qch] au tampon [*date, name*] (**on** sur); tamponner [*ticket, book*]; marquer [*goods*]; viser [*document, passport*]; **2 to ~ one's foot** (in anger) taper du pied; **3** affranchir [*envelope*].
III *vi* [*horse*] piaffer; **to ~ on** écraser (du pied) [*toy, foot*]; piétiner [*soil, ground*]; **to ~ out of a room** sortir d'une pièce à grands pas furieux.
■ **stamp out**: **~ out [sth], ~ [sth] out** éliminer.

stamp: **~-collecting** *n* philatélie *f*; **~-collector** *n* philatéliste *mf*; **~ed addressed envelope, sae** *n* enveloppe *f* timbrée à votre/son etc adresse.

stampede I *n* (of animals) débandade *f*; (of humans) ruée *f*.
II *vi* [*animals*] s'enfuir (pris d'affolement); [*people*] se précipiter.

stance *n* position *f*.

stand I *n* **1** (support, frame) support *m*; (for coats) portemanteau *m*; **2** (stall) (in market) éventaire *m*; (kiosk) kiosque *m*; (at exhibition, trade fair) stand *m*; **3** (in stadium) tribunes *fpl*; **4** (witness box) barre *f*; **to take the ~** aller à la barre; **5** (stance) **to take a ~ on sth** prendre position sur qch; **6** (**to make**) **a last ~** (livrer) une dernière bataille.
II *vtr* **1** (place) mettre [*person, object*] (**against** contre; **in** dans; **on** sur); **2** (bear) supporter [*cold, weight*]; tolérer [*nonsense, bad behaviour*]; **I can't ~ him** je ne peux pas le supporter or le sentir; **I can't ~ jazz/this town** je déteste le jazz/cette ville; **I can't ~ doing** je déteste faire; **3**° (pay for) **to ~ sb a drink** payer un verre à qn; **4 to ~ trial** passer en jugement.
III *vi* **1** (also **~ up**) se lever; **2** (as opposed to sitting) [*person*] se tenir debout; **3** [*object*] tenir debout; **to remain ~ing** rester debout; **4** (be positioned) [*building, village*] se trouver, être; (clearly delineated) se dresser; **5** (step) **to ~ on** marcher sur [*insect, foot*]; **6** (be) **as things ~**... étant donné l'état actuel des choses...; **the total ~s at 300** le total est de 300; **to ~ in sb's way** (figurative) faire obstacle à qn; **7** (remain valid) [*offer, agreement, statement*] rester valable; **8** (be a candidate) se présenter (**as** comme); **to ~ for election** se présenter aux élections.
■ **stand about, stand around** rester là (**doing** à faire).
■ **stand back 1** [*person, crowd*] reculer (**from** de); (figurative) prendre du recul (**from** par rapport à); **2** [*house*] être en retrait (**from** par rapport à).
■ **stand by**: ¶ **~ by** [*doctor, army, emergency services*] être prêt à intervenir; ¶ **~ by [sb/sth]** soutenir [*person*]; s'en tenir à [*principles, decision*].
■ **stand for**: **~ for [sth] 1** (represent) représenter [*ideal*]; **2** (denote) [*initials*] vouloir dire; **3** (tolerate) tolérer.
■ **stand in**: **to ~ in for sb** remplacer qn.
■ **stand out** [*person*] sortir de l'ordinaire; [*work, ability*] être remarquable.
■ **stand up**: ¶ **~ up 1** (rise) se lever; **2** (stay upright) se tenir debout; **3** [*theory, story*] tenir debout; **4** (resist) **to ~ up to** tenir tête à [*person*]; **5** (defend) **to ~ up for** défendre [*person, rights*]; ¶ **~ [sth] up** redresser [*object*]; ¶ **~ [sb] up**° poser un lapin à° [*girlfriend, boyfriend*].

standard I *n* **1** (level of quality) niveau *m*; **~s of service have declined** la qualité du service a baissé; **by any ~s** incontestablement; **to have high/low ~s** (in one's work) être très/peu consciencieux; **2** (official specification) norme *f* (**for** de); **3** (requirement) (of student, work) niveau *m* requis (**for** pour); (of hygiene, safety) critères *mpl*; **not to be up to ~** ne pas avoir le niveau requis; **by today's ~s** selon les critères actuels; **4** (banner) étendard *m*.
II *adj* **1** (normal) [*size, rate, pay*] standard; [*procedure*] habituel/-elle; [*image*] traditionnel/-elle; **it's ~ practice** c'est l'usage; **2** [*work, manual*] de référence.

standardize *vtr* normaliser, standardiser.

standard: **~ lamp** *n* (GB) lampadaire *m*; **~ of living** *n* niveau *m* de vie.

standby I *n* (person) remplaçant/-e *m/f*; **to be on ~** [*army, emergency services*] être prêt à intervenir; (for airline ticket) être en stand-by.
II *noun modifier* [*passenger, ticket*] en stand-by.

stand-in *n* remplaçant/-e *m/f*.

standing I *n* **1** (reputation) réputation *f*, rang *m* (**among** parmi; **with** chez); **2** (length of time) **of long ~** de longue date.
II *adj* **1** [*army, committee, force*] actif/-ive; **2** [*invitation*] permanent.

standing: **~ order** *n* virement *m* automatique; **~ room** *n* places *fpl* debout.

stand: **~-off** *n* (US) (stalemate) impasse *f*; **~point** *n* point *m* de vue.

standstill *n* (of traffic) arrêt *m*; (of economy, growth) point *m* mort; **to be at a ~** [*factory, port*] être au point mort; [*talks*] être arrivé à une impasse.

staple I *n* **1** (for paper) agrafe *f*; **2** (basic food) aliment *m* de base.
II *adj* [*product, food, diet*] de base.
III *vtr* agrafer (**to** à; **onto** sur).

stapler *n* agrafeuse *f*.

star I *n* **1** (in sky) étoile *f*; **2** (celebrity) vedette *f*, star *f*; **3** (asterisk) astérisque *m*; **4** (award) (to hotel, restaurant) étoile *f*; (to pupil) bon point *m*; **a three-~ hotel** un hôtel (à) trois étoiles; **5 ~s** (horoscope) horoscope *m*.
II *vtr* [*film, play*] avoir [qn] pour vedette [*actor*]; **~ring Fay Wray** avec Fay Wray en vedette.
III *vi* [*actor*] jouer le rôle principal (**in** dans).

starch I *n* **1** (carbohydrate) féculents *mpl*; **2** (for clothes) amidon *m*.
II *vtr* amidonner, empeser.

starchy *adj* **1** [*food, diet*] riche en féculents; **2**° [*person*] guindé.

stardom *n* célébrité *f*; **to rise to ~** devenir une vedette.

stare I *n* regard *m* fixe.
II *vi* regarder fixement; **to ~ at sb/sth** regarder fixement qn/qch.

starfish *n* étoile *f* de mer.

staring *adj* [*eyes*] fixe; [*people, crowd*] curieux/-ieuse.

stark *adj* [*landscape*] désolé; [*room, decor*] nu; [*reality*] cru; **in ~ contrast to** en opposition totale avec.
IDIOMS **~ naked** tout nu; **~ staring mad**° (GB) complètement cinglé°.

starlet *n* starlette *f*.

starry *adj* [*night, sky*] étoilé; [*eyes*] brillant.

starry-eyed *adj* ébloui (**about** par).

start I *n* **1** (beginning) début *m*; **at the ~ of** au début de; (**right**) **from the start** dès le début; **to make a ~ on doing** se mettre à faire; **from ~ to finish** du début à la fin; **for a ~** pour commencer; **2** (in sport) (advantage) avantage *m*; (in time, distance) avance *f*; (departure line) ligne *f* de départ; **3** (movement) **with a ~** en sursaut.
II *vtr* **1** (begin) commencer [*day, activity*]; entamer [*bottle, packet*]; **to ~ doing** commencer à faire; **2** (cause, initiate) déclencher [*quarrel, war*]; instaurer [*custom*]; lancer [*fashion, enterprise, rumour*]; **3** faire démarrer [*car*]; mettre [qch] en marche [*machine*].
III *vi* **1** (begin) commencer (**by doing** par faire); (in job) débuter (**as** comme); **to ~ again** recommencer; **2** [*car, engine, machine*] démarrer; **3** (depart) partir; **4** (jump nervously) sursauter (**in** de).
IV **to start with** *phr* **1** (firstly) d'abord, premièrement; **2** (at first) au début.
■ **start off**: ¶ **~ off 1** (set off) [*train, bus*] démarrer; [*person*] partir; **2** (begin) [*person*] commencer (**by doing** par faire; **with** par); [*business, employee*] débuter (**as** comme; **in** dans); ¶ **~ [sth] off**, **~ off [sth] 1** (begin) commencer [*visit, talk*] (**with** par); **2** mettre [qch] en marche [*machine*].
■ **start out** (on journey) partir.
■ **start over** (US) recommencer (à zéro).
■ **start up**: ¶ **~ up** [*engine*] démarrer; ¶ **~ [sth] up**, **~ up [sth]** faire démarrer [*car*]; ouvrir [*shop*]; créer [*business*].

starter *n* **1** (of race) starter *m*; **2** (on menu) hors-d'œuvre *m inv*.

starting: **~ line** *n* ligne *f* de départ; **~ salary** *n* salaire *m* de départ.

startle *vtr* **1** (take aback) surprendre; **2** (alarm) effrayer.

startling *adj* [*resemblance, contrast*] saisissant.

starvation I *n* famine *f*; **to die of ~** mourir de faim.
II *noun modifier* [*rations*] de survie; [*wages*] de misère.

starve I *vtr* affamer; (figurative) priver (**of** de); **to ~ sb to death** laisser qn mourir de faim.
II *vi* mourir de faim.

starving *adj* [*person, animal*] affamé; **I'm ~!** je meurs de faim!

state I *n* **1** état *m*; **the present ~ of affairs** l'état actuel des choses; **to be in a good/bad ~ (of repair)** être en bon/mauvais état; **he's not in a fit ~ to drive** il n'est pas en état de conduire; **a ~ of emergency** un état d'urgence; **2** (government, nation) (also **State**) État *m*; **3 she will lie in ~** sa dépouille sera exposée.
II **States** *n pl* **the States** les États-Unis *mpl*.
III *noun modifier* **1** [*school, sector*] public/-ique; [*enterprise, pension, secret*] d'État; [*subsidy*] de l'État; **2** (ceremonial) [*occasion*] d'apparat; [*funeral*] national; [*visit*] officiel/-ielle.
IV *vtr* **1** (declare) exposer [*fact, opinion*]; indiquer [*age, income*]; **to ~ that** [*person*] déclarer que; **2** (specify) spécifier [*amount, time, terms*]; exprimer [*preference*].
IDIOMS **to be in a ~** être dans tous ses états.

State Department *n* (US) ministère *m* des Affaires étrangères.

stately *adj* imposant.

stately home *n* (GB) château *m*.

statement *n* **1** déclaration *f* (**by** de; **on, about** à propos de); (official) communiqué *m*; **2** (also **bank ~**) relevé *m* de compte.

state: **~ of the art** *adj* [*equipment*] ultramoderne; [*technology*] de pointe; **~-owned** *adj* [*company*] étatique; **~-run** *adj* [*newspaper, radio, television*] contrôlé par l'État; [*company, factory*] géré par l'État; **~side** *adj* aux États-Unis; **~sman** *n* homme *m* d'État; **~ trooper** *n* (US) policier *m* d'État.

static I *n* **1** (also **~ electricity**) électricité *f* statique; **2** (interference) parasites *mpl*.
II *adj* **1** (stationary) [*image*] fixe; [*traffic*] bloqué; **2** (stable) [*population, prices*] stationnaire.

station I *n* **1** (also **railway ~** (GB)) gare *f*; **2** (radio, TV, channel) station *f*; (TV channel) chaîne *f*; **3** (also **police ~**) commissariat *m*; (small) poste *m* de police.
II *vtr* poster [*officer, guard*]; stationner [*troops*].

stationary *adj* [*queue, vehicle*] à l'arrêt; [*traffic*] bloqué.

stationer ▶ 805 *n* (also **~'s**) papeterie *f*.

stationery *n* **1** (writing materials) papeterie *f*; (for office) fournitures *fpl* de bureau; **2** (writing paper) papier *m* à lettres.

station: **~master** ▶ 805 *n* chef *m* de gare; **~ wagon** *n* (US) break *m*.

statistic *n* (figure) statistique *f* (**on** de); **~s** (field) la statistique.

statistical *adj* statistique.

statue *n* statue *f*.

statuesque *adj* sculptural.

stature *n* **1** (height) taille *f*; **2** (status) envergure *f*.

status *n* **1** (position) position *f*; **2** (prestige) prestige *m*; **3** (legal, professional) statut *m* (**as** de); **refugee ~** statut de réfugié; **financial ~** situation *f* financière.

status: **~ quo** *n* statu quo *m*; **~ symbol** *n* signe *m* de prestige.

statute *n* texte *m* de loi; **by ~** par la loi.

statutory *adj* [*powers, requirements, sick pay*] légal; [*body*] officiel/-ielle.

staunch *adj* [*supporter, defence*] loyal; [*Catholic, communist*] fervent.

stave *n* (Mus) portée *f*.
■ **stave off**: **~ off** [**sth**] tromper [*hunger, fatigue*]; écarter [*threat*].

stay I *n* **1** (visit, period) séjour *m*; **'enjoy your ~!'** 'bon séjour!'; **2 ~ of execution** sursis *m*.
II *vi* **1** (remain) rester; **to ~ for lunch** rester (à) déjeuner; **to ~ in business** rester à flot; **2** (have accommodation) loger; **to ~ in a hotel/with a friend** loger à l'hôtel/chez un ami; **to ~ overnight** passer la nuit; **3** (visit) **he's gone to ~ with his aunt** il est allé passer quelques jours chez sa tante.
■ **stay away 1** (stop coming) [*tourists*] ne plus venir; **to ~ away from** éviter [*place*]; **2** (not attend) **to ~ away from school/work** ne pas aller à l'école/à son travail.
■ **stay in** rester à la maison.
■ **stay out**: **to ~ out late/all night** rentrer tard/ne pas rentrer de la nuit; **to ~ out of trouble** éviter les ennuis.
■ **stay up 1** (waiting for sb) veiller; **2** (as habit) se coucher tard; **3** (not fall down) tenir.

staying-power *n* endurance *f*; **to have ~** (Sport) avoir du fond.

STD *n* (*abbr* = **sexually transmitted disease**) MST *f*.

steadfast *adj* [*determination, belief, refusal*] tenace.

steadily *adv* **1** (gradually) progressivement; **2** [*work, rain*] sans interruption.

steady I *adj* **1** (continual) [*stream, increase*] constant; [*rain*] incessant; [*breathing, progress*] régulier/-ière; **2** (stable) stable; **to hold** [**sth**] **~** bien tenir [*ladder*]; **3** [*voice, hand*] ferme; [*gaze*] calme; **4** (reliable) [*job*] stable; [*relationship*] durable.
II *vtr* **to ~ one's nerves** se calmer les nerfs.

steak *n* (of beef) steak *m*; **~ and chips** steak frites; **cod ~** darne *f* de colin.

steak: **~house** *n* (restaurant *m*) grill *m*; **~ knife** *n* couteau *m* à steak.

steal I *vtr* voler (**from sb** à qn); **to ~ a glance at sth** jeter un coup d'œil furtif à qch.
II *vi* **1** (thieve) voler; **to ~ from sb** voler qn; **2** (creep) **to ~ into/out of a room** entrer/quitter une pièce subrepticement.

stealing *n* vol *m*.

stealthy *adj* [*step, glance*] furtif/-ive.

steam I *n* **1** (vapour) vapeur *f*; (in room, on window) buée *f*; **2 full ~ ahead!** en avant toute!
II *vtr* faire cuire [qch] à la vapeur [*vegetables*].
III *vi* fumer, dégager de la vapeur.
IDIOMS **to run out of ~** s'essouffler; **to let off ~** décompresser.
■ **steam up** [*window, glasses*] s'embuer.

steam engine *n* locomotive *f* à vapeur.

steamer *n* (boat) (bateau *m* à) vapeur *m*.

steam: **~ iron** *n* fer *m* à vapeur; **~roller** *n* rouleau *m* compresseur.

steamy *adj* **1** [*bathroom, window*] embué; [*climate*] chaud et humide; **2**° (erotic) [*affair, scene*] torride.

steel I *n* **1** (metal) acier *m*; **2** (knife sharpener) aiguisoir *m*.
II *v refl* **to ~ oneself** s'armer de courage (**to do** pour faire; **for** pour).

steel: **~ industry** *n* sidérurgie *f*; **~works, ~yard** *n* installations *fpl* sidérurgiques.

steely *adj* [*determination, will power*] inébranlable; [*look*] dur.

steep I *adj* **1** [*slope, stairs*] raide; [*street, path*] escarpé; [*roof*] en pente raide; **2** (sharp) [*rise, fall*] fort (*before n*); **3**° [*price*] exorbitant.
II *vtr* **to ~ sth in** faire tremper qch dans.
III *vi* tremper (**in** dans).

steeple *n* (tower) clocher *m*; (spire) flèche *f*.

steeply *adv* **1** [*rise, drop*] à pic; **2** (of prices) [*rise*] en flèche.

steer I *n* (animal) bouvillon *m*.
II *vtr* **1** piloter [*ship, car*]; **2** (guide) diriger [*person*].
III *vi* (in car) piloter; (in boat) gouverner.
IDIOMS **to ~ clear of sth/sb** se tenir à l'écart de qch/qn.

steering *n* (Aut) direction *f*.

steering: **~ lock** *n* (Aut) blocage *m* de direction; **~ wheel** *n* volant *m*.

stem I *n* **1** (of flower, leaf) tige *f*; (of fruit) queue *f*; **2** (of glass) pied *m*.
II *vtr* arrêter [*flow*]; enrayer [*advance, tide*].
III *vi* **to ~ from** provenir de.

stencil I *n* **1** (card) pochoir *m*; **2** (pattern) dessin *m* au pochoir.
II *vtr* décorer [qch] au pochoir [*fabric, surface*].

stenography *n* (US) sténographie *f*.

step I *n* **1** pas *m*; **to take a ~** faire un pas; **I was a few ~s behind her** je la suivais de près; **to fall into ~ with sb** se mettre au même pas que qn; **a ~ in the right direction** un pas dans la bonne voie; **2** (measure) mesure *f*; (course of action) démarche *f*; **to take ~s** prendre des mesures; **3** (stage) étape *f* (**in** dans); **to go one ~ further** aller plus loin; **4** (stair) marche *f*; **~s** (small ladder) escabeau *m*.
II *vi* marcher (**in** dans; **on** sur); **to ~ into** entrer dans [*lift*]; monter dans [*dinghy*]; **to ~ off** descendre de [*pavement*]; **to ~ over** enjamber [*fence*].
IDIOMS **one ~ at a time** chaque chose en son temps.
■ **step aside** (in job transfer) céder sa place (**in favour of** à).
■ **step back** (figurative) prendre du recul (**from** par rapport à).
■ **step down** se retirer; (as electoral candidate) se désister.
■ **step in** intervenir (**and do** pour faire).
■ **step up**: **~ up** [**sth**] accroître [*production*]; intensifier [*campaign*].

stepbrother *n* demi-frère *m*.

step-by-step I *adj* [*guide*] complet/-ète.
II **step by step** *adv* [*explain*] étape par étape.

step: **~child** *n* beau-filsbelle-fille *m/f*; **~father** *n* beau-père *m;* **~ladder** *n* escabeau *m*; **~mother** *n* belle-mère *f;* **~ping stone** *n* pierre *f* de gué; (figurative) tremplin *m*; **~sister** *n* demi-sœur *f*.

stereo I *n* **1** (technique) stéréo *f*; **in ~** en stéréo; **2** (also **~ system**) chaîne *f* stéréo; **personal ~** baladeur *m*.
II *noun modifier* [*cassette, cassette player*] stéréo *inv*; [*broadcast*] en stéréo.

stereotype *n* stéréotype *m*.

sterile *adj* stérile.

sterilize *vtr* stériliser.

sterling *n* ▶ 748 livre *f* sterling *inv*; **in ~** en livres sterling.

stern I *n* (of ship) poupe *f*.
II *adj* [*person, measure, warning, look*] sévère; [*message*] grave.

steroid *n* stéroïde *m*.

stew I *n* ragoût *m*; (with veal) blanquette *f*.
II *vtr* cuire [qch] en ragoût [*meat*]; faire cuire [*fruit*]; **~ed apples** compote *f* de pommes.
III *vi* [*meat*] mijoter; [*fruit*] cuire (dans son jus).
IDIOMS **to ~ in one's own juice**○ mijoter dans son jus○.

steward ▶ 805 *n* (on plane, ship) steward *m*; (of club)intendant/-e *m/f*; (at races) organisateur *m*.

stewardess ▶ 805 *n* (on plane) hôtesse *f* (de l'air).

stick I *n* **1** (piece of wood) bâton *m*; (for kindling) bout *m* de bois; **2** (also **walking ~**) canne *f*; **3 a ~ of chalk/dynamite** un bâton de craie/dynamite; **a ~ of celery** une branche de céléri; **4** (in hockey) crosse *f*; **5** (conductor's) baguette *f*.
II *vtr* **1 to ~ sth into sth** planter qch dans qch; **he stuck a knife in her** il l'a poignardée; **2**○ (put) mettre; **3** (fix in place) coller [*poster, stamp*] (**in** dans; **on** sur; **to** à); **4**○ (GB) **I can't ~ it any longer** je n'en peux plus.
III *vi* **1 the thorn stuck in my finger** l'épine m'est restée dans le doigt; **2** [*stamp, glue*] coller; **to ~ to the pan** [*sauce, rice*] attacher○; **3** [*drawer, door, lift*] se coincer; **4** (remain) rester; **to ~ in sb's memory** or **mind** rester gravé dans la mémoire de qn.
■ **stick at**: **~ at** [**sth**] persévérer dans [*task*]; **~ at it!** persévère!
■ **stick out**: ¶ **~ out** [*nail, sharp object*] dépasser (**of** de); **his ears ~ out** il a les oreilles décollées; ¶ **~** [**sth**] **out**, **~ out** [**sth**]: **to ~ out one's hand/foot** tendre la main/le pied; **to ~ one's tongue out** tirer la langue.
■ **stick to**: **~ to** [**sth**] **1** (keep to) s'en tenir à [*facts, point*]; maintenir [*story, version*]; **2** (follow) suivre [*river, road*].
■ **stick together 1** [*pages*] se coller; **2**○ (be loyal) être solidaires; **3**○ (not separate) rester ensemble.
■ **stick up** (project) se dresser; **to ~ up for sb** défendre qn.

sticker *n* autocollant *m*.

stick: **~ing plaster** *n* pansement *m* adhésif, sparadrap *m*; **~-on** *adj* [*label*] adhésif/-ive.

sticky *n* **1** [*floor, fingers*] poisseux/-euse; [*label*] adhésif/-ive; **2** [*weather, day*] lourd; **3** (sweaty) [*hand, palm*] moite.

sticky tape○ *n* (GB) Scotch® *m*, ruban *m* adhésif.

stiff I *adj* **1** raide; (after sport, sleeping badly) courbaturé; **~ neck** torticolis *m*; **to have ~ legs** (after sport) avoir des courbatures dans les jambes; **beat the egg whites until ~** battre les œufs en neige ferme; **2** [*lever, handle*] dur à manier; **3** [*manner, style*] compassé; **4** (tough) [*sentence*] sévère; [*exam, climb*] difficile; [*competition*] rude; **5** (high) [*charge, fine*] élevé; **6 a ~ drink** un remontant.
II○ *adv* **to bore sb ~** ennuyer qn à mourir; **to be scared ~** avoir une peur bleue.

stiffen I *vtr* renforcer [*card*]; empeser [*fabric*].
II *vi* **1** [*person*] se raidir; **2** [*egg white*] devenir ferme; [*mixture*] prendre de la consistance.

stiffness *n* (physical) raideur *f*; (of manner) froideur *f*.

stifle *vtr* étouffer; **it's stifling!** on étouffe!

stigma *n* stigmate *m*.

stile *n* (on wall, hedge) échalier *m*.

still[1] *adv* **1** encore, toujours; **he's ~ as crazy as ever!** il est toujours aussi fou!; **they're ~ in town** ils sont encore en ville; **eat this bread while it's ~ fresh** mange ce pain pendant qu'il est (encore) frais; **you're ~ too young** (you're not old enough yet) tu es encore trop jeune; (you were and still are too young) tu es toujours trop jeune; **are you ~ here?** tu es toujours or encore là?; **2** (referring to the future) encore; **it has ~ to be decided** c'est encore à décider; **there is ~ a chance that** il est encore possible que (+ *subj*); **3** (nevertheless) quand même; **it ~ doesn't explain why** cela n'explique toujours pas pourquoi; **~, it's the thought that counts** enfin, c'est l'intention qui compte; **4** (with comparatives) encore; **better/worse ~** encore mieux/pire.

still[2] I *n* **1** (distillery) distillerie *f*; **2** (photograph) photo *f* de plateau.
II *adj* **1** (motionless) [*air, water*] calme; **totally ~** immobile; **2** (peaceful) [*countryside, streets*] tranquille; **3** [*drink*] non gazeux/-euse.
III *adv* [*lie, stay*] immobile; **to sit ~** se tenir tranquille; **to stand ~** ne pas bouger.

still life *n* nature *f* morte.

stilted *adj* guindé.

stimulate *vtr* stimuler [*appetite, creativity, person*]; encourager [*demand*].

stimulating *adj* stimulant.

stimulus *n* **1** (physical) stimulus *m*; **2** (boost) impulsion *f*; **3** (incentive) stimulant *m*.

sting I *n* **1** (part of insect) aiguillon *m*; **2** (result of being stung) piqûre *f*.
II *vtr* **1** [*insect*] piquer; **2** [*wind*] cingler.
III *vi* [*eyes*] piquer; [*cut*] cuire; [*antiseptic*] piquer; **it ~s!** ça pique!

stinging *adj* [*sensation*] de brûlure; [*pain*] cuisant.

stingy *adj* [*person*] radin○; [*amount*] mesquin.

stink I *n* (mauvaise) odeur *f*; **there's an awful ~!** ça pue!

II *vi* puer; **to ~ of petrol** puer l'essence; **it ~s** ça pue.

stinking *adj* puant.

stint I *n* **to do a three-year ~** travailler trois ans.
II *vi* **to ~ on** lésiner sur [*drink, presents*].

stipulate *vtr* stipuler (**that** que).

stir I *n* **to cause (quite) a ~** faire sensation.
II *vtr* **1** remuer [*liquid, sauce*]; mélanger [*paint, powder*]; **to ~ sth into sth** incorporer qch à qch; **2** [*breeze*] agiter [*leaves, papers*].
III *vi* **1** [*leaves, papers*] trembler; [*curtains*] remuer; **2** (budge) bouger.
■ **stir up**: ¶ **~ [sth] up, ~ up [sth]** provoquer [*trouble*]; attiser [*hatred, unrest*]; ¶ **~ [sb] up, ~ up [sb]** exciter [*crowd*].

stir-fry I *n* sauté *m*.
II *vtr* faire sauter [*beef, vegetable*].

stirring *adj* [*story*] passionnant; [*music, speech*] enthousiasmant.

stirrup *n* étrier *m*.

stitch I *n* **1** (in sewing, embroidery) point *m*; (in knitting, crochet) maille *f*; **2** (in wound) point *m* de suture; **to have one's ~es out** se faire retirer les fils; **3** (pain) point *m* de côté.
II *vtr* **1** coudre (**to, onto** à); **hand-~ed** cousu (à la) main; **2** recoudre [*wound*].

stoat *n* hermine *f*.

stock I *n* **1** (in shop, warehouse) stock *m*; **to have sth in ~** (in shop) avoir qch en magasin; (in warehouse) avoir qch en stock; **we're out of ~** nous n'en avons plus; **2** (supply, store) (on large scale) stock *m* (**of** de); (on domestic scale) provisions *fpl*; **3** (descent) souche *f*, origine *f*; **of peasant ~** de souche paysanne; **4** (for cooking) bouillon *m*; **beef ~** bouillon *m* de bœuf.
II **stocks** *n pl* **1** (GB) (in finance) valeurs *fpl*, titres *mpl*; **~s and shares** valeurs *fpl* mobilières; **2** (US) actions *fpl*; **3 the ~s** le pilori.
III *adj* [*size*] courant; [*answer*] classique; [*character*] stéréotypé.
IV *vtr* **1** (sell) avoir, vendre; **2** remplir [*fridge*]; garnir [*shelves*]; approvisionner [*shop*]; **well-~ed** [*garden, library*] bien fourni.
IDIOMS **to take ~** faire le point (**of** sur).
■ **stock up** s'approvisionner (**with, on** en).

stock: **~broker** ▷805 *n* agent *m* de change; **~-cube** *n* bouillon-cube® *m*.

stock exchange *n* (also **Stock Exchange**) **the ~** la Bourse.

Stockholm ▷574 *pr n* Stockholm.

stocking *n* bas *m*; **Christmas ~** ≈ soulier *m* de Noël.

stock-in-trade *n* spécialité *f*.

stockist *n* dépositaire *mf*.

stock market *n* **1** (stock exchange) Bourse *f* (des valeurs); **to be quoted on the ~** être coté en Bourse; **2** (prices, trading activity) marché *m* (des valeurs).

stock: **~pile** *vtr* stocker [*weapons*]; faire des stocks de [*food, goods*]; **~ room** *n* magasin *m*.

stocktaking *n* **to do the ~** faire l'inventaire.

stocky *adj* [*person*] trapu.

stodgy *adj* [*food*] bourratif/-ive; [*person, speech*] ennuyeux/-euse.

stoical *adj* stoïque.

stoke *vtr* (also **~ up**) alimenter [*fire, furnace*]; (figurative) entretenir [*flames*].

stolid *adj* [*person, character*] flegmatique; [*book, style*] sans relief.

stomach I *n* estomac *m*; (belly) ventre *m*; **to have a pain in one's ~** avoir mal au ventre or à l'estomac; **to lie on one's ~** être à plat ventre; **to do sth on an empty ~** faire qch à jeun; **to have a strong ~** avoir l'estomac bien accroché○.
II *noun modifier* [*ulcer, operation*] à l'estomac; [*cancer*] de l'estomac; **~ trouble** troubles *mpl* gastriques.
III *vtr* supporter [*person, attitude*].

stomp *vi* **to ~ in/out** entrer/sortir d'un pas lourd.

stone ▷738 I *n* **1** pierre *f*; (pebble) caillou *m*; **2** (in fruit) noyau *m*; **3** (GB) (weight) ≈ *6,35 kg*.
II *vtr* dénoyauter [*peach*].

stone: **Stone Age** *n* âge *m* de pierre; **~ circle** *n* cromlech *m*.

stoned○ *adj* défoncé○; **to get ~** se défoncer○ (**on** à).

stone: **~-deaf** *adj* sourd comme un pot○; **~ mason** ▷805 *n* tailleur/-euse *m/f* de pierre; **~wall** *vi* (filibuster) faire de l'obstruction; **~ware** *n* (poterie *f* en) grès *m*.

stony *adj* **1** (rocky) pierreux/-euse; **2** [*look, silence*] glacial.

stool *n* tabouret *m*.

stoop I *vi* être voûté; (bend down) se baisser; **to ~ so low as to do sth** s'abaisser jusqu'à faire qch.
II **stooping** *pres p adj* [*person*] courbé; **~ing shoulders** épaules *fpl* voûtées.

stop I *n* **1** (halt, pause) arrêt *m*; (short stay) halte *f*; (stopover) escale *f*; **to come to a ~** [*vehicle, work, progress*] s'arrêter; **to put a ~ to** mettre fin à; **2** (stopping place) arrêt *m*; **I've missed my ~** (on bus) j'ai loupé○ mon arrêt; (on train) j'ai loupé○ ma gare; **3** (in telegram) stop *m*.
II *vtr* **1** (cease) arrêter; (temporarily) interrompre [*activity*]; **~ it!** (don't do that) arrête!; (that's enough) ça suffit!; **to ~ doing** arrêter de faire; **I can't ~ thinking about her** je n'arrête pas de penser à elle; **rain ~ped play** la pluie a interrompu la partie; **2** (prevent) empêcher; **what's ~ping you?** qu'est-ce qui t'en empêche?, qu'est-ce qui te retient?; **to ~ sb (from) doing** empêcher qn de faire; **3** supprimer [*allowance*]; **to ~ a cheque** faire opposition à un chèque; **4** (plug) boucher [*gap, hole, bottle*].
III *vi* [*person, machine, heart, breathing, noise, rain*] s'arrêter; [*pain, worry*] cesser.
IV *v refl* **to ~ oneself** se retenir.
■ **stop by**○ passer; **to ~ by Brad's place** passer chez Brad.
■ **stop off** (on journey) faire un arrêt; **to ~ off at Paul's house** passer chez Paul.
■ **stop over** (breaking journey) s'arrêter; (in boat, plane) faire escale.

stopgap I *n* bouche-trou *m*.
II *noun modifier* [*measure*] provisoire.

stop: **~-off** *n* (quick break) arrêt *m*; (longer) halte *f*; **~over** *n* escale *f*.

stoppage *n* (strike) arrêt *m* de travail.

stopper *n* (for flask, jar) bouchon *m*.

stopwatch *n* chronomètre *m*.

storage I *n* (of food, fuel) stockage *m* (**of** de); **to be in ~** [*furniture*] être au garde-meuble.
II *noun modifier* [*compartment, space*] de rangement.

storage heater *n* radiateur *m* électrique à accumulation.

store I *n* **1** ▶805| (shop) magasin *m*; (smaller) boutique *f*; **the big ~s** les grands magasins; **2** (supply) provision *f* (**of** de); **3** (place) (for food, fuel) réserve *f*; (for furniture) garde-meuble *m*; **4** **what does the future have in ~ for us?** qu'est-ce que l'avenir nous réserve?
II *vtr* **1** conserver [*food, information*]; ranger [*furniture*]; **2** (Comput) mémoriser [*data*] (**on** sur).

store: **~keeper** ▶805| *n* (US) commerçant/-e *m/f*; **~ manager** ▶805| *n* directeur/-trice *m/f* de (grand) magasin; **~room** *n* (in house, school, office) réserve *f*; (in factory, shop) magasin *m*.

storey (GB), **story** (US) *n* étage *m*; **on the third ~** (GB) au troisième étage; (US) au quatrième étage.

stork *n* cigogne *f*.

storm I *n* **1** tempête *f*; (thunderstorm) orage *m*; **2** **she took Broadway by ~** elle a remporté un succès foudroyant à Broadway.
II *vtr* prendre [qch] d'assaut [*citadel, prison*].
III *vi* **he ~ed off in a temper** il est parti furibond.

storm: **~ belt** *n* zone *f* de tempêtes; **~cloud** *n* (figurative) nuage *m* noir.

stormy *adj* orageux/-euse.

story *n* **1** (account) histoire *f* (**of** de); **a true ~** une histoire vécue; **2** (tale) histoire *f* (**about, of** de); (short, literary) conte *m* (**of** de); **a detective/ghost ~** une histoire policière/de fantômes; **3** (in newspaper) article *m* (**on, about** sur); **4** (rumour) rumeur *f* (**about** sur); **the ~ goes that** on raconte que; **5** (US) (floor) étage *m*.

storybook *n* livre *m* de contes.

stout *adj* **1** (fat) corpulent; **to grow ~** s'épaissir; **2** (strong) [*wall*] épais/-aisse.

stove *n* **1** (cooker) cuisinière *f*; **electric/gas ~** cuisinière électrique/à gaz; **2** (heater) poêle *m*.

stow *vtr* ranger [*baggage*].

stowaway *n* passager/-ère *m/f* clandestin/-e.

straddle *vtr* [*person*] enfourcher [*horse, bike*]; s'asseoir à califourchon sur [*chair*].

straggle *vi* **1** **to ~ along** [*houses, villages*] être disséminé le long de [*road, beach*]; **2** (dawdle) traîner.

straggler *n* traînard/-e *m/f*.

straggly *adj* [*beard*] clairsemé; [*hair*] mou.

straight I *n* (part of racetrack) ligne *f* droite; **home ~** dernière ligne droite.
II *adj* **1** [*line, nose, road*] droit; [*hair*] raide; **in a ~ line** en ligne droite; **2** (level, upright) bien droit; [*tablecloth*] bien mis; **the picture/your tie isn't ~** le tableau/ta cravate est de travers; **3** (tidy, in order) en ordre; **4** (clear) **to get sth ~** comprendre qch; **now let's get one thing ~** que ce soit bien clair; **to set the record ~** mettre les choses au clair; **5** (honest, direct) [*person*] honnête, droit; [*answer, question*] clair; **to be ~ with sb** jouer franc-jeu avec qn; **6** [*majority, profit*] net/nette; [*choice*] simple; **7** [*spirits, drink*] sec, sans eau; **8** (consecutive) [*wins, defeats*] consécutif/-ive; **to win in ~ sets** gagner en deux (or trois) sets; **9** [*actor, role*] sérieux/-ieuse.
III *adv* **1** droit; **stand up ~!** tenez-vous droit!; **sit up ~!** asseyez-vous convenablement!; **to go/keep ~ ahead** aller/continuer tout droit; **to look ~ ahead** regarder droit devant soi; **he headed ~ for the bar** il s'est dirigé droit vers le bar; **the car was coming ~ at me** la voiture se dirigeait droit sur moi; **he fired ~ into the crowd** il a tiré en plein dans la foule; **they drove ~ through the red light** ils ont brûlé le feu rouge; **they drove ~ past me** ils sont passés droit devant moi; **2** (without delay) directement; **to go ~ back to Paris** rentrer directement à Paris; **to come ~ to the point** aller droit au fait; **3** (frankly) tout net; **I'll tell you ~**° je vous le dirai tout net; **~ out** carrément; **4** (neat) [*drink*] sec, sans eau.
IDIOMS **to keep a ~ face** garder son sérieux; **the ~ and narrow** le droit chemin.

straightaway *adv* tout de suite.

straighten *vtr* **1** tendre [*arm, leg*]; redresser [*picture, teeth*]; ajuster [*tie, hat*]; défriser [*hair*]; arrondir [*hem*]; **to ~ one's shoulders** se redresser; **2** (tidy) mettre de l'ordre sur [*desk*].
■ **straighten out**: **to ~ things out** (resolve) arranger les choses.
■ **straighten up**: ¶ **~ up** [*person*] se redresser; ¶ **~ up [sth]**, **~ [sth] up** (tidy) ranger [*objects, room*].

straight: **~-faced** *adj* sérieux; **~forward** *adj* [*answer, person*] franc/franche; [*account*] simple; **~-laced** *adj* collet-monté *inv*.

strain I *n* **1** (weight) effort *m* (**on** sur); (from pulling) tensions *fpl* (**on** de); **to put a ~ on** fatiguer [*heart, lungs*]; **2** (pressure) (on person) stress *m*; (in relations) tension *f*; **to put a ~ on** avoir un effet néfaste sur [*relationship*]; créer des tensions au sein de [*group, alliance*]; **3** (of virus, bacteria) souche *f*; **4** (style) **in the same ~** dans la même veine.
II **strains** *n pl* (of music) accents *mpl*.
III *vtr* **1** **to ~ one's eyes** (to see) plisser les yeux; **to ~ one's ears** tendre l'oreille; **2** (try) mettre [qch] à rude épreuve [*patience*]; **3** (injure) **to ~ a muscle** se froisser un muscle; **to ~ one's eyes** se fatiguer les yeux; **to ~ one's back** se faire un tour de reins; **4** (sieve) passer [*sauce*]; égoutter [*vegetables, pasta, rice*].
IV *vi* **to ~ at** tirer sur [*leash, rope*].

strainer *n* passoire *f*.

strait *n* détroit *m*; **the Straits of Gibraltar** le détroit de Gibraltar.

IDIOMS **to be in dire ~s** être aux abois.
straitjacket *n* camisole *f* de force; (figurative) carcan *m*.
strand I *n* (of hair) mèche *f*; (of fibre, web, wire) fil *m*; (of beads) rangée *f*.
II *vtr* **to be ~ed** rester en rade○; **to leave sb ~ed** laisser qn en rade○.
strange *adj* **1** (unfamiliar) inconnu; **a ~ man** un inconnu; **2** (odd) bizarre; **it is ~ (that)** il est bizarre que (+ *subj*).
strangely *adj* [*behave, react*] d'une façon étrange; [*quiet, empty*] étrangement; **she looks ~ familiar** c'est curieux, son visage ne m'est pas étranger; **~ enough,...** chose étrange,...
stranger *n* (from elsewhere) étranger/-ère *m/f*; (unknown person) inconnu/-e *m/f*; **a complete** or **total ~** un parfait inconnu.
strangle *vtr* étrangler.
stranglehold *n* (figurative) mainmise *f*.
strap I *n* (on shoe) bride *f*; (on case, harness) courroie *f*; (on watch) bracelet *m*; (on handbag) bandoulière *f*; (on bus, train) poignée *f*; (on dress, bra, overalls) bretelle *f*.
II *vtr* attacher (**to** à); **to ~ sb into** attacher qn dans [*pram, car seat*]; **to ~ sb/sth in** attacher qn/qch.
strapless *adj* [*bra, dress*] sans bretelles.
strapping *adj* costaud.
stratagem *n* stratagème *m*.
strategic *adj* stratégique.
strategy *n* stratégie *f*; **business ~** stratégie (des affaires).
stratify *vi* [*rock*] se stratifier; **a stratified society** une société pleine de clivages.
stratum *n* (social) couche *f*; (in geology) strate *f*.
straw *n* (substance) paille *f*; (single stem) brin *m* de paille; (for thatching) chaume *m*; (for drinking) paille *f*.
IDIOMS **to clutch at ~s** se raccrocher à n'importe quoi; **the last ~** la goutte qui fait déborder le vase.
strawberry I *n* fraise *f*; **strawberries and cream** fraises à la crème.
II *noun modifier* [*tart*] aux fraises; [*ice cream*] à la fraise; [*jam*] de fraises.
stray I *n* (dog) chien *m* errant; (cat) chat *m* vagabond.
II *adj* [*dog*] errant; [*cat*] vagabond; [*bullet*] perdu; [*tourist*] isolé.
III *vi* **1** (wander) s'égarer; **to ~ from the road** s'écarter de la route; **2** [*eyes, mind*] errer; **to ~ from the point** [*person*] s'écarter du sujet.
streak I *n* **1** (in character) côté *m*; **2** (period) **a winning/losing ~** une bonne/mauvaise passe; **3** (of paint) traînée *f*; (of light) rai *m*; **~ of lightning** éclair *m*; **4** (in hair) mèche *f*.
II *vtr* **1** strier [*sea, sky*]; **2 to get one's hair ~ed** se faire faire des mèches.
III *vi* **to ~ past** passer comme une flèche.
streaky bacon *n* (GB) bacon *m* entrelardé.
stream I *n* **1** (brook) ruisseau *m*; **2 a ~ of** un flot de [*traffic, customers, questions*]; **a ~ of abuse** un torrent d'insultes; **3** (GB Sch) groupe *m* de niveau.
II *vi* **1** (flow) ruisseler; **water was ~ing down the walls** l'eau ruisselait sur les murs; **sunlight was ~ing into the room** le soleil entrait à flots dans la pièce; **people ~ed out of the theatre** un flot de gens sortait du théâtre; **2** [*banners, hair*] **to ~ in the wind** flotter au vent; **3** [*eyes, nose*] couler.
streamer *n* (of paper) banderole *f*.
streamline *vtr* **1** (in design) caréner; **2** rationaliser [*production*]; dégraisser [*company*].
streamlined *adj* **1** (in design) [*cooker, furniture*] aux lignes modernes; [*hull, body*] caréné; **2** [*production, system*] simplifié.
street I *n* rue *f*; **in** or **on the ~** dans la rue; **to take to the ~s** [*population, rioters*] descendre dans la rue; **the man in the ~** l'homme de la rue.
II *noun modifier* **1** [*musician*] des rues; **2** [*culture*] de la rue.
IDIOMS **it's right up your ~**○ (taste) c'est exactement ce qui te plairait; (ability, dexterity) c'est ton rayon.
street: **~ directory** *n* répertoire *m* des rues; **~lamp** *n* (old gas-lamp) réverbère *m*; (modern) lampadaire *m*; **~ market** *n* marché *m* en plein air; **~ plan** *n* indicateur *m* des rues.
strength *n* **1** (of wind, person, government, bond, argument) force *f*; (of lens, magnet, voice, army) puissance *f*; (of structure, equipment) solidité *f*; (of material) résistance *f*; (of feeling) intensité *f*; **to build up one's ~** reprendre des forces; **2** (of solution) titre *m*; (of dose medicine) concentration *f*; **3** (asset) (of person, team, novel) qualité *f*; **4** (total size) **at full ~** au complet.
strengthen *vtr* renforcer [*building, argument, love, position*]; consolider [*bond, links*]; affirmer [*power, role*]; fortifier [*muscles*]; raffermir [*dollar*].
strenuous *adj* [*exercise*] énergique; [*work, activity, job*] ardu; [*protest, disagreement*] vigoureux/-euse.
stress I *n* **1** (nervous) tension *f*, stress *m*; **mental ~** tension nerveuse; **to be under ~** être stressé; **2** (emphasis) **to lay ~ on** insister sur [*fact, problem*]; **3** (in physics) effort *m*; **4** (in pronouncing) accent *m*.
II *vtr* mettre l'accent sur, insister sur; **to ~ the importance of sth** souligner l'importance *f* de qch; **to ~ (that)** souligner que.
stressed *adj* **1** (also **~ out**) (emotionally) stressé; **2** [*syllable*] accentué.
stressful *adj* stressant.
stretch I *n* **1** (section) (of road, track) tronçon *m*; (of coastline, river) partie *f*; **2** (of water, countryside) étendue *f*; **3** (period) période *f*; **to work for 12 hours at a ~** travailler 12 heures d'affilée.
II *adj* [*cover, fabric, waist*] extensible.
III *vtr* **1** (extend) tendre [*rope, net*]; **to ~ one's arms** s'étirer les bras; **to ~ one's legs** (figurative) se dégourdir les jambes; **2** (increase size of) étirer [*elastic*]; élargir [*shoe*]; (undesirably) déformer [*garment, shoe*]; **3** déformer [*truth*]; **4** (push to the limit) utiliser [qch] au maximum [*budget, resources*]; **the system is ~ed to the limit** le système est surchargé.

IV *vi* **1** [*person*] s'étirer; **2** [*road, track*] s'étaler (**for, over** sur); [*beach, moor*] s'étendre (**for** sur); **3** (become larger) [*elastic*] s'étendre; [*shoe*] s'élargir; (undesirably) [*fabric, garment*] se déformer.

■ **stretch out**: ¶ **~ out** s'étendre; ¶ **~ out [sth]**, **~ [sth] out** (extend) tendre [*hand, foot*] (**towards** vers); étendre [*arm, leg*]; étaler [*nets, sheet*].

stretcher *n* brancard *m*.

strew *vtr* éparpiller [*litter, paper*] (**on** sur); semer [*flowers*] (**on** sur); **~n with** jonché de [*leaves, litter*].

stricken *adj* **1** [*face*] affligé; [*area*] sinistré; **~ by** frappé de [*illness*]; pris de [*fear*]; accablé de [*guilt*]; **2** [*plane, ship*] en détresse.

strict *adj* [*person*] strict (**about** sur); [*view, principle*] rigide; [*silence, privacy*] absolu; [*Methodist, Catholic*] de stricte observance; **in ~ confidence** à titre strictement confidentiel; **in ~ secrecy** dans le plus grand secret.

strictly *adv* **1** [*treat*] avec sévérité; **2** [*confidential*] strictement; **'~ prohibited'** 'strictement interdit'; **~ speaking** à proprement parler.

stride I *n* enjambée *f*.
II *vi* **to ~ out/in** sortir/entrer à grands pas; **to ~ across sth** enjamber qch.
IDIOMS **to take sth in one's ~** prendre qch calmement.

strife *n* conflits *mpl* (**among** au sein de; **in** dans).

strike I *n* **1** grève *f*; **to come out on ~** se mettre en grève; **2** (attack) attaque *f*.
II *vtr* **1** (hit) frapper [*person, vessel*]; heurter [*rock, tree, pedestrian*]; **to ~ sth with** frapper qch avec; **he struck his head on the table** il s'est cogné la tête contre la table; **to be struck by lightning** être frappé par la foudre; **2** (afflict) frapper [*area, people*]; **to ~ terror into sb** frapper qn de terreur; **3** [*idea, thought*] venir à l'esprit de [*person*]; [*resemblance*] frapper; **to ~ sb as odd** paraître étrange à qn; **4**○ (discover) tomber sur○ [*oil, gold*]; **5** conclure [*accord, bargain*]; **to ~ a balance** trouver le juste milieu (**between** entre); **6** (ignite) frotter [*match*]; **7** [*clock*] sonner.
III *vi* **1** [*person, storm, disease*] frapper; **to ~ at** attaquer; **disaster struck** la catastrophe s'est produite; **2** [*workers*] faire (la) grève.

■ **strike back** riposter (**at** à).

■ **strike down**: **~ [sb] down**, **~ down [sb]** terrasser; **to be struck down by** (by illness) (affected) être frappé par; (incapacitated) être terrassé par.

■ **strike off**: **~ [sb] off** (from list) rayer [*candidate*]; radier [*doctor*].

■ **strike out**: ¶ **~ out** (hit out) frapper; **to ~ out at** attaquer [*adversary*]; s'en prendre à [*critics*]; ¶ **~ [sth] out**, **~ out [sth]** rayer [*name, paragraph*].

■ **strike up** [*orchestra*] commencer à jouer; **to ~ up a conversation with** engager la conversation avec; **to ~ up a friendship with** se lier d'amitié avec.

strike: **~breaker** *n* briseur/-euse *m/f* de grève; **~breaking** *n* retour *m* au travail.

striker *n* **1** (person on strike) gréviste *mf*; **2** (in football) attaquant/-e *m/f*.

striking *adj* [*person*] (good-looking) beau/belle (*before n*); [*design, contrast*] frappant.

striking distance *n* **to be within ~ of London** être près de Londres.

string I *n* **1** (twine) ficelle *f*; **a piece of ~** un bout de ficelle; **tied up with ~** ficelé; **2** (on bow, racket) corde *f*; (on puppet) fil *m*; **3** (series) **a ~ of** un défilé de [*visitors*]; une succession de [*successes, awards*]; **4** (set) **~ of onions** chapelet *m* d'oignons; **~ of pearls** collier *m* de perles; **5** (in bean) fil *m*.
II strings *n pl* (in orchestra) **the ~s** les cordes *fpl*.
III *vtr* enfiler [*beads, pearls*] (**on** sur).
IDIOMS **to pull ~s**○ faire jouer le piston○; **with no ~s attached** sans conditions.

■ **string along**○ (GB): ¶ **~ along** suivre; ¶ **~ [sb] along** mener qn en bateau○.

■ **string together**: **~ [sth] together**, **~ together [sth]** aligner [*words*].

string bean *n* haricot *m* à écosser.

stringency *n* (of law, measure) sévérité *f*; (of test) rigueur *f*.

stringent *adj* [*measure, standard*] rigoureux/-euse.

string: **~ instrument**, **~ed instrument** ▶753 *n* instrument *m* à cordes; **~ orchestra** *n* orchestre *m* à cordes; **~-pulling**○ *n* piston○ *m*.

strip I *n* **1** (narrow piece) bande *f* (**of** de); **2** (sports clothes) tenue *f*.
II *vtr* **1** déshabiller [*person*]; vider [*house, room*]; défaire [*bed*]; **to ~ sb of** dépouiller qn de [*belongings, rights*]; **to ~ sb of his/her rank** dégrader qn; **2** (remove paint from) décaper; **3** (dismantle) démonter.
III *vi* se déshabiller; **to ~ naked** se mettre tout/-e nu/-e.
IV stripped *pp adj* [*pine*] décapé.

strip cartoon *n* bande *f* dessinée.

stripe *n* **1** (on fabric, wallpaper) rayure *f*; (on crockery) filet *m*; **2** (on animal) (isolated) rayure *f*; (one of many) zébrure *f*.

striped *adj* rayé.

strip: **~ light** *n* lampe *f* au néon; **~ lighting** *n* éclairage *m* au néon *m*.

strive *vi* s'efforcer (**to do** de faire).

stroke I *n* **1** coup *m*; **on the ~ of four** à quatre heures sonnantes; **at a single ~** d'un seul coup; **a ~ of luck** un coup de chance; **a ~ of genius** un trait de génie; **2** (in swimming) mouvement *m* des bras; (particular style) nage *f*; **3** (mark of pen) trait *m*; (of brush) touche *f*; **4** (Med) congestion *f* cérébrale; **5 a 2-~ engine** un moteur à 2 temps.
II *vtr* caresser.

stroll I *n* promenade *f*, tour *m*; **to go for a ~** aller se promener.
II *vi* (also **~ about**, **~ around**) (walk) se promener; (more aimlessly) flâner.

stroller *n* (US) (pushchair) poussette *f*.

strong *adj* **1** (powerful) [*arm, person, current, wind*] fort; [*army, swimmer, country, state*] puissant; **2** [*heart, fabric, table*] solide; [*bond*] profond, étroit; [*candidate, argument*] de poids; [*market*] ferme; [*currency*] forte; **3** (concentrated) [*tea, medicine, glue*] fort; [*coffee*] serré; **4** [*smell, taste*] fort; [*colour*] soutenu; **5** (heartfelt) [*conviction*] intime; [*desire, feeling*] profond; [*opinion*] arrêté; [*criticism, opposition*] vif/vive; **6** (resolute) [*ruler, leadership*] à poigne; [*action, measure*] sévère; **7** [*chance, possibility*] fort (*before n*); **8 it's not my ~ point** ce n'est pas mon fort.

IDIOMS **to be still going ~** [*person*] se porter toujours très bien; [*relationship*] aller toujours bien.

strong: **~box** *n* coffre-fort *m*; **~hold** *n* forteresse *f*; (figurative) fief *m*.

strongly *adv* **1** [*criticize, oppose, advise*] vivement; [*protest, deny*] énergiquement; [*support, suspect*] fortement; [*believe*] fermement; **I feel ~ about this** c'est quelque chose qui me tient à cœur; **2** (solidly) solidement.

strong: **~-minded** *adj* obstiné; **~room** *n* chambre *f* forte; **~-willed** *adj* obstiné.

structural *adj* [*reform, change, problem*] structurel/-elle; [*defect*] de construction; **~ damage** dégâts *mpl* matériels.

structurally *adv* **~ sound** sain.

structure I *n* **1** (organization) structure *f*; **2** (building) construction *f*.

II *vtr* structurer [*argument, essay, novel*]; organiser [*day, life*].

struggle I *n* **1** lutte *f*; (scuffle) rixe *f*; **2** (difficult task) **it was a ~** cela a été dur; **they had a ~ doing** ils ont eu du mal à faire.

II *vi* **1** (put up a fight) se débattre (**to do** pour faire); (tussle, scuffle) se battre; **to ~ free** se dégager; **2** (try hard) lutter; (stronger) se démener; **to ~ with one's conscience** être aux prises avec sa conscience; **to ~ to keep up** avoir du mal à suivre.

■ **struggle along, struggle on** avancer à grand-peine; (figurative) persévérer.

struggling *adj* [*writer, artist*] qui essaie de percer.

strum *vtr* (carelessly) gratter [*guitar, tune*]; (gently) jouer doucement de [*guitar*].

strut I *n* montant *m*.

II *vi* (also **~ about**, **~ around**) se pavaner.

stub I *n* bout *m*; (of cheque, ticket) talon *m*.

II *vtr* **to ~ one's toe** se cogner l'orteil.

■ **stub out**: **~ [sth] out, ~ out [sth]** écraser [*cigarette*].

stubble *n* (straw) chaume *m*; (beard) barbe *f* de plusieurs jours.

stubborn *adj* [*person, animal*] entêté; [*behaviour*] obstiné; [*refusal*] opiniâtre; [*stain*] rebelle.

stubbornly *adv* obstinément.

stucco *n* (outside plasterwork) enduit *m*; (decorative work) stuc *m*.

stuck *adj* **1** (jammed, trapped) coincé; **to get ~ in** rester coincé dans [*lift*]; s'enliser dans [*mud*]; **2 to be ~ with**○ se coltiner○ [*task, person*]; **3 to be ~ for an answer** ne pas savoir quoi répondre.

stuck-up○ *adj* bêcheur/-euse○.

stud *n* **1** (on jacket) clou *m*; (on door) clou *m* à grosse tête; (on boot) crampon *m*; **2** (stallion) étalon *m*; (horse farm) haras *m*.

studded *adj* **1** [*door*] clouté; [*boots*] à crampons; **2 ~ with** parsemé de [*flowers, stars*]; constellé de [*jewels*].

student I *n* étudiant/-e *m/f*.

II *noun modifier* [*life, unrest*] étudiant; [*population*] d'étudiants.

student: **~ grant** *n* bourse *f* d'études; **~ ID card** *n* carte *f* d'étudiant; **~ nurse** *n* élève *mf* infirmier/-ière; **~ teacher** *n* enseignant/-e *m/f* stagiaire; **~ union** *n* (union) syndicat *m* étudiant; (building) maison *f* des étudiants.

studied *adj* étudié.

studio *n* studio *m*; (of painter) atelier *m*; (film company) société *f* de production.

studious *adj* studieux/-ieuse.

study I *n* **1** étude *f* (**of, on** de); **2** (room) bureau *m*.

II *noun modifier* [*leave, period, group, visit*] d'étude.

III *vtr* étudier; **to ~ to be sth** faire des études pour être qch.

IV *vi* **1** (revise) réviser; **2** (be educated) faire ses études.

stuff I *n* (things) choses *fpl*, trucs○ *mpl*; (personal belongings) affaires *fpl*; (rubbish, junk) bazar○ *m*; (substance) truc○ *m*; **she loves the ~** elle adore ça; **who wrote this ~?** qui a écrit ça?; **there's some good ~ in this article** il y a de bonnes choses dans cet article.

II *vtr* **1** rembourrer [*cushion*] (**with** de); bourrer [*suitcase, room*] (**with** de); **2** [*shove*] fourrer○ (**in, into** dans); **to ~ food into one's mouth** se bâfrer○; **3** (Culin) farcir [*turkey, chicken*]; **4** empailler [*dead animal, bird*].

III **stuffed** *pp adj* [*turkey, chicken*] farci; [*toy animal*] en peluche; [*bird, fox*] empaillé.

stuffing *n* **1** (Culin) farce *f*; **2** (of furniture, pillow) rembourrage *m*; (of stuffed animal) paille *f*.

stuffy *adj* **1** (airless) étouffant; **2** (staid) guindé.

stumble *vi* **1** (trip) trébucher (**against** contre; **on, over** sur); **to ~ in/out** entrer/sortir en chancelant; **2** (in speech) hésiter; **to ~ over** buter sur.

■ **stumble across**: **~ across [sth]** tomber par hasard sur [*rare find*].

stumbling block *n* obstacle *m*.

stump I *n* (of tree) souche *f*; (of candle, pencil, cigar) bout *m*; (of tooth) chicot *m*; (part of limb, tail) moignon *m*.

II○ *vtr* **to be ~ed by sth** être en peine d'expliquer qch; **to be ~ed for an answer** ne pas trouver de réponse; **I'm ~ed!** (in quiz) je sèche○!; (nonplussed) aucune idée!

stun *vtr* (daze) assommer; (amaze) stupéfier.

stunned *adj* **1** (dazed) assommé; **2** (amazed) [*person*] stupéfait; [*silence*] figé.

stunning *adj* (beautiful) sensationnel/-elle.

stunt I *n* (for attention) coup *m* organisé, truc○ *m*; (dangerous fall) cascade *f*.

II *vtr* empêcher [*development*]; nuire à [*plant growth*]; rabougrir [*crops*].
stunted *adj* [*tree, plant*] rabougri; [*body*] chétif/-ive.
stupefying *adj* stupéfiant.
stupendous *adj* [*achievement*] prodigieux/-ieuse; [*view*] fantastique.
stupid *adj* bête, stupide; **I've done something ~** j'ai fait une bêtise.
stupidly *adv* bêtement.
stupor *n* stupeur *f*; **in a drunken ~** hébété par l'alcool.
sturdy *adj* robuste, solide.
stutter *vtr, vi* bégayer.
St Valentine's Day *n* la Saint-Valentin.
sty *n* **1** (for pigs) porcherie *f*; **2** (also **stye**) orgelet *m*.
style I *n* **1** (manner) style *m*; **~ of life** style de vie; **Italian ~** à l'italienne; **2** (elegance) classe *f*; **to travel in ~** voyager princièrement; **to do things in ~** faire les choses en grand; **3** (design) (of car, clothing) modèle *m*; (of house) type *m*; **4** (fashion) mode *f*; **in the latest ~** à la dernière mode; **5** (approach) genre *m*; **that's not my ~** ce n'est pas mon genre.
II *vtr* couper [*hair*].
styling I *n* **1** (design) conception *f*; **2** (contours) ligne *f*; **3** (in hairdressing) coupe *f*.
II *noun modifier* [*gel, mousse*] fixant.
stylish *adj* [*car, coat, person*] élégant; [*resort, restaurant*] chic *inv*.
stylist ▶**805** *n* **1** (hairdresser) coiffeur/-euse *m/f*; **2** (designer) concepteur/-trice *m/f*.
stylistic *adj* [*detail, variety, development*] stylistique; [*similarity*] de style.
stylized *adj* stylisé.
stylus *n* pointe *f* de lecture.
suave *adj* [*person*] mielleux/-euse.
subconscious I *n* **the ~** le subconscient.
II *adj* inconscient; (in psychology) subconscient.
subconsciously *adv* inconsciemment.
subcontinent *n* sous-continent *m*.
subcontract *vtr* sous-traiter (**out to** à).
subdivide *vtr* subdiviser [*house, site*].
subdue *vtr* soumettre [*people, nation*].
subdued *adj* [*person*] silencieux/-ieuse; [*excitement*] contenu; [*lighting*] tamisé.
subeditor ▶**805** *n* (GB) secrétaire *m/f* de rédaction.
subject I *n* **1** (topic) sujet *m*; **to change the ~** parler d'autre chose; **2** (at school, college) matière *f*; (for research, study) sujet *m*; **3 to be the ~ of an inquiry** faire l'objet d'une enquête; **4** (citizen) sujet/-ette *m/f*.
II *adj* **1** (liable) **to be ~ to** être sujet/-ette à [*flooding, fits*]; être passible de [*tax*]; **2** (dependent) **to be ~ to** dépendre de [*approval*]; être soumis à [*law*].
III *vtr* **to ~ sb to sth** faire subir qch à qn.
subjective *adj* subjectif/-ive.
subject matter *n* sujet *m*.
sub judice *adj* devant les tribunaux.
subjugate *vtr* subjuguer [*country, people*].
subjunctive I *n* subjonctif *m*.
II *adj* [*form, tense*] du subjonctif; [*mood*] subjonctif/-ive.
sublet *vtr, vi* sous-louer.
sublime I *n* **the ~** le sublime.
II *adj* [*beauty, genius*] sublime; [*indifference*] suprême.
subliminal *adj* subliminal.
submarine *n* sous-marin *m*.
submerge *vtr* [*sea, flood*] submerger; [*person*] immerger (**in** dans).
submission *n* soumission *f* (**to** à).
submissive *adj* [*person*] soumis; [*behaviour*] docile.
submit I *vtr* soumettre [*report, plan, entry, script*] (**to** à); présenter [*bill, application*].
II *vi* se soumettre; **to ~ to** subir [*indignity, injustice*]; céder à [*will, demand*].
subnormal *adj* [*person*] arriéré.
subordinate *n, adj* subalterne (*mf*).
subpoena *vtr* assigner [qn] à comparaître.
subscribe *vi* **1 to ~ to** partager [*view, values*]; **2** s'abonner; **to ~ to** être abonné à [*magazine*].
subscriber *n* abonné/-e *m/f* (**to** de).
subscription *n* abonnement *m* (**to** à).
subsequent *adj* (in past) ultérieur; (in future) à venir.
subsequently *adv* par la suite.
subservient *adj* servile (**to** envers).
subside *vi* **1** [*storm, wind, noise*] s'apaiser; [*emotion*] se calmer; [*fever, excitement*] retomber; **2** [*building, land*] s'affaisser.
subsidence *n* affaissement *m*.
subsidiary I *n* (also **~ company**) filiale *f*.
II *adj* [*reason, character, question*] secondaire (**to** par rapport à).
subsidize *vtr* subventionner.
subsidy *n* subvention *f* (**to, for** à).
subsist *vi* subsister.
subsistence *n* subsistance *f*.
subsistence: **~ farming** *n* agriculture *f* de subsistance; **~ level**, **~ wage** *n* minimum *m* vital.
substance *n* **1** (matter) substance *f*; **2** (of argument, talks) essentiel *m*; (of claim, accusation) fondement *m*.
substandard *adj* de qualité inférieure.
substantial *adj* **1** [*sum, quantity*] important; [*majority*] appréciable; [*meal*] substantiel/-ielle; [*evidence*] solide; **2** (considerable) considérable.
substantially *adv* considérablement; [*better, less*] nettement.
substantiate *vtr* justifier [*allegation*]; appuyer [qch] par des preuves [*view*].
substitute I *n* **1** (person) remplaçant/-e *m/f*; **2** (product, substance) succédané *m*; **coffee ~** succédané de café; **there is no ~ for a good education** rien ne remplace de bonnes études.
II *vtr* substituer (**for** à).
substitution *n* substitution *f* (**for** à).
subterranean *adj* souterrain.

subtext *n* (figurative) message *m* sous-jacent.
subtitle *n* sous-titre *m*.
subtle *adj* [*change*] imperceptible; [*analysis, person*] subtil; [*humour*] très fin; [*hint*] voilé; [*lighting*] tamisé.
subtlety *n* **1** (of idea, approach, feeling) subtilité *f*; **2** (of film, book, style) complexité *f*; (of flavour) délicatesse *f*.
subtly *adv* [*influence*] imperceptiblement; [*flavoured, coloured*] délicatement.
subtotal *n* sous-total *m*.
subtract I *vtr* soustraire (**from** de).
II *vi* faire des soustractions.
subtraction *n* soustraction *f*.
suburb I *n* banlieue *f*; **inner ~** faubourg *m*.
II **suburbs** *n pl* **the ~s** la banlieue; **the outer ~s** la grande banlieue.
suburban *adj* [*street, shop, train*] de banlieue; (US) [*shopping mall*] à l'extérieur de la ville.
suburbia *n* banlieue *f*.
subversive I *n* élément *m* subversif.
II *adj* subversif/-ive.
subway *n* **1** (GB) (for pedestrians) passage *m* souterrain; **2** (US) (underground railway) métro *m*.
succeed I *vtr* succéder à [*person*]; **she ~ed him as president** elle lui a succédé à la présidence.
II *vi* **1** [*person*] réussir; **to ~ in doing** réussir à faire; **2** (in dynasty, hierarchy) succéder (**to** à).
succeeding *adj* qui suit, suivant.
success *n* succès *m*, réussite *f*; **to make a ~ of** réussir [*dish, life*]; mener [qch] à bien [*venture*]; **to be a ~** [*party*] être réussi; [*film*] avoir du succès; [*person*] avoir du succès (**with** auprès de; **as** comme)
successful *adj* [*attempt, operation*] réussi; [*plan, campaign*] couronné de succès; [*policy*] efficace; [*film, book, writer*] (profitable) à succès; (well regarded) apprécié; [*businessman*] prospère; [*career*] brillant; **to be ~** réussir (**in doing** à faire).
successfully *adv* [*try, campaign, argue*] avec succès.
succession *n* **1** (sequence) série *f* (**of** de); **in ~** de suite; **in close ~** coup sur coup; **2** (inheriting) succession *f* (**to** à).
successive *adj* [*attempt, government, victory*] successif/-ive; [*day, week*] consécutif/-ive.
successor *n* successeur *m*; **to be sb's ~ as** succéder à qn en tant que.
success: **~ rate** *n* taux *m* de réussite; **~ story** *n* réussite *f*.
succinct *adj* [*statement, phrase*] succinct; [*person*] concis.
succulent *adj* succulent.
succumb *vi* succomber (**to** à).
such I *det* **1** (of kind previously mentioned) (replicated) tel/telle; (similar) pareil/-eille; (of similar sort) de ce type (*after n*); **~ a situation** une telle situation; **in ~ a situation** dans une situation pareille; **a mouse or some ~ animal** une souris ou un animal semblable; **some ~ remark** quelque chose comme ça; **there's no ~ thing** ça n'existe pas; **you'll do no ~ thing!** il n'en est pas question!; **2** (of specific kind) **to be ~ that** être tel/telle que; **in ~ a way that** d'une telle façon que; **3** (any possible) **~ money as I have** le peu d'argent or tout l'argent que j'ai; **until ~ time as** jusqu'à ce que; **4** (so great) tel/telle; **5** (of such small worth, quantity) **you can borrow my boots, ~ as they are** ces bottes ne sont pas géniales○ mais tu peux les emprunter.
II *adv* **1** (to a great degree) (with adjectives) si, tellement; (with nouns) tel/telle; **in ~ a persuasive way** d'une façon si convaincante; **~ a nice boy!** un garçon si gentil!; **~ good quality as this** une telle qualité; **I hadn't seen ~ a good film for years** je n'avais pas vu un aussi bon film depuis des années; **it was ~ fun** on s'est tellement amusé; **~ a lot of problems** tant de problèmes; **there were (ever○) ~ a lot of people** il y avait beaucoup de monde.
III **such as** *phr* comme, tel/telle que; **~ a house as this, a house ~ as this** une maison comme celle-ci; **a person ~ as her** une personne comme elle; **~ as?** (as response) quoi par exemple?; **have you ~ a thing as a screwdriver?** auriez-vous un tournevis par hasard?
such and such *det* tel/telle; **on ~ a topic** sur tel ou tel sujet.
suck I *vtr* **1** sucer [*thumb, fruit, lollipop, pencil*]; (drink in) aspirer [*liquid, air*]; **2** [*current, mud*] entraîner; **to be ~ed under** être entraîné au fond.
II *vi* **to ~ at** sucer; **to ~ on** tirer sur [*pipe*].
III **sucking** *pres p adj* [*noise*] de succion.
■ **suck up**: ¶ **~ up**○ faire de la lèche○; **to ~ up to sb** cirer les pompes à qn○; ¶ **~ [sth] up, ~ up [sth]** pomper [*liquid*]; aspirer [*dirt*].
sucker *n* **1**○ (dupe) bonne poire○ *f*; **2** (on plant) surgeon *m*; **3** (pad) ventouse *f*.
suction *n* succion *f*.
sudden *adj* [*impulse, death*] soudain; [*movement*] brusque; **all of a ~** tout à coup.
suddenly *adv* [*die, grow pale*] subitement; [*happen*] tout à coup.
suds *n pl* (also **soap ~**) (foam) mousse *f* (de savon); (soapy water) eau *f* savonneuse.
sue I *vtr* intenter un procès à; **to ~ sb for divorce** demander le divorce à qn; **to ~ sb for damages** réclamer à qn des dommages-intérêts.
II *vi* intenter un procès.
suede I *n* daim *m*.
II *noun modifier* [*shoe, glove*] en daim.
suet *n* graisse *f* de rognon de bœuf.
Suez *pr n* Suez *m*; **the ~ Canal** le Canal de Suez.
suffer I *vtr* subir [*loss, consequences, defeat*]; souffrir de [*hunger*]; **she ~ed a great deal of pain** elle a beaucoup souffert; **to ~ a heart attack** avoir une crise cardiaque.
II *vi* **1** souffrir; **to ~ from** souffrir de [*rheumatism, heat*]; avoir [*headache, blood pressure, cold*]; **to ~ from depression** être dépressif/

-ive; **2** (do badly) [*company, profits*] souffrir; [*health, quality, work*] s'en ressentir.

sufferer *n* victime *f*; **leukemia ~s** les leucémiques.

suffering I *n* souffrances *fpl* (**of** de).
II *adj* souffrant.

sufficient *adj* suffisamment de, assez de; **to be ~** suffire.

sufficiently *adv* suffisamment, assez (**to do** pour faire).

suffocate I *vtr* [*smoke, fumes*] asphyxier; [*person, anger*] étouffer.
II *vi* **1** (by smoke, fumes) (crowd) être asphyxié; (by pillow) être étouffé; **2** (figurative) suffoquer (**with** de).

suffocating *adj* [*smoke*] asphyxiant; [*atmosphere, heat*] étouffant.

suffocation *n* (by smoke, fumes) asphyxie *f*; (by pillow) étouffement *m*.

suffrage *n* (right) droit *m* de vote; (system) suffrage *m*.

sugar *n* sucre *m*; **brown ~** sucre *m* roux.

sugar: **~ beet** *n* betterave *f* à sucre; **~ bowl** *n* sucrier *m*; **~ cane** *n* canne *f* à sucre; **~ lump** *n* morceau *m* de sucre.

sugary *adj* sucré; (figurative) [*person, smile*] mielleux/-euse; [*sentimentality*] mièvre.

suggest *vtr* **1** suggérer; **what are you ~ing?** qu'est-ce que vous insinuez?; **I am not ~ing that he's innocent** je ne dis pas qu'il est innocent; **2** (recommend) suggérer; **to ~ sb/sth for sth** suggérer qn/qch pour qch; **they ~ed that I (should) leave** ils m'ont suggéré de partir; **3** (evoke) évoquer.

suggestion *n* **1** (proposal) suggestion *f*; **any ~s?** vous avez des idées?; **at sb's ~** sur le conseil de qn; **2** (hint) soupçon *m* (**of** de); (of smile) pointe *f*; **3** (psychological) suggestion *f*; **the power of ~** la puissance de la suggestion.

suggestive *adj* suggestif/-ive; **to be ~ of sth** évoquer qch.

suicidal *adj* suicidaire.

suicide *n* (action) suicide *m*; (person) suicidé/-e *m/f*; **to commit ~** se suicider.

suit I *n* **1** (man's) costume *m*; (woman's) tailleur *m*; **a ~ of armour** une armure (complète); **2** (lawsuit) procès *m*; **3** (in cards) couleur *f*; **to follow ~** (figurative) faire de même.
II *vtr* **1** [*colour, outfit*] aller à [*person*]; **2** [*date, climate, arrangement*] convenir à; **3** (adapt) **to ~ sth to** adapter qch à.
III *vi* convenir.
IV *v refl* **to ~ oneself** faire comme on veut.

suitability *n* (of person) aptitude *f* (**for** pour); (of site, location) commodité *f*.

suitable *adj* [*accommodation, clothing, employment*] adéquat; [*candidate*] apte; [*gift, gesture*] approprié; **to be ~ for** convenir à [*person*]; bien se prêter à [*climate, activity, occasion*]; être fait pour [*role*]; **now seems a ~ time** il semble que ce soit le moment opportun.

suitably *adv* [*dressed, equipped, qualified*] convenablement.

suitcase *n* valise *f*.

suite *n* **1** (furniture) mobilier *m*; **2** (rooms) suite *f*; **3** (retinue) suite *f*; **4** (Mus) suite *f*.

suited *adj* **to be ~ to** [*place, clothes*] être commode pour; [*game, style*] convenir à; [*person*] être fait pour; **they are well ~** ils sont faits l'un pour l'autre.

sulk *vi* bouder (**about, over** à cause de).

sulky *adj* boudeur/-euse; **to look ~** faire la tête.

sullen *adj* [*person, expression*] renfrogné; [*day, sky, mood*] maussade.

sulphur (GB), **sulfur** (US) *n* soufre *m*.

sulphuric acid *n* acide *m* sulfurique.

sultana *n* (Culin) raisin *m* de Smyrne.

sultry *adj* **1** [*day*] étouffant; [*weather*] lourd; **2** [*look, smile*] sensuel/-elle.

sum *n* **1** (of money) somme *f*; **2** (calculation) calcul *m*; **to be good at ~s** être bon en calcul; **to do one's ~s** (figurative) faire ses comptes.
■ **sum up**: ¶ **~ up** récapituler; ¶ **~ up [sth]** [*judge*] résumer.

summarize *vtr* résumer [*book, problem*]; récapituler [*argument, speech*].

summary *n* résumé *m*.

summer I *n* été *m*; ▶ **autumn**.
II *noun modifier* [*evening, resort, clothes*] d'été; **~ visitor** estivant/-e *m/f*.

summer: **~ camp** *n* (US) colonie *f* de vacances; **~ holiday** (GB), **~ vacation** (US) (gen) vacances *fpl* (d'été); (Sch, Univ) grandes vacances *fpl*; **~house** *n* pavillon *m* (de jardin); **~ school** *n* université *f* d'été; **~ term** *n* troisième trimestre *m*.

summertime *n* **1** (period) été *m*; **2** (GB) **summer time** (by clock) heure *f* d'été.

summery *adj* estival.

summit *n* sommet *m* (**on** sur); **peace ~** sommet *m* pour la paix.

summon *vtr* **1** (call for) faire venir [*employee, police, doctor*]; convoquer [*ambassador*]; **to ~ a taxi** appeler un taxi; **2** (Law) citer.
■ **summon up**: **~ up [sth] 1** rassembler [*energy*] (**to do** pour faire); **2** évoquer [*image*].

summons I *n* **1** (Law) citation *f* (**to do** à faire; **for** pour); **to serve sb with a ~** citer qn à comparaître; **2** (gen) (order) injonction *f* (**from** de; **to** à).
II *vtr* citer (**to** à; **to do** à faire; **for** pour).

sumptuous *adj* somptueux/-euse.

sum total *n* (of money) montant *m* total; (of achievements) ensemble *m*.

sun I *n* soleil *m*; **in the ~** au soleil.
II *v refl* **to ~ oneself** [*person*] prendre le soleil; [*animal*] se chauffer au soleil.

sun: **~bathe** *vi* se faire bronzer; **~bather** *n* personne *f* qui prend un bain or des bains de soleil; **~bathing** *n* bains *mpl* de soleil; **~beam** *n* rayon *m* de soleil; **~bed** *n* (lounger) chaise *f* longue; (with sunlamp) lit *m* solaire; **~ block** *n* crème *f* écran total; **~burn** *n* coup *m* de soleil.

sunburned, **sunburnt** *adj* (burnt) brûlé par

le soleil; (tanned) (GB) bronzé; **to get ~** attraper un coup de soleil.

sun cream *n* crème *f* solaire.

Sunday ▶ 584 *pr n* dimanche *m*.

Sunday best *n* (dressed) **in one's ~** endimanché.

sun: **~dial** *n* cadran *m* solaire; **~dress** *n* robe *f* bain de soleil.

sundries *n pl* articles *mpl* divers.

sundry *adj* [*items, objects, occasions*] divers; (**to**) **all and ~** (à) tout le monde.

sun: **~flower** *n* tournesol *m*; **~glasses** *n pl* lunettes *fpl* de soleil; **~ hat** *n* chapeau *m* de soleil.

sunken *adj* **1** [*treasure, wreck*] immergé; **2** [*cheek*] creux/creuse; [*eye*] cave; **3** [*bath*] encastré; [*garden*] en contrebas.

sunlamp *n* (gen) lampe *f* à bronzer; (Med) lampe *f* à rayons ultraviolets.

sunlight *n* lumière *f* du soleil; **in direct ~** en plein soleil.

sun lotion *n* = **suntan lotion**.

sunny *adj* **1** ensoleillé; **it's going to be ~** il va faire (du) soleil; **2** [*child, temperament*] enjoué.

sun: **~ oil** *n* = **suntan oil**; **~ray treatment** *n* héliothérapie *f*; **~rise** *n* lever *m* du soleil; **~roof** *n* toit *m* ouvrant; **~set** *n* coucher *m* du soleil; (figurative) crépuscule *m*; **~shade** *n* (parasol) parasol *m*; (awning) auvent *m*; (in car) pare-soleil *m inv*.

sunshine *n* soleil *m*; **12 hours of ~** 12 heures d'ensoleillement.

sun: **~spot** *n* tache *f* solaire; **~stroke** *n* insolation *f*.

suntan *n* bronzage *m*; **to get a ~** bronzer.

sun: **~tan lotion** *n* lotion *f* solaire; **~tanned** *adj* bronzé; **~tan oil** *n* huile *f* solaire; **~trap** *n* coin *m* ensoleillé.

super○ *adj, excl* formidable.

superb *adj* superbe.

supercilious *adj* dédaigneux/-euse.

superficial *adj* superficiel/-ielle.

superfluous *adj* superflu (**to sth** pour qch; **to do** de faire).

superhuman *adj* surhumain.

superimpose *vtr* superposer [*picture, soundtrack*] (**on** à).

superintend *vtr* surveiller [*person, work*]; diriger [*organization*].

superintendent *n* **1** (supervisor) responsable *mf*; **2** (also **police ~**) ≈ commissaire *m* de police; **3** (US) (for apartments) concierge *mf*; **4** (US) (also **school ~**) inspecteur/-trice *m/f*.

superior I *n* supérieur/-e *m/f*.
II *adj* **1** [*person, team, intelligence, officer*] supérieur (**to** à; **in** en); [*product*] de qualité supérieure; **2** (condescending) condescendant.

superiority *n* supériorité *f* (**over, to** sur; **in** en).

superlative I *n* superlatif *m*.
II *adj* **1** [*performance, service*] superbe; **2** (in grammar) superlatif.

supermarket *n* supermarché *m*.

supernatural I *n* surnaturel *m*.
II *adj* surnaturel/-elle.

superpower *n* superpuissance *f*.

supersonic *adj* supersonique.

superstition *n* superstition *f*.

superstitious *adj* superstitieux/-ieuse.

supervise *vtr* superviser [*activity, staff*]; surveiller [*child, patient*]; diriger [*thesis, organization*].

supervision *n* **1** (of staff, work) supervision *f*; **2** (of child, patient) surveillance *f*.

supervisor ▶ 805 *n* **1** (for staff) responsable *m*; **shop ~** chef *m* de rayon; **2** (GB) (for thesis) directeur/-trice *m/f* de thèse; **3** (US Sch) directeur/-trice *m/f* d'études.

supper *n* (evening meal) dîner *m*; (late snack) collation *f* (du soir); (after a show) souper *m*; **the Last Supper** la Cène *f*.

supplant *vtr* supplanter [*product, system, method*]; évincer [*lover, rival*].

supple *adj* souple.

supplement I *n* **1** (fee) supplément *m*; **2** (to diet, income) complément *m* (**to** à); **3** (in newspaper) supplément *m*.
II *vtr* compléter [*diet, resources, training*] (**with** de); augmenter [*income, staff*] (**with** de).

supplementary *adj* supplémentaire; **~ charge** supplément *m*.

supplier *n* fournisseur *m* (**of, to** de).

supply I *n* **1** (stock) réserves *fpl*; **a plentiful ~ of money** des réserves abondantes d'argent; **in short ~** difficile à obtenir; **to get in a ~ of sth** s'approvisionner en qch; **2** (of fuel, gas, oxygen) alimentation *f* (**of** en); (of food) approvisionnement *m*; (of equipment) fourniture *f* (**to** à).
II supplies *n pl* **1** (food, equipment) réserves *fpl*; **food supplies** ravitaillement *m*; **to cut off sb's supplies** couper les vivres à qn; **2** (for office, household) (machines, electrical goods) matériel *m*; (stationery, small items) fournitures *fpl*.
III *vtr* **1** (provide) fournir (**to, for** à); (with raw materials) approvisionner [*factory, company*] (**with** en); (with fuel, food) ravitailler [*town, area*] (**with** en); **2** (fulfil) subvenir à [*needs, wants*].

supply: **~ and demand** *n* l'offre *f* et la demande; **~ teacher** *n* (GB) suppléant/-e *m/f*.

support I *n* **1** (moral, financial, political) soutien *m*, appui *m*; **to give sb/sth (one's) ~** apporter son soutien à qn/qch; **in ~ of sb/sth** [*campaign, intervene*] en faveur de qn/qch; **in ~ of this theory** pour appuyer cette théorie; **means of ~** (financial) moyens *mpl* de subsistance; **2** (physical, for weight) support *m*; (for limb) appareil *m* de maintien; **neck ~** minerve *f*; **3** (person) soutien *m*; **to be a ~ to sb** aider qn.
II *vtr* **1** (morally, financially) soutenir [*person, cause, organization, currency*]; donner à [*charity*]; **2** (physically) supporter [*weight*]; soutenir [*person*]; **3** confirmer [*argument, theory*]; **4** (maintain) [*breadwinner, farm*] subvenir aux besoins de; [*charity*] aider; **he has a wife and**

children to ~ il a une femme et des enfants à charge.

III *v refl* **to ~ oneself** subvenir à ses propres besoins.

support band *n* (at concert) groupe *m* passant en vedette américaine.

supporter *n* (gen) partisan *m*; (Sport) supporter *m*; (of political party) sympathisant/-e *m/f*.

supporting *adj* **1** [*actor, role*] de second plan; **2** [*wall, beam*] de soutènement.

suppose I *vtr* **1** (assume) supposer (**that** que); **I ~ so/not** je suppose que oui/non; **~ (that) it's true, what will you do?** imagine que ce soit vrai, qu'est-ce que tu feras?; **2** (think) **to ~ (that)** penser or croire que.

II **supposed** *pp adj* **1** [*father, owner*] présumé (*before n*); [*advantage*] prétendu (*before n*); **2 to be ~d to do/be** être censé faire/être; **it's ~d to be a good hotel** il parait que c'est un bon hôtel.

supposing *conj* **~ (that) he says no?** et s'il dit non?; **~ your income is X, you pay Y** supposons que ton revenu soit de X, tu paieras Y.

supposition *n* (guess) supposition *f*; (assumption) hypothèse *f*.

suppress *vtr* supprimer [*evidence, information*]; réprimer [*smile, urge, rebellion*]; étouffer [*scandal, yawn*]; dissimuler [*truth*].

suppression *n* (of evidence) suppression *f*; (of revolt) répression *f*; (of scandal) étouffement *m*; (of party) interdiction *f*.

supremacy *n* **1** (power) suprématie *f*; **2** (greater ability) supériorité *f*.

supreme *adj* [*ruler, power, achievement*] suprême; [*importance*] capital; **to reign ~** régner en maître.

sure I *adj* **1** (certain) sûr (**about, of** de); **I'm not ~ when he's coming** je ne sais pas trop quand il viendra; **I wouldn't be so ~ about that!** ce n'est pas si sûr que ça!; **we'll be there tomorrow for ~!** on y sera demain sans faute!; **nobody knows for ~** personne ne (le) sait au juste; **to make ~ that** (ascertain) s'assurer que; (ensure) faire en sorte que; **he's a ~ favourite (to win)** (Sport) c'est le grand favori; **2** (bound) **he's ~ to fail** il va sûrement échouer; **3** (confident) sûr; **to be ~ of oneself** être sûr de soi; **4** (reliable) [*friend*] sûr; [*method, remedy*] infaillible; **the ~st way to do** le moyen le plus efficace de faire; **5** (steady) [*hand, footing*] sûr; **to have a ~ aim** bien viser.

II *adv* **'~!'** (of course) 'bien sûr!'; **~ enough** effectivement.

sure-footed *adj* agile.

surely *adv* sûrement, certainement; **~ we've met before?** nous nous sommes déjà rencontrés, n'est-ce pas?; **~ you don't think that's true!** tu ne penses quand même pas que c'est vrai!; **'it was in 1991'—'1992, ~'** 'c'était en 1991'—'1992, tu veux dire'.

surf I *n* (waves) vagues *fpl* (déferlantes); (foam) écume *f*.

II **▶649** *vi* faire du surf; **to go ~ing** aller faire du surf.

surface I *n* **1** surface *f*; **on the ~** (of liquid) à la surface; (of solid) sur la surface; **to skim the ~ of** effleurer [*problem, issue*]; **2** (of solid, cube) côté *m*; **3** (worktop) plan *m* de travail.

II *vi* **1** [*person, object*] remonter à la surface; [*submarine*] faire surface; **2** [*tension, racism*] se manifester.

surface area *n*, **surface measurements** *n pl* superficie *f*.

surfboard *n* planche *f* de surf.

surfer *n* surfeur/-euse *m/f*.

surfing **▶649** *n* surf *m*.

surge I *n* **1** (of water, blood, energy) montée *f* (**of** de); (of anger, desire) accès *m* (**of** de); (of enthusiasm) élan *m* (**of** de); **2** (rise) (in prices, unemployment) hausse *f* (**in** de); (in demand) accroissement *m* (**in** de).

II *vi* **1** [*water, waves*] déferler; [*blood, energy, emotion*] monter; **to ~ forward** [*crowd*] s'élancer en avant; **2** [*prices, demand*] monter en flèche.

surgeon **▶805** *n* chirurgien *m*.

surgery *n* **1** (Med) (operation) chirurgie *f*; **to have ~** se faire opérer; **2** (GB Med) (premises) cabinet *m*; **3** (GB) (consultation time) (of doctor) (heures *fpl* de) consultation *f*; (of MP) permanence *f*.

surgical *adj* [*instrument*] chirurgical; [*boot, stocking*] orthopédique.

surgical: **~ spirit** *n* alcool *m* (à 90 degrés); **~ ward** *n* service *m* de chirurgie.

surly *adj* revêche.

surname *n* nom *m* de famille.

surplus I *n* surplus *m*; (in business) excédent *m*.

II *adj* [*clothes*] en trop; [*money, food, labour*] excédentaire; **~ milk** excédents *mpl* de lait.

surprise I *n* **1** (unexpected event, gift) surprise *f*; **that's a bit of a ~** c'est surprenant; **it came as a complete ~ to me** je ne m'y attendais pas du tout; **2** (astonishment) surprise *f*, étonnement *m*; **much to my ~** à ma grande surprise; **to take sb by ~** (gen) prendre qn au dépourvu; (Mil) surprendre qn.

II *noun modifier* [*visit, holiday*] surprise (after *n*); [*announcement, result*] inattendu; **to pay sb a ~ visit** aller voir qn sans le prévenir.

III *vtr* **1** surprendre, étonner; **it ~d them that no-one came** ils ont été surpris que personne ne vienne; **you (do) ~ me!** tu m'étonnes!; **2** surprendre [*intruder*]; attaquer [qch] par surprise [*garrison*].

surprised *adj* étonné; **I'm not ~** ça ne m'étonne pas; **I'm ~ at him!** je ne m'attendais pas à cela de sa part!

surprising *adj* étonnant, surprenant.

surprisingly *adv* [*well, quickly*] étonnamment; **~ frank** d'une franchise étonnante.

surreal *adj* surréaliste.

surrealist *n*, *adj* surréaliste (*mf*).

surrender I *n* **1** (of army) capitulation *f* (**to** devant); (of soldier, town) reddition *f* (**to** à); **2** (of territory, rights) abandon *m* (**to** à); (of weapons, document) remise *f* (**to** à).

II *vtr* **1** (Mil) livrer [*town*] (**to** à); **2** (give up)

céder [*weapons*] (**to** à); racheter [*insurance policy*]; rendre [*passport*] (**to** à).
III *vi* [*army, soldier*] se rendre (**to** à); [*country*] capituler (**to** devant).

surrogate mother *n* mère *f* porteuse.

surround *vtr* [*fence, trees*] entourer; [*police*] encercler [*building*]; cerner [*person*]; [*secrecy*] entourer [*event*].

surrounding *adj* environnant; **the ~ area** les environs *mpl*.

surroundings *n pl* cadre *m*; (of town) environs *mpl*; **natural ~** milieu *m* naturel.

surveillance *n* surveillance *f*.

survey I *n* **1** (of trends, prices) enquête *f* (**of** sur); (by questioning people) sondage *m*; (study, overview of work) étude *f* (**of** de); **2** (GB) (in housebuying) (inspection) expertise *f* (**on** de); (report) rapport *m* d'expertise; **3** (of land) étude *f* topographique; (map) levé *m* topographique.
II *vtr* **1** (investigate) faire une étude de [*market, trends*]; **2** (GB) (in housebuying) faire une expertise de; **3** (surveyor) faire l'étude topographique de [*area*]; **4** contempler [*scene, landscape*].

surveyor ▶805 *n* **1** (GB) (in housebuying) expert *m* (en immobilier); **2** (for map-making) topographe *mf*; (for industry, oil) ingénieur *m* topographique.

survival I *n* (of person, animal) survie *f* (**of** de); (of custom, belief) survivance *f* (**of** de).
II *noun modifier* [*kit, equipment, course*] de survie.

survive I *vtr* **1** survivre à [*winter, heart attack*]; réchapper de [*accident*]; surmonter [*crisis*]; **2** survivre à [*person*].
II *vi* survivre; **to ~ on sth** vivre de qch; **I'll ~** je m'en tirerai.

surviving *adj* survivant.

survivor *n* **1** (of accident, attack) rescapé/-e *m/f*; **2** (Law) survivant/-e *m/f*.

susceptible *adj* (to cold, pressure) sensible (**to** à); (to disease) prédisposé (**to** à).

suspect I *n* suspect/-e *m/f*.
II *adj* [*claim, person, vehicle*] suspect; [*foodstuff*] douteux/-euse.
III *vtr* **1** (believe) soupçonner [*murder, plot*]; **to ~ that** penser que; **2** douter de [*truth, motives*]; **she ~s nothing** elle ne se doute de rien; **3** (have under suspicion) soupçonner [*person*].

suspend *vtr* **1** (hang) suspendre (**from** à); **2** (call off) suspendre [*talks, trade*]; interrompre [*transport services, meeting, match*]; **3** (sanction) suspendre [*employee, sportsman*] (**from** de); exclure [qn] temporairement [*pupil*] (**from** de).

suspended sentence *n* condamnation *f* avec sursis.

suspender belt *n* (GB) porte-jarretelles *m inv*.

suspenders *n pl* **1** (GB) (for stockings) jarretelles *fpl*; **2** (US) (braces) bretelles *fpl*.

suspense *n* (in film, novel) suspense *m*; **to leave sb in ~** laisser qn dans l'expectative.

suspension *n* **1** (of meeting, services, match) interruption *f*; (of talks) suspension *f*; **2** (of player, employee) suspension *f*; (of pupil) exclusion *f* temporaire; **3** (Aut) suspension *f*.

suspicion *n* méfiance *f* (**of** de); **to arouse ~** éveiller des soupçons; **to be arrested on ~ of murder** être arrêté sur présomption de meurtre; **to fall under ~** devenir l'objet de soupçons; **to have ~s about sb/sth** avoir des doutes *mpl* sur qn/qch.

suspicious *adj* **1** méfiant; **to be ~ of** se méfier de [*person, motive*]; **2** [*person, object*] suspect; [*behaviour, activity*] louche.

suspiciously *adv* **1** (warily) d'un air soupçonneux; **2** (oddly) [*act*] de façon suspecte.

sustain *vtr* **1** (maintain) maintenir [*interest, success*]; **2** (Mus) soutenir [*note*]; **3** (physically) donner des forces à; (morally) soutenir; (support) soutenir; **to ~ life** rendre la vie possible; **4** recevoir [*injury, burn*]; éprouver [*loss*]; **5** (Law) admettre [*objection*].

sustenance *n* (nourishment) valeur *f* nutritive; (food) nourriture *f*.

swab I *n* (Med) (for cleaning) tampon *m*; (specimen) prélèvement *m*.
II *vtr* **1** (Med) nettoyer [qch] avec un tampon; **2** (also **~ down**) laver.

swagger *vi* **1** (walk) se pavaner; **2** (boast) fanfaronner.

swallow I *n* **1** (bird) hirondelle *f*; **2** (gulp) gorgée *f*.
II *vtr* **1** (eat) avaler; **2** encaisser° [*insult*]; ravaler [*pride*]; **3**° (believe) avaler°.
III *vi* avaler; (nervously) avaler sa salive.
■ **swallow up**: **~ up [sth]**, **~ [sth] up** engloutir.

swallow dive *n* (GB Sport) saut *m* de l'ange.

swamp I *n* marais *m*, marécage *m*.
II *vtr* inonder; **to be ~ed with** être inondé de [*applications*]; être débordé de [*work*].

swan *n* cygne *m*.

swanky° *adj* **1** (posh) rupin°; **2** (boastful) frimeur/-euse°.

swap° I *n* échange *m*.
II *vtr* échanger.
■ **swap around**: **~ [sth] around**, **~ around [sth]** permuter.

swarm I *n* (of bees) essaim *m*; (of flies) nuée *f*.
II *vi* [*bees*] essaimer; **to be ~ing with** grouiller de [*people, maggots*].

swarthy *adj* basané.

swastika *n* svastika *m*.

swat I *n* tapette *f* à mouches.
II *vtr* écraser [*fly, wasp*] (**with** avec).

sway I *n* **to hold ~** avoir une grande influence; **to hold ~ over** dominer.
II *vtr* **1** (influence) influencer; **2** (rock) osciller.
III *vi* [*tree, bridge*] osciller; [*vessel, carriage*] tanguer; [*person*] chanceler; (to music) se balancer.

swear I *vtr* jurer; **to ~ sb to secrecy** faire jurer le secret à qn.
II *vi* **1** (curse) jurer; **2** (attest) **to ~ to having done** jurer avoir fait.
■ **swear in**: **~ in [sb]**, **~ [sb] in** faire prêter serment à; **to be sworn in** prêter serment.

swearword *n* juron *m*, gros mot *m*.

sweat I *n* sueur *f*; **to be in a ~** être en sueur; **to break out into a ~** se mettre à suer; **to be in a cold ~ about sth** avoir des sueurs froides à l'idée de qch.
II **sweats** *n pl* (US) survêtement *m*.
III *vi* [*person, feet, cheese*] transpirer.
■ **sweat over**°: **to ~ over [sth]** suer° pour faire or écrire.

sweater *n* pull *m*.

sweat: **~ pants** *n pl* (US) pantalon *m* de survêtement; **~shirt** *n* sweatshirt *m*.

sweaty *adj* [*person*] en sueur; [*hand, palm*] moite; [*foot, cheese*] qui transpire.

swede *n* (GB) rutabaga *m*.

Swede ▶712 *n* Suédois/-e *m/f*.

Sweden ▶574 *pr n* Suède *f*.

Swedish ▶712 I *n* (language) suédois *m*.
II *adj* [*culture, food, politics*] suédois; [*teacher, lesson*] de suédois; [*ambassador, embassy*] de Suède.

sweep I *n* **1 to give sth a ~** donner un coup de balai à qch; **2** (movement) **with a ~ of his arm** d'un grand geste du bras; **3** (of land, woods) étendue *f*; **4** (of events, novel) ampleur *f*; **5** (also **chimney ~**) ramoneur *m*.
II *vtr* **1** (clean) balayer [*floor, path*]; ramoner [*chimney*]; **2** (push) **to ~ sth off the table** faire tomber qch de la table (d'un grand geste de la main); **to ~ sb off his/her feet** (figurative) faire perdre la tête à qn; **to ~ sb overboard** entraîner qn par-dessus bord; **3** [*beam, searchlight*] balayer.
III *vi* **1** (clean) balayer; **2 to ~ in/out** (majestically) entrer/sortir majestueusement; **to ~ through** [*disease, crime, panic*] déferler sur; [*fire, storm*] ravager.
IDIOMS **to ~ sth under the carpet** (GB) or **rug** (US) escamoter qch.
■ **sweep along**: **~ [sb/sth] along** entraîner.
■ **sweep aside**: **~ [sb/sth] aside, ~ aside [sb/sth]** écarter [*person, objection*].
■ **sweep up**: ¶ **~ up** balayer; ¶ **~ up [sth], ~ [sth] up** balayer [*leaves*].

sweeping *adj* **1** [*change, review*] radical; **2 ~ generalization** généralisation *f* à l'emporte-pièce.

sweet I *n* (GB) **1** (candy) bonbon *m*; **2** (dessert) dessert *m*.
II *adj* **1** [*food, tea*] sucré; [*fruit*] (not bitter) doux/douce; [*wine, cider*] (not dry) doux/douce; [*taste*] sucré; [*scent*] (pleasant) doux/douce; (sickly) écœurant; **to have a ~ tooth** aimer les sucreries; **2** (kind) [*person*] gentil/-ille; [*face*] doux/douce; **3** (pure) [*breath, smell*] bon/bonne (*before n*); [*sound*] mélodieux/-ieuse; **4** (cute) [*baby, cottage*] mignon/-onne.
III *adv* **to taste ~** avoir un goût sucré; **to smell ~** sentir bon.

sweet-and-sour *adj* aigre-doux/-douce.

sweet chestnut *n* **1** (nut) marron *m*; **2** (also **~ tree**) châtaignier *m*.

sweetcorn *n* maïs *m*.

sweeten *vtr* **1** (Culin) sucrer (**with** avec); **2** rendre [qch] plus tentant [*offer*].
■ **sweeten up**: **~ [sb] up, ~ up [sb]** amadouer [*person*].

sweetener *n* **1** (in food) édulcorant *m*; **2**° (bribe) incitation *f*; (illegal) pot-de-vin° *m*.

sweetheart *n* (boyfriend) petit ami *m*; (girlfriend) petite amie *f*.

sweetly *adv* [*say, smile*] gentiment; [*sing*] d'une voix mélodieuse.

sweet: **~ potato** *n* patate *f* douce; **~-talk**° *vtr* baratiner°; **~-tempered** *adj* [*person*] doux/douce; **~ trolley** *n* (GB) chariot *m* des desserts.

swell I *n* (of waves, sea) houle *f*.
II *vtr* gonfler [*crowd, funds*]; augmenter [*membership*]; [*flood water*] grossir [*river*].
III *vi* [*balloon, tyre, stomach*] se gonfler; [*wood*] gonfler; [*ankle, gland*] enfler; [*river*] grossir; [*crowd*] s'accroître.

swelling *n* (on limb, skin) enflure *f*; (on head) bosse *f*.

sweltering° *adj* [*conditions*] accablant; [*day, heat, climate*] torride.

swerve *vi* faire un écart; **to ~ off the road** sortir de la route.

swift I *n* martinet *m*.
II *adj* rapide, prompt; **to be ~ to do** être prompt à faire.

swill *n* pâtée *f* (des porcs).
■ **swill down**: **~ [sth] down, ~ down [sth]** laver [qch] à grande eau.

swim I *n* baignade *f*; **to go for a ~** (in sea, river) aller se baigner; (in pool) aller à la piscine.
II *vtr* nager [*distance, stroke*]; faire [qch] à la nage [*race*].
III *vi* **1** nager (**in** dans; **out to** vers, jusqu'à); **to ~ across sth** traverser qch à la nage; **2 to be ~ming in** baigner dans [*sauce, oil*]; **3** [*scene, room*] tourner.

swimmer *n* nageur/-euse *m/f*.

swimming ▶649 I *n* natation *f*.
II *noun modifier* [*contest, lessons, course*] de natation.

swimming: **~ costume** *n* (GB) maillot *m* de bain; **~ instructor** ▶805 *n* maître-nageur *m*; **~ pool** *n* piscine *f*; **~ trunks** *n pl* slip *m* de bain.

swimsuit *n* maillot *m* de bain.

swindle *n* escroquerie *f*.

swindler *n* escroc *m*.

swing I *n* **1** (of pendulum, needle) oscillation *f*; (of hips, body) balancement *m*; (Sport) swing *m*; **2** (in voting, public opinion) revirement *m* (**in** de); (in prices, economy) fluctuation *f* (**in** de); (in mood) saute *f* (**in** de); **a ~ away from** (in opinions) un mouvement contre; **3** (in playground) balançoire *f*.
II *vtr* **1** (to and fro) balancer; **to ~ a child round and round** faire tournoyer un enfant; **2** (cause to change) faire changer d'opinion [*voters*]; **to ~ a match sb's way** faire basculer un match en faveur de qn.
III *vi* **1** (to and fro) [*rope, object*] se balancer; [*pendulum*] osciller; **to ~ on the gate** se balancer sur le portillon; **2 to ~ open** s'ouvrir; **the car swung into the drive** la voiture

s'est engagée dans l'allée; **to ~ around** [*person*] se retourner (brusquement); **3** (change) **to ~ from optimism to despair** passer de l'optimisme au désespoir; **the party swung towards the left** le parti a basculé vers la gauche.

IDIOMS **to get into the ~ of things**○ se mettre dans le bain○; **to be in full ~** battre son plein○.

swing door (GB), **swinging door** (US) *n* porte *f* battante.

swinging *adj* [*music, step*] rythmé; [*rhythm*] entraînant; [*nightlife*] branché○.

swipe○ *vtr* (steal) piquer○, voler.

swirl I *vi* tourbillonner.

II swirling *pres p adj* [*snow, water, skirt*] tourbillonnant; [*pattern*] ondoyant.

Swiss ▶712 **I** *n* Suisse *mf*.

II *adj* [*culture, people, politics*] suisse; [*ambassador, embassy*] de Suisse.

Swiss: **~ French** ▶712 *n* (dialect) suisse *m* romand; **~ German** ▶712 *n* (dialect) suisse *m* allemand; **~ Italian** ▶712 *n* (dialect) suisse *m* italien.

switch I *n* **1** (change) changement *m* (**in** de); **a ~ to the Conservatives** un glissement en faveur des conservateurs; **2** (for light) interrupteur *m*; (on radio, appliance) bouton *m*.

II *vtr* **1** (change) reporter [*support, attention*] (**to** sur); **to ~ products/flights** changer de produit/de vol; **2** intervertir [*objects, roles*]; **I've ~ed the furniture round** j'ai changé la disposition des meubles.

III *vi* **1** (change) changer; **to ~ from German to French** passer de l'allemand au français; **we have ~ed (over) from oil to gas** nous sommes passés du mazout au gaz; **can we ~ back to BBC 2?** est-ce qu'on peut remettre BBC 2?; **2** (change positions) changer; (change scheduling) permuter (**with** avec).

■ **switch off**: ¶ **~ off** (turn off) s'éteindre; ¶ **~ off [sth]**, **~ [sth] off** éteindre [*appliance, light, engine*]; couper [*supply*].

■ **switch on**: ¶ **~ on** (turn on) s'allumer; ¶ **~ on [sth]**, **~ [sth] on** allumer.

■ **switch over** (on TV) changer de chaîne.

switch: **~board** *n* standard *m*; **~board operator** ▶805 *n* standardiste *mf*; **~over** *n* passage *m* (**from** de; **to** à).

Switzerland ▶574 *pr n* Suisse *f*.

swivel *vtr* faire pivoter [*chair, camera*]; tourner [*head, body*].

■ **swivel round** pivoter.

swivel chair, **swivel seat** *n* fauteuil *m* tournant, chaise *f* tournante.

swollen *adj* [*ankle, gland*] enflé; [*eyes*] gonflé; [*river*] en crue.

swoop I *n* (police raid) rafle *f*.

II *vi* **1** [*bird, bat, plane*] plonger; **to ~ down** descendre en piqué; **to ~ down on** fondre sur; **2** [*police, raider*] faire une descente.

sword *n* épée *f*.

swordfish *n* espadon *m*.

sworn *adj* **1** [*statement*] fait sous serment; **2** [*enemy*] juré; [*ally*] pour la vie.

swot○ **I** *n* bûcheur/-euse○ *m/f*.

II *vi* bûcher○.

sycamore *n* (also **~ tree**) sycomore *m*.

sycophant *n* flagorneur/-euse *m/f*.

syllable *n* syllabe *f*.

syllabus *n* programme *m*.

symbol *n* symbole *m* (**of, for** de).

symbolic *adj* symbolique (**of** de).

symbolism *n* symbolisme *m*.

symbolize *vtr* symboliser (**by** par).

symmetric(al) *adj* symétrique.

sympathetic *adj* (compassionate) compatissant (**to, towards** envers); (understanding) compréhensif/-ive; (kindly) gentil/-ille; (well disposed) bien disposé (**to, towards** à l'égard de).

sympathetically *adv* (compassionately) avec compassion; (kindly) avec bienveillance; (favourably) favorablement.

sympathies *n pl* **to have left-wing/right-wing ~** être de gauche/de droite.

sympathize *vi* **1** témoigner de la sympathie (**with** à); **I ~ with you in your grief** je compatis à votre douleur; **2** (support) **to ~ with** souscrire à [*aims, views*].

sympathy *n* **1** (compassion) compassion *f*; **2** (solidarity) solidarité *f*; **to be in ~ with sb** être d'accord avec qn.

symphony *n* symphonie *f*.

symphony orchestra *n* orchestre *m* symphonique.

symptom *n* symptôme *m*.

synchronize *vtr* synchroniser.

syndicate *n* **1** (of people) syndicat *m*; (of companies) consortium *m*; **2** (news agency) syndicat *m* de distribution.

syndrome *n* syndrome *m*.

synonymous *adj* synonyme (**with** de).

synopsis *n* (of play) synopsis *m*; (of book) résumé *m*.

syntax *n* syntaxe *f*.

synthesis *n* synthèse *f*.

synthesizer *n* synthétiseur *m*.

synthetic I *n* (textile) (fibre *f*) synthétique *m*; (substance) produit *m* synthétique.

II *adj* synthétique.

syringe I *n* seringue *f*.

II *vtr* **to have one's ears ~d** se faire déboucher les oreilles (avec une seringue).

syrup *n* sirop *m*; **cough ~** sirop *m* contre la toux.

system *n* système *m* (**for doing, to do** pour faire); **filing ~** système de classement; **road ~** réseau *m* routier; **reproductive ~** appareil *m* reproducteur.

systematically *adv* [*work, list*] méthodiquement; [*arrange, construct, destroy*] systématiquement.

systems: **~ analyst** ▶805 *n* analyste *mf* (de) systèmes; **~ programmer** ▶805 *n* programmeur *m* d'étude.

Tt

t, T *n* t, T *m*.

tab *n* **1** (on garment) (decorative) patte *f*; (loop) attache *f*; **2** (on can) languette *f*; **3** (label) étiquette *f*.

tabby (cat) *n* chat/chatte *m/f* tigré/-e.

table I *n* **1** table *f*; **to set the ~** mettre le couvert; **2** (list) table *f*, tableau *m*; **3** (in mathematics) table *f*.
II *vtr* **1** (GB) présenter [*bill, amendment*]; **2** (US) (postpone) ajourner.
IDIOMS **to turn the ~s on sb** renverser les rôles aux dépens de qn; **to lay** or **put one's cards on the ~** jouer cartes sur table.

table: **~cloth** *n* nappe *f*; **~ mat** *n* (under plate) set *m* de table; (under serving-dish) dessous-de-plat *m inv*.

tablespoon *n* **1** (object) cuillère *f* de service; **2** (also **~ful**) cuillerée *f* à soupe.

tablet *n* comprimé *m* (**for** pour).

table tennis *n* tennis *m* de table, ping-pong® *m*.

tabloid *n* tabloïde *m*.

taboo *n, adj* tabou (*m*).

tacit *adj* tacite.

tack I *n* **1** (nail) clou *m*; **2** (US) (drawing pin) punaise *f*; **3** (stitch) point *m* de bâti.
II *vtr* **1** (nail) **to ~ sth to** clouer qch à; **2** (in sewing) bâtir.
III *vi* [*sailor*] faire une bordée; [*yacht*] louvoyer.

tackle I *n* **1** (in soccer, hockey) tacle *m*; (in rugby, American football) plaquage *m*; **2** (for fishing) articles *mpl* de pêche; **3** (on ship) gréement *m*; (for lifting) palan *m*.
II *vtr* **1** s'attaquer à [*task, problem*]; **2** (confront) **to ~ sb about** parler à qn de; **3** (in soccer, hockey) tacler; (in rugby, American football) plaquer.

tact *n* tact *m*.

tactful *adj* [*person, letter*] plein de tact; [*enquiry*] discret/-ète.

tactfully *adv* [*say, behave*] avec tact; [*refuse, refrain*] par tact.

tactic *n* tactique *f*; **a delaying ~** une tactique dilatoire.

tactical *adj* tactique; **~ voting** vote *m* utile.

tactless *adj* [*person, question, suggestion*] indélicat; **to be ~** [*person, remark*] manquer de tact.

tadpole *n* têtard *m*.

tag I *n* **1** (label) étiquette *f*; (on cat, dog) plaque *f*; (on file) onglet *m*.
II *vtr* (label) étiqueter [*goods*]; marquer [*clothing, criminal*].
■ **tag along** suivre.

tail I *n* queue *f*.
II **tails** *n pl* **1** (tailcoat) habit *m*; **2** (of coin) pile *f*; **heads or ~s?** pile ou face?
■ **tail off** **1** [*figures, demand*] diminuer; **2** [*voice*] s'éteindre.

tail: **~gate** *n* hayon *m*; **~light** *n* feu *m* arrière.

tailor ▶805 I *n* tailleur *m*.
II *vtr* **to ~ sth to** adapter qch à [*needs, person*].
III **tailored** *pp adj* [*garment*] ajusté.

tailor-made *adj* [*garment*] fait sur mesure; (figurative) conçu spécialement.

taint *vtr* souiller [*politician, reputation*]; polluer [*air, water*]; gâter [*meat, food*].

tainted *adj* [*food*] avarié; [*water, air*] pollué (**with** par); [*reputation*] entaché.

take I *n* (in film-making) prise *f* (de vues); (Mus) enregistrement *m*.
II *vtr* **1** (take hold of) prendre [*object*]; **to ~ sb by the hand/throat** prendre qn par la main/à la gorge; **to ~ sb's hand** prendre la main à qn; **2** (remove) prendre; (steal) prendre, voler; (extract) tirer (**from** de); **he took the book off the shelf** il a pris le livre sur l'étagère; **she took a chocolate from the box** elle a pris un chocolat dans la boîte; **he took a pen out of his pocket** il a sorti un stylo de sa poche; **3** (carry with one) emporter, prendre [*object*]; (carry to a place) emporter, porter [*object*]; **to ~ sb sth, to ~ sth to sb** apporter qch à qn; **he took his umbrella with him** il a emporté son parapluie; **he took his books into his room** il a emporté ses livres dans sa chambre; **to ~ a letter to the post office** porter une lettre à la poste; **to ~ the car to the garage** emmener la voiture au garage; **to ~ sth upstairs/downstairs** monter/descendre qch; **4** (accompany, lead) emmener [*person*]; **to ~ sb to** [*bus*] emmener qn à [*place*]; [*road*] conduire or mener qn à [*place*]; **I'll ~ you to your room** je vais vous conduire à votre chambre; **he took her home** il l'a raccompagnée; **to ~ a dog/a child for a walk** promener un chien/emmener un enfant faire une promenade; **~ me with you!** emmène-moi!; **5** (go by) prendre [*bus, plane, train, taxi*]; prendre [*road*]; **he took the plane to Paris** il a pris l'avion pour aller à Paris; **~ the first turn on the right** prenez la première rue à droite; **6** (have) prendre [*bath, shower, holiday, milk, sugar, medicine*]; **we ~ a newspaper every day** nous prenons le journal tous les jours; **I'll ~ a pound of apples, please** donnez-moi une livre de pommes, s'il vous plaît; **7** (accept) [*person*] accepter [*job, bribe*]; [*shop*] accepter [*credit card, cheque*]; [*doctor, school*] prendre [*patients, pupils*]; [*machine*] accepter [*coins*]; [*person*] supporter [*pain, criticism*]; [*person*] accepter [*punishment*]; **she can't ~ a joke** elle ne comprend pas la plaisanterie; **I can't ~ any more!** je n'en peux plus!; **8** ▶915 (require) demander, exiger [*patience, skill, courage*]; prendre [*direct object*];

être suivi de [*case*]; **it ~s patience to do** il faut de la patience pour faire; **it ~s three hours to get there** il faut trois heures pour y aller; **it won't ~ long** ça ne prendra pas longtemps; **it took her ten minutes to repair it** elle a mis dix minutes pour le réparer; **to have what it ~s** avoir tout ce qu'il faut (**to do** pour faire); **9** (react to) prendre [*news, comments*]; **to ~ sb/sth seriously** prendre qn/qch au sérieux; **to ~ sth well/badly** bien/mal prendre qch; **to ~ sth as an insult** percevoir qch comme une insulte; **10** (adopt) adopter [*view, attitude*]; prendre [*measures, steps*]; **11** (assume) **I ~ it that** je suppose que; **he ~s me for a fool** il me prend pour un imbécile; **what do you ~ me for?** pour qui me prends-tu?; **12** (consider) prendre [*example*]; **~ Jack (for example)** prends Jack; **13** prendre [*notes, statement, letter, photograph*]; prendre [*pulse, temperature*]; **to ~ sb's measurements** (for clothes) prendre les mesures de qn; **14** (hold) [*hall, bus*] pouvoir contenir [*50 people*]; [*tank, container*] avoir une capacité de [*quantity*]; **15** (Sch, Univ) (study) prendre, faire [*subject*]; suivre [*course*]; prendre [*lessons*] (**in** de); passer [*exam, test*]; [*teacher, lecturer*] faire cours à [*pupils*]; **16** (negotiate) [*driver, car*] prendre [*corner*]; [*horse*] sauter [*fence*]; **17** (capture, win) [*army*] prendre [*fortress, city*]; (in games) [*player*] prendre [*piece*]; (in cards) faire [*trick*]; **18** (wear) **what size do you ~?** (in clothes) quelle taille faites-vous?; (in shoes) quelle pointure faites-vous?; **I ~ a size 10** (in clothes) je m'habille en 36; **I ~ a size 5** (in shoes) je chausse du 38; **19** (subtract) soustraire [*number, quantity*] (**from** de).

III *vi* [*drug*] faire effet; [*dye*] prendre; [*plant*] prendre.

IDIOMS **that's my last offer, ~ it or leave it!** c'est ma dernière proposition, c'est à prendre ou à laisser!; **to ~ a lot out of sb** fatiguer beaucoup qn.

■ **take aback**: **~ [sb] aback** interloquer; **to be ~n aback** rester interloqué.

■ **take after**: **~ after [sb]** tenir de [*person*].

■ **take along**: **~ [sb/sth] along** emporter [*object*]; emmener [*person*].

■ **take apart**: **~ [sth] apart 1** démonter [*car, machine*]; **2**○ (criticize) descendre [qch] en flammes○ [*essay, film, book*].

■ **take aside**: **~ [sb] aside** prendre [qn] à part.

■ **take away**: **~ [sb/sth] away, ~ away [sb/ sth] 1** (carry away) emporter; **2** (remove) enlever [*object*]; emmener [*person*]; **3** (subtract) soustraire [*number*]; **that doesn't ~ anything away from his achievement** ça n'enlève rien à ce qu'il a accompli.

■ **take back**: ¶ **~ [sth] back, ~ back [sth] 1** (to shop) rapporter [*goods*]; **2** retirer [*statement, words*]; ¶ **~ [sb] back** (accompany) ramener [*person*]; ¶ **~ [sb/sth] back, ~ back [sb/sth]** (accept again) reprendre.

■ **take down**: **~ [sth] down, ~ down [sth] 1** enlever [*picture, curtains*]; démonter [*tent, scaffolding*]; **2** noter [*name, details*].

■ **take hold** [*disease, epidemic*] s'installer; [*idea, ideology*] se répandre; **to ~ hold of** prendre [*object, hand*]; [*feeling*] envahir; [*idea*] prendre.

■ **take in**: ¶ **~ [sb] in, ~ in [sb] 1** (deceive) tromper; **I wasn't taken in by him** je ne me suis pas laissé prendre à son jeu; **2** recueillir [*refugee*]; prendre [*lodger*]; ¶ **~ in [sth] 1** (understand) saisir, comprendre [*situation*]; **2** (observe) noter [*detail*]; **3** (encompass) inclure; **4** (absorb) absorber [*nutrients, oxygen*]; **5** [*boat*] prendre [*water*]; **6** (in sewing) reprendre [*garment*].

■ **take off**: ¶ **~ off 1** [*plane*] décoller; **2** [*idea, fashion*] prendre; [*product*] marcher; [*sales*] décoller; ¶ **~ [sth] off**: **1 to ~ £10 off (the price)** réduire le prix de 10 livres sterling; **2 to ~ two days off** prendre deux jours de congé; ¶ **~ [sth] off, ~ off [sth]** enlever [*clothing, shoes, lid*]; ¶ **~ [sb] off, ~ off [sb] 1**○ (imitate) imiter [*person*]; **2** (remove) **to ~ sb off the case** [*police*] retirer l'affaire à qn.

■ **take on**: **~ [sb/sth] on, ~ on [sb/sth] 1** (employ) embaucher [*staff, worker*]; **2** jouer contre [*team, player*]; (fight) se battre contre [*person*]; **3** (accept) prendre [*responsibilities, work*]; **4** (acquire) prendre [*look, colour, meaning*].

■ **take out**: ¶ **~ [sth] out, ~ out [sth] 1** sortir [*object*] (**from, of** de); extraire [*tooth*]; enlever [*appendix*]; retirer [*money*]; **2 to ~ [sth] out on sb** passer [qch] sur qn [*anger, frustration*]; **to ~ it out on sb** s'en prendre à qn; ¶ **~ [sb] out** sortir avec [*person*]; **to ~ sb out to dinner** emmener qn dîner.

■ **take over**: ¶ **~ over 1** [*army, faction*] prendre le pouvoir; **2** (be successor) [*person*] prendre la suite; **to ~ over from** remplacer [*predecessor*]; ¶ **~ over [sth]** prendre le contrôle de [*town, region*]; reprendre [*business*].

■ **take part** prendre part; **to ~ part in** participer à [*production, activity*].

■ **take place** avoir lieu.

■ **take to**: **~ to [sb/sth] 1** se prendre de sympathie pour [*person*]; **2** (begin) **to ~ to doing** se mettre à faire; **3** (go) se réfugier dans [*forest, hills*]; **to ~ to the streets** descendre dans la rue.

■ **take up**: ¶ **to ~ up with** s'attacher à [*person, group*]; ¶ **~ up [sth] 1** (lift) enlever [*carpet, pavement*]; prendre [*pen*]; **2** (start) se mettre à [*golf, guitar*]; prendre [*job*]; **to ~ up one's duties** entrer dans ses fonctions; **3** (continue) reprendre [*story, cry, refrain*]; **4** (accept) accepter [*offer, invitation*]; relever [*challenge*]; **5 to ~ sth up with sb** soulever [qch] avec qn [*matter*]; **6** (occupy) prendre [*space, time, energy*]; **7** prendre [*position, stance*]; **8** (in sewing) raccourcir [*skirt, curtains*]; ¶ **~ sb up on 1** reprendre qn sur [*point, assertion*]; **2 to ~ sb up on an offer** accepter l'offre de qn.

take-away *n* (GB) **1** (meal) repas *m* à emporter; **2** (restaurant) restaurant *m* qui fait des plats à emporter.

take-home pay *n* salaire *m* net.

taken *adj* **1 to be ~** [*seat, room*] être occupé; **2** (impressed) **to be ~ with** être emballé○ par [*idea, person*].

take-off *n* **1** (by plane) décollage *m*; **2**○ (imitation) imitation *f* (**of** de).

take-out *adj* (US) [*food*] à emporter.

takeover *n* (of company) rachat *m*; (of political power) prise *f* de pouvoir.

takeover bid *n* offre *f* publique d'achat, OPA *f*.

taker *n* preneur/-euse *m/f*.

takings *n pl* recette *f*.

talc, talcum (powder) *n* talc *m*.

tale *n* (story) histoire *f*; (fantasy story) conte *m*; (narrative, account) récit *m*.

talent *n* talent *m*; **to have a ~ for** être doué pour.

talented *adj* doué, talentueux/-euse.

talisman *n* talisman *m*.

talk I *n* **1** (talking, gossip) propos *mpl*; **they are the ~ of the town** on ne parle que d'eux; **2** (conversation) conversation *f*, discussion *f*; **3** (speech) exposé *m* (**about, on** sur); (more informal) causerie *f*; **to give a ~** faire un exposé.
II **talks** *n pl* négociations *fpl*; (political) pourparlers *mpl*; **peace ~** pourparlers de paix.
III *vtr* parler; **to ~ business** parler affaires; **to ~ nonsense** raconter n'importe quoi; **to ~ sb into/out of doing** persuader/dissuader qn de faire; **he ~ed his way out of it** il s'en est tiré grâce à son bagout○.
IV *vi* parler; (gossip) bavarder; **to ~ to oneself** parler tout/-e seul/-e.
■ **talk over**: **~ [sth] over** discuter de [*matter, issue*].

talkative *adj* bavard.

talked-about *adj* **the much ~ group** le groupe dont on parle beaucoup/on a beaucoup parlé.

talker *n* **to be a good ~** avoir de la conversation.

talking I *n* **I'll do the ~** c'est moi qui parlerai; **'no ~!'** 'silence!'
II *adj* [*bird, doll*] qui parle.

tall ▶ 738 *adj* [*person*] grand; [*building, tree, chimney*] haut; **he's six feet ~** ≈ il mesure un mètre quatre-vingts; **to grow ~er** grandir.

tallness *n* (of person) grande taille *f*; (of building, tree, chimney) hauteur *f*.

tally I *n* compte *m*; **to keep a ~** tenir le compte (**of** de).
II *vi* concorder.

tambourine ▶ 753 *n* tambourin *m*.

tame I *adj* **1** [*animal*] apprivoisé; **2** [*story, party*] sage; [*reform*] timide.
II *vtr* **1** apprivoiser [*bird, wild animal*]; dompter [*lion, tiger*]; **2** soumettre [*person*].

tamper *vi* **to ~ with** tripoter [*machinery, lock*]; trafiquer [*accounts, evidence*].

tan I *n* **1** (also **sun~**) bronzage *m*; **to get a ~** bronzer; **2** (colour) fauve *m*.
II *adj* fauve.
III *vtr* **1** bronzer [*skin*]; **2** tanner [*animal hide*].
IV *vi* [*skin, person*] bronzer.

tandem *n* tandem *m*; **in ~** en tandem.

tang *n* (taste) goût *m* acidulé; (smell) odeur *f* piquante.

tangent *n* tangente *f*; **to go off on a ~** (in speech) partir dans une digression.

tangerine ▶ 559 *n* tangerine *f*.

tangible *adj* tangible.

tangle I *n* (of hair, string, wires) enchevêtrement *m*; (of clothes, sheets) fouillis *m*.
II *vi* [*hair, string, cable*] s'emmêler.
■ **tangle up**: ¶ **~ up** s'embrouiller; ¶ **~ up [sth], ~ [sth] up** embrouiller.
■ **tangle with**: **~ with [sb/sth]** se frotter à.

tangled *adj* [*hair, wool, wire*] emmêlé; [*brambles, wreckage*] enchevêtré.

tango I *n* tango *m*.
II *vi* danser le tango.
IDIOMS **it takes two to ~** tous les torts ne peuvent pas être du même côté.

tank *n* **1** (gen, Aut) réservoir *m*; (for oil) cuve *f*; (for water) citerne *f*; (for processing) cuve *f*; (small) bac *m*; (for fish) aquarium *m*; **2** (Mil) char *m* (de combat).

tankard *n* chope *f*.

tanker *n* **1** (ship) navire-citerne *m*; **oil ~** pétrolier *m*; **2** (lorry) camion-citerne *m*.

tanned *adj* (also **sun~**) bronzé.

tantalizing *adj* [*suggestion*] tentant; [*possibility*] séduisant; [*glimpse*] excitant.

tantamount *adj* **to be ~ to** équivaloir à, être équivalent à.

tantrum *n* crise *f* de colère; **to throw a ~** piquer une crise○.

tap I *n* **1** (for water, gas) robinet *m*; **on ~** [*beer*] pression *inv*; [*wine*] en fût; (figurative) disponible; **2** (blow) petit coup *m*; **to give sth a ~** donner un petit coup à qch.
II *vtr* **1** (knock) [*person*] taper (doucement); (repeatedly) tapoter; **to ~ a rhythm** battre la mesure; **2** mettre [qch] sur écoute [*telephone*]; **3** inciser [*rubber tree*]; exploiter [*resources*].

tap dance *n* (also **~ dancing**) claquettes *fpl*.

tape I *n* **1** bande *f* (magnétique); (cassette) cassette *f*; (video) cassette *f* vidéo; (recording) enregistrement *m*; **on ~** en cassette; **2** (also **adhesive ~**) scotch® *m*.
II *vtr* **1** (record) enregistrer; **2** (stick) **to ~ sth to** coller qch à [*surface, door*].

tape: **~ deck** *n* platine *f* cassette; **~ measure** *n* mètre *m* ruban.

taper *vi* [*sleeve, trouser leg*] se resserrer; [*column, spire*] s'effiler.
■ **taper off** diminuer.

tape recorder *n* magnétophone *m*.

tapered, tapering *adj* [*column, wing*] fuselé; [*finger*] effilé.

tapestry *n* tapisserie *f*.

tapeworm *n* ver *m* solitaire, ténia *m*.

tap water *n* eau *f* du robinet.

tar I *n* (substance, in cigarettes) goudron *m*; (on roads) bitume *m*.
II *vtr* goudronner [*road, roof*].

target I *n* **1** (gen) cible *f*; (Mil) objectif *m*; **to be right on ~** avoir tapé dans le mille; (figurative) [*sales, production*] correspondre exactement aux

objectifs; **2** (butt) cible *f*; **to be the ~ of abuse/ridicule** être insulté/ridiculisé.
II *noun modifier* [*date, figure*] prévu; [*audience, group*] visé, ciblé.
III *vtr* **1** (aim) diriger [*weapon, missile*]; (choose as objective) prendre [qch] pour cible [*city, site*]; **2** (in marketing) viser [*group, sector*].

target practice *n* exercices *mpl* de tir sur cible.

tariff *n* **1** (price list) tarif *m*; **2** (customs duty) droit *m* de douane.

tarmac *n* **1** (also **Tarmac**®) macadam *m*; **2** (GB) (of airfield) piste *f*.

tarnish I *vtr* ternir.
II *vi* se ternir.

tarpaulin *n* (material) toile *f* de bâche; (sheet) bâche *f*.

tarragon *n* estragon *m*.

tart *n* **1** (small) tartelette *f*; (GB) (large) tarte *f*; **2**○ (derogatory) pute● *f*.

tartan *n, adj* écossais (*m*).

tartar *n* (deposit) tartre *m*.

task *n* tâche *f*; **a hard ~** une lourde tâche.

tassel *n* (ornamental) gland *m*.

taste I *n* **1** goût *m*; **to leave a bad ~ in the mouth** laisser un arrière-goût; **to acquire a ~ for sth** (figurative) prendre goût à qch; **she has exquisite ~ in clothes** elle s'habille avec un goût exquis; **that's a matter of ~** ça dépend des goûts; **to be in bad ~** être de mauvais goût; **2** (brief experience) expérience *f*; (foretaste) avant-goût *m*; **a ~ of life in a big city** un aperçu de la vie dans une grande ville.
II *vtr* **1 I can ~ the brandy in this coffee** je sens le (goût du) cognac dans ce café; **2** (try) goûter [*food, drink*]; **3** (experience) goûter à [*freedom, success*].
III *vi* **to ~ sweet** avoir un goût sucré; **to ~ horrible** avoir mauvais goût; **to ~ like sth** avoir le goût de qch; **to ~ of** avoir un goût de [*vanilla, lemon*].

taste bud *n* papille *f* gustative.

tasteful *adj* de bon goût.

tasteless *adj* **1** [*remark, joke*] de mauvais goût; **2** [*food, drink*] insipide.

tasty *adj* [*food*] succulent.

tatters *n pl* lambeaux *mpl*; **to be in ~** [*clothing*] être en lambeaux; [*career, reputation*] être en ruines; [*hopes*] réduit à néant.

tattoo I *n* tatouage *m*.
II *vtr* tatouer (**on** sur).

taunt *vtr* railler [*person*] (**about, over** à propos de).

Taurus *n* Taureau *m*; ▶ **Aquarius**.

taut *adj* tendu.

tax I *n* (on goods, services, property) taxe *f*; (on income, profits) impôt *m*.
II *vtr* **1** imposer [*earnings, person*]; taxer [*luxury goods*]; **2** (Aut) **to ~ a vehicle** payer la vignette; **3** mettre [qch] à l'épreuve [*patience*].

taxable *adj* imposable.

tax: **~ allowance** *n* abattement *m* fiscal; **~ arrears** *n pl* arriérés *mpl* fiscaux.

taxation *n* **1** (imposition of taxes) imposition *f*; **2** (revenue from taxes) impôts *mpl*.

tax: **~ collector** *n* percepteur *m*; **~ disc** *n* vignette *f* (automobile); **~ evasion** *n* fraude *f* fiscale; **~-free** *adj* [*income*] exempt d'impôt.

taxi *n* taxi *m*; **by ~** en taxi.

taxing *adj* épuisant.

taxi rank (GB), **taxi stand** *n* station *f* de taxis.

tax: **~ office** *n* perception *f*; **~payer** *n* contribuable *mf*.

tax return *n* **1** (form) feuille *f* d'impôts; **2** (declaration) déclaration *f* de revenus.

TB ▶ **686** *n* (*abbr* = **tuberculosis**) tuberculose *f*.

te *n* (Mus) (also **ti**) si *m*.

tea *n* **1** (drink) thé *m*; **2** (GB) (light afternoon meal) thé *m*; (for children) goûter *m*; (evening meal) dîner *m*.

tea bag *n* sachet *m* de thé.

teach I *vtr* enseigner à [*children, adults*]; enseigner [*subject*]; **to ~ sb** enseigner [qch] à qn [*academic subject*]; apprendre [qch] à qn [*practical skill*]; **to ~ school** (US) être instituteur/-trice; **to ~ sb a lesson** [*person*] donner une bonne leçon à qn; [*experience*] servir de leçon à qn.
II *vi* enseigner.
III *v refl* **to ~ oneself Spanish** apprendre l'espagnol tout/-e seul/-e.

teacher ▶ **805** *n* (in general) enseignant/-e *m/f*; (secondary) professeur *m*; (primary) instituteur/-trice *m/f*; (special needs) éducateur/-trice *m/f*.

teacher training *n* formation *f* pédagogique.

teaching I *n* enseignement *m*; **to go into ~** entrer dans l'enseignement.
II *noun modifier* [*career*] d'enseignant; [*method, qualification*] pédagogique.

teacup *n* tasse *f* à thé.

teak *n* teck *m*.

team *n* **1** (of people) équipe *f*; **2** (of animals) attelage *m*.

team: **~ member** *n* équipier/-ière *m/f*; **~ spirit** *n* esprit *m* d'équipe.

teamwork *n* collaboration *f*.

teapot *n* théière *f*.

tear[1] I *n* (gen) accroc *m*; (Med) déchirure *f*.
II *vtr* déchirer [*garment, paper*]; mettre [qch] en pièces [*flesh, prey*]; **to ~ sth out of** arracher qch de [*book, notepad*]; **to ~ sth to pieces** mettre qch en morceaux; (figurative) démolir○ qch; **to be torn between** (figurative) être tiraillé entre [*options, persons*].
III *vi* **1** (rip) se déchirer; **2** (rush) **to ~ out/off** sortir/partir en trombe; **3 to ~ at** [*animal*] déchiqueter [*flesh, prey*]; [*person*] s'attaquer à [*rubble*].

■ **tear apart**: ¶ **~ [sth] apart, ~ apart [sth] 1** mettre [qch] en pièces [*prey*]; déchirer [*country*]; démolir○ [*film, novel, essay*]; **2** (separate) séparer; ¶ **~ [sb] apart 1**○ (criticize) descendre [qn] en flammes; **2** (dismember) mettre [qn] en pièces.

■ **tear away**: ¶ **~ away [sth]** arracher

[*wrapping, bandage*]; ¶ ~ **[sb] away** arracher [*person*].

■ **tear off**: ~ **[sth] off**, ~ **off [sth]** (carefully) détacher; (violently) arracher.

■ **tear open**: ~ **open [sth]**, ~ **[sth] open** ouvrir [qch] en le/la déchirant.

■ **tear out**: ~ **[sth] out**, ~ **out [sth]** détacher [*coupon, cheque*]; arracher [*page*].

■ **tear up**: ~ **[sth] up**, ~ **up [sth]** déchirer [*letter, document*].

tear[2] *n* larme *f*; **to burst into ~s** fondre en larmes.

tearful *adj* [*person, face*] en larmes; [*voice*] larmoyant.

tear gas *n* gaz *m* lacrymogène.

tease *vtr* taquiner [*person*] (**about** à propos de); tourmenter [*animal*].

teasing I *n* taquineries *fpl*.
II *adj* taquin, moqueur/-euse.

tea: **~spoon** *n* petite cuillère *f*, cuillère *f* à café; **~spoonful** *n* cuillerée *f* à café; ~ **strainer** *n* passoire *f* (à thé).

teat *n* **1** (of cow, goat, ewe) trayon *m*; **2** (GB) (on baby's bottle) tétine *f*.

tea: **~time** *n* (in the afternoon) l'heure *f* du thé; (in the evening) l'heure *f* du dîner; ~ **towel** *n* (GB) torchon *m* (à vaisselle).

technical *adj* **1** (gen) technique; **2** (Law) [*point, detail*] de procédure.

technical: ~ **college** *n* institut *m* d'enseignement technique; ~ **drawing** *n* dessin *m* industriel.

technicality *n* **1** (technical detail) détail *m* technique (**of** de); **2** (minor detail) point *m* de détail; **3** (technical nature) technicité *f*.

technically *adv* **1** (strictly speaking) théoriquement; **2** (technologically) techniquement; **3** (in technique) [*good, bad*] sur le plan technique.

technician ▶805 *n* technicien/-ienne *m/f*.

technique *n* technique *f*.

technological *adj* technologique.

technology *n* technologie *f*; **information ~** informatique *f*.

teddy *n* (also ~ **bear**) ours *m* en peluche.

tedious *adj* ennuyeux/-euse.

tedium *n* **1** (boredom) ennui *m*; **2** (tediousness) manque *m* d'intérêt.

teem *vi* **to be ~ing with** grouiller de [*people*]; abonder en [*wildlife*]; fourmiller de [*ideas*].

teenage *adj* [*daughter, son*] qui est adolescent/-e; [*singer, player*] jeune (*before n*); [*pregnancy*] précoce; [*fashion*] des adolescents.

teenager *n* jeune *mf*, adolescent/-e *m/f*.

teens *n pl* adolescence *f*; **to be in one's ~** être adolescent/-e.

tee-shirt *n* tee-shirt, T-shirt *m*.

teeter *vi* vaciller; **to ~ on the brink of sth** (figurative) être au bord de qch.

teethe *vi* faire ses dents.

teething troubles *n pl* difficultés *fpl* initiales.

teetotaller (GB), **teetotaler** (US) *n* personne *f* qui ne boit jamais d'alcool.

TEFL *n* (*abbr* = **Teaching of English as a Foreign Language**) enseignement *m* de l'anglais langue étrangère.

telecommunications *n pl* télécommunications *fpl*.

telegram *n* télégramme *m*.

telegraph I *n* télégraphe *m*.
II *noun modifier* [*pole, post, wire*] télégraphique.
III *vtr* télégraphier.

telepathy *n* télépathie *f*.

telephone I *n* téléphone *m*; **on** or **over the ~** au téléphone; **to be on the ~** (connected) avoir le téléphone; (talking) être au téléphone.
II *noun modifier* [*conversation, message*] téléphonique.
III *vtr* téléphoner à [*person*]; téléphoner [*instructions*]; **to ~ France** appeler la France.
IV *vi* appeler, téléphoner.

telephone: ~ **booth**, ~ **box** (GB) *n* cabine *f* téléphonique; ~ **call** *n* appel *m* téléphonique; ~ **directory** *n* annuaire *m* (du téléphone); ~ **number** *n* numéro *m* de téléphone.

telephonist ▶805 *n* (GB) standardiste *mf*.

telephoto lens *n* téléobjectif *m*.

telescope I *n* télescope *m*; (more technically) lunette *f*.
II *vi* [*stand, umbrella*] être télescopique; [*car, train*] se télescoper.

telescopic *adj* télescopique; ~ **sight** (on gun) lunette *f* de visée.

teletext *n* télétexte *m*.

televise *vtr* téléviser.

television I *n* **1** (medium) télévision *f*; **on ~** à la télévision; **2** (set) téléviseur *m*.
II *noun modifier* [*broadcast, camera, studio*] de télévision; [*film*] pour la télévision; [*interview*] à la télévision.

television: ~ **licence** (GB) *n* redevance *f* télévision; ~ **personality** *n* vedette *f* de la télévision; ~ **programme** (GB), ~ **program** (US) *n* émission *f* de télévision; ~ **screen** *n* écran *m* de télévision; ~ **set** *n* téléviseur *m*, poste *m* de télévision.

telex ▶805 I *n* télex *m*.
II *vtr* télexer.

tell I *vtr* **1** [*person*] dire [*lie, truth*]; raconter [*joke, story*]; prédire [*future*]; [*manual, gauge*] indiquer; **to ~ sb about sth** parler de qch à qn; **to ~ sb to do** dire à qn de faire; **to ~ sb how to do/what to do** expliquer à qn comment faire/ce qu'il faut faire; **to ~ the time** [*clock*] indiquer or marquer l'heure; [*person*] lire l'heure; **can you ~ me the time please?** peux-tu me dire l'heure (qu'il est), s'il te plaît?; **I was told that** on m'a dit que; **I told you so!** je te l'avais bien dit!; **do as you are told!** fais ce qu'on te dit!; **2** (deduce) **you can ~ (that) he's lying** on voit bien qu'il ment; **I can ~ (that) he's disappointed** je sais qu'il est déçu; **you can ~ a lot from the clothes people wear** la façon dont les gens s'habillent est très révélatrice; **3** (distinguish) distinguer; **can you ~ the difference?** est-ce que vous

voyez la différence?; **how can you ~ them apart?** comment peut-on les distinguer l'un de l'autre?
II *vi* **1** (reveal secret) **don't ~!** ne le répète pas!; **2** (be evidence of) **to ~ of** témoigner de; **3** (know) savoir; **as far as I can ~** pour autant que je sache; **how can you ~?** comment le sais-tu?; **4** (show effect) **her age is beginning to ~** elle commence à faire son âge.
III *v refl* **to ~ oneself** se dire (**that** que).
■ **tell off**: **~ [sb] off** réprimander [*person*].
■ **tell on**: **~ on [sb] 1** dénoncer [*person*] (**to** à); **2 the strain is beginning to ~ on him** on commence à voir sur lui les effets de la fatigue.

teller ▶805| *n* **1** (in bank) caissier/-ière *m/f*; **2** (in election) scrutateur/-trice *m/f*.

telling *adj* [*remark, omission*] révélateur/-trice.

telling-off *n* réprimande *f*.

tell-tale I *n* rapporteur/-euse *m/f*.
II *adj* [*sign*] révélateur/-trice.

temp° (GB) I *n* intérimaire *mf*.
II *vi* travailler comme intérimaire.

temper I *n* **1** (mood) humeur *f*; **to be in a good/bad ~** être de bonne/mauvaise humeur; **to be in a ~** être en colère; **to lose one's ~** se mettre en colère (**with** contre); **2** (nature) caractère *m*; **to have a foul ~** avoir un sale caractère.
II *vtr* **1** (moderate) tempérer; **2** tremper [*steel*].

temperament *n* **1** (nature) tempérament *m*; **2** (excitability) humeur *f*.

temperamental *adj* (volatile) capricieux/-ieuse.

temperamentally *adv* (by nature) psychologiquement; **they were ~ unsuited** il y avait entre eux incompatibilité de caractère.

temperance *n* **1** (moderation) modération *f*; **2** (being teetotal) tempérance *f*.

temperate *adj* [*climate, zone*] tempéré; [*person, habit*] modéré.

temperature *n* température *f*; **to have a ~** avoir de la température or de la fièvre; **to have a ~ of 39°** avoir 39° de fièvre.

tempest *n* tempête *f*.

tempestuous *adj* [*relationship, sea*] turbulent.

temple *n* **1** (building) temple *m*; **2** (Anat) tempe *f*.

tempo *n* (Mus) tempo *m*; (figurative) rythme *m*.

temporal *adj* temporel/-elle.

temporarily *adv* (for a limited time) temporairement; (provisionally) provisoirement.

temporary *adj* [*job, contract*] temporaire; [*manager, secretary*] intérimaire; [*arrangement, accommodation*] provisoire; **on a ~ basis** à titre provisoire.

tempt *vtr* tenter; **to ~ sb into doing sth** inciter qn à faire qch.

temptation *n* tentation *f*; **to give in to ~** céder à la tentation.

tempting *adj* [*offer*] alléchant; [*food, smell*] appétissant; [*idea*] tentant.

ten ▶492|, 554| I *n* dix *m inv*; **in ~s** [*sell*] par dizaines; **~s of thousands** des dizaines de milliers.
II *pron, det* dix *inv*.

tenacious *adj* tenace.

tenacity *n* ténacité *f*.

tenancy *n* location *f*; **six-month ~** bail *m* de six mois.

tenancy agreement *n* bail *m*.

tenant *n* locataire *mf*.

tend I *vtr* soigner [*patient*]; entretenir [*garden*]; s'occuper de [*stall, store*].
II *vi* **to ~ to do** avoir tendance à faire; **it ~s to be the case** c'est en général le cas.

tendency *n* tendance *f* (**to, towards** à; **to do** à faire); **there is a ~ for people to arrive late** les gens ont tendance à arriver en retard.

tender I *n* soumission; **to put work out to tender** mettre un ouvrage en adjudication.
II *adj* **1** [*meat*] tendre; **2** [*kiss, love, smile*] tendre; **3** [*bruise, skin*] sensible.
III présenter [*apology, fare*]; donner [*resignation*].
IV *vi* soumissionner, faire une soumission.

tenderness *n* **1** tendresse *f*; **2** (soreness) sensibilité *f*; **3** (of meat) tendreté *f*.

tendon *n* tendon *m*.

tendril *n* (of plant) vrille *f*; (of hair) mèche *f* folle.

tenement *n* (also **~ building** GB, **~ house** US) immeuble *m* ancien.

tenfold *adv* **to increase** or **multiply ~** décupler.

tennis ▶649| *n* tennis *m*; **a game of ~** une partie de tennis.

tennis court *n* court *m* de tennis, tennis *m inv*.

tenor *n* (Mus) ténor *m*.

tenpin bowling (GB), **tenpins** (US) ▶649| *n* bowling *m* (à dix quilles).

tense I *n* temps *m*; **the present ~** le présent (**of** de); **in the past ~** au passé.
II *adj* [*person, atmosphere, conversation*] tendu; [*moment*] de tension; **to make sb ~** rendre qn nerveux.
III *vtr* tendre [*muscle*]; raidir [*body*].
■ **tense up** [*person*] se crisper.

tension *n* **1** (gen, Tech) tension *f*; **2** (suspense) suspense *m*.

tent *n* tente *f*.

tentacle *n* tentacule *m*.

tentative *adj* [*smile, suggestion*] timide; [*conclusion, offer*] provisoire.

tentatively *adv* [*agree, conclude*] provisoirement; [*smile, speak*] timidement.

tenth ▶584|, 642| I *n* **1** (in order) dixième *mf*; **2** (of month) dix *m inv*; **3** (fraction) dixième *m*.
II *adj, adv* dixième.

tenuous *adj* [*link*] ténu; [*distinction, theory*] mince.

tenured *adj* [*professor*] titulaire; [*job*] de titulaire.

term I *n* **1** (period of time) (gen) période *f*, terme *m*; (Sch, Univ) trimestre *m*; **~ of office** mandat *m*; **~ of imprisonment** peine *f* de prison; **to have reached (full) ~** (of pregnancy) être à terme; **autumn/spring/summer ~** (Sch, Univ)

premier/deuxième/troisième trimestre; **2** (word, phrase) terme *m*.
II terms *n pl* **1** (conditions) termes *mpl*; (of will) dispositions *fpl*; (of financial arrangement) conditions *fpl* de paiement; **~s of reference** attributions *fpl*; **2 to come to ~s with** assumer [*identity, past, disability*]; accepter [*death, defeat, failure*]; affronter [*issue*]; **3** (relations) termes *mpl*; **to be on good ~s with** être en bons termes avec.
III *vtr* appeler, nommer.
IV in terms of *phr* **1** (as expressed by) en fonction de; **2** (from the point of view of) du point de vue de, sur le plan de; **the novel is weak in ~s of plot** ce roman est faible sur le plan de l'intrigue.

terminal I *n* **1** (at station) terminus *m*; (in airport) aérogare *f*; **ferry ~** gare *f* maritime; **2** (Comput) terminal *m*; **3** (for electricity) borne *f*.
II *adj* [*stage*] terminal; [*illness*] (incurable) incurable; (at final stage) en phase terminale.

terminally *adv* **the ~ ill** les mourants *mpl*.

terminate I *vtr* mettre fin à [*meeting, phase, relationship*]; résilier [*contract*]; annuler [*agreement*].
II *vi* se terminer.

termination *n* **1** (of discussion, relations, scheme) fin *f*; (of contract) résiliation *f*; **2** (Med) (also **~ of pregnancy**) interruption *f* de grossesse.

terminology *n* terminologie *f*.

terminus *n* (GB) terminus *m*.

terrace I *n* **1** (patio) terrasse *f*; **2** (row of houses) alignement *m* de maisons.
II terraces *n pl* (GB) (in stadium) gradins *mpl*.

terracotta ▶559 *n* **1** (earthenware) terre *f* cuite; **2** (colour) ocre brun *m*.

terrain *n* terrain *m*.

terrestrial *adj* terrestre.

terrible *adj* **1** [*pain, noise, sight*] épouvantable; [*accident, fight*] terrible; [*mistake*] grave; **2**○ [*food, weather*] affreux/-euse.

terribly *adv* **1** (very) [*pleased, obvious*] très; [*clever*] extrêmement; **I'm ~ sorry** je suis navré; **2** (badly) [*suffer*] horriblement; [*sing, drive*] affreusement mal.

terrific *adj* **1** (huge) [*amount*] énorme; [*noise*] épouvantable; [*speed*] fou/folle; [*accident, shock*] terrible; **2**○ (wonderful) formidable; **to look ~** (healthy) avoir l'air en pleine forme○; (attractive) être superbe.

terrified *adj* [*animal, face, person*] terrifié; [*scream*] de terreur; **to be ~ of** avoir une peur folle de.

terrify *vtr* terrifier.

terrifying *adj* (frightening) terrifiant; (alarming) effroyable.

territorial *adj* territorial.

territory *n* territoire *m*; (figurative) domaine *m*; **I'm on familiar ~** je suis sur mon terrain.

terror *n* terreur *f*.

terrorism *n* terrorisme *m*.

terrorist I *n* terroriste *mf*.
II *noun modifier* [*group, plot*] terroriste; **a ~ bombing** un attentat à la bombe.

terrorize *vtr* terroriser.

terry *n* (also **~ towelling** GB, **~ cloth** US) tissu *m* éponge.

terse *adj* [*style*] succinct; [*person, statement*] laconique.

tertiary *adj* [*era, industry, sector*] tertiaire; [*education, college*] supérieur.

test I *n* **1** (of person, ability) (gen) test *m*; (Sch, Univ) (written) contrôle *m*; (oral) épreuve *f* orale; **to put sb/sth to the ~** mettre qn/qch à l'épreuve; **to stand the ~ of time** résister à l'épreuve du temps; **2** (of equipment, machine, new model) essai *m*; **3** (Med) (of blood, urine) analyse *f*; (of organ) examen *m*; (to detect virus, cancer) test *m* de dépistage; (chemical analysis) analyse *f*; **to have a blood ~** se faire faire une analyse de sang; **4** (Aut) (also **driving ~**) examen *m* du permis de conduire.
II *vtr* **1** (gen) évaluer [*intelligence, efficiency*]; (Sch) (in classroom) interroger (**on** en); (at exam time) contrôler; [*psychologist*] tester; **2** (new model, product) essayer; (Med) analyser [*blood, sample*]; expérimenter [*new drug*]; **to have one's eyes ~ed** se faire faire un examen des yeux; **3** mettre [qch] à l'épreuve [*strength, patience*].
III *vi* **to ~ for starch/for alcohol** (in laboratory) faire une recherche d'amidon/d'alcool; **to ~ for an infection/allergy** faire des analyses pour trouver la cause d'une infection/allergie.

testament *n* **1** (proof) témoignage *m*; **to be a ~ to sth** témoigner de qch; **2 the Old/the New Testament** l'Ancien/le Nouveau Testament.

test: **~ ban** *n* interdiction *f* d'essais nucléaires; **~ case** *n* (Law) procès *m* qui fait jurisprudence; **~ flight** *n* vol *m* d'essai.

testicle *n* testicule *m*.

testify I *vtr* témoigner (**that** que).
II *vi* témoigner; **to ~ to** attester, témoigner de.

testimony *n* témoignage *m*, déposition *f*.

test: **~ tube** *n* éprouvette *f*; **~-tube baby** *n* bébé-éprouvette *m*.

tetanus ▶686 **I** *n* tétanos *m*.
II *noun modifier* [*injection, vaccine*] antitétanique.

tether *vtr* attacher (**to** à).
IDIOMS **to be at the end of one's ~** (exhausted) être au bout du rouleau○.

text *n* texte *m* (**by** de).

textbook *n* manuel *m* (**about, on** sur).

textile *n* textile *m*.

texture *n* texture *f*.

Thames *pr n* **the (river) ~** la Tamise.

than

■ **Note** When *than* is used as a preposition in expressions of comparison, it is translated by *que* (or *qu'* before a vowel or mute 'h'): *he's taller than me* = il est plus grand que moi; *London is bigger than Oxford* = Londres est plus grand qu'Oxford.
– For other uses, see the entry below.

I *prep* **1** (in comparisons) que; **thinner ~ him** plus mince que lui; **he has more ~ me** il en

a plus que moi; **I was more surprised ~ annoyed** j'étais plus étonné que fâché; **2** (expressing quantity, degree, value) de; **more/less ~ 100** plus/moins de 100; **more ~ half** plus de la moitié; **temperatures lower ~ 30 degrees** des températures de moins de 30 degrés.
II *conj* **1** (in comparisons) que; **he's older ~ I am** il est plus âgé que moi; **it took us longer ~ we expected** ça nous a pris plus de temps que prévu; **it was further away ~ I remembered** c'était plus loin que dans mon souvenir; **2** (expressing preferences) **I'd sooner** or **rather go to Rome ~ go to Venice** je préférerais aller à Rome que d'aller à Venise, j'aimerais mieux aller à Rome qu'à Venise; **3** (when) **hardly** or **no sooner had he left ~ the phone rang** à peine était-il parti que le téléphone a sonné; **4** (US) **to be different ~ sth** être différent de qch.

thank *vtr* remercier [*person*]; **~ God!** Dieu merci!

thankful *adj* (grateful) reconnaissant; (relieved) soulagé.

thankfully *adv* **1** (luckily) heureusement; **2** (with relief) avec soulagement; (with gratitude) avec gratitude.

thankless *adj* [*task, person*] ingrat.

thanks **I** *n pl* remerciements *mpl*; **with ~** avec mes/nos remerciements.
II° *adv* merci; **~ a lot** merci beaucoup; **no ~** non merci.
III thanks to *phr* grâce à.

Thanksgiving (Day) *n* (US) jour *m* d'Action de Grâces.

thank you **I** *n* (also **thank-you, thankyou**) merci *m*; **to say ~ to sb** dire merci à qn.
II *noun modifier* [*letter, gift*] de remerciement.
III *adv* merci; **~ for coming** merci d'être venu; **~ very much** merci beaucoup.

that ▶ **905** **I** *det* **at ~ moment** à ce moment-là; **at ~ time** à cette époque-la; **you can't do it ~ way** tu ne peux pas le faire comme ça; **he went ~ way** il est allé par là; **those patients (who are) able to walk** les patients qui sont capables de marcher; **~ lazy son of yours** ton paresseux de fils.
II *dem pron* **what's ~?** qu'est-ce que c'est que ça?; **who's ~?** qui est-ce?; (on phone) qui est à l'appareil?; **is ~ Françoise?** c'est Françoise?; **who told you ~?** qui t'a dit ça?; **~'s how he did it** c'est comme ça qu'il l'a fait; **what did he mean by ~?** qu'est-ce qu'il entendait par là?; **~'s the kitchen** ça, c'est la cuisine; **before ~, he had always lived in London** avant cela, il avait toujours vécu à Londres; **those who...** ceux qui...
III *rel pron* **the house ~ they live in** la maison dans laquelle ils vivent; **the day ~ she arrived** le jour où elle est arrivée.
IV *conj* que; **he said ~ he had finished** il a dit qu'il avait fini; **it's likely ~ they are out** il est probable qu'ils sont sortis.
V *adv* **it's about ~ thick** c'est à peu près épais comme ça; **I can't do ~ much work in one day** je ne peux pas faire autant de travail dans une journée; **he can't swim ~ far** il ne peut pas nager aussi loin.
IDIOMS **~ is (to say)...** c'est-à-dire...; **~'s it!** (that's right) c'est ça!; (that's enough) ça suffit!; **I don't want to see you again and ~'s ~!** je ne veux pas te revoir point final!

thatch *n* chaume *m*.

thatch: **~ed cottage** *n* chaumière *f*; **~ed roof** *n* toit *m* de chaume.

thaw **I** *n* dégel *m*.
II *vtr* faire fondre [*ice, snow*]; décongeler [*frozen food*].
III *vi* **1** [*snow*] fondre; [*ground, frozen food*] dégeler; **2** (figurative) se détendre.

the ▶ **906** *det* le/la/l'/les; **two chapters of ~ book** deux chapitres du livre; **I met them at ~ supermarket** je les ai rencontrés au supermarché; **~ opera** l'opéra; **~ French** les Français; **~ wounded** les blessés; **she buys only ~ best** elle n'achète que ce qu'il y a de mieux; **he didn't have ~ courage to refuse** il n'a pas eu le courage de refuser; **~ fifties** les années cinquante; **~ Hapsburgs** les Habsbourg; **the news made her all ~ sadder** la nouvelle n'a fait que la rendre encore plus triste; **~ more I learn ~ less I understand** plus j'apprends moins je comprends; **~ longer he waits ~ harder it will be** plus il attendra plus ce sera difficile; **~ sooner ~ better** le plus tôt sera le mieux; **~ fastest train** le train le plus rapide; **~ prettiest house in the village** la plus jolie maison du village; **THE book of the year** le meilleur livre de l'année; **do you mean THE Charlie Parker?** tu veux dire le célèbre Charlie Parker?

theatre, theater (US) **I** *n* **1** théâtre *m*; **to go to the ~** aller au théâtre; **2** (US) (cinema) cinéma *m*; **3** (Mil) théâtre *m*; **~ of operations** théâtre des opérations.
II *noun modifier* [*audience, seat, ticket*] de théâtre; [*company*] théâtral.

theatrical *adj* [*group*] de théâtre; [*agency, gesture, production, technique*] théâtral.

theft *n* vol *m* (**of** de).

their *det* leur/leurs.

■ **Note** In French, determiners agree in gender and number with the noun that follows. So *their* is translated by *leur* + masculine or feminine singular noun (*leur chien, leur maison*) and by *leurs* + plural noun (*leurs enfants*).
– When *their* is stressed, *à eux* is added after the noun: THEIR house = leur maison à eux.
– For *their* used with parts of the body ▶ **523**.

---

theirs *pron*

■ **Note** In French, possessive pronouns reflect the gender and number of the noun they are standing for; *theirs* is translated by *le leur, la leur, les leurs*, according to what is being referred to.

---

my car is red but ~ is blue ma voiture est rouge mais la leur est bleue; **my children are older than ~** mes enfants sont plus âgés que les leurs; **which house is ~?** c'est laquelle leur maison?; **the money wasn't ~ to give**

that

As a determiner

In French, determiners agree in gender and number with the noun that follows; ***that*** is translated by ***ce*** + *masculine singular noun* (***ce monsieur***), ***cet*** + *masculine singular noun beginning with a vowel or mute 'h'* (***cet homme***) and ***cette*** + *feminine singular noun* (***cette femme***). The plural form ***those*** is translated by ***ces*** (*ces livres, ces histoires*).

Note, however, that the above translations are also used for the English ***this*** (plural ***these***). So when it is necessary to insist on ***that*** as opposed to another or others of the same sort, the adverbial tag ***-là*** is added to the noun:

I prefer ***that*** *version*	= je préfère **cette** version-**là**

As a pronoun

- In French, pronouns reflect the gender and number of the noun they are standing for. So ***that*** (meaning *that one*) is translated by ***celui-là*** for a masculine noun, ***celle-là*** for a feminine noun and ***those*** (meaning *those ones*) is translated by ***ceux-là*** for a masculine noun and ***celles-là*** for a feminine noun:

all the dresses are nice but I like ***that*** *best*	= toutes les robes sont jolies mais je préfère **celle-là**

- When used as a relative pronoun, ***that*** is translated by ***qui*** when it is the subject of the verb and by ***que*** when it is the object:

the man ***that*** *stole the car*	= l'homme **qui** a volé la voiture
the film ***that*** *I saw*	= le film **que** j'ai vu

  Remember that in the present perfect and past perfect tenses, the past participle agrees in gender and number with the noun that ***que*** is referring back to:

the girl ***that*** *I met*	= la fille **que** j'ai rencontrée
the apples ***that*** *I bought*	= les pommes **que** j'ai achetées

- When ***that*** is used as a relative pronoun with a preposition, it is translated by ***lequel*** when standing for a masculine singular noun, by ***laquelle*** when standing for a feminine singular noun, by ***lesquels*** when standing for a masculine plural noun, and by ***lesquelles*** when standing for a feminine plural noun:

the chair ***that*** *I was sitting on*	= la chaise sur **laquelle** j'étais assis
the children ***that*** *I bought the books for*	= les enfants pour **lesquels** j'ai acheté les livres

  If the preposition would normally be translated by ***à*** in French (***to***, ***at*** etc), the translation of the whole (*preposition + relative pronoun*) will be ***auquel***, ***à laquelle***, ***auxquels***, ***auxquelles***:

the girls ***that*** *I was talking* ***to***	= les filles **auxquelles** je parlais

  If the preposition used would normally be translated by ***de*** in French (***of***, ***from*** etc), the translation of the whole (*preposition + relative pronoun*) will be ***dont*** in all cases:

the people ***that*** *I've talked* ***about***	= les personnes **dont** j'ai parlé

As a conjunction

When used as a conjunction, ***that*** can almost always be translated by ***que*** (***qu'*** before a vowel or mute 'h'):

she said ***that*** *she would do it*	= elle a dit **qu'**elle le ferait

In certain verbal constructions, ***que*** is followed by a subjunctive. For more information, consult the appropriate verb entry. For particular usages see the entry **that**.

the

- In French the definite article, like determiners, agrees in gender and number with the noun that follows; so ***the*** is translated as follows:

le or **l'** + masculine singular noun	**le** chien, **l'**ami
la or **l'** + feminine singular noun	**la** chaise, **l'**amie
les + masculine plural noun	**les** hommes, **les** avions
les + feminine plural noun	**les** femmes, **les** autos

- When ***the*** is used after a preposition in English, the two words (*preposition* + ***the***) are often translated by one word in French. If the preposition would normally be translated by ***de*** in French (***of***, ***about***, ***from*** etc), the *preposition* + ***the*** is translated according to the number and gender of the noun:

de + **le** or **l'** + masculine singular noun	**du** chien, **de l'**ami
de + **la** or **l'** + feminine singular noun	**de la** chaise, **de l'**amie
de + **les** + masculine plural noun	**des** hommes, **des** avions
de + **les** + feminine plural noun	**des** femmes, **des** autos

If the preposition would usually be translated by ***à*** (***at***, ***to*** etc) the *preposition* + ***the*** is translated according to the number and gender of the noun:

à + **le** or **l'** + masculine singular noun	**au** chien, **à l'**ami
à + **la** or **l'** + feminine singular noun	**à la** chaise, **à l'**amie
à + **les** + masculine plural noun	**aux** hommes, **aux** avions
à + **les** + feminine plural noun	**aux** femmes, **aux** autos

- Other than this, there are few problems in translating ***the*** into French. The following cases are, however, worth remembering as not following exactly the pattern of the English:

the *good,* ***the*** *poor,* ***the*** *unemployed etc*	= **les** bons, **les** pauvres, **les** chômeurs etc
Charles ***the*** *First, Elizabeth* ***the*** *Second etc*	= Charles Ier (Premier), Elizabeth II (Deux) etc
she's ***the*** *violinist of the century*	= c'est **la plus grande** violoniste du siècle
the *Tudors,* ***the*** *Batemans,* ***the*** *Kennedys etc*	= **les** Tudor, **les** Bateman, **les** Kennedy etc.
the *sporting event of the year*	= **le grand** événement sportif de l'année
it's ***the*** *film to see*	= c'est **le** film à voir

- This dictionary contains usage notes on such topics as *days of the week, illnesses, the human body*, and *musical instruments*, many of which use ***the***; for the index to these notes see ▶ 1024.

For other particular usages, see the entry **the**.

away ils or elles n'avaient pas à donner cet argent.

them ⊳908 *pron* **both of ~** tous/toutes les deux; **both of ~ work in London** ils/elles travaillent à Londres tous/toutes les deux; **some of ~** quelques-uns d'entre eux/quelques-unes d'entre elles; **none of ~ wants it** aucun d'entre eux/aucune d'entre elles ne le veut.

theme *n* thème *m*.

theme: **~ park** *n* parc *m* de loisirs (à thème); **~ song, ~ tune** *n* (of film) musique *f*; (of radio, TV programme) indicatif *m*.

themselves *pron*

■ **Note** When used as a reflexive pronoun, direct and indirect, *themselves* is translated by *se* (or *s'* before a vowel or mute 'h').
– When used for emphasis, the translation is *eux-mêmes* in the masculine and *elles-mêmes* in the feminine: *they did it themselves* = ils l'ont fait eux-mêmes or elles l'ont fait elles-mêmes.
– After a preposition, the translation is *eux* or *elles* or *eux-mêmes* or *elles-mêmes*: *they bought the painting for themselves* = (*masculine or mixed gender*) ils ont acheté le tableau pour eux *or* pour eux-mêmes; (*feminine gender*) elles ont acheté le tableau pour elles *or* pour elles-mêmes.

1 (reflexive) se, s'; **they washed ~** ils se sont lavés; **2** (emphatic) eux-mêmes/elles-mêmes; **3** (after preposition) eux/elles, eux-mêmes/elles-mêmes; **(all) by ~** tous seuls/toutes seules.

then

■ **Note** When *then* is used to mean *at that time*, it is translated by *alors* or *à ce moment-là*: *I was working in Oxford then* = je travaillais alors à Oxford *or* je travaillais à Oxford à ce moment-là. Note that *alors* always comes immediately after the verb in French.
– When *then* is used to mean *next*, it can be translated by either *puis* or *ensuite*: *a man, a horse and then a dog* = un homme, un cheval puis *or* et ensuite un chien.
– When *then* is used to mean *in that case*, it is translated by *alors*: *then why worry?* = alors pourquoi s'inquiéter?
– For all other uses, see the entry below.

I *adv* **1** (at that point in time) alors, à ce moment-là; (implying more distant past) en ce temps-là; **people were idealistic ~** en ce temps-là les gens étaient idéalistes; **from ~ on, life became easier** à partir de ce moment-là la vie est devenue plus facile; **since ~** depuis; **by ~ the damage had been done** le mal était déjà fait; **if things haven't changed by ~** si d'ici là les choses n'ont pas changé; **we won't be in contact until ~** nous ne serons pas en contact avant (ce moment-là); **2** (afterwards, next) puis, ensuite; **~ came the big news** puis or ensuite on nous a annoncé la grande nouvelle; **3** (in that case, so) alors; **~ why did you tell her?** mais alors pourquoi est-ce que tu le lui as dit?; **if it's a problem for you ~ say so** si ça te pose un problème dis-le; **it's all arranged ~?** tout est arrangé alors?; **that's all right ~** ça va alors; **now ~ what's all this?** bon, qu'est-ce qui se passe?; **4** (therefore) donc; **these ~ are the results of the policy** voici donc les résultats de cette politique; **overall ~ it would seem that** en résumé il semble donc que; **5** (in addition, besides) puis, aussi; **and ~ there's the fare to consider** et puis il faut aussi tenir compte du prix du billet; **6** (on the other hand) d'un autre côté; **she's good but ~ so is he** elle est bonne mais lui aussi; **he looks anxious but ~ he always does** il a l'air inquiet mais de toute façon il a toujours cet air-là.

II *adj* **the ~ prime minister** le premier ministre de l'époque; **the ~ mayor of New York, Mr X** M. X, qui était alors maire de New York.

thence *adv* **1** (from there) de là; **2** (therefore) de cela.

theologian *n* théologien/-ienne *m/f*.

theology *n* théologie *f*.

theorem *n* théorème *m*.

theoretical *adj* théorique.

theoretically *adv* théoriquement; **~ speaking** en théorie.

theorize *vi* théoriser.

theory *n* théorie *f*; **in ~** en théorie.

therapeutic *adj* thérapeutique.

therapist *n* thérapeute *mf*.

therapy *n* thérapie *f*; **to have ~** suivre une thérapie.

there

■ **Note** *there* is generally translated by *là* after prepositions (*near there* = près de là) and when emphasizing the location of an object/a point etc visible to the speaker: *put them there* = mettez-les là.
– *voilà* is used to draw attention to a visible place/object/person: *there's my watch* = voilà ma montre, whereas *il y a* is used for generalizations: *there's a village nearby* = il y a un village tout près.
– *there*, when unstressed with verbs such as *aller* and *être*, is translated by *y*: *we went there last year* = nous y sommes allés l'année dernière, but not where emphasis is made: *it was there that we went last year* = c'est là que nous sommes allés l'année dernière.
– For examples of the above and further uses, see the entry below.

I *pron* **~ is/are** il y a; **~ must be some mistake** il doit y avoir erreur; **~ isn't any room** il n'y a pas de place; **~ are many reasons** il y a beaucoup de raisons; **~ are two** il y en a deux; **~ is some left** il en reste; **~ seems to be** il semble y avoir; **once upon a time ~ was a king** il était une fois un roi; **~'ll be a speech later** il y aura un discours plus tard.

II *adv* **1** là; **up to ~, down to ~** jusque là; **put it in ~** mettez-le là-dedans; **in ~ please** (ushering sb) par là s'il vous plaît; **stand ~** mettez-vous là; **go over ~** va là-bas; **since we were last ~** depuis la dernière fois que nous y sommes allés; **to go ~ and back in an hour** faire l'aller et retour en une heure; **when do they get ~?** quand est-ce qu'ils arrivent là-bas?; **the train won't be ~ yet** le train ne sera pas encore là; **we get off ~** c'est là qu'on

them

◆ When used as a direct object pronoun, referring to people, animals or things, ***them*** is translated by ***les***:

*I know **them***	= je **les** connais
*I don't know **them***	= je ne **les** connais pas
*do I know **them**?*	= est-ce que je **les** connais?

◆ Note that the object pronoun normally comes before the verb in French and that, in compound tenses like the present perfect and past perfect, the past participle agrees in gender and number with the direct object pronoun:

*he's seen **them***	= il **les** a vus (***them*** being masculine or of mixed gender)
	= il **les** a vues (***them*** being all feminine gender)
*he hasn't seen **them***	= il ne **les** a pas vus = il ne **les** a pas vues
*has he seen **them**?*	= est-ce qu'il **les** a vus? = est-ce qu'il **les** a vues?

◆ In imperatives, the direct object pronoun is translated by ***les*** and comes after the verb:

*catch **them**!*	= attrape-**les**!*
*take **them**!*	= prenez-**les**!*

But in negative commands, ***les*** comes before the verb:

*don't take **them**!*	= ne **les** prenez pas!
*don't hit **them**!*	= ne **les** frappe pas!

◆ When used as an indirect object pronoun, ***them*** is translated by ***leur***:

*I gave it **to them***	= je le **leur** ai donné
*I didn't give it **to them***	= je ne le **leur** ai pas donné
*did I give it **to them**?*	= est-ce que je le **leur** ai donné?

◆ In imperatives, the indirect object pronoun is translated by ***leur*** and comes after the verb:

*write **to them**!*	= écris-**leur**!*
*say it **to them**!*	= dis-le-**leur**!*

But in negative commands, ***leur*** comes before the verb:

*don't show it **to them**!*	= ne le **leur** montre pas!

◆ After prepositions and the verb ***to be***, the translation is ***eux*** for masculine or mixed gender and ***elles*** for feminine gender:

*he did it **for them***	= il l'a fait **pour eux** (***them*** being masculine or of mixed gender)
	= il l'a fait pour **elles** (***them*** being all feminine gender)
*it's **them***	= ce sont **eux** ce sont **elles**

* Note the hyphen(s).

❑ For particular usages see the entry **them**.

descend; **will she be ~ now?** est-ce qu'elle y est maintenant?; **we must finish ~** nous devons nous arrêter là; **2** (to draw attention) (to person, activity) voilà; (to place) là; **what have you got ~?** qu'est-ce que tu as là?; **~ goes the coach** voilà le car qui s'en va; **~ you are** (seeing somebody arrive) vous voilà; (giving object) tenez, voilà; (that's done) et voilà; **~'s a bus coming** voilà un bus; **that paragraph ~** ce paragraphe.

III *excl* **~ ~!** allez! allez!; **~, I told you!** voilà, je te l'avais bien dit!; **~, you've woken the baby!** c'est malin, tu as réveillé le bébé!

IV **there again** *phr* (on the other hand) d'un autre côté.

thereabouts (GB), **thereabout** (US) *adv* **1** (in the vicinity) par là; **2** (roughly) **100 dollars or ~** 100 dollars environ.

thereby *conj* ainsi.

therefore *adv* donc, par conséquent.

thermal *adj* [*energy, insulation, reactor*] thermique; [*spring, treatment*] thermal; [*garment*] triboélectrique.

thermometer *n* thermomètre *m*.

Thermos® *n* (also **~ flask**) bouteille *f* thermos®.

thermostat *n* thermostat *m*.

thesaurus *n* dictionnaire *m* analogique.

these *pl* ▶ **this**.

thesis *n* **1** (Univ) (doctoral) thèse *f*; (master's) mémoire *m*; **2** (theory) thèse *f*.

they *pron*

■ **Note** *they* is translated by *ils* (masculine) or *elles* (feminine). For a group of people or things of mixed gender, *ils* is always used. The emphatic form is *eux* (masculine) or *elles* (feminine).

~ have already gone (masculine or mixed) ils sont déjà partis; (feminine) elles sont déjà parties; **here ~ are!** les voici!; **there ~ are!** les voilà!; **she bought one but ~ didn't** elle en a acheté un mais eux pas.

thick I *adj* **1** [*piece, garment, liquid, hair, make-up*] épais/épaisse; [*forest, vegetation, fog*] dense, épais/épaisse; **to be 6 cm ~** faire 6 cm d'épaisseur; **to be ~ with** être plein de [*smoke, noise*]; **2**○ (stupid) bête.

II *adv* **don't spread the butter on too ~** ne mets pas trop de beurre; **the snow lay ~ on the ground** il y avait une épaisse couche de neige sur le sol.

IDIOMS **to be in the ~ of** être au beau milieu de.

thicken I *vtr* épaissir.

II *vi* [*sauce, fog, clouds, waistline*] s'épaissir; [*voice*] s'enrouer; [*traffic*] devenir plus dense.

IDIOMS **the plot ~s!** l'affaire se corse!

thicket *n* fourré *m*.

thickly *adv* [*spread*] en une couche épaisse; [*cut*] en morceaux épais; [*say, speak*] d'une voix enrouée; **the grass grew ~** l'herbe poussait dru.

thickness *n* épaisseur *f*.

thick: **~set** *adj* trapu; **~-skinned** *adj* insensible.

thief *n* voleur/-euse *m/f*.

thieve *vtr*, *vi* voler.

thieving I *n* vol *m*.

II *adj* **~ children** enfants qui volent.

thigh *n* cuisse *f*.

thimble *n* dé *m* à coudre.

thin I *adj* **1** [*nose, lips, wall*] mince; [*line, stripe, wire*] fin; [*slice, layer*] fin, mince; **2** [*mixture*] liquide; [*soup, sauce*] clair; **3** [*person, body*] maigre; **to get ~** maigrir; **4** (fine) [*paper*] fin; [*fabric, mist*] léger/-ère; **5** [*crowd, hair*] clairsemé; **6 to wear ~** [*joke, excuse*] être usé.

II *vtr* **1** diluer [*paint*]; allonger [*sauce, soup*]; **2** = **thin out**.

III *vi* (also **~ out**) [*crowd*] se disperser; [*hair*] se clairsemer.

IV **thinning** *pres p adj* [*hair, crowd*] clairsemé.

■ **thin out**: **~ [sth] out, ~ out [sth]** éclaircir [*seedlings, hair*].

thing I *n* **1** (object) chose *f*, truc○ *m*; (action, task, event) chose *f*; **the best ~ (to do) would be to go and see her** le mieux serait d'aller la voir; **that was a silly ~ to do** c'était stupide de faire cela; **the ~ to do is...** ce qu'il faut faire c'est...; **it's all right if you like that sort of ~** ce n'est pas mal pour ceux qui aiment ça; **the ~ to remember is...** ce dont il faut se souvenir c'est...; **I couldn't hear a ~ (that) he said** je n'ai rien entendu de ce qu'il a dit; **the ~ is, (that)...** ce qu'il y a, c'est que...; **the only ~ is,...** la seule chose, c'est que...; **the good ~ (about it) is...** ce qu'il y a de bien, c'est que...; **2** (person, animal) **she's a pretty little ~** c'est une jolie petite fille; **you lucky ~**○! veinard/-e○!

II **things** *n pl* **1** (personal belongings, equipment) affaires *fpl*; **2** (situation, circumstances, matters) les choses *fpl*; **to see ~s as they really are** voir les choses en face; **~s are getting better** ça s'améliore; **how are ~s with you?** comment ça va?; **to worry about ~s** se faire du souci; **as ~s stand** dans l'état actuel des choses; **all ~s considered** tout compte fait.

IDIOMS **it's not the done ~ (to do)** ça ne se fait pas (de faire); **he's on to a good ~** il a trouvé le bon filon○; **for one ~... (and) for another ~...** premièrement... et deuxièmement...; **to make a big ~ (out) of it**○ en faire toute une histoire; **I must be seeing ~s!** je dois avoir des visions!; **one ~ led to another and...** et, de fil en aiguille...

think I *vtr* **1** (believe) croire, penser; **I ~ so** je crois; **I don't ~ so** je ne crois pas; **what do you ~ it will cost?** combien ça va coûter à ton avis?; **2** (imagine) imaginer, croire; **who'd have thought it!** qui l'aurait cru?; **who do you ~ you are?** pour qui vous prenez-vous?; **what on earth do you ~ you're doing?** mais qu'est-ce que tu fais?; **I thought as much!** je m'en doutais!; **that's what you ~!** (ironically) tu te fais des idées!; **and to ~ that I believed him!** (GB) et dire que je l'ai cru!; **3** (have opinion) **to ~ a lot/not much of** penser/ne pas penser beaucoup de bien de.

II *vi* **1** penser; (carefully) réfléchir; **I'll have to ~ about it** il faudra que j'y réfléchisse; **to ~ hard** bien réfléchir; **to ~ clearly** avoir les idées claires; **to be ~ing of doing** envisager de faire; **to ~ about doing** penser à faire; **come to ~ of it...** maintenant que j'y pense...; **2** (take into account) **to ~ about** or **of sb/sth** penser à qn/qch; **I can't ~ of everything!** je ne peux pas penser à tout!; **3** (consider) **to ~ of sb as** considérer qn comme; **he ~s of himself as an expert** il se prend pour un spécialiste; **4** (remember) **to ~ of** se rappeler.

■ **think ahead** bien réfléchir (à l'avance).

■ **think back** se reporter en arrière (**to** à).

■ **think out**: **~ out [sth]**, **~ [sth] out** bien réfléchir à.

■ **think through**: **~ through [sth]**, **~ [sth] through** bien réfléchir à [*proposal, action*]; faire le tour de [*problem, question*].

thinker *n* penseur/-euse *m/f*.

thinking **I** *n* **1** (reflection) réflexion *f*; **2** (way one thinks) pensée *f*; **to my way of ~** à mon avis.

II *adj* [*person*] réfléchi.

thinly *adv* **1** [*slice*] en tranches fines; [*spread*] en couche mince; **2 ~ disguised** à peine déguisé.

thinner *n* (also **thinners**) diluant *m*.

thin-skinned *adj* susceptible.

third ▶ 584, 642 **I** *n* **1** (in order) troisième *mf*; **2** (of month) trois *m inv*; **3** (fraction) tiers *m*; **4** (also **~-class honours degree**) (GB Univ) ≈ licence *f* avec mention passable; **5** (Mus) tierce *f*; **6** (also **~ gear**) (Aut) troisième *f*.

II *adj* troisième.

III *adv* **1** [*come, finish*] troisième; **2** (also **thirdly**) troisièmement.

third-class *adj* de troisième classe.

thirdly *adv* troisièmement.

third: **~ party** *n* tiers *m*; **~ person** *n* troisième personne *f*; **Third World** *n* tiers-monde *m*.

thirst *n* soif *f* (**for** de).

thirsty *adj* assoiffé; **to be ~** avoir soif; **to make sb ~** donner soif à qn.

thirteen ▶ 492, 554 *n, pron, det* treize (*m*) *inv*.

thirteenth ▶ 584, 642 **I** *n* **1** (in order) treizième *mf*; **2** (of month) treize *m inv*.

II *adj, adv* treizième.

thirties ▶ 584, 492 *n pl* **1** (era) **the ~** les années *fpl* trente; **2** (age) **to be in one's ~** avoir entre trente et quarante ans.

thirtieth ▶ 584 **I** *n* **1** (in order) trentième *mf*; **2** (of month) trente *m inv*.

II *adj, adv* trentième.

thirty ▶ 492, 554 *n, pron, det* trente (*m*) *inv*.

thirty-first ▶ 584 **I** *n* (of month) trente et un *m*.

II *adj* trente et unième.

this

■ **Note**

As a determiner

– In French, determiners agree in gender and number with the noun that follows; *this* is translated by *ce* + masculine singular noun (*ce monsieur*) BUT by *cet* + masculine singular noun beginning with a vowel or mute 'h' (*cet arbre, cet homme*) and by *cette* + feminine singular noun (*cette femme*). The plural form *these* is translated by *ces* (*ces livres, ces histoires*).

– Note, however, that the above translations are also used for the English *that* (plural *those*). So when it is necessary to insist on *this* as opposed to another or others of the same sort, the adverbial tag *-ci* (*this one here*) is added to the noun: *I prefer* THIS *version* = je préfère cette version-ci.

As a pronoun (*meaning this one*)

– In French, pronouns reflect the gender and number of the noun they are standing for. So *this* (meaning *this one*) is translated by *celui-ci* for a masculine noun, *celle-ci* for a feminine noun; *those* (meaning *those ones*) is translated by *ceux-ci* for a masculine plural noun, *celles-ci* for a feminine plural noun: *of all the dresses this is the prettiest one* = de toutes les robes celle-ci est la plus jolie.

– This dictionary contains usage notes on such topics as ***time units*** and ***dates***. For the index to these notes ▶ 1008.

– For other uses of *this*, see the entry below.

I *det* **~ paper** ce papier; **~ lamp** cette lampe; **do it ~ way not that way** fais-le comme ça et pas comme ça.

II *pron* **what's ~?** qu'est-ce que c'est?; **who's ~?** qui est-ce?; (on telephone) qui est à l'appareil?; **whose is ~?** à qui appartient ceci?; **~ is the dining room** voici la salle à manger; **~ is my sister Moira** (introduction) voici ma sœur Moira; (on photo) c'est ma sœur, Moira; **~ is not the right one** ce n'est pas le bon; **what did you mean by ~?** qu'est-ce que tu voulais dire par là?; **who did ~?** qui a fait ça?; **what's all ~ about?** qu'est-ce que c'est que cette histoire?; **~ is what happens when** voilà ce qui se passe quand.

III *adv* **it's ~ big** c'est grand comme ça; **having got ~ far it would be a pity to stop now** maintenant qu'on est arrivé jusque-là ce serait dommage de s'arrêter; **I didn't realize it was ~ serious** je ne m'étais pas rendu compte que c'était sérieux à ce point-là.

IDIOMS **to talk about ~ and that** parler de tout et de rien.

thistle *n* chardon *m*.

thong *n* **1** (on whip) lanière *f*; **2** (on shoe, garment) lacet *m*.

thorn *n* épine *f*.

IDIOMS **to be a ~ in sb's side** être une source d'irritation pour qn.

thorough *adj* **1** (detailed) [*analysis, knowledge*] approfondi; [*search, work*] minutieux/-ieuse; **2** (meticulous) minutieux/-ieuse.

thoroughbred **I** *n* pur-sang *m*.

II *adj* de pure race.

thoroughfare *n* rue *f*; **'no ~'** 'passage interdit'.

thoroughly *adv* **1** (meticulously) [*clean, examine, read*] à fond; [*check, search*] minutieusement; **2** (completely) [*clean, reliable, dangerous*] tout à fait; [*agree*] parfaitement; [*recommend*] chaleureusement.

thoroughness *n* minutie *f*.

those *pl* ▶ **that**.

though I *conj* bien que (+ *subj*); **talented ~ he is, I don't like him** il a beau être doué, je ne l'aime pas; **a foolish ~ courageous act** un acte stupide quoique courageux.
II *adv* quand même, pourtant; **it's very expensive, ~** c'est très cher, pourtant.

thought *n* **1** (idea) idée *f*, pensée *f*; **2** (reflection) pensée *f*; **deep in ~** plongé dans ses pensées; **3** (consideration) considération *f*; **to give ~ to sth** considérer qch; **we never gave it much ~** nous n'y avons pas beaucoup réfléchi.

thoughtful *adj* **1** (reflective) (gen) pensif/-ive; [*silence*] profond; **2** (considerate) [*person, gesture*] prévenant; [*letter*] gentil/-ille.

thoughtfully *adv* **1** [*stare, smile*] d'un air pensif; **2** (considerately) avec prévenance.

thoughtless *adj* irréfléchi; **to be ~ towards** manquer de considération pour.

thoughtlessly *adv* (insensitively) sans considération; (unthinkingly) sans réfléchir.

thought-out *adj* **well/badly ~** bien/mal conçu.

thought: **~ process** *n* mécanismes *mpl* de la pensée; **~-provoking** *adj* qui fait réfléchir.

thousand I *n* (figure) mille *m inv*; **a ~ and two** mille deux; **about a ~** un millier.
II *pron, det* mille *inv*; **four ~ pounds** quatre mille livres.

thousands *n pl* milliers *mpl* (**of** de); **in their ~** par milliers.

thousandth I *n* (in order, sequence) millième *mf*.
II *adj* millième.

thrash *vtr* **1** (whip) rouer [qn] de coups; **2**○ (Mil, Sport) écraser.
■ **thrash about, thrash around** se débattre.
■ **thrash out**: **~ out [sth]** venir à bout de [*problem*]; réussir à élaborer [*plan*].

thrashing *n* raclée *f*.

thread I *n* **1** (for sewing) fil *m*; **2** (of screw) filetage *m*; **3** (of story, argument) fil *m*.
II *vtr* enfiler [*bead, needle*].

threadbare *adj* usé jusqu'à la corde.

threat *n* menace *f* (**to** pour); **to pose a ~ to** être une menace pour.

threaten I *vtr* menacer; **to be ~ed with extinction** risquer de disparaître.
II *vi* [*danger, bad weather*] menacer; **to ~ to do** risquer de faire.

threatening *adj* [*expression, atmosphere*] menaçant; [*letter*] de menaces.

three ▶ **492**, **554** *n, pron, det* trois (*m*) *inv*.

three-dimensional *adj* en trois dimensions.

threefold I *adj* triple.
II *adv* triplement; **to increase ~** tripler.

three: **~-piece suit** *n* (costume *m*) trois-pièces *m inv*; **~-piece suite** *n* salon *m* trois pièces.

three-quarters ▶ **915**, **554** I *n* trois-quarts *mpl*; **~ of an hour** trois-quarts d'heure.
II *adv* [*empty, full, done*] aux trois-quarts.

thresh *vtr* battre.

threshold *n* seuil *m*; **to cross the ~** franchir le seuil.

thrift *n* économie *f*.

thrifty *adj* [*person*] économe (**in** dans).

thrill I *n* **1** (sensation) frisson *m*; **2** (pleasure) plaisir *m*.
II *vtr* (with joy) transporter [qn] de joie; passionner [*readers, viewers*].
III *vi* frissonner (**at, to** à).
IV **thrilled** *pp adj* ravi; **~ed with** enchanté de.

thriller *n* thriller *m*.

thrilling *adj* [*adventure, match, story*] palpitant; [*concert, moment, sensation*] exaltant.

thrive *vi* [*plant*] pousser bien; [*business, community*] prospérer; **she ~s on hard work** le travail lui réussit.

thriving *adj* [*business*] florissant; [*person*] prospère; [*plant*] en pleine santé.

throat *n* gorge *f*; **to have a sore ~** avoir mal à la gorge.

throb *vi* **1** [*heart, pulse*] battre; **my head is ~bing** ça me lance dans la tête; **2** [*motor*] vibrer; [*music, building*] résonner.

throbbing I *n* (of heart, pulse, blood) battement *m*; (of motor) vibration *f*.
II *adj* **1** [*pain, ache, sound, music*] lancinant; **2** [*engine, motor*] qui vibre.

throes *n pl* **death ~** agonie *f*.

throne *n* trône *m*; **on the ~** sur le trône.

throng I *n* foule *f* (**of** de).
II *vtr* envahir [*street, town*].

through I *prep* **1** (from one side to the other) à travers; **the nail went right ~ the wall** le clou a traversé le mur; **to poke sth ~ a hole** enfoncer qch dans un trou; **he was shot ~ the head** on lui a tiré une balle dans la tête; **it has a crack running ~ it** il est fêlé; **to fly ~ the clouds** voler au milieu des nuages; **2** (via, by way of) **to go ~ the town centre** passer par le centre-ville; **to look ~** regarder avec [*telescope*]; regarder par [*hole, window*]; **it was ~ her that I got this job** c'est par son intermédiaire que j'ai eu ce travail; **3** (past) **to go ~** brûler [*red light*]; **to get** or **go ~** passer à travers [*barricade*]; passer [*customs*]; **she's been ~ a lot** elle en a vu des vertes et des pas mures○; **4** (because of) **~ carelessness** par négligence; **~ illness** pour cause de maladie; **5** (until the end of) **all** or **right ~ the day** toute la journée; **6** (up to and including) jusqu'à; **from Friday ~ to Sunday** de vendredi jusqu'à dimanche; **open April ~ September** (US) ouvert d'avril à fin septembre.
II *adj* **1** [*train, ticket, route*] direct; [*freight*] à forfait; **'no ~ road'** 'voie sans issue'; **2** (successful) **to be ~ to the next round** être sélectionné pour le deuxième tour; **3**○ (finished) fini; **are you ~ with the paper?** as-tu fini de lire le journal?; **we're ~** (of a couple) c'est fini entre nous.

III *adv* **the water went right ~** l'eau est passée à travers; **to let sb ~** laisser passer qn; **cooked right ~** bien cuit; **to read sth right ~** lire qch jusqu'au bout.
IV **through and through** *phr* **English ~ and ~** anglais jusqu'au bout des ongles.

throughout I *prep* **1** (all over) **~ France** dans toute la France; **~ the world** dans le monde entier; **2** (for the duration of) tout au long de; **~ his life** toute sa vie; **~ history** à travers l'histoire.
II *adv* (in every part) partout; (the whole time) tout le temps.

throughway *n* (US) voie *f* rapide or express.

throw I *n* (in football) touche *f*; (of javelin) lancer *m*; (in judo, wrestling) jeté *m*.
II *vtr* **1** (with careful aim) lancer; (downwards) jeter; (with violence) projeter; **to ~ sth at sb** lancer qch à qn; **she threw her arms around my neck** elle s'est jetée à mon cou; **to ~ a six** (in dice) faire un six; **2** [*horse*] désarçonner [*rider*]; **3** (figurative) lancer [*punch, question*]; jeter [*glance*]; envoyer [*kiss*]; projeter [*image, light, shadow*] (**on** sur); **4** (disconcert) désarçonner; **5**° **to ~ a fit** piquer une crise°; **6**° (organize) **to ~ a party** faire une fête°; **7** (in pottery) tourner.
III *vi* lancer.
IV *v refl* **to ~ oneself** se jeter (**onto** sur); **to ~ oneself into one's work** se plonger dans son travail.
■ **throw away**: **~ [sth] away, ~ away [sth]** jeter [*paper, old clothes*]; gâcher [*chance, life*].
■ **throw back**: **~ back [sth], ~ [sth] back** rejeter [*fish*]; relancer [*ball*].
■ **throw in**: **~ in [sth], ~ [sth] in 1** (give free) faire cadeau de; **2** (add) ajouter [*ingredient*]; **3** faire [*remark*].
■ **throw off**: ¶ **~ off [sth], ~ [sth] off 1** écarter [*bedclothes*]; **2** se débarrasser de [*cold, handicap, pursuers*]; ¶ **~ off [sb], ~ [sb] off** (eject) (from bus, train, plane) expulser.
■ **throw on**: **~ on [sth], ~ [sth] on** enfiler [qch] en vitesse [*garment*].
■ **throw out**: ¶ **~ out [sb/sth], ~ [sb/sth] out** jeter [*rubbish*]; expulser [*person*] (**of** de); ¶ **~ out [sth], ~ [sth] out** rejeter [*application, decision*].
■ **throw together**: **~ [sb] together** réunir [*people*].
■ **throw up**: ¶ **~ up**° vomir; ¶ **~ up [sth], ~ [sth] up 1** lever [*arms, hands*]; lancer [*ball*]; **2**° (abandon) laisser tomber [*job*].

throwback *n* survivance *f* (**to** de).

thrush *n* (Zool) grive *f*.

thrust I *n* **1** (gen, Mil, Tech) poussée *f*; **sword ~** coup *m* d'épée; **2** (of argument) portée *f*.
II *vtr* **to ~ sth towards** or **at sb** mettre brusquement qch sous le nez de qn; **to ~ sth into sth** enfoncer qch dans qch.
■ **thrust out**: **~ [sth] out, ~ out [sth]** tendre brusquement [*hand*]; projeter [qch] en avant [*jaw, chin*].

thrusting *adj* [*person*] agressif/-ive; [*ambition*] puissant.

thud I *n* bruit *m* sourd.
II *vi* faire un bruit sourd.

thug *n* (hooligan) voyou *m*; (hired heavy) casseur *m*.

thumb I *n* pouce *m*.
II *vtr* **1** (also **~ through**) feuilleter [*book, magazine*]; **2**° **to ~ a lift** faire du stop°.
IDIOMS **to be under sb's ~** être sous la domination de qn.

thumbtack *n* punaise *f*.

thump I *n* **1** (blow) (grand) coup *m*; **2** (sound) bruit *m* sourd.
II *vtr* taper sur; **he ~ed me** il m'a tapé dessus.
III *vi* [*heart*] battre violemment; [*music, rhythm*] résonner.

thunder I *n* **1** tonnerre *m*; **a peal of ~** un roulement de tonnerre; **2** (of hooves) fracas *m*; (of applause) tonnerre *m*.
II *vtr* (shout) (also **~ out**) hurler.
III *vi* **1** (roar) [*person, cannon*] tonner; **2 to ~ past** passer dans un vacarme assourdissant.

thunder: **~bolt** *n* foudre *f*; (figurative) coup *m* de tonnerre; **~storm** *n* orage *m*; **~struck** *adj* abasourdi.

thundery *adj* orageux/-euse.

Thursday ▶ 584 *pr n* jeudi *m*.

thus *adv* ainsi; **~ far** jusqu'à présent.

thwart *vtr* contrarier [*plan*]; contrecarrer les desseins de [*person*].

thyme *n* thym *m*.

thyroid *n* (also **~ gland**) thyroïde *f*.

ti *n* (Mus) si *m*.

tiara *n* (woman's) diadème *m*; (Pope's) tiare *f*.

tick I *n* **1** (of clock) tic-tac *m*; **2** (mark) coche *f*; **3** (Zool) tique *f*.
II *vtr* cocher [*box, name, answer*].
III *vi* [*bomb, clock, watch*] faire tic-tac.
■ **tick away** [*time*] passer; [*clock, meter*] tourner.
■ **tick off**: **~ [sth] off, ~ off [sth]** cocher [*name, item*].
■ **tick over** (GB) tourner.

ticket *n* **1** (for plane, train, cinema, exhibition) billet *m* (**for** pour); (for bus, underground, cloakroom, left-luggage) ticket *m*; (for library) carte *f*; (label) étiquette *f*; **2**° (Aut) (for fine) PV° *m*; **3** (US) (of political party) liste *f* (électorale); (platform) programme *m*.

ticket: **~ agency** *n* agence *f* de spectacles; **~ inspector** ▶ 805 *n* contrôleur *m*; **~ office** *n* (office) bureau *m* de vente (des billets); (booth) guichet *m*.

tickle I *n* chatouillement *m*.
II *vtr* **1** [*person, feather*] chatouiller; [*wool, garment*] gratter; **2**° (gratify) chatouiller [*palate, vanity*]; **to ~ sb's fancy** amuser qn.

tidal wave *n* raz-de-marée *m inv*.

tide *n* marée *f*; (figurative) (of emotion) vague *f*; (of events) cours *m*; **the ~ is in/out** c'est la marée haute/basse; **to go against the ~** aller à contre-courant.
■ **tide over**: **~ [sb] over** dépanner.

tidily *adv* [*arrange, fold*] soigneusement; [*dress*] de façon soignée.

tidiness *n* (of place) ordre *m*; (of appearance) aspect *m* soigné.

tidy I *adj* **1** [*house, room, desk*] bien rangé; [*garden, work, appearance*] soigné; [*habits, person*] ordonné; [*hair*] bien coiffé; **2**○ [*amount*] beau/belle (*before n*).
II *vtr, vi* = **tidy up**.
■ **tidy up**: ¶ **~ up** faire du rangement; **to ~ up after** ranger derrière [*person*]; ¶ **~ up [sth], ~ [sth] up** ranger [*house, room, objects*]; arranger [*appearance, hair*].

tie I *n* **1** (piece of clothing) cravate *f*; **2** (bond) lien *m*; **family ~s** liens *mpl* familiaux; **3** (constraint) contrainte *f*; **4** (gen, Sport) (draw) match *m* nul.
II *vtr* **1** attacher [*label, animal*] (**to** à); ligoter [*hands*]; ficeler [*parcel*] (**with** avec); nouer [*scarf, cravate*]; attacher [*laces*]; **to ~ a knot in sth** faire un nœud à qch; **2** (link) associer (**to** à); **3 to be ~d to** être rivé à [*job*]; être cloué○ à [*house*].
III *vi* **1** (fasten) s'attacher; **2** (gen, Sport) (draw) (in match) faire match nul; (in race) être ex aequo; (in vote) [*candidates*] obtenir le même nombre de voix.
■ **tie back**: **~ [sth] back, ~ back [sth]** nouer [qch] derrière [*hair*].
■ **tie down**: **~ [sb] down, ~ down [sb]** attacher [*person*]; **she feels ~d down** elle se sent coincée○; **to ~ sb down to sth** (limit) imposer qch à qn.
■ **tie in with 1** (tally) concorder avec [*fact, event*]; **2** (have link) être en rapport avec.
■ **tie on**: **~ [sth] on, ~ on [sth]** attacher.
■ **tie up**: **~ [sb/sth] up, ~ up [sb/sth] 1** ligoter [*prisoner*]; ficeler [*parcel*]; attacher [*animal*]; **2** (freeze) immobiliser [*capital*]; **3 to be ~d up** (busy) être pris.

tie break(er) *n* (in tennis) tie-break *m*; (in quiz) question *f* subsidiaire.

tier I *n* (of cake, sandwich) étage *m*; (of system) niveau *m*; (of seating) gradin *m*.
II tiered *pp adj* [*seating*] en gradins; **~ed cake** pièce *f* montée.

tiger *n* tigre *m*.

tight I *adj* **1** [*grip*] ferme; [*knot*] serré; [*rope, voice*] tendu; **2** [*space*] étroit; [*clothing*] serré; (closefitting) [*jacket, shirt*] ajusté; **my shoes are too ~** mes chaussures me serrent; **it was a ~ squeeze** c'était très serré; **3** (strict) [*security, deadline*] strict; [*discipline*] rigoureux/-euse; [*budget, credit, schedule*] serré.
II *adv* [*hold, grip*] fermement; **hold ~!** cramponne-toi!; **sit ~!** ne bouge pas!

tighten I *vtr* serrer [*lid, screw*]; resserrer [*grip*]; renforcer [*security, restrictions*].
II *vi* **1** [*lips*] se serrer; [*muscle*] se contracter; **2** [*screw, nut*] se resserrer.

tight: **~-fisted**○ *adj* radin○; **~-fitting** *adj* ajusté.

tightly *adv* [*grasp, hold*] fermement; [*embrace*] bien fort; [*fastened*] bien.

tightness *n* (of space) étroitesse *f*; (of restrictions, security) rigueur *f* (**of** de).

tight: **~rope** *n* corde *f* raide; **~rope walker** *n* funambule *mf*.

tights *n pl* (GB) collant *m*.

tile I *n* (for roof) tuile *f*; (for floor, wall) carreau *m*.
II *vtr* poser des tuiles sur [*roof*]; carreler [*floor, wall*].

till[1] ▶ **until**.

till[2] *n* caisse *f*; **to have one's hand in the ~** piocher dans la caisse.

tiller *n* barre *f*.

tilt I *vtr* pencher [*table, sunshade*]; incliner [*head*]; rabattre [*hat, cap*].
II *vi* (slant) pencher.

timber *n* (for building) bois *m* (de construction); (trees) arbres *mpl*; (beam) poutre *f*.

timbered *adj* [*house*] en bois; **half-~ house** maison *f* à colombage.

timbre *n* timbre *m*.

time ▶**915**, **554** **I** *n* **1** temps *m*; **as ~ goes/went by** avec le temps; **at this point in ~** à l'heure qu'il est; **flight/journey ~** durée *f* du vol/voyage; **I was waiting for you here all the ~** je t'attendais ici et je n'ai pas bougé; **she was lying all the ~** elle mentait depuis le début; **you've got plenty of ~** tu as tout ton temps; **you took a long ~!** tu en a mis du temps!; **we had to wait for a long ~** nous avons dû attendre longtemps; **a long ~ ago** il y a longtemps; **I haven't seen him for some ~** ça fait un moment que je ne l'ai pas vu; **in five days' ~** dans cinq jours; **2** (hour of the day, night) heure *f*; **what ~ is it?, what's the ~?** quelle heure est-il?; **10 am French ~** 10 heures, heure française; **this ~ last week/year** il y a exactement huit jours/un an; **by this ~ next year** d'ici un an; **on ~** à l'heure; **the bus/train ~s** les horaires *mpl* des bus/des trains; **it's ~ for bed** c'est l'heure d'aller au lit; **it's ~ we started** il est temps de commencer; **about ~ too!** ce n'est pas trop tôt!; **in ~ for Christmas** à temps pour Noël; **twenty minutes ahead of ~** vingt minutes avant l'heure prévue; **3** (era, epoch) époque *f*; **at the ~** à l'époque; **there was a ~ when one could...** à une certaine époque on pouvait...; **in former ~s** autrefois; **it's just like old ~s** c'est comme au bon vieux temps; **4** (moment) moment *m*; **at ~s** par moments; **at the right ~** au bon moment; **this is no ~ for jokes** ce n'est pas le moment de plaisanter; **at all ~s** à tout moment; **any ~ now** d'un moment à l'autre; **the ~ has come for action** l'heure est venue d'agir; **by the ~ I finished the letter the post had gone** le temps de finir ma lettre et le courrier était parti; **some ~ next month** dans le courant du mois prochain; **for the ~ being** pour le moment; **from that** or **this ~ on** à partir de ce moment; **when the ~ comes** le moment venu; **in ~s of crisis** dans les périodes de crise; **5** (occasion) fois *f*; **nine ~s out of ten** neuf fois sur dix; **three ~s a month** trois fois par mois; **three at a ~** trois à la fois; **from ~ to ~** de temps en

temps; **6** (experience) **to have a hard ~ doing** avoir du mal à faire; **he's having a hard ~** il traverse une période difficile; **we had a good ~** on s'est bien amusés; **the good/bad ~s** les moments heureux/difficiles; **she enjoyed her ~ in Canada** elle a beaucoup aimé son séjour au Canada; **7** (Mus) mesure *f*; **to beat** or **mark ~** battre la mesure; **8 ten ~s longer/stronger** dix fois plus long/plus fort; **eight ~s as much** huit fois autant.
II *vtr* **1** (schedule) prévoir [*holiday, visit, attack*]; fixer [*appointment, meeting*]; **to be well-/badly-timed** être opportun/inopportun; **2** (judge) calculer [*blow, shot*]; **3** chronométrer [*athlete, cyclist*]; **to ~ oneself** se chronométrer.
IDIOMS **there is a ~ and place for everything** il y a un temps pour tout; **there's always a first ~** il y a un début à tout; **only ~ will tell** l'avenir nous le dira; **long ~ no see**○! ça fait un bail○ (qu'on ne s'est pas vus)!

time: **~ bomb** *n* bombe *f* à retardement; **~-consuming** *adj* [*activity*] qui prend du temps; **~ difference** *n* décalage *m* horaire; **~-lag** *n* décalage *m*.

timeless *adj* éternel/-elle.

time-limit *n* **1** (deadline) date *f* limite; **within the ~** dans les délais; **2** (maximum duration) durée *f* maximum.

timely *adj* opportun.

time off *n* (leave) congé *m*; (free time) temps *m* libre.

timer *n* (on light) minuterie *f*; (for cooking) minuteur *m*.

time: **~-scale** *n* période *f* (de temps); **~share** *n* (house) maison *f*/appartement *m* en multipropriété; **~span** *n* durée *f*; **~table** *n* (schedule) emploi *m* du temps; (for plans, negotiations) calendrier *m*; (for buses, trains) horaire *m*.

timid *adj* [*person, decision, reform*] timide; [*animal*] craintif/-ive.

timidity *n* timidité *f*.

timing *n* **1** (gen) **the ~ of the announcement was unfortunate** le moment choisi pour la déclaration était inopportun; **2** (Aut) réglage *m* de l'allumage; **3** (Mus) sens *m* du rythme.

tin I *n* **1** (metal) étain *m*; **2** (GB) (can) boîte *f* (de conserve); **3** (container) (for biscuits, cake) boîte *f*; (for paint) pot *m*; (for baking) moule *m*; (for roasting) plat *m* (à rôtir).
II *noun modifier* [*mug, bath*] en étain.
III **tinned** *pp adj* (GB) [*meat, fruit*] en conserve, en boîte.

tin: **~ can** *n* boîte *f* en fer-blanc; **~ foil** *n* papier *m* (d')aluminium.

tinge I *n* nuance *f*.
II *vtr* teinter (**with** de).

tingle I *n* (physical) picotement *m*; (psychological) frisson *m*.
II *vi* (physically) picoter; (psychologically) frissonner.

tinker *vi* **to ~ with** bricoler [*car*]; faire des retouches à [*document*].

tinkle I *n* tintement *m*.
II *vi* tinter.

tin: **~ opener** *n* (GB) ouvre-boîtes *m inv*; **~pot**○ *adj* (GB) [*dictatorship*] de pacotille.

tinsel *n* (decoration) guirlandes *fpl*; (figurative, derogatory) clinquant *m*.

tint I *n* (trace) nuance *f*; (pale colour) teinte *f*; (hair colour) shampooing *m* colorant.
II *vtr* teinter; **to get one's hair ~ed** se faire faire un shampooing colorant.
III **tinted** *pp adj* [*colour*] teinté; [*glass, spectacles*] fumé; [*hair*] teint.

tiny *adj* [*person, object, house*] tout petit; [*improvement*] très faible.

tip I *n* **1** (of stick, sword, pen, shoe, spire) pointe *f*; (of branch, leaf, shoot, tail, feather) extrémité *f*; (of finger, nose, tongue) bout *m*; (protective) (on shoe heel) bout *m* ferré; **2** (gratuity) pourboire *m*; **3** (practical hint) truc○ *m*, conseil *m*; (in betting) tuyau○ *m*.
II *vtr* **1** (tilt) incliner; (pour) verser; (dump) déverser [*waste, rubbish*]; **to ~ the scales** (figurative) faire pencher la balance; **2** (predict) **to ~ sb/sth to win** prédire que qn/qch va gagner; **3** donner un pourboire à [*waiter, driver*].
III *vi* **1** (tilt) s'incliner; **2** (figurative) [*balance, scales*] pencher (**in sb's favour** en favour de qn).
■ **tip off**: **~ off [sb]**, **~ [sb] off** avertir.
■ **tip over**: **~ over [sth]**, **~ [sth] over** faire basculer [*chair*]; renverser [*bucket, pile*].

tiptoe I *n* **on ~** sur la pointe des pieds.
II *vi* marcher sur la pointe des pieds.

tire I *n* (US) pneu *m*.
II *vtr* fatiguer.
III *vi* **1** (get tired) se fatiguer; **2** (get bored) **to ~ of** se lasser de.
■ **tire out**: **~ [sb] out** épuiser; **to be ~d out** être éreinté.

tired *adj* **1** (weary) [*person, face, legs*] fatigué; [*voice*] las/lasse; **2** (bored) **to be ~ of sth/of doing** en avoir assez de qch/de faire; **to grow ~ of sth/of doing** se lasser de qch/de faire.

tiredness *n* fatigue *f*.

tireless *adj* [*person*] inlassable, infatigable; [*efforts*] constant.

tirelessly *adv* sans relâche.

tiresome *adj* [*person, habit*] agaçant; [*problem, duty*] fastidieux/-ieuse.

tiring *adj* fatigant (**to do** de faire).

tissue *n* **1** (handkerchief) mouchoir *m* en papier; **2** (also **~ paper**) papier *m* de soie; **3** (Anat, Bot) tissu *m*; **4** (figurative) tissu *m*; **a ~ of lies** un tissu de mensonges.

tit *n* (Zool) mésange *f*.
IDIOMS **~ for tat** un prêté pour un rendu; **~ for tat killings** meurtres en représailles (d'autres meurtres).

titbit *n* (GB) (of food) gâterie *f*; (of gossip) cancan○ *m*.

titillating *adj* émoustillant.

title I *n* titre *m*.
II **titles** *n pl* (in film) générique *m*.
III *vtr* intituler [*book, play*].

titled *adj* titré.

Talking about Time

❑ For time by the clock, ▶ 554; for days of the week, months and dates, ▶ 584.

How long?

Note the various ways of translating ***take*** into French:

how long does it take?	= combien de temps faut-il?
it took me a week	= cela m'a pris / il m'a fallu une semaine
it'll take at least a year	= il faudra au moins un an / une bonne année
it'll only take a moment	= c'est l'affaire de quelques instants

Use ***dans*** for ***in*** when something is seen as happening in the future:

*I'll be there **in** an hour*	= je serai là **dans** une heure
***in** three weeks' time*	= **dans** trois semaines

Use ***en*** for ***in*** when expressing the time something took or will take:

*he did it **in** an hour*	= il l'a fait **en** une heure

The commonest translation of ***for*** in the 'how long' sense is ***pendant***:

*I worked in the factory **for** a year*	= j'ai travaillé à l'usine **pendant** un an

But use ***pour*** to translate ***for*** when the length of time is seen as being still to come:

*we're here **for** a month*	= nous sommes là **pour** un mois

And use ***depuis*** to translate ***for*** when the action began in the past and is still going on:

*she has been here **for** a week*	= elle est ici **depuis** une semaine
*I haven't seen her **for** years*	= je ne l'ai pas vue **depuis** des années

Note the use of ***de*** when expressing how long something lasted or will last:

an eight-hour day	= une journée **de** huit heures

When?

when did it happen?	= quand est-ce que c'est arrivé?
a month ago	= il y a un mois
a week ago yesterday	= il y a eu huit jours hier
when will you see him?	= quand est-ce que tu le verras?
in a few days	= dans quelques jours

(See above, the phrases with ***in*** translated by ***dans***.)

a month from tomorrow	= dans un mois demain

How often?

how often does it happen?	= cela arrive tous les combien?
every year	= tous les ans
five times a day	= cinq fois par jour
once every three months	= une fois tous les trois mois

How much an hour (etc)?

*how much do you get **an** hour?*	= combien gagnez-vous **de l'**heure?
*to be paid $20 **an** hour*	= être payé 20 dollars **de l'**heure
*to be paid **by the** hour*	= être payé **à l'**heure
*how much do you get **a** week / a month?*	= combien gagnez-vous **par** semaine / **par** mois?
*$3,000 **a** month*	= 3 000 dollars **par** mois

Forms in -ée: an / année, matin / matinée etc.

The ***-ée*** forms are often used to express a rather vague amount of time passing or spent in something, and so tend to give a subjective slant to what is being said, as in:

a long day / evening / year	= une longue journée / soirée / année
a whole day	= toute une journée / une journée entière

When an exact number is specified, the shorter forms are generally used, as in:

it lasted six days	= cela a duré six jours

title: **~holder** *n* tenant/-e *m/f* du titre; **~ role** *n* rôle *m* titre.

titter I *n* ricanement *m*.
II *vi* ricaner.

titular *adj* [*president, head*] nominal; [*professor, status*] titulaire.

to ▶917, ▶554 **I** *infinitive particle* **1** (expressing purpose) pour; **to do sth ~ impress one's friends** faire qch pour impressionner ses amis; **2** (linking consecutive acts) **he looked up ~ see**... en levant les yeux, il a vu...; **3** (after superlatives) à; **the youngest ~ do** le or la plus jeune à faire; **4** (avoiding repetition of verb) **'did you go?'—'no I promised not ~'** 'tu y es allé?'—'non j'avais promis de ne pas le faire'; **'are you staying? '—'I want ~ but...'** 'tu restes?'—'j'aimerais bien mais...'; **5** (following impersonal verb) **it is difficult ~ do sth** il est difficile de faire qch; **it's difficult ~ understand** c'est difficile à comprendre.
II *prep* **1** (in direction of) à [*shops, school*]; (with purpose of visiting) chez [*doctor's*]; (towards) vers; **she's gone ~ Mary's** elle est partie chez Mary; **to Paris** à Paris; **to Spain** en Espagne; **~ town** en ville; **the road ~ the village** la route qui mène au village; **trains ~ and from Paris** les trains à destination et en provenance de Paris; **turned ~ the wall** tourné vers le mur; **with his back ~ them** en leur tournant le dos; **2** (up to) jusqu'à; **~ the end/this day** jusqu'à la fin/ce jour; **3** (in telling time) **ten (minutes) ~ three** trois heures moins dix; **it's five ~** il est moins cinq; **4** (introducing direct or indirect object) [*give, offer*] à; **give the book ~ Sophie** donne le livre à Sophie; **be nice ~ your brother** sois gentil avec ton frère; **~ me it's just a minor problem** pour moi ce n'est qu'un problème mineur; **5** (in toasts, dedications) à; **~ prosperity** à la prospérité; **~ our dear son** (on tombstone) à notre cher fils; **6** (in accordance with) **is it ~ your taste?** c'est à ton goût?; **to dance ~ the music** danser sur la musique; **7** (in relationships, comparisons) **to win by three goals ~ two** gagner par trois buts à deux; **next door ~ the school** à côté de l'école; **8** (showing accuracy) **three weeks ~ the day** trois semaines jour pour jour; **~ scale** à l'échelle; **~ time** à l'heure; **9** (showing reason) **to invite sb ~ dinner** inviter qn à dîner; **~ this end** à cette fin; **10** (belonging to) de; **the key ~ the safe** la clé du coffre; **a room ~ myself** une chambre pour moi tout seul; **personal assistant ~ the director** assistant du directeur; **there's no sense ~ it** ça n'a aucun sens; **11** [*tied*] à; [*pinned*] à [*noticeboard*]; sur [*lapel, dress*]; **12** (showing reaction) à; **~ his surprise/dismay** à sa grande surprise/consternation.
IDIOMS **that's all there is ~ it** (it's easy) c'est aussi simple que ça; (that's that) un point c'est tout; **there's nothing ~ it** ce n'est pas compliqué.

toad *n* crapaud *m*.

toadstool *n* champignon *m* vénéneux.

to and fro *adv* [*swing*] d'avant en arrière; **to go ~** [*person*] aller et venir.

toast I *n* **1** (bread) toast *m*; **a slice of ~** un toast; **2** (drink) toast *m*; **to drink a ~** lever son verre.
II *vtr* **1** faire griller [*bread*]; **2** porter un toast à [*person, success*].

toaster *n* grille-pain *m inv*.

tobacco *n* tabac *m*.

toboggan *n* luge *f*, toboggan *m*.

today ▶584 **I** *n* aujourd'hui *m*; **~ is Monday** (aujourd'hui) nous sommes lundi.
II *adv* aujourd'hui; (nowadays) de nos jours; **~ week** dans une semaine aujourd'hui; **a week ago ~** il y a une semaine aujourd'hui; **later ~** plus tard dans la journée.

toddler *n* bébé *m* (*qui fait ses premiers pas*).

toe ▶523 *n* **1** (Anat) orteil *m*; **big/little ~** gros/petit orteil; **2** (of sock, shoe) bout *m*.
IDIOMS **to ~ the line** marcher droit; **from top to ~** de la tête aux pieds.

toffee *n* caramel *m* (au beurre).

together I *adv* **1** ensemble; **to get back ~ again** se remettre ensemble; **to be close ~** être rapprochés; **she's cleverer than all the rest of them put ~** elle est plus intelligente que tous les autres réunis; **they belong ~** (objects) ils vont ensemble; (people) ils sont faits l'un pour l'autre; **the talks brought the two sides closer ~** les négociations ont rapproché les deux parties; **2** (at the same time) à la fois; **all my troubles seem to come ~** tous mes ennuis semblent arriver en même temps.
II together with *phr* (as well as) ainsi que; (in the company of) avec.
IDIOMS **to get one's act ~** s'organiser.

togetherness *n* (in team, friendship) camaraderie *f*; (in family, couple) intimité *f*.

toil I *n* labeur *m*.
II *vi* **1** (also **toil away**) (work) peiner; **2** (struggle) **to ~ up the hill** monter péniblement la côte.

toilet *n* toilettes *fpl*; **public ~(s)** toilettes publiques.

toilet: **~ bag** *n* trousse *f* de toilette; **~ paper**, **~ tissue** *n* papier *m* toilette; **~ roll** *n* (roll) rouleau *m* de papier toilette; (tissue) papier *m* toilette; **~ seat** *n* lunette *f* de WC.

toilet-train *vtr* **to ~ a child** apprendre à un enfant à être propre.

token I *n* **1** (for machine, phone) jeton *m*; **2** (voucher) bon *m*; **book/record ~** chèque-cadeau *m* pour livre/pour disque; **3** témoignage *m*; **as a ~ of** en signe de.
II *adj* symbolique; **to make a ~ gesture** faire un geste pour la forme.

tolerable *adj* (bearable) tolérable; (adequate) acceptable.

tolerance *n* (gen, Med) tolérance *f*.

tolerant *adj* tolérant.

tolerate *vtr* (permit) tolérer; (put up with) supporter.

toll I *n* **1 death ~** nombre *m* de victimes (**from** de); **2** (levy) (on road, bridge) péage *m*; **3** (of bell) son *m*; (for funeral) glas *m*.
II *vtr* sonner [*bell*].

to

❑ This dictionary contains usage notes and appendices on such topics as *The Clock, Length and Weight Measurements, Games and Sports* etc. Many of these use the preposition ***to***. For the index to these notes ▶ **1024**.

As a preposition

◆ When ***to*** is used as a preposition with verbs of movement (*go, travel* etc), it is often translated by ***à*** (*à Paris, à Londres*), but remember to use ***en*** with feminine countries (*en France*) and ***au*** with masculine countries (*au Portugal*) ▶ **574**.

Remember when using ***à*** in French that ***à*** + *le* always becomes ***au***:

***to the** office*	= **au** bureau

and ***à*** + *les* always becomes ***aux***:

***to the** shops*	= **aux** magasins

◆ When ***to*** is used as a preposition with verbs such as *speak, give, say* etc, it is usually translated by ***à***:

*give the book **to** Jane*	= donne le livre **à** Jane
*I'll speak **to** the headmistress*	= je vais parler à la directrice
*she said it **to** my father*	= elle l'a dit **à** mon père
*show it **to** the policeman*	= montre-le **à** l'agent
*I pointed it out **to** the stewardess*	= je l'ai signalé **à** l'hôtesse
*give the ball **to** the little boy*	= donne le ballon **au*** petit garçon
*we gave it **to** the children*	= nous l'avons donné **aux*** enfants

* Remember that ***à*** + *le* = ***au*** and ***à*** + *les* = **aux**

◆ When ***to*** is used as a preposition with personal pronouns (*me, you, him, her, us, them*), the two words (*preposition* + *pronoun*) are translated by ***me/te/lui/lui/nous/vous/leur***:

*she gave it **to them***	= elle le **leur** a donné
*I'll say it **to her***	= je vais le **lui** dire

As part of an infinitive

◆ When ***to*** forms the infinitive of a verb taken alone, it needs no translation:

***to** go* = aller

However, when ***to*** is used as part of an infinitive giving the meaning ***in order to***, it is translated by ***pour***:

*he's gone into town **to buy** a shirt*	= il est parti en ville **pour acheter** une chemise

◆ ***to*** is also used as part of an infinitive after certain adjectives: ***easy to read*** etc. Here ***to*** is usually translated by ***à***:

*her writing is easy **to** read*	= son écriture est facile **à** lire

However, when the infinitive has an object, ***to*** is usually translated by ***de***:

*it's easy **to** lose one's way*	= il est facile **de** perdre son chemin

❑ To find out more about this point, see the note at ***it*** ▶ **699**.

◆ ***to*** is also used as part of an infinitive after certain verbs: ***she told me to wash my hands, I'll help him to tidy the room*** etc. Here the translation, usually either ***à*** or ***de***, depends on the verb used in French. To find the correct translation, consult the appropriate verb entry: **tell, help** etc. For all other uses, see the entry **to**.

III *vi* [*bell*] sonner.
IDIOMS **to take a heavy ~** (on lives) faire beaucoup de victimes; (on industry, environment) causer beaucoup de dégâts; **to take its** or **their ~** faire des ravages.

toll: **~booth** *n* poste *m* de péage; **~ bridge** *n* pont *m* à péage; **~ call** *n* (US) communication *f* interurbaine.

tomato I *n* tomate *f*.
II *noun modifier* [*puree*] de tomate; [*juice, salad*] de tomates; [*soup*] à la tomate; **~ sauce** sauce *f* tomate.

tomb *n* tombeau *m*.

tomboy *n* garçon *m* manqué.

tombstone *n* pierre *f* tombale.

tomcat *n* matou *m*.

tomorrow ▶584, 584 **I** *n* demain *m*; **I'll do it by ~** je le ferai d'ici demain; **~ will be the tenth of May** demain nous serons le 10 mai.
II *adv* demain; **see you ~!** à demain!; **~ week** demain en huit; **a week ago ~** il y aura une semaine demain; **early ~** tôt dans la journée de demain.
IDIOMS **~ is another day** demain il fera jour.

tomorrow: **~ afternoon** *n, adv* demain après-midi; **~ evening** *n, adv* demain soir; **~ morning** *n, adv* demain matin.

ton ▶738 *n* **1** (in weight) (GB) (also **gross ~** or **long ~**) ≈ *1016 kg*; (US) (also **net ~** or **short ~**) ≈ *907 kg*; **metric ~** tonne *f*; **2**○ (a lot) **~s of** des tas de○ [*food, paper, bands*].

tone I *n* **1** (gen, Mus) (quality of sound) timbre *m*; (on phone) tonalité *f*; **2** ton *m*; **his ~ of voice** son ton; **in angry ~s** avec colère; **3** (of letter, speech, meeting) ton *m*; **to set the ~** donner le ton à (**for** à); **to lower the ~ of** rabaisser le niveau de [*conversation*]; dégrader l'image de [*area*]; **4** (colour) ton *m*; **5** (firmness of muscle) tonus *m*.
II *vtr* (also **~ up**) tonifier [*body, muscles*].
III *vi* (also **~in**) (blend) [*colours*] s'harmoniser.
■ **tone down**: **~ down [sth]**, **~ [sth] down** atténuer [*colours, criticism*]; adoucir le ton de [*letter, statement*].

tone-deaf *adj* **to be ~** ne pas avoir l'oreille musicale.

tongs *n pl* (for coal) pincettes *fpl*; (in laboratory, for sugar) pince *f*.

tongue *n* **1** (gen, Anat, Culin) langue *f*; **to stick one's ~ out at sb** tirer la langue à qn; **to lose one's ~** (figurative) avaler sa langue; **2** (flap on shoe) languette *f*; **3** (language) langue *f*; **native ~** langue *f* d'origine.
IDIOMS **I have his name on the tip of my ~** j'ai son nom sur le bout de la langue; **to loosen sb's ~** délier la langue de qn; **a slip of the ~** un lapsus; **watch your ~!** surveille tes paroles!

tongue: **~-in-cheek** *adj, adv* au deuxième degré; **~-tied** *adj* muet/-ette; **~-twister** *n*: *phrase amusante pour exercice de diction*.

tonic I *n* **1** (also **~ water**) eau *f* tonique; **a gin and ~** un gin tonic; **2** (Med) remontant *m*; **to be a ~ for sb** (figurative) remonter le moral de qn.
II *adj* tonique.

tonight I *n* **~ will be overcast** le temps sera couvert ce soir.
II *adv* (this evening) ce soir; (after bedtime) cette nuit.

tonne ▶738 *n* tonne *f*.

tonsil *n* amygdale *f*; **to have one's ~s out** se faire opérer des amygdales.

tonsillitis ▶686 *n* amygdalite *f*.

too *adv*

■ **Note** When *too* means *also* it is generally translated by *aussi*: *me too* = moi aussi; *can I have some too?* = est-ce que je peux en avoir aussi?
– When *too* means *to an excessive degree* it is translated by *trop*: *too dangerous* = trop dangereux.

1 (also) aussi; **have you been to India ~?** (like me) est-ce que toi aussi tu es allé en Inde?; (as well as other countries) est-ce que tu es allé en Inde aussi?; **2** (excessively) trop; **~ big** trop grand; **~ many/~ few people** trop de/trop peu de gens; **I ate ~ much** j'ai trop mangé; **he was in ~ much of a hurry to talk** il était trop pressé pour parler; **it was ~ little ~ late** c'était trop peu trop tard; **you're ~ kind!** vous êtes trop aimable!; **I'm not ~ sure about that** je n'en suis pas si sûr.

tool I *n* (gen, Comput) outil *m*; **a set of ~s** un jeu d'outils.
II *vtr* travailler, repousser [*leather*].

tool: **~box** *n* boîte *f* à outils; **~ house** *n* (US) = **tool shed**; **~ kit** *n* trousse *f* à outils; **~ shed** *n* cabane *f* à outils.

tooth I *n* dent *f*; **set of teeth** (false) dentier *m*; **to cut one's teeth** [*baby*] faire or percer ses dents; **to cut one's teeth on** (figurative) se faire les dents sur.
II **-toothed** *combining form* **fine-/wide-~ed comb** peigne *m* fin/à dents larges.
IDIOMS **to get one's teeth into sth** s'investir (à fond) dans qch; **to lie through one's teeth** mentir effrontément.

toothache *n* mal *m* de dents; **to have ~** (GB) or **a ~** avoir mal aux dents.

tooth: **~brush** *n* brosse *f* à dents; **~ decay** *n* carie *f* dentaire; **~paste** *n* dentifrice *m*; **~pick** *n* cure-dents *m inv*.

top I *n* **1** (of page, ladder, stairs, wall) haut *m*; (of list) tête *f*; (of mountain, hill) sommet *m*; (of garden, field) (autre) bout *m*; (of vegetable) fane *f*; (of box, cake) dessus *m*; (surface) surface *f*; **at the ~ of** en haut de [*page, stairs, street, scale*]; au sommet de [*hill*]; en tête de [*list*]; **at the ~ of the building** au dernier étage de l'immeuble; **at the ~ of the table** à la place d'honneur; **to be at the ~ of one's list** (figurative) venir en tête de sa liste; **to be at the ~ of the agenda** être une priorité; **2** (highest position) **to aim for the ~** viser haut; **to get to** or **make it to the ~** réussir; **to be ~ of the class** être le premier/la première de la classe; **to be ~ of the bill** être la tête d'affiche; **3** (cap, lid) (of pen) capuchon *m*; (of bottle) bouchon *m*; (with serrated

edge) capsule *f*; (of paint-tin, saucepan) couvercle *m*; **4** (item of clothing) haut *m*; **5** (toy) toupie *f*.
II *adj* **1** (highest) [*step, storey*] dernier/-ière; [*bunk*] de haut; [*button, shelf*] du haut; [*layer, lip*] supérieur; [*speed*] maximum; [*concern, priority*] majeur; **in the ~ left-hand corner** en haut à gauche; **to pay the ~ price for sth** [*buyer*] acheter qch au prix fort; **to get ~ marks** (Sch) avoir dix sur dix or vingt sur vingt; **2** (furthest away) [*field, house*] du bout; **3** (leading) [*adviser, politician*] de haut niveau; [*job*] élevé; [*wine, restaurant*] haut de gamme; **to be in the ~ three** être dans les trois premiers.
III *vtr* **1** (head) être en tête de [*charts, polls*]; **2** (exceed) dépasser [*sum, figure*]; **3** (finish off) compléter (**with** par); (Culin) recouvrir [*cake*].
IV on top of *phr* **1** (on) sur [*cupboard, fridge, layer*]; **2** (in addition to) en plus de [*salary, workload*].
IDIOMS **on ~ of all this, to ~ it all** par-dessus le marché°; **from ~ to bottom** de fond en comble; **to be over the ~, to be OTT**° [*behaviour, reaction*] être exagéré; **to be/stay on ~** avoir/garder le dessus; **to be ~ dog** être le chef; **to come out on ~** (win) l'emporter; (survive) s'en sortir; **to feel on ~ of the world** être aux anges; **to shout at the ~ of one's voice** crier à tue-tête.
■ **top up**: **~ up [sth], ~ [sth] up** remplir (à nouveau) [*tank, glass*].

topaz *n* topaze *f*.

top: **~ class** *adj* de premier ordre; **~ hat** *n* haut-de-forme *m*; **~-heavy** *adj* [*structure, object*] lourd du haut.

topic *n* (of conversation, conference) sujet *m*; (of essay, research) thème *m*.

topical *adj* d'actualité.

topless *adj* [*model*] aux seins nus.

top: **~-level** *adj* [*talks, negotiations*] au plus haut niveau; **~ management** *n* (haute) direction *f*.

topography *n* topographie *f*.

topping *n* (of jam, cream) nappage *m*.

topple I *vtr* renverser.
II *vi* (sway) [*vase, pile of books*] vaciller; (fall) (also **~ over**) [*vase, person*] basculer; [*pile of books*] s'effondrer; **to ~ over the edge of** tomber de [*cliff, table*].

top: **~-ranking** *adj* important; **~ secret** *adj* ultrasecret; **~soil** *n* couche *f* arable.

topsy-turvy° *adj, adv* sens dessus dessous.

torch I *n* **1** (burning) flambeau *m*, torche *f*; **2** (GB) (flashlight) lampe *f* de poche.
II *vtr* mettre le feu à [*building*].

torchlight I *n* **by ~** (burning torches) à la lueur des flambeaux; (GB) (electric) à la lueur d'une lampe électrique.
II *noun modifier* (also **torchlit**) [*vigil*] aux flambeaux; **~ procession** retraite *f* aux flambeaux.

torment I *n* supplice *m*; **to suffer ~s** souffrir le martyre.
II *vtr* tourmenter.
III *v refl* **to ~ oneself** se tourmenter.

tormentor *n* persécuteur/-trice *m/f*.

torn *adj* déchiré.

tornado *n* tornade *f*.

torpedo I *n* torpille *f*.
II *vtr* torpiller.

torpid *adj* torpide.

torrent *n* torrent *m*; (figurative) flot *m*.

torrential *adj* torrentiel/-ielle.

torrid *adj* torride.

torso *n* torse *m*.

tortoise *n* tortue *f*.

tortuous *adj* tortueux/-euse.

torture I *n* torture *f*; (figurative) supplice *m*.
II *vtr* torturer; (figurative) tourmenter.

Tory *n* (GB) Tory *mf*, conservateur/-trice *m/f*.

toss I *n* **1** (throw) jet *m*; **a ~ of the head** un mouvement brusque de la tête; **2 to decide sth on the ~ of a coin** décider qch à pile ou face.
II *vtr* **1** (throw) lancer [*ball, stick, dice*]; faire sauter [*pancake*]; tourner [*salad*]; **to ~ sth into the air** lancer qch en l'air; **to ~ sb sth** lancer qch à qn; **to ~ a coin** jouer à pile ou face; **2** (throw back) [*animal*] secouer [*head, mane*]; **to ~ one's head** [*person*] rejeter la tête en arrière; **3** [*horse*] désarçonner [*rider*]; **4** [*wind*] agiter [*branches, leaves*].
III *vi* **1** [*person*] se retourner; **I ~ed and turned all night** je me suis tourné et retourné toute la nuit; **2** (flip a coin) tirer à pile ou face; **to ~ for first turn** tirer le premier tour à pile ou face.

toss-up° *n* **let's have a ~ to decide** décidons à pile ou face; **it's a ~ between a pizza and a sandwich** il faut choisir entre une pizza et un sandwich.

tot *n* **1**° (toddler) tout/-e petit/-e enfant *m/f*; **2** (GB) (of whisky, rum) petite dose *f*.
■ **tot up** (GB): ¶ **~ up** [*person*] additionner; ¶ **~ up [sth], ~ [sth] up** faire le total de [qch].

total I *n* total *m*; **in ~** au total.
II *adj* **1** [*cost, amount, profit*] total; **2** (complete) [*effect*] global; [*disaster, eclipse*] total; [*ignorance*] complet/-ète.
III *vtr* **1** (add up) additionner [*figures*]; **2** [*bill*] se monter à [*sum*].

totalitarian *n, adj* totalitaire (*mf*).

totally *adv* [*blind, deaf*] complètement; [*unacceptable, convinced*] totalement; [*agree, change, new, different*] entièrement.

totem *n* (pole) totem *m*; (symbol) symbole *m*.

totter *vi* [*person, regime, government*] chanceler; [*drunk person*] tituber; [*baby*] trébucher; [*pile of books, building*] chanceler.

tottering *adj* [*person, pile of books, regime*] chancelant; [*step*] mal assuré.

touch I *n* **1** contact *m* (physique); **the ~ of her hand** le contact de sa main; **at the slightest ~** (of button) à la moindre pression; **2** (tactile sense) toucher *m*; **3** (style, skill) (of artist, writer) touche *f*; (of musician) toucher *m*; **to lose one's ~** perdre la main; **this house lacks the feminine ~** on voit qu'il n'y a pas de femme dans cette maison; **that's a clever ~!** ça, c'est génial!; ▶ **finishing touch**; **4** (little) **a ~** un

petit peu; **there's a ~ of class/of genius about her** elle a quelque chose d'élégant/de génial; **a ~ of garlic** une pointe d'ail; **5** (communication) **to get/stay in ~ with** se mettre/rester en contact avec; **he's out of ~ with reality** il est déconnecté de la réalité; **6** (Sport) touche *f*.
II *vtr* **1** toucher; (interfere with) toucher à; **to ~ sb on the shoulder** toucher l'épaule de qn; **to ~ ground** atterrir; **I never ~ alcohol** je ne prends jamais d'alcool; **2** (affect) toucher; (adversely) affecter; (as matter of concern) concerner; **we were most ~ed** nous avons été très touchés.
III *vi* [*wires, hands*] se toucher; **'do not ~'** 'ne pas toucher'.
IDIOMS **to be a soft ~**○ être un pigeon○; **it's ~ and go whether he'll make it through the night** il risque fort de ne pas passer la nuit.
■ **touch down 1** [*plane*] atterrir; **2** (Sport) (in rugby) marquer un essai.
■ **touch (up)on [sth]** effleurer [*problem, topic*].

touchdown *n* **1** (by plane) atterrissage *m*; **2** (Sport) essai *m*.

touched *adj* **1** (emotionally) touché; **2**○ (mad) dérangé○.

touching *adj* touchant.

touchingly *adv* de façon touchante.

touch: **~ line** *n* (Sport) ligne *f* de touche; **~stone** *n* pierre *f* de touche; **~-type** *vi* taper au toucher; **~-typing** *n* dactylographie *f* au toucher.

touchy *adj* susceptible (**about** sur la question de).

tough I *adj* **1** [*businessman*] coriace; [*criminal*] endurci; [*policy, measure, law*] sévère; [*opposition, competition*] rude; **a ~ guy** un dur○; **to get ~ with sb** se montrer dur avec qn; **~ luck!** manque de pot○!; (unsympathetically) tant pis pour toi!; **2** (difficult) difficile; **3** (robust) [*person, animal*] robuste; [*plant, material*] résistant; **4** [*meat*] coriace; **5** (rough) [*area, school*] dur.
II○ *excl* tant pis pour toi!

toughen *vtr* renforcer [*leather, plastic*]; tremper [*glass, steel*]; durcir [*skin*]; (also **~ up**) endurcir [*person*]; renforcer [*law*].

toughness *n* **1** (of businessman, criminal, life) dureté *f*; (of law, measure) sévérité *f*; **2** (robustness) (of person, plant) résistance *f*; (of material) robustesse *f*; **3** (of meat) dureté *f*; **4** (of work, question) difficulté *f*.

toupee *n* postiche *m*.

tour I *n* **1** (of country) circuit *m*; (of city) tour *m*; (of building) visite *f*; (trip in bus) excursion *f*; **to go on a ~ of** visiter [*one thing*]; faire le circuit de [*several things*]; **a ~ of inspection** une tournée d'inspection; **2** (by team, band, theatre company) tournée *f*.
II *vtr* **1** visiter [*building, country, gallery*]; **2** [*band, team*] être en tournée en [*country*]; [*theatre production*] tourner en [*country*].
III *vi* **1 to go ~ing** faire du tourisme; **2** [*orchestra, play, team*] être en tournée.

touring I *n* **1** (by tourist) tourisme *m*; **2** (by team, theatre company, band) tournée *f*.
II *adj* [*exhibition*] itinérant; [*company, show*] en tournée; [*production*] de tournée.

tourism *n* tourisme *m*.

tourist I *n* touriste *mf*.
II *noun modifier* [*resort, season*] touristique; **the ~ trade** le tourisme.

tourist: **~ class** *n* (on flight) classe *f* touriste; **~ (information) office** *n* (in town) syndicat *m* d'initiative; (national organization) office *m* du tourisme; **~ trap** *n* piège *m* à touristes.

tournament *n* tournoi *m*.

tousle I *vtr* ébouriffer [*hair*].
II **tousled** *pp adj* [*hair*] ébouriffé; [*person, appearance*] débraillé.

tout I *n* **1** (GB) (selling tickets) revendeur *m* de billets au marché noir; **2** (soliciting custom) racoleur/-euse○ *m/f* (derogatory); **3** (racing) vendeur *m* de tuyaux.
II *vtr* (GB) (illegally) revendre [qch] au marché noir [*tickets*].

tow I *n* (Aut) **to be on ~** être en remorque; **to give sb a ~** remorquer qn.
II *vtr* remorquer, tracter [*trailer, caravan*].
■ **tow away**: **~ away [sth], ~ [sth] away** [*police*] emmener [qch] à la fourrière; [*recovery service*] remorquer.

toward(s) *prep*

■ **Note** When *towards* is used to talk about direction or position, it is generally translated by *vers*: *she ran toward(s) him* = elle a couru vers lui.
– When *toward(s)* is used to mean *in relation to*, it is translated by *envers*: *his attitude toward(s) his parents* = son attitude envers ses parents. For further examples, see the entry below.

---

1 vers; **~ the east** vers l'est; **he was standing with his back ~ me** il me tournait le dos; **~ evening** vers le soir; **~ the end of** vers la fin de [*month, life*]; **2** envers; **to be friendly/hostile ~ sb** se montrer cordial/hostile envers qn; **3** (as contribution) **the money will go ~ a new car** l'argent servira à payer une nouvelle voiture.

tow bar *n* (on car) crochet *m* d'attelage; (on recovery vehicle) barre *f* de remorquage.

towel *n* serviette *f* (de toilette); ▶ **bath towel, tea towel**.
IDIOMS **to throw** or **chuck**○ **in the ~** jeter l'éponge.

towel: **~ rail** *n* porte-serviettes *m inv*; **~ ring** *n* anneau *m* porte-serviettes.

tower I *n* tour *f*.
II *vi* **to ~ above** or **over** dominer [*village, street*].
IDIOMS **to be a ~ of strength** être solide comme un roc.

tower block *n* (GB) tour *f* (d'habitation).

towering *adj* [*building, cliffs*] imposant; [*performance*] excellent.

town *n* ville *f*; **to go into ~** aller en ville.
IDIOMS **to go to ~ on** ne pas lésiner sur [*decor, catering*]; exploiter [qch] à fond [*story,*

scandal]; **he's the talk of the ~** on ne parle que de lui.

town: **~ centre** (GB), **~ center** (US) *n* centre-ville *m*; **~ council** *n* (GB) conseil *m* municipal; **~ hall** *n* mairie *f*; **~ house** *n* petite maison *f* en centre ville; (mansion) hôtel *m* particulier; **~ planning** *n* (GB) urbanisme *m*; **~ship** *n* commune *f*; (in South Africa) township *m*; **~speople** *n pl* citadins *mpl*.

tow: **~path** *n* chemin *m* de halage; **~ truck** *n* dépanneuse *f*.

toxic *adj* toxique.

toxic waste *n* déchets *mpl* toxiques.

toxin *n* toxine *f*.

toy I *n* jouet *m*.
II *noun modifier* [*plane, train*] miniature; [*car, boat*] petit (*before n*); [*gun*] d'enfant.
III *vi* **to ~ with** jouer avec [*object, feelings*]; caresser [*idea*]; **to ~ with one's food** chipoter.

toyshop *n* magasin *m* de jouets.

trace I *n* **1** (evidence) trace *f*; **there is no ~ of** il ne reste aucune trace de; **2** (hint) (of irony, flavour, garlic) soupçon *m*; (of accent) pointe *f*; (of chemical, drug) trace *f*.
II *vtr* **1** (locate) retrouver [*person, weapon, car*]; dépister [*fault*]; déterminer [*cause*]; **to ~ sb to** retrouver la trace de qn dans [*hiding place*]; **the call was ~d to a London number** on a pu établir que le coup de téléphone venait d'un numéro à Londres; **2** (also **~ back**) faire remonter [*origins, ancestry*] (**to** à); **3** (draw) tracer; (copy) décalquer [*map, outline*].

tracing paper *n* papier-calque *m*.

track I *n* **1** (print) (of animal, person, vehicle) traces *fpl*; **2** (course, trajectory) (of person) trace *f*; (of missile, aircraft, storm) trajectoire *f*; **to cover one's ~s** brouiller les pistes; **to be on the wrong ~** faire fausse route; **to keep ~ of** [*person*] se tenir au courant de [*developments, events*]; suivre le fil de [*conversation*]; [*police*] suivre les mouvements de [*criminal*]; [*computer*] tenir [qch] à jour [*bank account, figures*]; **to lose ~ of** perdre de vue [*friend*]; perdre la trace de [*document, aircraft, suspect*]; perdre le fil de [*conversation*]; **to lose ~ of (the) time** perdre la notion du temps; **3** (path, road) sentier *m*, chemin *m*; (Sport) piste *f*; **(motor-)racing ~** (open-air) circuit *m*; (enclosed) autodrome *m*; **cycling ~** vélodrome *m*; **dog-racing ~** cynodrome *m*; **4** (railtrack) voie *f* ferrée; (US) (platform) quai *m*; **to leave the ~(s)** [*train*] dérailler; **5** (song on record, tape, CD) morceau *m*; **6** (of tank, tractor) chenille *f*; **7** (US Sch) (stream) groupe *m* de niveau.
II *noun modifier* (Sport) [*event, race*] de vitesse.
III *vtr* suivre la trace de [*person, animal*]; suivre la trajectoire de [*rocket, plane*].
■ **track down**: **~ [sb/sth] down, ~ down [sb/sth]** retrouver [*person, object*].

track and field events *n pl* épreuves *f* d'athlétisme.

tracker dog *n* chien *m* policier.

track record *n* **to have a good ~** avoir de bons antécédents; [*professional person*] avoir de bons antécédents professionnels; **a candidate with a proven ~ in sales** un candidat ayant une bonne expérience commerciale.

track: **~ shoe** *n* chaussure *f* de course à pointes; **~suit** *n* survêtement *m*.

tract *n* (Anat) **digestive/respiratory ~** appareil *m* digestif/respiratoire.

traction engine *n* locomobile *f*.

tractor *n* tracteur *m*.

trade I *n* **1** (activity) commerce *m*; **to do a good ~** faire de bonnes affaires; **2** (sector of industry) industrie *f*; **3** (profession) (manual) métier *m*; (intellectual) profession *f*; **by ~** de métier.
II *noun modifier* [*route, agreement, balance, deficit*] commercial; [*sanctions*] économique; [*association, journal*] professionnel/-elle; [*barrier*] douanier/-ière.
III *vtr* échanger (**for** contre).
IV *vi* faire du commerce; **to ~ at $10** s'échanger à $10.
■ **trade in**: **~ [sth] in, ~ in [sth]**: **he ~d in his old car for a new one** on lui a repris sa vieille voiture et il en a acheté une nouvelle.
■ **trade off**: **~ [sth] off, ~ off [sth]** échanger.

trade: **Trade and Industry Secretary** *n* (GB) ministre *m* du commerce et de l'industrie; **~ discount** *n* remise *f* professionnelle; **~ fair** *n* salon *m*.

trade-in I *n* reprise *f* (*d'un article usagé à l'achat d'un article neuf*).
II *adj* [*price*] avec reprise; [*value*] de reprise.

trade: **~mark** *n* (also **Trademark, Registered Trademark**) marque *f* déposée; **~ name** *n* nom *m* (de marque).

trader *n* **1** (shopkeeper, stallholder) commerçant/-e *m/f*; **2** (at stock exchange) opérateur/-trice *m/f* (en Bourse).

trade: **~ secret** *n* secret *m* de fabrication; **~sman's entrance** *n* entrée *f* de service; **Trades Union Congress, TUC** *n* (GB) Confédération *f* des syndicats (britanniques).

trade union I *n* syndicat *m*.
II *noun modifier* [*activist, leader, movement*] syndical.

trade: **~ union member** *n* syndiqué/-e *m/f*; **~ wind** *n* alizé *m*.

trading I *n* **1** (business) commerce *m*; **2** (at stock exchange) transactions *fpl* (boursières); **at the end of ~** à la fermeture du marché.
II *adj* [*nation*] commerçant; [*partner*] commercial.

tradition *n* tradition *f*.

traditional *adj* traditionnel/-elle.

traffic I *n* **1** (on road) circulation *f*; (air, sea, rail) trafic *m*; **~ into/out of London** la circulation vers/en sortant de Londres; **to hold up the ~** provoquer un bouchon; **2** (in drugs, arms, slaves, goods) trafic *m* (**in** de).
II *noun modifier* [*accident, regulations*] de la circulation; **~ flow** circulation *f*.
III *vi* **to ~ in** faire du trafic de [*drugs, arms, stolen goods*].

traffic duty *n* **to be on ~** faire la circulation.

traffic: **~ island** *n* refuge *m*; **~ jam** *n* embouteillage *m*.

trafficker *n* trafiquant/-e *m/f* (**in** de).

traffic: **~ lights** *n pl* feux *mpl* (de signalisation); **~ policeman** *n* agent *m* de la circulation; **~ warden** ▶805 *n* (GB) contractuel/-elle *m/f*.

tragedy *n* tragédie *f*.

tragic *adj* tragique.

trail I *n* **1** (path) chemin *m*, piste *f*; **to be on sb's ~** être sur la piste de qn; **2** (of blood, dust, slime) traînée *f*, trace *f*; **3** (trace) trace *f*, piste *f*.
II *vtr* **1** (follow) [*animal, person*] suivre la piste de; [*car*] suivre; **2** (drag) traîner.
III *vi* **1** [*skirt, scarf*] traîner; [*plant*] pendre; **2** (shuffle) **to ~ in/out** entrer/sortir en traînant les pieds; **3** (lag) traîner; **our team were ~ing by 3 goals to 1** notre équipe avait un retard de 2 buts; **to ~ badly** [*racehorse, team*] être à la traîne.

trail: **~ bike** *n* moto *f* tout-terrain; **~ blazer** *n* pionnier/-ière *m/f*.

trailer *n* **1** (vehicle, boat) remorque *f*; **2** (US) (caravan) caravane *f*; **3** (for film) bande-annonce *f*.

trailer park *n* (US) terrain *m* de caravaning.

trailing *adj* [*plant*] rampant.

train I *n* **1** (means of transport) train *m*; (underground) rame *f*; **on** or **in the ~** dans le train; **slow ~** omnibus *m*; **a ~ to Paris** un train pour Paris; **to go to Paris by ~** aller à Paris en train; **2** (succession) (of events) série *f*; **my ~ of thought** le fil de mes pensées; **3** (procession) (of animals, vehicles, people) file *f*; (of mourners) cortège *m*; **4** (of dress) traîne *f*.
II *noun modifier* [*crash, station*] ferroviaire; [*timetable*] des trains; [*driver, ticket*] de train; [*strike*] des chemins de fer.
III *vtr* **1** (prepare, educate) former [*staff, worker, musician*] (**to do** à faire); entraîner [*athlete, player*] (**to do** à faire); dresser [*circus animal, dog*]; **to be ~ed on the job** être formé sur le tas; **to ~ sb as a pilot/an engineer** donner à qn une formation de pilote/d'ingénieur; **2** (aim) braquer [*gun, binoculars*] (**on** sur).
IV *vi* **1** (for profession) être formé, étudier; **he's ~ing to be/he ~ed as a doctor** il suit/il a reçu une formation de docteur; **2** (Sport) s'entraîner.

trained *adj* [*staff*] qualifié; [*professional*] diplômé; [*voice, eye, ear*] exercé; [*singer, actor*] professionnel/-elle; [*animal*] dressé.

trainee *n* stagiaire *mf*.

trainer *n* **1** (of athlete, horse) entraîneur/-euse *m/f*; (of circus animal, dogs) dresseur/-euse *m/f*; **2** (GB) (shoe) (high) basket *f*; (low) tennis *m*.

training I *n* **1** (gen) formation *f*; (less specialized) apprentissage *m*; **~ in medicine** formation à la médecine; **2** (Mil, Sport) entraînement *m*; **to be in ~** s'entraîner; (following specific programme) suivre un entraînement.
II *noun modifier* (gen) [*course, period, scheme*] de formation; [*manual*] d'instruction; (Mil, Sport) d'entraînement.

training: **~ college** *n* (GB) école *f* professionnelle; (for teachers) centre *m* de formation pédagogique; **~ ground** *n* (Sport) terrain *m* d'entraînement; **~ ship** *n* navire-école *m*.

train: **~ set** *n* petit train *m*; **~ spotter** *m* passionné/-e *m/f* de trains.

trait *n* trait *m*.

traitor *n* traître/traîtresse *m/f* (**to** à); **to turn ~** trahir.

tram *n* (GB) tramway *m*.

tramp *n* (rural) vagabond *m*; (urban) clochard/-e *m/f*.

trample *vtr* piétiner; **to ~ sth underfoot** piétiner qch.

trampoline *n* trampoline *m*.

trance *n* transe *f*; (figurative) état *m* second; **to go into a ~** entrer en transe.

tranquil *adj* tranquille.

tranquillizer, **tranquilizer** (US) *n* tranquillisant *m*.

transaction *n* (in business) transaction *f*; (on stock exchange) opération *f*; **cash/credit card ~** transaction en liquide/effectuée avec une carte de crédit.

transatlantic *adj* [*crossing, flight*] transatlantique; [*accent*] d'outre-atlantique *inv*.

transcript *n* **1** (copy) transcription *f*; **2** (US Sch) duplicata *m* de livret scolaire.

transfer I *n* **1** (of information, skills, power, heat) transfert *m*; (of property, debt) cession *f*; (of funds) virement *m*; **2** (relocation) (of player, patient, prisoner) transfert *m*; (of employee) mutation *f*; **3** (GB) (on skin, china, paper) décalcomanie *f*; (on T-shirt) transfert *m*.
II *vtr* **1** transférer [*data, baggage*]; virer [*money*]; céder [*property, power*]; reporter [*allegiance, support*]; **I'm ~ring you to reception** je vous passe la réception; **2** (relocate) transférer [*office, prisoner, player*]; muter [*employee*].
III *vi* **1** [*player, passenger*] être transféré; [*employee*] être muté; **2** [*traveller*] changer d'avion; **3** (Univ) (change university) changer d'université; [*student*] (change course) changer de cours.

transfer: **~ lounge** *n* salle *f* de transit; **~ passenger** *n* passager/-ère *m/f* en transit; **~red charge call** *n* appel *m* en PCV.

transform *vtr* transformer.

transformation *n* transformation *f*.

transformer *n* transformateur *m*.

transfusion *n* transfusion *f*.

transient *adj* [*phase*] transitoire; [*emotion, beauty*] éphémère; [*population*] de passage.

transistor *n* transistor *m*.

transit I *n* transit *m*; **in ~** en transit.
II *noun modifier* [*camp, lounge*] de transit; [*passenger*] en transit.

transition I *n* transition *f*.
II *noun modifier* [*period, point*] de transition.

transitive *adj* transitif/-ive.

translate I *vtr* traduire; **to ~ theory into practice** mettre la théorie en pratique.
II *vi* [*person*] traduire; [*word, phrase, text*] se traduire; **this word does not ~** ce mot est intraduisible.

translation *n* (profession) traduction *f*; (school exercise) version *f*.

translator *n* traducteur/-trice *m/f*.

transmissible *adj* transmissible.

transmission *n* transmission *f*.

transmit I *vtr* transmettre.
II *vi* émettre.

transmitter *n* (in radio, TV) émetteur *m*; (in telecommunications) capsule *f* microphonique; **radio ~** émetteur *m* radio.

transparency *n* **1** (quality) transparence *f*; **2** (slide) diapositive *f*; (for overhead projector) transparent *m*.

transparent *adj* transparent.

transplant I *n* (operation) transplantation *f*; (organ, tissue transplanted) transplant *m*; **to have a heart ~** subir une transplantation cardiaque.
II *vtr* (gen) transplanter [*plant, tree*]; repiquer [*seedlings*]; (Med) transplanter, greffer.

transport I *n* (also **transportation** US) transport *m*; **air/road ~** transport aérien/par route; **to travel by public ~** utiliser les transports en commun; **I haven't got any ~ at the moment** je n'ai pas de moyen de locomotion en ce moment.
II *noun modifier* (also **transportation** US) [*costs, ship*] de transport; [*industry, strike, system*] des transports.
III *vtr* transporter [*passengers, goods*] (**from** de; **to** à).

transportation *n* **1** (US) = **transport I, II**; **2** (of passengers, goods) transport *m*.

transporter *n* (Mil) transport *m*.

transsexual *n, adj* transsexuel/-elle (*m/f*).

transvestite *n* travesti/-e *m/f*.

trap I *n* **1** (snare) piège *m*; **to set a ~ for** poser un piège pour [*animal*]; tendre un piège à [*person*]; **2** (vehicle) cabriolet *m*.
II *vtr* **1** (snare) prendre [qn/qch] au piège; **2** (catch) coincer [*person, finger*]; retenir [*heat*].

trapdoor *n* trappe *f*.

trapper *n* trappeur *m*.

trappings *n pl* **the ~ of** les signes *mpl* extérieurs de [*wealth, success*].

trash *n* **1** (US) (refuse) (in streets) déchets *mpl*; (from household) ordures *fpl*; **2** (low-grade goods) camelote° *f*; **3** (nonsense) âneries *fpl*; **the film is (absolute) ~** le film est (complètement) nul°.

trash: **~can** *n* (US) poubelle *f*; **~ heap** *n* tas *m* d'ordures.

trauma *n* traumatisme *m*.

traumatic *adj* (psychologically) traumatisant; (Med) traumatique.

traumatize *vtr* traumatiser.

travel I *n* voyages *mpl*; **foreign ~** voyages à l'étranger.
II *noun modifier* [*plans*] de voyage; [*brochure, company*] de voyages; [*expenses*] de déplacement; [*writer*] de récits de voyage; **the ~ business** l'industrie *f* du tourisme.
III *vtr* parcourir [*country, road, distance*].
IV *vi* **1** (journey) voyager; **he ~s widely** il voyage beaucoup; **to ~ abroad/to Brazil** aller à l'étranger/au Brésil; **2** (move) [*person, object, plane, boat*] aller; [*car, train*] aller, rouler; [*light, sound*] se propager; **bad news ~s fast** les mauvaises nouvelles vont vite; **to ~ at 50 km/h** rouler à 50 km/h; **to ~ a long way** [*person*] faire beaucoup de chemin; **to ~ back in time** remonter le temps; **3 to ~ well** [*cheese, wine*] supporter le transport.

travel: **~ agency** *n* agence *f* de voyages; **~ agent** ▶805, 805 *n* agent *m* de voyages; **~ card** *n* (GB) carte *f* de transport; **~ insurance** *n* assurance *f* voyage.

traveller (GB), **traveler** (US) *n* **1** (voyager) voyageur/-euse *m/f*; **2** (GB) (gypsy) nomade *mf*.

traveller's cheque (GB), **traveler's check** (US) *n* chèque-voyage *m*.

travelling (GB), **traveling** (US) **I** *n* (touring) voyages *mpl*; (on single occasion) voyage *m*; **to go ~** partir en voyage; **the job involves ~** le poste exige des déplacements.
II *adj* **1** [*actor, company, circus*] itinérant; [*bank*] mobile; **the ~ public** les usagers des transports en commun; **2** [*companion, rug*] de voyage; [*conditions*] (on road) de route; **3** [*scholarship*] de voyage; [*allowance, expenses*] de déplacement.

travelling: **~ clock** *n* réveil *m* de voyage; **~ library** *n* bibliobus *m*; **~ salesman** ▶805 *n* voyageur *m* de commerce.

travels *n pl* voyages *mpl*.

travel-sick *adj* **to be** or **get ~** souffrir du mal des transports.

travel-sickness *n* mal *m* des transports.

trawler *n* chalutier *m*.

tray *n* plateau *m*; **baking ~** plaque *f* à pâtisserie; **ice ~** bac *m* à glaçons; **in-/out-~** corbeille *f* arrivée/départ.

treacherous *adj* traître/traîtresse.

treachery *n* traîtrise *f*.

treacle *n* (GB) (black) mélasse *f*; (golden syrup) mélasse *f* raffinée.

tread I *n* (of tyre) (pattern) sculptures *fpl*; (outer surface) chape *f*.
II *vtr* fouler [*street, path, area*]; **to ~ water** nager sur place; **a well-trodden path** un sentier bien tracé; (in career) un parcours classique.
III *vi* (walk) marcher; **to ~ on** (walk) marcher sur; (squash) piétiner; **to ~ carefully** être prudent.

treadmill *n* (dull routine) train-train *m*.

treason *n* trahison *f*; **high ~** haute trahison.

treasure I *n* **1** trésor *m*; **2** (prized person) (woman) perle *f*; (man) homme *m* en or.
II *vtr* **1** (cherish) chérir [*person, gift*]; **2** (prize) tenir beaucoup à [*friendship*].
III treasured *pp adj* précieux/-ieuse.

treasurer *n* **1** (on committee) trésorier/-ière *m/f*; **2** (US) (in company) directeur *m* financier.

treasure trove *n* trésor *m*.

Treasury *n* (also **~ Department**) ministère *m* des finances.

treat I *n* (pleasure) (petit) plaisir *m*; (food) gâterie *f*; **I took them to the museum as a ~** je

les ai emmenés au musée pour leur faire plaisir; **oysters! what a ~!** des huîtres! vous nous gâtez!; **it's my ~**○ c'est moi qui paie; **to stand sb a ~**○ offrir qch à qn.
II *vtr* **1** (deal with) traiter [*person, animal, object, topic*]; **to ~ sb well/badly** bien traiter/maltraiter qn; **to ~ sb/sth with care** prendre soin de qn/qch; **they ~ the house like a hotel** ils prennent la maison pour un hôtel; **to ~ the whole thing as a joke** tourner toute l'affaire en plaisanterie; **2** (Med) traiter [*patient, disease*]; **3** (process) traiter [*chemical, fabric, water*]; **4** (pay for) **to ~ sb to sth** payer or offrir qch à qn; **to ~ oneself to** s'offrir [*holiday, hairdo*].
III **a treat**○ *phr* (GB) **the plan worked a ~** le projet a marché comme sur des roulettes○.

treatment *n* **1** (of person) traitement *m*; **special ~** (preferential) traitement de faveur; **it won't stand up to rough ~** ça ne résistera pas aux mauvais traitements; **2** (Med) (by specific drug, method) traitement *m*; (general care) soins *mpl*; **a course of ~** un traitement; **to receive ~ for sth** être sous traitement pour qch, recevoir des soins pour qch; **to undergo ~** être en traitement.

treaty *n* **1** (political) traité *m*; **peace ~** traité de paix; **2** (commercial, legal) contrat *m*; **for sale by private ~** à vendre de gré à gré.

treble I *adj* triple; **to reach ~ figures** atteindre la centaine.
II *vtr, vi* tripler.

tree *n* arbre *m*; **an apple/a cherry ~** un pommier/un cerisier.
IDIOMS **he can't see the wood** (GB) or **forest** (US) **for the ~s** il se perd dans les détails; **to be at the top of the ~** être arrivé au sommet.

tree: **~-lined** *adj* bordé d'arbres; **~ ring** *n* cerne *m*; **~ stump** *n* souche *f*; **~top** *n* cime *f* (d'un arbre); **~ trunk** *n* tronc *m* d'arbre.

trek I *n* (long journey) randonnée *f*; (laborious) randonnée *f* pénible.
II *vi* **to ~ across** traverser péniblement [*desert*]; **to go ~king** faire de la randonnée pédestre.

trekking ▶ 649 *n* randonnée *f* pédestre.

tremble *vi* trembler.

trembling *n* tremblement *m*.

tremendous *adj* [*effort, improvement, amount*] énorme; [*pleasure*] immense; [*storm, explosion*] violent; [*success*] fou/folle○.

tremor *n* **1** (in voice) tremblement *m*; **2** (in earthquake) secousse *f*.

trench *n* tranchée *f*.

trenchant *adj* incisif/-ive.

trench coat *n* imperméable *m*, trench-coat *m*.

trend *n* **1** (tendency) tendance *f*; **a ~ in** une tendance dans le domaine de [*medicine, education*]; **a ~ towards computerization** une tendance à l'informatisation; **2** (fashion) mode *f*; **to set a new ~** lancer une nouvelle mode.

trendy○ *adj* branché○.

trespass *vi* s'introduire illégalement; **to ~ on** (gen) pénétrer sans autorisation dans [*property*]; (Law) violer [*property*]; **'no ~ing'** 'défense d'entrer'.

trespasser *n* intrus/-e *m/f*; **'~s will be prosecuted'** 'défense d'entrer sous peine de poursuites'.

trial I *n* **1** (Law) procès *m*; **to be on ~** être jugé; **to go on ~, to stand ~** passer en jugement; **to come up for ~** [*person*] comparaître en justice; [*case*] être jugé; **to put sb on ~** (Law) juger qn; [*press, public*] condamner qn; **2** (test) (of machine, vehicle) essai *m*; (of drug, new product) test *m*; **to put sth through ~s** soumettre qch à des essais or tests; **by ~ and error** [*learn*] par l'expérience; [*proceed*] par tâtonnements; **3** (Sport) épreuve *f*; **4** (trouble) épreuve *f*; (less strong) difficulté *f*; **to be a ~** [*person*] être pénible à supporter.
II *noun modifier* [*period, separation*] d'essai; **on a ~ basis** à titre expérimental.

trial run *n* essai *m*; **to take a car for a ~** essayer une voiture.

triangle *n* triangle *m*.

tribe *n* tribu *f*.

tributary *n* affluent *m*.

tribute *n* hommage *m*; **to pay ~ to** rendre hommage à; **as a ~ to** en hommage à; **floral ~** (spray) gerbe *f*; (wreath) couronne *f*.

trick I *n* **1** tour *m*; (dishonest) combine *f*, truc○ *m*; **a clever ~** un tour habile; **a mean ~** un sale tour; **a ~ of the light** un effet de lumière; **2** (by magician, conjurer, dog) tour *m*; **to do a ~** faire un tour; **3** (knack, secret) astuce *f*; **to know a few ~s** s'y connaître (**about** en); **4** (habit, mannerism) manie *f*; **5** (in cards) pli *m*; **to take** or **win a ~** faire un pli.
II *noun modifier* [*photo, shot*] truqué.
III *vtr* duper, rouler○; **to ~ sb into doing sth** amener qn à faire qch par la ruse.
IDIOMS **the ~s of the trade** les ficelles du métier; **that'll do the ~** ça fera l'affaire.

trickery *n* tromperie *f*.

trickle I *n* (of liquid) filet *m*; (of powder, sand) écoulement *m*; (of investment, orders) petite quantité *f*; (of people) petit nombre *m*.
II *vi* **to ~ down** dégouliner le long de [*pane, wall*]; **to ~ into** [*liquid*] s'écouler dans [*container*]; [*people*] s'infiltrer dans [*country, organization*]; **to ~ out of** [*liquid*] suinter de [*crack, wound*].

trick question *n* question *f* piège.

tricky *adj* **1** [*decision, task*] difficile; [*problem*] épineux/-euse; [*situation*] délicat; **2** (wily) malin/-igne.

tricolour (GB), **tricolor** (US) *n* drapeau *m* tricolore.

tricycle *n* (cycle) tricycle *m*.

trifle I *n* (GB Culin) ≈ diplomate *m*.
II *vi* **to ~ with** jouer avec [*feelings, affections*]; **to ~ with sb** traiter qn à la légère.

trifling *adj* [*sum, cost, detail*] insignifiant.

trigger *n* **1** (on gun) gâchette *f*; **to pull the ~** appuyer sur la gâchette; **2** (on machine) manette *f*.
■ **trigger off**: **~ off [sth]** déclencher.

trigger-happy○ *adj* **1** à la gâchette facile; **2** (figurative) impulsif/-ive.

trilogy *n* trilogie *f*.

trim I *n* **1** (cut) (of hair) coupe *f* d'entretien; (of hedge) taille *f*; **2** (good condition) **to keep oneself in ~** se maintenir en bonne forme physique; **3** (border) (on clothing) bordure *f*; (on woodwork) moulure *f*; **4** (Aut) **exterior ~** finition *f* extérieure; **interior ~** garniture *f* intérieure.
II *adj* [*garden*] soigné; [*boat, house*] bien tenu; [*figure*] svelte; [*waist*] fin.
III *vtr* **1** (cut) couper [*hair, grass, material*]; tailler [*beard, hedge*]; ébouter [*wood*]; **2** (reduce) réduire [*budget, expenditure, workforce*] (**by** de); **3** (Culin) dégraisser [*meat*]; **4** (decorate) décorer [*tree, furniture*]; border [*dress, handkerchief*].

trimming *n* (on clothing) garniture *f*; **~s** (Culin) (with dish) accompagnements *mpl* traditionnels.

Trinidad *pr n* (l'île *f* de) la Trinité *f*.

Trinity *n* **the ~** la Trinité *f*.

trinket *n* babiole *f*.

trio *n* trio *m* (**of** de).

trip I *n* (journey) (abroad) voyage *m*; (excursion) excursion *f*; **business ~** voyage d'affaires; **to be away on a ~** être en voyage; **we did the ~ in five hours** nous avons fait le trajet en cinq heures.
II *vi* **1** (also **~ over**, **~ up**) (stumble) trébucher, faire un faux pas; **to ~ on** or **over** trébucher sur [*step, rock*]; se prendre les pieds dans [*scarf, rope*]; **2** (walk lightly) **to ~ along** [*child*] gambader; [*adult*] marcher d'un pas léger.
■ **trip up**: ¶ **~ up** (stumble) trébucher; (make an error) se tromper; ¶ **~ [sb] up, ~ up [sb]** faire trébucher; (with foot) faire un croche-pied à.

triple *adj* (gen) triple; (Mus) **in ~ time** à trois temps.

triplet *n* (child) triplé/-e *m/f*.

triplicate: **in ~** *phr* en trois exemplaires.

tripod *n* trépied *m*.

trip: **~ switch** *n* commutateur *m* à bascule; **~ wire** *n* fil *m* de détente.

triumph I *n* triomphe *m*.
II *vi* triompher (**over** de).

triumphant *adj* [*person, team*] triomphant; [*return, success*] triomphal.

trivia *n pl* futilités *fpl*.

trivial *adj* [*matter, scale, film*] insignifiant; [*error, offence*] léger/-ère; [*conversation, argument, person*] futile.

trolley *n* **1** (GB) (on wheels) chariot *m*; **drinks ~** chariot *m* à boissons; **2** (US) tramway *m*.

trolley: **~ bus** *n* trolleybus *m*; **~ car** *n* tramway *m*, tram *m*.

troop I *n* troupe *f*.
II *noun modifier* [*movements, carrier*] de troupes; [*train, plane*] de transport de troupes.
III *vi* **to ~ in/out** entrer/sortir en masse.

trooper *n* **1** (Mil) homme *m* de troupe; **2** (US) (policeman) policier *m*.
IDIOMS **to swear like a ~** jurer comme un charretier or troupier.

trophy *n* trophée *m*.

tropic *n* tropique *m*; **the ~ of Cancer/of Capricorn** le tropique du Cancer/du Capricorne; **in the ~s** sous les tropiques.

tropical *adj* tropical.

trot I *n* trot *m*; **at a ~** au trot.
II *vi* [*animal, rider*] trotter; [*person*] courir, trotter○; [*child*] trottiner.
IDIOMS **on the ~**○ (one after the other) coup sur coup; (continuously) d'affilée.
■ **trot out**○: **~ out [sth]** débiter [*excuse, explanation, argument*].

trotter *n* **pigs' ~s** (Culin) pieds *mpl* de cochon.

trouble I *n* **1** (problems) problèmes *mpl*; (personal) ennuis *mpl*; **engine ~** problèmes de moteur; **to get sb into ~** créer des ennuis à qn; **to make ~ for oneself** s'attirer des ennuis; **to be asking for ~** chercher des ennuis; **back ~** mal *m* de dos; **what's the ~?** qu'est-ce qui ne va pas?; **2** (difficulties) difficultés *fpl*; **to be in** or **get into ~** [*person*] avoir des ennuis; [*company*] avoir des difficultés; **to have ~ doing** avoir du mal à faire; **to get sb out of ~** tirer qn d'affaire; **to stay out of ~** éviter des ennuis; **3** (effort, inconvenience) peine *f*; **it's not worth the ~** cela n'en vaut pas la peine; **to take the ~ to do, to go to the ~ of doing** se donner la peine de faire; **to save sb the ~ of doing** épargner à qn la peine de faire; **to go to a lot of ~** se donner beaucoup de mal; **it's no ~** cela ne me dérange pas; **not to be any ~** [*child*] être sage; [*task*] ne poser aucun problème; **if it's too much ~, say so** si ça t'ennuie, dis-le-moi; **4** (discord) problèmes *mpl*; (with personal involvement) ennuis *mpl*; **I don't want any ~** je ne veux pas d'ennuis; **to be looking for ~** chercher les ennuis; **to get into ~** s'attirer des ennuis; **to make ~** faire des histoires○; **there'll be ~** il y aura du remous; **it will lead to ~** ça va mal finir.
II troubles *n pl* soucis *mpl*; **money ~s** problèmes *mpl* d'argent.
III *vtr* **1** (disturb, inconvenience) [*person*] déranger [*person*]; **may** or **could I ~ you to do?** puis-je vous demander de faire?; **2** (bother) **to be ~d by** être incommodé par [*cough, pain*]; **3** (worry) tracasser [*person*]; **don't let that ~ you** ne te tracasse pas pour cela.

troubled *adj* [*person, expression*] soucieux/-ieuse; [*mind*] inquiet/-iète; [*sleep, times, area*] agité.

trouble: **~maker** *n* fauteur/-trice *m/f* de troubles; **~shooter** *n* conciliateur/-trice *m/f*; (Tech) expert *m*; (in management) consultant/-e *m/f* en gestion des entreprises; **~some** *adj* [*person*] ennuyeux/-euse; [*problem*] gênant; [*cough, pain*] désagréable.

trough *n* **1** (for drinking) abreuvoir *m*; (for animal feed) auge *f*; **2** (between waves, hills, on graph) creux *m*; **3** (in weather) zone *f* dépressionnaire.

trousers *n pl* pantalon *m*; **short ~** culotte *f* courte.
IDIOMS **to wear the ~** (GB) porter la culotte○.

trouser suit *n* (GB) tailleur *m* pantalon.

trout I *n* truite *f*.
II *noun modifier* [*fishing*] à la truite; [*stream*] à truites.

trowel *n* **1** (for cement) truelle *f*; **2** (for gardening) déplantoir *m*.

truancy *n* absentéisme *m*.

truant *n* **to play ~** faire l'école buissonnière.

truce *n* trêve *f*.

truck *n* **1** (lorry) camion *m*; **2** (rail wagon) wagon *m* de marchandises.

truck driver, **trucker**○ ▶ 805 *n* routier *m*.

trucking *n* (transporting) transport *m* routier.

truckload *n* (of goods) chargement *m* (**of** de); (of people) camion *m* (**of** de).

truck stop *n* (restaurant *m*) routier *m*.

truculent *adj* agressif/-ive.

trudge *vi* marcher d'un pas lourd; **to ~ through the snow** marcher péniblement dans la neige; **to ~ round the shops** se traîner de magasin en magasin.

true I *adj* **1** (based on fact) [*news, fact, story*] vrai; (from real life) [*story*] vécu; **it is ~ to say that** on peut dire que; **the same is ~ of the new party** il en va de même pour le nouveau parti; **it can't be ~!** ce n'est pas possible!; **that's ~** (when agreeing) c'est juste; **2** (real, genuine) [*cost, meaning, democracy, American*] vrai (*before n*); [*identity, age*] véritable (*before n*); **to come ~** se réaliser; **an artist in the ~ sense of the word** un artiste dans toute l'acception du terme; **3** (heartfelt, sincere) [*feeling, repentance, understanding*] sincère; **~ love** le véritable amour; **4** (accurate) [*copy*] conforme; [*assessment*] correct, juste; **to be ~ to life** être vrai; **5** (faithful, loyal) fidèle; **to be ~ to sth** être fidèle à qch; **6** (Mus) [*note, instrument*] juste.
II *adv* [*aim, fire*] juste.
IDIOMS **to be too good to be ~** être trop beau pour être vrai; **to be/remain ~ to type** [*person*] être/rester semblable à lui-même/elle-même etc.

truffle *n* truffe *f*.

truly *adv* **1** (extremely) [*amazing, delighted, sorry*] vraiment; **2** (really, in truth) [*belong, think*] vraiment; **really and ~?** vraiment?; **well and ~** bel et bien; **3** (in letter) **yours ~** je vous prie d'agréer l'expression de mes sentiments distingués (formal).

trump I *n* (also **~ card**) atout *m*; (figurative) carte *f* maîtresse.
II trumps *n pl* (in cards) atout *m*; **spades are ~s** atout pique.

trumpet ▶ 753 **I** *n* **1** (instrument, player) trompette *f*; **2** (elephant call) barrissement *m*.
II *vtr* vanter les mérites de [*lifestyle, success*].
III *vi* [*elephant*] barrir.
IDIOMS **to blow one's own ~** vanter ses propres mérites.

trumpeter, **trumpet player** ▶ 805, 753 *n* trompettiste *mf*.

truncheon *n* matraque *f*.

trunk I *n* **1** (of tree, body) tronc *m*; **2** (of elephant) trompe *f*; **3** (for travel) malle *f*; **4** (US) (car boot) coffre *m*.
II trunks *n pl* maillot *m* de bain (*pour hommes*).

truss *n* **1** (of hay) botte *f*; **2** (Med) bandage *m* herniaire.
■ **truss up**: **~ up [sth], ~ [sth] up** brider, trousser [*chicken*]; ligoter [*person*].

trust I *n* **1** (faith) confiance *f*; **to put one's ~ in** se fier à; **to take sth on ~** croire qch sur parole; **2** (Law) (arrangement) fidéicommis *m*; (property involved) propriété *f* fiduciaire.
II *vtr* **1** (believe) se fier à [*person, judgment*]; **2** (rely on) faire confiance à; **3** (entrust) **to ~ sb with sth** confier qch à qn.
III *vi* **to ~ in** faire confiance à [*person*]; croire en [*God, fortune*]; **to ~ to luck** se fier au hasard.
IV trusted *pp adj* [*friend*] fidèle.

trust company *n* société *f* fiduciaire.

trustee *n* **1** (who administers property in trust) fiduciaire *m*; **2** (who administers a company) administrateur/-trice *m*/*f* (**of** de).

trust fund *n* fonds *m* en fidéicommis.

trusting *adj* [*person*] qui fait facilement confiance aux gens; **you're too ~** tu es trop naïf/naïve.

trustworthy *adj* [*staff, firm*] sérieux/-ieuse; [*friend, lover*] digne de confiance.

truth *n* **1** (real facts) **the ~** la vérité; **the whole ~** toute la vérité; **the ~ (of the matter) is that** la vérité, c'est que; **to tell you the ~**○ à vrai dire; **nothing could be further from the ~** c'est absolument faux; **2** (accuracy, veracity) **to confirm/deny the ~ of sth** confirmer/nier l'exactitude de qch; **3 there is no ~ in that** c'est absolument faux; **there is some ~ in it** il y a du vrai dans cela.
IDIOMS **~ is stranger than fiction** la réalité dépasse la fiction; **to tell sb a few home ~s** dire à qn ses quatre vérités.

truth drug *n* sérum *m* de vérité.

truthful *adj* [*person*] honnête; [*account, version*] vrai.

try I *n* **1** (attempt) essai *m*; **to have a ~** essayer (**at doing** de faire); **2** (Sport) essai *m*.
II *vtr* **1** (attempt) essayer de répondre à [*exam question*]; **to ~ doing** or **to do** essayer de faire; **to ~ hard to do** faire de gros efforts pour faire; **to ~ one's best to do** faire tout son possible pour faire; **let's ~ and phone them** essayons de leur téléphoner; **2** (test out) essayer [*tool, product, method, activity*]; prendre [qn] à l'essai [*person*]; [*thief*] essayer d'ouvrir [*door, window*]; tourner [*door knob*]; **to ~ one's hand at pottery/weaving** s'essayer à la poterie/au tissage; **~ that for size** essaie pour voir si ça te va; **3** (taste) goûter [*food*]; **4** (consult) demander à [*person*]; consulter [*book*]; **~ the library** demandez à la bibliothèque; **5** (subject to stress) **to ~ sb's patience** pousser qn à bout; **6** (Law) juger [*case, criminal*].
III *vi* (make attempt) essayer; **to ~ again** (to perform task) recommencer; (to see somebody) repasser; (to phone) rappeler; **~ and relax**

essaie de rester calme; **to ~ for** essayer d'obtenir [*loan, university place*]; essayer de battre [*world record*]; essayer d'avoir [*baby*]; **keep ~ing!** essaie encore!

■ **try on**: **~ [sth] on, ~ on [sth]** essayer [*hat, dress*]; **to ~ it on**○ bluffer.

■ **try out**: **~ [sth] out, ~ out [sth]** essayer [*machine, theory, language, recipe*].

trying *adj* [*person*] pénible; [*experience*] éprouvant.

T-shirt *n* T-shirt *m*.

tub *n* **1** (large) (for flowers, water) bac *m*; (small) (for ice cream, pâté) pot *m*; **2** (contents) pot *m*; **3** (US) (bath) baignoire *f*.

tubby○ *adj* grassouillet/-ette○.

tube *n* **1** (cylinder, container) tube *m*; **2**○ (GB) **the ~** le métro (londonien); **3**○ (US) (TV) télé○ *f*; **4** (in TV set) tube *m* cathodique; **5** (in tyre) chambre *f* à air.

IDIOMS **to go down the ~s** [*plans*] tomber à l'eau; [*economy*] tomber en ruines.

tuberculosis ▶ 686 *n* tuberculose *f*.

tubing *n* tuyauterie *f*.

tuck I *n* (in sewing) pli *m*; (to shorten) pli *m* horizontal.

II *vtr* glisser; **to ~ one's shirt into one's trousers** rentrer sa chemise dans son pantalon; mettre; **to ~ a card into one's pocket** glisser une carte dans sa poche.

■ **tuck away**: **~ [sth] away, ~ away [sth]** (put away) ranger; (hide) cacher; **the house was ~ed away in the wood** la maison se cachait or était cachée dans le bois.

■ **tuck in**: ¶ **~ in [sth], ~ [sth] in** rentrer [*garment, shirt*]; border [*bedclothes*]; ¶ **~ [sb] in, ~ in [sb]** border.

Tuesday ▶ 584 *pr n* mardi *m*.

tuft *n* touffe *f*.

tug I *n* **1** (pull) (on fishing line) secousse *f*; **to give sth a ~** tirer sur qch; **to feel a ~ of loyalties** se sentir partagé; **2** (also **tug boat**) remorqueur *m*.

II *vtr* (pull) tirer.

III *vi* **to ~ at** or **on** tirer sur [*rope, hair*].

tug-of-war *n* (Sport) gagne-terrain *m*; (struggle) lutte *f*.

tuition *n* cours *mpl*.

tuition fees *n pl* frais *mpl* de scolarité.

tulip *n* tulipe *f*.

tumble I *n* **1** (fall) chute *f*; **to take a ~** [*person*] faire une chute; **2** (of clown, acrobat) culbute *f*.

II *vi* **1** (fall) [*person, object*] tomber (**off, out of** de); **2** [*price, share, currency*] chuter; **3** (Sport) [*clown, acrobat, child*] faire des culbutes.

■ **tumble down** [*wall, building*] s'écrouler.

■ **tumble out** [*contents*] se renverser; [*words, feelings*] jaillir en désordre.

tumble: **~down** *adj* délabré; **~-drier, ~-dryer** *n* sèche-linge *m inv*.

tumbler *n* verre *m* droit.

tumour (GB), **tumor** (US) *n* tumeur *f*.

tumult *n* **1** (noise) tumulte *m*; **2** (disorder) agitation *f*.

tuna *n* (also **~ fish**) thon *m*.

tune I *n* air *m*; **to be in/out of ~** [*instrument*] être/ne pas être en accord; **to sing in/out of ~** chanter juste/faux.

II *vtr* accorder [*musical instrument*]; régler [*engine, radio, TV*].

IDIOMS **to call the ~** mener la danse; **to change one's ~** changer d'avis.

■ **tune in**: ¶ **~ in** mettre la radio; **to ~ in to** se mettre à l'écoute de [*programme*]; régler sur [*channel*]; ¶ **~ [sth] in** régler (**to** sur).

tuner *n* ▶ 805 accordeur *m*; **piano ~** accordeur *m* de piano.

tunic *n* (for gym) tunique *f*; (for nurse, schoolgirl) blouse *f*; (for soldier) vareuse *f*.

tuning *n* (of musical instrument) accord *m*; (of radio, TV, engine) réglage *m*.

tuning fork *n* diapason *m*.

tunnel I *n* tunnel *m*; **to use a ~** emprunter un tunnel.

II *vtr, vi* creuser.

tuppence *n* deux pence.

turbine *n* turbine *f*.

turbo *n* (engine) turbo *m*; (car) turbo *f*.

turbocharged *adj* turbo *inv*.

turbot *n* turbot *m*.

turbulence *n* (of air) turbulences *fpl*; (of waves) turbulence *f*.

turbulent *adj* **1** [*water*] agité; **2** [*times, situation*] agité; [*career, history*] mouvementé; [*passions, character, faction*] turbulent.

tureen *n* soupière *f*.

turf I *n* (grass) gazon *m*; (peat) tourbe *f*.

II *vtr* gazonner [*lawn, patch, pitch*].

■ **turf out**○: **~ out [sb/sth], ~ [sb/sth] out** virer○.

Turk ▶ 712 *n* Turc/Turque *m/f*.

turkey *n* **1** (bird) dinde *f*; **2**○ (US) (flop) bide○ *m*; (bad film) navet○ *m*.

Turkey ▶ 574 *pr n* Turquie *f*.

Turkish ▶ 712 **I** *n* (language) turc *m*.

II *adj* [*culture, food, politics*] turc/turque; [*teacher, lesson*] de turc; [*ambassador, embassy*] de Turquie.

Turkish: **~ bath** *n* bain *m* turc; **~ delight** *n* loukoum *m*; **~ towel** *n* serviette *f* éponge.

turmeric *n* (plant) curcuma *m*; (spice) safran *m* des Indes.

turmoil *n* (political, emotional) désarroi *m*.

turn I *n* **1** (in games, sequence) tour *m*; **whose ~ is it?** c'est à qui le tour?; **'miss a ~'** 'passez votre tour'; **to be sb's ~ to do** être au tour de qn de faire; **it was his ~ to feel rejected** il se sentait rejeté à son tour; **to have a ~ on** or **at the computer** utiliser l'ordinateur à son tour; **to take ~s at doing, to take it in ~s to do** faire qch à tour de rôle; **we took ~s at driving** nous avons conduit à tour de rôle; **take it in ~s!** chacun son tour!; **by ~s** tour à tour; **to speak out of ~** commettre un impair; **2** (circular movement) tour *m*; **to give sth a ~** tourner qch; **to do a ~** [*dancer*] faire un tour; **3** (in vehicle) virage *m*; **to make** or **do a left/right ~** tourner à gauche/à droite; **to do a ~ in the road** faire un demi-tour; **'no left ~'** 'défense de tourner à gauche'; **4** (bend, side road) tournant *m*, virage *m*; **take the next right ~, take the next ~ on the right** prenez la prochaine (rue) à droite; **5** (change, development) tournure *f*; **to take a ~ for the better** [*person, situation*] s'améliorer; [*things, events*] prendre une meilleure tournure; **to take a ~ for the worse** [*situation*] se dégrader; [*health*] s'aggraver; **6**○ (GB) (attack) crise *f*; **a dizzy ~** un vertige; **to have a funny ~** se sentir tout/-e chose○; **it gave me quite a ~, it gave me a nasty ~** ça m'a fait un coup○; **7** (act) numéro *m*.

II *vtr* **1** (rotate) [*person*] tourner [*wheel, handle*]; serrer [*screw*]; [*mechanism*] faire tourner [*cog, wheel*]; **to ~ the key in the door** or **lock** (lock up) fermer la porte à clé; (unlock) tourner la clé dans la serrure; **2** (turn over, reverse) retourner [*mattress, soil, steak, collar*]; tourner [*page*]; **to ~ one's ankle** se tordre la cheville; **it ~s my stomach** cela me soulève le cœur; **3** (change direction of) tourner [*chair, head, face, car*]; **to ~ one's back on** (abandon) laisser tomber [*friend, ally*]; abandonner [*homeless, needy*]; **4** (focus direction of) **to ~ [sth] on sb** braquer [qch] sur qn [*gun, hose, torch*]; **5** (transform) **to ~ sth white/black** blanchir/noircir qch; **to ~ sth opaque** rendre qch opaque; **to ~ sth into** transformer qch en [*office, car park, desert*]; **to ~ water into ice** changer de l'eau en glace; **to ~ a book into a film** adapter un livre pour l'écran; **to ~ sb into** [*magician*] changer qn en [*frog*]; [*experience*] faire de qn [*extrovert, maniac*]; **6** (deflect) détourner [*person, conversation*] (**towards** vers; **from** de); **7**○ (pass the age of) **he has ~ed 50** il a 50 ans passés; **she has just ~ed 30** elle vient d'avoir 30 ans; **8** (on lathe) tourner [*wood, piece*].

III *vi* **1** (change direction) [*person, car, plane, road*] tourner; [*ship*] virer; **to ~ down** or **into** tourner dans [*street, alley*]; **to ~ towards** tourner en direction de [*village, mountains*]; **the conversation ~ed to Ellie** on en est venu/ils en sont venus à parler d'Ellie; **2** (reverse direction) [*person, vehicle*] faire demi-tour; [*tide*] changer; [*luck*] tourner; **3** (revolve) [*key, wheel, planet*] tourner; [*person*] se tourner; **to ~ in one's chair** se retourner dans son fauteuil; **to ~ and walk out of the room** faire demi-tour et sortir de la pièce; **4** (hinge) **to ~ on** [*argument*] tourner autour de [*point, issue*]; [*outcome*] dépendre de [*factor*]; **5** (spin round angrily) **to ~ on sb** [*dog*] attaquer qn; [*person*] se retourner contre qn; **6** (resort to) **to ~ to** se tourner vers [*person, religion*]; **to ~ to drink/drugs** se mettre à boire/se droguer; **I don't know where to ~** je ne sais plus où donner de la tête○; **7** (change) **to ~ into** [*person, tadpole*] se transformer en [*frog*]; [*sofa*] se transformer en [*bed*]; [*situation, evening*] tourner à [*farce, disaster*]; **to ~ to** [*substance*] se changer en [*ice, gold*]; [*fear, surprise*] faire place à [*horror, relief*]; **8** (become by transformation) devenir [*pale, cloudy, green*]; **to ~ white/black/red** blanchir/noircir/rougir; **the weather is ~ing cold/warm** le temps se rafraîchit/se réchauffe; **9**○ (become) devenir [*Conservative, Communist*]; **business-woman ~ed politician** ancienne femme d'affaires devenue politicienne; **10** (go sour) [*milk*] tourner; **11** [*trees, leaves*] jaunir.

IV in turn *phr* [*answer, speak*] à tour de rôle; **she spoke to each of us in ~** elle nous a parlé chacun à notre tour.

IDIOMS **to do sb a good ~** rendre un service à qn.

■ **turn about** faire demi-tour.

■ **turn against**: ¶ **~ against [sb/sth]** se retourner contre; ¶ **~ [sb] against** retourner [qn] contre.

■ **turn around**: ¶ **~ around 1** (to face other way) [*person*] se retourner; [*bus, vehicle*] faire demi-tour; **2** (revolve, rotate) [*object, windmill, dancer*] tourner; **3** (change trend) **the market has ~ed around** il y a eu un renversement de situation sur le marché; ¶ **~ [sth] around, ~ around [sth] 1** (to face other way) tourner [qch] dans l'autre sens [*object*]; **2** (reverse decline in) redresser [*situation, economy, company*]; **3** (rephrase) reformuler [*question, sentence*].

■ **turn aside** se détourner (**from** de).

■ **turn away**: ¶ **~ away** se détourner; ¶ **~ [sb] away, ~ away [sb]** refuser [*spectator, applicant*]; ne pas laisser entrer [*salesman, caller*].

■ **turn back**: ¶ **~ back 1** (turn around) (on foot) rebrousser chemin; (in vehicle) faire demi-tour; **there's no ~ing back** il n'est pas question de revenir en arrière; **2** (in book) revenir; ¶ **~ [sth] back, ~ back [sth]** reculer [*dial, clock*]; ¶ **~ [sb] back, ~ back [sb]** refouler [*people, vehicles*].

■ **turn down**: ¶ **~ [sth] down, ~ down [sth] 1** (reduce) baisser [*volume, radio, gas*]; **2** (fold over) rabattre [*sheet, collar*]; retourner [*corner of page*]; ¶ **~ [sb/sth] down, ~ down [sb/sth]** refuser [*person, request*]; rejeter [*offer, suggestion*].

■ **turn in**: ¶ **~ in**: **to ~ in on oneself** se replier sur soi-même; ¶ **~ in [sth], ~ [sth] in**○: **to ~ in a profit** rapporter un bénéfice; **to ~ in a good performance** [*player*] bien jouer; ¶ **~ [sb] in, ~ in [sb]** livrer [*suspect*]; ¶ **~ oneself in** se livrer.

■ **turn off**: ¶ **~ off 1** (leave road) tourner; **~ off at the next exit** prends la prochaine sortie; **2** [*motor, fan*] s'arrêter; ¶ **~ off [sth], ~ [sth] off 1** (stop) éteindre [*light, oven, TV, radio*]; fermer [*tap*]; couper [*water, gas, engine*]; **2** (leave) quitter [*road*]; ¶ **~ [sb] off**○ rebuter.

■ **turn on**: ¶ **~ on [sth], ~ [sth] on** allumer [*light, oven, TV, radio, gas*]; ouvrir [*tap*]; ¶ **~ [sb] on, ~ on [sb]**○ exciter.

■ **turn out**: ¶ **~ out 1** (be eventually) **to ~ out well/badly** bien/mal se terminer; **to ~ out differently** prendre une tournure différente; **to ~ out all right** s'arranger; **it depends how things ~ out** cela dépend de la façon dont les choses vont tourner; **to ~ out to be wrong/easy** se révéler faux/facile; **it**

~s out that they know each other already il se trouve qu'ils se connaissent déjà; **as it ~ed out** en fin de compte; **2** (come out) [*crowd, people*] venir; ¶ **~ [sth] out, ~ out [sth] 1** (turn off) éteindre [*light*]; **2** (empty) vider [*pocket, bag*]; (Culin) démouler [*mousse*]; **3** (produce) fabriquer [*goods*]; former [*scientists, graduates*]; ¶ **~ [sb] out, ~ out [sb]** (evict) mettre [qn] à la porte.

■ **turn over**: ¶ **~ over 1** (roll over) [*person, vehicle*] se retourner; **2** (turn page) tourner la page; **3** [*engine*] se mettre en marche; ¶ **~ [sth/sb] over, ~ over [sth/sb] 1** (turn) tourner [*page, paper*]; retourner [*card, object, mattress, soil, patient*]; **2** (hand over) remettre [*object, money, find, papers*]; livrer [*person*] (**to** à); remettre la succession de [*company*]; **3** (reflect) **I've been ~ing it over in my mind** j'y ai bien réfléchi.

■ **turn round** (GB) = **turn around**.

■ **turn up**: ¶ **~ up 1** (arrive, show up) arriver, se pointer○; **don't worry—it will ~ up** ne t'inquiète pas—tu finiras par le retrouver; **2** (present itself) [*opportunity, job*] se présenter; **3** (point up) [*corner, edge*] être relevé; ¶ **~ up [sth], ~ [sth] up 1** (increase, intensify) augmenter [*heating, volume, gas*]; mettre [qch] plus fort [*TV, radio, music*]; **2** (point up) relever [*collar*].

turnaround *n* **1** (in attitude) revirement *m*; **2** (of fortune) revirement *m* (**in** de); (for the better) redressement *m* (**in** de).

turning *n* **1** (GB) (in road) virage *m*; **to take a wrong ~** tourner au mauvais endroit; **the next ~ on the right** la prochaine (rue) à droite; **I've missed my ~** j'aurais dû tourner plus tôt; **2** (work on lathe) tournage *m*.

turning point *n* tournant *m* (**in, of** de).

turnip *n* navet *m*.

turnoff *n* (in road) embranchement *m*.

turn of phrase *n* (expression) expression *f*; (way of expressing oneself) façon *f* de parler.

turnout *n* (to vote, strike, demonstrate) taux *m* de participation; **there was a magnificent ~ for the parade** beaucoup de gens sont venus voir le défilé.

turnover *n* **1** (of company) chiffre *m* d'affaires; **2** (rate of replacement) (of stock) rotation *f*; (of staff) taux *m* de renouvellement.

turn: **~pike** *n* (tollgate) barrière *f* de péage; (US) (toll expressway) autoroute *f* à péage; **~stile** *n* (gate) tourniquet *m*; (to count number of visitors) compteur *m* pour entrées.

turntable *n* (on record player) platine *f*.

turnup *n* (GB) (of trousers) revers *m*.

turpentine, turps○ *n* térébenthine *f*.

turret *n* tourelle *f*.

turtle *n* (GB) tortue *f* marine; (US) tortue *f*.

turtle: **~ dove** *n* tourterelle *f*; **~neck (sweater)** *n* pull-over *m* à col cheminée.

Tuscany *pr n* Toscane *f*.

tusk *n* défense *f*.

tussle *n* empoignade *f* (**for** pour).

tutee *n* (Univ) (in tutorial) étudiant/-e *m/f*; (individual) élève *mf* particulier/-ière.

tutor ▶805| **I** *n* **1** (private teacher) professeur *m* particulier; (in family) précepteur/-trice *m/f*; **2** (GB Univ) (teacher) chargé/-e *m/f* de travaux dirigés; (for general welfare) conseiller/-ère *m/f* d'éducation; **3** (US Univ) assistant/-e *m/f*; **4** (GB Sch) (of class) professeur *m* principal; (of year group) responsable *mf* pédagogique d'année.

II *vtr* donner des leçons particulières à (**in** de).

tutorial *n* (Univ) (group) classe *f* de travaux dirigés; (private) cours *m* privé.

tuxedo *n* (US) smoking *m*.

TV○ *n* (*abbr* = **television**) télé○ *f*.

TV: **~ dinner** *n* plateau *m* télé; **~ screen** *n* écran *m* télé.

twang *n* (of string, wire) vibration *f*; (of tone) ton *m* nasillard.

tweak *vtr* tordre [*ear, nose*]; tirer [*hair, moustache*].

twee○ *adj* (GB) [*house, decor*] mièvre; [*manner*] emprunté.

tweezers *n pl* pincettes *fpl*; (for eyebrows) pince *f* à épiler.

twelfth ▶584|, 642| **I** *n* **1** (in order) douzième *mf*; **2** (of month) douze *m inv*.

II *adj, adv* douzième.

twelve ▶492|, 554| *n, pron, det* douze (*m*) *inv*.

twenties ▶584|, 492| *n pl* **1** (era) **the ~** les années *fpl* vingt; **2** (age) **to be in one's ~** avoir entre vingt et trente ans.

twentieth ▶584| **I** *n* **1** (in order) vingtième *mf*; **2** (of month) vingt *m*.

II *adj, adv* vingtième.

twenty ▶492|, 554| *n, pron, det* vingt (*m*) *inv*.

twenty-first I *n* **1** (birthday) vingt et unième anniversaire; **2** (of month) vingt et un *m*.

II *adj* vingt et unième.

twenty: **~-one** ▶649| *n* (card game) vingt-et-un *m*; **~-twenty** *adj* [*vision*] de dix à chaque œil.

twice *adv* deux fois; **~ a day** or **daily** deux fois par jour; **she's ~ his age** elle a le double de son âge; **~ as much, ~ as many** deux fois plus; **~ as many people** deux fois plus de monde; **you need to be ~ as careful** il faut redoubler de prudence.

IDIOMS **once bitten ~ shy** chat échaudé craint l'eau froide (Proverb).

twiddle *vtr* tripoter; **to ~ one's thumbs** se tourner les pouces.

twig *n* brindille *f*.

twilight *n* crépuscule *m*.

twilight zone *n* zone *f* d'ombre.

twin I *n* jumeau/-elle *m/f*.

II *noun modifier* **1** [*brother, sister*] jumeau/-elle; **my ~ sons** mes fils jumeaux; **2** (two) [*masts, propellers*] jumeaux/-elles (*after n*); [*speakers*] jumelés.

III *vtr* jumeler [*town*] (**with** avec).

twine *n* ficelle *f*.

twinge *n* (of pain) élancement *m*; (of conscience, doubt) accès *m*; (of jealousy) pointe *f*.

twinkle *vi* [*light, star, jewel*] scintiller; [*eyes*] pétiller.

twinning *n* jumelage *m*.

twin town *n* ville *f* jumelle.

twirl **I** *n* tournoiement *m*; **to do a ~** [*person*] tournoyer.
II *vtr* faire tournoyer [*baton, partner*]; entortiller [*ribbon, vine*].
III *vi* [*dancer*] tournoyer; **to ~ round** (turn round) se retourner brusquement.

twist **I** *n* **1** (action) **he gave the cap a ~** (to open) il a dévissé le bouchon; (to close) il a vissé le bouchon; **2** (in rope, cord, wool) tortillon *m*; (in road) zigzag *m*; (in river) coude *m*; **3** (in play, story) coup *m* de théâtre; (episode in crisis, events) rebondissement *m*; **4** (small amount) (of yarn, thread, hair) torsade *f*; **a ~ of lemon** une tranche de citron.
II *vtr* **1** (turn) tourner [*knob, handle*]; (open) dévisser [*cap, lid*]; (close) visser [*cap, lid*]; **to ~ sth off** dévisser qch [*cap, lid*]; **he ~ed around in his chair** il s'est retourné dans son fauteuil; **to ~ sb's arm** (to hurt) tordre le bras à qn; **2** (wind) enrouler; **to ~ threads together** torsader des fils; **3** (bend, distort) tordre [*metal, rod, branch*]; déformer [*words, facts, meaning*]; **his face was ~ed with pain** son visage était tordu de douleur; **4** (injure) **to ~ one's ankle/wrist** se tordre le bras/le poignet; **to ~ one's neck** attraper un torticolis.
III *vi* **1** [*person*] **to ~ round** (turn round) se retourner; **2** [*rope, flex, coil*] s'entortiller; **to ~ and turn** [*road, path*] serpenter.
IDIOMS **to go round the ~**○ devenir fou/folle.

twisted *adj* **1** [*wire, metal, rod*] tordu; [*rope, cord*] entortillé; [*ankle, wrist*] tordu; **2** [*sense of humour*] malsain.

twisting *adj* sinueux/-euse.

twit○ *n* idiot/-e *m/f*.

twitch **I** *n* **1** (tic) tic *m*; **to have a ~ in one's eye** avoir un tic à l'œil; **2** (spasm) soubresaut *m*; **to give a ~** avoir un soubresaut.
II *vtr* tirer sur [qch] d'un coup sec [*fabric, curtain*].
III *vi* [*person*] avoir des tics; [*mouth*] trembler; [*eye*] cligner nerveusement; [*limb, muscle*] tressauter.

twitchy *adj* agité.

two ▶554, 492 **I** *n* deux *m inv*; **in ~s and threes** par deux ou trois, deux ou trois à la fois.
II *det* deux *inv*; **~ cars/students** deux voitures/étudiants.
III *pron* deux *inv*; **I bought ~ of them** j'en ai acheté deux; **to break sth in ~** casser qch en deux.
IDIOMS **to be in ~ minds about doing** hésiter à faire; **to put ~ and ~ together** faire le rapprochement.

two-faced *adj* hypocrite, fourbe.

twofold **I** *adj* double.
II *adv* doublement; **to increase ~** doubler.

two: **~-party system** *n* système *m* bipartite; **~-penny-halfpenny**○ *adj* (GB) de rien du tout; **~-piece** *n* (also **~-piece suit**) (woman's) tailleur *m*; (man's) costume *m* (deux-pièces); **~-pin** *adj* [*plug, socket*] à deux fiches; **~-seater** *n* (car) voiture *f* à deux places; (plane) avion *m* à deux places; **~-star (petrol)** *n* (GB) (essence *f*) ordinaire *f*; **~-star hotel** *n* hôtel *m* deux étoiles; **~-storey** (GB), **~-story** (US) *adj* à deux étages; **~-stroke** *adj* [*engine*] à deux temps; **~-time**○ *vtr* être infidèle envers, tromper [*partner*]; **~-way** *adj* [*street*] à double sens; [*traffic*] dans les deux sens; [*communication, exchange*] bilatéral; **~-way mirror** *n* glace *f* sans tain; **~-way radio** *n* émetteur-récepteur *m*.

tycoon *n* magnat *m*; **publishing ~** magnat de l'édition.

type **I** *n* **1** (variety, kind) type *m*, genre *m* (**of** de); **you're not my ~** tu n'es pas mon genre; **they're our ~ of people** c'est le genre de personnes que nous aimons bien; **I'm not that ~** ce n'est pas mon genre; **I know his ~** je connais les gens de son espèce; **you know the ~ of thing I mean** vous voyez à peu près ce que je veux dire; **to play** or **be cast against ~** jouer à contre-emploi; **2** (in printing) caractères *mpl*; **printed in small/large ~** imprimé en petits/gros caractères.
II *vtr* taper (à la machine) [*word, letter*]; **a ~d letter** une lettre dactylographiée.
III *vi* taper (à la machine).
■ **type in**: **~ in [sth]**, **~ [sth] in** taper [*word, character*].
■ **type out**: **~ out [sth]**, **~ [sth] out** taper (à la machine) [*letter*].
■ **type up** taper.

type: **~cast** *vtr* cataloguer [*person*]; **~face** *n* police *f* (de caractères); **~setter** ▶805 *n* typographe *mf*; **~setting** *n* composition *f*; **~writer** *n* machine *f* à écrire; **~written** *adj* tapé (à la machine), dactylographié (formal).

typhoid ▶686 *n* (also **~ fever**) (fièvre *f*) typhoïde *f*.

typhoon *n* typhon *m*.

typical *adj* [*case, example, day, village*] typique; [*generosity, compassion*] caractéristique; **it's ~ of him to be late** cela ne m'étonne pas de lui qu'il soit en retard.

typically *adv* [*react, behave*] (of person) comme à mon/ton etc habitude; **~ English** [*place, behaviour*] typiquement anglais; **she's ~ English** c'est l'Anglaise type.

typing **I** *n* **1** (skill) dactylo *f*; **my ~ is slow** ma frappe est lente; **2** (typed material) **two pages of ~** deux pages dactylographiées.
II *noun modifier* [*course*] de dactylo; [*error*] de frappe.

typing pool *n* **to work in the ~** travailler au service dactylo.

typing: **~ skills** *n pl* pratique *f* de la dactylo; **~ speed** *n* vitesse *f* de frappe.

typist *n* dactylo *mf*.
typographic(al) *adj* typographique.
typography *n* typographie *f*.
tyrannize *vtr* tyranniser.
tyranny *n* tyrannie *f* (**over** sur).
tyrant *n* tyran *m*.

tyre (GB), **tire** (US) *n* pneu *m*; **spare ~** (for car) pneu *m* de rechange; (fat) bourrelet *m*.
tyre: **~ lever** *n* démonte-pneu *m*; **~ pressure** *n* pression *f* des pneus; **~ pressure gauge** *n* manomètre *m* (pour pneus).

Uu

u, U *n* **1** (letter) u, U *m*; **2** (GB) (*abbr* = **universal**) (of film) ≈ tous publics.

U-bend *n* (in pipe) courbure *f* en U; (in road) virage *m* en épingle à cheveux.

udder *n* pis *m*.

UFO *n* (*abbr* = **unidentified flying object**) ovni *m inv*.

ugliness *n* laideur *f*.

ugly *adj* **1** [*person, building*] laid; [*wound*] vilain (*before n*); **2** [*situation*] dangereux/-euse; **to be in an ~ mood** [*mob*] gronder; [*individual*] être d'une humeur massacrante○.
IDIOMS **an ~ customer**○ un sale type○; **as ~ as sin** laid comme un pou.

UK ▶574 *pr n* (*abbr* = **United Kingdom**) Royaume-Uni *m*.

ulcer *n* ulcère *m*.

ulterior *adj* **without any ~ motive** sans arrière-pensée.

ultimate I *n* **the ~ in** le nec plus ultra de [*comfort, luxury*].
II *adj* [*result, destination*] final; [*sacrifice*] ultime (*before n*).

ultimately *adv* en fin de compte, au bout du compte.

ultimatum *n* ultimatum *m*; **to issue an ~** adresser un ultimatum (**to** à).

ultramarine *n, adj* outremer (*m*) *inv*.

ultrasound *n* ultrasons *mpl*.

ultrasound: **~ scan** *n* échographie *f*; **~ scanner** *n* échographe *m*.

ultraviolet *adj* ultraviolet/-ette.

umbilical cord *n* cordon *m* ombilical.

umbrella *n* parapluie *m*; **under the ~ of** (authority) sous l'égide *f* de.

umpire *n* arbitre *m*.

umpteen○ *adj* des tas de○; **~ times** trente-six fois.

UN *n* (*abbr* = **United Nations**) **the ~** l'ONU *f*.

unable *adj* **to be ~ to do** (lacking means or opportunity) ne pas pouvoir faire; (lacking knowledge or skill) ne pas savoir faire; (incapable, not qualified) être incapable de faire.

unacceptable *adj* [*proposal*] inacceptable; [*behaviour*] inadmissible.

unaccompanied *adj* **1** [*child, baggage*] non accompagné; [*man, woman*] seul; **2** (Mus) sans accompagnement.

unaccounted *adj* **to be ~ for** [*money*] être introuvable; [*person*] être porté disparu.

unacknowledged *adj* [*genius, contribution*] non reconnu; **her letter remained ~** on n'a pas accusé réception de sa lettre.

unadventurous *adj* [*person, production, style*] qui manque d'audace.

unaffected *adj* **1 to be ~** ne pas être affecté (**by** par); **2** (natural) tout simple.

unafraid *adj* [*person*] sans peur.

unaided *adv* [*stand, sit, walk*] sans aide.

unambiguous *adj* sans équivoque.

unanimity *n* unanimité *f* (**between, among** entre).

unanimous *adj* unanime.

unanimously *adv* [*agree, condemn*] unanimement; [*vote*] à l'unanimité.

unannounced *adv* [*arrive, call*] sans prévenir.

unanswerable *adj* [*question*] à laquelle il n'y a pas de réponse possible; [*remark, case*] irréfutable.

unanswered *adj* [*letter, question*] resté sans réponse.

unappetizing *adj* peu appétissant.

unappreciative *adj* [*person, audience*] ingrat.

unapproachable *adj* inaccessible [*place, person*].

unarmed *adj* [*person*] non armé; [*combat*] sans armes.

unashamedly *adv* ouvertement.

unasked *adv* [*come, attend*] sans être invité; **to do sth ~** faire qch spontanément.

unassuming *adj* modeste.

unattached *adj* **1** [*part, element*] détaché; **2** (single) [*person*] célibataire.

unattainable *adj* inaccessible.

unattractive *adj* [*person*] peu attirant; [*proposition*] peu intéressant (**to** pour).

unavailable *adj* **to be ~** [*person*] ne pas être disponible.

unavoidable *adj* inévitable.

unaware *adj* **1** (not informed) **to be ~ that** ignorer que; **2** (not conscious) **to be ~ of sth** ne pas être conscient de qch; **to be politically ~** ne pas être politisé.

unawares *adv* **to catch** or **take sb ~** prendre qn au dépourvu.

unbalanced *adj* **1** [*person, mind*] instable; **2** (biased) [*reporting*] partial.

unbearable *adj* insupportable.

unbeatable *adj* imbattable; **it's ~ value** c'est un prix imbattable.

unbeaten *adj* [*player, team*] invaincu; [*score, record*] qui n'a pas été battu.

unbelievable *adj* incroyable.

unbending *adj* inflexible.

unbias(s)ed *adj* impartial.

unblock *vtr* déboucher [*pipe, sink*].

unbolted *adj* **to be ~** ne pas être verrouillé.

unborn *adj* [*child*] à naitre; [*generation*] à

venir; **her ~ child** l'enfant qu'elle porte/portait etc.

unbreakable *adj* incassable.

unbroken *adj* **1** [*sequence, silence, view*] ininterrompu; **2** [*pottery*] intact.

unbuckle *vtr* déboucler [*belt*]; défaire la boucle de [*shoe*].

unbutton *vtr* déboutonner.

uncalled-for *adj* [*remark*] déplacé.

uncanny *adj* [*resemblance*] étrange; [*accuracy*] étonnant; [*silence*] troublant.

uncaring *adj* [*world*] indifférent.

uncensored *adj* [*film, book*] non censuré; [*version*] intégral.

uncertain I *adj* **1** (unsure) incertain; **to be ~ about** ne pas être certain de; **2** (changeable) [*temper*] instable; [*weather*] variable.
II in no ~ terms *phr* [*state*] en termes on ne peut plus clairs.

uncertainty *n* incertitude *f* (**about** en ce qui concerne).

uncertified *adj* [*document*] non certifié.

unchallenged *adj* incontesté; **to go ~** ne pas être récusé.

unchanged *adj* inchangé.

uncharacteristic *adj* [*generosity*] peu habituel/-elle; **it was ~ of him to give up** ce n'est pas son genre d'abandonner.

uncharitable *adj* peu charitable (**to do** de faire).

unchecked *adv* [*develop, grow, spread*] de manière incontrôlée.

uncivilized *adj* **1** (inhumane) [*treatment, conditions*] inhumain; **2** (uncouth, rude) grossier/-ière; **3** (barbarous) [*people, nation*] non civilisé.

unclaimed *adj* [*lost property, reward*] non réclamé.

unclassified *adj* [*document, information*] non classifié; [*road*] non classé.

uncle *n* oncle *m*.

unclear *adj* **1** [*motive, reason*] peu clair; **it is ~ how/whether...** on ne sait pas très bien comment/si...; **to be ~ about sth** [*person*] ne pas être sûr de qch; **2** [*instructions, voice*] pas clair; [*answer*] peu clair; [*handwriting*] difficile à lire.

uncollected *adj* [*mail, luggage*] non réclamé; [*taxes*] non perçu; [*refuse*] non ramassé.

uncomfortable *adj* **1** [*shoes, seat*] inconfortable; [*journey, heat*] pénible; **you look ~ in that chair** tu n'as pas l'air à l'aise dans ce fauteuil; **2** [*feeling, silence, situation*] pénible; **to make sb (feel) ~** mettre qn mal à l'aise; **to be ~ about** se sentir gêné par [*role, decision, fact*].

uncomfortably *adv* **1** [*seated*] inconfortablement; [*loud, bright*] désagréablement; **it's ~ hot** il fait une chaleur pénible; **2** [*say, laugh*] d'un air gêné.

uncommon *adj* rare; **it is not ~ to do** il n'est pas rare de faire.

uncommunicative *adj* peu communicatif/-ive.

uncompromising *adj* [*person, attitude*] intransigeant.

unconcerned *adj* (uninterested) indifférent (**with** à); (not caring) insouciant; (untroubled) imperturbable.

unconditional *adj* [*obedience, support, love*] inconditionnel/-elle; [*offer, surrender*] sans condition.

unconnected *adj* **1** [*incidents*] sans lien entre eux/elles; **to be ~ with** [*event, fact*] n'avoir aucun rapport avec; [*person*] n'avoir aucun lien avec; **2** [*phone, gas*] pas branché.

unconscious I *n* **the ~** l'inconscient *m*.
II *adj* **1** (insensible) sans connaissance; **to knock sb ~** assommer qn; **2** (unaware) **to be ~ of sth** ne pas être conscient de qch; **3** [*bias, hostility*] inconscient.

unconsciously *adv* inconsciemment.

unconsciousness *n* inconscience *f*.

unconstitutional *adj* inconstitutionnel/-elle.

uncontested *adj* [*leader, fact*] incontesté; [*seat*] non disputé.

uncontrollable *adj* [*emotion*] incontrôlable; [*tears*] qu'on ne peut retenir.

uncontrollably *adv* [*laugh, sob*] sans pouvoir se contrôler.

unconventional *adj* peu conventionnel/-elle.

unconvinced *adj* **to be ~** ne pas être convaincu (**of** de; **that** que).

unconvincing *adj* peu convaincant.

uncooked *adj* non cuit.

uncooperative *adj* peu coopératif/-ive.

uncoordinated *adj* [*efforts, service*] désordonné; **to be ~** [*person*] manquer de coordination.

uncork *vtr* déboucher [*bottle, wine*].

uncorrected *adj* [*error, proofs*] non corrigé.

uncorroborated *adj* non corroboré.

uncountable *adj* [*noun*] indénombrable.

uncouth *adj* [*person*] grossier/-ière; [*accent*] peu raffiné.

uncover *vtr* dévoiler [*scandal*]; découvrir [*evidence, body*].

uncritical *adj* peu critique; **to be ~ of sb/sth** ne pas être critique envers qn/qch.

unctuous *adj* onctueux/-euse, mielleux/-euse.

uncut *adj* **1** [*film, version*] intégral; **2** [*gem*] non taillé.

undamaged *adj* [*crops*] non endommagé; [*building, reputation*] intact.

undecided *adj* [*person*] indécis; [*outcome*] incertain; **the jury is ~** le jury n'a pas encore décidé.

undemanding *adj* [*task*] peu fatigant; [*person*] peu exigeant.

undemocratic *adj* antidémocratique.

undeniable *adj* indéniable.

under I *prep* **1** sous; **~ the bed** sous le lit; **a newspaper ~ his arm** un journal sous le bras; **~ it** en dessous; **it's ~ there** c'est là-dessous; **to come out from ~ sth** sortir de dessous qch; **~ letter D** sous la lettre D; **2** (less than) **~ £10** moins de 10 livres sterling;

children ~ five les enfants de moins de cinq ans or au-dessous de cinq ans; **a number ~ ten** un nombre inférieur à dix; **temperatures ~ 10°C** des températures inférieures à or au-dessous de 10°C; **3** (according to) **~ the law** selon la loi; **fined ~ a rule** condamné à une amende en vertu d'une règle; **4** (subordinate to) sous; **I have 50 people ~ me** j'ai 50 employés sous mes ordres.
II *adv* **1** [*crawl, sit, hide*] en dessous; **to go ~** [*diver, swimmer*] disparaître sous l'eau; **2** (less) moins; **£10 and ~** 10 livres sterling et moins; **children of six and ~** des enfants de six ans et au-dessous; **3** (anaesthetized) **to put sb ~** endormir qn.

underage *adj* **~ drinking** la consommation d'alcool par les mineurs; **to be ~** être mineur/-e.

under: **~body** *n* (Aut) dessous *m* de caisse; **~carriage** *n* train *m* d'atterrissage.

undercharge *vtr* faire porter un débit moindre à [*account*]; **he ~d me for the wine** il m'a fait payer le vin moins cher qu'il n'aurait dû.

under: **~clothes** *n pl* sous-vêtements *mpl*; **~coat** *n* couche *f* de fond.

undercooked *adj* pas assez cuit; **the meat is ~** la viande n'est pas assez cuite.

under: **~cover** *adj* [*activity, group*] clandestin; [*agent*] secret; **~current** *n* (in water) courant *m* profond; (in sea) courant *m* sous-marin; (figurative) courant *m* sous-jacent; **~developed** *adj* [*country*] sous-développé; [*negative*] pas assez développé; **~dog** *n* (in society) opprimé/-e *m/f*; (in game, contest) perdant/-e *m/f*; **~done** *adj* [*food*] pas assez cuit; [*steak*] (GB) saignant; **~estimate** *vtr* sous-estimer; **~expose** *vtr* sous-exposer; **~fed** *adj* sous-alimenté.

underfoot *adv* sous les pieds; **the ground was wet ~** le sol était humide.

underfunded *adj* insuffisamment financé.

undergo *vtr* subir [*change, test, operation*]; suivre [*treatment, training*]; **to ~ surgery** subir une intervention chirurgicale.

undergraduate *n* ≈ étudiant/-e *m/f* (*de première, deuxième ou troisième année*).

underground I *n* **1** (GB) (subway) métro *m*; **on the ~** dans le métro; **2 the ~** (political) la clandestinité; (artistic) l'underground *m*.
II *adj* **1** (below ground) souterrain; **2** (secret) clandestin; **3** (artistic) underground *inv*.
III *adv* **1** (below ground) sous terre; **2** (secretly) **to go ~** passer dans la clandestinité.

undergrowth *n* sous-bois *m*.

underhand *adj* **1** (also **underhanded** US) [*person, method*] sournois; **~ dealings** magouilles○ *fpl*; **2** (Sport) **to have an ~ serve** servir à la cuillère.

under: **~insure** *vtr* sous-assurer; **~line** *vtr* souligner; **~ling** *n* subordonné/-e *m/f*; **~lying** *adj* [*problem*] sous-jacent; **~mine** *vtr* saper [*foundations, authority, efforts*]; ébranler [*confidence, position*].

underneath I *n* dessous *m*.
II *adv* dessous, en dessous.
III *prep* sous, au-dessous de; **from ~ a pile of books** de dessous une pile de livres.

undernourished *adj* sous-alimenté.

underpants *n pl* slip *m*; **a pair of ~** un slip.

under: **~pass** *n* (for traffic) voie *f* inférieure; (for pedestrians) passage *m* souterrain; **~pay** *vtr* sous-payer [*employee*]; **~populated** *adj* sous-peuplé; **~privileged** *adj* [*area, background, person*] défavorisé; **~rate** *vtr* sous-estimer; **~-secretary** *n* (also **~-secretary of state**) (GB) sous-secrétaire *mf* d'État; **~shirt** *n* (US) maillot *m* de corps; **~signed** *n* soussigné/-e *m/f*.

understaffed *adj* **to be ~** manquer de personnel.

understand I *vtr* **1** comprendre; **is that understood?** c'est compris?; **to make oneself understood** se faire comprendre; **to ~ sb doing** comprendre que qn fasse; **as I ~ it** si je comprends bien; **2** (believe) **to ~ that** croire que; **it was understood that** on pensait que; **he was given to ~ that** on lui a donné à entendre que; **3 I thought that was understood** je pensais que c'était entendu.
II *vi* comprendre (**about** à propos de); **I quite ~** je comprends tout à fait.

understandable *adj* compréhensible; **it's ~** ça se comprend.

understandably *adv* naturellement.

understanding I *n* **1** (grasp of subject, issue) compréhension *f*; **to show an ~ of** faire preuve d'une bonne compréhension de; **our ~ was that** nous avions compris que; **2** (arrangement) entente *f* (**about** sur; **between** entre); **3** (sympathy) compréhension *f*; **4** (powers of reason) entendement *m*.
II *adj* [*tone*] bienveillant; [*person*] compréhensif/-ive.

understatement *n* litote *f*; **that's an ~!** c'est le moins qu'on puisse dire!

understudy *n* doublure *f* (**to** de).

undertake *vtr* **1** entreprendre [*search, study, trip*]; se charger de [*mission, offensive*]; **2 to ~ to do** s'engager à faire.

undertaker *n* **1** (person) entrepreneur *m* de pompes funèbres; **2** (company) entreprise *f* de pompes funèbres; **at the ~'s** aux pompes funèbres.

undertaking *n* **1** (venture) entreprise *f*; **2** (promise) garantie *f*.

under-the-counter *adj* [*goods, trade*] illicite; [*payment*] sous le manteau.

undertone *n* **1** (low voice) voix *f* basse; **in an ~** à voix basse; **2** (hint) nuance *f*.

undervalue *vtr* **1** (financially) sous-évaluer; **2** sous-estimer [*person, quality*].

underwater I *adj* [*cable, exploration*] sous-marin; [*lighting*] sous l'eau.
II *adv* sous l'eau.

underway *adj* **to get ~** [*vehicle*] se mettre en route; [*season*] commencer.

under: **~wear** *n* sous-vêtements *mpl*;

~weight *adj* trop maigre; **~world** *n* milieu *m*, pègre *f*.

underwrite; *vtr* **1** (in insurance) souscrire [*policy, risk*]; assurer [*property*]; **2** financer [*project*]; prendre en charge [*expense, loss*].

underwriter *n* **1** (of share issue) soumissionnaire *m*; **2** (in insurance) assureur *m*, souscripteur *m*.

undeservedly *adv* [*blame, punish*] injustement; [*praise*] de façon imméritée.

undesirable *adj* [*aspect, habit, result*] indésirable; [*influence*] néfaste; [*friend*] peu recommandable; **~ alien** (Law) étranger/-ère *m/f* indésirable.

undetected *adv* [*break in, listen*] sans être aperçu; **to go ~** [*person*] rester inaperçu; [*cancer*] rester non décelé; [*crime*] rester non découvert.

undeterred *adj* **to be ~ by sth/sb** ne pas se laisser démonter par qch/qn.

undeveloped *adj* [*person, organ, idea*] non développé; [*land*] inexploité; [*country*] sous-développé.

undignified *adj* [*behaviour, person*] indigne; [*language*] choquant.

undisciplined *adj* indiscipliné.

undiscovered *adj* [*secret*] non révélé; [*land*] inexploré; [*species*] inconnu; [*crime, document*] non découvert; [*talent*] méconnu.

undiscriminating *adj* sans discernement.

undisguised *adj* [*anger, curiosity*] non déguisé.

undisputed *adj* [*capital, champion, leader, fact*] incontesté.

undisturbed *adj* [*sleep*] paisible, tranquille; **to leave sb/sth ~** ne pas déranger qn/qch.

undivided *adj* **to give sb one's ~ attention** accorder à qn toute son attention.

undo *vtr* **1** défaire [*button, lock*]; ouvrir [*parcel*]; **2** annuler [*good, effort*].

undone *adj* **1 to come ~** [*parcel, button*] se défaire; **2 to leave sth ~** ne pas faire qch.

undoubtedly *adv* indubitablement.

undress **I** *vtr* déshabiller; **to ~ oneself** se déshabiller.
II *vi* se déshabiller.

undressed *adj* déshabillé; **to get ~** se déshabiller.

undrinkable *adj* **1** (unpleasant) imbuvable; **2** (dangerous) non potable.

undue *adj* excessif/-ive.

unduly *adv* [*optimistic, surprised*] excessivement; [*neglect, worry*] outre mesure.

unearthly *adj* [*light, landscape*] surnaturel/-elle; [*cry, silence*] étrange; **at an ~ hour** à une heure indue.

uneasily *adv* **1** (anxiously) avec inquiétude; **2** (uncomfortably) avec gêne; **3** (with difficulty) avec difficulté.

uneasy *adj* **1** [*person*] inquiet/-iète (**about, at** au sujet de); [*conscience*] pas tranquille; **I had an ~ feeling that** j'avais le sentiment désagréable que; **2** [*compromise*] difficile; [*peace*] boiteux/-euse; [*silence*] gêné; **3** [*sleep*] agité.

uneconomical *adj* **1** (wasteful) pas économique; **2** (not profitable) pas rentable.

uneducated *adj* **1** [*person*] sans instruction; **2** [*person, speech*] inculte; [*accent, tastes*] commun.

unemotional *adj* [*person*] impassible; [*account, reunion*] froid.

unemployed **I** *n* **the ~** les chômeurs *mpl*.
II *adj* au chômage, sans emploi

unemployment *n* chômage *m*; **with ~ at 20%** avec un chômage de 20%.

unemployment benefit (GB), **unemployment compensation** (US) *n* allocations *fpl* de chômage.

unenthusiastic *adj* peu enthousiaste (**about** au sujet de).

unenviable *adj* peu enviable.

unequal *adj* [*amounts, contest, pay*] inégal.

unequivocal *adj* [*person, declaration*] explicite; [*answer, support*] sans équivoque.

unethical *adj* **1** (gen) contraire à la morale (**to do** de faire); **2** (Med) contraire à la déontologie (**to do** de faire).

uneven *adj* [*hem, teeth*] irrégulier/-ière; [*contest, surface*] inégal.

uneventful *adj* [*day, life, career*] ordinaire; [*journey, period*] sans histoires.

unexciting *adj* sans intérêt.

unexpected *adj* [*arrival, success*] imprévu; [*ally, outcome*] inattendu; [*death*] inopiné.

unexpectedly *adv* [*happen*] à l'improviste; [*large, small, fast*] étonnamment.

unexplored *adj* inexploré.

unfailing *adj* [*support*] fidèle; [*optimism*] à toute épreuve; [*efforts*] constant.

unfair *adj* [*person, decision, advantage*] injuste (**to, on** envers; **to do** de faire); [*play, tactics*] irrégulier/-ière; [*trading*] frauduleux/-euse; [*competition*] déloyal.

unfair dismissal *n* licenciement *m* abusif.

unfairness *n* injustice *f*.

unfaithful *adj* [*partner*] infidèle (**to** à).

unfamiliar *adj* **1** [*face, name, place*] inconnu (**to** à); [*concept, feeling, situation*] inhabituel/-elle (**to** à); **2 to be ~ with sth** ne pas connaître qch.

unfamiliarity *n* **1** (strangeness) caractère *m* insolite; **2 his ~ with sth** sa mauvaise connaissance de qch.

unfashionable *adj* [*place, garment*] qui n'est pas à la mode.

unfasten *vtr* défaire [*clothing, button*]; ouvrir [*bag*].

unfavourable *adj* défavorable (**for sth** à qch; **to** à).

unfinished *adj* [*work*] inachevé; **to have ~ business** avoir des choses à régler.

unfit *adj* **1** (out of condition) qui n'est pas en forme; **2** [*housing*] inadéquat; [*pitch, road*] impraticable (**for** à); **~ for human consump-**

tion impropre à la consommation humaine; **~ for work** inapte au travail.

unflattering *adj* [*clothes, portrait*] peu flatteur/-euse.

unfold I *vtr* déplier [*paper, map, deck, chair*]; déployer [*wings*]; décroiser [*arms*].
II *vi* **1** [*leaf*] s'ouvrir; **2** [*scene*] se dérouler; [*mystery*] se dévoiler.

unforeseeable *adj* imprévisible.

unforeseen *adj* imprévu.

unforgettable *adj* inoubliable.

unforgivable *adj* impardonnable.

unforgiving *adj* impitoyable.

unfortunate *adj* **1** (pitiable) malheureux/-euse; **2** (regrettable) [*incident, choice*] malencontreux/-euse; [*remark*] fâcheux/-euse; **3** (unlucky) malchanceux/-euse; **those ~ enough to fall ill** ceux qui ont/ont eu etc la malchance de tomber malade.

unfortunately *adv* **~, she...** malheureusement, elle...

unfounded *adj* sans fondement.

unfriendly *adj* [*person, attitude, reception*] peu amical; [*place*] inhospitalier/-ière.

unfulfilled *adj* [*ambition*] non réalisé; [*desire, need*] inassouvi; [*promise*] non tenu; [*condition*] non rempli; [*prophecy*] inaccompli; **to feel ~** se sentir insatisfait.

unfurnished *adj* [*accommodation*] non meublé.

ungracious *adj* désobligeant (**of** de la part de).

ungrammatical *adj* incorrect.

ungrateful *adj* ingrat (**of** de la part de; **towards** envers).

unhappily *adv* **1** (miserably) d'un air malheureux; **~ married** malheureux en mariage; **2** (unfortunately) malheureusement; **3** (inappropriately) malencontreusement.

unhappiness *n* **1** (misery) tristesse *f*; **2** (dissatisfaction) mécontentement *m*.

unhappy *adj* **1** [*person, childhood, situation*] malheureux/-euse; [*face, occasion*] triste; **2** (dissatisfied) mécontent; **to be ~ with sth** ne pas être satisfait de qch; **3** (concerned) inquiet/-iète (**about** à propos de); **to be ~ about doing** ne pas aimer faire.

unharmed *adj* [*person*] indemne; [*object*] intact.

unhealthy *adj* **1** [*person*] maladif/-ive; [*diet*] malsain; [*conditions*] insalubre; **2** (unwholesome) malsain.

unheard-of *adj* **1** (shocking) inouï; **2** [*price*] record *inv*; [*actor*] inconnu.

unheeded *adj* **to go ~** [*warning, plea*] rester vain.

unhelpful *adj* [*employee*] peu serviable; [*attitude*] peu obligeant.

unhindered *adj* **~ by** sans être entravé par [*rules*]; sans être encombré par [*luggage*].

unhurried *adj* [*person*] posé; [*pace, meal*] tranquille.

unhurt *adj* indemne.

unhygienic *adj* [*conditions*] insalubre; [*way, method*] peu hygiénique.

unidentified *adj* non identifié.

unification *n* unification *f* (**of** de).

uniform *n* uniforme *m*; **out of ~** (Mil) en civil.

uniformity *n* uniformité *f*.

unify *vtr* unifier.

unilateral *adj* unilatéral.

unimaginable *adj* inimaginable.

unimaginative *adj* [*style*] sans originalité; **to be ~** manquer d'imagination.

unimportant *adj* sans importance (**for, to** pour).

unimpressed *adj* peu enthousiaste; **to be ~ by** ne pas trouver [qn/qch] extraordinaire [*person, performance*]; n'être guère convaincu par [*argument*].

uninhabitable *adj* inhabitable.

uninhibited *adj* [*attitude*] direct; [*person*] sans complexes (**about** en ce qui concerne); **to be ~ about doing** n'avoir aucun complexe à faire.

uninitiated *n* **the ~** le profane.

uninjured *adj* indemne; **to escape ~** sortir indemne.

unintelligible *adj* incompréhensible (**to** pour).

unintentional *adj* involontaire.

uninterested *adj* indifférent (**in** à).

uninteresting *adj* sans intérêt.

uninvited *adj* [*attentions*] non sollicité; [*remark*] gratuit; **~ guest** intrus/-e *m/f*.

uninviting *adj* [*place*] rébarbatif/-ive; [*food*] peu appétissant.

union *n* **1** (also **trade ~**) syndicat *m*; **to join a ~** se syndiquer; **2** (uniting) union *f*; (marriage) union *f*, mariage *m*; **3** (GB Univ) ▶ **student union**.

Unionist *n, adj* unioniste (*mf*).

unionize *vtr* syndicaliser.

unique *adj* **1** (sole) unique (**in that** en ce que); **to be ~ in doing** être seul à faire; **to be ~ to** être particulier à; **2** (remarkable) unique, exceptionnel/-elle.

unit *n* **1** (whole) unité *f*; **~ of measurement** unité de mesure; **2** (group) groupe *m*; (in army, police) unité *f*; **3** (department) (gen, Med) service *m*; (in factory) unité *f*; **4** (piece of furniture) élément *m*; **5** (Univ) unité *f* de valeur; **6** (in textbook) unité *f*.

unite I *vtr* unir (**with** à).
II *vi* s'unir (**with** à; **in doing** en faisant; **to do** pour faire).

united *adj* [*group, front*] uni (**in** dans); [*effort*] conjoint.

united: **United Kingdom** ▶**574** *pr n* Royaume-Uni *m*; **United Nations (Organization)** *n* (Organisation *f* des) Nations *fpl* unies; **United States (of America)** ▶**574** *pr n* États-Unis *mpl* (d'Amérique).

unity *n* unité *f*.

universal *adj* [*reaction*] général; [*education*] pour tous; [*principle*] universel/-elle.
universally *adv* [*believed*] par tous, universellement; [*known, loved*] de tous.
universe *n* univers *m*.
university **I** *n* université *f*.
II *noun modifier* [*degree, town*] universitaire; [*place*] à l'université.
unjust *adj* injuste (**to** envers).
unjustifiably *adv* [*claim, condemn*] sans justification.
unjustified *adj* injustifié.
unkempt *adj* [*appearance*] négligé; [*hair*] ébouriffé; [*beard*] peu soigné.
unkind *adj* [*person, thought, act*] pas très gentil/-ille; [*remark*] désobligeant; **to be ~ to sb** (by deed) ne pas être gentil avec qn; (verbally) être méchant avec qn.
unkindness *n* (of person) dureté *f*; (of fate) cruauté *f*.
unknown **I** *n* **1** **the ~** l'inconnu *m*; **2** (person) inconnu/-e *m/f*.
II *adj* inconnu; **~ to me,...** à mon insu...
unlace *vtr* délacer.
unlawful *adj* [*activity*] illégal; [*detention*] arbitraire; **~ killing** meurtre *m*.
unlawfully *adv* illégalement.
unleaded petrol (GB), **unleaded gasoline** (US) *n* essence *f* sans plomb.
unleash *vtr* lâcher [*animal*]; déchaîner [*violence, passion*]; déverser [*torrent*].
unleavened *adj* sans levain.
unless *conj* à moins que (+ *subj*), à moins de (+ *infinitive*); **he won't come ~ you invite him** il ne viendra pas à moins que tu (ne) l'invites; **she can't take the job ~ she finds a nanny** elle ne peut pas accepter le poste à moins de trouver une nourrice; **it won't work ~ you plug it in**! ça ne marchera pas si tu ne le branches pas!; **~ I'm very much mistaken** à moins que je (ne) me trompe; **~ otherwise agreed** sauf accord contraire.
unlicensed *adj* [*activity*] non autorisé; [*vehicle*] non immatriculé.
unlike *prep* **1** (in contrast to) contrairement à, à la différence de; **~ me, he...** contrairement à moi, il...; **2** (different from) différent de; **they are quite ~ each other** ils ne se ressemblent pas du tout; **3** (uncharacteristic of) **it's ~ her (to be so rude)** ça ne lui ressemble pas (d'être aussi impolie).
unlikelihood *n* improbabilité *f*.
unlikely *adj* **1** (unexpected) improbable, peu probable; **it is ~ that** il est peu probable que (+ *subj*); **they are ~ to succeed** il est peu probable qu'ils réussissent; **2** [*partner, choice, situation*] inattendu; **3** [*story*] invraisemblable.
unlimited *adj* [*quantity, power, resources*] illimité; [*access*] libre (*before n*).
unlined *adj* **1** [*garment, curtain*] sans doublure; **2** [*paper*] non réglé.
unlit *adj* [*room, street*] non éclairé; **to be ~** ne pas être éclairé.
unload **I** *vtr* **1** décharger [*goods, vessel, gun, camera*]; **2** (get rid of) se décharger de [*feelings*] (**on(to)** sur); se débarrasser de [*goods*].
II *vi* [*truck, ship*] décharger.
unlock *vtr* ouvrir [*door*]; **to be ~ed** ne pas être fermé à clé.
unloved *adj* **to feel ~** [*person*] se sentir mal aimé.
unloving *adj* [*person, behaviour*] peu affectueux/-euse.
unluckily *adv* malheureusement (**for** pour).
unlucky *adj* **1** [*person*] malchanceux/-euse; [*event*] malencontreux/-euse; [*day*] de malchance; **to be ~ enough to do** avoir la malchance de faire; **you were ~ not to get the job** c'est pure malchance que tu n'aies pas obtenu le poste; **2** [*number, colour*] néfaste, maléfique; **it's ~ to do** ça porte malheur de faire.
unmade *adj* [*bed*] défait; [*road*] non goudronné.
unmanageable *adj* [*child, dog*] difficile; [*system*] ingérable; [*hair*] rebelle.
unmarried *adj* célibataire; **~ mother** mère *f* célibataire.
unmentionable *adj* [*activity*] inracontable; [*subject*] tabou.
unmistakable *adj* **1** (recognizable) caractéristique (**of** de); **2** (unambiguous) sans ambiguïté; **3** (marked) net/nette.
unmoved *adj* indifférent (**by** à); (emotionally) insensible (**by** à).
unnamed *adj* [*company, source*] dont le nom n'a pas été divulgué.
unnatural *adj* **1** (odd) anormal; **it is ~ that** ce n'est pas normal que (+ *subj*); **2** [*style, laugh*] affecté; **3** [*silence, colour*] insolite.
unnecessarily *adv* inutilement.
unnecessary *adj* **1** (not needed) inutile; **it is ~ to do** il est inutile de faire; **it is ~ for you to do** il est inutile que tu fasses; **2** (uncalled for) déplacé.
unnerve *vtr* décontenancer, rendre [qn] nerveux/-euse.
unnerving *adj* [*experience, habit, reaction*] perturbant.
unnoticed *adj* inaperçu.
unobstructed *adj* [*view, exit, road*] dégagé.
unobtrusive *adj* [*person*] effacé; [*site, object, noise*] discret/-ète.
unoccupied *adj* **1** [*house, shop*] inoccupé; [*seat*] libre; **2** (Mil) [*territory*] libre.
unofficial *adj* [*figure*] officieux/-ieuse; [*candidate*] indépendant; [*strike*] sauvage.
unofficially *adv* [*tell, estimate*] officieusement.
unorthodox *adj* peu orthodoxe.
unpack *vtr* défaire [*suitcase*]; déballer [*belongings*].
unpaid *adj* [*bill, tax*] impayé; [*debt*] non acquitté; [*work*] non rémunéré; **~ leave** congé *m* sans solde.
unpalatable *adj* [*truth*] inconfortable; [*advice*] dur à avaler.
unparalleled *adj* **1** [*strength, luxury*] sans

égal; [*success*] hors pair; **2** (unprecedented) sans précédent.

unpasteurized *adj* [*milk*] cru; [*cheese*] au lait cru.

unplanned *adj* [*stoppage, increase*] imprévu; [*pregnancy, baby*] non prévu.

unpleasant *adj* désagréable.

unpleasantness *n* **1** (of odour, experience, remark) caractère *m* désagréable; **2** (bad feeling) dissensions *fpl* (**between** entre).

unplug *vtr* débrancher [*appliance*]; déboucher [*sink*].

unpopular *adj* impopulaire; **to be ~ with sb** ne pas avoir la cote○ auprès de qn.

unpopularity *n* impopularité *f*.

unprecedented *adj* sans précédent.

unpredictability *n* imprévisibilité *f*.

unpredictable *adj* [*event*] imprévisible; [*weather*] incertain; **he's ~** on ne sait jamais à quoi s'attendre avec lui.

unprepared *adj* **1** [*person*] pas préparé (**for** pour); **to catch sb ~** prendre qn au dépourvu; **2** [*speech*] improvisé; [*translation*] non préparé.

unprepossessing *adj* peu avenant.

unpretentious *adj* sans prétention.

unprincipled *adj* sans scrupules.

unproductive *adj* improductif/-ive.

unprofessional *adj* peu professionnel/-elle.

unprofitable *adj* [*company, venture, service*] non rentable.

unpromising *adj* peu prometteur/-euse.

unprotected *adj* (unsafe) [*person, area*] sans protection (**from** contre).

unpublishable *adj* impubliable.

unpublished *adj* non publié.

unpunished *adj* [*crime, person*] impuni; **to go ~** [*crime*] rester impuni.

unqualified *adj* **1** [*person*] non qualifié; **to be ~** ne pas être qualifié (**for** pour; **to do** pour faire); **2** [*support, respect*] inconditionnel/-elle; [*success*] grand.

unquestionable *adj* incontestable.

unravel **I** *vtr* défaire [*knitting*]; démêler [*thread, mystery*].

II *vi* [*knitting*] se défaire; [*mystery, thread*] se démêler; [*plot*] se dénouer.

unreal *adj* **1** (not real) irréel/-éelle; **2**○ (unbelievable) incroyable.

unrealistic *adj* irréaliste, peu réaliste.

unreasonable *adj* **1** [*behaviour, expectation*] qui n'est pas raisonnable; **he's being very ~ about it** il n'est vraiment pas raisonnable; **2** [*price, demand*] excessif/-ive; **at an ~ hour** à une heure indue.

unreasonably *adv* [*behave*] de façon peu raisonnable; **not ~** à juste titre.

unrecognizable *adj* méconnaissable.

unrecognized *adj* méconnu (**by** de); **to go ~** rester méconnu.

unredeemed *adj* [*mortgage*] non purgé; [*debt*] non remboursé.

unregistered *adj* [*birth*] non déclaré; [*letter*] non recommandé; [*vehicle*] non immatriculé.

unrelated *adj* **1** (not connected) sans rapport (**to** avec); **2** (as family) **to be ~** ne pas avoir de lien de parenté.

unrelenting *adj* [*heat, stare, person*] implacable; [*pursuit, zeal*] acharné.

unreliability *n* (of person) manque *m* de sérieux; (of machine, method, technique) manque *m* de fiabilité.

unreliable *adj* [*evidence*] douteux/-euse; [*method, employee*] peu sûr; [*equipment*] peu fiable; **she's very ~** on ne peut pas compter sur elle.

unremitting *adj* [*hostility*] implacable; [*pressure*] continu; [*struggle*] sans relâche.

unrepentant *adj* impénitent; **to remain ~** n'avoir aucun repentir.

unrepresentative *adj* non représentatif/-ive.

unrequited *adj* [*love*] sans retour.

unresolved *adj* irrésolu.

unrest *n* **1** (dissatisfaction) malaise *m*; **2** (agitation) troubles *mpl*.

unrestricted *adj* [*access*] libre (*before n*); [*power*] illimité.

unrewarding *adj* (unfulfilling) peu gratifiant; (thankless) ingrat.

unrivalled *adj* sans égal.

unroll *vtr* dérouler.

unruffled *adj* **1** imperturbable; **to be ~** ne pas être perturbé; **2** [*hair*] lisse.

unruly *adj* [*crowd, behaviour, hair*] indiscipliné.

unsafe *adj* **1** [*environment*] malsain; [*drinking water*] non potable; [*goods, working conditions*] dangereux/-euse; **2** (threatened) **to feel ~** ne pas se sentir en sécurité; **3** (Law) [*conviction, verdict*] douteux/-euse.

unsaid *adj* **to leave sth ~** passer qch sous silence.

unsatisfactory *adj* insatisfaisant.

unsatisfied *adj* [*person*] insatisfait; [*need*] inassouvi.

unsatisfying *adj* peu satisfaisant.

unsavoury (GB), **unsavory** (US) *adj* [*individual*] louche, répugnant.

unscheduled *adj* [*appearance, speech*] surprise (*after n*); [*flight*] supplémentaire; [*stop*] qui n'a pas été prévu.

unscientific *adj* [*approach*] non scientifique; **to be ~** [*method, theory*] ne pas être scientifique; [*person*] ne pas avoir l'esprit scientifique.

unscrew *vtr* dévisser.

unscrupulous *adj* [*person*] sans scrupules; [*tactic*] peu scrupuleux/-euse.

unseat *vtr* désarçonner [*rider*].

unseen *adv* [*escape, slip away*] sans être vu.

unselfconscious *adj* **1** (natural) naturel/-elle; **2** (uninhibited) sans complexes.

unselfish *adj* [*person*] qui pense aux autres; [*act*] désintéressé.

unsentimental *adj* [*speech, account, film,*

novel] qui ne donne pas dans la sensiblerie; [*person*] qui ne fait pas de sentiment.

unsettle *vtr* troubler [*person*]; perturber [*economy, process*].

unsettled *adj* **1** [*weather, climate*] instable; [*person*] perturbé; **2** [*account*] impayé.

unsettling *adj* [*question, experience*] troublant; [*work of art*] dérangeant.

unshaken *adj* [*person*] imperturbable (**by** devant); [*belief*] inébranlable.

unshaven *adj* pas rasé.

unsigned *adj* [*document, letter*] non signé.

unskilled *adj* [*worker, labour*] non qualifié; [*job, work*] qui n'exige pas de qualification professionnelle.

unsociable *adj* peu sociable.

unsocial *adj* **to work ~ hours** travailler en dehors des heures normales.

unsolicited *adj* non sollicité.

unsolved *adj* [*problem*] non résolu; [*murder*] non éclairci.

unsophisticated *adj* [*person*] sans façons; [*mind*] simple; [*analysis*] simpliste.

unsound *adj* [*roof, ship*] en mauvais état; [*argument*] peu valable; [*investment*] douteux/-euse; **to be of ~ mind** (Law) ne pas jouir de toutes ses facultés mentales.

unspeakable *adj* **1** (dreadful) [*pain, sorrow*] inexprimable; [*act*] innommable; **2** (inexpressible) indescriptible.

unspecified *adj* non spécifié.

unspoiled, **unspoilt** *adj* [*landscape, town*] préservé intact.

unspoken *adj* **1** (secret) inexprimé; **2** (implicit) tacite.

unstable *adj* instable.

unsteadily *adv* [*walk, rise*] en chancelant.

unsteady *adj* [*steps, legs, voice*] chancelant; [*ladder*] instable; [*hand*] tremblant; **to be ~ on one's feet** marcher de façon mal assurée.

unstoppable *adj* [*force, momentum*] irrésistible; [*athlete, leader*] imbattable.

unstressed *adj* [*vowel, word*] non accentué.

unstuck *adj* **to come ~** [*stamp*] se décoller; [*person*] connaître un échec.

unsubstantiated *adj* non corroboré.

unsuccessful *adj* **1** [*attempt, campaign*] infructueux/-euse; [*novel, film*] sans succès; [*lawsuit*] perdu; [*effort, search*] vain; **to be ~** [*attempt*] échouer; **2** [*candidate*] (for job) malchanceux/-euse; (in election) malheureux/-euse; [*businessperson*] malchanceux/-euse; [*artist*] inconnu; **to be ~ in doing** ne pas réussir à faire.

unsuccessfully *adv* [*try*] en vain; [*challenge, bid*] sans succès.

unsuitable *adj* [*location, clothing, accommodation, time*] inapproprié; [*moment*] inopportun; [*friend*] peu convenable; **to be ~** ne pas convenir (**for sb** à qn); **to be ~ for a job** ne pas convenir pour un travail.

unsuitably *adv* **he was ~ dressed** sa tenue était inappropriée; **they are ~ matched** [*couple*] ils sont mal assortis.

unsuited *adj* [*place, person*] inadapté (**to** à); **posts ~ to their talents** des postes qui ne conviennent pas à leurs aptitudes; **she was ~ to country life** elle n'était pas faite pour la vie à la campagne.

unsure *adj* peu sûr (**of** de); **to be ~ about how/why/where** ne pas savoir très bien comment/pourquoi/où; **to be ~ of oneself** manquer de confiance en soi.

unsweetened *adj* sans sucre, non sucré.

unsympathetic *adj* **1** (uncaring) [*person, attitude, tone*] peu compatissant; **to be ~ to sb** se montrer peu compatissant envers qn; **2** (unattractive) [*person, character*] antipathique; **3** (unsupportive) **to be ~ to** être opposé à [*cause, movement, policy*].

untaxed *adj* [*income*] non imposable; [*goods*] non taxé.

untenable *adj* [*position*] intenable; [*claim, argument*] indéfendable.

unthinkable *adj* impensable; **it is ~ that** il est impensable que (+ *subj*).

untidiness *n* désordre *m*.

untidy *adj* [*person*] (in habits) désordonné; (in appearance) peu soigné; [*habits, clothes*] négligé; [*room*] en désordre; **he looks very ~** il a l'air très négligé.

untie *vtr* défaire, dénouer [*knot, rope, laces*]; défaire [*parcel*]; délier [*hands, hostage*].

until

Note When used as a preposition in positive sentences, *until* is translated by *jusqu'à*: *they're staying until Monday* = ils restent jusqu'à lundi.

– Remember that *jusqu'à* + *le* becomes *jusqu'au* and *jusqu'à* + *les* becomes *jusqu'aux*: *until the right moment* = jusqu'au bon moment; *until the exams* = jusqu'aux examens.

– In negative sentences, *not until* is translated by *ne...pas avant*: *I can't see you until Friday* = je ne peux pas vous voir avant vendredi.

– When used as a conjunction in positive sentences, *until* is translated by *jusqu'à ce que* + *subjunctive*: *we'll stay here until Maya comes back* = nous resterons ici jusqu'à ce que Maya revienne.

– In negative sentences where the two verbs have different subjects, *not until* is translated by *ne…pas avant que* + *subjunctive*: *we won't leave until Maya comes back* = nous ne partirons pas avant que Maya revienne.

– In negative sentences where the two verbs have the same subject, *not until* is translated by *pas avant de* + *infinitive*: *we won't leave until we've seen Claire* = nous ne partirons pas avant d'avoir vu Claire.

– For more examples and particular usages, see the entry below.

I *prep* jusqu'à; (after negative verb) avant; **~ Tuesday** jusqu'à mardi; **~ the sixties** jusqu'aux années soixante; **~ a year ago** jusqu'à il y a un an; **~ now** jusqu'à présent; **~ then** jusqu'à ce moment-là, jusque-là; **(up) ~ 1901** jusqu'en or jusqu'à 1901; **valid (up) ~ April 1998** valable jusqu'en avril 1998; **~**

the day he died jusqu'à sa mort; **~ well after midnight** bien au-delà de minuit; **to wait ~ after Easter** attendre après Pâques; **to work from Monday ~ Saturday** travailler du lundi au samedi; **put it off ~ tomorrow** remets-le à demain; **I won't know ~ Tuesday** je n'aurai pas la réponse avant mardi; **they didn't ring ~ the following day** ils n'ont pas appelé avant le lendemain; **it wasn't ~ the 50s that**... ce n'est qu'à partir des années cinquante que...
II *conj* jusqu'à ce que (+ *subj*); (in negative constructions) avant que (+ *subj*), avant de (+ *infinitive*); **we'll stay ~ a solution is reached** nous resterons jusqu'à ce que nous trouvions une solution; **let's watch TV ~ he's ready** regardons la télévision en attendant qu'il soit prêt; **I'll wait ~ I get back** j'attendrai d'être rentré (**before doing** pour faire); **she waited ~ they were alone** elle a attendu qu'ils soient seuls; **don't look ~ I tell you to** ne regarde pas avant que je te le dise.

untimely *adj* [*arrival, announcement*] inopportun; [*death*] prématuré.

untrained *adj* **1** [*worker*] sans formation; **2** [*voice*] non travaillé; [*eye*] inexercé; [*artist, actor*] non formé; **3** [*animal*] non dressé.

untranslatable *adj* intraduisible (**into** en).

untreated *adj* [*sewage, water*] non traité; [*illness*] non soigné.

untroubled *adj* [*face, life*] paisible; **to be ~** (by news) ne pas être troublé (**by** par).

untrue *adj* **1** (false) faux/fausse; **2 it is ~ to say that** il est faux de dire que.

untypical *adj* [*person, behaviour*] peu typique; **to be ~ of sb** ne pas ressembler à qn (**to do** de faire).

unused[1] *adj* **to be ~ to sth/to doing** ne pas être habitué à qch/à faire.

unused[2] *adj* [*machine, building*] inutilisé; [*stamp*] neuf/neuve.

unusual *adj* [*colour, animal, flower*] peu commun; [*feature, occurrence, skill*] peu commun, inhabituel/-elle; [*dish, dress, person*] original; **it is ~ to find/see** il est rare de trouver/voir; **there's nothing ~ about it** cela n'a rien d'extraordinaire.

unusually *adv* exceptionnellement.

unveiling *n* **1** (of statue) dévoilement *m*; **2** (ceremony) inauguration *f*.

unwaged *adj* [*work, worker*] non salarié.

unwanted *adj* [*goods, produce*] superflu; [*pet*] abandonné; [*visitor*] indésirable; [*child*] non souhaité; **to feel ~** se sentir de trop.

unwarranted *adj* injustifié.

unwary I *n* **the ~** ceux qui ne se méfient pas.
II *adj* [*person*] sans méfiance.

unwelcome *adj* [*visitor, interruption*] importun; [*news*] fâcheux/-euse.

unwell *adj* souffrant; **he is feeling ~** il ne se sent pas très bien.

unwilling *adj* [*attention, departure*] forcé; **he is ~ to do it** il n'est pas disposé à le faire; (stronger) il ne veut pas le faire.

unwind I *vtr* dérouler [*cable, bandage, scarf*].
II *vi* **1** [*tape, cable, scarf*] se dérouler; **2** (relax) se relaxer.

unwise *adj* [*choice, loan, decision*] peu judicieux/-ieuse; [*person*] imprudent.

unwisely *adv* imprudemment.

unwittingly *adv* **1** (innocently) innocemment; **2** (without wanting to) involontairement; **3** (accidentally) accidentellement.

unworthy *adj* indigne (**of** de).

unwrap *vtr* déballer [*parcel*].

unwritten *adj* **1** [*rule, agreement*] tacite; **2** [*story, song*] non écrit.

unzip *vtr* défaire la fermeture à glissière de [*garment, bag*].

up I *adj* **1** (out of bed) **she's ~** elle est levée; **we were ~ very late last night** nous nous sommes couchés très tard hier soir; **they were ~ all night** ils ont veillé toute la nuit; **I was still ~ at 2 am** j'étais toujours debout à 2 heures du matin; **2** (higher in amount, level) **sales are ~ (by 10%)** les ventes ont augmenté (de 10%); **numbers of students are ~** le nombre d'étudiants est en hausse; **tourism is ~ (by) 5%** le tourisme a augmenté de 5%; **sales are 10% ~ on last year** les ventes ont augmenté de 10% par rapport à l'an dernier; **3**° (wrong) **what's ~?** qu'est-ce qui se passe?; **what's ~ with him?** qu'est-ce qu'il a?; **4** (erected, affixed) **the notice is ~ on the board** l'annonce est affichée sur le panneau; **is the tent ~?** est-ce que la tente est déjà montée?; **he had his hand ~ for five minutes** il a gardé la main levée pendant cinq minutes; **5** (open) **the blinds were ~** les stores étaient levés; **when the lever is ~ the machine is off** si le levier est vers le haut la machine est arrêtée; **6** (finished) **'time's ~!'** 'c'est l'heure!'; **when the four days were ~** à la fin des quatre jours; **7** (facing upwards) **'this side ~'** 'haut'; **she was floating face ~** elle flottait sur le dos; **8** (pinned up) **her hair was ~** elle avait les cheveux relevés.
II *adv* **1 ~ here/there** là-haut; **~ on the wardrobe** sur l'armoire; **~ in the tree/the clouds** dans l'arbre/les nuages; **~ in London** à Londres; **~ to/in Scotland** en Écosse; **~ to Aberdeen** à Aberdeen; **~ North** au Nord; **four floors ~ from here** quatre étages au-dessus; **I live two floors ~** j'habite au deuxième étage; **on the second shelf ~** sur la deuxième étagère en partant du bas; **I'll be right ~** je monte tout de suite; **2** (ahead) d'avance; **to be four points ~ (on sb)** avoir quatre points d'avance (sur qn); **she's 40–15 ~** (in tennis) elle mène 40–15; **3** (upwards) **T-shirts from £2 ~** des T-shirts à partir de deux livres; **from 14 ~** à partir de 14 ans.
III *prep* **~ the tree** dans l'arbre; **the library is ~ the stairs** la bibliothèque se trouve en haut de l'escalier; **he ran ~ the stairs** il a monté l'escalier en courant; **the shops are ~ the road** les magasins sont plus loin dans la rue; **he lives just ~ the road** il habite juste à côté; **to walk/drive ~ the road** remonter la

rue; **he put it ~ his sleeve** il l'a mis dans sa manche.

IV up above *phr* au-dessus; **~ above sth** au-dessus de qch.

V up against *phr* contre [*wall*]; **to come ~ against** rencontrer [*opposition*].

VI up and about *phr* debout; **to be ~ and about again** être de nouveau sur pied.

VII up and down *phr* **1** (to and fro) **to walk ~ and down** aller et venir, faire les cent pas; **2** (throughout) **~ and down the country** dans tout le pays.

VIII up to *phr* **1** (to particular level) jusqu'à; **~ to here/there** jusqu'ici/jusque là; **I was ~ to my knees in water** j'étais dans l'eau jusqu'aux genoux; **2** (as many as) jusqu'à, près de; **~ to 20 people/50 dollars** jusqu'à 20 personnes/50 dollars; **reductions of ~ to 50%** des réductions qui peuvent atteindre 50%; **to work for ~ to 12 hours a day** travailler jusqu'à 12 heures par jour; **3** (until) jusqu'à; **~ to 1964** jusqu'en 1964; **~ to 10.30 pm** jusqu'à 22 h 30; **~ to now** jusqu'à maintenant; **4 I'm not ~ to it** (not capable) je n'en suis pas capable; (not well enough) je n'en ai pas la force; (can't face it) je n'en ai pas le courage; **5 it's ~ to him to do** c'est à lui de faire; **it's ~ to you!** c'est à toi de décider!; **6** (doing) **what is he ~ to?** qu'est-ce qu'il fait?; **they're ~ to something** ils mijotent○ quelque chose.

IDIOMS **to be one ~ on sb** faire mieux que qn; **to be (well) ~ on** s'y connaître en [*art, history*]; être au courant de [*news*]; **the ~s and downs** les hauts et les bas (**of** de); **~ the workers!** vive les travailleurs!

upbringing *n* éducation *f*.

update I *n* mise *f* à jour (**on** de); **news ~** dernières nouvelles *fpl*.

II *vtr* **1** (revise) mettre or remettre [qch] à jour [*database, information*]; actualiser [*price, value*]; **2** (modernize) moderniser; **3** mettre [qn] au courant (**on** de).

upgrade *vtr* **1** (modernize) moderniser; (improve) améliorer; **2** promouvoir [*employee*].

upheaval *n* **1** (disturbance) bouleversement *m*; **2** (instability) (political, emotional) bouleversements *mpl*; (physical) remue-ménage *m inv*.

uphill I *adj* **1** [*road*] qui monte **~ slope** côte *f*, montée *f*; **2** [*task*] difficile.

II *adv* **to go/walk ~** monter; **the path led ~** le sentier montait.

uphold *vtr* soutenir [*right*]; faire respecter [*law*]; confirmer [*decision*].

upholsterer ▶ 805 *n* tapissier/-ière *m/f*.

upholstery *n* **1** (covering) revêtement *m*; **2** (stuffing) rembourrage *m*.

upkeep *n* **1** (of property) entretien *m* (**of** de); **2** (cost) frais *mpl* d'entretien.

uplifting *adj* tonique.

upmarket *adj* [*car, hotel*] haut de gamme; [*area*] riche.

upon *prep* **1** ▶ **on I 2, 6**; **2** (linking two nouns) **thousands ~ thousands of people** des milliers et des milliers de personnes.

upper I *n* (of shoe) empeigne *f*; **'leather ~'** 'dessus en cuir'.

II *adj* **1** [*shelf, cupboard*] du haut; [*floor, deck*] supérieur; [*lip*] supérieur; [*teeth*] du haut; **2** (in rank, scale) supérieur; **3 the ~ limit** la limite maximale (**on** de).

IDIOMS **to have/get the ~ hand** avoir/prendre le dessus.

upper case *adj* **~ letters** (lettres *fpl*) majuscules *fpl*.

upper circle *n* deuxième balcon *m*.

upper class *n* (*pl* **~es**) **the ~, the ~es** l'aristocratie *f* et la haute bourgeoisie.

Upper House *n* Chambre *f* haute.

upper middle class *n* **the ~, the ~es** la haute bourgeoisie *f*.

uppermost *adj* **1** (highest) [*branch*] le plus haut; (in rank) [*echelon*] le plus élevé; **2 to be ~ in sb's mind** être au premier plan des pensées de qn.

upright I *adj* **1** (physically) droit; **to stay ~** [*person*] rester debout; **2** (morally) droit.

II *adv* **to stand ~** se tenir droit; **to sit ~** (action) se redresser.

uprising *n* soulèvement *m* (**against** contre).

uproar *n* (noise) tumulte *m*; (protest) protestations *fpl*; **to cause (an) ~** déclencher un tumulte de protestations; **to be in ~** être dans la plus vive agitation.

uproot *vtr* déraciner.

upset I *n* **1** (surprise, setback) revers *m*; **to suffer an ~** subir un revers; **to cause an ~** causer la surprise; **2** (upheaval) bouleversement *m*; **3** (distress) peine *f*; **4** (Med) **to have a stomach ~** avoir un problème d'estomac.

II *adj* **to be** or **feel ~** (distressed) être très affecté; (annoyed) être contrarié; **to get ~** (angry) se fâcher (**about** pour); (distressed) se tracasser (**about** pour).

III *vtr* **1** (distress) [*sight, news*] bouleverser; [*person*] faire de la peine à; **2** (annoy) contrarier; **3** bouleverser [*plan*]; déjouer [*calculations*]; **4** (destabilize) rompre [*balance*]; **5** (Med) rendre [qn] malade [*person*]; perturber [*digestion*].

upsetting *adj* (distressing) navrant, affligeant; (annoying) contrariant.

upside down I *adj* à l'envers; sens dessus dessous.

II *adv* à l'envers; **to turn the house ~** mettre la maison sens dessus dessous.

upstage *vtr* éclipser.

upstairs I *n* haut *m*; **there is no ~** il n'y a pas d'étage.

II *noun modifier* [*room*] du haut; **an ~ bedroom** une chambre à l'étage.

III *adv* en haut; **to go ~** monter (l'escalier).

upstart *n, adj* arriviste (*mf*).

upstream *adv* [*travel*] vers l'amont; **~ from here** en amont d'ici.

upsurge *n* (of violence) montée *f* (**of** de); (in debt, demand) augmentation *f* (**in** de).

uptight○ *adj* **1** (tense) tendu; **2** (inhibited) coincé○.

up-to-date *adj* **1** [*music, clothes*] à la mode; [*equipment*] moderne; **2** [*records, timetable*] à jour; [*information*] récent; **to keep sth up to date** tenir qch à jour; **3** (informed) [*person*] au courant; **to keep up to date with** se tenir au courant de [*developments*]; **to bring sb up to date** mettre qn au courant (**about** de).

upturn *n* reprise *f*.

upward I *adj* [*push, movement*] vers le haut; [*path, road*] qui monte; [*trend*] à la hausse.
II *adv* [*look, point*] vers le haut; **to go** or **move ~** monter.

upwards *adv* [*look, point*] vers le haut; **to go** or **move ~** monter; **from five years/£10 ~** à partir de cinq ans/10 livres sterling.

uranium *n* uranium *m*.

Uranus *pr n* Uranus *f*.

urban *adj* (gen) urbain; [*school*] en ville; **~ dweller** citadin/-e *m/f*.

urbanization *n* urbanisation *f*.

urchin *n* gamin *m*; **street ~** gamin des rues.

Urdu ▶ 712 *n* urdu *m*.

urge I *n* forte envie *f*, désir *m* (**to do** de faire).
II *vtr* conseiller vivement, préconiser [*caution, restraint, resistance*]; **to ~ sb to do** conseiller vivement à qn de faire; (stronger) pousser qn à faire; **to ~ that sth (should) be done** insister pour que qch soit fait.

urgency *n* (of situation, appeal, request) urgence *f*; (of voice, tone) insistance *f*; **a matter of ~** une affaire urgente; **to do sth as a matter of ~** faire qch d'urgence.

urgent *adj* **1** (pressing) [*case, need*] urgent, pressant; [*message, demand*] urgent; [*meeting, measures*] d'urgence; **to be in ~ need of** avoir un besoin urgent de; **2** [*request, tone*] insistant.

urgently *adv* [*request*] d'urgence; [*plead*] instamment.

urinal *n* (place) urinoir *m*; (fixture) urinal *m*.

urinate *vi* uriner.

urine *n* urine *f*.

urn *n* urne *f*.

us *pron* nous.

■ **Note** The direct or indirect object pronoun *us* is always translated by *nous*: *she knows us* = elle nous connaît. Note that both the direct and the indirect object pronouns come before the verb in French and that, in compound tenses like the present perfect and past perfect, the past participle agrees in gender and number with the direct object pronoun: *he's seen us* (*masculine or mixed gender object*) il nous a vus; (*feminine object*) il nous a vues.
– In imperatives *nous* comes after the verb: *tell us!* = dis-nous!; *give it to us* or *give us it* = donne-le-nous (note the hyphens).
– After the verb *to be* and after prepositions the translation is also *nous*: *it's us* = c'est nous.

---

both of ~ tous/toutes les deux; **both of ~ like Balzac** nous aimons Balzac tous/toutes les deux; **every single one of ~** chacun/-e d'entre nous; **people like ~** des gens comme nous; **some of ~** quelques-uns/-unes d'entre nous; **she's one of ~** elle est des nôtres.

US *pr n* (*abbr* = **United States**) USA *mpl*.

USA *pr n* (*abbr* = **United States of America**) USA *mpl*.

use I *n* **1** (act of using) (of substance, object, machine) emploi *m*, utilisation *f* (**of** de); (of word, expression) emploi *m*, usage *m* (**of** de); **the ~ of force** le recours à or l'usage de la force; **for ~ as/in** pour être utilisé comme/dans; **for the ~ of** à l'usage de [*customer, staff*]; **for my own ~** pour mon usage personnel; **to make ~ of sth** utiliser qch; **to put sth to good ~** tirer bon parti de qch; **while the machine is in ~** lorsque la machine est en service or en fonctionnement; **'for external ~ only'** 'à usage externe'; **2** (way of using) (of resource, object, material) utilisation *f*; (of term) emploi *m*; **to have no further ~ for sth/sb** ne plus avoir besoin de qch/qn; **3 to have the ~ of** avoir l'usage de [*house, car, kitchen*]; avoir la jouissance de [*garden*]; **to lose the ~ of one's legs** perdre l'usage de ses jambes; **4** (usefulness) **to be of ~** être utile (**to** à); **to be (of) no ~** [*object*] ne servir à rien; [*person*] n'être bon à rien; **what ~ is a wheel without a tyre?** à quoi sert une roue sans pneu?; **what's the ~ of crying?** à quoi bon pleurer?; **it's no ~ (he won't listen)** c'est inutile (il n'écoutera pas).
II *vtr* **1** se servir de, utiliser [*object, car, room, money*]; employer [*method, word*]; profiter de, saisir [*opportunity*]; faire jouer [*influence*]; avoir recours à [*blackmail*]; utiliser [*knowledge, talent*]; **to ~ sth/sb as** se servir de qch/qn comme; **to ~ sth to do** se servir de qch pour faire; **2** (consume) consommer [*fuel, food*]; utiliser [*water, leftovers*]; **3** (exploit) se servir de [*person*].
III used *pp adj* [*car*] d'occasion; [*envelope*] qui a déjà servi.
■ **use up**: **~ [sth] up, ~ up [sth]** finir [*food*]; dépenser [*money*]; épuiser [*supplies*].

used

■ **Note** To translate *used to do*, use the imperfect tense in French: *he used to live in York* = il habitait York.
– To emphasize a contrast between past and present, you can use *avant*: *I used to love sport* = j'adorais le sport avant.

I *modal aux* **I ~ to read a lot** je lisais beaucoup; **he didn't ~ to** or **he ~ not to smoke** il ne fumait pas avant; **she ~ to smoke, didn't she?** elle fumait avant, non?; **she doesn't smoke now, but she ~ to** elle ne fume plus maintenant, mais elle fumait avant; **it ~ to be thought that** avant on pensait que; **there ~ to be a pub here** il y avait un pub ici (dans le temps).
II *adj* **to be ~ to sth** avoir l'habitude de qch, être habitué à qch; **to get ~ to** s'habituer à; **I'm not ~ to it** je n'ai pas l'habitude; **you'll get ~ to it** tu t'y habitueras; **it takes a bit of getting ~ to** il faut du temps pour s'y habituer.

useful *adj* utile; **to be ~ to sb** être utile à qn; **it is ~ to do** il est utile de faire; **to make oneself ~** se rendre utile.

usefully *adv* utilement.

useless *adj* **1** (not helpful) inutile; **it's ~ to do** or **doing** il est inutile de faire; **2** (not able to be used) inutilisable; **3**° (incompetent) incapable, nul/nulle°; **to be ~ at sth/doing** être nul en qch/pour (ce qui est de) faire.

user *n* (of public service) usager *m*; (of product, machine) utilisateur/-trice *m/f*.

user-friendly *adj* (Comput) convivial; (gen) facile à utiliser.

usher *vtr* conduire, escorter; **to ~ sb in/out** faire entrer/sortir qn.

usherette ▶ 805 *n* ouvreuse *f*.

USSR *pr n* (*abbr* = **Union of Soviet Socialist Republics**) URSS *f*.

usual **I**° *n* **the ~** la même chose que d'habitude.

II *adj* [*attitude, procedure, route, place, time*] habituel/-elle; [*word, term*] usuel/-elle; **it is ~ for sb to do** c'est normal pour qn de faire; **it is ~ to do** il est d'usage de faire; **they did all the ~ things** ils ont fait tout ce qu'il est d'usage de faire; **she was her ~ cheerful self** elle était gaie, comme d'habitude; **as ~** comme d'habitude; **'business as ~'** 'la vente continue'; **more/less than ~** plus/moins que d'habitude.

usually *adv* d'habitude, normalement.

utensil *n* ustensile *m*.

uterus *n* utérus *m*.

utility **I** *n* **1** (usefulness) utilité *f*; **2** (also **public ~**) (service) service *m* public.

II utilities *n pl* (US) factures *fpl*.

utmost **I** *n* **to do** or **try one's ~ to come** faire tout son possible pour venir; **to do sth to the ~ of one's abilities** faire qch au maximum de ses capacités.

II *adj* [*caution, ease, secrecy*] le plus grand/la plus grande (*before n*); [*limit*] extrême; **it is of the ~ importance that** il est extrêmement important que (+ *subj*).

utter **I** *adj* [*disaster, boredom, despair*] total; [*honesty, sincerity*] absolu; [*fool, stranger*] parfait (*before n*).

II *vtr* prononcer [*word, curse*]; pousser [*cry*]; émettre [*sound*].

utterly *adv* complètement; [*condemn*] avec vigeur.

U-turn *n* demi-tour *m*; (figurative) volte-face *f inv*; **to do a ~** faire volte-face.

UV *adj* (*abbr* = **ultraviolet**) [*light, ray, radiation*] ultraviolet/-ette.

Vv

v, **V** *n* **1** (letter) v, V *m*; **2 v** (*abbr* = **versus**) contre; **3 v** (*abbr* = **vide**) voir; **4 v** (*abbr* = **volt**) V, volt *m*.

vacancy *n* **1 'vacancies'** 'chambres libres'; **'no vacancies'** 'complet'; **2** (unfilled job) poste *m* à pourvoir, poste *m* vacant; **to advertise a ~** faire paraître une offre d'emploi.

vacant *adj* **1** (unoccupied) [*flat, room, seat*] libre, disponible; [*office, land*] inoccupé; **2** (available) [*job, post*] vacant, à pourvoir; **'Situations ~'** 'offres d'emploi'; **3** (dreamy) [*look, stare*] absent; [*expression*] vide.

vacant: **~ lot** *n* (US) terrain *m* vague; **~ possession** *n* (GB) jouissance *f* immédiate.

vacate *vtr* quitter [*house, premises, job*].

vacation I *n* vacances *fpl*; **the long ~** (GB), **the summer ~** les grandes vacances; **on ~** en vacances; **to take a ~** prendre des vacances.
II *vi* (US) **he's ~ing in Miami** il est en vacances à Miami.

vacationer *n* (US) vacancier/-ière *m/f*.

vaccinate *vtr* vacciner (**against** contre).

vaccination *n* vaccination *f* (**against** contre).

vaccine *n* vaccin *m* (**against** contre).

vacillate *vi* hésiter (**between** entre; **over** au sujet de).

vacuum I *n* **1** vide *m*; **to create a ~** faire le vide; **emotional ~** vide affectif; **2** (also **~ cleaner**) aspirateur *m*.
II *vtr* passer [qch] à l'aspirateur [*carpet*]; passer l'aspirateur dans [*room*].

vacuum: **~ flask** *n* bouteille *f* thermos®; **~ packed** *adj* emballé sous vide.

vagrant *n*, *adj* vagabond/-e (*m/f*).

vague *adj* **1** (imprecise) [*person, account, idea, memory, rumour, term*] vague; **2** (evasive) **to be ~ about** rester vague sur or évasif/-ive au sujet de [*plans, past*]; **3** (distracted) [*person, expression*] distrait; **4** (faint, slight) [*sound, smell, taste*] vague, imprécis; [*fear, feeling, embarrassment, unease*] vague (*before n*); [*doubt*] léger/-ère (*before n*).

vaguely *adv* **1** (faintly, slightly) vaguement; **it seems ~ familiar** cela me dit vaguement quelque chose; **2** (distractedly) [*smile, gaze, say, gesture*] d'un air distrait or vague; **3** (imprecisely) [*remember, understand, imagine, reply*] vaguement.

vain I *adj* **1** (conceited) vaniteux/-euse, vain (*after n*); **to be ~ about sth** tirer vanité de qch; **2** (futile) [*attempt, promise, hope*] vain (*before n*).
II in vain *phr* en vain.
IDIOMS **to take sb's name in ~** parler de qn (derrière son dos).

vainly *adv* [*try, wait, struggle*] vainement, en vain.

valance *n* (on bed base) tour *m* de lit; (above curtains) cantonnière *f*.

valentine card *n* carte *f* de la Saint-Valentin.

valet ▶805 *n* **1** (employee) valet *m* de chambre; **2** (US) (rack) valet *m* de nuit.

valiant *adj* [*soldier*] vaillant; [*attempt*] courageux/-euse; **to make a ~ attempt to do** tenter courageusement de faire; **to make a ~ effort to smile** s'efforcer bravement de sourire.

valiantly *adv* [*fight*] vaillamment; [*try*] courageusement.

valid *adj* **1** (still usable) [*passport, licence*] valide; [*ticket, offer*] valable (**for** pour); **2** (well-founded) [*argument, excuse, method*] valable; [*complaint*] fondé; [*point, comment*] pertinent.

validate *vtr* **1** prouver le bien-fondé de [*claim, theory, conclusion*]; **2** valider [*document, passport*].

validity *n* (of ticket, document, argument, method) validité *f*; (of complaint, objection) bien-fondé *m*.

valley *n* vallée *f*; (small) vallon *m*.

valour (GB), **valor** (US) *n* bravoure *f*.
IDIOMS **discretion is the better part of ~** prudence est mère de sûreté (Proverb).

valuable *adj* **1** [*commodity, asset*] de valeur; **to be ~** avoir de la valeur; **a very ~ ring** une bague de grande valeur; **2** [*advice, information, lesson, member*] précieux/-ieuse.

valuables *n pl* objets *mpl* de valeur.

valuation *n* (of house, land, company) évaluation *f*; (of antique, art) expertise *f*; **to have a ~ done on sth** faire évaluer qch.

value I *n* **1** (monetary worth) valeur *f*; **of little/great ~** de peu de/de grande valeur; **of no ~** sans valeur; **it has a ~ of £50** cela vaut 50 livres sterling; **to the ~ of** pour une valeur de; **2** (usefulness, general worth) valeur *f*; **to have** or **be of educational ~** avoir une valeur éducative; **I don't see the ~ of that** je n'en vois pas l'utilité; **novelty/entertainment ~** caractère nouveau/divertissant; **3** (worth relative to cost) **to be good/poor ~** avoir un bon/mauvais rapport qualité-prix; **to be good ~ at £5** ne pas être cher/chère à 5 livres sterling; **to get ~ for money** en avoir pour son argent; **4** (standards, ideals) valeur *f*; **family ~s** valeurs traditionelles (de la famille).
II *vtr* **1** (assess worth of) évaluer [*house, asset, company*] (**at** à); expertiser [*antique, jewel, painting*]; **2** (appreciate) apprécier [*person, friendship, opinion, help*]; tenir à [*independence, life*]; **to ~ sb as a friend** apprécier qn en tant qu'ami.

valve *n* **1** (in machine, engine) soupape *f*; (on tyre, football) valve *f*; **2** (Anat) valvule *f*.

van *n* **1** (small, for deliveries) fourgonnette *f*, camionnette *f*; (larger, for removals) fourgon *m*; **2** (US) (camper) auto-caravane *f*, camping-car *m*.

vandal *n* vandale *mf*.

vandalism *n* vandalisme *m*.
vandalize *vtr* vandaliser.
van driver ▶805| *n* chauffeur *m* de camionnette.
vanguard *n* avant-garde *f*; **in the ~** à l'avant-garde.
vanilla *n* vanille *f*.
vanilla: **~ essence** *n* extrait *m* de vanille; **~ sugar** *n* sucre *m* vanillé.
vanish *vi* disparaître (**from** de); **to ~ into the distance** disparaître au loin; **to ~ into thin air** se volatiliser.
vanishing *adj* [*species*] en voie de disparition.
vanity *n* vanité *f*.
vantage point *n* point *m* de vue, position *f* élevée; **from my ~ I could see...** de ma position je voyais...; **from the ~ of** du haut de.
vapid *adj* [*person, expression, remark, debate*] mièvre, fade; [*style, novel*] insipide, fade.
vaporizer *n* vaporisateur *m*.
vapour (GB), **vapor** (US) *n* vapeur *f*.
vapour trail *n* traînée *f* de condensation, traînée *f* d'avion.
variable *n*, *adj* variable (*f*).
variance *n* **to be at ~ with** ne pas concorder avec [*evidence, facts*].
variant *n* variante *f* (**of** de; **on** par rapport à).
variation *n* **1** (change) variation *f*, différence *f* (**in, of** de); **regional ~** variations régionales; **~ between A and B** différence entre A et B; **2** (new version) variante *f* (**of** de); (in music) variation *f* (**on** sur).
varied *adj* varié; **many and ~** divers et variés.
variegated *adj* **1** [*assortment, landscape*] varié; **2** (flower, leaf) panaché.
variety I *n* **1** (diversity, range) variété *f* (**in, of** de); **for a ~ of reasons** pour diverses raisons; **a ~ of sizes/colours** un grand choix de tailles/de coloris; **2** (type) type *m*; (of plant) variété *f*.
II *noun modifier* [*artist, act*] de variétés; **~ show** spectacle de variétés.
various *adj* **1** (different) différents (*before n*); **2** (several) divers; **at ~ times** (several times) à diverses reprises; (from time to time) de temps en temps; **in ~ ways** de diverses manières.
varnish I *n* vernis *m*.
II *vtr* vernir [*woodwork*]; **to ~ one's nails** se vernir les ongles.
varnishing *n* vernissage *m*.
vary I *vtr* varier [*menu, programme*]; faire varier [*temperature*]; changer de [*method, pace, route*].
II *vi* [*objects, people, tastes*] varier (**with, according to** selon); **it varies from one town to another** cela varie d'une ville à l'autre; **they ~ in cost/in size** ils varient quant au coût/à la taille; **to ~ greatly** varier considérablement.
varying *adj* [*amounts, degrees, opinions*] variable; **with ~ (degrees of) success** avec plus ou moins de succès.
vase *n* vase *m*; **flower ~** vase à fleurs.
vasectomy *n* vasectomie *f*.
vast *adj* **1** (quantitatively) [*amount, sum, improvement, difference*] énorme; [*number*] très grand (*before n*); **the ~ majority** la très grande majorité; **2** (spatially) [*room, area, plain*] vaste (*before n*), immense.
vastly *adv* [*improved, increased, superior*] considérablement, infiniment; [*different*] complètement.
vat *n* cuve *f*; **beer/wine ~** cuve à bière/vin.
VAT *n* (GB) (*abbr* = **value-added tax**) TVA *f*, taxe *f* à la valeur ajoutée.
Vatican *pr n* Vatican *m*; **~ City** cité *f* du Vatican.
vaudeville *n* variétés *fpl*.
vault I *n* **1** (roof) voûte *f*; **2** (also **~s**) (of house, for wine) cave *f*; (of bank) chambre *f* forte; (for safe-deposit boxes) salle *f* des coffres.
II *vtr* sauter par-dessus [*fence, bar*].
III *vi* sauter (**over** par-dessus).
vaulted *adj* [*roof*] voûté.
VCR *n* (*abbr* = **video cassette recorder**) magnétoscope *m*.
VD ▶686| *n* (*abbr* = **venereal disease**) MST *f*.
VDU *n* (*abbr* = **visual display unit**) écran *m* de visualisation.
VDU operator ▶805| *n* opérateur/-trice *m*/*f* de terminal de visualisation.
veal *n* veau *m*.
veer *vi* **1** (change direction) [*ship*] virer; (also **~ off**) [*person, road*] tourner; **2** [*person, opinion, emotion*] changer; **to ~ (away) from sth** se détourner de qch; **to ~ towards sth** se tourner vers qch.
vegan *n*, *adj* végétalien/-ienne (*m*/*f*).
veganism *n* végétalisme *m*.
vegetable I *n* **1** (edible plant) légume *m*; **2** (as opposed to mineral, animal) végétal *m*; **3**° (figurative) **to become a ~**° être réduit à l'état de légume.
II *noun modifier* [*knife, dish*] à légumes; [*soup, patch*] de légumes; [*fat, oil*] végétal; **~ garden** potager *m*.
vegetarian *n*, *adj* végétarien/-ienne (*m*/*f*).
vegetarianism *n* végétarisme *m*.
vegetate *vi* végéter.
vegetation *n* végétation *f*.
vehemence *n* (of speech, action) véhémence *f*; (of feelings) intensité *f*.
vehemently *adv* [*speak, react*] avec véhémence.
vehicle *n* **1** véhicule *m*; **'closed to ~s'** 'interdit à la circulation'; **2** (medium) véhicule *m* (**for** de); **3 to be a ~ for** être destiné à mettre en valeur [*actor*].
vehicular *adj* **'no ~ access'**, **'no ~ traffic'** 'circulation interdite'.
veil I *n* **1** voile *m*; (on hat) voilette *f*; **to take the ~** prendre le voile; **2** (figurative) voile *m*; **a ~ of secrecy** le voile du secret; **let's draw a ~ over that episode** oublions cet épisode.
II *vtr* [*mist, cloud*] voiler.

vein *n* (blood vessel) veine *f*; (on insect wing, leaf) nervure *f*; (in marble) veine *f*; (in cheese) veinure *f*; (of ore) veine *f*; **to continue in a similar ~** continuer dans la même veine.

velocity *n* vitesse *f*; (formal context) vélocité *f*.

velour(s) *n* velours *m*.

velvet I *n* velours *m*; **crushed ~** velours frappé.
II *noun modifier* [*garment, curtain, cushion*] en velours.

velvety *adj* velouté.

vending machine *n* distributeur *m* automatique.

vendor ▶805| *n* **1** (in street, kiosk) marchand/-e *m/f*; **2** (as opposed to buyer) vendeur/-euse *m/f*.

veneer *n* **1** (on wood) placage *m*; **2** (figurative) (surface show) vernis *m*.

venerable *adj* vénérable.

venereal disease ▶686| *n* maladie *f* vénérienne.

venetian blind *n* store *m* vénitien.

vengeance *n* vengeance *f*; **to take ~ (up)on sb** se venger de qn (**for** pour); **with a ~** de plus belle.

Venice ▶574| *pr n* Venise.

venison *n* (viande *f* de) chevreuil *m*.

venomous *adj* venimeux/-euse.

vent I *n* (outlet for gas, pressure) bouche *f*, conduit *m*; **air ~** bouche d'aération; **to give ~ to** décharger [*anger, feelings*].
II *vtr* décharger [*anger, frustration*] (**on** sur).

ventilate *vtr* aérer [*room*].

ventilation *n* **1** aération *f*, ventilation *f*; **~ shaft** puits *m* d'aérage; **2** (of patient) ventilation *f* artificielle.

ventilator *n* (for patient) respirateur *m* artificiel.

ventriloquism *n* ventriloquie *f*.

ventriloquist ▶805| *n* ventriloque *mf*; **~'s dummy** pantin *m* de ventriloque.

venture I *n* **1** (undertaking) aventure *f*, entreprise *f*; **a commercial ~** une entreprise commerciale; **2** (experiment) essai *m*; **a scientific ~** un coup d'essai en matière scientifique.
II *vtr* hasarder [*opinion, suggestion*]; **to ~ the opinion that** hasarder l'opinion selon laquelle; **might I ~ a suggestion?** puis-je me permettre une suggestion?; **to ~ to do** se risquer à faire.
III *vi* **to ~ into** s'aventurer dans [*place, street, city*]; **to ~ out(doors)** s'aventurer dehors.
IDIOMS **nothing ~d nothing gained** qui ne risque rien n'a rien.

venue *n* lieu *m*; **a change of ~** un changement de lieu.

Venus *pr n* Vénus *f*.

verb *n* verbe *m*.

verbally *adv* verbalement.

verbatim I *adj* [*report, account*] textuel/-elle.
II *adv* [*describe, record*] mot pour mot.

verbena *n* verveine *f*; **lemon ~** verveine citronnelle.

verbose *adj* verbeux/-euse.

verdict *n* **1** verdict *m*; **to return a ~** rendre un verdict; **to reach a ~** arriver au verdict; **a ~ of guilty/not guilty** un verdict positif/négatif; **the ~ was suicide** l'enquête a conclu au suicide; **2** (figurative) (opinion) verdict *m*; **well, what's the ~**○**?** eh bien, qu'est-ce que tu en penses?

verge *n* **1** (GB) (by road) accotement *m*, bas-côté *m*; **2** (brink) **on the ~ of** au bord de [*tears*]; au seuil de [*adolescence, death*]; **on the ~ of success** sur le point de réussir; **on the ~ of doing** sur le point de faire.
■ **verge on**: **~ on [sth]** friser [*panic, stupidity, contempt*].

verification *n* vérification *f*.

verify *vtr* vérifier.

vermicelli *n* vermicelles *mpl*.

vermilion ▶559| *n*, *adj* vermillon (*m*) *inv*.

vermin *n* **1** (rodents) animaux *mpl* nuisibles; **2** (lice, insects) vermine *f*.

vernacular I *n* (language) **the ~** la langue vulgaire; **in the ~** (in local dialect) en dialecte.
II *adj* [*architecture*] local.

verruca *n* verrue *f* plantaire.

versatile *adj* **1** (flexible) [*person*] plein de ressources, aux talents divers (*after n*); [*mind*] souple; **2** (with many uses) [*vehicle*] polyvalent; [*equipment*] à usages multiples.

versatility *n* **1** (flexibility) (of person) adaptabilité *f*; **2** (of equipment) polyvalence *f*.

verse *n* **1** (poems) poésie *f*; **to write ~** écrire des poèmes; **2** (form) vers *mpl*; **in ~** en vers; **3** (part of poem) strophe *f*; (of song) couplet *m*.

version *n* version *f* (**of** de).

versus *prep* contre.

vertebra *n* vertèbre *f*.

vertebrate *n*, *adj* vertébré (*m*).

vertical *adj* [*line, take-off*] vertical; [*cliff*] à pic; **a ~ drop** un à-pic.

vertically *adv* verticalement.

vertigo *n* vertige *m*; **to get ~** avoir le vertige.

verve *n* brio *m*, verve *f*.

very I *adj* **1** (actual) même (*after n*); **this ~ second** immédiatement; **2** (ideal) **the ~ person I need** exactement la personne qu'il me faut; **the ~ thing I need** exactement ce qu'il me faut; **3** (ultimate) tout; **from the ~ beginning** depuis le tout début; **at the ~ front** tout devant; **to the ~ end** jusqu'au bout; **on the ~ edge** à l'extrême bord; **4** (mere) [*mention, thought, word*] seul (*before n*); **the ~ idea!** quelle idée!
II *adv* **1** (extremely) très; **I'm ~ sorry** je suis vraiment désolé; **~ well** très bien; **she couldn't ~ well do that** elle ne pouvait pas vraiment faire cela; **that's all ~ well but who's going to pay for it?** c'est bien beau, tout ça, mais qui va payer?; **~ much** beaucoup; **I didn't eat ~ much** je n'ai pas mangé grand-chose; **2** (absolutely) **the ~ best/worst thing** de loin la meilleure/pire chose; **the ~ best hotels** les meilleurs hôtels; **at the ~**

latest au plus tard; **at the ~ least** tout au moins; **the ~ first** le tout premier; **the ~ next day** le lendemain même; **a car of your ~ own** ta propre voiture.

vessel *n* **1** (ship) vaisseau *m*; **2** (Anat) **blood ~** vaisseau sanguin.

vest *n* **1** (underwear) maillot *m* de corps; **2** (for sport, fashion) débardeur *m*; **3** (US) (waistcoat) gilet *m*.

vested interest *n* **to have a ~** être personnellement intéressé (**in** dans).

vestige *n* (trace) vestige *m*; (of truth, stammer) trace *f*.

vest pocket (US) I *n* poche *f* de gilet.
II **vest-pocket** *adj* [*dictionary, calculator*] de poche.

vet I *n* **1** ▶805 (*abbr* = **veterinary surgeon**) vétérinaire *mf*; **2**° (US Mil) ancien combattant *m*, vétéran *m*.
II *vtr* mener une enquête approfondie sur [*person*]; passer [qch] en revue [*plan*]; approuver [*publication*].

veteran I *n* vétéran *m*.
II *noun modifier* [*sportsman, politician*] chevronné; **a ~ peace campaigner** un vieux routier de la campagne pour la paix.

veteran car *n* (GB) voiture *f* ancienne (*construite avant 1905*).

veterinarian ▶805 *n* (US) vétérinaire *mf*.

veterinary surgeon ▶805 *n* vétérinaire *mf*.

veto I *n* **1** (practice) veto *m*; **2** (right) droit *m* de veto (**over, on** sur); **to exercise one's ~** exercer son droit de veto.
II *vtr* mettre or opposer son veto à.

vetting *n* contrôle *m*; **security ~** enquête *f* de sécurité.

vex *vtr* (annoy) contrarier; (worry) tracasser.

vexed *adj* **1** (annoyed) mécontent (**with** de); **2** (problematic) [*question, issue*] épineux/-euse.

VHF *n* (*abbr* = **very high frequency**) VHF.

via *prep* **1** (by way of) (on ticket, timetable) via; (other contexts) en passant par; **we came ~ Paris** nous sommes venus en passant par Paris; **2** (by means of) par; **transmitted ~ satellite** transmis par satellite.

viability *n* (of company, government, farm) viabilité *f*; (of project, idea, plan) validité *f*.

viable *adj* **1** (gen) [*company, government, farm*] viable; [*project, idea, plan*] réalisable, valable; **2** (Med) [*foetus*] viable.

viaduct *n* viaduc *m*.

vibrant *adj* [*person, place, personality*] plein de vie; [*colour*] éclatant.

vibrate *vi* vibrer (**with** de).

vibration *n* vibration *f*.

vicar *n* pasteur *m*.

vicarage *n* presbytère *m*.

vicarious *adj* (indirect) indirect.

vicariously *adv* **to live ~** vivre par procuration.

vice I *n* **1** vice *m*; (amusing weakness) faiblesse *f*; **2** (also **vise** US) (tool) étau *m*.
II *noun modifier* [*laws*] sur les mœurs.

vice: **~-captain** *n* capitaine *m* en second; **~-chancellor** ▶805 *n* président/-e *m/f* d'Université; **~-president** *n* vice-président/-e *m/f*; **~-presidential** *adj* [*candidate, race*] à la vice-présidence; **~roy** *n* vice-roi *m*; **~ squad** *n* brigade *f* des mœurs.

vicinity *n* voisinage *m*; **in the (immediate) ~ of Oxford** à proximité (immédiate) d'Oxford.

vicious *adj* [*animal*] malfaisant; [*speech, attack, price cut, revenge*] brutal; [*rumour, person, sarcasm, lie*] malveillant.

vicious circle *n* cercle *m* vicieux.

viciously *adv* brutalement.

victim *n* victime *f*; **to fall ~ to** être victime de [*disease, disaster, deceit*]; succomber à [*charm*].

victimization *n* persécution *f*.

victimize *vtr* persécuter.

victor *n* vainqueur *m*; **to emerge the ~** sortir vainqueur.

Victorian *adj* victorien/-ienne.

victorious *adj* victorieux/-ieuse (**over** sur).

victory *n* victoire *f*; **to win a ~** remporter une victoire.

video I *n* **1** (also **~ recorder**) magnétoscope *m*; **2** (also **~ cassette**) cassette *f* vidéo; **on ~** en vidéo; **3** (also **~ film**) vidéo *f*.
II *noun modifier* [*footage*] de vidéo; [*market*] de la vidéo; [*channel, evidence, link, equipment, graphics, game, recording*] vidéo; [*interview*] en vidéo.
III *vtr* **1** (from TV) enregistrer [qch]; **2** (on camcorder) filmer [qch] en vidéo.

video: **~ camera** *n* caméra *f* vidéo; **~ clip** *n* extrait *m*; **~ shop** (GB), **~ store** (US) ▶805 *n* vidéoclub *m*.

videotape I *n* bande *f* vidéo.
II *vtr* enregistrer [qch] en vidéo.

Vienna ▶574 *pr n* Vienne.

view I *n* **1** vue *f*; **you're blocking my ~!** tu me bouches la vue!; **to get a better ~** pour mieux voir; **to have a front/back ~ of sth** voir qch de face/de derrière; **to take the long(-term)/short(-term) ~ of sth** avoir une vision à long terme/à court terme de qch; **to do sth in (full) ~ of sb** faire qch devant qn or sous les yeux de qn; **to keep sth in ~** ne pas perdre qch de vue; **to disappear from** or **be lost to ~** disparaître; **2** (personal opinion, attitude) avis *m*, opinion *f*; **point of ~** point *m* de vue; **in his ~** à son avis; **in the ~ of Mr Jones** selon M. Jones.
II *vtr* **1** (consider) considérer; (envisage) envisager; **2** (look at) voir [*scene, building, collection, exhibition*]; visiter [*house, castle*]; regarder [*programme*].
III **in view of** *phr* (considering) vu, étant donné; **in ~ of this, they...** cela étant, ils...
IV **with a view to** *phr* **with a ~ to doing** en vue de faire, afin de faire.

viewer *n* **1** (of TV) téléspectateur/-trice *m/f*; **2** (of property) visiteur/-euse *m/f*; **3** (on camera) visionneuse *f*.

viewing I *n* **1 'Saturday night's ~'** 'notre/votre etc programme du samedi soir'; **essential ~ for teachers** à voir impérativement par les enseignants; **the film makes compulsive ~** le film est captivant; **2** (of house) visite *f*; (of film) projection *f*; **'~ by appointment only'** 'visite sur rendez-vous uniquement'.
II *noun modifier* [*trends, patterns*] d'écoute; [*habits, preferences*] des téléspectateurs; **~ figures** taux *m* d'écoute; **the ~ public** les téléspectateurs *mpl*.

viewpoint *n* (all contexts) point *m* de vue.

vigil *n* veille *f*; (by sickbed) veillée *f*; (by demonstrators) manifestation *f* silencieuse.

vigilante *n* membre *m* d'un groupe d'autodéfense.

vigorous *adj* [*person, attempt, exercise*] vigoureux/-euse; [*campaign*] énergique; [*denial*] catégorique.

vigorously *adv* vigoureusement; [*defend, campaign, deny*] énergiquement.

vigour (GB), **vigor** (US) *n* vigueur *f*; (of campaign, efforts) énergie *f*.

vile *adj* [*smell*] infect; [*weather*] abominable; [*place, colour*] horrible; [*mood*] exécrable.

villa *n* (in town) pavillon *m*; (in country, for holiday) villa *f*.

village I *n* village *m*.
II *noun modifier* [*shop, fête, school*] du village.

village: **~ green** *n* terrain *m* communal (*au centre d'un village*); **~ hall** *n* salle *f* des fêtes.

villager *n* villageois/-e *m/f*.

villain *n* (in book, film) méchant *m*; (child) coquin/-e *m/f*.

vindicate *vtr* justifier [*action, claim, judgment*].

vindictive *adj* [*person, behaviour*] vindicatif/-ive (**towards** envers).

vindictiveness *n* esprit *m* de vengeance.

vine *n* **1** (producing grapes) vigne *f*; **2** (climbing plant) plante *f* grimpante.

vinegar *n* vinaigre *m*.

vineyard *n* vignoble *m*.

vintage I *n* (wine) millésime *m*.
II *adj* **1** [*wine, champagne*] millésimé; [*port*] vieux/vieille; **2** [*comedy*] classique.

vintage: **~ car** *n* voiture *f* d'époque; **~ year** *n* grande année *f*.

vinyl I *n* vinyle *m*.
II *noun modifier* [*paint*] vinylique.

viola ▶ **753** *n* (violon *m*) alto *m*.

violate *vtr* **1** (infringe) violer; **2** profaner [*sacred place*]; troubler [*peace*].

violation *n* **1** violation *f*; **2** (of sacred place) profanation *f*; **3 traffic ~** infraction *f* au code de la route.

violence *n* violence *f*; **two days of ~** deux jours d'incidents violents.

violent *adj* **1** [*crime, behaviour, film, storm, emotion*] violent; **2** [*contrast*] brutal; **3** [*colour*] criard.

violently *adv* **1** [*shake*] violemment; [*struggle*] furieusement; **to be ~ ill** or **sick** (GB) avoir de violentes nausées; **2** [*brake*] brusquement; **3** [*react, object*] violemment.

violet ▶ **559** I *n* **1** (flower) violette *f*; **2** (colour) violet *m*.
II *adj* violet/-ette.

violin ▶ **753** *n* violon *m*.

violinist ▶ **805** *n* violoniste *mf*.

VIP (*abbr* = **very important person**) I *n* personnalité *f* (en vue).
II *adj* [*area, lounge*] réservé aux personnalités; **~ guest** hôte *mf* de marque; **to give sb (the) ~ treatment** recevoir qn en hôte de marque.

viper *n* vipère *f*.

virgin *n, adj* vierge (*f*).

Virgo *n* Vierge *f*; ▶ **Aquarius**.

virile *adj* viril.

virtual *adj* **1** (almost complete) quasi-total; **he was a ~ prisoner** il était pratiquement prisonnier; **2** (Comput) virtuel/-elle.

virtually *adv* pratiquement, presque; **it's ~ impossible** c'est quasiment° impossible.

virtual reality *n* réalité *f* virtuelle.

virtue I *n* **1** (goodness) vertu *f*; **2** (advantage) avantage *m*; **to extol the ~s of sth** vanter les mérites de qch.
II **by virtue of** *phr* en raison de.

virtuoso I *n* virtuose *mf* (**of** de).
II *adj* de virtuose.

virus ▶ **686** *n* virus *m*.

visa *n* visa *m*; **tourist ~** visa de touriste.

vis-à-vis *prep* (in relation to) par rapport à; (concerning) en ce qui concerne.

visceral *adj* viscéral; [*performance*] qui vous prend aux tripes°.

viscous *adj* visqueux/-euse, gluant.

visibility *n* **1** (good conditions for seeing) visibilité *f*; **2** (conspicuousness) visibilité; **light clothes improve your ~** des vêtements clairs vous rendent plus visible la nuit.

visible *adj* **1** (able to be seen) visible; **clearly ~** bien visible; **2** (concrete) [*improvement, sign*] évident; **with no ~ means of support** sans ressources apparentes.

visibly *adv* [*moved, shocked*] manifestement.

vision *n* **1** (idea, mental picture, hallucination) vision *f*; **to appear to sb in a ~** apparaître à qn; **Rousseau's ~ of the ideal society** l'idée de la société idéale selon Rousseau; **2** (imaginative foresight) sagacité *f*; **a man of ~** un visionnaire; **3** (ability to see) vue *f*; **to have blurred ~** voir trouble; **4** (visual image) image *f*; **a ~ of loveliness** l'image de la beauté; **5** (quality of a TV) image *f*.

visionary *n, adj* visionnaire (*mf*).

visit I *n* (call) visite *f*; (stay) séjour *m*; **a state ~** une visite officielle; **a home ~** une visite à domicile; **a flying ~** une visite éclair; **on her first ~ to China, she...** pendant son premier séjour en Chine, elle..., la première fois qu'elle est allée en Chine, elle...; **to pay a ~ to sb, to pay sb a ~** aller voir qn; (more formal) rendre visite à qn; **to have a ~ from** recevoir la visite de.
II *vtr* **1 to ~ Paris** (see) visiter Paris; (stay)

faire un séjour à Paris, aller passer quelques jours à Paris; **to ~ sb** (call) aller voir qn; (more formal) rendre visite à qn; (stay with) aller (passer quelques jours) chez qn; **2** (US) **to ~ with sb** aller voir qn.

visiting: **~ card** *n* (US) carte *f* de visite; **~ hours** *n pl* heures *fpl* de visite; **~ team** *n* visiteurs/-euses *mpl/fpl*; **~ time** *n* heures *fpl* de visite.

visitor *n* **1** (caller) invité/-e *m/f*; **we have ~s** nous avons de la visite; **2** (tourist) visiteur/-euse *m/f*.

visitor: **~ centre** (GB), **~ center** (US) *n* centre *m* d'accueil et d'information des visiteurs; **~s' book** *n* (in exhibition) livre *m* d'or; (in hotel) registre *m*.

visor *n* visière *f*.

vista *n* panorama *m*; (figurative) perspective *f*.

visual *adj* visuel/-elle.

visual: **~ aid** *n* support *m* visuel; **~ arts** *n pl* arts *mpl* plastiques.

visualize *vtr* **1** (picture) s'imaginer; **2** (envisage) envisager.

visually *adv* visuellement.

visually handicapped *adj* (partially-sighted) malvoyant; (non-sighted) nonvoyant.

visually impaired *n* **the ~** les malvoyants *mpl*.

visuals *n pl* (photographs, pictures) images *fpl*.

vital *adj* **1** (essential) [*asset, document, expenditure, information, research, industry, supplies, issue, need, interest*] primordial; [*match, point, support, factor*] décisif/-ive; [*service, help*] indispensable; [*treatment, organ, force*] vital; **of ~ importance** d'une importance capitale; **2** [*person*] plein de vie.

vitality *n* vitalité *f*.

vitally *adv* [*important*] extrêmement; [*needed*] absolument.

vital statistics *n* (of woman) mensurations *fpl*.

vitamin I *n* vitamine *f*; **with added ~s, ~ enriched** vitaminé.
II *noun modifier* [*requirements*] en vitamines; **to have a high/low ~ content** être riche/pauvre en vitamines; **~ deficiency** carence *f* en vitamines.

vitriolic *adj* [*editorial*] au vitriol; [*attack, response*] violent.

viva I *n* oral *m*.
II *excl* vive!

vivacious *adj* plein de vivacité.

vivacity *n* vivacité *f*.

vivid *adj* **1** (bright) [*colour, light*] vif/vive; **2** (graphic) [*imagination*] vif/vive; [*memory, picture*] (très) net/nette; [*dream, impression, description, example, imagery*] frappant.

vividly *adv* [*describe, illustrate, demonstrate*] de façon très vivante; [*remember, recall*] très bien.

vivisection *n* vivisection *f*.

vixen *n* **1** (fox) renarde *f*; **2** (woman) mégère *f*.

viz *adv* (*abbr* = **videlicet**) à savoir.

vocabulary *n* **1** (of a language) vocabulaire *m*; **2** (book) lexique *m*.

vocal *adj* (concerning speech) vocal.

vocalist *n* chanteur/-euse *m/f* (*dans un groupe pop*).

vocals *n pl* chant *m*; **who did the ~?** qui a assuré la partie vocale?; **to do the backing ~** faire les chœurs.

vocation *n* vocation *f*.

vocational *adj* professionnel/-elle; **~ course** stage *m* de formation professionnelle.

vociferous *adj* [*person, protest*] véhément.

vogue *n* vogue *f* (**for** de); **to go out of ~** se démoder; **to be out of ~** être démodé.

voice I *n* **1** (speaking) voix *f*; **in a loud ~** à haute voix; **in a low ~** à voix basse; **in a cross ~** d'une voix irritée; **keep your ~ down!** baisse la voix!; **his ~ is breaking** sa voix mue; **to have lost one's ~** (when ill) être aphone; **at the top of one's ~** à tue-tête; **2** (for singing) voix *f*; **to have a good ~** avoir une belle voix; **3** (opinion, expression) **to have a ~** avoir voix au chapitre (**in sth** en matière de qch); **4** (representative organization) porte-parole *m* (**of** de); **5** (in grammar) **in the active ~** à la voix active.
II *vtr* exprimer [*concern, grievance*].
IDIOMS **to like the sound of one's own ~** s'écouter parler.

voice: **~-over** *n* voix-off *f*; **~ training** *n* entraînement *m* de la voix.

void I *n* vide *m*; **to fill the ~** combler le vide.
II *adj* **1** (Law) [*contract, agreement*] nul/nulle; [*cheque*] annulé; **2** (empty) vide; **~ of** dépourvu de.

volatile *adj* (figurative) [*situation*] explosif/-ive; [*person*] lunatique; [*mood*] changeant; [*market, exchange rate*] instable.

volcanic *adj* volcanique.

volcano *n* volcan *m*.

volition *n* **of one's own ~** de son propre gré.

volley I *n* **1** (in tennis) volée *f*; **2** (of gunfire) salve *f* (**of** de); (of missiles) volée *f* (**of** de); **3** (series) **a ~ of** un feu roulant de [*questions*]; une bordée de [*insults, oaths*].
II *vtr* (in tennis) prendre [qch] de volée [*ball*].
III *vi* (in tennis) jouer à la volée.

volleyball ▶ 649 *n* volley(-ball) *m*.

volt *n* volt *m*; **nine-~ battery** pile *f* de neuf volts.

voltage *n* tension *f*.

volume *n* **1** (in measurement) volume *m* (**of** de); (of container) capacité *f*; **by ~** au volume; **2** (book) volume *m*; (part of set) tome *m*.
IDIOMS **to speak ~s (about sth)** en dire long (sur qch).

volume control *n* (bouton *m* de) réglage *m* du volume.

voluntarily *adv* de plein gré, volontairement.

voluntary *adj* **1** (not imposed) [*consent, control, recruit, euthanasia, redundancy*] volontaire; [*agreement, ban*] librement consenti; [*sanction*] non obligatoire; **2** (unpaid) bénévole; **to work on a ~ basis** travailler bénévolement; **3** [*movement*] volontaire.

volunteer I *n* **1** (offering to do sth) volontaire *mf*; **2** (unpaid worker) bénévole *mf*.
II *noun modifier* (unpaid) [*driver, fire brigade, helper, work*] bénévole.
III *vtr* **1** (offer) offrir; **to ~ to do** offrir de faire, se porter volontaire pour faire; **2** (divulge) fournir [qch] spontanément [*information*].
IV *vi* **1** se porter volontaire (**for** pour); **2** (as soldier) s'engager comme volontaire.

voluptuous *adj* voluptueux/-euse.

vomit I *n* vomi *m*.
II *vtr, vi* vomir.

voodoo *n, noun modifier* vaudou (*m*).

voracious *adj* vorace.

vortex *n* tourbillon *m*.

vote I *n* **1** (choice) vote *m*; **to cast one's ~** voter; **2** (franchise) **the ~** le droit de vote; **3** (ballot) vote *m*; **to have a ~** voter; **to take a ~ on** voter sur; **4** (body of voters) voix *fpl*; **the Scottish ~** les voix des Écossais; **by a majority ~** à la majorité des voix; **to increase one's ~ by 10%** recevoir 10% de voix en plus.
II *vtr* **1** (affirm choice of) voter; **to ~ sb into/out of office** élire/ne pas réélire qn; **2°** (propose) proposer.
III *vi* voter (**on** sur; **for sb** pour qn; **against** contre); **to ~ on whether** voter pour décider si; **let's ~ on it** mettons-le aux voix; **to ~ to strike** voter la grève.
IDIOMS **to ~ with one's feet** exprimer son mécontentement par son départ.

vote: **~ of confidence** *n* vote *m* de confiance (**in** en); **~ of thanks** *n* discours *m* de remerciement.

voter *n* électeur/-trice *m/f*.

voting I *n* scrutin *m*; **~ is by secret ballot** le vote se fait au scrutin secret.
II *noun modifier* [*intentions, rights*] de vote.

voting: **~ age** *n* majorité *f* électorale; **~ paper** *n* bulletin *m* de vote.

vouch *v* ■ **vouch for**: **~ for [sb/sth] 1** (informally) répondre de [*person*]; témoigner de [*fact*]; **2** (officially) se porter garant de.

voucher *n* (for gift, concession) bon *m*.

vow I *n* (of honour) serment *m*.
II **vows** *n pl* **1** (in religion) **to take one's ~s** prononcer ses vœux; **2 marriage** or **wedding ~s** promesses *fpl* du mariage.
III *vtr* faire vœu de; **to ~ to do** jurer de faire; (privately) se jurer de faire.

vowel *n* voyelle *f*.

voyage *n* voyage *m*; **on the ~** pendant le voyage; **to go on a ~** partir en voyage; **the outward/homeward ~** le voyage aller/de retour.

V-sign *n* **1** (victory sign) V *m* de la victoire; **2** (GB) (offensive gesture) geste *m* obscène.

vulgar *adj* **1** [*furniture, clothes*] de mauvais goût; [*behaviour, curiosity*] déplacé; [*taste*] douteux/-euse; [*person*] vulgaire; **2** (rude) grossier/-ière.

vulgarity *n* **1** (of furniture, clothes) mauvais goût *m*; (of person, behaviour) vulgarité *f*; **2** (rudeness) grossièreté *f*.

vulgarly *adv* [*called, known as*] vulgairement.

vulnerable *adj* vulnérable (**to** à).

vulture *n* vautour *m*.

w, **W** *n* w, W *m*.

wad *n* **1** (bundle) liasse *f* (**of** de); **2** (lump) boule *f* (**of** de).

wadding *n* **1** (padding) ouatage *m*; **2** (for gun) bourre *f*.

waddle *vi* [*duck, person*] se dandiner.

wade *vi* **1** (in water) **to ~ into the water** entrer dans l'eau; **to ~ ashore** marcher dans l'eau jusqu'au rivage; **to ~ across** traverser à gué; **2 he was wading through 'War and Peace'** il lisait 'Guerre et Paix', mais ça avançait lentement.

waders *n pl* cuissardes *fpl*.

wafer *n* (Culin) gaufrette *f*.

wafer-thin *adj* [*slice*] ultrafin.

waffle I *n* **1** (Culin) gaufre *f*; **2**○ (empty words) verbiage *m*; (in essay) remplissage *m*.
II○ *vi* (also **~ on**) (speaking) bavasser○; (writing) faire du remplissage.

waffle iron *n* (Culin) gaufrier *m*.

waft *vi* **to ~ towards** flotter vers; **to ~ up** monter.

wag I *vtr* remuer [*tail*]; hocher [*head*]; **to ~ one's finger at sb** (as threat) menacer qn du doigt.
II *vi* [*tail*] remuer, frétiller; **tongues will ~** ça va faire jaser.

wage I *n* (also **~s** *n pl*) salaire *m*.
II *noun modifier* [*agreement, claim, inflation, negotiations, rate, settlement, talks*] salarial; [*increase, rise*] de salaire; [*policy, restraint, freeze*] des salaires.
III *vtr* mener [*campaign*]; **to ~ (a) war against sth/sb** faire la guerre contre qch/qn.

wage: **~ bargaining** *n* négociations *fpl* salariales; **~ bill**, **~s bill** *n* facture *f* salariale; **~ costs** *n pl* coûts *mpl* salariaux.

wage earner *n* **1** (person earning a wage) salarié/-e *m/f* (hebdomadaire); **2** (breadwinner) soutien *m* de famille.

wage packet *n* **1** (envelope) enveloppe *f* de paie; **2** (money) paie *f*.

wager *n* pari *m*; **to make** or **lay a ~** parier, faire un pari.

wage: **~ round** *n* réajustement *m* des salaires; **~s council** *n* ≈ commission *f* des salaires; **~ sheet**, **~ slip** *n* feuille *f* de paie; **~ structure** *n* échelle *f* salariale.

waggon (GB), **wagon** *n* **1** (horse-drawn) chariot *m*; **2** (GB) (on rail) wagon *m* (de marchandises).
IDIOMS **to be on the ~**○ être au régime sec.

wail I *n* (of person) gémissement *m*; (of siren) hurlement *m*; (of musical instrument) son *m* plaintif.
II *vi* [*person, wind*] gémir; [*siren*] hurler; [*music*] pleurer.

wailing *n* (of person) gémissements *mpl*; (of wind) gémissements *mpl*; (of siren) hurlement *m*; (of music) son *m* plaintif.

waist *n* taille *f*; **to have a 70 cm ~** faire 70 cm de tour de taille; **to be ~-deep in water** avoir de l'eau jusqu'à la taille.

waist: **~band** *n* ceinture *f*; **~coat** *n* (GB) gilet *m*; **~line** *n* taille *f*; **~ measurement** *n* tour *m* de taille.

wait I *n* attente *f*; **an hour's ~** une heure d'attente; **to have a long ~** devoir attendre longtemps; **it will only be a short ~** ce ne sera pas long.
II *vtr* **1** (await) attendre [*turn*]; **don't ~ dinner for me**○ (US) ne m'attendez pas pour dîner; **2** (US) **to ~ table** servir à table.
III *vi* **1** (remain patiently) attendre; **to keep sb ~ing** faire attendre qn; **to ~ for sb/sth** attendre qn/qch; **it was worth ~ing for** cela valait la peine d'attendre; **to ~ for sb/sth to do** attendre que qn/qch fasse; **to ~ to do** attendre de faire; **I'm ~ing to use the phone** j'attends de pouvoir me servir du téléphone; **she can't ~ to start** elle a hâte de commencer; **you'll just have to ~ and see** attends et tu verras; **just you ~!** (as threat) tu vas voir○!; **~ for it!** tiens-toi bien○!; **2** (be left until later) [*meal, action*] attendre; **can't it ~?** ça ne peut pas attendre?; **3** (serve) **to ~ at** or **on table** servir à table.
IDIOMS **to lie in ~ for sb** [*attackers*] guetter qn.
■ **wait around**, **wait about** (GB) attendre.
■ **wait behind** attendre un peu; **to ~ behind for sb** attendre qn.
■ **wait in** (GB) rester à la maison.
■ **wait on**: **~ on [sb]** (serve) servir; **to be ~ed on** être servi; **to ~ on sb hand and foot** être aux petits soins pour qn.
■ **wait up 1** (stay awake) veiller; **to ~ up for sb** veiller jusqu'au retour de qn; **2** (US) (stay patiently) **~ up!** attends!

waiter ▶805 *n* serveur *m*; **'~!'** 'monsieur!'

waiter service *n* service *m* à table.

waiting *n* attente *f*; **'no ~'** 'arrêt et stationnement interdits'.

waiting game *n* **to play a ~** attendre son heure; (in politics) faire de l'attentisme.

waiting: **~ list** *n* liste *f* d'attente; **~ room** *n* salle *f* d'attente.

waitress ▶805 *n* serveuse *f*; **'~!'** 'madame!', 'mademoiselle!'

waive *vtr* (gen, Law) déroger à [*rule*]; renoncer à [*claim, demand, right*]; supprimer [*fee, condition*].

waiver *n* (Law) renonciation *f*.

waiver clause *n* **1** (Law) (in contract) clause *f* libératoire; **2** (in insurance) clause *f* de rachat.

wake I *vtr* réveiller; **to ~ sb from a dream** tirer qn d'un rêve.

II *vi* se réveiller; **I woke (up) to find him gone** à mon réveil, il était parti; **to ~ (up) from a deep sleep** sortir d'un profond sommeil.
■ **wake up**: ¶ **~ up** se réveiller; **~ up!** réveille-toi!; (to reality) ouvre les yeux!; ¶ **~ up [sb]**, **~ [sb] up** réveiller.

wakeful *adj* éveillé; **to have a ~ night** passer une nuit blanche.

wake-up call *n* réveil *m* téléphoné.

waking *adj* **in** or **during one's ~ hours** pendant la journée.

Wales *pr n* pays *m* de Galles.

walk I *n* **1** promenade *f*; (shorter) tour *m*; (hike) randonnée *f*; **it's about ten minutes' ~** c'est à environ dix minutes à pied; **on the ~ home** sur le chemin de la maison; **to go for** or **on a ~** (aller) faire une promenade; **to have** or **take a ~** faire une promenade; (shorter) faire un tour○; **to take sb for a ~** emmener qn faire une promenade or (shorter) un tour○; **to take the dog for a ~** promener le chien; **it's a long ~ back to the hotel** ça fait loin pour rentrer à l'hôtel à pied; **2** (gait) démarche *f*; **3** (pace) pas *m*; **at a brisk ~** d'un pas vif; **4** (path) allée *f*; **people from all ~s of life** des gens de tous les milieux; **5** (Sport) épreuve *f* de marche.
II *vtr* **1** faire [qch] à pied [*path, road*]; parcourir [qch] à pied [*district, countryside*]; (patrol) parcourir; **I can't ~ another step** je ne peux pas faire un pas de plus; **shall we take the bus or ~ it?** on prend le bus ou on y va à pied?; **2** (lead, escort) conduire [*horse*]; promener [*dog*]; **to ~ sb home** raccompagner qn chez lui/elle.
III *vi* (in general) marcher; (for pleasure) se promener; (not run) aller au pas; (not ride or drive) aller à pied; **to ~ with a limp/a swing** marcher en boitant/se dandinant; **it's not very far, let's ~** ce n'est pas très loin, allons-y à pied; **we go on holiday to ~** nous allons en vacances pour faire de la marche; **to ~ across** or **through sth** traverser qch (à pied) (*see note*); **a policeman ~ed by** un policier est passé; **he ~ed up/down the road** il a remonté/descendu la rue (à pied) (*see note*); **we've been ~ing round in circles for hours** nous tournons en rond depuis des heures; **someone was ~ing around upstairs** quelqu'un allait et venait à l'étage supérieur; **I'd just ~ed in at the door when...** je venais à peine de passer la porte, quand...; **suddenly in ~ed my father** soudain voilà que mon père est entré; **to ~ in one's sleep** (habitually) être somnambule; **to ~ up and down** faire les cent pas; **to ~ up and down a room** arpenter une pièce; **shall I ~ with you to the bus?** veux-tu que je t'accompagne au bus?; **he ~ed under a bus** il est passé sous un bus.
IDIOMS **take a ~**○! (US) dégage○!; **you must ~ before you can run** il ne faut pas brûler les étapes; **to ~ sb off their feet** mettre qn sur les rotules○.

■ **Note** *à pied* is often omitted with movement verbs if we already know that the person is on foot. If it is surprising or ambiguous, *à pied* should be included.

■ **walk across**: ¶ **~ across** traverser; **to ~ across to sth/sb** s'approcher de qch/qn; ¶ **~ across [sth]** traverser.
■ **walk around**: ¶ **~ around** se promener; (aimlessly) traîner; ¶ **~ around [sth]** (to and fro) faire un tour dans; (make circuit of) faire le tour de.
■ **walk away 1** s'éloigner (**from** de); **2** (refuse to face) **to ~ away from** se désintéresser de [*problem*]; **3** (survive unscathed) sortir indemne (**from** de); **4** (win easily) **to ~ away with** gagner [qch] haut la main [*game, tournament*]; remporter [qch] haut la main [*election*]; décrocher [*prize, honour*].
■ **walk back** revenir sur ses pas (**to** jusqu'à); **we ~ed back (home)** nous sommes rentrés à pied.
■ **walk in** entrer; **I'd just ~ed in when** je venais à peine d'entrer quand.
■ **walk into**: **~ into [sth] 1** (enter) entrer dans; **2** tomber dans [*trap*]; se fourrer dans [*tricky situation*]; **you ~ed right into that one**○! tu es tombé dans le panneau○!; **3** (bump into) rentrer dans [*door, person*].
■ **walk off**: ¶ **~ off 1** partir brusquement; **2**○ **to ~ off with sth** (innocently) partir avec qch; (as theft) filer○ avec qch; ¶ **~ off [sth]**, **~ [sth] off** se promener pour faire passer [*hangover, large meal*].
■ **walk out 1** sortir (**of** de); **2** (desert) partir; **to ~ out on** laisser tomber○ [*lover*]; rompre [*contract, undertaking*]; **3** (as protest) partir en signe de protestation; (on strike) se mettre en grève.
■ **walk over**: ¶ **~ over** (a few steps) s'approcher (**to** de); ¶ **~ over [sb]**○ **1** (defeat) battre [qn] à plates coutures; **2** (humiliate) marcher sur les pieds de.
■ **walk round**: ¶ **~ round** faire le tour; ¶ **~ round [sth]** (round edge of) faire le tour de; (visit) visiter [*town*].
■ **walk through**: **~ through [sth]** traverser [*house, forest*]; passer [*door*]; parcourir [*streets*]; marcher dans [*snow, mud, grass*].
■ **walk up**: **to ~ up to** s'approcher de.

walkie-talkie *n* talkie-walkie *m*.

walk-in *adj* (US) [*apartment*] de plain-pied sur la rue; [*clinic*] qui reçoit les clients sans rendez-vous.

walk-in closet *n* dressing *m*.

walking *n* (for pleasure) promenades *fpl* à pied; (for exercise) marche *f* à pied.

walking boots *n pl* chaussures *fpl* de marche.

walking distance *n* **to be within ~** être à quelques minutes de marche (**of** de).

walking: **~ frame** *n* (Med) déambulateur *m*; **~ holiday** *n* vacances *fpl* de randonnée; **~ race** *n* épreuve *f* de marche; **~ shoes** *n pl* chaussures *fpl* de marche; **~ stick** *n* canne *f*; **~ tour** *n* randonnée *f* à pied.

walk: **~man®** *n* walkman® *m*, baladeur *m*; **~-on** *adj* [*role*] de figurant; **~out** *n* (strike) grève *f* surprise; **~over** *n* victoire *f* facile (**for** pour); **~way** *n* allée *f*.

wall *n* **1** (construction) mur *m*; **2** (of cave, tunnel) paroi *f*; **3** (Anat) paroi *f*; **the stomach ~** la paroi stomacale; **4** (of tyre) flanc *m*.
IDIOMS **to be a fly on the ~** être une mouche; **to drive sb up the ~**○ exaspérer qn; **to go to the ~** faire faillite.
■ **wall off**: **~ off [sth]**, **~ [sth] off** (block off) condamner; (separate by wall) séparer [qch] par un mur.

wall: **~ chart** *n* affiche *f*; **~ covering** *n* revêtement *m* mural; **~ cupboard** *n* élément *m* (mural).

walled *adj* [*city*] fortifié; [*garden*] clos.

wallet *n* (for notes) portefeuille *m*; (for documents) porte-documents *m inv*.

wallflower *n* giroflée *f* jaune.
IDIOMS **to be a ~** faire tapisserie.

wall: **~ hanging** *n* tapisserie *f*; **~ heater** *n* radiateur *m* mural; **~ light** *n* applique *f* murale.

wallop○ *n* (punch) beigne○ *f*.

wallow *vi* **to ~ in** se vautrer dans [*mud, luxury*]; se complaire dans [*self-pity, nostalgia*].

wall painting *n* peinture *f* murale.

wallpaper I *n* papier *m* peint.
II *vtr* tapisser [*room*].

wallpaper stripper *n* décolleuse *f* (de papier peint).

wall-to-wall carpet *n* moquette *f*.

walnut I *n* **1** (nut) noix *f*; **2** (also **~ tree**) noyer *m*; **3** (wood) noyer *m*.
II *noun modifier* [*cake, yoghurt*] aux noix; [*oil*] de noix; [*furniture*] en noyer.

walrus *n* morse *m*; **~ moustache** moustache *f* à la gauloise.

waltz I *n* valse *f*.
II *vi* danser la valse (**with** avec).

wand *n* baguette *f*.

wander I *n* promenade *f*; **to have** or **take a ~** faire une balade○; **to have a ~ round the shops** faire un tour dans les magasins.
II *vtr* parcourir; **to ~ the streets** traîner dans la rue.
III *vi* **1** (walk, stroll) se promener; **to ~ around town** se balader en ville; **2** (stray) errer; **to ~ into the next field** s'égarer dans le champ voisin; **to ~ away** or **off** s'éloigner (**from** de); **3** (more casually) **to ~ in** arriver tranquillement; **to ~ over to** or **up to sb** s'approcher tranquillement de qn; **4** [*attention*] se relâcher; **her mind is ~ing** [*old person, patient*] elle divague; [*eyes, hands*] errer (**over** sur); **to ~ off the point** s'éloigner du sujet.
■ **wander about**, **wander around** (stroll) se balader; (when lost) errer.

wanderer *n* voyageur/-euse *m/f*.

wanderings *n pl* **1** (journeys) vagabondages *mpl*; **2** (confusion) divagations *fpl*.

wanderlust *n* envie *f* de voyager.

wane *vi* [*moon*] décroître; [*enthusiasm, popularity*] diminuer.

wangle○ I *n* combine○ *f*.
II *vtr* soutirer [*money, promise*]; se débrouiller pour avoir [*leave*]; **to ~ sth for sb** se débrouiller pour faire avoir qch à qn.

waning I *n* (of moon) déclin *m*; (weakening) déclin *m* (**of** de).
II *adj* [*moon*] décroissant; [*enthusiasm, popularity*] en baisse.

want I *n* **1** (need) besoin *m*; **to be in ~ of** avoir besoin de; **2** (lack) défaut *m*; **for ~ of** à défaut or faute de; **it's not for ~ of trying** ce n'est pas faute d'avoir essayé.
II *vtr* **1** (desire) vouloir; **I ~** (as general statement) je veux; (would like) je voudrais; (am seeking) je souhaite; **how much do you ~ for this chair?** combien voulez-vous pour ce fauteuil?; **do you ~ to come?** tu veux venir?; **I ~ the job finished** je veux que ce travail soit fini; **I don't ~ to** je n'en ai pas envie; (flat refusal) je ne veux pas; **to ~ sb to do** vouloir que qn fasse; **why does she ~ me to come?** pourquoi veut-elle que je vienne?; **I ~ the machine working by 11 o'clock** je veux que la machine soit en état de marche d'ici onze heures; **they just don't ~ to know** ça ne les intéresse pas; **2**○ (need) avoir besoin de; **you won't ~ a raincoat** tu n'auras pas besoin d'un imperméable; **to ~ to do**○ devoir faire; **you ~ to watch out** tu devrais faire attention; **what do they ~ with all those machines?** pourquoi est-ce qu'ils ont besoin de toutes ces machines?; **what do you ~ with me?** qu'est-ce que vous me voulez?; **3** (require presence of) demander; **if anyone ~s me** si quelqu'un me demande; **you're ~ed on the phone** on vous demande au téléphone; **the boss ~s you** le patron veut te voir; **to be ~ed by the police** être recherché par la police.
III *vi* **to ~ for** manquer de.

want ad *n* (US) petite annonce *f*.

wanted list *n* liste *f* des suspects.

wanting *adj* **to be ~** faire défaut; **to be ~ in** manquer de; **to be found ~** s'avérer décevant.

wanton *adj* [*cruelty, damage, waste*] gratuit; [*disregard*] délibéré.

war I *n* **1** (armed conflict) guerre *f*; **~ broke out** la guerre a éclaté; **in the ~** à la guerre; **to wage ~ on** faire la guerre contre; **to be at ~ with a country** être en guerre avec un pays; **a ~ over** une guerre pour [*land, independence*]; une guerre sur [*issue, problem*]; **2** (fierce competition) guerre *f*; **price ~** guerre des prix; **a ~ of words** un conflit verbal; **3** (campaign) lutte *f* (**against** contre); **to wage ~ on** or **against** mener une lutte contre.
II *noun modifier* [*correspondent, crime, film, widow, wound*] de guerre; [*cemetery, leader, grave, zone*] militaire; [*hero*] de la guerre; **~ deaths** victimes *fpl* de la guerre.

ward *n* **1** (in hospital) (unit) service *m*; (room) unité *f*; (separate building) pavillon *m*; **maternity ~** service de maternité; **hospital ~** salle *f* d'hôpital; **2** (electoral) circonscription *f* électorale; **3** (also **~ of court**) (Law) pupille *m*; **to**

be made a ~ of court être placé sous tutelle judiciaire.
■ **ward off**: **~ off [sth]** chasser [*evil, predator*]; faire taire [*accusations, criticism*]; écarter [*attack, threat*]; éviter [*bankruptcy, disaster*].

warden ▶805 *n* (of institution, college) directeur/-trice *m/f*; (of park, estate) gardien/-ienne *m/f*.

warder *n* (GB) gardien/-ienne *m/f*.

wardrobe *n* **1** (furniture) armoire *f*; **2** (set of clothes) garde-robe *f*; (for theatre) costumes *mpl*.

wardrobe: **~ assistant** ▶805 *n* assistant/-e *m/f* costumier/-ière; **~ director** ▶805 *n* costumier/-ière *m/f*; **~ mistress** ▶805 *n* costumière *f*.

ward: **~ round** *n* visite *f* (*du médecin hospitalier*); **~ sister** *n* (GB) infirmière *f* en chef.

warehouse *n* entrepôt *m*.

wares *n pl* marchandise *f*, marchandises *fpl*.

warfare *n* **modern ~** conflits *mpl* modernes; **chemical ~** guerre *f* chimique.

war: **~ games** *n pl* (Games) guerre *f* simulée; **~head** *n* ogive *f*.

wariness *n* **1** (caution) prudence *f* (**of** à l'égard de); **2** (distrust) méfiance *f* (**of** à l'égard de).

warlike *adj* [*people*] guerrier/-ière; [*mood, words*] belliqueux/-euse.

warm I *adj* **1** (not cold) [*place, food, temperature, water, day*] chaud; **in ~ weather** quand il fait chaud; **to be ~** [*person*] avoir chaud; **it's ~** il fait bon or chaud; **are you ~ enough?** as-tu assez chaud?; **it's nice and ~ in here** on est bien au chaud ici; **in a ~ oven** (Culin) à four très doux; **this beer is ~** cette bière est tiède; **it's ~ work** c'est un travail qui donne chaud; **to get ~** [*person, weather, object*] se réchauffer; **you're getting ~er!** (in guessing game) tu chauffes!; **to get sb/sth ~** réchauffer qn/qch; **to keep (oneself) ~** (wrap up) ne pas prendre froid; (take exercise) se réchauffer; (stay indoors) rester au chaud; **to keep sb ~** [*blanket*] tenir chaud à qn; **to keep sth ~** tenir [qch] au chaud [*food*]; chauffer [qch] (en permanence) [*room*]; **2** (enthusiastic) [*person, atmosphere, welcome*] chaleureux/-euse; [*admiration, support*] enthousiaste; **to have a ~ heart** être chaleureux/-euse; **~(est) regards** meilleures amitiés; **3** (mellow) [*colour*] chaud.
II *vtr* chauffer [*plate, food, water*]; réchauffer [*implement, bed*]; **to ~ oneself** se réchauffer; **to ~ one's hands** se réchauffer les mains.
III *vi* [*food, liquid, object*] chauffer.
■ **warm to, warm towards**: **~ to [sb/sth]** se prendre de sympathie pour [*person*]; se faire à [*idea*]; prendre goût à [*task*].
■ **warm up**: ¶ **~ up 1** [*person, room, house*] se réchauffer; [*food, liquid, engine, radio*] chauffer; **2** (become lively) s'animer; **3** [*athlete*] s'échauffer; [*singer*] s'échauffer la voix; [*orchestra, musician*] se préparer; ¶ **~ up [sth], ~ [sth] up 1** (heat) réchauffer [*room, bed, person*]; faire réchauffer [*food*]; **2** (prepare) chauffer○ [*audience*]; échauffer [*athlete, player*]; [*musician*] chauffer [*instrument*].

warm: **~ front** *n* front *m* chaud; **~-hearted** *adj* chaleureux/-euse.

warming *n* réchauffement *m*.

warming-up exercises *n pl* exercices *mpl* d'échauffement.

warmly *adv* [*smile, thank, recommend*] chaleureusement; [*speak, praise*] avec enthousiasme.

warmth *n* chaleur *f*.

warm-up *n* échauffement *m*.

warn I *vtr* avertir (**that** que), prévenir (**that** que); **to ~ sb about** or **against sth** mettre qn en garde contre qch; **to ~ sb to do** conseiller or dire à qn de faire; **to ~ sb not to do** déconseiller à qn de faire; **you have been ~ed!** tu es prévenu!
II *vi* **to ~ of sth** annoncer qch.
■ **warn off**: **~ [sb] off, ~ off [sb]** décourager; **to ~ sb off doing** déconseiller à qn de faire; **to ~ sb off one's land** demander à qn de quitter ses terres.

warning I *n* avertissement *m*; (by an authority) avis *m*; (by light, siren) alerte *f*; **a ~ against sth** une mise en garde contre qch; **a ~ about sth** une mise en garde à propos de qch; **to give sb ~** avertir qn (**of** de); **advance ~** préavis *m*; **health ~** mise en garde; **flood ~** avis de crue.
II *noun modifier* **1** [*siren, bell, device*] d'alarme; **~ light** voyant *m* lumineux; **~ notice** avis *m*, avertissement *m*; **~ shot** coup *m* de semonce; **~ sign** (on road) panneau *m* d'avertissement; (of illness, stress) signe *m* annonciateur; **2** [*glance, gesture, tone*] de mise en garde; (stronger) menaçant.

warp I *n* (deformity) déformation *f* (**in** de).
II *vtr* **1** déformer [*metal, wood, record*]; **2** pervertir [*mind, personality*].
III *vi* se déformer.

warped *adj* **1** [*metal, wood, record*] déformé; **to become ~** se déformer; **2** [*mind, humour*] tordu; [*personality, sexuality*] perverti; [*account, view*] faussé.

warplane *n* avion *m* militaire.

warrant I *n* **1** (Law) mandat *m*; **to issue a ~** établir un mandat; **a ~ is out for his arrest** un mandat d'arrêt a été lancé contre lui; **2** (for shares) bon *m* de souscription; **dividend ~** coupon *m* de dividende.
II *vtr* justifier [*action, measure*].

warranty *n* (guarantee) garantie *f*; (Law) simple garantie *f*.

warren *n* **1** (rabbits') garenne *f*; **2** (building, maze of streets) labyrinthe *m*.

warring *adj* [*factions, parties, nations*] en conflit.

Warsaw ▶574 *pr n* Varsovie.

warship *n* navire *m* de guerre.

wart *n* (on skin) verrue *f*; (on plant) excroissance *f*.

wartime *n* **in ~** en temps de guerre.

war-torn *adj* déchiré par la guerre.

wary *adj* **1** (cautious) prudent; **to be ~** montrer de la circonspection (**of** vis à vis de);

to be ~ of doing hésiter à faire; **2** (distrustful) méfiant; **to be ~** se méfier (**of** de).

wash I *n* **1** (by person) **to give [sth] a ~** laver [*window, floor*]; nettoyer [*object*]; lessiver [*paintwork, walls*]; **to give [sb] a ~** débarbouiller [*child*]; **to have a quick ~** faire un brin de toilette○; **2** (laundry process) lavage *m*; **weekly ~** lessive *f* hebdomadaire; **in the ~** (about to be cleaned) au sale; (being cleaned) au lavage; **3** (from boat) remous *m*; **4** (coating) couche *f* (de peinture); **5** (in art) lavis *m*; **6** (for face) lotion *f*.
II *vtr* **1** (clean) laver [*person, clothes, floor*]; nettoyer [*object, wound*]; lessiver [*paintwork, surface*]; **to get ~ed** se laver; **to ~ one's hands/face** se laver les mains/le visage; **to ~ the dishes** faire la vaisselle; **2** (carry along) **to ~ sb/sth overboard** emporter qn/qch par-dessus bord; **3** (in art) laver.
III *vi* **1** [*person*] se laver, faire sa toilette; [*animal*] faire sa toilette; **2** (do laundry) faire la lessive; **3** [*garment*] se laver; **to ~ easily** se laver facilement.
■ **wash away**: ¶ **~ [sth] away, ~ away [sth] 1** (clean) faire partir; **2** (carry off) emporter [*structure, debris*]; (by erosion) éroder; ¶ **~ [sb] away** emporter.
■ **wash down**: **~ [sth] down, ~ down [sth] 1** (clean) laver [qch] à grande eau [*surface, vehicle*]; lessiver [*paintwork*]; **2**○ arroser [*food*].
■ **wash off**: ¶ **~ off** partir au lavage; ¶ **~ [sth] off, ~ off [sth]** faire partir [qch] à l'eau; **to ~ the mud off the car** laver la voiture pour faire partir la boue.
■ **wash out**: ¶ **~ out** [*stain*] partir au lavage; [*colour*] passer; ¶ **~ [sth] out, ~ out [sth] 1** (remove by cleaning) faire partir [qch] au lavage [*stain*]; faire passer [*colour*]; **2** (rinse inside) rincer; **3** (clean quickly) passer [qch] à l'eau.
■ **wash through**: **~ [sth] through** passer [qch] à l'eau.
■ **wash up**: ¶ **~ up 1** (GB) (do dishes) faire la vaisselle; **2** (US) (clean oneself) faire un brin de toilette○; ¶ **~ [sth] up, ~ up [sth] 1** (clean) laver [*plate*]; nettoyer [*pan*]; **2** [*tide*] rejeter.

washable *adj* [*material, paint, ink*] lavable.

wash: **~-and-wear** *adj* d'entretien facile; **~basin** *n* lavabo *m*; **~bowl** *n* (US) lavabo *m*; **~cloth** *n* (US) lavette *f*; **~day** *n* jour *m* de lessive.

washed-out *adj* **1** (faded) délavé; **2** (tired) épuisé, lessivé○.

washer *n* (Tech) (as seal) joint *m*.

washer-dryer *n* lave-linge/sèche-linge *m inv*.

wash: **~-hand basin** *n* lavabo *m*; **~house** *n* buanderie *f*.

washing *n* (laundry) (to be cleaned) linge *m* sale; (when clean) linge *m*; **to do the ~** faire la lessive.

washing: **~ facilities** *n pl* douches-lavabos *fpl*; **~ line** *n* corde *f* à linge; **~ machine** *n* machine *f* à laver; **~ powder** *n* (GB) lessive *f* (en poudre); **~-up** *n* (GB) vaisselle *f*; **~-up liquid** *n* (GB) liquide *m* à vaisselle.

washout *n* **1**○ (project, system) fiasco *m*; **2**○ (person) nullité○ *f*; **3** (game, camp) fiasco *m* dû à la pluie.

wash: **~room** *n* toilettes *fpl*; **~-stand** *n* (US) lavabo *m*.

wasp *n* guêpe *f*.

waspish *adj* acerbe.

wastage *n* **1** (of money, resources, talent) gaspillage *m*; (of heat, energy) déperdition *f*; **2** (also **natural ~**) élimination *f* naturelle.

waste I *n* **1** (of food, money, energy) gaspillage *m* (**of** de); (of time) perte *f* (**of** de); **a ~ of effort** un effort inutile; **that car is such a ~ of money!** cette voiture, c'est vraiment de l'argent jeté par les fenêtres!; **it's a ~ of time trying to explain it** on perd son temps à essayer de l'expliquer; **that's a good opportunity gone to ~** voilà une bonne occasion de perdue; **to let sth go to ~** gaspiller qch; **2** (detritus) (also **wastes** US) déchets *mpl* (**from** de).
II wastes *n pl* **1** (wilderness) étendues *fpl* sauvages; **2** (US) = **waste I 2**.
III *adj* **1** [*food*] inutilisé; [*heat, energy*] gaspillé; [*water*] usé; **~ matter** déchets *mpl*; **~ products** (industrial) déchets *mpl* de fabrication; (bodily) déchets *mpl*; **2** [*land*] inculte; **3 to lay ~ (to)** dévaster.
IV *vtr* **1** (squander) gaspiller [*food, resources, energy, money, talents*]; perdre [*time, opportunity*]; user [*strength*]; **all our efforts were ~d** tous nos efforts ont été vains; **he didn't ~ words** il a été franc et direct; **subtlety is ~d on her** la subtilité lui passe au-dessus de la tête; **good wine is ~d on him** il n'est pas capable d'apprécier un bon vin; **2** (make thinner) décharner; (make weaker) atrophier.

waste: **~basket** *n* corbeille *f* à papier; **~bin** *n* (GB) (for paper) corbeille *f* à papier; (for rubbish) poubelle *f*.

wasted *adj* **1** [*care, effort, expense, life, vote*] inutile; [*commodity, energy, years*] gaspillé; **2** (fleshless) [*body, limb*] décharné; [*face*] émacié; (weak) [*body, limb*] atrophié.

waste: **~ disposal** *n* traitement *m* des déchets; **~ disposal unit** *n* (GB) broyeur *m* d'ordures; **~ dump** *n* dépotoir *m*.

wasteful *adj* [*product, machine*] qui consomme beaucoup; [*method, process*] peu économique; [*person*] gaspilleur/-euse.

wastefulness *n* (extravagance) gaspillage *m*; (inefficiency) manque *m* de rentabilité.

waste: **~land** *n* (urban) terrain *m* vague; (rural) terre *f* à l'abandon; **~paper** *n* papier *m* or papiers *mpl* à jeter; **~paper basket, ~paper bin** (GB) *n* corbeille *f* à papier; **~ pipe** *n* tuyau *m* de vidange.

wasting *adj* [*disease*] débilitant.

watch I *n* **1** (timepiece) montre *f*; **my ~ is slow/fast** ma montre retarde/avance; **to set one's ~** mettre sa montre à l'heure; **2** (surveillance) surveillance *f* (**on** sur); **to keep ~** monter la garde; **to keep (a) ~ on sb/sth** surveiller qn/qch.
II *noun modifier* [*chain, spring*] de montre.
III *vtr* **1** (look at) regarder; (observe) observer; **is**

there anything worth ~ing on television? y a-t-il quelque chose à voir à la télévision?; **I've ~ed these children grow up** j'ai vu grandir ces enfants; **2** (monitor) suivre [*career, development*]; surveiller [*situation*]; **3** (keep under surveillance) surveiller [*person, movements*]; **~ this noticeboard for further details** lire ce panneau d'affichage pour plus de détails; **to ~ the clock** surveiller la pendule; **4** (pay attention to) faire attention à [*obstacle, dangerous object, money*]; surveiller [*language, manners, weight*]; **to ~ the time** surveiller l'heure; **~ you don't spill it** fais attention de ne pas le renverser; **~ what you're doing** fais attention à ce que tu fais; **~ it**○! fais gaffe○!; **to ~ one's step** (figurative) faire attention; **5** (look after) garder [*person, property*].

IV *vi* regarder (**from** de); **they are ~ing to see what will happen next** ils attendent pour voir ce qui va se passer maintenant.

■ **watch for**: **~ for [sb/sth]** guetter [*person, chance*]; surveiller l'apparition de [*symptom*].

■ **watch out** (be careful) faire attention (**for** à); (keep watch) guetter; **~ out!** attention!

■ **watch over**: **~ over [sb/sth]** veiller sur [*person*]; veiller à [*interests, rights, welfare*].

watchband *n* (US) bracelet *m* de montre.

watchdog *n* **1** (dog) chien *m* de garde; **2** (organization) organisme *m* de surveillance; **consumer ~** service *m* de protection du consommateur.

watch: **~maker** ▶805 *n* horloger/-ère *m/f*; **~man** ▶805 *n* (guard) gardien *m*; **~ strap** *n* bracelet *m* de montre.

water I *n* eau *f*; **drinking ~** eau potable; **by ~** par bateau; **under ~** (submerged) sous l'eau; (flooded) inondé; **at high/low ~** à marée haute/basse; **to let in ~** prendre l'eau; **to pass ~** uriner; **to turn the ~ on/off** ouvrir/fermer le robinet; **to keep one's head above ~** (when swimming) garder la tête hors de l'eau; (financially) faire face à ses engagements.

II *noun modifier* [*jug, tank*] à eau; [*filter*] à eau; [*pipe, shortage*] d'eau.

III *vtr* arroser [*lawn, plant*]; irriguer [*crop, field*]; abreuver [*livestock*].

IV *vi* **the smell of cooking makes my mouth ~** l'odeur de cuisine me fait venir l'eau à la bouche; **the smoke made her eyes ~** la fumée l'a fait pleurer.

■ **water down**: **~ down [sth] 1** couper [qch] d'eau [*beer, wine*]; diluer [*syrup*]; **2** atténuer [*effect, plans, policy*]; édulcorer [*description, story*].

water: **~ authority** *n* compagnie *f* des eaux; **~ bed** *n* matelas *m* d'eau; **~ bird** *n* oiseau *m* aquatique; **~ bottle** *n* (for cyclist) bidon *m*; **~ cannon** *n* canon *m* à eau; **~colour** (GB), **~color** (US) *n* (paint) peinture *f* pour aquarelle; (painting) aquarelle *f*; **~cress** *n* cresson *m* (de fontaine).

watered-down *adj* **1** [*beer, wine*] coupé d'eau; **2** [*measures, policy*] atténué; [*version*] édulcoré.

water: **~fall** *n* cascade *f*; **~ filter** *n* filtre *m* à eau; **~front** *n* (on harbour) front *m* de mer; (by lakeside, riverside) bord *m* de l'eau; **~-heater** *n* chauffe-eau *m inv*.

watering can *n* arrosoir *m*.

water: **~ jump** *n* (Sport) rivière *f*; **~ level** *n* niveau *m* d'eau; **~ lily** *n* nénuphar *m*; **~ line** *n* ligne *f* de flottaison; **~logged** *adj* [*ground, pitch*] détrempé; **~ main** *n* canalisation *f* d'eau; **~mark** *n* (of sea) laisse *f*; (of river) ligne *f* des hautes eaux; (on paper) filigrane *m*; **~ meadow** *n* prairie *f* inondable; **~melon** *n* pastèque *f*; **~ power** *n* énergie *f* hydraulique.

waterproof *adj* [*coat*] imperméable; [*make-up*] résistant à l'eau.

waterproofs *n pl* vêtements *mpl* imperméables.

water: **~ rates** *n pl* (GB) taxe *f* sur l'eau; **~-resistant** *adj* qui résiste à l'eau.

waters *n pl* **1** (territory) eaux *fpl*; **2** (spa water) **to take the ~** faire une cure thermale; **3** (Med) eaux *fpl*; **her ~ have broken** elle a perdu les eaux.

water-ski (Sport) **I** *n* ski *m* nautique.

II *vi* faire du ski nautique.

water: **~-skiing** ▶649 *n* ski *m* nautique; **~ slide** *n* toboggan *m* de piscine; **~-soluble** *adj* soluble dans l'eau; **~ sport** *n* sport *m* nautique; **~ supply** *n* (in an area) approvisionnement *m* en eau; (to a building) alimentation *f* en eau; **~ system** *n* (for town) système *m* d'approvisionnement en eau; (for building) système *m* d'alimentation en eau; **~ table** *n* niveau *m* hydrostatique.

watertight *adj* **1** [*container, seal*] étanche; **2** (irrefutable) [*argument, case*] incontestable; [*alibi*] irréfutable.

water: **~ tower** *n* château *m* d'eau; **~ trough** *n* abreuvoir *m*; **~way** *n* voie *f* navigable; **~ wings** *n pl* bracelets *mpl* de natation.

watery *adj* **1** [*sauce, paint*] trop liquide; [*coffee*] trop léger/-ère; **2** [*colour, smile*] pâle; **3** [*vegetables*] mal égoutté.

watt *n* watt *m*; **100-~ bulb** ampoule de 100 watts.

wave I *n* **1** (hand gesture) signe *m* (de la main); **she gave him a ~ from the bus** elle lui a fait signe du bus; **2** (of water) vague *f*; **to make ~s** [*wind*] faire des vagues; (cause a stir) faire du bruit; (cause trouble) créer des histoires○; **3** (outbreak, surge) vague *f* (**of** de); **a ~ of strikes** une vague de grèves; **to occur in ~s** se produire par vagues.

II *vtr* **1** (move from side to side) agiter [*flag, ticket, banknote*]; brandir [*umbrella, stick, gun*]; **2 to ~ goodbye to sb** faire au revoir de la main à qn; **you can ~ goodbye to your chances of winning** tu peux dire adieu à tes chances de gagner; **3** (direct) **they ~ed us on/away** ils nous ont fait signe d'avancer/de nous éloigner.

III *vi* **1** (with hand) **to ~ to** or **at sb** saluer qn de la main; **2** [*branches*] être agité par le vent; [*corn*] ondoyer; [*flag*] flotter au vent.

■ **wave around, wave about**: **~ [sth]**

around brandir [*weapon, object*]; **to ~ one's arms around** agiter les bras dans tous les sens. ■ **wave aside**: **~ [sth] aside, ~ aside [sth]** repousser [qch] d'un geste [*suggestion*].

wave: **~ band** *n* bande *f* de fréquence; **~length** *n* (on radio) longueur *f* d'onde.

waver *vi* **1** (weaken) [*person*] vaciller; [*courage, love*] faiblir; [*voice*] trembler; **2** (hesitate) hésiter (**between** entre; **over** sur).

wavering I *n* **1** (hesitation) hésitation *f*; **2** (of voice) tremblement *m* (**of** dans).
II *adj* [*person, politician, voice*] hésitant; [*voter*] indécis; [*confidence, courage, faith, flame*] vacillant.

wavy *adj* [*hair, line*] ondulé.

wax I *n* (for candle, seal) cire *f*; (for skis) fart *m*; (in ear) cérumen *m*.
II *vtr* **1** cirer [*floor*]; lustrer [*car*]; farter [*ski*]; **2** (depilate) épiler [qch] à la cire [*legs*].
III *vi* [*moon*] croitre.

waxed jacket *n* (GB) ciré *m*.

waxing *n* **1** (of floor, table) cirage *m*; **2** (of car) lustrage *m*; **3** (of skis) fartage *m*; **4** (of legs) épilation *f* à la cire.

way I *n* **1** (route, road) chemin *m* (**from** de; **to** à); **the quickest ~ to town** le chemin le plus court pour aller en ville; **if we go this ~** si nous prenons cette route; **to ask the ~ to the station** demander le chemin pour aller à la gare; **the ~ ahead looks difficult** (future) l'avenir s'annonce difficile; **there is no ~ around the problem** il n'y a pas moyen de contourner le problème; **on the ~ back** sur le chemin du retour; **on the ~ back from the meeting** en revenant de la réunion; **the ~ forward is to negotiate** l'avenir est dans la négociation; **the ~ in** l'entrée (**to** de); **'~ in'** 'entrée'; **the ~ out** la sortie (**of** de); **the quickest ~ out is through here** c'est par ici que l'on sort le plus vite; **a ~ out of our difficulties** un moyen de nous sortir de nos difficultés; **the ~ up** la montée; **on the ~** en route; **we're on the ~ to Alison's** nous allons chez Alison; **I'm on my ~** j'arrive; **to send sb on his ~** (tell to go away) envoyer promener qn○; **to be on the ~ out** [*hats*] passer de mode; [*government, person*] être sur son déclin; **to be out of sb's ~** [*place*] ne pas être sur le chemin de qn; **don't go out of your ~ to do** ne te donne pas de mal pour faire; **out of the ~** (isolated) isolé; (unusual) extraordinaire; **along the ~** (to place) en chemin; (in process) en cours de route; **by ~ of** (via) en passant par; **to make one's ~ towards** se diriger vers; **to make one's ~ along** avancer le long de; **to make one's own ~ there** y aller par ses propres moyens; **to push one's ~ through sth** se frayer un chemin à travers qch; **to lie one's ~ out of trouble** se sortir d'affaire en mentant; **2** (direction) direction *f*, sens *m*; **which ~ did he go?** dans quelle direction est-il parti?; **he went that ~** il est parti par là; **come this ~** suivez-moi, venez par ici; **'this ~ for the zoo'** 'vers le zoo'; **'this ~ up'** 'haut'; **to run this ~ and that** courir dans tous les sens; **to look the other ~** (to see) regarder de l'autre côté; (to avoid seeing unpleasant thing) détourner les yeux; (to ignore wrongdoing) fermer les yeux; **to go every which ~** partir dans tous les sens; **the other ~ up** dans l'autre sens; **the right ~ up** dans le bon sens; **the wrong ~ up** à l'envers; **to turn sth the other ~ around** retourner qch; **to do it the other ~ around** faire le contraire; **I didn't ask her, it was the other ~ around** ce n'est pas moi qui le lui ai demandé, c'est l'inverse; **the wrong/right ~ around** dans le mauvais/bon sens; **if you're ever down our ~** si jamais tu passes près de chez nous; **she's coming our ~** elle vient vers nous; **an opportunity came my ~** une occasion s'est présentée; **3** (space in front, projected route) passage *m*; **to be in sb's ~** empêcher qn de passer; **to be in the ~** gêner le passage; **to get out of the ~** s'écarter (du chemin); **to get out of sb's ~** laisser passer qn; **out of my ~!** pousse-toi!; **once the election is out of the ~** une fois les élections passées; **to keep out of the ~** rester à l'écart; **to keep out of sb's ~** éviter qn; **to keep sth out of sb's ~** (to avoid injury, harm) garder qch hors de portée de qn; **to make ~** s'écarter; **to make ~ for sb/sth** faire place à qn/qch; **4** (distance) distance *f*; **it's a long ~** c'est loin (**to** jusqu'à); **my birthday is still some ~ off** mon anniversaire est encore loin; **we still have some ~ to go** nous avons encore du chemin à faire (**before doing** avant de faire); **to go all the ~ to China** aller jusqu'en Chine; **all the ~ along the road** tout le long de la route; **I'm behind you all the ~** je suis de tout cœur avec toi; **5** (manner) façon *f*, manière *f*; **do it this/that ~** fais-le comme ceci/cela; **to do/explain sth another ~** faire/expliquer qch autrement; **to do sth the French ~** faire qch à la française; **to do sth the right/wrong ~** faire bien/mal qch; **you're going about it the wrong ~** tu t'y prends mal or de travers; **try to see it my ~** mets-toi à ma place; **in his/her/its own ~** à sa façon; **to have a ~ with words** savoir manier les mots; **to have a ~ with children** savoir s'y prendre avec les enfants; **a ~ of doing** (method) une façon or manière de faire; (means) un moyen de faire; **that's the ~ to do it!** voilà comment il faut s'y prendre!; **what a ~ to run a company!** ce n'est pas comme ça qu'on gère une entreprise!; **I like the ~ he dresses** j'aime la façon dont il s'habille; **whichever ~ you look at it** de quelque façon que tu considères les choses; **either ~, she's wrong** de toute façon, elle a tort; **one ~ or another** d'une façon ou d'une autre; **I don't care one ~ or the other** ça m'est égal; **you can't have it both ~s** on ne peut pas avoir le beurre et l'argent du beurre; **no ~**○! pas question○!; **6** (respect, aspect) sens *m*; **in a ~ it's sad** en un sens c'est triste; **in a ~ that's true** dans une certaine mesure c'est vrai; **can I help in any ~?** puis-je faire quoi que ce soit?; **without wanting to criticize in any ~** sans vouloir le moins du monde critiquer; **in many ~s** à bien des égards; **in some ~s** à certains égards; **in no ~, not in any ~** aucunement; **this is in no ~ a criticism**

cela n'est en aucune façon une critique; **what have you got in the ~ of drinks?** qu'est-ce que vous avez comme boissons?; **by ~ of light relief** en guise de divertissement; **in a general ~** en général; **in the ordinary ~** d'ordinaire; **7** (custom, manner) coutume *f*, manière *f*; **that's the modern ~** c'est ce qui se fait de nos jours; **I know all her little ~s** je connais toutes ses petites habitudes; **that's just his ~** il est comme ça; **it's the ~ of the world** c'est la vie; **8** (will, desire) **to get one's ~, to have one's own ~** faire à son idée; **she likes (to have) her own ~** elle aime n'en faire qu'à sa tête; **if I had my ~** si cela ne tenait qu'à moi; **have it your (own) ~** comme tu voudras.

II *adv* **we went ~ over budget** le budget a été largement dépassé; **to be ~ out** (in guess, estimate) être loin du compte; **that's ~ out of order** je trouve ça un peu fort.

III by the way *phr* en passant; **by the ~,...** à propos,...; **what time is it, by the ~?** quelle heure est-il, au fait?

waylay *vtr* [*attacker*] attaquer; [*beggar, friend*] arrêter, harponner°.

waymark *n* balise *f*.

wayside *n* IDIOMS **to fall by the ~** (stray morally) quitter le droit chemin; (fail, not stay the course) abandonner en cours de route; (be cancelled, fall through) tomber à l'eau.

we *pron* nous.

■ **Note** In standard French, *we* is translated by *nous* but in informal French, *on* is frequently used: *we're going to the cinema* = nous allons au cinéma *or more informally* on va au cinéma.
– *on* is also used in correct French to refer to a large, vaguely defined group: *we shouldn't lie to our children* = on ne devrait pas mentir à ses enfants.

~ saw her yesterday nous l'avons vue hier; **~ left at six** nous sommes partis à six heures; (informal) on est partis° à six heures; **~ Scots like the sun** nous autres Écossais, nous aimons le soleil; **WE didn't say that** nous, nous n'avons pas dit cela; (informal) nous, on n'a pas dit ça°; **~ four are agreed that** nous quatre sommes convenus que; **~ all make mistakes** tout le monde peut se tromper.

weak *adj* **1** [*person, animal, muscle, limb*] faible; [*health, ankle, heart, nerves*] fragile; [*stomach*] délicat; [*intellect*] médiocre; [*memory*] défaillant; [*chin*] fuyant; **to have a ~ chest** avoir les poumons fragiles; **to have ~ eyesight** avoir la vue faible; **to be ~ with** or **from hunger** être affaibli par la faim; **to grow** or **become ~(er)** [*person*] s'affaiblir; [*pulse, heartbeat*] faiblir; **2** (Tech) [*beam, support*] peu solide; [*structure*] fragile; **3** (lacking authority, strength) [*government, team, pupil, president*] faible; [*parent, teacher*] (not firm) qui manque de fermeté; (poor) piètre (*before n*); [*script, novel*] inconsistant; [*plot*] mince; [*actor, protest, excuse, argument*] peu convaincant; [*evidence*] peu concluant; **~ link** or **spot** point *m* faible; **to grow** or **become ~er** [*government, team*] s'affaiblir; [*position*] devenir de plus en plus précaire; **4** (faint) [*light, current, concentration, sound*] faible; [*tea, coffee*] léger/-ère; [*solution*] dilué; **5** [*economy, dollar*] faible (**against** par rapport à); [*share*] à bas prix.

weaken I *vtr* **1** (through illness, damage) affaiblir [*person, heart, structure*]; diminuer [*resistance*]; rendre [qch] moins solide [*joint, bank, wall*]; **2** (undermine) nuire à l'autorité de [*government, president*]; affaiblir [*team, company, authority, defence*]; diminuer [*support, influence*]; amoindrir [*argument, power*]; nuire à [*morale*]; **3** (dilute) diluer; **4** (Econ) affaiblir [*economy, currency*]; faire baisser [*prices, demand*].

II *vi* **1** (physically) s'affaiblir; **2** [*government, resolve*] fléchir; [*support, alliance*] se relâcher; **3** (Econ) [*economy, currency*] être en baisse.

weakening *n* **1** (of health, eyesight) affaiblissement *m*; (of structure) dégradation *f*; **2** (of government, authority, resolve) affaiblissement *m*; (of ties, alliance) relâchement *m*.

weakling *n* (physically) gringalet *m*; (morally) mauviette *f*.

weakness *n* **1** (weak point) point *m* faible; **2** (liking) faible *m* (**for** pour); **3** (physical, moral) faiblesse *f*; **4** (lack of authority) faiblesse *f*; (of evidence, position) fragilité *f*; **5** (of light, current, sound) faiblesse *f*; (of tea, solution) légèreté *f*; **6** (of economy, currency) faiblesse *f*.

weak-willed *adj* **to be ~** manquer de fermeté.

wealth *n* **1** (possessions) fortune *f*; **2** (state) richesse *f*; **3** (large amount) **a ~ of** une mine de [*information*]; une profusion de [*detail*]; énormément de [*experience, talent*]; un grand nombre de [*documents*].

wealth tax *n* (GB) impôt *m* sur la fortune.

wealthy *adj* riche.

wean *vtr* sevrer [*baby*]; **to ~ sb away from** or **off sth** détourner qn de qch.

weapon *n* arme *f*.

weaponry *n* matériel *m* de guerre.

wear I *n* **1** (clothing) **children's/sports ~** vêtements *mpl* pour enfants/de sport; **2** (use) **for everyday ~** de tous les jours; **for summer ~** pour l'été; **I've had three years' ~ out of these boots** ces bottes m'ont duré trois ans; **3** (damage) usure *f* (**on** de); **~ and tear** usure *f*; **to show signs of ~** commencer à être usé; **to be somewhat the worse for ~** (drunk) être ivre; (tired) être épuisé.

II *vtr* **1** (be dressed in) porter; **to ~ blue** s'habiller en bleu; **to ~ one's hair long/short** avoir les cheveux longs/courts; **to ~ one's skirts long** s'habiller long; **to ~ one's clothes loose** aimer les vêtements lâches; **2** (put on, use) mettre; **I haven't got a thing to ~** je n'ai rien à me mettre; **to ~ make-up** se maquiller; **3** (display) **he wore a puzzled frown** il fronçait les sourcils d'un air perplexe; **4** (damage by use) user; **to ~ a hole in** trouer [*garment, sheet*].

III *vi* [*carpet, shoes*] s'user; **my patience is ~ing thin** je commence à être à bout de patience.

■ **wear away** [*inscription*] s'effacer; [*tread, cliff, façade*] s'user.

■ **wear down**: ¶ **~ down** s'user; **to be worn down** être usé; ¶ **~ down [sth]**, **~ [sth] down** user [*steps*]; saper [*resistance, resolve*]; ¶ **~ [sb] down** épuiser.

■ **wear off 1** [*drug, effect*] se dissiper; [*sensation*] passer; **2** (come off) s'effacer.

■ **wear out**: ¶ **~ out** s'user; ¶ **~ out [sth]**, **~ [sth] out** user; **to ~ out one's welcome** lasser l'amabilité de ses hôtes; ¶ **~ [sb] out** épuiser.

■ **wear through** [*elbow, trousers*] se trouer; [*sole, metal, fabric*] se percer.

weariness *n* lassitude *f*.

weary I *adj* [*person, smile, sigh, voice, gesture*] las/lasse; [*eyes, limbs, mind*] fatigué; **to grow ~** se lasser (**of** de; **of doing** de faire).
II *vi* se lasser (**of** de; **of doing** de faire).

weasel *n* **1** (Zool) belette *f*; **2** (sly person) sournois/-e *m/f*.

weather I *n* temps *m*; **what's the ~ like?** quel temps fait-il?; **the ~ here is hot** il fait chaud ici; **in hot/cold ~** quand il fait chaud/froid; **you can't go out in this ~!** tu ne peux pas sortir par un temps pareil!; **when the good ~ comes** quand il fera beau; **if the ~ breaks** si le temps change; **if the ~ clears up** si le temps s'arrange; **~ permitting** si le temps le permet; **in all ~s** par tous les temps.
II *noun modifier* [*chart, check, conditions, map, pattern, satellite, station*] météorologique; [*centre, bureau, study*] de météorologie.
III *vtr* survivre à [*crisis, upheaval*]; **to ~ the storm** (figurative) surmonter la crise.
IDIOMS **to be under the ~** ne pas se sentir bien; **to make heavy ~ of sth** avoir du mal à faire qch; **he made heavy ~ of it** il en a fait tout un plat○.

weather: **~beaten** *adj* [*face*] hâlé; [*rocks, landscape*] battu par les vents; **~cock** *n* girouette *f*; **~ forecast** *n* bulletin *m* météorologique; **~ forecaster** ▶805 *n* (on TV) présentateur/-trice *m/f* de la météo; (specialist) météorologue *mf*, météorologiste *mf*; **~proof** *adj* [*garment, shoe*] imperméable; [*shelter, door*] étanche.

weave I *vtr* **1** tisser [*rug, fabric*]; **2** (interlace) tresser [*cane, basket, wreath*]; [*spider*] tisser.
II *vi* **to ~ in and out** se faufiler (**of** entre); **to ~ towards sth** (drunk) s'approcher en titubant de qch.
III **woven** *pp adj* [*fabric, cloth, jacket, upholstery*] tissé.

weaving I *n* tissage *m*.
II *noun modifier* [*frame, machine*] à tisser; [*factory*] de tissage.

web *n* **1** (also **spider's ~**) toile *f* (d'araignée); **2** (network) **a ~ of** un réseau de [*ropes, lines*]; **a ~ of lies** or **deceit** un tissu de mensonges.

webbing *n* (material) sangles *fpl*.

web foot *n* patte *f* palmée.

wed *n* **the newly ~s** les jeunes mariés *mpl*.

wedding I *n* mariage *m*; **a church ~** un mariage religieux.
II *noun modifier* [*anniversary, cake, ceremony, present*] de mariage.

wedding: **~ breakfast** *n* repas *m* de mariage; **~ day** *n* jour *m* des noces; **~ dress**, **~ gown** *n* robe *f* de mariée; **~ guest** *n* invité/-e *m/f* au mariage; **~ night** *n* nuit *f* de noces; **~ reception** *n* repas *m* de mariage; **~ ring** *n* alliance *f*.

wedge I *n* **1** (to insert in rock, wood) coin *m*; (to hold sth in position) cale *f*; (in rock climbing) piton *m*; **2** (of cake, pie, cheese) morceau *m*; **a ~ of lemon** une tranche de citron; **3** (in golf) cocheur *m* de sable.
II *vtr* **1** (make firm) **to ~ sth in place** caler qch; **to ~ a door open** caler une porte pour la tenir ouverte; **the door is ~d shut** (stuck) la porte est coincée; **2** (jam) **to ~ sth into** enfoncer qch dans; **to be ~d against/between** être coincé contre/entre.
IDIOMS **that's the thin end of the ~** c'est le commencement de la fin.

Wednesday ▶584 *n* mercredi *m*.

wee○ *vi* (GB) faire pipi.

weed I *n* mauvaise herbe *f*; (in water) herbes *fpl* aquatiques.
II *vtr, vi* désherber.
■ **weed out**: **~ [sb] out**, **~ out [sb]** éliminer [*candidates, dissidents*]; se débarrasser de [*employee*].

weedkiller *n* désherbant *m*, herbicide *m*.

weedy○ *adj* [*person, build*] malingre; [*character, personality*] faible.

week ▶915 *n* semaine *f*; **last/next ~** la semaine dernière/prochaine; **this ~** cette semaine; **the ~ before last** il y a deux semaines; **the ~ after next** dans deux semaines; **every other ~** tous les quinze jours; **for ~s** pendant des semaines; **twice a ~** deux fois par semaine; **I'll do it some time this ~** je le ferai dans le courant de la semaine; **~ in ~ out** toutes les semaines; **a ~ today/on Monday** (GB), **today/Monday ~** aujourd'hui/lundi en huit; **a ~ yesterday** (GB), **a ~ from yesterday** (US) il y a eu huit jours or une semaine hier; **a ~ ago** il y a une semaine; **in three ~s' time** dans trois semaines; **a ~'s wages** une semaine de salaire; **to pay by the ~** payer à la semaine; **during the ~** pendant la semaine; (Monday to Friday) en semaine; **the working** or **work** (US) **~** la semaine de travail; **the ~ ending June 10** la semaine du 3 au 10 juin.

weekday I *n* jour *m* de (la) semaine; **on ~s** en semaine.
II *noun modifier* **~ train/flight** train circulant/vol assuré du lundi au vendredi.

weekend I *n* week-end *m*; **the ~ after (that)** le week-end suivant; **at the ~** (GB), **on the ~** (US) pendant le week-end; **at ~s** (GB), **on ~s** (US) le week-end.
II *noun modifier* [*break, excursion*] de week-end; [*performance, programme*] du samedi et du dimanche; **~ bag** petit sac *m* de voyage; **~ cottage** résidence *f* secondaire; **~ ticket** ticket *m* valable (uniquement) le week-end.

weekly I *n* (newspaper) journal *m* hebdomadaire; (magazine) (revue *f*) hebdomadaire *m*.

II *adj* hebdomadaire; **on a ~ basis** à la semaine.

weep I *n* **to have a little ~** verser quelques larmes.
II *vi* **1** (cry) pleurer (**over** sur); **2** (ooze) suinter.

weepy *adj* [*mood, film*] larmoyant; **to feel ~** avoir envie de pleurer.

weigh ▶738 I *vtr* **1** (on scales) peser; **to ~ 10 kilos** peser 10 kilos; **how much** or **what do you ~?** combien pèses-tu?; **to ~ oneself** se peser; **2** (assess) évaluer [*arguments, advantages, options*]; peser [*consequences, risks, words*]; **to ~ sth against sth** mettre en balance qch et qch.
II *vi* **1** (have influence) **to ~ against sb** faire du tort à qn; **to ~ in sb's favour** jouer en faveur de qn; **2** (be a burden) **to ~ on sb** peser sur qn; **to ~ on sb's mind** préoccuper qn.
■ **weigh down**: ¶ **~ down on [sb/sth]** peser sur; ¶ **~ down [sth/sb], ~ [sth/sb] down** surcharger [*vehicle, boat*]; [*responsibility, debt*] accabler; **to be ~ed down with** crouler sous le poids de [*luggage*]; être accablé de [*worry, guilt*].
■ **weigh in** [*boxer, wrestler*] se faire peser; [*jockey*] aller au pesage.
■ **weigh out** peser [*ingredients, quantity*].
■ **weigh up**: **~ up [sth/sb], ~ [sth/sb] up** évaluer [*prospects, situation*]; juger [*person*]; mettre [qch] en balance [*options, benefits, risks*].

weighing machine *n* (for people) balance *f*; (for luggage, freight) bascule *f*.

weight I *n* **1** (heaviness) poids *m*; **to put on/lose ~** prendre/perdre du poids; **to put one's full ~ on sth** appuyer de tout son poids sur qch; **2** (heavy object) poids *m*; **to lift ~s** (Sport) faire des haltères; **3** (figurative) **not to carry much ~** ne pas peser lourd (**with** pour); **to add one's ~ to sth** faire jouer son influence en faveur de qch; **to throw one's ~ behind sth** soutenir qch à fond.
II *vtr* **1** lester [*net, arrow*]; **2** (bias) **to ~ sth against sb/sth** faire jouer qch contre qn/qch; **to ~ sth in favour of sb/sth** faire jouer qch en faveur de qn/qch.
IDIOMS **to be a ~ off one's mind** être un grand soulagement; **to pull one's ~** faire sa part de travail; **to throw one's ~ about** or **around** faire l'important/-e *m/f*.

weightlessness *n* (in space) apesanteur *f*.

weight: **~-lifting** ▶649 *n* haltérophilie *f*; **~ training** ▶649 *n* musculation *f* (en salle).

weir *n* (dam) barrage *m*.

weird *adj* (strange) bizarre; (eerie) mystérieux/-ieuse.

welcome I *n* accueil *m*; **to give sb a warm ~** faire un accueil chaleureux à qn.
II *adj* **1** (gratefully received) bienvenu; **that's a ~ sight!** ça fait plaisir à voir!; **2** (warmly greeted) **to be ~** être le bienvenu/la bienvenue *m/f*; **to make sb ~** (on arrival) réserver un bon accueil à qn; **3 'thanks'—'you're ~'** 'merci'—'de rien'.
III *excl* (to respected guest) soyez le bienvenu/la bienvenue *m/f* chez nous!; (greeting friend) entre donc!; **~ back!**, **~ home!** je suis content que tu sois de retour!
IV *vtr* accueillir [*person*]; se réjouir de [*news, decision, change*]; être heureux/-euse de recevoir [*contribution*]; accueillir favorablement [*initiative, move*].
IDIOMS **to wear out one's ~** abuser de l'hospitalité de qn.
■ **welcome back**: **~ back [sb], ~ [sb] back** accueillir [qn] à son retour; (more demonstratively) faire fête à [qn] à son retour.
■ **welcome in**: **~ in [sb], ~ [sb] in** faire entrer [qn] chez soi.

welcoming *adj* [*atmosphere, person*] accueillant; [*ceremony, committee*] d'accueil.

weld *vtr* (also **~ together**) souder; **to ~ sth on** or **to** souder qch à.

welfare I *n* **1** (well-being) bien-être *m inv*; (interest) intérêt *m*; **to be concerned about sb's ~** se faire du souci pour le sort de qn; **2** (state assistance) assistance *f* sociale; (money) aide *f* sociale.
II *noun modifier* [*system*] de protection sociale; (US) [*meal*] gratuit.

welfare: **~ benefit** *n* prestation *f* sociale; **~ services** *n* services *mpl* sociaux.

well[1] **I** *adj* **1** (in good health) **to feel ~** se sentir bien; **are you ~?** vous allez bien?, tu vas bien?; **she's not ~ enough to travel** elle n'est pas en état de voyager; **she doesn't look at all ~** elle n'a pas l'air en forme du tout; **to get ~** se rétablir; **2** (in satisfactory state) bien; **all is not ~ in their marriage** il y a des problèmes dans leur mariage; **that's all very ~, but** tout ça c'est bien beau, mais; **it's all very ~ for you to laugh, but** tu peux rire, mais; **3** (advisable, prudent) **it would be just as ~ to check** il vaudrait mieux vérifier; **it would be as ~ for you not to get involved** tu ferais mieux de ne pas t'en mêler; **4** (fortunate) **the flight was delayed, which was just as ~** le vol a été retardé, ce qui n'était pas plus mal.
II *adv* **1** (satisfactorily) bien; **he isn't eating very ~** il ne mange pas beaucoup; **that boy will do ~** ce garçon ira loin; **he hasn't done as ~ as he might** il n'a pas réussi aussi bien qu'il aurait pu; **to do ~ at school** être bon/bonne élève; **mother and baby are both doing ~** la mère et l'enfant se portent bien; **the operation went ~** l'opération s'est bien passée; **you did ~ to tell me** tu as bien fait de me le dire; **we'll be doing ~ if we get there on time** on aura de la chance si on arrive à l'heure; **~ done!** bravo!; **she didn't come out of it very ~** (of situation) elle ne s'en est pas très bien sortie; (of article, programme) ce n'était pas très flatteur pour elle; **he is ~ able to look after himself** il est assez grand pour se débrouiller tout seul; **2** (used with modal verbs) **you may ~ be right** il se pourrait bien que tu aies raison; **I can ~ believe it** je veux bien le croire, je n'ai pas de mal à le croire; **it may ~ be that they are right** il se pourrait bien qu'ils aient raison; **I couldn't very ~ say no** je pouvais difficilement dire non; **we may as ~**

go home on ferait aussi bien de rentrer; **3** (intensifier) bien, largement; **it was ~ worth waiting for** ça valait vraiment la peine d'attendre; **the weather remained fine ~ into September** le temps est resté au beau fixe pendant une bonne partie du mois de septembre; **she was active ~ into her eighties** elle était toujours active même au-delà de ses quatre-vingts ans; **profits are ~ above average** les bénéfices sont nettement supérieurs à la moyenne; **4** (approvingly) **to speak/think ~ of sb** dire/penser du bien de qn; **5 to wish sb ~** souhaiter beaucoup de chance à qn.

III *excl* **1** (expressing astonishment) eh bien!; (expressing indignation, disgust) ça alors!; (expressing disappointment) tant pis!; (qualifying statement) enfin; **~, you may be right** après tout, tu as peut-être raison; **~, that's too bad** c'est vraiment dommage; **~ then, what's the problem?** alors, quel est le problème?; **very ~ then** très bien.

IV as well *phr* aussi.

V as well as *phr* aussi bien que; **they have a house in the country as ~ as an apartment in Paris** ils ont à la fois une maison à la campagne et un appartement à Paris.

IDIOMS **to be ~ in with sb**○ être bien avec qn○; **to be ~ up in sth** s'y connaître en qch; **to leave ~ alone** (GB) or **~ enough alone** (US) ne pas s'en mêler.

well² *n* (sunk in ground) puits *m*; (pool) source *f*.

well-attended *adj* **the meeting was ~** il y avait beaucoup de monde à la réunion.

well: **~-balanced** *adj* équilibré; **~-behaved** *adj* [*child*] sage; [*dog*] bien dressé; **~-being** *n* bien-être *m inv*; **~-defined** *adj* [*outline*] net/nette; [*role*] bien défini.

well-disposed *adj* **to be ~ towards** être bien disposé envers [*person*]; être favorable à [*regime, idea, policy*].

well: **~ done** *adj* [*steak*] bien cuit; [*task*] bien fait; **~-educated** *adj* (having a good education) instruit; (cultured) cultivé; **~-formed** *adj* bien modelé; **~-groomed** *adj* [*person, appearance*] soigné; [*hair*] bien coiffé; [*horse*] bien pansé.

well-informed *adj* bien informé (**about** sur); **he's very ~** il est très au courant de l'actualité.

wellington (**boot**) *n* (GB) botte *f* de caoutchouc.

well-kept *adj* [*house, garden, village*] bien entretenu.

well-known *adj* **1** [*person, place*] célèbre; **to be ~ to sb** être connu de qn; **2 it is ~ that, it is a ~ fact that** il est bien connu que.

well: **~-liked** *adj* très apprécié; **~-made** *adj* bien fait; **~-mannered** *adj* bien élevé; **~-meaning** *adj* [*person*] bien intentionné; [*advice*] qui part d'une bonne intention.

well-meant *adj* **his offer was ~** sa proposition partait d'une bonne intention.

well-off **I** *n* **the ~** les gens *mpl* aisés; **the less ~** les plus défavorisés *mpl*.

II *adj* (wealthy) aisé; **to be ~ for** avoir beaucoup de [*space, provisions*].

well: **~-read** *adj* cultivé; **~-respected** *adj* très respecté; **~-rounded** *adj* [*education, programme*] complet/-ète; [*individual*] qui a reçu une éducation complète; **~-thought-out** *adj* bien élaboré; **~-to-do** *adj* aisé; **~-tried** *adj* [*method, remedy*] éprouvé; **~-wisher** *n* personne *f* qui veut témoigner sa sympathie; **~-worn** *adj* [*carpet, garment*] élimé; [*steps*] usé; [*joke*] rebattu.

Welsh ▶712 **I** *n* **1** (language) gallois *m*; **2** (people) **the ~** les Gallois *mpl*.

II *adj* [*culture, people*] gallois; [*teacher, lesson*] de gallois.

welt *n* (on skin) marque *f* (de coup).

welterweight *n* poids *m* welter.

west **I** *n* **1** (compass direction) ouest *m*; **the West** l'Ouest *m*, l'Occident *m*; **2** (part of country) l'Ouest *m*; (political entity) l'Occident *m*.

II *adj* (gen) ouest *inv*; [*wind*] d'ouest.

III *adv* [*move*] vers l'ouest; [*lie, live*] à l'ouest (**of** de).

western **I** *n* (film) western *m*.

II *adj* **1** [*coast*] ouest *inv*; [*town, accent*] de l'ouest; **~ France** l'ouest de la France; **2** [*politics*] occidental.

westerner *n* Occidental/-e *m/f*.

westernize *vtr* occidentaliser; **to become ~d** s'occidentaliser.

west-facing *adj* exposé à l'ouest.

West Indian ▶712 **I** *n* Antillais/-e *m/f*.

II *adj* antillais.

West Indies ▶574 *pr n pl* Antilles *fpl*.

wet **I** *n* **1** (dampness) humidité *f*; **the car won't start in the ~** la voiture ne veut pas démarrer par temps humide; **2**○ (GB) (derogatory) chiffe *f* molle○.

II *adj* **1** (damp) [*hair, clothes, grass, surface*] mouillé; **~ with rain** mouillé par la pluie; **~ with blood** mouillé de sang; **~ with sweat** trempé de sueur; **to get ~** se faire mouiller; **to get one's feet ~** se mouiller les pieds; **to get the floor ~** tremper le sol; **~ through** trempé; **2** (freshly applied) [*cement, varnish*] humide; **'~ paint'** 'peinture fraîche'; **3** (rainy) [*weather, season, day, night, area*] humide; [*conditions*] d'humidité; **when it's ~** quand il pleut; **4** (GB) [*person*] qui manque de caractère.

III *vtr* **1** mouiller [*floor, object, clothes*]; **2** (urinate in) **to ~ one's pants/the bed** [*adult*] mouiller sa culotte/le lit; [*child*] faire pipi dans sa culotte/dans son lit; **to ~ oneself** [*child*] faire pipi dans sa culotte.

wet: **~ blanket**○ *n* rabat-joie *mf inv*; **~ suit** *n* combinaison *f* de plongée.

whack **I** *n* **1** (blow) (grand) coup *m*; **2**○ (try) essai *m*; **to get first ~ at** avoir la primeur de.

II *excl* paf!

III *vtr* **1** (hit) battre [*person, animal*]; frapper [*ball*]; **2**○ (GB) (defeat) piler○.

whacky° *adj* [*person*] dingue°; [*sense of humour*] farfelu°.

whale **I** *n* **1** (Zool) baleine *f*; **2**° (emphatic) **to have a ~ of a time** s'amuser comme un fou.
II° *vtr* (US) (thrash) donner une raclée° à.

wharf *n* quai *m*.

what ▶ 963 **I** *pron* **with ~?** avec quoi?; **and ~ else?** et quoi d'autre?; **~'s the matter?** qu'est-ce qu'il y a?; **~'s her telephone number?** quel est son numéro de téléphone?; **~'s that machine?** qu'est-ce que c'est que cette machine?; **~'s that button for?** à quoi sert ce bouton?; **~'s it like?** comment c'est?; **~'s the Flemish for this?** comment dit-on cela en flamand?; **~ did it cost?** combien est-ce que ça a coûté?; **do ~ you want** fais ce que tu veux; **take ~ you need** prends ce dont tu as besoin; **do you know ~ that device is?** sais-tu ce que c'est que cet appareil?; **~ I need is** ce dont j'ai besoin c'est; **and ~'s more** et en plus; **and ~'s worse** et en plus; **~'s that?** quoi? qu'est-ce que tu as dit?; **he did ~?** il a fait quoi?; **George ~?** George comment?
II *det* **do you know ~ train he took?** est-ce que tu sais quel train il a pris?; **~ a nice dress/car!** quelle belle robe/voiture!; **~ a strange thing to do!** quelle drôle d'idée!; **~ use is that?** à quoi ça sert?; **~ money he earns he spends** tout ce qu'il gagne, il le dépense; **~ few friends she had** les quelques amis qu'elle avait.
III **what about** *phr* **1** (to draw attention) **~ about the children?** et les enfants (alors)?; **2** (to make suggestion) **~ about a meal out?** et si on dînait au restaurant?; **~ about Tuesday?** qu'est-ce que tu dirais de mardi?
IV **what if** *phr* et si; **~ if I bring the dessert?** et si j'apportais le dessert?
V *excl* quoi!, comment!
IDIOMS **well, ~ do you know** tout arrive; **~ do you think I am**°! tu me prends pour quoi!; **~ with one thing and another** avec ceci et cela.

what-d'yer-call-it° *n* machin° *m*.

whatever **I** *pron* **1** (that which) (as subject) ce qui; (as object) ce que; **to do ~ is required/one can** faire ce qui est exigé/ce qu'on peut; **2** (anything that) (as subject) tout ce qui; (as object) tout ce que; **do ~ you like** fais tout ce que tu veux; **~ you say** (as you like) tout ce qui vous plaira; **3** (no matter what) quoi que (+ *subj*); **~ happens** quoi qu'il arrive; **~ she says, ignore it** quoi qu'elle dise n'en tiens pas compte; **~ it costs it doesn't matter** quel que soit le prix, ça n'a pas d'importance.
II *det* **1** (any) **they eat ~ food they can get** ils mangent tout ce qu'ils trouvent à manger; **2** (no matter what) **~ their arguments** quels que soient leurs arguments; **~ the reason** quelle que soit la raison; **for ~ reason** pour je ne sais quelle raison.
III *adv* (also **whatsoever**) **to have no idea ~** ne pas avoir la moindre idée; **'any petrol?'—'none ~'** 'il y a de l'essence?'—'pas du tout'.

what's-his-name° *n* Machin° *m*.

wheat *n* blé *m*.

wheat: **~ germ** *n* germe *m* de blé; **~meal** *n* farine *f* complète.

wheedle *vtr* **to ~ sth out of sb** soutirer qch à qn par la cajolerie.

wheel **I** *n* **1** (on vehicle) roue *f*; (on trolley, piece of furniture) roulette *f*; **2** (for steering) (in vehicle) volant *m*; (on boat) roue *f* (de gouvernail); **to be at** or **behind the ~** être au volant; **3** (in watch, mechanism, machine) rouage *m*; **4** (for pottery) tour *m*.
II *vtr* pousser; **they ~ed me into the operating theatre** ils m'ont emmené dans la salle d'opération sur un chariot.
III *vi* **1** (also **~ round**) [*bird*] tournoyer; **2** (turn sharply) [*person, regiment*] faire demi-tour; [*car, motorbike*] braquer fortement; [*ship*] virer de bord.
IDIOMS **to ~ and deal** magouiller°.

wheel: **~ alignment** *n* (Aut) parallélisme *m*; **~barrow** *n* brouette *f*; **~base** *n* (Aut) écartement *m* des essieux; **~chair** *n* fauteuil *m* roulant; **~clamp** *n* (Aut) sabot *m* de Denver.

wheeler dealer° *n* magouilleur/-euse° *m/f*.

wheezy *adj* [*voice, cough*] rauque; **to have a ~ chest** avoir la respiration sifflante.

when

■ **Note** *When* in questions is usually translated by *quand*.
– Note that there are three ways of asking questions using *quand*: *when did she leave?* = quand est-ce qu'elle est partie?, elle est partie quand?, quand est-elle partie?
– When talking about future time, *quand* will be used with the future tense of the verb: *tell him when you see him* = dis-lui quand tu le verras.

I *adv* **1** (in questions) quand; **~ are we leaving?** quand est-ce qu'on part?; **~ is the concert?** c'est quand le concert?; **I wonder ~ the film starts** je me demande à quelle heure commence le film; **we met once—I forget exactly ~** nous nous sommes rencontrés une fois—j'ai oublié la date exacte; **say ~** dis-moi stop; **2** (whenever) quand; **he's only happy ~ he's moaning** il n'est content que quand il rouspète; **~ I eat ice cream, I feel ill** quand or chaque fois que je mange de la glace, j'ai mal au cœur.
II *rel pron* où; **the week ~ it all happened** la semaine où tout cela s'est produit; **there are times ~ it's too stressful** il y a des moments où c'est trop stressant; **those were the days ~ we had no TV** c'était l'époque où il n'y avait pas de télévision.
III *conj* **1** (expressing time) quand; **~ you're in your teens** quand on est adolescent; **~ he was at school** quand il était à l'école, lorsqu'il était à l'école; **~ I reach 18** quand j'aurai 18 ans; **~ he arrives, I'll let you know** quand il arrivera or dès qu'il arrivera, je te le dirai; **2** (expressing contrast) alors que; **why buy their products ~ ours are cheaper?** pourquoi acheter leurs produits alors que les nôtres sont moins chers?

what

As a pronoun

In questions

- When used in questions as an object pronoun, ***what*** is translated by ***qu'est-ce que*** (***qu'est-ce qu'*** in front of a vowel or mute 'h'):

***what** is he doing?*	= **qu'est-ce qu'**il fait?
***what** did you say?*	= **qu'est-ce que** tu as dit?
***what** are we going to do?*	= **qu'est-ce que** nous allons faire?

- Alternatively, you can use ***que*** (***qu'*** before a vowel or mute 'h'), but note that, after ***que***, the order of subject and verb is reversed and a hyphen is inserted between them if the subject is a pronoun:

***what** is he doing?*	= **que** fait-il?
***what** did you say?*	= **qu'**as-tu dit?
***what** are we going to do?*	= **qu'**allons-nous faire?

- When used in questions as a subject pronoun, ***what*** is translated by ***qu'est-ce qui***:

***what** is happening?*	= **qu'est-ce qui** se passe?
***what** happened?*	= **qu'est-ce qui** s'est passé?
***what** is going to happen?*	= **qu'est-ce qui** va se passer?

Again, if you use ***que***, the order of subject and verb is reversed, the subject becomes ***il*** and a hyphen is inserted between them:

***what** is happening?*	= **que** se passe-t-il?*
***what** happened?*	= **que** s'est-il passé?
***what** is going to happen?*	= **que** va-t-il se passer?

* In this case, an additional *-t-* is required for the liaison between the two vowels to be made.

To introduce a clause

- When used to introduce a clause as the object of the verb, ***what*** is translated by ***ce que*** (***ce qu'*** before a vowel or mute 'h'):

*I don't know **what** he wants*	= je ne sais pas **ce qu'**il veut
*did they have **what** you wanted?*	= est-ce qu'ils avaient **ce que** tu voulais?
***what** he said was that . . .*	= **ce qu'**il a dit c'est que . . .

- When ***what*** is the subject of the verb, it is translated by ***ce qui***:

*tell me **what** happened*	= raconte-moi **ce qui** s'est passé
*I want to know **what**'s happening*	= je veux savoir **ce qui** se passe
***what** matters is that . . .*	= **ce qui** compte, c'est que . . .

With prepositions

What, when it is used with a preposition in English, is translated by ***quoi***. In French, however, the preposition always comes before ***quoi***:

***what** are you thinking about?*	= à **quoi** penses-tu?
*I don't know **what** he is talking about*	= je ne sais pas de **quoi** il parle

As a determiner

When ***what*** is used as a determiner, it is translated by ***quel***, ***quelle***, ***quels*** or ***quelles***, according to the gender and number of the noun that follows:

***what** train did you catch?*	= **quel** train as-tu pris?
***what** time is it?*	= **quelle** heure est-il?
***what** books do you like?*	= **quels** livres aimes-tu?
***what** colours do you like?*	= **quelles** couleurs aimes-tu?

❑ For further usages, see the entry **what**.

IV *pron* quand; **until/since ~?** jusqu'à/depuis quand?; **1982, that's ~ I was born** 1982, c'est l'année où je suis né; **that's ~ I found out** c'est à ce moment-là que j'ai su.

whenever *adv* **1** (no matter when) **~ you want** quand tu veux; **I'll come ~ it is convenient** je viendrai quand cela vous arrangera; **2** (every time that) chaque fois que; **~ I see a black cat, I make a wish** chaque fois que je vois un chat noir, je fais un vœu.

where

■ **Note** *where* in questions is usually translated by *où*: *where are the plates?* = où sont les assiettes?; *I don't know where the plates are* = je ne sais pas où sont les assiettes; *do you know where he is?* = est-ce que tu sais où il est?; *do you know where Paul is?* = est-ce que tu sais où est Paul?
– Note that *où + est-ce que* does not require a change in word order: *where did you see her?* = où est-ce que tu l'as vue?

I *adv* où; **~ is my coat?** où est mon manteau?; **~ do you work?** où est-ce que vous travaillez; **~ would I be if I'd married him?** où est-ce que je serais si je l'avais épousé?; **ask him ~ he went** demande-lui où il est allé; **do you know ~ she's going?** est-ce tu sais où elle va?; **the village ~ we live** le village où nous habitons; **sit ~ you like** asseyez-vous où vous voulez; **it's cold ~ we live** il fait froid là où nous habitons; **~ necessary** si nécessaire; **~ possible** dans la mesure du possible.
II *pron* **from ~?** d'où?; **that's ~ I fell** c'est là que je suis tombé; **that is ~ he is mistaken** c'est là qu'il se trompe; **this is ~ the situation becomes complicated** c'est là que la situation se complique.

whereas *conj* **she likes dogs ~ I prefer cats** elle aime les chiens mais moi je préfère les chats; **he chose to stay quiet ~ I would have complained** il a choisi de ne rien dire alors que moi je me serais sûrement plaint.

whereby *conj* **a system ~ all staff will carry identification** un système qui prévoit que tous les membres du personnel auront une carte.

wherever *adv* **1** (in questions) **~ has he got to?** où est-ce qu'il a bien pu passer?; **2** (anywhere) **~ she goes I'll go** où qu'elle aille, j'irai; **~ you want** où tu veux; **we'll meet ~'s convenient for you** nous nous retrouverons là où ça t'arrange; **3** (whenever) **~ necessary** quand c'est nécessaire; **~ possible** dans la mesure du possible.

whet *vtr* (stimulate) **to ~ the appetite** stimuler l'appétit; **the book ~ted his appetite for travel** les livres lui donnèrent envie de voyager.

whether *conj*

■ **Note** When *whether* is used to mean *if*, it is translated by *si*: *I wonder whether she got my letter* = je me demande si elle a reçu ma lettre.
– In *whether...or not* sentences, *whether* is translated by *que* and the verb that follows is in the subjunctive.

1 (when outcome is uncertain) si; **I wasn't sure ~ to answer or not** or **~ or not to answer** je ne savais pas s'il fallait répondre; **can you check ~ it's cooked?** est-ce que tu peux vérifier si c'est cuit?; **2** (no matter if) **you're coming ~ you like it or not!** tu viendras que cela te plaise ou non!; **~ you have children or not, this book should interest you** que vous ayez des enfants ou non, ce livre devrait vous intéresser.

whew *excl* (in relief) ouf!; (in hot weather) pff!; (in surprise) hein!

which ▶ 965 I *pron* **show her ~ you mean** montre-lui celui/celle etc que tu veux dire; **do you mind ~ you have?** est-ce que tu as une préférence?; **I don't mind ~** ça m'est égal; **can you tell ~ is ~?** peux-tu les distinguer?; **the contract ~ he's spoken about** le contrat dont il a parlé; **~ reminds me...** ce qui me fait penser que...
II *det* **~ books?** quels livres?; **she asked me ~ coach was leaving first** elle m'a demandé lequel des cars allait partir le premier; **~ one of the children...?** lequel or laquelle des enfants...?; **you may wish to join, in ~ case...** vous voulez peut-être vous inscrire, auquel cas...

whichever I *pron* **1** (the one that) (as subject) celui *m* qui, celle *f* qui; (as object) celui *m* que, celle *f* que; **'which restaurant?'—'~ is nearest'** 'quel restaurant?'—'celui qui est le plus proche'; **come at 2 or 2.30, ~ suits you best** viens à 14 h ou 14 h 30, comme cela te convient le mieux; **2** (no matter which one) (as subject) quel *m* que soit celui qui, quelle *f* que soit celle qui; (as object) quel *m* que soit celui que, quelle *f* que soit celle que; **'do you want the big piece or the small piece?'—'~'** 'est-ce que tu veux le gros ou le petit morceau?'—'n'importe'.
II *det* **1** (the one that) **let's go to ~ station is nearest** allons à la gare la plus proche; **2** (no matter which) **I'll be happy ~ horse wins** quel que soit le cheval qui gagne je serai content.

while I *conj* **1** (during the time that) pendant que; **he made a sandwich ~ I phoned** il s'est fait un sandwich pendant que je téléphonais; **~ in Spain, I visited Madrid** pendant que j'étais en Espagne, j'ai visité Madrid; **I fell asleep ~ watching TV** je me suis endormi en regardant la télé; **close the door ~ you're at it** ferme la porte pendant que tu y es; **2** (although) bien que (+ *subj*), quoique (+ *subj*); **3** (whereas) alors que, tandis que; **she likes dogs ~ I prefer cats** elle aime les chiens mais moi je préfère les chats.
II *n* **a ~ ago** il y a quelque temps; **a ~ later** quelque temps plus tard; **for a good ~** pendant longtemps; **a short ~ ago** il y a peu de temps; **it will take a ~** cela va prendre un certain temps; **after a (short) ~** au bout d'un moment; **once in a ~** de temps en temps.
■ **while away**: **~ away [sth]** tuer [*time*] (**doing, by doing** en faisant).

whilst *conj* = **while** I.

which

As a pronoun

In questions

◆ When ***which*** (meaning *which one* or *which ones*) is used as a pronoun in questions, it is translated by ***lequel***, ***laquelle***, ***lesquels*** or ***lesquelles***, according to the gender and number of the noun it is standing for:

*there are three peaches, **which** do you want?* = il y a trois pêches, **laquelle** veux-tu?

◆ When ***which*** is followed by a superlative adjective, then the translation is ***quel***, ***quelle***, ***quels*** or ***quelles***, according to the gender and number of the noun it is standing for:

(of the apples) ***which** is the biggest?* = **quelle** est la plus grosse?
(of the books) ***which** are the cheapest?* = **quels** sont les moins chers?

In relative clauses

◆ When used as a relative pronoun, ***which*** is translated by ***qui*** when it is the subject of the verb, and by ***que*** when it is the object:

*the book **which** is on the table* = le livre **qui** est sur la table
*the book **which** Tina is reading* = le livre **que** lit Tina

Note the different word order of subject and verb; this is the case where the subject is a noun but not where the subject is a pronoun:

*the book **which** I am reading* = le livre **que** je lis

Remember that in the present perfect and past perfect tenses, the past participle agrees in gender and number with the noun ***que*** is referring back to:

*the books **which** I gave you* = les livres **que** je t'ai donnés
*the dresses **which** she bought yesterday* = les robes **qu'**elle a achetées hier

◆ When ***which*** is used as a relative pronoun with a preposition, it is translated by ***lequel***, ***laquelle***, ***lesquels*** or ***lesquelles*** according to the gender and number of the noun it is standing for:

*the road **by which** we came* = la route **par laquelle** nous sommes venus
*the crates **behind which** he hid* = les caisses **derrière lesquelles** il s'est caché

If the preposition would normally be translated by ***à*** in French (***to***, ***at*** etc), the ***preposition + which*** is translated by ***auquel***, ***à laquelle***, ***auxquels*** or ***auxquelles***:

*the addresses **to which** we sent letters* = les adresses **auxquelles** nous avons envoyé des lettres

With prepositions normally translated by ***de*** in French (***of***, ***from*** etc), the translation of *preposition* + ***which*** becomes ***dont*** in all cases:

*a blue book, the title **of which** I've forgotten* = un livre bleu **dont** j'ai oublié le titre

As a determiner

When ***which*** is used as a determiner in questions, it is translated by ***quel***, ***quelle***, ***quels*** or ***quelles*** according to the gender and number of the noun that follows:

***which** car is yours?* = **quelle** voiture est la vôtre?
***which** dress did she buy?* = **quelle** robe a-t-elle achetée?*
***which** books did he borrow?* = **quels** livres a-t-il empruntés?*

Note that, in the second and third examples, the object precedes the verb so that the past participle agrees in gender and number with the object.

* In these cases, an additional *-t-* is required for the liaison between the two vowels to be made.

For particular usages see the entry **which**.

whim *n* caprice *m*; **on a ~** sur un coup de tête.

whimper I *n* gémissement *m* (**of** de).
II *vi* **1** [*person, animal*] gémir; **2** (whinge) [*person*] pleurnicher.

whimsical *adj* [*person*] fantasque; [*play, tale, manner, idea*] saugrenu.

whine *vi* (complain) se plaindre (**about** de); (snivel) pleurnicher; [*dog*] gémir.

whining I *n* (complaints) jérémiades *fpl*; (of dog) gémissements *mpl*.
II *adj* [*voice*] geignard; [*child*] pleurnicheur/-euse; [*letter*] de réclamation.

whinny *vi* [*horse*] hennir doucement; [*person*] hennir.

whip I *n* **1** (for punishment) fouet *m*; (for horse) cravache *f*; **2** (Culin) mousse *f*.
II *vtr* **1** (beat) fouetter; **2** (Culin) fouetter [*cream*]; battre [qch] en neige [*egg whites*]; **3**○ (remove quickly) **I ~ped the key out of his hand** je lui ai arraché la clé des mains.
■ **whip in**: **~ in [sth], ~ [sth] in** (Culin) incorporer [qch] (*avec un fouet*).
■ **whip out**: **~ out [sth]** sortir [qch] brusquement.
■ **whip up**: **~ up [sth] 1** (incite) attiser [*hatred, enthusiasm*]; provoquer [*fear*]; ranimer [*indignation, hostility*]; éveiller [*interest*]; rallier [*support*]; inciter [*strike, unrest*]; **2** (Culin) battre [qch] au fouet; **3** (produce quickly) préparer [qch] en vitesse.

whip: **~lash injury** *n* (Med) coup *m* du lapin; **~-round**○ *n* (GB) collecte *f*.

whirl I *n* **1** (of activity, excitement) tourbillon *m* (**of** de); **2** (spiral motif) spirale *f*.
II *vi* [*dancer*] tournoyer; [*blade, propeller*] tourner; [*snowflakes, dust, thoughts*] tourbillonner.
IDIOMS **to give sth a ~**○ essayer qch.
■ **whirl round** [*person*] se retourner brusquement; [*blade, clock hand*] tourner brusquement.

whirl: **~pool** *n* tourbillon *m*; **~pool bath** *n* bain *m* bouillonnant; **~wind** *n* tourbillon *m*.

whirr I *n* (of motor) vrombissement *m*; (of toy, camera, insect) bourdonnement *m*; (of wings) bruissement *m*.
II *vi* [*motor*] vrombir; [*camera, fan*] tourner; [*insect*] bourdonner; [*wings*] bruire.

whisk I *n* (also **egg ~**) (manual) fouet *m*; (electric) batteur *m*.
II *vtr* **1** (Culin) battre; **2** (transport quickly) **he was ~ed off to meet the president** on l'a emmené sur le champ rencontrer le président; **she was ~ed off to hospital** elle a été emmenée d'urgence à l'hôpital.

whisker I *n* (of animal) poil *m* de moustache.
II **whiskers** *n pl* (of animal) moustaches *fpl*; (of man) (beard) barbe *f*; (moustache) moustache *f*.

whisper I *n* chuchotement *m*; **to speak in a ~** or **in ~s** parler à voix basse; **his voice dropped to a ~** il a baissé la voix et s'est mis à chuchoter.
II *vtr* chuchoter (**to** à); **to ~ sth to sb** chuchoter qch à qn; **'she's asleep', he ~ed** 'elle dort', dit-il en chuchotant; **it is ~ed that** (figurative) on dit que.
III *vi* chuchoter; **to ~ to sb** parler à voix basse à qn.

whistle I *n* **1** (object) sifflet *m*; **to blow the** or **one's ~** donner un coup de sifflet; **2** (sound) (through mouth) sifflement *m*; (by referee) coup *m* de sifflet; (of bird, train) sifflement *m*.
II *vtr* siffler; (casually) siffloter.
III *vi* siffler; **to ~ at sb/sth** siffler qn/qch; **to ~ for** siffler [*dog*].
IDIOMS **to blow the ~ on sb** dénoncer qn; **to blow the ~ on sth** révéler qch.

white ▶559 I *n* **1** (colour) blanc *m*; **2** (of egg) blanc *m*; **the ~s of sb's eyes** le blanc des yeux de qn; **3** (also **White**) (Caucasian) Blanc/Blanche *m/f*; **4** (in chess, draughts) blancs *mpl*.
II **whites** *n pl* **tennis/chef's ~s** tenue *f* de tennis/de chef-cuisinier.
III *adj* **1** blanc/blanche; **bright ~ teeth** dents d'un blanc éclatant; **to go** or **turn ~** devenir blanc, blanchir; **to paint sth ~** peindre qch en blanc; **2** [*race, child, skin*] blanc/blanche; [*area*] habité par des Blancs; [*culture, prejudice, fears*] des Blancs; **a ~ man/woman** un Blanc/une Blanche; **3** (pale) pâle (**with** de); **to go** or **turn ~** pâlir (**with** de).

whitebait *n* (raw) blanchaille *f*; (fried) petite friture *f*.

white coffee *n* (at home) café *m* au lait; (in café) (café *m*) crème *m*.

white-collar *adj* [*job, work*] d'employé de bureau; [*staff*] de bureau; **~ worker** col *m* blanc, employé/-e *m/f* de bureau.

white elephant *n* **1** (item, knicknack) bibelot *m*; **2** (public project) réalisation *f* coûteuse et peu rentable.

white: **~ gasoline** *n* (US) essence *f* sans plomb; **~ horses** *n pl* (waves) moutons *mpl*.

White House *n* **the ~** la Maison Blanche.

white lie *n* pieux mensonge *m*.

whiten I *vtr* blanchir.
II *vi* [*sky, face, cheeks*] pâlir; [*knuckles*] blanchir.

whitener *n* **1** (for clothes) agent *m* blanchissant; **2** (for shoes) produit *m* pour blanchir; **3** (for coffee, tea) succédané *m* de lait en poudre.

whiteness *n* blancheur *f*.

white spirit *n* white-spirit *m*.

whitewash I *n* **1** (for walls) lait *m* de chaux; **2** (figurative) (cover-up) mise *f* en scène.
II *vtr* **1** blanchir [qch] à la chaux [*wall*]; **2** (also **~ over**) blanchir [*facts*].

white: **~ water** *n* eau *f* vive; **~ wedding** *n* mariage *m* en blanc.

Whitsun *n* (also **Whitsuntide**) Pentecôte *f*.

Whit Sunday *n* Pentecôte *f*.

whittle *vtr* tailler [qch] au couteau.
■ **whittle away**: ¶ **~ away [sth]** réduire [*advantage, lead, profits*]; ¶ **~ away at [sth]** tailler [*stick*]; réduire [*advantage, lead, profits*].
■ **whittle down**: **~ down [sth], ~ [sth] down** réduire (**to** à).

whizz-kid○ *n* jeune prodige *m*.

who *pron*

■ **Note** Note that there are three ways of asking questions using *qui* as the object of the verb: *who did he call?* = qui est-ce qu'il a appelé?, qui a-t-il appelé?, il a appelé qui?

1 (in questions) (as subject) qui (est-ce qui); (as object) qui (est-ce que); (after prepositions) qui; **~ knows the answer?** qui connaît la réponse?; **~ did you invite?** qui est-ce que tu as invité?, qui as-tu invité?; **~'s going to be there?** qui sera là?; **~ was she with?** avec qui était-elle?; **~ did you buy it for?** pour qui l'as-tu acheté?; **~ did you get it from?** qui te l'a donné?; **2** (relative) (as subject) qui; (as object) que; (after prepositions) qui; **his friend, ~ lives in Paris** son ami, qui habite Paris; **his friend ~ he sees once a week** l'ami qu'il voit une fois par semaine; **those ~ have something to say** quiconque a quelque chose à dire or ceux/celles qui ont quelque chose à dire; **3** (whoever) **bring ~ you like** tu peux amener qui tu veux; **~ do you think you are?** tu te prends pour qui?

whodun(n)it *n* polar○ *m*, roman *m* policier.

whoever *pron* **1** (the one that) **~ wins the election** celui ou celle qui gagnera les élections; **2** (anyone that) (as subject) quiconque; (as object) qui; **~ saw the accident should contact us** quiconque a assisté à l'accident devrait nous contacter; **invite ~ you like** invite qui tu veux; **3** (no matter who) **~ you are** qui que vous soyez.

whole I *n* **1** (total unit) tout *m*; **as a ~** (not in separate parts) en entier; (overall) dans l'ensemble; **taken as a ~** pris dans l'ensemble; **for the country as a ~** pour le pays dans son ensemble; **2** (all) **the ~ of** tout/-e; **the ~ of the weekend/August** tout le week-end/mois d'août; **the ~ of London is talking about it** tout Londres en parle; **nearly the ~ of Berlin was destroyed** Berlin a été presque entièrement détruit.
II *adj* **1** (entire) tout, entier/-ière; (more emphatic) tout entier/-ière; **a ~ hour** une heure entière; **a ~ day** toute une journée; **for three ~ weeks** pendant trois semaines entières; **his ~ life** toute sa vie, sa vie entière; **they searched the ~ country** ils ont cherché dans tout le pays or dans le pays tout entier; **~ cities were destroyed** des villes entières ont été détruites; **the ~ truth** toute la vérité; **the most beautiful city in the ~ world** la plus belle ville du monde; **this doesn't give the ~ picture** ceci ne dit pas tout; **let's forget the ~ thing!** oublions tout ça!; **she made the ~ thing up** elle a tout inventé; **2** (emphatic use) **a ~ new way of life** un mode de vie complètement différent; **that's the ~ point of the exercise** c'est tout l'intérêt de l'exercice; **I find the ~ idea absurd** je trouve cette idée complètement absurde; **3** (intact) intact.
III *adv* [*swallow, cook*] tout entier.
IV on the whole *phr* dans l'ensemble.

wholefood *n* (GB) produits *mpl* biologiques.

wholehearted *adj* [*approval, support*] sans réserve; **to be in ~ agreement with** être en accord total avec.

whole: **~heartedly** *adv* sans réserve; **~meal** *adj* complet/-ète; **~ milk** *n* lait *m* entier; **~ note** *n* (US Mus) ronde *f*; **~ number** *n* (nombre *m*) entier *m*.

wholesale I *n* vente *f* en gros.
II *adj* **1** [*business*] de gros; **2** (large-scale) [*destruction*] total; [*acceptance, rejection*] en bloc; [*attack*] sur tous les fronts.
III *adv* **1** [*buy, sell*] en gros; **2** [*accept, reject*] en bloc.

wholesaler *n* grossiste *mf*, marchand/-e *m/f* en gros; **wine ~** marchand de vin en gros.

wholesome *adj* **1** (healthy) sain; **2** (decent) [*person, appearance*] bien propre; [*entertainment*] innocent.

wholewheat *adj* = **wholemeal**.

wholly *adv* entièrement, tout à fait.

whom *pron* **1** (in questions) qui (est-ce que); (after prepositions) qui; **~ did she meet?** qui a-t-elle rencontré?, qui est-ce qu'elle a rencontré?; **to ~ are you referring?** à qui est-ce que vous faites allusion?; **2** (relative) que; (after prepositions) qui; **the person to ~/of ~ I spoke** la personne à qui/dont j'ai parlé.

whooping cough ▶686 *n* coqueluche *f*.

whorl *n* (of cream, chocolate) spirale *f*; (on fingerprint) volute *f*; (shell pattern) spire *f*; (of petals) verticille *m*.

whose I *pron* **1** (in questions) à qui; **~ is this?** à qui est ceci?; **2** (relative) **the boy ~ dog was killed** le garçon dont le chien a été tué; **the man ~ daughter he was married to** l'homme dont il avait épousé la fille.
II *det* **~ pen is that?** à qui est ce stylo?; **do you know ~ car was stolen?** est-ce que tu sais à qui appartenait la voiture volée?; **~ coat did you take?** tu as pris le manteau de qui?

why

■ **Note** Note that there are three ways of asking questions using *why*: *why did you go?* = pourquoi est-ce que tu y es allé?, pourquoi y es-tu allé?, tu y es allé pourquoi?

I *adv* **1** (in questions) pourquoi; **~ do you ask?** pourquoi est-ce que tu me poses la question?, pourquoi me poses-tu la question?; **~ bother?** pourquoi se tracasser?; **~ the delay?** pourquoi ce retard?; **~ not?** pourquoi pas?; **'tell them'—'~ should I?'** 'dis-le-leur'—'et pourquoi (est-ce que je devrais le faire)?'; **2** (making suggestions) pourquoi; **~ don't we go away for the weekend?** pourquoi ne pas partir quelque part pour le week-end?; **~ don't I invite them for dinner?** et si je les invitais à manger?
II *conj* pour ça; **that is ~ they came** c'est pour ça qu'ils sont venus; **I need to know the reason ~** j'ai besoin de savoir pourquoi.

wick *n* mèche *f*.

wicked *adj* **1** (evil) [*person*] méchant; [*heart, deed*] cruel/-elle; [*plot*] pernicieux/-ieuse; [*intention*] mauvais; **2** [*grin, humour*] malicieux/

-ieuse; [*thoughts*] pervers; **3** (vicious) [*wind*] méchant; [*weapon*] redoutable; [*sarcasm*] cinglant; **to have a ~ tongue** être mauvaise langue.

wicker I *n* (also **wickerwork**) osier *m*.
II *noun modifier* [*basket, furniture*] en osier.

wide ▶738 I *adj* **1** (broad) [*river, opening, mouth*] large; [*margin*] grand; **how ~ is your garden?** quelle est la largeur de votre jardin?; **it's 30 cm ~** il a 30 cm de large; **the river is 1 km across at its ~st** le fleuve fait or atteint 1 km à son point le plus large; **her eyes were ~ with fear** ses yeux étaient agrandis par la peur; **2** (immense) [*ocean, desert, expanse*] vaste; **3** (extensive) [*variety, choice*] grand (*before n*); **a ~ range of opinions** une grande variété d'opinions; **a ~ range of products** une vaste gamme de produits; **in the ~st sense of the word** au sens le plus large du mot; **4** (Sport) [*ball, shot*] perdu.
II *adv* **to open one's eyes ~** ouvrir grand les yeux; **to open the door/window ~** ouvrir la porte/la fenêtre en grand; **his eyes are (set) ~ apart** il a les yeux très écartés; **his legs were ~ apart** il avait les jambes écartées; **open ~!** ouvrez grand (la bouche)!; **to be ~ of the mark** [*ball, dart*] être à côté; [*guess*] être loin de la vérité.
III **-wide** *combining form* **a country~ search** une recherche menée dans tout le pays; **a nation~ survey** un sondage à l'échelle nationale.

wide: **~-angle lens** *n* objectif *m* à grand angle; **~ awake** *adj* complètement éveillé.

wide-eyed *adj* **1** (with surprise, fear) **he was ~** il ouvrait de grands yeux; **~ with fear/surprise** les yeux écarquillés de peur/surprise; **she stared/listened ~** elle regardait/écoutait les yeux écarquillés; **2** (naïve) [*person, innocence*] ingénu.

widely *adv* **1** (commonly) [*accepted, used*] largement; **it is ~ believed that** beaucoup de gens pensent que; **a country ~ admired for its technology** un pays qui fait l'admiration générale pour sa technologie; **this product is now ~ available** on trouve maintenant ce produit partout; **to be ~ known** être bien connu (**for** pour); **these are not ~ held views** ce ne sont pas des opinions très répandues; **2** [*spaced, planted*] à de grands intervalles; [*travel, differ, vary*] beaucoup.

widely-read *adj* [*student*] qui a beaucoup lu; [*author*] très lu.

widen I *vtr* **1** élargir [*road, gap*]; **2** élargir [*debate*]; étendre [*powers*]; **this has ~ed their lead in the opinion polls** ceci a renforcé leur position dominante dans les sondages.
II *vi* **1** [*river, road*] s'élargir; **his eyes ~ed** il a ouvert grand les yeux; **2** (increase) **the gap is ~ing between rich and poor** le fossé entre riches et pauvres s'élargit.

wide open *adj* **1** [*door, window, eyes, mouth*] grand ouvert; **2 the race is ~** l'issue de la course est indécise; **3 to lay oneself ~ to criticism** prêter le flanc à la critique.

wide-ranging *adj* [*reforms*] de grande envergure; [*interests*] très variés.

wide screen *n* grand écran *m*.

widespread *adj* [*epidemic*] généralisé; [*devastation*] étendu; [*belief*] très répandu.

widow I *n* veuve *f*; **war ~** veuve de guerre.
II *vtr* **to be ~ed** devenir veuf/veuve *m/f*; **she has been ~ed for two years** elle est veuve depuis deux ans.

widower *n* veuf *m*.

width ▶738 *n* **1** largeur *f*; **it is 30 metres in ~** il fait or mesure 30 mètres de large; **2** (of fabric) lé *m*.

wield *vtr* **1** brandir [*weapon, tool*]; **2** exercer [*influence, authority*] (**over** sur).

wife *n* femme *f*; (more formally) épouse *f*; **the baker's/farmer's ~** la boulangère/la fermière.

wig *n* (whole head) perruque *f*; (partial) postiche *m*.

wiggle○ I *n* **a ~ of the hips** un roulement des hanches.
II *vtr* faire bouger [*tooth, wedged object*]; **to ~ one's hips** rouler les hanches; **to ~ one's fingers/toes** remuer les doigts/orteils.
III *vi* [*snake, worm*] se tortiller.

wild I *n* **in the ~** [*conditions, life*] en liberté; **to grow in the ~** pousser à l'état sauvage; **the call of the ~** l'appel de la nature.
II *adj* **1** [*animal, plant*] sauvage; **~ bird/animal** oiseau/animal sauvage; **the pony is still quite ~** le poney est encore assez farouche; **2** [*landscape*] sauvage; **3** [*wind*] violent; [*sea*] agité; **it was a ~ night** c'était une nuit de tempête; **4** [*party, laughter, person*] fou/folle; [*imagination*] délirant; [*applause*] déchaîné; **to go ~** se déchaîner; **his hair was ~ and unkempt** il avait les cheveux en bataille; **5**○ (furious) furieux/-ieuse; **he'll go** or **be ~!** ça va le mettre hors de lui!; **6**○ (enthusiastic) **to be ~ about** être un fana○ de; **I'm not ~ about him/it** il/ça ne m'emballe○ pas; **7** (outlandish) [*idea, plan*] fou/folle; [*claim, promise, accusation*] extravagant; [*story*] farfelu○.
III *adv* **1** [*grow*] à l'état sauvage; **the garden had run ~** le jardin était devenu une vraie jungle; **those children are allowed to run ~!** on permet à ces enfants de faire n'importe quoi!; **to let one's imagination run ~** laisser libre cours à son imagination.

wild boar *n* sanglier *m*.

wildcat I *n* chat *m* sauvage.
II *adj* (US) [*scheme, venture*] risqué.

wild dog *n* dingo *m*.

wilderness *n* (wasteland) étendue *f* sauvage et désolée; **the garden has become a ~** le jardin est devenu une vraie jungle.

wild-eyed *adj* au regard égaré.

wildfire *n* **to spread like ~** se répandre comme une traînée de poudre.

wild flower *n* fleur *f* des champs, fleur *f* sauvage.

wild-goose chase *n* **it turned out to be a ~** ça n'a abouti à rien; **to lead sb on a ~** mettre qn sur une mauvaise piste.

wild: **~life** *n* (animals) faune *f*; (animals and plants) faune *f* et flore *f*; **~life park**,

~life reserve, **~life sanctuary** *n* réserve *f* naturelle.

wildly *adv* **1** [*invest, spend, talk*] de façon insensée; [*fire, shoot*] au hasard; **to hit out/run ~** envoyer des coups/courir dans tous les sens; **2** [*wave, gesture*] de manière très agitée; [*applaud*] à tout rompre; **to fluctuate ~** subir des fluctuations violentes; **to beat ~** [*heart*] battre à tout rompre; **3** [*enthusiastic, optimistic*] extrêmement.

wildness *n* **1** (of landscape, mountains) aspect *m* sauvage; (of wind, waves, weather) violence *f*; **2** (of person, behaviour) caractère *m* débridé; (of appearance) désordre *m*; (of evening, party) folie *f*; **3** (of idea, plan, scheme) extravagance *f*; (of imagination) délire *m*.

wilds *n pl* **to live in the ~ of Arizona** habiter au fin fond de l'Arizona.

Wild West *n* Far West *m*.

wilful (GB), **willful** (US) *adj* **1** [*person, behaviour*] volontaire; **2** [*damage, disobedience*] délibéré.

wilfully (GB), **willfully** (US) *adv* **1** (in headstrong way) obstinément; **2** (deliberately) délibérément.

will[1] I *modal aux* **1** (expressing the future) **it won't rain** il ne pleuvra pas; **~ there be many people?** est-ce qu'il y aura beaucoup de monde?; **they'll come tomorrow** ils vont venir demain; **what ~ you do now?** qu'est-ce que tu vas faire maintenant?; **2** (expressing willingness or intention) **~ you help me?** est-ce que tu m'aideras?; **we won't stay too long** nous ne resterons pas trop longtemps; **he won't cooperate** il ne veut pas coopérer; **I ~ not be insulted** je n'accepte pas qu'on m'insulte; **3** (in requests, commands) **~ you pass the salt please?** est-ce que tu peux me passer le sel s'il te plait; **~ you please be quiet!** est-ce que tu vas te taire?; **wait a minute, ~ you!** attends un peu!; **4** (in invitations) **~ you have some tea?** est-ce que vous voulez du thé?; **won't you join us for dinner?** est-ce que tu veux dîner avec nous?; **what ~ you have to drink?** qu'est-ce que tu prends?; **5** (in assumptions) **he'll be about 30 now** il doit avoir 30 ans maintenant; **you'll be tired, I expect** tu dois être fatigué je suppose; **they won't know what's happened** ils ne doivent pas savoir ce qui s'est passé; **6** (indicating sth predictable or customary) **they ~ ask for a deposit** ils demandent une caution; **these things ~ happen** ce sont des choses qui arrivent; **you ~ keep contradicting her!** il faut toujours que tu la contredises!; **7** (in short answers and tag questions) **you'll come again, won't you?** tu reviendras, n'est-ce pas?; **you won't forget, ~ you?** tu n'oublieras pas, n'est-ce pas?; **that'll be cheaper, won't it?** ça sera moins cher, non?; **'they won't be ready'—'yes, they ~'** 'ils ne seront pas prêts'—'(bien sûr que) si'; **'~ you call me?'—'yes, I ~'** 'est-ce que tu me téléphoneras?'—'bien sûr que oui'; **'she'll be furious'—'no, she won't!'** 'elle sera furieuse'—'bien sûr que non!'; **'I'll do it'—'no you won't!'** 'je le ferai'—'il n'en est pas question!'

II *vtr* **1** (urge mentally) **to ~ sb to do** supplier mentalement qn de faire; **to ~ sb to live** prier pour que qn vive; **2** (wish, desire) vouloir; **3** (Law) léguer (**to** à).

will[2] I *n* **1** volonté *f* (**to do** de faire); **to have a strong/weak ~** avoir beaucoup/peu de volonté; **to have a ~ of one's own** n'en faire qu'à sa tête; **strength of ~** force de caractère; **against my ~** contre mon gré; **to do sth with a ~** faire qch de bon cœur; **to lose the ~ to live** ne plus avoir envie de vivre; **2** (Law) testament *m*; **to leave sb sth in one's ~** léguer qch à qn.

II at will *phr* [*select, take*] à volonté; **you can change it at ~** tu peux le changer quand tu veux; **they can wander about at ~** ils peuvent se promener comme ils veulent.

willing *adj* **1** (prepared) **to be ~ to do** être prêt à faire; **I'm quite ~** je veux bien; **I'm more than ~ to help you** j'accepte volontiers de vous aider; **2** (eager) [*pupil, helper*] de bonne volonté; [*slave*] consentant; [*recruit, victim*] volontaire; **to show ~** faire preuve de bonne volonté; **3** [*donation*] bénévole; [*sacrifice*] volontaire.

willingly *adv* [*accept, help*] volontiers; [*work*] avec bonne volonté; **did she go ~?** est-elle partie de son propre gré?

willingness *n* **1** (readiness) volonté *f* (**to do** de faire); **2** (helpfulness) bonne volonté *f*.

willow *n* **1** (also **~ tree**) saule *m*; **2** (wood) (bois *m* de) saule *m*; **3** (for weaving) osier *m*.

will power *n* volonté *f* (**to do** de faire).

willy-nilly *adv* **1** (regardless of choice) bon gré mal gré; **2** (haphazardly) au hasard.

wilt I *vtr* faire dépérir [*plant*].

II *vi* **1** [*plant, flower*] se faner; **2** [*person*] (from heat, fatigue) se sentir faible; (at daunting prospect) perdre courage.

III wilted *pp adj* fané.

win I *n* victoire *f* (**over** sur).

II *vtr* **1** gagner [*match, bet, battle, money*]; remporter [*election*]; **2** (acquire) obtenir [*delay, reprieve*]; gagner [*friendship, heart*]; s'attirer [*sympathy*]; s'acquérir [*support*] (**of** de); **it won him the admiration of his colleagues** cela lui a valu l'admiration de ses collègues; **to ~ sb's love/respect** se faire aimer/respecter de qn.

III *vi* gagner; **to ~ against sb** l'emporter sur qn; **to ~ by a goal** gagner d'un but; **I've done my best to please her, but you just can't ~** j'ai tout fait pour lui faire plaisir, mais en vain.

■ **win back**: **~ [sth] back, ~ back [sth]** reconquérir [*support, votes, title, territory*] (**from sb** sur qn); regagner [*affection, respect*]; reprendre [*prize*] (**from** à).

■ **win over, win round**: **~ [sb] over** convaincre.

wince I *n* grimace *f*.

II *vi* grimacer, faire une grimace.

winch I *n* treuil *m*.

II *vtr* **to ~ sth down/up** descendre/hisser qch au treuil.

wind[1] **I** *n* **1** vent *m*; **North ~** vent du nord; **the ~ is blowing** il y a du vent; **which way is the ~ blowing?** d'où vient le vent?; **a high ~** un vent fort; **2** (breath) **to knock the ~ out of sb** couper le souffle à qn; **to get one's ~** reprendre souffle; **to get one's second ~** (figurative) reprendre ses forces; **3** (flatulence) vents *mpl*; **to break ~** lâcher un vent; **to suffer from ~** avoir des gaz.

II *vtr* **1** (make breathless) [*blow, punch*] couper la respiration à; [*climb*] essouffler; **2** faire faire son rot à [*baby*].

wind[2] **I** *n* **1** (of road) tournant *m*; **2** (movement) (of handle) tour *m*; **to give the clock a ~** remonter la pendule.

II *vtr* **1** (coil up) enrouler [*hair, rope, wire*] (**on, onto** sur; **round** autour de); **2** (also **~ up**) remonter [*clock, toy*]; **3** donner un tour de [*handle*]; **4 to ~ one's** or **its way** [*procession, road, river*] serpenter.

III *vi* [*road, river*] serpenter (**along** le long de); [*stairs*] tourner.

■ **wind down**: ¶ **~ down 1** [*organization*] réduire ses activités; [*activity, production*] toucher à sa fin; [*person*] se détendre; **2** [*clockwork*] être sur le point de s'arrêter; ¶ **~ down [sth], ~ [sth] down 1** baisser [*car window*]; **2** mettre fin à [*activity, organization*].

■ **wind in**: **~ in [sth], ~ [sth] in** remonter [*cable, line, fish*].

■ **wind on**: ¶ **~ on** [*film*] s'enrouler; ¶ **~ on [sth], ~ [sth] on** enrouler.

■ **wind up**: ¶ **~ up 1** (finish) [*event*] se terminer (**with** par); [*speaker*] conclure; **2**○ (end up) finir, se retrouver; ¶ **~ up [sth], ~ [sth] up 1** liquider [*business*]; fermer [*account, club*]; mettre fin à [*debate, meeting, project*]; **2** remonter [*clock, car window*]; ¶ **~ [sb] up, ~ up [sb] 1** (tease) faire marcher [*person*]; **2** (make tense) énerver.

winder *n* (for watch) remontoir *m*; (for window) lève-glace *m inv*.

windfall *n* fruit *m* tombé par terre; (figurative) aubaine *f*.

winding *adj* [*road, river*] sinueux/-euse; [*stairs*] en spirale.

wind instrument ▶753 *n* instrument *m* à vent.

windmill *n* moulin *m* à vent.

window *n* **1** (of house) fenêtre *f*; (of shop, public building) vitrine *f*; (of vehicle) (gen) vitre *f*; (of plane) hublot *m*; (stained glass) vitrail *m*; **to look out of** or **through the ~** regarder par la fenêtre; **2** (for service at bank or post office) guichet *m*.

window: **~ box** *n* jardinière *f*; **~ cleaner** *n* laveur/-euse *m/f* de carreaux; **~ display** *n* vitrine *f*; **~ ledge** *n* appui *m* de fenêtre; **~pane** *n* carreau *m*.

window seat *n* **1** (in room) banquette *f*; **2** (in bus, train) place *f* côté vitre.

window-shopping *n* **to go ~** faire du lèche-vitrines○ *m inv*.

windowsill *n* rebord *m* de fenêtre.

wind: **~pipe** *n* trachée-artère *f*; **~screen** *n* (GB) pare-brise *m inv*; **~screen wiper** *n* (GB) essuie-glace *m inv*; **~shield** *n* (US) = **windscreen**; **~surf** ▶649 *vi* faire de la planche à voile; **~surfer** *n* (person) véliplanchiste *mf*; (board) planche *f* à voile; **~swept** *adj* venteux/-euse.

windy *adj* [*place*] venteux/-euse; [*day*] de vent; **it was very ~** il faisait beaucoup de vent.

wine ▶559 *n* **1** (drink) vin *m*; **2** (colour) lie-de-vin *m*.

wine: **~ bar** *n* bar *m* à vin; **~ box** *n* ≈ cubitainer® *m*; **~ cellar** *n* cave *f*; **~ glass** *n* verre *m* à vin; **~ grower** *n* viticulteur/-trice *m/f*.

wine growing I *n* viticulture *f*.

II *noun modifier* [*region*] vinicole.

wine: **~ list** *n* carte *f* des vins; **~ merchant** ▶805 *n* négociant *m* en vins; **~ producer** ▶805 *n* viticulteur/-trice *m/f*; **~ rack** *n* casier *m* à bouteilles; **~ taster** ▶805 *n* dégustateur/-trice *m/f* de vins; **~ tasting** *n* dégustation *f* de vins; **~ vinegar** *n* vinaigre *m* de vin; **~ waiter** ▶805 *n* sommelier/-ière *m/f*.

wing I *n* **1** (of bird, insect) aile *f*; **to be on the ~** être en vol; **2** (of building, plane, car) aile *f*; (of armchair) oreille *f*; **3** (of political party) aile *f*; **4** (Sport) (player) ailier *m*; (side of pitch) aile *f*; **to play on the right ~** être ailier droit.

II **wings** *n pl* (in theatre) **the ~s** les coulisses *fpl*; **to be waiting in the ~s** (figurative) attendre son heure.

wink I *n* clin *m* d'œil; **to give sb a ~** faire un clin d'œil à qn; **we didn't get a ~ of sleep all night** nous n'avons pas fermé l'œil de la nuit.

II *vtr* **to ~ one's eye** cligner de l'œil.

III *vi* cligner de l'œil; **to ~ at sb** faire un clin d'œil à qn.

winner *n* **1** (victor) gagnant/-e *m/f*; **to be on to a ~** jouer gagnant; **2** (success) **to be a ~** [*film, book, song*] avoir un gros succès.

winning *adj* **1** (victorious) gagnant; **2** [*smile*] engageant; **to have ~ ways** avoir du charme.

winnings *n pl* gains *mpl*.

winning streak *n* **to be on a ~** [*gambler*] être dans une bonne passe; [*team*] remporter victoire sur victoire.

winter I *n* hiver *m*; ▶ **autumn**.

II *noun modifier* [*sports, clothes, weather*] d'hiver.

III *vi* passer l'hiver.

wintertime *n* hiver *m*.

wipe I *n* **1 to give sth a ~** (clean, dust) donner un coup de chiffon à qch; (dry) essuyer qch; **2** (for face, baby) lingette *f*.

II *vtr* essuyer [*table, glass*] (**on** sur; **with** avec); **to ~ one's hands/feet** s'essuyer les mains/les pieds; **to ~ one's nose** se moucher; **to ~ one's bottom** se torcher; **to ~ the dishes** essuyer la vaisselle; **to ~ sth clean** essuyer qch.

■ **wipe away**: **~ away [sth], ~ [sth] away** essuyer [*tears, sweat*]; faire partir [*dirt, mark*].

■ **wipe down**: **~ down [sth]**, **~ [sth] down** nettoyer [*wall, floor*].
■ **wipe off**: **~ off [sth]**, **~ [sth] off 1** faire partir [*dirt, mark*]; **2** effacer [*recording*].
■ **wipe out**: **~ out [sth]**, **~ [sth] out 1** nettoyer [*container, cupboard*]; **2** annuler [*inflation*]; anéantir [*species, enemy, population*].
■ **wipe up**: ¶ **~ up** essuyer la vaisselle; ¶ **~ up [sth]**, **~ [sth] up** essuyer.

wire I *n* **1** (length of metal) fil *m*; **electric/telephone ~** fil électrique/téléphonique; **2** (US) (telegram) télégramme *m*.
II *vtr* **1 to ~ a house** installer l'électricité dans une maison; **to ~ a plug/a lamp** connecter une prise/une lampe; **to ~ a room for sound** sonoriser une pièce; **2** (telegraph) télégraphier à [*person*]; télégraphier [*money*].

wire: **~ brush** *n* brosse *f* métallique; **~ cutters** *n pl* cisailles *fpl*; **~ mesh** *n* treillis *m* métallique; **~ netting** *n* grillage *m*; **~ wool** *n* paille *f* de fer.

wiring *n* (in house) installation *f* électrique; (in appliance) circuit *m* (électrique).

wiry *adj* **1** [*person, body*] mince et nerveux/-euse; **2** [*hair*] rêche.

wisdom *n* sagesse *f*; **to doubt** or **question the ~ of doing** douter qu'il soit sage de faire.

wisdom tooth *n* dent *f* de sagesse.

wise I *adj* **1** (prudent) [*person, words, precaution, saying*] sage; [*choice, investment*] judicieux/-ieuse; [*smile, nod*] avisé; **a ~ man** un sage; **a ~ move** une décision judicieuse; **it is ~ of sb to do** il est prudent de la part de qn de faire; **you would be ~ to do** tu ferais bien de faire; **was that ~?** était-ce bien raisonnable?; **to be ~ after the event** être sage après coup; **to be none the ~r** (understand no better) ne pas être plus avancé; (not realize) ne s'apercevoir de rien; **2**○ (aware) **to be ~ to sth** être au courant de qch; **to get ~ to** prendre le coup de [*situation*]; **to get ~ to sb** saisir○ à qui on a affaire.
II -wise *combining form* **1** (direction) dans le sens de; **length-~** dans le sens de la longueur; **2** (with regard to) pour ce qui est de; **work-~** pour ce qui est du travail.

wise guy○ *n* gros malin○ *m*.

wisely *adv* judicieusement.

Wise Men *n pl* **the three ~** les Rois *mpl* Mages.

wish I *n* **1** (request) souhait *m* (**for** de); **to make a ~** faire un vœu; **her ~ came true** son souhait s'est réalisé; **2** (desire) désir *m* (**for** de; **to do** de faire); **to express a ~ for sth** exprimer un désir de qch; **to go against sb's ~es** aller contre la volonté de qn; **it is my dearest ~ to visit Capri** mon vœu le plus cher est de visiter Capri; **I have no ~ to disturb you** je n'ai pas l'intention de vous déranger.
II wishes *n pl* vœux *mpl*; **good** or **best ~es** meilleurs vœux; (ending letter) bien amicalement; **best ~es on your birthday** meilleurs vœux pour votre anniversaire; **please give him my best ~es** je vous prie de lui faire toutes mes amitiés.
III *vtr* **1** (expressing longing) **I ~ he were here/had been here** si seulement il était ici/avait été ici; **I just ~ we lived closer** si seulement nous habitions plus près; **he ~ed he had written** il regrettait de ne pas avoir écrit; **he bought it and then ~ed he hadn't** il l'a acheté et puis a regretté de l'avoir fait; **I ~ed myself single again** j'aurais voulu être à nouveau célibataire; **2** (express congratulations, greetings) souhaiter; **I ~ you good luck/a happy birthday** je vous souhaite bonne chance/un bon anniversaire; **we ~ed each other goodbye and good luck** nous nous sommes dit au revoir et bonne chance; **I ~ him well** je souhaite que tout aille bien pour lui; **3** (want) souhaiter, désirer.
IV *vi* **1** (desire) vouloir; **just as you ~** comme vous voudrez; **what more could one ~ for?** qu'est-ce qu'on pourrait espérer or souhaiter de plus?; **2** (make a wish) faire un vœu.

wishful thinking *n* **that's ~** c'est prendre ses désirs pour des réalités.

wisp *n* (of hair) mèche *f*; (of straw) brin *m*; (of smoke, cloud) volute *f*.

wispy *adj* [*hair, beard*] fin; [*cloud, smoke*] léger/-ère.

wisteria *n* glycine *f*.

wistful *adj* (sad) mélancolique; (nostalgic) nostalgique.

wit I *n* **1** (sense of humour) esprit *m*; **to have a quick/ready ~** avoir la répartie facile/l'esprit d'à-propos; **2** (witty person) personne *f* spirituelle.
II to wit *phr* à savoir.

witch *n* sorcière *f*.

witch: **~craft** *n* sorcellerie *f*; **~ doctor** *n* shaman *m*.

with *prep*

■ **Note** This dictionary contains Usage Notes on such topics as the human body which use the preposition *with*. For the index to these Notes ▶ **1008**.

---

1 avec; **a meeting ~ sb** une réunion avec qn; **to hit sb ~ sth** frapper qn avec qch; **~ difficulty/pleasure** avec difficulté/plaisir; **to be patient ~ sb** être patient avec qn; **delighted ~ sth** ravi de qch; **to travel ~ sb** voyager avec qn; **to live ~ sb** (in one's own house) vivre avec qn; (in their house) vivre chez qn; **I'll be ~ you in a second** je suis à vous dans un instant; **take your umbrella ~ you** emporte ton parapluie; **bring the books back ~ you** ramène les livres; **~ the introduction of the reforms** avec l'introduction des nouvelles réformes; **~ that, he left** sur ce, il est parti; **you're safe ~ us** tu es en sécurité avec nous; **the blame lies ~ him** c'est de sa faute; **2** (in descriptions) à; avec; de; **a girl ~ black hair** une fille aux cheveux noirs; **the boy ~ the broken leg** le garçon à la jambe cassée; **a boy ~ a broken leg** un garçon avec une jambe cassée; **a TV ~ remote control** une télévision avec télécommande; **furnished ~ antiques** meublé avec des meubles anciens; **covered ~ mud** couvert de boue; **to lie ~ one's eyes closed**

être allongé les yeux fermés; **to stand ~ one's arms folded** se tenir les bras croisés; **filled ~ sth** rempli de qch; **surrounded ~ sth** entouré de qch; **3** (according to) **to increase ~ time** augmenter avec le temps; **to vary ~ the temperature** varier selon la température; **4** (owning, bringing) **passengers ~ tickets** les passagers munis de billets; **people ~ qualifications** les gens qualifiés; **somebody ~ your experience** quelqu'un qui a ton expérience; **have you got the report ~ you?** est-ce que tu as (amené) le rapport?; **5** (as regards) **how are things ~ you?** comment ça va?; **what's up ~ you?** qu'est-ce que tu as?; **what do you want ~ another car?** qu'est-ce que tu veux faire d'une deuxième voiture?; **6** (because of) **sick ~ worry** malade or mort d'inquiétude; **he can see better ~ his glasses on** il voit mieux avec ses lunettes; **I can't do it ~ you watching** je ne peux pas le faire si tu me regardes; **7** (suffering from) **people ~ Aids/leukemia** les personnes atteintes du sida/de la leucémie; **to be ill ~ flu** avoir la grippe; **8** (employed by, customer of) **a reporter ~ the Gazette** un journaliste de la Gazette; **he's ~ the UN** il travaille pour l'ONU; **I'm ~ Chemco** je travaille chez Chemco; **we're ~ the National Bank** nous sommes à la National Bank; **9** (in the same direction as) **to sail ~ the wind** naviguer dans le sens du vent; **to drift ~ the tide** dériver avec le courant.

withdraw I *vtr* retirer [*hand, money, application, permission, troops*]; renoncer à, retirer [*claim*]; rétracter [*accusation, statement*]; **to ~ sth from sb** retirer qch à qn.
II *vi* **1** [*person, troops*] se retirer (**from** de); [*applicant, candidate*] se retirer; **2** (psychologically) se replier sur soi-même.

withdrawal *n* **1** (of money, application, troops, statement) retrait *m* (**of, from** de); **he has made several ~s from his account recently** il a effectué plusieurs retraits de son compte récemment; **2** (psychological reaction) repli *m* sur soi; **3** (of drug addict) état *m* de manque.

withdrawal symptoms *n pl* symptômes *mpl* de manque; **to be suffering from ~** être en état de manque.

withdrawn *adj* [*person*] renfermé, replié sur soi-même.

wither I *vtr* flétrir.
II *vi* se flétrir.

withered *adj* [*plant, skin, cheek*] flétri; [*arm*] atrophié.

withering *adj* [*look*] plein de mépris; [*contempt, comment*] cinglant.

withhold *vtr* différer [*payment*]; retenir [*tax, grant, rent*]; refuser [*consent, permission*]; ne pas divulguer [*information*].

within I *prep* **1** (inside) **~ the city walls** dans l'enceinte de la ville; **~ the party** au sein du parti; **it's a play ~ a play** c'est une pièce dans la pièce; **2** (in expressions of time) **I'll do it ~ the hour** je le ferai en moins d'une heure; **15 burglaries ~ a month** 15 cambriolages en (moins d')un mois; **'use ~ 24 hours of purchase'** 'à consommer dans les 24 heures'; **~ minutes he was back** quelques minutes plus tard il était de retour; **they died ~ a week of each other** ils sont morts à une semaine d'intervalle; **3** (not more than) **to be ~ several metres of sth** être à quelques mètres seulement de qch; **it's accurate to ~ a millimetre** c'est exact au millimètre près; ▶**inch**; **4 to be ~ sight** [*coast, town*] être en vue; **to be ~ range of** être à portée de [*enemy guns*]; **to live ~ one's income** vivre selon ses moyens.
II *adv* à l'intérieur; **seen from ~** vu de l'intérieur.

without I *prep* **1** (lacking, not having) sans; **~ a key** sans clé; **~ any money** sans argent; **she left ~ it** elle est partie sans; **they left ~ me** ils sont partis sans moi; **2** (not) sans; **~ looking** sans regarder; **it goes ~ saying** cela va de soi; **~ saying a word** sans dire un mot.
II *adv* à l'extérieur; **from ~** de l'extérieur.

withstand *vtr* résister à.

witness I *n* **1** (gen, Law) (person) témoin *m*; **she was a ~ to the accident** elle a été témoin de l'accident; **~ for the prosecution/the defence** témoin à charge/à décharge; **to call sb as a ~** citer qn comme témoin; **2** (testimony) témoignage *m*; **to be** or **bear ~ to sth** témoigner de qch.
II *vtr* **1** (see) être témoin de, assister à [*incident, attack*]; **we are about to ~ a transformation of the economy** nous sommes sur le point d'assister à une transformation de l'économie; **2** (at official occasion) servir de témoin lors de la signature de [*will, treaty*]; être témoin à [*marriage*].

witness box (GB), **witness stand** (US) *n* barre *f* des témoins.

wits *n pl* (intelligence) intelligence *f*; (presence of mind) présence *f* d'esprit; **to have** or **keep (all) one's ~ about one** (vigilant) rester attentif/-ive; (level-headed) conserver sa présence d'esprit; **to collect** or **gather one's ~** rassembler ses esprits; **to frighten sb out of their ~** faire une peur épouvantable à qn; **to pit one's ~ against sb** se mesurer (intellectuellement) à qn; **to live by one's ~** vivre d'expédients; **a battle of ~** une joute verbale.
IDIOMS **to be at one's ~ end** ne plus savoir quoi faire.

witticism *n* bon mot *m*.

witty *adj* spirituel/-elle.

wizard *n* **1** (magician) magicien *m*; **2** (expert) **to be a ~ at chess/computing** être un as○ aux échecs/en informatique.

wizened *adj* ratatiné.

wobble I *vtr* faire bouger [*table, tooth*].
II *vi* [*table, chair*] branler; [*pile of books, plates*] osciller; [*voice*] trembler; [*jelly*] trembloter; [*person*] (on bicycle) osciller; (on ladder, tightrope) chanceler; **his legs were wobbling under him** ses jambes flageolaient.

wobbly *adj* [*table, chair*] bancal; [*tooth*] branlant; [*chin, voice, jelly*] tremblotant; [*handwriting, line*] tremblant; [*theory, plot*] boiteux/-euse.

woe *n* malheur *m*; **a tale of ~** une histoire pathétique.

woeful *adj* **1** (mournful) [*look, smile*] affligé; [*story, sight*] affligeant; **2** (deplorable) [*lack*] déplorable.

wolf *n* loup *m*; **she-~** louve *f*.
IDIOMS **to cry ~** crier au loup.

wolf-whistle I *n* sifflement *m* (*au passage d'une femme*).
II *vi* siffler (*au passage d'une femme*).

woman I *n* femme *f*; **the working ~** la femme active.
II *noun modifier* **a ~ Prime Minister** une femme premier ministre; **he's always criticizing women drivers** il est toujours en train de critiquer les femmes au volant; **he has lots of women friends** il a beaucoup d'amies; **women voters** électrices *fpl*; **women writers** femmes *fpl* écrivains.

womanizer *n* coureur *m* (de jupons°).

womb *n* (Anat) uterus *m*; **a baby in its mother's ~** un bébé dans le ventre de sa mère.

wonder I *n* **1** (miracle) merveille *f*; **to do** or **work ~s** faire des merveilles (**for** pour; **with** avec); **it's a ~ that** il est extraordinaire que; **(it's) no ~ that he's late** (ce n'est) pas étonnant qu'il soit en retard; **small** or **little ~ that she left** ce n'est guère étonnant qu'elle soit partie; **the ~s of modern medicine** les prodiges de la médecine moderne; **2** (amazement) émerveillement *m*; **in ~** avec émerveillement; **lost in ~** émerveillé.
II *noun modifier* [*cure, drug*] miracle (*after n*).
III *vtr* **1** (ask oneself) se demander; **I ~ how/why/whether** je me demande comment/pourquoi/si; (as polite request) **I ~ if you could help me?** pourriez-vous m'aider?; **it makes you ~** cela donne à penser; **it makes you ~ why/if/how** c'est à se demander pourquoi/si/comment; **2** (be surprised) **I ~ that** cela m'étonne que (+ *subj*).
IV *vi* **1** (think) **to ~ about sth/about doing sth** penser à qch/à faire qch; **2** (be surprised) **to ~ at sth** s'étonner de qch; (admiringly) s'émerveiller de qch.

wonderful *adj* [*book, film, meal, experience, holiday*] merveilleux/-euse; [*musician, teacher*] excellent; **to be ~ with** savoir comment s'y prendre avec [*children, animals*]; **I feel ~** je suis en pleine forme; **you look ~!** (healthy) tu as l'air en pleine forme!; (attractive) tu es superbe!

wonderfully *adv* [*funny, exciting, clever*] très; [*work, cope, drive*] admirablement.

wont *adj* **to be ~ to do** avoir coutume de faire; **as is his/their ~** comme à son/leur habitude.

woo *vtr* courtiser.

wood I *n* **1** (timber) bois *m*; **beech ~** bois de hêtre; **made of solid ~** en bois massif; **2** (forest) bois *m*; **oak ~** bois de chênes.
II **woods** *n pl* bois *mpl*.
III *noun modifier* [*fire, smoke*] de bois; **~ floor** plancher *m*.
IDIOMS **touch ~!** (GB), **knock on ~!** (US) touchons du bois!; **we are not out of the ~ yet** on n'est pas encore sorti de l'auberge.

wooded *adj* boisé; **heavily** or **thickly ~** très boisé.

wooden *adj* **1** [*furniture, object, house*] en bois; [*leg*] de bois; **2** [*expression*] figé.

wooden: **~ horse** *n* cheval *m* de Troie; **~ spoon** *n* cuillère *f* de bois.

woodland I *n* bois *m*.
II *noun modifier* [*animal, plant*] des bois.

wood: **~louse** *n* cloporte *m*; **~pecker** *n* pic *m*; **~ pigeon** *n* pigeon *m* ramier.

woodwind I *n pl* bois *mpl*.
II *noun modifier* [*instrument*] à vent (en bois); [*player*] d'instrument à vent; **the ~ section** les bois.

woodwork *n* **1** (carpentry) menuiserie *f*; **2** (doors, windows) boiseries *fpl*.

woodworm *n* ver *m* du bois; **to have ~** être vermoulu.

woody *adj* [*hill, landscape*] boisé; [*plant, stem*] ligneux/-euse; [*smell*] de bois.

wool I *n* laine *f*; **pure (new) ~** pure laine (vierge).
II *noun modifier* [*carpet, coat, shop*] de laine; [*trade*] lainier/-ière.
IDIOMS **to pull the ~ over sb's eyes** duper qn.

woollen (GB), **woolen** (US) I *n* (garment) lainage *m*.
II *adj* [*garment*] de laine.

woolly (GB), **wooly** (US) I° *n* lainage *m*.
II *adj* **1** [*garment*] de laine; [*animal coat, hair*] laineux/-euse; [*cloud*] cotonneux/-euse; **2** [*thinking*] flou.

word I *n* **1** mot *m*; **those were his very ~s** ce sont ses propres mots; **to have no ~s to express sth** ne pas trouver les mots pour exprimer qch; **long ~s** mots savants; **in your own ~s** avec tes propres mots; **to have the last ~** avoir le dernier mot; **it's the last ~ in chic/comfort** c'est ce qu'il y a de plus chic/confortable; **the last ~ in technology** le dernier cri en technologie; **I couldn't get a ~ in** je n'ai pas pu placer un mot; **not in so many ~s** pas exactement; **in other ~s** en d'autres termes; **the spoken/written ~** la langue parlée/écrite; **to put one's feelings** or **thoughts into ~s** exprimer ce qu'on ressent; **there's no such ~ as 'can't'** 'impossible' n'est pas français; **what's the Greek ~ for 'table'?** comment dit-on 'table' en grec?; **a ~ of warning** un avertissement; **a ~ of advice** un conseil; **I've said my last ~ on the subject** j'ai dit tout ce que j'avais à dire là-dessus; **too sad for ~s** trop triste; **in the ~s of Washington** pour reprendre l'expression de Washington; **I believed every ~ he said** je croyais tout ce qu'il me disait; **I mean every ~ of it** je pense ce que je dis; **a man of few ~s** un homme peu loquace; **not a ~ to anybody** pas un mot à qui que ce soit; **I don't believe a ~ of it** je n'en crois pas un mot; **not to have a good ~ to say about sb** n'avoir rien de bon à dire de qn; **I didn't say a ~!** je n'ai pas ouvert la bouche!; **he won't hear a ~ against her** il ne supporte pas qu'on dise quoi que ce soit contre elle; **the article didn't say a ~ about it** l'article n'en a pas parlé; **2** (information) nouvelles *fpl* (**about** concernant); **there is no ~ of the missing climbers** on est sans nouvelles des alpinistes disparus; **~ got out that...** la nouvelle a transpiré que...; **to bring/send ~ that** annoncer/faire savoir que; **he left ~ at the desk that...** il a laissé un message à la réception disant que...; **3** (promise, affirmation) parole *f*; **he gave me his ~** il m'a donné sa parole; **to break one's ~** ne pas tenir parole; **to hold sb to his/her ~** obliger qn à tenir parole; **a woman of her ~** une femme de parole; **to take sb's ~ for it** croire qn sur parole; **to doubt sb's ~** ne pas croire qn; **take my ~ for it!** crois-moi!; **to go back on one's ~** revenir sur sa promesse; **to be as good as one's ~** tenir parole; **4** (rumour) **~ has it that he's a millionaire** on dit qu'il est millionnaire; **~ got round** or **around that...** le bruit a couru que...; **5** (command) ordre *m*; **to give the ~ to do** donner l'ordre de faire; **if you need anything just say the ~** si tu as besoin de quoi que ce soit, dis-le; **just say the ~ and I'll come** tu n'as qu'un mot à dire et je viendrai; **their ~ is law** ils font la loi.

II **words** *n pl* (of play) texte *m*; (of song) paroles *fpl*.

III **-worded** *combining form* **a carefully-~ed letter** une lettre soigneusement formulée; **a strongly-~ed statement** un communiqué ferme.

IV *vtr* formuler [*reply, letter, statement*].

IDIOMS **my ~!** (in surprise) ma parole!; **right from the ~ go** dès le départ; **to have a ~ with sb about sth** parler à qn à propos de qch; **to have ~s with sb** s'accrocher avec qn; **to put in a good ~ for sb** glisser un mot en faveur de qn.

word-for-word I *adj* [*translation*] mot à mot *inv*.

II **word for word** *adv* [*copy, translate*] mot à mot; [*repeat*] mot pour mot.

wording *n* formulation *f*.

word-of-mouth I *adj* verbal.

II **by word of mouth** *phr* verbalement.

word: **~ order** *n* ordre *m* des mots; **~ processing, WP** *n* traitement *m* de texte; **~ processor** *n* machine *f* à traitement de texte.

wordy *adj* verbeux/-euse.

work I *n* **1** (physical or mental activity) travail *m* (**on** sur); **to put a lot of ~ into** travailler [*essay, speech*]; passer beaucoup de temps sur [*meal, preparations*]; **to put** or **set sb to ~** faire travailler qn; **it was hard ~ doing** ça a été dur de faire; **to be hard at ~** travailler dur; **your essay needs more ~** tu dois travailler davantage ta rédaction; **there's still a lot of ~ to be done** il reste encore beaucoup à faire; **to make short** or **light work of sth** expédier qch; **it's hot/thirsty ~** ça donne chaud/soif; **2** (occupation) travail *m*; **to be in ~** avoir du travail or un emploi; **place of ~** lieu *m* de travail; **to be off ~** (on vacation) être en congé; **to be off ~ with flu** être en arrêt de travail parce qu'on a la grippe; **to be out of ~** être au chômage; **3** (place of employment) **to go to ~** aller au travail; **don't phone me at ~** ne me téléphone pas à mon travail; **4** (building, construction) travaux *mpl* (**on** sur); **5** (essay, report) travail *m*; (artwork, novel, sculpture) œuvre *f* (**by** de); (study) ouvrage *m* (**by** de; **on** sur); (research) recherches *fpl* (**on** sur); **he sells his ~ to tourists** il vend ses créations aux touristes; **is this all your own ~?** est-ce que vous l'avez fait tout seul?; **to mark students' ~** noter les devoirs des étudiants; **his ~ isn't up to standard** son travail n'est pas du niveau requis; **a ~ of reference** un ouvrage de référence; **a ~ of fiction** une œuvre de fiction; **the ~s of Racine** l'œuvre *m* de Racine; **this attack is the ~ of professionals** l'attaque est l'œuvre de professionnels.

II **works** *n pl* **1** (factory) usine *f*; **~s canteen** cantine *f* de l'usine; **2** (building work) travaux *mpl*; **public ~s** travaux publics; **3**° (everything) **the** (**full** or **whole**) **~s** toute la panoplie°.

III *noun modifier* [*clothes, shoes*] de travail; [*phone number*] au travail.

IV *vtr* **1** (drive) **to ~ sb hard** surmener qn; **2** (labour) **to ~ shifts** travailler en équipes (de travail posté); **to ~ days/nights** travailler de jour/de nuit; **to ~ a 40 hour week** faire la semaine de 40 heures; **he ~ed his way through college** il a travaillé pour payer ses études; **3** (operate) se servir de [*computer, machine*]; **4** (exploit commercially) exploiter [*mine, seam*]; **5** (have as one's territory) [*sales rep*] couvrir [*region*]; **6** (consume) **to ~ one's way through** (use) utiliser [*amount, quantity*]; **7** (bring about) **to ~ wonders** or **miracles** faire des merveilles; **8** (use to one's advantage) **to ~ the system** exploiter le système; **how did you manage to ~ it?** comment as-tu pu arranger ça?; **I've ~ed things so that...** j'ai arrangé les choses de sorte que...; **9** (fashion) travailler [*clay, metal*]; **10** (manoeuvre) **to ~ sth into** introduire qch dans [*slot, hole*]; **to ~ a lever up and down** actionner un levier; **11** (exercise) faire travailler [*muscles*]; **12** (move) **to ~ one's way through** se frayer un passage à travers [*crowd*]; **to ~ one's way along** avancer le long de [*ledge, windowsill*]; **to ~ one's hands free** se libérer les mains; **it ~ed its way loose, it ~ed itself loose** cela s'est desserré peu à peu; **to ~ its way into** passer dans; **start at the top and ~ your way down** commencez par le haut et continuez jusqu'en bas.

V *vi* **1** (do a job) travailler (**doing** à faire); **to ~ at home** travailler à domicile; **to ~ for a living** gagner sa vie; **to ~ in advertising** travailler dans la publicité; **to ~ for sb** travailler pour qn; **to ~ in oils** [*painter*] travailler à l'huile; **2** (strive) lutter (**against** contre; **for** pour; **to do** pour faire); **to ~ towards** aller vers [*solution*]; s'acheminer vers [*compromise*]; négocier [*agreement*]; **3** (function) fonctionner; **to ~ on electricity** marcher or fonctionner à l'électricité; **to ~ off the mains** marcher sur secteur; **the washing machine isn't ~ing** la machine à laver est en panne; **4** (act, operate) **it doesn't** or **things don't ~ like that** ça ne marche pas comme ça; **to ~ on the assumption that** présumer que; **to ~ in sb's favour**, **to ~ to sb's advantage** tourner à l'avantage de qn; **to ~ against sb**, **to ~ to sb's disadvantage** jouer en la défaveur de qn; **5** (be successful) [*treatment*] avoir de l'effet; [*detergent, drug*] agir (**against** contre; **on** sur); [*plan*] réussir; [*argument, theory*] tenir debout; **flattery won't ~ with me** la flatterie ne marche pas avec moi; **I didn't think the novel would ~ as a film** je ne pensais pas qu'on pouvait tirer un bon film de ce roman; **6** [*face, features*] se contracter.

VI *v refl* **1 to ~ oneself too hard** se surmener; **to ~ oneself to death** se tuer à la tâche; **2 to ~ oneself into a rage** se mettre dans une colère folle.

IDIOMS **to ~ one's way up** gravir tous les échelons; **to ~ one's way up the company** faire son chemin dans l'entreprise.

■ **work around**: **~ around to [sth]** aborder; **it took him ages to ~ around to what he wanted to say** il lui a fallu un temps fou pour exprimer ce qu'il avait à dire; **to ~ the conversation around to sth** amener la conversation sur qch.

■ **work in**: **~ in [sth]**, **~ [sth] in 1** glisser [*joke, reference*]; mentionner [*fact, name*]; **2** (Culin) incorporer [*ingredient*].

■ **work off**: **~ [sth] off**, **~ off [sth] 1** (remove) retirer [*lid*]; **2** (repay) travailler pour rembourser [*loan, debt*]; **3** (get rid of) se débarrasser de [*excess weight*]; dépenser [*excess energy*]; passer [*anger, frustration*].

■ **work on**: ¶ **~ on** continuer à travailler; ¶ **~ on [sb]** travailler° [*person*]; ¶ **~ on [sth]** travailler à [*book, report*]; travailler sur [*project*]; s'occuper de [*case, problem*]; chercher [*cure, solution*]; examiner [*idea, theory*]; **'have you found a solution?'—'I'm ~ing on it'** 'as-tu trouvé une solution?'—'j'y réfléchis'.

■ **work out**: ¶ **~ out 1** (exercise) s'entraîner; **2** (go according to plan) marcher; **3** (add up) **to ~ out at** (GB) or **to** (US) s'élever à; ¶ **~ out [sth]**, **~ [sth] out 1** (calculate) calculer [*amount*]; **2** (solve) trouver [*answer, reason, culprit*]; résoudre [*problem*]; comprendre [*clue*]; **3** (devise) concevoir [*plan, scheme*]; trouver [*route*]; ¶ **~ [sb] out** comprendre [*person*]; **I can't ~ her out** je n'arrive pas à la comprendre.

■ **work to**: **~ to [sth]** s'astreindre à [*budget*]; **to ~ to deadlines** travailler en respectant des délais; **to ~ to tight deadlines** avoir des délais très serrés.

■ **work up**: ¶ **~ up [sth]** développer [*interest*]; accroître [*support*]; **to ~ up the courage to do** trouver le courage de faire; **to ~ up some enthusiasm for** s'enthousiasmer pour; **to ~ up an appetite** s'ouvrir l'appétit; ¶ **~ up to [sth]** se préparer à [*confrontation, announcement*]; ¶ **~ up [sb]**, **~ [sb] up 1** (excite) exciter [*child, crowd*]; **he ~ed the crowd up into a frenzy** il a mis la foule en délire; **2** (annoy) énerver; **to get ~ed up**, **to ~ oneself up** s'énerver; **to ~ oneself up into a state** or **frenzy** se mettre dans tous ses états.

workable *adj* **1** (feasible) [*idea, plan, suggestion*] réalisable; [*system*] pratique; [*arrangement, compromise*] possible; **2** [*land, mine*] exploitable; [*cement*] maniable.

worker I *n* (in manual job) ouvrier/-ière *m/f*; (in white-collar job) employé/-e *m/f*; **she's a good/slow ~** elle travaille bien/lentement.

II *noun modifier* [*ant, bee*] ouvrier/-ière.

work: **~ experience** *n* stage *m*; **~force** *n* (in industry) main-d'œuvre *f*; (in service sector) effectifs *mpl*.

working I *n* **1** (of machine) fonctionnement *m*; **2** (shaping, preparation) travail *m* (**of** de).

II *adj* **1** [*parent, woman*] qui travaille; [*conditions, environment, methods*] de travail; [*population, life*] actif/-ive; [*breakfast, lunch, day*] de travail; **during ~ hours** (in office) pendant les heures de bureau; (in shop) pendant les heures d'ouverture; **the ~ woman** la femme active; **we have a good ~ relationship** nous avons de bons rapports professionnels; **2** (provisional) [*document*] de travail; [*definition, title*] provisoire; **3** (functional) [*model*] qui fonctionne; [*farm, mine*] en exploitation; **to have a ~ knowledge of** connaître les éléments de base de; **in full ~ order** en parfait état de marche; **4** (Econ) [*expenses, plant, ratio, stock*] d'exploitation.

working: **~ agreement** *n* modus *m* vivendi; **~ capital** *n* fonds *m* de roulement.

working class I *n* classe *f* ouvrière; **the ~es** les classes *fpl* laborieuses.

II **working-class** *adj* [*area, background, family, life*] ouvrier/-ière; [*culture, London*] prolétarien/-ienne; [*person*] de la classe ouvrière.

working: **~ group** *n* groupe *m* de travail; **~ majority** *n* majorité *f* suffisante; **~ party** *n* groupe *m* de travail.

workings *n pl* rouages *mpl*.

working week *n* semaine *f* (de travail).

workload *n* charge *f* de travail; **to have a light/heavy ~** avoir peu/beaucoup de travail.

workman *n* ouvrier *m*.

workmanship *n* **a carpenter famous for sound ~** un menuisier connu pour la qualité de son travail; **furniture of the finest ~** des meubles d'une belle facture; **a piece of poor** or **shoddy ~** du travail mal fait or bâclé.

work: **~ of art** *n* œuvre *f* d'art; **~ permit** *n* permis *m* de travail; **~place** *n* lieu *m* de travail; **~shop** *n* atelier *m*; **~top** *n* plan *m* de travail; **~-to-rule** *n* grève *f* du zèle.

world I *n* monde *m*; **throughout the ~** dans le monde entier; **to go round the ~** faire le tour du monde; **the biggest in the ~** le plus grand du monde; **more than anything in the ~** plus que tout au monde; **this ~ and the next** le monde d'ici-bas et l'au-delà; **to lead the ~ in electronics** être à la pointe de l'électro-

nique; **the ~ of politics** le monde de la politique; **the business ~** le monde des affaires; **to go up in the ~** faire du chemin; **to go down in the ~** déchoir; **for all the ~ to see** devant tout le monde; **the outside ~** le reste du monde; **the Eastern/Western ~** les pays de l'Est/occidentaux; **the Roman ~** la civilisation romaine; **the ancient ~** l'antiquité; **he lives in a ~ of his own** il vit dans un monde à part.
II *noun modifier* [*events, market, leader, politics, rights, scale*] mondial; [*record, tour, championship*] du monde; [*cruise*] autour du monde.
IDIOMS **to be on top of the ~** être aux anges; **to get the best of both ~s** gagner sur les deux tableaux; **a man/woman of the ~** un homme/une femme d'expérience; **out of this ~** extraordinaire; **there's a ~ of difference** il y a une différence énorme; **it did him the** or **a ~ of good** ça lui a fait énormément de bien; **to think the ~ of sb** penser le plus grand bien de qn; **what/where/who in the ~?** que/où/qui etc diable?; **~s apart** diamétralement opposé.

world: **World Bank** *n* Banque *f* mondiale; **~-class** *adj* de niveau mondial; **World Cup** *n* Coupe *f* du Monde; **World Fair** *n* Exposition *f* universelle; **~-famous** *adj* mondialement connu.

world leader *n* **1** (politician) chef *m* d'État; **2** (athlete) meilleur/-e *m/f* du monde; (company) leader *m* mondial.

worldly *adj* **1** (not spiritual) matériel/-ielle; **~ goods** les biens matériels; **~ wisdom** la sagesse des nations; **2** (experienced) [*person*] avisé, qui a de l'expérience; **3** (materialistic) matérialiste.

worldly-wise *adj* avisé, qui a de l'expérience.

world power *n* puissance *f* mondiale.

world war *n* guerre *f* mondiale; **the First/Second World War** la Première/Seconde Guerre mondiale.

world-wide I *adj* mondial.
II *adv* dans le monde entier.

worm *n* ver *m*.

worn *adj* [*carpet, clothing, shoe, tyre*] usé; [*stone*] abimé; [*tread*] lisse.

worn-out *adj* **1** [*carpet, brake*] complètement usé; **2** [*person*] épuisé.

worried *adj* [*person, face*] inquiet/-iète; **to be ~ about sb/sth** se faire du souci or s'inquiéter pour qn/qch; **I'm ~ (that) he might get lost** j'ai peur qu'il ne se perde; **he's ~ that he hasn't heard from them** il s'inquiète de ne pas avoir de leurs nouvelles.

worrier *n* anxieux/-ieuse *m/f*.

worry I *n* **1** (anxiety) soucis *mpl* (**about, over** à propos de); **2** (problem) souci *m* (**about, over** au sujet de); **that's the least of my worries** c'est le dernier de mes soucis; **he's a ~ to his parents** il cause des soucis à ses parents.
II *vtr* **1** (concern) inquiéter; **I ~ that he won't come** j'ai peur qu'il ne vienne pas; **it worried him that he couldn't find the keys** ça l'a inquiété de ne pas trouver les clés; **2** (bother) ennuyer; **would it ~ you if I opened the window?** est-ce que ça vous ennuierait que j'ouvre la fenêtre?; **3** [*dog*] harceler [*sheep*].
III *vi* (be anxious) s'inquiéter; **to ~ about** or **over sth/sb** s'inquiéter or se faire du souci pour qch/qn; **don't ~!** ne t'inquiète pas!; **there's nothing to ~ about** il n'y a pas lieu de s'inquiéter; **he said it's nothing to ~ about** il a dit qu'il n'y avait là rien d'inquiétant.
IV *v refl* **to ~ oneself** s'inquiéter, se faire de souci (**about sb** au sujet de qn; **about sth** à propos de qch); **to ~ oneself sick over sth** se ronger les sangs○ au sujet de qch.
■ **worry at**: **~ at [sth]** [*dog*] mordiller, jouer avec [*toy*]; [*person*] retourner [qch] dans tous les sens [*problem*].

worry beads *n pl* chapelet *m* antistress.

worrying I *n* **all this ~ is making you ill** tout ce souci que tu te fais te rend malade; **stop your ~!** arrête de te faire du souci!
II *adj* inquiétant; **the ~ thing is that** ce qu'il y a d'inquiétant c'est que.

worse I *adj* pire (**than** que); **there's nothing ~ than** il n'y a rien de pire que; **there are ~ things in life than doing** il y a pire dans la vie que de faire; **the noise is ~** il y a plus de bruit; **to go from bad to ~** aller de mal en pis; **to get ~** [*pressure, noise*] augmenter; [*conditions, weather*] empirer; [*illness, conflict*] s'aggraver; **he's getting ~** (in health) il va plus mal; **the cough is getting ~** la toux empire; **to feel ~** (more ill) se sentir plus malade; (more unhappy) aller moins bien; **and what is ~** et le pire, c'est que; **to be made ~** être aggravé (**by** par); **you'll only make it ~!** tu ne feras qu'empirer les choses!; **and to make matters ~, he lied** et pour ne rien arranger, il a menti; **he is none the ~ for the experience** il ne se porte pas plus mal après cette expérience; **he couldn't have chosen a ~ place to meet** il n'aurait pas pu choisir un lieu de rendez-vous moins approprié; **the decision couldn't have come at a ~ time** la décision n'aurait pas pu arriver à un moment plus inopportun.
II *n* **there is ~ to come** ce n'est pas encore le pire; **to change for the ~** empirer.
III *adv* [*play, sing*] moins bien (**than** que); **to behave ~** se conduire plus mal; **she could do ~ than follow his example** ce ne serait pas si mal si elle suivait son exemple.

worsen I *vtr* aggraver [*situation, problem*].
II *vi* [*condition, health, weather, situation*] se détériorer; [*problem, crisis, shortage, flooding*] s'aggraver.

worsening I *n* aggravation *f* (**of** de).
II *adj* [*situation*] en voie de détérioration; [*problem, shortage*] en voie d'aggravation.

worse off *adj* **1** (less wealthy) **to be ~** avoir moins d'argent (**than** que); **to end up ~** finir avec moins d'argent; **I'm £10 a week ~** j'ai dix livres de moins par semaine; **2** (in a worse situation) **to be ~** être dans une situation pire; **to be no ~ without sth** pouvoir parfaitement se passer de qch.

worship I *n* **1** (religious devotion) culte *m*; **sun/ancestor ~** culte du soleil/des ancêtres; **freedom of ~** liberté *f* de culte; **place of ~** lieu *m* de culte; **an act of ~** un acte de dévotion; **2** (veneration) vénération *f*.
II **Worship** ▶642 *pr n* (GB) **Your Worship** (to judge) Monsieur le juge; (to mayor) Monsieur le maire; **his Worship the mayor** Monsieur le maire.
III *vtr* **1** (venerate) vénérer [*God, Buddha*]; (give praise) rendre hommage à; **2** adorer, avoir un culte pour [*person*]; avoir le culte de [*money, success*].
IV *vi* pratiquer sa religion.

worshipper *n* fidèle *mf*.

worst I *n* **1** (most difficult, unpleasant) **the ~** le/la pire *m/f*; **the storm was one of the ~ in recent years** la tempête était parmi les pires qu'il y ait eu ces dernières années; **they're the ~ of all** (people) c'est eux les pires; (things, problems, ideas) c'est ce qu'il y a de pire; **we're over the ~ now** nous avons passé le pire; **the ~ was yet to come** le plus dur était encore à venir; **the ~ of it is, there's no solution** le pire c'est qu'il n'y a pas de solution; **during the ~ of the recession** au plus fort de la crise; **to be at its ~** [*relationship, tendency*] aller au plus mal; **when the heat is at its ~** au plus fort de la chaleur; **these are fanatics at their ~** ce sont des fanatiques dans ce qu'ils ont de pire; **to think the ~ of sb** avoir une mauvaise opinion de qn; **if the ~ came to the ~** (in serious circumstances) dans le pire des cas; (involving fatality) si le pire devait arriver; **2** (most negative trait) **to bring out the ~ in sb** mettre à jour ce qu'il y a de plus mauvais chez qn; **3** (of the lowest standard, quality) **the ~** le plus mauvais/la plus mauvaise *m/f*; **he's one of the ~** c'est un des plus mauvais; **to be the ~ at French** être le plus mauvais en français.
II *adj* **1** (most unsatisfactory, unpleasant) pire, plus mauvais; **the ~ book I've ever read** le plus mauvais livre que j'aie jamais lu; **hypocrites of the ~ kind** des hypocrites de la pire espèce; **the ~ thing about the film is** ce qu'il y a de pire dans le film c'est; **she rang at the ~ possible time** elle a téléphoné au plus mauvais moment; **it's the ~ thing you could have said!** c'était vraiment la chose à ne pas dire!; **2** (most serious) plus grave; **one of the ~ recessions** une des crises les plus graves.
III *adv* **the children suffer (the) ~** ce sont les enfants qui souffrent le plus; **they were (the) ~ hit by the strike** ce sont eux qui ont été les plus touchés par la grève; **the ~-off groups in society** les groupes les plus démunis de la société; **~ of all,...** le pire de tout, c'est que...

worth I *n* **1** (quantity) **five pounds' ~ of sth** pour cinq livres de qch; **thousands of pounds' ~ of damage** des milliers de livres de dégâts; **a week's ~ of supplies** une semaine de provisions; **to get one's money's ~** en avoir pour son argent; **2** (value) valeur *f*; **of great ~** de grande valeur; **of no ~** sans valeur.
II *adj* **1** (of financial value) **to be ~ sth** valoir qch; **how much is it ~?** combien cela vaut-il?; **the pound is ~ 10 francs** la livre vaut 10 francs; **it's not ~ much** ça ne vaut pas grand-chose; **he is ~ £50,000** sa fortune s'élève à 50 000 livres; **2** (of abstract value) **to be ~ sth** valoir qch; **an experienced worker is ~ three novices** un travailleur expérimenté vaut trois débutants; **to be ~ a mention** mériter une mention; **to be ~ a try** valoir la peine d'essayer; **to be ~ it** (en) valoir la peine; **the book isn't ~ reading** le livre ne vaut pas la peine d'être lu; **that suggestion is ~ considering** la suggestion mérite réflexion; **that's ~ knowing** cela est bon à savoir; **everyone ~ knowing had left town** tous ceux qui comptaient avaient quitté la ville; **those little pleasures that make life ~ living** ces petits plaisirs qui rendent la vie agréable.
IDIOMS **for all one is ~** de toutes ses forces; **for what it's ~** pour ce que cela vaut; **to be ~ sb's while** valoir le coup.

worthless *adj* sans valeur; **he's ~** c'est un bon à rien.

worthwhile *adj* [*discussion, undertaking, visit*] qui en vaut la peine; [*career, project*] intéressant; **to be ~ doing** valoir la peine de faire; **it's been well ~** cela en valait vraiment la peine.

worthy *adj* **1** (deserving) **to be ~ of sth** mériter qch, être digne de qch; **the idea's not ~ of your consideration** l'idée ne mérite pas réflexion; **~ of note** digne d'intérêt; **to be ~ of doing** [*person*] être digne de faire; **2** (admirable) [*cause*] noble; [*citizen, friend*] digne; **3** (appropriate) **~ of sth/sb** digne de qch/qn; **a speech ~ of the occasion** un discours digne des circonstances.

would *modal aux* **1** (expressing the conditional) **it ~ be nice if everyone were there, wouldn't it?** ce serait bien si tout le monde était là, n'est-ce pas?; **if he had more money, he'd buy a car** s'il avait plus d'argent il achèterait une voiture; **we ~ have missed the train if we had left later** si nous étions partis plus tard, nous aurions raté le train; **we wouldn't have succeeded without him** nous n'aurions pas réussi sans lui; **2** (in indirect statements or questions) **we thought he'd forget** nous pensions qu'il oublierait; **did she say she ~ be coming?** est-ce qu'elle a dit qu'elle viendrait?; **I was sure you'd like it!** j'étais sûr que ça te plairait!; **I wish he ~ be quiet!** il ne pourrait pas se taire!; **3** (expressing willingness to act) **she wouldn't listen to me** elle ne voulait pas m'écouter; **he wouldn't do a thing to help us** il n'a rien voulu faire pour nous aider; **they asked me to leave but I wouldn't** ils m'ont demandé de partir mais j'ai refusé; **of course you ~ contradict him!** bien sûr il a fallu que tu le contredises!; **4** (in requests) **~ you give her the message?** est-ce que vous voulez bien lui transmettre le message?; **switch off the radio, ~ you?** éteins la radio, tu veux bien?; **~ you excuse me for a moment?** excusez-moi un instant; **5** (expressing one's wishes) **~ you like something to eat?** désirez-vous or voulez-vous manger quelque chose?; **I ~ like a**

beer je voudrais une bière; **we ~ like to stay another night** nous aimerions rester une nuit de plus; **she'd have liked to stay here** elle aurait aimé rester ici; **I wouldn't mind another slice of cake** je prendrais bien un autre morceau de gâteau; **6** (offering advice) **if I were you, I wouldn't say anything** à ta place, je ne dirais rien; **it ~ be better to write** il vaudrait mieux écrire; **it ~ be a good idea to wait** ce serait une bonne idée d'attendre; **you ~ do well to check the timetable** tu ferais bien de vérifier l'horaire; **7** (in assumptions) **I ~ have been 12** je devais avoir 12 ans; **it ~ have been about midday** il devait être à peu près midi; **8** (used to) **she ~ talk for hours** elle parlait pendant des heures.

would-be *adj* **1** (desirous of being) **~ emigrants/investors** personnes or ceux qui désirent émigrer/investir; **2** (so-called) **~ intellectuals** les soi-disant intellectuels; **3** (having intended to be) **the ~ thieves were arrested** les voleurs ont été arrêtés avant qu'ils aient pu passer à l'acte.

wound I **1** (injury) blessure *f*; (cut) plaie *f*; **bullet ~** blessure par balle; **knife ~** coup *m* de couteau; **a ~ to** or **in the head** une blessure à la tête; **2** (figurative) blessure *f*.
II *vtr* blesser.
IDIOMS **to lick one's ~s** panser ses blessures; **to rub salt into the ~** remuer le couteau dans la plaie.

wounded I *n* **the ~** les blessés/-es *m/f*.
II *adj* blessé; **~ in the arm** blessé au bras.

wounding *adj* [*sarcasm, comment*] blessant.

wpm *n pl* (*written abbr* = **words per minute**) mots/min.

wrangle I *n* querelle *f*.
II *vi* se quereller (**over, about** sur, à propos de; **with** avec).

wrangling *n* disputes *fpl* (**over** à propos de).

wrap I *n* (shawl) châle *m*; (stole) étole *f*.
II *vtr* (in paper) emballer (**in** dans); (in blanket, garment) envelopper (**in** dans); **to ~ a book in paper** envelopper un livre dans du papier; **I ~ped a handkerchief around my finger** je me suis noué un mouchoir autour du doigt; **to be ~ped in** être emmitouflé dans [*blanket*]; être enveloppé dans [*newspaper*]; être enveloppé de [*mystery*]; **would you like it ~ped?** je vous fais un paquet?
IDIOMS **to keep sth/to be under ~s** garder qch/être secret.
■ **wrap up**: ¶ **~ up** se couvrir; **~ up well** or **warm!** couvre-toi bien!; ¶ **~ up [sth], ~ [sth] up 1** faire [*parcel*]; envelopper [*gift, purchase*]; emballer [*rubbish*]; **2 to be ~ped up in** ne s'occuper que de [*person, child*]; être absorbé dans [*activity, work*]; **they are completely ~ped up in each other** ils ne vivent que l'un pour l'autre; **3** dissimuler [*meaning, facts, ideas*] (**in** derrière).

wrap: **~-around** *adj* [*window, windscreen*] panoramique; [*skirt*] portefeuille; **~-over** *adj* [*skirt*] portefeuille; [*dress*] croisé.

wrapper *n* (of sweet) papier *m*.

wrapping *n* emballage *m*.

wrapping paper *n* (brown) papier *m* d'emballage; (decorative) papier *m* cadeau.

wreak *vtr* assouvir [*revenge*] (**on** sur); **to ~ havoc** or **damage** infliger des dégâts; **to ~ havoc** or **damage on sth** dévaster qch.

wreath *n* couronne *f*; **to lay a ~** déposer une gerbe.

wreck I *n* **1** (car, plane) (crashed) épave *f*; (burnt out) carcasse *f*; **2** (sunken ship) épave *f*; **3** (sinking) (of ship) naufrage *m*; **4** (person) épave *f*.
II *vtr* **1** [*explosion, fire, vandals*] dévaster [*building, machinery*]; [*person, driver, impact*] détruire [*vehicle*]; **2** ruiner [*career, chances, health, life, marriage*]; gâcher [*holiday, weekend*].

wreckage *n* **1** (of plane, car, ship) épave *f*; (of building) décombres *mpl*; **2** (of hopes, plans) naufrage *m*.

wrecked *adj* **1** [*car, plane*] accidenté; [*ship*] naufragé; [*building*] démoli; **2** [*life, career, marriage*] ruiné.

wren *n* roitelet *m*.

wrench I *n* **1** (tool) tourne-à-gauche *m inv*; **2** (emotional upheaval) déchirement *m*.
II *vtr* tirer violemment sur [*handle*]; **to ~ one's ankle/knee** se tordre la cheville/le genou; **to ~ sth from sb** arracher qch à qn; **to ~ sth away from sth** arracher qch de qch.

wrestle I *vtr* **to ~ sb for sth** lutter contre qn pour qch; **to ~ sb to the ground** terrasser qn.
II *vi* **1** (Sport) faire du catch; **2** (struggle) **to ~ with** se débattre avec [*person, problem, homework, conscience*]; se battre avec [*controls, zip, suitcase*]; lutter contre [*temptation*].

wrestler *n* catcheur/-euse *m/f*.

wrestling ▶ 649 I *n* catch *m*.
II *noun modifier* [*match, champion, hold*] de catch.

wretched *adj* [*person*] infortuné; [*existence, appearance, conditions*] misérable; [*weather*] affreux/-euse; [*accommodation*] minable; [*amount*] dérisoire.

wriggle I *vtr* **to ~ one's toes/fingers** remuer les orteils/doigts; **to ~ one's way out of sth** se sortir de qch.
II *vi* [*person*] s'agiter, gigoter; [*snake, worm*] se tortiller; [*fish*] frétiller; **to ~ along the ground** ramper en se tortillant; **to ~ under sth** se glisser sous qch; **to ~ free** arriver à se dégager; **to ~ out of** se défiler devant [*duty, task*].

wring *vtr* **1** (also **~ out**) essorer [*clothes, cloth*]; **2** (extract) arracher [*confession, money*] (**from, out of** à); **3** (twist) **to ~ sb's/sth's neck** tordre le cou à qn/qch; **to ~ one's hands** se tordre les mains; (figurative) se lamenter.

wrinkle I *n* (on skin) ride *f*; (in fabric) pli *m*.
II *vtr* **1** rider [*skin*]; **to ~ one's nose** faire la grimace (**at** devant); **2** froisser [*fabric*].
III *vi* [*skin*] se rider; [*fabric*] se froisser; [*wallpaper*] gondoler.

wrinkled *adj* **1** [*person, face, skin*] ridé; [*brow*] froncé; **2** [*fabric, clothing*] froissé; [*stockings*] qui font des plis.

wrist ▶523 *n* poignet *m*.

wristwatch *n* montre-bracelet *f*.

writ *n* assignation *f* (**for** pour); **to issue** or **serve a ~ against sb, to serve sb with a ~** assigner qn en justice.

write I *vtr* **1** écrire [*letter, poem, novel*] (**to** à); composer [*song, symphony*]; rédiger [*business letter, article, report, prescription*]; faire [*cheque*]; écrire [*software, program*]; élaborer [*legislation*]; **he wrote me a cheque for £100** il m'a fait un chèque de 100 livres sterling; **I wrote home** j'ai écrit à ma famille; **2** (US) écrire à [*person*].
II *vi* écrire (**to sb** à qn); **to ~ in pencil** écrire au crayon; **to ~ neatly** écrire bien; **I have nothing to ~ with** je n'ai rien pour écrire; **I ~ for a living** je suis écrivain de métier.
■ **write back** répondre (**to** à).
■ **write down**: **~ [sth] down, ~ down [sth]** noter [*details, name*]; mettre [qch] par écrit [*ideas, suggestions*]; consigner [qch] par écrit [*information, findings*].
■ **write off**: ¶ **~ off** écrire une lettre (**to** à); **to ~ off for** écrire pour demander; ¶ **~ [sth/sb] off** **1** (wreck) bousiller complètement○ [*car*]; **2** (in bookkeeping) passer [qch] aux pertes et profits [*bad debt, loss*]; amortir [*capital*]; **3** (end) annuler [*debt, project, operation*].
■ **write out**: **~ [sth] out, ~ out [sth]** **1** (put down on paper) écrire; **2** (copy) copier.

write-off *n* **1** (US) (in taxation) somme *f* déductible de la déclaration des revenus; **2** (wreck) épave *f*.

writer ▶805 *n* (author) (professional) écrivain *m*; (nonprofessional) auteur *m*; **sports/travel ~** journaliste *mf* spécialisé/-e en sport/voyages; **he's a neat/messy ~** il écrit avec/sans soin.

writer's block *n* l'angoisse *f* de la page blanche.

write-up *n* **1** (review) critique *f*; **2** (account) rapport *m* (**of** sur).

writhe *vi* (also **~ about, ~ around**) se tortiller; **to ~ in agony** se tordre de douleur.

writing *n* **1** (activity) **~ is her life** écrire, c'est sa vie; **2** (handwriting) écriture *f*; **his ~ is poor/good** il écrit mal/bien; **3** (words and letters) écriture *f*; **to put sth in ~** mettre qch par écrit; **4** (literature) littérature *f*; **modern/American ~** littérature moderne/américaine; **the ~s of Colette** l'œuvre *m* de Colette; **it was an excellent piece of ~** c'était très bien écrit.

writing: **~ pad** *n* bloc *m* de papier à lettres; **~ paper** *n* papier *m* à lettres; **~ table** *n* bureau *m*.

written *adj* [*reply, guarantee, proof*] écrit; **he failed the ~ paper** il a échoué à l'écrit; **~ evidence** or **proof** (Law) preuves *fpl* écrites; **the ~ word** l'écriture.

wrong I *n* **1** (evil) mal *m*; **no sense of right or ~** aucun sens du bien ou du mal; **2** (injustice) tort *m*; **to right a ~** réparer un tort; **the rights and ~s of the matter** les aspects moraux de la question.
II *adj* **1** (incorrect) faux/fausse; (ill-chosen) mauvais; **he took the ~ key** il a pris la mauvaise clé; **it's the ~ wood/glue for the purpose** ce n'est pas le bois/la colle qu'il faut; **she was the ~ woman for you** ce n'était pas la femme qu'il te fallait; **to go the ~ way** se tromper de chemin; **to take the ~ road** se tromper de route; **to take the ~ turning** (GB) or **turn** (US) ne pas tourner au bon endroit; **to give the ~ answer** ne pas donner la bonne réponse; **everything I do is ~** je ne fais jamais rien de bien; **it was the ~ thing to say** c'était la chose à ne pas dire; **to say the ~ thing** faire une gaffe; **don't get the ~ idea** ne te méprends pas; **I dialled the ~ number** je me suis trompé de numéro, j'ai fait un faux or mauvais numéro; **you've got the ~ number** vous faites erreur; **2** (reprehensible, unjust) **it is ~ to cheat** c'est mal de tricher; **she hasn't done anything ~** elle n'a rien fait de mal; **it was ~ of me to do** je n'aurais pas dû faire; **it is ~ that** c'est injuste que; **there's nothing ~ with** or **in sth** il n'y a pas de mal à qch; **what's ~ with trying?** quel mal y a-t-il à essayer?; (**so**) **what's ~ with that?** où est le mal?; **3** (mistaken) **to be ~** [*person*] avoir tort, se tromper; **that's where you're ~** c'est là que tu te trompes; **I might be ~** il se peut que je me trompe; **to be ~ about** se tromper sur; **she was ~ about him** elle s'est trompée sur son compte; **am I ~ in thinking that...?** ai-je tort de penser que...?; **to prove sb ~** donner tort à qn; **4** (not as it should be) **there is something (badly) ~** il y a quelque chose qui ne va pas (du tout); **there's something ~ with this computer** il y a un problème avec cet ordinateur; **the wording is all ~** la formulation ne va pas du tout; **what's ~ with your arm?** qu'est-ce que tu as au bras?; **what's ~ with you?** (to person suffering) qu'est-ce que tu as?; (to person behaving oddly) qu'est-ce qui t'arrive?; **your clock is ~** votre pendule n'est pas à l'heure.
III *adv* **to get [sth] ~** se tromper de [*date, time, details*]; se tromper dans qch [*calculations*]; **I think you've got it ~** je pense que tu te trompes; **to go ~** [*person*] se tromper; [*machine*] ne plus marcher; [*plan*] ne pas marcher; **what's gone ~ between them?** qu'est-ce qui n'a pas marché entre eux?; **you can't go ~** (get lost) tu ne peux pas te tromper; (fail) tu peux être tranquille.
IV *vtr* (treat unjustly) faire du tort à [*person, family*].
IDIOMS **to be in the ~** être dans mon/ton etc tort; **to get on the ~ side of sb** se faire mal voir de qn; **to go down the ~ way** [*food, drink*] passer de travers; **to jump to the ~ conclusions** tirer des conclusions hâtives.

wrong: **~doer** *n* malfaiteur *m*; **~doing** *n* méfait *m*; **~foot** *vtr* (Sport) prendre [qn] à contre-pied; (figurative) prendre [qn] au dépourvu.

wrongly *adv* mal; **he concluded, ~, that...** il a conclu, à tort, que...; **rightly or ~** à tort ou à raison.

wrought *adj* [*silver, gold*] travaillé.

wrought iron *n* fer *m* forgé.

wry *adj* [*smile, look, humour*] narquois; **to have a ~ sense of humour** être pince-sans-rire; **to make a ~ face** faire une drôle de tête.

x, **X** *n* **1** (letter) x, X *m*; **2** (standing for number) **for x people** pour x personnes; **3 Ms X** Mme X; **X marks the spot** l'endroit est marqué d'une croix; **4** (kisses ending letter) grosses bises.

X-certificate *adj* [*film*] interdit aux moins de 18 ans.

xerox® *vtr* photocopier.

X-rated *adj* [*film, video*] interdit aux moins de 18 ans.

X-ray **I** *n* **1** (ray) rayon *m* X; **2** (photo) radiographie *f*, radio○ *f*; **to have an ~** se faire radiographier; **to give sb an ~** faire une radiographie à qn.
II *vtr* radiographier.

y, **Y** *n* y, Y *m*.

yacht I *n* yacht *m*.
II *noun modifier* [*crew*] de yacht; [*race*] de yachts; **~ club** yacht-club *m*.

yachting ▶649| I *n* yachting *m*.
II *noun modifier* [*clothes*] de yachtman; [*holiday*] en yacht.

yak *n* yack *m*.

Yale lock® *n* serrure *f* de sûreté.

yank *vtr* tirer [*person, rope*].
■ **yank out**: **~ [sth] out, ~ out [sth]** arracher.

Yankee *n* yankee *m*.

yap *vi* **1** [*dog*] japper (**at** après); **2** [*person*] piailler.

yapping I *n* jappements *mpl*.
II *adj* [*dog*] jappeur/-euse.

yard *n* **1 ▶738|** yard *m* (= *0.9144 m*); **2 ~s of room!** plus de place qu'il n'en faut!; **3** (of house, farm, prison, hospital) cour *f*; **4** (US) (garden) jardin *m*; **5** (for storage) dépôt *m*; (for construction) chantier *m*; **builder's ~** dépôt *m* de matériaux de construction.

yardstick *n* (figurative) critères *mpl*.

yarn *n* **1** (fibre) fibre *f* textile; (wool) laine *f*; **2** (tale) histoire *f*.

yashmak *n* voile *m* islamique.

yawn I *n* **1 to give a ~** bâiller; **2** (bore) **what a ~○!** que c'est barbant○!
II *vtr* **'see you tomorrow,' he ~ed** 'à demain,' dit-il en bâillant.
III *vi* **1** [*person*] bâiller; **2** [*abyss, chasm*] béer.

yeah○ *particle* ouais○, oui; **oh ~?** vraiment?

year ▶915| I *n* **1** (period of time) an *m*, année *f*; **two ~s ago** il y a deux ans; **all (the) year round** toute l'année; **over the ~s** au cours des ans or des années; **the ~ before last** il y a deux ans; **~ in ~ out** tous les ans; **they have been living in Paris for ~s** ils habitent Paris depuis des années; **they lived in Paris for ~s** ils ont habité Paris pendant des années; **for the first time in ~s** pour la première fois depuis des années; **it's a ~ since I heard from him** je n'ai plus de ses nouvelles depuis un an; **to earn £30,000 a ~** gagner 30000 livres sterling par an; **2** (indicating age) **to be 19 ~s old** or **19 ~s of age** avoir 19 ans; **a two-~-old child** un enfant de deux ans; **3** (pupil) **first/second-~** ≈ élève *mf* de sixième/cinquième.
II years○ *n pl* (a long time) **that would take ~s!** ça prendrait une éternité!; **it's ~s since we last met!** ça fait un siècle qu'on ne s'est pas vus!
IDIOMS **this job has put ~s on me!** ce travail m'a vieilli de 10 ans!

yearly I *adj* [*visit, account, income*] annuel/-elle.
II *adv* annuellement.

yearn *vi* **to ~ for** désirer (avoir) [*child*]; aspirer à [*freedom, unity*]; attendre [*season, event*]; **to ~ to do** avoir très envie de faire.

yearning I *n* désir *m* ardent (**for** de; **to do** de faire).
II yearnings *n pl* aspirations *fpl*.
III *adj* [*expression*] plein de désir.

yeast *n* levure *f*.

yell I *n* (shout) cri *m*; (of rage, pain) hurlement *m*.
II *vtr* crier [*warning*]; (louder) hurler [*insults*].
III *vi* crier; **to ~ at sb** crier après qn.

yelling I *n* cris *mpl*.
II *adj* [*mob, crowd*] vociférant.

yellow ▶559| I *n* jaune *m*.
II *adj* **1** (in colour) jaune; **to go** or **turn ~** jaunir; **2○** (cowardly) trouillard○.
III *vi* jaunir.

yellow-belly○ *n* trouillard/-e○ *m/f*.

yellowish ▶559| *adj* tirant sur le jaune; (unpleasantly) jaunâtre.

yelp I *n* (of animal) (of pain, fear) glapissement *m*.
II *vi* [*animal*] glapir.

yelping *n* (of animal) glapissements *mpl*.

yen *n* **1 ▶748|** yen *m*; **2○** (craving) **to have a ~ for sth/to do** avoir grande envie de qch/de faire.

yeoman *n* (also **~ farmer**) franc tenancier *m*.

yeoman of the guard *n* (GB) membre *m* de la garde royale.

yep○, **yup○** *particle* (US) ouais○, oui.

yes *particle* oui; (in reply to negative question) si.

■ **Note** *yes* is translated by *oui*, except when used in reply to a negative question in which case the translation is *si* or, more emphatically, *mais si*: *'did you see him?'—'yes (I did)'* = 'est-ce que tu l'as vu?'—'oui (je l'ai vu)'; *'you're not hungry, are you?'—'yes I am'* = 'tu n'as pas faim?'—'si (j'ai faim)'.
– Note that there are no direct equivalents in French for tag questions and short replies such as *yes I did, yes I am*.
– For some suggestions on how to translate these, see the note at **do**.

---

yes-man○ *n* lèche-bottes *m inv*.

yesterday ▶584|, 584| I *n* hier *m*; **~'s newspaper** le journal d'hier; **~ was a sad day for all of us** la journée d'hier a été triste pour nous tous; **~ was the fifth of April** hier nous étions le cinq avril; **the day before ~** avant-hier.
II *adv* hier; **only ~** pas plus tard qu'hier; **all day ~** toute la journée d'hier; **a week ago ~** il y a eu une semaine hier; **early/late ~** tôt/tard dans la journée d'hier; **only ~ he was saying to me...** hier encore il me disait...

yesterday: **~ afternoon** *n, adv* hier après-

you

◆ In English ***you*** is used to address everybody, whereas French has two forms: ***tu*** and ***vous***. The usual word to use when you are speaking to anyone you do not know very well is ***vous***. This is sometimes called the polite form:

would ***you*** *like some coffee?*	= voulez-**vous** du café?
can I help ***you****?*	= est-ce que je peux **vous** aider?
what can I do for ***you****?*	= qu'est-ce que je peux faire pour **vous**?

The more informal pronoun ***tu*** is used between close friends and family members, within groups of children and young people, by adults when talking to children and always when talking to animals; ***tu*** is the subject form, the direct and indirect object form is ***te*** (***t'*** before a vowel or mute 'h') and the form for emphatic use or use after a preposition is ***toi***:

would ***you*** *like some coffee?*	= veux-**tu** du café?
can I help ***you****?*	= est-ce que je peux **t'**aider?
there's a letter for ***you***	= il y a une lettre pour **toi**

As a general rule, when talking to a French person use ***vous***, wait to see how they address you and follow suit. It is safer to wait for the French person to suggest using ***tu***. The suggestion will usually be phrased as *on se tutoie?* or *on peut se tutoyer?*

Note that ***tu*** is only a singular pronoun and ***vous*** is its plural form.

Remember that in French the object and indirect object pronouns are always placed before the verb:

she knows ***you***	= elle **vous** connaît
	= elle **te** connaît
I'll give ***you*** *my address*	= je **vous** donnerai mon adresse
	je **te** donnerai mon adresse

◆ In compound tenses like the present perfect and the past perfect, the past participle agrees in number and gender with the direct object:

I saw ***you*** *on Saturday*	
(to one male: polite form)	= je **vous** ai vu samedi
(to one female: polite form)	= je **vous** ai vu**e** samedi
(to one male: informal form)	= je **t'**ai vu samedi
(to one female: informal form)	= je **t'**ai vu**e** samedi
(to two or more people, male or mixed)	= je **vous** ai vu**s** samedi
(to two or more females)	= je **vous** ai vu**es** samedi

When ***you*** is used impersonally as the more informal form of ***one***, it is translated by ***on*** for the subject form and by ***vous*** or ***te*** for the object form, depending on whether the comment is being made amongst friends or in a more formal context:

you *can do as* ***you*** *like here*	= **on** peut faire ce qu'**on** veut ici
you *could easily lose your bag here*	= **on** pourrait facilement perdre son sac ici
these mushrooms can make ***you*** *ill*	= ces champignons peuvent **vous** rendre malade
	= ces champignons peuvent **te** rendre malade

For a guide to the correct verb forms with **vous**, **tu** and **on**, consult the verb in the French-English part of the dictionary and check the number in square brackets, which will refer you to the French verb tables at the back of the dictionary.

For particular usages, see the entry for **you**.

midi; **~ evening** *n, adv* hier soir; **~ morning** *n, adv* hier matin.

yet I *conj* pourtant.
II *adv* **1** (up till now, so far) encore; (in questions) déjà; (with superlatives) jusqu'ici; **it's not ready ~** ce n'est pas encore prêt; **has he arrived ~?** est-il (déjà) arrivé?; **not ~** pas encore, pas pour l'instant; **it's the best ~** jusqu'ici, c'est le meilleur; **2** (also **just ~**) tout de suite, encore; **don't start ~** ne commence pas tout de suite; **3** (still) encore; **they may ~ come** ils pourraient encore arriver; **he'll finish it ~** il va le finir; **he won't come for hours ~** il ne viendra pas avant quelques heures; **4** (even, still) encore; **~ more cars** encore plus de voitures; **~ another attack** encore une autre attaque; **~ again** encore une fois.

yew *n* **1** (also **~ tree**) if *m*; **2** (wood) bois *m* d'if.

YHA *n* (GB) (*abbr* = **Youth Hostels Association**) association *f* des auberges de jeunesse.

yield I *n* rendement *m*.
II *vtr* **1** (produce) produire; **2** (provide) donner, fournir [*result, meaning*]; fournir [*clue*]; **3** (surrender) céder (**to** à); **to ~ ground** (figurative) céder du terrain.
III *vi* **1** (give in) (to person, temptation, pressure, threats) céder (**to** à); **to ~ to persuasion** se laisser persuader; **2** (under weight, physical pressure) céder (**under** sous); **3** (be superseded) **to ~ to** [*technology, phenomenon*] céder le pas à; **4** (US) (driving) céder le passage.

yodel *vi* jodler, iodler.

yoghurt *n* yaourt *m*, yoghourt *m*.

yoke I *n* (harness, burden) joug *m*.
II *vtr* **1** (also **~ up**) atteler; **2** (also **~ together**) (figurative) joindre.

yokel *n* péquenaud/-e○ *m/f*, plouc○ *mf*.

yolk *n* jaune *m* (d'œuf).

yonks○ *n pl* (GB) **I haven't seen him for ~** ça fait une éternité que je ne l'ai pas vu.

you ▶983 *pron* **1** (addressing sb) **YOU would never do that** (polite) vous, vous ne feriez jamais cela; (informal) toi, tu ne ferais jamais ça; **~ English** vous autres Anglais; **~ idiot**○**!** espèce d'imbécile○!; **~ two can stay** vous deux, vous pouvez rester; **2** (as indefinite pronoun) (subject) on; (object, indirect object) vous, te; **~ never know!** on ne sait jamais!; **it makes ~ sleepy** ça fait dormir.

you: **~-know-what**○ *pron* vous-savez-quoi, tu-sais-quoi; **~-know-who**○ *pron* qui-vous-savez, qui-tu-sais.

young I *n* **1** (young people) **the ~** les jeunes *mpl*, la jeunesse *f*; **for ~ and old (alike)** pour les jeunes comme pour les vieux; **2** (animal's offspring) petits *mpl*.
II *adj* (not very old) jeune; **to be ~ at heart** avoir l'esprit jeune; **she is ten years ~er than him** elle a dix ans de moins que lui; **I feel ten years ~er** j'ai l'impression d'avoir rajeuni de dix ans; **in my ~er days** quand j'étais jeune; **you're only ~ once!** on n'est jeune qu'une fois; **the night is ~** la nuit ne fait que commencer; **Mr Brown the ~er** M. Brown le jeune; (Mr Brown's son) M. Brown fils; **~ lady** jeune femme *f*; **~ people** jeunes gens *mpl*; **~ person** jeune *m*; **the ~er generation** la jeune génération; **her ~er brother** son frère cadet; **the two ~er children** les deux cadets; **I'm not as ~ as I used to be** je n'ai plus 20 ans; **we're not getting any ~er** nous ne rajeunissons pas.

youngish *adj* assez jeune.

young-looking *adj* **to be ~** faire (très) jeune.

young: **~ offender** *n* délinquant/-e *m/f*; **~ professional** *n* jeune salarié/-e *m/f*.

youngster *n* **1** (young person) jeune *m*; **2** (child) enfant *mf*.

your ▶985 *det* votre/vos; (more informally) ton/ta/tes.

yours *pron*

Note For a full note on the use of the *vous* and *tu* forms in French, see the boxed note for the entry *you*.
– In French, possessive pronouns reflect the gender and number of the noun they are standing for. When *yours* is referring to only one person, it is translated by *le vôtre, la vôtre, les vôtres* or, more informally, *le tien, la tienne, les tiens, les tiennes*. When *yours* is referring to more than one person, it is translated by *le vôtre, la vôtre, les vôtres*.

my car is red but ~ is blue ma voiture est rouge mais la vôtre or la tienne est bleue; **her children are older than ~** ses enfants sont plus âgés que les vôtres or les tiens; **which house is ~?** votre or ta maison c'est laquelle?; **he's a colleague of ~** c'est un de vos or tes collègues; **it's not ~** ce n'est pas à vous or à toi; **the money wasn't ~ to give away** vous n'aviez pas à donner cet argent.

yourself *pron*

Note For a full note on the use of the *vous* and *tu* forms in French, see the entry *you*.
– When used as a reflexive pronoun, direct and indirect, *yourself* is translated by *vous* or familiarly *te* (or *t'* before a vowel or mute 'h'): *you've hurt yourself* = vous vous êtes fait mal *or* tu t'es fait mal.
– In imperatives, the translation is *vous* or *toi*: *help yourself* = servez-vous *or* sers-toi. (Note the hyphens).
– When used for emphasis, the translation is *vous-même* or *toi-même*: *you yourself don't know* = vous ne savez pas vous-même *or* tu ne sais pas toi-même.
– After a preposition, the translation is *vous* or *vous-même* or *toi* or *toi-même*: *you can be proud of yourself* = vous pouvez être fier de vous *or* vous-même, tu peux être fier de toi *or* toi-même.

1 (reflexive) vous, te, t'; **have you hurt ~?** est-ce que tu t'es fait mal?; **2** (in imperatives) vous, toi; **3** (emphatic) vous-même, toi-même; **you ~ said that...** vous avez dit vous-même que..., tu as dit toi-même que...; **4** (after prepositions) vous, vous-même, toi, toi-même; **5** (expressions) **(all) by ~** tout seul/toute seule; **you're not ~**

your

❑ For a full note on the use of the *vous* and *tu* forms in French, see the note on *you* ▶ 983.

◆ In French, determiners agree in gender and number with the noun that follows:

your + masculine singular noun (chien *m*, ami *m)*

(to one person: polite form) (to two or more people)	**votre** chien, **votre** ami
(to one person: informal form)	**ton** chien, **ton** ami

your + feminine singular noun (pomme *f*, orange *f)*

(to one person: polite form) (to two or more people)	**votre** pomme, **votre** orange
(to one person: informal form)	**ta** pomme, **ton*** orange

* Note that *ton* is used with a feminine noun beginning with a vowel or mute 'h'.

your + plural noun

(to one person: polite form) (to two or more people)	**vos** chiens, **vos** amis, **vos** pommes, **vos** oranges
(to one person: informal form)	**tes** chiens, **tes** amis, **tes** pommes, **tes** oranges

When ***your*** is stressed, ***à vous*** or ***à toi*** is added after the noun:

(to one person: polite form) **your** house (to two or more people)	= **votre** maison **à vous**
(to one person: informal form) **your** house	= **ta** maison **à toi**
(to one person: polite form) **your** parents (to two or more people)	= **vos** parents à **vous**
(to one person: informal form) **your** parents	= **tes** parents à **toi**

◆ When used impersonally to mean ***one's***, ***your*** is translated by ***son***, ***sa*** or ***ses***, when ***you*** is translated by ***on***:

*you pay **your** bills at the end of the week*	= on paie **ses** factures à la fin de la semaine
*you buy **your** tickets at the door*	= on prend **ses** billets à l'entrée
*you get good value for **your** money*	= on en a pour **son** argent

The translation after an impersonal verb in French is ***son***, ***sa***, ***ses***:

*you have to buy **your** tickets at the door*	= il faut prendre **ses** billets à l'entrée
*you should always look after **your** health*	= il faut prendre soin de **sa** santé

Note, however, the following:

*smoking is bad for **your** health*	= le tabac est mauvais pour **la** santé
*sweets are bad for **your** teeth*	= les bonbons sont mauvais pour **les** dents
***your** average student*	= **l'**étudiant moyen

❑ For ***your*** used with *parts of the body*, see the usage note on **The Human Body** ▶ 523.

today tu n'as pas l'air dans ton assiette aujourd'hui.

yourselves *pron*

■ **Note** When used as a reflexive pronoun, direct and indirect, *yourselves* is translated by *vous*: *help yourselves* = servez-vous.
– When used for emphasis, the translation is *vous-mêmes*: *do it yourselves* = faites-le vous-mêmes.
– After a preposition, the translation is *vous* or *vous-mêmes*: *did you buy it for yourselves?* = est-ce que vous l'avez acheté pour vous *or* pour vous-mêmes?

1 (reflexive) vous; **2** (emphatic) vous-mêmes; **3** (after prepositions) vous, vous-mêmes; **all by ~** tous seuls/toutes seules.

youth **I** *n* **1** (young man) jeune homme *m*; **a gang of ~s** une bande de jeunes gens; **2** (period, state of being young) jeunesse *f*; **because of his ~** à cause de son jeune âge; **3** (young people) jeunes *mpl*.
II *noun modifier* [*club*] de jeunes; **~ culture** culture *f* des jeunes.

youthful *adj* **1** (young) jeune; **2** (typical of youth) **his ~ looks** son air jeune; **she's a very ~ 65** elle fait très jeune pour ses 65 ans.

youth: **~ hostel** *n* auberge *f* de jeunesse; **~ hostelling** *n* loger en auberge de jeunesse; **~ work** *n* travail *m* social auprès des jeunes; **~ worker** ▶ 805 *n* éducateur/-trice *m/f*.

Yule log *n* bûche *f* de Noël.

yuppie *n* jeune cadre *m* dynamique, yuppie *m* (derogatory).

Zz

z, Z *n* z, Z *m*.
zany *adj* loufoque°.
zap° **I** *excl* paf!
II *vtr* **1** (destroy) détruire [*town*]; tuer [*person, animal*]; **2** (fire at) tirer sur [*person*]; **3** (delete from computer screen) supprimer.
III *vi* **to ~ into town/a shop** faire un saut° en ville/dans un magasin; **to ~ from channel to channel** zapper°.
zapper° *n* (TV remote control) télécommande *f*.
zeal *n* **1** (fanaticism) zèle *m*; (religious) ferveur *f*; **2** (enthusiasm) ardeur *f*, zèle *m*.
zealot *n* fanatique *mf*.
zebra *n* zèbre *m*.
zebra crossing *n* (GB) passage *m* (protégé) pour piétons.
zenith *n* (figurative) apogée *m*.
zero I *n* zéro *m*.
II *noun modifier* [*altitude, growth, inflation, voltage*] zéro *inv*; [*confidence, interest, involvement, development*] nul/nulle; **sub-~ temperatures** des températures en dessous de zéro.
■ **zero in**: **to ~ in on [sth]** (figurative) (pinpoint) cerner [*key issue*].
zero: **~ hour** *n* heure *f* H; **~-rated** *adj* (GB) exempté de TVA.
zest *n* (enthusiasm) entrain *m*; **his ~ for life** sa joie de vivre.
zigzag I *n* zigzag *m*.
II *noun modifier* [*design, pattern*] à zigzags; [*route, road*] en zigzag.
III *vi* [*person, vehicle, road*] zigzaguer; [*river, path*] serpenter; **to ~ up/down** monter/descendre en zigzag.
zilch° *n* que dalle●.
zing° *n* (energy) entrain *m*.
zip I *n* **1** (also **~ fastener, zipper** (US)) fermeture *f* à glissière, fermeture *f* éclair®; **to do up/undo a ~** tirer/défaire une fermeture à glissière; **2**° (energy) tonus *m*; **3** (US) (also **~ code**) code *m* postal.
II *vtr* **to ~ sth open/shut** ouvrir/fermer qch en tirant la fermeture à glissière.
III° *vi* **to ~ along, to ~ past** filer à toute allure; **to ~ past sb/sth** dépasser qn/qch à toute allure.
■ **zip through**°: **to ~ through a book** lire un livre en diagonale°.
■ **zip up**: ¶ **~ up** [*garment, bag*] se fermer par une fermeture à glissière; ¶ **~ [sb/sth] up, ~ up [sb/sth]** remonter la fermeture à glissière de qn/qch.
zipper *n* (US) = **zip I 1**.
zodiac *n* zodiaque *m*.
zombie *n* (figurative) abruti/-e° *m/f*.
zone I *n* zone *f*.
II *vtr* (divide) diviser [qch] en zones.
zonked° *adj* (also **zonked out**) (tired) crevé°.
zoo *n* zoo *m*.
zoo keeper ▶**805** *n* gardien/-ienne *m/f* de zoo.
zoologist ▶**805** *n* zoologue *mf*, zoologiste *mf*.
zoology *n* zoologie *f*.
zoom I *n* (also **~ lens**) zoom *m*.
II *vi* **1**° (move quickly) **to ~ past** passer en trombe; **to ~ around** passer à toute vitesse dans; **he's ~ed off to Paris** il a foncé° à Paris; **I'll just ~ out to the shop** je vais faire un saut° au magasin; **2**° (rocket) [*prices, profits*] monter en flèche.
zucchini *n* (US) courgette *f*.

French verbs

Standard verb endings

	-er	-ir	-r, -re
INDICATIVE Present			
Singular 1	-e	-is	-s *or* -e
2	-es	-is	-s *or* -es
3	-e	-it	-t *or* -e
Plural 1	-ons	-(iss)ons	-ons
2	-ez	-(iss)ez	-ez
3	-ent	-(iss)ent	-ent
INDICATIVE Imperfect			
Singular 1	-ais	-(iss)ais	-ais
2	-ais	-(iss)ais	-ais
3	-ait	-(iss)ait	-ait
Plural 1	-ions	-(iss)ions	-ions
2	-iez	-(iss)iez	-iez
3	-aient	-(iss)aient	-aient
INDICATIVE Past historic			
Singular 1	-ai	-is	-s
2	-as	-is	-s
3	-a	-it	-t
Plural 1	-âmes	-îmes	-mes
2	-âtes	-îtes	-tes
3	-èrent	-irent	-rent
INDICATIVE Future			
Singular 1	-erai	-rai	-rai
2	-eras	-ras	-ras
3	-era	-ra	-ra
Plural 1	-erons	-rons	-rons
2	-erez	-rez	-rez
3	-eront	-ront	-ront
INFINITIVE			
Present	-er	-ir	-r *or* -re

	-er	-ir	-r, -re
SUBJUNCTIVE Present			
Singular 1	-e	-(iss)e	-e
2	-es	-(iss)es	-es
3	-e	-(iss)e	-e
Plural 1	-ions	-(iss)ions	-ions
2	-iez	-(iss)iez	-iez
3	-ent	-(iss)ent	-ent
SUBJUNCTIVE Imperfect			
Singular 1	-asse	-sse	-sse
2	-asses	-sses	-sses
3	-ât	-ît	-ît *or* -ût
Plural 1	-assions	-ssions	-ssions
2	-assiez	-ssiez	-ssiez
3	-assent	-issent	-ssent
IMPERATIVE Present			
Singular			
3	-e	-s	-s
Plural 1	-ons	-(iss)ons	-ons
2	-ez	-(iss)ez	-ez
CONDITIONAL Present			
Singular 1	-erais	-rais	-rais
2	-erais	-rais	-rais
3	-erait	-rait	-rait
Plural 1	-erions	-rions	-rions
2	-eriez	-riez	-riez
3	-eraient	-raient	-raient
PARTICIPLE			
Present	-ant	-(iss)ant	-ant
Past	-é	-i	-i *or* -u

1 aimer

INDICATIVE

Present
j' aim**e**
tu aim**es**
il aim**e**
nous aim**ons**
vous aim**ez**
ils aim**ent**

Imperfect
j' aim**ais**
tu aim**ais**
il aim**ait**
nous aim**ions**
vous aim**iez**
ils aim**aient**

Past historic
j' aim**ai**
tu aim**as**
il aim**a**
nous aim**âmes**
vous aim**âtes**
ils aim**èrent**

Future
j' aim**erai**
tu aim**eras**
il aim**era**
nous aim**erons**
vous aim**erez**
ils aim**eront**

Perfect
j' ai **aimé**
tu as **aimé**
il a **aimé**
nous avons **aimé**
vous avez **aimé**
ils ont **aimé**

Pluperfect
j' avais **aimé**
tu avais **aimé**
il avait **aimé**
nous avions **aimé**
vous aviez **aimé**
ils avaient **aimé**

Past anterior
j' eus **aimé**
tu eus **aimé**
il eut **aimé**
nous eûmes **aimé**
vous eûtes **aimé**
ils eurent **aimé**

Future perfect
j' aurai **aimé**
tu auras **aimé**
il aura **aimé**
nous aurons **aimé**
vous aurez **aimé**
ils auront **aimé**

IMPERATIVE

Present
aim**e**
aim**ons**
aim**ez**

Past
aie **aimé**
ayons **aimé**
ayez **aimé**

SUBJUNCTIVE

Present
(que) j' aim**e**
(que) tu aim**es**
(qu')il aim**e**
(que) nous aim**ions**
(que) vous aim**iez**
(qu')ils aim**ent**

Imperfect
(que) j' aim**asse**
(que) tu aim**asses**
(qu')il aim**ât**
(que) nous aim**assions**
(que) vous aim**assiez**
(qu')ils aim**assent**

Perfect
(que) j' aie **aimé**
(que) tu aies **aimé**
(qu')il ait **aimé**
(que) nous ayons **aimé**
(que) vous ayez **aimé**
(qu')ils aient **aimé**

Pluperfect
(que) j' eusse **aimé**
(que) tu eusses **aimé**
(qu')il eût **aimé**
(que) nous eussions **aimé**
(que) vous eussiez **aimé**
(qu')ils eussent **aimé**

CONDITIONAL

Present
j' aim**erais**
tu aim**erais**
il aim**erait**
nous aim**erions**
vous aim**eriez**
ils aim**eraient**

Past I
j' aurais **aimé**
tu aurais **aimé**
il aurait **aimé**
nous aurions **aimé**
vous auriez **aimé**
ils auraient **aimé**

Past II
j' eusse **aimé**
tu eusses **aimé**
il eût **aimé**
nous eussions **aimé**
vous eussiez **aimé**
ils eussent **aimé**

PARTICIPLE

Present aim**ant**

Past **aimé, -e**
ayant **aimé**

INFINITIVE

Present aim**er**

Past avoir **aimé**

2 plier

INDICATIVE

Present
je pli**e**
tu pli**es**
il pli**e**
nous pli**ons**
vous pli**ez**
ils pli**ent**

Imperfect
je pli**ais**
tu pli**ais**
il pli**ait**
nous pli**ions**
vous pli**iez**
ils pli**aient**

Past historic
je pli**ai**
tu pli**as**
il pli**a**
nous pli**âmes**
vous pli**âtes**
ils pli**èrent**

Future
je pli**erai**
tu pli**eras**
il pli**era**
nous pli**erons**
vous pli**erez**
ils pli**eront**

Perfect
j' ai **plié**
tu as **plié**
il a **plié**
nous avons **plié**
vous avez **plié**
ils ont **plié**

Pluperfect
j' avais **plié**
tu avais **plié**
il avait **plié**
nous avions **plié**
vous aviez **plié**
ils avaient **plié**

Past anterior
j' eus **plié**
tu eus **plié**
il eut **plié**
nous eûmes **plié**
vous eûtes **plié**
ils eurent **plié**

Future perfect
j' aurai **plié**
tu auras **plié**
il aura **plié**
nous aurons **plié**
vous aurez **plié**
ils auront **plié**

IMPERATIVE

Present
pli**e**
pli**ons**
pli**ez**

Past
aie **plié**
ayons **plié**
ayez **plié**

SUBJUNCTIVE

Present
(que) je pli**e**
(que) tu pli**es**
(qu')il pli**e**
(que) nous pli**ions**
(que) vous pli**iez**
(qu')ils pli**ent**

Imperfect
(que) je pli**asse**
(que) tu pli**asses**
(qu')il pli**ât**
(que) nous pli**assions**
(que) vous pli**assiez**
(qu')ils pli**assent**

Perfect
(que) j' aie **plié**
(que) tu aies **plié**
(qu')il ait **plié**
(que) nous ayons **plié**
(que) vous ayez **plié**
(qu')ils aient **plié**

Pluperfect
(que) j' eusse **plié**
(que) tu eusses **plié**
(qu')il eût **plié**
(que) nous eussions **plié**
(que) vous eussiez **plié**
(qu')ils eussent **plié**

CONDITIONAL

Present
je pli**erais**
tu pli**erais**
il pli**erait**
nous pli**erions**
vous pli**eriez**
ils pli**eraient**

Past I
j' aurais **plié**
tu aurais **plié**
il aurait **plié**
nous aurions **plié**
vous auriez **plié**
ils auraient **plié**

Past II
j' eusse **plié**
tu eusses **plié**
il eût **plié**
nous eussions **plié**
vous eussiez **plié**
ils eussent **plié**

PARTICIPLE

Present pli**ant**

Past **plié, -e**
ayant **plié**

INFINITIVE

Present pli**er**

Past avoir **plié**

3 finir

INDICATIVE

Present	
je	fin**is**
tu	fin**is**
il	fin**it**
nous	fin**issons**
vous	fin**issez**
ils	fin**issent**

Imperfect	
je	fin**issais**
tu	fin**issais**
il	fin**issait**
nous	fin**issions**
vous	fin**issiez**
ils	fin**issaient**

Past historic	
je	fin**is**
tu	fin**is**
il	fin**it**
nous	fin**îmes**
vous	fin**îtes**
ils	fin**irent**

Future	
je	fin**irai**
tu	fin**iras**
il	fin**ira**
nous	fin**irons**
vous	fin**irez**
ils	fin**iront**

Perfect		
j'	ai	fin**i**
tu	as	fin**i**
il	a	fin**i**
nous	avons	fin**i**
vous	avez	fin**i**
ils	ont	fin**i**

Pluperfect		
j'	avais	fin**i**
tu	avais	fin**i**
il	avait	fin**i**
nous	avions	fin**i**
vous	aviez	fin**i**
ils	avaient	fin**i**

Past anterior		
j'	eus	fin**i**
tu	eus	fin**i**
il	eut	fin**i**
nous	eûmes	fin**i**
vous	eûtes	fin**i**
ils	eurent	fin**i**

Future perfect		
j'	aurai	fin**i**
tu	auras	fin**i**
il	aura	fin**i**
nous	aurons	fin**i**
vous	aurez	fin**i**
ils	auront	fin**i**

IMPERATIVE

Present	fin**is**	
	fin**issons**	
	fin**issez**	
Past	aie	fin**i**
	ayons	fin**i**
	ayez	fin**i**

SUBJUNCTIVE

Present	
(que) je	fin**isse**
(que) tu	fin**isses**
(qu')il	fin**isse**
(que) nous	fin**issions**
(que) vous	fin**issiez**
(qu')ils	fin**issent**

Imperfect	
(que) je	fin**isse**
(que) tu	fin**isses**
(qu')il	fin**ît**
(que) nous	fin**issions**
(que) vous	fin**issiez**
(qu')ils	fin**issent**

Perfect		
(que) j'	aie	fin**i**
(que) tu	aies	fin**i**
(qu')il	ait	fin**i**
(que) nous	ayons	fin**i**
(que) vous	ayez	fin**i**
(qu')ils	aient	fin**i**

Pluperfect		
(que) j'	eusse	fin**i**
(que) tu	eusses	fin**i**
(qu')il	eût	fin**i**
(que) nous	eussions	fin**i**
(que) vous	eussiez	fin**i**
(qu')ils	eussent	fin**i**

CONDITIONAL

Present	
je	fin**irais**
tu	fin**irais**
il	fin**irait**
nous	fin**irions**
vous	fin**iriez**
ils	fin**iraient**

Past I		
j'	aurais	fin**i**
tu	aurais	fin**i**
il	aurait	fin**i**
nous	aurions	fin**i**
vous	auriez	fin**i**
ils	auraient	fin**i**

Past II		
j'	eusse	fin**i**
tu	eusses	fin**i**
il	eût	fin**i**
nous	eussions	fin**i**
vous	eussiez	fin**i**
ils	eussent	fin**i**

PARTICIPLE

Present	fin**issant**
Past	fin**i, -e**
	ayant fin**i**

INFINITIVE

Present	fin**ir**
Past	avoir fin**i**

4 offrir

INDICATIVE

Present	
j'	offr**e**
tu	offr**es**
il	offr**e**
nous	offr**ons**
vous	offr**ez**
ils	offr**ent**

Imperfect	
j'	offr**ais**
tu	offr**ais**
il	offr**ait**
nous	offr**ions**
vous	offr**iez**
ils	offr**aient**

Past historic	
j'	offr**is**
tu	offr**is**
il	offr**it**
nous	offr**îmes**
vous	offr**îtes**
ils	offr**irent**

Future	
j'	offr**irai**
tu	offr**iras**
il	offr**ira**
nous	offr**irons**
vous	offr**irez**
ils	offr**iront**

Perfect		
j'	ai	offert
tu	as	offert
il	a	offert
nous	avons	offert
vous	avez	offert
ils	ont	offert

Pluperfect		
j'	avais	offert
tu	avais	offert
il	avait	offert
nous	avions	offert
vous	aviez	offert
ils	avaient	offert

Past anterior		
j'	eus	offert
tu	eus	offert
il	eut	offert
nous	eûmes	offert
vous	eûtes	offert
ils	eurent	offert

Future perfect		
j'	aurai	offert
tu	auras	offert
il	aura	offert
nous	aurons	offert
vous	aurez	offert
ils	auront	offert

IMPERATIVE

Present	offr**e**	
	offr**ons**	
	offr**ez**	
Past	aie	offert
	ayons	offert
	ayez	offert

SUBJUNCTIVE

Present	
(que) j'	offr**e**
(que) tu	offr**es**
(qu')il	offr**e**
(que) nous	offr**ions**
(que) vous	offr**iez**
(qu')ils	offr**ent**

Imperfect	
(que) j'	offr**isse**
(que) tu	offr**isses**
(qu')il	offr**ît**
(que) nous	offr**issions**
(que) vous	offr**issiez**
(qu')ils	offr**issent**

Perfect		
(que) j'	aie	offert
(que) tu	aies	offert
(qu')il	ait	offert
(que) nous	ayons	offert
(que) vous	ayez	offert
(qu')ils	aient	offert

Pluperfect		
(que) j'	eusse	offert
(que) tu	eusses	offert
(qu')il	eût	offert
(que) nous	eussions	offert
(que) vous	eussiez	offert
(qu')ils	eussent	offert

CONDITIONAL

Present	
j'	offr**irais**
tu	offr**irais**
il	offr**irait**
nous	offr**irions**
vous	offr**iriez**
ils	offr**iraient**

Past I		
j'	aurais	offert
tu	aurais	offert
il	aurait	offert
nous	aurions	offert
vous	auriez	offert
ils	auraient	offert

Past II		
j'	eusse	offert
tu	eusses	offert
il	eût	offert
nous	eussions	offert
vous	eussiez	offert
ils	eussent	offert

PARTICIPLE

Present	offr**ant**
Past	offert, -e
	ayant offert

INFINITIVE

Present	offr**ir**
Past	avoir offert

5 recevoir

INDICATIVE

Present
je reç**ois**
tu reç**ois**
il reç**oit**
nous rec**evons**
vous rec**evez**
ils reç**oivent**

Imperfect
je rec**evais**
tu rec**evais**
il rec**evait**
nous rec**evions**
vous rec**eviez**
ils rec**evaient**

Past historic
je reç**us**
tu reç**us**
il reç**ut**
nous reç**ûmes**
vous reç**ûtes**
ils reç**urent**

Future
je rec**evrai**
tu rec**evras**
il rec**evra**
nous rec**evrons**
vous rec**evrez**
ils rec**evront**

Perfect
j' ai reç**u**
tu as reç**u**
il a reç**u**
nous avons reç**u**
vous avez reç**u**
ils ont reç**u**

Pluperfect
j' avais reç**u**
tu avais reç**u**
il avait reç**u**
nous avions reç**u**
vous aviez reç**u**
ils avaient reç**u**

Past anterior
j' eus reç**u**
tu eus reç**u**
il eut reç**u**
nous eûmes reç**u**
vous eûtes reç**u**
ils eurent reç**u**

Future perfect
j' aurai reç**u**
tu auras reç**u**
il aura reç**u**
nous aurons reç**u**
vous aurez reç**u**
ils auront reç**u**

IMPERATIVE

Present
reç**ois**
rec**evons**
rec**evez**

Past
aie reç**u**
ayons reç**u**
ayez reç**u**

SUBJUNCTIVE

Present
(que) je reç**oive**
(que) tu reç**oives**
(qu')il reç**oive**
(que) nous rec**evions**
(que) vous rec**eviez**
(qu')ils reç**oivent**

Imperfect
(que) je reç**usse**
(que) tu reç**usses**
(qu')il reç**ût**
(que) nous reç**ussions**
(que) vous reç**ussiez**
(qu')ils reç**ussent**

Perfect
(que) j' aie reç**u**
(que) tu aies reç**u**
(qu')il ait reç**u**
(que) nous ayons reç**u**
(que) vous ayez reç**u**
(qu')ils aient reç**u**

Pluperfect
(que) j' eusse reç**u**
(que) tu eusses reç**u**
(qu')il eût reç**u**
(que) nous eussions reç**u**
(que) vous eussiez reç**u**
(qu')ils eussent reç**u**

CONDITIONAL

Present
je rec**evrais**
tu rec**evrais**
il rec**evrait**
nous rec**evrions**
vous rec**evriez**
ils rec**evraient**

Past I
j' aurais reç**u**
tu aurais reç**u**
il aurait reç**u**
nous aurions reç**u**
vous auriez reç**u**
ils auraient reç**u**

Past II
j' eusse reç**u**
tu eusses reç**u**
il eût reç**u**
nous eussions reç**u**
vous eussiez reç**u**
ils eussent reç**u**

PARTICIPLE

Present rec**evant**

Past reç**u, -e**
ayant reç**u**

INFINITIVE

Present rec**evoir**

Past avoir reç**u**

6 rendre

INDICATIVE

Present
je rend**s**
tu rend**s**
il rend
nous rend**ons**
vous rend**ez**
ils rend**ent**

Imperfect
je rend**ais**
tu rend**ais**
il rend**ait**
nous rend**ions**
vous rend**iez**
ils rend**aient**

Past historic
je rend**is**
tu rend**is**
il rend**it**
nous rend**îmes**
vous rend**îtes**
ils rend**irent**

Future
je rend**rai**
tu rend**ras**
il rend**ra**
nous rend**rons**
vous rend**rez**
ils rend**ront**

Perfect
j' ai rend**u**
tu as rend**u**
il a rend**u**
nous avons rend**u**
vous avez rend**u**
ils ont rend**u**

Pluperfect
j' avais rend**u**
tu avais rend**u**
il avait rend**u**
nous avions rend**u**
vous aviez rend**u**
ils avaient rend**u**

Past anterior
j' eus rend**u**
tu eus rend**u**
il eut rend**u**
nous eûmes rend**u**
vous eûtes rend**u**
ils eurent rend**u**

Future perfect
j' aurai rend**u**
tu auras rend**u**
il aura rend**u**
nous aurons rend**u**
vous aurez rend**u**
ils auront rend**u**

IMPERATIVE

Present
rend**s**
rend**ons**
rend**ez**

Past
aie rend**u**
ayons rend**u**
ayez rend**u**

SUBJUNCTIVE

Present
(que) je rend**e**
(que) tu rend**es**
(qu')il rend**e**
(que) nous rend**ions**
(que) vous rend**iez**
(qu')ils rend**ent**

Imperfect
(que) je rend**isse**
(que) tu rend**isses**
(qu')il rend**ît**
(que) nous rend**issions**
(que) vous rend**issiez**
(qu')ils rend**issent**

Perfect
(que) j' aie rend**u**
(que) tu aies rend**u**
(qu')il ait rend**u**
(que) nous ayons rend**u**
(que) vous ayez rend**u**
(qu')ils aient rend**u**

Pluperfect
(que) j' eusse rend**u**
(que) tu eusses rend**u**
(qu')il eût rend**u**
(que) nous eussions rend**u**
(que) vous eussiez rend**u**
(qu')ils eussent rend**u**

CONDITIONAL

Present
je rend**rais**
tu rend**rais**
il rend**rait**
nous rend**rions**
vous rend**riez**
ils rend**raient**

Past I
j' aurais rend**u**
tu aurais rend**u**
il aurait rend**u**
nous aurions rend**u**
vous auriez rend**u**
ils auraient rend**u**

Past II
j' eusse rend**u**
tu eusses rend**u**
il eût rend**u**
nous eussions rend**u**
vous eussiez rend**u**
ils eussent rend**u**

PARTICIPLE

Present rend**ant**

Past rend**u, -e**
ayant rend**u**

INFINITIVE

Present rend**re**

Past avoir rend**u**

7 être

INDICATIVE

Present

je	suis
tu	es
il	est
nous	sommes
vous	êtes
ils	sont

Imperfect

j'	étais
tu	étais
il	était
nous	étions
vous	étiez
ils	étaient

Past historic

je	fus
tu	fus
il	fut
nous	fûmes
vous	fûtes
ils	furent

Future

je	serai
tu	seras
il	sera
nous	serons
vous	serez
ils	seront

Perfect

j'	ai	été
tu	as	été
il	a	été
nous	avons	été
vous	avez	été
ils	ont	été

Pluperfect

j'	avais	été
tu	avais	été
il	avait	été
nous	avions	été
vous	aviez	été
ils	avaient	été

Past anterior

j'	eus	été
tu	eus	été
il	eut	été
nous	eûmes	été
vous	eûtes	été
ils	eurent	été

Future perfect

j'	aurai	été
tu	auras	été
il	aura	été
nous	aurons	été
vous	aurez	été
ils	auront	été

IMPERATIVE

Present sois
soyons
soyez

Past aie été
ayons été
ayez été

SUBJUNCTIVE

Present

(que) je	sois
(que) tu	sois
(qu')il	soit
(que) nous	soyons
(que) vous	soyez
(qu')ils	soient

Imperfect

(que) je	fusse
(que) tu	fusses
(qu')il	fût
(que) nous	fussions
(que) vous	fussiez
(qu')ils	fussent

Perfect

(que) j'	aie	été
(que) tu	aies	été
(qu')il	ait	été
(que) nous	ayons	été
(que) vous	ayez	été
(qu')ils	aient	été

Pluperfect

(que) j'	eusse	été
(que) tu	eusses	été
(qu')il	eût	été
(que) nous	eussions	été
(que) vous	eussiez	été
(qu')ils	eussent	été

CONDITIONAL

Present

je	serais
tu	serais
il	serait
nous	serions
vous	seriez
ils	seraient

Past I

j'	aurais	été
tu	aurais	été
il	aurait	été
nous	aurions	été
vous	auriez	été
ils	auraient	été

Past II

j'	eusse	été
tu	eusses	été
il	eût	été
nous	eussions	été
vous	eussiez	été
ils	eussent	été

PARTICIPLE

Present étant

Past été (invariable)
ayant été

INFINITIVE

Present être

Past avoir été

8 avoir

INDICATIVE

Present

j'	ai
tu	as
il	a
nous	avons
vous	avez
ils	ont

Imperfect

j'	avais
tu	avais
il	avait
nous	avions
vous	aviez
ils	avaient

Past historic

j'	eus
tu	eus
il	eut
nous	eûmes
vous	eûtes
ils	eurent

Future

j'	aurai
tu	auras
il	aura
nous	aurons
vous	aurez
ils	auront

Perfect

j'	ai	eu
tu	as	eu
il	a	eu
nous	avons	eu
vous	avez	eu
ils	ont	eu

Pluperfect

j'	avais	eu
tu	avais	eu
il	avait	eu
nous	avions	eu
vous	aviez	eu
ils	avaient	eu

Past anterior

j'	eus	eu
tu	eus	eu
il	eut	eu
nous	eûmes	eu
vous	eûtes	eu
ils	eurent	eu

Future perfect

j'	aurai	eu
tu	auras	eu
il	aura	eu
nous	aurons	eu
vous	aurez	eu
ils	auront	eu

IMPERATIVE

Present aie
ayons
ayez

Past aie eu
ayons eu
ayez eu

SUBJUNCTIVE

Present

(que) j'	aie
(que) tu	aies
(qu')il	ait
(que) nous	ayons
(que) vous	ayez
(qu')ils	aient

Imperfect

(que) j'	eusse
(que) tu	eusses
(qu')il	eût
(que) nous	eussions
(que) vous	eussiez
(qu')ils	eussent

Perfect

(que) j'	aie	eu
(que) tu	aies	eu
(qu')il	ait	eu
(que) nous	ayons	eu
(que) vous	ayez	eu
(qu')ils	aient	eu

Pluperfect

(que) j'	eusse	eu
(que) tu	eusses	eu
(qu')il	eût	eu
(que) nous	eussions	eu
(que) vous	eussiez	eu
(qu')ils	eussent	eu

CONDITIONAL

Present

j'	aurais
tu	aurais
il	aurait
nous	aurions
vous	auriez
ils	auraient

Past I

j'	aurais	eu
tu	aurais	eu
il	aurait	eu
nous	aurions	eu
vous	auriez	eu
ils	auraient	eu

Past II

j'	eusse	eu
tu	eusses	eu
il	eût	eu
nous	eussions	eu
vous	eussiez	eu
ils	eussent	eu

PARTICIPLE

Present ayant

Past eu, -e
ayant eu

INFINITIVE

Present avoir

Past avoir eu

9 aller

INDICATIVE

Present

je	vais
tu	vas
il	va
nous	allons
vous	allez
ils	vont

Imperfect

j'	allais
tu	allais
il	allait
nous	allions
vous	alliez
ils	allaient

Past historic

j'	allai
tu	allas
il	alla
nous	allâmes
vous	allâtes
ils	allèrent

Future

j'	irai
tu	iras
il	ira
nous	irons
vous	irez
ils	iront

Perfect

je	suis	allé
tu	es	allé
il	est	allé
nous	sommes	allés
vous	êtes	allés
ils	sont	allés

Pluperfect

j'	étais	allé
tu	étais	allé
il	était	allé
nous	étions	allés
vous	étiez	allés
ils	étaient	allés

Past anterior

je	fus	allé
tu	fus	allé
il	fut	allé
nous	fûmes	allés
vous	fûtes	allés
ils	furent	allés

Future perfect

je	serai	allé
tu	seras	allé
il	sera	allé
nous	serons	allés
vous	serez	allés
ils	seront	allés

IMPERATIVE

Present va, allons, allez

Past sois allé, soyons allés, soyez allés

SUBJUNCTIVE

Present

(que) j'	aille
(que) tu	ailles
(qu')il	aille
(que) nous	allions
(que) vous	alliez
(qu')ils	aillent

Imperfect

(que) j'	allasse
(que) tu	allasses
(qu')il	allât
(que) nous	allassions
(que) vous	allassiez
(qu')ils	allassent

Perfect

(que) je	sois	allé
(que) tu	sois	allé
(qu')il	soit	allé
(que) nous	soyons	allés
(que) vous	soyez	allés
(qu')ils	soient	allés

Pluperfect

(que) je	fusse	allé
(que) tu	fusses	allé
(qu')il	fût	allé
(que) nous	fussions	allés
(que) vous	fussiez	allés
(qu')ils	fussent	allés

CONDITIONAL

Present

j'	irais
tu	irais
il	irait
nous	irions
vous	iriez
ils	iraient

Past I

je	serais	allé
tu	serais	allé
il	serait	allé
nous	serions	allés
vous	seriez	allés
ils	seraient	allés

Past II

je	fusse	allé
tu	fusses	allé
il	fût	allé
nous	fussions	allés
vous	fussiez	allés
ils	fussent	allés

PARTICIPLE

Present allant

Past allé, -e; étant allé

INFINITIVE

Present aller

Past être allé

10 faire

INDICATIVE

Present

je	fais
tu	fais
il	fait
nous	faisons
vous	faites
ils	font

Imperfect

je	faisais
tu	faisais
il	faisait
nous	faisions
vous	faisiez
ils	faisaient

Past historic

je	fis
tu	fis
il	fit
nous	fîmes
vous	fîtes
ils	firent

Future

je	ferai
tu	feras
il	fera
nous	ferons
vous	ferez
ils	feront

Perfect

j'	ai	fait
tu	as	fait
il	a	fait
nous	avons	fait
vous	avez	fait
ils	ont	fait

Pluperfect

j'	avais	fait
tu	avais	fait
il	avait	fait
nous	avions	fait
vous	aviez	fait
ils	avaient	fait

Past anterior

j'	eus	fait
tu	eus	fait
il	eut	fait
nous	eûmes	fait
vous	eûtes	fait
ils	eurent	fait

Future perfect

j'	aurai	fait
tu	auras	fait
il	aura	fait
nous	aurons	fait
vous	aurez	fait
ils	auront	fait

IMPERATIVE

Present fais, faisons, faites

Past aie fait, ayons fait, ayez fait

SUBJUNCTIVE

Present

(que) je	fasse
(que) tu	fasses
(qu')il	fasse
(que) nous	fassions
(que) vous	fassiez
(qu')ils	fassent

Imperfect

(que) je	fisse
(que) tu	fisses
(qu')il	fît
(que) nous	fissions
(que) vous	fissiez
(qu')ils	fissent

Perfect

(que) j'	aie	fait
(que) tu	aies	fait
(qu')il	ait	fait
(que) nous	ayons	fait
(que) vous	ayez	fait
(qu')ils	aient	fait

Pluperfect

(que) j'	eusse	fait
(que) tu	eusses	fait
(qu')il	eût	fait
(que) nous	eussions	fait
(que) vous	eussiez	fait
(qu')ils	eussent	fait

CONDITIONAL

Present

je	ferais
tu	ferais
il	ferait
nous	ferions
vous	feriez
ils	feraient

Past I

j'	aurais	fait
tu	aurais	fait
il	aurait	fait
nous	aurions	fait
vous	auriez	fait
ils	auraient	fait

Past II

j'	eusse	fait
tu	eusses	fait
il	eût	fait
nous	eussions	fait
vous	eussiez	fait
ils	eussent	fait

PARTICIPLE

Present faisant

Past fait, -e; ayant fait

INFINITIVE

Present faire

Past avoir fait

INFINITIVE	Rules	INDICATIVE Present	Imperfect	Past Historic	Future
11 créer	*always* é	je crée, -es, -e, -ent nous créons, -ez	je créais ...	je créai ...	je créerai ...
12 placer	c	je place, -es, -e, -ez, -ent	nous placions, -iez	ils placèrent	je placerai ...
	ç *before* a *and* o	nous plaçons	je plaçais, -ais, -ait, -aient	je plaçai, -as, -a, -âmes, -âtes	
13 manger	g	je mange, -es, -e, -ez, -ent	nous mangions, -iez	ils mangèrent	je mangerai ...
	ge *before* a *and* o	nous mangeons	je mangeais, -eais, -eait, -eaient	je mangeai, -as, -a, -âmes, -âtes	
14 céder	è *before silent final syllable*	je cède, -es, -e, -ent			
	é	nous cédons, -ez	je cédais ...	je cédai ...	je céderai ...
15 assiéger	è *before silent final syllable*	j'assiège, -es, -e, -ent			
	ge *before* a *and* o	nous assiégeons	j'assiégeais, -eais, -eait, -eaient	j'assiégeai	
	é *before silent syllable*				j'assiégerai ...
16 lever	è *before silent syllable*	je lève, -es, -e, -ent			je lèverai ...
	e	nous levons, -ez	je levais ...	je levai ...	
17 geler	è *before silent syllable*	je gèle, -es, -e, -ent			je gèlerai ...
	e	nous gelons, -ez	je gelais ...	je gelai ...	
18 acheter	è *before silent syllable*	j'achète, -es, -e, -ent			j'achèterai ...
	e	nous achetons, -ez	j'achetais ...	j'achetai ...	
19 appeler	ll *before mute* e	j'appelle, -es, -e, -ent			j'appellerai ...
	l	nous appelons, -ez	j'appelais ...	j'appelai ...	
20 jeter	tt *before mute* e	je jette, -es, -e, -ent			je jetterai ...
	t	nous jetons, -ez	je jetais ...	je jetai ...	
21 payer	i *before mute* e	je paie, -es, -e, -ent			je paierai ...
	or y	je paye, -es, -e, -ent nous payons, -ez	je payais ...	je payai ...	je payerai ...

CONDITIONAL	SUBJUNCTIVE		IMPERATIVE	PARTICIPLE		
Present	Present	Imperfect		Present	Past	
je créerais ...	que je crée ...	que je créasse ...	crée créons, -ez	créant	créé, -e	11
je placerais ...	que je place ...		place, -ez		placé, -e	12
		que je plaçasse ...	plaçons	plaçant		
je mangerais ...	que je mange ...		mange, -ez		mangé, -e	13
		que je mangeasse ...	mangeons	mangeant		
	que je cède, -es, -e, -ent		cède			14
je céderais ...	que nous cédions, -iez	que je cédasse ...	cédons, -ez	cédant	cédé, -e	
	que j'assiège ...		assiège			15
j'assiégerais ...	que nous assiégions , -iez	que j'assiégeasse ...	assiégeons	assiégeant	assiégé, -e	
je lèverais ...	que je lève, -es, -e, -ent		lève			16
	que nous levions, -iez	que je levasse ...	levons, -ez	levant	levé, -e	
je gèlerais ...	que je gèle, -es, -e, -ent		gèle			17
	que nous gelions, -iez	que je gelasse ...	gelons, -ez	gelant	gelé, -e	
j'achèterais ...	que j'achète, -es, -e, -ent		achète			18
	que nous achetions, -iez	que j'achetasse ...	achetons, -ez	achetant	acheté, -e	
j'appellerais ...	que j'appelle, -es, -e, -ent		appelle			19
	que nous appelions, -iez	que j'appelasse ...	appelons, -ez	appelant	appelé, -e	
je jetterais ...	que je jette, -es, -e, -ent		jette			20
	que nous jetions, -iez	que je jetasse ...	jetons, -ez	jetant	jeté, -e	
je paierais ...	que je paie, -es, -e, -ent		paie			21
je payerais ...	que je paye, -es, -e, -ent	que je payasse ...	paye			
	que nous payions, -iez		payons, -ez	payant	payé, -e	

INFINITIVE	Rules	INDICATIVE Present	Imperfect	Past Historic	Future
22 essuyer	i *before mute* e	j'essuie, -es, -e, -ent			j'essuierai ...
	y	nous essuyons, -ez	j'essuyais ...	j'essuyai ...	
23 employer	i *before mute* e	j'emploie, -es, -e, -ent			j'emploierai ...
	y	nous employons, -ez	j'employais ...	j'employai ...	
24 envoyer	i *before mute* e	j'envoie, -es, -e, -ent			
	y	nous envoyons, -ez	j'envoyais ...	j'envoyai ...	
	err				j'enverrai ...
25 haïr	i	je hais, -s, -t			
	ï	ns haïssons, -ez, -ent	je haïssais ...	je haïs ... (haïmes, haïtes)	je haïrai ...
26 courir		je cours ...	je courais ...	je courus ...	je courrai ...
27 cueillir		je cueille, -es, -e, nous cueillons ...	je cueillais ...	je cueillis ...	je cueillerai ...
28 assaillir		j'assaille, -es, -e, nous assaillons, -ez, -ent	j'assaillais ...	j'assaillis ...	j'assaillirai ...
29 fuir	i *before consonants and* e	je fuis, -s, -t, -ent		je fuis ...	je fuirai ...
	y *before* a, ez, i, o	nous fuyons, -ez	je fuyais ...		
30 partir	*without* t	je pars ...			
	with t	il part ...	je partais ...	je partis ...	je partirai ...
31 bouillir	ou	je bous, s, t			
	ouill	nous bouillons ...	je bouillais ...	je bouillis ...	je bouillirai ...
32 couvrir		je couvre, -es, -e, nous couvrons ...	je couvrais ...	je couvris ...	je couvrirai ...
33 vêtir		je vêts ...	je vêtais ...	je vêtis ...	je vêtirai ...
34 mourir	eur	je meurs, -s, -t, -ent			
	our	nous mourons, -ez	je mourais ...	je mourus ...	je mourrai ...
35 acquérir	quier	j'acquiers, -s, -t, -ièrent			
	quer	nous acquérons -ez	j'acquérais ...		j'acquerrai ...
	qu			j'acquis ...	

CONDITIONAL	SUBJUNCTIVE		IMPERATIVE	PARTICIPLE		
Present	Present	Imperfect		Present	Past	
j'essuierais ...	que j'essuie, -es, -e, -ent		essuie			22
	que nous essuyions, -iez	que j'essuyasse...	essuyons, -ez	essuyant	essuyé, e	
j'emploierais ...	que j'emploie, -es, -e, -ent		emploie			23
	que nous employions, -iez	que j'employasse ...	employons, -ez	employant	employé, -e	
	que j'envoie, -es, -e, -ent		envoie			24
	que nous envoyions, -iez	que j'envoyasse ...	envoyons, -ez	envoyant	envoyé, -e	
j'enverrais ...						
			hais			25
je haïrais ...	que je haïsse, qu'il haïsse	que je haïsse, qu'il haït	haïssons, haïssez	haïssant	haï, -e	
je courrais ...	que je coure ...	que je courusse ...	cours, courons, -ez	courant	couru, -e	26
je cueillerais ...			cueille			27
	que je cueille ...	que je cueillisse ...	cuillons, -ez	cueillant	cueilli, -e	
			assaille			28
j'assaillirais ...	que j'assaille ...	que j'assaillisse	assaillons, -ez	assaillant	assailli, -e	
je fuirais ...	que je fuie, -es, -e, -ent	que je fuisse...	fuis		fui, -e	29
	que nous fuyions, -iez		fuyons, -ez	fuyant		
			pars			30
je partirais ...	que je parte ...	que je partisse ...	partons, -ez	partant	parti, -e	
			bous			31
je bouillirais ...	que je bouille ...	que je bouillisse ...	bouillons, -ez	bouillant	bouilli, -e	
	que je couvre, -es, -e,		couvre			32
je couvrirais ...	que nous couvrions ...	que je couvrisse ...	couvrons, -ez	couvrant	couvert, -e	
je vêtirais ...	que je vête ...	que je vêtisse ...	vêts vêtons, vêtez	vêtant	vêtu, -e	33
	que je meure ...		meurs		mort, -e	34
je mourrais ...		que je mourusse ...	mourons, -ez	mourant		
	que j'acquière, -es, -e, -ent		acquiers			35
j'acquerrais ...	que nous acquérions, -iez		acquérons, -ez	acquérant		
		que j'acquisse ...			acquis, -e	

INFINITIVE	Rules	INDICATIVE			
		Present	Imperfect	Past Historic	Future
36 venir	i	je viens, -s, -t, -nent		je vins ... ils vinrent	je viendrai ...
	e	nous venons, -ez	je venais ...		
37 gésir	*Defective*	je gis, tu gis, il gît, nous gisons, -ez, -ent	je gisais ...		
38 ouïr	*Archaic*	j'ois ... nous oyons ...	j'oyais ...	j'ouïs ...	j'ouïrai ...
39 pleuvoir		il pleut	il pleuvait	il plut	il pleuvra
		ils pleuvent	ils pleuvaient	ils plurent	ils pleuvront
40 pourvoir	i	je pourvois, -s, -t, -ent			je pourvoirai ...
	y	nous pourvoyons, -ez	je pourvoyais ...		
	u			je pourvus ...	
41 asseoir	ie	j'assieds, -ds, -d			j'assiérai ...
	ey	nous asseyons, -ez, -ent	j'asseyais ...		
	i			j'assis ...	
asseoir (oi/oy *replace* ie/ey)	oi	j'assois, -s, -t, -ent			j'assoirai ...
	oy	nous assoyons, -ez	j'assoyais ...		
42 prévoir	oi	je prévois, -s, -t, -ent			je prévoirai ...
	oy	nous prévoyons, -ez	je prévoyais ...		
	i/u			je prévis ...	
43 mouvoir	eu	je meus, -s, -t, -vent			
	ou	nous mouvons, -ez	je mouvais ...		je mouvrai ...
	u			je mus, -s, -t, -(û)mes, -(û)tes, -rent	
44 devoir	û *in the past participle masc. sing.*	je dois, -s, -t -vent nous devons, -ez	je devais ...	je dus ...	je devrai ...
45 valoir	au, aille	je vaux, -x, -t			je vaudrai ...
	al	nous valons, -ez, -ent	je valais ...	je valus ...	
prévaloir					

CONDITIONAL	SUBJUNCTIVE		IMPERATIVE	PARTICIPLE		
Present	Present	Imperfect		Present	Past	
je viendrais …	que je vienne, -es, -e, -ent	que je vinsse …	viens			36
	que nous venions, -iez		venons, -ez	venant	venu, -e	
						37
				gisant		
j'ouïrais …	que j'oie …	que j'ouïsse …	ois		ouï, -e	38
	que nous oyions …		oyons, -ez	oyant		
il pleuvrait	qu'il pleuve	qu'il plût		pleuvant	plu	39
ils pleuvraient	qu'ils pleuvent	qu'ils plussent				
je pourvoirais …	que je pourvoie, -es, -e, -ent		pourvois			40
	que nous pourvoyions, -iez		pourvoyons, -ez	pourvoyant		
		que je pourvusse …			pourvu, -e	
j'assiérais …			assieds			41
	que j' asseye … que nous asseyions …		asseyons, -ez	asséyant		
		que j'assisse …			assis, -e	
j'assoirais …	que j'assoie, -es, -e, -ent		assois			
	que nous assoyions, -iez		assoyons, -ez	assoyant		
je prévoirais …	que je prévoie, -es, -e, -ent		prévois			42
	que ns prévoyions, -iez		prévoyons, -ez	prévoyant		
		que je prévisse …			prévu, -e	
	que je meuve, -es, -e, -ent		meus			43
je mouvrais …	que nous mouvions, -iez		mouvons, -ez	mouvant		
		que je musse …			mû, mue	
	que je doive, -es, -e, -ent	que je dusse …	dois		dû, due	44
je devrais …	que nous devions, -iez		devons, -ez	devant		
je vaudrais …	que je vaille, -es, -e, -ent		vaux			45
	que nous valions, -iez	que je valusse …	valons, -ez	valant	valu, -e	
	que je prévale, -es, -e					

INFINITIVE	Rules	INDICATIVE			
		Present	Imperfect	Past Historic	Future
46 voir	oi	je vois, -s, -t, -ent			
	oy	nous voyons, -ez	je voyais ...		
	i/e/u			je vis ...	je verrai ...
47 savoir	5 forms	je sais, -s, -t, nous savons, -ez, -ent	je savais ...	je sus ...	je saurai ...
48 vouloir	veu/veuil	je veux, -x, -t, veulent			
	voul/voudr	nous voulons, -ez	je voulais ...	je voulus ...	je voudrai ...
49 pouvoir	eu/u(i)	je peux, -x, -t, peuvent		je pus ...	
	ouv/our	nous pouvons, -ez	je pouvais ...		je pourrai ...
50 falloir	*Impersonal*	il faut	il fallait	il fallut	il faudra
51 déchoir	choir *and* échoir *are defective*	je déchois, -s, -t, -ent nous déchoyons, -ez	je déchoyais ...	je déchus ...	je décherrai ...
52 prendre	prend	je prends, -ds, -d			je prendrai ...
	pren	nous prenons, -ez ils prennent	je prenais ...		
	pri(s)			je pris ...	
53 rompre		je romps, -ps, -pt, nous rompons ...	je rompais ...	je rompis ...	je romprai ...
54 craindre	ain/aind	je crains, -s, -t			je craindrai ...
	aign	nous craignons, -ez, -ent	je craignais ...	je craignis ...	
55 peindre	ein	je peins, -s, -t			je peindrai ...
	eign	nous peignons, -ez, -ent	je peignais ...	je peignis ...	
56 joindre	oin/oind	je joins, -s, -t			je joindrai ...
	oign	nous joignons, -ez, -ent	je joignais ...	je joignis ...	
57 vaincre	ainc	je vaincs, -cs, -c			je vaincrai ...
	ainqu	nous vainquons, -ez, -ent	je vainquais ...	je vainquis ...	
58 traire	i	je trais, -s, -t, -ent		(*obsolete*)	je trairai ...
	y	nous trayons, -ez	je trayais ...		

CONDITIONAL	SUBJUNCTIVE		IMPERATIVE	PARTICIPLE		
Present	Present	Imperfect		Present	Past	
	que je voie, -es, -e, -ent		vois			**46**
	que nous voyions, -iez		voyons, -ez	voyant		
je verrais ...		que je visse ...			vu, -e	
je saurais ...	que je sache ...	que je susse ...	sache, -ons, -ez	sachant	su, -e	**47**
	que je veuille, -es, -e, -ent		veux (veuille)			**48**
je voudrais ...	que nous voulions, -iez	que je voulusse ...	voulons, -ez (veuillez)	voulant	voulu, -e	
	que je puisse ...	que je pusse ...	(*obsolete*)		pu	**49**
je pourrais ...				pouvant		
il faudrait	qu'il faille	qu'il fallût	(*no form*)	(*obsolete*)	fallu	**50**
	que je déchoie, -es, -e, -ent		déchois	(*no form but* échéant)		**51**
je décherrais ...	que nous déchoyions, -iez	que je déchusse ...	déchoyons, -ez		déchu, -e	
je prendrais ...			prends			**52**
	que je prenne ...		prenons, -ez	prenant		
		que je prisse ...			pris, -e	
je romprais ...	que je rompe ...	que je rompisse ...	romps -pons, -pez	rompant	rompu, -e	**53**
je craindrais ...			crains		craint, -e	**54**
	que je craigne ...	que je craignisse ...	craignons, -ez	craignant		
je peindrais ...			peins		peint, -e	**55**
	que je peigne ...	que je peignisse ...	peignons, -ez	peignant		
je joindrais ...			joins		joint, -e	**56**
	que je joigne ...	que je joignisse ...	joignons, -ez	joignant		
je vaincrais ...			vaincs		vaincu, -e	**57**
	que je vainque ...	que je vainquisse ...	vainquons, -ez	vainquant		
je trairais ...	que je traie, -es, -e, -ent	(*obsolete*)	trais		trait, -e	**58**
	que nous trayions, -yiez		trayons, -ez	trayant		

INFINITIVE	Rules	INDICATIVE			
		Present	Imperfect	Past Historic	Future
59 plaire	ai	je plais, tu plais, il plait (*but* il tait) nous plaisons ...	je plaisais ...		je plairai ...
	u			je plus ...	
60 mettre	met	je mets, nous mettons	je mettais ...		je mettrai ...
	mis			je mis ...	
61 battre	t	je bats, -ts, -t			
	tt	nous battons ...	je battais ...	je battis ...	je battrai ...
62 suivre	ui	je suis, -s, -t			
	uiv	nous suivons ...	je suivais ...	je suivis ...	je suivrai ...
63 vivre	vi/viv	je vis, -s, -t, nous vivons ...	je vivais ...		je vivrai ...
	véc			je vécus ...	
64 suffire		je suffis, -s, -t, nous suffisons ...	je suffisais ...	je suffis ...	je suffirai ...
65 médire		je médis, -s, -t, nous médisons, vous médisez (*but* vous dites, redites)	je médisais ...	je médis ...	je médirai ...
66 lire	i	je lis, -s, -t			je lirai ...
	is	nous lisons, -ez, -ent	je lisais ...		
	u			je lus ...	
67 écrire	i	j'écris, -s, -t			j'écrirai ...
	iv	nous écrivons, -ez, -ent	j'écrivais ...	j'écrivis ...	
68 rire		je ris, -s, -t, nous rions ...	je riais ... nous riions, -iez	je ris ... nous rîmes ...	je rirai ...
69 conduire		je conduis ...	je conduisais ...	je conduisis...	je conduirai ...
70 boire	oi	je bois, -s, -t, -vent			je boirai ...
	u(v)	nous buvons, -ez	je buvais ...	je bus ...	
71 croire	oi	je crois, -s, -t, ils croient			je croirai ...
	oy	nous croyons, -ez	je croyais ...		
	u			je crus ...	

CONDITIONAL	SUBJUNCTIVE		IMPERATIVE	PARTICIPLE		
Present	**Present**	**Imperfect**		**Present**	**Past**	
je plairais …	que je plaise …		plais plaisons, -ez	plaisant		**59**
		que je plusse …			plu	
je mettrais …	que je mette …		mets mettons, -ez	mettant		**60**
		que je misse …			mis, -e	
			bats			**61**
je battrais …	que je batte …	que je battisse …	battons, -ez	battant	battu, -e	
			suis			**62**
je suivrais …	que je suive …	que je suivisse …	suivons, -ez	suivant	suivi, -e	
je vivrais …	que je vive …		vis vivons, -ez	vivant		**63**
		que je vécusse …			vécu, -e	
je suffirais …	que je suffise …	que je suffisse …	suffis suffisons, -ez	suffisant	suffi (*but* confit, déconfit, frit, circoncis)	**64**
je médirais …	que je médise … que nous médisions, -iez	que je médisse …	médis médisons médisez (*but* dites, redites)	médisant	médit	**65**
je lirais …			lis			**66**
	que je lise …		lisons, -ez	lisant		
		que je lusse …			lu, -e	
j'écrirais …			écris		écrit, -e	**67**
	que j'écrive …	que j'écrivisse …	écrivons, -ez	écrivant		
je rirais …	que je rie …	que je risse …	ris, rions, riez	riant	ri	**68**
	que nous riions, -iez	que nous rissions …				
je conduirais …	que je conduise …	que je conduisisse …	conduis conduisons, -ez	conduisant	conduit, -e (*but* lui, nui)	**69**
je boirais …	que je boive, -es, -e, -ent		bois			**70**
	que nous buvions, -iez	que je busse …	buvons, -ez	buvant	bu, -e	
je croirais …	que je croie …		crois			**71**
			croyons, -ez	croyant		
		que je crusse …			cru, -e	

INFINITIVE	Rules	INDICATIVE			
		Present	Imperfect	Past Historic	Future
72 croître	oi	je croîs, -s, -t			je croîtrai ...
	oiss	nous croissons, -ez, -ent	je croissais ...		
	û			je crûs ...	
73 connaître	je connais, -s,	-ssons, -ssez, -ssent	je connaissais ...	je connus ...	
	i *before* t	il connaît			je connaîtrai ...
74 naître		je nais, nais,			
	i *before* t	naît			je naîtrai ...
	naisse	nous naissons, -ez, -ent	je naissais ...		
	naqu			je naquis ...	
75 résoudre	ou/oudr	je résous, -s, -t		(absoudre *and* dissoudre *have no past historic*)	je résoudrai...
	ol/olv	nous résolvons, -ez, -ent	je résolvais ...		
	olu			je résolus ...	
76 coudre	oud	je couds, -ds, -d			je coudrai ...
	ous	nous cousons, -ez, -ent	je cousais ...	je cousis ...	
77 moudre	moud	je mouds, -ds, -d			je moudrai ...
	moul	nous moulons, -ez, -ent	je moulais ...	je moulus ...	
78 conclure		je conclus, -s, -t, nous concluons, -ez, -ent	je concluais ...	je conclus ...	je conclurai ...
79 clore	*Defective*	je clos, -os, -ôt ils closent	(*obsolete*)	(*obsolete*)	je clorai ...
80 maudire		je maudis, -s, -t nous maudissons, -ez, -ent	je maudissais ...	je maudis ...	je maudirai ...

CONDITIONAL	SUBJUNCTIVE		IMPERATIVE	PARTICIPLE		
Present	**Present**	**Imperfect**		**Present**	**Past**	
je croîtrais...	que je croisse ...	que je crûsse ...	crois croissons, -ez	croissant	crû, crue (*but* accru, -e)	**72**
je connaitrais ...	que je connaisse ...	que je connusse ...	connais, -ssons, -ssez	connaissant	connu, -e	**73**
je naitrais ...	que je naisse ...	que je naquisse ...	nais naissons, -ez	naissant	né, -e	**74**
je résoudrais ...	que je résolve ...	que je résolusse ...	résous résolvons, -ez	résolvant	(absous, -oute; dissous, -oute) résolu, -e	**75**
je coudrais ...	que je couse ...	que je cousisse ...	couds cousons, -ez	cousant	cousu, -e	**76**
je moudrais ...	que je moule ...	que je moulusse ...	mouds moulons, -ez	moulant	moulu, -e	**77**
je conclurais ...	que je conclue ...	que je conclusse ...	conclus concluons, -ez	concluant	conclu, -e (*but* inclus, -e)	**78**
je clorais ...	que je close ...	(*obsolete*)	clos	closant	clos, -e	**79**
je maudirais ...	que je maudisse qu'il maudisse	que je maudisse qu'il maudît	maudis -ssons, -ssez	maudissant	maudit, -e	**80**

Numbers

Cardinal numbers in French

0	zéro*	80	quatre-vingts‡§
1	un†	81	quatre-vingt-un¶
2	deux	82	quatre-vingt-deux
3	trois	90	quatre-vingt-dix‡
4	quatre	91	quatre-vingt-onze
5	cinq	92	quatre-vingt-douze
6	six	99	quatre-vingt-dix-neuf
7	sept	101	cent un†
8	huit	102	cent deux
9	neuf	110	cent dix
10	dix	187	cent quatre-vingt-sept
11	onze	200	deux cents
12	douze	250	deux cent◊ cinquante
13	treize	1 000	∞mille
14	quatorze	1 001	mille un†
15	quinze	1 002	mille deux
16	seize	1 020	mille vingt
17	dix-sept	1 200	mille** deux cents
18	dix-huit	2 000	deux mille††
19	dix-neuf	1 0000	dix mille
20	vingt	100 000	cent mille
21	vingt et un	100 200	cent deux mille
22	vingt-deux	1 000 000	un million‡‡
30	trente	1 264 932	un million deux cent soixante-quatre mille neuf cent trente-deux
40	quarante		
50	cinquante		
60	soixante	1 000 000 000	un milliard‡‡
70	soixante-dix‡	1 000 000 000 000	un billion‡‡
71	soixante et onze		

* In English *0* may be called ***nought***, ***zero*** or even ***nothing***; French is always *zéro*: ***a nought*** = ***un zéro***.

† ***one*** is ***une*** in French when it agrees with a feminine noun, so ***un crayon*** but ***une table***, ***une des tables***, ***vingt et une tables***, etc.

‡ (70) Also ***septante*** in Belgium and Switzerland. (80) Also ***octante*** in Switzerland and Canada, ***huitante*** in Switzerland. (90) Also ***nonante*** in Belgium and Switzerland.

§ Note that when *80* is used as a page number it has no *s*: ***page eighty*** = ***page quatre-vingt***.

¶ ***vingt*** has no *s* when it is in the middle of a number. The only exception to this rule is when ***quatre-vingts*** is followed by ***millions***, ***milliards*** or ***billions***, eg ***quatre-vingts millions***, ***quatre-vingts billions*** etc.

◊ ***cent*** does not take an *s* when it is in the middle of a number. The only exception to this rule is when it is followed by ***millions***, ***milliards*** or ***billions***, eg ***trois cents millions***, ***six cents billions*** etc. It has a normal plural when it modifies other nouns: ***200 inhabitants*** = ***deux cents habitants***.

∞ Where English would have a comma, French has simply a space. A full stop (period) can be used, e.g. ***1.000***. As in English, there is no separation in dates between thousands and hundreds: ***in 1995*** = ***en 1995***.

** In dates, the spelling ***mil*** is preferred to ***mille***, i.e. ***en 1200*** = ***en mil deux cents***. However, when the year is a round number of thousands, the spelling is always ***mille***, so ***en l'an mille***, ***en l'an deux mille*** etc.

†† ***mille*** is invariable; it never takes an *s*.

‡‡ The French words ***million***, ***milliard*** and ***billion*** are nouns, and when written out in full they take ***de*** before another noun, eg ***a million inhabitants*** = ***un million d'habitants***. However, when written in figures, ***1,000,000 inhabitants*** = ***1 000 000 habitants***, but is still spoken as *un million d'habitants*. When *million* etc. is part of a complex number, *de* is not used before the nouns, eg ***6,000,210 people*** = ***six millions deux cent dix personnes***.

Use of en

Note the use of ***en*** in the following examples:

there are six	= il y en a six
I've got a hundred	= j'en ai cent

en must be used when the thing you are talking about is not expressed (the French says literally *there of them are six, I of them have a hundred* etc.). However, ***en*** is not needed when the object is specified:

there are six apples = il y a six pommes

Approximate numbers

When you want to say *about* ... , remember the French ending ***-aine***:

about ten	= une dizaine
about ten books	= une dizaine de livres
about fifteen	= une quinzaine
about fifteen people	= une quinzaine de personnes

Similarly ***une trentaine***, ***une quarantaine***, ***une cinquantaine***, ***une soixantaine*** and ***une centaine*** (and ***une douzaine*** means ***a dozen***). For other numbers, use ***environ*** (***about***):

about thirty-five	= environ trente-cinq
about four thousand pages	= environ quatre mille pages

Note the use of ***centaines*** and ***milliers*** to express approximate quantities:

hundreds of books	= des centaines de livres
thousands of books	= des milliers de livres
I've got thousands	= j'en ai des milliers

Phrases

numbers up to ten	= les nombres jusqu'à dix
to count up to ten	= compter jusqu'à dix
almost ten	= presque dix
less than ten	= moins de dix
more than ten	= plus de dix
all ten of them	= tous les dix
all ten boys	= les dix garçons

Note the French word order:

my last ten pounds	= mes dix dernières livres
the next twelve weeks	= les douze prochaines semaines
the other two	= les deux autres
the last four	= les quatre derniers

Calculations in French

$10 + 3 = 13$	dix et trois font *or* égalent treize
$10 - 3 = 7$	trois ôté de dix il reste sept *or* dix moins trois égale sept
$10 \times 3 = 30$	dix fois trois égale trente
$30 : 3 = 10$	($30 \div 3 = 10$) trente divisé par trois égale dix

Note how the French division sign differs from the English.

5^2	cinq au carré
5^3	cinq puissance trois
5^{100}	cinq puissance cent
$\sqrt{12}$	racine carrée de douze
$\sqrt{25} = 5$	racine carrée de vingt-cinq égale cinq
$B > A$	B est plus grand que A
$A < B$	A est plus petit que B

Decimals in French

Note that French uses a comma where English has a decimal point.

	say
0,25	zéro virgule vingt-cinq
0,05	zéro virgule zéro cinq
0,75	zéro virgule soixante-quinze
3,45	trois virgule quarante-cinq
8,195	huit virgule cent quatre-vingt-quinze
9,1567	neuf virgule quinze cent soixante-sept *or* neuf virgule mille cinq cent soixante-sept
9,3456	neuf virgule trois mille quatre cent cinquante-six

Percentages in French

	say
25%	vingt-cinq pour cent
50%	cinquante pour cent
100%	cent pour cent
200%	deux cents pour cent
365%	trois cent soixante pour cent
4,25%	quatre virgule vingt-cinq pour cent

Fractions in French

	say
$\frac{1}{2}$	un demi*
$\frac{1}{3}$	un tiers
$\frac{1}{4}$	un quart
$\frac{1}{5}$	un cinquième
$\frac{1}{6}$	un sixième
$\frac{1}{7}$	un septième
$\frac{1}{8}$	un huitième
$\frac{1}{9}$	un neuvième
$\frac{1}{10}$	un dixième
$\frac{1}{11}$	un onzième
$\frac{1}{12}$	un douzième (*etc*)
$\frac{2}{3}$	deux tiers†
$\frac{2}{5}$	deux cinquièmes
$\frac{2}{10}$	deux dixièmes (*etc*)
$\frac{3}{4}$	trois quarts
$\frac{3}{5}$	trois cinquièmes
$\frac{3}{10}$	trois dixièmes (*etc*)
$1\frac{1}{2}$	un et demi
$1\frac{1}{3}$	un (et) un tiers
$1\frac{1}{4}$	un et quart
$1\frac{1}{5}$	un (et) un cinquième
$1\frac{1}{6}$	un (et) un sixième
$1\frac{1}{7}$	un (et) un septième (*etc*)
$5\frac{2}{3}$	cinq (et) deux tiers
$5\frac{3}{4}$	cinq (et) trois quarts
$5\frac{4}{5}$	cinq (et) quatre cinquièmes
45/100ths of a second	= quarante-cinq centièmes de seconde

Ordinal numbers in French§

1st	1er‡	premier (*fem.* première)
2nd	2^{e}	second *or* deuxième
3rd	3^{e}	troisième
4th	4^{e}	quatrième
5th	5^{e}	cinquième
6th	6^{e}	sixième
7th	7^{e}	septième
8th	8^{e}	huitième
9th	9^{e}	neuvième
10th	10^{e}	dixième
11th	11^{e}	onzième
12th	12^{e}	douzième
13th	13^{e}	treizième
14th	14^{e}	quatorzième
15th	15^{e}	quinzième
16th	16^{e}	seizième
17th	17^{e}	dix-septième
18th	18^{e}	dix-huitième
19th	19^{e}	dix-neuvième
20th	20^{e}	vingtième
21st	21^{e}	vingt et unième
22nd	22^{e}	vingt-deuxième
23rd	23^{e}	vingt-troisième
24th	24^{e}	vingt-quatrième
25th	23^{e}	vingt-cinqième
30th	30^{e}	trentième
31st	31^{e}	trente et unième
40th	40^{e}	quarantième
50th	50^{e}	cinquantième
60th	60^{e}	soixantième
70th	70^{e}	soixante-dixième¶
71st	71^{e}	soixante et onzième
72nd	72^{e}	soixante-douzième
73rd	73^{e}	soixante-treizième
74th	74^{e}	soixante-quartorzième
75th	75^{e}	soixante-quinzième
79th	79^{e}	soixante-dix-neuvième
80th	80^{e}	quatre-vingtième¶
81st	81^{e}	quatre-vingt-unième
90th	90^{e}	quatre-vingt-dixième¶
91st	91^{e}	quatre-vingt-onzième
99th	99^{e}	quatre-vingt-dix-neuvième
100th	100^{e}	centième
101st	101^{e}	cent et unième
102nd	102^{e}	cent-deuxième
196th	196^{e}	cent quatre-vingt-seizième
200th	200^{e}	deux centième
300th	300^{e}	trois centième
400th	400^{e}	quatre centième
1,000th	$1\,000^{e}$	millième
2,000th	$2\,000^{e}$	deux millième
1,000,000th	$1\,000\,000^{e}$	millionième

Like English, French makes nouns by adding the definite article:

the first	= le premier (*or* la première, *or* les premiers *m pl* *or* les premières *f pl*)
the second	= le second (*or* la seconde *etc*)
the first three	= les trois premiers *or* les trois premières

Note the French word order in:

the third richest country in the world	= le troisième pays le plus riche du monde

* Note that ***half***, when not a fraction, is translated by the noun ***moitié*** or the adjective ***demi***; see the dictionary entry.

† Note the use of ***les*** and ***d'entre*** when these fractions are used about a group of people or things: ***two-thirds of them*** = ***les deux tiers d'entre eux***.

‡ This is the masculine form; the feminine is ***1re*** and the plural ***1ers*** (*m*) or ***1res*** (*f*). All the other abbreviations of ordinal numbers are invariable.

§ All the ordinal numbers in French behave like ordinary adjectives and take normal plural endings where appropriate.

¶ (70e) Also ***septantième*** in Belgium and Switzerland. (80e) Also ***octantième*** in Switzerland and Canada, and ***huitantième*** in Switzerland. (90e) Also ***nonantième*** in Belgium and Switzerland.

Index of lexical and grammar notes

Lexical notes

Age *492*
The Clock *554*
Colours *559*
Countries, Cities, and Continents *574*
Currencies and Money *748*
Dates, Days, and Months *584*
Forms of Address *642*
Games and Sports *649*
The Human Body *523*
Illnesses, Aches, and Pains *686*
Languages and Nationalities *712*
Length and Weight Measurements *738*
Musical Instruments *753*
Quantities *813*
Shops, Trades, and Professions *805*
Talking about Time *915*

Grammar notes

after *491*
before *515*
do *599*
for *639*
have *671*
her *675*
it *699*
might *743*
not *762*
should *857*
since *861*
that *905*
the *906*
them *908*
to *917*
what *963*
which *965*
you *983*
your *985*